2001

WOMEN IN WORLD HISTORY

A Biographical Encyclopedia

WOMEN IN WORLD HISTORY

A Biographical Encyclopedia

VOLUME

4

Cole-Dzer

Anne Commire, Editor

Deborah Klezmer, Associate Editor

YORKIN PUBLICATIONS

GALE GROUP

Detroit
San Francisco
London
Boston
Woodbridge, CT

Yorkin Publications

Anne Commire, *Editor*
Deborah Klezmer, *Associate Editor*
Barbara Morgan, *Assistant Editor*

Eileen O'Pasek, Gail Schermer, Patricia Coombs, James Fox,
Catherine Cappelli, Karen Rikkers, *Editorial Assistants*
Karen Walker, *Assistant for Genealogical Charts*

Special acknowledgment is due to Peg Yorkin who made this project possible.

Thanks also to Karin and John Haag, Bob Schermer, and to
the Gale Group staff, in particular Dedria Bryfonski, Linda Hubbard, John Schmittroth, Cynthia Baldwin,
Tracey Rowens, Randy Bassett, Christine O'Bryan, Rebecca Parks, and especially Sharon Malinowski.

The Gale Group

Sharon Malinowski, *Senior Editor*
Rebecca Parks, *Editor*
Linda S. Hubbard, *Managing Editor, Multicultural Team*

Margaret A. Chamberlain, *Permissions Specialist*
Mary K. Grimes, *Image Cataloger*

Mary Beth Trimper, *Production Director*
Evi Seoud, *Assistant Production Manager*

Cynthia Baldwin, *Product Design Manager*
Tracey Rowens, *Cover and Page Designer*

Barbara Yarrow, *Graphic Services Manager*
Randy Bassett, *Image Database Supervisor*
Robert Duncan and Michael Logusz, *Imaging Specialists*
Christine O'Bryan, *Graphics Desktop Publisher*

Library of Congress Catalog Card Number 99-24692
A CIP record is available from the British Library

ISBN 0-7876-4063-8
Printed in the United States of America.

Library of Congress Cataloging-in-Publication Data

Women in world history : a biographical encyclopedia / Anne Commire, editor, Deborah Klezmer, associate editor.
    p. cm.
    Includes bibliographical references and index.
    ISBN 0-7876-3736-X (set). — ISBN 0-7876-4080-8 (v. 1). —
    ISBN 0-7876-4061-1 (v. 2) — ISBN 0-7876-4062-X (v. 3) — ISBN 0-7876-4063-8 (v. 4)
    1. Women—History Encyclopedias. 2. Women—Biography Encyclopedias.
    I. Commire, Anne. II. Klezmer, Deborah.
        HQ1115.W6 1999   99-24692
        920.72'03—DC21

10 9 8 7 6 5 4 3 2 1

Cole

Cole, Margaret (1893–1980)

British political activist and writer. Name variations: Dame Margaret Cole. Born Margaret Isabel Postgate in 1893; died in 1980; daughter of (John) Percival Postgate (1853–1926, a classical scholar); granddaughter of John Postgate (1820–1881, a reformer); educated at Roedean School and Girton College, Cambridge (degree in classics, 1914); married G.D.H. Cole (a socialist and scholar), in 1918 (died 1949); children: two daughters and one son.

Born into a liberal family, Dame Margaret Cole would influence many significant Labour politicians as a leading socialist. Her grandfather was John Postgate, a famous reformer, and her father was a Cambridge Classics don. After her graduation from Girton College, Cambridge, where she earned a degree in classics in 1914, Cole taught at St Paul's Girls' School in London for two years. Her belief in socialism was strengthened when her brother Raymond was imprisoned as a conscientious objector during World War I. Cole joined the Fabian Society's Research Department, which was under the domination of Guild Socialists seeking worker control of factories.

In 1916, she met G.D.H. Cole, a socialist and scholar who had authored *The World of Labour* (1913) and was the leader of the radical opposition to Fabian leaders Sidney and *Beatrice Webb. The Coles broke away from the Fabian Society in 1918, the year they were married, and formed the Labour Research Department.

This Department, however, became dominated by the British Communist Party, after which the Coles abandoned it and moved to Oxford where G.D.H. was appointed a university reader in economics. But Margaret Cole disliked Oxford and from 1929 on they maintained a house in London. Reunited with the Webbs, in the late 1920s they rejoined the Fabian Society. The Coles organized a special strike committee in the General Strike of 1926, and were responsible for influencing many future Labour leaders, including Hugh Gaitskell.

Margaret Cole was a defender of egalitarian education and during the 1930s organized classes for the Workers' Education Association, an organization for which she taught from 1925 to 1949. In 1935, the Coles founded the new Fabian Research Bureau, which collected a good deal of the data for postwar Labour reforms. They wrote *Review of Europe of Today* (1933) and *The Condition of Britain* (1937). Margaret was a member of the London County Council (1943–65), of which she was alderman from 1952 to 1965, and she was with the Inner London Education Authority from 1965 to 1967 and served as president of the Fabian Society from 1963.

Among her many writings are *Makers of the Labour Movement* (1948) and *Beatrice and Sidney Webb* (1955). She also edited two volumes of Beatrice Webb's diaries. Prior to G.D.H.'s death in 1949, Margaret wrote more than 30 critically acclaimed detective novels with her husband. In 1965, she was created OBE; in 1970, she was created DBE (Dame of the British Empire).

SUGGESTED READING:
Cole, Margaret. *Life of G.D.H. Cole.* 1971.

Cole, Rebecca J. (1846–1922)

African-American physician. Born in Philadelphia, Pennsylvania, on March 16, 1846; died in Philadelphia on August 14, 1922; graduated from the Institute for Colored Youth, Philadelphia, 1863; graduated from the Female Medical College of Pennsylvania (now The Medical College of Pennsylvania), 1867.

Enduring the double prejudice of race and gender, Rebecca Cole was the first black woman to graduate from the Female Medical College of Pennsylvania. She then became resident physician at the New York Infirmary for Women and Children (established in 1857 by *Elizabeth Blackwell), where she worked with the poor, dispensing practical information on infant and family health. She later practiced in Columbia, South Carolina, and was a superintendent of the

Government House for Children and Old Women in Washington, D.C. Cole eventually returned to Philadelphia where she established a practice and served as superintendent of a homeless shelter. With another physician, **Charlotte Abby**, she conducted a Woman's Directory that gave legal and medical aid. Rebecca Cole died in 1922, after 50 years in medicine.

Coleman, Bessie (1892–1926)

First African-American woman pilot in the world who earned an international license in France in 1921 and spent the next five years touring the U.S., giving exhibition flights and speaking in theaters, churches, and schools to exhort blacks to seek their future in aviation. Born on January 26, 1892, in Atlanta, Texas; killed in fall from plane on April 30, 1926, in Jacksonville, Florida; daughter of George (a day laborer) and Susan Coleman (a domestic worker); attended one-room school for blacks in Waxahachie, Texas, to the eighth grade; spent one year at preparatory school of Colored Agricultural and Normal University in Langston, Oklahoma (now Langston University); married Claude Glenn, on January 30, 1917, but at no time did she inform her family, reside with Glenn, or use his name.

Family moved to Waxahachie, Texas (1894); with exception of school year at Langston (1910–11), resided in Waxahachie until 1915, when she moved to Chicago; was manicurist there until 1920 when she went to France for flight lessons (November 1920–September 1921); was issued license by Fédération Internationale Aéronautique (June 15, 1921); returned to France from Chicago for advance aerobatic lessons (February–August 1922); gave first exhibition flight in the world by a black woman, in New York (September 3, 1922); performed further flights in Memphis and Chicago (1922), distributed advertising leaflets by air in California (1923); was badly injured in plane crash in Santa Monica (February 4, 1923) and hospitalized until May; that same month, gave lecture series on aviation at Los Angeles YMCA (May 1923); had flight in Columbus, Ohio (1923), and flights and lectures in Houston, Galveston, San Antonio, Fort Worth, Dallas, Wharton and Waxahachie, Texas (summer 1925); gave lecture tour and exhibition flights in Savannah and Augusta, Georgia, and St. Petersburg, West Palm Beach, Orlando and Jacksonville, Florida (1926).

On July 15, 1921, Bessie Coleman, an African-American flying a French Nieuport, landed on the runway of France's finest flight school, l'École d'Aviation des Frères Caudron at Le Crotoy in the Somme. The manicurist from Chicago had won her wings from the Fédération Aéronautique Internationale to become the first black woman pilot in the world. The license was duly recognized the following September in the magazine *l'Aérophile* in a list of 61 successful candidates, among whom Coleman was the only woman. The license-winning flight marked the end of the first 29 years of her life, starting with childhood in a Texas town where the segregated, one-room grade school closed whenever the students were needed to pick cotton. By 1915, she was working as a manicurist in a South Side Chicago barbershop. But it was only the beginning of an odyssey to show the world that a black woman could compete with the best of stunt pilots and to convince the members of her race that they, too, could seize the opportunities opening up for employment in the new technology of flight.

Born in a dirt-floored, one-room cabin in Atlanta, Texas, on January 26, 1892, Coleman was one of nine surviving children born to **Susan Coleman**, a domestic worker, and her husband George, a day laborer. When Bessie was two, her father moved his family to Waxahachie, Texas, where he bought one quarter of an acre of land in the segregated east side of town. On it, he built a three-room "shotgun" house, characterized by a series of doors opening from one room to the next so that one "could shoot a shotgun through the length of the house." For the next seven years, Bessie enjoyed a frugal but happy childhood, sharing household tasks with her two older brothers, who were still at home, and playing with the three younger sisters born after her. Coleman's childhood ended at nine when George Coleman proposed another move, this time to Indian Territory in Oklahoma. There, his status as the grandchild of three Native Americans assured him of the citizen's rights denied him in Texas, where both blacks and Indians were feared or despised by the majority of the white residents. When Susan refused to go, he left alone. Coleman's two brothers, Walter and John, soon departed for Chicago, leaving the nine-year-old Bessie to serve as homemaker and caretaker for her three younger sisters while her mother worked as a domestic for a white couple in Waxahachie.

Coleman's schooling was sporadic, limited by the needs of her siblings and the demand for labor in the cotton fields where whole African-American families worked whenever such seasonal labor offered additional income. The

Bessie
Coleman

school, one room for all eight grades, was hot in the summer and cold in the winter, a four-mile walk from home for instruction from a teacher whose own education was limited to eight grades. Yet Coleman soon became an accomplished reader, entertaining the family at night by reading aloud from the books her illiterate mother borrowed from a wagon library. They were stories of African-American heroes, among them Paul Laurence Dunbar, *Harriet Tubman and Booker T. Washington. Although *Uncle Tom's Cabin* was one of her favorites, after reading it Coleman once declared: *"I'll* never be a Topsy *or* an Uncle Tom!"

A gifted math student as well, Bessie became the family's bookkeeper, toting up the weight of the cotton picked by Susan and her children. She proved a reluctant picker who sometimes sat on the long bag as it was dragged along the rows by some unsuspecting adult. However, she demonstrated her worth at the scales, where she not only calculated the family's wages but put her foot on the scale whenever "the man" looked away. Beautiful, healthy, intelligent and with a sense of self-worth unmarred by poverty and racism, Coleman was determined to "amount to something," as her ambitious church-going mother had adjured her.

Her first escape from Waxahachie came in 1910 when she left for Langston, Oklahoma, to attend the Colored Agricultural and Normal University with tuition earned and saved from her labor as a laundress. But records reveal that she needed further work at the preparatory school before starting undergraduate studies, and at the end of the year, her funds exhausted, she returned to Waxahachie to labor again as a laundress, delivering her work at the back doors of her white employers.

By 1915, when she was 23, Coleman left for Chicago, where her brother Walter, a Pullman porter, offered her shelter until she could find a job. Balking at becoming a domestic, as most African-American women with limited educations were in Chicago, she became a manicurist. Within a year, she won a contest sponsored by the black weekly, the *Chicago Defender,* as the best and fastest manicurist in black Chicago. But this was not, in Coleman's view, "amounting to something" in the eyes of her own people or the whole world.

I point to Bessie Coleman and say without hesitation that here is a woman, a being who exemplifies and serves as a model to all humanity, the very definition of strength, dignity, courage, integrity, and beauty.

—*Mae Jemison, MD and first black woman astronaut

Not until the age of 28 did she find the goal she sought. On a fall day in 1920, her brother John, a World War I veteran who had served in France, entered the barber shop where she worked and began telling the customers that the women in France were better than the women in black Chicago. The French women, he said,

could even fly airplanes! "That's it," she said. "You just called it for me!" Undoubtedly she had already seen newsreels and films glorifying World War aviators, but the Coleman family credited John's taunt as providing the ultimate motivation in her decision to become a flier.

Within days, she sought someone to teach her but soon discovered that while it was hard enough for even white women to get flying instruction, for a black woman it was impossible. Coleman turned for help to one of Chicago's most influential African-Americans, Robert Abbott, editor and publisher of the *Defender.* Abbott advised her to go to France, a recognized national leader in aviation, where racism did not exist. If she would learn French, he said, he would help her apply to a school there. She did, at a Michigan Avenue language school, and by November of 1920 she sailed for France.

Coleman learned to fly in six months at the best school in France, managed by plane designers and aviators Gaston and René Caudron. But on her return to the United States in September, she soon realized that just being a pilot was not enough to gain the attention of a public avid for the stunts of daredevil circus fliers. Determined as ever, she returned to Europe the following February to take aerobatic lessons in France. She then journeyed to Holland where Anthony Fokker taught her to fly the world-renowned planes that he himself had designed, and finally to Germany, where one of her teachers was a World War I flying ace.

Arriving back in New York in August of 1922, on September 3 she gave an exhibition flight in Long Island, attended by several thousand spectators and praised by critics in both black and white newspapers. Coleman's race, gender and flying skill all contributed to the attention that followed. In addition, she possessed a sense of drama, her beauty augmented by the costume she had designed: military jacket, riding breeches, a long leather coat and a leather helmet with goggles pushed up so the audience could see her face as she climbed into the cockpit of her plane. Her poise and self-assurance were also evident in interviews for the press, and, like most aviators of the period, she was not averse to exaggeration in declaiming her adventures in Europe. Her debut in Long Island was followed by successful shows in Memphis and Chicago.

Not long after that, her promising career stalled when she broke a contract with a black movie company that had hired her to star in a film. The company had failed to tell her that she was to play an ignorant black girl who comes from the country to the big city, a role she viewed as demeaning to the women of her race and particularly to those she had known in Texas. A year later, she met and gave flying lessons to an advertising executive for an automobile tire company in California. He offered to buy her a plane if she in turn would airdrop advertising leaflets for his company. She bought the plane in Coronado, a war surplus JN-4, or "Jenny," army trainer. But on her first flight in it, the plane stalled and crashed soon after take-off. She spent the next four months in a Santa Monica hospital recuperating from a broken leg and other injuries. Yet, before she left California, Coleman gave a series of lectures at the Los Angeles YMCA, revealing her growing determination to open a school for black aviators.

She returned to Chicago without a job or a plane and, with the exception of one show in Columbus, Ohio, it was more than a year before she could find the backing for an exhibition tour in Texas, during the summer of 1925. The tour was a resounding success, with appearances in Houston, Dallas, Wharton, Richmond, San Antonio, Fort Worth, and Waxahachie, where she insisted there be a non-segregated main gate for ticket holders. In addition to stunt flying and parachute jumping, she also lectured on aviation in African-American theaters, churches, and schools.

After a brief return to Chicago, Coleman left in January of 1926 for theatrical engagements in Savannah and Augusta, Georgia, and followed this by engagements and exhibition flights in St. Petersburg, Tampa, and West Palm Beach, Florida. At the invitation of Baptist minister Hezakiah and **Viola Hill** , his wife, Coleman next spent two months in Orlando, when she wrote to her sister, **Elois**, that she was at last nearing her goal of raising enough capital to open a flight school. She left Orlando for Jacksonville, Florida, for an engagement sponsored by the Negro Welfare League, an exhibition flight scheduled for May 1, 1926. With money from an Orlando benefactor, she paid for another army surplus "Jenny" to be flown by a mechanic-pilot from Love Field, Texas, to Jacksonville—a trip that required three forced landings.

On April 30, the day before the exhibition was to take place, Coleman asked the mechanic-pilot to fly her over the field where she was to make a parachute jump. Too short to see over the cockpit's edge, she wore no safety belt, and, as she leaned out to survey the field below, the plane suddenly accelerated and flipped over. She fell 1,500 feet to her death. The plane crashed nearby, killing the pilot.

In her efforts to raise money for an aviation school open to blacks and to convince members of her race that there were opportunities for them in aviation, Coleman found countless obstacles. There were black men who resented a black woman doing what they could not. There were also many black women, often the most effective activists for civil liberties and better schools, who were too socially conservative to accept the colorful Coleman. African-American newspapers covered her appearances when possible but were limited in size, circulation, and money. The white press not only failed to give her the publicity she needed but often belittled her as well. Even in the story of her death, two Jacksonville newspapers referred to her as "the Coleman woman," or just "the woman," while identifying the pilot as "Mr. Wills."

Only in death was Bessie Coleman finally honored. She was given three funerals, one in Jacksonville, another in Orlando, and the last in Chicago, where 10,000 people filled the Pilgrim Baptist Church and spilled out into the surrounding streets. Coleman left a heritage of growing interest in aviation on the part of both men and women of her race. She was the founder of a movement that embraced Chicago's Checkerboard Field pilots of the 1930s, the visionary Lt. William J. Powell, founder of Bessie Coleman flying clubs, and the renowned Tuskegee U.S. Army fighter pilots of World War II. Bessie Coleman is buried at Lincoln Cemetery in Chicago.

SOURCES:

"Chicago Colored Girl Learns to Fly," in *Aerial Age Weekly*. October 17, 1921.

"Colored Aviatrix Bobs Up Again," in *Air Service Newsletter*. February 20, 1926.

Hardesty, Von and Dominic Pisano. *Black Wings: The American Black in Aviation*. Washington, DC: Smithsonian Institution Press, 1987.

King, Anita. "Family Tree: Brave Bessie, First Black Pilot," in *Essence*. Part 1, May 1976; part 2, June 1976.

Patterson, Elois. *Memoirs of the Late Bessie Coleman, Aviatrix*. Privately printed, 1969.

Rich, Doris L. *Queen Bess: Daredevil Aviator*. Washington and London: Smithsonian Institution Press, 1993.

COLLECTIONS:

African-American newspapers (originals and/or microfilms) at: Moorland-Spingarn Research Center, Howard University, Washington, D.C.; City of Dallas Public Library, Dallas, Texas; Eartha White Collection, Thomas F. Carpenter Library, University of North Florida, Jacksonville, Florida; Eugene C. Barker Texas History Center, University of Texas,

Austin, Texas; Houston Metropolitan Research Center, Houston Public Library, Houston, Texas; Lilly Library, Indiana University, Bloomington, Indiana; Memphis Shelby County Public Library, Memphis, Tennessee; Pennsylvania State University Library, University Park, Pennsylvania; Rosenberg Library, Galveston Public Library, Galveston, Texas; Schomberg Center for Research in Black Culture, New York Public Library, New York, New York; Soper Library, Morgan State University, Baltimore, Maryland; State Historical Society of Wisconsin, Madison, Wisconsin.

PAPERS AND MEMORABILIA:
DuSable Museum of African American History, Chicago, Illinois; National Air and Space Museum, Smithsonian Institution, Washington, D.C.

Doris L. Rich, author of *Amelia Earhart: A Biography* (Smithsonian Institution Press, 1989) and *Queen Bess: Daredevil Aviator* (Smithsonian Institution Press, 1993)

Coleman, Kit (1864–1915)

Canadian journalist. Name variations: Kathleen Coleman. Born Kathleen Blake near Galway in Western Ireland, in 1864; died in Hamilton, Ontario, Canada, in 1915; married George Willis (a wealthy country squire), in 1880 (died 1884); married Edward Watkins, in 1884 (died 1889): married Theobald Coleman (a physician), in 1898; children: (second marriage) son Thady and daughter Pat.

In 1889, as a concession to Canada's emerging "New Woman" movement, Christopher Bunting, the managing editor of the *Toronto Mail*, hired Kathleen "Kit" Coleman to create what he envisioned as a harmless little column of recipes and fashion tips for his Saturday issue. Before long, Coleman was producing some of the most imaginative and thought-provoking journalism ever seen in Canada. Over the next 21 years, through her popular and controversial column "Woman's Kingdom," Coleman commented on a host of topics, from Canadian politics ("After you meet an Ottawa veteran, you sometimes wonder if in the beginning God did not create three species—man, woman and politician.") to fashion trends ("The new hats are weird. But we say that every spring and still wear them."). She initiated Canada's first advice to the lovelorn ("Arlene: We have not yet arrived at the era where women can propose marriage. Remember, paper child: man proposes, woman disposes.") and joined the press corps to cover the Spanish-American War in spite of a ban imposed on women journalists by the U.S. military. In 1893, she traveled to the Chicago World Columbian Exposition and, in 1898, covered Queen *Victoria's Diamond Jubilee. She interviewed some of the most prominent personalities of her day, including William Randolph Hearst and *Sarah Bernhardt, whom, it was said, she slightly resembled. In 1904, Coleman helped found the Canadian Women's Press Club and was elected its first president.

Born near Galway in Western Ireland in 1864 into a well-established Irish family (her uncle was the noted Dublin orator Reverend Tom Burke), Kit Coleman apparently adopted her father's liberal views. When she was 16, her parents arranged her marriage to George Willis, a wealthy country squire 40 years her senior. Willis provided for her education in Dublin and Brussels but appeared to have little affection for his young bride. When he died in 1884, leaving his money to his mother, Coleman went to England, then Canada, where she took a job as a secretary in Toronto. Shortly thereafter, she married her boss, Edward Watkins. The couple moved to Winnipeg, where Coleman had two children, Thady and Pat; the youngsters later provided fodder for her column until they reached adolescence and complained that her remarks were making them the targets of schoolyard teasing. When Watkins died suddenly in 1889, Coleman returned to Toronto and pursued her childhood interest in writing. With little experience, she began submitting articles to Canadian magazines. A piece on the bohemians she had observed in Paris during a summer holiday caught the eye of Bunting, who made her Canada's first full-time woman's-page editor.

Coleman produced her early columns from her rooms in a shabby boarding house, writing while her children were in school. Once a week, she traveled by streetcar to the newspaper office to gather her mail and supervise the setting of her column, which she submitted in almost illegible handwriting, possibly the result of nearsightedness that forced her to hold the pen an inch from her nose. If the printers complained, she would show up the following week with the column pasted together in a 20-foot strip, just to aggravate them further. The initial columns, entitled "Fashion Notes and Fancies for the Fair Sex," were half-pages but soon blossomed into her seven-column "Woman's Kingdom" format.

Although Bunting did not always approve of Coleman's comments on inept politicians or corrupt businessmen, he gave her free reign. Although her brash attacks, often directed at men, thrust her headlong into the New Woman movement, Coleman was a reluctant member of the sisterhood. Equality was fine in the workplace, but private life was quite another matter. "The

New Woman movement is a fine one in moderation," she wrote.

> But it overshoots its mark when it makes a vain effort to equalize the sexes, the chief charm of which is that they can never be equalized. They are each the beautiful component of the other. Until nature changes her laws and God alters His creation, it will always be thus. Two unequal sexes fitting wonderfully together.

Coleman, while the purveyor of beauty hints and fashion forecasts, had little regard for her own appearance, often wearing the same wrinkled blouse and run-down shoes that she wore in the newspaper composing room to an important interview or event. She ignored her permanently ink-stained fingers, twisted her naturally curly red hair into a casual upsweep, and frequently made up her face with a heavy hand. Warm and sympathetic by nature, she was nonetheless given to outbursts of temper. Coleman once physically accosted a gentleman who had stormed into the newspaper office to protest something she had written, threatening to cut off his beard with the scissors she was using to clip items from a paper. (Coleman later apologized in a note, explaining that she had no intention of harming his beard. "I was aiming for your nose," she wrote, "which I felt required trimming as it was so large it could not help poking into other people's affairs.") Coleman was also a tyrant about smoking and drinking, although she was known to be slightly more tolerant of these habits in males than in females. If a woman lit up a cigarette or became inebriated in her presence, she offered a vigorous scolding regardless of the setting. She once asked the waiter in a posh Ottawa restaurant to remove a woman smoker at the next table to the alley, "where the rest of the trash is kept." In spite of her temper and dowdy appearance, Coleman was adored by her colleagues, who stood in awe of her intelligence, wit, and unfailing dedication.

Known to go to any lengths to get a story, Coleman traveled to Cleveland, Ohio, in an effort to interview the notorious swindler *Cassie Chadwick. She hung around the city jail for days, until she and a handful of reporters were finally allowed access to Chadwick's cell. When Chadwick would not cooperate and insisted that the guard remove the reporters, Coleman tricked her way back into the cell by telling the guard she had dropped her glove. In 1898, when war on Spain was declared, Coleman literally haunted the office of Secretary of War Russell Alger until he gave in and signed the papers making her an accredited correspondent (the only woman among 134 men). She had an equally difficult time reaching her destination. After waiting six weeks in a dank hotel in Tampa, Florida, she was denied passage on the special press boat for Cuba. She was even turned away from a Red Cross Ship leaving from Key West, reportedly because *Clara Barton took an instant dislike to her. Coleman finally made it to Cuba by talking her way onto a decrepit U.S. government freighter carrying war supplies. Once she reached her destination, she was given no special allowances as a woman. Bedding on the ground, and eating when and where she could, Coleman filed vivid and poignant accounts of the war. After the crucial battle at Santiago, she wrote: "Here in Santiago, men, nobles and commoners alike, dying in filth and stench, and uttermost squalor; lying out there on the hills for the buzzard and the crab to feed upon. There was heartbreak in the thought of it; in the sight of all this hopeless suffering. We are very little creatures. Very small and cheap and poor."

> *Why do men look ashamed if they are caught reading the woman's page in a newspaper? Are women utter idiots? Do men believe that there is not a word to be written for our sex beyond frills and fopperies?*
>
> —**Kit Coleman, 1891**

In 1898, after professing that she'd never take a third husband, Coleman married her relentless suitor, Dr. Theobald Coleman, and for two years lived in an isolated mining town before settling in Hamilton, Ontario. There, in addition to covering stories, she took up horseback riding and raised prizewinning Bedlington terriers. In 1911, when she was denied a small raise from the newspapers for an additional front-page column she was ordered to write, Coleman quit her job and began selling "Woman's Kingdom" (renamed "Kit's Column") to dozens of newspapers across Canada. Charging five dollars a column, she earned more than she ever had at the *Mail*.

In 1915, Coleman went to bed one evening with a cold, expecting to produce another column from her sickbed the next day. The cold developed into pneumonia, from which she died at age 51. By that time, she had won the respect of her colleagues and paved the way for other female journalists like Faith Fenton (*Alice Freeman), who covered the Klondike Gold Rush, ❧▶ Cora Hind, named the first agricultural editor in Canada by the *Winnipeg Free Press*, and poet **Jean Blewett**, who was hired by the *Toron-*

❧▶
See sidebar
on the
following page

Hind, Cora (b. 1861)
Canadian journalist. Born in 1861.

When Cora Hind began writing for the *Winnipeg Free Press* in 1901, she had already served as a wheat inspector for three years. Her judgment of crops and possible yield were so accurate that for the next 25 years her estimates influenced the advance price of Canadian wheat.

to Globe to compete with Coleman. Instead of becoming arch rivals, Coleman and Blewett disappointed everyone by becoming good friends. It was Blewett who dubbed Coleman "the Queen of Hearts" and in a *Globe* column wrote that Kit "not only writes of the affairs of the heart when she renders romantic advice, but she touches our hearts with everything she does."

SOURCES:

Ferguson, Ted. *Kit Coleman: Queen of Hearts*. NY: Doubleday, 1978.

Barbara Morgan,
Melrose, Massachusetts

Coleridge, Mary Elizabeth
(1861–1907)

British poet, novelist, and critic. Born in London, England, on September 23, 1861; died in Harrogate, Yorkshire, England, on August 25, 1907; daughter of Arthur Duke Coleridge (clerk of the Assize on the midland circuit) and Mary Anne (Jameson) Coleridge; educated at home; never married; no children.

Selected writings: The Seven Sleepers of Ephesus *(novel, 1893);* Fancy's Following *(poems, 1896);* Fancy's Guerdon *(poems, 1897);* The King with Two Faces *(novel, 1897);* Non Sequitur *(sketches, 1900);* The Fiery Dawn *(novel, 1901);* The Shadow on the Wall *(novel, 1904);* The Lady on the Drawing-Room Floor *(novel, 1906);* Life of Holman Hunt *(biography, 1908);* Last Poems *(1905);* Poems New and Old *(1907);* Gathered Leaves *(stories and essays, 1910).*

The great-great-niece of Samuel Taylor Coleridge, Mary Coleridge was educated at home, where she was influenced by a steady stream of literary visitors. Tutored by her father's friend, poet William Johnson Cory (1823–1892), Coleridge began writing verses and stories at an early age, although as a young girl she was more interested in becoming a painter than a writer. In 1893, she published her first novel, *The Seven Sleepers of Ephesus,* which was highly praised by Robert Louis Stevenson, though it went un-

noticed by the critics. Two collections of poems, *Fancy's Following* (1896) and *Fancy's Guerdon* (1897), both published under a pseudonym, met with more success. Her breakthrough came with *The King with Two Faces* (1897), a historical romance based on the assassination of Gustavus III of Sweden, which established her reputation and was followed by a number of successful novels, mostly historical in nature. Coleridge also contributed articles to the *Monthly Review*, the *Guardian*, the *Cornhill Magazine*, and the *Times Literary Supplement*.

Coleridge, who never married, devoted a great deal of time teaching working women in her home and at the Working Women's College. She died suddenly of appendicitis in 1907, just short of her 46th birthday. A volume of work, *Poems New and Old,* was published the year of her death, and additional poems were added to a 1954 edition. Coleridge's poetry, recognized today over her novels and essays, is seen as a precursor to 20th-century poetry in its preoccupation with dreams, psychic states, and the problems of identity. In appraising her work, poet and critic Robert Bridges wrote: "It is the intimacy and spontaneity of her poems that will give them their chief value."

Coleridge, Sara (1802–1852)

*English writer. Born at Greta Hall, near Keswick, England, on December 23, 1802; died on May 3, 1852; fourth child and only daughter of Samuel Taylor Coleridge and **Sara Fricker Coleridge** (whose sister Edith Fricker married Robert Southey); married her cousin Henry Nelson Coleridge (1798–1843; a lawyer), in 1829; children: four, including Herbert Coleridge (1830–1861); lived in Hampstead, London, later in Chester Place, Regent's Park.*

Sara Coleridge was born at Greta Hall, near Keswick, England, on December 23, 1802, the fourth child and only daughter of Samuel Taylor Coleridge and Sara Fricker. The Fricker sisters had a penchant for artists. Sara Fricker married poet and critic Samuel Taylor Coleridge; **Edith Fricker** (d. 1837) married poet Robert Southey; and another sister married Robert Lovell, a Quaker poet. After 1803, all three couples lived together. William and *Dorothy Wordsworth at Grasmere were their neighbors. Because of his wanderings and opium habit, Samuel Coleridge was often away from home, and "Uncle Southey" became the pater familias. Wordsworth, in his poem, the *Triad,* left a description, or "poetical glorification," as Sara Coleridge calls it, of the three little girls growing up in this milieu—his own daughter Dora, **Edith May Southey**, and Sara Coleridge the younger, the "last of the three, though eldest born." Greta Hall was Sara Coleridge's home until her marriage; and the literati of the Lake colony seem to have been her only teachers.

With the help of Southey and his library, Sara Coleridge was a successful autodidact whom William Wordsworth deemed "remarkably clever." Before she was 25, she had read the chief Greek and Latin classics and had learned French, German, Italian and Spanish. In 1822, she translated from the Latin Martin Dobritzhoffer's *Account of the Abipones;* in 1825, she translated the *Memoirs* of the Chevalier Bayard.

In September 1829, Sara Coleridge married her cousin, Henry Nelson Coleridge, at Crosthwaite Church, Keswick, after a seven-year engagement. He was then a chancery barrister in London. The first eight years of their married life were spent in a little cottage in Hampstead where four of her children were born, two of whom survived. In 1834, Sara Coleridge published *Pretty Lessons for Little Children,* which was primarily designed for her own children but speedily passed through several editions. After the Coleridges moved to Chester Place in Regent's Park, she also wrote her longest work, the romantic fairy tale *Phantasmion* (1837). Considered her best work, *Phantasmion* contained songs that were greatly admired at the time by Leigh Hunt and other critics.

On the death of Samuel Coleridge in 1834, Sara's husband was appointed his literary executor; Sara then took on these duties following the demise of her husband in 1843. She edited *Aids to Reflection, Notes on Shakespeare and the Dramatists,* and *Essays on his own Times*; the elaborate discourses that she appended to these works illustrate the scope of her knowledge as well as her critical and analytical ability. She labored over her father's works for the rest of her life, until illness intervened in 1850. She died in London on May 3, 1852.

Shortly before her death, Sara Coleridge wrote an autobiographical fragment, covering her first nine years, for her daughter. This work was then completed by her daughter and published in 1873, together with some of her letters, under the title *Memoirs and Letters of Sara Coleridge.* Providing a view into a cultured and highly speculative mind, the letters contain many fitting appraisals of known people and books, and are especially interesting for their allusions to Wordsworth and the Lake Poets.

SUGGESTED READING:

Coleridge, Sara. *Memoirs and Letters.* London, 1873.

Woolf, Virginia. "Sara Coleridge," in *Death of the Moth and Other Essays.*

Coleridge-Taylor, Avril (1903—)

English conductor, composer, and pianist who founded and conducted two orchestras and composed numerous orchestral, chamber, piano, and vocal works. Born Avril Gwendolen Coleridge-Taylor in South Norwood, England, on March 18, 1903; daughter of Samuel Coleridge-Taylor, distinguished African-British composer.

The daughter of noted composer Samuel Coleridge-Taylor, Avril Coleridge-Taylor seemed destined to write music. Her first composition was penned at age 12, and she won a scholarship to attend the Trinity College of Music to study piano and composition the same year. Gordon Jacob and Alec Rowely taught her composition while she learned conducting from Sir Henry Wood, the famous founder of the *Proms* concerts. Coleridge-Taylor founded two orchestras—the Coleridge-Taylor Symphony Orchestra, which she conducted from 1946 until 1951, and the Malcolm Sargent Symphony Orchestra. She also founded and directed the New World Singers, a male voice ensemble. In addition, she frequently conducted. Coleridge-Taylor was the first woman to conduct the H.M. Royal Marine band. She also conducted the BBC Symphony Orchestra and the London Symphony Orchestra. During her conducting career, she continued to compose. Some of her works include *Ceremonial March for Independence of Ghana* (1957), *Comet Prelude* (1952), *Symphonic Impression* (1942), and a Piano Concerto in F-minor (1938).

John Haag, Athens, Georgia

Colet, Louise (1810–1876)

French journalist and poet who was Flaubert's lover and the model for his **Madame Bovary**. *Born Louise Revoil at Aix, France, on September 15, 1810; died on March 8, 1876; daughter of a Provençal family named Revoil; educated at home; married Hippolyte Colet (1808–1851, a musician), on December 5, 1834; children: (with Victor Cousin)* **Henriette Cousin**.

Selected works: Lui: roman contemporain (Lui: A View of Him, 1859).

Louise Colet was born in 1810 at Aix, France, of a middle-class Provençal family; she was the daughter of a wine merchant. Considered an outstanding beauty, she married the music composer and violinist, Hippolyte Colet, who was a professor of harmony and counterpoint at the Paris Conservatoire. The couple arrived in Paris in 1835. There, Colet concentrated on her poetry. Her volume of verse, *Fleurs du Midi,* appeared in 1836, followed by another *Penserosa* in 1839. She also wrote *La Jeunesse de Goethe* (1839), a one-act comedy; *Les Funerailles de Napoléon* (1840), a poem; and the novels *La Jeunesse de Mirabeau* (1841) and *Les Coeurs brisés* (1843). In 1837, she received a government pension. Two years later, she won the Academie Française poetry prize. Only the fifth woman winner since the prize's establishment in 1671, she drew national attention, including that of Academician Victor Cousin, later the minister of public instruction in France. Though her works would be endowed five or six times by the Institute, it is thought that she owed this distinction to the influence of Cousin rather than to the quality of her work. The criticism of her books and the prizes conferred on her by the Academy exasperated Colet, and in 1841 Paris was diverted by her counterattack on Alphonse Karr for his reviews in *Les Guêpes* (she stabbed him). In 1840, she had to defend an action brought against her by Madame **Récamier**'s heirs, after Colet published correspondence between Benjamin Constant and Récamier in her columns in the *Presse.*

A prolific writer of prose and verse, Colet is known more for her intimate connections with some of her famous contemporaries—Abel Villemain, Gustave Flaubert, and Victor Cousin—than for her own writing. Cousin and Colet became lovers, and she gave birth to a daughter, Henriette, whom Cousin publicly acknowledged as his and supported. In 1846, she met and began a liaison with Flaubert, 12 years her junior, which lasted for two years. Flaubert was an influential editor of her writing and later modeled his best-known fictional character, Madame Bovary, after her. When Colet became pregnant from a relationship with another man, both the affair with Flaubert and her marriage ended. The infant died shortly after birth. After her separation, Colet's government pension did not sustain her comfortably and fell far short when her husband Hippolyte returned to her, riddled with consumption (tuberculosis). She supported him until his death in April 1851.

Colet and Flaubert resumed their stormy relationship in 1851. Desperate to marry Flaubert but harshly rebuffed, the hot-tempered Colet be-

came resentful and published scathing novelized accounts of her lover while continuing to pursue him: *Une Histoire de soldat* (*A Soldier's Story,* 1856) and *La Servante* (*The Maidservant,* 1854). An affair with Alfred de Musset did not distract her from Flaubert, but did provide new material for a successful publication in 1859. *Lui: roman contemporain* (*Lui: A View of Him*) was in part a fictionalized account of the Musset-*George Sand affair, and in part a fictionalized account of Colet's life. **Francine du Plessix Gray** describes Colet as a "19th-century Erica Jong who recklessly splashed her life and loves across her poetry and prose."

Because of her tarnished reputation, as well as ill health, Colet moved to Italy in 1859, where she worked as a journalist and correspondent. She returned to France at the outbreak of the Franco-Prussian War and had some success giving lectures to sold-out audiences: she was an ardent supporter of the Paris Commune of 1871 and a fervent critic of the Catholic Church. In later years, says Gray, she became "a militant born-again moralist." Colet, who suffered from chronic respiratory difficulties, contracted anthrax and bronchitis. She died March 8, 1876, at the age of 65.

SOURCES:
Buck, Claire, ed. *The Bloomsbury Guide to Women's Literature.* NY: Prentice Hall, 1992.
Rose, Marilyn Gaddis. "Foreword." *Lui: A View of Him.* Athens, GA: University of Georgia Press, 1986.

SUGGESTED READING:
Gray, Francine du Plessix. *Rage and Fire: A Life of Louise Colet.* NY: Simon and Schuster, 1994.

Crista Martin,
Boston, Massachusetts

Colette (1381–1447)

Flemish religious reformer and saint. Name variations: Saint Coletté. Born Nicolette Boelet at Corbie, near Amiens, on January 13, 1381; died at Ghent on March 6, 1447; daughter of Robert Boelet (an artisan) and a mother who was dutifully religious.

Of the Franciscan order of the Poor Clares, Colette instituted reforms in its rules and administration. Eighteen when her parents died within a short time of each other, she was left under the guardianship of Dom de Roye, the Benedictine abbot of Corbie. Though de Roye wished to see her safely married, Colette preferred to seek the life of a religious, but she was soon disappointed. She lived in one convent then another, leaving both because she found the life too soft. She then entered the convent of the Poor Clares of

Moncel, near Pont-Saint-Maxence, but once again found the rules too lax for her needs.

On September 17, 1402, authorized by her guardian to take the vow of seclusion, she took up residence in a cell between two buttresses of Notre Dame de Corbie, accessed from the church by a grill. She lived there for three years. While there, St. Francis of Assisi and St. *Clare of Assisi appeared to her and commanded her to reform the Franciscan order. After an audience with Pope Benedict XIII, Colette was named superior general of all the convents of Poor Clares.

She traveled, worked miracles, endured suffering, and collaborated with St. Vincent Ferrer to eradicate schism. The Colettine reform spread through France, Spain, Flanders, and Savoy.

Colette (1873–1954)

French novelist, short-story writer, journalist, essayist, memoirist, actress and music-hall performer who created some of the most memorable female characters in literature. Name variations: Sidonie-Gabrielle Colette; Colette Willy; la baronne de Jouvenel. Born

Colette
(1873–1954)

in Saint-Sauveur-en-Puisaye (Yonne), France, on January 28, 1873; died in Paris on August 3, 1954; youngest child of Jules-Joseph Colette and Adèle-Eugenie Sidonie ("Sido") Landoy Robineau-Duclos Colette; married Henry ("Willy") Gauthier-Villars, in Saint-Sauveur, May 15, 1893; married Henry Bertrand Léon Robert de Jouvenel des Ursins (called "Sidi"), in Paris, on December 19, 1912; married Maurice Goudeket, in Paris, on April 3, 1935; children: one daughter, Colette de Jouvenel, known as "Bel-Gazou" (b. in Paris, July 3, 1913).

Began writing first of Claudine novels (1894); made debut as a mime (1906); had affair with "Missy" (1906–11); began career in journalism (1911); was first awarded the Legion of Honor (1920); opened Institute of Beauty in Paris (June 1932); made voyage to New York (June 1935); elected to Belgian Royal Academy of Language and Literature (1936); husband Maurice Goudeket arrested by Gestapo, in Paris (December 12, 1941); elected to Academy Goncourt (May 1945), voted president (1948); given a state funeral (August 7, 1954).

Selected publications: The Vagrant *(1912);* Barks and Purrs *(1913);* Cats, Dogs, and I *(1924);* Chéri *(1929);* Claudine at School *(1930);* Mitsou *(1930);* The Gentle Libertine *(1931);* The Other One *(1931);* Young Lady of Paris *(published in England as* Claudine in Paris; *1931);* A Lesson in Love *(1932);* Recaptured *(1932);* The Ripening *(1932);* The Last of Chéri *(1932);* Morning Glory *(1932);* The Pure and the Impure *(1933);* The Innocent Wife *(1934);* The Indulgent Husband *(1935);* Duo *(1935);* Cat *(1936);* Mother of Claudine *(1937).*

"If I were famous, I would know," Colette once remarked to her daughter. Without doubt, she was famous, and infamous too. An innocent provincial village girl, Colette had three husbands, a daughter, and several women lovers; she was vulnerable and resilient, audacious and disciplined, maligned and admired. And she created some of the most unforgettable female characters in French literature. "To know Colette, the woman, one need only read her novels," a friend stated. "She tells more about herself to those who read her than she ever told to those who knew her in person."

Born in the Burgundian village of Saint-Sauveur, Sidonie-Gabrielle Colette was the youngest of four children. Her pragmatic, strong mother Adèle-Eugenie Sidonie Robineau-Duclos, known as Sido, was a widow with two children when she married Captain Jules-Joseph Colette, a graduate of the military academy of St-Cyr who had lost a leg in the Crimean War. The family was financially comfortable for many years, but Captain Colette made poor investments and was forced to sell much of his wife's property and to borrow money. Colette's secure and stable childhood ended abruptly when she was 12; her strange, morose half-sister Juliette married a young doctor, and the family, unable to provide the dowry as stated in the marriage contract, was forced to sell their house and furniture at public auction. Colette's idyllic childhood was shattered by the humiliation of poverty. The family moved to Châtillon-Coligny and lived with Colette's half-brother, Achille Robineau-Duclos, a doctor. If Colette clung to memories of the halcyon days of her youth in Saint-Sauveur, her brother Léopold lived in the minutia of the past, recalling the sound of the rusty gate in Sido's garden.

Captain Colette, a man with literary pretensions, frequently corresponded with an acquaintance from his military days, Albert Gauthier-Villars, a science publisher in Paris whose son Henry visited the Colettes, fell in love with Sidonie-Gabrielle, and eventually asked for her hand. Sido did not entirely approve of this Parisian sophisticate who already had an illegitimate son, was "highly-sexed and patently a man of the world," and 14 years older than his fiancée. Known as Willy, he "wrote" reviews of literature and music for various Paris papers. Actually, he retained numerous "assistants" who wrote articles that Willy edited and signed as his own. Colette later toiled in "the factory," as she called it, writing best-selling books (the Claudine series) that Willy also claimed as his own. Willy's charm was matched by his physical repulsiveness: "M. Willy was not huge, he was bulbous," Colette recalled. "It has been said that he bore a marked resemblance to Edward VII. To do justice to a less flattering but no less august truth, I would say that, in fact, the likeness was to Queen Victoria."

In May 1893, 20-year-old Colette married the man she admitted she never really knew. In her memoirs (*My Apprenticeships*, 1936), a mature Colette remembered: "My life as a young woman began with this freebooter. . . . Before that—except for my parents' ruin, the money gone, the furniture sold by public auction—it had been roses all the way. But what would I have done with everlasting roses?" Willy carried off his young bride to a cramped, dark apartment in Paris, a city, she said, that filled her with dread. Her response to the bottle-green and chocolate walls, to the "ugly dream" of marital sex, and the alien atmosphere of Paris, was to become ill for two months. Colette was desperately unhappy, but she resolved "that whatever happened I must hide the truth from Sido. I kept my word." If Colette ever had any illusions about marriage, they were destroyed when she received an anonymous letter that led her to **Charlotte Kinceler**'s apartment where she found Willy and his mistress. Without uttering a word, Colette left. Curiously, she came to like the woman and learned from her "my first notions of tolerance and concealment and the possibility of coming to terms with an enemy." When a few years later Charlotte committed suicide, Colette sadly noted, "She was twenty-six years old and had saved money." Colette's "girlhood" had died too.

Willy may have been a failure as a husband, but through him Colette was introduced to the Parisian intellectual elite and the brilliant café society of the Belle Epoque, and she became a writer. Her "insecure, useless life," as she described it, was changed forever when Willy insisted that she write down recollections of her school days. *Claudine at School* appeared in 1900 under Willy's name alone and sold 40,000 copies in two months. Though considered by some to be "wickedly licentious," it was not pornographic. *Claudine* became a sensation as clothing, soaps, lotions, and other products capitalized on the schoolgirl image. Three more Claudine novels were followed by two works based on the female character, Minne, all attributed to "Willy." Colette's literary career had been launched. Adapted for the stage, Claudine was personified by the young actress **Polaire**. To generate publicity, Willy coerced Polaire and Colette into appearing with him in public dressed identically as Claudines, intimating a lesbian bond between the two young women. In fact, Colette's name was already associated with some of the most noted lesbians in Paris, relations encouraged by Willy to promote public scandal and attention.

By 1905, their marriage was over. Locked in her room each day and forced to write, Colette developed a career, and living in Paris she acquired a number of illustrious friends. Her interest in the theater and music hall prompted her to take lessons in mime from Georges Wague. Willy encouraged her to go on tour with Wague's company, a not too subtle "notice to quit" the house, as Colette realized. "While I was dreaming of escape, someone beside me had been dreaming of conveniently showing me the door." In February 1906, Colette made her debut as a mime in the role of a faun. At the same time, she became the mistress of the Marquise **Mathilde de Belboeuf**, known as Missy, great-granddaughter of the Empress **Josephine** (Napoleon I's wife), descendant of Louis XV of France, and a transvestite. Such affairs conducted with some discretion were tolerated, even fashionable, among the Parisian *beau monde*. But Colette, having already appeared half-naked on stage in several mimes, caused outrage and a near riot at the Moulin Rouge theater. In "Dream of Egypt," a pantomime about an Egyptian mummy come to life, Colette slowly emerged from her wrappings to receive a passionate kiss from an Egyptian scholar, played by Missy. A police order forbade a second performance.

From 1906 to 1911, Colette made her living in music halls and the café-concert circuit, in Paris and on tour. She continued to live with Missy and to write novels based on her experiences. *Tendrils of the Vine* (1908) describes her affair with Missy, and *The Vagabond* (1910), an autobiographical account of her music-hall years, was nominated for the prestigious Prix Goncourt. Scandal and recognition as an accomplished writer defined Colette as a notable public figure. Her tempestuous personal life became even more complex when she added Auguste Hériot, heir to a department store fortune, to her ménage. Polaire's former lover, Hériot was doggedly devoted to Colette for two years and served as a model for a character in *The Vagabond*. Involved with both Missy and Hériot, Colette continued to perform on stage, and to write. But at age 38, Colette entered a new phase in her career and personal life.

I am no thinker, I have no *pensées* (thoughts). . . . Perhaps the most praiseworthy thing about me is that I have known how to write like a woman.

—Colette

This third career, in journalism, commenced in December 1910, when she began writing regular articles for the leading Paris newspaper, *Le Matin,* using a pseudonym; for many readers, the name Colette was associated with a libidinous lifestyle. Her reputation did not prevent the editor-in-chief of *Le Matin* from becoming involved with his talented contributor. Baron Henry de Jouvenel (called "Sidi") was "handsome . . . elegant, charming, and highly intelligent," father of two sons, one (Bertrand) from his ex-wife, the second (Renaud) from his current mistress, the **Countess de Comminges**, who threatened to kill Colette. But this melodramatic episode quickly passed, and Comminges and

Hériot sought mutual consolation on a six-week cruise. The shuffle among lovers never interfered with Colette's pursuit of her careers.

In September 1912, Colette's mother Sido died of cancer. Colette's reaction was peculiar and evoked charges of a lack of feeling. She refused to wear mourning or to attend the funeral. Sido had been the bedrock of her daughter's life, but Colette seldom dwelt on the past, or those who inhabited it. Her sister Juliette's suicide in 1908, the death of her brothers and her first two husbands likewise elicited no reaction, no sense of loss or mortality. To Colette, death was no more than a "banal defeat." Nearly 40 years old, Colette's life suddenly changed; she was pregnant. In December 1912, she married Henry de Jouvenel, and six months later gave birth to a daughter, **Colette de Jouvenel**, known as Bel-Gazou (beautiful gazelle). Marriage and motherhood limited Colette's freedom; in *The Shackle* (1913), she describes love as the shackle for "one is no longer 'free'." Instead, as she wrote, "I have become [Sidi's] watcher, anchored at his side forever." No doubt Colette was in love with the dynamic de Jouvenel, but was she capable of subordinating her desires and needs to those of a man? Colette's stepson, Renaud de Jouvenel, accused her of calumniating men in her novels, portraying them as "stupid, irresponsible and incomprehensible." "She is so inward-looking that she does not see him," he concluded, and her "monstrous ego" prevents her from loving them. Indeed, in a stinging reproof, he characterized Colette as "intellectually lesbian," as "fascinated by homosexuality," and having "almost exclusively feminine friendships."

Colette's additional career as lecturer ended abruptly in August 1914, when war broke out. Her daughter was sent to live at Castel-Novel, the Jouvenel family estate in Corrèze. Sidi enlisted in the army, while Colette remained in Paris working as a night nurse in a military hospital and writing newspaper articles. In December, she joined her husband at Verdun for three months; she also served as war correspondent in Italy at various times in 1915–16. War and separation strained their marriage as did de Jouvenel's attraction to other women. However, Colette and Sidi continued to work at *Le Matin*, and, in 1919, he made her literary editor of the paper. That same year, Colette began writing one of her best works, *Chéri*. Chéri is one of the few well-developed male characters in her fiction, an amalgam of men Colette knew: a fragile, rather effete young man who has a love affair with Léa, a strong, older woman who in many ways re-sembled Colette herself. Acclaimed as one of France's most distinguished writers, Colette was awarded the Legion of Honor by the French government.

"What I write comes to pass," Colette noted, and in the summer of 1920 the plot of *Chéri* was played out at Colette's house (Rozven) on the coast of Brittany; Colette had an affair with her 16-year-old stepson, Bertrand de Jouvenel. Her account of the affair provided the plot for *The Ripening Seed* (1923). Meanwhile, Sidi pursued a political career and was elected to the French Senate. He also served as French representative to the League of Nations in Geneva. A succession of mistresses and his demanding career widened the rift in their marriage. Colette was upset, but she was not an innocent victim, for she too was unfaithful. Eventually, Sidi became aware that his son and wife were lovers, and in the autumn of 1923, while Colette was on a lecture tour, Sidi "left without a word." Personal turmoil never affected Colette's literary production, however. *Chéri* and *The Vagabond* were adapted for the stage, a book of memories of her mother was completed, and a sequel to *Chéri* was begun. Further, she resumed acting and continued working for *Le Matin* until 1923. Despite her unconventional lifestyle, Colette's literary reputation grew. She never intentionally wrote to shock or titillate, but some critics and readers were offended by her realistic portrayal of male/female relations: "Can't you ever write a book that isn't about love or adultery . . . or half-incestuous goings-on? Aren't there other things in life?" Sidi had asked. But love, in all its manifestations, was what interested Colette. In her life, and in her novels, she "eagerly picked the fruits of the earth, without discriminating those which were forbidden," as Bertrand de Jouvenel saw it.

Colette's preoccupation with love in her writing was reflected in her personal life: "love has never been a question of age," Colette said in an interview. One of her biographers states that Colette's affair with Bertrand "taught her that she needed a man who was younger than herself, a man whose career was manifestly second to her own, a man who would devote himself entirely to her service." At age 52, Colette found such a man, Maurice Goudeket, who was 35. They met through mutual friends, were lovers for ten years, married for 19 more, forever "best friends." Colette was a vagabond, constantly moving from one lover-husband to another, from one place to another. After selling her house in Brittany, she bought another near

Saint-Tropez, and frequently changed apartments in Paris. If Colette's life as wife and lover, and as writer and performer, was unconventional, her role as mother verged on the unacceptable. To Colette and de Jouvenel, the pursuit of satisfying careers and love affairs left their daughter largely out of their lives. Bel-Gazou, who bore a strong resemblance to her father, resented her mother's lack of attention and overtly disliked Goudeket. Like many successful artists, Colette was self-centered, unwilling to sacrifice her career for a daughter who represented a past she preferred to forget. Colette was only secondarily a mother, wife, or lover; she was Colette, "both legally and familiarly. . . . I now have only one name, which is my own."

Writing was always laborious for her, and she complained that it made her ill and bored her. But she persisted because, she said, "I do feel the honour of my profession . . . [though] I never work easily." This may explain in part Colette's fictional characters who are based on people she knew and reflect her own prejudices and attitudes. Henry de Jouvenel and his various mistresses (in *The Other One*, 1929) and Colette's gay friends (in *The Pure and the Impure*, 1932) were thus made immortal. The latter, "a study of sexual inversion," produced a public furor and was withdrawn from serialization after only four installments. Colette considered it her best book—an opinion not universally shared by critics.

Eager to supplement her income during the worldwide depression of the 1930s, Colette opened an Institute of Beauty in June 1932, in a fashionable section of Paris. Her skill with words did not transfer into a skill for applying cosmetics to her customers, and, despite her dedication to the enterprise, it closed in 1933.

Though Colette had "a horror of writing," she never contemplated giving up the profession that made her famous. While running her business, she had written one of her most original works, *The Cat* (1933). A love triangle involving a man, his cat, and his young bride serves as the vehicle for Colette to express her love for animals; the young woman competes with the cat for the love of her husband, and she loses. "Our perfect companions never have fewer than four feet," Colette wrote. Voted "the greatest living writer of French prose" by French writers in 1935, Colette's place in literature was secured when she was elected to the Royal Academy of Belgium. Membership in the prestigious French Academy would elude her due to her gender; founded in 1635, no woman would be elected until *Marguerite Yourcenar in 1981.

Colette and Goudeket maintained separate residences and avoided the subject of marriage. But when invited to write an account of the maiden voyage of the *Normandie* to New York, they decided to marry rather than create a scandal in the more prudish United States. A ten-minute civil ceremony in Paris united Colette and her "best friend." Colette was not well-known in the States, but she enjoyed the sights of New York and the attention she received.

Bel-Gazou's "unsettled life" had caused her mother some concern. Moreover, Bel-Gazou's marriage to the dull Dr. Denis Dausse in August 1935 (Colette did not attend), ended in disaster. Two months later, they divorced. Colette blamed the breakup on "physical revulsion" on her daughter's part; Henry de Jouvenel cited boredom as the compelling reason. "I left many women because of that," he told Bel-Gazou. Many years later, Renaud de Jouvenel asked Bel-Gazou why she had married at all. "To normalize myself," she told him. From this remark, he speciously concluded that "she must have begun very early to have relations with girls or women." At least one of Colette's biographers agreed that "Colette had damaged her more than she knew." There is no question but that Colette herself was bisexual—"There *are* no unisexuals," she had written to a friend.

In early 1936, Colette published her memoirs of Willy, her first marriage, and on becoming a writer (*My Apprenticeships*). Her often poignant observations reveal much about her novitiate as wife and writer. Married to a "man I never understood," she admitted that "to have worked for him and beside him taught me to dread, not to know him better." Unhappy, exploited, and lonely, Colette was, however, "learning to live. . . . To endure without happiness and not to droop, not to pine, is a pursuit in itself, you might almost say a profession." Willy had also taught her that discipline was a virtue, and she was grateful for that. Time and distance had not dimmed her recollections of marriage where she discovered that "the worst thing in a woman's life [is] her first man, the only one you die of." Colette states frankly that she "did not think highly" of the four Claudine books she wrote under Willy's tutelage and had not changed her mind. But she still resented that he had sold all rights to the books without consulting her and had kept the proceeds.

Despite being promoted to Commander of the Legion of Honor and initiated into the Belgian Royal Academy, Colette retained doubts about her talent; she prided herself on her self-doubt: "When a writer loses self-doubt, the time has come to lay aside his pen." This is not false modesty, for Goudeket confirms that Colette was constantly amazed and delighted by public appreciation of her work.

At age 65, Colette finally relinquished her nomadic ways, moved into an apartment overlooking the charming courtyard of the Palais Royal in Paris, and sold her house near Saint-Tropez. Filled with *nouveau riche* and celebrities, the resort town had impinged on her privacy. Further, Europe appeared poised for war, and its proximity to Italy was dangerous.

After war was declared on September 3, 1939, Colette began to broadcast overseas for Paris Mondial, describing Parisian daily life. In June 1941, before German troops entered Paris, Colette, Goudeket, and her longtime maid and companion, Pauline, fled by car to the de Jouvenel château in Corrèze, now owned by Bel-Gazou. Safe but restless, they returned to occupied Paris in September. "I am used to spending

From the movie Gigi, *starring Louis Jordan, Leslie Caron, and Maurice Chevalier.*

my wars in Paris," Colette explained. Her apartment and the Palais-Royal were Colette's retreat in the empty, hungry city where she recreated her own "little province." Increasingly immobile due to crippling arthritis, her world was shrinking. Two novellas, *Looking Backwards* and *From My Window,* reflect her pensive mood, the need to reconsider times past. The horror of the German occupation appeared at her door at 7:30 AM on Friday, December 12, 1941, when the Gestapo arrested Maurice Goudeket who was Jewish. Colette contacted everyone who might have influence with the German authorities, including French collaborators. Without explanation, Maurice was released in early February 1942 and soon left to stay with friends in the unoccupied zone of France. During the war years, Colette wrote her last fictional work, *Gigi,* later a successful stage play and movie. Set in the late 19th century, an age of famous courtesans, the story is about love and youth, with a happy ending. Several years later, Colette was spending a summer in Monte Carlo when she met a young actress doing a scene for a French film. "There is our

Gigi for America," she told Maurice; *__Audrey Hepburn__ consequently played the role in the comedy on Broadway.

The liberation of Paris in August 1944 brought a rapid return to normal living. A few days before the war ended in Europe (May 1945), Colette was elected to the Academy Goncourt, only the second woman ever to be so honored; she became its president in 1948. After a series of medical treatments for arthritis, Colette was able to attend a revival of her play _Chéri_ and began to assemble her voluminous writings for the publication of her collected work, a rare distinction for a living author. Colette also received the star of "Grand Officier" of the Legion of Honor, the highest rank ever accorded a woman. And as France's most eminent literary figure, she was given the Gold Medal from the City of Paris and an award from the American ambassador.

Fiction was replaced with four books of reminiscences and reflections on the past, on Saint-Sauveur and life in Paris. She conceded that "forty-five years in Paris haven't made me anything but a provincial, searching twenty _arrondissements_ [districts] and two river banks for her lost province." But Colette had created her own "province," described in _From My Window._ She sustained a zest for living that characterized her 81 years: "Throughout my existence I have studied flowering more than any other manifestation of life," she told a group of university students. "There is never a time when discoveries end . . . and I shall cease to flower when I cease to live." To Colette observing and recording the wonders of nature and of humanity constituted living. "We never look enough," she lamented, "never exactly enough, never passionately enough." Just before she died on a warm and sultry day in early August 1954, some swallows flew past her window: "Look, Maurice, look!" were her last words. As one critic wrote, "One doesn't read Colette. One sees what she sees. One breathes what she breathes; one touches what she touches."

Colette was the first Frenchwoman ever given a State funeral; ceremonies were held in the court of honor of the Palais-Royal (just beneath her window). There would be no religious service, no priest officiating at the funeral. Archbishop of Paris Feltin refused Maurice's request for the service to be held in the Église (church) Saint-Roch, on the grounds that Colette had been twice divorced. Colette was buried in a private service in Père Lachaise cemetery in Paris, among the most renowned figures of France.

The Place Colette, located at the entry to the Palais-Royal, celebrates her memory, her lasting presence in the city.

In 1952, Colette had attended the première of a documentary film of her life. "What a wonderful life I've had!" she declared, "What a pity I didn't realize it sooner."

SOURCES:
Belles Saisons: A Colette Scrapbook. Edited by Robert Phelps. NY: Farrar, Straus and Giroux, 1978.
Colette. _My Apprenticeships._ Translated by Helen Beauclerk. NY: Farrar, Straus and Giroux, 1978.
Crosland, Margaret. _Colette: The Difficulty of Loving._ Indianapolis, IN: Bobbs-Merrill, 1973.
Richardson, Johanna. _Colette._ NY: Dell, 1983.

SUGGESTED READING:
Colette. _Earthly Paradise._ Edited by Robert Phelps. NY: Farrar, Straus and Giroux, 1966.
Cottrell, Robert D. _Colette._ NY: Frederick Ungar, 1978.
Lottman, Herbert. _Colette: A Life._ Boston, MA: Little, Brown, 1981.
Sarde, Michèle. _Colette: Free and Fettered._ Translated by Richard Miller. NY: William Morrow, 1980.

RELATED MEDIA:
Colette (play), starring __Zoe Caldwell__, opened at the Ellen Stewart Theater in New York City in May 1970.
Gigi was adapted as a French film in 1950, starring __Daniele Delorme__ and directed by *__Jacqueline Audry__; adapted as a stageplay by *__Anita Loos__ and presented on Broadway in 1951, starring Audrey Hepburn; produced as musical by MGM, 1958, starring __Leslie Caron__, Maurice Chevalier, and *__Hermione Gingold__, music by Alan Jay Lerner.
Mitsou was also brought to the screen by Jacqueline Audry in 1957, again with Delorme in the title role.

__Jeanne A. Ojala__, Professor of History, University of Utah, Salt Lake City, Utah

Coligny, Henriette de (1618–1683)

_French writer and poet. Name variations: Comtesse de la Suze; countess of La Suze. Born Henriette de Coligny in 1618; died in 1683; eldest daughter of Gaspard III de Coligny, maréchal de Châtillon (1584–1646, a marshal of France under Louis XIII and nephew of *__Louise de Coligny__); great granddaughter of Gaspard II de Coligny (1519–1572, an admiral and leader of the Huguenots); married Thomas Hamilton, earl of Haddington (died one year later); married compte de La Suze._

With Paul Pellisson and others, Henriette de Coligny wrote _Recueil de pièces galantes_ (also known as _Recueil La Suze-Pellisson_) in 1663; it became one of the most popular miscellanies of 17th-century verse and prose. Born a Protestant, Henriette turned Catholic. Soon after, her marriage to the comte de La Suze, notorious for his drunken debauches and jealous temperament, was over. The countess is said to have been a cosmopolitan beauty who corresponded with Balzac and Saint-Evremond; her salon was a kind of extension of Hôtel de Rambouillet.

Coligny, Louise de (1555–1620)

Princess of Orange and countess of Nassau. Name variations: Luise of Bourbon-Montpensier. Born in 1555 (some sources cite 1546); died at the Château de Fontainebleau on November 15, 1620; daughter of Gaspard II de Coligny, Maréchal de Châtillon (1519–1572, an admiral and leader of the Huguenots), and Charlotte de Laval (d. 1568); granddaughter of ◄❧ Louise de Montmorency, Madame de Châtillon (fl. 1498–1525); sister of François de Coligny (1557–1591, a follower of Henry IV) and aunt of Gaspard III (1584–1646, a marshal of France under Louis XIII and father of *Henriette de Coligny); married Charles de Téligny (who died in the Massacre of St. Bartholmew); became fourth wife of William I the Silent (1533–1584), prince of Orange, count of Nassau (r. 1544–1584), stadholder of Holland, Zealand, and Utrecht (r. 1572–1584), on April 12, 1583 (assassinated in 1584); children: Frederick Henry (1584–1647), prince of Orange (r. 1625–1647, who married *Amelia of Solms); and others.

Louise de Coligny was born into an important and influential French family. Her father Gaspard II de Coligny, maréchal de Châtillon (1519–1572), an admiral of France, had served honorably and courageously until he was defeated and imprisoned in Spain. While a captive, he converted to Protestantism and became a joint leader of the Huguenots with Louis I, prince of Condé, in 1560. Gaspard's influence over Charles IX, king of France, earned him the enmity of Catholics and the dukes of Guise.

As queen regent for Charles IX, *Catherine de Medici hoped to improve the volatile relations with the Huguenots by offering her daughter *Margaret of Valois in marriage to Calvinist Henry of Navarre (the future Henry IV). The wedding festivities were marked by a general uneasiness, until an assassination attempt against a Calvinist leader sparked the infamous St. Bartholomew's Day Massacre of the Huguenots in Paris in 1572. That day, 3,000 Huguenots were killed in Paris alone, including Louise de Coligny's father and her first husband Charles de Téligny.

Louise fled France and took refuge in Switzerland. While spending a life in exile away from her children, she wrote over 200 letters to her family and influential Protestants asking for their help, letters that reflected her profound suf-

fering. In 1583, she married William I the Silent, prince of Orange; he was assassinated the following year. From afar, Louise and her brother François were devoted followers of Henry IV, king of France, in establishing the Protestant faith. Following Henry's assassination in 1610, Louise returned to France, but was soon back at The Hague. Ten years later, she died in France at the Château de Fontainebleau.

SUGGESTED READING:
Marchegay, P., ed. *Correspondence de Louise de Coligny.* 1887.

Colledge, Cecilia (1920—)

British figure skater. Born on November 28, 1920, in England.

Invented many features of figure skating, including the parallel spin, the layback, the one-foot axle; was the first to perform a double jump in competition; won a silver medal in figure skating in the 1936 Garmisch-Partenkirchen Olympics, narrowly losing to Sonja Henie who took the gold; won the World Championship (1937).

Cecilia Colledge was an extremely inventive skater. The first to perform the parallel spin or "camel," the layback, and the one-foot axle, she was also the first to execute a double jump in competition. Competitive skating was initially limited to carving precise figures on the ice. Skaters soon tired of this rigid routine, however, and aspired to the moves of ballet artists, leaping and turning in the air. Colledge performed the first free-skating program to a specific piece of music, choreographing her moves. Her model was the American skater, *Theresa Weld, who caused a commotion in 1920 when she included "unfeminine" jumps on the ice, including a salchow, in her program. Judges often warned women to "control" their athletic prowess on the ice, but this advice was usually ignored.

Cecilia Colledge began skating at age 11 and was the youngest Olympian in the 1932 Lake Placid Winter Olympics where she placed eighth. In 1933, she was a close second to *Sonja Henie for the European championship. In 1935, Colledge won the silver medal in the world championships and the first of eight consecutive national titles. She was British national champion from 1935–39 and from 1946–48. In the 1936 Berlin Games, following the compulsory figures, she was just 3.6 points behind Henie, the closest anyone had come to the incomparable skater for some time. Henie, who barely beat out Colledge

❧►
Louise de Montmorency (fl. 1498–1525).
See Margaret of Angoulême for sidebar.

in the freestyle with a score of 5.8 to Colledge's 5.7, took the gold and Colledge the silver.

In 1937, after Henie's retirement, Colledge finally won the World Championship, Henie's title for the previous ten years. In 1951, Colledge immigrated to the United States and taught at the Skating Club of Boston, which has formed so many champions. She was elected to figure skating's Hall of Fame in 1980. Although Sonja Henie remains better known, many of the moves that continue to thrill fans were originated by the innovative Cecilia Colledge.

Karin Loewen Haag,
Athens, Georgia

Collett, Camilla (1813–1895)

Pioneering Norwegian feminist and Norway's first feminist-realist novelist. Pronunciation: KOL-let. Born (Jacobine) Camilla Wergeland on January 23, 1813, in the small Norwegian city of Kristiansand; died on March 6, 1895; daughter of Nicolai (a cleric) and Alette Dorothea (Thaulow) Wergeland; sister of poet Henrik Wergeland (1808–1845); educated at home until 1827, when she spent two years at the Herrnhuters' school in Christiansfeld, Germany; married Peter Jonas Collett (a lawyer), July 14, 1841 (died, December 1851, age 38); children: four sons, Robert (b. 1842), Alf (b. 1844), Oscar (b. 1845), Emil (b. 1848).

Had first meeting with the poet Johan Sebastian Welhaven (early 1830); traveled on the Continent (1834 and 1836–37); published first independently written article (1842); published first (and only) novel (1854–55); awarded a literary gold medal (1863); made first honorary member of Norsk Kvinnesaksforening (The Norwegian Women's Cause, 1884).

Selected writings: "Nogle Strikketøjsbetraktninger" ("Musings while Knitting"—a collection of articles first published in Den Constitutionelle; 1862); Amtmandens Døttre (The District Governor's Daughters; her only novel, published in two parts 1854 and 1855); Fortællinger (stories; 1860); I de lange Nætter (In the Long Nights; 1862); Sidste Blade (Last Leaves; 1868, 1872, 1873); Fra de Stummes Lejr (From the Camp of the Mutes; 1877); Mot Strømmen (Against the Current; I: 1879, II: 1885).

It was the end of January 1830 and in Christiania (as the Norwegian capital of Oslo was then called) the streets were cold and dreary. Seventeen-year-old Camilla Wergeland pushed open the gate to the wealthy merchant Herre's townhouse and was about to ascend the steps when she heard the voices of two men who were just leaving. One voice belonged to the son of the house, a devoted friend of hers. The other man's voice, resonant and with a Bergen accent, was that of a stranger. Shyly, she hid behind the corner of the house while the two men passed.

The young girl guessed that the visitor was the poet Johan Sebastian Welhaven (1807–1873), already at 22 enjoying a considerable reputation among the capital's intelligentsia. But although the incident impressed itself on her mind, she had no way of guessing that he would be the catalyst for her long battle for open, honest relations between men and women, and for women's rights in society. Most Norwegians know that the torment of her protracted relationship with Welhaven was made worse because her family held publicly opposed views to those of his circle. What is often overlooked, however, is that the ideas propounded by Welhaven and his friends happened to express her own opinions. And those opinions had little to do with love and everything to do with her own character and talents, with her background and education, and with historical developments in Norway.

Camilla Collett was born Camilla Wergeland in the small town of Kristiansand in 1813, at the southern end of a country that stretches from about 58°N all the way to 71°N, with a landscape of stark, soul-searing contrasts. At the time of her birth, the Norwegian economy was largely pre-industrial, "unless one counts the large number of small distilleries," as the historian R.G. Popperwell puts it. But great change was in the making, and Collett's writing came to reflect closely the altering economic and cultural patterns and the social dislocations she observed while her country lumbered towards industrialization. She saw the plight of those whom progress did not seem to touch, of the people who remained fettered by poverty, ignorance, gender, or sheer physical isolation.

To understand the independence of Camilla Collett's mind and the forces behind the bitter political and cultural debates that became a part of her daily existence, we must consider both Norway's precarious economic position and the high feelings generated by the provisions made at the Peace of Kiel on January 14, 1814, after Napoleon's final defeat at Leipzig.

In 1807, at the height of the Napoleonic wars, the British had reacted to an impending Dano-Norwegian alliance with Napoleon by bombarding Copenhagen and forcing the Danes to hand over their fleet. When the Danish government declared war on Britain and solidarity with Napoleon, British warships blocked Norway's access to the open sea. Not only was shipping essential to the Norwegian economy, but the country was dependent on import for basic necessities such as grain. A crop failure in Norway in both 1807 and 1808 resulted in widespread famine, and the year before Camilla was born, both the crops and the fishing had failed. Norwegian bankruptcies were frequent between 1813 and 1816.

In a series of moves designed by the victorious powers to punish Denmark and strengthen Sweden (now ruled by King Charles XIV John, a politically astute former marshal of the defeated Napoleon), Norway's long union with Denmark was dissolved, and the country was placed under Swedish hegemony instead. This move infuriated those Norwegian political leaders who felt greater kinship with the Danes than with the Swedes, whose French-born king they distrusted. But it pleased those who (like Camilla's father) saw the alliance as a change from Danish oppression and a way to remain in the major powers' good graces, and who believed that their new Constitution's provisions for Norwe-

Camilla Collett

gian decision-making would prevent the country from becoming too unequal a partner in the union with Sweden.

Camilla's father, the cleric Nicolai Wergeland, was one of the signatories to that Constitution at Eidsvoll on May 17, 1814, a day the Norwegians still celebrate as the beginning of their modern nationhood. This made him a public figure; so it created quite a stir when, two years later, he published a treatise in which he joined those who were outraged by the Treaty of Kiel's provision that Norway should help pay the war debt of Denmark-Norway, and in which he showed his staunch belief in Norwegian national uniqueness, thought to manifest itself especially in the peasant culture.

His private and public convictions proved fateful for his family. When Camilla was barely four years old, he obtained a living at Eidsvoll parsonage, where he so recently had helped midwife the birth of a self-conscious new Norway, and where his passionate, romantic nature envisioned a perfect setting for his own work as well as for the rearing of his family.

But nationhood had been conceived and baptized in the heady rush of a northern spring as well as in the flattering glow of a late-blooming and peculiarly Norwegian national romanticism. Dean Wergeland soon found the peasants crude and the physical and intellectual isolation of inland Eidsvoll (a long day's ride north of Oslo) devastating, and he grew dark and brooding. Little Camilla witnessed an even greater change in her mother **Alette Wergeland**, now responsible for a big rural household and deprived of almost all human contact outside her family. In "Night Six" of the autobiographical work *I de lange Nætter,* Camilla writes of her mother: "Thus she vegetated next to Father, the two of them forming the greatest contrasts ever devised by Nature, without absorbing anything from him. He protected her in the same way an overhanging cliff protects and shelters the quivering flower it also deprives of sunshine."

Collett never raised the issue of whether her mother had been consulted about the move to Eidsvoll. She was not concerned with the division of power between a man and wife who had chosen to live together, as her parents had done, but with every woman's lack of power within a social, cultural, and economic framework that made it difficult for women to follow their hearts and control their own marital fate in the first place. It has often and accurately been noted that Collett addressed a problem especial-

ly affecting women of her own privileged class. Some see this as regrettable insularity on her part, while others consider it honest reporting of the *Jane Austen school.

Austen and other 19th-century novelists taught that solitude was prized by young women who needed time away from the prying, censorious eyes that followed them everywhere, and Camilla Collett's writing was no different. But she never romanticized the rural isolation that was the lot of so many Norwegians, for she knew the stress of living in small, isolated communities. The fear of gossip may truly govern people's lives, as Collett later demonstrated in *The District Governor's Daughters.* Even with a modern population of almost 4.5 million people, Norway is a sparsely inhabited country. At the time Collett wrote her novel, the country had scarcely 1.5 million, and only about 163,000 of those lived in the urban areas that had chiefly grown up around waterborne trade.

> *You're a man.* You're free. You may seize life and be active, you may create things, in a word: you may *live!*
> —Camilla Collett in a letter to her brother

At the beginning of the 19th century, the ancient fish-trading city of Bergen still had more people than the capital's population of around 12,000. Compared with most of the rest of the country, however, both cities were bustling metropolitan areas. In great part owing to the Constitution's stipulation that *Stortinget* (Parliament) was to meet in Christiania, the capital began to grow as a political, cultural, and economic center during precisely those years when young Camilla gained her footing among the city's intellectual and mercantile elite. Both her fiction and her nonfiction reflect these changes.

In rural as well as urban areas of Norway, the literary climate during Camilla's formative years was lit by the rays of late romanticism from Danish and German writers such as Oehlenschläger, Novalis, Tieck and Steffens. In addition, a uniquely Norwegian brand of national romanticism in art and literature flourished. But Aagot Benterud, a modern biographer of Collett, notes that a growing admiration for the classical style, which stressed simplicity, virile strength, restraint, and control, ran parallel to the current of late Continental romanticism in Norway in the years after 1814. Females were expected to be passive, and it was a terrible breach of etiquette for a woman to show tender feelings for a man before he had revealed serious intentions. Collett later named this constraint the "Law of Femininity" and claimed that it blighted all her adult life.

While Dean Collett and his wife were languishing in their rural existence, their children enjoyed great physical freedom at the Eidsvoll parsonage, and household discipline was haphazard. Until she was about 13, Camilla led a rough-and-tumble life interspersed with bouts of tutoring by her father and the teachers secured for her brothers. This was because primary education, until the School Act of 1827, was left entirely to local initiative and private exertion, while any family that could afford it sent their children abroad for their secondary education until a Latin School for boys and the Nissen School for Girls were founded in Christiania in 1843 and 1848 respectively.

Camilla's often bizarre tutors furnished her with a rogue's gallery that any writer would envy, but they did not provide the polish Dean Wergeland wanted for his beautiful youngest daughter, his pride and joy. In 1826, he enrolled her in Miss Pharo's school for girls in the capital, where Camilla felt very much out of place. Later (1837), she explained in a letter to her close friend **Emilie Diriks** that she and her siblings had grown up in all innocence with faults that came home to roost when they finally were turned loose among other people.

After a year, Camilla was sent to Christiansfeld in Schleswig, to a school run by the Herrnhuters, a sect of the Moravian Brethren. Here she stayed for two years. Private correspondence shows that those were difficult years for the shy country girl from Norway, although she did well in her studies. Her later reminiscences dwell more on friendships formed and on her gratitude for this first exposure to Continental culture and sophistication. Here, she began a lifelong journey of self-discovery. In "Night Eight" of *I de lange Nætter,* she describes her unformed self just at the outset of this period: "I was . . . a good-natured, obedient, well-brought up child, insignificant to look at and shapeless in all my ways, and I understood the secret of my innermost self about as much as I understand mathematics to this day."

A far from robust child, she jeopardized her health when betting with her school friends that she could live for a week on food purchased for four shillings a day, but she discovered in the process that she possessed pride, fortitude, and willpower, all qualities that stood her in good stead later. In every way, her years at Christiansfeld had a profound influence on her later development. She remained deeply religious all her life, although without much outward demonstration of piety. According to her son Alf, she never rid herself of a tendency to use German words and phrases; a modern reader will certainly find her prose difficult at times. Most important, her experiences and mental horizon were expanded beyond Norway. This made her less willing to accept status quo back home, and better equipped to explore new solutions to what she regarded as age-old and peculiarly Norwegian problems.

She returned to Eidsvoll in 1829 and was prepared for confirmation that autumn by her father. That same year, her elder sister was married off, at age 19, to a man she did not want. Collett's horror at her sister's fate is delineated in the character of Louise in *The District Governor's Daughters,* and it put her on notice regarding the rigid code by which she and the other women in her circle were expected to live, and which her own mother passively supported.

Louise's sister Sofie Kold, the young heroine of Collett's only novel, reflects the author's own experience in returning home as a smoothly polished lure intended to catch a desirable husband who will take her off her family's hands. The trouble with both the fictional Sofie and the real-life Camilla was that they returned to an isolated rural setting where they had plenty of opportunity to think and brood, and where eligible young men were thin on the ground. Trips to the capital were called for.

In Camilla's case, visits to Christiania became increasingly frequent during the next several years, although such journeys meant a day's travel by horse and carriage via a system of relay stations. In winter, snow and ice smoothed the roads, so that was the season for markets and social events requiring travel. Thus it was that the 17-year-old Camilla found herself in Christiania in January of 1830, escaping from the deep gloom that had descended anew on her father's parsonage once the Christmas festivities were over.

Her beauty, talents, and excellent connections gave her instant social success, which she was far from rejecting. She was extremely fond of dancing and very musical (she sang and played both the piano and the guitar), and her passionate nature suited her well for both friendship and love. She encountered the latter when she met Johan Sebastian Welhaven formally in the Herres' drawing room soon after she had watched the handsome, reserved young poet leaving the family's house by the stairs.

Their meeting resulted in a seemingly mutual *coup de foudre,* which he immortalized in a poem describing the impact on everyone when she entered the room—and which she kept in her heart for a lifetime. His romantic looks and deep, expressive voice immediately captured her imagination, while her fastidious temperament as well as her firm grounding in Continental culture drew her towards his camp of people dedicated to maintaining the cultural influences and connections formerly obtained through Denmark. She fell deeply in love. Welhaven was also strongly attracted to Camilla, but he was poor, proud, ambitious, and cautious, and the stern moral climate that made it impossible for Camilla so much as to hint at an attachment until he had declared his intention to marry her, added greatly to the strain of their relationship.

As Alf Collett noted many years later, his mother's social success was not due to the considerable reputation of her father and of her brother, the barnstorming young poet Henrik Wergeland (1808–1845). On the contrary, the circles in which she traveled, and of which Welhaven was an important part, used their literary organ *Den Constitutionelle* to attack Henrik Wergeland as a person, politician, and poet. Unfazed, their target continued to champion the need for general education, the virtues of simple, peasant-style living, the need to cleanse the Norwegian language of foreign influence, and the right of Jews to enter the Norwegian realm, to name but a few of his passions.

Camilla's father shared his son Henrik's political ideas and the attacks made upon him, and both of them forged sharp arrows aimed back at Johan Sebastian Welhaven and his followers. Camilla, who was well aware that her family (and just about everybody else) knew of her emotional and intellectual involvement with Welhaven, stood her ground, but the conflicts with her family and the uncertainties of her protracted relationship with Welhaven made her ill. Early in the spring of 1834, her father took her to Paris to cheer her up and obtain medical help.

They stayed in Paris for several months. Camilla formed a lasting admiration for French writers (she especially admired *George Sand*'s style) and took lessons in singing, drawing, and painting. She had inherited her parents' keen aesthetic sense, and her father always encouraged her to develop her artistic talents with the exception of her deep yen for acting, which he

was dead set against. Despite the Parisian diversions, Camilla's health remained poor. On their journey home, she became so ill that her father feared for her life. After a lengthy stay in Hamburg, they returned to Eidsvoll late in the autumn of 1834, where old problems lay waiting and fresh ones were brewing.

Each new controversy between Welhaven and Henrik Wergeland added to Camilla's burden. In 1833, Norwegian farmers had begun to demand the use of powers granted them in the Constitution of 1814, causing a debate in which Welhaven and Camilla's brother took opposite sides. In addition, Welhaven was an exponent of the "romantic realism" associated with *das junge Deutschland,* as fresh romantic breezes were reaching Norway from Denmark and Germany. This new form of romanticism brought with it a different feminine ideal from the neoclassical one, but the movement did not succeed in making life easier for Norwegian women in general or Camilla in particular, since modern factory-based industry was also making itself felt by this time. The latter stressed materialistic achievements and left little admiration for qualities in which women supposedly excelled, such as a talent for selfless love.

Camilla met Welhaven again in Christiania in the winter of 1834–35, at which time the battle raging around her brother's poem *Norges Dæmring* (*The Dawn of Norway*) was in full cry and grew worse when Dean Wergeland published a highly polemical work defending his son and attacking Welhaven. In her diary for February of 1836, Camilla wrote that Welhaven had said the mere fact that she was her father's daughter made him bitter towards her. They exchanged only a few awkward letters while she visited friends in Hamburg from August of 1836 until the summer of 1837.

Upon her return home, her mood was one of despair—much of it due to her father's anger that she had refused an offer of marriage from a wealthy Hamburg man. She poured out her heart in letters to Emilie Diriks, whose quick intelligence, well-formed literary tastes, and bruising experiences with a domineering mother made her an accepting and sensitive friend. At the same time, Diriks (who died in 1843) became the testing ground for Camilla's developing literary style, in which a lifelong preoccupation with the plight of women forced into marriage was already taking form. In a letter written from Hamburg at Whitsuntide in 1837, Camilla wondered why even loving parents were in such a hurry to get rid of their children that they began planning for it while the children were still small. Another recurring theme in Camilla's correspondence is the repression of young girls and the consequences of an education and training that make them unable to cope with life's vicissitudes.

Before going abroad in the spring of 1837, Camilla had written: "My love for Welhaven is extinguished. I love him no more." Later, events show that this was untrue, but her statement suggests that she was ready to form a new attachment. In January of 1838, she met the lawyer Peter Jonas Collett, a well-known and articulate member of the pro-Welhaven faction, who saw no reason to discontinue his attacks on Henrik Wergeland even after he fell in love with Camilla. The latter again stood her ground against her family, and on July 14, 1841, she and Collett were married.

Their Christiania household was considered somewhat eccentric, but that did not prevent it from becoming a gathering place for the capital's intellectual élite. Despite this stimulation, and despite enjoying a marriage of inclination, Camilla—who had inherited her father's tendency to brood—suffered recurring bouts of melancholy during the next ten years. Four small sons eventually clamored for her attention, and the practical details of running a household frustrated her. She was fortunate in having a mate who not only assumed some of those daily responsibilities, but who understood that the root of her frustration was her increasing need to develop artistically and intellectually. He encouraged her to write for publication, and they collaborated on several pieces. Her first independently written article appeared in *Den Constitutionelle* in 1842.

Peter Jonas Collett was appointed professor of law at the University of Christiania in 1848. In addition, he took on much outside work in order to meet the financial demands of his growing family. His health suffered in consequence, and just before Christmas of 1851 he succumbed to typhoid fever.

Camilla Collett refused to enter into the secluded, penurious widowhood awaiting women in her position. She declined an offer of financial help from two of her husband's brothers, but allowed her eldest son to become the ward of an uncle and sent her youngest son to another. After selling the house in Uranienborgveien, she went to Denmark with her two remaining sons, and here (in the summer of 1853) she completed Part I of *The District Governor's Daughters*, which she had begun before her husband's death. It was published anonymously in 1854; the second

part followed in 1855. It was the first Norwegian novel to address social problems directly, and it caused an uproar. Some reviewers missed the point of the book entirely, while others found it too accurate for comfort.

The novel tells the story of two young people, Sofie Ramm and Georg Kold, who believe that only a love freely given is a worthy foundation for marriage, but who have reached their convictions by such different avenues that in the end, their hearts and lives are forced apart. Neither of them is a match for the ruthless "realism" of Sofie's mother, who uses every stratagem afforded by her society to get her daughters respectably married as expeditiously as possible. The novel's influence upon the works of such male Norwegian writers as Bjørnstjerne Bjørnson, Jonas Lie, Alexander Kielland, and Henrik Ibsen, was profound, and of all Collett's works, *The District Governor's Daughters* has remained the most widely read. Now a classic in Norwegian literature, it introduced realism and everyday concerns into fiction writing and began a strong tradition of women writers addressing a rapidly growing circle of women readers.

The storm raging around her novel could hardly have come as a surprise to Camilla Collett. Her husband had warned her that the time was probably not yet ripe for the things she wanted to say; a warning that must have grown out of his own involvement with drafting legislation to improve the economic conditions of Norwegian women. In 1854, just after the publication of Part I, Norwegian women were given equal inheritance rights with men, thanks in no small part to Jonas Collett. But that was just a beginning. Goaded by her sense of social injustice, by the public reaction to her book, and by old emotional wounds she would not permit to heal, Camilla was no longer willing to remain anonymous in speaking out for women's rights. She produced no more fiction, but wrote essays and engaged in newspaper discussions until the year she died.

In a peripatetic existence that repeatedly took her back and forth between Norway and the Continent (where she formed a lasting friendship with Henrik Ibsen and his wife **Susannah Thoresen Ibsen**), Camilla became increasingly occupied with the growing struggle to improve the conditions for women, and she became a public figure. In her private life, she found it as hard as ever to create a balance between the emotional demands made upon her by her writing, by her sons, by her sense that she had failed her gentle husband, and by her attempts to reach some kind of *modus vivendi* with Welhaven, who had married a friend of hers and become the father of six children. After a period of strained relations in Christiania, she resumed her gypsy existence and had only occasional, though friendly, contact with Welhaven until he died in 1873.

Her anger and frustration never cooled, however, and she once declared that had it not been for the great turmoil she had been forced to endure in consequence of her relationship with Welhaven, she would never have written a word. While that surely was an exaggeration, she certainly was determined that future generations of women should not suffer as she had done.

Camilla Collett thought that women must first of all be educated to see themselves in a different light, and that they must be free of economic bondage. Political privileges would then follow of their own accord. Not everyone within the women's movement agreed with her, but progress was made on all fronts. In 1863, unmarried women above the age of 25 were declared legally competent. By 1875, Camilla had helped form a Women's Reading Society, and, in 1882, women gained the right to take the *examen artium,* the series of final exams from the gymnasium that also serve as entrance exams to the university. After 1884, they could obtain university degrees. That was also the year the Women's Cause Association was formed, and Camilla Collett was made its first honorary member. Recognition for her work in securing women's rights began to replace the reputation for social and literary bohemianism that followed her even after King Charles XV of Sweden and Norway presented her with the gold medal *Literibus et artibus* in 1863.

The Cause gained further momentum when the Women's Suffrage Association was formed by *Gina Krog in 1885. The first women's journal, *Nylænde* ("Newly Cleared Land"), was started in 1887, and in 1889 the old marriage vows dating from 1688, which declared that a wife should be subservient to her husband, were changed. In 1901, six years after Collett's death, Norwegian women won limited rights to vote in municipal elections (since 1884 the franchise had been extended to all men above 25 years of age and with a certain minimum income). Norwegian women obtained full suffrage in 1913.

Much of Camilla Collett's writing gives the impression that she considered herself born in the wrong place at the wrong time. Seen in historical perspective, however, she came along at a perfect time. Her life coincided with the eventful period in which the Norwegians redefined themselves as a nation after more than four centuries of Danish hegemony, and her struggle for women's rights not only paralleled, but in many ways helped shape the social and legal developments that enabled Norway to meet the 20th century as a modern European state.

SOURCES:

Benterud, Aagot. *Camilla Collett: En skjebne og et livsverk*. Oslo: Dreyer, 1947.

Bergsøe, Clara. *Camilla Collett*. Copenhagen: Gyldendalske Boghandel, 1902.

Collett, Alf. *Camilla Colletts Livs Historie*. Copenhagen: Gyldendalske Boghandel, 1911.

Collett, Camilla. *Breve fra Ungdomsaarene*. Oslo: Gyldendal, 1930.

———. *The District Governor's Daughters*. Translated with an introduction by Kirsten A. Seaver. Norwich: Norvik Press, 1992.

———. *Før Brylluppet. Brevveksling med P.J. Collett og andre 1840-41*. Oslo: Gyldendal, 1933.

———. *Frigjørelsens Aar. Brevveksling med. J. Collett og andre 1838-39*. Oslo: Gyldendal, 1932.

———. *I de lange Nætter*. Oslo: Gyldendal.

———. *Optegnelser fra Ungdomsaarene*. Oslo: Gyldendal, 1926.

Collett, Peter Jonas. *Studenteraar: Optegnelser og Refleksioner 1831-38*. Oslo: Gyldendal, 1934.

"Diktning og demokrati. Camilla Collett 150 år—Full kvinnestemmerettighet 50 år—1813-1913-1963," in *Samtiden*. Hefte I. Oslo: Aschehoug, 1963.

Garton, Janet. *Norwegian Women's Writing 1850–1900*. London: Athlone Press, 1993.

Popperwell, R.G. *Norway*. Nations of the Modern World Series. London: Ernest Benn, 1972.

SUGGESTED READING:

Engelstad, Irene, and Janneken Overland. *Frihet til å skrive*. Oslo: Pax, 1981.

———, et al., eds. *Norsk kvinnelitteraturhistorie*. Vol. I: 1600–1900. Oslo: Pax, 1988.

Møller Jensen, Elisabeth. *Emancipation som lidenskab: Camilla Colletts liv og værk*. Charlottenlund: Rosinante, 1986.

Steen, Ellisiv. *Den lange strid: Camilla Collett og hennes senere forfatterskap*. Oslo: Gyldendal, 1954.

———. *Diktning og virkelighet: En studie i Camilla Colletts forfatterskap*. Oslo: Gyldendal, 1947.

Wergeland, Agnes Mathilde. *Leaders in Norway*. Freeport, NY: Books for Libraries Press, 1966 (first published in 1916).

COLLECTIONS:

Amundsen, Leiv, ed. Camilla Collett, and P.J. Collett, *Dagbøker og Breve* (Diaries and Letters). 4 vols. Oslo: Gyldendal, 1926-33. Vol. 1: *Optegnelser fra Ungdomsaarene* (Youthful Memoranda); Vol. 2: *Breve fra Ungdomsaarene* (Letters from Youth); Vol. 3: *Frigjørelsens Aar: Brevveksling med P.J. Collett og andre 1838-1839* (The Years of Liberation: Correspondence with P.J. Collett and Others 1838–39); Vol. 4: *Før Brylluppet: Brevveksling med P.J. Collett og andre 1840–41* (Before the Wedding: Correspondence with P.J. Collett and Others 1840–41).

Collett, Camilla. *Samlede Verker* (Collected Works). 3 vols. Kristiania (Oslo) and Copenhagen: Gyldendalske Boghandel (Nordisk Forlag), 1912–13.

Kirsten A. Seaver, historian, novelist and translator, including Camilla Collett's *The District Governor's Daughters* (Norvik Press, 1992)

Collett, Glenna (1903–1989).

See Vare, Glenna Collett.

Colley, Sarah Ophelia (1912–1996).

See Pearl, Minnie.

Collier, Constance (1878–1955)

*British actress. Born Laura Constance Hardie in Windsor, England, on January 22, 1878; died in Hollywood, California, on April 25, 1955; daughter of C.A. Hardie (an actor) and Lizzie (Collier) Hardie (an actor); granddaughter of **Leopoldina Collier**, who brought one of the first ballet companies to England; married actor Julian L'Estrange, c. 1905 (died 1918).*

Selected films: Intolerance (1916); Tongues of Men (1916); The Code of Marcia Gray (1916); Macbeth (1916); Bleak House (UK, 1920); The Bohemian Girl (UK, 1922); Shadow of Doubt (1935); Professional Soldier (1936); Girls' Dormitory (1936); Little Lord Fauntleroy (1936); Wee Willie Winkie (1937); Stage Door (1937); A Damsel in Distress (1937); Zaza (1939); Susan and God (1940); Kitty (1946); The Dark Corner (1946); Monsieur Beaucaire (1946); The Perils of Pauline (1947); Rope (1948); An Ideal Husband (UK, 1948); Whirlpool (1950).

$\mathcal{C}$onstance $\mathcal{C}$ollier

The daughter of actors, Constance Collier was named after a character in Shakespeare's *King John*, the play in which her parents were touring at the time of her birth. Her mother **Lizzie Hardie** rejoined the company when Constance was only three weeks old, supposedly leaving the infant wrapped up in a blanket on her dressing table while she performed. As a youngster, when Collier was not appearing with her parents on stage (at three, as a fairy in *A Midsummer Night's Dream*; at six, as one of the children in *The Silver King*), she was often left in the care of the landlady of whichever theatrical boarding house they were able to find. Her father C.A. Hardie was an alcoholic who was often ill, and her mother was never steadily employed, so Constance's young life was a constant round of agents' offices, tours, and education on the move. She attended a single term in boarding school (described as the most horrible experience of her life), after which her formal education ended.

Collier's theatrical career got under way when, after lying about her age, she was employed by George Edwardes, who trained her as one of his famous Gaiety Girls (a chorus of beautiful young women named for the Gaiety Theatre). After singing and dancing lessons, she made her first appearance in *A Gaiety Girl* (1894), which was followed by *The Shop Girl* (1895). Life began to change for the young teenager when, like all the Gaiety girls, she was showered with public adoration, attended the best parties, and won the attention of a number of men. During those heady years, she was engaged twice: once to a millionaire 35 years her senior and once to a married man. Finally deciding that she wanted to become a serious actress, she signed on for a provincial tour in the second company of *An Ideal Husband*, an experience she hated. After roles in two flops, she became an artist's model to support herself between short-lived stage engagements. In 1898, after a chance meeting with playwright H.V. Esmond, she was offered the part of Chiara the Gypsy in *One Summer's Day*, her breakthrough role.

In 1901, Collier was engaged by actor-manager Beerbohm Tree to play at His Majesty's Theatre, where, after a resounding success as Pallas Athene in *Ulysses*, she was rewarded with a long-term contract. (During the run of *Ulysses*, she was still under contract at the Drury Lane Theatre to play in *Ben Hur* and for a time managed to perform in both plays each night.) Her success in *Ulysses* was followed by the role of Roma in *The Eternal City*, a performance that the actress found beyond her experience. Although the public appreciated her efforts, the critics were less impressed. J.T. Grien found her talent limited: "She may disturb but she does not move us. She imposes but she rarely impresses." Adding to Collier's woes was a lunatic extra who, during the run of the show, threatened and nearly killed her.

While with Tree, Collier played numerous roles, including Mistress Ford in *The Merry Wives of Windsor*, Viola in *Twelfth Night*, Julie de Noirville in *A Man's Shadow*, and Portia in

Julius Caesar. Around 1905, while on tour with the company as Nancy in Comyns Carr's version of Dickens' *Oliver Twist*, she married Julian L'Estrange, an irresistible—and irresponsible—young actor. Collier claimed that their careers kept them apart so much that the marriage seemed more like "an intermittent love affair." The arrangement may have been for the best, given L'Estrange's reputation. (He died in 1918, during an influenza epidemic.)

In 1908, Collier made her first appearance in New York, as Ann Marie in *Samson*. From then until 1914, she divided her time between London and New York. Throughout the years of the First World War, she played in a number of all-star revivals to raise money for charities. She produced *Peter Ibbetson* and also played Mary, Duchess of Towers, which remained her favorite role of her career. In 1916, she made her Hollywood film debut in D.W. Griffith's *Intolerance* and would continue to make infrequent appearances in films through the 1940s. In 1918, she again toured the United States and appeared with her husband in *An Ideal Husband*.

In the early 1920s, Collier became seriously ill, possibly because of diabetes. Partially blind and barely able to stand unassisted, she was sent to Switzerland for treatment, the first patient in Europe ever to be treated with the drug insulin. By September 1923, after a full recovery, she was playing the Duchesse de Surennes in Somerset Maugham's comedy *Our Betters*. During the run, she collaborated with Ivor Novello on a play called *The Rat*, which they then produced. She joined forces with Novello again for *Downhill*, which drama critic James Agate attacked harshly as "the purest trash put together for the purpose of exploiting Mr. Novello's personal attractions." Criticism aside, the play made them both a lot of money.

In 1928, Collier returned to New York for a revival of *Our Betters*, her first comedy role in the States. For the next ten years, she traveled back and forth between England and America, enchanting audiences in hits like *Hay Fever*, *Dinner at Eight*, *The Torch Bearers*, *Aries is Rising*, and *Curtain Going Up*. Noel Coward, visiting the actress at her New York hotel during this time, described her as "presiding from her bed, attired in a pink dressing gown, with a Pekinese in one hand and a cigarette in the other." Collier spent her later years in Hollywood, where she continued to make movies, mostly playing irascible eccentrics.

Barbara Morgan,
Melrose, Massachusetts

Collingwood, Elizabeth (1924—)

English royal. Name variations: Elizabeth Colvin; Elizabeth Lascelles. Born Elizabeth Ellen Collingwood on April 23, 1924, in Wimbledon, London, England; daughter of Sydney Collingwood and Charlotte Annie (Oughterson) Collingwood; married a man named Colvin; became second wife of Hon. Gerald David Lascelles (b. 1924, grandson of King George V and *Mary of Teck), on November 17, 1978; children: Martin David Lascelles (b. 1962). Gerald Lascelles' first wife was *Angela Dowding.

Collins, Addie Mae (d. 1963).

See Davis, Angela for sidebar.

Collins, Cardiss (1931—)

U.S. Congresswoman (January 5, 1973–January 3, 1997). Born Cardiss Hortense Robertson in St. Louis, Missouri, on September 24, 1931; only child of Finley (a laborer) and Rosia Mae (Cardiss) Robertson (a nurse); attended Bishop and Lincoln Elementary Schools, Detroit, Michigan; graduated from High School of Commerce, Detroit; attended Northwestern University, Chicago, Illinois; married George Washington Collins, in 1958 (died, December 8, 1972); children: one son, Kevin.

Cardiss Collins was elected to fill her husband's unexpired Congressional term after his death in 1973. She went on to become the longest-serving black woman in the history of Congress and devoted herself to providing better living and working conditions in her predominantly black district in Illinois. As evidence of her popularity, she ran unopposed in 1988.

Collins was born in St. Louis, Missouri, and moved to Detroit as a child. After attending Northwestern University, she remained in Chicago, where she worked for the Illinois Department of Labor and later as an auditor in the Department of Revenue. With her marriage to rising politician George Collins in 1958, she began her political career, serving as a Democratic committeewoman and supporting her husband's campaigns. By the time he was elected to Congress, she was so immersed in his career that when he was killed in a plane crash in 1972 she seemed the perfect candidate to fill his unexpired term. It was difficult, however, for Collins to leave her son in the care of his grandmother so that she might work in Washington; she always regretted the lost time with him. Perhaps the biggest stumbling block to her first years in Congress, however, was her intense shyness. "I was basically an introvert, but once people learned I had something to say, I gained confidence. But it took a long time to come out of my shell and realize I was here, doing this alone." Eventually, she was respected among her peers not only for her toughness, but for her wit, candor, and homespun charm.

Collins' long tenure in Congress was marked by several firsts. She was the first woman and the first black to chair the House Government Operations Subcommittee on Man-

power and Housing, and the first woman to chair the Congressional Black Caucus. She was also the first black and the first woman to serve as a Democratic whip-at-large. From 1981, she was a member of the Committee on Energy and Commerce and also sat on the Select Committee on Narcotics Abuse and Control. She was reelected to 11 succeeding Congresses.

Collins, Eileen Marie (b. 1956).
See Astronauts: Women in Space.

*C*ardiss
*C*ollins

Collins, Janet (1917—)

First African-American dancer to find considerable success in ballet, becoming a premiere danseuse for the Metropolitan Opera in the 1950s, who later gained notice in modern dance and as a teacher. Born Janet Collins on March 2, 1917, in New Orleans, Louisiana; daughter of Ernest Lee Collins (a tailor) and Alma (de Lavallade) Collins (a seamstress); completed high school in Los Angeles; attended Los Angeles City College; never married; no children.

Studied dance in Los Angeles and performed on early television shows and with various companies; first New York solo concert debut (1949); was principal ballet dancer of the Metropolitan Opera (1951–54); gave solo concert tours in U.S. and Canada (1952–55); taught at Marymount College, Harkness House, School of American Ballet, San Francisco Ballet School. Awards: Donaldson Award for best dancer of the Broadway season (1951–52); Dance Magazine Award (1959).

Works choreographed: Blackamoor *(1947);* Eine Kleine Nachtmusik *(1947);* Spirituals *(1947);* Protest *(1947);* Après le Mardi Gras *(1947);* Juba *(1949);* Three Psalms of David *(1949);* Moi l'Aime Toi, Chère *(1951);* The Satin Slipper *(1960);* Genesis *(1965);* Cockfight *(1972);* Birds of Peace and Pride *(1973);* Song *(1973);* Fire Weaver *(1973);* Sunday and Sister Jones *(1973).*

In mid-20th-century America, ballet was still a snowy, white world, a pristine playground of snowflakes, sylphs, and swans that required money for years of training. Without sponsorship, most African-Americans could ill afford the financial burden. More important, many thought that African-Americans were physically incapable of mastering ballet technique because of the structure of their bodies. Janet Collins opened the door. Though it remains an area of dance with relatively few blacks, she set a precedent that began to enlarge the possibilities for African-Americans in the field.

Born in New Orleans, Louisiana, on March 2, 1917, Collins was of mixed African and French ancestry. Her father was a tailor; her mother was a seamstress. All the children—four girls and one boy—proved successful, attending college and attaining professional careers in education, social work, and the army. When Collins was four, the family moved to Los Angeles where she spent the rest of her formative years. She took her first dance lessons at the age of ten at a local Catholic social center and was still in junior high school when she danced in vaudeville and in the Los Angeles casts of productions by Hall Johnson of *Run Little Chillun* and *Mikado in Swing*. She even briefly joined the touring company of *Katherine Dunham. Thus, she became extremely versatile, a characteristic that led to a very diverse career and for which she would be heralded in the competitive dance world.

Perhaps recognizing the difficulties she would face as a black, Collins did not limit her dance training. She took ballet and Spanish dance classes from *Carmelita Maracci, ballet from Adolph Bolm, *Mia Slavenska, Carlotta Tamon, and Dorothy Lyndall, and modern dance from Lester Horton. Later in New York, after her first solo recital in 1949, she received a scholarship to study composition with *Doris Humphrey. She also took modern dance classes with Humphrey and *Hanya Holm, and ballet with Margaret Craske and Anthony Tudor. At a time when loyalty was highly prized and spite widely rampant amid the members of the nascent and struggling young American dance world, Collins defied the system and gained invaluable, broad experience.

> ⊤o me Dance is not an 'I' but a truth. As all truth is derived from simple, fundamental laws of nature, thus we, ourselves, do not create a truth, but rather, put forth a conscious effort to find it.
>
> —Janet Collins

While still in Los Angeles, Collins auditioned for the world-renowned ballet company, Ballets Russes. She was offered acceptance into the company on two conditions: first, that she would be used only in small parts, and second, that she would have to use "Caucasian" make-up to make her look white. "[I] cried for an hour," Collins told an interviewer. "And went back to the barre."

This incident was only a small indication of the discrimination that awaited the young dancer. John Martin, the influential critic of *The New York Times*, promulgated the common misconception of the capabilities of African-Americans. In *John Martin's Book of Dance*, revised in 1963, he wrote: "By and large, [the Negro] has been wise enough not to be drawn into [ballet], for its wholly European outlook, history, and technical theory are alien to him culturally, temperamentally, and anatomically." In his view, however, Janet Collins was the exceedingly rare exception. She was the *only* instance of a "Negro" ballerina, "beautifully equipped physically, technically and stylistically."

Collins received accolades in ballet, however, after she had achieved success in other dance styles. In 1949, she was 32 when she made her choreographic and solo debut at the 92nd St. YMHA, earning a chance to appear on the annual Audition Winners Concert, which chose outstanding newcomers in the dance field. Walter Terry, critic of the *New York Herald Tribune*, wrote of this debut: "It took no more (and probably less) than eight measures of movement in the opening dance to establish her claim to dance distinction as the most highly gifted newcomer in many a season."

Soon thereafter, Hanya Holm employed her in the Cole Porter musical, *Out of This World* (1950), to dance a role called "Night." Collins received ecstatic reviews. In a Broadway season where the competition included the premieres of Jerome Robbins' *The King and I* (with its well-received ballet "The Little House of Uncle Tom"), *A Tree Grows in Brooklyn*, and *Guys and Dolls*, Collins was given the Donaldson Award for the best Broadway dancer of the season. During this period, she also appeared on early television variety shows, including "The Admiral Broadway Review" (NBC, 1949), "This is Show Business"

Janet
Collins

(CBS, 1951), and the Paul Draper and Jack Haley shows. Overcoming significant racism, she established herself as a preeminent, talented dancer.

Collins' crowning achievement was being named a principal dancer at the Metropolitan Opera. From 1951–54, while already in her mid-30s, she performed starring roles in *Aïda, Carmen, La Gioconda,* and *Samson et Delila.* During time off from the Metropolitan Opera's seasons, she conducted extensive tours around the United States and Canada. Although she never received much critical acclaim for her choreography, she performed diverse programs of modern dance, ballet, and dancing to black spirituals and had both pianist and drumming accompanists. Again, her strength and rarity lay in her very diverse abilities.

Most dance aficionados recognized Collins' uniqueness, particularly in her success in both the ballet and modern styles. Asked about the inherent conflict between ballet and modern dance that many believed existed, Collins replied: "There is no conflict. You need both to extend the range of the body." In a brochure issued by her agent, Columbia Artists Management, she elaborated:

> This great difference in the approach to dance between the Ballet and Modern schools is not necessarily a conflicting one, provided the dancer approaches both with an open-minded attitude, and learns, and absorbs and assimilates the vast and enriching science and art at the heart of each.

Indeed, Collins was teaching both ballet and modern at this time. At George Balanchine's prestigious School of American Ballet, she taught modern dance from 1950 to 1952. She also taught at Marymount College, Harkness House, and the San Francisco Ballet School.

It was her inspiration as a role model for African-Americans, however, that proved to be her lasting contribution to dance. The next generation of African-Americans in dance, including Geoffrey Holder and Arthur Mitchell, held her in awe. Closer to home, her own cousin **Carmen DeLavallade** greatly benefitted from Collins' successes. Following directly in her footsteps, DeLavallade was the next great African-American woman ballet dancer, and even took over Collins' principal roles at the Metropolitan Opera. Then Arthur Mitchell, the first African-American accepted in the New York City Ballet in 1956, left that company to start the Dance Theatre of Harlem in 1968. From then on, African-Americans have at least had a prominent, though isolated, place in bal-

let. The hard-fought successes can be attributed to the pioneering work and talent of Janet Collins.

SOURCES:
Biographical Dictionary of Dance. NY: Schirmer Books, 1982.
Chujoy, Anatole. *The Dance Encyclopedia.* NY: Simon and Schuster, 1967.
"Interview with Janet Collins," in *Dance Magazine.* February 1954, pp. 27–29.
Janet Collins and Her Company. Souvenir Program [1953?]. Dance Collection, Performing Arts Library at Lincoln Center, New York Public Library.
Phonotape of interview with Walter Terry, 1953, in the Dance Collection, Performing Arts Library at Lincoln Center, New York Public Library.

SUGGESTED READING:
Emery, Lynne Fauley. *Black Dance From 1619 to Today.* NJ: Princeton Book Company, rev. ed. 1988.
Long, Richard. *The Black Tradition in American Dance.* NY: Rizzoli, 1989.
Thorpe, Edward. *Black Dance.* London: Chatto and Windus, 1989.

COLLECTIONS:
Scrapbooks, manuscripts, programs, photographs, costume designs, and clippings at the Dance Collection, Performing Arts Library at Lincoln Center, New York Public Library.

RELATED MEDIA:
"Eye on Dance: Dancing Families," hosted by **Celia Ipiotis** with Geoffrey Holder, Carmen DeLavallade, and Christian Holder, WNYC, original airdate February 7, 1983, in Dance Collection, Performing Arts Library at Lincoln Center, New York Public Library.

Julia L. Foulkes,
University of Massachusetts at Amherst

Collins, Kathleen (1942–1988)

African-American independent filmmaker and playwright. Name variations: Kathleen Collins Prettyman. Born Kathleen Conwell Collins on March 18, 1942, in Gouldtown, New Jersey; died of cancer on September 18, 1988; attended Skidmore College and Middlebury Graduate School of French in Paris; married; children: a daughter, and two sons from a previous relationship, as well as a stepdaughter and stepson.

Filmography: The Cruz Brothers (1979); Losing Ground (1982); Gouldtown: A Mulatto Settlement (1988). Selected plays: In the Midnight Hour, The Brothers, Only the Sky is Free (a fictional account of the life of African-American aviator *Bessie Coleman). Professor of film history and production at City College New York; finalist for the Susan Blackburn International Prize for Playwrighting.

Kathleen Collins was just coming into her own as a creative force within the African-American independent filmmaking community when she died from cancer at age 42. Collins was born in Gouldtown, a village in southern New Jersey that was founded by four separate families, each of mixed race, nearly 400 years ago. She traced her ancestry to 1623, and it was about her ancestral home that she made her last film in 1988, *Gouldtown: A Mulatto Settlement.*

As a child, she moved from Gouldtown to Jersey City, New Jersey, where she grew up. Collins took an undergraduate degree from Skidmore College, majoring in philosophy and religion, then did graduate work in Paris at the Middlebury School of French where she studied French literature and the cinema.

Though she is most known as a filmmaker, at first Collins considered herself a writer. In her short career, she wrote six plays, all produced, including a production of "The Brothers," which was staged during the American Place Theatre's 1982–83 season. She also wrote several short stories and four screenplays; at the time of her death, she had completed most of a novel titled *Black and White Imagery.*

After considerable struggle, Collins became a filmmaker during the last years of her life. She had written a script called *Women, Sisters and Friends,* but her attempts to raise money to produce and direct the film were futile. "This was 1971," she told David Nicholson in an interview for *Black Film Review.* "Nobody would give money to a black woman to direct a film."

Collins temporarily gave up and went back to writing plays. To support her children, she took a job as film editor for NET. In 1974, she was hired by City College of New York (CCNY) to teach production and screenwriting, a fortuitous move. There, she met Ronald Gray. Then a student at CCNY, Gray had so much faith in Collins' ability as a director that he put together $5,000 to finance her first film, thus becoming her co-producer. Gray was also her cinematographer on this film as he would be on later projects. Collins was not at all sure they could pull off the film on that tiny budget. "I had this crazy script by this good friend, Henry Roth, from a novel called, *The Cruz Chronicles: A Novel of Adventure,*" Collins told Nicholson. "It was frightening . . . but we did it. [Ronald] and I have incredible tenacity." Titled *The Cruz Brothers and Miss Malloy,* the film was a success, though the African-American Collins was criticized for making a film about Puerto Ricans and a dying Irish woman. That type of criticism, however, was likely regarded as irrelevant by Collins. She was, in her words, a "literary filmmaker" whose creative vision was never limited by race, national boundaries or color. "I am much more concerned with how people resolve their inner dilemma in the face of external reality."

The relative success of *Cruz Brothers* helped Gray and Collins raise the $125,000 for what became arguably Collins' most important work, *Losing Ground,* possibly the first independent film to feature an African-American professional woman as the protagonist. Though it is one of the few feature films that depict a black woman with a growing feminist consciousness, Collins was quick to add that her point of view, though considered feminist, was first and always African-American. "I would like to think that there is a black aesthetic among black women filmmakers," Collins told writer **Loretta Campbell**. "Black women are not white women by any means; we have different approaches to life and different attitudes. Historically, we come out of different traditions."

Collins cherished her identity as a part of the larger community of black women, part of a tradition that is shared and passed on, and she was inspired by her predecessor, *Lorraine Hansbury, author of *Raisin in the Sun,* another black woman who died young. "I have this feeling of being very connected to Lorraine Hansbury," Collins told Nicholson. "I've never found another black writer who I felt was asking the same questions. . . . She was able to encompass this wide range of experience from Jewish intellectuals to black middle class to Africa." The same could be said of Collins.

Kathleen Collins' premature death in 1988 was deeply felt by her friends and colleagues in the filmmaking community. The staff of *Black Film Review,* joining others at her memorial in New York City, spoke of the loss: "There is no other voice like Kathleen Collins' among filmmakers. Her vision 'goes to the bone' and we stand before her naked and grateful."

SOURCES:

Aker, Ally. *Reel Women: Pioneers of the Cinema 1896 to the Present.* NY: Continuum 1991.

Campbell, Loretta. "Reinventing Our Image: Eleven Black Women Filmmakers," in *Heresies.* Vol. 4, 1983, p. 62.

Foster, Gwendolyn A. *Women Film Directors: An International Biocritical Dictionary.* Westport, CT: Greenwood Press, 1995.

Klotman, Phyllis Rauch, ed. *Screenplays of African-American Experience.* Bloomington: Indiana University Press, 1981.

Nicholson, David. "A Commitment to Writing: A Conversation with Kathleen Collins Prettyman," in *Black Film Review.* Vol. 5, no. 1. Winter 1988–89, p. 2–15.

Reid, Mark A. *Redefining Black Film*. Berkeley, CA: University of California Press, 1993.

Steward, William. *Gouldtown: A Very Remarkable Settlement of Ancient Date*. Philadelphia, PA: Lippincott, 1913.

Deborah Jones,
Studio City, California

Colomba.

Variant of Columba.

Colon, Maria (1958—)

Cuban javelin thrower, who was the first person from her country to win an Olympic gold medal. Name variations: María Caridad Colón. Born María Caridad Colón on March 25, 1958, in Cuba; married Angel Salcedo (her coach).

Born on March 25, 1958, in Cuba, Maria Colon was considered one of her nation's finest female athletes by the late 1970s, after winning several medals at the Pan American Games. Her greatest success took place during the 1980 Olympics in Moscow, where she won the gold medal in javelin on her first try. Luck as well as her own talent favored her on this occasion, given the fact that East Germany's *Ruth Fuchs, the "queen of javelin throwing," turned in a disappointing performance. With her victory, Maria Colon became the first woman of color to gain an Olympic gold medal in a throwing event. A favorite with the crowds, she was a solid performer in major meets but sometimes vanished from the public eye for long stretches of time. When not competing, she teaches physical education in Havana. She is married to her coach, Angel Salcedo.

John Haag,
Athens, Georgia

Colonna, Catherine (d. around 1440)

*Countess of Montefeltro. Name variations: Cattarina Colonna. Died around 1440; niece of Pope Martin V; married Guido Sforza, count of Montefeltro; children: *Seraphina Sforza (1434–1478).*

Colonna, Vittoria (c. 1490–1547)

*Italian poet and religious reformer whose friendships and correspondence with notable writers of the day contributed to her fame. Name variations: Marchioness of Pescara. Born probably 1490 (some sources cite 1492) in Marino, Italy; died in Rome on February 25, 1547; daughter of Fabrizio Colonna (member of the powerful Colonna family and an influ-ential soldier) and **Agnese da Montefeltro** also known as Anna da Montefeltro (daughter of Federico, duke of Urbino); betrothed at age four to Francesco Ferrante d'Avalos (son of an important Spanish family resident in Italy); they were married in 1509; children: none, although she raised her husband's orphaned nephew.*

*Wrote poetry throughout her adult life, although most poems were composed after the death of her husband (1525); active in reform of Catholic Church; corresponded with many notable contemporaries. Her biography was written by *Isabella Albrizzi in 1836.*

The events that shaped Vittoria Colonna's life serve also to obscure her contributions. Although she wrote some poems early in adulthood, by far the greatest number of her poems were composed in response to the death of her husband, who was killed in one of the many battles of the 16th century in which control of the Italian peninsula was being contested. Her wanderings after his death, and his friendships with literary people of her day, spurred her into correspondence. Yet historians have tended to focus their attention on the wars that were the cause of her writings, and literary critics have been so overawed by the accomplishments of her correspondents that they see Colonna as a footnote on the page of Cardinal Pietro Bembo, Baldassare Castiglione, even Michelangelo, whose fame surely rests on his accomplishments in the figurative arts, not poetry.

The record of her early life is blank. She was probably born in 1490, although some records say 1492. Judging by her later literary output, she was evidently well educated in both classical and contemporary literature. Her father's family had long been important in Rome, as her mother's had in nearby Urbino. In the storm that was brewing for control of the Italian peninsula, young Colonna was used as a pawn: she was betrothed at the age of four to Ferrante d'Avalos, son of the marquis of Pescara, scion of a powerful Spanish family residing in Italy (at that time, Spain was the center of the Holy Roman Empire). Ferrante I, the king of Naples, had a hand in arranging this match. One tradition holds that she went to live with her future in-laws at an early age, and this certainly would not have been unusual at the time. What *is* known for certain is that the marriage was celebrated when Colonna was in her late teens, on December 29, 1509, in a magnificent ceremony in Rome.

The young couple immediately went to live in Ischia, a small island off Naples, then the most populous city on the peninsula, where they are known to have visited the humanist Jacopo

Sannazzaro at his Neapolitan villa. Although most of Vittoria's early work is lost, it is likely that she began to write her poems during this time. In 1510, her father left Marino to fight on the side of the Spaniards and Pope Julius II (best known today as Michelangelo's patron) against the French, and her husband left shortly afterwards to join in the struggle. In his absence, Colonna took charge of her husband's young orphaned nephew Alfonso d'Avalos.

As with most educated, upper-class women of the day, Colonna was expected to run the household in her husband's absence. She was probably accustomed to seeing her mother fulfill this role, but, nonetheless, it must still have been a heavy responsibility. Her husband, who participated in many battles, was wounded and taken prisoner at the battle of Ravenna. In 1525, he died of his wounds in Milan, while being held hostage. Colonna was on her way to him when news of his death reached her in Viterbo (near Rome), and she turned back to Ischia.

Vittoria Colonna

A childless widow, with more than enough money to live on, had several options. At first, after turning down several suitors, she thought of entering a convent, but Pope Julius' successor, Clement, convinced her otherwise. Instead, she spent the rest of her life traveling from convent to convent (in the Renaissance, convents frequently served as high-class hotels for unattached gentlewomen), writing poems, and involving herself in religious matters and in the arts. In 1544, she settled in the Benedictine convent of St. Anne in Rome.

Shortly after her husband's death, Colonna began writing the enormous corpus of poems that occupied much of her time. She says in her poetry that writing was an outlet for the tremendous grief she felt at her loss. Modern critics have sometimes cast doubt on the sincerity of her grief, citing her husband's long absences and his open relationships with mistresses in various cities during his military campaigns. It must be remembered, however, that this was an arranged marriage, that the couple, who had known each other all their lives, knew from early childhood that they were to be married. Even if, as is probable, their marriage did not correspond to the modern ideal, the two had close ties. Colonna, in fact, continued after her husband's death in her role as adoptive mother of her husband's young nephew and maintained a close friendship with Ferrante's aunt for the rest of her life.

As time went on, Colonna idealized her dead husband and used her future meeting with him as an analogy for the mystical union with Christ. Gradually, her theme turned to religion and philosophy; the poems were widely circulated and eventually published. As befits a "gentlewoman," Colonna never involved herself directly in their publication, although five editions appeared in her lifetime (the first in 1538). The poems remained popular, with many more editions appearing throughout the 16th and 17th centuries.

As she traveled, Colonna took pains to meet the poets in the various cities where she stopped. When she moved on, she remained in contact with many of them, writing letters and exchanging poems. Many of these letters, which have been preserved, show her deep interest in the arts as well as her relationships with other writers. She also was friendly with many of the women who, like her, were in charge of their households while their husbands were at war. Some of these women ran literary circles that were the precursors of the "salons" that were to arise on the Continent in the next century. Though, in comparison, Colonna's correspondence with other notable women is scanty. The early Renaissance was an important era in the development of women writers, and *Veronica Gambara and *Gaspara Stampa contributed important works to Italian literature. They certainly knew of each other, and Colonna possibly met Stampa.

Colonna was highly regarded by her fellow writers. Baldassare Castiglione, in fact, entrusted her with the manuscript of his most famous work, *The Courtier*, before it was printed (she appears to have violated his trust, circulating the manuscript until he grew so afraid that someone else would print it that he ordered a rush revision and printing). Among her literary friends, she numbered such giants as Bembo, Luigi Alamanni, Pietro Aretino, Lodovico Ariosto, as well as writers of lesser rank.

Colonna's most famous literary friendship was with Michelangelo Buonarotti, who, aside from his genius in the figurative arts, was an accomplished poet and neo-Platonist philosopher. In fact, although most agree that Colonna was the superior poet of the two, her accomplishments have long been overshadowed by an evaluation of her as "Michelangelo's friend." Their first meeting probably took place in 1538, when she was 47 and he was 63. Their passionate friendship appears to have been immediate. She sent him her poems. He addressed some of his finest sonnets to her, made drawings for her, spent long hours as her companion, and asked her opinion of his works. She wrote glowingly of them, including his Pietà and a Crucifixion that he made especially for her. Her move to Orvieto and Viterbo in 1541, when her brother Ascanio Colonna rebelled against Pope Paul III, did not lessen the intensity of their relationship, and they continued to visit and correspond as before. She returned to Rome in 1544, staying as usual at the convent of San Silvestro.

Though Colonna continued to write sonnets lamenting the loss of her husband, many of her poems written later in life were religious in theme, depicting the vanity of human attachments and the importance of religious faith. Well versed as she was in the humanist neo-Platonic philosophy (as was Michelangelo), she managed to balance this viewpoint with orthodox Christianity, seeing this philosophy as a way of returning the church to its original principles. Aside from her shorter poems, she is the author of a long poem, "Trionfo di Cristo" ("Triumph of Christ"), modeled on Petrarch's "I Trionfi" ("The Triumphs"). Like Petrarch, she used the difficult rhyme scheme, called the "terza rima," invented by Dante for the *Divine Comedy*. In this verse, the lines (all of 11 syllables) have an interlocking rhyme scheme: ABA BCB CDC DED, etc.

Colonna was an advocate of church reform. The early 16th century was a period of political and religious turmoil. The Catholic Church had become increasingly corrupt, with popes openly keeping mistresses, priests accepting bribes, monks and nuns living riotously in their monasteries. At various times, reforms had been attempted. Various religious orders were founded in a bid to return to the simplicity and charity envisioned by Christ (most notably, the Franciscans and the Poor Clares in the Middle Ages), but even these orders were subject to the same corruption that infected the main church. The Franciscans, in an attempt to return to the principles of their founders, formed a splinter group, nicknamed the "Capuchins," and Colonna was vigorous in her defense of this group. Unfortunately, these small efforts at reform did not halt the steady decline of the church, and the Inquisition and the Reformation followed shortly after her death.

Oh what a magnanimous maiden, oh what a truly famous and divine name!

—**Cardinal Pompeo Colonna**

After a brief illness, Vittoria Colonna died at the convent of San Silvestro on February 25, 1547. At the time of her death, 22 volumes of her poems were in print. The most celebrated of her literary output appears to have been her early poems concerning her husband. For a time, her popularity diminished, many found her style cold and formal. Recently, however, critics have begun reevaluating Colonna's writings, recognizing her contribution to literature and philosophy.

SOURCES:
Colonna, Vittora. *Rime*. Edited by Alan Bullock. Florence: Gius. Laterza and Figli, 1982.
Jerrold, Maud F. *Vittoria Colonna, With Some Account of Her Friends and Her Times*. NY: Dutton, 1906.
Reumont, Alfred von. *Vittoria Colonna, marchesa di Pescara: Vita, fede e poesia nel secolo decimosesto*. Torino: E. Loescher, 1892.

SUGGESTED READING:
Luzio, A. *Vittoria Colonna*. Modena, 1885.
Roscoe, T. *Vittoria Colonna*. London, 1868.
Visconti, P.E. *Le Rime di Vittoria Colonna*. Rome, 1846.

Tracy Barrett,
Vanderbilt University, Nashville, Tennessee

Colquhoun, Ithell (1906–1988).

See Agar, Eileen for sidebar.

Colt, Ethel (1912–1977).

See Barrymore, Ethel for sidebar.

Colter, Mary Elizabeth (1869–1949)

American architect and designer. Born Mary Elizabeth Jane Colter in Pittsburgh, Pennsylvania, on April 4, 1869; died in 1949; graduated from the California School of Design, San Francisco, California, 1890.

Along with the breathtaking vistas, visitors to Arizona's Grand Canyon, one of the most awe-inspiring sites on the American landscape, will encounter six ancient-looking buildings designed by Mary Elizabeth Colter, one of the few American women architects working before World War I. Colter was an avid student of Native American culture who worked for the Fred Harvey Company, an enterprise that prospered by providing food, accommodations, and services for the Santa Fe Railroad. Although most of the buildings Colter designed and decorated throughout the Southwest and Midwest have disappeared, the building projects at the canyon have endured, and four have been designated National Historic Landmarks.

Mary Elizabeth Colter

Colter was raised in St. Paul, Minnesota, and attended the California School of Design in San Francisco, where she also apprenticed to a local architect. After graduating in 1890, she returned to Minnesota and taught art to support her mother and a sister. She was first hired by Fred Harvey as a consultant to design and decorate two buildings at the canyon: an emporium selling Indian-made goods, and Hopi House, a building for housing Indian crafts. Harvey hired her as a permanent architect and designer in 1910. The eccentric Colter worked for the enterprise for the next four decades, keeping an apartment near Harvey headquarters in Kansas City, Missouri, but mostly living in Harvey motels on the road. Described as windswept in appearance and a chain smoker, Colter was considered difficult and outspoken, constantly annoying her crews by demanding to be involved in the smallest detail of a project. Colter's biographer **Virginia L. Grattan,** quoted one of the architect's colleagues as saying, "Everyone hated to see her come on the job."

Colter was almost theatrical in her approach to a design project. Like an actor preparing for a role by envisioning an elaborate life story for her character, Colter began by creating a history for her building, complete with inhabitants. Michael Durham, in an article about the architect for *American Heritage*, describes how she tackled one of her favorite works, a hotel in Winslow, Arizona, by imagining it as the rambling rancho of an early 19th-century don. Her inspiration for the canyon's Hermit's Rest, which stands at the head of Hermit's Trail and now functions as a rest stop for tourists and hikers, was the vision of the 19th-century prospectors and guides who inhabited the canyon. She elaborated on this image until Hermit's Rest looked, in Durham's words, like "an elaborate shelter built stone by stone by some hoary recluse according to the dictates of his own eccentric vision." For the interior, dominated by a massive stone fireplace, Colter ordered the stones for the vaulted ceiling blackened with soot, to look as though an open fire had been burning for years. A weathered tree limb was lodged between the exposed beams in the ceiling to make the ceiling appear hand built. Colter's final flourish was the addition of cobwebs in the corners to make the building look old.

In 1914, the year she finished Hermit's Rest, she also designed Lookout Studio, an eccentric building that hangs over the edge of the canyon wall. Before the roof line was altered, it resembled a prehistoric cliff dwelling. Colter's final Grand

Canyon projects, The Watchtower and Bright Angel Lodge, are striking achievements. The Lodge incorporated features that Durham calls "pure Colter." The exterior color was taken from a weathered telephone pole that she had spotted in Mexico, and the stones on the floor-to-ceiling fireplace represent billions of years of the canyon's geological history, "from stones worn smooth by the Colorado River to the more recent Kaibab limestone found at the canyon's rim."

The Watchtower at Desert View, completed in 1935, remains Colter's masterpiece. A 70'-high circular structure, it is a re-creation of towers built by the prehistoric Anasazi people throughout the Grand Canyon region. In preparation for the work, Colter visited ruins of the Anasazi towers, then had a wooden tower erected to visualize how the building would appear on the site and check on the views it would provide. The completed structure, 30' wide at the base, is larger and stronger than any of those constructed by the Anasazi; its masonry walls are supported by a steel frame provided by Santa Fe Railway engineers. Several exterior stones on the lower level bear authentic carved symbols and drawings, and the tower is further related to its prehistoric past by a small "ruin" Colter built just behind it. In the large circular first level, she created a ceremonial room of an Indian pueblo, complete with chairs created out of tree burls and a log ceiling salvaged from the first Grand Canyon hotel. On the second floor, she duplicated a Hopi room, with a snake altar at the center (used for rain dances), and a large round wall painting by a tribal artist, Fred Kabotie, who respected the architect, in spite of her willfulness. "Miss Colter was a very talented decorator with strong opinions," he said. ". . . I admired her work, and we got along well . . . most of the time."

Colter retired in 1948, at age 79, and died one year later. One of her first buildings at the canyon, Hopi House, was newly renovated in 1995, having deteriorated after an inexpert renovation around 1935. It was necessary to replace 40% of the exterior rock of the building, which was obtained from the same quarry as the origi-

The Watchtower, 1932, designed by Colter.

nal stone. The entire interior was replastered by two Hopi men, who worked in the traditional manner, using their bare hands. The inside of the building was cleaned and polished, and the second floor opened up to allow tourists more browsing room in the shop area. Though the renovation was deemed an unqualified success, Colter might not have been so pleased; one can envision her, hairdo askew, aghast at the polyurethaned floors and impatiently demanding that a precise quality of sand be brought in to give the place the old dusty look it had in 1905.

SOURCES:

Durham, Michael S. "Landmarks on the Rim," in *American Heritage.* April 1996, pp. 137–144.

SUGGESTED READINGS:

Grattan, Virginia L. *Mary Colter, Builder Upon the Red Earth.* Flagstaff AZ: Northland Press, 1980.

Barbara Morgan,
Melrose, Massachusetts

Coltrane, Alice (1937—)

American pianist, organist, and harpist. Name variations: Alice McLeod; Lady Trane; Turiya Sagittinanda. Born Alice McLeod in Detroit, Michigan, on August 27, 1937; sister of Ernie Farrow; married John Coltrane, around 1965 (died 1967).

Rippling, rhythmically free arpeggios are said to characterize the piano and harp playing of Alice Coltrane, wife of jazz great John Coltrane. Alice Coltrane's organ work, described as less flowing than her piano and harp playing, is known for the use of trills and dramatic pauses. Her musical development began at the age of seven with the study of classical music. She studied jazz with Bud Powell and gained experience with church groups. In these early years, Coltrane developed her talents with the jazz ensembles of Kenny Burrell, Lucky Thompson, Yusef Lateef, and Johnny Griffin. In 1962 and 1963, she toured and recorded with **Terry Gibbs,** and it was at this time that she met John Coltrane. They were married around 1965. In 1966, she joined her husband's group, replacing McCoy Tyner. John Coltrane died the following year (1967), and Alice went on to lead many ensembles. Among the saxophonists who played in her groups were Pharoah Sanders, Joe Henderson, Archie Shepp, Frank Lowe, and Carlos Ward; double bass players included Cecil McBee and Jimmy Garrison; and drummers included Rashied Ali, Roy Haynes, and Ben Riley. Following Coltrane's move to California (1972), she founded a retreat for the study of Eastern religions, the Vedantic Center, in 1975, later publishing a book of spiritual texts called *Endless*

Wisdom. After founding the Vedantic Center, she seldom performed but recorded an album in 1978 with Roy Haynes and Reggie Workman called *Transfiguration.* In a tribute to her husband, in 1987 Coltrane performed with a quartet that included her sons at New York's Cathedral of St. John the Divine.

Colum, Mary Gunning
(1884–1957)

Irish-born American author who was a highly regarded literary critic in New York in the 1920s. Name variations: Molly Colum. Born Mary Catherine Maguire in Ireland in 1884 (some sources cite 1887); died in New York City on October 22, 1957; daughter of Charles Maguire and Maria (Gunning) Maguire; married Padraic Colum in 1912; children, none. Immigrated to U.S. (1914).

Irish-born Mary Gunning Colum was both a participant in, and witness to, some of the most important and exciting literary events of the first half of the 20th century. Born in 1884 as Mary Catherine Maguire, she was soon drawn into the intellectual and political turmoil that convulsed Ireland in the first years of the 20th century. A Gaelic cultural Renaissance went hand in hand with increasingly vehement demands for political freedom from Great Britain, and a youthful Mary Maguire found the city of Dublin during these years to be a fascinating place in which ideas were argued with energy; brilliant new poems, plays and novels appeared virtually every week; and life in general was exciting and full of surprises.

While still a student at University College, Dublin, she moved with confidence in the Irish capital's literary circles, meeting—and sometimes sparring with—such emerging giants as William Butler Yeats, A.E. (George William Russell) and James Joyce. Decades later, when Mary Maguire had become Mary Colum and had established herself as one of the best critics in the United States, she noted that critics were "best developed during their formative period when they are surrounded by writers, saturated in literature, rocked and dandled to its sounds and syllables from their earliest years, as composers have to be rocked and dandled to the sounds of music."

In 1912, Mary Maguire married Padraic Colum, a struggling poet and playwright who was associated with Yeats and *Lady (Augusta) Gregory in their efforts to create a national stage tradition at Dublin's recently founded Abbey

Theater. Mary wrote articles and reviews, but since these earned little money, she taught at St. Enda's, a school operated by a fervent Irish nationalist, Padraic Pearse, who was executed by the British for being a leader of the 1916 Easter Rebellion. Padraic Colum was not so much a political firebrand as a dreamy, impractical poet with poor financial prospects, but his bride "Molly" loved him and had faith in the future. Both she and her husband were passionately involved in the Dublin literary scene and both were founders of *The Irish Review,* a journal that quickly became a major voice in Irish intellectual life.

In 1914, the Colums sailed for the United States, leaving behind a European continent that was plunging into the madness of fratricidal warfare, with Ireland itself on the brink of open insurrection against the hated British overlords. The Colums found America exhilarating from the day of their arrival, and they brimmed with ideas about their future careers. Fortunately what all immigrants found to be a difficult time of adjustment was made considerably less painful in their case by the fact that they were able to spend their first months living with a relative in Pittsburgh. Mary took a teaching job that brought in a modest but steady income, while Padraic luckily got a commission from the Carnegie Institute to help in the production of several Irish plays. From the start of their arrival in the United States, their financial situation was better than it had been in Ireland. The Colums yearned for broader horizons and moved to New York City, where Mary continued to teach for a while. Soon, however, her desire to put words on paper became a dominant goal, and she found a job writing editorials for the trade journal *Women's Wear.*

During the next years, Mary and Padraic Colum expanded their circle of friendships. In the summers of 1917 and 1918, they spent several months at the MacDowell Colony in upstate New York where they met a number of leading writers of the day, including Edwin Arlington Robinson, DuBose Heyward, and *Elinor Wylie. The years after World War I saw the careers of both Mary and Padraic Colum grow and prosper. While he wrote many poems of note and produced a highly popular series of books on legends and mythology, she contributed articles to the leading American literary journals, including *Scribner's, Saturday Review, The Nation, The New Republic,* and the *Yale Review.* Her reputation as an expert on modern literature made her one of the regular reviewers for *The New York Times,* and her assessments were often reprinted in other journals.

From 1933 to 1940, Mary Colum wielded considerable power in American literary life through her monthly contributions to *Forum* magazine. By the late 1930s, she was regarded as one of the leading critics in the United States. Recognition of her work during these years included two Guggenheim fellowships, as well as awards from Georgetown University and the American Institute of Arts and Letters.

Despite her busy schedule, Colum was able in 1937 to publish *From these Roots,* a sweeping interpretation of modern literature that received generally high marks from her fellow critics. During the next years, she worked on her autobiography, *Life and the Dream,* which received enthusiastic reviews at the time of its publication in 1947. Carl van Doren described it as "the best chronicle I know of an individual Irish contribution to the intellectual life of America." Edmund Wilson praised Colum for having presented a superb portrait of Irish writers, "the nobility and the fire of the movement, and her pictures of its personalities have . . . humanity and . . . dignity."

In the mid-1950s, Mary decided to work with her husband on a collaborative project, a study of James Joyce as they had known him. It was while working on this book that Mary Colum died suddenly at her desk on October 22, 1957. It was a classic writer's death, ending literally in mid-sentence. Fortunately the manuscript had been almost completed at the time, and it appeared in print the year after her death as *Our Friend James Joyce.*

Some years before his death, Padraic Colum told an interviewer that he never knew, given his poverty and poor prospects in 1912, why "Molly ever married me." It was clear that, both as fellow writers as well as husband and wife, they had been a superb team. On one occasion in the 1920s, when both were in Hawaii to start one of his writing projects, he suddenly suffered a major loss of confidence and decided to "slip off to Australia." Fortunately Molly was there to save the day, telling Padraic in no uncertain terms, "Now's the time to get your self-confidence. . . . No, you are not going to Australia. You'll have to stay here." Recalling the incident many decades later, Padraic Colum said: "So I did [stay] and worked it out." Padraic Colum died in Enfield, Connecticut, on January 11, 1972, at the age of 90.

SOURCES:
Bowen, Zack R. "Ninety Years in Retrospect: Excerpts from Interviews with Padraic Colum," in *Journal of*

Irish Literature. Vol. 2, no. 1. January 1973, pp. 14–34.

———. *Padraic Colum: A Biographical-Critical Introduction.* Carbondale, IL: Southern Illinois University Press, 1970.

Colum, Mary. *From these Roots: The Ideas that Have Made Modern Literature.* NY: Scribner, 1937.

———. *Life and the Dream.* Rev. ed. Chester Springs, PA: Dufour Editions, 1966:

———, and Padraic Colum. *Our Friend James Joyce.* Garden City, NY: Doubleday, 1958.

Hoehn, Matthew, ed. *Catholic Authors: Contemporary Biographical Sketches 1930–1947.* Newark, NJ: St. Mary's Abbey, 1948.

"Mary Colum Dies; A Literary Critic," in *The New York Times.* October 23, 1957, p. 33.

Rimo, Patricia A. "Mollie Colum and Her Circle," in *Irish Literary Supplement.* Fall 1985, p. 26.

Sternlicht, Sanford. *Padraic Colum.* Boston, MA: Twayne Publishers, 1985.

John Haag,
University of Georgia, Athens, Georgia

Columba of Cordova (d. 853)

Saint. Executed in 853 in Cordova, Spain.

At the time of Columba's birth, Christians and Muslims had been locked in conflict for over 500 years. During one persecution of Catholics by the Muslims, Columba, a nun at Cordova, purposefully left her convent to declare her faith before the cadi's tribunal (Muslim magistrates). For this, she was beheaded in 853. Her feast day is celebrated on September 17.

Columba of Rieti (1467–1501)

Italian mystic of the Third Order of Penance who promoted a project to reform the religious female life in the early modern age. Name variations: Angela or Angelella; Columba de Rieti; Colomba da Rieti; called Columba ("dove") because of a miraculous event that took place during her baptism. Born in Rieti, Italy, in 1467 in a merchants' family; died on May 20, 1501; daughter of Angelo Antonio and Giovanna Guadagnali, called Vanna.

Columba of Rieti took her vows at age 18. At 21, she left her hometown and moved to Perugia, where she founded the nunnery of the Colombe and engaged in social and political reform. According to tradition, when Perugia was struck by the plague in 1494, it was Columba's intercession that ended the epidemic and saved the population. Known as the co-patron of Rieti and Perugia with the title of protector, Columba died on May 20, 1501, at age 34; the cause of death was said to be her continued fasts and physical penances.

SOURCES:

Bontempi, S. Angeli De'. *Legenda B. Columbae,* in AA.SS. Maii, V, Anversa: 1865 p. 319–398.

———. *Legenda Volgare.* Perugia: Augusta Library, ms. D. 62.

Una santa, una citta. Proceedings of the historical congress for the 5th centenary of the coming in Perugia of Columba from Rieti, Florence: 1990.

Zarri, G. *Le sante vive: Cultura e religiosità femminile nella prima et moderna.* Torino: Rosemberg and Sellier, 1989.

SUGGESTED READING:

Il Territorio, special issue, Vol. VIII, no. 2–3. January–August 1992.

Tozzi, I. *Colomba da Rieti: Sacro e parola di donna.* Demian: Teramo, 1993.

Ileana Tozzi,
member of the Società Italiana delle Storiche,
lives in Rieti, Italy

Columba of Sens (d. 274?)

Saint. Born in Spain. Executed around 274.

It is said that from birth Columba of Sens had a horror of pagan idols (idols were popular in the Roman Empire of the 3rd century). As a child in Spain (Hispania), she heard stories of France (Gaul) and its Christian religion. Fleeing Spain, she settled in Sens, a city in northeast France, where she was baptized and welcomed by the populace. When the Roman emperor Aurelian passed through Sens in 274 CE on his mission to reconquer Gaul, he had all the Christians of the town put to death except Columba. Aurelian was attracted by her beauty and noble origins. That day, however, she spurned him, and he handed her over for execution. Legend has it that, as she was about to die, a bear came out of the woods and knelt before her. The Roman soldiers kept a respectful distance until Columba dismissed the bear, her protector. The executioners then carried out their orders, and Columba was beheaded. Her feast day is celebrated on December 31st.

Colwin, Laurie (1944–1992)

American fiction and food writer. Born on June 14, 1944, in New York, New York; died of a heart attack on October 24, 1992, in New York; daughter of Estelle Snellenberg; educated at Bard College and Columbia University; married Juris Jurjevics (an editor), in 1981; children: Rosa Audrey Jurjevics.

Selected works: Passion and Affect *(1974);* Shine on, Bright and Dangerous Object *(1975);* Happy All the Time *(1978);* Family Happiness *(1982);* Home Cooking *(1988);* A Big Storm Knocked It Over *(1993);* More Home Cooking *(1993).*

Laurie Colwin was born in New York but spent her youth in Long Island, Chicago and Philadelphia. She returned to Manhattan as an adult and attended Bard College and Columbia University before quitting school and going into publishing. Colwin worked her way through four publishing houses, moving up from a clerical position to assistant editor at Dutton. She wrote at night, publishing her first story in *The New Yorker* (1969). When Dutton fired her for insubordination, she took it as a sign. "If I hadn't been fired, I don't know what would have happened to me because I was very unwilling to make that gesture of saying, 'Forget the job. I'm a writer.'"

Colwin's short-story collection *Passion and Affect* was published in 1974 and was followed by several novels. Food played a prominent role in her writing; as a columnist for *Gourmet*, she could make the successes and failures of a typical kitchen her central theme. Her frank acknowledgment of the mess that can accompany cooking earned her a devoted following. Several of Colwin's columns were collected in 1988's *Home Cooking*. In 1987, she was awarded a Guggenheim Fellowship.

Colwin married Soho Press editor Juris Jurjevics in 1981, and they had a daughter, Rosa. Eleven years later, in 1992, Laurie Colwin died at age 48. At the time of her death, she had two books in production. *A Big Storm Knocked It Over* and *More Home Cooking* were released in 1993.

SOURCES:

The New York Times (obituary). October 26, 1992, D10.

Pearlman, Mickey, and Katherine Usher Henderson. *A Voice of One's Own*. Boston, MA: Houghton Mifflin, 1990.

Schwarz, Karen. "The Writing Life," in *Writer's Digest*. December 1983, pp. 22–23.

Crista Martin,
Boston, Massachusetts

Comaneci, Nadia (1961—)

Rumanian gymnast who was the first woman in the history of international gymnastics to score a perfect 10.0. Pronunciation: Co-ma-NEETCH. Born on November 12, 1961, in Onesti, Rumania; daughter of Gheorghe (an auto mechanic) and Stefania Comaneci; married Bart Conner (an Olympic gymnast), on April 27, 1996, in Rumania.

Became overall European Champion (1975, 1977, 1979); won Olympic gold medals in all-around, uneven bars, and balance beam as well as team silver and bronze in floor exercise in Montreal (1976); won the Chunichi Cup in Japan (1976); won the World Championship (1978); won Olympic gold medals in floor exercises and balance beam, won a silver team medal and silver in the all-around in Moscow (1980); won the all-around, uneven bars, and floor exercise in World University Games (1981).

By age six, Nadia Comaneci was studying gymnastics; at 14, she was the first woman in the history of international gymnastics to score a perfect 10.0; by 19, she had about reached the end of her competitive career and was heading for serious trouble.

Born in 1961 in the factory town of Onesti in Rumania's Carpathian mountains, Comaneci was only in kindergarten when gymnastic coaches, Béla and **Marta Károlyi**, spotted her as she played with a classmate on the school grounds. "They were running and jumping and pretending to be gymnasts," said Béla. "Then the bell rang. Before I could find out who they were, all the children rushed together for the door to go inside. I lost them in the crowd." Convinced he had

Nadia Comaneci

seen something special, he returned to the school and went from class to class but after a time all the little girls began to look alike. A few days later, he returned to each class, this time asking, "Who loves gymnastics here?" In the third room, two girls jumped up and shouted, "We do!" One of the two would go on to become a ballet dancer; the other was Nadia Comaneci.

In those days of the Cold War and government-sponsored sports programs, in order to get financing, eager young gymnasts first had to first pass the beam test. Fear of the beam was a sure way to weed out potentially inferior gymnasts. When Béla placed six-year-old Comaneci on the 4"-wide piece of spruce, she sauntered across, fearless. By 1968, she was gymnast-in-residence at the Károlyis' fledgling sports lycée, the National Institute of Gymnastics, in her hometown. She received lodging, meals, training, equipment, and education—all paid for by the Rumanian government. One year later, in 1969, Béla entered her in the Rumanian national junior championships. The youngest there, the eight-year-old Nadia finished 13th. By 1971, she was junior national all-around champion, a title she successfully defended in 1972, now age 11.

In 1975, Nadia Comaneci moved into international senior competition. Her first win came in April at the Champions All tournament at Wembley, England. Four months later, to everyone's surprise, the 13-year-old took the European championships held at Skein, Norway, coming in well ahead of Russia's five-time European champion *Ludmila Tourischeva who finished 4th. For meticulous execution of intricate vaults and her personal version of the difficult Radochla somersault on the uneven bars, Comaneci won a gold medal in the all-around, the vault, the uneven bars, and the balance beam, while also taking second to Russia's ❧▸ Nelli Kim in the floor exercise. With this extraordinary performance, the young Rumanian was voted 1975 Sportswoman of the Year by European sportswriters and the International Gymnastic Federation.

In March 1976, she toured the United States with the Rumanian team. During this first visit to a country she would eventually adopt, Comaneci won every competition, including the American Cup. While performing the difficult Tsukahara vault—a full twist into a back somersault—Comaneci scored a perfect 10.0, the first 10.0 ever scored in a U.S. gymnastics competition; she also scored a 10.0 in the floor exercise. At the end of the tournament, she shared the press podium with another young gymnastics winner, America's Bart Connor, who, when egged on by photographers, gave her a peck on the cheek. Connor was infatuated; Nadia, at 13, was unfazed.

Though Nadia Comaneci entered the 1976 Olympics in Montreal as the top gymnast in the world, expectations were also high for the successful and more experienced Russian team who had sauntered off with the 1972 Olympics, especially the international sweetheart *Olga Korbut and the always looming Ludmila Tourischeva.

On July 18, 1976, in Montreal's Forum, teams met for the first day of the compulsories for the combined event, which includes the balance beam, the horse vault, floor exercises, and uneven bars. Considered too physically demanding, the uneven bars had not been a woman's event until the Helsinki Olympics in 1952; the contest requires coarsened hands, enormous strength in the arms and shoulders, and fearlessness while executing dangerous moves; it also inflicts a spirited lashing on thighs and groins as gymnasts whip through a crowded program where pauses must not be noticeable.

By the time Comaneci approached the bars, the Russians had scored well. Olga Korbut had executed a spellbinding program and held the highest score with a 9.90; Nelli Kim had earned a 9.80 and Tourischeva a 9.75. Comaneci's fellow Rumanians had also done well: ❧▸ Gabriela Trusca was tied with Tourischeva, ❧▸ Mariana Constantin was ahead of Kim with a 9.85, and Comaneci's friend and constant competitor ❧▸ Teodora Ungureanu had tied Korbut at 9.90. Sporting her trademark ponytail, bangs, and serious demeanor, Comaneci hoisted herself up and worked between the bars for 23 seconds of dazzling loops and twists, which concluded in a flawless dismount. Awarded a 10.0, she was the first gymnast to receive a perfect score in Olympic history. The scoreboard, unequipped to register the moment, could only manage a 9.99. That day Comaneci also scored highest in the beam event with a 9.90, topping Korbut's 9.80, but on the floor exercises Tourischeva held her own. By the end of the first day, Comaneci led the combined competition in points.

On the afternoon of the second day, the gymnasts went through the optional exercises while Comaneci fidgeted on the sidelines. In the vault, she came in third behind Nelli Kim and ❧▸ Maria Filatova of Russia. In the bars, Olga Korbut repeated her performance of the day before, another outstanding 9.90, while Kim (9.85) and Tourischeva (9.80) improved. When it was Comaneci's turn, she approached the bars, her bangs meeting her brows in knitted concentration. Hoisting herself up, she did 23 seconds of handstands, somersaults, twists and turns, released and landed another flawless dismount. Though the scoreboard stubbornly stuck at 9.99, the judges had given her another 10.0. Onlookers were enthralled.

Comaneci then catapulted onto the balance beam. At first, the audience was audibly gasping as she executed dangerous maneuvers with darting moves, but her confidence began to bolster their confidence, and they were soon riveted on the amazing skills of this 86-pound, 4'11", 14-year-old. Another perfect 10.0. "With no more strain than it would take to raise a hand to a friend, she is airborne," wrote a *Time* staffer, "a backflip, landing on the sliver of a bar with a thunk so solid it reverberates; up, backward again, a second blind flip, and a landing. No 747 ever set itself down on a two-mile runway with more assurance or aplomb." ABC's commentator, Jim McKay, rhapsodized, she "swims in an ocean of air." The eyes of the world had turned from the ever-smiling, crowd-pleasing Olga Korbut, to the dour, concentrated, ever-serious Nadia Comaneci. Olympic history was being made.

The third and final day of the combined exercises, known as the voluntary leg of the competition, was held in front of 18,000, the largest crowd that had ever assembled for a gymnastics event. Comaneci occasionally walked the arena clutching a large doll, a worn seal-skin Eskimo figure given her years earlier by Béla. On the horse event, Nelli Kim led off with a 10.0, the first perfect vault ever achieved; Tourischeva placed second with a 9.95, and Comaneci came in third with a 9.80. The uneven bars were hotly contested: 9.90s went to Korbut, Ungureanu, ❧▸ **Márti Egervári** of Hungary, and Nelli Kim. As Comaneci approached the bars, observers knew that the likelihood of her reaping three successive perfect scores was almost nonexistent. She hoisted herself up, did 23 seconds of swinging, turning, circling, and landed another flawless dismount. 10.0. She followed that with her second successive perfect 10.0 on the balance beam. The gold medal in the combined individual exercises was indisputably hers. Nelli Kim placed second and Tourischeva third. (Team medals went to the Soviet Union first, Rumania second, and East Germany third.)

The individual events were held that afternoon. The only entrants allowed in each specialty are the six gymnasts with the highest scores in the two rounds (compulsory and voluntary) of

❧▸ **Kim, Nelli** (1957—)
Russian gymnast. Born in the central Asian city of Chimkent, Russia, on July 19, 1957; daughter of Korean parents.

Won World Championship in horse vault (1978) and floor exercises (1978); won four Olympic medals: two gold in horse vault and floor exercises, one team gold, and one silver (1976).

Nelli Kim was Nadia Comaneci's chief competition at the 1976 Games in Montreal. Awarded two perfect 10s, Kim won four Olympic medals: two gold in horse vault and floor exercises, one team gold, and one silver, attacking the bars and beams with singular determination.

❧▸ **Trusca, Gabriela** (1957—)
Rumanian gymnast. Born on July 28, 1957.

In 1976, Gabriela Trusca won the silver medal in the team all-around in the Montreal Olympics.

❧▸ **Constantin, Mariana** (1960—)
Rumanian gymnast. Born on August 3, 1960.

Mariana Constantin won the silver medal in the team all-around in the Montreal Olympics in 1976.

❧▸ **Ungureanu, Teodora** (1960—)
Rumanian gymnast. Born on November 13, 1960.

In 1976, in the Montreal Olympics, Teodora Ungureanu won a bronze medal for the balance beam, a silver in the uneven parallel bars, and a silver in the team all-around.

❧▸ **Filatova, Maria** (1961—)
Soviet gymnast. Born on July 19, 1961.

In 1976, Maria Filatova won the gold medal in the team all-around in the Montreal Olympics. Four years later in the Moscow Olympics, she won the bronze medal in the uneven parallel bars and another gold medal in the team all-around.

❧▸ **Egervári, Márti** (1956—)
Hungarian gymnast. Name variations: Marta or Marti Egervari. Born in August 1956.

In the 1976 Montreal Olympics, Márti Egervári won the bronze medal in the uneven parallel bars.

the team competition. Comaneci continued domination of the uneven bars with another 10.0, winning the gold; her teammate Ungureanu took the silver and Egervári the bronze. On the beam, Comaneci achieved her 7th 10.0, finishing with a 19.95 total out of a possible 20; she took the gold in this event while Korbut took the silver, and Ungureanu the bronze. In the floor exercises, Nelli Kim received her second 10.0 for the gold, while Tourischeva took the silver and Comaneci the bronze. Kim also took the vault, with ◄❀ **Carola Dombeck** of East Germany placing second and Tourischeva third.

Over the three-day competition, Comaneci was awarded seven perfect 10.0s and had won five medals, three of them gold. "The tiny point spreads she won by don't begin to indicate how much better she is than her nearest rivals," said Frank Bare, executive director of the U.S. Gymnastics Federation. "There has never been anyone like her, never been anyone who approaches her." Said the eclipsed Olga Korbut, "I gave all I had."

But at Comaneci's press conferences, audiences were disappointed that Nadia was not like the beloved Olga. Unlike Korbut, Comaneci was expressionless and still; she did not celebrate her victories. Continually prodded to smile, or questioned about her lack of a smile, Nadia responded: "I don't come here to smile, I come here to do a job." Embarrassed by all the attention, she just wanted to go home.

Though thousands of Rumanians were standing at the Bucharest airport to welcome her back and she was awarded the Hero of Socialist Labor (her country's highest honor), things were not all that perfect at home. The Rumanian officials and press went out of their way to extol the

entire team and not single out the extraordinary performance of Comaneci, while internationally, expectation for her perfect scores continued. The following year, her parents separated (1977). Worse yet, to the consternation of enthusiasts, she did what all little girls do, she began to grow up; at 16, she added 20 pounds to her frame and 4" to her height. Rumors circulated that she was tired of practice, quitting the school, had fallen in love.

Through the 1970s, Comaneci continued to compete, but Cold War politics prohibited her from traveling to the West, where she was wildly popular, for fear she might defect. She won the Chunichi Cup and the World Cup in Tokyo in 1978; that same year, she was also beaten badly by her 14-year-old teammate ◄❀ **Emilia Eberle** during a meet in West Germany.

In the 1980 Olympics in Moscow, Comaneci performed well, winning gold medals in the balance beam and floor exercise. Controversially low scores from two judges in the balance beam, however, cost her the all-around, which went to Soviet ◄❀ **Yelena Davydova**. But the games had been boycotted by the United States and other nations, limiting the competition and exposure.

At her last major tournament, the 1981 World University Games in Bucharest, Comaneci won the all-around, uneven bars, and floor exercise. By then, her longtime coach Béla Károlyi had defected to the U.S., opened a school in Houston, and was training gymnasts of the future like *Mary Lou Retton. It was said Comaneci was having an affair with the son of dictator Nicolae Ceausescu, an assertion she denies. Retiring in 1984, at age 23, she signed on as an international gymnastics judge and was a coach of the Rumanian team when it competed in the 1984 Olympics in Los Angeles. She then took a job coaching for the government until 1989. But Comaneci longed for escape from the obscurity she was facing in her own country; she'd "rather die in a free country than die in a Communist one," she would later tell reporters.

In 1989, under cover of darkness, she walked six hours to the Hungarian border. There, she met Rumanian émigré Constantin Panait, a 38-year-old Florida roofer, married with four children, who had agreed to help her defect to his new country. Traveling by way of Vienna, she entered the United States.

The defection was costly. With Panait, she toured the United States but the news media began to notice the weight gain, the heavy make-

❀► **Dombeck, Carola** (1960—)

East German gymnast. Born on June 25, 1960.

In the Montreal Olympics, 1976, Carola Dombeck won a silver medal in the horse vault and a bronze in the team all-around.

❀► **Eberle, Emilia** (1964—)

Rumanian gymnast. Born on March 4, 1964.

In the Moscow Olympics in 1980, Emilia Eberle took the silver medal in the uneven parallel bars and the team silver in the all-around.

❀► **Davydova, Yelena** (1961—)

Soviet gymnast. Name variations: Elena Davidova. Born on August 7, 1961.

In the Moscow Olympics, in 1980, Yelena Davydova won gold medals in both the individual and team all-around. She also won bronze medals for the floor exercise and balance beam.

up, the married man at her side. Americans, too, were finding it hard to forgive her for not remaining that harmless 14-year-old. Though it was quickly assumed Comaneci was involved with Panait, she maintains this was not true.

But fellow gymnasts saw more than the media, and some knew she was in trouble. Panait was keeping Comaneci a virtual prisoner, misrepresenting the relationship, threatening the withdrawal of his sponsorship and deportation, if she told anyone of his actions. He was also pocketing all her performance fees. Under the pretense of a lucrative job offer, Alexandru Stefu, a former Rumanian rugby coach living in Montreal, called Panait and Comaneci to a meeting. In the safety of his presence, Nadia told Stefu that Panait was mistreating her. Panait fled. For the next 18 months, Comaneci lived with Stefu and his wife while working out and getting back in shape.

After Stefu's death in a snorkeling accident, Comaneci turned to gymnastic coach Paul Ziert, who arranged her appearances and let her stay in a room in his home. At the time, Ziert was also coaching Bart Conner, with whom Comaneci fell in love. Comaneci and Conner were together for four years, living in Norman, Oklahoma, where Conner ran a gymnastics school and the two coached, before they married in Rumania in 1996.

In the 1970s and '80s, gymnasts like Olga Korbut, Nadia Comaneci, and Mary Lou Retton effectively transformed the sport of gymnastics from one of grace to one of power, from one dominated by ballerinas to one dominated by athletes. Many of Comaneci's moves were dangerous, including the Salto Comaneci, a twisting back-somersault dismount off the uneven bars. She was the first gymnast in the world to perform the Radochla somersault on the higher of the uneven bars, a feat which, upon seeing, said one reporter, is not necessarily believing. She was also responsible for the now almost obligatory three back handsprings in a row on the balance beam. Comaneci's career was a cornerstone of gymnastic history, and her influence is still apparent as athletes continue to enhance and reinvent one of the most popular disciplines of the sports world.

SOURCES:

Gutman, Bill. *Modern Women Superstars* (juvenile). NY: Dodd, Mead, 1977.

"Head over Heels," in *People Weekly*. March 27, 1995, pp. 105–106.

Time. August 2, 1976, p. 44.

Woolum, Janet. *Outstanding Women Athletes*. Phoenix, AZ: Oryx Press, 1992.

RELATED MEDIA:

ABC's "Wide World of Sports" (March 18, 1995) presented a 90-minute documentary of Comaneci's first return to Rumania (with commentators Bart Conner and *Donna de Varona).

Comden, Betty (1915—)

American playwright, lyricist, screenwriter, and performer, best known for her work with Adolph Green, with whom she wrote the screenplay and lyrics for the movie classic Singin' in the Rain. *Born Basya Astershinsky Simselyevitch-Simselyovitch Cohen on May 3, 1915, in Brooklyn, New York; daughter and one of two children of Leo (an attorney) and Rebecca (Sadvoransky) Cohen (a teacher); attended Brooklyn Ethical Culture School; graduate of Erasmus Hall High School; New York University, B.S., 1938; married designer Steven Kyle (d. 1979), on January 4, 1942; children: daughter Susanna Kyle; son Alan Kyle (d. 1990).*

Theater musicals (in collaboration with Adolph Green): On the Town *(book and lyrics, 1944);* Billion Dollar Baby *(book and lyrics, 1945);* Two on the Aisle *(sketches and lyrics, 1951);* Wonderful Town *(lyrics, 1953);* Peter Pan *(lyrics, 1954);* Bells Are Ringing *(book and lyrics, 1956);* Say, Darling *(lyrics, 1958);* Do Re Mi *(1960);* Subways Are for Sleeping *(1961);* Fade Out—Fade In *(book and lyrics, 1964);* Hallelujah, Baby! *(lyrics, 1967);* Applause *(book, 1970);* On the Twentieth Century *(book and lyrics, 1978);* A Doll's Life *(book and lyrics, 1982);* The Will Rogers Follies: A Life in Revue *(co-lyricist, 1991).*

Films (in collaboration with Green): Good News! *(screenplay, 1947);* The Barkleys of Broadway *(screenplay, 1949);* On the Town *(screenplay and lyrics, 1949);* Take Me Out to the Ball Game *(lyrics, 1949);* Singin' in the Rain *(screenplay and lyrics, 1952);* The Band Wagon *(screenplay, 1953);* It's Always Fair Weather *(screenplay and lyrics, 1955);* Auntie Mame *(screenplay, 1958);* Bells Are Ringing *(screenplay and lyrics, 1960);* What a Way to Go *(screenplay and lyrics, 1964).*

Betty Comden's collaboration with Adolph Green, likely the longest and closest collaboration in American musical theater history, has produced librettos, screenplays, and lyrics for Broadway and Hollywood for over 50 years. Beginning as performers as well as writers, they were part of the evolution of the musical—from the thinly plotted shows of the 1940s with clever showstopping numbers and catchy ballads, to modern almost operatic plays with musical numbers so integrated with plot and character that a single popular tune rarely emerges. Through the years, Comden and Green have teamed up with a number of different composers and countless performers, but they have always worked together. In her memoirs, *Off Stage,* Comden writes that her long association with Adolph Green has led people to assume they are married, though he has been married for years to actress **Phyllis Newman.** Comden, married to Steven Kyle since 1942, was widowed in 1979. "Confusion still reigns," she quips. "I always say as long as we are not confused, everything is all right."

Born Basya Astershinsky Simselyevitch-Simselyovitch Cohen (changed to Betty Comden around the time her "distinguished" nose was altered), she grew up in Brooklyn, in the arms of a loving Jewish family. Fascinated by words even as a child, Comden wrote and acted as early as grammar school, her most vivid memory being a seventh-grade dramatization of Sir Walter Scott's *Ivanhoe,* in which she played an undersized Rebecca. Though she shunned her high school plays because she felt she was not pretty enough, by 1938 when she received her degree in drama from New York University, she wanted only to perform.

While making the rounds of theatrical agents, she met the similarly unemployed actor, Adolph Green, a toothy, brilliant eccentric whom she once described as "a man who reads while crossing the street." They joined forces, and with a couple of Green's friends, including Judy Tuvim (who would become *Judy Holliday*), formed the Revuers, a satirical group that wrote and performed topical sketches and songs. Leonard Bernstein, another friend and Green's sometime roommate, often sat in as the group's accompanist. Their first show, called *Where To Go in New York,* included the first Comden and Green song "The Subway Opening," a melodic history of the Sixth Avenue line. This, as well as other songs from these early revues, mostly about New York City and show business, typify the satirical, sophisticated, and urbane approach that would become the hallmark of the Comden-Green lyric. The Revuers' Sunday night performances at Greenwich Village's Vanguard theater were soon expanded to three nights, then six. By 1939, they were appearing five nights a week at the Rainbow Room atop the RCA Building. They made weekly appearances on NBC radio and performed at the Blue Angel, Radio City Music Hall, and Loew's State Theatre. "We turned into a New York institution," said Comden.

In the mid-1940s, Bernstein called on them to write the book and lyrics for *On the Town,* a stage musical based on his popular ballet *Fancy Free,* which told the story of three sailors on 24-hour leave in New York City. Considered one of the most literate shows Broadway had produced, it opened on December 28, 1944, to critical acclaim. Lewis Nichols of *The New York Times* called it "the freshest and most engaging musical show since the golden days of Oklahoma! Everything about it is right. . . a perfect example of what a well-knit fusion of the respectable arts can provide for the theatre." The musical also marked the debut of Comden and Green as performers. Comden played Claire de Loon, an anthropology student who falls in love with Ozzie, a sailor played by Green. *Cue* magazine called Comden faintly reminiscent of a young *Fannie Brice.*

Their second show, *Billion Dollar Baby* (1945), with music by Morton Gould, enjoyed only a modest run, and a third, *Bonanza Bound,* closed in Philadelphia. But with their names now established on Broadway, Comden and Green found themselves courted by Hollywood. Their first film assignment was a new scenario for the 1947 film remake of the stage musical *Good News* (1927), for which they created lyrics for the memorable song "The French Lesson," introduced by *June Allyson* and Peter Lawford. Three other films followed in 1949: *The Barkleys of Broadway,* the last partnering of Fred Astaire and *Ginger Rogers*; the film adaptation of *On the Town* (1949), for which they received their first Screenwriters Award for lyrics; and *Take Me Out to the Ball Game.* Although Comden and Green returned to New York in 1951, they would script other Hollywood musicals throughout their career. Perhaps most memorable was the screenplay and lyrics for *Singin' in the Rain* (1952), a satire of Hollywood in the late 1920s, that noted film critic **Pauline Kael** called "about the best Hollywood musical of all time." They created the screenplay for *The Band Wagon* (1953) and *It's Always Fair Weather* (1955), for which they received a second Screenwriters Award. Later films included *Auntie Mame* (1958), *Bells Are Ringing* (1960), and *What a Way to Go* (1964).

Meeting each day from one to five in the afternoon, Comden and Green established a working pattern early in their career that endured. "We meet daily on the great theory that nothing is wasted," Comden once explained. "I usually sit at the typewriter with a carbon in the machine for Adolph to take home. Sometimes we just sit staring at each other for hours without saying a word." Comden also refers to a "kind of radar" between them, "based on stuff we have both read or heard or shared." She further describes the lyric-writing process as requiring long sessions with the composer and then further work alone. When a show finally reaches the rehearsal stage, it becomes an around-the-clock ordeal, with each assignment bringing its own particular problems.

Wonderful Town (1953), another collaboration with Bernstein, is considered by some to be Comden and Green's finest work. It contains some of their sharpest lyrics, including "One Hundred Easy Ways (To Lose a Man)," a specialty number created for *Rosalind Russell's limited singing talents, and the comic dance number "Conga!" with its delightful kooky rhymes (rhythm bands/ monkey glands/ hot-dog stands). Comden and Green won a Tony and a Donaldson Award for their lyrics. However, they would not work with Bernstein again, though the composer remained one of Comden's dearest friends until his death in 1990.

Sketches and lyrics for the musical revue *Two on the Aisle* (1951) launched Comden and Green's first collaboration with composer Jule Styne and a relationship that endured for three decades. With him, they created a new production of *Peter Pan* (1954) and the book and lyrics for *Bells Are Ringing* (1956), which proved not only to be a starring vehicle for their old friend Judy Holliday, but also the greatest box-office success of their Broadway career—with a run of 924 performances, a nationwide tour, and a motion-picture adaptation. The show boasted a number of satirical songs, including "It's a Simple Little System," a comic number based on *The Racing Form,* and "Drop That Name," a parody on the guests at exclusive parties. Comden and Green produced the lyrics for two songs from the show that became standards: "The Party's Over" and "Just in Time." Following this triumph came lyrics for the more moderately successful *Say Darling* (1958).

In December 1958, Comden and Green returned to performing with a successful Off-Broadway revue, *A Party with Betty Comden and Adolph Green,* which included a repertoire of their own songs dating back to the Greenwich Village days. After 82 performances, the show toured, then returned to New York in 1959, where it won an Obie. In 1975, an expanded version was performed at the Loeb Center at Harvard University, before it returned to New York in 1977. In his review of the show for *The New York Times,* Clive Barnes summed up Comden's and Green's talents as both writers and performers. "They have a manic dexterity with words," he wrote, "a gift for rhyme and an ear for reason. As performers they have this dazzling charm, which makes them the kind of people you would really like to invite into your home."

At the height of her professional success, Comden's life also included a husband and two children, Susanna and Alan, who were raised amid a busy work schedule and numerous separations from their mother. Of her 37-year marriage to designer Steven Kyle, she says "We were deeply, closely happy with each other and about each other." Their happiness did not preclude unresolved issues including that of her more prominent and lucrative career and the strain and complications of working with Adolph—not romantic complications, as she is quick to point out, but every other kind. These problems paled, however, alongside the tragic death of Comden's talented artistic son Alan, who died of AIDS in 1990 after a troubled childhood and years of drug addiction. Of the many poignant

From the movie Singin' in the Rain, *starring Debbie Reynolds and Gene Kelly, screenplay and lyrics by Betty Comden and Adolph Green.*

referrals to Comden's children in her book, none is considered more heart-wrenching than the chapter in which she replays motherhood, changing the script at various junctures to reflect a more favorable outcome.

Beginning in the 1960s, the narrow scope of Comden and Green's standard musical conventions began to grow stale, especially with the advent of tighter librettos and character lyrics in shows like *Hello Dolly!*, *A Funny Thing Happened on the Way to the Forum*, *Cabaret*, *Company*, and *A Chorus Line*. Their next two shows with Styne, *Do Re Mi* (1960) and *Subways Are for Sleeping* (1961), managed respectable runs in spite of weak librettos and unimpressive scores. After *Fade Out—Fade In* (1964), a comic vehicle for **Carol Burnett**, Comden and Green worked again with Styne on one of their more ambitious projects, *Hallelujah, Baby!* (1967), about the plight of black Americans from 1900 to the 1960s. An uneasy mixture of musical comedy and politics, the show never quite jelled, and the score was regarded as merely pleasant, with no bite. The team floundered until the hit *Applause* (1970), starring **Lauren Bacall**, with its tight, smart libretto based on the 1950 film *All About Eve*.

A fresh approach was evident in *On the Twentieth Century* (1978), with composer Cy Coleman, for which they received Tony Awards for both the book and lyrics. Everything about the show, which provided a comeback role for *Imogene Coca, was larger than life, including sets by **Robin Wagner** that included replicas of the streamlined Twentieth Century Limited train. Comden and Green's animated lyrics, including pastiche numbers "Veronique" and "Babette," were reminiscent of their work in the two Bernstein musicals. The best song from the show, "Our Private World," was considered their most imaginative work in years. The show, however, proved too stylized for most audiences and enjoyed only a limited run.

In 1982, the team showed their range with a serious musical *A Doll's Life*, designed as a sequel to Ibsen's *A Doll's House*. With music by Larry Grossman, the story traces Nora's life after she leaves her husband and children. "This show," explained Comden, "is closer to the kind of thing we want to be doing, having arrived at this stage of our lives. It examines things we hadn't gone into very much in other works— human relationships and sexuality." The show did not survive unfavorable reviews and closed after five performances. Undaunted, Comden and Green supplied the lyrics for another Cy Coleman musical, *The Will Rogers Follies*, in 1991, which ran for 983 performances and won the New York Drama Critics Award as Best Musical of 1990–91.

Armed with a fax machine and a long-resisted computer, Betty Comden maintains her optimism while admitting that in her youth she would not have believed that life could be so full of "wrenching sadness." Amid gloomy predictions that the American musical is a dying art form, she and Green, as they used to say, are "back at the old fruit stand," creating yet another happy ending.

SOURCES:

Comden, Betty. *Off Stage*. NY: Simon and Schuster, 1995.
Current Biography. NY: H.W. Wilson, 1945.
Ewen, David. *American Songwriters*. NY: H.W. Wilson, 1987.
Gottfried, Martin. *Broadway Musicals*. NY: Harry N. Abrams, 1979.
Smith, Cecil. *Musical Comedy in America*. NY: Theatre Arts Books, 1950.

Barbara Morgan,
Melrose, Massachusetts

Comingore, Dorothy (1913–1971)

American actress. Name variations: acted under the names Kay Winters and Linda Winters. Born in Los Angeles, California, on August 24, 1913; died in 1971; attended University of California.

Selected films: Campus Cinderella *(1938);* Comet over Broadway *(1938);* Prison Train *(1938);* Trade Winds *(1938);* Blondie Meets the Boss *(1939);* North of the Yukon *(1939);* Scandal Sheet *(1939);* Mr. Smith Goes to Washington *(1939);* Cafe Hostess *(1939);* Pioneers of the Frontier *(1940);* Citizen Kane *(1941);* The Hairy Ape *(1944);* Any Number Can Play *(1949);* The Big Night *(1951).*

Dorothy Comingore made the transition from stage to screen under the name Linda Winters. She appeared in comedy shorts during the mid-1930s, along with an appearance or two with the Three Stooges and in some low-budget Westerns. Her breakthrough role was in Orson Welles' *Citizen Kane* (1941), playing Kane's pathetic second wife Kate. Seemingly destined for stardom, Comingore nevertheless faded in a series of supporting roles. Her career ended in 1951, when she was blacklisted in the wake of the House Un-American Activities Committee hearings.

Comito or Comitona (fl. 500s).

See Anastasia and Comitona.

Comnena, Anna (1083–1153/55).

See Anna Comnena.

Compagnoni, Deborah (1970—)

Italian skier. Name variations: dubbed "Tombagnoni" by the Italian press. Pronunciation: Kome-pah-NYO-nee. Born in Bormio, Sondrio, Italy, on June 4, 1970; coached by Tino Pietrogiovanna.

Won the gold medal in the giant slalom at the World Championships in Sierra Nevada, Spain (1996); took the World Cup giant slalom race in Cortina and became the first Italian woman to win a World Cup title (1996–97), finishing fourth overall; won the gold in the slalom and the giant slalom at the World Championships (1997).

After recuperating from two knee operations and stomach surgery in which 22 inches of her intestine had been removed, Deborah Compagnoni won the Olympic gold medal in the women's super giant slalom (known as the Super G) at Albertville in 1992. Until then, she had

never finished higher than fourth in any World Cup event. One day later, she crashed into a gate in the giant slalom and skidded off the course, tearing a ligament in her left knee.

In 1994 in Lillehammer, she earned a gold medal in the giant slalom, one of only 24 of 47 starters who arrived at the finish. Compagnoni came into the Nagano Olympics in 1998 as reigning world champion. She took the silver in the slalom, placing second to *Hilde Gerg of Germany, then won another gold medal in the giant slalom. "I stay calm. It's in my character," she said.

Compton, Fay (1894–1978)

English actress. Born Virginia Lillian Emmeline MacKenzie in London, England, on September 18, 1894; died on December 12, 1978; one of five children of Edward (an actor and founder of the Compton Old English Company) and Virginia (Bateman) Compton (an actress and daughter of American impresario H.L. Bateman); sister of novelist Sir Comp-

From the movie Citizen Kane, starring Dorothy Comingore.

ton Mackenzie; attended Leatherhead Court School, Surrey, and a school in Paris; married producer H.G. Pelissier, in 1911 (died 1913); married comedian Lauri de Frece (died 1921); married actor Leon Quartermaine (divorced 1942); married actor Ralph Michael (divorced 1946); children: (first marriage) one son, director Anthony Pelissier.

Selected films: She Stoops to Conquer (1914); One Summer's Day (1917); Judge Not (1920); A Woman of No Importance (1921); The Old Wives' Tale (1921); A Bill of Divorcement (1922); This Freedom (1923); The Loves of Mary Queen of Scots (1923); The Eleventh Commandment (1924); The Happy Ending (1925); London Love (1926); Robinson Crusoe (1927); Zero (1928); Fashions in Love (US, 1929); Cape Forlorn (Love Storm, 1931); Tell England (The Battle of Gallipoli, 1931); Waltzes from Vienna (Strauss' Great Waltz, 1933); Autumn Crocus (1934); The Mill on the Floss (1937); So This Is London (1939); The Prime Minister (1941); Odd Man Out (1946); Nicholas Nickleby (1947); London Belongs to Me (Dulcimer Street, 1948); Britannia Mews (The Forbidden Street, 1949); Blackmailed (1950); Laughter in Paradise (1951); Othello (1952); Lady Possessed (1952); Aunt Clara (1954); Town on Trial (1956); The Story of Esther Costello (1957); The Haunting (1963); Uncle Vanya (1963); The Virgin and the Gypsy (1970).

Born into one of England's long-established theatrical families, Fay Compton made her debut at 12 in a Christmas play called Sir Philomir or Love's Victory; from then on, she was never out of work. Reaching worldwide audiences very late in her career, with her portrayal of Aunt Ann on "The Forsyte Saga" television series, her varied and distinguished career embraced stage, film, and television, and afforded her the opportunity to work with some of the greatest playwrights, directors, and actors of her time.

Compton was in The Follies (1911) when she met and married her first husband, the show's producer, H.G. Pelissier, who was 20 years her senior. He died in 1913, at age 39, leaving the 19-year-old Compton with a son. She played in a series of farces before marrying comedian Lauri de Frece and traveling with him to the United States, where, in 1914, she made her New York debut as Victoria, in the musical Tonight's the Night. The couple toured the States, returning to England during World War I.

Compton then moved away from musicals, attempting a variety of roles and working with directing giants Charles Hawtrey, H.B. Irving, and George Alexander. This period was highlighted by her appearances in the title role in Peter Pan (1917), as Blanche Wheeler in Fair and Warmer (1918), and as the lead in Somerset Maugham's Caesar's Wife (1919), a plum emotional role.

In 1920, she played the title role in J.M. Barrie's Mary Rose, a play about a young mother who disappears and returns years later to find that the world has changed though she has remained the same. Critic W.A. Darlington described the arc of Compton's portrayal as "radiant at the beginning of the play and almost unbearably pathetic at the close." Compton played opposite actor Leon Quartermaine, whom she married after being widowed for a second time. They appeared together again in Maugham's The Circle (1921), as well as in Barrie's Quality Street (1921). In 1925, they co-starred in Ashley Duke's comedy The Man with a Load of Mischief, which was followed by This Woman Business, The White Witch, and a revival of Mary Rose (all 1926). Compton divorced Quartermaine in 1942. Her fourth and last husband was actor Ralph Michael; they also divorced in 1946.

Compton did not undertake a Shakespearean role until she opened as Ophelia to John Barrymore's Hamlet in 1925. She repeated the role with Sir Godfrey Tearle in 1931 and with John Gielgud in 1939, prompting James Agate to call her the best Ophelia he had ever seen. Critic J.C. Trewin was more explicit: "This was no chit around Elsinore, but the true 'rose of May,' a girl profoundly hurt; someone who might indeed have mourned as she did for the Hamlet she had lost. . . . [S]he was herself a noble mind o'erthrown. I have not forgotten Fay Compton's Ophelia and those wide, reproachful eyes." In 1935, at the Open Air Theatre in Regent's Park, Compton played Titania in A Midsummer Night's Dream and Rosalind in Love's Labour's Lost. Her Ophelia found numerous revivals, and Shakespearean roles continued to be a mainstay of her career.

Compton's later work included performances with the Old Vic, for which she won particularly good reviews for her Regan in Gielgud's King Lear (1940). A subsequent portrayal of Constance of Britagne (*Constance of Brittany) in King John brought accolades from Audrey Williamson, who called her work "all that her long experience, silver voice and emotional range had led us to anticipate—grief and distraction truly blent, with both the flash of imperiousness and tenderness of affection." Other later successes included Ruth in Noel Coward's Blithe Spirit (1941) and Martha Dacre in *Esther McCracken's No Medals (1941). In 1948, Compton received the Ellen Terry Award for her role as

Mary in *Family Portrait.* In 1959, she appeared on Broadway for the first time in 20 years in the lackluster *God and Kate Murphy.* Joining Laurence Olivier at the first Chichester Festival in 1962, she played Marya in Chekhov's *Uncle Vanya* and Grausis in *The Broken Heart.*

Early in her career, Compton made a number of silent films in England, then went to Hollywood in 1928 for her first American film *Fashions in Love,* co-starring Adolph Menjou. Her only other American film was *Lady Possessed* in 1952. With her debut on the London music-hall stage in *Songs* (1939), her career was also peppered with performance in pantomimes and variety-show tours.

In 1959, when Fay Compton was 65, her memory began to fail, evoking criticism of her Lady Bracknell in *The Importance of Being Earnest,* in which she was forced to paraphrase speeches. A year later, however, she was considered back in form for her role as Comtesse de la Brière in *What Every Woman Knows.* Peter Roberts, in *Plays and Players,* called the role "beautifully done," adding: "Drama students who want to learn to laugh naturally on the stage and at the same time to adopt a French accent that is not an embarrassment should hie them to the Waterloo Road." Fay Compton was awarded a CBE in 1975 and continued to perform up to her death in 1978.

SUGGESTED READING:
Compton, Fay. *Rosemary,* 1926.

Barbara Morgan,
Melrose, Massachusetts

Compton-Burnett, Ivy (1884–1969)

English novelist, author of psychological thrillers set in an earlier time, whose works are almost entirely composed of dialogue. Name variations: I. Compton-Burnett. Born Ivy Compton-Burnett on June 5, 1884, at Pinner, a village in Middlesex, England; died on August 27, 1969, at Braemar Mansions, London; daughter of James Compton Burnett (a homeopathic physician) and Katharine (Rees) Compton-Burnett; tutored at home; attended Assiscombe College for the Daughters of Gentlemen; Howard College, Bedford; Royal Holloway College, London University, Egham, Surrey; lived with Margaret Jourdain (d. 1951, a writer and expert on furniture); never married; no children.

Awards: Commander of the Order of the British Empire; James Tait Black Memorial Prize (1956); honorary Doctor of Letters, University of Leeds (1960).

Father died (1901); entered Royal Holloway College to study classics (1902); favorite brother Guy died (1905); passed Bachelor of Arts honors examination (1906); first novel published (1911); mother died (1911); brother Noel killed fighting in France (1916); two sisters died, possibly by suicide (1917); began life with Margaret Jourdain, writer and expert on furniture (1919); Margaret died (1951).

Selected publications—novels: Dolores *(1911);* Pastors and Masters *(1925);* Brothers and Sisters *(1929);* Men and Wives *(1931);* More Women Than Men *(1933);* A House and Its Head *(1935);* Daughters and Sons *(1937);* A Family and a Fortune *(1939);* Parents and Children *(1941);* Elders and Betters *(1944);* Manservant and Maidservant *(published in U.S. under title* Bullivant and the Lambs, *1947);* Two Worlds and Their Ways *(1949);* Darkness and Day *(1950);* The Present and the Past *(1953);* Mother and Son *(1955);* A Father and His Fate *(1957);* A Heritage and Its History *(1959);* The Mighty and Their Fall *(1961);* A God and His Gifts *(1963); (unfinished and published posthumously)* The Last and the First *(1971).*

The critic Charles Burkhardt maintains that all serious writers are eccentric, writers of "extreme individuality whose audiences remain small." Ivy Compton-Burnett was one of that breed, but she was never quite content with her limited readership. Of *Agatha Christie, translated and read round the world, she said wistfully, "Think of the pleasure she must give. Think of the pleasure." Yet she admitted that she would have written "for a dozen."

Ivy Compton-Burnett had apparently always expected to be a writer. "We come of a booky family," she said. For Compton-Burnett, her early years held unusually great significance, foreshadowing the world to be created in her novels. Ivy's father James Compton Burnett, a man of great energy, ardent convictions, and considerable charm, was born in 1840 at Redlynch near Salisbury. The family legend held that the Burnetts were directly descended from Gilbert Burnet, bishop of Salisbury, a notable 17th-century writer of church history. The descent may be uncertain. James Burnett himself was the son of a Redlynch coal dealer. His childhood was impoverished, but his vitality and talent propelled him into a medical career. He obtained training on the Continent and early in his professional life became an ardent champion of homeopathic medicine, writing extensively as well as maintaining a large and lucrative practice.

James' first wife, the daughter of a homeopathic chemist, gave birth to five children before she died. His second wife, with whom he was deeply in love, was golden-haired **Katharine**

Rees Compton-Burnett, daughter of the mayor of Dover. Ivy, born in 1884, was the first of Katharine's seven children. James' career flourished, and the family settled in Hove, Sussex, in a splendid red-brick house of 13 bedrooms with a large staff of servants. Despite prosperity, the inner tensions in the house were many. Ivy, sensitive, observant, and always somewhat delicate, must have felt them keenly. Olive, the eldest of the first group of little Burnetts, eight years old at the time of her father's remarriage, keenly resented her stepmother and would always call her

"Mrs. Burnett." Olive's siblings were apparently scarcely happier under the new regime.

Katharine, though proud of her own clever brood and anxious that both daughters and sons should be well educated, was not fond of small children. "She loved us," Ivy would later report, "but she did not like us." She was apparently a highly emotional woman, concerned with her personal beauty, wardrobe, and social status. It was she who hyphenated the family name. James enjoyed his children and played delightful games that they long remembered, but his thriving practice, as well as his extensive popular writings and his editorship of the *Homeopathic World,* kept him much from home.

Ivy seems not to have been close to her sisters but was deeply attached to her beloved brothers Guy and Noel; she was convinced they would also take up writing. The children were tutored for some years at home. Later Ivy was sent to day school at Assiscombe College for the Daughters of Gentlemen, still later to Howard College, Bedford, but duty to family and home would long be a strong moral imperative for her. The center of her life remained with the large and insulated household at Hove.

The pillar of that household was abruptly removed when Dr. Burnett died in 1901. Katharine went at once into a mourning that was excessive even for a Victorian widow, dressing the entire household black, down to the baby in her crib. Ivy would for many years wear long black gowns, though perhaps for different motives than those of her grieving mother.

In 1902, Compton-Burnett was sent to study classics at the Royal Holloway College at Egham in Surrey, founded not many years previously to educate the daughters of the middle- and upper-middle classes. The college, which contained some 800 rooms, was housed in a newly built château patterned after Chambord in the Loire Valley in France. The furnishings were elaborate and the food excellent, by no means usual characteristics of women's schools of the period. Ivy seems not to have taken a particularly active part in the busy college life, but she was a good student whose own writing would always be influenced by the austere economy, though not the cathartic tragic sense, of the Greeks whom she studied.

In 1905, she was called briefly home to Hove because of the death of her beloved brother Guy. It was a loss that she seems to have felt to the end of her life, a loss that left Katharine, her mother, still more emotionally uncontrol-lable than she had been since her husband's death. Though Compton-Burnett returned to Holloway, where in 1906 she passed the Bachelor of Arts honors examination, there was no escape from the dark house at Hove, and she was assigned the task of tutoring her sisters. She seems not to have been an eager teacher and apparently sat at table busy with her own writing while the younger girls quietly occupied themselves in their own way.

In 1911, Compton-Burnett's first novel *Dolores,* a tale of a daughter's determined self-sacrifice, was published. It was the only one of her books in which critics found the marked influence of another author—in this case George Eliot (*Mary Anne Evans). It was also the only one of her books that she later repudiated, even suggesting that her brother Noel had a considerable hand in writing it. **Hilary Spurling**, her major biographer, has rejected this suggestion.

But now the family life was changing. Katharine died in 1911, soon after the publication of *Dolores.* Compton-Burnett took over control of the household at Hove, relaxing only slightly her mother's stern regimen, refusing to allow her musical younger sisters to practice their instruments at home. She herself disliked music. In 1915, the sisters declared their independence and moved to quarters of their own choosing, with the noted pianist *Myra Hess. In 1916, the second brother Noel, friend of Rupert Brooke and other talented classmates at King's College, Cambridge, was killed fighting in France. "[Guy and Noel] dying like that quite smashed my life up, it quite smashed my life up," Compton-Burnett would say many times. The household at Hove was dismantled.

Further tragedy was to ensue. In 1917, the two youngest sisters died of an overdose of veronal, possibly suicides. The tight family world was gone forever. Adrift and homeless, Compton-Burnett lived from 1916 to 1917 with **Dorothy Beresford**, the beautiful sister-in-law of her dead brother Noel. In the summer of 1918, like so many other Londoners, Ivy was stricken with influenza and, living alone, was discovered and saved almost by chance. The illness induced a long lassitude. In October 1919, **Margaret Jourdain**, author and expert on fine furnishings and embroideries, joined Compton-Burnett in her flat at Leinster Square. It was a major turning point in both lives. Margaret was gifted, vigorous, gregarious, unorthodox and, like Compton-Burnett, an atheist. She created a beautiful setting at Braemar Mansions, their longtime home.

Compton-Burnett said that she and Margaret were "neuters." Margaret claimed that she had never felt sexual passion, perhaps, she suspected, because of the frightening hereditary paralysis that had crippled two of her siblings. No matter what the details of their relationship, the two women found peace and stability together. Compton-Burnett was long considered by the many friends who came into their life to be the "dull" one of the pair, quietly pouring tea as the brilliant Margaret shone. But Ivy was writing again. In 1925, 14 years after the publication of *Dolores,* she found her own unique voice with her second novel, the highly original *Pastors and Masters.* For the rest of her life, with the exception of trips to the Continent with Jourdain to study art and pick Alpine flowers, writing would be her major preoccupation. She had few other interests.

In her own eccentric way, Compton-Burnett is a radical thinker, one of the few modern heretics.

—Mary McCarthy

As reported by her friend and biographer, **Elizabeth Sprigge,** Compton-Burnett seems to have spent considerable time thinking about each novel before beginning actual composition. When she was ready to commit words to paper, or, as she said, when a book "seemed to be trying to come out," she wrote on a series of penny exercise books. She used a pencil and erased frequently, since she had, she said with characteristic understatement, "nothing against corrections." When she had completed the first draft of a novel, she threw it away. She then proceeded to write a second draft rather quickly, though still amending. This manuscript, also in pencil on penny exercise books, went to her typist, then on to her publisher.

With the exception of the early *Dolores,* Compton-Burnett's 20 novels show little influence from other writers. She had in her girlhood been introduced to the major English novelists, especially those of the 19th century—Eliot, Thackeray, Hardy, *Charlotte Brontë, and *Mrs. Gaskell. She was particularly fond of *Jane Austen, though little of Austen surfaced in her own work. Some critics found echoes of Henry James, but such echoes were muted. She did not reflect the other great 19th-century novelists, Dickens and Trollope, who awakened only her guarded admiration.

Compton-Burnett's style has been called abstract and intellectual. Her books are composed largely of dialogue, "something," she said, "between a play and a novel." Descriptions of place are almost nonexistent and descriptions of persons are brief, though often striking, usually appearing when characters are first introduced. The cast of characters is typically large. One would-be novelist has said that he would have practiced the genre if he had ever learned to move characters from one place to another. The problem does not concern Compton-Burnett; her people don't move. They simply *are,* from paragraph to paragraph, in one place or another. Settings, fragmentarily described, are schools or, more frequently, large country houses in a somewhat decaying state. The country house has been a familiar milieu in English fiction, and it gives scope for the story of Compton-Burnett's major interest—the family.

The presentation is witty, closely observed, and scalpel sharp. Fraud, domestic tyranny, death, bastardy, incest and even murder occur in an atmosphere of outer decorum with the criminal never brought before a court of law. Homosexual relationships are calmly and matter-of-factly explored. Other than money, almost no influence from the outside worlds of politics, public events, and professional activity seep into the hermetic family existence. Clergy appear but not the comforts of religion. One dying character says, "I don't feel I am going to meet my Maker. And if I were, I should not fear Him. He has not earned the feeling." Ultimately, Compton-Burnett's people must live, for better or more frequently for worse, with such disheartening knowledge as they have gained of themselves and of each other.

Though never a bestselling author, Compton-Burnett attracted an appreciative, even ardent core of readers and critics. The novel *Manservant and Maidservant,* published in the United States in 1947 under the title *Bullivant and the Lambs,* was generally conceded to be her most satisfying work.

With most of her contemporary women novelists she had little contact, literary or personal. Leonard and *Virginia Woolf's Hogarth Press rejected her third novel, *Brothers and Sisters,* published eventually by **Heather Cranton.** Woolf would speak later of "the bitter truth and intense originality of Miss Compton-Burnett," but the two met seldom and never became friends. Ivy seems to have thought poorly of *Iris Murdoch, and, at a dinner party requested by *Rebecca West, Ivy is said to have downed even that formidable conversational opponent with her wit.

In 1951, the greatest loss "I could have had" came to Compton-Burnett with the death of Margaret Jourdain. In June of that year, she was made a CBE—Commander of the Order of the British Empire—an honor that was dulled by her grief. Her *Mother and Son* won the James Tait Black prize in 1955, and in 1960 she received an honorary doctorate from the University of Leeds, this time to her satisfaction. Too frail to accept the awards in person, she became a Dame in the Queen's Birthday Honors in 1967 and in 1968 was named a Companion of Literature of the Royal Society of Literature.

In her last years, Compton-Burnett was visited by loyal friends and by her surviving sisters, with whom she was at last reconciled. She died in 1969, leaving unfinished a novel, *The First and The Last,* which was edited and appeared in 1971 under the imprint of Victor Gollancz, her publisher since 1937. When asked to write her autobiography, Compton-Burnett had refused, since "I have had such an uneventful life that there is little to say." To another correspondent she wrote, "I have not been deedy." Few personal papers of any kind and no letters dating before 1919 survive, and even at her death she left hardly more. She kept no journals, wrote no notes and no self-revealing letters. To a singular degree, for Ivy Compton-Burnett, her life and her books were one.

SOURCES:

Baldanza, Frank. *Ivy Compton-Burnett.* NY: Twayne, 1964.

Burkhardt, Charles. *I. Compton-Burnett.* London: Victor Gollancz, 1965.

Powell, Violet. *A Compton-Burnett Compendium.* London: Heinemann, 1973.

Sprigge, Elizabeth. *The Life of Ivy Compton-Burnett.* NY: Braziller, 1973 (originally published in England by Victor Gollancz).

Spurling, Hilary. *Ivy, the Life of I. Compton-Burnett.* NY: Alfred Knopf, 1984.

SUGGESTED READING:

Grieg, Cicely. *Ivy Compton-Burnett, A Memoir.* Garnstone Press, 1972.

Johnson, Pamela Hansford. *I. Compton-Burnett.* British Council, Longmans, 1951.

Liddell, Robert. *The Novels of Ivy Compton-Burnett.* London: Victor Gollancz, 1955.

Margery Evernden, Professor Emerita, English Department, University of Pittsburgh, and freelance writer

Comstock, Ada Louise (1876–1973)

American educator. Born on December 11, 1876, in Moorhead, Minnesota; died on December 12, 1973, in New Haven, Connecticut; educated at University of Minnesota (1892–1894), Smith College (B.L., 1897), Columbia University (A.M. in English, history and education, 1899); married Wallace Notestein, in 1943.

Ada Comstock had a long and distinguished career as an American educator. Born in Minnesota in 1876, she was a student at the University of Minnesota in Minneapolis from 1892 to 1894, before graduating Phi Beta Kappa with a B.L. from Smith College in 1897. She then attended Columbia University in New York City, from which she earned her A.M. in English, history, and education in 1899. Returning to Minneapolis, Comstock began teaching at the University of Minnesota; she remained there for 12 years, from 1900 to 1912, becoming full professor of rhetoric and dean of women (Comstock was the only woman in the university to serve as an administrator).

In 1912, she became the first woman dean of Smith College and would serve in that capacity for 11 years. When the Association of Collegiate Alumnae and the Southern Association of College merged to become the American Association of University Women (AAUW), Comstock was the first president of the new organization (1921), a position she would hold until 1923, the year she became president of Radcliffe College. Comstock is credited with developing a much closer working relationship between Radcliffe and Harvard University.

Herbert Hoover appointed Comstock as the only woman of the 11-member Wickersham Commission to study problems in law enforcement, particularly the problems resulting from Prohibition. Rather than vote in favor of repealing the 18th Amendment, she voted to modify it. As chair of the AAUW's International Relations Department, Comstock urged American intervention against totalitarian aggressors. She was also a member of the National Committee for Planned Parenthood, for which she led fundraising in 1941. Comstock died in New Haven, Connecticut, on December 12, 1973.

Comstock, Anna Botsford

(1854–1930)

First woman professor at Cornell University, leader of the nature-study movement, and author or illustrator of many natural science books. Name variations: Anna Botsford. Born Anna Botsford on September 1, 1854, on the family farm near Otto, in Cattaraugus County, New York; died on August 24, 1930, at her home in Ithaca, New York; only child of Marvin and Phebe (Irish) Botsford (a farm couple); attended a rural elementary schoolhouse, a "select" high school in Otto, and two years at the Chamberlin Institute and Female College in Randolph; enrolled in Cornell

University in 1875, left to marry her zoology instructor John Henry Comstock in 1878, returned in 1882, graduated in 1885.

Along with husband, spent entire career at Cornell, except for three years at the Department of Agriculture in Washington, D.C. (1879–81); appointed first woman assistant professor at Cornell, in nature study (1899), full professor (1920). Awards: Sigma Xi, national honor society of the sciences, one of the first four women (1888); Phi Kappa Phi honor society (1922); named one of the 12 greatest women in America by the League of Women Voters (1923); honorary Ph.D. from Hobart College (1930).

Anna Comstock's illustrations and wood engravings appeared in John Henry Comstock's An Introduction to Entomology *(1888) and* A Manual for the Study of Insects *(1895). Her engravings were also exhibited at the New Orleans (1885), Chicago (1893), Paris (1900) and Buffalo (1901) expositions and won her election to the American Society of Wood-Engravers. She and her husband collaborated on* Insect Life *(1897) and* How To Know the Butterflies *(1904). She also wrote* The Handbook of Nature-Study *(1911), as well as* Ways of the Six-Footed *(1903),* How To Keep Bees *(1905),* Dreams of a Heathen Idol *(1906),* The Pet Book *(1914), and* Trees at Leisure *(1916).*

In 1899, a visitor passing through White Hall at Cornell University might have seen two desks side by side, positioned in front of two east windows overlooking the green of the main quadrangle. One was the plain, orderly desk of John Henry Comstock, professor of entomology. The other belonged to Anna Botsford Comstock, professor of nature study, the first woman named as a professor to the faculty of the young university where science was given a place of honor equal to that accorded the classics in older institutions of learning. Her roll-top desk was equipped with many irregular pigeon-holes, identified by neat titles in white ink: "Entomology Department," "Extension," "Handbook." A special gas-light illuminated the workspace where she did her wood-engraving, and her tools were laid out ready for use. On an adjoining table were prints and proofs, as well as an early typewriter. A hand-cranked telephone hung from the wall nearby, something of a luxury in a time when there was no mail delivery and she had to walk to Ithaca for her letters. The telephone enabled the couple to communicate with each other whenever one was working unusually early or late, which was often the case for the Comstocks of Cornell who, during a half-century of collaboration,

published a shelf-full of books, authored jointly and separately.

Anna Comstock was widely esteemed not only for the seven science books and the novel she wrote, but for her work in popularizing the study of nature among schoolchildren and their teachers. In 1923, she was named one of the 12 greatest women in America, along with social worker *Jane Addams and author *Edith Wharton. Her success was due to her ability to integrate the study of animal, plant, and insect life and to make the subject understandable as no other professional scientist had done.

Anna Botsford Comstock always traced her feeling for the natural world to the influence of her mother, **Phebe Irish Botsford**, a Hicksite Quaker who, because of her religious beliefs, did not sing her daughter to sleep but instead lulled her by reciting poetry. Phebe and her husband Marvin moved when their only child was three to a frame house on the edge of what Anna in her memoir called "a primeval forest." Until after the Civil War, the farm was self-sufficient: they raised wheat and corn for bread, as well as vegetables and fruit, cattle, pigs, and sheep; Phebe made maple sugar and cheese, spun wool and made their clothes. She was "an exquisite needlewoman" claimed Anna. In spite of her busy life, Phebe always had time to read to the child and to impart her passionate love of beauty in nature, teaching Anna to recognize dozens of flowers, to cure wild herbs, to observe wild creatures and the constellations. Phebe was an advanced thinker who adopted the costume of bloomers for herself and her daughter. She also instilled the habit of work: Anna learned to sew when she was four and knit at six; thereafter, she had to make her own stockings.

Anna was close friends with the neighbor boy and felt that a girl was fortunate "who learns early in life that men are good." She attended a rural schoolhouse taught by a man for three months in the winter, and by a woman for three months in the summer, as was common for rural children of the time. Since the school had been built on their property, teachers often boarded with the Botsfords, and Anna had the advantage of their company. She was a talkative girl, with a good memory, who became fractious in school as she grew older, probably because of the lack of challenge.

When Anna was 13, the family moved to a large new house nearer the town of Otto. There was no public high school, but her father, a progressive farmer who was among the first to buy

farm machinery, could afford to send her to a "select school" with superior teachers where she began to study drawing. A wealthy woman friend in town encouraged Comstock to go to college. After graduation from preparatory school, she taught for a year in Otto, then applied to Cornell University, which had just begun to admit women. In high school, she had had some romantic liaisons, but her ambition had prevented any "sentimental entanglements;" one of her reasons for attending Cornell was the rumor that men there ignored the women, and Anna thought it would be good to have the "combined advantages of a university and a convent."

Cornell had been established for eight years. There were a few women students, many of whom went on to distinguished careers in women's colleges. During her first term in the winter of 1875–76, Anna was instructed in zoology by a young man who had himself just graduated from Cornell the year before, John Henry Comstock. Young Henry's childhood had been far more difficult than Anna's. His father had gone west in 1849 with the gold rush, soon after the boy's birth, but had died in a cholera epidemic on the way. His mother, **Susan Allen Comstock**, of the family of the Revolutionary patriot Ethan Allen, had worked her way back east. She suffered a long illness, and then turned to nursing to support her son, who lived with a variety of foster families. While working on a schooner that sailed the Great Lakes, the teenaged boy had encountered a *Treatise on Some of the Insects Injurious to Vegetation*, which captured his interest. He entered Cornell in 1869, the year after it opened, drawn by the status given to the study of science there, and by the opportunity its founder guaranteed to boys who wanted to work their way through. By the end of his sophomore year, he was instructing other students in entomology, as there was no qualified lecturer in the field. Immediately after graduation, he joined the faculty.

I've heard her give a lesson in cross-fertilization in flowers that had all the wonder and poetry of the creation itself.

—**Unidentified student of Anna Comstock**

Anna Botsford was interested in English and history, but took a course in invertebrate zoology to balance her curriculum. At the time of their meeting, Anna and Henry Comstock were each engaged to others. Anna's relationship ended by mutual consent; Henry's fiancée developed tuberculosis and decided against marriage. When Anna took a second course from Henry, in field and laboratory entomology, he made her a present of a drafting board, a T-square, and sticks of India ink, and encouraged her to begin to draw insects. Their mutual interest developed into an interest in each other, and they were married on October 7, 1878. Anna, who did all her own housework, had to interrupt her studies, but then as later they worked as a team: Henry helping with the dishes, and Anna helping in the lab.

The following spring, Henry was appointed chief entomologist for the U.S. Department of Agriculture, and they moved to Washington, D.C. There the couple was able to afford a housekeeper, and Anna worked in the Department with her husband. Despite a rule against two in the same family being employed in one governmental office, the Commissioner of Agriculture insisted on paying Anna for doing research, answering queries for agricultural papers, and running the office when her husband was in the field. When he returned, Anna, using a microscope, made detailed drawings of the scale insects (coccidae) that preyed on the citrus groves. Her drawings illustrated differences upon which Henry Comstock was later able to base classifications of the insects. In his annual report, published in 1881, her drawings were highly praised.

A change of administration brought a new commissioner, and the Comstocks returned to Cornell. A boarder did the housework, so Anna could work in the lab on drawings for the coccid report. The following year, 1882, she returned to the university to pursue a degree in science, taking the minimum number of courses so she could continue to work in the lab. Henry was writing *An Introduction to Entomology*, and to illustrate it Anna began to study wood engraving from the instructions that came with her tools. Her work was interrupted by a nine-week illness, during which her hair fell out. When it grew back, she continued to wear it short for two or three years, until her husband gently remarked that "One member of the family must have long hair—shall it be you or I?" They also took their meals in the dormitory to free her from domestic chores. In 1885, Comstock received her degree. Her engravings won the first honorable mention at the New Orleans Exposition that year, which encouraged her to go to New York to study wood engraving with John P. Davis; she became the third woman elected to the American Society of Wood Engravers. "My work was original," Anna Comstock explained. "I always worked with the insect before me."

In the 1890s, the Comstocks began to spend the winter term at Stanford, in Palo Alto, California, so they could collect insects throughout the year. Henry was working on two large books, the *Introduction to Entomology* and *A Manual for the Study of Insects*. He rose at 4 AM to have three hours to write every day before his classes. She worked on the engravings from 8 AM to 6 PM, and then indulged in the novel sport of bicycling for recreation and exercise. They published the *Manual* themselves, as the Comstock

Publishing Company, so they could offer it at a low rate to students. It remained in print for nearly 50 years.

The Comstocks were disappointed to have no children, but their house was always full. Relatives attending Cornell often boarded with them. Anna entertained students and faculty, customarily reading poetry or essays after dinner; the Quaker poet John Greenleaf Whittier and the naturalist Henry Thoreau were among her favorites. She also made time to care for the ill or bereaved among her family and friends. The two were described by their fellow faculty member James Needham in the *Scientific Monthly* as a "complemental pair": he was "short, quick-spoken, alert, even fidgety," while she was tall, slow-spoken, gracious and dignified. But their work and their goals were completely intertwined.

Cornell University was a land-grant college. Ezra Cornell believed in the importance of educated farm people for agricultural progress, and his university pioneered extension teaching, although its College of Agriculture was not established until 1904. As early as 1876, Henry Comstock addressed farmers at a meeting of the New York State Horticulture Society on insects injurious to fruits. By 1879, Cornell had established an Agricultural Experiment Station. In 1886, the university held the first Farmers' Institute; invitations addressed laboriously in script by Anna Comstock were sent to all farmers whose addresses were known, and 85 attended the first meeting, at which Henry Comstock lectured.

An agricultural depression affecting the East in the early 1890s was causing farm children to migrate to New York City, and a conference was called by a group of charities there to seek solutions. Anna Comstock was the only person to attend from Cornell. The conference resolved on an educational program designed to attract rural children to farm life, and a course of nature study was proposed. In 1894, the state appropriated $8,000 for Cornell to conduct a pilot project. The faculty was overwhelmed by an unexpectedly large response, and Anna Comstock was drafted, at first on a volunteer basis, to begin the program together with Liberty Hyde Bailey, who headed the Department of Horticulture. Bailey relied on her not only to develop materials but also to negotiate the introduction of nature study into the public schools. Anna wrote leaflets for the teachers in rural schools and met with educators in the State Department of Education at Albany and with Teachers' Institutes. In 1897, the first annual report on the merits of the different university extension courses ranked the nature study program number one. The leaflets did more than instruct rural teachers, they also established the pattern whereby state colleges came to recognize their obligations to people in the state through the extension services.

In 1899, Anna Comstock was made assistant professor of nature study at the Cornell University Extension Division, the first time a woman had held the title of professor, but the following year her title lapsed because conservative trustees objected to a woman professor. Instead, she was named as lecturer with the same salary. During the summers of 1899 and 1900, she taught a Nature Study School at Cornell to 100 teachers, with lectures, field and lab work, but most of the teachers were from urban areas. Thereafter, she taught summer sessions at state normal schools attended by rural teachers, and at Chautauqua. During the school year, she lectured at Columbia Teachers' College, Stanford, and the University of Virginia. In 1903, she gave lectures to teachers from the black high school in Lynchburg, Virginia, and found them "better observers of nature than the white teachers." She also taught courses at Cornell for farm men and women, including a course on the farm library, where she cultivated an appreciation of natural history, U.S. history, and nature poetry. According to **Ruby Bell Smith**, Anna's many travels showed "a spirit of adventure and a burning desire for public service in her willingness to accept discomforts in the horse and buggy days."

After the *Manual* was finished, the Comstocks began to write *Insect Life,* designed for children's teachers, also published by Comstock Publishers in 1897 and still in use 30 years later. In 1903, Ginn and Co. published Anna Comstock's *Ways of the Six-Footed,* a collection of her writings in various publications. The following year, she and Henry collaborated once more to produce *How to Know the Butterflies,* published in 1904. In the fall, she was busy again on *How to Keep Bees* (1905) as well as with the monthly leaflets for the extension class in nature study.

During her illness in the 1880s, she had developed insomnia, so she began to keep a journal of philosophical reflections. A novel based on this journal, *Confessions of a Heathen Idol,* was published in 1906 under a pseudonym because she "thought it would be scandalous for a scientific woman to write a novel." Her husband was supportive but not effusive. The book was popular enough to have a second printing under her own name.

The Comstocks spent the winter of 1907–08 in Egypt, Greece, and Europe, on their first and only sabbatical leave. After their return, Anna thought that the leaflets and other material she had written should be compiled to form the basis for a comprehensive manual. In 1909, she began work on her *Handbook of Nature Study,* which would run to almost 1,000 pages. No commercial publisher would handle it, so her husband agreed to have Comstock Publishing produce it, prepared to lose money on what he called "a desk book with a thousand pictures." The *Handbook,* published in 1911, was translated into eight languages, became Comstock's biggest financial asset, and was still in print in the 1990s. In addition to her work lecturing and writing, Anna Comstock served as a trustee for the William Smith College for women, opened in 1908, and for its co-ordinate college, Hobart.

The Cornell Agricultural College created the Department of Rural Education in 1911, and in 1913 Anna Comstock was again made an assistant professor of the Cornell faculty, joining two other women professors who were in home economics. Comstock was made a full professor in 1920. She continued to publish, producing *The Pet Book* in 1914 and *Trees at Leisure* in 1916, as well as field notebooks for children on birds, flowers, trees, and common animals. In 1917, she became editor of the *Nature Study Review,* for which she had written since its founding in 1905. Junior Naturalist Clubs were also started under her guidance, which eventually evolved into the 4-H Clubs. Comstock, however, was never active in the fight for women's suffrage that challenged so many women of her generation. She did not believe women's votes would change national policy, and she felt all her efforts were necessary "to fight narrowness and injustice in the schools."

Henry Comstock retired in 1914, at age 65, and worked for the next ten years on his massive *Introduction to Entomology,* the climax of his work. When it was published with illustrations by Anna, he told her, "This is our book." Although they had not published jointly after the *Manual for the Study of Insects* and *How to Know the Butterflies,* there was "mutual help in every book by either," according to Needham. "He was as proud of her achievements as she was of his." Anna observed, "Our writing was the thread on which our days were hung." A portrait of both was painted by Olaf Brauner for the university library. Cornell recognized their partnership in naming Comstock Hall and the Comstock Graduate Fellowships. Needham remarked in 1946, "It has been said that many an institution is the lengthened shadow of a man. The Department of Entomology at Cornell is the lengthened shadow of a man and his wife."

In 1926, Henry Comstock suffered a brain hemorrhage that left him partially paralyzed and unable to talk. Although Anna continued to work, writing her memoir, *The Comstocks of Cornell,* which was published posthumously, and giving occasional lectures up until shortly before her death, she wrote on the last page of her last book that with his stroke, life had ended for them both; the rest was "mere existence."

For 30 years, Anna Comstock profoundly influenced the field of education. The nature-study movement, of which she was a pioneer, continued into the 1950s, and the American Nature Study Society attracted a new generation of naturalists like Roger Tory Peterson. During the 1970s, nature study merged with the burgeoning environmental movement; state and county nature centers were established to promote the close observation of nature, which was the trademark of the work of Anna Botsford Comstock.

SOURCES:

Comstock, Anna Botsford. *The Comstocks of Cornell.* Ithaca, NY: Cornell University Press, 1953.

Needham, James. G. "The Lengthened Shadow of a Man and His Wife," in *Scientific Monthly.* February–March 1946, p. 140–150; 219–229.

Sawyer, Ruth. "What Makes Mrs. Comstock Great?," in *Woman Citizen.* September 20, 1924, p. 8.

Smith, Ruby Bell. *The People's Colleges: A History of the New York State Extension Service in Cornell University and the State, 1876–1948.* Ithaca, NY: Cornell University Press, 1949.

Wanamaker, John. "The Story of A Rolltop Desk," in *Nature Magazine.* October 1950, p. 429–430.

COLLECTIONS:

Anna Botsford and John Henry Comstock Collection, Rare Book and Manuscript Division, Cornell University Library, Ithaca, New York.

Kristie Miller, author of *Ruth Hanna McCormick: A Life in Politics 1880–1944* (University of New Mexico Press, 1992)

Comyn, Alice (fl. 1318)

Baroness Beaumont. Name variations: Alice Beaumont. Flourished around 1318; daughter of Alexander Comyn, 6th earl of Buchan; married Henry Beaumont, 1st baron Beaumont, around 1311; children: five, including John Beaumont (1318–1342), 2nd baron Beaumont; ***Isabel Beaumont*** *(d. 1368, mother of* ***Blanche of Lancaster****).*

Conboy, Sara McLaughlin
(1870–1928)

American labor leader. Born Sara Agnes McLaughlin on April 3, 1870, in Boston, Massachusetts; died on January 7, 1928, in Brooklyn, New York; married Joseph P. Conboy (a Boston letter carrier).

Known as Aunt Sara to thousands of workers, Sara Conboy was one of the first women to rise to prominence in the upper echelons of organized labor. She was born in Boston in 1870 and by age 11 was working in a candy factory. The next several years brought employment in a button factory and in various carpet mills, as Conboy became a skilled weaver. Her marriage to a Boston letter carrier ended with his death only two years into their marriage.

While working in a Roxbury mill, Conboy successfully led the employees in a strike for increased wages and union recognition; this success brought her to prominence in labor circles, and she became an organizer for the United Textile Workers of America, of which she also served as secretary-treasurer (beginning in October 1915). Conboy was an effective lobbyist for protective legislation for women and children in factories, and achieved strong results as a fund raiser. When Woodrow Wilson called a conference on labor in 1918, Conboy was the only woman in attendance. In Portsmouth, England, she represented the American Federation of Labor in 1920 at the conference of the British Trades Union Congress. Conboy was among four women who participated in a conference on employment, called by President Warren G. Harding, in September 1921. The National Committee on Prisons and Prison Labor and the New York State Housing Commission were among the organizations of which Conboy was an active member. A leader in the labor movement, Sara Conboy died in Brooklyn, New York, on January 7, 1928.

Concannon, Helena (1878–1952)

Irish scholar of works on Irish religious and women's history. Born Helena Walsh in Maghera, County Derry, Ireland, on October 28, 1878; died on February 27, 1952; educated at Loreto College, Dublin, the Royal University of Ireland, the Sorbonne, and the University of Berlin; married Thomas Concannon, in 1906.

Published first book (1915); member of Dail Eireann (1933–37) and of Seanad Eireann (1937–52).

Selected writings: Life of St. Columban (1915); The Defence of Gaelic Civilisation (1919); Women of '98 (1919); Daughters of Banba (1922); Defenders of the Ford (1925); A Garden of Girls (1928); The Poor Clares in Ireland (1929); White Horsemen (1930); Irish Nuns in Penal Days (1931); At the Court of the Eucharistic King (1931); St. Patrick: His Life and Mission (1932); Blessed Oliver Plunket (1935); The Queen of Ireland (1938); The Cure of La Courneuve (1944); Poems (1953). *With Thomas Concannon:* Eamhain Macha (undated), Fianna Eireann (undated), Inis Fail (undated), Seoda na Sean (1924).

Born in Maghera, County Derry, on October 28, 1878, Helena Walsh was one of seven children of a close-knit and deeply religious family. The standards inculcated in her home would guide her throughout her days: according to her friend, **Mary Macken**, her life "was an amalgam of the human and the divine, embracing fatherland and family, husband and home, the Creator and his Creation as they stood revealed in the faith and practices of the Catholic Church."

The young Helena showed an outstanding intelligence and was fortunate in being one of the first generation of university-educated women. Having received her early education at the local national school, she went on to Loreto College in Dublin, and in 1897 won a Royal University scholarship in Modern Languages. In 1900, she took a BA with first-class honors, and her MA two years later. In 1929, her book, *The Poor Clares in Ireland*, won her a D.Litt from the National University of Ireland.

In 1900, Helena met Thomas Concannon, whom she married in 1906. The Concannons lived for a time in County Monaghan, and later moved to Galway, where Thomas was a civil servant. Among the many interests that they shared was the restoration of the Irish language. Thomas was a prominent figure in the Gaelic League, and Helena made extensive use of Irish-language sources in her historical works; she published a number of works in Irish in collaboration with her husband.

A fervent nationalist, Concannon supported Eamon de Valera in his opposition to the Anglo-Irish Treaty of 1921. In 1933, she was elected to the Dail as representative for the National University of Ireland, and in 1937 to the Senate, in which she served until her death in 1952. As a public representative, she took pride in her regular attendance in the House, but **Mary Clancy**, in her assessment of the part played by female members in debates in the Dail and Senate during this period, takes a critical view of her contributions, which she describes as "regular though by no means impressive." As a member of de Valera's Fianna Fail party, Concannon committed herself to unwavering support for its policies "in a back-bench way." In her response to legislation relating to women, she subscribed to the conservative consensus that regarded the female role as primarily maternal and domestic. Thus, in 1936, she stated in the House: "Everybody has his or her own way of solving Ireland's ills. My method would be to make these rural domestic economy schools general . . . and make a course of six months compulsory on all Irish girls before they would be allowed to marry." In the following year, de Valera introduced a draft Constitution, which incorporated elements unacceptable to feminists, notably in its insistence on the primacy of women's domestic role. Although the Women Graduates' Association, of which she was a member, spearheaded the campaign against the new Constitution, Concannon herself fully approved the measure and spoke in its favor in the House.

Over these years, Concannon produced a steady stream of books and articles on religious and women's history. Her first work, *Life of St. Columban* (1915), was a scholarly biography that utilized her expertise as a linguist and historian, and was awarded a prize of $1,000 by the Catholic University of America. Two of her books, *Daughters of Banba* (1922) and *St. Patrick* (1932), received the Tailteann Medal for Literature, and *The Poor Clares in Ireland* (1929) won the National University Prize for Historical Research.

Concannon's historical writings reflected her belief that women had a distinctive, albeit circumscribed, role to play in the achievement of independence and in the shaping of independent Ireland. She dedicated her *Daughters of Banba* "to the memory of the unknown women, faithful and unnumbered, who in every age of Ireland's age-long struggle, have died of hunger and hardship, but ere they were gathered into their forgotten graves passed on still-living the unconquerable spirit of the Irish race." In this collection of biographies of distinguished Irishwomen, she remarked that "it is usually around the men of a country that its history is written; when it comes to pass that but half of its history is written, and that half, perhaps, not the more important." Her consciousness of this disparity set her apart from her contemporaries and has earned her the gratitude of her successors in this field. Though conservative in other aspects of her life, Concannon was a pioneering figure in the recovery of women's history in Ireland.

SOURCES:

Brady, Anne M., and Brian Cleeve. *A Biographical Dictionary of Irish Writers.* Mullingar: Lilliput Press, 1985.

Clancy, Mary, "Aspects of women's contribution to the Oireachtas debate in the Irish Free State, 1922–37," in M. Luddy and C. Murphy, eds. *Women Surviving: Studies in Irish Women's History in the 19th and 20th Centuries.* Dublin: Poolbeg Press, 1990, pp. 206–232.

Hoehn, Matthew, ed. *Catholic Authors: Contemporary Biographical Sketches, 1930–1947.* Newark, NJ: St Mary's Abbey, 1948.

Macken, Mary M. "Musings and memories: Helena Concannon," in *Studies.* Vol. XLII, March 1953, pp. 90–97.

Rosemary Raughter,
freelance writer in women's history, Dublin, Ireland

Condé, Princesse de (fl. 1600–1621).

See Longueville, Anne for sidebar on Charlotte of Montmorency.

Condé, Princesse de (1757–1824).

See Louise Adelaide de Bourbon.

Condorcet, Sophie Marie Louise, Marquise de (1764–1822)

French salonnière. Name variations: *Mademoiselle de Grouchy; Sophie de Grouchy; also known as Grouchette. Born Sophie Marie Louise de Grouchy at the Château Villette, near Meulan, France, in the spring of 1764; died in Paris on September 8, 1822; married Marie Jean Antoine de Caritat, marquis de Condorcet (a mathematician), in 1778 (died March 29, 1794); children: at least one daughter.*

The philosopher **Marie Jean de Caritat,** marquis de Condorcet, fell in love with Sophie de Grouchy, known as Grouchette, while watching as she attended an infant suffering from rabies. In 1778, she married the marquis, a world renowned mathematician, reformer, and adviser of Turgot, who was 20 years her senior. Known as virtuous people, the Marquis and Marquise Condorcet were fierce defenders of Protestants, slaves, and women.

Sophie opened a salon shortly after her marriage. Located at the Quai di Conti in the Hôtel des Monnaies (her husband was the director there), her group drew many foreigners, particularly the English, whose language Condorcet spoke fluently. Her salon became the "center of an enlightened Europe." Completely self-taught, the thin, delicate Sophie had observed her brothers' tutoring and, while canoness at the convent of Neuville, read an entire encyclopedia.

In turbulent 18th-century France, the Condorcets were republicans, radical social reformers who called for the monarchy's end and the start of a constitutional government. To impugn the Condorcets' reputation, in July 1791 Royalists began a salacious press campaign against them, which insinuated that Sophie was a prostitute. In one edition of their propaganda sheet, there was a nude drawing of her with the caption: *res publica* (public property).

The Marquis Condorcet's pamphlet attacking the Constitution led to his impeachment by the Assembly. He was facing arrest when he fled his home on July 8, 1793, and was secretly sheltered by **Madame Vernet** at the Rue des Fossoyeurs, near Saint Sulpice. In an effort to safeguard her daughter's inheritance from the possible seizure of her husband's assets, Sophie filed for divorce from her absent husband in January 1794. Even though she had advised him of her intent to have the decree annulled on his return, the move pained Sophie.

But on the day the decree was finally granted in May 1794, she was unaware that her husband had been dead for two months. His body had been found on March 29 in his cell at Bourg Egaliè prison in a town formerly known as Burgh la Reine, but the authorities did not know his identity. Upon being arrested as a suspected fugitive, he had given a false name to protect Madame Vernet.

Sophie purchased a lingerie shop but lived in poverty until 1799 when she was able to recover some of her property. Reopening her salon, she continued to maintain her republican views and alienate imperial authorities. From 1801 to 1804, she published her husband's writings. Sophie died in 1822 and was buried at Père Lachaise cemetery in Paris without a religious ceremony.

Cone, Carin (b.1940).

See Grinham, Judith for sidebar.

Cone, Claribel and Etta

American art collectors.

Cone, Claribel (1864–1929). Born on November 14, 1864, in Jonesboro, Tennessee; died on September 20, 1929, in Lausanne, Switzerland; daughter of German immigrants; graduated from the Woman's Medical College of Baltimore, 1890; advanced training at Johns Hopkins University Medical School in Baltimore.

Cone, Etta (1870–1949). Born on November 30, 1870, in Jonesboro, Tennessee; died on August 31, 1949, in Blowing Rock, North Carolina; daughter of German immigrants.

Housed in a separate wing of the Baltimore Museum of Art, the Cone Collection is considered one of the world's great assemblages of modern art, especially the work of Matisse. The women responsible, Claribel and Etta Cone, were born in Jonesboro, Tennessee, daughters of German immigrant parents. They grew up in Baltimore, where they attended public schools before Claribel began studies at the Woman's Medical College of Baltimore. After her graduation, Claribel then interned in Philadelphia at the Blockley Hospital for the Insane. Returning to Baltimore, she received advanced training at the new Johns Hopkins University Medical School and researched there under Dr. William H. Welch. Claribel served as a pathology teacher at the Woman's Medical College until the school closed in 1910 and her medical career drew to its end.

Claribel and her sister Etta ran an informal salon that was open to artists, musicians, intellectuals, and professionals of the 1890s. Claribel was known for her eccentricities and her eye for antiques, while her sister Etta, the shyer of the two, was known for her cooking and her taste in art. Etta's interest in the French Impressionists can perhaps be traced to her acquaintance with Leo and *Gertrude Stein, with whom the sisters were friends.

In 1896, Etta began purchasing paintings, and after the death of their parents the sisters had the funds to become ardent collectors. They began amassing in earnest from 1902. Their travels to Europe included visits to Stein's apartment in Paris where they came into contact with French contemporary art and artists. The purchase of their first Picasso in 1905 was followed by their first Matisse in 1906.

When World War I broke out in August of 1914, Claribel was in Munich, and she decided to remain there to avoid wartime travel. She made her way back to Baltimore in 1921. Upon her return, she rented another apartment in their building to serve as a private museum to house their collection, which came to include works of Renoir, Manet, Cézanne, Degas, and Bonnard. Accented with Renaissance furniture and textiles, the collection also contained many pieces by Matisse, an artist with whom Etta enjoyed an enduring friendship.

In 1929, Claribel died suddenly in Lausanne, Switzerland. In her will, she had bequeathed her portion of the collection to her sister. Etta, disconsolate over the loss of her sister, lived out a quiet life. She spent summers in Europe—particularly in Italy—wintered in Baltimore, and continued to care for their museum, which sometimes served as the site of small shows and concerts. When Etta died in 1949 at Blowing Rock, North Carolina, the Baltimore Museum of Art was given the Cone Collection and $400,000 for the new wing to be built for the purpose of housing it.

SUGGESTED READING:

Gabriel, Mary. *The Art of Acquiring: A Portrait of Etta and Claribel Cone.* Baltimore, MD: Bancroft, 1999.

Cone, Etta (1870–1949).

See Cone, Claribel and Etta.

Cones, Nancy Ford (1869–1962)

American photographer. Born Nancy Ford in Milan, Ohio, in 1869; died in 1962; married James Cones (a photographer), in 1897 (died 1939); children: Margaret Cones.

In 1905, Eastman Kodak received 28,000 entries for their photographic competition; first prize went to a young photographer named Edward Steichen. Taking second above another hopeful, Alfred Stieglitz who took third, was a farmwife from Loveland, Ohio, named Nancy Ford Cones. After becoming interested in photography in her 20s, she had married James Cones, a fellow photographer, and moved to a 25-acre farm in Loveland. There they worked together, with James printing negatives, until his death in 1939. While she also photographed celebrated figures such as William Howard Taft, most of Cone's work celebrated the life of the farm. Her rural scenes were utilized in advertising campaigns for Eastman Kodak and Bausch and Lomb; they also appeared in *Country Life in America* and *Woman's Home Companion.* Fifteen years after her death, a Cincinnati art dealer discovered and purchased her legacy of 4,000 prints and 15,000 glass-plate negatives. "The

"Milking Time." Photo by Nancy Ford Cones (1912).

name of Nancy Ford Cones is not now commonly known even to the most ardent devotees of photography," wrote an *American Heritage* contributor, "an obscurity thoroughly undeserved. . . . At once precise and soft with summer light, they recall the steady toil and small pleasures of farm life three-quarters of a century ago."

SOURCES:

"Loveland Summer," in *American Heritage*. August 9, 1981.

COLLECTIONS:

Walt Burton Galleries, Cincinnati, Ohio.

Connaught, duchess of.

See Louise Margaret of Prussia (1860–1917).

Connaught, queen of.

See O'Malley, Grace.

Connolly, Maureen (1934–1969)

Teenage tennis sensation and first woman to complete the Grand Slam, winning all four major tournaments in the same calendar year, whose life was cut short by cancer. Name variations: (nickname) "Little Mo"; Maureen Connolly Brinker. Born Maureen Catherine Connolly on September 17, 1934, in San Diego, California; died on June 21, 1969, in Dallas, Texas; daughter of Martin and Jessamine Connolly; married Norman Brinker, in 1955; children: Brenda Lee Brinker (b. 1957); Cynthia Anne Brinker (b. 1960).

Named female athlete of the year three times by the Associated Press; won the Wightman Cup nine times; was Wimbledon singles champion (1952, 1953, 1954); won the singles championship in U.S. Open (1951, 1952, 1953); won the singles title in the French Open (1953, 1954); won the singles title in the Australian Open (1953); with N. Hopman, won the French Open women's doubles (1954); with Julia Sampson, won the Australian women's doubles (1953); youngest national junior champion, youngest male or female to make the national top ten professional rankings, first and youngest to complete the Grand Slam at the age of 18 (1953).

"Tennis has been the most important thing in my life ever since I first picked up a racquet at the tender age of ten," wrote Maureen Connolly, but her real love was horseback riding. She played tennis partially because her mother couldn't afford riding lessons or the horse Maureen dreamed about. At the beginning of her career, when her mother attempted to finance a small ranch, Connolly offered to trade her increasing fame on the courts for the opportunity to ride and be around horses. Luckily for tennis fans, the ranch deal fell through. Instead of moving to the country, Maureen Connolly competed at country clubs, rising as high as it is possible to rise, faster than any woman had ever risen in women's tennis. Ironically, the sensational tennis career, once nearly traded for the chance to be around horses, ended because of a tragic horseback riding accident.

Nobody will ever know how many more tennis championships Connolly would have won or whether the teenage superstar would have matured into the greatest player in the history of the sport, just as nobody can guess what she might have accomplished on the equestrian circuit if she had started riding horses at a young age. What the record books show is that a teenager, playing professionally for three years, accomplished enough to rank as one of the all-time best in women's tennis.

Born and raised in San Diego, California, Maureen Connolly lived with her mother Jessamine and an aunt. Her father, a sailor, left the family when Maureen was three or four. Her mother, who had once dreamed of becoming a concert pianist, worked as a piano player and church organist. An active, brown-eyed, light-haired, only child, Maureen attended ballet class, took singing lessons, learned to draw, and liked to write. Her writing eventually helped her meet her future husband, and, though the ballet training never led to the stage, Connolly later displayed great footwork and graceful movements in another arena.

On her way to play tag with friends among the sand piles at San Diego's University Heights playground, Connolly stopped to watch the tennis players on the three municipal courts. Befriended by Wilbur Folsom, the park's instructor, she started working for pocket money as a ball girl, picking up tennis balls during Folsom's lessons. Eventually, Folsom invited her to join in. Connolly, who quickly learned the basic strokes, began helping the instructor by returning balls to his pupils.

Some reports claim that a leg prosthesis limited Folsom's mobility, forcing him to learn terrific ground strokes and passing shots, which in turn became his legacy to Connolly. Maureen wrote that she was naturally left-handed but switched because Folsom convinced her that there had never been a left-handed tennis champion. Playing right handed, she quickly absorbed Folsom's instructions and thrived on his encouragement. As a ten-year old, she developed solid ground strokes and learned how to scramble from side to side on the court.

Armed with a $1.50 racquet purchased by her mother, ten-year-old Connolly entered her first tournament, the La Jolla playground's 13-and-under division. Reaching the finals, she hung tough in the first set before being decisively beaten by **Anne Bissell** in the second set to lose the match, 8–6, 6–2. Connolly never forgot the name of her opponent, or the thrills and the jangled nerves she experienced during her first competition. Disappointed by defeat, she channeled her frustration into desire. Aspiring to be a champion, convinced that practice and determination were the routes to attaining her goals, she dedicated herself to long, regular workouts.

Connolly began to win every tournament she entered, even though she was almost always the youngest competitor in her age group. Her enormous talent was soon noticed, and she received encouragement. When the Balboa Tennis Club presented 11-year-old Connolly with a complimentary membership in their junior development program, she continued to improve, playing against both women and men in the program, practicing with and getting advice from older club members.

In 1947, while playing in the Southern California Invitational Tennis Championship tournament, the 12-year-old met the controversial coach ◄❧ **Eleanor "Teach" Tennant** at the Beverly Hills Tennis Club. Though admittedly nervous during the tryout, Connolly impressed the coach and began a relationship that lasted six years. Tennant, who worked with tennis greats Bobby Riggs, **Alice Marble* and **Pauline Betz*, had an enormous influence on every aspect of Connolly's tennis game and considered her the best player she'd ever drilled. She concentrated on Connolly's ground strokes, taught her young student game strategy, and challenged her to concentrate on footwork. Tennant also put Connolly through strength exercise drills but avoided developing a spectacular serve because her student was still growing.

Connolly quickly became more than a curiosity. Maintaining average grades in high school, she began a serious tournament career in 1949. She collected 50 junior trophies, traveling to dozens of tournaments. At 14, she was the youngest player to win the national girls' championship. At 15, she ranked tenth among U.S. women's players, making her the youngest woman to ever break the women's top-ten rankings. "She was way ahead of her time, she had a cockiness, or overbearing, that always gave you the feeling that she was in charge and you were just the onlooker," said tennis legend Jack Kramer, surprised by the power of her game while facing her in a social game of doubles. Under Tennant's tutelage, Connolly played a base-line game based on superb ground strokes and her ability to cover the entire court. She had strong passing shots. Her devastating lobs and drop shots made up for her limitations at the net. Ultimately her biggest weapon was her willpower and her ability to concentrate.

Tennant didn't limit herself to the physical side of Connolly's game. Perhaps her strongest, though highly questionable influence, involved her psychological approach. Coach Tennant convinced Connolly that her game required she be a little nervous before a match. Connolly wrote that Tennant started "keying me up" before big matches. She wanted Maureen protected from distractions, cocooned in a private exclusion zone. As Connolly matured and her confidence grew, Tennant became convinced that she was becoming more social, consequently less competitive and less ruthless against her competition, particularly when it came to **Doris Hart*, one of the highest-ranked players in the country.

As a child, Connolly idolized Hart, who was ten years her senior. Eventually, Hart took the newcomer under her wing, and Connolly took great pride in their friendship. Convinced Connolly would not have the heart to beat someone she revered, Tennant duped Connolly into think-

---

❧► **Tennant, Eleanor** (fl. 1920–1940)

American tennis coach. Name variations: Teach Tennant.

Often called "Hollywood's best-known coach," Eleanor Tennant ranked third among American women tennis players in 1920, before becoming a highly regarded professional tennis coach. Her pupils included champions **Maureen Connolly, *Alice Marble, *Pauline Betz*, and Bobby Riggs, as well as such non-champions as Clark Gable and **Carole Lombard*. Tennant was innovative and tough, pushing Marble to practice five sets a day, rather than the usual three, because she felt that five sets in practice equaled three in a match. When Marble came down with what was thought to be tuberculosis, Tennant put her in a sanatorium for five months and worked overtime to pay the bills. When her winning protege Maureen Connolly called a press conference and publicly fired Tennant, it is said that Tennant never fully recovered from the shock.

Maureen
Connolly

ing that Hart perceived her to be a spoiled brat. Connolly was devastated. "No idol fell faster or with a more shattering crash than Doris Hart," she wrote. "I was shocked, stunned, then I saw blinding red. This was no passing dislike, but a virulent, powerful and consuming hate. . . . I be-lieved I could not win without hate, and win I must because I was afraid to lose. So, tragically, this hate, this fear became the fuel of my obses-sion to win." Hart and Connolly did not com-municate for two years. Programmed to win and thoroughly practiced, Connolly won and won.

By the time she turned 16 and graduated from Cathedral Catholic High School, Maureen Connolly had become good enough not only to compete at the professional level but to dominate international competition. In September 1951, she won the U.S. title at the West Side Tennis Club in Forest Hills, her first major championship, and ruled the women's tennis tour for three tumultuous years. She never lost a singles match in major competitions.

There is nothing like competition. It teaches you early in life to win and lose, and, when you lose, to put your chin out instead of dropping it.

—Maureen Connolly

Allison Danzig, a tennis reporter for *The New York Times,* said of the 5'5", 130-pound teenager: "Maureen, with her perfect timing, fluency, balance and confidence, has developed the most overpowering stroke of its kind the game has known." The world wasn't quite ready for Connolly's meteoric rise. The public respected her talent and liked her color and panache, but her youth made her somewhat a freak of nature. Connolly's three main American opponents were roughly ten years her senior. The image of a bubbling teenager off the court, and a cold, powerful, emotionless assassin on the courts, didn't mesh. The teenage tennis star sported a nickname more suitable for a linebacker or home-run hitter: "Little Mo," stemmed from "Big Mo," short for the U.S.S. *Missouri* battleship based in San Diego.

Teenage tennis stars were not the norm in Connolly's time. In the early 1950s, women's sports rarely received attention, even the major men's events were not yet televised. Connolly paved the way and left headlines in her wake. The prodigy's powerful game intrigued the international press. However, the confidence, concentration and willpower that made her a champion, also made her a media target. Her unsmiling, unrelenting and seemingly unforgiving court demeanor resulted in her being depicted by cartoonists as a grim-faced automaton.

Coach Tennant's greatest student also showed a soft, but no less confident, side. Embroidered kittens and puppies or butterfly wings adorned her knee-length outfits. After Connolly helped the U.S. to victory in her first Wightman Cup competition, she brazenly informed Ted Tinling, the famed clothing designer for women's tennis stars, that he should begin making outfits for her on the tour. Tinling recalled,

"She just marched in and said: 'I like your clothes; I'm going to wear them.'"

Connolly wasn't in it for the money—the women's tour paid little in the early '50s—but privately she craved popularity. Her first great international challenge, Wimbledon, was also her first major welcome in the public arena. The British press surrounded Connolly, and she did not disappoint. Expecting a shy teenager, they found Little Mo willing to answer questions and pose for all picture requests. But Connolly raised eyebrows when she announced plans to go straight from the airport to watch a boxing match. "I don't believe in strict training," she declared. "Bed by eleven o'clock is early enough and an occasional night out until one in the morning is all right too."

Then, Connolly startled the press by publicly firing Coach Tennant after an argument about how to treat a nagging shoulder injury. Tennant had suggested she withdraw from Wimbledon and rest the shoulder in order to prolong her career; Connolly adamantly refused. The press wondered whether she was acting hastily and precociously, but in hindsight perhaps Connolly somehow sensed her limited time. (Connolly, who later learned of Tennant's fabrication regarding Doris Hart, apologized to Hart, putting their friendship back on track.)

Without her coach and with her liberal training habits, the cocky American nearly needed an early return ticket from her first visit to Wimbledon. In a fourth-round match against British favorite **Susan Partridge,** down 4–5 in the third set, trailing 15–30, and serving her second serve, Connolly was one point away from match point and defeat. She won the next point. "At 30-all," she wrote, "suddenly piercing the tense silence, a young voice rang out clear and bold: 'Give 'em hell, Mo!' . . . I stood stunned, paused, looked and saw a U.S. Air Force boy. His face was a flash of youth, shining, glowing." The voice from home helped Connolly turn the tide. The final score read 6–3, 5–7, 7–5, and she went on to the semifinals where she bested *Shirley Fry. By defeating *Louise Brough in the finals, Connolly became the youngest Wimbledon champion in more than 60 years.

During a civic ceremony celebrating her return, the San Diego Jaycees presented Connolly with Colonel Merryboy, a Tennessee Walker horse. "I thought it was a contentious, ill-tempered beast myself, and so did a lot of others," said Ted Tinling. "But Mo loved that horse, and no one could tell her anything about it." Now ranked number one, Connolly began to collect her trophies. Her game improved under the coaching of tennis greats Harry ("Hop") Hopman, an Australian Davis Cup champion, and Lester Stoefen, a former men's doubles world champion. She considered Hop and his wife **Nell**, who traveled with her as a business manager and chaperon, her two closest friends on the tour. She credited Stoefen with improving her serve.

Connolly worked hard to improve her game and to maintain her mental sharpness. She practiced three hours a day, five days a week. She dedicated herself to physical conditioning but also recommended an easy day "off" every so often, concentrating on the ball and on having fun, instead of the score, so as not to become "overplayed." Her age, her success, and her unorthodox habits—she often practiced only with men—alienated some of the American women on the tour. At times, she also distanced herself from members of the press, earning a reputation as a snob. Frustrated by bad press, at one point she wrote an editorial headlined: "I Am No Swell Head."

By the summer of 1953, top seeded at Wimbledon, Connolly lost only eight games in five matches on her way to the finals. At Centre Court, she defeated American Doris Hart 8–6, 7–5, in a match still regarded to be one of the greatest women's finals ever played. On September 7, 1953, she again defeated Hart to win the U.S. Championship at Forest Hills, making her, at age 18, the youngest player, and the first player to complete the Grand Slam of all four major tennis titles in a calendar year: a feat matched only by *Margaret Court (1970) and *Steffi Graf (1988). The only humiliating loss in Connolly's Grand Slam year was a 6–0, 6–0 beating from Hart and Fry, shared with partner **Julie Sampson** in the women's doubles final.

After the Grand Slam victory, still only 19, Connolly won a third successive Wimbledon crown. She loved everything about Centre Court at Wimbledon and only lost five sets on the way to winning 18 consecutive matches at the All-English club. "Here was the realm of my hopes, my fears, my dreams," she wrote, "and, as long as I live, I shall be there in spirit, savoring the glory, tasting the heartbreak." But her straight-set demolition of Louise Brough at Wimbledon that summer of 1954 would be her last public appearance on a tennis court.

Back in San Diego, while she was riding Colonel Merryboy alongside another equestrian, a speeding cement truck swerved to avoid hitting them. Both the horses and the other rider were unharmed, but the cement chute swung wide of the truck and cut into Connolly's right leg just above the ankle, digging into the bone. While waiting for an ambulance, a nurse happened by and kept Connolly from using her blouse as a tourniquet, a move that probably saved the leg.

The wound eventually healed but arterial damage lessened the flow of blood to her lower leg, and Connolly's quickness never returned. Rehabilitation programs for the leg, even ballet classes, failed. With her movement-based game severely restricted, Connolly attempted several comebacks but never again played professional tennis. She announced her retirement in February 1955.

For a while, she lingered in the spotlight. In a pioneering move, unheard of for a female athlete in the 1950s, she joined Jack Kramer as a representative for the Wilson Sporting Goods Company. She also received a payment of $110,734 from the truck driver's insurance company. Tennis experts conjecture that Connolly would have dominated the tennis circuit for years. None of the three American women—Doris Hart, Louis Brough, and Shirley Fry—who ruled the tour for the two years following Connolly's retirement had ever been able to handle Connolly.

For Connolly, the year 1955 had its consolation. Beginning in 1951, to help earn spending money, she had filed a series of "Letters from Little Mo," for publication in the *San Diego Union,* during her tennis travels. Then, her aunt suggested she write a story about the 1952 Olympic equestrian team. Always eager to be near horses, Connolly arranged to interview Norman Brinker, an Olympic equestrian team member and San Diego entrepreneur, at the stable where he kept his horses. Finding Brinker appealing, Connolly "kind of dragged" out the interview. The press followed the romance, and the stories added to her public appeal. When Connolly asked Ted Tinling to design a wedding dress for her marriage, Trans World Airlines scored free publicity by flying the gown from England in a package marked "special cargo," placed across three first-class seats.

Maureen Connolly and Norman Brinker married in 1955 and settled in San Diego. Two years later, in 1957, they had their first child, a daughter named **Brenda Lee Brinker. Cynthia Anne Brinker**, a second daughter, completed the family in 1960. In the early 1960s, the Brinkers moved to Dallas where Norman directed the

Steak 'N Ale restaurant chain and owned Brink's Coffee Shop. The family lived in a house on three acres outside Dallas, with a swimming pool, pond, and stable, and a barn large enough to shelter seven polo ponies. Connolly lived a private, though active life. She occasionally assisted her husband, finding decorations for the coffee shop. She worked as a columnist and feature writer, studied history at Southern Methodist University, and devoted time to the Texas Junior Wightman Cup team. Friends and acquaintances knew her to be a warm and generous, far from the grim competitor portrayed by the media.

But in 1965, at age 31, Connolly experienced another abrupt turn. Doctors discovered a malignancy in her stomach. She battled disease with the same determination she displayed on the court, and the struggle lasted nearly as long as her professional career. Over a three-year period, Connolly endured three major stomach operations. "My sister and I never knew she was dying," said Cindy Brinker, Connolly's youngest daughter who was only six at the time of her mother's diagnosis. "Being the champion she was, she thought she could beat it." Cindy remembers that on the day of her death, Maureen Connolly was practicing an acceptance speech for one more award that she was scheduled to give later that summer. She died on June 21, 1969, at the age of 34.

A few months earlier, in December of 1968, the Maureen Connolly Brinker Tennis Foundation had been co-founded by Mo and **Nancy Jeffett**, with Norman Brinker, Jeffett, and Robert C. Taylor as trustees. The foundation, incorporating a number of tennis activities that had been started by Connolly and her associates in the 1960s, officially launched a myriad of programs, all created to promote women's tennis. With the backing of a large endowment via fund-raising by the Virginia Slims of Dallas, the non-profit foundation has assisted hundreds of players around the world.

SOURCES:
Conklin, Mike. "Programmed to Win," in *Chicago Tribune*. September 4, 1988, section C, p. 31.
Connolly, Maureen. *Power Tennis*. NY: A.S. Barnes, 1954.
Frayne, Trent. *Famous Women Tennis Players*. NY: Dodd, Mead, 1979.
Higdon, Hal. *Champions of the Tennis Court*. Englewood Cliffs, NJ: Prentice-Hall, 1971.
Horner, Peter. "The Legacy of 'Little Mo,'" in *United States Tennis Association Magazine*. January 1991, p. 12.
Interviews with Nancy Jeffett, president, and Carol Weyman, executive director, Maureen Connolly Brinker Tennis Foundation.

Obituary. "Maureen Connolly, Tennis Star, Dies," in *The New York Times*. June 22, 1969, section 1, p. 69.
Parsons, John. "Maureen Connolly," in *Official 1993 Wimbledon Program*. All-England Lawn Tennis and Croquet Club, p. 13.
Philip, Robert. "Lawn Tennis: Tragedy of the Teenage Prodigy," in *The Daily Telegraph*. September 6, 1993, p. 37.
Roth, Anna. *Current Biography*. NY: H.W. Wilson, 1951.
COLLECTIONS:
Maureen Connolly Brinker Tennis Foundation, P.O. Box 7065, Dallas, Texas.

Jesse T. Raiford,
President of Raiford Communications, Inc.,
New York, New York

Connolly, Olga Fikotová (b. 1932).

See Fikotová, Olga.

Conolly, Louisa (1743–1821).

See Lennox Sisters.

Conrad-Martius, Hedwig
(1888–1966)

German philosopher and member of the Göttingen Circle. Name variations: Hedwig Martius. Born Hedwig Martius in 1888 to a medical family in northern Germany; died in 1966; studied with Edmund Husserl at the University of Göttingen 1911–1912; Ph.D. University of Munich, 1913; married Theodor Conrad in 1912.

Awarded essay prize from the Philosophische Fakultat at the University of Göttingen (1912); was a lecturer, University of Munich from 1949.

Selected works: Ursprung und Aufbau des Lebendigen Kosmos *(1938);* Der Selbstaufbau der Natur: Entelechien und Energien *(1944);* Naturwissenschaftlich-metaphysische Perspectktiven; Drei Vortrage *(1948);* Das Lebendige; die Endlichkeit der Welt; der Mench Drei Dispute *(1951);* Die Zeit *(1954);* Das Sein *(1954);* Der Raum *(1958);* Brief an Hedwig Conrad-Martius *(1960);* Die Geistseele des Menschen *(1960);* Schriften zur Philosophie *(1963).*

Hedwig Martius was one of the first women to be a professional academic. In 1888, she was born in the north of Germany to an established medical family, who sent her to study literature at the University of Göttingen in 1911. She soon became interested in the philosophical movement of phenomenology that was centered in the university, however, and later burned her early attempts at writing drama and poetry.

Martius was introduced to phenomenology through attending the lectures of Moritz Geiger. He recommended her to Edmund Husserl, the philosopher who led the movement of phenomenology in continental European philosophy. The study of how we perceive the world, phenomenology was one of the most important philosophical approaches in the 20th century. As one of Husserl's students, Martius participated in the philosophical discussion group that became known as the Göttingen Circle, which included such notable philosophers as Max Scheler, Adolf Reinach, Fritz Kaufmann, *Edith Stein, Roman Ingarden, and Alexandre Koyre.

In 1912, Martius left the University of Göttingen for the University of Munich to pursue her Ph.D. in Philosophy. Her thesis grew out of a paper written at the University of Göttingen for which she had won a prize from the Philosophische Fakultat. (She did not pursue the Ph.D. at Göttingen because they required fluency in Latin.) That same year, she married Theodor Conrad, who supported her academic work with an orchard farm, as women were not permitted to hold paid academic positions at the time. Conrad-Martius lived alternately at the farm in Bergzabern (Palatinate) and in Munich while she studied.

Her work was characteristic of the Göttingen Circle. Conrad-Martius' doctoral thesis was a critique of positivism, the approach to philosophy that was then flourishing in Vienna and would continue to dominate British and American philosophy throughout the 20th century. Positivism considers the world in terms of discrete units that map onto the truths expressed in language. For Conrad-Martius, as a phenomenologist, this approach to ontology (the study of the grounds of reality) was mistaken, and she took the position that we must look for deeper structures in our experience. Her later work concerned nature and the forms, or "essences," which underlie our experience of it. After the completion of her Ph.D. in 1913, she continued to read natural science and the great philosophers, especially the German idealists. World War I left the farm unproductive and the Conrads struggled to make ends meet. Nonetheless, Conrad-Martius frequently hosted the meetings of the Göttingen Circle at the farm.

In 1930, Conrad-Martius returned to philosophical work, though she continued to struggle financially. Although women were now permitted to lecture at German universities, the economy was weak. After the Nazis came into power, she was prohibited from academic employment and publication because she had a Jewish grandparent. Conrad-Martius nonetheless published in German magazines and abroad, and the end of World War II unleashed a torrent of her academic publications. In 1949, she was granted a lectureship at the University of Munich. She died in 1966.

SOURCES:

Kersey, Ethel M. *Women Philosophers: a Bio-critical Source Book*. NY: Greenwood Press, 1989.

Spiegelberg, Herbert. *The Phenomenological Movement*. Boston: Martin Nijhoff, 1982.

Waithe, Mary Ellen, ed. *A History of Women Philosophers, vol. 3*. Boston: Martinus Nijhoff Publications, 1987.

Catherine Hundleby, M.A. Philosophy, University of Guelph, Guelph, Ontario, Canada

Constance.

Variant of Constantia.

Constance (d. 305 CE).

See Catherine of Alexandria for sidebar.

Constance (c. 321–354).

See Constantina.

Constance (c. 1066–1090).

See Matilda of Flanders for sidebar.

Constance (fl. 1100)

*Viscountess of Beaumont. Possibly illegitimate daughter of *Sybilla Corbert and Henry I (1068–1135), king of England (r. 1100–1135); married Richard, viscount of Beaumont; children: *Ermengarde de Beaumont; Raoul VI de Beaumont.*

Constance (c. 1374–1416)

*Duchess of Gloucester and Kent. Name variations: Constance Plantagenet. Born around 1374; died on November 28, 1416; daughter of Edmund of Langley, 1st duke of York, and *Isabel of Castile (1355–1392); married Thomas Despenser, 1st earl of Gloucester, in 1379; married Edmund Holland, 4th earl of Kent; children: (first marriage) three, including *Isabel Despenser (1400–1439) and Richard Despenser, lord Despenser (d. 1414).*

Constance-Anna of Hohenstaufen

*Byzantine empress. Name variations: Anna-Constance of Hohenstauffen; Anna Constanza. Daughter of Frederick II, Holy Roman emperor (r. 1215–1250) and *Constance of Aragon (d. 1222); second wife of John III Dukas Vatatzes, Nicaean [Byzantine] emperor (r. 1222–1254); children: Basil Vatatzes. John III's first wife was *Irene Lascaris (fl. 1222–1235).*

Constance Capet, countess of Toulouse (c. 1128–1176).

See Adelaide of Maurienne for sidebar.

Constance de Cezelli (d. 1617)

French noble and military leader. Name variations: Constance of Leucates. Birth date unknown; died in 1617 in Leucates, France; married the lord of Leucates; children: at least one.

Constance was a woman of the lower nobility who married the lord of Leucates. Leucates was a small region located in Languedoc, what is now southern France. During the invasion of France by the Spanish in 1590, Constance's husband was taken prisoner. He had left her in charge of defending Leucates when he went to join the French armies, and she acquitted herself well. Constance led the defense of the town personally, and tried to arrange for her husband's release by negotiating with the Spanish. However, they refused to free him unless she relinquished Leucates. Constance refused, and her husband was killed by his captors when they realized she would not yield the town. This served only to increase her resolve, and several months later the Spanish armies gave up the siege. For her bravery and loyalty, the French king Henry IV awarded Constance the position of governor of Leucates, which she held until her death in 1617.

Laura York,
Riverside, California

Constance Enriques, Enriquez or Henriques (1290–1313).

See Constance of Portugal.

Constance Jones, E.E. (1848–1922)

British philosopher whose ideas were misrepresented by Bertrand Russell as his own. Born Emily Elizabeth Constance Jones in Wales in 1848; died in 1922; daughter of the squire of the parish of Llangarron; tutored at home; attended boarding school in Cheltenham; Moral Sciences Tripos at Girton College, Cambridge University, 1880.

Was a lecturer at Girton College from 1884; served as librarian of Girton College (1890–93); was vice-mistress of Girton College (1896–1903); was mistress of Girton College (from 1903); served as executive member of the Aristotelian Society (1914–16); published prolifically, particularly on logic.

Selected works: Elements of Logic as a Science of Propositions *(1890);* An Introduction to General Logic *(1892);* "Symposium: Character and Circumstance," *in* Proceedings of the Aristotelian Society, *New Series 3 (1902–03);* "Character and Circumstance" *in* International Journal of Ethics 9; Primer of Logic *(1905);* "Logic and Identity in Difference" *in* Proceedings of the Aristotelian Society *(1907);* "Precise Number and Numerical Identity," *in* Mind *(1908);* A Primer of Ethics *(1909);* "Mr. Russell's Objections to Frege's Analysis of Propositions," *in* Mind *(1910);* "A New 'Law of Thought' and Its Implications," *in* Mind *(1911);* A New Law of Thought and Its Logical Bearings *(1911);* As I Remember *(1922).*

Although Emily Elizabeth Constance Jones spent her childhood and most of her life in Britain, where her father was squire of the parish of Llangarron, Herefordshire, she spent her early adolescence with her family just outside Capetown, South Africa, and received much of her early education there. In the Constance Jones' large servant-filled house in Capetown, Emily was tutored by governesses in French and German and read the philosophers of the time who wrote in these languages: Schiller, Goethe, Voltaire, Moliere, Racine, and Corneille.

Having acquired a thirst for knowledge, Emily began earnest study upon her return to England. She went to a boarding school for girls in Cheltenham, where she continued to study languages (now including Italian) and mathematics. At age 19, when her basic schooling was complete, she returned home. Emily joined an essay society and was inspired to go to university by a friend of her brothers; this friend was studying Moral Science and shared with her some of his philosophical readings by Fawcett and Mill.

As the family put greater priority on their sons' educations, most of the support for Emily's education came from an aunt on her father's side, a Mrs. Collins. Emily attended the only women's college she knew of, Girton College, Cambridge, with periodic interruptions when her aunt had difficulty providing the financing. At Girton, she prepared for the Moral Science Tripos, a program that included all of the traditional areas of philosophy as well as political economics and psychology, and studied under Henry Sidgwick, James Ward, and John Neville Keynes. Despite having to miss terms, which hurt her academic career, she was so accomplished that recommendations from Sidgwick and Ward earned her the job of completing the translation of Herman Lotze's *Mikrokosmos.*

In 1880, Constance Jones completed her studies and passed her examinations Class 1.

When she returned to Cambridge in 1884, she studied logic and began to pursue the philosophy of language. These topics were the focus of the "analytic" movement that was overtaking philosophy at the time and which dominated 20th-century philosophy in Britain and North America. Constance Jones' ideas, particularly her view of categorical propositions (statements that characterize objects, such as "the cat is black"), were very influential and admired by her colleagues as original and important contributions to the field of logic. Her professional career was spent developing her view that categorical propositions are composed of a subject and a predicate related by identity or non-identity. Bertrand Russell, who had also recently graduated from Cambridge, is known to have presented her ideas as his own without crediting her. Because Constance Jones did not publish any books until 1890, and because she was very modest, Russell's plagiarism was not recognized for some time.

Constance Jones was closely involved with the Aristotelian Society, a prestigious organization for the discussion of philosophy. A great deal of her work showed up in their publications and in the philosophical journal *Mind*. From 1890 to 1893, she acted as the librarian of Girton College, because the position was hard to fill. She became vice-mistress of the college in 1896, and mistress in 1903. From 1914 to 1916, she served on the executive committee of the Aristotelian Society. Constance Jones continued to publish philosophy prolifically, and in 1922, the year of her death, published her autobiography, *As I Remember*.

Catherine Hundleby, M.A. Philosophy,
University of Guelph, Guelph, Ontario, Canada

Constance of Antioch (1128–c. 1163).

See Melisande for sidebar.

Constance of Aragon (d. 1222)

*Holy Roman empress and queen of Sicily. Died on June 23, 1222; daughter of *Sancha of Castile and Leon (1164–1208) and Alphonso II (1152–1196), king of Aragon (r. 1164–1196); married Emeric, king of Hungary (r. 1196–1204); became first wife of Frederick II (1194–1250), Holy Roman emperor (r. 1212–1250) and king of Sicily (r. 1197–1250), in February 1210; children: (first marriage) Ladislas III, king of Hungary (r. 1204–1205); (second marriage) Henry VII, king of Germany (d. 1242); *Constance-Anna of Hohenstaufen (who married John III Dukas Vatatzes, Nicaean emperor [r. 1222–1254]). Frederick*

II's second wife was *Yolande of Brienne (1212–1228); his third was *Isabella of England (1214–1241).*

Constance of Aragon (d. 1327)

*Duchess of Penafiel. Died on August 19, 1327, at Château de Garci Munoz; daughter of *Blanche of Naples (d. 1310) and Jaime or James II, king of Sicily and Aragon (r. 1291–1327); married John Manuel or Juan Manuel de Villena "el Scritor" of Castile, duke of Penafiel, on April 2, 1312; children: *Constance of Castile (1323–1345), queen of Portugal. Juan Manuel's second wife was *Blanche de la Cerda (c. 1311–1347).*

Constance of Aragon (c. 1350–?)

*Queen of Sicily. Name variations: Constanza of Aragón. Born around 1350; daughter of *Eleanor of Sicily (d. 1375) and Pedro IV also known as Peter IV the Ceremonious (b. 1319), king of Aragon (r. 1336–1387); married Frederick III the Simple, king of Sicily (r. 1355–1377); children: *Maria of Sicily (d. 1402).*

Constance of Arles (c. 980–1032)

*Capetian queen of France. Name variations: Constance of Provence. Born around 980 (some sources cite 973); died on July 25, 1032, in Melun; daughter of William, count of Toulouse (William I of Provence); became third wife of Robert II the Pious (972–1031), king of France (r. 996–1031), in 1005; children: Hugh (1007–1025); *Adela Capet (c. 1010–1079), countess of Flanders (mother of *Matilda of Flanders); Henry I (1008–1060), king of France (r. 1031–1060); Robert I (1011–1076), duke of Burgundy (r. 1031–1076).*

In 998, Pope Gregory V excommunicated Robert II the Pious, king of France, and voided his second marriage to his cousin ☙ Bertha of Burgundy (964–1024) because they were too closely related. Robert then married Constance of Arles, daughter of the count of Toulouse, and she gave birth to four children. On her husband's death, Constance was determined to put her youngest son Robert I, duke of Burgundy, on the throne of France, rather than the appointed successor, her eldest living son Henry. With the support of the duke of Normandy, the count of Anjou, and the count of Flanders, Henry overthrew his brother. Crowned Henry I, he then pardoned Robert and granted him the duchy of

Bertha of Burgundy (964–1024). See Matilda of Flanders for sidebar.

Burgundy. In the meantime, however, the conflict weakened the French monarchy.

Constance of Brittany (1161–1201)

Duchess of Brittany and countess of Chester. Name variations: Constance de Bretagne; Constance of Britagne. Born in 1161; died in Nantes, Anjou, France, on September 5, 1201, while giving birth to twins; daughter of Conan IV, duke of Brittany, and *Margaret of Huntingdon (c. 1140–1121); married Geoffrey Plantagenet, duke of Brittany, in July 1181; married Ranulf de Blondville, 4th earl of Chester, in 1187 (divorced 1199); married Guy, viscount of Thouars, in 1199; children: (first marriage) *Eleanor, the Maid of Brittany (1184–1241); Matilda (1185–1186); Arthur, duke of Brittany (1187–1203); (third marriage) twins *Alice (1201–1221), duchess of Brittany, and Katherine de Thouars (b. 1201, who married Andrew de Vitre of Brittany).

Constance of Burgundy (1046–c. 1093).

See Urraca (c. 1079–1126) for sidebar.

Constance of Castile (d. 1160)

Queen of France. Born after 1140; died in childbirth on October 4, 1160; daughter of Alphonso VII, king of Castile and Leon (r. 1126–1157), and *Berengaria of Provence (1108–1149); became second wife of Louis VII (1120–1180), king of France (r. 1137–1180), before November 18, 1153; children: *Margaret of France (1158–1198, who married Bela III, king of Hungary) and *Alais of France (b. 1160).

Constance of Castile, duchess of Lancaster (1354–1394).

See Beaufort, Joan (c. 1379–1440) for sidebar.

Constance of Castile, queen of Portugal (1323–1345).

See Castro, Ines de for sidebar.

Constance of France (fl. 1100s)

Princess of Antioch and countess of Blois. Name variations: Constance Capet. Born between 1072 and 1092; daughter of *Bertha of Holland (1055–1094) and Philip I the Fair (1052–1108), king of France (r. 1060–1108); sister of Louis VI (c. 1081–1137), king of France (r. 1108–1137); married Bohemond II or Bohemund I of Taranto (d. 1111), prince of Antioch (r. 1098–1111); married Hugh I, count of Blois, in

1104; children: (first marriage) Bohemond or Bohemund II of Antioch (r. 1126–1130).

Constance of Germany (1154–1198).

See Constance of Sicily.

Constance of Hungary (d. 1240).

See Agnes of Bohemia (1205–1282) for sidebar.

Constance of Leucates (d. 1617).

See Constance de Cezelli.

Constance of Portugal (1290–1313)

Queen of Castile and Leon. Name variations: Constance Henriques, Enriques or Enriquez. Born on January 3, 1290; died on November 17, 1313, in Sahagun; interred at Valladolid; daughter of Diniz also spelled Dinis or Denis (1261–1325), king of Portugal (r. 1279–1325), and *Elizabeth of Portugal (1271–1336); married Ferdinand IV (1285–1312), king of Castile and Leon (r. 1295–1321), in 1301 or 1302; children: Alphonso XI, king of Castile and Leon (r. 1312–1350); *Eleanor of Castile (1307–1359); Constanza (c. 1309–c. 1311).

Constance of Provence (c. 980–1032).

See Constance of Arles.

Constance of Rabastens (fl. 1384).

See Women Prophets and Visionaries in France at the End of the Middle Ages.

Constance of Sicily (1154–1198)

Holy Roman empress and queen of Sicily. Name variations: Constance d'Altavilla; Constance of Germany; (German) Konstanz. Born in 1154 in Sicily; died on November 27, 1198, in Germany; daughter of Roger II the Great, king of Sicily (r. 1103–1154), duke of Apulia (r. 1128–1154), and Beatrice of Rethel; married Henry VI (1165–1197), king of Germany and Holy Roman emperor (r. 1190–1197), king of Sicily (r. 1194–1197), on January 27, 1186; children: Frederick II (b. 1194), Holy Roman emperor (r. 1215–1250).

Constance of Sicily was born a princess of the Sicilian royal house. Her father, King Roger II, died shortly before her birth, and her mother, *Beatrice of Rethel, died of complications after her birth, leaving Constance to begin life as an orphan. The throne was assumed by her nephew who became king of Sicily as William II. Constance was raised at the Sicilian court, where she remained until 1186 when she married the Holy

Roman emperor's son, Prince Henry Hohenstaufen of Germany (later Holy Roman Emperor Henry VI). Though it remains unclear why she married at such a late age, it is possible that her position as only the aunt of the reigning Sicilian king made her a less valuable marriage prospect than other princesses. However, her marriage to the future emperor of Germany was likely regarded as an excellent ending to what was probably a long search for a suitable husband.

Three years after her marriage, the new princess of Germany also became queen of Sicily, when William II died without children and named Constance as his heir. Although she claimed the title, Constance could not actually take the throne for some time because the people of Sicily did not want Henry Hohenstaufen, a foreigner, as their king, and because Constance was also opposed by the pope, who was an enemy of her husband. Therefore, Tancred of Lecce, one of Constance's nephews, set himself up as ruler of Sicily with the approval of the Sicilians and the pope. A war of succession quickly developed.

The coronation of Henry and Constance as emperor and empress in 1190 tilted the balance of the war in their favor, due to the vast resources now at the new emperor's disposal. Tancred remained entrenched for several more years, primarily because Henry's new duties kept him away from Sicily. On Tancred's death in 1194, Constance was finally able to claim the throne as her own. In that year as well, she gave birth to her first and only child, Frederick, later Holy Roman Emperor Frederick II. But Constance's fortunes turned in 1197, when her husband Henry, an extremely severe emperor who counted the pope and many kings among his mortal enemies, died suddenly that September, and not many mourned his passing. Overnight Constance's position changed from that of a powerful empress to a woman who feared for her safety and that of her infant son Frederick, Henry's heir.

The leading nobles of Germany opposed the succession of Constance's son because it would mean a long minority, a political situation always best avoided. They convened to choose a new emperor, settling on Otto of Brunswick, who was crowned as Emperor Otto IV in January 1198. Constance fled Germany with her son and returned to Sicily. She died in November of that year, about age 44, leaving her son in the pope's custody. The pope, Innocent III, at first favored Otto but, in 1212, reversed his decision and had the boy Frederick reinstalled as Emperor Frederick II.

Laura York,
Riverside, California

Constance of Sicily (d. 1302)

Queen of Aragon. Died in 1302; daughter of Manfred, king of Naples and Sicily (r. 1258–1266, illegitimate son of Frederick II, Holy Roman emperor) and Beatrice of Savoy; married Pedro III also known as Peter III, king of Aragon (r. 1276–1285), in 1262; children: Alphonso III (1265–1291), king of Aragon (r. 1285–1291); Elizabeth of Portugal (1271–1336); Jaime or James II (d. 1327), king of Aragon (r. 1291–1327); Frederick II (1271–1336), king of Sicily (r. 1296–1336).

In many historical accounts of the late Medieval period, Constance, queen of Aragon (located in the western Mediterranean, and including Sicily and Sardinia), is never mentioned. The limited information about her life tells us that she was the daughter and heir of Manfred, king of Sicily, and his first wife ❦➤ **Beatrice of Savoy**. In 1262, Constance married Peter III, king of Aragon, who ruled from 1276 to 1285. Shortly after the marriage, her father Manfred lost his throne in 1266 to Charles of Anjou (son of Louis VIII of France), who was subsequently driven out of Sicily in a bloody revolt known as the Sicilian Vespers (1282). As Constance's husband, Peter III now had entrée to the throne, although the papacy still recognized Charles as king of Naples and Sicily. After defeating Charles at Callo, Peter recaptured the throne in Constance's name, maintaining his refusal to pay homage to the pope. The ensuing struggle to maintain the family right to ascendancy continued even after Peter's death in 1285. Constance apparently spent the rest of her life seeing that her children were established as rulers of Sicily. She was fairly successful: Alphonso III succeeded to the throne of Aragon; James I succeeded to the throne of Sicily under his mother's regency and later succeeded to the throne of Aragon; and Frederick II, appointed a regent in 1291 when James took over Aragon, was elected king of Sicily four years later and eventually was recognized by the pope. Constance's daughter *Elizabeth of Portugal** left the kingdom and married Denis (Diniz), king of Portugal.

❦➤ **Beatrice of Savoy** (fl. 1240s)
*Queen of Naples and Sicily. Name variations: Beatrix of Savoy. Flourished around the 1240s; married Manfred, king of Naples and Sicily (r. 1258–1266, illegitimate son of Frederick II, Holy Roman emperor); children: *Constance of Sicily* (d. 1302).*

Constance of Styria (1588–1631)

*Queen of Poland. Name variations: Constance of Austria. Born on December 24, 1588; died on July 10, 1631; daughter of Charles, archduke of Austria, and *Mary of Bavaria (1551–1608); sister of *Margaret of Austria (c. 1577–1611) and Anna of Styria (1573–1598); became second wife of Zygmunt III also known as Sigismund III, king of Poland (r. 1587–1632), king of Sweden (r. 1592–1599), on December 11, 1605; children: Casimir V also known as John II Casimir (1609–1672), king of Poland (r. 1648–1668); John Albert also known as Jan Albert (1612–1634), bishop of Warmia and Cracow; Charles Ferdinand (1613–1655), bishop of Breslau; Alexander Charles (1614–1634); *Anna Constancia (1619–1651, who married Philip William, elector of the Palatinate). Sigismund III's first wife was *Anna of Styria, sister of Constance.*

Constance of Toulouse

*Queen of Navarre. Daughter of Raymond VI (b. 1156), count of Toulouse, and **Beatrice of Beziers**; married Sancho VII (b. after 1170), king of Navarre (1194–1234), after 1195.*

Constancia or Constantia.

Variant of Constance.

Constantia (c. 293–?)

Roman empress. Name variations: Constantina. Born Flavia Valeria Constantia around 293 CE; died before 330; daughter of Constantius I Chlorus (r. 305–306) and Theodora (fl. 290s); half-sister of Constantine I the Great, Roman emperor (r. 306–337); married C. Valerius Licinius (primary Roman emperor of the East), in 312; children: Licinius Caesar.

The daughter of Constantius Chlorus and ◄❦ Theodora (stepdaughter of Maximian, the senior Roman Emperor of the West), Constantia was born about the time her father was named Maximian's junior emperor with duties along the Rhine and the northern Roman frontier. She was the younger half-sister of the famous Constantine I the Great, who was Constantius Chlorus' son by his long-time consort *Helena (c. 255–329). Constantia also had two full brothers, Flavius Dalmatius and Flavius Julius Constantius, but they never rivalled the importance of Constantine the Great. Although Constantius Chlorus married Theodora for political advancement (a union that forced him to leave Helena), there appears to have been no resentment of Constantia on Constantine's behalf. Too young to have a political marriage arranged for her while her father was still alive (Constantius Chlorus died in 306), Constantia became a pawn in her half-brother Constantine's ambitious plan to reunify the entire empire under his sole authority.

Diocletian, the most prominent Roman political figure between 284 and 305, had divided the empire into four parts—the *Tetrarchy*—each dominated by an emperor, two (Diocletian and Maximian) of senior rank (called the Augusti) and two (Constantius Chlorus and Galerius) of junior rank (the Caesars), so as to bring an imperial presence to bear on the multiple problems facing the empire at the time. After Diocletian and Constantius Chlorus died, however, Constantine asserted his ambitions against several imperial rivals and by 312 he had already unified the West under his reign. In that year, Constantine married Constantia to Licinius, the primary emperor of the East, who was at the time Constantine's ally against two additional imperial competitors named Maxentius and Maximinus. After these rivals were removed by Constantine and Licinius (313), however, their own competition only intensified. The opening salvo in the following conflict occurred in 316, leaving Licinius battered but not overthrown. Ironically, their fallout had been precipitated by Constantia giving birth to Licinius' son, a younger Licinius. Constantine, now an Augustus and seeking to establish his authority in the naming of Caesars before Licinius could act to elevate his own heir to that status, proposed to elevate a kinsman-in-law named Bassianus to the rank of Caesar. Not caring for Constantine's unilateral action, and not wanting to see his own position hedged in by Constantinian supporters, Licinius objected. There followed a brief war in which Constantine won some territory from Licinius, but Constantine could not crush his eastern rival. In the subsequent treaty (317), which established an un-

❦► **Theodora** (fl. 290s)

*Roman noblewoman. Flourished in late 200s CE; daughter of *Eutropia (fl. 270–300 CE) and Afranius Hannibalianus; stepdaughter of Maximian, the senior Roman emperor of the West; half-sister of *Fausta (d. 324); second wife of Constantius I Chlorus, Roman emperor (r. 305–306); children: *Constantia (c. 293–?); Flavius Dalmatius; Flavius Julius Constantius; Hannibalianus; *Eutropia (who married Nepotianus); and Anastasia (who married Bassianus).*

easy peace, it was agreed that Constantine's two sons (Crispus and Constantinus) along with the younger Licinius should all become Caesars, although the oldest of the lot (Crispus) was only a teenager at the time.

A precarious truce ensued, during which Constantine increasingly championed the Christian cause—in large part to win over the political loyalty of that organized minority. Although Licinius was no die-hard enemy of Christians and had even, with Constantia, favored certain Church officials (especially the Arian bishop, Eusebius of Nicomedia), he could not be described as a good friend of the Church. In fact, knowing that the greater number of Christians lived in the East (where he ruled), and suspecting that Constantine was wooing Christians for political reasons, Licinius began to take precautions against the formation of a pro-Constantinian/Christian faction in the East by dismissing Christians from his imperial service. This, however, only provided Constantine with an excuse to renew his attack eastward (in 323–324). Constantine's victory was decisive this time, for in a single campaign he overthrew Licinius and assumed a position of unrivaled authority over the entire empire. Licinius "retired" from office upon the promise of his own personal safety, but along with his son he was immediately put under house arrest. Within a year, both were executed at Constantine's command, despite Constantia's plea for their lives. With Licinius' reign declared an usurpation and his law declared void, Constantine became sole ruler of the Roman Empire.

Whatever emotions privately consumed Constantia in the wake of her half-brother's ruthlessness (also wreaked upon other members of his immediate family in 325), neither Constantia nor her two full-brothers publicly broke with the emperor. In fact, they continued to enjoy Constantine's largesse, a sure sign that they kept any displeasure to themselves. For her part, Constantia maintained a public presence and a formal association with Constantine's interests.

As attracted to Christianity as was Constantine, Constantia had been a friend and confidant of many church leaders. In fact, it is probably no exaggeration to say that the prominence that Eusebius of Nicomedia had realized at the court of Licinius was due largely to Constantia. After Constantine's victory, Eusebius continued as a figure of some importance, albeit a controversial one, because he (along with many others) was long inclined to embrace the theological arguments of Arius on the nature of Christ, which were revolutionary concepts at the time, especially the proposition that Christ was not one with the Father, but of a "similar" substance. This position generated heated discussion within the Church and produced the Council of Nicaea in 325 presided over by Constantine. Here, the view of Arius was rejected as heretical and the "orthodox" understanding of the Trinity was articulated. Although many Arians subsequently confessed their "error," the issue of the nature of Christ did not go away, and many—including Constantia's and Constantine's mother, Helena—continued to associate closely with those like Eusebius of Nicomedia, who, even after his reconciliation with the forces of orthodoxy, tended to skirt the issue of Christ's essence.

Although Constantia thus flirted with heresy, her beliefs never officially alienated her from Constantine, and she may even (in part because of her unwillingness to provoke Constantine on other issues) have helped to protect the more circumspect of one-time Arians from persecution. Regardless, Constantia's devotion was famous enough for Constantine to rename the city of Maiuma (the port city of Palestinian Gaza) "Constantia" in her honor after it had converted to Christianity. The date of Constantia's death is not known precisely, but it seems that she was dead before 330. As such, perhaps the renaming of Maiuma (c. 327) can be helped to date her passing, for the creation of a new "Constantia" would have been an appropriate dedication to the memory of a devoted and loyal partisan of the Empire's first Christian emperor.

William S. Greenwalt, Associate Professor of Classical History,
Santa Clara University, Santa Clara, California

Constantia (c. 321–c. 354).

See Constantina.

Constantin, Mariana (b. 1960).

See Comaneci, Nadia for sidebar.

Constantina.

Variant of Constantia.

Constantina (c. 321–c. 354)

Roman empress and saint. Name variations: Constance; Constantia. Born around 321; died in Bithynia around 354; buried in a mausoleum attached to the basilica of St. Agnes; elder daughter of Constantine I the Great (285–337), Roman emperor (r. 306–337), and Fausta (d. 324); sister of Constantius II; married her cousin Hannibalianus, in 335 (divorced 337); married Flavius Claudius Constantius Gallus also known as Gallus Caesar, Roman emperor (r. 351–354), in 350.

There are two versions of the story of Constantina (or there may be two daughters of Constantine the Great whose stories have become intertwined). In the first, she is the elder daughter of *Fausta and Constantine I the Great, and briefly married to her cousin Hannibalianus from 335 to 337. In 350, when a senior Roman army officer named Magnentius usurped the Western emperor Constans, Constantina convinced Vetranio, the aging Master of the Infantry, to rebel and block Magnentius as he progressed eastward. Magnentius wanted to marry Constantina and form an alliance with her brother, the Eastern emperor Constantius II, but Constantius offered her to a cousin, Gallus, an Arian Christian like herself, instead. Historian Ammianus describes her as a "mortal fury," who encouraged her second husband's cruelty as he suppressed conspiracies and a Jewish rising when he became Roman emperor from 351 to 354. When Constantius II accused Gallus of treason, Constantina hurried to Bithynia to plead her husband's case. She died there and was buried in an exquisite porphyry sarcophagus in a mausoleum attached to the basilica of *St. Agnes (d. 304?), a church she had founded. The mausoleum, now known as S. Costanza, still exists.

In the second version, Constantina—a daughter, or possibly a niece, of Constantine I the Great and Fausta (or possibly ◄ Minervina)—was a leper who learned of miracles taking place at the tomb of the Christian martyr St. Agnes. Constantina had a vision from St. Agnes on a pilgrimage to the tomb and was promised a cure if she converted to Christianity. Baptized and restored to health, Constantina dedicated herself to her new religion and was intent on remaining a virgin.

When General Vulcacius Gallicanus, conqueror of the Persians, sought her hand in marriage, she refused. The Emperor Constantine, though Christian, was annoyed by her refusal; to please him, Constantina agreed to marry the general after he had warded off the Scythians who were invading Thrace. When Gallicanus left on his mission, he placed his daughters **Attica** and **Artemia** in Constantina's care and took two of her servants with him to further strengthen their bond.

While he was away, Constantina begged God to free her from her pledge to Gallicanus. Meanwhile, her servants convinced Gallicanus that he would be invincible in his campaign against the Scythians if he embraced Christianity. Following his victory, Gallicanus remained a Christian, gave up all thought of marrying Constantina, and

Minervina. See *Helena (c. 255–329) for sidebar.*

turned his attention toward good works. He was later martyred, along with Constantina's servants (around 361–363), under the reign of Julian the Apostate. Constantina passed her life in the company of Attica and Artemia, who had also been converted, near the church of St. Agnes and was buried there. Her feast day is February 18th.

Constantina (fl. 582–602).

See Sophia (c. 525–after 600 ce) for sidebar.

Constanza.

Variant of Constance.

Contat, Louise (1760–1813)

French actress. Born Louise Françoise Contat in 1760; died in 1813; sister of Marie Contat (1769–1846); married a nephew of the poet de Parny.

French actress and sister of *Marie Contat, Louise Françoise Contat made her debut at the Comédie Française in 1766 as Atalide in *Bajazet*. Her initial successes, however, were in comedy, playing Suzanne in Beaumarchais' *Mariage de Figaro* and lending importance to several other minor parts. As the soubrette in the plays of Molière and Marivaux, she found opportunities fitted specifically to her talents. Contat retired in 1809 and married a nephew of the poet de Parny.

Contat, Marie (1769–1846)

French actress. Born Marie Émilie Contat in 1769; died in 1846; sister of Louise Françoise Contat (1760–1813).

French soubrette and sister of *Louise Contat, Marie Contat was known especially for her roles as the pert servant in the plays of Molière and Jean François Regnard. She made her debut in 1784 and retired in 1815.

Content, Marjorie (1895–1984)

American photographer. Born in New York, New York, in 1895; died in Doylestown, Pennsylvania, in 1984; married Harold Loeb, in 1914 (divorced 1921); married Michael Carr (an artist and set designer), in 1924 (died 1927); married Leon Fleischman, in 1929 (divorced 1934); married Jean Toomer (a poet and novelist), in 1934 (died 1967); children: (first marriage) Harold Albert (who legally changed his name to James); and Mary Ellen (who legally changed her name to Susan).

Marjorie Content, who did not begin photographing seriously until the late 1920s, was strongly influenced by Alfred Steiglitz and probably *Consuelo Kanaga, who became her friend during the early 1920s. Specializing in portraits, still lifes, flowers, cityscapes, and landscapes, Content traveled intermittently in the West to photograph the life of Native Americans. Between 1933 and 1934, she photographed for the Bureau of Indian Affairs. Several of her pictures appeared in the Parisian photography annual *Photographie* between 1932 and 1935. Content, who was married four times, moved to Doylestown, Pennsylvania, with her fourth husband, the poet and novelist Jean Toomer, in 1934. There, she became a member of the Religious Society of Friends.

Conway, Anne, Viscountess Conway (1631–1679).

See Finch, Anne.

Cook, Edith Maud (d. 1910)

British aviator and parachutist. Name variations: Spencer Kavanagh; Violet Spenser. Killed in July 1910.

Edith Cook learned to fly on a Blériot monoplane in early 1910 at the Grahame-White School at Pau, France, under the name Spencer Kavanagh. She was already well-known as a parachute jumper under another pseudonym Violet Spenser. In July 1910, Cook was killed while making a descent from a balloon over Coventry.

Cook, Eliza (1818–1889)

English poet. Born on December 24, 1818, in Southwark, England; died at Wimbledon, England, on September 23, 1889; daughter of a London tradesman (brasier).

Eliza Cook grew up in London the youngest of 11 children. On her father's retirement in 1827, the family moved to a farm in Sussex. As a girl, the self-taught Cook contributed poetry to the *Weekly Dispatch* and *New Monthly* and, at 17, published *Lays of a Wild Harp* (1835). She published *Melaia and other Poems* in 1838, the same year that her poem "The Old Armchair" caught the fancy of working and middle-class readers on both continents, making her a household name. Written in memory of her beloved mother, the poem was known for a commonsensical domestic viewpoint that was considered unpretentious, moral, but never sentimental. Be-

ginning in 1849, Cook edited and published *Eliza Cook's Journal* until the magazine failed in 1854; many articles in the magazine were republished in *Jottings from My Journal* (1860). Cook followed this with *New Echoes and Other Poems* (1864) and was given a civil list pension of £100 per annum (1863). Both her popularity and health declined in her later life and, for a number of years, she was an invalid. Her complete collected poems were published in 1870.

Cook, Lady (1846–1923).

See Claflin, Tennessee.

Cook, Madge Carr (1856–1933).

See Belmont, Eleanor Robson for sidebar on Carr-Cook, Madge.

Cook, Tennessee (1846–1923).

See Claflin, Tennessee.

Cooke.

See also Coke and Cook.

Cooke, Anna Rice (1853–1934)

Hawaiian philanthropist and founder of the Honolulu Academy of Arts. Born Anna Charlotte Rice in Honolulu, Hawaii, on September 5, 1853; died in Honolulu on August 8, 1934; youngest of five children of William Harrison (an American missionary) and Mary Sophia (Hyde) Rice (also a missionary); attended Punahou School, Honolulu; attended Mills' Young Ladies Seminary, Benicia, California; married Charles Montague Cooke (a businessman), April 29, 1874; children: Charles Montague Cooke, Jr. (b. 1874); Clarence Hyde Cooke (b. 1876); William Harrison Cooke (1879–1880); George Paul Cooke (b. 1881); Richard Alexander Cooke (b. 1884); Alice Theodora Cooke (b. 1888); twins Dorothea Cooke (1891–1892) and Theodore Atherton Cooke.

In 1874, Anna Rice, the daughter of American missionaries, married Charles Cooke, also of a missionary family. The couple would remain true to the ethics of their childhoods by using their ensuing good fortune to improve Hawaii, their adopted home. With money amassed from Charles Cooke's successful business enterprises, including the Bank of Hawaii, they founded the Aquarium at Waikiki, Rice Hall (a dormitory), and the Cooke Library at Punahou School. Through the Charles M. and Anna C. Cooke Trust, a charitable enterprise, their fortune was further distributed to benefit the community. The couple also built a large wooden-frame Victorian house on property that covered a block in the center of the city of Honolulu, in which they raised five sons and a daughter (two other children died in infancy). They also traveled extensively, purchasing art objects and furnishings for their home from the Orient and British Columbia. When Charles died in 1909, Anna Cooke continued to travel with her daughter **Alice Cooke**, the last of her children to leave home. When she neared 70, and the house began to overflow with her treasures, Cooke decided to tear down the house and build a museum in its place. In addition to displaying her vast collection, the museum was to be used to educate and inspire the people of the islands, especially the children. The Honolulu Academy of Arts opened its doors on April 8, 1927.

In a building designed in the style of Hawaiian architecture, the Academy's galleries flanked a center court representing Hawaii's location in the Pacific, with the Oriental Court placed west and the Occidental Court east. In addition to planning the building and participating in cataloguing her collection, Cooke also pioneered an educational program to help the youth of Hawaii, composed of many ethnic groups, appreciate their cultural heritages. With input from the school systems, she oversaw the design of art exhibits planned to assist teachers in enriching their regular classes with art history. Concerned that some children might not have access to the museum, Cooke traveled to them, bringing paintings and other art objects to the rural country schools.

Rose Terry Cooke

Cooke spent her later years in a new home she built in the style of a Chinese farmhouse. Remaining active in the academy's work, she was known for her lively conversation (often centering on the near poverty days of her youth) and by her gentle manner of persuasion. She was fond of games, especially cards, and a form of Fan Tan known as "Foxy Grandma" became popular in Honolulu because she was so good at it. When Cooke died at age 80, people of all ages, races, and economic groups attended her funeral.

The Honolulu Academy of Arts is a monument to her quiet philanthropy.

Cooke, Rose Terry (1827–1892)

American author. Born Rose Terry in West Hartford, Connecticut, on February 17, 1827; died in Pittsfield, Massachusetts, on July 18, 1892; married Rollin H. Cooke, in 1873.

Though Rose Cooke's first published work was a volume of *Poems* (1860), she was best known for her fresh and humorous stories, which dealt primarily with New England country life: *Happy Dodd* (1878), *Somebody's Neighbors* (1881), *Rootbound* (1885), *The Sphinx's Children* (1886), *Steadfast* (1889) and *Huckleberries* (1891).

Cookson, Catherine (1906–1998)

British novelist whose books often depict the working-class country or mind-set of Northern England, where she was raised. Name variations: Catherine Marchant; Dame Catherine Cookson. Born Catherine McMullen on June 20, 1906, in Tyne Dock, South Shields, England; died of a heart ailment in Jesmond Dene, Newcastle, England, on June 11, 1998, at age 91; daughter of Catherine Fawcett and a father she never knew; educated at parochial schools; married Thomas Cookson, in June 1940; no children.

Awarded an Order of the British Empire (OBE, 1985); made Dame Commander of the British Empire (CBE, 1993).

Selected works: Kate Hannigan (1950); The Round Tower (1968); Our Kate (1969); Catherine Cookson Country (1986); The Cultured Handmaid (1988); Let Me Make Myself Plain (1988).

Catherine Cookson was born in Northern England, on June 20, 1906. Her mother was an unmarried 24-year-old barmaid who endured the reputation of a "fallen woman" when she became pregnant. Her father was thought a gentleman for not speaking ill of her or the circumstances. "If I in her womb had been aware of what she was suffering during those nine months that she carried me," wrote Cookson, "then I should surely have been born mental." The child grew up in her grandparents' home in the industrial port of Tyne Dock in South Shields, England. Her grandmother died when she was seven, and her grandfather and alcoholic mother had a tenuous relationship. They took lodgers into their small home for extra money, and young Catherine made frequent trips to the In-and-Out Pawn Shop, selling and retrieving their belongings.

Cookson began writing at age 11 and saving money gleaned from odd jobs. At 14, she quit school to begin working, and, determined to leave Tyne Dock, at 23 she took a job in Hastings, a seaside resort, managing the laundry at a workhouse for inmates and indigents. With her salary and savings, Cookson bought The Hurst and opened it as a boarding house for gentlemen. In 1940, she married a teacher, Thomas Cookson, six years her junior. They longed for children, but Catherine miscarried three times (a fourth was stillborn) and attributed several depressions requiring hospitalization to the disappointment.

Begun in 1950, Cookson's publishing career soon came to support the couple. Thomas retired from teaching to assume the majority of the household duties, providing Cookson with more writing time. She published over 50 novels, including her 7-novel "Mary Ann" series. Her stories have been adapted to stage, screen, television and radio, and her annual reading figure of five million on Britain's lending library charts eclipsed her nearest rival, *Agatha Christie, who stood at two million.

Cookson's mother died in 1956; that same year, Cookson began the autobiography *Our Kate*, which she wrote and rewrote for 12 years. After almost 50 years away, Cookson returned to the Northern country of England in 1975, where she was enthusiastically welcomed home. The visit led to a memoir of the area, *Catherine Cookson Country* (1986). Cookson's manuscripts are held in the special collection at Boston University.

Crista Martin,
Boston, Massachusetts

Coolbrith, Ina Donna (1841–1928)

American poet. Name variations: began using her mother's maiden name Coolbrith in 1862. Born Josephine Donna Smith in Nauvoo, Illinois, on March 10, 1841; died in Berkeley, California, on February 29, 1928; niece of Joseph Smith, founder of Mormonism; attended school in Los Angeles; married Robert B. Carsley, in 1858 (divorced 1861).

Shortly after her birth, Ida Coolbrith's widowed mother took her children to live in St. Louis; about ten years later, the family continued on to California by wagon train. (Coolbrith was the first white child to cross the Beckwourth Pass through the Sierra Nevada.)

Catherine Cookson

After attending school in Los Angeles, marrying, and quickly divorcing, Coolbrith moved to San Francisco in 1862 where she taught school, continued to write, and joined the bay area's literary circle. Associated with Bret Harte in editing the *Overland Monthly* (1868), Ina Coolbrith also worked as a librarian for the Oakland Public Library (1873–1906) and was named poet laureate of California (1915). Her poetry collections included *The Perfect Day and Other Poems* (1881) and *Songs of the Golden Gate.*

Coolidge, Elizabeth Sprague
(1863–1953)

American patron of music, whose benefactions greatly assisted many contemporary composers and introduced chamber music to thousands of Americans. Born Elizabeth Penn Sprague in Chicago, Illinois, on October 30, 1864; died in Cambridge, Massachusetts, on November 4, 1953; daughter of Albert Arnold Sprague and

Nancy (Atwood) Sprague; married Frederic Shurtleff Coolidge; children: Albert Sprague Coolidge.

One of the most generous "angels" in the musical life of the 20th century was a tall, substantially built, distinctly autocratic woman who had to rely on a hearing aid to enjoy the music she so loved. Her name, Elizabeth Sprague Coolidge, had a distinctly patrician ring to it, which was appropriate since she came from the most significant aristocracy the United States was able to produce in the final decades of the 19th century, the aristocracy of wealth. The families of both of her parents, the Spragues and the Atwoods, had lived as hardy, independent farmers in Vermont, but in 1861, after graduating from Yale, her father Albert Sprague and his brother founded what quickly became the largest wholesale grocery business in the world.

Born in Chicago in 1864, Elizabeth had several siblings. Since all of them died in infancy, her parents spent a great deal of time with her and were deeply concerned about her education and future. Her mother **Nancy Atwood Sprague**, with whom Elizabeth enjoyed a warm relationship, was energetic and intellectually alert. Mother Sprague was delighted that, from her earliest years, her daughter exhibited these same qualities in abundance. Conventional wisdom meant little to a young girl who simply had to discover things through her own experiences. In her memoirs, Elizabeth's cousin *****Lucy Sprague Mitchell** characterized the young Elizabeth Sprague as being very much "a determined individualist, with 'social' leanings that were rather confusing to her conservative father, who greatly admired her, though a bit uncomprehendingly."

Enjoying the benefits of an excellent private education, Elizabeth Sprague began to take piano lessons at age 11. Strongly drawn to music because of its beauty, the young girl also looked upon it as an opportunity to build up mechanical skills that would give her the power to produce beautiful, meaningful sounds. As a result, Elizabeth became an accomplished pianist, in later years noting that she owed much of her moral and mental strength to her piano teacher's "exaction from me, throughout my girlhood, of reverence for duty, of coordinated self-control, and uncompromising fidelity to standards."

Long hours of difficult piano practice was clearly therapeutic for Elizabeth, who de-

scribed it as "a mechanical stabilizer"—one that gave her a strong "sense of power and balance" and helped her maintain emotional stability. Beginning in the 1890s, she began to compose music, some of which would later be performed in public, but was written mainly as a refuge from the worst affliction possible for a musician—deafness. Sprague began to lose her hearing in the 1890s and for much of her life used hearing aids.

Elizabeth Sprague married orthopedic surgeon Frederic Shurtleff Coolidge in 1891, and the couple resided in Chicago until 1904 when they moved to Pittsfield, Massachusetts. Their only child, Albert Sprague Coolidge, was born in 1894. The marriage was by all accounts a happy one, its only major difficulties being the often precarious state of Albert's health, which had to withstand several crises; he died of tuberculosis in 1915. That same year her parents died, and it seems probable that her intense devotion to matters musical helped her to deal with the stresses brought on by the multiple traumas.

Just prior to her mother's death, the Sprague family gave a joint contribution of $200,000 to Yale University for the construction of that institution's first music building, Sprague Memorial Hall. In 1916, in memory of her parents, Elizabeth endowed the first pension fund for the Chicago Symphony Orchestra. The same year, she agreed to contribute up to $50,000 annually in support of the Bureau of Educational Experiments, a project headed by her cousin Lucy. Another munificent gift went to local efforts in Pittsfield to halt the spread of tuberculosis, but closest to her heart during this early stage of her philanthropical career was her underwriting of performances by a string quartet.

Elizabeth Coolidge's fortune enabled her to bestow generous gifts in behalf of various musical projects she regarded as desirable. The string quartet she sponsored became the renowned Berkshire Quartet. To create a perfect setting for great chamber music, she built a Temple of Chamber Music near her Pittsfield estate, and from 1918 through 1924 she sponsored annual South Mountain Chamber Music Festivals at this pleasant site. Chamber music in the United States made a quantum leap as a result of the Coolidge initiatives, with each festival featuring new compositions, announcements of commissions for additional works, and the award of prizes. Besides serving as patron and manager of the festivals, Elizabeth Coolidge occasionally performed as pianist as well. Sometimes her own compositions would be featured. Her musical vigor was undiminished even in the last years of her life; in 1943, she amazed her friends by performing at a Library of Congress recital at the age of 79, playing with remarkable energy the solo piano part of Robert Schumann's quintet, accompanied by the Kolisch Quartet.

Taking advantage of the start of the great economic boom of the 1920s, Coolidge increased her musical expenditures by crossing the seas and sponsoring a festival in Rome. In time, she would sponsor concerts spanning the globe from London to Moscow to Hawaii. In 1925, she established the Elizabeth Sprague Coolidge Foundation at the Library of Congress. She had already written about her purpose in fostering the development of chamber music, to make possible "the triumph of Spirit over Brute Force . . . the immortality of Human Inspiration in the face of threatened mechanical destruction."

As the details of the Coolidge Foundation's organization were worked out, it became clear that the Music Division of the Library of Congress would administer the income from two substantial trust funds, which ensured a yearly income (in the 1920s) of $25,000. An additional $60,000, which was later increased substantially, made it possible for the Library of Congress to construct a chamber music hall, appropriately named the Coolidge Auditorium. Enjoying excellent acoustics, it boasted a seating capacity of 511.

To bring new music to these superb facilities, Coolidge commissioned chamber music from virtually all of the distinguished composers of the day, some of them famous, others barely known but showing promise; a highly abridged listing of them range from Samuel Barber, Béla Bartók, and Benjamin Britten to Aaron Copland, Luigi Dallapiccola, Paul Hindemith, Bohuslav Martinu, Walter Piston, Francis Poulenc, Sergei Prokofiev, Maurice Ravel, Ottorino Respighi, and on through the alphabet to Arnold Schoenberg, Virgil Thomson, and Heitor Villa-Lobos.

The Great Depression that began in October 1929 slowed down but did not end Coolidge's support of chamber music in America. Defaults in her Chicago municipal bonds reduced the income of several of her trust funds, and changes in her tax assessment forced her to cut back on her contributions. Nevertheless, she continued to support a number of composers including Frank Bridge, a talented British composer who was also the teacher of Benjamin Britten; in Italy, Coolidge support enabled Gian Francesco Malipiero to continue his creative efforts. To those fortunate enough to benefit from her generosity, she was truly "the fairy godmother of chamber music."

Interested in the progress of modern dance as well, Coolidge commissioned a number of ballet scores by major composers. These included Igor Stravinsky's *Apollon Musagète*, Darius Milhaud's *Imagined Wing*, Paul Hindemith's *Mirror Before Me* (retitled *Herodiade*), and Aaron Copland's *Appalachian Spring*. The Milhaud, Hindemith, and Copland works were all given their world premieres in 1944 by the *Martha Graham* Dance Company. The late 1930s to late 1940s were a particularly creative period for performers, in part due to the fact that many talented musicians had fled from Fascist-controlled nations. Some of the performers sponsored during these years by the Coolidge Foundation included *Myra Hess*, Rudolf Serkin, Ralph Kirkpatrick, and Alexander Schneider; the eminent string quartets included the Budapest, Pro Arte, and Kolisch.

By the 1930s, Elizabeth Coolidge's robust health began to falter so she spent winters in California both for health reasons and to be near her son. Here, she enjoyed not only music but movies and long automobile rides. The approach of old age did not diminish her innate sense of humor. She enjoyed jokes at her own expense, whether it was about her height (at 5'11", she was tall for her generation), her deafness, or her habitual dropping of handbags, gloves and concert programs. Often witty, she once responded to the question of why she did not support modern art with the reply, "I may be deaf but I am not blind." Some of her friends claimed that during concerts of dissonant modern chamber music, which she had commissioned but did not particularly enjoy, she would simply turn off her hearing aid.

Although certainly wealthy, Elizabeth Sprague Coolidge was not as rich as some believed her to be. She managed her fortune astutely in order to give generously to those in need. This included not only musicians but nurses, who received both her own and her parents' Chicago houses, and crippled children, who were given her Pittsfield home. Another Pittsfield facility, for tuberculosis patients, received her generous support. Generally shunning publicity, she finally accepted the Cobbett Medal of London, the Order of the Crown of Belgium, became a member of the French Legion of Honor, and was made an honorary citizen of Frankfurt am Main, Germany.

A woman of strong character, Elizabeth Sprague Coolidge was a feisty and flinty American original. Unafraid of majority opinions, she was a convinced atheist who had hoped that the opening event of the festival celebrating the inaugural of her foundation in 1925 would not be a prayer but a performance of Charles Martin Loeffler's *Canticle of the Sun*, a composition commissioned for the occasion. Coolidge was certain that this was "surely a more exultant hymn of praise and devotion than would be likely to issue from the Senate or the House of Representatives." As the program was finally worked out, the festival opened with Bach's "To God on High All Glory Be."

Elizabeth Sprague Coolidge died in Cambridge, Massachusetts, on November 4, 1953. The year following her death, a "memorial festival" lasting two days and sponsored by the South Mountain Association was held at Pittsfield in the Temple of Music that she had built so many decades earlier. Her contribution to the evolution of music in the 20th century was immense and is still being assessed. With little exaggeration, Olin Downes, music critic of *The New York Times*, gave a fair estimate of this remarkable woman's role as benefactor and patron in the musical life of the 20th century when he described it as being "without parallel in the modern period on either side of the Atlantic."

SOURCES:

Barr, Cyrilla. "The Musicological Legacy of Elizabeth Sprague Coolidge," in *Journal of Musicology*. Vol. 11, no. 2. Spring, 1993, pp. 250–268.

Bedford, William C. "Elizabeth Sprague Coolidge, the Education of a Patron of Chamber Music: The Early Years" (Ph.D. dissertation, University of Missouri, 1964).

Elizabeth Sprague Coolidge Papers, Library of Congress, Washington, D.C.

"Godmother of Chamber Music," in *Newsweek*. Vol. 24, no. 20. November 13, 1944, pp. 102, 104.

Keefer, Lubov. *Music Angels: A Thousand Years of Patronage*. Baltimore, MD: Sutherland Press, 1976.

Neuls-Bates, Carol. "Elizabeth Sprague Coolidge, twentieth-century benefactress of chamber music," in Judith Lang Zaimont, ed. *The Musical Woman: An International Perspective*, Vol. II: 1984–1985. Westport, CT: Greenwood Press, 1987, pp. 136–144.

"Patroness," in *Time*. Vol. 52, no. 2. July 12, 1948, pp. 32, 34.

Temianka, Henri, and Donald L. Leavitt. "The Boundless Legacy of Elizabeth Sprague Coolidge," in *Chamber Music Magazine*. Vol. 2, no. 1, 1985, pp. 14–17.

John Haag, University of Georgia, Athens, Georgia

Coolidge, Grace Goodhue

(1879–1957)

First lady of the U.S., from 1923 to 1929, who became a popular cultural leader and a symbol of American womanhood during the Jazz Age. Born Grace Anne Goodhue on January 3, 1879, in Burlington, Vermont; died on July 8, 1957, in Northampton, Massachusetts; daughter of Lemira Goodhue and Andrew Issachar Goodhue (an engineer and steamboat inspector); married Calvin Coolidge, on October 4, 1905; children: John Coolidge (b. 1906); Calvin Coolidge, Jr. (1908–1924).

During the 20th century, Grace Goodhue Coolidge, one of the most glamorous and popular first ladies of the United States, complemented well the thrifty, stern public image of Calvin Coolidge, encouraged and promoted the artistic life of Washington, D.C., and gave her charitable energies to the education of the deaf.

Born January 3, 1879, Grace Anne Goodhue was the only child in a middle-class Vermont family. "Never was a babe more tenderly loved and cared for than I," she wrote. Her father Andrew Goodhue worked as an engineer and later as an inspector of steamboats. He was, said Grace, her mother **Lemira Goodhue**'s constant companion. With few children nearby for playmates, Grace learned to cook and sew at an early age under Lemira's tutelage. She went to local schools, graduated from Burlington (Vermont) High School in 1897, then attended the University of Vermont, where she started a chapter of Pi Beta Phi, then a woman's fraternity. Following her graduation in 1902, Grace began training at the Clarke School for the Deaf in Northampton, Massachusetts. "I thought," she later recalled, "that I should like to learn to teach little deaf children when I grew up." At the Clarke School, she was fascinated with "this highly specialized teaching" that stressed lip-reading. Her lifelong interest in the deaf had begun.

During her second year of teaching at the Clarke School, Grace inadvertently glimpsed through a window and beheld a young lawyer, Calvin Coolidge, shaving, clad only in his union suit and a hat. Her laughter attracted his attention. A mutual friend arranged a meeting between Grace and Calvin, who was already locally famous as a man who said as little as possible. One friend quipped that since she had been able to teach the deaf to hear, Grace Goodhue might now be able to teach the mute to speak.

The courtship proceeded slowly, but Grace and Calvin soon found common interests despite

Grace
Goodhue
Coolidge

their very different temperaments, and Calvin proposed. Though Grace's mother opposed the marriage, she gave in because of the determination of the young couple. They were married on October 4, 1905, in a small ceremony in the Coolidge home in Burlington. After a brief honeymoon in Canada, they returned to Northampton to set up their new home. Grace left her job at the Clarke School, regarding it her duty, as she said in her recollections, to make adjustments that would "contribute to efficiency and permanency."

The Coolidges had two sons: John, born in 1906, and Calvin, Jr., born in 1908. During the ten years after their wedding, Grace adapted to Calvin's political ambitions as a rising figure in Massachusetts Republican politics. For the most part, she was not seen on the hustings. When she sought to attend one of her husband's speeches, he discouraged her. Instead, Grace Coolidge raised her children, did charitable work for the Congregational Church, and spent much time working with Pi Beta Phi. She attended the national conventions of what was now a sorority and was chosen vice-president for the eastern seaboard region in 1915. Meanwhile, her husband was elected governor of Massachusetts in 1918. Despite Grace's low profile, their friends agreed that she was one of Calvin's greatest political assets. Her charm and intelligence had already impressed observers of the state's political scene.

She was a practical woman with high ideals, a warm-hearted woman with common sense, a woman with rare charm and good will.

—Ishbel Ross

Events soon carried Grace Coolidge onto a wider stage. The Republican Party nominated Calvin to run for vice president in 1920. When Warren G. Harding was elected president, the Republican victory sent Grace Coolidge to Washington, D.C., as the wife of the vice president in March 1921. Though Grace was on friendly terms with the new first lady, *Florence K. Harding, the two women were not close. But Washington society warmed to the Coolidges quickly, and they soon found themselves at the center of a busy social life. They lived in the Willard Hotel where Grace received visitors every Wednesday afternoon. As the wife of the vice president, she in turn presided over the weekly meetings of The Ladies of the Senate, a group that gave the wives of senators an opportunity for social occasions and enabled them to do charitable good works.

During the summer of 1923, President Harding suffered a heart attack; he died on August 2. Calvin Coolidge was sworn in as president early in the morning of August 3, and Grace Coolidge was now the first lady. She recalled "a sense of detachment—this was I and yet not I, this was the wife of the President of the United States and she took precedence over me."

By 1923, the institution of the first lady had not yet developed into its modern form. Presidential wives were not expected to endorse a social

program or identify themselves with a national problem. In the case of both *Edith Bolling Wilson, wife of Woodrow Wilson, and Florence Harding, these first ladies had not been popular figures or social leaders in Washington. As motion pictures and the mass media became more influential during the early 1920s, curiosity about the presidency and the White House grew. Despite her lack of previous experience, Grace Coolidge had a natural charm and appeal to the public that soon translated into a growing popularity. Fascination with her personal style raised interest in the first lady to levels that made her a national celebrity.

In the White House, Grace supervised a staff of 18 domestic servants. She had only one personal secretary to handle all the mail that she received. **Laura Harlan** held the post until October 1925. **Mary Randolph** succeeded her and stayed until the end of the president's term in March 1929. Randolph's memoir, *Presidents and First Ladies*, is an excellent source about Grace Coolidge. Despite her new fame, Grace continued to correspond with the friends she had made in Pi Beta Phi, even though most of her mail received a routine acknowledgement from her secretary. An apprehensive Grace took to her new role with the help of her husband who instructed her to avoid talking politics and dancing in public. When press stories appeared that she had learned horseback riding, Calvin warned her to eschew trying anything new. She proved to be a gracious White House host with an ability to put nervous guests at ease quickly. When a clerk in a Washington store once asked her: "Did anyone ever tell you before that you look like Mrs. Coolidge?" Grace answered "yes," but remembered that she said so "with never a smile."

Family tragedy struck the Coolidges during their first year in the White House. Their younger son Calvin became ill from an infected blister and his condition soon worsened. Antibiotics had not yet been discovered, and blood poisoning set in. He died on July 7, 1924, and his parents never fully recovered from their loss. His father later said that the presidency meant little to him after young Calvin died. His mother composed a poem about the loss five years later that now appears in her memoirs. In part it reads:

> You, my son,
> Have shown me God.
> Your kiss upon my cheek
> Has made me feel the gentle touch
> Of Him who leads us on.

With little time for private grieving, the Coolidge victory in the 1924 campaign gave the couple another four years in the White House. During those years, Grace, who especially enjoyed music and the theater, did much to promote the fine arts. Her goal, she said, was "to gather a company of people who knew and appreciated the best in music." She had Sergei Rachmaninoff, the Russian composer and pianist, play three times at the White House for one of her many musicales to which as many as 300 guests were invited. The tenor John McCormack also sang on these occasions. Grace attended operas and plays in Washington avidly and was a special fan of Gilbert and Sullivan.

In dress and appearance, Grace Coolidge was more glamorous than most of her immediate predecessors as first lady. She wore large stylish hats and conservative, soft dresses. A portrait of her in a long red dress with her collie Rob Roy at her side captured her slim figure and shining hair. It now hangs in the White House. President Coolidge encouraged his wife to dress well, and she soon became a fashion leader for women of the time.

Grace devoted a good deal of her time to improving the physical appearance of the White House. The building, not refurbished for a quarter of a century, needed renovation. The work was done in 1927 while the Coolidges lived at Dupont Circle. The first lady added period furniture from the time that the White House was first constructed, and she had other furnishings, pictures, and china installed from previous administrations. She asked the public to send in rare pieces of period furniture for exhibition in the White House and also encouraged beautification plans for Washington, D.C.

Her interest in the education of the deaf remained strong. *Helen Keller, the most famous blind, deaf, and mute American of that time visited her at the White House. Toward the end of the Coolidge presidency, the president and first lady, who believed in the lip-reading techniques rather than sign language, lent their names to a $2 million fund-raising campaign for the Clarke School's endowment. By the time they left the White House, the goal had been achieved.

Grace Coolidge did not discuss public business with her husband. When asked to intercede with the government, she told each petitioner to take their case up with the president directly. What she knew about events, she said in her autobiography, came from the daily papers and other sources of information open to everybody. This would explain her surprise, along with that of the nation, in the summer of 1927. By then, both of

the Coolidges were in uncertain health, and the president worried whether his wife could survive another four years in the White House. At their vacation retreat in the Black Hills of South Dakota, the president issued a terse statement to the press on August 2, 1927: "I do not choose to run for President in 1928." Grace learned of the decision only after it was announced. To those who expressed dismay that she had not been consulted, she remarked in her memoirs that she was "rather proud of the fact that after nearly a quarter of a century of marriage, my husband feels free to make his decisions and act upon them without consulting me or giving me advance information concerning them."

Making way for their successors, President Herbert Hoover and *Lou Henry Hoover, the Coolidges left Washington when the president's term ended on March 4, 1929, and returned to their home in Northampton. "Gone were the men of the Secret Service," she said, "the aides, the valet, the maid, and we were homeward bound." The public remained curious about the Coolidges. "As many tourists pass our door as drove through the spacious grounds of the White House," she wrote. During the next four years, the Coolidges traveled and lived quietly in their retirement. She composed several autobiographical articles about her White House experiences and published more of her poems. On January 5, 1933, Grace went upstairs to call Calvin for lunch and came down to tell his secretary that her husband was dead.

During the next 24 years, Grace Coolidge pursued an extensive round of charitable work. She was a member of the board of trustees of Mercersburg Academy where the Coolidge boys had been educated. She continued her work with the deaf when she became president of the board of the Clarke School in 1935. With the onset of World War II, she raised money for children refugees from Germany and Holland, and she was active in civil defense, Red Cross, and war-bond sales between 1942 and 1945. She maintained a special love for baseball, listening faithfully to the broadcasts of the Boston Red Sox games and following the strategy of a game closely. When she went to Fenway Park or to games in Washington, she impressed major-league players with her knowledge of the sport. Grace Coolidge died on July 8, 1957, of the effects of old age on her weakened heart. Her ashes were buried in Plymouth, Vermont.

All first ladies are to some degree political celebrities. To that demanding and public position, Grace Coolidge brought a winning combination of good humor and personal style that made her a popular favorite during the 1920s when media coverage of the White House became more intense. Within the limits that her husband set for her, she used her influence to act as a symbol of fashion and patron of the arts to the nation. Few first ladies have been more admired during their days in the White House.

SOURCES:

Caroli, Betty. *First Ladies*. Oxford University Press, 1986.

Coolidge, Calvin. *The Autobiography of Calvin Coolidge*. Cosmopolitan, 1929.

McCoy, Donald R. "Grace Anna Goodhue Coolidge," in Barbara Sicherman and Carol Hurd Green, eds., *Notable American Women*. Harvard University Press, 1980, pp. 162–163.

Randolph, Mary. *Presidents and First Ladies*. D. Appleton, 1936.

Ross, Ishbel. *Grace Coolidge and Her Era*. Calvin Coolidge Memorial Foundation, 1988 (paperback reprint of original edition published by Dodd, Mead, 1962).

Wikander, Lawrence E., and Robert H. Ferrell, eds. *Grace Coolidge: An Autobiography*. High Plains Publishing, 1992.

SUGGESTED READING:

Anthony, Carl Sferrazza. *First Ladies: The Saga of the Presidents' Wives and Their Power, 1789–1961*. NY: William Morrow, 1990.

Gutin, Myra G. *The President's Partner: The First Lady in the Twentieth Century*. Greenwood, 1989.

Lewis L. Gould,
Eugene C. Barker Centennial Professor
in American History, University of Texas at Austin, Texas

Coolidge, Susan (1835–1905).

See Woolsey, Sarah Chauncey.

Cooney, Joan Ganz (1929—)

American television executive and president of Children's Television Workshop, who originated the revolutionary children's program "Sesame Street." Name variations: Joan Ganz. Born Joan Ganz in Phoenix, Arizona, on November 30, 1929; one of three children of Sylvan C. (a banker) and Pauline (Reardan) Ganz; attended Dominican College, San Rafael, California; B.A. cum laude, University of Arizona, 1951; married Timothy J. Cooney (treasurer of the Equal Employment Council), in February 1964 (divorced); married Peter G. Peterson (former U.S. secretary of commerce and former chair of Lehman Brothers), on April 26, 1980.

Joan Ganz Cooney, founder and director of the Children's Television Workshop (CTW) and the mastermind behind the revolutionary children's show "Sesame Street," was raised and educated in Phoenix, Arizona. Born to a Jewish father and Catholic mother, Cooney and her

brother and sister were raised in their mother's religion. She credits the message of Father Keller's Christopher movement, that if right-thinking people did not get into mass communications others would, as a major influence on her life. After graduating from the University of Arizona, she worked as a reporter for the *Arizona Republic* for a year before moving to New York, where Ganz broke into television as a publicist for NBC and the "U.S. Steel Hour." She later produced documentaries for public television and, in 1966, won an Emmy for her program "Poverty, Anti-poverty and the Poor." At age 34, well established in her career, she married Timothy J. Cooney, then treasurer of the Equal Employment Council.

Her journey to "Sesame Street" began during a dinner party at the Cooney home in February 1966, when the conversation turned to television's educational potential. One of Cooney's guests, Lloyd Morrisett, then vice president of the Carnegie Corporation, asked if she would be willing to undertake a study exploring public television's potential for preschool education. Intrigued by the idea, Cooney agreed. Her preliminary research proved that 96% of American homes had television sets and that youngsters sat in front of them some 60 hours a week. In perhaps her most meaningful discovery, she also found that children were definitely learning from the medium, though primarily through the fast-paced imaginative musical jingles of the commercial spots. In the report that Cooney submitted to the Carnegie Corporation the following November, she concluded that a well-designed television program would fulfill the National Education Association's recommendation that all children be given the opportunity to begin schooling at age four, while accomplishing this goal at a fraction of the $3 billion or more it would cost the federal government to provide the necessary classroom space.

After receiving initial funding of $8 million from foundations and federal agencies to establish the Children's Television Workshop, Cooney and her associates undertook three additional years of exhaustive planning, including extensive seminars with educational and entertainment experts to establish curriculum goals, which included raising the level of awareness of young, and particularly disadvantaged, as well as teaching numbers, the alphabet, and basic reasoning skills. After testing five pilot shows in the summer of 1969, the first hourlong "Sesame Street" (the title alluding to the "Open, Sesame!" command in the Arabian Nights story of Ali Baba) aired on November 10, 1969, over

*J*oan
*G*anz
*C*ooney

the National Educational Television network, which consisted of some 190 stations.

Utilizing the fast-paced technique of commercials to "sell" the alphabet and numbers, the show employed animation, soft rock music, and the irrepressible Muppets of Jim Henson (who at first wanted nothing to do with children's shows), along with live actors. The basic set simulated an East Harlem neighborhood, with brownstones and an integrated population. The initial reviews were overwhelmingly positive.

Barbara Delatiner wrote in *Newsday* (November 10, 1969): "Today's opening show is an exciting example of what can be accomplished when inventive attention is paid to the care and feeding of young minds." Les Brown of *Variety* (December 24, 1969) praised the program as "the most naturally integrated show on television," adding, "if racial peace and harmony ever visit this country, 'Sesame Street' may be one of the reasons why."

President of CTW until 1990, then chair of its executive committee, Cooney considered herself part hardheaded businesswoman, part crusader, as she struggled to develop a business acumen equal to her idealism. The show's success increased her workload with a products business (books, records, and toys), fundraising, and planning for a new show. She viewed the labor as simply part of the ebb and flow of life. "I think there are seasons of life," she stated in *Particular Passions*. "I've gone through very austere periods where I've just worked, and then less austere times when I felt I could let up and concentrate more on my personal life." Cooney credits a serious illness around the time of her separation and divorce with helping her realize the need to balance her work with personal relationships. She subsequently remarried into a large family and helped raise several of her younger stepchildren.

Through the years, "Sesame Street" has won numerous awards, including countless Emmies, and Cooney has received wide recognition as an innovator and outstanding executive. Under her watchful eye, the show continued to evolve and grow with the times. Within the first ten years, it slowed in pace and increased its curriculum, adding bilingual and bicultural education, and including children with developmental difficulties in the cast. While expanding health, safety, and nutrition topics, the program has not shied away from more serious concerns like sibling rivalry, divorce, and death. Throughout her tenure, Cooney continued to pioneer and set an example, although it was sometimes difficult to equal or top the success of "Sesame Street." In 1971, the Children's Television Workshop introduced *The Electric Company* for ages 7 to 10 and, in 1980, *3-2=1 Contact* for ages 8 to 12. *Square One TV* and *Ghostwriter* were later productions, as well as a number of commercial television specials.

SOURCES:

Brown, Les. *Les Brown's Encyclopedia of Television.* Detroit, MI: Visible Ink Press, 1992.

Gilbert, Lynn, and Gaylen Moore. *Particular Passions: Talks with Women Who Have Shaped Our Times.* NY: Clarkson N. Potter, 1981.

Moritz, Charles, ed. *Current Biography 1970.* NY: H.W. Wilson, 1970.

"The 25 Most Powerful Women in America," in *Biography Magazine.* April 1999, p. 9.

Barbara Morgan,
Melrose, Massachusetts.

Cooper, Anna J. (c. 1858–1964)

African-American educator, scholar, feminist, and writer. Name variations: Annie. Born Anna Julia Haywood Cooper in Raleigh, North Carolina, on August 10, 1858 or 1859; died in Washington, D.C., on February 27, 1964; daughter of Hannah Stanley (a slave) and possibly George Washington Haywood (her owner); attended Saint Augustine's Normal School and Collegiate Institute (now Saint Augustine's College), Raleigh; A.B., Oberlin College, 1884; M.S. in mathematics, Oberlin College, 1887; attended Guilde Internationale, Paris, France, summers of 1911, 1912, and 1913; attended Columbia University, summers 1914–17; Ph.D., Sorbonne, 1925; married George A.C. Cooper, in 1877 (died 1879).

During the years following the Emancipation Proclamation, Anna Cooper, the daughter of a slave, became a student at the newly opened Saint Augustine's Normal School and Collegiate Institute, where she remained to become a teacher. In 1877, she married fellow teacher George A.C. Cooper, who died just two years later. As a young widow, Cooper went on to attend Oberlin College, one of the few institutions at the time that accepted blacks and women. After earning a master's degree in mathematics (1887), she took a position in Washington, D.C., at the Preparatory High School for Colored Youth, later renamed the Paul Laurence Dunbar High School. A teacher at the Dunbar High School, Cooper also served as principal from 1902 until 1906 when she left over a dispute with school board members who wished to dilute the curriculum of "colored" schools; she returned in 1910 to teach Latin. After several summers at the Guilde Internationale in Paris and three summers at Columbia University, she received her doctorate degree at the Sorbonne on March 23, 1925, at age 66. She was only the fourth African-American woman to earn a Ph.D. and was among the first women to do so in France. While teaching and pursuing her studies, Cooper raised two foster children as well as her half-brother's five orphaned grandchildren.

Throughout her career, she was concerned with women's rights and the status of African-Americans. During a period of racial terrorism in the 1890s, Cooper and other black intellectuals were instrumental in arousing public consciousness of race relations and providing direction. During the decade, she presented papers and addressed a number of diverse groups and organizations, including the American Conference of Educators (1890), the Congress of Representative Women (1893), The National Conference of Colored Women (1895), and the National Federation of Afro-American Women (1896). Her earliest writing, *A Voice from the South* (1892), contains her views as a dedicated feminist and an advocate for her race.

In her later years, Cooper was involved with Washington's Frelinghuysen University, an institution providing adult educational opportunities for blacks, of which she served as president for a short time. Anna Julia Cooper died on February 27, 1964, at the age of 105.

SUGGESTED READING:

Cooper, Anna Julia. *A Voice from the South: By a Black Woman from the South.* NY: Oxford University Press, 1988.

Hutchinson, Louise Daniel. *Anna J. Cooper, a Voice from the South.* Washington, DC: Smithsonian Press, 1981.

COLLECTIONS:

The papers of Anna J. Cooper are in the Moorland-Spingarn Research Center, Howard University.

Cooper, Charlotte (1871–1966)

British tennis player who was a five-time winner at Wimbledon and the first woman to win a gold medal in the Olympic Games. Name variations: Mrs. A. Sterry; (nickname) "Chattie." Born in Ealing, Middlesex, England, on September 22, 1870; died on October 10, 1966.

Won singles championships at Wimbledon (1895, 1896, 1898, 1901, and 1908); won the gold medal for singles and mixed doubles-outdoors at the Olympic Games in Paris (1900).

Officially the first woman to win a gold medal in the Olympic Games, Charlotte "Chattie" Cooper was already a three-time Wimbledon champion before appearing at the Paris Olympics in 1900. Noted for her strength and her attack (unusual in the "ladylike" matches of the time), Cooper defeated French champion **Helen Prevois** in straight sets to take the gold. She then went on to win a second gold medal in the mixed-doubles competition, partnered with Reginald Doherty. Cooper attributed her success to her "lenient" mother, who allowed her the freedom to pursue the sport. She won two more

Wimbledon titles, capturing her last championship in 1908, at age 38.

Cooper, Christin (1961—)

American skier. Born in California in 1961.

Won national slalom championship (1977) and the slalom, giant slalom, and overall (1980) and giant slalom (1984); placed 2nd in the slalom at the World Cup (1981) and 2nd in the slalom and giant slalom and 3rd overall (1982); won Olympic silver medal in giant slalom in the 1984 Sarajevo Winter Olympics; reported for CBS television during Nagano games.

When Christin Cooper's family moved from California to Idaho, she began skiing and proved adept on the slopes. She won the Canadian-American title at 15, and by 16 she was national slalom champion. In three World Cup finishes, Cooper was in the top ten. She won the slalom, giant slalom, and overall in the 1980 nationals. That same year, she competed in the 1980 Winter Olympics at Lake Placid where she was 7th in the giant slalom and 8th in the slalom, the best finishes for any American skier during the 1980 games.

In the 1981 World Championships, Cooper continued to finish among the top scorers: she was 2nd in the slalom and 4th overall; in the 1982 Worlds, she took a silver in the slalom and giant slalom and a bronze in the combined. A broken leg and subsequent surgery took Christin Cooper out of competition for the 1983 season. When the 1984 Olympics arrived, she made a dramatic comeback: righting herself when her skis slipped out from under her five gates from the top, she won a silver in the giant slalom, 40 seconds behind her gold-medaling teammate *Debbie Armstrong. Cooper was also national champion in giant slalom that year.

SOURCES:

Howe, N. "The Courage of Christin," in *Skiing.* Vol. 33. January 1981, pp. 123–125.

Markel, Robert, Nancy Brooks, and Susan Markel. *For the Record: Women in Sports.* NY: World Almanac Publications, 1985.

Karin Loewen Haag,
Athens, Georgia

Cooper, Cynthia (1963—)

American basketball player, known for her "raise the roof" gesture, who was named Most Valuable Player during the premiere season of the WNBA. Born April 14, 1963; one of eight children of Mary Cobbs; graduated University of Southern California, 1986.

Named to the NCAA Final Four All-Tournament Team (1986); played for the U.S. in the Goodwill

Games (1986, 1990), the World Championship (1986, 1990), and Pan Am Games (1987); played overseas for Segovia in Spain (1986–87); named MVP of the European All-Star Game (1987); played overseas for Alcamo (1994–96), and Parma in Italy (1987–94 and 1996–97); made the 1996 Italian League All-Star Team; over first ten pro seasons, was leading scorer eight times and second leading scorer twice; won the gold medal (1988) and the bronze medal (1992), playing with the U.S. Olympic teams; was leading scorer (37.5 ppg) in the European Cup (1996); signed on with the WNBA's Houston Comets; was voted the WNBA's MVP (1997 and 1998).

Cynthia Cooper did not grace a basketball court until she was 16. A few years later, she was majoring in physical education at the University of Southern California and playing guard on their winning Lady Trojan team that took the NCAA national championships in 1983 and 1984. Cooper made three NCAA Final Four appearances and was named to the 1986 NCAA Final Four All-Tournament Team. Following college, like all top-notch women's basketball college players, Cooper had to find a career overseas, playing professionally in Spain and Italy for the next 13 years. Always close to her mother, Cooper claimed her proudest moment came in 1988 when she won the Olympic gold medal on her mother's birthday, then presented it to her.

In 1997, the inaugural WNBA season, Cooper finally came home, and it was none too soon. Cooper had learned that her mother had breast cancer. Playing for the Houston Comets, with her mother generally in attendance, Cynthia Cooper was unanimously voted the WNBA's Most Valuable Player for the 1997 season. With her expertise and team leadership, Cooper guided her team to the WNBA finals. She then posted a game-high 25 points, 4 rebounds and 4 assists in a 65–51 win over the New York Liberty for the WNBA championship on August 30, 1997. In 1998, she scored 23 points over Phoenix to lead her team to its second consecutive title and her second consecutive MVP award; she was the first WNBA player to reach 1,000 career points (July 1998). In 1998, Cooper was honored as Sportswoman of the Year by the Women's Sports Foundation.

SUGGESTED READING:
Cooper, Cynthia. *She Got Game: My Personal Odyssey.* Warner, 1999.

Cooper, Lady Diana Duff (1892–1986).

See Bagnold, Enid for sidebar.

Cooper, Gladys (1888–1971)

English actress-manager and musical-comedy star, best known for her roles in drawing-room comedy, who was the most popular actress on the London stage by 1914 and darling of British "Tommies" as they went into battle in the First World War. Name variations: Dame Gladys Cooper. Born Gladys Constance Cooper in Lewisham, England, on December 18, 1888 (some sources erroneously cite 1890); died at her home in Henley-on-Thames on November 17, 1971; daughter of Charles William Frederick Cooper (a journalist who founded The Epicure magazine) and Mabel Barnett Cooper; married Henry Buckmaster (an actor), on December 12, 1908 (divorced 1922); married Sir Neville Charles Pearson (a magazine editor and publisher), on June 15, 1928 (divorced, October 1936); married Philip Merivale (an actor), on April 30, 1937 (died 1946); children: (first marriage) John Buckmaster (an actor) and **Joan Buckmaster Morley** (who married the popular character actor Robert Morley); (second marriage) **Sally Pearson Hardy** (who married the actor Robert Hardy). Awards: Dame Commander of the Order of the British Empire (1967).

Made stage debut at Theater Royal, Colchester, England, as Bluebelle in Bluebelle in Fairyland (1905); London debut at the Gaiety Theater as one of the Gaiety Girls; played in The Belle of Mayfair and Babes in the Wood (1906); The Girls of Gottenburg (1907); Havana *and* Our Miss Gibbs (1908); The Dollar Princess (1909); Half a Crown (1911); The Pigeon and Milestones (1912); Diplomacy (1913); My Lady's Dress (1914); entertained troops in France (1914–16); on tour in scenes from Shakespeare with Ellen Terry (1918); Home and Beauty (1919); The Betrothal, If, *and* The Sign on the Door (1921); The Second Mrs. Tanqueray (1922); Magda (1923); Diplomacy (1924); Iris (1925); The Last of Mrs. Cheyney (1925–26); The Letter (1927); The Sacred Flame (1929); Cynara (1930); The Rats of Norway (1933); The Shining Hour (1934); Othello (1935); Macbeth (1935); Call It a Day (1936); Dodsworth (1938); Twelfth Night, As You Like it, *and* A Midsummernight's Dream (all summer, 1938); Spring Meeting (1938–39); The Morning Star *(New York, 1942)*; The Indifferent Shepherd (1947); The Hat Trick (1950); Relative Values (1951–52); The Night of The Ball (1955); The Chalk Garden (1955–56); A Passage to India (1962).

Filmography: The Eleventh Commandment *(U.K., 1913)*; Dandy Donovan *(U.K., 1914)*; The Gentleman Cracksman *(U.K., 1914)*; The Real Thing at Last *(U.K., 1916)*; The Sorrows of Satan *(U.K., 1916)*; Masks and Faces *(U.K., 1917)*; My Lady's

Gladys Cooper

Dress *(U.K., 1917)*; Unmarried *(U.K., 1920)*; The Bohemian Girl *(U.K., 1922)*; Bonnie Prince Charlie *(U.K., 1923)*; The Iron Duke *(U.K., 1934)*; Rebecca *(1940)*; Kitty Foyle *(1940)*; *(as* Lady Nelson*)* That Hamilton Woman *(1941)*; The Black Cat *(1941)*; The Gay Falcon *(1941)*; This Above All *(1942)*; Eagle Squadron *(1942)*; Now Voyager *(1942)*; Forever and a Day *(1943)*; Mr. Lucky *(1943)*; Princess O'Rourke *(1943)*; The Song of Bernadette *(1943)*; The White Cliffs of Dover *(1944)*; Mrs. Parkington *(1944)*; Valley of Decision *(1945); Love Letters (1945); The Green Years (1946); The Cockeyed Miracle (1946); Green Dolphin Street (1947); The Bishop's Wife (1947); Beware of Pity (U.K., 1947); Homecoming (1948); The Pirate (1948); The Secret Garden (1949); Madame Bovary (1949); Thunder on the Hill (1950); At Sword's Point (1952); The Man Who Loved Redheads (1955); Separate Tables (1958); The List of Adrian Messenger (1963); My Fair Lady (1964); The Happiest Millionaire (1967); A Nice Girl Like Me (U.K., 1969).*

Gladys Constance Cooper was born in Lewisham, England, a then unfashionable southeast suburb of London, on December 18, 1888. Her father Charles William Cooper was a journalist who founded *The Epicure* magazine, her mother **Mabel Barnett Cooper** was a housewife. Raised in Chiswick in western London with her two younger sisters, Cooper appeared early in school and other amateur theatricals, beginning her professional career on her 16th birthday in the provincial town of Colchester, where she had gone with one of her friends who was auditioning for a part at the Theater Royal there. Struck by her fresh, blonde beauty, the management immediately hired young Gladys to play the title role of Bluebelle in a touring company of a Christmas "pantomime" (holiday musical extravaganzas popular in Britain), *Bluebelle in Fairyland.*

It is ten times easier to play a good part than a poor one. . . . [Audiences] will rave about an actor or an actress who has a scene in which nobody could fail; but someone who is making an exceptionally good job of a thankless part gets very little credit.

—Gladys Cooper

Although her father deplored her going on the stage, Cooper persisted and, two years later, made her debut in London at the Gaiety Theater as one of George Edwardes' "Gaiety Girls," at that time, the most celebrated chorus line in Europe. In later years, however, Cooper apparently felt that this debut was insufficiently dignified for the serious actress that she had become and dropped all references to it in her biographical data. From the Gaiety, she soon began appearing in small roles in such Edwardian musical froth as *The Belle of Mayfair* (1906), *The Babes in the Wood* (1906), *The Girls of Gottenburg* (1907), and *Havana* (1908). It was in the latter musical comedy that Gladys Cooper made her name, and soon she was one of the most popular young

actresses featured on the theatrical cards of the day. Before she was much past 20, she was starring in such productions as *Our Miss Gibbs* (1908) and the London staging of the American musical *The Dollar Princess* (1909).

The years immediately before the First World War saw a dramatic change in what was considered the ideal in feminine beauty. The late 19th century had appreciated the larger woman, exemplified in Britain by the voluptuous *Lily Langtry and in the U.S. by the buxom *Lillian Russell. The turn of the century brought in the Edwardian beauty, known in America as "the Gibson Girl" after the drawings of artist Charles Dana Gibson, who excelled in the depiction of the type; the cool, elegant, aristocratic beauty crowned with an air of haughtiness was modeled after his wife *Irene Gibson. About 1910, however, the taste turned towards a softer, gentler, more demure look; the shy young maiden with soft, low-piled hair and large eyes modestly downcast, her face a mirror of child-like sweetness. It was to this latter type that Gladys Cooper belonged, and in Britain, with her blue eyes and golden hair, she came to epitomize the new style until, in turn, it, too, was swept away by the flappers of the 1920s, known in Britain as "the bright young things." In the decade that encompassed the First World War, then, Gladys Cooper was hailed as the ideal of English womanhood and her countenance became the standard against which the beauty of British women would be judged for years to come. She was the favorite "pin-up" of the British "Tommies" in France, and they were said to have gone into the trenches with her picture in their wallets. Her first name, Gladys, is Welsh, and her fame did much to popularize it in the England of her day.

For several years, it seemed that Gladys Cooper would become a permanent fixture in British musical comedies and operettas. George Edwardes, who produced such fare, early secured her under contract and would not release her to appear in straight plays even when other producers requested her services. In later years, Cooper attached enormous importance to her early career in musical comedy, asserting that it was a training unsurpassable in the development of grace, poise, and stage presence. Nevertheless, she was a highly intelligent woman and had aspirations to be something more than a glamour girl or even a celebrated musical comedy star; she wished to become a serious actress, and, in 1911, as soon as she was free of her contract with Edwardes, she appeared in her first non-musical, a farce entitled *Half a Crown*. The play only lasted ten performances, but a year later she was appearing as Ann Welwyn in *The Pigeon* by the popular and respected playwright John Galsworthy (1912), and then as Dora in an all-star revival of *Diplomacy* (1913) by the French playwright Victorien Sardou, a play that she was to revive with considerable success a decade later. Then, in Edward Knobloch's *My Lady's Dress*, she played the role of five different characters, a feat that earned her recognition as one of the most promising actresses on the English stage.

With the outbreak of World War I in 1914, Gladys Cooper went to France to entertain the troops with what was called a "concert party" headed by Seymour Hicks, a career move that did much to endear her to the young men of her generation. Returning to London and remembering her years tagged as a musical star, Cooper determined that never again would she allow herself to be typecast. "Familiarity," she later said, "breeds [theatrical] trickery but variety constantly calls for fresh effort and breeds versatility." Deciding that the best way in which to grow as an artist was to play as many and as varied roles as possible, she assumed direct control of her own career. Thereafter, associating herself with various managements, she undertook the production of classic and modern plays that gave her the range that she felt was necessary for her maturation as an actress.

Beginning in 1917, she and Frank Curzon, a noted London producer, launched the production of a series of old and new plays in many of which Cooper herself starred, such as W. Somerset Maugham's *Home and Beauty* (1919), Maurice Maeterlinck's fantasy *The Betrothal*, Lord Dunsany's *If* and *The Sign on the Door* by her good friend Channing Pollock (all in 1921). Shortly thereafter, she managed to wring additional mileage out of such theatrical antiques as Hermann Sudermann's *Magda*, a play over 80 years old but which had some theatrical curiosity in having been an Ibsenesque "problem play" written some 30 years before Ibsen virtually created the genre. In so doing, she challenged comparison with no less than *Sarah Bernhardt, *Eleonora Duse, and *Mrs. Patrick Campbell, all of whom had essayed the role a generation and more before. Cooper then revived *The Second Mrs. Tanqueray* by Sir Arthur Wing Pinero, which had passed as a rather daring "modern" drama when it was first performed in the 1890s. This vehicle served Cooper for an impressive 221 performances in 1922 and, for the first time, earned her wide critical recognition as a dramatic actress. In 1923–24, she delighted London

theatergoers in *Peter Pan* at the Adelphi Theater, becoming the first Peter to "fly" in through the window (on a suspension wire), a feat now taken for granted. She then revived Pinero's *Iris* (1925) and also produced a number of other contemporary plays, especially Frederick Lonsdale's *The Last of Mrs. Cheyney*, which ran for almost a year (1925) and in which she starred opposite Sir Gerald du Maurier. In time, Cooper became celebrated for her ability to turn a good play into box-office gold, and, over the years, just about every practicing British playwright of her era came to write plays expressly for her.

An astute business woman and a good judge of what would work on the modern stage, Cooper, together with Curzon, now assumed the management of The Playhouse Theater in London, where she would produce eight plays in the next eight years, the first being Somerset Maugham's *The Letter*, a melodrama set in Malaya, in which she played the adulterous and murderous wife Leslie Crosbie, a role reprised on the screen by *Bette Davis in 1940. One of Cooper's greatest successes, this production ran for 338 performances and established her as the leading actress-manager in English theater. Somerset Maugham was so impressed with her production of his drama that he immediately gave Cooper the first option on his two new plays *The Sacred Flame* and *The Painted Veil,* the first of which she both staged and played in in 1929. This was followed by her production of H.M. Harwood's and R. Gore-Browne's *Cynara* (1930). Cooper enjoyed being a manager, reveling in the conferences and the decision-making that went with the work. "Being a manager alters an actress' whole point of view," she once observed. "She stops reading scripts to find parts and [instead] reads to find plays. Her own part becomes a secondary consideration. As a producer I have often cast myself for parts that no [other] manager would have engaged me for."

Frank Curzon died in 1927, but Cooper continued to manage The Playhouse Theater alone until 1934, when a combination of factors, not the least of which were the enormous work involved, the distraction from her acting, the needs of her children, the increasing competition from the talking films, and the Great Depression, caused her to cease operating her project. Her years as a manager stood her in good stead as an actress, however, long after her years at The Playhouse had come to an end. She learned, for example, that it was important to open a play during a "good" season, when one critical success was following another, for the sense of the critics and of the audience that they were in the midst of a glittering season rubbed off on every other production that opened. If a season was seen to be poor, one's own production, even if good, could be greeted as just another mildly interesting feature in an otherwise lackluster year.

In 1933, Raymond Massey, best remembered for his film role as Abraham Lincoln, who had directed the New York production of *The Sacred Flame*, brought to Cooper's attention the dramatization of *The Rats of Norway,* a novel by the youthful Keith Winter that had created a stir when it had first appeared in 1932. Cooper was extremely impressed by Winter's work, especially by what she called "his comprehension of women's psychology." Impressed, as well, by the play's theatrical possibilities, Cooper staged *The Rats of Norway* in London with herself, Massey, and a youthful Laurence Olivier in the cast. Although it received mixed reviews, it was one of the successes of the season. The following year, Cooper again appeared with Massey in the London production of Robert E. Sherwood's *Acropolis,* which was considerably less successful. At this time, however, Keith Winter approached Cooper with a second play, *The Shining Hour*. After consultation with Massey, who agreed to appear with her in the drama together with his wife, the actress *Adrianne Allen, Cooper decided to do the play. On the advice of Noel Coward, however, she and Massey opted to premiere the work in New York.

Gladys Cooper arrived in New York for her American debut in the spring of 1934, together with Keith Winter and the entire cast of *The Shining Hour*, which had already been rehearsed in London. The play was both a critical and popular success and the New York critics, agreeing that Cooper was worthy of her reputation, were soon comparing her to the celebrated American actress, *Katharine Cornell, a comparison that would be made over and over.

It was now, in mid-life, that Gladys Cooper undertook her first Shakespearean roles. Wisely, she chose to make her debut in New York, where the local critics had less emotional involvement with the Bard, playing at the Plymouth Theater opposite Philip Merivale, her future husband, in *Othello* and *Macbeth* in 1935. In assaying the roles of Desdemona and Lady Macbeth, Cooper had the advantage of having seen *Othello* only once (in the Paul Robeson version in London in which *Peggy Ashcroft had distinguished herself as Desdemona), and *Macbeth* not at all, so that, uninfluenced as well as

unintimidated by the interpretations of her predecessors, she simply played the parts as she thought they should best be played. Although neither production satisfied the critics, Cooper managed to garner good personal reviews especially for her sleepwalking scene in *Macbeth*. Cooper worked well with Merivale and enjoyed working in New York, so much so that she took a house in Darien, Connecticut, for the run of the plays. True to her determination never to become typecast, Cooper immediately followed her Shakespearean adventure with an appearance with Merivale in a modern British play, *Dodie Smith's *Call It a Day*, which was staged by the Theater Guild in the seasons of 1935–36 and 1936–37 and which ran for 194 performances on Broadway. Now wed, the Merivales took an apartment on Park Avenue for themselves and Cooper's daughter Sally from a previous marriage. Returning to London, Cooper and Merivale appeared in the London production of *Dodsworth* (1938), based on Sinclair Lewis' 1935 dramatization of his 1929 novel. The couple then appeared together that summer doing Shakespeare in the open-air theater in Regent's Park, with Cooper starring as Olivia in *Twelfth Night*, as Rosalind in *As You Like It*, and as Oberon in *A Midsummer Night's Dream*. Returning to New York, Cooper now chose a modern play as her vehicle, Emlyn Williams' *The Morning Star*.

In 1938, Gladys Cooper and her husband formed a managerial partnership, together with the London producer Lee Ephraim and the American performer Georgie Jessel, to produce *Spring Meeting* in New York, a play that had had a most successful run in London. The play opened that fall and ran through the season into 1939. It was at this time in her life, however, that Gladys Cooper made another abrupt career move. Suddenly becoming serious about work in motion pictures, she decided to settle in California. Cooper had made her first British talking film as early as 1935, but now, from 1940 through the 1950s, she became a regular in American motion pictures. Highly esteemed for the quiet elegance that she brought to her characterizations, she was much in demand to play society women, both English and American, both virtuous and villainous, moving effortlessly from one studio to another—United Artists, Warner Bros., RKO, MGM—although most of her films were made for the last two. Her appearances in *Rebecca* (1940), in which *Judith Anderson and *Joan Fontaine also appeared, and *That Hamilton Woman* (1941) were well-received, as was her brief but important role in *The Song of

Bernadette (1943). Her greatest success was as Bette Davis' possessive and domineering mother in *Now Voyager* (1942), for which she was nominated for an Academy Award for the Best Supporting Actress of the year. Cooper's last important appearance on the screen in her later years was as the mother of Henry Higgins in *My Fair Lady* (1964). Her last American film, *The Happiest Millionaire,* would be made in 1967.

Having returned to postwar London in 1947, Cooper resumed her career on the stage as Melanie Aspen in Peter Ustinov's *The Indifferent Shepherd* (1948). A number of modest successes followed, among them her role as a lady cricketer in Thomas Browne's farce *The Hat Trick* (1950), but it was in Noel Coward's *Relative Values* (1951), that Cooper was "discovered" by a new generation of London theater audiences. In 1953, Gladys Cooper starred in Wynyard Browne's *A Question of Fact* and, two years later, returned to the New York stage for the first time since 1943 in the role of Mrs. St. Maugham in *Enid Bagnold's popular play *The Chalk Garden,* which had served as a successful vehicle for both of her great contemporaries, Peggy Ashcroft and *Edith Evans. Cooper received enthusiastic reviews for her performance, one of the memorable events of the season. She marveled at the warmth and affection of her reception in a city where she did not consider herself to have had much of a following. Back in London, she appeared in a number of other plays, then returned to New York one final time in 1962 for the role of Mrs. Moore in a stage adaptation of E.M. Forster's novel *A Passage to India,* a role immortalized on the screen in 1984 by Ashcroft.

Cooper excelled in drawing-room comedy but handled herself equally well and often quite brilliantly in Shakespeare and Shaw. "Earnestness," "consistent insight," "extraordinarily vivacious," "resplendent" were typical terms with which her various appearances were greeted by the critics, who, while they were not always satisfied by her choice of vehicles, were almost always enthusiastic about her performances. Indeed, her talents were not only recognized by the critics and her peers but also attracted the attention of Queen *Elizabeth II, who, in 1967, awarded Cooper the coveted title of Dame of the Order of the British Empire, an honor accorded to relatively few ladies of the theater, and which placed Gladys Cooper in the highest theatrical rank among such major British actresses as *Ellen Terry, *May Whitty, *Sybil Thorndike, Ashcroft, and Evans.

As an actress, Dame Gladys Cooper is remembered not so much for her ability to master a play or a role but rather for her ability to select the roles that were perfect for her and which permitted her to excel. Though she attempted to grow as an actress and to expand her horizons, as her appearances in Shakespearean comedy and tragedy attest, she was less versatile than Ashcroft and less inclined to challenge herself. As the years passed, however, and the Edwardian period from which she had sprung became clouded with nostalgia, Dame Gladys Cooper attracted increasing affection as one of the last famous representatives of her era and one of the last theatrical links to the age of Terry. Audiences flocked to see her perform, and she became increasingly revered by the British. "Retire?" she is quoted as having said in her later years. "Whatever for?"

Only towards the end of her life did Cooper become involved with television, and her last role was that of the mistress of a gang of sophisticated international jewel thieves on the American TV series "The Rogues" in 1963, in which she played with David Niven, Charles Boyer, and Gig Young. Reviewing the series for *The New York Times,* Jack Gould wrote that her "portrayal of the doyenne of cultural rascality is an absolute gem."

Gladys Cooper married three times. Her first marriage to an actor, Henry Buckmaster, on December 12, 1908, ended in divorce in 1922 but left her with two children, son John Buckmaster, who later became an actor, and daughter Joan, who married the popular character actor Robert Morley. During her second marriage to Sir Neville Charles Pearson, magazine editor and publisher, on June 15, 1928, she had a daughter Sally, who married the actor Robert Hardy. A devoted mother, despite the demands of her career, Cooper brought her youngest daughter to America with her on both of her first two appearances in New York. In October 1936, she divorced Pearson and on April 30, 1937, wed Philip Merivale in Chicago; the marriage lasted until his death in 1946.

Cooper had homes in both England and California and communicated between them regularly. She evinced no snobbery in connection with performing in the U.S., a country that she claimed to love, and cheerfully worked in New York and Hollywood as easily as she did in London. Her pastimes included gardening and traveling, and she enjoyed overseeing the construction of her homes. She had a fondness for Welsh corgis, a breed of dog made fashionable by the queen, had a taste for yogurt, and loved to drive, once motoring across the United States from coast to coast. Like many theater people, she was quite superstitious, carrying with her all sorts of good luck charms from her earliest years on the stage and, following British theatrical custom, always traveling with a large wicker hamper in which she kept her costumes.

Cooper was 5'5" and weighed approximately 112 pounds, but, slim and perfectly proportioned, she gave the impression of being taller than she actually was. Her eyes were a deep blue, and she held her aristocratic head with its rather prominent nose characteristically high, her chin jutting forward. No one played the English grande dame better than she. On stage, she was noted for her glamorous wardrobe and was often cited as one of the most beautifully dressed women, but in private life she cared little for clothes and dressed simply. In later years, she preferred pastel colors that she believed best set off her delicate beauty, a beauty that aged gracefully and remained with her until the end of her life. Bright and alert, Gladys Cooper never lost her interest in the theater or in current events. She talked easily and gave a good interview. A religious woman and a true Edwardian until the end, she deplored the decline in morals, standards, and taste in the modern world, especially in the theater and films, and openly joined the chorus of protests that accompanied the advent of *Jesus Christ Superstar*, a production that she detested. Scorning retirement, Dame Gladys Cooper worked continuously and was planning a tour of Canada in *The Chalk Garden*, when she fell ill with pneumonia. Ten weeks later, she died in her sleep at her home in Henley-on-Thames on November 17, 1971, just a few weeks before her 83rd birthday. Gladys Cooper had written her own memoirs as early as 1931 but in 1953 was the subject of a more up-to-date biography by Sewell Stokes for which Somerset Maugham wrote the preface.

SOURCES:
Current Biography. NY: H.W. Wilson, 1946.
Philadelphia Free Library, Theater Collection.
Stokes, Sewell. *Without Veils*. London, 1953.

SUGGESTED READING:
Cooper, Gladys. *Gladys Cooper*. London, 1931.
Wyndham, H. *Chorus to Coronet*. London, 1951.

Robert H. Hewsen, Professor of History,
Rowan University, Glassboro, New Jersey

Cooper, Sarah Ingersoll

(1835–1896)

American educator and first president of the International Kindergarten Union. Born Sarah Brown Ingersoll in Cazenovia, New York, on December 12, 1835;
died in San Francisco, California, on December 10, 1896; cousin of orator and agnostic Robert C. Ingersoll; attended Cazenovia Seminary, 1850–53; Troy Female Seminary, 1854; married Halsey F. Cooper (a newspaper editor), in 1855 (died 1885); children: two daughters, including Harriet Cooper (d. 1896).

Sarah Ingersoll Cooper was a schoolteacher and governess before her marriage to the editor of Tennessee's *Chattanooga Advertiser*, Robert C. Ingersoll. In 1869, after she had suffered several years of poor health and the loss of a daughter, the family moved to San Francisco, where Sarah began a popular Bible study class in her Presbyterian church. In 1881, however, she was expelled from the congregation over her refusal to accept the doctrines of infant damnation and eternal punishment. She removed herself and her Bible class to the Congregational Church, where in 1879 she and members of the class opened the Jackson Street Kindergarten. The success of the venture led to other kindergartens and ultimately to the organization of the Golden Gate Kindergarten Association, which, under Cooper's direction, guided the incorporation of 40 kindergartens in the San Francisco area, enrolling nearly 3,600 children. Numerous kindergartens based on Cooper's model sprang up across the country and abroad. In 1891, the Association opened the Golden Gate Kindergarten Free Normal Training School, and in 1892 Cooper helped found and was elected the first president of the International Kindergarten Union.

Involved in many other civic and charitable organizations, Cooper was in demand as a public speaker. She spoke at the World's Columbian Exposition of 1893 and was one of five women delegates to the Pan-Republic Congress. In 1895, she was elected first president of the Woman's Congress. Following the suicide of Cooper's husband in 1885, her daughter **Harriet Cooper** became her constant companion and secretary. In 1896, Harriet suffered a deep depression during which she made several unsuccessful attempts to take both her own and her mother's lives. On December 10, 1896, Harriet turned on the gas in their San Francisco apartment and asphyxiated them both.

Cooper, Susan Fenimore

(1813–1894)

American naturalist, author, philanthropist, and biographer of her father, James Fenimore Cooper. Name variations: (pseudonym) Amabel Penfeather. Born Susan Augusta Fenimore Cooper on April 17, 1813, in

Mamaroneck, New York; died of possible stroke in Cooperstown, New York, on December 31, 1894; daughter of Susan Augusta (De Lancey) Cooper and James Fenimore Cooper (a writer); educated privately at home in Cooperstown, New York, until 1817, when the family moved to New York City; attended private schools in the City, 1817–26; attended a French boarding school; never married; no children.

Family moved from Mamaroneck, New York, to Cooperstown, New York (1813); moved with family to New York City (1817); lived with family in Europe (1826–33); lived with parents, working as her father's amanuensis until his death (1851); death of mother (1854); devoted much time to charitable work including work with the Christ Church Charity House for destitute families; organized the Christ Church Sewing School (1860); helped establish Thanksgiving Hospital in Cooperstown (1868) and Orphan House of the Holy Savior, also in Cooperstown (1871).

Selected publications: (novel) Elinor Wyllys; or, the Young Folk of Longbridge *(published in America under pseudonym Amabel Penfeather and edited by her father, 1845);* Rural Hours. By a Lady *(1850); "The Lumley Autograph," in* Graham's Magazine *(1851); "A Dissolving View," in* The Home Book of the Picturesque: or, American Scenery, Art, and Literature *(Putnam, 1852); (edited)* John Leonard Knapp's Country Rambles in England; or Journal of a Naturalist *(1853);* The Rhyme and Reason of Country Life: or, Selections from Fields Old and New *(Putnam, 1854);* Rural Rambles, or, Some Chapters on Flowers, Birds, and Insects: By a Lady *(Willis P. Hazard, 1854);* Mount Vernon: A Letter to the Children of America *(D. Appleton, 1859); "Sally Lewis and Her Lovers," in* Harper's New Monthly Magazine *(1859); (edited)* Pages and Pictures, from the Writings of James Fenimore Cooper *(W. A. Townsend, 1861); "Fragments from a Diary of James Fenimore Cooper," in* Putnam's Magazine *(1868); "Passages from a Diary by James Fenimore Cooper," in* Putnam's Magazine *(1868); "Bits," in* Putnam's Magazine *(1868); (edited) "The Battle of Plattsburgh Bay: An Unpublished Manuscript of J. Fenimore Cooper," in* Putnam's Magazine *(1869); (edited) "The Eclipse: From an Unpublished MS. of James Fenimore Cooper," in* Putnam's Magazine *(1869); "Village Improvement Societies," in* Putnam's Magazine *(1869); (edited)* Appletons' Illustrated Almanac for 1870 *(D. Appleton, 1869); "The Magic Palace," in* Putnam's Magazine *(1870); "The Chanting Cherubs," in* Putnam's Magazine *(1870); "Insect-Life in Winter," in* Putnam's Magazine *(1870); "Madame Lafayette and Her Mother," in* Putnam's Magazine *(1870); "Female Suffrage: A Letter to the*

Christian Women of America," in Harper's New Monthly Magazine *(1871); "Two of My Lady-Loves," in* Harper's New Monthly Magazine *(1872); "Rear Admiral William Branford Shubrick," in* Harper's New Monthly Magazine *(1876); introduction to* Household Edition *of 15 of James Fenimore Cooper's novels (Houghton-Mifflin, 1876–84); "Mrs. Philip Schuyler: A Sketch," in* Worthy Women of Our First Century *(J.B. Lippincott, 1877); "The Wonderful Cookie: A True Story," in* Wide Awake Pleasure Book *(D. Lothrop, 1879); "The Hudson River and Its Early Names," in* Magazine of American History *(1880); "The Adventures of Cocquelicot," in* St. Nicholas *(1881); "Small Family Memories (1883)," in* Correspondence of James Fenimore Cooper *(Yale University Press, 1922); "Orphan House of the Holy Savior," in* A Centennial Offering: Being a Brief History of Cooperstown, with a Biographical Sketch of James Fenimore Cooper *(Freeman's Journal Office, 1886); "The Thanksgiving Hospital,"* A Centennial Offering *(Freeman's Journal Office, 1886); a chief contributor to* Appletons' Cyclopaedia of American Biography *(D. Appleton, 1886–1889); "A Glance Backward," Atlantic Monthly (1887); "A Second Glance Backward,"* Atlantic Monthly *(1887); (edited) "Financial Condition of New York in 1833,"* Magazine of American History *(1889); (edited)* William West Skiles: A Sketch of Missionary Life at Valle Crucis in Western North Carolina, 1842–1862 *(James Pott, 1890); "A Lament for the Birds,"* Harper's New Monthly Magazine *(1893); "An Outing on Lake Otsego,"* The Freeman's Journal *(1894); "The Cherry-Colored Purse (A True Story),"* St. Nicholas *(1895).*

For American Romantics and Transcendentalists, nature played a central role in the way they looked at themselves, God, and their place in the grand scheme of things. The American 19th-century "nature" writers who have achieved prominence in university curricula are Ralph Waldo Emerson ("Nature," 1836) and Henry David Thoreau (*Walden*, 1854). Women, too, expressed a keen interest in nature, wrote about it at great length, and turned a fine observational eye to describing the particulars of their locale. Not only did these women record the minutiae of the place they observed, but they also demonstrated the same acuity of perception in drawing correlations between the natural routine and order and ways of humankind. Susan Fenimore Cooper, along with her English counterpart *Dorothy Wordsworth, was such a woman.

Cooper's most important book, *Rural Hours* (1850), a chronicle of one year's natural cycle at her home near Lake Otsego in central New York, remained in print for almost 40 years, even issued in a color-plate illustrated edition in 1851. The book was originally published anonymously "by a Lady," but in later editions Cooper took credit for her popular work. *Rural Hours* predates its now well-known counterpart, Thoreau's *Walden* (1854), by four years—a book considered by scholars as the measuring stick for natural chronicles. Ironically, *Rural Hours* outsold *Walden* and Thoreau's other chronicle, *A Week on the Concord and Merrimack Rivers* (1849); Cooper's book was also better known and in print longer than *Walden*, appearing in its final revised edition in 1887. Thoreau's own journal entry for October 8, 1852, indicates that he had read *Rural Hours,* at least in part. The book received favorable reviews from William Cullen Bryant and Washington Irving and was published in England as *Journal of a Naturalist in the United States* (1855). Cooper served as the editor of renowned British naturalist John Leonard Knapp's *Journal of a Naturalist; with Notes and Additions, by the Author of "Rural Rambles"* (1853), principally because of the enthusiastic public regard for her own book.

We admire the strange and brilliant plant of the green-house, but we love most the simple flowers we have loved of old, which have bloomed many a spring, through rain and sunshine, on our native soil.

—Susan Fenimore Cooper

Susan Cooper also edited *The Rhyme and Reason of Country Life: or, Selections from Fields Old and New* (1854), an anthology of poetry and some prose on the subject drawn from American, European, and Asian sources. The customs, history, and plant and animal life of rural New York form the basis for much of what she wrote, including "Village Improvement Societies" (1869), "The Magic Place" (1870), "Insect-Life in Winter" (1870), "The Hudson River and Its Early Names," (1880), "A Lament for the Birds" (1893), and "An Outing on Lake Otsego" (1894); she also contributed to *Appletons' Illustrated Almanac for 1870* (1869).

Susan Fenimore Cooper's life was that of a traditional woman born into an established New York family: her grandfather, William Cooper, had founded Cooperstown, New York; her father James Fenimore Cooper became a prolific writer of popular novels, including the "Leatherstocking" series—*The Pioneers* (1823), *The Last*

of the Mohicans (1826), *The Prairie* (1827), *The Pathfinder* (1840), and *The Deerslayer* (1841). Her mother **Susan Augusta Cooper**'s family, the De Lanceys, were well-to-do landholders descended from French Huguenots. As a young girl, Susan Fenimore Cooper and her family lived near Cooperstown, eventually moving to their fine country house, Angevine, near Scarsdale, in 1818. Cooper claimed that her original inspiration for *Rural Hours* came from the country buggy rides she took as a young child with her grandfather De Lancey on which he taught her forest and meadow lore.

In 1822, James Fenimore Cooper relocated his family to New York City—in part due to friction with his in-laws, but also so that he could be closer to his publisher and the children could attend good schools. In 1823, with James in debt and in poor health and longing for a change, Susan learned French with her father in preparation for a move to Europe. Three years later, the family set sail on the *Hudson*; they would remain in Europe for the next seven years. Settling in Paris, the Coopers moved in the highest social circles that included Sir Walter Scott and the Marquis de Lafayette. James served as U.S. Consul for the city of Lyon, France, a position secured for him by DeWitt Clinton. While living with their parents, Susan and her two sisters—**Anne Charlotte Cooper** and **Caroline Martha Cooper**—attended an exclusive boarding school run by Madames Trigant de la Tour and Kautz where they studied geography, history, arithmetic, music, drawing, and dancing. In other words, the Cooper daughters were schooled to be fine Victorian ladies. Besides residing in France, the family traveled to Switzerland, lived in Florence, Naples, Rome, Dresden, and England for short periods of time; in each instance, the Cooper children continued their education with private tutors.

No evidence exists to indicate that Susan was actively interested in securing a husband; it is clear, however, that the young girl was courted by several men while the family lived in Europe, including Samuel F.B. Morse, the American inventor of the telegraph, Dr. Ashbel Smith of North Carolina (1805–1886), then a medical student in Paris, and a European noble. In all instances, Cooper's father rejected their proposals, claiming that he did not want her marrying until she was at least 20 and that he did not want any of his family marrying a European. Susan, like her younger sister, Anne Charlotte, remained single her entire life. Although James Cooper was a possessive father, her other sister, Caroline Martha, defied her parents' wishes—and her father's anger—to marry her longtime sweetheart, Henry Phinney.

In 1833, the family returned to New York City, settling in Cooperstown, New York, in 1836. Susan remained a devoted daughter. At age 18, she had become her father's copyist-secretary. When her cousin William, James' amanuensis, died of tuberculosis in 1831, Susan had also filled this position and would remain her father's secretary until his death in 1851, becoming then his literary executor. That year, she moved to Byberry Cottage in Cooperstown, where she lived with her sister Anne Charlotte, and where she resided until the end of her life. Cooper began her long writing career in earnest after her father's death, in part to supplement a meager inheritance.

Much of what Susan Cooper produced had to do with her father, including selections from his work (*Pages and Pictures, from the Writings of James Fenimore Cooper*, 1861, and "Passages from a Diary of James Fenimore Cooper," 1868), previously unpublished correspondence and manuscript material ("The Battle of Plattsburgh Bay: An Unpublished Manuscript of J. Fenimore Cooper," 1869, and "The Eclipse: From an Unpublished MS. of James Fenimore Cooper," 1869), selections from his journal ("Fragments from a Diary of James Fenimore Cooper," 1868), short articles about her father ("The Chanting Cherubs," 1870, "A Glance Backward," 1887, and "A Second Glance Backward," 1887), and introductory sections to 15 of his novels published as the Household Edition between 1876 and 1884: *The Deerslayer, The Last of the Mohicans, The Pathfinder, The Pioneers, The Prairie, Afloat and Ashore, The Crater, Jack Tier, Miles Wallingford, The Pilot, The Red Rover, The Sea Lions, The Two Admirals, The Water-Witch, The Wing-and-Wing*. As his executor, Cooper also had to wrestle with her father's deathbed prohibition against publishing his biography; by publishing the aforementioned materials, however, Susan Cooper did her best to provide information about her father while at the same time honoring his request. Later in life, she also wrote a reminiscence for her nieces and nephews recounting her earliest years, which was later published by her nephew, James Fenimore Cooper, as "Small Family Memories" in his heavily abridged *Correspondence of James Fenimore Cooper* (1922).

Besides pieces about her father, natural history, and central New York, Susan Cooper also wrote short stories for magazines. These narratives are sentimental and moralistic, like her first published piece, the novel *Elinor Wyllys: A Tale* (1845), about a homely young woman who suffers a series of disappointments but whose life holds the promise of better things to come at the book's conclusion. Cooper's short stories include "The Lumley Autograph" (1851), "Sally Lewis and Her Lovers" (1859), "Two of My Lady-Loves" (1872), and "The Wonderful Cookie: A True Story" (1879). Several of her stories were written specifically for a children's audience, including "The Adventures of Cocquelicot: A True History" (1881), the tale of her family's orange Angora cat whom they acquired while living in Paris and brought back with them to New York, and "The Cherry-Colored Purse: A True Story" (published posthumously, 1895).

Cooper responded to the American Women's Suffrage Movement in her article, "Female Suffrage: A Letter to the Christian Women of America" (1870). In it, she exhorts women to cease their demands, basing her argument on biblical traditions: "Let men make the laws [and women] promote by all worth means the moral civilization of the country [by exemplary work in their homes]."

Other works by Cooper are principally biographical in nature, and, aside from those dealing with her father, they include *Mount Vernon: A Letter to the Children of America* (1859), which briefly summarizes the first president's life and seeks financial support for the preservation of his home, "Madame Lafayette and Her Mother" (1870), "Rear-Admiral William Branford Shubrick" (1876), "Mrs. Philip Schuyler: A Sketch" (1877), entries in *Appletons' Cyclopaedia of American Biography* (1886–89), and *William West Skiles: A Sketch of Missionary Life at Valle Crucis in Western North Carolina, 1842–1862* (1890).

Beginning in the 1860s, Susan Cooper actively involved herself in charitable work for her community. In 1860, she organized the Christ Church Sewing School, which, by its second year, had 80 young women enrolled. She was also one of the five trustees of Thanksgiving Hospital, which she helped establish in 1868 to assist the impoverished of Cooperstown. Perhaps one of her greatest accomplishments was establishing The Orphan House of the Holy Savior (1871) which, by 1885, housed over 100 homeless children. Cooper's writing reflects her devotion to these charities, including "Orphan House of the Holy Savior" (1886) and "The Thanksgiving Hospital" (1886).

Susan Fenimore Cooper spent almost her entire adult life living in Cooperstown, New

York; for the 15 years prior to her death, she did not leave her hometown except between 1875 and 1881 for trips to care for her mother's ailing sister in Geneva, New York. Susan Fenimore Cooper died in her home, perhaps of a stroke, on December 31, 1894, and is buried in Cooperstown next to her parents in Christ Church where a stained-glass window commemorates her devotion to the poor of that town.

SOURCES:

Baym, Max I., and Percy Matenko. "The Odyssey of the Water-Witch and a Susan Fenimore Cooper Letter," in *New York History.* Vol. 51, 1970, pp. 33–41.

Beard, James Franklin, ed. *The Letters and Journals of James Fenimore Cooper.* 6 vols. Cambridge, MA: Harvard University Press, 1968.

Cooper, Susan Fenimore, "Small Family Memories" in *Correspondence of James Fenimore Cooper.* Ed. by James Fenimore Cooper. New Haven, CT: Yale University Press, 1922, pp. 7–72.

Cunningham, Anna. "Susan Fenimore Cooper—Child of Genius," in *New York History.* Vol. 25, 1944, pp. 339–350.

Jones, David. "Introduction," in *Rural Hours.* Syracuse: Syracuse University Press, 1968.

Kurth, Rosaly T. "Susan Fenimore Cooper: An Annotated Checklist of Her Writings," in *New York History.* Vol. 58, 1977. pp. 173–193.

———. "Susan Fenimore Cooper: A Study of Her Life and Works," Dissertation, Fordham University, 1974.

Levin, Susan M. "Romantic Prose and Feminine Romanticism," in *Prose Studies: History, Theory, Criticism.* Vol. 10, no. 2, 1987, pp. 178–195.

Maddox, Lucy B. "Susan Fenimore Cooper and the Plain Daughters of America," in *American Quarterly.* Vol. 40, no. 2, 1968, pp. 131–146.

COLLECTIONS:

Correspondence and papers located in the Clifton Waller Barrett Library of American Literature, University of Virginia; and the Cooper Collection in the Beinecke Rare Book and Manuscript Library, Yale University.

Melissa E. Barth, Coordinator of the Office of Women's Concerns and Women's Studies and Professor of English, Appalachian State University, Boone, North Carolina

Cooper, Whina (1895–1994)

Maori leader and Mother of the People, beloved by both Maoris and whites, who was prominent in native land rights in New Zealand, active in other reform movements, and became Dame Whina Cooper toward the end of her life. Name variations: Mrs. Richard Gilbert; Mrs. William Cooper. Pronunciation: SEE-nah KOO-per. Born Josephine Te Wake on the shores of Hokianga Harbor, New Zealand, on December 9, 1895; died in Panguru on March 26, 1994; daughter of Heremia Te Wake, chief of the Hokianga tribes, and Kare Pauro; attended St. Joseph's School for Maori Girls; married Richard Gilbert, in 1916; married William Cooper, in 1940; children: (first marriage) four; (second marriage) two.

Became a prominent businesswoman, owning several farms and stores; became active in land reform plan instituted by Sir Apirana Ngata (1929); elected first woman president of a New Zealand rugby association (1947); founded the Maori Women's Welfare League (1951); led a 700-mile march to preserve Maori land (1975); honored as a Commander of the British Empire (CBE) for her services to the Maori people (1979); raised to the rank of Dame of the British Empire (DBE, 1981).

During the 1940s, New Zealanders often saw a boat, truck, or bus filled with children on their way to a rugby game. They were coached by a feisty Maori woman who frequently challenged the referees' decisions with: "I'm not satisfied with your interpretation of the rules. That's not how we see them." In fact, Whina Cooper was not above taking disagreements off the playing field and into the meeting hall; the entire North Hokianga Rugby Union once met to review her objections. In 1946, she became president of the Hokianga Rugby Union, the first woman to hold a position previously occupied exclusively by men. Though rugby is a tough, physical game, she was not averse to instructing children in its play. Her life, after all, reflected her attitude on the field. In addition to rugby, Cooper enjoyed hockey, netball, table tennis, fishing, and was a keen shot. Known first among the Maoris as the Mother of the People, she was also a farmer, a postal clerk, and owner of several businesses. During her long life, she would not only lead the Maoris, she would become a leader among all New Zealanders.

Whina Te Wake was born on December 9, 1895, in a tiny Maori settlement on the shores of Hokianga Harbor. Her father was Heremia Te Wake, a chief of the Hokianga tribes, and a devout Catholic. Whina was a child of his second family. A widower with grown children, Heremia was 57 when he married a young girl of 15 named **Kare Pauro**. When Whina was born, the women delivering her thought she was a still-born boy. Grabbing the limp infant, Heremia began to put holy water on her, saying, "I baptize you Joseph," at which point the newborn began to scream. When her sex was discovered, the name was changed to Josephine, although she would always be called Whina, a Maori abbreviation of the name. When Whina was two, her younger sister **Heretute Te Wake** was born, completing the family.

Whina's upbringing reflected the cross fertilization then occurring between Europeans and

Maoris. A member of the Catholic Church, she grew up accustomed to European housing, clothes, and utensils, but she was also at home with her Maori heritage, able to fish and hunt with the best. During her early years, Whina walked six miles each day to attend school. There, Maori children were allowed to speak only English and were punished severely for speaking their own language. Whina was a quick student, and her father relied on his daughter's literacy. She read the newspaper to him daily, and in return he taught her Maori chants, tribal traditions, and traditional medi-

cines and remedies. When Whina was nine, the family moved to Whakarapa, and the journey to school was less distant. There she loved fishing and the canoe races that were often held.

As a chief, Heremia frequently associated with members of the government. While with Sir James Carroll, the Maori minister of Native Affairs, Heremia expressed his wish to send his daughter to boarding school but feared that he could not afford the expense. Heremia's attitude was somewhat unusual. Maori women were not necessarily considered equal with men, but he

Whina Cooper, first president of the Maori Women's Welfare League, addressing the inaugural conference in Wellington, 1951.

had a high regard for Whina, clearly favoring her over her older stepbrothers.

When Whina reached the age of 12, Carroll arranged for her to enter St. Joseph's Maori Girls' College at Napier. At the end of her long journey to Napier, she encountered more people gathered in one place than she had ever seen in her life. An excellent student, she quickly adjusted to life at the convent school. She learned to play hockey, basketball, and tennis, and to swim. St. Joseph's introduced Cooper to European life, giving her an understanding of this culture that would later prove invaluable.

Cooper finished school at 18, and her father arranged a marriage for her with an older chief. When she refused the marriage, her father accepted her decision, and for the next few years she held various jobs. Teaching school at Pawarenga, clerking in a local store, and serving as housekeeper for the local parish priests, she showed her willingness to try her hand at almost anything. During her tenure as parish housekeeper, she became extremely close to Father Kreijmborg, and for a time entertained thoughts of entering a convent. Close association with the Catholic hierarchy was important to Cooper spiritually throughout her life.

𝓜en come out of [women], all men, never mind who they are, the King, the Governor, the big chiefs—everybody. They all come out of a woman. Without women they wouldn't even be alive.

—Whina Cooper

In 1916, Whina met and married a young Maori surveyor named Richard Gilbert, who was considered a "good catch." The couple settled on her father's farm, where the first of their four children was soon born. Two years later, they began to endure a series of setbacks. Whina contracted the flu during the great worldwide influenza epidemic. That same year, her father died at the age of 80, and Whina felt the loss as a great blow. Soon, she was shocked to discover that the farm and house she and Gilbert had assumed they would inherit would actually go to Heremia's sons by his first marriage, because he had never changed his will. There was already a rift in the family, as the stepbrothers had long resented the favored treatment they felt Whina and her sister had received, and now the Gilberts and their young children found themselves without a home or source of income. The family moved from the spacious farmhouse into a small shack, and

Whina began to dig for gum, used in preparation of paint, varnish, and linoleum, to earn a living.

Whina had continued to maintain close contact with Father Kreijmborg. When the priest, who came from a wealthy family, received an inheritance, he wanted to use it to help individuals among the Maori. It was natural, therefore, that Whina and Richard Gilbert were among the first to whom he offered aid with a small loan. Whina was willing to accept the money only after the priest convinced her that taking out a loan and paying it back could actually benefit others. She used the money to buy back her father's farm from her brothers, and it was soon a profitable enterprise; when Father Kreijmborg made her another loan to buy a local store, she turned the venture into a similar success. Over the next few years, through investments in a number of farms and businesses, Whina's grasp of finances, imports, and the importance of buying in bulk led to prosperity beyond her dreams.

As the daughter of an important chief, Whina fell naturally into the role of leadership. She founded a branch of the Farmers' Union and became its first president in an effort to improve the quality of livestock and seed used on Maori farms. She then built a health clinic and brought in Dr. George McCall Smith, an eccentric Scot and excellent physician, who established a unique health service that he intended to use as a blueprint for a national system of health care. Whina also built a Parish Hall for tribal meetings, which she came increasingly to dominate. As men showed resentment and began to challenge her authority, she would remind them that all men were born of women, and therefore it was natural for them to make important decisions. During this time, her many community efforts began to include coaching the local rugby team.

In 1928, Whina discovered that her sister Heretute had become romantically involved with her husband. Not long after, she experienced another loss when Father Kreijmborg was killed in an auto accident. She then had to challenge an attempt by the church to confiscate her properties by proving she had long since paid back her loans. She also began the work of repairing her marriage.

In 1929, new opportunities began to open up for the Maoris when Sir Apirana Ngata became minister of Native Affairs. Ngata proposed a land-reform program for his people that would allow Maoris to develop land into farms and produce wool and dairy products. Not surprisingly, the new minister was drawn to the dynamic and successful businesswoman from the northern provinces to help him in instituting the program, and Whina was soon deeply enmeshed in organizing meetings for Ngata to present the plan to the Maoris.

Barely nine months after the scheme was implemented in Whina's district, Ngata returned with other members of Parliament to see what had been accomplished. The group was amazed by all that had been done with little outside funding. The *Auckland Star* reported:

> A full ceremonial reception was given the official party on arrival at Panguru, where 5,000 out of 7,000 acres are under development. This is the biggest scheme of its kind among the Nagapuhi property. It carries 1,400 head of cattle and comprises 50 units. The expenditure to date is £7,500. Its development has reached a high standard, due largely to the unbounded enthusiasm of Mrs. R. Gilbert, who is almost on speaking terms with every batten in the high grade fences that subdivide holdings.

From this point forward, Whina's name was known throughout New Zealand.

Tragedy followed triumph in 1934, when the government fell and Ngata was no longer in power. That same year, Richard Gilbert, who had always supported his wife's ventures, grew ill, and surgery revealed extensive cancer. During her involvement with the land development program, Whina had met William Cooper, who had been Maori representative to the 1926 Royal Commission investigating confiscation of Maori land. Although William was married, the couple became involved, and, at the time of Gilbert's death in March 1935, Whina was seven months pregnant with Cooper's child. William divorced his wife and moved in with Whina. Her behavior, straying so far from the precepts of her church, was at odds with Whina's ardent Catholicism and profoundly shocked the Maoris. She left Panguru for seven years and set up a home with Cooper outside Whangarei. The couple eventually had two children and were married in the church after William succeeded in having his first marriage annulled.

In 1940, at age 45, Whina Cooper was asked to organize a national celebration commemorating the signing of the Treaty of Waiangi, in which the Maoris had ceded their native sovereignty of New Zealand in return for the protection of British law. Back in her element, Whina arranged for a carved meeting house to be constructed, met with government officials, and arbitrated disputes. Not long after, when New Zealand was drawn into World War II, she and her husband returned to Panguru, where they gradually became immersed in local affairs and were active in parish activities, rugby, and the war effort.

In 1947, Whina Cooper made New Zealand history when she was elected the first woman president of a rugby union branch. Her inspection of the union books uncovered the fact that Maoris had to underwrite many of their expenses, while the whites did not, and led to a policy change so that the union's money was shared by everyone. When nuns were brought to the area to establish a school, the Cooper family gave up their farmhouse and lived for a while in a barn in order to assist in the project.

In 1949, Whina Cooper's husband William died suddenly of a heart attack, another terrible blow. By 1951, she had decided to move to Auckland so that her children would have better educational opportunities. Since the end of World War II, increasing numbers of Maoris were leaving rural New Zealand for better jobs in the city, where they often faced discrimination in housing and employment. In Auckland, Cooper found slums inhabited by a vast number of underpaid Maoris from throughout New Zealand. There she also became a friend of Bishop James Liston who had never closely associated with Maoris before and distrusted them. Influenced by his friendship with Cooper, the bishop became committed to offering a special Catholic ministry to urban Maoris.

The urban ministry became one of a number of new areas into which Cooper invested her energies. In September 1951, after attending a conference of welfare committees, she became the representative for its 300 delegates, who organized to found the Maori Women's Welfare League to promote the general health and well being of women and children. Soon she was president of the organization, traveling around the country to assess conditions in Maori communities. It was in the urban areas that she discovered the most shocking evidence of substandard dwellings and overcrowding. When bureaucrats of the Department of Maori Affairs maintained that no one ever requested housing, Cooper went to Parliament and received permission to document the need for Maori housing in Auckland. Using volunteers, she conducted a street-by-street survey compiled in a massive report that finally resulted in the building of adequate housing. Through Cooper, the league became the first Maori organization to speak with a national voice about issues of racial and legal discrimination, health and child care.

In 1957, at age 61, Cooper retired as president of the Maori Women's Welfare League. Always an active church member, she now threw her energies behind building a church center in Auckland. A Dutch priest, Father van Enckevort, was in charge of such a project, which he had been unable to get underway, and gave Cooper permission to raise money for it while he made a brief visit home to Holland. When he returned, Cooper had already raised £500 and more was to follow. She organized concerts, raffles, dances, games, bring-and-buys, and other fundraisers. Her Queen Carnivals, in particular, became famous, in which various groups entered a female contestant who did not win on the basis of beauty but on how much money her sponsors raised for the Catholic Center. In two years, Cooper raised £44,000, and in 1966 the Auckland Catholic Maori Center was finally built, with a plaque installed in the foyer declaring, "This place is the fruits of the efforts of the people, and of their Mother, Whina Cooper."

By this time, Cooper's works were being acknowledged beyond the boundaries of New Zealand. For her efforts on behalf of the Maoris, she was awarded the rank of Member of the British Empire. In 1974, at age 79, she was elderly, frail, and sometimes tired, when she was given the rank of Commander of the British Empire, but her contribution to public life was still not ended. When the Maoris ceded New Zealand to the British, 2.5 million acres of land had been set aside for them, but over time, much of it was being seized by the whites under one pretext or another. In March 1975, Cooper attended a Maori meeting where she listened with increasing concern to stories of the disappearance of their lands. Following her suggestion to stage a march on Parliament, young Maoris organized under Cooper's leadership over the next few months. On September 14, 1975, with her three-year-old granddaughter at her side, Cooper took her place at the head of a 700-mile march that would take 30 days. The 5,000 marchers moved from one Maori community to the next, gathering 60,000 signatures demanding the return of their land. Many marveled at the presence of Whina Cooper, now 80 years old, and the demonstration ultimately made her a heroine of many environmentalists as well as the Maoris.

Throughout the next 18 years, Whina Cooper remained active. In 1982, she moved back to Panmure, to be near her children. At this point, her extended family numbered some 130. Having lived simply throughout her life, she could move easily from a large farmhouse to a barn, and she dwelled quite happily in a small trailer before moving to a house.

In 1981, in recognition of her many contributions, she had attained the British government's highest rank of honor as a Dame of the British Empire, the equivalent of a knight, and was known henceforth as Dame Whina Cooper. In 1986, she enjoyed observing the return of Halley's Comet, which she had watched in May 1910 as a student at St. Joseph's Maori School.

Born a poor child of illiterate parents, Whina Cooper nevertheless had many assets from the moment of her birth. Her proud Maori heritage, strong family, intelligence, and enthusiasm took her from a small village to the halls of Parliament. She raised a large family, founded prosperous businesses, organized sports teams, and created national organizations that addressed the issues of poverty, the environment, gender and racial equality, and quality of life. When she died, on March 26, 1994, at age 98, in Panguru, she was returned to the earth beneath the mountains of Panguru and Papata, where she sleeps with her ancestors.

SOURCES:

Craig, Robert. *Historical Dictionary of Polynesia.* Metuchen, NJ: Scarecrow Press, 1993.

"Dame Whina Cooper," in *The New York Times.* Tuesday, March 29, 1994, p. A 13.

"Dame Whina Cooper," in *The Times* [London]. March 30, 1994, p. 21.

King, Michael. *Whina: A Biography of Whina Cooper.* London: Hodder and Stoughton, 1983.

———. *Maori: A Photographic and Social History.* Auckland, NZ: Heinemann, 1984.

McLauchlan, Gorden, ed. *The Illustrated Encyclopedia of New Zealand.* Auckland, NZ: David Bateman, 1989.

Rice, Geoffrey W., ed. *The Oxford Encyclopedia of New Zealand.* 2nd ed. Auckland, NZ: Oxford University Press, 1992.

Sinclair, Keith, ed. *The Oxford Illustrated History of New Zealand.* Auckland, NZ: Oxford University Press, 1990.

Karin Loewen Haag, freelance writer, Athens, Georgia

Cooper, Mrs. William (1895–1994).
See Cooper, Whina.

Coosaponakeesa (c. 1690– c. 1763).
See Musgrove, Mary.

Cope, Mother Marianne
(1838–1918)
German-born American member of the Third Order of St. Francis who ministered to the lepers of Hawaii

for more than 35 years. Name variations: Barbara Koob; Sister Mary Anna Cope; Marianna; Mother Cope; Mother Marianne of Molokai. Born Barbara Koob in Germany on January 23, 1838; died in Hawaii on August 9, 1918; daughter of Peter (a farmer) and Barbara (Witzenbacher) Koob; attended St. Joseph's Parish School.

Relocated from Germany to Utica, New York (1839); invested in the habit of a novice (November 9, 1862), becoming Sister Mary Anna; pronounced her vows (November 19, 1863); appointed temporary superior for the Immaculate Conception Convent in Rome, New York (1866), then superior of St. Teresa's and principal of St. Peter's School in Oswego, New York; appointed superior of St. Joseph's Hospital in Syracuse (June 1870); elected second provincial superior of the Sisters of St. Francis (December 1877); arrived in Hawaii (November 8, 1883); the Kapiolani Home for Girls at Kakaako opened (November 1885); arrived in Kalaupapa to live among a thousand lepers (November 1888).

Mother Marianne Cope dedicated more than 35 years of her life to helping the sufferers in Hawaii's leper colonies in the late 19th and early 20th centuries. Born on a farm in Germany, she was baptized Barbara Koob in Heppenheim, in the Grand Duchy of Hesse-Darmstadt. In search of a prosperous life, her parents, **Barbara Witzenbacher Koob** and Peter Koob, brought their nine surviving children, of whom Barbara was the fifth, to America in 1839. The family took up residence in the growing city of Utica, New York, which had many German-speaking Catholics and a "German Church," St. Joseph's, where the services were conducted in German. There, ten-year-old Barbara received the Sacrament of Confirmation and Holy Communion. It is assumed that she attended local schools before completing St. Joseph's Parish School in 1851. Bilingual, she spoke in English at school and German at home. According to Utica's census records, Barbara was working "in factory," and it is likely that she was employed at the Utica Steam Woolen Mills located across the street from her home. In addition to caring for her younger siblings and executing household tasks, she worked for nine years, supplementing the family income.

She was about 15 when she came under the spell of St. Francis' maxim: "I am not here to be served, but to serve." **Sister Bernardina**, a sister of the Third Order of St. Francis, established a convent in Utica and counseled young Barbara: "Hope for God's reward when He is ready to grant it." Following the death of her father in July 1862, Barbara requested admittance to the Sisters of the Third Order of St. Francis. Accepted, she was sent to Syracuse where she trained at the St. Francis Convent and was invested with the habit of a novice on November 19, 1862. She took the name Sister Mary Anna (Mary for the Virgin and Anna for Sister Bernardina whose name had been Anna before she became a nun). On November 18, 1863, she renounced all her worldly possessions, and the following day, November 19, she pronounced her vows. With the Americanized version of the German Koob, she signed her name Sister Mary Anna Cope. Various spellings of her names were used, and in the German community the name became Marianna, then Marianne, the latter of which she used by 1871 almost exclusively.

Now dedicated to the Third Order of St. Francis, Marianne Cope first served as a teacher before becoming an administrator in 1866 when she became temporary superior for the Immaculate Conception Convent in Rome, New York. She was then appointed superior of St. Teresa's and principal of St. Peter's School (Oswego, New York). In June 1870, she was appointed superior of St. Joseph's Hospital in Syracuse, a newly opened facility, the running of which was entirely under her wing. When elected second provincial superior of the Sisters of St. Francis, she succeeded Mother Bernardina and supervised 62 sisters, nine school missions, and two hospitals.

In June 1883, public concern about the spread of leprosy in the Kingdom of Hawaii, as well as demand for containment of the disease and for the government to provide for the lepers, prompted Father Leonor Fouesnel, who was assigned to the Catholic Mission in Hawaii, to request that Sisters of Charity come to "take charge of our hospitals" in Hawaii. Mother Marianne replied to his letter: "I am hungry for the work and I wish with all my heart to be one of the chosen ones, whose privilege it will be to sacrifice themselves for the salvation of the souls of the poor Islanders. . . . I am not afraid of any disease, hence it would be my greatest delight even to minister to the abandoned 'Lepers.'"

Selected to lead the mission, she chose six sisters to accompany her to Hawaii (**Sister M. Bonaventure Caraher, Sister M. Crescentia Eilers, Sister M. Renata Nash, Sister M. Rosalia McLaughlin, Sister M. Ludovica Gibbons,** and **Sister M. Antonella Murphy**). On November 8, 1883, they arrived in Hawaii aboard the *Mariposa*. As they were taken in five carriages provided for by King Kalakaua to the Cathedral of Our Lady of Peace, bells rang out to welcome them.

Horrible health conditions greeted Mother Marianne when she toured the Branch Hospital at Kakaako, Oahu; the hospital served as a "receiving station" for individuals who were suspected of having leprosy. When the Act to Prevent the Spread of Leprosy (or the Segregation Law) went into effect in 1866, a leprosarium had been established at Kalawao on the island of Molokai, and it was to this facility that those diagnosed with the disease at the Branch Hospital were removed. At the hospital, Mother Marianne met with "the ravaged mutilated bodies of the patients far advanced in the disease; the blinded eyes, the parts of faces eaten away, leaving gaping holes where the noses had been, lost fingers and toes, hands contracted into claws, legs ending in stumps." These horrors, however, in no way deterred her from her sense of purpose. On January 3, 1884, she and the sisters who accompanied her were moved from temporary housing into a two-story convent that had been constructed for them near the hospital compound. Sister M. Ludovica Gibbons was assigned by Mother Marianne to remain at the convent and prepare the food for the sisters, a careful task because it was known that leprosy might be contracted by way of mouth. Their mission, the Convent of St. Francis, was the first Franciscan mission in Hawaii; it was also the first mission, independent of affiliation with a European community, that was established outside the United States by women.

Among Mother Marianne's projects was the Kapiolani Home for Girls at Kakaako, a home for healthy girls whose parents suffered from leprosy. She worked with Queen *Kapiolani (1834–1899) to establish the home, and it opened in November 1885. Mother Marianne and her charges worked their way through the Kakaako hospital's cookhouse, dining room, and patients' cottages to clean away the filth. With compassion, they dressed the sores of the lepers whose beds and clothing they cleaned. Asked to travel to Wailuku, Maui, to prepare a newly built government hospital for opening, Mother Marianne accepted the task. She purchased supplies and saw the hospital to a general state of readiness at which time Queen *Liliuokalani came to inspect the facility, requesting Mother Marianne as her guide. When Mother Marianne asked the queen to name the hospital, Liliuokalani gave it the name "Malulani," meaning "under the protection of Heaven." After Mother Marianne's return to the hospital

at Kakaako, Franciscan sisters would continue to run the Malulani Hospital until 1929.

Mother Marianne had arrived in Hawaii in 1883 with the intent of returning to Syracuse after seeing the other sisters established in their headquarters, but in 1885, after more than 20 months, she decided to remain. She and her sisters would be paid $20 a month from the years 1883 to 1917, the year in which their pay would double. At Kakaako, she asked the Board of Health to remove the superintendent of the hospital, Henry Van Giesen, who had brutalized the patients, and she was placed in control. During July 11–16, 1886, Mother Marianne was visited by Father Damien; he had contracted the disease after working with the lepers on Molokai and wanted to know more about a new form of treatment that involved bathing in hot water with herbs and minerals. He requested Mother Marianne's assistance on Molokai, fearing what might happen to the lepers there after his death. Accompanied by only Sister Leopoldina and Sister Vincent, Mother Marianne, now 50 years old, traveled to Kalaupapa to live among a thousand lepers; there, she would feel her life fulfilled.

She took over the running of the Bishop Home, a home for women and girls, and lived in a tiny convent, St. Elizabeth's. Mother Marianne planned new housing facilities, kept health records, ordered supplies, and tended to the patients. The sisters did their own laundry, as well as that of the patients, in the stream, and planned surprises for the children. Mother Marianne also made dresses for the girls who in 1905 numbered 80 and were all dressed in wine-colored uniforms. She also worked in a garden, growing fruits and vegetables for use in the two cookhouses, and she was pleased when asked for plants by patients who wished to start their own gardens. Robert Louis Stevenson visited Mother Marianne in May 1889 and lived in the settlement's guest cottage for a week. He composed a poem to Mother Marianne, the last two lines of which show his impression of the work at the leper settlement: "He marks the sisters on the painful shores, and even a fool is silent and adores." When Stevenson returned to Honolulu, he sent a piano to Kalaupapa. Mother Marianne spent 30 years at this settlement and helped to establish a new convent at Kalawao called the Convent of Our Lady of Mercy. A home for boys, later called the Baldwin Home, was also built at Kalawao.

During her 35 years of working with lepers, Mother Marianne did not contract the disease, nor did any of the sisters in her charge. In 1917, the director of the Royal Hawaiian Band, Henry Berger, composed his "An Ode to St. Anne" to honor her. Mother Marianne Cope died at age 80 and was buried at Kalaupapa, on a hillside beneath orange trees she had planted. A monument stands nearby to commemorate her.

SOURCES:

Petersen, Barbara Bennett, ed. *Notable Women of Hawaii.* Honolulu: University of Hawaii Press, 1984.

Copeland, Lillian (1904–1964)

American track and field star. Born in New York City on November 25, 1904; died on February 7, 1964.

Competitor in the shot put, discus, and javelin; won a silver medal in the discus in the Olympics (1928) and a gold in the same event in the Olympics (1932).

At the University of Southern California, Lillian Copeland played tennis and basketball, participated in track and field, and won every track event she entered. Her first national title was in the shot put in 1925; that year, she would win eight more. In 1926, she broke two world records, throwing the javelin 112'5½" and the discus 101'1". In the 1928 Amsterdam Games, Copeland competed only in the discus because the shot put was not an Olympic women's event. She threw the discus 121'7⅞" to win a silver medal. Copeland continued to win national titles and in the 1932 Los Angeles Olympics won a gold medal in the discus with a throw of 133'1⅝", which set a world record. She was inducted into the Helms Athletic Hall of Fame and the Jewish Sports Hall of Fame. After retiring from competition, Copeland served as a juvenile officer with the Los Angeles County Sheriff's Department from 1936 to 1960.

Karin Loewen Haag,
Athens, Georgia

Copley, Clara (d. 1949)

Irish entrepreneur who ran a prize-fighting ring. Name variations: Ma Copley. Died in 1949.

Called a "woman in a man's world—the world of prize fighting," Clara Copley, who came from a circus family, made her home in a Romany caravan. Known as Ma Copley, she embarked on her career in the world of prize fighting in the 1930s. With the shortage of work during these years, young men were lured to fighting with hopes of winning money. Copley started with a boxing booth and later held boxing matches in a large, wooden building in Belfast. Among those who fought in her tourna-ments were fly-weight champion of 1948 Rinty Monaghan; Irish champion Bunty Doran; Tommy Armour, who knocked out British champion Eric Boon; and Jimmy Warnock who triumphed over world fly-weight champion Benny Lynch. Copley died in 1949.

Coppi, Hilde (1909–1943)

German anti-Nazi activist who was a member of the Berlin support group of the "Red Orchestra" spy network. Born Hilde Rake in Berlin, Germany, on May 30, 1909; executed at Plötzensee on August 5, 1943; married Hans Coppi (1916–42); children: one son Hans.

Hilde Rake was born a child of working-class Berliners on May 30, 1909. As was true for many Berlin workers of the pre-Nazi era, Socialist ideas and ideals were part of her daily life. With the coming of the Nazi dictatorship, she felt it natural to continue working for the Marxist cause in various underground organizations, despite the great risk of discovery and the price—confinement in a concentration camp or death—if caught. The Communists were the most implacable enemies of the Hitler regime in the years after 1933. In a Communist cell, Hilde met and fell in love with another young activist, Hans Coppi. Also from a poor family, Hans had to support himself as an unskilled worker during the depression years of the early 1930s; despite his lack of formal education, he was an intelligent Socialist who had earlier joined the Communist Youth organization. In 1934–35, he served a year in prison for participating in the distribution of anti-Nazi literature. After his release, he upgraded his skills, finding employment as a turner while Hilde worked as a secretary and receptionist. Following their marriage, the couple's political commitments increased, as their small apartment became a center of underground activities, including the writing and printing of pamphlets, and a refuge for anti-Nazis on the run from the Gestapo. Many of these fugitives were helped to escape to Denmark or Czechoslovakia.

By 1940, the Coppis established contacts with the Schulze-Boysen-Harnack resistance circle. Hilde spent much of her spare time listening to Moscow Radio and other anti-Nazi foreign broadcasts, carefully taking notes to be passed on to various underground cells. Hans used a boat on Berlin's many lakes to send coded radio messages to the USSR, containing important data gathered by the "Red Orchestra" organization. When the couple was arrested in September 1942, along with virtually all other members of the "Red Orchestra" organization, Hilde was in her third trimester of pregnancy. Sentenced to death soon after his arrest, Hans was executed on December 22, 1942, never having seen his son Hans, who had been born on November 27. Determined to end treasonous activity, on January 20, 1943, the special Nazi war tribunal sentenced Hilde Coppi to death. Although she was permitted to nurse her infant in her cell, no clemency was ever shown in her case and she was executed at Plötzensee on August 5, 1943. Her last letter to her mother bespoke the courage with which she had lived:

> The hardest part, the separation from my little Hans, is behind me. How happy he made me! I know that he will be well taken care of in your loyal, dear maternal hands, and for my sake, Mama—promise me—remain brave. . . .

SOURCES:

Biernat, Karl Heinz, and Luise Kraushaar. *Die Schulze-Boysen-Harnack-Organisation im antifaschistischen Kampf.* Berlin: Dietz Verlag, 1970.

Gollwitzer, Helmut, Käthe Kuhn, and Reinhold Schneider, eds. *Dying We Live: The Final Messages and Records of the Resistance.* NY: Pantheon Books, 1956.

Kraushaar, Luise. *Deutsche Widerstandskämpfer 1933–1945: Biographien und Briefe.* 2 vols. Berlin: Dietz Verlag, 1970.

John Haag,
Athens, Georgia

Coppin, Fanny Jackson (1837–1913)

American teacher and missionary who became the first black woman in the U.S. to head an institution of higher learning.

Name variations: (pseudonym) Catherine Casey. Pronunciation: KOP-in. Born Fanny Marion Jackson in 1837 in Washington, D.C.; died of arteriosclerosis at her home in Philadelphia on January 21, 1913; daughter of unknown father and Lucy Jackson, a slave; attended public school briefly and received private tutoring; attended Rhode Island State Normal School in Bristol, 1859; A.B., Oberlin College, 1865; married Reverend Levi Jenkins Coppin, in 1881.

Fanny Jackson Coppin

Worked as domestic (1851–59); served as principal of the female department and teacher of Greek, Latin, and mathematics, Institute for Colored Youth in Philadelphia (1865–69); served as principal of the Institute (1869–1902); served as AME missionary, South Africa (1902–04); wrote autobiography, Reminiscences of School Life and Hints on Teaching *(1913).*

At the age of 14, Fanny Jackson took a job as a domestic servant in the household of George Henry Calvert, author and great-grandson of Lord Baltimore, the founder of Maryland. For the next six years, the recently freed slave used money she earned in the Calvert's Newport, Rhode Island, home to hire a tutor. For one hour, three days a week, she pursued her studies. This preparation allowed her to attend a year of public school for black children, Rhode Island State Normal School in Bristol, and, ultimately, the Ladies Department of Oberlin College. Driven by a dream to "get an education and become a teacher to my people," Fanny Jackson graduated from Oberlin in 1865. Four years later, she became the first black woman in the United States to head an institution of higher learning.

Fanny Marion Jackson was born in 1837 in Washington, D.C. Her father's identity is not known, but her mother's name was **Lucy Jackson**. Her aunt, **Sarah Orr Clark**, purchased Fanny's freedom for $125 when Fanny was a young girl, then sent her to New Bedford, Massachusetts, to live with another aunt and perform domestic service outside the home. Fanny moved to Newport in 1852, where she went to work for the Calverts. Although working as a domestic did not provide her with funds for further education, she was able to attend Oberlin College in Ohio, one of very few schools that admitted black students during this period, thanks in part to scholarships—one from Bishop Daniel Payne of the African Methodist Episcopal Church, the other from Oberlin. Her Aunt Sarah continued to assist her, as well.

Fanny Jackson turned out to be an exceptional student who within a year moved from the "literary" course usually pursued by women to the "gentlemen's" classical course leading to the A.B. degree. In her junior year, the faculty selected her to serve as a pupil-teacher in the preparatory department, a position in which no black student had ever before served. Each year, 40 students were chosen from the junior and senior classes to teach these preparatory classes, but Jackson quickly became the most popular instructor. While at Oberlin, she was named senior class poet, gave music lessons, and also organized an evening literacy class for recently freed slaves.

In 1865, the Institute for Colored Youth in Philadelphia hired Jackson as principal of the female department and teacher of Greek, Latin, and mathematics. The Institute had been established by Richard Humphreys, a member of the Society of Friends, in 1837 as a classical high school. It was considered one of the nation's most prestigious black educational institutions, a reputation that would only increase during Jackson's tenure there. In 1869, when the Institute's principal Ebenezer Bassett was appointed U.S. minister to Haiti, the board of managers named Jackson principal of the school, making her the first African-American woman to hold such a position in the United States.

Jackson proved to be an active and imaginative leader of the Institute for Colored Youth. In 1871, she responded to the growing need for public-school teachers by initiating a normal-school program. She also became a prominent advocate of industrial and technical education, often lecturing on the subject or writing about it under the pseudonym "Catherine Casey" for the *Christian Recorder*. After years of her pressuring the board of managers, the Institute added an industrial department in 1889. By 1900, the department offered training in ten fields, including printing, bricklaying, tailoring, and sewing.

When speaking to Institute students or other African-American groups, Jackson often stressed the virtues of self-help and self-denial. As she told the Institute class of 1879:

> You can do much to alleviate the condition of our people. Do not be discouraged. The very places where you are needed most are those where you will get least pay. Do not resign a position in the South which pays you $12 a month as a teacher for one in Pennsylvania which pays $50.

The fact that Jackson practiced what she preached by dedicating her life to others added great weight to her argument.

Fanny Jackson married Reverend Levi J. Coppin, pastor of the Philadelphia Bethel Church, in 1881. He transferred to a Baltimore congregation soon after the marriage, so the couple often lived apart until his return to Philadelphia in 1885. Fanny Coppin became quite active in the African Methodist Episcopal (AME) Church in subsequent years, serving as national president of its Home and Foreign Missionary Society. When Levi was elected an AME bishop

in 1900, he was assigned to Cape Town, South Africa. Fanny resigned her position as principal two years later to join him in Africa. She threw herself into missionary work, traveling hundreds of miles to establish new missions and to "talk to the women upon the subjects of righteousness, temperance, and the judgement to come."

A hundred men can lift a log together very easily, but when only a few take hold at a time very little is accomplished.

—Fanny Jackson Coppin

Fanny Coppin returned to Philadelphia in 1904 with her health failing. Though she was often confined to her home during her remaining years, she remained on the board of managers of the Home for the Aged and Infirmed Colored People in Philadelphia. She also worked on an autobiography, *Reminiscences of School Life* (1913), which appeared in the year she died. In 1909, a Baltimore normal school was named in her honor. This institution became Coppin State College.

SOURCES:

Coppin, Fanny Jackson. *Reminiscences of School Life and Hints on Teaching.* Philadelphia: AME Book Concern, 1913.

Perkins, Linda M. "Heed Life's Demands: The Educational Philosophy of Fanny Jackson Coppin," in *Journal of Negro Education.* Vol. 51, 1982, pp. 181–190.

SUGGESTED READING:

Sterling, Dorothy, ed. *We Are Your Sisters: Black Women in the Nineteenth Century.* NY: W.W. Norton, 1984.

COLLECTIONS:

Institute for Colored Youth Papers, Friends Historical Library, Swarthmore College, Swarthmore, Pennsylvania

John Craig, Professor of History, Slippery Rock University, Slippery Rock, Pennsylvania

Corbaux, Fanny (1812–1883)

English artist. Name variations: Fanny Corbeaux. Born Marie Françoise Catherine Doetter Corbaux in 1812; died in 1883.

Fanny Corbaux' father was reduced to poverty when she was 15. Though she was without any formal artistic training, she was determined to support herself and her father by painting and won the gold medal of the Society of Arts by the time she was 18. Staying primarily with portraits, she painted small pictures in oil and watercolors. A self-taught artist, she was among the first to advocate on behalf of women for their admission as students to London's Royal Academy. Corbaux was also a distinguished Biblical scholar who wrote a series of letters on "The Physical Geography of the Exodus."

Corbert, Sybilla

*Mistress of Henry I. Name variations: Corbet. Daughter of Sir Robert Corbert or Corbet; mistress of Henry I, king of England (r. 1068–1135); children: *Matilda, duchess of Brittany (fl. 1000s); *Sybilla (d. 1122, who married Alexander I, king of Scots); *Constance (who married Richard, viscount de Beaumont, and was the mother of *Ermengarde de Beaumont).*

Corbett, Cicely (1885–1959).

See Fisher, Cicely Corbett.

Corbett, Marie (1859–1932)

*British suffragist. Born Marie Gray in Tunbridge Wells, England, in 1859; died in 1932; daughter of George (a fruit importer and candy manufacturer) and Eliza Gray; married Charles Corbett (a lawyer), in 1881; children: *Margery Corbett-Ashby (1882–1981); *Cicely Corbett Fisher (1885–1959).*

Political activism was very much a part of Marie Corbett's life from an early age. Her mother **Eliza Gray** and her father George Gray, a successful fruit importer and candymaker, were staunch Liberals who supported numerous progressive causes. In 1881, Marie married the radical lawyer Charles Corbett and settled on his large estate at Woodgate in the village of Danehill in Sussex. For many years, the couple put their combined social conscience into action by providing free legal advice for those living in their area. They also raised two daughters, **Margery Corbett-Ashby** and **Cicely Corbett Fisher**, educating them at home with the help of a language tutor.

Marie's political career began following the passage of the Municipal Franchise Act, when she joined the Uckfield Board of Guardians and subsequently became the first woman to serve on the Uckfield District Council. A champion of women's rights, she was instrumental in founding the Liberal Women's Suffrage Society, which was organized to persuade the Liberal government to give women the vote. When the efforts of the Society failed, she joined ranks with the National Union of Women Suffrage Societies. In 1906, when Charles Corbett became the first Liberal elected to represent East Grinstead in the House of Commons, he also supported women's

suffrage, even though it distanced him from his Liberal colleagues.

Corbett continued as an early voice for suffrage, and when the Liberal Party did not advance the cause sufficiently, she and her daughters helped form the Liberal Women's Suffrage Group. Marie also enlisted her daughters as speechmakers. On their campaign rounds, the women often met with hostile crowds, especially in the Conservative seat of East Grinstead, where less than 20% of the women supported the suffrage movement. In 1911, Marie joined **Muriel, countess de la Warr**, and **Lila Durham** to form the East Grinstead Suffrage Society, but membership remained small and meetings were poorly attended.

As the suffrage movement grew in numbers and intensity, hostility sometimes erupted into violence. On July 23, 1923, at a pre-rally on East Grinstead High Street to prepare for a mass rally at Hyde Park on July 26, a crowd of 1,500 had gathered to hear speeches. Joining Corbett on the platform were Edward Steer, a local politician in favor of women's rights, and Laurence Housman, a writer and campaigner for the Suffrage Union. As the speeches got under way, a group of rowdy boys began hurling eggs and tomatoes at the speakers. Eventually the crowd turned ugly and threw rocks, forcing Corbett and the others to take cover in a nearby house. Only after the crowd began breaking into the building did the police intervene.

Following passage of the Equal Franchise Act in 1928, which gave all women over the age of 21 the right to vote, Marie Corbett set out to reform the workhouse system. Before her death in 1932, she was successful in closing down the Uckfield Workhouse and finding homes for all the orphans therein.

SUGGESTED READING:

Corbett-Ashby, Margery. *Memoirs.* 1996.

Hamilton, Mary Agnes. *Remembering Good Friends.* 1944.

Harrison, Brian. *Prudent Revolutionaries.* Oxford: Clarendon, 1987.

Roberts, Marie, ed. *The Suffragists.* 1995.

Corbett-Ashby, Margery (1882–1981)

*British suffragist and politician. Born Margery Corbett at Danehill, Sussex, England, in 1882; died at Danehill, Sussex, on May 22, 1981; eldest of two daughters of Charles Corbett (a lawyer) and *Marie (Gray) Corbett; elder sister of Cicely Corbett Fisher (1885–1959); educated at home; attended Newnham*

College, Cambridge University; attended Cambridge Teachers Training College; married Brian Ashby (a barrister), in 1910; children: one.

One of the few women to be involved in Britain's earliest suffrage campaigns, Margery Corbett-Ashby had a political career that spanned three-quarters of a century and included seven thwarted bids for election to the House of Commons. Still going strong at 98, she attended the Women's Day of Action in London in 1980.

The daughter of suffragist *Marie Gray Corbett and radical lawyer Charles Corbett, Margery Corbett-Ashby was born and raised at Danehill, Sussex. As a child, she and her younger sister *Cicely Corbett Fisher were educated by their parents at home with the assistance of a local woman who tutored them in French and German. Following in their mother's footsteps, the girls supported women's rights and, in 1900, joined with a group of teenage friends to form a society called the Younger Suffragists.

Corbett-Ashby attended Newnham College, Cambridge University, where she was active in the Cambridge branch of the National Union of Women Suffrage Societies and became secretary of the Constitutional Suffrage Movement. Although she successfully completed her studies and passed her examinations, Cambridge University did not grant degrees to women at the time, so she went on to prepare for a teaching career at Cambridge Teachers Training College. (Cambridge University began awarding degrees to women in 1947.)

Margery eventually gave up her plans to teach, but she did not abandon the suffrage cause. In 1907, she was appointed secretary of the National Union of Women Suffrage Societies and, as such, edited their journal. Discouraged by the Liberal Party's record on women's suffrage, she left the Women's Liberal Federation and, with her mother and sister, helped form the Liberal Women's Suffrage Group. She also became a member of the National Committee of the National Union of Women Suffrage Societies. In 1909, she joined the International Women Suffrage Alliance and spoke at conferences in Berlin and Stockholm.

In 1910, Margery married Brian Ashby, a barrister, and four years later gave birth to her only child. For several years thereafter, her activities were curtailed, though she did engage in hospital work during World War I and also ran a canteen at Woodgate that provided nourishing meals for the local schoolchildren.

Following the passage of the Qualification of Women Act in 1918, Corbett-Ashby was one of 17 women who stood as candidates in the postwar election. Running as the Liberal candidate for Ladywood, Birmingham, she campaigned on a feminist platform advocating full political equality between men and women. Suffering her first defeat (she would subsequently make six more unsuccessful runs for the House of Commons), she went on to serve as a member of the International Alliance of Women, representing the organization at the Versailles Peace Conference. In 1920, she participated in the first postwar congress of the International Woman Suffrage Alliance, serving as its president from 1923 to 1946. She was also a British delegate to the Geneva Disarmament Conference but resigned the post in 1935, in protest over the government's refusal to back a practical plan for mutual security and defense.

Margery Corbett-Ashby stayed active in politics after World War II. In 1952, at age 70, she became editor of International Women's News. She died in Danehill, Sussex, on May 22, 1981, at the age of 99.

SUGGESTED READING:

Corbett-Ashby, Margery. Memoirs. 1996.

Hamilton, Mary Agnes. Remembering Good Friends. 1944.

Harrison, Brian. Prudent Revolutionaries. Oxford: Clarendon, 1987.

Roberts, Marie, ed. The Suffragists. 1995.

Corbin, Alice (1881–1949).

See Monroe, Harriet for sidebar on Alice Corbin Henderson.

Corbin, Margaret.

See "Two Mollies."

Corday, Charlotte (1768–1793)

Norman whose passion for justice so far exceeded the capacity or will of the Revolution to separate justice from politics that she individually indicted, judged, and executed the radical journalist Jean Paul Marat, by murdering him in his bath. Name variations: Marie-Anne-Charlotte de Corday d'Armont. Born Marie-Anne-Charlotte de Corday d'Armont at Champeaux in the Calvados of Normandy, France, on July 27, 1768; executed in Paris on July 17, 1793, for the murder of Jean Paul Marat, revolutionary journalist; daughter of Jacques-François de Corday (a minor aristocrat in serious economic decline) and a mother who died in childbirth when Charlotte was quite young; never married; no children.

Attended the convent school at Caen and read deeply in the plays of her ancestor, the tragedian Corneille, as well as Plutarch, Raynal, and Rousseau; inspired by the eruption of the French Revolution (1789), her sympathies came to be with the faction known as the Girondins; upon the fall of that faction from power in Paris (spring, 1793) and the arrival of several Girondin leaders in Caen, she sensed a major part for herself in the Revolution; traveled to Paris (July 1793) and murdered Jean Paul Marat, radical editor of Ami du Peuple, *whom she blamed for the Girondins' fate.*

I have avenged many innocent victims, I have prevented many other disasters. The day will come when the people, undeceived, will rejoice at being delivered from a tyrant . . . rejoice at my fate. The cause of it is beautiful.

—Charlotte Corday, imprisoned after murdering Jean Paul Marat

Charlotte Corday, like several other assassins of prominent political figures, is known to history exclusively for the criminal act she performed. Also like others, including John Wilkes Booth, she acted to avenge the defeat of a cause she had passionately embraced. Having steeped herself in the accounts of the heroic deeds of republican Greece and Rome, and being a woman of both intellect and feeling, she saw in the death of Jean Paul Marat the salvation of both the Revolution and the Girondins, the moderate republicans of her time. She also sought the inevitable martyrdom that must follow upon her act. In her death, she would do for France what she could not do, as a woman, in the political assemblies in Paris. She would, by her sacrifice and by her example, turn her nation away from the murderous, divisive, and populist policies of the Jacobin regime and lead it back to moderate, rational, constitutional government by those of talent and position. Ironically, her violent act only intensified the terroristic policies of the Parisian regime and precluded any peaceful, legislative resolution of the political crisis of the time. One author, J. Mills Whitham, has even speculated that Corday's knife may have prevented moderate Jacobins like Jacques Danton from ending the Terror before they were themselves proscribed.

Corday was descended from an aristocratic French family in Normandy and could claim the prominent 17th-century dramatist, Corneille, as

an ancestor. Her biographer **Marie Cher** believes that she was much like Corneille's ideal characters: pure, faithful, willful, and prone to fanaticism. When she was born in 1768, however, the family was struggling to make ends meet. Her father was the victim of primogeniture laws that effectively left him with insufficient acreage to play the aristocrat. Even so, he embraced politics, generally leaning toward a reformed France under a limited monarchy. Charlotte, one of five children, inherited little from her father but his pride and his devotion to affairs of state.

She was a quiet child, given to moods, studious and serious. Her modest, unremarkable childhood was ended, however, by a sharp blow when both her mother and sister died. Having lost, therefore, her only family support by age ten, she grew all the more introverted and detached. Eventually, she left her family and moved in temporarily with her uncle, the Abbe de Corday, who may have introduced her to classical literature. In the meantime, her mind turned to the attractions of doubt and disputation. Perhaps it was with the intent to counter this course that the **Abbess of the Abbaye-aux-Dames** at Caen consented to take Charlotte into the *abbaye* (abbey) to educate and provide for her. This opportunity opened a new world for Corday, for it gave her access to the institution's library. It was a world she explored intently.

Charlotte was most interested in the accounts of the stern republicans of the world of antiquity. Apparently, her own proclivities to simplicity, virtue, and self-sacrifice were stimulated by Plutarch's biographies of communal heroes, men and women who preferred death over compromise of principle. Similarly, Rousseau's call for resistance to civilization's corruptions may have led her to renounce the attractions of sexual love. In any event, she appears to have had no intimates, male or female, but matured into a self-sufficient, dedicated, brisk young woman.

The onset of the French Revolution in 1789 was for Corday, as it was for all French, the beginning of profound changes. Fired by the news from Paris and other centers, and eager for every scrap of information, the young woman of 21 sought freedom outside the abbey. Taken in by **Madame de Bretteville**, a wealthy widowed cousin in Caen, Charlotte was soon preoccupied by the ebb and flow of the Revolution. As the early moderate phase of the insurrection was succeeded by foreign war and a swing toward popular egalitarianism, bitter internal factional struggles became the essence of the Revolution. Constitutional monarchists gave way to moder-

Charlotte Corday

ate republicans, and they, in turn, criticized by urban populists, were discredited by defeat in foreign war after 1792. In August 1792, Louis XVI, the king of France, was overthrown, largely by the force of Parisian radicals in the city government, the Commune, and the national political faction known as the Jacobins. A key figure in these events was Jean Paul Marat, the writer and editor of the popular newspaper, *Ami du Peuple* (*Friend of the People*). At that time, the leading faction in the Legislative Assembly was the Girondins, a loosely associated group of politicians from the provinces of France who resented the influence of Paris and its radical leaders over the Revolution. Marat and others, especially the rival faction, the Jacobins, believed the Girondins were actually monarchist and opposed to the ambitions of the common people. When a new assembly, the National Convention, was elected late in 1792, Marat and the Jacobins forced the trial and execution of Louis XVI and in June of 1793 expelled the Girondins from the national legislature. Some Girondins were executed, but some escaped to stimulate a number of so-called Federalist revolts in various parts of the country.

The Girondin collapse shocked Charlotte Corday in provincial Caen. Perhaps because of her aristocratic heritage and the prospect of her cousin's legacy, she had come to regard the Jacobins and the Parisian radicals as murderous oppressors of true liberty. Events like the September Massacres in Paris in 1792, when thousands of unarmed captives in Parisian prisons were slaughtered, seemed a degradation of the Revolution and its earlier ideals of personal liberty and constitutional government. Corday accepted accounts of Marat and the Jacobins as the cruel instigators of these mass murders. Should this monster, as she saw him, continue to promote such outrages, France would collapse and the Revolution, with all its opportunities for virtue's triumph, would be lost.

The young woman's sense of justice was deeply offended. Having seen the past of her imagination, of the righteous Romans and Spartans, seemingly come to life in the brave new world of France, she could not bear to see it sullied by the *canaille* or ignorant, filthy common inhabitants of the Parisian slums. She was sure the Jacobins, and especially Marat, had roused this barbaric element for their personal power and had used it against the true republicans, the men of talent and virtue of the Gironde. Patriots, she decided, must save the country. It was a time for a true Roman, a true Spartan, for someone willing to sacrifice herself for the salvation of the community.

Actually, the Jacobins were, in many respects, of the same views and social strata as the Girondins. Its leaders, however, such as Maximillien Robespierre and Jacques Danton, had been willing to embrace the urban radicals and some of their proposals to prevent defeat in the foreign war, prevent the return of royalist power, offset the centrifugal forces of internal separatism, and halt counter-revolution. To Corday, however, they were dangerous levelers and tyrants.

Her predilections to detest the Jacobins were reinforced by the political climate of Caen. Officials in the city, as in others, feared and protested the rising power of Paris and the move toward centralization of all authority in the capital. Thus, when the Girondins were proscribed in the Convention in mid-1793, some of their leaders, including the handsome Charles Barbaroux from Marseilles, made their way to Caen. Immediately, Corday made contact with them. They were intent on raising forces to march on Paris and overthrow the Jacobins. The prospect both repelled and intrigued the young woman. She certainly desired the destruction of the Jacobins, but she hated the thought of her beloved France sinking into civil war. There had to be a way to prevent it. In short order, ideas took form. If the archfiend Marat could be re-

moved, the Girondins could rouse the French nation to unity and bring peace. It was her call. She must go to Paris and do the deed; she must kill Marat.

It appears irrational to think that the death of a single individual could change the fate of an entire nation. Whether irrational or not, the idea has motivated many assassins. To Corday, immersed in her books and obsessed with her own purity and sense of destiny, the act would not be murder as such, and, in fact, she denounced the prosecutor who described her as a murderess at her trial. She regarded the strike at Marat as an act of communal defense. That her own death must follow almost immediately, she knew and accepted with equanimity. Her demise would complete her contribution to France by providing the example for other patriots. Of course, for the example to have the greatest impact, it must be known that her actions were planned and carried out deliberately and earnestly. Hence, every step of the drama was recorded by Corday herself in letters to Barbaroux and her father and in a written testament she attached to her clothes on the day of the assassination. If vanity had its role in the affair, Corday, described as an attractive woman, was, for all her guarded virtue and alleged desire for anonymity, as flattered by personal attention as anyone.

Carefully, Charlotte Corday made her preparations, but she informed no one. She would not let anyone stop her. From Barbaroux, she obtained a letter of introduction to a Girondin still in the Convention by the name of Deperret. Through him, she hoped to gain admission to the Convention and to kill Marat on the spot. She expected to be torn to pieces immediately after assailing the hated journalist.

To associates in Caen, and to her father, Charlotte said she was going to England because she could no longer live in a country so torn by violence. After burning her papers. she took the coach to Paris on June 9 and arrived on June 11. On the way, according to her account, a young man made a proposal of marriage to her; she ignored him. In Paris, she took a room at the Hôtel de la Providence and then made her way to Deperret. She said nothing directly about her plans, but she did ask him if Marat normally attended the sessions of the Convention. The deputy read Barbaroux's letter but told her Marat was ill and confined to his lodgings. Apparently not interested in the young woman, he did not pay her much attention even when she warned him to leave Paris while he could. In fact, her pride was hurt by Deperret's indiffer-

Charlotte Corday and Marat. *Painting by Paul-Jacques-Aimé Baudry.*

ence, and her hopes for a public assassination were diminished, but having come so far, she would not turn back.

Early on the morning of Saturday, July 13, the day before the fifth anniversary of the storm-ing of the royal fortress, the Bastille, Corday arose and went to the market area called the Palais Royale. There she paid 40 sous for a black-handled kitchen knife and concealed it in her clothing. Hiring a coach, she went straight to Marat's house in the Rue des Cordeliers. Marat's wife, **Simonne Evrard,** met Corday at the door and asked her business. Openly suspicious, Evrard stared at the well-dressed woman and told her Marat was not receiving visitors. Charlotte had expected such a reception, however, and had written a note, which she left with Simonne, declaring that she had vital information for Marat concerning certain Girondin conspiracies at Caen. She said that she would expect an answer from the *Friend of the People.*

After returning to the Hôtel de la Providence, Charlotte sent another letter to Marat seeking an interview. She also wrote diverse letters, apparently intended for all of France, explaining her motives and her proposed action. In one of these she wrote: "I can offer you nothing but my life, and I thank heaven that I am free to dispose of it; I desire only that . . . my head, carried through Paris, may be a rallying standard for all the friends of law."

In the evening, Corday again hired a coach and arrived at Marat's house a little after seven o'clock. She had her knife with her. At the door the visitor from Caen, dressed in a brown dress and a black hat, was blocked by two of Marat's housekeepers. Shortly, Simonne came to the door and saw the same woman whom she had spoken to that morning. She allowed Charlotte to wait in the dining room while she asked Marat if he would see her. He agreed, and Charlotte stepped into the bathroom to see a small, emaciated man of 50, suffering from a painful skin disease, seated in a shoe-like tub, wearing a loose dressing gown with a bandanna around his head. Wearily, he asked her to state her business. Well prepared, and exhibiting incredible self-control, Corday sat on a hard wooden chair and began to tell him of the machinations at Caen. Awaiting the departure of Simonne from the room, she gave him names of officials, Girondin refugees, and their sympathizers. Marat took up a pen to record the names on a paper on a board. Apparently content, Simonne left the room. At that moment, Marat said that all the persons named would soon be guillotined. Rising to her feet, Corday drew the knife and, with fanatical force, plunged it through the invalid's ribs into his lung and heart. Marat cried out in pain and sank back in the tub. He died within a minute or two.

The women rushed into the room, but Charlotte raced past them, heading for a door. Another visitor, Laurent Bas, one of the distributors of the *Ami du Peuple,* seized her before she could escape. One of the women, screaming in rage and grief, repeatedly struck Corday with her fists, and only the arrival of the police spared her from immediate death. Perhaps, Charlotte had meant to save her life after all, or, possibly, she sought martyrdom in the more public arena of the streets. In any event, she was roughly searched, and her testimony was found pinned to her clothes. Amid the commotion and recriminations, deputies from the Convention reached the Rue des Cordeliers to question her on behalf of the Committee of Public Safety. Stoically, she insisted that she had acted alone and refused to implicate the Girondins. All she asked was that she not be tortured before her inevitable ride to the scaffold.

As the shocking news of the murder spread across the city, thousands of indignant citizens took to the streets. Corday was taken by cab, under great security, to the Abbaye prison, but the poor, who adored Marat, surrounded the coach and cursed her and shrieked for her head. Only narrowly did the police keep her alive on the journey. Ironically, even as she was arrested, the Girondin rebellion, hatched at Caen, was being easily broken by Jacobin forces.

At the Abbaye, awaiting her trial, Corday was allowed to write and composed a letter to Barbaroux explaining her deed and, in a letter to the Committee of Public Safety, complained of the close guard attending her and her lack of privacy. Naturally, the letter never reached Barbaroux, but it is likely that Charlotte knew that would be the case and was consciously preparing her own eulogy. Poor Barbaroux, the handsome young Marseillaise. After the rebellion failed, he fled the encircling Jacobin forces but, close to capture in an open field, shot himself. Still alive, he was dragged away to be guillotined before he could die.

Charlotte Corday stayed only briefly at the Abbaye. Soon she was taken to the Conciergerie, the prison where political suspects were held to await trial before the Revolutionary Tribunal. To complement the record, the Committee of Public Safety sent an artist, Hauer, to sketch her, and the sketch would later be a full painting. She appears calm, even somewhat smug, in the final painting. If she betrayed any fear, much less remorse, the artist has not shown it to posterity. In her cell, she also wrote a last letter to her father, apologizing for not consulting with him concerning the use she had made of her life.

On July 17, Corday was escorted to the Revolutionary Tribunal. She asked for an old acquaintance, a certain Doulcet, as her counsel. He did not know of her arrest, however, and, meanwhile, the court appointed Chaveau de la Garde, a Jacobin, to defend her. Simonne Evrard was the first to give evidence, and she repeated the details of the crime. Asked by the prosecutor, Fouquier-Tinville, why she had killed Marat, Corday shouted that she was punishing his crimes. She denied she had rehearsed the act, saying only that she had intended to kill the writer at the Convention and to die at the hands of the mob. Did she suppose that in killing Marat, she had destroyed all who shared his views? She answered that in taking his life she would save France and the lives of thousands. Her defender could only suggest that fanaticism had driven the young woman to the desperate circumstances in which she now found herself. About noon, the tribunal found her guilty of premeditated murder and sentenced her to death on the guillotine.

At mid-afternoon, the public executioner, Sanson, appeared at Charlotte's cell with his assistants. They cut her hair far up the back of her neck, dressed her in a red shirt to symbolize her role as a murderer, tied her hands, and took her to a tumbrel, an open cart, for the ride across the city to the Place de la Revolution where the guillotine awaited her. She refused the ministrations of a priest, believing she had no sin to confess.

Night was coming on when Corday was brought to the scaffold. A huge throng turned out for the execution, and along the entire route she was cursed and condemned by the angry Parisians. Ignoring them, she conversed quietly with the man who would soon decapitate her. Told it was a considerable distance to the Place de la Revolution, she replied that they would, even so, surely get there. A brief rainstorm passed over the city, but the sky cleared when the cart stopped at the scaffold. Briefly, she hesitated; then she climbed the steps. Her shawl was removed, she was placed on the board, and the board was slid into place. Her head rested in the slot, and the blade fell. One of Sanson's assistants seized the severed head and slapped the pale face. Later, some claimed that the dead cheeks blushed.

Charlotte Corday achieved her goal. She killed Marat, the man she regarded as a monster who had betrayed the Revolution. Yet it is clear that her higher purpose, the ending of Jacobin control and the success of the Girondin cause was not accomplished. Indeed, the death of Marat intensified the suspicions of the Commune and the Jacobin Convention and ushered in an even bloodier phase of the political terror that did not end for another year. In the mean-

time, thousands died, including most of the Girondin leaders she had intended to redeem France. Sadly, one of the condemned Girondins exclaimed that Corday had "destroyed us, but she has taught us how to die." And, in fact, Charlotte Corday had never really known what to do but to kill her nemesis and then die. Her courage cannot be disputed, and her will to justice must impress any modern observer. Yet, as in many another attempt to alter the forces of history by wielding the assassin's weapon, Corday's attack actually strengthened the hand of her enemies. Her crime, undoubtedly a political one, was no less and no more a crime than the judicial murders perpetrated by her enemies at the tribunals of the Revolution. But her undertaking, like the greater drama of which it was a part, the Revolution itself, raises a fundamental question: can any society be positively changed in any permanent way by the use of willful violence against other human beings?

SOURCES:

Cher, Marie. *Charlotte Corday and Certain Men of the Revolutionary Torment.* NY: D. Appleton, 1929.

Sokolnikova, Galina Osipovna. *Nine Women Drawn from the Epoch of the French Revolution.* Translated by H.C. Stevens. NY: Books for Libraries Press, 1932, reprinted 1969, pp. 35–63.

Whitham, J. Mills. *Men and Women of the French Revolution.* NY: Books for Libraries Press, 1933, reprinted 1968, pp. 152–184.

SUGGESTED READING:

Gottschalk, Louis R., and Jean Paul Marat. *A Study in Radicalism.* Greenberg, 1927.

C. David Rice, Professor of History, Central Missouri State University, Warrensburg, Missouri

Cordière, La Belle (c. 1523–1566).

See Labé, Louise.

Corelli, Marie (1855–1924)

English novelist, one of the most popular in late-19th-century England. Name variations: Mary MacKay or Mackay; Minnie Mackay. Born Mary Mills in Bayswater, London, England, in 1855; died of heart disease in Stratford-upon-Avon, England, on April 21, 1924; daughter of Charles Mackay (1814–1889, a poet and journalist) and Mary Ellen Mills; lived with Bertha Vyver (who later wrote Corelli's memoirs) in Stratford-upon-Avon.

For years, Marie Corelli maintained that she was the daughter of an Italian father and Scottish mother but was adopted in infancy by Charles Mackay, a poet and journalist. In actuality, Corelli was the daughter of Mackay and **Mary Ellen Mills**, a servant who became his sec-

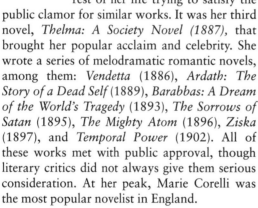

Marie
Corelli

ond wife in 1859. The family moved to Fern Dell, near Box Hill, Surrey, where Corelli was encouraged to pursue music by her neighbor George Meredith. The name Corelli was chosen as appropriate for a musical career.

But in 1886, Mary Mackay under the name Marie Corelli published *A Romance of Two Worlds*, a clever, well-written narrative concerning a psychic experience connecting the Christian Deity with a world force in the form of electricity. The book had an immediate impact and large sale, and Corelli devoted the rest of her life trying to satisfy the public clamor for similar works. It was her third novel, *Thelma: A Society Novel (1887)*, that brought her popular acclaim and celebrity. She wrote a series of melodramatic romantic novels, among them: *Vendetta* (1886), *Ardath: The Story of a Dead Self* (1889), *Barabbas: A Dream of the World's Tragedy* (1893), *The Sorrows of Satan* (1895), *The Mighty Atom* (1896), *Ziska* (1897), and *Temporal Power* (1902). All of these works met with public approval, though literary critics did not always give them serious consideration. At her peak, Marie Corelli was the most popular novelist in England.

SUGGESTED READING:

Bigland, E. *Marie Corelli.* 1953.

Masters, Brian. *Now Barabbas was a Rotter: The Extraordinary Life of Marie Corelli.* 1978.

Scott, W.S. *Marie Corelli.* 1955

Vyver, Bertha. *Memoirs of Marie Corelli.* 1930.

Corey, Martha (d. 1692).

See Witchcraft Trials in Salem Village.

Cori, Gerty T. (1896–1957)

American physician and biochemist, known for her research on the metabolism of carbohydrates in animals, who was co-recipient of the Nobel Prize for medicine in 1947 for discovering the process by which glycogen is converted to sugar. Pronunciation: KOR-ee. Born Gerta Theresa Radnitz on August 15, 1896, in Prague, Austro-Hungarian Empire (now Czech Republic); died in St. Louis, Missouri, on October 26, 1957; daughter of Otto Radnitz (a chemist and businessman) and Martha (Neustadt) Radnitz; Realgymnasium of Tetschen, 1914; German University of Prague Medical School, M.D., 1920. married Carl Ferdinand Cori, on August 5, 1920; children: Carl Thomas Cori, 1936.

Was a student assistant at German University of Prague (1917–19); worked as assistant at the Children's Hospital of Vienna (1920–22); was assistant pathologist (1922–25) and assistant of biochemistry (1925–31) at the New York State Institute for the Study of Malignant Diseases; was assistant professor, University of Buffalo (1930–31) and Washington University School of Medicine, St. Louis; worked as a research associate in pharmacology (1931–43); was an associate professor of biochemistry (1943), and full professor (1947).

In 1947, Gerty Cori and her husband Carl were awarded the Nobel Prize for discovering the enzymes that convert glycogen into glucose and then back again into glycogen. They shared the award with Bernardo Houssay who was honored for his work with pituitary hormones. Gerty Cori was the first woman from America and the third woman worldwide to earn the Nobel Prize. It was common knowledge within the American scientific community that the Coris worked as a closely knit team and considered each other as equal partners; the pair studied together, shared a laboratory, worked on the same projects, and co-published numerous scientific papers. Gerty was known as the lab genius, while Carl was the visionary. "Our efforts have been largely complementary," said Carl, as he thanked the Nobel committee, "and one without the other would not have gone as far as in combination."

Their discovery was considered to be one of the most brilliant and important contributions to modern biochemistry, yet throughout her career Gerty was often assumed to be Carl's assistant and was employed in lesser positions than her husband. Even after she received the Nobel Prize, some prominent scientific organizations, including the American Chemical Society (ACS), honored Carl but not Gerty, though in 1948 the ACS did award Gerty the Garvan Medal, the society's prize to an outstanding woman chemist. She was also honored with other prizes and awards, received several honorary degrees, and belonged to several professional groups. In addition, President Harry Truman appointed her to the board of directors of the National Science Foundation, and she was posthumously inducted into the National Women's Hall of Fame in 1998.

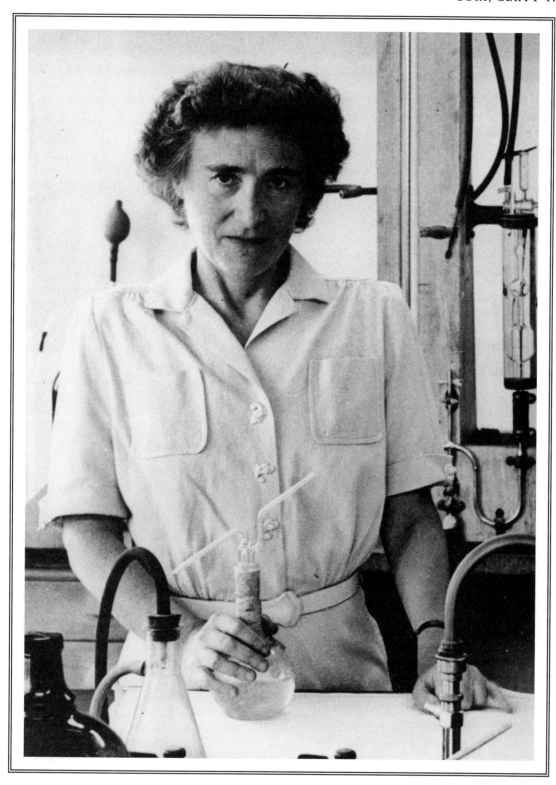

Gerty
T. Cori

Tragically, just as Gerty's many years of research were finally recognized in the form of the prestigious Nobel Prize, she was diagnosed with a fatal form of anemia. For the remaining years of her life, she maintained her relentless style of research and devoted herself to studying glycogen storage diseases in children. During this time, she identified four different diseases and essentially generated the field of genetic diseases, a major scientific achievement that was described by Herman Kalckar as "unmatched."

Gerty Theresa Cori was born on August 15, 1896, in Prague, which at the time belonged to the Austro-Hungarian Empire. Raised in a moderately wealthy Jewish family, she was the eldest of three daughters born to Otto and **Martha Neustadt Radnitz**. When Gerty was a child, girls from her social class were expected to learn the social graces and enough cultural trivia to carry on an informed conversation. Gerty had private tutors for her primary education and then went to a Lyceum for girls for high school. Her uncle, who was a professor of pediatrics, encouraged Gerty to obtain the necessary education to attend medical school. At that time, girls' schools did not offer the courses required to enter the university, such as Latin, mathematics, chemistry, and physics. Gerty solved that problem by studying these subjects on her own, with the aid of a teacher whom she had met while on vacation with her family. By 1914, when she was 18 years old, she passed the medical school entrance exam.

Art and science are the glories of the human mind. I see no conflict between them.

—**Gerty Cori**

Although Gerty was primarily interested in medical research, it was customary to obtain the training of a medical doctor, and she subsequently enrolled in the medical school at the German University of Prague. There, she met Carl Cori, who was also a medical student, but Carl's education, and his relationship with Gerty, was interrupted by the First World War when he was drafted into the Sanitation Corps of the Austrian army. Upon his return, the couple resumed their courtship and both graduated from medical school. They married in 1920 against the wishes of Carl's family. The senior Coris felt that their son's career would be jeopardized by his marrying a Jew, even though Gerty converted to Catholicism so that their wedding could take place in the Roman Catholic Church.

At this time, Eastern Europe was in the midst of hardship: the political situation was unstable, starvation was rampant, and anti-Semitism on the rise. Medical research was given low-priority, but medical doctors were in high demand, so Gerty worked as a physician at the Karolinen Children's Hospital in Vienna, where she also researched and published several papers on cretinism (congenital thyroid deficiency). Carl secured employment at the University of Graz, where, in order to get the job, he had to prove that he was not Jewish. Life, for the Coris,

was not easy: they lived in two different cities, and Gerty, who was basically working for meals, wanted to be involved with medical research. In addition, the political climate was volatile, with anti-Semitism continually escalating. Consequently, the Coris decided to leave Europe. Carl took a position with the Institute for the Study of Malignant Diseases in Buffalo, New York. Gerty remained behind for six months until Carl secured a position for her at the Institute as assistant pathologist.

For the next several years, the Coris established themselves within the medical research community and became American citizens. Although they had well-equipped laboratories and the freedom to collaborate, pursue, and publish their own research, Gerty struggled against a single-minded director. Because he believed that parasites were the causative agent of cancer, Gerty spent fruitless hours searching for parasites in the stool of cancer patients until she refused to look any longer. Angry that she failed to support his etiological theories, the director threatened to fire her and warned her to stay out of her husband's laboratory. Gerty complied for a short time and was soon back collaborating with Carl. Carl, too, received pressure not to work with Gerty. At a job interview, he was told that it was "un-American for a man to work with his wife." Likewise, the same university called Gerty in for an interview and told her that she was "standing in the way" of her husband's career. Fortunately, neither wife nor husband accepted these attitudes, and they continued to conduct their investigations as research partners.

During their years in Buffalo, the Coris became interested in glycogen and glucose synthesis, and, by the late 1920s, they were able to explain the cycle by which, upon physiological demand, glycogen in the muscles is converted to glucose. The muscles use most of the glucose as a source of energy and what is not used is left in the muscles in the form of lactic acid. The body then recycles the lactic acid by way of the liver, which converts the lactic acid into blood glucose for return to the muscle where it is changed back into glycogen. This important discovery became known as the "Cori cycle." Later in their careers, the Coris discovered the specific enzymes that were responsible for the glycogen/glucose conversions, the hormones that affect the enzymes, and diseases that can be caused by an alteration of the enzymes.

The Coris' research did not fully belong in an institute that was specifically devoted to cancer research, so the couple searched for other positions, at a time when women scientists were anything but highly regarded. In addition, many institutions had strict nepotism rules, although husband and wife research teams were not uncommon; typically, the husband would be hired as a tenured professor, while the wife would assume the post of an assistant or low-level instructor. A woman's job was safe as long as her relationship with the tenured male endured. Carl was fully aware of the prevailing sexist conditions and, in 1931, managed to find employment at the Washington University School of Medicine in St. Louis, which had already hired several female scientists. Carl was director of the pharmacology department, and Gerty was hired as a research associate.

Gerty was known for her precise methods in the laboratory and demanded perfection from herself as well as those around her. The Coris worked six days a week, but during the evenings and on weekends they entertained a great deal and managed to avoid talking about their research. The work that had been accomplished in Buffalo served as the groundwork for her discoveries in St. Louis. The Coris had already demonstrated the glycogen-glucose cycle but aspired to study each step of the cycle on a molecular level. To do so, Gerty and Carl extracted soluble components from frog muscle and analyzed them. In 1936, they isolated a new glucose compound called glucose-1-phosphate from the frog muscle tissue; this new compound became known as the Cori ester. That same year, Gerty gave birth to their only child, Thomas Carl Cori. She worked until it was time for her to be admitted to the maternity hospital and returned to work in her laboratory three days postpartum.

A few years later, the Coris shifted their focus to studying enzymes. At that time, it was known that enzymes control chemical reactions, but very few enzymes had been identified. According to Cori's biographer, Joseph Larner, it was Gerty who provided the decisive influence to study enzymes and was the major contributor to most of the Coris' papers during 1938 and 1939. In 1939, the Coris discovered the enzyme phosphorylase, which breaks down glycogen into the Cori ester. This discovery led to the enzymatic synthesis of glycogen in a test tube, which was the first bioengineering of a large molecule in a test tube, an event of great import because it disproved the thought that large molecules could only be made in living cells. The Coris isolated several enzymes and studied the correlation between the structure and function of a specific enzyme to its ability to start or stop

a chemical reaction. The Coris were among a small group of scientists whose research proved how many biological and medical phenomena were a result of a biochemical imbalance and whose findings served as a basis for modern molecular biology.

World War II drastically altered the American workplace as women filled men's jobs. Carl's work shifted toward defense projects while Gerty was left to run the lab on her own. Women scientists were in high demand; as a result, many were finally given positions that matched their credentials. In 1944, Gerty was made associate professor and given tenure at Washington University. As the war was ending, both Gerty and Carl were offered professorships at Harvard University and at the Rockefeller Institute in New York City, but Washington University offered Gerty a professorship while Carl was made chair of a new and enlarged biochemistry department. By the late 1940s, the Coris' lab, a hub of activity, was considered to be the center for enzyme research. While Gerty ran the labs, Carl primarily wrote and supervised the younger researchers. Gerty was kind, caring, intense, and explosive. In addition to reading all the newest scientific discoveries, she also read five to seven books a week on a wide range of subject matter, from art to zoology. She could converse knowledgeably about anything, from literature, art, shopping, and child rearing to the structure of a molecule. Carl spoke five languages, played the cello, and wrote poetry.

The Cori lab was known for its nondiscriminatory practices and hired many Jews and women. Gerty focused only on an individual's intellectual integrity, ignoring gender or religion. She encouraged women scientists and provided extra support to those who had children. Outspoken, she was an activist who was very sensitive to women's issues. Generally, in an attempt to appear as serious as their male counterparts, women working in the scientific community usually dressed the part. Gerty and her female coworkers characteristically dressed in dowdy suits. Once in jest, Gerty's co-workers staged a competition for the worst dressed: Gerty won unanimously.

In 1947, Gerty was diagnosed with an unknown form of fatal anemia. It is postulated that the cause was due to the excessive exposure to x-rays that she received during her early years in Buffalo when she was studying the effects of x-radiation on the skin and on the metabolism of certain body organs. The Coris traveled the world in search of a treatment for her anemia, and she tried many curative therapies, a number of which had damaging side effects. She became dependent on blood transfusions which, because the transfusion was composed of whole blood, caused her body to produce antibodies that made Gerty feel very sick. At one point, she had her spleen removed, which probably prolonged her working years. Sometimes Carl had to carry her around her lab.

Gerty lived for ten years following her diagnosis. In public, she ignored her illness and rarely spoke of it, although she once confided to her friend, **Mildred Cohn**, "If something like this happens to you, it would be better if a ton of bricks fell on you." During her last days, she was forced to stay in bed. She became frustrated and sad, but she still read voraciously. When she could no longer read anything "serious," she switched to mysteries.

Gerty Cori died at the age of 61 on October 26, 1957. Her funeral was attended by scientists from all over the world. A string quartet played Beethoven and a television excerpt from Gerty's appearance on "This I Believe" was shown: "Honesty, which stands mostly for intellectual integrity, courage, and kindness are still the virtues I admire," she had told her interviewer, newscaster Edward R. Murrow, "though with advancing years the emphasis has been slightly shifted and kindness now seems more important to me than in my youth. The love for and dedication to one's work seems to me to be the basis for happiness. For a research worker, the unforgotten moments of his life are those rare ones, which come after years of plodding work, when the veil over nature's secret seems suddenly to lift and when what was dark and chaotic appears in a clear and beautiful light and pattern."

SOURCES:

Joseph, Bea, and Charlotte Warren Squires, eds. *Current Biography.* NY: H.W. Wilson, 1947.

Kass-Simon, G., and Patricia Farnes, eds. *Women of Science: Righting the Record.* Indiana University Press, 1990.

McGrayne, Sharon Bertsch. *Nobel Prize Women in Science.* Birch Lane Press, 1993.

Singer, Charles, and E. Ashworth Underwood. *A Short History of Medicine.* 2nd ed. NY: Oxford University Press, 1962.

SUGGESTED READING:

Ochoa, S., and H. Kalckar. "Gerty T. Cori, Biochemist," in *Science.* Vol. 128, 1958, pp. 16–17.

Christine Miner Minderovic,
B.S., freelance writer, Ann Arbor, Michigan

Corinna (fl. 5th or 3rd c. BCE)

Ancient Greek poet of Boeotia who is said to have been the teacher of the lyric poet Pindar and to have defeated him in competition. Name variations: Korinna; nicknamed Myia, "Fly." Pronunciation: KOR-inna. Born in either the 5th or the 3rd century BCE in Tanagra or Thebes in Boeotia; daughter of Acheloodorus and Procatia; pupil of Myrtis(?), another female poet of Boeotia. Almost all details of Corinna's career and dates are doubtful or disputed.

Verse: in antiquity, five books of her poetry, perhaps called weroia, "Tales" or "Narratives" on mythical subjects were collected. Only fragments remain, three of which are fairly large and continuous. These are collected (with a translation) in Greek Lyric IV: Bacchylides, Corinna, and Others, *Loeb Classical Library, ed. and trans. D.A. Campbell (Cambridge: Harvard University Press, 1992).*

Our appreciation of female poets in antiquity is hampered by the scant remnants of their work. One of the most intriguing aspects of the Boeotian poet Corinna is the disparity between the ancient testimonials that describe a grand career in her lifetime and an extant corpus that bears surprisingly little relation to the literary tradition in which she stands. Her fragments manifest such an atypical poetic voice, in fact, that scholars are still debating—with no decisive arguments on either side—whether to place her as an older contemporary of Pindar in the 5th century BCE or some 200 years later in the 3rd century.

The various ancient accounts of her life and activities all date to 50 BCE or later; most of these, though fantastic and amusing, are less than factually reliable. Her relationship with Pindar of Thebes (518–438 BCE), the greatest lyric poet of Greece, is the grounds for the most tantalizing and frustrating evidence about her career. The Greeks celebrated many of their athletic and religious festivals with competitive choral presentations of lyric poetry on mythical themes. Several testimonials state that Corinna defeated Pindar in competition at Thebes as many as five times. The accuracy of this assertion is impossible to verify, but the story of Pindar's sour grapes, which tells of his revenge by calling Corinna a "sow," has been shown by C.M. Bowra to be based on late misreading of Pindar's notoriously difficult verse. The notion that the two poets were acquainted in some way has always been attractive. A humorous passage of Plutarch, for example, describes an elder Corinna's criticism of a young Pindar's work: apparently he preferred bombastic ornament to well-told myth, the true substance of poetry. This story is probably at the root of the popular (and apparently post-classical) supposition that Corinna was actually Pindar's teacher. Whatever their actual connection, it should be noted that when Corinna herself names Pindar in a couple of brief fragments, she shows clear admiration for him.

The debate over Corinna's dates revolves around an issue internal to the texts themselves. Her poems are written in a Boeotian dialect, but the texts we possess use a system of spelling that dates to within 25 years before or after 200 BCE. Those scholars who like to preserve the spirit of the ancient testimonials claim that what we have are late transcriptions of Corinna's original compositions in 5th-century orthography; those who reject the ancient consensus claim that she actually wrote in the Hellenistic era. Even if it is impossible to decide how her dialect is relevant to dating, it does say a good deal about the idiosyncrasies of her work. In addition to using a dialect that is not often found in other authors in this genre, Corinna seems to preoccupy herself almost exclusively with Boeotian myth and myth variants. This fact, coupled with her limpid, uncomplicated narrative style and simple, though not naive, meters, has led some to speculate on the correctness of seeing her work as choral lyric at all. Scholars West and Kirkwood have suggested that it might have been composed to serve the cause of regional patriotism.

Of the three best preserved fragments of her poetry, the first tells of a singing competition between the personified Boeotian mountains Helicon and Cithaeron. Judged by the gods in a secret ballot, Cithaeron's song about the concealment of the infant Zeus from Cronus wins the day. The last readable lines of this fragment (some 17 connected lines) has the defeated Helicon ripping rock from himself and hurling it to the ground. The second continuous fragment (about 40 complete lines) narrates the prophecies of a certain Acraephen to the river-god Asopus concerning the marriages of his nine daughters to Zeus, Poseidon, Apollo, and Hermes. The third discernible nugget of text (about 20 lines) appears to be autobiographical in nature; it begins, "Terpsichore [a muse] bids me sing my lovely tales to the women of Tanagra gowned in white, and the city takes great delight in my clear-chattering voice." The fragment continues with a list of some of the stories that the poet has told in the past.

Though reference to Tanagrian women (and further on, "maidens") in the quoted fragment suggests a context of choral performance, it is very difficult to place Corinna in the wider context of Greek literature at either of the time periods proposed for her. There is no doubt that she gained a fair degree of renown in antiquity: she was a late addition to the canonical list of nine Greek lyricists and was popular enough throughout the classical world to receive the unequivocal praise of the Latin poets Propertius and Statius. It is also probable that Ovid named the central female figure of his *Amores* after her. Yet Corinna's individualistic subject matter and style make it difficult either to pinpoint definite precursors to her work or to identify later authors who show her influence. In this she differs markedly from *Sappho, the most famous Greek woman poet, who not only defined the genre of love lyric for the rest of antiquity but also manifested a distinctive feminine voice. Corinna tells us little about the place of a woman poet in society, with the exception of one rather disheartening fragment on *Myrtis, a 5th-century BCE poet dubiously said to have been Corinna's teacher: "I reproach also clear-voiced Myrtis, because, a woman, she went into competition with Pindar." This fragment goes against the grain of those ancient accounts of Corinna's own competition with Pindar.

> *A*re you forever asleep? You were not drowsy in the past, Corinna.
>
> —Corinna

The fact that we have so few reliable materials for placing Corinna is grounds enough for calling her one of the greatest enigmas of ancient Greek literature; the fact that she is a rare female name in a genre and epoch dominated by men only increases the mystery. Barring the possibility of the discovery of more papyrus fragments of her works, it seems likely that Corinna and her "Tales" will remain an open book.

SOURCES:

Bowra, C.M. *Pindar*. Oxford: Clarendon Press, 1964.

Campbell, D.A., ed. and trans. *Greek Lyric IV: Bacchylides, Corinna, and Others*. Cambridge, MA: Harvard University Press, 1992.

Clayman, Dee Lesser. "The Meaning of Corinna's Weroia," in *Classical Quarterly*. n.s. 28, 1978, pp. 396–397.

Kirkwood, G.M. *Early Greek Monody: The History of a Poetic Type*. Ithaca, NY: Cornell University Press, 1974.

Lefkowitz, Mary R., and Maureen B. Fant. *Women's Life in Greece and Rome: A source book in translation*. 2nd. ed. Baltimore, MD: Johns Hopkins University Press, 1992.

Segal, Charles. "Choral lyric in the fifth century," in *The Cambridge History of Classical Literature*, vol. 1.1: *Early Greek Poetry*. Edited by P.E. Easterling and B.M.W. Knox. Cambridge: Cambridge University Press, 1989.

Caterina Cornaro

COLLECTIONS:

Campbell, David A. *Greek Lyric Poetry.* 2nd. ed. Bristol: Bristol Classical Press, 1982.

———, ed. and trans. *Greek Lyric IV: Bacchylides, Corinna, and Others.* Cambridge, MA: Harvard University Press, 1992.

Page, D.L. *Poetae Melici Graeci.* Oxford: Clarendon Press, 1962.

SUGGESTED READING:

Lattimore, Richmond, trans. *Greek Lyrics.* 2nd. ed. Chicago, IL: University of Chicago Press, 1960.

RELATED MEDIA:

Portraits of Corinna in H. von Heintze, *Das Bildnis der Sappho* (Mainz, 1966), plates 11–15.

Peter O'Brien, Department of Classical Studies, Boston University

Cork, countess of.

See Monckton, Mary (1746–1840).

Cornaro, Caterina (1454–1510)

Queen of Cyprus. Name variations: Catherine Cornaro. Born in 1454 in Venice; died on July 5, 1510, in Asolo, Italy; married James II the Bastard, king of Cyprus (r. 1460–1473), in 1472; children: James III (b. 1472), king of Cyprus (r. 1473–1474).

Caterina Cornaro came from the powerful Cornaro family of Venice, which held large estates in Italy. As was the custom of her age, she was educated in the liberal arts and languages at a school for noble girls run by Benedictine nuns. When she was 14, a marriage was arranged between Caterina and the king of Cyprus, James II. Four years later, when she had finished her schooling, she moved to Cyprus; her married life ended a few months later when James died suddenly in 1473. The widowed queen gave birth to a son James III of Cyprus some months after her husband's death.

The birth of James III began a power struggle between queen Caterina and the Cyprian nobility, each of whom wanted to control the regency of the infant. After two years of war, Caterina was restored to the throne with the aid of her native Venice; however, the small boy for whom she had struggled died soon afterwards of malaria. Caterina retained her position as sole ruler of the island for 14 more years, but she increasingly found herself merely a puppet of the Venetian government. In 1488, she was forced to abdicate and deed the island of Cyprus to Venice. Caterina returned to Italy and took up residence on her fief of Asolo, where she established a brilliant court, patronizing Italian artists, humanist scholars, and writers whose lives were described by the Italian scholar Pietro Bembo in his dialogue *Gli Asolani* (1505). She also became known as a founder of hospitals and a generous benefactor to charities. Caterina Cornaro died at age 56.

Laura York,
Riverside, California

Cornaro Piscopia, Elena Lucretia (1646–1684)

Italian philosopher and writer. Name variations: Helena. Born Elena Lucretia Cornaro Piscopia in 1646; daughter of John Baptist Cornaro Piscopia (procurator of St. Mark's); Ph.D., University of Padua, 1678; first woman to receive a doctorate in Philosophy.

The intellectual capabilities of Elena Lucretia Cornaro Piscopia were recognized early on by her father, John Baptist, who sought out the best tutors for her. Carlo Rinalin, the first professor in philosophy at the University of Padua, taught her philosophy, and from Fr. Hippolytus Marchetti she learned theology. Though Cornaro Piscopia became fluent in Spanish, Latin and Greek, as well as her native Italian, the academic drive was not hers, but her father's. Her scholarly work seems to have been motivated more by the prestige it would bring to her family—women intellectuals being almost unheard of—than from a passion for philosophy or from personal ambition.

On June 25, 1678, at age 32, she became the first woman to receive a doctorate in philosophy. (The University of Padua did not award a doctorate to another woman for 70 years.) Given a choice of philosophers on which to be examined, she had chosen Aristotle. Cornaro Piscopia presented philosophical positions in reflection of two passages from Aristotle's work (probably the *Posterior Analytics* and the *Physics*) and almost fainted during the proceedings.

Despite the great admiration others had for her philosophical capabilities, she published no works. She had become a Benedictine oblate at a very young age, but never a full nun, wearing her habit underneath her fine clothing. Her vows of humility made it difficult for her to accept the many honorary awards that were offered to her in the scant six years before she died in her late 30s.

Catherine Hundleby, M.A. Philosophy,
University of Guelph, Guelph, Ontario, Canada

Cornelia (c. 195–c. 115 BCE)

Roman wife of Tiberius Sempronius Gracchus (one of the most powerful Romans of his generation), mother of the Gracchi (whose careers sparked the revolution that overthrew the Roman Republic), and one of the most influential political and cultural figures of her day. Name variations: Cornelia Sempronii. Pronunciation: Cor-NEE-lia. Born around 195 BCE; died around 115 BCE; second daughter of Publius Cornelius Scipio Africanus (the Roman victor over Hannibal in the Second Punic War) and Aemilia; married Tiberius Sempronius Gracchus, around 175 (died 154 BCE); children: 12, though only Sempronia, Tiberius Gracchus, the younger, and Gaius Gracchus, survived to adulthood.

Cornelia was the product of a marriage linking the Cornelii (through her father) and the Aemilii (through her mother), two of Rome's most established patrician families in the generations before her birth. Cornelia's family on both sides constituted a virtual who's who of prominent Roman politicians and generals in the period of the middle Republic. Some of these had patriotically sacrificed their lives; others were among the greatest war-heroes Rome had ever produced. Cornelia's father, Publius Cornelius Scipio, who, after his victory over Carthage in the Second Punic War, was awarded the honorific name "Africanus," was the greatest of them all, but her family's service to Rome was not limited to the charismatic conqueror of Hannibal. To name only the most prominent of the others: Cornelia's paternal grandfather and great uncle had both died fighting Carthage in Spain, and her maternal grandfather, as one of Rome's two serving consuls, had been slaughtered with sword in hand, along with tens of thousands of others, fighting Hannibal at Cannae in the greatest military defeat any Roman army would ever experience.

At the time of Cornelia's birth, Scipio Africanus was enjoying the height of his popularity and political influence—an influence that left, as its greatest legacies, the transformation of the Roman army from a militia into a semi-professional force and imperial expansion throughout the Mediterranean basin. Nevertheless, no republic can long function under the dominance of only one man or faction. While Rome's influence was spreading as a result of its victory over Carthage in the Second Punic War (218–201), there arose an increasing concern that foreign ways would undermine the traditional institutions and morality that had been credited with Rome's success. Conservative, perhaps even reactionary, anxieties began to influence the electorate. These were successfully tapped by Scipio's political arch-enemy, Marcus Porcius Cato, often referred to as the "Elder" or "Censor," to distinguish him from his equally famous great-grandson. Cato made a virtue of "Romaness" by attacking everything foreign. In addition to ending every one of his speeches with the exhortation "but first . . . Carthage *must* be destroyed!," Cato, though well versed in Greek himself, attacked everything Hellenic as degenerate and socially dangerous. Over time, Cato's fulminations had an effect upon Scipio's popularity, for there

was no greater philhellene in Rome than Scipio. Scipio was a devotee of Greek literature and art, surrounding himself with as many hellenic manuscripts and intellectuals as possible. When serving Rome in regions heavily populated by Greeks, such as Sicily and the East, he was even famous for "going native" by adopting Greek dress and customs. In addition to the fears such habits engendered, Scipio's infamous love of extravagant living, and an almost unprecedented 20-year-long political ascendancy that fed his arrogance, undermined his popularity at home. By the 180s, he and his brother, Lucius, came under increasing attack and ultimately under indictment for alleged abuses of power and the misuse of public funds. Although neither Scipio was convicted, the influence of Cornelia's father was broken. He withdrew from Rome and politics to die at Liternum a bitter man in 184.

Cornelia's mother ◀❧ **Aemilia** had at least four children—two sons and two daughters—who lived to adulthood. Although we know little about Aemilia, she appears to have shared her husband's interests in Greek culture and high living. At least, she appears to have been no miser, for she was famous for the rich, religious rituals she underwrote and for the expensive attire she donned, even during the bleakest hours of the Second Punic War when such dress was considered inappropriate. As far as her sons were concerned, neither ever approached Scipio's stature. The older, Publius, was denied a political career by ill-health and is most famous for the adoption of Scipio Aemilianus. The younger, Lucius, began a political career, reaching the praetorship in 174, but for unknown reasons fell afoul of powerful interests and never attained Rome's highest magistracy. Of Aemilia's daughters, we know only of the youngest Cornelia, who married Tiberius Sempronius Gracchus (c. 175), after her brothers negotiated a political alliance between their interests and his.

This match surprised many, both because the Sempronii and the Cornelii had long been at political odds, and because Tiberius had previously attacked some of the policies of Cornelia's father. Apparently, however, his had been more a principled protest of specific policies than an out and out attack, for as a tribune in 184 Tiberius twice vetoed actually bringing Scipio to trial on trumped up charges. Cornelia's husband was of a plebeian, but noble, family. Tiberius' grandfather had attained the consulship in 238. Tiberius himself would become one of the greatest figures of his generation, reaching the consulship twice, in 177 and 163, and also serving as censor in

❧▶ **Aemilia** (fl. 195 BCE)

*Roman patrician. Flourished in 195 BCE; daughter of Lucius Aemilius Paullus (consul in 219 and 216 BCE); sister of Lucius Aemilius Paullus (consul in 182 and 168 BCE); married Publius Cornelius Scipio Africanus (the Roman victor over Hannibal in the Second Punic War); children: two sons and two daughters who lived to adulthood, including Publius (who adopted Scipio Aemilianus); Lucius (praetor in 174); and *Cornelia (c. 195–c. 115 BCE).*

Aemilia had four brothers. Her father Aemilius Paullus allowed two of them to be adopted by sonless friends to keep alive their family name. Ironically, the two brothers who were not adopted died before their father. Thus, legally, Aemilia's family died out when her father expired.

169. In addition, he triumphed twice for military conquests in Spain and Sardinia, and was elected as an augur, an important religious office with political implications. Undoubtedly, therefore, as Cornelia's brothers saw their political fortunes waning, they sought to hitch their futures to that of a rising "star." Although it is clear that at one level this was a thoroughly political union, it is equally clear that Tiberius and Cornelia came to love one another deeply. They jointly produced 12 children, though only three survived childhood, and immersed them in phil-

> ❧▸ **Sempronia** (c. 168 BCE–?)
>
> *Roman noblewoman. Born around 168 BCE; daughter of *Cornelia (c. 195–c. 115 BCE) and Tiberius Sempronius Gracchus; married Scipio Aemilianus, around 155 (died 129 BCE); no children.*

hellenism. Subsequently as a highly sought after widow (Tiberius died in 154), she would refuse all proposals of marriage (one of which even came from a King Ptolemy of Egypt) to remain a *univira* (literally, a "one-man" woman) and thus, faithful to her husband.

Cornelia was the ideal Roman matron, steadfast in upholding the honor of her husband, efficient in running the household, and dedicated to the rearing of her children. Tiberius' and Cornelia's marriage appears to have been idyllic by Roman standards. He tended to the affairs of the state and the family's public interests, while she reigned over the domestic scene, charged with overseeing a substantial establishment composed of children, slaves, and free attendants. That she was well suited to her responsibilities by ability, personality, and education, no one doubted. Cornelia was of strong character, forceful opinion, and she inherited her father's fabled charisma. She was also educated in the arts as well as the practical skills necessary to oversee a sizeable household and to enhance the political ambitions of a Roman Senator. The resulting combination made her the intellectual and emotional, if not legal, equal of any spouse. Her personal advantages, together with the formidable status and reputation of her family, insured Tiberius' devotion to and appreciation of his wife. As a result, Cornelia's and Tiberius' relationship surpassed the formal expectations of a traditional Roman political marriage.

Of Cornelia's relationship with her children, the sources are also clear: they always remained close. Unlike some of her station, Cornelia was personally diligent in the raising of her children. Their upbringing began with a thorough indoctrination in the traditional Roman virtues—piety, patriotism, honesty, self-sacrifice, knowing the value of thrift and dedication, a sense of responsibility, a sense of justice, a sense of proper restraint—and then proceeded to the magnificence of the classical Greek literary canon. No expense was spared to supply them with the best Greek tutors, with well-known intellectuals such as Diophanes of Mitylene and Blossius, the Stoic

philosopher from Cumae, invited into her household for the sake of her children. Rhetoric was especially emphasized so that when each was in a position to make a public mark, it would be an eloquent one, steeped in hellenic humanitas.

❧▸ **Sempronia** was the oldest of Cornelia's offspring to survive childhood, and although no beauty, her status and training garnered a proposal of marriage around 155 from Scipio Aemilianus, perhaps the most eligible bachelor of his day. This union was probably one of the last accomplishments of Cornelia's husband before his death, and, despite whatever emotions were involved, it reeked of politics. By birth, Scipio Aemilianus was the second son of L. Aemilius Paullus, under whom he served when the Romans conquered the Macedonians in the Third Macedonian War in 168. Scipio, however, had already been adopted by Publius Scipio, the sonless son of Aemilia and Scipio Africanus and the brother of Cornelia. In addition, Aemilius Paullus was the brother of Scipio Africanus' wife, Aemilia. Thus, Sempronia married a man who was biologically her mother's uncle's son and legally her cousin. The marriage reinforced links with two established political allies of the Sempronian clan and two families renowned for their staunch support of Roman imperialism and phil-hellenic attitudes. With the death of Tiberius, Scipio Aemilianus became the dominant figure of Cornelius' family circle. Shortly after his marriage to Sempronia, Aemilianus' career sky-rocketed. Serving in Spain in the late 150s, he insured his place in history with an early consulship (147) after which he defeated Carthage in the Third Punic War (146). This was Rome's final conflict with its fiercest rival, for Carthage was thereafter obliterated in order to preclude a fourth clash. A censorship followed for Aemilianus (142), as did a second consulship (134), and another command in Spain (133) where his younger brother-in-law, Tiberius, served under him, and where he was again victorious. Aemilianus' private life, however, withered as his public fortunes blossomed. He and Sempronia did not have children, and over time the two proved incompatible. In fact, when he was murdered in 129, some accused Sempronia—and through her, Cornelia—of complicity. Personal ties aside, however, it was politics that would drive a wedge between Aemilianus and his in-laws.

Tiberius Gracchus the Younger was ten and Gaius Gracchus less than a year old when their father died. Thus, just at the time when a young Roman noble would begin to look to his father for guidance in the rough political arena of the world's greatest city, Tiberius the Younger had no father. Cornelia assumed the duties of a father as well as a mother to her two "jewels," as she referred to her sons, and by all accounts, she did so impeccably. It was said that although both were "well endowed by nature, they were thought to owe their virtues more to education than to nature." Ambitious through and through, Cornelia held up Aemilianus' success as a model for her maturing sons, even reproaching them as they grew older "because the Romans still called her the mother-in-law of Scipio, but not the mother of the Gracchi." When old enough to begin his military service, Tiberius the Younger did so under Aemilianus in Africa against Carthage (146). In 137, as a quaestor in Spain, to which he had been assigned thanks to his father's earlier service in the region, Tiberius the Younger experienced something that would radically affect his future and that of his immediate family.

To understand the significance of Tiberius the Younger's Spanish service, however, we must digress somewhat. Since the end of the Second Punic War in 201, Rome had become an imperial power, conquering lands and adding them as provinces to the Republic. In the process, Rome found it constantly necessary to maintain large armies outside of Italy—armies that both protected Roman interests and stimulated further conquest. These armies were mostly composed of Roman citizens, who legally owed the state military service if they owned a minimum of landed property. Of course, as the distances between Italy and wherever these armies fought increased, it became necessary to keep the soldiers under arms for longer and longer periods, thus preventing the men who constituted Rome's draftable population away from their small, family farms for increasingly extended periods. This, in turn, made it more and more difficult for the farms of the absentee legionnaires to maintain their profitability. Over time, unable to maintain a traditional lifestyle, tens of thousands of these farmers sold off their ancestral lands and their families moved into rapidly growing cities, especially Rome. Unfortunately, with no industrial base in the modern sense, there were few jobs in the cities. So, when whatever profits from the sale of these farms had been spent, these Romans became destitute and absolutely reliant on rich patrons and/or the state for survival.

To this festering social dislocation other factors contributed. For one thing, Hannibal's presence in Italy for 16 years during the Second Punic War had already damaged extensive areas of the Italian countryside, again worsening the plight of the small farmer. For another, with Rome's military successes against Carthage, in Spain, in Sardinia, Corsica, and Sicily, in the Balkans, and in Anatolia came extensive financial profits, which rolled into Italy in the form of booty, and continued to be imported through increasing revenues reaped from provincial taxation. Unfortunately, most of the money fell into the hands of Rome's Senatorial nobility, opening up a wider and wider chasm between the haves and the have-nots. By law, no Senator could be engaged in any business but farming, thus as the rich got richer, they tended to invest their money in land, which their poorer compatriots sold off. Huge plantations were amassed, and these came to be worked by a large population of imported slaves—slaves that the many Roman wars made relatively inexpensive. In other words, Rome's imperial growth greatly, and adversely, affected the social structure of Roman Italy.

> *You* will say that it is glorious to take vengeance on one's enemies. That seems to no one greater and more glorious than it does to me, but only if it can be done without injury to one's country.
>
> —**Cornelia, excerpt of a letter from the *Fragments* of Cornelius Nepos**

Serious ramifications followed, not the least of them being the great slave revolts that began to wreak havoc over the Italian countryside, but as far as Tiberius the Younger's career is concerned, we can focus on three things. First, when Romans became landless, legally they retained most of their rights, including the right to vote in elections, but they ceased to be eligible for service in the Roman army. As a result, the number of men on the draft roles plummeted at exactly the time when Rome's military commitments abroad were at their most extended. More commitments meant the need for more men—but legally the military manpower supply was drying up. Second, as the pool of potential draftees shrank, Roman generals were less willing to impose the harsh discipline traditionally associated with military service. As a result, those armies that did exist proved to be less efficient in the field than their predecessors. And third, with so many destitute Romans having no ethical way to earn a living in the cities, in large numbers they began to sell their votes to the Senators most willing to pay to get elected to political offices—offices, which invariably put them into a position to tap the financial flow from Rome's growing number of provinces. Thus, a vicious cycle of political corruption and moral decay—an age of "bread and circuses"—had begun.

Such was the situation when Tiberius the Younger journeyed to Spain to assume his official responsibilities as quaestor (137). On the way, as he traversed northern Italy, Tiberius was struck by the number of slaves he saw working the land in lieu of the free population he knew had once tilled that soil. When he arrived in Spain, Tiberius' chief duty was to negotiate the freedom of an incompetent general, Hostilius Mancinus. Mancinus had led his less-than-disciplined army into ambush and captivity as he sought to collect booty and win a cheap victory, one he could turn into a triumph back at home. After playing upon his father's connections and reputation, Tiberius the Younger accomplished his mission, negotiating in good faith, but in so doing found it necessary to treat Mancinus' captors as if they were Rome's equals. When he returned to Rome with Mancinus, his army and a treaty that guaranteed that Rome would henceforth treat these Spaniards as free allies, his own brother-in-law led the Senate to accept the army, reject the treaty, and return Mancinus to Spain to be dealt with in any way his one-time captors wished. Eventually, the Spaniards returned him to Rome unharmed, reasoning that Mancinus and Rome deserved one another.

Scipio apparently acted as he did because he thought that an inexperienced Tiberius had given away too much by treating one Spanish tribe as Rome's equal. (Perhaps this was another factor in the deteriorating marriage of Aemilianus and Sempronia.) Regardless, Tiberius the Younger, having lost face, was furious with Aemilianus for what he considered a major betrayal, and, as a result, married the daughter of one of Aemilianus' most bitter political rivals, Appius Claudius. Further, a few years later in 133, when Tiberius was elected to the tribunate, he introduced his famous Land Bill, backed initially by Claudius and a few other eminent Senators. This bill was meant to deal with several problems at once. It called for the distribution of Rome's extensive *public* lands strewn about Italy to *landless* citizens. By doing so, on the idealistic plane Tiberius the Younger hoped to repopulate rural Italy with Roman citizens: 1) to increase the number of those who would be eligible for military service; 2) to introduce an effective counterbalance to the growing slave threat to the free population of Italy; and 3) to stem the tide of political corruption that resulted when the Roman poor sold their votes to the rich.

Although on the surface Tiberius' bill appeared enlightened, it met immediate and stout resistance from the majority of his Senatorial peers, including Aemilianus. There were two reasons for this. First, the extensive tracts of publicly owned land that dotted the Italian peninsula and which had been acquired piece by piece as Rome extended its domination over its Italian neighbors had not been allowed to lie fallow since their initial acquisition. Indeed, to generate revenue for the state, the land had been leased to those willing to pay for its use. It should come as no surprise that by far the largest share of this public land was leased to Senators, who thereby augmented their privately owned plantations. Some of this public land had been leased out to powerful interests for generations before Tiberius' bill, and these stood to lose the cost of any improvements that had been made, as well as substantial future revenues if the state reclaimed them for another use. Greed, pure and simple, motivated much opposition. But there was also a political side to this proposal. That is, if Tiberius the Younger was successful, he could look forward to the political support of those who would thereby reacquire farms. The size of this clientage had the potential of redefining the shape of the existing Roman factions, and everybody who would not benefit from the scheme—including Aemilianus—howled at the prospect. Much rhetoric was expended and much political maneuvering attempted before it became clear that Tiberius had the upper hand among the Roman poor, if not the Senate. His rhetorical ability had won the day. Admitting temporary defeat, Tiberius' enemies nevertheless swore that they would reverse their fortunes when Tiberius the Younger surrendered his magistracy at the end of the year (all regular Roman offices were annual). Fearing that his magisterial successors might overturn his reforms, however, Tiberius announced that he would run for an unprecedented second consecutive tribunate. This unexpected development ignited his opposition. A force, led by the *pontifex maximus* (Rome's highest religious official), met the faction of Tiberius in the Roman forum. A riot ensued and when the dust settled, Tiberius the Younger and many of his supporters lay dead in the city's streets—the first loss of life in a civil disturbance in Rome since the foundation of the Republic, over 350 years earlier.

What role did Cornelia play in these affairs? Although Roman law prohibited a woman from holding public office, it is clear that Cornelia not only stood beside her older son—literally as well as figuratively, for she appeared with him in public as he emotionally appealed to the electorate—but actually helped to shape his political agenda. Nevertheless, with Tiberius the Younger dead and Aemilianus alienated, Cornelia had no access to the public forum until her younger son, Gaius, was old enough to join in the political fray. Thus, with one exception, she cultivated her cultural interests, furthered her younger son's education, and lived in relative obscurity for the next decade. That exception came in the year 129, when Aemilianus was assassinated, after a bold attempt of his own to advance the causes of justice and political expediency (he also wanted more clients) by championing the extension of Roman citizenship to long time Italian allies. The prospect was not only opposed by the most conservative Senators, but also by Rome's masses who feared that their own privileges would, as a result, be watered down. Although no more than slander, some accused both Cornelia and Sempronia of complicity in Aemilianus' death.

An active role for Cornelia was resurrected when Gaius, less disciplined than his brother but his rhetorical equal, ran for the tribunate in 123. The motives behind Gaius' political agenda were more complex than those that had spurred his brother a decade earlier, as indeed was the agenda itself. It is apparent, however, that Gaius was at least as motivated by a desire to avenge his brother's death as he was by anything else. His reform package contained many things that benefitted the have-nots in Roman society: it reinforced Tiberius' land bill; established colonies in and beyond Italy; subsidized a series of benefits for the urban poor; and, through road building, facilitated the bringing of food to markets, among others. Several aspects of his program, however, hint at a sinister purpose behind his seemingly progressive program. For example, he threw provincials to the wolves by effectively creating a system that prevented Roman governors from enforcing Roman law over Roman businessmen in the provinces. Thereafter, not only could honest governors *not* bring miscreants to heel but, those few who tried, ran the risk of being convicted by their businessmen/adversaries of provincial maladministration in courts controlled by the businessmen themselves. Also, in a series of laws, Gaius sought legal vengeance on those whom he knew to have been associated with the murder of the brother he had adored, even if stacked courts had convicted no one; he even sought to debase the entire Senatorial order for its perceived complicity in Tiberius' death.

Taking all of Gaius' legislation into account during his two tribunates, it seems clear that he was motivated less by idealism of any sort than by a sheer hatred of the entire class that had precipitated Tiberius' death. Although many of his laws benefitted non-Senators, they appear to have done so primarily to win those constituencies as allies so that the Senate could be assaulted. Regardless, in 123 and 122 Gaius' drive elevated him to the position of Rome's uncrowned king. His opponents, realizing that he was winning support through the dispensing of political pork, abided by the old maxim, "if you can't beat them, join them," and began to outbid Gaius for the loyalty of Rome's non-Senatorial classes.

During this period, Cornelia stood by her son's more progressive legislation while publicly decrying his irrational attacks upon the entire Senatorial order. She is known to have made him desist from attacks on one notable rival. Disregarding Cornelia's attempts to temper Gaius' activities, his political opponents lumped her with everything he attempted to do. In an almost unprecedented fashion, she became the object of public attack. One charge levelled against her was that she had organized agricultural workers to come to Rome, not to participate legitimately in Rome's political process but to act as goons to break up legitimate assemblies of Gaius' opponents. Given her known disapproval of her son's more radical tactics, this almost certainly was untrue, but Gaius was forced to defend Cornelia openly and, in the process, was able to win some sympathy from those who thought only the lowest of the low would publicly assail a prominent politician's mother. Nevertheless, it remains clear that Cornelia was actively partisan on both her sons' behalf to a degree that was unprecedented in her day. Thus, she set an example that influenced other women of her station to become more politically active.

Despite, or perhaps because of, her activism—not all of Rome welcomed women to politics—the tide flowed against Gaius by the end of 122. Outbid by his cynical rivals for the loyalty of the masses, and foolishly away from Rome to establish a colony on the old cite of Carthage at a crucial time, Gaius returned to discover some of his legislation already overturned. Acting precipitously to disrupt his enemies, he resorted to physical violence. Peace was restored only after Gaius and hundreds of his supporters had been butchered in the riots that followed.

The violence that surrounded the two Gracchi polarized Roman society and led to the intense factionalism that so disrupted law and order that it overthrew the Republic, the process coming to fruition with the victory of Octavian

(Augustus) over Marc Antony and *Cleopatra (VII) in 31—over a century of open civil strife in all. Bereft of her sons, Cornelia retired to the small town of Misenum, where she retained a high social and cultural profile presiding over perhaps the era's most influential literary salon, in the process fostering the Greco-Roman amalgam that would dominate the Mediterranean cultural scene for almost 500 years after her death. Kings exchanged gifts with her as they had for decades, friends visited, and intellectuals, especially Greek, dropped by to enjoy her hospitality. Cornelia seems to have made the most of her situation, although she clearly grieved the personal losses she had suffered.

In the few years between Gaius' death and her own, Cornelia began the process of her sons' political deification, speaking of them, tearlessly, in tones previously reserved for the legendary heroes of early Rome. Throughout, she also maintained a copious correspondence with friends beyond Misenum, expressing herself as a dedicated mother and loyal patriot in a style that was lofty enough to warrant publication and literary praise. In the generations that followed, her letters had a significant impact, and she came to be remembered more for her refined statements on what it was to be a philhellenic—but intensely patriotic—Roman matron than for the specific policies she and her sons once supported.

SOURCES:

Cornelius Nepos. *Fragments*. Trans. by J.C. Rolfe. Cambridge, MA: Harvard, 1929.

Plutarch, *Makers of Rome: Lives of Tiberius and Gaius Gracchus*. Penguin, 1965.

SUGGESTED READING:

Astin, A.E. *Scipio Aemilianus*. Oxford, 1967.

Lefkowitz, M.R., and M.B. Fant. *Women's Life in Greece and Rome*. Baltimore, MD: Johns Hopkins, 1992.

Stockton, D. *The Gracchi*. Oxford, 1979.

W.S. Greenwalt, Associate Professor of Classical History, Santa Clara University, Santa Clara, California

Cornelia (c. 100–68 BCE)

Roman noblewoman and wife of emperor Julius Caesar. Born around 100 BCE; died in 68 BCE; daughter of Lucius Cornelius Cinna; married Gaius Julius Caesar (c. 100–44 BCE), Roman emperor, in 84 BCE; children: daughter Julia (d. 54 BCE).

Cornelia was the daughter of the patrician, Lucius Cornelius Cinna, who, despite his ancient family, was a liberal by the standards of the 1st century BCE. Between the years 87 and 84, Cinna was elected to an impressive four consulships, although he was not universally popular as these

were years of Roman civil war pitting the liberal *populares* against the conservative "Optimates." Leading the Optimates was the brilliant but ruthless Lucius Cornelius Sulla, while Cinna and his even more illustrious colleague, Gaius Marius, championed the *populares* faction until both died: Cinna the victim of a military mutiny and Marius of old age. Bereft of such talented leadership, the *populares* cause floundered and eventually fell before Sulla who thereafter did his best (unsuccessfully, as it turned out) to prevent its resurrection.

Before her father's death and Sulla's ascendancy, Cornelia was destined to link Cinna's political interests with those of a promising political ally in a highly charged political atmosphere. The appropriate match for Cornelia turned out to be the soon-to-be-famous Gaius Julius Caesar, because he had two especially attractive qualities at the time of their union. First, like Cornelia he was a patrician; and second, Caesar's family had been intimately associated with the *populares* faction since Cinna's colleague Marius had married Caesar's great-aunt, *Julia (d. 68 BCE). Together the marriages of Marius to Julia and of Cornelia to Caesar (in 84) helped to rehabilitate the political fortunes of Caesar's branch of his ancient family, for, despite the family's long history, none of Caesar's immediate forefathers had been distinguished.

Religion as well as politics were instrumental in bringing Cornelia and Caesar together. The polytheistic Romans believed that their gods demanded honor before any important business—public or private—could be transacted. In Rome, there were many important priesthoods (with varying expertises and responsibilities) significant to the running of the state, and each of these was much coveted because of the high status a priesthood conferred upon its holder. The most ancient of these religious offices were reserved for patricians who were married to patricians, because that class had at one time maintained a monopoly on all Roman political and religious authority. By the 1st century, however, the number of prominent patrician families had declined precipitously. Thus, when the position of *flamen Dialis* (an ancient priesthood, steeped in ritualistic taboo but nevertheless prestigious) came open in 84 and Caesar became the leading candidate for that office, it became necessary to procure for him a patrician spouse. Cornelia was a perfect choice, politically expedient and from the right social stratum for Caesar's political-religious advancement. Although theirs was an arranged marriage, it seems that it pleased both principals—especially Caesar, for he weathered stormy times on Cornelia's behalf.

Sulla's victory over the remnants of the *populares*' faction came in late 82, at which time he forbade on political grounds Caesar's completion of the ceremonies necessary to establish the younger man as the *flamen Dialis*. Thus, Caesar never held that priesthood. Ironically, however, the fact that Caesar had begun the process by which the *flamen Dialis* was made eligible to assume his duties probably saved his life, for a religious aura was perceived as surrounding such candidates. Although Sulla had his way with Caesar in regard to this priesthood, he was not successful in his demand that Caesar divorce Cornelia. Standing up to the dictator, Caesar insisted that he had no intention of shedding his wife. Such defiance at a time when Sulla *was* the political authority in Rome so endangered Caesar's life that he went into hiding in the nearby Sabine territory. Hunted down by a Sullan patrol, Caesar was able to escape Italy (making his way to Anatolia) only by buying off its officer with a significant bribe. Even so, Sulla had a modicum of revenge for Caesar's audacity, when he seized Cornelia's marriage dowry and severed all of her claims to her family's estate—a considerable financial loss to both Cornelia and Caesar. Nevertheless, Caesar's faithfulness did have a political payoff, for the remnants of the *populares* faction remembered his bravery and loyalty to his wife and, as a result, would later rally around his leadership.

Although little is known about their intimate relationship, Cornelia remained very important to Caesar throughout his early political career because she linked her husband's fortunes to her father's political faction. The marriage produced a daughter named *Julia (d. 54 BCE), and, since no known animosity split the couple, it is likely that the union was congenial to both parties.

In 68, the year after he obtained his first elective office, Caesar's great-aunt, Julia, died. Using her funeral in a political fashion to reinforce his claims to the loyalties of the remaining *populares*, Caesar delivered a famous eulogy. Soon thereafter, Cornelia also died at a young age. Although it was unusual to make an event out of the funeral of such a young woman, Caesar nevertheless broke with tradition to present another public oration. Under most circumstances, the Romans disliked such innovation, but Caesar's emotionally delivered eulogy for Cornelia moved his audience to admiration. As a result, the virtues attributed to Cornelia circulated widely after her demise among a respectful public, thus winning her an association in death with the most famous heroines from the Roman past.

William S. Greenwalt, Associate Professor of Classical History, Santa Clara University, Santa Clara, California

Cornelia (c. 75–after 48 BCE)

Roman noblewoman and wife of Pompey the Great. *Born around 75 BCE; died after 48 BCE; daughter of Metellus Scipio; married Publius Licinius Crassus, in 55 (died 53 BCE); married Pompey the Great (106–48 BCE), Roman consul, in 52 BCE.*

The daughter of Metellus Scipio, a partisan of the First Triumvirate (the political alliance consisting of Julius Caesar, Pompey the Great, and Crassus), Cornelia was famous for her lineage, education, character, beauty and charm. She was first married in 55 to Publius Licinius Crassus, the son of Caesar's political ally; this union ended when her husband was killed in 53 (in modern Syria) along with his father, during their abortive campaign against the Parthian Empire. In a second political marriage (52), Cornelia wed Pompey the Great, although many in Rome thought her better suited by age to be the bride of one of Pompey's sons. When the political friendship of Caesar and Pompey the Great deteriorated into civil war, Cornelia strongly supported Pompey, who doted upon his young spouse. After Pompey lost the battle of Pharsalus to Caesar in 48, Pompey fled the battlefield and mainland Greece to join his wife at Mytilene on the island of Lesbos. Cornelia blamed his misfortune on herself, claiming to be the jinx that had ruined both Pompey and her first husband, the younger Crassus. When, in an effort to resuscitate his rivalry with Caesar, Pompey made his way to Egypt, Cornelia witnessed Pompey's murder from the deck of the ship that had carried them to Alexandria. The assassination of Pompey had been orchestrated by the Egyptian pretender, Ptolemy XIII, in his effort to win over Caesar's gratitude, with hopes that Caesar would intervene on his behalf in Ptolemy's civil war against his famous sister *Cleopatra VII.

William S. Greenwalt, Associate Professor of Classical History, Santa Clara University, Santa Clara, California

Cornelia (fl. 1st c. BCE)

Roman noblewoman. Flourished in the 1st century BCE; daughter of Scribonia and one of her two unknown husbands, possibly Cornelius Scipio; married Paullus Aemilius Lepidus (a consul); children: two sons, Paullus and Lepidus.

Cornelia was the daughter of *Scribonia and one of her two unknown husbands (Scribonia's third husband was Octavian, who later became Augustus). Cornelia married Paullus Aemilius Lepidus, the nephew of the Lepidus who with Marc Antony and Octavian constituted the "Second Triumvirate." This triumvirate was the political junta that formed to unite the Caesarian faction in the wake of Julius Caesar's assassination (44 BCE) and to avenge his murder by striking down his assassins. Despite his kinship to one of the triumvirs, Cornelia's husband initially sided with the assassins in the wars that followed Caesar's murder; for this, his life was declared forfeit by the triumvirs in 43 BCE. In 42, Cornelia's husband won Crete for Brutus, one of Caesar's assassins, but after Brutus' defeat at the hands of Antony and Octavian at Philippi in the same year Aemilius Lepidus Paullus made his peace with Octavian, under whose patronage his career flourished. Cornelia and Lepidus had two sons, Paullus and Lepidus, before Cornelia died at a young age. After her death, the famous poet Propertius was commissioned to write an elegy to help assuage her husband's grief.

William S. Greenwalt, Associate Professor of Classical History, Santa Clara University, Santa Clara, California

Cornell, Katharine (1893–1974)

American actress of extraordinary range who competed for the title "First Lady of the American Theater" and helped create its Golden Age, a period dominated almost exclusively by great actresses. Name variations: first name Katharine is often misspelled Katherine. Born Katharine Cornell in Berlin, Germany, on February 16, 1893 (and not in 1898 as she had previously claimed); died of pneumonia at her home in Vineyard Haven, Massachusetts, on June 9, 1974; daughter of Peter C. Cornell (a physician who at one time managed the Majestic Theater in Buffalo, New York) and Alice Gardner Plimpton Cornell; educated in Buffalo schools and at Oakmere School in Mamaroneck, New York; married Guthrie McClintic, on September 8, 1921; no children.

Awards: Chancellor's Medal University of Buffalo (1935); Drama League Award for her performance as Juliet in Romeo and Juliet (1935); gold medal of the National Achievement Award (1937); Jane Addams Medal Award, Rockford College (1950); Doctorate of Letters, Wisconsin University (1936), Elmira College, Hobart College, and the University of Pennsylvania (1937–39); Doctorate in Humane Letters, Smith College (1937); Doctorate in Literature, Cornell University (1937); Doctorate in Fine Arts, Clark University (1941), Ithaca College (1947), Princeton University

(1948); Doctorate in Humane Letters, Middlebury College (1955).

*Theater (unless otherwise noted, all appearances were in New York City): made debut with Washington Square Players in Bushido (November 13, 1916), also in The Death of Tintagiles, Plots and Playwrights, The Life of Man (1916–18); with the **Jessie Bonstelle** Stock Company in Buffalo and Detroit, appeared in The Gypsy Trail, Daybreak, Broken Threads, Fanny's First Play, Captain Kidd, Jr., Lilac Time, Cheating Cheaters (1918); toured in The Man Who Came Back (1918–19); made London debut as Jo in Little Women (November 10, 1919); appeared as Eileen Baxter-Jones in Nice People, as Sydney Fairfield in A Bill of Divorcement (1921), as Mary Fitton in Will Shakespeare (1923), as Laura Pennington in The Enchanted Cottage (1923), as Henriette in Casanova (1923), as Shirley Pride in The Way Things Happen (1924), as Lalage Sturdee in The Outsider (1924), as Suzanne Chaumont in Tiger Cats (1924); played the title role in Candida (1924), Iris Fenwick in The Green Hat (1925), Leslie Crosbie in The Letter (1927), Ellen Olenska in The Age of Innocence (1928), Madeline Carey in Dishonored Lady, Elizabeth Barrett Browning in The Barretts of Wimpole Street (1931); appeared in the title role in Lucrece, as Elsa Brandt in Alien Corn (1933); toured as Juliet in Romeo and Juliet (1933–34); appeared as Juliet in New York (December 1934); revived The Barretts of Wimpole Street (1935); appeared as Joan of Arc in Saint Joan (1936), as Oparre in Wingless Victory (1936), as Mariamne in Herod and Mariamne (1938), as Linda Easterbrook in No Time for Comedy (1939), as Jennifer Dubedat in The Doctor's Dilemma (1941), as Masha in The Three Sisters (1942), as Stella Boswell in Lovers and Friends (1943); toured overseas in The Barretts of Wimpole Street (1944), ending tour in New York (March 1945); appeared in title role in Antigone (1946), as Cleopatra in Antony and Cleopatra (1947), as Anna de Mendoza in That Lady (1949); toured as Smilja Darde in Captain Carvallo (1950); appeared as Constance Middleton in The Constant Wife (1951), as Mary Prescott in The Prescott Proposals (1953), as The Countess Rosmarin in The Dark is Light Enough (1955), as Mrs. Patrick Campbell in Dear Liar (1959–60); retired (1961).*

Katharine Cornell was born on February 16, 1893, in Berlin, Germany, where her father Peter Cortelyou Cornell was a post-graduate medical student studying surgery. Her mother **Alice Cornell,** a depressed alcoholic, died when Katharine was 22. A few years after returning to

Katharine
Cornell

the U.S., Peter Cornell became part owner and manager of the Star Theater in Buffalo, New York, where Katharine grew up. Her childhood appears to have been a somewhat unhappy one, and in later years she admitted to being shy, introverted, and essentially fearful, very much afraid of being hurt. Nevertheless, the theatrical world to which she was introduced through her father's second profession fascinated her from her earliest years, and she found refuge in the production of amateur theatricals and school plays. At her father's theater, she was able to see the greatest stars of the day, and, by her own account, it was from watching a performance of *Maude Adams as Peter Pan, that she decided that the theater was to be her life.

> The First Lady of the American Theater.
>
> —Alexander Woolcott

At age 15, Katharine Cornell was sent to Miss Merrill's School in Mamaroneck, New York, where she studied dramatic arts, returning there to teach for the school year 1915–16. On one occasion, Edward Goodman of the Washington Square Players, a semi-professional theatrical company staging plays in Greenwich Village, came up to Mamaroneck from New York City to help in the direction of a play that Cornell had written, and he suggested that she audition for the Players on her next trip to the city. Unfortunately, Cornell's mother died shortly before her scheduled tryout, and Cornell was so overwhelmed with stage fright that she virtually lost her voice and failed to make an impression. A few months later, however, she was given one line ("My son, my son") as a mother in a Japanese Noh drama entitled *Bushido*. Thereafter, Katharine Cornell remained with the Washington Square Players for two years earning the pathetic sum of $40 throughout that time, otherwise supporting herself with the income from a small estate left by her mother. In 1917, she was given a part in the play *Plots and Playwrights* for which she obtained her first notice, a critic observing "there is a new girl who stands out—Katharine Cornell. . . . A tall girl with a fine strong head, broadly spread eyes and full mouth—mentality, physical control and simplicity." From the Washington Square players, Cornell went on to the *Jessie Bonstelle Stock Company in Chicago, where she honed her craft in a variety of roles in widely different productions. She then toured with *The Man Who Came Back*, which was taken to London. This vehicle turned out to be Cornell's London debut and farewell performance at one and the same time, for, even though she regularly vacationed in Europe, she never performed there again.

The decisive point in Cornell's career came in 1921, when the young casting director, Guthrie McClintic, saw her during the casting of *Rachel Crother's play, *Nice People*, and wrote in his notebook: "Interesting. Monotonous. Watch." On September 8th, the two were married and remained so until his death 40 years later. From the time of their marriage onwards, McClintic took charge of his wife's career, aiding her in her selection of vehicles, directing her in all of them from *The Green Hat* onwards, and encouraging her to reach greater heights as an actress. On her part, Cornell never hesitated to give her husband full credit for all that she had achieved:

> If not for Guthrie, I think that I would have continued just drifting. . . . He wanted to be an actor and my career was a sublimation of his desire, because he could pour his talents through me and that was a great advantage to me. . . . I continued in the theater buoyed up mostly by his enthusiasm for it. He was one of those people who fascinated you always. You were never bored; sometimes upset, but never bored.

Though less than a Svengali, McClintic dominated his wife's professional life, and it seems certain that their marriage was an unusual one, perhaps even asexual. McClintic was known to be bisexual, and, in his book *The Sewing Circle*, Axel Madsen openly cites Cornell as being gay. Nevertheless, there seems to be no doubt that the two were devoted to one another. Early in their marriage they rented, then purchased, a large house in Manhattan on Beekman Place, which they gradually furnished largely with pieces selected from the productions in which Cornell appeared. Vastly different in both temperament and habits, Cornell arranged for the third floor of their home to be exclusively hers; the fourth, exclusively her husband's, the lower floors open to both. An unusual arrangement for an unusual marriage but for the McClintics it worked for those 40 years. Later they acquired a summer home at Vineyard Haven on Martha's Vineyard Island, Massachusetts. When Guthrie McClintic died, Katharine Cornell, unwilling to continue her career without him, simply retired.

A few weeks after their marriage, Katharine Cornell opened in New York in *A Bill of Divorcement*, a play by the British author *Clemence Dane that made her a star and that, adapted as a film in 1931, would do the same for *Katharine Hepburn. Alexander Woolcott, drama critic for *The New York Times*, was highly laudatory about the play and called Cornell's performance "superb." It was his review that largely guaranteed the success of the production, which thus gave Cornell a lengthy run and time to impress the public. *A Bill of Divorcement* was followed by *Will Shakespeare,* another play by Dane, with Otto Kruger in the title role, **Haidée Wright* as Queen Elizabeth, and Cornell as the "Dark Lady of the Sonnets." Though less successful than *A Bill of Divorcement,* once again, her reviews were excellent. The same year, she opened in *The Enchanted Cottage,* a sentimental melodrama by the veteran English playwright Arthur Wing Pinero. Cornell then appeared as Henriette in *Casanova.* John Corbin's review of her performance in *The New York Times* was typical of the notices that Cornell was now receiving as a matter of course: "Katharine Cornell suffuses her scenes with the lure of feminine sensibility and courageous adventure." Kenneth Macgowan wrote in *Vogue:* "Miss Cornell's is a finished art, characteristic of everything she has ever done and filled with rich potentialities of the future."

In January 1924, Cornell appeared in her first play produced by McClintic, *The Way Things Happen,* again, a work by Dane. Critic Burns Mantle wrote in the *New York News:* "Katharine Cornell seems to have the certain subtle something that makes great actresses. . . . [E]xternally, at least, she is not at all the actressy type. And yet she has more of the Duse quality than any of the other younger women of the stage." *The Way Things Happen* was followed by *The Outsider* and *Tiger Cats,* but it was not until she appeared in the title role of George Bernard Shaw's *Candida,* with Pedro de Cordoba and **Clare Eames,* that Cornell experienced her first theatrical triumph. Typical was the review of H.T. Parker in the *Boston Transcript:* "Candida was Miss Katharine Cornell, who achieved the part by mental and spiritual sensibility, gave it limpid outlet; poeticized along the way; filled it with a nervous or a tranquil beauty. Beyond Mr. Shaw was it transfigured." Even Shaw himself was captivated, if only by Cornell's original kind of beauty:

> Your success in *Candida* and something blonde and expansive about your name, had created an ideal suburban British Candida in my imagination. Fancy my feeling on seeing in the photograph a gorgeous dark lady from the cradle of the human race! . . . If you look like that, it doesn't matter a rap whether you can act or not. Can you? Yours, breath-bereaved, —G. Bernard Shaw.

On September 15, 1925, Cornell opened as Iris March in the New York production of Michael Arlen's *The Green Hat,* a play that had been a sensation in London where **Tallulah Bankhead* had created the role. Essentially a shallow depiction of a "modern" young woman of the day and her various difficulties, the play captured the imagination of the public, being a clear expression of the spirit of the era. For the first time, at age 32, Katharine Cornell saw her name up on the marquee.

Katharine Cornell's triumph in *The Green Hat* was followed by her success as Leslie Crosbie in Somerset Maugham's *The Letter,* a play that **Gladys Cooper* had made a success in London and which would be one of the roles confirming **Bette Davis* as a serious actress when she starred in the film version in 1940. Cornell then appeared in a dramatization of **Edith Wharton*'s 1919 novel of the New York high society of her youth, *The Age of Innocence,* with a young Franchot Tone as the hero Newland Archer, and then in *Dishonored Lady* (1930), another critical and popular success.

From 1931 onwards, Katharine Cornell appeared only under her own management. That year, with the Great Depression in full swing, she and McClintic established their own production association called "Katharine Cornell Presents." Disliking the star system, so ubiquitous in the theater of her youth and still somewhat entrenched in the 1930s, Cornell was content to have her name in the heading as presenter and otherwise placed her name at the bottom of the cast list in the program and other advertisements for the play. The McClintic's first joint production turned out to be one of Cornell's greatest successes, *The Barretts of Wimpole Street* by Rudolf Besier, which opened at the old Empire Theater on February 9, 1931. On its surface, the drama seems less than arresting. The story details how poet Robert Browning entered into a correspondence with poet **Elizabeth Barrett Browning* and, upon meeting her, discovers a 39-year-old unmarried invalid dominated by her father. The two fall in love, and Robert convinces Elizabeth to shake off her father's yoke and run away with him to Italy. As played by Cornell and her co-star Brian Aherne, however, the play took on a far richer texture and a deeper meaning. In his review of the play, Brooks Atkinson, drama critic for *The New York Times* and a lifelong admirer of Cornell's work, wrote:

> [This play] introduces us to Katharine Cornell as an actress of the first order. Here the disciplined fury that she has been squandering on catch-penny plays becomes the vibrant beauty of finely-wrought character. By the crescendo of her playing, by the wild

sensitivity that lurks behind her ardent gestures and her piercing stares across the footlights she charges the drama with a meaning beyond the facts it records. Her acting is quite as remarkable for the carefulness of its design as for the fire of her presence.

The Barretts of Wimpole Street ran for a year on Broadway after which Cornell followed with *Lucrece*, a translation of a French drama set in ancient Rome, in which she appeared with Pedro de Cordoba, Brian Aherne and *Blanche Yurka; and next with *Alien Corn*, with Luther Adler. It was then that she undertook her famous and near legendary touring production of *The Barretts of Wimpole Street* (1933–34). Gathering a company of first-rate actors, including Basil Rathbone and an 18-year-old Orson Welles, and alternating the play with *Candida* and *Romeo and Juliet*, Cornell embarked on a grand tour of America, traveling 20,853 miles across the country and giving 225 performances in 77 cities. On this tour, in spite of the Depression, the competition from radio, and the increasingly sophisticated talking films, Cornell played to packed theaters and showed that the "road" was still a viable theatrical medium.

Returning to New York in December 1934, Katharine Cornell assayed the role of Juliet, thereby attempting to rank herself among the great classical actresses of her day, *Ellen Terry, *Sybil Thorndike, *Edith Evans, and *Peggy Ashcroft. The great problem of portraying this most beautiful and poignant of Shakespeare's heroines has always been that by the time an actress becomes mature enough in her craft to attempt it, she is usually too old to play the role convincingly. This is what defeated *Ethel Barrymore in 1919, and it was her relative youth that enabled *Jane Cowl to enjoy a greater success in the part the same year. Yet, Katharine Cornell, at 41, had not only reached the stage of her career when she could master the role, but was one of those rare actresses who was able to capture the youthfulness of the part in a thoroughly convincing manner. In the words of critic John Mason Brown:

> Of all the Juliets we have seen, Cornell's is the only one that satisfactorily embodies the descriptions of Juliet's movements as given in the script. Her "fair daughter of rich Capulet" may be adult in form but she is young in motion and in heart. She literally runs . . . with her arms outstretched to love. As she glides, free-limbed and lovely, across the stage, one feels instinctively the young girl Shakespeare saw in his Poet's mind come to life.

The Cornell *Juliet* was followed by *Flowers of the Forest*, a modern play by John Van Druten that was one of Cornell's few unqualified failures; it ran but five weeks. She returned, however, to critical acclaim with a revival of *Romeo and Juliet* followed by her success in *St. Joan* by George Bernard Shaw, which opened at the Martin Beck Theater on March 9, 1936. Directed, as usual, by McClintic, it became one of Cornell's greatest triumphs. Once again, she was credited for her remarkable ability to portray the innocence and vibrancy of youth as easily as if they were costumes to be donned or doffed with each performance of the play. Presenting the very blend of modesty and assurance that Shaw's text required, she was a radiant village girl at the opening of the play but one who matures, scene by scene, to the brink of sainthood at the drama's close. Shaw's play, perhaps his best work, was wonderfully served in this production.

In the years that followed, Katharine Cornell continued to add to her list of great performances, appearing successfully in Maxwell Anderson's *Wingless Victory*, which ran for 108 performances (1936–37), a revival of *Candida* (1937), Clemence Dane's adaptation of a German play *Herod and *Mariamne* (1937), S.N. Behrman's *No Time For Comedy* (1939), which she performed for 24 weeks in New York and on a tour of 56 cities for the rest of the season of 1940. Returning to New York, she next starred in a revival of Shaw's comedy *The Doctor's Dilemma*. Now at the height of her career, Katharine Cornell sallied forth into Chekhov with her famous all-star production of *The Three Sisters* (December 1942), with herself as Masha and *Judith Anderson as Olga. After a brief appearance as Stella Boswell in *Lovers and Friends* (November 1943), she went on an overseas tour, daring to entertain soldiers with *The Barretts of Wimpole Street* (1944)—and succeeding—on a trip that did not end until her return to New York in March 1945. After the war, she appeared in the title role of Jean Anouilh's *Antigone* (1946), an adaptation of Sophocles' Greek tragedy staged in modern dress as it had been in Paris during the war, where Antigone's struggle against the tyrant was read (as its author intended) as the struggle of the French against the German occupation. This was followed by another revival of *Candida* again in April of the same year, with a young Marlon Brando as Marchbanks.

In 1947, Cornell returned to Shakespeare—at age 54—boldly attempting the part of Shakespeare's *Cleopatra VII in *Antony and Cleopatra*, a role that had sunk Tallulah Bankhead a decade before, and in which both *Julia Marlowe and Jane Cowl were widely considered to have failed. A rambling and disjointed piece of dramaturgy, far-ranging in scope and uncannily varied in mood, it is a devilishly difficult play to interpret on the stage but one which, as magnificent in conception as it is in its verse, has consistently drawn great actresses to its challenge. Under McClintic's direction, Cornell achieved yet another triumph. Again, in the words of John Mason Brown:

> No actress playing Cleopatra can hope to realize in every scene the various Cleopatras that Shakespeare wrote. To be wanton and witty, lustful and regal, mischievous and sublime as the part demands that Cleopatra must be, is to ask the impossible away from the printed page. Yet Cornell succeeds in being all these things to an amazing degree. . . . Vocally and in her person, she captures nearly all the changing moods of the chameleon. . . . [S]he looks her loveliest. She walks with a panther's grace. And she dies magnificently.

Cornell's production of *Antony and Cleopatra* broke all previous records for the run of the play. It was followed by Cornell's appearance as Anna de Mendoza in *That Lady* (1949); and on tour as Smilja Darde in *Captain Carvallo* (1950).

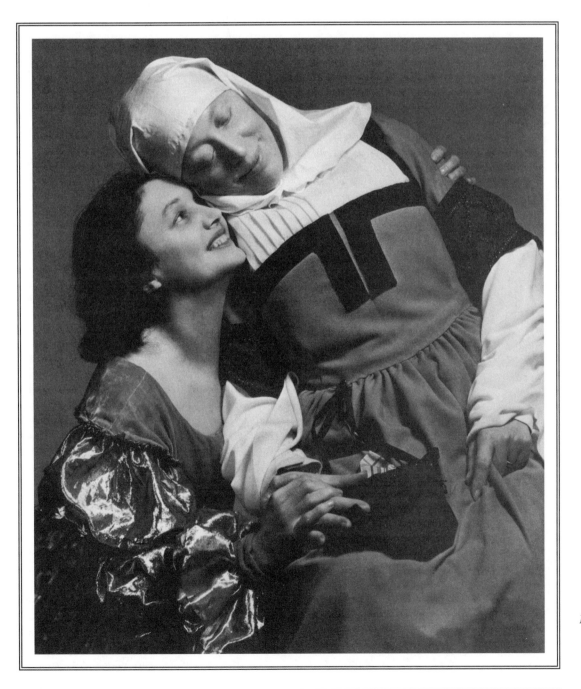

Katharine Cornell and Edith Evans (as the nurse), in Romeo and Juliet *(1934).*

In 1951, Cornell opened in a notable revival of Somerset Maugham's 1928 comedy *The Constant Wife* with George Brent as her co-star and with the role of her mother played by the esteemed *Grace George, who had been one of the great beauties of the New York stage at the turn of the century. Cornell then appeared as Mary Prescott in *The Prescott Proposals* (1953) and as the Countess Rosmarin in Christopher Fry's *The Dark is Light Enough* (1955). In 1959 and 1960, Cornell starred as *Mrs. Patrick Campbell both on tour and in New York, in *Dear Liar,* a dramatization of the platonic affair between the English actress Stella Campbell and the Anglo-Irish playwright George Bernard Shaw. This was Cornell's last appearance on the stage.

A dedicated actress, Katharine Cornell, alone among her contemporaries, took the responsibilities of "the road" seriously and did more than any other actress to raise the standards of provincial audiences across America, in an era when theater had largely given way to the motion picture everywhere outside of the very largest cities in the country. Audiences, for their part, responded with the same warmth to her personality as to her presentations. Once, in Seattle, when her train was delayed due to flood conditions, a capacity audience waited for her arrival until the curtain finally rose at 1:05 AM.

As an artist, Katharine Cornell had the utmost respect of her peers: "She elevated theater throughout the world," claimed The American National Theater and Academy. Far from surrounding herself with mediocrities in order to enhance her own impression on an audience—a not uncommon practice among stage stars of an earlier era and some of her own—Cornell sought only the finest players for her productions and never had trouble inducing them to work with her. Thus, during the 30 years under her own management, she appeared with most of the significant actors of the New York and London stages: Aherne, Judith Anderson, Dudley Digges, Clare Eames, Edith Evans, Maurice Evans, Grace George, **Margalo Gilmore**, *Ruth Gordon, Edmund Gwenn, *Ann Harding, Cedric Hardwicke, Leslie Howard, Raymond Massey, Burgess Meredith, Philip Merivale, *Mildred Natwick, Laurence Olivier, Tyrone Power, Basil Rathbone, **Florence Reed**, Ralph Richardson, Franchot Tone, and Orson Welles—a veritable who's who of the theater of the period. Critics, too, held her in the highest regard: "Something electric happened when she stepped on stage," wrote Atkinson.

A lady of the theater to her fingertips, Katharine Cornell never made a motion picture, save for a brief appearance as herself in the all-star *Stage Door Canteen,* asserting that nothing could replace the intimacy of a theater audience, a decision that ultimately deprived her of the international recognition that she assuredly deserved. She did, however, appear on radio from time to time, where she was able to utilize the richness of her deep voice to full advantage. Again, despite her success in London as early as 1919, Cornell never returned to the English stage, so that of all the great American actresses of her day, she was the least known to British audiences.

In her appearance, Katharine Cornell was a woman of unusual features and, as a child, considered herself to be "terribly ugly" to the point that she avoided contact with children of her own age. Her cheekbones were high and protruding, her mouth overly large and full, and her eyes too big for her face and set far apart. Yet, while not a beauty in the conventional sense, she was nevertheless a remarkably handsome woman and, like all great actresses, could command beauty when the part required it. Over and over again, critics cited her striking looks and how they never failed to enrich her interpretation of a role. An athletic woman, she played tennis and golf and enjoyed traveling and vacationing in Europe, but her off-stage personality, like that of many performing artists (e.g. *Greta Garbo, with whom she was often compared) tended to be rather bland, and she was always difficult to write about. In the words of her biographer, the Pulitzer Prize-winning playwright Tad Mosel, "There were no anecdotes, no funny stories, no crazy peccadillos, no Bohemian whims . . . and those who bore grudges against her could not be found." Her greatest fault was perhaps a lack of real ambition. That she became one of the first ladies of the American theater is certain, but that she ever intended this to be the case is far less so. If she assayed many great roles—Candida, Juliet, Cleopatra, for example—there were just as many that she never approached and should have—Lady Macbeth, Hedda Gabler, and Nora in *A Doll's House.* Towards the end of her career, she tended to repeat herself in earlier triumphs, and her last plays were unworthy of her genius.

In her later years, the career of Katharine Cornell faltered. Something seemed to have gone out of her acting, and audiences found her performances less magnetic. Her last three productions were received with reservation, and after the death of her husband in 1961, she ceased to perform. Her natural shyness, her stage fright, and the burdens of managing her own career appeared too daunting for her without McClintic by her side. Thereafter, she spent the last 13 years of her life in retirement at her summer home on Martha's Vineyard or in a small house that she kept in New York. Katharine Cornell died of pneumonia at her home in Vineyard Haven, Massachusetts, at age 81, and was cremated in Boston. A memorial service was held in the 300-year-old Association Hall, the former Vineyard Haven Town Hall that she had helped restore.

SOURCES:

Brown, John Mason. *Dramatis Personae.* NY: Viking Press, 1963.

Cornell, Katharine. *I Wanted to Be an Actress.* 2nd ed. NY: Random House, 1941.

Herbert, Ian, ed. *Who's Who in the Theater.* 16th ed. NY: Pitman.

Madsen, Axel. *The Sewing Circle.* NY: Birchlane Press, 1995.

Mosel, Tad, with Gertrude Macy. *The World and Theater of Katharine Cornell.* Boston, MA: Atlantic-Little Brown, 1978.

SUGGESTED READING:

Cornell, Katharine. *Curtain Going Up.* New York, 1943.

McClintic, Guthrie. *Me and Kit.* Boston, MA: Little, Brown, 1955.

Robert H. Hewsen, Professor of History, Rowan University, Glassboro, New Jersey

Cornelys, Theresa (1723–1797)

British madame. Name variations: Madame Cornelys. Born in Venice in 1723; died in Fleet Prison on August 19, 1797.

At one time Madame Cornelys directed all the theaters in the Austrian Netherlands. As a noted manager of public assemblies at Carlisle House (Soho, London), she organized balls, concerts, and masquerades, and performed as a singer. Cornelys, who also provided beautiful ladies of the night at hefty prices, ran one of the most celebrated "salons" in Europe, attended by royalty and members of Parliament. As a pretext for further investigation, Magistrate Sir John Fielding closed down her house, charging that she had presented dramatic performance without a license. A grand jury later found: "she does keep and maintain a common disorderly house, and does permit and suffer divers, loose and idle persons, as well as men and women, to be and remain during the whole night, rioting and otherwise misbehaving themselves." Ruined, Cornelys sold the Carlisle House furniture for needed cash, fell into obscurity, and, under the name of Mrs. Smith, sold donkey's milk at Knightsbridge for some time before she was sent to debtor's prison in Fleet Street. She died there in 1797.

Cornwall, countess of.

See Clare, Margaret de (1249–1313).
See Clare, Margaret de (c. 1293–1342).

Cornwall, duchess of.

See Sancha of Provence (c. 1225–1261).

Cornwallis, C.F. (1786–1858)

English author. Name variations: Caroline Frances Cornwallis. Born in 1786; died at Lidwells, in Kent, on January 8, 1858; daughter of William Cornwallis (rector of Wittersham and Elham in Kent).

C.F. Cornwallis acquired a thorough knowledge of Latin and Greek and, from an early age, carried on a correspondence with many eminent persons. Her initial work, *Philosophical Theories and Philosophical Experience by a Pariah* (1842), was the first of a series of 20 "Small Books on Great Subjects," which included the *Connection of Physiology and Intellectual Science, Ragged Schools, Criminal Law, Greek Philosophy,* and the *History and Influence of Christian Opinions.* Cornwallis also published *Pericles, a Tale of Athens* (1847). Her letters were printed in 1864.

Cornwallis-West, Mrs. George (1854–1921).

See Churchill, Jennie Jerome.

Corombona, Vittoria (c. 1557–1585).

See Accoramboni, Vittoria.

Coronado, Carolina (1820–1911)

Spanish writer of the 19th century. Name variations: Victoria Carolina Coronado Romero; Carolina Coronado de Perry. Born on December 12, 1820, in Almendralejo, near Badajoz, Spain; died on January 15, 1911; daughter of Nicolás Coronado Gallardo and María Antonia Romero; married Horatio Justus Perry (an American diplomat), in 1852; children: Carlos Horacio (b. 1853); Carolina (b. 1857); Matilde (b. 1861).

Carolina Coronado was born into a solidly middle-class family on December 12, 1820, in Almendralejo, near Badajoz, Spain. She showed an early predilection for poetry, composing and memorizing verses before she had even learned to write. Her first published poem appeared in 1839, in the magazine *El Piloto* of Madrid. Other poems and articles quickly followed, to widespread praise. Coronado's fame grew with the publication of her first volume of poetry in

1843. A year later, however, a sudden illness nearly took her life, and her family was ready to bury her when a doctor detected catalepsy. Though her health remained somewhat fragile, she wrote profusely for periodicals throughout the Hispanic world and the United States.

The person with whom she had a long romance, identified only as Alberto, died in 1847. Coronado then moved to Madrid and, in 1848, received from the Artistic and Literary Lyceum a crown of gold and laurel at the hands of Queen *Isabella II. In 1851, Coronado met an American diplomat, Horatio Justus Perry. They quietly married in a Protestant ceremony in Gibraltar on April 10 of the following year. Her desire to have her marriage confirmed by public Catholic rites was frustrated, however, by a relative who announced that Carolina had taken a vow of perpetual chastity in 1848. To the dismay of Spanish conservatives, she and her husband went to France where a Catholic ceremony was celebrated. Perry's position gave her access to wider social circles in Madrid, and Coronado became a fixture in the city's literary circles.

Domestic responsibilities and the birth in 1853 of her first child, Carlos Horacio, cut her literary output. She also accompanied her husband on diplomatic assignments. When the United States attempted to buy or forcibly annex Cuba, she and her husband worked to decrease tensions. Pro-slavery American senators called for Perry's resignation, and the couple decided to remain in Spain as private citizens. He turned to the business of laying trans-Atlantic underwater cables and later rejoined the U.S. diplomatic corps. She devoted more time to her family, while continuing to write lyrical poetry noted for its liberalism and love of nature. In 1857, her first daughter, Carolina, was born, followed four years later by a second, Matilde. Her home remained a gathering place for Madrid's literary figures.

Coronado spent her later life in Portugal. Her eldest daughter died in 1873, causing the poet's emotional collapse. After her recovery, the family moved to Lisbon. Perry's cable business failed during a financial panic, ruining him. He died in 1891. Carolina Coronado lived until January 15, 1911, and her remains, along with her husband's, were interred in Badajoz. In addition to romantic poetry, Coronado left a legacy of plays and novels.

SOURCES:

Castilla, Alberto. *Carolina Coronado de Perry: biografía, poesía e historia en la España del siglo XIX.* Madrid: Ediciones Beramar, 1987.

Kendall W. Brown, Chair, Department of History, Brigham Young University, Provo, Utah

Corrigan, Mairaid (b. 1944).

See joint entry under Williams, Betty.

Corson, Juliet (1841–1897)

American cookery instructor. *Born on January 14, 1841 (some sources cite 1842), in Roxbury, Massachusetts; died on June 18, 1897, in New York City; privately educated.*

Selected writings: Fifteen Cent Dinners for Families of Six *(1877);* Cooking Manual *(1877);* Training Schools of Cookery *(1879);* Twenty-five Cent Dinners for Families of Six *(1878);* Cooking School Text-Book *(1879);* Juliet Corson's New Family Cook Book *(1885);* Miss Corson's Practical American Cookery *(1886);* Family Living on $500 a Year *(1887).*

Juliet Corson was born in Massachusetts in 1841 but lived in New York City from the time she was six. Kept from school due to fragile health, she was educated privately, largely in her uncle's extensive library, and was earning a living as a librarian for the Working Woman's Library by the age of 18. She published verse and other writings in periodicals to supplement her income and eventually had a regular column in the *New York Leader* on subjects of interest to women. The *National Quarterly Review* hired Corson as an indexer, a position that led to a job as a staff writer.

Corson was an organizer and secretary of the Free Training School for Women in 1873. The school initially provided lessons in bookkeeping, sewing, and proofreading, and Corson added a cooking course in 1874. She hired a chef to demonstrate while she gave the lectures. In November 1876, she opened the New York Cooking School, which was an instant success. The following year, she wrote the textbook for the course entitled *Cooking Manual* (1877). Her success was furthered by her pamphlet *Fifteen Cent Dinners for Families of Six*, which Corson published and distributed at her own expense during a time of economic crisis in America. By 1878, Corson was traveling widely to lecture, and the next year she was responsible for the important circular *Training Schools of Cookery*. As a consultant on founding and operating cooking schools, Corson was contacted by government organizations. She worked as editor of *Household Monthly* during 1890–91. At the World's Columbian Exposition in Chicago in 1893, Corson was honored for her work and presided over the exhibit of the New York State cooking school.

Costa, Maria Velho de (b. 1938).

See Three Marias, The.

Costanza.

Variant of Constance and Constanza.

Costanza (1182–1202)

Portuguese princess. Born in May 1182; died on August 3, 1202, at Lorvano; daughter of *Douce of Aragon (1160–1198) and Sancho I (1154–1211 or 1212), king of Portugal (r. 1185–1211 or 1212).

Costello, Dolores (1905–1979)

American actress. Born on September 17, 1905, in Pittsburgh, Pennsylvania; died in 1979; daughter of Maurice Costello (1877–1950, a silent-screen actor) and his leading lady; sister of ❧➤ Helene Costello (1903–1957, an actress); married John Barrymore, in 1928 (divorced 1935); married John Vruwink (her obstetrician), in 1939 (divorced 1951); children: (first marriage) John Barrymore, Jr. (b. 1932, an actor); Dolores Ethel Mae Barrymore (b. 1933).

Filmography: The Sea Beast (1926); Manon Lescaut (1926); Bride of the Storm (1926); A Million Bid (1927); When a Man Loves (1927); The Third Degree (1927); Tenderloin (1928); Old San Francisco (1928); Glorious Betsy (1928); Noah's Ark (1928); Show of Shows (1929); The Redeeming Sin (1929); Madonna of Avenue A (1929); Glad Rag Doll (1929); Expensive Woman (1931); Breaking the Ice (1931); Little Lord Fauntleroy (1936); Yours for the Asking (1936); Girls on Probation (1938); Whispering Enemies (1939); The Magnificent Ambersons (1942); This is the Army (1943).

As children, Dolores and her sister Helen (later Helene) were first seen in the Vitagraph films (c. 1911) that starred their father Maurice Costello, a matinée idol who began in films in 1907. After attending private schools and a stint at modeling for top illustrators including James Montgomery Flagg, 17-year-old Dolores began acquiring bit parts in East Coast movie productions.

In 1924, following a dance duet in George White Scandals, she and her sister were signed by Warner Bros. Two years later, John Barrymore chose Dolores, a fragile blonde beauty, for his leading lady in The Sea Beast (a silent adaptation of Moby Dick). By the time the movie was remade by Barrymore as a talkie in 1930, Costello had become Barrymore's wife (1928)

❧➤ Costello, Helene (1903–1957)

American actress. Born in 1903; died in 1957; daughter of Maurice Costello (1877–1950, a silent-screen actor) and his leading lady; sister of Dolores Costello (1905–1979); married, in 1930.

For a short time in the 1920s, Helene Costello's film career rivaled that of her sister *Dolores Costello. Helene was the star of the first Vitaphone all-talking feature Lights of New York (1928). Her other films include The Man on the Box (1925), Don Juan (1926), In Old Kentucky (1927), The Heart of Maryland (1927), Midnight Taxi (1928), and The Circus Kid (1928). But Helene Costello married in 1930 and, with the advent of sound, effectively disappeared from the screen. In her later years, she was hospitalized while her sister Dolores supported her. Helene died in 1957.

and was pregnant, so *Joan Bennett was given the lead. "The first version, was, at least, excitingly romantic," wrote *Pauline Kael; "this talkie is much less so—Barrymore is 48 and isn't wildly in love with his leading lady (as he quite clearly was in the first), and he's working with a whale that resembles a vast mattress."

As a result of The Sea Beast, Dolores Costello became a headliner throughout the 1920s, starring in Manon Lescaut (1926), Bride of the Storm (1926), A Million Bid (1927), When a Man Loves (1927), The Third Degree (1927), Tenderloin (1928), Old San Francisco (1927), Glorious Betsy (1928), Noah's Ark (1928), The Redeeming Sin (1929), Madonna of Avenue A (1929), Glad Rag Doll (1929), and Expensive Woman (1931). After the birth of her daughter in 1933, she retired. Two years later, however, following her divorce in 1935, she returned to the screen, taking on more mature roles, such as Freddie Bartholomew's mother in Little Lord Fauntleroy (1936). Her last starring role was that of Isabel Amberson in The Magnificent Ambersons (1942), directed by Orson Welles. Except for a small role in This is the Army the following year, she retired once more, living on a ranch in Del Mar, 100 miles south of Los Angeles. In 1951, Costello attempted a stage comeback with The Great Man.

Cotrubas, Ileana (1939—)

World-famous Rumanian soprano, known especially for her Mozart roles. Born Ileana Galati in Rumania on June 9, 1939; studied in Budapest with Elenescu and Stroescu.

❧➤
See illustration
on the
following page

*Dolores
Costello*

Ileana Cotrubas made her debut in Bucharest in 1964 after studying singing there for several years. She then went to Vienna for further study and three years at the Frankfurt Opera from 1968 to 1971. In 1967, she sang the Second Boy in *Die Zauberflöte* (*The Magic Flute*), and two years later she was performing at Glyndebourne. Appearances at Covent Garden, the Paris Opéra, La Scala, and the Metropolitan followed. Her sweet-toned, agile voice conveyed vulnerability to great effect and as a result Cotrubas often played young, gentle heroines.

She sang Tatyana, Violetta, Adina, Norina, Amina, Antonia, and Manon among other characters. Many of her roles were recorded, especially those written by Mozart, before her retirement in 1989.

Cottee, Kay (1954—)

Australian yachtswoman who became the first woman to sail nonstop around the world, solo. Born in Australia in 1954.

Sailed nonstop around the world for 189 days, solo (November 1987–June 1988), covering 25,000 nautical miles; because of courage that endeared her to fellow Australians, she was the recipient of several honors, including the Australian of the Year Award.

Kay Cottee was born in 1954 with a congenital heart defect (a murmur, as well as pulmonary stenosis). Though her condition caused occasional fatigue, she proved it would never prevent her from living life to the fullest. Like many Australians, Cottee grew up fascinated by the sea; when only a child, she vowed to be the first woman to sail around the world nonstop and alone. Until the 1970s, Australian yachtswomen faced deeply entrenched prejudice, barriers that began to deteriorate just as Cottee entered the arena of women's competitive sailing. In 1978, Poland's *Krystyna Chojnowska-Liskiewicz** had successfully completed a solo trip around the world, and by the mid-1980s the idea of a woman sailing solo around the globe was no longer regarded as outlandish or ridiculous. After years of preparation, in 1986 Cottee signaled the seriousness of her plans to break major solo sailing records by entering both the Two-Handed Trans-Tasman and Solo Trans-Tasman races.

Kay Cottee sailed out of Sydney harbor aboard her 38-foot yacht *Blackmore's First Lady* on November 29, 1987. Although only a handful of family and friends were on hand to wave farewell, she was convinced that, come what may, she would succeed in achieving her goals, the first of which was to circle the globe and the second of which was to raise money to combat drug addiction among Australian youths. Much of what Cottee experienced during the next six months was of a routine nature for a seasoned sailor, but on three occasions she thought she might not return home alive. Near Cape Horn, mountainous seas swamped her boat, breaking the boom; in the Indian Ocean, a sudden squall turned *Blackmore's First Lady* on its side. She faced her third scrape with death

upon awakening from sleep to see a commercial fishing ship bearing down on her vulnerable yacht. Cottee fired a flare into the darkness, alerting the crew of the behemoth to change course just in time to miss her.

On June 5, 1988, 189 days later, she sailed *Blackmore's First Lady* back into Sydney harbor to complete the epic journey. An estimated quarter of a million cheering Australians, including her parents and boyfriend, were on hand to greet her, while the band of the Royal Australian Navy played "Waltzing Matilda." Hundreds of yachts and small boats sailed out under the famous Harbor Bridge to salute Cottee in a breathtaking pageant, while ferries sounded their horns and firefighting tugboats sprayed great plumes of water. Her voyage over, Cottee had set a number of world records. She was the first woman to circumnavigate the globe solo and nonstop without assistance. She also recorded the fastest speed and fastest time by a woman for a circumnavigation, the longest time at sea

Ileana Cotrubas

by a woman, and the greatest distance at sea by a woman. Cottee's voyage also made her the first woman to sail around the five main Capes in the southern hemisphere.

SOURCES:

Morris, Christopher. "Solo yachtswoman's record: Non-stop around the world," in *The Times* [London]. June 6, 1988, pp. 1, 24.

Stell, Marion K. *Half the Race: A History of Australian Women in Sport.* North Ryde, New South Wales: Angus and Robertson, 1991.

Vamplew, Waray *et al.*, eds. *The Oxford Companion to Australian Sport.* Melbourne: Oxford University Press, 1992.

"Woman Circles Globe," in *The New York Times.* June 6, 1988, p. C4.

John Haag, Associate Professor,
University of Georgia, Athens, Georgia

Cotten, Elizabeth (c. 1893–1987)

African-American folk singer and composer—known for her composition "Freight Train" and her left-handed, upside-down guitar picking—who began performing at age 60. Name variations: Libba Cotten; Elizabeth Cotton; Sis Nevilles. Born in early January 4 (or 5), 1893 or 1895, in Chapel Hill, North Carolina; died on June 29, 1987, in Syracuse, New York; daughter of George Nevilles (or Nevills, a miner and mill worker) and Louisa Price Nevilles (a cook, launderer, and midwife); married Frank Cotten, around 1910; children: daughter, Lillie (or Lily).

Taught herself banjo and guitar on her brother's instruments around age seven; left school at age nine; bought a guitar with own money at about age 12; was a domestic worker until she retired at age 70; after moving to Washington, D.C. (1940s), met the Seeger family and began working in their home; encouraged by Seegers, began to perform publicly (late 1950s); "Freight Train," composed at age 11 or 12, became popular during the folk-music revival period and a lawsuit was required for her to get credit and royalties; recorded several folk-music albums and appeared at many colleges, festivals and clubs (1958–80s); received Burl Ives Award from National Folk Festival Association (1972), National Endowment for the Arts National Heritage Fellowship Award, and several honors from the city of Syracuse, including city's first "Living Treasure"; was oldest person honored with Grammy Award, for Elizabeth Cotten Live! *(1984/85?); included among 75 influential African-American women in photo documentary* I Dream a World. *Famous songs, in addition to "Freight Train," are "Shake, Sugaree," "Oh, Babe, It Ain't No Lie," "I'm Going Away," and "Washington Blues."*

George and **Louisa Price Nevilles** did not give their newest child a formal name when she was born in early January 1895 in Chapel Hill, North Carolina. Around the house, she was known as Babe, Sis, or sometimes Short. On her first day of school, when the teacher asked if she had a name, she answered: "Yes, Elizabeth." Later in life, she told an interviewer, "I don't know if I'd ever heard the name, but I had to say something!" The name became her own.

Raised as farmers, both her parents had moved to Chapel Hill before Elizabeth's birth. George was a laborer, usually working in the mines or mills around the area; Louisa was a launderer, cook, and midwife. Elizabeth and her siblings did chores together and roamed the area near their home. As they worked and played, the children made up songs. "Freight Train," known to her family and friends as "Elizabeth's song," would later become identified with her in folk-music annals.

Composed when she was 11 or 12 as one of these "makeup songs," "Freight Train" invoked the spirit of the three-coach train that went by her home en route to the University of North Carolina in Chapel Hill. "We kids be always goin' watchin' that train," she remembered. "We'd get sheets and wave. You couldn't see faces, just handkerchiefs wavin' back. The train'd be so loaded with students it'd get stuck. It had to go up a little hill and it'd stall and have to wait for another engine to come push it." When a freight train hauling furniture took to the route, the same problems occurred. Cotten recalled the "chug-a, chug-a, chug-a, chug-a" sound of the train as it went by the house and "the clanking of the cars as they went up the hill."

In spite of the danger, or maybe because of it, train tracks were a popular playground. "We used to go over to the railroad track and play," Cotten said. "We used to watch the train come in . . . and I always wanted a train ride, I just wanted to know how did it feel. Just a level ride. [The ticket agent] says to me, 'Do you all want a little ride?' And that was exactly what we was going after. So he put us on the coach and that's when they backed up and shifted around. Take one off and put one on. Well, I got that little ride. And I got to ride on the freight train, too." After the ride, said Cotten, "me and my brother, we'd have to do the night work. We'd cut wood and sing. We would each have a song, he had his and I had mine. We used to sing about trains. That was the beginning of me writing 'Freight Train,' right along then."

In addition to the train tracks, the university—the main business of Chapel Hill—was also a center of activity and interest. Each year, even those who had no one graduating would dress up and go downtown to celebrate. "[T]hey'd buy their children little new slippers . . . dresses . . . hats . . . going to the commencement," Cotten reminisced. The graduates "would have a beautiful march," she continued. "If there would be room they would let us in but there was never no room. So we used to hang in the window. I didn't, but my brothers did, just to get to see them march in." At the university commencement ceremonies, young Elizabeth learned another tune, "Graduation March," that she arranged for guitar. When the graduates marched in, "they'd play that band song that I pick on the guitar; that's what they'd march to."

Cotten's brothers and sisters, all of whom could play instruments and sing, made fiddles out of corn cobs, played on a comb through paper, and used mouth harps. "At Christmas," she recalled, "we'd go serenadin' folks, and sometimes they'd give us a apple or a drink of locust beer. We used to make up songs ourselves and see who can do it fastest." Her older brother sang and played his banjo when he came in at night. By listening to him, Cotten learned the tunes and how to pick the strings. Despite the obstacle of being left-handed (at that time, all string instruments were built to be played in right-handed fashion), she had created her own style for playing and could pick out popular tunes on the banjo by the time she was seven.

When her brother bought a guitar, he put it under the bed to hide it from her, but Cotten soon found it and would sneak the instrument out to practice when he was gone: sometimes a broken string gave her away. Playing and learning tunes became almost as important to her as eating, as Cotten taught herself the left-handed picking pattern she later became famous for.

> The first thing I'd do, I laid the guitar flat in my lap and worked my left hand till I could play the strings backwards and forwards. And then after I got so I could do that, then I started to chord it and get the sound of a song that I know. And if it weren't but one

Elizabeth Cotten

string I'd get that. Then finally I'd add another string to that, and keep on till I could work my fingers pretty good. And that's how I started playing with two fingers. And after I started playing with two fingers for a while, I started using three. I was just trying to see what I could do. I never had any lessons, nobody to teach me anything. I just picked it up.

Cotten only needed to hear a song once to pick out the tune on the guitar or banjo. Chapel Hill had many musicians, so she had ample opportunity to hear the folk songs of the region. When strumming with her brothers, she played melody while one brother played bass and the other chords. They made music for family and friends.

Like many African-American children of her era, Elizabeth Cotten had to leave school to begin working. By age 9, she was a day worker and live-in helper in the Chapel Hill area. At 12, she was earning one dollar per month, "carrying wood and minding children for a Chapel Hill family." Her mother saved the money and bought her a guitar that cost four months' wages.

She was a creative songster and musician, a smooth, subtle instrumentalist, and possessed a very special grace which she communicated so well to her friends and public audience.

—Mike Seeger

When she was a young teenager, Elizabeth "got religion," as she put it, and joined the Baptist church. There she was told she could no longer play the songs she'd grown up with: "The Deacon . . . told me, 'You got to stop and serve God.' Sometimes I played them, but I weaned myself away." From then until age 58, she played guitar only occasionally, in church. When she was 15, she married Frank Cotten and had a daughter whom she named Lillie. Elizabeth worked as a cook and housekeeper in Chapel Hill with one sojourn in New York City.

In the early 1940s, when Cotten was in her 40s, she moved to Washington, D.C., to be near her daughter and grandchildren. She continued working as a housekeeper and had a seasonal job at Lansburgh's department store. Near Christmas, folk-song scholar *Ruth Crawford (Seeger) was shopping at Lansburgh's, with her baby and young daughter ◄▒ **Peggy Seeger** in tow. When Peggy wandered away from her mother, a search was launched and Cotten found her. "She was crying so hard," said Cotten. Ruth liked Eliza-

Seeger, Peggy (b. 1935). See *Crawford, Ruth* for sidebar.

beth immediately and offered her a job as housekeeper and cook for the Seeger family, which included Peggy's siblings, Mike, **Barbara** and **Penny Seeger**, and their father, ethnomusicologist Charles Seeger. It was Penny who nicknamed Cotten "Libba"; "Elizabeth" was too much to say. Cotten would remain with them for a decade, helping the family through Ruth Seeger's illness and death from cancer in 1953.

Some years after Cotten began working for the Seegers, Peggy discovered their housekeeper playing the guitar. "I didn't say word," recalled Cotten. "I didn't know how she'd feel about it. I was playing her guitar. . . . 'Well,' she said, 'what were you playing?' I said, '"Freight Train."' So she said, 'Play it for me,' and I sang and played 'Freight Train.' And that's the beginning, how they learned I could play a guitar." That day, Mike Seeger returned from school and learned Cotten's secret. Said Mike: "It was one of those rare moments. Peggy said, 'Did you know Libba could play?' or something like that. We went into the music room and she played 'In the Sweet Bye and Bye,' which is a church song. She played it first in the very four-square church manner and then . . . there was a brief pause and . . . she played it in the ragtime style. And it was *incredible*, a cross between a classical parlor style and blues, which is what I think makes her music so charming; it's sparse and reserved but also just a little bit loose."

Intrigued by her upside-down, two-finger playing style, the children made deals to clear the table, wash the dishes, and do other house work so that Cotten would play for them. Peggy and Mike were blossoming as folk singers themselves and listened avidly to Cotten's repertoire of songs.

In 1957, Peggy Seeger performed "Freight Train" on a tour of Europe. While in England, she allowed a recording of the song and thus unwittingly promoted its commercial debut at the beginning of the great folk-song boom. The tune was popularized in England by **Nancy Whiskey** but no mention was given of a composer. Cotten first knew of the liberties taken when she heard her song on television. "I was sitting at home one night and . . . they announced Nancy Whiskey was going to sing it. When I heard it," she continued, "I said, 'That's my song.' I felt terrible 'bout it. Everybody knew it was my song." Although the Seeger children helped her get a settlement for the unacknowledged recordings, Cotten felt she would never get the same monetary compensation others received from the song. By the early 1980s, over 25 recordings of the song had been made by different singers, including **Rusty Draper**, Peter, Paul and Mary, Peter and Gordon, Dick and DeeDee, and Cotten herself. Pete Seeger, older half-brother of Peggy and Mike, recorded the song, and guitarists added "Freight Train" to their repertoires. Later, it was recorded by country music performers like Chet Atkins, Jimmy Dean, and Jim and Jesse (the latter set new words to Cotten's tune). In 1974, Cotten was an invited witness at the Senate's hearings on the American Folklife Preservation Act. Performing "Freight Train," she had senators and onlookers joining the singing.

Elizabeth Cotten began her own performance and recording career after the misadventure with "Freight Train." In 1957 and 1958, Mike Seeger taped Cotten singing at her home in Washington, D.C. The first album was released in 1958 by the Smithsonian's Folkways Recordings and led to bookings. Her first concert appearance was shared with Mike Seeger at Swarthmore College in 1960. The following year, Cotten was one of several amateur musicians who appeared at the first University of Chicago Folk Festival. Traveling across the United States and Canada, Cotten appeared on college campuses, at festivals, and in clubs, coffee houses and auditoriums. Interest in her music inspired further remembrances of folk songs from her youth and the composition of new ones, aided by her great-grandchildren. Most of the latter songs were included on her second album from Folkways, *Shake Sugaree.*

Cotten developed her own stage persona, using the name "Libba." She would play her music, tell about her life while continuing to pick background music, then urge audiences to sing along. "Libba Cotten, seventy-two years old and black, got a standing ovation from 3,000 white students at Duke University in March," wrote a proud Peter Seeger. How she performed "broke all the rules of show business." The album *Elizabeth Cotten Live,* for which she won a Grammy, exemplifies her stage programs from the early 1980s. Yet another album, Folkways' *When I'm Gone,* contains more of her older songs as well as songs she learned on the concert circuit.

Cotten's unusual method of playing guitar or banjo produced the unique sound for which she was renowned. She had several styles of playing on both guitar and banjo, but is best known for her adaptation of the southeastern country ragtime picking, also known as single string guitar picking. "Freight Train" is played in this style, which was a great influence on the next generation of folk singers such as **Judy Collins** and **Joan Baez**. Mike Seeger noted that "a lot of guitar picking where you play a bass chord and some kind of melody goes back to the influence of Elizabeth Cotten."

Around 1970, Elizabeth Cotten retired from domestic service. Although she had appeared with some frequency at musical events in the '60s and '70s, she did not begin touring regularly until the late '70s when John Ullman, of Traditional Arts Services, began handling her bookings. By 1978, she had done well enough to purchase a house in Syracuse, New York, to be near her family. In addition to recordings and personal appearances, she was also featured in a 1974 video, *Grass Roots Series #1—Old Time Music,* and appeared on the syndicated PBS television program "Me and Stella" in 1977.

Several honors came Cotten's way in her 80s and early 90s. She received the National Endowment for the Arts National Heritage Fellowship Award, and several tributes from the city of Syracuse. She was also included among the 75 influential African-American women in the photo documentary *I Dream a World.* In 1993, Cotten was listed among "The 100 Greatest Guitarists of the 20th Century" by *Musician* magazine.

"She was warm, solid in her identity and belief," wrote Mike Seeger. "She was my friend and teacher as we travelled and played music together. She will always be warmly remembered by all of us whom she touched." Elizabeth Cotten continued to do live shows until May 1987, just weeks before her death. She died in Syracuse on June 29, 1987, after a short hospitalization that included surgery after brain seizures. A few years before, she had told an interviewer: "Every time my agent sends me, I'm ready to go. I'm not going to retire till I get so I can't use my singing or my guitar strings."

SOURCES:

Cohen, Norm. *Long Steel Rail: The Railroad in American Folksong.* Urbana, IL: University of Illinois Press, 1981.

Gaume, Matilda. *Ruth Crawford Seeger: Memoirs, Memories, Music.* Composers of North America, No. 3. Metuchen, NJ: Scarecrow Press, 1986.

Harrington, Richard. "Celebrating Elizabeth Cotten," in *The Washington Post.* January 7, 1983, sec. D, p. 7.

Harris, Sheldon. *Blues Who's Who: A Biographical Dictionary of Blues Singers.* NY: Da Capo Press, 1991.

Hine, Darlene Clark, ed. *Black Women in America: An Historical Encyclopedia.* Vol. I. Brooklyn, NY: Carlson, 1993.

Lawless, Ray M. *Folksingers and Folksongs in America: A Handbook of Biography, Bibliography, and*

Discography. New rev. ed. NY: Duell, Sloan and Pearce, 1965.

Lornell, Kip. Telephone interview. January 29, 1996.

Obituary. *Facts on File World News Digest with Index.* Vol. 47, no. 2432. July 3, 1987, p. 488.

Obituary, *The New York Times,* June 30, 1987, sec. B, p. 8.

"The 100 Greatest Guitarists of the 20th Century," in *Musician.* February 1993.

Seeger, Mike. Brochure notes for Elizabeth Cotten, *Freight Train and Other North Carolina Folk Songs and Tunes.* Smithsonian Folkways C-SF 40009. Audio recording, originally issued as Folkways FG 3526.

Seeger, Pete. *The Incompleat Folksinger.* Edited by Jo Metcalf Schwartz. NY: Simon and Schuster. 1972.

Vinton, John. "'Freight Train' Carried Elizabeth Cotten to Success," in *The Sunday Star.* Washington, D.C. January 8, 1967, sec. E.

Warner, Anne. *Traditional American Folk Songs from the Anne and Frank Warner Collection.* Syracuse, NY: Syracuse University Press, 1984.

SUGGESTED READINGS:

Badeaux, Ed. "Please Don't Tell What Train I'm On," in *Sing Out!* September 14, 1964, pp. 6–11.

Baggelaar, Bristin, and Donald Milton. *Folk Music: More Than a Song.* NY: Thomas Y. Crowell, 1976.

Bastin, Bruce. *Red River Blues: The Blues Tradition in the Southeast.* The Music in American Life Series. Champaign, IL: University of Illinois Press, 1986.

Coy, Carol. "Elizabeth Cotten," in *Folk Scene.* April 1974, p. 17.

Journal of American Folklore. Published for the American Folklore Society. Boston, MA: Houghton, Mifflin, 1888–present.

March, Stephen. "Elizabeth Cotten, Gentle genius of the Guitar," in *Southern Voices.* Vol. 1. August–September 1974, pp. 69–72.

Sonnier, Austin M. *A Guide to the Blues: History, Who's Who, Research Sources.* Westport, CT: Greenwood, 1994.

COLLECTIONS:

More information about Elizabeth Cotten, as well as American folk songs and folksingers, may be found at the Office of Folklife Programs of the Smithsonian Institution, 955 L'Enfant Plaza, Suite 2600, Washington, D.C. 20560.

Margaret L. Meggs, writer of essays, articles and short stories about women's lives, teaches women's studies in college and continuing education courses

Cotten, Libba (c. 1893–1987).

See Cotten, Elizabeth.

Cotton, Elizabeth (c. 1893–1987).

See Cotten, Elizabeth.

Couchman, Elizabeth (1876–1982)

Australian politician. Name variations: Dame Elizabeth Couchman. Born on April 19, 1876, at Geelong, Australia; died on November 18, 1982; daughter of Elizabeth Mary (Ramsay) Tannock and Archibald Tannock (a confectioner); attended Girls' High School, Geelong, and University of Western Australia (B.A., 1916); married Claude Couchman (a businessman), 1917 (died, 1927); no children.

Elizabeth Couchman, an influential politician at a time when political opportunities for women were circumscribed, helped provide a political base for women in Australia. Born in 1876 to Scottish immigrants, she would later remember the political discussions between her mother and grandmother as being her earliest recollections. After matriculating from Girls' High School, Geelong, in 1895, she was a teacher at Methodist Ladies' College and at Tintern. Couchman headed to Perth for the free education available from the University of Western Australia, where she studied political science and maintained interests in constitutional law and economics. In the year following her B.A. in 1916, she married Claude Couchman in Melbourne. Widowed in 1927, she participated fully in public life as a justice of the peace, through volunteer work, and by way of the Australian Women's National League. Formed in 1904, the League was established to support loyalty to the throne and empire, battle socialism, educate women in the political arena, and protect the interests of women and children. The largest continuing non-Labor political organization, it provided the launching pad for Couchman's career.

Known for her political astuteness, insight, and administrative abilities, Couchman became president of the League in 1927. In 1932, she became the first woman to be appointed to the Australian Broadcasting Commission (ABC), a post she would hold for a decade. In this capacity, she was often on the minority side where policy was concerned; for example, her recommendation that the ABC do a report on conditions to which the Aborigines were subjected was considered too controversial. In 1934, she was a member of the Australian delegation to the League of Nations.

When the new Liberal Party was formed in December of 1944, Couchman was provided with a position of strength from which to negotiate, and she succeeded in securing structural equality for the party women. She was a member of the State Executive and State Council as well as the party's Victorian vice-president (1949–55). Sir Robert Menzies described Couchman, who at State Council raised points of order into her 80s, as "the greatest statesman of them all." She was appointed DBE (Dame of the British Empire) in 1961. Couchman died on November 18, 1982, having paved the way for other women in politics, including **Margaret Guilfoyle** whom she nominated for preselection for the Senate (1970).

SOURCES:
Radi, Heather, ed. *200 Australian Women*. NSW, Australia: Women's Redress Press, 1988.

Coucy, Isabella de (1332–1382).
See Isabella.

Coucy, Mary de (c. 1220–?).
See Mary de Coucy.

Coucy, Mary de (fl. 1300s).
See Mary de Coucy.

Coucy, Philippa de (fl. 1378).
See Philippa de Coucy.

Courland, Anne of (1693–1740).
See Anna Ivanovna.

Court, Margaret Smith (1942—)

Australian tennis player who won 24 major singles championships and was the fourth player in history to win the Grand Slam. Name variations: Margaret Smith; Margaret Court; Mrs. Barry M. Court; Reverend Margaret Court. Born on July 16, 1942, in Albury, New South Wales, Australia; daughter of Lawrence William Smith (a foreman in a cheese-and-butter processing plant) and Maud (Beaufort) Smith; attended St. Augustine's Convent, around 1956, and Albury Technical College; married Barry M. Court (a yachtsman and wool broker, later Western Australia agricultural minister), on October 28, 1967; children: Daniel Lawrence (b. 1971); Marika Margaret (b. 1974); Teresa Ann; and another daughter.

Began playing tennis at age eight at the Albury Tennis Club (1950); trained as a teenager in Melbourne; won the Australian Senior International Championship (1960); toured with the Australian team (1961); won the French, Italian and American titles (1962), and seeded first at Wimbledon but lost to Billie Jean King in their inaugural match (the first top seed in London to lose the opening round); won the Australian title again and was ranked first in women's world tennis; won the Australian title (1963) and defeated King at Wimbledon; won the Australian, Italian, and German titles (1964); won the American and All-England titles (1965); opened a boutique, called "Peephole" in Perth, Western Australia; married (1967); returned to tennis, traveling with husband who had become her manager (1968); lost all major championships except Wimbledon (1968–69); won the Grand Slam (1970); left tennis to have a child

(1971); returned to win 16 out of 18 tournaments and 78 out of 80 singles matches, 8 out of 10 tournaments on the Virginia Slims Tour (1972–April 1973); in a much publicized match, lost to Bobby Riggs, a former U.S. tennis professional (May 1973); in a world tour, defeated Chris Evert in a close match (1973); defeated Evonne Goolagong in the U.S. Open Championship (1973); won the 1973 Virginia Slims Trophy; retired after participating in the 1975 Virginia Slims Tour.

Publications: The Margaret Smith Story (1965); Court on Court: A Life in Tennis (1975), and several monographs on playing tennis.

Major titles: Australian singles (1960–66, 1969–71, 1973); French singles (1962, 1964, 1969, 1970, 1973); Wimbledon singles (1963, 1965, 1970); U.S. singles (1962, 1965, 1969–70, 1973); Australian doubles (1961–63, 1965, 1969–71, 1973); French doubles (1964–66, 1973); Wimbledon doubles (1964, 1969); U.S. doubles (1963, 1968, 1970, 1973, 1975); Australian mixed (1963–64); French mixed (1963–65, 1969); Wimbledon mixed (1963, 1965–66, 1968, 1975); U.S. mixed (1961–65, 1969–70, 1972); Federation Cup (1963–65, 1968–69, 1971. Inducted into the International Tennis Hall of Fame, International Women's Sports Hall of Fame.

Movement is my game.
—**Margaret Smith Court**

The youngest of four children, Margaret Smith Court grew up in a modest house in Albury, New South Wales, Australia, the daughter of **Maud Smith** and Lawrence Smith, a foreman in a cheese-and-butter processing plant. No one in the family was particularly interested in tennis, but two of her siblings were bicycle racers. As a child, Court was a roughneck and the leader of the "Smith Gang," a group of neighborhood boys who took pleasure in climbing trees, swinging on ropes over the river, and hitching free rides on trucks as they slowed for the sharp curves on the nearby road. At St. Bridget's, the local parochial school, she felt restricted and was the first out the door at the end of the day to play cricket, soccer, basketball, or softball with the boys. Court was so fast on her feet that she was once approached by a coach who thought she had potential as an Olympic runner.

Court's initial experience with tennis took place in the street, with makeshift boards and discarded balls. When she was eight, a friend of her mother's gave her an old, heavy tennis racket, which she used for illicit games at the nearby Albury Tennis Club. Wally Rutter, the owner of the club, was so impressed with Court's skill that

Margaret Smith Court

tralian Junior Championship, which she lost to ✤▶ **Jan Lehane** and **Lesley Turner**. In 1960, however, she defeated Lehane in the Australian Senior International Championship and went on to successfully defend her title against Lehane the following year. During the early days of her career, Court was still shy and awkward. In a 1970 interview, tennis star John Newcombe spoke of Court's teenage image: "She wasn't the sort you'd notice at a party. . . . But you certainly noticed her determination at tennis. She used to be a skinny girl, but she lifted weights, ran, trained hard and played hard."

In 1961, on a world tour with an Australian team, captained by **Nell Hopman**, Court fared badly, winning only the Kent (England) All-Comers Championship and suffering defeats in the semifinals of the Italian championship and the quarterfinals of the English and French. The following year, 1962, traveling independently of the Australian team (because of some friction with Hopman), Margaret Court was far more successful, amazing everyone by winning the Italian, French, and American titles. Seeded #1 at Wimbledon that year, she suffered an attack of nerves and lost her initial match to *Billie Jean King, thus becoming the first top seed in the prestigious tournament ever to lose on the first round. Back on home turf, however, Court won the Australian title and was ranked as the top player in the world.

Court won the Australian singles for the third consecutive time in 1963, then defeated Billy Jean King at Wimbledon, seemingly having conquered her nerves. In 1964, she won the Australian, Italian, and German championships, but lost in France, the United States, and England. The following year, she won the American and All-England titles, but confessed to being "tired and bored with everything." In 1966, after losing to **Nancy Richey** in Paris and Billie Jean King at Wimbledon, she retired, saying that she wanted to catch up on some of the social life she had sacrificed for the game.

Moving to Perth, Australia, Court shared a house with **Helen Plaisted**, an Australian squash star, and **Ann Edgar**, a teacher. Court and Plaisted opened a boutique called "Peephole," which specialized in sports gear and clothing. The business thrived, as did Court's new-found social life. Through her business contacts, she met and married Barry Court, a yachting enthusiast, wool broker, and son of the Minister of Industrial Development for Western Australia. It was Barry who introduced Court to the world of sailing and also encouraged her to return to the ten-

he made her an official member when she was ten. He also gave her her first formal tennis instruction and encouraged her to attend the Saturday afternoon tennis workshops he held for the young people in the area. Instead of paying for lessons, Court worked around the club, cutting grass, serving food, and painting lines on the courts. Rutter and his wife had no children of their own and treated Court like a daughter.

By the time she had reached adolescence, Court had collected some 50 trophies in local championships and was part of the Albury team for Country Week in Sydney, an annual competition where she regularly competed and won against older competitors. Tennis began to absorb more and more of her time, especially after she came to the attention of world champion Frank Sedgman. Apprised of her potential by Rutter, Sedgman invited Court to Melbourne. There, she lived with her older sister and worked as a receptionist at Sedgman's athletic center. Training with Stan Nicholes, who put her on a strict physical fitness program, and Keith Rogers, who coached her in her game, Court became a member of the Wilson Cup Team for the state of Victoria and won all of the state titles on the Australian junior circuit, except for the Aus-

nis tour in 1968. "Traveling with Barry was a joy," she said. "We seemed to have adventures everywhere we went. Things had never been this much fun for me when I went abroad on my own and finally I was learning to relax between matches and really enjoy life."

Although she lost all four of the major championships in 1968, Court came back strong in 1969, winning everywhere but at Wimbledon. In *Great Women Tennis Players*, Owen Davidson and C.M. Jones speculate that Court's temperament had improved. "It seemed at last that her will was now strong enough to force her to play her best tennis in crises," they wrote, "where once she would have crumbled through anxiety." Indeed, 1970 was the year of her first Grand Slam, which got under way with an easy win in the Australian singles. Court then went on to beat **Helga Niessen** in Paris and former rival Billie Jean King in London. Davidson and Jones called the match against King "the finest ever played by two women at Wimbledon—or elsewhere." Court then completed her Grand Slam with a win over the fiery *Rosemary Casals** in the American Open.

After the Grand Slam, Court went into a slump, during which she suffered muscle and stomach problems, and a persistent throat infection. After losing the Melbourne, Paris, and Wimbledon championships in 1971, she left the tour to await the arrival of her son Danny who was born in 1972. Within weeks, she joined the pro tour, and, by April 1973, Court had won 16 out of 18 tournaments and 78 out of 80 singles matches. In the first half of the lucrative Virginia Slims tour that year, she won prizes totaling $59,850.

While Court enjoyed her winning streak, Bobby Riggs, a 55-year-old former Wimbledon champion and professed "male chauvinist," was mounting a battle against women's liberation in general, and women's demands for equal purses in tennis in particular. In February 1973, he issued a challenge to play any woman in the world for a $5,000 prize (later doubled). After five major players turned Riggs down, including Billie Jean King, Court took on the challenge, which was set for May 13. "My feeling was that as the top woman player in the world I should defend women's tennis from Riggs and his insults," Court wrote in her autobiography. "I also felt confident I could beat him." She later admitted that she had been much too casual in preparing for the match, which was blown out of proportion by the media and took on a circus atmosphere. Although Court expected Riggs'

❧ Lehane, Jan (1941—)

Australian tennis champion. Name variations: Jan O'Neill. Born in Grenfell, New South Wales, in 1941.

For a brief time, from 1959 to 1960, Jan Lehane was ranked number one in senior tennis in Australia, winning the hard-court title in 1959. Margaret Court's arrival and dominance effectively placed Lehane second in her next four bids for Australian Open titles.

game to be weak, she did not expect it to be as slow as it was. Keeping the game at a snail's pace, "like a teen-ager in a Sunday afternoon doubles match," wrote Court, Riggs destroyed her rhythm and her confidence and won 6–2, 6-1. For Court, the only positive aspect of the match, and the follow-up in the Houston Astrodome four months later when Billie Jean King beat Riggs in three straight sets, was that it brought tennis into the lives of millions for the first time. This was Court's only foray into the ongoing concerns of women activists in tennis.

On the world tour in 1973, traveling with her husband and son, Court won the Australian title, then went on to face and defeat 18-year-old *Chris Evert** in the finals of the French open, one of the toughest matches of her career. In September 1973, Court won her fifth U.S. Open, defeating *Evonne Goolagong**. Cliff Gewecke described Court's performance as "the picture of steady, refined, unflamboyant play," while Phil Elderkin observed, "It is Margaret's style to hit every ball as though it were set point. . . . The big serve, the ground strokes, the ability to volley are all part of her arsenal." Her concentration, he wrote, was "wonderful to behold."

In 1974, Court dropped out of the game to have her second child, Marika, born in July of that year. After a difficult battle to get back in shape, she returned to play in the South African tournament that year, reaching the semifinals in singles but losing to **Dianne Fromholtz**. In the West Australian championships in Perth, she was seeded #3, behind **Olga Morozova**, of Russia, and Evonne Goolagong, but went on to defeat **Kerry Melville** in the semifinals and take the final from Morozova. Feeling overly confident, Court let down a bit in training for the Australian Open, which she lost to 18-year-old *Martina Navratilova**. In 1975. Court, now traveling with her husband, two children, and a nanny, joined her last Virginia Slims tour, scoring her first victory by defeating Navratilova in a three-setter 6–3, 3–6, 6–2.

Although a superb tennis player with an outstanding record, Court was never popular among her colleagues, especially the Americans. "Maybe it's because she's naturally quiet and withdrawn," speculated reporter Barry Lorge. "Maybe it's because she developed her game and her career individually, not as part of a clique. Maybe it's envy. Maybe it's resentment of Margaret's diffidence. . . . Tennis is growing as a spectator sport and the women are battling and scratching for their share of prize money. Many of them are frustrated that the number one player in the world has very little conception of promotion and virtually no glamour." Her trainer Stan Nicholes thought Court, like many other athletes, was misunderstood. "Many people think that Margaret is stuck up, or aloof," he said. "But this is just humble shyness. . . . I'll always remember when Margaret won Wimbledon for the first time. Over TV she thanked Keith Rogers and myself. For her in the moment of her tremendous triumph to remember us—I thought it was something." Court, who consistently passed up offers for television commercials and hated haggling for expense money, never enjoyed her fame. "My dislike of the spotlight inhibited me," she admitted, "and prevented me from cashing in on my tennis talent."

Upon her retirement in 1975, at age 32, Court had achieved an extraordinary record, ranking number one in world standings six times and becoming the second woman in history to complete the Grand Slam. (*Maureen Connolly was the first, in 1953.) At the end of the 1972 season, Court had a record of 20 victories in the four major international tournaments, 13 doubles championships, and 16 mixed doubles. Perhaps more important to her, however, was the fact that she had also managed to combine her career with marriage and motherhood (which later included a third child). "I'm just a wife and mother who plays tennis," she wrote. In 1982, Court began studying for the ministry; as of 1999, she was a senior minister at the Victory Life Church in Perth.

SOURCES:
Brown, Gwilym. *Sports Illustrated*. September 14, 1970.
Court, Margaret Smith. with George McGann. *Court on Court: A Life in Tennis*. NY: Dodd, Mead, 1975.
Elderkin, Phil. *Christian Science Monitor*. May 11, 1973.
Gewecke, Cliff. *Christian Science Monitor*. February 26, 1973.
Hickok, Ralph. *Sports Champions, Their Stories and Records*. NY: Houghton Mifflin, 1995.
Lorge, Barry. *Sport*. July 1971.
"Margaret Smith Court," in *Current Biography*. NY: H.W. Wilson, 1973.
Smith, Margaret. *The Margaret Smith Story*. London: Stanley Paul, 1965.

SUGGESTED READING:
Collins, Bud. *Modern Encyclopedia of Tennis*. Detroit, MI: Gale Research, 1994.

Evelyn Bender, Ed.D., Librarian,
School District of Philadelphia, Pennsylvania

Courtenay, Eleanor (c. 1395–1418).

See Mortimer, Eleanor.

Courtenay, Margaret (fl. 1330)

*Countess of Devon. Name variations: Margaret Bohun. Flourished around 1330; daughter of Humphrey Bohun, 4th earl of Hereford, 3rd of Essex, and *Elizabeth Plantagenet (1282–1316, daughter of Edward I of England); married Hugh Courtenay (1303–1377), 2nd earl of Devon; children: Hugh Courtenay (d. around 1374), 3rd baron Courtenay.*

Courtneidge, Cicely (1893–1980)

British comedian. Name variations: Dame Cicely Courtneidge. Born Esmeralda Cicely Courtneidge on April 1, 1893, in Sydney, Australia; died on April 26, 1980, in London, England; daughter of Robert Courtneidge (an actor, manager, and producer); educated in London and Switzerland; married Jack Hulbert (an actor), in 1915 (died 1978).

Films: Elstree Calling (1930); The Ghost Train (1931); Jack's the Boy (Night and Day, 1932); Soldiers of the King (The Woman in Command, 1933); Aunt Sally (Along Came Sally, 1934); Me and Marlborough (1935); The Perfect Gentleman (US, 1935); Things Are Looking Up (1935); Everybody Dance (1936); Take My Tip (1937); Under Your Hat (1940); Miss Tylip Stays the Night (1955); Spider's Web (1960); The L-Shaped Room (1962); The Magnificent Men in Their Flying Machines (1965); The Wrong Box (1966); Not Now, My Darling (1973).

Comedian and musical comedy star Dame Cicely Courtneidge credited half her success to her husband Jack Hulbert, her acting partner, producer, and, often times, director from 1913 until his death in 1978. Known affectionately as Cis and Jack, the couple were beloved by British theatergoers. By all accounts, the energy with which they performed was remarkable right to the end. At a performance of the revival of *Dear Octopus* in 1967, a young man, who had never seen the couple before, was overheard remarking to his equally young companion, "The

Mother, you know, Cicely what's-her-name—she's got such fantastic, such extraordinary . . . vitality!"

Courtneidge, daughter of theater impresario Robert Courtneidge, was born in Australia. Her given first name, Esmeralda, was the title of the comic opera in which her father was playing when she arrived. Little is known about her mother. Her father's influence was strong, and it was assumed that she would follow in his footsteps. As a child, Courtneidge received dancing, elocution, and singing lessons along with her regular education. She made her stage debut at age eight, as one of the fairies in *A Midsummer Night's Dream* (her one and only Shakespearean role). After touring with her father in Australia, she returned to England and continued to work under his management. Her London debut came as Rosie Lucas in the production of *Tom Jones* (1907), which was followed by a string of ingenue roles in musical comedies, including *The Pearl Girl* (1913), opposite then newcomer Hulbert. Although Courtneidge admitted that she was not overly impressed with him at first, she eventually succumbed to his enthusiasm for rehearsing the love scenes. They married three years later.

Around 1916, when a series of flops drove her father into debt, Courtneidge was forced for the first time to look for employment independent of him. Unable to find anything in musical comedy, she set aside her dream of becoming the second *Gertie Millar (one of the famous "Gaiety Girls") and went to work putting together a music-hall act. Courtneidge, who never envisioned herself a comedian, was an instant success, especially with her male impersonations that she would continue to perform in shows for over 30 years. Her most popular number was the Guardsman singing "There's Something About a Soldier," although she was also cited for her impersonation of Noel Coward in the revue *Over the Moon*.

While Courtneidge toured the variety circuit, her husband, recently returned from World War I, reestablished his career. The couple first appeared together in a revue called *Ring Up*, but it was not until 1923 that their stage partnership began to take off, with successes like *Little Revue Starts at Nine O'Clock* (1923), *By the Way* (1925, and in New York, 1926), *Clowns in Clover* (1927), and *The House That Jack Built* (1929). Although they became one of the top draws at the West End and should have been a very rich couple, their business manager was less than capable, and they found themselves seri-

Cicely Courtneidge

ously in debt. In order to double their income potential, Courtneidge went back to the music halls, while Hulbert took theater roles.

During the 1930s, film work also helped them achieve solvency. Courtneidge mostly co-starred with her husband, but also did several solo films, including one of her biggest successes, *Soldiers of the King* (1933), in which she played both mother and daughter. In 1935, she appeared in *Things Are Looking Up*, considered by some to be her best film, in which she played a circus equestrian who impersonates her twin sister, a prim schoolteacher. Less successful was an MGM effort, *The Perfect Gentleman*, which was released as *The Imperfect Woman* in Britain. In her memoirs, *Cicely* (1953), Courtneidge assessed the film: "I didn't think the result very good. I will go further. I thought it was rubbish. We remade the rubbish, twice with different directors." Her ebullience and broad comedy did not appeal to everyone, especially American audiences, and, according to some critics, it did not transfer well to film. In America, André Sennwald of *The New York Times* wrote: "Frequently her humour is down around its old level of elephantine burlesque and vaudeville athleticism. But she can be surprisingly effective on occasion." Of her few later films, Courtneidge's featured role of the aging and lonely lesbian in *The L-Shaped Room* (1962) is considered outstanding.

The couple returned to the stage in *Under Your Hat* (1938), written and directed by Hulbert, which enjoyed a two-year run (it was later made into a film). During World War II, they had success in *Hulbert Follies* (1941), *Full Swing* (1942), and *Something in the Air* (1943). After the war, Hulbert produced a solo vehicle for his wife called *Under the Counter*, a topical satire on the black market during the war. They took the show to New York in 1947, where the British humor fell flat.

From the first days of her marriage, Courtneidge relied on her husband to help guide her career. She credited Hulbert with believing in her even when she doubted herself. "Only Jack firmly believed I could switch from romantic parts to the hurly-burly of the music halls," she said. When they began their work together on the stage, he became her best critic, possessing what she called a "critical faculty which leaves a sweet taste in the mouth." Offstage, Courtneidge's hobby was her home in Mayfair, where she indulged her actor friends with late-night dinners and shop talk. She also managed the couple's business affairs, which included deciphering complicated performing contracts.

In 1951, Courtneidge and Hulbert starred in the Ivor Novello musical *Gay's the Word*, in which Courtneidge sang "Vitality." This number, delivered in her characteristic "singing speech," became her theme song. (Novello died suddenly just three weeks into the run.) Courtneidge then returned to revue with *Over the Moon*, followed by a tour with Hulbert in Scotland. In 1960, the couple appeared together in the farce *The Bride Comes Back*, their first partnership in a non-musical play. A reviewer in *Plays and Players* praised Courtneidge for her pacing and the use of devices that were beyond actresses half her age: "I shall not soon forget the brilliant technique with which she 'stumbles' down the staircase on high stiletto heels on the morning after the night before."

In 1961, at age 65, Courtneidge took on her first solo leading part in a straight play (and without her husband directing), *The Bride and the Bachelor*, by Ronald Millar. This production was a difficult undertaking for her, as she was surrounded by new faces and confronted with a challenging script that had to be rewritten during its pre-London tour. Millar was overwhelmed by her professionalism. "Nothing mattered to Cis except the job at hand," he said. "She was prepared to work night and day and try any suggestions that looked promising." Although initial press was poor, television clips enticed audiences for a run of 500 performances. (Courtneidge avoided reviews of her work, saying she was easily hurt and that she needed to remained buoyed up, especially if a show was not an immediate success.) In 1967, with her husband beside her, she triumphed in another straight role, that of Dora Randolph in *Dodie Smith's Dear Octopus*. The reviews were glowing. Wrote John Russell Taylor: "Jack Hulbert and Cicely Courtneidge play with the sort of splendid confidence that only a lifetime of being applauded at every entrance can give."

Courtneidge went on to play in *Move Over, Mrs. Markham* (1971), her last appearance in the West End. In 1972, she was made a Dame of the British Empire (DBE). In 1976, she toured with Hulbert in the autobiographical *Once More with Music*. When Hulbert died in 1978, Courtneidge could not regroup. On what would have been her husband's 88th birthday, she fell into a coma and never regained consciousness. She died on April 26, 1980.

Barbara Morgan,
Melrose, Massachusetts

Cousins, Margaret (1878–1954)

Irish suffragist, theosophist, and vegetarian who immigrated to India in 1915, and was active in Indian women's and nationalist movements, and became the first woman magistrate in India. Name variations: M.E.C.; Gretta. Born Margaret Elizabeth Gillespie on November 7, 1878, in Boyle, Co. Roscommon, Ireland; died in Adyar, India, on March 11, 1954; attended local National (elementary) School in Boyle and Boyle Intermediate School; won a scholarship to Victoria High School for Girls in Derry; studied at the Royal Academy of Music in Dublin; received a Bachelors degree in Music at the Royal University of Ireland in 1902; married James Cousins (a poet, teacher, lecturer, and government adviser), in 1903; no children.

Awards: elected to be the first non-Indian member of the Indian Women's University at Poona (1916); invited to become first woman magistrate in India (1922); awarded Founders' Silver Medal of the Theosophical Society (1928); granted scholarship by the International Institute of the Teachers' College in Columbia University, New York (1931); awarded 5,000 rupees by the Madras government for being a "political sufferer for Indian freedom" (1949).

Helped organize the Irish Vegetarian Society (1904–05); was one of the four founders of the Irish Women's Franchise League (1908); served one month in prison in Holloway jail for stone throwing (1910); served one month in Tullamore jail for breaking windows (1913); moved to Liverpool with husband (June 1913); became founder member of the Church of the New Ideal (March 1914); sailed for India (October 1915); served as founder member of the Women's Indian Association (July 1917); appointed foundation head-mistress of the National Girls' School in Mangalore (1919–20); became first honorary woman magistrate in Madras (1922); initiated first All-Asia Women's Conference at Lahore (January 1931); addressed mass meeting in New York to protest imprisonment of Gandhi (February 1932); sentenced to one year's imprisonment at Vellore for addressing a public meeting (December 1932).

Selected publications: The Awakening of Asian Womanhood *(Madras: Ganesh, 1922);* The Music of Orient and Occident *(Madras: B.G. Paul, 1935);* Indian Womanhood Today *(Allahabad: Kitabistan, 1941); (with James Cousins)* We Two Together *(Madras: Ganesh, 1950).*

Vastly different in size and population, and geographically thousands of miles apart, Ireland and India have experienced common dilemmas as a result of their colonization by Britain. Their women have had similar tugs of loyalties; whether to fight for their countries freedom or put their energies into the women's suffrage and other feminist causes at the risk of being labeled unfeminine and unpatriotic. A woman who recognized the similarities and was a supporter of nationalist and feminist causes in both countries was Irishwoman Margaret Cousins, born Margaret Elizabeth Gillespie.

In 1878, the year of Cousins' birth, Charles Stuart Parnell, the leader of the Irish Parliamentary Party at Westminster, was wielding constitutional nationalists into a force to be reckoned with, and Home Rule for Ireland was becoming a possibility at some point in the future. The revolutionary nationalists, the Fenians, were planning to gain independence by more violent means. In India, seven years later in 1885, the Indian National Congress was formed to fight for Indian Home Rule. By this stage, John Stuart Mill, an English Liberal member of Parliament,

had already raised the issue of women's suffrage at Westminster when he attempted to add a women's suffrage amendment to the 1867 Reform Bill. Despite his failure, his efforts did not go unrewarded as they inspired the foundation of women's suffrage movements in both Britain and Ireland. These three issues, Irish independence, Indian independence, and women's rights would be major influences in Cousins' life.

As a girl growing up in the west of Ireland, Cousins, the eldest of 12 children in a Protestant Unionist household, quickly became politically aware; one of her daily tasks was to read the newspaper to her father. In the joint autobiography she later wrote with her husband James H. Cousins, she recalls seeing Parnell addressing a meeting in her town of Boyle, County Roscommon, and later observed the condemnation that was poured upon him by the clergy when he was named as co-respondent with *Katherine O'Shea in a divorce case that cost him his political career. Despite her Protestant background, Cousins very much sympathized with the Home Rule cause.

Within my first year of landing on Indian soil I was dedicated to the service of India via service to that half of India—its womanhood—which seemed to me the most direct instrument for leverage of the whole people.

—Margaret Cousins

Her experiences as a daughter and her observations of her own and her sisters' different treatment from their younger brothers brought home to her the injustice of women's unequal position in the world. This was reinforced by her sympathy for her mother who had little say in running the household. Mrs. Gillespie was not given a weekly or monthly allowance, only accounts at local stores. When bills had to be paid, she always encountered complaints and "black looks" from her husband. To Cousins, who, nevertheless, seemed to hold great affection for her father, this situation was indicative of the plight of many women. "And it was there and then that my girlish determination began to try and change the financial status of wives and mothers, who all worked so hard and got no money for themselves. I saw that it was a kind of curse in those days to be born a girl; and I used to wish deeply that I had been born a boy."

A successful student, Cousins appeared to have enjoyed her schooling and was particularly astute at music. She developed her talents in this direction and obtained a scholarship to a high school in Derry. It is significant that, on leaving this institution, her headmistress warned her: "I should not be so independent." Independence of spirit was a characteristic that was to remain with her throughout her life.

After high school, she went to Dublin to study music. This was in the first years of the 20th century when the atmosphere in Dublin was invigorating for young intellectuals. The Celtic revival and Irish literary Renaissance were in full swing and writers like James Joyce, W.B. Yeats, and J.M. Synge were making their names known in literature, poetry, and drama. The nationalist movement, too, which was not unconnected, was also gathering force. These were the circles that Margaret got drawn into, and she met her future husband, schoolteacher and rising poet James Cousins, during this period. According to her memoirs, there seems to be an initial period when she had to persuade herself that he would be a suitable partner. In time, however, their common interests in poetry, music, literature, and theosophy created a bond that was to last 50 years.

At the time of their marriage, she declared that she would join her spouse in his vegetarianism and now was "happy to look the animal kingdom innocently in the face." In the ensuing years before the First World War, James taught high school, and she taught music part-time. Three issues dominated their attention: vegetarianism, theosophy, and women's suffrage. They helped found the Irish Vegetarian Society in 1905, and Margaret Cousins was its honorary secretary. They were regulars at the vegetarian restaurant in College Street, Dublin, which, writes C.P. Curran, "was a rendezvous for the literary set" and became "a place of propaganda." There, they and their friends would discuss life and politics. Some were fascinated by the supernatural and claimed to have psychic experiences.

This led the couple into theosophy, a study of the mysticism of the East, and also into participation in seances. They went to hear and meet *Annie Besant, the renowned theosophist, on her visit to Dublin in 1902 to give a lecture on "Theosophy and Ireland." This portentous meeting with an Englishwoman who claimed to be three-quarters Irish would later lead Margaret and James to a new life in India in 1915. After another visit by Besant in 1909, the couple helped resurrect the Dublin Lodge of the Theosophical Society.

All of Margaret Cousins' interests very much overlapped and had an impact upon each other. When she went to Manchester in 1906 to attend a vegetarian conference, she also ended up attending a conference of the National Council of Women. There, she made contacts with English women suffragists and was deeply interested in their campaign for the enfranchisement of women. So much so that in the following years she was to make return visits to attend meetings of the Women's Social and Political Union that was led by the *Pankhursts. Cousins participated in their campaigns and, indeed, in their violence.

Fired up by her English contacts with suffragism, Cousins and her husband, along with another couple, Frank and *Hanna Sheehy-Skeffington, founded the Irish Women's Franchise League (IWFL) in November 1908. This was not the first, or only, suffrage movement in Ireland. The Irish Women's Suffrage and Local Government Association (IWSLGA) had been founded by Quaker *Anna Haslam and her husband back in 1867, shortly after John Stuart Mill's failed attempt to amend the Second Reform Bill, and there were other organizations reflecting different denominations and political orientations. However, the new, militant IWFL deemed them all to be too mild and asserted that the IWSLGA had failed entirely to awaken popular enthusiasm or sympathy, and that the masses of the population had never heard of it.

Cousins, who was determined that she would wake up the Irish public, took to speaking on the back of trucks, in parks, in meeting halls, outside churches, before university students, and anywhere else she could find a crowd gathering. She later recalled her tours around the country: "In rousing and educating opinion in country towns our experiences were very varied. Usually we set off two by two on tours. There were difficulties in securing places for meetings, difficulty in finding hotel accommodation or a press that would urgently print our notices of a meeting. Very rarely did we find a local man or woman who would preside." It did not take her long to get used to public speaking, although at first she practiced "in a field behind our house with only an ass for my audience."

Between 1908 and 1913, Margaret Cousins was very much involved in the suffrage movements in both England and Ireland. She was a regular contributor to the weekly newspaper of the IWFL, *The Irish Citizen*, and wrote columns on a wide number of issues. She was in contact with international suffragists and played a role in bringing foreign suffragists to Ireland for lecture tours.

The problems facing suffragists in Ireland were more complex than those facing women in England. Irish women did not have a domestic parliament to appeal to. They had to petition the Parliament at Westminster along with English women for a women's suffrage bill. They also had an alternate route of petitioning Irish politicians who had seats there and tried to persuade them to have a women's suffrage amendment included in a Home Rule Bill for Ireland. However, the Irish members of Parliament were reluctant to include anything that might jeopardize the Home Rule Bill. And it was unlikely that as long as the British Parliament was unwilling to give the vote to English women that they would give it to Irish women.

Cousins and her fellow suffragists were not deterred by these obstacles and were determined to make their voices heard. In 1910, Margaret served a month in Holloway, the women's prison in London, for throwing stones at No. 10 Downing Street, the residence of the Liberal prime minister, Herbert Henry Asquith. She was again sentenced for the cause in 1913. This time it was in Tullamore jail in Ireland for breaking windows in Dublin Castle, the center of British administration in Ireland. Her stay in Tullamore was marked by a hunger strike that was carried out in order to get political status. In a letter to the chair of the prison board, she asserted: "I am not a criminal but a political prisoner—my motives were neither criminal nor personal—being wholly associated with the agitation to obtain Votes for Women. I shall fight in every way in my power against being branded a criminal." Cousins was successful in her fight for political status and was released after a month.

In June 1913, Margaret and James moved to Liverpool, England. Although they were very much part of Dublin life and active in many spheres, their financial situation was not a happy one. In their joint autobiography, James Cousins talks about being a bankrupt and unable to manage upon his meager teacher's salary. He was offered a position in Liverpool with a much higher salary by a businessman with vegetarian interests. This was to be an interim step on their way to India to pursue their interests in theosophy.

While in England, Margaret Cousins continued her activities with the WSPU and also became president of the Liverpool Vegetarian Society. She blended her interests in feminism and spiritualism when she became a founder member of a church for women called the Church of the New Ideal. "I was not myself an enthusiastic churchgoer," she recalled. "Yet psalms and hymns stirred something in my background, and where responses did not agree with my conviction, I left on others the responsibility of making them." She was aware of dissatisfaction among other women with their churches, particularly Church of England women, and argued that, "Preaching has been a masculine monopoly, but the women's time to preach is coming. Women would no doubt preach the same things as men, but they would view them from a different angle." She asserted that if the churches did not voluntarily change their attitudes towards women, "women will organize their own churches." There are few known records on this church, and Cousins only gives it a small space in her autobiography. However, its services did seem to be recognizably Christian and there was an emphasis on women preaching.

World War I had been going on for more than a year when the couple finally set sail for India in October 1915. They had been informed by Annie Besant that she had use for their skills. Margaret Cousins' experiences in England and Ireland in many ways prepared her for her next 40 years in India. The same causes and issues evident in her early life were to consume her as the years went by.

Women's education at all levels became a major commitment for Cousins. She was the first non-Indian member of the women's university at Poona in 1916 and worked hard to improve the curriculum. In 1919, she traveled 1,000 miles to start a girls' school at Mangalore. It was here she came up against the reality of child marriage that she was later to campaign against. She was appalled at the lack of girls' schools in India and reckoned that for every ten boys' schools there was only one for girls. Her arguments were shrewd; she questioned how uneducated women could make good wives for educated men. She campaigned hard for compulsory education for girls, and largely through her efforts it was introduced in Madras in 1932. In 1934, she was appointed to the board of Studies in Western Music at Madras University. Subsequently, she published a book, *The Music of Orient and Occident* (Madras, 1935), which was based upon a collection of articles she had written for the Indian press. She offered to "the Goddess of Music this humble endeavor to promote mutual appreciation between East and West through the medium of sweet sound."

When she first came to India, Cousins believed that women's suffrage was at least one hundred years away. Within a year or two, however, she changed her mind and began actively campaigning for the vote for Indian women. Her experience in the Irish and English suffrage movements came in handy, especially when she had to speak to the British, petition politicians, organize, lecture, and produce a journal. She helped found the Women's India Association (WIA) in 1917 and was editor of its monthly journal *Stri Dharma*. There were similarities with the Irish suffrage campaign: India was not yet independent and there were disputes among women in the WIA whether or not women's suffrage was detracting from the nationalist cause. There were differences of opinion between Annie Besant, its president, and Margaret Cousins on this matter. Nevertheless, Cousins and a number of supporters persisted, and in 1917 Madras became the first Indian region to grant women full suffrage rights. Other sections of India followed over the next ten years. In fact, Cousins proudly claimed that women in India had full suffrage earlier than British women who had to wait until 1928 to qualify for the vote at the age of 21.

Women's suffrage was only one of Cousins' feminist concerns. She wrote two books, *Awakening of Asian Womanhood* (1922) and *Indian Womanhood Today* (1941), and numerous journal and newspaper articles that outlined the areas that could be focused upon to improve the quality of women's lives. Child marriage, the *purdah* system, the plight of young widows, the scarcity of education for women, and vocational training were all issues that claimed her attention. Her heart went out to little girls as young as five or six who were married off and producing babies by the time they were 12 or 13. Then there were those females who were widowed in their teens and for the rest of their lives had no status and were treated as no better than servants by their in-laws and families. Purdah or the enclosure of Muslim women was, she declared, both physically and mentally oppressive, and the society as a whole could not advance if women were continued to be kept in this manner.

These were not problems that Cousins could solve alone or in the immediate future, but they were focused upon at several conferences she helped to organize. In 1927, the first All-India Women's Conference was held at Poona, concentrating on educational reform. Other such conferences followed, and in 1931 the first All-Asia Women's Conference was held at Lahore, largely due to the efforts of Cousins who had been inspired when she attended a session of the Pan-Pacific Women's Conference in the United States in 1930. Another All-India Women's conference was held at Ahmedabad in December 1936, which Cousins presided over.

She did not just write and lecture on women's issues. Cousins was very much involved in philanthropic work and was instrumental in setting up child, maternity, and welfare clinics to improve the lot of Indian women, as well as encouraging the setting up of networks of women's organizations, and calling for the establishment of teacher-training colleges for women. With her community services widely recognized, she was appointed first woman magistrate in Madras, as well as India, in 1922. As magistrate, she was in a position to observe the general injustices in society and have a role in correcting the behavior of individuals.

Coming from Ireland, Margaret Cousins had full sympathy with the cause of Indian nationalism. She had close associations with the Indian National Congress and was a friend and associate of Mohandas Gandhi. She spoke on behalf of the Indian National Congress and in defense of Gandhi and his imprisonment at a mass meeting in New York in 1932. Several months later, she pleaded at the League of Nations in Geneva for Indian independence: "In those centers of international opinion I laid bare the dual game Britain is playing; its pretence of making a Constitution to give India freedom, but its determination to hold tight to everything essential to India's self-government."

When she returned to India after a year-and-a-half's absence towards the end of 1932, she found that things had tightened up considerably and that British rule was becoming paranoid about Indian nationalism. She particularly objected to the Ordinances that prevented public speaking. These she felt must be challenged, and after getting legal advice and meeting with several prominent nationalist individuals, including Gandhi who was in prison, she decided to address a public meeting of more than a thousand people on a beach. Arrested shortly after, she gave an impassioned courtroom speech pleading the cause of Indian nationalism. She concluded by saying, "If it is their intention to strike me dumb for a year, are we to deduce that their new Constitution is going to be so unsatisfactory that I must be locked up for all time to prevent my criticism of it? If this is British justice and democracy, then I am proud of free speech and Indian national freedom, and I am ashamed that English idealism has fallen to the present depths of oppression."

She spent ten and a half months in prison, and, while there, true to form, attempted to improve the lot of her fellow prisoners. She took over part of the prison courtyard to plant flowers, and she started classes in civics, singing, and needlework. She was also able to persuade prison authorities to allow her to give weekly recitals for "our other sisters" (women under life sentences) using Indian records and an old gramophone. The reality of capital punishment was brought before her when a woman in the second next cell was hanged for a domestic murder for which she claimed innocence. Cousins was to campaign against this when she came out of prison.

During the remainder of the 1930s and part of the 1940s, Cousins continued pursuing issues that had always interested her. She and James began writing their joint autobiography in 1940. Over 700 pages, this volume is an invaluable resource on the suffrage movements in Ireland and England and the woman's movement in India, as well as being a fascinating account of the Indian nationalist movement and providing insight for scholars of theosophy. She campaigned for election candidates who were members of the National Congress Party. Likewise, she supported women candidates in a variety of elections. She continued her philanthropic and educational work and her advocacy of female education. Theosophy remained important for the rest of her life, as well as music. Throughout, a piano was never far from her side. Her reputation spread nationally and internationally, and wherever she traveled she was asked to lecture.

Bad health finally slowed Cousins down in the 1940s. She had high blood pressure and suffered from a stroke. Her husband and good friends took care of her in her remaining years. Nevertheless, she lived long enough to see Indian Independence in 1947, though it was somewhat soured by the partition of the country and the creation of Pakistan. The new Indian government recognized her contributions to the state by awarding her 5,000 rupees in 1949, a great help to the financially strapped couple. She also lived to witness an increasing number of Indian women participate in politics, and female education become more widespread and acceptable. While there was still much to be done at the time of her death in 1954, Margaret Cousins had initiated numerous reforms and improvements for Indian womanhood.

SOURCES:

Cousins, Margaret. *The Awakening of Asian Womanhood.* Madras: Ganesh, 1922.

——. *Indian Womanhood Today.* Allahabad, Kitabistan, 1941.

—— and James Cousins. *We Two Together.* Madras, Ganesh, 1950.

——. *The Music of Orient and Occident.* Madras, B.G. Paul, 1935.

Curran, C.P. *Under the Receding Wave.* Dublin: Gill and MacMillan, 1970.

Denson, Alan. *James H. Cousins and Margaret E. Cousins: A Biobibliographical Survey.* Kendal: Alan Denson, 1967.

Murphy, Cliona. *The Women's Suffrage Movement and Irish Society in the Early Twentieth Century.* Philadelphia, PA: Temple University Press, 1989.

One Who Knows: Mrs Margaret Cousins and Her Work in India. Madras: Women's Indian Association, 1956.

P.L.P. "James Cousins and Margaret Cousins. An Appreciation," in *Dublin Magazine.* April–June 1956, pp. 29–32.

Ramusack, Barbara. "Cultural Missionaries, Maternal Imperialists, Feminist Allies: British Women Activists in India, 1865–1945," in *Women's Studies International Forum.* Vol. 13, no. 4, 1990. pp. 309–321.

COLLECTIONS:

All-India Women's Conference Archives, Margaret Cousins Library, New Delhi; annual Reports of the Irish Women's Franchise League, National Library of Ireland.

Cliona Murphy, History Department, California State University, Bakersfield, and author of *The Women's Suffrage Movement and Irish Society in the Early Twentieth Century*

Coutts, Angela Burdett (1814–1906).

See Burdett-Coutts, Angela.

Coventy, countess of.

See Gunning, Maria (1733–1760).

Cowan, Edith (1861–1932)

Australian politician and the first woman in Australian Parliament, who worked on behalf of women's rights and services for children. Born on August 2, 1861, at Glengarry near Geraldton, Western Australia; died on June 9, 1932; daughter of Mary Eliza Dircksey (Wittenoom) Brown (a teacher) and Kenneth Brown (a pastoralist); granddaughter of **Eliza Brown** *(d. 1896), a colonist who documented Australian colonial life through letters home to her family in England; married James Cowan, on November 12, 1879; children: four daughters and a son.*

After the death of her mother **Mary Eliza Brown** in 1868, Edith Cowan's father, a pastoralist, remarried. But Kenneth Brown was an alcoholic, and he would later be sentenced to hang for the shooting of his second wife. Cowan would dedicate her life to social reforms to improve the status of women and enhance their dignity.

She married James Cowan on November 12, 1879, and the couple had four daughters and a son. James went from registrar and master of the Supreme Court to an appointment as police magistrate in Perth; the new position brought both social and economic security. Edith became the first secretary of the Karrakatta Women's Club, where women mastered public speaking and exchanged books on women's rights, health, and literature. She would later become vice-president and president of the organization. For a number of terms, she served on the North Fremantle Board of Education (which was among the few public offices open to women at the time); worked with the Ministering Children's League; and lent her efforts to the House of Mercy for unmarried mothers (Alexandra Home for Women). Cowan served as a foundation member of the Children's Protection Society and was a pioneer in the field of day nurseries for children of working mothers. In 1915, she was appointed a justice of the Children's Court and in 1920 became one of the first women to be appointed justice of the peace.

Instrumental in the creation of the Western Australian National Council of Women, Cowan served as president of the council from 1913 to 1920. When the women's movement was bitterly divided by the Health Act of 1917, which introduced compulsory notification of venereal disease, Cowan approved the act calling it "the fairest yet offered between men and women."

In 1920, she was awarded the OBE for her war work. After the ban on women in Parliament was removed, Cowan was an endorsed Nationalist candidate for West Perth (1921). She defeated the sitting member and became the first woman to enter Australian Parliament. During her term, she promoted migrant welfare, infant health centers, sex education in the State's schools, and women's rights, arguing that women should be legally entitled to a portion of their husbands' income. It was Cowan who introduced the Women's Legal Status Act, which opened the legal profession to women in Western Australian. She was defeated in the elections of 1924 and 1927.

Acting as an Australian delegate to the 7th International Conference on Women, Cowan traveled to the United States in 1925. She died on June 9, 1932, having been instrumental in making the women's movement in Western Australia a political force.

Cowden-Clarke, Mary (1809–1898).

See Clarke, Mary Cowden.

Cowen, Lenore (c. 1897–1984).

See Coffee, Lenore.

Cowl, Jane (1883–1950)

American actress and playwright. Name variations: (pseudonym) C.R. Avery; (joint pseudonym with Jane Murfin) Alan Langdon Martin. Born Grace Bailey in Boston, Massachusetts, on December 14, 1883; died in Santa Monica, California, on June 22, 1950; attended Erasmus Hall, 1902–04, and Columbia University; married Adolph Klauber (an American theatrical producer), in 1908.

Selected films: The Garden of Lies (1915); The Spreading Dawn (1917); Stage Door Canteen (1943); Once More, My Darling (1949); No Man of Her Own (1949); The Secret Fury (1950); Payment on Demand (1950).

Selected writings: (with Jane Murfin) Lilac Time (1917); (with Murfin) Daybreak (1917); Information Please (1918); (with Murfin under joint pseudonym Alan Langdon Martin) Smilin' Through (1919); (with Theodore Charles) The Jealous Moon (1928); (under name C.R. Avery) Hervey House (1935).

Once considered the most beautiful woman on the American stage, Jane Cowl made her theatrical debut in David Belasco's *Sweet Kitty Bellairs* in 1903, while still a schoolgirl. Over the next few years, she played numerous small parts while perfecting her acting technique under Belasco's direction. Her first major role in *Is Matrimony a Failure?* (1910) was greeted with critical acclaim, and she went on to star billing in *Within the Law* (1912), which enjoyed a run of 540 performances.

Cowl wrote most of her plays, many of which she also starred in, with *Jane Murfin, a friend from her Belasco days. Their first effort, *Lilac Time* (1917), was a moderate hit, but the later *Smilin' Through* (1919) turned into a Broadway phenomenon, running for 1,170 performances. (The play was written under the joint male pseudonym Alan Langdon Martin, because Cowl and Murfin suspected that sex discrimination might have contributed to the failure of two earlier plays, *Daybreak* and *Information Please*.)

In 1923, Cowl reached the peak of her acting career as Juliet in *Romeo and Juliet*, which ran for 856 consecutive performances (157 in New York, the remainder on tour), establishing the world record for Shakespearean productions. In 1924, she appeared in *Pelleas and Melisande*. A brief dry spell was followed by two hits: Noel

Coward's *Easy Virtue* (1925) and Robert Sherwood's comedy *The Road to Rome* (1927).

Subsequent efforts floundered, including a production of *The Jealous Moon*, which she wrote with Theodore Charles, and a 1930 revival of *Twelfth Night*, which she also designed. Cowl's last substantial run was in John Van Druten's *Old Acquaintance*, which opened in 1940. After some years playing stock and revivals around the country, she made her last New York stage appearance in *The First Mrs. Fraser*, in 1948.

Most of Cowl's films were undistinguished. In 1943, she appeared as herself in the movie *Stage Door Canteen*, of interest mainly because she was a co-director of the actual Stage Door Canteen operated by the American Theatre Wing during World War II. The actress died in Santa Monica, California, on June 22, 1950.

Barbara Morgan,
Melrose, Massachusetts

Cowles, Fleur (1910—)

American magazine editor, journalist, artist, and author who was founding editor of the innovative and short-lived Flair *magazine. Born Fleur Fenton in Montclair, New Jersey, on January 20, 1910; eldest of two daughters of Matthew (a businessman and manufacturer) and Eleanor (Pearl) Fenton; graduated from Montclair High School, 1926; attended School of Fine and Applied Arts, New York; married Atherton Pettingell (an advertising executive), on February 13, 1932 (divorced 1946); married Gardner Cowles (a publishing magnate), on December 27, 1946 (divorced 1955); married Tom Montague Meyer (an English millionaire), on November 18, 1955.*

Fleur Cowles is best remembered in America as the flamboyant and innovative genius behind the short-lived magazine *Flair*, which ran for just 12 issues between February 1950 and January 1951. *Flair*, however, does not tell the whole story of Cowles, who also rescued *Look* magazine from certain disaster and became a writer, painter, and philanthropist of some note. In an October 1996 article in *Vanity Fair*, coinciding with the publication of her latest book as well as a lavish volume called *The Best of Flair*, a longtime acquaintance likened Cowles to "a comet from nowhere" and commented on her fascinating self-styled life. "She invented herself, never making a false step. She has an amazing power within herself to make anything she wants happen."

Jane Cowl

Cowles grew up in Montclair, New Jersey, and has called her childhood "too painful to discuss." At the age of 11, she was keeping a secret journal under her mattress and dreaming of becoming a great writer like her idol *Katherine Mansfield. While attending New York's School of Fine and Applied Arts, she began what she refers to as "spasmodic" work in advertising by bluffing her way into a job as senior copywriter for Gimbels' department store. Cowles then moved to Boston, where she worked in a similar capacity for another store, C. Crawford Hollidge. Back in New York by 1932, she married Atherton Pettingell, an advertising executive. In 1935, the couple formed Pettingell and Fenton, a lucrative advertising agency of which she was executive vice president. Producer Harold Prince, who worked at Pettingell and Fenton in the summer of 1942 as an office boy, recalls, "it was all very theatrical, atmospheric, and glossy, with models like **Lisa Fonssagrives** stalking in and out. I liken Fleur physically to *Gertrude Lawrence** in *Lady in the Dark*. And Pettingell was a very tall, handsome, dashing fellow—very Errol Flynn-y." The marriage, however, did not endure, and they divorced in 1946.

During World War II, Cowles reinvented herself as a dollar-a-year volunteer, writing speeches for the War Production Board and other government agencies. At the end of the war, she wangled herself a permit to fly to Europe, thus becoming the first civilian woman to enter several liberated countries. Cowles says this distinction gave her status and paved her way into the White house in 1946, as Special Consultant to the Famine Emergency Committee, assisting Herbert Hoover, the committee's chair. Her Oval Office connections would continue with President Dwight D. Eisenhower, who in 1954 offered her an ambassadorship to Greece, or possibly Formosa. Thinking it might put undue strain on her then second marriage, she declined, telling the *New York Post*, "I am probably the only woman in history to turn down an ambassadorship." Eisenhower later appointed her as special envoy to Queen *Elizabeth II*'s coronation.

No matter what you've got, it takes more than that.

—Sign opposite Fleur Cowles' desk at *Look* magazine.

Her career in publishing began in 1946, with her marriage to Gardner "Mike" Cowles, president of Cowles Magazines, publishers of the floundering *Look* magazine as well as several newspapers. Eight months into the marriage, she was directing the new women's department of the magazine and representing the female point of view on the executive editorial board. Hoping to turn *Look* into a family magazine—and to compete on an equal footing with *Life*—she introduced sections on food, fashion, and family problems, thus doubling *Look*'s advertising core and circulation within two years. Her frank, demanding style, however, made enemies along the way. In spite of incredibly long work days, the Cowleses maintained a glamorous lifestyle, which included high-powered and celebrity friends like *Marilyn Monroe* and Bernard Baruch (who for a time telephoned Cowles daily to drill her on world affairs). They further enlarged their social circle with a yearly trip around the world.

All the while, Cowles was formulating plans for *Flair*, a monthly "class" magazine that turned out to be one of the most beautiful, eclectic publications ever seen in the United States. In one of her several memoirs, Cowles describes *Flair* as "a phenomenon in American magazine publishing. . . . the first honestly general magazine of all the arts." With the support and financial backing of her husband (who, according to his son, could not resist a gamble), *Flair* was launched in 1950 and advertised as the "magazine for moderns." It was distinguished by state-of-the art features, and the use of advanced graphic techniques, including a variety of paper stocks and printing processes, and pages of varying sizes. *Flair* also featured the first double fold-out cover, die cuts, and a new binding method that did away with staples and allowed the pages to lay flat. The publication was so chock-full of gimmicks that it inspired several cartoons, including a famous one by Charles Addams in which a three-handed creature is simultaneously reading the magazine and its accordion foldouts. Another cartoonist depicted one writer telling a colleague, "My story was in *Flair* but it fell out."

Although *Flair* dazzled its limited audience, it also drew its share of detractors, mostly from the media and advertising worlds. *Time* dismissed the preview issue as "a fancy bouillabaisse of *Vogue*, *Town and Country*, *Holiday*, etc." *Business Week* called it "a highly impractical business venture." Subsequent issues inspired further attacks, some blistering. S.J. Perelman, in an article in *The New Yorker* titled "The Hand That Cradles the Rock," likened Fleur Cowles' personality to "a Kansas cyclone successfully wedded to Devonshire clotted cream." In January 1951, after just 12 issues, the magazine had accrued losses totaling $2 million, and Mike Cowles, against his wife's wishes, shut down the operation. In an effort to keep the magazine alive, Cowles brought out a hardback edition, *Flair Annual 1953*, which included many of the stories that were left unpublished when the magazine folded. Although she went on to other things, she remained wedded to her brainchild, which subsequently became a collectors' item. The 1996 publication, *The Best of Flair*, was the culmination of a project that had been Cowles' dream and mission for 50 years.

During her heyday, with her trademark ash-blonde hair and black horn-rimmed glasses, Cowles appeared to go everywhere and know everyone. (Some of her travel was done in an Ercoupe plane that she flew herself after getting her pilot's license in 1944.) A prolific writer, she authored 16 books. As a result of her stay in Argentina in 1950, she wrote *Bloody Precedent* (1952), a comparative study of the Argentinean dictatorships of Juan and *Evita Perón* and their

Fleur Cowles

predecessors Manuel and **Encarnación de Rosas**. Although criticized by some reviewers as uneven, the work was called by *The New York Times* "perhaps the most perceptive and accurate picture of Evita Perón published to date." Cowles also wrote *The Case of Salvador Dali*, whom she call's "Surrealism's most curious character," and was a contributor to several other volumes. Her memoir *Friends and Memories* (1978) contains sketches about her impressive array of friends and acquaintances, including Gamal Abdel Nasser, Bernard Baruch, **Margaret**

Thompson Biddle, Madame Chiang Kai-shek (*Song Meiling), Marilyn Monroe, *Conchita Cintrón, *Isak Dinesen, and *Jacqueline Auriol. There is also a chapter on the noted plastic surgeon John Converse and the Institute of Reconstructive Plastic Surgery of the New York University Medical Center, which Cowles helped establish through years of fund-raising.

In 1955, Cowles divorced for the second time and later that same year married English millionaire Tom Montague Meyer (Cary Grant was best man). She then moved to England, where she took up painting, lining the walls of three residences with her oils. In 1969, she began to paint professionally and was encouraged by the young Italian painter Dominico Gnoli, who died tragically in 1970. Surrealistic in style, Cowles' images usually take the form of flowers and animals. Her work, first exhibited in 1965, has subsequently been viewed in over 50 one-woman shows, several of them in important museums in the United States and Brazil. Her paintings accompany several parables written by Robert Vavra. One of her paintings is also included in a book by Beverly Nicols, *The Art of Flower Arrangements*.

Fleur Cowles resided in England in an 18th-century suite of rooms in Albany that was once Lord Melbourne's palace. In 1996, her party to launch her book, *She Made Friends and Kept Them,* an anecdotal memoir, had an impressive guest list, including writers, artists, scientists, and titled aristocrats from Europe and Asia. Though content with her life, she admitted that if someone wanted to publish *Flair* again, she would be ready. As she told *Vanity Fair,* "My blood's not red—it's blue ink. I would create a section, edited by me, maybe an insert in another magazine, called 'Flair by Fleur.' It would be Flair for art, for food, for fashion, and for entertainment. I'd design it and give it my ideas. I have an idea a second."

SOURCES:

Collins, Amy Fine. "A *Flair* for Living," in *Vanity Fair.* October 1996, pp. 202–222.

Cowles, Fleur. *Friends and Memories.* NY: Reynal, 1978.

Current Biography. NY: H.W. Wilson, 1952.

SUGGESTED READING:

Cowles, Fleur. *She Made Friends and Kept Them: An Anecdotal Memoir.* HarperCollins, 1996.

Barbara Morgan,
Melrose, Massachusetts

Cowles, Virginia (1912–1983)

American war correspondent. Born Virginia Spencer Cowles in Brattleboro, Vermont, on August 12, 1912; *died in an automobile accident on September 17, 1983, near Bordeaux, France; daughter of Edward Spencer Cowles (an author and physician, as well as psychiatrist at the Bloodgood Cancer Foundation at Johns Hopkins and director of the Body and Mind Foundation) and Florence (Jaquith) Cowles; grew up in Massachusetts; educated at private schools.*

A Boston debutante during the 1928–29 season, Virginia Cowles quickly rebelled against the lifestyle of her class and sought work as a journalist. After apprenticing with a column on the *Boston Breeze,* she moved to New York and found work for a fashion magazine, where she tried to "write awfully well," she said, "about absolutely nothing." Joining the Hearst syndicate, she traveled to Europe and the Far East, then arrived in Spain, a week after the battle of Guadalajara, in 1936. "The only way for a woman to cover a war," she wrote, "is to tell the paper of her choice that she is going anyway and would they like some stories." While in Spain, she latched on to fellow-correspondents *Martha Gellhorn and Ernest Hemingway, until a close brush with imprisonment as a spy hastened her return to Paris.

Cowles continued sending dispatches to the United States during her second trip to Spain in August 1937, accompanied by Tommy Thompson, an attaché of the British Embassy, and Rupert Belville, an English flyer with Franco's army. Hired by the London *Sunday Times* as a roving correspondent, Virginia traveled to Berlin and was given lessons on Hitler from his devotee, ◄ Unity Mitford. Cowles was in Prague when Czechoslovakia was overrun with Germans. She then went to Moscow where she was soon disenchanted with Stalin's claims of gender equality: he allowed no interviews with female journalists. Cowles was in Finland when Russia invaded and interviewed Mussolini in Italy. She arrived in Paris only days before the occupation to find that everyone had fled; she hastily returned to England. Her book, *Looking for Trouble* (1941), a plea for the U.S. to aid Britain, was a bestseller and published before Pearl Harbor. In 1947, she was named to the Order of the British Empire (OBE).

SOURCES:

Current Biography. New York: H.W. Wilson, 1942.

Cowley, Hannah (1743–1809)

English dramatist. Name variations: (pseudonym) Anna Matilda. Born Hannah Parkhouse in Devonshire, England, in 1743; died in Devonshire on March 11, 1809; daughter of Philip Parkhouse (a bookseller);

Mitford, Unity. See Mitford, Jessica for sidebar.

married Captain Cowley (in the East India Company's service), around 1768.

Hannah Parkhouse was about 25 when she married Captain Cowley of the East India Company's service. It would be another seven years before the idea of writing occurred to her. While witnessing a theatrical performance, she turned to her husband and groaned, "Why, I could write as well!" Her answer to his laugh of incredulity was the first act of her play *The Runaway*. She finished writing the entire drama in two weeks and sent the script to David Garrick, who produced it with complete success at Drury Lane in February 1776. During the next 20 years, Cowley wrote a number of plays, one of which, the popular *Belle's Strategem* (1780), was frequently revived by Henry Irving and *Ellen Terry. She also wrote *A Bold Stroke for a Husband* (1783) and, under the pseudonym Anna Matilda, contributed sentimental verse to the *World*.

Cowper, Emily, countess of (d. 1869).

See Lamb, Emily.

Cowper, Mary (1685–1724)

English diarist and lady of the bedchamber to Caroline of Ansbach. Name variations: Countess Mary Cowper. Born Mary Clavering in 1685; died in 1724; daughter of John Clavering, Esquire, of Chopwell, Durham; married Lord William Cowper (lord keeper of the Great Seal and later lord chancellor to King George I), in 1706; children: several.

Described as well-educated, ambitious, and beautiful, Mary Cowper married Lord William Cowper, who became chancellor to King George I, in 1706, then spent several years caring for her family as well as translating her husband's writings into French. She also corresponded dutifully with Princess *Caroline of Ansbach (future wife of George II), and in 1714, was named a lady of the bedchamber to Caroline, who had since become princess of Wales. Mary then began a diary of her observations of court life, which she hoped one day to present in more polished form. However, when her husband resigned his office in 1722, after being falsely accused of conspiring against the crown, Mary Cowper destroyed much of the diary in order to protect him. Only two portions of the work survived: entries from 1714 to 1716, and a section from 1720.

Amid a description of the coronation of George I in the earlier entries, Cowper included details of a poison pen plot to break up her marriage to Lord William. "[M]y Lord had a Letter every Day, some of whole Sheets of Paper, filled with Lies about me; to say I was a mean Wretch; that I was Coquette, and should be more so; that my playing so well was, and would be, a Temptation to bring all the Rakes in Town about me; that it had been so thus far in my Life." Further entries reveal that Cowper did not suffer fools gladly: "Mademoiselle Schutz is a very unreasonable Body, and would take no Hints that I wished to be alone, but took a Pleasure in staying, because I was uneasy at it." Nor did she approve of the behavior she sometimes encountered: "The Duchess of Roxburgh is certainly an ill Woman. She does not care what she says of Anybody to wreak her Malice or Revenge."

SOURCES:

Blodgett, Harriet, ed. *The Englishwoman's Diary*. London: Fourth Estate, 1991.

Barbara Morgan,
Melrose, Massachusetts

Cox, Elizabeth Margaret Beath (b. 1932).

See Beath, Betty.

Cox, Ida (1896–1967)

American blues singer, known as the "Queen without a Crown," whose unusually long recording career lasted from 1923 to 1940 and was revived in 1961. Name variations: Velma Bradley; Kate Lewis; Julia Powers; Julius Powers; Jane Smith. Born Ida Prather in Toccoa, Georgia, on February 25, 1896 (some sources cite 1889); died on November 10, 1967, in Knoxville, Tennessee; married Adler Cox of Florida Blossoms Minstrel Show in the 1920s; married Jesse Crump (a singer-pianist, in the 1920s and 1930s); reportedly married a third time; children: one.

Ida Cox launched her career by touring with her own tent show in the South. In 1923, she began recording for Paramount, becoming one of the most successful blues recording artists in America. Her "Rambling Blues"—made with her second husband, Jesse Crump, at the piano and Tommy Lanier playing the coronet—is an archetypal blues. Its musical form is standard as is its state of mind:

> Early this morning the blues came walkin' in my room,
> I said, "Blues, please tell me what you're doin' makin' me feel so blue."

Although she specialized in blues, not all the songs she sang were of this genre. "I've Got the

Blues for Rampart Street," for example, is actually a ragtime-Dixieland piece. In 1939, John Hammond brought Ida Cox to New York for the legendary concert *From Spirituals to Swing*. She made several more recordings at that time. In 1945, she suffered from a stroke and returned to Knoxville in 1949. Cox came out of retirement in 1961 to record once more. She wrote many songs that have been preserved on recordings.

SOURCES:

Harris, Sheldon. *Blues Who's Who: A Biographical Dictionary of Blues Singers*. New Rochelle, NY: Random House, 1987.

Herzhaft, Gérard. *Encyclopedia of the Blues*. Trans. by Brigitte Debord. Fayetteville: University of Arkansas Press, 1992.

Tirro, Frank. *Jazz: A History*. NY: W.W. Norton, 1993.

John Haag,
Athens, Georgia

Cox, Louise H.K. (b. 1865)

American painter. Born in San Francisco, California, in 1865; studied at the New York Academy under Kenyon Cox; married Kenyon Cox, in 1892.

Though skilled at decorative work, Louise Howland King Cox was considered at her best in her naturalistic portraits of children. Cox was elected a member of the National Academy of Design, and in 1900 was awarded a bronze medal at the Paris Exposition.

Cox, Lynne (1957—)

American long-distance swimmer. Born on January 2, 1957, in Manchester, New Hampshire; daughter of Estelle Cox (an artist) and Albert Cox (a radiologist); attended the University of California, Santa Barbara, where she majored in history.

Set a new English Channel record for both men and women (1972); was the first woman to successfully swim Cook Strait (1975); crossed the Bering Strait (1987); swam ten miles across Peru's Lake Titicaca (1992); completed 14-mile swim across the Gulf of Aqaba (1994); also swam the Nile, Africa's Cape of Good Hope, and Siberia's Lake Baikal.

Lynne Cox was the first woman to successfully swim Cook Strait. Separating New Zealand's North and South islands, this 13½-mile, shark-infested waterway is considered one of the most demanding of all long-distance swims. Only three swimmers had conquered this swim before Cox, at 18, made history in 1975.

Lynne was born into a family of swimmers. Her grandfather swam across the Hudson River,

and both her parents swam for recreation. "My husband and I taught the children how to swim when they were very young," said Cox's mother Estelle. Cox credits her older brother David, a successful long-distance swimmer, with inspiring her. "He started competitive swimming and got me into it," she recalled. When the siblings swam the same waterways, they did so from opposite directions to avoid rivalry. Their father Albert sponsored Lynne and David's marathon swims at a cost for each foreign swim of approximately $3,000. With Lynne's success, she could have found another sponsor but was determined not to mix her passion for swimming with prize money: "One of my biggest disappointments was meeting some of my childhood idols. Somehow when they started swimming strictly for money rather than the challenge, it really disturbed me. It wasn't sport anymore." Almost every day, Cox swam ten miles in the Pacific, near the family home in Los Alamitos, California.

In 1972, with the memory of *Gertrude Ederle motivating her, Cox attempted the English Channel, considered the Mt. Everest of marathon swims. Before her, only 200 of the 1,400 swimmers who had attempted the swim between England and France had succeeded. The young Cox set the record on July 20 with a time of 9 hours and 57 minutes. When Richard David, an Army lieutenant, broke her record by 13 minutes, Cox faced the swim a second time and again set the record with a time of 9 hours and 36 minutes.

Although she'd crossed the English Channel twice and swam the muddy waters of the River Nile in 1974 (swimming past alligators and dead dogs), her New Zealand swim of 1975 was by far her toughest. Five hours into her battle with the 40-knot winds, 58-degree water, and 8-foot swells, Cox was ready to quit: "I was physically and mentally exhausted. It was dark out there and I couldn't see the land I was swimming to. I tried to keep myself busy by counting strokes and singing John Denver songs . . . usually singing about the sunshine because it was cold. I tried to keep the negative thoughts out of my head but they started grabbing me." Then the pilot spotted what were thought to be sharks. As it turned out, Cox was greeted by dolphins instead. "They swam up to me and would dive in and out of the water," she recalled. "They kept me company. Just like they were friends urging me on." Just over seven hours later, Cox was triumphant.

In 1987, Cox crossed the frigid waters of the 40-degree Bering Strait, a 2.7 mile swim between Little Diomede Island in the United States

Opposite page

𝓛otta
𝓒rabtree

to Big Diomede Island in the former Soviet Union. "In 2 hours and 6 minutes, I swam across the international dateline," said Cox. "I made the swim to show that our countries are neighbors." The symbolism did not go unnoticed. When the Soviet Union's president Mikhail Gorbachev began treaty negotiations with the U.S. soon after, he mentioned her name in his opening remarks.

In 1992, she swam ten miles across Peru's Lake Titicaca, the world's highest navigable lake, and was fodder for aquatic organisms that left huge welts all over her body; in 1994, she completed a 14-mile swim, against the current, across the Gulf of Aqaba to symbolically unite Jordan, Egypt, and Israel. A woman whose goal it was to swim every conquerable distance of water between landmarks, Cox once remarked: "I don't know what I'd do with myself if I didn't swim."

SOURCES:

Havens, F.M. "Lynne Cox: Out of the Pool and Into the Swim," in *Pittsburgh Press*. June 1, 1975.

Los Angeles Times. October 16, 1994.

San Francisco Chronicle. March 3, 1994.

Coyne, Colleen (1971—).

See Team USA: Women's Ice Hockey at Nagano.

Crabtree, Lotta (1847–1924)

American actress. Born Charlotte Crabtree in New York City on November 7, 1847; died in Boston, Massachusetts, on September 25, 1924; attended Miss Hurley's Spring Valley School; never married.

Born in New York City in 1847, Comedian Lotta Crabtree grew up from the age of four in California, where her father pursued a dream of hitting it big in the Gold Rush. In 1855, she began touring the mining camps, entertaining miners with songs, dances, and recitations. Chaperoned by her mother, the red-headed moppet played barrooms, schools and grocery stores and, according to a correspondent to the *Brooklyn Eagle*, became "the pet of the miners."

By 1857, Crabtree had refined her routine and was touring theaters in and around San Francisco. Her first legitimate role was Gertrude in *Loan of a Lover* in 1858, during which time she also spent six months at Miss Hurley's Spring Valley School, the longest period of uninterrupted schooling she would have. In 1859 and 1860, she performed at the Opera House and Eureka theaters billed as "Miss Lotta, the San Francisco Favorite." Her first appearance in New York was not successful, but, after a three-

year tour, she returned to a sensational reception in the premiere of *Little Nell and the Marchioness,* a play written especially for her by John Brougham. *Frank Leslie's Illustrated Magazine* compared her to "California wine, bright, sparkling, piquant." Crabtree was an established star; playwrights rushed to write for her, and she won enormous success in plays like *Heartsease, Zip,* and *Musette.* From 1870, she toured with her own company, becoming one of the first actresses to travel with supporting players instead of relying on local stock companies to supply them.

Crabtree took *Musette* to London in 1883, where audiences had trouble following the plot and resorted to harassing the actors with catcalls and insulting remarks (not unusual behavior for 19th-century theatergoers). Undaunted, she is reported to have enlisted Dickens' son to write her an adaptation of *The Old Curiosity Shop,* which both critics and audiences adored. She followed that triumph with a comic vaudeville called *Mam'zelle Nitouche,* in which she performed an opera parody, did a turn on the snare drums, and sang a Japanese song.

Returning to the United States, Crabtree purchased the Park Theatre in Boston for a huge sum and embarked on another successful tour. One reviewer, upon seeing her 1885 season opener at New York's Grand Opera House, described her distinctive talent: "No one can wink like Lotta. No woman can perform so wide a variety of contortions with her features . . . no one can kick higher or oftener." In 1887, David Belasco and Clay Green wrote a play for her called *Pawn Ticket 210,* which she introduced in Chicago. Throughout her career, she was distinguished by a perpetual childlike innocence, no matter how daring her dances or risqué her repartee, and her naturalness and grace won the hearts of audiences.

During a tour in 1890, Crabtree fell on stage, injured her back, and never fully recovered. Then 45, she retired, returning to the stage only briefly during World War I to entertain soldiers and veterans. She traveled, took up painting, and after her mother's death bought the Brewster Hotel in Boston and moved in. Having amassed a fortune, she invested in racehorses, theaters, office buildings, and jewelry. Crabtree died on September 25, 1924, leaving over $4 million to charity, much of which went to aid veterans, ex-convicts, and abandoned animals. One million was designated for the Lotta Agricultural Fund and bequeathed to Massachusetts Agricultural College (now the University of Massachusetts), where it provided interest-free farm loans and agricultural scholarships. Lotta Crabtree scholarships continue to be given to University of Massachusetts students. There is also a dormitory named for her on the Amherst campus.

Barbara Morgan,
Melrose, Massachusetts

Craft, Ellen (1826–c. 1891)

Escaped slave, abolitionist activist and educator. Born Ellen Smith in 1826 in Clinton, Georgia; died around 1891 in Charleston, South Carolina; buried at Woodville; daughter of James Smith (a slave-master, lawyer, and surveyor) and Maria (Smith's slave); illiterate until adulthood, then attended Ockham School, Ockham, England; married William Craft, on November 7, 1850; children: Charles Estlin; William, Jr.; Brougham; **Ellen Crum;** *Alfred.*

Given as a wedding present to half-sister Eliza Collins and moved to Macon, Georgia (1837); escaped slavery masquerading as a white master of her black slave husband (1848); settled in Boston; active in New England abolitionist work; fled to England after passage of U.S. Fugitive Slave Act (1850); studied three R's and taught sewing at Ockham School (pioneering venture in industrial education), founded by Lord Byron's daughter; appeared with abolitionist groups; cared for her five children, often single-handedly as her husband undertook trading and abolitionist work in Dahomey, Africa; family returned to U.S. (1870); established Woodville plantation and school south of Savannah, Georgia; taught domestic science, reading and arithmetic; moved to Charleston, South Carolina, to live with activist daughter Ellen and her physician husband William Crum (1890).

In 1826, 50 years after the signing of the Declaration of Independence, a teenaged house slave in Clinton, Georgia, gave birth to a baby girl who would become for a brief time the most famous black woman in the United States. Of the several hundred 19th-century narratives of escape from slavery, hers was to be probably the most dramatic. She would be proclaimed a heroine by such noted former slaves as William Wells Brown, America's first black man of letters, and Frederick Douglass, black orator and anti-slavery activist. She would be acclaimed also by Boston abolitionists Wendell Phillips, William Lloyd Garrison and Theodore Parker. The baby was named Ellen. Her young mother Maria was the light-skinned slave of Major James Smith, a lawyer, surveyor and one of the richest men in central Georgia. He was also Ellen's father.

Ellen Craft spent her first 11 years on the Smith plantation unkindly treated by her mistress because she bore so strong a resemblance to her father. When in 1837 her white half-sister **Eliza** was married to Dr. Robert Collins of Macon, Ellen was sent as a wedding gift to the Collins home. The gift was not unusual. In Virginia, the mulatto half-sister of Thomas Jefferson's bride had been sent to Monticello as a slave.

Craft later asserted that her life in the Collins' fine house was easier than the life of most slaves. A trusted lady's maid, she was not ill-treated by her mistress-sister. She was allowed her own quarters and taught to sew, a skill that would be of lifelong benefit to her. She was not taught to read and write, however; Georgia law expressly forbade anyone to teach reading and writing to a slave.

In Macon, a growing town of some 4,000 inhabitants, half white and free, half black and slave, Craft had somewhat greater freedom of movement than she would have had on a country plantation. Sunday was free, as was, with permission, the precious holiday week between Christmas and New Year. Macon had a number of slaves who were trained as skilled artisans. They were allowed to receive money for their work, though required to give a specified annual sum to their masters. Clever and hard-working slaves could thus accumulate some money of their own.

Among these Macon black men was a cabinet maker named William Craft. As a child and teenager, William had seen his parents and siblings sold separately to owners in different parts of Georgia. A deeply poignant memory was of the sale of his 14-year-old sister, taken away without a moment for goodby. He later recalled:

> The thought of the harsh auctioneer not allowing me to bid my dear sister farewell sent red-hot indignation darting like lightning through every vein. It quenched my tears, and appeared to set my brain on fire, and made me crave for power to avenge our wrongs! But, alas! we were only slaves, and had no legal rights; consequently we were compelled to smother our wounded feelings, and crouch beneath the iron heel of despotism.

Ellen and William met in the slave society of Macon and fell in love. She was allowed to take him into her cabin, and, with their shared skills, they made a simple home. Yet as slaves they could not have a legal or religious marriage. Also, Ellen seems to have been resolved not to bear children who would by law belong to her slave master.

Ellen Craft

Illiterate but intelligent and high-spirited, the young couple dreamed of freedom. The dream was daring. A generation earlier desperate and adventurous black Georgians had made their way to the Seminole Indians in Florida and to Mexico. In mid-century, those escape routes were closed. Further north, slaves were escaping, aided by the abolitionists of the "underground railroad" who harbored them when they reached free territory.

Flight from Macon in the deep South would require a thousand-mile journey across slave states. The punishment for failure would be severe—jail, whipping, torture, perhaps even sale to a house of prostitution for Ellen. Wrote William:

> The greatest excitement prevails at a "slave hunt." The slave holders and their hired ruffians appear to take more pleasure in this inhuman pursuit than English sportsmen do in chasing a fox or stag. . . . But the mere idea that we were held as chattels, and deprived of all legal rights—the thought that we could not call on the bones and sinews God gave us as our own: but above all, the fact that another man had the power to tear from our cradle the new-born babe and sell it in the shambles like a brute, and then

scourge us if we dared to lift a finger to save it from such a fate, haunted us for years.

In December 1848, the Crafts conceived of an escape plan whose chance of success seemed to justify the risk. Ellen was so light-skinned that among strangers she could pass as white. A black man could not travel alone on public transportation in the South, but he *could* travel as the slave of a white man. The Crafts' plan was that Ellen should disguise herself as a young male in poor health traveling north to Philadelphia for medical treatment. Dark-skinned William would travel as her/his slave.

*W*e could not understand by what right we were held as "chattels."

—**William Craft**

In a few hectic days the two gathered the clothing Ellen would need, William purchasing garments from several white merchants, Ellen making herself a pair of trousers. With much persuasion, they obtained from their masters passes that would allow them to be absent from home during the Christmas holiday.

Just how the young couple, illiterate and without travel experience, knew what their escape route should be remains something of a mystery. What is known is that, very early on the morning of December 21, the two left Ellen's cabin to go by different routes to the Macon railroad station. There a delicate looking young man in trousers, jacket, fashionable fringed cloak and stove-pipe hat, face half masked with green glasses and right arm in sling and poultice, bought two tickets for Savannah. When William took his place in the car for black passengers, he was frightened to see his master on the station platform but was able to hide until the train glided down the tracks.

Ellen, in her fine accommodations for whites only, had a greater fright. The passenger who seated himself beside her was a close friend of the Collins family and had eaten dinner at their home only the evening before. The young "slavemaster" pretended to be deaf and so escaped having to engage in the general conversation. For the first time in her life, Ellen, silently listening, came to realize from the lively talk of cotton, slaves, and abolitionists that abolitionists were not thieving monsters but white men and women who fought against the oppression of slavery.

That knowledge was of little assistance during the next perilous days. At Savannah, the

Crafts went on board a steamer bound for Charleston, South Carolina. In Charleston, they registered at a leading hotel, then bought tickets for a steamer trip to Wilmington, North Carolina. From Wilmington, a train took them to Washington, D.C., where they transferred to the Baltimore line. At last, on Christmas morning, they reached free Philadelphia.

Each hour of the journey presented perils: first there was young "Mr. Johnson's" illiteracy (only the sling on her right arm and her assumed rheumatism hid Ellen's inability to sign her name). Then there were the inquisitive fellow passengers who invited "Mr. Johnson" to share drinks and cigars and wondered at "his" staying apart from them. Others warned against taking a bright and attentive slave to the North where "the boy" would surely attempt to run away. An aggressive woman traveler mistook William for one of her own slaves, of whom ten had taken flight since her husband's recent death, she declared indignantly. Officials at Baltimore, the last slave port, demanded extensive information from any white man taking a slave into the North.

Even in the City of Brotherly Love danger lurked. The Fugitive Slave Law of 1793, still in force, required that slaves captured in free states be returned South to their masters. Ellen, now truly ill after the sleepless nights of the journey, could not believe that any white person, even in Pennsylvania, could be kind to her. William was more trusting. Following the advice of a fellow train passenger, he hailed a cab and gave directions to a boarding house owned by an abolitionist. There, Ellen shed her disguise. Soon the couple were taken to the farm home of Quakers who sheltered them and at once set about teaching them to sign their names.

Word spread rapidly in the abolitionist community, and the Crafts had an unexpected and intriguing visitor, an escaped slave named William Wells Brown. Brown would become known as America's first black man of letters, a novelist, playwright, historian and songwriter. He was, in 1848, a lecturer for the Massachusetts Anti-Slavery Society. Clever dramatist and propagandist, he saw at once that the Crafts' unique story would draw large audiences, and he persuaded them to come to Massachusetts to lecture with him.

For some months, they criss-crossed the state of Massachusetts, appearing at numerous Anti-Slavery Society meetings. At first, it was William who spoke, but audiences, who had never before seen a woman fugitive, began to demand that Ellen tell her story. Women who spoke in public were generally derided—a mid-century Unitarian minister said of a noted suffragist orator that "tomorrow the hen will crow"—but Ellen's presentation was sympathetically received. Newspaper accounts were published as far away as Macon's *Georgia Telegraph*.

The Crafts' decision to reveal their true names was a bold move taken because they wanted to make sure that their story would be believed. Frederick Douglass, after escaping from his Maryland master, had at first hidden his real identity. Other fugitives had been equally secretive.

The Crafts' frank revelation did them no immediate harm. Leaving the lecture tour, they settled in Boston. They were welcomed by the orator Wendell Phillips, by the Unitarian and Congregationalist minister Theodore Parker and by others active in the anti-slavery cause, as well as by the community of free blacks. Yet their hope of leading a peaceful life using their own skills was not to be realized. Despite the ardor of the abolitionists, Bostonians did not hire black artisans. Ellen was able to work as a seamstress, but William found no job as a cabinet maker and was obliged to open a used-furniture store.

Graver difficulties awaited. In 1850, Congress passed a new Fugitive Slave Law that made more stringent the provisions of the original bill. The new legislation was intended to nullify the laws by which several free states, Massachusetts among them, had sought to contravene the long-standing federal statute.

Now, if any white man took an oath that a particular black man was his runaway slave, federal marshals and U.S. Commissioners were required to deliver the runaway to his master, real or reputed. "All good citizens were commanded to aid and assist them." Accused blacks could not speak for themselves or demand a jury trial, and anyone who helped them could be subject to imprisonment. Commissioners were paid twice as much for turning in a black man than for setting him free. During the next six years, more than 200 arrests of fugitives would be recorded, with other captures probably going unnoted.

In 1850, two slave hunters appeared in Boston, bent upon seizing William and Ellen. Some advisors suggested that, for their protection, the couple be arrested by the state of Massachusetts and charged with fornication. Arrest by the state would presumably place them beyond federal control. The Crafts did not accept the desperate proposal. They chose instead to be legally married by the fiery Theodore Parker, who gave William a Bible and a sword to protect both soul and body, then set out at once for Canada where they planned to sail for refuge in England. The winter journey to Halifax was difficult, and the fleeing couple met prejudice along the way. At last in late November, ill and weary, they boarded the *S.S. Cambria* as steerage passengers. In mid-December, they reached Liverpool.

The fugitives arrived in a country that had freed its own West Indian slaves and where abolitionists—though, in fact, only a few, Ellen was soon to decide—were actively supporting the anti-slavery movement in the United States. Prince Albert, Queen *Victoria's consort, was president of the English Anti-Slavery Society, and other notables were involved.

The Crafts joined their friend William Wells Brown, also now in England, on a lecture tour through Scotland. As a woman, Ellen was not allowed to speak, but she received much attention, seated on the platform before Brown's dramatic panorama depicting the life of American slaves. Ellen was shrewd enough to see that racial prejudice existed even in the British Isles and that abolitionists quarreled among themselves, often misunderstanding their American counterparts. Yet, at last, the Crafts could begin a peaceful and productive life.

They went to live in the village of Ockham some 20 miles from London. There they were enrolled in the Ockham School, a pioneering venture in industrial education founded by *Ada Byron Lovelace (1815–1852), Lord Byron's daughter. In the mornings, the Crafts studied reading and writing, the skills so long denied them. In the afternoons, William taught carpentry while Ellen taught sewing. In 1852, Charles Estlin Phillips Craft was born, the first of the couple's five children.

At the end of their second Ockham year, the Crafts were offered positions as superintendent and matron of the industrial department of the school, but William had other ambitions. He would go to London and seek his fortune. His new friends were shocked. William was called "proud and secretive," also "suspicious and self-willed," although "really a good fellow" to whom his wife, despite her "natural good sense," yielded entirely. Two people who had undergone so many trials to gain their liberty were not to be deterred by the disapproval of well-meaning benefactors. In London, where Ellen tended their growing family, William embarked on a variety of uncertain business ventures. Eventually the sale of boots and raincoats made of the newly invented vulcanized rubber allowed the couple to buy their first home, in the London suburb of Hammersmith.

In 1860, William published *Running a Thousand Miles for Freedom*, an account of the escape story he and Ellen had told so often. Such slave narratives were popular reading. Some of the stories were written by white abolitionist authors, retelling the accounts given them by escaped slaves. Some were dictated by ex-slaves to white scribes. Some, like the autobiography of William Wells Brown, were written by the escaped slaves themselves with minimal help from white advisors. The sale of such narratives at Anti-Slavery Society meetings and elsewhere might earn for their black authors money to purchase the freedom of relatives still enslaved or to establish a new life in the North. William Craft sent a copy of *Running a Thousand Miles* to Massachusetts, asking that any revenues not used for the anti-slavery cause be sent to him for the education of his children.

Fighting an impulse to return to the United States and enlist in the Union army during the Civil War, William set out on a quite different adventure. He went to Dahomey on Africa's west coast to try to promote trade with England and to persuade the king of Dahomey to give up the slave trade and cease human sacrifice. William had scant luck with the king, although he was presented with three slave boys whom he brought back to England to free and educate. He had more luck with his trading venture, importing palm oil and other African products. In 1864, he undertook a second journey that would keep him in Africa for three years but bring him little profit. This time the king presented him with 60 slaves whom William felt honor bound to take from Dahomey and free.

Left in London, Ellen had the responsibility for her own children and for the education of the three young African boys. She brought her mother Maria to England. In addition, Ellen was busy with a variety of organizations set up to aid freed slaves and black children. The years in England had developed her self-confidence and a willingness to speak her mind in public, which made one American report that "Ellen is a kind of missionary among the grandees here."

But the United States was not forgotten. The news was heartening. Not only was slavery abolished and the Civil War ended but black men were holding offices of which they could not previously have dreamed. The 15th Amendment, guaranteeing the vote to all males regardless of color, was making its way through the state legislatures and would soon be a part of the federal constitution. Many suffragists had joined in the struggle to grant the ballot to black men, letting their own demands for women's rights take second place.

With what must have been high hopes, the Crafts returned to Massachusetts where they were welcomed as celebrities by the happily disbanding Anti-Slavery Society. In 1870, they went South, determined to help educate their people for freedom. But they found the Georgia they had known impoverished. Great plantations had been destroyed. Sherman's pillaging "march to the sea" had left devastation and bitter memories. A few blacks prospered, but many worked for their former masters in a kind of economic slavery. Others roamed the countryside, homeless and unemployed.

The Crafts themselves had resources quite unequal to their dreams, and fund raising for benevolent causes aiding freed blacks was growing increasingly difficult. William was accused of soliciting money for his personal use, and his libel suit against his attackers went badly, eating up time and money and ending in legal defeat. At Hickory Hill, the South Carolina home that they leased, crops were planted, and Ellen set up a small school, but after a single season the plantation was torched by the Ku Klux Klan.

In 1872, the Crafts leased a second plantation, Woodville, 19 miles south of Savannah. Woodville had once been a splendid property, producing rice and long-staple cotton. Abandoned at the approach of Sherman's army, both "big house" and slave cabins were badly deteriorated, and the fertile 1,800 acres were overgrown with weeds. For 18 years, the Crafts struggled at Woodville to develop a cooperative farming community and an industrial school modeled on Ockham School in England. William traveled to raise funds, played a part in Georgia's Republican politics, and continued to write and lecture. Ellen managed the plantation, gradually purchasing the necessary animals and attracting new families, some from white plantations that exacted harsher sharecropping terms.

Rural postwar Georgia offered little or no education to black children. Ellen, with the help of two of her grown sons and her young daughter, taught the children of Woodville and neighboring plantations the basics of reading and writing, geography, arithmetic, and history.

She also taught black women, many of them former field hands, gentle child-raising practices, sewing, and other household skills. She established a Sunday School and welcomed itinerant preachers. Dogged by a crippled economy, as were their white neighbors, the Crafts nevertheless managed to maintain the only black-owned plantation in their county. There Ellen, though often overshadowed in public life by her husband, proved her skills as administrator and educator.

Sometime in 1890, the Crafts moved to South Carolina to live with their daughter, **Ellen Craft Crum**, a founder of the National Federation of Afro-American Women and wife of Dr. William Crum, a physician, Republican, and future U.S. Minister to Liberia.

Probably in 1891—the exact date is uncertain—Ellen Craft died in Charleston. As she had wished, she was buried at Woodville in Georgia soil. As the Boston *Liberator* had reported in 1849, Wendell Phillips declared that "we could look in vain through our Revolutionary history looking for an instance of courage and noble daring to equal that of the escape of W. and E.C.; and future historians and poets will tell this story as one of the most thrilling of the nation's annals." It would, in fact, be well over a century after Phillips' prediction when a biographer began to seek out the details of Ellen Craft's largely forgotten story.

SOURCES:

Craft, William. *Running a Thousand Miles for Freedom*. London, England: William Tweedie, 1860.

Sterling, Dorothy. *Black Foremothers*. Old Westbury, NY: The Feminist Press, 1979 (includes excellent bibliography).

The William and Ellen Craft Papers. Donated by Department of Black Community Education Research and Development. Black Studies Department, University of Pittsburgh, 1978.

SUGGESTED READING:

Child, Lydia Maria. *The Freedmen's Book*. Boston, 1865.

Siebert, William. *The Underground Railroad from Slavery to Freedom*. New York, 1898.

Weiss, John. *Life and Correspondence of Theodore Parker*. Boston, 1863.

COLLECTIONS:

Boston Public Library Anti-Slavery Collection contains letters from Ellen Craft, William Craft and others active in the anti-slavery movement; the National Archives in Washington, D.C. holds letters from William Craft.

Margery Evernden, Professor Emerita, English Department, University of Pittsburgh, and freelance writer

Craig, Isa (1831–1903).

See Knox, Isa.

Craig, May (c. 1889–1972)

Irish actress. Born in Dublin, Ireland, around 1889; died in a Dublin nursing home on February 8, 1972; married Vincent Power-Fardy (an American), around 1916 (died 1930); children: five.

May Craig appeared in the original production of John Millington Synge's *The Playboy of the Western World* in 1907. She joined the Abbey Theatre in 1916, remained with the company for the rest of her life, and made six U.S. tours. After her husband died in 1930, Craig raised five young children on her own. She is best remembered for roles as Mrs. Tancred in Sean O'Casey's *Juno and the Paycock* and Mrs. Henderson in William Butler Yates' drama about Jonathan Swift, *The Words upon the Windowpane*.

Craigie, Pearl Mary Teresa (1867–1906)

Anglo-American novelist and dramatist. Name variations: (pseudonym) John Oliver Hobbes. Born Pearl Richards in Boston, Massachusetts, on November 3, 1867; died in London, England, on August 13, 1906; eldest child of John Morgan (a New York merchant) and Laura Hortense (Arnold) Richards; educated by private tutors and at schools in Paris and London; attended University College, London; married Reginald Walpole Craigie, in February 1887 (divorced, July 1895); children: one son.

Selected writings: Some Emotions and a Moral (1891); The Sinner's Comedy (1892); A Study in Temptations (1893); The Gods, Some Morals and Lord Wickenham (1894); A Bundle of Life (1894); The Herb-Moon, A Fantasia (1896); The School for Saints (1897); The Ambassador (1898); Robert Orange (1899); A Repentance (1899); The Wisdom of the Wise (1900); The Serious Wooing, a Heart's History (1901); Tales About Temperaments (1902); The Bishop's Move (1902); The Vineyard (1903); Love and the Soul Hunters (1903); Imperial India, Letters from the East (1903); Letters from a Silent Study (1904); The Science of Life (1904); The Artist's Life (1904); The Flutes of Pan, A Romance (1905); The Dream and the Business (1906); Tales (1909).

Pearl Mary Teresa Craigie, who wrote under the pseudonym John Oliver Hobbes, enjoyed a 15-year literary career that was cut short by her death at age 38. Born in Boston, she moved to London as a child and remained there for most of her life. Although she began writing at the age of nine, she did not seriously pursue her career until the end of an unhappy marriage. Craigie left her husband Reginald Craigie in 1890 and, in 1895, was granted a divorce and custody of her son. With her first novel, *Some Emotions and a Moral* (1891), she established a formula from which she seldom digressed. Utilizing the theme of self-knowledge through love, she created stock characters and portrayed them over and over again. Critics, for the most part, admired her wit and musical style more than her plots or characters. "She could paint a scene concisely, analyze character pungently, and deal neatly with the ironies of life," commented a reviewer for *The Athenaeum*. "Her limitation was that she hardly ever dealt with anything else." Her dramas, like her novels, met with varying degrees of success. *The Ambassador* (1898), ran for a full season, mainly due to the wit of the dialogue. Her later efforts, with the exception of *The Bishop's Move* (1902), were not nearly as successful. She also wrote many miscellaneous essays and sketches.

A handsome woman with a great deal of charm, Craigie was active in London society and had a large circle of friends in literary and musical circles. She also had a mystical side and would often withdraw to a convent for religious meditation. (After suffering through her public divorce trial, Craigie joined the Roman Catholic Church and acquired the names "Mary" and "Teresa.") She was also active in philanthropic activities and served as president of the Society of Women Journalists in 1895–96. Although Craigie never enjoyed robust health, her death from heart failure in 1906, was unexpected.

Barbara Morgan,
Melrose, Massachusetts

Craik, Dinah Maria Mulock

(1826–1887)

English Victorian who earned her living by writing and who believed in greater freedom of opportunity for women, especially those unmarried. Name variations: Miss Mulock; Mrs. Craik. Born Dinah Maria Mulock on April 20, 1826, in Stoke-on-Trent, Staffordshire; died on October 12, 1887, at Bromley, Kent; first child and only daughter of Thomas Samuel (an unstable dissenting preacher) and Dinah (Mellard) Mulock; educated at Brampton House Academy, with possibly sporadic tutoring by her father; married George Lillie Craik, in 1865; children: adopted abandoned baby girl, 1869.

Father lost job and family moved to Newcastle-under-Lyme (1831); helped mother to keep a school (183?–39); family moved to London (summer 1839); published verses in Staffordshire Advertiser, *(1841); her mother died (1845); published first novel* The Ogilvies *(1849); lived with Frances Martin (1850); published* John Halifax, Gentleman *(1856); published* A Woman's Thoughts about Women *(1857); awarded Civil List Pension of £60 per annum (1864); published* The Little Lame Prince and his Travelling Cloak *(1875); wrote text for* Fifty Golden Years *(1887).*

The ideal Victorian woman was a wife and mother, devoted to, and utterly dependent on, her husband. Dinah Mulock Craik believed in this ideal, but early experience and later observation taught her that for many women it was an impossibility. Her way of life and her writings advocated a fairer deal for all such women, while never losing sight of romantic love.

There are many question marks in piecing together Dinah Mulock Craik's life. She wrote no autobiography, actively disapproving of biographies of female celebrities. She maintained that it was unseemly for women to court any sort of publicity when alive, and that, when dead, their private lives were no business of the general public. Such information as remains is sketchy, often biased, occasionally open to more than one interpretation, and sometimes frankly inaccurate.

Dinah Mulock's father Thomas was born in Dublin, of minor Irish gentry. He was a lawyer, a journalist, a merchant, a lecturer, a Baptist preacher, a pamphleteer, a secretary, a dabbler, never sticking to anything. As a young man, he was handsome and a brilliant speaker. But he was also quarrelsome, stubborn (the poet Byron dubbed him Muley Mulock) and litigious. He was imprisoned for libel, for debt, and for contempt of court. At one stage, he was confined to a lunatic asylum. According to letters to her brother, Craik found it difficult not to hate him in later life.

Craik's mother, **Dinah Mellard Mulock**, seems to have been a woman of strong character. She married Thomas Samuel Mulock, the charismatic Baptist preacher who was lodging next door, on June 7, 1825. At the time, she was over 30 and living between Stoke-on-Trent and Newcastle-under-Lyme with her two unmarried sisters and her widowed mother. Her father had been a prosperous tanner. It may not be too far-fetched to suggest that neither received from the other what they had hoped when they married. She did not make him rich. He did not bring her the position she had envisaged.

On April 20, 1826, their daughter Dinah Maria was born. By 1829, following the birth of two sons, the family was complete. At first, Thomas Mulock's career prospered. He was minister of a fine new chapel in Stoke-on-Trent and popular as a powerful preacher. But extravagance and quarrelsomeness were his undoing, and by 1831 he had lost his position. It seems certain that it was around this time that he was committed to a lunatic asylum but doubt surrounds how long he stayed there. Some believe that it was Mrs. Mulock who had Thomas committed when, six years into their marriage, he proved himself unfit to support his family.

Either with, or more likely without Thomas, the Mulock family returned to Mrs. Mulock's birthplace of Newcastle-under-Lyme and there remained until 1840 in a terraced house opposite one of the fields where the poor of the town were allowed to pasture their animals. Wherever he was, Thomas Mulock does not seem to have supported his family financially during this time. Mrs. Mulock's father had left her some money when he died, and this she augmented by running a school. Enough money was found to send Dinah to a local private day school, Brampton House Academy, but by 12 she was helping to support the family by looking after a child and by 13 she was teaching in her mother's school.

Stoke-on-Trent where Dinah Mulock Craik was born and Newcastle-under-Lyme where she spent much of her childhood are in that part of England called the Potteries. Until about the middle of the 18th century, the area had been mainly agricultural, though there was some coal mining, and pottery had been made there since about 1700 BCE. However, the completion of the Trent and Mersey Canal in 1770 provided cheap reliable transport equally suitable for carrying delicate wares such as china, and heavy goods such as coal and clay. This, combined with a concentration in the area of such skilled manufacturers as Wedgewood, Minton, Adams and Spode, caused an industrial explosion. According to Hugh McKnight in *The Shell Book of Inland Waterways*, "in 1760 the population of the area was about 7,000, but by 1800 it had reached 25,000 and in 1861 some 120,000." Stoke must have been something of a boom town when the Mulocks were living there—it was created a Parliamentary borough with the right to send two members to Parliament, by the Reform Bill of 1832. In contrast, Newcastle was less affected for, although it was only a few miles away, it did not lie directly on the main Trent and Mersey Canal. The connecting branch, built

Dinah Maria Mulock Craik

at the end of the 18th century, came too late to enable Newcastle to benefit from the earlier dramatic expansion in trade.

As babies in Stoke, the young Mulocks were looked after by their mother (even then there was no money to pay a nursemaid), but in Newcastle they had to entertain themselves for much of the time. According to two of Craik's essays in *Studies from Life,* their chief occupations, when not at school, were reading and acting out, with acting out being far the more popular of the two.

> *A*nything is a woman's business which she feels herself impelled to do, and which . . . she feels capable of doing.
>
> —Dinah Mulock Craik

To go outdoors, all three children wore long, blue-print pinafores tied with a leather belt over their other clothes. These other clothes were a hat, "stout shoes, merino stockings," she wrote, "and those substantial under-vestments which we were then not ashamed to call 'trousers.'" For middle-class children, they seem to have had a great measure of freedom—Craik suggests it was because they were provincial rather than London dwellers. They were allowed to play freely on the Green, in the garden, and in the aforementioned field when suitable. They were at "full liberty to run, jump, climb, scramble, or crawl." In the winter, they skated on the frozen canal. At other times, they played whip and top, ball games and marbles. They made bonfires, dug holes, and built play-dens. Craik especially remembered how they killed an ash tree by making it into the chimney of one of their huts and then actually using "fire and a good deal of gunpowder."

As with many another household of limited means, all available money was needed for life's necessities. Craik noted that they did not "live in a reading community," so she and her friends preferred playing to reading. Furthermore, very few books specifically for children were being published this early in the 19th century, so any books or periodicals that came their way tended to be adult. When their next-door neighbor began lending them *Chamber's Edinburgh Journal*, the young Mulocks quarrelled so fiercely over it that they were forbidden to bring it into the house. Problem solved, they read it in the garden.

The first book Craik recalls reading was about a family of robins. She was six and it was lent to her by a seven-year-old friend. She graduated to cheap editions of *Sinbad the Sailor* and *Jack the Giant Killer* and thence to more factual travel stories. After geography came an interest in science, though this had its limitations. As Craik writes, "Many books of this era come to mind: *Endless Amusements*—which would have deserved its name with us, save for the unfortunate fact that the experiments therein were quite impracticable for want of capital."

Dinah Mulock Craik makes tantalizing reference to how her interest in the "romantic element" was awakened by being read to "during one summer, and at intervals during several other summers and winters." By whom and at what age she does not say. It could not have been her mother for "the treat of being read to was quite impossible in our busy household." One chore familiar to many a 19th-century child, but spared the little Mulocks, was learning religious poetry and chunks of the Bible by heart although, according to Dinah, "we all read [the Bible] aloud reverently, verse by verse, elders and youngers alternately, every Sunday evening." Her final succumbing to the unconstrained pleasures of reading came when she and her brothers were forced to spend the whole of one winter indoors by a succession of childish ailments. They were rescued from total boredom by "the bookseller of the town, who granted us free range of his circulating library."

Craik was finally released from the unpleasant task of trying to make unruly schoolboys respect her while still only a child herself by the reconciliation of her parents. In 1840, the family moved to London, and thanks to Mrs. Mulock's inheritance on the death of her mother, lived comfortably for a while. Mrs. Mulock's inheritance had been put into Trust (some claim at her instigation), thus preventing her husband from taking control of it. Otherwise, until the Married Women's Property Act of 1870, any money or property belonging to a woman automatically became her husband's. Dinah learned Italian, Greek and drawing. She went to the theater, to dances, and to parties. The family entertained and were entertained in return. But the setting up of the Trust had prevented Thomas Mulock from getting his hands on the capital sum of money left to his wife, and they were soon living way beyond the means of the interest. By 1844, Mrs. Mulock and Dinah had left Mr. Mulock and the boys in London and returned to Staffordshire, possibly intending to start up another school. But this never happened. Mrs. Mulock had been ill for some time and on October 3, 1845, she died.

By now Thomas Mulock was bankrupt. It is sometimes claimed that he entirely abandoned his children, but a letter from Dinah to her father seems to suggest that the arrangement was more mutual than is often implied. Ben, the youngest, was 16. Tom was 18 and studying painting. Dinah was 19. By the terms of the Trust, no money was available to them until their 21st birthdays. Middle-class females who had fallen on hard times often sought refuge in the home of a wealthier relation. Those sufficiently educated often became governesses. Dinah Mulock Craik did neither of these. The three Mulocks set up house together in cheap lodgings. Tom left art school and joined the merchant navy (sadly he fell into the dry dock during preparations for his second voyage, broke both thighs, and died on February 12, 1847). Ben studied to become a civil engineer, while Dinah took to professional writing.

Before the death of her mother, Craik had had several of her poems published, but now she wrote stories for children and adults. She learned how to produce both the simple moral tales that appealed to the educated working-class readership of the weekly *Chamber's Edinburgh Journal* and the romantic and exotic stories favored by the middle-class readers of the monthly magazines springing up in the wake of more widespread literacy and cheaper printing techniques. Late in 1849, her first novel *The Ogilvies* was published and was an instant success. The romantic tale of three girl cousins seeking after love and marriage perfectly suited the popular taste of the time.

As soon as Ben received his inheritance in 1850, he immigrated to Australia. On being left alone, Dinah took lodgings in Camden Town with another independently minded young woman, Frances Martin. Such a thing was almost unheard of at this time and the novelty seems to have amused her. She wrote in a letter to her novelist friend, *Elizabeth Gaskell, "She, 22—I, 25.—Are we not a steady pair of elderly women?" About this time, **Margaret Ogilvie** described her as being "a tall young woman with a pliant figure and eyes that had a way of fixing the eyes of her interlocutor . . . as if she meant to read the other on which she gazed . . . but Dinah was always kind, enthusiastic, somewhat didactic and apt to teach."

She continued contributing to magazines, writing children's books and popular novels until, in 1856, she published *John Halifax, Gentleman*, which critics hailed as a masterpiece and which has never since been out of print. Perhaps significantly, the main character is male. The story of a poor boy rising to middle-class respectability by honesty and hard work has been likened in sentiment to a book published three years later by Samuel Smiles entitled *Self-Help*. *John Halifax, Gentleman* was probably the novel critics had in mind when they began to compare the up-and-coming George Eliot (*Mary Anne Evans) to her, causing Eliot to write rather pettishly to a friend, "the most ignorant journalist in England would hardly think of calling me a rival of Miss Mulock—a writer who is read only by novel readers, pure and simple, never by people of high culture."

It is only fair to say George Eliot did have a point. Although Dinah Mulock Craik continued to write and her novels remained popular (she was demanding £2,000 a novel at the height of her career), she never produced another *John Halifax, Gentleman*. Its success, however, gave her the confidence and authority to speak out about her own beliefs. In 1858, *A Woman's Thoughts about Women* was published. In this series of essays, Craik sets down the mores upon which she lived her life. Happy marriage and motherhood is best. However, no woman—married or unmarried—should be idle, for activity brings self-respect. Girls ought to be brought up in such a way that, should happy marriage be denied them, they are capable of supporting themselves. Women have a special responsibility towards one another that transcends class distinctions.

For the next few years, Craik continued to write, living as an independent woman and succeeding in a man's world. In 1859, she moved to Hampstead. In 1864, she was awarded a Civil List Pension for her services to literature. Intermittently, she supported her father (who did not die until 1869) and her brother, Ben. There seems to have been much of the father in the son's make-up. For 13 years, he traveled about the world, doing various jobs but settling at nothing. From time to time, he came back to Dinah until in 1863 he returned once again but this time so mentally ill that she was unable to look after him. He was committed to an asylum, tried to escape, was injured, and died on June 17. After this, Craik left London for a while to live at Wemyss Bay on the River Clyde in Scotland.

Then, in 1865, Dinah Mulock married. While she was still living in London, there had been a railway accident nearby. One of the injured was George Lillie Craik, a young man belonging to a family with whom she had been friendly for many years. He was the nephew of George Lillie Craik, Sr., a well-known writer. For some time, George the younger was nursed at her house. When he was sufficiently recovered, he returned to Glasgow where he was an accountant. Now they were man and wife. It was an unconventional match, for the groom was 11 years her junior and physically disabled.

Not everyone approved of the alliance. George's mother accused her of abusing the role of elderly aunt while he was a guest in her house and saw her as lacking in that deference expected of a Victorian wife towards her husband. Dinah certainly continued to work as hard as ever and used her own money to have a house designed for them both by Norman Shaw, a leading architect of the day. Be that as it may, the marriage seems to have been a happy one. The couple lived in London where George had become a partner in Macmillan's publishing firm. In 1869, the Craiks adopted a daughter whom they called Dorothy (meaning gift of God). This was another act that flew in the face of convention. The baby had been found abandoned near their home and nothing was known about her background. Medical scientists at this time still believed in "bad blood" and the strength of heredity, but the Craiks were undeterred.

Throughout her life, Craik tried to live according to her beliefs. From time to time, she wrote on behalf of "good causes," for example, the Governesses Benevolent Institution (1852) and the Edinburgh Children's Hospital (1865), donating the proceeds to them. She encouraged and befriended women attempting to live independently. For instance, she gave financial help to

Laura Herford, the first woman student at the Royal Academy of Art, and used her Civil List Pension to help struggling women writers. She invited women of all classes to her home, from groups of young, middle-class admirers, to London shop girls and local reformatory girls. As biographer **Shirley Foster** writes, she had "no desire for revolution" but she whole-heartedly championed the right of women to fulfil their potential, unhindered by the blind conventions of the times.

Perhaps surprisingly, Craik did not travel beyond Britain until 1867. On her return, she began to add travel articles to her other writings. Although she wrote children's stories all her life, the one for which she is best remembered, *The Little Lame Prince*, was not written until 1875. This has not lost its appeal. In 1990, **Rosemary Wells** adapted it for younger, modern-day readers because, as it says on the fly-leaf, it was one of Wells' "favorite books as a child." Craik's later novels were written for specific purposes. *A Brave Lady* (1870) argued for married women's property rights, *King Arthur: Not a Love Story* (1886) was a propaganda novel about adoption, *Hannah* (1871) championed the right of a husband to marry his dead wife's sister. Four years later, Craik accompanied **Edith Waugh** to Switzerland so that Edith could marry William Holman Hunt, her brother-in-law, because such marriages were illegal in England. Holman Hunt had been a friend since the days when he and Tom Mulock had been art students together. In 1887, Craik wrote the text for *Fifty Golden Years*, a souvenir publication for Queen *Victoria's Jubilee celebrations. In October of the same year, Dinah Mulock Craik died of heart failure in the midst of preparations for her daughter's wedding.

SOURCES:

Craik, Dinah Maria Mulock. *Studies from Life*. London: Hurst and Blackett, 1861.

———. *A Woman's Thoughts about Women*. London: Hurst and Blackett, 1858.

Foster, Shirley. "Dinah Mulock Craik: Ambivalent Romanticism," in *Victorian Women's Fiction: Marriage, Freedom and the Individual*. London: Croom Helm, 1985.

Mitchell, Sally. *Dinah Mulock Craik*. Boston: Twayne Publishers, 1983.

Barbara Evans, research associate in women's studies at Nene College, Northampton, England

Craik, Mrs. (1826–1887).

See Craik, Dinah Maria Mulock.

Crain, Jeanne (1925—)

American actress. Born on May 25, 1925, in Barstow, California; eldest of two daughters of George A. (a teacher) and Loretta (Carr) Crain; attended St. Mary's Academy; graduated from Inglewood High School, 1941; attended University of California at Los Angeles, 1952; married Paul Frederick Brinkman (former actor under name of Paul Brooks), on December 31, 1945; children: seven.

Films: The Gang's All Here *(1943);* Home in Indiana *(1944);* In the Meantime, Darling *(1944);* Winged Victory *(1944);* State Fair *(1945);* Leave Her to Heaven *(1945);* Centennial Summer *(1946);* Margie *(1946);* You Were Meant for Me *(1948);* Apartment for Peggy *(1948);* A Letter to Three Wives *(1949);* The Fan *(1949);* Pinky *(1949);* Cheaper by the Dozen *(1950);* I'll Get By *(cameo, 1950);* Take Care of My Little Girl *(1951);* People Will Talk *(1951);* The Model and the Marriage Broker *(1952);* Belles on Their Toes *(1952);* O. Henry's Full House *("The Gift of the Magi" episode, 1952);* Dangerous Crossing *(1953);* City of Bad Men *(1953);* Vicki *(1953);* Duel in the Jungle *(1954);* Man Without a Star *(1955);* Gentlemen Marry Brunettes *(1955);* The Second Greatest Sex *(1955);* The Fastest Gun Alive *(1956);* The Tattered Dress *(1957);* The Joker Is Wild *(1957);* Guns of the Timberland *(1960);* Twenty Plus Two *(1961);* Madison Avenue *(1962);* Ponzio Pilato *(Pontius Pilate, It./Fr., 1962);* Neferite Regina del Nilo *(Queen of the Nile, It., 1962);* Col Ferro e col Fuoco *(also titled* Invasion 1700 *and* Daggers of Blood, *It./Fr./Yug., 1962);* Hot Rods to Hell *(52 Miles to Terror, 1967);* Skyjacked *(1972);* The Night God Screamed *(1975).*

Jeanne Crain, whose exquisite features and wholesome image graced the films of the 1940s and 1950s, was first discovered by Orson Welles, while she was touring RKO Studios with her high school class. Welles, who at the time was casting his film *The Magnificent Ambersons* (1942), had the 15-year-old tested for the role of Lucy but seeing the results felt that she was too immature and did not project well on the screen. Crain, intent on an acting career since her first role in an eighth-grade play, went on to win a number of beauty contests. She was on her way to a successful modeling career ("Camera Girl of 1942") when Hollywood beckoned once again.

Crain made her film debut adorning a swimming pool in the 20th Century-Fox musical *The Gang's All Here* (1943), starring *Alice Faye and *Carmen Miranda. She landed her first major role (third billing) in the racing story *Home in Indiana* (1944), with Walter Brennan and another studio hopeful, *June Haver. Of her early films, however, Crain is probably best remembered for her starring role in the remake

Jeanne Crain in
Margie *(1946).*

of the musical *State Fair* (1945). *Variety* called her a perfect foil for Technicolor and also remarked on her excellent voice, perhaps unaware that her singing was dubbed by **Louanne Hogan**. On the strength of her performance, she was named a star of tomorrow by *Motion Pic-* *ture Herald* and given a new, more lucrative, Fox contract.

Crain's marriage in 1945 to actor Paul Frederick Brinkman, who would later leave the profession to become a furniture manufacturer, had a great impact on her career. Over the course of the next 18 years, she would give birth to seven children, often losing plum roles to pregnancy or family responsibilities. Devoted to motherhood, she once said: "You have to decide which is more important to you, an armful of babies or a scrapbook full of screen credits." In 1956, Crain was separated temporarily from her husband (there were rumors of other women), but the two reunited on the eve of their 11th anniversary. She credited their strong Catholic faith as the reason the marriage survived.

Crain's popularity rose considerably in 1946, with the release of *Margie*, a sentimental story about the loves of a young high school girl that earned her a *Life* magazine cover. By now, Crain was receiving over 2,000 fan letters a week (second only at the time to *Betty Grable), but she took the next year off to have her first child, forcing the cancellation of a proposed film. After excellent notices as William Holden's wife in *Apartment for Peggy* (1948), she was again forced out of several projects due to pregnancy. She made three films in 1949: *A Letter to Three Wives*, *The Fan*, and *Pinky*, the last of which won her the only Academy Award nomination of her career and gave her some credibility as an actress. The film, which co-starred heavy hitters *Ethel Waters and *Ethel Barrymore, dealt with the subject of racial intolerance, telling the story of a light-skinned black nurse (Crain) who passes for white in the North, then returns to her southern black roots. Crain had written Darryl Zanuck asking for the role and tested for the part just two weeks after her second child was born. Although many Southern cities refused to show the controversial film, it was a landmark movie in its treatment of a contemporary issue. (At the time, no one seemed to question the casting of a white woman for a light-skinned black, even though *Lena Horne was in Hollywood and available.) The role made Jeanne Crain the #1 box-office earner of 1949 and secured for her another four-year contract with Fox.

What the studio offered, however, were films featuring sweet young girl roles, including *Cheaper by the Dozen* (1950), the biopic on *Lillian Moller Gilbreth, and *I'll Get By* (1950). Perhaps the most noteworthy of Crain's films of this period was the George Cukor-directed comedy *The Model and the Marriage Broker* (1951), though *Thelma Ritter, as a lonely-hearts advisor, ran away with the laughs. By 1953, Crain had wearied of the image Fox had created for her, and, after losing the leads in *Quo Vadis* and *Carrie*, she finally broke with the studio, commenting, "I've been cute long enough. I can't take a chance of being forced to play somebody's daughter again. I'm not another *Mae West, but then I'm not the washed-face pigtail type people think I am either."

Hiring a new publicist, Crain also dyed her hair red, in hopes of winning sexier roles. After *Duel in the Jungle* (1954) for Warner Bros., she signed a five-year contract with Universal, which specified that she appear in one movie a year. Her first venture with the new studio was the western *Man Without a Star* (1955), in which she played an unscrupulous rancher, a role *The New York Times* found her "a bit too haughty and polished for." She was more successful in promoting her new image in *Gentlemen Marry Brunettes* (1955), co-starring *Jane Russell, and prompting William Zinsser of the New York *Herald Tribune* to remark: "She has been hiding her light under a pinafore far too long. She turns out to be a fine song and dance girl from head to toe."

Crain's last film for Universal was the courtroom melodrama *The Tattered Dress* (1957). The studio ended her contract because she had been unable to report for a film due to the birth of her fifth child (she later sued for back pay). She was off the screen for three years, during which time she appeared in a television production of "Meet Me in St. Louis" and also made an unsuccessful pilot for "The Jeanne Crain Show," which cast her as an ex-New York model and mother of two, married to a magazine editor. Other television appearances included "The Great Gatsby" (1958), "My Dark Days," a two-part drama on "G.E. Theater" (1962), and "The Other Woman" on "U.S. Steel Hour" (1960).

Her return to films included a western and three undistinguished pictures in Europe, before she returned to the United States to appear in the low-budget *Twenty Plus Two* (1961) and *Madison Avenue* (1962), which had potential as an exposé of the advertising industry but was not favorably received. One of her last feature films was *Hot Rods to Hell* (1967). Crain busied herself with other interests, mainly painting and sculpting, and made only scattered appearances. Her final films were *Skyjacked* (1972) and *The Night God Screamed* (1975).

Barbara Morgan,
Melrose, Massachusetts

Cranch, Mary Smith (1741–1811).

See Adams, Abigail for sidebar.

Crandall, Ella Phillips (1871–1938)

American nurse. Born on September 16, 1871, in Wellsville, New York; died on October 24, 1938, in New York City; graduated from Philadelphia General Hospital School of Nursing, 1897.

Ella Phillips Crandall was dedicated to establishing public nursing as a recognized profession with high standards. She was born in Wellsville, New York, but grew up in Dayton, Ohio. Two years after her graduation from Philadelphia General Hospital School of Nursing (1897), she returned to Dayton, taking positions as assistant superintendent of the Miami Valley Hospital and as director of the hospital's school of nursing, which was then newly founded. Moving to New York City in 1909, Crandall entered the New York School of Philanthropy. She worked for a year in the visiting nurse service of *Lillian Wald's Henry Street Settlement House, as a superintendent.

Crandall served on the graduate nursing faculty of Columbia University's Teachers College from 1910 to 1912, and in 1911 on a commission charged with researching the need for organized public-health work as well as the as yet unclarified role of nurses. As a result of the commission's work, the National Organization for Public Health Nursing emerged in 1912, and Crandall became executive secretary. She worked for the association for eight years, laboring to develop the field of public-health nursing into a recognized profession. Crandall traveled often, giving addresses, and contributed to the organization's *Public Health Nurse* (subsequently *Public Health Nursing*).

She worked on the American Red Cross' nursing committee during the First World War and served as executive secretary of the National Emergency Committee on Nursing of the General Medical Board of the Council of National Defense. In 1920, she resigned from her post as head of the Public Health Nursing organization but remained active on behalf of public-health nursing. From 1922 to 1925, Crandall served as associate director of the American Child Health Association and in 1927 was named executive secretary of the Payne Fund, a newly formed philanthropic foundation that sponsored research in the field of education. She died on October 24, 1938, in New York City.

Crandall, Prudence (1803–1890)

Anti-slavery educator whose attempt to open a boarding school for African-American girls in Con-necticut grew into one of the great race controversies of the antebellum era. Pronunciation: CRAN-del. Born Prudence Crandall on September 3, 1803, in Hopkinton, Rhode Island; died of influenza in Elk Falls, Kansas, on January 28, 1890; buried in Elk Falls; daughter of farmer Pardon Crandall and Esther (Carpenter) Crandall; attended New England Friends Boarding School in Providence, Rhode Island, 1825–26, 1827–30; married Calvin Philleo (a Baptist minister), on August 19, 1834.

Taught school in Plainfield, Connecticut (1830–31); appointed principal, Canterbury Female Boarding School (1831–32); appointed principal, High School for Young Colored Ladies and Misses in Canterbury (1833–34); tried under Connecticut's notorious "Black Law" (1834), won on appeal; moved to Ithaca, New York (1834); moved to Troy Grove Township, La Salle County, Illinois (1842); moved to Cordova, Illinois (1865); moved to Elk Falls, Kansas (1874); voted a pension of $400 by Connecticut Legislature (1886).

A year after Prudence Crandall opened an exclusive female boarding school in Canterbury, Connecticut, she received a visitor who asked for a substantial "favor." **Sarah Harris**, the teenage daughter of a local black farmer, told Crandall that she wanted "to get a little more learning, enough if possible to teach colored children, and if you will admit me to your school, I shall forever be under the greatest obligation to you." Crandall knew that she risked criticism within the community if she admitted Harris to her school, but, certain that the white girls already in attendance would welcome the school's first black student, she approved her entrance. In January 1833, the Canterbury Female Boarding School thus became an integrated institution, an event that exploded into one of the great race controversies of the antebellum era.

Prudence Crandall was born on a farm in Hopkinton, Rhode Island, in 1803, the second of four children and oldest daughter of Pardon and **Esther (Carpenter) Crandall**. Raised in a Quaker family, Prudence attended the New England Friends Boarding School in Providence during the late 1820s. Her parents would move to Canterbury in Windham County, and, in 1830, Crandall began teaching in nearby Plainfield, Connecticut. In 1831, community leaders in Canterbury asked her to open a "genteel female seminary for the young ladies of the village." Advanced educational opportunities were very limited for American women during this period. Older girls were often unwelcome in public schools, as was the case in Canterbury. The opening of boarding schools for young women represented a rather new, though growing, phenomenon that would ultimately lead to a dramatic increase in the number of women who received a serious education. The Canterbury Female Boarding School, which was housed in a large home in the center of town, quickly became one of the most respected in Connecticut after its opening in November 1831.

As was common for unmarried women, Crandall continued to live with her parents, though she was 27 when she founded the boarding school. At this time, the Crandall's Canterbury household included a black servant, **Marcia**, who shared with Crandall copies of William Lloyd Garrison's new publication, *The Liberator*. Impressed by Garrison's uncompromising demand for an immediate end to slavery and his belief in racial equality, Crandall resolved to "serve the people of color." She would soon get her chance. Marcia's fiancée was Charles Harris, the son of a successful and respected African-American farmer, William Harris. Charles' younger sister, Sarah, had gone to district school with white children, but had no opportunity to further her education. Thus Sarah approached Crandall about attending the Canterbury Female Boarding School.

I have put my hand to the plough and will *never* no *never* look back.

—**Prudence Crandall**

Some of the girls in attendance knew Sarah as a former classmate, and thus no student voiced any opposition to her enrollment. So in January 1833, she began her studies there. Many leading members of the community, however, immediately began to complain and threatened to withdraw their children from the school. Prudence Crandall, for her part, refused to back down, so most disgruntled parents removed their daughters. Forced to confront the issue of racial injustice directly for the first time in her life, Crandall chose to follow a dramatic and courageous course. On January 18, she wrote to Garrison, explaining her new found determination to "change white scholars for colored ones" and open a school for black girls. Garrison embraced the idea, and the great battle was on.

Crandall traveled to Boston, Providence, New York, and Philadelphia to recruit students whose parents could afford the $25 per quarter tuition and board. After this successful trip, she returned to Connecticut to complete plans for transforming her school. On February 20, 1833, she dismissed the white pupils who remained at her institution. But before she could get the new "High School for Young Colored Ladies and Misses" started, extensive organized opposition began to crystallize in Canterbury.

After a town meeting, a committee of "the most powerful men" in the town visited Crandall. They expressed a fear that the opening of the school would lead to interracial marriages and injure property values. Crandall, however, would not yield to pressure to abandon her plan. Instead, on March 2, *The Liberator* carried an advertisement for the new institution, noting that classes would begin April 1. On March 9, a huge public meeting took place in Canterbury where two resolutions were passed, one stating that "the inhabitants of Canterbury protest against [the opening of the school] in the most earnest manner," while the other called on Crandall "to abandon the project." Fiery speeches followed, including one by lawyer and prominent Democratic politician Andrew T. Judson, who lived next door to the boarding school. Judson was a leader of the local branch of the American Colonization Society, which advocated sending free blacks to Liberia in Africa. The man who would come to lead the fight against the school claimed that Prudence Crandall was a part of a radical anti-slavery conspiracy that would turn New England into the "Liberia of America," and he promised legal action to stop the venture. His pledge met with wild applause.

As a woman, Prudence Crandall was not allowed to attend the town meeting. Therefore, she designated Reverend Samuel T. May of nearby Brooklyn (a close friend of Garrison's who became Crandall's most loyal and effective supporter) and Arnold Buffum, New England Anti-Slavery Society agent, to represent her. But led by Judson, the crowd, threatening violence, refused to let them speak, an action that *The Liberator* would later condemn under the heading "Heathenism Outdone." Garrison placed the names of the principal antagonists in bold black letters to signify the dark crime against humanity their intolerance had brought to Canterbury.

Faced with fanatical opposition, Crandall nonetheless remained firm, and the school opened on April 1 with 15 students. She remained unmoved even when local shopkeepers refused to sell her supplies, doctors failed to visit sick children, and the Congregational church barred black students from attending services. Manure was thrown into the school's well, windows were broken with rocks, and various ani-

 Prudence Crandall

mal parts (mainly from chickens and cats) were hurled at Crandall and her pupils.

With help from Quakers and local blacks, however, Crandall kept the school open. Supplies were brought in from outside Canterbury, many by other members of the Crandall family, and William Harris transported water from his farm. So the town turned toward legal action, invoking an old, long-ignored Connecticut law barring paupers and vagrants. Penalty for the offense was corporal punishment "on the naked body." They then arrested **Anna Eliza Hammond**, a 17-year-old student from a prominent African-American family in Providence, Rhode Island. But Judson and his allies feared the negative publicity should the punishment actually be carried out, and leading abolitionists put up a large cash bond. Consequently, this threat failed to work against Crandall and her pupils. "I have put my hand to the plough," she promised, "and I will *never* no *never* look back."

The boarding school remained open throughout April and most of May 1833. Then, the town convinced the state legislature to act. On May 24, it passed the notorious "black law" (as it came to be labelled): "no person shall set up or establish in this state any school, academy, or literary institution, for the instruction or education of colored persons who are not inhabitants of the state . . . without the consent, in writing, first obtained of a majority of the civil authority, and also of the select-men of the town." The citizens of Canterbury could hardly contain themselves in their joy, as people celebrated in the streets and fired off cannon.

But Prudence Crandall would not send her students home and, on June 21, was arrested for violating the new law. Taken to Brooklyn, Crandall refused to accept bond money and spent a night in jail. *The Liberator* and other anti-slavery forces used the imprisonment to great advantage, and the stance of Prudence Crandall became a national (and even international) *cause célèbre*. The wealthy abolitionist Arthur Tappan of New York provided money for the legal defense and established a newspaper, *The Unionist,* published in Brooklyn, which supported Crandall's position. The trial itself began on August 23 with Andrew Judson leading the prosecution and a number of Connecticut's most prominent lawyers defending Crandall. The defense argued that the "black law" was unconstitutional because it denied blacks their equal rights as citizens. This trial ended in a hung jury, but a second convicted her; the judge in the case claimed the new law was constitutional because "it would be a perversion of terms . . . to say that slaves, free blacks, or Indians, were citizens, within the meaning of the term, as used in the constitution."

As Prudence Crandall appealed the decision, the school remained open. In the summer of 1834, she had 32 students. The legal debate itself, in many ways, foreshadowed the question of African-American citizenship addressed in the *Dred Scott* decision two decades later. But in the Crandall case, the state supreme court skirted the controversial citizenship issue by simply reversing her conviction on a technicality—and thus the great controversy in Canterbury continued.

Facing Crandall's intransigence and legal defeat, some of the townspeople of Canterbury turned to more overt violence. First, someone tried to burn down the school. Then, during the night of September 9, the house "was assaulted by a number of persons with heavy clubs or iron bars," as *The Liberator* reported; "five window sashes were destroyed, and more than ninety panes of glass were dashed to pieces." Faced with a mounting threat to the safety of the girls, Crandall finally closed the school and moved away. The town had "won." But as William H. Burleigh, an abolitionist and teacher in Cran-

dall's school, remarked about this apparent victory, "Twenty harmless girls, whose only offence against the peace of the community is that they have come together to obtain useful knowledge," were sent home. "I felt ashamed of Canterbury, ashamed of Connecticut, ashamed of my country."

Just before Crandall moved, she married a Baptist minister from Ithaca, New York, Calvin Philleo. Most of her friends disapproved of a union to this outsider 16 years her senior, though Philleo was an anti-slavery advocate. They thought him lazy, domineering, and unpleasant, and, though they seem to have been right, Crandall loved him. The Philleos considered opening another school for black girls in a major city, but the plan never materialized. Instead, for over 50 years Prudence Crandall lived the typical life of a married woman of the era— unfulfilled and suffocated. The freedom she enjoyed in the early 1830s disappeared. In 1842, she moved with her husband to Illinois where she faded into obscurity. After Calvin's death in 1872, she moved to Elk Falls, Kansas, to live with her brother. She worked locally for temperance, international arbitration, and women's rights, but so far removed from the major centers of population, few Americans noticed. In 1886, she told a visitor:

My whole life has been one of opposition. I never could find anyone near me to agree with. Even my husband opposed me, more than anyone. He would not let me read the books that he himself read, but I did read them. I read all sides, and searched for the truth, whether it was in science, religion, or humanity. Here, in Elk Falls, there is nothing for my soul to feed upon. Nothing, unless it comes from abroad in the shape of books, newspapers, and so on. There is no public library, and there are but one or two persons in the place that I can converse with profitably for any length of time. No one visits me, and I begin to think they are afraid of me.

That same year, the Connecticut State Legislature voted to give Prudence Crandall an annuity of $400. Led by Samuel Clemens (Mark Twain), 112 people petitioned to have some compensation given to "the noble Christian woman" who had suffered "cruel outrages" at the hands of her fellow citizens many years before. Crandall accepted the money "as the settlement of a 'just debt' for the destruction of her 'hopes and prospects.'" Four years later, the woman of great principal and conviction died of influenza in Elk Falls. There now stands at Howard University a dormitory named after Prudence Crandall, an honor that she no doubt would have appreciated more than any apology or money.

SOURCES:

Foner, Philip S., and Josephine F. Pacheco. *Three Who Dared: Prudence Crandall, Margaret Douglas, Myrtilla Miner—Champions of Antebellum Black Education.* Westport, CT: Greenwood Press, 1984.

Fuller, Edmund. *Prudence Crandall: An Incident of Racism in Nineteenth-Century Connecticut.* Middletown, CT: Wesleyan University Press, 1971.

SUGGESTED READING:

Litwack, Leon F. *North of Slavery: the Negro in the Free States, 1790–1860.* Chicago, IL: University of Chicago Press, 1961.

Yellin, Jean Fagan. *Women and Sisters: The Antislavery Feminists in American Culture.* New Haven, CT: Yale University Press, 1989.

COLLECTIONS:

Prudence Crandall Museum, Canterbury, Connecticut.

John M. Craig, Professor of History, Slippery Rock University, Slippery Rock, Pennsylvania, author of *Lucia Ames Mead and the American Peace Movement* and numerous articles on activist American women

Crane, Caroline Bartlett

(1858–1935)

American Social Gospel minister and municipal reformer, known nationally as "America's Housekeeper." Name variations: Caroline Bartlett; Carrie. Born Caroline Julia Bartlett on August 17, 1858, in Hudson, Wisconsin; died on March 24, 1935, of a heart attack at her home in Kalamazoo, Michigan; daughter of Lorenzo Dow Bartlett (a riverboat owner-captain) and Julia (Brown) Bartlett; attended public then private school; graduated valedictorian from Carthage College in Illinois; studied privately for the ministry under the tutelage of the Reverend Oscar Clute, a Minnesota Unitarian Conference missionary; also guided in her theological studies by the Reverends William Channing Gannett, Samuel McChord Crothers, and Henry M. Simmons; graduate courses in sociology at the University of Chicago; married Augustus Warren Crane (a physician and early radiology pioneer) on December 31, 1896; children: adopted Warren Bartlett Crane in February 1914 and, about a year later, adopted Juliana Bartlett Crane, giving both children the birth date of May 25, 1913, in order to make them twins.

Family moved to LeClair, Iowa (1873), then to Hamilton, Illinois (1874); following graduation from Carthage College (1879), worked at various jobs in Iowa, Illinois, the Dakota territory, Minnesota, and Wisconsin; first assignment as a Unitarian minister in Sioux Fall, Dakota Territory (1887); accepted a ministerial position in Kalamazoo, Michigan; had formal ordination (1889); took on additional duties in nearby Grand Rapids and also traveled to England where she was profoundly moved by many urban social problems (1890); active in woman suffrage activities and served on many local, regional, and national committees; named to the Michigan Women's Hall of Fame (1985).

Caroline Bartlett Crane's interest in religious questions began when she was young, and she became a Unitarian minister in her late 20s. Because she instigated reforms nationwide that would help "clean up" America's cities, she became nationally known, by mid-life, as "America's Housekeeper." Her prime adult years coincided with the optimistic reform efforts of the Progressive Era. During that time, Crane was one of the nation's most prominent reformers. She would remain a national figure and a symbol of reform until her death of a heart attack in 1935.

Caroline Bartlett, known to her childhood friends and family as Carrie, was born in Hudson, Wisconsin, in 1858, the third of four children. Early aware of the child's intelligence, her family encouraged her to focus on education rather than domesticity. She learned to read at age four. While she enjoyed a loving relationship with her mother, her intelligence caught the interest of her father who became her childhood mentor. She enjoyed school and would later recall that she was "eager to learn and sincerely fond of those who could help me," which led to her being the subject of the childhood taunt, "teacher's pet." Her father's strong focus on her school record made her "unduly anxious to excel." From family stories, Carrie learned that the "Bartlett women" had a history of strong will and independence. Few women during this time combined marriage and a career; as an "independent Bartlett woman," young Carrie never entertained the possibility of marriage. A spirited, intelligent, thoughtful child, she instead looked forward to a career.

Prior to Crane's birth, her mother and father had left the Methodist Church when the minister told them it was "God's will" that their first two children had died of scarlet fever. Carrie attended the Congregationalist Sunday school as a child, and by the age of seven she was disturbed by what she saw as illogic in biblical teachings. By 1874, the family was living in Hamilton, Illinois. Because of Carrie's interest in spiritual matters, and her continued unease with conservative Christian beliefs, her father arranged for a Unitarian minister to speak in town. That evening, to her parents' dismay, she announced her plans to become a Unitarian minister. Her father termed the idea "idiotic." She broached the topic again in 1876. When they still would not support her goal, she instead went to Carthage College, in Illinois. Although Carthage usually limited women students to an easier course of study than men, Crane insisted on completing the more difficult, male curriculum. She graduated valedictorian of her class in 1879.

After graduation, she asked her parents for financial assistance in order to attend a theological seminary. They refused. Since scholarships were not available for women, she temporarily put aside this ambition. For the next few years, Crane worked at various jobs, including private tutoring, serving as principal of the public schools in Montrose, Iowa, working as a reporter for the *Minneapolis Tribune,* and functioning as city editor of the *Oshkosh Morning Times* in Wisconsin. When her mother died in 1883, Crane briefly homesteaded with her father in the Dakota territory.

We must do something for others as well as for ourselves. And the more we have done for others, the more in the end, we shall find we have done for ourselves.

—Caroline Bartlett Crane

In 1886, when she repeated her desire to become a Unitarian minister, her father finally gave his blessing. For six months, she went into seclusion to meditate on and write about spiritual matters. In the fall of 1886, the Iowa State Unitarian Conference accepted her as a candidate for the ministry. Although women ministers were rare in most of the country, the Iowa Conference during the 1880s ordained women ministers, known collectively as the "Iowa Sisterhood," in order to provide an adequate number of spiritual leaders for the frontier.

Her first assignment, in 1887, was in Sioux Falls, Dakota (then still a territory), where she expressed a commitment to the Social Gospel. Primarily an urban movement, the Social Gospel combined congregational activism with a belief in scientific and social progress. Since God existed in all things, Crane argued, God also existed in the processes that could improve society. Her ministry would focus on those social processes throughout her life. The Social Gospel afforded Progressive Era women (who did not yet have the vote) the opportunity to affect institutional development or reform in government and education, allowing all people a chance for greater involvement in shaping their community.

In 1889, Crane accepted the pastorate at the First Unitarian Church in Kalamazoo, Michigan, a state in which women ministers were not common. This congregation—which was in conflict and had been without a pastor for five years—was seeking a minister primarily to have someone to conduct funerals. Crane transformed the church into a large, cohesive organization that embraced her enthusiasm for the Social Gospel. She renamed it the People's Church. The leaders of the "seven day a week" church tried out institutional reforms, such as the first free kindergarten in Michigan, and then urged government institutions to take over those reforms that proved successful. During this time, Crane continued her education by taking summer classes at the University of Chicago, a leader in the new, exciting field of sociology. As one of the sociology department's first graduate students, she learned to use systematic analysis to define social problems and find possible solutions.

In 1896, well-known agnostic Robert Ingersoll visited Kalamazoo, Michigan. Evangelicals nationwide had recently instituted a prayer campaign for his conversion. Ingersoll proclaimed Crane's church to be the "grandest thing in the state" and added that if it were in his community he would become a member. As Crane's congregation included agnostics, transcendentalists, Christians, Jews, Muslims, Christian Scientists, and anyone else who felt the need to express spirituality through community action, Ingersoll could have joined without causing a ripple. Her name gained national prominence when the press, misunderstanding the nature of Ingersoll's enthusiasm, mistakenly reported that America's most famous heretic had been converted by Caroline Bartlett. While denying his conversion, Ingersoll re-emphasized his admiration for Crane and her church, and the national attention made her the most widely known woman minister of her day.

In 1896, she surprised her friends, congregation, and the general public by marrying Dr. Augustus Warren Crane. Though Augustus would become a well-known pioneer in the field of radiology and one of the first to suggest that radiology might be used as a treatment for cancer, at the time of their marriage he was ten years younger than Caroline (a fact that raised local eyebrows), and he was yet unknown. The decision to marry was difficult for her because she had long held the common assumption that women who pursued careers should not also attempt marriage and family. After the wedding made national news, suffragist *Susan B. An-*

Caroline
Bartlett
Crane

thony wrote Crane to express both her best wishes and reservations about the union. While Anthony hoped the marriage would multiply the happiness and productivity of both partners, she felt marriage did not often produce those results. For the Cranes, however, marriage would indeed encourage both private happiness and public productivity.

For health reasons, Crane resigned as minister of the People's Church shortly after her marriage. Working her schedule around her health needs, she expanded her Social Gospel activities to include "Municipal Housekeeping," or improving the quality of life in urban areas by cleaning up the elements that adversely affect it. Using a sociological survey that critically examined municipal services and hygiene, she investigated the aspects of Kalamazoo that most affected community health, including meat and milk industries, sanitation, water supply, and various social agencies. Crane not only exposed the unsanitary meat packing conditions in the Kalamazoo area but also the city's legal inability to regulate these industries. As a result of her findings, she initiated state regulations that would allow cities to better control the meat coming in from outlying areas.

Kalamazoo benefitted from these, and other reforms, instituted by Crane, and soon other cities asked her to conduct "Sociological and Sanitary Surveys." As her reputation grew nationally, she traveled extensively, completing 62 city surveys between 1907 and 1916. Her largest surveys included a 12-city inspection of Kentucky and a 17-city survey of Minnesota. Insisting on community-wide support for her work before she would accept an assignment, Crane was typically paid $100 a day to personally inspect water systems, sewage processing, street sanitation, garbage collection, food processing, and institutions such as schools, prisons, hospitals and poor houses. She always presented her findings at large public meetings where citizens could ask questions and become involved in the process of reform.

In 1914, the Cranes adopted an infant son, Warren. Within a year, they adopted a second infant, Juliana. While the care of the children, as well as health problems, limited her role as "America's Housekeeper," Crane continued to be in the public eye. During World War I, she was appointed president of the Michigan Women's Committee of National Defense. Pairing this patriotic work with a campaign for women's suffrage, she helped garner public support for the passage of the 19th amendment, which would grant women the vote.

In the 1920s, Crane became associate editor of the *Woman's Journal*, a magazine for civic-minded women. In 1923–24, President Calvin Coolidge encouraged community leaders to plan and build single family dwellings as part of the "Better Homes in America Contest," a national competition for home designs. Secretary of Commerce Herbert Hoover urged Crane to head the project for Kalamazoo. As a result, Crane designed and oversaw the building of "Every-

man's house." The house, affordable to the working class and designed for easy and efficient childcare, won first prize out of 1,500 submissions. In 1925, Doubleday published a book by Crane about "Everyman's House." Among her last civic contributions, before she died of a heart attack in 1935, were Crane's work on prison reform, service on the boards of the National Municipal League, the American Civic Association, and the Michigan Housing Association, and her position as chair of the Michigan Association for Old Age Security. Caroline Bartlett Crane was inducted into the Michigan Women's Hall of Fame in 1985.

SOURCES:

Crane Papers, Western Michigan University Archives and Regional History Collections, Kalamazoo, MI.

Hathaway, Richard, ed. *Michigan: Visions of our Past.* East Lansing, MI: Michigan State University Press, 1989.

Troester, Rosalie Riegle, ed. *Historic Women of Michigan: A Sesquicentennial Celebration.* Lansing, MI: Michigan Women's Association, 1987.

SUGGESTED READINGS:

Rickard, O'Ryan. *A Just Verdict: The life of Caroline Bartlett Crane.* Kalamazoo, MI: New Issues Press, 1994.

COLLECTIONS:

The papers of Caroline Bartlett Crane are located at Western Michigan University Archives and Regional History Collections, Kalamazoo, MI..

JoAnne Thomas, Western Michigan University, Kalamazoo, Michigan

Cranz, Christl (1914—)

German Alpine skier. Born July 1, 1914, in Germany.

Won the Olympic gold medal in the combined event (1936); won more titles (12) than anyone before her—male or female—in the World Championships (1934–39): in the downhill (1935, 1937, 1939), the slalom (1934, 1937, 1938, 1939), and the combined (1934, 1935, 1937, 1938, 1939).

In the 1936 winter Olympics in Garmisch-Partenkirchen, the women's Alpine consisted of a combined event that included a downhill and a slalom. Christl Cranz won the gold; her teammate **Kathe Grasegger** took the silver. The bronze was won by a 16-year-old Norwegian named **Laila Schou-Nielsen**. Between the years 1934 and 1939, Cranz won 12 World Championship titles, more than any previous athlete—male or female.

Crapp, Lorraine J. (1938—)

Australian swimmer. Born in 1938 in Australia; married Bill Thurlow (a physician).

First woman to swim the 400-meter freestyle in under five minutes; first Australian—male or female—to hold world records in all freestyle races at the same time; broke 23 world records and won 9 Australian championships; won three gold, one silver, and two bronze medals in the British Empire and Commonwealth Games; won Olympic gold in the 400-meter freestyle (1956) and team gold in the 4x100-meter freestyle relay (1956); won an Olympic silver in the 400-meter freestyle (1960).

Shortly before the 1956 Olympics in Melbourne, Australia, Lorraine Crapp became the first woman to swim the 400-meter in less than five minutes. During the Games, she took the 400-meter freestyle from teammate *Dawn Fraser with a time of 4:54.6, a new Olympic record. Fraser's turn came in the 100-meter, which she won in 1:02.0. Along with teammates Fraser, ❦➤ **Faith Leech**, and **Sandra Morgan**, Crapp was also the recipient of a gold medal in the 4x100-meter freestyle relay; the U.S. team took the silver.

When Crapp arrived for the 1960 Olympics in Rome, she had secretly married Dr. Bill Thurlow the night before. Officials and the Australian press greeted the news like indignant parents, and the morale of the quiet, introspective swimmer suffered. She returned home with only a silver in the 400-meter freestyle and retired after the Rome Olympics.

Craven, Louisa, countess of
(c. 1785–1860).

See Brunton, Louisa.

Crawford, Ann (1734–1801).

See Barry, Ann Street.

Crawford, Cheryl (1902–1986)

American producer-director. Born in Akron, Ohio, on September 24, 1902; died in New York City on October 7, 1986; daughter of Robert K. Crawford and Luella Elizabeth (Parker) Crawford; attended Butchel College and Smith College; never married; no children.

Awards: Doctor of Fine Arts, Smith College (1962); Brandeis University Medal of Achievement for Distinguished Contribution to American Theater Arts (1964); Lawrence Langner Award for Lifetime Achievement in the Theater (1977).

Theatrical credits include: (as director) The House of Connelly (1931), Night Over Taos (1932), Success Story (1932), Big Night (1933), Till the Day I Die (1935), Weep for the Virgins (1935); (as producer)

The School for Scandal, Ah, Wilderness, The Second Mrs. Tanqueray, Biography, The Royal Family, The Emperor Jones, The Male Animal, Elmer the Great, The Time of Your Life (1940); Twelfth Night, Charlie's Aunt, Native Son, Johnny Belinda, Golden Boy, Anna Christie (1941); Porgy and Bess, The Flowers of Virtue, A Kiss for Cinderella, The Little Foxes, Watch on the Rhine, Pal Joey (1942); One Touch of Venus (1943); The Perfect Marriage (1944); The Tempest (1945); Henry VIII, What Every Woman Knows, John Gabriel Borkman, Androcles and the Lion (1946); Brigadoon, Galileo (1947); Love Life, Ballet Ballads (1948); Regina (1949); Tower Beyond Tragedy (1950); The Rose Tattoo, Paint Your Wagon, Peer Gynt (1951); Camino Real (1953); The Thirteen Clocks (1954); The Honeys, Reuben Reuben (1955); Mister Johnson, Girls of Summer (1956); Good as Gold (1957); Comes a Day, The Shadow of a Gunman (1958); The Rivalry, Sweet Bird of Youth (1959); Period of Adjustment (1960); Brecht on Brecht (1961); Mother Courage and Her Children, Jennie, Strange Interlude (1963); Blues for Mister Charlie, The Three Sisters, Doubletalk (1964); The Freaking out of Stephanie Blake (1967); Celebration (1969); Colette (two productions, 1970); The Web and the Rock (1972); Yentl (1975); Do You Turn Somersaults (1978). Published memoirs in 1977 entitled One Naked Individual: My Fifty Years in the Theatre.*

While in grammar school, Cheryl Crawford skipped a grade; consequently, she never learned the Pledge of Allegiance. The following year, when she stood with her new classmates proudly reciting, "and to the republic for which it stands," Crawford went on loudly with, "*one naked individual* with liberty and justice for all." Traumatic? Probably. Her memoirs bear that title. "One naked individual," she claimed, was an accurate description of her 50 years as a woman producer in the American theater.

Born into a well-to-do, midwestern family in 1902, Crawford knew early on she wanted a career in the theater. In June of 1924, following her junior at Smith College, she headed for Cape Cod, intent on spending the summer in Provincetown, where Eugene O'Neill worked with the famous Provincetown Players. On arrival, she was met with the news that the theater had burned down. Fortunately, a wealthy patron agreed to fund a new theater that was to be housed on a wharf, and the group was to meet that night. With the help of her playwright friend Harry Kemp, Crawford found herself at the first meeting of the new theater company. By the end of summer, she was hooked.

❦ *Leech, Faith.* See *Fraser, Dawn* for sidebar.

After graduating cum laude from Smith in 1925, Crawford talked her way into a job as an assistant stage manager for producer *Theresa Helburn at the prestigious Theatre Guild. With Helburn as a mentor, Crawford worked on several Guild productions, including George Bernard Shaw's *Pygmalion*, starring *Lynn Fontanne, and Eugene O'Neill's *Marco's Millions* and *Strange Interlude*.

In 1926, Crawford met Harold Clurman and Lee Strasberg. The threesome were soon close and spent hours discussing not only the future of the American theater but their proposed contributions. "Naturalism" had come to America. Actors of bygone days had been theatrical if not grandiose in their stage personas, but the trend in the late 1920s leaned decidedly towards what Russian auteur Constantin Stanislavski dubbed "The Method."

Crawford, Clurman and Strasberg were converts, at one point traveling to Moscow to study under the master. In 1930, with the imminent demise of the Theatre Guild, the troika decided to form their own company, called The Group Theatre, composed of 28 actors and several playwrights. Wrote Clurman: "If the theater is to be an art one must have a permanent company trained in a unified method of work to which all elements, sets, costumes, music contribute. And the plays one does should reflect our social and cultural life." Though The Group only existed for five years (1931–36), it produced several landmark plays, including Sidney Kingsley's Pulitzer prize-winning, *Men In White*, Maxwell Anderson's *Winterset*, and four plays by Clifford Odets, one of which was the groundbreaking *Waiting for Lefty*.

The importance of The Group in the history of the American theater can not be underestimated. Wrote Crawford: "The Group Theatre became the seed which supplied the inspiration for many theater projects that followed. Various groups sprang up all over the country. . . . I didn't know . . . that there would be an Actor's Studio but I do know it would never have been born had not the Group preceded it."

In the fall of 1937, Crawford set out on her own as an independent producer and had five failures in a row. Finally, in 1942, she had her first hit, a revival of George and Ira Gershwin's *Porgy and Bess*. When she produced two more dramas that same year and neither were successful, Crawford was convinced that her forte was the musical theater. She went to work with German expatriate Kurt Weill on a musical called *One Touch of Venus*. Directed by Elia Kazan, the production, starring *Mary Martin, opened in October 1943 and became, bannered *Variety*, "Broadway's first musical smash of the season." Having two successful musicals allowed Crawford the financial means to experiment. With director *Margaret Webster and producer-actor *Eva Le Gallienne, Crawford produced Shakespeare's daunting *The Tempest*. The production opened on Broadway at the Alvin Theater on January 25, 1945, and had a longer run than any other American production of the play to date.

On the heels of their success, Webster, Le Gallienne, and Crawford founded The American Repertory Theater. Webster had grown up in England where repertory companies were the norm. In fact, England's Old Vic had just played New York, and the trio had the opportunity to see Laurence Olivier in four different classical roles. The threesome believed a company modelled after the Old Vic would be welcomed by audience and critics, and even more so by writers and actors. "With plays rotating," wrote Crawford, "the actors could stay fresh and develop their talents in a variety of roles."

On November 6, 1946, the American Rep opened its season with *Henry VIII* starring Victor Jory and Le Gallienne. *What Every Woman Knows, John Gabriel Borkman,* and *Androcles and the Lion* followed. Unfortunately, only *Androcles* was a critical success. Though the company managed to hang on for one more season, by the end of 1947 the American Rep was over. Crawford hooked up with the American National Theater and Academy (ANTA), a not-for-profit company partially funded by Congress, much like the National Endowment for the Arts and PBS. She continued her association with ANTA until 1951 when it too lost funding. Once again, she was on her own. "Ever since the Group days I had truly wanted to be involved in theater that had a core and continuity," she wrote. "When ART and ANTA died . . . I became again that naked individual I had tried to avoid."

Once again musical theater saved her. In 1946, she joined hands with Alan Jay Lerner and Frederick Lowe to present *Brigadoon*. When the show opened in New York, it was enormously successful. From then on, though she had her share of flops, Crawford became one of the most highly regarded producers on the Broadway stage. She followed the success of *Brigadoon* with another Lerner and Lowe collaboration, *Paint Your Wagon*. And though her earlier attempts at producing drama were less than successful, Crawford produced four of playwright

Tennessee Williams' works, including *The Rose Tattoo* and *Sweet Bird of Youth*.

Though Crawford would always remain an independent producer, she never fully relinquished her dream of having an American repertory company. In 1947, Crawford, Elia Kazan, Lee Strasberg and director Robert Lewis formed the famous Actor's Studio. The idea, wrote Crawford, was "to offer a sort of artistic home to the many young actors and actresses who wanted to stretch their capabilities, a sympathetic atmosphere in which they could tackle their limitations." Set up as a non-profit organization, the group was, and is, a school for actors. It became Hollywood's premiere training facility, producing such stars as *Marilyn Monroe, Paul Newman, and Marlon Brando, as well as the next generation of actors like **Sally Fields** and Sean Penn. Though the original goal of the Actor's Studio was to nurture new talent, the board of directors branched out with the Actor's Studio Theater. Unfortunately, the experiment ended with a disastrous New York production of Chekhov's *Three Sisters*, which essentially ended Crawford's association with the group.

Though Crawford was never to be a part of a successful repertory company, her attempts and those of her colleagues certainly laid the foundation for the dozens of theater companies that now exist coast to coast. Crawford continued to produce successful Broadway shows well into the 1970s. Her last production was *Yentl* starring **Tovah Feldshuh**. Based on the Isaac Bashevis Singer novel, it was eventually made into a movie by **Barbra Streisand**.

Crawford never married, but during the Group Theatre years she was linked romantically to actress **Dorothy Patten**. Born into a wealthy Southern family, Patten had a reasonably successful Broadway career before she joined the Group. Historian **Wendy Smith** claims that the liaison with Patten was an established and accepted fact to other members of the Group. In her autobiography, Crawford is circumspect about her private life, and it may be, as she claims, that her work was her first and all consuming passion. Crawford died in New York City at the age of 84.

SOURCES:

Crawford, Cheryl. *One Naked Individual: My Fifty Years in the Theatre*. NY: Bobbs-Merrill, 1977.

Herbert, Ian, ed. *Who's Who in the Theatre: A Biographical Record of the Contemporary Stage, Volume 1*. Detroit, MI: Gale Research, 1981.

Obituary. *The New York Times*. October 8, 1986.

Smith, Wendy. *Real Life Drama: The Group Theatre and America, 1931–1940*. NY: Grove Weidenfeld, 1990.

Deborah Jones, Studio City, California

Crawford, Joan (1906–1977)

Hollywood actress and icon, who appeared in 80 films and received an Academy Award for Mildred Pierce, *and whose humble beginnings, haughty manner, and impeccable grooming inspired a generation of young women. Name variations: Billie Cassin. Born Lucille Fay LeSueur on March 23, 1906, in San Antonio, Texas; died on May 10, 1977, in New York City; daughter of Thomas LeSueur (a laborer) and Anna Bell (Johnson) LeSueur; married Douglas Fairbanks Jr., on June 3, 1929 (divorced 1933); married Franchot Tone, on October 11, 1935 (divorced 1939); married Phillip Terry, on September 20, 1942 (divorced 1946); married Alfred Steele, on May 10, 1955 (died, April 1959); children:* **Christina Crawford** *(adopted, June 1940); Christopher (adopted, 1942); Cathy (adopted, 1947); Cynthia (adopted, 1947).*

Filmography: Lady of the Night *(1925);* Proud Flesh *(1925);* Pretty Ladies *(1925);* Old Clothes *(1925);* The Only Thing *(1925);* Sally lrene and Mary *(1925);* The Boob *(1926);* Tramp Tramp Tramp *(1926);* Parts *(1926);* The Taxi Dancer *(1927);* Winners of the Wilderness *(1927);* The Understanding Heart *(1927);* The Unknown *(1927);* Twelve Miles Out *(1927);* Spring Fever *(1927);* West Point *(1928);* Rose Marie *(1928);* Across to Singapore *(1928);* The Law of the Range *(1928);* Four Walls *(1928);* Our Dancing Daughters *(1928);* Dream of Love *(1928);* The Duke Steps Out *(1929);* The Hollywood Revue of 1929 *(1929);* Our Modern Maidens *(1929);* Untamed *(1929);* Montana Moon *(1930);* Our Blushing Brides *(1930);* Paid *(1930);* Dance Fools Dance *(1931);* Laughing Sinners *(1931);* This Modern Age *(1931);* Possessed *(1931);* Grand Hotel *(1932);* Letty Lynton *(1932);* Rain *(1932);* Today We Live *(1933);* Dancing Lady *(1933);* Sadie McKee *(1934);* Chained *(1934);* Forsaking All Others *(1934);* No More Ladies *(1935);* I Live My Life *(1935);* The Gorgeous Hussy *(1936);* Love on the Run *(1936);* The Last of Mrs. Cheyney *(1937);* The Bride Wore Red *(1937);* Mannequin *(1938);* The Shining Hour *(1938);* Ice Follies of 1939 *(1939);* The Women *(1939);* Strange Cargo *(1940);* Susan and God *(1940);* A Woman's Face *(1941);* When Ladies Meet *(1941);* They All Kissed the Bride *(1942);* Reunion in France *(1942);* Above Suspicion *(1943);* Hollywood Canteen *(1944);* Mildred Pierce *(1945);* Humoresque *(1946);* Possessed *(1947);* Daisy Kenyon *(1947);* Flamingo Road *(1949); (cameo)* It's a Great Feeling *(1949);* The Damned Don't Cry *(1950);* Harriet Craig *(1950);* Goodbye My Fancy *(1951);* This Woman Is Dangerous *(1952);* Sudden Fear *(1952);* Torch Song *(1953);* Johnny Guitar *(1954);* Female on the Beach *(1955);* Queen Bee *(1955);* Autumn

Leaves *(1956)*; The Story of Esther Costello *(1957)*; The Best of Everything *(1959)*; What Ever Happened to Baby Jane? *(1962)*; The Caretakers *(1963)*; Straight Jacket *(1964)*; I Saw What You Did *(1965)*; Berserk *(UK, 1967)*; Trog *(1970)*.

Joan Crawford lived a Cinderella story. Abandoned early in life by her father, she was abandoned again, at age 11, by her stepfather, after which she began to scrub and sweep her way through life. She never quite found her prince, but her good looks and vivacious personality attracted many men who helped her find her way to fame. By age 22, she was a star, and through tenacity and hard work she remained a star for half a century.

Crawford was born Lucille Fay LeSueur in San Antonio, Texas, not on March 23, 1908, as she had said, but in 1906, to Tom LeSueur, a French Canadian laborer from whom she inherited her large brown eyes, and **Anna Johnson LeSueur**, a local woman of Irish and Scandinavian descent. The LeSueurs had three children—Daisy (who died in infancy), Hal Hayes LeSueur (born in 1904), and Lucille—before the pressures of family proved too much for Tom LeSueur, and he left.

$\mathcal{S}$he was the perfect image of the movie star, and, as such, largely the creation of her own indomitable will.

—George Cukor

It is not certain how long Anna LeSueur kept her family in San Antonio. At different times, Crawford gave the figure as three months, six months, and one year, but she did remember "a woman in a checkered apron who gave her round cookies with fat currants in them." At any rate, Anna LeSueur moved her two children to the tiny town of Lawton, Oklahoma, when Crawford was a small child.

Anna soon married Henry Cassin, "a small man who dressed with flamboyance and wore glittering rings on his stubby fingers," according to Crawford biographer Bob Thomas. Cassin was a show man, owner of the Lawton Opera House. Lucille, whose stepfather called her "Billie" because of her roughneck ways, adored him and adored the opera house. As the boss' daughter, she was allowed to stand backstage, and the performers smeared her face with greasepaint and taught her how to dance the cakewalk and the buck-and-wing. "She listened wide-eyed to their tales," writes Thomas, "and she didn't realize that her heroes were the dregs of vaudeville, rejected misfits with scant talent who were reduced to touring Oklahoma for little more than subsistence."

When she was six, however, a series of events shook her small world, and Crawford was never quite an innocent again. While jumping off her porch, she cut her foot on a jagged piece of glass and was told she would not be able to walk without a limp. With Henry's encouragement, she refused to believe it and, a few months later, could dance for 30 minutes before collapsing in pain.

During her confinement, while Crawford was prowling around the basement, she came upon a large burlap bag filled with gold coins. But when she showed them to her mother, Anna was more upset than excited. Crawford and her brother Hal were sent to their grandparents the following day; when they returned, Henry Cassin had been charged as an accomplice to a gold embezzler. Though he was acquitted, the residents of Lawton, already suspicious of the showman, were never convinced of his innocence. Anna soon persuaded her husband to move his family to Kansas City.

It was the beginning of the end of the Cassin family. During the gold incident, Crawford's brother had broken the news that Henry was not her real father. She was crushed. In Kansas City, the Cassins leased a third-rate hotel and worked such long hours that they enrolled Crawford in a convent school. One weekend when she went home, Henry Cassin was gone. Her mother told her she could not afford to keep her at Saint Agnes, but when Crawford protested, Anna worked out an agreement with the Mother Superior: Crawford could stay at school and wait on tables in exchange for room and board.

So at age 11, she began to support herself. After Crawford graduated from grammar-school, Anna found another school willing to educate her daughter in exchange for light housekeeping. Crawford's three years at Rockingham Academy were anything but light. She was up at dawn every day, bathing, dressing, and cooking for 30 children. She also cleaned the 14-room mansion that housed the school. If she failed, she was beaten with a broom. Crawford would fall in bed at midnight, exhausted.

In her last year at Rockingham, she began to blossom. Crawford was turning into a beautiful young woman; she was also turning heads. Boys began asking her to dances, and as much as she enjoyed the boys, she enjoyed dancing even more. One of her dates, an ambitious, intelligent fellow named Ray Sterling, convinced her to as-

Joan
Crawford

pire to more than the job at a local department store that she had taken after graduating from Rockingham. She would go to college.

At Stephens College in Columbia, Missouri, Crawford settled into the same arrangement she had at Saint Agnes and Rockingham Academy: education in exchange for chores. But she had worked so hard at both institutions that she had learned next to nothing and lacked adequate preparation for college classes. Even worse, she did not fit in with the more sophisticated girls.

Three months after her arrival, on the day she discovered that as a working girl she could not join a sorority, she decided to return home.

But Kansas City could not hold her. Crawford left her training as a telephone operator, then left three successive department-store jobs. She was offered work as a "chorus girl" in Springfield, Missouri, and did not hesitate. When she told the manager her name was Lucille LeSueur, he said, "Well, honey, you sure picked a fancy one!"

The show folded after two weeks, but Crawford used her connections to find similar work in Chicago, Oklahoma City, and Detroit. At only 5'4", she was small for the chorus, a bit overweight and not the most beautiful girl on the line, but her energy and engaging manner made her a favorite. One night in Detroit, J.J. Shubert, the theatrical tycoon, was in the audience; recognizing her appeal, he offered her a spot in the chorus of *Innocent Eyes,* a musical set to open on Broadway ten days later, on March 20, 1924, three days before her 18th birthday.

Crawford spent ten months in New York City, dancing in *Innocent Eyes* and, after it went on the road, a Shubert musical called *The Passing Show of 1924.* She shared a room at a respectable boarding house with another chorus girl and hoped to become a famous dancer. In December, just as Crawford was planning to return to Kansas City for Christmas, an executive from Metro-Goldwyn-Mayer, the studio created eight months earlier from the merger of three film companies, spotted her on stage. She declined his offer for a screen test. But a kind stage manager intervened, insisting that a screen test was an important opportunity, and she relented, took the test and left for Kansas City. On Christmas Day, she received a telegram: "YOU ARE PUT UNDER A FIVE-YEAR CONTRACT STARTING AT SEVENTY-FIVE DOLLARS A WEEK. LEAVE IMMEDIATELY FOR CULVER CITY, CALIFORNIA. CONTACT MGM KANSAS CITY FOR TRAVEL EXPENSES." On New Year's Day, 1925, Lucille LeSueur boarded the Sunset Limited for California.

Nothing prepared her for Los Angeles, with its pastel bungalows, tall palm trees and balmy weather. She had only seen eight movies in her entire life and had never heard of most of the movie stars at the MGM studio. Because of the merger, there were many young beauties around the studio lot who, like Crawford, were collecting substantial paychecks for doing little more than posing for publicity photographs and hoping for occasional roles on the silent screen. Crawford instinctively knew that most would never make it in the movies and resolved to avoid that fate.

As always, she took matters into her own hands. She became a constant visitor on MGM sets, arriving early each morning even though she had nothing to do. She studied the scenes, and at night, back in her hotel room, she would replay them in the mirror. She pressed the producer who had seen her on Broadway, and he used his influence to get Crawford her first screen role. *Pretty Ladies* was the story of the *Ziegfeld Follies,* and Crawford was in the chorus. She quickly got a second, tiny role in *The Only Thing,* followed by *Old Clothes,* which would prove to be a big step. Crawford shared some scenes with Jackie Coogan, who was, as Bob Thomas notes, "Metro's most important contribution to the merger with Mayer and Goldwyn."

As Crawford was making something of a name for herself at MGM, the publicity chief decided that she needed a new one. He thought Lucille LeSueur too "stagy," even if authentic. A fan magazine, *Movie Weekly,* agreed to sponsor a contest and ran photographs of her with entry blanks for submission of new names. The winner: "Joan Arden," until someone else claimed it as her own. So after three days as Joan Arden, Lucille LeSueur became, by studio decree, Joan Crawford. She hated it.

The young starlet had made the first cut, but there was much work to be done. She did most of it on the dance floor. Hollywood had lunch dances at the Montmarte and tea dances at the Coconut Grove. The Pom Pom Club and the Garden Court Hotel had evening orchestras. There were plenty of willing escorts, and Joan Crawford became something of an expert in the Charleston, dancing all day long.

Her energy did not go unnoticed, and the attention led to more roles. In 1927, she made six movies and learned much along the way. She lost weight, which allowed her fine facial bones to emerge, with improved dramatic effect. She allowed her co-stars to teach her what they knew about acting, and some of them, like actor Lon Chaney, knew quite a bit. She accepted gifts of designer dresses from admirers eager to impart their good tastes.

The most important man who took notice of Joan Crawford, budding starlet, was MGM head Louis B. Mayer, who ordered up a new contract for $250 a week. Joan felt rich, and for the times she *was* rich. She already had moved from her hotel to a tiny bungalow, and her brother Hal had come to stay. Now she rented a three-bedroom bungalow and sent for her mother.

Any lingering illusions about her family were quickly dispelled. Hal wanted to be a star, too, and had the same good looks as his sister, but he was lazy. He spent his days dating, drinking, and wrecking his sister's car. Her mother, who could at least, Joan thought, take over as housekeeper, continued to side with Hal in any argument. Hal and Anna began to run up high department-store bills in Crawford's name and hide them from her. The house was so often filled with dinner guests that Joan could not get to sleep early enough to be rested for her early calls at the studio. She realized she needed a house of her own and bought one in Beverly Hills for $18,000. She supported her mother and brother for the rest of their lives, but the mutual animosity remained. They hardly ever saw one another.

Crawford became well established as one of the dozen or so best-known actresses on the MGM lot but continued to look for the roles

From the movie Rain, *starring Joan Crawford and Walter Huston.*

that would make her a true star. She had no intention of fading when her youthful beauty faded, as she knew it would. Her breakthrough came in 1928. *Our Dancing Daughters* was a huge success and catapulted Crawford from "sweetheart to the stars" to "the star." Mayer doubled her salary. Letters from adoring young women began to pour into the studio, and she answered each one herself.

With her career in order, Joan Crawford was ready to perfect her personal life. Since coming to California, she had enjoyed many romances but longed for something more stable. Douglas Fairbanks, Jr., was the son of one of the film industry's most famous actors. Though only a fledgling actor himself, his family was Hollywood royalty. He was also considerate and cultivated, and he and Joan were very much in love. They married in 1929, when Crawford was 23 (although she was already claiming to be two years younger). She was intimidated by Doug's family, especially his stepmother, actress *Mary Pickford, but, characteristically, rose to the occasion. She began to read voraciously and to dress in a more demure, sophisticated style. During the early years of their marriage, the Fairbanks were a handsome, captivating couple, and captivated by each other.

Crawford was changing, and so was her industry. The stock-market crash of 1929 altered the national mood and suddenly the "jazz baby" silent films were no longer much in demand. Americans were lining up to see "talkies," and soon the stars were taking diction lessons. Crawford was luckier than some: her husky voice was a perfect complement to her looks. Her career continued its climb; when rival *Norma Shearer became pregnant, Crawford won the dramatic lead in *Paid,* a film about a woman wrongly imprisoned, which won her high marks from critics and audiences alike. That triumph was followed by another, *Grand Hotel,* in 1932, with the great *Greta Garbo. There were inevitable ups and downs in the roles that followed, but Crawford always worked. At MGM, in Hollywood and all across the country, Joan Crawford was a star.

As such, she was able to arrange her private life as she pleased. When, after four years, her marriage became somewhat stale, she announced her intention to divorce in a *Louella Parsons gossip column. Crawford had numerous affairs, most notably with actor Clark Gable. She began to practice Christian Science; its dogma perfectly fit her impatience with minor illnesses. She became known among colleagues and film crews as a generous giver of gifts. She continued her tradition of answering every fan letter, and was always the most accessible of stars. Her insistence on cleanliness, which no doubt had its roots in her childhood, became an obsession. At home or on the set, she was always scrubbing, knitting, working with her hands.

In 1935, she married for the second time, to Franchot Tone, a sophisticated, if little known, New York actor and member of the Group Theater. Tone introduced her to plays, poetry and literature; she opened the doors of Hollywood for him. They also were in love, and in 1937, when *Life* proclaimed Joan Crawford the first Queen of the Movies, her life must have seemed complete.

But a string of uninspired films left her on somewhat shaky ground. *Mannequin,* in 1938, promised an end to her slump: it was a return to the working-girl roles that had served her well, and Crawford was co-starring with veteran actor Spencer Tracy, with whom she began an illicit romance. The film was not met with much interest, however, and later that year a film journal listed her in an article entitled "Box Office Poison." Louis Mayer, taking advantage of her slipping status, cut her salary from $125,000 to $100,000 per film in her new, five-year contract.

Four years after her marriage to Tone, she announced a divorce, once again in a Parsons gossip column. But she longed for children and, after several miscarriages, decided to adopt. **Christina** arrived in 1940; brother Christopher followed two years later. Joan seemed, on the surface, to be a devoted and delighted mother; at home, however, she was a strict disciplinarian, apparently unable to avoid inflicting her own unfortunate childhood on her children.

There were only a few bright spots in what were otherwise disappointing years: working on the film version of *Clare Boothe Luce's play, *The Women*; appearing in her first comedic role in *Susan and God,* and portraying a disfigured woman in *A Woman's Face.* In 1941, Joan Crawford was 35, and the stars who had been on the silent screen were being replaced with fresher faces: *Judy Garland, *Greer Garson, and *Lana Turner. Mayer rid MGM of its older stars by offering them bad pictures, and Crawford had some terrible ones: *When Ladies Meet, They All Kissed the Bride, Reunion in France.* In 1943, she asked to be released from her contract, walking away from the studio that had been her home for 18 years. She had been in 56 pictures.

Crawford accepted a three-picture contract with Warner Bros., where Jack Warner was looking for someone to threaten his difficult star, *Bette Davis. But two years later, Crawford had appeared in only one film, *Hollywood Canteen,* in which she briefly played herself helping in the war effort. *Mildred Pierce,* the film version of a popular James M. Cain novel, was her comeback. The drama opened in 1945 to good reviews and earned Crawford her only Academy Award for Best Actress.

In 1942, she had married for the third time, to actor Phillip Terry, and, as with her first two marriages, its demise after four years was announced by Parsons. For the next nine years, until her fourth and final marriage, Crawford was never without escorts and enjoyed her share of romances. But her friends could not help notice that her behavior had become erratic. Despite her continued belief in Christian Science, she began to smoke and drink for the first time. Alcohol probably contributed to the odd behavior: she was known to greet dates at her door wearing nothing but a slip and to leave dinner parties between courses.

In 1947, she adopted two more children, Cathy and Cynthia, and although she was more lenient with them than with her first two, much of her strange behavior was directed at her children. She beat them for minor transgressions and humiliated them in front of company. Joan Crawford was very generous in many other respects, giving graciously of her time and money to others, but not to her children. Actress *Helen Hayes once said, "Joan tried to be all things to all people. I just wish she hadn't tried to be a mother."

While other actresses of her age and accomplishments were willing to retire, Crawford was not. She was not vain about roles, and her career showed surprising strength after the success of *Mildred Pierce.* That triumph was followed by steady work through the late 1940s. She continued to play an excellent publicity game, staying on good terms with reporters, photographers, and her devoted fan club. She was still quite attractive, trim, and looking taller, as always, than her 5'4''. She had another major success in 1952 with *Sudden Fear,* a thriller that earned her a third Academy Award nomination (the second

From the movie Mildred Pierce, *starring Joan Crawford.*

was for *Possessed* in 1947). The following year, she made her first film for MGM in ten years. *Torch Song* was essentially a one-woman show, full of song and dance, and shot in Technicolor. One critic said, "Here is Joan Crawford, all over the screen, in command . . . a real movie star."

In 1955, she married Alfred Steele, head of Pepsi-Cola. He was strong and secure, and although she continued to make movies she began to enjoy a life apart from Hollywood. They bought a huge apartment in New York City, and Crawford began a second career as a Pepsi ambassador. Steele arrived too late to be of much help with Crawford's two elder children, who by that time were troublesome teenagers, but provided her with much needed companionship. When he died suddenly of a heart attack in 1959, after four years of marriage, he left her lonely and also broke. The man who had guided Pepsi through its growth years had not handled his own finances as well. Two days after his death, his widow was elected to fill his vacancy on the Pepsi board of directors. She also accepted a small role in *The Best of Everything*. She knew she had to work.

It was her idea to make a movie with arch-rival Bette Davis. *Whatever Happened to Baby Jane?* grossed nine million dollars in 1962 and became a cult classic that introduced the aging stars to a new generation. Crawford's four final movies were all in same horror genre.

Her last work was in television; she was once directed by a 21-year-old Steven Spielberg for an episode of "Night Gallery." In 1973, at age 65, she was asked to leave her post at Pepsi because of a bitter rivalry with the new boss. The last five years of her life were spent alone in New York, in a smaller and then even smaller apartment. She was close to her two younger children but not her elder ones (the eldest, Christina, wrote a devastating book, *Mommie Dearest*, which was made into a hit movie.) Crawford enjoyed an active social life until 1974, when an unflattering newspaper photo caused her to decline all further public appearances. On the morning of May 10, 1977, with her weight down to 85 pounds, she rose and prepared breakfast for her maid. Returning to bed to watch soap operas, she called to make sure the breakfast had been eaten, and then she died, most likely of liver cancer, although she had never sought treatment.

SOURCES:

Considine, Shaun. *Bette and Joan: The Divine Feud*. NY: E.P. Dutton, 1989.

Crawford, Christina. *Mommie Dearest*. NY: William Morrow, 1978.

Crawford, Joan, with Jane Kesner Ardmore. *A Portrait of Joan*. NY: Doubleday, 1962.

Friedrich, Otto. *City of Nets: A Portrait of Hollywood in the 1940s*. NY: Harper and Row, 1986.

Quirk, Lawrence J. *The Films of Joan Crawford*. Secaucus, NJ: Citadel Press, 1968.

Rothe, Anna, ed. *Current Biography 1946*. NY: H.W. Wilson, 1946.

Thomas, Bob. *Joan Crawford*. NY: Simon and Schuster, 1978.

Elizabeth L. Bland, reporter, *Time* magazine

Crawford, Ruth (1901–1953)

American composer and pioneering folk-song archivist who was the first woman to be awarded a Guggenheim Foundation Fellowship in composition. Name variations: *Ruth Crawford Seeger or Ruth Crawford-Seeger. Born Ruth Porter Crawford on July 3, 1901, in East Liverpool, Ohio; died of cancer in Chevy Chase, Maryland, on November 18, 1953; daughter of Clara Alletta (Graves) Crawford (a teacher) and Clark Crawford (a Methodist minister); graduated American Conservatory of Music in Chicago, Bachelor of Music (B.M.), 1924, Master of Music (M.M.), 1927; married Charles Louis Seeger, in 1932; children: Michael known as Mike Seeger (b. August 1933, a singer and multi-instrumentalist); ✧▸* Peggy *Seeger (b. 1935); Barbara Seeger (b. 1937); Penelope known as* Penny Seeger *(b. 1943, a singer).*

Began piano lessons at age six; taught piano at the School of Musical Art in Jacksonville during and after completion of high school; entered the American Conservatory of Music in Chicago (fall 1920); completed and premiered earliest musical compositions in public performance (beginning 1924); won first prize in a composition contest sponsored by Sigma Alpha Iota (1927); was in residence at MacDowell Colony in Peterborough, New Hampshire (summer 1929); left Chicago for New York City (fall 1929); studied composition with Charles Seeger (1929–30); awarded Guggenheim Foundation Fellowship (1930); spent year in Europe (1930–31); returned to New York (November 1931); associated with the Composers Collective (1932–33); began collecting, transcribing, and arranging folk songs (1933); moved to Washington, D.C. area (1935); gave private piano lessons and taught music in several nursery schools (1935–53); published folk-song collections (1948–53). Awards: first prize, composition contest, Sigma Alpha Iota (1927); Guggenheim Foundation Fellowship (1930).

Published compositions: Four Preludes for Piano *(San Francisco: New Music Edition, 1932);*

Piano Study in Mixed Accents *(San Francisco: New Music Edition, 1932)*; Three Songs for Contralto, Oboe, Piano, and Percussion *(San Francisco: New Music Edition, 1933)*; String Quartet 1931 *(Bryn Mawr, PA: Merion Music, 1941)*; Suite for Wind Quintet *(New York: Continuo Music Press, 1969)*; Chant *(NY: Continuo Music Press, 1971)*; Chinaman, Laundryman, and Sacco Vanzetti *(Bryn Mawr, PA: Merion Music, 1976)*; Diaphonic Suites *(NY: Continuo Music Press, 1972)*.

Published folk-song anthologies: American Songbag *(NY: Harcourt, Brace, 1927)*; Our Singing Country *(NY: Macmillan, 1941)*; Coal Dust on the Fiddle *(Philadelphia: University of Pennsylvania Press, 1943)*; Folk Song U.S.A. *(NY: Duell, Sloan and Pearce, 1947)*; American Folk Songs for Children *(Garden City, NY: Doubleday, 1948)*; Anthology of Pennsylvania Folklore *(Philadelphia: University of Pennsylvania Press, 1949)*; Animal Folk Songs for Children *(Garden City, NY: Doubleday, 1950)*; Treasury of Western Folklore *(NY: Crown, 1951)*; American Folk Songs for Christmas *(Garden City, NJ: Doubleday, 1953)*; Let's Build a Railroad *(NY: Aladdin Books, 1954)*; Folklore Infantil do Santo Domingo *(Madrid, Spain: Ediciones Cultura Hispanica, 1955)*.

Selected discography: Diaphonic Suite No. 3 for Two Clarinets, *CPO 999111-2*, *"Clarinet Counterpoints" (1930)*; Five Songs, *Cambria CD-1037 (1929)*; Quartet, *Gramavision R4S-79440 (1931)*; Two Movements for Chamber Orchestra, *Delos DCD-1012 (1926)*; Music of Ruth Crawford-Seeger, *Musical Heritage Society MHC 312229X*.

Widely recognized as one of the most innovative American composers of the first half of the 20th century, Ruth Crawford became an influential member of the musical avant-garde during the 1920s, and in 1930 she was the first woman to win a Guggenheim Foundation Fellowship in composition. She was born in East Liverpool, Ohio, into a family of upper-middle-class standing both socially and economically. Her father Clark Crawford was a Methodist minister, and her mother **Clara Crawford** was an occasional teacher. The family moved frequently, eventually settling in Jacksonville, Florida. Beginning in the fall of 1912, a serious kidney ailment forced Clark to spend considerable time at the Mayo Clinic in Rochester, Minnesota. His death occurred less than two years later, leaving Clara with sole financial responsibility for her daughter Ruth and son Carl.

Ruth Crawford began piano lessons when about six years of age and soon exhibited unusu-

al musical talent. During her high school years, she took harmony lessons and wrote her first compositions (none of which survive). At the beginning of her senior year, the director of the School of Musical Art in Jacksonville offered Crawford a teaching position, which she held for three years. She also continued her own study of composition and piano.

Ruth Crawford

Seeger, Peggy (b. 1935)
American folk singer and songwriter. Born in 1935; daughter of *Ruth Crawford (1901–1953) and Charles Louis Seeger; sister of Penny Seeger (1943—); half-sister of Pete Seeger; married Ewan MacColl (died).

Peggy Seeger writes and sings folk ballads, mostly with a feminist slant, as represented by the song "I'm Gonna Be an Engineer." Many of her albums, including *At the Present Moment* for Rounder, were collaborations with her husband Ewan MacColl, British folk artists, or her brother and sister. With her brother Mike Seeger, she recorded the album *American Folk Songs for Children* for Rounder; with Mike and her sister Penny, she recorded the album *American Folk Songs for Christmas*, also for Rounder.

A bequest of money, possibly from her father's family, allowed Crawford to enroll at the American Conservatory in Chicago in the fall of 1921. Though not an overly large sum, it supported her for one year. Her goal was simple: she wanted to become a concert pianist. But in 1922, muscle spasms and tension in her arms forced her to reduce the time spent practicing piano. In frustration, she wrote her mother on March 14, 1922:

> I cannot practice! My left arm has gone on strike. I have kept thinking that with my letting up on practising—with the rest it would thus be getting, it would be all right. But for the past week I have done this: got in only two hours Friday, an hour Saturday, (etc.). . . . I took an electric treatment Saturday, but it made me worse instead of better.

Fortunately, Crawford's affinity for harmonization exercises and composition provided much needed solace during this difficult period.

She returned to the Conservatory for a second year, this time supported by teaching piano lessons. Her muscular difficulties continued to preclude extended practice, and she instead concentrated on composition. Her assignments completed under the tutelage of Adolf Weidig earned Crawford high praise. In the two years that followed, Weidig assumed a role of increasing prominence in Crawford's education, eventually serving as her private composition instructor. Crawford later recalled her lessons in a January 29, 1933, letter to Nicolas Slonimsky:

> Sprinkling sevenths and ninths plentifully and insistently, and observing or breaking the solemn rules of harmony with equal regularity, I was guided with great understanding during the next years by Adolf Weidig, . . . who seems to me to have had an unusual balance between necessary discipline and necessary allowance for individuality.

Upon completion of her bachelor's degree in 1924, Crawford continued on at the Conservatory, earning her master's degree in composition, *summa cum laude,* in 1927. Years later, in a letter to Slonimsky (January 29, 1933), she recalled other important influences she experienced as a student: "Contact in 1925 with Djane Lavoie Herz, with whom I studied piano, and with Dane Rudyar, and later with Henry Cowell, established a definite turning-point in my work." It enabled her to "see far along the way" toward which she "had been groping" with her numerous student compositions. Rudyar later rendered significant support in Crawford's application for a Guggenheim Fellowship. Through Herz, Crawford made the acquaintance of Henry Cowell, her first publisher, and Alfred Franken-

stein, later the music and art critic for the *San Francisco Chronicle*. Frankenstein maintained a lifelong enthusiasm for avant-garde music, especially Crawford's, and also introduced Crawford to Carl Sandburg, who collaborated with Crawford in various creative projects.

Crawford spent the summer of 1929 in residence at the MacDowell Colony in Peterborough, New Hampshire—a secluded haven for artists, writers and musicians. Supported by a grant, she worked on several song settings for the poetry of Carl Sandburg, including "Joy," "Loam," and "Sunsets." Near the end of her stay, she met the composer and author *Marion Bauer (1887–1955), whose friendship and advice Crawford valued highly. She wrote in a diary entry dated August 16, 1929:

> One thing I learned from this beautiful afternoon with Marion Bauer was that I had been forgetting that craftsmanship was also art. I have not been composing and have felt tense, partly because I relied on inspiration only. I was not willing to work things out. . . . Courage, Marion Bauer tells me—work. You have a great talent. You must go ahead.

In the fall of 1929, Crawford moved to New York City and began a year of study with the noted musicologist, composer, and teacher Charles Seeger. The compositions she completed preceding her arrival represented a synthesis of experimental procedures supported by a keen awareness of more well-established and traditional techniques. Marion Bauer noted that Crawford's music of this period was "distinctly in a cerebral stage," but her warm emotional nature was "threatening to break through." During her studies with Seeger, Crawford explored the potential of an innovative procedure known as "dissonant counterpoint." No longer lingering at a creative crossroads, she rapidly developed her own unique style that combined atonal melodies and angular rhythmic lines in delicate counterpoint. She wrote relatively few compositions while in New York, but the high quality and exquisite technical development evident in her work convinced the Guggenheim Foundation committee to select her as a recipient—the first woman ever—of a grant to study composition in Europe for a year.

While in Europe, Crawford met many renowned and influential musicians, most notably Albert Roussel, Maurice Ravel, Bela Bartók, Alban Berg and *Nadia Boulanger. Rather than studying with these or any other well-established composers, Crawford set out on her own. She completed the celebrated *String Quartet 1931*, arguably the most influential composition of the first half of the 20th century. Composer and critic George Perle was among the first to observe its "marked advance in technical complexity and musical interest," which far surpassed music written some 30 years later. She also wrote the fourth and final *Diaphonic Suite,* which was premiered in Berlin on April 8, 1931. Wrote Edward Ansel Mowrer:

> Crawford allows a viola and cello to talk simultaneously, with the effect of hearing two telephone voices at once. At the end of the second movement the two speakers begin to coalesce. Her aim, so she stated, was to achieve new effects in atonal music and her success was apparent.

In late 1931, Crawford returned to New York City and immediately faced the challenge of finding living quarters and employment. She sought piano students and found some time for composition. Her relationship with Charles Seeger, kept viable during her absence through frequent correspondence, now extended far beyond the boundaries of teacher and pupil. They were married on October 2, 1932, and the first of their four children, folk singer Michael Seeger, was born a year later.

At the instigation of Henry Cowell, Crawford and Seeger became involved, in the early 1930s, with a small group of New York musicians and intellectuals called the Composer's Collective. The organization focused on the economic hardship of the Depression and sought to give musical expression to a variety of political and social ills. Two important protest songs—"Sacco, Vanzetti" and "Chinaman, Laundryman"—completed by Crawford in 1933, reflect her association with the Collective. These were among the last pieces of art music she composed. With musical opportunities becoming increasingly scarce in New York City, Crawford and Seeger moved their family to the Washington, D.C., area.

After 1933, Crawford turned her creative energy solely to the collection and transcription of folk music, working in collaboration with Seeger, Carl Sandburg, folk archivists John and Alan Lomax, and Pete Seeger (Charles Seeger's son from his first marriage). In a letter to composer Edgard Varèse on May 29, 1948, Crawford wrote:

> I am not sure whether the road I have been following the last dozen years is a main road or a detour. I have begun to feel, the past year or two, that it is the latter—a detour, but a very important one to me, during which I have descended from the stratosphere onto a solid well-traveled highway, folded my wings and breathed good friendly dust as I travelled along in and out of the thousands of fine traditional folk-tunes which I have been hearing and singing and transcribing from field recordings.

Crawford assumed a variety of roles in these projects, including music consultant, arranger, editor, or transcriber, all of which resulted in several published volumes of songs. Alan Lomax described his collaboration with Crawford in a taped interview with biographer **Matilda Gaume:**

> It was a wonderful experience to work with her because she was tireless . . . she had a wonderful ear and she cared very, very, very much. And of course was the nicest woman that could possibly be imagined. You couldn't help loving her. She was like my older sister, or like my aunt, or like my best friend, and it was *Our Singing Country* that we worked on so long and hard together that was a testament about how good it can get if it's a folk song book.

In 1941, Crawford accepted a teaching position at the cooperative nursery school attended by her children and drew upon arrangements of folk songs for much of her teaching material. In her introductory essay for *American Folk Songs for Children,* Crawford summarized her philosophical, educational, and aesthetic reasons for choosing folk music:

> This kind of traditional or folk music is thoroughly identified with the kind of people who made America as we know it. Some of it came . . . from other countries and has been little changed. . . . All of it has partaken of the making of America. . . . It belongs to our children—it is an integral part of their cultural heritage.

During the late spring or early summer of 1953, Crawford began to experience ill health, which was eventually diagnosed as cancer. An operation in the early fall temporarily relieved her symptoms and she rallied briefly. Her attempts to resume teaching and composing proved futile, however, and her condition gradually worsened. She died on November 18, 1953, in Chevy Chase, Maryland.

"For all her great creative gifts and wide musical knowledge," writes Sidney Robertson Cowell, Ruth Crawford "was a sturdy personality of the utmost simplicity and naturalness. She had the widest possible sympathies, the quickest loyalty and kindness—a memorably rich and generous human being who was a most rewarding friend."

SOURCES:

Cowell, Sidney Robertson. "Ruth Crawford Seeger, 1901–1953," in *International Folk Music Journal.* Vol 8, 1955, pp. 55–56.

Gaume, Matilda. "Crawford (Seeger), Ruth (Porter)," in *The New Grove Dictionary of American Music*. 4 vols. Ed. by H. Wiley Hitchcock and Stanley Sadie. NY: Macmillan, 1986, Vol. 1, pp. 531–532.

———. "Ruth Crawford: A Promising Young Composer in New York, 1929–30," in *American Music*. Spring 1987, pp. 74–84.

———. "Ruth Crawford Seeger," in *Women Making Music: The Western Art Tradition, 1150–1950*. Ed. by Jane Bowers and Judith Tick. Urbana, IL: University of Illinois Press, 1986, pp. 370–388.

———. *Ruth Crawford Seeger: Memoirs, Memories, Music*. Metuchen, NJ: Scarecrow Press, 1986.

Karpf, Juanita. "'Pleasure in the Very Smallest Things': Trichordal Transformation in Ruth Crawford's *Diaphonic Suites*," in *The Music Review*, 1995.

———. "Tradition and Experimentation: An Analytical Study of Two *Diaphonic Suites* by Ruth Crawford," unpublished D.M.A. dissertation, University of Georgia, Athens, GA, 1992.

Nicholls, David. *American Experimental Music, 1890–1940*. Cambridge, England: Cambridge University Press, 1990.

Perle, George. "Atonality and the Twelve-Note System in the United States," in *The Score*. Vol. 27, July 1960, pp. 51–66.

"Ruth Crawford's Settings of Sandburg Poems Issued by *New Music*," in *Musical America*. May 25, 1933, p. 53.

Seeger, Ruth Crawford. *American Folk Songs for Children*. Garden City, NY: Doubleday, 1948.

Wilding-White, Ray. "Remembering Ruth Crawford Seeger: An Interview with Charles and Peggy Seeger," in *American Music*. Vol. 6, Winter 1988, pp. 442–454.

SUGGESTED READING:

Ammer, Christine. *Unsung: A History of Women in American Music*. Westport, CT: Greenwood Press, 1980.

Jepson, Barbara. "Ruth Crawford Seeger: A Study in Mixed Accents," in *Feminist Art Journal*. Vol. 6, no. 1. Spring 1977, pp. 13–16.

Mantel, Sarah, and Susan Wheatley. "Reflections of Change: A Comparative View of Crawford and Larsen," in *International League of Women Composers Journal*. June 1993, pp. 1–5.

Nelson, Mark D. "In Pursuit of Charles Seeger's Heterophonic Ideal: Three Palindromic Works by Ruth Crawford," in *Musical Quarterly*. Vol. 72, 1986, pp. 458–475.

Neuls-Bates, Carol, ed. *Women in Music: An Anthology of Source Readings from the Middle Ages to the Present*. NY: Harper and Row, 1982.

Nicholls, David. "Ruth Crawford Seeger: An Introduction," in *The Musical Times*. Vol. 124, 1983, pp. 421–425.

Seeger, Charles. "On Dissonant Counterpoint," in *Modern Music*. Vol. 7, June–July 1930, pp. 25–31.

———. "Ruth Crawford," in *American Composers on American Music*. Ed. by Henry Cowell. Palo Alto, CA: Stanford University Press, 1933, pp. 110–118.

Slonimsky, Nicolas, ed. *Baker's Biographical Dictionary of Musicians*, 8th ed. NY: Schirmer Books, 1992.

Tick, Judith. "Dissonant Counterpoint Revisited: The First Movement of Ruth Crawford's *String Quartet 1931*," in *A Celebration of American Music: Words and Music in Honor of H. Wiley Hitchcock*. Ed. by Richard Crocker, R. Allen Lott and Carol J. Oja. Ann Arbor, MI: University of Michigan Press, 1990, pp. 405–422.

———. *Ruth Crawford Seeger: A Composer's Search for American Music*. NY: Oxford University Press, 1997.

———. "Ruth Crawford Seeger (1901–1953)," in *Historical Anthology of Music by Women*. Ed. by James R. Briscoe. Bloomington, IN: Indiana University Press, 1987, pp. 268–290.

———. "Ruth Crawford Spiritual Concept: The Sound-Ideals of an Early American Modernist, 1924–1930," in *Journal of the American Musicological Society*. Vol. 44, no. 2. Summer 1991, pp. 221–261.

COLLECTIONS:

Correspondence, papers, diaries and manuscripts located in the Music Division, Library of Congress, Washington, D.C.

Juanita Karpf, Assistant Professor of Music and Women Studies, University of Georgia, Athens, Georgia

Crayencour, Marguerite de (1903–1987).

See Yourcenar, Marguerite.

Crazy Bet (1818–1900).

See Van Lew, Elizabeth.

Crescentii (892–932).

See Marozia Crescentii.

Crespé, Marie-Madeleine
(1760–1796)

French ballerina. Name variations: Mlle Théodore; Marie-Madeleine Crespe. Born in 1760; died in 1796; studied with Lany; married Jean Bercher, known as Dauberval, 1782.

Debut in Myrtil et Lycoris *(December 1777); created the part of Lise in the original production of Dauberval's* La Fille mal gardée.

In 1776, the 16-year-old Marie-Madeleine Crespé left the *corps de ballet* to pursue other options. Known as "the philosopher in satin ballet slippers," she was an inveterate reader, especially of Jean-Jacques Rousseau's writings. When she returned to the Opéra and was apprised of the usual backstage machinations, she wrote to Rousseau for advice as to how to handle them. He wrote her a long reply filled with solemn warnings. Throughout most of her career, Crespé was cognizant of his alarums, except for the time she challenged **Mlle Beaumesnil** to a duel. The nature of the conflict between the two women remains unknown, though there is a strong possibility it concerned a duplicate love interest—namely Dauberval. The dueling party arrived at the field near the Porte Maillot just outside Paris with their seconds; an assistant conductor wisely placed the weapons on the damp grass and the pistols misfired. The duelists, at first stunned, reportedly laughed and made up.

In 1781, Crespé went to London with Jean Georges Noverre, dancing the title role in his production of *Rinaldo and Armida*. Wrote a thankful Noverre: "She performed with such lightness that without even leaping, by the mere elasticity of her instep, one had the impression that she never touched the ground." Because she enjoyed London and the distance from Dauberval, Crespé had her Paris Opera contract canceled with the help of *Marie Antoinette. She made the mistake, however, of summering in France at a château of Dauberval's, and the directors of the Opera had a change of mind, fearful other dancers might find it easy to break their contracts. Arrested, Crespé was put in La Force prison, and the public was incensed. In a missive from prison, she pointed out to the minister that there was a clause "with no conditions or restrictions" that had been in the letter apprising her of her release from the Opera. She also mentioned that she had married Dauberval the week before she was arrested. Crespé and Dauberval left for Bordeaux where he was ballet master and choreographer and she was premiere danseuse. She died there at age 36.

SOURCES:

Migel, Parmenia. *The Ballerinas: From the Court of Louis XIV to Pavlova*. NY: Macmillan, 1972.

Cresson, Edith (1934—)

French economist and politician who was France's first woman prime minister. Born in France in 1934.

Edith Cresson joined the Socialist Party (PS) in 1975. She served as mayor of Thure (1977) and from her seat in the European Parliament (1979) became known as an expert in agriculture. The first woman to head the Ministry of Agriculture (1981–83), Cresson then moved into positions as trade minister (1983–84 and 1984–86) and minister for European affairs (1988). She resigned in 1990 and took a senior post with the Schneider engineering group. Cresson was regarded as a steadfast fighter and a French trade protectionist who was staunchly pro-business. In May 1991, François Mitterand appointed her prime minister, and Cresson had the distinction of being the first woman in the country's history to hold this post. Her stay as prime minister, however, would prove short-

lived. Mitterand had hoped that Cresson would build the country's economic strength, but she was forced to resign after the Socialist Party's defeat in regional elections in April 1992, only ten months into her appointment.

In 1994, she was nominated to be one of France's members of the European Commission, the administrative and executive arm of the European Union (EU), to serve from January 1995. In March 1998, Cresson resigned, along with 20 other members of the Commission, after a damning report found several of them guilty of "favoritism." Cresson had appointed her personal, hometown dentist to be her science adviser, an ill-advised move that drew charges of nepotism. When not holding public office, Cresson works as a business consultant.

Cripps, Isobel (1891–1979)

Wife of Sir Stafford Cripps, British diplomat, who was famous in her own right. Name variations: Dame Isobel Cripps. Born Isobel Swithinbank in 1891; died in 1979; second daughter of Commander Harold William (a landowner) and Amy (Eno) Swithinbank; educated privately and at Heathfield, near Ascot; married Sir Stafford Cripps (1889–1952), in 1911; children: one son John (who became editor of the Countryman*) and three daughters, including Peggy (who married Joe Appiah).*

The wife of the brilliant lawyer and diplomat Sir Stafford Cripps, Dame Isobel Cripps supported her husband's political career and cared for him in his poor health. Married in 1911, Cripps accompanied her husband to the USSR, where he served as ambassador in Moscow from 1940 to 1942. During World War II, she served as president of the British United Aid to China Fund. After receiving the CBE in 1946, she toured China as the guest of General Chiang Kai-shek and Madame Chiang (*Song Meiling). That year, she also visited Yenan at the invitation of Mao Zedong and was presented with the Special Grand Cordon of the Order of the Brilliant Star of China and the award of the National Committee of India in celebration of International Women's Year.

Crisler, Lois (1897–1971)

American writer whose observations provided some of the first detailed descriptions of wolves' social interactions. Born Lois Brown in 1897; died on June 4, 1971, in Seattle, Washington; married Herb "Cris" Crisler (divorced); no children. Taught at the University of Washington.

Lois Crisler's observations of the wolves with whom she shared her Arctic tundra home in the mid-20th century were called by A. Starker Leopold in 1958 "the most meticulous and complete description of wolf mannerisms and behaviour that has been written." In an age when the wolf was still a largely misunderstood and widely feared creature, Lois Crisler and her husband Herb (known as Cris) spent more than eight years observing and living with wolves. While filming wildlife for a Disney movie that featured caribou, they began their journey in the Arctic wilds of the Brooks Range where they were to spend 18 months. At a secluded lake in the Range, Crisler posed a question to herself: "'What *do* I want?' My answer was instant. 'To be where "the people that walk on four legs" are. For the rest I can pick myself up, get off the couch of uncorseted slackness. Tauten my muscles and take the direction of the desire under the desires.'" Her purpose was not to be challenged by survival in the wild, as it was for many who came to such harsh environments before her, but rather to establish communication with other species.

Lois
Crisler

Reluctant to take guns with them, or to film any set-up scenes, the Crislers were looking to document the real action of Arctic wildlife while setting ethical boundaries for their imposition on the land. In addition to living among the free creatures of the Arctic during their time on the Range, the Crislers brought two wolves into their home for the purposes of observation, filming, and, most paramount, friendship. During the beginning of their first summer camp, two cubs, Trigger and Lady, were obtained from Eskimos, and Lois began writing descriptions of the wolves' interactions with each other and with their adoptive family; hers were detailed, intimate, and extended observations and notes. Attempting to "try to live in a degree of freedom with animals not human-oriented," Crisler worked to shape her life to the needs of the wolves and assumed that her venture with Trigger and Lady was marked by a moral correctness that included respect for the wolves as free beings, "neither doglike nor humanlike, but wolf and wild." She was amazed when, given opportunities to roam out of the pen and off-leash, the young wolves returned voluntarily to the Crislers.

The 1958 work *Arctic Wild* is Crisler's account of the months spent sharing a cabin with Trigger and Lady. Providing unprecedented details of these social creatures, she described wolves "smiling," "talking," and, at particularly rewarding moments, sharing eye contact with her. "The wolf had read my eyes!" she said of Trigger:

> The thing happens so fleetingly, the animal's wild inexorable intelligence seizes the knowledge so instantaneously that the wonder is I ever blundered into awareness of this deepest range of communication . . . your true feeling looks out of your eyes, the animal reads it. The wolf has a characteristic way of looking at your eyes. He does not stare, his eyes merely graze yours in passing. I learned at last to have my eyes ready for that unguarded instant when the wolf's eyes brushed mine.

*Rachel Carson, in a letter to Dorothy Freeman, repeated a description of Lois provided by their friend Elizabeth Lawrence: "Lois and Cris are exactly the people you would expect and hope them to be. She is more beautiful than the photographs indicate—her eyes perhaps are a difficult color. Not large or small, but with a kind of magnificence about her." In another letter to Freeman, Carson elaborates on Crisler's character: "I think we must remember that she lives in a world almost wholly without companionship, something hard for us to conceive. There is no 'small talk' in her—she has forgotten the easy chatting and exchange of not-so-important comment that makes up social intercourse. She thinks deeply—when she speaks the thoughts come from far down in the recesses of that solitude-bound mind and personality. 'Like someone from another world.'"

In their efforts to produce a marketable film, the Crislers wanted to show the true social nature of wolves, and it was thought that views of family life among a wolf pack could achieve this purpose while also displaying the emotion and intelligence the Crislers had witnessed in the wolf. Hoping to film wild cubs in a den, Herb was unsuccessful in his first attempt. He then raided a den. Late one evening, he surprised Lois with the cubs. Greeted by the stolen cubs, Lois "involuntarily . . . shrank," as her relationship with the world of the "people who walk on four legs" was altered irrevocably. While she and Lady nurtured the cubs, Crisler was haunted by images of the she-wolf from whom the young cubs had been taken. Before their time on the tundra was out, Lady was killed by a female rival. Another female wolf who hung about the camp prompted Crisler to question if she might be the cubs' mother, but when Trigger attempted to lead the cubs off the tundra toward this wolf the Crislers prevented him from doing so.

After Trigger left them to form his own family with another wolf pack, the Crislers continued to parent the pups and encouraged them to stake out their territory. But upon the film's completion, the Crislers had to return to the States. Knowing the cubs would starve to death if left on their own, or be forced to live in captivity if brought to America, Lois Crisler faced the violation the couple had committed: "What was right to do," she said, "in a situation unright from its beginning—the hour the pups were stolen from their den?" Determined not to destroy the cubs, the couple shipped them to their cabin in Colorado, where several acres were used to construct a pen. Writes Carson to Freeman: "[Lois] wrote such a heartbreaking, revealing thing . . . about the morning after her return—that when she awoke she lay abed for a while, moaning from time to time, and that the dog who is her special companion came and laid his muzzle across her face, trying to comfort. I could see that it was agony for her to return to that life." When the wolves escaped the safety of the pen, all but one were killed by locals.

For the next seven years, Lois Crisler's life was dedicated to the lone surviving wolf, Alatna, with whom she had a private, exclusive bond. Crisler's purpose was to protect Alatna from the crippling effects of captivity and to provide some semblance to the life of a wolf in the wild. Alatna was given a series of dog mates with whom she produced several litters of puppies. Unlike wolves, wolf-dog hybrids have been shown to be potentially vicious and unpredictable; many of Alatna's hybrid pups had to be destroyed because they were dangerous or for the purpose of controlling the population in the pens.

Rachel Carson begged Crisler to give the world the story of Alatna, and Crisler would publish *Captive Wild* to document her seven years with the wolf. Crisler's impending divorce from her husband forced her to leave the cabin in Colorado. Finding no other way to honor her friendship with Alatna given the possibilities she saw for the wolf's future, Crisler euthanized Alatna and her family. Writes the naturalist Barry Lopez: "Lois Crisler . . . killed the wolves she raised from pups because she couldn't stand what captivity had done to them. And her." Confronted with the choices of death or life as a captive for the animals they studied, women who were to come after Crisler—*Jane Goodall, *Dian Fossey, and *Biruté Galdikas—saw a third alternative that reintroduced the wildlife into their home terrain. In Crisler's day, however, this alternative was not yet in common practice. Crisler's narrative *Captive Wild* ends at the moment she kills Alatna while recalling her "free with her fellow wolves on the tundra in the old big days of her youth." By returning Alatna to the wild in this literary gesture, Crisler conceptualized the obligation that the next generation of observationalists would honor by returning borrowed animals to the wild.

Wrote Crisler of her experience with the wolf: "I had not dreamed until now that I had something to give Alatna—and she had been able to receive it—besides my main effort and preoccupation, which had been, so passionately, to keep her as herself, to keep her heart confident and free. But I had given her something—I did not know what in a wolf's mind. I had given her of my humanness. She had given me of her wolfness. We were both different. She was still all wolf. I was, I thought, more human."

SOURCES:

Freeman, Martha, ed. *Always Rachel: The letters of Rachel Carson and Dorothy Freeman.* Boston, MA: Beacon, 1995.

Norwood, Vera. *Made from This Earth.* Chapel Hill, NC: University of North Carolina, 1993.

Cristina (1965—)

Spanish princess and duchess of Palma. Name variations: Christina or Christine; Cristina Bourbon. Born

*Cristina Frederica Victoria on June 13, 1965, in Madrid, Spain; daughter of *Sophia of Greece (b. 1938) and Juan Carlos I, king of Spain (r. 1975—); married Inaki Urdangarín y Liebaert (a professional athlete), October 4, 1997.*

Third in line to the Spanish throne, Princess Cristina married a Basque commoner in a 13th-century cathedral in Barcelona in October of 1997. It was the city's first royal wedding in over 600 years. The service was in Spanish, Catalan, and Basque. Her husband Inaki Urdangarin is a professional athlete.

Cristina I of Naples (1806–1878).

See Isabella II for sidebar on Maria Cristina I of Naples.

Crochet, Evelyne (1934—)

French pianist. Born in 1934; studied with Yvonne Lefébure, Edwin Fischer and Rudolf Serkin.

Evelyne Crochet won a first prize in **Yvonne Lefébure**'s class at the Paris Conservatory in 1954. Her American debut saw her partnered with Francis Poulenc in the American premiere of his Concerto for Two Pianos and Orchestra; the Boston Symphony was conducted on the occasion by Charles Munch. She has made acclaimed recordings of the complete piano works of Gabriel Fauré and has also revealed an affinity for lesser-known works of German composers, particularly Franz Schubert.

John Haag, Athens, Georgia

Croly, Jane Cunningham (1829–1901)

English-born American writer and editor, founder of the women's club movement in America, and champion of women's right to work, who syndicated her work and created the first newspaper "women's pages." Name variations: Jennie June (journalistic pseudonym, sometimes spelled Jenny June). Pronunciation: Crow-lee. Born Jane Cunningham on December 19, 1829, in Market Harborough, Leicestershire, England; died on December 23, 1901, of heart failure in New York City; moved to United States in 1841, at age 12; daughter of Joseph Cunningham (a Unitarian minister) and Jane (Scott) Cunningham (a homemaker); married David Goodman Croly, on February 14, 1856; children: Minnie Croly; Viola Croly; Herbert Croly (founding editor of The New Republic); Alice Cary Croly; and a son who died in infancy.

Jane
Cunningham
Croly

Became first woman reporter at a U.S. daily newspaper (New York Tribune, 1855); became first woman syndicated newspaper columnist in America (1857); created first "women's pages" in a U.S. newspaper (New York World, 1862); formed women's club Sorosis (1868), serving as its president (1870, 1875–86); was instrumental in the founding of the General Federation of Women's Clubs (1889); founded the Woman's Press Club of New York City (1889), serving as its president (1889–1901); awarded honorary doctorate by Rutger's Women's College (1892), where she was appointed chair of journalism and literature.

Newspaper articles published in: New York Tribune, *beginning in 1855;* (New York) Sunday Times *and* Noah's Weekly Messenger, *beginning in 1855;* New York Herald, *beginning in 1856;* (New York) Graphic Daily Times *and* Weekly Times, *beginning in 1861;* New York World, *1862–72; and* (New York) Daily Graphic, *beginning in 1873. Syndicated columns published, beginning in 1857, in* New Orleans Picayune, New Orleans Delta, Baltimore American, Richmond Enquirer, Chicago Times, Louisville Journal, *and other periodicals. Chief staff writer for* Mme. Demorest's Mirror of Fashions, *later* Demorest's Monthly Magazine, *1860–87. Editor of* Godey's Lady's Book, *1887–88, and the magazine of the General Federation of Women's Clubs (titled variously as the* Woman's Cycle, *the* Home-Maker, *and the* New Cycle), *1889–96.*

Books: Jennie June's American Cookery Book *(1866);* Jennie Juneiana: Talks on Women's Topics *(1869);* For Better or Worse: Talks for Some Men and All Women *(1875);* Knitting and Crochet: A Guide to the Use of the Needle and the Hook *(1885);* Ladies' Fancy Work: A Manual of Designs and Instructions in All Kinds of Needle-Work *(1886);* Sorosis: Its Origin and History *(1886);* Thrown on Her Own Resources, Or, What Girls Can Do *(1891);* The History of the Women's Club Movement in America *(1898).*

Jane Cunningham Croly is memorialized in journalism history as the first syndicated woman newspaper columnist in America and as the initiator of newspaper "women's pages"; she is remembered by women's-studies historians chiefly as the founder of the women's club movement in America. Her contributions to club organization as well as newspaper journalism—a career she shared with her husband David Croly—were indeed considerable. But perhaps an equally important contribution in both fields was her tireless championship of women's right to work. At the same time other women activists of the late 19th century agitated for suffrage, Jane Cunningham Croly—known to most of her readers as Jennie June—believed that women's emancipation lay in their professional and financial independence rather than the vote. She also believed that women could combine a career with marriage and motherhood, as she did quite successfully.

Jane Cunningham arrived in America at the age of 12. Her Unitarian-minister father's support of the working classes—the same issue that would dominate much of her later writing—was considered too liberal by the community where he preached in Leicestershire, England, so the Reverend Joseph Cunningham moved his family to upstate New York (first Poughkeepsie and then the town of Wappingers Falls). Despite limited schooling, Jane was well-read thanks to her use of her father's extensive library. As a teenager, she taught school and wrote a semi-monthly newsletter for the congregation led by her brother John, another minister, for whom she also did housekeeping.

When her father died in 1854, however, 25-year-old Jane went to New York City to seek a more substantial income. She sold her first article to Charles A. Dana, then assistant editor of the *New York Tribune*, who hired her as a staff writer—the first woman in such a position at a U.S. daily newspaper. Rather than writing columns or essays from home, as other women newspaper writers did, Jane Cunningham reported stories and then wrote them on deadline from her desk in the city room; in this sense, according to journalism historian *Ishbel Ross*, she was a "forerunner of the [20th-century] trained reporter." From the start of her newspaper career in 1855, she used an alliterative pseudonym as her byline, taking her cue from contemporaries, including "Fanny Fern" (*Sara Willis Parton), "Grace Greenwood" (*Sara Clarke Lippincott), and "Minnie Myrtle" (Nancy Johnson); she chose "Jennie June" from Benjamin F. Taylor's poem "The Beautiful River."

Jane wrote primarily about women's topics, including fashion and manners, and, because of the growing female readership of newspapers in the mid-19th century, she was soon contributing to several New York newspapers. At one of them, the *New York Herald*, she met reporter David Croly, whom she married on February 14, 1856. The next year, she began reselling her columns to newspapers in New Orleans, Richmond, Baltimore, Louisville, and Chicago—thus becoming the first American woman newspaper writer to syndicate her work.

In 1859, the Crolys moved to Rockford, Illinois, where David briefly served as editor and publisher of the *Rockford Daily News* and where their first child, **Minnie Croly**, was born. Within a year, they returned to New York City, where both David and Jane found work at a new daily, the *New York World*. In 1862, David became managing editor of the paper, and Jane began what would later be known as "women's pages," a regular section devoted to fashion, homemaking, shopping, and entertaining. While producing this section for the *World* during the 1860s and early 1870s, she took on several additional responsibilities, writing dramatic and literary criticism for various newspapers, serving as the chief staff writer for *Ellen Curtis Demorest's* *Mme. Demorest's Mirror of Fashion* (later *Demorest's Monthly Magazine*), and authoring a cookbook. Croly continued to syndicate her newspaper articles and began to issue collections of them in book form.

Much of her newspaper and magazine work was what would later be known as "service journalism," offering actual instructions for cooking, sewing, and decorating, and giving shoppers specific information about merchandise. But she also offered broader advice to her women readers. She counseled mothers about the education of their daughters, complaining that the finishing schools of the day produced young women ill-prepared for life. In the early 1860s, she noted that:

> A fashionably educated young lady knows all about the last new opera, and is able to give the correct etiquette for an evening party, but it is doubtful if she can tell the boundaries of her own country, or spell the commonest words with accuracy . . . . [Rather than] the studious cultivation of all the absurd nonsense concerning dress, style, fortune, . . . [w]hat we want is educational institutions which will teach girls what they ought to know when they take their places as women, and make them active, sensible, useful wives and mothers.

She believed that good health, common sense, and practical preparation led ultimately to women's long-term happiness, especially in marriage: "If [girls] can run, jump, skate, swim, ride, and mend their own torn dresses," she wrote, "they are in better condition to be married . . . than if they had been confined to a daily promenade in the most fashionable of bonnets."

Croly also turned her editorial attention to the circumstances of a growing category of young women: "working girls." She advocated better working conditions for women factory and shop employees while also promoting women's entry into the professions, maintaining that careers made women "self-sustaining, self-reliant, and respected." She urged her middle-class female readers to enter fields then just opening for women, including office secretarial work and department-store sales. Later in her life, she published a collection of her earlier newspaper columns on the subject of women and work, the 1891 *Thrown on Her Own Resources, Or, What Girls Can Do*, probably the first book of career advice for women. In one of those columns, she set forth her belief that the economic independence that resulted from working—not political power gained through the vote—was the key to women's equality:

> This equal performance of contract between men and women, as between man and man, is the greatest step in advance that has been taken or conceded to women in this age of advancement. It lifts them out of dependence into independence; it gives them the equal chance; it puts money-power into their hands, and that is what women must have if they are to achieve a place in this money-worshipping world. . . . The reason why the inferior man is practically superior to a woman infinitely beyond him in all essential attributes, is because he has assumed his right to earn money, while she has not.
>
> The silly pride which makes a virtue of helplessness, which considers money given better than money earned, is fast disappearing, and the pace becomes accelerated with every financial success achieved by women on their own account.

She dismissed the notion that women were constitutionally incapable of surviving in the business world, pointing out that—to the contrary—in their home lives women regularly proved that they possessed "the primary qualities necessary for success . . . —courage, persistence, elasticity, and mental grasp of a situation." Croly believed that "Work, and work for pay, is the motto of to-day for girls who wish to prove themselves true daughters of the nineteenth century, and ready for the responsibility which the twentieth century will be sure to bring."

I have never done anything that was not helpful to women, so far as it lay in my power.

—**Self-written epitaph of Jane Cunningham Croly**

At the same time, she also assured her readers that they could work and still be good wives and mothers. Indeed, in her own peak period of professional production, Croly was managing a growing household. During the 1860s, she had three more children: a son who died in infancy, another daughter, **Viola Croly**, and another son, Herbert Croly. (Herbert would later become famous in Progressive political and journalistic circles, as the author of the 1909 book *The Promise of American Life* and as the founding editor of *The New Republic*, begun in 1914.) Jane's fifth and last child, **Alice Cary Croly**, was named for the feminist writer of that name. *Alice and *Phoebe Cary were among the several women writers with whom Croly formed important and lasting friendships; others included **Louisa May Alcott**, Sara Willis Parton, **Miriam Squire** (Mrs. Frank) Leslie, **Ella Wheeler Wilcox**, and **Kate Field.**

The support and encouragement of other talented women led to Jane Cunningham Croly's second career, that of clubwoman. She had already demonstrated her talents as an organizer by calling a "Woman's Congress" of activists in New York in 1856. In 1868, after she and other women writers in New York were excluded from a journalists' dinner in honor of the visiting Charles Dickens, they founded their own club, calling it Sorosis (a botanical term). The goal of the new organization was to "promote agreeable and useful relations among women of literary and artistic tastes" and to provide "an opportunity for the discussion among women, of new facts and principles, the results of which promise to exert an important influence on the future of women and the welfare of society."

While Alice Cary was the first president of Sorosis, and other members served in that capacity during its early years, Croly headed the group through most of the 1870s and 1880s. Though founded by women writers—its other such members included Phoebe Cary, Kate Field, Fanny Fern, and Ellen Demorest—the organization was open to women outside the literary field as well. The club was widely criticized and ridiculed in the press, alternately derided as a silly feminine vanity and as an inappropriately masculine endeavor. In her 1886 history of the organization, Croly explained the significance of the group and the reason for the controversy:

> The young members of to-day will wonder why all this fuss could have been made about a mere society of women. But they must remember that eighteen years ago social and secular organization among women did not exist. There were no State Aid Societies, no Women's Exchanges, no Kitchen Garden Associations, or Industrial Unions, or Workingwomen's Clubs, no Church or Missionary Societies officered and carried on exclusively by women. No purely women's societies at all, outside of the sewing circle. . . . [A]nd it was doubted, by many good men and women, whether a secular society of women, of different tastes, habits and pursuits, and with no special object to bind them, could hang together for any length of time.

But "hang together" Sorosis did. In its first two years, its membership grew from a dozen women to nearly a hundred, and the group became involved not only with professional concerns, but also with broader social issues, examining and publicizing problems including infant mortality, prison reform, and the health aspects of women's dress reform. Another ongoing activity of the club was its agitation for the admission of young women to American colleges. In its structure and its goals, Sorosis became a model for other professional women's clubs that were springing up across the country in the late-19th century.

During the 1870s and early 1880s, Croly continued her extensive newspaper and magazine work and published two books on needlework. From 1887 to 1888, she took the helm of the failing, 57-year-old *Godey's Lady's Book*, briefly holding a half-interest in the magazine. This proved to be her final staff move in journalism, as she became more and more involved in the cause of clubwomen. Her involvement did not flag despite the death, on April 29, 1889, of her husband, whose health had been failing for a decade. That same year, Croly founded the Woman's Press Club of New York City (serving as its president for the rest of her life) and helped to create the General Federation of Women's Clubs. For the next eight years, she also edited the first three incarnations of the General Federation's variously named magazine, first the *Woman's Cycle,* then the *Home-Maker,* and then the *New Cycle* (the magazine continued into the 20th century under still other titles, and other editors).

In 1892, Jane Cunningham Croly was awarded an honorary doctor of literature degree by Rutger's Women's College in New Jersey, where she served as chair of journalism and literature and became the first woman to teach college-level journalism in America. She remained active in club activities throughout the 1890s, publishing her *History of the Women's Club Movement in America* in 1898. The following year, she broke her hip in a bad fall, an injury that never fully healed and led to her physical decline. She died of heart failure in New York City on December 23, 1901.

SOURCES:

Ashley, Perry J., ed. *American Newspaper Journalists, 1873–1900. Dictionary of Literary Biography.* Vol. 23. Detroit, MI: Gale, 1983.

Croly, Jane Cunningham ["Jennie June"]. *Jennie Juneiana: Talks on Women's Topics.* Boston, MA: Lee and Shepard, 1884.

———. *Sorosis: Its Origin and History*. NY: J.J. Little, 1886.

———. *Thrown on Her Own Resources, Or, What Girls Can Do*. NY: Thomas Y. Crowell, 1891.

Mathews, Fannie Aymar. "The Woman's Press Club of New York City," in *Cosmopolitan Magazine*. Vol. XI, no. 4. August 1891, pp. 455–461.

Mott, Frank Luther. *A History of American Magazines*. Vols. I–V. Cambridge, MA: Harvard University Press, 1957.

Ross, Ishbel. *Ladies of the Press*. NY: Harper and Brothers, 1936.

SUGGESTED READING:

Croly, Jane Cunningham. *The History of the Women's Club Movement in America*. NY: H.G. Allen, 1898.

Woman's Press Club of New York City. *Memories of Jane Cunningham Croly, "Jennie June."* NY: Putnam, 1904.

COLLECTIONS:

Four collections at the Schlesinger Library, Radcliffe College: Jane Cunningham Croly Papers, Elizabeth Bancroft Schlesinger Papers, Strickland Autograph Collection (also contains photos and correspondence), and American Women Writers Collection.

Woman's Press Club of New York City Papers, Rare Book and Manuscript Library, Columbia University.

Carolyn Kitch, former editor for *Good Housekeeping* and *McCall's*, and Assistant Professor at the Medill School of Journalism at Northwestern University, Evanston, Illinois

Crompton, Richmal (1890–1969).

See Lamburn, Richmal Crompton.

Cromwell, Bridget (1624–c. 1660)

*Daughter of English soldier and Lord Protector Oliver Cromwell. Name variations: Bridget Fleetwood. Baptized on August 5, 1624, in Huntingdon, England; died soon after the Restoration (1660), date of death unknown; daughter of Oliver Cromwell and *Elizabeth (Bourchier) Cromwell; sister of *Mary, Countess of Falconberg (1636–1712); married General Henry Ireton (1611–1651); married Charles Fleetwood, (c. 1618–1692), on June 8, 1652; children: (first marriage)* ❦▸ *Bridget Bendish (c. 1650–1726); Jane Ireton; Elizabeth Ireton; (second marriage) Anne (died young), possibly others who also died young.*

Bridget Cromwell was the eldest daughter of Oliver Cromwell, Lord Protector of England, Scotland, and Ireland from 1653 to 1658, during the Commonwealth. At age 22, Bridget married Henry Ireton, a soldier and her father's loyal supporter. Ireton was killed in 1652, a victim of Irish warfare, and shortly thereafter Bridget married Charles Fleetwood, who helped Cromwell govern England from 1655 to 1657. Upon Oliver Cromwell's death, Fleetwood initially supported Richard Cromwell (the son of Oliver, who was

❦▸ **Bendish, Bridget** (c. 1650–1726)

*English celebrity. Born Bridget Ireton about 1650; died in 1726; daughter of General Henry Ireton (1611–1651) and *Bridget Cromwell (daughter of Oliver Cromwell); granddaughter of Oliver Cromwell.*

Bridget Bendish was mostly famed for her physical resemblance to her grandfather Oliver Cromwell.

named Protector after his father's death), but later joined a group of officers, including Richard's brother Henry, who deposed him. Bridget was often torn in her loyalties between her husband and her brothers. Although she stood staunchly by her husband, she agonized over the rift between Richard and Henry. In one of many letters to Henry, she wrote: "I am very unfit and unapt to write, and yet I would not altogether neglect to stir up the affection which ought to be betwixt so near relations, and is very apt to decay. I blame none but myself."

SOURCES:

Wolfe, Don M. *Milton and His England*. NJ: Princeton University Press, 1971.

Cromwell, Elizabeth (1598–1665)

*Lady Protectress. Name variations: Elizabeth Bourchier; though her name was Elizabeth she was called Joan by the cavaliers. Born Elizabeth Bourchier in 1598; died at Northborough Manor, in Northamptonshire, England, the home of her son-in-law John Claypole, in 1665; buried in the local church; eldest of six children of Sir James Bourchier (a merchant of the shire of Essex but no relation to the noble Bourchiers of Essex) and *Frances Crane Bourchier; married Oliver Cromwell (1599–1658), on August 22, 1620; children: Robert (b. October 1621); Oliver (b. February 1623); *Bridget Cromwell (1624–c. 1660); Richard (b. October 1626–1712); Henry (b. January 1628); Elizabeth Cromwell, later Lady Claypole, known as Bettie (b. July 1629–d. August 6, 1658); *Mary Cromwell (1636–1712), countess of Fauconberg; Frances Cromwell (1638–1721), also known as Lady Rich, later known as Lady Russell.*

The plump and pretty Elizabeth Cromwell, wife of the Lord Protector Oliver Cromwell, endured a great deal of mockery from the scandalmongers and satirists. They called her Protectress Joan—Joan then being a generic term for a rustic. Along with the absolutely unproved accusations of "drunkenness," she was seen as a conventional domestic, a stingy one at that. But "there was more to Mrs. Cromwell than mere household management," writes **Antonia Fraser**. Rather, she was shrewd, with the ability to manage her husband and steer him in political affairs.

SOURCES:

Fraser, Antonia. *Cromwell: The Lord Protector*. NY: Alfred Knopf, 1973.

Cromwell, Mary (1636–1712)

Countess of Fauconberg. Name variations: Mary of Falconberg; Mary, countess of Falconberg; Mary Fauconberg. Born in February 1636 in Ely, England; died in 1712 in London, England; daughter of Oliver Cromwell, later Lord Protector of England, and Elizabeth (Bouchier) Cromwell; married Thomas Belayse, Viscount Fauconberg, in November 1657 (died 1700); no children.

Mary Cromwell was the seventh of eight surviving children of Oliver Cromwell and *Elizabeth Bouchier Cromwell. At the time of her birth, her father, who would later gain permanent renown as one of England's most important rulers, had just begun his climb to fame as a newly elected member of Parliament. Her mother was the daughter of a wealthy London merchant. By all accounts, the Cromwells were the model of a contented and affectionate Puritan family; both Elizabeth and Oliver were loving and devoted parents, despite the demands and dangers of Oliver's political and military career. Mary had a particularly close relationship with her father, revealed in their letters and in the letters of those who knew them. Oliver admired his daughter, whom he and everyone called Mall, for her intelligence and high-spirited nature. By the time she was 16, it was clear Mary resembled her father physically and in her character—dark hair and eyes, outgoing, aggressive, and strong-minded.

In 1653, Oliver Cromwell began looking for a suitable husband for Mary. By this time the Puritan party, with Oliver as its military and political leader, was winning the long English Civil War against the Anglican royalists. King Charles I had been executed four years earlier, and Cromwell was consolidating his power over England as head of the Parliament. He wanted his children's marriages to be part of this consolidating process by arranging alliances with powerful and influential families. Negotiations for Mary's hand were opened between several powerful potential allies, including the sons of the duke of Buckingham and the Prince of Condé,

the French noble leading a revolt against the French king. These maneuverings went on for four years; as Oliver's power grew, his political needs changed, and he sought new alliances. In the end, Oliver, now installed as Lord Protector of the Realm and the most powerful man in England, finally concluded a marriage arrangement for Mary, now 20 years old.

Mary's new husband was a widower, Thomas Belayse, Viscount Fauconberg. He was an Anglican, not a Puritan, and although he was not a Royalist himself, he came from a family who opposed Cromwell's Puritan Party. This alliance reveals Cromwell's move toward reconciliation with his enemies as his hold on power became secure. But Cromwell was not only thinking of himself in arranging this marriage; he saw Belayse as an intelligent man of high moral character whose high social position would make him a good husband for his beloved daughter. Rumors that Belayse was impotent (he had no children from his first marriage) were treated as a joke by Oliver, and did not deter the Cromwells from the proposed wedding.

Mary and Viscount Fauconberg were married in November 1657 in a private Anglican ceremony at the royal palace of Hampton Court. The Cromwells provided the new Viscountess Fauconberg with a large dowry and welcomed the couple to remain in London at the Cromwell court, rather than moving up north to Fauconberg's estates. Thus Mary did not have to part from her family even after her wedding. In some ways the rumors about the Viscount proved to be correct; in four decades of marriage, only once did Mary suspect herself to be pregnant, and she never gave birth to any children.

The next year, Mary and Thomas left London for a long political tour of northern England. The trip was designed to improve Cromwell's image and support among the north's prominent families, many of whom were staunch Royalists, by demonstrating the alliance between Cromwell and the Royalists that their marriage represented. As always, Mary would be a loyal daughter and valuable political asset to her father, concerned with helping him maintain his position.

In August 1658, Mary took care of her father after the death from cancer of his favorite child, her older sister **Elizabeth (Bettie) Cromwell**. Oliver, himself in poor health, was devastated by Bettie's death, so much so that Mary refused to leave him even to attend her sister's funeral. Only a few weeks later, Mary faced another personal tragedy when Oliver died in September. In his letters, her husband describes Mary's intense grief for weeks after the loss of her beloved father.

The remaining Cromwells were treated well by the royalists who regained power after Oliver Cromwell's death, despite their connection to the Lord Protector. Even the newly crowned king Charles II, son of the king whom Cromwell had executed, refused to punish Cromwell's wife and children. The family retained its property and much of its wealth.

However, in death Oliver himself was deeply hated by the royalists. After the restoration of Charles II in 1660, Oliver's body was disinterred from its vault in Westminster Abbey and thrown into a common grave pit to be burned. Among the many different versions of what happened to his body after that is one popular story concerning Mary Cromwell. Countess Fauconberg is said to have bribed the soldiers guarding the grave pit to give her her father's body. She then had the body transported to northern England and reburied in a tomb (which still survives) on her husband's estate of Newburgh. The actual fate of the body is unknown, but the legend, true or not, certainly shows that Mary's lasting devotion to her father was widely recognized.

Of all the Cromwells, Mary prospered the most after the Lord Protector's death. Her husband Thomas remained in favor in the new administration and served King Charles as an ambassador. He went on to become a Privy Councilor to King William III, who made him an earl as well. Mary remained a popular figure at the royal court for the rest of her life; always loyal to her own family first, she used her influence to help her many relatives and improve her family's fortunes. Mary was widowed in 1700, at the age of 63. She survived her husband by 12 years, living well into the reign of Queen *Anne, the third monarch to rule after Cromwell. Countess Fauconberg was buried at St. Nicolas Church in Chiswick, near her estates at Sutton Place.

SOURCES:

Fraser, Antonia. *Cromwell: The Lord Protector.* NY: Alfred Knopf, 1973.

Laura York,
Riverside, California

Crosby, Caresse (1892–1970)

English philanthropist and founder of the Black Sun Press. Born Mary Phelps Jacob in New York, New York, in 1892; died in Rome, Italy, in 1970; married a Peabody; married Harry Crosby (died); married a third time.

Caresse Crosby came from a "crystal chandelier background" and could claim such ancestors as Plymouth Colony governor William Bradford and Civil War general Robert Fulton. She was also related to a minister to the Court of St. James's. When she was presented at Court, King George V chased and secured her hat that had blown off in the wind during a garden party. Crosby was early drawn to the arts, and the magazine *St. Nicholas* purchased one of her drawings. She wrote and printed her own newspaper, using a gelatin board.

Crosby first married into the Peabody family, which led to wealth and the acquisition of J.P. Morgan as an uncle. But it was with her second husband, Harry Crosby, that she entered the creative world to which she would become inextricably bound. Harry gave her the name Caresse, and the two, both wealthy, had high times in Paris where their address was the Rue de Lille. Caresse was known to appear at tea in Paris with her dog, a whippet who sported a gold necklace and gold-lacquered toenails.

Caresse and Harry founded the Black Sun Press, which printed their own poetry, the letters of Henry James and Marcel Proust to Walter Berry (Caresse's cousin), and the work of writers D.H. Lawrence, James Joyce, Hart Crane, Ezra Pound, and *Gertrude Stein; their Crosby Continental Editions, launched in the 1930s, would introduce American writers to the French, including *Kay Boyle, William Faulkner, and Ernest Hemingway. The couple purchased an old mill near Chantilly, which at one time had been Jean-Jacques Rousseau's home; they called the place "Le Moulin du Soleil" and entertained widely. Following the death of her husband, Crosby dedicated her time and finances to several causes, in particular the World Citizenship Movement, centered at Delphi. She married a third time, and her husband purchased Hampton Manor, designed by Thomas Jefferson, in America. Located near Fredericksburg, Virginia, the Manor became a refuge for some of the most creative minds in history. The sculptor David Hare, Salvador and **Gali Dali**, Henry Miller, and Ezra Pound were among those who stayed. Crosby helped edit Dali's memoirs and exhibited Miller's Hampton Manor watercolors in a gallery she had opened in Washington.

Known for her aristocratic nature, generosity, and ready wit, she was described by her late husband Harry in a poem as also having "way-

ward eyes," "girlish loveliness," and "slender legs." Crosby, the owner of a *pied-à-terre* in Rome, entertained at her vast castle in the Rieti province, where her usual number of guests, 12, had at times stretched to as many as 30. (When 30 members of New York's Living Theater enjoyed her hospitality upon being stranded in her neighborhood for two months, they chopped all available wood to warm themselves from the icy mountain winds, including an occasional chair.)

Although Crosby's finances rescued many artists from difficult times, "it's not a question of being a do-gooder," she remarked. "When I helped writers and artists I benefited more than they did. I think everybody should chip in and do whatever can be done." She elaborated on her system of dispersement: "If he is a good artist and a bad fellow, he doesn't get as many meals as if he is a good artist and good fellow." The library of Southern Illinois University purchased Crosby's large collection of papers and books, prompting her comment, it was "the only time I ever made any money on one of my deals with artists and writers." She reaped even less with another deal. In November 1914, she had patented and sold a "backless brassiere," consisting of two handkerchiefs and ribbon sewn together, to Warner Brothers Corset Company of Bridgeport, Connecticut. The value of the patent was later estimated at $15 million. Crosby, now considered the first to patent a brassiere, saw none of the profit.

SOURCES:
Rogers, W.G. *Ladies Bountiful*. NY: Harcourt, Brace, 1968.

SUGGESTED READING:
Conover, Anne. *Caresse Crosby: From Black Sun to Roccasinibalda*. Capra.
Crosby, Caresse. *The Passionate Years*. 1953.

Crosby, Fanny (1820–1915)

American blind poet, hymn writer, and worker in the Mission Movement. Born Frances Jane Crosby in Southeast Putnam County, New York, on March 24, 1820; died in Bridgeport, Connecticut, on February 12, 1915; only child of John (a farmer) and Mercy (Crosby) Crosby; attended the New York Institution for the Blind, New York City, 1835–43; married Alexander Van Alstyne (a blind teacher), on March 5, 1858 (died 1902); children: one (died in infancy).

Blind from infancy, Fanny Crosby became a popular poet and a prominent figure in American evangelical religious life at the end of the 19th century. Recognized primarily as the author of as many as 9,000 hymns, she was also a well-known speaker and devoted mission worker. In her later years, she was often referred to as "the Protestant saint" or "the Methodist saint," because of the large number of the faithful throughout the world that made pilgrimages to receive her prayers and advice.

Fanny, the only child of John and **Mercy Crosby**, was born in rural Southeast, New York, where eight members of the extended family shared one small cottage. At the age of six weeks, she contracted an eye infection, for which a doctor prescribed hot poultices that left her completely blind. Before the end of her first year, she lost her father to illness. (Her mother would later remarry and have three additional children.) While her widowed mother worked as a domestic, Crosby spent much of her time in the care of her grandmother Eunice, who was determined that the child not grow up to be a helpless invalid. Eunice became her granddaughter's eyes, describing the physical world to her in terms she hoped Fanny would understand. "My grandmother was more to me than I can ever express by word or pen," said Crosby. Although the family attended church every Sunday, it was Eunice who endlessly read to Crosby from the Bible and patiently answered her stream of questions. Crosby's blindness never stopped her from being an active, spirited girl, who learned to ride a horse bareback, climbed trees, and was as mischievous as any of her playmates.

Her mother Mercy, remaining hopeful that something could be done for her daughter's condition, scraped together enough money to take Fanny to New York. About age five, Fanny was examined there by several ophthalmologists, who confirmed that the damage to her eye tissue was irreversible. Mercy changed jobs around this time and took Fanny to the Quaker village of North Salem, where they lived in the home of her new employer. This was the first time Fanny had been solely in the care of her mother, and Mercy, although devoted to her daughter, was much stricter than Eunice. Around 1828, they moved to a boarding house in Ridgefield, Connecticut. Mercy took another job as a domestic while Fanny was enrolled in school. The teachers found it difficult to attend to her needs, so she spent most of her time in the care of the landlady, Mrs. Hawley, who set the child to the task of memorizing the Bible. Crosby would repeat what Hawley read to her line by line, chapter by chapter. Gifted with a phenomenal memory, within two years Crosby had mastered all four Gospels, as well as many of the psalms, all of Proverbs, all of Ruth, and the Song of Solomon.

As an adolescent, Crosby began to suffer bouts of moodiness and depression, which increased with Eunice's death in 1831. Still unable to attend school on a regular basis, she nonetheless developed a beautiful singing voice and mastered the guitar well enough to accompany herself. An excellent storyteller, Crosby was much in demand at local gatherings. Around this time, she started writing poems about events in the neighborhood, some of which were published in the local newspaper. Crosby's chance for a full education finally came in 1835. Although devastated by the knowledge that she'd have to leave her mother, the 15-year-old Crosby enrolled in the newly founded New York Institution for the Blind.

After overcoming initial homesickness, she embraced the institute as her new home and, for the next two decades, experienced what she called "the brightest joys I e'er have known." Outgoing and bright, she quickly made friends and easily mastered her lessons. Crosby's early talent for writing verse was encouraged by her teachers, especially after she visited Scottish phrenologist Dr. George Combe, who examined her skull and pronounced that she had great potential as a poet and should be given every opportunity to develop her talent. During her eight years at the institute, Crosby became one of its prize students and something of a celebrity as "The Blind Poetess." Many of her works were published in the poetry columns of local New York papers, and some poems found their way into *The Saturday Evening Post*. In 1941, the New York *Herald* published her poetic eulogy on President William Henry Harrison, after his untimely death just one month after taking office. She was often called on to recite for famous visitors to the school and was part of a student group that made public appearances in the area to demonstrate the educability of the blind and to encourage parents of blind children to send them to the school. The group also appeared before a joint session of Congress in January 1844 and again in April 1847. After her graduation, Crosby stayed on at the institute as a teacher of English grammar, rhetoric, and ancient history.

In April 1844, while she was still a student, Crosby had published her first small volume of poetry under the title *The Blind Girl and Other Poems*. It was followed by a second and third volume: *Monterey and Other Poems* (1851) and *A Wreath of Columbia's Flowers* (1858). Crosby, writing in the sentimental style of the day, belonged to a cadre of popular poets that have been relegated to the historical basement. Bernard Ruffin, in his biography *Fanny Crosby*,

Opposite page

Caresse

Crosby

Fanny Crosby

Brooklyn. As Crosby's interests outside the marriage increased, the couple grew apart and separated amicably around 1885. Van Alstyne died in 1902.

Crosby began writing verses to be set to music in 1851, when she and George F. Root, a music instructor at the institute, collaborated on a cantata called "The Flower Queen," which they were successful in publishing. She contributed lyrics to 60 or so other songs, some of which went on to become popular favorites of her day, like "Hazel Dell," "There's Music in the Air," and "Rosalie, the Prairie Flower." Around 1864, she began writing hymns; although like her poetry they suffered from cliché and sentimentality, a few displayed qualities beyond ordinary talent. Crosby is often credited with producing 9,000 hymns, but the exact number is unknown because, out of modesty, she wrote under many different pseudonyms (possibly as many as 200). For many years, she was employed by William Bathchelder Bradbury, the most prolific hymn writer of the period and the publisher of Sunday school hymnbooks. (Following Bradbury's death, the company was reorganized by Sylvester Main and Lucius Horatio Biglow.) In addition to producing her own verses to be set to music and writing words to a given melody, Crosby also revised the work of other hymn writers. Among the 20 or so musicians she collaborated with was the singing evangelist Ira D. Sankey, partner and colleague of renowned preacher Dwight L. Moody. Sankey and Moody often said that the success of their evangelical campaigns was due in most part to Fanny Crosby's hymns.

Of the huge volume of hymns Crosby produced, her best known include "Rescue the Perishing," "Jesus the Water of Life Will Give," "Blessed Assurance," "The Bright Forever," "Savior, More Than Life to Me," "Pass Me Not, O Gentle Savior," and her personal favorite "Safe in the Arms of Jesus." Although her hymns are non-denominational, they were especially popular with the Methodist Church, which for a time observed Fanny Crosby Day. (Crosby converted from Calvinistic Presbyterianism to the Methodist Church in 1850.)

At age 80, Crosby moved to Bridgeport, Connecticut, where she lived with her widowed sister, **Carolyn (Carrie) Ryder**, who also served as her secretary and amanuensis. After Carrie's death in 1906, Crosby spent the remainder of her life with her niece **Florence Booth**, who also lived in Bridgeport. Active into advanced age, Crosby produced yet another book of poems,

describes much of her verse as undistinguished and banal, but he also cites several champions of her work. Henry Adelbert White (1880–1951), a poet and longtime professor of English at various universities, called Crosby a first-class writer. Literary critic and editor Henry Sandison (1850–1900) said she was "naturally a classical poet," and maintained that her secular verse was frequently of excellent quality. Most critics, however, agree that although Crosby occasionally rose above the conventional, much of her notoriety as a poet had more to do with her blindness than her poetic gifts.

In 1858, Crosby married Alexander Van Alstyne, another blind teacher, and ended her long association with the Institution for the Blind. The couple settled on Long Island, where they lived in rented rooms in a small country town. Van Alstyne made what money he could giving piano lessons and playing the organ in various churches in the area. Crosby, meanwhile, seemed to blossom away from the city and her notoriety. Around 1859, the couple had a child who died in infancy, and a grief-stricken Crosby longed to return to a familiar setting. The couple moved back to Manhattan and took a room a few blocks from the institute; they later settled in

Bells at Evening and Other Verses (1897), and wrote two volumes of autobiography, *Fanny Crosby's Life-Story* (1903) and *Memories of Eighty Years* (1906).

Although she continued to produce hymns, Crosby's later years were also spent in service at the Bridgeport Christian Union and the Bowery Mission in New York City. From 1867 to 1915, she established schools for the poor in New York City. Crosby was constantly booked for speeches for the Railroad Branch of the YMCA and at local churches and grange halls. She also participated in the annual summer educational and recreational assemblies held in Chautauqua, New York (under the auspices of the Methodist Church), and received visitors from around the world. Crosby was 95 when she died of arteriosclerosis and a cerebral hemorrhage on February 12, 1915. After the largest funeral ever held in Bridgeport, surpassing even that of P.T. Barnum, she was buried in Mount Grove Cemetery.

SOURCES:

James, Edward T, ed. *Notable American Women 1607–1950*. Vol. 1. Cambridge, MA: The Belknap Press of Harvard University Press, 1971.

McHenry, Robert, ed. *Famous American Women: A Biographical Dictionary from Colonial Times to the Present.* Springfield, MA: G. and C. Merriam, 1980.

Ruffin, Bernard. *Fanny Crosby.* A Pilgrim Press Book from United Church Press, 1956.

SUGGESTED READING:

Burger, Dolores. *Women Who Changed the Heart of the City: The Untold Story of the City Rescue Mission Movement.* Kregel, 1995.

Barbara Morgan,
Melrose, Massachusetts

Cross, Mrs. George (1844–1926).

See Cambridge, Ada.

Cross, Joan (1900–1993)

British soprano, opera administrator and teacher who was highly respected in British musical circles. Born in London, England, on September 7, 1900; died in Aldeburgh, Suffolk, on December 12, 1993; never married.

Closely identified with the music of Benjamin Britten (1913–1976); created the role of Ellen Orford at the 1945 world premiere of Britten's opera Peter Grimes; *also created major roles in other Britten operas, including* Albert Herring, Gloriana *and* The Turn of the Screw; *was a founding member of the English Opera Group; began directing operas at Covent Garden (1946); founded the Opera School (later the London Opera Centre, 1948); honored as a Commander of the British Empire (1953).*

Much more than a talented singer during her long career, Joan Cross left a permanent mark on British musical life. An artist of strong convictions, in the last decades of her life she delighted in discussing the pluses and minuses of the contemporary musical scene while lunching at one of Aldeburgh's charming pubs. She had much about which to reminisce as a key figure in the popularization of the music of Benjamin Britten, a pioneer of British opera, and one of the most inspiring and influential singing teachers in the United Kingdom.

Born in London on September 7, 1900, Cross studied first at St. Paul's Girls School, where one of her teachers was the noted composer Gustav Holst. Her advanced musical training took place at the Trinity College of Music, first studying violin but soon studying singing with Dawson Freer. Upon graduation, her first job was singing in the chorus of *Lilian Baylis' Old Vic Theater. Her interest in opera came late—Cross did not attend her first opera, Gounod's *Faust,* until she was 18. She initially found opera to be dull until hearing Puccini. Thrilled by his music, she decided to aim for a career in the theater.

Remaining at the Old Vic, Cross was a seasoned singer by the late 1920s, having appeared in numerous opera productions of Mozart, Verdi and Wagner. By 1931, she had advanced to the position of principal soprano of the Sadler's Wells Opera, a new theater bravely inaugurated by Lilian Baylis in the depths of the world economic depression. In that year, Cross made her debut as Mimi in Puccini's *La Boheme.* Throughout the 1930s, she was a mainstay of the Sadler's Wells company, constantly adding new and demanding roles to her repertoire. In addition to standard roles, she appeared in a number of premieres of contemporary works including Arthur Benjamin's *The Devil Take Her,* as well as in rarely performed older works such as Rimsky-Korsakov's *Snow Maiden* and *Tsar Saltan.* By the start of World War II, she had become a major vocal artist and enjoyed a reputation as one of the most popular performers on the Sadler's Wells operatic stage. During this period, she also sang occasionally at London's prestigious Covent Garden Opera House, performing the star roles in a number of operas including *Carmen, Lohengrin* and *Otello.* She sang a number of other demanding Wagnerian roles and, in March 1939, successfully added the role of the Marchallin in Richard Strauss' *Der Rosenkavalier* to her large repertoire.

The beginning of World War II in September 1939 did not halt Cross' determination to continue her career in music. Even though the Sadler's Wells theater was bombed during the Blitz, she and her colleagues continued to perform in war-scarred London. In the fall of 1940, the Sadler's Wells singers began touring, not only to avoid the dangers of further bombardment but as part of a morale-building effort in other British cities and towns. The tours were fraught with problems inherent in being on the road as well as with the unique dangers of modern warfare directed against a civilian population, but Cross and her colleagues came through the ordeal with flying colors. Critical notices were usually highly enthusiastic, and she starred in a number of new productions including Smetana's *The Bartered Bride* and Mozart's *Cosi fan tutte*.

Soon after the Sadler's Wells Opera departed from London to tour the provinces, its executive director, Tyrone Guthrie of the Old Vic Theater, appointed Joan Cross manager of the company. Cross had already taken on an informal administrative role after the death of Lilian Baylis in 1937, and Guthrie's conviction that she possessed strong talents in this area was quickly proven to be correct. As excellent an administrator as she was a singer, Cross was known to be decisive, fair and often witty. During these years, she used her position to strike a blow on behalf of affordable and accessible music for average citizens, a concept in which she strongly believed. From 1943 to 1945, she ran the company under the most difficult of conditions, bringing opera to regions starved of the arts in wartime. Cross spent most of her time on the myriad details of administration, appearing on stage only on those occasions when a singer was ill or had been kept from showing up in the theater by a bombing raid.

In 1945, Cross' decision as Sadler's Wells manager to reopen the opera house in London with a work by a contemporary composer, Benjamin Britten, set the stage for the final and most important phase of her career. She had met Britten through his companion, Peter Pears, and was deeply impressed by the shy young composer. Britten had just completed the score of his opera *Peter Grimes*, which Cross first heard in a dingy Liverpool attic with Britten playing it for her on the piano. Then and there, she determined that this would be the work with which the postwar Sadler's Wells Opera would begin its season. Though many of the Sadler's Wells singers received the Britten score with little enthusiasm, regarding it as too modernly dissonant, Cross retained her belief that Britten's score was a masterpiece of "new music." Within the opera company, opposition to the new opera was fierce.

One faction whispered the absurdity that Cross was planning to use the opera to advance her career. Another objection was grounded in the fact that both Pears and Britten had been conscientious objectors during the just ended war, and also that both men were gay and lovers. Totally indifferent to such opposition, Cross pushed ahead, determined to make operatic history. *Peter Grimes* received its world premiere performance on June 7, 1945, with Cross in the role of Ellen Orford. The critics praised her singing and acting; they declared Britten's opera to be the dawn of a new era in British music.

Despite the brilliant success of the premiere of *Peter Grimes*, the bitter divisiveness among her colleagues that had led up to the premiere performance could neither be forgotten nor always easily forgiven by Cross. Severing her links with Sadler's Wells, she threw in her lot with a new company soon to be known as the English Opera Group. After 1945, she became increasingly identified with the music of Benjamin Britten. In 1946, she created the role of the Female Chorus in Britten's opera *The Rape of Lucretia*. The next year, 1947, she created the role of Lady Billows in his *Albert Herring*. In 1953, she created the star role in yet another Britten opera, *Gloriana*. This work, which premiered at Covent Garden in 1953 as part of the national celebration of the coronation of Queen *Elizabeth II*, was a profound psychological study of Queen *Elizabeth I*.

In 1955, Cross sang the last of her five Benjamin Britten operatic premieres, creating the role of the housekeeper Mrs. Grose in his *The Turn of the Screw*. That same year, she starred as the Countess in Mozart's *Marriage of Figaro* at Covent Garden, a performance that prompted the critic Andrew Porter to write, "Joan Cross's Countess . . . is a wonderful example of a character created *through* the music." In September of the same year, she appeared on stage for the last time, singing the role she had created only a few months earlier, that of Mrs. Grose. Noting that even during Cross' last stage appearance she remained "in fine voice," opera critic Desmond Shawe-Taylor lamented her decision to retire, pointing out how her skilled and subtle performance of Britten's opera had assured its success with the audience. Cross' performance in *The Turn of the Screw* was recorded by Decca in a definitive interpretation conducted by the composer.

Following her retirement as a singer, Cross pursued a new facet of her musical career. Within weeks of her last stage appearance, she was busy managing a production of *Cosi fan tutte* for the Opera Studio. In 1956, she produced Britten's *Albert Herring,* and on the reputation gained from this and other successes she found herself increasingly in demand as an opera director. Cross worked on various productions not only in the United Kingdom but also in Canada, The Netherlands, and Scandinavia. By passing on her decades of stage experience, she was able to play a significant role in the artistic growth of the Norwegian National Opera.

As the years went by, Cross spent more time teaching at the Opera School in London (later the London Opera Centre), which she and **Anne Wood** had founded in 1948. During the last decades of her long life, Cross lived in the town of Aldeburgh, Suffolk, in a small cottage packed with operatic memorabilia. Residents as well as visitors to Aldeburgh—where the music festivals organized by Benjamin Britten drew music lovers from all over the globe—could count on seeing the elderly but still vivacious Joan Cross vigorously discussing music with friends and strangers in the local pub. Although she was honored with the rank of Commander of the British Empire in 1951, she never was awarded a Dameship, which many of her admirers believed she richly deserved; some suspected she was denied this due to opinions strongly expressed throughout her long career. Only days before her death in Aldeburgh on December 12, 1993, EMI issued a compact disc set of her classic 1948 recording of Britten's *Peter Grimes.* With her passing, British musical life lost one of its most distinctive artists and ardent champions.

SOURCES:

Baker, Frank Granville. "A Leading Role in the Opera," in *Guardian.* December 14, 1993, sec. 2, p. 18.

Carpenter, Humphrey. *Benjamin Britten: A Biography.* London: Faber and Faber, 1992.

Hardy, C. "Joan Cross," in *Opera.* Vol. 1, no. 1. February 1950, pp. 22–28.

Harewood, Lord. "Joan Cross—a birthday celebration," in *Opera.* Vol. 41, no. 9. September 1990, pp. 1032–1039.

"Joan Cross," *The Times* [London]. December 15, 1993, p. 19.

RELATED MEDIA:

Decca CD 425 672-2 (Benjamin Britten, *The Turn of the Screw*).

EMI British Composers CD CMS7-64727-2 (Recordings of the Music of Benjamin Britten).

John Haag, Associate Professor, University of Georgia, Athens, Georgia

Cross, Mrs. John W. (1819–1880).

See Evans, Mary Anne.

Cross, Mary Ann or Marian (1819–1880).

See Evans, Mary Anne.

Cross, Zora (1890–1964)

Australian poet and journalist. Born Zora Bernice May Cross on May 18, 1890, at Eagle Farm, Brisbane, Australia; died on January 22, 1964, at Glenbrook in the Blue Mountains; daughter of Mary Louisa Eliza Ann (Skyring) Cross and Ernest William Cross (an accountant); married Stuart Smith (an actor), on March 11, 1911 (marriage dissolved, 1922); lover of David McKee Wright (an author and journalist); children: (with Wright) two daughters; (with another) one son who was adopted by Wright.

Selected works: A Song of Mother Love (1916); Songs of Love and Life (1917); The Lilt of Life (1918); (children's verse) The City of Riddle-me-ree (1918); Elegy on an Australian Schoolboy (1921); (pamphlet) An Introduction to the Study of Australian Literature (1922); Daughters of the Seven Mile: The Love Story of an Australian Woman (1924); The Lute Girl of Rainyvale: A Story of Love, Mystery and Adventure in North Queensland (1925); The Victor (serialized in the Sydney Morning Herald, 1933); This Hectic Age (1944).

Known as a woman much in advance of her time, Zora Cross was responsible for what biographer **Dorothy Green** has called the "first sustained expression in Australian poetry of erotic experience from a woman's point of view." Cross was born in Brisbane, Australia, in 1890. Her parents influenced her literary ambitions; she is said to have inherited a sense of poetic mission from her mother and threads of Celtic fantasy from her father. Cross received her early education at Gympie and Ipswich Girls' Grammar School, followed by high school in Sidney where she went on to attend the Teachers' College. After starting to teach primary school, she left her position to give birth to a daughter who did not survive. Cross married an actor by the name of Stuart Smith in 1911; she refused to live with him, however, and the marriage would be dissolved in 1922, eight years after the birth of her son who was the result of a love affair.

To earn a living, Cross taught elocution and acted in one of Philip Lytton's companies before turning to freelance journalism. She submitted her poetry to literary magazines, and, in addition to writing as a drama critic for *Green Room* and *Lone Hand,* she worked as a columnist for the *Brisbane Daily Mail.* Following the outbreak of war, Cross traveled through north Queensland, touring with a concert party to help raise war funds. Although her first novel was refused by T.C. Lothian in 1916, her first book of poems, *A Song of Mother Love,* was published in the same year in Brisbane.

In 1917, Cross returned to Sydney. That year, she published *Songs of Love and Life* which comprised 60 love sonnets. In expressing the erotic experience of a woman, Cross is said to have fused sensuousness and religiosity. *Songs* received what Green has described as "favourable if somewhat startled reviews." The sonnets in this work, and other poems in the 1918 work *The Lilt of Life*, were inspired by her love affair with David McKee Wright, a well-known author and journalist, who fathered two daughters by Cross and adopted her son. The affair scandalized the Sydney literary establishment, as the inspiration of her poems became evident. Contributing to the scandal was the mistaken belief that Wright had neglected previous paternal obligations, which in fact Cross helped him to honor. Nonetheless, Wright was shut out of his editorship of the *Bulletin's* Red Page, placing a strain on their finances.

In 1918, Cross published *The City of Riddle-me-ree*, a work of children's verse said to perhaps best exemplify her lyric gift. This work was followed in 1921 by the more somber *Elegy on an Australian Schoolboy*, in which the poet mourns the World War I death of her young brother John Skyring Cross. In addition to poetry, she published several works of fiction including *Daughters of the Seven Mile: The Love Story of an Australian Woman* (1924); *The Lute Girl of Rainyvale: A Story of Love, Mystery and Adventure in North Queensland* (1925); and *This Hectic Age* (1944). She also authored a pamphlet entitled "An Introduction to the Study of Australian Literature" (1922), which is now considered outdated but was a useful resource in her day. In 1933, Cross' novel *The Victor* was serialized in the *Sydney Morning Herald*.

When Wright died suddenly in 1928, Cross was left in financial peril as she worked to provide for her children with freelance writing. Despite her struggles to support her family, she is said to have remained cheerful and diligent. Cross' younger daughter would later describe her mother as "a delightful and amusing parent, who never for one moment lost sight of her priority as a writer and a poetess." From 1930, Cross received a Commonwealth Literary Fund pension of £2 a fortnight, but the family still often went without bare necessities. An intended trilogy of Roman novels was never completed, and Cross died on January 22, 1964, at Glenbrook in the Blue Mountains.

SOURCES:

Radi, Heather, ed. *200 Australian Women*. NSW, Australia: Women's Redress Press, 1988.

Wilde, William H., Joy Hooton, Barry Andrews. *Oxford Companion to Australian Literature*. Melbourne: Oxford, 1985.

Crothers, Rachel (1878–1958)

One the most successful and prolific American playwrights of the early 20th century. Born in Bloomington, Illinois, on December 12, 1878; died in Redding, Connecticut, on July 5, 1958; youngest child of Eli Kirk (a physician) and Marie Louise (dePew) Crothers (a physician); graduated from Illinois State Normal School, 1892.

Principle works (dates of production): Nora (1903); The Point of View (1904); Criss Cross (1904); Rector (1905); The Three of Us (1906); The Coming of Mrs. Patrick (1907); Myself-Bettina (1908); Kiddies (1909); A Man's World (1909); He and She (1911); The Herfords (1912); Ourselves (1913); The Heart of Paddy Whack (1914); Old Lady 31 (1916); (with Kate Douglas Wiggin) Mother Carey's Chickens (1917); Once upon a Time (1918); A Little Journey (1918); 39 East (1919); Nice People (1921); Everybody (1921); Mary the Third (1923); Expressing Willie (1924); A Lady's Virtue (1925); Venus (1927); Let Us Be Gay (1929); As Husbands Go (1931); When Ladies Meet (1932); Caught Wet (1932); Susan and God (1937).

In a career that bridged four decades, Rachel Crothers wrote 24 full-length plays that were produced on the New York stage, making her the most successful and prolific American playwright of the early 20th century and an important, though often overlooked, contributor to the emergence of the modern American drama. Crothers' plays were crafted around contemporary problems and social issues, as she focused on women's search for freedom in a man's world, providing, as she put it, a "*Comédie Humaine de la Femme*, or a Dramatic History of Woman." As early as 1912, she observed, "If you want to see the sign of the times, watch women. Their evolution is the most important thing in modern life."

The daughter of two physicians (her mother **Marie dePew Crothers** was the first woman doctor of note in Bloomington, Illinois), Crothers displayed an early talent for drama. At age 13, Rachel wrote, produced, and acted in her first play, *Every Cloud Has a Silver Lining; or The Ruined Merchant*. In high school, her activities with the Bloomington Dramatic Club often took precedence over her studies; after graduation in 1891, she was off to Boston to study elocution at the New England School of Dramatic Instruction. But a career on the "wicked" stage did not sit well with her family, so after receiving her certificate in 1892, Crothers returned to Bloomington to teach and perform an occasional recital. Around 1896, she made her way to New York, where she enrolled in the Stanhope-Wheatcroft School of Acting. After her first year, she joined the staff and would spend the next four years teaching and acting with several stock companies and in a touring company of *The Christian*.

While continuing to teach, Crothers wrote, staged, and directed many one-act plays, several of which were produced in some of the city's smaller theaters. Many of these early plays were published in popular periodicals of the day such as *Smart Set*. She later credited this intense period with teaching her the production aspects of her craft. Her first professional play, *Nora*, was unsuccessfully produced by **Carlotta Nielson** in 1903. Crothers' first full-length effort, *The Three of Us*, received a successful Broadway production in 1906. After her first two plays, Crothers staged and directed all of her own works, also serving as her own manager, agent, and occasionally producer. In 1920, she returned to acting to play the lead in *He and She*.

Rachel Crothers

Her plays were noted for their careful construction, with Joseph Wood Krutch once calling her, "almost the only remaining composer of what used to be called 'a well made play.'" In *Twentieth Century American Dramatist*, writer Lynn D. Todd divides Crothers' oeuvre into three distinct categories. The early plays, social-problem dramas written between 1906 and 1914, focus on the New Woman, the term applied to those women seeking emancipation during the first two decades of the 20th century. These plays include *The Three of Us*, *A Man's World*, and *He and She*, as well as several other less significant works. *A Man's World*, considered Crothers most fully developed portrayal of the New Woman, is the story of Frank Ware, a successful woman writer. Ware is raising an adopted son, Kiddie, whose unwed mother died in childbirth after being deserted by her lover. Ware's fiancé turns out to be Kiddie's father, and he refuses to accept responsibility for his conduct. At the close of the play, unable to accept the double standard and wanting to uphold her convictions, Ware sends her fiancé away. This unhappy ending, unusual for that time, drew praise from critics.

A group of social comedies, written from 1921 to 1927, focused on women's continuing pursuit of freedom and chronicled the youthful rebellion of the flapper. In *Nice People* (1921), Crothers' immodest leading character Theodora (Teddy) Gloucester smokes, drinks, dances, and is hellbent on doing exactly as she pleases. Although the play was a commercial success, critics decried Teddy's reformation in the final act. Louis V. De Foe of the *New York World* wrote that Crothers "should have allowed Theodora, her heroine, to plunge straight to the unhappiness which is the logical end of the course she pursues." The play, however, was very much in keeping with Crothers' optimistic view that the wild extremes of the 1920s would eventually even out. Although admittedly shocked by some of the things she witnessed, she told a *New York Herald* reviewer: "I predict also that these very girls who claim independence, who want to see 'life' and go to look at its dangerous places, will recover balance. Love is by no means worn out; they will fall in love and marry."

Also from this period, *Mary the Third* (1923), is another look at love and marriage. To discover which of her two boyfriends will make the better marriage partner, Mary plans a weekend camping trip with them both. She tells Mary the First (her grandmother) and Mary the Second (her mother), "People don't know each other before they're married. That's why most marriages are merely disappointing experiments instead of lifetime mating. That's why the experimenting ought to be done before marriage." Although Mary ultimately abandons her trip rather than hurt her family, she remains faithful to her convictions. When she finally decides to marry, she vows to stay financially independent in order to escape entrapment and also makes a pact with her intended marriage partner to divorce before love dies. The end of the play finds Mary and her fiancé exchanging the same emotional endearments that had been uttered by the other Marys and their suitors in the prologue, thus expressing Crothers' own belief that romance finds its way into the life of even the most rational women. Another interesting play of this period, *Venus* (1927), explores the existence on another planet of an advanced egalitarian society without sexual differences.

Between 1929 and 1937, Crothers' plays examined women's new-found sexual freedom and its sometimes disastrous results. *When Ladies Meet* (1932), judged the best work of Crothers' career, is among these urbane social comedies. The heroine of the play, Mary Howard, is a successful writer who falls in love with her married publisher, Rogers Woodruff. Mary naively believes that Rogers' wife Claire will give him up when she hears of the affair. When Mary meets Claire at a weekend house party, the two women come to respect one another and decide to confront Rogers. Mary is unprepared, however, for Rogers' refusal to acknowledge his love for her in front of Claire. The play ends with Claire divorcing Rogers, and Mary realizing the pitfalls of sexual encounters in a man's world. In 1938, the play was awarded the Megrue Prize for Comedy by the Dramatists Guild.

Early in her career, Crothers also produced a string of sentimental comedies, all box-office hits, mainly from 1914 to 1919. Her output included some genuine farces as well, like *Expressing Willie* (1924), satirizing Freudianism, and a *genre* piece, *Old Lady 31* (1916). In 1934, Crothers spent a few disastrous months in Hollywood as a screenwriter.

Never married, she divided her time between New York and a beloved refurbished farmhouse in Connecticut. She spent mornings writing in bed, in a room purposely kept free of distracting furnishings. Crothers was said to let the rough draft of a play mellow before reading it to friends to see if they liked it. "I must feel the reactions of an audience," she once said.

In addition to her own work, Crothers devoted considerable time to philanthropies and causes related to the theater. During World War I, she founded the Stage Women's War Relief Fund, composed of over 2,000 women of the theater who undertook a variety of war-relief activities. During the Depression, she supervised the formation of the United Theatre Relief Committee, which established the Stage Relief Fund, for which she served as president. In the period from 1932 to 1951, the Relief Fund distributed close to $800,000 to needy theater artists. Finally, during World War II, Crothers organized the American Theatre Wing for War Relief, best known for its Stage Door Canteen, of which she was executive director until the age of 72.

Starring *Gertrude Lawrence, Crothers' last play, *Susan and God*, was cited by the Theatre Club as the 1938 season's most outstanding play; it was also the longest running play of her career. The plot centers on Susan Trexel, a rich and sophisticated woman in her 30s, who after joining a new religious movement attempts to convert everyone around her. It turns out to be the glorification of self rather than spiritual fulfillment that captures Susan's zeal, and Crothers' message becomes a warning against selfishness in one's pursuit of independence and self-fulfillment.

As Lynn Todd points out, critics have viewed Crothers' work "as, at best, interesting social history or at worst, skillful box-office artistry." The denigration of her plays based on their commercial appeal dismisses Crothers' integrity and complete devotion to the art of the theater. The assessments of America's dramatic historians—who have, for the most part, either ignored Rachel Crothers completely or relegated her to the status of a minor playwright—are called into question as Crothers' views continue to provide important social documentation, particularly of women's lives in the early 20th century.

SOURCES:

Hartnoll, Phyllis, and Peter Found, eds. *The Concise Oxford Companion to the Theatre*. NY: Oxford University Press, 1993.

Kunitz, Stanley, and Howard Haycraft. *Twentieth Century Authors*. NY: H.W. Wilson, 1941.

MacNicholas, John, ed. *Twentieth Century American Dramatists*. Detroit, MI: Gale Research, 1981.

Barbara Morgan,
Melrose, Massachusetts

Crouch, Anna Maria (1763–1805).

See Caroline of Brunswick for sidebar.

Crouch, Eliza (c. 1837–1886).

See Pearl, Cora.

Crowdy, Rachel Eleanor.

See Furse, Katharine for sidebar.

Crowe, Mrs. George (1842–1917).

See Bateman, Kate.

Crowe, Sylvia (b. 1901)

British landscape architect and designer, who was one of the leading theorists and practitioners in her field in the 20th century. Name variations: Dame Sylvia Crowe. Born Sylvia Crowe on September 15, 1901, in Banbury, Oxfordshire, England; daughter of Eyre Crowe and Beatrice (Stockton) Crowe; attended Berkhamsted Girls' School; graduated from Swanley Horticultural College, Kent, 1922; studied under Edward White; shared an office with **Brenda Colvin**.

Selected writings: The Landscape of Power *(London: Architectural Press, 1958);* Tomorrow's Landscape *(London: Architectural Press, 1963);* Forestry in the Landscape *(London: Her Majesty's Stationery Office, 1966);* Garden Design *(3rd ed., Wappingers Falls, NY: Garden Art Press, 1994);* The Landscape of Forests and Woods *(London: Her Majesty's Stationery Office, 1978).*

Destined to become a true pioneer in the profession of landscape architecture, Sylvia Crowe spent her most formative years in the beautiful English countryside of the Sussex Weald. Her father Eyre Crowe was an engineer who retired from his profession in order to become a fruit farmer. He was a restless man whose health was poor, and as part of his search for both a healthier climate and new experiences took his family on trips to Europe. Both of her parents loved the countryside, and her mother was an enthusiastic gardener. One of Sylvia Crowe's first memories of childhood was celebrating her fourth birthday "in a Corsican forest sitting revelling in the carpet of wild cyclamen." She grew up in near-idyllic circumstances, with her parents' farm located next to a beautiful lake and near a picturesque village named Felbridge. When Sylvia developed tuberculosis, she had to remain isolated from other children and so received an unconventional education; her "classroom" was the unspoiled countryside and the barns and stables of the Crowe family farm, and she "read in the book of nature" by wandering in the countryside and working on the farm.

With the start of World War I in the summer of 1914, all able-bodied men were called to the front, making her labor essential to the functioning of the family farm. She woke at half past five in the morning to drive the small herd of cows to the barn and milk them. Almost 70 years later, she fondly recalled that these years on the Sussex farm served to deeply imbue her "with country-side values and an intense love of landscape."

Crowe worked as a landscape designer from 1926 until the eve of World War II and, after war service, became one of the world's best known landscape architects. In addition to creating harmonious plans for several of the United Kingdom's new cities, she became a leader in landscaping power plants and other industrial facilities, creating realistic and aesthetically pleasing designs that helped alleviate the scars of industry's intrusion into nature. Universally respected in her profession throughout the world, she received many awards, including that of Order of the British Empire in 1967. She became a Dame Commander of the British Empire in 1973.

SOURCES:
Edwards, Susan. "Report: Dame Sylvia Crowe," in *Landscape Architecture*. Vol. 76, no. 2. March–April 1986, pp. 96–97.

Festing, Sally. "Lady in the Landscape," in *New Scientist*. Vol. 81, no. 1138. January 18, 1979, pp. 180–182.

Fischer, Thomas. "Books," *Horticulture: The Magazine of American Gardening*, Vol. 72, no. 10. December 1994, pp. 54–59.

Harvey, Sheila, ed. *Reflections on Landscape: The Lives and Work of Six British Landscape Architects*. Aldershot, Hants., Eng: Gower Technical Press, 1987.

Plumptre, George. *The Garden Makers: The Great Tradition of Garden Design from 1600 to the Present Day*. NY: Random House, 1993.

Titchmarsh, Alan. "Dame Sylvia Crowe," *The Garden*, Vol. 111, part 8. August 1986, pp. 389–392.

John Haag, Associate Professor, University of Georgia, Athens, Georgia

Crump, Diane (1949—)

American jockey who was the first woman to race against men in a U.S. parimutuel race and the first to ride in a Kentucky Derby. Born in Connecticut in 1949; has managed thoroughbred horse farms, including the training barn at Calumet Farms in Kentucky; later barn manager at Keysville Post Stables in Flint Hill, Virginia.

On February 7, 1969, in Hialeah, Florida, a shy, 104-pound exercise groom by the name of Diane Crump made history as the first woman to compete with men in a parimutuel race. Riding a 50-to-1 shot, Bridle N' Bit, Crump finished 10th in a 12-horse field. She went on to become the first woman to compete in the historic Kentucky Derby, at Churchill Downs, in the spring of 1970. Astride her three-year-old colt, Fathom, Crump finished 15th in a field of 17. Her maiden Derby gallop paved the way for **Patricia**

Cooksey in 1984, who finished 11th on So Vague; Cooksey also became the first woman to compete in the Preakness, finishing 6th on Tajawa in 1985.

Crump enjoyed a 17-year career as a jockey with total earnings of over $1 million. She compiled an impressive record of 1,614 starts, with 235 wins, 204 seconds, and 203 thirds. One of her starts was the historic Lady Godiva Stakes at Suffolk Downs in Boston, on April 29, 1969, the first parimutuel horse race featuring all females. More unusual than the race was the fact that in 1969 Massachusetts had six other fully licensed women, in addition to Crump, who could compete—**Penny Ann Early, Tuesdee Testa, Brenda Wilson, *Robyn Smith, Barbara Adler,** and **Connie Hendricks.** Diane Crump retired in 1986 to become a trainer.

Cruso, Thalassa (1908–1997)

English-born American gardening expert, author, and television personality. Born in London, England, on January 7, 1908 (some sources cite 1909); died in Wellesley, Massachusetts, in June 1997; daughter of Antony Alford and Mildred S. (Robinson) Cruso; granted acad. diploma anthropology and archeology, London School of Economics, 1932; married Hugh O'Neill Hencken, on October 12, 1935; children: Ala Mary (who married William S. Reid); Sophia (who married David L. Stone); Thalassa (who married Thomas J. Walsh, Jr.).

Member of several international horticultural societies; recipient of many awards for gardening.

Selected publications: Making Things Grow (1969); A Small City Garden (1972); To Everything There Is a Season (1973); Making Things Grow Outdoors (1974); The Cape Cod Dunes (1974); Making Vegetables Grow (1975).

Through her appearances on Johnny Carson's "Tonight Show," as well as her own television show and books, Thalassa Cruso became a familiar figure to Americans as an expert gardener and gardening instructor. Born in England in 1908, she made her home in Boston, Massachusetts, from 1935, where her program "Making Things Grow" aired on Boston's acclaimed public-television station, WGBH, bringing her to the public's attention. As she became known for her practical approach, humor, and candor in coping with gardening failures, her show aired throughout the educational television network as well as on commercial television. After the show had been running for two years, Cruso recorded her principles in the book *Making Things Grow,* which appeared in 1969. Soon a standard for indoor gardeners, this book was followed by several more. Her views—with their references to English gardening and orders to establish a plant's care in accordance with its native environment—proved pertinent even to the experienced gardener, while her style encouraged the novice. Cruso held memberships in several international horticultural societies and received numerous awards for gardening. She was a columnist for the *Boston Sunday Globe* and a frequent contributor to *McCall's, Country Jour-* *nal,* and *Horticulture.* Cruso practiced "tough love," wrote a correspondent for *Time.* "She poked, prodded and downright bullied fading philodendrons and pooped polypodies until they stood at attention."

SOURCES:

Time. June 30, 1997, p. 23.

Cruvelli, Sofia (1826–1907)

German soprano. Born Sophie Crüwell in Bielefeld, Prussia, on March 12, 1826; died in Monaco on November 6, 1907; sister of Friederika Marie Crüwell

Thalassa

Cruso

(1824–1868), a mezzo-soprano; studied in Paris with Bordogni, and in Milan with Lamperti; married Baron Vigier, in 1856.

Of Italian descent, Sofia Cruvelli was born in Bielefeld, Prussia, in 1826. Thought to be one of the finest dramatic sopranos of her day, she was first successful in Vienna in 1847 in Oddabella's *Attila,* and later in Paris and London. In 1854, she appeared at the Grand Opera in Paris and was widely lauded for her performance in Verdi's *Les Vêpres siciliennes,* which had been written for her. Her disappearance during rehearsals, however, had caused a stir when it was learned that she had taken a brief "honeymoon" with a Baron Vigier. She married him in 1856 and retired from the stage.

Cruz, Celia (1924—)

Cuban singer. Born in 1924 in Havana; studied at the Conservatory of Music; married Pedro Knight (her director and manager), in 1962; defected to the United States.

Destined to be known as the "Queen of Salsa," Celia Cruz was born in Havana in 1924. Her singing career began in the 1940s on local radio stations, and she studied at the Conservatory of Music. From 1950 to 1965, as the lead singer with La Sonora Matancera, the most popular orchestra in Cuba, Cruz toured, made recordings, and headlined with the group at The Tropicana, a famed nightclub in Havana. Among her scores of hit songs were "Bemba Colora," "del Cocoye," "Yerbero," "Moderno," and "Burundanga" (which went gold in 1957).

In 1962, Cruz married her music director and manager, Pedro Knight. She then defected to the United States where she joined Tito Puente, the "King of Latin Swing," in 1966. Cruz toured the country with his orchestra. In 1974, she won a Grammy for *Celia and Johnny,* an album that she recorded with the orchestra of Johnny Pacheco. *Celia-Ray-Adalberto-Tremendous Trio!, De Nuevo,* and *The Winners* (with Willie Colon) are among her other popular albums. Cruz has been highly regarded for her improvisation.

Cruz, Juana Inés de La (1651–1695).

See *Juana Inés de la Cruz.*

Csák, Ibolya (b. 1915).

See *Lambert, Margaret Bergmann for sidebar.*

Cudworth, Damaris (1658–1708).

See *Masham, Damaris.*

Cullberg, Birgit (b. 1908)

Swedish dancer, choreographer, and director. Born in Nyköping, Sweden, in 1908; studied at Stockholm University; attended the Jooss-Leeder School at Dartington Hall, England (1935–39).

Following her studies in choreography with Kurt Jooss at the Jooss-Leeder School at Dartington Hall in England, Birgit Cullberg returned to Sweden in 1939 to learn ballet techniques and form her own dance group for commercial revues. Her initial ballets, especially *Propaganda* and *Offensive,* were known for their humor, satire, and behavioral studies. With Ivo Cramér, she directed the Swedish Dance Theatre from 1946 to 1947. Cullberg was a resident choreographer of the Royal Swedish Ballet from 1952 to 1959 and then served as director and choreographer of Stockholm City Theatre. She was awarded the Swedish King's fellowship in 1958 and the Order of Vasa in 1961.

Her choreographic works include *Miss Julie* (1950), *Medea* (1951), *Romeo and Juliet* (1955), *Moon Reindeer* (1957), *Odysseus* (1959), *The Lady from the Sea* (1960), *Eden* (a *pas de deux,* 1961) and the television ballet "The Evil Queen" (1961), which won the Prix d'Italia.

Cullberg's dances were a frequent staple of Scandinavian companies as well as of the American Ballet Theatre, the New York City Ballet, and the Chilean National Ballet, among others. She is the author of *The Ballet and We, The Ballet School,* and many articles on dance (all in Swedish). In June 1963, she was appointed a member of the artistic council to the Royal Swedish Ballet, where she staged her *Seven Deadly Sins.*

Cullberg would choreograph approximately one page of music a day, writes *Agnes de Mille, "sometimes only one movement a day, writing in Swedish and French classical terminology and drawing in colored crayon every position, step, and transition beside each bar. This is the most complete preparation on record and so graphic (she studied painting) that a stranger could read back the figure designs." Cullberg estimated that it took 400 hours to prepare a 40-minute work.

SOURCES:
de Mille, Agnes. *The Book of the Dance.* NY: Golden Press, 1963.

Cullis, Winifred Clara (1875–1956)

British physiologist who was the first woman in the United Kingdom to serve as a professor of physiology. Born in 1875 in Gloucester, England; died in 1956;

educated at King Edward VI High School for Girls, Birmingham, and Mason College; attended Newnham College, Cambridge University; doctorate, University of London, 1908; never married.

Demonstrator in physiology, Royal Free Hospital Medical School (1901); lecturer and head of physiology department (1908–41); awarded D.Sc. (1908); taught at the University of Toronto (1908–12); reader at University of London (1912), became professor of physiology (1919), and first holder of Jex-Blake chair of physiology (1926–41); carried out important research in the early part of her career; an ardent feminist, played a leadership role in several organizations including British Federation of University Women (president, 1925–29) and the International Federation of University Women (president, 1929–32); retired from teaching (1941) but remained active in the field of physiology; headed women's section, British Information Services, New York (1941–43); lectured in Middle East (1944–45); was one of the first women to be elected membership in the Physiology Society; awarded CBE (1929).

Winifred Clara Cullis grew up in a time of changing attitudes about the desirability of women being admitted to institutions of higher learning and choosing careers as professors in these institutions. Born in Gloucester in 1875, Cullis was educated in Birmingham and at Mason College, where she took classes in physics, biology and physiology. An outstanding student, she was admitted to Cambridge University on a Sidgwich Scholarship. Cullis was awarded a doctorate by the University of London in 1908, by which time she was already a productive researcher. Starting that year, she published a number of collaborative papers in the *Journal of Physiology*; these included important contributions to knowledge in the field, such as a new method of determining oxygen and carbon dioxide in small volumes of fluid in order to study the gas metabolism of gut. Other significant work included studies of the mammalian heart, which were based on meticulously detailed investigations of its nerves.

Winifred Cullis began her teaching career in 1901 as a demonstrator in physiology and became known as an effective and popular teacher. From 1908 until 1912, she taught at the University of Toronto, returning to England in 1912 to accept a full-time lectureship at the University of London, a post that became a professorship in 1919. As the first woman to receive appointments as either a demonstrator, lecturer or professor of physiology in the United Kingdom, she

played an important role in the acceptance of women in the field. Her great talent and non-confrontational personality did much to win over those males in her field who resisted the idea of female equality. On July 3, 1915, she became one of the first six women to be elected to membership in the Physiological Society of Great Britain. An ardent feminist, Cullis served as president of the British Federation of University Women from 1925 through 1929. She also had the distinction of being president of the International Federation of University Women from 1929 through 1932. Convinced that intellectual exchange served the cause of international understanding, Cullis became vice-president in 1937 of the British-American Associates, a trans-Atlantic academic exchange organization.

Cullis did not slow down her activities upon her retirement from teaching in 1941. As she had done in World War I, she traveled extensively to lecture to troops on health and hygiene. She remained associated with research in physiology, particularly work being done at London's Royal Free Hospital. Cullis received many honors for her achievements, including appointment in 1919 to the Order of the British Empire. In 1929, she was made Commander of the British Empire. A superb scholar and meticulous researcher, Winifred Cullis did not believe that knowledge should be the property of only a small elite. To prove her point, she wrote two books meant for a mass audience, *The Body and its Health* (1935) and *Your Body and the Way it Works* (1949); these were intended to present accurate information about human physiology so that average men and women could practice preventative medicine by living healthier lives. Winifred Clara Cullis died in 1956.

SOURCES:

Cullis, Winifred, and Muriel Bond. *The Body and its Health*. London: Allen and Unwin, 1935.

———. *Your Body and the Way it Works*, London: George Unwin and Allen, 1949.

O'Connor, W.J. *British Physiologists 1885–1914: A Biographical Dictionary*. Manchester: Manchester University Press, 1991.

John Haag, Associate Professor, University of Georgia, Athens, Georgia

Cumberland, countess of.

See Clifford, Margaret (c. 1560–1616).

Cumberland, duchess of.

See Mary Tudor for sidebar on Eleanor Brandon (c. 1520–1547).

See Horton, Ann (1743–1808).

See Frederica of Mecklenburg-Strelitz (1778–1841).

See Thyra Oldenburg (1853–1933).

Cummins, Maria Susanna

(1827–1866)

American author of the 1854 bestseller The Lamp-lighter, *which drew attention to the rising popularity of women novelists. Born Maria Susanna Cummins on April 9, 1827, in Salem, Massachusetts; died on October 1, 1866, in Dorchester, Massachusetts; daughter of Mehitable (Cave) Cummins and David Cummins (a lawyer and judge); educated at Mrs. Charles Sedgwick's Young Ladies School; never married; no children.*

Selected works: The Lamplighter *(1854);* Mabel Vaughan *(1857);* El Fureidîs *(1860);* Haunted Hearts *(1864).*

Born in Salem, Massachusetts, in 1827, Maria Susanna Cummins was the first child of David and **Mehitable Cummins**; three more children would follow. Maria's father was a Norfolk Country Court judge with four children from two previous marriages. Maria led a privileged life and was formally educated in Lenox, Massachusetts, at the residential Mrs. Charles Sedgwick's Young Ladies' School. The school mistress' sister-in-law, author *Catharine Maria Sedgwick, was the first fiction writer to whom Cummins was introduced. Following her graduation, Cummins returned to live with her parents in Salem, Massachusetts, where she began writing. At age 27, she published *The Lamplighter*. Within a month, the book sold 20,000 copies, then tripled those sales within a year (earning the enmity of Nathaniel Hawthorne, who was then struggling for commercial success). Although her articles and three subsequent novels never achieved the same popularity, Cummins was financially well-established. After her father's death, she moved to the Dorchester home of a sibling, taught Sunday school, and wrote. An abdominal illness that began in 1864 led to her death in 1866 at age 39.

SOURCES:
Baym, Nina. "Introduction." *The Lamplighter.* New Brunswick, NY: Rutgers University Press, 1988.

SUGGESTED READING:
Estes, Glenn E., ed. *Dictionary of Literary Biography, v. 42.* Detroit, MI: Gale Research, 1985.

Crista Martin,
Boston, Massachusetts

Cunard, Emerald (1872–1948).

See Cunard, Nancy for sidebar on Lady Maud Cunard.

Cunard, Grace (c. 1891–1967)

American actress, writer, and filmmaker. Born Harriet Mildred Jeffries in Columbus, Ohio, on April 8, *1891 (some sources cite 1893); died on January 19, 1967, in the Motion Picture Home in Woodland Hills, California; sister of Myna Seymour (Cunard), an actress; married actor Joe Moore (d. 1926, divorced); married Jack Shannon, real name Tyler (an actor/stuntman), in 1925; no children.*

Filmography: The Duke's Plan *(1910);* Dante's Inferno *(1912);* The She Wolf *(1913);* The Madonna of Slums *(1913);* Bride of Mystery *(1914);* Lady Raffles *(1914);* Lucille Love *(1914); (serial)* Girl of Mystery *(1914);* The Mysterious Leopard Lady *(1914);* The Mysterious Rose *(1914); (serial)* The Broken Coin *(1915);* The Campbells Are Coming *(1915);* The Doorway of Destruction *(1915);* The Hidden City *(1915);* Nabbed *(1915);* One Kind of Friend *(1915);* The Bandit's Wager *(1916);* Behind the Mask *(1916);* Brennon O'the Moor *(1916);* Born of the People *(1916);* The Elusive Enemy *(1916);* Her Better Self *(1916);* Her Sister's Sin *(1916);* Heroine of San Juan *(1916);* His Majesty Dick Turpin *(1916);* Lady Raffles Returns *(1916);* The Madcap Queen of Crona *(1916);* Phantom Island *(1916); (serial)* Peg O'the Ring *(1916);* The Powder Trail *(1916);* The Princely Bandit *(1916); (serial)* The Purple Mask *(1916);* The Sham Reality *(1916);* The Strong Arm Squad *(1916);* Circus Sarah *(1917);* Her Western Adventure *(1917);* In Treason's Grasp *(1917);* The Puzzle Woman *(1917);* Society's Driftwood *(1917);* True to Their Colors *(1917);* Unmasked *(1917);* The Spawn *(1918);* The Daughter of Law *(1920);* The Man Hater *(1920);* The Woman of Mystery *(1920);* The Girl in the Taxi *(1921);* Her Western Adventure *(1921); (serial)* A Dangerous Adventure *(1922);* The Kiss Barrier *(1925);* Outwitted *(1925);* Exclusive Rights *(1926); (serial)* Fighting with Buffalo Bill *(1926); (serial)* The Winking Idol *(1926); (serial)* Blake of Scotland Yard *(1927);* The Denver Dude *(1927); (serial)* The Return of the Riddle Rider *(1927);* The Rest Cure *(1927); (serial)* The Haunted Island *(1928);* The Masked Angel *(1928);* The Price of Fear *(1928);* The Ace of Scotland Yard *(1929);* A Lady Surrenders *(1930);* Ex-Bad Boy *(1931);* Resurrection *(1931);* The Bride of Frankenstein *(1935).*

When Harriet Jeffries was a child, traveling by ship was the only way to see the world. She must have had the wanderlust at an early age, because after her stage debut at 13 she took the stage name "Grace Cunard," naming herself after the two most glamorous ocean-liners of the day—the "Grace" and the "Cunard." Accompanied by her mother, she hired on with a traveling stock company and toured the United States.

By 1910, the 17-year-old Cunard found herself unemployed. Desperate to continue her budding acting career, she accepted a job in "moving pictures," a choice "legitimate" actresses would never consider. Her first job was for the infamous D.W. Griffith in a movie called *The Duke's Plan* (1910). Though Cunard was an immediate success, she did not like working for the mercurial Griffith. Whether or not she had already started formulating her own ideas about filmmaking is unclear, but by 1915 she had formed a production company with actor-director Francis Ford, brother of the famed director, John Ford. On their earliest efforts, Cunard is credited as writer and actress; Ford is credited as director and actor. Soon, Cunard took a co-director credit and finally a director credit as well.

Cunard and Ford were best known for their action-adventure serials that were popular from 1915–1925. Similar to what is known to modern-day audiences as "episodic" television, different episodes of serials were shown each week at the local movie house. The most popular storylines of that period were female action-adventure dramas nicknamed "cliff-hangers." Each week as heroine, Cunard had to outwit a nefarious villain in order to save a hapless victim from imminent peril. Just 5'4" with auburn hair and green eyes, she was athletic and fearless, and insisted on doing her own stunts though it occasionally landed her in the hospital.

In the movies that Cunard directed and starred, women were never the stereotypical victims seen most often in silent films directed by men. In *Lady Raffles*, she appears as a seductive jewel thief with a cavalier attitude, who eludes capture by fleeing on an elephant. In *The Purple Mask*, as a Robin Hood type, she successfully outmaneuvers the detective who is determined to end her career. One of her most interesting roles came in a 1929 science-fiction film, *The Last Man on Earth*. Cunard portrays a gangster who kidnaps the last male on the planet and holds him for ransom from an all-woman government.

Cunard's films made clear early on that women were credible in action-adventure roles and, like her contemporaries *Lois Weber, *Ida May Park, and *Jeanie MacPherson, Grace Cunard proved women could be as successful behind the camera as in front of it.

SOURCES:

Acker, Ally. *Reel Women: Pioneers of the Cinema, 1896 to the Present.* NY: Continuum, 1993.

Foster, Gwendolyn A. *Women Film Directors: An International Biocritical Dictionary.* Westport, CT: Greenwood Press 1995.

"Grace Cunard, 73, Silent Film Star," in *The New York Times* (obituary). January 24, 1967.
Moving Picture World. September 14, 1915, p. 26.
Weaver, John, comp. *Twenty Years of Silents.* Methuen, NJ: Scarecrow Press, 1971.

Deborah Jones,
Studio City, California

Grace Cunard

Cunard, Maud (1872–1948).

See Cunard, Nancy for sidebar.

Cunard, Nancy (1896–1965)

English poet, journalist, publisher, and aristocrat who crusaded against racial and class prejudices and fascist oppression. Name variations: Nancy Fairbairn. Born Nancy Clara Cunard at Nevill Holt, in Leicestershire, England, on March 10, 1896; died at Hôpital Cochin in Paris, France, on March 16, 1965; buried in Père Lachaise Cemetery, Paris; only daughter of Sir Bache Cunard and Maud Alice (Emerald) Burke Cunard; married Sydney Fairbairn, London, on November 15, 1916 (divorced, mid-1925); no children.

Published Wheels *(November 1922); published book of poems,* Outlaws *(1921); had affair with Aldous Huxley (1922); published* Sublunary *(1923); published* Parallax *(1925); had affair with Louis Aragon (1926–28); established Hours Press in Paris (1928); met Henry Crowder (1928); visited U.S. (1931 and 1932); published anthology* Negro *(February 1934); journeyed to Moscow (August 1935); covered Spanish Civil War (1936–39); traveled to Chile (February 1940); spent World War II in London (1941–45); traveled to liberated Paris (February 1945); published* Grand Man: Memories of Norman Douglas *(1954); published* G.M.: Memories of George Moore *(1956); declared insane, committed to Holloway Sanatorium, London (1960).*

Nancy Cunard was the archetypical spoiled English upper-class rich girl, a 1920s "new woman," sophisticated, unconventional, and in-

---

&► **Cunard, Maud** (1872–1948)

English-American socialite and patron of the arts. Name variations: Lady Maud; Lady Emerald Cunard. Born Maud Alice Burke in San Francisco, California, on August 3, 1872; died in England on July 10, 1948; her father was related to the Irish patriot, Robert Emmett; her mother was half French; married Sir Bache Cunard (grandson of the founder of the shipping line), in April 1895 (separated 1911); children; *Nancy Cunard *(1896–1965).*

When Lady Maud Cunard married Sir Bache Cunard, grandson of the founder of the shipping line, she became mistress of his estate Nevill Holt in the heart of fox-hunting country in Leicestershire, England. British country life before the turn of the century, however, was a little too pastoral for the ex-Miss Burke, late of San Francisco. After a dalliance with the writer George Moore, she ran off with conductor Sir Thomas Beecham and changed her name to Emerald. A patron of the arts and friend of artists and royalty, Lady Maud regularly gave dinner parties at the Dorchester during the London blitz, in defiance of the falling bombs. In those early days, her pals were **Violet Rutland**, American portrait painter **Pansy Cotton**, and ***Jennie Jerome Churchill**. Emerald Cunard was the subject of many books and paintings, including a portrait by ***Marie Laurencin**.

SOURCES:
Fielding, Daphne. *Emerald and Nancy: Lady Cunard and her Daughter.* London: Eyre and Spotteswoode, 1968 (published in America as *Those Remarkable Cunards,* Atheneum).

SUGGESTED READING:
Moore, George. *Letters to Lady Cunard, 1895–1933.* Edited by Rupert Hart-Davis. 1957.

---

dependent. A published poet at age 20, a crusader for "causes," an advocate of the avant-garde, and an inveterate traveler, she often suffered from lack of direction and purpose in life. She engaged in shocking behavior, alienated friends and family, and treated her many lovers as sexual objects to be used and discarded. However, Cunard's commitment to racial equality for blacks and her abhorrence of social inequality were genuine. Even those who knew her best could not agree on the motivation behind her undaunted "crusading" efforts on behalf of those who suffered injustices. In a collection of remembrances of Cunard, a friend remarked on her "profound love for humanity [which] compelled her to participate . . . in every drama that burst out in this, our sad world." However, another friend could state that "there was no universal love of humanity about [Cunard]." She was an enigma: who she was is obvious, what she was is not so evident. But there is general agreement on the impression Cunard made on people. She was beautiful, tall, slender, aggressive, reckless, sexually promiscuous, unconventional to an extreme, and an immutable hater.

Daughter of an English country gentleman, Nancy Cunard was born on the family's 13,000-acre estate of Nevill Holt and raised among the exclusive upper class that she came to despise. Great-granddaughter of the American steamship line magnate, Samuel Cunard, she also had American ties through her wealthy mother, the lovely socialite Maud Alice Burke (Lady ◄► **Maud Cunard**) of San Francisco. Despite wealth and privilege, Nancy received only sporadic attention and little affection from her parents. Lady Cunard found motherhood distasteful, "a low thing—the lowest," but relished her role as host to writers, prime ministers, and even the prince of Wales (later Edward VIII). Nancy's father Sir Bache Cunard was more interested in hunting and the outdoors than in his brilliant houseguests. Intelligent and curious, Nancy listened avidly to her mother's friends talk of literature and public affairs.

Nancy's life drastically changed when she was 15. Lady Cunard fell in love with Sir Thomas Beecham, separated from her husband, and moved with her daughter to a fashionable address in London. Nancy never experienced a normal, settled existence from that time until her death. Her peripatetic lifestyle as an adult was one of her most enduring traits. Enrolled at Miss Woolf's exclusive school in London, Cunard excelled in her classes and won several prizes. In 1912, she went to Munich to study German and

music; the following spring, she attended a girls' finishing school in Paris. Having visited Italy with her parents in 1909, she was an experienced traveler at an early age. Her fluency in French, German, Italian, and Spanish allowed her to move easily around Europe, and later in Mexico and Latin America. She also knew some Russian. As an adult, Nancy Cunard was more European than English.

Typical of her class and time, Cunard had her "coming out" as a London debutante in 1914. Elegant balls and parties, attended by the "proper" young men and women, bored her. She was drawn to a group of more rebellious upper-class friends who composed the "Corrupt Coterie." This rather bohemian set included her friend **Iris Tree** with whom she rented a room in the Bloomsbury area of London. Cunard wrote poetry, frequented clubs that featured American jazz, and gained a reputation as a modern, independent "New Woman." Occasionally, she attended her mother's brilliant social gatherings; the Irish writer George Moore, Lady Cunard's platonic admirer, had great influence on Nancy's promising career as a poet. Nancy was greatly impressed by Ezra Pound and admired his poetry, but not his politics. After the Second World War, Pound was declared insane for his wartime support of the Fascists in Europe, brought back to the United States and confined in St. Elizabeth's Hospital in Washington, D.C. In 1946, Nancy wrote him, saying, "It is inconceivable to me that an 'intellectual' should collaborate with Fascism."

You have the conviction, a rather despairing one, that she didn't fit in anywhere, to any class, nay, to any nationality. . . . She was just herself.

—Michael Arlen

Lady Cunard approved of Nancy's writing, but that did not preclude marriage. What is surprising is not that Nancy became engaged to the handsome, rather prosaic, Sydney Fairbairn, but that she married him. Fairbairn was an army officer, wounded in the war (1914–18), and was on leave after recuperating in Cairo. Lady Cunard had assumed Nancy would marry a wealthy, well-born gentleman; Fairbairn, a graduate of Eton and a German university, was acceptable but not "top-drawer." According to Cunard, she married in order to get away from her mother and to have an independent life of her own. The wedding, in November 1916, received a great deal of attention in the London society pages; ignoring convention and fashion, Nancy wore a gold dress and dispensed with bridesmaids and bouquets. Less than two years later, the marriage collapsed. Cunard was a spirited non-conformist, who found marriage stifling and Fairbairn a philistine. Moreover, she had fallen in love with Peter Broughton Adderley, an officer on leave from the western front. Adderley was killed one month before the war ended.

At the end of the war, Nancy told Fairbairn their marriage was over: "I had married a foul man. . . . I loathed him." In early 1919, after contracting flu and pneumonia, she went with a friend to southern France to convalesce. From her diary of 1919, one glimpses the mature Nancy Cunard: her need to shock, her melancholy and restlessness, and concern over her future—what kind of career, where to live, how to give purpose to her life. These concerns were never resolved satisfactorily through a lifetime of searching and experimenting; "I seem to want too much," she confessed, "hence a mountain of unhappiness." At this time, Cunard drank to excess and picked up strangers for casual sex. Already her health was affected by alcohol, cigarettes, and not eating. Dissatisfied and longing to escape the narrow confines of English society, Cunard decided to move to France, a decision that would change and define her life for the next 45 years. "I had determined to leave England," she wrote in 1955, "and leave I did—on January 7th 1920, I went to France—alone 'for ever'."

There were frequent visits to London, but France was her home. Her interest in the avant-garde brought her into contact with Dadaism and Surrealism and its founders, Tristan Tzara, André Breton, Louis Aragon, and others. Cunard considered herself a poet, and her unorthodox tastes drew her into the maelstrom of Parisian culture and the liberated lifestyle of the 1920s. Affairs with the writers Michael Arlen and Aldous Huxley were brief and unsatisfying. To Cunard, Arlen was too materialistic, seeking fame and wealth, and Huxley was sexually repugnant. Both novelists used Cunard as a character in their novels; she was portrayed as Iris March in Arlen's *The Green Hat,* a woman who "gave you a sense . . . that she was somehow outside the comic, squalid, sometimes, almost fine laws by which we judge as to what is and what is not conventional." In one of Huxley's works, he described her as "bleak, magnetic, destructive." In truth, Cunard tended to separate her carnal appetites from love and warmth, with what **Anne Chisholm** called "masculine detachment." And often her lovers, including Arlen and Huxley, suffered from her "detachment." (She was also said to be Hemingway's model for Lady Brett in *The Sun Also Rises.*)

The year 1920 was certainly momentous for Nancy. She left England, began her affair with Arlen, and had a hysterectomy in a Paris clinic, from which she almost died. The reason for the operation is obscure. She may have had a miscarriage or an abortion, or perhaps it was simply to prevent future pregnancy. In her letters, Cunard makes it clear that she never wanted children. And she achieved what she desired—sexual freedom. She scorned the double-standard imposed on women, refused to conform to feminine conventions, and threw aside discretion in sexual relations.

In France, Cunard began to give some order to her life. She took an apartment on the Ile Saint Louis in Paris, filled it with modern art and friends from the international literary and artistic community, and continued to write poetry. She published two collections in 1921 and 1923. But to say she settled down would be inaccurate. From the end of summer to December 1921, Cunard spent time in Paris, Normandy, Monte Carlo, Berkshire (England), Deauville (France), Spain, Venice, the south of France, and London. By constantly moving about, she hoped to fill a void that existed in her life, but as she admitted, "There's a vague promise of excitement in the air and nothing ever happens. *C'est la mal des voyageurs.*" Nancy Cunard considered herself a poet, but was writing a vocation or an avocation in her case? There is no question that she had talent and the technical skill required of an artist; *Parallax*, published in 1925, is one of her best works and was well-received by the critics. At the same time, Cunard discovered an interest in African art—ivories, masks, fetishes, and especially ivory bracelets, the latter worn from wrist to elbow, which became her trademark. Louis Aragon, the young Surrealist intellectual, shared her interest in primitive art and admired her taste and enthusiasm. Unfortunately, he also fell in love with her. Cunard was unfaithful despite her genuine affection for him: "I don't think anyone has ever loved me save Louis," she wrote years later, "I, on the other hand have truly and entirely loved many. . . . So much for love." Aragon had become a communist, and though Cunard never joined the party, any party, she identified with the political left. Like Aragon, and many other French intellectuals, she became an ardent anti-Fascist.

In the late '20s, Nancy bought a house in Réanville, about 60 miles from Paris, where she lived until the Nazi occupation of France in 1940. Shortly, Cunard's new business venture, a small publishing house, occupied an outbuilding on the property. She purchased a rare century-old hand press and hired a French printer to teach her how to operate it. The Hours Press was born. Cunard intended to publish works in limited editions of high quality, works that would not appeal to commercial publishers. Ezra Pound, Norman Douglas, and the first published work of Samuel Beckett made a reputation for her press among the numerous small publishing houses flourishing at this time. Nancy handled all aspects of the business; she operated the hand press, chose the authors and books, wrote publicity, and kept the accounts. Eventually, she moved the press to Paris but gradually lost interest in the enterprise that had realized a small profit. Money was not a factor in her decision to abandon the press. Publishing was time consuming, and Nancy needed to be on the move.

Cunard and Aragon were on holiday in Venice when their affair ended with his attempted suicide. This act of sad desperation left Nancy untouched, unmoved. After he left for Paris, Cunard stayed on and continued to party with her cousin Edward Cunard and his friends. Here she met the African-American Henry Crowder who played piano in a jazz group called Eddie South and His Alabamians. Cunard initiated an affair that would change her life and Crowder's. Her biographer states that she had found a new lover, one of color, and "she found a cause, a symbol, a weapon, a victim." Cunard intended to help Crowder; she encouraged him to write music, and she aided him financially for many years. They returned to Paris together, but Cunard never intended to have an exclusive affair. Her casual sex with other black American musicians in Paris made Crowder threaten to end their affair. But he was no match for Nancy's strong will. She was said to lack "sexual warmth," and she often treated Crowder badly, not because of his color, but as a lover.

From Crowder, Nancy became aware of American racism, segregation, and black culture, and she began planning to edit a black anthology "to demonstrate the dignity and genius of the black race and to expose the injustice of prejudice." To experience first hand the black experience in America, Cunard made two trips to the United States (1931 and 1932). She sailed to New York and stayed in a hotel in Harlem where she was impressed with the Harlem Renaissance then in full flower. But she was vocally critical of American blacks' lack of interest in their African heritage. She met W.E.B. DuBois, Langston Hughes and other eminent blacks whom she persuaded to contribute to her anthology. While in America, she learned of the case of the Scottsboro Boys, the nine black youths wrongfully accused of raping two white girls, **Victoria Price** and *Ruby Bates, in Alabama. As a crusader for racial justice, Cunard embraced the blacks' cause, collected money in Europe, and rallied support for their legal defense. Race and class prejudice were anathema to her. Lady Cunard had been furious to learn of Nancy's affair with Crowder, and Nancy reacted savagely by attacking her mother's perceived bigotry in *Black Man and White Ladyship,* which she had privately printed and distributed to friends. She and her mother never communicated in any way from this time on.

Nancy's second trip to the United States caused a sensation in the press. It was alleged that she had come to New York because she was attracted by the black singer Paul Robeson. She received hate mail and was hounded by reporters. During a short visit to Jamaica, she met Marcus Garvey and agreed with him that blacks should return to Africa. On her return to France, Cunard plunged into the work of collecting and editing articles, poems, and music for the anthology. In spring 1933, she went to London to find a publisher. *Negro* appeared in February 1934, dedicated to Henry Crowder. This impressive book contained 250 contributions from 150 authors, two-thirds of whom were black, and covered all aspects of black culture and history. Crowder criticized the collection as "shallow and empty," and his estrangement from Nancy led him to charge that white women could never understand the black man's feelings towards them. Crowder's version of their troubled, often absurd, "love" affair became the subject of his book, *As Wonderful as All That?*

In August 1935, Nancy visited Moscow, possibly because of her sympathy with communist ideals. That fall, she began work as a correspondent for the Associated Negro Press (Chicago), which took her to Geneva to report on the League of Nations meetings and to Spain to cover the Civil War. From 1936 to 1939, this brutal conflict consumed her time and attention. She also wrote articles for the *New Times* (London) and the *Manchester Guardian,* determined to inform the world of Fascist atrocities inflicted on innocent civilians. She collected money for Spanish refugees and helped settle them in London and in France, many at her house in Normandy.

With war in Europe imminent, Cunard sailed for Chile in January 1940. France was soon occupied by the Nazis, and Nancy realized that she too was a refugee. She decided to return to London. During the war years, she wrote articles for various British journals, reviewed plays, wrote poetry, and worked for General Charles De Gaulle's Free French organization in London. In early 1945, six months after the liberation of Paris, she returned to France; she had heard that her house in Réanville had been ransacked by German soldiers and local French collaborators,

but the extent of the damage shocked and distressed her. Her collection of African art, her valuable books and paintings had been vandalized, not stolen, and her house was in ruins. Even the large thyme bush behind her house had been destroyed, which led her to remark, "The missing bush seemed to say: 'No more, no more of any of this for you. Don't try to come back'." It was obvious she could not live there any longer, not among those who had maliciously ravaged her house, her only home. Despite repeated attempts to secure compensation for her losses from the French government, she ultimately failed. Restless and rootless, alone and without a career, Cunard wandered around France, England, and Mexico. She finally bought an isolated, primitive farm house at La Mothe-Fénélon in the Dordogne.

Poetry and articles continued to pour forth from her much maligned French typewriter, but her life still lacked direction and meaning. Cheap wine, chain-smoking, and numerous meaningless affairs undermined her health and fueled her depression. Despite her unstructured lifestyle, Cunard wrote and had published two books (in 1954 and 1956) on her friends Norman Douglas and George Moore. While working on the latter, she wrote: "My idea of writing, of really writing and enjoying it, is when ideas, etc. come so fast that there is barely time to pick up another sheet to put into the typewriter. . . . Some kind of fluid is there and oneself merely the transmitter." She dreaded solitude and tried, as usual, to fill the emptiness of her existence with travel. Unfortunately, she began to exhibit signs of mental instability that led to serious altercations involving the police in various countries; she was arrested and detained and eventually expelled from Spain in the spring of 1960. Shortly after, she was incarcerated in London for being drunk and disorderly.

Cunard became increasingly violent, babbled incoherently, and made sexual advances to strangers. She was declared insane and incompetent and was committed to Holloway Sanatorium (outside London) for four months. After 30 years of alcoholism and promiscuity, Nancy Cunard had self-destructed. While confined, she wrote to her friend *Janet Flanner in July 1960, "not being one who wants to go through life entirely alone in every sense and at every hour, I have loathed my life, all of it, and spit on it, at present, for the future and the past." Within a few months of her release from the sanatorium, she returned to France with her new lover Tomás, a young Spanish blacksmith. He left her in July 1961, for which she was grateful. But she was alone again, often ill, and in need of money. Never had Cunard earned a living. Like so many upper-class women of her time, she lived off family inheritances, in Nancy's case from her father and then one-third of her mother's estate after her death in 1948. In the summer of 1963, Nancy began work on a book about the Hours Press with an American scholar, Hugh Ford. To escape loneliness and the isolation of La Mothe during the winter of 1963–64, she lived with her friend, Jean Guerin, in his villa at Saint-Jean-Cap-Ferrat. She wrote poetry, corresponded with friends, drank, and flew into uncontrollable rages. The following winter, she fell and broke her leg while living again at Guerin's villa. Alcohol and erratic behavior forced Guerin to ask her to leave.

In early March, on board a train for Paris, Cunard drank heavily and behaved irrationally—she ate her ticket rather than give it to the ticket collector. Without warning, she arrived at a friend's house in a village near Paris. The next morning, she was sent off in a taxi, to be met in Paris by Janet Flanner and taken to a doctor. Instead, Nancy ordered the driver to take her to the apartment of a former lover. From there, she checked into a small hotel; when she called for a taxi, the driver turned her over to the police. Ill and muttering incoherently, the gendarmes brought her to the Hôpital Cochin where she died three days later—alone. Nancy Cunard was cremated and buried in the Père Lachaise cemetery in Paris, this talented, lonely woman who, as she wrote in a poem, "walked alone . . . defiant, of single mind" and who "has no epitaph."

SOURCES:

Chisholm, Anne. *Nancy Cunard*. NY: Penguin Books, 1979.

Ford, Hugh. *Nancy Cunard: Brave Poet, Indomitable Rebel, 1896–1965*. Philadelphia, PA: Chilton, 1968.

SUGGESTED READING:

Burkhart, Charles. *Herman and Nancy and Ivy: Three Lives in Art*. London: Victor Gollancz, 1977.

Crowder, Henry. *As Wonderful as All That? Henry Crowder's Memoir of His Affair with Nancy Cunard*. Navarro, CA: Wild Tree Press, 1987.

Cunard, Nancy. *These Were the Hours*. Carbondale: Southern Illinois University Press, 1969.

Fielding, Daphne. *Emerald and Nancy: Lady Cunard and her Daughter*. London: Eyre and Spottewoode, 1968 (published in America as *Those Remarkable Cunards*, Atheneum).

COLLECTIONS:

Correspondence, papers, diaries, scrapbooks, photographs and memorabilia are located at the Harry Ransom Humanities Research Center, University of Texas, Austin, Texas.

Jeanne A. Ojala, Professor of History, University of Utah, Salt Lake City, Utah

Cunegond.

Variant of Cunegunde or Cunigunde.

Cunegunda or Cunegunde.

See also Cunigunde.

Cunegunde (fl. 800s)

Queen of Italy. Name variations: *Cunegonde or Kunigunda. Married Bernhard or Bernard (c. 797–818), king of Italy (r. 810–818), in 813; children: Pepin II, count of Perrone (b. 817).*

Cunegunde (1234–1292)

Saint and queen of Poland. Name variations: Kinga. Born in 1234; died in 1292; daughter of Bela IV, king of Hungary (r. 1235–1270), and *Maria Lascaris (fl. 1234–1242); married Boleslaus or Boleslav V the Chaste, king of Poland (r. 1243–1279).

Cunegunde (d. 1357)

Electress of Brandenburg. Name variations: Kunegunda. Died in 1357; daughter of Kazimierz also known as Casimir III the Great, king of Poland (r. 1333–1370), and one of his four wives, *Aldona of Lithuania (d. 1339), Adelaide of Hesse, Krystryna Rokizanska, or *Jadwiga of Glogow; married Louis VI the Roman, duke of Bavaria, elector of Brandenburg (r. 1350–1365).

Cunegunde (d. after 1370)

Duchess of Saxony. Died after 1370; daughter of Ladislas I Lokietek, king of Poland (r. 1306–1333), and *Elizabeth of Bosnia (d. 1339); sister of Casimir III, king of Poland (r. 1333–1370), and *Elizabeth of Poland (c. 1310–1386); married Bernard, duke of Swidnica; married Rudolf, duke of Saxony.

Cunegunde (1465–1520)

Duchess of Bavaria. Name variations: Cunigunde, Kunigunde. Born on March 16, 1465, in Wiener Neustadt; died on August 8, 1520, in Munich; daughter of *Eleanor of Portugal (1434–1467) and Frederick III, king of Germany and Holy Roman emperor (r. 1440–1493); sister of Maximilian I, Holy Roman emperor (r. 1493–1519); married Albert II, duke of Bavaria.

Cunigunde (d. 1040?)

Saint and Holy Roman empress. Name variations: Cunegunda; Cunigunde of Hungary; Cunigunda of

Luxemburg; Kunegunde or Kunigunde. Died on March 3, 1039, or 1040 (some sources cite 1030 or 1033) in Germany; interred at Bamberg; daughter of Siegfried of Luxemburg (c. 922–998), count of Ardennes (r. 963–998), and possibly *Hedwig of Eberhard (930–992); granddaughter of *Cunigunde of France (c. 900–?); married Henry II (972–1024), Holy Roman emperor and king of Germany (r. 1002–1024), in 1002 or 1003; children: some sources claim that she was the mother of Agatha of Hungary who married Edward the Atheling (more likely, however, Agatha was the daughter of Cunigunde's brother-in-law Bruno, bishop of Augsburg).

Around 1002 or 1003, Cunigunde, daughter of Siegfried of Luxemburg, married the Holy Roman emperor Henry II. Though Henry had longed to be a monk, the prior Richard of Verdun convinced him that he would better serve God as a ruler. Cunigunde was his ideal mate. Wrote *Anna Brownell Jameson in *Legends of the Monastic Orders*, Cunigunde "not only set an example of piety and charity but of industry, working continuously with her hands when not engaged in prayer."

The marriage of Cunigunde and Henry was a mystical union, one of love and respect; both vowed to remain chaste throughout their life together. After several years, Cunigunde was accused by scandalmongers of adultery. Henry, though convinced of his wife's purity, was upset by the malicious rumors. According to legend, in an attempt to refute these accusations, Cunigunde requested a "trial by ordeal" and walked unhurt over burning ploughshares (hot irons). In doing so, she was immediately vindicated.

After Henry's death in 1024, Cunigunde entered the Benedictine Convent at Kaufungen, near Cassel, as a nun. She died there on March 3, in 1039 or 1040. Henry was canonized in 1152. Pope Innocent III canonized Cunigunde in 1200. Effigies of Cunigunde and Henry, lying side by side under a canopy in their imperial robes, can be found in the Cathedral of St. Stephen at Bamberg. Scenes of the royal couple are engraved on the pedestal: Cunigunde paying architects with her dower to build the church in Bamberg; Cunigunde walking over the fiery ploughshares; Henry leaving Cunigunde at the time of his death. The story of St. Cunigunde lives on in German poetry, art, and in numerous ballads and legends.

Eileen O'Pacek,
Northport, New York

Cunigunde of Bohemia (d. 1321)

Bohemian princess. Died in 1321; daughter of Cunigunde of Hungary (d. 1285) and Otakar or Ottokar II the Great (b. 1230?), king of Bohemia (r. 1253–1278), duke of Austria and Styria (r. 1252–1276); married Boleslaw II (divorced 1302); children: Euphrosyne or Eufrozyna; Waclaw of Poland (d. 1336); Berta (died after 1341).

Cunigunde of France (c. 900–?)

Countess of Verdun. Born around 900; daughter of Ermentrude of France; grandmother of St. *Cunigunde (d. 1040?); married her second husband Richwin (b. around 885), count of Verdun, in 920; children: Siegfried of Luxemburg (b. around 922), count of Ardennes.

Cunigunde of Hohenstaufen (fl. 1215–1230)

Queen of Bohemia. Name variations: Cunigunda; Kunegund of Staufen; Cunigunde von Hohenstaufen. Flourished around 1215 to 1230; daughter of Philip of Hohenstaufen also known as Philip of Swabia (c. 1176–1208), Holy Roman emperor (r. 1198–1208), and probably *Irene Angela of Byzantium (d. 1208); sister of *Beatrice of Swabia (1198–1235) and *Marie of Swabia (c. 1201–1235); married Wenzel also known as Wenceslas I (1205–1253), king of Bohemia (r. 1230–1253); children: Otakar or Ottokar II (c. 1230–1278), king of Bohemia (r. 1253–1278), duke of Austria and Styria (r. 1252–1276).

Cunigunde of Hungary (d. 1285)

Queen of Bohemia. Name variations: Cunigunde of Hungary; Kunegunda of Chernigov. Died on September 9, 1285; daughter of *Anna of Hungary (daughter of Bela IV, king of Hungary) and Rastislav, ex-prince of Novgorod; became second wife of Otakar or Ottokar II the Great (c. 1230–1278), king of Bohemia (r. 1253–1278), duke of Austria and Styria (r. 1252–1276), on October 25, 1261; married Javisza von Rosenberg, in June 1284; children: (first marriage) *Agnes of Bohemia (1269–1297); Wenzel also known as Wenceslas II (1271–1305), king of Bohemia (r. 1278–1305); *Cunigunde of Bohemia (d. 1321). Ottokar II's first wife was *Margaret of Babenberg.

Cunigunde of Swabia (fl. 900s)

Holy Roman empress. Name variations: Kunigunde. Flourished in the 900s; daughter of Berthold, pfalz-

graf of Swabia; married Liutpold of Bavaria, margrave of Bavaria; married Conrad I, Holy Roman emperor (r. 911–918); children: (first marriage) Arnulf the Bad, duke of Bavaria (r. 907–937); Berthold, duke of Bavaria (r. 938–947); (second marriage) **Cunigunde of Germany** *(who married Werner, count of Worms). Liutpold's first wife was* ***Hildegarde of Bavaria** *(c. 840–?).*

Cunigunde Sobieska (fl. 1690s)

Electress of Bavaria. Flourished in the 1690s; married Maximilian II Emmanuel, elector of Bavaria (r. 1679–1726); children: Charles VII (1697–1745), Holy Roman emperor (r. 1742–1745). Maximilian's first wife was ***Maria Antonia** *(1669–1692).*

Cunigundes.

Variant of Cunegunde or Cunigunde.

Cunitz, Maria (1610–1664)

German astronomer noted for her simplification of Kepler's tables of planetary motion. Name variations: Marie. Born Maria Cunitz in 1610 in Schweidnitz, Silesia; died in 1664 in Pitschen, Silesia; daughter of Dr. Heinrich Cunitz; educated by father and tutors; married Dr. Elias von Löven, 1630; no children.

Selected publications: Urania Propitia *(1650).*

Maria Cunitz devoted her life to correcting the troublesome problems inherent in Johannes Kepler's *Rudolphine Tables* of planetary motion, which were based on the lifelong observations of Tycho Brahe. However, Cunitz was no mere calculator; her mastery of astronomical theory was evident in her work.

Cunitz was born in 1610 in Schweidnitz, Silesia, the eldest daughter of Heinrich Cunitz, a wealthy physician and landowner. Guided by her father, she learned seven languages (including Latin, Greek and Hebrew) and studied medicine, art, music, mathematics, history and astronomy. At age 20, she married one of her tutors, Elias von Löven, a physician and amateur astronomer.

Von Löven encouraged his wife's mathematical and astronomical talents, especially her interest in Kepler's *Rudolphine Tables* used to calculate planetary positions. It was a well-established fact at the time that the complicated tables contained a number of errors. Cunitz set about to simplify them and correct as many mistakes as possible. Her work was hampered,

however, by lack of funds and astronomical equipment, as well as by interruptions caused by the Thirty Years' War (1616–48). Indeed, she spent most of her life as a refugee in Poland and sought shelter in a cloister with her husband for a time. Despite these conditions, Cunitz succeeded in publishing her results as *Urania Propitia (Sive Tabulae Astronomicae Mire Faciles)* in 1650, in both Latin and German. Although she did correct a number of errors in the original tables, she simplified Kepler's work by neglecting higher order terms in the formulae, thus introducing new errors. Her work, nonetheless, clearly demonstrated her mastery of both mathematics and astronomical theory. Cunitz' publication of the work under her maiden name did not prevent the common assumption that her husband had in fact done most of the work. In response to the misattribution, her husband added a preface to the later editions in which he denied any part in the work.

Cunitz died in Pitschen, Silesia, in 1664, again a refugee from war. Although called by some contemporaries the "Second *Hypatia," Cunitz had her critics. In 1706, Johann Eberti (in his *Eroffnetes Cabinet des gelehrten Frauenzimmers*) charged that she was "so deeply engaged in astronomical speculation that she neglected her household." This charge was often repeated throughout the 18th century.

SOURCES:

Alic, Margaret. *Hypatia's Heritage.* Boston, MA: Beacon Press, 1986.

Krupp, E.C. "Astronomical Musings," in *Griffith Observer.* Vol. XXXIX. May 1975, p. 8–18.

Mozans, H.J. *Women in Science.* Notre Dame: University of Notre Dame Press, 1991.

Ogilvie, Marilyn Bailey. *Women in Science.* Cambridge, MA: MIT Press, 1986.

Schiebinger, Londa. *The Mind Has No Sex?* Cambridge, MA: Harvard University Press, 1989

Kristine Larsen, Associate Professor of Physics and Earth Sciences, Central Connecticut State University, New Britain, Connecticut

Cunningham, Ann (d. 1647)

English noble and rebel. Died in 1647 in England.

Although Lady Ann Cunningham was one of many religious activists during the Protestant Reformation in England, not many women pursued their activism as militantly as she. A member of the lower nobility, she was a devoted convert to the strict doctrine of Calvinism. She believed that England should be converted to her faith, by force if necessary. To accomplish this, she rode across the countryside accompanied by other Calvinist women rebels, terrorizing the populace. She rode fully armed with daggers and pistols, as did her women companions. Their militaristic ways were not supported by the rest of the Calvinist minority in England, and they accomplished very little for their cause.

Laura York,
Riverside, California

Cunningham, Ann Pamela

(1816–1875)

American who, through her efforts to preserve George Washington's home at Mount Vernon, began the movement for historic preservation in the U.S. Name variations: (pseudonym) The Southern Matron. Born August 15, 1816, at "Rosemont," Laurens County, South Carolina; died at her home "Rosemont" on May 1, 1875; buried in the churchyard of the First Presbyterian Church; daughter of Robert and Louisa Cunningham (wealthy plantation owners); educated by a governess and at the Barhamville Institute near Columbia, South Carolina; never married.

Founded Mount Vernon Ladies Association of the Union (1853); completed purchase of Mount Vernon (February 22, 1859); served as first regent of the Ladies Association (1853–74).

Though we slay our forests, remove our dead, pull down our churches . . . let them see that we know how to care for the home of our hero.

—Ann Pamela Cunningham

It was the custom of boat captains navigating the Potomac in the 19th century to ring their bells when they passed George Washington's home at Mount Vernon. On one such occasion, in 1853, **Louisa Cunningham**, traveling home to South Carolina, felt compelled to write to her invalid daughter whom she had just left in Philadelphia:

> It was a lovely moonlit night that we went down the Potomac. I went on deck as the bell tolled and we passed Mount Vernon. I was painfully distressed at the ruin and desolation of the home of Washington, and the thought passed through my mind: Why was it that the women of his country did not try to keep it in repair, if the men could not do it? It does seem such a blot on our country.

Upon receiving the letter, Ann Pamela Cunningham, in Philadelphia to be treated for a spinal injury (suffered in a riding accident) that would plague her for the rest of her life, resolved to accept her mother's challenge. Thus was born the Mount Vernon Ladies Association of the Union.

With Cunningham leading the effort—she was the association's first "regent" until her resignation in 1874—the women of the association publicized and raised money for the cause all over the country. In a very real sense, the hundreds of thousands who continue to enjoy the restored mansion and outbuildings, and who stroll the gardens and grounds, have the women of the association to thank.

By creating the Mount Vernon Ladies Association of the Union, Cunningham stepped in to do a job the nation's male politicians had been unable to do. Because George Washington was seen as a hero of the Revolution and Father of his country, suggestions for a suitable memorial came with regularity following his death in 1799. But while sentiment was strong, action was not forthcoming. That year, Congress resolved to build a marble monument to Washington in the capital city; the House and Senate, however, could not agree on an appropriation. In 1833, a private association formed to build the memorial, but it only raised $87,000 in 13 years. In 1848, Congress authorized the private Washington Monument Society to build the monument, and at last work began. The monument would not be completed until 1876.

Congress also considered the purchase of Mount Vernon in 1846, and, in the 1840s, the governor of Virginia suggested that the state buy the property and turn it to some good use, possibly as an asylum for soldiers, an agricultural school, or a literary institution. Neither legislative body acted, and the estate remained in the hands of John A. Washington, in whose possession it continued to deteriorate.

While the idea for preserving Mount Vernon had been discussed for some years, the impetus behind Cunningham's 1853 decision to champion the cause was the rumor that John A. Washington had offered the property for sale, essentially to the highest bidder. The home and tomb of George Washington seemed in danger of being bought by Northern real-estate speculators. On December 2, 1853, Cunningham, writing as "The Southern Matron," published the first of what would prove to be many rousing "Appeals" for the rescue of Mount Vernon. In "To the Ladies of the South," the readers of the *Charleston Mercury* were reminded that, "Congress has virtually declined to purchase and preserve Mount Vernon in behalf of the nation." She went on to warn her readers in the most emphatic way:

> Yet there is now necessity for immediate action, as schemes are on foot for its purchase

Ann
Pamela
Cunningham

Mount Vernon, east front, before renovations.

by Northern capital, and its devotion to money-making purposes. . . . [C]an you be still, with closed souls and purses, while the world cries "Shame upon America," and suffer Mount Vernon, with all its sacred associations, to become, as is spoken of and probable, the seat of manufacturers and manufactories; noise and smoke, and the "busy hum of *men*," destroying all sanctity and repose around the tomb of *your* own "world's wonder?". . . Never! Forbid it, shades of the dead, that the Pilgrims of the shrine of true patriotism should find thee forgotten, and surrounded by blackening smoke and deafening machinery, where money, money, only money ever enters the thought, and gold, only gold, moves the heart or moves the arm!

The Southern Matron hoped that by alerting people to this potential calamity, the national love of Washington might move them to contribute the money necessary for the purchase of Mount Vernon.

Cunningham judged correctly. Contributions poured in, and on the fifth anniversary of her appeal in the *Mercury*, the Mount Vernon Ladies Association of the Union, chartered by the State of Virginia, purchased the estate. Though a great deal of work remained to restore the property, in the space of five years Mount Vernon had been saved from speculators through the private contributions of patriotic Americans.

From the beginning, Cunningham aimed her appeals specifically at the women of America, and many people, both male and female, saw the preservation of Mount Vernon as an appropriate form of woman's work. It was thought that, removed as they were from the messy world of public life, women would bring to the project the dignity necessary to properly honor Washington's memory. In the hands of women, Mount Vernon would be elevated above the corrupting influences of party politics that seemed to have paralyzed the effort.

The purity of the endeavor was guaranteed in part because the women involved were not out to make money for themselves. Cunningham wrote to John Washington in 1859 to assure him of this:

Mount Vernon, east front, 1999.

Our whole enterprise is based upon the *voluntary system* in order to make our tribute to the memory of Washington "the heart felt offering of a greatful [sic] people!" Therefore as the sentiment has met with decided approval—our work is done by the voluntary self consecration of the women of our land—aided as they nobly are by the sterner sex.

Further, Cunningham did not feel it was proper for her or any of the Association Ladies to receive any individual publicity for their efforts. She signed her first several appeals "The Southern Matron" for just this reason.

Motivated by the lofty ideals of patriotism, and proceeding in a virtuous and selfless way, the ladies of the Mount Vernon Association exemplified the "true woman" of the antebellum period. The members of the association saw themselves as embodying the cardinal virtues of true womanhood: piety, purity, submissiveness, and domesticity (**Barbara Welter** was perhaps the first historian to describe these characteristics in her influential article, "The Cult of True Womanhood, 1820–1860," in *American Quar-*

terly 18, 1966). Far from handicapping them, these womanly virtues contributed to the association's success, according to one contributor to *Godey's Lady's Book*. In 1859, she wrote: "Our feminine ways of doing business are shown to be rather more expeditious and certain than those of masculine management, chiefly because we put our hearts' energies into the work, and do not ask any compensation save success!" Without resorting to the "unwomanly tones" and demands of the suffragists, the Ladies of the Association did push the boundaries of the "domestic sphere," and they created new public opportunities for themselves.

This did not go unnoticed, and the Mount Vernon Ladies Association had its detractors. Some years after the fact, Cunningham remembered problems the association had organizing in Philadelphia. At first, things went splendidly: "in 1855 Philadelphia awoke; great enthusiasm prevailed; . . . boxes for contributions were allowed in Independence Hall." But then, said Cunningham, the movement was squelched when influential men in the city realized that women were behind it: "because it was woman's effort and they disapproved of women mixing in public affairs." What seemed like appropriately feminine behavior to Cunningham and her ladies was clearly not seen that way by everybody.

So, while their efforts generally met with approval—and while they were usually seen as consonant with the roles prescribed for women within their sphere—such efforts also took these women into the public world, otherwise off-limits to them. The novelty was not lost on them at the time. ◀ **Sara Agnes Pryor**, writing in the June 1895 *American Historical Register*, looked back to her childhood and recalled:

> I remember the first meeting of the Mount Vernon Association in my town. The most beautiful and dignified member of the family was missing at the noon-day dinner. "Where have you been?" was the chorus that greeted her when she appeared with flushed cheeks and kindling. "Where have I been? To the Town Hall! And more, to a meeting of ladies—yes *ladies*! Making speeches and passing resolutions like men!" If a vote had been taken from the younger members of the family, the verdict would have been that surely the world was coming to an end!

By any measure, but certainly by that of the mid-19th century, the association accomplished a great deal in a brief period. National fundraising, a monthly publication, members around the country, negotiations with politicians, the successful purchase of Mount Vernon—all this without violating the proscriptions of female behavior.

The women of the association felt that they were answering a sacred call on behalf of the na-

tion. It is no accident that the call should be to rescue Washington's home, not a battlefield or his Executive Office. Within their domestic sphere, women had been entrusted with the safe-keeping of American homes; through the Mount Vernon Ladies Association, women took on the guardianship of the national home. The ladies of the Mount Vernon Association endeavored to rescue what surely was the site of perfect domesticity, because it had produced the perfect American. Regardless of what kind of home an ordinary American might have actually come from, he or she could journey to Mount Vernon and view the ideal. At Mount Vernon, George Washington, the greatest public figure in American history and the abstract embodiment of every American virtue, became domesticated.

By domesticating Washington in this way, the ladies of the association hoped to redeem more than individuals. In the 1850s, the rescue and preservation of Mount Vernon served a greater purpose. Many believed this effort would help heal sectional wounds and bring the national family together again, symbolically, under the same roof. Ann Pamela Cunningham had addressed her initial appeals specifically to the "Ladies of the South." In her first article, she warned her Southern sisters of the "schemes" to purchase Mount Vernon by "Northern capital." Shortly thereafter, however, Cunningham changed her strategy and began appealing to all American women. As she wrote in 1858: "When I started the Mount Vernon movement it was a Southern affair altogether. . . . A call was made to the women of *the South* to gather around Washington's grave. . . . The motives were pure, the intentions were generous, but it failed! . . . *Washington belonged not alone to the South*!" By 1856, the Mount Vernon Ladies Association became the Mount Vernon Ladies Association *of the Union*.

In a Fourth of July speech in 1859, association member **Mary Cutts** applauded the unifying effect the preservation of Mount Vernon might have:

> Miss Cunningham, Regent of the Mount Vernon Ladies Association, with her strong love for the Union and the whole Union, proposes that from the North to the South, from the East to the West of the United States, the people should join together as a band of brothers, in a simultaneous effort to advance this truly national enterprise.

Cunningham may have begun her project motivated by sectional animus, but, with the crisis growing closer, Mount Vernon became the site where the two sections might forget about their

---

⊰▶ Pryor, Sara Agnes (b. 1830)

American author and social leader. Name variations: Mrs. Roger Pryor. Born on February 19, 1830, in Halifax County, Virginia; tutored at home and attended a female seminary in Charlottesville, Virginia; married Roger Atkinson Pryor (a lawyer, member of the New York Supreme Court, and U.S. congressional representative); children: seven.

Sara Agnes Pryor founded the National Society of the Daughters of the American Revolution and was a charter member of the Colonial Dames of America. Though always a writer and a frequent contributor to magazines, her first book was not published until she was 73; six years later, she published *My Day: Reminiscences of a Long Life.*

---

squabbles. In an event heavy with symbolism, on February 23, 1858, the women presented gifts to Massachusetts Senator Edward Everett and Alabama Senator William Lowndes Yancey, representative figures of North and South, for their efforts to save Mount Vernon.

Explaining why the association, and precisely not Congress, should act as guardian of Mount Vernon, Cunningham told readers of the May 1855 *Southern Literary Messenger* that the politicians in Congress would make Mount Vernon "the great yearly battle ground of pro and anti slavery antipathies. The heart sickens at the mere thought of such a 'future' for it."

Just as North and South spiralled toward disunion, the women who worked to save Mount Vernon believed that the two sections, like siblings who have fallen out, could be brought back together around its hearth. Cunningham went on to reiterate that, under the care of the nation's women, Mount Vernon could serve as the nurturing, national home:

> Devoted woman would neither be baffled nor conquered; but she alone triumphs when common homestead can be procured as a common heritage, for the estranged children of a common father, the spell of whose memory will yet have the power to reunite them around *his* hallowed sepulchre.

At the moment when Washington was being used by men for purposes of divisive sectional politics, the ladies of the association insisted that Washington, and those who would honor his memory, should stand above politics.

Despite their efforts, of course, Mount Vernon did not exert the healing influence the association hoped it would. Yet whatever else the war may have destroyed, it left Mount Vernon intact. At the outset of the fighting, generals Scott, McClellan, and Lee agreed that Mount Vernon would be treated as neutral territory. As **Mrs. Comegys**, the vice-regent from Delaware, explained to Honorable Nicholson in 1868:

> By order of Generals Scott and McClellan, no soldier with arms was permitted to tread upon our enchanted 200 acres, and General Lee (Heaven rain blessings on his head) gave an order that the first man in his armies who went there at all, should be shot. So it was the Ararat of the day—the only spot held to be sacred or not in dispute; and I may add, not without pride, that our Association was the only one in the land, whose national organization was preserved.

Though the association she headed would continue its work after the end of the fighting, the war had a profound impact on Ann Pamela Cun-

ningham. In November 1865, she penned a long, rambling lament to her doctor in Philadelphia. Having spent the war at her home in South Carolina, her sectional loyalties, which she hid as regent of the Association, resurfaced: "O! How changed I am! Where is the *enthusiasm* to come from needed to re-kindle extinguished fires? . . . I have become a broken spirited woman whose inspiration is gone because the fountain from which I drew it is dried up forever!" Cunningham felt personally betrayed by the savagery of the war. Her enthusiasm gone, her faith in the nation destroyed, she wrote to Dr. Hodge: "My 'idol' is broken! I see now, it is made of villainous clay and not porcelain." But when Mount Vernon opened to the public again in the spring of 1865, the *Boston Semi-Weekly Advertiser* announced: "It is one of the pleasantest features of the return of peace, that the sacred home of the father of his country is once more accessible to the people of all sections of the nation."

Cunningham seems to have been possessed with an unusual fascination with the past, and one that represents a new historical consciousness that would make Mount Vernon's preservation possible. In 1845, she had published an article-length history of her family in which she tried to redeem the reputation of her Loyalist ancestors. Appearing as an appendix in George Ward's *Journal and Letters of the Late Samuel Curwen, . . . A Loyalist Refugee in England, During the American Revolution*, Cunningham's piece received harsh criticism, most notably from William Gilmore Simms. The attack angered Cunningham, and Simms apologized for having "given pain to a creature so delicately constituted." Cunningham responded that "mind has no sex," and that it was her "misfortune to be made of sterner stuff."

In her letter to Hodge, Cunningham remembered nostalgically: "As a mere child of 10 years my eyes would flash—face flush & my soul fill with ardor, as I would recite from American history." Similarly, she began a business letter to **Sarah Tracy** in 1866 by telling her:

> I have been bewitched tonight. I believe my dear Miss T the "spirit of the past" came over me & my pen has flown—jotting down "remembrances" as they crossed the mind pretty much at hap-hazard I fear—I did not intend to do as I have but I went "on & on" almost unconsciously, for without knowing why I could not get rid of the past.

With the coming of the Civil War, however, it had become clear that the relentless forces of change from which Cunningham would rescue Mount Vernon were not simply invaders from the North.

Change came inevitably in both North and South, and that realization gave new urgency to the association's work. When she resigned her position as regent of the association in 1874, her farewell address underscored her desire to insulate Mount Vernon and protect it from all the forces of the outside world. She told the vice regents:

> Such was the pledge made to the American heart when an appeal was made to it to save the home and tomb of Washington, the Father of His Country, for all change, whether by law or desecration. . . . The mansion and the grounds around it should be religiously guarded from change—should be kept as Washington left them.

Looking to the future, she advised them more directly:

> Ladies, the home of Washington is in your charge—see to it that you keep it the home of Washington. Let no irreverent hand change it; no vandal hands desecrate it with the fingers of progress. . . . Let one spot in this grand country of ours be saved from change. Upon you rests this duty.

This sentiment has become the guiding principle of Mount Vernon, and Cunningham's address is read each year at the annual meeting of the Ladies Association.

The association's vision of what Mount Vernon might be has been largely realized. Restored in exact duplication of the original and filled with original artifacts, Mount Vernon has, for over 100 years, remained a mecca for worshipers of the secular religion of Washington. The estate is seen annually by well over one million visitors, and former curator Charles Cecil Wall has written of them: "If asked why they come, they might well echo the words of Ann Pamela Cunningham: 'They come to see how and where George Washington lived.'"

Though committed to preserving an unchanging past, the Mount Vernon Ladies Association of the Union did, in one sense, point the way toward the future. As the 19th century wore on, more and more Americans felt the need to take refuge in the simplicity of the past, to escape, at least temporarily, the confusion of the present. When they did so by preserving the relics of the past, they followed the model developed at Mount Vernon. Those who would later preserve Andrew Jackson's home, The Heritage, and Jefferson's Monticello looked to the Mount Vernon Ladies Association for inspiration.

SOURCES:
Page, Thomas Nelson. *Historical Sketch of Ann Pamela Cunningham.* Mount Vernon Ladies Association, 1903.

———. *Mount Vernon and Its Preservation, 1858–1910.* NY: Knickerbocker Press, 1932.

SUGGESTED READING:
Hosmer, Charles. *The Presence of the Past: A History of the Preservation Movement in the United States Before Williamsburg.* NY: Putnam, 1965.

Kammen, Michael. *A Season of Youth: The American Revolution and the Historical Imagination.* NY: Knopf, 1978.

Marling, Karal Ann. *George Washington Slept Here: Colonial Revivals and American Culture.* Cambridge: Harvard University Press, 1988.

COLLECTIONS:
Manuscript and archival material about Ann Pamela Cunningham and her efforts to preserve Mount Vernon can be found in the library at Mount Vernon.

Steven Conn, Assistant Professor of History, Ohio State University, Columbus, Ohio

Cunningham, Imogen (1883–1976)

American photographer whose work did not receive widespread critical attention and public recognition until she was well into her 80s. Born Imogen Cunningham in Portland, Oregon, on April 12, 1883; died on June 24, 1976, in San Francisco, California; daughter of Isaac Burns Cunningham (a farmer and businessman) and Susan Elizabeth Burns Cunningham (a homemaker); graduated with honors, University of Washington, Seattle, 1907; married Roi Partridge (an etcher), in 1915 (divorced 1934); children: Gryffyd, Rondall, and Padraic.

Worked in the portrait studio of Edward S. Curtis (1907–09); studied photochemistry in Dresden, Germany (1909–10); set up a portrait studio in Seattle and began to work professionally (1910); moved to Oakland, California (1920); created her extended photographic study of plants and flowers (1921–25); began photographing for Vanity Fair *magazine (1931); was a founding member of f/64 Group (1932); moved to San Francisco (1947); taught at California School of Fine Arts (1947–50); named a fellow of the National Academy of Arts and Sciences (1967); published* Imogen Cunningham: Photographs *(1970); had photo exhibit of her work, Metropolitan Museum of Art (1973); published* Imogen!: Imogen Cunningham Photographs, 1910–1973, *a second collection of photographs (1974).* After Ninety *was published posthumously (1977).*

Imogen Cunningham, whose career spanned seven decades, beginning around 1906 and ending only with her death in 1976, was among the most accomplished and original photographers of the 20th century. The range of her photographic subjects was vast: she moved easily from studies of plants and landscapes to formal portraits and figures. So closely did her techniques and aesthetic approaches mirror those in the photographic arts at large that her career virtually provides a history of American photography.

Imogen Cunningham was born on April 12, 1883, in Portland, Oregon, one of ten children. Her father Isaac Cunningham had moved to Portland from Texas with his three children following the death of his first wife. He then married **Susan Burns (Cunningham)**, a widow from Mississippi, and Imogen was the first of six children born of this union. She was named after Cymbeline's daughter, her father's favorite female character in Shakespeare.

Isaac Cunningham was an idealistic, self-educated free thinker; he practiced vegetarianism, studied theosophy, and was fanatically opposed to organized religion. A grocery clerk turned farmer, he dabbled unsuccessfully in communal farming before moving his family to Seattle in 1889 and landing in the wood and coal business. His advanced ideas did not extend, however, to women's liberation. Imogen's mother was almost completely illiterate and worked 14 hours a day cooking, cleaning, and caring for the children. Determined to escape her mother's dismal fate, Imogen actively pursued an alternative life for herself.

In 1901, while a still a high school student, she decided on a career in photography after seeing reproductions of *Gertrude Kasebier's photographs, including the classic "Blessed Art Thou among Women." Although Isaac was skeptical of her career choice, he nonetheless built her a darkroom in the woodshed. Imogen purchased a 4x5 camera and a course of instructions for $15 from a correspondence school, and she began to photograph.

In 1903, Cunningham enrolled at the University of Washington in Seattle with the intention of studying art. At that time, the school had no art curriculum, so she majored in chemistry, wrote her thesis on "The Scientific Development of Photography," and graduated with honors in 1907. Her first job after college was in the Seattle studio of Edward S. Curtis, who at the time was compiling a now famous photographic portfolio of American Indian portraits. While working in Curtis' studio, Cunningham learned commercial platinum printing.

In 1909, she received a national Pi Beta Phi scholarship to study photochemistry at the Technische Hochschule in Dresden, Germany. While there, she developed a technique of coating printing paper, substituting cheap salts of lead for platinum, and published her method in a German technical magazine. Cunningham returned to Seattle a year later in 1910 and opened a successful portrait studio. Of her early professional work little remains, as the heavy glass negatives she used for portraiture were destroyed when she moved to San Francisco. But of her personal work that did survive, it is clear that Cunningham was also seriously exploring more artistic forms of photography. She was deeply influenced by the then-fashionable "pictorialist" movement of the Photo-Secession Group, and her romantic predilections were also revealed in her admiration of pre-Raphaelite poetry and William Morris. Her self-conscious attempts to elevate photography to a fine art are reflected in the images she produced. She was fond of dressing her subjects in costumes and photographing them in soft-focus, dream-like poses as she recreated scenes and characters from literature and poetry. One of her photographs from this period, "Eve Repentant," features a naked Eve placing her hand on Adam's shoulder as he turns away. The photograph was the subject of great controversy after it was published in a Seattle magazine in 1910.

I photograph anything that light falls on.

—Imogen Cunningham

In 1915, Imogen Cunningham married Roi Partridge, an etcher, in Seattle. The nude photographs she took of him that year on Mt. Rainier caused such a public scandal that she removed them from view for more than 50 years. Nine months after their marriage, her first son Gryffyd was born. Twin sons, Rondall and Padraic, followed in 1917, the year the family moved to San Francisco, where Roi began teaching at Mills College. In 1920, the family settled near the campus in Oakland, and Cunningham spent the next few years trying to balance her duties as a mother and faculty wife with her ambitions as a serious photographer. Though she no longer had a formal studio and only occasionally accepted professional commissions, she continued her work. With "one hand in the dishpan, the other in the darkroom," she incorporated her domestic life into her photography by turning her camera on her sons and the strange objects and animals they brought to her. Cunningham was also an enthusiastic gardener, an interest she began to incorporate into her art. Around 1921, she started photographing flora, particularly the plants and flowers in her own garden. Over the next few years, she created the plant studies that are often considered her finest work. Cunningham later remarked that "the reason I really turned to plants was because I couldn't get out of my own backyard when the children were small." These sharply focused, close-up photographs of individual plants and flowers are strongly reminiscent of the work of *Georgia O'Keeffe, though Cunningham did not see O'Keeffe's work until years later. From 1923 to 1925, Cunningham made an extended study of magnolia flowers, often considered as including her most arresting images.

Throughout this period she maintained a relationship with her photographer friends, including Edward Weston, whom she had met in 1923. Years later in 1932, Cunningham, along with Weston, Ansel Adams, Paul Strand, and several other West Coast-based photographers organized a photography reform association, the "f/64 Group," to promote a new aesthetic direction in photography. The Group opposed the older Photo-Secession Group whose work dominated photography in the first part of the century and had heavily influenced Cunningham's earlier work. Until this time, artists had used the photographic medium to create soft-focus, painterly images. The f/64 Group wanted instead to use sharp focus and a wide depth of field to create photographs that would offer a window onto the real world. It was a move away from self-conscious romanticism towards an uncompromising, sharply detailed realism. Though the group only existed formally for two years and held but one major exhibit, it had an enormous influence on the future of photography. Cunningham, however, was less philosophically wedded to the ideology of this new approach than were her associates. She had always exhibited an experimental streak, and her innate curiosity and wide-ranging interests would always lead her to eschew any convention or orthodoxy in the pursuit of innovative techniques and unexpected images. She drew on dada and surrealism for inspiration and later experimented with a variety of techniques, most notably the use of double exposure. Her finest example of this technique is perhaps her 1962 portrait of poet and filmmaker James Broughton entitled "The Poet and His Alter Ego." Double images recur throughout her work partly as a result of her keen appreciation of the special relationship subsisting between her twin sons. She often photographed two similar objects side by side—two symmetrical trees, two humans, two plant forms. She also used the technique of "sandwiching" negatives (a technique of exposing two or three layered negatives on an enlarger) to produce interesting double images.

In 1931, Cunningham began taking photographs for the magazine *Vanity Fair*. Three years later, when the magazine invited her to New York for an assignment, she accepted the offer against her husband's wishes; the disagreement aggravated the couple's growing marital problems, which culminated in a divorce later that year. The two remained on good terms, and Cunningham never remarried.

Throughout the 1940s and 1950s, Cunningham continued to pick up occasional magazine assignments for *Vanity Fair* and other publications, but it was mainly through her portrait work that she supported herself. By this time, she had developed into a highly accomplished and talented portrait photographer; and today some of her portraits, including a series of photographs of dancer *Martha Graham*, remain her most well-known and recognizable images.

Never one to obsess over the technical aspects of portraiture, she concentrated on revealing the character of the person she was photographing. She did so in part by interacting freely with her subject throughout the photo session in an effort to break down the self-consciousness of the sitter so that the real person could be captured on film. As she explained, "You must be able to gain an understanding at short notice and at close range of the beauties of character, intellect, and spirit, so as to be able to draw out the best qualities and make them show in the face of the sitter." One observer of Cunningham's unique style of work noted in a 1951 issue of the magazine *Modern Photography*: "When you've been photographed by Imogen Cunningham, you haven't just had a sitting, you've had an experience."

In 1947, Cunningham moved to a small cottage in San Francisco, a few blocks from the California School of Fine Arts where she taught in the photography department under the directorship of Minor White until 1950. Her income from photography had never amounted to much, and during these years she lived frugally and worked in relative obscurity. It was not until the 1960s—by which time Cunningham was well into her 80s—that her work began to receive widespread critical attention and public recognition. In 1964, the influential photography magazine *Aperture* devoted an entire issue to her work, and increasingly her photographs were exhibited at the more prestigious galleries. In 1967, she was one of only two women (the other was Martha Graham) to be named fellows of the National Academy of Arts and Sciences.

Imogen Cunningham, Self-Portrait with Camera 2 (late 1920s).

Two collections of her photographs were published: *Imogen Cunningham: Photographs* (1970) and *Imogen!: Imogen Cunningham Photographs, 1910–1973* (1974). In 1973, to mark her 90th year, the Metropolitan Museum of Art held an exhibit of her photographs. In an article for *The New York Times*, art critic Hilton Kramer wrote: "Others may have brought a deeper and a more concentrated vision to photography, or a more flamboyant sense of drama, but Miss Cunningham brought a love and appetite for life."

Imogen Cunningham's eccentric appearance—her trademark flowing black capes, brightly beaded hats, and large peace signs—coupled with her straightforward, no-nonsense manner, made her an instantly recognizable figure around San Francisco. She identified with and befriended the bohemian 1960s generation, and they, in turn, transformed her into a cult figure. She was the subject of three films: *Two Photographers, Imogen Cunningham and Wynn Bullock* (Fred Padula, 1966); *Imogen Cunningham: Photographer* (John Korty, 1967); and *Never Give Up: Imogen Cunningham* (Ann Hershey, 1974). Cunningham even acted in James Broughton's 1967 film *The Bed*.

Throughout her last years, Imogen Cunningham remained disciplined, focused, and optimistic. She always believed that her best photograph would be made tomorrow, and she worked steadily until her death. Concerned with the presentation of her work after her death, in 1974 she established the Imogen Cunningham Trust to preserve her negatives and exhibit and publish her prints. In 1975, at age 92, she began the ambitious project that would be published posthumously as *After Ninety* (1977). The book contains photographs of aged people like herself who remained vital and actively engaged in life. Imogen Cunningham died on June 24, 1976, in San Francisco, California.

SOURCES AND SUGGESTED READING:

Cunningham, Imogen. *After Ninety*. Seattle, WA: University of Washington Press, 1977.
———. *Imogen Cunningham: Photographs*. Seattle: University of Washington Press, 1970.
Dater, Judy. *Imogen Cunningham: A Portrait*. Boston, MA: New York Graphic Company, 1979.
Lorenz, Richard, and Imogen Cunningham. *Imogen Cunningham: Flora*. Boston, MA: Bulfinch Press, 1996.
The New York Times, June 26, 1976.

COLLECTIONS:

Cunningham's papers are in the Smithsonian Institution's Archives of American Art, Washington D.C.; her negatives and a collection of prints are in the Imogen Cunningham Trust, Berkeley, California.

RELATED MEDIA:

Imogen Cunningham at 93 (13 min.), Carousel Film and Video, 1972.
Imogen Cunningham: Photographer, directed by John Korty, 1967.
Never Give Up: Imogen Cunningham, (28 min.) directed by Ann Hershey, Phoenix Films and Video, won the American Film Festival blue ribbon award, 1974.
Portrait of Imogen, documentary directed by Meg Partridge, Imogen Cunningham's granddaughter, Pacific Pictures, 1995.
Two Photographers, Imogen Cunningham and Wynn Bullock, Fred Padula, 1966.

Suzanne Smith, freelance writer, Decatur, Georgia

Cunningham, Kate (1876–1948).

See O'Hare, Kate Richards.

Cunningham, Minnie Fisher
(1882–1964)

American politician and suffragist. Name variations: Minnie Fisher. Born Minnie Fisher in New Waverly, Texas, on March 19, 1882; died on December 9, 1964; seventh child of Captain Horatio White Fisher and Sallie (Abercrombie) Fisher; obtained teacher's certificate; attended the school of pharmacy of the University of Texas Medical Branch, becoming one of the first women to graduate in pharmacy in Texas; married Beverly Jean Cunningham (a lawyer), on November 27, 1902 (died 1927).

Known throughout Texas as "Mrs. Democrat," Minnie Cunningham grew up in a liberal household; her mother once commented that the freedom of the slaves took the white race out of bondage. Influenced by **Annette Finnegan**, one of the founders of the suffrage movement in Texas, Cunningham became president of the Galveston Equal Suffrage Association and began touring the state as a speaker.

In 1915, Cunningham replaced Finnegan as president of the Texas Equal Suffrage Association, and was active in the impeachment proceedings of anti-suffrage governor James Ferguson. (*See Miriam A. Ferguson.*) In 1918, with the passage of a Texas suffrage bill, Cunningham registered to vote. "You'll never know how I felt when I walked out with that piece of paper," she wrote a friend. She then became involved in passing federal suffrage and served as executive secretary on the National League of Women Voters.

In 1927, Cunningham ran for the U.S. Senate, though she only carried her home county in the primary. In 1944, at age 62, she ran in the primary for governor of Texas, challenging the views of the seated Democratic governor Coke Stevenson. Though defeated by a ratio of two-to-one, "her ability to carry the progressive banner through the gubernatorial race," wrote Crawford and Ragsdale, "and her headline-worthy speeches gave the liberal movement in Texas decided gains in their fight against the mounting conservative domination of state politics."

SOURCES:

Crawford, Ann Fears, and Crystal Sasse Ragsdale. *Women of Texas*. Austin, TX: State House Press, 1992.

Cuppi or Cupis, Marie-Anne de (1710–1770).

See Camargo, Marie-Anne Cupis de.

Curie, Éve (b. 1904)

French journalist who traveled more than 40,000 miles covering Allied action during World War II and wrote a prize-winning biography of her mother, famed scientist Marie Curie. Name variations: Eve. Born Éve Denise Curie in Paris, France, on December 6, 1904; daughter of Pierre and Marie (Sklodowska) Curie, both Nobel Prize-winning scientists; sister of Irène Joliot-Curie (1897–1956); received education by childhood governesses and a private school established by her mother for children of Sorbonne professors; graduated from Collège Sevigné; married Henry Labouisse (an American diplomat), on November 19, 1954; no children.

Had brief career as a concert pianist, then writer and critic of music, movies, and books for several French newspapers and journals; wrote biography of her mother, which won the American National Book Award for nonfiction (1937); awarded the Polonia Restitua and Chevalier de la Legion d'Honneur for the book (1939); forced from France by the Nazi invasion, joining the Free French in London (1940); began travel as a journalist to Allied battlefields around the world (1941); published widely acclaimed writings from the military front (1943); awarded the croix de guerre for her wartime service to France (1944); was co-publisher of Paris-Presse (1945–49); made seven lecture tours to the U.S. (1939–49); served as special adviser to the secretary general of the North Atlantic Treaty Organization (1952–54); posted in Beirut, Caracas, and other cities with her husband. Publications: Madame Curie (Doubleday, 1939); Journey Among Warriors (Doubleday, 1943).

Near the small Russian village of Mozhaisk, the temperature was 47° below zero as a car crept across the snowswept landscape amid gunfire and bursting shells. When it came to a stop, Éve Curie, the first Western reporter to reach the battlefield, emerged and carefully picked her way forward to avoid land mines, in order to inspect German tanks standing still in their tracks. The corpses of hundreds and hundreds of Germans, their uniforms stiff with frozen blood, littered the landscape, mingling with dead horses and shattered weapons. Careful not to touch bodies that might be booby-trapped, she noted that the soldiers' thin uniforms were no protection against the bitter Russian winter. Back in the car, she

Éve Curie

moved on past burned-out villages and listened to Russian peasants tell about the 200 members of their village who had been rounded up by the soldiers and then dynamited inside the church. All around lay death, horror, and destruction; yet this was the scene of a great victory. For here at the village of Mozhaisk, the Soviet troops had stopped Hitler's armies in what would prove to be the turning point of World War II. When Éve Curie relayed news of the battle to the outside world, she was telling the Allies that Hitler's doom was ultimately sealed.

The upbringing of Éve Curie would hardly seem to have prepared her for this job. She had grown up surrounded by the insulated world of scientific research, the daughter of the famous scientists Pierre and *Marie Curie. One year before Éve's birth, the Curies became world famous when they were awarded the Nobel Prize for their discovery of the radioactive element, radium. Born on December 6, 1904, Éve never really knew her father, who died in a traffic accident on April 19, 1906. Marie Curie had grown up in Poland in an academic family of slender means, and she kept her household uncomplicated so that maintenance would not rob her of time for her scientific research. Éve and her older sister, *Irène (Joliot-Curie), were brought up largely by their paternal grandfather, Dr. Eugène Curie, and a succession of governesses. Since the governesses were usually from Poland, the girls were fluent in French, Polish, and English and also excelled in science and mathematics. Because their mother believed women should be physically fit, they got daily exercise, especially in performing gymnastics, and both brought home prizes for their gymnastic achievements.

As a child, Éve did not know her mother well. "My mother was terribly occupied by her work and her lectures," wrote Éve; "my father had just died, and she had to carry a crushing load. It was not until my adolescence, and towards the end of her life that an intimacy grew up between us which enabled me to understand the grandeur, and the simplicity, of her character." Éve was very different from the Curies, whose lives were dominated by academic pursuits. Irène, seven years older than Éve, was shy, scholarly, and very much like her parents. Marie Curie and Irène never troubled about their appearance or surroundings; Éve, on the other hand, was born with a sense of style. She loved fashionable clothes and tasteful surroundings, and enjoyed discussing literature and the events of the day. But on holidays the three bicycled, swam and hiked together, and the mother encouraged a spirit of intellectual and physical independence in her younger daughter that allowed Éve to pursue her own interests with self-confidence.

> She would not be the daughter of Marie [Curie] if she did not have an open and compassionate heart.
>
> —Henry C. Wolfe

After attaining her degree at the Collège Sevigné, Éve Curie performed in France and Belgium as a concert pianist, then turned to writing as a music, theater, and movie critic for various French newspapers and periodicals. Once she earned her own income, she began to enjoy late nights out in Paris. In contrast to her mother and sister, who hated being in the public eye, Éve enjoyed the parties, banquets, and travel associated with fame, and was sometimes cast as Marie Curie's representative in public. Éve also took increasing care of her mother as Marie Curie's health began to be eroded by her years of exposure to radiation. Irène, now a physicist, took over her mother's work at the Radium Institute and was appointed director in 1932. Meanwhile, Éve stayed at her mother's side as she became progressively weaker. She was with her mother when she died on July 4, 1934.

Several publishers encouraged Éve to write her mother's biography, but she was not sure she was capable of the task. When she approached André Maurois for advice, he encouraged her to get on with the job. The manuscript was completed in two years. Extremely well written, the book became a classic of its kind. Documenting the difficulties of a young Polish woman determined to pursue a career in science, it describes the mutual love and respect Marie shared with Pierre Curie, as well as the poverty, interminable work, and fatigue they endured in their quest for the elusive radioactive element, radium. *Madame Curie* reads like a novel but is also scientifically meticulous. It won the National Book Award for nonfiction in the United States in 1937 and became a worldwide bestseller.

Two years after Irène and her husband were awarded a Nobel Prize in chemistry, Éve had established outstanding credentials in a very different field. Between 1939 and 1949, she made seven U.S. lecture tours. Easily mistaken for a model, she was pursued by journalists and appeared on the cover of *Independent Woman* and in magazines like *Vogue*. In 1939, her biography was awarded the Clement Cleveland Medal and the Polonia Restituta medal, and she was made a Chevalier de la Legion d'Honneur.

In 1939, however, war clouds loomed over Europe. After the German invasion of Poland in September, Éve wrote many articles begging the nations of Europe to come to the aid of her mother's homeland. She was appointed director of women's activities for the Ministry of Information to rally French women in defense of their country, but crisis followed crisis, and, in May 1940, Germany invaded France. While Irène Joliot-Curie was considered a scientific asset to the German Reich and initially offered semi-official protection that was later withdrawn, Éve was regarded as a threat to the Nazis and fled to Spain in fear for her life. Boarding a crowded ship for England, she was forced to sleep in a chair on deck and watch as German planes dive bombed the ship. On her arrival in Britain, she learned that she had been deprived of her French citizenship by the German puppet Vichy government controlling France, and her biography of her mother was on the list of books to be burned.

From fashionable figure to stateless refugee, Éve Curie embarked after a few months on a 40,000-mile journey as a combat reporter covering the action of Allied troops. In November 1941, she boarded a transatlantic clipper in New York for the first leg of the trip that eventually carried her from Brazil to Nigeria, Cairo and the

Libyan front, then Alexandria, Beirut, Damascus, Teheran, Kuibyshev, Moscow, Mozhaisk and back to Iran, then to Mandalay and Rangoon, up to Chunking and Chentu in China, and back to India, with stops in Calcutta and New Delhi. Her travels encompassed steamy jungles and subarctic battlefields, and the conditions were often appalling. Suffering malaria in Cairo and frostbite in Russia, she kept sending out her firsthand reports, and while it was true that her mother's name often allowed her access to the famous, there were also times she was the only one on the scene because she went where few dared to venture. Whether interviewing Chiang Kai-shek, Charles de Gaulle, Mohandas Gandhi, or German prisoners of war, she was a master of the art of storytelling, and exacting in all details. In 1943, her journalistic accounts were compiled in a book, *Journey Among Warriors*, gaining her even wider recognition. One critic wrote, "It is one of those rare reports on the war that keep you riveted to the sentence you are reading, fearful that you may miss a word, while at the same time straining to get on to the fascinating chapters that must lie ahead."

Returning eventually to Britain, Curie took up what she described as "the banal, unheroic, unglorious, unthrilling work which is the part of women in wars." Donning the khaki uniform of a private, she joined General Charles de Gaulle's Voluntaires Françaises (Fighting French Women's Corps), following a path similar to that of her mother, who drove an ambulance in World War I. In Éve's job there were no barracks at first, so she slept on a mattress on the floor of an empty house, which she and the other women transformed bit by bit into a headquarters.

In 1944, Curie was awarded France's medal, the croix de guerre, for her wartime service to her country. After the liberation, she returned to Paris and became co-publisher of the *Paris-Presse* from 1945 to 1949, while continuing to lecture worldwide. From 1952 to 1954, she was special adviser to the secretary general of the North Atlantic Treaty Organization. At age 50, she married Henry Labouisse, a widower and native of New Orleans, who was an official of the U.S. State Department and the United Nations. The couple moved to Beirut, where Henry directed the U.N. Relief and Works Agency for Palestine Refugees, a job complicated by negotiations between Israelis and Palestinians. Labouisse was highly regarded for his diplomacy, and the couple later moved to Venezuela, where he was chief of the Economic Survey and Development, before heading President John Kennedy's task force on foreign aid. In 1979, he oversaw UNICEF's relief efforts in Cambodia. Happily married, Curie enjoyed her life out of the limelight and the stepdaughter and grandson she had gained. "The only thing that matters to me is for us to live well—and together," she said. From time to time, she would reappear publicly, featured in a magazine as elegant and ever wise.

After the death of her husband in 1987, Curie continued to live in New York, as America had become her adopted country. Many children of famous parents flounder, but Éve Curie had become all her mother could have desired. If anything, her mother's shadow seemed an inspiration to her daughter.

SOURCES:

Avery, Marjorie. "Pvt. Eve Curie Sounds a Call," in *The New York Times Magazine*. November 28, 1943, pp. 14, 41.

Curie, Éve, Phillip Barrès, and Raoul de Roussy De Sales, eds. *Journey Among Warriors*. NY: Doubleday, 1943.

———. *Madame Curie*. NY: Doubleday, 1939.

———. *They Speak for a Nation: Letters from France*. NY: Doubleday, 1941.

Curie, Marie. *Pierre Curie*. NY: Macmillan, 1923.

Duffield, Marcus. "The Same World Only Different," in *Commonweal*. June 4, 1943, p. 173.

"Eve Curie Now," in *Vogue*. Vol. 138. August 15, 1961, pp. 92–93.

"Eve Curie Punished for Opposing Vichy," in *The New York Times*. May 4, 1941, p. 32.

Fadiman, Clifton. "Mlle. Curie Sees the World," in *The New Yorker*. May 8, 1943, pp. 81–82.

Giroud, Françoise. *Marie Curie: A Life*. NY: Holmes and Meier, 1986.

"In Exile," in *The New York Times*. June 23, 1940, sec. IV, p. 2.

Maurois, André. "Mademoiselle Eve Curie," in *Vogue*. Vol. 91. April 15, 1938, pp. 74–77, 172.

Pace, Eric. "Henry R. Labouisse Dies; Former Chief of Unicef," in *The New York Times*. March 27, 1987, sec. IV, p. 18.

"This Month's Cover—A Curie Carries On," in *Independent Woman*. Vol. 18, no. 5. May 1939.

Wolfe, Henry C. "The Compassionate Voyager," in *Saturday Review of Literature*. Vol 26, no. 19. May 8, 1943, p. 7.

Karin Haag, freelance writer, Athens, Georgia

Curie, Irène (1897–1956).

See Joliot-Curie, Irène.

Curie, Marie (1867–1934)

Polish-born research scientist and discoverer of the element radium, the first woman to win a Nobel prize and the first person to win a second Nobel, who ranks with Albert Einstein in scientific influence and achievement during the 20th century. Name varia-

tions: Madame Curie; Marie Sklodowska or Sklodovska. Born Marya or Manya Sklodowska in Warsaw, Poland, on November 7, 1867; died of leukemia on July 4, 1934, in Saint-Gervais, France; daughter of Wladyslaw Sklodowski (a high school physics teacher) and Bronislava or Bronislawa Sklodowska (director of a girls' school); educated at a Gymnasium in Warsaw and father's laboratory; began university study at the Sorbonne at age 24; married Pierre Curie (a physicist), on July 26, 1895, in Sceaux, France; children: Irène Joliot-Curie (1897–1956); Éve Curie (b. 1904).

Moved to Paris to attend the Sorbonne (1891); awarded First for master's examination for physics (1893); awarded Second for master's examination in mathematics (1894); began work on dissertation (1894); announced the possibility of a new radioactive element (1898); awarded Bertholet Medal of the French Academy of Sciences (1902); awarded Davy Medal of the Royal Society of London (1903); shared the Nobel Prize for physics with husband Pierre and Henri Becquerel (1903); received Elliott Cresson Medal of the Franklin Institute (1909); husband Pierre killed in traffic accident (1906); awarded second Nobel Prize, for chemistry, for isolation of metallic radium (1911); developed medical use of X-ray technology on the wounded of WWI (1914–18); visited the U.S. and met President Warren G. Harding (1921); made second trip to U.S. and was guest of President Herbert Hoover and Lou Henry Hoover (1929); was a member of 85 scientific societies throughout the world; was a member of the French Academy of Medicine; received 20 honorary degrees; served 12 years on the International Commission on Intellectual Cooperation of the League of Nations; enshrined in France's Pantheon (1995).

The idea of choosing between family life and the scientific career did not even cross Marie's mind. She was resolved to face love, maternity and science, all three, and to cheat none of them.

—Éve Curie

In 1902, Marie Sklodowska Curie and her husband Pierre returned one night to their darkened laboratory and discovered tiny glass containers glowing on the shelves. In the glimmering vials, the Curies instantly recognized the success of their long and arduous research, "the mysterious source of radiation . . . radium—their radium." For four years, the couple had been engaged in the exhausting labor of extracting and isolating their new discovery from huge quantities of clumsy pitchblende ore; while there had

been times when Pierre had believed the struggle was not worth the time and effort, Marie had always refused to stop. That night, as aware as they were of their awesome achievement, neither could have realized its full ramifications.

Marya, or Manya, as she had been called in her native Poland, was born in Warsaw on November 7, 1867, the youngest of the five children of Wladyslaw Sklodowski and Bronislawa Sklodowska. Her father was a high school teacher of physics, her mother the director of a girls' school, and she had three sisters—Zosia, Bronislava, and Helena—and a brother Jozef. The family lived under the harsh conditions of Russian control. Once an independent nation, Poland had been carved into three parts under the rule of Germany, Austria, and Russia since the late 18th century, and in Warsaw the Russians made regular inspections of the schools to guarantee that the Polish language was not being taught. Because of the strict Russian edicts, Wladyslaw Sklodowski was harassed, then demoted. After his salary was reduced, the family had to move to poorer lodgings, where they took in boarders to make ends meet. But the parents of the curly-haired little girl valued academic achievement, and her fascination with the mineral specimens, electroscope, tubes, scales, and other instruments of her father's workroom were taken for granted.

In 1873, Marie's oldest sister Zosia died of typhus contracted from a boarder; two years later, her mother died of tuberculosis, but Marie remained an excellent student, following the success of her sister Bronya and her brother Jozef in winning a gold medal for academic achievement at the gymnasium, or secondary school. In the Russian Empire, however, women were not admitted to universities, and there was no hope of her attending university in Warsaw. Following her graduation, she spent a year with relatives in the country, a period of happy memories she would recall throughout her life. One vivid recollection was of a *kulig*, or all-night carnival and fancy dress ball, for which Marie disguised herself as a peasant and danced all night, followed by a wild sleigh ride home. At the end of the year, she returned to her father's house in Warsaw, planning to support herself by giving private lessons and to join the "floating university" where sympathetic teachers gave private instruction to gifted individuals. Marie and Bronya also became active in underground political movements bent on reform and freeing the Polish people from Russian rule.

Longing to go to Paris, where being a woman did not hinder attendance at the univer-

Marie
Curie

sity, Marie and her sister Bronya hit upon a plan. Marie would work as a governess to help pay for Bronya's studies to become a doctor, and, once Bronya had her degree, she would help to pay for Marie's turn at studies. Eventually Marie landed a good position with a family on a dis- tant country estate in Szczuke, and became both teacher and friend to the family's eldest daugh- ter, Bronka. The two taught illiterate children in the village, and Marie found time to continue her studies in physics and mathematics on her own. She also fell in love, but the romance ended when the parents of the young man opposed the marriage. For three years, Marie stayed on, earning the money to support Bronya's studies, until her sister was at last a doctor, and it was Marie's turn.

In November 1891, at age 24, Marie Sklodowska reached Paris and enrolled at the Faculty of Science at the Sorbonne. Finding great gaps in her knowledge of mathematics and physics, she was nevertheless stubborn, persistent, and obsessed with perfection. In 1893, she passed First in the master's examination in physics and, in 1894, passed Second in mathematics, a feat made all the more remarkable by the fact that she was mastering the French language at the same time. Her work was so demanding that she had given up any thought of marriage, but in January 1894, a Polish professor, Joseph Kowalski, was in Paris on his honeymoon and introduced her to Pierre Curie, already recognized as a physicist of note at the youthful age of 35. Working in the School of Physics and Chemistry at the Sorbonne, Pierre was in the process of developing new equipment that would eventually be essential in all physics laboratories, as well as experimenting with problems of crystallography. He and his brother Jacques had discovered the phenomenon of piezoelectricity and had invented the piezoelectric quartz balance, an apparatus for making precise measurements of small quantities of electricity. The night they met, Marie Sklodowska and Pierre Curie became deeply involved in a discussion about quartz crystals, the first of many, and their ensuing courtship was carried out in true scientific style: Pierre's first gift to Marie was a copy of his pamphlet, "On Symmetry in Phenomena: Symmetry of an Electric Field and of a Magnetic Field." When he asked her to marry him, Marie declined, on the grounds that Poles should not abandon their country when it was struggling against Russian tyranny. In 1895, Pierre successfully defended his doctoral thesis and once more urged Marie to marry him. Finally she consented, and the wedding took place in the city hall of the Parisian suburb of Sceaux, on July 26, 1895.

The couple settled in a Paris apartment, and Marie found work in the laboratory of the Sorbonne's School of Physics, still determined to complete her doctorate. Two years later, she was pregnant when the couple set out on a long bicycle trip, which was cut short by the birth of their daughter *Irène (Joliot-Curie), delivered by Pierre's father, Dr. Eugène Curie. After the birth, Marie returned to work on her dissertation, de-

ciding to further her study of the experiments previously done by Henri Becquerel on X-rays, which seemed to indicate a new type of radiation. To investigate the nature and origin of radiation, she chose to work with uranium, and the School of Physics offered a glassed-in storeroom on the ground floor where she could conduct her experiments.

Steaming in summer and freezing in winter, the room had many drawbacks as a laboratory, but Curie equipped it with the instruments designed by her husband for making precise electric measurements and set to work. The Curie electrometer, ionization chamber, and the piezoelectric quartz balance, all invented by Pierre and his brother, were critical to her success.

In follow-up to Becquerel, who had observed that uranium compounds cause air to conduct electricity, Curie measured the conductivity of air around other compounds and gradually became convinced that radiation was an atomic property. To test whether it occurred elsewhere, she examined every other known element, in compounds as well as the pure state, and discovered that compounds of thorium also emitted rays like those in uranium. This led to the more remarkable discovery that a mineral ore called pitchblende emitted more Becquerel radiation than the compounds of either uranium or thorium, and Curie began to suspect that the powerful radioactive substance might be an element hitherto unknown. On April 12, 1898, in a preliminary note to the Academy of Sciences, she made her scientifically stunning announcement about the possibility of a powerful new radioactive element, present in ordinary pitchblende. The Atomic Age was born.

At this point, Pierre entered into a formal collaboration with his wife. The couple speculated that radioactivity in pitchblende was probably caused by the presence of two new elements, one of which they called radium, and the other of which Marie named polonium after her homeland. Although the discovery drew considerable scientific attention, the couple knew that the existence of the two materials would not be proved until they obtained samples in pure form.

To extract even small amounts of the elements took huge quantities of crude ore. The Austrian government offered a ton of residue ore from the St. Joachimsthal mines in Bohemia if the Curies would pay the transportation costs. A ton of the material eventually arrived in enormous coarse sacks, and the backbreaking work began. For four years, while Pierre worked on identifying the properties of radium, his wife smelted the ore for study in its pure state. There were times when Pierre, believing they had invested too much time and effort, prodded Marie to give up the task, but she refused, continuing the work of purification and concentration. Finally, by 1902, Marie had obtained a decigram of the pure element, about enough to fill the tip of a teaspoon, and calculated its atomic weight to be 225. (Subsequently she isolated a few milligrams of polonium, a highly unstable element that would never prove to be as important as radium.)

In the couple's home, meanwhile, Pierre's father had become special teacher and friend to their daughter Irène. In 1900, since Pierre's salary did not support the family, Marie had also taken a job as a lecturer in physics at the Girls' Normal School in Sèvres, combining long hours in the laboratory with a long commute on a slow train, while still working on her doctoral dissertation. In June 1903, she passed her doctoral examination, with what might well be the most astounding scientific dissertation ever submitted, entitled "Researches on Radioactive Substances." In August of that year, the Curies' second child was born prematurely and died. Of these years of great difficulties and discovery, Marie later wrote, "We had no money, no laboratory, and no help. . . . And yet . . . the best and happiest years of our lives were spent, entirely consecrated to work."

In November 1903, the Curies were awarded the Nobel Prize for Physics, and Marie Curie became the first woman to receive the honor. Thanks to the prize money, the family could finally live in some comfort, but the couple renounced all material profit from their discovery, believing it should be shared with the world. In October 1904, Pierre was appointed professor of physics at the Sorbonne, and a month later Marie was appointed superintendent of his laboratory; that December, she gave birth to their daughter *Éve Curie. Of this period, Marie wrote she had found, "all I could have dreamed at the moment of our union and more." A mere two years later, in April 1906, tragedy struck

From the movie Madame Curie, starring Greer Garson.

when Pierre was killed in a traffic accident, leaving Marie with two young children to support. Though devastated, Curie refused a pension from the Ministry of Public Education because she wanted to continue her research work. Appointed to fill Pierre's chair of physics, she became the first woman professor at the Sorbonne.

For several years, Curie continued her efforts to isolate the pure, uncombined element of metallic radium. In 1910, with the assistance of André Debierne, she succeeded, and the following year she became the first recipient of two Nobels, this time in chemistry. At the deeply conservative and all-male French Academy of Sciences, however, the honor of membership was withheld. Pierre had been elected to the institution a year before his death, but the submission of his wife's name resulted in months of bitter wrangling. Her admittance was denied, finally, by one vote. Ignoring the slight, Curie continued her work, and in 1914 the University of Paris and the Pasteur Institute jointly established the Radium Institute, with Marie Curie as director of the research division.

That year also saw the outbreak of World War I, causing Curie to turn her research to practical wartime use. Demonstrating how radiology could be used to locate shrapnel fragments in battlefield wounds, Curie oversaw the design and equipment of 20 radiological cars, nicknamed "Little Curies," which followed the troops, and 200 radiological rooms, fixed and mobile posts, where more than a million wounded men received X-rays in the course of the war. Devoted to the war effort, Curie made many visits to the battlefront to supervise medical use of radiology, often accompanied by her daughter, Irène. She also used the money from her second Nobel Prize to purchase war bonds and offered her medals to be melted down, but this sacrifice was refused by the Bank of France.

In 1918, at the end of World War I, Curie saw Poland reinstated as a nation, a moment she considered one of the high points in her life. Now called Madame Curie, she was at the height of her fame, known throughout the world. In 1921, she traveled with her daughters to the United States to receive a gram of radium to continue her research. While there, she attended a huge gathering of the American Association of University Women at Carnegie Hall in New York and received honorary degrees from many American institutions. In 1923, she wrote a biography of her husband Pierre, and in 1925 she fulfilled a longstanding dream when she traveled to Warsaw to lay the cornerstone for an institute for radium research in her homeland. In 1929, she returned to the United States to receive more funding and was a guest at the White House at the invitation of President Henry Hoover and First Lady *Lou Henry Hoover.

Curie's daughters brought her great joy. Irène followed in her mother's footsteps, obtaining her Ph.D. with a thesis on polonium, and worked at the Radium Institute. She married an assistant in her mother's laboratory, Frédéric Joliot, and in 1935 the Joliot-Curies received a Nobel Prize. Her second daughter Éve became an internationally acclaimed journalist and wrote a biography of her mother, cited by the American Library Association as the best nonfiction book for 1937.

Ironically, the discovery that made Marie Curie famous also eroded her health and resulted in her death. At a time when no one realized the dangers of radioactivity, she was constantly and repeatedly exposed to materials in huge doses. Even now, her notebooks, desk, and laboratory equipment are highly radioactive and will be for hundreds of years to come. In later years, the exposure caused Madame Curie to suffer fatigue and increasing blindness due to cataracts, and her hands were pitted from handling the element. On July 4, 1934, with her daughters at her side, she succumbed to leukemia; she was buried at her husband's side.

Over 60 years later, in April 1995, the French government officially recognized the work of one of their most brilliant scientists. In one of his last acts, outgoing president François Mitterand announced that the ashes of Marie Curie and her husband Pierre would be carried in wood coffins from a small-town cemetery to the Pantheon, to be enshrined as the 70th and 71st immortals so honored there. Though one other woman, **Sophie Bertholet**, rests in the Pantheon alongside her husband, renowned chemist Marcellin Bertholet, Marie Curie was "the first lady in our history," noted Mitterand, "honored for her own merits." Throughout its history, the Pantheon has been known as the home of the nation's "great men."

Marie Curie's discovery of radium launched the Atomic Age, which has brought both good and evil. Today, no one could conceive of medicine without X-rays and many other techniques made possible by her work. But the destructive nature of radiation, which she also grew to understand, brought grave dangers to the human race. Her hope was always that humanity would choose the good and shun the evil—a choice humans are now continually forced to confront.

SOURCES:

Curie, Éve. *Madame Curie*. NY: Doubleday, Doran, 1939.

Curie, Marie. *Pierre Curie*. NY: Macmillan, 1923.

Giroud, Françoise. *Marie Curie: A Life*. NY: Holmes and Meier, 1986.

Opfell, Olga S. *The Lady Laureates: Women Who Have Won the Nobel Prize*. 2nd ed. Metuchen, NJ: Scarecrow Press, 1986.

Pflaum, Rosalynd. *Grand Obsession: Marie Curie and Her World*. NY: Doubleday, 1989.

Reid, Robert W. *Marie Curie*. NY: Collins, 1974.

Karin Haag, freelance writer, Athens, Georgia

Curry, Denise (1959—)

American basketball player who, in the mid-1980s, held the record for the most points in a single game. Born in Davis, California, on August 22, 1959; attended University of California at Los Angeles.

Although some were quicker, stronger, or jumped higher than Denise Curry, she was known as a universal player, effective in any position, who outshone her fellow athletes overall. No player who came before her in UCLA basketball history, male or female, had more points than Curry. She qualified for the 1980 Olympic team, but the United States boycotted the games when the former Soviet Union invaded Afghanistan. Curry joined the U.S. national team playing on its East European tour in 1982; the team upset the Soviet Union 85–83 that year. As opportunities for women to play basketball once they left college were extremely limited, Curry played for a West German club in 1983. The following year, she finally made it to the Los Angeles Olympics, and her basketball team won the gold. During her career, Curry scored 3,198 points. In the mid-1980s, she held the record for the most points in a single game at 47.

Karin Loewen Haag, Athens, Georgia

Curtis, Ann (1926—)

American swimmer. Name variations: Ann Curtis Cuneo. Born Ann Elisabeth Curtis in Rio Vista, California, on March 6, 1926; daughter of Florence Gertrude (Donohue) and Marvin Curtis, Jr.; married Gordon Cuneo (a basketball star), in 1949; children: four.

First woman to swim 100 yards in less than a minute (59.4 seconds); set four world freestyle records and 18 American records; won 31 national championships; won a gold in the 400 meter, a gold medal in the relay, and a silver in the 100 meter in the 1948 London Olympics; first woman to win the James E. Sullivan Memorial Trophy.

When Ann Curtis first entered the 1943 AAU girls' freestyle, no one took much notice of the 11-year-old swimmer. Taught to swim at the Sisters of the Ursuline Convent in Santa Rosa, she had not had professional coaching. But the young Curtis surprised everyone by winning the race, in the first of what would be many triumphs.

Charlie Sava, the famous West Coast coach of champion swimmers, invited Curtis to train with him at his Crystal Plunge pool. The regimen was tough—three miles of swimming each day with no time off on Sundays. To develop her leg power, he threaded a rope through a pulley above the pool; one end of the rope was lashed to her ankles, the other to a nine-pound weight. For 30 minutes each day, she kicked against this restraint, cutting through the water without using her hands. Two months later, Sava felt she was ready for competitive swimming.

At 17, Curtis won her first national championship in Shakamak Park, Indiana, setting records in both the 400- and 880-yard freestyle. She continued to shatter national records in the next 11 consecutive meets she entered. In 1944, a year after winning her first national championship, Curtis won the James E. Sullivan Memorial Trophy, the first woman to do so.

In subsequent years, she continued to set records—4 world freestyle and 18 American. With a 59.4 time, Curtis became the first woman to swim 100 yards in less than a minute. She won 31 national championships. In the 1948 Olympics in London, she won a gold in the 400 meter, a second gold in the relay (setting a new Olympic record of 4:29.2), and a silver in the 100 meter.

After Ann Curtis retired from swimming competition in 1949, she married Gordon Cuneo, a basketball star, and had four children. Founder of her own swim club, Curtis taught a new generation the many skills she acquired during her career, including what came to be known as the "Curtis crawl."

Karin L. Haag, Athens, Georgia

See illustration on the following page

Curtis, Doris Malkin (1914–1991)

American geologist. Born on January 12, 1914, in Brooklyn, New York; died on May 26, 1991, in Houston, Texas; Brooklyn College, B.S., Columbia University, Ph.D.

In an age when comparatively few women made careers in the sciences, Doris Malkin Cur-

Ann Curtis

tis rose in the field of geology to become the first woman president of the Geological Society of America, an organization of 17,000 members. She spent the majority of her career as a geologist exploring for Shell Oil Company, where she worked from 1942 to 1979. The late 1970s en-

ergy crisis made the need for oil exploration more apparent, and in 1979 Curtis opened her own consulting firm. She was a teacher at Houston's Rice University, president of the Society of Economic Paleontologists and Mineralogists, and the first woman president of the American

Geological Institute (a federation of societies in earth sciences founded in 1848). In 1990, Curtis took her post as president of the Geological Society of America. She died in 1991 during her term, age 77.

Curtis, Harriot and Peggy

American golfers and tennis players.

Harriot Curtis (1881–1974). Born Harriot S. Curtis on June 30, 1881, in Manchester-by-the-Sea, Massachusetts; died on October 25, 1974, in Manchester-by-the-Sea.

> *Won the USGA Women's Championship (1906).*

Peggy Curtis (1883–1965). Name variations: Margaret Curtis. Born Margaret B. Curtis on October 8, 1883, in Manchester-by-the-Sea, Massachusetts; died in Boston on December 24, 1965.

> *Runner-up in the U.S. Women's Amateur Championship (1900 and 1905) and winner (1907, 1911, 1912); with Evelyn Sears, won the National Women's doubles title in tennis (1908); received USGA's Bobby Jones Award for "sportsmanship"; was one of the first to be inducted in the Women's Golf Hall of Fame (1951).*

The sisters Curtis played significant roles in chipping women's golf out of its sandtrap. Peggy Curtis, who could belt a brassie farther than many of her male counterparts, was two-time runner-up in the U.S. Women's Amateur Championship. In 1907, she finally took the title by defeating the defending champion, her older sister Harriot, in the finals. In 1908, Peggy Curtis crossed over for a game of tennis, winning the National Women's doubles title with **Evelyn Sears.**

Along with several other top players, the Curtis sisters sailed to England in 1905 to play an informal team match and take part in the British Ladies' Championship, the first American women to take on the British opposition. They had hoped to establish an international competition, but another 25 years passed before the idea was resurrected. Then nearing middle age, the Curtises donated a trophy, thus beginning the Curtis Cup. The first match officially took place at Wentworth, Surrey, in 1932, with the Americans winning five matches to two. Since then, the Cup has been awarded every other year (excluding the World War II years).

During World War I, Peggy, known as a large, competitive woman who was oblivious to fashion, immersed herself in Red Cross Work and established food clinics for children in the war-torn countries of Europe. She died in Boston

Peggy Curtis

in 1965. Harriot was a civil-rights activist, dean of women at Hampton Institute in 1927, and, for many years, secretary of the New England United Negro College Fund campaign. At age 93, she died in Manchester-by-the-Sea in the same room in which she had been born.

Curtis, Margaret (1883–1965).
> *See Curtis, Harriot and Peggy.*

Curtis, Nell (1824–1898).
> *See Demorest, Ellen Curtis.*

Curzon, Grace Hinds.
> *See Glyn, Elinor for sidebar.*

Curzon, Irene (1896–1966).
> *See Curzon, Mary for sidebar.*

Curzon, Mary Leiter (1870–1906)

Vicereine of India. Name variations: Baroness Curzon of Kedleston. Born Mary Victoria Leiter in Chicago,

burn to the ground once more in 1877. Even so, Mary grew up in luxury, for the family was exceedingly rich. They lived in a Chicago townhouse, as well as a $500,000 mansion, Linden Lodge, on Wisconsin's Lake Geneva, where they moored their steam-yacht *Daisy*. They socialized with the Fields and Mr. and Mrs. Potter Palmer (*Bertha Honoré Palmer).

In 1881, Levi Leiter split with Marshall Field. That same year, the Leiters moved to Washington D.C. and settled into the majestic Blaine house on Dupont Circle. Mary grew up to be a slender, 5'8", appealing debutante. She could boast a friendship with many of the city's elite, including Henry and *Clover Adams. The 18-year-old Mary was also a firm friend of first lady *Frances Folsom Cleveland, then only 23.

In 1890, Mary met George Curzon, then a Member of Parliament, at a ball in London; they were married in 1895. That same year, Lord Curzon was made undersecretary of state for Foreign Affairs. Three years later, he was named viceroy of India. The Curzons were in India for six years. Though Mary appeared fully up to the task of vicereine of India, fulfilling the role with grace and distinction, the years, three pregnancies, the stress, and the climate took a toll. By the time the couple returned to England, her health was failing; Mary Curzon died in July 1906, age 36. The *Chicago Tribune* reported in her obituary: "It was remarked that she had none of the aggressive self-confidence which, rightly or wrongly, is usually attributed to ambitious American girls, but she attracted by reserve and a thoughtful, studious manner and an engaging sympathy."

SUGGESTED READING:

Nicolson, Nigel. *Mary Curzon.* NY: Harper and Row, 1977.

Cusack, Dymphna (1902–1981)

Australian novelist and playwright whose writings have been translated for publication in 31 countries. Name variations: LND; EDC. Born Ellen Dymphna Cusack on September 22, 1902, in Wyalong, New South Wales, Australia; died in 1981; daughter of Bridget (Crowley) Cusack and James Cusack (a sheep farmer); attended St. Ursula's College, 1917–20; University of Sydney, BA (with honors), 1925, diploma of education, 1925; married Norman Freehill (a journalist and writer); no children.

Awarded the West Australian drama prizes (1942) for Morning Sacrifice and (1943) Comets Soon Pass; awarded the Playwrights' Advisory Board drama prizes (1945) for Shoulder the Sky and (1946)

Illinois, on May 27, 1870; died in London, England, on July 18, 1906; daughter of Levi Z. Leiter (a merchant and partner with Marshall Field) and Mary Theresa (Carver) Leiter (granddaughter of Judge Samuel Fish); educated by governesses, tutors, and attended the school of Madame Cléophile Burr in Washington, D.C.; married diplomat George Nathaniel Curzon (1859–1925), later marquess Curzon of Kedleston, viceroy of India, in 1895; children: ❧▸ *Irene Curzon, Baroness Ravensdale (1896–1966);* ❧▸ *Cynthia Curzon Mosley (1898–1933); and* ❧▸ *Alexandra Curzon Metcalfe (b. 1903).*

Mary Leiter Curzon was one of the most famous women of her time. The daughter of Levi Leiter, an early partner of Marshall Field, she was born in Chicago, Illinois, in 1870. Mary had one brother Joseph and two sisters, **Nancy Leiter**, who married Colin Campbell, and **Marguerite Leiter**, known as Daisy, who married the earl of Suffolk. One year after Mary's birth, the Great Fire of Chicago destroyed the emporium of Field and Leiter; the store was rebuilt only to

Stand Still Time; *received the* Sydney Daily Telegraph *novel award (1948) for* Come in Spinner; *given the Coronation Medal for services to Australian literature (1953); granted the British Arts Council Award for* The Golden Girls; *granted a Commonwealth literary fellowship, for* Southern Steel.

Selected works: Jungfrau *(1936); (with Miles Franklin)* Pioneers on Parade *(1939); (play)* Red Sky at Morning *(1942), filmed (1944); (with Florence James)* Come in Spinner *(1951);* Say No to Death *(1953);* Southern Steel *(1953);* The Sun in Exile *(1955);* Chinese Women Speak *(1958);* Heatwave in Berlin *(1961);* Picnic Races *(1962);* Holidays among the Russians *(1964);* Black Lightning *(1964); (with James)* Four Winds and a Family *(1965); (with T. Inglis Moore and Barrie Ovendeu)* Mary Gilmore: A Tribute *(1965);* Ilyria Reborn *(1966);* The Sun Is Not Enough *(1967);* The Half-Burnt Tree *(1969); (play)* The Golden Girls *(1970);* A Bough in Hell *(1971); (with husband Norman Freehill)* Dymphna Cusack *(autobiography, 1975).*

Ellen Dymphna Cusack's middle name—Celtic for singer or poet—foretold her career as a storyteller. She was born on a sheep run, near the True Blue gold mine, which her father staked and worked. Called Nell by her family, she was a sickly child and was sent to the preferable climate of Coom, Narrandera, to live with her namesake, her aunt **Ellen Leahy.**

Cusack enrolled at St. Ursula's convent school in Armindale and was often asked to lead the lower grades when a teacher was absent; the experience fostered her fondness for education. By accepting a scholarship to the University of Sydney, she was committed to teaching at least five years in the public schools; she began as an English and history teacher at Neutral Bay High School and gave nearly 20 years of service. Her retirement in 1944 was largely due to poor health, though her leaving was expedited by her candid remarks about the Department of Education's sexist treatment of the faculty. *A Window in the Dark,* edited by **Debra Adelaide** and published in 1991, contains Cusack's writings on her teaching career, but it reveals little personal information about the intensely private author.

Dymphna Cusack began publishing while she was still teaching. Neuralgia forced her to dictate the first draft of her work, which was then typed and returned for editing and rewriting. Known as a progressive, her many books dealt with social injustice. Cusack, a lifelong member of Australia's Communist Party, died in 1981. Her manuscripts are held at the National Library of Australia.

Curzon, Irene (1896–1966)

Baroness Ravensdale. Born January 20, 1896; died in 1966; daughter of *Mary Leiter Curzon (1870–1906) and Lord George Curzon (1859–1925, a diplomat); never married; no children.

Irene Curzon, who inherited her father's secondary title Baroness Ravensdale, never married. She devoted her days to women's rights, social causes, music, and travel.

Mosley, Cynthia (1898–1933)

English socialite. Name variations: Lady Cynthia Mosley. Born Cynthia Curzon on August 28, 1898; died in 1933; daughter of Mary Leiter Curzon (1870–1906) and Lord George Curzon (1859–1925, a diplomat); married Sir Oswald Mosley (1896–1980), 6th baronet.

Like her mother before her, Cynthia Mosley died young. She was only 35 at the time of her death in 1933. Cynthia's husband, Fascist leader Sir Oswald Mosley, would marry **Diana Mitford* in 1936 and go on to become a national pariah.

Metcalfe, Alexandra (b. 1903)

English reformer. Name variations: Lady Alexandra Metcalfe. Born Alexandra Curzon in 1903; daughter of *Mary Leiter Curzon (1870–1906) and Lord George Curzon (1859–1925, a diplomat); married Edward Dudley Metcalfe, equerry to the prince of Wales.

Lady Alexandra Metcalfe became an advocate for children's welfare throughout the world.

SOURCES:

Adelaide, Debra. "Introduction," in *A Window in the Dark.* Canberra, Australia: National Library of Australia, 1991.

Buck, Claire, ed. *The Bloomsbury Guide to Women's Literature.* NY: Prentice Hall, 1992.

RELATED MEDIA:

Caddie, based on Cusack's *Caddie, the Story of a Barmaid,* starring **Helen Morse** and Jack Thompson, directed by Donald Crombie, was filmed in 1976.

"Come in Spinner" was produced as a television series by the Australian Broadcasting Commission, 1989.

Red Sky at Morning was filmed in 1944.

Crista Martin,
Boston, Massachusetts

Cusack, Margaret Anne
(1832–1899)

Irish nun, reformer, and writer. Name variations: Sister Mary Frances Clare; the Nun of Kenmare. Born

Margaret Anne Cusack near Dublin, Ireland, in 1832; died in Warwickshire, England, in 1899.

Margaret Anne Cusack began her religious life by joining the Anglican sisterhood in London, England. She converted to Roman Catholicism in 1858, taking the religious name Sister Mary Frances Clare. From 1861 to 1884, Cusack conducted the celebrated convent of Poor Clares, which she established at Kenmare, County Kerry, and organized for the purpose of providing poor and friendless girls with an education. When in 1884 she established the Sisters of Peace, a similar order but with a wider range, not only did Leo XIII sanction the work but Cusack received the hearty support of Christians, both Catholic and Protestant. Cusack visited the United States in 1886. Embittered in later life, she reverted to Anglicanism and attacked Catholicism. Among her many published works are the *Students' History of Ireland* and *Woman's Work in Modern Society.* Cusack also published pamphlets on women, biographies of saints Patrick, Columba, and *Bridget, as well as works of fiction, such as *Ned Rusheen* (1871) and *Tim O'Halloran's Choice* (1877). Her autobiography *The Nun of Kenmare* was published in 1889, the year before her death.

Cushing Sisters

Fosburgh, Minnie Astor (1906–1978). American socialite, philanthropist. Name variations: *Mary Cushing; Minnie Astor. Born Mary Benedict Cushing on January 27, 1906; died of cancer in Manhattan on November 4, 1978; second child and first daughter of Henry Cushing (a prominent neurosurgeon) and Katherine "Kate" (Crowell) Cushing (a socialite); sister of *Betsey Cushing Roosevelt Whitney (1908–1998) and *Babe Paley (1915–1978); married Vincent Astor (b. 1891, real estate tycoon); married James Whitney Fosburgh (a painter); no children. Vincent Astor's first wife was Helen Huntington Astor (the former Helen Dinsmore), later Helen Huntington Hull.*

Paley, Babe (1915–1978). American socialite. Name variations: *Barbara Cushing; Barbara Mortimer. Born Barbara Cushing on July 5, 1915; died on July 6, 1978; fifth child and third daughter of Henry Cushing (a prominent neurosurgeon) and Katherine "Kate" (Crowell) Cushing (a socialite); sister of *Betsey Cushing Roosevelt Whitney (1908–1998) and *Minnie Astor Fosburgh (1906–1978); married Stanley Grafton Mortimer, Jr. (Standard Oil heir), on September 21, 1940 (divorced 1946); married William Paley (chair of the board of CBS television); children: Stanley Grafton*

*Mortimer III (b. 1942); **Amanda Joy Mortimer** (b. 1943); William Cushing Paley (b. 1948); **Kate Paley** (b. 1950); (stepchild by second marriage) Hilary Paley; (stepchild by second marriage) Jeffrey Paley.*

Whitney, Betsey Cushing Roosevelt (1908–1998). American socialite and philanthropist. Name variations: *Betsey Cushing; Mrs. James Roosevelt; Mrs. John Hay Whitney. Born Betsey Maria Cushing on May 18, 1908; died in Manhasset, New York, on March 25, 1998; third child and second daughter of Henry Cushing (a prominent neurosurgeon) and Katherine "Kate" (Crowell) Cushing (a socialite); sister of *Babe Paley (1915–1978) and *Minnie Astor Fosburgh (1906–1978); married James Roosevelt (eldest son of Franklin Delano and Eleanor Roosevelt), in June 1930 (divorced 1940); married John Hay (Jock) Whitney; children: Sara Roosevelt; Kate Roosevelt.*

The Cushing sisters—Minnie, Betsey, and Babe—captured the hearts and imaginations of the American public as the most glittering socialites of the mid-20th century. Known for their beauty, wealth, and glamorous marriages, they led seemingly charmed lives that represented the dream of middle-class America, and their influence on trends and fashions spanned four decades between the 1930s and the 1970s.

These three women grew up with their two brothers comfortably ensconced in the upper-middle-class society of Boston. Their father Henry Cushing held a position at Harvard and had earned a reputation as the father of modern brain surgery, while their mother **Kate Crowell Cushing** came from a socially distinguished Cleveland family. The prominence of his position and her family name kept the Cushings in wealthy society circles, despite the fact that the Depression had wiped out most of the family fortune. Kate, as the matriarch, became determined to see her daughters well-married. She groomed them from an early age on how to act as proper blue-blooded wives, and made sure that they attended the rounds of dances and coming-out parties that were critical to meeting prospective husbands. The girls' beauty and natural charm, not to mention their social standing, worked heavily in their favor.

Betsey, who was their third child and second daughter, married first, in June of 1930, choosing James Roosevelt as the groom. James was the son of the powerful political couple, *Eleanor Roosevelt and Franklin Delano Roosevelt, who were, at the time of the marriage, first lady and governor of New York. Although James brought the prestige and social prominence that Kate desired for her daughters, he was also virtually penniless with no actual prospects for financial advancement. However, his familial ties led the young couple into the White House when Franklin Delano Roosevelt ascended to the presidency and made his son a trusted advisor. The president also favored the quiet, ladylike charm of his daughter-in-law and recruited Betsey to act as White House hostess during Eleanor's frequent absences. Although she proved to be an able host, Betsey disliked the media attention associated with her position and did her best to shield her young daughters, Sara and Kate, from the public eye. But even as they rose through Washington society's ranks, Betsey's marriage to James quickly disintegrated, and they divorced in 1940.

As Betsey's marriage came to an end, her youngest sister, Babe, marched up the aisle with Stanley Grafton Mortimer, Jr., heir to the immense Standard Oil fortune, on September 21, 1940. Kate Cushing was ecstatic over the match, since not only was Stanley sure to inherit a vast fortune, he was also handsome and much admired. Kate had pinned most of her hopes for a good marriage on Babe, who was the most beautiful of the trio of girls. However, Babe had initially seemed more intent on her career as a fashion editor—working first for *Glamour* magazine and later for *Vogue*—than on finding a suitable husband. She fit comfortably in the world of fashion as one of New York's most beautiful women—a remarkable accomplishment given the fact that a 1934 car wreck had nearly destroyed her face. Although reconstructive surgery repaired the damage, it was Babe's own intelligence and charm that finished the picture of perfection as New York society celebrated the vivacious young woman. Her marriage to one of the world's most eligible bachelors seemed like a fairy-tale to the public, and the couple had two children, Stanley Grafton Mortimer III, born in 1942, and **Amanda Joy Mortimer**, born in 1943.

A mere six days after Babe's wedding, Minnie fulfilled her mother's hopes by marrying Vincent Astor. Minnie was introduced to the astronomically wealthy real estate tycoon by her sister Betsey at a White House party, and Minnie had been his longtime mistress since that time. When Vincent finally secured a divorce from his wife, **Helen Huntington Astor**, he and Minnie married three weeks later. Unfortunately, the differences between Vincent and Minnie, which had gone unnoticed during their long courtship, came glaringly to the surface after their marriage. The somber, awkward nature of the older

gentleman clashed with the gay, blithe spirit of his younger bride (although she was 35 when they married), and they were soon spending their time apart. While Vincent spent long months sailing, Minnie set up a glittering salon as a patron of the arts. Rumors existed that neither of Vincent's marriages had actually been consummated, along with hints that Minnie was a lesbian—rumors that were fueled further by the close ties she would later maintain with New York's artistic, homosexual community.

Having seen all three of her daughters enter into respectable first marriages, Kate set out to find a suitable second husband for her recently divorced daughter, Betsey, and landed on John Hay "Jock" Whitney of the staggeringly wealthy Whitney clan. He and Betsey married in 1941, and this union was to prove the most amiable of the Cushing sisters' marriages. By all accounts, the couple genuinely loved each other, and thanks to Betsey's influence, Jock deserted the playboy life he had led prior to the marriage and settled down. He developed close ties to the Republican Party and became the U.S. ambassador to England in 1957, by the appointment of President Dwight Eisenhower. The move to England delighted Betsey, an ardent Anglophile, and they became the toast of London, hosting royalty and dignitaries with elegance and simplicity. They returned to the United States when the four-year appointment ended and devoted themselves to business and philanthropic interests. Betsey kept busy through her fundraising work for the Museum of Modern Art, Yale University, and the North Shore Hospital.

Babe, the second daughter to marry, was also the second to break free of her first marriage and enter into a second union. She and Stanley Mortimer divorced in 1946, and she remarried a year later, this time to Bill Paley, the head of Columbia Broadcasting. Although as a self-made millionaire and a Jew, Paley did not qualify as a "blue-blood," his ambition was unmistakable, and Babe left her job at *Vogue* to settle down with him on an estate in New York. In addition to her children from her first marriage and his two children from his first marriage, the couple had children of their own—William Cushing Paley, born in 1948, and **Kate Paley**, born in 1950. Unfortunately, this marriage proved as unfulfilling as her first. Bill Paley's quest for power and glamour included showcasing his beautiful wife in the designer gowns that had landed her on "Best Dressed" lists for more than a decade, and she felt she was little more than a possession to him. Babe found comfort from her loveless marriage in her friendship with Truman Capote, the renowned writer and gossip, who became a fixture at all the Paley gatherings. This friendship ended when Capote published scandalous details of her life and the lives of other society women in a thinly-veiled excerpt from *Answered Prayers*, a book of fiction he was writing, which was published in *Esquire* magazine.

After a six-week illness brought on by a severe heart condition, Kate Cushing died on May 8, 1949, secure in the knowledge that her daughters had, indeed, settled into storybook marriages of wealth and prestige. However, Minnie rebelled against her mother's upbringing by divorcing Vincent Astor in 1953 and marrying James Whitney Fosburgh, a painter of modest reputation and means who was also an openly practicing homosexual. This choice of a husband—so far removed from Kate Cushing's prescribed definition of a "suitable match"—inspired no small amount of speculation as to the marriage's chances for success, but Minnie initially adored the artistic atmosphere that her painter-husband cultivated. Minnie's salons became famous for their glittering guest lists, which included such notables as composer Leonard Bernstein, playwright Tennessee Williams, and Princess *Margaret Rose of England. Minnie used her influence to benefit the arts, serving as a trustee of the Metropolitan Museum of Art and supporting struggling young artists. Later, however, the platonic relationship between Minnie and James soured as he painted less and drank more. The quality of Minnie's salons deteriorated along with the health of the two partners and their marriage; by the 1970s, both Minnie and James were dying of cancer.

Cancer struck Babe at the same time. In 1973, she became ill with pneumonia while on a whirlwind tour of China. Her doctors advised her to quit her lifelong smoking habit, but her compliance with their orders came too late to halt the growth of a malignant tumor on her right lung. The full removal of the cancerous lung in 1975 severely curtailed her activities. She died in early July of 1978, three months after the death of James Fosburgh, and four months before Minnie also succumbed to cancer. Both women left vast inheritances of jewels, stock, and other assets to family members and treasured friends. Betsey lived for another 20 years, outliving her beloved husband Jock by 16 years, before passing away in 1998 at the age of 89.

SOURCES:

Grafton, David. *The Sisters: The Lives and Times of the Fabulous Cushing Sisters*. Villard Books, 1992.

Rebecca Parks,
Detroit, Michigan

Cushman, Charlotte Saunders
(1816–1876)

American actress. Born Charlotte Saunders Cushman in Boston, Massachusetts, on July 23, 1816; died in Boston in 1876; elder daughter and the first of five children of Elkanah (a merchant in the West Indies trade) and his second wife Mary Eliza (Babbitt) Cushman.

Destined to be known as America's first great actress, Charlotte Cushman was born into a distinguished Boston family. Her father was a descendant of Robert Cushman, business manager for the group of Pilgrims who settled in Plymouth in 1620. When Charlotte was 13, her childhood ended abruptly with the failure of the family business, which forced her to leave school and take work as a domestic. Intent upon a career as an opera singer, she studied with several teachers, including James G. Maeder, music director of Boston's Tremont Theater, who arranged her first professional appearance as Countess Almaviva in *The Marriage of Figaro* (April 1835). She then joined Maeder on tour, but her voice failed to live up to its early promise. Cushman then turned to acting and made her debut as Lady Macbeth at New Orleans' St. Charles Theatre in April 1836.

Her performance led to a contract at the Bowery Theatre in New York, but a week after her first appearance the theater burned to the ground. She had better luck in her next engagement in Albany and was hired in 1837 by the Park Street Theatre in New York, where she played a variety of roles. Most notable were her portrayals of Meg Merrilees, the Gypsy fortuneteller in the popular *Guy Mannering*, a dramatization of Sir Walter Scott's Gothic novel, and Romeo, the first of the male roles that would figure so prominently in her repertoire. Early in her career, Cushman became known for the meticulous preparation of her roles. To research the character of Nancy Sykes in *Oliver Twist* (1839), she is said to have traveled to the city's Five Points region to study the speech and mannerisms of the slum dwellers and to collect pieces of tattered clothing for her costume.

In 1842, still relatively unknown, Cushman became manager of Philadelphia's Walnut Street Theatre, where she became a local favorite, in spite of fellow actor George Vandenhoff, who thought her talent was crude and "uncultivated." During the 1843–44 season, she played Lady Macbeth opposite the English Shakespearean actor William Macready, a role that would later be considered one of her finest. In

1845, Cushman went to London and enjoyed a triumphant debut at the Princess Theatre, starring as Bianca in the tragedy *Fazio*. The reviews were glowing, comparing her debut to that of Edmund Kean. Even the conservative *Times* hailed her as "a great acquisition to the London stage" and called her a worthy successor to England's legendary *Sarah Siddons. A subsequent tour of the provinces was so successful that Cushman was able to bring her family over to join her. In December 1845, after a triumphant engagement at London's Haymarket Theatre, she played the male lead in *Romeo and Juliet* op-

posite her sister **Susan Cushman,** who was said to be more beautiful than Charlotte but less talented. In 1848, Charlotte performed for Queen *Victoria, then returned to America in 1849 for a three-year tour, during which she portrayed Cardinal Wolsey in *Henry VIII* and added Hamlet to her repertoire of male roles.

In appearance, Cushman was a commanding presence; tall, with an ample figure, she had rather plain features dominated by a high forehead and piercing eyes. Her enormous physical energy and remarkable vocal versatility lent

Charlotte Saunders Cushman

themselves to her more flamboyant, tragic roles, and were especially effective in her masculine portrayals. However, even allowing for the declarative style of 19th-century acting, she was thought by some to be over the top at times (to "chew the scenery" in theatrical parlance), though her style is considered to have mellowed somewhat as her career progressed. Cushman did not excel in subtle character portrayals nor in comedy, and critics often accused her of "pointing," or concentrating her energy in a few dramatic scenes, while routinely acting the rest of the play.

*Mary Anderson, another American actress, recalled Cushman's performances of the gypsy in *Guy Mannering*, one of her signature roles: "When in the moonlight of the scene, she dashed from her tent on to the stage, covered with the gray, shadowy garments of the gypsy sibyl, her appearance was ghost-like and startling in the extreme. In her mad rushes on and off stage she was like a cyclone." Anderson went on to describe the climactic scene. "When Dick Hatterick's fatal bullet entered her body, and she came staggering down the stage, her terrible shriek, so wild and piercing, so full of agony and yet of the triumph she had given her life to gain, told the whole story of her love and her revenge."

In 1852, having shrewdly invested her earnings, Cushman announced the first of a number of retirements from the stage and returned to England. Thereafter, her American appearances were limited to several tours and a few benefit performances for the U.S. Sanitary Commission during the Civil War. From 1853 to 1870, at her house in London and winter retreat in Rome, she entertained a wide circle of expatriated artists and helped many of them advance their careers. Most accounts of the actress describe her as deeply religious (a Unitarian by upbringing) and overly solicitous, especially toward her family. Her romantic involvements appear to have been limited to a girlhood engagement and a brief love affair in 1836. Aside from some raised eyebrows over her penchant for portraying men, the public held her in high esteem. There are a few published recollections, however, that characterize her as possessive and domineering; one associate recalled that she occasionally slugged performers who particularly annoyed her.

In 1870, after an operation in Switzerland to remove a cancerous tumor, Cushman returned to the States with her close friend sculptor *Emma Stebbins and established residences in Boston, Massachusetts, and Newport, Rhode Island. She continued to perform, although ill health and constant pain forced her to abandon traditional acting in favor of dramatic readings, usually consisting of pieces from Shakespeare, Browning, and Tennyson. On November 7, 1874, Cushman gave an emotional farewell performance of Lady Macbeth in New York, which was followed by an outpouring of affection from a crowd of 25,000 well-wishers that had gathered outside her hotel. Her final performance was a reading in Easton, Pennsylvania, in 1875. Charlotte Cushman died in Boston a year later, at age 59. Funeral services were held in Boston's King's Chapel, followed by burial in Mount Auburn Cemetery in Cambridge. In 1907, as a tribute to her, the first Charlotte Cushman Club was established in Philadelphia as a hotel for traveling actresses. As late as the 1940s, other Cushman clubs continued to flourish in Boston, Chicago, and other American cities.

SUGGESTED READING:

Leach, Joseph. *Bright Particular Star*. New Haven, CT, 1970.

Waters, Clara Erskine Clement. *Mrs. Charlotte Cushman*. Boston, MA: J.R. Osgood, 1882.

Barbara Morgan,
Melrose, Massachusetts

Cushman, Pauline (1833–1893)

American actress who won fame as a Union spy in the Civil War. Name variations: Major Pauline Cushman; Pauline Cushman Fryer. Born in New Orleans, Louisiana, on June 10, 1833; died in poverty in San Francisco, California, on December 7, 1893; her father was a dry goods merchant from Spain; her mother was from France (both immigrated to U.S. in 1830s); married Charles Dickinson, in the late 1850s (died 1861); married Jere Fryer, in 1879 (divorced 1888); children: (first marriage) two, both died young.

Began stage career at 18 (1851); volunteered as Union spy (1861–63); recounted her spy story in concert halls and on vaudeville stages (1870s); ran hotels in San Francisco and Casa Grande, Arizona (1880s); granted the honorary title of "Major of Cavalry" by the Union army for her work as a spy.

On a sweltering June afternoon in 1863, Pauline Cushman lay prostrate in a tent, surrounded by armed guards of the Confederate Army of Tennessee. She was feverish, exhausted, and suffering from the terrible heat. Far worse, she knew that as soon as her health recovered, her only reward would be death by military execution. Cushman, a beautiful young actress, had once proclaimed herself a loyal friend of the Southern rebellion. But a Confederate military

Pauline Cushman

court had concluded that she was actually a Union spy. Confederate detectives caught her trying to carry sensitive military documents over to the Union lines. Convicted of this crime against the Confederacy, Cushman had been sentenced to hang.

But that afternoon the rebel camp suddenly broke into wild confusion. Union troops, led by General Rosencrans, were approaching, and the Confederates were thrown into retreat. In the midst of this panic, the prisoner was forgotten by all of her captors, save one. A gallant young captain came to Cushman's bedside and told her that she would be left behind and that her life would thus be spared. He went on to confess that he was in love with her and promised to find her once the war was over.

When the Union troops arrived, they were greeted by the still feeble but jubilant woman who would soon be hailed across the North as "the spy of the Cumberlands." Just like the Confederate captain, these soldiers fell in love with her, particularly after they learned the story of her daring acts of espionage and her flirtation with death. Union officers regaled her with candy and flowers, and two generals carried her to the ambulance that brought her safely behind Union lines. Still confined to her bed, Cushman was visited by a parade of admiring officers and local dignitaries. Among them was Brigadier General James Garfield, the future president, who took a particular interest in Cushman's heroics and granted her the honorary title of "Major of the Cavalry."

Pauline Cushman was so much the perfect woman spy of melodrama that some of her doings seem amusingly improbable. But if all the doubtful incidents of her great adventure are discarded, her story is still a startling one.

—**Agatha Young**

The dramatic story of the cavalry's rescue of "Miss Major Cushman" soon became well known to the American public, told to them most often by Cushman herself. For years after the war, she recounted the event in concert halls and on vaudeville stages, thrilling audiences with a tale that sparkled with ingenious disguises, daring chases, passionate but chaste love scenes, and her last minute redemption from the jaws of death. With each incident punctuated by Cushman's commanding stage presence, many in the audience found this true story more incredible than any fictional melodrama.

Pauline Cushman's recent biographers all agree that her story is a very good one; in fact, they find the legend of the alluring actress turned daredevil spy a bit too good, too romantic and dramatic, to be entirely believed. These skeptics look beyond the tale and take a more objective look at the teller. Throughout her life, they remind us, Pauline Cushman made her living through the art of deception, first as an actress, then as a spy, and finally as a self-publicist. She was such a master of disguise, in fact, that most who have explored her story finally conclude that

the line between truth and legend is almost impossible to discern. "A story like hers is a research worker's nightmare," historian **Agatha Young** has complained, "for the whole story is bestrewn with falsehoods, errors and half truths."

One point on which all of Pauline Cushman's chroniclers agree is that she was a striking woman. She was born in New Orleans in 1833, the daughter of a Spanish father and a French mother who eloped and then immigrated to America. To American eyes, this "creole" blood gave her an exotic look. The faded daguerreotypes that have survived show a dark-complexioned woman with long black curls, a striking figure posed dramatically before the camera's eye.

Cushman's natural beauty was tempered by strength, both physical and emotional. When she was ten years old, her father went bankrupt, after making some reckless speculations in the cotton trade. Like many American families in the 19th century, the Cushmans tried to recoup their fortune by striking out for the frontier, the land of fresh starts. In this case, the frontier was Grand Rapids, Michigan, where Cushman's father opened a trading post, doing most of his business with Native Americans. Growing up in this rustic environment, Cushman became an expert rider, learned to handle a gun and a canoe with ease, and developed the bodily strength and spirit of self-reliance that would someday help her survive several dangerous ordeals.

As legend has it, all of the young Indian braves in her community fell in love with the beautiful creole maiden. Supposedly, one even proposed, only to be told by her that "the Indian and the pale face cannot mingle!" At age 18, Cushman felt drawn back to the white man's civilization, particularly to the glamour of the stage. Traveling to New York, she soon caught the eye of theater managers and moved quickly from bit parts to leading roles in popular shows. Now a star attraction, she enjoyed a triumphant return to her hometown of New Orleans. "Her form is perfect," one writer rhapsodized, "so perfect that the sculptor's imagination would fail to add a single point, or banish a single blemish." Theater critics wrote far more about her "form" than they did about her acting ability, but Cushman evidently had remarkable charisma on stage and was always a favorite with her audiences.

While her career was flourishing in the late 1850s, her personal life was marked by tragedy. She married Charles Dickinson, a musician and actor. The couple had two children who both died of disease at a young age. Her husband would follow not long after. Volunteering for the Union army, he died of "camp fever" only a few months into the war.

Two years later, in 1863, Cushman was performing in Louisville, Kentucky, when she stumbled on her opportunity to enlist in the Union cause. Louisville was controlled by Union troops, but they struggled to maintain order in a city with many Southern sympathizers. A couple of these Southerners—paroled Confederate officers—mistakenly assumed that the famed actress from New Orleans was on their side, and they approached her with a proposition. At the time, she was starring in a play that ended each night with a rousing toast to the Union cause. They agreed to pay her a large sum—accounts vary from $300 to $3,000—to give that toast to the Confederacy instead.

A few days later, Cushman agreed to go through with the plan. Rumors spread along Louisville's Confederate grapevine that something exciting would happen at the theater that evening. The house was packed with friends of the South, and, as the play progressed, sporadic bouts of violence broke out between them and the Unionists in the audience. At last, in the play's grand finale, Cushman raised her glass and declared, "Here's to Jeff Davis and the Southern Confederacy! May the South always maintain her honor and her rights!" Before she had time to drink down the toast, the theater broke into battle, with Confederates leading the charge.

Caught up in this frenzy of fist fighting, chair throwing, and rebel yelling, these Southern sympathizers did not realize that they were being watched, their names recorded by Union intelligence officers stationed in the audience. They could not have known that, when the Confederate officers had first asked Cushman to make the toast, she had gone straight to a Union officer, Colonel Moore. Moore advised her to go ahead with the toast, as a way for his police force to uncover those disloyal to the Union. The toast that marked Cushman as a Southern loyalist was, in fact, her first act of deception as a Union spy.

Outraged by the destruction of his theater as well as by Cushman's secessionist sentiments, the manager fired her on the spot. But this only made her a more valuable employee of the Union army. To all appearances, she was a proud and defiant martyr who lost her job defending Confederate honor. Colonel Moore advised her to keep playing this role on the public "stage" of Louisville's streets, and she apparently did so quite convincingly. Before long she was surrounded by dozens of underground Confederates, all anxious to express their admiration and give her their support. At the same time, they gave her a surfeit of valuable information about smuggling, spy rings, and other covert operations, stories that Cushman promptly reported to Union officers.

Notoriety is often an asset for a stage performer, and Cushman soon got a new job offer from a stage manager in Nashville who was anxious to cash in on the actress' recent scandal. Since Nashville was much closer to enemy lines and had an even larger population of Confederates, the army encouraged her to take the job and resume her spying operations. On stage in Nashville, Cushman was a sensation, while offstage she continued to play the role of a friend of the Southern rebellion, all the while passing valuable information to the Union's Colonel Truesdail, chief of espionage for the Army of the Cumberland.

Then Truesdail asked Cushman to consider "an undertaking of unusual and extreme danger." With spring approaching, General Rosencrans, head of the Union's Army of the Cumberland, was preparing to move southward, taking the offensive against the Confederate General Braxton Bragg's smaller force. But Rosencrans did not know exactly where Bragg was, how many men he had, and how well-fortified and supplied they were. He desperately needed more information, and Truesdail thought that Cushman was the one who could get it.

His plan was to send her into enemy territory. This would be easy, since Southern sympathizers were regularly rounded up and "expelled" from the Union side. Once among the Confederates, she was to play the role of a worried sister, searching for her brother among their soldiers. Cushman really did have a brother in the Southern army, so she would find the part easy to play. Using this pretext, Truesdail wanted her to ingratiate herself with the Southern officers and then survey as many fortifications and army camps as she could. He warned her that she should not write anything down, but make a mental note of all that she saw.

This was a far more daring and sophisticated mission than any Cushman had done before, but, inspired by patriotism, she readily accepted. Armed only with her good looks, her acting ability, and a six-shooter, she allowed the Union army to "expel" her into enemy territory. There, in the no-man's land along the military border, she met a disreputable smuggler who agreed, for the price of her fine horse, to take her to the Confederate camp in Columbia, Tennessee.

Cushman took a room in the hotel there and, just as Truesdail had expected, soon enjoyed the attentions of a host of gallant Confederate officers. Inspired by her physical attractions, her sad story about a lost brother, and her reputation as a friend of the South, these men soon lined up for a chance to brag about their military accomplishments and their plans, providing much useful information to their charming new companion. Though they regretted her departure, one officer provided her with a "letter of safeguard" that allowed her to pass on to Shelbyville, the site of General Bragg's headquarters.

There she befriended an engineering captain who helped to design Confederate forts. Cushman feigned disinterest in the subject, but when the man left his office to run an errand she snatched some blueprints from his table. Ignoring Truesdail's advice, she hid them in the lining of a spare pair of shoes, along with some drawings she had made of forts and camps she had seen. Though this would eventually be her downfall, all was going according to plan. She traveled freely from camp to camp, guided everywhere by infatuated officers. One quartermaster even had a Confederate uniform specially tailored for her and tried to convince her to work as his special aide. She played her part beautifully and was apparently thriving in what Agatha Young has called a "dream world of romantic adventure."

But the dream turned into a nightmare when the time came for her to return to the Union lines with all the information she had gathered. Locating the smuggler who had carried her South, she asked him to take her to Nashville, explaining that she needed to retrieve some dresses. But he grew suspicious and, perhaps hoping for a reward, turned her over to a Confederate agent who soon discovered the documents that she had artlessly concealed in her shoes. What the agent did not discover was her revolver, still hidden on her person. As he brought her into custody, Cushman had the opportunity to shoot him and perhaps escape north. But she could not pull the trigger, could not cross the line from acting into true warfare.

Her situation looked bleak as she was passed from one guard to another on her way to a military trial. After a desperate and almost successful escape attempt, she was brought before General Nathan Bedford Forrest, one of the most formidable and uncharmable men in the Confederacy. Forrest tried to scare her, then passed her on to General Bragg himself. The evidence against Cushman was clear, and the guilty verdict came swiftly. Legend suggests that a "light-hearted heroine" took the sentence of death in stride, bantering with Bragg: "Come, now, general, I don't think I'll be either useful nor ornamental dangling at the end of a rope." The same aura of melodramatic fantasy abounds with stories that her guards fell in love with her, that they fanned her to keep her cool, and that she enjoyed regular visits from generals Bragg and Forrest while awaiting her execution. Historians, who doubt that the execution order would have been carried out against a woman, turn a cold eye on these romantic scenes and suggest that Cushman was deeply unnerved by the prospect of hanging. Exhausted by the mental and physical strain, she seemed to suffer a nervous breakdown that confined her to her tent until she was rescued by the Union advance weeks later.

Pauline Cushman's spying days were over, and, after a slow recovery from nervous exhaustion, she returned to the safer and more glamorous world of the theater. Decked out in a military uniform, the "major" recalled her "startling adventures" before eager audiences in places such as P.T. Barnum's famed American Museum. Cushman was still a stunning presence on stage. One of her admirers remembered her as "a woman of magnificent physique, with large, lustrous, slow black eyes, raven ringlets falling almost to her waist, with the profile of a Madonna and a voice as melodious as a lute." Cushman was almost as much of a sensation offstage. She once publicly horsewhipped a man for spreading false rumors about her sex life; another time, she smashed plates on the head of a particularly annoying suitor.

Eventually, American audiences grew tired of Civil War stories. Cushman tried running her own theater company and then went into the hotel business in San Francisco. In 1879, she married a younger man named Jere Fryer, and the couple opened a hotel in the frontier boomtown of Casa Grande, Arizona. There she embarked on another round of larger-than-life adventures, mediating gun battles on the town's main street, wielding a pistol to keep order in her saloon, and developing a reputation among the ranchers, homesteaders, and cowboys for being a generous host most of the time, and a formidable enemy when crossed.

Fryer turned out to be an unfaithful husband. Supposedly, when Cushman confronted one of her romantic rivals, the two ended up in a knock down fistfight in a mule corral. Cushman lost badly, suffering two black eyes. A few years later, she lost her husband as well. She returned to San Francisco and tried in vain to make a comeback on the stage. But her beauty and her fortune were gone, and there was no longer a flock of admirers around her. She was also suffering from terrible bouts of arthritis, made worse by the fact that she now had to make a meager living scrubbing floors. The landlady in the boardinghouse where she lived found her dead on December 7, 1893, killed by an accidental overdose of morphine, taken to relieve her arthritic pain.

Pauline Cushman seemed destined for an unmarked pauper's grave until the landlady alerted a local veterans' group. The aging soldiers of the Grand Army of the Republic remembered the daring exploits of the "spy of the Cumberlands" and honored her with a full military funeral.

SOURCES:
Horan, James D. *Desperate Women.* NY: Putnam, 1952.
Huddleston, Ed. *The Civil War in Middle Tennessee.* Nashville, TN: Parthenon Press, 1965.
Kane, Harnett T. *Spies for the Blue and Gray.* NY: Hanover House, 1954.
Moore, Frank. *Women of the War: Their Heroism and Self-Sacrifice.* Hartford, CT: S.S. Scranton, 1866.
Sarmiento, F.L. *Pauline Cushman, Union Spy and Scout.* NY: John E. Potter, 1865.
Young, Agatha. *The Women and the Crisis: Women of the North in the Civil War.* NY: McDowell, Obolensky, 1959.

Ernest Freeberg, historian, Atlanta, Georgia

Custis, Eleanor Calvert.
See Washington, Martha for sidebar.

Custis, Martha (1731–1802).
See Washington, Martha.

Custis, Nelly (1779–1852).
See Washington, Martha for sidebar.

Cuthbert, Betty (1938—)

Australian sprinter. Born in 1938 in Ermington, Sydney, Australia.

Won gold medals in the 100 meters, the 200 meters, and the 4x100 at the Melbourne Olympics (1956); won a gold medal in the 400 meters at the Tokyo Olympics (1964).

Soon to be Australia's Golden Girl, her nation's greatest woman sprinter, Betty Cuthbert was so successful in school sports that she caught the attention of **June Maston** (June Maston Ferguson), a sprinter who ran with *Shirley Strickland, Betty McKinnon, and ✦ Joyce King for a silver medal in the 4x100 meters in the 1948 Olympics. Cuthbert joined the Western Suburbs Athletic Club and, in 1953, while

coached by Ferguson, won the national junior 100-yard championships in 11.3. Before the Melbourne Olympics in 1956, she broke the world record for the 200 meters at 23.2. A rivalry with **Marlene Matthews**, another Sydney runner, helped both athletes to arrive at the Olympics in peak condition.

In the Games, 18-year-old Betty Cuthbert won the gold medal in the 100 meters in 11.5, arriving ahead of **Christa Stubnick** of East Germany who took silver and teammate Matthews who took bronze. The 200 meters ended with the three women in the same order, and Cuthbert's winning time was 23.4. She also anchored the Australian team in the 4x100 meter relay (following teammates Shirley de la Hunty-Strickland, **Norma Croker**, and **Fleur Mellor**) to another gold medal and a world record of 44.5. Great Britain's team—**Anne Pashley, Jean Scrivens, June Paul-Foulds**, and **Heather Armitage**—took the silver, while the U.S. team—*Mae Faggs, *Margaret Matthews, *Wilma Rudolph**, and **Isabelle Daniels**—took the bronze. It was the year of the Aussies. The women's track team was composed of only 16% of their nation's contingent but won more than half of Australia's gold medals, putting Australia third behind the U.S. and the Soviet Union for most medals won.

Though the unassuming Cuthbert was named Australia Broadcasting's Sportstar of the year (1956), internationally it was Australia's swimmer *Dawn Fraser, winning the first of her eight career gold medals at Melbourne, who became the bigger star. Allen Guttmann theorizes in *Women's Sports* that ambivalence about women's track-and-field stars remained strong through the early part of the 20th century: "The public continued in these years to prefer exemplars of conventionally 'feminine' sports. The preference was observable in the careers of two of the Australian stars—Cuthbert, a runner, and Fraser, a swimmer. . . . Australian officialdom had a much harder time with [Fraser] than with Betty Cuthbert, . . . but Fraser's antics, which included an attempt to steal the Japanese flag from Emperor Hirohito's palace, made her seem 'one of the girls.' She was not at all conventionally beautiful, . . . but she appeared 'curvaceous' in a swimsuit and the public loved her. Photographs of Cuthbert, on the other hand, revealed sinewy limbs and a face contorted to a breathless grimace. The message was clear: the watery way to a man's heart was preferable to the cinder track."

Troubled by injury, Cuthbert lost the 100 and 200 meters to America's *Wilma Rudolph** in the Rome Olympics in 1960 and did not

King, Joyce. See *Blankers-Koen, Fanny for sidebar.*

place. For the next four years, the Australian retired to work in her father's nursery. In 1964, she came out of hiding to compete once more, in the Tokyo Olympics. To the surprise of all, the 26-year-old took the gold in the new 400 meters in a record 52 seconds, beating *Ann Packer of Great Britain by two tenths of a second. **Judith Amoore** took the bronze. It was Betty Cuthbert's greatest win, and she was given the coveted Helms Award on her return home. Since retirement, Cuthbert has had to deal with the debilitating effects of multiple sclerosis.

SOURCES:
Guttmann, Allen. *Women's Sports: A History.* NY: Columbia University Press, 1991.

Cutpurse, Moll (c. 1584–1659).

See Frith, Mary.

Cuzzoni, Francesca (c. 1698–1770)

Italian soprano. Born in Parma, Italy, around 1698; died in Bologna in 1770; married Sandoni (a harpsichordist); studied with Lanzi.

Made debut in Parma (1716); made debut in London, creating Teofane in Handel's Ottone *(1723); created several other Handel roles, including Rodelinda, Cleopatra in* Giulio Cesare, *Asteria in* Tamerlano, *and Lisaura in* Allesandro.

In 1716, Francesca Cuzzoni made her debut in Parma. In 1722, after her Italian success, she arrived for a London engagement having married in transit the harpsichordist who had been sent to retrieve her. She scored a sensation in her 1723 London debut, creating the role of Teofane in Handel's *Ottone.* Though Cuzzoni was described physically as "short and squat" and of negligible acting ability, her voice was reputed to be of the highest quality. Joining Handel's Royal Academy company, she was its leading prima donna until the arrival of *Faustina Bordoni in 1726. The subsequent rivalry, spurred on by a titillated public and eager press, culminated in a slugging match between the two divas during a performance of Bononcini's *Astianatte* in 1727. Soon after, Cuzzoni returned to Italy. Through the years, she made two more appearances in London, the last in 1750. By then, she was nearly voiceless and heavily in debt. It has been reported that she was bailed out of prison by the prince of Wales. After another incarceration in Holland, she returned to Italy and supported herself with button-making; she died in poverty in Bologna in 1770.

Cybo, Maddalena (d. 1519).

See Medici, Maddalena de.

Cymbarka or Cymburga (c. 1396–1429).

See Cimburca of Masovia.

Cynane (c. 357–322 BCE).

See Cynnane.

Cynethryth (fl. 736–796)

*Queen of Mercia. Flourished 8th century; married Offa II, king of Mercia, around 756; children: at least three, including Eadburgh (c. 773–after 802) and possibly *Etheldreda (d. around 840).*

Born into an important Saxon family of Mercia (a kingdom of west England), Cynethryth was one of the most famous queens of the early Middle Ages. This does not mean, however, that she was popular; instead, Cynethryth had a terrible reputation for cruelty. She married King Offa II of Mercia around 756 and ruled with him until his death in 796. In those years, Cynethryth reigned with almost the same powers as a queen-regnant (one who inherits the crown herself), though she had only married into the royal house of Mercia. As queen, she oversaw many aspects of the kingdom's administration, passing edicts and legislation, and making foreign-policy decisions. Offa and Cynethryth even struck coinage bearing the queen's name and image, a highly unusual act. She had several children, including *Eadburgh, who grew up to be as despised a queen as her mother. After Offa's death, Cynethryth became an abbess.

Laura York,
Riverside, California

Cynisca (fl. 396–392 BCE)

First Greek woman to breed horses and race them in the Olympic chariot races. Name variations: Kyniska. Pronunciation: coo-NISS-ka. Born in Sparta, birth date unknown, but probably close to that of her brother Agesilaus in 444 BCE; daughter of Archidamus or Archidamos II, king of Sparta, and his second wife.

Owner of the victorious four-colt chariot in the 96th and 97th Olympic games (396 and 392 BCE).

Although we know somewhat more about *Bilistiche, who won Olympic chariot races in the 3rd century BCE, Cynisca of Sparta was better known in antiquity as the first woman to have done so. She was the daughter of King Archidamus II (reigned 469–427 BCE), the famous leader of the Spartans in the first years of the Peloponnesian War, and sister to his son and successor Agesilaus

(444–360 BCE), who would lead his country against the Persians and other Greek states in the years of Spartan hegemony following the war. Sparta, where a girl's education included rigorous physical and athletic training, was unique among the other Greek states in the relative equality of status between men and women. A woman's participation in the Olympic chariot races, however, was limited to financial sponsorship of team, vehicle and driver, and our ancient sources are quite neatly divided in their accounts of Cynisca's interest in the sport.

On one side we have Plutarch and Xenophon, who mention Cynisca in the course of biographies on her brother Agesilaus. Both claim that she participated in the Olympics only at her brother's instigation, and that he wished her to enter horses in the competition for the sole purpose of teaching his subjects a moral lesson. Plutarch describes Agesilaus' reasoning:

> Seeing that some of the citizens thought themselves to be somebody and gave themselves great airs because they kept a racing stud, he persuaded his sister Cynisca to enter a chariot in the races at Olympia, for he wished to demonstrate to the Greeks that this sort of thing was no sign of excellence, but only of having money and being willing to spend it.

While we do not know whether this alleged admonition was heeded, we do know that to later generations Cynisca was highly esteemed for her achievement. The Greek author Pausanius, who wrote his travel book *Description of Greece* in the 2nd century CE, says nothing about Agesilaus' agency, but only that she was "exceedingly ambitious to succeed at the Olympic games, and was the first woman to breed horses and to win an Olympic victory." Pausanius also reports that in his day a hero-shrine to Cynisca stood in Sparta and that a statue depicting chariot, horses, charioteer and Cynisca herself existed in Olympia. Part of the stone base on which this latter statue group was placed has been excavated in modern times, and its four-line epigraph is preserved whole in the *Greek Anthology*. The fact that these tangible memorials survived and were considered worthy attractions some five centuries after her death is ample testimony to the favor with which ancient Greece viewed her individual accomplishments; this high esteem likely outbalances the pessimistic opinion of Plutarch and Xenophon as to Cynisca's motivation.

SOURCES:

The Greek Anthology. Edited and translated by W.R. Patton. Vol. 5. Loeb Classical Library. London: William Heinemann, 1926. p. 11.

The Oxford Classical Dictionary. Edited By N.G.L. Hammond and H.H. Scullard. Oxford: The Clarendon Press, 1970.

Paulys Real-Encyclopädie der Classischen Alterumswissenschaft. Edited by Georg Wissowa. Stuttgart: J.B. Metzlersche Buchhandlung, 1897—.

Pausanius. *Description of Greece.* Edited and translated by W.H.S. Jones and H.A. Ormerod. Vols. 2 and 3. Loeb Classical Library. London: William Heinemann, 1960.

Plutarch. *Plutarch's Moralia.* Edited and translated by F.C. Babbitt. Vol. 3. Loeb Classical Library. London: William Heinemann, 1961.

———. *Plutarch's Lives.* Edited and translated by Bernadotte Perrin. Vol. 5. Loeb Classical Library. London: William Heinemann, 1968. p. 53.

Xenophon. *Scripta Minora.* Edited and translated by E.C. Marchant. Loeb Classical Library. London: William Heinemann, 1971.

SUGGESTED READING:

Fantham, Elaine, *et. al. Women in the Classical World: Image and Text.* Chapter 2: "Spartan Women: Women in a Warrior Society." Oxford: Oxford University Press, 1994.

Peter H. O'Brien,
Boston University

Cynnane (c. 357–322 BCE)

Macedonian half-sister of Alexander the Great who attempted to avenge her husband's death and win power following Alexander's death. Name variations: Cynane. Born around 357 BCE; died in 322 BCE; daughter of Philip II, king of Macedonia (r. 359–336 BCE), and Audata (the first of Philip's seven wives); half-sister of Alexander III the Great (356–323 BCE), king of Macedonia; married Amyntas, around 337; children: (first marriage) Adea (337–317 BCE, later renamed Eurydice).

The daughter of Philip II of Macedonia and **Audata** (the first of Philip's seven wives), Cynnane was the half-sister of Alexander the Great. Cynnane's mother Audata was the daughter of Bardylis, an Illyrian chieftain whom Philip defeated in battle to guarantee Macedonia's control of their mutual frontier (358). This victory was an important event in Macedonian history, for the Illyrians under Bardylis had long overshadowed Macedonia and had even pillaged that realm several times. It also began the rise of Philip who thereafter went on both to secure Macedonia and to unite the rest of Greece under his power. In the wake of Philip's victory, he married Audata, his rival's daughter, to help secure the peace between Macedonia and Illyria that followed.

Cynnane, probably the oldest child of polygamous Philip, seems to have been Audata's only offspring. Following Illyrian custom, Audata trained Cynnane as a warrior—a training Cynnane would pass on to her own daughter when the time came. Beyond her education (which was unusual for women in Macedonia), nothing is known of Cynnane until Philip arranged her marriage (c. 337) to his nephew, Amyntas. This Amyntas was the son of Perdiccas II who had preceded Philip on the throne. It appears that Amyntas briefly succeeded Perdiccas as king, but his extreme youth at the time of his father's death invited the Illyrians and several other foreign enemies (as well as domestic rivals) to ravage the Macedonian countryside. To bring a competent soldier to the throne, Philip replaced Amyntas as king, although—in a gesture of kindness uncharacteristic of his dynasty—Philip spared Amyntas' life and even reared him as a son.

The marriage of Cynnane and Amyntas produced a daughter Adea (later renamed *Eurydice). Amyntas, however, was not to live long. In 336, Philip was assassinated. During the confusion that followed the king's death, Philip's not-yet-great son Alexander had Amyntas murdered in order to prevent any challenge to his smooth accession. Amyntas' execution left Cynnane embittered toward Alexander and all associated with his direct line. Not long after Amyntas' death, probably in order to see the hostile Cynnane and her infant daughter removed from Macedonia, Alexander betrothed Cynnane to one Langarus, a leader of the Agriani (lesser allies of the Macedonians). Before this marriage took place, however, Langarus died. Since Cynnane did not wish to marry again, especially if Alexander was to have any part in the arrangements, she withdrew from the Macedonian court to a private estate, where she trained Eurydice in military matters, brooded over the injustice done to her husband, and bided her time.

There Cynnane stayed until she learned of Alexander the Great's death (323) and the resulting political fallout. For over 300 years, the Argead Dynasty had ruled over a Macedonian state that was extremely primitive in political organization. Argead kingship was "personal" in nature, with only the king holding any real power or authority. All positions except that of the king were held ad hoc, and at the monarch's whim. Influence within Argead Macedonia depended entirely upon access to the king's person; if a king wished to delegate authority, he did so for as long as the agent so honored kept the king's confidence. The realm was little more than an extension of the royal household, in which the king assumed the rights and responsibilities associated with fatherhood as these were understood throughout the Greek world. As such, his authority was as much founded upon a religious, moral authority as it was upon any constitutional power. The Argeads

Roxane
(d. 311/310 BCE).
See Olympias for
sidebar.

never had a well-defined principle of succession, and it appears that the only two conditions a would-be monarch had to meet in order to be considered for the throne were that he be a male and that he be of the Argead family. Sons often succeeded fathers, but what really mattered for kingship was competence and ruthlessness, since Macedonia was almost never free of significant foreign threat. As such, although sons had strong claims upon the people's loyalty when their royal fathers passed away, the throne almost always was quickly occupied by the strongest adult Argead male then available.

Since Alexander had been guilty of removing royal rivals at the beginning of his reign, however, and, since he had not been overly concerned with fathering an heir, the only adult Argead male living at the time of Alexander's death was his mentally deficient half-brother Arrhidaeus (neither Cynnane, Alexander, nor Arrhidaeus shared a common mother). Although, Alexander's Bactrian wife ◄ Roxane (d. 311/310 BCE) was pregnant when Alexander the Great died, no one knew whether the pregnancy would produce a son, and even more important, even if a son resulted, no one knew exactly what to do with the Argead throne before such time as he could assume authority in his own right. The Macedonians faced an unprecedented situation at a dangerous time, before the enormous Persian Empire had been fully pacified. As it turned out, Roxane would give birth to a son (Alexander IV). But well before his birth, a near civil war among factions within the Macedonian army gave rise to a precarious solution to the successional dilemma. Under the leadership of a Perdiccas, one of the ranking officers at Babylon (where Alexander the Great died), it was agreed that the incompetent Arrhidaeus would become the king—mostly to perform important religious rituals associated with the post—but that if Roxane had a son, that child would also be recognized as a king. Thus, after Alexander IV was born, an unprecedented joint kingship was established. Since both kings needed a guardian, Perdiccas parlayed his fortuitous possession of Alexander the Great's body and signet ring into a general recognition of his role as the kings' protector. In order to secure this recognition, however, Perdiccas had to oversee a general distribution of powerful appointments to his military peers, a distribution that eventually assured the dismemberment of Alexander the Great's Empire.

Not knowing what the future would bring, Cynnane saw in the elevation of Arrhidaeus—who assumed the name Philip (III) along with his throne—an opportunity both to return to the thick of court intrigue and to extract revenge for the murder of Amyntas. Keeping abreast of affairs, in 322 Cynnane prepared to act decisively. Although it had been less than a year since the joint kingship had been established, the compromise that had brought the kings into Perdiccas' care was beginning to unravel. This was chiefly because many, especially the generals Antigonus in western Turkey and Ptolemy I Soter in Egypt, were beginning to question whether the decrees Perdiccas was issuing under the kings' names were as much for the good of the empire as they were for the good of Perdiccas. Wishing to deal with several problems, but especially to squash the open hostility of Antigonus, Perdiccas and the kings proceeded to western Turkey. With Perdiccas and the kings so near to Macedonia, Cynnane (with Eurydice in tow) decided to pay a visit. Despite an attempt by Antipater (who had served as the Macedonian in charge of Europe) to forcibly restrain her, Cynnane fought her way out of Macedonia with the intention of arranging Eurydice's marriage to Arrhidaeus. Cynnane's plan was simple: she intended to invoke Eurydice's ties to Perdiccas III and Philip II (Eurydice was the granddaughter of both) as a prelude to demanding before the Macedonian army that Eurydice be allowed to marry Arrhidaeus. Although the prospect of such a marriage was especially anathema to Perdiccas, none of the generals at the time looked forward to such a union. However, Cynnane knew that the marriage of the still unwed Arrhidaeus to the doubly Argead Eurydice would be very popular among the rank and file of the army, who would look forward to any children the union might produce.

More ominously—although Cynnane would not have admitted this to the troops whom she needed to support her power play—it seems clear that her intention, upon seeing Eurydice married to Arrhidaeus, would be for her and her daughter to "free" the kings from Perdiccas so as to allow the kings to "reign" on their own behalf; this ploy fell within the realm of possibility because very few Macedonians knew the extent of Arrhidaeus' mental incapacity. If that stage of their plan could be reached, then it would be possible for Cynnane and Eurydice to rule through the incompetent Arrhidaeus. Of course, Eurydice would attempt to become pregnant as soon as possible in order to anchor her status. One can only imagine what accident they had in mind for the young Alexander once he had fallen into their hands, but it is certain that his life would have been quickly forfeited once Cynnane and Eurydice were in control. What revenge against the shade of Alexander the Great could possibly surpass the exquisite pleasure of cutting off his direct line and royally supplanting it with the seed of his onetime victim, Amyntas?

Things, however, did not proceed exactly as planned. Learning that the pair was on their way to undermine his command of the joint kings, Perdiccas sent his younger brother, Alcetas, with a squad to head off the determined women before they could force a public confrontation. In the disturbance that ensued between Alcetas and Cynnane, Cynnane was killed. When the main part of Perdiccas' army learned to its horror that the daughter of Philip II and the half-sister of Alexander III had been murdered as she attempted to secure an Argead wife for the reigning Arrhidaeus, it demanded that the marriage of Arrhidaeus to Eurydice proceed as envisioned by Cynnane. (*See also* Eurydice [337–317 BCE].)

William S. Greenwalt,
Associate Professor of Classical History,
Santa Clara University, Santa Clara, California

Cynthia (1910–1963).
See Brousse, Amy.

Cypros (fl. 28 CE).
See Berenice (28 CE–after 80 CE) for sidebar.

Cyprus (c. 90 BCE–?).

*Mother of Herod. Name variations: Cypros. Born an Arab in Nabatea, a kingdom east of Judea, around 90 BCE; married Antipater the Idumaean (d. 43 BCE, minister to the Hasmonian queen *Alexandra); children: sons Phasael, governor of Jerusalem (d. 40 BCE); Herod the Great, king of Judea (73–4 BCE).*

Czerny-Stefanska, Halina (1922—)

Polish pianist, best known for her renditions of Chopin. Born in Cracow in 1922; winner of the 1949 Chopin Competition in Warsaw.

Halina Czerny-Stefanska studied with Alfred Cortot in Paris. She was the co-winner, with *Bella Davidovich, of the 1949 Chopin Competition in Warsaw. Her London debut took place in 1949 during the centennial year of Chopin's death. Czerny-Stefanska is best known for her Chopin, especially her mazurka playing. A celebrated recording of the Chopin E minor Concerto thought to be by the legendary Rumanian pianist Dinu Lipatti (1917–1950) was discovered to be a 1955 recording by Czerny-Stefanska.

SUGGESTED READING:

Tanasescu, Dragos, and Grigore Bargauanu. *Lipatti.* Ed. by Carola Grindea; trans. by Carola Grindea and Anne Goosens. London: Kahn and Averill, 1988.

John Haag,
Athens, Georgia

Dabrowska, Maria (1889–1965)

Polish writer, regarded as one of the leading writers of the school of critical realism, whose masterwork Noce i dnie *is one of the greatest novels in 20th-century Polish literature. Born Maria Szumska in Russów near Kalisz, Russian Poland, on October 6, 1889; died in Warsaw on May 19, 1965; read philosophy and sociology at Lausanne and Brussels; married Marian Dabrowski (a Polish Socialist), in 1911 (died 1925).*

Selected works: Dzieci Ojczyzny *(Children of the Fatherland, 1918);* Galaz czeresni *(The Cherry Branch, 1922);* Usmiech dziecinstwa *(The Smile of Childhood, 1923); (short stories)* Ludzie stamtad *(Folk from Over Yonder, 1926);* Noce i dnie *(Nights and Days, 1932–34); (memoirs)* Pilgrimage to Warsaw *(1969);* Przygody czlowiecka myslacego *(The Adventures of a Thinking Man, published posthumously as a fragment, 1970); postwar diaries, covering the years from 1945 to 1965, began to appear in print in Warsaw (1996).*

Maria Dabrowska, universally regarded as Poland's outstanding woman prose writer of the 20th century, was born into the lower *szlachta* (gentry), the daughter of an estate manager in what was then Russian Poland. After completing her preparatory studies in local private schools, she moved to Western Europe, studying science, economics, and sociology at the universities of Brussels and Lausanne. Typical of her generation, she combined being a student with intense political activity designed to free Poland of for-

eign rule. In 1911, she married **Marian Dabrowski,** a Polish Socialist who had been forced into temporary exile because of his activities during the failed anti-Russian revolt of 1905. To her already deep sense of social justice was added a sense of heightened political militancy. For a number of months in 1913–14, Maria was able to study social conditions in England while on a fellowship provided by the cooperative movement. Unlike many Polish intellectuals, Dabrowska was never attracted to Marxism, believing instead that the path of gradual reform taken by nations like Great Britain was preferable to that of a bloody revolution.

Returning to Poland in 1914, Dabrowska experienced the privations of World War I while earning a living as a journalist for *Spolem* (*United*), the journal of the national cooperative movement. Convinced that Poland was only as strong as the millions of souls at the bottom of society, the impoverished peasantry, she became their passionate defender, demanding for them elementary social justice based on sweeping land reforms and an intellectual-moral transformation of all aspects of rural life. Besides her polemical writings, Dabrowska began to publish short stories about rural life, the earliest of which appeared in print in 1911. The collections included *Dzieci Ojczyzny* (*Children of the Fatherland,* 1918) and *Galaz czeresni* (*The Cherry Branch,* 1922). After Poland achieved independence in 1918, she took a job in the newly formed Ministry of Agriculture in Warsaw, working there until 1924. One of her first major critical successes was the cycle of short stories based on her own memories of rural life, *Usmiech dziecinstwa* (*The Smile of Childhood,* 1923), which caught the attention of avant-garde literary circles because of its innovative, essentially Proustian, form of narration.

Already in the early 1920s and particularly after the establishment of a military dictatorship by Marshal Jozef Pilsudski in a bloody coup d'etat in 1926, Maria Dabrowska was identified with the liberal wing of Polish literary and political life. Her strong sense of social justice put her on a collision course with the Pilsudski elements whose extremist views and Polish chauvinism made many of them defenders of the social status quo and often vehemently anti-Semitic. Identified with the political opposition to the dictatorship, she fought against the demagogues. Dabrowska's writings of the 1920s and early 1930s were realistic depictions of rural working-class privation and suffering. She portrayed people who retained their humanity despite the injustices under which they lived and labored in countless villages and estates. In another noteworthy book, *Ludzie stamtad* (*Folk from Over Yonder*), a collection of short stories published to critical acclaim in 1926, Dabrowska presented another realistic and, at times, even harsh portrait of the lives of peasants. Refusing to romanticize their misery, she aspired to create both a work of genuine literary art and a signal for political and social action on their behalf.

In Dabrowska's masterpiece, the tetralogy *Nights and Days* (*Noce i dnie*, 1932–34), she matched the quality of the great Russian novels by blending realism with an epic story, depicting the profound changes that had transformed Polish life from the 1860s through 1914. Detailing the inexorable decline of the gentry class, *Nights and Days* is a chronicle of the social and intellectual upheavals that impacted on both individuals and an entire nation. While showing sympathy for her protagonists, Dabrowska's basic view was that the wrenching social changes they endured were not only inevitable but necessary. She depicted men and women as part of an emerging moral order, better than that of the past; a society based on social justice and moral responsibility. Hailed by critics as a milestone in modern Polish literature, *Nights and Days* has been widely admired for its stylistic elegance; its clear and effortless style having been judged by guardians of the language as an example of standard Polish to be emulated by writers and editors.

Originally structured as a psychological novel, *Nights and Days* greatly outgrew its original framework, becoming instead a vast panorama of a half-century of Polish history. It matches the epic breadth of Tolstoy but belongs to the genre of family chronicle. The contemporary novels it most strongly resembles are Thomas Mann's *Buddenbrooks* and John Galsworthy's *Forsyte Saga*. Dabrowska was also deeply influenced by the Danish writer Jens Peter Jacobsen, whose novel *Niels Lyhne* she translated into Polish. The two main characters of *Nights and Days*, Bogumil Niechcic and Barbara Ostrzenska, are more than isolated individuals, but rather function as representatives of their family, social caste and generation. The finely drawn characterizations are part of a much larger portrait of an entire society convulsed by profound changes leading to ever more turbulent ones. Many critics have commended Dabrowska for her skill in drawing a subtle portrait of Barbara, a highly complex woman whose life is a clear reflection of the social transformation that affected her not only as an individual but also as a

representative figure of altered family relations. The meticulous realism of *Nights and Days* gives the work a spirit of authenticity, which is not surprising in view of the fact that much of it is autobiographical, and the character Marcin is modeled after Dabrowska's husband Marian Dabrowski.

Maria Dabrowska

Politically sympathetic to the left but never a doctrinaire member of any political party or faction, Maria Dabrowska fought intolerance and injustice with her pen until the very last day of interwar Polish independence. Like her fellow Poles, she mourned for her nation when German troops occupied Poland in September 1939. Over six million Poles, half of them Jews, died during more than five years of brutal Nazi occupation. Dabrowska wrote no original works during this period, remaining active instead in the rich underground cultural life that flourished despite German attempts to destroy Polish culture. Her only literary production during these years was a translation of the classic *Diary* of Samuel Pepys.

Dabrowska remained in Poland after 1945, despite the fact that by the late 1940s the government of the Polish People's Republic had imposed a harshly Stalinist regime of intellectual censorship and repression. She maintained her artistic integrity, refusing to provide the government with either statements of support or literary productions of propaganda value. Instead, she continued to write works that measured up to her own high artistic and ethical standards. Unfortunately, she was unable to complete her second family saga intended as a sequel to *Nights and Days*, *Przygody czlowieka myslacego* (*The*

Adventures of a Thinking Man); it was published posthumously as a fragment in 1970. Fully aware of her unchallenged reputation as Poland's *grande dame* of letters, Maria Dabrowska was able in the final years of her life to speak out in defiance of the chilly blasts of censorship that regularly swept across Polish intellectual life. In 1964, she joined 33 other writers and scholars to sign a letter addressed to Premier Jozef Cyrankiewicz protesting ever-increasing censorship. While many of her colleagues abandoned their protest efforts at this point, Dabrowska continued to press the authorities for a significant change in policy. Later in 1964, she spoke out about the lack of intellectual freedom for writers at an open meeting of the Polish Writers Union, receiving a standing ovation from the 500 authors in attendance. Because of her incredible popularity at home and her considerable international reputation, the government took no measures against her. In fact, after her death in May 1965, she was given a state funeral, and there was extensive coverage in the media.

Maria Dabrowska's artistic reputation remains unassailable in Poland. Her finely drawn depictions of Poland's poor, particularly its long-exploited peasantry, continues to find resonance with readers. The endurance of the rural poor, particularly women, so movingly portrayed in *Nights and Days*, guarantees that this epic novel will continue to be a national classic in Poland, appearing in literally dozens of editions; it was also made into a film and a television series. A number of posthumous works appeared after her death, including a volume of memoirs published in 1969 entitled *Pilgrimage to Warsaw*. In 1996, her extensive postwar diaries, covering the years from 1945 to 1965, began to appear in print in Warsaw to considerable critical and public interest.

SOURCES:
Dabrowska, Maria. *A Village Wedding, and Other Stories.* Warsaw: Polonia Publishing House, 1957.
Folejewski, Zbigniew. *Maria Dabrowska.* NY: Twayne Publishers, 1967.
———. "Maria Dabrowska's Place in European Literature," in *Books Abroad.* Vol. 38, no. 1. Winter 1964, pp. 11–13.
Kridl, Manfred. *A Survey of Polish Literature and Culture.* The Hague: Mouton Publishers, 1956.
Kuncewicz, Maria. "A Great Provincial," in *Polish Review.* Vol. 10, no. 4. Autumn 1965, pp. 3–7.
Milosz, Czeslaw. *The History of Polish Literature.* NY: Macmillan, 1969.
Polanowski, Edward. *Maria Dabrowska: 1889–1965.* Wroclaw: Zaklad Narodowy im. Ossolinskich, 1990.
Scherer-Virski, Olga. *The Modern Polish Short Story.* The Hague: Mouton, 1955.

John Haag,
Athens, Georgia

Dacier, Anne (1654–1720)

French scholar, linguist, and translator. Name variations: Anne LeFèvre, Lefevre, Lefebvre, or Le ferre; Anne Tanneguy Lefèvre; Madame Dacier. Born Anne Lefebvre in Saumur, France, in March 1654; died in Paris on August 17, 1720; buried beside her husband in the Church of Saint Germain l'Auxerrois; daughter of (Latinized) Tanquillus Faber also known as Tannegui or Tanneguy Lefebvre (1615–1672, a humanist, classical scholar, teacher at the Protestant Academy at Saumur, and editor) and Madame Lefebvre; educated by her father; married Jean Lesnier (a printer and bookseller); married André Dacier (a scholar), in 1683 (died 1722); children: two daughters, **Henriette-Susanne Dacier** *and* **Marie Dacier**; *one son, Jean-Andre.*

Appointed to the Ricrovati Academy in Padua. Selected works: translations of Marcus Aurelius; the first French translations of Sappho, Plautus, Aristophanes, Terence, Anacreon, and Homer (possibly in conjunction with her mother and husband).

Anne Lefebvre was born in Saumur, France, to a learned family. Her father Tanneguy Lefebvre was a classical scholar who taught at the Protestant Academy in the town. Her mother Madame Lefebvre was also schooled. Though Anne's brothers were not interested in the Greek and Latin taught them by their father, Anne, overhearing their lessons, took well to the studies. Upon seeing his daughter's extraordinary capacity for learning, Tanneguy devoted himself to her education, making Anne unusually well versed for a woman of her time. She became one of the most accomplished scholars in Europe. Following the death of her father in 1672, and facing financial difficulties, she married Jean Lesnier, a printer and bookseller. Anne was soon on her own again, although it is unknown whether he died or left her.

She moved to Paris, where she began working as a translator, publishing an edition of the works of the 3rd-century Greek scholar Callimachus, head of the Alexandrian library. The reputation acquired by this work gained her an invitation to assist in the preparation of the Delphin editions of the classics. In 1683, she married André Dacier, a member of the French Academy who had been a favorite pupil of her father; for many years, André and Anne had shared his classroom. This union was dubbed "the marriage of Greek and Latin." They lived in Paris for 45 years, mostly in an apartment in the Louvre, a fashionable indulgence granted to them by the king. Anne's three children, including a gifted daughter, died before she did, and her ensuing sorrow led her to abandon scholarship for the remainder of her life.

Despite the brevity of her intellectual career, Dacier is recognized as one of the most accomplished French scholars of the 17th century. She corresponded with Queen *Christina of Sweden, among others, and translated several plays of Plautus, the whole of Terence, the *Plutus* and *Clouds* of Aristophanes, Plutarch's *Lives,* and the whole of Anacreon and *Sappho. She is particularly known for her translation of Marcus Aurelius and Homer. Although Dacier was aided by her mother and her husband in the Marcus Aurelius translation, the preface, which drew most of the praise, is thought to be hers alone.

Dacier's classical interpretation of Homer's *Iliad* was at odds with the travestied *Iliad,* based on her work, that was published by her contemporary Houdar de La Motte. Provoked, Dacier defended the ancient text. The longstanding controversy between Ancients and Moderns was thus rekindled, and others joined in the heated debate concerning their comparative merits. Dacier and La Motte reconciled in 1716, and both of their translations have seen modern-day reissues.

SOURCES:

Atherton, Margaret. *Women Philosophers of the Early Modern Period.* Indianapolis: Hackett, 1994.

Kersey, Ethel M. *Women Philosophers: a Bio-critical Source Book.* CT: Greenwood Press, 1989.

Smith, Christopher. "Anne Lefebvre Dacier," in Katharina Wilson, ed., *Encyclopedia of Continental Women Writers.* CT: Garland, 1991.

Catherine Hundleby, M.A. Philosophy,
University of Guelph, Guelph, Ontario, Canada

Dafovska, Ekaterina (c. 1976—)

Bulgarian biathlon champion. Born around 1976.

An administrator from Tchepelare, Bulgaria, Ekaterina Dafovska did not take up the biathlon, an event that combines cross-country skiing and shooting, until 1992; one year later, she made the national team. In the 1994 Lillehammer Olympics, she came in 29th in the 15-kilometer competition.

Dafovska was ranked only 51st in World Cup standings when she entered the 1998 Nagano Olympics in Japan. Fighting off wind-driven snow that severely reduced visibility for shooting, she surprised everyone by winning Bulgaria's first-ever Winter Olympic gold medal with a race time of 54:52, 17.8 seconds ahead of **Elena Petrova** of the Ukraine who took the silver. **Ursula Disl** of Germany repeated as bronze medalist. All three shot 19 out of 20 targets.

Dagmar (1847–1928), empress of Russia.

See Marie Feodorovna.

Dagmar of Bohemia (d. 1212)

*Queen of Denmark. Name variations: Margaret of Bohemia. Died on May 24, 1212; daughter of Ottokar I (d. 1230), king of Bohemia (r. 1198–1230), and *Adela of Meissen; first wife of Valdemar also known as Waldemar II the Victorious, king of Denmark (r. 1202–1241), in 1205; children: Valdemar or Waldemar the Younger (1209–1231), joint-king of Denmark with his father (r. 1215–1231).*

The daughter of Ottokar I, king of Bohemia, and *Adela of Meissen, Margaret of Bohemia was married to Waldemar II the Victorious, king of Denmark, in 1205. The day after her marriage, she petitioned the king to repeal the ploughtax, which was then a heavy burden on the Danes. She also begged for the release of all prisoners. Having rapidly won the love of the Danes because of her beauty, goodness, and saintly life, Margaret was rechristened Dagmar ("the mother of the day") by a grateful nation. To the end of her life, she was constantly striving to ease suffering and relieve distress.

Following Dagmar of Bohemia's death around 1212, Waldemar married *Berengaria (1194–1221). Since his daughter, *Sophia of Denmark (1217–1248), and three of his sons—Eric IV, Abel, and Christopher I, all kings—were born after 1213, they are presumed to be the offspring of Waldemar and Berengaria.

Dagmar of Denmark (1847–1928).

See Marie Feodorovna.

d'Agoult, Marie (1805–1876).

See Wagner, Cosima for sidebar on Marie d'Agoult.

Dagover, Lil (1897–1980)

German actress who was a major star of stage and screen for over 50 years and made over 100 films. Born Marta Maria Lillits Seubert (some sources give her name as Marie Antonia Sieglinde Marta Seubert), on September 30, 1897, in Madioen, Java, Netherlands East Indies; died in Munich, Germany, on January 30, 1980; daughter of Adolf Seubert and Marta (Herf) Seubert; married Fritz Daghofer, in 1914 (divorced 1919); married Georg Witt.

Born to German parents on the island of Java where her father was a forestry expert employed by the government of the Netherlands East Indies, Marta Maria Lillits Seubert was taken to Germany at the age of six. Orphaned by the death of both parents when she was 13, she was raised by family members in various German cities. Marta Maria matured into a young woman of astonishing beauty during the next few years. She began to study acting while at boarding school in Weimar and, at age 17, married the actor Fritz Daghofer, a man 35 years her senior. Though the marriage ended in 1919, it was through Daghofer that she met leaders of a German film industry that was going through changes as revolutionary as those that were convulsing the nation's political landscape. Having changed her name to Lil Dagover, the neophyte actress appeared in two films in 1919: Fritz Lang's *Harakiri* (*Butterfly*) and Robert Wiene's pathbreaking expressionist film *The Cabinet of Dr. Caligari*, in which she appeared in the small role of Jane.

Dagover's brief film appearances alerted the public to the emergence of a new star, a woman of considerable dramatic talent and beauty. In the 1920s, she starred in Lang's *Der müde Tod* (*Destiny*, 1921), as well as in a number of well-received films directed by the brilliant F.W. Murnau, including *Phantom* (1922) and *Chronik von Grieshuus* (*At the Grey House*, 1925). She also co-starred in 1925 with Emil Jannings in *Tartuffe*. In 1925, Dagover's talent and stunning looks brought her to the attention of Germany's leading theater impresario Max Reinhardt, who invited her to represent "Beauty" at his recently founded festival in Salzburg, Austria, in the Calderon-von Hofmannsthal play *The Great Theater of the World*. Reinhardt chose well, and Dagover personified Beauty for thousands of fascinated playgoers at the Salzburg Festival for the next six years.

During the last years of the silent film era, Lil Dagover was a star not only in Germany and Austria but in Sweden and France. She appeared in several Swedish films, including Gustav Molander's *Hans engelska Fru* (*Discord*, 1928). In France, she starred in Julien Duvivier's *Le Tourbillon de Paris* (*The Whirlwind of Paris*, 1928) as well as in *La Grande Passion* (1929) and *Monte Cristo* (1929), an unusually long film that was presented in two parts. As Dagover matured in years, her screen image became well defined: she was the handsome woman who was no longer young and accepted the fact that she would have to compete with younger women who sometimes proved alluring to men simply because of their youth and physical perfection. In two films released in 1932, *Die letzte Illusion* (*The Last Illusion*) and *Das Abenteuer der Thea Roland* (*The Adventures of Thea Roland*), Dagover embodied the dilemmas of an older woman in love with a younger man. In *The Last Illusion,* she superbly portrayed a woman of 40 who loses her chance at love when the younger man she is infatuated with is seduced by her own daughter. Another fine performance was given in *The Adventures of Thea Roland,* a role in which Dagover was willing to show how a woman confronts her own fading beauty, made all the more touching because of dark circles under her eyes and facial lines that could no longer be concealed by makeup.

By 1931, Lil Dagover had become an international film star. That year, Warner Bros. invited her to Hollywood for the lead in *The Woman from Monte Carlo*. The film, which premiered in Indianapolis in America's heartland, was a success, depicting as it did an actress who was considerably more animated and sparkling than she had been in some of her European productions. Well read, fluent in five languages, with a pleasant voice, Dagover had no problems making the transition from silent to sound films, and she was ready to continue her career as the 1930s began. In 1931, she made a brief but memorable appearance in Erik Charell's extravaganza *Der Kongress tanzt* (*The Congress Dances*). In the early years of the Nazi regime, she avoided appearing in propaganda films, starring instead in such clever comedies as *Ich heirate meine Frau* (*I'm Marrying My Wife*, 1934) and a German version of Oscar Wilde's *Lady Windermere's Fan*, which was released in 1935. In 1935, she also appeared in *Der höhere Befehl* (*The Higher Command*), set in the period of the Napoleonic Wars, in which she played a French actress and spy. Dagover revealed previously untapped depths in *Schlussakkord* (*Closing Chord*, 1936), portraying a mother desperately searching for her lost son.

In her 1937 starring role in *Die Kreuzersonate* (*The Kreuzer Sonata*), adapted from the short story by Leo Tolstoy, Dagover gave an excellent performance as Yelena, a woman destroyed for breaking society's moral code by slipping into an adulterous relationship. As an upholder of middle-class morality, the Nazi regime encouraged and subsidized art that made a case for traditional virtues. Even though he was himself a notorious philanderer, Nazi propaganda chief Joseph Goebbels praised *The Kreuzer Sonata* and Dagover's performance in it,

seeing to it that she was rewarded with the coveted title of *Staatsschauspielerin* ("State Actress"). At age 40, Dagover was at the pinnacle of her fame and from this point on increasingly began to take character parts. During the war years, she appeared in supporting roles in many so-called *Kostümfilme*—extravaganzas based on heroic periods in German history as seen through the distorting lens of Nazi ideology. She appeared in the 1943 propaganda film *Wien 1910* (*Vienna 1910*), which glorified the career of anti-Semitic mayor Karl Lueger. For her work in entertaining German troops, she received a War Service Cross in 1944.

Given the fact that she had remained relatively untainted by Nazism, Lil Dagover was able to resume her acting career soon after 1945. Not all of the films she appeared in were distinguished, but in several instances she displayed the star qualities that her fans of the 1920s and 1930s remembered. These performances included her roles in *Königliche Hoheit* (*Royal Highness,* 1953), *Bekenntnisse des Hochstaplers Felix Krull* (*The Confessions of Felix Krull,* 1957), and Alfred Weidemann's television dramatization of *Buddenbrooks* (1957); all productions were based on writings of Thomas Mann. After a long absence, Dagover returned to the stage in the 1950s, receiving rave reviews for her leading roles in *Colette's *Gigi* and Jean Giraudoux's *The Madwoman of Chaillot.* The range of her interests extended from the classic German plays of Heinrich von Kleist to the plays of Anton Chekhov and Tennessee Williams.

The last phase of Lil Dagover's career was rich in achievements. In 1967, she was awarded the Cross of Merit of the Federal Republic of Germany. Despite her venerable age, she gave some of the most distinguished performances of her career in a number of carefully chosen roles in such films as Hans-Jürgen Syberberg's *Karl May* (1961), as well as in Maximilian Schell's *Der Fussgänger* (*The Pedestrian,* 1974), *Der Richter und sein Henker* (*The Judge and His Hangman,* 1975) and *Geschichten aus den Wienerwald* (*Tales from the Vienna Woods,* 1979). Lil Dagover died in Munich on January 30, 1980.

SOURCES:

Aros. *Lil Dagover: Der Werdegang einer schönen Frau.* Berlin: Verlag August Scherl, 1932.

Dagover, Lil. *Ich war die Dame: Erinnerungen.* Munich: Schneekluth Verlag, 1979.

Kreimeier, Klaus. *The Ufa Story: A History of Germany's Greatest Film Company 1918–1945.* Translated by Robert and Rita Kimber. NY: Hill and Wang, 1996.

"Lil Dagover," in *The Times* [London]. February 9, 1980, p. 14.

Romani, Cinzia. *Tainted Goddesses: Female Film Stars of the Third Reich.* Translated by Robert Connolly. NY: Sarpedon Publishers, 1992.

John Haag,
Athens, Georgia

Dahiyah Kahinah (fl. 695–703).

See Kahina.

Dahl-Wolfe, Louise (1895–1989)

*American photographer who excelled at fashion, still lifes, portraits, and documentation. Born in San Fran-*cisco, California, in 1895; died in Allendale, New Jersey, in 1989; attended California School of Design (now the San Francisco Art Institute); studied painting with Frank Van Sloan; married Meyer (Mike) Wolfe (a sculptor), in 1928 (died 1985); no children.*

Acclaimed for her impeccable color sense and her innovative use of naturalistic decors in fashion photography, Louise Dahl-Wolfe was probably the foremost female fashion photographer during the early postwar period. Born and raised in San Francisco, California, she attended the California School of Design (now the San Francisco Art Institute), where she studied painting with Frank Van Sloan. Her work at the time was also greatly influenced by artist Rudolph Schaeffer, an expert on color. Dahl-Wolfe's interest in photography began when she met *Anne W. Brigman in 1921, but she did not actually purchase a camera until 1927, when she toured Italy and Morocco with *Consuelo Kanaga. In the interim, she designed electric signs in New York and worked for a decorator in San Francisco.

In 1928, Dahl-Wolfe met and married sculptor Meyer Wolfe, whom she later credited with fostering her career by helping with her work and sharing household duties. They spent their early years together in San Francisco, where Dahl-Wolfe was employed as a photographer for an interior decorator. In 1932, she moved to a cabin in the Tennessee Smoky Mountains and produced still lifes and portraits of the mountain people. Returning to New York in 1933, she met Frank Crowninshield, then publisher of *Vanity Fair,* who ran the photographs in his magazine. Receiving favorable notices, Dahl-Wolfe began working freelance, producing advertising and fashion photographs for *Women's Home Companion* and various department stores, such as Saks Fifth Avenue and Bonwit Teller.

In 1936, she became a staff photographer for *Harper's Bazaar,* a post she held until 1958. In deference to her talent, the magazine allowed her the privilege of working out of her New York studio, although she also traveled extensively on fashion shoots. During her tenure, *Harper's* featured her photographs on 86 covers, used over 600 of her color images, and printed hundreds more of her black-and-white shots. In addition to her extraordinary use of color, Dahl-Wolfe was known for the naturalness of her settings and a delicacy of style that was attributed, at the time, to her gender. (She felt that her style had more to do with her studies at the California School of Design than with any female trait.) Dahl-Wolfe also worked for *Sports Illustrated* and *Vogue* before retiring to New Jersey in the mid-1960s. She died in 1989.

Dahlbeck, Eva (1920—)

Swedish actress, best known for her work in films of Ingmar Bergman. Born in Saltsjö-Duvnäs, Sweden, on March 8, 1920; trained at Royal Dramatic Theater, Stockholm.

Selected films: Ride Tonight *(1942);* Black Roses *(1945);* Eva *(1948);* Only a Mother *(1949);* Unser Dorf *(The Village, Switzerland, 1952);* Defiance *(1952);* Secrets of Women *(1952);* Barabbas *(1953);* A Lesson in Love *(1954);* Dreams *(1955);* Smiles of a Summer Night *(1955);* Brink of Life *(1957);* A Matter of Morals *(U.S./Sweden, 1960);* The Counterfeit Traitor *(U.S., 1962);* All These Women *(1964);* Loving Couples *(1964);* Morianna *(I the Body, 1965);* The Cats *(1965);* Les Créatures *(France/Sweden, 1966);* The Red Mantle *(Hagbard and Signe, Denmark/Sweden, 1967);* People Meet and Sweet Music Fills the Heart *(Den./Sw., 1967);* Tintomara *(1970).*

Eva Dahlbeck made her stage debut in 1941. In 1958, she was named Best Actress at Cannes Festival for her performance in Ingmar Bergman's *Brink of Life*. A writer as well as an actress, she has also written a play, a film script, a book of poetry, and more than ten novels.

Daini no sanmi (999–after 1078).

See Murasaki Shikibu for sidebar.

Dalassena, Anna (c. 1025–1105).

See Anna Dalassena.

d'Albret, Jeanne (1528–1572).

See Jeanne d'Albret.

d'Albret, Jeanne III (1528–1572).

See Jeanne d'Albret.

Dale, Kathleen (1895–1984)

English pianist, widely known for her newspaper and journal articles, as well as a book about music. Born Kathleen Richards in London, England, on June 29, 1895; died in Woking, England, on March 3, 1984; studied piano with Fanny Davies (1861–1934) and York Bowen (1884–1961); studied composition with Benjamin Dale; married Benjamin Dale (1885–1943).

Kathleen Dale studied piano with *Fanny Davies and York Bowen and was a composition student of Benjamin Dale, whom she later married. A highly regarded accompanist and cham-

ber-music performer, Kathleen Dale made many radio broadcasts in the 1920s and 1930s. She taught at the Matthay Piano School and the Workers' Educational Association. As a musical scholar, she edited and was the first to publish Schubert's Piano Sonata in E minor. For decades she wrote stimulating newspaper and journal articles and, in 1954, published *Nineteenth-Century Piano Music*. Dale's obituary in *The Times* of London noted that her diminutive stature "seems to have acted as a spur to achievement and she commanded a rare intellectual authority."

SOURCES:
Melville, Derek. "Mrs. Kathleen Dale," in *The Times* [London]. March 16, 1984, p. 16.

John Haag, Athens, Georgia

d'Alençon, Emilienne.

See Uzès, Anne, Duchesse d' for sidebar.

Dalila.

Variant of Delilah.

Dall, Caroline Wells (1822–1912)

American author, reformer, and women's rights advocate. Name variations: Caroline H. Dall. Born Caroline Wells Healey in Boston, Massachusetts, on June 22, 1822; died in Washington, D.C., on December 17, 1912; married Charles H.A. Dall (a Unitarian minister), in September 1844 (some sources cite 1843); children: two, including William Healey Dall (b. 1845, a naturalist and author).

Selected writings: Essays and Sketches *(1849);* Woman's Right to Labor *(1860);* Historical Pictures Retouched *(1860);* The College, the Market, and the Court; or, Woman's Relations to Education, Labor, and Law *(1867);* Egypt's Place in History *(1868);* Patty Gray's Journey to the Cotton Islands *(a three-volume children's book, 1868–1870);* The Romance of the Association; or, One Last Glimpse of Charlotte Temple and Eliza Wharton *(1875);* My First Holiday; or, Letters Home from Colorado, Utah, and California *(1881);* What We Really Know about Shakespeare *(1886);* Sordello—a History and a Poem *(1886);* Barbara Fritchie—a Study *(1892);* Margaret and Her Friends *(1895);* Transcendentalism in New England *(1897);* Alongside *(a privately printed memoir of her childhood, 1900);* Nazareth *(1903);* Fog Bells *(1905).*

Born into a well-to-do family, the intellectually gifted Caroline Wells Healey began contributing essays on religion and moral issues to various periodicals by age 13. Her father provided her with an excellent private-school education

Caroline Wells Dall

were well received. Much of her writing focused on the progress of the women's movement and many of her papers were read at the annual Woman's Rights Conventions. Her best-known book, *The College, the Market, and the Court,* went through two editions. In an essay on sex and education written in 1874, Dall pointed out the necessity for women to fit their intellectual pursuits into lives of family responsibilities: "So far, women have written in the nursery or the dining room, often with one foot on the cradle. They must provide for their households, and nurse their sick, before they can follow any artistic or intellectual bent."

For many years, Dall conducted a class in literature and morals from her home in Washington, D.C. In 1865, she founded the American Social Science Association, of which she served as director and vice president. She died on December 17, 1912, in Washington.

Barbara Morgan,
Melrose, Massachusetts

Dal Monte, Toti (1893–1975)

Italian coloratura soprano. Born Antonietta Meneghel on June 27, 1893; died at Pieve di Soligo on January 26, 1975, in Treviso, Italy; studied with Barbara Marchesio; married Enzo de Muro Lomanto (a singer); children: one daughter.

Debuted at La Scala (1921), at the Metropolitan Opera (1924), and at Covent Garden (1926); retired (1949).

After studying for five years with **Barbara Marchesio**, Antonietta Meneghel made her debut in *Francesca di Rimini* in the Teatro alla Scala, on February 22, 1916. She made ten lire a day. During rehearsals, when conductor Gino Marinuzzi had suggested that she change her name, she chose her nickname, Toti, and her grandmother's maiden name, Dal Monte. Following her debut, Toti Dal Monte sang Cio-Cio San in *Madame Butterfly* at the Teatro Lirico of Milan on September 14, 1918. Dal Monte's first foreign engagements were in South America where she sang in Argentina, Uruguay, and Brazil.

The famous Italian conductor Arturo Toscanini engaged her to sing Lucia at La Scala in 1921 and Beethoven's Ninth Symphony in June 1922. Toscanini then asked her to sing in the cast, and his endorsement won Dal Monte a permanent place at La Scala. She became well known in the world's major opera houses. In 1924, she debuted at the Metropolitan Opera as Lucia and in 1926 at Covent Garden as Lucia

in hopes that she would pursue a literary career, but Dall was more interested in religion and working with the underprivileged. At age 15, she started one of the first nursery schools for working mothers in Boston. At 19, a year before her father went bankrupt, she was invited to participate in *Margaret Fuller's public conversations. Fuller, a Transcendentalist, held her famous Conversations while she was in Boston between 1839–40. The participants, a who's who of eminent Bostonians, met regularly and discussed such topics as mythology, art, ethics, health, education, great men, and women's rights. Heavily influenced by Fuller, Dall would later recount the experience in *Margaret and Her Friends* (1895).

In 1844, after serving for several years as a vice-principal of a girls' school in Georgetown, Washington, D.C., Caroline married Charles Dall, a Unitarian minister. Over the next decade, she taught, lectured, raised two children, and served as a corresponding editor of *Paulina Wright Davis' women's rights monthly, *The Una*. In 1849, Dall published a collection of her own early writings called *Essays and Sketches*. Her marriage was not happy, and in 1855 Charles left to become the first Unitarian missionary to Calcutta, India. From then on, the couple lived apart except for occasional visits.

Left on her own, Dall threw her efforts behind the women's rights cause but found that she was unsuited to public leadership. She turned once again to writing and produced an impressive body of work that included histories, biographies, and children's books, all of which

and Rosina. That same year, she was engaged for a four-month tour of Australia and New Zealand with the renowned Australian singer *Nellie Melba. Off and on, between 1924 and 1928, Dal Monte criss-crossed the United States from coast to coast. In 1931, a five-month tour took her from Moscow to Hong Kong, Manila, Shanghai, and five cities in Japan.

Dal Monte's coloratura soprano was light, clear, and brilliant but with more weight than most. Her voice had great purity, and she could float a note and a focused tone at any dynamic level. Wide ranging, her voice allowed Dal Monte to shade it according to the role. She was able to darken her voice enough to sing as a light mezzo. In addition to a beautiful voice, Dal Monte was known as an accomplished actress whose roles were credible and appealing. She made several recordings for RCA Victor and His Master's Voice, which remain collectors' items.

Dal Monte suffered from high blood pressure, which ultimately caused her to retire from singing in 1949, but she continued to act. In January 1975, she was hospitalized for circulatory problems and died at Pieve di Soligo on January 26.

John Haag,
Athens, Georgia

Dalrymple, Jean (1910–1998)

American theatrical publicist, producer, and director who was a driving force behind the New York City Center. Born in Morristown, New Jersey, on September 2, 1910; died in New York City, on November 15, 1998; daughter of George (a businessman) and Elizabeth (Collins) Dalrymple; attended public school in Newark, New Jersey, for six months; tutored at home; married Ward Morehouse (a drama critic for the New York Sun*), in 1932 (divorced 1937); married Major-General Philip de Witt Ginder, on November 1, 1951 (died 1968); no children.*

One of the most respected women in the American theater, Jean Dalrymple was a driving force behind the New York City Center for three decades. The antithesis of the hard-driving, cigar-chomping male producer usually associated with Broadway's heyday, Dalrymple was once described by a reporter as "fragile as a Fragonard painting, but hep with a sense of timing like a Garrand rifle." She apparently could lure just about anyone into performing on her terms and convinced a host of stars, including *Gertrude Lawrence, *Helen Hayes, Jose Ferrer, and Maurice Evans, to appear at the City Center for salaries considerably lower than they might otherwise command. "Jean always had a kind of solid serenity about her," said producer Robert Whitehead. But "she had a great determination to get things done."

Raised in the well-to-do suburb of Morristown, New Jersey, Dalrymple attended public school for only six months, then was tutored at home by a cousin and governess. She began writing stories at an early age and decided to become a stage director after seeing her first play, *Snow White and the Seven Dwarfs*. At age 16, after completing a secretarial course, Dalrymple landed a plum job at a Wall Street brokerage house but left after four years to tour in a vaudeville act she had created with her boyfriend Dan Jarrett. She and Jarrett subsequently collaborated on a play, *Salt Water*, which was produced by John Golden. It was Golden who recognized her potential and launched her career, hiring her to work in his office as a general assistant in all aspects of the play production business.

Joti
Dal
Monte

In 1940, Dalrymple opened her own publicity office in New York, out of which she handled publicity for such hit plays as *Mr. and Mrs. North*, *The Green Pastures*, *Porgy and Bess*, *One Touch of Venus*, *The Voice of the Turtle*, and *Anna Lucasta*. In addition, she managed and publicized such stars as *Lily Pons, *Vera Zorina, *Tallulah Bankhead, *Mary Martin, Leopold Stokowski, and Norman Bel Geddes. She also served as a concert-tour manager, accompanying singer *Grace Moore and the pianist Jose Iturbi on several visits to South America and Europe. In 1945, Dalrymple produced her first play, *Hope for the Best*, a comedy by journalist William McCleery. The production, starring Franchot Tone and *Jane Wyatt, ran for three months, after which Dalrymple produced the John Cecil Holm comedy *Brighten the Corner*, which starred Charles Butterworth in his last Broadway role. A successful production of the comedy *Burlesque*, with Burt Lahr and **Jean Parker**, followed.

Jean
Dalrymple

she soon began taking an active role in producing for the Theater and Light Opera Companies.

During her long tenure with the City Center, Dalrymple produced the plays of Shakespeare and Shaw, as well as more contemporary works. She also brought to the stage revivals of the musicals by Cole Porter, the Gershwins, Frank Loesser, Rogers and Hart, and Rogers and Hammerstein. One of her earliest productions at the City Center was *Porgy and Bess* (1944), which she was able to book after it completed a national tour. In 1961, she mounted another production of *Porgy and Bess*, this time restoring the work to its original operatic form exactly as George Gershwin and DuBose Heyward had intended. In her 1975 memoir, *From the Last Row*, Dalrymple recalled that although she was proud of the production, it got mixed notices. "Howard Taubman of *The New York Times*, who had formerly been that paper's music critic and editor, loved it. Judith Crist of the *Herald Tribune* said she liked 'the old Broadway version better.' I wrote and told her she had a tin ear."

Dalrymple was married for five years to Ward Morehouse, drama critic for the *New York Sun*, with whom she collaborated on the screenplay *It Happened in New York*, produced by Universal. She divorced Morehouse in 1937 and later married Major General Philip de Witt Ginder, who died in 1968. A lifelong resident of New York City, Dalrymple lived in a brownstone across the street from the City Center. She died there in 1998, at the age of 96.

Although Franchot Tone once characterized Dalrymple as "the tenderest little lady," she was nonetheless a powerful force in the theater world. Much of her success can be credited to a missionary's zeal for bringing theater to the public. "I can do absolutely nothing I don't believe in," she once said, "but I can do *anything* I do believe in."

SOURCES:

Current Biography 1953. NY: H.W. Wilson, 1953.

Dalrymple, Jean. *From the Last Row.* Clifton, NJ: James T. White, 1975.

Severo, Richard. Obituary in *The New York Times News Service.* November 17, 1998.

Barbara Morgan,
Melrose, Massachusetts

Dalrymple's next production, Jean-Paul Sartre's *Red Gloves*, adapted by Daniel Taradash and starring Charles Boyer, proved to be one of her most controversial, provoking a storm of protest from the French playwright and his supporters who claimed that it was "vulgar" and contained a strong anti-Communist bias. Although Sartre even brought suit against his agent for authorizing the translation without permission, Dalrymple went ahead with her production, contending that the American version captured the tone and key points of the original play.

Meanwhile, Dalrymple was also involved in the New York City Center, which was established in 1943 by Mayor Fiorello LaGuardia and City Council president Newbold Morris who wanted to found a "temple for the performing arts." (The City Center was housed in the old Shriner's Mecca Temple that had been taken over by the city for nonpayment of taxes.) Her early work with the Center was as a volunteer public relations director and board member, but

Dalrymple, Learmonth White

(1827–1906)

New Zealand feminist and educational reformer.
Born in Port Chalmers, New Zealand, in 1827; died in 1906.

Learmonth Dalrymple began her career as a teacher, during which time she was in touch with *Dorothea Beale and *Frances Mary Buss, British innovators in girls' education. Following their lead, Dalrymple crusaded for secondary education for females in her own country. Through her efforts, the Otago Girls' High School was opened in 1871 and served as a model for 70 later schools. During early discussions about founding a University of New Zealand, Dalrymple successfully petitioned for the admission of women. (The first woman graduate of the university was **Kate Edger**, who earned a degree in mathematics in 1877.) By 1890, close to half the students in New Zealand universities were women. Dalrymple was also an advocate for preschool and primary education. Her book *The Kindergarten* (1879) dealt with the ideas of Friedrich Wilhelm Froebel, who founded the kindergarten system. Dalrymple was active in the temperance and suffrage movements as well.

d'Alvarez, Lili.

See Aussem, Cilly for sidebar.

Dalyell, Elsie (1881–1948).

See Chick, Harriette for sidebar.

d'Amboise, Francise (1427–1485).

See Amboise, Francise d'.

Dame aux Camélias, La (1824–1847).

See Plessis, Alphonsine.

Damer, Anne Seymour (1748–1828)

English sculptor. Born Anne Conway in 1748 (some sources cite 1749); died on May 28, 1828; daughter of Field Marshal Henry Seymour Conway (1721–1795); friend of Nelson, Walpole, and Napoleon; married John Damer, in 1767 (died 1776).

Anne Damer, while engaged in conversation with Scottish philosopher and historian David Hume, criticized some plaster casts they had seen. When Hume remarked that it was easier to criticize than create, Damer rose to the challenge by obtaining some wax and sculpting a head that she then showed him. Her work had enough merit to surprise him, but Hume renewed his challenge by suggesting that the difficulty of chiseling outweighed that of working with wax. Damer executed a bust in stone, which, though crude, elicited his admiration. From then on, she devoted herself to the practice of sculpture.

Damer traveled considerably and kept a journal. She studied under Ceracchi, acquired technique in the studio of Bacon, and learned the elements of anatomy from George Cruikshank. After visiting Italy in order to observe Grecian art, she began to imitate its pure, simple style. She married the Honorable John Damer in 1767, but the marriage was unhappy. He committed suicide in 1776.

Damer executed a number of works, including an eight-foot marble statue in the Registry Office, Edinburgh; two colossal heads in Portland stone, which ornament the keystone of the bridge at Henley-upon-Thames; a statue of George III; a bust of Fox, which she personally presented to her friend Napoleon Bonaparte in 1815 (in return, she received a snuffbox with the portrait of the emperor set in diamonds); a bust of another friend Lord Horatio Nelson, who sat for the work immediately after his return from the Battle of the Nile (she presented this sculpture to the city of London); busts of her father, of Sir Humphry Davy, of her mother, and of herself.

Anne Damer died on May 28, 1828. Though she at one time intended to publish her journal, in her will she commanded all her papers be destroyed; among them were not only her manuscripts but many interesting and valuable letters. Maintaining that the distinction of being an artist was all that she wanted in life, she requested that her working apron and her tools be placed beside her in her coffin.

D'Amica, Suso Cecchi (b. 1914).

See Cecchi D'Amico, Suso.

Damita, Lili (c. 1901–1994)

French-born leading lady who, though celebrated as a popular movie actress, achieved even greater celebrity as a result of her tempestuous marriage to the swashbuckling Errol Flynn. Born Liliane Marie Madeleine Carré in Bordeaux, France, on July 19, 1901 (some sources state she was born in Paris on July 10, 1904); died in Miami Beach, Florida, on March 21, 1994; married Errol Flynn (an actor), in 1935; married Allen Loomis; children: (first marriage) Sean Flynn.

Born in Bordeaux, France, Liliane Carré was a beautiful girl who became a music-hall star at age 16 at the Folies Bergère, soon succeeding the famous *Mistinguett as the star of the Casino de Paris revue. Educated at convent schools in Portugal, Spain and Greece, she studied dancing in Belgium and entertained Allied troops during World War I. Her name change took place when King Alphonso XIII of Spain, a notorious womanizer, saw her in a red bathing suit on the beach in Biarritz, and asked who the "*damita del maillo rojo*" (girl in the red bathing suit) was. Liliane Carré was now Lili Damita, and her acting career flourished in the mid-1920s in French, German, Austrian, and British silent films.

Damita spoke five languages, but it was for her stunning looks, not her linguistic talents, that Samuel Goldwyn summoned her from Berlin to Hollywood in 1928 to play opposite Ronald Colman in the movie version of Joseph Conrad's "Rescue." The film was a success, prompting the *New York Times* reviewer to describe her as an actress who was "fascinatingly handsome and gives an intelligent performance" in a role generally regarded as being difficult. The films she starred in during the next few years included *The Bridge of San Luis Rey* (1929), based on the Thornton Wilder novel, *The Cockeyed World* (1929), one of Hollywood's last silent films, and *Fighting Caravans* (1931), a lively adventure comedy in which she shared top billing with Gary Cooper. She was also in 1931's *Friends and Lovers,* with Adolphe Menjou, Laurence Olivier, and Erich von Stroheim. Two more hit films followed in 1932: *The Match King*, based on the life of Swedish "match king" Ivar Kreuger, and *This is the Night,* with Cary Grant, in which she starred as a philandering married woman.

Lili Damita found herself increasingly at the center of the American cult of celebrity during the ensuing years. Fan magazines and newspapers alike chronicled every detail of her life, her rumored or genuine love affairs, changes of hairdo, and new film roles. By the mid-1930s, she was an established superstar and had been romantically linked with many men, including Prince Louis Ferdinand of Prussia, grandson of German ex-Kaiser Wilhelm II and great-great-grandson of Queen *Victoria. In 1929, the prince spent several years in the United States, working for Henry Ford in Detroit, obtaining a pilot's license, and meeting Franklin D. Roosevelt and Charlie Chaplin. In Hollywood, Louis Ferdinand met and fell in love with Damita. He planned to elope with her to Tijuana but decided at the last moment that she had been exploiting their relationship for publicity reasons and broke off the affair. Damita's comment on the episode was curt, noting simply that "I will never marry royalty, they are too self-centered, and so am I." Louis Ferdinand would marry *Kira of Russia in 1938.

In 1935, Damita completed work on what turned out to be her last film, the farce *Brew-*ster's Millions. That same year, she married the Tasmanian-born actor Errol Flynn, who had pursued her with great ardor after spotting her in the company of *Merle Oberon on a transatlantic liner. Damita soon discovered that Flynn's charms were superficial. He was a compulsive womanizer, an alcoholic, and spent his income as fast as it was acquired, compelling him to earn money by carrying out spy missions against the U.S. for a Nazi agent, Austrian-born Dr. Hermann Erben.

But Damita and Flynn were suited to each other in at least some ways. Both enjoyed music, dancing, and social life, and both were endowed with enough intelligence and intellectual curiosity to enjoy good books. She taught him about French wines and French cooking, while he instructed her in the basics of English cookery. Yet from the outset, their union was doomed. Emotionally insecure, Flynn needed constant praise, something Damita was not willing to do. Soon, minor tensions turned into major clashes. Tempers flared, and years later Flynn recalled that "Only by great nimbleness of foot did I avoid a weekly fractured skull." Both Flynn and Damita broke their marriage vows, and some in Hollywood believed that both actors were bisexual.

The Damita-Flynn marriage, punctuated by quarrels, separations, and acrimonious attempts at reconciliation, somehow lasted until 1941, the same year Damita gave birth to her only child, a son named Sean. After Sean's birth, she began divorce proceedings against Flynn, who found himself accused at the time of statutory rape by two adolescent members of his fan club. Although he was acquitted of the rape charges, in 1942 the divorce judge awarded Damita half of Flynn's property and $1,500 a month. The dissipated Flynn died in October 1959. Damita remarried in 1962, her second husband being Allen B. Loomis, a wealthy Iowan. This marriage would also end in divorce.

Her son Sean attempted an acting career in the 1960s but was drawn to the war in Vietnam as a photographer. He disappeared in Cambodia in 1970 and was declared legally dead by a Palm Beach court in 1984. It was not until almost three decades after his disappearance that the mystery of what happened to him was explained. Declassified CIA documents released in the 1990s told how Sean Flynn and another photojournalist, Dana Stone, were captured near the Vietnamese-Cambodian border. They were held in a small village for months, marched north with the villagers into Cambodia, then taken back to Vietnam and finally, when they pressed

MOTION PICTURE CLASSIC

JANUARY

25¢

Hollywood
Sob-Stories
(Greta Garbo)

Nancy Carroll *on*
Lessons in Love

*Lili
Damita*

for their release by going on a hunger strike, Flynn and Stone were beaten to death with hoes by a squad sent in by the Khmer Rouge.

Despite her determined efforts over many years to find out, Lili Damita never knew what happened to her son. She died of Alzheimer's disease in Palm Beach, Florida, on March 21, 1994, too late to comprehend any CIA report.

SOURCES:

Bergan, Ronald. "The Lady in Red," in *The Guardian* [London]. April 7, 1994, p. 13.

Boxer, Sarah. "Eyes on a War: Fixed Images, Stilled Shutters," in *The New York Times*. November 3, 1997, pp. B1, B8.

Higham, Charles. *Errol Flynn: The Untold Story*. Garden City, NY: Doubleday, 1980.

"Lili Damita," in *The Times* [London]. April 4, 1994, p. 17.

Madsen, Axel. *The Sewing Circle: Hollywood's Greatest Secret—Female Stars Who Loved Other Women*. Secaucus, NJ: Carol, 1995.

Niven, David. *Bring on the Empty Horses*. NY: Putnam, 1975.

———. *The Moon's a Balloon: Reminiscences*. London: Hamilton, 1971.

"Prince Louis Ferdinand of Prussia," in *Daily Telegraph*. September 28, 1994, p. 21.

Saxon, Wolfgang. "Lili Damita, Actress from France Who Starred in Hollywood, Dies," in *The New York Times Biographical Service*. March 1994, p. 430.

John Haag, Athens, Georgia

Damo (fl. 6th c. BCE)

Pythagorean philosopher. Born in Crotona, Italy; daughter of Pythagoras of Samos (a philosopher, mathematician, politician, spiritual leader) and Theano of Crotona (a Pythagorean philosopher); sister of Arignote, Myia, Telauges, and Mnesarchus; educated at the School of Pythagoras.

In some accounts, Damo is the only daughter of *Theano and Pythagoras, the ancient Italian philosopher, but she is generally considered to have had two sisters *Arignote and *Myia. Two brothers, Telauges and Mnesarchus, are also noted. All became members of the sect established by their father Pythagoras. Pythagoreanism ascribed to the precept of metempsychosis and the teaching that earthly life is only a purification of the soul. It stressed moderation and the study of mathematics. Devotees believed that the order of the world was derived from numbers.

Although Damo is not noted for any works herself, it is quite likely that she contributed to the doctrines ascribed to Pythagoras. In testimony to his greatness, it was the tradition of the sect to credit him with authorship. Some of the content of Pythagoras' writings comes to us through Damo's preservation. Based on the commentaries of their father, her sister Arignote and her brother Telauges composed the *Sacred Discourses*, which were central to the development of the Pythagorean tradition as it continued to flourish for the next few centuries. The commentaries were in Damo's care after Pythagoras' death in a fire at Myia's house.

It is not clear the social status to which Damo would have been accustomed prior to her father's death, as early accounts of Pythagoras and the Pythagoreans come primarily from followers who tended to glorify and romanticize their lives. But it is certain that she suffered great hardship following his death. Though the Pythagoreans were expelled from Crotona and Damo was exceedingly poor, she refused to sell her father's writings because he had prohibited the communication of their teachings to strangers.

SOURCES:

Coppleston, Frederick, S.J. *A History of Philosophy*. London: Search Press, 1946.

Guthrie, W.K.C. "Pythagoras and Pythagoreanism," in *Encyclopedia of Philosophy*. Vol. 7. Edited by Paul Edwards. NY: Macmillan, 1967.

Jamblichus, C. *Life of Pythagoras*. London: John M. Watkins, 1926.

Kersey, Ethel M. *Women Philosophers: a Bio-critical Source Book*. CT: Greenwood Press, 1989.

Philip, J.A. *Pythagoras and Early Pythagoreanism*. Toronto: University of Toronto Press, 1966.

Schure, Edouard. *The Ancient Mysteries of Delphi: Pythagoras*. NY: Rudolf Steiner, 1971.

Waithe, Mary Ellen, ed. *A History of Women Philosophers*. Vol. 1. Boston: Martinus Nijhoff, 1987.

Catherine Hundleby, M.A. Philosophy, University of Guelph, Guelph, Ontario, Canada

Damoreau, Madame (1801–1863).

See Cinti-Damoreau, Laure.

Dampierre, Emmanuela del (b. 1913)

Duchess of Segovia. Born Emmanuela Vittoria del Dampierre on November 8, 1913, in Rome, Italy; daughter of Roger del Dampierre, 2nd duke of San Lorenzo, and Vittoria Emilia di Poggio Suasa; became first wife of Jaime (1908–1975), duke of Segovia (renounced claim to the throne of Spain in 1939), on March 4, 1935; married Antonion Sozzani, on November 21, 1949; children: (first marriage) Alfonso Jaime (b. 1936), duke of Cadiz; Gonzalo (b. 1937).

Damsel of Brittany (1184–1241).

See Eleanor, the Maid of Brittany.

Dananir al Barmakiyya (fl. late 8th c.)

Arabian singer who wrote the Book of Choice Songs. Flourished in the late 8th to early 9th centuries; dates of birth and death are uncertain.

Dananir al Barmakiyya was a slave who was sold to the household of Yahya ibn Khalid al-Barmaki, where she was taught music. The Barmak family came from Persia, and many of its members received high positions in the government during the reign of al-Mansur (r. 754–755). Although Dananir was only a slave, the opportunity to learn to perform vocally meant a chance at fame and fortune. Singers often married their own masters, achieving high positions and immense wealth. Her teachers included Ibrahim and Ishaf al-Mausuli, Ibn Jami, Fulaih, and Badhl. Dananir's voice was so beautiful that the Abbasid ruler, Caliph Harun al-Rashid, hero of the *Arabian Nights*, took great pleasure in hearing her sing at his minister's house in Baghdad and gave her extravagant gifts, including a necklace worth 30,000 gold coins. When Om Jafar, al-Rashid's wife, became jealous of the singer and the gifts she was receiving, she insisted on meeting Dananir. But upon hearing her sing, Om Jafar told her husband that his gifts were worth the cost. Also a composer, Dananir al Barmakiyya authored *Kitab mujarrad al-aghani* (*Book of Choice Songs*).

John Haag, Athens, Georgia

Dancer, Ann (1734–1801).

See Barry, Ann Street.

Danco, Suzanne (1911—)

Belgian coloratura soprano. *Born in Brussels, Belgium, on January 22, 1911; studied at the Brussels Conservatory and with Fernando Carpi in Prague.*

Won the International Bel Canto Prize in Venice (1936); debuted at the Genoa Opera as Fiodiligi in Mozart's Cosi fan tutte (1941); appeared in Teatro alla Scala (1948), Glyndebourne (1948–51), and Covent Garden (1951).

Suzanne Danco is remembered primarily as one of the most aristocratic and accomplished recitalists, but she also had a wide-ranging experience in many operatic roles. During her career, Danco appeared in *Cosi fan tutte, Peter Grimes, Oedipus Rex,* and *Wozzeck.* Although she received high praise for her roles, she lacked the temperament for operatic singing, which calls for a certain glamour. Danco chose, instead, to concentrate on a modern repertory as a recitalist.

Best described as a "slender soprano," her voice was light, and she found it difficult to make an impression on listeners in some roles. Though her singing was supple and attractive and her musicianship meticulous, at times the character of her voice did not seem fully formed. Certain roles, however, were perfectly suited to Danco's voice. In *Cosi fan tutte* under Karl Böhm's direction, she was at her best, with a liquid tone quali-

ty and fluid coloratura. French opera also suited her talents. Her lyric soprano, lighter than is usually encountered, was a perfect voice for the recitals for which she became widely known.

John Haag, Athens, Georgia

Suzanne Danco

Dandridge, Dorothy (1923–1965)

African-American actress, singer and dancer, one of the first black actresses to enter the Hollywood mainstream and the first to be nominated for an Oscar for Best Actress. Name variations: Dottie. Pronunciation: DAN-dridj. Born Dorothy Dandridge on November 9, 1923, in Cleveland, Ohio; died by her own hand in her Hollywood apartment on September 8, 1965; daughter of Ruby and Cyril Dandridge; attended public schools sporadically but did not complete high school; married Harold Nicholas, in 1941 (divorced 1946); married Jack Denison, on June 22, 1959 (divorced 1962); children: (first marriage) Harolyn ("Lynn").

Appeared in black vaudeville with sister as "The Wonder Kids" throughout the South from the age of three; moved with family to Los Angeles (1930); began appearing in nightclubs and revues by her late teens, and in small film parts soon after; given the leading role in Carmen Jones *(1954), a lavish, all-black adaptation of the Bizet opera, for which she was nominated for Best Actress; starred in the film version of* Porgy and Bess *(1959), for which she won the Golden Globe award for Best Actress.*

Filmography: A Day at the Races *(1937);* Lady from Louisiana *(1941);* Sundown *(1941);* Sun Valley Serenade *(1941);* Bahama Passage *(1941);* Drums of the Congo *(1942);* Hit Parade of 1943 *(1943);* Since You Went Away *(1944);* Atlantic City *(1944);* Tarzan's Peril *(1951);* Jungle Queen *(1951);* The Harlem Globetrotters *(1951);* Bright Road *(1953);* Remains To Be Seen *(1953);* Carmen Jones *(1954);* Island in the Sun *(1957);* The Decks Ran Red *(1958);* Porgy and Bess *(1959);* Tamango *(1959);* Moment of Danger *(Malaga, U.K., 1960).*

I was the first Negro that thousands of whites ever met.

—Dorothy Dandridge

In 1953, 20th Century-Fox assigned Austrian-born Otto Preminger his first musical, *Carmen Jones,* a lavish adaptation of the Bizet opera that was to feature an entirely African-American cast. Oddly, the problem for Preminger had nothing to do with being a 45-year-old Austrian directing an all-black film based on a French opera (there were no mainstream black directors in those days), the problem was finding a suitable leading lady for his Carmen. Most of the other lead roles had already been cast with some of the top African-American entertainers of the day—Harry Belafonte, *Pearl Bailey, Brock Peters, and a young **Diahann Carroll**. So far, however, the right Carmen had eluded him—until the day a tall, strikingly beautiful woman with luxurious, jet black hair sauntered into his office, wearing a slit skirt and low-cut blouse. It

took Preminger several minutes to recognize an actress that he knew well under the wig and provocative clothing; one he had considered too refined to play the earthy Carmen. Dorothy Dandridge was given the part that would prove to be her breakthrough role.

Dandridge was certainly no stranger to the limitations imposed on an African-American woman in a business run by white men. She had learned it first from her mother **Ruby Dandridge**, a singer and dancer who brought young Dottie and her sister **Vivian** along with her on the black Southern vaudeville circuit of the mid-1920s. Dorothy's father Cyril had left Ruby before Dottie was born in Cleveland, Ohio, in 1923. Struggling to earn a living for herself and her daughters, Ruby put Vivian and three-year-old Dottie on stage as "The Wonder Kids," playing throughout the South to African-American audiences in church halls and segregated auditoriums. The duo would recite poetry and perform skits their mother wrote for them. Ruby also brought along her friend **Eloise Matthews**, whom Dottie and Vivian came to call "Auntie Ma-Ma," as both piano-player and guardian for the two girls. Many years later, Dorothy claimed in her autobiography that she had been physically abused by Matthews, who kept the girls in line with violent threats that often became painfully real. "She did everything she could to destroy me," Dorothy wrote.

After several years on the road, Ruby heard that there were jobs for African-Americans in Hollywood, and in 1930 seven-year-old Dorothy found herself in California, attending school for the first time while her mother auditioned for bit parts in radio plays and films as the black "mammy" or the wealthy white people's maid. Jobs were not as plentiful as Ruby had expected, and before long Dottie and Vivian—now joined by a third girl, ◂ **Etta Jones**—began appearing as The Dandridge Sisters, playing nightclubs and revues up and down the West Coast. The act was well-received, and all eyes fastened on Dottie who, with her lighter skin and Caucasian features, was the most "white-looking" of the three. By the mid-1930s, the girls were appearing at the Cotton Club in Harlem, although Dandridge—now 14—confessed she felt "small-town and raw" next to the professional chorus girls and singers they met on the New York circuit. Appearing on the same bill were the Nicholas Brothers, a successful song-and-dance act of the time. Harold and Fayard Nicholas befriended the girls, but it was Harold who seemed particularly cordial toward Dorothy.

❧▸ **Jones, Etta** (1928—)

African-American jazz and pop singer. Born in 1928.

Often confused with **Etta James**, Etta Jones sang jazz and pop, in an understated, vibrant fashion. She was a frequent partner of saxist Houston Person in the 1970s and 1980s. Her albums include: *Don't Go to Strangers* (1960), *Something Nice* (1960), *Fine and Mellow* (1987), and *Sugar* (1989).

Dorothy
Dandridge

In actuality, Dandridge was beginning to be noticed for her distinctive singing style and what one critic termed her "puma-lithe figure." When the Dandridge Sisters act broke up in the early 1940s, Dorothy found work in revues, like Duke Ellington's "Jump for Joy," and in feature films.

In fact, her very first film appearance had been in 1937, when she was given a small walk-on in the Marx Brothers' *A Day at the Races*. Similar small roles followed, always as a maid, a "mammy," or in musical shorts that were, by any generation's standards, outrageous racial slurs. These were the only parts open to African-American actors in mainstream films of the time, with pay scales far below those of white actors, since blacks were barred from the actors' unions. But Dandridge needed to work and took what she could find.

In 1941, she and Harold Nicholas appeared in *Sun Valley Serenade,* attracting favorable attention for their rendition of "Chattanooga Choo Choo." During the shoot, Nicholas proposed marriage and Dandridge accepted. She would later claim the marriage was never happy; nonetheless, the following year, a child was born to the couple, a daughter named Harolyn, though Dandridge would call her "Lynn." Nicholas and Dandridge publicly disputed the events surrounding the day of Lynn's birth, with Dorothy claiming, and Harold denying, that he was out with another woman the night her labor pains began. Dandridge maintained she waited until morning for Harold to come home, by which time the baby had to be delivered using forceps. Whatever the truth, it became evident within two years that something was seriously wrong with the child. Although physically normal and beautiful like her mother, Lynn had not begun speaking by the time she was two, and tests revealed brain damage. Told that Lynn would never mature mentally, Dandridge was advised to institutionalize her. But she refused, choosing instead to place her daughter in the care of none other than Eloise Matthews, who would faithfully take care of Lynn for nearly 20 years. Not long after, Dandridge and Nicholas were divorced.

Dandridge turned all her attention on her career. While on a nightclub tour, she played New York's legendary La Vie en Rose; there, she attracted the attention of Harry Belafonte, with whom she would remain friends. She was on the cover of *Look* magazine, and her popularity and national attention brought her acceptance in all-white venues across the country. In Miami Beach, for example—where African-Americans lived in a segregated section of Miami and had to travel back and forth to their jobs at the large, beachside hotels—Dandridge threatened to quit her engagement at the Fontainbleau unless she was given a room at the hotel. The management relented. She also claimed to be the first black performer to play the Waldorf Astoria's Empire Room.

Dandridge began to see herself as a "flying wedge," a bridge between white-and-black audiences. "The audience," she wrote in her autobiography, "could 'integrate' with a colored woman who had Caucasian features." She also convinced herself that marrying a white man was inevitable, a way to affirm her standing as racial peacemaker—all this, at a time when America had yet to seriously face its deep racial divisions. "Color was the major tragedy in Dottie's life," her close friend **Geri Branton** told journalist **Gail Lumet Buckley**.

Her watershed year was 1953. Hollywood had by now discovered the largely untapped black moviegoing audience, and two films starring Dorothy Dandridge appeared that year, both for MGM: *Bright Road,* in which she played opposite Belafonte, and *Remains To Be Seen.* It was also the year that she landed the lead role in *Carmen Jones* and began a long-running affair with Preminger that she hoped would end in marriage. She had had the same hope for an earlier affair with actor Peter Lawford, which ended when Dandridge suggested marriage—a move that, in the mid-1950s, would surely have ended both their careers.

When *Carmen Jones* was released in 1954, Dandridge found herself the toast of Hollywood for her performance, becoming the first African-American with an Oscar nomination for Best Actress. (***Hattie McDaniel** had won for Best Supporting Actress for *Gone With the Wind* in 1939.) Although Dandridge lost the award to ***Grace Kelly** for *The Country Girl,* she felt vindicated in her role as integration's pioneer.

But Hollywood saw it differently. Studio heads preferred seeing Dandridge as a black sex goddess; it gave them a way to titillate audiences with forbidden interracial love that, while plainly indicated, was never actually portrayed explicitly on screen. She was, in fact, the latest in a long line of stereotyped feminine "mulattos," cast as tragic figures caught between their African-American heritage and their Caucasian features. In her next three films—*Island In The Sun, The Decks Ran Red,* and *Tamango*—she portrayed just such a character, falling in love with a white man only to be rejected and cast aside. Far from being the bridge between black and white, Dandridge found herself reinforcing on screen the very barriers she thought she was demolishing. *Island In The Sun,* in fact, was banned in Alabama for promoting "race mongrelization," and *Tamango* had to be shot in France when an American studio and distributor could not be found. Before long, Dandridge had to admit to herself that her dream would be unrealized. "Nothing that I had—beauty, money, recognition as an artist—was sufficient to break through the powerful psychological bind of racist thinking," she wrote.

But there was one more triumph in store. Columbia Pictures had hired Rouben Mamoulian to direct its production of *Porgy and Bess*. Mamoulian chose Dandridge as his female lead to play opposite Sidney Poitier's Porgy. Soon after casting was completed, however, Mamoulian was replaced by Preminger. Although their affair had cooled, Dandridge and Preminger had remained professionally friendly, and Dorothy still had hopes for their future. But Preminger seemed intent on calling an end to it all. Years later, Poitier recalled the first day of shooting, reporting that Preminger, as if to warn Dandridge

that any further relations were out of the question, went out of his way to humiliate her before cast and crew. She was "stripped naked" by Preminger's abuse and insults, said Poitier. Nevertheless, when the film was released the following year, Dandridge's performance was hailed as her best work to date. In 1959, she won the Golden Globe award—the Hollywood Foreign Press' version of the Oscar—as Best Actress.

That same year, she married again. The groom, this time, was white. He was Jack Denison, a former Las Vegas maitre d' who had re-

From the movie Carmen Jones, *starring* Dorothy Dandridge.

cently purchased a night club on Hollywood's Sunset Strip in partnership with Sammy Davis, Jr. Denison suggested Dandridge return to her show-business roots by performing at his club, hoping her name would bring in an audience and give his business venture a successful launch. Despite her film successes, however, her name failed to draw the crowds, and it was not long before Denison's club was forced to close. In 1962, she and Denison divorced amid speculation in the press that he had been physically abusing her.

Dandridge's downward spiral quickened. Movie offers had stopped. She lost nearly all her savings in a get-rich-quick oil scheme, then discovered she owed nearly $130,000 to creditors. She was forced to declare bankruptcy, and, on the day she was being evicted from her Hollywood Hills home, her daughter Lynn—now grown—was returned to her. For 20 years, Dandridge had refused to institutionalize her daughter, but now, with no money for home care, she had no choice.

Taking a small apartment, cushioning her pain with pills and liquor, Dandridge made one last effort to go back to work. She took whatever singing jobs she could find and signed a contract with a $10,000 advance for her autobiography, *Everything and Nothing*, which didn't materialize until five years after her death. One of her final public appearances was in a stage production of *Show Boat*, but the drugs and alcohol had taken their toll. Dandridge barely made it through the run of the show.

By spring 1965, she told an old friend and former manager that she felt she was dying and asked him to make sure she was cremated in whatever she was wearing at the time of her death. She struggled on through the summer, but it was this same friend who, on September 8, discovered Dandridge's body on the bathroom floor of her apartment. The Los Angeles County coroner reported that she had died of an overdose of an anti-depressant prescribed by her psychiatrist. She was 42.

In the early 1950s, when Dandridge's career was beginning its meteoric climb, she was invited to a dinner for Achmed Sukarno, then the president of Indonesia, who is reported to have told her, "Never forget, with the white man you will never be equal." But it was Dorothy Dandridge's tragedy that she dedicated herself to showing the world that African-Americans and whites *could* be on an equal footing. The reality of her era, on the eve of the fight for civil rights, finally crushed her. "Dorothy was at the mercy of fantasies," said Geri Branton. "She thought that because she ate in the dining room with the big shots, she had conquered racism."

SOURCES:
Buckley, Gail Lumet. "Dorothy's Surrender," in *Premiere*. Vol. 6, no. 13. September 15, 1993.
Dandridge, Dorothy, with Earl Conrad. *Everything and Nothing*. NY: Abelard-Schuman, 1970.

SUGGESTED READING:
Bogle, Donald. *Dorothy Dandridge*. Amistad Press, 1997.
Null, Gary. *Black Hollywood: The Negro In Motion Pictures*. NY: Citadel Press, 1975.

RELATED MEDIA:
Introducing Dorothy Dandridge, starring Halle Berry, HBO, August 1999.

Norman Powers, writer-producer, Chelsea Lane Productions, New York, New York

Dane, Clemence (1888–1965)

English novelist and playwright. Name variations: also wrote under real name Winifred Ashton; acted under Diana Cortis. Born Winifred Ashton on February 21, 1888, in Greenwich, London; died on March 28, 1965, in London; daughter of Arthur Charles (a commission merchant) and Florence (Bentley) Ashton; educated in England, Germany, and Switzerland; studied art in Dresden and at the Slade School, London.

Selected writings: Regiment of Women *(1917);* Legend *(1919);* Broome Stages *(1931); (collection of feminist essays)* The Woman's Side *(1926);* Tradition and Hugh Walpole *(1929); (detective story written with Helen Simpson)* Sir John *(1930); (with Helen Simpson)* Enter Sir John *(1932); (biography of* *Mary Kingsley)* A Woman Among Wild Men *(1938);* London Has a Garden *(1964).*

Plays: A Bill of Divorcement *(1921);* Will Shakespeare *(1921);* Naboth's Vineyard *(1926);* Granite *(1926);* Adam's Opera *(1928);* Wild Decembers *(1932);* Come of Age *(1933);* Mariners *(1927);* Eighty in the Shade *(1959).*

Clemence Dane began writing after ill health cut short an acting career. Born Winifred Ashton, she took her pseudonym from the Church of St. Clement Danes in the Strand, in the area of London where she lived for most of her life. Her first novel, *Regiment of Women* (1917), about life at a girls' school, met with critical acclaim, as did *Legend* (1919), about a woman writer, and *Broome Stages* (1931), the story of a theatrical family. Dane teamed with the Australian-born novelist *Helen Simpson to write several detective stories that featured an actor-manager as the main character. Her last book, *London Has a Garden* (1964), is a history of Covent Garden that also contains some of her reminiscences.

Dane's first play, *A Bill of Divorcement* (1921), dealt with the issues of divorce on the grounds of insanity. The play had a long run in London and in New York where it provided *Katharine Cornell with one of her first major roles on Broadway. It also provided *Katharine Hepburn her first role in film. However, Dane's subsequent plays were not as well received. Three of her plays were based on literary lives: *Will Shakespeare* (1921), *Wild Decembers* (1932, about the Brontës), and *Come of Age* (1933, based on the life of Thomas Chatterton). In 1934, she adapted Rostand's *L'Aiglon* for the stage, followed by adaptations of Max Beerbohm's *The Happy Hypocrite* (1936) and Friedrich Hebbel's *Herodes and Mariamne* (1938). Her last play, *Eighty in the Shade* (1958), was written especially for *Sybil Thorndike. Dane also produced seven film scripts, including the screenplay for *Anna Karenina* (1935).

In addition to writing, Dane, who had studied art as a girl, was known as an excellent sculptor. Her bust of the famed actor Ivor Novello stands in the foyer of the Theater Royal in Drury Lane. She received the CBE in 1953.

d'Angeville, Henriette (1795–1871)

French mountaineer. Born in 1795; died in Lausanne, Switzerland, in 1871; member of the Beaumonts, a prestigious French family (her father was imprisoned during the French Revolution); lived at Ferney, near Geneva, Switzerland; never married.

The first woman to organize and undertake her own climb, Henriette d'Angeville successfully ascended Mt. Blanc (15,771 ft.) in September 1838, at age 44. She was not, however, the first woman to reach the summit. In 1809, ⚜➤ **Marie Paradis**, an 18-year-old Chamonix maid, made the ascent, but the attempt was not officially acknowledged because she was apparently dragged up the last several stages by her companions while in an altitude-induced semicoma. Noted d'Angeville: "When I went up Mont Blanc it had not been ascended by any woman capable of remembering her impressions."

In the mid-19th century, women did not ride bicycles much less scale mountains. Compounding the dangers of the climb was a prejudice against independent-minded women that might have defeated a less resolute individual. As **Durvla Murphy** relates in an introduction to d'Angeville's diary, even a robust constitution in a woman was "generally regarded as a peasant quality, not an attribute of which ladies should boast, and cer-

Clemence Dane

tainly not one to be displayed by climbing a mountain most gentlemen preferred to admire from afar." Undaunted by her critics, d'Angeville planned her trek in just 15 days, including hiring her retinue and gathering provisions.

She set off on a Monday morning with six guides, six porters, a mule driver, and a well-stocked caravan of wine, mutton, fowl, and chocolate. Murphy speculates that d'Angeville's

⚜➤ **Paradis, Marie** (fl. 1808)

French mountaineer who made the first female ascent of Mt. Blanc. Flourished around 1808.

Chamonix's 18-year-old Marie Paradis climbed Mt. Blanc (15,771 ft.) in 1808. Unfortunately, little is known about the young adventurer who has been identified either as the owner of tearooms in Les Pèlerins or as a Chamonix maid. She was lured into making the climb by guides who promised that as the first woman to reach the peak, she would become rich and famous. Reports that she had been dragged half dead to the top turned out to be quite correct. "I just remember it was white all around," she said, "and black down away below, but that's all."

Henriette
d'Angeville

forced to stop and nap every 20 steps until she finally found the strength to drag herself to the peak. Her guides offered to carry her, but she staunchly refused. As she drove her stick into the summit, she experienced a complete revival and, for the next hour, marveled at the spectacle before her. While enjoying the remarkable views, d'Angeville wrote a number of letters to her friends and relatives "to serve as a constant reminder that I had not forgotten them even on the summit of Mont Blanc." Before leaving the peak, her guides formed a seat with their hands and lifted her as high as they could, thus elevating her four feet above the peak, to a height never attained by her predecessors. With rising winds and a storm approaching, the party made its way back to base camp where they witnessed a spectacular avalanche before completing the journey back to Chamonix the next day.

D'Angeville returned home to "a position she enjoyed, having a morbid passion for self-advertisement," notes Claire Elliane Engle in *Mountaineering in the Alps.* After the climb, one of her first visitors was Marie Paradis (now an old woman), who came to offer congratulations and compare notes. Over the next 25 years, d'Angeville made 21 more ascents, climbing the 10,250-ft. Oldenhorn in the Alps at the age of 69. She died in 1871, the same year *Lucy Walker became the first woman to climb the Matterhorn (14,690 ft.).

SOURCES:

d'Angeville, Henriette. *My Ascent of Mont Blanc.* Translated from the French by Jennifer Barnes. London, England: HarperCollins, 1991.

Barbara Morgan, Melrose, Massachusetts

d'Angoulême, Margaret or Marguerite (1492–1549).

See Margaret of Angoulême.

Daniel, Jessie Ames (1883–1972).

See Ames, Jessie Daniel.

Daniels, Bebe (1901–1971)

American actress. Born Phyllis (sometimes cited as Virginia) Daniels in Dallas, Texas, on January 14, 1901; died in 1971; daughter of Melville Daniels (a Scottish-born manager of a touring theater company) and Phyllis (Griffin) Daniels (a Spanish-born actress); educated under private teachers; attended Sacred Heart Convent, Los Angeles, California; married Benjamin Bethel Lyon, Jr. (an actor), on June 14, 1930; children: Barbara Bebe Lyon; (adopted) Richard Lyon.

21 pounds of clothing may have posed as much of a hazard as any she would meet on the mountain. "Under a voluminous belted cloak she wore fleece-lined plaid, peg-top trousers and thick woolen stockings over silk stockings. A close fur-trimmed bonnet with a green veil matched a long black boa, a black velvet facemask and deep fur cuffs." Unable to contain the elation of getting under way, she began the trek at a fast pace. "My feet seemed winged," she recorded. "I scarcely walked, I ran! . . . 'Slowly, slowly!' cried the guides. 'Think of tomorrow.'"

In her detailed account of the experience, d'Angeville noted that it was not the first ninetenths of the climb, but the final ascent to the summit that posed the greatest challenge. After conquering the Mimont rocks, traversing the Bossons glacier, and facing a variety of menacing avalanches and seracs, she was almost defeated by altitude sickness just as her goal was within grasp. Beset by a pounding heart, muscle weakness, and intervals of leaden sleepiness, she was

Bebe
Daniels

Selected films: Male and Female *(1919);* Why Change Your Wife? *(1920);* The Affairs of Anatol *(1921);* The Speed Girl *(1921);* Pink Gods *(1922);* Unguarded Women *(1924);* Monsieur Beaucaire *(1924);* Campus Flirt *(1926);* She's a Sheik *(1927);* Rio Rita *(1929);* Alias French Gertie *(1930);* Love Comes Along *(1930);* Reaching for the Moon *(1931);* The Maltese Falcon *(1931);* Forty-Second Street *(1933);* Counsellor at Law *(1933);* The Return of Carol Dean *(1935);* Hi Gang *(GB, 1940);* Life with the Lyons *(GB, 1953);* The Lyons in Paris *(GB, 1955).*

Bebe Daniels, the dark-eyed movie star, reinvented herself several times in a career that spanned over 50 years. She was on stage at the age of four, played juveniles in the silents, and made over 200 shorts before appearing in a major film. When Paramount, her studio for ten years, refused to put her in the talkies, she signed with RKO and not only talked but sang her way into a second series of successful films. When her career declined in the 1930s, she and her husband, actor Ben Lyon, traveled to London, where they enjoyed success on the music-hall circuit and in a popular radio and television series.

Born in Dallas, Texas, in 1901, Daniels was still a baby when her theatrical parents moved to Los Angeles. Billed as "The World's Youngest Shakespearean Actress," the four-year-old appeared in her father's stock company as one of the princes in *Richard III*. She went on to juvenile roles in various stock companies and at nine made her screen debut in the Selig Company two-reeler *The Common Enemy*. At 14, Daniels signed with Hal Roach and began her adult career paired in comedies with Harold Lloyd and Snub Pollard, including many of the "Lonesome Luke" and the "Winckle" series. In 1919, she signed a four-year contract with Paramount, where she worked for Cecil B. DeMille who was then associated with Realart, a subsidiary of Paramount. When her initial contract expired, she signed once more with Paramount, working there until 1928. Her first role with DeMille was a bit-part in *Male and Female* (1919). Before long, she had star status, trailing only third behind Paramount's *Gloria Swanson and *Pola Negri.

Daniels was adored by colleagues as well as fans. When she was arrested and jailed for speeding in 1921, she reportedly enjoyed an elaborately appointed cell, catered meals, and visitations by a cadre of Hollywood legends during her incarceration. After her release, she was rushed by her studio into production of a movie based on the experience called *The Speed Girl* (1921). Her popularity continued through a variety of roles, mainly light comic leads opposite Wallace Reid, Rudolph Valentino, and Ricardo Cortez. She also occasionally tackled more worldly playgirl types such as the hard-drinking flapper in *Nice People*, the film version of *Rachel Crothers' play.

When Paramount refused to test her for talkies, Daniels bought out the remaining nine months of her contract and moved to RKO, where she was cast in the lavish film version of the Ziegfeld musical *Rio Rita* (1929). Although many in Hollywood felt her career was finished, Daniels proved that she could not only manage a heavy Spanish accent but was up to the singing the role demanded. The picture became one of the year's box-office hits, and she enjoyed a rekindled career in sound, beginning with *Love Comes Along* (1930), in which she also sang. Another of her musicals, *Reaching for the Moon* (1931), co-starred Bing Crosby in his first important role. In 1931, Daniels played the shifty character, a role later to be made famous by *Mary Astor, in the original version of *The Maltese Falcon*. She followed this with *Counsellor at Law* and the wildly popular *42nd Street* (both 1933).

In 1930, Daniels disappointed a battalion of male admirers by marrying actor Ben Lyon, her co-star in *Alias French Gertie* (1930) and several subsequent films and stage productions. In the mid-1930s, with both of their careers in a slump, the couple journeyed to London for a three-week stint at the London Palladium. Well received, they remained there throughout World War II, headlining in music halls and entertaining the troops. (In 1946, Daniels was awarded the U.S. Medal of Freedom for her work with soldiers.) During this period, they also began the BBC radio show "Hi Gang!," which became immensely popular and led to a film by the same name. They also did a West End revue, *Gangway*, and Daniels appeared solo in the British version of Cole Porter's *Panama Hattie*.

Upon returning to America in 1946, Lyon took an executive position with 20th Century-Fox, while Daniels wrote and produced a low-budget comedy for Hal Roach called *The Fabulous Joe* (1948). The couple missed England, however, and returned in 1949. Failing to resurrect "Hi Gang," they started a new radio series, "Life with the Lyons," in which their daughter Barbara and son Richard also appeared. The show became a popular television series and inspired two films: *Life with the Lyons* (1955) and *The Lyons in Paris* (1955). Daniels suffered a series of strokes in the 1960s and died in 1971. Ben Lyon later married actress **Marion Nixon**.

Barbara Morgan,
Melrose, Massachusetts

Daniels, Mabel Wheeler

(1878–1971)

American composer who cofounded the MacDowell Colony. Born in Swampscott, Massachusetts, in 1878; died in Cambridge, Massachusetts, in 1971; only child of George Frank Daniels (a businessman) and Sarah (Wheeler) Daniels; graduated cum laude from Radcliffe College, 1900; studied orchestration at the New

England Conservatory of Music; attended Munich's Royal Conservatory, 1902.

Mabel Wheeler Daniels' early talent for music was encouraged both by her father, a businessman and president of the Handel and Haydn Society, and her mother, who oversaw piano lessons for her daughter at an early age. Daniels later blossomed at Radcliffe, where she composed and conducted operettas and sang in the Glee Club. She continued her studies at the New England Conservatory of music and in 1902 traveled to Munich to attend the prestigious Royal Conservatory. Upon her return, she published a book on her experiences called *An American Girl in Munich* (1905). From 1911 to 1918, she was based in Cambridge, Massachusetts, where she directed the Glee Club at Radcliffe (1911–13) before becoming the musical director at Simmons College in Boston (1913–18). With her friend ***Marian MacDowell**, Daniels helped establish the MacDowell Colony in Peterborough, New Hampshire, a peaceful retreat where she worked on her own compositions, including several operettas, choral and vocal works, and orchestral and chamber music. Her cantata *The Desolate City* (1913) was first performed at the Colony and became one of her more popular works.

Although conservative in her politics as well as her music, Daniels felt strongly about women's rights and supported the suffragists. She insisted that her music be judged on merit alone, saying it made no difference whether the work was "written by a man or a woman or a Hottentot or a Unitarian." Daniels continued to compose into her 80s and died in 1971 at age 93.

Daniels, Margaret Truman (b. 1924).

See Truman, Bess for sidebar.

Danilova, Alexandra (1903–1997)

One of the leading ballerinas of the 20th century who combined a four-decade dancing career in Soviet Russia, Western Europe, and the U.S. with a subsequent career as a distinguished teacher. Nickname: Choura (pronounced Shura), Shura. Pronunciation: Da-NEEL-ova. Born Alexandra Dionisevna Danilova on November 20, 1903 (she sometimes claimed to be uncertain of the precise year and even admitted being less than forthright about it), in Peterhof near St. Petersburg, Russia; died in New York on July 12, 1997; daughter of Dionis Danilov and Claudia (Gototzova or Gototsova) Danilova (possibly servants of the im-

perial court); taught by governesses and in private schools to 1911, student at Imperial Ballet School, 1911–20; married Giuseppe Massera (an engineer), in 1931 (died 1935); married Casimir Kokitch (a ballet dancer), in 1941 (divorced 1948); no children.

Death of her parents (c. 1905); studies disrupted by revolution (1917); returned to ballet school (1918); joined Soviet State Ballet (1920); promoted to soloist (1922); joined friends for tour of Germany and remained in Western Europe (1924); joined Diaghilev's Ballets Russes (1925); began love affair with Balanchine (1926); promoted to star ballerina in Diaghilev's troupe (1927); because of death of Diaghilev, Ballets Russes dissolved (1929); joined Colonel W. de Basil's Ballets Russes de Monte Carlo (1933); toured the U.S. (1933–34); joined new Ballets Russe de Monte Carlo (1938); settled in U.S. (1939); became an American citizen (1946); left Ballets Russe (1951); formed own ballet troupe (1956); gave farewell ballet performance (1957); began efforts as choreographer (1958); joined faculty of School of American Ballet (1964); appeared in film, The Turning Point *(1977); ended teaching career, received Kennedy Center Award (1989); returned for visit to Russia (1993).*

Selected roles: The Street Dancer in Le Beau Danube; *Swanhilda in* Coppélia; *title role in* The Firebird; *title role in* Giselle; *Odette-Odile in* Swan Lake.

Alexandra Danilova, called "Choura" by her close friends, was one of the most significant figures in the world of 20th-century ballet. Educated in the last years of the Russian Imperial Ballet School prior to the Bolshevik Revolution of 1917, she danced on the Soviet stage, brought her training and talents to Western Europe in the 1920s and, starting in the 1930s, toured the United States as well. She led the migration of top-ranking ballet talent to the U.S. at the start of World War II, and she continued to dance with distinction through the 1950s. Her tours made her the most famous ballerina of the time in America and helped to popularize ballet in much of the country. Following the traditional pattern, she then shifted her interests into teaching and played a significant role in the training of young dancers until the late 1980s.

As a performer, Danilova was famous for her combination of brilliant technique and visible pleasure in dancing. Moreover, she was a living testimony to the role of tradition in ballet. As **Olga Maynard** wrote at the close of Danilova's years on the stage, "She is the link with the Maryinsky in St. Petersburg and the theatre Diaghilev created

*A*lexandra
*D*anilova

possibility of learning ballet. She soon became a student noted for her consistently high ranking in her class.

As her biographer A.E. Twysden has noted, Danilova experienced the Russian style of training in which a youngster was immersed for ten years of daily effort in learning the technique of dance. This was far different from the less extensive schooling of dancers in other countries. It was to give Danilova and other Russians of her generation an unmatched artistic range, technical ability, and ease of bodily expression. Part of the curriculum for the students included participating in children's roles in operas and ballets put on by the Maryinsky Theater. By the time young Alexandra was a second-year student, she was taking on such duties. Thus, she was able to see, at close range, the leading ballerinas of the era such as *Matilda Kshesinskaia and *Tamara Karsavina.

According to Danilova's memoirs, the young ballerina had a brush with violent death during the chaos of 1917. Despite orders forbidding students to look out from the school during times of unrest, she and her classmates gave in to curiosity and clustered in front of a window. A soldier fired, and the bullet nearly struck her. On the larger stage of Russian life, the Bolshevik Revolution of November 1917 brought a radical Marxist government to power. For a time, Danilova and members of her family fled the capital for the Kuban.

Nonetheless, the ballet remained a respected institution, and her school reopened. She returned to it in 1918. Although food was scarce and the rooms could not be heated, the aspiring ballerina found that it was possible to continue her training without serious interruption. Upon graduation in 1920, she and her small group of classmates were taken on as professional dancers, becoming members of the old Maryinsky Theater, now renamed the State Ballet Company by the Soviet government.

The hardships of the time included a lack of transportation in St. Petersburg. Danilova had to make a round trip of nearly an hour and a half by foot in order to reach the theater. She soon made an impression on the ballet's directors, moving into the front row of the ballet corps for rehearsals. It was a significant honor for someone who had been a student only a few months before. She had the opportunity to work with the rising young artistic director of the company, Fedor Lopukhov. In the last perfor-

early in the twentieth century. . . . [N]ot a ghost, but a warm, sparkling, laughing woman."

The future ballet star was born in Peterhof, the site of one of the great palaces for Russia's monarchs, outside St. Petersburg on November 20, 1903. There is some uncertainty about the year of her birth. Orphaned at an early age, she had no clear information about her parents' background. It is possible her father was a servant or a low-ranking official at the imperial court. She was fortunate enough to be taken in by a wealthy woman, **Lydia Gototsova**, who soon married the prominent Russian general Mihail Batianov. The pair adopted her. Some sources refer to Gototsova as her aunt, but Danilova seemed unsure of this in her memoirs.

Danilova began her formal ballet training in 1911, when she was accepted into St. Petersburg's prestigious Imperial Ballet School. She was not yet nine years of age, but she entered the school in the rigorous category of a boarding student. It was an unconventional choice for a child of a privileged family, but the young girl's schoolteachers had noticed her physical skills. Moreover, young Alexandra herself had already become intrigued by the

Alexandra Danilova in Firebird.

mance of her initial ballet season, she was given a solo role in *Coppélia*.

Despite the Soviet government's radical course in many areas after 1917, it did not encourage experimentation in the ballet. Instead, it clung to a repertory that Danilova described as "very Victorian." Since her days as a student, Danilova was the close friend of George Balanchine, who entered the Imperial Ballet School a year after she did. A talented choreographer, he reveled in the creation of new ballet possibilities.

Balanchine arranged concert performances in his spare time, featuring his modern, acrobatic style of choreography and asked Danilova to join his group, the Young Ballet. She soon found that official disapproval of Balanchine extended to her. She was forced to leave the Young Ballet or face expulsion from the roll of the State Ballet. Nonetheless, she spent her free hours visiting theaters where imaginative leaders in the world of the arts, like Vsevolod Meyerhold, were challenging longstanding traditions.

$\mathcal{F}$irst as a dancer and later as a teacher . . . she ran through our ballet century like a steel-tough thread of gold.

—Clive Barnes

Danilova's breakthrough to prominence in the Soviet State Ballet Company came in 1922, at the close of her second season. She was handed the title role in *The Firebird* and, in short order, was given other soloist roles. In her initial performance of *The Firebird,* she expended her physical energy so lavishly during the first part of the evening that she was exhausted to the point of fainting by the final curtain. It was a preview of the exuberance for which she was to become famous.

In June 1924, Balanchine, Danilova, and a number of other figures in the Soviet ballet world received permission to tour Western Europe. They went only for the vacation months of the Maryinsky's season, from June to September, intending to sample the freer and more lively artistic world outside Russia. Danilova later wrote that she left expecting to return to play a major role promised her for the next season in *Don Quixote.* But she never went back.

The small troupe performed successfully in Berlin and other German cities, although they were humiliated to discover they sometimes had to perform in vaudeville theaters. As Twysden put it, they were "sandwiched in between the performing animals and the clowns." They went on to London where Danilova was surprised to find that Communist speakers could orate in Hyde Park free of government interference.

Ignoring urgent telegrams from the Soviet government demanding that they return home, the wandering troupe decided to see Paris first. In the French capital, they received job offers from Sergei Diaghilev, the prominent Russian musical impresario who had centered his efforts in France and Britain since 1909. In their first meeting, Diaghilev had asked Danilova to dance for him even though she was wearing her street clothes and regular shoes. As a soloist and a vet-

❧➤
Irina Baronova
and *Tatiana
Riabouchinska.*
See Toumanova,
Tamara for
sidebars.

eran of the Imperial Ballet School, the young ballerina was offended at the suggestion she needed an audition but reluctantly complied. She passed the test and, with her small group of companions, was invited to join Diaghilev's company in London.

In joining the company, Danilova defied orders to return to the Soviet Union; in effect, she was choosing the permanent role of an exile. She soon discovered that Diaghilev was hard to please. After her first solo, he told her bluntly, "Well, you are much too fat and you danced abominably." In fact, she had gained 15 pounds since leaving Russia. As she put it, "Life in Russia had been a diet in itself."

Despite this shaky start, Danilova rose to stardom in Diaghilev's company. The sudden departure of the company's star ballerina, ❧➤ **Vera Nemchinova,** in 1927 created a vacancy that Diaghilev chose her to fill. Danilova's long legs, her small head, and her splendid carriage made her the natural center of attention on any stage. Some of her greatest successes, including the first ballet created for her, *The Triumph of Neptune,* came in works Balanchine choreographed. Years later, Anton Dolin, her frequent partner in these ballets, remarked that Danilova had been a bad influence on Balanchine. She was so talented that she could perform even the most extreme movements he required; thus, Balanchine was not prepared to revise his choreography thereafter for less capable ballerinas. Her relationship with Balanchine was also a personal one: they were lovers from 1926 to 1931.

With the death of Diaghilev in 1929, Danilova found herself without an institutional home. "The Diaghilev company," she wrote in later years, "was a big Russian family. We had our squabbles, but they didn't last long." Only in 1933, after a period of personal and professional disruption, including an end to her affair with Balanchine, did she establish a new tie with a ballet company. The Ballets Russes de Monte Carlo was an offshoot of Diaghilev's company, and gradually Danilova found her place in it. Initially, she was overshadowed by a trio of youthful female dancers known as "the baby ballerinas" (*Tamara Toumanova, ◄❧ Irina Baronova, and ◄❧ Tatiana Riabouchinska). Beside these teenagers, she seemed a veteran, and she found herself unable to gain access to the new ballets being developed for the company. In time, however, she emerged as its star, but she did so without Balanchine. He had originally been hired by the impresario, Colonel W. de Basil, but he was fired just as Danilova was arriving. She now established a lasting professional relationship with another gifted choreographer, Léonide Massine.

In 1933, the de Basil company came to America under the auspices of the American theater promoter, Sol Hurok. Danilova was pleased to find that she and her colleagues were introducing enthusiastic audiences to a new art form. "Most American audiences," she wrote in her memoirs, "had never seen ballet." The company returned during each of the next four years, each time with a more extended tour.

In 1938, Danilova took on a new tie, moving with Massine to the new Ballets Russe de Monte Carlo, an offshoot of the Ballets Russes. Here she stood as the unchallenged star. With the start of World War II, the Ballets Russe de Monte Carlo and Danilova immediately relocated to the United States. Their extensive tours of the 1940s and 1950s continued to promote an interest in ballet in large regions in the United States. American critics lauded her combination of impeccable technique and vivacious personality. Wrote Edwin Denby, "She seems suddenly to be happy to be dancing, with a pleasure like a little girl's." Leon Danielian, one of her younger dance partners, noted in 1992: from the early 1930s onward, "Shura was the first real ballerina I saw," and she was "the image of what every American girl who studied ballet looked up to and wanted to be."

In 1941, Danilova married Casimir Kokitch, one of the soloists in the company. Her earlier marriage to Italian engineer Giuseppe Massera, in 1931, had quickly led to a separation. Before she could get him to agree to a divorce, Massera died in 1935. Kokitch, whom she called "Koscha," was a Yugoslav. He soon departed along with most of the other male dancers in the company for military service. Over the next years, Danilova found herself involved in the war effort, performing for USO clubs throughout America. In the frantic touring of the war years, Danilova and her colleagues sometimes traveled to more than one hundred towns in six months. In 1946, she applied for American citizenship.

Within a few years, she found herself in a new (albeit professional) relationship with Balanchine; he was now a guest choreographer for the company, and he created a number of new roles for her. Meanwhile, her marriage collapsed. When Kokitch returned from his military service, Danilova found their life together strained by his drinking and his jealousy of her professional success. In 1948, they separated, then divorced.

Danilova left her permanent position in the company in 1951. By then, the Ballets Russe had lost many of its stars to other companies, and Sol Hurok had ceased to arrange their tours. Moreover, Danilova had grown impatient with the unorthodox interpretations of the new artistic director, a Polish dancer named ✤➤ **Nina Novak**. In 1956, Danilova formed her own small troupe of four dancers and took it on worldwide tours. Her last performance as a dancer took place in Japan in September 1957.

Her career took a new turn, appropriate to an aging but highly regarded figure in the ballet world. In 1958, she became a choreographer, starting with modest success in a Broadway show. She first made her mark staging the dances for the Metropolitan Opera's production of *La Gioconda*. Her success led her to a longterm relationship with the Metropolitan, as well as contracts with a variety of other companies.

Danilova had begun to teach ballet in the late 1950s; she now turned to full-scale teaching

---

✤➤ **Nemchinova, Vera** (1899–1984)

Russian ballerina. Name variations: Nemtchinova. Born Vera Nicolayevna Nemchinova in Moscow, Russia, in 1899; died in 1984; studied with Lydia Nelidova in Moscow, then Elizabeth Anderson; married Anatole Oboukhov.

Engaged by the Diaghilev's Ballets Russes in 1915, Vera Nemchinova made her first appearance in the corps de ballets, rising soon to soloist, then ballerina. She created the female roles in *Les Biches* (1924), *Les Tentations de la Bergère* (1924), and *Les Matelots* (1925). Partnering with Anton Dolin, she formed the Nemchinova-Dolin Ballet company, which appeared in London and then toured England. From 1931 to 1925, Nemchinova was prima ballerina with the Lithuanian State Ballet, then joined the Ballets Russe de Monte Carlo in 1936, creating the lead role in *L'Epreuve d'Amour*. In 1943, she danced the title role of Princess Aurora with the American Ballet Theatre.

✤➤ **Novak, Nina** (1927—)

Polish dancer. Born in Warsaw, Poland, in 1927; general ballet training in the school of the Warsaw Opera House; studied with *Bronislava Nijinska, Leon Woizikowski, and others; married Roman Rojas Cabot (a Venezuelan diplomat), in 1962; settled in Caracas, Venezuela.

Beginning in 1948, Nina Novak danced solo with the Ballets Russe de Monte Carlo. She was promoted to ballerina in 1952 and continued working with the Ballets Russe for the next nine years.

---

in 1964 when she became a regular faculty member for the School of American Ballet. In this position, her path again crossed that of George Balanchine, who was the director of the school. In 1974, he asked her to collaborate with him at the New York City Ballet in staging a production in which she had once starred: *Coppélia*. In a way that impressed the company's dancers, who must have been well aware of the couple's longtime relationship, Danilova and Balanchine, both in their 70s, demonstrated every part for the company. They also, it was noted, treated each other with comfortable informality.

In 1976, Danilova was offered a part in the film *The Turning Point* by director Herbert Ross, himself an erstwhile dancer, in which she portrayed a former prima ballerina who devoted her energies to training the young stars of tomorrow. Even so, said Danilova, "I wasn't about to pack my bag and leave for Hollywood." Instead, she threw even more of her energy into her teaching at the School of American Ballet.

Ten years later, now in her 80s, Danilova published her memoirs, *Choura*. In summing up her life as a dancer, she wrote that she had made her art her highest priority. To it she had sacrificed everything—without regrets. The final line of her book read: "I gave one hundred percent of myself to my art, and my art has repaid me." Her colleagues and institutions showered Danilova with honors. In December 1989, for example, she was presented with a gold medallion by the Kennedy Center in Washington, D.C. In 1991, the New York City Ballet helped her celebrate her birthday with an opening night gala performance.

Danilova retired from her teaching in 1989. Her advancing age brought her a variety of injuries: a broken knee cap in 1989 and a fractured shoulder in 1991. Nonetheless, she remained open to new adventures. In the summer of 1993, the veteran dancer made a return visit to Russia, the first time she had seen her homeland since 1924. That November, in New York City, she celebrated her 90th birthday. Alexandra Danilova died in New York, age 93, on July 12, 1997.

SOURCES:

"The Ballets Russes, 1932–1962: A Symposium," in *Dance Chronicle: Studies in Dance and the Related Arts.* Vol. 15. Fall 1992, pp. 191–221.

Barnes, Clive. "Danilova at Ninety," in *Dance Magazine.* Vol. 68. March 1994, p. 90.

Clarke, Mary, and Clement Crisp. *Ballerina: The Art of Women in Classical Ballet.* London: BBC Books, 1987.

Danilova, Alexandra. *Choura: The Memoirs of Alexandra Danilova.* NY: Alfred A. Knopf, 1986.

Maynard, Olga. *The American Ballet.* Philadelphia, PA: Macrae Smith, 1959.

Montague, Sarah. *The Ballerina: Famous Dancers and Rising Stars of Our Time.* NY: Universe Books, 1980.

Twysden, A.E. *Alexandra Danilova.* NY: Kamin Dance Publishers, 1947.

SUGGESTED READING:

Au, Susan. *Ballet & Modern Dance.* London: Thames and Hudson, 1988.

Mason, Francis, ed. *I Remember Balanchine: Recollections of the Ballet Master by Those Who Knew Him.* NY: Doubleday, 1991

Spencer, Charles. *The World of Diaghilev.* Harmondsworth, Eng.: Penguin, 1979.

Taper, Bernard. *Balanchine: A Biography.* NY: Times Books, 1984.

RELATED MEDIA:

The Turning Point (119 min), starring **Anne Bancroft, Shirley MacLaine,** and Tom Skerritt, directed by Herbert Ross, 20th Century-Fox, 1977.

Reflections of a Dancer: Alexandra Danilova (52 min), directed by **Anne Belle,** Direct Cinema, 1990.

Neil M. Heyman, Professor of History, San Diego State University, San Diego, California

Danilova, Olga

Russian cross-country skier. Married and mother of twins.

Olga Danilova finished 6th at Lillehammer in the 5K classical cross-country race in 1992. In 1998, she won a gold medal at Nagano in the 15K classical with a time of 46:55.4, beating out her teammate *Larissa Lazutina of Russia in a close contest. **Anita Moen-Guidon** of Norway went home with the bronze. A few days later, positions reversed. Danilova won a silver medal in the women's 10-kilometer race while Lazutina placed first. They then came together in the 4x5-kilometer relay, along with **Nina Gavriliuk,** and **Yelena Välbe,** to win a gold medal for the Russian team with a time of 55:13.5. Norway finished second (**Bente Martinsen, Marit Mikkelsplass, Elin Nilsen, Anita Moen-Guidon**) with a time of 55:38.0; Italy third (**Karin Moroder, Gabriella Paruzzi, Manuela di Centa,** and **Stefania Belmondo**) with a time of 56:53.3.

Danton, Louise (1777–1856).

See Desmoulins, Lucile for sidebar.

Danvers, Lady (1561–1627).

See Guiney, Louise Imogen for sidebar.

Danzi, Maria Margarethe (1768–1800)

German composer and singer. Born Maria Margarethe Marchand in 1768 in Frankfurt am Main,

Germany; died in Munich on June 11, 1800; daughter of Theobald Marchand, director of the Munich Theater; married Franz Danzi, in 1790.

At age ten, Maria Danzi began singing lessons with *Franziska Lebrun, sister of the noted composer Franz Danzi. She would marry Danzi in 1790. From 1781 to 1784, Maria lived with her brother Heinrich in Salzburg in the house of Leopold Mozart, the father of Wolfgang Amadeus Mozart, taking lessons in piano and composition. She began her singing career in 1786 at the Munich Court Opera.

Although renowned singers rarely excel at other areas of music, Maria Danzi was gifted and confident enough in her talents to become a composer as well. Along with her husband, she went on many concert tours, but she also found time to compose chamber works of charm and structural strength. These include an *Andante and Variations* for keyboard and a set of three sonatas for piano and violin. In recent years, the sonatas have been republished and recorded, and listeners have found these works eminently listenable. Maria Danzi's talents were not given the chance to come to full fruition due to her death at age 32. Many of her piano compositions have unfortunately been lost.

John Haag,
Athens, Georgia

D'Aquino, Iva Toguri (b. 1916).

See Toguri, Iva.

d'Arblay, Madame (1752–1840).

See Burney, Fanny.

Darc or d'Arc, Jeanne (c. 1412–1431).

See Joan of Arc.

d'Arconville, Geneviève

(1720–1805)

French essayist, novelist, moralist, translator, scientist, and implacable enemy of the French revolution who lost one of her sons to the guillotine and was in hiding during the worst months of Robespierre's Reign of Terror. Name variations: Geneviève-Charlotte d'Arlus; Dame Thiroux d'Arconville. Born Marie-Geneviève-Charlotte d'Arlus in Paris, October 17, 1720; died in Paris, France, on December 23, 1805; married Louis-Lazare Thiroux d'Arconville; children: three sons, including Thiroux de Crosne.

Still relatively little known, Geneviève d'Arconville was one of the most intellectually pro-

ductive women in France during the second half of the 18th century. Born in Paris into a family of tax collectors, she was married at the age of 14 in February 1735, to Louis-Lazare Thiroux d'Arconville, a wealthy advisor to the parlement of Paris. Despite the fact that she had three sons, d'Arconville was intellectually curious in many disciplines, attending lectures in various scientific fields—including anatomy—at the Jardin du Roi. Always an individualist, starting at age 23 she began to dress like an old woman because her face had been disfigured by an attack of smallpox. Despite this, she was able to charm the leading figures of the Enlightenment, appearing in the prominent salons of Paris and carrying on an extensive correspondence with such literary and scientific figures of the day as Voltaire, Turgot, Lavoisier, Fourcroy, Anquetil, and Sainte-Palaye.

Some of her earliest publications included a 1759 translation into French of Alexander Monro's *Treatise on Osteology*. Many excellent translations of contemporary English books flowed from her pen over the next decades including novels, plays, books of poetry as well as such unusual works as Kenneth Macaulay's history of Saint Kilda and Peter Shaw's chemistry textbook. Her translations introduced the French reading public to *Aphra Behn's *History of Agnes de Castro* (*Inez de Castro) and John Gay's *The Beggar's Opera*. D'Arconville's own scientific investigations resulted in a 1766 volume entitled *A Treatise on Putrefaction*. She also carried out extensive research into the medicinal value of the chamomile herb (*Anthemis nobilis*).

Madame d'Arconville's restless mind led her to investigations of archives and volumes of official records, the final result being a series of biographies of great historical personalities including *Marie de Medici, Cardinal d'Ossat, and François II (Frances II), king of France and Navarre. Not only did she master the biography genre, d'Arconville also published several essay collections on such popular subjects of the day as friendship (*De l'amitie*, 1764), the passions (*Des passions*, 1775), and "Moral Thoughts and Reflections on Diverse Subjects" (1760). In all of her works, an elegant style was as important as the clarity of her reasoning. One of her most remarkable efforts was the seven-volume *Melange of Literature, Ethics and Physics*, which appeared in print in 1775 at the start of the ill-fated reign of Louis XVI.

Emotionally and intellectually attached to the Old Regime, d'Arconville hated and feared the French Revolution that began in 1789. Her warnings of its potential for destructiveness were borne out when one of her three sons, Thiroux de Crosne, who had served the state as Intendant of Rouen and lieutenant general of the Paris police, was guillotined. In mortal danger herself, d'Arconville spent the worst months of Robespierre's Reign of Terror with her sister Mme **Angran d'Alleray** in the small town of Piepus. Despite the infirmities of old age, d'Arconville continued to read and write, working up to the last days of her life while on her deathbed. This remarkable woman died on December 23, 1805. She still lacks a major biographical study, and her probable authorship of some writings, originally published anonymously, still has not been definitively linked to her name.

SOURCES:

Girou-Swiderski, Marie-Laure. "Vivre la Révolution: L'Incidence de la Révolution sur la carriere et la vie de trois femmes de lettres," in Marie-France Brive, ed. *Les Femmes et la Révolution française, II: L'Individu et le social, apparitions et representations.* Toulouse: PU du Mirail, 1990, pp. 239–249.

Phyllis Dare

La Porte, Hippolyte, Marquis de. *Notices et observations à l'occasion de quelques femmes de la société du dix-huitième siècle.* Paris: H. Fournier, 1835.

John Haag,
Athens, Georgia

Dare, Grace (1873–1953).

See Bondfield, Margaret.

Dare, Phyllis and Zena

British stage actresses.

Phyllis Dare (1890–1975). Born Phyllis Dones in Fulham Park Gardens, London, England, on August 15, 1890; died on April 27, 1975; youngest daughter and one of three children of Arthur Dones (a clerk in a divorce court who later managed his daughters' careers) and Haddie Dones; sister of Zena Dare.

Zena Dare (1887–1975). Born Florence Harriette Zena Dones in Fulham Park Gardens, London, England, on February 4, 1887; died on March 11, 1975; one of three children of Arthur Dones (a clerk in a divorce court) and Haddie Dones; sister of Phyllis Dare; married Maurice Vyner Baliol Brett (second son of the 2nd Viscount Esher), in 1911 (died 1934); children: one son and two daughters.

Two of the most stunning and popular actresses of Edwardian England were the sisters Dare, Phyllis and Zena, who for decades delighted audiences in London's West End and on tour. At the height of their fame, their likenesses graced hundreds of picture postcards, which were sold across the country. As a boy, the famed critic James Agate was said to have harbored a picture of Zena Dare in his school locker.

Daughters of a judge's clerk, the sisters made their stage debut in 1899 in the pantomime *Babes in the Wood.* In 1900, Phyllis went on to make her first provincial appearance at the Theater Royal, in Manchester, in *Little Red Riding Hood.* She was then engaged by actor-manager Seymour Hicks to play at the Vaudeville Theater in London, where she charmed audiences in *Bluebell in Fairyland* and *The Catch of the Season.* Her big break came in 1906, when she took over the lead in the musical comedy *The Belle of Mayfair* after the renowned actress **Edna May** left the show. Though she was triumphant in the role, Phyllis' success was short-lived because she had also signed a contract to appear in an Edinburgh Christmas pageant. (The lead in *The Belle of Mayfair* was subsequently taken over by *Billie Burke.) In 1909, after her appearance in Edinburgh and a tour in *The Dairymaids*, Phyllis appeared in the highly acclaimed Robert Courtneidge musical comedy *The Arcadians*, which played 809 performances at the Shaftesbury Theater. In 1911, the legendary theatrical manager George Edwardes tapped her for the title role in *Peggy*. During the run of the show, Phyllis recorded "Ladies Beware" for the fledgling recording company, His Master's Voice. She also recorded four songs from the show *Tina*, which opened at the Adelphi in 1915. Her career continued throughout the war years, both in variety and review. In 1919, she was in *Kissing Time*, followed by *The Lady of the Rose*, *The Street Singer*, and *The Maids of the Mountains*. During the 1930s and 1940s, she appeared in show after show, straight comedies as well as musicals.

Phyllis Dare never married, though at age 22, while playing in *The Sunshine Girl*, she met and fell in love with the show's composer Paul A. Rubens. The couple announced their engagement, but Rubens fell ill with tuberculosis. With no hope of recovery and not wanting to burden Phyllis, he broke off the engagement. He died in 1917, at age 40.

Zena Dare's career paralleled her sister's. As a young girl, she appeared in pantomime in Scotland, toured in *An English Daisy*, and played Cinderella at the Shakespeare Theater in Liverpool. In 1904, she was cast in her first adult role in Seymour Hicks' *The Catch of the Season*, a part originally intended for Hicks' wife *Ellaline Terriss, who temporarily retired due to pregnancy. A great success, the show ran for 621 performances, although after a year Zena was replaced by her sister Phyllis because of another contract commitment. Like Phyllis, Zena also worked for George Edwardes, playing in the musicals *Lady Madcap*, *The Little Cherub*, and *The Girl on Stage*. In 1906, she rejoined Seymour Hicks, playing a variety of roles, including Victoria Siddons in *The Gay Gordons* and Peter Pan.

In 1911, at the peak of her success Zena retired from the stage to marry Maurice Brett, second son of the second Viscount Esher. They had a son and two daughters. Zena returned to the stage in 1926, at age 39. Rather than continuing in musicals, she enjoyed great success in straight roles, including Mrs. Cheyney in *The Last of Mrs. Cheyney* and a role opposite Noel Coward in *The Second Man*. In 1926, she formed her own company and toured South Africa. On her return, Zena teamed with Ivor Novello in *Proscenium*, in which she enjoyed her greatest success since her preretirement musical days. She also paired with Novello in 1936, playing the

manager of a beauty parlor in his musical *Careless Rapture*. The *Times* of London described her roles with Novello as "exactly suited to her years and to her bent for mild caricature."

In 1940, Zena and Phyllis appeared together on stage in a tour of a revival of Novello's *Full House*. Zena followed this with a comic performance of Lady Caroline in a revival of *Dear Brutus*, after which she took the role of the Red Queen in *Alice through the Looking Glass*. In 1949, the sisters were joined again on stage in Novello's musical *King's Rhapsody*, with Zena playing Novello's mother and Phyllis his mistress. An enormous success, the play even ran seven months after Novello's death in 1951. Following *King's Rhapsody*, Phyllis retired to Brighton, at age 61. Zena remained on stage for another ten years, in a variety of popular plays, including *Sabrina Fair*, *Double Image*, and *Nude with Violin*. Her last appearance was as Rex Harrison's mother, Mrs. Higgins, in *My Fair Lady*, which opened in April 1958 and played in

Zena Dare

London for five years before going on tour. Zena retired in 1965 and died on March 11, 1975. Six weeks later, on April 27, her sister Phyllis also passed away.

SOURCES:
Cliffe, Peter. "Stars of Yesterday: Phyllis Dare," in *This England*. Autumn 1990.

Barbara Morgan,
Melrose, Massachusetts

Dare, Virginia (b. 1587)

Colonial figure and first child born of English parents in America. Born on August 18, 1587, on Roanoke Island (now North Carolina); date of death unknown; daughter of Ananias Dare (a bricklayer) and Elyonor also seen as Ellinor or Elenor (White) Dare (daughter of Governor John White).

Virginia Dare, daughter of Ananias and **Elenor Dare**, was the first child born of English parents in America. Elenor and Ananias were among the 116 pilgrims to accompany cartographer and painter John White on his British expedition to Sir Walter Raleigh's Virginia colony, so named after Queen *Elizabeth I, the "Virgin Queen." When the expedition left Plymouth, England, on May 8, 1587, Elenor Dare, daughter of White, was one of only 17 women on board and was probably six months pregnant with her first child. After an arduous journey, the expedition missed its intended destination of mainland Virginia, landing instead on Roanoke Island, where Virginia Dare was born a month later. The child was christened on Sunday, August 24; three days later, John White sailed for England to report on the settlement.

War between Spain and England delayed his return to Roanoke for four years, and when he landed again in 1590 there was no trace of the settlement or its inhabitants. Reputedly, the only clue left was a cryptic inscription of the word "Croatoan" carved on a tree. Some historians believe that the message may have meant that the colonists had joined a friendly Croatoan tribe on the mainland, while others argue that the word was hurriedly scratched into the tree as the Croatoans attacked. Although the fate of the "lost colony" was never determined, Virginia Dare came to symbolize faith in the throes of adversity. Some have suggested that Elenor Dare, the colonist who undertook the sea voyage while pregnant, should also be remembered as a symbol of courage.

Dare, Zena (1887–1975).

See Dare, Phyllis and Zena.

Dark, Eleanor (1901–1985)

Australian novelist, mainly of contemporary fiction, whose historical trilogy brought her fame and fortune.

Name variations: (pseudonyms) P.O'R. and Patricia O'Rane. Born Eleanor ("Pixie") O'Reilly in the year of Australian Federation 1901 in Sydney, Australia; died of osteoporosis in Katoomba, New South Wales (NSW), in 1985; daughter of Dowell O'Reilly (a poet, short-story writer, and sometime Labor politician) and Eleanor (McCulloch) O'Reilly (a housewife); attended several private schools before boarding at Redlands, an exclusive all-girls' school in Sydney, where she graduated, 1919; married Eric Payten Dark (a medical doctor and Military Cross recipient in the Great War), in 1922; children: one son, Michael.

Lived most of her 63 years of married life in Katoomba, a small town in the Blue Mountains southwest of Sydney; wrote verse from age seven but turned eventually and solely to prose; published Slow Dawning (1932), the first and least successful of ten published novels; published The Timeless Land (1941), bringing her wide acclaim at home and overseas; published last novel Lantana Lane (1959), which closed with a flourish one of the most successful writing careers of an Australian woman writer of her generation.

Awards: twice-winner of Australia's then most coveted literary prize, the Australian Literature Society's gold medal for best novel (1936 and 1938); The Timeless Land selected U.S. Book-of-the-Month (October 1941); awarded the Order of Australia for "services to Australian literature" (1977).

Selected publications: (contemporary fiction) Slow Dawning (1932, only known surviving copy in Humphrey McQueen papers in National Library of Australia), Prelude to Christopher (1934), Return to Coolami (1936), Sun Across the Sky (1937), Waterway (1938), The Little Company (1945), Lantana Lane (1959); (historical trilogy) The Timeless Land (1941), Storm of Time (1948) and No Barrier (1953). Early verse of the 1920s and early '30s published in Australia in a wide variety of journals (The Triad, Bulletin, Woman's Mirror); some 20 short stories also published in journals, such as the Bulletin, The Triad, Motoring News, Home and Ink. Selected nonfiction: "Caroline Chisholm and Her Times" in Flora S. Eldershaw, ed., The Peaceful Army: A Memorial to the Pioneer Women of Australia, 1788–1938 (Sydney, Women's Executive Committee and Advisory Council of Australia's 150th Anniversary Celebrations, 1938); "Australia and the Australians," in Australian Week-End Book (No. 3, 1944); "Drawing a Line Around It," in Writer (U.S., Vol. 59, October 1946); "A world damned a man, but what does it mean?" in Daily Telegraph *(April 23, 1948); (introduction) G. Farwell and F.H. Johnston, eds.,* This Land of Ours: Australia *(Sydney, 1949); "They All Come Back," in* Walkabout *(Vol. 17, 1951) and "The Blackall Range Country," in* Walkabout *(Vol. 21, 1955).*

Eleanor Dark was born Eleanor O'Reilly in Sydney, Australia, in 1901. Her life and work spanned most of the 20th century. For the artist she thought herself to be, this "coincidence of birth," as she called it, continued to shape the way she perceived her world and her role in it. The fact that 1901 was also the year of Australia's Federation, the birth of the nation, placed other sets of challenges upon her. She was an Australian writer whose offerings were intended equally for art and country. It is only fitting that her most celebrated novel should have been the artist's rendition of the essence of her Australia: the timeless land. Unlike most of her fellow writers, Dark did not pine for other lands and cultures. Australia was her spiritual, as well as physical, home. A most enduring tribute to the woman and artist is a residential writers' center established in her memory and housed in "Varuna," the "flash but not too flash" mountain residence that was home for most of her adult life.

In 1942, at the height of Dark's writing career, an American academic wrote requesting a brief biographical sketch. Though Dark expressed herself "very willing to help," she explained there was "hardly material for such a thing, as my life has been uneventful to the point of being humdrum." Throughout her life, she sought futilely to deflect attention from the personal to her work. This was partly to protect her privacy and partly because of a firm conviction that the text was all. She loathed publicity and once wrote to her American literary agent that: "If I could arrange the literature world to my satisfaction writers would never be photographed, and would be known by numbers instead of names." She may also have preferred to keep certain aspects of her personal experience away from the scrutiny of the public. Her life may not have been one of high drama, but it had elements of Greek tragedy. From childhood to old age, recurring themes of marriage breakups, insanity, and suicide, stalked her. It is in the story beneath the "uneventful" and "humdrum" texture of her days that the essence of the individual and her art are mostly found.

Long before writing became for Eleanor Dark her art, profession, or calling, it had been the daily bread of the young Eleanor, known as Pixie O'Reilly. It had belonged to the world of

magic and play of the young child, of intellect and peer competition of the schoolgirl, of romance and fanciful illusions of the budding woman. It had been the flapper's principal weapon of rebelliousness, and the young bride's unit of barter for the little extra needed around the house. From the start, Dark later admitted, she had had "a remarkable facility" for verse, which "once broken into print" she had "no difficulty in selling." This skill allowed her to establish "a good trade in sonnets" which, at seven-and-sixpence each, were "the same price as a bag of manure for the garden." In time, as the young Mrs. Eric Payten Dark, she would extend her "flippant" attitude to her prose. Written in 1923, her first novel *Slow Dawning* would be produced "deliberately . . . with the object of making money," Dark confessed contritely at the peak of her literary career. "I regard it as a judgment upon me that it was not published till many years later, in 1932, which meant that what money I did make out of it—and it did as well as I expected—I did not get at the time I wanted it."

> *An accident of birth had invited her to see her life in a slick, chronological pattern; the century had grown with her.*
> —Eleanor Dark, *The Little Company*

Plaything, magic wand, protest banner, pocket-money and many other things became elevated to "art," writing had woven itself into the fabric of the little girl's life even before she could read or write. Like Lesley Channon of *Waterway,* one of many young heroines in her fiction whom she styled after herself: "Her earliest recollections were of lively debates between her father and any one of a dozen friends who haunted their home to talk to him. . . . Ideas and the words with which to express them, had been toys of her childhood along with books and dolls." The love and habit of books were things she acquired not through mother's milk but on father's lap. By the tender age of three, when she taught herself to read, Pixie had begun to internalize her father Dowell O'Reilly's hunger for the written word. His "habit with books," Dowell acknowledged, was not that of "the winetaster, the gourmet" but of "a glutton, a drunkard." Indeed, to the little girl, the written word, either in the form of her own compositions or in her father's imposing library, appears to have been the beacon of an otherwise bleak childhood. By the time a confident and poised

Eleanor Dark stepped out of her private world into the public limelight in 1936 as winner of Australia's most coveted literary award, the relationship had undergone a fundamental change. It had been formalized and consecrated. The little girl and one of the "toys of her childhood" were now a solemn pair: the artist and her art.

The story of Eleanor Dark—individual and artist—orders itself naturally into three parts. Two halves of the "private years" (1901–30 and 1950–85) frame her "public years" (1930s–1940s) as writer and would-be social reformer.

Until recently, the conventional view of Dark's early years among historians was of a quaint, unruffled and virtually motherless childhood spent amidst literary and political enthusiasms generated by a father to whom she was a devoted disciple. Dark herself encouraged and reinforced this singular version of her childhood, through the family anecdotes she fed those requesting biographical material.

Material released since her death explodes the myth of a happy, father-centered household. Pixie O'Reilly did not, it suggests, live in a house where literature and politics set the general tone of family discussions and social life. These were elements, but more as temporary and welcome distractions from a family life scarred by anxieties over health, finances, and the parents' basic incompatibilities. Hers was not in any sense a normal or happy childhood. The virtual absence of **Eleanor McCulloch (O'Reilly)** from the story of her daughter's young years does signify the mother's lack of influence upon her daughter's real and imagined lives. An aura of mystery and intrigue surrounds Eleanor McCulloch's history, fostered partly by the fact that her voice is utterly silent from the historical record and partly by the general lack of sources relating to her. Little is known about McCulloch, including the circumstances surrounding her last illness and her death in 1914, reportedly of thyrotoxis, a disease of the thyroid gland. Through the latter period of her life was she mentally ill (as her husband sometimes hinted) or merely emotionally distraught (as most of the evidence suggests)? Was she driven to despair by an unhappy marriage, or did she harbor the seeds of madness? One thing is clear; McCulloch was a disturbing presence in her daughter's life—her absence in many ways a far more potent presence than Dowell O'Reilly.

A loving but weak father, he was too insecure and preoccupied with his own misfortunes to be of much support to his daughter. There was also a definite emotional schism between father and mother, though they were clearly fond of one another. The sensitive question of Eleanor McCulloch's mental state remained a barrier between them. Over half a century later, the matter resurfaced when Dark, in her 60s, set out to compile and compose family histories for her son. "D O'Reilly says in letter that during last ten days her mind failed," she noted. A disturbing issue was involved. Its demons lay at the heart of *Prelude to Christopher*, dealing with the origins and manifestations of insanity, "particularly of hereditary insanity." With her first self-styled heroine, Anne of "Pilgrimage," Dark seemed to share "that strange, instinctive fear of her own mind which she had dimly realized in her far too early in childhood."

In terms of her work the role of the father has been overestimated at the expense of the mother. Dowell O'Reilly's influence on his daughter's thinking and writing remain undisputed. It was his influence that prompted Dark to take "the political scene for granted equally with the literary atmosphere." An early advocate of women's suffrage in the N.S.W. Parliament, Dowell O'Reilly endowed the "woman question" with keen relevance to Pixie. Distinct resonances of his Australia can be heard in her later evocations of the timeless land. Both shared an abiding love for an Australia mature and self-assured, without anger or nostalgia towards a Mother Country or Mother Culture. They also shared a conception (and celebration) of Australia as a fugitive from Western Civilization and its rigid and life-negating strictures of convention and tradition. Note, for example, Dowell O'Reilly's poem "Australia" (1894), which reads in part:

> When Nature's heart was young and wild
> She bore in secret a love-child,
> And weeping, laughed—too glad to dress
> Its lawless, naked loveliness.

O'Reilly offered his daughter one gift that had no equal, and which she cherished through her darkest moments. Offsetting the fears of mental illness from the McCulloch strain was the knowledge that through her blood also ran a very different kind of madness. She belonged to a long and honorable family tradition of artists, a fact to which she referred several times in the family history.

> My father was a writer, and had some gift for drawing; his brother, Tom, and his sister, Rose, also did some writing though I think none of it was published except a very small book of verse. . . . My brother Pat drew well and, when he died, left among his belong-

ings a few pages of MS, evidently the beginning of a novel; I have produced some books, Bim [her younger brother and a painter] you know about. My cousin . . . has written at least one play.

Ultimately, however, it was not "atmosphere," matters of sexual politics, love of country, or even an empowering heritage but more subterranean influences that fed the artist's Muse. It was McCulloch, and her complex legacy to her daughter of anxiety and shame, that appears to have been the principal animating force behind the writing itself. McCulloch's legacy to her daughter was an unhappy one. But while an artist's real and imagined lives are ultimately inextricable, elements that impoverish one often enrich the other. Such appears to have been the case with Dark. Her mother's legacy of suffering became a moving force behind her finest works, in many of whose characters, relationships, and passages reside the demons of Eleanor McCulloch. The prime example lies in her portrait of Linda Hendon in *Prelude to Christopher,* and her futile struggles to retain a grip on the two most precious and poisoned parts of her life: her sanity and her marriage.

With the mother's death in 1914, the family was split into its four surviving parts. Henceforth, the family history records, "there was no real home or family life." Dowell O'Reilly moved to a boarding house, the older son Pat worked on a farm, and the younger boy Bim boarded at a preparatory school. Thirteen-year-old Eleanor went to live with her maternal grandmother. A year later, she became a boarder at Redlands, her first happy home. The refugee from a broken home and veteran of five schools abandoned herself utterly to this new world. "I wouldn't leave for anything," she wrote a cousin a year after arriving there. Hopeless in mathematics, Dark excelled in the humanities, particularly literature. One of her compositions so impressed her teacher that she felt sure her student "must unmistakably possess the divine spark." But there was a price to pay when graduation day came. The school and its privileged popula-

Eleanor Dark, with her husband Eric.

tion of students had raised expectations—of university, overseas travel, a literary career—none of which her family could meet. A brief training course in secretarial work fitted her for her first (and only) salaried employment: as typist in a solicitors' firm in Sydney. Dark hated everything about her new life: from the working-class types she was forced to rub shoulders with, to the grimy crowded streets of the city, to the undercurrents of sexual harassment she sensed between the male boss and the "girls in the office." The essence of this anger is distilled in her "flapper" literature of the '20s and early '30s.

Marriage to Eric Payten Dark, medical doctor and an old family friend 12 years her senior, rescued her immediately and permanently from what had become unbearable. For all her sneers at the tendency of women towards "compulsive domesticity," Dark slipped easily into her new domestic roles as doctor's wife and mistress of "Varuna." Eric Dark never quite recovered from the tragedy of his first wife's death, soon after the birth of their first child, but his grief was a life-affirming force. After his loss, Eleanor seemed all the more precious to him. From all accounts, it was a most successful partnership. Looking back on some six decades of their married life, Eric described the relationship simply as "Perfect love from her to me and from me to her." From the start, it was an orderly and conservative household with no blurring of the edges between the man's and the woman's place in the home. Eric was the breadwinner, and she, the one responsible for any social entertainment, sewing, curtain-mending, scone-baking, jam-preserving, and the many other activities that filled her life. Eleanor Dark's domestic circumstances stood well apart from the norm, however, in one critical aspect: her husband's recognition of her right to her own career. As much in love with the woman as the artist, Eric Dark and his doctor's earnings gave her *carte blanche* to shape her literary life as she wished. The result was a decade-long apprenticeship from which she emerged in her own good time.

To a life that had borne so much tragedy and alienation, Eric Dark brought comfort and support, stability and security. Eleanor, it seems, never again lacked material or emotional riches. But there was a price for this bonanza. Eric's politics underwent a dramatic conversion during the Great Depression. As the Tory became a socialist, his process of "moving from Right to Left" seemed never ending—to his own and his family's detriment. Thus, the 1930s–1940s belonged to the public figure Eleanor Dark became

against her better instincts. Even the family home, originally a quaint, small, weatherboard house, was replaced by a large imposing residence befitting her new stature (if not her new radical profile in Depression-scarred Australia). Driven by the advent of fascism, Dark joined in protest campaigns against State repression, particularly censorship, her *bête noire*. But her heart was never in politics, and it showed. She aimed to strike a radical pose in her novels of the late '30s and failed. She learned her lesson and never again attempted to write in the social-realist tradition. Her next project took her to a safe and distant past, a period far enough from contemporary reality to allow her natural bent towards giving philosophy and "long-term problems" full and honest scope. In *The Timeless Land,* she explored Australia's early European beginnings to find where and how early visions of the good society had soured and, in so doing, sought to revive them. The success of *The Timeless Land* in 1941 made her almost a household name in her own country.

The book was well received overseas. The timing of the American publication proved providential. Just when the American-Australian military alliance began to crystalize in the minds of both nations, Dark's tale of the birth of a British colony "down under" offered glimpses of shared bonds of British culture and oppression. Richard Casey, then Australian diplomatic envoy to Washington, D.C., thought the book created "a very good public for Australia"; its appeal was so widespread that on a train ride to New York one day, he had observed "several Americans absorbed in the book."

The outbreak of another world war paralyzed Dark's creative energies. It was only towards the end that she emerged from the cursed "artistic paralysis" to write *The Little Company,* one of her least successful novels. A disappointed colleague expressed what others must have felt of this unworthy successor to *The Timeless Land*: "Fancy wasting her lovely talent on such stuff as the mental and moral gropings of a pettybourgeois writer in days like these! It's being stuck in that beautiful home on top of a mountain."

The advent of the atom bomb, even before the peace agreement was signed, suddenly raised the specter of a nuclear holocaust. Dark—and an entire generation of Western radical intellectuals—watched helplessly as the promised land turned instead into a wasteland, where mass culture ruled and mass destruction threatened a population apparently oblivious to the dangers posed by either. Unlike the war, which had galvanized the citizen at the expense of the artist, the immediate postwar period sent electric shocks through both at once. H.G. Wells' call for fellow runners in the "race between education and disaster" captured her imagination.

While Eric Dark brandished his communist sympathies to all and sundry, in the process attracting powerful enemies that eventually thrust him from political, sentimental, and professional associations precious to him, Eleanor preferred to do her work quietly and unobtrusively. *Storm of Time* (1949), the second volume in the trilogy, proved an even greater *tour de force* than the first. Critics at home, in the States and England generally raved about it. It too, it seems, may have been selected by the U.S. Book-of-the-Month Club had it not been for its massive length at a time of serious paper shortages. Even after several cutting sessions, the book she called "The Monster" finished at an extraordinary 300,000 words.

The "public years" came to an abrupt and premature end in late 1949 when Cold War politics so soured community life with rumors and innuendoes of supposed subversive communist activities that in half-disgust, half-trepidation the Darks left for warmer climes—physical and political—in Australia's Deep North in the state of Queensland. *No Barrier*, the third volume in the trilogy, was written in this interlude and reflects the unsettled and unsatisfactory circumstances in which it was written. At its conclusion, Dark swore she would never write another historical novel.

During the second half of the "private years" (1950–85), Dark tasted some of the sweetest and most bitter fruits of her long life. The 1950s were largely sunlit years. In Montville, Queensland—a small farming village "round the corner from the world"—Dark found a rural Australia untouched by and largely unaware of the escalating political and military tensions throughout the West. The life of a hobby-farmer suited her. Every aspect of it—family, community, creativity—thrived in the carefree existence that was life at "The Lane." *Lantana Lane* is a witty and charming recreation of what were possibly her happiest years. Even as the inevitable march of progress signalled the beginning of the end of their little idyllic world, she and fellow farmers had no regrets. "The world and his wife will come whizzing past our doors, but we shall know, if they do not, that this mile-long strip of glassy bitumen was once Lantana Lane." A family crisis brought the Montville years to an abrupt end, and she re-

turned permanently to Katoomba. She never published again.

Instead, the 1960s belonged to Dark, the family historian, whose carefully crafted and documented stories of the O'Reilly and Dark families constitute, among other things, an integral part of her own story. It is no accident that her diaries, punctiliously kept for some 40 years, fell silent. Life and its many blows had finally snuffed the one flame—the impulse to write and communicate her feelings—that had been her lifeline since childhood. An interview given by Eric Dark to **Giulia Giuffre** on his wife's behalf shortly before her death throws rare light into her mood in this last stage of her life. She regretted having written anything at all, he said; her books had caused more trouble than they were worth.

Drained of creative energies and bitter about the lack of community support she and others in Australian "high" literary society had received over the years, Dark turned instinctively to the source of her greatest comfort from childhood onwards: fellow artists of other times. Tchaikovsky's "Pathetique" Symphony had been a favorite. So had William Blake's poetry, particularly his "Songs of Innocence and Experience." In her last communion with a kindred spirit, Eleanor Dark turned fittingly to Wordsworth's "Intimations of Immortality."

SOURCES:

Boyd, J. "'That Dark Lady's Husband': The Forgotten Life of Dr Eric Payten Dark," B.A. Honors Thesis (University of Western Sydney, Macarthur, 1992).

Eleanor Dark papers, Mitchell Wing, State Library of New South Wales, Australia, ML MSS 4545.

Eleanor Dark papers, National Library of Australia, NLA MS 4998.

Giuffre, G. "Eric Dark—for Eleanor Dark," in *A Writing Life: Interviews with Australian Women Writers.* Sydney: Allen & Unwin, 1990.

Papers relating to Eleanor and Eric Dark, in private collection of Michael Dark, Katoomba, N.S.W.

Papers relating to Eric Dark, in private collection of John Dark, Sydney, N.S.W.

Wyndham, M., "Eleanor Dark, 'the hard and lonely alternative,'" B.A. Honors Thesis (Australian National University, 1987).

SUGGESTED READING:

Devanny, J., "Writers at Home: Eleanor and Eric Dark," in *Bird of Paradise*. Sydney: Frank Johnson, 1945.

Ferrier, C., ed. *As good as a yarn with you: letters between Miles Franklin, Katharine Susannah Prichard, Jean Devanny, Marjorie Barnard, Flora Eldershaw and Eleanor Dark.* Cambridge University Press, 1992.

Grove Day, A. *Eleanor Dark.* Boston: Twayne, 1976.

Modjeska, D. *Exiles at Home: Australian Women Writers 1925-1945.* Sirius Books, 1984.

Murray-Smith, S. "Darkness at Dark," in *Australian Book Review.* Vol. 2. September 1963.

Tennant, K. "A Little Company against the Bulldozer Mentality," in *Sydney Morning Herald*. February 14, 1974.

Thomson, A.K. *Understanding the Novel: The Timeless Land*. Brisbane, Jacaranda, 1966.

Wilkes, G.A. "The Progress of Eleanor Dark," in *Southerly*. Vol. XII, no. 3, 1951.

COLLECTIONS:

Correspondence, papers, memorabilia, photographs and portraits located in the Mitchell Wing, State Library of New South Wales, Sydney; and the National Library of Australia, Canberra, Australia.

Marivic Wyndham, Ph.D.
scholar and author of *Eleanor Dark: A World-Proof Life*
(Australian National University, 1995)

Dark Lady, The (c. 1578–1647).

See Fitton, Mary.

Darling, Grace (1815–1842)

British hero who, with her father, rescued nine survivors of the steamer Forfarshire *when it was wrecked in a violent storm in September 1838. Born Grace Horsley Darling at Bamburgh, Northumberland, England, on November 24, 1815; died on October 20, 1842; seventh of nine children (including two sets of twins) of William (a lighthouse keeper) and Thomasin (Horsley) Darling.*

$\mathcal{G}$race
$\mathcal{D}$arling

On the night of September 6, 1838, during a violent storm, the *Forfarshire*, one of the first luxury steamships, was bound from Hull to Dundee with 63 people on board when it struck Harcar Rock in the Farne Islands, off the coast of Northumberland. In the first light of morning on September 7, William Darling, the keeper of the Longstone Lighthouse, and his 22-year-old daughter Grace caught sight of the movement of survivors on Harcar Rock. Grace and her father rowed three-quarters of a mile to rescue the nine survivors, four crew members and five passengers, including one woman. Since all nine would not fit into their boat, two trips were necessary, and Grace went out only once. After returning to the lighthouse with the woman and four crew members, she attended to the injured while William Darling and two of the ship's crew members went back for the remaining survivors.

The daring rescue brought immortality to Grace Darling, described by *Jessica Mitford as "the first 'media' heroine." "She seems to have been the right girl in the right place at the right time to usher in the Victorian era," Mitford wrote in *Grace Had an English Heart*. "What could be a more appropriate ornament to the beginning of the eighteen-year-old Queen's reign than 'an English maid;/ Pure as the air around her,/ Of danger ne'er afraid'?" From the time of "the Deed," Darling was besieged by reporters, who spread her story across the country, often taking liberty with the facts. She received medals from the Humane Society, as well as a grant from the treasury, and became the subject of countless biographies, two of which were published with astonishing speed in 1839: *Grace Darling, or the Heroine of the Farne Islands*, by G.M. Reynolds, and *Grace Darling, or The Maid of the Isles*, by Jerrold Vernon, a local writer. In addition to paintings, poems, and even a song honoring her valor, a romanticized likeness of Darling graced Staffordshire commemorative pottery as well as a Cadbury chocolate tin. In 1884, a hybrid Grace Darling rose, creamy white shaded with pink, made its way into English gardens. As late as 1987, Royal Doulton issued a Grace Darling statuette.

Although she is only dimly remembered in modern-day Britain, the small village of Bamburgh abounds with memorials to her, among them her birthplace, the house where she died (transformed into a gift shop), a two-room museum, and her monument in the Bamburgh churchyard. Built in 1844 by C. Raymond Smith, a London sculptor, the monument did not hold up well and underwent numerous restorations, one of which was helped along by *Ida Lewis, the "Grace Darling of America," who contributed money to the repair effort.

The perpetuation of the Grace Darling legend may have been due in part to her early death from influenza on October 20, 1842, several years short of her 30th birthday. Her funeral, four days later, was attended by mourners from every walk of life, some coming from miles away to pay their respects. Queen *Victoria contributed to Darling's memorial, and William Wordsworth composed an 100-line poetic tribute to her, from which 17 lines were chosen for a memorial stone in St. Cuthbert's Chapel on the Inner Farne Island.

SOURCES:

Mitford, Jessica. *Grace Had an English Heart*. NY: E. P. Dutton, 1988.

Barbara Morgan,
Melrose, Massachusetts

Darmesteter, Mary F. (1856–1944).

See Duclaux, Agnes Mary F.

Darnell, Linda (1921–1965)

American actress. Born Monetta Eloyse Darnell in Dallas, Texas, on October 16, 1921; died from injuries sustained in a house fire in Glenview, Illinois, on April 10, 1965; third of five children of a postal clerk; attended public schools in Dallas; attended Central High School in Los Angeles and had studio tutoring; married Peverell Marley (a cinematographer), on April 18, 1943 (divorced 1951); married Philip Liebmann, on February 25, 1954 (divorced 1955); married Merle Roy Robertson (a pilot), on March 3, 1957 (divorced 1963); children: Charlotte Mildred, called Lola (adopted in 1948).

Selected films: Hotel for Women (1939); Daytime Wife (1939); Stardust (1940); Brigham Young (1940); The Mark of Zorro (1940); Chad Hanna (1940); Blood and Sand (1941); Rise and Shine (1941); The Loves of Edgar Allan Poe (1942); The Song of Bernadette (1943); Buffalo Bill (1944); It Happened Tomorrow (1944); Summer Storm (1944); Sweet and Lowdown (1944); The Great John L. (1945); Fallen Angel (1945); Hangover Square (1945); Anna and the King of Siam (1946); Centennial Summer (1946); My Darling Clementine (1946); Forever Amber (1947); The Walls of Jericho (1948); Unfaithfully Yours (1948); A Letter to Three Wives (1949); Slattery's Hurricane (1949); Everybody Does It (1949); No Way Out (1950); The Thirteenth Letter (1951); The Lady Pays Off (1951); The Guy Who Came Back (1951); Saturday Island (1952); Night without Sleep (1952); Blackbeard the Pirate (1952); Second Chance (1953); This Is My Love (1954); Dakota Incident (1956); Zero Hour (1957); Black Spurs (1965).

Linda Darnell may have been one of the most reluctant film stars of the 1940s. "I had no great talent, and I never wanted to be a movie star," she once recalled. "But my mother had always wanted it for herself, and I guess she projected through me. I was going to become a movie star or mom was going to burst in the attempt." By age four, Darnell was taking tap-dancing lessons and was enrolled in every local talent contest. At 11, she was modeling for a local department store and, at 14, entered her first beauty contest. Two years later, she won a regional "Gateway to Hollywood" contest and was screentested by RKO, but she was sent home to Dallas within a short time to grow up a bit. In 1939, a talent scout from Fox remem-

bered her from the Gateway contest and wired her to come to Hollywood, where she became a contract player. After only three weeks of acting lessons, her first role in the movie *Hotel for Women* (1939) prompted one critic to remark that she would not be a challenge to *Bette Davis for quite some time.

With her delicate, even features and dark hair and eyes, Darnell was perfect for the innocent heroines and faithful wives of her early pictures, such as *Daytime Wife* (1939) with Tyrone Power. Her role in *The Mark of Zorro* (1940), again with Power, was her first Technicolor film, and the close-ups boosted her star status. All the while, Darnell's mother continued to meddle in her career, requesting that Fox transfer her husband from the Dallas postal system to Beverly Hills and arranging for her daughter's contract to place much of her pay in a Darnell family trust.

Linda Darnell moved from her parents' home in 1942 and a year later eloped to Las Vegas with cinematographer Peverell Marley, who was already twice divorced and 20 years her senior. "I need an older, experienced man to guide me," she told the press. "Everyone else on the lot pampered me and treated me as if I were a baby." The couple adopted a little girl in 1948, three years before the marriage ended. A second marriage in 1954 to Philip Liebmann (of the New York brewery family) would only last a year. Her last marriage, to pilot Merle Robertson in 1957, would end in a bitter divorce in 1963. During the hostile proceedings, Robertson charged Darnell with continual drunkenness and neglect of marital duties. Darnell countered with accusations that Robertson had fathered a child with a Yugoslavian actress.

During the 1940s, Darnell turned to more sultry roles, beginning with Olga the woodcutter's daughter in an adaptation of a Chekhov story called *Summer Storm* (1944). She hoped the role would serve as a more dramatic vehicle, but the film was considered mediocre, as was *Hangover Square* (1945), a horror movie in which she played a music-hall trollop who is murdered by an insane composer. This was followed by her portrayal of a siren in *Fallen Angel* (1945). In 1946, Darnell was paired with *Jeanne Crain and Cornel Wilde in the popular musical *Centennial Summer*.

The best opportunity of her career came when she replaced British import Peggy Cummins as the arrogant hussy in *Forever Amber* (1947), a film based on *Kathleen Winsor's best-selling novel set in the reign of Charles II. Under the direction of Otto Preminger, the long-awaited and much-hyped film premiered on October 22, 1947, but received only a lukewarm reception from audiences. Darnell made several other films for Fox, including *Unfaithfully Yours* (1948), *A Letter to Three Wives* (1949), which was probably the best of the lot, and *No Way Out* (1950), before the termination of her contract in 1952.

She appeared in low-budget minor films during the remainder of the 1950s (including several in Italy) and made an inauspicious stage debut in *A Roomful of Roses* (1956) in Phoenix, Arizona, far enough off the beaten track to avoid big-city critics. In addition to a subsequent tour in *Tea and Sympathy*, she was also seen on television, appearing on "Playhouse 90," "Climax," "77 Sunset Strip," "Rawhide," and the "Jane Wyman Theater." In October 1956, Darnell joined the cast of an ill-fated Broadway production called *Harbor Lights*, in which she played a Staten Island housewife opposite Robert Alda and Paul Langton. Unfortunately, this time she did not escape notice. Critic Brooks Atkinson of *The New York Times* was unmerciful: "As the Mother, the beautiful Linda Darnell . . . goes through each scene with the same distaste for the story, the symbolism and the scenery." The play closed after four performances.

Darnell's later career included further stage tours and a nightclub act that received a fair review from *Variety*. By some accounts, the fading of her beauty and the downward spiral of her career led to a drinking problem. The actress died unexpectedly in April 1965, the result of injuries sustained in a fire at the home of her onetime secretary, whom she was visiting after touring in *Janus*. Her last film, a mini-budgeted western called *Black Spurs*, opened shortly after her death. *The New York Times* review provided a sad epitaph: "Poor departed Linda Darnell. The actress did her last turn yesterday—playing the small role of a saloon hostess that almost anybody could have ambled through."

SOURCES:

Halliwell, Leslie. *The Filmgoer's Companion.* NY: Hill and Wang, 1974.

Katz, Ephraim. *The Film Encyclopedia.* NY: HarperCollins, 1994.

Parish, James Robert. *The Fox Girls.* New Rochelle, NY: Arlington House, 1971.

Barbara Morgan,
Melrose, Massachusetts

Darragh, Lydia Barrington

(1729–1789)

American nurse and midwife who was a Revolutionary War hero. Born Lydia Barrington in Dublin, Ireland, in 1729; died in Philadelphia, Pennsylvania, on December 28, 1789; daughter of John Barrington; married William Darragh (a tutor), in November 1753 (died 1783); children: nine, of which five reached maturity, Charles, Ann, John, William, and Susannah.

Lydia Barrington Darragh immigrated to America from Ireland in 1753, shortly after her marriage. Settling in Philadelphia, she and her husband William became members of the Monthly Meeting of Friends and parented nine children (five of whom reached maturity). In addition to caring for her children, Darragh worked as a nurse and midwife, making a significant contribution to the support of her large family.

Her status as a hero of the American Revolution developed from a story first published in 1827, long after her death, which later received elaboration. Accordingly, during the period of the British occupation of Philadelphia (September 1777–June 1778), Darragh's house faced the headquarters of General William Howe and was commandeered for a secret meeting held on the night of December 2, 1777. Listening at a keyhole, Darragh learned of the British plan to attack General George Washington two nights later at Whitemarsh, eight miles away. On the morning of December 4, Darragh obtained a pass to leave the city to purchase flour but instead made her way toward the American camp, where she encountered Col. Thomas Craig and relayed the information. Craig passed the word along, and when the British troops marched out of Philadelphia they found the Continental Army ready to repel them, forcing Howe's return to the city. Unrecognized as a hero in her lifetime, Darragh continued to reside in Philadelphia, where, after her husband's death in 1783, she was suspended from the Quaker church for failing to attend meetings and for not adhering to church policies. She appears to have been reinstated, however, for when she died in 1789 she was buried in the Friends' cemetery in Philadelphia.

Darré, Jeanne-Marie (1905–1999)

French pianist. Name variations: Darre. Born in Givet, France, a town near the Belgian border, on July 30, 1905; died on January 26, 1999, in Port Marly, France; studied with Marguerite Long and Isidor Philipp (1863–1958) in Paris; taught at the Paris Conservatoire and concertized widely.

Studying with *Marguerite Long and Isidor Philipp, two of the most important piano teach-

Opposite page

Linda
Darnell

sic films, including Mayerling *(1936) and* La Ronde *(1950). Born in Bordeaux, France, on May 1, 1917; daughter of Jean and Marie-Louise Witkowski Darrieux; married Henri Decoin (a film director), in 1934 (divorced 1940); married Porfirio Rubirosa, in 1942 (divorced 1947); married Georges Mitsinkides (an author), in 1948; children: (third marriage) one son, Mathieu.*

Born in Bordeaux in 1917, Danielle Darrieux and her family moved to Paris when she was two years old. When she was seven, her father, an ophthalmologist and military physician, died. A cello student at the Paris Conservatory, Darrieux was only 14 when she made her film debut in *Le Bal* (1931), in which she depicted a willful adolescent. Although she abandoned whatever plans she might have had of a musical career as an instrumentalist, Darrieux's considerable vocal talents were quickly discovered, and in 1934 she appeared in a highly successful musical, *La Crise est finie*. Another 1934 film that showcased Darrieux's emerging talent was *Mauvaise Graine*. Based on a Billy Wilder story and co-directed by Wilder, Darrieux played a girl who acted as a decoy for her brother's gang; her portrayal gave the film much of its special flavor. Taking advantage of her newfound fame, Darrieux made another film in 1934, *Volga en flammes*. Set in Russia during the Bolshevik revolution, this epic was mostly filmed in Prague.

In 1935, Darrieux took on her first truly dramatic role in *Le Domino vert*, depicting a heroine under both emotional and—significant for the 1930s—financial stress. At the same time, she continued to work in musical comedies with established stars like the Polish tenor Jan Kiepura. It was the 1936 film *Mayerling*, in which she co-starred with the prominent actor Charles Boyer, that brought Danielle Darrieux to world attention. Based on the true story of the 1889 suicide of Austro-Hungarian crown prince Rudolph of Habsburg and his young mistress *Marie Vetsera, this film revealed Darrieux's astonishing talent to a global audience and remains the most moving and popular of the many screen versions of the Mayerling story. Critics were at a loss to describe the intensity and depth of the performance given by an actress not yet 20 when the film was released in France. The entire film world was now interested in Danielle Darrieux.

In 1934, she married film director Henri Decoin, who appreciated his wife's talents, seeing to it that she could choose from not only excellent scripts but from a variety of styles including mu-

Jeanne-Marie Darré

ers of the period, Jeanne-Marie Darré won first prizes in both their classes. Her concert career began in 1920, and she had a long, distinguished teaching career at the Paris Conservatoire. Darré's American recital debut in 1962 was an unqualified success. Her favorite pieces were the Ravel G major concerto, Weber's *Konzertstück*, and the five concerti of Saint-Saëns. In 1926, at the very start of her illustrious career, she delighted Paris by performing all five of the Saint-Saëns concerti in one marathon evening. Darré's dry, brilliant style was perfect for the great works of French pianism. Of her many recordings, one of the most distinguished is an acclaimed reading of the Liszt Piano Sonata, controversial because of her strongly analytical approach to the work.

John Haag,
Athens, Georgia

Darrieux, Danielle (1917—)

French actress who, in an international career lasting more than six decades, appeared in a number of clas-

sicals. In 1937, she starred in Decoin's *Mademoiselle ma mere,* portraying a woman who, after rejecting her parent's advice not to marry an older man, then proceeds to have a passionate affair with her new husband's son. At this time, Darrieux made her stage debut in *Jeux Dangereux,* a

play by her husband that she performed in both Paris and Brussels. In January 1937, she accepted a generous offer by Universal Studios to work in Hollywood, signing a nine-year contract, with options, at $4,000 a week. But she was not happy in California, and the only starring film she made there, *The Rage of Paris* (1938), is generally not considered one of her significant achievements. Litigation over breach of contract with Universal Studios and other American film firms clouded the late 1930s for Darrieux and dimmed prospects that she would ever return to America. Despite the war clouds on the immediate horizon, Darrieux made several more films to delight her millions of loyal fans, including *Katia* (1938), which was filmed in Hungary. The movie reestablished a Mayerling mood of doomed European aristocracy by sketching the tragic life of Tsar Alexander II and *Ekaterina Dolgorukova, the woman who loved him.

German troops defeated France in a few weeks in the late spring of 1940 and by June of that year had occupied Paris. Darrieux and her husband Henri Decoin, whom she divorced that same year, established a production company, Continentale, and set about to make films. In the first movie to be made under German occupation, *Premier Rendezvous* (1941), Darrieux is an orphan who runs away to join her pen pal, but finding him unattractive and middle-aged fortunately meets his nephew (Louis Jourdan) who is young, handsome and interested. Dramatic changes took place during the war in Darrieux's private life. In 1942, she married the notorious playboy from the Dominican Republic, Porfirio Rubirosa. Apparently unaware, or at least uninterested, in the Nazi persecution of Jews and French patriots, Darrieux and most of her fellow stars were more than willing to collaborate with the Nazi occupation forces. In March 1942, she and other glamorous celebrities, including **Junie Astor**, **Suzy Delair**, and *Viviane Romance, accepted a German offer to visit Berlin, where they were wined and dined and became valuable grist for the Nazi propaganda mills of Joseph Goebbels.

In 1945, after the liberation of France, Darrieux resumed her film career. That year, her adoring public was pleased with her performance in *Adieu Chérie*, a light entertainment perfect for a nation only too ready to forget the sufferings—and moral compromises—of the previous five years. Her next several films were unsuccessful, but Darrieux had a smashing success on stage starring in *L'Amour Vient en Jouant*. When she and Rubirosa divorced in 1947, rumors swirled through France asserting that American tobacco heiress **Doris Duke** had "bought" him from the French actress for the price of $1 million. In 1948, Darrieux married the author Georges Mitsinkides, a union that would last. Her one child, Mathieu, was born from this, her third and final marriage.

A major triumph for Darrieux was her starring role in *La Ronde,* a 1950 film directed by Max Ophüls and based on the 1903 play *Der Reigen* by the Austrian naturalist playwright Arthur Schnitzler. As a married woman in bed with her student lover who is embarrassed by his temporary impotence, Darrieux won rave reviews for the exquisite subtlety of her acting. Her triumph in *La Ronde* led to two further well-received roles in films directed by Ophüls, as Rosa in *Le Plaisir* (*The House of Pleasure,* 1952), and as Madame Louise de . . . in *The Earrings of Madame de . . .* (1953). In the latter film, regarded by many critics as the one in which Darrieux gave her greatest cinema performance, she portrayed a dazzling but debt-ridden socialite married to a general (Charles Boyer). To get money, she sells the diamond earrings her husband gave her as a wedding gift, telling him that she had lost them. Her unhappy marriage leads her into an affair with an Italian diplomat (Vittorio de Sica), who bestows on her the same earrings. One admiring critic wrote that "Darrieux covers the spectrum of aristocratic femininity—she goes from being a heartbreaker to being heartbroken without missing a halftone."

Exhibiting remarkable versatility, Darrieux was able at all stages of her career to star in both films and on stage while also carrying the day as a singer and a television performer. In the 1956 film epic *Alexander the Great,* she gave a fine performance as Alexander's mother *Olympias. Willing to forget her earlier unpleasant experiences in Hollywood, Darrieux more than held her own as a co-star with James Mason in the 1952 spy thriller *Five Fingers.* Her singing talent by no means discarded, she turned in excellent performances in the 1951 musical *Rich, Young, and Pretty,* a Hollywood extravaganza in which, at age 34, she was featured as *Jane Powell's mother. In Jacques Demy's 1967 musical *The Young Girls of Rochefort,* Darrieux expertly handled the role of café proprietor Yvonne, mother to twin sisters Delphine and Solange (played in the film by real-life sisters **Catherine Deneuve** and *Françoise Dorléac). In this film, Darrieux turned out to be the only performer who sang well enough to use her own voice, all of the others having to depend on dubbed singing voices.

As she gracefully entered middle age, Danielle Darrieux showed little sign of slowing down. She continued to accept film roles that usually earned her strong reviews and the loyalty of her many fans. At the same time, she increasingly turned her attention to the theater and quality television roles. Just to prove that she still possessed star quality, in the 1980s she returned to the screen to turn in a series of superb performances. These included her depiction of Françoise Canavaggia in the 1983 film *En Haut des marches,* a role that displayed the full range of human emotions as a Frenchwoman attempting to revenge her husband's death at the hands of Nazi collaborators. Equally impressive was her portrayal in the 1982 film *Une Chambre en ville (A Room in Town)* of Baroness de Neuville, an unhappy alcoholic factory owner determined to crush a strike launched by her angry workers.

After more than 60 years of acting, Danielle Darrieux remained the star she had become in her late teen years. In 1991, she appeared on French television in "Plège infernal," in 1992 in the film *les Mamies,* and on the Paris stage in 1995 in *Harold et Maude.* A grateful French nation rewarded her for lifetime achievements in the dramatic arts on numerous occasions, including the granting of the Chevalier de la legion d'honneur (1962), the rank of Officier de la legion d'honneur (1977), as well as the film industry's César d'honneur (1985) and the prix de l'Amicale des cadres de l'industrie cinématographique (1987). In a remarkable career extending over seven decades, Danielle Darrieux won the admiration of several generations of film fanciers both in France and abroad, earning for herself the title of a cherished *artiste dramatique.*

SOURCES:
Chateau, René. *Le Cinema français sous l'Occupation, 1940–1944.* Courbevoie: Éditions René Chateau/La Mémoire du Cinema, 1995.
Halimi, André. *Chantons sous l'Occupation.* Paris: O. Orban, 1976.
Le Boterf, Hervé. *La Vie Parisienne sous l'Occupation 1940–1944 (Paris bei Nacht).* Vol. 1. Paris: Éditions France-Empire, 1974.
Webster, Paul. "Hand in glove with the Nazis," in *Manchester Guardian Weekly.* Vol. 154, no. 13. March 31, 1996, p. 27.
Whitehall, Richard. "Danielle Darrieux," in *Films and Filming.* December 1961.

John Haag, Associate Professor of History, University of Georgia, Athens, Georgia

Darton, Patience (1911–1996)

British nurse in the Spanish Civil War and political activist. Name variations: Patience Edney. Born Patience Darton in Orpington, Kent, England, on August 27, 1911; died in Madrid, Spain, on November 6, 1996; had a sister, Hillary Darton; married Eric Edney; children: one son, Robert.

Patience Darton was born into a prosperous publishing family in 1911, but, by the time she was in her mid-teens, her father's business declared itself bankrupt, and the family had to live in straitened economic circumstances. Although she had hoped to study medicine, the shrunken family purse made this an impossibility. Consequently, she chose instead a career in nursing. Even this modest goal was not easily achieved. Darton had to save for fully three years from her sparse earnings as a nanny and later as a cook in a tea restaurant, in order to have the more than £8 needed to pay the admission fees and purchase the uniform that would enable her to enroll in a course of nursing.

As she began her studies, Darton found herself facing the Great Depression of the 1930s. Her social consciousness developed rapidly during these years. She found herself confronting massive injustices on a daily basis. For instance, many of the patients who came to her hospital for treatment were dying women who, because they lacked the one shilling and six pence needed to pay for a physician's services, had delayed going to hospital until it was too late. Employed men, on the other hand, were covered by health insurance and could therefore choose to go to their physicians on a much more frequent basis, often saving their lives as a consequence of early detection and treatment.

By the time civil war broke out in Spain in the summer of 1936, Darton had completed training as a midwife at University College Hospital, London. She worked in midwifery around Woolwich Arsenal, and it was here that the full force of suffering and social injustice in the economic depression became clear to her. Darton was furious every time hand grenades were tested at the nearby Arsenal. Each test cost £300, a vast sum that could, if budgeted for social programs, provide much-needed medical services for the poor. At the same time, her hatred of Fascism made her realize that British rearmament was probably a necessary evil. But the inequities overwhelmed her. On one occasion, she tried to calm the fears of a dying mother who was deeply concerned about the future of her seven children. Almost as distressing to Darton were the working conditions of midwives and nurses, who were poorly paid for long work weeks that were physically and emotionally draining.

Darton decided that if her nursing skills were of any value to the hard-pressed Republican forces of Spain, she would gladly go to the war and offer her assistance. Unable at first to find out how to join a nurses' volunteer unit, she contacted reporters at both the *Daily Herald* and *News Chronicle*, newspapers sympathetic to the Spanish Republican cause. Through them, she came in contact with the appropriate medical support committee. A clear indication of the desperate nature of the situation was the fact that, in February 1937, she was sent to Spain on only two days' notice.

Within days of her arrival, Darton's medical skills proved to be of great value for a wounded British volunteer, Tom Wintringham. The dubious quality of Spanish medicine, made much worse by the defection of most doctors for Fascist-occupied territory, was made clear when she discovered Wintringham, lying ill in a fly-infested hospital room, diagnosed with typhus by local doctors and quite obviously not recovering. Darton quickly concluded that Wintringham's condition had been misdiagnosed, that he was in fact suffering from malnutrition and a serious abscess. Denied help by the medical staff of the hospital, she took the initiative to lance the man's wounds and was able to provide him with a steady supply of nourishing food from visiting Britishers. The results of her ministrations were an amazing recovery from a veteran near death who could now return home.

Like all of the nurses who worked for the International Brigades in Spain, Darton put in long hours with little rest under the most dangerous conditions possible. Despite the inadequacies of the situation, she and other members of her staff were able to save many lives. Somehow, despite the pace of her life, Darton met and fell in love with a Brigade soldier, Robert Aaquist. Aaquist was born in Germany of a Norwegian father and a German-Jewish mother, and the family fled the Nazis, first to North Africa and finally to Palestine. Lieutenant Robert Aaquist died in the summer of 1938 during the Ebro offensive, the Spanish Republic's last, and unsuccessful, military gamble. Though Darton was enormously grieved when informed of Aaquist's death, she was transferred to the front lines, where her work in the midst of death and bombardment proved to be therapeutic.

The Ebro offensive was the tragic last gasp of Republican Spain. Lacking weapons, the Republican forces, strengthened by the International Brigades, hoped that their courage and military experience would match or better the firepower of the Fascists. For a few days, the situation appeared promising, but soon the tide of battle turned. Darton, working in a primitive hospital dug into a cave, cared as best she could for the rapidly growing number of wounded men.

Darton participated in the final parade of the International Brigades in October 1938 as they departed from Spain in the vain hope that Franco would reciprocate by asking his German and Italian allies to depart as well. *Dolores Ibarruri*, known as La Pasionaria, gave an emotional speech before the assembled veterans, declaring "You are history, you will one day return to Spain!" Darton arrived back in London in December 1938, with her memories and private grief. Soon after, more determined than ever to fight Fascism, she joined the British Communist Party but was content to remain in the rank and file of a tiny movement that was never able to gain mass support. Darton's belief in Communism was based on her idealism and clearly ignored the Machiavellian aspects of Stalinism. Besides joining committees dedicated to helping the thousands of desperate Spanish refugees in France, she devoted her medical talents to taking care of the Czech refugees, many of them Jewish, who now streamed into the United Kingdom after Hitler's most recent aggression, the annexation of Bohemia and Moravia in March 1939.

By the end of World War II, Darton was working in an important post for the United Nations Relief and Rehabilitation Agency (UNRRA). She had the responsibility of getting foodstuffs to the starving civilian population of the newly liberated European Continent. Although much was accomplished by UNRRA, Darton also had many frustrations on the job, including clashes with American military officers who seemed more concerned with getting luxury supplies to American troops than shipping bare necessities to Europe's civilians. Soon after the war ended, Darton returned to her nursing job. The paranoid tensions of the Cold War dismayed her, but she remained a Communist, convinced that the Soviet Union had found the best path for its future.

In the early 1950s, she married Eric Edney, a Communist Party official, and belatedly started a family. Besides remaining a social activist in her profession in and around London, Darton believed that the Chinese too had made the right decision in 1949 by creating the Chinese People's Republic and attempting to build Socialism. Rather naively, Darton and her husband went to China, hoping to contribute to the efforts to change society. Her son Robert was born there. Soon after, however, Darton and her family found itself enmeshed in China's domestic turmoil. Eric was arrested, and for a time it appeared that Patience and her son too would find themselves behind bars. She discovered to her regret that, despite its Socialist government, China remained China. But Darton remained stubbornly committed to the Communist ideal and did not quit, as many had, the tiny British Communist Party.

Always extremely frank in voicing her opinions, in her last years Patience Darton expressed regrets about some of the things she had done—or not done—in her long life. On one theme, however, she expressed great satisfaction, the time she had spent in Spain during the Civil War. This had been, she continued to believe, "a great cause" and she remained proud of having played a role, if only a small one, in that great and tragic drama of the 1930s. While admitting that the Spanish conflict had been full of complexities, she asserted that for her it was a wonderfully clear-cut affair, one simply went to Spain to take a stand against the spread of Fascism.

Fearing that she would one day linger on and eventually die in a nursing home, she told an interviewer that if faced with that choice, she would prefer to take a fatal dose of sleeping pills. Fortunately for Patience Darton, death came in the most triumphant form possible. Along with about 700 survivors of the International Brigades (out of perhaps 1,000 worldwide), she traveled to Spain in November 1996 to participate in celebrating the 60th anniversary of the Civil War. Aged and frail as she and virtually all of her comrades were, they were elated by the reception given them in Madrid, which included the granting of honorary Spanish citizenship. Fulfilling La Pasionaria's 1938 prophecy, Darton had finally returned to Spain. It was there, at age 85, that the veteran nurse suddenly died. On the previous evening, she had attended a Madrid concert given in honor of the International Brigade veterans, an emotional festivity attended by 35,000 citizens of the Spanish capital.

SOURCES:

Alexander, Bill. *British Volunteers for Liberty: Spain 1936–1939*. London: Lawrence and Wishhart, 1982.

Barker, Dennis and Shen Liknaitzky. "Patience Edney: Great Exit for a Fighter," in *The Guardian* [London]. November 12, 1996, p. 16.

Green, Martin. "Patience Edney," in *The Independent* [London]. December 2, 1996, p. 16.

Lataster-Czisch, Petra. *Eigentlich rede ich nicht gern über mich: Lebenserinnerungen von Frauen aus dem Spanischen Bürgerkrieg 1936–1939*. Leipzig and Weimar: Gustav Kiepenheuer Verlag, 1990.

Tarvainen, Sinikka. "Visit of 'last Romantic' war veterans opens old wounds in Spain," in *Deutsche Presse-Agentur*. November 11, 1996.

John Haag, Associate Professor of History, University of Georgia, Athens, Georgia

Darusmont or d'Arusmont, Frances (1795–1852).

See Wright, Frances.

Darvas, Lili (1902–1974)

Hungarian-born American actress who topped off a distinguished career by starring in the internationally acclaimed Hungarian film Love. *Born in Budapest, Hungary, in 1902; died in New York City on July 22, 1974; married Ferenc Molnar (a playwright), in 1926 (separated around 1932).*

In a career on both sides of the Atlantic Ocean that spanned more than 50 years and revealed a total mastery of three very different languages and cultural traditions, Lili Darvas proved to be a durable, superb actress. Born in Budapest, Hungary, she grew up in prosperous circumstances, her father being a successful physician. When his stagestruck daughter was 19, he financed a performance of *Romeo and Juliet* with a repertory theater that allowed her to take the lead. This, he said, was no more unusual than paying for the publication of a child's first book. Lili's performance was a sensation and one of Budapest's leading theatrical managers offered her a contract. Soon, she was a star not only in Budapest but throughout Hungary. In 1925, the famous German impresario Max Reinhardt invited her to Salzburg to audition for him. Despite the fact that Darvas knew no German and was famous only in Hungary, Reinhardt saw star quality in the young actress. He made her an offer she did not refuse, namely he would pay for an apartment for her and her mother in Vienna so that she could study German intensively with a tutor for one year, all expenses paid. The year over, she would make her debut in his Vienna theater. In return, she would sign a four-year contract with Reinhardt.

In that year, Lili Darvas completely mastered German, making her Vienna debut at the famous Theater in der Josefstadt. It was a complete triumph, and Otto Preminger, manager of the theater who was as delighted by the young Hungarian's performance as the audience, would note with astonishment decades later that Lili Darvas was the only foreigner he had ever encountered who had learned to speak German without an accent. Another turn in direction during this period of Darvas' life was her 1926 marriage to Ferenc Molnar. Almost a quarter-century older than his bride, Molnar was a world-famous playwright and almost as well known in Budapest for his practical jokes as for his plays. Darvas' career prospered during the next dozen years, and she worked in Reinhardt's theaters in Vienna, Salzburg, and Berlin. Her husband took an interest in her career by writing several plays for her to star in, including *Delilah, Olympia* and *Still Life*. In 1927, Darvas visited New York City on tour but, since she found the English language to be odd—she was particularly struck by a sign for a gift shop, since in German *gift* means poison—she made no plans to learn a third language, thinking it would be quite irrelevant to her career.

The Nazi occupation of Austria in March 1938 forced the Molnars to flee their beloved Vienna. Ferenc Molnar was Jewish and since Nazi racial legislation defined Lili Darvas as "a half blood-Jewess," their lives were in danger. Fortunately, they were able to flee to Switzerland by train. After a short stay in the United Kingdom, Darvas and her husband arrived in New York. Wealthy from his royalties, Molnar took a suite at the Plaza Hotel. Darvas rented an apartment nearby that she shared with a friend, a Viennese actor and director who had followed her into exile. Although the erotic part of their marriage was over, Darvas and her husband remained on the closest possible terms. Every day, she went to the Plaza to lunch with him and engage in lively discussions.

Determined to create a stage career for herself in New York, Darvas took the advice of friends like Walter Slezak and worked hard to perfect her English. Although she could never shake an accent as she had done when she learned German, Darvas nevertheless became fluent in the language of her new country. Having an accent was a distinct disadvantage in her career, for now she was called only to play "foreigner" roles. Still, her European reputation and her obvious talent landed her more than a few good stage roles, including that of a celebrated European actress in George S. Kaufman and *Edna Ferber's *Bravo*, as well as jobs in radio soap operas. Her first Broadway role in English was in Ferdinand Bruckner's *The Criminals,* followed by *Soldier's Wife,* which ran for almost a year. In Henry Denker's drama "A Far Country," she portrayed **Amalia Nathansohn Freud**, the formidable mother of Sigmund Freud, receiving positive reviews from the New York critics.

Lili Darvas continued her acting career after her husband died in 1952. Besides roles in the new medium of television, she could still be seen on the Broadway stage, portraying the grandmother in *Lillian Hellman's *My Mother, My Father and Me* and Mme. St. Pé in the 1958 revival of Jean Anouilh's *The Waltz of the Toreadors.* Starting in the 1950s, she also began to make regular trips to

Europe. She often spent her summers in Austria, and occasionally acted in Europe, including an appearance in a Berlin production of Chekhov's *The Cherry Orchard.* In the 1960s, she began to travel to her native Hungary. One of the most meaningful aspects of her Hungarian trips was being reunited with her stepdaughter—Ferenc Molnar's daughter by his first wife **Margit Veszi**. (Molnar's second wife was actress **Sari Fedak**; his longtime domestic partner, **Wanda Bartha**, committed suicide in 1947.) Since Lili's stepdaughter was a woman her own age, this enabled Darvas to meet with her stepdaughter's children and grandchildren. During the next years, Darvas spent pleasant summers with her newly discovered family in a cottage on Lake Balaton.

In 1970, she was invited to appear in an Hungarian film being produced in Budapest. She flew to Europe and filmed her part, that of a bedridden woman aged 96 who does not know that her adored son is serving time in prison for a political offense. To protect the old lady, her daughter-in-law fakes letters from the son, telling his mother that he is in New York successfully working as a film director. The pretense is maintained until the old woman dies. The poignant story, based on novellas by Tibor Dery, gave Darvas an opportunity to once again star in a Hungarian-language drama. When the film was released in 1971 under the title *Love,* Darvas' depiction of the old woman living out her last days in a world of memory and fantasy was universally acclaimed as revealing "a fully developed character, although an invalid whose only backdrop is her bed." The film critic Stanley Kauffmann, a friend of Darvas, was overwhelmed by the quality of her performance in *Love,* praising the entire work as being "of all wonders, an exquisite political film, exquisite in its art, political because government policies sift out three lives."

Although in fragile health during her final years, Lili Darvas also appeared in the critically acclaimed role of the elderly Rachel in Hans Werner Henze's "Rachel, la Cubana," which was broadcast by New York television station WNET. Lili Darvas died in her Manhattan home on July 22, 1974.

SOURCES:
"Hungarian Film, 'Love,' May Set a Trend," in *The New York Times.* March 3, 1971, p. 34.

Kauffmann, Stanley. "Album of Lili," in *Michigan Quarterly Review.* Vol. 23, no. 4. Fall 1984, pp. 563–575.

"Lili Darvas," in *Variety.* July 24, 1974.

Saxon, Wolfgang. "Lili Darvas, Actress of Stage and Film, Dies at 72," in *The New York Times Biographical Edition.* July 1974, p. 935.

John Haag, Associate Professor of History, University of Georgia, Athens, Georgia

Jane
Darwell

Darwell, Jane (1879–1967)

American actress who won an Academy Award for Best Supporting Actress for her characterization of Ma Joad in The Grapes of Wrath. *Born Patti Woodward in Palmyra, Missouri, on October 15, 1879;* died of a heart attack at the Motion Picture Country Home on August 13, 1967; daughter of W.R. Woodward (a railroad tycoon and president of the Louisville Southern Railroad); attended Miss Loring's private school, Chicago, a girls' school in Louisville,

Kentucky, and Dana Hall, Boston; apprenticed with the Chicago Opera House.

Selected films: Rose of the Rancho *(1914);* Brewster's Millions *(1920);* Tom Sawyer *(1930);* Back Street *(1932);* Design for Living *(1934);* Life Begins at 40 *(1935);* Captain January *(1936);* Slave Ship *(1937);* Three Blind Mice *(1938);* Jesse James *(1939);* The Rains Came *(1939);* Gone with the Wind *(1939);* The Grapes of Wrath *(1940);* All That Money Can Buy *(1941);* Private Nurse *(1941);* The Ox-Bow Incident *(1942);* The Impatient Years *(1944);* Captain Tugboat Annie *(1946);* My Darling Clementine *(1946);* Three Godfathers *(1948);* Wagonmaster *(1950);* Caged *(1950);* The Lemon Drop Kid *(1951);* Fourteen Hours *(1951);* We're Not Married *(1952);* The Sun Shines Bright *(1952);* Hit the Deck *(1955);* The Last Hurrah *(1958);* Mary Poppins *(1964).*

In 1940, a plump, middle-aged actress named Jane Darwell received an Academy Award for Best Supporting Actress for her characterization of Ma Joad in the film version of John Steinbeck's *Grapes of Wrath*, a performance that is still considered one of the best character portrayals to ever come out of Hollywood. For Darwell, the award marked a quarter-century in films, but she still had another 20 years of work ahead of her. Recognized more by her peers than the public, Darwell's name is associated with the cadre of actors whose outstanding performances hold films together by providing support for the more richly rewarded stars with whom they share the screen.

Darwell was raised at the family ranch near Iron Mountain, Missouri, and in the cities where her father had business interests—Chicago, St. Louis, and Louisville. Her early ambition was to become a bareback rider. After a prestigious education at some of the finest schools in the country, she decided to become an actress. Compromising with her parents who wanted her to pursue a more respectable career in light opera, Darwell spent two years apprenticing at the Chicago Opera House, after which she took up acting studies in London and Paris, where she also played some minor roles.

From 1913 to 1915, Darwell was a member of the pioneering Lasky Film Company, appearing in the early silent films *Rose of the Rancho, The Master Mind,* and *Brewster's Millions.* Most of her early career was spent alternating between stage and film work, and the resulting wide range of experience eased her later transition into talkies. During a two-season stint on Broadway, Darwell had a role in Sidney Howard's first play, *Swords* (1921). She also appeared with Henry Duffy's company in San Francisco and on tour in Portland, Seattle, and other cities along the West Coast. From 1930 on, however, most of her work would be in film.

Darwell started and ended her career in character roles. She appeared in countless films throughout the 1930s, usually cast as domineering motherly types that she came to despise. "Those mealy-mouthed women," she called them, "how I hated them. I played so many of them—those genial small-town wives. I was getting awfully tired of them, and the studio didn't have anything else for me, so we were preparing regretfully to part." As she faced this juncture, 20th Century-Fox tested her for the part of Ma Joad only out of politeness. With 53 actresses in contention, Darwell's test was viewed after the studio executives had decided on someone else. Director John Ford requested that they see Darwell before finalizing their decision, and her characterization turned out to be so outstanding that they cast her. Darwell found much to admire in Ma Joad. "She is such a fine strong character," she said, "able to endure anything. All these terrible things happen to her. She still manages to go on. . . . Oh, it's a grand part."

In 1940 when she received the Academy Award, Darwell lived on an estate outside Hollywood with her brother's grandnieces, 14 dogs, and 17 cats. Comfortable with middle age because it allowed her to forget about her figure and the vagaries of love, she looked forward to years of acting. Darwell continued to grace the screen until 1964, three years before her death.

Barbara Morgan,
Melrose, Massachusetts

Dash, countess.
See Saint Mars, Gabrielle (1804–1872).

Dashkoff, Ekaterina (1744–1810).
See Dashkova, Ekaterina.

Dashkova, Ekaterina (1744–1810)

Russian princess, philologist, writer, and confidante of Catherine the Great, who became the first woman president of the St. Petersburg Academy of Science and of the Russian Academy. Name variations: Princess Katerina or Catherine Dashkoff; Ekaterina Vorontsova or Worontsova; wrote articles on moral and ethical problems under the pen-name Rossianka, and a number of dramas have been attributed to her. Pronunciation: KAT-eh-REEN-a Dosh-KOV-a. Born Ekaterina Romanovna Vorontsova on March 17, 1744, in St. Petersburg, Russia; died on January 4, 1810, in Trotskoye, Russia; daughter of prince Roman I. Vorontsov and Marfa Surmina; sister of Elizabeth Vorontsova; educated in the home of her uncle, as well as self-taught reader of serious literature and the philosophers of the enlightenment; married Prince Michail Dashkov, in 1760; children: a first son, and Paul (Pavel) and Anastasia.

Participated in the palace revolution that brought Catherine the Great to the Russian throne (1762); rejected by Catherine, left the court in disgrace, and retired with her husband to Trotskoye, where he died, leaving her to pay off his debts (1764); granted permission to travel in Europe (1769); accompanied her son to study in Edinburgh (1775); returned to St. Petersburg, and the good graces of Empress Catherine, where she was made director of St. Petersburg Academy of Science (1782); was founder and first president of the Russian Academy (1783); unofficially dismissed from academy positions (1794); after Catherine's death, exiled to Novgorod by the new tsar (1796); reinstated by the new tsar but rejected invitation to return to academic posts (1801).

When young **Catherine Willmot** traveled from England to visit the formidable Princess Ekaterina Dashkova on her Russian estate at Trotskoye early in the 19th century, she wrote home to relatives about the multifaceted talents of her vigorous host who knew how to feed cows and teach bricklayers to build a house. Dashkova also wrote plays and poems, composed music, had considerable knowledge of the theater, and demonstrated a willingness during Sunday services to correct the mistakes of the local priest. "Not only have I never met such a personality," wrote the young Englishwoman, "I have never heard about such a creature."

In addition, Ekaterina Dashkova was a recognized philologist, who had founded the journal *Interlocutor of Russian Word-lovers*, for which she had invited literary contributions from many distinguished Russian writers; she had also initiated the publication of the first Russian dictionary. Her progressive views on education and study of the works of contemporary philosophers had led her to work out her own program for the education and upbringing of Russian young men; and her memoirs were highly regarded by the famous Russian literary critic and writer, Aleksandr Herzen.

Princess Dashkova was fond of folk songs, and by all accounts she could sing well; she was an enthusiastic naturalist, collected numerous minerals, and made a herbarium during her European travels; at home, she was accomplished at gardening and planting orchards, and her opinions on architectural monuments and works of art were considered exact and profound.

In Dashkova one can feel a force, not quite organized yet bursting to free life out of the mustiness of Moscow stagnation—something strong, versatile, energetic.
—**Aleksandr Herzen**

Unfortunately, what this intellectually energetic woman never quite mastered was the ability to sail safely through the sea of political intrigues that ruled the Russian imperial court. While Voltaire and Diderot were among the great thinkers of the time she could claim as friends, she never quite adapted to the world of courtly gossip, servility, and dull routine; in later years, she wrote that she always felt ill at ease at court. At the time of her birth, family connections made her the godchild of Russia's Empress *Elizabeth Petrovna, and the future emperor, Peter III, and, for a period during her youth, she considered herself a close confidante of the German princess who was to become the Empress *Catherine II the Great, but a habit of outspokenness destined the Princess Dashkova to spend much of her life in exile.

Ekaterina was born in 1744 in St. Petersburg. Little is known about her mother, **Marfa Surmina**, who died when Ekaterina was only two, except that she was reputed to have been a very rich and beautiful woman and may have given money often to the empress, who was known for her prodigality. Ekaterina's father was Prince Roman Vorontsov, a lieutenant-general and senator who cared little about his children. After the death of his wife, only his eldest son, Alexander, remained with the prince, while his second son (a future ambassador to England) was brought up by his grandfather, and two elder daughters were appointed maids of honor at the imperial court; one of them, **Elizabeth Vorontsova**, became the favorite mistress of Peter III. Ekaterina, the youngest child, was raised in the household of her uncle, M. Vorontsov, who was a chancellor and spared no money in engaging the best teachers for his daughter and niece. The young Princess Ekaterina thus learned the elegant manners of the nobility, to draw and to dance, and to speak four foreign languages as well as Russian. She wrote later, however, that "nothing had been done" for her moral and spiritual education and believed this had begun for her only after she left her uncle's house.

When she was 14, Ekaterina fell ill with the measles and was sent to the country to recover. Thanks to the good library in the house where she stayed, reading became her passion. Voltaire, Bayle, Boileau, and Montesquieu became her favorite authors, with their Enlightenment faith in the power of reason. Under their influence, she began to question the political order of the time and a number of other social and political issues.

Returning to her uncle's house a more mature person, Ekaterina often sought solitude and wrote in her memoirs later about that period, "Profound melancholy meditations about myself and my relations changed my lively and mocking mind." In those years, she showed herself to be independent and touchy, proud and sensitive, trustful, but sometimes short-tempered. She abhorred society gossip, was bored at parties and balls, and cared little about being pretty or graceful. In her attempt "not to be like others," she refused to wear makeup, which was in common use among women of her position. Instead, Ekaterina preferred to collect books. "Never," she wrote, "had any jewelry given more delight than books," and she became one of the best-educated women of her time. Fortunately, her ever-inquiring mind could be satisfied by many of the outstanding people who visited her uncle's house, giving her opportunities to discuss law, forms of government, and culture.

Ekaterina was 16 when she fell in love with a handsome guardsman, Prince Michail Dashkov. According to a story related by Claude de Rulhieres, then the French ambassador in St. Petersburg, the marriage came about after the prince ventured to pay a few compliments to young Ekaterina, who went to her uncle and told him that the prince had proposed; since the young man did not dare to admit to the first official of the state that he hadn't meant to marry his niece, the marriage took place. True or not, the story fairly represents the quick wit and resoluteness that were widely recognized as Dashkova traits.

The wedding took place on February 12, 1760. Unfortunately, Dashkova did not feel well received at her husband's Moscow estate. According to her memoirs, "A new world, a new way of life opened before me. It was quite different from the life I was used to. I was frightened and embarrassed because my mother-in-law could not speak any foreign languages and my Russian was rather poor." To please her mother-in-law, she studied Russian again, and the first years of her marriage, lived far from the royal court, were apparently happy. By the time the prince was ordered to St. Petersburg by the grand duke, the future Emperor Peter III, Ekaterina was pregnant and "inconsolable" at the thought of separation.

Prince Dashkov was on his way back to his wife when he fell ill and, not wishing to worry her, stayed for a while at the home of an aunt. By chance, Dashkova learned of his illness and set off for the house where he was staying, accompanied by a midwife. Enduring attacks of pain along the way, she reached the house and fainted at the sight of her sick husband. The next day, she gave birth to their first son. "A woman who was capable of such love," wrote Herzen, "who could fulfill her will despite dangers, fears and pain, was destined to play a great role in the society she belonged to."

In 1761, the couple had returned to St. Petersburg when the Grand Duke Peter was pronounced heir to the throne, as the reign of Empress Elizabeth Petrovna neared its end. Peter was an unstable man who openly disliked his wife, the German Princess Catherine, and made no secret of his affair with the sister of Ekaterina Dashkova, Elizabeth Vorontsova, whom he called "Romanovna." At court, Peter failed to maintain even a minimum of decorum, he antagonized many by ignoring the practices of the Russian Orthodox Church, and he was generally unpopular throughout the country. Because his idol was Frederick II the Great of Prussia, he had appointed Holshtinia generals to head the Russian guard units, and Dashkova wrote that there had never been generals in Russia "less deserving of their position." In her memoirs, she describes the "barracks-like" behavior of Peter at parties with disgust.

As Empress Elizabeth Petrovna, Peter's aunt, neared death, Peter attempted to widen his following by drawing more guardsmen and courtiers, including Prince Dashkov, into his retinue. When the prince was ordered to attend Peter's court at Oranenbaum, the Princess Dashkova followed her husband, but she never hid her antipathy for the grand duke, and she never hesitated to argue with him. This straightforwardness and bravery quick-

Ekaterina
Dashkova

ly made her popular among the officers of the military guard.

While Dashkova clearly disliked Peter, she was fascinated by his wife, whom she had first met in the home of her uncle. Indeed, the German-born Princess Catherine charmed many people. Much has been written about the appeal of her smile, her sober mind, and her equanimity; the Princess Dashkova was also impressed by her intelligence and erudition. When they first met, Dashkova was 15, half the age of the future empress; Catherine had heard about the chancellor's erudite young niece and showed she was favorably impressed by presenting the girl with her

fan. The two subsequently exchanged small confidences and books, and, when Dashkova wrote verse in rapturous praise of the empress-to-be, Catherine considered Dashkova a talented poet. At court, the two became known as the Catherines "Big" and "Small" and exchanged notes and messages of devotion and love. Both were interested in the French philosophers and writers of the Enlightenment and believed in the importance of education for the future well-being of society. But when Peter recognized the extent of Dashkova's adoration of his wife, he warned her: "My dear child, you should remember that it is much safer to deal with such honest simpletons like your sister and myself than with certain clever ones, who will squeeze juice out of an orange and then throw away the peel."

In December 1761, Empress Elizabeth Petrovna died and was mourned by all of St. Petersburg except Peter, who did not even try to hide his joy at finally becoming tsar. His reign was not to last long, however. The following June, he was dethroned by the military officers and replaced by his wife, who became Russia's Empress Catherine II, known in history as Catherine the Great.

Some historians, including S. Solovyev, believe Dashkova's role in the coup was less significant than Dashkova imagined it to be. There were many officers furious with Peter III's adoration of the German emperor and his treacherous policies as well as his inane orders and immoral private life. Dashkova's familiarity with the officers may have helped to strengthen their resolve; without question, she was determined to see her friend brought to the Russian throne, and she helped to stir up discontent by speaking of the danger to Catherine if Peter were to divorce her.

As a foreigner, Catherine also knew the value of being backed by the Princess Dashkova, a member of the Russian aristocracy whose father was a senator and whose uncle was chancellor. Dashkova, at age 18, was elated by the revolution and dreamed of working with Catherine to spread the influence of the Enlightenment philosophers in Russia. "I was happy that the revolution happened without bloodshed," she later wrote, and she even tried to engage experienced diplomats, including Kirill Rosomovsky and Nikita Panin, in the overthrow. But they were too shrewd politically to become directly involved, and disillusionment for Dashkova set in once she saw the role Catherine intended for her lover, Gregory Orlov.

Panin had agreed to the dethronement of Peter III but had wanted Peter's son Paul to be made tsar, with his mother as regent. Catherine had listened to Panin bare this plan without revealing her own intentions, or being frank with Dashkova. Panin was, in fact, given responsibility for the upbringing of Paul as successor to the throne, but, once the overthrow of Peter was achieved, Dashkova, who had never concealed her distaste for Orlov, found herself, with what Herzen describes as "the quickness of truly regal ingratitude," estranged from the new empress.

Catherine II expressed her gratitude to Dashkova by mandating that she be awarded the Order of St. Catherine "for her excellent services" and given 24,000 rubles. This "payment" was, of course, an insult; not at all what the idealistic Dashkova desired. During the coronation, Dashkova, as the wife of a colonel, found herself standing in the last row according to court etiquette (a very modest place). Gradually, her friendship with the empress was painfully shattered.

The empress had other reasons for showing her former friend such shabby treatment. On June 28, after Peter III had been dethroned (and later died under mysterious circumstances), the two women had appeared together, dressed in the same military uniforms worn many years before by guards during the reign of Peter the Great, and had ridden from St. Petersburg to Peterhof at the head of a regiment about to engage in battle against Peter's few remaining supporters. What the empress could not afford to forget about that day of her triumph was the sight of soldiers carrying Dashkova across the square to the Winter Palace. It was a show of obvious affection for her that could also be taken as a demonstration of their approval of Dashkova's hostile attitude toward Orlov.

After the coronation, Dashkova moved with the court to St. Petersburg but was treated there with distrust and suspicion. She was also alienated now from her family, who had hoped that her sister Elizabeth Vorontsova, the lover of the now defunct tsar, would become empress. Even after reports of foreign ambassadors labeled Dashkova "an instigator and conspirator," and she and her husband were forced to leave St. Petersburg for Moscow, she never said a resentful word against Catherine II.

In 1764, at age 20, Dashkova endured the greatest sorrow of her life; both her husband and her elder son died. Widowed with two children, she found that her husband had also left behind massive debts. "For 15 days," she later wrote, "I was between life and death." Once she recovered, she settled onto her estate at Trotskoye, not far from Moscow, and applied her energy to paying off her husband's creditors and restoring her family to well-being. When the house on the estate proved too decrepit to live in, she had strong logs cut and a smaller house built for her and her children; to meet expenses, she was forced to sell her jewelry, and most of her silver and other valuables. Brought up in luxury and extravagance, she now lived in a modest country house and became practical and economical in the day-to-day management of the estate, wearing the simplest of clothes and acting as nurse and governess to her children. In five years, she was able to settle her husband's debts.

In 1769, Dashkova requested permission to go abroad for the sake of her children's health. In fact, she was eager to see the cities, picture galleries and museums of Europe, without wasting time attending court receptions and other social affairs required of someone of her status. By traveling unofficially, she was able to investigate scientific collections and make serious observations on agriculture, industries, and public institutions.

While visiting a picturesque Belgian spa, Dashkova met two English families, named Morgan and Hamilton, with whom she made friendships that lasted to the end of her life. Many years later, two nieces of the Hamilton family, Cat and **Martha Willmot**, paid visits to Dashkova and became closer to her than her own children. In England, when Dashkova was shown the library at Oxford University, her attention was drawn to Russian manuscripts and a Russian-Greek dictionary, which may have led to her compilation of a Russian grammar and a Russian dictionary.

In France, according to Dashkova's memoirs, she met the philosopher Diderot and enjoyed daily talks, which "started at dinner time and lasted until two or three in the morning." Dashkova was rather short and far from pretty, with a high, open forehead, plump cheeks, deepset eyes, a large mouth, dark hair and black eyebrows. She was slightly stooped, her movements were quick and not graceful, but Diderot wrote of her that she was "Russian soul and body." It is possible that their acquaintance led him to visit Russia. In Switzerland, she was also received by Voltaire, the famous free thinker, who was then 76.

Dashkova returned to Russia. There, she led a solitary life, reading a great deal, particularly about the sciences and education, and took part in founding the Free Russian Society, a scientific group at Moscow University. She contributed articles on various topics to its journal. As her son Paul Dashkov grew older, she plunged into problems of pedagogy and worked out a program of education for her children. She viewed the English system of higher education as the best, and, in 1775, she asked permission of Catherine II to accompany Paul while he completed his education at Edinburgh University. In the British Isles, she made friends with many scientists and professors, studied political economy and composed music, some of which was performed in a Dublin church. One who appreciated the elegant simplicity of her musical compositions was the great English actor David Garrick.

In 1779, after Paul Dashkov had completed his study at Edinburgh, his mother wrote to Prince Gregory Potemkin, the powerful Russian diplomat and favorite of Catherine the Great, in search of a career for her son but received no answer. Discouraged, she traveled in Europe with her son until December 1781, when she received a letter from the Empress Catherine saying that Paul could be enlisted in any regiment his mother chose for him. In 1782, after seven years abroad, Dashkova returned to Russia, where she was received warmly by the empress and presented with an estate and houses in St. Petersburg and Moscow. That same year, she was appointed director of the St. Petersburg Academy of Science, the first woman ever to occupy the post.

The reputation of the academy had suffered under its president Kirill Rosomovsky, who had occupied the post for a half-century since his appointment at age 18. Rosomovsky had little interest in the development of science but was a "person inviolable" because of his support of the Empress Catherine during the coup of 1762, when he had been in command of the Izmilovsky regiment. Dashkova's post of director had been instituted in order to get the work done that was not being carried out by the president, and the princess received wide powers, including the right to address the empress directly on all problems. Also, she was now politically more shrewd than she had been 20 years before. Before entering the academy, she paid a visit to the respected mathematician, Leonard Euler, who had not attended sessions at the academy for several years, and persuaded him to go with her and introduce her to other academicians and professors.

In the history of the academy, there had been many developments in physics, chemistry, geography, astronomy, geology, and metallurgy, as well as considerable study of the country's natural resources, very little of which had been implemented. Taking a thoroughly practical approach, Dashkova began by balancing the academy's budget (which had been in a deplorable condition), improving the working conditions of scientists, and promoting and organizing scientific expeditions. She also enlarged the library, adding many books from her private collection, and reorganized its printing house so that many academicians were finally paid wages long overdue. Recognizing the literary and scientific achievements of one of its most important past members, Mikhail Lomonosov, Dashkova also arranged for the academy to publish his complete works.

Not a scientist herself, Dashkova utilized her exceptional administrative skills to motivate the academicians. Her economic policies yielded savings that were used to sponsor a series of public lectures on the main branches of exact and natural sciences, and she increased the number of students admitted into the academy gymnasium. During this same period, she also founded *The Interlocutor of Russian Word-lovers*, a journal that contributed much to the development of Russian literature and journalism.

In 1783, she became president of the new Russian Academy, founded on her initiative, which was to play an important role in the history of Russian philology and literature. Where the previous position had demonstrated her administrative skills, this one gave greater latitude to her own creativity. Taking the time to write the new institution's regulations, she made the enrichment and purification of the Russian language its top priority and insisted that its members become familiar with Russia's great literary works and important events in Russian history. She also oversaw the compilation of a Russian grammar and the first Russian dictionary, for which she personally contributed many entries in the six volumes, produced 1789–94.

In a poem honoring the founding of the Russian Academy, Dashkova was described as "the Minerva of our day." Her straightforward, sometimes even quarrelsome nature drew contradictory opinions from her contemporaries, however, and she continued to provoke members of the imperial court, even criticizing Empress Catherine and the procurator-general for political closed-mindedness and poor ethics. In 1793, when the French Revolution was still recent enough to have a frightening impact on the monarchs of Europe, including Catherine, the Russian writer Aleksandr Radischev had already been exiled to Siberia for writing about the terrible conditions of Russian serfs. That year, Dashkova again antagonized the empress by authorizing the Russian Academy to publish *Vadim of Novgorod*, by Knyzhnin, the tragic story of a republican leader in the popular assembly of an ancient Russian city that paralleled conditions in the current regime. The incensed monarch again made life in St. Petersburg difficult for Dashkova, and in 1794,

given a two-year leave from her duties, which was actually an unofficial dismissal, she returned to her home in Trotskoye. No less energetic at age 50, Dashkova now turned her attention to improving the living conditions for her serfs, building parks, orchards, and better homes for their use.

In 1796, Dashkova learned of the death of Catherine, her old friend and foe. The empress was succeeded by her son Paul, who had never forgiven his mother for her participation in dethroning his father. Now he took out his wrath on Dashkova, as Catherine's accomplice in the coup, by exiling her to a remote village in the Novgorod district. Confined to a small log cabin with a shortage of writing paper and few books, Dashkova lived cut off from the rest of the world, since writing letters to a disgraced lady-in-waiting could be dangerous. To occupy herself, she painted landscapes on a wooden table top, which she would wipe clean for reuse after the completion of each painting. A secret letter from an influential relative advised Dashkova to appeal to the Empress Marie Feodorovna (*Sophia Dorothea of Wurttemberg), who was wife of the tsar. The empress Marie interceded on her behalf, and Dashkova was allowed to return to her residence in Trotskoye but could visit Moscow only when the court was not in the city, effectively cutting her off from members of the court and political life.

The reign of the new tsar lasted only five years. After his death in 1801, Dashkova was no longer in disfavor, and members of the Russian Academy requested her return to her former post, but she was now in her late 50s, and declined the honor. She did attend the coronation of Alexander II, grandson of Catherine the Great, but left the court soon after, never to return. Known by then as "Moscow's most famous person," she spent the rest of her days in Trotskoye except for occasional visits to Moscow.

Dashkova's relations with her son and daughter were complicated. Her daughter **Anastasia Dashkova** was an extravagant woman, and mother and daughter often quarreled; Dashkova's son married against her will, and she did not meet her daughter-in-law until after his death, in 1807. She had closer relationships with the nieces of her English friend, Mrs. Hamilton, and her last years in Trotskoye were brightened by the visits of Martha and Catherine Willmot. It was largely for them that she wrote her memoirs, which reveal her rich spiritual world, her wide-ranging interest in political, military, and social events, and her valuable comments on the achievements of Russian and foreign science. At the end of the 20th century, Ekaterina Dashkova remained the only woman to have occupied the post of the president of the Academy of Science.

SOURCES AND SUGGESTED READING:

Feinstein, M.Sh. *Raised to a Pedestal*. Moscow, 1992.

Losinskaya, L.Ya. *At The Head of Two Academies*. Moscow, 1978.

Memoirs of Princess E.R. Dashkova. Moscow, 1990 (English edition: London: Trubner and Co., 60 Paternoster Row, 1859).

The Russian journals of Martha and Catherine Willmot.

Solovyev, S. *The History of Russia*. Vol. 25, Moscow, 1978, pp. 102–124.

SUGGESTED READING:

Fitzlyon, Kyril, ed. and trans. *The Memoirs of Princess Dashkova: Russia in the Time of Catherine the Great*. Durham, NC: Duke University Press, 1995.

Galina Kashirina, teacher of the English language at State Gymnasium #11, St. Petersburg, Russia

Dashwood, Elizabeth Monica

(1890–1943)

British author and radio personality famous for her "Provincial Lady" series. Name variations: (pseudonym) E.M. Delafield. Born Edmée Elizabeth Monica de la Pasture on June 9, 1890, in Steyning, Sussex, England; died on December 2, 1943, in Cullompton, Devon, England; daughter of Elizabeth Lydia Rosabelle (Bonham) de la Pasture (a writer of numerous novels under Mrs. Henry De La Pasture, who was later known as Lady Clifton) and Count Henry Philip Ducarel de la Pasture; married Paul Dashwood, on July 17, 1919; children: Lionel Dashwood (1920–1940); Rosamund Dashwood (b. 1924).

Selected writings: Zella Sees Herself *(Heinemann, London, 1917);* The War-Workers *(Heinemann, 1918);* The Pelicans *(Heinemann, 1919);* Consequences *(Hodder & Stoughton, London, 1919);* Tension *(Hutchinson, London, 1919);* The Heel of Achilles *(Hutchinson, 1921);* Humbug: A Study in Education *(Hutchinson, 1921);* The Optimist *(Hutchinson, 1922);* A Reversion to Type *(Hutchinson, 1923);* Messalina of the Suburbs *(Hutchinson, 1924);* Mrs. Harter *(Hutchinson, 1924);* The Chip and the Block *(Hutchinson, 1925);* Jill *(Hutchinson, 1926);* The Entertainment and Other Stories *(Hutchinson, 1927);* The Way Things Are *(Hutchinson, 1927);* The Suburban Young Man *(Hutchinson, 1928);* What Is Love? *(Macmillan, London, 1928, republished as* First Love, *Harper, 1929);* Turn Back the Leaves *(Macmillan, 1930);* Diary of a Provincial Lady *(Macmillan, 1930);* Women Are Like That *(Harper, London, 1930);* Challenge to Clarissa *(Macmillan, 1931, republished as* House Party, *Harper, 1931);* To See Ourselves: A Domestic Comedy in Three Acts *(Gollancz, London, 1931);* Thank Heaven Fasting *(Macmillan, 1932, republished as* A Good Man's Love, *Harper, 1932);* The Provincial Lady Goes Further *(Macmillan, 1932, republished as* The Provincial Lady in London, *Harper, 1933);* The Time and Tide Album *(Hamilton, London, 1932);* Gay Life *(Macmillan, 1933);* General Impressions *(Macmillan, 1933);* The Glass Wall: A Play in Three Acts *(Gollancz, 1933);* The Provincial Lady in America *(Macmillan, 1934);* Faster! Faster! *(Macmillan, 1936);* Straw without Bricks: I Visit Soviet Russia *(Macmillan, 1937, republished as* I Visit the Soviets, *Harper, 1937);* Nothing Is Safe *(Macmillan, 1937);* Ladies and Gentleman in Victorian Fiction *(Hogarth Press, London, 1937);* As Others Hear Us: A Miscellany *(Macmillan, 1937);* When Women Love *(Harper, 1938, republished as* Three Marriages, *Macmillan, 1939);* Love Has No Resurrection and Other Stories *(Macmillan, 1939);* The Provincial Lady in Wartime *(Macmillan, 1940);* No One Now Will Know *(Macmillan, 1941);* Late and Soon *(Macmillan, 1943).*

Well known under her pseudonym E.M. Delafield, Elizabeth Monica Dashwood was a highly prolific fiction writer who achieved her greatest success with her Provincial Lady, a character whose popularity earned her a large following in both England and America.

Known as Emmie, she was born Edmée Elizabeth Monica de la Pasture on June 9, 1890, in Steyning, Sussex, England, the daughter of **Elizabeth Bonham de la Pasture**, a novelist who published from 1900 to 1918. Never outgoing or attractive enough to lure suitors, Emmie was criticized by her mother and would later recall: "I was the victim of an emotionally loving, terribly possessive parent who had . . . not the slightest idea of . . . her unconscious determination that I should grow up to be nothing but an extension of her own personality." Emmie was raised bilingual in both French and English, and attended boarding schools in Belgium and Britain. Her closest relationship was with her younger sister **Yolande,** with whom she moved from school to school according to their mother's whim. Emmie's father, Henry de la Pasture, a more gentle parent, died of a heart attack in October of 1908, before Dashwood was 20. Two years after his death, while Emmie and Yolande were away on holiday, their mother married Sir Hugh Clifton, the colonial secretary of Ceylon. The sisters were advised of the wedding on their return home and sent to live with their maternal aunt Connie in Cornwall. Dashwood remained there until she joined a French order of nuns in Belgium, at age 21.

The order was run on strict rules: no talking 23 hours a day, no friendships, and no written endearments or confidences kept, even with family. Those who broke the rules were physically punished. A letter written by Emmie to Yolande, which advised her against becoming a nun, was intercepted by the nuns and destroyed, an act that cemented Dashwood's unhappiness with the order. She left the convent just short of her second year, less socially equipped than when she had entered.

On her return to England, she joined the Volunteer Aid Detachment (VAD) and began using the name Elizabeth. For the first time in her life, Dashwood's popularity increased, and her creativity flourished. She published *Zella Sees Herself* in 1917 under the pseudonym E.M. Delafield (an Anglicization of de la Pasture intended to prevent confusion between Emmie and her mother).

The author received a fan letter from Major Paul Dashwood, who asked to meet her. The two were wed in 1919 and moved first to Hong Kong and then to Singapore, where Paul was an engineer in several British harbor-building projects. Elizabeth Dashwood continued to write from Asia, but she did not find the isolation of military life agreeable. By 1922, she convinced her husband that they and their two young children, Lionel and Rosamund, had to move home. Their return to England effectively ended Paul's engineering career, and Elizabeth became the family's primary breadwinner.

Dashwood, who had never learned to cook or clean because her mother had deemed these chores beneath her, was ill-equipped as a homemaker, but she was always available to her children and wrote constantly. Paul, meanwhile, took work as the land agent for the estate on which their home, Croyle, was situated. Dashwood joined the writing staff of *Time and Tide* magazine, where she quickly advanced to an editorial position and introduced her most famous character. Popularity for the Provincial Lady, a member of the nobility and keen observer of vanity and hypocrisy, was so high that the author wrote *Diary of a Provincial Lady*, which debuted in 1930 and has since become a classic.

Elizabeth took a flat in London while Paul remained in Kentisbeare, and she returned home when her children were on holiday from boarding school. Their son Lionel attended his father's alma mater, Rugby, and their daughter Rosamund followed in her mother's footsteps, moving from school to school as her mother searched for the right influences. The Dashwood marriage was strained but cordial, though they presented a familial front to frequent literary visitors.

Lionel was his mother's most frequent male companion, and his death from a self-inflicted, possibly accidental, gunshot wound in 1940 devastated her. Dashwood's declining health forced her permanent return to Croyle in 1941, and the reunion with her husband renewed the relationship. After a colostomy in November of 1941, Dashwood's health worsened. She collapsed during a lecture and died at home two days later, on December 2, 1943. She was buried next to her son.

SOURCES:

McCullen, Maurice L. *E.M. Delafield*. Boston: Twayne, 1985.

Powell, Violet. *The Life of a Provincial Lady*. London: Heinemann, 1988.

Crista Martin,
Boston, Massachusetts

Daskam, Josephine Dodge (1876–1961).

See Bacon, Josephine Dodge.

Dassault, Madeleine (1901–1992)

French industrialist who played a crucial role in advancing her husband's career, then controlled their vast business empire after his death. Born in 1901 as Madeleine Minckès in Salonika, Greece; died on July 12, 1992; married Marcel Bloch (name later changed to Marcel Dassault); children: two sons, Claude and Serge.

Madeleine Dassault, who died in 1992 at the age of 91 as one of the richest women in Europe, lived a long and colorful life mostly in the shadow of her husband, industrialist Marcel Dassault who was born Marcel Bloch. Madeleine married the talented young aircraft designer in July 1919. Dassault persuaded her father, a French-Jewish furniture merchant, to finance Marcel's first ventures in aviation. By the start of World War II, he was head of a formidable manufacturing enterprise. Because of the family's wealth and prominence, Marcel was long able to avoid being arrested by the French collaborationist regime, but in 1944 he was finally deprived of his freedom for refusing to assist the Nazi occupation authorities, eventually being deported to the Buchenwald concentration camp in Germany. Soon after, Madeleine and her two young sons Claude and Serge were also deported to Buchenwald, but they were released in August 1944. As a Jew and an anti-Nazi, Marcel narrowly escaped death. The family was reunited in April 1945.

It was soon after the end of World War II that the Bloch family name was changed. Marcel's brother Paul was one of the first supporters of General Charles De Gaulle after De Gaulle broadcast from London his defiance of the Nazi occupiers of France in July 1940. Paul Bloch signed his pledge of Resistance support for De Gaulle with the code name "Char d'Assault"

(assault tank), a nom-de-guerre that he would proudly retain. After the war, both Paul and his brother Marcel changed their names from Bloch to Dassault. Another change wrought by the war on the Dassault family was that Marcel and Madeleine converted from Judaism to Roman Catholicism.

By the 1950s, the Dassault business empire was vast and growing, and Marcel reigned as the undisputed sovereign of France's aerospace industry. Madeleine avoided publicity despite her husband's international fame, but in May 1964,

Madeleine Dassault

she involuntarily made headlines when she was kidnapped and held for ransom. Fortunately, she survived the ordeal, and the culprits were in time arrested and imprisoned. For decades, Madeleine Dassault's keen business sense had remained in the background, but after her husband's death in April 1986, she quickly emerged as a force to be reckoned with. Along with her sons, she controlled vast industrial interests, including fighter aircraft and business jets, electronics, pharmaceuticals (Merieux), Europe 1 Radio, financial and real estate companies, and, last but certainly not least, the Chateau Dassault vineyard. Despite her advanced age, she played an active management role by serving on a number of corporate boards until her death in Paris on July 12, 1992.

SOURCES:

Assouline, Pierre. *Monsieur Dassault.* Paris: Balland, 1983.

Barfield, Norman. "Madeleine Dassault," in *The Guardian* [London]. August 10, 1992, p. 33.

Carlier, Claude. *Marcel Dassault: La Legende d'un siècle.* Paris: Perrin, 1992.

"Madeleine Dassault," in *The Times* [London]. July 31, 1992, p. 15.

John Haag,
Athens, Georgia

d'Assisi, Clara (c. 1194–1253).

See Clare of Assisi.

Dat So La Lee (c. 1835–1925)

Native American Washo basket maker whose work was not introduced to the world until she reached age 60. Name variations: Dat-So-La-Lee; Datsolalee; Dabuda; Louisa Kayser (or Kaiser); Big Hips, Wide Hips. Born Dabuda around 1835 in a Washo village near present-day Sheridan, Nevada, near Lake Tahoe (since there is no written record of her birth, contemporary estimates placed her age at death between 75 and 90); died on December 6, 1925, in Carson City, Nevada; Washo parents unknown; married Assu of Washo tribe who died of consumption early into their marriage; married Charley Kayser (Kaiser), in 1888, a man of mixed Washo-Miwok blood; children: (first marriage) two who died in infancy.

Known as the finest of the Washo basket makers, for whom basketry is an art as well as a craft, the woman nicknamed Dat So La Lee was said to have sewn legends into her baskets. Born in the Carson Valley of Nevada and called from her girlhood days "magic fingers," Dat So La Lee created some of her best designs from dreams or visions.

Not much is known about her childhood and early adult life, although when she was older she liked to tell the story of seeing white soldiers for the first time. After the death of her first husband and two children, Dat So La Lee, a 300-pound, hard-living woman, worked for miners and their wives as a cook and washerwoman. In her spare time, she loved to gamble. In 1871, she moved to Monitor, California, another mining community, to work for the Harris Cohn family. Her relationship with the family was a productive one that would last the rest of her life.

Until the mid-1890s, it was assumed that traditional Washo basketry had died out. Though Dat So La Lee seems to have neglected her basketmaking for many years as well, it is believed she returned to it out of financial necessity. In 1895, she showed her wares to Abe Cohn, son of her former employer. As the owner of the Emporium in Carson City, Nevada, Cohn, along with his wife, was a modest collector of Indian art. He recognized Dat So La Lee's ability and quickly agreed to market her baskets; some were featured in the St. Louis Exposition of 1919.

Washo baskets are unusual because the coiled baskets are sewn not woven. Made entirely from willow, mountain fern, and water birch, these baskets derive their colors only from these natural fibers. In a painstaking process, Dat So La Lee handpicked the materials, and, once they were cured, she split the fibers by hand. Because of the meticulous labor involved, many of the baskets took up to a year to make and often had as many as 34 stitches per inch.

As Europeans have heraldic shields, Washo basket makers used traditional symbols to signify family crests. One of Dat So La Lee's most famous baskets, called "Our Ancestors Were Hunters," is stitched with arrow points and generation marks that signify her people had been hunters for many years. Made in 1902, the basket is one of approximately 40 unusually large and well-made pieces that are dubbed her "great treasures." Many of Dat So La Lee's finest works were purchased by private collectors for as much as $10,000. Twenty of the baskets were bought by the state of Nevada and are now housed in the Nevada State Museum.

SOURCES:

Cohodas, Marvin. "Dat-So-La-Lee and the 'Degikup,'" in *Halycon: A Journal of the Humanities.* Vol. 4, 1982, pp. 119–140.

Hickson, Jane Green. *Dat-So-La-Lee, Queen of the Washo Basket Makers.* Carson City, NV: Nevada State Museum, 1967.

Deborah Jones,
Studio City, California

Daubenton, Jeanne or Peronne
(d. 1372).

See Women Prophets and Visionaries in France at the End of the Middle Ages.

d'Aubigné, Françoise (1635–1719).

See Maintenon, Françoise d'Aubigné, Marquise de.

D'Aulnoy, Comtesse (c. 1650–1705).

See Aulnoy, Marie Catherine, Comtesse d'.

Dauser, Sue (b. 1888)

American superintendent of the Navy Nurse Corps. Born Sue Sophia Dauser in Anaheim, California, on September 20, 1888; daughter of Francis X. Dauser and Mary Anna (Steuckle) Dauser; graduated from the Fullerton High School, 1907; attended Leland Stanford University, 1907–09; graduated from California Hospital School of Nursing, Los Angeles.

In September 1917, five months after the United States entered World War I, 29-year-old Sue Dauser, joined the Naval Reserve as a nurse. Immediately appointed a chief nurse in charge of Base Hospital No. 3, a medical facility organized in Los Angeles, she was then mobilized in Philadelphia for shipment overseas. Eight months later, Dauser was appointed nurse in the Regular Navy and, once again, immediately promoted to chief nurse, U.S. Navy. After duty with Base Hospital No. 3 in Edinburgh, Scotland, she served at naval hospitals in Brooklyn, San Diego, and aboard ship. In 1923, when President Warren G. Harding made his Alaskan cruise on the *Henderson*, she tended the president aboard ship during his final illness. Her later tours included "tropical duty" in Guam and the Philippines, after which she served in San Diego and Puget Sound, Washington. Dauser subsequently served at Mare Island, California, and at the U.S. Naval Dispensary at Long Beach, where she was in charge of nursing activities from 1935 to 1939.

In 1939, she was named superintendent of the Navy Nurse Corps. Dauser was given the twofold task of organizing and administering the expanded Nurse Corps in preparation for and during World War II, as well as securing equitable rank and privileges for navy nurses. (At the time, the navy offered its nurses only vague "officer's privileges" in lieu of relative rank, thus making it difficult to recruit reserves.) In July 1942, Congress provided for relative rank (title and uniform, but not commission, pay, or other benefits of regular rank), and Dauser received the relative rank of lieutenant commander. The pay discrepancies ($90 for a nurse ensign as compared to $150 for a male counterpart) were addressed in December 1942. A year later, in December 1943, Dauser was promoted to the relative rank of captain, equivalent to *Florence A. Blanchfield's army rank of colonel, making her the first American woman entitled to wear four gold stripes on the sleeve of her uniform. In February 1944, temporary commissions were authorized for all army and navy nurses.

Dauser, who outranked all other women commanders in the armed forces, continued her leadership of some 8,000 nurse officers until November 1945, when she stepped down as superintendent. She retired from the navy in April 1964 and took up residence in La Mesa, California.

Davenport, Dorothy (1895–1977).

See Reid, Dorothy Davenport.

Davenport, Fanny (1850–1898)

American actress-manager, one of the most successful of the late-19th century. Born Fanny Lily Gypsy Davenport in London, England, on April 10, 1850; died in South Duxbury, Massachusetts, on September 26, 1898; eldest daughter and one of seven children of Edward L. (an actor) and Fanny Elizabeth (Vining) Gill Davenport (an English actress); attended Boston public schools; married Edwin H. Price (an actor and later her business manager), on July 30, 1879 (divorced 1888); married William Melbourne MacDowell, on May 19, 1889.

Fanny Davenport, the most popular and successful actress-manager of the late-19th century, was born in London in 1850. Brought to Boston as a child, she followed her famous parents into the theater there, often appearing with her father's company. She made her New York debut at age 11 as King Charles in *Faint Heart Never Won Fair Lady*, a play produced by her father and J.W. Wallack, Jr. Her first adult role came in *Still Waters Run Deep* (1865), another Davenport-Wallack production. She then joined a Louisville stock company, where among other roles she portrayed Carline in *The Black Crook*, a play considered by some theater scholars to be the first musical comedy. In 1869, while playing in Philadelphia's Arch Street Theater under the management of *Louisa Lane Drew, she attracted the attention of Augustin Daly, who engaged her for the Fifth Avenue Theater. Davenport appeared there in leading roles from 1869 to 1877, enjoying particular success in W.S. Gilbert's

Charity (1874), which showcased her powerful dramatic ability. Daly then starred her in his own *Pique* (1876), a production which ran for 238 consecutive performances and secured her reputation as a fine actress.

Davenport acquired a keen business sense along the way and started her own touring company in 1877, becoming both actress and manager. She toured the principle theaters in cities across the United States, surrounding herself with superb supporting players while always retaining her star status. She undertook a wide range of roles, including Shakespeare's heroines as well as more contemporary women like Polly Eccles in *Caste* and Lady Gay Spanker in *London Assurance*. While in London in 1882, she purchased rights to Victorien Sardou's *Fedora* (at the time a great hit for *Sarah Bernhardt in Paris). After premiering the play in New York in 1883, Davenport toured it with great success for four years. She later played in four additional Sardou plays: *Tosca, Cleopatra*, and *Gismonda*, all melodramas that lent themselves to her declamatory and somewhat uncontrolled style. Her final undertaking, a lavish production of *A Soldier of France* in 1897, was a failure, and Davenport lost the large investment she had made from her own funds. In March 1898, physically exhausted and broken in spirit, she retired to her vacation home in Duxbury, Massachusetts. She died there on September 26, 1898, at age 48, and was buried in Forest Hills Cemetery, Boston.

Barbara Morgan,
Melrose, Massachusetts

Davenport, Marcia (1903–1996)

American author and music critic, known for her popular biography of Mozart and the 1942 bestseller Valley of Decision. *Born Marcia Gluck in New York on June 9, 1903; died in Pebble Beach, California, on January 16, 1996; daughter of Alma Gluck (the lyric soprano) and Bernard Gluck; stepdaughter of Efrem Zimbalist (the celebrated violinist); educated at the Friends School in Philadelphia, the Shipley School at Bryn Mawr; also attended Wellesley for two years, and graduated with a bachelor's degree from University of Grenoble in France; married Frank D. Clarke, in April 1923 (divorced 1925); married Russell W. Davenport (managing editor of* Fortune *and key advisor to Wendell Willkie), on May 11, 1929 (died 1954); children: (first marriage) Patricia Delmas Clarke (b. March 1924); (second marriage) Cornelia Whipple Davenport (b. April 1934).*

Marcia Davenport was the daughter of the famous lyric soprano *Alma Gluck. "I was fitted into my mother's existence along with the other exigencies," wrote Davenport. "If I wanted companionship I had to come up to adult standards." Though Marcia was hopelessly untalented at the piano, her mother signed her up for lessons because "she believed, as I do, that to permit a child to grow up illiterate in music is as bad as to permit general illiteracy." Davenport was also allowed free roam of books, which would later serve her well.

After her first marriage, she took a job as an advertising copywriter. From 1928 to 1931, she was on the editorial staff of *The New Yorker*. She was a music critic for *Stage* magazine (1934–39) and a radio commentator on the Metropolitan Opera broadcasts (1936–37). Her first book *Mozart*, which appeared in 1932, was a great success. It was translated into French, German, Spanish and Portuguese and has been continuously in print.

Most of Davenport's life was divided between New York and Europe, with second homes in Milan, Lake Como, Salzburg, and Vienna. She lived in Prague throughout the postwar crisis in Czechoslovakia, which culminated in the communist coup d'état and the mysterious death of Jan Masaryk. These experiences are recounted in her autobiographical *Too Strong for Fantasy* (Scribner, 1967), in which she also creates portraits of her mother, Maxwell Perkins, *Lotte Lehmann, and *Marjorie Kinnan Rawlings, and describes her 50-year friendship with Arturo Toscanini.

Her bestseller, *The Valley of Decision*, was a sharp break from her music-centered books. Published in 1942, the huge, sprawling, highly praised novel revolves around a steel-mill-owning family in Pittsburgh. The book, successfully adapted for the screen by MGM in 1945, was edited by **Blanche Sewell** and starred Gregory Peck, *Gladys Cooper, *Jessica Tandy, and *Greer Garson. Because of her performance, Garson was handed her fifth Best Actress Oscar nomination in a row. Davenport also wrote *Of Lena Geyer* (fiction, 1936) and *The Constant Image* (fiction, 1960). She died, age 92, in Pebble Beach, California, on January 16, 1996.

SOURCES:
Current Biography. NY: H.W. Wilson, 1944.

Davey, Constance (1882–1963)

Australian psychologist who specialized in work with children with special needs. Born Constance Muriel Davey at Nuriootpa, South Australia, on December 4, 1882; died on December 4, 1963; daughter of Stephen

Henry (a bank manager) and Emily Mary (Roberts) Davey; educated at country schools; B.S., University of Adelaide, 1915; M.A., 1918; Ph.D., University College, London, 1924.

From 1908 to 1921, Constance Davey studied part time at the University of Adelaide and taught mathematics and economics at a girls' school. While working on her Ph.D. in psychology at University College in London, she traveled throughout England, the United States, and Canada to observe teaching methods for children with special needs. From 1924 to 1942, she was a psychologist in the South Australian Education Department, where she established the state's first "opportunity class" for children with developmental difficulties. She also organized an extended-care program to provide vocational guidance and introduced a plan to train special-education teachers. In addition to her work at the Education Department, Davey assisted outside agencies as a consultant in handling children with problems. From 1927 to 1950, she lectured at the university and in 1934 helped establish courses to train social workers. In 1938, she was appointed to the government committee examining child delin-

Marcia Davenport

quency, during which time she recommended reforms based on guardianship.

Also a political activist and a feminist, Davey was a 30-year member of the Women's Non-Party Political Association (League of Women Voters), working to see women represented on public boards and commissions. She helped draft a bill for the Guardianship of Infants Act in 1940, which supported equal parental guardianship. Davey championed reforms in the Children's Court, seeking the right for women to serve as jurors. From 1945, as senior research fellow at the university, she worked on a historical study of South Australian laws relating to children, which was published in 1956 as *Children and Their Law-makers*. She was elected a fellow of the British Psychological Society in 1950 and was appointed OBE in 1955. Constance Davey died of cancer on December 4, 1963.

SOURCES:

Radi, Heather, ed. *200 Australian Women*. NSW, Australia: Women's Redress Press, 1988.

David, Caroline Edgeworth

(1856–1951)

English-born educator, feminist, and social reformer who was active in Australia for more than 50 years. Name variations: Mrs. Edgeworth David, Lady Caroline Edgeworth David; Cara David (the name she preferred and always signed). Born Caroline Martha Mallett in Southwold, on the East Anglian coast of England, in 1856; died at her home outside Sydney, Australia, on December 25, 1951; daughter of Samuel (a fisherman) and Pamela (Wright) Mallett; attended a village dame school and St. Edmund National School, Southwold, where she became a pupil-teacher at age 13; won a Queen's Scholarship to Whitelands College, 1874, admitted there 1875 and remained as a lecturer from 1876 to 1882; married Tannatt William Edgeworth David (knighted in 1920), on July 30, 1885; children: Margaret (Madge) Edgeworth David (1886–1948); Mary (Molly) Edgeworth David (b. 1889); William (Billy) Edgeworth David (b. 1891).

Departed England for a school administrative post in Australia (1882); became first principal of Hurlstone Training College for Women, Ashfield, Sydney, New South Wales (1883–85); was the only woman to accompany a geology expedition headed by her husband to the Ellice Islands (1897); was a founding member of the Feminist Club, a founding member and vice president of the Women's Club, a member of the National Council of Women, a founder and presi-

dent of the Women's National Movement for Reform, and division commissioner for North and West Metropolitan Divisions of the NSW Girl Guides (1926–28); served as state commissioner of Girl Guides NSW (1928–38); was president of Bush Book Club.

Major publications: "Mission Work in Funafuti," in *Australian Christian World (1897); Funafuti, or Three Months on a Coral Island: An Unscientific Account of a Scientific Expedition (Murray, London, 1899, also published in abridged school edition, by Sir Isaac Pitman & Sons, London, 1913).*

In 1897, on a grey day threatening rain, Cara David set eyes for the first time on the tiny coral island of Funafuti, part of the Ellice Islands in the Pacific Ocean and now named Tuvalu, after a rough four-day voyage aboard the SS *Maori* from the island of Fiji. At sea for the past three weeks, she was the only woman accompanying a geology expedition led by her husband Tannatt William Edgeworth David, and she was to remain on the island for three months. Her role, as noted in a diary she kept while on Funafuti, was to attend to the stores, collect flora, nurse the sick, cook and care for herself and husband, make friends with the Funafutians, and keep a record of her observations. Tiring quickly of these restrictive and routine roles, she also moved into a close and easy relationship with the Funafutians, especially the women, and immersed herself in their customs, lifestyles, and environment, which she studied with great energy and gusto.

But she had left three children—ages eleven, eight, and six—back in Sydney and missed them dearly. The David children experienced similar pangs, writes daughter Molly (**Mary Edgeworth David**) in her book *Passages of Time*: "Victorian fathers, however kindly were august beings never really in touch with their children as mothers were. Home without our mother was indeed a desolate place." There is little evidence in Cara David's diary, however, of a languishing, pining mother or dependent wife. Clearly delighted by the opportunity to live among people of a different culture, this adventurous woman demonstrated the inquiring characteristics of mind, body and spirit that were to last throughout her long life.

Cara David's childhood and adolescence in England were marked by family tragedy, deprivation and poverty. She was born Caroline Martha Mallet in the working-class fishing village of Southwold on the coast of East Anglia, facing the North Sea. Since Roman times, Southwold had been invaded by the Romans and the Danes and was later under constant threat of

*C*aroline
*E*dgeworth
*D*avid

French and Dutch incursions. With a legacy of Flemish, Dutch, English, and Roman architecture, the town remains a charming visual feast. In the 19th century, it was still predominantly a fishing village, but as sea bathing became a fashionable pastime, its character changed to accommodate a continuing influx of summer tourists.

A childhood in these beautiful surroundings was no preparation for the lower-middle-class social world of teaching she was to aspire to later. School inspectors in Southwold argued that the absence of many fathers as fishermen at sea caused children to run wild, allowed too much freedom by their mothers. In reality, in homes where the father was absent up to nine months of the year, working for low financial rewards in a fishing industry notorious for its instability, children tended to work as often as possible to supplement the low family income and were thus less likely to go to school. Boys went to sea at a very young age, and girls were employed gutting herring or stayed at home to help mothers overburdened by the care of large families, poor living conditions, and the grinding daily life of poverty.

Cara's mother **Pamela Wright (Mallett)** was the daughter of a schoolmaster and probably educated to live at a higher social level than what was offered by Samuel Mallett, the man she chose to marry. In 1860, when Cara was four, Samuel drowned. The brief influence of her mother before she also died, and the influence of her grandparents, from an educated, lower-middle-class background, gave the child opportunities to avoid what might have been a very different future if her parents had lived. Her maternal grandmother, aware of the economic and social struggles the girl faced as an orphan in class-ridden Victorian England, is reputed to have recognized her outstanding learning abilities and encouraged her to become a pupil-teacher. Many young women in Cara's position turned to teaching as a means of earning a livelihood, but her career was to put her on a pathway that carried her well beyond the Common Board school.

In 1875, Cara entered Whitelands Ladies College, situated in the fashionable suburb of Chelsea, in London. The school occupied a three-story Georgian building surrounded by a large garden, described as having an iron gate and a "little gravelly lilacly, sparrowy path with flower beds on either side." At 19, Cara had not been outside her native town of Southwold, but she adapted well. She won many prizes for her school work, went to night school to upgrade her science qualifications, and was considered outspoken. One inspector is reported to have said she had a "sharp tongue," a reference that may have exaggerated a forceful personality and a capacity to voice an opinion. Both traits, not considered readily acceptable in women at the time, were to be trademarks of Cara David in her later years.

At the end of her training, Cara remained for six years as a governess (lecturer) at Whitelands, where every inspection of her work was reported in positive and flattering terms. By 19th-century standards, she was no longer young, but she was considered a personable and good-looking woman when she decided, at age 29, to leave England to take the position of principal at Hurlstone Training College for Women in Sydney, Australia. At the interview held in England, Henry Parkes, the premier of New South Wales and under secretary for education, was so impressed that he did not consider it necessary for her to be bound to the usual service contract of three years. Mr. Mundella, the English member of the selection panel, thought Parkes was being a little generous, "I say Parkes, you had better bind her . . . or else she will be married before she gets there." Parkes responded by addressing Cara, "You will not make a fool of the colony will you Miss Mallett?" to which she replied, "No sir, I will not."

Setting sail on the SS *Potosi* in October 1882, Cara was a few days out of the port of Gravesend when she met Tannatt Edgeworth David, a geologist and the eldest son of the Reverend William David of South Wales. When the *Potosi* docked at Sydney in November, Tannatt and the attractive schoolteacher went their separate ways, neither of them suspecting that they would marry within three years. Until June 1885, Cara was principal of Hurlstone, where she introduced radical reform to the curriculum and upgraded the role of science for female teachers, drawing on her wide experience at Whitelands to improve the standards of teacher training and classroom facilities. Encountering considerable opposition to her ideas, she was frustrated by the shortsightedness of some of her superiors but met their resistance with equanimity and a wry sense of humor.

After her marriage in July 1885, Cara David's life became both more political and more adventurous. Her first child, **Madge Edgeworth David**, was born in a tent on the coal diggings at Maitland, a small town upriver from Newcastle on the New South Wales coast. Her second and third were born in the same town, but by this time in a house. In 1891, the Davids moved to Sydney. Restless and inquisitive, David cared deeply about her home and family but was always looking for new challenges. At one time or another, she pursued new food fads, physical culture, and religion. Not content with mere lip service, she threw herself whole-heartedly into her inquiries about the Christadelphian, Methodist, Seventh-Day Adventist, Unitarian, Quaker, and Baptist sects. Most were found wanting, but not before she had shocked her family by considering being rebaptized according to the practice of total immersion.

Ambiguity about their role in society was common among those Victorian women who became notable as travelers and public figures. Seeking adventure and exploration, often courting danger and exposing themselves to all kinds of privation, they frequently felt duty bound at the same time to live out the domestic and filial duties demanded of them. David loved her home and the domestic environment it framed, but if she had not married it is likely that the traveler in her would have surfaced even more than it did. As it was, her marriage to a scientist, who was an adventurer himself, provided some opportunities for her to realize her restless ambitions. She would accompany Tannatt and his students on many field trips to snowcapped Mount Kosciusko, the highest mountain in Australia; she would also return to England twice, once in 1916, at age 60, via Canada, where she was trapped for six months in Halifax by the events of World War I; ten years later, in 1926, she would travel via the Cambridge Gulf and Capetown. She is reported to have been the first woman to ride on horseback to the summit of Mount Kosciusko, wearing a divided skirt, which shocked the locals; she would also allow her daughters to ride astride and would prevent their wearing the whalebone stays then fashionable.

At the time of the trip to Funafuti in 1897, David was 42 years old. She had been appointed an examiner to Sydney Technical College, and, from 1895 to 1897, she vetted candidates for the teaching diploma in kindergarten and primary grades at the University of Sydney. Writing about her experiences on Funafuti, she was frank, lively, and for some of her contemporaries, shocking. In the second edition of the book abridged for schools, parts were excised, including references to bathing with her husband in lagoons and pools (since these swimming excursions took the place of normal bathing, there may have been a suspicion some found disturbing, that the Davids swam naked), and the chapters describing the laws and customs of the Funafutians.

All her life, David took an intense interest in education and social reform. In the 1890s, she joined the National Council of Women (New South Wales Branch) and became actively involved, along with the nation's suffragists, in supporting compulsory domestic science education for girls. Her professional background as a trained educator and administrator gave her a good deal of credibility with the bureaucrats and allowed her to have direct influence on many policy decisions made within the Department of Public Instruction of New South Wales.

In 1901, a meeting held in the Women's College at the University of Sydney led to the formation of the Women's Club. Elected a vice-president, Cara David declared at that meeting: "[I]t would do brainy women good to mix with one another, and others who were not brainy would be none the worse! Men could take it easy in their clubs and women need a place for that."

In June 1916, David founded The Women's National Movement and became its first president. This body, many of whom came from the ranks of the Women's Club members who had joined together to stop the sale of liquor after 6

PM, now made it their goal to close hotels at the same hour. When David led a procession of some 2,000 women in a march on Parliament House, in Macquarie Street, Sydney, many well-known Australian women activists marched with her—including **Annie Golding**, the radical teacher unionist and member of the Womanhood Suffrage League, and ***Mary Gilmore**, poet and tireless worker for the Australian Community Party—and signed a leather-bound testimonial to David's leadership. When the government subsequently decided to outlaw the sale of liquor after 6 PM, the credit went to David.

In 1914, David was a founding member of the Feminist Club. Until the more radical ***Jessie Street** made a bid for the club's presidency in 1928, its primary outlook was focused around what was termed exaggerated reverence for motherhood. Nonetheless, it is doubtful if the Feminist Club was any more conservative than the suffragists or other bourgeois women's groups. Most supported "educated motherhood," as opposed to a real version of liberated womanhood. Issues of concern in the Feminist Club closely paralleled those of the National Council of Women, including maternal and child welfare, custody of children, and the legal status of women. In the 1930s, the Feminist Club supported the union-inspired Council of Action for Equal Pay (CAEP), which was more directly associated with trade unions and women workers. The CAEP, representing women workers from 53 trade unions, had a broad political framework clearly in line with the more radical political platforms of the Australian labor movement and the Australian Labor Party.

True to her reputation of liberal-mindeness and lack of social pretension, Cara David is said to have dissuaded Tannatt from accepting knighthood twice before 1920, when his superiors at the University of Sydney exerted pressure to compel the distinguished scholar and scientist to acknowledge the honor of being named a Knight of the British Empire. Cara feared the elevation of her status as Lady David would damage her ability to interact with the many individual women and women's organizations she had supported throughout her life. Most of all, she loathed the snobbery associated with such titles, and at age 64, she was furious to be forced to accept it, even in her husband's honor. In the remaining 31 years of her life, she continued her work in the public sphere, supporting women's groups at a local level. Nationally, she became state commissioner of Girl Guides in New South Wales (1928–38), her last major public role, which she took on at age 72. When she retired, at age 82, she could look back on a life of extraordinary leadership through two half-centuries of social, political, and educational history in Australia. Known as a gifted public speaker, she was praised in 1930 in *The Lone Hand* for her personality, tact, capacity to debate, and organizing abilities.

Convinced that the means to benefit the status and education of women would be developed only from outside the organized educational and political systems of the day, Cara David believed that women needed a place—a "club"—to meet and develop policies for change. She was at her best when talking to women, and she sought out their company at both formal and informal levels to test ideas and weld important friendships. She maintained long-term friendships with a number of similarly independent-minded women with wide interests throughout her life, and she often said that women friends were preferable to men friends, because you could talk more openly to women, and about more things. She was vigorously opposed to the double standards weighted against women; and her endeavors to change the liquor laws were aimed at limiting the male drunkenness that aggravated the misery and poverty of many innocent women and children. Knowing how difficult it could be to wring changes in girls' schooling from a male hierarchy, she brought her power to bear as an activist able to speak cogently and fluently on a range of issues.

Tannatt died in 1934. In her remaining years, Cara David lived with her daughter Molly, who never married, at Hornsby, an outer suburb of Sydney. Her eldest daughter Madge, became the first woman to be elected to the Tasmanian Parliament. She was killed in a plane crash in 1948, when returning from a conference of the National Council of Women in Brisbane, Queensland. Although frail in her last few years, Cara David remained in good health until her death on Christmas Day, 1951.

SOURCES:

Cole, M. *Whitelands College: The History.* Whitelands College: Whitelands College Monographs, 1982.

David, Mrs. Edgeworth. "Housewifery Schools," in *The Australasian Nurses Journal.* Vol. 4, no. 12, 1906, pp. 397–405.

David, Mary Edgeworth. *Passages of Time: an Australian Woman 1890–1974.* St. Lucia: University of Queensland Press, 1975.

Hooper, F.E. *The Story of the Women's Club.* Sydney: 1964.

Kyle, Noeline. "Can You Do as You're Told? The Nineteenth Century Preparation of a Female Teaching in England and Australia," in *Comparative Education Review.* Vol. 36, no. 4, 1992, pp. 467–586.

SUGGESTED READING:

Biklen, S.K., and M.B. Brannigan, eds. *Women and Educational Leadership.* Toronto: Lesington Books, 1980.

Huie, S.F. *Tiger Lilies: Women Adventurers in the South Pacific.* North Ryde: Angus and Robertson, 1990.

COLLECTIONS:

Private Archives, Cara David Correspondence (diary notes, miscellaneous) and David Family Papers, located with Anne Edgeworth (Godfrey-Smith), the granddaughter of Cara David, Canberra, Australian Capital Territory.

Whitelands College Archives, Roehampton Institute, West Hill, London, England.

Women's Club. *Annual Reports.* 1906–1920, Mitchell Library, State Library of New South Wales, Macquarie Street, Sydney, Australia.

Noeline J. Kyle, Professor of History, Queensland University of Technology, Australia, and author of *The Family History Writing Book* (with R. King, Allen & Unwin, Sydney, 1993), and other works of women's history and education

David, Catherine.
See French "Witches."

David, Mrs. Edgeworth (1856–1951).
See David, Caroline Edgeworth.

David, Elizabeth (1914–1992)

English cookery writer who sparked British interest in foreign cuisine and lent stylish, literate writing to the preparation of food and selection of wine. Born Elizabeth Gwynne in 1914; died in 1992; studied French history and literature at the Sorbonne; married Ivor David (a career army officer).

Selected works: A Book of Mediterranean Food *(1950);* French Country Cooking *(1951);* Italian Food *(1954);* Summer Cooking *(1955);* French Provincial Cooking *(1960);* English Cooking *(1970);* English Bread and Yeast Cookery *(1977);* Harvest of the Cold Months: The Social History of Ice and Ices *(published posthumously, 1995).*

Five years after World War II, as a beleaguered England slowly weaned itself off years of food rationing, Elizabeth David wrote a cookery book entitled *A Book of Mediterranean Food* (1950) that became a bestseller. A year later, she published *French Country Cooking*, which she followed with several others, hurling the combined weight of her books "against the drab tyranny of 'meat and two veg,'" wrote **Ingrid Rowland** in *The New York Review of Books* (April 4, 1996). With the publication of *French Provincial Cooking* in 1960, ten years after her first success, David's "characteristic mix of tart practicality and deep erudition had already begun to work its changes on the English palate." She had become England's premiere epicure, with an OBE (1976), a CBE (1986), the Order of Chevalier du Mérité Agricole from France (1977), and title of Fellow of the Royal Society of Literature.

David's passion for cooking started at 16, while she studied French history and literature at the Sorbonne and boarded with a gastronomic French family. She married a career army officer and revelled in the dishes she discovered while living in the many parts of the world where he was posted. A dedicated researcher who wrote with a large dollop of English wit, she was fascinated not only with food but its history and philosophy. "Far more than collections of recipes," wrote Rowland of her books, "they are really treatises on human civility."

David died in 1992 before completing her last book, *Harvest of the Cold Months: The Social History of Ice and Ices.* This work, started in the mid-1970s, began as a simple look at early European ice-cream recipes but soon moved into the area of early refrigeration and the demand for ice brought on by the Industrial Age. Edited by **Jill Norman** and published posthumously in 1995, the book could have been an "intellectual sorbet," writes Rowland. "But Elizabeth David was never that kind of writer. Food and its history have long been the domain of keenly intelligent, physically imposing, mature women—it is no accident that Juno, their archetype, was the goddess of memory as well as domestic virtue." Like her American counterpart and friend *Julia Child, David was definite about her opinions. While Child called *nouvelle cuisine* Cuisinart cooking, David referred to it as "those airy little nothings accompanied by their *trois sauces* served in doll's house swimming pools round one side of the plate."

SOURCES:
Rowland, Ingrid D. "The Empress of Ice Cream," in *The New York Review of Books.* Vol XLIII, no. 6. April 4, 1996, p. 54–56.

David-Neel, Alexandra

(1868–1969)

French explorer and expert on Tibetan Buddhism who became the first Western woman to visit the forbidden city of Lhasa. Name variations: Alexandra Neel; attempted career as opera singer under name Alexandra Myriel. Born in Saint-Mandé, France, on October 24, 1868; died in Paris in 1969, a celebrity at the age of 100; daughter of a radical journalist living in exile in Belgium; married distant cousin, Philippe Neel (split up within days, though corresponding regularly until his death in 1941); children: (adopted) Yongden, a Sikkimese monk and companion on her journeys.

Lived an unhappy childhood, both at convent school and with her family; briefly attempted career as an opera singer, before taking up journalism and studying Eastern religions; set sail for India (August 3, 1911) to embark on a series of Asiatic journeys, culminating with her visit to Lhasa in disguise (1923); returned to France as a hero (1925); immersed in writing about her journeys and studying Buddhism until her death (1969).

Selected writings: My Journey to Lhasa *(1927);* With Mystics and Magicians in Tibet *(1931);* Tibetan Journey *(1936).*

One night in Tibet, on a particularly high pass, 100 miles north of Lhasa, Alexandra David-Neel and her adopted son Yongden found themselves in danger of freezing. They desperately needed to warm themselves if they were to survive until morning. Unfortunately, the flint and steel they carried to light a fire had become wet and would not ignite. In desperation, David-Neel resolved to dry the tools by means of *thumo reskiang*—the Tibetan art of increasing internal body heat. She had been initiated into this practice some years before while living as a hermit. She had seen, she wrote: "Hermits seated night after night, motionless on the snow, entirely naked, sunk in meditation, while the terrible blizzard whirled and hissed around them." She had witnessed: "The test given to their disciples who, on the shore of a lake or river in the heart of winter, dried on their bodies, as on a stove, a number of sheets dipped in the icy water."

I craved to go beyond the garden gate, to follow the road that passed it by.
—Alexandra David-Neel

Sending Yongden off to gather fuel to keep warm by exercise, David-Neel placed the flint and steel under her clothes and began to concentrate intensely on the ritualistic practice. Soon, in her mind's eye, she saw flames rising around her. "They grew higher and higher," she wrote; "they enveloped me, curling their tongues about my head. I felt deliciously comfortable." Coming out of her trance, she found a bitter wind still blowing, but her body was glowing, and the flint and steel were dry. By the time the astonished Yongden returned, she had made a fire and was boiling tea.

As a child in France, Alexandra David-Neel was strong-willed but unhappy. Her parents were ill-matched and difficult, and she loathed her convent schooling. Indeed, she ran away more than once, on one occasion getting as far as England. After an unsuccessful attempt to become an opera singer, Alexandra began to attend lectures on Buddhism and other Eastern religions at the Theosophical Society in Paris. She also studied journalism and the Tibetan language, for she was by now determined to travel and write about the East.

It was at this time that she made a rather curious marriage with Philippe Neel, a distant cousin. Given Alexandra's independence and lust for travel, it seems odd that she should ever have thought of marriage as a viable proposition. Indeed, it was not. Within a couple of days, the couple had split up. Nevertheless, they would correspond and respect each other for the rest of their lives. Stranger still, Philippe would provide the money without which David-Neel's years of travel would not have been possible. He also became her literary agent.

David-Neel set sail for India on October 3, 1911, and was not to return to Europe for 14 years. She managed to obtain an interview with the Dalai Lama, then in exile in Darjeeling—the first Western woman to be so privileged. The experience increased her eagerness to learn more about Tibetan Buddhism and the customs of the inhabitants of this remote land.

The situation in Tibet at the end of the 19th century was one to whet the appetite of explorers, mystics, surveyors, and botanists alike—for the country had been sealed off from Western foreigners for almost 100 years. Before the borders were closed, anyone could make the journey if they were brave enough to face the icy passes and the murderous brigands who infested the border areas. Few did, except a handful of Jesuit priests and Franciscan missionaries.

However, by the early 19th century, the steadily expanding empires of Britain and Russia, on her south and northern borders, convinced the Tibetan authorities of the need to close the kingdom to protect the country's religious and political integrity. The result was that during the last two decades of the century, an assortment of intrepid travelers were attempting to penetrate the forbidden land, about which almost nothing was known. Above all, there was a race of sorts to reach that most forbidden place of all—the holy city of Lhasa, spiritual home of the highest lama in Tibet—the Dalai Lama.

Three of these were women—**Annie Royle Taylor** (1891), **Mrs. St. George Littledale** (1895), and **Susie Rijnhart** (1898)—and all were detected by the Tibetans and turned back after epic and dangerous journeys. Two of the women—Taylor and Rijnhart—were missionaries, naive enough to think they could convert the Dalai Lama to Christianity. In her effort, Susie Rijnhart lost both a husband and a baby.

By 1904, the race was over. Fearing Russian influence in Lhasa (which would prove nonexistent), the Indian viceroy, Lord Curzon, sent Colonel Sir Francis Younghusband across the Himalayan passes at the head of a small army. By the beginning of August, the "most mysterious city on earth" was entered by Western soldiers and journalists. The foreign correspondents relayed the secrets of Lhasa to an eager world.

Although deeply humiliated by the invasion, Tibetan enmity toward the British did not last long, since the British had no intention of staying. Having discovered no Russians and having established the right to set up a small trading mission in the town of Gyantse, the British expedition left for India. In fact, Tibet's danger came from a different quarter. In 1910, the Chinese invaded Tibet and occupied Lhasa amid much slaughter, and the Dalai Lama fled to exile in India. Here his ties with Britain were strengthened, and he became a lifelong friend of the British administrator Sir Charles Bell. After the Chinese were ousted from Tibet in 1913, Bell was invited to Lhasa as the Dalai Lama's personal guest and stayed for over a year. Some of the mysteries of the strange land had been dispelled.

This in no way diminishes Alexandra David-Neel's achievements. Trespassers in Tibet were still not welcome, particularly women, and Lhasa was strictly out of bounds except by direct invitation of the Dalai Lama. The British, determined to maintain their warmer relations with the Tibetan administration, were also keen to enforce this ban.

Alexandra David-Neel began her Tibetan adventures in 1914, when she illegally crossed the border and a spent a winter studying at a monastery a few miles from the frontier. A year later, after living for some months as a hermit in a cave in Sikkim in northern India, she again crossed into Tibet, journeying as far as Shigatse and the great monastery of Tashilumpo. This was the home of the Panchen Lama—the second highest lama in Tibet. "I was most cordially welcomed," she wrote later. "The high lama wished me to stay with him for a long time, if not forever.

He offered me free access to all libraries and lodgings in the town." David-Neel knew, however, that she was in no position to enjoy his largesse. Indeed, on returning to Sikkim, she found that the British had learned of her illicit travels and had ordered her to leave northern India.

Years later, she was to write angrily of the British: "What right had they to erect barriers around a country which was not even legally theirs." She felt she was being prevented from pursuing her quite legitimate interest in Tibetan culture, literature, and religion. This differenti- ated her from many of the early participants in the race for Lhasa. "Strange as the fact may appear," she wrote, "I must confess that, unlike most travellers who have attempted to reach Lhasa, and have failed to reach their goal, I never entertained a strong desire to visit the sacred lamaist city. . . . [A]nd as for researches regarding the literature, philosophy, and secret lore of Tibet, these things could be pursued more profitably amongst the literati and mystics in the freely accessible and more intellectual parts of north-eastern Tibet, than in the capital." So David-Neel set out for northeastern Tibet.

Alexandra David-Neel

Journeying eastward through Burma, Japan, and Korea, staying in Buddhist monasteries and constantly studying the ways of the East, David-Neel eventually reached Peking in October 1917. She had now been joined by a young Sikkimese lama named Yongden, who would eventually become her adopted son.

The two travelers set out to cross 2,000 miles of a China racked by civil war and banditry, to the great Tibetan monastery of Kumbum on Tibet's northeastern border. Here they remained for almost three years, steeping themselves in the life of the monastery, translating sacred texts, while all the time David-Neel was perfecting her almost faultless Tibetan. They also made several excursions into the Tibetan borderland. It was on one of these, when David-Neel was again made to leave at the behest of the local British consul, that she finally resolved to travel to Lhasa. "Before the frontier post to which I had been escorted," she wrote, "I took an oath that in spite of all obstacles I would reach Lhasa and show what the will of a woman could achieve!"

David-Neel's plan was that she and Yongden travel disguised as beggar pilgrims on their way to visit the holy city. The fact that Yongden was a well-read lama would add color to their story, for thousands of such mendicant monks and their families ramble across Tibet throughout the year, going from one sacred place to another. As David-Neel wrote: "A lama capable of reading the Scriptures, who can perform the different lamaist ceremonies, and can, above all, act as exorcist and fortune-teller, may at any time find himself so well provided with food, clothing, and even money, that he may dispense with begging for several months." David-Neel would pose as Yongden's aged and beggarly mother, but she carried a small bag of gold and a revolver for emergencies. In addition to wearing ragged clothes, David-Neel dyed her hair with Chinese ink and darkened her face. They would thus dispense with the need for immense caravans of pack animals that would give them away.

So at last, in the winter of 1923, now aged 55, Alexandra David-Neel set out on her greatest adventure of all. For the next four months, she and her companion struggled towards Lhasa through atrocious weather and across some of the most inhospitable terrain on earth. Sometimes to avoid settlements and government posts, they slept out in the forest, using a small tent they concealed in their baggage. At other times, they shared the primitive hospitality of Tibetan hovels. Their staple diet was *tsampa*—a mixture of barley and butter tea.

But David-Neel was in no way deterred. Indeed, she revelled in her surroundings. As she wrote in *My Journey to Lhasa:*

> I should have to eat in the way of the poor, dipping my unwashed fingers in the soup and in the tea, to knead the tsampa, and to do any number of things which disgusted me. Yet I knew that such a penance would not be without reward, and that under cover of my inconspicuous garb of a poor pilgrim I should gather a quantity of observations which would never have come within the reach of a foreigner, or even perhaps, of a Tibetan of the upper classes. I was to live near the very soul and heart of the masses of that unknown land, near those of its womenfolk whom no outsider had ever approached. To the knowledge I had already acquired about the religious people of the country I would add another and quite intimate one, concerning its humblest sons and daughters.

In her account of her epic journey, David-Neel shows perception and great good humor. She avoids over-romanticizing the ordinary Tibetan. She also shows a sense of mischief—almost of glee—in the way that she and Yongden were able to hoodwink self-important officials, for the dangers of detection, by other pilgrims as well as officials, were very real. Had she been found out, she would have been ignominiously returned to the border, and Yongden would have been severely punished, perhaps even executed.

One evening as they approached Lhasa, a strange lama seemed "to spring out of the ground" in front of them and sat down uninvited at their campfire. After remaining silent for a while, during which darkness fell, he slowly drew out a bowl made from a skull and asked for tea. Then staring fixedly at David-Neel, he asked why she was no longer wearing the costume she had customarily worn in Eastern Tibet. "My heart stopped beating," she wrote later. "This man knew me! But from where I did not know." Seeing her apprehension, the strange lama added even more mysteriously: "Do not try to remember me. I have as many faces as I desire, and you have never seen this one." They then conversed far into the night on Tibetan philosophy and mysticism, and David-Neel knew intuitively that this uninvited guest would not betray her. "Finally," she wrote, "he arose, and staff in hand, vanished like a phantom, as he had come. His footsteps made no sound on the stony path. He entered the jungle, and seemed to melt away in it."

The last stage of Alexandra David-Neel's journey to Lhasa was now at hand. Fortuitously, the companions had arrived just as the great New Year Festivals were beginning, and the road to the city was thronged with pilgrims just like themselves. Added to this, a huge dust storm blew up as they were entering the gates, hiding everyone. Slipping into the city was easy. "For two months," David-Neel recounts, "I was to wander freely in the lamaist Rome, with none to suspect that, for the first time in history, a foreign woman was beholding the Forbidden City." The two travelers found accommodation in a "ramshackle cottage occupied by beggarly people," where the idea of looking for a foreign woman would have occurred to no one.

Now David-Neel was free to reap the rewards of her hardships on the road. She could wander the busy streets, enjoying the bazaars, tea shops and temples, and gossip with other pilgrims, who never suspected her identity. She could observe the shoddy foreign goods on sale and be amused by the bands playing English tunes or the khaki-clad soldiers (some of them carried European rifles that were specially doctored by British holy men, she was told, so as not to harm Westerners).

She was also able to visit the Potala Palace, the massive building—part palace, part temple, part fortress—which towers over the city and was only open to pilgrims during the New Year Festivals. There she saw the "sumptuous suites of apartments" of the Dalai Lamas surrounded by temples, tombs, and shrines, and all lit up by thousands of yak-butter candles (indeed the whole of Lhasa smelt of yak butter). There were also fearsome shrines to evil demons and deities that pre-dated the arrival of Buddhism in Tibet that needed constant tending, she was told, if their escape was to be prevented. David-Neel saw the Dalai Lama officiate at the Butter Festival, where he inspected the great statues carved from butter. She also visited the three great monasteries of Lhasa—Sera, Draping, and Garden—each housing over 500 monks, and paid her respects at the Jokhang, the holiest temple in Tibet.

After living undetected in Lhasa for two months, Alexandra and Yongden were forced to leave in a hurry. They had witnessed a drunken domestic quarrel in the hovel where they lived and were being called to give evidence before the magistrate. David-Neel did not believe that even her perfect Tibetan disguise could stand up to that sort of scrutiny. Reluctantly, they set out on the road south to British India. David-Neel later recalled looking back on Lhasa for the last time from some miles away: "From that distance the Potala alone could be seen . . . a tiny castle suspended, it seemed, in the air like a mirage."

On her return to France in 1925, David-Neel found she was famous. She was showered with honors, being awarded the coveted Gold Medal of the Geographical Society of France and made a Chevalier of the Legion of Honor. She was also awarded a silver medal by the Royal Geographical Society of Belgium. Britain gave her nothing, perhaps because they were piqued at how successfully she had hoodwinked their authorities, or more likely because her travels had not actually contributed to the scientific exploration of Tibet. Tibetan experts such as Younghusband and David Macdonald, a dumbfounded British trade agent who had met her in Gyantse after she left Lhasa, were generous in their praise of her extraordinary fortitude and courage. David-Neel did have some detractors, however. A disparaging book was published in France in 1972—three years after her death—claiming that she neither went to Lhasa nor spoke Tibetan. Such allegations are easily dismissed. Indeed, David Macdonald, the first British official to see her after she left Lhasa, had no hesitation in confirming in writing where she had come from, and that she spoke fluent Tibetan—as he did himself.

David-Neel's great travels were over, but her interest in Tibetan Buddhism was lifelong. She wrote many esoteric tracts on the subject, as well as highly popular books such as *With Mystics and Magicians in Tibet* (in which her claim that she actually once witnessed a monk flying stretches credibility). Her great hardships do not appear to have affected her health in any way. Indeed, she was to survive her adopted son Yongden by 14 years. Alexandra David-Neel died in 1969, at age 100.

SOURCES:

Avedon, John. *Tibet Today*. Wisdom Publications, 1987.

David-Neel, Alexandra. *My Journey to Lhasa*. London: Virago Press, 1983.

Gibb, Christopher. *The Dalai Lama*. London: Exley, 1990.

Hicks, Roger, and Ngakpa Chogyam. *Great Ocean: The Dalai Lama*. London: Element Books, 1984.

Hopkirk, Peter. *Trespassers on the Roof of the World*. London: John Murray, 1982.

Christopher Gibb, writer, historian, volunteer with Tibetan refugees in Northern India, who made it to Lhasa under his own steam in 1985

Davidova, Elena (b. 1961).

See Comaneci, Nadia for sidebar on Yelena Davydova.

Davidovich, Bella (1928—)

Soviet pianist, widely recorded, who often performed chamber music with her son Dmitry Sitkovetsky. Born in Baku, Azerbaijani, in the Soviet Socialist Republic, on July 16, 1928; studied with Konstantin Igumnov (1873–1948) at the Moscow Conservatory as well as with Yakov Flier (1912–1978); immigrated to the United States in 1978; children: Dmitry Sitkovetsky.

Bella Davidovich studied with Konstantin Igumnov at the Moscow Conservatory as well as with Yakov Flier and shared first prize with *Halina Czerny-Stefanska at the 1949 Chopin Competition in Warsaw. Her first appearance in Western countries was with the Leningrad Philharmonic Orchestra in 1966. She enjoyed a successful career in the Soviet Union, particularly as a Chopin specialist, before emigrating to the United States in 1978, where she continued to reap critical praise. David Dubal wrote that her "pianistic diction is immaculate, each phrase being well tailored and finely calibrated." Some critics detected in her playing a poetic strain sometimes lacking elements of rapture or humor. Her recordings of the four Chopin Ballades, several Beethoven sonatas, and the Saint-Saëns G minor Concerto received positive reviews. She showed great sympathy for the piano music of Scriabin, and her treatment of his Second Sonata elicited some of her best playing. She often performed chamber music with her son, the gifted violinist Dmitry Sitkovetsky.

SOURCES:

"Davidovich, Bella," *Current Biography Yearbook 1989.* NY: H.W. Wilson, 1989, pp. 129–133.

Dubal, David. *The Art of the Piano.* NY: Summit Books, 1989.

Gruen, John. "A Different Kind of Family Affair," in *The New York Times.* March 16, 1986, section 2, p. 21.

John Haag,
Athens, Georgia

Davidow, Ruth (1911—)

Russian-born American nurse and political activist who was one of the nurses with the Abraham Lincoln Brigade during the Spanish Civil War. Born in Volkavisk, Russia, on September 11, 1911; grew up in New York City; married Fred Keller; children: one daughter.

Born in 1911 into a poor Jewish family in Tsarist Russia, Ruth Davidow immigrated with her mother and brother to the United States in 1914. Her father, an artist, had arrived in New York City several years earlier. Living in Brooklyn, the struggling family was dealt a severe blow when Ruth's father contracted tuberculosis. Her mother, never complaining, kept the family from destitution by working as a seamstress. The Bolshevik revolution of 1917 inspired Ruth's mother to ever greater political involvement, believing as she did that the "world needed to be changed." Memories of pogroms in Tsarist Russia made many Russian-Jewish immigrants in New York believe that the Bolsheviks would not only create a better, Socialist society, but end the scourge of anti-Semitism. Ruth Davidow grew up in a militantly Marxist home, with her mother not only passionately discussing politics but actively proselytizing the revolutionary message in her neighborhood by selling the Communist newspaper, *The Daily Worker.* Although Ruth loved her father, who had little interest in politics, it was obvious that her mother served as a role model both for herself and her siblings, a brother and a sister.

After dropping out of school to help support her family because of her father's lingering illness, Ruth found work as a waitress and also took odd jobs. At first, Davidow wanted to study law, but her family's poverty precluded this. Told that there would be no tuition fees if she studied nursing, she embarked on this career path despite her father's disapproval. By the early 1930s, Ruth Davidow received her diploma as a registered nurse.

In a time of economic depression and immense human suffering, Davidow regarded her increasing political involvement during those years as being no more than normal and appropriate to the challenges of the times. Only the Communist Party and its revolutionary agenda, she felt, would be able to change the world sufficiently to prevent another catastrophe like the world economic depression. Working as a visiting nurse, she took advantage of the travel opportunities her profession opened up, including work in California in the mid-1930s. Politically, Davidow was determined to do all she could to halt the spread of Fascism, which had captured Germany in 1933. Being Jewish, she was particularly outraged by the overt anti-Semitism displayed by Hitler's Third Reich. Her daily work as a nurse served to heighten her political consciousness during these years of struggle and achievement, which she analyzed many decades later: "I felt part of a long chain of what happens every day. One needs this background, this feeling of being connected to somebody. . . . I always considered it more important to work with people than with institutions."

Ruth Davidow's opportunity to play a role in the world struggle against Fascism came in

1936, with the start of the civil war in Spain. Supported by "volunteer" forces from Nazi Germany and Fascist Italy, Francisco Franco's Fascist rebel army attacked the legally elected leftist government of the Spanish Republic in July 1936. Within weeks, an International Brigade was formed by anti-Fascist volunteers from many countries, including those who had escaped from prisons and concentration camps in Germany, Italy, Poland, Hungary and Yugoslavia. Although she had hated Fascism for years, until 1936 Davidow did not believe that the United States could do much to halt its spread. Now, however, a concrete opportunity presented itself. Sixty years later, she explained her rationale for volunteering to go to Spain as a nurse: "When [the Fascists and Nazis] got to Spain, I realized, we're next. So I turned overnight. I was always an anti-fascist and I figured, 'This is my fight, and there's no such thing as a piecemeal fight'." Although the U.S. government warned against going to Spain to fight for the Republic, hundreds of men and women went there illegally, endangering not only their lives and health, but their citizenship as well. In time, 2,800 Americans would fight and nurse in Spain.

Working with the medical staff of the American volunteer unit, the Abraham Lincoln Brigade, Davidow found that medical conditions in Spain ranged from difficult to tragically inadequate. Medical supplies were rarely available due to the blockade imposed by the Western powers. But medical volunteers like Davidow and the physician she assisted, Dr. Irving Busch, performed hundreds of operations and saved the lives of many gravely wounded Americans and other International Brigade soldiers. Working at an improvised medical facility in the small town of Bella Casa, situated about 20 miles behind the front lines, Davidow and other American volunteer nurses worked long hours, week after week, to treat the wounded. She had to fight not only her exhaustion, but a debilitating case of malaria as well, Bella Casa being situated in a malarial region. But Davidow and her fellow nurses usually ignored their own exhaustion and illnesses.

After working at Bella Casa for about six months, Davidow was transferred to front-line duty. Medical conditions at the front were often shockingly primitive, and the wounded men had to be treated under constant danger of enemy attack from the air. The emergency hospital she worked in was little more than a hastily excavated cave in the side of a mountain, its entrance camouflaged from observation from the air by a tarpaulin. Many gravely wounded soldiers died of shock, loss of blood and infection, but the heroic efforts of Davidow and others often saved lives. Because of her leadership skills, she was transferred from the front to the hospital at Castellejo, where she was able to raise staff and patient morale dramatically. In the last, tragic phase of the war, she worked at a front-line hospital during the Ebro offensive of 1938.

In the two years that she spent as a nurse in Spain, Davidow witnessed much heroism but also learned that idealism alone was not enough to save the Spanish Republic. The Republicans were under-equipped and relied on soldiers who displayed courage but often carried only antiquated weapons. She also came to realize that human beings were complex creatures who did not always behave rationally. And she sometimes encountered treachery, as when one of the hospital cooks was found to be watering down the precious milk allotted for patients in order to sabotage their recovery. Regarding him as a Fascist sympathizer and Fifth Columnist, Davidow warned him with a kitchen knife, letting him know that one more incident would justify her cutting his throat (the milk supply was never again tampered with).

In the summer of 1938, Davidow worked in a front-line hospital close to the Ebro river where the Republican forces made a desperate gamble to change the tide of war. Constant Fascist bombing raids on her hospital convinced her that she would never return to the United States alive. Though she started to leave the front lines, she returned within the hour, greeted by her staff with tears in their eyes. But the war was lost, and in the fall of 1938 Davidow returned to the United States. The Spanish Republic was defeated in the spring of 1939, and, in September of that same year, Nazi Germany triggered World War II. One of the 49 American nurses who served with the Abraham Lincoln Brigade in Spain, Davidow's political odyssey did not end with her return to the United States.

Refusing to be demoralized by the defeat of the Left in Spain, Davidow remained active in radical politics and emerged as a leading personality in the West Coast sections of the Veterans of the Abraham Lincoln Brigade, the organization representing the survivors' interests after 1939. Unapologetic about her political and social militancy, Davidow settled in San Francisco where she soon became a personality to be reckoned with on the activist scene. She married Fred Keller, an official of the Electricians' Union, whose radical brand of trade unionism caused him to be persecuted during the McCarthy era for "un-American" attitudes. Davidow too refused to be intimidated by the FBI agents who often visited her home and spread negative stories about her to the neighbors. Raising her daughter to be socially conscious, Ruth was extremely proud when at age seven that daughter accompanied a black friend to what had been until then a segregated public swimming pool. She reminded her daughter that more than a decade before integration began in the U.S. armed forces, a black man named Oliver Law had been commander of a fully integrated American fighting unit in Spain. Leading his men into battle, Oliver Law died at the battle of Brunete in July 1937.

As the placid 1950s changed into the more rebellious mood of the 1960s, Davidow was active in San Francisco in organizing public protests against racism, sexism, the Vietnam War, and the old nemesis of Spanish Civil war veterans, the House Un-American Activities Committee. In the 1960s, she went to Mississippi to render assistance to blacks fighting for their civil rights in that state. She also worked in Cuba for a period of 18 months to upgrade the public-health delivery system of Havana. In Cuba, the tensions between Washington and Havana made her believe that a U.S. invasion might once again transform her into a combat nurse, but in the end she returned home safely.

Despite her advancing years, in the 1980s Davidow was actively engaged with groups demanding American initiatives on a nuclear weapons freeze. She also found time to agitate for abortion rights, and used every opportunity to sharply criticize the Central American policies of the Reagan administration. Ever the champion of the underdog, she was the only volunteer to look after the medical needs of the militant Native Americans who occupied Alcatraz as a dramatic protest. Back in San Francisco, she launched a health clinic in the Haight-Ashbury district to minister to the stricken youth of a drug culture gone out of control. In early 1991, almost 80, Davidow marched to protest American military involvement in the Gulf War.

In November 1996, Ruth Davidow and about 700 other aging and often frail International Brigade veterans of the Spanish Civil War gathered in Madrid to receive the homage of a now-democratic Spain, which granted them all honorary Spanish citizenship. Several years earlier, Ruth Davidow had reflected: "I knit and someone rips. You make progress slowly. It's a long historical process. And nothing is won forever unless you fight for it."

SOURCES:

Guthmann, Edward. "They Fought for Ideals in the Spanish Civil War," in *San Francisco Chronicle*, May 12, 1991, p. 28.

King, Brett Allan. "Camaradas in Arms: Spain Thanks Those Who Sacrificed to Help the Republic Against Franco," in *Chicago Tribune*. January 5, 1997, Womanews section, p. 1.

Lataster-Czisch, Petra. *Eigentlich rede ich nicht gern über mich: Lebenserinnerungen von Frauen aus dem Spanischen Bürgerkrieg 1936–1939*. Leipzig and Weimar: Gustav Kiepenheuer Verlag, 1990.

Patai, Frances. "Heroines of the Good Fight: Testimonies of U.S. Volunteer Nurses in the Spanish Civil War, 1936–1939," in *Nursing History Review*. Vol. 3, 1995, pp. 79–104.

Walker, Martin. "The Old Glory of America's Left," in *The Guardian* [London]. October 8, 1994, p. 31.

John Haag, Associate Professor of History, University of Georgia, Athens, Georgia

Davidson, Lucretia Maria

(1808–1825)

American poet. Born in Plattsburg, New York, on September 27, 1808; died at age 17 of tuberculosis in Plattsburg on August 27, 1825; daughter of a physician; sister of Margaret Miller Davidson (1823–1838).

An American poet, Lucretia Maria Davidson was considered remarkably precocious, writing her first poem, "Epitaph on a Robin," at age nine. Before she died of tuberculosis at age 17, her work included 278 poems of various lengths. In 1829, Samuel F.B. Morse collected and published her writings under the title *Amir Khan and Other Poems*. She was the sister of *Margaret Miller Davidson.

Davidson, Margaret Miller

(1823–1838)

American poet. Born in Plattsburg, New York, on March 26, 1823; died at age 15 of tuberculosis in Saratoga, New York, on November 25, 1838; buried in the village graveyard at Saratoga; daughter of a physician; sister of Lucretia Maria Davidson (1808–1825).

When Margaret Miller Davidson was born, her 15-year-old sister *Lucretia Maria Davidson* was already a poet of some renown. Seven of the nine siblings of the Davidson family died young, including Lucretia who died at age 17 of tuberculosis. Margaret was only two and a half. Educated by her mother, Margaret too was encouraged to write poetry. but soon the beautiful, delicate child was also wasting away from the dreaded disease. Washington Irving, who met the girl when she was 12, noted: "The soul was wearing out the body. I felt convinced that she was not long for the world; in truth, she already appeared more spiritual than mortal." Edgar Allan Poe described her as a "fairy child." The works of the two sisters were published collectively in 1850, along with a biography of Margaret by Irving. For a time, the entire nation was enthralled with the romantic tragedy of the frail sisters.

Davies, Christian (1667–1739).

See Cavanaugh, Kit.

Davies, Emily (1830–1921)

English educationalist, principal founder of Girton College, Cambridge, and suffrage campaigner who devoted her long life to the struggle for equal rights for women. Born Sarah (a name she did not use) Emily Davies on April 22, 1830, in Southampton on the English south coast; died in London on July 13, 1921; daughter of John (a Church of England cleric and headmaster of a private school) and Mary (Hopkinson) Davies; educated mainly at home by mother and tutors; never married; no children.

Family moved from southern England to Gateshead (1839); lived in London (1862–1921); edited Victoria Magazine (1864–65); involved in a suffrage movement (1862–67); served as member of the London School Board (1870–73); opened a college to provide women with university-level education (1869); was the main founder of Girton College near Cambridge (1873); was mistress of Girton College (1873–75); associated with the college for the rest of her life; resumed suffrage activities (1886); served as vice-president of Conservative and Unionist Women's Franchise Association (1912). Awards: honorary LLD degree, University of Glasgow (1901).

Selected publications: The Higher Education of Women (Strahan, 1866); Thoughts on some Questions relating to Women (Bowes & Bowes, 1910, contains reprints many of her essays and pamphlets).

On a sunny Friday afternoon in May 1897, hundreds of undergraduates gathered around Senate House Yard, near the center of the great English university at Cambridge. Full of high spirits, many leaned from windows, shouting and cheering as banners and posters were hung along college walls. An effigy of a woman student, clad in voluminous blue bloomers and astride a bicycle, was suspended from the top story of an adjoining bookshop. As the university dons, there to vote, emerged into the area from Senate House, they faced a barrage of flour, rotten eggs, confetti and fireworks. By late afternoon, the atmosphere had become wilder. A university proctor, employed to enforce the regulations governing students, was mobbed and, along with his bulldog, had to be rescued by the police. Nearby shops were raided for boxes and shutters, merchants' carts were seized, fences were pulled down: heaped together, they made a bonfire. Riotous activity continued until midnight when the fire brigade both extinguished the bonfire and hosed down the surrounding throng of undergraduates. The cause of the disturbance was a ballot, campaigned for by Emily Davies and others, to determine whether women should be awarded University of Cambridge degrees on the same terms as men.

In many respects, the household into which Emily Davies was born ill-fitted her for a life of political and educational campaigning. Her father John Davies was a scholarly man but one who shared those prejudices about the place of women that were common at the time. He also had a difficult personality; he could be self-righteous, disdainful and pedantic—traits that were to some extent shared by his daughter.

> *In all that concerned women, she was a revolutionary; in all else, a conservative.*
>
> —Barbara Stephen

John Davies was born in Wales in 1795 and in 1823 married **Mary Hopkinson**, the daughter of a businessman of Derby. (In a letter of 1868, Emily Davies suggested that unfortunate people such as herself, "who are made up of an ill-assorted compound of Celtic and Anglo-Saxon blood, are by the nature of their constitution continually impelled to say and do what they are sorry for afterwards.") After an education at the University of Cambridge, her father became a cleric and for a time proprietor and head of a boarding school for boys. He was running his school in Southampton when Emily, the fourth of five children, was born on April 22, 1830. John Davies, who wrote a number of books on theological topics, taught from economic necessity rather than a sense of vocation and was glad in 1839 to become the vicar of Gateshead, in the northeast of England. (He was offered the post by a friend and fellow Evangelist, the bishop of Durham—in keeping with the tradition that most clerical appointments in the Anglican Church were made through personal contacts.) Soon after arriving in Gateshead, he recommended that a local school run by one of his curates should no longer admit girls, as they had the effect of lowering its status. True to this precept, Emily and a sister were mainly educated by their mother, apart from a brief period at a local girls' school and some instruction in French and Italian by a tutor. Her three brothers were sent away to fee-paying schools and (except for one brother who articled to a solicitor) to Cambridge University. It is likely that an autobiographical element is present in an article of 1868 in which Davies wrote:

> Probably only women who have laboured under it can understand the weight of discouragement produced by being perpetually told that, as women, nothing much is ever to be expected of them, and it is not worth their while to exert themselves. . . . Every effort to improve the education of women which assumes that they may, without reprehensible ambition, study the same subjects as their brothers and be measured by the same standards does something towards lifting them out of the state of listless despair of themselves into which so many fall.

Even though her early years were spent in constrained and genteel circumstances, Emily Davies did find outlets for her intelligence and energy. She helped her father in charitable and other duties about the parish. In 1848, she befriended **Jane Crow**, the daughter of a local businessman, who was later to introduce her to a schoolfriend, Elizabeth Garrett (later *****Elizabeth Garrett Anderson**), whose attempts to follow a medical career were greatly encouraged by Emily. Several months of 1851 were spent with her parents in Geneva, a holiday that improved her knowledge of other languages and broadened her horizons. Another foreign visit in 1858 to Algiers, where a brother had gone in the hope of improving his health, led to a meeting with **Anne Leigh Smith**, who was to introduce her to her sister Barbara Leigh Smith (later known as the artist and educational reformer *****Barbara Bodichon**).

An older brother, John Llewelyn Davies, had also become a cleric. He became vicar of St. Mark's, Whitechapel, in the east end of London in 1852 and was occasionally visited there by Emily. Though the family background was both socially and politically conservative, her brother became involved with the progressive circle surrounding F.D. Maurice, a leading Christian Socialist. (*****Margaret Llewelyn Davies**, who through the Women's Co-operative Guild spent her life trying to improve the lot of working-class women, was John Llewelyn Davies' daughter.)

Thus, even in a Gateshead rectory, Emily Davies was becoming acquainted with some reformist ideas. She acted as the organizer of a local branch of the Society for Promoting the Employment of Women, which was founded in 1859. Jane Crow became first secretary of the society's London office, which was in the same building in which the *Englishwoman's Journal* was edited. Launched in 1858, this publication soon came to Emily Davies' attention and during visits to her brother she helped with the day-to-day work of the office. She was present at lectures delivered by *****Elizabeth Blackwell**, the only legally registered woman physician in Britain (she had obtained her training in the United States); it was at this time that Emily Davies began to help Elizabeth Garrett along her often difficult path of medical training—one successfully trodden despite the many obstacles put in her way.

The death of John Davies allowed Emily to take up residence, along with her mother, in London, where she moved in 1862. For about six months, she acted as editor of the *Englishwoman's Journal*. In 1864, she edited for about a year the *Victoria Magazine,* a monthly established by *****Emily Faithfull**. Though mainly of a literary character, the magazine also included articles on women's issues, notably Emily Davies' "The Influence of University Degrees on the Education of Women." To improve the standards of education in schools—necessary if women were to progress to higher education—she advocated examinations that were set and marked by external examiners. Some heads of girls' schools, who approved of the efforts of Emily Davies and others to organize such examinations, provided candidates. One supportive head was *****Frances Mary Buss**, though *****Dorothea Beale**, whose name is often linked with hers as a progressive headmistress, had reservations about examining girls. In this, Beale was not unusual. One schoolmistress, referred to by Emily Davies, believed examinations would "foster the spirit of confidence and independence which is too common amongst girls of the present day." Even an advocate of girls' examinations, the dean of Canterbury (Emily Davies was adept at recruiting supporters of the highest respectability), wrote to warn her that education should not result in the "sacrifice of that unobtrusiveness which is at the same time the charm and the strength of our Englishwomen." In 1865, the Senate of the University of Cambridge voted narrowly, by 55 votes to 51, to accept a recommendation that local examinations set by members of the university for boys' schools should be available also to girls' schools. This was to be for a trial period of three years, but once the precedent had been established opponents had

Opposite page

Emily

Davies

to accept that the situation could not be reversed. Also in 1865, Emily Davies was invited to give evidence, along with Frances Mary Buss, to the government-appointed Schools Enquiry Commission, an indication of the reputation she had established in the field of education.

In the 1860s, Emily Davies was involved in activities to promote women's suffrage. She supported the radical Liberal candidate for the Westminster seat, John Stuart Mill, in the general election of 1865, and became friendly with his stepdaughter, the campaigner for women's rights *Helen Taylor. John Mill warmly supported the emancipation of women and this aspect of his philosophy perhaps weighed more heavily with Davies than some of his other progressive ideas. She later left the women's suffrage campaign, in part because of the way some of its leaders associated it with the advanced wing of the Liberal Party. Emily Davies, whose views on many questions were highly conventional, wanted to avoid the identification of women's suffrage with one of the two main political parties, and she was always disinclined to compromise her opinions in order to retain a facade of agreement.

In any case, by the late 1860s she was deeply involved in the question of women's education. At the heart of her philosophy was the conviction that there should be no differences in the standards applied to men and women. She rejected the belief, widespread among the middle and upper classes, that such subjects as Greek, Latin, and mathematics were suitable for boys and young men while girls and young women were intended for nothing more intellectually demanding than music, needlework, and the basics of reading and writing. Women with ambitions to go beyond this level were often regarded as "masculine," while no husband, according to popular prejudice, would want a wife who appeared to be as clever as he was. In a similar vein, women were generally regarded as "the weaker sex," both physically and intellectually, and often women themselves accepted this as axiomatic and deferred to the dominant masculine ideology. Many parents equated ignorance with innocence at a time when polite society had a horror of indecorousness. Though Emily Davies could in 1864 present a paper at a meeting of the National Association for the Promotion of Social Science, she could not deliver it herself: to do so would have been considered "unladylike," and it was read on her behalf.

Her paper, "On Secondary Instruction Relating to Girls," argued both for improvements in the standards of girls' education and the value

of the same types of examination for boys and girls. This latter position put her at odds with some supporters of educational reform who believed it would be asking too much of girls to compete on the same terms as boys. Similarly, those sympathetic to the idea of university education for women often believed it would have to be at a lower level.

However, a commitment to equal standards was maintained by Emily Davies in the protracted and complex developments that led to the founding of Girton College, near Cambridge. Family tradition might have inclined her towards forming links with Cambridge, where her father and brothers had studied; perhaps too, she preferred what in a letter to Barbara Bodichon of 1868 she called "the cool Cambridge manner," adding: "It is not half as pleasant as the kind, gushing way Oxford men have, but it comes to more." The details of how those links were made need not be given, though to begin with the college was opened, in 1869, with five women students at Benslow House, Hitchen, roughly half way between London and Cambridge. The students' examination papers were those sat by candidates at the University of Cambridge, an arrangement that was made privately with the examiners who had set the papers; the university authorities somewhat loftily announced that such a matter was none of their concern. This system, despite Emily Davies' tireless secretarial work, did not always operate smoothly. On one occasion, two candidates traveled to Cambridge to sit a paper (in a room in a hotel), only to wait for over an hour before the examination could start—the messenger carrying the paper had gone to a wrong address.

In 1873, following much effort to raise funds for a new building in the village of Girton, the college moved to within about two miles of Cambridge (the distance was carefully chosen as it was decided that contact with undergraduates at the male colleges should be discouraged). At Girton, some of the previous arrangements continued. Dons sympathetic to the idea of women's education provided informal assistance—in 1873, 22 out of 34 professors allowed women (chaperoned, of course) to attend their lectures—and papers were still marked outside the control of the university statutes. This meant that women did not receive degrees.

An effort was made in 1881 by supporters of degrees for women to improve the position. It was pointed out that the University of London had begun in 1878 to award degrees to women and that this disadvantaged those who studied at

Girton and Newnham (the other Cambridge college for women, which Emily Davies always viewed with unfriendly rivalry). The outcome represented a compromise: women were formally allowed access to examinations; if successful, their names were published in the class lists, and they were awarded a certificate. It was an example of the piecemeal reform characteristic of modern Britain, as celebrated in the self-congratulatory verse of the Poet Laureate, Alfred Tennyson:

> A land of settled government,
> A land of just and old renown,
> Where Freedom slowly broadens down
> From precedent to precedent.

Freedom to be awarded degrees on the same terms as men, however, was slow to arrive. Even the much commented on achievement of Girton's **Agnata Frances Ramsay**, who in the classics examination of 1887 was the only first-class candidate, did little to change things. In March 1897, the Syndicate of the university produced a report recommending that women who passed their examinations should receive degrees. At that time, all men who had become Masters of Arts of the university (by the simple expedient of paying a fee a few years after the award of their Bachelors' degrees) could take part in votes concerning the university's statutes. Many were encouraged to believe that women and their supporters were asking for too much: the press frequently employed the phrase "the thin end of the wedge" and drew comparisons with the demands of the suffrage movement. Within Cambridge, the minority of dons who had opposed the higher education of women regrouped over the issue of the Syndicate's recommendations, and gained the support of those who held that the agitation on the women's behalf was disrupting the work of the university and bringing unwanted publicity. Old prejudices were revived about the fitness of women for intellectual activity. One flysheet put into circulation referred to the way men were favored by "Divine Providence," while a letter to the press was hostile to change on the more prosaic grounds that "to darn a stocking well and sew on buttons" would "contribute more to the general well-being than an ability to discuss the binomial theorem or the differential calculus."

Even many undergraduates were drawn into this spasm of reaction. A vote of the Union Society on May 11 condemned the proposed concessions by 1,083 votes to 138. This result anticipated a similar outcome when university MAs gathered to vote later that month; amid the uproar previously described, 1,713 men voted against the Syndicate's recommendations and 662 in favor. The more equal treatment of women at Cambridge was thus blocked for what was to be another quarter of a century.

Since the mid-1830s, Emily Davies had gradually become less involved in the running of Girton College. In the absence of a more suitable candidate, she had acted as its mistress from 1873 to 1875. It was her view that the head of the college should be a woman of some standing, and she declared herself delighted to be succeeded by **Frances Bernard**, a niece of Lord Lawrence who had spent some time in India assisting her uncle while he was viceroy there. A period of illness in 1876 led her to resign as secretary of the committee that administered the college, though she was given the title of honorary secretary, which she held until 1904. A person of decided opinions and persistent in seeking to apply them, Emily Davies inevitably disagreed with the approach of some of those with whom she worked. She was reluctant to allow the teaching staff at Girton a voice in the college's administration, while she did all she could to insist that available funds should be used to provide places for undergraduates rather than develop the sort of postgraduate activities that were becoming a feature of other Cambridge colleges.

Even at the height of her involvement with Girton, Emily Davies retained an interest in the work of other bodies, such as the London School Board (she was elected to it in 1870 and served for three years) and the London Schoolmistresses' Association, of which she was the secretary from its formation (after a meeting at her home) in 1866 until it was disbanded in 1888. In 1886, she joined the London National Society for Women's Suffrage and, in keeping with her apparently unlimited capacity for administrative work, joined its general committee in 1889. She took part in various constitutional methods of agitation for the parliamentary franchise—deputations, letter-writing, the gathering of signatures on petitions, public meetings—but deplored the militancy of those women who tried to force the granting of the vote through such tactics as chaining themselves to railings, smashing windows and setting fire to pillar-boxes.

When in 1912 the National Union of Women's Suffrage Societies, to which the London group was affiliated, declared that candidates of the Labour Party (the only party pledged to women's suffrage) should be supported, she resigned. She then joined the Conservative and Unionist Women's Franchise Association, of which she became a vice-president. In 1918, at the age of 88, she cast her first parliamentary vote. It was also her last. She died on July 13, 1921, at Hampstead in north London. Had she lived another two years, she would have seen Cambridge concede the award of degrees to women, but with other restrictions maintained. It was not until 1948 that the end came to all formal distinctions between men and women at the University of Cambridge, in a reform that also abolished most of the old statutes that allowed graduates a voice in university affairs.

Emily Davies' papers, which were deposited in Girton College, contain her note objecting to any memoir of her work "of an intimate personal nature," while adding that "there are not materials for it." No study of her has revealed more than a record of a life of work on behalf of women. It would seem, to paraphrase the contemporary rhyme, that like "Miss Buss and Miss Beale, Cupid's darts she did not feel." **Margaret Forster** has suggested that "her sharp tongue and steely eye" made most men afraid of her. This might be true, but social convention—and practical considerations—allowed few Victorian women of similar background to have both a family and a public life. If not out of respect for her wish for nothing of an "intimate personal nature" but because it is fruitless to speculate on what might have been, the life of Emily Davies has to be estimated in terms of her efforts to improve the education, employment, and political position of women.

SOURCES:

Bennett, Daphne. *Emily Davies and the Liberation of Women 1830-1921.* London: Audre Deutsch, 1990.

Bradbrook, M.C. *"That Infidel Place": A Short History of Girton College 1869–1969.* London: Chatto & Windus, 1969.

Forster, Margaret. *Significant Sisters: The Grassroots of Active Feminism, 1839–1939.* London: Secker & Warburg, 1984.

Megson, B., and J. Lindsay. *Girton College 1869–1959: An Informal History.* Cambridge: Heffer, 1960.

Rosen, Andrew. "Emily Davies and the Women's Movement, 1862–1867," in *Journal of British Studies.* Vol. 19, no. 1. Fall 1979, pp. 101–121.

Stephen, Barbara. *Emily Davies and Girton College.* London: Constable, 1927.

———. *Girton College 1869-1932.* Cambridge: Cambridge University Press, 1933.

SUGGESTED READING:

Levine, Philippa. *Victorian Feminism, 1850–1900.* London: Hutchinson, 1987.

McWilliams-Tullberg, Rita. *Women at Cambridge: A Men's University—Though of a Mixed Type.* London: Victor Gollancz, 1975.

COLLECTIONS:

Emily Davies papers, Girton College, Cambridge.

D.E. Martin, Lecturer in History, University of Sheffield, Sheffield, England

formance of *Ethel Smyth's violin sonata in Leipzig. In the late 1920s, she made one of the first electrical recordings of Robert Schumann's concerto. She also played the then almost unknown Elizabethan composers. Davies excelled as a recital accompanist and also collaborated with world-class virtuosos like Pablo Casals. In 1921, she was the first musician to give a piano recital in Westminster Abbey; she also gave many recitals in the church of St. Martin-in-the-Fields and is believed to be the first woman to play piano in a church. Sir Edward Elgar dedicated his Concert Allegro Op. 46 to her. One of her students was *Kathleen Dale.

John Haag, Athens, Georgia

Davies, Gwendoline and Margaret

Welsh philanthropists, art collectors, patrons of art, fine printing and music who were known as The Ladies of Gregynog.

Davies, Gwendoline (1882–1951). Name variations: The Ladies of Gregynog. Born Gwendoline Elizabeth Davies in Llandinam, Montgomeryshire, Wales, on February 11, 1882; died in Oxford at the Radcliffe Infirmary on July 3, 1951; daughter of Edward Davies (1852–98) and Margaret Jones Davies (d. 1888); educated at Highfield School, Hendon, and privately; never married; no children.

Awarded Companion of Honor (1937).

Davies, Margaret (1884–1963). Name variations: The Ladies of Gregynog. Born Margaret Sidney Davies in Llandinam, Montgomeryshire, Wales, on December 14, 1884; died in London on March 13, 1963; daughter of Edward Davies (1852–98) and Margaret Jones Davies (d. 1888); educated at Highfield School, Hendon, and privately; never married; no children.

Awarded Hon. LL.D. (University of Wales), 1949.

Collected art from 1908; were major benefactors of charities and cultural institutions in Wales (c. 1914–50); ran canteen for allied troops at Troyes and Rouen (1916–18); purchased Gregynog Hall, Montgomeryshire, as an art center (1920); organized concerts and festivals of music and poetry (1921–38); founded Gregynog Press (1922); founded Gwendoline and Margaret Davies Trusts (1934); Gwendoline Davies Bequest to National Museum of Wales (1951); gift to National Library of Wales (1951); gift of Gregynog Hall to University of Wales (1960); Margaret Davies Bequest to National Museum of Wales (1963).

Gwendoline and Margaret Davies were born in Llandinam, Montgomeryshire, Wales, in

Fanny Davies

Davies, Fanny (1861–1934)

English pianist who was particularly known for her interpretation of Schumann. Born on June 27, 1861, in Guernsey, Channel Islands, England; died in London on September 1, 1934; studied with Karl Reinecke, Oscar Paul, and Clara Schumann.

One of the most celebrated of English pianists, Fanny Davies studied first with Karl Reinecke and Oscar Paul. From 1883 through 1885, she was tutored by *Clara Schumann and is now considered to have been one of Schumann's most gifted and distinguished pupils. During the 1888 season, George Bernard Shaw attended a performance by Davies' which led him to remark that her playing was "full of speed, lilt, life, and energy. She scampered through a fugue of Bach's with a cleverness and jollity that forced us to condone her utter irreverence." The Beethoven Fourth Concerto was one of her specialties, and her Schumann playing was highly respected, particularly because it derived directly from the great tradition of Clara Schumann herself. Davies championed the classical works of Beethoven and Chopin as well as what were then new compositions by Brahms and British composers. In 1887, she and Adolf Brodsky gave the first per-

1882 and 1884, respectively. They were the granddaughters of David Davies of Llandinam (1818–1890), a self-made man who had amassed a fortune from contracting, coal-owning, and building railways and docks, and was elected a Liberal Member of Parliament in 1874. Their brother David Davies (1880–1944; created Baron Davies in 1932) was also a Liberal MP, parliamentary private secretary to the Prime Minister David Lloyd George in 1916–17, a founder of the League of Nations, and the greatest Welsh public benefactor of his day, closely associated with Aberystwyth University College, the National Library of Wales, and the campaign against tuberculosis. Following the early death of their mother **Margaret Jones Davies** in 1888, their father married their mother's sister, Elizabeth Jones (1853–1942). After his death ten years later, in 1898, their stepmother was responsible for the upbringing of the sisters. **Elizabeth Jones Davies** was active in public affairs, became the first woman magistrate in Montgomeryshire, and was a supporter of numerous charities and good causes.

In their youth, the Davies sisters lived with their stepmother at Plas Dinam, Llandinam, and in their London flat at 3 Buckingham Gate, SW1. They were educated at Highfield School, Hendon, and at home, and brought up in the family faith. As Calvinistic Methodists, they were teetotal and strict sabbatarians. Their upbringing forbade dancing and the opera, but permitted tennis, riding, and even fox-hunting. Neither enjoyed good health, and from 1924 onwards Gwendoline suffered increasingly from a blood disease. She was a competent violinist—the owner of a Stradivarius violin—and played the organ. Margaret sang and played the harp; she also briefly attended the Slade School of Art in London as an external pupil, and later received private instruction in painting. The sisters enjoyed travel, initially in the company of their governess **Jane Blaker**. After leaving school, Gwendoline visited the United States, and both sisters regularly traveled abroad, usually for periods of a month during the spring, frequenting Paris and Italy, and venturing further afield to the Mediterranean, Egypt, and the Middle East. Neither made close personal attachments and were generally uncomfortable in the presence of strangers.

By 1907, the joint fortune of the Davies sisters was around £1,000,000, partly invested in family businesses. During the booming years before the First World War, their annual income may have exceeded £40,000. Such means did not compare with those of millionaire collectors such as Henry E. Huntington or William Hesketh Lever, but the sisters were among the wealthiest young women in the United Kingdom. They inherited a family tradition of philanthropy, and in 1911 shared with their brother in the gift of £150,000 to endow the campaign against tuberculosis. In 1914, David Davies and his sisters jointly contributed £5,000 to the building fund for the recently founded National Museum of Wales in Cardiff; a gift that Gwendoline and Margaret repeated in 1916.

> *The tragedy is that we have so much to give that is not money.*
> —**Gwendoline Davies, March 26, 1929**

The Davies family had little interest in works of art, and the sisters were introduced to collecting by Jane Blaker's brother Hugh (1873–1937), an artist and critic, who was curator of the Holburne of Menstrie Museum in Bath from 1905. In 1908, Gwendoline and Margaret began to collect through Blaker's agency, spending over £13,850 on a pair of sea scenes by J.M.W. Turner and £4,930 on two oils by Corot. The following year, they spent over £18,000 on four paintings by Romney, Millet, Corot, and Anton Mauve. The conservative tone of these purchases of works by well-established British and French artists is confirmed by Margaret's diary of the sisters' visit to Paris in 1909: "There is a very good collection by Corot . . . some very beautiful tiny gems by Millet of peasant life . . . and also many I do not care for, they are too impressionist to suit me." In 1910–11, the sisters spent over £37,000 on 20 paintings of similar character. This included four Turners, a Raeburn, and a small Meissonier, as well as two large works by Millet, *The Sower* and *The Peasant Family*. Writing in July 1910, Blaker acknowledged his indebtedness and requested to provide any future services without a fee. Thereafter, he seldom acted formally on their behalf but remained an adviser.

In 1912, the Davies sisters visited Italy, and almost certainly viewed Claude Monet's exhibition of recent Venetian views in Paris on the return journey. Blaker wrote approvingly: "I . . . am delighted that you think of getting some examples of the Impressionists of 1870. Very few English collectors, except Hugh Lane, have bought them at all, although much of their best work is in America." While their expenditure in 1912 remained fairly constant, at £19,343 on 25 works of art, its range widened considerably to include a monumental Auguste Rodin bronze of *The Kiss* and three Monet oils of Venice, as well as a small Manet, a trio of works by Millet, two Daumiers and a group of Turners. At the suggestion of the painter Murray Urquhart (1880–1972), a friend of Blaker and their brother, the sisters exhibited their collection at their own expense, at Cardiff and Bath between February and May 1913. Few comparable displays of French art had been seen in Britain, causing Blaker to exclaim that "the exhibition is the greatest artistic event in the history of Wales." The year 1913 proved a milestone in the history of the Davies collection, in which they spent over £30,000 on 18 works. These included five Monets, Rodin's *St. John the Baptist,* Renoir's *The Parisienne,* purchased from the distinguished Rouart collection, and a Mathis Maris. The following year, their collecting activities were much more modest, and ceased altogether with the outbreak of the First World War.

Gwendoline Davies

Following the German invasion in August 1914, the Davies sisters and their mother financed the travel and resettling in Wales of 91 Belgian refugees "of the better class." These included the sculptor George Minne (1866–1941), the painters Gustave van de Woestijne (1881–1947) and Valerius de Saedeleer (1867–1941), and several musicians, including the brothers Marcel and Nicholas Lavoureux. Gwendoline had recently founded a School of Instrumental Music at Aberystwyth University College, and the sisters sought "to invite Belgian artists to come to Wales, where they would not only be able to continue their work but also to bring a specific talent to the Welsh people." This transplanted colony helped foster appreciation of the visual arts in Aberystwyth, where an Arts and Crafts Department was later established, with the support of the Davies sisters. In the summer of 1916, Gwendoline purchased Rodin's life-size bronze *Eve* for £1,500 and spent £2,350 on ten oil paintings and a drawing by Augustus John. The latter purchase was probably inspired by Blaker, who had recently published an article on

John, a Welshman widely regarded as the leading progressive painter in the United Kingdom. In appreciation, the artist agreed to present a complete set of his etchings to the National Museum of Wales.

Two of the Davies sisters' cousins had died in combat and their brother David had served two years in France before the failure of the British offensive in 1916 dashed allied hopes of an imminent end to the war. That year, like many other upper- and middle-class women, they decided to make a personal contribution to the war effort by opening a Red Cross canteen. Gwendoline remained until the end of the war at the "Cantine des Dames Anglais" at Troyes, catering for French troops, who were notoriously poorly supplied. After working with her sister for a while, Margaret moved on to work at a canteen in Rouen. In 1917, now in direct contact with the leading French dealer Emile Bernheim, Gwendoline spent £8,440 on six paintings, including Manet's *The Rabbit* and Monet's *Rouen Cathedral: setting sun.* Early the following year, she broke entirely new ground with the purchase from Bernheim Jeune for £3,750 of two major oil paintings by Cézanne, *Midday, L'Estaque* and *Provençal Landscape,* followed by Daumier's *Don Quixote Reading,* acquired for £811 from the collection of Edgar Degas. As Paris was within range of German artillery, these new acquisitions were dispatched to the Victoria Art Gallery in Bath, where they remained on display until 1920.

In 1918, the Davies sisters endowed the new museum in the Arts and Crafts Department at Aberystwyth University College with a sum of £5,000, and from 1920 until 1936 they funded the architect and designer Sydney Greenslade (1866–1955) to purchase studio pottery, prints and applied art for it. At the end of the war, the sisters once again employed Blaker as an agent. In 1919, they spent £10,900 on a miscellany of pictures, including a Raeburn and a religious scene by Rembrandt's pupil Gebrandt van den Eeckhout, as well as Turner watercolors and Augustus John drawings. Mindful of the financial difficulties of the National Museum of Wales, Gwendoline purchased John's portrait of the Welsh poet W.H. Davies for £550 with the specific intention of lending it to the national collection and offered help towards the purchase of his monumental *Canadian War Memorial* cartoon. Even with her assistance, its purchase price remained well beyond the museum's means. The following year, the sisters spent over £29,000 on paintings and drawings, more than in any other years except 1910 and 1913. These acquisitions included Cézanne's *Still Life with teapot,* Van Gogh's *Rain—Auvers* and Manet's *Argenteuil,* as well as two groups of work by Camille Pissarro and Maurice de Vlaminck. Much the most expensive purchases were a Botticelli workshop *Virgin and Child* and a Dutch school *Portrait of a Woman* attributed to Frans Hals, bought from Hugh Blaker at a cost of £5,000 and £9,000, respectively. Thereafter, their collecting tailed off rapidly. In November 1921, Gwendoline expressed her inability to continue buying works of art "in face of the appalling need everywhere—Russian children . . . ex soldiers, all so terribly human. After all, it is humanity that needs help & sympathy." She made a few further acquisitions, such as Turner's *Beacon Light* at £2,625 in 1922 and a pair of Degas bronzes for £800 and an El Greco workshop *Disrobing of Christ* at £6,000 in 1923, but stopped entirely after 1926. Margaret continued to make modest purchases, mainly of paintings by recent British painters, such as Gilman and Sickert, until 1939. Her principal acquisition during the interwar years was Millet's *The Gust of Wind,* which she obtained from Blaker in 1937, apparently in settlement of a debt.

The immediate reason for the curtailment of the Davies sisters' activities as art collectors was their purchase in July 1920, for £33,599, of Gregynog Hall and its adjoining estate of 311 acres. Gregynog is a large property, essentially of mid-19th-century date, situated a few miles northeast of the Davies family home at Plas Dinam. As early as 1916–17, Gwendoline had speculated on the possibility of making Gregynog the home of a community of artisans, but this project only became feasible with the end of the war, which provided the additional motive of the rehabilitation of ex-soldiers. For advice and practical assistance, the sisters turned to an old friend, Dr. Thomas Jones (1870–1955), then assistant secretary to the Cabinet and editor of the current affairs magazine *The Welsh Outlook,* who became closely associated with the new art center. Gwendoline confided to him: "Gregynog must have an atmosphere of its own if it is to be what we *hope* it will be . . . so any decoration or furniture must have this end in view; it must be beautiful, but the beauty of simplicity & usefulness." The sisters initially intended the house to serve as a center for cultural activities, and it was several years before family circumstances required them to vacate Plas Dinam and move into residence at Gregynog. In April 1924, Gwendoline wrote "we have never looked upon it as 'home' before," and a month later noted that "All our pictures & other treasures have been moved to Gregynog & will remain there in future."

Even before the purchase of Gregynog was finalized, in April 1920 Gwendoline was assembling a library of "1000 and one volumes . . . for the education of plumbers and paper hangers" and purchasing four baby grand and five upright pianos. Shortly after, the sisters commissioned suites of arts and crafts furniture from the leading cabinetmaker Peter Waals (1870–1937), who was also consulted on the possibility of adding furniture-making to the curriculum at Gregynog. In February 1921, on Blaker's recommendation, the sisters engaged the painter and architect Robert Ashwin Maynard (1888–1966) as controller at Gregynog and sent him to London to study printing, wood engraving, and pottery, before taking up his position. Although progress was delayed by the sisters' promise to contribute £58,000 to a trust for improving housing in Wales, a printing workshop was ready by June 1922. Six months later, the Gregynog Press was inaugurated with an edition of 120 Christmas cards.

M argaret
D avies

Gwendoline acknowledged from the outset that "anything like a commercial enterprise at Gregynog would be quite impracticable, even if it were desirable," and that the press should specialize in "small editions & small books . . . specimens of fine workmanship & also of literary value." Its first book, published in December 1923, aptly fulfilled these criteria: a volume of the poems by the 17th-century Welsh author George Herbert in an edition of 300 copies on hand-made paper. The following July, Gwendoline defined the primary objective of the press as "to unlock the door of the treasure house of Welsh literature, romance & legend & make it accessible to the English speaking public . . . that it must inevitably attract attention & win for the little country that tardy recognition of cultured nations. . . . But we must bring to this task a strong critical sense & permit nothing which is not of *the best*."

Under Maynard and his successors Blair Hughes-Stanton (1902–1981) and James Wardrop (1905–1957), the Gregynog Press published 45 books and over 200 pieces of ephemera between 1923 and 1940. Editions were small, between 150 to 475 copies, many illustrated with wood engravings by leading artists including David Jones (1895–1974) and ◆❧ **Gertrude Hermes** (1901–1983). Deluxe copies were provided with hand-made bindings by the master binder George Fisher (1879–1970). Their subject matter ranged from poems by historic and contemporary Welsh authors to Milton and Cervantes, and from Euripedes to Omar Khayyâm. Eight books were in Welsh and eleven others had Welsh authors or were otherwise associated with Wales. Prices varied from 10s. 6d. to £10. 12s. for standard editions and from £1. 11s. 6d. to £21 for specially bound copies. The sisters took no part in the running of the press and declined "to make any *personal* profit out of the books," while hoping that "some day the press will be able to pay its own way." On account of the high production costs of hand-made books and their limited demand, which was exacerbated from 1929 by the Depression, it remained dependent upon their financial support. Thanks to their belief that "it is worth while producing a beautiful thing for its own sake," the Gregynog Press earned an international reputation for its standards of craftsmanship and design.

From 1921, Gregynog served as a center for student retreats and the residential conferences of bodies such as the Welsh School of Social Service, the League of Nations, and the Council of Music for Wales, whose founding director was the organist and choirmaster Sir Henry Walford Davies (1869–1941), Gregynog Professor of Music at Aberystwyth. Informal concerts and services were held frequently to coincide with such events, and in 1929 the Gregynog Choir was founded. Comprising the Davies sisters, their family, friends and neighbors, it held annual Easter concerts of choral music, which gradually attracted the participation of conductors and composers of international repute, including Sir Adrian Boult (1889–1983) and Dr. Ralph Vaughan-Williams (1872–1958). These essentially amateur gatherings were succeeded, between 1933 and 1938, by annual Festivals of Music and Poetry on themes such as "The Commemoration of Famous Men." The Gregynog Summer festivals were performed by professional musicians and singers before invited audiences of around 200 visitors. Held in a country house with a superlative art collection in a rural set-ting, when opportunities to hear musicians of the highest class were severely restricted, the Festivals made a great impact. Although reviewed in the press and frequently recalled by visitors and participants, these performances remain the most elusive area of the Davies sisters' patronage. As an art form in which they directly participated—as singers and musicians—their significance for Gwendoline and Margaret was undoubtedly profound.

The outbreak of the Second World War in 1939 marked the end of the Gregynog Press and the Festivals of Music and Poetry. The house provided refuge for evacuees and was requisitioned as a Red Cross convalescent home. By the time peace returned, Gwendoline was too ill to make major new initiatives, although Margaret resumed purchasing works of art in 1948, seldom spending more than £500 in a year on established British artists such as J.D. Innes and Jacob Epstein and moderately progressive younger painters including Ivon Hitchens and John Piper. The sisters had given a group of works, including sculptures by Rodin and paintings by Augustus John to the National Museum of Wales in 1940, but it is unclear when they decided to leave the bulk of their art collection to the nation. Following Gwendoline's death in 1951, her collection of 109 paintings, drawings, and sculpture was bequeathed to the museum, whose *Annual Report* observed: "By this princely benefaction the character of the Department of Art has been transformed, so that it now takes a high place among the major art-collections of Great Britain." In May 1960, Margaret presented Gregynog Hall to the University of Wales as "a centre for the appreciation of the visual arts, music, and dramatic art," together with an annual endowment of £12,000. The same month, she sold Monet's *Grand Canal, Venice* and a number of minor works by Daumier, Pissarro, and Vlaminck at auction for £48,870. Over the following two years, advised by John Steegman, a former curator at the National Museum, she spent almost the whole of this sum on artists previously unrepresented in the Davies collection, including Marquet, Bonnard, Sisley, Utrillo, and Mathew Smith. Early in 1963, Margaret died, bequeathing 151 works of art to the museum, and reuniting the spectacular collection that she and Gwendoline had assembled.

The Davies family had become rich through the Victorian industrialization of Wales, and Gwendoline and Margaret had a profound sense of indebtedness to the working classes upon which their wealth depended. Following a min-

Hermes,
Gertrude. See
Agar, Eileen for
sidebar.

ing accident in 1927, Gwendoline wrote: "We *must* do something for these brave men who risk their lives by day & night & keep us in luxury. We've *got* to build Jerusalem somewhere or other in the Rhondda." Together with their brother David, they sought to repay this debt through donations to causes such as the campaigns against tuberculosis and to improve working-class housing. Because the sisters were recognized as extremely generous towards good causes, they constantly received appeals for aid, and in 1924 Gwendoline ruefully observed: "we are fast coming to the conclusion that indiscriminate, wholesale giving of money or things is bad in the extreme & does much more harm than good." The sisters were earnestly concerned that their money should be well spent, and went to some length to ensure this. A minor but characteristic instance occurred when they resolved to help a young Welsh soldier who had tried to save the life of their nephew Mike, who was killed in action in Holland in 1944. Visiting the soldier's mother, they ascertained that he was fond of gardening and set him up in business as a market gardener. Notwithstanding the sisters' wealth, their expenditure seems to have remained fairly constant and was probably limited to the interest of their investments.

Although Gwendoline and Margaret regularly consulted Hugh Blaker, he was not the architect of their collection, but rather an adviser who facilitated access to the art world and confirmed their developing tastes. In January 1925, shortly before she ceased acquiring works of art, Gwendoline observed "the great joy of collecting anything is to do it *yourself,* with expert opinion granted, but one does like to choose for oneself. All the time we have been collecting our pictures we have never bought one without having seen it or at least a photograph before purchasing." The greatest financial investment that the sisters made in an individual artist was the £26,732, which they spent on eight oil paintings by J.M.W. Turner. Fashionable Barbizon school painters were almost as expensive; six oils by Corot cost £15,156 and eight by Millet £18,788. The prices of contemporary French artists were more modest, and the sisters spent £12,845 on six Rodin sculptures and £11,530 on nine Monet oils. At a time when the reputation of the Post-Impressionists remained hotly debated, they secured a trio of oils by Cézanne for £5,750, and a major landscape by Van Gogh for £2,020. By comparison, the generally indifferent old master paintings that the sisters acquired from Hugh Blaker in 1919–22 seem distinctly expensive. The French pictures and sculpture

constitute but one major element in the Davies collection, but its reputation as a whole is ultimately dependent upon them. With the exception of the collection of Realist and Impressionist paintings assembled by the Irishman Sir Hugh Lane in 1905–13, the Davies sisters formed the first collection of avant-garde French art in the United Kingdom. Samuel Courtauld, who began his own remarkable collection in 1923, acknowledged his debt to their example.

In their settlement of a colony of Belgian refugee artists in Aberystwyth and their development of Gregynog Hall as an arts center, the Davies sisters were inspired by the Arts and Crafts Movement, which flourished in late Victorian England. Designers such as E.W. Gimson and C.R. Ashby established workshops in rural settings from 1895 to 1902, providing precedents for such a foundation, while the Gregynog Press itself was modelled upon the Kelmscot Press, founded by William Morris in 1890. Although there were antecedents for many of the Davies sisters' activities, their range remains extraordinary. Gwendoline alluded to their cultural aspirations for the Welsh people in July 1924: "We have led the Welsh horse to the clearest brook we could possibly get, yet he has only tossed his head & walked straight through, stirring up all the mud & stones he could in doing so—He is so self-complacent, so self-sufficient—so ignorant—how are we ever to convince him that he is thirsty?" In short, the Davies sisters sought nothing less than to reform the entire artistic life of Wales through the visual arts, music, and literature. They were only partially successful in this objective, but their achievements were spectacular and their ambition remains an inspiration.

SOURCES:

Charles, R.L., and John Ingamells. *Catalogue of the Margaret S. Davies Bequest.* Cardiff: National Museum of Wales, 1963.

Evans, Mark. *Impressions of Venice from Turner to Monet.* Cardiff and London: National Museum of Wales/Lund Humphries, 1992.

Gregynog. Edited by G.T. Hughes, P. Morgan, and J.G. Thomas. Cardiff: University of Wales Press, 1977.

Harrop, Dorothy A. *A History of the Gregynog Press.* Pinner, Middlesex: Private Libraries Association, 1980.

Ingamells, John. *The Davies Collection of French Art.* Cardiff: National Museum of Wales, 1967.

Parrott, Ian. *The Spiritual Pilgrims.* Narberth & Tenby, Pembrokeshire: H.G. Walters, 1969.

Shen, Lindsay. "Philanthropic Furnishing: Gregynog Hall, Powys," in *Furniture History.* Vol. 21, 1995, pp. 217–235.

Steegman, John. *Catalogue of the Gwendoline E. Davies Bequest.* Cardiff: National Museum of Wales, 1952.

Unpublished papers at the National Library of Wales and the National Museum of Wales.

Vincintelli, Moira. "The Davies Family and Belgian Refugee Artists & Musicians in Wales," in *The National Library of Wales Journal*. Vol. 23, 1981–82, pp. 227–232.

—— and Anna Hale. *Catalogue of the Early Studio Pottery in the Collections of University College of Wales Aberystwyth*. Aberystwyth 1986.

White, Eirene, Lady. *The Ladies of Gregynog*. Newtown, Powys: University of Wales Press, 1985.

Dr. Mark L. Evans, Assistant Keeper (Fine Art), Department of Art, National Museum and Gallery of Cardiff, Cathays Park, Cardiff, Wales

Davies, Lilian May (1915—)

Duchess of Halland. Name variations: Princess Lilian May of Sweden. Born on August 30, 1915, in Swansea, Wales; daughter of William John Davies and Gladys Mary (Curran) Davies; married Walter Ivan Craig, on September 27, 1940 (divorced); married Bertil Gustaf Oscar Bernadotte (1912–1997), prince of Sweden and duke of Halland, on December 7, 1976.

Davies, Mandy Rice (b. 1944).

See Keeler, Christine for sidebar.

Davies, Margaret (1884–1963).

See Davies, Gwendoline and Margaret.

Davies, Margaret Llewelyn

(1861–1944)

British radical and women's rights advocate. Born in Marylebone, England, in 1861; died in 1944; daughter of John Llewelyn Davies and Mary (Crampton) Llewelyn Davies; niece of *Emily Davies (1830–1921); attended Queen's College, London, and Girton College, Cambridge.

Influenced by her father, a cleric with Christian Socialist connections, and her mother, a suffragist, Margaret Davies became a lifelong advocate for women. A member of the Women's Co-operative Guild for 33 years, Davies championed a minimum wage for women co-operative employees, equal divorce rights for women, and improved maternity care and benefits. She also helped found the International Women's Co-operative Guild in 1921 and served as the first woman president of the Co-operative Congress in 1922. Her numerous publications include *Maternity: Letters from Working Women*, an influential book detailing experiences of childbirth and rearing. A supporter of the Russian Revolution, Davies was also chair of the Society for Cultural Relations with the USSR (1924–28).

Davies, Marion (1897–1961)

American film star of the 1920s and 1930s whose relationship with newspaper magnate William Randolph Hearst eclipsed her career. Born Marion Cecilia Douras on January 3, 1897, in Brooklyn, New York; died on September 22, 1961; youngest of four daughters and one son of Bernard (a lawyer and politician) and Rose (Reilly) Douras; attended public school in Brooklyn and the convent of the Sacred Heart, Hastings, New York; married Horace G. Brown (a merchant marine officer), on October 31, 1951.

Films: Runaway Romany (1918); Beatrice Fairfax (serial, 1918); Cecilia of the Pink Roses (1918); The Burden of Proof (1918); The Belle of New York (1919); Getting Mary Married (1919); The Dark Star (1919); The Cinema Murder (1919); April Folly (1920); The Restless Sex (1920); Buried Treasure (1921); Enchantment (1921); The Bride's Play (1922); Beauty's Worth (1922); The Young Diana (1922); When Knighthood Was in Flower (1922); Adam and Eva (1923); Little Old New York (1923); Yolanda (1924); Janice Meredith (1924); Zander the Great (1925); Lights of Old Broadway (1925); Beverley of Graustark (1926); The Red Mill (1927); Tillie the Toiler (1927); Quality Street (1927); The Fair Co-ed (1927); The Patsy (1928); The Cardboard Lover (1928); Show People (1928); Marianne (1929); The Hollywood Revue of 1929 (1929); Not So Dumb (1930); The Florodora Girl (1930); The Bachelor Father (1931); It's a Wise Child (1931); Five and Ten (1931); Polly of the Circus (1932); Blondie of the Follies (1932); Peg o' My Heart (1933); Going Hollywood (1933); Operator 13 (1934); Page Miss Glory (1935); Hearts Divided (1936); Cain and Mabel (1936); Ever Since Eve (1936).

Marion Davies may be remembered as much for her 30-year relationship with newspaper magnet William Randolph Hearst as she is for her movie career, which encompassed the heyday of the silents and the transition into talkies. From 1918, when Davies was just gaining recognition as a young "Ziegfeld girl," Hearst dominated her life and career, not only selecting her roles and financing her movies but also backing each film with favorable publicity from his vast newspaper empire. Ironically, as her benefactor, Hearst may have undermined her career, because the question of whether or not she could have attained stardom on her own was to color her every accomplishment. Although a gifted comedian and one of the most popular women in Hollywood, Davies was her own worst critic. "All my life I wanted to have tal-

ent," she wrote in her autobiography *The Times We Had*. "Finally I had to admit there was nothing there. I was no *Sarah Bernhardt.*" Among the many who believed that Davies had more than enough talent to maintain her career without assistance was Orson Welles, whose contro-versial movie *Citizen Kane* (written by Herman J. Mankiewicz, a frequent guest of Hearst and Davies at the San Simeon mansion) caricatured the Hearst-Davies affair. "Marion Davies was one of the most delightfully accomplished come-diennes in the whole history of the screen,"

Welles wrote in 1975. "She would have been a star if Hearst had never happened. She was also a delightful and very considerable person."

A precocious and spirited child, Marion Davies was the youngest of five children of Bernard and **Rose Douras**. Her three sisters—**Ethel Douras, Rose Douras,** and **Reine Douras (Lederer)**—all had brief stage careers. A brother Charles died in a drowning accident when Marion was a baby. Her education was complicated by a childhood stutter that would remain with her throughout her life, eventually becoming a disarming asset. After several public schools refused to take her, Davies was sent away to a convent school in Hastings, New York. During her weekends at home, she studied ballet with her sisters and, beginning in the summer of 1912, took tap-dancing lessons for a year or so, although she lacked concentration and believed that daily practice was bad for her system. Her earliest stage appearances were in the "pony" (chorus) lines of a few small-time reviews and in a musical version of Maeterlinck's *The Bluebird*. By 1914, now a stunning blonde with a slightly wicked smile, Davies began to draw attention. That year, she made her Broadway debut as one of some 500 hoofers in a show called *Chin-Chin* and embarked on the frenetic social life of a popular New York chorine.

> [Marion Davies] was never one of Hearst's possessions: he was always her suitor, and she was the precious treasure of his heart for more than thirty years, until his last breath of life. Theirs is truly a love story. Love is not the subject of *Citizen Kane*.
>
> —Orson Welles

Throughout 1915, Davies appeared in a number of revues. Her affair with the 52-year-old Hearst began when she was 19, during the run of *The Ziegfeld Follies of 1916*, and was at first kept secret because Hearst's wife **Millicent Hearst**, a former showgirl herself, was pregnant. During the early courtship, Davies saw other men, but by 1917, when she was put on the Hearst payroll, she had become his mistress. For Hearst, a complicated and inhibited man in spite of his immense wealth and power, Davies was the perfect foil. Providing the warmth and humanity he lacked, she became his intermediary with the outside world. Hearst idolized Davies, giving her everything she wanted, except the opportunity to become his wife. Millicent would not agree to a divorce on religious grounds and remained very much in the picture.

Hearst divided his time between Davies, his wife and sons, and his business and political dealings, which meant that Davies was on her own for long periods.

Davies' career in the theater continued on the upswing, resulting in a number of film offers. In 1918, with the backing of her ex-brother-in-law, George Lederer (who had been married to her sister Reine), Davies made her first film, *Runaway Romany*, a poorly written, poorly executed movie even by the standards of early feature-film production. Even so, after viewing an early screening, Hearst announced that he would make her a star, and from that day forward he took over every aspect of her career. Her 1918 film, *Cecilia of the Pink Roses*, was given a less than enthusiastic review in *The New York Times*, but Hearst's *New York American* ran a three-column headline announcing the arrival of a new cinema star: "Marion Davies Wins Triumph in Cecilia." Each Hearst review outdid the previous one, a pattern that would continue for over 20 years.

In 1919, Hearst formed an agreement with Paramount to release Davies' pictures, which were produced through his Cosmopolitan Production Company. The films that followed, including *The Dark Star* (1919), *April Folly* (1920), *The Restless Sex* (1920), and *Buried Treasure* (1921), all lost money, mostly due to Hearst's enormous production budgets. In April 1920, Davies made her last stage appearance in Ed Wynn's *Carnival*. The film *Enchantment* followed in 1921, her best to date as well as *Photoplay's* pick as best picture of the month. In 1922, Hearst spent an extraordinary $1.5 million to produce *When Knighthood Was in Flower* and commissioned Victor Herbert to write two songs to accompany the film. Davies' performance as *Mary Tudor was praised in both Hearst and non-Hearst papers alike, particularly for its comic moments. *Louella Parsons, writing for the Hearst rival *New York Telegraph*, saw great potential in Davies and posed a question to Hearst within her review: "Why don't you give Marion Davies a chance?" Davies solidified her reputation with her next film, *Little Old New York* (1923), which premiered in a theater Hearst bought and renovated especially for the event.

In 1924, Cosmopolitan moved to the Goldwyn lot. When Goldwyn subsequently merged with Metro to form MGM, Cosmopolitan went along. Realizing the value of the Hearst association, MGM head Louis B. Mayer financed all of Cosmopolitan's films and paid Davies an unprecedented $10,000 a week. The Goldwyn partnership produced several moderately profitable movies: *Yolanda* (1924), *Zander the Great* (1925), and *Lights of Old Broadway* (1925), which resulted in a growing following for Davies. However, Hearst continued to limit her roles to fragile, virginal heroines, even though she was more suited to gutsy comic roles. It is generally agreed that only a few of Davies' films ever fully displayed her gifts as an actress, among them two directed by King Vidor in 1928: *The Patsy*, in which she impersonated *Pola Negri, *May Murray, and *Lillian Gish; and *Show People*, a burlesque chronicling the career of a movie star known for slapstick who eventually triumphs as a dramatic actress.

In addition to idolizing Davies and controlling her career, Hearst provided her with a luxurious lifestyle. She divided her time between her own beach house at Santa Monica (the largest house on the southern California beach, with some 15 bathrooms), a 14-room bungalow provided for her on the MGM lot, and several Hearst properties, including the monument to his mother *Phoebe Apperson Hearst, the castle at San Simeon, which was designed over a 27-year period by *Julia Morgan, a San Francisco architect trained in classical architecture at École des Beaux-Arts in Paris. Perched atop La Cuesta Encantade (The Enchanted Hill), overlooking the California coastline, the Mediterranean Revival palace and its surrounding grounds (including several "castlettes," an indoor and outdoor pool, and a private zoo) was Davies' vacation home during the 1920s; there, she and Hearst entertained a steady stream of royalty, heads of state, artists, authors, and film stars. It was not unusual for upwards of 70 Hollywood guests to appear on a weekend, transported from the city on Hearst's own train. Davies' extensive social life and the constant round of parties may have exacerbated a drinking problem that had begun in her teens and would eventually take its toll. Hearst, who was adamantly opposed to drinking, tried for years to get Davies to stop; it has been speculated, however, that he may have been the source of an underlying unhappiness that fueled her addiction.

In the 1920s, a social consciousness awakened in Davies that would eventually earn her a reputation as Hollywood's most generous star. In addition to her benevolence to family and friends, she contributed over $2 million to the Marion Davies Children's Clinic, which was established in 1932. The facility was later expanded and became part of the UCLA Medical

❧➤ Hearst, Millicent (1882–1974)

*American socialite. Name variations: Millicent Willson; Mrs. William Randolph Hearst. Born in 1882; died at age 92 at her home in New York City in December 1974; daughter of George H. Willson (a popular vaudeville performer); married William Randolph Hearst (a newspaper publisher), on April 28, 1903; children: five sons, including George Hearst, John Randolph Hearst, and twins Elbert Willson Hearst and Randolph Apperson Hearst (b. 1915); grandmother of **Patricia Campbell Hearst**, known as Patty Hearst.*

As members of a dancing group called "The Merry Maidens," 16-year-old Millicent Willson and her older sister **Anita Willson** were appearing in *The Girl from Paris* at the Herald Square Theater when they met William Randolph Hearst. At first, Hearst was seen squiring both sisters around Manhattan, and there was speculation as to which he would marry. In 1903, the 40-year-old publisher wed 21-year-old Millicent. Twelve years and five sons later, Hearst became infatuated with another chorine, *Marion Davies.

As the marriage broke down publicly (Hearst gave up the pretext of a happy family life and was always in the company of Davies), Millicent Hearst continued to hold her head high. She was a devoted war worker during World War I, heading the women's division of the Mayor's Committee on National Defense in New York. Even though she would not grant her husband a divorce, Millicent remained on friendly terms with William, and they occasionally consulted on business and family matters until his death in 1951.

In her autobiography *Every Secret Thing*, Patty Hearst writes that during her 1974 ordeal in the hands of the Symbionese Liberation Army, as she was locked in a closet for 57 days, she would think of her grandmother Millicent, then in her 80s, whom she called Mamalee: "She was a very special person in my life, whom my sisters and I would visit for ten days or two weeks every summer in Southampton, New York. Sitting in the dark in that hot sweaty closet, I could visualize Mamalee's big, beautiful house and its huge rolling lawn just off the Atlantic Ocean, . . . and the fresh flowers throughout the house, clipped daily from the garden. We would go bicycle riding, swim, or play tennis for most of the day and then join Mamalee and her sister, Aunt Anita, who lived with her there, for a late-afternoon tea."

SOURCES:
Hearst, Patricia Campbell, with Alvin Moscow. *Every Secret Thing*. NY: Doubleday, 1982.

SUGGESTED READING:
Swanberg, W.A. *Citizen Hearst*. NY: Scribner, 1961.

School. She also contributed large sums to other institutions helping children of the poor. On a more personal level, she was also directly involved in the lives of those around her, providing for the education of the daughter of her cook and helping a movie electrician by supplying funds for his son's medical expenses. When Hearst faced financial difficulties during the late 1930s, Davies would give him $1 million of her own fortune.

Davies' last silent movie, *The Cardboard Lover* (1928), was warmly received, but her career was about to take a dip with the advent of sound. Before they heard her speak, moviegoers heard Davies sing in MGM's star-studded extravaganza, *The Hollywood Revue of 1929*. Her next film, *Marianne* (1929), featured her delightful imitations of Sarah Bernhardt and Maurice Chevalier, which were added to the movie as an afterthought on the last day of filming. In 1934, after Davies was passed over for several roles, she moved to Warner Bros., where she starred in *Page Miss Glory* (1935), playing comic scenes opposite *Patsy Kelly. But her age, now 38, was beginning to work against her. Her film *Hearts Divided* (1936) was a stretch, as was *Cain and Mabel* (1936), with Clark Gable. *Newsweek* quipped: "Clark Gable and Marion Davies fit in this picture like a fat hand squeezed into a small glove."

When Davies made her last picture *Ever Since Eve* in 1936, the Hearst empire was struggling financially and several unflattering biographies had appeared about the newspaper tycoon. The film received a scathing review from Frank Nugent of *The New York Times:* "The film comes so close to being the year's worst. We won't quibble. Let's call it the worst." Later, Davies would make her last professional appearance as an actress in a "Lux Radio Theater" broadcast of *Peg o' My Heart*. Although Davies was subsequently offered the role of the mother in *Claudia,* Hearst refused to let her take a character part, especially that of a character who dies.

Hearst, forced to cut back on spending, lived relatively quietly with Davies at San Simeon until the bombing of Pearl Harbor. Fearing the castle might be shelled by the Japanese, they then moved to Wyntoon, a residence in the middle of a wilderness, 700 miles from Hollywood on the Oregon line. Davies referred to Wyntoon as "Spittoon" and found the exile intolerable. In 1944, they returned to San Simeon, where she once again immersed herself in Hollywood's social scene. As Hearst's health declined, Davies was frequently escorted by Horace G. Brown, a merchant marine officer who was divorced from **Grace Tibbett.**

William Randolph Hearst died on the morning of August 14, 1951, while Davies was sleeping. Having been given a strong barbiturate by one of his attending doctors, she awoke to learn that Hearst's sons had already removed his body for burial. (There were published rumors of a conspiracy on the part of the Hearst sons and corporate executives to drug Marion to get her out of the way when death came.) "His body was gone, whoosh, like that," she told a reporter. "Old W.R. was gone, the boys were gone. I was alone. Do you realize what they did? They stole a possession of mine. He belonged to me. I loved him for thirty-two years and now he was gone. I couldn't even say good-bye." Although omitted from his will, Davies benefitted from a stock agreement that brought her an estimated $150,000 yearly income.

Ten weeks after Hearst's death, Davies married Captain Horace Brown in Las Vegas. The marriage was not a happy one; there were several separations and rumors of divorce, though it never materialized. Through the years, Davies enjoyed several successful real-estate ventures, as well as a profitable return from an investment on the musical *Kismet,* which ran 583 performances on Broadway and spawned countless roadshows and revivals. In 1960, she appeared briefly on *Hedda Hopper's television show "This Is My Hollywood," which included a tour of her Beverly Hills home, but her later years were marred by bouts of depression and increased drinking. In the summer of 1960, after refusing surgery for what would turn out to be a malignant growth in her jaw, she attended the Democratic National Convention, turning her house and the houses of her relatives over to the Kennedy family. After President John F. Kennedy was elected, she attended the inaugural ceremonies and ball. In the spring of 1961, Davies entered the hospital and underwent surgery for malignant osteomyelitis. Although the operation was initially successful, she later fell and broke her leg, severely complicating her recovery.

Marion Davies died on September 22, 1961, and was buried in the Douras family crypt in Hollywood Cemetery. Shortly after her death, film critics rediscovered her as a genuine comic performer. In a 1971 article on the making of *Citizen Kane,* film critic *Pauline Kael asserted that "Marion Davies had been a major leading lady who had not needed the drum-beaters of the Hearst empire to remain in the movies." The affirmation of her talent would no doubt have pleased Davies, who is said to have come to terms with both her career and her controversial relationship with Hearst before her death. Shortly before her final coma, she called her husband

Horace over to her bed and told him that she had no regrets.

SOURCES:

Anderson, Earl, "Marion Davies," in *Films in Review.* Vol. XXIII, no. 6. June–July 1972.

Davies, Marion. *The Times We Had: Life with William Randolph Hearst.* Indianapolis: Bobbs-Merrill, 1975.

Guiles, Fred Lawrence. *Marion Davies.* NY: McGraw-Hill, 1972.

Shipman, David. *The Great Movie Stars: The Golden Years.* Boston: Little, Brown, 1970.

Barbara Morgan,
Melrose, Massachusetts

Davies, Moll.

See Gwynn, Nell for sidebar.

Davis, Adelle (1904–1974)

Pioneering and controversial American nutritionist who was an early proponent of a "health food" diet. Name variations: (pseudonym) Jane Dunlop. Born Daisie Adelle Davis on February 25, 1904, in Lizton, Indiana; died in California on May 31, 1974, of bone cancer; youngest of five children of Charles Eugene Davis and Harriet (McBroom) Davis; graduated from the University of California at Berkeley, 1927; University of Southern California, Master's in biochemistry, 1938; married George Edward Leisey, in 1946 (divorced 1953); married Frank V. Sieglinger, in 1960; children: (first marriage) two adopted, George Davis Leisey and Barbara Adelle Leisey.

Established a private nutritional counseling practice (1931); began publishing books calling for nutritional reform (1940s) and became the nation's leading advocate of the health benefits of foods grown without pesticides, chemical fertilizers, and extensive refining; became a leading figure in the growing "health food" movement, but her work came under increased scientific criticism, particularly her claims that most social ills were the direct result of poor nutrition (1960s); her lax methodology and the discovery of hundreds of errors in her books called her reputation into question, though she remained a popular media figure and continued to espouse her theories freely.

In 1942, as many of America's young were marching off to World War II, a slim volume on a subject about which the nation had little time to think appeared on the bookshelves of school libraries. Called *Vitality Through Planned Nutrition,* it urged readers to pay closer attention to the food they were eating. Written by a "consulting nutritionist" named Adelle Davis, the book claimed that scientifically planned nutrition could assure vitality and good health well past middle-age and warned against the blandishments of "food racketeers" who "sprinkle their vocabulary freely with scientific terms which are not understood by the untrained person." The book's author could hardly have imagined at the time that, 20 years later, the same charge would be made against her.

Daisie Adelle Davis had every right to consider herself among the well-trained. The youngest of five daughters born to Charles and Harriet Davis, on February 25, 1904, she was one of the relatively few women in the early part of the century who held degrees from two of the nation's leading universities, in "household science" and in biochemistry. Both were the result of a fascination with food that began in early childhood, and which she suspected had something to do with her mother's death when Davis was only 17 months old. "Maybe I wanted to make up for the good mother I never had, to become the good mother myself," she once said. She often claimed that the strict upbringing Charles Davis gave to his youngest daughter was because he had wanted a boy; she described her childhood as lonely and unhappy.

> *A*mericans are the most abundantly fed people in the world, but their diets are far from the best nutritionally.
>
> —**Adelle Davis**

But there was always food, fresh from the fertile Indiana soil of the Davis farm. Adelle said she could cook before she could read and had to ask her sisters to recite aloud the recipes from the *Fanny Farmer cookbook that was the unofficial bible of the Davis kitchen. Throughout her public schooling, Davis repeatedly won 4-H ribbons for her canning and baking skills and received her best grades in home economics, though she remembered the pain of these years just as well as the recognition. "I was round and roly-poly and I felt so alone," she once remembered. "I felt so hated inside." The first thing she did upon leaving home for Purdue University in 1923 was to drop the name her father had given her: Daisie. It reminded her, she said, of pigs and cows.

As if going off to college weren't bold enough for a young woman in the early 1920s, Davis distanced herself even further from her childhood memories by moving to California, where she continued her studies at the University of California at Berkeley and received her bachelor's degree in 1927. Then she crossed the country to New York, where she acquired more training in dietetics at New York City's Bellevue and

Fordham hospitals before finding a job as the superintendent of nutrition for the Yonkers, New York, school system. Throughout her training, Davis became convinced that Americans weren't paying enough attention to their diets and were, in fact, making themselves sick by committing what she later called "slow murders in the kitchen." So convincing were her arguments that she was able to set up a successful nutritional counseling practice in Manhattan with several prominent obstetricians as clients.

By 1931, Davis had moved her counseling practice back to California and had begun studies at the University of Southern California that would lead to her master's degree in biochemistry in 1938. Her research further convinced her of the importance of scientific principles of nutrition, especially the value of Vitamin A in helping the body to resist disease. Her first published work, in fact, was a 1932 promotional brochure for a milk company that extolled the virtues of the high Vitamin A content of her client's product. Two more privately printed brochures followed, *Optimal Health* in 1935 and *You Can Stay Well* in 1939. But a Depression-ridden America was having a hard enough time finding sufficient food to go around, leaving Davis' theories and rallying cries for better nutrition largely unheeded. *Vitality Through Planned Nutrition,* published in 1942 while the nation's attention was focused on the war, contained an entire chapter devoted to Vitamin A in which Davis urged her readers to consume large doses of carotene-rich vegetables, drink at least a quart of milk a day, and take substantial quantities of supplements. "Massive doses of Vitamin A have caused no ill effects," she assured her public. "A group of babies fed 166,666 international units of carotene daily for five months suffered no ill effects," though she offered no attribution for the study to which she referred. Claiming that the body could easily store excess amounts of the nutrient and that what could not be stored was destroyed in the intestinal tract, Davis confidently asserted that "it seems wise to err on the side of taking too much rather than too little."

Postwar prosperity and its resulting "baby boom" meant America had more mouths to feed than ever. Agricultural scientists began to introduce the first of scores of newly synthesized chemical fertilizers and additives designed to boost production, but Adelle Davis saw danger ahead and once again took up her pen to write the first of her four "Let's" books, *Let's Cook It Right,* published in 1947. It was followed by *Let's Have Healthy Children* (1951), *Let's Eat Right to Keep Fit* (1954), and *Let's Get Well* (1965). The books, still in print, sold well over ten million copies in various revisions during Davis' lifetime; *Let's Eat Right to Keep Fit* alone went through 33 hardcover editions before a paperback version finally appeared in 1970. Throughout the series, Davis' sound warnings that chemicals and over-refining were destroying the nutritional value of America's food became increasingly strident. She called most cookbooks "treatises on how to produce diseases," claimed that "the whole country is at the mercy of people making money off our food," and urged Americans to eat unprocessed, unrefined foods that had been grown without chemical pesticides or additives.

A growing number of Americans were ready to listen. By the mid-1950s, the undercurrent of dissatisfaction with mainstream America's smug comforts began erupting in various forms, California being one of the most active breeding grounds for questioners of prevailing social values. Davis' call for returning to natural ways of eating and living fit neatly into these groups' beliefs. Her growing fame was not without its disadvantages, however, as her claims came under increasingly critical scrutiny from the scientific community of which she still considered herself a member. "In the early days, I'd get so discouraged I'd cry," she once recalled. "For years, people thought I was a kooky crank."

There were problems in her personal life, too. Although the initial stability of her first marriage to George Leisey in 1946 had marked the beginning of the "Let's" series, the marriage was foundering by the early 1950s. The adoption of two children, George Davis Leisey and **Barbara Adelle Leisey,** failed to help matters, and in 1953, the couple divorced. That same year, Davis began seven years of psychotherapy under three successive analysts, the first two male. "Then I realized I needed to have a good mother figure, too, so I found a woman," she remembered years later. "Believe me, it was the best money I ever spent." She said that her work with Jungian, Reichian, and Freudian techniques all showed that she had deep-seated fears of failure that she traced to her father's disappointment at not having a son. "A lot of us do things because of neurotic patterns," she said. "Unless you've had a lot of deep analysis you don't see that."

Despite the rigors and pain of her therapy, Davis kept up an active writing and lecturing schedule and accepted a growing number of patients at her nutritional counseling practice. One of them was a retired lawyer and accountant named Frank Sieglinger, who came to her for advice in 1958, the year she closed her practice under pressure from her growing popularity. The two were married in 1960, providing the anchor Davis felt she had been missing. "He wears well, my Frank does," she told an interviewer in 1971, after 11 years of marriage. "He says he doesn't have much to do with Adelle Davis, but he likes Mrs. Sieglinger just fine."

The 1960s marked the peak of Davis' fame as "the High Priestess of the new nutrition religion" as *Time* called her. But she steadfastly insisted that her theories were hardly a fad. "Up to fifty years ago," she said, "organic food was the only kind anybody knew of. Time was in this country that when you opened your mouth, you put in good food. That was when the real brains got developed—Washington, Jefferson, people like that. These days, we don't grow enough skulls to put a brain in anymore." Such pithy observations, coupled with her bright blue eyes, gray hair, and deep voice (she sang tenor in her church choir) made her a favorite with the media, for whom she was always willing to provide a pearl of natural-grown wisdom. Her "You are what you eat" entered the national lexicon, and she became even more of a cult figure when she admitted experimenting with LSD in the late 1950s, "when it was still legal," she was careful to point out. "It scared the bejesus out of me," she said, "but I learned so much!" (She recounted her experiences in 1961's *Exploring Inner Space*, written under the name Jane Dunlop.)

Davis continued to lose ground, however, with her medical colleagues. As the nation's "food guru" was adopted by nature movements, ashrams, communes, and other groups then considered on the American fringe, Davis' claims seemed to be more and more out of step with accepted medical knowledge. By the mid-1960s, she was asserting that such disparate misfortunes as impotence, alcoholism, drug addiction, along with a host of social ills—from high divorce rates and spiraling crime rates to economic upheavals and racial tensions—were the direct result of bad eating. In numerous revisions of her "Let's" books, she continued to recommend massive doses of vitamins A, D, and E, despite evidence of toxicity leading to some of the very diseases they were supposed to prevent. She claimed that epilepsy could be cured simply with treatments of large doses of magnesium; advised readers that potassium chloride, highly toxic in large doses, could cure kidney disorders; and warned that pasteurized milk was dangerous, especially for pregnant women who ran the risk, she said,

of having their babies born with cataracts. Such statements enraged the mainstream medical profession and detracted from Davis' main message of good, sensible nutrition. "Let them call me anything they want," Davis responded. "I have facts to back up everything I say."

After a closer examination, Davis' critics disagreed. Dr. Russell Randall, who headed the Medical College of Virginia's Department of Renal Diseases in the late 1960s and early 1970s, took issue with her recommendation of potassium chloride as a treatment for nephrosis and baby's colic. "This could kill them," he said in print. "A person with bad kidney function taking her advice could have a cardiac arrest." Davis denied she had advised the use of such a dangerous chemical, but the edition of *Let's Have Healthy Children* used by a Florida couple to treat their two-month-old colicky son did, indeed, contain such advice. After several days of Davis' prescribed three grams a day, the baby died. Davis' publishers settled quietly out of court.

Another leading physician, Dr. Edward Rynearson, professor emeritus at the Mayo Clinic, also took Davis to task in print, charging that her books were "larded with inaccuracies, misquotations, and unsubstantiated statements" and speculated that the only reason her books were so popular was that Americans "loved hogwash." An analysis of one of her books, he said, turned up an average of one factual error per page, with scores of inaccuracies found in the references, and he called attention to permanent stunting of a young girl's growth after her parents claimed they had followed Davis' advice and given her massive doses of vitamin A. "I have squillions of references to research that indicates or proves my statements are true," Davis said. "Most physicians have not studied nutrition and there isn't one medical school in the United States that teaches nutrition seriously." Nonetheless, in 1969, the White House Conference on Food, Nutrition and Health labelled her the single most harmful source of false information in the country; and, in 1972, the Chicago Nutrition Association placed three of her "Let's" books on its "not recommended" list. "Oh, these doctors with their mother problems!" Davis complained. "I guess they have to have someone to take it out on and I guess I'm as good as anyone."

Still, laudatory articles about her continued to appear in national publications, and she was relentlessly pursued by natural food restaurant chains, organic food producers, and vitamin makers to endorse their products—lucrative offers that she steadfastly refused, often citing religious grounds. "My church [The Church of Religious Science] believes that since you're part of God, you've got the power to function nobly, and therefore you'd better do it," she explained.

Her supporters said that Davis was the best proof of her theories' efficacy. In 1970, at age 66, she was playing tennis five days a week (singles, she stressed, because doubles didn't provide enough exercise), swimming every morning (naked, she recommended, which was better for the circulation), tending to the organic garden and orchards she and Frank had planted at their home in Palos Verdes Estates, California, and maintaining a heavy travel and lecture schedule. When a reporter from *Look* arrived to interview her, she whipped up an organic lunch of a fresh green salad, zucchini, cabbage cooked in milk, a filet of sole coated with powdered skim milk and wheat germ, and huge glasses of fresh, unpasteurized milk. "It was delicious," the reporter later wrote, "but on the way to the airport afterward I nearly exploded from the gas it produced." Davis recommended B vitamins and hydrochloric acid to help his digestion.

No one seemed more surprised than Davis when, in 1973, she shocked her millions of fans by announcing that she had been diagnosed with bone cancer, which she variously blamed on too many X-rays that had been taken for "insurance purposes" or on the processed foods she had eaten as a young woman, before her nutritional enlightenment. Reminded by a reporter of the statement in one of her books that she had never known a single adult who drank a quart of milk a day to develop cancer, she curtly replied, "Well, I was wrong," and stressed that her illness in no way disproved any of her nutritional beliefs. Certainly, although her health was weakened, her enthusiasm was not. "Frankly, I'd be very surprised if I died of cancer," she said. "I'm eating better than ever and my resistance is high." She admitted having undergone an operation for her disease earlier in the year but refused to say what self-prescribed regimen of vitamins and minerals she was following. "What's it anybody's business what I'm taking," she said, perhaps recalling the criticisms that still plagued her, "unless I have proof whether it will work?"

Because of the increasing discomfort caused by her cancer, Davis curtailed her lecture schedule but continued to make television appearances and grant interviews, looking her usual bright-eyed, grandmotherly self. But by the winter of 1974, the pain was too much even for Davis. She returned to her home for the last time and died on May 31, 1974, aged 70.

Although many of Davis' pronouncements are still in dispute, an equal number have since formed the basis for ongoing revelations of the delicate balance between body chemistry and good health that mark contemporary nutritional theory. Perhaps more important, Adelle Davis' remarkable resilience and determination in the face of challenges to her work and, ultimately, her very life, was exemplary. In one of her last interviews that determination was still very much in evidence. "Don't worry about me," she called out cheerily as the reporter was leaving. "I've had a good life, a rich life," she said, "and there's plenty more to go."

SOURCES:
Davis, Adelle. *Vitality Through Planned Nutrition.* NY: Macmillan, 1942.
Howard, Jane. "Earth Mother to the Food Faddists," in *Life.* October 22, 1971.
Poppy, John. "Adelle Davis and the New Nutrition Religion," in *Look.* December 15, 1970.
Sicherman, Barbara, and Carol Hurd Green, eds. *Notable American Women: A Biographical Dictionary.* Cambridge, MA: Belknap Press, 1980.
Wixen, Jean. "Ill With Cancer, Adelle Davis Still Sticks to Her Preaching," in the *Chicago Sun Times.* December 23 and 24, 1973.

Norman Powers, writer-producer, Chelsea Lane Productions, New York

Davis, Angela (1944—)

African-American revolutionary activist, scholar, and Communist who gained fame in the early 1970s when prosecutors claimed she had assisted a courtroom rebellion by radical black prisoners. Name variations: Angela Y. Davis. Born Angela Yvonne Davis on January 26, 1944, in Birmingham, Alabama; daughter of B. Frank Davis (a gas station owner) and Sallye B. Davis (a teacher); attended Birmingham public schools until 1959, and Elizabeth Irwin High School in New York City, 1959–61; graduated Brandeis University, 1961–65, B.A. magna cum laude and Phi Beta Kappa; attended Goethe University, Frankfurt, Germany, 1965–67; attended University of California at San Diego, 1967–69; married Hilton Braithwaite, in 1980 (divorced several years later); no children.

Lived in New York (1959–61); attended Eighth World Festival for Youth and Students in Helsinki (1962); spent year in France (1963–64); joined Communist Party (July 1968); traveled to Cuba (1969); taught at UCLA (1969–70); went underground (August 9, 1970); arrested in a New York motel (October 13, 1970); acquitted of all charges (June 4, 1972); served as co-chair of the National Alliance Against Racist and Political Repression (1973); was full-time lecturer, San Francisco State University (1978); was vice-presidential

candidate on the Communist Party ticket (1980 and 1984); served on board of directors, National Black Women's Health Project (1983); challenged Communist Party (1991); endorsed Committees of Correspondence (1992). Awards: Lenin Peace Prize (1979).

Selected publications: "Reflections on the Black Woman's Role in the Community of Slaves," in The Black Scholar (December 3, 1971, pp. 2–15); If They Come in the Morning (The Third Press, 1971); Women, Race and Class (Random House, 1981); Women, Culture and Politics *(Random House, 1989);* Blues Legacies and Black Feminism: Gertrude "Ma" Rainey, Bessie Smith, and Billie Holiday *(Pantheon, 1998).*

When Angela Davis, disguised in a wig and make-up, disappeared underground and fled from California in August 1970, she became only the third woman in U.S. history to be placed on the F.B.I.'s "Ten Most Wanted" list. Davis' decision to evade prosecution and adopt a clandestine existence was the last in a series of events stemming from her acts of solidarity with black prisoners. Her arrest in New York City two months later culminated in a highly publicized political trial that paradoxically made Davis the most well-known radical black woman in a period when a new generation of leftists considered the Communist Party, to which she belonged, moribund and discredited.

We must fight for your life as though it were our own—which it is—and render impassable with our bodies the corridor to the gas chamber. For, if they take you in the morning, they will be coming for us that night.
—**James Baldwin, "Open Letter to My Sister, Angela Y. Davis"**

Early in 1970, Davis became a vocal defender of George Jackson, John Clutchette, and Fleeta Drumgo, who were incarcerated in Soledad Prison, one of the toughest facilities in California. The Soledad Brothers, as the three became known, were black radicals accused of a prison murder. On January 13, 1970, a white guard, O.G. Wilson, had shot and killed three unarmed prisoners from his watchpost far above the prison yard when an altercation broke out between inmates. When a grand jury ruled that Wilson's actions had been "justifiable homicide," a spontaneous rebellion broke out in Soledad, and another guard who inadvertently stumbled upon an angry group of convicts was pushed over a railing to his death. There was no evidence that Jackson, Clutchette, and Drumgo committed the killing, and it appeared that they were being targeted simply because of their political views. They faced a death sentence.

Davis, who had been active in the black liberation movement for several years in Los Angeles, agreed to coordinate the efforts of the Soledad Brothers Defense Committee for all of L.A. She spoke before community groups and on dozens of campuses. In the course of the campaign, Davis became intimate with George Jack-

son, and the two expressed their love as much as they could through prison bars. Radicals saw in Jackson a symbol of the racist core of the American legal system. He had received a one-year-to-life sentence at age 18 simply for being in the car when his friend robbed $75 from a gas station. As of 1969, he had already served 10 years for the petty theft. Jackson developed revolutionary consciousness inside the prison system, and the publication of a collection of his letters, *Soledad Brother* (1970), gave him a literary reputation as an intelligent autodidact while unveiling to the world his feelings for Davis. "I'm thinking about you," he wrote to her on May 29, 1970. "I've done nothing else all day."

With the encouragement of George Jackson, Davis took his 17-year-old younger brother Jonathan under her wing. Jonathan admired his brother tremendously, embraced his radicalism, worked for his release, and was deeply angered by the injustice of the penal system. He also served as a bodyguard for Davis at a time when she was receiving persistent death threats. He therefore knew that Davis kept some guns in her closet. On August 7, 1970, Jonathan Jackson used those guns in an attempt to free three radical black prisoners—James McClain, Ruchell Magee, and William Christmas—from a trial in a courtroom in Marin County. He armed the convicts, took as hostages the judge, district attorney, and several jurors, and attempted to escape in a rented van that he had left parked outside. Bullets fired by law enforcement officers riddled the van, however, and Jonathan Jackson, the judge, McClain and Christmas were killed. Davis had been nowhere near the courthouse, but authorities sought to charge her with murder, kidnapping, and conspiracy to commit murder and rescue prisoners. On August 9, she vanished underground.

Racism, and the struggle against it, had shaped Davis' experience since her childhood in the segregationist South. Born in 1944 at the Children's Home Hospital in Birmingham, Alabama, Davis was the oldest of four children, including sister **Fania Davis** and brothers Benny and Reginald. (Ben later became a professional football player, and Fania was later active in defense efforts on Angela's behalf and would coauthor an article with her.) Davis' college-educated father Frank Davis had given up teaching high school and owned a service station in the black section of downtown Birmingham. **Sallye Davis,** her mother, was also a college graduate who, as a student in the 1930s, had been a leader of the Southern Negro Youth Congress and was involved in defense campaigns for the Scottsboro Boys, nine blacks unjustly accused of raping two white girls (*Ruby Bates and Victoria Price). The Davises had cordial friendships with black friends in Alabama and New York who had joined the Communist Party, some of whom went underground to avoid anticommunist repression in the 1950s.

When Davis was four, the family moved out of Birmingham's housing projects and into a Victorian house in a neighborhood electric with racism. In 1949, the area became known as "Dynamite Hill" when an explosion destroyed the home of a black minister and his wife who were the first to buy a house on the "white side" of Center Street. Davis attended inferior, segregated schools, but was a good student and enjoyed reading at the public library. At age 15, she was accepted by a scholarship program of the American Friends Service Committee to stay with a white family and attend school in New York. While living in Brooklyn with the family of Episcopalian Reverend William H. Melish, himself under criticism for his refusal to renounce the Soviet Union, Davis attended high school in Greenwich Village from 1959 to 1961.

At Elizabeth Irwin High School, uniquely progressive and experimental, left-wing students and teachers introduced Davis to socialist and communist writings. In her 1974 autobiography, Davis recalled the excitement she felt at the time to find that the analysis of capitalism in Marx and Engels' *Communist Manifesto* accounted for the social divisions of racism: "What had seemed a personal hatred of me, an inexplicable refusal of Southern whites to confront their own emotions, and a stubborn willingness of Blacks to acquiesce, became the inevitable consequence of a ruthless system which kept itself alive and well by encouraging spite, competition and the oppression of one people by another." Davis attended lectures by the Communist historian Herbert Aptheker and went to some meetings of Advance, a Communist Party youth organization.

In September 1961, she entered Brandeis University on a scholarship, as one of a handful of black students. In summer 1962, she attended the Eighth World Festival for Youth and Students in Helsinki, Finland, traveling to Paris and Geneva on the way. She majored in French literature and in 1963–64 spent her junior year at the Sorbonne in France on a special program. Meanwhile, the civil-rights movement for racial equality had revived throughout the South, and, while she was still in France, Davis learned that four girls she had known had died in the bombing of the 16th St. Baptist Church in Birmingham on September 15, 1963. The girls (known for years as the 🐦▶ **Birmingham Four**), **Denise McNair, Cynthia Wesley, Addie Mae Collins,** and **Carol Robertson,** who ranged in age from 11 to 14, were killed while attending Sunday School.

After her return to Brandeis, Davis began to attend lectures by the neo-Marxist philosopher Herbert Marcuse, and she took a graduate seminar from him on Kant's *Critique of Pure Reason.* An excellent student, Davis graduated magna cum laude and Phi Beta Kappa in 1965. Her work with Marcuse had interested her in philosophy, so she decided to attend Goethe University in Frankfurt, Germany, where she studied under critical theorists Theodor Adorno and Jürgen Habermas, among others. Davis attended rallies against the Vietnam War held by the German socialist student group, SDS, and visited East Germany for a May Day rally. In 1967, desiring to return to the U.S. and participate in the mushrooming radical movements, Davis decided to rejoin Marcuse, who had by then moved to the University of California at San Diego.

At UC San Diego, Davis helped establish a Black Student Union on campus and became active in campaigns centered in Los Angeles against police brutality. She joined the Black Panther Political Party (BPPP), a distinct group with a similar name to the Black Panther Party initiated by Huey P. Newton and Bobby Seale. The BPPP soon joined the Student Non-Violent Coordinating Committee (SNCC), a national group then in the process of collapse, and became its L.A. chapter. Davis resigned from the group when it expelled Franklin Alexander, a leading activist with whom Davis had worked closely, simply because he was a Communist. In July 1968, tired of the "irresolution, inconsistency and ineffectiveness" of the ad-hoc left, as she

🐦▶ Birmingham Four

Denise McNair (11), **Cynthia Wesley** (14), **Addie Mae Collins** (14), and **Carol Robertson** (14) were in the Sixteenth Street Baptist church basement in Birmingham, Alabama, preparing to attend Sunday school and the monthly Youth Day service, when a bomb went off, killing all four (September 15, 1963). For years, they were known as the Birmingham Four, victims of racial hatred; their individual names were rarely given. This trend ceased when Spike Lee produced the documentary *4 Little Girls* for HBO in 1998, detailing each girl's life.

later put it, Davis resolved to consider joining the Communist Party, USA (CPUSA).

In *An Autobiography,* Davis writes that even though she knew she was a Marxist, she had at first resisted joining the CPUSA because she thought it was guilty of "not paying sufficient attention to the national and racial dimensions of the oppression of Black people, and therefore submerging the special characteristics of our oppression under the general exploitation of the working class." In L.A., however, the party had a special group composed exclusively of people of color, the Che-Lumumba Club, named after the Third World revolutionaries Che Guevara and Patrice Lumumba. After long discussions with black Communists Franklin and **Kendra Alexander** and **Charlene Mitchell**, as well as with Southern California district organizer **Dorothy Healey**, Davis decided in July 1968 to join the CPUSA. She was convinced that capitalism had to be abolished before black liberation could be achieved.

In the 1968–69 academic year, Davis devoted herself to a successful struggle at UC San Diego for a Third World college and completed her coursework and oral exams, leaving only her dissertation to finish. In the summer of 1969, Davis traveled for the first time to Cuba. Far more than the Soviet Union, Cuba was a revolutionary inspiration for young Communists in the 1960s, because it seemed fresh and uncompromised compared to the staid societies of Eastern Europe. In a 1970 prison interview, Davis mentioned that in Cuba she had observed "vestiges of cultural racism which have to be combatted," but her belief in Communism was sustained by her visit, and she would revisit Cuba repeatedly in the 1970s.

When she returned to the United States, Davis found herself at the center of a controversy. In the spring, she had been hired to teach philosophy at the University of California at Los Angeles (UCLA), but that summer an FBI informant had written to the campus daily with the news that she was a Communist. Governor Ronald Reagan and the UC Regents were in an uproar. A McCarthy-era state law prevented Communists from teaching at state universities. When Davis received a letter from the UC chancellor asking whether she was a member of the Communist Party, she decided to openly declare her affiliation. "Yes, I am a Communist," she replied. "And I will not take the Fifth Amendment against self-incrimination, because my political beliefs do not incriminate me; they incriminate the Nixons, Agnews and Reagans." Davis

was fired, but she continued to teach anyway as the case wound its way through the courts. Eventually the courts found the law unconstitutional, but UCLA did not reappoint Davis for the following year (she had signed only a one-year contract), despite her approval by the Philosophy Department.

As it turned out, Davis could not possibly have taught in Los Angeles that fall of 1970. It was the year of the Soledad Brothers, of Jonathan Jackson's courthouse liberation attempt, of Davis' underground flight and arrest and incarceration in New York City. At the Women's House of Detention in Greenwich Village, Davis was held in the psychological ward and then in solitary confinement until she went on a hunger strike and outside pressure convinced authorities to place her in the regular jail. Davis fought unsuccessfully against her extradition to California. In December 1970, she was transported to the Marin County Jail.

As Davis awaited trial, she became a cause célèbre. Black, young, revolutionary, with her hair in a natural Afro, Davis seemed to raise the clenched fist for an entire generation. If found guilty, she might well have been executed. A battery of lawyers, including Leo Branton and Howard Moore, built her legal defense, while the National United Committee to Free Angela Davis mobilized popular support for her. Davis did not seek out attention as did other movement "stars" like Jerry Rubin and Eldridge Cleaver. In her prison writings, she eschewed a "cult of personality" in favor of a united front among all political prisoners. Yet Angela Davis became a household name. Dorothy Healey later wrote, "Because she was not simply a Communist, but a Black in a time of racial upheaval, and because she was not simply a Black Communist but a beautiful woman, the media turned its full focus on her, and for the next few years she was never long out of the headlines." Many prominent intellectuals, cultural personalities and civil-rights leaders from around the world—including writer James Baldwin, philosopher Georg Lukács, entertainers **Aretha Franklin** and Herbie Hancock, Reverends Jesse Jackson and Ralph Abernathy, U.S. Representative Ronald Dellums, and ***Coretta Scott King**—called eloquently for her release and for a fair trial. Even a song for her, "Angela," appeared on the album *Sometime in New York City* (March 1972) by John Lennon, **Yoko Ono** and the Plastic Ono Band.

During her incarceration, Davis suffered further setbacks. On July 19, 1971, the cases of Davis and Ruchell Magee were severed from one another because the codefendants could not agree upon a legal strategy, feeding media speculation about personal and political differences. On August 21, 1971, Davis was dealt a much more serious blow when George Jackson was shot in the back and killed by guards at San Quentin. They alleged that Jackson had tried to smuggle a pistol in under a wig from the visitation room. Lastly, Davis sheltered private doubts about the Communist Party. During a jailhouse visit, she told Healey that she was thinking of resigning from CP because the party newspaper in New York, the *Daily World,* had repeatedly denounced Jonathan Jackson's act as "adventurist" and sought to dissociate Davis from him in that way. However, *Bettina Aptheker,** an acquaintance of Davis' since they first met at meetings of the Communist youth group Advance in New York in the early 1960s, believed Healey must be referring to the period after George Jackson was killed, when Davis was "very depressed, totally disheartened, just hanging on, trying to keep her sanity."

Rather than quit the party, Davis emerged from her trial an apparent diehard loyalist. On June 4, 1972, she was acquitted on all three counts by the jury. The prosecution had presented no evidence apart from the guns' registration (which Davis freely admitted) to link Davis to Jonathan Jackson's actions. Davis believed she owed her freedom to the defense efforts of the CPUSA and other Communist parties around the world. After a quick round of speeches to her U.S. supporters, she embarked on a tour of Communist states. Arriving in Moscow in August 1972, she said, "It was no accident that I began my tour of many countries by coming first to the Soviet Union, the first land of socialism." Davis became practically uncritical of the governments of Eastern Europe and Cuba, and in 1979 was given the Lenin Peace Prize by the USSR. She took a seat on the National Committee of the Communist Party, and ran twice, in 1980 and 1984, as the running mate of Communist leader Gus Hall in his presidential bids. She also became co-chair of the National Alliance Against Racist and Political Repression, the renamed incarnation of her defense committee, with the aim of aiding political prisoners and fighting racism.

Although her public fame has faded, in the 1980s Davis achieved a new status in controversies over curricula and culture on campus. In 1978, she had obtained a job as a full-time lecturer at San Francisco State University, and in the 1980s she began to travel the college circuit, speaking on a range of political and cultural topics. Despite her training under Marcuse, Davis

has published nothing philosophical. Her most-discussed book, *Women, Race and Class* (1981), is a historical and political essay that builds upon an article on women under slavery that Davis wrote in 1971 for the *Black Scholar.* Widely used in women's studies courses, *Women, Race and Class* delivers an indictment of the feminist movement with its dual theme that recurrent racism and class bias have marred American feminism and that the abolition of monopoly capitalism and establishment of socialism are necessary for the liberation of women.

In 1987, Davis told a British interviewer in the *New Statesman* that she was reluctant to call herself a feminist because the term "originated in white, middle-class circles and for a long time was used to connote women who worked on issues which concerned only them—isolated from the larger context." Feminists have returned Davis' criticism. One, who reviewed Davis' collected essays and speeches, *Women, Culture and Politics* (1989), for *The Nation,* found Davis' style boring, uninsightful and disjointed. "Davis's structuralism is like an unassembled Tinkertoy set," wrote Jackie Stevens. "All the pieces are there (the defense industry, homophobia, consumerism, sexism, denial, racism), but Davis never puts them together in a coherent model."

Davis is still a political and cultural radical. Her Afro is gone, but it has been replaced by dreadlocks. She joined the board of directors of the National Black Women's Health Project, formed in 1983, and has quit a four-pack-a-day cigarette habit to become a vegetarian and runner. Her brief marriage in 1980 to Hilton Braithwaite, a colleague at San Francisco State, ended in divorce. In 1985, she was arrested with students at Berkeley in an anti-apartheid rally, and that same year she joined hundreds of women in Nairobi to lead a protest against the appointment of **Maureen Reagan,** the president's daughter, as head of the U.S. delegation to the U.N. Conference on Women. "I still consider myself a revolutionary," she told the *L.A. Times* in 1988. "I think that I am militant." Davis joined the faculty at the University of California at Santa Cruz, specifically the History of Consciousness department, and was awarded a three-year Presidential Chair and $75,000 to increase feminist and ethnic studies at the school. She also began work on her book on black women's music of the 1920s and 1930s, focusing on *Ma Rainey, *Bessie Smith, and *Billie Holiday, which would be published in 1998.

As the bureaucratic states in Eastern Europe disintegrated in 1989, Davis expressed hopes that a new and more democratic variety of socialism would be the outcome. At the 25th National Convention of the CPUSA in December 1991, Davis sent a letter stating that she could not attend because of illness and the need to care for a friend dying of AIDS, but she challenged the political course of unreconstructed Stalinism proposed by Gus Hall and endorsed a reform initiative underway to unite democracy and socialism: "I believe the Communist Party will become ever more rapidly obsolescent—mere fossilized evidence of past struggles won and lost, past theoretical stances effective and not, past modes of practice with their limitations as well as their strengths—if it is afraid to engage in rigorous self-evaluation, radical restructuring and democratic renewal." For that stance, Davis was summarily stripped of her position on the National Committee of the Communist Party. No longer a member of the CPUSA, she endorsed the Committees of Correspondence, a breakaway group with a core of former CPUSA members that attracted and welcomed some socialists from different traditions, including Maoism and Trotskyism.

SOURCES:

Abbott, Diane. "Revolution by Other Means (interview with Angela Davis)" in *New Statesman*. August 14, 1987, pp. 16–17.

"Angela Davis: Still on the Front Line," in *Ebony*. Vol. 45. July 1990, pp. 56, 58.

Beyette, Beverly. "Angela Davis Now," in *Los Angeles Times*. March 8, 1988.

Bhavnani, Kum-Kum. "Complexity, Activism, Optimism: An Interview with Angela Y. Davis," in *Feminist Review*. Vol. 31. Spring 1989, pp. 66–81.

Davis, Angela. *An Autobiography.* NY: International, 1988.
——. *If They Come in the Morning.* NY: Signet, 1971.

Healey, Dorothy and Maurice Isserman. *Dorothy Healey Remembers.* NY: Oxford University Press, 1990.

Keerdoja, Eileen, and Michael Reese. "Davis: Campaigning As a Communist," in *Newsweek*. Vol. 95. June 9, 1980, pp. 12, 17.

Stevens, Jackie. "Talking About a Revolution," in *The Nation*. Vol. 248. February 27, 1989, pp. 279–281.

SUGGESTED READING:

Coombs, Orde. "Angela Davis Keeps the Faith," in *New York* magazine. April 17, 1978, pp. 43–47.

Davis, Angela. *Women, Culture and Politics.* NY: Random House, 1989.
——. *Women, Race and Class.* NY: Vintage, 1983.

Elbaum, Max. "De-Stalinizing the Old Guard," in *The Nation*. February 10, 1992, pp. 158–162.

Jackson, George. *Soledad Brother.* NY: Bantam, 1970.

Christopher Phelps, Editorial Director at *Monthly Review Press*, New York, New York

Davis, Bette (1908–1989)

Two-time Oscar-winning actress known as "the first lady of the American screen." Born Ruth Elizabeth Davis in Lowell, Massachusetts, on April 5, 1908; died of cancer on October 6, 1989, in Paris, France; *second of two children of Harlow and Ruth (Favor) Davis; sister of Barbara ("Bobby") Davis; married Harlan (Ham) Nelson, in August 1932 (divorced 1938); married Arthur Farnsworth, on December 30, 1941 (died August 1943); married William Grant Sherry (an ex-Navy man), on November 29, 1945 (divorced); married Gary Merrill (an actor), on July 28, 1950; children: (third marriage) Barbara Davis Sherry (called "B.D."); (fourth marriage) adopted two children, Margot and William.*

Enjoyed first public exposure in summer repertory performances (1927), followed by Broadway appearances (1929–30); after a screentest with Universal, embarked on a 55-year film career (1931–86), with more than 80 films; awarded Oscar as Best Actress (1935 and 1938); was the first woman awarded the American Film Institute's Lifetime Achievement Award (1977).

Films: Bad Sister *(1931)*; Seed *(1931)*; Waterloo Bridge *(1931)*; Way Back Home *(1932)*; The Menace *(1932)*; Hell's House *(1932)*; The Man Who Played God *(1932)*; So Big *(1932)*; The Rich Are Always With Us *(1932)*; The Dark Horse *(1932)*; Cabin in the Cotton *(1932)*; Three on a Match *(1932)*; 20,000 Years in Sing Sing *(1933)*; Parachute Jumper *(1933)*; The Working Man *(1933)*; Ex-Lady *(1933)*; Bureau of Missing Persons *(1933)*; Fashions of 1934 *(1934)*; The Big Shakedown *(1934)*; Jimmy the Gent *(1934)*; Fog over Frisco *(1934)*; Of Human Bondage *(1934)*; Housewife *(1934)*; Bordertown *(1935)*; The Girl from Tenth Avenue *(1935)*; Front Page Woman *(1935)*; Special Agent *(1935)*; Dangerous *(1935)*; The Petrified Forest *(1936)*; The Golden Arrow *(1936)*; Satan Met a Lady *(1936)*; Marked Woman *(1937)*; Kid Galahad *(1937)*; That Certain Woman *(1937)*; It's Love I'm After *(1937)*; Jezebel *(1938)*; The Sisters *(1938)*; Dark Victory *(1939)*; Juarez *(1939)*; The Old Maid *(1939)*; The Private Lives of Elizabeth and Essex *(1939)*; All This and Heaven, Too *(1940)*; The Letter *(1940)*; The Great Lie *(1941)*; The Bride Came C.O.D. *(1941)*; The Little Foxes *(1941)*; The Man Who Came to Dinner *(1941)*; In This Our Life *(1942)*; Now, Voyager *(1942)*; Watch on the Rhine *(1943)*; Thank Your Lucky Stars *(1943)*; Old Acquaintance *(1943)*; Mr. Skeffington *(1944)*; Hollywood Canteen *(1944)*; The Corn Is Green *(1945)*; A Stolen Life *(1946)*; Deception *(1946)*; Winter Meeting *(1948)*; June Bride *(1948)*; Beyond the Forest *(1949)*; All About Eve *(1950)*; Another Man's Poison *(UK, 1951)*; Payment on Demand *(1951)*; Phone Call from a Stranger *(1952)*; The Star *(1952)*; The Virgin Queen *(1955)*; Storm Center *(1956)*; A Catered Affair *(1956)*; (cameo) John Paul Jones *(1959)*; The Scapegoat *(UK, 1959)*; A Pocketful

Bette
Davis

of Miracles *(1961)*; Whatever Happened to Baby Jane? *(1962)*; The Empty Canvas *(Italian, 1964)*; Dead Ringer *(1964)*; Where Love Has Gone *(1964)*; Hush, Hush . . . Sweet Charlotte *(1965)*; The Nanny *(UK, 1965)*; The Anniversary *(UK, 1967)*; Connecting Rooms *(UK, 1970)*; Bunny O'Hare *(1971)*; Madame Sin *(1972)*; Burnt Offerings *(1976)*; Return from Witch Mountain *(1978)*; Death on the Nile *(1978)*; The Watcher in the Woods *(UK, 1980)*; The Whales of August *(1987)*.

One afternoon in 1931 in Hollywood, on the Universal lot, a young actress nervously waited for the screening of her first film. Before the film was half over, she ran out of the darkened theater in tears. She hated her performance, hated what she looked like, and hated herself for giving up what had been a promising career on Broadway for the movies. The producer Carl Laemmle seemed to confirm her feelings when he remarked to an associate that the new young actress had "as much sex appeal as Slim Summerville," comparing her to a gawky vaudeville comedian then appearing in slapstick comedies. But more than 50 years later, Bette Davis would be the reigning queen of American cinema, known for her portrayals of strong-willed females capable of overcoming tragedy and outwitting domineering men. Her career would be declared over at least twice, but Davis would fight her way back with such fierce determination that film critic E. Arnot Robinson would note, "I think Bette would probably be burned as a witch if she had lived two or three hundred years ago."

I don't take the movies seriously, and anyone who does is in for a headache.

—Bette Davis

Even Davis' childhood seemed fraught with dramatic overtones. She had been born Ruth Elizabeth Davis in Lowell, Massachusetts, on April 5, 1908, the eldest daughter of Harlow and **Ruth Davis**. Harlow had been smitten with the artistic, dreamy Ruth Favor as soon as they had met at a Baptist-run summer camp in Maine at the turn of the century. All went well with the marriage while Harlow went to law school and Ruthie raised their two daughters (Barbara, or "Bobby," had been born in 1909). But when the girls were barely out of grammar school, Harlow and Ruthie became estranged and, by 1918, divorced. Ruthie blamed Harlow's philandering for the separation, while Harlow disapproved of Ruthie's flights of artistic fancy, from dance to drama to painting to poetry. Whatever the reasons, Davis would later say she couldn't remember even a moment of affection between her parents. Bette and Bobby found themselves the talk of Lowell's conservative Baptist community, in which divorce was rare.

In 1921, Ruthie, no doubt anxious to leave her gossiping neighbors behind, decided her future lay with photography and enrolled in a course offered in New York City, taking her two girls with her. Davis hated the dirt and grime of the city, but she said later that she learned her first important lesson there—how to play to a camera. Ruthie's assignments for her photography classes continually demanded a model, and she chose Bette as her favorite. Bobby was told to sit quietly in a corner while her mother and her sister worked. It was during their time in New York that Davis, enamored of Balzac's *Cousin Bette,* changed the spelling of her name from Betty to Bette. When Ruthie's money ran out, the girls were taken back to Massachusetts and entered in Newton High School, where Bette was noted for her poise, self-confidence, and for the scandalous fact that her parents were divorced. No one seemed to take much notice of Bobby.

By 1927, Ruthie was becoming alarmed at reports that her eldest daughter was "boy crazy," and endeavored to harness Bette's energies with dancing and drama lessons. A trip to Boston to see a production of Ibsen's *The Wild Duck* inspired Davis to be an actress. She would, in fact, appear in a production of the same play on Broadway a few years later. Despite Ruthie's efforts, a young beau of Bette's, Harlan (Ham) Nelson, asked for Bette's hand in marriage. Ruth's answer was to wrangle a scholarship at the John Murray Anderson School of Drama in New York, where Davis was sent to study under a youthful *Eva Le Gallienne. While she was still in school, Davis successfully auditioned for a part in a production of Virgil Geddes' *The Earth Between,* then being mounted at The Provincetown Playhouse in Greenwich Village. The show's opening was delayed, however, and in the interim Davis took a job with The Temple Players, a repertory company rehearsing for its summer season in Rochester, New York, under the direction of George Cukor—later one of Hollywood's most successful directors. Cukor was not impressed with the willowy young woman from Lowell and fired her. Fortunately, *The Earth Between* was now ready. Davis' reviews were respectful and, in light of her later career, ironic; she was cited for her "soft, unasserting style." Summer stock and her first Broadway appearance in a play called *Broken Dishes* followed, along with her work in *The Wild Duck.*

Hollywood, meanwhile, had come to Broadway. The studio system that would rule the movie industry for the next four decades needed a constant supply of young contract players, and the legitimate stage was a fertile hunting ground. By 1930, Davis had become sufficiently noticed in New York for several of the studios to invite her to screentest. Her first test, for Sam Goldwyn, was a failure, but Universal offered her a three-

From the movie Of Human Bondage, starring Bette Davis and Leslie Howard.

year contract, at $300 a week, a considerable increase over what Davis could make on the stage. Ruthie urged her daughter to accept.

Davis' first assignment for Universal was the movie that so upset her at the screening—a film called *Bad Sister,* based on Booth Tarkington's story *The Flirt,* which opened in 1931 and was poorly reviewed. One critic called her performance "lugubrious." Davis announced her intention to break her contract with Universal and return to New York and the stage. But her sister Bobby had begun to display signs of emotional disturbance, perhaps exacerbated from the constant strain of living in her sister's shadow. (Bobby would recover, however, and settle down to a quiet married life.) Her medical bills demanded the steady income provided by Davis' contract, and there followed a string of mostly forgettable roles in Universal's "B" films. But Davis was getting exposure and experience and soon came to the attention of Jack Warner, who bought out her Universal contract and signed her to appear in Warner's 1932 production *The Man Who Played God*. It was the beginning of a long and stormy relationship with Warner Bros., but one that would ultimately bring her international stardom. This was also the year of Davis' first marriage, to none other than the young beau whose intentions back East had propelled her into a film career. Harlan Nelson had followed her to California, and the two were married in August as Davis was shooting *The Man Who Played God*.

Davis was convinced she was better than the roles Warner offered her, but it took her four years to win the first part she felt suited her talents—the role of the mean-spirited Mildred in *Of Human Bondage*, which was released in 1936 and was the first film that made the critics take notice. Her work was solid enough to convince Warner to cast her in the lead of the melodrama *Dangerous*, a tearjerker that proved immensely popular and won Davis her first Oscar as Best Actress. But it was her next film that would make her a star.

Director William Wyler had been assigned a script called *Jezebel* and was casting the lead role of Julie Marsden, an antebellum vixen who wreaks havoc in the lives of several lovers. Wyler and Davis had met six years earlier, at Universal, when he was still directing screentests. On that day, wardrobe had given Davis a low-cut blouse to wear to one of the endless tests she had to endure under her Universal contract. Just as she entered the studio in the revealing top, Wyler happened to ask an associate, "So what do you think of these dames who show off their chest and think they'll get jobs?" Mortified, her screentest was a disaster. She reminded Wyler of this first meeting when she tested for *Jezebel*. "I'm nicer now," Wyler said, and proved it by giving her the part. Even though Davis would later claim that Wyler was demanding and often rude, the two became lovers during the filming, no small contribution to the budget and schedule problems that plagued the production. The strain on Davis was intense, especially when she

discovered she was pregnant with Wyler's child. Rumors began to fly, and Warner was forced to put out a press release when shooting finally wrapped, saying Miss Davis would be taking time off due to a nervous collapse from the stress of a particularly difficult role. Davis quietly disappeared and had an abortion.

Jezebel opened in 1938 and won her a second Oscar as Best Actress. But the conflicts of the film's history were not yet over. As Davis was being acclaimed Hollywood's major new discovery, Harlan filed for divorce on grounds of "cruel and inhuman treatment." He told friends that Davis had continually criticized him for what she perceived as a lack of ambition and had flaunted her infidelity. The divorce was finalized later that year.

For the next six years, Davis would work constantly, sometimes appearing in as many as four films a year, many of them to become classics, and many marked by rumored affairs with her leading men. In later life, she would often cite 1942's *Now, Voyager* as her favorite film, one that combined all the right elements of script, cast, and director (Irving Rapper). It is the film in which her co-star, Paul Henreid, chivalrously lights two cigarettes at once and proffers one to Davis. Three of the films in this period (*Mrs. Skeffington, Now, Voyager,* and *Juarez*) included Claude Rains, the man Davis called her favorite actor; and it was during the shooting of 1939's *The Private Lives of Elizabeth and Essex* that Charles Laughton wandered over from another sound stage and gave her the advice she said ruled her career from then on: "Never stop daring to hang yourself." She fought continually with Warner over everything from working conditions to wardrobe, and even sued the studio for holding her to her contract when she announced her intention to appear in two European films (she lost her case). By the beginning of World War II, Davis had become the most popular, respected, vexing, fearsome, and successful female star in Hollywood.

In 1939, exhausted after completing *The Private Lives of Elizabeth and Essex*, Davis took a much-needed vacation in her beloved New England. At a New Hampshire inn, she met Arthur Farnsworth, a handsome scion of a wealthy New England family. "He was as removed from the theater as anyone could be," Davis said later, "and had no interest in competing with me in any way." She married "Farney" on December 30, 1941, and he became her anchor in the sometimes tempestuous seas of a Hollywood career. But the relationship came to a tragic, abrupt end in August of 1943. Farney collapsed from a cerebral hemorrhage on Hollywood Boulevard and died the next day. It would be the last stable relationship Davis was to know.

When the war came to Hollywood, Davis was instrumental in creating the Hollywood Canteen for GIs on Sunset Boulevard, calling it one of the few things in her life of which she was truly proud. But the war changed Hollywood, and Davis' career. Now, it was patriotic war stories the public wanted, while the melodramas and so-called "women's films" of the '30s became less popular. While Davis had done ten pictures between 1937 and 1939, she appeared in only five between 1945 and 1948 and did not work at all during 1947.

Another factor in the downturn in her career was her marriage during this period to a husky ex-Navy man named William Sherry. Sherry had a reputation as a hard-living womanizer, and Davis was warned about him, even by Sherry's own mother, who said her son was cruel. A detective's report on Sherry commissioned by Bobby confirmed the mother's statement, but Davis refused to read the report and became Mrs. William Grant Sherry on November 29, 1945. The physical abuse began on their wedding night, when Davis claimed Sherry threw a suitcase at her. The marriage produced a daughter, **Barbara Davis Sherry**, whom Bette always called "B.D.," but Sherry's outbursts of violent anger, some of them on the sets of her films, grew worse. Davis began to fear for her daughter's safety, not to mention her own. She left her husband and filed for divorce, even agreeing to pay Sherry alimony if he'd stay away.

Hollywood insiders claimed that Davis' career was over. But Bette did not agree and knew exactly the role she wanted to use for her comeback. When *Claudette Colbert injured her back and had to withdraw from the Darryl Zanuck film she had been working on, Davis mounted a successful campaign for the role of Margot Channing in Zanuck's All About Eve, the story of a reigning actress who is brutally shoved aside by the ambitions of a younger woman, Eve Harrington, played by *Anne Baxter. The film, directed by Joseph Mankiewicz, opened in 1950 and was nominated for 14 Academy Awards, including Best Actress nominations for both Baxter and Davis, though neither won. During the shooting, Davis began an affair with the film's leading man, Gary Merrill; when her divorce from Sherry was finalized, she and Merrill were married on July 28, 1950.

"I considered Gary my last chance at love and marriage," she wrote in her autobiography, This 'n That. But the ten years with him, she said, were the ten darkest years of her life. Professionally, she was out of work for three of those ten years because of health problems, and the pictures in which she appeared when she was able to work were poorly received. Personally, the marriage was a troubled one. The studio public relations department depicted them as a happy new couple, especially when they adopted two children, Margot and William. But privately, Davis claimed Merrill was "mean and cruel" to her own daughter, B.D. There was further anguish when Margot was later diagnosed with a severe learning disability and was institutionalized. Perhaps as a diversion from these troubles, she and Merrill kept up a frantic social life that began to take its toll. Although Davis had called Merrill "a good drinker," he was rumored to be a borderline alcoholic, and the couple's raucous parties became the talk of Hollywood. The strain finally became too much, and a divorce was announced in July of 1960. "Divorce is failure," Bette said. "But it is better to fail than to continue in an unhappy marriage." She listed four reasons why marriages fail: money, having only one bathroom, an inability to communicate, and sex—the last of which she called "God's joke on human beings."

By the time of her divorce from Merrill, it was again being said that Davis' career was over. There were few parts offered her now, and during the last years of her marriage, she had even placed advertisements in trade magazines offering her services. But she found yet another "comeback picture"—1962's Whatever Happened to Baby Jane? The Henry Farrell novel was brought to her by *Joan Crawford, Davis' contemporary, who was also having difficulty finding good parts. The book, with its story of two middle-aged sisters with a decidedly bizarre relationship, had possibilities. Director Robert Aldrich saw its potential and took the project to Seven Arts Films, which now owned Davis' old studio, Warner Bros. Shooting began in mid-1961. The stories told of the shoot are legion, especially the maneuverings and plottings of its two stars, but there is little doubt that Davis was the driving force behind the production. She considered it a revolutionary breakthrough in feminine drama, a startling next step from her "women's" pictures of the '30s and '40s. She insisted on doing her own, clown-like makeup, a parody of her glamorous image of 25 years before, demanded that the film was shot in stark black and white, and even took a lower salary in exchange for a percentage of the film's profits. The picture was shot for well under a million dollars and grossed well over that figure in its first two weeks in theaters. Davis was once again nominated for Best Actress but lost the award to **Anne Bancroft** in what Bette claimed was a campaign against her mounted by Joan Crawford. Even so, at 54, Davis had a new career. She teamed up again with Aldrich for the camp classic of Southern Gothic, *Hush, Hush . . . Sweet Charlotte,* released in 1965. Crawford was to have played in the film, too, but withdrew because of illness after only ten days of shooting and was replaced, after personal pleas from Davis, by *Olivia de Havilland. Once again, in an eerie imitation of real life, Davis played a woman disturbed by her past who triumphs in the end.

For the rest of her life, Davis worked fairly regularly, lending prestige to a string of otherwise mundane pictures in the U.S. and Britain. She was quick to seize on television as another provider of steady work, appearing on talk shows and everything from the "Andy Williams Show" to "Perry Mason." The American Film

From the movie Whatever Happened to Baby Jane?, *starring Joan Crawford and Bette Davis.*

Institute recognized her perseverance and her contributions to the industry by making her the first woman to receive its Lifetime Achievement Award in 1977.

In 1983, Davis suffered two more setbacks. The first was a book published by B.D., *My Mother's Keeper*. In the tradition of **Christina Crawford**'s *Mommy, Dearest*, B.D.'s book professed to reveal the "truth" about her famous mother, although it contained none of the devastating revelations of the sort that filled the Crawford book. Instead, it attempted to portray Davis as a power-driven, ambition-mad mother who had little time for her family except when publicity demanded it. B.D., who had married, raised a family, and distanced herself from Davis over the past 15 years, now wrote, "Mother was a destroyer, and the thing that amazes me is that I wasn't destroyed." According to friends, Davis had doted on B.D. and never stopped talking about her even when the two women became estranged. She claimed to have had no inkling of her daughter's plans and was deeply hurt by *My Mother's Keeper*.

Not long after the book was released, Davis was diagnosed with breast cancer and underwent a mastectomy. Complications from the operation led to a stroke. Once again, it seemed that she would never work again. But in 1986, Davis gave a luminous performance in what would be her last film, *The Whales of August*, in which she starred opposite the venerable *Lillian Gish. Even at 78, Davis found it hard to let go of her former glory days, demanding that her trailer be turned to face away from everyone else's and trying to tell the film's director, Lindsay Anderson, just how a scene should be played. When the two elderly stars were required to play a scene on a ledge some distance down a cliff on the rocky Maine coast, 88-year-old Gish allowed herself to be carried to the location while Davis stubbornly insisted on getting there on her own, slipping and hurting a hip in the process. Lillian Gish, who had been playing in silent films when Davis was in grammar school back in Lowell, remained aloof. Her only comment about Bette was, "She must be a very unhappy woman."

In 1989, Davis was invited to open a film festival in Spain, but during the ceremonies she began to feel unwell. She was flown to the American Hospital in Paris, where it was discovered that the cancer of six years earlier had reappeared and spread throughout her body. She died on October 6, 1989, at the age of 81. With her at her death was her secretary and traveling companion,

Kathryn Sermak, who summed up ten years with Davis by simply saying, "She inspired pride in everyone." Despite her tumultuous, sometimes controversial life, it was Davis' pride in her work, and the power she wielded in a male-dominated industry, for which she is ultimately remembered. "I have decided," Davis wrote not long before she died, "that work is the one great hope, the one anchor, for a satisfying life."

SOURCES:

Davis, Bette, with Michael Herskowitz. *This 'n That*. NY: Putnam, 1987.
———. *The Lonely Life*. NY: Putnam, 1962.
Leaming, Barbara. *Bette Davis: A Biography*. NY: Simon & Schuster, 1992.
Stein, Whitney. *Mother Goddam*. NY: Hawthorne Books, 1974.

SUGGESTED READING:

Spada, James. *More Than a Woman: An Intimate Biography of Bette Davis*. Bantam, 1993.

Norman Powers, writer-producer, Chelsea Lane Productions, New York, New York

Davis, Dorothy Hilliard

(1917–1994)

American pilot, member of the Women's Air Service Pilots (WASP) during World War II, who played a crucial role in the campaign to gain official government recognition for the WASPs as military veterans, which was successfully achieved in 1977. Born Dorothy Hilliard Davis in 1917; died in San Francisco, California, on May 25, 1994; daughter of Oscar Harris Davis and "Dottie" Davis; graduated in 1944 from Class 44-W-10, the last group of WASPs to graduate before the organization was deactivated.

One of the most serious problems of military aviation during World War II was the loss of trained pilots in combat and the immense difficulties of replacing this highly skilled "manpower" pool. As early as 1939, *Jacqueline Cochran had interested *Eleanor Roosevelt in the possibility of using women in the U.S. military services in the event of war, in order to release all male pilots for combat duty. By the late 1930s, with about 3,000 American women licensed to fly, there could be little doubt that a previously unused corps of skilled pilots was available. After Pearl Harbor, two relatively independent programs for women pilots emerged. One, created in September 1942 and headed by ❧➤ **Nancy Love**, was the Women's Auxiliary Ferrying Squadron (WAFS), an experimental squadron of experienced women pilots assigned to the task of ferrying aircraft for the Air Transport Command. The other unit, headed by the noted aviator Jacqueline Cochran and launched in Novem-

❧➤ Love, Nancy. See Cochran, Jacqueline for sidebar.

ber 1942, was the Women's Flying Training Detachment (WFTD), essentially a training program established to provide pilots for the squadron. Although both of these organizations were organized under civil service rules and were not regarded as part of the military, Cochran's goal was that they be upgraded as quickly as possible to full military status including commissions for its graduates.

In August 1943, the two organizations were merged to form the Women's Airforce Service Pilots (WASP). Both Love and Cochran were disappointed when initially WASP pilots, many of them with long years of prewar flying experience, found themselves restricted to daytime flights in liaison aircraft and primary trainers. Nancy Love broke the barrier by receiving permission to check out in B-17s and P-51 Mustangs. Jacqueline Cochran made her contribution to expanding the duties of WASP pilots by receiving official clearance from General Henry "Hap" Arnold, commanding general of the U.S. Army Air Forces (USAAF), for her graduates to tow targets as well as ferry aircraft. At the anti-aircraft training base of Camp Davis, North Carolina, WASP volunteers flew old and dangerous A-24 and A-25 dive bombers, freeing male pilots for other duties, including combat. Engine failure cost the lives of two WASPs at Camp Davis and several others barely survived when their planes were hit by friendly fire from the ground.

With the barriers down, WASPs soon were flying every first-line fighter, bomber, trainer and transport plane in the USAAF. By the end of 1944, fully half of Ferrying Division's fighter pilots were WASPs. By this time, they were making three out of four domestic fighter deliveries, and with a lower accident rate than that of male pilots. In its first year of existence, WASP pilots set a new safety record in military aviation, flying the equivalent of 3,000,000 miles for each fatal accident, a rate equal to .05 fatal accidents for each 1,000 hours of flying time (the overall USAAF fatality rate during this period was significantly higher at .07). WASP pilots quickly earned reputations among male pilots in the USAAF of being highly competent and professional under many different flight conditions and challenges. They were particularly impressive in handling the B-26 Marauder, generally regarded at the time to be an aircraft that was difficult and even dangerous to fly. WASPs outperformed their male counterparts both on the ground in flight school and in the air when many of them flew B-26s on tow-target missions to train aerial gunners.

Often WASP pilots, not being members of the military, were able to cut through red tape because of their skills and courage. One such instance was when ☙➤ Ann Baumgartner, assigned to Wright Field as a consultant on new flying equipment, persuaded top brass at the base to let her fly some of the planes on hand. Soon she was flying P-51s, P-47 Thunderbolts, and a rare captured Japanese Zero. Ann Baumgartner made history when clearance came through for her to fly the experimental Bell YP-59A jet pursuit plane, thus becoming the only American female jet pilot of World War II. Baumgartner would remain the only American woman with military jet flying credentials for almost a decade.

On December 20, 1944, with victory in World War II in sight and with the demand for combat pilots matched by the supply, the WASPs were officially deactivated. In its 28 months of existence, the WASP and its precursor units had drawn more than 25,000 applications for flight training. Of these, 1,830 were accepted and 1,074 won their wings. These women, from all walks of life, ferried more than 12,000 aircraft of 78 different types, flying millions of miles. Not part of the military services, their pay was only two-thirds that of the male civilian ferry pilots they had replaced. Despite the obvious discrimination, many offered to continue their work ferrying aircraft for a dollar a year.

At the graduation of the last class of WASP cadets at Sweetwater, Texas, on December 7, 1944, General "Hap" Arnold commented:

> Frankly, I didn't know in 1941 whether a slip of a young girl could fight the controls of a B-17 in the heavy weather they would naturally encounter in operational flying. Those of us who had been flying for 20 or 30 years knew that flying an airplane is something you do not learn overnight. . . . Well, now in 1944, more than two years since WASPs first started flying with the Air Forces, we can come to only one conclusion—the entire operation has been a success. It is on the record that women can fly as well as men.

Told they were no longer needed, the women pilots now searched for new roles. Some returned to their prewar lives, but others hoped to build new careers in the military. They were deeply disappointed when legislation on their behalf failed to secure passage in Congress because of strong lobbying from male flight instructors. Now eligible for the draft when their government-contract flight schools shut down, the men coveted the flight assignments that had previously been held by WASPs.

Dorothy Davis, "Dottie" to her many friends, had graduated a WASP in Class 44-W-10, the last class to receive diplomas before the WASPs became a part of American history in December 1944. Raised in Virginia, she eventually moved to San Francisco where she worked as a claims adjudicator for the Veterans Administration. Like almost all WASPs, she retained warm memories of her wartime experiences, but they began to seem like "ancient history" with the passage of time. Many veterans traveled to Sweetwater, Texas, in 1972 for a stirring reunion. Few regretted having served in wartime despite the unequal status that had defined their terms of service. Some remained bitter because since 1945 they had been denied the disability and health benefits available to all male pilot veterans of the war. In 1976, Dorothy Davis and her fellow-WASPs became deeply angered when the Pentagon, after having decided to train women for military flying operations, issued a statement describing the prospective female pilots as "the first women to fly for the military."

Remembering how they had been paid less, often ignored, and were now being turned into virtual nonpersons, Davis and others set about to achieve justice once and for all. They recruited "Hap" Arnold's son, Colonel Bruce Arnold, who fully agreed with his father's wishes, namely that the WASPs be militarized in recognition of their services. A strong ally was found in Senator Barry Goldwater, who had respected WASPs since World War II, having witnessed their flying skills when he was a Ferry Command pilot. Powerful groups organized to lobby against the WASPs. The American Legion and the Veterans Administration argued that militarizing the WASP organization would serve as a precedent for doing the same for every civilian body of World War II—the Civil Air Patrol, the Merchant Marines, etc.—and that the financial obligations resulting from such a redefinition would simply be too large a drain on the Federal treasury.

As one of the most enthusiastic activists among the WASP veterans, Dorothy Davis joined the campaign for Congressional lobbying, using all her spare hours to gather petitions. At first her successes were slight. Many Americans had never heard of the WASPs. She devised a fact sheet to hand out; few took the time to read it. Undaunted, Davis found the strategic moment to make her case: the opening in San Francisco of the film *Star Wars*. With long lines stretching around the blocks of local theaters, she had a captive audience. Rain or shine, she would be there, wearing her old WASP uniform.

✤▸ **Baumgartner, Ann** (c. 1923—)

American aviator. Born around 1923; formerly a journalist.

In October 1944, at Wright Field in Dayton, Ohio, 21-year-old Ann Baumgartner flew a YP-59A, America's first experimental jet, reaching 350 miles per hour and an altitude of 35,000 feet.

The fact sheet gave moviegoers something to read while waiting in line. Furthermore, Davis was happy to explain details and even tell about her own personal part in the story of the WASPs. These efforts paid off with thousands of signatures that were sent to Washington. Energized, other organizers throughout the country were able to gather support for their petitions. The mood throughout America was changing as a new, all-volunteer military force was being created. Increasingly aware of the need to recruit women as well as men into the armed services, the Pentagon supported the WASPs in their efforts to gain belated military status.

Success for Dorothy Davis and her fellow WASPs came in 1977 when Congress passed the G.I. Improvement Act and President Jimmy Carter recognized these aging proud veterans retroactively as having once been on active military service. They did not receive retroactive pay or death insurance, but symbolically these remarkable women were now accepted as part of the great family of World War II veterans. Although they had not seen combat, WASPs had risked their lives every day while on duty. Thirty-eight of them had died while flying for their country during World War II (*see* *Cornelia Fort), and now, more than three decades later, they were receiving recognition for their courage, devotion to duty, and a job well done. Dorothy Davis was deeply mourned by a dwindling band of WASPs when she died in San Francisco on May 25, 1994.

SOURCES:

Bollow, John. "Remembering the WASPS," in *Saturday Evening Post*. Vol. 267, no. 3. May–June 1995, pp. 58–59, 65, 73, 77.

Cole, Jean Hascall. *Women Pilots of World War II*. Salt Lake City: University of Utah Press, 1995.

"Dorothy Davis, 77, World War II Pilot," in *The New York Times Biographical Service*. May 1994, p. 794.

Frisbee, John L. "The WASPS of World War II," in *Air Force Magazine*. Vol. 78, no. 11. November 1995, p. 37.

Granger, Byrd H. *On Final Approach: The Women Airforce Pilots of W.W. II*. Scottsdale, AZ: Falconer, 1991.

Gruhzit-Hoyt, Olga. *They Also Served: American Women in World War II*. Secaucus, NJ: Carol, 1995.

Holden, Henry M., and Lori Griffith. *Ladybirds II: The Continuing Story of American Women in Aviation*. Mt. Freedom, NJ: Black Hawk Publishing, 1993.

Jaros, Dean. *Heroes without Legacy: American Airwomen, 1912–1944*. Niwot, CO: University Press of Colorado, 1993.

Kageleiry, Jamie. "War and Reunion," in *Yankee*. Vol. 55, no. 12. December 1991, pp. 82–89.

Noggle, Anne. *For God, Country, and the Thrill of It: Women Airforce Service Pilots in World War II, Photographic Portraits*. College Station: Texas A&M University Press, 1990.

Verges, Marianne. *On Silver Wings: The Women Airforce Service Pilots of World War II, 1942–1944*. NY: Ballantine Books, 1991.

Williams, Vera S. *WASPS: Women Airforce Service Pilots of World War II*. Osceola, WI: Motorbooks International, 1994.

John Haag, Associate Professor of History, University of Georgia, Athens, Georgia

Davis, Hallie Flanagan (1889–1969).

See Flanagan, Hallie.

Davis, Hilda (b. 1905).

See Cobb, Jewell Plummer for sidebar.

Davis, Joan (1907–1961)

Popular American actress and comedian of the 1940s. Born Madonna Josephine Davis in St. Paul, Minnesota, on June 29, 1907; died of a heart attack in Palm Springs, California, on May 22, 1961; only daughter of LeRoy (a train dispatcher) and Nina Davis; graduated from Mechanic Arts High School, St. Paul; married Serenus (Sy) Wills (a comedian), in 1931; children: one daughter, Beverly Wills (b. 1933, an actress).

Selected films: Millions in the Air *(1935);* The Holy Terror *(1937);* On the Avenue *(1937);* Wake Up and Live *(1937);* Angel's Holiday *(1937);* Thin Ice *(1937);* Life Begins in College *(1937);* Love and Hisses *(1937);* Sally, Irene and Mary *(1938);* Josette *(1938);* My Lucky Star *(1938);* Hold That Co-Ed *(1938);* Just Around the Corner *(1938);* Tail Spin *(1939);* Daytime Wife *(1939);* Free Blonde and 21 *(1940);* Hold That Ghost *(1941);* Sun Valley Serenade *(1941);* Two Latins from Manhattan *(1941);* Yokel Boy *(1942);* Sweetheart of the Fleet *(1942);* Two Senoritas from Chicago *(1943);* Around the World *(1943);* Beautiful but Broke *(1944);* Show Business *(1944);* Kansas City Kitty *(1944);* She Gets Her Man *(1945);* George White's Scandals *(1945);* She Wrote the Book *(1946);* If You Knew Susie *(1948);* Make Mine Laughs *(1949);* Traveling Saleswoman *(1950);* Love That Brute *(1950);* The Groom Wore Spurs *(1951);* Harem Girl *(1942).*

Once hailed as the world's funniest woman, Joan Davis was known for her rubber-faced grimaces, sublime sense of timing, and broad slapstick style. In describing the comic gridiron scene from her 1938 movie *Hold That Co-Ed*, Kyle Crichton wrote: "Miss Davis makes flying tackles. . . . She takes off into space in an array of limbs and arms resembling nothing other than an octopus taking a flying test; she ends by falling on her caboose with a crash that not only shakes the stadium but shakes the inherent faith of man in the frailty of woman." After establishing herself as a talented screen comedian, Davis later reinvented herself for radio audiences, then in the 1950s produced the highly popular television series, "I Married Joan," in which she portrayed the zany wife of a beleaguered judge, played by Jim Backus.

As early as the age of three, Joan Davis was performing at community events. She turned to comedy after being laughed at during a serious recitation, and she was still quite young when talent scouts persuaded her family to allow her to tour the Pantages Theater Circuit as "The Toy Comedienne." After putting her career on hold while she finished high school (valedictorian of her class), Davis then took up the tour again, playing the vaudeville circuit as well as amusement parks, summer camps, and Elks lodges. In 1931, she created a new act with comedian Sy Wills, whom she married five months after meeting, and continued to tour with him for another three years. Around 1934, with vaudeville on the wane, they made their way to Hollywood, where Davis signed a long-term contract with 20th Century-Fox. From 1937 to 1941, she made about 25 films for Fox, then freelanced for another three years. In 1944, RKO and Universal signed her to similar contracts, each giving her star billing and allowing her to make one picture a year with another studio.

In 1941, Davis made a reluctant debut on the radio, concerned that so much of her comedy would be lost to a listening audience. On her first show, she parodied the popular novelty song "Hey, Daddy," singing a few lines then finishing it as a monologue. The number was a huge success. A similar interpretation of the ballad "My Jim," performed on the Rudy Vallée program "Village Store," resulted in her becoming a regular member of the show. When Vallée left the show in 1943 for a stint in the Coast Guard, she replaced him. With comedian Jack Haley acting as her co-star, the show grew rapidly in popularity, and by the end of the year Davis was voted radio's top comedienne. By 1945, she was third in the ratings, just behind Bob Hope and the team of Fibber McGee and Molly (*Marian Jordan). In September 1945, boasting the largest team of writers in radio, Davis moved from NBC to CBS with a new show to replace the popular George Burns and *Gracie Allen in their Monday-night slot. Rounding out her career in the 1950s, Davis formed her own production company to produce her hit television show "I Married Joan," which ran from 1952 to 1957.

Green-eyed with reddish brown hair, Davis was said to be much prettier than her screen persona and was known as one of Hollywood's best-dressed. Fond of sports, she swam, biked, and played golf, and she was a regular at the weekly boxing show at the American Legion Stadium in Hollywood. Her husband wrote much of the material for her shows, and daughter **Beverly Wills**, born in 1933, also acted. Wills played Fuffy Adams on the popular radio program "Junior Miss," starring *Shirley Temple (Black). Joan Davis succumbed to a heart attack in Palm Springs, California, at age 53, on May 22, 1961.

Barbara Morgan,
Melrose, Massachusetts

Davis, Katharine Bement
(1860–1935)

American penologist and social worker. Born on January 15, 1860, in Buffalo, New York; died on December 10, 1935, in Pacific Grove, California; eldest of three girls and two boys of Oscar Bill (a businessman) and Frances (Bement) Davis; graduated from the Rochester Free Academy, 1879; taught for ten years at the Dunkirk High School before entering the junior class at Vassar College in 1890, graduating with honors, 1892; attended Columbia University, 1892–93; attended the University of Chicago (spending one year abroad at the universities of Berlin and Vienna), graduating with a Ph.D. in economics, 1900.

Born in Buffalo, New York, in 1860, Katharine Davis spent her childhood in Dunkirk and in Rochester, where she graduated from the Rochester Free Academy in 1879. A family financial crisis delayed her college education for ten years, during which time she taught school while taking night courses. In 1890, she entered Vassar as a junior, graduating in 1892 with honors. She went on to study food chemistry and nutrition at Columbia while teaching science at Brooklyn Heights Seminary for Girls. In the summer of 1893, she was director of the New York State Exhibit of a model worker's home at the World's Columbian Exposition in Chicago, which demonstrated how a family could maintain adequate dietary and living conditions on a small salary. That same year, she became the head of the St. Mary's Street College Settlement in Philadelphia, where she put the Chicago model into practice within the settlement's low-income black and immigrant population. In 1897, she began doctoral studies in political economics at the University of Chicago, which incorporated a year abroad at the universities of Berlin and Vienna.

After receiving her Ph.D. in 1900, Davis was appointed superintendent of the newly opened Reformatory for Women at Bedford Hills, New York, a post she would hold for 13 years. During her tenure, the reformatory was cited as "the most active penal experiment station in America." Davis was instrumental in establishing a prison farm, a cottage system of housing, and vocational training courses for the women inmates. Her pioneering work in identifying and separating reformable from repeat offenders so impressed John D. Rockefeller, Jr. that he established the Laboratory of Social Hygiene in 1912 on property adjacent to the reformatory, with the purpose of furthering her research.

During a European trip in 1909, Davis received international recognition for organizing an emergency self-help relief program following an earthquake in Messina, Sicily. For her efforts, she won medals from the Red Cross and the Italian government, as well as a Papal commendation.

In 1914, she was appointed commissioner of correction for New York City by the newly elected reform mayor John Purroy Mitchel, making her the first woman to serve at a cabinet level in that municipality. Davis quickly moved to improve conditions within the city's penal institutions: she established the New Hampton Farm School for Boys in Orange County, removing delinquents from the confined city reformatory and providing them with open-air work; initiated plans for the New York City Detention Home for Women (which opened in 1932); took steps to abolish striped clothing among city inmates; and worked to eliminate narcotic peddling within the city's institutions and to upgrade dietary and medical facilities. In the summer of 1914, she was instrumental in suppressing a riot among convicts at Blackwell's Island, through her intelligent and sensitive handling of the situation. In 1915, in response to her efforts, the New York legislature enacted a program of indeterminate sentencing and parole supervision, and named Davis first chair of the city's parole board, a post she held until the end of the reform administration in 1918.

From 1918 until her retirement in 1928, Davis was general secretary and a member of the board of directors of the Bureau of Social Hygiene, a branch of the Rockefeller Foundation, where she continued the bureau's work in investigating commercialized vice and prostitution. She directed research into narcotic addiction and the "international white slave trade," as well as the broader fields of public health and hygiene. During World War II, she headed the women's section for social hygiene of the Commission on Training Camp Activities. After the war, she crossed Europe on an inspection tour for the Young Women's Christian Association and raised over $2 million in relief funds. An active contributor to scholarly and professional journals, she published a study, *Factors in the Sex Life of Twenty-two Hundred Women*, in 1929. In 1930, Davis moved to Pacific Grove, California, where she took up residence with her two sisters. She died there on December 10, 1935, at age 75.

Davis, Knox (1814–1835).

See Davis, Varina for sidebar on Knox Taylor.

Davis, Lady (1923–1990).

See Davis, Pa Tepaeru Ariki.

Davis, Marguerite (b. 1889).

See Spyri, Johanna for sidebar.

Davis, Moll.

See Gwynn, Nell for sidebar on Moll Davies.

Davis, Nancy (b. 1921).

See Reagan, Nancy.

Davis, Pa Tepaeru Ariki (1923–1990)

Cook Islands traditional leader and president of the House of Ariki from 1980 until her death. Name variations: Lady Davis. Born in 1923; died in February 1990; married Thomas (Tom) Davis; children: two sons.

Settled by migrants from Tahiti, Samoa, and the Marquesas by the 1200s CE, the Cook Islands are spread over 750,000 square miles of the Pacific Ocean between American Samoa to the west and French Polynesia to the east. The inhabitants were influenced by the Maori culture of New Zealand and to this day speak a Maori dialect besides English. The total land mass of 13 inhabited and 2 uninhabited islands consists of 91.5 square miles. The largest of the islands, Rarotonga, is home to about half of the population of less than 19,000. European explorers including Captain James Cook, for whom the islands are named, made infrequent visits before the 1820s when British missionaries introduced Christianity and trade began with New Zealand. Fearful of French designs on the islands, in 1888 Ariki **Makea Takau**, the "Queen" who dominated political affairs in the town of Avarau on the main island of Rarotonga, petitioned the British government to establish a protectorate over the most important of the Cook Islands.

In 1900, the local Council of Ariki (chiefs) petitioned for annexation to New Zealand, which formally took place on June 11, 1901. Over the next decades, significant improvements took place in health and education. In the mid-1990s, with life expectancy at birth 69.8 years, adult literacy at 99% and per capita GDP $US 3,500+, the Cook Islands quality of life was the highest of any of the states of Polynesia. In August 1965, the Cook Islands became a sovereign self-governing state in free association with New Zealand, the latter nation retaining responsibility for foreign affairs and defense. Cook Islanders were extended New Zealand citizenship, the right of unrestricted immigration to New Zealand, and generous economic assistance.

With the achievement of self-government in 1965, Cook Islanders had to come to grips with the problem of how best to blend their Polynesian traditions with the patterns of the modern world. In the political realm, one of the ways to build a stronger sense of nationhood was to incorporate traditional leadership into a postcolonial imagined community. Thus in 1965, under the political leadership of Albert Henry, local Ariki (paramount chiefs) were accorded a symbolic position as local royalty, while at the same time being excluded from actual political power. At the most general level, the traditional polity of Rarotonga is triadic in structure, comprising three confederations or *vaka* (literally canoes): Takitumu, Te Au-o-Tonga, and Puaikura (also known as Arorangi). Each "canoe" is composed of a number of genealogically related *ngati,* cognatic descent groups with rights to areas of land stretching from the mountainous interior of islands down to the sea. The Takiktumu *vaka* is represented by two Ariki titles, Pa and Kainuku.

Pa Tepaeru Ariki received the title of Pa Ariki at the age of nine. She spent much of her early childhood in New Zealand. Her marriage to Tom Davis (Pa Tuterangi Ariki), later knighted as Sir Thomas Davis, placed Pa Tepaeru in the center of not only Cook Islands but international affairs. Also educated in New Zealand, Tom became a government medical official on Rarotonga but decided to continue his career abroad. The Davises and their two sons sailed to America on a boat Tom had built. After completing his postgraduate studies at Harvard, he did medical research for the U.S. military and the space program. In the early 1970s, the Davis family returned to the Cook Islands. Tom Davis became premier in 1978, serving almost uninterruptedly until 1987. Pa Tepaeru Ariki Davis was elected president of the House of Ariki in 1980.

Although the House of Ariki wielded virtually no substantive power in Cook Islands politics, it nevertheless was accorded a certain amount of respect by most of the citizens of the new nation. The Ariki were seen as living links with the pre-European, pre-Christian past of the islands, a source of distinctive and deeper humanity and a more authentic culture. The links to the past were actively fostered by the Ministry of Cultural Development, which encouraged the performance of investiture ceremonies and educating the public—including interested tourists—of their meaning. It was argued in the 1960s when the House of Ariki was created that the retention of recognition of the "royal heritage" of the Cook Islands would associate their remote and little-known nation with such better known states as Samoa, Tonga, and even Great Britain, each of which was able to retain strong sovereign identities because of monarchical traditions refurbished for the modern world. Ariki, it was argued, were individuals who because of their royal status were able to remain above the mundane concerns of daily politics.

Although theoretically above politics, the House of Ariki never gained the power and prestige of another traditional body some of its members hoped they could emulate, namely the British House of Lords. The Cook Islands House of Ariki, despite the personal popularity of Pa Tepaeru Ariki Davis, never was granted such a constitutional role. Its power was symbolic and served to emphasize cultural traditions. Many of its members were politically active women like **Makea Nui** Ariki, who was known for her vigorous opposition to the regime of Premier Albert Henry. In March 1983, **Fanaura Kingstone** became the first woman elected to the Cook Islands Parliament. Pa Tepaeru Ariki Davis, on the other hand, was a quietly conciliatory personality who was much respected by Cook Islanders both at home and in New Zealand, where more than 30,000 lived on a permanent basis. Although the Cook Islands were relatively prosperous because of generous subsidies from the New Zealand treasury to create public-sector jobs, it was unlikely that many of the Cook Islanders who had migrated to New Zealand to seek work would ever return home (by the 1990s nearly 70% of all Cook Islanders lived in New Zealand). Try as they might to retain them, the old cultural patterns no longer seemed appropriate to their urban lifestyles. It was clear that on Rarotonga and the other inhabited Cook Islands the forces of modernity had deeply eroded the traditional values represented by the Ariki and their ancient "canoe" ways of life.

Pa Tepaeru Ariki Davis (Lady Davis) died in February 1990. Her death was marked by two days of official mourning in the Cook Islands, the only such official mourning ever recognized there. Her body lay in state in Auckland, New Zealand, where Sir Graham Latimer, chair of the New Zealand Maori Council, after greeting "the canoes, friends and all the good people gathered here," spoke movingly of his mourning "for you at this time. Go, our mother, join Sir James Henare and all those who have gone before. Sleep well in your eternal rest."

SOURCES:

Craig, Robert D. *Historical Dictionary of Polynesia.* Metuchen, NJ: Scarecrow Press, 1993.

Crocombe, Ron, ed. *Cook Islands Politics: The Inside Story*. Auckland, NZ: Polynesian Press, 1979.

Davis, Thomas R.A.H. *Island Boy: An Autobiography*. Auckland, NZ: Institute of Pacific Studies, University of the South Pacific, 1992.

Denoon, Donald *et al.*, eds. *The Cambridge History of the Pacific Islanders*. Cambridge: Cambridge University Press, 1997.

Hoadley, Steve. *The South Pacific Foreign Affairs Handbook*. North Sydney, Australia: Allen & Unwin/New Zealand Institute of International Affairs, 1992.

Phelan, Nancy. *Pieces of Heaven: In the South Seas*. St. Lucia: University of Queensland Press, 1996.

Sissons, Jeffrey. "Royal Backbone and Body Politic: Aristocratic Titles and Cook Island Nationalism since Self-Government," in *The Contemporary Pacific: A Journal of Island Affairs*. Vol. 6, no. 2. Fall 1994, pp. 371–396.

"Understanding What Living Together Really Means," in *New Zealand Herald*. February 7, 1990.

John Haag, Associate Professor of History,
University of Georgia, Athens, Georgia

Davis, Paulina Wright (1813–1876)

American feminist, reformer and suffragist. Born Paulina Kellogg on August 7, 1813, in Bloomfield, New York; died on August 24, 1876, in Providence, Rhode Island; one of two daughters and three sons of Captain Ebenezer (a volunteer in the War of 1812) and Polly (Saxton) Kellogg; married Francis Wright (a merchant), in January 1833 (died 1845); married Thomas Davis (a jewelry maker and politician), in April 1849; children: (second marriage) two adopted daughters.

In 1817, when Paulina Wright Davis was five years old, her family moved to a tract of land near Niagara Falls; she spent several years of early childhood enjoying the freedom and adventure of frontier life. In 1820, however, after the death of both her parents, she was sent to live in LeRoy, New York, in the care of her orthodox Presbyterian aunt. In the strict religious environment of her new home, she joined the church and prepared for missionary service in the Hawaiian Islands. Her plans were interrupted in 1833 by her marriage to Francis Wright, a young, upcoming businessman from Utica who had courted her for five years.

Of a similar outlook, Davis and her young husband embarked on work for abolition, temperance, and women's rights. They helped organize an anti-slavery convention held in Utica in October 1835 and, as a consequence, suffered a mob attack on their house. In the late 1830s, Davis joined *Ernestine Rose in petitioning the New York legislature for a married women's property law. After her husband's death in 1845, she used her sizable inheritance to continue her reform work. Davis was an attractive woman with blonde hair and clear blue eyes, whose appearance added considerably to her gentle, earnest appeals. She toured the East and Midwest lecturing on physiology and hygiene, using an unclad female mannequin imported from Paris which, when produced during her talks, was said to have caused some in the audience to faint, and others to flee the room.

In 1849, she married Thomas Davis, a widower and jewelry manufacturer from Rhode Island, who was also a politician. When he was elected to Congress on a Democratic ticket in 1852, Davis accompanied him to Washington for his single term. She then turned her energies to the cause of women's rights, taking the lead in plans for the first National Woman's Rights Convention, over which she presided in October 1850. In February 1853, she began publishing, at her own expense, the monthly periodical *Una*, one of the first publications devoted to women's rights. With editorial assistance from *Caroline Dall, the publication continued to appear until late 1855.

In 1859, Davis toured Europe, devoting time to the study of painting. The Civil War temporarily suspended the women's movement, and it was not until 1868 that Davis helped found the New England Woman Suffrage Association, of which she was president until 1870. With the split in the national suffrage movement in 1869, Davis lent her support to the National Woman Suffrage Association of *Susan B. Anthony and *Elizabeth Cady Stanton (whom she was said to resemble). After participating in suffrage conventions in Washington and New York, she went abroad for a second time to continue her art studies.

In her later years, Davis became an enthusiastic spiritualist, finding comfort from her painful rheumatic gout by communicating with what she called the Other World. She died in Providence, Rhode Island, at age 63, and was buried in Swan Point Cemetery. By her request, Elizabeth Cady Stanton spoke at her memorial service.

Barbara Morgan,
Melrose, Massachusetts

Davis, Pearl (1899–1962).
See Adler, Polly.

Davis, Rebecca Harding (1831–1910).
See Olsen, Tillie for sidebar.

Davis, Varina Howell (1826–1906)

First lady of the Confederacy during the Civil War. Name variations: Mrs. V. Jefferson Davis. Born Vari-

na Anne Banks Howell on May 7, 1826, on Marengo plantation in Louisiana, near Natchez, Mississippi; died in New York City on October 16, 1906; buried at Hollywood Cemetery in Richmond, next to her husband; second child of William Burr Howell and Margaret Louisa (Kempe) Howell of The Briers plantation in Natchez, Mississippi; attended private boarding school in Philadelphia, around 1836, later tutored by Judge George Winchester; married Jefferson Davis (1808–1889), on February 26, 1845; children: Samuel Emerson (b. 1852); Margaret Howell Davis (b. 1855); Jefferson Davis, Jr. (b. 1857); Joseph Evan Davis (b. 1859); William Howell Davis (b. 1861); Varina Anne Davis, called Winnie Davis (1864–1898).

Married Jefferson Davis and moved to Brierfield plantation (1845); moved to Washington where her husband would eventually serve in the House of Representatives, Senate, and would be appointed secretary of war (1845–61); was first lady of the Confederacy (1861–65); traveled in Canada and Europe (1865–77); collaborated with her husband in writing The Rise and Fall of the Confederate Government (1878–81); moved to New York (1892). Selected publications: Jefferson Davis: Ex-President of the Confederate States: A Memoir by His Wife (1890).

Born May 7, 1826, into the small, tightly-knit oligarchy of planters clustered around the Mississippi River before the Civil War, Varina Howell Davis was the second child of William and **Margaret Howell** of Natchez, Mississippi, both of whom were descended from distinguished Southern families. Varina had one older brother William and later three younger siblings, Margaret, Becket, and Jefferson (whom she referred to affectionately as "Jeffy D"). Like many daughters of privileged Southern families, a ten-year-old Varina was sent North for schooling, where she impressed her teachers at an exclusive boarding school in Philadelphia as being "smart and capable." After only two terms, however, she returned to The Briers, her family home near Natchez, where she received the remainder of her education from a private tutor, Judge George Winchester. Winchester, a graduate of Harvard, gave Varina an education that exceeded the level of most women of her day. She studied French, Latin and the English classics, and by the time she was a teenager she read the *National Intelligencer* regularly. She later credited Winchester with instilling in her a "pure, high standard of right."

Varina met Jefferson Davis through his brother Joseph, who owned a huge plantation some 30 miles south of Vicksburg called "The Hurricane." Jefferson Davis had already distin-

guished himself as an army officer and owned a plantation nearby called "Brier-field." In 1835, he had married **Knox Taylor**, the daughter of his commanding officer, Colonel Zachary Taylor, and had left his military career to settle down as a planter. Within three months of their wedding, however, Knox took sick and died. Jefferson fell into a deep depression and for the next eight years seldom left his plantation. In an effort to bring his brother out of self-enforced exile, in 1843 Joseph suggested to Varina's parents that she be allowed to spend time at the Hurricane over the Christmas holiday.

Varina's first impression of her 36-year-old suitor was mixed. She described Jefferson to her mother as "a remarkable kind of man, but of uncertain temper. . . . the kind of person" who would "rescue one from a mad dog at any risk," but "insist upon a stoical indifference to the

Varina Howell Davis

Taylor, Knox (1814–1835)

American; daughter of Zachary Taylor. Name variations: Sallie Knox Taylor; Sarah Knox Taylor; Knox Davis. Born Sarah Knox Taylor in 1814; died on September 15, 1835; daughter of Zachary Taylor (army major, Mexican war hero, and president of the U.S.) and Margaret Mackall Smith Taylor; married Jefferson Davis, on June 17, 1835, in Louisville, Kentucky.

Knox Taylor was born in 1814, the daughter of Zachary Taylor, an army major and future president of the United States, and *Margaret Smith Taylor. In 1835, while her family was stationed at Fort Crawford at Prairie du Chien, Wisconsin, Knox Taylor met one of her father's subordinates, the future Confederate president Jefferson Davis. Because Zachary Taylor did not want his daughter subjected to the family dislocations of the military life, the courtship was carried on at an aunt's home. Jefferson Davis resigned from the army and married Knox on June 17, 1835, in Louisville, Kentucky, with neither family present. Tragically, both Davis and his bride developed malaria during a summer visit to a sister's plantation in southern Mississippi, and Knox died on September 15.

fright afterwards." Despite her initial misgivings and the 18-year difference in their ages, Varina and Jefferson soon discovered many common interests. They often slipped away from the family to ride together, and in the evenings they could be seen bent together over some political treatise or classical work while they debated issues and philosophy. Jefferson was quickly impressed by Varina's intelligence and wit, as well as her beauty. By the time Varina returned home in February 1844, Jefferson had proposed. Varina's mother was at first hesitant about the difference in ages, but when Jefferson visited the family in the spring of 1844 Margaret quickly gave her approval.

Soon after their engagement became official, Jefferson left to attend to political duties as elector-at-large, campaigning for James K. Polk. A disconsolate Varina grew pale and thin. She worried obsessively about his fragile health and was distressed by criticism of his party in the newspapers. By the time Jefferson returned in early 1845, Varina was too weak to stand. Both families suggested that the wedding be postponed, but Varina was determined that Jefferson never leave her again. On February 26, 1845, Varina and Jefferson were married in a simple private ceremony in the Howell home. In many ways, the marriage would prove successful; the tall brunette's impressive personality proved a major asset for her rather formal husband. Her friend in wartime Richmond, *Mary Boykin Chesnut, wrote, "She is as witty as he is wise."

But after the wedding, Varina was plagued by the shadow of Knox. Her honeymoon was marred by Jefferson's insistence that they visit his first wife's grave in Louisiana, and by tales related by members of Jefferson's family there of his abiding love for Knox, including the story of how, years after her demise, Jefferson had happened upon one of Knox's slippers in an old trunk and fainted away with grief. Varina's health and spirits were greatly improved when the couple arrived at their destination in New Orleans, where they spent several weeks at the St. Charles Hotel, rubbing shoulders with the city's upper crust.

When the couple returned to Brierfield, they moved into the rough, unpretentious home that Jefferson had built there. Although he would build a more elaborate home for his wife five years later, Varina recalled their original home fondly, with its deep fireplaces and doorways six feet wide, designed to let in the breeze. During these early years, Varina described herself as a "loving but useless wife." She worked hard at

beautifying their home and supervising the household servants. Unlike many Southern women of her generation, Varina never questioned the institution of slavery. Joseph and Jefferson Davis were well known throughout the area for what was considered at the time "humane treatment" of their slaves, and overseers at the Hurricane and Brierfield were not allowed to use corporal punishment. The 1860 census indicated that there were 113 slaves at Brierfield belonging to the master. This large number reflected both the success of the plantation and the fact that Davis considered inhuman the practice of selling slaves. Despite it being illegal to allow slaves to handle weapons, Jefferson Davis hunted with slaves. He also shook hands with them against convention, provided a slave hospital, and allowed slave juries to handle most cases of wrong doing. While he thought the institution a positive good, Jefferson did not believe it to be permanent. In a speech on Oregon on July 12, 1848, he talked of emancipation in several generations and said it was an "institution for the preparation of that race for civil liberty and social enjoyment." After the Civil War, Davis is reported to have been upset over the oppressive circumstances of former slaves.

In the fall of 1845, Jefferson was elected to the House of Representatives, and in December the couple moved to a boarding house in Washington. Jefferson worked hard as a legislator and soon earned a reputation as a man on the way up. Varina, always concerned for her husband's health, worried over his habit of working until 2 or 3 AM. In the stimulating atmosphere of the capital, she grew up quickly. She frequently attended Congressional debates and learned to hold her own in social affairs.

When the Mexican War broke out in 1846, Jefferson accepted the colonelcy of a Mississippi regiment, and Varina returned to Brierfield. During her husband's absence, her management of the plantation provoked criticism from her brother-in-law Joe, and a distraught Varina fled to her parents' plantation. Jefferson was on leave for two weeks in November and did what he could to calm his young wife.

When the war ended, Davis returned a hero, having received a wound in the foot that put him on crutches for two years. His war exploits bolstered his political career. Two months later, he was appointed to a vacant seat in the Senate. The Davises returned to Washington where they were often entertained by his ex-in-laws, the new president Zachary Taylor and *Margaret Smith Taylor. In the Senate, Davis distinguished himself as a staunch defender of States Rights and the institution of slavery. Varina supported him unquestioningly but later wrote: "He was so impervious to the influence of anything but principle in shaping his political course that he underrated the effect of social intercourse in determining the action of public men and never sought to exert it in behalf of his own policy."

Davis resigned his Senate seat in 1851 to run for governor but lost to Henry S. Foote by 999 votes. Varina was relieved to return to Brierfield, confiding to her mother, "You know my heart never went with Jeff in politics or soldiering." She settled down to a more domestic life, and on July 30, 1852, gave birth to a son, Samuel Emerson. Jefferson and Varina's quiet days at Brierfield were brief. In late 1852, the newly elected president, Franklin Pierce, appointed Jefferson secretary of war. Varina at first urged him to decline the offer on the basis of his delicate health but eventually relented, and the family returned to Washington.

The happiness of the next four years was marred by the death of Samuel, just short of his second birthday. The loss of their first son was eased somewhat by the birth of a daughter, **Margaret Howell Davis**, on February 25, 1855. Jefferson was a great success in his cabinet position, and Varina earned a reputation as a poised and vivacious host. The birth of another son, Jefferson Jr., on January 16, 1857, impaired Varina's health for several months, but a brief vacation on the Gulf Coast did much to improve her spirits.

When the Davis family returned to Washington in late 1857, their contingent was expanded still further by the addition of Varina's two youngest siblings, Maggie and Jeffy D. Jefferson generously accepted them as part of the Davis household and put them in school at his own expense. Although Varina continued to appear in capital society, she found herself devoting more of her time to the care of her growing family. The acrimonious debates over the Kansas question in 1858 took their toll on Jefferson's health; he developed glaucoma and lost all vision in his left eye. On April 18, 1859, Varina gave birth to another son. She proposed naming him William, after her father, but Jefferson insisted on christening him Joseph Evan, after his brother Joe. Varina was angered by his insistence on naming the child after someone whom she considered unkind, but she soon forgave him.

By the time Congress reassembled in December 1859, the debates over slavery had become intense. Jefferson continued to argue for the extreme Southern position as the Southern states moved inexorably toward secession. In his valedictory speech to the Senate on January 21, 1861, he concluded, "May God have us in his holy keeping, and grant that before it is too late peaceful councils may prevail."

Three weeks after the Davises returned to Brierfield, a telegram arrived informing Jefferson that he had been elected president of the newly formed Confederate States of America. Varina later recalled that Jefferson's face reflected "profound grief" at the news and that he "neither desired nor expected" the office, but that his deep sense of responsibility would not allow him to shirk his duty. Jefferson left Brierfield the next day, and soon afterward Varina and the family took up residence at the Confederate capital in Montgomery, Alabama. The Davis family received a warm reception, but Jefferson soon found himself beaten down under the pressures of his new position and the outbreak of war in April 1861. He was not only plagued by chronic insomnia but by hordes of office-seekers.

Montgomery's distance from the battlefront prompted the Confederate government to move the capital to Richmond, Virginia, in May. At first, Varina expressed relief at leaving behind the heat and congestion of Montgomery, but she soon found the ladies of Virginia's old aristocracy to be cool and distant. The failure of the Confederate troops to quickly win the war brought heavy criticism upon Jefferson by late 1861, which Varina could never abide. Quarrels over military commissions alienated the Davises from many of their former friends, who soon began calling Varina "a coarse western woman" or "Queen Varina." Varina was also "utterly upset," according to Mary Chesnut, at "the carping and fault-finding to which the President is subjected."

On December 16, 1861, another son, William Howell, was born, and on February 22, 1862, Jefferson was inaugurated as president under the new permanent Confederate constitution. These temporary lifts to their spirits were dampened by news of military reverses in early 1862. Varina did what she could to salvage Jefferson's reputation, but the heavy burden of government administration severely curtailed the number of entertainments she could give, and she blamed this for Jefferson's declining influence in Confederate government.

When Federal troops pushed close to Richmond, Jefferson sent Varina and the children to Raleigh, North Carolina, an action that earned Varina a flood of criticism in the press. By early

1863, they received word that Brierfield had been pillaged and the Hurricane burned to the ground by Union soldiers. Varina's spirits were buoyed by her friendship with Mary Chesnut, who had moved to Richmond, and by knitting and distributing money and clothing to the Confederate troops in the hospitals.

Varina's father, who had settled in Montgomery after fleeing Mississippi, fell ill and died in March 1863. Soon after she returned from his funeral, a bread riot broke out in Richmond on April 2, which was quelled only after Jefferson threatened to have the mob shot by the military. As food became ever scarcer, Varina received mounting criticism for sponsoring social engagements while much of Richmond starved. Jefferson's health continued to decline, and throughout the spring he was bedridden with fever and bronchitis.

The summer of 1863 brought further disaster. Robert E. Lee was defeated at Gettysburg and Vicksburg fell to Union troops. Later that year, Jefferson traveled South to try to smooth relations between his battle-weary officers. Upon his return, Varina began sponsoring weekly public receptions at the Southern White House in an attempt to improve public relations. They were discontinued in January 1864, after a fire was set during one of the receptions.

Jefferson and Varina were devastated by the death of their five-year-old son Joe on April 30, 1864. He had slipped while climbing a bannister on a White House balcony and fallen 30 feet to the brick pavement below. Two months later, on June 27, 1864, Varina gave birth to daughter Varina Anne, called "Winnie." As the only spark of happiness during an otherwise black time, **Winnie Davis** was a blessing. For decades after the war, she was fondly referred to by Southerners as "the daughter of the Confederacy."

The fall of Atlanta in September was a further blow to Jefferson's prestige. "I am so tired [of] hoping, fearing and being disappointed," Varina wrote Mary Chesnut, "that I have made up my mind not to be disconsolate even though thieves break through and steal. . . . People do not snub me any longer, for it was only while the lion was dying that he was kicked, dead, he was beneath contempt."

As the condition of the Confederate forces continued to deteriorate, Jefferson sent his wife and children south, telling Varina, "If I live you can come to me when the struggle is ended, but I do not expect to survive the destruction of constitutional liberty." He gave her a small pistol and showed her how to fire it and then sent his family by train through South Carolina and into Georgia. Fleeing the capital, he was reunited with his family early in May. On May 10, the family was captured by Union forces at Irwinsville, Georgia. Jefferson was charged with conspiring in the assassination of Abraham Lincoln and imprisoned at Fort Monroe. Varina and the children were kept under guard at the Savannah hotel for about two months, after which they were allowed to move to Mill View, a plantation outside Augusta.

But Varina Davis received word that her husband's poor health was being made worse by manacles and constant guards. Although the chains were removed a few weeks later, Jefferson was still not allowed to leave his damp, vermin-infested cell, and a light was shone continually in his eyes. Fearing for her husband's life and afraid that he would go blind under such treatment, Varina immediately wrote letters to all the congressmen and senators who had known Davis before the war, begging them to intercede with President Andrew Johnson on his behalf. In May 1866, when she was finally allowed to visit him, she was appalled at his "shrunken form and glassy eyes" and quickly released an account of his condition to the press. She traveled to Washington to plead for his release, but Johnson insisted that his hands were tied by a recalcitrant Congress.

When no evidence linking Davis to Lincoln's assassination emerged, Federal authorities indicted him on charges of treason to the U.S. government. Varina tirelessly traveled the country to drum up support for her husband's parole. Responding to her campaign, a writ of *habeas corpus* was entered in May 1867 and $100,000 bail met by *New York Tribune* editor Horace Greeley and abolitionist Gerrit Smith. After two years of incarceration, Jefferson Davis was released and never called to trial; the general amnesty signed by President Johnson on December 25, 1868, nullified the charges against him.

Jefferson's release did not end the difficulties faced by his family. Like many Southern planters, they had lost almost everything. Still weak and plagued by ill health from his imprisonment, he determined to go to England to seek gainful employment. In 1868, the family moved overseas, and Varina enrolled the children in school in England and France. Jefferson attempted to set up a business as a cotton broker in Liverpool. The family was welcomed warmly by other Confederate expatriots, like Judah P. Benjamin and John Slidell, but Jefferson was never able to get his business off the ground.

In late 1869, Jefferson returned to the United States and moved to Memphis, Tennessee, to take a position as president of the Carolina Insurance Company. Not relishing the prospect of living in Memphis, Varina stayed in Europe near her children for another year before finally reuniting the family in 1871. But the move to Memphis did not solve their financial woes; the Carolina Insurance Company went bankrupt in 1873. To add to their misfortune, their ten-year-old son Billy died of diphtheria in 1872, and Varina's beloved younger brother, Jeffy D, was drowned in the Pacific when his ship collided with another in 1875.

Soon after the wedding of her daughter Margaret to J. Addison Hayes, a Memphis banker, in January 1876, Varina, Jefferson, and their daughter Winnie, now 13, returned to England, where Jefferson hoped to establish a trading company. When he was unable to secure investors, he was forced to abandon the project. The constant strain of financial worries and frequent upheavals took their toll. Varina developed heart problems and was forced to convalesce at her sister's home in Liverpool while Jefferson returned to America.

Upon his return, Jefferson decided to compile and publish a history of the Confederacy. A wealthy widow, ❧▶ **Sarah Dorsey**, who owned a plantation called Beauvoir, just outside Biloxi, Mississippi, offered Jefferson a house on her estate and her assistance as secretary if he would undertake the project. After his failures in the business world, Jefferson believed he had few options. Varina, dejected after months of illness, quickly grew jealous of Dorsey, and her suspicions were raised by tidbits of gossip released by the press. In late 1877, she sent Jefferson an angry letter expressing her disapproval of the arrangement:

> I am grateful for the kindness to you and my children, but do not desire to be under any more obligation to her. When people here ask me what part of your book she is writing, and such things, I feel aggravated nearly to death.

When Varina recovered enough to travel home, she returned to Memphis but refused to join Jefferson at Beauvoir. When he pleaded with her to change her mind, she retorted:

> Do not, please do not let Mrs. Dorsey come to see me. I cannot see her and do not desire ever to do so again, beside[s] I do not wish to be uncivil and embarrass you and would certainly be so against my will. Let us agree to disagree about her and I will bear my separation from you as I have the last six months.

Finally relenting, Varina moved to Beauvoir in the summer of 1878, but soon after she was stricken with a "brain fever" upon receiving word that their last son, Jefferson Jr., had died of yellow fever on October 16, 1878.

The following year, Dorsey died of cancer, and Jefferson purchased Beauvoir from her estate for $5,500. Jefferson and Varina poured all of their energies into completing the history, which was finally published in 1881 as *The Rise and Fall of the Confederate Government*. Varina penned a note to Winnie, then attending school in Germany, "Well, dear love, the book is done and coming out—'whoop la.'"

To celebrate the book's completion, the couple traveled to Europe for a two-month vacation in Paris. When they returned, they brought 16-year-old Winnie with them. Winnie quickly became her father's chief assistant, taking over from Varina much of the secretarial responsibilities and, in 1885, joining her father on a speaking tour through Alabama and Georgia. Father and daughter received tremendous support from their audiences, which were made up mostly of old Confederate soldiers.

Varina's close friend Mary Chesnut died in 1886. In 1889, 81-year-old Jefferson Davis developed bronchitis and malaria while en route between Beauvoir and Brierfield. Varina met him in New Orleans, where for three weeks he struggled against growing weakness. Finally on December 6, he died and was buried in Metairie Cemetery, and in 1893 his remains were moved to Richmond. Varina determined to publish a memoir of her husband, as a last attempt to clear his reputation. She worked steadily until at last in 1890 she completed a 1,638-page book entitled *Jefferson Davis, Ex-President of the Con-*

❧▶ **Dorsey, Sarah Anne** (1829–1879)

American prose writer. Born in Natchez, Mississippi, on February 16, 1829; died in New Orleans, Louisiana, on July 4, 1879; owned a plantation called Beauvoir, just outside Biloxi, Mississippi.

A linguist and student of Sanskrit, Dorsey's literary work began with the (Episcopal) *Churchman*. Her writings include: *Lucia Dare* (1867); *Panola: A Tale of Louisiana* (1877); *Atalie* and *Agnes Graham*. She was amanuensis to Jefferson Davis in the preparation of his *Rise and Fall of the Confederate Government*.

federate States: A Memoir by His Wife. Much of the publication was copied from Jefferson's earlier publication. Though strongly biased in his favor, it contained some interesting material never recorded elsewhere.

In the following years, Varina and Winnie scrambled to stay financially afloat. The book never sold enough to bring in any real income, and Beauvoir and Brierfield were both deeply encumbered by debt. A failed romance with Alfred Wilkinson, a Syracuse lawyer, along with the death of her father, had a detrimental effect on Winnie's health. Margaret, now living in Colorado Springs, Colorado, occasionally sent financial assistance to her mother and sister. Never completely comfortable at Beauvoir, Varina determined in 1892 to move to New York City, where she hoped to use her connections with Joseph Pulitzer's family to launch herself and Winnie into a writing career. Varina contributed articles to the *Sunday World* while Winnie worked on novels. But Winnie's health continued to deteriorate, and on September 18, 1898, she died at 33 from malarial gastritis.

After Winnie's death, Varina concentrated on her one remaining child, Margaret, and on her grandchildren. In 1902, Varina sold Beauvoir to the United Confederate Veterans for $10,000. In October of 1906, she caught pneumonia and on October 16 breathed her last with the words, "Oh Lord in thee have I trusted, let me not be confounded."

SOURCES:

Ross, Ishbel. *First Lady of the South: The Life of Mrs. Jefferson Davis.* NY: Harper, 1958.

Van der Heuvel, Gerry. *Crowns of Thorns and Glory: Mary Todd Lincoln and Varina Howell Davis: The Two First Ladies of the Civil War.* NY: E.P. Dutton, 1988.

Wiley, Bell Irvin. *Confederate Women.* NY: Greenwood Press, 1975.

Woodward, C. Vann and Elisabeth Muhlenfeld. *The Private Mary Chesnut: The Unpublished Civil War Diaries.* NY: Oxford University Press, 1984.

Peter Harrison Branum, Ph.D. Philosophy, Auburn University, Auburn, Alabama

Davison, Emily (1872–1913)

English militant suffragist. Born Emily Wilding Davison in Blackheath, England, in 1872; died on June 8, 1913; daughter of Charles and Margaret Davison; graduated B.A. from London University; obtained a first at Oxford in English Language and Literature.

Emily Davison was born in Blackheath, England, in 1872, the daughter of a Northumbrian couple. Productive at school, she won a place at Holloway College to study literature. Two years later following her father's death, she was forced to leave Holloway because her mother could not afford the £20 term fees. Instead, Davison took a job as a schoolteacher in Worthing.

In 1906, she joined the Pankhursts' Women's Social and Political Union (WSPU) and, by 1908, was one of the chief leaders in the June WSPU demonstration in London. Becoming deeply enmeshed in the militant activities of the group, she eventually gave up full-time teaching. She was also involved with the Worker's Educational Association.

In March 1909, Davison was arrested while attempting to hand a petition to Herbert Asquith, then prime minister. Found guilty of disturbance, she was sentenced to one month in prison. Four months later, for trying to enter a London hall where the chancellor of the exchequer, Lloyd George, was making a speech, she was again imprisoned. After a five-day hunger strike, she was released.

A few days later, along with **Mary Leigh** and *****Constance Lytton**, Davison was arrested for stone throwing. The stones, wrapped in paper with the words "Rebellion against tyrants is obedience to God," were being hurled at Lloyd George's motorcar as it wended its way toward Newcastle. Sentenced to one-month hard labor in Strangeways Jail, the women went on a hunger strike and were force-fed 49 times. Davison, to thwart the force-feeding and prison brutalization, barricaded herself in her cell. When a prison officer climbed a ladder, inserted a hose pipe through a window, and blasted icy water at her, slowly filling the cell, she still refused to allow access. Before the cell had been completely gorged with water, the door was broken down.

Keir Hardie, leader of the Labour Party, expressed concern in the House of Commons over the treatment of Davison. Public sympathy was also on her side. She litigated against the men at Strangeways who had been responsible for the hosepipe incident, and damages were awarded in her favor on January 19, 1910. Then Davison's militant attacks escalated. In 1911, she was sentenced to six months for setting fire to a mailbox. To draw attention to the cause, she attempted suicide by throwing herself down an iron staircase at Holloway in 1911; she landed on wire-netting, 30 feet below, and suffered severe spinal injuries.

Emily Davison became convinced that the conscience of Parliament would only be awakened by the sacrifice of a life. Thus at the Epsom

Derby on June 4, 1913, in full view of King George V and Queen *Mary of Teck, Davison rushed onto the course wrapped in a WSPU banner, grabbed the reins of Anmer, the king's horse, and was trampled; she died four days later. Her skull had been fractured, and she never regained consciousness.

Though the British at large generally dismissed Davison's actions as that of a mentally ill fanatic, representatives of many unions, including the gas workers', dockers' and general laborers', attended her funeral, as well as graduates and clergy. Though the police had banned the procession, the streets were lined by respectful crowds as her coffin was escorted through London by 2,000 suffragists. Buried at her mother's home in Morpeth in Northumberland, her tombstone is inscribed "Deed, not words." *Emmeline Pankhurst was arrested during the march.

SUGGESTED READING:

Colmore, Gertrude. *The Life of Emily Davison.* Women's Press, 1913.

Morley, Ann, and Liz Stanley. *The Life and Death of Emily Davison.* Women's Press, 1988.

Roberts, Marie, ed. *The Militants,* 1995.

Davydova, Yelena (b. 1961).

See Comaneci, Nadia for sidebar.

Dawes, Sophia (1705–1840).

See Feuchères, Sophie, Baronne de.

Dawidowicz, Lucy (1915–1990)

American historian of the Holocaust, whose major work The War Against the Jews *(1975) argued that virtually all of the policies of Nazi Germany were rooted in Adolf Hitler's racism. Born Lucy Schildkret in New York, New York, on June 16, 1915; died in New York City on December 5, 1990; daughter of Max Schildkret and Dora (Ofnaem) Schildkret; sister of* **Eleanor Schildkret***; married Szymon M. Dawidowicz.*

Selected writings: From that Time and Place: A Memoir 1938–1947 *(NY: W.W. Norton, 1989);* The Golden Tradition: Jewish Life and Thought in Eastern Europe *(NY: Henry Holt, 1967);* The Holocaust and the Historians *(Cambridge, MA: Harvard University Press, 1981);* The Jewish Presence: Essays on Identity and History *(NY: Henry Holt, 1977);* The War Against the Jews 1933–1945 *(NY: Henry Holt, 1975).*

Born in New York City as the daughter of Yiddish-speaking Polish-Jewish immigrants, Lucy Schildkret Dawidowicz was a quintessential New Yorker, energetic and always ready to engage in a heated argument over any and all points of Jewish history. Short in stature, she was a colorful personality with a thick Bronx accent and, as a leading historian of the Holocaust, did not suffer fools at all. Despite her contentious nature, she gained the respect of many of her fellow historians for her deep knowledge of her subject and her defense of views that remain controversial to this day. In her major work, *The War Against the Jews* (1975), Dawidowicz argued that Hitler's ideological goals—the achievement of German racial purity and the annihilation of the Jews—determined his political and military goals. Thus, the energy for Nazi Germany's drive towards war and the attempt to achieve world domination came from its murderous campaign against the Jews. Dawidowicz was 60 when she published this book, having lived a life rich in experiences both rewarding and tragic.

After graduating from New York's Hunter College in 1936, Dawidowicz made attempts to travel to Europe to experience Yiddish culture at its source in Poland. Fortunate during the Depression era to receive a research fellowship, she sailed from New York in the summer of 1938 to spend a year in Vilna working at the YIVO Institute, the leading Yiddish cultural research center. Called "the Jerusalem of Lithuania," Vilna in 1938 remained remarkably intact as a medieval city, a fabled center of Jewish learning with cobbled streets and ancient, crumbling arches. The YIVO Institute, founded in 1925, had by 1938 become the nerve center of a vibrant Yiddish-based cultural Renaissance, and it was here that Dawidowicz met dozens of brilliant young men and women determined to help create a new Jewish tradition appropriate for the 20th century. Without her knowing it, the year Dawidowicz spent in Vilna represented the last flowering of Jewish cultural life in Poland before the onset of the Holocaust. She left Vilna on the eve of war, traveling through Nazi Germany in the last days of August 1939 and then on to Copenhagen, from which she sailed for the United States, arriving in Boston on September 28.

From 1940 through 1946, Dawidowicz worked in New York as the assistant to the research director of the Institute for Jewish Research, the American branch of YIVO. These were years of hope and anguish, hope that somehow the Jews of Nazi-occupied Europe might survive the oppression that grew greater with each passing day, and anguish when it became clear in 1942 that an unparalleled disaster of genocidal proportions was taking place. Although Dawidowicz's life during these years was busy and productive, she also experienced a profound sense of anguish for the countless victims of Nazi murder squads. Toward the Germans, there was a growing feeling of rage and a desire for revenge. Many years later, in her 1989 memoir *From that Time and Place*, Dawidowicz recalled that during these years she "felt as if I were living in disconnected universes—in a real world of normal obligations and pastimes and in a phantasmagoric world of my fevered imagination, in which I partook of its agony and death as if it were my real world."

In 1946–47, Dawidowicz lived in occupied Germany as an educational officer for displaced persons' camps, working for the American Jewish Joint Distribution Committee. Helping Holocaust survivors set up and run Jewish schools, libraries, newspapers as well as dramatic and musical groups gave Dawidowicz hope that a new life could flourish in the ruins of a morally as well as physically devastated Europe. One of her most satisfying experiences was to supervise the launching of a Yiddish-language journal, using the same Munich printing press that had once been used to print the infamous *Völkischer Beobachter,* the official newspaper of the Nazi Party. Having lost virtually all of her Vilna friends in the Holocaust, Dawidowicz felt a visceral hatred for Germans during her year in that ruined and defeated territory. She saw them as being as "craven in defeat as they had been insolent in victory." In January 1948, soon after her return to the U.S., Dawidowicz married Szymon Dawidowicz, a Polish-Jewish activist who had miraculously escaped from the Nazi net.

From 1946 through 1967, Dawidowicz held the post of research analyst for the American Jewish Committee, finally being promoted to director of research in 1968. During these years, she continued to immerse herself in the often baffling—and almost always horrifying—details of the Holocaust. It was on this subject that she wrote her 1961 master's thesis at Columbia University. A "late bloomer" in terms of publishing her scholarship, Dawidowicz produced her first major work in Jewish history in 1967, a well-received anthology of readings on Jewish life and thought in pre-Holocaust Eastern Europe entitled *The Golden Tradition.* Although she would never earn a doctorate, by 1969 Lucy Dawidowicz's credentials as a scholar were sufficiently impressive for her to receive an appointment as an associate professor at New York's Yeshiva University. During this period, when much of her energy went into writing a major study of the Holocaust, she received a number of prestigious research grants and fellowships, including ones from the Gustave Wurzweiler Foundation and the Guggenheim Foundation.

In 1975, at an age when many scholars begin to look longingly toward leisurely years of retirement, Lucy Dawidowicz finally published what would be her magnum opus. Her book, *The War Against the Jews, 1933–1945,* received many enthusiastic reviews from newspaper critics but in numerous instances professional historians were less positive in their assessment of her work. Some questioned her basic thesis, namely that Hitlerian ideology was the sole explanation of the Holocaust, while others noted critically her refusal to either explain or pass judgment on the apparent failure of most of Europe's Jews to actively resist the Nazis during the various stages of the Holocaust. Over the next years, Dawidowicz would often bitterly clash with her critics, either in print or at various scholarly gatherings. She asked whether historians, who had not personally experienced the terrors of Nazi rule, could even be asked to write on such issues, which she regarded as being morally inappropriate for non-victims to render judgment on. Secondly, she noted that under any circumstances Jewish resistance to the Nazis was doomed anyway given the isolation of Jews, their weak organization and lack of weapons, and the overwhelming military superiority of the Nazis and their allies. Nothing of consequence could have been done, she claimed, and to think otherwise was simply to ignore the reality of the times.

In her 1981 book *The Holocaust and the Historians,* Dawidowicz set off a veritable firestorm by attacking the views of a number of prominent intellectuals, most of them Jewish, on the topic of Jewish passivity during the Holocaust. Among others, she sharply criticized *Hannah Arendt, Bruno Bettelheim, and Raul Hilberg for painting portraits of a European Jewish community that with few exceptions was not only weakly led but often cowardly in its relationship to the Nazis and their collaborators. She was particularly vehement in her defense of the various Jewish Councils—*Judenräte*—set up by the Nazis to help govern Jewish communities in the occupied nations of Hitler's Europe. Rather than indicting these self-governing boards as de facto Nazi collaborators as Arendt and the others had done, Dawidowicz presented a viewpoint in which the terrible dilemmas of wartime were emphasized. She also vehemently defended the American Jewish community against the charge that it had often been complacent during World War II and had missed many opportunities to alert the world to the Holocaust.

Many of Lucy Dawidowicz's contemporaries were taken aback by the direct and blunt nature of her polemics, which were rarely if ever diplomatic. Her unwillingness to clothe her arguments in the often bland language of standard academic discourse may have stemmed from the essential nature of her personality, or it may have been a defense mechanism related to the fact that she never received a doctorate, the "union card" of the modern academic world. Possibly her spiky personality was made even more so in her last years because of grief over the death of her husband Szymon in 1979. There was, however, another Lucy Dawidowicz who was quite different from the implacable debater and sometimes harsh polemicist. Relaxing in her leisure hours, Dawidowicz was a passionate operagoer, a devotee of the Metropolitan Opera and a connoisseur of great vocal art, who in the summer brought the same kind of unbridled enthusiasm to her rooting for the New York Mets at Shea Stadium or watching them in front of her television in her book-filled apartment on 200 West 86th Street. This, too, was Lucy Dawidowicz, a quintessential New Yorker both at work and play.

Lucy Dawidowicz's last book, her 1989 memoir *From that Time and Place*, was a fitting capstone to her remarkable career as a scholar and Jewish activist. Richly evocative of her youth and early adulthood, it is a bittersweet recollection of her year in the doomed city of Vilna, of her emotional turmoil during the final years of the Holocaust when she and millions of other American Jews were powerless to halt the tragic events in Europe. Possibly the most moving section of this book is Dawidowicz's recollection of her work among Holocaust survivors in a shattered postwar Germany. During her last years, Dawidowicz not only enjoyed her considerable success as a scholar and publicist but also seems to have found a measure of personal peace. In October 1985, she visited Berlin for the first time since 1947 and was able to pass a dispassionate judgment on the German nation's rehabilitation from the burdens of its Nazi past. Her postwar feelings of revulsion and desire for personal revenge for Nazi crimes had now been replaced by the idea that reconciliation between Germans and Jews could in fact begin to take place. While walking down West Berlin's crowded Kurfürstendamm, she suddenly realized that most of the crowd she was in had not even been born in 1945. These young Germans were not the Nazis of the 1930s and 1940s but "ordinary young people, too young to be charged with the burden of Germany's terrible history. They were not the ghosts of the Nazi past."

In her personal life, Dawidowicz had traveled a long and often complicated path over the decades. Raised in a Jewish home that was centered on Yiddish culture but indifferent to Judaism as a religion, Dawidowicz had as a student at Hunter College rebelled against her "mildly socialist" parents by joining the Young Communist League. Disillusioned with Marxist rigidity, she quit after a year. By the final years of her life, her political views had moved to the neoconservative Right, her religion had become Orthodox Judaism, and her former indifference to Zionism had metamorphosed to one of being a passionate defender of a militarily strong Israel. Lucy Dawidowicz was working on an extensive chronicle of the Jewish presence in the United States that, had it been completed, would surely have elicited further lively debates when she died in New York City on December 5, 1990.

SOURCES:

Bernstein, Richard. "Lucy S. Dawidowicz, 75, Scholar Of Jewish Life and History, Dies," in *The New York Times Biographical Service*. December 1990, p. 1150.

Dawidowicz, Lucy S. "Lies About the Holocaust," in *Commentary*. Vol. 70, no. 6. December 1980, pp. 31–37.

———. "In Berlin Again," in *Commentary*. Vol. 82, no. 2. August 1986, pp. 32–41.

Gelles, Walter. "PW Interviews: Lucy Dawidowicz," in *Publishers Weekly*. Vol. 235. May 12, 1989, pp. 264–265.

Kozodoy, Neal. "In Memoriam: Lucy S. Dawidowicz," in *Commentary*. Vol. 93, no. 5. May 1992, pp. 35–40.

Marrus, Michael R. *The Holocaust in History*. NY: Meridian, 1989.

John Haag, Associate Professor of History, University of Georgia, Athens, Georgia

Day, Doris (1924—)

American singer-actress whose warm and outgoing persona made her one of the most popular film stars of the 1950s. Born Doris von Kappelhoff in Cincinnati, Ohio, on April 3, 1924; second of three children and only daughter of Frederick Wilhelm (a music teacher) and Alma Sophia (Welz) von Kappelhoff; attended Our Lady of Angels High School through sophomore year; married Al Jorden (a trombone player in Gene Krupa's band), in March 1941 (divorced 1943); married George Weidler (a saxophone player and brother of the child movie actress Virginia Weidler), in 1946 (divorced 1949); married Marty Melcher (a producer-manager), on April 3, 1951 (died 1968); married restaurateur Barry Comden (divorced 1981); children: (first marriage) son, Terry Melcher (b. 1942).

Filmography: Romance on the High Seas *(1948);* My Dream is Yours *(1949);* It's a Great Feeling *(1949);* Young Man with a Horn *(1950);* Tea for Two *(1950);* The West Point Story *(1950);* Storm Warning

(1951); Lullaby of Broadway *(1951)*; On Moonlight Bay *(1951)*; I'll See You in My Dreams *(1951)*; *(cameo)* Starlift *(1951)*; The Winning Team *(1952)*; April in Paris *(1952)*; By the Light of the Silvery Moon *(1953)*; Calamity Jane *(1953)*; Lucky Me *(1954)*; Young at Heart *(1955)*; Love Me or Leave Me *(1955)*; The Man Who Knew Too Much *(1956)*; Julie *(1956)*; The Pajama Game *(1957)*; Teacher's Pet *(1958)*; Tunnel of Love *(1958)*; It Happened to Jane *(1959)*; Pillow Talk *(1959)*; Please Don't Eat the Daisies *(1960)*; Midnight Lace *(1960)*; Lover Come Back *(1962)*; That Touch of Mink *(1962)*; Jumbo *(1962)*; The Thrill of It All *(1963)*; Move Over, Darling *(1963)*; Send Me No Flowers *(1964)*; Do Not Disturb *(1965)*; The Glass-Bottom Boat *(1966)*; Caprice *(1967)*; The Ballad of Josie *(1968)*; Where Were You When the Lights Went Out? *(1968)*; With Six You Get Eggroll *(1968)*.

When singer-actress Doris Day engaged A.E. Hotchner to help write her autobiography in 1973, she longed to dispel the golden-girl image that had followed her throughout her career. "I'm tired of being thought of as Miss Goody Two-Shoes . . . the girl next door, Miss Happy-Go-Lucky," she told him. "I'm not the All-American Virgin Queen and I'd like to deal with the true, honest story of who I really am." Whether it was simply because of her blonde, freckle-faced good looks, the winsome appeal of her singing voice, or the romantic nature of many of her films, Doris Day had an aura of good will surrounding her that nothing could shake. Occasional departures into darker movie roles did little but confuse her fans. (After her portrayal of *Ruth Etting in Love Me or Leave Me, she was deluged with mail castigating her for drinking and playing a lewd woman.) Off-screen, Doris Day's life was an on-going challenge, with every professional success seemingly countered by a personal tragedy.

There must be something about me, about whatever it is that I give off, that accounts for this disparity between who I am and who I appear to be.

—Doris Day

She was born Doris von Kappelhoff in Cincinnati, Ohio, on April 3, 1924, and named for her mother's favorite silent-screen star, *Doris Kenyon. Her parents were opposites: her mother Alma was warm and outgoing; her father Frederick was an introverted music teacher, who paid more attention to his piano and other women than his family. Doris was 11 when her father became involved with her mother's best

friend, and the resulting separation and divorce of her parents created a scandal that confused and humiliated her. She and her older brother Paul (another brother Richard died before she was born) remained with her mother, who took them to live in suburban Evanston where she went to work in the family bakery.

While still in kindergarten, Day made her stage debut at the local Masonic hall, after which she pestered her mother for dancing lessons. Following several years of tap, ballet, and acrobatics, as well as performances at local clubs and city events, she met another 12-year-old hoofer, Jerry Doherty. Teaming up, they won the $500 grand prize as the best dance team in Cincinnati in a contest run by one of the local department stores. Their mothers, buoyed by prospects of show-biz careers for their children, used the money to finance a four-week trip to Hollywood, where the young hopefuls studied briefly with Louis DaPron at the famous Fanchon & Marco dancing school. At the end of four weeks, prospects looked so favorable that the two mothers decided to move to California permanently, and the foursome wound their way back to Cincinnati to convince Doherty's father to move his dairy business west. At a party given by hometown friends on October 13, 1937, Day bid farewell to her life in Ohio, then went out for a final hamburger with her boyfriend Larry Doherty (Jerry's brother) and several friends. On the way home, while crossing railroad tracks in rainy weather, their car was struck by a locomotive. Day suffered a compound fracture of her right leg, ending her promising dancing career and nearly crippling her for life.

To help ease the boredom of her 14-month convalescence (during which she fell and rebroke the partially healed bone a second time), Day convinced her mother to allow her voice lessons. She made her first radio appearance on the Saturday morning amateur program "Carlin's Carnival," with the help of her singing teacher, and subsequently landed a weekend gig singing at Charlie Yee's Shanghai Inn, a local Chinese restaurant. Later, Day was hired to sing for Barney Rapp, a small-town bandleader who had a club opening in Cincinnati. It was Rapp who convinced her to change her name from Kappelhoff to Day, after the song *Day after Day*, one of her most frequently requested numbers. Day then toured with Bob Crosby's band out of Chicago and later joined Les Brown for a three-month tour of one-nighters. Although she could not read music, Day relied on memory and ear, much like Bing Crosby and Frank Sinatra. "She

was every band leader's dream," said Les Brown, "a vocalist who had natural talent, a keen regard for the lyrics, and an attractive appearance."

At age 17, just as her career was hitting its stride, Day left the Brown band to marry Al Jor-den, a trombone player she had met while singing with Rapp. Although both her mother and Les Brown urged her not to destroy her promising career by marrying so young, Day refused to listen. "Singing was just something to do until that time came," she said later. "Home and marriage was the only career I wanted. And the only career I have ever really wanted." But Jorden turned out to be a batterer during jealous rages, even through her pregnancy with their son Terry, who was born in February 1942. After enduring repeated assaults, followed by scenes of contrition, Day left him and returned to Cincinnati with her son.

Following her divorce in 1943, Day went back on the road with Les Brown, leaving her son with her mother in Cincinnati. During the tour, she introduced the song "Sentimental Journey." "I *always* feel a rise in my scalp or on the backs of my wrists when something is special," she said, "whether it be song or man. I stepped to the microphone, and on the second run-through I sang the lyrics. I loved the song. I loved singing it, and we all thought it was going to be a big hit." Recorded on the Okey label, "Sentimental Journey" became a million-seller, a song that would forever be associated with Doris Day.

During that second stint with Les Brown, Day met and married George Weidler, a saxophone player, and became a trailer-housewife while Weidler worked in Hollywood. The couple parted after only eight months, possibly because Weidler feared Day's career might surpass his. (Their relationship continued after the divorce, and it was Weidler who would introduce Day to the Christian Science religion, which she would then embrace as her own.)

In 1946, Day's agent secured an interview for her with Michael Curtiz, who was looking for a singer to replace a pregnant *Betty Hutton as the lead in his movie *Romance on the High Seas*. Still shaky from her recent breakup with Weidler, Day was distracted and teary-eyed during most of the interview but still managed to secure a screentest. Convinced that she had blown the test, she booked a ticket back to Cincinnati before receiving the news that the part was hers. Although the finished picture was considered banal, Day received good reviews. Acting came as naturally to her as singing. "From the first take onward," she said, "I never had any trepidation about what I was called on to do. Movie acting came to me with greater ease and naturalness than anything else I had ever done." She then embarked on a series of 14 pictures for Warner Bros., managing to squeeze in a tour of duty with Bob Hope's concert and radio troupe between her first and second film.

After a few romantic musicals, Day was labeled Hollywood's girl-next-door, even though she would occasionally take on dramatic roles in such movies as *Young Man with a Horn* (1950), *Love Me or Leave Me* (1955), and *The Man Who Knew Too Much* (1956), which also produced the Oscar-winning song "Que Sera, Sera." In 1951, she received the Laurel Award as "the leading new female personality in the motion picture industry" and was named by *Motion Picture Herald* as one of the top ten bankable film stars of 1952. Her singing career kept pace with her burgeoning film career. Day was a leading moneymaker for Columbia Records for over four years, producing about 12 records yearly with annual sales of around 5 million.

But success and constant work came at a price. In 1954, after the release of *Calamity Jane* (in which she sang the Academy Award-winning song "Secret Love"), Day began to suffer shortness of breath and heart palpitations, which culminated in nervous collapse. Still recovering, she scarcely remembered making her next picture, *Lucky Me* (1954). Her film career hit its peak in the 1960s when she starred in a series of sophisticated bedroom farces opposite romantic co-stars such as Rock Hudson, Cary Grant, and James Garner. She was nominated for an Academy Award for the first of these films, *Pillow Talk*, in 1959.

In 1951, after romances with several of her co-stars, including Jack Carson and Ronald Reagan, Day had married her agent Marty Melcher, who at one time had been married to *Patti Andrews of the Andrews Sisters. Melcher seemed to provide the serene, steady relationship Day needed, as well as some stability for her son Terry, whom he adopted. He converted to Christian Science, becoming almost fanatical in his observances. But Melcher had a reputation in show-business circles as a hustler who worshipped money over people, and some believed his marriage to Day had been monetarily motivated. Over the course of their up-and-down marriage (during which his relationship with Terry disintegrated), Melcher and his lawyer Jerry Rosenthal managed and invested all of Day's earnings. When Melcher died in 1968, it was discovered that $20 million of her earnings had been squandered, leaving her heavily in debt. In the midst of her grief and attempts to ascertain whether her husband had been a thief or a dupe because of his association with Rosenthal, Day discovered that one of Melcher's final acts before his death was to commit her to a television series. "The Doris Day Show," based on the premise of a widow with two children living on a farm, had just started production when

From the movie
Calamity Jane,
starring Doris
Day.

Day's son Terry became tangentially involved in the notorious Charles Manson case; the brutal murders took place at a house he had once owned. A music producer, Terry had at one time auditioned Manson, who was interested in recording his own music, and had turned him down. Some believed that Manson had sent his followers to the house looking for Terry rather than the house's new occupant **Sharon Tate**.

Thus Day was thrust into one of the most frightening periods of her life. For the next year, a guard patrolled her house day and night. Her son Terry, also under heavy security, became reclusive and increasingly dependent on drugs and alcohol, an addiction that culminated in a near fatal motorcycle accident that shattered both his legs. Through his long and torturous recovery, Day established a mother-son relationship with him that had been impossible when he was a child. "Although he was thirty years old," she said, "it was the first time I had really taken care of him." Terry battled his way back, resumed his job, and subsequently married and had a son.

Day also bounced back. She hired a new producer for her floundering television show, which ran, with a new format, from 1968 to 1973. In 1974, after a long and costly court trial, she was awarded more than $22 million in damages from Rosenthal. There was also a fourth marriage to restaurateur Barry Comden, which ended in divorce in 1981. Day then left show business. Moving to Carmel, California, she devoted herself to the animal-rights movement and the Doris Day Animal League, a national organization she established in 1987. After an absence of a decade, she returned briefly to the spotlight as the host of a cable television show, "Doris Day and Friends" (1985–86).

SOURCES:

Candee, Marjorie Dent, ed. *Current Biography.* NY: H.W. Wilson, 1954.

Clarke, Donald, ed. *The Penguin Encyclopedia of Popular Music.* NY: Viking, 1989.

Hartigan, Patti. "The Mysterious Adoration of Doris Day," in *The Boston Globe.* October 4, 1996. Section E, p. 10.

Hotchner, A.E. *Doris Day: Her Own Story.* NY: William Morrow, 1976.

Katz, Ephraim. *The Film Encyclopedia.* NY: Harper-Collins, 1994.

Barbara Morgan,
Melrose, Massachusetts

Day, Dorothy (1897–1980)

American pacifist and radical who founded the Catholic Worker *newspaper and ran the movement's New York House of Hospitality. Born Dorothy Day on November 8, 1897, in Brooklyn, New York; died on November 29, 1980; third of five children and eldest daughter of John and Grace (Saterlee) Day; married Barkeley Tobey (divorced); married (common law) Forster Batterham; children: (second marriage) Tamar (b. 1926).*

Was first jailed, after a suffrage march (1917); published autobiographical novel The Eleventh Virgin *(1924); converted to Catholicism (1927); issued first* Catholic Worker *(May 1, 1933); published* From Union Square to Rome *(1937); published autobiography,* The Long Loneliness *(1952); jailed with Mexican migrant workers, California (1973).*

Dorothy Day spent her youth as a hard-drinking radical journalist in Greenwich Village and had love affairs with several literary celebrities of her day, including the playwright Eugene O'Neill. But after her conversion to Catholicism, she became a different kind of radical, as dedicated as before to social justice but now in the context of strict religious orthodoxy. Many American Catholics in the early years of the Catholic Worker movement disliked and mistrusted her, but by the last years of her life in the 1970s she was a widely acclaimed figure, taken by Catholic activists as a prophet and forerunner of the modern church.

Day was born in November 1897, the daughter of a journalist who wrote horse-racing columns and tried periodically to become a novelist. He was a rather unstable man, emotionally cold, often drunk, sometimes unable to work, and the family moved frequently during Day's youth, from New York to Oakland, California, then back to Chicago. She was in San Francisco, aged eight, at the time of the 1906 earthquake and recalled later how the emergency had led people to work together for once as they recovered from the catastrophe. At age 12, having had no religious education but with an eagerly religious temperament, Dorothy Day began to study the Bible and attend an Episcopalian church with her sister **Della.** Her mother's nervous breakdown when Dorothy was 15 increased an already stressful home life, but one from which she found it hard to break. She attended the University of Illinois in Champagne-Urbana for two years but left college when the family moved to New York rather than staying to graduate. Under the influence of her college professors, she declared herself an atheist.

In New York, she became a journalist for *The Call* and *The Masses,* met Floyd Dell, Max Eastman, and other militant Greenwich Village socialists. She endorsed their sexual radicalism too and entered into a destructive relationship with a bullying writer named Lionel Moise, which led to her becoming pregnant and getting an abortion, only to be deserted by him. She may even have attempted suicide in the backwash of this humiliating affair. She later gave a graphic fictional account of it in her one published novel, *The Eleventh Virgin* (1924), which she later regretted having ever written. Meanwhile, as a radical jour-

Dorothy
Day

nalist she roamed the
poorest sections of New
York's slums, writing about
strikes, hunger, and the struggle of impoverished immigrant workers for living
wages. She also volunteered for the Anti-Con-
scription League, which tried to prevent young
men from being drafted to fight in the First
World War. Always willing to join demonstrations and picket lines, Day was arrested in
1917 in a confrontation with Washington,
D.C., police during a women's suffrage rally.
She was sentenced to 30 days in jail and served
16 of them before President Woodrow Wilson
pardoned her and her fellow inmates. Ironically, as the feminist scholar **June O'Connor** has

shown, Day was not re-
ally devoted to the cause
that led to her arrest. O'Connor
writes:

> Not only was Day not an advocate of
> women's suffrage, she was not a feminist in
> any self conscious, intentional, or public
> way. She spurned sociopolitical feminism,
> refusing to march on behalf of women's
> rights; she was no closet feminist either,
> since she regularly critiqued the movement
> in both its early and later twentieth century
> forms as being too self-centered.

Day was jailed again in 1922, this time after a
police raid on a house owned by the Industrial
Workers of the World (IWW), where she was

wrongly accused of prostitution. She was released after a humiliating series of body searches and taunts.

A person can start out aiming to be righteous and end up self-righteous; we can become so earnestly the doers of works of charity that we think the Lord has given us a special blessing. . . . I remember a nun who came to visit us [who said] . . . 'This is dangerous work.' I'll remember her words until my dying day.

—Dorothy Day

After a stay in London, Paris, and Capri, during which a short, unsuccessful marriage to a literary promotor named Barkeley Tobey was unraveling, Day returned to America and went to work in Chicago for two years on the Communist newspaper *The Liberator,* then to New Orleans for a job with the *New Orleans Item.* While she was there, her novel was published. Though it was no great literary success, Day did manage to sell the movie rights for $5,000, with which she was able to return to New York and buy a house. She finally found a more durable relationship with Forster Batterham, a biologist, and lived with him as his common-law wife from 1924 until 1927. Together they had a child, Tamar, but were drawn apart by Day's growing determination to have the child, and then herself, baptized in the Catholic faith. Batterham, a principled atheist, would have nothing to do with organized religion, and on this irreconcilable difference the couple split up. Day later described their intense relationship in *The Long Loneliness* and explored the irony that, through loving him, she came to love God, though that in turn took her away from the man she loved:

> Forster had made the physical world come alive for me and had awakened in my heart a flood of gratitude. The final object of this love and gratitude was God. No human creature could receive or contain so vast a flood of love and joy as I often felt after the birth of my child. With this came the need to worship, to adore.

The breakup was stormy and painful; at one point, Batterham broke into the room where she was staying and almost strangled her after a raging argument.

At first, conversion did not help in pointing Day towards her life's work, and she continued to move restlessly, signing on for a time as a Hollywood scriptwriter, then touring Mexico with her young daughter and sending articles about peasant Catholics' everyday life

to the Catholic journals *America* and *Commonweal.* As the Great Depression worsened, however, she became determined to aid the suffering people of America directly, rather than simply writing about them. Until then, her mid-30s, she had seen herself primarily as a writer. From this point on, she continued to write copiously but now most of her writing went into a new newspaper, *The Catholic Worker,* which she launched on May Day 1933 and sold for one cent per issue. Day also decided to live among the poor by running a House of Hospitality, always open, in which hungry men and women were fed, clothed, and sheltered, with no questions asked about their origins or experiences, and no effort to feed them religion before dinner (as did the Salvation Army). As she wrote in *Loaves and Fishes,* her book about her work:

> We never ask people why they are here. They just come from the streets to eat, to wait, to find some place for themselves, to have someone to talk to, someone with whom to share and so to lighten their troubles.

Day ran her Mott Street House of Hospitality solely on voluntary contributions. Enough idealistic people (mainly but not all Catholics) contributed the money, time, blankets, clothes and food supplies to enable the experiment to survive, while Day's growing circle of admirers opened Houses of Hospitality in other cities across the United States. Her monthly articles in the *Catholic Worker* were almost always directly autobiographical, many of them anecdotes about life in the House, and, although an inevitable aura of romance soon surrounded it, she tried to discourage sentimentality by insisting on the horribleness of some of the people she welcomed there. Her constantly repeated theme was that the hand of Christian love must be held out especially to the people who are most unlovable, even if they are dishonest, unkind, and physically repellent. She was robbed repeatedly by people she had helped.

From the beginning, the Catholic Worker movement was influenced by Peter Maurin, a French immigrant from a peasant background (the oldest of 22 children) who preached and practiced an ascetic brand of Catholicism. An itinerant philosopher much given to cryptic utterances, Maurin published many of his thoughts in the *Catholic Worker,* but Day was careful not to surrender control of its editorial policy to him. Although the paper covered strikes and other issues of national and labor politics, it showed from the beginning a mystical tendency and carried "Easy Essays" by Maurin and philosophical ruminations by several other authors. With Maurin's encouragement, the Catholic Worker movement also bought a farm in upstate New York, but the group's lack of agricultural experience made it a hopeless failure except as a rural "flophouse." Maurin himself toured the country discussing the ideas of the movement but consistently returned to Dorothy Day in New York until he died in 1949. She always claimed that he was the mastermind behind the operation, though most historians of the movement doubt it. As one of them, Mel Piehl, points out:

It was personally comforting to Day, as well as strategically useful to her as a woman leading a social movement in the sexually conservative Catholic Church, to be able to point to the male co-founder of the movement and to emphasize that she was merely carrying out Maurin's program.

As a link with a venerable tradition of European Catholic social thought, moreover, he was a genuinely important figure. Like Day, he had a vision of sanctification through suffering and failure; at a time when most American Catholics wanted nothing more than an end to the Depression and

Dorothy Day

a revived prosperity, the two of them eagerly embraced the "privilege" of poverty and the chance to suffer a little of the pain Christ had known.

In 1891, Pope Leo XIII had issued an "encyclical" letter, *Rerum Novarum* ("The Conditions of Labor"), which condemned many of the characteristics of industrial capitalism and outlined the need for a just society. The encyclical also condemned socialism and communism as atheistic systems, and it upheld the right to private property. These two features had made it unacceptable to the growing American left at the turn of the century, but Catholic trade unionists quoted it to show that theirs was not a "reactionary" church. In 1931, the 40th anniversary of the first encyclical, Pope Pius XI issued a new encyclical, *Quadragesimo Anno* ("The Reconstruction of the Social Order"), confirming the older Pope's declarations and updating his indictment of a heartless, materialist capitalism. The American Catholic bishops had also made a statement pledging themselves to "social reconstruction" at the beginning of the 1920s. This collection of official declarations gave Day and her followers ample justification for their work, though the pontiffs and bishops had not foreseen the kind of radical self-abnegation Day brought to her program. The *Catholic Worker,* then, was pledged to fight for social justice and against communism along papally approved lines. As historian James Fisher has shown, many of Day's Catholic contemporaries feared that it was "a potential Trojan Horse for Communist infiltration, while on the Left, Day's former associates scorned it as a tool of clerical fascism."

Day enriched her own religious life by becoming involved in frequent meditative retreats, conducted in strict silence and featuring severe self-mortification, led by Fathers Onesimus Lacouture and John Hugo. These priests, dismayed by the materialism and complacency of many American Catholics, saw in Day a true believer in their idea of salvation through suffering. Their ideals were so extreme that the church hierarchy itself censured them in 1943, arguing that they were taking a "Jansenist" position that condemned nature itself as corrupt. To Dorothy Day, however, they remained inspirational, and she wrote a massive collection of retreat articles based on their ideas.

In the interwar years, most American Catholics were either themselves immigrants, or were descended from people who had migrated to America in the last hundred years, and whose ethnic identity was still strong—Irish, German, Polish, Italian, and Slavic. Typical Catholic laypeople were docile and deferential towards the church hierarchy so that lay Catholic movements usually accepted leadership and guidance from priests. Day was no immigrant (she had Puritan ancestors) and did not want priests telling her what to do. Instead, she threw down constant challenges to the clergy and bishops, demanding that they live up to the church's high ideals, spend less on their own creature comforts and more on the urban poor all around them, and fulfil the honorable vow of poverty. She was sufficiently eloquent and impressive that even some of the important church patriarchs, such as New York's Cardinal Francis Spellman, who could have made life very difficult for her organization, put up with her criticisms and contributed both money and words of encouragement to her work. Spellman remarked to another priest that, despite her odd ways, she might turn out to be a saint.

In 1936, the outbreak of the Spanish Civil War forced an early crisis on the *Catholic Worker.* Most of the American Catholic press was fervently enthusiastic about Francisco Franco's uprising—some newspapers referred to him as "The George Washington of Spain." The reason was that the Spanish republic of the early 1930s was anti-clerical, and, when the war began, republicans in some communities massacred priests and nuns. Rebelling against the republic, Franco posed as the defender of the church against bloodthirsty atheism. Day, however, was implacably opposed to war under any circumstances and refused to endorse Franco. She was still close enough to the American secular left to know that it had its own string of atrocity stories, of massacres committed by Franco-ists, and this knowledge hardened her determination to speak out for neither combatant. This pacifist-neutrality enraged mainstream Catholic editors, and Day became the object of their editorial wrath.

Catholics who could tolerate her neutrality in that comparatively remote war had a more difficult time accepting her continued antiwar position during World War II when America was directly involved. The Japanese attack on Pearl Harbor and the news of Nazi atrocities in Europe convinced many Catholic Workers that they must fight in the war. About 80% of the Catholic Worker men eligible for military service accepted the call and went to fight. Day never wavered in her absolute pacifist convictions, however, and remained highly controversial on the issue during the 1950s when the government tried to compel citizens' cooperation in civil-defense schemes against possible nuclear attacks. Day coolly refused to move to a fallout shelter during trial runs and was prosecuted for her resistance in 1955 (but given a suspended sentence). She and several sympathizers protested against these drills in each of the next four years, sometimes serving a few days in prison after having their day in court (where they condemned the immorality of a nuclear weapons-based military policy) but more often released with suspended sentences right away. Day also condemned a declaration by Pope Pius XII in 1956 when he spoke in favor of the Catholic "just war" tradition and against the idea that a Catholic could be a conscientious objector or pacifist.

The Second Vatican Council (1962–65) and the social turmoil of the 1960s transformed American Catholicism. Priests and nuns began to participate in civil-rights marches and anti-Vietnam war demonstrations, even to be arrested for civil disobedience. A young man named Roger LaPorte, who had worked occasionally at one of the Houses of Hospitality, burned himself alive in front of the United Nations in protest over the American escalation of the Vietnam War. As he lay dying, he declared that he was one of the Catholic Workers. To the Catholic left of that decade, Day was already a legend, and her life's work an inspiring example. She did not always see eye to eye with the Catholic left, however, especially when some of its members seemed less devoted to strict religious orthodoxy than she. For example, the Jesuit priest, writer, and activist Daniel Berrigan held informal celebrations of the mass at the Catholic Worker house but horrified Day by casually breaking ordinary bread for communion and letting crumbs fly (even though priests were taught that every particle of the bread, transformed by transubstantiation into the Body of Christ, must be accounted for). She never endorsed the clamor of young Catholics for a relaxation of the papal prohibition on contraception; to her, indeed, the strict sexual code of Catholicism had beckoned her away from what she saw as a dissolute life.

The Catholic Worker movement was still thriving when Dorothy Day died in 1980. By then, tens of thousands of Americans had been affected by it, some as recipients of food, clothing, and shelter, others as volunteers or temporary residents. Day knew that many people who came for short stays, especially students and intellectuals, became impatient at the impracticality of the Workers' system, and its inability to touch the roots of the problems it tried to remedy. Responding to critics of this kind, Day answered:

We *are* impractical, as impractical as Calvary. . . . We feed the hungry, yes; we try to shelter the homeless and give them clothes, if we have some, but there is a strong faith at work; we pray. If an outsider who comes to visit doesn't pay attention to our praying and what that means, then he'll miss the whole point of the thing.

For Day, participation in a community of suffering, which she often thought of and referred to as the Mystical Body of Christ, was certain to seem illogical to purely secular observers. To it, nevertheless, she dedicated the second and more successful half of her life.

SOURCES:

Coles, Robert. *Dorothy Day: A Radical Devotion*. Reading, MA: Addison-Wesley, 1987.

Fisher, James T. *The Catholic Counter-Culture in America: 1933–1962*. Chapel Hill, NC: University of North Carolina Press, 1989.

Miller, William. *Dorothy Day: A Biography*. San Francisco, CA: Harper and Row, 1982.

O'Connor, June. *The Moral Vision of Dorothy Day: A Feminist Perspective*. NY: Crossroad, 1991.

Piehl, Mel. *Breaking Bread: The Catholic Worker and the Origin of Catholic Radicalism*. Philadelphia, PA: Temple University Press, 1982.

Roberts, Nancy L. *Dorothy Day and the Catholic Worker*. Albany, NY: SUNY Press, 1984.

Patrick Allitt, Professor of History, Emory University, Atlanta, Georgia

Day, Lady (c. 1915–1959).

See Holiday, Billie.

De Acosta, Mercedes.

See Garbo, Greta for sidebar.

de Almania, Jacqueline Felicia
(fl. 1322)

Parisian doctor. Name variations: Jacoba Felicie de Almania; Jacqueline Felicie de Almania; Jacoba d'Alamanie. Flourished in 1322 in Paris.

Jacqueline de Almania is one of the most well known of medieval women doctors. A French noblewoman, she practiced medicine in Paris and became involved in a long court battle over her right to practice. In 1322, the faculty of the medical school in Paris issued a ban on all physicians working without a license (which the masters of the school asserted could only be properly granted by their establishment). This move was designed to protect the interests of Paris' university-trained physicians, who were more scarce, more expensive, and often less knowledgeable than midwives and healers, and thus less sought after by the ill. De Almania was herself a popular healer, which may be why the masters prosecuted her so vigorously. She was arrested, fined, and excommunicated for her violation of the ban.

Unwilling to honor the ban and lose her livelihood, she prepared a spirited and well-argued defense of her medical capabilities, and she arranged for the testimony of eight former patients who attested that her superb skills had cured them even when male doctors had given up hope of their recovery. De Almania argued her case from several vantage points. First, she agreed with the law banning unlearned people from the healing trades but said such a law did not exclude experienced, wise women like herself. She proposed that women were necessary in the field of medicine to help other women, who were too modest to be examined by a male physician. Lastly, de Almania submitted that she was a fair and honest doctor, for she did not charge patients until after they were cured, and that she remained with patients for the duration of their recovery rather than simply prescribing cures and departing.

After several weeks of hearings, the court decided in favor of the university faculty. The magistrate, undoubtedly aware of the immense political clout the faculty held in the city, agreed that medical school was an absolute prerequisite to the practice of medicine. The court upheld the fine against Jacqueline de Almania and refused to lift the ban of excommunication. After the decision, de Almania disappears from the court documents, so it is uncertain whether she complied with the ban, left the city, or kept practicing her trade illegally.

SOURCES:

Amt, Emilie. *Women's Lives in Medieval Europe.* NY: Routledge, 1993.

LaBarge, Margaret W. *Women in Medieval Life.* London: Hamish Hamilton, 1986.

Laura York, Riverside, California

de Almeida, Julia (1862–1934).

See Almeida, Julia Lopes de.

Dean, Jennie (1852–1913)

African-American missionary and school founder. Name variations: Jane Serepta Dean. Born in Prince William County, Virginia, in 1852 (some sources cite 1854); died in 1913; daughter of Charles and Annie Dean.

Jennie Dean was born a slave in 1852 to parents who were owned by the Cushing and Newson families in Prince William County, Virginia. Details of her early life are few, but it is thought that Jennie's father taught her to read and write, and that she attended a country school for a few months. After the Civil War, her father settled near Sudley Springs. Dean moved to Washington, D.C., and took a job, the earnings from which she sent to her family to help support their farm. Her weekend trips home were spent establishing Sunday schools or missions, and Dean gave industrial training to the community's children.

Returning to Prince William County to live, Dean was concerned by the flight of black children from rural areas to the cities. The social development of black children was paramount to her, and she encouraged parents to purchase land and keep their children home. In 1896, she wrote "Jennie Dean's Rules for Good Behavior among Her People," a pamphlet that included instructions such as "Politeness Home and Abroad," "Don't Be Late in Going to Church; If You Are Late, Take a Seat Nearest the Door," and "Don't Address an Audience with Your Hands in Your Pockets."

Dean's leadership in the community prompted the establishment of the Mount Calvary Church, which initially met in the house her father had built. Her pleas to the community for funds to build a church, fashioned after her guiding philosophy of "You do your part and I'll do mine," were successful. Stephen Johnson Lewis in his biography of Dean entitled *Undaunted Faith* detailed her urgings: "You can each give something if only a day's work. . . . Whenever you sell something, lay aside a small sum, if only a few pennies, for the building fund. Those who have nothing to sell, come and give your labor when we raise the building. After my day's work, I will go out and try to collect money for the fund." In 1880, the church was built and consecrated.

Convinced that African-Americans could not advance without education, after 12 years of mission work Dean secured both local and national funding for the establishment of Manassas Industrial School for Colored Youth. Members of local communities assisted in the construction of the school building, and in September 1894 Frederick Douglass addressed the audience during the school's dedication ceremony. Designed to teach vocational and life skills as well as academics, Manassas Industrial School opened with 6 students and would enroll a total of 75 during its first year. In addition to academics, boys were instructed in masonry, blacksmithing, carpentry, wheelwrighting, machinery, and agriculture, while girls were instructed in housekeeping, cooking, sewing, and laundry work. To help cover the cost of the modest tuition fee, part-time jobs and scholarships were available to students. A trades building and a new library were added by 1915, thanks to funding from Andrew Carnegie and friends in the North, and in 1933 Manassas entered the public-school system.

Although Dean's direct involvement with the school decreased over the years, her interest in the school's advancement remained unwavering until her death, following a long illness, in 1913. She was buried in the cemetery of the church she'd helped to build. At the site of her family's original farmhouse stands a stone marker with a bronze plaque.

SOURCES:

Smith, Jessie Carney, ed. *Notable Black American Women*. Detroit, MI: Gale Research, 1992.

Dean, Julia (1830–1868)

*American actress. Born on July 22, 1830, in Pleasant Valley (now Cahoonzie) near Port Jervis, Orange County, New York; died soon after childbirth in New York on March 6, 1868; buried with her infant daughter; daughter of **Julia Drake** Dean (d. 1832, an actress known for her work in Western theaters) and Edwin Dean (an actor-manager); niece of **Frances Denny Drake** (an actress); married Dr. Arthur P. Hayne (son of Senator Robert Y. Hayne of South Carolina), on January 21, 1855 (divorced); married James G. Cooper (a federal official in Utah Territory), 1865; children: (first marriage) Arthur Hayne; **Julia Hayne**; two others died in infancy.*

An American actress, Julia Dean first appeared at the Bowery Theater as Julie in *The Hunchback*. The role was to remain her specialty. She was also the original Norma in Epes Sargent's *Priestess* and the original ***Leonora de Guzman**, mistress of Alphonso XI, king of Castile, in Boker's tragedy *Leonor de Guzman*.

SUGGESTED READING:

James, Edward T., ed. *Notable American Women*. Cambridge, MA: Belknap Press, 1971.

Dean, Vera Micheles (1903–1972)

Russian-born American author and international relations analyst who opposed the worst excesses of McCarthyism to argue for a world peace based on a rationally realized U.S.-Soviet détente. Born Vera Micheles in St. Petersburg, Russia, on March 29,

1903; died in New York City on October 10, 1972; daughter of Alexander Micheles and Nadine (Kadisch) Micheles; married William Johnson Dean; children: Elinor and William.

Selected writings: Europe in Retreat (NY: Alfred A. Knopf, 1941); On the Threshold of World Order (NY: Foreign Policy Association, 1944); The Four Cornerstones of Peace (NY: Whittlesey House, 1946); The United States and Russia (Cambridge, MA: Harvard University Press, 1948); Foreign Policy Without Fear (NY: McGraw-Hill, 1953); The Nature of the Non-Western World (NY: New American Library, 1957); Roads to Peace (NY: Public Affairs Committee, 1962).

Born in Tsarist Russia into a liberal and culturally assimilated Jewish family, Vera Micheles and her sister and brother were educated for a cosmopolitan world. Not only philosophically but practically as well, the three Micheles children were well-equipped to survive in an unstable world, being tutored in a number of languages. Vera became fluent in seven languages besides Russian, including French, German and English. Decades later, her linguistic abilities would enable her to not only discuss matters of state with high officials but the grubby details of

Jennie Dean

daily life with cab drivers and flea market vendors. Vera's father, of German-Jewish background, had worked in New York City from 1888 to 1896 as a reporter and thus had fully mastered English, while her mother, though of Polish and German Jewish background, had been baptized in the Russian Orthodox Church and educated in England and Germany. **Nadine Kadisch** after her 1899 marriage to Alexander Micheles not only assisted her husband with his business affairs but also translated English novels into Russian (besides raising three children).

As a bourgeois intellectual and capitalist, Alexander Micheles did not dare return to Bolshevik Russia after November 1917 from Finland where he had taken his family that summer. In 1919, the family succeeded in going to London. Vera was sent to live in Boston under the care of William Nickerson, an executive of the Gillette Company for whom her father had worked in Russia. Trained by her family to be practical, Vera attended a business school in order to support herself and worked briefly as a stenographer. In 1921, however, she enrolled at Radcliffe College. In her junior year at Radcliffe, she earned Phi Beta Kappa honors and graduated with distinction in 1925. Supported by a Carnegie Endowment fellowship, she attended Yale University, from which she received a master's degree in 1926. Now it was back to Radcliffe, which in 1928 awarded Vera Micheles a doctorate in fields that were then quite novel, international relations and international law.

In 1928, Vera Micheles became a citizen of the United States and moved to New York City to work for the Foreign Policy Association. In August 1929, she married William Johnson Dean, a New York attorney. Unlike many Americans, the Deans were fortunate during the Great Depression, remaining relatively affluent and secure. A daughter, **Elinor Dean**, was born in 1933. Tragedy struck in 1936 when William Dean died, but Vera had little time to mourn. Five weeks later, she gave birth to her son William. Extensive lecture tours, writing and teaching kept family finances healthy and required that Vera Dean organize every minute of every working day.

By 1938, Dean had been promoted to the post of research director of the Foreign Policy Association. At the heart of the FPA goal of educating the public were a series of informative publications, including *Foreign Policy Reports,* the monthly *Foreign Affairs Bulletin,* and the "Headline" series of books. Dean's numerous writings focused on the threat posed to U.S. security by isolationist attitudes. She argued force-

fully that only a policy of collective security could halt the drift toward war and chaos. The dangers of Fascism were also made clear, and the urgent necessity of the United States to take an increasingly active role in world affairs was spelled out in publications she wrote or edited for the Foreign Policy Association.

After Pearl Harbor, Dean became an ardent advocate of preparing for a postwar world in which strong world organizations stabilized not only the political but also the social and economic foundations of nations as well. In recognition of her efforts, the U.S. Department of State invited her to serve as an advisor to the American delegation at the founding conference of the United Nations in San Francisco in 1945. Deeply concerned by the rapid increase of American-Soviet tensions after 1945, Dean spent much time and energy over the next decade writing about the necessity of achieving a solid basis for East-West understanding and détente. Fearing that the Cold War could suddenly erupt into a nuclear catastrophe, she wrote in 1947 that the only "inevitable" between the two superpower victors of World War II should be "the war against hunger, disease, illiteracy, poverty and fear. In this war there are no frontiers, and there should be no ideological differences. In this war the United States and Russia can fight side by side as peace-time allies."

Exhibiting considerable courage in her 1953 book *Foreign Policy Without Fear,* Dean challenged the fearmongering spirit most strongly associated with Senator Joseph McCarthy by asserting that "As long as any American who does not agree one hundred percent with a given set of doctrines can be called 'subversive' . . . the United States will find it increasingly difficult to inspire confidence in its common sense, its integrity, and its reliability in time of crisis." Described as "a stately, dark blonde" with a "brusque and direct" manner, Vera Micheles Dean displayed an incredible amount of energy. Besides her many duties at the Foreign Policy Association, she taught over the years at such noted schools as Harvard University, Barnard College, Smith College, the University of Rochester, and the Graduate School of Public Administration of New York University. Desiring to address as large an audience as possible, she published in countless journals, including *The New Republic* and *The Christian Century.*

Resigning as FPA research director in 1961, Dean continued to teach at New York University for another decade until her health began to decline. Besides being awarded more than a dozen honorary doctorates, she received the French Legion of Honor in 1947 and the *Jane Addams Medal in 1954. She died in New York City on October 10, 1972, after a heart attack. A memorial service was held in her honor at the United Nations Chapel.

COLLECTIONS:

Vera Micheles Dean Papers, Schlesinger Library, Radcliffe College.

John Haag, Associate Professor of History, University of Georgia, Athens, Georgia

Deane, Martha (1899–1976).

See McBride, Mary Margaret.

de Ayala, Josefa (1630–1684)

Portuguese painter of the 17th century. Name variations: Josefa de Obidos; Josefa Aiala Figueira. Born Josefa Aiala Figueira in 1630, probably in Seville, Spain; died on July 22, 1684; buried in the church of São Pedro in Obidos; daughter of Baltazar Gomes Figueira and Catalina de Ayala y Cabrera.

Details of Josefa de Ayala's early years remain obscure. She was born in 1630, probably in Seville, Spain, although some have placed her birth in Obidos (Portugal). She seems to have been the daughter of a minor Portuguese painter, Baltazar Gomes Figueira, and his Spanish wife, **Catalina de Ayala y Cabrera.** In 1640, Portugal asserted its independence from Spain, and shortly thereafter the family apparently moved to Obidos. Living in the Quinta da Capeleira outside the walls of Obidos, Josefa became a fixture in her father's studio and early showed artistic talent.

It was soon evident that her abilities surpassed his. At 19, she made engravings for the *Estatutos* for the University of Coimbra. She worked with a broad variety of mediums: oils, water colors, ceramics, metals, and drawings. Her still life's were considered especially good. Among Josefa's portraits was that of the Portuguese queen *Marie Françoise of Savoy (1646–1683). Many of the churches and monastic houses near Obidos commissioned works from de Ayala. As her fame spread, visitors to the spa at the Caldas da Rainha made it a point to visit her studio. She died on July 22, 1684, and was buried in the church of São Pedro in Obidos.

SOURCES:

Costa, Luis Xavier da. *Uma Aguafortista do Século XVII (Josefa Ayala).* Coimbra: Imprensa da Universidade, 1931.

Hernández Díaz, José. *Josefa de Ayala, pintora ibérica del siglo XVII.* Sevilla: Ayuntamiento de Sevilla, 1967.

Kendall W. Brown, Professor of History, Brigham Young University, Provo, Utah

de Beauharnais, Hortense (1783–1837).

See Hortense de Beauharnais.

de Beauharnais, Josephine (1763–1814).

See Josephine, Empress.

de Beauvoir, Simone (1908–1986).

See Beauvoir, Simone de.

de Bettignies, Louise (d. 1918)

French spy during World War I. Name variations: Alice Dubois. Born Louise de Bettignies in Lille, France; died in prison on September 27, 1918.

In 1914, at the onset of World War I, Louise de Bettignies, an attractive, intelligent French woman, fled the German invasion of her country along with many other French refugees. Crossing the Channel into England, she brought with her military information from French officials as well as from her own observations. She was enlisted by the British as a spy and returned to France under the name of Alice Dubois. The system of espionage that she organized and operated was in place until shortly before the war ended.

Posing as a lace peddler, de Bettignies worked out of her hometown of Lille and enlisted some 40 agents to work with her. Among them was Paul Bernard, who at one time wrote in coded shorthand a 1,600-word spy report that fit beneath a stamp on a postcard, and **Marie-Leonie Vanhoutte,** who, posing as a cheese peddler named Charlotte, worked with de Bettignies gathering information. De Bettignies made trips to Holland once a week carrying hidden information. Said to be ingenious at devising ways to hide her messages—using toys, bars of chocolate, umbrellas, and even the frame of a pair of glasses—she once carried a message written in invisible ink on transparent paper placed beneath the glossy surface of a photograph. De Bettignies and her partner Vanhoutte were eventually arrested by German secret agents. Although convicted and sentenced to die, both women were spared from execution at the last minute. De Bettignies died in prison on September 27, 1918, a few weeks before the end of the war.

Debo, Angie (1890–1988)

Prize-winning historian whose works described the tragic fate of North American Indians, especially the Five Tribes of Oklahoma, and whose interest in justice led her to become an activist on their behalf. Pronunciation: DEE-bo. Born Angie Elbertha Debo on

See illustration on the following page

Louise de Bettignies

January 30, 1890, near Beattie, Kansas; died in Enid, Oklahoma, on February 21, 1988; buried in Marshall, Oklahoma, her home most of her life; daughter of Edward Peter Debo (a farmer) and Lina (Cooper) Debo; graduated University of Oklahoma, 1918; University of Chicago, M.A. in history, 1924; University of Oklahoma, Ph.D. in history, 1933; never married; no children.

Awards: numerous, including John H. Dunning Prize from the American Historical Association (AHA) for The Rise and Fall of the Choctaw Republic; Career Award for Distinguished Scholarship from the AHA (1987); first woman to have her portrait hung in the State capital rotunda in Oklahoma City.

Family moved to Marshall, Oklahoma Territory (1899); taught in rural schools; taught at West Texas State Teachers College (1924–1933); was curator of Panhandle-Plains Historical Museum (1933–34); was an independent scholar (1934–41); served as state director for the Oklahoma Federal Writers Project (1941–42); served as lay minister for the Methodist Church (1943–44); was curator of maps for Oklahoma State University Library (1947–54); was a scholar and activist on behalf of American Indians (1954–81).

Selected publications: The Rise and Fall of the Choctaw Republic (Oklahoma, 1934); And Still the Waters Run (Princeton, 1940); The Road to Disappearance *(1941)*; Oklahoma: A Guide to the Sooner State *(1942)*; Tulsa: From Creek Town to Oil Capital *(1943)*; Prairie City *(Knopf, 1944)*; Oklahoma: Footloose and Fancy-free *(1949)*; The Five Civilized Tribes of Oklahoma *(1951)*; Indians of the United States *(Oklahoma, 1970)*; Geronimo *(Oklahoma, 1976)*; *author of nine other books (including one coauthored and three edited volumes) and numerous articles.*

Angie Debo was born on January 30, 1890. Her parents, Edward and **Lina Cooper Debo**, were tenant farmers who managed through unremitting labor and frugality, despite the depression of 1893, to acquire railroad land near Manhattan, Kansas. Then news of a "great commercial awakening" brought them into Oklahoma Territory, ten years after the famous land rush of 1889. Throughout her long life, Debo's most vivid memory was of November 8, 1899, when as a nine-year-old, she had sat on the seat of a covered wagon beside her mother, peering out at the tall "green wheat stretching to the low horizon," in Marshall, Oklahoma Territory, her new home.

Despite meager resources and her own lack of education, Lina Debo imbued her two children—Angie and her eight-year-old brother Edwin—with high aspirations. Described as a "practical feminist" who thought wives were entitled to an equal voice in family matters, Lina raised turkeys to pay for Angie's parlor organ and music lessons. She also encouraged her children's love for books and learning and instilled in them her Christian faith.

For Angie, growing up in Oklahoma Territory proved both exciting and frustrating. As her mother's apprentice, she learned the household and farm tasks so vital to settlers. From Lina, she also derived her love of flowers and gardening. But the young girl soon discovered that Oklahoma offered fewer educational opportunities than Kansas. When Debo completed eighth grade, with no high school nearby, she waited for an opening to teach in the rural areas. A resignation brought her into her own one-room schoolhouse, where she discovered that, in addition to dealing with children of widely varying ages and skills, she faced unruly boys who sought to drive 17-year-old instructors out of the classroom. Exerting firm control from the beginning, Debo attained the self assurance that led others to describe her later as a woman of "authority."

At last, in 1910, three years after Oklahoma had achieved statehood, Marshall opened its first high school. Angie graduated in 1913 at age 23. Two years later, she entered the University of Oklahoma, where she "came under the influence" of Edward Everett Dale. In his late 30s, the tall, slim unprofessorial figure illustrated his points with humorous tales drawn from his own pioneering and ranching experiences. At Harvard, where he had recently obtained his master's, he had studied under Frederick Jackson Turner, the historian whose famous essay, "On the significance of the Frontier in American History," had laid the basis for studying the West as a distinct region. Dale, having lived through many of the events described, credited his mentor with having "opened up a new Heaven and a new earth in the field of American history" and sought to inspire the same enthusiasm among the offspring of Oklahoma pioneers seated before him. Debo, whose background was similar, concluded that if Dale could become a college professor despite his late entry into college, she too could aspire to a similar career.

When I start on a research project I have no idea how it will turn out. I simply want to dig out the truth and record it. I am not pro-Indian, or pro-anything, unless it is pro-integrity.

—Angie Debo

In 1918, after earning her bachelor's degree, Angie saved her salary as a schoolteacher and principal, and by fall of 1923 she was attending the University of Chicago. Her disappointment over the defeat of Woodrow Wilson's plans for America's participation in the League of Nations led Debo, a lifelong Democrat, to study international relations. At that time, prompted by the decline in male enrollment with the U.S. involvement in World War I, higher education began to welcome women, and female enrollment in graduate schools rose dramatically.

When Angie's master's thesis, "The Historical Background of the American Policy of Isolation," was published by Smith College's "Studies in History" series in 1924, she was "greatly encouraged." Debo needed the reassurance. While the master's in that era was the desired degree for college-level teaching, most institutions stated flatly they would hire a woman only when men were not available. Nonetheless, West Texas State Teachers' College (now West Texas State) employed her. For the next decade—minus a year spent in residency at the University of Oklahoma—Canyon, Texas, became her home. While working on her doctorate under Dale who had obtained his in 1922, Debo was advised that the Choctaw Nation's archives in the Oklahoma University library had never been used. She had found her dissertation topic.

The year Debo received her Ph.D.—1933—was the same year she lost her teaching position, partly because of budget cuts necessitated by the Great Depression and partly because of personality conflicts with her department head, a man who never earned his doctorate. After serving as part-time curator of the newly opened Panhandle Plains Historical Museum, she decided to quit in summer 1934 and spend a year writing another book before seeking another professorship. She wrote Dale that she preferred to "do one year of creative work than to spend the rest of an ordinary lifetime just marking time." Based on her own quietly held but deeply felt religious faith, she was certain "that if we are committed to use [our] life in the best way that our special talents will permit us . . . we will be divinely guided into the kind of use that we were intended for."

Angie Debo

For Debo, whose dissertation was published as *The Rise and Fall of the Choctaw Republic* (Oklahoma, 1934), that use was in writing the history of her homeland, Oklahoma, especially as it concerned the Five Tribes—the Cherokees, Choctaws, Creeks, Chickasaws, and Seminoles. A few months later, when her work received the John H. Dunning Award as "the most important contribution to American historical studies in 1934," her decision to become an independent scholar, despite the ongoing Depression, seemed warranted.

Without employment and relying on a small grant, Debo traveled to Muskogee, Oklahoma, and Washington, D.C., where she painstakingly searched Native American records and governmental archives to complete her third book. In this work, which she viewed as her most important, she uncovered a "criminal conspiracy." Through chicanery and manipulation of the legal system, prominent Oklahomans had taken most of the land and oil holdings from 70,000 Native Americans who had once owned the eastern half of what became the State of Oklahoma, leaving them largely impoverished. It was a startling discovery for a woman in her mid-40s. Growing up in western Oklahoma, Debo had known nothing about events in eastern Oklahoma, an area more distant to her, she noted, than "the most remote portion of the globe" and "farther away," in terms of her understanding.

Debo also acknowledged that had she known what she would find, she would never have started her study. Once into her subject, however, "I felt an obligation to go on with it." She worked rapidly, hoping that Oklahomans could profit from her findings as they debated whether to accept a state version of the federal Indian Reorganization Act (IRA) of 1934. Under the IRA, the older policy of forcing native peoples to give up their communal lands and traditions in order to become assimilated was being reversed. The new policy emphasized the rebuilding of tribal land bases and Native American traditions. Debo, knowing that her study demonstrated the consequences of forcing the Five Tribes to give up their holdings, wanted her work published quickly so that the public could benefit from her insights as debate unfolded.

Unfortunately, when University of Oklahoma president William Bizzell decided that the university press should not publish her study, Debo's contract was canceled. Bizzell, acting on the advice of his assistant, history professor Morris Wardell (also a student of Dale), feared that Debo's identification of powerful individuals involved in defrauding Native Americans could bring retaliation from the state legislature or lawsuits against the university or its press.

For the next three years, barely subsisting on small grants, Debo lived a hand-to-mouth existence, while Joseph A. Brandt, director of the Oklahoma University Press, sought another publisher for her work. Her 1939 manuscript, *The Road to Disappearance,* which traced the history of the Creek republic until its termination, again told a tale of white duplicity. The Oklahoma Press, short on funds, was unable to set a publication date. Nor had Brandt found a publisher for her work on the betrayal of the Five Tribes. In her correspondence, Debo, who seldom indulged in self pity, uncharacteristically described herself as "completely at the end of my financial and spiritual resources," and still "desperately trying to find something to do—teaching, lecturing, research, *anything,*" as she approached 50.

A year later, Princeton University Press published her work on the Five Tribes as *And Still the Waters Run.* Shortly thereafter, *The Road to Disappearance* appeared. Though neither enjoyed a large sale, they, along with her earlier work on the Choctaws, incorporated anthropological studies and, unlike many works of that era, examined tribal people in all their complexity instead of presenting them as stereotyped savages or victims without true historical identity. Finally, unlike many scholars who ended their accounts with the late 19th century, Debo carried hers—always with Native Americans at center stage—well into the 20th.

Six years after losing her teaching position, Debo, still impoverished, borrowed train fare to travel to Oklahoma City. Boarding at the YWCA for fifty cents a day, she sought to become the administrative head of the Oklahoma Federal Writers' Project. Gaining this position staved off destitution for another year, but her independent spirit and impatience with the writing skills of her staff guaranteed frustration. By 1941, with the WPA's *Oklahoma: A Guide to the Sooner State* almost finished, Debo returned to her parents' home in Marshall, where she resumed writing. By 1943, her book *Tulsa: From Creek Town to Oil Capital* was fast disappearing from Oklahoma bookstores.

Shortly after, Debo, having obtained an Alfred A. Knopf Fellowship, was at work on *Prairie City,* the story of an Oklahoma town, a composite of Marshall and nearby communities. By tracing its development up to U.S. entry and participation in World War II, she provided a humorous and affectionate account of her community. Conscientiously honest, she also discussed the nativism, racism, religious bigotry, and greed that had marred local life and fortunes.

During World War II, given the shortage of teachers and ministers, Debo taught high school history and served as Marshall's lay Methodist minister. By 1947, the 57-year-old writer and her widowed mother were living in Stillwater, where Debo served as curator of maps at Oklahoma Agricultural and Mechanical College (now Oklahoma State University). That year, she turned down the chance to join the university's history department. Although teaching was her favorite pastime, producing books was her highest priority. This was true even though she found writing grueling labor, which she enjoyed as much as a "galley slave enjoyed rowing." Two years later, she published *Oklahoma: Foot-loose and Fancy-free,* still one of the best interpretative studies of the state. Again, while her love for her homeland was evident, she took residents to task for engaging in environmentally destructive practices and neglecting many of the state's cultural and educational resources.

In 1951, the Indian Rights Association published the results of her field work among the fullbloods of the Five Tribes, an update on conditions since the publication of *And Still the Waters Run.* In *The Five Civilized Tribes of Oklahoma,* Debo revealed that these tribes were losing their remaining lands at a rate of about 35,000 acres annually. To reverse this trend, she called for the expansion of economic and social services, especially in public health and education.

At that time, Debo's diary recorded her struggle as she tried to meet her job responsibilities while her mother, suffering from arteriosclerosis and diabetes, faded in and out of senile dementia. Nonetheless, despite the burdens of caretaking, Lina's death in June 1954 left Angie bereft and convinced that "creative work" was "the only antidote to grief and loneliness." But new concerns impeded Debo's progress as a writer. In the early 1950s, Congress and the federal government had inaugurated the policy of Termination, an attempt to end federal relations with tribes while placing them under state jurisdiction in matters of law and order. To counter what she saw as a gross violation of national trust and responsibility, Debo bombarded representatives and senators with letters and spoke frequently to clubs and church groups. Eventually, when Termination proved disastrous for those tribes that underwent the process, such as the Menominee of Wisconsin, federal policy changed and Termination ended.

Beginning in 1958, Debo satisfied her pent up desires to travel the world, visiting Europe and Mexico. In 1966, at age 76, she journeyed through Africa, touring Uganda, Kenya, Tanzania, and Egypt before returning home. Four years later, Debo's still popular work, *Indians of North America*, appeared (1970). Partly the outcome of a summer institute offered to teachers of Indian students, it was also inspired by her desire to write a book describing America's "true imperialism," its shameful treatment of its native peoples.

By now Debo had transformed her Christmas mailing into an activist network on behalf of indigenous people. From Marshall, she coordinated an effort in which she received information from unidentified agencies and then sent an ever-widening circle of correspondents the salient facts about the impact that Congressional bills would have on Native Americans and advice about approaching local and national politicians. As she related in a 1974 article, she had always begun her research with an open mind, wanting only "to discover the truth." Earlier, she had thought that when her work appeared in print, her job was done. "Later I came to see that after my findings were published I had the same obligation to correct abuses as any other citizen." Debo's ever-expanding network played a vital role in the Alaskan Native Claims Settlement Act of 1971, in which the Native peoples were given 40 million acres of land to continue their traditional way of life. Her group later helped win water rights for the Papago Indians and campaigned for similar rights for the Pima Indians, both Arizona tribes.

In 1972, Debo began a biography of Geronimo, the Apache chief who had long been portrayed as a bloodthirsty warrior clothed in a blanket of human scalps. Basing her study on her interviews of the 1950s with his descendants and other Apaches, she sought to dispel the libelous myths surrounding this figure. *Geronimo: The Man, His Time, His Place* (1976) won the prestigious Wrangler Award and a prize from the Southwestern Library Association.

The last decade of her life brought more honors as the Oklahoma American Civil Liberties Union, in which she was a founding member, created the Angie Debo Civil Liberties Volunteer Award. She received an honorary degree from Wake Forest College and the Outstanding Alumni Award from the University of Oklahoma. These years, however, also brought increasing

pain and infirmities, for by 1978, she was crippled from osteoporosis and her sight and hearing were failing.

Nonetheless, between 1981 and 1985, Debo worked with her friend from the ACLU, **Gloria Valencia-Weber**, along with historian **Glenna Matthews**, on an oral history project. They were assisted by **Aletha Rogers**. Debo recorded her experiences growing up in Oklahoma and the difficulties she had encountered later as a female historian. In 1985, the State of Oklahoma honored Debo by displaying her portrait, the first woman to be so acknowledged, in the Capitol rotunda, alongside that of such figures as Sequoyia, Will Rogers, and former speaker of the House of Representatives, Carl Albert. The oral history project, having received a number of grants, resulted in a film, "Indians, Outlaws and Angie Debo," produced by **Barbara Abrash** and **Martha Sandlin**. Focusing primarily on Debo's struggle to publish *And Still the Waters Run* and her work on behalf of Indians, the film appeared on the PBS series "The American Experience" in the fall of 1988. Unfortunately, however, Debo had died on February 21, 1988, only weeks after Glenna Matthews had accepted the Career Award for Distinguished Scholarship on Debo's behalf from the American Historical Association.

Nonetheless, Native American leaders, such as *Wilma T. Mankiller, formerly the principal chief of the Cherokee Nation, continue to honor Debo, and Oklahoma newspaperwoman **Edith Gaylord Harper** has established the biennial Angie Debo Prize for the most significant book on the Southwest published by the University of Oklahoma Press. Finally, Debo's works, meticulously researched, have proved so reliable that they have formed the basis of court decisions favoring Native American rights. Her example of courage and integrity continues to inspire those who remember her as a friend and those who meet her for the first time through her writings.

SOURCES:

Angie Debo Collection, Special Collections-University Archives, Edmund Low Library, Oklahoma State University, Stillwater, Oklahoma.

Valencia-Weber, Gloria. *Angie Debo 1890–1988: An Autobiographical Sketch, Eulogy and Bibliography.* Published by The College of Arts and Sciences and Department of History, Oklahoma State University, June 1988.

SUGGESTED READING:

Matthews, Glenna and Gloria Valencia-Weber. "Against Great Odds: The Life of Angie Debo," in *OAH Newsletter.* Vol. 13. May 1985, pp. 8–11.

McIntosh, Kenneth. "Geronimo's Friend: Angie Debo and the New History," in *Chronicles of Oklahoma.* Vol. 66. Summer 1988, pp. 164–177.

Schrems, Susan and Cynthia Wolff. "Politics and Libel: Angie Debo and the Publication of *And Still the Waters Run*," in *The Western Historical Quarterly*. Vol. 22. May 1991, pp. 184–203.

RELATED MEDIA:

Indians, Outlaws and Angie Debo, produced by Barbara Abrash and Martha Sandlin, Institute for Research in History, 1988.

Shirley A. Leckie, Professor of History, University of Central Florida and author of *Elizabeth Bacon Custer and the Making of a Myth* (University of Oklahoma Press, 1993)

Deborah (fl. 12th c. BCE)

Prophet and judge of Israel, considered to be a historical figure, who stands out among women in both Jewish and Christian history because of her power and influence. Name variations: Deborah the Judge. The literal meaning of Deborah is "honey bee"; the Hebrew for Deborah is close to the Hebrew dabar, *meaning word, often referring to the word of God, and to the Aramaic root,* dbr, *meaning to lead; names in Hebrew culture and narrative expressed anticipation of a person's destiny; Deborah was associated with the presumed enlightening and courage-producing potential of honey.*

As with most Biblical women, we do not know the specifics of Deborah's early life. As a child, she would have grown up within a strong extended family and clan. Her parents and elders would have taught her the sagas of their tradition, including an understanding of God that contrasted with the Canaanite fertility gods and goddesses. Though boys' education would have been favored over girls', this was before the days of formal schooling. As a girl, Deborah would early on have assumed domestic responsibilities; however, it seems possible that special attention might have been given to her religious education. Perhaps she demonstrated a propensity for gathering wisdom, or perhaps there were no sons in her family to prime for leadership roles. Whatever the reason, this woman—who would have been considered a man's property and prevented from inheriting land—emerged as a leader who was subject to no one and was responsible for the securing of land for her people.

There are two accounts of Deborah's leadership in the book of Judges (chapters 4 and 5). The first, a prose rendering, which shows the hand of one or more editors, is later than the second account, a piece of poetry (known as "Deborah's Song") that was possibly an eyewitness account and is one of the oldest examples of extant Hebrew literature. Reading the story of Deborah feels more like a leap into the future rather than a peek into the quite distant past.

Deborah is first introduced as a leader who displays authority over all men in the narrative and speaks for God—without a literary bat of the eye. Apparently, she rose to power by common consent of the people, who recognized her wisdom and sought her counsel and guidance in important matters. Though the narrative speaks from a patriarchal milieu in which women are presumed subordinate to and owned by men, there is, in Deborah's case, a surprising suspension of some key aspects of patriarchy. A significant handful of women emerge as heroines in Biblical narrative, but they are usually in stereotypic female roles: seductive tricksters, or faithful wives, daughters, and sisters. Most surprisingly, though Deborah's husband may be alluded to (it is unclear whether she is "wife of Lapidoth" or "woman of fire"; Hebrew meaning could go either way), and though she is given the title "mother of Israel," she functions in the story apart from any role as wife to a husband, mother to a son, or sister to a brother. Finally, in contrast to other Biblical war finales, Deborah sings to celebrate her own victory, rather than that of returning male heros. "Deborah stands out as a unique figure in the Hebrew Bible," writes **Cheryl Ann Brown**. "She is at once a prophetess, a poetess, a great military leader on a par with male military leaders, and even a judge, not simply like others, but a judge to whom Israelites turned for legal counseling and settling of court cases" (Judg. 4:5).

At that time Deborah, a prophetess, woman of fire, was judging Israel. She used to sit under the palm of Deborah . . . and the Israelites came to her to dispense justice.

—*Judges 4:4,5*

Deborah's exceptional nature, in fact, has been too much to swallow for some commentators and retellers. First-century historian Josephus diminished Deborah's stature, and a later legendary rendition of her tale censures Deborah for behaving unseemly. Some rabbis nicknamed her "the hornet" or "buzzing bee" because they thought she was arrogant. Modern commentators as well have obscured Deborah's preeminence and attributed her rise to an absence of leaders in Israel. Because the military leader Barak takes a strong role in the narrative, however, we can assume that Deborah is not judge because there was no one else available. Furthermore, other brave men are vaunted in Deborah's song for their readiness to protect Israel. Interpretive stutterings notwithstanding, the narrative eloquently portrays this woman as a leader *extraordinaire*.

Deborah emerges as judge during a time when the people of Israel have fallen into idolatry and suffered decades of cruel oppression from the hands of the Canaanites—"in those days caravans ceased and travelers kept to the byways" (5:6). The rustic Hebrews were then a loose federation, and they rejected Canaan's absolutism of the city-states and the extreme hierarchy that created sharp divisions between the privileged elite and the subjected others. Considered intruders and revolutionaries from the perspective of the indigenous Canaanites, the alien Israelites were continually in conflict with the inhabitants of the land. Because warfare was the universal paradigm for handling territorial disputes, battles figure prominently in the sagas of the Judges. The dynamics of this political strife were complicated by religious overtones; in the ancient world, religious fervor and national allegiance were linked. In Israel's understanding, God was on the side of the suffering minority, and interaction with the other nations (who "followed other gods") was believed a key source of religious apostasy. The identity of this Iron Age woman-of-fire is forged within this paradigm, and she emerges as one who has credibility and prowess in this setting.

The battle for which Deborah is remembered took place around 1125 BCE. The technologically advanced Canaanites, boasting an army of nearly a thousand chariots of iron, controlled a strategically located stronghold that threatened to strangle the main route of Israelite trade. Deborah follows three earlier leaders, referred to as judges, who functioned primarily as warrior-liberators for victims of military aggression; but she alone fulfills the additional roles of prophet and judicial arbitrator. It was Deborah's habit to sit under a particular palm tree (the "palm of Deborah") to counsel and dispense justice. As tribal judge, her task was to rally the people together to defend their customs and territory. As a prophet, her call was to bring God's word and gather the wayward back to Him.

In her capacity as God's messenger, Deborah beckons Barak, Israel's general, and conveys to him God's command that he mobilize the troops to confront the Canaanites in battle. Her oracle contains a strategic plan and the promise of divinely accomplished victory. Barak entreats Deborah to go with him into battle ("If you will go with me, I will go; but if you will not go with me, I will not go."). Deborah chides his hesitance but complies, and against overwhelming odds God delivers the enemy into Israel's hands by means of a torrential downpour that creates a mud trap for the chariots. The enemy troops are routed; however, Sisera, the Canaanite general, escapes on foot. The story ends when the desperate general finds apparent refuge in the tent of ◂❧ Jael, the wife of a man whose clan is at peace with Sisera's. Evidently Jael, in a surprising display of independence from her husband and clan (emphasized in the phrasing "the tent of Jael" rather than, as would be expected, the tent of Heber, her husband), makes her own decision as to whose side she will be on. She entices Sisera into her tent in feigned hospitality. Adept at the women's work of staking tents to the ground, she uses her skill to kill this general by hammering a tent peg through his skull. In pursuit of Sisera, Barak reaches Jael's tent and learns of her exploit. Victory over Canaan complete, Deborah and Barak sing a gloating and celebratory ballad that congratulates the brave warriors who offered themselves, chastises the tribes who did not come to Israel's aid, extols the bravery and wiles of Jael, and praises the God who crushed the enemy.

Within the book of Judges, Deborah stands out as one of few judges whose character is never sullied by some moral lapse. Modern critics, however, are somewhat uncomfortable with Deborah's character. Although she seems not to be confined by the power structures and expectations of patriarchy, neither does she stand against some of its questionable assumptions. In song, Deborah glorifies the protective aggression of her army and celebrates the violent demise of Sisera and his people. As **Danna Fewell** and David Gunn note, "The authority of violence is justified. And in the face of that authority, the woman, Deborah, has offered no real alterna-

---

❧▸ **Jael** (fl. c. 1125 BCE)

Biblical heroine who killed Sisera, Israel's mighty enemy. Name variations: Jahel; Yael. Flourished around 1125 BCE; wife of Heber the Kenite (Judg. 4:17–22).

After the defeat of the Canaanites by Barak, Sisera, the captain of Jabin's army, fled and took refuge with the tribe of Heber. Jael, a Kenite woman and the wife of Heber, welcomed Sisera into her tent with the offer of milk and a promise to guard against intruders while he slept. When he fell asleep, Jael killed him by driving a tent nail into his temples with a mallet. Jael was later honored in the song of *Deborah as "most blessed above women."

---

tive." These authors conclude that Deborah and Jael, as women in a man's world, find their place within its structures—they offer no alternative. *Elizabeth Cady Stanton, in *The Woman's Bible*, severely condemns Jael's behavior as that "more like the work of a fiend than a woman."

There is justification for this social critique. The ultimate test of faithfulness to Israel's God is just and merciful treatment of those on the margins (widows, orphans, strangers, and poor). Indeed, as one progresses through the book of Judges, the tactics of oppressors and oppressed are sometimes indistinguishable; trust in God's compassionate presence becomes commandeered by national fervor. God's enemies and God's friends appear to be defined. The narrative depicts an us/they, win/lose worldview: Israel's victory is celebrated and Canaan's demise is legitimated. Deborah, as the mother of Israel, shows a fierce and exclusive protection toward her own. Though her song expresses an awareness of the grief that will come upon the "other" mother—Sisera's—awaiting her son's return from war, the lyrics are short on transformative vision.

Though modern readers cannot fail to see the exclusiveness and brutality of the narrative, we must be careful of too easily pressing Deborah into the service of our contemporary agendas. If we consider the story in its context, we discern glimpses—if not realizations—of an alternate vision. There are places where Deborah's story strains against and indeed sits in judgment upon its own reality. There are four such places of renewal in Deborah's story: movement toward and realization of gender equality, gropings toward peace, the suggestion of partnership, and hints of solidarity with the ravished.

The first, the movement toward gender equality, is evidenced by Deborah's very presence as a judge. However, her relationship to Barak may reveal more of the texture in which such equality was wrestled. Though many male commentators are embarrassed by Barak's refusal to go into battle without Deborah (one legend called him an ignoramus), his reticence may point to his courage rather than his cowardice. He is not afraid to defer to a woman's authority, and he is not above seeking a woman's counsel in battle. It is a tribute to Deborah's character that Barak seeks her presence, and it is to Barak's credit that he does not denounce or bypass Deborah's judgment. Deborah's plan for battle no doubt seemed unwise in light of Canaan's overwhelming technological advantage. However, asking only for her presence alongside, Barak is willing to proceed with her

strategy. Deborah apparently upbraids Barak for handing the glory of killing Sisera over to a woman ("I will surely go with you; nevertheless, the road on which you are going will not lead to your glory, for the Lord will sell Sisera into the hand of a woman."). Although her words are more a portent of what is to take place than an attempt to humiliate her general, it is possible that Barak exposed and challenged remnants of patriarchy even in Deborah. The "road" that he goes on does not lead to his personal glory, but Barak surely prepares the way for what turns out to be their mutual glory. This leads into the broader theme of partnership that is suggested in the overall narrative.

Though in some ways Deborah may seem "larger than life," her story is as striking for the number of players that she brings onto center stage with her as it is for the number of laurels that she accumulates. The three-part cooperation between Deborah, an Israelite woman, Barak, an Israelite man, and Jael, a Kenite woman (a people aligned with the Canaanites), is an interesting study in partnership. Typically in the judge stories, a single man is identified as the military deliverer. In this story, three characters are responsible for the nation's deliverance. Each is indispensable for the delivery of the suffering nation, and all three share the glory of Israel's victory. Though Deborah is remembered as the judge, Barak and Jael also take center stage. Deborah's unique role as leader does not seem to be at the expense of, or in exclusion of, other heros.

In fact, the first-century writer of *Biblical Antiquities*, known as Pseudo-Philo (his work was erroneously attributed to Philo), compares Deborah's unique leadership to that of the incomparable Moses. Moses and Deborah, in the range and significance of their calling and competencies, seem to stand apart from all other leaders. However, there is a twist in the parallelism. While, according to the Moses narratives, a similar triad formed between Moses, his brother Aaron, and his sister *Miriam the Prophet, God jealously protected Moses' pre-eminence—to the near demise of Miriam. However, in the Deborah narrative, sustained partnership, including perhaps mutual correction, is the trajectory. It has even been suggested that in Judges 4 Deborah and Jael are described in such a way as to evoke recollection of Canaanite partner goddesses whose joint efforts eventually became inseparable. Though this is a partnership of power, it is undergirded by a commitment to the powerless. This theme, though not always recognized, is central to the narrative.

It has frequently been noted that "Deborah's Song" brings in aspects of a woman's perspective on battle. In the last stanzas, the singer paints a powerful verbal picture of the scene on the home front of Sisera's family. Deborah imagines the noble women waiting, peering out their windows, wondering what is taking so long; Sisera's mother and her ladies presume that Sisera and his men, victorious, are dividing spoil, including the customary booty ("Are they not finding and dividing the spoil?—A girl or two for every man").

Why does the composer of this song include this scene? Those who decry the violence of the passage maintain that the stanzas are taunting, insinuating that the proud will soon fall, and the plunder will go in the other direction. Surely, "Deborah's Song" gloats over the "poetic justice" rendered when a band of ill-prepared peasants bests a rich and powerful army and a lone woman fells its general. But, rather than taunting, it is equally possible that these stanzas represent a brief but significant suspension of the us/they perspective so pervasive in the ancient world. If only for a moment, these mothers share a common experience.

Deborah's war-victory song ends with the poignant awareness that women suffer the long-term consequences of war-defeat. While that awareness includes a fleeting empathy for "the other" mother, the real empathy is for Israel's daughters. Sisera's victory would give every male victor an Israelite "woman or two" (literally, a *womb* or two); Sisera's defeat protects Israel's daughters from this sexual slavery. There is an implicit but profound celebration for the women and girls who were spared from Canaan's ravishment. Jael is "most blessed of women," not because she was so bravely violent, but rather because she has redeemed the Israelite wombs. We are brought to eavesdrop on the Canaanite hearth so that we do not miss the often hidden story of equal opportunity of suffering during war—sons *and* daughters are lost, and sons *and* daughters are spared.

However, more than mere celebration for the fortunate daughters, there is a hint of protest in these odd stanzas. The brute recitation of the Canaanite despoiling of women is not endorsement or even resignation to the custom. Interestingly (although it may well have taken place), Israel's counter-plundering is neither celebrated nor mentioned. In a culture where bragging over booty was a familiar theme in war epics, the silence may be significant. Though one might argue that the reserve in detailing Israel's booty-taking reflects an unwillingness to admit to reci-

procal brutality, it is still a move beyond the usual male bravado. Bellicose and indignant though she may be, Deborah does not engage in power politics as usual; she is within a tradition of those groping toward a vision a peace.

"Would Deborah rather have accomplished the deliverance of the people by peaceful means?" asks **Margaret Wold**. The pastoral scene of Deborah adjudicating justice beneath a palm tree signals that neither holy war nor treachery was Deborah's chief modus operandi. In fact, Deborah's oracle itself represents a movement beyond the traditional glorification of human might and control. Her message, though it still ensues in brutal consequences for "the enemy," is framed in what **Susan Niditch** calls "an ideology of non-participation." The task of Israel is not to muster its power and vanquish its enemy; it is rather to relinquish control and trust in God, who "loves the weak and controls the war." When it comes down to it, this is the story of a man deferring to and following a woman who is leaving it up to God. Yairah Amit comments that the hero of the story is neither Deborah, nor Barak, nor even Jael, but rather God. Certainly, we could critique this theory for its apparent lack of realism and responsibility (which is one interpretation for Barak's hesitance). But it is groping toward an alternative understanding of war, perhaps even, as Niditch sees it, a "breakthrough toward an ideology of peace."

Any breakthrough, however, recedes after Deborah's death. Pseudo-Philo portrayed Deborah as a visionary leader and enlightener whose impending death threatens to leave a great void in her community. "To whom do you commend your sons whom you are leaving? Pray therefore for us, and after your departure your soul will be mindful of us forever," the people implore. In Pseudo-Philo's retelling, Deborah exhorts the people to live as she has taught them. Sadly, though she established peace for 40 years, Deborah's accomplishments seemed to have been reversed by subsequent judges. The next judge, Gideon, requested the gold taken as booty from war be fashioned into an idol of sorts. Jepthah ended up sacrificing his own daughter in his bid for power. And Samson depended on his physical prowess to the exclusion of wisdom and responsibility, brandishing his power in personal vendettas and foolish escapades. Gender equality, peace, partnership, and solidarity with the weak fade. Tragically, the epic ends as it began—in chaos, war, and violence.

Yet, in world history, Deborah's vision and enlightenment did not die. Israel itself continued to nurture pockets of equality, peace, and justice, as Deborah's spirit reemerged in prophets, wise women, and liberators. And Deborah, woman of fire, miracle of her time, inspires women to look beyond the actual to the possible, to refuse victimization and imagine a new future.

SOURCES:

Judges. Contained in *The New Oxford Annotated Bible.* New Revised Standard Version. York: Oxford University Press, 1991.

SUGGESTED READING:

Amit, Yairah. "Judges 4: Its Content and Form," in *Journal of the Study of the Old Testament.* Vol. 39, 1987, pp. 89–111.

Brenner, Athalya. *The Israelite Women: Social Role and Literary Type in Biblical Narrative.* Sheffield: JSOT Press, 1985.

Brown, Cheryl Anne. *No Longer Be Silent: First Century Jewish Portraits of Biblical Women.* Louisville, KY: Westminster-John Knox Press, 1992.

Fewell, Danna Nolan. "Judges." in *The Women's Bible Commentary.*

Newsom, Carol A., and Sharon H. Ringe, eds. Louisville: Westminster-John Knox Press, 1992.

———, and David M. Gunn. "Controlling Perspectives: Women, Men, and the Authority of Violence in Judges 4 & 5," in *Journal of the American Academy of Religion.* Vol. LVIII, no. 3, pp. 389–411.

Niditch, Susan. *War in the Hebrew Bible.* NY: Oxford University Press, 1993.

Wilson, Lois Miriam. *Miriam, Mary and Me: Women in the Bible.* Winnipeg: Wood Lake books, 1992.

Wold, Margaret. *Women of Faith & Spirit.* Minneapolis: Augsburg Press, 1987.

> **Carol Lakey Hess**, faculty member at Princeton Theological Seminary, who works on issues relating to theology and gender

de Bourbon, Anne Geneviève (1619–1679).

See Longueville, Anne Geneviève de.

de Brabant, Marie (c. 1530–c. 1600).

See Marie de Brabant.

de Brinvilliers, Marguerite d' (1630–1676).

See Brinvilliers, Marie de.

DeBucq de Rivery, Aimée de (c. 1762–1817).

See de Rivery, Aimee Dubucq.

de Burgh, Cecily (d. before 1273).

See Balliol, Cecily.

de Burgh, Elizabeth (1295–1360).

See Clare, Elizabeth de.

de Burgh, Elizabeth (d. 1327).

See Elizabeth de Burgh.

de Burgh, Elizabeth (1332–1363).

See Elizabeth de Burgh.

de Burgh, Margaret (d. 1243).

See Margaret de Burgh.

de Burgh, Margaret (d. 1259).

See Margaret de Burgh.

de Burgh, Margaret (d. 1303).

See Margaret de Burgh.

de Burgos, Julia (1914–1953)

Puerto Rican poet and political activist whose work celebrated Puerto Rican culture, explored woman's experience, and denounced injustice and exploitation. Name variations: Julia Burgos de Rodriguez, Julia Burgos. Pronunciation: WHO-lee-uh day BOOR-goes. Born Julia Constanza de Burgos on February 17, 1914 (some sources cite 1917) in the town of Carolina, Puerto Rico; died on July 6, 1953, at Harlem Hospital, New York City; daughter of Francisco Burgos Hans (a farmer) and Paula García de Burgos; graduated from Muñoz Rivera Primary School, 1928; graduated from University High School in Río Piedras, 1931; granted degree in education from the University of Puerto Rico, 1933; took postgraduate studies in languages at the University of Havana; married Rubén Rodríguez Beauchamp, in 1934 (divorced 1937); married Armando Marín, in 1943; no children.

Awards: Puerto Rican Institute of Literature Award for best book of the year for Canción de la verdad sencilla (1939); Journalism Prize of the Institute of Puerto Rican Literature (1946).

Grew up in rural Puerto Rico (1914–27); family moved to Río Piedras to further daughter's education (1928); worked as rural grade-school teacher and social worker (1934–36); published first poems in the newspaper El Imparcial (1937); published first volume of poetry Poema en veinte surcos (1938); published second book, Canción de la verdad sencilla (1939); traveled to New York and then settled in Havana, Cuba (1940); returned to New York (1942); worked as journalist for the weekly Pueblos Hispánicos (1943–44); suffered repeated bouts of alcoholism, depression and hospitalization (1946–53); collapsed on Fifth Avenue and died anonymously (1953); posthumous publication of final volume of poetry, El mar y tú (1954).

Poetry: Poema en veinte surcos (Poem in Twenty Furrows, 1938); Canción de la verdad sencilla (Song of the Simple Truth, 1939); El mar y tú (The Sea and You, 1954). Collections: Antología poética (San Juan,

Puerto Rico: Editorial Coquí, 1979); Canción de la verdad sencilla (2nd ed., Río Piedras, Puerto Rico: Ediciones Huracán, 1982); El mar y tú: otros poemas (2nd ed., Río Piedras, Puerto Rico, 1981); Obra poética (San Juan, Puerto Rico: Institute of Puerto Rican Culture, 1961); Poema en veinte surcos (2nd ed., Río Piedras, Puerto Rico: Huracán, 1982).

Julia de Burgos, Puerto Rico's short-lived but beloved poet, was born in the countryside near the Rio Grande de Loíza and the town of Carolina on February 17, 1914. She was the youngest of thirteen siblings, only six of whom survived to adulthood. It is said that as a child she wanted to place the body of one of her departed siblings on a flower-strewn raft and float it down the Loíza in hopes that the water spirits would offer a more hospitable reception than the earth. On August 28, 1960, seven years after her death, other Puerto Rican poets would gather on the banks of the Loíza and, accompanied by the Chorus of the University of Puerto Rico, launch a flower-covered boat into the waters. According to **María Solá** in her introduction to Burgos' *Yo misma fui mi ruta*, Julia de Burgos "has become more than a writer and more than a national poet; she has become a legendary figure, with all that legend has of enchantment, fantasy and false illusion."

I was the strong roar of the jungle and the river and voice between two echoes, I ascended the hills.

—**Julia de Burgos**

The precarious economic situation of the de Burgos family mirrored the dismal economic conditions of Puerto Rico in the 1920s. Julia was raised by **Paula García de Burgos**, a sensitive, generous mother, and Francisco Burgos, a creative but alcoholic father. Julia shared many adventurous outings on horseback with her father, who entertained his daughter with the tales of heroes from life and literature, such as Don Quixote, Robinson Crusoe, Napoleon, and Latin America's liberator, Simón Bolívar. Ironically, these pleasant overnight camping trips paralleled other outings in which a young Julia had to search for her father who often disappeared when he became drunk.

While de Burgos' father represented independence and adventure, it was her mother who first lead the young poet towards a love of reading and writing. Julia's mother was the center of the family, its strength, and the force that guided Julia and her siblings towards a better life. Paula de Burgos often sacrificed to provide an educa-

tion for her children. She was Julia's spiritual center throughout life and her greatest source of inspiration and love. Raised in her mother's beloved garden, surrounded by the green hills of rural Puerto Rico, and nurtured by the presence of the Loíza River, Julia was from infancy inextricably tied to the land.

At the age of five, Julia began first grade in her neighborhood public school. For several years, in response to the family's economically motivated moves, she attended a series of schools in the area. For seventh and eighth grade, she was forced to leave her parents and live in the town of Carolina at the home of the Rosenda Romero family. Julia stood out as a scholar and won several prizes as an athlete. After she graduated from the Muñoz Rivera School, her parents sold their land and moved the family to Río Piedras, home of the University of Puerto Rico, in order to pave the way for a university education for their youngest daughter.

The move meant more economic hardship for the family and a loss of daily contact with the land Julia so loved, but she was able to enter University High School in 1928. Julia's mother struggled to pay her daughter's tuition. At times, Julia climbed through windows to attend classes that had been closed to her because of her family's poverty. These were years of hard work and isolation for de Burgos since social life with more wealthy peers was nearly impossible. She lived for her studies. Free time was dedicated to her beloved sports—basketball, track, and swimming. In May of 1931, she graduated with superior grades, having completed the four-year high school course in three years.

The following August, Julia de Burgos entered the University of Puerto Rico, graduating in May of 1933 with a degree in education. Almost immediately, she obtained her first full-time job, a position with the Puerto Rico Economic Reconstruction Administration, distributing food and milk and offering child-care education in poor neighborhoods. By 1935, the agency was closed, and Julia became a primary teacher in the town of Cedro Arriba de Naranjito. This signaled a return to the rural life that she so loved; it was also to be the last time that de Burgos would live in rural Puerto Rico.

While she had studied at the university, Julia's contacts with fellow students had introduced her to the Puerto Rican movement for independence from the United States. She would be an active proponent of Puerto Rican nationalism for the rest of her life. While this movement was

WOMEN IN WORLD HISTORY

Julia de Burgos

not widespread among the general population of Puerto Rico, many writers, artists and educators believed that Puerto Rico would best safeguard its special cultural heritage and thrive economically as an independent nation. Quite a few of this century's most famous and respected Puerto Rican writers and thinkers were, and remain, strong and vocal supporters of independence.

It was during de Burgos' initial years as a schoolteacher that Puerto Rico's revolutionary Nationalist Party, lead by the charismatic Pedro Albizu Campos, began to rise in prominence to coordinate the struggle for independence. In re-sponse to her own commitment to the nationalist movement, Julia de Burgos began writing poetry. She apparently completed a first book of verses, *Poemas exactos a mí misma* (Precise poems to myself) but the volume was never published and is now considered lost. In October of 1936, she addressed the first major convention of a coalition of groups working for Puerto Rican independence with a speech entitled "Women and the Suffering of the Homeland."

During these active years in which de Burgos habitually endured economic hardship, she continued to polish her poetry. In 1938, with the publication of *Poema en veinte surcos* (Poem in

Twenty Furrows), she suddenly emerged as a mature voice in Puerto Rican poetry. The poems portray both a woman rebelling against her limiting circumstances and a recognition of the economic and cultural injustices that limited Puerto Rico and its people. Hand in hand with this indignant strength, however, the poems also reveal an inner struggle between a desire for personal freedom and the fears and insecurities this necessarily involves. Julia herself called this conflict "a game of hide-and-seek with my being."

Between 1935 and 1939, de Burgos looked for ways to publish her work, always the poet's hardest task. She was, however, determined, using funds saved from her own small salary to support her writing and publication. In order to distribute her verses, she traveled by bus throughout the Island of Puerto Rico, selling her first volumes wherever she could find willing vendors or a gathering of people.

During these years, she confronted a series of personal challenges. She married Rubén Rodríguez Beauchamp in 1934; by 1937, they were divorced. In 1935, her mother became ill with cancer, and after she lost a leg to the disease the cancer spread to her stomach. Julia had to deal with the emotional and financial burden of her mother's illness. Much of the money she had earned selling her books from town to town went to pay doctors. From a creative standpoint, however, these were among the happiest days of de Burgos' life. She formed part of the group of famous Puerto Rican artists and writers who were instrumental in the nationalist movement. Her friends included the leader of the group, Luís Llorens Torres, and poets Luís Palés Matos and Evaristo Ribera Chevremont, all stellar intellectuals who influenced the creation of contemporary Puerto Rican culture. In 1936–37, de Burgos worked with a radio "School of the Air" as a writer of educational materials for children. Her public support of nationalism caused her to lose the position, but not before she had written a series of dramas.

The year 1939 was a tragic and joyous one for de Burgos. In October, her mother finally succumbed to cancer. Days later, influential poets held a recital in honor of Julia de Burgos at the Puerto Rican *Ateneo* (institute of culture). The scholar Manuel Rivera Matos read an essay on "The Theme of the River in the Poetry of Julia de Burgos," and Julia recited the poem "My Mother and the River." On December 8, she published a new book of verses, *Canción de la verdad sencilla* (Song of the Simple Truth), for which she received the Puerto Rican Institute of

Literature's award for best book of the year. This second book of poetry abandoned the historic themes related to nationalism to deal entirely with the question of love. It is dedicated, in de Burgos' words, to "the simple truth of loving you in yourself and in all else." Some of the poems speak of the ecstasy of fulfilled love; others foresee the difficulties and, finally, the anguish caused by love and the loss of individual freedom it entails.

In fact, much of de Burgos' life at this time was dedicated to projects she shared with Juan Isidro Jiménez Grullón, a doctor and political activist from the Dominican Republic. Identified by most as the great love of her life, Jiménez Grullón probably inspired the verses of her second published volume. From 1939 to 1942, de Burgos and Jiménez Grullón shared daily life and political activism in Puerto Rico, and later New York and Cuba. Jiménez Grullón's circumstances as an impoverished political exile only added to the economic instability that had always been part of Julia's life.

Her mother's death convinced Julia to leave Puerto Rico and follow Jiménez Grullón to New York early in 1940. January in New York was both stimulating and devastating for the poet. Impressed by the "fantastic" cultural opportunities, she also expressed distaste at the city, which she likened to "an enormous military barracks" where "there is very little family life." Her lifelong struggle between loneliness and independence began to play itself out in her poetry and life. Here, she continued to be involved in the movement for Puerto Rican independence. For a short time, she worked with the U.S. Census in order to send money back home to her family.

Finally in April, de Burgos left for Havana, again following Jiménez Grullón who had gone to the Cuban capital several months earlier. As she traveled from New York to Miami to catch a boat for Cuba, the past months of isolation led to pressing thoughts of suicide. Nevertheless, after visits to several Caribbean Islands, Julia settled in Havana and was fortunate to live in an apartment overlooking the sea. After traveling to various Cuban cities with Jiménez Grullón, she began studies of Greek, Latin, and French at the University of Havana in 1941 but was unable to complete her course work when she ran out of money for tuition. During this period, she spent a great deal of time with other Caribbean writers and artists and gave a series of interviews to local newspapers.

According to **Yvette Jiménez de Baez**, it is from Cuba that Julia "sang with her most authentic voice" and from this period came her book *El mar y tú* (The Sea and You). Due to lack of funds, she was unable to publish this third volume of poetry. Publication would have to wait until 1954, a year after her death. While in Havana, she also began another book of poetry, *Campo* (Countryside), which she never completed.

The poetry of *El mar y tú* speaks again of love both as a voyage on a rough sea and an eventual shipwreck. De Burgos expresses feelings of anguished rejection over love lost and finally turns again towards the possibility of death. Only poetry seems to give meaning to life:

Forgive me, my love, if I speak your name
Except for your song I am a bare wing
Death and I sleep together
Only my song to you awakens me. (*Canción amarga*)

In 1942, Julia and Jiménez Grullón resolved the legal impediments to marriage, but relations between the two had suffered, and they abruptly separated. In response, Julia left for the United States, this time alone. She went to New York, hoping to earn enough money to eventually return to Puerto Rico. She also dreamt of publishing more books of poetry that would live up to her early works so she could return home in triumph. But life in New York proved difficult. De Burgos was unable to find employment as a writer or teacher, and she held brief, low-paying jobs as secretary, translator, salesperson, seamstress, and machine operator. Ethnic and political discrimination often closed doors, and she frequently felt defeated and alone. By this time, de Burgos had begun to suffer from the alcoholism that would eventually lead to her death.

For a time, stability returned. In 1943, she met and married Armando Marín, worked for the weekly magazine *Pueblos Hispánicos,* regained contact with her family in Puerto Rico, and composed new poetry. In 1944–45, she lived with her husband for a year in Washington, D.C., working in an office during the day and attending night school to learn Portuguese. In 1946, she returned to New York where word reached her that one of her articles had received the journalism prize of the Institute of Puerto Rican Literature. A series of public homages were held for her in New York City.

But alcoholism continued to undermine her physically and creatively. In 1949, de Burgos was diagnosed with cirrhosis of the liver. From this point on, she was in and out of various hospitals and grappled with long bouts of depression. On one occasion, she filled out the admission papers to the hospital and wrote "writer, journalist and translator" in the space for profession. Later, hospital staff crossed out those words and inserted "suffers from amnesia." They were unable to believe this thin, ill Puerto Rican woman could be telling the truth.

Finally in 1953, after another hospitalization, Julia de Burgos was released to family friends with whom she stayed for a few days. At the beginning of July, she disappeared into the streets of Manhattan. For over a month, friends and family searched for her, until they were informed of her death by the Bureau of Missing Persons. According to official records, Julia de Burgos was found unconscious on Fifth Avenue, taken to Harlem Hospital, and died shortly thereafter. Since no identifying documents could be found on her person, her body was deposited in the city morgue, and she was buried in a pauper's grave in Potter's Field. It was said that the poet was so tall that city workers had to amputate her legs to fit her body into the conventional pine coffin. She had died of pneumonia.

Julia's remains were exhumed through the intercession of the Puerto Rican Institute of New York. On September 6, 1953, they arrived in San Juan where, after much pomp and ceremony, Julia de Burgos was reburied in the cemetery in Carolinas, the town of her birth. She had never returned to Puerto Rico after her first trip to New York some 13 years earlier, but with death she was finally home: "I was a star open to all dreams/ Today I close myself from the world, and my songs are silent." In 1954, friends compiled some of Julia de Burgos' final poems from those last years in exile in New York. These were published along with *El mar y tú*, the volume she had written in Cuba but had never been able to publish in her lifetime.

The poetry of Julia de Burgos speaks often of love and the striking landscape of Puerto Rico. Because of this, her verses are sometimes compared to the early writings of the 1971 Nobel Prize winner, Chilean poet Pablo Neruda (1904–1973). She also shared with Neruda a view of Puerto Rican reality that led her to protest against colonialism, injustice, exploitation and war. Some works are marked by pessimism. At times, de Burgos felt unable to bear the burden of so much personal disappointment and failed political struggle. Death became a tragic presence particularly in the poems from her final years.

Throughout her poems, as in her life, Julia de Burgos chafed against the role that Puerto Rican society had prescribed for women—the resigned passivity of the "good" wife and mother. More drawn to a spirit of rebellion, she chose to live in exile. Her poems often convey the impression of a free and sensuous spirit, joyously celebrating womanhood and nature. A few literary critics have identified in her work examples of militant feminism, which differentiate her from most of the other women poets of Latin America, with the exception, perhaps, of Argentinean *Alfonsina Storni (1892–1938).

Her production was limited to three books, totalling about 150 poems, and a few more verses and articles that appeared in newspapers. Because her poetry sings about so many human emotions and still presents the social reality of Puerto Rico, Julia de Burgos continues to be recognized and appreciated. Perhaps her greatest gift to Puerto Rican culture was the creation of a new option for women's literary voices. As María Solá wrote in her study of de Burgos' poetry:

> The lyric voice created by Burgos at times expresses fury, audacious challenge, or ironic mockery; in all her texts she displays pride in her intelligence, talent and freedom. It is this new image of women that forms her greatest contribution, a vision that makes her a forerunner of the literature of today.

SOURCES:

de Burgos, Julia. *Yo misma fui mi ruta.* Edited by María M. Solá. Río Piedras, Puerto Rico: Ediciones Huracán, 1986.

Fox Lockert, Lucía. "Vida, pasión y muerte de Julia de Burgos," in *Letras Femininas.* Vol. XVI, no. 1–2, 1990, pp. 121–124.

Jiménez de Baez, Yvette. *Julia de Burgos, vida y poesía.* Río Piedras, Puerto Rico: Editorial Coquí, 1966.

SUGGESTED READING:

Acosta Belén, Edna. *La mujer en la sociedad puertorriqueña.* Río Piedras, Puerto Rico, 1980.

Perez, Janet. "The Island, the Mainland and Beyond: Literary Space in Puerto Rican Women's Poetry," in *Revista canadiense de estudios hispánicos.* Vol. 14, no. 3, Spring 1990.

Torres-Robles, Carmen L. "Social Irredentism in the Prose of Julia de Burgos," in *The Bilingual Review.* Vol. 17, no. 1, 1992. p. 43.

RELATED MEDIA:

Bernstein, Leonard (vocal score), *Songfest: a cycle of American poems for six singers and orchestra,* Jalna Publications, 1988 (one of the songs is based on Julia de Burgos' poem, "A Julia de Burgos").

Julia de Burgos (16 mm) film biography with readings of her poetry, produced in New York by the Cinema Guild, around 1975.

Virginia Gibbs, Assistant Professor of Spanish Language and Literature, Luther College, Decorah, Iowa

De Camp, Miss (1774–1838).

See Kemble, Maria Theresa.

de Carvajal, Luisa (1568–1614).

See Carvajal, Luisa de.

de Castro, Inez (c. 1320–1355).

See Castro, Inez de.

de Castro, Rosalía (1837–1885).

See Castro, Rosalía de.

Decaux, Lucile (1887–1973).

See Bibesco, Marthe Lucie.

De Chambrun, Josée.

See Laval, Josée.

Decker, Mary (b. 1958).

See Slaney, Mary Decker.

de Clare, Isabel (c. 1174–1220).

See Clare, Isabel de.

de Clare, Matilda (d. 1315).

See Matilda de Burgh.

de Clere.

Variant of de Clare.

de Cleyre, Voltairine (1866–1912)

*Political theorist and feminist whose work made a significant contribution to the development of the Anarchist movement in the United States. Name variations: (pseudonym) Fannie Fern (not to be confused with journalist Sara Payson Willis Parton who changed her name legally to *Fanny Fern). Pronunciation: Vol-TAIR-ean dee CLARE. Born Voltairine de Claire on November 17, 1866, in Leslie, Michigan; died on June 12, 1912, in Chicago, Illinois; third daughter of Hector Auguste de Claire and Harriet (Clarke) de Claire (a seamstress); attended the convent of Our Lady of Lake Huron, Sarnia, Ontario, Canada; never married; children: Harry (b. 1890).*

Embarked on first lecture tour in Michigan (1884); influenced by events surrounding the Haymarket riot, Chicago (1886); traveled to Great Britain on lecture tour (1897); affected by the assassination of President McKinley in Buffalo, New York, by anarchist sympathizer (1901); shot and seriously wounded in Philadelphia (1902); traveled to Norway (1903); supported peasants after outbreak of Mexican revolution (1911).

Selected publications: (poems) The Burial of My Yesterday (1885); (pamphlet) "The Gates of Freedom" (1891); (pamphlet) "In Defence of Emma Goldman and the Right of Expropriation" (1893); (poems) The Gods and the People (1896); (pamphlet) "The Question of Women vs. Orthodoxy" (1896); (pamphlet) "The Modern Inquisition in Spain"

(1897); (pamphlet) "The Worm Turns" (1900); (pamphlet) "The Catechism of Anarchism" (1902); (pamphlet) "The Making of an Anarchist" (1903); (pamphlet) "Anarchism and American Traditions" (1908); (pamphlet) "The Dominant Idea" (1910); (pamphlet) "The Mexican Revolution" (1911); (pamphlet) "Francisco Ferrer" (1911); (pamphlet) "Direct Action" (1912). Many of these pamphlets are reprinted in her Selected Works, edited by Hippolyte Havel (1914).

On the evening of December 19, 1902, a young man named Herman Helcher walked on to a platform in a hall in Philadelphia where Voltairine de Cleyre was delivering a lecture. As he approached, Helcher drew a revolver from his pocket and shot her three times from close range. Although seriously wounded, de Cleyre refused to identify the assailant, who was known to her, to the police. Later, when Helcher was apprehended, Voltairine wrote that his actions should be attributed to temporary mental instability and that he should not be sent to prison.

De Cleyre's remarkable response to her erstwhile assassin was not due to any feelings of sympathy towards Helcher, whose amorous overtures she had previously rejected. Rather, her actions were consistent with her belief as an anarchist that all legal and administrative institutions of the state (such as the police and prisons) only seek to exercise an illegitimate power of coercion over the individual. Such power is illegitimate because it is incompatible with the anarchist ethical ideal of personal freedom mediated by a respect for the autonomy and liberty of others. In her mind, though Helcher's actions were wrong in failing to regard the rights of another, it would have been equally wrong to subject his freedom to the coercive power of the state.

Voltairine de Cleyre was born in 1866 into a poor, working-class family in Leslie, Michigan. Her father Hector de Claire (who had emigrated from Belgium in 1854) and mother **Harriet de Claire** appear to have been active in the abolitionist movement, helping escaped slaves from the South to pass over the border into Canada. Both prided themselves on being "freethinkers" and celebrated this fact by naming their youngest daughter after the famous nonconformist philosopher of the French Enlightenment, Voltaire.

In 1867, the family moved to Little Village, Clinton County, Michigan, but shortly thereafter Hector and his wife separated. Voltairine then moved with her mother and sister **Adelaide de Claire** (her other sister had previously died in a drowning accident) to nearby St. Johns where, in 1872, she entered Clinton County elementary school. By all accounts, Voltairine was a precocious and intelligent child who, even at this early age, was deeply affected by the plight of the factory laborers in the surrounding communities. In a school notebook, written when she was no more than 11 years of age, she noted with feeling that the "degradation of the workers is horrible" and expressed a desire to do something to alleviate their condition.

Voltairine's mother only worked intermittently as a seamstress, and as a result the family's life in St. Johns was often marked by extreme poverty. This difficult situation was exacerbated by the fact that Harriet seems to have had few feelings of warmth or affection for her daughters. Voltairine, in particular, became increasingly difficult to control as she began to rebel against the harsh disciplinary regime that her mother sought to impose.

> *I die, as I have lived, a free spirit, an Anarchist, owing no allegiance to rulers, heavenly or earthly.*
>
> **—Voltairine de Cleyre**

Following completion of elementary school in 1878, Voltairine left St. Johns and went to live with her father in Port Huron, Michigan. By this time, Hector had abandoned his earlier secular beliefs and had once again taken up the Catholic faith of his youth. Over the strenuous objections of Harriet (who had originally been brought up as a Protestant), he enrolled his daughter in the convent of Our Lady of Lake Huron in Sarnia, Ontario. A story subsequently arose that he had chosen the convent in order that Voltairine should eventually become a nun. In fact, however, it appears that Hector was more concerned to find an educational institution that would both develop his daughter's recognized intellectual capacities as well as provide an environment of emotional and physical self-control, two qualities that she clearly lacked.

The next five years proved to be a testing time. Although she was an excellent scholar, Voltairine found herself in a state of constant disagreement with the nuns and the discipline they attempted to enforce. On a number of occasions, she fled the convent for her mother's home in St. Johns only to be fetched back each time by her father. Although she was deeply unhappy, Voltairine refused to be cowed by her circumstances and instead wrote to her sister that she was full of an "immortal spirit of rebellion." It was perhaps one of the manifestations of that spirit that prompted her, at this time, to alter the spelling of her surname from *de Claire* to *de Cleyre*.

After graduating in December 1883, Voltairine broke with her father completely and returned to live with her sister and mother in St. Johns. For the next three years, she attempted to establish a living for herself as a private teacher of English and music. Her lack of success was not due to her lack of teaching abilities but, rather, to the lack of teaching opportunities in the confines of the small town. Voltairine filled her spare time constructively, however, by reading extensively from a variety of classical and scientific literature. She soon put this reading to use in a series of public lectures, given at locations throughout Michigan, in which she spoke on a variety of anti-religious topics. In 1885, de Cleyre published her first volume of poems, which she pointedly entitled *The Burial of My Yesterday* and which included the lines, "And now humanity, I turn toward you/ I consecrate my life to the service of the world."

De Cleyre's political beliefs began to be focused in 1886 in the aftermath of the Haymarket affair in Chicago in which a bomb was thrown which killed or injured several policemen. In the aftermath, four anarchists (who were widely considered to be innocent of the crime) were hanged. The entire incident rapidly became a *cause célèbre* and drew many, including Voltairine, to sympathy with the radical cause.

The following year, she moved briefly to Grand Rapids, Michigan, where she combined her activities as a public lecturer with a new vocation as writer for the anti-establishment journal the *Progressive Age* (under the pseudonym of Fannie Fern). It was not, however, until she attended a talk by Clarence Darrow (best known for his role as defense attorney at the 1925 Scopes "monkey" trial in Dayton, Tennessee) that she began to identify herself openly as a socialist.

In 1888, de Cleyre met two men who had a significant impact on her future. The first, Dyer D. Lum (born in Geneva, New York, in 1839) was the author of *The Economic Aspects of Anarchism*. He advocated a theory known as "anarcho-syndicalism," a position that views industrial associations or trade unions as the organizational germ of a future non-authoritarian society and advocates the use of mass strikes as the most effective means of attaining that goal. Lum had a crucial influence in molding Voltairine's intellectual development (she was later to refer to him as her "spiritual father"). He gradually won her over to the anarchist cause by encouraging her to read the works of such distinguished theoreticians as the American Benjamin Tucker and, in particular, France's Pierre-Joseph Proudhon. Lum also influenced her to move to Philadelphia, then the major center of anarchism in North America, where she eventually came into contact with such famous contemporary anarchists as *Emma Goldman and Alexander Berkman. In the same year, 1888, Voltairine met James Elliott (1849–1935), a Philadelphia carpenter who was active, albeit in a minor way, in the radical movement. The nature of their early relationship is obscure, but it is known that by late 1889 Voltairine was pregnant. Early the following year, she gave birth to a son, Harry.

After Voltairine's death, a spurious story would circulate claiming that Elliott had prevented her from living with the child. On the contrary, from the beginning, motherhood seems to have played no role in Voltairine's self-image. Thus, immediately following the birth, she left her partner and son and went to live in Kansas for a year. Although, on her return, she once again went to live with Elliott, she refused to acknowledge any responsibility for Harry. When de Cleyre and Elliott eventually parted (in 1894), their son continued to live solely with his father who, as time went on, displayed increasing signs of mental instability. It was only a few years before her own death that Voltairine was able to bring herself to affect a partial reconciliation with Harry. Remarkably, the young man appears to have borne her no ill-will for the treatment he had been afforded.

One positive outcome of this affair was to galvanize de Cleyre to reflect more deeply on the issue of the role of women in society. She produced two important pamphlets, "The Gates of Freedom" (1891) and "The Case of Women vs. Orthodoxy" (1896), which, in the words of **Margaret Marsh**, represent "the most complete articulation of the anarchist-feminist position to appear in the nineteenth century."

De Cleyre argued that there is an inextricable link between the economic structure of society and the social institution of marriage. Only by breaking that link will women be able to achieve the goal of true equality and be in a position to assert their individual autonomy and freedom of control over their own person. This is a difficult task that ultimately requires nothing less than the complete abolition of prevailing capitalist relations of ownership and control of society's means of production. An important start can be made, however, if women begin to acknowledge a belief in the possibility of personal autonomy and freedom. De Cleyre rejected the notion that this could be achieved through the medium of organized groups. Rather, she advocated individual acts of rebellion in which each woman sought to challenge, in her own way, the customary roles that society demanded of her (for instance, the pressure to marry and bear children). Such acts, de Cleyre believed, would create the conditions for a fundamental restructuring of all the traditional social relationships between men and women.

Throughout the 1890s, Voltairine continued to expand her circle of radical friends. In 1892, she met and collaborated with Saverio Merlino, an important Italian anarchist recently arrived in the United States, in the production of the bimonthly journal *Solidarity*. De Cleyre suffered a hard blow in the following year, however, with the death of Dyer Lum. Despite their difference in age, they enjoyed a deep emotional and intellectual affinity that was partially revealed in 1896 in de Cleyre's second volume of poems, *The Gods and the People*.

Apart from one theoretical work on anarchism (a defense of her friend Emma Goldman published in 1893), Voltairine's most significant activity at this time remained public lecturing. She spoke frequently before large, if sometimes skeptical, audiences, urging them to find in the radical principles of anarchism a continuation of the work of more conventional American thinkers such as Thomas Jefferson and Ralph Waldo Emerson. At the same time, because she always refused to accept payment for her lectures, Voltairine was forced to earn what she could as a private teacher. She taught English to the children of Russian-Jewish immigrants and, in turn, learned Yiddish so well that she was able to contribute to that community's anarchist journal, *Freie Arbeiter Shtimme*.

In 1897, de Cleyre traveled to London and from there embarked on an extensive lecture tour of England and Scotland. She made the acquaintance of a number of important figures, including Peter Kropotkin (widely regarded as the leading anarchist theoretician of the period) and Max Nettlau, the anarchist historian, who later described her as the "pearl of anarchist literature." Somewhat to her surprise, she discovered that her reputation as an anarchist-feminist theoretician had preceded her, and that she was held in considerable regard by the European radical movement.

The highlight of this trip, however, was her meeting with several Spanish anarchists (the "Montjuich deportees," named after the prison in Barcelona where they had been held). These were the survivors of a group who had been arrested, tortured, and in some instances executed following a bomb attack in which they had played no part. Their brutal treatment at the hands of the Spanish authorities was widely condemned by the general public in Britain. On her return to the United States later the same year, de Cleyre published an important pamphlet on their experiences, "The Modern Inquisition in Spain." From this time on, she was increasingly regarded as the most important link bridging the European and North American anarchist movements.

Despite her increasing reputation, the turn of the century proved a difficult time for de Cleyre. She began to suffer from a chronic ear-and-throat infection that often left her bedridden for weeks at a time. Moreover, following the assassination of President William McKinley in 1901 by an anarchist sympathizer, the anarchist movement fell into public disrepute, and it became increasingly difficult for de Cleyre to carry on her work as a lecturer. She became emotionally depressed, and there is some evidence to suggest that she considered committing suicide.

In 1903, as she was recuperating from Helcher's attempt on her life, de Cleyre was invited to Norway by Kristofer Hansteen, a leading European anarchist. In many ways, this seems to have been her happiest period, as she gradually emerged from the depths of her physical, emotional, and intellectual despair. When she returned to the U.S. in 1907, she was ready to resume her career as a lecturer and, more significantly, make her most important theoretical contributions to anarchist thought.

In two pamphlets, "Anarchism and American Traditions" (1908) and "The Dominant Idea" (1910), Voltairine developed what can now be recognized as one of the earliest critiques of modern consumer culture. She argued that modern society can be principally characterized by its love of material possessions. The desire to own and consume such possessions has effectively become, for the great majority of people, their paramount goal. Moreover, although these individuals may claim that this quest is fulfilling, in reality, it only gives rise to an unremitting mood of personal dissatisfaction. The problem, therefore, is to convince these individuals that only a radically different style of life will result in a more satisfied self.

De Cleyre was less forthcoming in proposing concrete measures whereby such a transformation could occur. She was convinced that salvation did not lie in the capitalist system which, after all, had created the problem in first place. As an anarchist, she favored a decentralized economy run according to principles of workers' self-management, and she advocated programs of education and propaganda as the most conducive means whereby this might be achieved. Most important (and here she recalled her earlier feminist writings), individuals should seek personal freedom through the exercise of their own autonomy and respect for the rights and liberties of others.

In the last few years of her life, Voltairine became increasingly active in the anarchist movement. She left Philadelphia in 1910 and moved to Chicago where she became involved with an anarcho-syndicalist labor organization called the International Workers of the World (the "Wobblies"). The Wobblies championed a program of revolutionary change not dissimilar to that advocated by her old friend Lum, and in 1912 she published a pamphlet ("Direct Action") that strongly sympathized with their position.

When the Mexican revolution broke out in 1911, de Cleyre worked tirelessly organizing meetings in support of the peasants' cause. She began to learn Spanish with the aim of traveling to Mexico in order to participate in the rebellion at first hand. Before she could do so, she was subject to a recurrence of her ear infection. De Cleyre entered a hospital in Chicago in June 1912, and there, due to complications following surgery, she died at the age of 45.

SOURCES:

Avrich, Paul. *An American Anarchist: A Life of Voltairine de Cleyre.* Princeton, NJ: Princeton University Press, 1978.

de Cleyre, Voltairine. *Selected Works.* Edited by Hippolyte Havel. NY: Mother Earth, 1914.

Marsh, Margaret. *Anarchist Women, 1870–1920.* Philadelphia, PA: Temple University Press, 1981.

Muñoz, Vladimir. *Anarchists.* NY: Golden Press, 1981.

SUGGESTED READING:

Woodcock, George. *Anarchism.* Harmondsworth: Penguin Books, 1979.

Dave Baxter, freelance writer,
Waterloo, Ontario, Canada

De Costa, Maria Velho (b. 1938).

See The Three Marias.

DeCosta, Sara (1977—).

See Team USA: Women's Ice Hockey at Nagano.

de Crayencour, Marguerite (1903–1987).

See Yourcenar, Marguerite.

de Dia, Beatrice (c. 1160–1212)

French troubadour. Name variations: Contessa Beatrice de Dia. Born around 1160, lived in Provence; died in 1212; may have married William of Poitiers, count of Valentinois.

Beatrice de Dia is now known mainly for writing four ballads, all love elegies that still survive. She may have been the wife of William of Poitiers and the mistress of Rambaud of Orange (Raibaut d'Orange), also a troubadour. (Some accounts indicate that she may have married the count of Ambrunois and have been the mistress of Guillaume Adhermar.) A historical account by Father Millet confirms that most probably William was her husband and Rambaud her lover. De Dia's ballads indicate that Rambaud left her in later years, inspiring her to write her most acclaimed ballad, *Plang.* Passionate and sensual, this ballad documents the love of a woman who expresses her sentiments candidly. Beatrice de Dia's compositions document the important role women played in Europe's medieval musical world.

John Haag,
Athens, Georgia

Dee, Ruby (1923—)

*African-American actress, winner of an Obie and two Drama Desk awards, known for her dedication in the cause of civil rights. Born Ruby Ann Wallace on October 27, 1923, in Cleveland, Ohio; one of four children of Marshall Edward (a porter and waiter on the Pennsylvania Railroad) and Emma (Benson) Wallace; attended public schools in Harlem; graduated from Hunter High School, New York City; B.A. from Hunter College; married Ossie Davis (an actor), on December 9, 1948; children: two daughters, **Nora Davis** and **LaVerne Davis**; one son, Guy Davis.*

Selected stage credits: first appeared on stage with the American Negro Theater (at Library Theater) in Natural Man *(1941),* Starlight *(1942), and* Three's a Family *(1943); made Broadway debut as Ruth in Howard Rigsby and Dorothy Heyward's* South Pacific *(Cort Theater, 1943); appeared in title role of* Anna Lucasta *(Mansfield Theater, 1944); portrayed Ruth Younger in* A Raisin in the Sun *(Ethel Barrymore Theater, 1959),* Lutiebelle Gussie Mae Jenkins in Purlie Victorious *(Cort Theater, 1961),* Lena in Boesman and Lena *(1970); appeared in Alice Childress'* Wedding Band *(1973).*

Filmography: No Way Out *(1950);* The Jackie Robinson Story *(1950);* The Tall Target *(1951);* Go Man Go! *(1954);* Edge of the City *(1957);* St. Louis

Blues *(1958)*; Virgin Island *(1960)*; A Raisin in the Sun *(1961)*; Take a Giant Step *(1963)*; Gone Are the Days! *(Purlie Victorious, 1963)*; The Balcony *(1963)*; The Incident *(1967)*; Uptight *(1968)*; Buck and the Preacher *(1972)*; *(cameo)* Black Girl *(1972)*; Countdown at Kusini *(US/Nigeria, 1976)*; Do the Right Thing *(1988)*.

Elected to the Theater Hall of Fame in 1988, Ruby Dee has combined an extraordinary career as an actress with writing and an ongoing commitment to civil rights. Born in Cleveland, Ohio, she was raised in New York's Harlem, where the family moved when she was

an infant. Her mother **Emma Wallace**, a schoolteacher, was determined that her children would amount to something and saw to it that music and literature had a prominent place in their lives. Dee later described herself as a shy, nonaggressive child, but added: "I had wild feelings churning inside me I wanted to express." She became interested in acting in high school after her classmates applauded her classroom reading from a play. While studying languages at Hunter College, she apprenticed with the American Negro Theater, then housed in the basement of the West 135th Street branch of the New York

Ruby Dee

Public Library. She made her earliest stage appearances at the Library Theater, in productions of *Natural Man* (1941), *Starlight* (1942), and *Three's a Family* (1943). In December 1943, she made her Broadway debut in the short-lived World War II drama, *South Pacific,* by Howard Rigby and *Dorothy Heyward (no relation to the Rodgers and Hammerstein musical of the same name). Her performance in the title role of Philip Yordan's *Anna Lucasta* (1944), about a streetwalker transformed by true love, brought her to the attention of the critics, who also praised her portrayal of Marcy in the all-black production of *A Long Way from Home* (1948), an adaptation of Maxim Gorki's *The Lower Depths*. In 1948, during a break in rehearsals for *Smile of the World*, Dee married actor Ossie Davis, whom she had known since 1946.

During the 1950s, Dee continued to perform on the stage while launching her film career, which has included notable roles in *The Jackie Robinson Story* (1950), *Edge of the City* (1957), and Spike Lee's *Do the Right Thing* (1988). In 1959, Dee reached a high point in her stage career as Ruth Younger in *Lorraine Hansberry's prize-winning play, *A Raisin in the Sun*, the story of a struggling black family living in a Chicago tenement. The critics agreed that as the long-suffering wife and daughter-in-law, a role she repeated in the movie, Dee turned in an inspired yet seemingly effortless performance. She followed that success with a role opposite her husband in *Purlie Victorious* (1961), a satire on black-white relationships in the South, which Davis also wrote. She continued to expand her acting repertoire at the American Shakespeare Festival in Stratford, Connecticut, playing Katherina in *The Taming of the Shrew* (1965) and Cordelia in *King Lear* (1965). Other ventures into the classics have included starring performances at the Ypsilanti (Michigan) Greek Theater and the University of Michigan's professional theater program: she appeared with Bert Lahr in Aristophanes' *The Birds* (1966) and played Gertrude in *Hamlet* (1975), opposite Sam Waterston.

Dee turned in a riveting performance in Athol Fugard's important play *Boesman and Lena* (1970), about the plight of South Africa's Cape Coloureds—people of mixed race. As Lena, the wife of a defeated brute of a husband, Dee's portrayal impressed the critics. Clive Barnes wrote in *The New York Times* (June 23, 1970): "It is complete—it has the quickness of life about it. Never for a moment do you think she is acting—even, and this is the trick, when she is at her most stagey. . . . Her frail sparrow-figure, her bright, unsubdued eyes, her voice, . . .

her manner, her entire being, have a quality of wholeness that is rarely encountered in the theater." For Dee, who won the Obie and Drama Desk Award for the role, playing Lena was a liberating experience, freeing her from her stereotyped image as the black "*June Allyson." In an interview with **Patricia Bosworth** for *The New York Times*, Dee remarked, "I understand Lena. I relate to her particular reality because it is mine and every black woman's. . . . With Lena I am suddenly, gloriously free." She received a second Drama Desk Award in 1973 for her performance in *Alice Childress' *Wedding Band*.

Dee made her television debut in 1960 in "Actor's Choice" (on Camera Three) and went on to regular appearances as a guest performer. She received an Emmy nomination for her performance in an episode of "East Side, West Side," and also appeared with her husband on National Education Television programs, including the "History of the Negro People."

Dee's talent is not confined to acting; she has published a book of poetry called *Child Glow and Other Poems* (1973) and has written several plays, including *Twin Bit Gardens* (1976), the musical *Take It from the Top* (1979), and *Zora Is My Name* (1983), about Harlem Renaissance writer *Zora Neale Hurston. She also co-authored and starred in the film *Uptight* (1969).

Throughout her career, along with her husband, Dee has also focused much of her time to racial equality, serving on national committees and performing in benefits to raise money for civil rights and other related causes. To assist talented young black actresses, she has established the Ruby Dee Scholarship in Dramatic Art. In May 1970, she and Ossie Davis were presented the Frederick Douglass Award by the New York Urban League for bringing a "sense of fervor and pride to countless millions." In 1975, they were the recipients of Actors Equity's Paul Robeson Citation for their "outstanding creative contributions in the performing arts and to society at large."

In a show business marriage that has defied the statistics for longevity, Ruby Dee and Ossie Davis have produced three children, two daughters, Nora and LaVerne, and a son, Guy. She has referred to Ossie as her "best friend," and he has described her as a "primitive," a woman "whose style of life is original, not derivative."

SOURCES:

Katz, Ephraim. *The Film Encyclopedia.* NY: HarperCollins, 1994.

McGill, Raymond D., ed. *Notable Names in the American Theater.* Clifton, NJ: James T. White, 1976.

Moritz, Charles, ed. *Current Biography.* NY: H.W. Wilson, 1970.

SUGGESTED READING:

Dee, Ruby, and Ossie Davis. *With Ossie and Ruby: In This Life Together.* NY: Morrow, 1998.

Dee, Ruby. *My One Good Nerve* (a collection of verse based on her one-woman show of that title), Wiley, 1998.

Barbara Morgan,
Melrose, Massachusetts

de Erauso, Catalina (1592–1635).

See Erauso, Catalina de.

de Ergadia, Joan (fl. 1300s).

See Isaac, Joan.

Deffand, Marie du (1697–1780).

See Salonnières.

de Galard, Geneviève (1925—)

French nurse and hero of the Indo-Chinese war, known as the Angel of Dien Bien Phu. Born Geneviève de Galard-Terraube, on April 13, 1925, in Paris, France; youngest of two daughters of Vicomte Oger de Galard-Terraube (an army officer); attended the *Louise de Bettignies private school; received a baccalaureate degree from a Dominican convent in Toulouse; studied fine arts at the École du Louvre, Paris; studied English at the Sorbonne; received state nursing diploma from nurses training school as well as a diploma from the Paris School of Social Work; married paratrooper Captain Jean de Heaulme, on May 21, 1957; children: two.

Geneviève de Galard-Terraube was born in Paris and taken by her mother to Toulouse after the death of her father in 1940. At age 24, she entered nursing school, hoping to be of service to her nation. After training, she joined the Infirmières Pilotes et Secouristes de L'Air (IPSA), a specially trained corps of airborne pilot-nurses and first-aid workers. The detachment was officially established in 1946, under the French Military Air Transport Service, at the start of the French war in Indochina. One of only 35 young nurses to meet the stiff IPSA requirements—including tests in nursing, aviation, tropical medicine, geography, and English—in April 1953 de Galard began duty in Indochina as a nurse on a plane that flew into battle zones and brought back wounded French soldiers to Saigon.

In January 1954, as part of a second tour of duty, she began flying to Dien Bien Phu, in North Vietnam, to evacuate severely wounded soldiers to Hanoi. Built as an underground fortress by the French in 1953 to give mobile units a base from which to launch guerrilla attacks behind Vietminh lines, Dien Bien Phu was subsequently surrounded by two divisions of Vietminh guerrilla fighters, making it vulnerable to attack. On March 28, during a routine flight to airlift wounded from the base, the plane in which de Galard was flying was destroyed by enemy artillery during repairs, forcing her to remain at the base until it was once again safe enough to fly out.

For the next two months, she joined the all-male, 30-member medical staff, living and working in extreme conditions and surviving a steady barrage of enemy attacks. Trading her navy-blue uniform for a pair of boots and coveralls, she asked for no special favors, often sleeping on a stretcher on the floor among the wounded. As French outposts continued to fall to the Vietminh, casualties mounted daily causing the hospital, built to house 45 patients, to accommodate up to 250. Through the horrors of war and a rainy season that brought mud, rot, and an outbreak of maggots to the underground facility, de Galard worked tirelessly, risking her life to go out into the fields to attend the

Geneviève de Galard

long line of wounded. To the men she treated, who were often in critical condition, she became a lifeline. On April 29, the commander of Dien Bien Phu visited the hospital to award de Galard a Croix de Guerre and the red ribbon of the Legion of Honor. The next night, in a special ceremony, she was made an honorary Legionnaire, first class, amid the cheers of her patients.

On May 6, Dien Bien Phu was captured by the Vietminh soldiers, although its medical team was given special permission to return to the patients. On May 16, Ho Chi Minh, president of Vietnam, liberated 735 French wounded prisoners and soon after notified de Galard that she too would be freed. Although she postponed taking leave to stay with her "children," she was finally instructed by the French commander of aviation to proceed to Hanoi and left on May 25.

De Galard was greeted in Hanoi as a celebrity (one of the paratroopers who met her plane would later become her husband), and foreign publishers bid large sums for her memoirs. From Hanoi, she flew to Paris, where she was presented with the Air Medal and the Air Medical Service Silver Medal.

On July 26, 1954, de Galard was given a ticker-tape parade in New York City and received by Mayor Robert Wagner, who called her "the heroine of the entire world." Following the parade, she received awards from the American Nurses Association and the National League for Nursing and was later honored at a charity ball at the Waldorf-Astoria. A cross-country tour followed, with a stop in Washington, where President Dwight D. Eisenhower presented her with the Medal of Freedom. She then returned to France to resume work as a flight nurse, making an additional one-year trip to the United States in 1955 for in-service training at the Rusk Institute for rehabilitation. In 1957, de Galard married Captain Jean de Heaulme, and during the first year of her marriage worked as a rehabilitation nurse at Les Invalides, a veteran's hospital in Paris. She later had two children and disappeared from public life.

SOURCES:
Mckown, Robin. *Heroic Nurses.* NY: Putnam, 1966.

Barbara Morgan,
Melrose, Massachusetts

de Gaulle, Madame (1900–1975).

See de Gaulle, Yvonne.

de Gaulle, Yvonne (1900–1979)

French first lady who went into exile with her husband Charles de Gaulle when he headed the Free French resistance during WWII and was, in her later years, affectionately known in France as "Tante Yvonne" (Aunt Yvonne). Name variations: Madame de Gaulle. Born Yvonne Charlotte Anne-Marie Vendroux (pronunciation: Vahn-DROO) on May 22, 1900, in the family home in Calais, on the Channel coast of France; died on November 8, 1979, in the military hospital Val-de-Grâce, Paris; daughter of Jacques Vendroux (the head of a biscuit manufacturing company) and Marguerite (Forest) Vendroux; received primary and secondary education largely with private tutors at home; spent several years at a primary school, Notre-Dame in Calais; married Charles de Gaulle, on April 7, 1921 (a civil ceremony took place the previous day but it was the religious ceremony held April 7 that was regarded as their wedding by the de Gaulles); children: Philippe (b. December 28, 1921); Elisabeth de Boissieu (b. May 15, 1924); Anne de Gaulle (January 1, 1928–February 6, 1948).

Childhood years spent in family home in Calais; at age five, began primary education with private tutors (1905); as German forces advanced toward Calais at outset of WWI, Vendroux family took refuge in England (July–August 1914); family returned to Calais (December 1914); cared for war wounded in Calais (1915–16); left Calais, under threat of German bombs, for safety in Paris (1916); as renewed German offensive threatened Paris (March 1918), sent out of harm's way to Mortagne, Brittany, then Perigueux (summer and autumn, 1918); worked with mother among the wounded war veterans in Calais (1919–20); met Charles de Gaulle (October 1920); after marriage, lived together in Paris (1921); moved with Charles, who was promoted to major and placed in charge of 19th Battalion of Light Infantry in Trier, Germany (1927); moved with family to Beirut (then in Syria, a French mandate of the League of Nations, now Lebanon), where Charles was posted (1929); returned to Paris (1931); purchased La Boisserie, an estate in the village of Colombey-les-Deux-Églises, in the Haute-Marne department in eastern France (June 9, 1934); based in Metz where Charles commanded the 507th Tank Regiment (1937); outbreak of WWII (September 1, 1939); Germans entered Paris (June 14, 1940); de Gaulle family left France for London (June 17) where Charles' first BBC radio broadcast back to France called for resistance against Germany (June 18); moved to join Charles in liberated Algiers (July 1943); Allied invasion of Normandy (June 6, 1944); rejoined Charles, now head of the Provisional Government, in Neuilly, near Paris (September 1944); Charles resigned as head of the Provisional Government (January, 1946); moved back into La Boisserie

(May 1946); death of daughter Anne, caused by pneumonia (February 6, 1948); returned to Paris with recall of Charles to power during Algerian crisis (June 1, 1958); became "first lady" of France upon the inauguration of Charles as first president of the Fifth Republic (January 8, 1959); narrowly survived an assassination attempt in the company of her husband (August 22, 1962); retired to La Boisserie after referendum defeat of de Gaulle (April 1969); death of Charles de Gaulle (November 9, 1970).

On August 22, 1962, in the Paris suburb of Petit-Clamart, en route from the Élysée Palace to the town of Villacoublay, the French presidential car was ambushed by a commando who fired some 150 shots from automatic weapons. Fourteen bullets struck the car in which Charles and Yvonne de Gaulle, their son-in-law Alain de Boissieu, and the driver Francis Marroux were riding, on their way for a weekend at the presidential retreat in Colombey-les-Deux-Églises. No one was hit. The Petit-Clamart attack was but the closest call in a series of assassination attempts by groups opposed to Charles de Gaulle's ceding of independence to the rebellious colony of Algeria. The general, at least according to some accounts, had been too proud even to drop to the floor during the fusillade, and, even though a bullet passed between their heads, Yvonne de Gaulle had also remained seated erect during the attack. Upon their arrival at Villacoublay, the general turned to his wife and said: "Yvonne, you are brave."

Yvonne de Gaulle's behavior during and after the Petit-Clamart assassination attempt typified the stoicism, courage, and fidelity that characterized her entire adult life and for which she is remembered in France. Years after her death, President Richard Nixon remembered her having said in 1969, "the presidency is temporary, the family permanent." The product of a middle-class Catholic family from Calais, in Normandy, Yvonne de Gaulle exemplified the "dutiful wife and mother," silent in public but influential behind the scenes. Deeply religious and private, she kept to herself whatever complaints she might have had living with the self-assured and frequently cantankerous Charles de Gaulle. She lived so privately that, even as first lady in France during the 1960s, she was able to shop in Parisian stores without being recognized. Although her role came increasingly into question in the France of the 1960s, she nonetheless came to be respected in France as "Tante Yvonne" (Aunt Yvonne), during the presidency of her husband.

The daughter of Jacques and **Marguerite Vendroux**, Yvonne Vendroux was born on May 22, 1900, in the family home in Calais, on the Channel coast of France. Her father, who had gone into the biscuit-producing business, came from a long line of shipowners and local mayors and was himself vice president of the Chamber of Commerce, a municipal councilor, and the honorary consul of several foreign countries. He was, in French terms, a "notable," or local dignitary. His family, the Van Droog, tobacco producers, had moved in the late 17th century from Delft in Holland to Dunkirk, where the name was changed to Vandroux; later the family moved to Calais, where the name was changed to Vendroux. Yvonne's mother, Marguerite Forest Vendroux, was the granddaughter of a well-known notary of the town of Charleville.

Madame de Gaulle's importance was considerable not for what she said or did but for what she neither did nor said, by her silent presence.
—André Malraux

Yvonne Vendroux had a happy and stable childhood. Raised amid comfortable circumstances, the second of four children, she spent her early years with her family, in Calais in the winter and in a country estate in the Ardennes during the summer, where she went mountain climbing and developed a lifelong love of nature, especially flowers. Most of her schooling took place in the form of home tutoring. Dubious about the quality of the local schools after the 1905 separation of church and state in France, Yvonne's parents hired a tutor, **Mademoiselle Delannoy**, for her primary education. After 1907, she was sent for awhile as a day student to the local Notre-Dame boarding school, but her parents retained the tutor to supplement their daughter's education. Her secondary school education took place entirely at home.

Yvonne's first communion, in 1911, was followed by three relatively carefree years, broken with the onset of World War I in August 1914. As German forces advanced toward Calais and bombs fell on the town early in the war, the Vendroux family took refuge in Kent, in southern England. By the end of 1914, when it had become clear that the French forces would hold and Calais would be safe from German invasion, the Vendroux family returned. There, Yvonne's activities continued to revolve around the home as her mother cared for wounded war veterans. In 1916, seeking greater security, the family again left Calais for Paris, where Yvonne remained until March 1918, when a renewed German offensive led the family to send her and her sister **Suzanne** to Brittany. Now 18, Yvonne next went to Perigueux, where she spent the final days of World War I. With the end of the war, the Vendroux family turned to the restoration of their various properties in the Calais and Ardennes areas. Yvonne assumed an increasing role in household management, allowing her mother to continue to work in veterans' hospitals. Her older brother Jacques accompanied her as chaperon to the parties and balls in Paris and Calais. Yvonne soon joined her mother working among the war wounded, widows, and orphans.

In October 1920, at a tea arranged by family friends, Yvonne met Captain Charles de Gaulle, then on a brief leave from service with the French military mission in Poland. Shortly thereafter, he invited her to a ball at Saint-Cyr, the French military academy. Taken with Charles, Yvonne accepted and went in the company of Jacques. A few days later, asked directly about her feelings toward Charles, Yvonne replied, "It will be he or no one." The families met, and the couple was officially affianced on November 11, 1920. Charles had to return for two additional months' service in Poland, then returned to France in February. He was named professor of history at Saint-Cyr, a post that would keep him in Paris.

Yvonne Vendroux and Charles de Gaulle were married in a civil ceremony in Calais on April 6, 1921, and in a religious ceremony the next day at the Notre-Dame Church in that city. Following their marriage, the young couple settled in a modest Paris apartment and lived a relatively quiet life. Their son Philippe was born at the end of 1921. In 1924, their second child, Elizabeth, was born. Charles finished his studies at the War College, published his first book, *La Discorde chez l'Ennemi* (Discord in the Enemy), and was posted as an officer working with Marshal Philippe Pétain, the hero of World War I, with whose career his own would be dramatically crossed. In 1927, Yvonne de Gaulle joined her husband in a posting in Trier, Germany, where in 1928, their daughter Anne was born. Within months of Anne's birth, it had become clear that she was suffering from Down's syndrome. Anne was never to speak well or eat or dress unaided. Her illness was the great personal tragedy of the de Gaulles who cared for her tenderly.

In 1929, the de Gaulles were sent to Beirut, Lebanon, then part of French-controlled Syria, where they remained until 1931. In 1932, Yvonne's father died; her mother died the following year. At the end of 1933, Charles de Gaulle was promoted to lieutenant colonel. In June 1934, the de Gaulles bought "La Boisserie," the estate of Yvonne's late parents, located in the village of Colombey-les-Deux-Églises, in the gently rolling hills of the Haute-Marne department about midway between Paris and France's eastern frontier. The year 1934 also saw the publication of Charles' second book, *Vers l'armée de métier* (The Army of the Future), which argued, to little avail, that the French should adopt new mechanized forms of warfare. In 1937, Charles was given the command of the 507th Tank Regiment based in Metz. Life for the de Gaulle family revolved quietly around Paris, Metz, and La Boisserie.

Yvonne's domain was the family home at La Boisserie, her place of refuge from the turbulent political affairs surrounding her husband. She quietly endured the tragedy of Anne's disabilities while living with a man who was very much a lone rebel in political and military circles during the 1930s, and who clearly ruled as master of the household. Known for his arrogance, Charles was said to be a tyrant at home, with Yvonne silently bearing the brunt of his disappointment and frustration. Charles dominated conversations; Yvonne was told plainly, and sometimes publicly, that her opinion did not count. On more than one occasion Charles was observed telling his wife to be silent, that she could not possibly know anything about politics. Years later, an acquaintance said that compared to the cheerful if somewhat reticent young woman who had married Charles in 1921, the Yvonne of the late 1930s was profoundly sad.

The outbreak of war with Nazi Germany in September 1939 found Charles in command of his tank regiment. Poland was quickly crushed by the Germans, but the war with France involved little actual fighting in what became known as the *drôle de guerre*, or phony war. This changed with the German thrust westward of May 10, 1940. The force of the German onslaught was such that, within days, Charles was writing from the front to Yvonne at La Boisserie, warning her to be ready for quick flight in the event that the military situation turned disastrous. On June 1, Charles was promoted to brigadier-general. Five days later, he was appointed undersecretary of state for National Defense and War by Premier Paul Reynaud. The Germans entered Paris on June 14. On June 16, the Reynaud government was replaced by one headed by Marshal Pétain, who was committed to seeking peace with the Germans. A day later, Yvonne with her three children and their governess left for England to join her husband, a political exile.

For the second time in her life, Yvonne de Gaulle experienced wartime exile in England. On June 18, Charles broadcast back to France, calling on the entire nation to resist the Germans and any French authority that supported collaboration with them. In London, their son Philippe, then 18 years old, joined the newly created Free French Navy in July. In addition to the occupation of her homeland, Yvonne had to ac-cept the fact that her husband was now a rebel, standing almost alone against his country's legal government, which was headed by World War I hero and his own former sponsor, Marshal Pé-tain. Moreover, Pétain sentenced Charles to death in absentia for wartime desertion and trea-son. Yvonne set up a household in London as he organized what became the Free French resis-tance to Nazi Germany and the government of Vichy France. Whatever his other activities in wartime London, Charles was invariably present to tell Anne stories at her bedtime and to shield her from the press.

Yvonne de Gaulle, chatting with a group of lacemakers (Calais, 1959).

Together with other Londoners, Yvonne endured the German Blitz or air raids in the summer and fall of 1940, but ultimately her faith in her husband's vision was rewarded; the fortunes of war turned with the entry of the Soviet Union and the United States into combat against the Nazis. Following the liberation of French North Africa, the de Gaulle family returned to Algiers in June 1943. The liberation of metropolitan France, which began with the D-Day landings in Normandy, June 6, 1944, left the country under the Free French, reorganized as a Provisional Government and headed by Charles de Gaulle. In late August, Paris was liberated and by the end of September, almost all of metropolitan France had been cleared of Germans. Yvonne, now the wife of the leader of the Provisional Government, returned home to supervise the reconstruction of La Boisserie, which had been pillaged and partially burned during the Occupation. Charles, however, became increasingly dispirited as the politicians who had dominated prewar politics and, in his view, had brought on the catastrophe of 1940, regained strength, promising to recreate what he called the "regime of parties." On January 3, 1946, a few weeks after the marriage of daughter Elisabeth to Commander Alain de Boissieu, Charles abruptly resigned his position. The family lived until May in an uncomfortable house rented from the government while La Boisserie was being restored and Charles waited restlessly to be recalled to power.

In 1946, with the help of Georges Pompidou, who later served as one of Charles' prime ministers and was to become his successor as president, the de Gaulles established the **Anne de Gaulle** Foundation to help handicapped girls. The Foundation was to care for Anne in the event that her parents predeceased her. Supported financially by the income from Charles' books, the Foundation built a house on a wooded hill in the Chevreuse valley. Staffed by six nuns and a mother superior, the house eventually provided for some 40 handicapped girls. Yvonne helped select them.

In April 1947, Charles created the *Rassemblement du Peuple Français* (Rally of the French People), a political party that was to serve as a vehicle for his return to power. Then, on February 6, 1948, Anne died of bronchial pneumonia at age 20. With the death of Anne, the Anne de Gaulle Foundation occupied much of Yvonne's attention. She also accompanied Charles throughout France as he campaigned for his new *RPF,* but by 1952, the party was fading and he ended it the next year. These years were spent,

often with their grandchildren, at La Boisserie where Charles worked on his memoirs, with occasional trips abroad where he was received as the hero of the wartime French Resistance. To visitors at La Boisserie, Yvonne occasionally expressed the desire to protect her husband "for history," and keep him out of politics. The tranquil life was interrupted, however, when the government's inability to suppress the Algerian rebellion led to rioting by European Algerians in the streets of Algiers on May 13, 1958. La Boisserie was quickly turned into a command post as Charles and his advisors planned his return to office. On June 1, Charles de Gaulle was voted in as premier by the National Assembly with full powers to write a new constitution for France. The result was France's Fifth Republic, with a much stronger presidency, filled in 1959 by Charles de Gaulle.

Once again, Yvonne de Gaulle was a reluctant first lady of France. During the early 1960s, Charles survived several assassination attempts by opponents of independence for Algeria. The closest call was the Petit-Clamart fusillade in 1962. Profiting by the wave of sympathy engendered by the assassination attempt, Charles proposed a constitutional change to elect the president by universal suffrage, which was approved by popular referendum in October. In 1965, against Yvonne's will, he stood as a candidate for the presidency. Forced into a runoff with Socialist candidate François Mitterrand, Charles was elected in the second round to a seven-year term.

To many in 1960s France, "Aunt Yvonne" came to represent the wife of a previous era. She accompanied Charles to innumerable Paris Opera galas, where she sat through close to 30 performances of "Carmen," and hosted the Kennedys, Khrushchevs, and many other world leaders. The comparison of the prim and somewhat dowdy Yvonne, who scrupulously supervised the household affairs of France's presidential Élysée Palace, with the youthful and fashionable *Jacqueline Kennedy, who accompanied her husband, then president of the United States, on a visit to Paris in 1961, was played out in the international press. Wearing sedate black, gray, or mauve dresses designed by Paris couturier Jacques Heim, Yvonne avoided décolletage and shunned the more up-to-date fashions of *Coco Chanel. Yvonne's successor as France's first lady, **Claude Pompidou**, recalled later that Yvonne's only advice to her had been to wear hats. Yvonne arranged the floral decorations of the palace, and she loved to travel and accompany her husband on all his official trips abroad, but whenever possible, she returned

Yvonne de Gaulle, with Charles de Gaulle (1966).

to La Boisserie and the gardens that were her favorite pastime.

A strict Catholic, Yvonne set an austere tone at the Élysée Palace, making sure the private lives of those in her husband's entourage passed moral muster. Exerting a considerable, if private, influence, she saw to it that divorcees were weeded out of influential positions and excluded from presidential social functions. She was equally severe in her judgments of much of the literature and film of the 1960s and carefully scrutinized the selection of films to be shown in the palace. For her religious devotions, she had a special chapel built inside the Élysée Palace.

Yvonne was with Charles when, during the height of the student and worker unrest of May 1968, he traveled to Baden-Baden to consult with French generals about the possibility of his resigning. She shared his disappointment, when, in April 1969, in a referendum he had called on behalf of decentralizing political reforms, he was defeated. Having staked his political prestige on the referendum, Charles immediately resigned. The couple returned to La Boisserie, where on November 9, 1970, Charles died. Yvonne continued to live there, where she cooked, knitted, and tended her garden, visited often by her children and four grandchildren until the fall of 1978, when she withdrew to the Sisters of the Immaculate Conception convent in Paris. In July 1979, she was operated on in Paris for an intestinal obstruction. Readmitted to a Paris military hospital, she died November 8, 1979. She was buried beside Charles and Anne at the church cemetery in Colombey-les-Deux-Églises. Surviving Yvonne, in addition to her son Philippe and daughter Elisabeth, were her grandchildren and one great-grandson. Mourned as the symbol of moral rectitude and marital fidelity of a long gone era, "Tante Yvonne" was called the "minister of common sense" in the government of General Charles de Gaulle. Following her death, La Boisserie, which remained in the possession of Philippe, was converted into a museum, open to the public, in honor of the de Gaulles.

SOURCES:

Béliard, Jean. "Entretien avec Richard Nixon," in Institut Charles de Gaulle. *De Gaulle en son siècle. Vol. 1: Dans la mémoire des hommes et des peuples.* Paris: Plon/La Documentation Française, 1991, pp. 78–86.

Dulong, Claude. *La Vie quotidienne a l'Élysée au temps de Charles de Gaulle.* Paris: Hachette, 1974.

Jullian, Marcel. *Madame de Gaulle.* Paris: Stock, 1982 (in French).

Lassus, Robert. *Le mari de Madame de Gaulle.* Paris: J.C. Lattès, 1990.

Meyer-Stabley, Bertrand. *Les dames de l'Élysée, Celles d'hier et de demain.* Paris: Perrin, 1995.

Vendroux, Jacques. *Yvonne de Gaulle, ma soeur, l'enfant, la jeune fille, la jeune femme 1900–1932.* Paris: Plon, 1980.

SUGGESTED READING:

Behr, Edward. "The Silent First Lady of France, Yvonne de Gaulle is a lonely woman feared by many, known by few," in *Saturday Evening Post.* Vol. 237, No. 2. January 18, 1964, pp. 64–65.

Chapman, Robin. "Anne's Story," a fictional story in which Anne de Gaulle speaks, in *Wartimes.* London: Sinclair-Stevenson, 1995.

Cook, Don. *Charles de Gaulle: A Biography.* NY: Putnam, 1983.

De Gaulle, Charles. *The Complete War Memoirs of Charles de Gaulle.* 3 vols. Translated by Jonathan Griffin (vol. 1), Richard Howard (vols. 2 and 3). NY: Simon and Schuster, 1964.

——. *Memoirs of Hope: Renewal and Endeavor.* Translated by Terence Kilmartin. NY: Simon and Schuster, 1971.

Duquesne, Jacques. "De Gaulle Époux d'Yvonne, amant de Marianne," in *L'Express.* July 30, 1998, pp. 50–51.

Gordon, Bertram M. "Charles de Gaulle," in Frank W. Thackeray and John E. Findling, eds. *Statesmen Who Changed the World: A Bio-Bibliographical Dictionary of Diplomacy.* Westport, CT: Greenwood Press, 1993, pp. 157–168.

——. "Charles de Gaulle," in Anne Commire and Deborah Klezmer, eds., *Historic World Leaders.* Vol. II. Detroit, MI: Gale Research, 1994, pp. 482–487.

Lacouture, Jean. *De Gaulle.* 2 vols. Volume 1: *The Rebel, 1890–1944,* translated by Patrick O'Brian and II: *The Ruler, 1944–1970,* translated by Alan Sheridan. NY: Norton, 1991–92.

Prial, Frank P. "Yvonne de Gaulle, Widow of French Leader, Dead," in *The New York Times.* November 9, 1979, B4.

RELATED MEDIA

De Gaulle and France (180 min), portrait of de Gaulle with archival footage and interviews with people who knew him, Films for the Humanities and Sciences, Princeton, N.J., 1992.

De Gaulle, Republican Monarch (30 min), from the series "Leaders of the 20th Century," documentary, Learning Corporation of America, New York, 1978.

La Presidence de la Republique (29 min), the French presidency from 1875 through 1980 with emphasis on the presidency of de Gaulle, PICS, Iowa City, Iowa, 1981.

Bertram M. Gordon,
Frederick A. Rice Professor of History,
Mills College, Oakland, California;
author of *Collaborationism in Europe during the Second World War,*
and editor of *Historical Dictionary of World War II France*
(Westport, CT: Greenwood Press, 1998)

de Gautier, Felisa Rincon (1897–1994).

See Gautier, Felisa Rincon de.

De Genlis, Stephanie (1746–1830).

See Genlis, Stéphanie-Félicité, Comtesse de.

de Gouges, Olympe (1748–1793).

See Gouges, Olympe de.

de Gournay, Marie (1565–1645).

See Gournay, Marie le Jars de.

de Guzman, Luisa (1613–1666).

See Luisa de Guzmán.

de Havilland, Olivia and Joan Fontaine

English actresses and sisters who took on the Hollywood brass and shared eight Academy Award nominations between them.

Olivia de Havilland (1916—). Born Olivia Mary de Havilland on July 1, 1916, in Tokyo, Japan; daughter of Walter (a patent attorney) and Lillian (Ruse) de Havilland; sister of actress Joan Fontaine (1917—); attended public schools and Notre Dame Convent, Belmont, California; married Marcus Goodrich (a novelist), in 1946 (divorced); married Pierre Galante (editor of Paris-Match*), in 1955 (separated); children: (first marriage) one son, Benjamin; (second marriage) one daughter, Gisele.*

Selected films: A Midsummer Night's Dream *(1935);* Alibi Ike *(1935);* The Irish in Us *(1935);* Captain Blood *(1935);* Anthony Adverse *(1936);* The Charge of the Light Brigade *(1936);* Call It a Day *(1937);* The Great Garrick *(1937);* It's Love I'm After *(1937);* Gold Is Where You Find It *(1938);* The Adventures of Robin Hood *(1938);* Four's a Crowd *(1938);* Hard to Get *(1938);* Wings of the Navy *(1939);* Dodge City *(1939);* The Private Lives of Elizabeth and Essex *(1939);* Gone with the Wind *(1939);* Raffles *(1940);* My Love Came Back *(1940);* Santa Fe Trail *(1940);* Strawberry Blonde *(1941);* Hold Back the Dawn *(1941);* They Died with Their Boots On *(1941);* The Male Animal *(1942);* In This Our Life *(1942);* Princess O'Rourke *(1943);* Government Girl *(1943);* Devotion *(1946);* The Well-Groomed Bride *(1946);* To Each His Own *(1946);* The Dark Mirror *(1946);* The Snake Pit *(1948);* The Heiress *(1949);* My Cousin Rachel *(1953);* That Lady *(1955);* Not As a Stranger *(1955);* The Ambassador's Daughter *(1956);* The Proud Rebel *(1958);* Libel *(UK, 1959);* The Light in the Piazza *(1962);* Lady in a Cage *(1964);* Hush Hush Sweet Charlotte *(1965);* The Adventurers *(1970);* Pope Joan *(UK, 1972);* The Fifth Musketeer *(Behind the Iron Mask, 1977);* Airport '77 *(1977);* The Swarm *(1978).*

Joan Fontaine (1917—). Name variations: acted under the name Joan Burfield and Joan St. John. Born Joan de Beauvoire de Havilland on October 22, 1917, in Tokyo, Japan; daughter of Walter (a patent attorney) and Lillian (Ruse) de Havilland; sister of actress Olivia de Havilland (1916—); married Brian Aherne (an actor), in 1939 (divorced 1944); married William Dozier (a producer), in 1946 (divorced 1951); married Collier Young (a producer-screenwriter), in 1952 (divorced 1961); married Alfred Wright, Jr. (golf editor of Sports Illustrated *and former correspondent for* Life*), in 1964 (divorced); children: (second marriage) Deborah; (third marriage) adopted daughter Marita from Peru.*

Selected films: No More Ladies *(1935, her only credit as Joan Burfield);* Quality Street *(1937);* The Man Who Found Himself *(1937);* You Can't Beat Love *(1937);* Music for Madame *(1937);* A Damsel in Distress *(1937);* A Million to One *(1937);* Maid's Night Out *(1938);* Blonde Cheat *(1938);* Sky Giant *(1938);* The Duke of West Point *(1938);* Gunga Din *(1939);* Man of Conquest *(1939);* The Women *(1939);* Rebecca *(1940);* Suspicion *(1941);* This Above All *(1942);* The Constant Nymph *(1943);* Jane Eyre *(1944);* Frenchman's Creek *(1944);* The Affairs of Susan *(1945);* From This Day Forward *(1946);* Ivy *(1947);* The Emperor Waltz *(1948);* Kiss the Blood Off My Hands *(1948);* Letter from an Unknown Woman *(1948);* You Gotta Stay Happy *(1948);* Born to be Bad *(1950);* September Affair *(1951);* Darling How Could You! *(1951);* Something to Live For *(1952);* Ivanhoe *(UK-US, 1952);* Decameron Nights *(UK, 1953);* Flight to Tangier *(1953);* The Bigamist *(1953);* Casanova's Big Night *(1954);* Serenade *(1956);* Beyond a Reasonable Doubt *(1956);* Island in the Sun *(1957);* Until They Sail *(1957);* A Certain Smile *(1958);* Voyage to the Bottom of the Sea *(1961);* Tender Is the Night *(1961);* The Witches *(The Devil's Own, UK, 1966).*

Beginning in the mid-1930s, Hollywood fell under the spell of the de Havilland sisters, Olivia ("Livvy") and Joan (who would later borrow the name Fontaine from her mother's second husband). Remarkably beautiful and fiercely competitive, they were notorious for their sisterly feuds, both real and manufactured. Less remembered, but historically more important, were the wars they waged with their respective studio bosses for better roles and working conditions. While Joan battled a near hostage situation at Selznick International, Olivia's fight with Warner Bros. made it to the Supreme Court of California and resulted in a landmark decision that led to the demise of the antiquated and repressive studio system.

Born in Tokyo of British parents, the girls were sickly as babies. When Olivia was three and Joan two, the de Havillands separated (later to divorce), and the children sailed with their mother to America. There, they settled in Saratoga, California, located in the foothills of the Santa Cruz Mountains. Olivia proved the more resilient of the two youngsters, recuperating well from a bout of pneumonia following a tonsil operation. Joan, however, survived an attack of measles and strep only to be stricken with anemia that left her almost an invalid. Ill health would plague Joan throughout her life, including a six-year bout with toxoplasmosis, a parasite of the blood. While Olivia led an active life, swimming and playing field hockey, her sister was left behind. "Livvy can, Joan can't" was a taunt that haunted the younger sibling through childhood and sapped her confidence. But what Joan lacked in stamina, she made up for in intelligence, scoring over genius level on intelligence tests. Excelling in school, the sisters also studied voice and diction from an early age and occasionally gave living-room performances of Shakespeare, which Joan later called "just awful." At 15, Joan went to Tokyo to live with her father, while Olivia finished high school and planned to become an English and speech teacher. When Joan returned two years later, Olivia, who had won a scholarship to Mills College, had been "discovered" in a production of *A Midsummer Night's Dream* with the Saratoga Community Players. Chosen to play Hermia in Max Reinhardt's stage and screen versions of the play, she was subsequently signed by Warner Bros. to a seven-year contract.

Olivia de Havilland's early roles encompassed a series of sweet, demure heroines in films dominated by the studio's top male stars, among them Errol Flynn, with whom she was cast in a number of romantic adventures. Considered one of the best of her early movies was *Anthony Adverse* (1936), which won critical acclaim for the 19-year-old and boosted her stature as one of Hollywood's most beautiful and promising stars. Mervyn Le Roy, who directed her in the film, called her a born actress: "Her diction is superb. She can deliver a line with any inflection the director wants, as accurately as if it were played on a piano—and she has the greatest of arts—the ability to act as if she weren't acting at all." De Havilland's next big break came when, over studio boss Jack Warner's protestations, she accepted the role of Melanie in David Selznick's ground-breaking epic, *Gone with the Wind* (1939), the most profitable movie of all time. (Reputedly, Joan was also considered for the role, but Selznick dismissed her as too chic.) De Havilland's skill in turning the sugary, too-good-to-be-true character of Melanie into a real and moving woman won her an Oscar nomination. Later, she would struggle to rid herself of the "sweet Melanie" image, which her sister Joan may have helped to promulgate.

While Olivia was taking Hollywood by storm, Joan's career had yet to take off. She started on the stage, accepting roles in a mystery drama called *Kind Lady* and in a West Coast production of *Dodie Smith*'s *Call It a Day*, for which she received good reviews. Joan was of-

fered her first movie contract when delivering lunch to Olivia at the make-up department at Warner's. Although both her mother and sister were against her entering what was considered "Olivia's domain," Joan made her movie debut in MGM's *No More Ladies* (1935) with *Joan Crawford. Forbidden by her family to use the name de Havilland, Joan acted briefly under the name Burfield (after a street in Hollywood) before finally settling on Fontaine. She was eventually contracted under RKO and made a series of forgettable pictures, including *A Damsel in Distress* (1937), which she would later recall as aptly named. Cast opposite Fred Astaire in a singing and dancing role (she could do neither), she was described by one critic as "the weak spot in the picture . . . a wooden woman." Fontaine was then loaned out for a variety of small parts before being dropped by RKO when her contract ran out. Considering herself a failure at 22, she thought seriously of giving up her career, but the prospect of playing the second Mrs. de Winter in the movie *Rebecca*, from *Daphne du Maurier*'s bestselling novel, improved her outlook. Selznick, who had asked her to test shortly after purchasing the rights, considered countless actresses for the role, and Fontaine waited six months while he made up his mind. She landed a small part in *The Women* (1939) before learning that she had been chosen for the coveted role. In the interim, she also married her first husband, the actor Brian Aherne. The marriage ended in divorce as did three subsequent marriages.

For her work in *Rebecca*, astutely directed by Alfred Hitchcock, Joan won her first Oscar nomination and gained stature as a superb actress in her own right. She received a longterm contract from Selznick, although her relationship with him, much like Olivia's with Jack Warner, got off to a bad start. While Selznick continued to cast her as a defenseless heroine, she considered herself capable of more gutsy roles. Disagreement aside, her second movie under the Selznick contract, *Suspicion* (1941), was made while on loan to RKO, and won her an Oscar as well the New York Film Critics' Award. The occasion was made more dramatic by the fact that de Havilland had also been nominated for her work in *Hold Back the Dawn* (1941). The sisterly rivalry that had fueled Hollywood's rumor mill now appeared full blown, and the press, misinterpreting Joan's shyness, was not particularly sympathetic to her. (In 1943, she was selected by the Hollywood Women's Press Club as the least cooperative actress of the year.) After *Suspicion*, Fontaine be-

Olivia de Havilland

came more selective about her films, turning down role after role until *The Constant Nymph* (1943), which Selznick allowed her to make only after she had agreed to do *This Above All* as well. Joan later described *The Constant Nymph* as the happiest assignment of her career. She re- mained friends with her co-star Charles Boyer, whom she called "a kind, gentle, helpful actor." *The New York Times* called her portrayal of Tessa, a delicate teenager, "a superb achievement," and she was once again nominated for an Academy Award.

Joan
Fontaine

In 1943, after de Havilland was cast in a series of remakes (*Raffles* and *Saturday's Children*) and in a supporting role in *The Private Lives of Elizabeth and Essex* (playing second fiddle to *Bette Davis' Elizabeth), she brought suit against Warner's for release from her contract, claiming that her seven-year agreement with them had ended. The studio countered by saying that she had six months more to run as the result of five suspensions when she had refused to play assigned roles. The prolonged suit against the studio, which was later backed by the Screen Actors Guild, went all the way to the California Supreme Court. A landmark decision, known as the "De Havilland Decision," was handed down on February 3, 1945, and forever changed the history of studio and player relationships by setting the outside limit of a studio-player contract at seven years, including periods of suspension. As a result of the litigation, de Havilland was absent from pictures for over a year, though she appeared frequently in radio dramas and took an active part in supporting Franklin Roosevelt's bid for the presidency. She returned to films in *The Well-Groomed Bride* (1946), followed by the drama *To Each His Own* (1946), for which she won her first Oscar, as Best Actress. That year, she married Marcus Goodrich, becoming the author's fifth wife. The union produced a son before ending in divorce.

De Havilland's career peaked with her portrayal of a mental patient in the landmark film *The Snake Pit* (1948), which is often considered her finest, most developed role. Though she won the New York Film Critics' Award and was nominated for another Academy Award, de Havilland lost the Oscar to *Jane Wyman (*Johnny Belinda*). The following year, however, Olivia won her second Oscar and another Film Critics' Award for *The Heiress* (1949), even though many felt she was too pretty for the Ugly Duckling role. After an unsuccessful attempt to establish herself on the Broadway stage (playing Juliet and Candida), she returned to the screen in *My Cousin Rachel* (1953) and *That Lady* (1955), her last movies before she moved to Paris with her second husband Pierre Galante, the editor of *Paris-Match*. Maintaining that she was no longer interested in films, she nonetheless made several abroad. De Havilland returned to Hollywood to make two horror films, *Lady in a Cage* (1964), about an invalid trapped in an elevator, and *Hush Hush Sweet Charlotte* (1965), in which she reluctantly took over Joan Crawford's role when Crawford fell ill. Her later work included *The Adventurers* (1970), *Airport 77* (1977), and *The Swarm* (1978). She also appeared in a number of television productions, among them the series "Roots: the Next Generation" and "Anastasia: The Mystery of Anna"; her portrayal of the Dowager Empress in the latter brought her a Golden Globe. In 1961, she published *Every Frenchman Has One*, recollecting her life in Paris.

Joan Fontaine followed her success in *The Constant Nymph* with *Jane Eyre* (1944), which also drew raves. She continued to star in numerous films, occasionally trading in her innocent heroines for more sophisticated roles. Her relationship with Selznick continued to degenerate, and, after being suspended for most of 1945, she moved to RKO, where she embarked on a series of costume dramas. (In her biography *No Bed of Roses*, Fontaine faults Selznick for making huge profits by loaning her, as well as other stars, to other studios and for using bullying tactics when she refused a role.) Notable at RKO was *Letter from an Unknown Woman* (1948), a story of lost-remembered love co-starring Louis Jourdan that was considered by some to be one of her finest performances. During the 1950s, she made primarily conventional films, with the exception of her touching performance as a budding actress on the skids in *Something to Live For* (1952). In 1954, she replaced *Deborah Kerr in the Broadway play *Tea and Sympathy,* which she regarded as a terrifying experience in spite of excellent reviews. Of her later films, most notable are the wartime drama *Until They Sail* (1957) and *Tender Is the Night* (1962), in which her performance was the only aspect of the film that critics praised.

After three failed marriages, in 1964 Fontaine married for the fourth time, taking up residence in New York. Vowing that she no longer needed to make pictures, she remained content to wait until the right part came along. Her interests beyond acting led to success as a licensed pilot, an expert golfer, and a Cordon Bleu cook. In 1978, she published her memoir, *No Bed of Roses*, and also appeared in Vienna in *The Lion in Winter*. Most of her later work has been on television, often guesting. Fontaine had a substantial role in the telemovies "The Users" (1979) and "Crossings" (1986). She also played the matriarch in "Dark Mansions," a Gothic melodrama and pilot for a possible series.

SOURCES:

Fontaine, Joan. *No Bed of Roses.* NY: William Morrow, 1978.

Gray, Dorothy. "Olivia," in *Palm Beach Life.* June 1974.

"Joan Fontaine," in *Current Biography.* NY: H.W. Wilson, 1944.

Katz, Ephraim. *The Film Encyclopedia.* NY: Harper-Collins, 1994.

Shipman, David. *The Great Movie Stars: The Golden Years.* Boston: Little Brown, 1995.

SOURCES:

Higham, Charles. *Sisters: The Story of Olivia de Havilland and Joan Fontaine.*

Barbara Morgan, Melrose, Massachusetts

Dehner, Dorothy (1901–1994)

American sculptor of Surrealist and geometric abstractions who was a late bloomer as an artist, start-

ing to sculpt in her 50s and going on to becoming an acclaimed figure in the art world. Name variations: Dorothy Smith. Born in 1901 in Cleveland, Ohio; died in New York, New York, on September 22, 1994; married David Smith (an artist), in 1927 (divorced 1951); married Ferdinand Mann, in 1957; children: two stepchildren.

Born in Cleveland in 1901 into a family of German and Dutch ancestry, Dorothy Dehner learned to paint with the help of three talented aunts while in her teens. She also was a dance student, studying with a former member of the Denishawn Company. Family affluence enabled her to travel to Europe to become acquainted with avant-garde developments in the arts. A difficult stage in her life began in her late teens after the deaths of her parents and only sister. Therapy for young Dorothy was a career in the theater. "When I was in a play," she said, "I could be anybody but me. I could feel good about myself." Eventually, in 1924, she broke away from her Cleveland roots to move to New York City. Besides appearing in off-Broadway plays, she enrolled at the Art Students League. Originally interested in sculpture, she decided to study drawing. Her circle of friends during these years included painters John Graham, Stuart Davis, and Arshile Gorky, all of whom were pioneers of abstract art in an America that was culturally isolationist and generally hostile to "alien European" ideas. Among the interesting artists she met was a strong-willed and ambitious sculptor, David Smith, whom she married in 1927.

At first Dehner and her husband lived in Brooklyn, but in 1940 they moved to the small town of Bolton Landing in upstate New York where they bought an 18th-century farmhouse. Although David Smith was becoming nationally recognized for his works of abstract sculpture, Dehner refused to abandon her own artistic impulses. Among the works she created at Bolton Landing was a series of paintings of idyllic rural scenes entitled "Life on the Farm." Reflecting some of her deepest inner struggles, she also did a remarkable series of ink drawings of demonic figures surrounded by vultures and bats, which she entitled the "Damnation Series." Despite these often impressive and powerful works, Dehner chose to play second fiddle to David Smith, who had emerged as an artistic superstar by the late 1940s. On occasion, as when her 1948 drawing "Star Cage" was used by Smith as inspiration for one of his sculptures, the couple would be able to collaborate on a project.

But most of the time, Dehner felt overwhelmed and increasingly alienated by her husband's ego, his competitiveness, and in the final analysis by his indifference to her own artistic aspirations. The couple divorced in 1951. Although their marriage had failed, decades later Dehner continued to praise Smith as "America's greatest sculptor."

In 1955, Dorothy Dehner produced her first works of sculpture. "I'd always wanted to," she said. "Now I was free to do it." Small in scale and executed in bronze, these early works were seen by critics as owing something to David Smith's rangy, attenuated style, but other observers detected a special, Surrealist and lyrical touch that only Dehner possessed. Encouraged by what she was able to produce, Dehner now began to work in wood, and by 1957 she was able to exhibit her work at New York's prestigious Willard Gallery. Her second marriage in 1957, to Ferdinand Mann, was by all accounts a happy one. By 1965, her reputation in the art world enabled Dehner to enjoy a solo exhibition at the Jewish Museum in New York. Dehner was strongly inspired by African art, and her sculptures often reproduce the rough surfaces and totemlike quality of the art of Africa. Some of her most powerful works included *Cenotaph for Li Po* and *Egyptian King*, bronze sculptures described as being "tall ladder-like accumulations of disks and rectangles, . . . beautiful and successful in every way, like relics of some long-forgotten religion."

In the mid-1980s, Dorothy Dehner's eyesight deteriorated drastically, and she became legally blind. An error made with a prescription drug further weakened her sight to the point in the early 1990s that she was totally blind in one eye and had only limited vision in the other. But she refused to quit working ("I have come to accept my loss of vision and I just go on") and was able to work out a method of continuing to produce sculpture. She began to rely on a fabricator who could execute her ideas as described in maquettes that were in turn based on drawings she had done in the 1970s. Interviewed after she had become almost totally blind, Dorothy Dehner showed remarkable determination, asserting that she did not mind dying but did worry about pain. She had no illusions that her time had almost run out: "When you're seventy, you think you'll have another decade. When you're in your nineties, you know damn well you don't have much more time." She then added, "I love being old. Because I love what I am whenever I am, whether I'm four years old, or fifteen or thirty-two . . . no, I love my life."

Dorothy Dehner's art was spontaneous and central to her existence during the last four decades of her long and productive life. "I can never talk about my art," she once said. "Art historians can, but I really can't. Whatever that thing is on paper or in bronze, it came out of my fingers and my heart or soul." Dorothy Dehner died in New York City on September 22, 1994.

SOURCES:

Bethune, Elizabeth de. "Dorothy Dehner," in *Art Journal.* Vol. 53, no. 1. Spring 1994, pp. 35–37.

Cotter, Holland. "Dorothy Dehner: Conquering Metal at a Dauntless 91," in *The New York Times Biographical Service.* November 1993, pp. 1592–1593.

Diehl, Carol. "Dorothy Dehner," in *ARTnews.* Vol. 95, no. 6. June 1996, pp. 148–149.

"Dorothy Dehner, 92, Sculptor With a Lyrically Surreal Style," in *The New York Times Biographical Service.* September 1994, p. 1450.

John Haag, Associate Professor of History,
University of Georgia, Athens, Georgia

Déia, Maria (c. 1908–1938).

See Bonita, Maria.

dei Vigri, Caterina (1413–1463).

See Catherine of Bologna.

Déjazet, Pauline-Virginie (1797–1875)

French actress. Name variations: Dejazet. Born on August 30, 1797 (some sources cite 1798), in Paris, France; died on December 1, 1875.

One of the great names in the French theater, Pauline-Virginie Déjazet first appeared on stage at the age of five and subsequently became well-known in vaudeville for her male impersonations. In 1821, she began a seven-year association with the Gymnase, where her male roles (also called "breeches") became so famous that they were known as "Déjazets." In 1831, she went to the newly opened Palais-Royal, where she enjoyed 13 years of enormous popularity. After a salary dispute, Déjazet went on to play at the Variétés and the Gaîté, portraying great ladies and young peasant girls in addition to her repertoire of male roles. In 1859, she became manager of the Folies, which was later renamed the Théâtre Déjazet. She was successful playing youthful roles well into her 60s, especially in a number of Sardou's earlier plays. Her last appearance in Paris was in 1870. That same year, Déjazet was seen in a series of French plays at the Opera Comique in London.

Dejerine, Augusta (1859–1927).

See Klumpke, Dorothea for sidebar on Augusta Klumpke.

de Jesús, Carolina Maria (c. 1913–1977).

See Jesus, Carolina Maria de.

Deken, Aagje (1741–1804)

Dutch poet and novelist. Name variations: Agathe, Agatha. Born in 1741 in the northern Netherlands; died on November 14, 1804.

Born in the northern Netherlands in 1741, Aagje Deken would become a frequent collaborator with novelist ✥➤ **Elizabeth Bekker** on realistic stories of Dutch life. Deken was orphaned at an early age and lived in an Amsterdam orphanage before becoming a servant and governess. Employed by the Bosch family, she was befriended by their daughter **Maria Bosch**; the two wrote religious poetry together: *Stichtelijke gedichten* was published in 1775.

After Deken sent a letter to Elizabeth Bekker chastising her for her satirical poetry and worldly behavior, the two became close friends and collaborators. Bekker, widowed in 1777, persuaded Deken to quit her job and move in with her. The year 1777 is considered a turning point in the history of letters in the Netherlands, because it was the year that the two women came together. In 1778, they moved to Bur-

---

✥➤ **Bekker, Elizabeth (1738–1804)**

Dutch novelist. Name variations: Elisabeth Bekker; Elizabeth Betjen Wolff; Elizabeth Wolff-Bekker; Betje Wolff. Born at Vlissingen, northern Netherlands, on July 24, 1738; died in The Hague, on November 5, 1804; married Adriaan Wolff (a Reformed cleric at Beemster), in 1759 (died 1777).

Daughter of Calvinist merchants, Elizabeth "Betje" Bekker entered into a theoretical marriage with Adriaan Wolff, a vicar 31 years her senior. Her writing debut in 1763 consisted of poetry of moral contemplation, though her later poetry became satirical. After Adriaan's death in 1777, Bekker began to write with her close companion *Aagje Deken. While living in Burgundy with Deken, Bekker was exposed to some of the dangers of the Revolution, and she is said to have escaped the guillotine only by her presence of mind. She lived with Deken for nearly 30 years before her death on November 5, 1804. Deken died nine days later.

---

gundy, in part for political reasons, arriving just in time for the French Revolution.

Returning to Holland in 1797, they took up residence at The Hague until Bekker's death in 1804. They lived together for nearly 30 years, collaborating on novels, including the extremely popular works *De Historie van Mejuffrouw Sara Burgerhart* (History of Sara Burgerhart, 1782), *De Historie van den Heer Willem Leevend* (History of William Leevend, 1784–85), *Letters of Abraham Blankaart* (1787), and *Cornelia Wildschut* (1793–96). The pair, whose individual contributions to their novels were indistinguishable, also produced *Geschrift eener bejaarde vrouw* (Document of an Elderly Woman) in 1802. Deken died nine days after Bekker in 1804. Their correspondence was published in 1987 as *Briefwisseling van Betje Wolff en Aagje Deken* (Correspondence of Betje Wolff and Aagje Deken).

de Kooning, Elaine Fried

(1918–1989)

American painter and art critic who was an Abstract Expressionist of the New York School. Born Elaine Marie Catherine Fried in Sheepshead Bay, Brooklyn, on May 12, 1918; died on February 1, 1989; first of four children, two girls and two boys, of Marie and Charles Fried; graduated from Erasmus High School; attended Hunter College but left to enroll in the Leonardo da Vinci Art School and the American Artists School; married artist Willem de Kooning (1905–1997), in 1943; no children.

Elaine de Kooning, artist, writer, and wife of famous painter Willem de Kooning, was a central figure in the emergence of Abstract Expressionism in New York City during the 1940s and 1950s. Although she considered herself first and foremost a painter, de Kooning was also a talented writer whose contributions to *Art News* and other magazines established her as the foremost voice of the New York School. John Canaday, in a *New York Times* article, called her the "mascot, sybil, and recording secretary" of Abstract Expressionism.

De Kooning grew up in Brooklyn, the eldest child of a middle-class family. Her earliest influence was her mother **Marie Fried**, who took her on weekly excursions to the Metropolitan Museum and exposed her to literature, theater, and the opera. At the age of six, de Kooning was drawing constantly and by ten was referred to by her peers as "the artist." After high school, she attended Hunter College for about a month

before enrolling in both the Leonardo da Vinci Art School and the American Artists School, which were then two of the most popular art schools in New York. A beautiful young woman, with great intelligence and a quick wit, de Kooning was extremely popular and enjoyed the attentions of a number of men. One of her early liaisons was with painter Milton Resnick, after which she met Willem de Kooning, a strikingly attractive and gifted artist whose passions in life were, by his own admission, painting and women. Willem became her teacher, and they married in 1943, becoming the darlings of a colorful bohemian art scene that included Hans Hofmann, Arshile Gorky, Mark Rothko, Franz Kline, Barrett Newmann, and Jackson Pollock. Although the marriage was unconventional (the couple lived apart for some 20 years, and Willem fathered a child with another woman), de Kooning always credited Willem as her original teacher and greatest influence. Once when questioned about working in the shadow of a famous husband, she replied, "I don't work in his shadow. I work in his light."

In spite of the financial hardships of the 1940s, de Kooning drew and painted continuously, producing still lifes, cityscapes, and portraits, including many of her husband. Enduring a skimpy diet, and often forced to paint over old canvases because she couldn't afford new ones, she perfected her own "action painting" technique, consisting of the bold, slashing strokes seen in a series of paintings called "Faceless Men" (1949–1956), in which the subjects were recognizable only by their characteristic body stances. De Kooning's sister **Marjorie Luyckx**, in an essay on the artist, describes Elaine's technique as instinctive. "In doing a portrait she seemed to apply the brushstrokes in a wildly random manner and yet, sometimes suddenly, a startling likeness of the figure would emerge. If it didn't, she would set the canvas aside and begin on a second without changing the position of the sitter (and often a third or even a fourth)."

By the early 1960s, de Kooning was well known as a portrait painter, using as subjects members of her wide and impressive circle of friends and admirers, including critic Harold Rosenbert, poets Frank O'Hara and John Ashbery, artist Aristodimos Kaldis, and President John F. Kennedy. Commissioned to paint the president in 1962, she was still at work on the preliminary series of studies when he was assassinated. One of the 36 studies she produced now resides in the Truman Library in Missouri; another is housed at the John F. Kennedy Library in Boston.

De Kooning was encouraged in her early writing career by poet Edwin Denby, the music critic for the *New York Herald Tribune*, and Thomas Hess, then editor of *Art News*, who hired her in 1948. During the course of her career, she turned out some 100 articles for *Art News* as well as other magazines and was the first in the American art scene of the 1950s to take on the dual role of artist and critic. (Fairfield Porter joined her at *Art News* in 1955.) Her close proximity to artists of the New York School helped make her a successful critic, claims artist **Rose Slivka**: "As an Abstract Expressionist painter herself, she wrote from inside the group, sharing the special friendship and confidence of the artists in each other, having access to their studios, and learning the thoughts and techniques artists reserve only for each other." Two of de Kooning's finest essays were on fellow artists and personal friends Arshile Gorky ("Gorky: Painter of His Own Legend") and Franz Kline ("Franz Kline: Painter of His Own Life").

In the late 1950s, as the artists in the New York School became relatively prosperous, life in the city for de Kooning began to dissolve into rounds of gallery openings and parties, which she found self-destructive. Her paintings reflected her mood, with heavy colors and titles such as *Man in Hiding, Death of Johnny A,* and *Suicide*. In 1957, she left New York to teach at the University of New Mexico, the first of many guest teaching positions she would undertake throughout her career. During this period, she began a series of bullfight paintings (1957–63), brilliant works in slashing strokes of magenta, chartreuse, orange, and blue, executed in ink washes, watercolors, lithographs, and oils, which ranged in size from ten inches to ten feet. These were followed by a basketball and baseball series during the 1960s and a later series on the theme of Bacchus (1976–83), inspired by a 19th-century sculpture in the Luxembourg Gardens of Paris.

De Kooning's final series, begun in 1983, was inspired by the 25,000-year-old cave paintings in the Pyrenees mountains of France and would consume the artist for the rest of her life. In viewing the Paleolithic cave drawings, de Kooning felt she was accessing her own artistic roots as she discovered relationships between the methods of these earliest artists and those of the Abstract Expressionists. "They gave the affirmation to her own way of working," Slivka explains, "and became a culmination, a coming together from her whole life, of her ways of working, of action painting, with its ambigui-

ties, erasures, interplay of contour, surface, line, slash, smudge, dot, and drip."

De Kooning's first one-woman show was at the New York Stabel Gallery in 1954 and was followed by over 50 solo and group exhibitions in the U.S. and abroad during the course of her career. She received her widest recognition as a painter after she reached age 60; her cave paintings were the subject of ten one-woman shows between 1987 and 1988. The last exhibition of her work while she was alive opened in November 1988 at the Fischbach Gallery and included her cave series as well as *High Wall*, a triptych nine feet wide and almost twenty feet high, which is considered by many to be her masterpiece. She worked on *High Wall* for over a year, along with a series of small, simple Sumi paintings done with brush and ink.

SUGGESTED READING:

De Kooning, Elaine, *The Spirit of Abstract Expressionism: Selected Writings*. NY: George Braziller, 1994.

Barbara Morgan,
Melrose, Massachusetts

de Krüdener, Julie (1764–1824).

See Krüdener, Julie de.

de la Cerda, Blanche (c. 1311–1347)

*Duchess of Penafiel. Born around 1311; died in 1347; daughter of Fernando also known as Ferdinand de la Cerda (b. 1272) and **Juana Nunez de Lara** (1285–1351); became second wife of John Manuel also known as Juan Manuel "el Scritor," duke of Penafiel, in 1328; children: Beatriz (died young); *Joanna of Castile (1339–1381). Juan Manuel's first wife was *Constance of Aragon (d. 1327).*

Delafield, E.M. (1890–1943).

See Dashwood, Elizabeth Monica.

de la Guerre, Elisabeth-Claude Jacquet (c. 1666–1729).

See Jacquet de la Guerre, Elisabeth-Claude.

de Laguna, Grace Mead (1878–1978)

American philosopher. Name variations: Delaguna. Born Grace Mead Andrus on September 28, 1878; died on February 17, 1978; Cornell University, B.A., 1903; Cornell University, Ph.D., 1906; married Theodore de Laguna; children: Frederica de Laguna (b. 1906, an anthropologist); Wallace de Laguna (b. 1910, a nuclear scientist).

Was an assistant professor of philosophy, Bryn Mawr (1912–16); was an associate professor (1916–28), and professor of philosophy (from 1928); was cofounder, with Theodore, of the Fullerton Philosophy Club (1925).

Works: "The Mechanical Theory in Pre-Kantian Rationalism" (1906); (with Theodore de Laguna) Dogmatism and Evolution *(1910); "Sensation and Perception" (1916); "The Limits of the Physical," in* Philosophical Essays in Honor of James Edwin Creighton *(1917); "Phenomena and their Determination," in* Philosophical Review *(1917); "Dualism in Animal Psychology" (1918);* Speech: Its Function and Development *(1927); "Dualism and Gestalt Psychology," in* Psychological Review *(1930); "Knowing and Being: a Dialectical Study," in* Philosophical Review *(1936); "Professor Urban on Language," in* Philosophical Review *(1941); "Cultural Relativism and Science," in* Philosophical Review *(1942); "Democratic Equality and Individuality," in* Philosophical Review *(1946); "Communication, the Act and the Object with Reference to Mead," in* Journal of Philosophy *(1946); "Speculative Philosophy," in* Philosophy Review *(1951); "Existence and Potentiality," in* Philosophical Review *(1951); "The Lebenswelt and the Cultural World," in* Journal of Philosophy *(1960); "The Person," in* Review of Metaphysics *(1963);* On Existence and the Human World *(1963).*

Grace de Laguna spent over 60 years teaching philosophy to women at Bryn Mawr. She completed her undergraduate degree at Cornell University in 1903, at age 24, and went on to complete her Ph.D. there in 1906. In 1925, during her tenure at Bryn Mawr, she established the Fullerton Philosophy Club with her husband Theodore de Laguna, to foster philosophical discussion among philosophers and faculty members.

De Laguna published a large number of papers in academic journals and a few books on philosophy. Her intellectual interests were always wide-ranging. Early on, she focused on the traditional areas of philosophy—epistemology (theory of knowledge), metaphysics (theory of reality), and phenomenology (study of how we perceive the world)—as they relate to philosophy of mind and psychology. Later, she became interested in communication and the social sciences, and to these she turned her philosophical skills. She worked at improving the theoretical foundations of psychology, anthropology and sociology. Her daughter, **Frederica de Laguna**, was born in 1906 and followed her mother's interest in social science, pursuing anthropology and spending her life studying the native peoples

of the Arctic. De Laguna's other child, a son Wallace born in 1910, became a nuclear scientist. Grace de Laguna died in 1978, just a few months before she would have turned 100.

SOURCES:

Kersey, Ethel M. *Women Philosophers: a Bio-critical Source Book.* NY: Greenwood Press, 1989.

Waithe, Mary Ellen, ed. *A History of Women Philosophers, vol. 4.* Boston: Martinus Nijhoff Publications, 1987.

Catherine Hundleby, M.A. Philosophy,
University of Guelph, Guelph, Ontario, Canada

de la Haye, Charlotte (1737–1805).

See Montesson, Charlotte Jeanne Béraud de la Haye de Riou, marquise de (1737–1805).

de la Haye, Nicolaa (1160–1218).

See Siege Warfare and Women for sidebar.

de la Hunty-Strickland, Shirley (b. 1925).

See Strickland, Shirley.

de Lambert, Mme. (1647–1733).

See Salonnières for sidebar.

de la Mora, Constancia (1906–1950).

See Mora, Constancia de la.

Deland, Margaret (1857–1945)

American writer whose popular works often contrast the past with the present. Born Margaretta Wade Campbell (later shortened her name to Margaret) on February 23, 1857, near Allegheny, Pennsylvania; died on January 13, 1945; daughter of Sample and Margaretta Campbell; educated in Pittsburgh and at the Pelham Priory in New Rochelle, New York, then studied art and design in 1875 at Cooper Union in New York City; married Lorin Fuller Deland, on May 12, 1880 (died 1917); no children.

Became assistant instructor of drawing and design at Normal College of the City of New York (now Hunter College, 1876); her poem, "The Succory," appeared in Harper's New Monthly Magazine *(1885); published first book,* The Old Garden and Other Verses *(1886); published first novel,* John Ward, Preacher *(1888); following husband's death, did war-relief work in France (1917) and received the Legion of Honor for this work; elected to the National Institute of Arts and Letters (1926).*

Selected writings: The Old Garden and Other Verses *(1886);* John Ward, Preacher *(1888);* A Summer Day *(1889);* Florida Days *(1889);* Sidney *(1890);* The Story of a Child *(1892);* Mr. Tommy Dove and Other Stories *(1893);* Philip and His Wife *(1894);* The

Wisdom of Fools *(1897);* Old Chester Tales *(1899);* Dr. Lavendar's People *(1903);* The Common Way *(1904);* The Awakening of Helena Ritchie *(1906);* An Encore *(1907);* RJ's Mother and Some Other People *(1908);* Where the Laborers Are Few *(1909);* The Way to Peace *(1910);* The Iron Woman *(1911);* The Voce *(1912);* Partners *(1913);* The Hands of Esau *(1914);* Around Old Chester *(1915);* The Rising Tide *(1916);* Small Things *(1919);* The Promises of Alice: The Romance of a New England Parsonage *(1919);* An Old Chester Secret *(1920);* The Vehement Flame *(1922);* New Friends in Old Chester *(1924);* The Kays *(1926);* Captain Archer's Daughter *(1932);* If This Be I, As I Suppose It Be *(1935);* Old Chester Days *(1937); and* Golden Yesterdays *(1941).*

Margaretta Wade Campbell, who was named after her mother, was born near Allegheny, Pennsylvania, on February 23, 1857. Her mother died while giving birth to her, and her father, Sample Campbell, died when she was only about four years old. Margaretta, who shortened her name to Margaret when she was older, was raised by a maternal aunt, **Lois Wade Campbell.** (Like her sister, Margaret's mother, Lois had married a Campbell; though the two men were unrelated.) Margaret spent her childhood in a privileged household on the estate of Louis and Benjamin Bakewell Campbell in Manchester, Pennsylvania, on the Ohio River near Allegheny. She received her education in Pittsburgh and at the Pelham Priory in New Rochelle, New York. In 1875, she moved to New York City, where she attended classes in art and design at Cooper Union. The next year, she became an assistant instructor of drawing and design at the Normal College of the City of New York (now Hunter College), and stayed there until her marriage to Lorin Fuller Deland on May 12, 1880. Lorin Deland was the junior partner of the Boston printing house of Deland and Son.

Early in their marriage, the couple shocked some segments of the public by taking into their home, over the course of four years, about 60 unmarried mothers, helping them to understand, to accept, and to overcome society's censure. To assist in this effort, Margaret Deland painted china and then turned to writing verses for greeting cards. A friend sent some of her poems to *Harper's New Monthly Magazine,* which published "The Succory" in March 1885. More of her poems were published in magazines, and in 1886 Houghton, Mifflin published her first book, *The Old Garden and Other Verses,* which enjoyed great popularity. By 1899, Deland had also made a name for herself as a fiction writer,

and her first novel, *John Ward, Preacher* (1888), was a great success.

Around this time, the couple purchased a summer home in Kennebunkport, Maine, where Deland spent part of each year for the rest of her life. With Lorin Deland's success in advertising and the income from her books, the couple enjoyed a comfortable lifestyle, and both became leaders of Boston society.

Deland's fiction often contrasts the past with the present, comparing old values and customs with new ideas, urban and rural ways, and the goals of the individual and the community as a whole. Several of her novels, *Old Chester Tales* (1899), *Dr. Lavendar's People* (1903), *Around Old Chester* (1915), and *New Friends in Old Chester* (1924), are set in a town resembling Manchester, Pennsylvania, where Deland grew up; but most of the stories written before 1898 are set elsewhere. From this date until 1937, the inhabitants of Old Chester were well known and beloved by American readers.

Margaret Deland

Deland's insistence on writing about unpopular and controversial problems often earned her criticism as well as occasional praise. In her first novel, *John Ward, Preacher*, she attacks religious beliefs. To conclude that she was a pioneer and a rebel, however, would be a half-truth, because she held many traditional and conservative values about marriage, motherhood, and self-sacrifice. And although she examines divorce in *The Iron Woman* (1911), feminism in *The Rising Tide* (1916), pacifism in *The Kays* (1926) and adultery in *The Vehement Flame* (1922), she opposed universal female suffrage. In her essay "The Change in the Feminine Ideal" (*Atlantic Monthly*, March 1910), she advocates selective suffrage, based upon class, education, and economic conditions.

After Lorin Deland's death in May 1917, Margaret went to France to engage in war-relief work, and incorporated many of her experiences in *Small Things* (1919). For her accomplishments there, she was awarded the Legion of Honor. In 1926, she was among the first women elected to the National Institute of Arts and Letters. She also received honorary degrees from Rutgers University (1917), Tufts University (1920), Bates College (1920), and Bowdoin College (1921).

Margaret Deland lived to be nearly 90 years old. Her life spanned the Civil War and World War II, and she witnessed enormous cultural changes. Both her autobiographical volumes, *If This Be I, As I Suppose It Be* (1935) and *Golden Yesterdays* (1941), provide valuable historic insights into that time period.

SOURCES:

St. Andrews, B.A. "Margaret Deland" in *Dictionary of Literary Biography*. Vol. 78. Edited by Bobby Ellen Kimbel and William E. Grant. Detroit, MI: Gale Research, 1989, pp. 147–154.

Jo Anne Meginnes, freelance writer, Brookfield, Vermont

Delaney, Mary Granville (1700–1788).

See Delany, Mary Granville.

Delaney, Shelagh (b. 1939).

See Littlewood, Joan for sidebar.

Delano, Jane Arminda (1862–1919)

American nurse who unified the workings of the Army Nurse Corps and the Red Cross. Born on March 12, 1862, in Townsend, New York; died on April 15, 1919, in Savenay, France; youngest of two daughters of George and Mary Ann (Wright) Delano; attended Cook Academy, Montour Falls, New York; Bellevue Hospital Training School for Nurses, New York; 1884–86; *brief courses of study at the University of Buffalo Medical School and the New York School of Civics and Philanthropy.*

Graduating as a nurse in 1886, Jane Delano began her career during a yellow fever epidemic in 1887. That year, as a superintending nurse at an emergency center near Jacksonville, Florida, she insisted on the use of mosquito netting, though the cause of the outbreak had not yet been determined. She moved on to attend a typhoid fever epidemic in a mining company hospital in the Arizona Territory and, from 1890 to 1895, acted as assistant superintendent of nurses and as an instructor at the University of Pennsylvania Hospital School of Nursing. After further studies and various positions of employment (including at the New York City House of Refuge on Randall's Island and at the nursing school of Bellevue and its associated hospitals), she left professional life for two years to care for her mother in her last illness.

In 1909, Delano's reputation was such that she was named chair of the newly formed National Committee on Red Cross Nursing Services, which had been established to create a bridge between the Red Cross (then headed by *Mabel Boardman) and the nursing profession. That same year, she was elected president of the American Nurses' Association and superintendent of the Army Nurse Corps. Before leaving her army post in 1912 to devote herself full time to the Red Cross, she was successful in replacing the Army Nursing Reserves with a Red Cross nursing corps and in raising salaries for army nurses, thus attracting a higher caliber of graduates to its ranks.

In 1912, Delano locked heads with Boardman over the issue of keeping the American Red Cross Nursing Service a strictly professional service rather than voluntary. Although Delano prevailed, she allowed Boardman to develop the auxiliary Volunteer Nurses' Aides. With **Isabel McIsaac**, Delano also produced a book, *American Red Cross Textbook on Elementary Hygiene and Home Care of the Sick*, to help train the volunteers (1913).

Under Delano's leadership, the nursing service was able to provide 8,000 nurses to the Army Nurse Corps when the United States entered World War I in April 1917. During the course of the war, she administered the flow of 20,000 nurses for duty overseas, as well as large numbers of nurses aides and other workers. The added emergency of the influenza epidemic of 1918 was also met by the Red Cross nurses.

Delano's tireless work took a toll on her strength as well as her good nature. In 1919, on an inspection tour of postwar Red Cross work in France, she was stricken with mastoiditis and died in a hospital in Savenay, France. The U.S. Army and the Red Cross awarded her posthumous distinguished service medals, and her body was brought from France and reinterred at Arlington National Cemetery.

Barbara Morgan,
Melrose, Massachusetts

Delanoue, Jeanne (1666–1736)

Saint. Name variations: Joan Delanoue. Born in Saumur, in the French province of Anjou, in 1666; died in Saumur in 1736; daughter of a merchant.

Jeanne Delanoue was born in Saumur, in the French province of Anjou, in 1666. Her father, a small-time merchant, sold cloth, crockery, and religious curios to the faithful on pilgrimage to a nearby shrine. On his death, Jeanne inherited his house and shop and continued the practice. But Delanoue was a miser. She was notorious for driving a hard bargain, renting space in her house at exorbitant rates, and engaging in commerce on Sunday. "What changed her nature it is difficult to say," writes *Phyllis McGinley. "But saints have recovered from more picturesque depravities than stinginess and Joan did at length repent. She began in a small way by giving away one of her dresses. . . . Soon she was looking after several orphans in her little house and taking in off the street anyone who seemed destitute." Eventually, Jeanne Delanoue founded the Sisters of St. *Anne and spent her life in service to the poor. Her feast day is celebrated on August 17.

SUGGESTED READING:
McGinley, Phyllis. *Saint-Watching.* NY: Viking, 1969.

Delany, Bessie (1891–1995).

See joint entry under Delany, Sarah Louise and Delany, Annie Elizabeth.

Delany, Mary Granville (1700–1788)

English literary correspondent and artist who was a friend of Jonathan Swift. Name variations: Mrs. Delany or Delaney; Mary Granville; Mary or Mrs. Pendarves. Born Mary Granville on May 14, 1700, at Coulston, Wiltshire, England; died at Windsor, on April 15, 1788; niece of 1st Baron Lansdowne; married Alexander Pendarves, in 1718 (died 1724); married Patrick Delany or Delaney (an Irish cleric), in 1743 (died 1768).

An English woman of literary tastes, Mary Granville Delany first married Alexander Pendarves in 1718. Following his death in 1724, she left Cornwall a wealthy widow of 24 to live in London. In 1743, she married another widower, the eminent preacher Patrick Delany, who became the dean of Down through her influence. While they lived in Delville, at Glasnevin, near Dublin, she began to draw and write, describing the landscapes they encountered on their journeys. She also designed and embroidered fabrics. She and her husband were close friends of Jonathan Swift.

Mary Delany returned to London after her husband's death in 1768. Sought after socially, she was the friend of **Margaret Bentinck**, the second duchess of Portland, and King George III. The king called her his "dearest Mrs. Delany," gave her a house in Windsor and a pension of £300 a year. Delany was a great favorite with the royal family. She presented some of the "paper mosaic" for which she was famous to Queen *Charlotte of Mecklenburg-Strelitz. Delany's major work *Hortus Siccus*, 900 cut-paper depictions of plants, resides in the British Museum. When she died in 1788, Mary Granville Delany left behind six volumes of autobiography and letters, which present a detailed view of English society in the 18th century. They were published by her great-great niece in 1861–62; another edition, titled *Letters from Georgian Ireland,* was published by Angélique Day in 1991.

Delany, Sadie (1889–1999).

See joint entry under Delany, Sarah Louise and Delany, Annie Elizabeth.

Delany, Sarah Louise and Delany, Annie Elizabeth.

African-American sisters who as centenarians became best-selling authors.

Delany, Sarah Louise (1889–1999). Name variations: Sadie Delany. Born Sarah Louise Delany on September 19, 1889, in Raleigh, North Carolina; died at home in Mount Vernon, New York, on January 25, 1999; second daughter and two of ten children of Nanny James and Henry Beard Delany (a teacher and Episcopal priest); graduated from St. Augustine's College; attended Pratt Institute; Columbia University, B.A., 1920, M.Ed., 1925; never married; no children.

Delany, Annie Elizabeth (1891–1995). Name variations: Bessie Delany. Born Annie Elizabeth Delany on September 3, 1891, in Raleigh, North Carolina; died at home in Mount Vernon, New York, on September

Sadie Delany

25, 1995; third daughter and two of ten children of Nanny James Delany and Henry Beard Delany (a teacher and Episcopal priest); graduated from St. Augustine's College and Columbia University, D.D.S., 1923; never married; no children.

Selected works: Having Our Say, The Delany Sisters' First 100 Years (with Amy Hill Hearth, 1993); The Delany Sisters' Book of Everyday Wisdom (1994); (solo) Sarah L. Delany, On My Own at 107 (with Amy Hill Hearth, 1997).

African-American centenarians Sadie and Bessie Delany first came to national attention in 1993, with the publication of their book *Having Our Say: The Delany Sisters' First 100 Years*, an oral history tracing their family life and their remarkable achievements as pioneering professionals—one a dentist and the other a teacher—during a time when neither women nor blacks had many opportunities. The book, contextualized by **Amy Hill Hearth** who had previously written an article on the sisters for *The New York Times*, was on the *Times* best-seller list for 28 weeks, and inspired the award-winning Broadway play *Having Our Say* (1995) by **Emily Mann**. "Not bad for two old inky-dinks!," crowed Bessie over their success. Responding to a deluge of fan mail, the sisters came out with a second book in 1994, *The Delany Sisters' Book of Everyday Wisdom*.

Sadie and Bessie were two of ten children of Henry Beard Delany, an ex-slave who became America's first black Episcopal bishop, and **Nanny James Delany**, an issue-free black whose ancestry was mostly white. (Issue-free meant that although she had some black ancestry, her mother was not a slave.) The sisters grew up on the North Carolina campus of St. Augustine's College, a school for blacks in Raleigh, where their father was a teacher and an administrator and their mother was the supervising matron. The Delany children were well-educated, strictly disciplined, and held to high standards, although their environment was nurturing and somewhat protected. "We had unusual parents, " Bessie said. "Everyone thinks their parents were special, but I know ours were. Our father was wise and he was very proud of his family. We were and we are a loving family, very close to each other."

The sisters vividly recalled the changes in the South at the turn of the century, when the Jim Crow laws institutionalized segregation by race. They remembered the first day they were refused service at Johnson's Drug Store in Raleigh, where they customarily went for limeades, and the day they went to get water and found a divider placed over the middle of the spring with a sign on one side that read "Whites Only." "It was a terrible time," Sadie said. "People got lynched—it was terrible." Bessie, the more outspoken and confrontational of the sisters, would frequently sneak sips from the "white" water fountains and was almost lynched herself one day for speaking rudely to a "rebby boy" in a train station. They endured racism later in life, too. Bessie spoke of a particularly humiliating incident that occurred at the Hotel Pennsylvania in Manhattan in 1924, when she asked a man at the front desk to direct her to the room where she was to attend a medical conference. "That louse directed me to the men's room," she recalled, still angry after 65 years. "I have never gotten over that."

The Delanys left St. Augustine's as certified teachers, and both taught school until they had saved enough to pay for college. Sadie joined her brother Hap in New York in 1916, and attended a two-year program at Pratt Institute in Brooklyn before entering Teachers College at Columbia University. After receiving both a bachelor's and master's degree in education, she began her teaching career, eventually becoming the first black woman permitted to teach home economics at the high school level in New York City. (She later admitted that she skipped the mandatory interview for her first teaching job, fearing that she might be rejected because of her race. Instead, she just appeared on the first day of classes and began teaching.) Bessie followed her sister in 1918, entering the dental program at Columbia after being turned away from New York University's dental program because she was female. After graduating in 1923, she became only the second black woman to be licensed to practice dentistry in New York City. Known as "Dr. Bessie, Harlem's colored woman dentist," she never turned a patient away, no matter how poor or sick. "I remember a child with syphilis, and nobody else would touch her," she said. "I said, 'Well, somebody's got to help her,' so I did." Bessie charged $2 for a cleaning and $5 for a silver filling, never raising her prices in 27 years of practice.

The sisters, who socialized with the elite of the Harlem Renaissance, like W.E.B. DuBois, Paul Robeson, and Langston Hughes, never married, although they received many offers. "You see, in our day it didn't occur to anyone that you could be married *and* have a career," Sadie explained. They lived together in an apartment on 145th Street and Seventh Avenue until 1928, when they moved with their widowed mother into a house in the Bronx. After Nanny's death in 1956, they bought a two-family house in Mount Vernon, New York, where they were among the first to integrate the neighborhood.

The sisters attributed their longevity to simple clean living. "No drinking, no chewing, no smoking," said Sadie. They also joked that they probably lived so long because they didn't marry. "We never had husbands to worry us to death," said Bessie. They started each day with a spoonful of cod liver oil and a chopped clove of garlic, and never drank the tap water without boiling it first. They also performed yoga exercises every morning except Sunday, when they attended Episcopal church service in Mount Vernon. The sisters kept up with world events by reading the daily newspapers and watching the "MacNeil-Lehrer Newshour" each evening on a black-and-white television set. Independence was also an important aspect of their well-being, as was laughter, enjoyment, and a stress-free life. Mentally, the Delanys were as sharp as tacks. "There

Bessie Delany

was no date, name or other detail that the sisters could not recall about their century long lives," wrote Hearth in her first article on the pair.

Bessie Delany began to fail after breaking her hip in 1994 and was the first of the sisters to die, passing away quietly at home on September 25, 1995, at the age of 104. Sadie conceded to hiring a part-time cook and companion but remained in the Mount Vernon home tending Bessie's garden. Aided again by Amy Hill Hearth, Sadie expressed her profound loss in a new book *On My Own at 107: Reflections on Life Without Bessie*. "A few day after you left us Bessie," she wrote, "I started wearing one of your suit coats—you know, the gray one you loved so much. It made me feel good having it wrapped around me. I'm very conscious of being alone. I notice your absence in everything I do." Sadie survived to 109, dying peacefully in her sleep like Bessie on January 25, 1999.

SOURCES:

Bernstein, Amy. "Epitaph," in *U.S. News & World Report*. October 9, 1995.

Delany, Sarah L., with Amy Hill Hearth. *On My Own at 107*. San Francisco, CA: HarperCollins, 1997.

Hearth, Amy Hill. "Two 'Maiden Ladies' with Century-Old Stories to Tell," in *The New York Times*. September 22, 1991.

Jones, Charisse. "The Younger of Delany sisters, Bessie, dies in her sleep, at 104," in *The Day* (New London, CT). September 26, 1995.

Lyons, Christine and William Barnhill. "'We're Having Our Say'," in *AARP Bulletin*. Vol. 35, No. 3, March 1994.

"Obituary," in *The Day* (New London, CT). January 26, 1999.

RELATED MEDIA:

Having Our Say by **Emily Mann**, opened on Broadway in 1995.

"Having Our Say: The Delany Sisters' First 100 Years," starring ***Ruby Dee, Diahann Carroll**, and **Amy Madigan**, with a cameo appearance by **Della Reese**, first aired on CBS television on April 18, 1999.

Barbara Morgan,
Melrose, Massachusetts

Delany Sisters, The.

See joint entry under Delany, Sarah Louise and Delany, Annie Elizabeth.

de Lara, Adelina (1872–1961)

English pianist. Born in Carlisle, England, on January 23, 1872; died in Woking, England, on November 25, 1961; studied with Clara Schumann.

Adelina de Lara was among a select number of pianists fortunate enough to be a pupil of one of Europe's foremost pianists, ***Clara Schumann**. Schumann's unique Romantic style, which dated to the beginning of the 19th century when the piano was invented, was learned from her father Robert Schumann and passed on to her students. De Lara embraced Clara's style and technique, and her recordings are valued for their illumination of that earlier world.

de la Ramée, Louise (1839–1908).

See Ramée, Louise de la.

de la Rocha, Alicia (b. 1923).

See Larrocha, Alicia de.

de Laroche, Baroness (b. 1886).

See Quimby, Harriet for sidebar on Elise-Raymonde Deroche.

de la Roche, Mazo (1879–1961)

Popular and prolific Canadian writer. Born Mazo Roche ("de la" added later) on January 15, 1879, in Toronto, Ontario, Canada; died on July 12, 1961; *daughter of William Roche (a salesperson) and Alberta Lundy Roche (a carpenter); attended the Ontario School of Art in Toronto, Canada, and studied under George Agnew Reid; children: (adopted) Renee and Esme.*

Awarded the Atlantic Monthly *prize for fiction and received widespread recognition for her novel,* Jalna *(1927); traveled abroad for first time and remained in England, making her home there for a number of years (1929); with her cousin Caroline Clement, adopted two orphaned children of friends (1931); returned to Toronto and re-established a home there (1938).*

Selected writings: Explorers of the Dawn *(1922);* Possession *(1923);* Low Life: A Comedy in One Act *(1925);* Delight *(1926);* Come True *(1927);* Jalna *(1927);* Low Life and Other Plays *(1929);* The Return of the Emigrant *(1929);* Whiteoaks of Jalna *(1929);* Portrait of a Dog *(1930);* Finch's Fortune *(1931);* Lark Ascending *(1932);* The Thunder of New Wings *(1932);* The Master of Jalna *(1933);* Beside a Norman Tower *(1934);* Young Renny *(1935);* Whiteoaks: A Play *(1936);* Whiteoak Harvest *(1936);* The Very House *(1937);* Growth of a Man *(1938);* The Sacred Bullock and Other Stories of Animals *(1939);* White Oak Heritage *(1940);* Wakefield's Course *(1941);* The Two Saplings *(1942);* Quebec: Historic Seaport *(1944);* The Building of Jalna *(1944);* Return to Jalna *(1946);* Mary Wakefield *(1949);* Renny's Daughter *(1951);* A Boy in the House *(1952);* A Boy in the House and Other Stories *(1952);* Whiteoak Brothers: Jalna 1923 *(1953);* Variable Winds at Jalna *(1954);* The Song of Lambert *(1955);* Ringing the Changes: An Autobiography *(1957);* Bill and Coo *(1958);* Centenary at Jalna *(1958);* Morning at Jalna *(1960);* Selected Stories of Mazo de la Roche *(1979).*

Play productions: Low Life *(Trinity Memorial Hall, Toronto, May 14, 1925);* Come True *(Hart House Theater, Toronto, May 16, 1927);* The Return of the Emigrant, *(Hart House Theater, Toronto, March 12, 1928);* Whiteoaks, *by de la Roche and Nancy Price (Little Theater in the Adelphi, London, April 13, 1936);* The Mistress of Jalna *(New Theater, Bromley, Kent, United Kingdom, November 12, 1951).*

Mazo Roche was born January 15, 1879, the only child of William Roche, a salesperson, and **Alberta Lundy Roche**, a carpenter. Mazo adopted the French prefix *de la* to her family name when young. After spending several years in Newmarket, a village in Ontario north of Toronto, Canada, she and her family moved to Toronto and resided there from 1885 until 1910. Shortly after they had moved there, **Caroline Clement**, de la Roche's cousin, came to live with

them, and the two became constant, close companions, seldom separated in 70 years.

De la Roche attended the Ontario School of Art in Toronto for a period and studied under George Agnew Reid, the president of the Ontario Society of Artists. In 1910, her family moved to Rochedale, a fruit-and-stock farm west of Toronto, and they remained there until 1915, when William Roche died. Because of serious financial difficulties, the family was forced to move back to Toronto, and de la Roche, whose writing career had begun in 1902 with the publication of a short story in *Munsey's Magazine*, decided to develop a career for herself in writing. By 1927, she had achieved widespread recognition with her novel, *Jalna*, and had received the *Atlantic Monthly* prize for fiction. She also published a variety of works, including several plays, a collection of short stories, *Explorers of the Dawn* (1922), and two novels, *Possession* (1923) and *Delight* (1926). The latter story was written at her summer cottage near Clarkson, Ontario, and this setting provided the model for Jalna, the home of the Whiteoak family, the history of which was indelibly etched for de la Roche's readers in 16 novels from 1927 to 1960.

The chronicles of the Whiteoak family of Jalna made Mazo de la Roche one of Canada's most popular writers in the first half of the 20th century. More than 11 million copies in 193 English editions and 92 foreign editions of this family saga were sold during her lifetime. A sensitive and imaginative writer, she is associated with the movement toward greater realism in Canadian fiction during that period. The theme in all her work, including the Jalna series, is maintaining individual freedom but not at the expense of tradition.

In 1929, de la Roche went abroad for the first time. She made her home in England, and in 1931, de la Roche and Caroline Clement adopted two orphaned children of friends. They resided there until 1938, when rumors of war and de la Roche's poor health forced them to return to Toronto. During these years, Mazo mostly traveled and raised her two adopted children.

Besides the Whiteoak novels, she was also the author of varied works, including two children's books, *The Song of Lambert* (1955) and *Bill and Coo* (1958); a history of Quebec, published in 1944; an autobiography, *Ringing the Changes* (1957); two adaptations of the Whiteoak novels for the theater, *Whiteoaks* (produced and published 1936) and *The Mistress of Jalna* (produced in 1951); two collections of short stories; and four novels: *Lark Ascending* (1932), *The Thunder of New Wings* (1932), *Growth of a Man* (1938) and *The Two Saplings* (1942).

SOURCES:

Daymond, D.M. "Mazo de la Roche," in *Dictionary of Literary Biography*. Vol. 68. Edited by W.H. New. Detroit, MI: Gale Research, 1988, pp. 106–112.

Jo Anne Meginnes, freelance writer, Brookfield, Vermont

de la Rochefoucauld, Edmée (1895–1991).

See La Rochefoucauld, Edmée de.

Delarverié, Stormé.

See Arbus, Diane for sidebar.

de la Sablière, Mme. (1640–1693).

See La Sablière, Marguerite de.

De la Torre, Lillian (c. 1902–1993).

See McCue, Lillian.

Delaunay, Le Vicomte (1804–1855).

See Girardin, Delphine.

De Launay, Mademoiselle (1684–1750).

See Staal de Launay, Madame de.

Delaunay, Sonia (1885–1979)

Russian-born abstract artist who was intimately involved in the development of modern art movements, such as Orphism and Dadaism, and largely responsible for the utilization of modern artistic concepts in 20th-century design and fashion. Name variations: *Sonia Terk; Sonia Uhde; Sonia Delaunay-Terk or Terk-Delaunay. Born Sophie Stern on November 14, 1885, in Gradzihsk, Ukraine; died on December 5, 1979, in Paris; daughter of Elie Stern (a factory worker) and Anne (Terk) Stern; raised from age five by uncle Henri Terk (a lawyer); attended University in Karlsruhe, Germany, 1903–05; studied at the Académie de la Palette in Paris; married Wilhelm Uhde, in 1908 (divorced 1910); married Robert Delaunay, in 1910; children: Charles Delaunay (b. January 18, 1911).*

Moved to Paris (1905); established studio (1906); painted first Simultaneous Contrasts *(1912); produced first simultaneous clothing (1913); opened Casa Sonia and designed costumes for ballet* Cléopatre *(1918); designed costumes for production of* Aïda *(1920); established Atelier Simultané (1924); decorated Boutique Simultanée for the International Exhibition of Decorative Arts (1925); published* Sonia Delaunay: Compositions, Couleurs, Idées *(1930); portfolio of works by Delaunay, Arps, and Magnelli published (1950); had solo exhibition in Paris (1953); appointed Chevalier des Arts and des Lettres (1958); first major traveling exhibition in North America organized by National Gallery of Canada (1965); published* Colored Rhythms *(1966); received Legion of Honor (1975).*

Major works: (illustrations) Blaise Cendrars' La Prose du Transsibérien et de la Petite Jehanne de France *(1913), Tristan Tzara's* Juste Présent *(1961); (lithographs) "10 Origin" (1942), "Album With Six Prints" (1962); (murals)* Les Voyages lointains *(1937), Portugal (1937); (paintings)* Le Bal Bullier, 1913 *(Musée National d'Art Moderne, Paris),* Rythme col-

oré, 1946 (Collection of Cohen family, New York), and Triptyque, 1963 (The Tate Gallery, London).

On July 6, 1923, the Dadaist drama *The Evening of the Bearded Heart* was staged at the Théâtre Michel, in Paris, by Tristan Tzara, the champion of Dada. The Dada movement was being challenged for leadership of the avant-garde by the Surrealist movement, led by André Breton, and on the night of the show the conflict became heated. After repeated interruptions failed to stop the performance, Breton leapt on stage and broke the lead actor's arm with a blow from his cane. With that, Tzara joined Breton on stage, and the two fought until the police arrived. Shortly after the agitators were led off and the theater had been quelled, Paul Eluard bolted from his seat and dashed to the stage, smashing the footlights as he did so. Such was the volatile artistic community of 1920s' Paris, and at its heart was Sonia Delaunay, the designer of the radical costumes for the eventful performance.

𝓑eauty refuses to submit to the constraint of meaning or description.

—Sonia Delaunay

She was born Sophie Stern in a small rural Ukrainian village, Gradizhsk, and her early childhood was spent surrounded by the natural beauty of the region. At age five, however, for reasons unknown, she moved to St. Petersburg, and the bulk of the rest of her life was spent in urban environments. Sophie, who was always known as Sonia, became the adopted daughter of her maternal uncle Henri Terk, a prosperous lawyer, and took his surname. Her life in St. Petersburg was one of privilege and luxury. The Terk family, while Jewish, did not suffer directly from the repression of Jews in late 19th-century Russia. Sonia traveled in Europe with her family, and this, added to instruction from her governesses, resulted in her learning French, English, and German at a young age. She also showed promise as a painter and studied art with dedication and sensitivity. In 1903, on the recommendation of her drawing teacher, she went to study under Ludwig Schmid-Reutte, who emphasized drawing, at the university in Karlsruhe, Germany. Here, she first learned of the Impressionists. Finding their work close to her own feeling about art, she determined to expose herself to their environment and moved to Paris.

Like so many artists, Delaunay was captivated by the city and spent most of her life there. Arriving in 1905, she enrolled in classes at the Académie de la Palette, where the structured method of teaching a range of approaches was not comfortable for Delaunay, who had a firm vision of her only artistic direction. Instead, she left the school, set up her own studio, and became part of a circle of young artists and poets, many of them also from Russia, who were interested in the avant-garde. One of her friends, painter **Elizabeth Epstein**, introduced her to Franz Marc and Wassily Kandinsky, two of the most influential members of the Expressionist movement. Pressure from Sonia's family to re-

turn home and marry led her to propose marriage, of a convenient nature, to Wilhelm Uhde, a gallery owner and friend. They were married in London in 1908. That same year, she had her first solo exhibition, showing works influenced by Impressionist concerns with light and color but different in execution, principally because her concern was mainly with color. Delaunay was determined to find her own style at a time when Fauvism, a technique also focusing on the importance of pure color, was the rage in Paris. Her circle of acquaintances in artistic circles continued to widen, as she met both Picasso and Braque in 1909.

During the years 1907 to 1910, Sonia developed a relationship with Robert Delaunay that was initially based on mutual interests in the future of art, but which eventually led Sonia to divorce Wilhelm Uhde, who was as amicable about this as about the marriage. She married Robert Delaunay in November of 1910; in January 1911, their son Charles Delaunay was born. The work of Robert and Sonia Delaunay was for many years inseparably linked in the eyes of the art world, with most of the attention focused on Robert. This fact obscured the importance of Sonia Delaunay to modern art, as well as her role in the formation of the artistic style that they shared. Following her first exhibition, Delaunay did not show her work in a gallery again until 1953, but in that period she established herself as a major influence on modern art, and particularly design.

From 1910 to 1912, Delaunay devoted much of her time to exploring the avenues for artistic expression in embroidery and textiles. By 1912, however, she was returning to painting as her principal art form, her work concentrating on the use of color, free from figurative constraints. She was one of many artists and writers in Paris interested in reflecting the realities of the modern world in their art, among them Marc Chagall. Delaunay became close friends with Guillaume Apollinaire, one of the most prominent 20th-century French poets. In 1913, she also met Blaise Cendrars, referring to him in 1962 as "the truest and greatest poet of our time." Delaunay illustrated an edition of Cendrars' poem about the Eiffel Tower, the *Prose du Transsibérien,* with mainly abstract designs. Sixty-two copies were printed, each somewhat different, the culmination of Delaunay's interest in book-cover design. Evolving from this project, Delaunay developed the concept of poster-poems, merging words with her designs based on her theory of simultaneity. Her concept of simultaneous art was that art depicts the essence of movement; in this, she differed from the effort of the Futurists to portray a sequence of movement simultaneously. Cendrars, who was a great supporter of this work, referred to himself as the poet of the simultaneous.

Eventually, the letters themselves controlled the composition of her works, and Delaunay recognized the obvious commercial applicability of her posters. She began a series of designs for such companies as Pirelli and Dubonnet. In 1913, the Delaunays were included in the Erster Deutscher Herbstsalon, a major exhibition of avant-garde art and objects. Sonia Delaunay's paintings were shown along with her book covers, posters, and textile projects. About the same time, she began work on *Prismes électriques* ("Electric Prisms"), an oil painting reminiscent of her collage work, which was submitted to the Salon des Independants of 1914. By 1915, Apollinaire had popularized the term Orphic to describe the work of both of the Delaunays, and the brief movement associated with them remains known as Orphism. Orphism introduced pure color into Cubist-influenced art, exemplified most in the work of Robert Delaunay and Marc Chagall; Orphism also influenced the Futurists in Italy and the Expressionists in Germany and Russia. After visiting Delaunay in Paris in 1912, a young Russian academic named Smirnoff delivered a lecture on the simultaneous in St. Petersburg.

As part of their involvement with the fashionable artistic class in Paris, the Delaunays patronized the Bullier, a popular dance hall where the new rages of the tango and foxtrot could be observed. Delaunay, who did not care to dance, portrayed the dancers at the Bullier as a rolling sea of color, with the individuals undifferentiated, in her *Le Bal Bullier* of 1913.

In 1915, after some time spent in Spain, the Delaunays settled in Portugal, where they had found a circle of like-minded artists and intellectuals. Initially, they shared a villa with Sam and **Vianna Halpert** in Vila do Conde, then in 1916 they moved to Valenca do Minho, on the border with Spain. In Valenca, Delaunay designed the decoration for the façade of a local chapel; though the project was not completed, the designs rendered as part of the process were some of Delaunay's most interesting figurative works. The year 1916 saw a major exhibition of Delaunay's work in Oslo and Stockholm, for which she designed the cover of the exhibition catalogue. In October of 1917, the Delaunays' lives were drastically altered by the Russian Revolution; though she was a fervent supporter of the revolution, it cost Delaunay the income from the rent of 80 apartments in St. Petersburg, which in fact represented most of her total earnings. The Delaunays moved to Madrid, where they felt they could earn a better living as artists. Once again, Sonia was determined to explore the commercial value of her many experiments with artistic expression in design and decoration.

In Madrid, Delaunay made the acquaintance of Serge Diaghilev, head of the Russian Ballet, who eventually commissioned Robert to design the sets and Sonia the costumes for the company's revival of *Cleopatra,* which was to be staged in London. To create the costumes, which bore only slight resemblance to historical dress, Delaunay allowed the full expression of her approach to shape and color. The success of the ballet resulted in several other commissions for her, including costumes for a 1920 production of *Aïda* at the Teatro Liceo in Barcelona.

Sonia Delaunay became familiar with society circles in Madrid, a fact that encouraged her to start her own boutique, the Casa Sonia, to champion modern sensibilities in interior design. The shop was also to carry her jewelry, which like all her work embodied her approach to art, particularly her "simultaneous necklaces." Although this boutique is referred to by some authors as though it actually functioned, Delaunay herself noted in 1967 that it had never in fact opened. While engaged in this project, she also began accepting commissions to decorate homes, as well as the Petit Casino, a theater that opened in 1919. However, the Delaunays were drawn to the Paris art scene; they were excited by the ideas of the surrealists, with whom they corresponded. Also, despite her growing success as a designer, Delaunay was finding it difficult to progress as an artist in Spain. In 1921, the Delaunays returned to Paris.

There, the Delaunays' apartment became an example of the integration of art into all aspects of everyday life, a reflection of her approach, and compatible with the notions of the Dadaists that were in vogue. Thus, the Delaunays were more welcome in the Parisian artistic circle of the '20s than artists who had been Cubists, or followed other artistic modes declared dead by the Dadaists. Hosting weekly gatherings of like-minded artists, Sonia Delaunay invited the guests to contribute to the decor themselves; the results were a startling mix of Dada and Surreal efforts. Among the many prominent artists involved were Man Ray, Jean Arp, and Chagall. By 1922, Delaunay was again decorating professionally. She began to produce and sell simultaneous scarves that both displayed her characteristic artistic motifs and exemplified her dedication to the applied arts. So, also, did her "Dress-poems," in which original poems were an integral part of the design of clothes. She applied her concept of simultaneity to the costumes she designed for Tzara's ill-fated performance of *The Evening of the Bearded Heart.*

The turning point in Delaunay's career, the event that cemented her future as a crucial figure in 20th-century fashion, was the 1923 request from a fabric manufacturer that she submit some designs to them. Her involvement in applying her work on shape and color to textile design led Delaunay to set up her own printing workshop to control the quality of the resulting fabric. The Atelier Simultané was opened in 1924 and produced a unique line of designs, mostly on silk, which focused on the use of a small number of vibrant colors in each textile, and a range of geometric shapes more diverse than the circles of her earlier work. Delaunay's fabrics soon became popular among the highly fashion conscious in both Europe and America.

At the International Exhibition of Decorative arts in Paris in 1925, Delaunay provided her works for the *Boutique Simultanée,* including fabrics, clothes, and accessories. Distinct from the other Art Deco approaches to design, it was Delaunay's sensibility that became the most influential in the sphere of fashion. In 1927, she gave a lecture at the Sorbonne on the influence of painting on fashion design. She expressed the need for fashion to change, to emphasize "not inspiration derived from the past, but grappling with the subject as if everything begins anew each day." In 1930, the album entitled *Sonia Delaunay: Compositions, Couleurs, Idées* was published. Her era of greatest success, however, was cut short by the Depression, a fact that did not disappoint her that much, as business was not to her taste; after 1930, Delaunay returned to being primarily a painter.

Sonia Delaunay explored a number of unusual artistic mediums during the 1920s and '30s, including the use of electric lighting as media. Her project for an illuminated advertisement for Zig-Zag cigarettes won a prize for publicity murals in 1936. In 1937, she was involved again with an international exhibition in Paris, this time emphasizing "arts and technics." While Robert designed the air and railway pavilions for the exhibition, Sonia completed three murals for the air pavilion on the theme of the airplane, and two others for the railway pavilion: *Les Voyages lointains* (which earned a medal) and *Portugal.*

With the outbreak of war, the Delaunays moved south, first to Auvergne, then to Midi, and finally to Mougins. In 1941, Robert Delaunay died of cancer; Sonia spent many years organizing exhibitions to preserve and enhance his reputation as a painter. She moved to Grasse, where she lived with the Arps and Magnellis until 1943, and alone for a short period after they left. In 1942, Delaunay produced a series of lithographs with Jean Arp, *Sophie Tauber-Arp, and Alberto Magnelli, which were eventually published in 1950. In 1945, she returned to Paris and exhibited with the Art Concret group. In 1947, she participated in the "Tendencies of Modern Art" exhibition, which included 20 artists, including Arp. In 1948, she took part in two smaller exhibits, also including Arp and Tauber-Arp. She joined the artistic group Espace in 1952, and in the same year she had a solo exhibition at the Galerie Bing in Paris. In 1954, she exhibited again with the Grasse group (Arp, Tauber-Arp, and Magnelli) at the Galerie Bing. In 1955, she participated in the "Great Women Artists" exhibition at the Delius Gallery, New York, was awarded the Grand Prix Lissone from Italy in 1955, and a major exhibition of her works toured Italy, Austria, Belgium, Germany, France, Switzerland, the Netherlands, and Brazil. She was active in numerous other exhibitions during the late 1950s and early 1960s, including an exhibition devoted to international collage in Houston in 1958.

The first major Delaunay exhibition in North America, including works from Sonia and Robert, was mounted in 1965 by the National Gallery of Canada. In 1966, the book *Rhythms-Colors* was published, containing poems by Jacques Damase and *pochoirs* (stencils) by Sonia Delaunay; this work was indicative of Delaunay's long involvement with the integration of poetry and art. Another example of her diversity was the issue of two large tapestries of her design by Gobelins (the premier French tapestry factory) in 1966. A large retrospective exhibition, containing 197 of her works, was mounted at the Musée National d'Art Moderne, Paris, in 1967. In 1969, *Dress-Poems,* another collaboration with Damase, was published, and she received the international grand prize at the Salon International de la Femme, in Cannes.

In 1970, the album *With Myself* was published, containing ten of Delaunay's etchings, and in 1973 the volume *Illuminations* by Rimbaud was released, with 18 pochoirs by Delaunay. Her 1969 oil painting *Rhythme couleur, No. 1633* was presented by the president of

France to the president of the United States in 1970. She received the Grand Prize of the City of Paris in 1973, and in 1975 she was named officer of the Legion of Honor. Projects and exhibitions continued during the 1970s, including the 1977 publication of Tzara's *La coeur du gaz* illustrated with ten lithographs by Delaunay. Sonia Delaunay died on December 5, 1979, ending nearly 70 years of intense involvement with modern art. Her fascination with the methods of connecting art to all other aspects of culture led to her substantial impact on 20th-century notions of fashion and design.

SOURCES:

Buckberrough, Sherry A. *Sonia Delaunay: A Retrospective.* Buffalo, NY: Albright-Knox Art Gallery, 1980.

Cohen, Arthur A. *Sonia Delaunay.* NY: Harry Abrams, 1975.

———, ed. *The New Art of Colour: The Writings of Robert and Sonia Delaunay.* NY: Viking, 1978.

Damase, Jacques. *Sonia Delaunay: Rhythms and Colors.* Greenwich, CT: New York Graphic Society, 1972.

Madsen, Axel. *Sonia Delaunay: Artist of the Lost Generation.* NY: McGraw-Hill, 1989.

Nemser, Cindy. *Conversations with 12 Women Artists.* NY: Scribner, 1975.

SUGGESTED READING:

Delaunay, Sonia. *Nous Irons Jusqu'au Soleil.* Paris: Editions Robert Laffont, 1978.

Dorival, Bernard. *Sonia Delaunay.* Paris: Editions Jacques Damase, 1980.

Morano, Elizabeth. *Sonia Delaunay: Art Into Fashion.* NY: George Braziller, 1986.

RELATED MEDIA:

Sonia Delaunay: Prises de Vues pour une Monographie, film, 1972.

COLLECTIONS:

Bibliothèque Nationale, Paris; Musée National d'Art Moderne, Paris.

William MacKenzie, Department of History, University of Guelph, Guelph, Ontario, Canada

Delaye, Marguerite (fl. 1569)

French war hero. Flourished around 1569 in Montelimar, France.

The only records of Marguerite Delaye show that she was living in Montelimar, France, in 1569. It was a time when France was racked by civil wars, with Catholics led by Henry I, 3rd duke of Guise, and Huguenots led by the followers of Louis I, prince de Condé. In that year, the town was put under siege by the troops of Huguenot leader Admiral Gaspard de Coligny. Delaye was one of the brave defenders of Montelimar, eventually losing one arm during a battle. The town erected a one-armed statue of Delaye in her memory.

Laura York, Riverside, California

del Bene, Adriana Gabrieli
(c. 1755–1799).

See Bene, Adriana Gabrieli del.

Delbo, Charlotte (1913–1985)

French author whose books have been critically acclaimed for providing some of the most profound insights into the Holocaust era and whose masterwork, the trilogy Auschwitz and After, *has steadily grown in reputation, first in France and then in the English-speaking world. Name variations: Charlotte Dudach. Born on August 10, 1913, in Vigneux-sur-Seine, Seine-et-Oise, France; eldest of four children; father was a civil engineer; died in Paris in 1985; married Georges Dudach.*

Born in a Paris suburb on the eve of World War I, Charlotte Delbo grew up in a France that had won a pyrrhic victory in 1918 and was now a deeply divided nation and society. Like many in her generation, she believed Marxism to be the only correct response to the injustices of her time, and in the 1930s she became an ardent supporter of the French Communist movement. Joining the Young Communist League in 1932, two years later Delbo met Georges Dudach, a Marxist intellectual whom she would eventually marry. With her strong literary and artistic interests, it was only natural that she would find work in the theater. In 1941, she was on tour with the Theater de l'Athenee in South America working as an assistant to the theater's impresario Louis Jouvet. Despite the fact that German armies had invaded France and now occupied much of its territory, Delbo was determined to return home to be with her husband, who had joined one of the first cells of the Résistance. She was particularly angered by the news that one of her close friends, the architect and Communist activist André Woog, had been arrested by French authorities and guillotined for possession of anti-Fascist propaganda materials. Although Louis Jouvet had strongly argued against her trying to return, Delbo was able to travel an indirect route via Portugal, Spain, and the Unoccupied (Vichy) Zone of France. She met her husband at Pau on the French-Spanish border, and returning separately via different routes to avoid capture, the couple finally arrived back in Paris on November 15, 1941.

As a collaborator with her husband in his underground activities, Delbo shared the great risks he had assumed by producing anti-German leaflets. The Communist resistance network of which they were members took great precautions to help them elude arrest, and during the four months the couple worked together they lived in a number of Paris apartments using various assumed names. Their luck ran out at noon on March 2, 1942, when they were arrested in their apartment by French police. Soon turned over to the German Gestapo office in Paris, wife and husband were incarcerated in different prisons. Only once, on the morning of May 23, 1942, did Charlotte Delbo see her husband. On that occasion, she was escorted to his cell at Mont-Valérien prison to say farewell to him. A few hours later, he was executed by a firing squad. Georges Dudach was 28 years old.

Delbo remained in prison in Romainville in German-occupied France until January 24, 1943. On that day, along with 229 other French-women, she was deported to the infamous Auschwitz-Birkenau concentration and death camp. Here she was tattooed with the number that would be indelibly imprinted on her left forearm for the rest of her life: 31661. Delbo remained in Auschwitz for a time, being eventually transferred to a satellite camp called Raisko. In January 1944, along with a small group of her compatriots, she was transferred to the all-women's camp of Ravensbrück. A few weeks before the total collapse of Nazi Germany, Delbo was released to Red Cross officials, who transported her to Sweden to begin the process of physical and psychological rehabilitation. Of the group of 230 women in Delbo's group, most of whom were, like herself, not Jewish and had been arrested for anti-Nazi political activities, only 49 returned alive from the various German camps and prisons in the spring of 1945.

Back in Paris after the war, Delbo did not waste time grieving but instead wrote down her memories of the horrors she and others had experienced. Although *None of Us Will Return*, the first section of her memoir, had been completed by 1946, she chose not to publish her manuscript until it had proven it could withstand "the test of time, since it had to travel far into the future." Realizing every day how utterly transformed she had been by her experiences, Delbo wrote of herself soon after the war, "I'm not alive. I died in Auschwitz but no one knows it."

Delbo resumed working in the theater and wrote a number of plays during the next decades. Not until 1965 did she finally publish *Aucun de nous ne reviendra* (*None of Us Will Return*) as the first part of what would be the trilogy *Auschwitz et après* (*Auschwitz and After*). The second volume, *Une conaissance inutile* (*Useless Knowledge*), much of which was written as long

ago as 1946–47, appeared in print in Paris in 1970. The trilogy's third and concluding volume, *The Measure of Our Days,* was published in 1971. Critical reviews in the Francophone press of the world was positive, and by 1990 a German translation of the trilogy had been published in Basel, Switzerland. The English-speaking world began to discover the unique and powerful voice of Charlotte Delbo in 1968 when *None of Us Will Return* was published by Grove Press. The full text of the trilogy was published in an excellent translation in 1995 by Yale University Press to laudatory reviews.

Charlotte Delbo's ambition as a writer was to find her own unique voice in order to communicate the essential truths—her phrase is "to see the unthinkable"—about what she had experienced in the Nazi death camps. Readers of her works are made immediately aware of the stylistic originality and visual intensity of her writing, which is an artful combination of prose and free verse. The juxtaposition of prose and poetry, moving through a fragmentary and non-chronological narrative, serves to draw the reader into the terror and dehumanization that was the system of Nazi genocide. Small details tell of a larger tale of merciless racism and annihilation: in "The Teddy Bear," a section in *Auschwitz and After,* the inmates find a fluffy pink toy, which had once been held "in the arms of a little girl who will leave her toy with her clothing, carefully folded, at the entrance to the 'showers'." The reality she had known before her arrival at Auschwitz and what another author has called the "concentration camp universe" is a basis for the many contrasting impressions in her books. In *None of Us Will Return,* Delbo contrasted the scenes of greetings and farewells taking place at a normal train station with what happened daily for years at Auschwitz, "a station where those who arrive are those who are leaving . . . where those who arrive have never arrived, where those who have left never came back." *None of Us Will Return* ends with a deeply moving "Prayer to the Living to Forgive Them for Being Alive," an injunction to us all to justify our existences:

> because it would be too senseless
> after all
> for so many to have died
> while you live
> doing nothing with your life

In Charlotte Delbo's last book, *La mémoire et les jours* (*Days and Memory*, 1985), she made her final attempts to "explain the inexplicable." Here, as in her other works, she hoped to be true to the sovereign principle of her art, *Il faut donner a voir* ("they must be made to see.") The immense efforts Delbo made to create works of art that would speak to her own and future generations led her to plumb the deepest recesses of her own and her comrades' sufferings. She would speak of her two selves, the one that existed before Auschwitz, and the one that emerged after Auschwitz. The image of a snake shedding its skin was, she believed, most appropriate for conjuring up the reality of her "new" nature after the camp years. Unlike the snake-skin, however, which shrivels, disintegrates and vanishes, the skin of Auschwitz was now a permanent part of her being: "Auschwitz is so deeply etched on my memory that I cannot forget one moment of it. So you are living with Auschwitz? No, I live next to it. Auschwitz is there, unalterable, precise, but enveloped in the skin of memory, an impermeable skin that isolates it from my present self. Unlike the snake's skin, the skin of memory does not renew itself. . . . Thinking about it makes me tremble with apprehension." Delbo was willing to endure the pain of recalling and artistically recreating the most painful years of her life because to the end of her career as a writer she believed passionately that the death and suffering of those years had meaning. She ardently hoped that her writings would enable coming generations to see what had happened in order to prevent such deeds of degradation and inhumanity from ever taking place again.

Charlotte Delbo never remarried after losing her husband to the Nazis in 1942. From 1945 until her death in 1985, she played an active role in the literary life of Paris. In her final years, she lovingly nursed her dying, widowed father. Delbo was tall and physically striking. On first meeting her, some described her appearance as being that of Electra in the classic Greek play. This was a telling visualization, in view of the fact that one of her favorite plays was Jean Giraudoux's *Electra* in the production staged by her lifelong friend and theater colleague Louis Jouvet. The final poem of her trilogy, entitled "Envoi," in fact refers directly to the Giraudoux play. Viewing the Holocaust as much from an artistic as an historical perspective, Charlotte Delbo described it as "the greatest tragedy of the 20th century." Charlotte Delbo is increasingly regarded as one of the most eloquent survivors from the Holocaust's nightmare universe.

SOURCES:

Delbo, Charlotte. *Auschwitz and After*. Translated by Rosette C. Lamont. New Haven, CT: Yale University Press, 1995.

———. *Convoy to Auschwitz: Women of the French Resistance*. Translated by Carol Cosman. Boston, MA: Northeastern University Press, 1997.

———. *Days and Memory*. Translated by Rosette Lamont. Marlboro, VT: Marlboro Press, 1990.

———. *None of Us Will Return*. Translated by John Githens. Boston: Beacon Press, 1978.

Haft, Cynthia. *The Theme of the Nazi Concentration Camps in French Literature*. The Hague: Mouton, 1973.

Jones, Judy. "None of Us Will Return: A Musical Narrative" (Master's thesis, Washington State University, 1984).

Kessler-Harris, Alice and William McBrien, eds. *Faith of a (Woman) Writer*. Westport, CT: Greenwood Press, 1988.

Langer, Lawrence L., ed. *Art From the Ashes: A Holocaust Anthology*. New York and Oxford: Oxford University Press, 1995.

Rittner, Carol, and John K. Roth, eds. *Different Voices: Women and the Holocaust*. NY: Paragon House, 1993.

Van Gelder, Lawrence. "Who Will Carry the Word?," in *The New York Times*. November 10, 1993, p. B6.

John Haag, Associate Professor of History, University of Georgia, Athens, Georgia

Deledda, Grazia (1871–1936)

Leading Sardinian writer and recipient of the Nobel Prize for Literature in 1926 who presented, in her most noted works, a profoundly pessimistic view of the human condition. Name variations: Gracia. Pronunciation: GRATZ-ia de-LEAD-ah. Born Grazia Cosima Deledda on September 27, 1871, in Nuoro, Sardinia; died in Rome on August 16, 1936, of cancer; daughter of Giovantonio (Totoni) Deledda (a local landowner and businessman) and Francesca Cambosa (or Cambosu) Deledda; attended primary school in Nuoro, 1878–1882 (some sources indicate she finished in 1881); married Palmiro Modesani (or Madesani), a civil servant, on November 4, 1899; children: two sons, Sardus (b. 1900), Franz (b. 1904).

Published first short story (1886); published first novel, shortly before the death of her father (1892); moved to Cagliari, capital of Sardinia (1899); moved to Rome (1900); film version of her novel Cenere *appeared (1916); shifted writing themes from Sardinia to psychological introspection (1921); her novel* La Madre *(The Mother and the Priest) appeared in English with introduction by D.H. Lawrence (1922); received Nobel Prize for Literature (1926).*

Selected works: Anime oneste *(Honest Souls, 1895);* Elias Portolu *(1903);* Cenere *(Ashes, 1904);* Canne al vento *(Reeds in the Wind, 1913);* La Madre *(Mother or The Woman and the Priest, 1920).*

In the first decades of the 20th century, Grazia Deledda was an important Italian novelist and the most distinguished writer to emerge from the island of Sardinia. A prolific author, she completed 33 novels as well as approximately 250 works of lesser scope such as short stories and articles. Although she wrote in Italian, most of her work is set in Sardinia and rooted in the traditions of Sardinian culture. Her achievement as an author received the high honor of the Nobel Prize for Literature. Awarded to Deledda in 1926, it was only the second Nobel Prize in Literature to be given to a woman. *Selma Lagerlöf of Sweden had won the first in 1909. Although Deledda wrote mainly in an unadorned prose style about her Sardinian peasant neighbors, her work has been hailed by critics for its deep psychological insight. Recent analysis of her work has explored the particular concern she directed toward the role of women in Sardinian society at the turn of the century.

So long as I wrote children's stories, no one bothered much. But when the love stories started—with nighttime rendezvous, kisses, and sweet, compromising words—the persecution became relentless, from all my family, and was backed up by outsiders, who were the most frightening and dangerous of all.

—Grazia Deledda's "Grace" from *Unspeakable Women*

The Sardinia in which Deledda was born and grew to adulthood was a remote and special part of the newly created Kingdom of Italy. Its unique culture dated back to the Bronze Age, and, according to her biographer **Carla Balducci**, Deledda was profoundly influenced by traditional stories about Sardinia's past. After passing through many hands, the island came under the control of the northern Italian Kingdom of Savoy at the start of the 18th century. When Italy was united in 1860, Sardinia became a part of the new state.

In the latter part of the 19th century, the island remained a primitive region of poverty, illiteracy, and ingrown cultural traditions. It lacked electricity and sewers, and the vast majority of its population was illiterate. In a phrase that all students of her work cite, Deledda herself described her hometown as "a village of the Bronze Age." She did not leave it, even to travel to a larger city in Sardinia, until the age of 28.

The future author was born in the small town of Nuoro, in the mountainous area of central Sardinia known as Barbagia, on September 27, 1871. Deledda's birthplace in this remote region was tied to the outside only by horsedrawn transportation. She was the fourth child and the second daughter born to the Deleddas. Her paternal grandfather was a peasant who had become a small landowner. Her father Giovantonio Deledda (known as Totoni) attended a university, expanded the family's landholdings, and worked as a public notary. Her mother **Francesca (Chiscedda) Cambosu** was the illiterate daughter of a local family.

The young girl grew up speaking the local dialect, Logudoro, and received only a minimal education, attending a grammar school in Nuoro for four years. This was the basic stint of schooling offered to all Italian children including those on Sardinia. As Balducci has put it, for a typical Sardinian girl who would receive her practical education from her mother it was enough to learn "to count . . . to read and write in her dialect, and to read some Italian." Grazia left her formal education behind when, not yet 11 years old, she received her primary school diploma. Her future educational development owed much to her mother's brother, a priest named Don Sebastiano, who discerned her strong intellectual powers when she was still a small child.

Deledda had the advantage of a family with a literary bent: her father was an enthusiastic amateur poet. Despite the conventions that limited education for females, the bright young girl was able to continue her schooling in informal fashion. Sebastiano tutored her in Latin, and a neighbor, who taught literature at the local boys' school, taught her Italian grammar and composition. When the neighbor fled the community to avoid paying his sizable debts, Grazia inherited his books. She also remembered his words of encouragement. He had said that her writing, even at this early stage in her life, was good enough to be published. In addition, the local bishop, a friend of the Deleddas, willed his library to the family. Writes Balducci: "Through these books Grazia gave herself a diversified modern education." According to some authorities, she began to write poetry and short stories when she was only eight years old.

In this isolated community, Grazia aspired to be a great professional writer. Remarkably, her study of Italian, the vehicle for her renowned and popular novels, began only in her early teenage years. Her girlhood infatuation with a schoolmate of her brother led to the writing of her first short story, a romantic tale entitled "Sangue Sardo" ("Sardinian Blood"). Sent to the women's fashion magazine *Ultima Moda*, it was accepted and published in July 1887. Even

Grazia Deledda

more important for Deledda's future, the skill she had exhibited impelled the editors to invite her to submit additional work.

Much of her family as well as their neighbors in Nuoro reacted less favorably. Her father encouraged her to continue her writing, but many of her relatives were shocked that she had written for a corrupt popular magazine. The plot of "Sardinian Blood," in which a jealous young girl kills her sister's boyfriend, then escapes punishment by disappearing, bothered many members of the community. Over the next several years, young Grazia continued to write, although she received no money for her work, only the pride of being a published author. Still struggling to write proper Italian, she drew on a remarkable tenacity in learning the new words she needed to escape the vocabulary of her local dialect. By the time she was 20, she had produced novels and a set of short stories and was being published in Rome and Milan as well as in Cagliari, Sardinia's capital city.

Deledda's novel *Fior di Sardegna* (*Flower of Sardinia*), completed in 1891, depicted Sardinian life and society. Quickly accepted, it appeared in early 1892 and presented her work to a wide audience, bringing Deledda extensive correspondence with other authors, as well as editors and members of the reading public. Her letters to one reader revealed important aspects of her view of the future. "I write because I dream of fame," she told him, "which I know intuitively I shall never achieve." But she tempered this pessimism with an expectation that her success would cause her to leave her birthplace. "I foresee that one day I must leave my rock island, and this, indeed is one of my most ardent desires."

The death of Totoni Deledda in 1892 deprived the family of its mainstay and removed from the young author her most ardent supporter within both her family and the town of Nuoro. Now, the townspeople criticized her literary work more openly than ever before. Grazia's brothers, free of their father's supervision, ran wild in a burst of dissipation, squandering the family's resources and ruining their reputations with sexual liaisons among the community's farmwomen. Her brother, Andrea, ended up in prison, although Grazia was able to secure his release. A second brother, Santus, went insane. The death in childbirth of Enza, her elder sister, put an additional cloud over the family's fortunes. Meanwhile, Grazia had to take over the direction of the family's business affairs.

Balducci considers this set of misfortunes a basic influence on Deledda's literary career. In that critic's view, the Italian writer now went into a "pessimistic" decade from 1899 to 1909 "in which everything she wrote was imbued with a sense of the futility of the human condition." An earlier student of Deledda's work, Domenico Vittorini, wrote in 1900: "One feels that a gust of pessimism has passed over Deledda's spirit."

In the view of critic Mario Aste, there was another crucial influence on the young author's future: her work in collecting Sardinian folklore.

Between 1892 and 1895, Deledda gathered songs, poems, and other expressions of the culture and primitive beliefs of the average Sardinian for a journal that specialized in Italian popular traditions. The stock figure of the bandit, who loomed large in Sardinian tradition, as well as the average Sardinian's deep affection for the island's rugged landscape were two elements that she incorporated into her writing. Even her plain and sometimes awkward style, criticized by many students of her work, reflected her immersion in Sardinian culture. "As a true bilingual," writes Aste, "she thought both in Sardinian and Italian." In many passages in her work, it is possible to see how she took Sardinian forms, then translated them into standard Italian.

Another force shaping her career, in the view of several critics, was the influence of writers like Giovanni Verga. Verga was a Sicilian who abandoned the romantic tradition that had dominated Italian novels earlier in the 19th century. He presented realistic but psychologically penetrating depictions of the common people of Sicily. Notes **Martha King** in her introduction to *Cosima,* from Verga and the similar writer Luigi Capuana, Deledda "learned to curb the highly romantic tendencies absorbed from her early reading." She applied the lessons she learned to the common people of her own island.

While Deledda's writing may have drawn its inspiration from her recent tragedies, her personal life took a series of positive turns at the close of the decade. The financial success of her novel *Anime oneste,* first published in 1895, gave her a degree of financial independence. The novel had been well received in Italy, and translation rights had been sold to a French publisher for a substantial sum. She now found it possible to leave the limited world of Nuoro. In 1899, her thriving literary reputation brought her an invitation to visit Cagliari, the largest city on the island. Countess **Maria Manca**, the editor of *Donna Sarde* (*Sardinian Lady*), a magazine to which Deledda had long contributed, asked her to make the short journey to the southern coast of Sardinia. For the first time in her life, Deledda left Nuoro.

At one of the literary salons Countess Manca arranged, Grazia met Palmiro Madesani, an Italian government official stationed in Sardinia. They fell deeply in love and in early November, less than three weeks after her arrival in Cagliari, announced their engagement. On January 11, 1900, Grazia became a bride at the age of 28—old by Sardinian standards. Three months later, she accompanied her husband when he was transferred to Rome. Palmiro understood and supported her work, her novel *Elias Portolu* was soon completed, and she found herself pregnant. In her new surroundings and circumstances, Deledda experienced unprecedented joy. "I am happy with a happiness pure and serene," she declared in a letter. "He loves me. I love him. . . . We are masters of the entire world."

Deledda's literary career continued without interruption. Even as she became the mother of two sons, Sardus, born in late 1900, and Franz, born in 1904, she continued to write. Her husband muffled the noise he made playing the piano in order to give her the quiet her efforts required. At least two hours each day were devoted to continuing her literary production, and her children recalled in later life how the family was conditioned to provide her with this crucial time to write. Franz, her younger son, put his recollections in striking form when he was an adult: "Unconsciously, we understood that in that room, for those two hours, Genius was rising to creation."

The book she began in the early months of 1900, *Elias Portolu,* became the centerpiece of her literary reputation. Deledda's most renowned work of literature appeared in serial form in a Roman magazine in the second half of 1900, and it was published in its entirety in 1903. Critics such as Sergio Pacifici have analyzed it extensively to draw the essential themes of her view of human nature. It shows the inability of individuals to draw happiness from life even when such opportunities apparently exist.

The publication of *Elias Portolu* raised Deledda's standing to a new level, and in 1907 she was nominated for the first time for the Nobel Prize in Literature. Though he remained an Italian government official, her husband Palmiro acted as her financial manager and saw to it that Deledda's works were widely translated and published throughout Europe. The couple divided their time between Rome and a number of second homes ranging from locations on the Italian Riviera to the Adriatic coast. From 1900 to 1911, the two made regular trips back to Sardinia, but Grazia also had the advantage of foreign travel as her husband was assigned abroad. In 1910, for example, they spent the year in Paris. As one of Italy's most widely read authors, Deledda found her work translated into other forms. Her novel *Cenere,* written in 1904, was made into a film in 1916. Other works were adapted for the stage and for opera.

A notable achievement in her body of work was the novel *La Madre.* By the time it appeared in 1920, Deledda had already established herself as a best-selling author, but this book had an unusual impact. Translated into all the major European languages at once, its English translation, *The Woman and the Priest,* featured an introduction by D.H. Lawrence. The colorful and controversial English novelist greeted her achievement with enthusiasm, and Lawrence's sponsorship of her work played a major role in Deledda's growing international reputation. That reputation was now so well established that she became a perennial finalist for the Nobel Prize.

By the early 1920s, Sardinia's most famous writer had little direct contact with her homeland. Deledda's mother had died in 1916, and, in 1922, the last of her brothers also passed away. During the 1920s, Deledda's writing likewise took a new turn. Abandoning her vivid descriptions of Sardinia's people, landscape, and myths, she stressed what Aste has called "psychological introspection . . . and flights into the fantastic." Many critics now found that her work lost much of its power and originality. Nonetheless, her long-standing achievements earned her the Nobel Prize in Literature in 1926.

Deledda greeted the news with irony. When her husband rushed to tell her, she merely glanced up from working in the kitchen, said "It's about time," and went back to her cooking chores. She told one of the hordes of newspaper reporters who gathered at the Madesani home that her life and working routine would remain as before. "Nothing changes in the direction of my life," she said. "Today I am determined to stay here in my study for several hours." When Italian dictator Benito Mussolini insisted in honoring her at an elaborate reception, she took the opportunity to ask him for a single favor. She requested, and he granted, the release from prison of an anti-Fascist acquaintance.

Deledda traveled to Sweden to accept the honor in person. A shy woman, at the award ceremony she gave only a brief speech, the shortest on record for a Nobel Prize winner. Soon after receiving the award, Deledda found that she was ill with cancer. Despite severe pain and the trauma of two operations, she continued her literary production until her death on August 16, 1936. The noted author left important insights into her life in an autobiography, lightly disguised as a novel. This book, entitled *Cosima* (her middle name), appeared in the year following her death.

The body of Sardinia's leading author was buried in Rome wearing the suit in which she had accepted the Nobel Prize. Following World War II, officials in Nuoro successfully petitioned the Madesani family to consent to her reburial in Nuoro, her birthplace. The house in which she was born remains in existence, and the street where it stands has been renamed Via Gracia Deledda in her memory.

Recent appraisal of Deledda's work has examined her treatment of women in Sardinian society. In the world Deledda depicted, notes Bruce Merry, women "were prevented, even when they inherited middle-class status, from travel or education," and they had no role whatsoever in the professions or business. They escaped from their restricted circumstances with covert love affairs or a passion for literature or clothes. Deledda, whose own limited education was typical, frequently mentions the opportunities open for boys including the secondary school at Cagliari and the universities on the Italian mainland. Nonetheless, her female characters frequently rise above the adversity of life far better than their male companions. As Merry puts it, Deledda's women "were real creatures, adept at coping."

D.H. Lawrence saw Deledda as "fascinated by her island and its folks, more than by the problems of the human psyche." But characterizing Deledda essentially as a Sardinian writer does not tell the entire story for critics like Sergio Pacifici and Martha King. King finds Deledda's achievement resting in the Sardinian author's depiction of the general course of human trials and tribulations. Thus, while Deledda shows simple Sardinians who "play out their essentially tragic lives against a backdrop of mountains and bare plains, sheepfold and vineyards, . . . [h]er emphasis on character and the eternal conflicts of love, hate, and jealousy transcends time and place."

SOURCES:

Aste, Mario. *Grazia Deledda: Ethnic Novelist*. Potomac, MD: Scripta Humanistica, 1990.

Balducci, Carolyn. *A Self-Made Woman: Biography of Nobel-Prize-Winner Grazia Deledda*. Boston, MA: Houghton Mifflin, 1975.

King, Martha. Introduction to *Cosima*, by Grazia Deledda. Translated by Martha King. NY: Italica Press, 1988.

Lawrence, D.H. Foreword to *La Madre* (*The Woman and the Priest*), by Grazia Deledda. Translated by M.G. Steegman. London: Daedalus, 1987.

Merry, Bruce. *Women in Modern Italian Literature: Four Studies Based on the Work of Grazia Deledda, Alba De Céspedes, Natalia Ginzburg and Dacia Maraini*. Townsville, Australia: Department of Modern Languages, James Cook University of North Queensland, 1990.

Pacifici, Sergio. *The Modern Italian Novel: From Capuana to Tozzi*. Carbondale, IL: Southern Illinois University, 1973.

Vittorini, Domenico. *The Modern Italian Novel*. 1930.

Wasson, Tyler, ed. *Nobel Prize Winners*. NY: H.W. Wilson, 1987.

SUGGESTED READING:

Russell, Rinaldina, ed. *Italian Women Writers: A Bio-Bibliographical Sourcebook*. Westport, CT: Greenwood Press, 1994.

Wilkins, Ernest Hatch. *A History of Italian Literature*. Revised by Thomas G. Bergin. Cambridge, MA: Harvard University Press, 1974.

Neil M. Heyman, Professor of History, San Diego State University, San Diego, California

de Lempicka, Tamara (1898–1980).

See Lempicka, Tamara de.

de Lenclos, Ninon (1623–1705).

See Lenclos, Ninon de.

del Giocondo, Lisa (1474–?)

Florentine woman. Name variations: Mona Lisa; Monna Lisa; Lisa Ghevardini; Mona Lisa de' Gherardini; La Gioconda. Born Lisa Ghevardini in Naples, Italy, in 1474; death date unknown; married Francesco di Zanobi del Giocondo (a Florentine merchant), in 1495.

Lisa del Giocondo was a beautiful woman of Florence, whose face inspired one of the most famous paintings in the world—the *Mona Lisa*. Though del Giocondo was born in Naples, where she lived as a girl, her maiden name Ghevardini was that of an ancient, noble family of Florentines. In 1495, she married Francesco del Giocondo, a wealthy Florentine merchant; during the rest of her life, as far as is known, she lived in Florence, where she seems to have been a happy wife and mother, but of her later years there is no record.

It was probably in the first year of her marriage that she met Leonardo da Vinci, and a friendship began that grew into a platonic affection, about which many writers have woven romance. In 1503, according to a contemporary art critic Giorgio Vasari, da Vinci was commissioned by Francesco del Giocondo to paint his wife's portrait. "After toiling over it for four years, he left it unfinished" and refused to give it to Francesco.

Physically, morally and intellectually, Lisa del Giocondo fascinated da Vinci; he painted her again and again. The extent of her influence is manifest in much of his work, and his major paintings produce something of her personality. The Mona Lisa smile can be found over and over in Northern Italy where works of da Vinci and his pupils are to be seen; the painting, known as *La Gioconda* or *Mona Lisa* set a fashion in vitality and subtlety of expression absolutely unrivalled. "Some have speculated that she was pregnant at the time of the portrait, while others have claimed she was asthmatic," wrote Mervin and Prunhuber, "But no one has ever penetrated the mystery of her smile."

In 1516, da Vinci journeyed to France, to the court of Francis I, who cordially welcomed the artist and heaped him with honors. The artist brought with him the portrait, *La Gioconda,* for which the king paid him 4,000 gold ecus, an immense sum in those days. Three years later, da Vinci died, while his famous *Mona Lisa* remained at Fontainebleau for more than a century until Louis XIV took her to Versailles. After the French Revolution, the painting with "the irresistible enigmatic smile" found its final resting place on the walls of the Louvre.

On August 21, 1911, the artistic world was shocked by the news that the *Mona Lisa* had been stolen, but it was returned after several months. An Italian painter, employed by the museum, had walked off with the painting and tried to sell it in Italy. It now hangs as of old, one of the chief ornaments of the Louvre, and one of the most precious pictures in France.

SOURCES:

Mervin, Sabrina, and Carol Prunhuber. *Women: Around the World and Through the Ages.* Wilmington, DE: Atomium Books, 1990.

Delilah (1200–1000 BCE?)

Biblical woman. Name variations: Dalila. Delilah is portrayed in the Old Testament (Judges 16.4ff.) as the third romantic interest of the traditional Israelite hero, Samson.

It is possible, but unlikely, that the Biblical Delilah was a historical figure. As convention has it, she was a Philistine beauty from the Wadi Sorek (near modern Gaza) who attracted Samson's amorous attentions. According to our only source the Old Testament (*Judges* 16.4ff.), before meeting Delilah, Samson had already begun a deadly feud with the Philistines, Delilah's people. Seeking Samson's destruction, some Philistine leaders approached Delilah to enlist her in the cause of Samson's ruin. Convinced to betray Samson for a monetary reward, Delilah is said to have done everything within her wiles to bring about his fall. The element of the account that makes the story historically suspect are the three open betrayals of Samson that Delilah is said to

have arranged before her fourth attempt succeeded. Thus, Samson must be seen either as one of history's dimmer heroes, or as a figure whose portrayal was intended to provide a negative moral example about the dangers of chasing beautiful women.

In the first attempt, after Delilah asks Samson about the source of his strength, he replies that he can be successfully bound only by "seven fresh bowstrings," which, if discovered by his enemies, would lead to his destruction. Acting upon the information forwarded by Delilah, the Philistines attempt to trap Samson but fail. In the next attempt, Samson's enemies learn from Delilah that he could only be restrained by ropes that "had never been used." Acting on this information, again the Philistine's fail. After more of Delilah's inquiries (apparently made palatable by her charms), Samson then responds that he can only be imprisoned by a rope woven from seven locks of his own hair. When that attempt also fails, Delilah gears up once more, this time to be taken into Samson's confidence as he final-

Lisa del Giocondo, the inspiration for Leonardo da Vinci's Mona Lisa.

Delilah and
Samson.

ly reveals that he can only be overcome if his
hair is cut. (The belief in the magical potency of
hair was not unique to the Israelites; the Germans, for example, who settled in France during
the early medieval period long followed their
Merovingian monarchs because of the strength
represented in these "long-haired" kings.) The
truth thus revealed, the Philistines succeed: with
Samson asleep in Delilah's lap, a barber appears
to shave Samson, leaving him helpless.

Taking her blood money, Delilah then vili-
fies Samson before turning him over to his enemies. Laid low by his lust for women, Samson is thus enslaved by his enemies and
brought to Gaza, where he is put on public
display in the temple of the god Dagon. Praying for a modicum of revenge, Samson begs
for a return of his old strength, which God
grants him. Samson then kills himself and a
host of his enemies by pulling down, upon all,
the chief temple of Gaza.

The folktale elements of this story support
the ahistorical nature of the account. Available

evidence suggest that Delilah is most accurately
seen as an element in a morality tale meant to
warn men against beguiling sexuality.

William Greenwalt,
Associate Professor of Classical History,
Santa Clara University, Santa Clara, California

Delille, Henriette (1813–1862)

*African-American religious leader. Born a free Creole
of color in New Orleans, Louisiana, in 1813; died in
1862; youngest of three children of Jean Baptiste
Delille-Sarpy (a white creole) and his mistress Marie
Joseph "Pouponne" Dias (a free woman of color).*

So fair-skinned as to be mistaken for white
on census records, Henriette Delille seems to
have been "reared for *plaçage,* or for being the
kept woman of a wealthy man," writes Lester
Sullivan in *Notable Black American Women*;
she was given lessons in French literature,
dance, and music. But at age 11, Henriette entered a school for young girls run by the French
nun, Sister Saint **Marthe Fontier**, and became

deeply involved in charitable works. Delille eventually founded the Roman Catholic Sisters of the Holy Family, a society of free black women.

SUGGESTED READING:

Detiege, Sister Audrey Marie. *Henriette Delille: Free Woman of Color: Foundress of the Sisters of the Holy Family.* New Orleans, LA: Sisters of the Holy Family in New Orleans, 1976.

Hart, Sister Mary Francis. *Violets in the King's Garden: A History of the Sisters of the Holy Family of New Orleans.* New Orleans, LA: Sisters of the Holy Family in New Orleans, 1976.

Della Casa, Lisa (1919—)

Swiss lyric soprano. Born in Burgdorf near Berne, Switzerland, on February 2, 1919; studied with Margaret Haeser in Berne and Zurich; married Dragan Debeljevic, in 1947; children: one daughter.

Debuted as Cio-Cio San in Solothurn-Biel (1941); debuted as Zedenka in Salzburg (1947); debuted in Great Britain at Glyndebourne (1951); was a member of the Vienna State Opera (1947–73); debuted at the Metropolitan Opera (1953) and sang for 15 seasons until 1968.

Lisa Della Casa was born near Berne, Switzerland, on February 2, 1919. After studying with **Margaret Haeser**, she debuted as Cio-Cio San in 1941. Although she loved singing Italian opera, Della Casa was rarely cast in these roles. Instead, she sang Mozart more frequently, performing and recording Donna Elvira in *Don Giovanni*, the Countess in *Figaro*, and Fiordiligi in *Cosi fan tutte*. Somewhat of a Richard Strauss specialist, she performed Zedenka in *Arabella*, Ariadne in *Capriccio*, and Octavian, Sophie, and Marshallin in *Der Rosenkavalier*. She became the 20th century's acknowledged master interpreter in the title role of Strauss' *Arabella* and made complete recordings for Decca in 1957 and Deutsche Grammophon in 1963. Della Casa virtually owned the role of *Arabella* after she performed it for the first time.

Lisa Della Casa's lyric soprano was somewhat inconsistent. The upper notes were light and easy but the bottom of her range was weak and tinny. Her middle voice was never dependable or strong, even at the beginning of her career, and became weaker with the passage of time. Despite limited resources, she pushed her artistry to the utmost. At her best, her voice had a radiant quality that was nearly unmatched. Della Casa performed for the last time in 1974.

John Haag,
Athens, Georgia

Lisa Della Casa

della Rovere, Vittoria (d. 1694).

See Medici, Vittoria de.

della Scala, Beatrice (1340–1384)

Italian noblewoman. Name variations: Regina della Scala; Regina Visconti. Born Beatrice Regina della Scala in 1340 in Vicenza; died in June 1384 in Milan; daughter of Mastino II della Scala, count of Verona; married Bernarbò or Bernabo Visconti, lord of Milan, in August 1350; children: Marco (d. 1382); Ludovico (d. 1404); Carlo (d. 1404); *Thaddaea Visconti (d. 1381); *Virida Visconti (c. 1354–1414); *Catherine Visconti (c. 1360–1404); Rodolfo (d. 1389); Mastino (d. 1405); *Agnes Visconti (c. 1365–1391); Valentina Visconti (d. 1393); Antonia Visconti; Maddalena Visconti (d. 1404); *Elizabeth Visconti (d. 1432); Lucia Visconti; Anglesia Visconti.

Beatrice della Scala was born into the ruling family of Vicenza and Verona, the daughter of Count Mastino II of Verona. She was called Regina, the Latin word for queen, by her family because of her pride and assertiveness. As was usual for her time, Regina was married young, about age ten, though she did not live with her husband for several years. He was Bernabo Visconti, an Italian noble about 17 years her senior. The marriage was Count Mastino's attempt to secure the friendship of the powerful Visconti family, rulers of the Lombard region of northern Italy. His hopes were realized after 1354, when Bernabo became lord of Milan, making him one of the most powerful men in Italy.

Despite the difference in their ages, after Regina matured the marriage proved to be an excellent match. She had 15 children in their 34 years together. (Bernabo Visconti also boasted of at least 30 illegitimate children.) The couple shared similar interests in literature and the arts, and other characteristics as well. Like Bernabo, Regina was energetic, ambitious, and single-minded in her desire to create in Lombardy an ever larger and more prosperous state ruled by the Visconti. Regina contributed substantially to this common goal when, as Mastino's last surviving heir, she inherited Verona and Vicenza. The gain was not without a struggle, however; her illegitimate brothers claimed the cities for themselves and Regina and Bernabo were forced to attack and defeat them before adding the territories to the Visconti state.

There is considerable evidence of Bernabo's confidence in his young wife's administrative abilities. She advised him on matters of state, helped negotiate her children's marriages, and often accompanied him on his frequent military campaigns. Bernabo made her numerous land grants for her personal use and, in some cases, gave her authority over territories as well. One example is the territory of Reggio, which Bernabo acquired in 1371 and gave to Regina, who ruled it personally. She served as regent of Brescia for her son, and also ruled the cities of Parmigiana and Lunigiana. In addition, Regina sought to remedy the destruction of earlier warfare on the cities of Lombardy, and used her personal fortune to purchase and redevelop devastated areas, including reclaiming wastelands. She sought to help the poor in other ways as well, giving generously to charities and religious foundations in Milan.

Lady Regina died suddenly of a fever in June 1384 while preparing to join her husband on yet another campaign. She was 44 years old.

SOURCES:

de Mesquita, D.M. Bueno. *Giangaleazzo Visconti, Duke of Milan.* Cambridge: Cambridge University Press, 1941.

Muir, Dorothy. *A History of Milan Under the Visconti.* London: Methuen, 1924.

Laura York,
Riverside, California

della Scala, Costanza.
See Este, Costanza d'.

della Scala, Regina (1340–1384).
See della Scala, Beatrice.

della Scala, Verde.
See Este, Verde d'.

del Maino, Agnes (fl. 1420s)

*Milanese woman. Flourished in the 1420s; mistress of Filippo Maria Visconti (1392–1447), duke of Milan (r. 1402–1447); children: (with Filippo) *Bianca Maria Visconti (1423–1470). Filippo Visconti was married to Maria of Savoy.*

Deloria, Ella (1888–1971)

Yankton (Ihanktonwan) Sioux (Dakota) who was a linguist and ethnologist. Name variations: Anpetu Waste Win, meaning "Beautiful Day Woman," to commemorate the blizzard that raged on the day of her birth. Born Ella Carla Deloria on January 30, 1888, on the Yankton Sioux reservation in South Dakota; died on February 12, 1971, in South Dakota; first of four children of Philip Deloria (an Episcopal priest also known as Tipi Sapa or "Black Lodge" of Yankton-French descent) and Mary (Sully) Deloria of Yankton-Irish descent; aunt of the noted writer Vine Deloria, Jr., author of Custer Died for Your Sins; *attended St. Elizabeth's Mission School, Wakpala, South Dakota, and All Saint's School, Sioux Falls, South Dakota; attended University of Chicago, 1910–11, Oberlin College, 1911–13, Columbia University, 1913–15, where she received her B.S., 1915.*

Began association with noted anthropologist, Dr. Franz Boas, and worked with him until his death in 1942; awarded Indian Achievement Medal (1943).

Selected publications: "Sun Dance of the Oglala Sioux" in Journal of American Folklore *(1929);* Dakota Texts *(1932); (with Boas)* Dakota Grammar *(1941);* Speaking of Indians, *(1944).* Waterlily, *a novel about the life of a Teton Sioux woman, was written in the early 1940s and published posthumously (1988).*

Ella Deloria's research is considered some of the best ever published on her native Sioux (Dakota) culture. Her linguistic translations, including a bilingual collection of Sioux tales, gives us a description of Dakota life unparalleled by any other anthropologist. Particularly important in Deloria's research is her accurate portrayal of native women, a subject most often misinterpreted by other scholars. As a tribal member and as a woman, she had a personal as well as intellectual interest in interpreting native life to white society.

Deloria was born on the Yankton Sioux reservation in South Dakota, the eldest of four children. Her family moved to the Standing Rock Reservation when her father, Philip Deloria (Tipi Sapa), was assigned to St. Elizabeth's Mission as a deacon of the Episcopal Church. He was ordained to the priesthood in 1892. Though Deloria and her siblings were reared in the Christian faith, they were never expected to disregard their Sioux culture and language with which they lived.

An avid and serious student, Deloria graduated from New York's Columbia University with a B.S. in 1915. She returned to South Dakota and took a series of teaching assignments, none of which utilized her academic skills as much as she wished. But Deloria was dedicated to her family, in particular to her father who suffered from a long illness. A lifetime of correspondence reveals that she was often torn between her obligation to her family and her commitment to her work.

While attending Columbia, she had attracted the attention of Franz Boas, who was considered by academics as the dean of anthropologists and a leader in the study of Native American languages. In 1927, Boas asked her to translate and edit texts written in her native Sioux. Deloria was delighted with her new assignment for which she gathered additional stories and legends, and the resulting "Sun Dance of the Oglala Sioux" was published in *Journal of American Folklore* in 1929.

Deloria would continue her association with Boas until his death in 1942. Whenever possible, she devoted herself to field research, often traveling between the Dakota reservations to interview elders on traditional life. She sent the fieldwork, with translations, to Boas and, after his death, to *Ruth Benedict, another noted anthropologist. In 1932, the material gathered from these research trips was published as *Dakota Texts*. Boas and Deloria collaborated on *Dakota Grammar*, published in 1941. *Speaking of Indians*, an intimate and accurate portrait of native culture, particularly Sioux, was published in 1944.

For the rest of her life, Deloria devoted herself to writing and lecturing, most often in efforts to insure that her native Dakota would not fade into oblivion as had many native languages. At the time of her death, she was working on a Dakota dictionary. Her notes exist as the "Ella C. Deloria Project" at the University of South Dakota.

SOURCES:

Bataille, Gretchen, ed. *Native American Women: A Biographical Dictionary*. NY: Garland, 1993.

Murray, Janette K. *Ella Deloria: A Biographical Sketch and Literary Analysis*. Phd. dissertation: University of North Dakota, 1974.

Deborah Jones, freelance writer, Studio City, California

Delorme, Marion (c. 1613–1650)

Famous French courtesan at the time of Louis XIII. Name variations: de Lorme. Born near Champaubert, France, around 1613 (some sources cite 1611); death date established as 1650; daughter of Jean de Lou, sieur de L'Orme (president of the Treasurers of France in Champagne) and **Marie Chastelain***; possibly married Henri Coiffier de Ruzé, marquis de Cinq-Mars.*

The legendary courtesan Marion Delorme was possibly lured into the profession by the epicurean and atheist Jacques Vallée Desbarreaux. She soon left him, however, for the popular and successful Henri Coiffier de Ruzé, marquis de Cinq-Mars, whom she may have secretly married. (There was also a rumor about a later marriage to an English lord.) Delorme presided over one of the most famous salons of 17th-century Parisian society. She was the friend of *Ninon de Lenclos.

After Cinq-Mars was executed for conspiring against Cardinal Richelieu, Delorme purportedly entertained a who's who of lovers, including Saint-Évremond, the comte de Gramont, and even Cardinal Richelieu. In 1650, she was arrested under the orders of Cardinal Jules Mazarin for her complicity in the Fronde and was found dead by officers. This is thought, however, to have been a ruse. She is even said to have lived to the age of 137 years, spending her last years in poverty. A number of authors used her story for subject matter, including Alfred de Vigny in the novel *Cinq Mars* (1826), Victor Hugo in the play *Marion Delorme* (1831), Edward Bulwer-Lytton in *Richelieu* (1839), and G. Bottesini in an opera of the same name.

Delphine of Puimichel.

See Women Prophets and Visionaries in France at the End of the Middle Ages.

Del Rio, Dolores (1905–1983)

Mexican film actress of extraordinary versatility who charmed her audiences for better than half a

century. Pronunciation: doh-LOH-res del-REE-oh. Born Lolita Dolores Asunsolo y Martinez on August 3, 1905, in Durango, Mexico; died in April 1983; daughter of Jesus (a bank president and large landowner) and Antonia (Lopez Negrete) Asunsolo (a highly placed noblewoman who could trace her lineage to the Toltecs); married Jaime Martinez del Rio (scion of the one of the richest families in Mexico), in 1921 (died 1928); married Cedric Gibbons, in 1930 (divorced, January 1941); married Lewis Riley, in 1959; children: none.

Born into an extremely wealthy family in one of the poorest states of northwestern Mexico; moved to Mexico City (1910) to avoid the ravages of Pancho Villa's army and was educated in a prestigious Catholic academy; visited Europe with her family and was presented to the king of Spain (1919); married at age 15 (1921); with husband, spent more time in Paris and U.S. than in Mexico; cast in minor roles in several films; having recently been widowed, starred in a critically important film, Evangeline *(1929), the beginning of an impressive career in Hollywood that lasted throughout the 1930s and early 1940s; following a much-publicized falling-out with lover Orson Welles, returned to Mexico to work with the film industry there (1943); periodically returned to work in Hollywood films but made her permanent home in Mexico; became a figure of great repute, not just in film but on stage, where she was an unofficial godmother for a new generation of Mexican actors and actresses.*

Filmography: Joanna *(1925);* High Steppers *(1926);* The Whole Town's Talking *(1926);* Pals First *(1926);* What Price Glory? *(1926);* Resurrection *(1927);* The Loves of Carmen *(1927);* The Gateway of the Moon *(1928);* No Other Woman *(1928);* The Red Dance *(1928);* Revenge *(1928);* Ramona *(1928);* The Trail of '98 *(1929);* Evangeline *(U.A., 1929);* The Bad One *(1930);* The Girl of the Rio *(1932);* Bird of Paradise *(1932);* Flying Down to Rio *(1933);* Wonder Bar *(WB, 1934);* Madame Du Barry *(WB, 1934);* In Caliente *(1935);* I Live for Love *(WB, 1935);* Widow from Monte Carlo *(WB, 1936);* Accused *(UA, England, 1936);* Devil's Playground *(1937);* Lancer Spy *(1937);* International Settlement *(1938);* The Man from Dakota *(1940);* Journey into Fear *(1942);* Flor Silvestre *(Mexico, 1943);* Maria Candelaria *("Portrait of Maria," Mexico, 1943);* Bugambilia *(Mexico, 1944);* Los Abandonadas *(Mexico, 1944);* La Otra *(Mexico, 1946);* The Fugitive *(1947);* Historia de una Mala Mujer *(Argentina, 1948);* Dona Perfecta *(Mexico, 1950);* La Cucaracha *(Mexico, 1958);* Flaming Star *(U.S., 1960);* Cheyenne Autumn *(U.S., 1964);* C'era

Una Volta *("More Than a Miracle," Italian, 1967);* Rio Blanco *(1967);* The Children of Sanchez *(1978).*

Durango is a dry, dusty Mexican state noted chiefly for its harsh physical conditions and for the self-reliance of its people. Ironically, it was precisely in this rough environment that Dolores Del Rio, perhaps the brightest flower in 20th-century Mexican cinema, was born and spent her earliest years.

Young Dolores came from a privileged background. Her father was the president of the Bank of Durango and one of the state's wealthiest landowners. In the nearly feudal atmosphere prevalent at the time, Dolores could expect to enjoy the life of a princess with all manner of luxuries and attention just for the asking. That few other children could aspire to such a life, however, was something that the poor of the state found increasingly hard to bear.

In 1910, when revolution swept the country, Durango went over wholeheartedly to the radical guerrilla fighters of Pancho Villa. Dolores' family fled their properties, never to return. Instead of being brought up in the Durango hinterland, therefore, she was raised in an affluent suburb of Mexico City. In many ways, it was the best thing that happened to her, for now she had the benefits of living in a cosmopolitan city with its many sights and sounds and foreign residents.

Del Rio received her education at the French convent of Saint Joseph in Mexico City. All her teachers agreed that she was an exceptionally lovely child with a natural talent for singing and dancing. She captivated all around her. In 1919, while on a European tour with her family, she was presented to the king of Spain who had much the same reaction.

Upon her return to Mexico, she made the acquaintance of Jaime Martinez del Rio, scion of one of the country's oldest families. In 1921, they married. The 15-year-old bride then settled down with her husband to pursue a pampered and idle existence on his family's immense ranch. For any other young upper-class Mexican woman this might have been the end of the story, but Del Rio had no intention of limiting herself to tea parties, dancing, and bearing children. She was restless for a different kind of life.

About that time, a noted American film director, Edwin Carewe, came to Mexico City with his new bride to spend a few days of their honeymoon. The young couple made the rounds in cultural and diplomatic circles and, in the course of one such engagement, met the Del

Dolores
Del
Rio

Rios, who were of a similar age and disposition. Carewe was at once struck by the beauty and poise of Dolores. Half smiling but still very serious, he asked her whether she had ever considered a career in movies. In fact, in more whimsical moments, she *had* considered it, but she also knew that such a course presented some deep problems for someone of her class. Carewe shrewdly suggested that he work on the matter through Jaime. The latter had often thought of himself as a writer—and now, as a potential screenwriter. Jaime visited Hollywood at

Carewe's invitation in early 1925, and a few weeks later sent for Dolores. Her parents, with tears in their eyes, begged her not to go, weeping even at the Mexico City train station. For her part, Del Rio never looked back.

In truth, Dolores Del Rio had had little interest in the vagaries of the idle rich. She wanted a career that would demonstrate her talent, imagination, and scope. Hollywood offered this and more. In the mid-1920s, Tinsel Town was still only a small community hidden among the citrus groves of Southern California, but it nonetheless possessed great allure for the uninitiated. After all, thousands of fans crowded movie theaters every week to marvel at the likes of Douglas Fairbanks, *Gloria Swanson, *Mary Pickford, and John Gilbert. Hundreds of would-be actors and actresses were also arriving every week.

I thought she was the most beautiful woman I had ever seen. I used to follow her around—at a discreet distance, of course—just to admire her.

—Orson Welles

Del Rio showed much of the same naivete as all the rest. In the mid-1920s, film audiences were much attracted to the Latin lover stereotype, as with Ramon Novarro and Rudolph Valentino; could not she be the female Valentino? With this thought in mind, she signed a personal contract with Carewe and was rushed into the project that he was then filming at Burbank. In the film, *Joanna* (1925), Del Rio appeared as a society vamp who systematically mistreated the lily-white heroine. Greatly excited about this first experience before the camera, she urged friends and relatives to attend the film's premiere. She sat there horrified as she slowly learned that, after the ravages of the cutting room, her role had been reduced to a shadow of what she expected. The sensitive young woman nearly abandoned her career ambitions right then and there; it took all of Carewe's power of persuasion to convince her to stay.

He had less luck with her husband. Jaime, who had yet to find a screenwriting niche in Hollywood, was growing increasingly frustrated. As he struggled to define his identity in this environment, however, Dolores had already defined her own. Carewe could take much responsibility for this. Still enthralled with his discovery, he carefully molded and guided her through the various phases and contours of acting. He secured an interpreter for her and arranged for her to receive English lessons. She soon lost all of her initial roughness. Though her next few roles were certainly minor, her exotic beauty gained her considerable attention—and more and more, so did her acting skills. The gap between the reputation that she enjoyed and that of her husband widened.

Del Rio attained full-fledged star status in 1928 with the release of the film *Ramona*. This love story of Old California, based on *Helen Hunt Jackson*'s popular novel, featured Warner Baxter as Alessandro and Dolores in the title role as the tragic Spanish-Native American maiden. The public's reaction was extremely positive. Hollywood had found the perfect actress for the perfect role and the mass of filmgoers saw it immediately. Del Rio soon became the object of idolatrous fan mail. Film executives from every studio made offers. The upward shift that all this implied spelled the end for her marriage. Desperate for any work, Jaime had taken a writing position in New York, and in his absence Dolores filed for divorce. He died soon after in Berlin, purportedly of blood poisoning, though the fan magazines universally ascribed his death to a broken heart.

Though her personal life remained unsettled, Del Rio's film career blossomed. In 1929, she starred for United Artists in *Evangeline*, which she later referred to as her "finest screen role and most pretentious picture." The film was one of Hollywood's first productions to boast some sound sequences, and Del Rio actually sang a French chansonette and the title tune, which had been composed by Al Jolson. In the course of the film, she also aged from a young maiden to an elderly Sister of Mercy. In all, the film gave her room to display a great range of talents. The critics responded well (though many did fault her singing), and the public was again enthusiastic.

In the wake of her success with *Evangeline*, Del Rio made a surprising move. She broke with her longtime associate, Edwin Carewe, and signed a new agreement, which included a $9,000 weekly salary, with United Artists. Only weeks before, the fan magazines had linked Del Rio romantically with Carewe, who now withdrew, deeply hurt, another victim, so they said, of her ambitions. He died ten years later, a suicide.

In spite of the various canards, Del Rio's career did not suffer from these tribulations. In fact, she seemed to gain in popularity during times of personal conflict. In 1930, she met Cedric Gibbons, the shy, gentlemanly art director and set designer at MGM studios. They became involved very quickly, and, within just a few weeks, they wed in Santa Barbara.

Gibbons recognized something in Del Rio that her fans should have seen but did not: that despite being a part of the Hollywood star system, she was still fundamentally an aristocratic Latin with all of the prejudices and virtues associated with that class. Though flirtatious and sexy on screen and in front of the press, in her personal life she set a high value on decorum. These contradictions were often difficult for her to deal with. In the end, the pressures of her public image and the reality of her conservative, overly controlled private life were building in the weeks following her return from her honeymoon. In 1931, she suffered a nervous breakdown. This might have been the end for Del Rio, for Hollywood was notoriously fickle in such matters. Local wags simply passed her off as another spoiled has-been, but her husband stood loyally by her and nursed her back to health. By the end of the year, she had recovered sufficiently to resume her acting career.

In 1932, she starred in *Bird of Paradise*, a David O. Selznick production with a South Seas setting. Even the director, King Vidor, recognized that the story-line was trite, but Selznick insisted that Dolores Del Rio was too valuable an asset not to be used in it. "I don't care what story you use," he reportedly said, "as long as Del Rio jumps into a flaming volcano at the finish." Again the audiences loved what they saw. They were just as enchanted a year later when she appeared in a romantic role in the classic *Flying Down to Rio*, which also featured the first teaming of Fred Astaire and *Ginger Rogers.

Over the next four years, Del Rio starred in five films—*Wonder Bar* (1934), *Madame Du Barry* (1934), *I Live for Love* (1935), *Widow from Monte Carlo* (1936), and *Accused* (1936). The first four of these were made for Warner Bros. and the final picture for United Artists in England. These were not banner years for Del Rio, though she gave solid performances in all these films. Warner Bros. made little effort to develop her screen persona beyond what Carewe had done. And the pattern remained the same over the next three years when she worked for Columbia and for 20th Century-Fox.

From the movie The Fugitive, *starring Dolores Del Rio and Henry Fonda.*

Del Rio was aware of the problem; she hired a new drama coach and associated herself with the stage actors she had admired from a distance. But the good roles in film simply failed to materialize. Her wounded pride prevented her from accepting scripts that might tarnish her image any further (her 1940 part in *The Man from Dakota* was in every way a low point). During this period of decline, her second marriage fell apart. She divorced Gibbons, almost without an explanation, in January 1941.

Still without a clear direction in her work, Del Rio became the offscreen love interest of Orson Welles, ten years her junior and at that time the most controversial actor-filmmaker in Hollywood. Their romance was evidently ardent, though her studied discretion kept her from revealing much of anything to the press. Yet, when he abruptly left her for the much-younger *Rita Hayworth, the much-wounded Del Rio made a decision that scarcely hid her disappointment and anger. In carefully worded language, she announced that she was returning to her native country: "I wish to choose my own stories, my own director, and cameraman. I can accomplish this better in Mexico." She thus left the glitter of Hollywood behind, though she kept the door open in many ways; she had invested heavily in real estate and still owned hundreds of acres in and around Los Angeles, and she knew every important director and producer in the city.

In Mexico, Del Rio found much of what she had missed in the United States. There the critics treated her with tremendous respect. To them, she was less exotic than she was distinguished, and in this, her beauty was almost incidental. The Mexican public adored her. Del Rio also now contributed in a wide-ranging way to her art by working as producer, planner, adviser, and

unofficial godmother to the national film industry. Over the next three years, she won two Ariel Awards (the Mexican equivalent of the Oscar) and made five Spanish-language movies, including the famed *Maria Candelaria*. All were wildly successful on the Latin American film circuit. Now Del Rio could boast of being much more than a Hollywood creation; she could claim to be the ambassador of Mexican film to the world of cinema in general. She also realized a lifelong ambition by becoming a stage actress of much repute in Mexico.

Hollywood periodically beckoned. In 1947, John Ford paired her with Henry Fonda in *The Fugitive*, a suspenseful film with a spiritual theme shot in Mexico. During the McCarthyist period, Del Rio returned several times to the States, but, in spite of her strong anti-communist credentials, she never landed the right part. She made a curious comeback in the early 1960s when she played Elvis Presley's mother in the unusual film *Flaming Star*, a western "with a conscience." In the interim, she had made dramatic presentations on the Mexican and U.S. stage, guest-starred in television dramas, and continued her excellent work in Mexican film (winning several more Ariels). She opened a fully staffed nursery for the children of Mexican film actresses. (Having never had children of her own, she regarded her work with this nursery as especially fulfilling.)

In 1959, Del Rio remarried. The groom was Lewis A. Riley, an American film producer who had resided in Mexico for over 20 years. Unlike her previous marriages, this one endured and by all accounts was remarkably successful. Riley's appreciation of his wife's place in modern Mexican culture was well matched by her respect for his talents in film production.

Del Rio maintained a heavy work schedule well into her 70s. She appeared as the mother of Omar Sharif in Carlo Ponti's *C'era Una Volta* (1967) and eleven years later she starred with Anthony Quinn and ❧ Katy Jurado in *The Children of Sanchez*. This was to be her last film. She died in April 1983.

Dolores Del Rio was a key figure in modern cinema. By giving depth to the image of the Latin American woman, she also made it more human, more approachable, and, at the same time, more attractive. Her trailblazing opened the door for other Latin women seeking to explore the ever-changing world of film.

SOURCES:

King, John. *Magical Reels: A History of Cinema in Latin America.* Verso, 1990.

❧▸ Jurado, Katy (1927—)

Mexican-American actress. Born Maria Cristina Jurado Garcia on January 16, 1927, in Guadalajara, Mexico; married Ernest Borgnine, in 1959 (divorced 1964).

Following a Mexican film career, Katy Jurado moved to Los Angeles as a columnist for Mexican publications. Her acting credits include *High Noon* (1952), *Trapeze* (1956), *The Man from Del Rio* (1956), *One-Eyed Jacks* (1961), *Barabbas* (1961), *The Children of Sanchez* (1968), and *Under the Volcano* (1984). She was nominated for an Academy Award for Best Supporting Actress for her performance in *Broken Lance* (1954).

Parish, James Robert. *The Hollywood Beauties*. Arlington House, 1978.

SUGGESTED READING:

Michael, Paul, ed. *Movie Greats*. CT: Garland, 1969.

Thomas Whigham, Associate Professor of History, University of Georgia, Athens, Georgia

de Maintenon, Françoise (1635–1719).

See Maintenon, Françoise d'Aubigné, Marquise de.

Demandols de La Palud, Madeleine.

See French "Witches."

de Marillac, Louise (1591–1660).

See Marillac, Louise de.

de Martinez, Maria Cadilla (1886–1951).

See Cadilla de Martínez, Maria.

Dembo, Tamara (1902–1993)

Russian-born American psychologist, pioneer of psychological field theory and an important theorist in rehabilitation psychology, who developed a method of studying anger that emphasized the importance of understanding the context of each situation. Born in Baku, Azerbaijan, on May 28, 1902; died in Worcester, Massachusetts, on October 17, 1993; University of Berlin, doctorate in psychology, 1930; never married.

Came to the U.S. to escape Nazism; taught and carried out research work at a number of American universities including Harvard, spending the final decades of her productive career at Clark University.

Born into a prosperous Russian-Jewish family in Baku, Azerbaijan, in 1902, Tamara Dembo was diagnosed with a heart murmur as a young child. As a result, she spent many of her early years confined to her home and often to her bed. The irony is that she lived to be over 90 years of age and became one of the world's leading experts on the psychological problems of the handicapped. The experience of being treated as an invalid left an indelible mark on Dembo, causing her to accentuate the positive aspects in her own situation and the situations of others with various afflictions and handicaps. Among her earliest significant contributions to psychological theory was the idea of "asset-mindedness," the concept that after suffering serious injury some individuals were able to successfully rehabilitate themselves by focusing on the strengths they still possessed rather than on the problems and disabilities that set them apart from other human beings and from their earlier lives.

Tamara Dembo grew up in very comfortable circumstances in St. Petersburg (which became Petrograd in 1914 and Leningrad in 1924), but her world was radically transformed by the Bolshevik Revolution of 1917. Civil war, famine, and increasing political repression made a normal life impossible for young Dembo, who left Russia never to return in the mid-1920s. Moving to Berlin, which had a large community of Russian emigrés, she enrolled as a psychology student at the University of Berlin. There, Dembo was fortunate to study with Kurt Koffka, Wolfgang Köhler, Kurt Lewin, and Max Wertheimer, professors who were making fundamental investigations in the emerging discipline of Gestalt psychology. Dembo was able to thrive intellectually in such an exciting atmosphere and in 1930 was awarded her doctorate in psychology by the University of Berlin. Within a year of graduation, in 1931 she published a classic article on the dynamics of anger. This article helped to advance research in the field, prompting Kurt Lewin to redirect his analyses of personal activities from the individuals themselves to the situations in which they were involved. More than a half-century after its publication, Dembo's study of anger continued to stimulate and enrich research into this area of investigation.

Dembo, who was frustrated professionally and increasingly alarmed by the political situation in Berlin, decided to immigrate to the U.S. to continue her career, several years before Adolf Hitler and his Nazi movement seized power in Germany. Energetic and brilliant, the refugee scholar was able to find her first position at Smith College as a research associate of one of her former Berlin mentors, Kurt Koffka. For the next decade, she found work at Worcester State Hospital, Cornell University, and the University of Iowa. Her publications continued to emphasize the idea that human behavior was largely determined by current situations rather than past history. In 1941, she was a co-author with Kurt Lewin and Roger Barker of an important study, *Frustration and Regression: An Experiment with Young Children*.

By 1945, Dembo had become director of a research project at Stanford University studying the best ways in which to assist in the psychological rehabilitation of people who had lost limbs or been blinded. Working with **Gloria Ladieu Leviton** and **Beatrice Wright**, Dembo created a new theoretical understanding of how people adjust to misfortune, focusing on the notion of devaluation that took place when misfortune struck. Dembo's pioneering research in rehabilitation psychology helped change attitudes toward the handicapped. At the time of her work in the 1940s and 1950s, most people regarded a person without legs as being profoundly handicapped. Not Dembo, who simply observed an individual who could not get upstairs. It was the stairs that were handicapping the person, and thus she became a forceful advocate for ramps and elevators, instructing an entire generation that the disabilities were in the environment rather than in the persons.

After teaching and carrying out further research projects at the New School for Social Research and at Harvard, Tamara Dembo accepted an offer in 1953 from Clark University to become part of a research team developing new methods for families to cope with the problems of children with cerebral palsy. After nearly a decade of intensive work, Dembo's team published a detailed report on their findings, which many observers regarded as opening up new grounds of psychological terrain. Dembo remained at Clark for the rest of her life, living on campus and making important research contributions. Always eager to share her rich store of life experiences, she became a cherished member of the Clark academic community. Her concept of "asset-mindedness" would be a powerful inspiration to teachers, researchers, and millions of handicapped individuals the world over.

In the final decades of her life, Dembo warned of the dangers the psychological profession faced due to its having helped to create and maintain relationships of social domination in the contemporary world. She hoped that in a future world that was more democratic and humane, the unequal relationship between experimenter and subject in psychological research would be reduced and even eliminated. Recalling the horrors she had personally lived through both in Russia and Germany, she repeatedly warned her colleagues of the dangers of establishing an uncritical and dependent relationship with the military, particularly in a democracy. Although she had lost friends and family to Stalin's gulag and the Nazi Holocaust, Tamara Dembo remained to the end of her life an essential optimist, convinced that human beings can create situations of trust and profound respect for one another. Despite her failing health, she continued to the last years of her life to conduct a series of exciting *domashnye seminary* (home seminars), inspiring and sharpening the professional skills of young students and mature colleagues alike. Much loved and highly respected, Tamara Dembo died in Worcester, Massachusetts, on October 17, 1993.

SOURCES:
Kennedy, Randy. "Tamara Dembo, 91, Gestalt Psychologist Who Studied Anger," in *The New York Times Biographical Service.* October 1993, p. 1438.
Rivera, Joseph de. "Tamara Dembo (1902–1993)," *American Psychologist.* Vol. 50, no. 5. May 1995, p. 386.
Rosa, Alberto and James V. Wertsch. "Tamara Dembo and Her Work: An Introduction," in *Journal of Russian and East European Psychology.* Vol. 31, no. 6. November–December 1993, pp. 5–13.
Wertsch, James V. "In Memoriam," in *Journal of Russian and East European Psychology.* Vol. 31, no. 6. November–December 1993, pp. 3–4.

John Haag, Associate Professor of History, University of Georgia, Athens, Georgia

de Medici.

See Medici, de.

Demel, Anna (1872–1956)

Austrian proprietor of Vienna's world-famous "Demel's" pastry shop. Born in Vienna, Austria, on March 4, 1872; died in Vienna on November 7, 1956; married Karl Demel.

For more than half a century, Anna Demel reigned over one of traditional Vienna's most beloved sites of intellectual exchange, the famous "Ch. Demel's Söhne, k.k. Hofzuckerbäcker und Hoflieferant," a pastry shop whose exquisite creations were enjoyed not only by ordinary mortals but also by the exalted nobility who resided a stone's throw down the street in the vast Hofburg complex, the Imperial Palaces of the Habsburg dynasty. Even the collapse of the Austro-Hungarian monarchy in 1918 did not dim the luster of Demel's. Pastries, coffee and sandwiches were served there in good times and bad in a leisurely spirit that seemingly refused to accept most of the changes ushered in by a 20th century that often treated Vienna and traditional Austria in a brutal fashion. Owned by her husband Karl Demel's family since 1857 "*der Demel,*" as the shop is known affectionately to native Viennese, has been situated for generations in the Kohlmarkt, one of Vienna's most fashionable streets.

A Viennese institution by the closing decades of the 19th century, the unequaled quality of Demel's pastries earned it a commanding position in the highly competitive world of Vienna's pastry-cooks by achieving the signal distinction of being chosen as Court Pastry Baker, *Hoflieferant,* "by appointment to his Imperial and Royal Majesty Emperor Franz Josef I." For more than a century, Vienna's "best society" has met there to chatter, exchange the latest gossip while consuming immense quantities of delectable pastries washed down with various types of coffee. In a hectic and unstable world, Demel's has come to signify an unchanging world of tradition, perhaps best described by the late great Viennese cabaret artist Helmut Qualtinger in his song "Die Demelinerinnen" ("Demel's Waitresses"):

Solang wir da sind, ist ka Not. (As long as we're here, there will be no troubles.)
Ist fast all's im rechten Lot. (Almost everything will work out well.)
Wenn wir mal nimmer da sind, (When one day we are gone,)
ist die alte Zeit erst tot. (Only then will the good old days have died.)

SOURCES:

Ackerl, Isabella, and Friedrich Weissensteiner. *Österreichisches Personenlexikon.* Vienna: Verlag Carl Ueberreuter, 1992.

"Anna Demel 80 Jahre alt," in *Neues Österreich.* March 2, 1952.

Berzeviczy-Pallavicini, Federico von. *Die k.k. Hofzuckerbäckerei Demel: Ein Wiener Märchen.* Edited by Christian Brandstätter. Vienna: Molden Edition Graphische Kunst, 1976.

Eidlitz, Johannes. "Der Demel—altbacken?," in *profil: Das unabhängige Magazin Österreichs.* Vol. 10, no. 4. January 23, 1979, p.48.

John Haag,
Athens, Georgia

de Mello, Theresa (1913–1997)

*Princess of Hohenzollern. Born Theresa Lisboa Figueria de Mello on June 10, 1913, in Rome, Italy; died on March 30, 1997, in Madrid, Spain; daughter of Jeronymo de Avellar Figueira de Mello and Candida Riberia Lisboa; married Andres Bolton, on July 3, 1936 (divorced 1956); married Nicholas (1903–1978), prince of Hohenzollern and son of *Marie of Rumania, on June 13, 1967.*

de Méricourt, Théroigne (1762–1817).

See Théroigne de Méricourt, Anne-Josèphe.

de Merode, Cleo (1875–1966).

See Mérode, Cléo de.

Demessieux, Jeanne (1921–1968)

French composer, organist and pianist, who was the first woman to play the organ in Westminster Abbey. Born in Montpellier, France, on February 14, 1921; died in Paris on November 11, 1968; studied with Magda Tagliaferro, Jean and Noël Gallon, and Marcel Dupré at the Paris Conservatoire, graduating with distinction in 1941.

Served as organist at Saint-Ésprit Church in Paris (1933–62); appointed professor at Liège Conservatoire in Liege, Belgium (1948); enjoyed an artistically triumphant tour of the U.S. (1953); was the first woman to play the organ in Westminster Abbey, London.

French organists have dominated both performance and composition for the venerable instrument since the 19th century. Until the appearance of Jeanne Demessieux in the 1940s, however, the playing of the organ was largely a male preserve. Demessieux's talents as performer on, and composer for, the instrument could not be argued away, and by the 1950s she had become one of the undisputed masters of the field. A child prodigy, she began to perform at the services in the Saint-Ésprit Church in Paris before her 12th birthday, a position she was to hold for almost three decades. Her teachers at the Paris Conservatory included the legendary organist Marcel Dupré and the great pianist *Magda Tagliaferro. While there, Demessieux won first prize in harmony in 1937, in piano in 1938, and in fugue and counterpoint in 1940. Her first public recital was at the Salle Pleyel in Paris in 1946.

Demessieux began to concertize extensively in 1947 before becoming a professor of organ at Liège Conservatory. Most of her compositions were for the organ, and they included a set of 12 *Chorales and Preludes, Twelve Choral Preludes on Gregorian Themes* and an impressive *Te Deum* that has been recorded. Demessieux also composed choral music, chamber music and a *Poem for Organ and Orchestra,* which was published in Paris by Durand in 1952. Only 47 when she died, Jeanne Demessieux had not yet reached her zenith; nonetheless, few in the world had ever possessed her prodigious technique.

John Haag,
Athens, Georgia

de Mille, Agnes (1905–1993)

Dancer, choreographer, author, lecturer, and pioneer in the inclusion of American themes, gesture, and body language into classical ballet and the incorporation of classical ballet into musical comedy, whose dances for the Broadway show Oklahoma! *revolutionized the American musical. Name variations: de Mille, De Mille, DeMille. Born Agnes George de Mille in New York City on September 18, 1905 (and not in 1908 or 1909, as occasionally found); died of a stroke in her Greenwich Village, New York, apartment on October 7, 1993; daughter of William Churchill de Mille and Anna Angela (George) de Mille; educated in Hollywood, California, and at University of Califor-*

nia at Los Angeles (UCLA); studied ballet under Theodore Kosloff, a former member of the Moscow Imperial Theater, and later, in London, under Marie Rambert and Tamara Karsavina; made her debut in 1916; married Lieutenant Walter Prude of the Army Air Corps, on June 14, 1943; children: one son, Jonathan.

Awards: graduated with honors from the University of California cum laude; New York Critics Prize (1942–46); Donaldson Award (1943–47); Mademoiselle Merit Award (1944); named American Woman of the Year by the American Newspaper Woman's Guild (1946); Lord and Taylor Award (1947); Antoinette Perry ("Tony") award (1947, 1962); Dancing Masters Award of Merit (1950); Dance Magazine Award (1957); Capezio Award (1966); first president of the Society for Stage Directors and Choreographers (1965–66); elected to the Theater Hall of Fame (1973); Agnes de Mille Theater at the North Carolina School of the Arts at Winston-Salem named in her honor (1975); Handel Medallion (1976); Commonwealth Award in Dramatic Arts (1980); Kennedy Center Career Achievement Award (1980); National Medal of the Arts (1986). Honorary Doctorates in Letters from Mills College (1952), Smith College, (1954) Western College (1955), Hood College (1957), Northwestern University (1960), Goucher College and Nasson College (1961), Clark University (1962), UCLA (1964), Franklin and Marshall College (1965), Western Michigan University (1967); L.H.D., Dartmouth College (1974), Duke University (1975), the University of North Carolina (1980), and New York University (1981).

Made first appearance in her father's production The Ragamuffin (1916), first New York appearance in Mozart's La Finta Giardiniera (1927); concert debut at the Guild Theater (1928); appeared with the Grand Street Follies (1928); choreographed her first ballet, Black Ritual (1940); toured with the Agnes de Mille Dance Theater (1953–54); appeared at Covent Garden, London, in Three Virgins and the Devil and Rodeo (1955); Omnibus lectures and ballets (1956–57); appeared in Conversations about the Dance at the Hunter College Playhouse (Nov. 3, 1974 and 1975); performed with the Royal Winnipeg Ballet in her own ballet The Rehearsal (Hunter College, N.Y., Oct., 1965) and choreographed The Bitter Weird for the same company.

Choreographed: the revival of the 1864 musical The Black Crook (1929); (film) Romeo and Juliet (1935); (musical) Hooray for What (1937); (musical) Swingin' the Dream (1939); (ballet) Black Ritual (1940); (musical) Drums Sound in Hackensack (1941);

(ballet) Three Virgins and a Devil (1941); (ballet) Rodeo (1942); (musical) Oklahoma! and One Touch of Venus (both 1943); (ballet) Tally Ho; (musical) Bloomer Girl (1944); (musical) Carousel (1945); (musical) Brigadoon (1947); (musical) Allegro (also directed, 1947); (ballet) Fall River Legend (1948); (and directed ballet) Rape of Lucrecia (1949); (musical) Gentlemen Prefer Blondes (1949); (directed only) Out of This World (1950); (musical) Paint Your Wagon (1951); (ballet) The Harvest According (1952); (musical) The Girl in Pink Tights (1954); (ballet) Rib of Eve (1956); (ballet) Sebastian (1957); (musical) Goldilocks (1958); (musical) Juno (1959); (ballet) Bitter Weird and (musical) Kwamina (both 1961); (musical) 110 in the Shade (1963); (ballet) The Wind in the Mountains and The Four Shades (both 1965); (touring company only) Where's Charley? (1966); (also directed) Come Summer (1969); (ballet) A Rose for Miss Emily (1971); (ballet) Texas Fourth (1971); (ballet) The Informer (1988); (ballet) The Other (1992).

Selected writings: Dance to the Piper (1951); And Promenade Home (1957); To a Young Dancer (1962); Book of the Dance (1963); Lizzie Borden: A Dance of Death (1968); Dance in America (1970); Russian Journals (1970); Speak to Me, Dance with Me (1974); Conversations about the Dance (1974); Where the Wings Grow (1978); America Dances (1980); Reprieve (1981); Portrait Gallery (1990); Martha: The Life and Work of Martha Graham (1991). Also wrote numerous magazine articles for Atlantic, Esquire, Vogue, McCall's, Good Housekeeping, Horizon, and The New York Times Magazine.

Born in New York City on September 18, 1905, Agnes de Mille came from a distinguished middle-class background. Her maternal grandfather was the economist and social reformer Henry George, by her own account "probably the best known American [at that time], excepting Theodore Roosevelt and Mark Twain." According to Kenneth Galbraith, George remains one of the two 19th-century American writers still read in that field. Her paternal grandfather Henry C. de Mille and her father William C. de Mille (whose mother **Beatrice Samuel**, an Englishwoman of Jewish origin, was a prominent playwright's agent), were both successful playwrights, her father later working as a writer and director in Hollywood. The famed pioneer film director Cecil B. De Mille (as he spelled the family name) was her uncle. Raised first in New York but taken when young to Hollywood, California, where she attended local schools, de Mille, by her own account, had a happy childhood, spending her summers at Merriewood in Sulli-

van County, New York, a retreat for writers and theatrical people, an annual experience that she later described in her biographical work *See Where the Wings Grow*. There, she often danced alone in the woods and felt, even then, that her destiny was to be a great artist. Inspired by see-

ing a performance of the Russian ballerina *Anna Pavlova at the Metropolitan Opera House in New York in 1910, she staged her own dance concert in her back yard with a group of her friends. Later, she saw Nijinsky, *Isadora Duncan, and *Ruth St. Denis, but, as far as she was concerned, none of them cast the spell upon her that had been cast by the great Pavlova. By 1914, de Mille had decided to become a ballet dancer and began attending local ballet schools.

Her father was not sympathetic to his daughter going into the theater, a profession that he knew well as a playwright, and, under his influence, she attended the University of California at Los Angeles, graduating *cum laude* with a B.A. in English. Her mother **Anna de Mille** was much more sensitive to her daughter's ambitions and, after Agnes graduated in 1927, Anna took her and her younger sister **Margaret** to New York. There, while Margaret attended college, Agnes began seeking work in the theater. In 1928, she made her debut as a soloist doing a character sketch entitled "Stage Fright" based on a statue of a shy young dancer by the French impressionist artist, Dégas. The critics liked what they saw. "Like Chaplin, she sees tragedy through the lens of comedy," wrote John Martin in *The New York Times*. In these performances, which were really humorous choreographed character sketches, de Mille was accompanied by Louis Horst, a pianist who also worked for Ruth St. Denis and who accompanied *Martha Graham. This brought her in contact with the world of modern dance that was about to enter its golden age.

This is the story of someone who got not what she wanted, but better than she deserved.

—Agnes de Mille

Agnes de Mille's reputation as a choreographer began in 1929, when she staged the dances for the Hoboken revival of *The Black Crook*, an Anglo-American collaboration first produced in New York in 1866 and widely considered to have been the first true musical comedy; she then appeared with stock companies and variety shows. In 1931, she danced with Martha Graham, *Helen Tamiris, Charles Weidman, and *Doris Humphrey in programs sponsored by Dance Repertory, a group that briefly attempted to bring soloists and small dance groups together for joint performances. Although unsuccessful, Dance Repertory brought the classically trained de Mille into contact with the foremost modern dancers of her generation, and this led to her frequently being thought of as a modern dancer herself.

Now a recognized dancer and director, in 1932 Agnes de Mille went to Europe with her mother and began to give solo recitals, managing seven concerts in Paris, Brussels, and Lon-

don. She then moved to London, where for several years she gave recitals, staged dances for musical reviews—among them Cole Porter's great musical hit *Nymph Errant*, starring *Gertrude Lawrence—and aided in the establishment of the London Ballet Company. In England, de Mille studied ballet with *Marie Rambert, became friends with Lawrence, got to know the writer *Rebecca West, was visited backstage by *Tamara Karsavina, lunched with George Bernard Shaw, and otherwise hobnobbed with the theatrical, artistic, and cultural elite of prewar Britain. On May 9, 1933, she met Ramon Reed, a wealthy young man of 23, who suffered from a form of multiple sclerosis that had left him unable to walk since the age of 16. Although six years his senior, de Mille began dropping in on Reed at his London flat seeking refuge from the hurley-burley of her social life. Reed soon fell in love with de Mille, and she, while not requiting his feelings, developed a deep need for him on a level that she alone understood. He gave her love, a profound appreciation of her as an artist, and seemed, at least to her, to be the one person who appreciated the importance of her work. On her part, de Mille gave him intellectual stimulation, emotional comfort, a certain amount of affection, and, above all, a reason to live. With Reed paralyzed below the waist, their relationship was purely platonic, and this added to the pain for both of them. This friendship lasted for two years, during which Reed and de Mille vacationed together, and, when she returned to America, he joined her for a time in California. There, with still no offers even after a sold-out concert in Hollywood, she was badly in need of his emotional support. Upon her return to New York, Reed returned to England, where de Mille soon joined him. Soon after, however, Reed died, leaving a poignant and touching memory that de Mille carried with her the rest of her life, not revealing it until she told the story in her 1973 book *Speak to Me, Dance with Me*.

In England, Agnes de Mille's acquaintance with the Polish dancer and choreographer, Marie Rambert, director of the experimental Ballet Club, subsequently renamed the Ballet Rambert, led to an association with her protégé, Antony Tudor, later considered by many critics to have been the most important influence in ballet in the 20th century. In 1937, de Mille danced in the premier of his work *Dark Elegies*, a choreographical meditation on grief and mourning. During these London years, de Mille was often back in the U.S., where she choreographed the dances for Leslie Howard's Broadway appearance in *Hamlet* (1936), and the Leslie Howard–*Norma Shearer** film version of *Romeo and Juliet* (1937). Traveling to Hollywood, Agnes de Mille worked hard on the choreography for this film only to discover that hardly anyone at the studio took the dances seriously and that most of them were either not filmed at all or only in snippets. Bitterly disappointed, she at least found herself with $8,000 on hand and a renewed self-confidence in her ability to "produce really good professional work." In her own words, she felt "impregnable—not successful yet, but impregnable—I knew."

Despite her disappointment with Juliet, Agnes de Mille was undiscouraged. The example set by her father and her uncle, Cecil, had created a worldview for Agnes de Mille that did not permit the acceptance of failure. Returning to New York, she was immediately hired at a modest salary to stage the dances for a new musical comedy entitled *Hooray for What*, starring the popular comedian Ed Wynn, and, incidentally, the first directorial assignment for Vincente Minnelli, previously known only as a scenery and costume designer and later to be the husband of *Judy Garland** and father of **Liza Minnelli**. In 1939, de Mille choreographed her first ballet, *Black Ritual,* for the New York City Ballet. Set to the music of Darius Milhaud's *La Création du Monde* and attempting to recreate the atmosphere of some primitive ritual, this was an unusual production for that period in that it was performed by an all-black cast. It was followed by the comic and satirical *Three Virgins and a Devil,* a lusty work set in the Middle Ages (1941), and the now-legendary *Rodeo* (1942), a ballet set to the music of the American composer Aaron Copland.

Commissioned by the Ballet Russe de Monte Carlo, which, cut off from Europe by World War II, was forced to "Americanize" its repertoire by the encouragement of American choreographers creating ballets on American themes, *Rodeo* brought something new to classical ballet that, once assimilated, was to bring something new to musical comedy. In this work, de Mille devised a new balletic stance characterized by bent knees and widespread legs creating a distinctive bow-legged appearance, not only excellent as a depiction of cowboys but also successfully creating the impression of men on horseback. Opening night was a triumph with de Mille taking 20 curtain calls. Critic Burton Rascoe called *Rodeo* "the most original and most interesting innovation in the ballet in modern times," while John Martin wrote, "In nothing that she has previously done has de Mille exhibited so much pure choreographic skill and resourcefulness."

The success of *Rodeo* attracted the attention of *Theresa Helburn** and Lawrence Langner of the Theater Guild, who were planning to turn Lynn Riggs' successful play *Green Grow the Lilacs* into a musical to be called *Oklahoma!* They asked de Mille to do the choreography for the production. Until *Oklahoma!* came along in 1943, there was no such thing as serious dancing on the American musical stage. Such excellent shows as *The Boys From Syracuse* (1938) and even *Pal Joey* (1940), otherwise so ahead of their time, were characterized by choreography little removed from night-club jazz dancing of the type best remembered from such Busby Berkeley choreographed films as *42nd Street, Gold Diggers of 1933,* and *Gold Diggers of 1935.* Tap-dancing of the type purveyed by *Ruby Keeler** and later, in a more polished and sophisticated way, by *Eleanor Powell** held the stage until the Second World War; dances served as interludes between scenes and dialogue and frequently did little more than give the principals a chance to change their costumes. *Oklahoma!* changed all that. The choreography of Agnes de Mille was not only central to the production but integral, advancing the plot as much as the dialogue and songs, especially in the "dream" ballet in which the heroine, unable to choose between suitors, dances with both of them, at the end of which, she has determined her choice. In *Oklahoma!,* elements of ballet and modern dance were integrated with more traditional dance forms in an original and captivating way. The Broadway musical would never again be the same.

Justifying her fascination with Western themes, de Mille remarked, "American folk dances have always been my passion; they're a lot wilder and more exciting than the dancing we do today. That's why *Oklahoma!* was fun to do. People in Oklahoma in 1900 enjoyed dancing; they went lurching and careening around the floor, throwing themselves about with wonderful enthusiasm and abandon. Just watching them, you feel the same excitement." She was also fussy about casting. "*Oklahoma!* I believe, was the first musical show where every dancer was hired for just one reason—that he or she was the best available for the role," she wrote. "I stand on the record that this system, though prissy, worked."

The critics were unanimous in their praise of *Oklahoma!,* agreeing that in this work Agnes de Mille had surpassed her achievement in *Rodeo* both in depth and in sheer choreographic beauty.

In the words of the New York music critic Olin Downes, "You watch with excitement and delight, and with a lump in your throat, for this is something more than admirably stylized choreography." She has made the ballet "not only acceptable to the average theatergoer who would be bored to death by classical ballet but something he can get excited and shout about." The dean of American dance critics, Walter Terry, wrote: "With Agnes de Mille's dance for *Oklahoma!*, in 1943, the whole concept of musical comedy dancing was forever changed. De Mille used ballet, modern dance, folk dance, dramatic gesture. She also used artist-dancers, but, more than all of these, she made dancing a living part—not just a 'turn'—of the musical itself. Her now-famous dream sequence from the show was proof enough that dancing could say things that no words could convey and say them in terms that a non-dance audience could understand. Her dances were not rhythmic exercises, not tricks, not mere diversions. They spoke for the hearts of lovers, they revealed terrifying and wonderful secrets, they identified the characteristics of a people." The year 1943 proved to be an especially rewarding one for Agnes de Mille, who not only reached the summit of her career but who, on June 14, married an officer in the Army Air Corps, Walter F. Prude, with whom she had her only child, a son Jonathan. The marriage proved successful, and after the war Prude became a concert artist's manager until his death in 1988.

The result of the stunning success of *Oklahoma!* was the opening of a golden age of American musical comedy that made the form a major contribution to world theater. De Mille then followed this triumph with the choreography for a series of Broadway musicals: *One Touch of Venus* (1944), *Bloomer Girl* (1944), *Carousel* (1945), *Brigadoon* (1946), and *Allegro* (which she also directed, 1947). Other choreographers soon followed her lead in such now legendary productions as *Up in Central Park, South Pacific, Kiss Me Kate, The King and I,* and *West Side Story.* Meanwhile, *Oklahoma!* opened in London in 1946 where it achieved the same success and made a star of Howard Keel.

The third pinnacle of her career, after *Rodeo* and *Oklahoma!*, was reached by de Mille in her ballet *Fall River Legend*, a psychological study that dealt with the story of *Lizzie Borden, who, although acquitted of having brutally murdered both her parents with an axe in 1891, was widely considered to have gotten away with the crime. This ballet, perhaps her most ambitious work, probably represented the summit of her

achievement, leading her to be called "the most famous choreographer in the world." The story of Lizzie Borden fascinated de Mille, who, several years later, published a well-researched book on the subject.

Despite her success with this ballet, Agnes de Mille returned to the musical-comedy form. *Gentlemen Prefer Blondes*, starring *Carol Channing (1949) and set in the 1920s, was a Broadway musical of the traditional type for which de Mille did not hesitate to design appropriate dances, and her choreography for the production was delightful. She then went on to create the dances for such later musicals as *Paint Your Wagon* (1952), *The Girl in Pink Tights* (1954), *Goldilocks* (1958), *Juno* (1959), *Kwamina* (1961), and *110 in the Shade* (1963). Interspersed with these musical sorties, de Mille continued to create balletic works for the American Ballet Theater such as *Tally Ho* (1944), *The Harvest According* (1952), *Rib of Eve* (1956), *Sebastian* (1957), *The Wind in the Mountains* (1965), *The Four Marys* (1965), *A Rose for Miss Emily* (1969), *Texas Fourth* (1976), *The Informer*, based on the Irish rebellion against English rule from 1917 to 1921 (1988), and, her final work, *The Other*, a symbolic portrayal of a woman's encounter with death (1992). She also served as the narrator for the television broadcasts of the Bolshoi Ballet (1965).

As it turned out, however, Agnes de Mille had accomplished her greatest work in the 1940s. Thereafter, though she continued to choreograph, direct, and even perform, her work never achieved the same level of distinction. Nevertheless, what she had achieved by mid-century had so changed the dance in America that she remained a revered and respected figure in the dance world for the rest of her life. This was fortunate, for as her career gradually slowed, she was able to earn a decent living as a lecturer and also as an author, whose books were sure to find a ready market. In 1973, de Mille founded the Heritage Dance Theater that toured for two years, offering dances that drew heavily on the folk tradition.

Slender in her youth, Agnes de Mille was rather short (5'2") and as she grew older she became somewhat heavy so that it was a rather squat little woman who danced the lead in *Rodeo* at the Brussels World's Fair in 1958, in the special theater at the American pavilion that featured productions of American musical comedies.

A vigorous and determined woman and an indefatigable worker, de Mille extensively researched her dances and was remarkably eclectic in the sources upon which she drew for her choreography. She often recycled material, such as certain solo pieces on Western themes that were incorporated into *Rodeo,* and the Civil War ballet in *Bloomer Girl* that served as the inspiration for *A Harvest According.* She was also a gifted pianist, and an excellent and prolific writer, who found time to author 11 books, including *Martha: The Life and Work of Martha Graham* (1991) and her autobiographical works: *Dance to the Piper* (1951), *And Promenade Home* (1957). She wrote for magazines and maintained a voluminous correspondence, especially with her mother; her carefully preserved letters were published in *Speak to Me, Dance with Me* in 1973. A quintessential American, de Mille was anything but pompous or "arty," and her books, while well-written, are forthright, opinionated, witty, earthy, and laced with sly humor. Coy about her age, she managed to write more than one book of reminiscences without bothering to mention it.

A product of the Progressive era in American history and strongly influenced by her

From the Fall River Legend, *choreographed by Agnes de Mille, starring Lucia Chase and Alicia Alonso.*

grandfather, de Mille also became a social activist. She argued before government agencies for state and federal aid for the arts, was a founding member of the National Council on the Arts, and the first chair of its Dance Panel (1965), and, in the 1970s and '80s, often denounced "big business" in her curtain speeches. A "liberated woman" before her time, she could be arrogant and brutally candid, so much so that in the theater world she was known as the "virago." On the other hand, she was sensitive and ego-involved with her work. Easily hurt, she could become excessively defensive. A good speaker, she frequently appeared on television, and her public lectures were well-received.

In 1975, at age 70, Agnes de Mille was struck down by a cerebral hemorrhage that left her severely incapacitated. As determined as ever and unwilling to become an invalid, she immediately undertook a program of physical therapy during which she learned to write with her left hand. Her recovery proved to be a startling success that she described in her book *Reprieve*, written in collaboration with her doctor. She then returned to a life of lecturing and choreography until her death of a stroke in her Greenwich Village apartment on October 7, 1993. She was survived by her son Jonathan and two grandsons.

Taken as a whole, the choreography of Agnes de Mille, as well as her personal dancing style, were characterized by a lively and irreverent humor, but in *Rodeo* and in the Civil War ballet in *Bloomer Girl* they at times achieved considerable pathos while some of the dances designed for *Fall River Legend* successfully conveyed the elements of tragedy. Perhaps the greatest tribute to de Mille as an artist is that her works, *Rodeo* and *Fall River Legend*, so highly esteemed by George Balanchine, passed into the permanent repertory of his American Ballet Theater, where they have become enshrined as classics of choreography, a discipline that had been the least American of art forms until her time.

SOURCES:
de Mille, Agnes. *Dance to the Piper*. Boston, MA: Little, Brown, 1951.
———. *Speak to Me, Dance with Me*. Boston, MA: Little, Brown, 1973.
———. *Where the Wings Grow*. Garden City, NY: 1950.
Theater Collection, Philadelphia Free Library.

SUGGESTED READING:
Easton, Carol. *No Intermissions: The Life of Agnes de Mille*. Boston, MA: Little Brown, 1996.
Terry, Walter. *The Dance in America*. NY: Harper & Row, 1956.

Robert H. Hewsen, Professor of History, Rowan University, Glassboro, New Jersey

De Mille, Katherine (1911–1995)

American actress. Name variations: Katherine De Mille Quinn. Born Katherine Lester in Vancouver, British Columbia, Canada, on June 29, 1911; died of Alzheimer's disease on April 27, 1995, in Tucson, Arizona; orphaned as a child; at age nine, adopted by Cecil B. De Mille (1881–1959, the movie director) and Constance (Adams) De Mille (an erstwhile actress); attended the exclusive Hollywood School for Girls; sister of **Cecilia De Mille**; *became first wife of Anthony Quinn (the actor), in 1936 (divorced 1963); children: five.*

Filmography: Madam Satan (1930); Viva Villa! (1934); The Trumpet Blows (1934); Belle of the Nineties (1934); All the King's Horses (1935); Call of the Wild (1935); The Crusades (1935); Drift Fence (1936); The Sky Parade (1936); Ramona (1936); Banjo on My Knee (1936); Charlie Chan at the Olympics (1937); Love Under Fire (1937); Under Suspicion (1937); Blockade (1938); In Old Caliente (1939); Isle of Destiny (1940); Dark Streets of Cairo (1940); Ellery Queen, Master Detective (1940); Aloma of the South Seas (1941); Black Gold (1947); The Unconquered (1947); (bit) The Man from Del Rio (1956).

Katherine De Mille, the adopted daughter of the actress **Constance De Mille** and movie director Cecil B. De Mille, appeared in many movies of the 1930s and 1940s, including Jack London's *Call of the Wild* (1935) and *Helen Hunt Jackson*'s *Ramona* (1936). De Mille married actor Anthony Quinn in 1936; the couple had five children before divorcing in 1963. De Mille retired from acting in 1950.

Demorest, Ellen Curtis (1824–1898)

Arbiter of American fashion who democratized the availability of smart women's clothing through the development of paper patterns and was a strong supporter of women's achievements in business. Name variations: Nell Curtis; Mme. Demorest. Pronunciation: Dem-OR-est. Born Ellen Louise Curtis on November 15, 1824, in Schuylerville, Saratoga County, New York; died on August 10, 1898; daughter of Henry D. (a successful hat manufacturer) and Electa (Abel) Curtis; attended Schuylerville Academy; married William Jennings Demorest, on April 15, 1858; children: William Curtis (b. 1859) and Evelyn Celeste Caradora Louise (b. 1865).

Set up a millinery shop in Schuylerville and prospered (1843); moved her business to millinery center in Troy, NY, and eventually to New York City (1844); began distributing paper patterns and founded a quarterly fashion catalog Mirror of Fashions of which she

was editor (1860); continued publishing special fashion publications while the magazine appeared under various titles—Demorest's Illustrated Monthly and Mme. Demorest's Mirror of Fashions (1865–77), Demorest's Monthly Magazine (1878–89), Demorest's Family Magazine (1899–99); shifted editorial duties to sons (1882); founded, with other women professionals, the woman's club Sorosis (1868); established, with Susan King, the Woman's Tea Company to import tea to be sold by gentlewomen (1872); received patents for elevator shaft floor and dress improvements such as the Imperial Dress Elevator, a method of raising a long skirt while walking; won many awards at international expositions and at the Philadelphia Centennial (1876).

When young Nell Curtis was growing up at Old Saratoga, known as Schuylerville, in Saratoga County, New York, the area boasted a dual fame as revolutionary battleground and health spa. Half a century earlier, the surrender there of the British general John Burgoyne had been a turning point for the patriots during the American Revolution; long before that, the healing waters of the local springs had been a gathering place of the Mohawk tribe of Native Americans, and in 1767, when the pre-revolutionary British superintendent of Indian Affairs, the Hon. Sir William Johnson was introduced to them by tribal members, these "Medicine Waters of the Great Spirit" had entered colonial legend. By the 1820s, what Cleveland Amory has described as the "king" of the Northern watering holes, had become a fashionable resort. There the seemingly contradictory influences of patriotic history and the anti-democratic show of extravagance in the fashions of the resort town all played a part in the development of Ellen Curtis Demorest as fashion "interpreter" and designer, who attained international fame, and was considered, according to Russell Lynes, to be a prime cultural asset to America and one of the wonders of her age.

In childhood, Nell's interest in fashion was awakened by the annual arrival of visitors for the bathing and healing powers of the waters of Saratoga Springs. Watching the arrivals was a way of life for the natives who flocked to see the notable members of society, described by *Edna Ferber in her novel *Saratoga Trunk,* as they stepped off the train. The travelers arrived from Southern plantations and seaboard cities alike, and according to a column that appeared in *Demorest's Monthly Magazine* in 1865, "For a few weeks or months, these ordinarily dull and commonplace villages and hamlets . . . present the spectacle of a grand reunion of wealth, fashion, and beauty out of doors."

Nell Curtis was the second of eight children—six girls and two boys—born to Henry D. and **Electa Abel Curtis**. According to historian *Ishbel Ross, the families of both parents had settled in the region at the time of the American Revolution. Nell's father was a farmer and owner of a men's hat factory, able to provide well for his family; they lived in a comfortable home. After attending a local school and Schuylerville Academy, Nell set up a millinery shop, with the help of her father, and, after a prosperous year, she moved to Troy, New York, a leading millinery center, and later to the borough of Brooklyn in New York City.

*W*illiam and *E*llen *C*urtis *D*emorest

In 1858, Nell was 34 when she married William Jennings Demorest, a dry-goods merchant and widower with two children, in what was soon to be a formidable business partnership. As Mme. Demorest, the former milliner was to challenge the status of Paris as the center of fashion and, in the process, become an international phenomenon. Her sister **Kate Curtis** was also an important part of the family business team.

As the story is told, the seeds of their great success were sown when the new Mrs. Demorest was watching a maid cut out a dress from a crude brown-paper pattern. Because she and her sister Kate had been working on simplifying their system, watching the maid cut around the paper gave Nell the idea of accurate, mass-produced paper patterns. However, **Caroline Bird** refutes the idea that using paper pattern pieces as guide for cloth originated with the Demorests' maid. (Woman's magazine historian **Helen Woodward** claims the same story for the Buttericks.) Kate and Nell had been working on a dress chart that "would simplify the cumbersome and expensive cut-and-try method of making clothes fit," writes Bird. With their chart and simplified designs, the sisters did foresee the potential in selling the design of a garment separate from the garment itself. According to Bird, the system of paper patterns they devised was to be as American as the elitist couturiers were French, bringing aristocratic styles and cuts to all kinds of women. It was both an ingenious accomplishment and a contribution worthy of a democratic society.

William Demorest, who had both a talent for promotion and a willingness to support the work of the two, was quick to see the potential in Nell and Kate's ideas. Typical of his promotional abilities were his links to tours made by *Jenny Lind. When Lind toured the United States, she wore fashions donated by Demorest's Emporium.

By 1860, the paper patterns were being sold and publication of the quarterly fashion catalog *Mirror of Fashions* had begun, with Ellen Demorest as editor; the magazine proved to be a way of promoting a number of Demorest products. Some historians maintain that the goal of the magazine was to encourage home sewing, using the patterns stapled inside, and to build a network of local distribution agencies to sell the pattern; historian Frank Luther Mott, however, in his multivolume history of American magazines, looks upon the pattern as a kind of premium to sell the magazine. Whichever viewpoint is more valid, the fashion sense of Ellen Curtis Demorest was the key to both, and the combined venture was highly successful.

*P*arents, teach your daughters some remunerative business. Select for them as you do for your sons—according to natural or apparent capability.

—Ellen Curtis Demorest

With her sister Kate, Demorest was able to adapt foreign styles into patterns and made samples available at an establishment on Broadway. At the height of her success, her fashion patterns could reach farm wives before they were available to the Paris elite. According to Lynes, of all the "firms that made and scattered patterns abroad, none could hold a candle to Mme. Demorest's Emporium of Fashion in New York. It was the soul of elegance." Her biannual fashion openings at the Emporium were perfectly timed and became social events of the first order. On the labor end of the business, she hired blacks to work on the same terms as whites long before integration was generally considered acceptable, and minority employees were welcome on equal terms at gala occasions at the Emporium.

In 1860, the Demorests hired *Jane Cunningham Croly for their new *Mirror of Fashions.*

Croly, who wrote under the pen name Jennie June, was recently returned from Rockford, Illinois, where she and her husband David had attempted to start a newspaper. (Ishbel Ross wrote a combined biographical study of Croly and Demorest in *Crusades and Crinolines*.) Because Croly was the one writing about the beginnings of the women's club movement in New York City, she is frequently credited with an organizing impulse that by all rights should be shared with a number of other New York women professionals, including *Fanny Fern (whose copy was more precious to publisher Robert Bonner than that of Henry Ward Beecher or *Alice Cary). In the founding of the Sorosis woman's club, Nell Demorest was another of the organizers, and Ross gives an account of the famous 1868 meeting at Delmonico's, at which men of the press club were wined and dined but not allowed to speak. That night Nell Demorest gave a toast to "Man, the Monopolizer," reminding her audience that daughters, like sons, could inherit good qualities from their father, and then discussed the problem of a woman's services being recognized as a duty owed and subject to the caprice of her spouse. Further, according to Demorest, "Men have monopolized the right to declaim, lecture, preach, do public speaking, and women wound up with no experience that might be useful," adding that we should not wonder if our daughters learn to smile at suggestions of extravagance of dress. "She is none the poorer for the outlay, for ordinarily a wife owns only her wardrobe."

Nell Demorest also found it outrageous that some considered it a disgrace for women to work. In 1870, in a column in her magazine, she pointed out that useful, compensated labor affords the only means of independence and of physical, mental, and moral growth. "Men have learned the lesson long ago—no man is respectable, in the highest sense, who is an idler," she asserted, adding that a few working women couldn't force change but women by the thousands could strike at and annihilate the foundation of the false system created by women as a dependent class.

Although the columns of Croly as Jennie June are more consistently strident, Nell Demorest frequently made strong statements about the employment of women working and the need for them to learn how to be independent. She also took firm stands on child and wife abuse, on questions of prison reform and the treatment of the insane, and she was an advocate for the work of *Dorothea Dix. She applauded Queen *Margaret of Savoy (1851–1925) who had a woman on her staff of personal physicians, and she criticized Queen *Victoria for her unfriendliness to women doctors. According to the *Dictionary of Literary Biography,* the columns of Jennie June were primarily a forum for the Demorest reform philosophies. Clearly, the long, close working relationship between Demorest and Croly demonstrates that they held similar goals for women.

According to Ross, Demorest was an impressive figure, tall and erect, with dark hair, a high forehead, and aquiline features. In addition to presiding over an international pattern empire, she was particularly proud of the highly successful purchasing bureau, run primarily by her husband, to fill mail orders for all kinds of merchandise, a forerunner of the modern catalog business. Success in this area allowed him to speculate successfully in Manhattan real estate, and his additional publishing ventures resulted eventually in the management of five separate periodicals with a combined circulation of over one million.

Demorest's first child, William Curtis, was born the year after her marriage; a daughter Evelyn was born in 1865. William's two children by his previous marriage were Henry and Vienna. In the years that her children were young, Mme. Demorest, as she became known professionally, divided her time between the Emporium and her home. The family maintained a country place at Claremont, in northern Manhattan, but Saratoga also lured her back during the summers for a quieter life at the old Curtis homestead, where gardening and music were two of the family's primary interests.

According to Ross, the Demorests reached their peak during the 1870s, when they had agents all over the U.S., and their son Henry ran an office in Paris. In 1865, the *Mirror of Fashion* had become a general magazine, *Demorest's Illustrated Monthly and Mme. Demorest's Mirror of Fashions,* and continued under this long and cumbersome title until 1877 when it was simplified to *Demorest's Monthly Magazine.* Each issue included a tissue-paper pattern and hand-colored plates describing the fashions and how to make them. Illustrations of children's clothes and hats and accessories such as purses were also included, with instructions, along with architectural drawings, sheet music, lithographs of famous people, and poetry and fiction by famous writers. By 1882, its lineup of published women writers included *Julia Ward Howe, *Martha J.R. Lamb, *Margaret Sangster (1838–1912), and *Louisa May Alcott.

Demorest further enlarged the field of employment for women with her system of "agents"

for the magazines and with the Woman's Tea Company, started in 1872. According to Ross, the agents were very successful, while the latter enterprise, undertaken with **Susan A. King**, a New Yorker who had been successful in real estate, enjoyed a modest success. King made trips to the Orient to select the teas and to negotiate with growers and exporters, traveling on a clipper ship renamed the *Madam Demorest.*

In 1874, when New York businesses were generally failing, the Demorests continued to do well, and their showrooms and work studios were moved from three houses on Broadway to a fine old mansion at 17 E. 14th Street. According to Ross, their businesses had increased 15-fold in four years and two million patterns were mailed each year. In 1876, the year of the Philadelphia Centennial (where Demorest was awarded top honors in fashion), three million patterns were distributed through 1,500 agencies. At a time when dress reform was a popular issue and proponents were opposed to the inclusion of high-fashion ladies' clothing in the women's displays, the patterns remained successful anyway. In the next decade, however, this portion of the Demorest empire went into decline, in part due to the swamping effect of competition from Ebenezer Butterick, who had secured a patent on patterns for men's clothing that he began to distribute. In 1887, Demorest withdrew from the pattern business, and it was sold.

In 1885, William had retired to devote himself to the temperance movement and ran that year for lieutenant governor of New York on the Prohibition ticket; he was the Prohibition candidate for mayor of New York City in 1890 and died in 1895. Nell Demorest had meanwhile suffered a stroke and was an invalid. She moved into the Hotel Renaissance in New York where she died three years later of a cerebral hemorrhage, at age 73; she was buried in Kensico Cemetery in Valhalla, New York.

It is difficult to determine which Demorest was the real inventor; the pages of their magazines are full of ingenious devices and products—a spiral-spring bosom pad, a combination suspender and shoulder brace, special complexion cremes, fragrances, and the Imperial Dress Elevator. According to patent historian **Anne Macdonald**, Ellen Demorest invented, but did not patent, an inexpensive hoop skirt that won many prizes, and she did patent a few items, including an elevator shaft floor, a "puff" for arranging hair, and a dress improvement called the Imperial Dress Elevator, which raised a long skirt while walking. Although William patented most of his gadgets, neither he nor Ellen patented the paper pattern. Because of this, they were unable to establish their priority in court, even though they had been the first to put them on the market. Their success with them was phenomenal, nonetheless.

Like many outstanding women of her era, Ellen Curtis Demorest has been supplanted by the more political heroines of the suffrage movement; nonetheless, she was a heroine to many of her contemporaries. She is remembered for introducing international fashion sense and know-how to grassroots America. Her publications initiated simplified instructions for creating fashionable looks with products designed to ease the demands on time and money for being well-dressed. As a "fashion arbiter," she adapted couture to clean, modern lines available through her well-fitted and easy-to-use paper patterns, and she "Americanized" high fashion for anyone who could read.

SOURCES:

Bird, Caroline. *Enterprising Women*. NY: W.W. Norton, 1976.

Ferber, Edna. *Saratoga Trunk*. Greenwich, CT: Fawcett, 1972.

James, Edward T., Janet Wilson James, and Paul S. Boyer. *Notable American Women: A Biographical Dictionary*. Cambridge, MA: The Belknap Press of Harvard University.

Lynes, Russell. *The Tastemakers: The Shaping of American Popular Taste*. NY: Harper, 1955.

Macdonald, Anne L. *Feminine Ingenuity: How Women Inventors Changed America*. NY: Ballantine, 1992.

Mott, Frank Luther. *A History of American Magazines, 1865–1885*. Vol. III. Cambridge: Harvard University Press, 1938.

Riley, Sam G., ed. *American Magazine Journalists, 1850-1900*. Vol. 79 of the *Dictionary of Literary Biography*. Detroit, MI: Gale Research, 1989.

Ross, Ishbel. *Crusades and Crinolines: The Life and Times of Ellen Curtis Demorest and William Jennings Demorest*. NY: Harper and Row, 1963.

SUGGESTED READING:

Amory, Cleveland. *The Last Resorts: A Portrait of American Society at Play*. NY: Harper, 1952.

Blair, Karen J. *The Clubwoman as Feminist: True Womanhood Redefined, 1868-1914*. NY: Holmes and Meier, 1988.

Croly, Jane Cunningham. *History of the Women's Club Movement in America*. NY: Henry G. Allen, 1898.

McCabe, James D. *The Illustrated History of the Centennial Exhibition*. Philadelphia, PA: National Publishing, 1876.

Ann Mauger Colbert, Journalism Coordinator, Indiana University–Purdue University at Fort Wayne, Fort Wayne, Indiana

Deng (r. 105–121)

Dowager empress of China. Name variations: Teng. Ruled from 105 to 121; died in 121.

During the Eastern or Later Han Dynasty, Empress Deng ruled as dowager queen following the death of Emperor He Di (Ho Ti), who ruled from 88 to 105. Deng was regent for her infant son from 105 until her death in 121.

Deng, Cora (b. 1900).

See Deng Yuzhi.

Deng Yaping (1973—)

Chinese table tennis champion. Born on February 5, 1973, in Henan Province, China; daughter of a table tennis coach.

Though table tennis did not become an Olympic event until the Seoul Games in 1988, the Chinese have been dominating the sport since the 1950s. That summer, the Chinese took the gold, silver, and bronze in the singles.

In China, those who show unusual skills in the sport are selected to attend a school, where table tennis is the main curriculum: the daily routine consists of six hours of table tennis, one hour of running and exercise, and two hours of study. Born in 1973, Deng Yaping was playing table tennis by the time she was five; her father was a professional table tennis coach. By age 15, she was playing at a national level, but, because of her 4'10½" height, she was often missing from the list of China's national team during the later 1980s.

But Deng was quick and very determined. In 1992, in Barcelona, Spain, she upset the top-seeded players to win two Olympic gold medals for table tennis in singles and doubles—the first double-gold winner in that event in Olympic history. In the finals, she was up against her doubles partner, ⚭▶ Qiao Hong, who was No. 2 in the world. In 1995, at the 43rd World Table Tennis championships, Deng walked away with three gold medals. In 1996 in the Atlanta Olympics, Deng again placed first in women's singles and, with her partner Qiao Hong, took first in doubles as well. Notes *Amy Feng, the U.S. women's champion, Deng "has her own style. She has a great serve; 80–90 percent of the time, you get killed. And she's a real quick attacker, backhand and forehand. She can play offense and defense both ways, and she changes all the time."

Deng Yingchao (1903–1992)

Most prominent leader of the Chinese women's movement, who was also the revolutionary comrade and

wife of Premier Zhou Enlai. Name variations: Deng Yinzhao or Deng Yin-Zhao; Deng Wenxu; Teng Yingchao; Teng Ying-ch'ao; Teng Ying-chao. Pronunciation: Ying (rhymes with ring) Chao (rhymes with now). Born Deng Wenxu in 1903 (some sources say 1904) in the northcentral Chinese province of Henan (Honan); daughter of an officer in the imperial army under the late Qing Dynasty and a mother who became a schoolteacher; education was typical of Chinese students of the time in Beijing and Tianjin; married Zhou Enlai (Chou Enlai), later premier of Communist China, in 1925; children: none of her own, but did adopt.

Joined the radical students' movement, in particular "The Awakening Society" and met Zhou Enlai (1919); joined the Socialist Youth League (1924); became member of the new Chinese Communist Party and leader in the women's movement (1925); one of the few women to survive the epochal Long March, the formative event in Chinese Communist history (1934–35); worked in liaison groups between CCP and Chinese Nationalist Party (KMT) throughout Sino-Japanese War (1937–45); continued to direct the woman's movement and held many important offices following the success of the revolution (1949); assisted in drafting the Marriage Reform Law of 1950 (1950); gave last major policy speech, before the Eighth Party Congress (1956); perhaps the most honored woman in the People's Republic of China up to the time of her death.

Deng Yingchao was born in the closing years of the traditional Chinese Confucian society. Like many women of good family at that time, she became a supporter of women's rights and joined radical student groups in their efforts to overthrow the moribund Qing dynasty that had controlled the Chinese throne since the 17th century. As a member of the student movement, she met another young radical, Zhou Enlai. Through their marriage and their work for the Communist Party, the two became, in the words of historians Donald Klein and **Anne Clark**, "probably the most redoubtable couple in the history of the Chinese Communist movement." After Zhou became premier of China, and over the many decades that he remained the close ally of Mao Zedong, Deng Yingchao carried on her own role as a major leader of the Chinese women's movement. Although modest and unassuming throughout her career, the power of her position was evident as a member of the ruling Central Committee from 1956.

Born Deng Wenxu in 1903, in Henan (Honan) province, Deng Yingchao was the

❧▸ **Qiao Hong** (1968—)
Chinese table tennis champion. Born on November 21, 1968.

In 1989, at the 40th World Table Tennis championships, Qiao Hong walked away with titles in both women's singles and doubles. At Barcelona in 1992, she took an Olympic silver medal in table tennis singles and a gold medal in doubles.

daughter of an army officer in the Chinese imperial army and, some sources say, an unsuccessful landlord. The family's economic status was probably marginal during his life, and, at his death, her mother became a schoolteacher to support them. Little is known about Deng's mother, but she was of the same generation as **Yu Manzhen**, mother of the later female literary and revolutionary figure, *Ding Ling (1904–1985). The two mothers probably shared the aspirations of many in their generation, who wanted a modern education and a more egalitarian life for their daughters than they had themselves known.

Toward the mid-19th century, Confucian institutions and values had guided China for more than a thousand years. Confucianism prized a hierarchical social system, based above all on a respect for authority, which had produced a rigid society that provided for great stability and cultural continuity until it was forced to meet the many and deeply threatening challenges of the modern world. Then China found its sovereignty threatened by the Western powers, principally Great Britain, which gradually gained control over increasing chunks of Chinese territory. Germany, Japan, and France were also nibbling away at its lands and its resources.

Culturally, Chinese had long felt themselves to be at the very center of the world, the cynosure of civilization. But by the time Deng Yingchao was born, it was apparent to most Chinese people that their country was politically weak and extremely backward in a number of ways. One index of its backwardness, felt by many, was the relatively low status attributed to Chinese women. In the great works of Western fiction that became available in translation, Chinese women discovered striking contrasts between themselves and Western women, who were often presented as actively engaged in political and social reform.

Resolved that her daughter would be a modern woman, Deng Yingchao's mother sent her to college in Tianjin, which was the port city for Beijing, China's capital and cultural center. In 1919, Deng Yingchao was a student at the Hebei First Woman's Normal School in Tianjin, when the country was convulsed by the May Fourth Movement, named for the date when political events exposed the corruption and weakness of the government that had replaced the traditional Qing government in 1912. When events also revealed that the foreign powers, particularly Japan, intended to continue their aggression in China, people throughout China, particularly the students in the large cities, rose up in response and began to organize and agitate for real reform. Out of this ferment, modern China, and many of its leaders, grew.

*D*eng Yingchao, the wife of Zhou Enlai, is among the most important women in the history of the Chinese Communist Movement. Like most women CCP leaders, her political prominence is largely of her own making, rather than the reflection of her marriage to one of Communist China's greatest leaders.

—Donald W. Klein and Anne B. Clark

Deng Yingchao was active at first in helping to found radical organizations at her school. Like others, she saw that the key to success was to organize beyond the small circles of students and incite Chinese in general to join the reform movement, and her efforts expanded in Tianjin. In her words, as related by Chow Tse-tsung, the critical factor was "to awaken our fellow citizens." Deng Yingchao's special task was organizing speaker's groups to work among Chinese women. It was in the course of a street demonstration that Deng Yingchao met her future husband Zhou Enlai. In September 1919, they began working together in the "Awakening Society," a radical group. She edited a succession of papers and magazines that quickly came and went, suppressed by the military despots dominating the governments in Beijing. Like many students, Zhou and Deng were repeatedly imprisoned for brief periods.

An earlier generation of Chinese youth had been mobilized to desperate and ill-organized acts of violence in hopes that enough disorder would sweep away the Chinese government and with it China's problems. One representative of that group was *Qiu Jin (1875–1907), whose heroic martyrdom continued to inspire Chinese women but provided no useful model. The problem addressed by Deng's generation was how to create a revolution. Then, in 1917, occurred the event that was to catch the eyes of the world: The Russian Bolshevik revolution.

Most Chinese thought of Russia as an Asian nation, because so much of it lay in the East. Before its overthrow, the government was also a despotic monarchy, very similar to their own former imperial governments and the more recent warlord regimes. Eagerly studying events in Russia, students like Deng and Zhou learned the importance of organizing a vanguard political party led by dedicated professional revolutionaries. In addition to serving as a model and inspiration, the new radical Soviet Union was also interested in fomenting revolution worldwide. The Soviet government wanted to distract its Western enemies who were weak and vulnerable in Asia. Soviet leaders also believed that all the world would inevitably become Communist.

After 1919, the Chinese activists saw the Soviet example as more and more alluring. In 1920, Zhou left for France to work and study, while Deng Yingchao remained in the Beijing area to work and organize. In 1924, she joined the Socialist Youth League, a precursor to the Communist Party. In 1925, as a member of the new Chinese Communist Party, she became the head of party activities among women in the Beijing-Tianjin region, the political center of China. Following the return of Zhou Enlai to China, they married late that year, in Canton.

After Beijing and Shanghai, Canton became the third center of Communist Party activity. Located in the south, it was important for reaching the peasantry in China's great southern hinterland. Because the Communists were in alliance with the Chinese Nationalist Party, known as the Guomindang (or Kuomintang [KMT]), they could work fairly openly, but the alliance was an uneasy one and doomed to a violent end. The Guomindang, led by a military leader, Chiang Kai-shek, was chiefly interested only in political reform, seeking a strong central government freed of the many local warlord regimes. The Communists believed that nothing less than a thorough social and cultural revolution would fit China for the modern world. While they worked together, the Guomindang provided the military muscle, and the Chinese Communist Party (CCP) supplied the mass organizations such as the Peasant movement, increasingly dominated by Mao Zedong, and the women's movement, led by Deng Yingchao. Deng held high office in both the CCP and the Guomindang. After it was apparent that the Guomindang military arm would indeed conquer the warlord regimes and unite China, Chiang Kai-shek turned upon the Communists. The rift began in the summer of 1927, with a bloody massacre in Shanghai, which drove Communists everywhere underground.

Because the CCP was at that time controlled by its Soviet advisors, who wished above all to see a victory in China that would confirm the Russian model of revolution, little bands of workers and peasants controlled by the Communists were wasted in fruitless attacks on urban centers. But in the countryside, Mao Zedong and his ally Zhou Enlai were by then working toward a peasant-based rural revolution. Mao and others established a revolutionary base in the remote south, where Deng Yingchao arrived about mid-1932. There, she continued to be active in the women's movement.

In 1934, Chiang's troops broke Communist defenses and the survivors fled north for thousands of miles, in what became known as the Long March, to join another base area at Yenan. This terrible ordeal involved hundreds of small and large battles, great hardships, and thousands of casualties. Deng became one of the few women to complete the march, although she contracted tuberculosis along the way and often had to be carried on a stretcher. Out of this ordeal emerged the core party leadership, principally Mao Zedong and Zhou Enlai.

In 1937, the Japanese occupied Beijing, during the Sino-Japanese War, which was to last until 1945. That year, Deng Yingchao was in Beijing, seeking treatment for her tuberculosis. In fear of Japanese arrest, she contacted the American writer Edgar Snow, whom she knew from Yenan. In his work *The Battle for Asia,* Snow says that Deng "possessed one of the most astute political brains" he had "encountered among Chinese women." Snow's wife Nym Wales (**Helen Foster Snow**) noted the ordinariness of her looks, referring to her as "a competent-looking matronly woman," then in her mid-30s.

The Sino-Japanese war, which became part of the Pacific Theater of World War II after 1941, brought the Guomindang and the CCP back into uneasy alliance. Deng Yingchao worked in liaison groups, spending much time at the Chinese wartime capital in Chongqing (Chungking). After the Japanese defeat in 1945, the frequently violent partnership of the Guomindang and the CCP continued until civil war broke out again the following year.

The combination of its own corruption, the Japanese invasion, and CCP success at mobilizing mass movements of peasants and women under the banners of nationalism and reform proved too much for the Guomindang. In 1949, after losing a renewed civil war, its leadership fled to Taiwan. Mao was now chair of the CCP, Zhou Enlai was head of the state apparatus as China's new premier, and Deng Yingchao was one of the primary leaders of the women's movement.

In early 1959, Deng Yingchao assisted in the drafting of the most significant document to affect Chinese women since the original works of Confucius and later Neo-Confucian commentators had established the gender-biased balance of power against women in traditional China. After several millennia of dreadful oppression, the Marriage Reform Law of 1950 gave Chinese women equal rights. Chinese women could now at least seek legal redress for many of the injustices they continued to suffer, even after the Communist victory. Although the system had changed, the old values lingered, and in some regards still survive.

The recent past has revealed many weaknesses of the Communist system, in China and elsewhere. But for Deng Yingchao and other modern Chinese women, the Chinese Communist Party that they helped shape and lead was the beginning of the effort to redress the ancient gender inequality of Chinese society. Deng Yingchao continued to hold many important offices, including a membership on the governing Central Committee of the CCP from 1956. Although her address to the Eighth Party Congress that year was her last major policy speech, she served in many public and ceremonial posts after that time. Until her death in 1992, at the age of 88, she remained the most honored female political leader in China.

SOURCES:

Boorman, Howard L., ed. "Teng Ying-ch'ao," in *Biographical Dictionary of Republican China.* Vol. III. NY: Columbia University Press, 1970, pp. 264–265,

Chow Tse-tsung. *The May Fourth Movement: Intellectual Revolution in Modern China.* Stanford: Stanford University Press, 1960.

Klein, Donald W. and Anne B. Clark, eds. "Teng Ying-ch'ao," in *Biographical Dictionary of Chinese Communism 1921–1965.* Vol II. Cambridge, MA: Harvard University Press, 1971, pp. 838–843.

Snow, Edgar. *The Battle for Asia.* NY: 1941.

Wales, Nym. *Inside Red China.* NY: 1939.

"Widow of Late Premier Dies at 88," in *The Beijing Review.* July 20–26, 1992, p. 7.

SUGGESTED READING:

Hu Hsing-fen. *Mrs Li Zhifan: A Memoir about Deng Yingchao.* Edited by Israel Epstein and translated by Li Chaotseng and Deng Guangyin. Hong Kong: Joint Publishing, 1987.

Salisbury, Harrison. *The Long March*. NY: McGraw, 1987.

Snow, Edgar. "Red China's Gentle Hatchet Man," in *The Saturday Evening Post*. March 27, 1954.

———. *Red Star Over China*. NY: Bantam, 1978.

Jeffrey G. Barlow,
Professor in the Department of Social Studies,
Pacific University, Forest Grove, Oregon

Deng Yinzhao (1903–1992).

See Deng Yingchao.

Deng Yuzhi (b. 1900)

Radical feminist who took an active role in China's May 4th Revolution of 1919 and, through her work for the Young Women's Christian Association, improved working conditions for women, particularly in factories, while also organizing night schools that became a forum for feminism throughout China. Name variations: Cora Deng; Teng Yü-chih. Pronunciation: Ding YOU-zhee. Born Deng Yuzhi in Shashi, China, in 1900; daughter of a government official; attended Zhou Nan Girls' Middle School, Fuxiang School for Girls, Jinling College in Nanjing, and one year at London School of Economics; married but separated shortly afterward, in 1919; no children.

Orphaned at age ten (1910); sent by grandmother to Fuxiang School for Girls, where she joined the YWCA; as president of the student self-government association, became organizer in the May 4th Revolution (1919); forced into an arranged marriage, left her husband and his family to attend Jinling College in Nanjing (1919); pursued by her husband's family, fled to Shanghai where she worked several years for the YWCA; attended the London School of Economics (1929–30); returned to China, appointed head of the YWCA's Bureau of Labor (1930); began organizing night schools throughout China to raise women's political, social, and feminist consciousness; collaborated with the Chinese Communist Party (1930–40s); appeared with Mao Zedong in Tiananmen Square on the occasion of the founding of the People's Republic of China (1949); served in numerous organizations and as general secretary of the YWCA.

For a girl born in 1900 in the city of Shashi, China, Deng Yuzhi had unusual exposure to radical social ideas. Her father was a government official and a strict Confucian, but he was also a social progressive, who cut off his queue (pigtail) and joined the Anti-Footbinding Society. When Deng was eight, the family moved to Changsha, the most prominent city in Hunan province, and a political, cultural, and educa-

tional center known for its radicalism since the 1890s. The first government-sponsored schools for girls had been established only in 1906, and her parents were enthusiastic about the new opportunity for Deng and her sister, who were enrolled in the progressive Zhou Nan Girls' Middle School. According to Deng, "My parents wanted to send us to a modern school because the atmosphere in Changsha was very progressive at the time." Zhou Nan's students were known for their public defiance of traditional female roles. They bobbed their hair and appeared in public unescorted, shocking older Chinese. A number of Zhou Nan students, including **Yang Kaihui** (second wife of **Mao Zedong**), *Xiang Jingyu, *Cai Chang and *Ding Ling, later became leaders in the Chinese Communist Party.

Deng was still a young child, when her father became ill with tuberculosis. When she was only ten, both her parents died, and she went to live with her grandmother, a devout Buddhist who was converted to Christianity after witnessing the kindness of the missionaries who treated her son at Yale Hospital in Changsha. Her granddaughters became Christian as well.

After graduation from the Zhou Nan Middle School, Deng was sent to Fuxiang School for Girls, where she learned English, became familiar with Western culture, and joined the Young Women's Christian Association (YWCA), the beginning of a long affiliation. The YWCA belongs to the great era of Christian missions, when its outposts were established in more than 30 countries. The institution had been founded in London in 1855, by **Emma Robarts** and ❦▶ **Mary Jane Kinnaird**. Robarts wanted to help the thousands of young women pouring into cities, looking for work, who became victims of the harsh labor conditions of the early Industrial Revolution, while Kinnaird was particularly concerned about African slaves and Indian women whose status was unprotected; the two joined forces to found an organization run by women and for women. Broadly ecumenical in its philosophy, the YWCA quickly evolved from evangelism to social gospel, particularly as teachers, administrators, and social workers came into contact with women around the world. Although conditions were grim in European and American slums, they were grimmer still in China, India, Africa, and the Middle East where women had fewer rights, and the efforts of the YWCA to improve their status drew individuals like Deng Yuzhi into its ranks.

Deng Yuzhi was president of the student self-government association at Fuxiang School for Girls when the Revolution of May 4, 1919, erupted. The battles of World War I had ended the previous year, and, in the final settlements at the Versailles Peace Conference, parts of China were ceded to the Japanese. When news of this reached the public, Chinese students joined in demonstrations, and campuses throughout the country were soon engaged in the boycott of Japanese goods. At Fuxiang, Deng played a major role in demonstrations throughout the spring and summer, taking to the streets with her classmates, making speeches, and exhorting local shopkeepers not to buy Japanese goods.

At Fuxiang School, Deng's teachers were generally independent, unmarried women, whom she greatly admired. With the May 4th Movement, she became strengthened in her belief that she must set out on a new path, and declared her intention to "support myself and not depend on a father, husband, or son." Shortly after her high school graduation that year, her declaration of independence appeared to be short lived, when her grandmother informed her that she was to be wed, according to common practice, in a marriage arranged by her parents many years earlier. Wanting earnestly to continue her education, Deng extracted a promise from her in-laws that she would be permitted to finish college. As soon as the wedding had occurred and she was moved in with her husband's family, she found the promise broken. She fled her new home to take refuge at the Fuxiang School.

With the support of her former teachers, Deng was sent to Jinling College in Nanjing, one of a handful of colleges open to women, with only five or six faculty members and a hundred students. When the lawyer and family of Deng's husband discovered her whereabouts and insisted upon her return, the college president, *Matilda Thurston, intervened and sent Deng to Shanghai in 1921. For the next few years, Deng Yuzhi moved frequently, working for the YWCA for two years in Changsha, then another two years finishing her education at Jingling, followed by two more years of work for the YWCA.

In Shanghai, Deng began a working relationship with **Maud Russell**, who had come to China with the YWCA in the mid-1910s. Russell believed that Christianity must be combined with socialism if it were to have any effect on the everyday lives of the Chinese. "Whatever little knowledge I had about socialism at that time was started by my contact with Maud," said Deng, "and her helping me read those famous books about social revolution."

In 1929–30, Deng Yuzhi's introduction to radical Christian socialism was reinforced by a year of study at the London School of Economics. Promoted by Sidney and *Beatrice Webb, the school was the center of progressive socialism, and strongly influenced by freethinkers like George Bernard Shaw, who were then calling for a new social order that guaranteed workers rights and benefits.

> *A*s I went through the factories I saw the terrible living conditions and the long hours, the child labor, and all that. . . . I tried to describe why women were not able to earn their own living, why they were subject to oppression in the home as well as the factory.
>
> —Deng Yuzhi

In 1930, Deng returned from England and became head of the YWCA Labor Bureau. Thousands of workers had moved to large industrial cities like Shanghai to work in factories, and the working conditions were appalling, especially for women and children. Women, who comprised two-thirds of the Shanghai workforce, were loaded on carts, pushed by burly men, early in the morning, to work 19-hour days in filthy and life-threatening conditions. The modesty of the YWCA's demands for reform give a notion of just how awful conditions were: The organization asked for one day off a week, 13-hour days, safeguards on machinery, and a minimum age for hiring children. Most factory owners, who averaged profits of 50–150%, saw these demands as outrageous. In China, human lives, and especially women's lives, were cheap.

In one attempt at reforming working conditions, the YWCA offered classes in the hope of "developing workers who would carry on Christian work," an approach doomed to failure be-

Kinnaird, Mary Jane (1816–1888)

English philanthropist. Name variations: Lady Kinnaird; Mrs. Arthur Kinnaird. Born Mary Jane Hoare in 1816; died in 1888; married Arthur Fitzgerald Kinnaird, 10th baron Kinnaird (1814–1887, also a philanthropist).

In 1849, Lady Kinnaird edited *Servants Prayers*. Along with **Lady Canning**, she also sent aid to the wounded in the Crimea. With **Emma Robarts**, *et al.*, Kinnaird was one of the founders of the Young Women's Christian Association.

cause it did not address the fundamental problems. Deng Yuzhi began to suggest a different tack. Uneducated women could never be politically effective, she felt, and 80% of Chinese women were illiterate. In educating them about their condition, they would be motivated to demand change. Since many factories were owned by the Japanese, Deng's approach was also patriotic and nationalistic, a stance against the hated foreigners.

Like her actions during the May 4th Revolution, her leadership of the Labor Bureau was enthusiastic and intense. Deng Yuzhi established night schools for women in major industrial centers, offering courses in writing, mathematics, geography, history, and current affairs. The women learned James Yen's simplified form of writing, the 1,000 Chinese character method, and within a year they could read a newspaper and write simple letters.

Night-school classes were used to further a political agenda. With the help of several teachers, Deng wrote a text that explained "what imperialism was, how to be patriotic, why workers were oppressed, and why workers' lives are so inferior to those of the capitalists." Teachers organized discussions about Japanese imperialism, workers' rights, and women's place in society. Patriotic songs were sung and students were encouraged to join the National Salvation Movement, which advocated full independence for China. This blending of practical skills with nationalistic patriotism proved a potent combination, and the popularity of Deng Yuzhi's YWCA night-school program grew throughout the country.

Had it not been for Deng's Christian affiliation, the night-school program would have been prohibited by the Guomindang, the ruling political party then governing China. The Guomindang was adamantly opposed to social change, particularly of a radical or Marxist nature, and had outlawed the Chinese Communist Party. Despite this prohibition, the Communists thrived, partly because many felt only radical change could reform China. Deng's night schools were a perfect solution to the party's problem of reaching a wider audience. Deng and her teachers were devoted to radical reform, and since her relations with the Guomindang were amicable, socialist philosophy was allowed to be taught in her schools without government interference. Trusted by the Guomindang, Deng Yuzhi occupied a unique position, as a radical Christian also courted by the Communists.

During the 1930s and 1940s, Deng increasingly collaborated with the Communists whose power in China was growing. "The YMCA and YWCA are not churches," she explained. "They are social organizations with membership among the masses. So we got in touch with the more progressive groups, including the underground communist group. They wouldn't tell you they were Communists, but they would appear as patriotic workers. That we would welcome." By enlisting the help of party cultural workers and members to teach at the schools and to give special programs, she made the night-school program a vital link between the party and the people. She saw both the YWCA and the Communists as fighting for a free China, a bond more important than ideological differences. Wrote Deng:

> What held us together was that we wanted to be an independent country managed by our own people. That was in accordance with the communist idea of a free China as well. So on those terms we worked together. As far as religious beliefs are concerned, they were atheists and we had our own beliefs. They didn't ask us to become atheists and we didn't ask them to become Christians. Zhou Enlai made it very clear to us, "You go on with your own religious activities and we are atheists. But we won't bother you. That's your freedom."

Deng Yuzhi's blending of Christianity and Communism was not without precedent. Karl Marx borrowed much from his own Judeo-Christian heritage when formulating his social doctrine, and the Gospel was full of admonitions to share with the poor and help the oppressed, themes that Marx echoed. Fusion of these two Western ideologies seemed natural to Deng who never joined the Chinese Communist Party. "I was a Christian," she said, "so how could I be a communist?" She no doubt recognized that if she joined the party, her agenda for women's liberation would be subjugated to the requirements of the revolution. Male revolutionaries were generally more devoted to the overthrow of the current government than to furthering a feminist agenda.

Following the end of World War II, civil war broke out in China between the Guomindang and the Chinese Communist Party. Eventually the Guomindang was forced to flee to Taiwan, and the Communists took over, establishing the People's Republic of China. For two decades, Deng Yuzhi had been a revolutionary force in the country. As a Christian, her position could have been difficult, if not impossible, in the nascent People's Republic, had it not been for the service provided by the network of YWCA night schools in raising feminist consciousness.

On October 1, 1949, when Mao Zedong appeared on a reviewing platform in Tiananmen Square to celebrate the founding of the People's Republic, Deng Yuzhi was there as an honored guest. She was also invited to participate in meetings establishing the All-China Federation of Women and to join the People's Political Consultative Council.

Despite this acceptance, the Cold War made a neutral stance regarding the YWCA difficult. On January 8, 1950, the People's Republic of China confiscated the American consulate, and by July the last Americans had left the country; soon all the Western institutions that once operated in China, including missionary schools, churches, and other foreign institutions, were closed—except for the YWCA, which continued to function. Walking the line of radical Christianity, Deng managed to be tolerated by the new Communist government as she had by the Guomindang.

For Deng Yuzhi, long regarded as a radical, relations with the YWCA itself were not always easy. In 1950, she decided to attend the World Peace Conference in Warsaw, a meeting that the international YWCA decided to boycott. Deng felt strongly that her presence was required as a Chinese Christian, and she not only attended this conference but a second held in Warsaw in 1953. Despite these philosophical differences, Deng was ultimately promoted to general secretary of the China YWCA, which continued throughout the Cold War and the Cultural Revolution. Remaining a practicing Christian with a radical agenda, she was responsible for improvements in women's working conditions in the factories, including shorter hours, higher wages, vacations, and medical and child care, which became more common in the People's Republic. While some might label Deng as a compromiser, a more apt label is that of independent feminist. From the time of its founding, YWCA members maintained a notable independence that foreshadowed the women's liberation movement in a later era.

SOURCES:

Boyd, Nancy. *Emissaries: The Overseas Work of the American YWCA 1859-1970.* NY: The Women's Press, 1986.

Honig, Emily. "The Life and Times of Deng Yuzhi (Cora Deng)," in Cheryl Johnson-Odim and Margaret Strobel, eds., *Expanding the Boundaries of Women's History: Essays on Women in the Third World.* Bloomington, IN: Indiana University Press, 1992, pp. 122–143.

Hunter, Jane. *The Gospel of Gentility: American Women Missionaries in Turn-of-the-Century China.* New Haven, CT: Yale University Press, 1984.

Reed, James. *The Missionary Mind and East Asia Policy, 1911–1915.* Cambridge, MA: Council on East Asian Studies, 1983.

Varg, Paul A. *Missionaries, Chinese and Diplomats: The American Protestant Missionary Movement in China, 1890–1952.* Princeton, NJ: Princeton University Press, 1958.

Karin Loewen Haag,
freelance writer, Athens, Georgia

Denis, Louise (c. 1710–1790).

See Chatelet, Marquise for sidebar.

Denison, Flora MacDonald
(1867–1921)

Member of the Canadian reform and suffrage movements of the early 20th century, who was one of a few who argued for women's rights based on an image of women as equal and autonomous citizens. Name variations: Flora Merrill. Born Flora MacDonald Merrill in 1867 in the wilderness of Northern Ontario, Canada; died on May 23, 1921, from complications related to pneumonia; daughter of George Merrill (a teacher); sources do not mention her mother's name; attended a Collegiate Institute in Belleville until age 15; attended a Commercial school in Toronto; married Howard Denison, in August 1892; children: Merrill (b. 1893).

Moved to Detroit and began journalism career (late 1880s); returned to Toronto, began dressmaking career (1893); joined suffrage movement (1903); established independent dressmaking shop (1905); began writing for Toronto Sunday World *(1906); served as president of Canadian Suffrage Association (1910–14); established "Bon Echo" retreat in Central Ontario (1916).*

Selected publications: Mary Melville *(1900);* Women Suffrage in Canada *(1912); contributor to* Detroit Free Press *and* Saturday Night *(1890s to early 1900s); contributor to* Toronto Sunday World *(1906–14); published* Sunset of Bon Echo *(eight issues, 1916).*

In the midst of a battle between the two major suffrage organizations in Ontario, Canada, the president of the Canadian Suffrage Association received an unsigned letter addressed to "Flora MacDonald Denison, Dressmaker." Contained in the letter was a warning to Denison to keep to her "own class." According to its anonymous authors, it was only through the efforts of their kind that support for suffrage had been "lifted . . . out of the dressmaking class" and embraced by the "best people."

In many ways, the letter exemplified the conflict that lay at the heart of Canada's feminist movement, as well as those aspects of Canadian society that Denison fought against throughout her public career. For one thing, she abhorred the inequality and injustice that resulted from societal notions of a hierarchial class structure. Moreover, she must have realized that these women were also reacting to her "radical" views toward the issue of suffrage, which differed from those of many of her colleagues then in pursuit of the vote for women. Denison saw women as equal and autonomous members of society, entitled to the same rights as men, in contrast to the more accepted view, which assumed women and men were fundamentally different in "nature" and, therefore, destined to perform different societal roles. In her lifestyle as well as her writing, Denison exemplified an alternative vision of feminism, which sets her apart from her countrywomen involved in the women's movement of the early 20th century.

Of course, all my roads lead to the one goal— the goal of women's emancipation from all customs and prejudices that have made her discriminated against.

—Flora MacDonald Denison

The Merrill family was middle class, respectable and firmly established in Picton, Ontario, when Flora MacDonald Merrill was born into it, in 1867. Her father was George Merrill, who quit his job as master of the Picton Grammar School, packed up his family, and moved to the wilderness of Northern Ontario to improve the family's lot by trying his hand at mining. The mining venture proved to be a financial disaster from which the family never recovered. They moved back to Belleville, near Picton, where George worked sporadically and eventually became a heavy drinker.

No record exists of the impact of these early years on Denison's later thought and lifestyle. The Merrill family undoubtedly found their social status diminished, but the family appears to have been close, and, judging by his daughter's later life, it is reasonable to speculate that the adventurous and rebellious spirit of the father rubbed off on her. What is certain is that Denison acquired a lifelong interest in mysticism and parapsychology from her family. Her sister Mary, who died in 1880, was credited with extraordinary extrasensory powers, such as the ability to levitate chairs with her eyes. As an adult, Flora Denison rejected orthodox Chris-

Opposite page

Flora MacDonald Denison

tianity because Christian ideals, such as original sin, did not coincide with her own beliefs about human nature. In particular, she detested the "miserable position" women were given within the Christian church. In a suffrage speech, she castigated orthodox Christianity, asserting:

> The Church with its doctrine of the total depravity of the human race founded upon its assertion of the inherent wickedness of woman has built up a false morality, a mock modesty, a sneaking hypocrisy. It has murdered innocence. . . . The teaching of the Church is at the bottom of women's slavery.

Denison adhered instead to a number of mystical religions and philosophies such as Theosophy (espoused by *Annie Besant and *Helena Blavatsky) and the Free Thought movement of American poet *Ella Wheeler Wilcox.

After completing grammar school in Belleville, Flora moved to Picton to live with her aunt and uncle while attending the Collegiate Institute. By age 15, she was a school teacher. For unknown reasons, she shortly left teaching and moved to Toronto, Ontario, to train at a commercial school and work for an insurance company. By the late 1880s, she had moved to Detroit, Michigan, where she found work in an office. All occupations she had sought were common and acceptable for lower-middle-class women before marriage, and in her frequent moves she had always lived with relatives, thereby asserting no more independence than was considered "respectable" female behavior.

While in Detroit, Flora met Howard Denison, whom she married in August 1892, at age 25. Not much is known about their relationship, although it was not particularly close, at least after the initial courtship, and they eventually separated. Howard was a traveling salesman, an occupation that did not carry much status, and he was not consistent in supporting his family, which included a son Merrill, born in 1893. Wrote Denison:

> Girls took their position from what their fathers were, women took their position from what their husbands were. As long as they had a brother or a husband to support them they were respectable. They did not lose caste.

Clearly, Denison gained no "respectability" or class status from either her father or her husband. In Canadian society around 1900, it was expected that women would leave paid employment following the wedding to care for their homes and family; if working-class women were still forced to work, society had not come to terms with the causes of this situation and thus blamed the women indirectly.

In Detroit, Denison began to contribute articles to the *Detroit Free Press*. After the family moved to Toronto, Ontario, in 1893, she continued to write, contributing articles to the monthly magazine *Saturday Night*. Her most consistent source of income, however, came from dressmaking. By 1898, she had been hired as a "modiste" for the Robert Simpson Company, managing the custom-dress department. As a dressmaker, she was in the elite of the profession, considered a skilled worker, and made a decent income. She was self-supporting—a rarity in Canadian society, since most working women did not earn incomes sufficient to support themselves. This undoubtedly contributed to her growing independence, and the development of her views about women.

Dressmaking (including all the "needle trades") was notorious for its poor work conditions and pitifully low wages, however, and despite her own privileged position, Denison soon became an outspoken critic of the working conditions in an industry composed, almost entirely, of women workers. In her mind, it was unjust and cruel that women were paid starvation wages to make lavish clothing for the rich. In a column in *Saturday Night,* she offered the following poem:

> Pale blue lips—a ghastly picture
> Stitching she to dress a world
> That, perchance, does not dress her
> Nor indeed but barely feeds her,
> Hardly gives her bread enough
> To keep soul and flesh together
> This "The Woman with the Needle"

Denison's opposition stemmed from her beliefs about caste and work. *Caste* was the term she used to refer to both social inequality and the snobbery or elitism that went with it. Perhaps it was her experience of seeing her own status lowered, without feeling a reduction in her own self-worth, that led her to despise any class division predicated on the notion that some classes were superior to others. In her mind, all work, whether manual or intellectual, was equal, and what was necessary was for people to view and treat each other as equals. Her beliefs about caste were summed up in a pre-1910 speech:

> The thing that keeps the world moving is work. . . . It is labour that builds the castles, makes the carriages and paves the streets and yet the one that can play the best game of cards with labour's products to shuffle or he who by chance of birth . . . claims ownership, lives in castles, rides in the carriage over the paved streets.

In 1905, Denison quit her job at Simpsons to protest the introduction of time clocks. To

her, the clocks promoted class distinction and social inequality. Having established a name for herself as a creative dressmaker of high quality, she established her own shop, which she would run successfully until 1916.

A meeting with ◄❧ **Emily Howard Stowe**, a doctor and early Canadian suffragist, had led Denison to join the Dominion Women's Enfranchisement Association in 1903, one of the major national suffrage organizations in Canada. Suffrage had not yet gained widespread appeal, and the association was small, composed primarily of the few female doctors practicing in Canada. Denison quickly became prominent in the organization. By 1906, she was the association's secretary and acted as delegate to the Third World Conference of the International Suffrage Alliance in Copenhagen. From 1910 to 1914, she would be president of the organization, by then renamed the Canadian Suffrage Association. For several years, her house would serve as the association headquarters, and she would provide the movement with a prominent voice through her column in the *Toronto Sunday World,* a popular newspaper with a large circulation. Beginning sporadically in 1906, the column became a regular weekly feature in September 1909, and a platform for a variety of social issues, mostly related to women.

By the standards of the age, Denison's views about women, family, and home were radical, even to her colleagues within the Canadian women's movement. While the cause of suffrage that claimed women's right to vote had achieved widespread popularity by 1910, most middle-class women in support of it subscribed to what was called "maternal feminism." Along with the generally held contemporary view that women, due to their nature, were primarily responsible for care of the home and family, they saw the vote as a means of fulfilling their duties to home and children, since many political issues impinged on the privacy of the home. Women's "special" qualities, it was asserted, as the more caring, moral, and nurturing of the sexes, should be brought into public life in order to help steer the nation away from corruption and immorality. The vote was construed, in essence, as a form of social housekeeping. While Denison held that men and women differed in essential ways, she saw the vote as deserved by women simply because they were autonomous and equal citizens of the country. All citizens—women, the poor, and immigrants—should have the voice the vote gave them in public affairs. Rejecting the "public housekeepers" view, she argued for a more comprehensive equality, active in the public world of work and politics as well as the privacy of the home. "Men need women in politics," she wrote, "women need men in the home. The suffrage fight is not to separate the sexes but to join the sexes."

No doubt, her own personal experiences as a working woman separated from her husband influenced her views, which extended to issues of marriage and the family. In a society that did not provide decent jobs for women, and where women without men to support them were left on the fringe, she argued against the popular mythology that confined women to the home; in recognition of the value of child care, she advocated paying a wage to poor mothers, and she also supported divorce and abortion. In 1909, Denison alluded to abortion when she argued that it was better to "look after the children that are here than fuss too much about the ones that will never exist." She also argued that women should be able to propose marriage, and that titles for women that display marital status should be abolished. In one speech, she said:

> Women's sphere should only be limited by her capabilities and I believe there is no sex in the human brain. Women are at last in the commercial arena and each day becoming more independent. Their final salvation will be achieved when they become the financial equals of men.

The maternal feminists could not go this far; it was to be another 50 years before Denison's vision of equality would dominate the women's movement. Meanwhile, her outspoken advocacy of such ideas frequently led to friction with her associates in the suffrage movement. By 1912, suffrage organizations had grown substantially, but Denison's unorthodox views, combined with her lower-class status, were causing dissension, especially among the new members, who were

❧► **Stowe, Emily Howard** (1831–1903)

Canadian doctor and feminist. Born Emily Jennings in South Norwich, Upper Canada (now Ontario), in 1831; died in 1903; graduated from the New York College of Medicine for Women, M.D., 1867; married John Stowe; no children.

After graduating from New York's College of Medicine, Emily Howard Stowe returned to Canada and launched her 13-year fight to be admitted to the College of Physicians and Surgeons in Ontario. In 1880, she became the first woman to practice medicine in Canada. A leading suffragist, she was the founder and first president of the Dominion Woman Suffrage Association.

more conservative than their predecessors. In 1913, Denison again attended the International Suffrage Alliance conference, this time in Budapest. On her way home, she stopped in England, where she delivered a speech to the Women's Social and Political Union (WSPU). The WSPU was highly controversial in North America because of its radical views and tactics espoused by members. When Denison returned to Canada a member of the WSPU, it was the final straw for many in the association, and in 1914 Denison was compelled to resign her presidency.

Perhaps as a means of getting away from the tensions, Denison left Toronto and moved to the small town of Napanee, in Northern Ontario, where she worked as a dressmaker and remained plagued by financial difficulties. In 1916, she moved again, this time to New York state where she served as a speaker and organizer for the women's suffrage campaign. Her financial situation remained difficult, and she became deeply troubled by the outbreak of World War I, an anxiety that was escalated when her son Merrill decided to join the U.S. army. Denison and Merrill were exceptionally close, and, throughout his years in the army, she wrote him daily letters that he answered with regularity.

By 1910, Denison had returned to the Ontario countryside, where she and Howard purchased "Bon Echo," a property in the Ontario highlands. After 1916, she ran the place for a number of years as a summer hotel and spiritual retreat and also managed to publish eight issues of a magazine entitled *Sunset of Bon Echo*.

Denison's public activity centered at this time around a developing interest in socialism. In 1918, she helped organize the Social Reconstruction Group of the Toronto Theosophical Society. As its honorary president, she attended the 1918 convention, which launched the Ontario section of the Canadian Labour Party, one of a number of early socialist parties in the country. In 1918–19, she gave a number of speeches to the party membership on the women's movement and the ideas of Walt Whitman.

It is hard to say whether Denison ever fully embraced the tenets of socialism; the ideas expressed in her columns and as a member of the suffrage movement cannot be labeled as "socialist." Although she advocated equality and spoke out against injustice in work and the social system, she also promoted a vague notion of "brotherhood," and the idea of class antagonism inherent in socialism would probably not

have appealed to her. Her desire was for all people to regard and treat one another as equals.

Denison had suffered for years from declining health, and when she contracted pneumonia, she was unable to fight it. She died on May 23, 1921, at age 54. An obituary in the *Canadian Theophist* eulogized: "No one in the present generation of Canadians has done more for the 'institution of the dear love of comrades' than Flora MacDonald Denison."

SOURCES:

Gorham, Deborah. "Flora MacDonald Denison: Canadian Feminist," in *A Not Unreasonable Claim: Women and Reform in Canada 1880s–1920s*. Edited by Linda Kealey. Toronto: Women's Educational Press, 1979, pp. 47–70.

Roberts, Wayne. "Six New Women: A Guide to the Mental Map of Women Reformers in Toronto," in *Atlantis*. Vol. 3. Autumn 1977, pp. 145–164.

SUGGESTED READING:

Denison, Flora MacDonald. *Mary Melville: The Psychic*. Toronto: Austin, 1900.

——. *Women Suffrage in Canada*. Toronto: Toronto Suffrage Association, 1912.

MacDonald, Dick. *Mugwump Canadian: The Merrill Denison Story*. Montreal: Content, 1973.

COLLECTIONS:

Merrill Denison Collection located in the Douglass Library, Queens University, Kingston, Ontario.

Scrapbooks located in the University of Toronto Rarebooks Room, University of Toronto, Toronto, Ontario.

Catherine Briggs,
freelance writer and Ph.D. Candidate,
University of Waterloo, Waterloo, Ontario, Canada

Denmark, queen of.

Dennett, Mary Ware (1872–1947)

*American birth control advocate, women's suffragist, and pacifist whose 1929 landmark court case helped redefine the legal definition of obscenity. Pronunciation: DEN-et. Born Mary Coffin Ware on April 4, 1872, in Worcester, Massachusetts; died of myocarditis in a nursing home in Valatie, New York, on July 25, 1947; daughter of George Whitefield Ware (a wool merchant) and Livonia Coffin (Ames) Ware; niece of *Lucia Ames Mead; attended Boston public schools, Miss Capen's School for Girls, Northampton, Massachusetts, and Boston Museum of Fine Arts; married William Hartley Dennett, on January 20, 1900 (divorced 1913); children: three boys, two of whom, Carleton and Devon, survived past childhood.*

Taught decoration and design, Drexel Institute in Philadelphia (1894–97); opened handicraft shop in Boston (1898); councilor, Boston Society of Arts and Crafts (1899–1905); served as field secretary of Massachusetts Woman Suffrage Association (1908–10); named corresponding secretary, National American Woman Suffrage Association (1910–14); served as field

secretary, American Union Against Militarism (1916); founded, then directed, National Birth Control League (1915–18) and Voluntary Parenthood League (1919–25); published "The Sex Side of Life: An Explanation for Young People" in the Medical Review of Reviews *(1918); was editor for* Birth Control Herald *(1922–25); wrote* Birth Control Laws *(1926); won celebrated obscenity case, U.S. v. Dennett (1930); wrote* Who's Obscene? *(1930) and* The Sex Education of Children *(1931); named chair, World Federalists (1941–44).*

During the spring of 1929, Mary Ware Dennett became a reluctant national celebrity. Then a 53-year-old grandmother, her ordeal as the defendant in what would turn out to be a landmark free speech case received extensive coverage in the popular press. Dennett had been active in a variety of reform causes, including the women's suffrage, peace, and birth-control movements, but hers had hardly been a household name before the trial. But as she sat in a Brooklyn, New York, courtroom on the afternoon of April 23, anxiously awaiting the jury's verdict, this was all about to change. For the next 12 months, her life remained a whirlwind of excitement and turmoil.

Mary Dennett harbored "a deep aversion to being spotlighted," though she had devoted much of her life to political activism. Born in 1872 in Worcester, Massachusetts, to George Whitefield Ware and **Livonia Ames Ware**, she grew up in comfortable, middle-class surroundings. Her father was a wool merchant, while her mother's side of the family included some notable reform-minded writers, including Mary's great-uncle Charles Carleton Coffin, the famous Civil War correspondent, and her aunt *Lucia Ames Mead, the prominent peace activist. Mary went to public and private schools in the Boston area, attended the Boston Museum of Fine Arts school, and, upon graduation, taught decoration and design at the Drexel Institute in Philadelphia from 1894 until 1897. The following year, with her sister **Clara Ware**, she opened a handicraft shop that sold gilded leather. The Ware sisters revived the ancient art of making guadamaciles, gilded and tooled wall hangings that formed the major handcraft of Spain in the 15th and 16th centuries. In 1900, Mary married architect William H. ("Hartley") Dennett, with whom she had three boys, including two (Carleton and Devon) who survived past childhood. Mary and Hartley separated in 1909 and divorced in 1913. Around this time, Dennett became a leading member of the Massachusetts Woman Suffrage Associa-

Mary Ware Dennett, with her sons.

tion, serving as the group's field secretary from 1908 until 1910. She then accepted election as the National American Woman Suffrage Association's (NAWSA) corresponding secretary, and she remained one of this organization's chief publicists until 1914.

Dennett was also active in the Intercollegiate Socialist Society, the single-tax movement, and, particularly after World War I broke out in 1914, the American peace movement. She served as field secretary for the American Union Against Militarism, helped found the People's Council for

Peace and Democracy, and joined the New York City branch of the Woman's Peace Party. At the same time, Dennett emerged as a leader of the birth-control movement, helping to found the National Birth Control League (NBCL), and then leading the organization from 1915 until 1918. In 1919, she created the Voluntary Parenthood League (VPL), which became the principal rival of *Margaret Sanger's American Birth Control League (ABCL) during the 1920s.

Mary Dennett believed that denying individuals access to birth-control information violated First Amendment rights. Her focus on birth control as a civil liberties issue was inconsistent with Sanger's desire to pass "doctor's only" laws that would limit the distribution of birth-control information and devices to patients who consulted physicians. Recognizing that the "well-to-do educated class . . . obtained and utilized birth control knowledge, despite the laws," Dennett thought that the time had come for legislation to catch up with current practices and expand this "right" to all Americans.

I look forward to the day when we shall have a sex education that matches up to the time we live in, expressive as the time we live in, and as progressive as commerce and science.

—**Mary Ware Dennett**

The major federal anti-obscenity statute that Dennett condemned was, in fact, antiquated. Introduced in 1873 by anti-obscenity crusader Anthony Comstock, the "Comstock law" banned from the mails any "obscene, lewd, or lascivious" material and gave the postmaster general the power to identify such matter. Any writings that included information on "preventing conception" were included in the ban. Dennett's primary goal was to see these two words stricken from law, but the U.S. Congress, fearful of controversy on such a sensitive issue, refused to undertake any serious reconsideration of the postal obscenity statute.

Dennett, as head of the Voluntary Parenthood League, was openly critical of the postal service for continuing a selective, though often vigorous, enforcement of the Comstock law. It was this adversarial position that seems to have gotten her into trouble with the postmaster general who, in 1922, banned a Dennett-authored pamphlet as an obscene publication. The work in question, *The Sex Side of Life: An Explanation for Young People,* was a sex-education manual for children. Before it was labelled ob-

scene, Dennett had sold thousands of copies of the 24-page booklet written initially by the single mother in 1915 as a sex-education primer for her young sons. *The Sex Side of Life* was somewhat more explicit than most other sex-education manuals of the period. It included four diagrams, the use of the proper medical terminology for sex organs and functions, and a clear explanation of physiological and emotional aspects of sex. It was also very popular with some schools and youth groups like the YMCA, so she continued to send it out under first-class postage in defiance of the ban.

In August 1928, Dennett sent a copy to American Civil Liberties Union (ACLU) counsel Morris L. Ernst after reading an article he had written condemning censorship. He wrote back, asking if she "ever considered testing out the legality of the pamphlet in the courts." Ernst offered to take the case without compensation if Dennett wanted to fight the postal authorities in court, and she consented. Ironically, before Ernst finished devising a strategy to bring an injunction suit against the government, the Justice Department indicted Mary Dennett under the Comstock law of 1873. A post-office inspector "rigged up a decoy to order a pamphlet," which Dennett then sent to a post-office box in Grottoes, Virginia.

When the case went to trial, the sole issue, in the view of the judge, was whether or not the jury believed the sex manual offended "the common sense and modesty of the community." They decided that it did, and Dennett received a $3,000 fine. But when the birth-control advocate declared she would pay no fine, however small, and promised to appeal, the case began to receive considerable attention in newspapers and journals. Nearly every newspaper in the country covered the case. Editorial opinion was overwhelmingly sympathetic toward Mary Dennett and rebuked the government in pointed, often sarcastic, terms. A week after the trial, Dennett wrote that "support for the case is rolling up till it looks like a mountain range," and she noted that she knew of "only [a] single instance . . . of newspaper disparagement of me or my pamphlet," though Dennett opponents were often quoted in these articles.

On January 15, 1930, Morris Ernst presented Dennett's appeal before the U.S. Court of Appeals. Labelling the issue at hand "a test case of vital importance," he warned that if the conviction stood, "it will deal a disastrous blow to the cause of sex education." His appeal was based on the argument that the Comstock law violated the First Amendment and that the pamphlet was not obscene in the first place. The position of the Justice Department was straight forward because clear precedent seemed to be on its side. The courts had long held that a work was obscene even if only one isolated excerpt "depraved and corrupted" those who were most susceptible to immoral influences (which included children).

Two months after hearing oral arguments, the Appeals Court overturned the original Dennett conviction on the grounds that the pamphlet was not obscene. As justice Augustus Hand wrote, "any incidental tendency to arouse sex impulses which such a pamphlet may perhaps have, is apart from and subordinate to its main effect. The tendency can only exist in so far as it is inherent in any sex instruction and it would seem to be outweighed by the elimination of ignorance." Thus by redefining what constituted obscene, Hand and his colleagues toppled the major legal barrier restricting meaningful sex education for children in *U.S. v. Dennett*.

The importance of this landmark case would go further than this, however. A series of U.S. Circuit Court cases that built on the *Dennett* decision, culminating in the *Ulysses* (the James Joyce book long banned as obscene) case, extended the definition of obscene as applied in the *Dennett* case to novels. No longer did the courts consider the effect of an isolated excerpt on especially susceptible persons, but instead considered "whether to the average person, applying contemporary community standards, the dominant theme of the material taken as a whole appeals to prurient interest."

Ironically, the *Dennett* decision also had an impact on the process that removed the stigma of illegality from birth-control information and devices. Citing the *Dennett* case, in *Davis* v. *United States,* the court ruled that "the [Comstock] statute must be given a reasonable construction," which then paved the way for Morris Ernst to argue in the *Japanese Pessaries* case (1936) that birth control could be medically necessary. The court agreed, with Augustus Hand again providing the rationale: the Comstock law's framers lacked adequate information about the dangers of conception and the safety of contraception, knowledge that would have led them not to include the words "preventing conception" in the statute. The justices of the U.S. Circuit Court in New York thus accomplished what Mary Dennett had sought through legislative action for two decades, though some states failed to get in line with federal case law until the mid-1960s.

Following her tumultuous year of notoriety, Mary Dennett renewed her efforts to encourage legislative action to legalize the distribution of birth-control information. She was unsuccessful, though the courts ultimately effected what politicians refused to do. In the early 1930s, Dennett actually withdrew from active organizational work within the reproductive-rights movement. Over the next 15 years, she devoted much of her attention to the American peace movement. In 1941, at the age of 69, she was elected chair of a new organization, the World Federalists. She brought the same kind of commitment to peace work that she had devoted to the campaign to fully legalize sex education and birth control. Upon her death in 1947, she left behind many decades of skilled organizational activism and a landmark court case that had helped to clarify the place of the Bill of Rights in American society.

SOURCES:

Craig, John M., "'The Sex Side of Life': The Obscenity Case of Mary Ware Dennett," in *Frontiers: A Journal of Woman Studies.* Vol. 15, Fall 1995, pp. 145–166.

Dennett, Mary Ware. *Who's Obscene?* NY: Vanguard Press, 1930.

Gordon, Linda. *Woman's Body, Woman's Right: Birth Control in America.* NY: Penguin Books, 1990.

SUGGESTED READING:

Ernst, Morris, and Alan U. Schwartz. *Censorship: The Search for the Obscene.* NY: Macmillan, 1964.

Chesler, Ellen. *Margaret Sanger: A Biography.* NY: Simon and Schuster, 1992.

COLLECTIONS:

ACLU Cases, American Civil Liberties Archives, Seeley G. Mudd Manuscript Library, Princeton, University.

Mary Ware Dennett Papers, Arthur and Elizabeth Schlesinger Library, Radcliffe College, Cambridge, Massachusetts.

John M. Craig, Professor of History, Slippery Rock University, Slippery Rock, Pennsylvania, author of *Lucia Ames Mead and the American Peace Movement* and numerous articles on activist American women

Dennis, Clare (1916–1971)

Australian swimmer. Name variations: some sources incorrectly cite Claire. Born on April 14, 1916; died of cancer at age 55 in 1971; married George Golding (Olympic athlete), in 1941.

Clare Dennis, who trained at Clovelly Beach in Sydney, won her first New South Wales and Australian championships at age 14 in the 220-yard breaststroke. After breaking the world record at age 15, she became the youngest member of the Australian delegation to compete in the 1932 Olympics in Los Angeles. Dennis surprised everyone by winning the Olympic gold medal in the 200-meter breaststroke, breaking the Olympic record at 3:06.3. She was the only non-American gold medalist in the women's swimming competition. From 1931 to 1935, Dennis was the premiere swimmer in her specialty in the world. In 1934, she was the first Australian swimmer to win a gold medal in the British Empire Games.

Dennis, Sandy (1937–1992)

American actress who won an Academy Award for Best Supporting Actress for her role in Who's Afraid of Virginia Woolf. *Born Sandra Dale Dennis in Hastings, Nebraska, on April 27, 1937; died in Westport, Connecticut, of ovarian cancer on March 2, 1992; attended Capitol Grammar School, Lincoln, Nebraska; graduated from Lincoln High School; attended Nebraska Wesleyan University and the University of Nebraska; studied acting at the HB Studio and the Actors Studio, New York.*

Selected films: Splendor in the Grass *(1961);* Who's Afraid of Virginia Woolf? *(1966);* Up the Down Staircase *(1967);* The Fox *(1968);* Sweet November *(1968);* That Cold Day in the Park *(Can.-US, 1969);* A Touch of Love *(Thank You All Very Much, UK, 1969);* The Out-of-

Towners *(1970);* The Only Way Out Is Dead *(Can., 1971);* Mr. Sycamore *(1975);* God Told Me To *(1976);* Nasty Habits *(UK, 1977);* Demon *(1977);* The Three Sisters *(1977);* The Four Seasons *(1981);* Come Back to the Five and Dime, Jimmy Dean, Jimmy Dean *(1982);* Another Woman *(1988);* 976-EVIL *(1988);* Parents *(1989).*

Distinguished by her waif-like demeanor, nervous mannerisms, and a speech pattern once likened to that of an early *Katharine Hepburn, actress Sandy Dennis distinguished herself playing emotionally uncertain and vulnerable women. She grew up in Nebraska and worked in community theater and summer stock before making her way to New York, where, while window shopping in Greenwich Village, she was noticed by a Hungarian producer who cast her in a revival of Ibsen's *The Lady from the Sea*. After understudying *Tuesday Weld in Elia Kazan's production *The Dark at the Top of the Stairs*, she emerged as a Broadway star in the 1960s, winning back-to-back Tony Awards for roles as a young social worker in *A Thousand Clowns* (1963), with Jason Robards, Jr., and as the mis-

From the movie Up the Down Staircase, starring Sandy Dennis.

tress of a married businessman in the comedy *Any Wednesday* (1964). Although some critics found her acting overly mannered, most were enthusiastic in their praise. "Let me tell you about Sandy Dennis," Walter Kerr of the *New York Herald Tribune* began one review. "There should be one in every home." *Cue* magazine's Emory Lewis called her a top-ranked Broadway clown, "unquestionably a new star. Her timing is far too brilliant in one so young."

Although she preferred the stage to movies, Dennis went on to win an Academy Award for Best Supporting Actress for her first substantial film role in Mike Nichols' *Who's Afraid of Virginia Woolf* (1966). As Honey, the fragile bride in the younger of two faculty couples who engage in an all-night drinking spree, she held her own with heavyweights *Elizabeth Taylor, Richard Burton, and George Segal. A reviewer for the *National Observer* felt she portrayed "the most viable character in the film." Dennis described working with Nichols as the happiest experience of her life. "He let you do the outrageous things you're capable of," she said. "He let you do the crazy things." A number of interesting film performances followed, notably *Up the Down Staircase* (1967), for which she received the Moscow Film Festival's best-actress award, and in Robert Altman's *That Cold Day in the Park*. In 1968, she portrayed Celia, the confused wife of a drug addict, in an American television production of "A Hatful of Rain." Later films included *The Four Seasons* (1981), *Another Woman* (1988), and her last, *Parents* (1989).

Offstage, Dennis was known as unpretentious, uninhibited, and compulsively candid. An animal lover since childhood, she reputedly kept at least eight cats and two dogs at her home in Westport, Connecticut. Dennis had a ten-year relationship with jazz musician Gerry Mulligan, which ended in 1976. Her later stage work included roles in *How the Other Half Loves, Absurd Person Singular, Same Time Next Year*, and *Come Back to the Five and Dime, Jimmy Dean, Jimmy Dean* (she also appeared in the movie version). The actress died of ovarian cancer, at age 55, on March 2, 1992. Found among her papers was a personal memoir, which includes memories of her childhood on a farm and her battle with cancer. The book was published posthumously in 1997.

SOURCES:
Dennis, Sandy. *Sandy Dennis: A Personal Memoir.* Edited by Doug Taylor and Louise Ladd. Papier-Mache, 1997.

Barbara Morgan,
Melrose, Massachusetts

Denny, Arbella (1707–1792)

Irish philanthropist who initiated the reform of the Dublin Foundling Hospital and founded the first Magdalen Asylum, or home for penitent prostitutes.

Name variations: Arabella; Lady Arbella Denny. Born Arbella Fitzmaurice in Ireland in 1707; died in Dublin on March 18, 1792 (some sources incorrectly cite 1785); daughter of Thomas Fitzmaurice, 1st Earl of Kerry, and Anne (Petty) Fitzmaurice, countess of Kerry; married Arthur Denny of Tralee, on August 26, 1727 (died 1742); no children.

Undertook the reform and improvement of the Dublin Foundling Hospital (1759) and continued to be associated with it until 1778; member of the Ladies' Committee of the Dublin Lying-in Hospital (1760); received thanks from the Irish House of Commons for her work at the Foundling Hospital (1764); awarded freedom of the City of Dublin (1765); elected honorary member of the Dublin Society (1766); founded the Magdalen Asylum in Leeson Street, Dublin (1767) and supervised its management until her retirement (1790).

In 1767, a pamphlet announcing a plan for a new type of charitable institution was published in Dublin. Voicing a currently widespread concern about the extent and effects of prostitution, the anonymous author of the *Letter to the public on an important subject* called for the foundation of "an infirmary for wounded consciences, an asylum for penitent females, early seduced from the paths of virtue . . . but now willing, nay, eager to return to their duties to God, themselves, and the community." In place of the "diseases, poverty and brutal insults" to which prostitutes were subject, inmates would "be lodged, boarded and clothed in a decent, becoming and comfortable manner, carefully and conscientiously instructed in the principles of true religion, and powerfully assisted in their virtuous resolutions." A fund had already been set up for the establishment of such a house and support for the venture was sought from all concerned citizens, but particularly from "the ladies of this kingdom . . . who, with compassion equal to their own superior virtue, will certainly patronize an undertaking designed to restore many fallen and unhappy persons of their sex to chastity, decency and competence. The influence of such examples cannot fail to be universal." On June 9, 1767, a general meeting of supporters of the new charity was held, and two days later, on June 11, the Magdalen Asylum opened in Leeson Street in Dublin under the direction of Lady Arbella Denny.

Although Lady Arbella's name quickly became synonymous with that of the asylum, this was by no means her first involvement in the field of philanthropy. She had already won fame for her interest in improvement and reform, had been awarded the freedom of the city of Dublin, and had been formally thanked by the Irish House of Commons for her "extraordinary bounty and charity," which went far beyond the conventional good works in which aristocratic and leisured ladies commonly engaged. Her philanthropy was innovative as well as energetic: the Magdalen Asylum was the first institution of its kind, as well as the first charity founded and run by women for women in Ireland. As the "protectress of helpless infancy and penitent frailty," that is, of foundling children and of "fallen women," Denny addressed herself to sectors of society whose needs had previously been disregarded and, by demonstrating the capacity of women to carry on such work and by encouraging members of her own sex to follow her example, paved the way for greater involvement by women in public life.

[Lady Arbella Denny's] kindness, patience, and perseverance, which surmounted obstacles that would have appalled a more ordinary mind, cannot be recollected without admiration.

—*Biographia Hibernica*

Lady Arbella, born in 1707, was the fourth of five children of Lord and Lady Kerry. Thomas Fitzmaurice, her father, owned vast tracts of land in the remote and beautiful southwest corner of Ireland, and Arbella's childhood was probably spent at the family seat of Lixnaw, near Tralee, where the Fitzmaurices, lords of Kerry since the 12th century, lived in considerable splendor: Charles Smith, visiting Lixnaw in 1756, described its magnificent gardens and a private chapel, its walls covered by frescoes copied from Raphael. Despite her privileged upbringing, however, the young Arbella could hardly fail to be aware of the tensions within her family background. Her father was described by his grandson as an "obstinate and inflexible" man, poorly educated, an "excessive bad husband" and a despot who tyrannized over the surrounding countryside as well as over his own household and family. "In consequence, his children did not love him, but dreaded him." **Anne Fitzmaurice**, Lady Kerry, on the other hand, was a woman of "superior understanding, address and temper" and of "an ambitious, active disposition." She was the only daughter and favorite child of Sir William Petty, the scientist and diplomat, and, under his supervision, had received an unusually broad education. A friend of Jonathan Swift, who commended her wit and intelligence, she was also a shrewd businesswoman who, according to her grandson, brought into the family "whatever degree of sense may have appeared in it, or whatever wealth is likely to remain in it." It was clearly with the maternal side of her heritage that Lady Arbella most closely identified. From her mother, she inherited an interest in science and the arts as well as energy and a zeal for improvement, and she is on record as having declared herself "prouder of my grandfather Petty's struggles, and industry, and success in life, than of all the honours of the House of Lixnaw."

In 1727, at the age of 20, Arbella married a neighboring landowner, Colonel Arthur Denny, "a very good sort of man" but "uninformed and ignorant." The Dennys' marriage was childless, and for that reason, perhaps, a close and enduring relationship developed between Lady Arbella and her nephew, William Fitzmaurice, later Lord Shelburne, who, having been virtually abandoned by his parents, spent the first four years of his life in his grandfather's house at Lixnaw. In a fragment of autobiography, written many years later, Shelburne recorded the love and "unspeakable gratitude" that he owed to his aunt for her tenderness at that time, and noted her influence on him. "She was," he wrote, "the only example I had before me of the two qualities of mind which most adorn and dignify life— amiability and independence"; she impressed upon him the necessity of "order" in all things; above all, "she inculcated into me a sense of duty towards God, the public, and my neighbours." The bond between Lady Arbella and her nephew remained strong, and in later life, Lord Shelburne, a leading politician and prime minister in 1782–83, was able to repay his aunt's devotion by promoting and financially supporting some of her benevolent enterprises.

In 1742, Colonel Denny died. His estate passed to his brother, leaving Lady Arbella with "comparatively small means for her rank in life." Nevertheless, she is reported to have refused several offers of marriage, having acquired, so she said, "too much experience ever to become a slave again," and instead took advantage of the opportunity offered by widowhood to pursue her own inclinations and concerns. In 1745, she moved to Dublin, where she was to live for the rest of her life, creating around her house at Blackrock a garden, which

John Wesley, who visited her there in 1783, described as "one of the pleasantest spots I ever saw." She became a noted hostess and a leading figure in Dublin society, traveled in Ireland and England and in 1751 made a tour of Europe where she was entertained at a number of princely courts.

She also acquired a reputation for benevolence and was active in a variety of schemes to relieve need and to improve the living and working conditions of the Irish poor. As a young woman, she had engaged in the type of private charities appropriate to her station as the daughter and wife of local landowners, establishing, for instance, "a little apothecary's shop . . . for the benefit of the poor" at Lixnaw. In Dublin, where there was widespread concern about the incidence of poverty and the impact of urbanization, she involved herself in a wide range of initiatives. She was, for instance, a member of the Ladies' Committee of the recently founded Dublin Lying-in Hospital and was a keen supporter of the work of the Dublin Society, founded in 1731 to encourage Irish manufactures and agriculture. Projects that she promoted included the development of a stove "for drying . . . codfish without the heat of the sun," the export of Irish cheeses, and the cultivation of madder and of flax. She had a particular interest in the welfare of the Irish textile industry, submitting memoranda on such subjects as the production of linen damask and of woollen and worsted goods, and with a number of other aristocratic ladies was appointed patron of the "public warehouse" established by the Society to promote Irish silk manufacture; in pursuit of the same end, she planted mulberry trees and bred silkworms in her garden at Blackrock. In 1766, the Dublin Society, in recognition of her contribution, elected her as its first honorary, as well as its first female, member, and in 1788 it recorded its thanks to her for "her constancy in creating employment and alleviating poverty and distress" to which, "through the Society and in other ways, she had given her life." Among these "other ways" was certainly included Lady Arbella's involvement with the Dublin Foundling Hospital which, beginning in 1759 when she was already over 50, was to bring her to public prominence as a philanthropist and reformer, and present her with a challenge which, as an early biography in *Biographia Hibernica* remarked, "would have appalled a more ordinary mind."

Denny's intervention in the affairs of the Foundling Hospital is in hindsight, perhaps, less surprising than the fact that in the first half century of its existence she was the only individual to show any genuine and sustained will to deal with conditions there. Founded in 1730 by Act of Parliament to address the practices, largely arising from poverty, of infanticide and child abandonment, the hospital from the beginning gave cause for concern. Although it had been established as a department of the Dublin Workhouse, the hospital was, in fact, a national institution, accepting abandoned children from all over Ireland and even from Britain. During its first year, 165 infants were admitted; thereafter, numbers rose sharply, and by 1757 the hospital had 2,069 children in its care. The heavy demands made on its facilities were compounded by insufficient funding and by lax management procedures. The governors met only rarely, irregularities and embezzlement were common, discipline was strict and often brutal, care was inadequate, and mortality rates among the children were extremely high: of 4,025 admissions in the period 1730–37, for instance, at least 3,235 died, from a range of causes that included "cold, hunger, lying in the streets, scrofulous or other disease" and, in the case of babies brought from the countryside, their sufferings on the journey. While older children were kept in the hospital, babies under two were given out into the care of foster mothers. Many were subsequently reported to have died, some were believed to have been murdered by their nurses and others simply disappeared, with the hospital authorities apparently making little effort to ascertain their fate.

In 1757, the House of Commons was sufficiently concerned to appoint a committee to enquire into the state and management of the institution. Its report was an appalling catalogue of mismanagement, neglect, and active cruelty. The diet, clothing and accommodation of the foundlings were found to be wretched. The dormitories were damp with broken windows; because of the conditions and the shortage of nurses to care for them, "the children have been frequently almost eaten up with vermin and uncleanness." Those who complained about the conditions "have been put into the cells of Bedlam, where mad people are kept, and continued there for days, weeks and months, some put into the same cells with mad men, and others most severely corrected and whipped."

It was almost certainly the revelations contained in this report that prompted Lady Arbella to concern herself in the hospital's affairs. According to *Biographia Hibernica*:

> She promptly stepped forward and proposed . . . that it should be visited by some

ladies of consequence, in rotation, rightly judging that the wants of young children, the negligence of nurses, and the general management of such an institution, fell more within their sphere of observation than of any gentlemen, however wise or discerning they might be.

Such a committee was established shortly afterwards but, while the other ladies involved soon lost interest, Denny persevered in her initiative. For 20 years, she visited the hospital several times weekly, engaged extra nurses to whom she offered incentives to encourage greater care of their charges, reorganized the nursery and infirmary, and supervised the enlargement and improvement of the hospital premises. Much of this she funded herself, spending in all over £4,000 of her own and her friends' money on the project. Few details of the institution's routine escaped her attention. It was recorded, for instance, that she installed a clock in the nursery, "to mark, that as children reared by the spoon, must have but a small quantity of food at a time, it must be offered frequently; for which purpose this clock strikes every twenty minutes, at which notice, all the infants that are not asleep, must be discreetly fed." She also made use of her association with the Dublin Society to foster the manufacture of bone lace by the foundlings, thereby providing them with a skill as well as with a small income. The lace so produced was sold at her request in the Society's warehouse, and its records for the period 1764–77 chronicle a number of payments to her for distribution as prizes among the children.

Lady Arbella's efforts were reflected in a marked improvement in conditions at the hospital and in a decline in the death rate, from over 50% of the total admitted 1750–60 to under 25% of those received in the period 1760–70. A 1764 House of Commons report noted that the children in the nursery "were found to be usefully employed and carefully educated . . . well fed, clothed and in general healthy," while "by the extraordinary care of the nurses in the workhouse, excited by premiums given by the Right Honourable Lady Arbella Denny . . . many of their lives have been saved." In the following year, she received the freedom of the city of Dublin "as a mark of . . . esteem for her many great charities and constant care of the poor foundling children in the City Workhouse," and in 1778, when old age forced her to retire, the governors of the workhouse offered her their "sincere and grateful acknowledgement" of her work, which had been "the means of saving the lives of many innocents."

Despite these plaudits, however, Denny's initiatives received no legislative support and produced no fundamental reform in the organization or supervision of the hospital. The improvements that she introduced vanished with her departure, and in 1788 a report to the House of Commons noted the need for more "cleanliness and order" and the detrimental effects "of the loss of Lady Arbella Denny's visits." The short-lived nature of the reforms that she had introduced illustrate the constraints on women's potential for action. Forced to work within existing structures and dependent on the cooperation and goodwill of bodies and individuals who demonstrated little evidence of concern or will to reform, her achievement could only be a personal, and thus a temporary, one. The decision to establish her own charity may well have been prompted by frustration at these restrictions, as well as by an awareness, gained in the course of her association with the Foundling Hospital, of the necessity for a refuge "for unfortunate females . . . willing to prefer a life of penitence and virtue to one of guilt, infamy and prostitution." Such a home had been opened in London a few years before, providing a model for the new institution. However, a novel feature of the Dublin enterprise, one that set it apart from other charities in both Britain and Ireland and became the pattern for a new type of female philanthropy, was the major role played by women in its affairs.

The Magdalen Asylum opened its doors at Leeson Street in Dublin on June 11, 1767, and received its first inmate shortly afterwards; 11 penitents were admitted during the first year, and by 1795 a total of 388 applicants had entered the house. The charity was financed by subscriptions and donations and by the weekly collections and the proceeds of the annual charity sermon at its own chapel, which, as one of Dublin's most popular places of worship, attracted aristocratic and affluent congregations and fashionable preachers. A committee of "governesses," elected from the lady subscribers, was appointed to visit the house regularly and to oversee the welfare, instruction, and training of inmates, but the principal authority was Lady Arbella, who, assisted by her deputy, **Mrs. Usher**, was closely involved in every aspect of the charity's affairs. Lady Arbella was also responsible for drawing up the comprehensive and detailed regulations under which the house operated, and which showed a characteristic concern for order and for the proper use of time. The day, which began at six in summer and seven in winter and ended at ten o'clock at night, was to be passed in "private devotions," meditation and prayer, housework and other employments, such as reading and needlework. Even the duration of meals was stipulated, the time to be measured by an hour glass placed in the center of the table, an hour being allowed for dinner and half an hour each for breakfast, supper and relaxation after meals.

The regime within the house was strict and undoubtedly had a punitive aspect. Designed above all for "the distressed soul, who has . . . perceived the error of her ways, and loathes her former vileness," it strongly emphasized the horror of the women's past way of life and stressed the need for a complete break. Inmates were known as "penitents" or "magdalens," recalling the Biblical *Mary Magdalen; their letters were subject to examination by the superintendent and their spiritual welfare was in the charge of a chaplain, who "exhorts and reproves them when required." Their real names were not used in the asylum. On admission, they were assigned a number by which they were to be known throughout their stay, a practice designed to protect their anonymity, but which also tended to depersonalize them and to emphasize the break with their former existence. On the other hand, the regime, though strict, was not inhumane. The house rules, for instance, stipulated that "it is Lady Arbella's wish that no business should be done in the Kitchen or Laundry after Candlelight and that all should be collected in the workroom, that work, reading and good instruction might go on with comfort, order, and tranquility for the mutual advantage of the whole family." There was, too, a recognition that prostitution was a response to economic factors and that moral reform must be underpinned by social rehabilitation. The majority of those admitted were under 17 years of age; women over 20, regarded as "incapable of instruction," were theoretically not accepted, although the registers of the house show that exceptions were sometimes made to this rule. The usual "period of probation" was two to three years, and an inmate was only dismissed when she had either been reconciled with her family or furnished with "a means of honest livelihood." Training was given in skills such as needlework and housework, and most of the inmates who successfully completed their term appear to have found employment either in the needle trades or in domestic service. On leaving the house, they were given such clothes as were necessary, as well as a bounty of three guineas provided by Lady Arbella out of her own pocket.

Although Denny retired from her involvement with the Foundling Hospital in 1778, describing herself in a letter to Lord Shelburne at that time as "a cripple," she continued to be closely associated with the management of the asylum until at least 1790, when she made her final entry in the house register. She died two years later at the age of 85, expressing in her will her regret "that the smallness of my fortune will not, in justice and prudence, allow me to make any donation to charities so worthy of support" as the Foundling Hospital and the Magdalen Asylum. Never a wealthy woman, she had spent much of what she did possess on her various philanthropic endeavors. However, her will did reflect her charitable interests: in addition to legacies to family and friends, she left £20 to be distributed among "the most industrious and impotent" of the poor of Tralee, as well as bequests to the poorhouse and roomkeepers at Lixnaw and to the poor living near her house at Blackrock. Typically too, she left precise instructions with regard to the arrangements for her burial, directing that her body be left uncoffined for three days to make certain that she was dead, and that her coffin should have no ornament, "my name and age only on the top, with the date." Nevertheless, her funeral was a spectacular affair. Contemporary newspaper reports describe the passage of the hearse, drawn by six horses, from Dublin to Tralee, and the funeral itself, attended by a number of "wailing" mourners, 12 widows whom she had supported since her husband's death some 50 years earlier. In Dublin, the Royal Irish Academy offered "a prize medal, value 100 guineas, for the best monody on the death of the late Lady Arabella Denny," and a few months later such an elegy was published, eulogizing Lady Arbella's unbounded charity, and in particular her work for foundlings and for prostitutes. This aspect of her mission was also noted in a second poetic tribute, published in the *Dublin Chronicle* of September 22, 1792. Supposedly written by a magdalen, it mourned the loss of a "bless'd saint . . . our greatest friend," and anticipated the imminent end of the asylum itself. In fact, the institution did survive, becoming a home for unmarried mothers rather than for penitent prostitutes, but retaining until well into the present century many of the features that Lady Arbella had herself introduced.

Denny was, above all, a practical philanthropist, who left little indication of the impulses that fuelled her humanitarianism. One motivation was clearly her faith, which she summarized as a sense of duty "to God, my neighbours, and myself," and which she hoped to pass on to the objects of her charity. The Magdalen Asylum, she wrote, "was founded only for the shelter and advantage of . . . penitent Christians that in a state of peace and tranquillity they may learn their duty to God, to their neighbour and to themselves." Alongside this ran a second and more secular concern for order, which is evident both in small things, such as her passion for punctuality, and in the whole thrust of her work, which like most other philanthropic initiatives of the period, was pragmatic as well as humanitarian. Charity was not simply a Christian obligation; it was also a means of controlling the poor and marginalized, with the ultimate aim of safeguarding order within society itself. Within the Magdalen Asylum, penitents, through the development of personal discipline and an approved mode of behavior, were to become useful and virtuous members of the community, while society itself would be protected against the threat posed to its security by ignorance, vice, and license.

Lady Arbella's philanthropy, therefore, had clearly conservative elements. Yet she was also a pioneer, in initiating action on behalf of those, such as foundlings and prostitutes, who had previously attracted little attention from the benevolent, and in the claim that she staked for women in the field of organizational charity. The limitations on her potential for reform in relation to the Foundling Hospital may well have been instrumental in indicating to her the desirability of an institution over which she could exercise full control. The Magdalen Asylum provided such an opportunity, and in the process offered to other philanthropic women guidelines for organization and action, and a training that they could employ in subsequent decades in new institutions and in a variety of causes.

SOURCES:

Bayley Butler, Beatrice. "Lady Arbella Denny 1707–1792," in *Dublin Historical Record*. Vol. IX, no. 1, 1946–47, pp. 1–20.

Fitzmaurice, Edmond. *Life of William, Earl of Shelburne.* Vol. 1. London: Macmillan, 1875.

Peter, A. *A Brief Account of the Magdalen Chapel.* Dublin. 1907.

Ponsonby, Arthur. *Scottish and Irish Diaries.* First published 1927. Reissued NY: Kennikat Press, 1970.

Ryan, Richard. *Biographia Hibernica: A Biographical Dictionary of the Worthies of Ireland.* London: 1822.

SUGGESTED READING:

Robins, Joseph. *The Lost Children: A Study of Charity Children in Ireland, 1700–1900.* Dublin: I.P.A., 1980.

COLLECTIONS:

Registers of the Magdalen Asylum, Leeson Street, vols. I and II, 1766–1798, Denny House, Dublin.

Proceedings of the Dublin Society, vols. I–XXV, 1764–1789, Royal Dublin Society, Dublin.

Assorted material in the National Library of Ireland and in the Royal Irish Academy, Dublin.

Rosemary Raughter,
freelance writer in women's history, Dublin, Ireland

---

de Noailles, Anna (1876–1933).

See Noailles, Anna de.

Densmore, Frances (1867–1957)

American who was pioneer in the study of Native American music and a founder of the field of ethnomusicology. Born Frances Theresa Densmore in Red Wing, Minnesota, on May 21, 1867; died in Red Wing, Minnesota, on June 5, 1957; daughter of Benjamin (a civil engineer) and Sarah (Greenland) Densmore; attended Oberlin Conservatory of Music.

When Frances Densmore was growing up in Red Wing, Minnesota, she often heard the distant singing of the Sioux, an experience that would eventually shape her life's work. Frances was the oldest of two daughters in a prominent, well-to-do family; her grandfather was a judge and amateur scientist, and her father was a civil engineer. As a child, Densmore was given music lessons for which she showed an unusual aptitude. She began at home with keyboard and harmonic studies and, by age 17, journeyed to the Oberlin Conservatory of Music to continue her studies. From 1889 to 1890, Densmore took private instruction in Boston. For the next few years, she trained a boys' choir, lectured and published on musical topics, taught piano, and served as a church organist.

The turning point in Densmore's life came in 1893. Like thousands of Americans, she attended the Chicago World's Fair, which featured Native American song and dance. She was fascinated by the performances that took her back to her childhood. That same year, she read *Alice Cunningham Fletcher*'s book, *A Study of Omaha Music.* She contacted Fletcher who encouraged her interest in Native American music.

Densmore's interests were highly unusual in her day. In the late 19th century, American Indians were still considered savages; many had been annihilated and most of the remaining numbers had been relocated on Indian reservations. Few whites considered their traditions important or meaningful. With no guidelines existing for her study, Densmore had to create them as she went along. In 1905, she made her first field trip to a Chippewa (Ojibwa) village near the Canadian border with her sister **Margaret Densmore**, and one of the Native Americans, **Little Spruce**, enacted a private religious ceremony for her. A year later, two Sioux women dictated songs that Densmore transcribed. She began to publish her observations, her first article appearing in the April–June 1907 issue of the *American Anthropologist*.

Densmore soon realized transcriptions alone could not fully convey the spirit of the music and so turned to a new technology, wax cylinders. These turn-of-the-century devices were forerunners of phonograph records. Although crude by modern standards, wax cylinders did a creditable job of recording the human voice. Densmore would make nearly 2,500 wax cylinder recordings, a collection that remains one of the world's largest.

When she realized the enormity of the project, Densmore applied to the Bureau of American Ethnology at the Smithsonian Institution for assistance; she was urged to record the oldest singers before they died, so that their tradition would not die with them. In 1907, receiving a grant of $150, she purchased an Edison Home phonograph. This would be the first of many grants to follow in the next 50 years. She began working tirelessly among the Chippewa. By the time *Chippewa Music—II* (Bulletin 53) was published in 1913, Densmore had studied Teton Sioux music and had begun collecting Mandan and Hidatsa songs from North Dakota. Over her long career, she would collect songs from more than 30 tribes.

Not only was her interest in Native American music ahead of her time, but the research methods for a study such as hers demanded highly unorthodox practices for a woman of the period. The work was physically exacting and Densmore lived in the wilderness. In an era before transistors, she had to lug heavy recording equipment. Wherever she went, she had to set up a recording studio, sometimes in a coal shed full of mice, a vacant jail cell, or any available shack. Often tribes were inaccessible by car, necessitating travel by boat or canoe. As technology improved, Densmore adopted it. She returned to record the same Omaha singers who had been recorded 50 years earlier to determine if their songs had changed. In addition to documenting the songs and musical instruments used, Densmore recorded information about the singers, their costumes, and the ceremonies performed.

Frances Densmore worked into her late 80s before dying at age 90. As the 20th century progressed, there was increasing respect for Native Americans, and the importance of her pioneering effort became more and more apparent. Recognizing that her work would not be the final interpretation, Densmore said, "Other students, scanning the material, may reach other conclusions. My work has been to preserve the past, record observations in the present, and open the way for the work of others in the future."

SOURCES:

Frisbie, Charlotte J. "Frances Theresa Densmore (1867–1957)," in *Women Anthropologists: A Biographical Dictionary*. Edited by Ute Gacs, *et al.* NY: Greenwood Press, 1988, pp. 51–58.

Hoffman, Charles, ed. *Frances Densmore and American Indian Music*. Vol. XXIII. Heye Foundation, 1968.

Lurie, Nancy Oestreich. "Women in Early American Anthropology," in *Pioneers of American Anthropology: The Uses of Biography*. Edited by June Helm MacNeish. Seattle, WA: University of Washington Press, 1966, pp. 29–81.

Schusky, Ernest L. "Densmore, Frances," in *Dictionary of American Biography*. Edited by John A. Garraty. Supplement 6, 1956–1960. NY: Scribner, 1980, pp. 161–163.

John Haag, Associate Professor of History, University of Georgia, Athens, Georgia

d'Entragues, Catherine Henriette de Balzac (1579–1633).

See Medici, Marie de for sidebar on Entragues, Catherine Henriette de Balzac d'.

de Obidos, Josefa (1630–1684).

See de Ayala, Josefa.

Deoteria (fl. 535)

Queen of Metz (Austrasia). Name variations: Déoteria. Flourished around 535; married Theodebert or Thibert I (504–548), king of Metz (Austrasia, r. 534–548), in 535; children: Thibaud (d. 555), king of Metz (Austrasia, r. 548–555).

d'Epinay, Madame (1726–1783).

See Épinay, Louise, Madame la Live d'.

de Pisan or de Pizan, Christine (c. 1363–c. 1431).

See Christine de Pizan.

de Poitiers, Diane (1499–1566).

See Diane de Poitiers.

Deraismes, Maria (1828–1894)

French feminist, well-known writer, lecturer, and anti-clericalist. Pronunciation: der-REM. Born in Paris, France, on August 15, 1828; died in Paris on February 6, 1894; sister of Anna Féresse-Deraismes; never married.

Selected writing: Le théâtre chez soi (1863); Aux femmes riches (1865); Nos principes et nos moeurs (1867); Éve contre M. Dumas fils (1867); Les droits

des enfants *(1886);* Éve dans l'humanité *(1891).*
Founded Le Républican de Seine et Oise *(1881).*

Maria Deraismes was born in 1828 to a rich commercial family. Her parents, liberal republicans of a Voltairian stripe, were profoundly anticlerical and believed that girls should be as well educated as boys. Hence, she and her older sister, **Anna Féresse-Deraismes**, received educations quite out of the ordinary for the time. Maria studied all the classical subjects, taking particular interest in music, painting, drama, history, literature, and philosophy (both European and Asian), and thus brought to her life's work intellectual resources denied most women. Free—being unmarried by choice and very wealthy—she set out to become a writer, producing several comedies collected in *Théâtre chez soi* (1863), as well as some pamphlets and collected articles and speeches, including *Aux femmes riches* (1865), *Thérésa et son époque* (1865), *A propos des courtisanes* (1865), *Nos principes et nos moeurs* (1868), *L'Ancien devant le nouveau* (1869), *Ève contre Dumas fils* (1872), *France et progrès* (1873), *Lettre au clergé français* (1879), *Les Droits de l'enfant* (1887), *Épidémie naturaliste* (1888), and *Ève dans l'Humanité* (1891). She contributed to several periodicals, among them *Nain Jaune, L'Époque, Le National,* and *Le Grand Journal* early in her career, and later to *Le Semaine anti-cléricale, Le Rappel, L'Événement, Le Républicain de Seine-et-Oise* (which she directed, 1881–85), as well as *Le Droit des Femmes* (1869–71, 1879–90), renamed *L'Avenir des Femmes* (1871–79), with which through Léon Richer (1824–1911) she was closely associated.

Even more than a writer, however, Deraismes was a woman of speech and action. Her earliest writings already revealed an interest in women's education and their right to participate in all public spheres. This led Adolphe Géroult, Jules Labbé, and Léon Richer to invite her to speak in a lecture series, the Free-Thinkers Conferences, in 1866 at the Masonic Grand-Orient Lodge. She was about to decline the offer—public speaking by women in mixed assemblies on public issues was exceedingly rare, usually forbidden by authorities, and in any event regarded as unseemly—when she read an article by Jules Barbey d'Aurevilly in *Nain Jaune* savagely mocking women writers as "bluestockings." The diatribe so enraged her that she accepted the offer to lecture. Her debut was a triumph. An editor of Émile de Girardin's *La Liberté,* Édouard Siebecker, wrote:

> I expected to find a pedantic old spinster, affected and worthless.

> I was greatly surprised to see a young woman 24 or 25 years old. [She was 38.] She was slightly pale, with great refinement of shape and demeanor, of simple elegance, without ridiculous timidity or impudent self-assurance.

> She won her listeners over from the start. Her voice was of good timbre, her elocution easy, her language of great purity, her flashes of wit were shrewd without being spiteful, well cast. With all this a great deal of good sense and high erudition.

> I was seduced along with the others.

Henceforth, although she did not speak frequently, Deraismes became France's most celebrated female orator of the time.

At first, she spoke and wrote mostly on literary or philosophical subjects, but she soon began to address women's issues frequently and participated regularly in *André Léo's Society for the Claiming of the Rights of Women. In 1869, Deraismes helped Richer found the weekly *Le Droit des Femmes,* the longest-lived women's publication of its time; in 1870, they founded the Association for the Rights of Women, which in 1874, under conservative political pressure, was renamed the Society for the Amelioration of Woman's Condition. In 1881, Léo's group fused with the Amelioration to form the Society for the Amelioration of Woman's Condition and the Demand of Her Rights. A year later, for reasons never entirely clear, Richer formed another society, the French League for the Rights of Women, which still exists.

Deraismes and Richer were by all odds the dominant figures in the now burgeoning women's movement in the 1870s and 1880s. He concentrated on the paper while she mainly wrote and spoke and ran the Amelioration Society. Theirs was a hard struggle against entrenched attitudes and a web of constricting laws, and it was carried on while the Third Republic itself was continually being threatened by conservative and reactionary parties until the collapse of General Boulanger's movement in 1889. During the conservative era of the Moral Order (1873–77), the Amelioration was suppressed (December 1875–August 3, 1878). Deraismes waged a courageous fight for the Republic, turning her estate in Pontoise (Seine-et-Oise) into a resistance center during the *Seize mai* (May 16th) crisis (1877) and securing the election of the department's first republican deputy. Deraismes subsequently played important roles in getting educational reforms for women in the 1880s, the divorce law (1884), and the right of businesswomen to vote for judges of the commercial tribunals, which passed the Chamber of Deputies in 1894. She also was active in such causes as free thinking, anti-vivisection, protection of mothers and children, and societies and homes for mothers.

Deraismes and Richer organized France's first general women's conference, the International Congress of the Rights of Women (July 29–August 9, 1878), held at the Grand-Orient. Attendance was sparse, and the affair marked the split between Deraismes and ***Hubertine Auclert**, who advocated first obtaining the vote—a position Deraismes and Richer rejected as divisive and a danger to the republic because of the hold of the Roman Catholic Church on masses of women. A second assembly, the French and International Congress of the Rights of Women (June 25–29, 1889), sponsored by both Deraismes' and Richer's groups as an alternative to a government-sponsored conference in connection with the Paris Exposition, likewise had a small attendance but did attract participants from six foreign countries and some important politicians. Deraismes, a staunch laissez-faire liberal, used the occasion to come out against "protectionist" legislation for women, such as forbidding night work, saying that more basic reforms should be passed, which would install equality between the sexes. She was also an important participant in the General Congress of Feminist Societies (May 13–15, 1892), which, however, failed to form a policy capable of integrating socialist feminism with the mainstream liberal movement. In the meantime, during the years when education laws were a center of attention, she also organized with Victor Schoelcher the Anticlerical Congress (May 15, 1881), participated in the National Congress for the Separation of Church and State (1882), and was president of the Federation of Free-Thought Groups of Seine-et-Oise.

In her later years, Deraismes, whose contacts with Freemasonry were of long standing, put a great deal of energy into trying to convert the order—a politically powerful organization to which a large number of prominent republican politicians belonged—to the feminist cause by opening its membership to women. She got herself admitted to the lodge at Pecq (Seine-et-Oise) on January 14, 1882, but the Grand-Orient Lodge promptly expelled the lodge, which in turn had to expel her to be reinstated. Not to be denied, in 1893 with the aid of Senator Georges Martin, Deraismes finally succeeded in forming a new lodge open to both sexes, the Grand Scottish Rite Mixed Lodge of France—Human Rights.

Similar lodges soon formed at Lyon, Blois, Le Havre, then abroad, and the order still exists.

After Maria Deraismes' death from cancer in Paris in 1894, streets were named for her in Pontoise and Paris, a first there for a woman (17th arrondissement), and a statue of her was erected in the Square des Epinettes in 1898, of which, sadly, only the pedestal remains.

Maria Deraismes, with Leon Richer, began a new stage in the women's movement in France by firmly linking it to political life and issues. The most important early influences on her feminism stemmed from Saint-Simonianism through her family, John Stuart Mill, and her own full education, notably in philosophy. Her central themes were the education of women, their right to participate fully in all spheres of life, and the importance of a family life based upon rationality, justice, and an equal sharing by husband and wife, including even sexual fulfillment for the woman, hitherto a rare claim, but in Deraismes' case with a flat rejection of "free love" and any double standard for either partner: "We—women—we want to be what *we are*, not what you have made us" (1869). She presented these themes most effectively from the platform and in pungent, lively newspaper articles; her longer, more formal writing was far less successful. A woman of strikingly good looks, a fine voice, and distinguished bearing and style, she compelled attention by her appearance, her gifts for sharp debate and striking turns of phrase, and her brilliant intellect.

In the political struggle, she adopted the *"politique de la brèche,"* i.e., a focussed attack on the weakest part of the wall in order to open a breach and begin the demolition of sexual inequality, "the obstinate debris of the caste organization: man the high caste, woman the low caste" (1869). This tactic strongly resembled that of her many friends among the "Opportunists," the moderate republicans who came to power during the first two decades of the Third Republic and who, said Léon Gambetta, would enact reforms when "opportune." To her, this meant concentrating on obtaining women's social and civil rights first; the civic right to vote would then surely follow. Until 1879, she avoided the suffrage issue because it would divide the republicans and strengthen the conservatives, whose strongest support derived from the Catholic Church. The suffrage thus clashed with the anticlericalism in which she had been raised. After 1879, she relented (Richer much less so) and even allowed her name to be put up as a shadow candidate in 1885, but she never gave the suffrage pride of place; preservation of the Republic and rule by the republicans would have to come first, whatever the cost to feminist demands.

The causes for which she worked on the political scene principally included better education for women; revision of the Civil Code, which made women perpetual minors; the right to divorce; the right to file paternity suits; equal pay for equal work; the right of women to control their own income; the ending of state-supervised prostitution; the right of women to bear equal witness to private and public acts; the right of women to enter all professions; and the right of businesswomen to vote for and serve on commercial tribunals. Obviously, political and social concerns intermingled. Deraismes was a laissez-faire liberal and rejected socialism and communism, certainly of the Marxian variety. She called the Paris Commune (1871) "a collective crime," although she protested the harsh sentences meted out to Communards such as *Louise Michel. While she rejected talk of class (she preferred Gambetta's *couches*—strata) and class warfare, however, her Saint-Simonian background led her to criticize current social conditions, norms, and mores, and to pursue social betterment.

Neither Deraismes nor most other French feminist leaders of her time sought to build mass followings. Such was the status and outlook of most of these women that an enterprise of this ilk appeared chimerical at best if not downright dangerous. Rather, she worked among educated, bourgeois women to build pressure groups that could force the republican politicians to face up to the full implications of the new republic's motto, "Liberty, Equality, Fraternity," and recognize that half of the French population was still denied its rightful benefits. "In France," she chided her fellow republicans, "masculine supremacy is the last aristocracy" (1882).

It has been said that Deraismes' views contained at least two dilemmas. First, while maintaining women's natural equality with men, she held that women have certain innate qualities such as devotion, self-denial, balance, perseverance, and sagacity, and that women are by nature moral and virtuous. But by underlining differences that could so easily be linked to the care of family and children, she risked confining women to a role that ran contrary to her desire to see women participate equally in all walks of life. Secondly, if it was her special achievement to open to feminism a political dimension, she could hardly deny that the vote was fundamental to any truly effective political action. If she

wanted to strike at the weakest link, it has been argued, that link was not the multiple strictures on women embedded in the Civil Code, but the republicans' refusal to allow women to possess a free society's single, most basic right.

Maria Deraismes—intelligent, courageous, passionate, strident, self-assured, aggressive, compassionate, prone too often to pontificating and moralizing but always ready to cry out against injustice—played a huge role in launching feminism in France, a role not always appreciated by many who came afterward. She was too domineering and impatient and lacked talent in building organizations and encouraging the emergence of new leadership, they charged. Her politics were too partisan, too colored by a visceral anticlericalism and vehement republicanism, and too imbued with elitist assumptions. But Deraismes had thrust feminism into the arena and made it a public issue in which respectable women could engage. From the low estate to which the women's movement had fallen after the failure of the revolutions of 1848, Deraismes proudly proclaimed in 1883, "I have resuscitated it; I have once again put it into the limelight. I have examined it, studied it under all its points of view, under all its aspects." In 1921, a quarter century after her death, Léon Abensour justly remarked, "Many contemporary feminists have, without moreover always rendering unto Caesar that which belongs to him, borrowed ideas, facts, and arguments from the works of Maria Deraismes."

SOURCES:

Abensour, Léon. *Histoire générale du féminisme. Des origines à nos jours.* Paris: Resources, 1921 (Slatkine Reprints, 1979).

Albistur, Maïté, and Daniel Armogathe. *Histoire du féminisme français, du moyen âge à nos jours.* 2 vols. Paris: Éditions des Femmes, 1977.

Bidelman, Patrick K. *Pariahs Stand Up! The Founding of the Liberal Feminist Movement in France, 1858–1889.* Westport, CT: Greenwood Press, 1982.

Deraismes, Maria. *Ce que veulent les femmes: Articles et conférences de 1869 à 1891.* Préface et notes de Odile Krakovitch. Paris: Spyros, 1980.

Dictionnaire de biographie française. A. Balteau, M. Barroux, M. Prevost *et al.,* directeurs. Paris: Letouzey et Ané, 1933-.

Evans, Richard J. *The Feminists: Women's Emancipation Movements in Europe, America and Australasia 1840–1920.* London: Croom Helm, 1977.

Hause, Steven C., with Anne R. Kenney. *Women's Suffrage and Social Politics in the French Third Republic.* Princeton, NJ: Princeton University Press, 1984.

Historical Dictionary of the Third French Republic. 2 vols. Patrick H. Hutton, ed. Westport, CT: Greenwood Press, 1986.

Klejman, Laurence, and Florence Rochefort. *L'Égalité en marche: Le féminisme sous la Troisième République.*

Paris: Presses de la Fondation nationale des sciences politiques, 1989.

Moses, Claire Goldberg. *French Feminism in the Nineteenth Century.* Albany, NY: SUNY Press, 1984.

Rabaut, Jean. *Histoire des féminismes français.* Paris: Stock, 1978.

Sowerwine, Charles. *Sisters or Citizens? Women and Socialism in France Since 1876.* NY: Cambridge University Press, 1982.

David S. Newhall,
Professor Emeritus of History, Centre College;
author of <i>Clemenceau: A Life at War</i> (Edwin Mellen Press, 1991)</div>

de Ranfaing, Élizabeth (d. 1649).

See French "Witches."

Derbhorcaili.

Variant of Devorgilla.

Derby, countess of.

See Hastings, Anne (c. 1487–?).

See Siege Warfare and Women for sidebar on Charlotte Stanley (1599–1664).

See Farren, Elizabeth (c. 1759–1829).

Derby, Margaret, countess of.

See Beaufort, Margaret (1443–1509).

Deren, Maya (1908–1961)

Russian-born American experimental filmmaker often cited as the creator of the first film of the American avant-garde and the "choreo-cinema," a collaborative art between the dancer and the camera. Born Eleanora Derenkowsky in Kiev, Russia, on April 29, 1908 (some sources cite 1917); died of cerebral hemorrhage in St. Alban's Naval Hospital, Queens, New York, on October 13, 1961; daughter of Marie (a teacher) and Alexander (a Russian-Jewish psychiatrist called Solomon in some sources) Derenkowsky (name later shortened to Deren); attended the L'École Internationale (Geneva), Syracuse University, and the New School for Social Research; New York University, B.A.; Smith College, A.M. in literature, 1939; married a labor reformer (divorced in 1938 after three years); married Alexander Hackenschmied (a Czech filmmaker who worked under the name Alexander Hammid), in 1942 (divorced); married Teiji Ito (a composer), in 1960.

Awarded the first Guggenheim fellowship ever bestowed for creative filmmaking (1946); first woman and the first American to win the Cannes Grand Prix Internationale for Avant-Garde Film (for Meshes of the Afternoon*).*

Filmography: (with Alexander Hammid) Meshes of the Afternoon *(1943);* At Land *(1944);* A Study in Choreography for Camera *(1945); (home movie, with Hammid)* The Private Life of a Cat *(1945);* Ritual in Transfigured Time *(1946);* Meditation on Violence *(1948);* The Very Eye of Night *(1959);* The Witch's Cradle *(released incomplete, 1961).*

Books: An Anagram of Ideas on Art, Form and the Film (New York, 1946); The Divine Horseman: The Living Gods of Haiti (New York, 1953); Divine Horsemen: Voodoo Gods of Haiti (New York, 1970).

Articles: "Choreography of Camera" (Dance, October 1943); reply to Manny Farber in New Republic (November 11, 1946); "Creative Cutting: Parts I and II" (Movie Makers, May–June 1947); "Meditation on Violence" (Dance Magazine, December 1948); "Movie Journal" (Village Voice, August 25, 1960); "Cinema As an Art Form" (Introduction to the Art of the Movies, ed. Lewis Jacobs, 1960); "Adventures in Creative Filmmaking" (Home Movie Making, 1960); "Cinematography: The Creative Use of Reality" (Daedalus: The Visual Arts Today, 1960); "A Statement of Principles" (Film Culture, summer 1961); "Movie Journal" (Village Voice, June 1, 1961); "Chamber Films" (Filmwise, no. 2, 1962); "A Lecture . . ." (Film Culture, summer 1963); "The Very Eye of Night" (Film Culture, summer 1963); "Film in Progress" (Film Culture, winter 1965); "Notes, Essays, Letters" (Film Culture, winter 1965); "A Statement on Dance and Film" (Dance Perspectives, no. 30, 1967); "Tempo and Tension" (The Movies as Medium, ed. Lewis Jacobs, 1970).

Russian-born Maya Deren was America's best-known independent and experimental filmmaker in the era during and following the Second World War. As a director, actress, producer, writer, and lecturer, she was instrumental in helping experimental filmmaking in the United States achieve a position of respect in the international art world. Her works, seen as definitive American trance and ciné-dance films, used ritual and symbol to explore the relationships between real versus imagined time and space.

Deren was born in Kiev, Russia, in 1908. Her father had served as a medical corpsman in the Russian army and her mother was the graduate of a strenuous program in an arts conservatory. The family immigrated to America a few years after the Russian Revolution (1922), and the family name was shortened from Derenkowsky to Deren. In the United States, her psychiatrist father repeated his medical training, became a lecturer in mental hygiene in Syracuse, New York, and joined the staff of the State Institute for the Feeble-Minded in Syracuse, of which he was eventually the director. Deren's mother worked as a teacher and encouraged her daughter to seek out the best education possible. Deren received her high school education at L'École Internationale in Geneva, Switzerland, and rejoined her family following graduation. At Syracuse University, she studied journalism and would later be known for uncommonly articulate writings about the cinema. During her student years, Deren wrote for left-wing periodicals and entered into an early marriage to a labor reformer with whom she relocated to New York's Greenwich Village, where the couple became active in the American Socialist Party. After receiving her B.A. from New York University, she did graduate work in literature at Smith College with a master's thesis that discussed the influence of the French symbolists on the imagist poets. Later, Deren's film work would be noted for its resemblance to the Imagism movement in poetry. After three years of marriage, Deren divorced in 1938.

A year following her graduation from Smith in 1939, Deren became personal secretary to the African-American dancer-choreographer *Katherine Dunham. Although Deren was not a trained dancer, she and Dunham collaborated on a book of modern dance theory. Deren shared an interest in African and Haitian tribal dance, as well as in mythology and ritual, with the African-American dancers she met via Dunham. As Deren strayed from the ideas of Freudian psychoanalysis passed down to her by her father, she became increasingly interested in Jungian psychology, which along with Surrealism attached importance to "primitive" art, for its concepts regarding the archetypal symbol and "collective unconscious."

In 1941, Deren joined Dunham and her company on tour. She met Alexander Hammid, the Czech documentary filmmaker, in Los Angeles. Deren would remark that Hammid taught her "the mechanics of film expression and, more than that, the principle of infinite pains." The knowledge of film she acquired from Hammid was of large significance to Deren's creative development:

> I had been a poet up until then, and the reason that I had not been a very good poet was because my mind worked in images which I had been trying to translate or describe in words; therefore, when I undertook cinema, I was relieved of the false step of translating images into words, and could work directly so that it was not like discovering a new medium so much as finally coming home into a world whose vocabulary, syntax, grammar, was my mother tongue; which I understood, and thought in, but, like a mute, had never spoken.

Deren and Hammid were married in 1942. *Meshes of the Afternoon*, her first film, was

codirected by Hammid. The year was 1943, the 16mm equipment was borrowed, and Deren and Hammid lent themselves as actors to the 18-minute film with their Los Angeles house as the set. Shot in two-and-a-half weeks, *Meshes* was a silent film devoid of conventional plot. The initial sequence reveals a woman who is coming home after seeing what P. Adams Sitney, writing in Richard Roud's *Cinema: A Critical Dictionary,* describes as a "mysterious black-veiled figure before her. She observes the dislocation of several objects which will eventually assume symbolic dimensions: a key, a knife, a telephone, a record-player." The woman then falls asleep in an armchair before a window. As this action pattern is three times repeated, the objects become increasingly menacing. During the climax of the third repetition, writes Sitney, "three versions of herself perform a ritual around the dining-room table which ends in the election of one to attack the sleeping figure with a knife." At the point of the stabbing, the dream seems to end as she is awakened by her lover's kiss. She sees that the dislocated objects have been returned to their rightful places as she and her lover climb to the upper bedroom. Together they lie down. The woman, grabbing the knife, stabs it into her lover's face, which at the moment of contact is shown to have been an illusion. The woman has instead shattered a mirror that had held his reflection. "The pieces of the mirror fall mysteriously to the edge of a sea . . . ," writes Sitney. "In the final cycle of the film a man approaches and enters the house again in the same pattern as her previous entrances only to find her dead, her throat apparently cut, with seaweed clinging to her, and the fragments of the shattered mirror about her."

"The film begins in actuality," remarks Deren, "and, eventually ends there. But in the meantime the imagination, here given as a dream, intervenes." In this first film, Deren began to use the medium as a means to eclipse traditional notions of time and space, in favor of a constructed time-space reality, an exploration for which her work would become well known. *Meshes* maintained continuous action while severing time-space unities, and the result was what **Louise Heck-Rabi** has described as "a trance-like mood by the use of slow motion, swish-pan camera movements, and well executed point-of-view shots." Deren would later pen a letter to her friend James Card, which traced the evolution of her six films. In this correspondence, she described a sequence in *Meshes:*

> [T]he girl with the knife rises from the bale to go towards the self which is sleeping in

the chair. As the girl . . . rises, there is a close-up of her foot as she begins striding. The first step is in sand (with suggestion of sea behind), the second stride (cut in) is in grass, the third is on pavement, and the fourth is on the rug, and then the camera cuts up to her head with the knife descending towards the sleeping girl. What I meant when I planned that four-stride sequence was that you have to come a long way—from the very beginning of time—to kill yourself, like the first life emerging from the primeval waters. These four strides, in my intention, span all time.

The film became famous for this four-stride sequence. Regarded as a milestone in the history of American independent film, *Meshes* is widely considered to be the first film of the American avant-garde, responsible for introducing in America what Sitney has termed the "trance film" which he has called "the dominant avant-garde film genre of the late 40s and early 50s." While some critics have seen *Meshes* as among the tradition of European surrealism, Deren consistently denied that this was a surrealist film, wanting it to be viewed as "concerned with the relationship between the imaginative and objective reality."

Deren's next film, however, did indeed draw on surrealist notions and was planned as an exploration of surrealist artifacts as "the cabalistic symbols of the twentieth century" and of surrealist artists as modern magic-workers. This film, *The Witch's Cradle,* was shot in the Surrealist "Art of This Century" gallery with artists Marcel Duchamp and Pajarito Matta serving as actors. The film was released unfinished in 1961.

Hella Heyman and Alexander Hammid provided technical assistance for Deren's 1944 film *At Land* (15 minutes), which was described by Sitney as a "pure American trance film." During the film, waves land a woman, played by Deren, on a beach. Ascending a tree trunk, her head disappears out of the shot, to reappear at the bottom of the next frame where she is ignored by diners at a banquet table. Crawling to the end of the table, she finds a chess game, takes a chess piece that she then drops, and pursues the piece through different landscapes. Eventually, she is lost to sight in the dunes. Lewis Jacobs found the film's major cinematic value in its "fresh contiguities of shot relationships achieved through the technique of beginning a movement in one place and concluding it in another. Thus real time and space were destroyed. In its place was created a cinematic time and place." In this universe, remarked Deren, "the problem of the individual as the sole continuous element, is to relate itself to a fluid, apparently incoherent, universe. It is in a sense a mythological voyage of the twentieth century."

Deren, with her dark hair and sensual features, was known for her charismatic personality and dramatic appearance, and she was a central figure in the 1940s artistic community of Greenwich Village. Rabinovitz and Baumgarten in a Cinema Texas program note remark that her qualities alienated as well as attracted: "Rudolf Arnheim, *Anais Nin, and James Agee have labeled her everything from strong-willed, commanding, seductive and hypnotic to dogmatic, obstinate, restless, unsatisfied, and energetic to the point of violence."

Deren's use of created space and time figured in her next work *A Study in Choreography for the Camera* made in 1945. Collaborating with the dancer Talley Beatty, she filmed this three-minute piece by partnering the dancer with the camera. Sitney's account of the film describes its beginning with "a circular pan in a clearing in the woods. In making the one circle the camera periodically passes the dancer; at each encounter he is further along in his slow, up-stretching movement. At the end of this camera movement, he extends his foot out of the frame and brings it down in a different place; this time, inside a room." As the dance goes on, the dancer moves through various places until, Sitney continues, "he begins a pirouette, which changes, without a stopping of the camera, from very slow motion to very fast. Then he leaps, slowly, very slowly, floating through the air, in several rising, then several descending shots, to land in a speculative pose back in the wood clearing." By introducing the potential for isolating a single gesture as a complete cinematic form, Deren created what *New York Times* ballet critic John Martin called "the beginnings of a virtually new art of 'choreo-cinema,' in which the dancer and the camera collaborate on the creation of a single new work of art."

Deren saw and used ritual as an action different from all other actions because its purpose is realized through form. "In ritual," she said, "the form is the meaning. More specifically, the quality of movement is not a merely decorative factor; it is the meaning itself of the movement. . . . The quality of individual movements, and, above all, the choreography of the whole, is mainly conferred and created by filmic means—the varying camera speeds, the relating of gestures which were, in reality, unrelated, the repetition of patters. . . . Being a film ritual, it is achieved not in spatial terms alone, but in terms of a Time created by the camera."

*Maya Deren in
At Land.*

Her *Ritual in Transfigured Time* is generally considered to be the fullest realization of Deren's ideas. This 16-minute film, made in 1946, counted only two actual dancers among the cast (**Rita Christiani** and Frank Westbrook) while, in Deren's words, conferring "dance upon non-dancers." A more ambitious dance film than *Study in Choreography, Ritual* furthered her exploration of form. Deren used joined movements, as she had in *Choreography,* this time with one person beginning a movement, another continuing it, and another completing it. The film ultimately shows the metamorphosis of a woman from a widow in black to a bride in white, using the cinematic device of negative processing for the transformation.

Deren put forth her idea of the "personal film" in lectures and extensive writings as she traveled the United States and visited colleges, museums, and art schools. She published *An Anagram of Ideas on Art, Form and Film* in 1946. This work showed strong support of independent film following an analysis of American industrial and independent filmmaking activities. "Agony and experience" was Deren's description of her films: "subjective films concerned with personal feelings and problems in which the people are not individuals but symbols, abstractions or generalizations."

Kay and Peary noted in *Women and the Cinema* that "personal filmmaking meant personal film distribution" for Deren. Renting the Provincetown Playhouse on New York's Mac-Dougal Street in 1946, Deren held the first public screenings in the United States of 16mm films that had been privately made, and these attracted large audiences.

The same year, Deren was awarded the first Guggenheim fellowship ever given for creative filmmaking (she shared the distinction that year with the Whitney brothers). For her first four films, she became the first woman and the first American to win the Cannes Grand Prix Internationale for Avant-Garde Film.

In a departure from her earlier work, Deren traveled to Haiti for her next film to explore new avenues in ritual and myth. Although the film was never completed, her experiences in Haiti figured in her *Divine Horseman,* a book on Haitian cults (1953). Having gone to Haiti as, in her own words, "an artist, as one who would manipulate the elements of a reality into a work of art," she had been foiled by "the irrefutable reality and impact of Voudoun mythology. . . . I end by recording, as humbly and accurately as I can, the logics of a reality which had forced me to recognize its integrity and to abandon my manipulations."

She returned to filmmaking in 1948 with *Meditation on Violence* (12 minutes), which used movements from the training of Wu-tang and Shao-Lin, two ancient schools of Chinese boxing, and aimed to "abstract the principle of ongoing metamorphosis and change." This was her first film to use a soundtrack, which included Chinese flute and Haitian drums. Dissatisfied with the result, she spoke of reediting the film but never did.

Deren's third marriage, in 1960, was to composer Teiji Ito, who had provided the score for her last film, *The Very Eye of Night,* made in 1959. This 15-minute dance film included a fair amount of optical printing, and took Deren "out in space about as far as I can go."

In 1961, following a series of cerebral hemorrhages, Maya Deren died at age 53. Called the "mother of the underground film," she had paved the way for the future of American independent films. Rudolf Arnheim eulogized Deren as one of film's "most delicate magicians." In her letter to James Card (April 19, 1955), she wrote of a near-fatal operation that had inspired her last film: "I came out of it with a rapidity that dazzled," she wrote. "Then I actually realized that I was overwhelmed with the most wondrous gratitude for the marvelous persistence of the life force. . . . And then I had a sudden image: a dog lying somewhere very still, and a child, first looking at it, and then, compulsively, nudging it. Why? to see whether it was still alive. . . . To make it move to make it live. So I had been doing with my camera."

SOURCES:

Lyon, Christopher. *International Dictionary of Films and Filmmakers, Vol. II: Directors/Filmmakers.* Chicago, IL: St. James Press, 1984.

Roud, Richard, ed. *Cinema: A Critical Dictionary,* 1980.

Wakeman, John, ed. *World Film Directors.* Vol. I. NY: H.W. Wilson, 1987.

RELATED MEDIA:

Maya Deren: Experimental Films (1 hr. 16 mins.), video includes *Meshes of the Afternoon, Ritual in Transfigured Time, Meditation on Violence, At Land, A Study in Choreography for Camera,* and *The Very Eye of Night.*

de Rivery, Aimee Dubucq

(c. 1762–1817)

Legendary French woman who became Nakshedil Sultana in the Turkish harem of Abdul Hamid I. Name variations: de Riverie; Nakshedil Sultana. Born around 1762 on the French Caribbean island of Martinique; died in Constantinople (now Istanbul), Turkey, in 1817; daughter of a noble family; cousin of Josephine Tascher de la Pagerie (Empress *Josephine), who married Napoleon Bonaparte; attended a convent school in Nantes, France; children: (with Abdul

Hamid I) Mahmud II, sultan of the Ottoman Empire (r. 1808–1839).

It is difficult to separate fact from fiction in the life of Aimee Dubucq de Rivery, who disappeared during a sea voyage in 1788 and is said to have reappeared as Nakshedil Sultana in a Turkish Harem during the period of the Ottoman Empire. Although no one can be certain that Nakshedil and the fair, blue-eyed Aimee are one and the same, the story of a beautiful young girl's triumphant rise from slave to powerful sultana has become legendary.

Aimee was raised on the family sugar plantation on the French Caribbean island of Martinique. After her preliminary schooling on the island, she was sent to a convent school in Nantes, France, where she spent several years. After her schooling was completed, she and her governess were sailing home to Martinique when they were shipwrecked and picked up by a Spanish ship bound for Majorca. The Spanish ship was then captured by pirates and taken to Algiers, where Aimee Dubucq de Rivery was sold to the *dey* (the governor of the province). Sensing an opportunity to win political favor, the *dey* then gave de Rivery as a gift to Sultan Abdul Hamid I.

Locked within the imperial harem at Constantinople, de Rivery was taught the rules and hierarchy of the harem and given the name Nakshedil ("image of the heart"). She soon became the favorite of Abdul Hamid and gave birth to their son, Mahmud (II), who was in line to ascend the throne.

When Abdul Hamid died in April 1789, his 27-year-old nephew became Selim III. For the next 18 years, de Rivery shared Selim's life and exercised great influence. She taught him French, and he in turn started a French newspaper and allowed her to decorate the palace in the rococo style. He also authorized a permanent ambassador to be sent from Istanbul to Paris. Selim's liberalism, however, cost him his life. In 1807, he was assassinated by religious fanatics, who would have also killed de Rivery's son Mahmud had she not hidden him. Thus, Mahmud became the next sultan and accomplished many reforms that were attributed to the influence of his mother.

By one account, de Rivery then left the confines of the harem and, given the title *sultana valide* (queen mother), occupied a palace on the shores of the Bosporus, where she continued to advise her son. In another version of the story, she spent her final days within the harem. Although de Rivery had dutifully practiced Islam, as the laws of her confinement dictated, she had retained her Christian faith. Her final request was that a priest perform the last rites. Her son, in an unprecedented act, purportedly gave permission for a Catholic priest to enter the harem, in order to fulfill her mother's dying wish.

SUGGESTED READING:

Croutier, Alev Lytle. *Harem: The World Behind the Veil.* NY: Abbeville Press, 1989.

Barbara Morgan,
Melrose, Massachusetts

Dernbourg, Ilona Eibenschütz
(1872–1967).

See Eibenschütz-Dernbourg, Ilona.

Dernesch, Helga (1939—)

Austrian soprano and mezzo-soprano. Born February 3, 1939, in Vienna, Austria; studied at the Vienna Conservatory (1957–61).

Debuted at the Berne Opera (1961); appeared at Bayreuth (1965–69); debuted at Salzburg (1969), Chicago (1971), Vienna Staatsoper (1972), and Metropolitan (1985).

Aimee
Dubucq
de
Rivery

Helga Dernesch was one of the few singers to have considerable success as a soprano and mezzo-soprano. Yet, her recordings of Brünnhilde and Isolde, show that she would eventually be a mezzo-soprano, as her high notes never had the ease and openness of a true soprano. When Dernesch suffered a vocal breakdown in 1979 during rehearsals for *Die Frau ohne Schatten* in Hamburg, the conductor Christoph von Dohnanyi advised her to rework her voice in the mezzo-soprano range. This she accomplished in short order. She premiered in the operas of Aribert Reimann: *Lear* (1978) and *Troades* (1986). Her background as a Wagnerian singer was helpful in preparing these roles.

John Haag,
Athens, Georgia

Deroin, Jeanne-Françoise

(1805–1894)

French socialist feminist, prominent in the Revolution of 1848, who was the first woman in France to run for national office. Name variations: Deroin sometimes incorrectly spelled Derouin. Pronunciation: JHAN fran-SWAHZ der-RWEN. Born in Paris, France, on December 31, 1805, to working class parents; died in London, on April 2, 1894; self-educated; married M. Desroches, in 1832; children: two daughters, one son (d. 1887).

Became allied with Saint-Simonianism (early 1830s); conducted a school for poor children (1840s); during the Revolution of 1848, founded clubs and daily, weekly, and monthly journals promoting rights for women and workers; ran for the Legislative Assembly and founded the Union of Fraternal Associations of Workers (1849); arrested and sentenced for subversion (1850); released (1851) and fled to England (1852); published the Almanach des femmes *(1852–54); corresponded occasionally with feminist and socialist leaders (1850s–80s).*

In midlife, Jeanne Deroin was described as "a small, thin woman generally wearing a hooded coat capped with black plumes decorated with a rose-red ribbon," a puny figure who, despite a certain sickly air, possessed a tough body, that would endure for 88 years, and an even tougher will.

She was born to impoverished working-class parents in Paris on December 31, 1805. Because she was habitually silent about her private life, her known story has long gaps. Of her earliest years, she said only, "I knew little of the joys of childhood." Trained as a seamstress, she had no formal education. Her mother thought women needed none, an idea that may have turned Jeanne toward considering women's place in the scheme of things. She taught herself to read, and she read voraciously. By the 1830s, she was familiar with Morellet, Mably, Rousseau, and other philosophes, and had come under the influence of the "utopian" socialists Pierre Leroux, Fourier, Cabet, and especially Henri, Comte de Saint-Simon (1760–1825).

From the beginning, it seems, she loved liberty and hated domination of any kind. She dreamed of a chaste, sexless marriage, but when she married a M. Desroches, the treasurer of a state retirement home, in a civil ceremony in August 1832, she found sex was not part of the bargain when he said she would be free to act as she saw fit. She gave birth to two daughters and a son whom she loved even so. She wanted autonomy from men but not from children.

In the early 1830s, she turned from a conventional republicanism toward the Saint-Simonians because they, unlike the republicans, favored equality for women. In time she came to fear, however, that the eccentricities of utopian socialism would arouse hostility toward the feminist cause. She never wholly adopted Saint-Simonianism because she disagreed with its apolitical stance and above all because its odd religious cult was ruled by a male hierarchy headed by a kind of pope. The religious dimension of Deroin's thought nonetheless was very important, for she linked religion and politics indissolubly. She rejected institutional religion but strongly believed in a Creator God who is the sole Authority and the Father of social and sexual equality. After her own fashion, she was a Christian socialist: Jesus, a human reformer superior to the philosophers of antiquity, was the founder of socialism.

Amidst the social and intellectual ferment of the years 1830–34, Deroin (and other women) sent in a "declaration of faith" to *Le Globe* which contained the core of the views she held thereafter, notably including an attack on the practice of women taking their husbands' names, a custom never before challenged so bluntly. She was probably not, however, a staff member on the Saint-Simonian gazette *La Femme libre* and its successors, *L'Apostolat des femmes* and *La Tribune des femmes*, as is often asserted by those who believe she was the author of the "Jeanne-Victoire" articles. Apparently not until the Revolution of 1848 did she embark on public action to support her beliefs. In the meantime, during the 1840s, Deroin became a teacher. She founded a school for poor children and her own after one abbé Deguerry helped her in her struggle to obtain a license; she failed twice because she couldn't write in cursive, was poor in arithmetic, and held unorthodox religious ideas. She earned a meager living, because poor children, of course, often could not pay.

When the Revolution of February 1848 broke out, Deroin entrusted her children to friends, used only her maiden name, in order not to compromise her civil-servant husband, and began what became seven years of intense public activity. Aided by Olinde Rodrigues, a Saint-Simonian banker, she and *Eugénie Niboyet founded France's first feminist daily paper, *La Voix des femmes* (The Women's Voice, March 20–June 18). Parting ways with Niboyet, she and **Désirée Gay**, founded a weekly, *La Politique des femmes* (June 18–August 5), a more socialist paper emphasizing workers' solidarity more than feminism as such. Finally, she founded and directed a monthly, *L'Opinion des femmes* (August 1848, January 28–August 10, 1849). Limited resources, the need to make the government-required caution deposit, a flood of competing papers, and the unpopularity of feminism in most quarters held these papers to circulations under 300. Clubs, however, proliferated. The early Society of the Women's Voice, with Niboyet as president, Gay vice-president, and Deroin secretary-general, became the Women's Club on May 11 and met thrice weekly, sessions usually interrupted by jeering men. For reasons unknown, Deroin and Gay left and founded the Mutual Association for the Education of Women, an adjunct of the *Politique des femmes*, which also published brochures, including Deroin's eight-page *Cours de droit social pour les femmes* (Course in Social Law for Women; Imprimerie du Plan, n.d.) Some time in the summer of 1848, Deroin also founded, with a Fourierist, Dr. Malatier, and **Adèle Esquiros**, the short-lived Club of the Emancipation of Women. Female club activity suffered a mortal blow, however, when the Constituent Assembly—elected in April to replace the Provisional Government of February and write a constitution for the new Second Republic—decreed (July 26) during the crackdown after a largely working-class uprising (the June Days) that women could not speak in public debates nor join, nor attend, political clubs.

In the heady days of the spring of 1848, Deroin and many others believed the reign of God on earth would begin once the principles of Liberty, Equality, and Fraternity became embedded in hearts and laws, but that any such program would fail without equality for women. At the start, Deroin sent four petitions to the government and signed an appeal in *La Voix des femmes* in this vein, although at first it was proposed that men would choose the most worthy women to act as guardians of the principles of the revolution and of women's rights—hardly a radical idea. The paper called for the vote only for widows and single women, reflecting the common belief that votes for both husbands and wives might split families, the bedrock social organisms. In the same spirit, Deroin, Gay and **Anna Knight de Longueville** petitioned the National Assembly to name women as consultants to the constitution committee. They were groping for some way to help write the laws, especially laws to legalize divorce, revise the Civil Code, organize women's labor, and (particularly for Deroin) get equal pay with men and abolish state-sanctioned prostitution. These proposals went nowhere.

To Deroin, it was axiomatic that the true Republic was impossible as long as "the last of privileges remained, that is, the one of men." When the government grandly proclaimed that "the vote belongs to all with no exceptions," she replied that there were "17 million" exceptions. Men acting alone have made a mess, she observed, which proves that both sexes are needed for a proper republic to work. This must be done on a basis of equality throughout: "society is founded on the family: if the family remains founded on inequality, society will take its old course." To reach this goal, violence must be rejected. The awful bloodshed of the June Days appalled her. She appealed for peace and tried to persuade **Félicité de Lamennais** to mediate. She distrusted revolutionary leaders, who in her view became exploiters of the misery of others. But her own experience of attempting to lead brought frustration over the lack of response she received from the masses of ordinary women: "Woman, still slave," she wrote in *Cours de droit social*, "remains veiled in silence. . . . Held down by man's yoke, she has not even the aspirations toward liberty; man must liberate her."

Despite obstacles and unfazed by the retirement of many of her compatriots, Deroin pressed on and in early April 1849 made her most dramatic move. She announced her candidacy for the Legislative Assembly in the April 23 elections, becoming the first woman ever in France to run for national office. Her announcement proclaimed, "An assembly composed entirely of men is as incompetent to make the laws which govern a society composed of men and women as would be an assembly composed entirely of the privileged to discuss the interests of the workers or an assembly of capitalists to uphold the honor of the country." Besides rights for women, her platform called for a general amnesty, the organization of work and public education, and (a typical '48ist touch) a universal congress of peoples convoked to regularize production and exchange and to enable France to support oppressed peoples.

Deroin tried to persuade the left-wing Social Democrats to put her on their committee as a symbolic gesture or at least as an endorsement of her candidacy. The famous socialist P.-J. Proudhon, strongly anti-feminist, opposed this saying that the fact that women have organs intended to nourish the young makes them unfit for the polls. He apparently made no reply, writes **Priscilla Robertson**, when Deroin asked him to show her the organ that qualified him as an elector. The Social Democrats turned her down. She campaigned around Paris, sometimes being refused admission to meetings, at others allowed to speak. She became instant fodder for press mockeries, theater jokes, and caricatures by Daumier. Informed on April 16 that her candidacy was unconstitutional, she continued on anyhow and did win some sympathy in working-class districts. But most men did not want to waste a ballot, so only a pitiful handful wrote in her name. Ironically, *George Sand, who had flatly refused a nomination, received more votes.

The political dead end Deroin had reached convinced her to seek to "change the basis of society." Socialistic mutual-benefit associations had sprung up in the 1840s; the Revolution furnished exceptionally fertile soil. Deroin, not drawn to theorizing but to action, seized upon this apolitical means to build that new "basis." For once, she reaped some success, short-lived though it proved to be. On February 6, 1849, she had joined *Pauline Roland's Fraternal Association of Socialist Teachers and Professors and presently joined with Elisa Lemonnier and *Suzanne Voilequin to ask the Social Democrats to support a Fraternal Society of the United Workers, an ambitious project including a production cooperative, school, library, and courses for working women. The party turned a deaf ear. Undeterred, Deroin founded the Fraternal Association of the Social Democrats of the Two Sexes for Political and Social Enfranchisement of Women. In August 1849, she outlined a plan for a cooperative organization embracing all associations. Her monthly L' Opinion des femmes had

to cease publication because of the 1000-franc fine levied against it for publishing the plan.

Nevertheless, delegates from 83 associations met on August 23 and named a committee, including Deroin, to draw up a constitution, and on October 5 some 104 associations' delegates adopted the draft creating the Union of the Fraternal Associations of Workers. Deroin, the chief inspirer, sat on the central committee. The Union was a complicated, quite ingenious scheme to unite production and consumption among the associations so that individuals could be self-sufficient and not have to resort to public markets. The plan's leitmotif was not equal pay per se but the assurance of fair distribution to all according to their needs.

If such a union or unions were to spread, the need for a government at all would be undermined. The authorities decided to act. On May 29, 1850, the police broke into a meeting of the leaders and arrested all 47 men and 9 women present, of whom 27 men and 2 women (Deroin and Roland) were held for trial. At the trial, Deroin disclaimed being the inspirer of the organization in order to spare the male defendants embarrassment. She explained her socialist views with "social erudition," a reporter wrote, but the judges seemed more interested in her views on marriage, illegitimacy, and her use of her maiden name. Sentenced to six months on November 15, she was imprisoned at Saint-Lazare. While there, she wrote a 14-page pamphlet, Du Célibat (Paris: Les Marchands de nouveautés, 1851), arguing that marriage is not woman's sole destiny; an appeal (with Roland) for solidarity to American feminist "sisters," who in the Second National Women's Rights Convention delegated *Lucretia Mott to correspond with French feminists; and (with Roland) a letter to the Legislative Assembly protesting a projected law (passed in July) forbidding women the right to petition.

Deroin was released on June 3, 1851 (or in some accounts early July). The association had survived, and she addressed them in a 47-page brochure, Lettres aux associations sur l'organisation du crédit (Paris: G. Sandré, 1851), defending barter against the use of money. She resumed giving lessons, tried to start special classes for workers, and organized aid for families of political outlaws and exiles. Finally, disgusted by Louis-Napoléon's coup (Dec. 2, 1851) and police surveillance of herself, she fled to London in August 1852 and never returned. Her children joined her there, her eldest daughter staying with her to the end. Her son, sickly, died in 1887. As for her husband, he had lost his job for reading socialist literature and gone insane for a time. He recovered but could not join her and soon died of typhoid fever. Deroin eked out a living teaching poor children, retiring in 1861. She practiced vegetarianism and over time was drawn to spiritualism. In 1880, the Third Republic awarded her a 600-franc pension, which helped her through her last years.

In London, she continued writing, in 1852–54 publishing with the aid of friends three annual issues of the *Almanach des femmes*, the first (in Paris) in French, the latter two in French and English. The almanachs, reflecting the disappointments of 1848 when women had hoped for inclusion, devoted much space to the exploits of women and to societies serving good causes. Besides treating broad subjects of interest to women, she defended her ideas about the freeing of women and workers, the organization of production, and the abolition of the death penalty. Unfortunately, she failed to gain a sufficient circulation to continue. After that her writing faded. She issued a brochure, *Lettre aux travailleurs* (1856), a reworking of the *Lettres aux associations*; wrote a letter to Pierre Laroux, June 9, 1858, published in *L'Espérance*; corresponded with the First International Workingmen's Association in 1865; corresponded with the feminist advocate Léon Richer c. 1877; wrote a letter to his *Le Droit des femmes*, October 7, 1883, in which she opposed his call for the right of women to file paternity suits, saying it would increase infanticides; and wrote letters to the suffragist *Hubertine Auclert** in 1886. Deroin is also known to have projected or started on an *Essai sur la doctrine de Pythagore*; an *Évangile des femmes* combining "true" Christianity with "true" socialism; and a *Souvenirs de 1848* using notes from *L'Opinion des femmes*. Jeanne Deroin died in London on April 2, 1894. Her funeral was well attended, with the eulogy being delivered by the eminent English socialist William Morris.

Deroin's socialism sought to convert through example, not violence. Her activity focused upon freeing women and the working class generally from their historic bondage. Unlike most contemporaries, writes **Joan Wallach Scott**, she "turned sexual difference into an argument for equality." At the deepest level, her ideas turned upon finding again "the true law of God," wrongly interpreted by men, in order to "put back some order . . . in the big household that is the State." Order could be achieved only by establishment of equality between the sexes—which are at once complementary and autonomous—beginning in the family, the foundation of society: "Man is able to establish order only by despotism," she wrote; "woman is able to organize only through the power of maternal love; the two united will be able to reconcile order and liberty." Seeing marriage as "a state of servitude for women," she wanted it to be "purified, moralized, equalized, under the inspiration of the precepts posed by God himself."

Unfortunately for Deroin herself, she and the other female reformers in 1848 were greeted mostly with scorn and incomprehension, unjustly caricatured as "social and sexual misfits." In fact, she idealized—to excess, some would say—marriage and motherhood and denounced sexual promiscuity and prostitution. The women's movement failed in 1848 in France, not to revive until the late 1860s. Plainly, Deroin was born out of her time. Not until 1944 did women vote in France, nearly a century after she stood for election to the Parliament. Her ideas of sexual equality have become common currency, but only generations after her activist years. Her thought and actions displayed a remarkable consistency. As **Michèle Riot-Sarcey** notes, despite poverty, repeated failures, misunderstanding, and unmerited neglect, her "outstanding character . . . forces admiration. . . . The coherence of this individual . . . is flawless."

SOURCES:

Bidelman, Patrick K. *Pariahs Stand Up! The Founding of the Liberal Feminist Movement in France, 1858–1889*. Westport, CT: Greenwood Press, 1982.

Decaux, Alain. *Histoire des françaises*. Vol. 2: *La Révolte*. Paris: Librairie Académique Perrin, 1972.

Dictionnaire biographique du mouvement ouvrier français. Sous la direction de Jean Maitron. Paris: Éditions ouvrières, 1964—.

McMillan, James F. *Housewife or Harlot: The Place of Women in French Society, 1870–1914*. NY: St. Martin's Press, 1981.

Moses, Claire. *French Feminism in the Nineteenth Century*. Albany: SUNY Press, 1984.

Offen, Karen. "Deroin, Jeanne," in *An Encyclopedia of Continental Women Writers*. Ed. by Katherine M. Wilson. NY: Garland, 1991.

Rabaut, Jean. *Histoire des féminismes français*. Paris: Éditions Stock, 1978.

Rendall, Jane. *The Origins of Modern Feminism: Women in Britain, France and the United States, 1780–1860*. NY: Schocken Books, 1984.

Riot-Sarcey, Michèle. "De l'utopie de Jeanne Deroin," in *1848—révolutions et mutations au XIXe siècle*. No. 9, 1993, pp. 29–36.

———. *La Démocratie à l'épreuve des femmes: Trois figures critiques du pouvoir, 1830–1848* [Eugénie Niboyet, Jeanne Deroin, Désirée Gay]. Paris: Albin Michel, 1994.

———. "A Public Life Denied to History: Jeanne Deroin, or the Forgetfulness of Self," in *Turning Points in*

History. First International Conference, Amsterdam, 26–30 September 1988. History of European Ideas. Vol. 11 special, 1988, pp. 253–261.

Robertson, Priscilla. An Experience of Women: Pattern and Change in Nineteenth Century Europe. Philadelphia, PA: Temple University Press, 1982.

Scott, Joan Wallach. Only Paradoxes to Offer: French Feminists and the Rights of Man. Cambridge, MA: Harvard University Press, 1996.

SUGGESTED READING:

Agulhon, Maurice. The Republican Experiment, 1848 to 1852. Cambridge: Cambridge University Press, 1983.

Amann, Peter. Revolution and Mass Democracy: The Paris Club Movement in 1848. Princeton, NJ: Princeton University Press, 1975.

Bell, Susan Groag, and Karen Offen, eds. Women, the Family, and Freedom: The Debate in Documents, Vol. 1. Stanford: Stanford University Press, 1983.

Desroches, Henri. Solidarités ouvrières: Sociétaires et compagnons dans les associations coopératives (1831–1900). Paris: Éditions Ouvrières, 1981.

Dictionnaire de biographie française. A. Balteau, M. Barroux, M. Perrot, et al., directeurs. Paris: Letourzey et Ané, 1933-.

Langer, William L. Political and Social Upheaval, 1832–1852. NY: Harper & Row, 1969.

Price, Roger. The French Second Republic: A Social History. Ithaca: Cornell University Press, 1972.

Rabine, Leslie Wahl. Feminism, Socialism, and French Romanticism. Bloomington: Indiana University Press, 1993.

Ranvier, Adrien. "Une feministe de 1848: Jeanne Deroin." La Révolution de 1848. Vol. 4: 317–55, Vol. 5:421–430, 480–498. Paris: Cornély, 1907–8.

Riot-Sarcey, Michèle. "La Conscience féministe des femmes en 1848: Jeanne Deroin et Désirée Gay." Stephane Michaud, ed., Un fab11eux destin: Flora Tristan. Dijon: Presses Universitaires de Dijon, 1985.

Robertson, Priscilla Smith. Revolutions of 1848: A Social History. Princeton: Princeton University Press, 1952.

Serrière, Michèle. "Jeanne Deroin," in Femmes et travail. Paris: Éditions Martinsart, 1981.

Thomas, Edith. Les Femmes de 1848. Paris: Presses Universitaires de France, 1948.

———. Pauline Roland. Paris: Librairie M. Rivière, 1956.

DOCUMENTS:

Paris: Bibliothèque de l'Arsenal, Fonds Enfantin; Bibliothèque Historique de la Ville de Paris, Fonds Bouglé; Bibliothèque Marguerite-Durand, Dossier Deroin.

David S. Newhall, Professor Emeritus of History, Centre College, Danville, Kentucky, author of Clemenceau: A Life at War (Edwin Mellen, 1991)

de'Rossi, Properzia (c. 1490–1530).

See Rossi, Properzia de.

Derouin, Jeanne (1805–1894).

See Deroin, Jeanne-Françoise.

Derricotte, Juliette (1897–1931)

African-American university official and student leader whose accidental death in 1931 triggered a national outrage in the black community because her death was seen as one of the inevitable consequences of the Southern regime of racial segregation and inequality. Born Juliette Aline Derricotte in Athens, Georgia, on April 1, 1897; died in Chattanooga, Tennessee, on November 7, 1931; daughter of Isaac and Laura (Hardwick) Derricotte; never married.

Born in a small Georgia university town a generation after the abolition of slavery, Juliette Aline Derricotte grew up in a large and loving African-American family. Her father Isaac, a cobbler, and her mother **Laura**, a seamstress, had managed to create an emotionally caring environment for their nine children despite their modest incomes and having to live in a racially segregated society. Intellectually curious as well as emotionally sensitive, as a child Juliette wished one day to attend Athens' well-known Lucy Cobb Institute, but her mother was forced to tell her that this exclusive girls' school had a rule excluding "young girls of color." Juliette's sense of having been excluded because of the color of her skin rather than because of any lack of merit only strengthened her resolve to forge ahead. After successfully completing her secondary school education in Atlanta, she was accepted at Talladega College in Alabama.

Derricotte was shocked to discover that all of her professors at Talladega were white, but she quickly grew to love the small school and emerged as a student leader. She won prizes for public speaking, became president of the campus YWCA, and was often called on to settle disputes between students and faculty. Personable, warm, and mature beyond her years, Juliette made many friends among both her fellow students and her teachers at Talladega College. After her 1918 graduation, she went to New York City to take a summer course at the YWCA National Training School. Impressed by the young black woman from the South, YWCA officials appointed Derricotte in the fall of 1918 to the post of secretary of the organization's National Student Council.

The excellence of her YWCA work among students in New York brought her to the attention of other organizations, including the World Student Christian Federation (WSCF). Having been appointed a member of the WSCF general committee, in 1924 Derricotte was sent to England as one of two black delegates to represent American college students at an international conference. In 1928, she made what was then an epic trip to Mysore, India, to meet with Asian student leaders. Although Derricotte had read about the humiliations of colonialism and knew from her own experience the evils of racism, the trip to India nevertheless was a profound experience for her. Here, she saw firsthand how cruel imperialism's racial ideology could be to individuals. From a young Indian woman, Derricotte learned that only when all the whites in her church had been seated could she, as a non-white, expect to receive a seat. A young woman from Japanese-occupied Korea told Juliette of racial prejudice, discrimination, segregation, and repression by Asians against other Asians that more than matched the racism of the American South. The seven weeks Derricotte spent in India in 1928 gave her deep insights into many of the most profound unsolved dilemmas of the 20th century.

Rather than being depressed or demoralized, Juliette Derricotte found herself inspired by what she had seen, heard, and experienced. Writing some time later about the Mysore conference in the influential black American journal *The Crisis,* she chose to view the 90 or so delegates of the general committee that had met in Mysore as pointing the way to "what can happen to all the world. With all the differences and difficulties, with all the entanglements of international attitudes and policies, with all the bitterness and prejudice and hatred that are true between any two or more of these countries, you are here friends working, thinking, playing, living together in the finest sort of fellowship, fulfilling the dream of the World's Student Christian Federation, 'That All May be One'."

A perceptive observer during her travels, Derricotte recalled her trip to India not only in terms of personal friendships but of deeper issues that still needed to be explored further and understood more deeply: "the wealth as well as the physical poverty of India haunts me; I ache with actual physical pain when I remember the struggles of all India today."

After having received a master's degree in religious education from Columbia University in 1927, Derricotte began to think about returning to her native South in order to participate in black educational programs. In 1929, the year that she was chosen to be the only woman trustee of Talladega College, she accepted an offer as dean of women at Fisk University in Nashville, Tennessee. She walked into a troubled campus at Fisk, which was still attempting to enforce what had become in the 1920s increasingly anachronistic rules for regulating the personal lives of young women. In little over a year, however, Derricotte had succeeded in winning the confidence of the great majority of Fisk's female students and the overall situation on campus was becoming more tranquil. With this in mind, she decided to take a trip from Nashville to Athens, Georgia, in order to visit her mother.

On the way, the car driven by Derricotte, which had as passengers three Fisk students from Georgia, was involved in a serious accident about a mile outside Dalton, Georgia. Most grievously injured in the wreck were Derricotte and one of her passengers. After emergency treatment, it was decided that since the local tax-supported hospital did not admit black patients, it would be best if Derricotte and the student spent the night at the home of a black woman who provided beds for black patients. The seriousness of the situation was made clear when the student died during the night and Derricotte's condition did not improve. Driven by ambulance to Chattanooga's Walden Hospital, Juliette Derricotte died there on November 7, 1931. Besides mourning the premature and tragic death of a highly talented young woman who likely would have gone on to positions of national and international leadership, the special circumstances of Juliette Derricotte's death thrust a glaring spotlight on the evils of racial segregation in the American South. The full details of her death were never completely clarified, but it was clear that had she gained admittance to the hospital in Dalton, both she and the other injured passenger might have lived. Writing in *The Crisis* several months after her death, W.E.B. Du Bois noted that Derricotte and her three passengers were going to Georgia by automobile because of the Jim Crow railroad cars of the South, which were demeaning and humiliating to black travelers. A national debate was unleashed by her death, and one of her white friends, **Ethel Gilbert**, was prompted to note that Derricotte's death once again served to dramatize how "rotten and wicked and unspeakably cruel" the system of racial segregation really was, and how in this case it had resulted in two deaths.

SOURCES:

Cuthbert, Marion V. *Juliette Derricotte.* NY: The Womans Press, 1933.

Derricotte, Juliette. "The Student Conference in Mysore, India," in *The Crisis.* Vol. 36, no. 8. August 1929, pp. 267, 280–283.

Du Bois, W.E.B. "Dalton, Georgia," in *The Crisis.* Vol. 39, no. 3. March 1932, pp. 85–87.

Jeanness, Mary. *Twelve Negro Americans.* NY: Friendship Press, 1925.

"Juliette Derricotte: Her Character and Her Martyrdom," in *The Crisis.* Vol. 39, no. 3. March 1932, pp. 84–85.

Richardson, Joe M. *A History of Fisk University, 1865–1946.* University, AL: University of Alabama Press, 1980.

Smith, Jessie Carney. *Epic Lives: One Hundred Black Women Who Made a Difference.* Detroit, MI: Visible Ink Press, 1993.

John Haag, Associate Professor of History, University of Georgia, Athens, Georgia

Dervorgilla.

Variant of Devorgilla.

Derzhinskaya, Zeniya (1889–1951)

Russian soprano, who was one of the outstanding singers of her era. Born in Kiev, Russia, on February 6, 1889; died in Moscow on June 9, 1951; was made a People's Artists of the USSR (1937).

Zeniya Georgiyevna Derzhinskaya studied with F. Pash and *Mathilde Marchesi in Kiev. When Derzhinskaya sang Rachmaninov, the composer himself praised her performance. Moving to Moscow, she sang at the Narodnïy Dom opera house from 1913 to 1915, then went to the Bolshoi Theater where she remained until 1948. Under Václav Suk, Derzhinskaya created her best roles—Lisa in Tchaikovsky's *The Queen of Spades,* Nastasya in Tchaikovsky's *Sorceress,* and Fevroniya in Rimsky-Korsakov's *The Legend of the City of Kitezh.* Her voice had a wide range and beautiful timbre. Particularly successful in her portrayal of Russian women, she was also remembered as Mariya in Tchaikovsky's *Mazeppa* and as Marguerite in Gounod's *Faust.* In 1926, Derzhinskaya gave a concert performance of *Kitezh* at the Paris Opéra which was a great success. After her retirement in 1948, she taught at the Moscow Conservatory until her death in 1951. A much-beloved artist, Zeniya Derzhinskaya was made a People's Artist of the USSR in 1937.

John Haag, Athens, Georgia

de Sant Jordi, Rosa (b. 1910).

See Arquimbau, Rosa Maria.

Desbordes-Valmore, Marceline (1785–1859)

Romantic French poet and singer. Name variations: Marcelline; Marceline Valmore. Born Marceline Félicité Josèphe Desbordes at Douai, France, on June 20, 1785 (some sources cite 1786); died on July 23, 1859; daughter of a poor artisan; married François Prosper Lanchantin (an actor known as Valmore), in 1817; children: (with Henri Latouche) one son; (with Lanchantin) three daughters.

The poet Marceline Desbordes-Valmore was orphaned as a child when the French Revolution of 1789 wiped out most of her family. To support herself, she made her debut at age 16 in comic opera, but she soon quit the stage when an illness threatened the loss of her voice. In 1817, following an unfortunate love affair with writer Henri Latouche and the birth and death of their child, she married a kind, but minor, actor François Prosper Lanchantin, who was called Valmore. The couple remained together, touring the country as actors, and had three daughters.

Desbordes-Valmore consoled her many misfortunes by writing Romantic poetry of love and childhood, gentle work distinguished for its unaffected tenderness and melancholic air. Her writing was praised by Baudelaire and Sainte-Beuve, and Verlaine claimed her as an influence. Desbordes-Valmore wrote several stories as well as *Élégies et romances* (Elegies and Romances, 1818), *Élégies et poésies nouvelles* (New Elegies and Poems, 1824), *Les Pleurs* (Tears, 1833), *Pauvres Fleurs* (Poor Flowers, 1839) and *Bouquets et Prières* (Bouquets and Prayers, 1843). Her correspondence was published in 1896. The renowned French photographer Nadar, who shied away from the fad of deathbed pictures, made two exceptions: Victor Hugo and Mme Desbordes-Valmore. In 1959, an exhibition at the Bibliothèque Nationale in Paris honored the centenary of her death.

See illustration on the following page

Desgarcins, Magdeleine Marie (1769–1797)

French actress. Born Magdeleine Marie Louise at Mont Dauphin (Hautes Alpes) in 1769; died in Paris on October 27, 1797.

In her short career, Magdeleine Desgarcins was numbered among the greatest of French tragediennes. She was an associate of François Talma, with whom she almost always played. Desgarcins debut came at the Comédie Française on May 24, 1788, in *Bajazet,* a performance that was so successful that she was immediately made *sociétaire.* In 1791, she was one of the actresses who left the Comédie Française and followed Talma to the house in the rue Richelieu, which was soon to become the Théâtre de la République, where she triumphed in *King Lear, Otello,* and La Harpe's *Melanie et Virginie.* Desgarcins' health failed, however, and she died insane in Paris on October 27, 1797.

Deshayes, Catherine (d. 1680).

See French "Witches."

Marceline
Desbordes-
Valmore

Deshoulières, Antoinette

(1638–1694)

*French poet. Name variations: Des Houlières, Deshoulieres. Pronunciation: DAY-zoo-LYAIR. Born Antoinette du Ligier de la Garde in Paris, France, on January 1, 1638 (some sources cite 1637); died of cancer in Paris on February 17, 1694; daughter of Melchior du Ligier, sieur de la Garde, maître d'hôtel to the queens *Marie de Medici and *Anne of Austria (1601–1666); married Guillaume de Boisguérin, seigneur Deshoulières, in 1651; children: daughter Antoinette Thérèse Deshoulières (1662–1718).*

Born in Paris in 1638, Antoinette Deshoulières was given a thorough education, including Latin, Spanish and Italian, and was instructed in poetry by the poet Jean Hesnault. At 13, she married Guillaume de Boisguérin, Lord Deshoulières; about a year after the marriage, he followed the prince of Condé to Flanders as lieutenant-colonel of one of his regiments. Returned for a time to her parents' house, Madame Deshoulières wrote poetry and studied the philosophy of Pierre Gassendi. She joined her husband at Rocroi, near Brussels, where she became the object of embarrassing attentions on the part of the prince of Condé. Having annoyed the government by her urgent demand for the arrears of her husband's pay, she was imprisoned in the château of Wilworden. She was freed by her husband a few months later when he attacked the château, leading a small band of soldiers. An amnesty was proclaimed, and they returned to France.

Deshoulières, who soon became highly visible at the court of Louis XIV and in literary society, won the friendship and admiration of the most eminent literary women and men of her age. Some of her more devout flatterers went so far as to style her the tenth muse and the French Calliope. Her numerous poems included examples of almost all the minor forms, odes, eclogues, idylls, elegies, chansons, ballads, and madrigals. Of these, only the idylls—especially "The Sheep," "The Flowers," and "The Birds"—have endured. Voltaire pronounced Deshoulières the best of women French poets, and her reputation with her contemporaries is indicated by her election as a member of the Academy of the Ricovrati of Padua and of the Academy of Arles. In 1688, her long-standing poverty was relieved by a pension of 2,000 livres bestowed upon her by the king. But she had been battling cancer for the last 12 years of her life, and she died in Paris on February 17,

Antoinette Deshoulières

1694. Complete editions of her works were published at Paris in 1695 and 1747. These include a few poems by her daughter, **Antoinette Thérèse Deshoulières**, who inherited her talent for writing.

SUGGESTED READING:

Buck, Claire, ed. *The Bloomsbury Guide to Women's Literature*. NY: Prentice Hall, 1992.

Perkins, W. "Mme Deshoulières," in *Newsletter of the Society for French Seventeenth-Century Studies*. 1983, pp. 125–133.

Desiderata (d. 773)

*Queen of the Franks. Name variations: Desideria; Ermengarde. Birth date unknown; died in 773; daughter of Desiderius, king of the Lombards, and Queen Ausa; became second wife of Charlemagne (Charles I), king of the Franks (r. 768–814), Holy Roman emperor (r. 800–814), in 770 (annulled 771). Charlemagne had five wives: *Himiltrude; Desiderata (d. 773); *Hildegarde of Swabia (c. 757–783); *Fastrada (d. 794); and *Luitgarde (d. 800).*

The marriage of Desiderata, daughter of the Lombard king, and Charlemagne, Holy Roman emperor, was arranged by *Bertha (719–783), Charlemagne's mother. Daughter and mother-in-law exchanged a warm affection, but, within one year of the marriage, Charlemagne repudiated Desiderata in 771 for reasons unknown and sent her back to her family. When Desiderata heard of her husband's marriage to *Hildegarde of Swabia that same year, she retired to a monastery founded by her parents where her sister was abbess. Desiderata died two years later in 773.

Désirée (1777–1860)

*Queen of Sweden. Name variations: Desiree Clary; Bernhardine or Bernardine Eugenie Desiree. Born Bernardiné Eugénie Désirée Clary on November 9, 1777, in Marseille, France; died on December 17, 1860, in Stockholm, Sweden; buried in Stockholm; daughter of François Clary (a prosperous merchant of Marseille); sister of Julie Clary Bonaparte (1771–1845); married Jean Baptiste Jules Bernadotte also known as Karl XIV Johan or Charles XIV John (1763–1844), king of Sweden (r. 1818–1844), on August 17, 1798; children: Oscar I (1799–1859), king of Sweden (r. 1844–1859, who married *Josephine Beauharnais [1807–1876]).*

Queen Désirée was born Bernardiné Eugénie Désirée Clary on November 9, 1777, in Marseille, France, the daughter of François Clary, a prosperous merchant of Marseille. Before Désirée turned 20, she was pursued by Napoleon Bonaparte who wanted to marry her. Désirée's sister *Julie Clary Bonaparte had married Joseph Bonaparte, however, and their father felt that one Bonaparte in the family was enough. Désirée was forced to turn down Napoleon's proposal (the film *Desiree*, starring Marlon Brando and *Jean Simmons, was based on the incident).

In 1798, Désirée married the French soldier Jean Bernadotte who would rise from the ranks to become one of Napoleon's mar-

Désirée

shals and later be placed on the throne of Sweden by Napoleon and crowned Charles XIV John. Charles XIV and Désirée began the Bernadotte line that continued through the 20th century. Though Désirée visited Sweden in 1810 and 1811, she did not live there until 1823. She was queen of Sweden from 1818 to 1844.

Desiree Bernadotte (b. 1938)

*Baroness Silfverschiold. Name variations: Désirée of Sweden. Born Désirée Elizabeth on June 2, 1938, at Haga Palace, Stockholm, Sweden; daughter of Gustavus Adolphus (1906–1947), duke of Westerbotten, and *Sybilla of Saxe-Coburg-Gotha (1908–1972); sister of Carl XVI Gustavus, king of Sweden; married Niclas, baron Silferschiöld or Silfverschiold, on June 5, 1964; children: Carl Otto Edmund (b. 1965); Christina-Louise, baroness Silfverschiold (b. 1966); Helene Ingeborg, baroness Silfverschiold (b. 1968).*

Desjardins, Marie Catherine (1640–1683).

See Villedieu, Catherine des Jardins, Mme de.

Deslys, Gaby (1884–1920)

French actress and danseuse. Born Marie-Élise-Gabrielle Caire in 1884 in Marseille, France; died on February 11, 1920.

Around the turn of the century, Gaby Deslys was a well-known vaudeville star in Paris, appearing in the Folies-Bergére and at the Olympia where she introduced American dancing with her partner Harry Pilcer. In 1906, she made her first appearance in London as the Charm of Paris in *The New Aladdin*. She was first seen in New York in 1911 in *Les Debuts de Chichine*. Deslys' successful career afforded her a luxurious lifestyle which included a suite in the Rue Villebois-Mareuil, a private hotel in Paris, and a London residence in Kensington, where, according to *Janet Flanner, "the bed lay on a dais beneath an arch of black marble supported by marble pillars." The actress eschewed marriage, claiming that no amount of money could buy her liberty. Unfortunately, her career was cut short by her untimely death at the age of 36. Her estate, estimated at nine million francs, was divided between Pilcer, the poor and tubercular of Marseilles, and her family, the Caires. However, distribution of the estate was contested by a Hungarian family who insisted that Deslys was really one of theirs, a woman by the name of **Hedwige Navratil** of Hatvan, Hungary. Subse-

 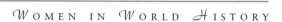

quently, two other women bearing this name appeared in the Paris courts, further complicating the issue.

RELATED MEDIA:

Deslys was portrayed by *Tamara Toumanova in the MGM musical *Deep in My Heart*, 1954.

Barbara Morgan,
Melrose, Massachusetts

Desmares, Christine (1682–1753).

See Champmesle, Marie for sidebar.

Desmares, Marie (c. 1642–1698).

See Champmesle, Marie.

Desmier, Eleanor (1639–1722)

*Countess of Williamsburg. Name variations: Eleanor d'Olbreuse. Born on January 17, 1639; died on February 5, 1722; daughter of Alexander II Desmier, Seigneur d'Olbreuse; married George Guelph, duke of Brunswick-Luneburg (elector of Hanover, 1648–1665, duke of Celle, 1665–1705), on September 15, 1665; children: *Sophia Dorothea of Brunswick-Celle (1666–1726, who married George I, king of England).*

One of the great beauties of Europe, Eleanor Desmier had a morganatic marriage with George, duke of Brunswick-Luneburg. Later, the union was made fully legal by the emperor of Germany.

Desmond, Astra (1893–1973)

English contralto who introduced many of the works of Edvard Grieg, Edward Elgar, and other modern composers to British audiences. Born in Torquay, England, on April 10, 1893; died in Faversham, England, on August 16, 1973; married Sir Thomas Neame, in 1920; made a Commander of the British Empire in 1949 for her musical contributions.

Astra Desmond studied singing at the Royal Academy of Music with *Blanche Marchesi and gave her first recital in London in 1915. Though she was the first to sing the title role in Rutland Boughton's opera *Alkestis*, Desmond concentrated mainly on concerts and oratorios. Particularly known for performing new works, she was one of the first to sing Edvard Grieg's works and gave numerous recitals in the original Norwegian. Desmond was awarded a medal of St. Olav for her serious study and performing of Scandinavian works. She also researched and wrote about Grieg, Dvorak, and Sibelius as well as other composers. Desmond was associated with the works of Sir Edward Elgar after 1920 and

was considered to be an outstanding interpreter of the Angel in Elgar's *The Dream of Gerontius*.

John Haag,
Athens, Georgia

Gaby
Deslys

Desmond, countess of.

See Fitzgerald, Katherine (c. 1500–1604).

Desmoulins, Lucile (1771–1794)

Victim of the Terror in the French Revolution whose devotion to her family, and particularly her husband Camille Desmoulins, transcended political posturing and evoked a nobility of spirit admirable even to her enemies. Name variations: Lucille. Born Lucile Duplessis in or near Paris in 1771; died on the guillotine in Paris on April 13, 1794; daughter of a wealthy official in the French Ministry of Finance and Madame Duplessis; married Camille Desmoulins (a poor law student who, upon the outbreak of the Revolution, became a famous activist and journalist), on December 29, 1790; children: son, Horace (b. July 6, 1792).

Supported her husband in his shifting political stances and played host to the Jacobins, a circle of his political associates in Paris (1790–94); exerted heroic efforts to secure husband's release upon his arrest by Revolutionary authorities; died by order of the Committee of Public Safety one week after her husband was executed (April 1794).

A number of women left a mark on the history of the French Revolution, a great political and social convulsion that shook France from 1789 to 1799. Those who did are known to us primarily for their capacity to exert some political influence and thus overcome their inherent disadvantage of being female in a time when women were regarded as naturally unfit for political activity. Lucile Desmoulins generally shared the prevailing attitude, and for most of her brief life conformed to all the expectations her family and husband held for her. At the last, however, she drew upon some inner will that allowed her to transform herself from the "gentle Lucile" to a woman of unforgettable defiance to injustice and tyranny.

𝒢ood night, my dear mother. A tear falls from my eyes; it is for you. I am going to sleep in the tranquillity of the innocents.

—**Lucile Desmoulins, on the eve of her execution during the French Revolution**

Lucile Desmoulins was in most respects a typical woman of her time and place. She was born Lucile Duplessis, the daughter of an official in the French Ministry of Finance in the government of Louis XVI in the 1780s. Her father was a wealthy man, possessing property in Paris and at his estate at Bourg La Reine. Her mother was a woman of high spirits, flirtatious, amorous, and probably not overly burdened with the idea of marital fidelity. Apparently, as Lucile grew from her privileged childhood into her teens, she acquired not only a striking physical beauty, but also a female confidant in the form of her mother who, true to the emerging romantic mood of the age, instilled in her daughter the conviction that the ideal of femininity was overpowering physical, intellectual, and spiritual love. Lucile became a young woman in Paris, a city brimming with young men in search of love as much as she, and who could not but be attracted to her beauty and the 100,000 franc dowry that would come with her.

It was near her father's house, in the fashionable Luxembourg Gardens, that Lucile met the man upon whom she bestowed her limitless devotion. In the last year before the outbreak of the French Revolution, Lucile fell in love with Camille Desmoulins, a young student who had studied law with Maximilien Robespierre, a future leader of revolutionary France. Camille frequented the Luxembourg, posing and extolling various sentiments to passersby. It could not be said that he was handsome or well established. In fact, his prospects were flimsy when Lucile met him, but that seemed unimportant to her. After a courtship in the Gardens, Camille asked Lucile to marry him, but her father, suspecting Camille's motives and his chances, would not hear the young man's petition. The couple, having no alternative, reverted to their meetings in the Luxembourg and dreamed of a future together.

When the Revolution exploded in Paris in the spring and summer of 1789, Camille recognized that a wonderful opportunity had come his way. Well read in the law and the classics and convinced that his star would lead him to greatness, Camille followed the opening events of the upheaval hungrily. In July 1789, as Paris was in turmoil because of the high expectations aroused by the establishment of a National Constituent Assembly at nearby Versailles, and equally agitated for fear of a royal reaction in force, Camille seized the moment. When fear gripped the city on July 12, he leapt upon a table in a café in the popular entertainment area, the Palais Royal, and, with a pistol in hand, shouted to the citizens to arm themselves against the king. In the next two days, Camille was in the forefront of crowds seeking weapons, donning revolutionary cockades, and demanding the arming of the population against royal repression. On the glorious 14th of July, the young orator was among the leaders of the attack on the Bastille, a royal fortress prison in the heart of the city. As a "victor" at the Bastille, Camille Desmoulins became a famous name among patriots and revolutionaries.

If the Revolution gave Camille his voice, it also presented him the opportunity to use another weapon, the pen. Forgetting the law, he became a journalist, publishing his *Révolutions de France et de Brabant*. Instantly popular in Paris and other locations, the journal attacked all counterrevolutionaries, foreign enemies, aristocrats, and, eventually, the king. Soon, Camille joined the popular Cordeliers Club and the Jacobin Club, an emerging power in Paris and in the National Assembly. Among others, Camille could count as friends, Maximilien Robespierre, Louis-Marie Freron, Jacques Danton, Jerome Pétion, Brissot de Warville, and other rising figures in the Revolution. The Revolution also gave him Lucile. Impressed with Camille's fame and prospects, in December 1789 Monsieur Duplessis bestowed his daughter's hand and dowry on the new child of fortune. Both Lucile and her fiancé were ecstatic, and they were married on December 29. Lucile was said to have been "joyfully weeping" as she accepted the congratulations of Robespierre and Brissot de Warville, both of whom would later be targets of Camille's criticisms.

As a married woman, partner to a man apparently touched by destiny, Lucile was more beautiful, more pleasant, more vivacious than ever. She and Camille became the center of a social circle of political leaders, mostly Jacobins, ever waxing in power as the Revolution veered in a more radical direction in the early 1790s. She never failed him. She helped him with his articles, she cooked for him, she sewed for him, she adored him, and she defended his every virtue and his every fault. No one, not even her father, was permitted to criticize Camille, even though, in fact, he could be factious, shallow, and pompous. Lucile did not see such failings: Camille was her great love, her ideal, her hero. When she gave birth to a son, Horace, on July 6, 1792, her happiness knew no bounds. Now she and Camille had achieved the ultimate fruit of their union.

Lucile's joy was shortly sullied, however, by raw fear. By August 1792, the struggle for control of the French government was coming to a crisis point. Loathing the changes forced upon him by the National Assembly and by the violence across France, Louis XVI attempted to escape France with his family in June 1791. He failed and was brought back to Paris. Louis, in these circumstances, publicly accepted the changes wrought by the Revolution and swore that he would abide by the new constitution. Few believed him, least of all the revolutionary press. Camille certainly doubted the king's sincerity and passed these views on to Lucile.

In April 1792, France went to war with the hostile German states of Prussia and Austria. Swearing enmity to kings, the French revolutionaries proposed to liberate Europe from all tyrants. The tyrants, however, fought back with professional armies against France's politicized divisions. By August, the enemy was marching on French soil, and Paris was threatened. Fear and suspicion against the king and queen, *Marie Antoinette, an Austrian by birth, led to a conspiracy between the Jacobins, the revolutionary city government, the Commune, and the popular assemblies in the Sections, or political divisions, of Paris to overthrow the king. Camille and his friend, Danton, took part in the attack on the royal palace, the Tuileries, on August 10. Lucile was paralyzed with fear. In her diary she wrote: "Camille arrived with a fusil. O God, I hid myself . . . covered my face with my hands and wept. . . . I realized that he was running into danger."

The conspirators' victory brought Camille into the new provisional government as secretary to Danton, who had become minister of justice. Lucile echoed Camille's denunciations of the dethroned king and was not critical when Danton, and perhaps Camille, played a part in the judicial murder of thousands of royalist suspects in Parisian jails in September. Then, when the faction known as the Girondins, mostly men from the provinces who resented the Parisian's dominance in the nation's affairs, and which included old friends like Brissot and Jerome Pétion, resisted the increasingly radical populist policies of the Jacobins, Lucile said nothing as they were denounced by Camille in imitation of Robespierre. The Girondists were proscribed and Brissot died on the guillotine; Pétion killed himself.

The suppression of the Girondins touched off civil war in France, and, combined with an expanding list of foreign enemies, meant that the National Convention, elected in late 1792 and controlled by the Jacobins, especially those associated with Robespierre, was at war with much of France and much of Europe. Everywhere there were rumors, fears, suspicions, and spontaneous violence. The Convention, to respond to the threat of chaos and uncontrolled terror, created the Committee of Public Safety and granted it extraordinary executive powers.

One group that now became a target of the Jacobin Committee of Public Safety was the urban proto-socialists known as the *Enragés*. Regarded as undisciplined and unreliable, they were soon arrested. More formidable than the *Enragés* was the group centered on the journalist, Jacques Hébert. Hébert published a scandalous paper called *Père Duchesne* which pressed for the destruction of the Christian religion as counterrevolutionary. When Camille began his new newspaper in December 1793, *Le Vieux Cordelier,* he joined the mounting attack led by Danton and Robespierre against the Hébertists. Lucile, typically, followed her husband's lead and added that Hébert had been rude and indecent toward her. In any event, Hébert's ideas on drastic taxation of the wealthy served to frighten Lucile and perhaps her newly rich husband as well. In March,

Hébert and his followers were sent to the guillotine. Hébert had once been Camille's comrade in the Cordeliers Club.

Following the Committee of Public Safety's destruction of the Hébertists, powerful elements in the National Convention, the Committee of Public Safety, and the Jacobins began to pressure Robespierre, the unofficial leader of the Committee, to move against the group now referred to as the Indulgents. This band of revolutionaries, led by Danton, demanded a moderation of the Terror. The Terror had succeeded, they argued, in suppressing internal rebellion, stabilizing the economy, and turning back the many foreign enemies of France. To continue the Terror would be to discredit the Revolution and foster ever more enemies. In *Le Vieux Cordelier*, Camille began to make similar appeals. It was a dangerous course for him, and Lucile sensed it, for he was pitting himself against the formidable Robespierre. The "Incorruptible," as Robespierre was called, was not prepared to relax the Terror. Even though hundreds were going to the guillotine each week in Paris and in the countryside, Robespierre and his closest associates thought that counterrevolution was still possible and that France had to be compelled to make the herculean efforts required to save the nation. It is likely that the "Incorruptible" also meant to remove "unvirtuous" men, a task of enormous proportions indeed.

Lucile Desmoulins sensed the danger. She urged Camille to leave Paris and let matters settle. Yet, even though very worried, Camille loved the role he played in shaping public opinion in his journal and in the clubs. As the days passed, however, the friendship between the two old schoolmates cooled. When Camille called for clemency and denounced the more ferocious laws of the Terror, Robespierre assumed that it was he under attack. He struck back at the Jacobins, denouncing *Le Vieux Cordelier*. Without reflection, Camille answered Robespierre by asserting that Maximilien was playing a double game. In March, Camille was expelled from the Cordeliers and the Jacobins. Lucile's fears were proving to be justified.

Actually, while Camille had angered Robespierre and other members of the Committee, his offenses were but a part of the larger crime of being associated with Danton. Openly demanding an end to the extraordinary decrees and power of the Committee, Danton made himself an enemy of Robespierre; there were others on the Committee who wanted Danton's head as payment for their support of Robespierre against the Hébertists. Camille knew he had misstepped, but it was too late to turn back. When his printer refused to publish his last issue of *Le Vieux Cordelier*, Camille succumbed to despair. It could only be a matter of time.

On March 30, pressured by others on the Committee, Robespierre consented to an arrest order for Danton, Camille Desmoulins, and others. Soldiers came in the middle of the night to take Camille to the Luxembourg Prison. Lucile was helpless and terrified. By morning, however, she had gained her composure. Now began her gallant, if futile, fight to save her husband. From one office to another, up this street and down that one, across the city she appealed, she implored, she begged for Camille's release. No one would help her. When exhausted, she stood silently outside the Luxembourg, yearning for the sight of him. With Danton's 16-year-old wife ✤➤ Louise, Lucile frantically appealed to Robespierre, the only man who could save Camille and Danton. Pitifully, without pride, she wrote to the "Incorruptible," reminding him of his old friendship, of *their* old friendship, of the nights Robespierre had been a part of the Desmoulins family circle. But Maximilien, who had attended Lucile's wedding, would not answer her letter, nor would he permit her to come to him at his house in the rue Saint-Honoré. He had already decided that Danton and Camille must die that the Revolution might live.

From prison, Camille wrote to Lucile begging her to live, to protect their son. "Adieu, Loulou," he wrote, "my life, my soul, my divinity on earth." The words stirred her to action. Across the city she rambled, damning the Committee, cursing Robespierre. Plots and schemes filled her head: she would bribe Camille's jailers; she would somehow raise an insurrection in the city; she would do something. To everyone and to no one she cried: "Why am I at liberty? Do people think that just because I am a woman I do not dare to raise my voice?" But no one listened.

On the day before the Dantonists were to die, Saint-Just, a close associate of Robespierre, accused Lucile of fomenting a rebellion in the prison and of conspiring with known counter-revolutionaries. She was soon under arrest. It is fortunate she did not see her husband's last journey across Paris to the guillotine. In the tumbrel with Danton, Camille completely broke down. Hysterically, he tore his clothes, shouted his name to the crowd lining the avenues, and, apparently, believed the citizens would surge forward to save him and Danton, or that somehow Lucile might rescue him. Danton tried to encourage his friend to display dignity, commenting with his usual dark humor on the mobs now calling for their blood who had a few weeks before all but worshipped them as idols. Camille could not, however, bring himself under control. As they passed Robespierre's house in the rue Saint-Honoré, Danton, defiant to the end, bellowed toward Robespierre's abode: "You will follow me!" At the scaffold, Danton hesitated, then reproached himself: "Come, Danton, no weakness!" Then, to the executioner, "Show my head to the people; it is worth showing." Camille followed, weeping over his lost Lucile.

Lucile was to live another week. Before the Revolutionary Tribunal, she made no defense. Her thoughts were on her coming death, and she believed intensely that she would be reunited with Camille in another world. On April 13, she mounted the tumbrel, ironically with ❧➤ **Madame Hébert**, whose husband she had hated. Lucile wore a white veil over her hair, just as she had on her wedding day, At the guillotine, she displayed no fear. She all but danced up the steps and quickly placed herself in the correct position. A moment later, she was dead.

SOURCES:

Cher, Marie. *Charlotte Corday and Certain Men of the Revolutionary Torment.* NY: D. Appleton, 1929, pp. 160–170.

Soboul, Albert. *The French Revolution 1787–1799.* NY: Vintage Books, 1975, pp. 364–368.

Sokolnikova, Galina Osipovna. *Nine Women Drawn from the Epoch of the French Revolution.* Translated by H.C. Stevens. Books for Libraries Press, 1932, reprinted 1969, pp. 193–220.

SUGGESTED READING:

Connally, Owen D. *French Revolution and Napoleonic Era.* Holt, Rinehart & Winston, 1979, pp. 157–167.

C. David Rice, Professor of History, Central Missouri State University, Warrensburg, Missouri

De Souza, Mme (1761–1836).

See Souza-Botelho, Adélaïde-Marie-Émilie-Filleul, marquise of.

Despard, Charlotte (1844–1939)

Feminist, socialist, and Irish republican activist. Born Charlotte French in Ripple, Kent, England, on June 15, 1844; died on November 9, 1939, in Belfast, Northern Ireland; third daughter of William French and Margaret (Eccles) French; educated privately; married Maximilian Despard, on December 20, 1870 (died, April 4, 1890); no children.

Selected publications: Chaste as Ice, Pure as Snow *(Tinsley, 1874);* A Modern Iago *(Griffith and Farnan, 1879);* The Rajah's Heir *(Tinsley, 1890);* Women in the

❧➤ Danton, Louise (1777–1856)

Young French wife of Jacques Danton. Name variations: Sebastienne-Louise Gély; Louise Gély; Louise Dupin. Born Sébastienne-Louise Gély in 1777; died at age 80 in Paris in 1856; daughter of Marc-Antoine Gély (a former Admiralty official); married Jacques Danton, in 1793 (guillotined, 1794); married Claude-François Dupin (prefect, officer of the Legion of Honor, under Napoleon).

Following the death of his first wife **Gabrielle Danton**, who had died giving birth to their fourth son in February 1793, and concerned about his motherless sons, Jacques Danton married 16-year-old Louise Gély, a friend of the family, on June 12, 1793. Less than one year later, she was a widow. Soon after, Louise Danton remarried but, in her sorrow, never mentioned Danton's name again.

❧➤ Hébert, Madame (d. 1794)

French Revolutionary. Died on the guillotine in Paris on April 13, 1794; married Jacques René Hébert (1757–1794).

Nation *(1909);* Women in the New Era *(1910);* Theosophy and the Women's Movement *(1913).*

In her long and eventful life, Charlotte Despard embraced a range of causes to which she gave enthusiasm, dedication, and considerable financial support: the plight of the poor, women's suffrage, socialism, Irish independence, and communism. The contradictions in her life were as varied as the causes she supported.

She was born Charlotte French into a wealthy Kent family of Irish antecedents, one of five sisters and one brother. Their mother became reclusive and mentally unstable, and when their father died the children were looked after by a strict guardian who was resented by Charlotte and her sisters. Charlotte tried to run away and become a servant in London. Educated at home, she began to write poetry. Charlotte was devoted to her only brother John, the youngest in the family, who would later distinguish himself as a soldier. During the First World War, he was Field Marshal Sir John French, commander of the British Expeditionary Force in France; in 1918, he was appointed viceroy of Ireland just as the Irish war of independence was starting, which brought him into conflict with his sister.

In 1857, the French children went to Edinburgh to live with their mother's family who were strict Presbyterians, an atmosphere not to Charlotte's taste. Her eldest sister **Mary French** came of age in 1863 and was able to take responsibility for the rest of the family. They moved to York and subsequently to London where they set up house on their own. After their mother's death, they had substantial private incomes that gave them an unusual degree of freedom for the time. Even so, Charlotte disliked intensely the conventions that hemmed in women. In an autobiographical fragment, she referred to the disadvantages of "an inferior, slipshod education" which she was determined to overcome. "We were taught a little music, a little drawing, no science or mathematics, but a little literature, geography and history. Manners of course! The impression left on the mind is of incompetent teachers and indifferent learners—nothing thorough." She longed to be of some use in the world, but for her and her sisters, as wealthy women born into a certain social position in Victorian England, "it was not thought necessary that we should do anything but amuse ourselves until the time and the opportunity of marriage came along."

Her own interest in social conditions had been awakened while living in York when she visited a rope factory and was appalled by the conditions of the women and children working there. In politics she took an interest in the cause of Italian independence and admired the leaders Giuseppe Mazzini and Giuseppe Garibaldi. Intellectually, she was greatly influenced by Percy Shelley's writings, especially his views on women and marriage, and would remain so for the rest of her life. She deeply resented the inferior position of women in society: "Heaven had decreed that I should be a woman. . . . I must prove my gratitude by gentleness, obedience and submission."

By 1866, two of her sisters were married and over the next three years Charlotte and her other sisters traveled in Europe. In 1870, after returning to England from France, she met Maximilian Despard, of Huguenot Irish extraction, and married him in December 1870. Despard, whose family came from the Irish midlands, had gone to Hong Kong in the early 1860s and made a fortune there trading in tea and gemstones. He also invested in the new Hong Kong and Shanghai Bank which was to repay considerably over the years. He was a man of liberal views and supported a wider franchise and reform in society generally. Charlotte wrote that she "married happily in the sense that my freedom in that relation, often so difficult, was always respected." Soon after their marriage, she started writing and her first novel was published in 1874. This work and subsequent novels were marred by improbable plotting and characters.

In 1879, the Despards bought an estate in Surrey, near London. They traveled extensively and after a visit to India Charlotte became interested in Buddhism as well as seances, which she attended. Maximilian continued to trade in tea and gemstones but throughout the 1880s his health, never good, declined. They were on another journey to India when he died on board ship in April 1890.

Charlotte Despard was left a very wealthy widow. She had already taken up charity in the Nine Elms area of south London, one of the poorest districts, and after her husband's death she moved to the area. It was only after his death, as she wrote later, that "I was able to give full expression to my ideals." She was attracted to Catholicism, though she retained her interest in Buddhism and spiritualism. Despard also became a vegetarian and wore a black lace mantilla that became something of a physical trademark. In 1892, she was elected to the Kingston Poor Law Board which supervised the running of the local workhouse. She did her best to alleviate the conditions in the workhouse, particularly in regard to the treatment of elderly inmates. She also helped to set up clinics and surgeries for poor children.

In the course of her work in south London, she met members of the Marxist Social Democratic Federation, including Edward Aveling and *Eleanor Marx, and became a socialist: "Socialism to me is a religion," she declared. But her work in south London had also brought home the conditions faced by working women, and she became actively interested in women's suffrage. Despard predicted that the 20th century would see the rise of two great movements—women and labor. In 1906, she joined the Pankhursts' Women's Social and Political Union (WSPU) and succeeded *Sylvia Pankhurst as secretary in June 1906. For a time, Despard enjoyed immunity from arrest during WSPU demonstrations because of the prestige that her brother, Sir John French, enjoyed as a military hero of the Boer War. Charlotte had bailed out her brother on several occasions when he got into debt, but he regarded her suffragist activities with increasing disapproval. In February 1907, she was sentenced to 21 days in Holloway Jail after a demonstration outside the Houses of Parliament. She loathed prison and this fuelled a growing disillusionment with the Pankhursts' leadership of the WSPU. In October 1907, she supported the formation of a new organization, the Women's Freedom League, of which she subsequently became president. The League did some valuable work, notably the setting up of watch committees to monitor the inequalities in the way the courts sentenced women. Administration, however, was not Despard's strong point. She often failed to consult members of her executive about policy and was accused of being too dictatorial. An attempt was made to unseat her as president but she survived.

Suffrage was not Despard's only interest. In 1909, she met Mohandas Gandhi who was on a visit to London and who would later describe her as "a wonderful person." That same year, she also met James Connolly, the Irish Marxist labor leader, when she visited Dublin and spoke to his Irish Socialist Republican Club. When the First World War broke out, Despard was strongly pacifistic and joined the British section of the Women's International League for Peace and Freedom. She and the League looked after the wives and families of men fighting at the front. They also strenuously resisted attempts to reintroduce the Contagious Diseases Acts which enforced compulsory medical inspection of women

suspected of having venereal disease. At the end of the war, she stood as a Labor candidate for the British Parliament in the general elections of December 1918 and was defeated.

Charlotte Despard maintained a consistent, if sporadic, interest in Irish affairs for many years. Her own antecedents were Irish as were her husband's; she had known James Connolly who was executed after the 1916 Rising in Dublin; she campaigned for the release of *Maud Gonne who had been arrested by the British authorities; last, but no means least, those same British authorities were symbolized in the person of her own brother, now the earl of Ypres, who had become the viceroy of Ireland and, as such, titular head of the British administration in Ireland. But it was the death in October 1920 of the Lord Mayor of Cork, Terence MacSwiney, which spurred her to more active participation in Irish affairs. Despard went to Ireland in January 1921, and she and Maud Gonne toured the southwest, a dangerous proceeding as the area was then under martial law.

Charlotte Despard

When stopped by British forces, Despard had no hesitation in using her brother's name, which infuriated him. To the great disapproval of her family, she gave up her houses and activities in England and moved to Dublin where she bought Roebuck House in south Dublin, which she shared with Maud Gonne. She became involved with the White Cross organization which helped the wives and families of Sinn Fein prisoners.

She and Maud Gonne opposed as inadequate the terms of the Anglo-Irish Treaty which gave independence to southern Ireland in December 1921. When civil war broke out in June 1922, they tried to effect an agreement between the opposing sides but to no avail. As more and more republican prisoners were arrested, Charlotte Despard became president of the Women's Prisoners' Defence League which helped families, gave information as to where prisoners were being held, and organized public demonstrations. The League was banned in January 1923, though the ban was ignored. Roebuck House became a base for Maud Gonne's children, for assorted republicans who were either on the run or just released from prison, and for refugees from Belfast. In 1924, a jam factory was set up in its grounds to give employment to former prisoners.

Despard's brother, Lord Ypres, died in 1925; he had refused to see her, despite her requests. She became increasingly attracted to Communism and she gave James Connolly's son, Roddy, money to set up the Irish Workers' Party and a newspaper *The Workers' Republic*. However, faced with political apathy and the opposition of the Catholic Church, the new party failed to make any headway. In 1930, at age 86, she visited the Soviet Union with the Friends of Soviet Russia, of whose executive she was a member, and was greatly impressed by what appeared to be a new socialist utopia. On her return to Ireland, she bought a house in Dublin which became the headquarters of the Friends of Soviet Russia and the Irish Workers' College. This was wrecked by a right-wing Catholic mob in 1933.

It was at the urging of *Hanna Sheehy-Skeffington that Despard decided to leave Dublin and go to Belfast. Sheehy-Skeffington told of the distress being caused there by unemployment and the attempts to unify Protestant and Catholic workers. These hopes of unity were short-lived and vanished in sectarian riots which erupted in 1935. Despard remained in Belfast but began to speak out against the rise of Fascism in Europe. On her 93rd birthday in 1937, there was a celebration in London attended by many distinguished guests including Sylvia Pankhurst,

*Nancy Astor, Paul Robeson and George Bernard Shaw. Despard died two years later in November 1939 and was buried in the republican plot at Dublin's Glasnevin Cemetery. Maud Gonne in her funeral oration described her friend as "a white flame in the defence of prisoners and the oppressed."

SOURCES:

Fox, R.M. *Rebel Irish Women*. Talbot Press, 1935.

French, Gerald. *The Life of Field-Marshal Sir John French, First Earl of Ypres*. Cassell, 1931.

Linklater, Andro. *An Unhusbanded Life: Charlotte Despard, Suffragette, Socialist and Sinn Feiner*. Hutchinson, 1980.

Ward, Margaret. *Unmanageable Revolutionaries: Women and Irish Nationalism*. Brandon, 1983.

Deirdre McMahon, Dublin, Ireland, Assistant Editor, *Dance Theatre Journal* (London), and author of *Republicans and Imperialists* (Yale University Press, 1984)

Despenser, Eleanor (1292–1337).

See Isabella of France for sidebar on Eleanor de Clare.

Despenser, Elizabeth (d. 1408)

English noblewoman. Name variations: Elizabeth Fitzalan. Died in 1408; daughter of Edward Despenser, 1st baron Despenser, and **Elizabeth Burghersh** *(daughter of Bartholomew, 4th baron Burghersh); married John Fitzalan, before 1385; children: John Fitzalan (1385–1421);* **Margaret Fitzalan** *(b. around 1388).*

Despenser, Isabel (1400–1439)

Baroness Burghersh and countess of Warwick. Name variations: Isabel le Despencer; Isabel Beauchamp. Born on July 26, 1400, in Cardiff; died on December 27, 1439, at Friars Minoresses, London; interred on January 13, 1439, at Tewkesbury Abbey, Gloucester; daughter of Thomas Despenser, 1st earl of Gloucester, and **Constance** *(c. 1374–1416, daughter of Edmund of Langley); married Richard Beauchamp, earl of Worcester (d. 1422); married Richard Beauchamp (1381–1439), 5th (or 13th) earl of Warwick, on November 26, 1423; children: (first marriage)* **Elizabeth Beauchamp,** *baroness Abergavenny; (second marriage) Henry Beauchamp (c. 1423–1445), 1st duke & 6th earl of Warwick;* **Anne Beauchamp** *(1426–1492).*

Isabel Despenser married Richard Beauchamp, earl of Worcester; he died in 1422. The following year, she married his cousin Richard Beauchamp, earl of Warwick. Her husbands' identical names are frequently the source of some confusion.

Desprès, Suzanne (1875–1951)

French actress. Born at Verdun, France, in 1875; died in 1951; studied at the Paris Conservatoire; married Aurelien Lugné-Poë (b. 1870, an actor-manager).

Suzanne Desprès received her training at the Paris Conservatoire where she took first prize for comedy and second prize for tragedy (1897). She married actor-manager Aurelien Lugné-Poë, founder of *L'Œuvre*, a new school of modern drama. Desprès had great success in several plays produced by him. She later played at the Gymnase and at the Porte Saint-Martin. In 1902, Desprès made her debut at the Comédie Française, where she appeared in important plays, including *Phèdre*.

Dessilava (fl. 1197–1207)

Tsarina of Bulgaria. Name variations: Princess Dessilava. Flourished between 1197 and 1207; married Kaloyan, tsar of Bulgaria.

Dessilava married Kaloyan, 3rd of the Asenid rulers who succeeded his elder brother Peter in 1197. Under Tsar Kaloyan's ruthless leadership, the Bulgarian empire was expanded, but in 1207 he was assassinated by one of his own followers.

de Staël, Germaine (1766–1817).

See Staël, Germaine de.

d'Este.

See Este, d'.

Destinn, Emmy (1878–1930)

Czech novelist, composer, and singer, who was one of the 20th century's greatest sopranos. Name variations: Destinnova. Born Ema Pavlína Kittlová or Kittl on February 26, 1878, in Prague; died on January 28, 1930, in Ceske Budjeovice; married Joseph Halsbach, in 1923.

Emmy Destinn ranks as one of the 20th century's greatest sopranos. A prodigious worker, she made over 1,500 appearances on the operatic stage. At the age of 20, she appeared in the Berlin Opera in 1898, debuting in the role of Santuzza in Mascagni's *Cavalleria rusticana*. Though she had been rejected by both the Prague and Dresden operas, her debut in Berlin was a success. Destinn, who took her stage name in tribute to her teacher, Marie Loewe-Destinn, soon moved from the Berlin Opera to the Hofoper where she remained for a decade.

Dessilava

In 1901, she was chosen by *Cosima Wagner to sing Senta at Bayreuth in *Der Fliegende Holländer* (*The Flying Dutchman*). In 1904, she debuted in Covent Garden as Donna Anna in Mozart's Don Giovanni. Critic Herbert Klein wrote: "An artist capable of success at the outset in this most exacting of roles will one day stand in the royal line of dramatic sopranos." The Bohemian star then sang the leading role in Giacomo Puccini's opera *Madame Butterfly* at its first performance in London (1905). "Hers was one of the greatest voices and she was one of the greatest singers. . . . [N]obody ever sang Butterfly as Destinn did," wrote *Frances Alda. "Her manner of singing was so perfect, her voice so divine . . . all these made her unforgettable." In 1907, Destinn created the leading role of Richard Strauss' *Salomé* in Paris and Berlin.

Destinn's nationality would prove problematic both in her career and personal life. It is likely that she adopted her stage name to disguise her Czech origins and secure more roles in the German-speaking world. Despite this concession to Germanic culture, she remained a fierce and outspoken nationalist. A passionate patriot, she had been frustrated in London, where she could not work up interest in compositions by compatriots

*Emmy
Destinn*

rare lyric beauty exhibited in *Und ob die Wolke* from *Der Freischütz* to the verve and bite she displays in Milanda's aria from *Dalibor.*

SOURCES:

Rketorys, A., and Dennis, J. "Emma Destinn," in *Record Collector.* Vol. 20, 1971, p. 5.

Sadie, Stanley, ed. *New Grove Dictionary of Music and Musicians.* 20 vols. NY: Macmillan, 1980.

John Haag, Associate Professor of History, University of Georgia, Athens, Georgia

d'Estraigues, Henriette (1579–1633).

See Medici, Marie de for sidebar on Entragues, Catherine Henriette de Balzac d'.

d'Estrées, Gabrielle (1573–1599).

See Estrées, Gabrielle d'.

de Tencin, Mme (1685–1749).

See Salonnières.

d'Eu, Maud (d. 1241).

See Maud of Lusignan.

Deutsch, Helen (1906–1992)

American screenwriter of such superhits as The Unsinkable Molly Brown, I'll Cry Tomorrow, *and* National Velvet, *who initiated the New York Drama Critics Circle Award. Born in New York, New York, on March 21, 1906; died in New York, New York, on March 15, 1992; daughter of Heyman and Ann (Freeman) Deutsch; a brief marriage was annulled.*

Wrote many prominent screenplays, including I'll Cry Tomorrow *and* The Unsinkable Molly Brown; *had initial success as co-writer of the adaptation of Enid Bagnold's* National Velvet, *one of the year's ten best (1944), which introduced a youthful Elizabeth Taylor to the American public; won a Golden Globe for screenplay* Lili, *about an orphan played by* **Leslie Caron.**

Smetana and Dvorák. She was interned by the Austro-Hungarian government for a time because of her undisguised sentiments.

In 1908, Destinn left the Berlin Hofoper which refused to give her leave to sing at the Metropolitan Opera in New York. However, her career had soared in Prague and, with contacts in the United States, Great Britain, and her own country, she had a busy life until World War I intervened. While at the Met, she performed 339 times between 1908 and 1920. She retired to a castle in southern Bohemia in 1921, where she wrote a play, a novel, and some poetry. In poor health for some time, she had a stroke in the room of a specialist she was consulting on January 27, 1930, and died the following day.

Destinn had an unmistakable voice, a warm throb in the middle range that was combined with a dramatic intensity. *Lotte Lehmann was "nearly distracted" as she "listened to that angelic voice." Destinn made over 250 recordings, which document her ability to move from the

An authentic New Yorker, Helen Deutsch was attracted to the theater during her years as a student at Barnard College and worked with the legendary Provincetown Players. Deutsch held several jobs while at the theater, including working as play reader, press secretary and—occasionally—serving in the box office, selling tickets. Determined to make her name on Broadway and in Hollywood, she supported herself during the Depression by writing short stories for magazines and feature articles for the *New York Herald Tribune,* while at the same time honing her skills as a playwright. Deutsch also reviewed plays, often as a ghost-writer. When Robert Garland, drama critic of the *New York World-*

Telegram was too drunk to write his assigned piece, she would be called on to write the review that appeared the next day under his name. Deutsch also began working as a press agent during these years, doing most of her work quietly on the telephone. ("I was a *shy* press agent. People knew my voice but had no idea what I looked like.")

Helen Deutsch's shyness did not prevent her from taking issue with what she felt were the often wrongheaded choices made by Pulitzer Prize judges when it came to drama. Accordingly, in 1934 she founded and became secretary of the New York Drama Critics Circle, whose purpose was to award a prize that more fairly honored the best American play of the preceding theater season. Although her reputation in New York's theater world was secure by the end of the 1930s, it was not until 1944 that Helen Deutsch achieved her first major success as a screenwriter. Her screenplay adaptation, which resulted in the 1944 motion-picture classic *National Velvet,* starring *Elizabeth Taylor** and Mickey Rooney, was judged perfect by critics and audiences alike. The *Enid Bagnold** story, of a young English girl who disguises herself as a male jockey in order to compete in—and win—the Grand National Steeplechase, remains a popular staple of family entertainment more than 50 years after its premiere. The same year, 1944, also saw the release of Deutsch's effective screenplay of *The Seventh Cross,* based on a bestselling anti-Nazi novel by exiled German writer *Anna Seghers.**

In her 1950 screenplay for the adventure film *King Solomon's Mines,* Deutsch produced a highly successful entertainment of an African safari that was full of exotic locales and thrills. Another hit was her 1953 musical *Lili,* about an innocent French orphan girl and her infatuation with a carnival magician. Lili is comforted by a crippled puppeteer in the carnival who cheers her up and with whom she eventually falls in love. Much of the credit for the success of *Lili* was due to Deutsch's screenplay which made of it a slight but beguiling fantasy. A radical departure from adventure and fantasy was Deutsch's 1956 screenplay for the film *I'll Cry Tomorrow* (1956), based on the autobiography of actress and singer *Lillian Roth.** A painful look at Roth's descent into personal disaster because of her alcoholism, *I'll Cry Tomorrow* featured *Susan Hayward** and was highly successful. The same year saw a popular television production on NBC of Deutsch's adaptation of "Jack and the Beanstalk." Over the years, Deutsch also wrote a number of successful song lyrics including "Hi-Lilli, Hi-Lo," which she dismissed as being "dreadful."

In 1964, Helen Deutsch produced one of her most memorable screenplays, *The Unsinkable Molly Brown,* based loosely on the life of *Molly Brown.** In this MGM movie, Brown is a strong-willed woman who aspires to high society after her husband Johnny makes them wealthy by discovering gold in his Western mine. Remaining in Europe after Johnny returns to the United States, she eventually realizes that she is not happy without him. Returning home on the *Titanic* in April 1912, Brown's unsinkable spirit enables her to save not only herself but others on her lifeboat. Saved, she is reunited with Johnny. With its well-crafted screenplay, *The Unsinkable Molly Brown* was praised by *The New York Times* as "big, brassy, bold and freewheeling," and the musical received six Academy Award nominations in various categories, thus becoming the third highest-grossing motion picture of 1964.

Helen Deutsch's 15th and last screenplay was *The Valley of the Dolls* (1967), based on the novel of the same title by *Jacqueline Susann.** Deutsch's career in Hollywood ended abruptly in the controversy that ensued over authorship of the screenplay, with Deutsch disavowing any involvement and claiming that Susann had meddled with the script. The film was a commercial success but a critical disaster. From this point on, Deutsch devoted her time to lecturing and teaching adult-education courses. She worked sporadically on both her autobiography (never finished) and "a 12th-century novel I shall never complete." She continued her lifelong study of the 12th century, reading passages in Middle Latin, Middle French, Middle German and Middle English. She donated her large collection of rare books, manuscripts and letters to Boston University. Other items, including rare recordings, were donated by her to the University of Wyoming. Helen Deutsch died in her Manhattan home on March 15, 1972.

SOURCES:

Deutsch, Helen, and Stella B. Hanau. *The Provincetown: A Story of the Theater.* NY: Farrar & Rinehart, 1931 (reprint ed., Atheneum, 1972).

"Helen Deutsch," in *The Times* [London]. April 9, 1972, p. 27.

Lambert, Bruce. "Helen Deutsch, 85, Screenwriter of 'Lili' and 'National Velvet'," in *The New York Times Biographical Service.* March 1992, p. 317.

COLLECTIONS:

Helen Deutsch Collection, Boston University.

John Haag, Associate Professor of History, University of Georgia, Athens, Georgia

Deutsch, Helene (1884–1982)

Polish-born psychoanalyst and pioneer theoretician in female psychology. Born Helene Rosenbach in the town of Przemyśl in Polish Galicia on the Ukrainian border of the Austro-Hungarian empire (present-day Poland), on October 9, 1884; died on March 29, 1982, in Cambridge, Massachusetts; daughter of Wilhelm Rosenbach (a lawyer) and Regina (Fass) Rosenbach; granted M.D. from the University of Munich Medical School, 1912; married Felix Deutsch, in 1912; children: Martin (b. 1917).

Worked as full-time assistant at the Wagner-Jauregg Clinic for Psychiatric and Nervous Disorders, Vienna (1912–18); admitted to the Vienna Psychoanalytic Society (1918); became founding member of the Vienna Training Institute (1925); made president of the Vienna Training Institute (1925–34); arrived in the U.S. (1934); joined the staff of the Boston Psychoanalytic Institute (1934); was a training analyst at the Boston Training Institute (1934–62).

Selected publications: The Psychology of Sexual Functions in Women *(1925);* Psychoanalysis of the Neuroses *(1932);* The Psychology of Women *(Volume I, 1944, Volume II, 1945);* Neuroses and Character Types *(1965);* Selected Problems of Adolescence *(1967);* A Psychoanalytic Study of the Myth of Dionysus and Apollo *(1969);* Confrontations With Myself *(1973).*

Though the relevance of Helene Deutsch's theoretical contributions to contemporary psychoanalysis is currently debated, her status as a central figure at the beginning of the psychoanalytic movement is beyond dispute. One of the first women admitted to the Vienna Psychoanalytic Society and a founding member and director of the Vienna Training Institute, she wielded enormous power and influence over the training of analysts and the future direction of psychoanalysis. She was also the first major theorist of feminine psychology, devoting numerous books and articles to the subjects of female sexuality and the unique psychological dilemmas posed by motherhood. Her own struggle to achieve professional success at a time when women were roundly discouraged from pursuing careers bears the hallmarks of a dedicated early 20th-century feminist: a strong drive to overcome a restrictive home life and seek higher education; an early flirtation with radical politics and unconventional relationships with men; a conflicted desire to balance her role as dutiful wife and mother with that of pioneering psychoanalyst. Yet her theoretical contributions have largely been dismissed by contemporary feminists as offering little more than a perpetuation of Freudi-

an phallocentrism and for unwittingly providing a biological basis for women's subjugation. In more recent years, however, revisionist scholars have begun to call for a new interpretation of her work as highly original in defining the complexities of maternal and paternal identification and in illustrating the role of identification in personality formation and disorders of narcissistic self-esteem.

Helene Deutsch's interest in psychoanalysis was informed by her own childhood struggles. She was born on October 9, 1884, the fourth and last child of a well-established Jewish family in Przemyśl, a garrison town in Polish Galicia on the Ukrainian border of the Austro-Hungarian Empire. Her father Wilhelm Rosenbach was a highly educated lawyer who achieved professional and public prominence despite the region's deep-rooted anti-Semitism. From an early age, Deutsch seems to have identified closely with her father. She took a genuine interest in his work and routinely accompanied him to court. As a young child, she even entertained the notion of becoming a lawyer, though at that time the practice of law was closed to women.

Deutsch's earliest difficulties in life revolved around her strained relationship with her mother. Later she would describe her childhood as classically "oedipal"—consisting of hatred for her mother and love for her father. **Regina Fass Rosenbach** indeed seems to have singled her youngest child out as the object of her maternal rage. Deutsch later wrote that she always disliked her mother whom she viewed as autocratic and preoccupied with social convention, and who beat her "not to punish me, but as an outlet for her own pent-up aggressions." Deutsch's siblings (a brother and two sisters) were a good deal older, and Regina Rosenbach seems to have had little interest in parenting her youngest. That job fell to a succession of nurses and to her older and much-beloved sister, **Malvina Rosenbach**, whom Deutsch credited with providing her with the love and maternal attention she craved.

Deutsch was a brilliant and imaginative child. Like many girls, she kept a diary during her early teenage years. But Deutsch's diary contained far more than the usual longings and emotional outpourings that typify adolescent diaries. Rather, hers was a novelistic, book-length narrative written as the journal of a modern Viennese Catholic girl named "Madi Fournier." In her journal, Deutsch created a life far more exciting and unconventional than her own. Yet interspersed throughout the long, engaging chronicles of Madi Fournier were dramatic expressions of

Helene Deutsch

her own ambitions and dreams for a future well beyond that which she could reasonably expect.

Deutsch's desperate longing for a richer, less restricted life, as well as her ongoing conflicts with her mother, stamped an indelible rebelliousness in her. As was then the fashion in a girl's education, she was formally schooled until the age of 14, after which she continued to pursue instruction through independent study and private tutoring. But around the time that she completed her formal schooling, she began a longterm relationship with Herman Lieberman, a married man 14 years her senior. Lieberman

was a committed socialist, active in the Polish labor movement, and a well-known public figure who awakened in Deutsch an interest in radical politics. She developed a deep commitment to revolutionary activism: she attended demonstrations, dispensed propaganda, and organized the first-ever strike of Przemyśl women. With Lieberman's help, she began writing articles for the *Pzyemyśl Voice*. As their professional collaboration and personal relationship deepened, and Deutsch openly accompanied Lieberman around town and to socialist conferences, her mother was horrified by her daughter's behavior and did what she could to thwart Helene's scandalous romantic and political entanglements. When Deutsch's ambitions for a life outside the bounds of bourgeois propriety met implacable familial hostility, she ran away from home. She returned only when her parents signed a contract agreeing to help their daughter gain university admission.

With financial support from her family, Deutsch left home in 1905 to devote her time to studying for the *abitur* in Lwow (Lemberg). During the following year, her romance with Lieberman seems to have cooled perceptibly, while the dual pressures of study and family strain took a toll. In 1906, she spent time in a sanatorium near Graz for treatment of depression. Although she recovered, physical and emotional ailments would continue to plague her over the next several years.

In February 1907, at age 22, she passed her college exams and received her *abitur*. That fall, she became one of the first women to enroll in the medical school at the University of Vienna. After a painful break with Lieberman in 1910, she left Vienna for Munich where she continued her medical studies. Shortly thereafter, she met Felix Deutsch, a physician who would later become a pioneer in the treatment of psychosomatic disorders. On April 14, 1912, the two were married in Vienna. (Their son Martin would be born in 1917.)

The year of Deutsch's marriage, she received her medical degree and accepted a job as a full-time assistant at the famous Wagner-Jauregg Clinic for Psychiatric and Nervous Disorders, where she worked for the next six years. Though her work at the clinic was lauded, her gender precluded her from gaining an official position, and she remained unpaid. Despite her marginal status, her responsibilities increased during the latter part of World War I when many of the male doctors were drafted into the army. She later recalled of those years that her most rewarding work involved treating the seriously disturbed, unresponsive patients who had been labeled as suffering from "stupor."

By 1918, Helene Deutsch had become familiar with the writings of Sigmund Freud and had developed a deep interest in psychoanalysis. She had first encountered Freud's work in 1907 and increasingly immersed herself in it. "As I absorbed Freud's teachings on the unconscious mind and began to believe in infantile sexuality and . . . the role of these forces in the formation of neuroses, I gradually became a devoted disciple." In August, Deutsch left the Wagner-Jauregg Clinic to undergo a yearlong analysis with Freud. That same year, she became the second female member of the Vienna Psychoanalytic Society and also began analyzing patients under Freud's direction. Freud's immediate confidence in Deutsch was evident. Her first patient was a member of Freud's own family and in 1919 she became his unofficial assistant, accompanying him the following year to the Sixth Congress of the International Psycho-Analytical Association in The Hague. Deutsch pursued the study of psychoanalysis with the same tenacity and single-mindedness that had marked her earlier conversion to socialism and her admittance to medical school. "Psychoanalysis," she later recalled, "was my last and most deeply experienced revolution; and Freud . . . became for me the greatest revolutionary of my life."

Helene Deutsch's particular interest in female psychology developed early in her career. "My intense interest in women stemmed from various sources: first, from my own narcissism, a wish to know myself; second from the fact that research until then had been chiefly concerned with men." The first lectures she presented to the Vienna Psychoanalytic Society focused on the problems of women and feminine sexuality. In 1925, she published *The Psychology of Sexual Functions in Women*, the first monograph devoted specifically to feminine psychology and one which offered a systematic description of female instinctual development and its relation to the reproductive function. In her book, Deutsch relied heavily on Freud's classic model of the stages of development. She characterized the first active stage of a girl's sexuality as phallic. The phallic stage, Deutsch believed, is succeeded by a passive stage brought on by the girl's recognition that she does not possess a penis. This realization is experienced as a loss and results in mourning. Deutsch's theories of puberty followed the same trajectory: an active state that gives way to passivity as a girl construes menstruation as both castration and a symbol of the lack of a baby. The longing for a baby and a penis, Deutsch believed, were the motivations behind the girl's desire for sexual intercourse. She also described the experience of pregnancy as being informed by early infantile oral and anal fantasies of incorporation and expulsion, the latter expressed in morning sickness and miscarriage. To her credit, Deutsch decried the practice of early 20th-century obstetrics which she believed created an unpleasant and uncaring atmosphere for birth, leaving new mothers feeling depleted rather than enhanced by the experience.

Shortly thereafter, she began a long study of the writer *George Sand in which she traced the patriarchal and maternal roots of femininity and identified a woman's "masculinity complex." Deutsch was drawn to Sand, who also bridled at bourgeois conventionality and who, like Deutsch, identified with her father and was estranged from her mother. In other writings of this period, Deutsch used literary sources, the experiences of patients, and her own difficult relationship with her mother and maternal struggles with her son to explore the ways sex and mothering affected a woman's self-esteem.

In 1925, Helene Deutsch was elected the first director of the newly created Vienna Training Institute. Modeled after the Berlin Training Institute, it was designed to formulate standards and to establish a formal training program for students of psychoanalysis. For the next nine years, Deutsch supervised the training of a new generation of analysts.

In 1934, Deutsch and her family moved permanently to the United States. She had briefly visited America once before, in 1930, at which time she had been heralded in the newspapers as "the first accredited ambassador of her sex to come here from the King of Psycho-Analysis." Now the family settled in Cambridge, Massachusetts, where Deutsch took up where she left off in Vienna, practicing psychoanalysis, delivering lectures at the Boston Psychoanalytic Institute, and working as a training analyst at the Boston Training Institute. As she had done on her earlier trip to America, she missionized throughout the country as Freud's intellectual emissary.

By this time, Deutsch had modified her earlier theories, recasting them in light of greater experience and observation. Deutsch's new theoretical framework provided a complete psychological overview of the development of women from menarche to menopause. She first described the young girl's psychological development into womanhood, a process that she deemed complete with the onset of menstruation. It is in the course of this process that Deutsch believed the "feminine core" is formed. Deutsch also defined the three "essential traits of femininity" as narcissism, passivity and masochism. But here she broke with Freud and provided a more liberating, less restrictive view of the interplay of these traits. Deutsch still saw passivity as an essential characteristic of woman, but she redefined it as "activity directed inward." This inward-directed activity, she believed, accounted for a woman's exaggerated fantasy life, her intuitive sensitivity, and her ability to empathize. A component of this passivity is feminine masochism which included self-sacrifice and tolerance of pain.

Deutsch saw female narcissism as a healthy and necessary trait to counteract the woman's tendency to be overly submissive and give her an independent sense of self.

Deutsch also saw motherhood as the "central problem of femininity." She viewed the new mother's altruistic readiness to sacrifice her own needs to that of her baby's as masochistic, but not necessarily self-damaging, as the mother's own narcissistic tendencies keep her from total self-abnegation. It was only when mothering led to a complete renunciation of erotic fulfillment or when the mother possessed unmastered masochistic tendencies that Deutsch believed conflicts arose.

Her theories of feminine psychology were published in 1944 and 1945 in her magnum opus, the two-volume *The Psychology of Women*, which at the time became the standard textbook of feminine psychology and remains important today. In it, she again sets her ideas of instinctual development against the background of biological determinism, although she also concedes that sociological and cultural factors affect female development. It was this insistence on the importance of biology that drew professional criticism from several of her contemporaries (including the German psychoanalyst *Karen Horney) who were beginning to research the societal, cultural, and educational factors resulting in women's subjugation.

Another of Helene Deutsch's important theoretical contributions to psychology was the notion of the "as if" personality. The term was designed to refer to those individuals who are capable of powerful identifications that are imitative and lacking in character. These people, Deutsch believed, "validate their existence by identification." The "as if" personality "behaves as if [he/she] possessed a fully felt emotional life" but in reality merely mimics the perceived feelings and experiences of others. Deutsch traced the origins of this personality type to an inability to develop a normal Oedipus complex in early childhood.

Despite advancing years, Deutsch remained professionally engaged, though she actively retired from the Boston Psychoanalytic Institute in 1954 at the mandatory retirement age of 70. Though she continued to analyze a few patients, she devoted most of her time to research and writing. Much of Deutsch's later published work involved the interplay of psychology and literature, and she wrote numerous psychoanalytic articles on literary topics, including *A Psychoanalytic Study of the Myth of Dionysus and Apollo* (1969).

Deutsch also traveled extensively throughout Europe and Israel in the 1950s and 1960s, and engaged in the amateur study of the chickens and cows that she raised at "Babayaga Farm," a rural property she owned in Wolfeboro, New Hampshire, and named after a witch from a Polish fairy tale. In 1973, she wrote her autobiography, *Confrontations With Myself,* and in it she reflected on the problem of motherhood in light of women's political and social progress in the 20th century:

> Social progress, while not eliminating all difficulties connected with motherhood, has increased women's opportunities as active members of society outside the home. A large measure of freedom and equality has been achieved; more is coming. I welcome all progress in the direction of women's liberation with pleasure, but also with a silent, sad realization: though woman is different now, she is forever the same, a servant of her biological fate, to which she has to adjust other pursuits.

Helene Deutsch remained intellectually vital to the end. In 1977, she helped **Nancy Friday** with her bestselling book, *My Mother, My Self.* Five years later, on March 29, 1982, Helene Deutsch died in Cambridge, Massachusetts, at the age of 97.

SOURCES:

Appignanesi, Lisa, and John Forrester. *Freud's Women.* London: Weidenfeld and Nicolson, 1992.

Deutsch, Helene. *Confrontations With Myself.* NY: W.W. Norton, 1973.

———. *The Psychology of Women.* NY: Grune & Stratton, 1944 (vol. I), 1945 (vol. II).

Roazen, Paul. *Helene Deutsch: A Psychoanalyst's Life.* Garden City, NY: Doubleday, 1985.

Sayers, Janet. *Mothers of Psychoanalysis.* NY: W.W. Norton, 1991.

Webster, Brenda S. "Helene Deutsch: A New Look," in *Signs: Journal of Women in Culture and Society.* Vol. 10, no. 31, 1985, pp. 553–571.

COLLECTIONS:

Helene Deutsch Archive, Schlesinger Library, Radcliffe College, Cambridge, Massachusetts.

Suzanne Smith,
freelance writer and editor, Decatur, Georgia

Deutscher, Tamara (1913–1990)

Polish-born British editor, researcher and author, who was the collaborator and wife of the socialist historian Isaac Deutscher. Born Tamara Lebenhaft in Lodz, Russian Poland, on February 1, 1913; died in London, England, on August 7, 1990; married Isaac Deutscher (a social historian); children: one son, Martin.

Played a crucial role in the research and writing of her husband's influential books and after his death edited his manuscripts; a believer in democratic socialism, she was highly critical of the repressive nature of the Soviet regime, and was active in British intellectual circles that defended the human rights of dissident elements in the Soviet bloc.

Although she was a talented writer and a respected intellectual in her own right, Tamara Deutscher chose to subordinate her own ambitions to those of her husband, the noted Marxist historian Isaac Deutscher. After his death in 1967, she divided her time and energy between her own writings and editing her late husband's manuscripts. Born Tamara Lebenhaft in Lodz, the leading industrial center of Poland, she grew up in an intellectual Jewish family fated to be almost entirely wiped out in the Holocaust. Educated in Poland and in Belgium, she escaped to Great Britain in 1940 and quickly began a promising career as a literary critic. Charming and attractive, Tamara Lebenhaft met fellow Pole Isaac Deutscher, a journalist like herself, in London during World War II. Like herself, Isaac was an ardent Marxist who had doubts about the Stalinist version of Socialism. They fell in love, married, and she gave birth to a son, Martin. Young and talented, both Tamara and Isaac Deutscher traveled together during some of the most dramatic years of the 20th century as war correspondents in Germany. After the defeat of Nazism, they remained in occupied Germany as reporters.

Convinced that her husband was destined to do serious work, Tamara Deutscher encouraged him to abandon journalism in order to devote his full time and energy to writing books from an independent Marxist perspective. The early 1950s were extremely busy years for the Deutschers. While Isaac spent virtually all of his time researching and writing, Tamara was not only a wife and mother but also an indispensable collaborator as research assistant, critic, and copy editor. These were difficult years for the couple, not only financially but emotionally. As committed but independent-minded Marxists living during the most intolerant years of the Cold War, they found themselves both personally and ideologically isolated from the intellectual life of the Western world. As his books began to appear in print, this isolation was eased considerably. Isaac Deutscher was fully aware of the immense debt he owed to his literary collaborator and wife, and he dedicated his biography of J.V. Stalin to her as "a link in our friendship," also noting that her "critical sense [had] contributed to the shaping of every paragraph" in the book. On another occasion, he paid tribute to Tamara as "my first, the severest and the most indulgent critic."

In 1954, Isaac Deutscher published the first volume of his definitive biography of Leon Trotsky. The critical response to the Trotsky project, which was completed in 1963 with the publication of a third and concluding volume, was highly favorable. By the mid-1960s, Isaac Deutscher had become an internationally recognized historian of Soviet leaders as well as a compelling advocate for an independent orientation within the Marxist ideology. A passionate critic of American involvement in Vietnam, he was well known in radical student circles both in Europe and in the United States.

Tamara Deutscher's world was shattered when her husband died suddenly in 1967. After the initial shock, she continued her life on the same path they had traveled on as a team since World War II. She organized his unpublished manuscripts and was able to see all of his major works published posthumously. She published a number of works of her own, including a well-received anthology on V.I. Lenin. A sharp observer of events in the Communist world, she remained highly critical of both the Soviet and Maoist versions of Socialism. Tamara Deutscher condemned Soviet intervention in Czechoslovakia in 1968 and spoke out to defend the rights of dissidents in that country in the 1970s. Her skills as a researcher were utilized by others besides her late husband. Her research assistance to the noted historian E.H. Carr enabled him to publish in 1984 a highly detailed study of Soviet involvement in the Spanish Civil War of 1936–39.

In London during the last decades of her life, Deutscher was the doyenne of a small but intellectually passionate circle of intellectuals who remained convinced that despite its many setbacks, Socialism was the only system capable of liberating humanity from its ancient enemies of ignorance, poverty and war. Among the friends she made in the years after her husband's death were a new generation of British leftist intellectuals, including a group that published its analyses and polemics in the well-regarded *New Left Review*. Despite the universally acknowledged horrors of Stalinism and the collapse of Communist states in Europe a few months before her death, Tamara Deutscher believed to the end of her life that Socialism, human decency and democracy were all compatible ideals. She died of emphysema in London on August 7, 1990, loved and respected by an international coterie of friends.

SOURCES:

Carr, Edward Hallett. *The Comintern and the Spanish Civil War.* Edited by Tamara Deutscher. London: Macmillan, 1984.

Deutscher, Isaac. *The Great Purges.* Edited by Tamara Deutscher. Oxford and NY: Basil Blackwell, 1984.

———. *Marxism in Our Time.* Edited by Tamara Deutscher. London: Jonathan Cape, 1972.

———. *The Non-Jewish Jew and Other Essays.* Edited and with an Introduction by Tamara Deutscher. NY: Hill and Wang, 1968.

Deutscher, Tamara , ed. *Not by Politics Alone: The Other Lenin.* London: Allen & Unwin, 1973.

———, et al. *Political Prisoners in Czechoslovakia and the USSR: The Struggle for Socialist Democracy.* Nottingham: Bertrand Russell Peace Foundation/ The Spokesman, 1975.

———, et al., eds. *Voices of Czechoslovak Socialists.* London: Committee to Defend Czechoslovak Socialists, 1977.

Horowitz, David, ed. *Isaac Deutscher: The Man and His Work.* London: Macdonald, 1971.

Ostrower, Heinz. "In Memoriam: Tamara Deutscher," in *Monthly Review.* Vol. 42, no. 11. April 1991, pp. 50–51.

Singer, David. "Tamara Deutscher," in *The Independent* [London]. August 10, 1990, p. 13.

"Tamara Deutscher, Writer, 77," in *The New York Times.* August 9, 1990, p. B12.

John Haag, Associate Professor of History, University of Georgia, Athens, Georgia

Deutschkron, Inge (1922—)

German-Jewish Holocaust survivor and author whose memoirs are considered to be among the most fascinating chronicles of survival to come out of the Holocaust. Born Ingeborg Deutschkron in Finsterwalde, Germany, on August 23. 1922; daughter of Martin and Ella (Mannhalt) Deutschkron.

Selected writings: Bonn and Jerusalem: The Strange Coalition *(Philadelphia, PA: Chilton, 1970); . . .* denn ihrer war die Hölle: Kinder in Gettos und Lagern *(Cologne: Verlag Wissenschaft und Politik, new ed., 1985);* Milch ohne Honig: Leben in Israel *(Cologne: Verlag Wissenschaft und Politik, 1988);* Outcast: A Jewish Girl in Wartime Berlin *(Translated by Jean Steinberg. NY: Fromm International, 1989);* Unbequem—:Mein Leben nach dem Überleben *(Cologne: Verlag Wissenschaft und Politik, 1992);* Sie blieben im Schatten: Ein Denkmal für "stille Helden" *(Berlin: Edition Hentrich, 1996).*

Born in 1922 during a period of political chaos and economic inflation, Inge Deutschkron grew up in a family of assimilated German Jews who felt themselves to be as loyal to the Fatherland as any other Germans.

Inge's father was a teacher and a committed Social Democrat who believed that German democracy had to be defended by all possible means against its enemies, particularly the violent Nazi movement led by Adolf Hitler. Among

Inge's earliest memories were the hours she and her father Martin spent in the smoke-filled back rooms of a Berlin taverns, folding political pamphlets. The annual May Day demonstrations of Berlin's workers and intellectuals gave her "a taste of the shared feeling of commitment and unity of politically engaged people." These heady years of her youth ended in 1933 for Inge Deutschkron and the rest of Germany's Jewish population when the Nazi Party seized power and set up a dictatorial regime vowing to cleanse the nation of the evils of Marxism, democracy, and liberalism. Not yet 11 in 1933, she learned from her parents, who were not religiously observant Jews, that she was Jewish and would thus be subjected to taunts and insults in the new Germany, the Third Reich.

In 1935, all German Jews, including the Deutschkron family, were classified as aliens by the infamous Nuremberg Laws. Now officially segregated, German Jews in the next few years suffered ever-increasing discrimination and humiliation. In 1938, all Jewish males had to add "Israel" as a new middle name; females had to add "Sara" as a middle name. The bloody *Kristallnacht* pogrom of November 1938 made it clear that Germany's Jews now faced a future that was bleak at best. Deutschkron's father, who had found work in a Jewish school, realized that the time had come for his family to flee Germany. In April 1939, believing that he would soon be able to secure permission for his family to follow, he was able to immigrate to England. In August 1939, Inge and her mother **Ella Mannhalt Deutschkron** received the good news from her father that he had been able to find work for both of them in the home of a professor in Glasgow. Unfortunately, within weeks Germany attacked Poland and this last avenue of escape was shut down. Although Inge still received an occasional letter from her father, he could now do nothing for his trapped wife and daughter. The harsh regime under which Jews lived became even worse as Jewish-owned radios were confiscated and telephones in Jewish homes were disconnected. Living in a state of permanent curfew, Jews were not allowed to leave their homes between the hours of 8 PM and 5 AM. Among other restrictions, Jews could no longer visit theaters, concert halls, and movies. Parks and public recreational areas were closed to them, except for specially segregated park benches marked by Stars of David.

Almost from the start of the punitive regime initiated against Germany's Jews in 1938–39, many of them began to depend on the support of non-Jewish friends and neighbors for assistance. Inge found domestic employment in the home of Dr. Conrad Cohen, an official of the Berlin Jewish Community. Although many Germans supported Nazi anti-Semitic policies, and even more remained indifferent to the fate of Jews, a small but significant minority helped Jews on the basis of religious, moral, and political principles. In the case of the Deutschkrons, some of the family's Socialist friends from pre-Nazi years continued to remain loyal despite the dangers.

Starting in April 1941, Deutschkron became subject to compulsory labor. At first she found work in an I.G. Farben plant that manufactured parachute silk. Although Jews at this point did not yet have to wear Jewish stars on their clothing on a mandatory basis, here they were required to do so. Ten hours daily work in front of a rotating spindle watching thread in a room that was hot and noisy was exhausting. The factory administration emphasized the segregated status of its Jewish workers by herding them into a separate canteen with only a table and no chairs. Within days of starting work for I.G. Farben, Inge's knee became excruciatingly inflamed and would not bend because of the long gruelling hours on the job and an additional three hours standing in the train to and from work. Needing medical certification to find a less stressful job, Deutschkron went to a non-Jewish physician other Jews had consulted and found trustworthy. Dr. Damm examined Deutschkron, quickly signing a form declaring that she was unable to perform work that required her to stand. He also certified that she urgently needed sick leave. After some weeks at minimum pay sick leave, she found a secretarial job at a workshop employing mostly blind Jewish workers that produced brooms and brushes for the German military.

By September 1941, German Jews were required to wear a Jewish star on their clothing when out in public. The process of isolation of Jews and Germans was now virtually complete, setting Inge and Ella Deutschkron apart from others who had once been neighbors and fellow Germans. When on the street, she noted, some individuals "looked at me with hostility, others with sympathy, and still others averted their eyes." Sometimes touching experiences took place without warning when a stranger would come up to Inge on the street and slip something into her pocket, an apple or some meat ration stamps. By October 1941, a small but growing number of Germany's Jews were being transported to the east as part of the Final Solution of the Jewish Question. After more than a year of watching the majority of Berlin's Jews being deported to their deaths, including her 85-year-old uncle and his unmarried sister who was taken from a Jewish old-age home, Inge was compelled in January 1943 to go underground when her place of employment was shut down. Even though they were blind and their work was of value to the war effort, virtually the entire work force of her workshop was deported to the death camps of the east.

For more than two years, Inge Deutschkron and her mother Ella depended on a number of families to provide them with shelter, food, and protection. Out of a sense of solidarity and humanity, they kept Inge and her mother alive. On several occasions, mother and daughter had to change residences, rarely staying in one place more than a few months because of the enormous burden of risk their presence placed on their rescuers' families. One of their protectors, **Lisa Holländer**, a Gentile whose Jewish husband had been murdered by the Nazis, not only did not hesitate to offer her home to the Deutschkrons, she welcomed the opportunity. For some months, Ella was even able to use forged identification papers to obtain work in a nearby textile factory.

After many brushes with death, including near misses from Allied bombing raids, Inge and Ella Deutschkron were still alive when the war ended in the spring of 1945. Both had survived the Holocaust due to incredible luck, their own resourcefulness, and the courage of a large number of non-Jewish friends and comrades. They also survived the chaos of the final days of Nazism, when all semblance of civilized life broke down, and many Soviet troops took German women as the natural booty of a victorious and bitterly fought war. Inge and Ella eventually went to England to be reunited with Martin Deutschkron, who had often wondered if his wife and daughter had somehow been able to survive the Nazi cauldron. At first, Inge had hoped to remain in Germany to be part of the democratic reconstruction of a physically and morally shattered nation. But she discovered that there was no future for a Social Democrat in a Soviet occupation zone dominated by Communists whose agenda included a rapid absorption of Social Democrats into a Socialist Unity Party controlled by German Bolsheviks loyal to Moscow.

Arriving in London with Ella in August 1946, Inge Deutschkron first enrolled at the University of London to study languages but dropped out to work in the offices of the Socialist International. By the early 1950s, she had traveled to a number of Asian countries on the invitation of their Socialist parties and written articles for several journals. Her growing reputation as journalist enabled her to move to Bonn in 1955 to write about the West German scene. In 1958, she became the Bonn reporter for the Israeli newspaper *Maariv*, a job that was upgraded in 1960 to that journal's correspondent for all Germany. In 1966, Inge Deutschkron became a citizen of Israel but remained in Bonn until 1972 when she moved permanently to Israel to work as member of *Maariv*'s editorial office in Tel Aviv.

Clearly torn between her strong feelings for both Berlin and Israel, a land that gave her "something that I had never known: security and protection," in 1989 Inge Deutschkron moved back to Berlin, where part of her remained rooted. Her return was bittersweet. She could not fail to forget that some Berliners had risked their lives to save her own and her mother's life, but also detected strong elements of racism, indifference, and ignorance of the past, particularly among the youth. At times, she despaired of Germany's capacity to ever rise above the horrible legacy of the Holocaust. Anti-Semitic incidents in the early 1990s made her pessimistic, and she accused some Germans of "closing their windows so as not to be burdened by the stench of smoke." Having herself received threatening telephone calls and letters, she seriously considered leaving Germany a final time, but her continuing belief that "the solidarity shown me during those terrible war years had become a covenant" made her decide to remain.

Energized by the need to alert the next generation of Germans to the evils of racism and ethnic intolerance, Deutschkron remained busy in the eighth decade of her life in countless classrooms and lecture halls, informing the young about her own wartime survival and decades of activity on behalf of German-Jewish reconciliation. She also visited Jewish cultural centers in Berlin, Munich, and other German cities to relate her extraordinary life story to Jews still struggling with memories of the past and concern for the future. Deutschkron continued to write books, including a 1996 volume honoring Righteous Gentiles in the Holocaust, *Sie blieben im Schatten: ein Denkmal für "stille Helden"* (*They remained in the shadows: A monument for "quiet heroes"*). Never one to underestimate the impact of the media for both ill and good, she worked with the film producer Wolfgang Kolneder to help create a documentary film about her life in the Berlin underground, *Daffke: Die vier Leben der Inge Deutschkron* (*Daffke:*

The Four Lives of Inge Deutschkron). In 1994, Inge Deutschkron was awarded the City of Berlin's Moses Mendelssohn Prize in honor of her unceasing efforts in "fostering tolerance toward those who think differently and as well as between peoples, races and religions."

SOURCES:

Boehm, Eric H. *We Survived: Fourteen Histories of the Hidden and Hunted in Nazi Germany.* New ed. Santa Barbara, CA: ABC-Clio Information Services, 1985.

"'Dann bin ich weg über Nacht'," in *Der Spiegel.* Vol. 46, no. 51. December 14, 1992, pp. 48–49, 51, 53, 56.

"'Der Holo ist beendet'," in *Der Spiegel.* Vol. 46, no. 47. November 16, 1992, pp. 65, 68, 70–71, 73.

Gross, Leonard. *The Last Jews in Berlin.* NY: Simon and Schuster, 1982.

Halter, Marek. *Stories of Deliverance: Speaking with Men and Women who Rescued Jews from the Holocaust.* Translated by Michael Bernard. Chicago: Open Court, 1998.

Kiersch, Gerhard, *et al. Berliner Alltag im Dritten Reich.* Düsseldorf: Droste Verlag, 1981.

Kolneder, Wolfgang. *Daffke—! Die vier Leben der Inge Deutschkron: 70 Jahre erlebte Politik.* Berlin: Edition Hentrich, 1994.

Ludwig, Volker. *Linie 1; Ab heute heisst du Sara.* Edited by Ingeborg Pietzsch. Berlin: Henschel Verlag, 1990.

RELATED MEDIA:

"Daffke: Die vier Leben der Inge Deutschkron: politische Dokumentation in drei Teilen," by Wolfgang Kolneder (videocassette); Berlin: Carsten Kruger Film- und Fernsehproduktion, 1994.

John Haag, Associate Professor of History, University of Georgia, Athens, Georgia

de Valera, Sinéad.

See Milligan, Alice for sidebar on Sinéad Flanagan.

de Valois, Ninette (b. 1898)

Irish-born teacher, choreographer, and founder of the Royal Ballet who helped to establish classical ballet in Britain. Pronunciation: VALL-wah. Born Edris Stannus on June 6, 1898, at Baltiboys, Blessington, Co. Wicklow, Ireland; daughter of T.R.A. Stannus (a lieutenant-colonel) and Lilith (Graydon-Smith) Stannus; educated at home and at Lila Field (Stage) Academy for Children; married Dr. Arthur B. Connell, in July 1935; no children.

Awards: Commander of the British Empire (CBE, 1947); Chévalier, Légion d'honneur (1950); Dame of the British Empire (DBE, 1951); fellow, Royal Academy of Dancing (1963); Gold Albert Medal, Royal Society of Arts (1964); (first woman recipient) Erasmus Prize Foundation Award (1974); Irish Community Award (1980); Companion of Honor (CH, 1982); Order of Merit (OM, 1992); granted Hon. Mus.Doc., London (1947), Hon. D.Litt., Reading (1951), Hon. D.Litt., Oxford (1955), Hon. D.Mus., Sheffield (1955), Hon. Mus.D., Dublin (1957), Hon. D.F.A., Smith College (1957), Hon. LL.D., Aberdeen (1958), Hon. LL.D., Sussex (1975), Hon. D.Litt., Ulster (1979), Hon. D.Mus., Durham (1982).

First performed professionally (1913); joined Diaghilev's Ballets Russes (1923); founded Academy of Choreographic Art, London (1926); hired by Lilian Baylis to work at the Old Vic (1926); worked at Festival Theater, Cambridge (1926–31) and Abbey Theater, Dublin (1927–35); founded the Vic-Wells (subsequently Sadler's Wells and Royal) Ballet (1931); founded Sadler's Wells (subsequently Royal) Ballet School (1931); moved company to Royal Opera House, Covent Garden (1946); made first American tour (1949); Sadler's Wells Ballet given Royal Charter (1956); retired as director of Royal Ballet (1963). Founder and director, Turkish School of Ballet (1948) and Turkish State Ballet (1956); founder, Iranian National Ballet (1958); patron, Irish Ballet Company (1974). Publications: Invitation to the Ballet (John Lane, 1937); Come Dance With Me (Hamish Hamilton, 1957); Step by Step (W.H. Allen, 1977).

Ninette de Valois spent the first years of her life at Baltiboys, a country house in the scenic surroundings of County Wicklow, just south of Dublin. Her mother's family had been long established in the county, and her great-grandmother, **Elizabeth Smith,** was a perceptive diarist whose chronicles were published in 1980. Her father, an army officer, was later killed in the First World War. A stage career was an unlikely prospect for someone from de Valois' background, but when the family moved to England in the early 1900s it became possible. She took dance lessons and also saw the first seasons of Diaghilev's Ballets Russes in London. When her mother decided that she should be trained properly, she went to the Lila Field Academy for Children whose previous alumni included Noel Coward and Micheál MacLiammóir. It was, she later wrote, a typical theatrical school, and she learned something of everything. Early in 1913, after changing her name from Edris Stannus to Ninette de Valois, she went on tour with a company of students from the school who were called "The Wonder Children." They performed programs of small ballets and plays in a variety of venues, and de Valois was later to boast that she danced in every seaside theater in England. One of her most popular pieces was an impression of *Anna Pavlova in The Dying Swan. The touring was gruelling but instilled into de Valois an iron discipline and stamina that never left her.

In autumn 1914, she secured her first London engagement at the Lyceum Theater and worked there every year for the following five years as well as on other concert engagements. In summer 1919, she was engaged for the opera ballet at Covent Garden which she found a valuable experience not just musically but later when she started to choreograph. De Valois was anxious to improve her technique and studied with some the most influential teachers of the time, among them Edouard Espinosa, Enrico Cecchetti, and Nicholas Legat. They each influenced her dancing: Espinosa gave her strong, clear footwork; from Cecchetti, she learned the importance of symmetry and detail, and the meaning of *ports de bras* (carriage of the arms); Legat made her less tense and gave her a sense of her own worth as a dancer. She later invited him to teach at Sadler's Wells in the 1930s.

In 1921, she had her first performing contact with the Russian ballet when she danced with Leonide Massine's company at the Royal Opera House. The standard of the choreography was far in advance of anything she had done previously, but a bigger challenge lay ahead. In

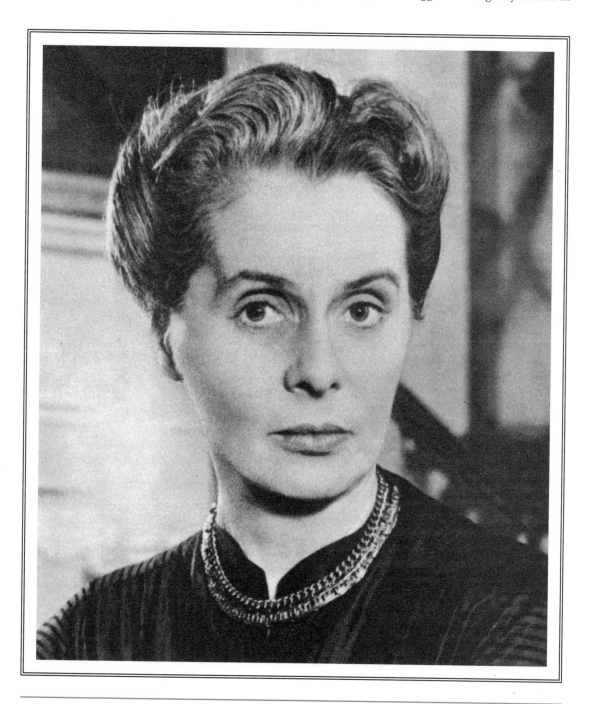

Ninette de Valois

September 1923, de Valois joined Diaghilev's Ballets Russes and for the next two years was part of a company that was at the forefront of theatrical dance, music, and design. De Valois absorbed as much of this creativity as she could, watching Diaghilev's genius "welding, molding, guiding and seeking." Performing with the company also gave her the opportunity to see the great cities of Europe and their theaters, galleries, and museums. She danced in many of Mikhail Fokine's ballets, but the two choreographers who made the most impression on her were *Bronislava Nijinska and George Balanchine. She admired Balanchine's endless dance invention and acute musicality; she was also fortunate to dance in Nijinska's two greatest ballets, which were choreographed during de Valois' first year with the company, *Les Noces* and *Les Biches,* in the latter creating the role of the Hostess. Nijinska also coached her in some of the variations from *The Sleeping Beauty,* but it took de Valois some time to appreciate the influence of the Russian classical tradition. She was bored when she saw *Swan Lake* until it was explained to her by *Vera Trefilova, one of the great ballerinas of the pre-revolutionary era in Russia. The Russian classics would later become a cornerstone of her own company in the 1930s.

> *My mind prefers adversity and complexity to any state of smooth living.*
>
> —Ninette de Valois

De Valois left the Ballets Russes in 1925 but returned as a guest artist in 1926 and 1928. She had gained immeasurably from her years with Diaghilev, but, when formulating plans for her own company, she was determined that in one respect she would not follow his example: she wanted a permanent company not a touring one. The very idea of an English ballet struck many people as ludicrous. The country may have produced some good dancers but, unlike the French, Italians, Danes, and Russians, it had no tradition of ballet. Ballet, to Diaghilev's English public in the 1920s, meant the Russian ballet in all its glamour and glory, and it would take decades for that prejudice to weaken. De Valois was aware of this and knew that if English ballet was to flourish it needed a repertory theater, a secure base from which to grow, and what better repertory theater with which to begin the process than the Old Vic.

In 1926, she approached *Lilian Baylis, the formidable director of the Old Vic, with a proposal to establish the nucleus of a ballet compa-ny under the auspices of her theater. Baylis was impressed with de Valois' practicality, and she hired her to teach movement to the drama students and to arrange short dances for plays and operas. In return, the ballet would be allowed to perform in some of the theater's programs. Baylis and de Valois were alike in important essentials: they had vision and the patience to wait for longterm plans to come to fruition. Baylis had great respect for de Valois which was reciprocated, and de Valois paid warm and perceptive tribute to Baylis in her memoirs. De Valois was grateful for the opportunity to work at the Vic but was paid very little and later in 1926 became resident choreographer at the Festival Theater in Cambridge, run by her cousin Terence Gray, which staged experimental drama. The *Oresteia,* in October 1926, was one of its most successful productions, and de Valois' movement for the chorus attracted particular praise. The poet W.B. Yeats saw her work at the Festival Theater and invited her to come to Dublin to help him restage his *Plays for Dancers* at the Abbey Theater. Their collaboration was to last until 1935, and de Valois wrote about Yeats with great insight in *Come Dance With Me* and *Step by Step.* For her, he was indisputably one of the world's greatest poets, and she regarded her work with him as a cherished experience; Yeats found their collaboration equally stimulating. Her work with Yeats led to her later appreciation of the plays of Samuel Beckett.

With drama, opera, and now ballet being performed at the Old Vic, space was at a premium, and in 1926 the dilapidated Sadler's Wells Theater in north London was purchased. It opened in 1931 and became the home of the opera and ballet companies. The first full evening of ballet took place in May 1931, and from then on the Vic-Wells Ballet, as it became known, gradually attracted a loyal and discriminating audience. Besides her work for the drama and opera companies, de Valois had been choreographing her own ballets since 1925. In July 1931, her ballet *Job,* using the best British talents, was hailed as a distinguished creation. Described as a "masque for dancing," the ballet had a libretto by Geoffrey Keynes based on William Blake, designs by *Gwen Raverat, and music by Ralph Vaughan-Williams. De Valois' best choreography was created in the 1930s, but when planning a repertoire for her company she knew she needed a more wide-ranging base. She wanted a choreographer who could create and develop a native English classical style; but the foundation for this style was the staging of the great Russian classical ballets that were hardly known in the West. The instruments for both were at hand.

In 1933, de Valois invited Nikolai Sergeyev, who had directed the Maryinsky Ballet in St. Petersburg just before the Revolution, to stage the Petipa-Ivanov masterworks for her company from the notations he had brought with him from Russia. Between 1933–39, he produced *Coppélia, Giselle, The Nutcracker, Swan Lake,* and *The Sleeping Beauty.* The productions were modest both in design and performance, but their significance for the company was enormous; they were the basis of later, grander productions that made the company's classical reputation in the 1940s and 1950s. Frederick Ashton joined the company as resident choreographer in the 1935–36 season. Ashton had started his career with *Marie Rambert's company and had also worked with Bronislava Nijinska and in the commercial theater. In Ashton, de Valois found a choreographer of lyrical classicism and sensitive musicality who was also full of wit and humor. For 40 years, Ashton's choreography shaped and defined English classical ballet and provided a wealth of wonderful roles for generations of dancers. With de Valois and Ashton, the third member of the triumvirate at the Vic-Wells company was the musical director Constant Lambert. A composer of considerable intellectual gifts, Lambert was an indispensable adviser. He had an innate understanding of dancers and their different styles, and this made him one of the finest dance conductors of his time.

In the early years of the Vic-Wells company, de Valois was fortunate in attracting several major guest stars including *Alicia Markova, Anton Dolin, *Lydia Lopokova, and Stanislas Idzikowski. But she was also anxious to build up the company's own stars and immediately spotted the potential of the young *Margot Fonteyn. As Fonteyn's gifts developed, she became the muse of Frederick Ashton who created a magnificent series of ballets for her in an artistic relationship that lasted, on and off, for over 40 years. But de Valois was also intent on developing male dancing and a strong male roster was built up in the 1930s, notably Robert Helpmann, Harold Turner, and Michael Somes. De Valois continued to dance until the late 1930s, and in 1937 she created the role of Webster, the bossy maid, in Ashton's *A Wedding Bouquet.* It was a humorous portrait of de Valois herself.

The seasons at Sadler's Wells lasted from September to May and thus gave the dancers a measure of financial security which was rare at the time but which de Valois considered vital for the future of the company. Looking back on that first decade, de Valois remembered the dedication and sense of purpose that inspired them. She also created some of her finest choreography: *The Haunted Ballroom* (1934), *The Rake's Progress* (1935) and *Checkmate* (1937). *Checkmate* was performed in Paris in 1937 when the company was invited to appear at an international exhibition, an indication of its growing reputation. There was further recognition when it appeared at a royal gala performance at Covent Garden in 1939.

After war broke out in September 1939, Sadler's Wells became a shelter for the homeless, and the company led a peripatetic existence on tour. One of the most dramatic moments in its history occurred in May 1940 when the company was on tour in Holland and narrowly escaped the German invasion (*see also Hepburn, Audrey*). As Britain awaited invasion in the summer of 1940, de Valois decided, with unerring instinct, to create a comedy ballet, *The Prospect Before Us,* which was a great audience favorite. But difficult as the war years were, they were the making of the Sadler's Wells Ballet (as the company was renamed in 1941). The regular tours to a huge range of venues made the company well-known. Another London base was found at the New Theater and the seasons there were extremely popular despite the dangers of German air-raids. In addition to her work with the company, de Valois also helped her husband most weekends at his London surgery. She had married Dr. Arthur B. Connell in July 1935.

The company emerged from the war with a healthy bank balance, most of which de Valois spent on new premises for the school that was reorganized in 1946–47 to include both academic and dance studies for its students. De Valois began regular, annual dance seminars for ballet teachers at the school which were particularly influential. But there were other momentous changes in store. In 1945, the Sadler's Wells Ballet was invited to become the resident company at the Royal Opera House, Covent Garden, which was due to reopen after the war. Despite initial reservations, due mainly to her gratitude to the Sadler's Wells Theater, de Valois accepted, knowing what an opportunity this represented in terms of greater space and prestige. However, a smaller company was retained at Sadler's Wells, the Sadler's Wells Theater Ballet, and became an important training ground for young dancers and especially for new choreographers, among them John Cranko and Kenneth MacMillan.

Covent Garden was reopened in February 1946 with a lavish new production of *The Sleeping Beauty* produced by de Valois; the lavishness was a major achievement since strict rationing was still in force. It became the company's signature ballet, and Fonteyn, now reaching the height of her powers, was one of the finest interpreters of Aurora. Frederick Ashton also created some of his best ballets in the years immediately after the reopening, *Symphonic Variations, Cinderella* (the first three-act ballet created for the company), *Scènes de ballet,* and *Daphnis and Chloe.* In 1949, the Sadler's Wells Ballet was invited to the Metropolitan Opera House in New York and had a triumphant reception. The United States became the company's most important touring destination, and there were almost annual visits until the 1960s. The American tours were also an important source of revenue at a time of severe financial difficulties in Britain. De Valois achieved personal success on the U.S. lecture circuit and found that her work with Yeats attracted considerable interest among college audiences.

The early death of Constant Lambert in 1951 was a personal and professional loss to de Valois. It also coincided with criticism that artistically the company had lost its way. In 1950, she had created her last major ballet, *Don Quixote,* to music by Roberto Gerhard. Though some critics thought it ahead of its time, it was a failure and has never been revived. Only *The Rake's Progress* and *Checkmate,* of all de Valois' ballets, have remained regularly in the repertory. Despite the company's artistic doldrums in the early 1950s, there were other achievements. In 1955, White Lodge, a former royal residence in Richmond Park, London, became the residential junior school of the ballet. The growing reputation of the school was due to the calibre of the teachers de Valois appointed, and in the late 1950s a particularly gifted generation of young dancers graduated, among them ◄ Antoinette Sibley, *Lynn Seymour, Merle Park, Anthony Dowell, and David Wall. At the Sadler's Wells Theater Ballet, de Valois was encouraging new choreography by Cranko and MacMillan. In 1957, she invited Cranko to create the first three-act ballet to a specially composed English score, Benjamin Britten's *The Prince of the Pagodas.* She later encouraged Cranko to take on the directorship of the Stuttgart Ballet in Germany. He was not the first to receive such encouragement. In 1951, *Celia Franca went to Canada and helped to found the National Ballet of Canada and its school. In 1963, *Peggy van Praagh became the director of the Australian Ballet. De Valois also took an active interest in the other companies she

had helped to found in the 1950s, the Turkish State Ballet and the Iranian National Ballet.

Although de Valois was pleased to be made a Dame of the British Empire by King George VI in 1951, she wanted recognition for her company; in 1956, to her great delight, it finally received a royal charter from Queen *Elizabeth II and became the Royal Ballet, with the school becoming the Royal Ballet School. That year, de Valois also paid her first visit to Russia at the invitation of the Soviet government. The Royal Ballet first visited Russia in 1961, and the Russian connection was strengthened the following year. Rudolf Nureyev had defected in June 1961, shortly after the Royal Ballet's visit, and in 1962 de Valois invited him to join the company. It was a decision that attracted some controversy as it was felt by some that he would overshadow the other male dancers. De Valois argued that Nureyev would have a stimulating effect and so it proved. He had a considerable influence on the development of male dancing; his partnership with Fonteyn was legendary; and in 1963 he produced for the Royal Ballet the Petipa masterpiece that was virtually unknown in the West at that time, "The Kingdom of Shades" from *La Bayadère.* It became just as much a signature piece for the Royal Ballet as *The Sleeping Beauty.*

After 32 years as director, de Valois retired in 1963 and was succeeded by Frederick Ashton. However, she remained closely involved with the Royal Ballet School until the early 1970s and, even after that, was frequently seen in its classrooms. In 1977, she supervised a new production of *The Sleeping Beauty* for the Royal Ballet. As she neared her centenary, she retained an active interest in the company and the school. There was also renewed scholarly interest in her choreography. In *Step by Step,* she wrote that the Royal Ballet "was never meant to be a personal effort in a particularly specialised direction. It was to become something that would have a root in the country's theater." Take root the Royal Ballet did and, that it did, was due to de Valois' personal effort and vision.

SOURCES:

De Valois, Ninette. *Come Dance With Me: A Memoir 1898–1956.* London: Hamish Hamilton, 1957.

———. *Invitation to the Ballet.* London: John Lane, 1937.

———. *Step by Step: The Formation of an Establishment.* London: W.H. Allen, 1977.

Walker, Kathrine Sorley. *Ninette de Valois: Idealist without Illusions.* London: Hamish Hamilton, 1987.

SUGGESTED READING:

Beaumont, Cyril. *The Sadler's Wells Ballet.* London: C.W.Beaumont, 1946.

◄►
Sibley, Antoinette. *See Fonteyn, Margot for sidebar.*

Bland, Alexander. *The Royal Ballet: The First 50 Years.* London: Threshold, 1981.

Clarke, Mary. *The Sadler's Wells Ballet: A History and an Appreciation.* London: Adam & Charles Black, 1955.

RELATED MEDIA:

"Madam," two-part documentary for Channel Four television, London, December 1982–January 1983.

Deirdre McMahon, Dublin, Ireland,
Assistant Editor, *Dance Theater Journal* (London)
and author of *Republicans and Imperialists*
(Yale University Press, 1984)

Devanny, Jean (1894–1962)

Australian author and political activist whose career was marked by the conflict between her devotion to the Australian Communist Party and her strong affiliation with feminism. Name variations: Jane, Jenny. Pronunciation: De-VANE-ee. Born Jane Crook on January 7, 1894, in Ferntown, New Zealand; died of leukemia at Townsville, Queensland, Australia, on March 8, 1962; daughter of a coal miner; her mother was the daughter of a British colonel; attended state primary school, 1898–1907; married Hal Devanny, in 1911; children: Karl Devanny (d. 1934); Patricia Devanny; Erin Devanny (d. 1919).

Moved to New Zealand capital of Wellington (1919); published her first novel (1926); moved to Sydney, Australia (1929); arrested for the first time, joined Communist Party (1930); became National Secretary of WIR and traveled in Germany and the Soviet Union (1931); participated in the northern Queensland sugar strike (1935); learned of her expulsion from the Australian Communist Party (1941); readmitted to the Communist Party (1943); resigned from Communist Party (1950); rejoined the Communist Party (1957).

Selected works: The Butcher Shop *(1926);* Sugar Heaven *(1936);* Cindie *(1949);* Travels in North Queensland *(1951); (posthumously published autobiography)* Point of Departure *(1986).*

Jean Devanny was a significant Australian writer during the first half of the 20th century. Committed to political radicalism, she moved from affiliation with the Labor Party in New Zealand to serve as an energetic organizer and agitator for the Communist Party in Australia. Committed as well to feminist ideals, Devanny found herself frequently at odds with the demands placed upon her by the party's structure and its directives. In the view of many of her fellow Australian Communists, her support for women's liberation combined with her public advocacy of birth control and devotion to children's welfare vitiated her political reliability.

The conflict came to a head with her expulsion from party membership in the early 1940s.

Although Devanny was later exonerated and readmitted to the Communist Party, the incident helped crystallize her desire to write a candid autobiographical account of her life, her political activities, and her personal affairs. The book, *Point of Departure*, went through a number of very different drafts and remained in manuscript form until one draft, edited by **Carole Ferrier**, was finally published in Australia in 1986.

The future Jean Devanny was born Jane Crook on January 7, 1894, at Ferntown, located in a coastal region on New Zealand's South Island. She would not be known as Jean until the 1920s. The eighth of ten children, she came from a colorful and troubled family. She was the granddaughter of a British army colonel whose career brought him assignments throughout the British empire, leading to a final mission in New Zealand to fight the local Maori tribes. In a country with few eligible men, the colonel's daughter was only 17 when she married the man who would become Jean's father. The marriage brought her a pregnancy every other year and residence with a husband who had a frightening weakness for strong drink and violent behavior.

Young Jean's father worked as a blacksmith and in other skills connected with the local mining industry, and his alcoholism and explosive actions terrified the entire family. She attended public schools in New Zealand, starting when she was only four years old. She later recalled the harshness of conditions there, notably the use of corporal punishment. Although a gifted student in subjects like English, her weakness in arithmetic made her the target for fierce beatings. One teacher, however, became a close friend and provided her with information about sexuality that she could not receive from her own, prudish mother. Early in her troubled childhood, the future writer became an insatiable reader, and music lessons, which made her a skilled amateur pianist, likewise gave variety to her rural existence. She received little encouragement, however, with her mother taunting her for such interests as her collection of insects. "Books," she later wrote, "became my refuge from the harassments of domestic life."

Devanny quit school at age 13 and went to work in a number of menial occupations such as maid in a local boardinghouse. She nonetheless continued to educate herself with a self-directed reading program. It included both the literary works of the time, as well as such provocative writers as Charles Darwin. She later recalled that her initial interest in socialism came partly as a result of her reading, especially books provided to her by a mining engineer and his wife who had only recently arrived from England. Another set of events in her childhood—her father's lingering death from phthisis, a miner's disease—also contributed to her political radicalism.

In 1911, at age 17, she married a miner named Hal Devanny, four years her senior. She later claimed that his political views took shape under her guidance as she piled books upon him. The future feminist author had three children in four years. She also came to an early understanding of the deep personality differences separating herself and her husband. She was mercurial and perpetually full of energy; despite his success as a labor organizer, he was a quiet and withdrawn figure at home.

An indication of Jean Devanny's growing interest in the ideas of Karl Marx came in 1912 when she named her first child Karl. As her husband became increasingly prominent in the miners' union, she soon found herself entertaining some of the most important figures in the New Zealand Labor Party, many of them headed for high posts in a future Labor government. She soon took on the role of Labor Party speaker herself.

A working class activist and agitator; a revolutionary socialist; a women's liberationist; a woman writer.

—Carole Ferrier

Devanny's restless energies, which many of her acquaintances remarked upon throughout her life, were not exhausted by her role of devoted mother and party activist. She studied music seriously, with lessons in the violin, piano, and singing. Her literary career also began in earnest, starting with a series of film scenarios. Mailed to Hollywood studios, they garnered only polite rejection letters. Her musical interests collapsed, however, in 1919 with the death of her youngest child and second daughter Erin. The girl was hospitalized for peritonitis; after seven weeks of lingering illness followed by apparent recovery, she died. Devanny was devastated. As she recovered emotionally, she turned her interests increasingly toward literature. Shortly thereafter, she sold her first piece, a description of the New Zealand countryside, to a local newspaper. She soon began to produce a flurry of short stories, although only a few of them got into print.

Devanny's first novel, *The Butcher Shop*, appeared in 1926, and three other novels and a book of short stories followed in short order. *The Butcher Shop* gave an early indication of how seriously Devanny would be criticized for her writing and the feminist posture it contained. Focusing on the role of women in the society of rural New Zealand, it was both sexually candid and graphic in describing the brutality to which females were subjected. In time, the book was to be banned in Boston as well as a number of countries, including Nazi Germany and Australia.

During the 1920s, husband and wife became increasingly involved with the labor movement in New Zealand. Hal's work as a skilled miner brought them a measure of prosperity, but their radical view of society remained unaffected. Sometimes they attended meetings of the New Zealand Communist Party, but they found it too snobbish and elitist. As she remembered the Communists of her birthplace, they "spoke and acted as if they were the intellectual chosen, and all others the despised beneath their feet." But the Devannys were uncomfortable with the Labor Party as well. It struck them as faction-ridden and dominated by its right wing.

In 1929, Hal and Jean Devanny moved to Sydney, Australia. Several years before, their son Karl had been diagnosed with heart disease, and the specialist they consulted recommended that the boy leave the cold climate of New Zealand for the more temperate weather of Australia. By now the full force of the Depression had struck Australia, and the family was reduced to desperate measures. Despite her slender stature, Jean sought and obtained a physically demanding position that was the only work readily available: cooking and cleaning at a sheep ranch deep in the Australian interior. Her experiences in this desolate region of New South Wales formed the background for her novel *Out of Such Fires*, which was published in 1934.

The Devannys continued their radical activities, and, in 1930, became members of the Australian Communist Party. Their children, Karl and Patricia, led the way. The precipitating event was a workers' march against the new Australian government. Even though the government was one composed of members of the Labor Party, it seemed nonetheless to be indifferent to workers' needs. Two of the Devanny children marched in a demonstration to get help for the unemployed and were arrested. Jean and Hal, although not physically present at the march, were nonetheless falsely identified by policemen as having been participants. At her trial, Jean Devanny proudly proclaimed to the journalists in attendance that she too was a writer, and that she would thereupon join the Communist Party partly in protest at the way marchers (and their sympathizers) were being treated. She refused on principle to pay a fine of £2, choosing instead to go to jail for four days.

When Devanny was released from prison, she began immediately to serve as a party activist. She was ordered to concentrate on public speaking, sometimes addressing as many as five meetings in a single day. In short order, she was put in charge of the Australian branch of the Workers International Relief (WIR) organization. This was a group supported by the Communist Party and intended to provide relief for workers in distress. Increasingly prominent in party circles, she was chosen in 1931 to travel to Europe to participate in the Berlin conference of the WIR. Following her stay in Germany, she went on to make a six-week tour of the Soviet Union.

Jean Devanny's role within the Australian Communist Party soon brought her feminist and individualistic personal views in conflict with her political loyalties. Determined to be a good, even well-disciplined member of the party, Devanny nonetheless became an outspoken critic of numerous party ideas and practices. On some of her tours, she gave lectures—for women only—on the issue of birth control. The party was an organization that permitted women to exercise only a minimum of power and influence, and Devanny was openly critical of such a situation. The party's political circumstances, in which it faced the likelihood it would be declared an illegal organization, made such internal criticism particularly unpopular. From her standpoint, although she was committed to accept party discipline, it was regrettable, she put it, that "the sanctity of leaders was an obsession." She noted that often untalented individuals, selected for leadership posts, thereby "were supposed to become magically invested with an immunity to make mistakes and therefore to stand above criticism." Although she accepted the party's strictures about writing in the style of socialist-realism, she also promoted cooperation between Communist and sympathetic writers in a broadly based organization. This contradicted the party policy of the time and led to a direct reprimand for her.

Meanwhile, Devanny continued her literary production in prolific fashion. In addition to several novels set in New Zealand but published only after she had settled in Australia, Devanny also produced 14 other novels and a number of works of nonfiction. Nonetheless, as a Communist writer, Devanny faced serious day-to-day difficulties. As **Drusilla Modjeska** has put it,

writers like her "needed long hours of solitude and contemplation," and the party's claim to every hour of a member's day for activities like public speaking, or even selling newspapers, took precedence over other activities.

During the 1930s, Devanny's marriage went into a decline. While she continued to live with Hal, their sexual intimacy came to an end. In *Point of Departure,* Jean was notably reticent in describing this shift in her home life. She was far more explicit in her account of her longtime, intimate relationship with J.B. Miles, the Communist Party's general secretary. Although she referred to him in her autobiography only as "Leader," she provided a detailed description of how they conducted themselves. She noted for example that their love affair did nothing to change her role as his party subordinate. He was sometimes scathing in his public criticism when her political views deviated from his understanding of the party line.

Ferrier suggests that Devanny's devotion to sexual freedom went well beyond what the author was willing to reveal in print. Devanny had not only worked assiduously in **Marian Piddington**'s birth-control clinic since her arrival in Sydney, but she also apparently had a number of sexual liaisons apart from her affairs with "Leader." She was explicit in her autobiography in declaring that a double standard of sexual conduct was contrary to Marxist principles.

In 1934, Devanny lost a second child: her son Karl finally succumbed to the heart problems from which he had suffered for more than a decade. Devanny herself was increasingly troubled by ill-health, including pleurisy, starting in the mid-1930s. Nonetheless, she took on exhausting work as a party speaker, traveling at length through the more remote regions of Australia. She supplemented her meager diet with massive doses of cod liver oil to give her some relief from her ailments. Photographs taken during these years show her distressingly frail appearance. Nonetheless, one of her listeners described her as "the best agitational speaker I ever heard," and another recalled her "words at express speed" as well as her "tongue like an axe in a woodchopping contest." Sure of herself and her views, she tore into any member of her audience who tried to ask a probing question.

Devanny later recalled how her reputation as a party workhorse sometimes led to her exploitation by her superiors. Despite her physical problems, she was called upon to fill in for other speakers when they wanted to do nothing more than take a day at the beach. Nonetheless, her devotion to Communist Party affairs never faltered. She was willing to go to jail again, this time under hard labor conditions, in 1933. The self-sacrificing Devanny, who was living a pinched existence on state welfare payments, gave up the royalties from her books so that money could go into the Communist Party's funds. Nonetheless, she found herself continually at odds with her party superiors over her claim that writing literature was valuable as direct political work.

Devanny's travels to the northern state of Queensland led to the publication of her most renowned novel, *Sugar Heaven,* in 1936. Its background is the 1935 strike of sugar cane workers in North Queensland, and the editors of *The Oxford Companion to Australian Literature* consider it "one of the earliest and most significant of the socialist-realist Australian novels." The book features two strong women characters whom the Communist Party treats badly. Dulcie, a shy, newly married bride of a sugar worker, becomes a successful militant. Devanny used her to make the point that the party was ignoring such valuable recruits by insisting that an acceptance of abstract political theory, not the experiences of individuals in their day-to-day lives, was the road to political radicalization. A second character, Eileen, is a talented local woman; she is refused the right to join the Communist Party because of her candor in conducting a love affair with an Italian sugar worker. Devanny used Eileen's plight to criticize both the party's sexual hypocrisy and its anti-Italian ethnic prejudice.

The supreme crisis in Devanny's political career came in the early 1940s. With the start of World War II, she returned to her old, grueling schedule of public speaking. Gritting her teeth, she reluctantly defended the alliance between Nazi Germany and the Soviet Union that lasted from the fall of 1939 to the summer of 1941. Despite her unflagging party loyalty, Devanny was increasingly disturbed by the crude attitudes male party members displayed toward women. During a stay in northern Queensland, where she had gone to recover from her on-going health problems, she openly criticized local Communist men for their dissolute sexual behavior and exploitation of local women. In a time of war, with many men off on military service, such boorish behavior by party members was common and widely accepted. In revenge, they accused her of licentious behavior and managed to get her expelled from the party in 1941.

To Devanny's dismay, her lover, "Leader," did nothing to assure her a fair hearing against such trumped up accusations.

Devanny's difficulties may have been heightened by the reaction of many close associates to her personality and what Modjeska calls "her strident, didactic, and abrasive manner." In any case, over a period of several years, Devanny found herself ostracized by her former party comrades. Her own loyalty to the party's historical role remained intact, however. As she put it, "the ideals of communism . . . came uppermost." She was subsequently exonerated in 1943 and offered reinstatement as a Communist Party member, but the episode rankled her so that it came to dominate the final third of the published version of her autobiography.

Devanny spent most of the World War II years working as a journalist and in what she cryptically described as "entertainment and educational work among the troops." After 1945, she returned to party work, but her relations with party leaders and members of the rank and file remained strained. In early 1950, she finally resigned from her once cherished membership in the Communist Party. The precipitating event was the harsh criticism she received for *Cindie,* her latest book. She then retired with her husband Hal to Townsville, a city located in Queensland that she had enjoyed visiting in the 1930s, after World War II. She spent the last years of her life writing radio scripts and short stories, and throwing herself energetically into gardening and the local musical scene. Her 1951 book, *Travels in North Queensland,* showed how far she had moved from her earlier political interests. In a revealing letter written in 1953, she looked back on her literary career with some bitterness. "I have not exploited the small measure of ability of writing I possess one whit," she complained. She had never really been able to think about her work: "Thought was reserved for politics." In fact, she had written her books either to make money for her struggling family or to promote the political causes to which she was so ardently attached.

In the aftermath of Nikita Khrushchev's 1956 denunciation of the crimes of Joseph Stalin, Devanny once again joined the Australian Communist Party. She died at Townsville on March 8, 1962, of leukemia. Her autobiography, which was published only in 1986, was a revealing account of the writer-activist's life. It described candidly such issues as her turbulent early years in a violent household, her sexual maturation, and the personality differences between her and her husband that burdened their marriage. But it also provided a vivid insight into the lifestyle of a self-proclaimed party activist and into the largely closed social and intellectual world in which such individuals functioned.

SOURCES:

Ferrier, Carole, ed. *Point of Departure: The Autobiography of Jean Devanny*. St. Lucia; University of Queensland Press, 1986.

Modjeska, Drusilla. *Exiles at Home: Australian Women Writers, 1925–1945*. London: Sirius Books, 1981.

Wilde, William H., Joy Hooton, and Barry Andrews, eds. *The Oxford Companion to Australian Literature*. 2nd ed. Melbourne: Oxford University Press, 1994.

SUGGESTED READING:

Clancy, Laurie. *A Reader's Guide to Australian Fiction*. Melbourne: Oxford University Press, 1992.

Ferres, Kay. "Written on the Body: Jean Devanny, Sexuality and Censorship," in *Hecate*. Vol. 20. May 1994, pp. 123–134.

Ferrier, Carole, ed. *Gender, Politics and Fiction: Twentieth Century Australian Women's Novels*. St. Lucia: University of Queensland, Press, 1985.

Goodwin. *A History of Australian Literature*. Houndmills, Basingstoke, Hampshire, England: Macmillan, 1986.

Neil M. Heyman, Professor of History, San Diego State University, San Diego, California

de Varona, Donna (1947—)

American swimmer who won two Olympic gold medals. Born on April 26, 1947, in San Diego, California; daughter of Martha and Dave de Varona (an insurance salesman); sister of actress Joanna Kerns *(who barely missed making the 1968 Olympic team in gymnastics); graduated University of California, Los Angeles, 1970; married John Pinto (a businessman).*

Won gold medals in the 400-meter individual medley and the 400-meter freestyle relay at the Tokyo Olympics (1964); won 37 national swimming titles; broke 18 national and world records; was the first female sports commentator on network television; was co-founder and president of the Women's Sports Foundation.

Champion swimmer Donna de Varona began her athletic career at age three when she started paddling around California pools. She and her older brother practiced swimming freestyle in the ocean and in public pools in Lafayette, California. When she was ten, de Varona entered the Far Western American Athletic Union (AAU) meet in California and finished last among ten contenders. Determined to work harder, she began to practice at the Berkeley YMCA and to train five to six hours a day at the Santa Clara Swim Club. Three years later,

she broke her first record in the 400-meter individual medley event at the Outdoor National AAU championships. The difficult medley—which includes one lap each of the backstroke, breaststroke, butterfly, and freestyle—was de Varona's best event, a testament to her versatility. In 1960, the 13-year-old was the youngest member of the American team at the Rome Summer Olympics, but her specialty, the 400 meter, was not approved for women at that time. As an alternate, she did not swim in competition.

But de Varona dominated women's swimming for the next four years, setting world records in backstroke, butterfly, and freestyle. In 1961, she posted a world record of 5:34.5 in the AAU medley, defending her previous title. She bested her own world record by a full 18 seconds at the world championships in Lima, Peru. The 400-meter individual medley was approved for women swimmers at the 1964 Tokyo Olympics, and Donna de Varona won the gold in that event (her Olympic Trial time of 5:14.9 stood as world's best until 1967). She also captured a gold medal, swimming the second leg of the 400-meter freestyle relay. Other members of the winning foursome were *Pokey Watson, *Sharon Stouder, and **Kathy Ellis.**

Throughout the early 1960s, de Varona, who was called the "Queen of Swimming," dominated the sport. In 1969, she was inducted into the International Swimming Hall of Fame, followed by induction into the International Women's Sports Hall of Fame in 1983 and the U.S. Olympic Hall of Fame in 1987. An attention-drawing swimmer, de Varona was constantly defined as "unusually attractive" and appeared on the covers of *Life, Time, Saturday Evening Post,* and *Sports Illustrated,* as well as foreign periodicals. "People thought it was unusual for a female athlete to be attractive," she commented. "We were still fighting that battle then. It got to the point where I was ashamed of my looks. I wanted to play them down."

In 1965, she retired from competitive swimming and enrolled at the University of California at Los Angeles where she majored in political science. At age 18, de Varona became an ABC sports commentator. "I was so young I needed a work permit," she recalled. In the next few years, she—along with *Suzy Chaffee and *Billie Jean King—led the fight for equality for women in all levels of sports. Said de Varona:

> Not all men like sports and not all women hate sports. Those are clichés that have become too widely accepted.... I'd like to

Donna de Varona

see the women who want to participate in sports, either for recreation or as a living, be treated with the same respect by the general public, by the press, by television, and so on, as male athletes. In my work for television I've sometimes been sent to interview a girl or woman who has just done something interesting or unique in a sport. Sometimes that interview never gets on the air. I believe it's because the producer feels that not enough people are interested in a woman doing something in sports. That's an attitude I'm always fighting to change.

De Varona was the first woman to cover the Olympics for U.S. network television. Her insightful commentary gained women a foothold in sports broadcasting. As a lobbyist, she played an important role in the passage of the Amateur Sports Act and in getting Title IX of the Education Amendments of 1972 implemented. This legislation ensured equal opportunity of women's sports in schools and colleges throughout the nation. She served on the President's Council on Physical Fitness and on President Jimmy Carter's Advisory Committee for Women. As a swimming star, sports commentator, and lobbyist for women's sports, Donna de Varona has worked to widen the margins of opportunity: "I had my dream, and I achieved it. Now I want to see it happen for other people."

SOURCES:

Bortstein, Larry. *After Olympic Glory.* NY: Frederick Warne, 1978.

Porter, David L., ed. *Biographical Dictionary of American Sports: Basketball and Other Indoor Sports.* NY: Greenwood Press, 1989.

Woolum, Janet. *Outstanding Women Athletes: Who They Are and How They Influenced Sports in America.* Phoenix, Arizona: Oryx Press, 1992.

Karin L. Haag, freelance writer, Athens, Georgia

De Vaux, Clotilde (1764–1846).

See Vaux, Clotilde de.

de Vere.

See Vere.

de Vere, Anne (d. 1559).

See Howard, Anne.

de Vere, Philippa.

See Philippa de Coucy.

Devereux, Frances (d. 1631).

See Walsingham, Frances.

Devereux, Frances (d. 1674).

See Stuart, Arabella for sidebar.

Devereux, Penelope (c. 1562–1607).

See Rich, Penelope.

Devers, Gail (1966—)

American track-and-field athlete who won three Olympic gold medals. Born on November 16, 1966, in San Diego, California; only daughter and one of two children of Larry Devers (a Baptist minister) and Alabe Devers; attended the University of California, Los Angeles; married and divorced R.J. Hampton (a track-and-field athlete).

Won silver medal in 100-meter hurdles at World championships (1991); won gold medal in 100-meter sprint (closest finish ever recorded in Olympic race) at Olympic Games, Barcelona, Spain (1992); won gold medal in 100-meter sprint at World championships (1993 and 1999); won 100-meter hurdles at U.S. Track championship (1995); won gold medals in 100-meter hurdles and 4x100 relay at Atlanta Olympics (1996).

The story of American track-and-field athlete Gail Devers has been called one of the most inspiring in the history of sport. In 1988, newly married and on the brink of a promising career, Devers was stricken with Graves' disease, a serious thyroid disorder that compromises the metabolic and nervous systems. In addition to the debilitating symptoms of the illness, she experienced such serious side effects from the treatments used to cure her that at one point doctors seriously considered amputating her feet. With the help of a new therapy, however, Devers made a dramatic recovery, then battled further to get her body and mind back into championship form. Her dramatic comeback was the subject of a television movie, "Run for the Dream: The Gail Devers Story," which first aired on June 16, 1996.

The daughter of a Baptist minister, Gail Devers was born and raised in San Diego, California. "We were a 'Leave It to Beaver' family," she recalled in a *Sports Illustrated* article. "We had picnics, rode bikes and played touch football together. We did Bible studies together. My father and brother played the guitar together." She also noted that her parents were fairly strict; she and her brother had to be in the house when the streetlights went on, and the only program they were allowed to watch on television was "I Love Lucy." (Devers became so addicted to the sitcom that she collected most of the 179 episodes.)

Gail dreamed of becoming a school teacher and only dabbled in sports before entering high school where she started out as a distance runner. By her senior year, she had developed into an impressive sprinter: she won the 100-meter sprint and the 100-meter hurdles at the California high school track championships and was offered a scholarship to the University of California at Los Angeles (UCLA).

Her college track coach turned out to be the dynamic Bob Kersee, who sized up her potential immediately. Predicting that she would some day break the U.S. record in the 100-meter hurdles and that she would make the 1988 Olympic team, he set about getting her into shape. "I hadn't had much coaching," Devers told *Sports Illustrated*. "So I thought that if he had all this faith in me, he'd coach me well. For quite a while Bobby believed in me more than I believed in myself."

In her senior year, Devers set a new American record for the 100-meter hurdles (12.61) and easily qualified for the Olympics in Seoul, Korea. Newly married to R.J. Hampton, another young track star, her future appeared to hold nothing but promise. But in Seoul, she failed to make the finals, a disappointment that she first attributed to over-training. Throughout the next two years, however, she experienced a series of mysterious and frightening symptoms that included weight fluctuations, severe headaches, memory loss, and nearly perpetual menstrual bleeding. Doctors, who were baffled for months, finally diagnosed Graves' disease and began chemotherapy and radiation treatments to shrink her enlarged thyroid. The treatment destroyed the gland completely, causing her skin to crack and bleed and her feet to swell and ooze to the point that she could only crawl or be carried around her apart-

ment. She later estimated that she came within 48 hours of losing her feet to amputation, before doctors decided to risk a new therapy. Devers responded instantly to the new protocol and, within a month, was back on her feet. A year later at the 1991 World championships, she won a silver medal in the 100-meter hurdles.

Devers also made a strong showing at the 1992 Olympics in Barcelona. In the hurdles, she took a commanding lead but tripped over the final hurdle to come in fifth; even so, she went on to win the 100-meters in the closest finish ever recorded—100th of a second. Devers' gold-medal triumph was somewhat dimmed when fellow American *Gwen Torrence implied that some of the 100-meter competitors were using performance-enhancing drugs. Devers avoided the ensuing controversy except to admit to using Synthroid to fool her body into thinking she had a thyroid gland. Bob Kersee was more emphatic in his reaction, calling the accusations "sour grapes." At the 1993 World championships, Devers had another close win in the 100-meter sprint, beating Jamaican ***Merlene Ottey-Page**

Gail Devers

by only several 100ths of a second. (Both runners were given the same time on the scoreboard, and it was only after the race that the judges awarded the win to Devers.)

Starting in 1994, when her world ranking in the 100-meters dropped considerably, Devers began to concentrate on the hurdles. She won the 100-meter hurdles at the 1995 national championships and received a gold medal in the event at the 1996 Olympics in Atlanta (along with a gold medal in the 4-by-100 relay). "It's obvious there is not a hurdler in the world as fast as Gail," said Kersee at the time about his star. "[E]very hurdler in the world has got to be intimidated by Gail because they all know rule No. 1: remove the hurdles and there's no way they can outsprint her."

Devers, who is further distinguished by her long and immaculately manicured fingernails (which she covers with athletic tape when performing), makes her home in Atlanta with her dogs. She is a voracious reader, whipping through long novels at a feverish clip, and possesses the quiet inner strength that comes from triumphing over enormous odds: "[T]here's nothing that can come up in my life that I can't get over after going through what I did," she says, looking back on her illness. "I wouldn't wish it on anyone, but I'm happy I went through it. I think back . . . to March of 1991, when I was wondering if I would ever walk again, let alone run."

SOURCES:
"Gail Devers Story Tells How a Sprinter Overcame Illness to win Olympic Gold," in *Jet*. June 3, 1996.

Johnson, Anne Janette. *Great Women in Sports*. Detroit, MI: Visible Ink, 1998.

Moore, Kenny. "Gail Force," in *Sports Illustrated*. May 10, 1993.

"Picks & Pans," in *People*. June 17, 1996.

Barbara Morgan,
Melrose, Massachusetts

Devi, Gayatri (c. 1897–1995).

See Gayatri Devi.

Devi, Phoolan (c. 1956—).

See Phoolan Devi.

de Vilmorin, Louise (1902–1969).

See Vilmorin, Louise de.

De Vito, Gioconda (1907–1994)

Italian-born British violinist who spent much time teaching and is known for her exquisite recordings. Born in Martina Franca, Lecce, Italy, on June 22, 1907; died in 1994.

Gioconda De Vito studied violin at Pesaro and later in Rome before winning the international violin competition in Vienna in 1932. This led to her appointment as principal professor of violin at the Accademia di St. *Cecilia in Rome where she remained until after 1945. De Vito first came to London to make records in 1947; a year later, she made her concert debut with the London Philharmonic Orchestra. She married and settled permanently in Great Britain. Concertizing until her retirement in 1961, De Vito was acclaimed for her expert technique and poetic imagination. Her Stradivarius violin, on loan from the Academy of St. Cecilia, produced a clear, rich tone under her touch. De Vito made numerous recordings that remain as a testimony to her art.

John Haag,
Athens, Georgia

Devlin, Bernadette (b. 1947).

See McAliskey, Bernadette.

Devon, countess of.

See Courtenay, Margaret (fl. 1330).
See Beaufort, Margaret (c. 1407–?).
See Talbot, Anne.

Devonshire, countess of.

See Cavendish, Christiana (1595–1675).

Devonshire, duchess of.

See Woodville, Elizabeth for sidebar on Katherine Plantagenet (1479–1527).

See Lamb, Caroline for sidebar on Georgiana Cavendish (1757–1806).

See Lamb, Caroline for sidebar on Cavendish, Elizabeth (1759–1824).

Devorgilla.

Variant of Dervorgilla.

Devorgilla (1109–1193)

Meath princess. Name variations: Dearbhfhorgaill; Dervorgilla. Born in 1109; died in religious retirement in Drogheda in 1193; daughter of Muirchertach Mac Lochlainn, king of Meath; married Tighearnán O'Rourke, king of Bréifne; abducted by Dermot MacMurrough, king of Leinster, 1152.

Devorgilla was the daughter of Muirchertach Mac Lochlainn, the king of Meath, who often aligned with Dermot MacMurrough to retain control over Dublin. Devorgilla married Tighearnán O'Rourke, a long-standing enemy of MacMurrough. In 1152, the rivalry of these two kings, O'Rourke and MacMurrough, was exacerbated by MacMurrough's abduction of Devorgilla. In 1166, O'Rourke dethroned Mac-Murrough. From exile, MacMurrough reconquered Dublin in 1169 and remained in control until his death in 1171. Devorgilla was benefactor of the Nuns' Church at Clonmacnoise, which she caused to be erected in 1167. She died at the convent in Drogheda in 1193.

Devorgilla (d. 1290)

Co-founder of Balliol College at the University of Oxford and mother of John Balliol, king of Scotland.
Name variations: Derbhorcaill; Dervorguilla; Devorgilla de Galloway; Devorgilla Balliol. Died on January 28, 1290; interred in Sweetheart Abbey, Kirkland; daughter of ***Margaret** *(d. 1228) and Alan of Galloway; married John Balliol (d. 1269), in 1233; children: Hugh Balliol (c. 1240–1271, who married* **Agnes de Valence***); Alan Balliol; Alexander Balliol (d. 1278, who married* **Eleanor of Geneva***); John Balliol, king of the Scots (c. 1250–1313, r. 1292–1296);* ***Cecily Balliol** *(d. before 1273, who married John de Burgh);* ***Ada Balliol** *(fl. 1256, who married William Lindsay of Lambarton);* ***Margaret Balliol** *(c. 1255–?, who married John Comyn).*

de Warrenne, Isabel.

See Isabel de Warrenne.

Dewhurst, Colleen (1924–1991)

Canadian-born actress who won Tony Awards for her work in **All the Way Home** *(1960) and* **A Moon for the Misbegotten.** *Born in Montreal, Quebec, Canada, on June 3, 1924 (some sources cite 1926); died of cervical cancer in South Salem, New York, on August 22, 1991; attended Downer College of Young Ladies (now Lawrence University), Milwaukee, Wisconsin, and Academy of Dramatic Arts; married James Vickery, in 1947 (divorced); twice married and twice divorced actor George C. Scott; children: (second marriage) two sons, Alexander and Campbell.*

Selected stage work: Made acting debut as student (1946); made professional debut as one of the neighbors in Desire Under the Elms *at the ANTA (1952); appeared as Lady Macbeth at the New York Shakespeare Festival (1957), Caesonia in* Caligula *at the 54th Street Theater (1960), Mary Follett in* All the Way Home, *for which she received the Tony Award (1960), Abbie Putnam in* Desire Under the Elms *at Circle in the Square (1963), Cleopatra in* Antony and Cleopatra *at the Delacorte (1963), Amelia Evans in Carson McCuller's* Ballad of the Sad Cafe *at the Martin Beck (1963), Sara in* More Stately Mansions *at the*

Broadhurst *(1965), Hester in* Hello and Goodbye *(1969), Shen Teh in* The Good Woman of Setzuan *at the Vivian Beaumont (1970), Gertrude in* Hamlet *at the Delacorte (1972), Christine Mannon in* Mourning Becomes Electra *at Circle in the Square (1972), Josie Hogan in* A Moon for the Misbegotten *at the Morosco, for which she received her second Tony Award (1973), Martha in* Who's Afraid of Virginia Woolf *at the Belasco (1977).*

Films: The Nun's Story (1959); Man on a String (1960); A Fine Madness (1966); The Last Run (1971); The Cowboys (1972); MCQ (1974); Annie Hall (1977); The Third Walker (Can., 1978); Ice Castles (1978); When a Stranger Walks (1979); Final Assignment (Can., 1980); Tribute (Can., 1980); The Dead Zone (1983); The Boy Who Could Fly (1986); Obsessed (Can., 1988); 11/4/1988 (1989); Bed and Breakfast (1989); Termini Station (1991); Dying Young (1991). Appeared regularly on television, including as Inez in No Exit, *Cleopatra in* Antony and Cleopatra, *and as Medea; played a running part as* **Candice Bergen***'s mother on the series "Murphy Brown."*

The daughter of a professional hockey player and a Christian Science practitioner, Colleen Dewhurst had an early ambition to be a pilot. Criticized for her lack of academic seriousness, she dropped out of Downer College for Young Ladies and worked as a dental receptionist before enrolling in New York's Academy of Dramatic Arts, where she studied with Harold Clurman and Joseph Anthony. To support herself, she worked as a switchboard operator, an usher at Carnegie Hall, and an instructor at a reducing gym. She made her New York debut in 1946, while still an acting student, playing the role of Julia Cavendish in *The Royal Family.* In 1952, she had a small part in a production of Eugene O'Neill's *Desire Under the Elms,* in which she would later play the leading role of Abbie Putnam. Dewhurst did not appear on Broadway again until January 1956, when she played both a Turkish concubine and a virgin of Memphis in *Tamburlaine the Great.* That same year, she met Joseph Papp, founder and director of the New York Shakespeare Festival, and he cast her as Tamora in his production of *Titus Andronicus.* This was the beginning of a long association with Papp, who was probably most responsible for launching her career.

Dewhurst was a passionate actress, tall, robust, with a throaty voice and a laugh that Walter Kerr of *The New York Times* once described as "wolverine." She won Tony Awards for her roles of Mary Follett in *All the Way Home* (1960) and Josie Hogan in a revival of O'Neill's *A Moon for*

*W*OMEN IN *W*ORLD *H*ISTORY

Colleen
Dewhurst

the Misbegotten (1973), as well as several Obies for her off-Broadway performances. Throughout her career, Dewhurst was closely identified with the plays of O'Neill; she played Christine in his *Mourning Becomes Electra* and Mary Tyrone in *Long Day's Journey into Night.* "I love the O'Neill women," she told Rex Reed in an interview for *Conversations in the Raw.* "They move from the groin rather than the brain. To play O'Neill you have to be big. You can't sit around and play little moments of sadness or sweetness. You cannot phony up O'Neill."

She was equally well suited to Shakespearean roles, notably Kate in *Taming of the Shrew*, Lady Macbeth, Cleopatra, and Gertrude in *Hamlet*. Other outstanding performances were in Athol Fugard's *Hello and Goodbye* (for which her portrayal of the embittered prostitute Hester won her the 1969–70 Drama Desk award), Brecht's *The Good Woman of Setzuan* (1970), and Betti's *The Queen and the Rebels* (1982). As well, she played *Lillian Hellman in Bentley's *Are You Now or Have You Ever Been . . . ?* (1978). Dewhurst made sporadic appearances in films (which she referred to as "my famous cameos") as well as on television. She was seen in a recurring role on the situation comedy "Murphy Brown," for which she won one of her three Emmys. In one of her final New York appearances, she portrayed *Carlotta O'Neill, wife of Eugene O'Neill, in the one-woman play *My Gene* (1987).

In 1947, while studying acting, Dewhurst had married fellow student James Vickery. The marriage ended 12 years later, after which she was twice married and twice divorced from actor George C. Scott, with whom she often performed. Her two closest friends were actresses **Zoe Caldwell** and *Maureen Stapleton. Dewhurst was the president of the Actors' Equity Association from 1985 to 1991 and was active in a number of theater causes, including those that lent support to actors afflicted with AIDS. The actress died of cancer, at age 67, in 1991.

SUGGESTED READING:

Dewhurst, Colleen, with Tom Viola. *Colleen Dewhurst: Her Autobiography*. NY: Scribner, 1997.

Barbara Morgan,
Melrose, Massachusetts

de Wolfe, Elsie (1865–1950)

American interior decorator, known as the Founding Mother of Decorating. Name variations: Lady Mendl. Born in New York, New York, in 1865; died in Paris, France, on July 12, 1950; one of five children of Stephen de Wolfe (a doctor); attended Mrs. Macauley's School for Young Ladies, New York, and a finishing school in Scotland; lived with Elisabeth "Bessie" Marbury (a theatrical agent), from 1887 to 1926; married Sir Charles Mendl (a British embassy functionary), on March 10, 1926.

Elsie de Wolfe, known as the Founding Mother of Decorating, rescued interior design from the stuffy, dark Victorian period and remained its arbiter of style for 50 years. Espousing a philosophy of simplicity, suitability, and proportion, she turned the design world upside down with her innovations—cotton chintz, mirrors, trellises, painted furniture, and decoupage. De Wolfe was also a legendary character, a master of self-invention, and one of the first international celebrities. She dieted before it was fashionable, maintained a live-in relationship with a woman for 40 years, was a front-line nurse during World War I, married at 60, and, at 70, tinted her hair blue and entered a fancy dress ball by way of a cartwheel.

De Wolfe's remarkable life and career appeared to be driven by a deep-rooted insecurity. She was one of five children of an engaging but irresponsible New York doctor, whose risky business ventures relegated the family to the fringes of New York society. A precocious and difficult child, de Wolfe was also exceedingly plain, a fact that her parents and schoolmates would not let her forget. To compensate, she escaped into fantasies, dreaming about "beautiful objects, about pictures and houses," she later recalled. She was educated in New York and at a finishing school in Scotland where she lived for three years with her mother's cousin, the wife of a chaplain to Queen *Victoria's chaplains. Through this connection, de Wolfe was presented at court during the social season of 1885, an occasion that determined her future course. "If I am ugly, and I am," she remembered saying to herself, "I am going to make everything around me beautiful. That will be my life." To that end, she dressed in stylish well-cut clothes, kept herself immaculately groomed, and embarked on a stringent diet and exercise program that she continued throughout her life. She also aligned herself with the American beauty, **Cora Potter**, whose own place in London society assured de Wolfe an entrée to the beautiful people.

In 1886, de Wolfe returned to New York with Potter and began performing as a drawing-room actress, then an acceptable route into New York society. With the death of her father, however, and the pressing need to earn a living, she embarked on a 10-year professional acting career that, according to biographer **Jane S. Smith**, "was marked by neither talent nor favorable reviews but provided a good income, the possibility of summers in France, and the commissioning there of the clothes she wore on the stage." Despite her "wooden" acting and poor notices, de Wolfe gained a loyal following of women who flocked to her plays to see her Paris clothes. The first Saturday of an Elsie de

Wolfe play came to be known as the "dress-makers' matinee." During her early acting career, de Wolfe also met ❧▶ **Elisabeth Marbury**, a wealthy, unmarried eccentric of high social standing who eventually became a theatrical agent. The two women became longterm companions, a relationship that would endure for 40 years, until de Wolfe's sudden marriage to an English diplomat in 1926. Marbury's devotion to de Wolfe was unfailing, though de Wolfe maintained an emotional detachment characteristic of all her relationships.

In 1892, the two women purchased a run-down house on the corner of 17th Street and Irving Place in New York City, and it was there that de Wolfe first tried her hand at interior decorating. Stripping away the dwelling's Victorian accumulation of heavy paneled walls and somber rugs, she painted much of the house white and introduced French cane chairs, soft-toned fabrics, tile floors, transparent lampshades, and muslin curtains. The transformation was revolutionary at the time, and news of it sent ripples through the New York social scene, in which the women, dubbed "the Bachelors," had become quite prominent. De Wolfe had cards printed up announcing that she was available to decorate other people's houses, and there were a few immediate takers. Then in 1905, Marbury, who was on the founding board of the Colony Club, a prestigious retreat for the wives of New York's elite businessmen, helped secure de Wolfe a commission to decorate the interior of the Club's new building, designed by Stanford White. De Wolfe patterned her decoration on her memories of English country houses, using chintzes, wicker furniture, and, most startling of all, trellises. She dressed the room off the main drawing room in a dark green trellis, with a fountain, and trellised cornices and friezes, reminiscent of an 18th-century conservatory. The two-year project was a triumph and established de Wolfe in a new profession. Among the important clients of her early career was tycoon Henry Clay Frick, who hired her to decorate the private rooms of his new mansion on Fifth Avenue and paid her a healthy commission. In 1913, she published her first book, *The House in Good Taste,* a collection of how-to articles on interior decoration that were mostly ghostwritten by **Ruby Ross Goodnow**, who later became her first competitor.

While working on the renovations of the Colony Club, de Wolfe planned for the restoration of what would become her masterpiece and

❧▶ **Marbury, Elisabeth** (1856–1933)

American author's representative, producer, and theatrical manager. Name variations: Bessie. Born in New York City on June 19, 1856; died in New York on January 22, 1933; privately educated, mostly by her father; never married; lived with Elsie de Wolfe, 1887–1926.

Elisabeth Marbury was twice decorated by the French government for services rendered to French authors. Born in New York in 1856, she was educated by her father and often attended the theater. At age 29, she organized a charity benefit for a theatrical producer that raised $5,000 and prompted him to recommend that she pursue a career in the theater. In 1888, she co-produced *Little Lord Fauntleroy* on Broadway and began to manage the career of its author *Frances Hodgson Burnett*. In 1891, she became the English and American representative for the Société de Gens de Lettres, a French writers' organization, and began to handle the English-speaking rights for French playwright Victorien Sardou. She would also represent the American interests of Georges Feydeau, Edmond Rostand, Ludovic Halévy, George Bernard Shaw, James M. Barrie, Jerome K. Jerome, and many others. Her American clients included *Rachel Crothers* and Clyde Fitch. Marbury had offices in Paris, London, Berlin, and Madrid. By the turn of the century, she was attaining prominence in New York as a producer of plays and musical comedies, including *Love o' Mike* (1916) with music by Jerome Kern, and *See America First* (1916), with music by Cole Porter. She was responsible for the American careers of Vernon and *Irene Castle.*

Marbury's live-in relationship with American interior decorator *Elsie de Wolfe* began in 1887 and was to endure for 40 years. With *Anne Morgan* and *Florence J. Harriman*, Marbury founded the Colony Club, the first women's social club in New York, which was a prestigious retreat for the wives of New York's elite businessmen (de Wolfe was commissioned to decorate the Club's building). When World War I broke out, the energetic and influential Marbury gave valuable aid to the Allied cause and was made honorary president of the Women's National Committee of the American Defense Society. In 1919, she was decorated by the Belgian government with the medal of Queen Elizabeth, "in recognition of services she has rendered to Belgium since 1914." Marbury, a 200-pound, five-packs-a-day smoker, died in 1933. Her funeral was held at St. Patrick's Cathedral in Manhattan and was attended by, among others, the mayor of New York City and the governor of New York state.

SUGGESTED READING:
Marbury, Elisabeth. *My Crystal Ball.* 1923.

the passion of her life, the Villa Trianon at Versailles, the house in France Marbury had purchased for them in 1905. It was part of the great Versailles palace complex built during the reign of Louis XIV). **Nancy Richardson**, who wrote of the designer for *House & Garden* (April 1982),

viewed the Villa Trianon as the ultimate example of de Wolfe's contribution to the 20th century. It reflected "her love of the way Europeans lived and of 18th-century furniture, which [suited] her own modern taste for comfort, light, and a certain bareness." It also illustrated "her lighthearted treatment of period furniture (she painted it, *used* it, tweaked it with the freshness of cotton rather than silk), [and] her underlying restraint and flair."

During World War I, de Wolfe and Marbury turned Villa Trianon over to the Red Cross to be used as a hospital (thus assuring it would be saved). At Marbury's insistence, de Wolfe returned to her New York decorating business, but she could not forget the devastation she had seen on a tour of the Marne battlefield. In 1916, she returned to France, volunteering as a nurse in the Ambrine Mission outside Paris, where she endured the worst aspects of war while tending to the injured French and British soldiers. At one point, she returned to America and used her celebrity and influence to raise money for the purchase of ambulances. Toward the end of the war, she helped the Ambrine flee the approaching Germans. The French government, in a tribute to her service, awarded her the *Croix de Guerre* and later the Legion of Honor.

After the war, de Wolfe ended her relationship with Marbury and spent increasingly more time in Europe, where she partied in *Elsa Maxwell's circle and plied her decorating schemes among a new set of rich clients. Now in her 60s, she married British diplomat Charles Mendl, whom she had met at a party on the Riviera. Theirs was a marriage of convenience and companionship, which also considerably enhanced de Wolfe's social contacts. Constantly seeking new decorating challenges, in 1931 she bought an apartment in Paris (once the home of Prince Roland de Bourbon) and created what she considered to be the perfect bathroom salon; this was described by biographers **Nina Campbell** and **Caroline Seebohm** as "a triumph of elegance and comfort, with fireplace, mirrored friezes, a divan upholstered in bold zebra skin, a tub surrounded with all-mirrored columns, taps in the shape of swans' heads, hooks in the form of dolphins, light fixtures gleaming the luster of oyster shells and mother-of-pearl." De Wolfe, perched on her zebra-skin sofa, often entertained visitors in the elegant salon de bain.

As the Depression took hold and deepened, de Wolfe's client pool began to dry up. In 1937, when her New York business declared bankruptcy, she was set loose into what Campbell and Seebohm have called "a kind of glittering limbo." Now 72, she invented herself anew with a face lift, blue-dyed hair, and an ever more strenuous regimen designed to stave off the rav-

ages of time. Her parties grew more costly and exotic. A circus ball in 1938 included animals, jugglers, acrobats, three orchestras, and a Hawaiian guitarist strumming from a boat in the swimming pool. When World War II interrupted the festivities of her life, de Wolfe took refuge in California, purchasing what was said to be the ugliest house in Hollywood and transforming it into a showplace. For the four years she resided there, the parties continued, attended now by movie stars, writers, musicians, and a growing list of male protégés, including James Amster, who later became a well-known New York decorator, and designer Tony Duquette, who became president of the Elsie de Wolfe Foundation after her death.

> *I* can't paint, I can't write, I can't sing. But I can decorate and run a house, and light it, and heat it, and have it like a living thing and so right that it will be the envy of the world, the standard of perfect hospitality.
>
> —Elsie de Wolfe

At the age of 81, crippled by arthritis and hardly able to walk, de Wolfe returned to France and undertook the daunting task of restoring her beloved Villa Trianon, which had not weathered well the effects of the Nazi officers who had inhabited the villa during the occupation. Restored to its prewar glory in spite of shortages of materials and artisans, the villa was the scene of a few more parties, although de Wolfe was beginning to fade. "There she was in a small wheelchair by the pool," recalled Jean-Louis Faucigny-Lucinge, "looking terribly pathetic . . . in great pain . . . surrounded by her dogs, very made-up, still, and determined not to give in." De Wolfe finally released her tenuous hold on life on July 12, 1950. By her request, there was no funeral. She bequeathed the bulk of her estate to her stalwart maid and companion **Hilda West**, with the remainder going to her foundation, established to provide scholarships for young designers and to carry on her charities. The Villa Trianon was left to her friend and neighbor Paul-Louis Weiller, who in 1981 put the contents of the house up for sale.

Elsie de Wolfe's innovations and personality continue to influence decorating and decorators to this day. Designer Albert Hadley recalled that de Wolfe's doctrine of suitability, style, and taste was an integral part of his training at the prestigious Parsons School of Design. "Lots of people were as talented as she was," he said, "but she was the first, she had endured and was the best known."

SOURCES:
Campbell, Nina, and Caroline Seebohm. *Elsie de Wolfe: A Decorative Life*. NY: Panache Press, 1992.
Richardson, Nancy. "Elsie de Wolfe," in *House & Garden*. April 1982, pp. 126–132, 197–199.

Barbara Morgan,
Melrose, Massachusetts

Dewson, Molly (1874–1962)

American politician, economist, and first prominent organizer of women voters for the Democratic Party. *Name variations: Mary Williams Dewson. Born Mary Williams Dewson in Quincy, Massachusetts, on February 18, 1874; died in Castine, Maine, on October 22, 1962; attended Miss Ireland's School; graduated from Wellesley College, 1897; lived with* **Mary G. Porter**.

After serving six years, from 1925 to 1931, as president of the Consumers' League of New York, Molly Dewson was urged by *Eleanor Roosevelt to organize the women in the Democratic Party as a viable force. Dewson had taken part in Franklin Roosevelt's New York gubernatorial campaign in 1930. By 1936, Dewson was vice-chair of the Democratic National Committee, actively lobbying President Roosevelt to appoint more women to Cabinet posts. One result was the appointment of *Frances Perkins as secretary of labor. Dewson also served on the President's Advisory Committee on Economic Security, involved in planning the Social Security system. She was the first woman to serve on the Social Security Board.

Dexter, Caroline (1819–1884)

Australian feminist. *Name variations: Caroline Lynch. Born in Nottingham, England, in 1819; died in 1884; daughter of a jeweller; educated in England and Paris, France; married William Dexter (a painter), in 1843 (died 1860); married William Lynch (a lawyer).*

Caroline Dexter was born in Nottingham, England, in 1819. In 1855, age 36, she sailed for Australia to join her husband, painter William Dexter, who had immigrated there three years previous. The couple founded an art school, but when it failed they moved to Gippsland. There, Caroline wrote *Ladies' Almanack: The Southern Cross or Australian Album and New Year's Gift* (1857), a book sympathetic to aboriginal culture which chronicled life in Australia.

Dexter left her husband and moved to Melbourne where she campaigned for dress reform and started the Institute of Hygiene. In 1861, she joined with *Harriet Clisby to found the *Interpreter*, a radical feminist journal. When her husband died in 1860, Dexter married a prosperous lawyer William Lynch and became a patron of artists and writers.

Dhabba the Cahina.

See Kahina.

d'Hericourt, Jenny Poinsard (1809–1875).

See Hericourt, Jenny Poinsard d'.

Dhouda or Dhoudha (fl. 820–841).

See Dhuoda of Septimania.

Dhuoda of Septimania (fl. 820–843)

Frankish noblewoman and writer. *Name variations: Dodane; Dhouda; Dhoudha. Flourished between 820 and 841; married Bernard, count of Septimania, around 824; children: two sons, including William (b. 826).*

A Frankish noblewoman, Dhuoda is one of the very earliest medieval women writers known. She married Count Bernard of Septimania (in southern France) in 824 and gave birth to a son William in 826. Soon after William's birth, Bernard sent Dhuoda and her child to a castle in a remote part of his province; his reasons for this separation are unknown. When William was a small boy, his father sent him to the court of King Charles I the Bald as a pledge of Bernard's loyalty to the monarch. Around 840, Bernard returned to Dhuoda briefly, and she gave birth to another son in 841. Again, this child was taken from her by Bernard for political purposes, and it is doubtful Dhuoda ever saw either son again. Despite her husband's callous treatment, Dhuoda remained a faithful wife and dedicated herself to preserving Bernard's estates for him, perhaps more for the future benefit of her sons than for Bernard. Apparently her husband had no administrative skills and spent money freely, and it was to her credit that he retained such a large province to bequeath to William.

Dhuoda's life, as she recorded, was one of loneliness and grief. To help ease her mind after her sons were taken from her, she composed a manual of instruction for her eldest son, now about 15, living at the king's court. She understood the temptations William would face at the splendid royal court, but believed she could aid him in making the right life choices, even if she could not see him. Written between 841 and 843, the work, called the *Manual of Dhuoda*, is the only source of information available on her life. It detailed two behavior codes she wanted him to follow. First and most important, she wanted her son to always be a good Christian and serve God constantly in word and deed. Secondly, she wanted him to know proper behavior for a noble; to this end, she urged him to respect and show gentleness to others, even if they were below his rank, and to give generously to charitable causes.

Dhuoda justified her authority for such a work from her position as a mother, writing that, even though she was a sinful and unworthy woman, she was still his only mother and he needed to heed her admonitions. The work also clearly shows an affectionate mother who was genuinely concerned about her son's welfare, and it is these moments that make the manual a touching document. At the end, Dhuoda included a short poem she had composed and wished to have engraved on her tomb.

As a book by a lay woman, the *Manual of Dhuoda* stands alone in the literature of 9th-century Europe; it gives the impression of a sad, lonely woman who refuses to be embittered by the trials she has faced and who trusts in God to reward her for her suffering. Unfortunately, her manual could not serve William for long; he joined a rebellion against the king in 849, five years after his father's execution for treason, and was executed.

SOURCES:

Amt, Emilie. *Women's Lives in Medieval Europe.* NY: Routledge, 1993.

LaBarge, Margaret W. *Women in Medieval Life.* London: Hamish Hamilton, 1986.

Laura York,
Riverside, California

Diana.

Variant of Diane.

Diana (1961–1997)

Princess of Wales who was a beloved international celebrity and one of the world's most charitable benefactors. Name variations: Lady Diana Spencer. Born Diana Frances Spencer on July 1, 1961, at Park House, the family's country home on the grounds of the royal estate at Sandringham in Norfolk, England; died, age 36, in Paris, France, in an automobile accident on August 31, 1997; interred at Althorp, Northamptonshire, on September 6, 1997; third of four children of Edward John VIII Spencer (b. 1924), viscount Althorp, and Frances Burke Ruth Roche (Fermoy) Spencer, viscountess Althorp, later known as Frances Shand Kydd; married Charles Philip Arthur

George Windsor (b. 1948), prince of Wales, July 29, 1981; children: William Arthur (b. 1982); Henry Charles (b. 1984).

After completing education in private schools, took a job as an assistant in a London kindergarten; married Charles, prince of Wales, royal family's oldest son (July 29, 1981), followed by the birth of two royal sons, Princes William and Harry, during the next decade; heard divorce announced in House of Commons (August 1996); began dating film producer and financier Dodi al-Fayed; was with al-Fayed in Paris at the time of the car crash that claimed both their lives (August 1997).

To speak of Lady Diana Spencer is to speak in contradictions. Although she was one of the world's most glamorous and aristocratic women, born to privilege and raised in wealth, the public perceived her as one of their own, as "the people's Princess" who bridged the gap between Britain's commoners and an aloof, cold monarchy. She embraced charitable causes, aiding the poor and diseased, yet reveled in designer gowns and expensive jewelry. She was seen as a beaming member of the international jet-set, yet she suffered from debilitating depression. And while she excoriated the reporters and photographers who hounded her relentlessly, she at the same time found ingenious ways to manipulate the image of her that they presented to the world. Now, her sanctification by a tragic death has left the world with only these fragmented glimpses, as blurred as the invasive tabloid photographs she loathed. Four years before her death, Diana pleaded with her public to "find it in your hearts to give me time and space," but there would not be enough of either.

In her death as in her life, Diana straddled the world where fairy tales come true and the world where babies die of AIDS; she was The Princess, and she was of the people, and she was gone.

—Sharon Begley and Christopher Dickey, *Newsweek*

Thirty years before, the need for such an impassioned statement would have seemed ludicrous, for she had been known in her childhood as a quiet, shy, rather serious-minded girl. The Honorable Diana Frances Spencer was born on July 1, 1961, the third of four children of the Viscount and Viscountess Althorp, otherwise known as John and Frances Spencer. Like her older siblings, Diana was born at Park House, the family's country home on the grounds of the royal estate at Sandringham in Norfolk. The Spencers had been enjoying royal favor since the early 16th century, when an enterprising ancestor had so successfully built his sheep farm into a linchpin of the immensely profitable British wool trade that a hereditary earldom had eventually been bestowed on the family. Diana's paternal lineage was a bewildering array of links to the throne from Charles II onward, mostly through a byzantine collection of royal mistresses and their illegitimate offspring. In later years, in fact, it would be noted that Diana carried more royal blood in her veins than her husband. Her mother, Lady Frances Fermoy (later **Frances Shand Kydd**), was the granddaughter of a willful American girl (**Frances Ellen Work**) who had, in the late 19th century, defied her jingoistic father by marrying a British noble, leading to much discussion among royal genealogists about Diana's own well-publicized stubborn streak and their determined attempts to relate her, however distantly, to famous Americans ranging from George Washington to *Gloria Vanderbilt.

Sir John and Lady Frances had been expecting, indeed praying for, a boy as their third child. Daughters ✥ **Sarah Spencer** and ✥ **Jane Spencer** had been born in 1955 and 1957, respectively, leaving Johnnie Spencer desperate for a male heir to inherit the title and keep its attendant riches out of the hands of relatives. The couple's joy at the birth of a boy in 1960 was dashed when the infant died just ten days later. Diana arrived the following year to barely disguised disappointment. "I was the girl who was supposed to be a boy," she once drily noted. The hoped-for male heir, Charles Spencer, finally arrived in 1964.

Having produced the required male after five childbirths in ten years, Lady Frances and her husband considered themselves relieved of further childbearing duties and turned their attention to a number of discreet extramarital affairs that led to a trial separation in 1966. Lady Frances' affair with Peter Shand Kydd, a wealthy wallpaper manufacturer, was by then well-known, as was Kydd's intention to leave his wife and three children to marry Frances. With Sarah and Jane in boarding school, Diana and her younger brother went to live with their mother in London's elegant, leafy Belgravia. Kydd's ensuing divorce, in which Frances was named by Kydd's wife as an adulteress, was followed by similar proceedings initiated by John Spencer against Frances. London society was electrified when Frances' mother, Lady **Ruth Fermoy**, testified in court against her own daughter and urged that her son-in-law be given custody of the children, the elder woman apparently of the opinion that the children's chances of good marriages were more favorable as Spencers than as Kydds. Among her set, Frances Kydd became known as "the bolter," although she would herself be abandoned by Kydd in later years. Diana's fractured home life as a child would later be cited as a factor in her adult struggles with depression. "Her childhood was hell," Diana's friend Peter Jensen once said. "Her parents despised each other. She grew up under that."

Five-year-old Diana weathered these domestic storms only to find herself back with her father in Norfolk with a succession of nannies and a suddenly empty house, bereft of the laughter and activity that had marked her earlier years in a two-parent household. Photographs of her at this period are of a rather somber, blonde-haired, rosy-cheeked country girl in corduroys and Wellies, keeping company with a procession of family pets against a background of ancient stone and mellowed brick. At the age of six, Diana was sent to Riddlesworth Hall, to which Spencer girls for generations had been packed off to begin their formal education. She was a mediocre student, but she excelled at team sports and was so well liked by the other girls that she was awarded a special school prize for helpfulness in her second year. She managed to do well enough at her schoolwork to advance in 1973 to West Heath School in Kent. It was at West Heath that she formed the friendships that

✥ **Spencer, Sarah** (1955—)

British royal. Name variations: Sarah McCorquodale; Lady Sarah Spencer. Born Elizabeth Sarah, Lady Spencer, in 1955; daughter of Edward John VIII Spencer (b. 1924), viscount Althorp, and Frances Burke Ruth Roche (Fermoy) Spencer, viscountess Althorp, later known as Frances Shand Kydd; married Neil Edward McCorquodale, in May 1980.

✥ **Spencer, Jane** (1957—)

British royal. Name variations: Jane Fellowes; Lady Jane Spencer. Born Cynthia Jane Spencer in 1957; daughter of Edward John VIII Spencer (b. 1924), viscount Althorp, and Frances Burke Ruth Roche (Fermoy) Spencer, viscountess Althorp, later known as Frances Shand Kydd; married Sir Robert Fellowes (the Queen's private secretary), in March 1978; children: Laura Jane Fellowes (b. 1980).

would last the rest of her life, while again winning a school service award. But she failed to pass four of her five "O level" tests, equivalent to American SATs, and ended her formal education with her graduation from West Heath in 1977, when she was 16.

By now she was Lady Diana Spencer, by virtue of the death of her paternal grandfather and her father's inheritance of the ancestral title of Earl Spencer. The change in status also required leaving the family's beloved Park House to take possession of the ancient Spencer family seat, Althorp, a sprawling country house set in a 600-acre park on a 13,000-acre estate north of London, near the village of Great Brington. Diana's memories of Althorp (perversely pronounced by the British as "ALL-trup") were not fond ones. Not long after the family's arrival there, her father was named as an adulterer in a divorce proceeding filed by Lord Dartmouth. The ex-countess of Dartmouth was **Raine Cartland**, the daughter of British romance novelist *Barbara Cartland whose books were among Diana's favorite reading as a young woman. Barbara Cartland was now Diana's stepgrandmother. None of the Spencer children attended their father's marriage to Raine in a quiet civil ceremony in London in July of 1976, for the simple reason that none of them were told about it. Further trouble ensued when Raine set about redecorating Althorp with money raised by selling off many of its renowned artistic treasures and by imposing strict rules of the house on Diana and young Charles (Sarah and Jane were now living in London on their own). "Raine stopped play" became one of Diana's favorite quips, but the strained relations seemed to go far beyond the usual ones between stepmother and daughter. Raine constantly criticized her husband's daughters, claiming that Jane was "only good for producing children" and that Sarah was "okay as long as she sticks to hunting and shooting, which is all she cares about." As for Diana, Raine said, "How can you have a single conversation with someone who doesn't have a single 'O' level? It's a crashing bore." Not surprisingly, Diana began to spend less time at Althorp and more in London, where she stayed with her mother and her other stepparent.

There were skiing vacations to Gstaad, a full schedule of balls and teas during the social season, and occasional visits to Althorp for weekend parties. At one of them, a shooting party in November of 1977 arranged by her sister Sarah, Diana first met the man who was the world's most eligible bachelor. It was Sarah, however, who was then attracting attention as a possible bride for Prince Charles, although the relationship would not advance beyond a brief infatuation. As generations of Spencers before them had done, Diana's family entertained visions of royal in-laws and made sure to include during that weekend a more intimate dance party at Althorp in the prince's honor that would provide further exposure to their daughters. "I remember thinking what fun she was," Charles later said of his first meeting with Diana, although the two would not see each other again for some time.

Despite these lofty social duties, Diana had to attend to practical matters as well, since her Spencer inheritance was many years away and a small allowance was her only support. There were, accordingly, several jobs minding the children of friends and acquaintances, followed by a ten-week cooking course that led to a position with a catering firm, where she prepared meals and served cocktails at private parties. A position at a dance school teaching ballet to children came next. By the time she was hired as a supervisor at the Young England kindergarten in Pimlico in southwest London, Diana had used the proceeds of an inheritance from the will of her American great-grandmother to rent a three-bedroom flat near fashionable Knightsbridge. She and two friends from West Heath with whom she shared the apartment each contributed about $34 a week toward the rent, becoming members in good standing of the collection of young aristocrats then called "Sloane's Rangers," after the central square in Knightsbridge surrounded by many of their favorite watering holes.

Along with her peers and most of the rest of England, Diana followed with interest the procession of what the press called "Charlie's Angels," the line of young women seen in Prince Charles' company who were publicly scrutinized in turn as potential princesses. Royal enthusiasts worried that Charles, in his early 30s when Diana moved to Knightsbridge, had waited the longest of any royal heir to take a wife, although the number of young women with whom he had been dallying over the years was impressive. "He's supposed to be an incurable romantic, although a late starter," one palace observer noted. "It wasn't until University that the interest in women took hold." Charles apparently compensated for his tardiness with such dispatch that the media quickly lost interest in his younger brother, Prince Andrew, who had been dubbed "Randy Andy" in the tabloids. Among Charles' paramours during the 1970s, besides Sarah Spencer, was actress **Susan George**, followed by the lead singer of a pop group called "The Three Degrees" and, more suitably from the Palace's standpoint, several titled women of good family. The press had been particularly fascinated with **Anna Wallace**, the daughter of a wealthy Scottish landowner whose sharp temper and stinging rebukes earned her their sobriquet of "Whiplash Wallace," but the relationship ended when Charles pointedly ignored her at a royal ball to spend much of the evening dancing with *Camilla Parker-Bowles, whom he had known for some years.

But by the late 1970s, careful observers began to notice that one name had been appearing consistently on the lists of Charles' invited guests to various functions. Diana was at Sandringham twice for royal shooting parties in 1979 and 1980, at Balmoral during the summers of those years, and was among the royal party invited to watch when Charles took to the polo field with his team, Les Diables Bleus. It was during this polo weekend in July of 1980 that Diana found herself sitting on a bale of hay at a lawn party following the game, chatting with the heir to the English throne. She later recalled for journalist Andrew Morton that she had told Charles how much she remembered and sympathized with the loss of his beloved "Uncle Dickie," Lord Louis Mountbatten, who had been killed by an IRA bomb the previous year. Charles, she said, had seemed moved by her compassion and responded by spending much of the rest of the afternoon in her company.

By the time of the pinnacle of the British summer social season, the Goodwood House Ball, marking the end of the Goodwood Races, even casual observers could not help but notice how much time Charles spent on the dance floor with Diana Spencer; or that she was again among his intimates aboard the royal yacht *Britannia* during the annual Cowes Week of yacht racing just a month later. When Charles and Diana were photographed at Balmoral in August of 1980 fishing together without a chaperon, the press was off and running.

"He's in love again!" trumpeted *The Sun*, while armies of photographers set up camp outside Diana's Knightsbridge flat or followed her red Mini Metro through snarls of London traffic. She once agreed to be photographed outside the Young England kindergarten on the hopeless promise she would then be left alone, only to find herself splashed across the pages of the world's newspapers with a strong sun shining from behind and through her thin summer dress, her shapely legs becoming the subject of earnest discussions in pubs across the land. "I cried like a baby to the four walls," Diana told journalist Morton 11 years later. "I just couldn't cope with it." The public attention was so intense by late 1980 that Diana's mother was obliged to write a letter to *The Times* asking Fleet Street's editors "whether, in the execution of their jobs, they consider it necessary or fair to harass my daughter daily, from dawn until well after dusk?"

Even with the constant snooping, the world did not immediately know of Charles' proposal of marriage to Lady Diana Spencer on February 6, 1981, offered in the nursery of Windsor Castle. Charles said that he had missed her terribly during a skiing vacation to Switzerland and then asked her, simply and plainly, to marry him. She later confessed to being overcome with a giggling fit before her suitor's earnest reminder that she might one day be queen of England brought home the enormous consequences of her answer. She said yes. Charles relayed the news of Diana's acceptance to his mother *Elizabeth II, then at Sandringham, only moments afterward; Diana's family was told the following day. "She looked as happy as I have ever seen her look," Diana's brother Charles remarked. "It wasn't the look of somebody who had just won the jackpot, but somebody who looked spiritually fulfilled as well." Diana's grandmother, Lady Ruth Fermoy, later denied reports that she had promoted the match, claiming she had, in fact, advised against it by telling her granddaughter that the difference in lifestyle would be too difficult an adjustment.

It was not until Diana had left England for an Australian vacation that the announcement was made public, on February 24, with the marriage scheduled for that summer. Charles was 33; Diana just 19 when the world learned of her engagement. The age difference was only one of the striking contrasts between them. Despite the string of women that preceded Diana, the prince of Wales was a rather introspective man, fond of architecture and painting, ruled by a rigid code of conduct instilled in him since childhood that had effectively shielded him from the public he was raised to serve. Diana, on the other hand, was still a free-spirited young woman much more immersed in the real world than her fiancé but nonetheless prone to the dreams and fantasies of youth. While Diana had fallen in love with her Prince Charming, Charles looked at the matter with the circumspection of his upbringing and his greater years. "Essentially, you must be good friends," he had once answered a reporter's question about the nature of marriage, "and love, I'm sure, will grow out of that friendship." Also unlike Charles, Diana's experience of the opposite sex was limited to the occasional date and a chaste kiss on the cheek, while Charles had frankly admitted to her his past liaisons, some with married women whom, he is said to have told her, were "safer" because they had husbands and families to protect and would remain silent. Then, too, there was the media exposure which, to Charles, had long been a fact of life but that, to Diana, was disturbing enough to have provoked her mother's indignant letter to the *Times*. It was merely a hint of what would become of Diana's privacy as a member of the royal family.

Diana's translation to the rarified atmosphere of the monarchy began at once. The red Mini Metro disappeared and was replaced by a chauffeured Rolls Royce from Buckingham Palace; Diana was required to officially adopt Clarence House, the traditional royal holding pen for future princesses, as her residence (although she still spent most nights in her own flat). She embarked on weeks-long courses in royal protocol and etiquette, including everything from where and how to sit during public appearances by the royal family, to the carriage of one's head and posture during public appearances and the proper method of waving to one's public from balconies or the back seats of limousines. The indoctrination into royal house rules was in addition, of course, to the preparations for the wedding itself, set for July 29.

Much time and discussion was focused on the design and manufacture of Diana's gown, which was made by hand by just one seamstress. It was, naturally, of English silk, featured pearl embroidery and mother-of-pearl sequins, lavishly ruffled sleeves, and a V-neck over a frilly laced bodice, all surmounted by a diamond tiara that was a Spencer family heirloom. The gown, which was immediately copied by the score for less exalted weddings, was ivory-colored rather than white to cut down on glare reflected to television cameras. But its most dramatic feature was its 25-foot train, the longest of any royal bridal gown in English history, requiring a small army of attendants moving in near-military precision for her merely to take a step, to say nothing of the even more formidable task of descending from the bridal carriage. Diana spent hours practicing her "wedding walk" up and down the cavernous ballroom of St. James's Palace with pounds of paper tissue attached to her head. There were endless alterations and modifications to the gown as the weeks passed, many because of considerable variations in Diana's weight as the pressures mounted.

Charles, meanwhile, with his much plainer wardrobe consisting merely of his royal naval uniform, had plenty of time to plan the first wedding of a prince of Wales since 1863, when Victoria's son, the future Edward VII, had married *Alexandra of Denmark. Details of that earlier occasion were closely studied, including the royal naval cadets' uniforms which were resurrected for Diana's two pageboys. Unlike the earlier wedding, however, which had taken place in the usual site for royal rites of passage, Westminster Abbey, Charles had chosen St. Paul's after deciding that its acoustics were more suited to the music of English composers like Purcell, Elgar, and Sir William Walton which would grace the ceremony. Three orchestras of which he was the royal patron would perform, while a choir of which he was president would be joined by opera diva **Kiri Te Kanawa** for the vocal segments of the program.

During the late winter and early spring of 1981, some 2,600 coveted invitations issued from the Lord Chamberlain's office while Charles and Diana were relentlessly photographed and interviewed, together and separately. Charles recalled for the press how he had thought Diana "a very jolly, amusing and attractive girl, great fun, bouncy and full of life" at their first meeting five years earlier. Diana related how her future husband had been "a tower of strength" in coping with the attention focused on her and how she looked forward to her new status as a way to improve herself as an individual by serving her nation. "As I'm only 20," she said, "I've got a good start." The only crack in Diana's shy, winsome demeanor that the public was to see came the weekend before the wedding, as Diana watched Charles play polo. She suddenly burst into tears, Charles rushing off the field to offer comfort and guide her to a waiting limousine.

The display was chalked up to pre-wedding nerves, neither the public nor the press knowing the details of Diana's harried, lonely life as a royal fiancee. Charles' constant round of royal appearances kept him away from his bride-to-be for most of the four months of their engagement, and Diana angrily claimed a dozen years later that on the few occasions when they were required to appear together, Charles criticized her clothes and made light of her discomfort at the loss of the privacy she had once cherished. It was during the engagement, Diana said, that the eating disorder known as bulimia began to plague her, marked by periods of deliberate, often secretive overeating followed by guilt-ridden bouts of purging and self-starvation. Although the cause of the disorder often lies in childhoods troubled by fractured domestic environments, it is exacerbated by the stresses of adult life. In Diana's case, the stresses of life as a public icon rather than a human being were disastrous.

In addition to these sorts of pressures, she later related, there was the package she discovered, just a week before the wedding, in the office at Buckingham Palace which she shared with several of Prince Charles' aides and secretaries. Diana insisted on opening it even though it was not addressed to her. It contained a gold bracelet with a blue enameled disk bearing the letters "F" and "G" intertwined. Diana needed no explanation, for it was common knowledge among royal intimates that "Fred" and "Gladys" were the nicknames Charles and Camilla Parker-Bowles had given each other and that their relationship had not ended with Charles' engagement, despite Diana's expectations.

Charles had been smitten with the former Camilla Shand since he had first met her in 1972, when his polo team mate Andrew Parker-Bowles was courting her. She was outgoing, buoyant, attractive, and shared Charles' passion for the pursuits of the country aristocracy. (Her great-grandmother, *Alice Keppel, had been the mistress of Edward VII.) Camilla had already married by the time Charles realized the depth of his feeling for her, but their friendship—and, some whispered, their adultery once Camilla had wed—continued unabated. Camilla's house, Middlewich, was only 12 miles from the prince's Highgrove, in Gloucestershire, and every reporter worth a tabloid salary knew the unmarked car that Charles used to pop over for a visit. "There were three of us in this marriage," was Diana's much-quoted assessment of the situation after it had all ended in a heap of accusations and innuendo. In those later years of bitterness, Diana even claimed she had seriously considered canceling the wedding, although it is hard to believe that she actually thought she could turn the prince of Wales into a jilted bridegroom by simply walking away a few days before a ceremony that bore the weight of centuries of national tradition. And it is hard to square Diana's angry rebukes in light of the note Charles sent to her the night before the wedding, enclosed with a signet ring engraved with his royal symbol. "I'm so proud of you and when you come up I'll be there at the altar for you tomorrow," he wrote to her. "Just look 'em in the eye and knock 'em dead."

She did just that on the morning of July 29, 1981, as she stepped Cinderella-like from the glass coach that had carried her and her father from Clarence House to St. Paul's; walked regally beside Earl Spencer for the three-and-a-half minutes it took to negotiate the aisle toward her waiting prince (although it was Diana who supported her father, much weakened by a stroke but insistent on taking her to the altar); and curtsied gracefully to the queen. She then turned to the archbishop of Canterbury to be transformed from Diana Spencer into Her Royal Highness, the princess of Wales. Seven hundred and fifty million people in 70 countries watched a ceremony that hardly seemed real, one that confirmed the future of a centuries-old institution that had lost much of its practical use but none of its capacity to enchant with the gleam of a fantasy world. "I was calm, deathly calm," Diana recalled to a friend a dozen years later, when the gleam had long been dulled. "I felt I was the lamb to the slaughter. I knew it, and I couldn't do anything about it."

Any hopes she might have held for a quiet honeymoon, first at the Mountbatten estate in Hampshire, Broadlands, and then during a Mediterranean cruise on the royal yacht, proved false. Even at sea, where it was more difficult for the media to follow, the couple was surrounded by the 200 officers and crew of the *Britannia* and were rarely alone together. When a few private moments were granted them, Charles preferred reading passages aloud to her from his favorite books and resisted Diana's persuasions to tell her more about himself. The couple joined the royal family at Balmoral on their return to England, the expectation being that Diana would now assume a less prominent role in the life of the monarchy and dedicate herself to producing an heir. No one, not even Diana, expected that the public would become so besotted with their fairy-tale princess.

Hardly a day passed without a photograph of "Shy Di" gracing the tabloids. Anything would do—a glimpse through an unguarded window, a wave while emerging from a palace limousine, a peep from a phalanx of security guards. The British public had never had a princess like this one, an attractive young woman who, if not exactly from a background like theirs, at least seemed at home in their world. It was as if she were their eyes and ears on the monarchy, who might one day report to them what those remote, untouchable demi-gods were up to in their palaces, yachts and private jets. Diana could have told them that except for their adulation and the stir she caused wherever she went, most of her royal life was, frankly, boring. Charles, when not traveling on his constant round of royal duties, spent his leisure time surrounded by cronies and courtiers with whom she had little in common. Indeed, she was by far the youngest member of the royal entourage. Even the queen, it was said, had come to recognize her new daughter-in-law's loneliness and had suggested that Diana invite some of her friends for overnight and weekend stays at the Palace.

Soon, Diana began to turn her energies to the charity work for which she would be most admired. She began with the usual royal patronage of hospitals, pensioners homes and, especially, children's charities, but it was to Diana's great credit that she turned, too, to causes that the Crown had so far passed over. She added drug addiction, mental illness, and childhood abuse to her growing list. She became the first member of the royal household to visit the psychiatric ward at Broadmoor prison, where some of the country's most violent and psychotic criminals were held. Most famously, she became the royal patron of several AIDS charities and made sure she was photographed touching and hugging AIDS victims at a time when most of the public feared to do so. "Anywhere I see suffering," she once said, "that is where I want to be, doing what I can." She often pointed out that the prince's official motto, *Ich Dien*, meant "I serve."

In late October of 1981, Diana appeared with Charles on a tour of Wales, highlighted by her first public speech, in Cardiff, which she delivered partly in Welsh. She then returned to London for the announcement from Buckingham Palace on November 5 that she was pregnant. Her first pregnancy was a difficult one, for more than the usual physical reasons since, as the months wore on, Diana was finding the expectations placed on her increasingly troublesome. Even to her closest friends, she was no longer "Di" or even the nickname she had borne since childhood, "Duch," but "Your Royal Highness" or "ma'am." Women she had gone to school with and with whom she had giggled her way through pajama parties were now required to curtsey to her, while a simple shopping trip involved at least 20 security guards, an ambulance in waiting in case of emergency, and the usual bevy of strident reporters. Worse, her Prince Charming was proving ever more distant, more impatient with her attempts for emotional intimacy and, it seemed, more fond of spending time with his bookish friends or with the women who had been his confidantes before his marriage—notably Camilla, who was a frequent visitor to Highgrove when Diana chose to remain in London and even served as host at Charles' parties there when Diana was not present. By spring of 1982, the royal couple were rarely seen in public in each other's company. What was not known outside the royal family was Diana's desperate reactions to her loneliness, cries for help from a young woman barely out of her teens. In addition to bulimic episodes that grew more and more frequent, Diana slashed her wrists on at least two occasions, and threw herself down a flight of stairs at Kensington Palace, although doctors determined that her baby had not been hurt. These incidents were quickly cloaked in the deepest royal security. All that became publicly known was that on June 21, 1982, England was given a new heir for the line of succession, named Prince William.

As that year wore on, however, the watchful press began to suspect that all was not well. The scarcity of joint public appearances, once attributed to Diana's pregnancy, now became intriguing portents of domestic turmoil. Much was made of Diana's appearance 15 minutes late in the royal box at a memorial concert for Britain's war dead in November of 1982—an unprecedented and shocking breach in etiquette that brought Charles' obvious displeasure. (Charles had insisted she attend; Diana had insisted on staying home with her baby, then had changed her mind at the last minute after everyone else had left for the event.) Careful observers also noticed two other breaches of protocol—first, the announcement that Prince William was not being raised by a nanny but by Diana personally, a sharp departure from tradition; second, that the child would accompany his parents on a tour of Commonwealth nations in the Pacific, rather than being left at home. Both were against the queen's express wishes. Even more disturbing, the family would actually travel on the same plane together, risking the loss of two heirs to the throne if disaster struck during the journey. Although the tour went well and Charles and Diana seemed happy in each other's company, these oddities were much pondered. Further departures from the usual followed. The changes in Charles' wardrobe, for example, were much discussed, it being noticed that the prince's tailoring became much more natty as the months passed, his choice of ties more colorful and, some sniffed, more flamboyant. Then there were Charles' appearances, in Diana's company, at rock concerts, particularly at performances by INXS, the princess' favorite.

Suspicions were temporarily put to rest with the news of Diana's second pregnancy. The announcement was made on February 14, 1984; on September 15, Prince Henry Charles Albert David, quickly and more conveniently referred to as Prince Harry, was born. Fleet Street happily quipped that Diana had now produced "an heir and a spare," although Diana's comment in private to Charles that "I'm not a production line, you know" was not reported. After the birth of her second son, Diana appeared increasingly drawn and thin, while much was made of her behavior during a state visit to Vancouver to open Expo '86, where she spoke sharply to reporters and later collapsed and fainted into

Charles' arms. "Even the Prince cannot paper over all the cracks that have begun to appear in his wife's persona," noted the *Daily Mail,* recalling Diana's undisguised irritation just a few weeks earlier in Vienna, when the wife of that city's mayor had playfully flirted with Charles during a state dinner.

Buckingham Palace began to sense a looming public relations disaster when Diana's friendship with *Sarah Ferguson, the ebullient and outspoken daughter of the manager of Charles' polo team, began to attract attention. "Fergie," as the press quickly dubbed her, was a member in good standing of a group of bored youngbloods who frequented night clubs of dubious reputation and occasionally got themselves into the papers for behavior the Palace considered unsuitable to the company kept by a royal princess. Even more alarming, Fergie's engagement to Andrew, Charles' younger brother and the duke of York, was announced in late 1985, after Diana had invited Fergie to the Royal Ascot during the summer and introduced them. With the marriage of Prince Andrew to his new duchess, the Palace now had two renegades on its hands. The British press obligingly produced its usual pungent sobriquet by referring to the two women as the "Throne Rangers," but the Palace was not amused. An annoyed Charles, in another unusual breach of etiquette, was heard to mutter "Come on, come on" to his wife and sister-in-law when the two clowned and giggled for the press during a ski vacation in Switzerland, stepping on each other's skis and digging each other in the ribs.

By 1987, Diana and her husband were inhabiting completely different worlds. Charles increasingly sought comfort with his old friend Camilla and with his traditional circle, much occupied with polo, foxhunting, dog breeding and other such country pursuits; Diana's cohorts were more interested in fashion, rock groups, and attending the right parties. When several of her friendships threatened to cross the line into full-blown affairs, the Palace hastily took measures. Her relationship, for example, with a sergeant assigned to the Palace security forces was quickly ended by his transfer away from royal duty. More worrisome was her much-reported friendship with dashing young stockbroker Philip Dunne, especially after she was photographed running her fingers through his hair at an elegant wedding reception at which Charles was also a guest. Other of Diana's friendships were less controversial, notably with Prince Juan Carlos, king of Spain, with whose family she often vacationed in the Mediterranean and of whose children she was particularly fond. Even then, Charles objected to the tabloid photographs of his bikini-clad princess taken during one such stay with the Spanish royal family.

By the late 1980s, Diana and Charles were only appearing in public when necessity demanded it. Gossip about the state of the marriage was so rampant that the queen herself, it was said, had decided to intervene by sternly lecturing her son and daughter-in-law about their public duty, whatever their private lives might be. Philip Dunne was induced by the Palace to stop seeing Diana; and when rumors began to spread of a relationship with James Hewitt, who was a member of the Royal Horse Guards and who had been giving the two young princes riding lessons, Hewitt was quietly reassigned to a more distant post. Charles, meanwhile, was reportedly told to consider the consequences of his relations with Camilla Parker-Bowles, whom Diana had boldly confronted at a party in 1988. "I would just like you to know that I know exactly what is going on between you and Charles," she was heard to tell her rival. A carefully devised series of public appearances was instituted for the royal couple, often in the company of their children, while the queen's admonitions, some said, were responsible for the Princess of Wales' announced patronage of a new national organization designed to offer counseling for troubled relationships. At least in public, where they were now seen more frequently, Charles and Diana appeared to have reconciled. The nation was particularly touched at Charles' obvious sympathy and support for Diana at the death of her father in March of 1992. But then came Andrew Morton's book.

Morton, a tabloid writer and the author of several books on the royals, claimed his *Diana: Her True Story* was based on conversations with some of Diana's closest friends and confidantes who, he said, "believed that for once the truth should be told about the difficult life Diana has led." Morton did not need to point out that his sources would hardly have spoken to him without Diana's explicit approval, and admitted after Diana's death that she herself had been the source for much of the book's information. His written questions were taken to her at Kensington Palace by one of Diana's friends. Diana would then tape record her answers and send the tapes back to Morton by the same route. "I was at the end of my tether," she answered Morton when he asked her why she had contacted him.

The book laid bare everything that had been so carefully hidden from public knowledge—Diana's belated doubts about the marriage, Charles' relationship with Camilla Parker-Bowles (referred to by Diana as "the rottweiler"), Diana's suicide attempts, and her struggles with bulimia (the royal family, it was said, complained she was wasting good food). "We are in danger of losing the Princess of Wales," Morton told a British newspaper, laying the blame squarely on the royal family who, he said, were doing nothing to help her. Morton's publisher, meanwhile, took care that statements from those interviewed appeared prominently in the newspapers, to confirm that Morton's reportage of their conversations was accurate. Buckingham Palace refused to comment on the book, except to say that Diana had granted no official interviews to Morton. More to the point, there was no official denial of the book's contents, while the invitation to tea Camilla Parker-Bowles received from the queen just a week after the book's appearance only made things worse. "I'm certainly not going to bury myself away because of what the papers say," Camilla defiantly said.

The public reaction to the book underscored Britain's ambiguous relationship to its monarchy. While the staid and loyal management of Harrod's refused to put the "scurrilous publication" on the store's shelves, the tabloids editorialized about the uselessness of an institution that displayed such a callous regard for Diana's suffering. Chat shows earnestly explored whether the book was a breach of royal privacy and whether Diana was simply not suited for royalty, while Diana herself burst into tears at the sight of supporters bearing signs saying "We Love You" during an official tour of a new cancer hospital. Pop psychologists volubly offered their analyses of Diana's condition on television and radio; the stairwell down which Diana had thrown herself during her first pregnancy attracted so many gawkers that it had to be roped off; and the archbishop of Canterbury said the royal couple, and especially their children, were in his prayers daily.

Buckingham Palace had already been shaken earlier in the year by Sarah Ferguson's separation (and later divorce) from Prince Andrew. Now, while it publicly remained silent about the latest scandal, the private discussions in the royal quarters of the Palace were long and intense. Prince Philip joined the queen in suggesting a cooling off period for Diana and Charles while, at the same time, getting them as much as possible in front of the public in a show of unity.

By mid-June, Diana and Charles appeared on a balcony of the Palace smiling and waving. They were seen at concerts and benefits, apparently enjoying each other's company, and a tour of South Korea that fall was announced.

It is not known if Diana was present at the strategy sessions designed to counter the damage done to Charles' image, or if she had advance knowledge of the first salvo in the public relations plan: the *Sunday Times*' front page "The Case For Charles," which appeared in late June. It was followed by *U.K. Today*'s "Charles: His True Story" in early July, written by a well-known biographer of the prince of Wales. Both articles were liberally sprinkled with interviews by Charles' intimates, who all stated that the Charles of Morton's book was not the Charles they knew. They stressed Charles' dedication to his country and the responsibilities of his position. More important, they implied that it was not Charles' behavior, but Diana's illness, that had led to the present state of the marriage. As for Camilla, the *Today* article claimed, Charles had naturally turned to an old friend in an effort to "maintain his sanity in a traumatic marriage," when his attempts to help his wife were met with "tears and shouting." The public spectacle of the couple's private affairs now had Diana on the defensive and under even more scrutiny.

It was a deliriously good story for Fleet Street, which now intensified the chase with more sophisticated means. In August of 1992, the *Times* printed the transcript of a telephone conversation between Diana and one James Gilbey, who had called her on his car phone. The call had been recorded, the paper said, in January of 1989 by a source the *Times* refused to identify. Gilbey professed undying love for his "Squidgy," while Diana described her relatives as "the royal twits." As usual, the Palace had no public comment but put it about that despite the call, Charles and Diana were still trying to patch things up. In November of that year, however, while Diana was away on an official visit to France, Prime Minister John Major offered the Commons a statement from the Palace informing the Honorable Members that the prince and princess of Wales had decided on a temporary separation, although they would continue to carry out their royal duties and there were no plans for a divorce. Then, in January of 1993, six months after "Squidgygate," *The Daily Mirror* scooped its rivals by printing the transcript of yet another supposedly private telephone conversation, this one between Charles and Camilla

Parker-Bowles. This call, too, had been recorded in 1989; but while Diana's and Gilbey's comments left much to interpretation, the talk between Charles and Camilla was embarrassingly, extravagantly sexual, leaving no doubt as to the adulterous nature of their relationship.

Less than a year later, on December 3, 1993, Diana publicly announced that she would be leaving public life to devote herself to charitable causes and to the raising of her sons. She delivered the news in an emotional speech to a charitable gathering, telling her audience that she would try to fashion a means "of combining a meaningful public role with, hopefully, a more private life." The ambiguous statement mirrored her own confusion at the ruins of what had once seemed a fairy tale come true. This time, the fickle press came down firmly on her side, excoriating Charles for going off foxhunting while his wife suffered. One tabloid published a poll it had taken indicating that more than 30% of the public now thought that the queen should remain on the throne until Prince William came of age, bypassing her eldest son as the country's next monarch. The publication of *Princess in Love,* a tell-all book in which James Hewitt, the princess' former riding instructor, described his affair with her from 1986 to 1991, failed to swing opinion toward Charles. Even the two-and-a-half-hour documentary *Charles: Private Man, Public Role* on Britain's ITV, during which Charles disingenuously claimed that he had turned to Camilla only after his marriage "became irretrievably broken down," did nothing to alter his image as a cold-hearted philanderer.

The next year, however, the pendulum began to swing the other way when two of Diana's affairs with married men became public, both marriages in question dissolving in divorce; while her attempt to portray herself as the wronged woman in a BBC documentary backfired. In the program, Diana said she had no intention of divorcing Charles and that any such idea would have to come from him. "I believe I have a public role to fulfill and I have two children to bring up," she said—which many took to mean that Diana needed the royal family's money, if not their respect. More dangerously, Diana admitted that while she had no expectation of becoming queen of England, it made no difference because, she claimed, Charles had no interest in becoming king. The reaction from an outraged Queen Elizabeth was swift and cutting. In a letter to her son and daughter-in-law, leaked by the Palace to the papers in December of 1995, the queen wrote of her "anger and frustra-

tion" at the couple's inability to reconcile their differences and their lack of respect for the institution to which they were privileged to belong. "An early divorce," the queen succinctly concluded, "is desirable." Privately, it was pointed out to Diana that the queen had a constitutional right to oversee the upbringing of potential heirs to the throne. The implication was clear. Her children could be taken away from her, with or without a divorce.

Diana spent that Christmas alone, at Kensington Palace, while the rest of the royal family, including her sons, celebrated the holiday elsewhere. Now there were rumors of her erratic temper, of bitter arguments with the boys' nanny, of pointless disputes with her staff. Both her private secretary and his assistant resigned just after Christmas, followed by Diana's chauffeur. Finally, on February 28, 1996, Diana announced that she had agreed to a divorce. But even this difficult decision was not without controversy, for Diana claimed that she would be keeping her royal title. The Palace icily responded that no such agreement had been made and that the actual terms of the divorce had not been settled. Charles, it was said, exploded in anger at Diana's rash claim. It took the next six months to agree to the terms, which were announced in August. Diana would receive a lump sum payment of $26 million, based on her average annual expenses while married of some $245,000 (although they had sometimes reached $1.5 million). The Palace would accept no further responsibility for her personal finances. She would be allowed to remain at Kensington Palace and to participate in the upbringing of her children. Finally, she would lose her title of "Her Royal Highness," and would henceforth be referred to as "Diana, Princess of Wales." By denying the royal title, the queen made sure that Diana's name would not appear in any official documents about the Windsors, making it plain to history that Diana Spencer had been removed from the royal lineage. It was said that the queen privately ordered that Diana's name never again be spoken in her presence.

Diana made no public comment immediately after her divorce, leaving the press to speculate on how the Palace would deal with the fact that the heir apparent to the throne was now a divorced man and technically ineligible for the honor. But it was the press itself that now became the target of growing public anger, despite the fact that it was the public who bought the papers. A photographer who accosted Diana outside a gym in West London was in turn at-

tacked by a passerby, who put the offender in an armlock while Diana removed the film from his camera; and Diana herself, after letting her personal bodyguards go as an economy measure, was not above swatting and flailing at *paparazzi* who came too close. At the same time, Diana

knew she needed the media's help in refashioning her public image. She was pleased with their coverage of the auction of 79 of her dresses at Christie's in New York, which raised over $5 million for AIDS and cancer charities; and she willingly posed and chatted with the press corps that followed her to Angola and to Bosnia in the first half of 1997 as part of the Red Cross campaign to ban land mines, which had long been an important cause for her.

Her separation from the royal family only seemed to increase the fascination with her love life, which intensified in July of 1997 during Diana's stay, with her two sons, in St. Tropez as a houseguest of Egyptian tycoon Mohammed al-Fayed and his eldest son, Emad Mohammed, nicknamed Dodi. The elder al-Fayed was not a well-liked figure in Britain. His purchase of Harrod's, the very symbol of British gentility, had been preceded by an ugly battle to keep it out of foreign hands which had fanned conservative xenophobia into full flame and had led to al-Fayed's petition to become a British citizen being firmly denied. Al-Fayed admitted to seeking revenge when he helped bring down *Margaret Thatcher's Tory government by revealing that conservative members of Parliament had accepted bribes from him. Diana's friendship with the al-Fayeds, and particularly with Dodi, whom she had first met in 1986, was portrayed in the press as her way of snubbing the old-line aristocrats who had rallied around Charles. Diana did, in fact, tell a French magazine interviewer during the early summer of 1997 that she would have left England for good if it had not been for William and Harry.

Dodi al-Fayed was known more for his ostentatious lifestyle than for his business acumen, although he had successfully dabbled in the movie business by co-financing such prominent films as *Chariots of Fire, The World According to Garp,* and Stephen Spielberg's *Hook.* When Dodi broke off his engagement with model **Kelly Fisher** to court Diana in earnest, the press broke into full cry. The papers were soon filled with hastily snapped shots of the two together. Not even Dodi's impressive flotilla of security boats surrounding his yacht during a Mediterranean cruise with Diana could defeat telephoto lenses the length of baseball bats. The two were captured, if somewhat indistinctly, embracing on deck or sitting wrapped in each others arms, fueling rumors that marriage was in the offing. It was said, in fact, that Dodi intended to formally propose to Diana during a planned visit to Paris in late August. The engagement ring, the papers breathlessly reported, had already been purchased. So it was that an army of photographers on motorcycles or in small, nimble sports cars converged on Paris' Ritz Hotel on August 30, 1997, and waited. During the evening, Diana spoke with *The Daily Mail's* Richard Kay, whom she had known since her marriage to Charles and who was one of the few journalists she trusted. She had sounded, Kay reported the next day, "as happy as I have ever known her. For the first time in years, all was well with her world."

The press corps' vigil lasted until past midnight. They had not been fooled by the chauffeur Dodi had sent downstairs to roar away in his Range Rover earlier in the evening, leaving the couple surrounded without a driver to spirit them away and forcing Dodi to recall the driver who had gone off duty earlier in the evening, Henri Paul. Paul returned to work shortly after ten with instructions to be ready to drive his employer and Diana to the al-Fayed private apartment. Finally, at 12:20, Diana, al-Fayed, and a bodyguard named Trevor Rees-Jones emerged from the hotel and clambered into the Ritz' armor-plated Mercedes, with Henri Paul at the wheel, Rees-Jones sitting next to him in the front seat, and Diana and Dodi in the rear. Rees-Jones was the only one to buckle his seatbelt as the Mercedes raced across the Place de la Concorde toward the Seine with the convoy of clicking *paparazzi* in hot pursuit, swarming around the car at a red light before it screeched away and sped onto a dual-lane carriageway running along the river. With the Eiffel Tower twinkling ahead, the Mercedes and its pursuers hurtled into a tunnel under Place d'Alma. Moments later, shortly after 12:35, the car ricocheted at full speed off one of the tunnel's supporting columns, whipped completely around from the force of the collision, and slammed into the opposite wall. Its roof and sidewalls were crushed, while the engine was rammed backwards into the passenger compartment. Dodi al-Fayed and Henri Paul were killed instantly. Diana and Rees-Jones were rushed to La Pitie-Salpetriere hospital, one of the city's best, where Rees-Jones' injuries, although severe, were found to be treatable. But frantic efforts to save Diana's life failed. She had sustained massive head injuries, while the impact to her chest had perforated her left lung and filled her chest cavity with blood. Her heart stopped beating moments after arriving at the hospital, and resuscitation efforts ultimately proved fruitless. At four o'clock on the morning of August 31, 1997, Lady Diana Spencer, princess of Wales, was officially pronounced dead. She was 36 years old. The news was relayed to Balmoral by the British Embassy. Charles' reaction was a cry of grief and pain so loud and anguished that the British Embassy official who placed the telephone call clearly heard it. "Who would ever believe me if I described the Prince's reaction?" he later said. "He uttered a cry of pain that was spontaneous and came from the heart, before breaking into uncontrollable sobs."

"We are today a nation in a state of shock, in mourning, in grief that is so deeply painful to us," British Prime Minister Tony Blair told a press conference hours later. But while similar sentiments from world leaders arrived at Buckingham Palace, the outpouring of grief was hard-edged with anger at the photographers who, it seemed, had hounded Diana literally to death. The public rage was so intense that the French government launched an official investigation, particularly aimed at what had happened in the 15 minutes between the emergency call placed by one of the photographers on a cellular phone and the arrival of the ambulances. Witnesses told of *paparazzi* pressed against the wreckage snapping the "death pictures" that were published the next day, while making no effort to rescue the car's occupants. "I was trying to push back the photographers, who were virulent," one of the first police officers on the scene later testified to the investigators. "At no time did a photographer come to give me a hand. They kept taking pictures the whole time." One of the nine photographers held and interrogated by police admitted "we didn't help the injured," although his failure to act was because, he said, he had been "paralyzed by the connection between me and the people in the car." Another claimed to have reached into the car to take Diana's pulse and to have comforted Trevor Rees-Jones, although the film taken from his camera proved he had also been taking pictures at the same time. Diana's brother Charles angrily told reporters that "every proprietor and editor of every publication that has paid for intrusive and exploitative photographs [of Diana] . . . has blood on his hands today." Rees-Jones, who did not regain consciousness for days afterward, was unable to recall the moments leading up to the crash. French investigators would later conclude that it had been the combination of the pursuing press corps and the amount of alcohol consumed by Henri Paul before he was called back to duty that had proved fatal.

Anger was directed, too, at the royal family itself. While crowds waited outside the gates of Buckingham Palace, while reporters waited in the Palace's press rooms, while millions of Britons sat by their televisions and radios, there was only silence after Prince Charles, his two sons, and Diana's sisters accompanied Diana's body home to London. Three days after her death, by which time 43 condolence books had

been signed by mourners and mounds of flowers and sympathy notes had been deposited outside the Palace, there was still no official word from the throne. Finally, a three-line statement was issued thanking the public for its sympathy and saying that the princess of Wales would be given "a unique funeral for a unique person." The statement's brevity and terse wording only increased the perception of a cold, unemotional monarchy. "Not one word has come from a royal lip, not one tear has been shed in public from a royal eye," complained *The Sun,* which had published some of the most scandalous pictures of Diana while she had lived. The paper neglected to mention that at no time in modern history had such public displays ever been observed in a member of the royal family, even while bombs fell or London burned or kings died, for it had long been intrinsic to the royal code that a calm, dignified image is a public duty of the highest order. Others were shocked that Diana would not be given a full, state funeral, forgetting that such a ceremony is reserved only for notable government leaders or members of the royal family, from which Diana had been removed by divorce.

But even royalty cannot be blind to public opinion, and it was clear that something needed to be done. "Speak to us, Ma'am!," pleaded *The Daily Mirror;* and on the evening of September 5, Queen Elizabeth II did just that in an extraordinary television address broadcast live to her subjects. She spoke, she said, not only as a monarch but "as a grandmother" who, she assured her audience, would see to it that her grandsons would be raised with love and respect. Her astonishingly personal tone was maintained when it came to the subject of her late daughter-in-law, of whom she had never before publicly spoken. Diana was, the queen said, "an exceptional and gifted human being" whom she "admired and respected," adding that she joined her subjects to "thank God for someone who made many, many people happy." As a further indication of the royal family's sense of loss, however guarded, the Palace announced that the Union Jack would be flown at half-mast on the day of Diana's funeral and that the route the funeral procession would take had been extended from one mile to three, to allow more of her public to pay their final respects as her coffin made its way to Westminster Abbey.

It was said that the crowd that lined the streets from Kensington Palace to the Abbey on September 6, 1997, was the largest public turnout in London since the end of World War

II. A worldwide television audience estimated at two billion joined in watching as the somber procession made its way east from Kensington, through a city eerily silent despite the throngs. In another tribute to Diana's memory, the coffin was allowed to pass under the Wellington Arch, near Hyde Park, an honor that had always been reserved for royalty; and in another remarkable display of regal grief, the queen bowed to the coffin as it passed the gates of Buckingham Palace, where she had been waiting with Prince Philip, Prince Charles, her grandsons, and Diana's brother, Charles Spencer. The younger men then joined the procession, walking slowly behind the coffin along the Mall to the Abbey, where 2,000 dignitaries and celebrities from around the world had gathered.

The ceremony that followed would be remembered for two things—Elton John's moving delivery of "Goodbye, England's Rose," adapted from his earlier song "Candle in the Wind"; and for Charles Spencer's emotional tribute to his sister, with his stinging rebuke to the media that had made Diana, he said, "the most hunted person of the modern age," and his unexpected snub to the royal family sitting in front of him. He promised his sister that her "blood family" would see to it that her sons were raised in "the imaginative and loving way in which you were steering these two exceptional young men, so that their souls are not simply immersed by duty and tradition, but can sing openly, as you planned." But even in death, the contradictions persist. The "people's princess" lies alone on a small island in the middle of a lake at Althorp, where her Spencer ancestors buried their hunting dogs and where only her immediate family can visit her grave.

"I have watched many, many hours of television in the aftermath of Diana's death," wrote **Barbara Grizzuti Harrison**, "and the images speak: She inclines her body and applies her hands and her lips to lepers, to babies with amputated limbs, to frail AIDS victims; she gathers her children to her heart with an almost violent ecstasy of tenderness. I can't believe that all of this was done in the name of public relations. . . . A doctor I know, a kind healer, was on the staff of Harlem Hospital when Diana visited. He said, 'They were literally untouchable, some of the people she touched; you wouldn't want to be anywhere near them. . . . But she touched them and welcomed them into her affection with absolute unself-consciousness.'. . . She loved the world and the world loved her back, and it was thrilling to have her among us."

SOURCES:

Anderson, Christopher. *The Day Diana Died.* NY: Morrow, 1998.

Begley, Sharon, and Christopher Dickey. "Horror in the Night," in *Newsweek.* September 8, 1997.

Buskin, Richard. *Princess Diana: Her Life Story.* Lincolnwood, IL: Publications International, 1997.

Harrison, Barbara Grizzuti. "The Princess We Loved," in *TV Guide.* September 20, 1997.

Lyall, Sarah. *Britain's Diana-Mania, Anniversary Edition,* in *The New York Times,* August 23, 1998.

Miles, Rosalind. "A Girl Like Diana," in *Saturday Night.* Vol. 112, no. 9. November 1997.

Morton, Andrew. *Diana: Her True Story.* NY: Simon & Schuster, 1992.

Pontaut, Jean-Marie and Jérôme Dupuis. *Investigation on the Death of Diana.* Paris: Éditions Stock, 1998.

Norman Powers, writer/producer,
Chelsea Lane Productions, New York

Dianda, Hilda (1925—)

Argentine composer, musicologist, professor, and titular conductor of the Chamber Orchestra of the National University of Córdoba, who conducted many international orchestras. Born in Córdoba, Argentina, on April 13, 1925.

Hilda Dianda studied in Buenos Aires under Honorio Siccardi from 1942 to 1950. She then went to Italy where she studied conducting with Hermann Scherchen in Venice. In 1958, the French Government invited her to join Pierre Schaeffer's Groupe de Recherches Musicales. A year later, she was in Italy at the invitation of Italian radio and television to study electronic music. In 1964, Dianda won the Medal of Cultural Merit in Italy for her work there. She returned to Argentina from 1967 to 1970 where she was professor of composition, instrumentation, orchestration, and technical and orchestral conducting at the National University's School of Fine Arts in Córdoba. Dianda often participated in international festivals as a conductor and composer.

John Haag,
Athens, Georgia

Diane de France (1538–1619).

See Medici, Catherine de for sidebar.

Diane de Poitiers (1499–1566)

French duchess who was married at 15 to a man old enough to be her grandfather, then became, at 37, the mistress of a king who, though young enough to be her son, made her the most powerful woman in France. Name variations: Dianne de Poytiers, la grande sénéchale de Normandie; Duchess of Valenti-

nois. Pronunciation: Di-ANN duh Pooah-TEAY. Born on December 31 (some cite September 3), 1499, in the province of the Dauphiné, France; died at Anet, Normandy, on April 25 (or April 22), 1566; daughter of Jeanne de Bastarnay and Jean de Poitiers, lord of Saint-Vallier and captain of the King's Guard; tutored at home; married Louis de Brézé, in 1515; children: daughters Françoise (b. 1520), and Louise.

Following the death of her mother, went to live with the family of the duke of Bourbon (1509); married and moved to Anet, Normandy (1515); became mistress of Henry II (1536); acquired Chenonceau (1555); following Henry's death, returned to Anet (1559).

Born on the eve of the 16th century, the life of Diane de Poitiers spans the end of the Renaissance and the beginning of the Reformation. Her father was Jean de Poitiers, the lord of Saint-Vallier. Her mother **Jeanne de Bastarnay** was the first of her father's three wives. Jeanne died when her three daughters were still young. At the age of ten, Diane, the oldest, went to live at Moulins with the duke and duchess of Bourbon (Charles II of Bourbon and ◄❧ **Suzanne of Bourbon**). There, she served as a maid-in-waiting to their daughter. Diane and the other girls were tutored in religion, Latin, dancing and playing the lute. They also studied manners from a book written by the duchess, who admonished: "Love as you will but marry well." Diane followed the advice but reversed the order. She married well, then she loved.

The duchess accomplished a matrimonial coup in arranging a marriage for Diane. However, when the wedding bells rang, the bride had little to celebrate. She hardly knew Louis de Brèzè, the man who was about to become her husband. He was 40 years older, short-tempered, stern, and not at all the handsome knight of her childhood tales. His severe features matched his character. It mattered little to her that he was admired for his courage as a soldier. In choosing the bridegroom, the fact that he was ill-suited for the lively, 15-year-old girl was outweighed in the duchess of Bourbon's mind by his

❧►
Suzanne of Bourbon. See Louise of Savoy for sidebar.

❧► **Brézé, Charlotte de** (c. 1444/49–?)
French princess. Name variations: Charlotte de France; Charlotte de Breze. Born between 1444 and 1449; murdered by her husband; daughter of Charles VII, king of France, and Agnes Sorel; married Jacques de Brézé; children: Louis de Brézé (who married Diane de Poitiers).

lineage. Louis was a gentleman of the blood royal, being the son of ◄❧ **Charlotte de Brézé**, daughter of Charles VII through his alliance with *Agnes Sorel.

On a wet and windy day in March, Louis de Brézé, count of Maulévrier, grand sénéchale de Normandie, brought the new bride to his home, the castle of Anet in Normandy, near Paris. After the art-filled castle of Moulins, the feudal fortress of her husband's ancestors looked dismal to Diane with its forbidding towers and moat. The room in which the bride and groom slept seemed to be haunted. Years before, Charlotte, Louis de Brézé's mother, had been brutally murdered there by her husband Jacques de Brézé, who, having discovered his Master of the Hounds in bed with his wife, had stabbed both of them to death on the spot. Shortly after the wedding, Diane, a teenager, was left in charge of the dreary fortress when Louis de Brézé went to war. Diane's father accompanied her husband, who was the older of the two men.

The year of Diane de Poitier's marriage, 1515, was also the year Francis I became king. Young Francis was the French counterpart of Henry VIII, his rival across the English Channel. Both princes of the Renaissance were "stirred by beauty," in art, music, literature, and women. Francis was crowned after the death of his cousin and father-in-law Louis XII. Louis had been married only three months to Henry VIII's 18-year-old sister, *Mary Tudor (1496–1533), and, it was reported unofficially, died from "kissing her too much."

When not fighting, Louis de Brézé took Diane to court, where she functioned as lady-in-waiting to the king's mother, *Louise of Savoy (1476–1531), and later, to Queen *Claude de France (1499–1524). From childhood, Diane had developed the habit of horseback riding every morning and soon joined the king's hunting parties at Fontainebleau. She was witty and attractive, her best features being golden hair, a fine figure, and a fresh complexion. She also shared the king's interest in the arts, and he introduced her to the Italian Renaissance. During his Italian campaigns, Francis had been dazzled by the works of the Renaissance artists and had convinced several to come to France. Among them were Benvenuto Cellini and the aging Leonardo da Vinci who had brought with him the famous *Mona Lisa*.

In March 1519, Louis de Brézé and Diane lit bonfires to celebrate the birth of the king's sec-

Diane de Poitiers

ond son, who was named Henry (II) to flatter the English king. Diane, of course, had no way of knowing that 17 years later this boy would fall passionately in love with her and change her life. The following year, Diane gave birth to her first daughter. Soon after, Louis de Brézé left to join the king at the Field of the Cloth of Gold, in Picardy. This spectacular meeting of the courts of France and England was designed by Francis to seduce Henry VIII into aligning with France against the Spanish king, Charles V. The French extravagance failed. Henry sided with Charles V. In 1523, the powerful duke of Bourbon (at whose house Diane had lived) committed an act of high treason by signing a secret treaty with Henry VIII and Charles V. Diane's father, as a friend of the duke, was implicated.

Louis de Brézé discovered the plot and informed the king, unaware that his father-in-law's name was on the list of traitors. Diane was 24 and the mother of two daughters when her father was arrested and found guilty of helping the duke escape. The public beheading was about to take place when a messenger announced that a royal pardon had been granted. Disappointed, the crowd dispersed slowly. Very likely, Louis de Brézé used his influence with the king to obtain his father-in-law's pardon. Some chroniclers,

Madeleine de la Tour d'Auvergne. See Medici, Catherine de for sidebar.

however, hinted that Diane had done more than shed tears. Protestant historians, who sought revenge from Diane de Poitiers for her persecution of the Huguenots, wrote that she had saved her father's life by offering herself to the king. The story was picked up by Victor Hugo and some early historians. The titillating element of this version was that it made Diane de Poitiers mistress to two kings of France, a father and his son.

In 1525, Charles V, king of Spain and Holy Roman emperor, captured France's king Francis I in Pavia, Italy. Francis' mother Louise of Savoy and sister, *Margaret of Angoulême (1492–1549), entered into a web of negotiations that involved most of the monarchs of Europe and even Suleyman the Magnificent, ruler of the Ottoman Empire. Charles V agreed to release the king but made the cruel demand that Francis' sons be sent as hostages until all conditions of the agreement were fulfilled. The boys, aged eight and seven, spent four traumatizing years in captivity. Of his two sons, Francis I preferred the older one who bore his name and resembled him. His youngest Henry was moodier and more introverted.

Madame . . . I entreat you will remember him who has never known but one God and one love.

—Henry II to Diane de Poitiers

A romantic account of Diane's first meeting with Henry places the event as early as 1525. According to this story, which appears in several texts, she was among those who accompanied the princes to Bayonne, near the French border, for the exchange with their father. The boys' mother, Queen Claude, had died recently, and shy Henry was particularly distraught. Diane kissed him before handing him over to his Spanish captors, and the memory of the embrace is said to have sustained Henry during the long imprisonment.

Three years after his sons' release, Francis I visited Louis de Brézé, at Anet, and from there wrote a letter concerning the negotiations for the marriage of his son Henry to *Catherine de Medici. It was dated April 24, 1531. That same year, Louis de Brézé died at age 72. Diane built a monument to her husband and vowed to wear nothing but black and white for the rest of her life. At 30, she found herself a titled widow and landowner. She had radiant good looks, a youthful body, and fine health. Most of all, she was well-informed, smart, and possessed grace and elegance. In 1533, having joined the court at

Paris, she attended the wedding of Henry and Catherine who were both 16 years old. It was a joyful occasion for everyone but the groom, who had never met his Italian bride. Catherine's life had been even sadder than Henry's. The daughter of Lorenzo de Medici, duke of Urbino, and *Madeleine de la Tour d'Auvergne, Catherine became an orphan days after her birth when her mother died from childbirth and her father from syphilis. Catherine was raised by her uncles, both popes: Leo X, who excommunicated Martin Luther in 1520, and Clement VII, who refused to grant Henry VIII a divorce to marry *Anne Boleyn.

Catherine seemed to have truly loved her young husband, but Henry, though always courteous, was sexually indifferent to her. When he was 17, his older brother died, making him the dauphin (next in line to the throne). Feeling unprepared for the role, he turned to Diane de Poitiers for help and guidance. Their relationship began as one of mentor and student. For Henry, his love would always be mixed with respect and gratitude. He found in Diane, who was 20 years older, the mother he had lost when he was a boy. Diane found in Henry the young husband she had never had. By 1536, it seems likely that they were lovers. Diarists of the day wrote that Henry's melancholy all but vanished at the start of his liaison. Some even claimed they had seen him laugh.

Those who failed to understand that the lonely, neglected second son had finally found a friend, accused Diane of seducing the young prince and using sorcery and satanism to keep him. Diane weathered gossip by ignoring it. The secret of her success, she said, was not witchcraft but healthy living. She attributed her slim figure to her devotion to exercise, and her clear complexion to the daily habit of bathing in cold water. She was an avid reader and collector of art. There is no doubt that she was influential in forming her lover's taste. The ambassador to the duke of Ferrara reported that His Majesty was preoccupied with Madame Diane with whom "he spends at least eight hours a day," adding that he was being led by the tip of his nose. Henry and Diane rode together, hunted, conversed, and read. One of the books they studied was Machiavelli's *The Prince*. Having managed a large estate in the absence of her husband, Diane had acquired a sound practical sense, and Henry relied on her judgment and on her pragmatic approach. In addition, she knew how to obtain her wants through reason rather then caprice, diplomacy rather than coercion. Catherine, on the other hand, was temperamental and given to outbursts. On an impulse, she once had a hole pierced in the floor above the room where Diane and Henry met.

After ten years of marriage, Catherine de Medici was still childless. She found herself a vestigial member of the royal family: not yet a queen, not yet a mother, and no longer needed at her husband's side. The question of her barrenness became her obsession and the great concern of the court. The matter was discussed at length and the possibility that Henry was at fault was rejected when he offered the argument that while campaigning in Piedmont, he had fathered a child. Born in 1538, she was named &➤ **Diane (de France)** and brought up at court. This led many to speculate that she was Diane and Henry's daughter.

The burden of infertility was on Catherine, who stopped at nothing to increase her chances of giving birth. She swallowed elixirs of mare's milk, rabbit's blood, and sheep's urine. Around her neck, she wore a small sack containing the ashes of a large frog. She even stopped riding a mule as it was known that a sterile animal could contaminate the rider. She finally gave birth to a son on January 19, 1543. Nine more children followed during the next 13 years. A physician was credited for having solved Catherine's problem, but an envoy from Venice claimed that Diane played a large part in the cure by periodically reminding the king of his marital duties toward his wife.

With the birth of the royal children, Diane might have taken second place to the new mother, but the mistress found a way of becoming indispensable to the royal couple. Not only did she ably assist the queen during her confinements, but she also took charge of the growing nursery. Diane's numerous letters to Jean III de Humières, the children's tutor, have survived. Cordial and to the point, they are filled with advice about the hiring of wet nurses, medicine to be given, and other problems. Henry's letters to the tutor are, by contrast, warm and more concerned with the happiness of the children than with household details.

Diane's political influence on the king began early and continued with the years. She was instrumental in bringing about the alliance of France and Scotland through the marriage of Henry's four-year-old son to four-year-old *Mary Stuart (1542–1587). Mary, the future queen of Scots, arrived in France two years later to join the royal children and immediately captivated the French court. Henry II, who reportedly said, "She is the most perfect child that I ever saw," asked Diane to supervise Mary's education.

When Henry showed his appreciation for his mistress by granting her the duchy of Valentinois, many objected. He came under even heavier criticism when he made her the recipient of a huge source of revenue called *la Paulette*, a tax placed on appointments to military, ecclesiastical, and civil offices. When Diane protested, "This seems to me to be all too great a gift," the king replied, "It is my royal pleasure to lay *la Paulette* as a nosegay at your feet." This new favor made her extremely wealthy and powerful; it also made her many enemies. Although some historians have exaggerated the influence she had over the king, undeniably Diane de Poitiers had great powers over him. The emissary of Edward VI of England wrote, "The Duchess of Valentinois ruleth the roast [sic]." Henry II was not a stupid man; if he relied on her political savvy and her experience it was because in many cases her advice was sound. Her fanatical Catholicism, however, led her to sway the king to use hideously repressive methods towards the Huguenots. Henry had been somewhat tolerant of these French Protestants, but, on this issue, he was opposed by wife and mistress who were able to sway him. Devoutly religious, both believed that anti-Catholic sentiment had to be plucked out immediately. With the backing of the clergy, this attitude caused Huguenots to be burned at the stake. Reportedly, after witnessing the burning of one man, Henry was so sickened that he vowed never to attend such an event again, though Diane thought the punishment fit the crime. On another occasion Diane and Catherine were also in agreement. Henry was not involved in affairs with many women, but he did have a very brief encounter with &➤ **Mary Flemming**, a woman

&
Diane de France (1538–1619). See Medici, Catherine de for sidebar.

&➤ **Flemming, Mary** (fl. 1540s)
Scottish attendant to Mary Stuart, queen of Scotland. Name variations: Lady Flemming, Madame de Flemming. Flourished in the 1540s; had liaison with Henry II; children: a boy, known as the Bastard of Angoulême.

Mary Flemming was an attendant for the child **Mary Stuart**, future queen of Scots. The facts seems to suggest that Flemming was encouraged to seduce the king by political rivals of Diane de Poitiers in an effort to minimize de Poitier's influence. But Flemming made the mistake of bragging about her coup to all who would listen, causing her removal from court.

who had accompanied Mary Stuart. This resulted in the birth of a boy who was raised in the royal nursery but was known as the Bastard of Angoulême. Wife and mistress acted in unison to demand the dismissal of Mary Flemming.

There is little question that Diane de Poitiers was Henry's only love. In a letter, he entreats her to "keep in remembrance him who has never loved, nor will love, anyone but you." Henry felt a constant need to display his love with concrete gifts. The most valuable was Chenonceau, a jewel of a castle in the Loire Valley. Because Henry's father had acquired the place in a somewhat shady deal, Diane feared future heirs might claim it, so she arranged a bizarre scheme in which the royal family relinquished its claims on Chenonceau. She then bought it back (with royal funds) at a rigged auction. This shrewd, calculating trait is also evident in the manner in which Diane acquired her fine collection of books. In order to stock the national library, Francis I had established the precedent of requiring that a copy of every published book be sent to the Royal Depot. Diane persuaded Henry to request two books—one of which ended up on her shelf. On another occasion, she reveals herself as being not only rapacious but callous. In a letter written in 1556 to the baron of Chalus, she asks him to negotiate the best price for 480 Spanish sailors captured by a French galley during a storm. Referring to them as slaves, she also suggests the manner of payment.

The only area in which she was extravagant and unrestrained was in the patronage of artists. Her most exceptional contribution was in architecture. Under the keen supervision of the gifted architect Philibert Delorme, the old gloomy fortress of Anet was converted to an immense and graceful castle that was included in a book entitled *The Most Excellent Buildings of France*. Delorme rejected the Renaissance style and adopted the purer lines of ancient Rome, anticipating the trend toward neo-classicism. When it was completed in 1554, the building was the only one of its kind in Europe since antiquity, and it was a sensation. Most of the grandiose edifice was torn to the ground during the French Revolution.

Château of Chenonceau, given to Diane de Poitiers by Henry II.

WOMEN IN WORLD HISTORY

Diane's improvement of Chenonceau made it a showcase. She spanned the river Cher with a bridge that connected the residence to both banks. Her delicately landscaped gardens were greatly admired and copied. She experimented with exotic plants that included mulberry trees to raise silkworms for the production of silk. She so embellished Chenonceau that when the king died, the queen appropriated it, giving Diane the less attractive château of Chaumont in exchange.

Henry II died shortly after celebrating his 40th birthday. Bravado killed him. On the occasion of the wedding of his daughter *Elizabeth of Valois (1545–1568) to Philip II of Spain, Henry had arranged festive events. The last was a jousting competition in which he performed in defiance of his wife Catherine who, having had a premonition of his death, had begged him tearfully not to participate. Henry received a blow in his right eye and the wooden lance remained embedded in his eye socket. The king took ten days to die, while his physicians dressed the wound with coagulated egg whites and tried everything from bleedings to purges. In a desperate attempt to relieve the king's suffering, they ordered four condemned prisoners to be executed prematurely. Their heads were brought to the surgeons who simulated the accident and proceeded to dissect the heads to determine the damage to the brain. In probably the cruelest act of revenge by the queen who had suffered 23 years of jealousy, Diane was excluded from the dying man's sickroom.

Following Henry's death, Catherine de Medici became the most powerful woman on the Continent. Not only was she mother to the new king, Francis II, but mother-in-law to two monarchs, Mary Stuart and Philip II of Spain. Her sons Charles (IX) and Henry (III) would also become kings. Except for having to return the crown jewels that Henry had given her, Diane was not persecuted or forced to end her life in a convent like previous royal mistresses. Allowed to retire to Anet, she spent the rest of her days doing charitable works, founding a hospital, a nursery for abandoned infants, a home for young women in trouble, and another for homeless women. Diane also arranged to train midwives so they would serve in the countryside and provided dowry money for needy girls.

Diane de Poitiers was unique and fascinating. She had charm and patience, was reasonable, calculating, frugal, manipulative, and, when necessary, could be chillingly detached and cold-blooded. Had she been born a man in the 16th century, she probably would have been a diplomat of some stature.

SOURCES:

Guiffrey, Georges. *Lettres Inédites, Publiées d'après les Manuscrits de la Bibliothèque Impériale avec une Introduction et des Notes.* Geneva: Slatkine Reprints (reprinted from 1866 Paris Edition), 1970.

Seely, Grace Hart. *Diane the Huntress: The Life and Times of Diane de Poitiers.* NY: D. Appleton-Century, 1936.

Strage, Mark. *Women of Power: The Life and Times of Catherine de' Medici.* NY: Harcourt Brace Jovanovich. 1976.

SUGGESTED READING:

Cartland, Barbara. *Royal Lovers.* England: Marwin Publishing, 1989.

Durant, Will. *The Reformation from The Story of Civilization: Part VI.* NY: Simon and Schuster, 1957.

COLLECTIONS:

Five letters written by Henry II (in his own hand) to Diane de Poitiers, the correspondence of six ambassadors of the Venetian Republic to France during the reign of Francis I and Henry II, and 106 letters written by Diane de Poitiers; all located in the Archives of the Bibliothèque Nationale in Paris.

Claire Hsu Accomando, author of *Love and Rutabaga: A Remembrance of the War Years* (St. Martin's Press, 1993); articles on art and history have appeared in *American History Magazine, The Christian Science Monitor, Ararat* and *Artweek.*

Diane of France (1538–1619).

See Medici, Catherine de for sidebar.

Dianti, Laura (fl. 1527)

*Italian woman of the Renaissance. Mistress of Alfonso I d'Este (1476–1534), 3rd duke of Ferrara and Modena; children: (with Alfonso I) Alfonso d'Este (1527–1587, who married Giulia della Rovere). Alfonso I d'Este was married to *Anna Sforza (1473–1497) and *Lucrezia Borgia (1480–1519).*

Diaz, Jimena (fl. 1074–1100)

Spanish hero and wife of El Cid. Name variations: Ximena. Daughter of the count of Oviedo; niece of Jimena Munoz (c. 1065–1128) and Alphonso VI, king of Castile; married Rodrigo Diaz de Vivar (c. 1043–1099), also known as El Cid Campeador, in 1074; children: twins Maria de Vivar (who married Peter of Aragon); Cristina de Vivar (mother of Garcia IV the Restorer, king of Navarre); son Diego.

The 1074 marriage between Jimena Diaz and Rodrigo Diaz de Vivar was a turning point for Rodrigo. Jimena was the daughter of the count of Oviedo and the niece of *Jimena Munoz and Alphonso VI, king of Castile. The wedding, probably arranged by the king, bound Rodrigo to Jimena's prominent family from Asturias with blood ties to the royal dynasty.

As a Castilian military commander, Rodrigo led Christian forces against invading Muslims and in 1094 captured the important coastal city of Valencia. For his efforts, he would be celebrated as a national hero of Spain, popularly known as El Cid.

When Rodrigo died in his bed on July 10, 1099, in Valencia, control of the town fell to Jimena, who struggled to defend what Rodrigo had fought so hard to possess. Three years later on the advice of Alphonso VI, Jimena evacuated Valencia and sought refuge in Castile. Many of the treasures, spoils, and possessions accumulated by Rodrigo were taken to the ancestral lands near Vivar. The most important item transported was the body of Rodrigo which Jimena reinterred near Burgos, in the Benedictine monastery of San Pedro de Cardeña.

SOURCES:

Fletcher, Richard. *The Quest for the Cid.* Knopf, 1989.

Pidal, Ramón Menéndez. *La España del Cid.* Espasa-Calpe, 1964 (English translation. *The Cid and His Spain.* John Murray, 1934).

SUGGESTED READING:

de Chasca, Edmund. *The Poem of the Cid.* Twayne, 1976.

Jimena Diaz is interred with her husband El Cid in the church of San Pedro de Cardeña in Burgos.

O'Callaghan, Joseph F. *A History of Medieval Spain.* Cornell University Press, 1975.

Dick, Gladys (1881–1963)

American physician and microbiologist who, with her husband, isolated the bacteria that causes scarlet fever and developed methods of diagnosis, prevention, and treatment of the disease. Born Gladys Rowena Henry on December 18, 1881; died of cerebral arteriosclerosis in Palo Alto, California, in 1963; received high school and college degrees in Nebraska; graduated Johns Hopkins, M.D., 1907; postgraduate work in Berlin; married George Dick (a physician); children: (adopted) Roger Henry Dick and Rowena Henry Dick.

In 1903, when Gladys Dick enrolled in medical school at Johns Hopkins, women were not yet provided housing by the school. (She eventually organized the small group of female students in residence to buy a group house.) After earning her M.D., she stayed on at the university to conduct research on experimental cardiac surgery and blood chemistry. In 1911, she moved to the University of Chicago where she began working on the etiology, or cause, of scarlet fever, a major public health hazard at the time that killed a quarter of its predominantly young victims. After marrying her collaborator, George Dick, she and her new husband continued their research at the university's John R. McCormick Memorial Institute for Infectious Diseases.

In 1923, after ten years of methodical research, the couple isolated hemolytic streptococci, previously considered a secondary invader, as the cause of the disease. Less than a year later, they developed a skin test ("the Dick test"), which was distributed throughout the world. They then turned their attention to developing an antiserum. Although their discoveries made them celebrities in the scientific community, they were criticized for patenting their methods of producing the toxin and an antitoxin. The Dicks maintained that they only sought to control the quality of others' use of their methods, but fellow scientists felt that patents would block further research and biological standardization. The controversy cooled in the 1940s, with the development of antibiotics.

When she was 49, Gladys and her husband adopted two children. In her later years, she divided her time between the Cradle Society (an adoption agency she had founded) and polio research. In 1953, weakened by cerebral arteriosclerosis, she retired with her husband to Palo Alto, California. Ten years later, in 1963, Gladys Dick succumbed to the disorder.

Barbara Morgan, Melrose, Massachusetts

Dickerson, Nancy (1927–1997)

American who was the first female correspondent for CBS News and the first woman to report from the floor of a national convention. Name variations: Nancy Hanschman. Born Nancy Conners Hanschman in Wauwatosa, a suburb of Milwaukee, Wisconsin, in 1927; died in New York City on October 18, 1997; awarded B.A. from the University of Wisconsin, 1948; took speech and drama classes at Catholic University of America, Washington D.C.; married C. Wyatt Dickerson, Jr., on February 24, 1962 (divorced 1983); married John C. Whitehead (a deputy secretary of state); children: (first marriage) five.

Nancy Dickerson, destined to become a pioneering woman in news television, taught school in Milwaukee for several years after college before moving East. Unable to find work in New York, she settled in Washington, D.C., where she took a clerical position at Georgetown University, then worked as a staff assistant to the Senate Foreign Relations Committee. In 1954, her growing interest in television led her to CBS, where she spent six years working off camera. In addition to producing the radio program "The Leading Question," she worked as the associate producer of "Face the Nation." Her knowledge of the Washington scene, as well as her friendships with many members of Congress, proved invaluable in obtaining stories for the show and won her the title "CBS' secret weapon."

Although CBS had yet to hire a woman for its news staff, Dickerson saw her chance in 1959 while in Europe to produce a story about the Women's Army Corps. Acting on her own initiative, she interviewed a number of European political leaders about Soviet Prime Minister Nikita Khrushchev's visit to the United States. Her stories proved of such superior quality that CBS aired them without hesitation. Six months later, she landed an exclusive interview with House Speaker Sam Rayburn, which was aired on the Douglas Edwards' news program. In 1960, as a result of these journalistic coups, Dickerson became the first woman correspondent for CBS and was also given a five-minute radio show called "One Woman's Washington." She was assigned to cover the civil-rights bill then in Congress as well as Senate Majority Leader Lyndon Johnson. That fall in Los Angeles, she became the first woman to cover the televised Democratic Convention.

Nancy Dickerson

With her marriage to C. Wyatt Dickerson, Jr., in 1962, Nancy stopped using her maiden name Hanschman. In 1963, she moved to NBC, where she appeared regularly on "The Huntley-Brinkley Report" and "The Today Show," in addition to anchoring her own daily news show. Dickerson covered many of the major events of the decade, including John F. Kennedy's funeral, the civil-rights marches on Washington, and Martin Luther King's "I Have a Dream" speech, and the inaugurals of three presidents: Kennedy, Johnson, and Richard Nixon.

At the height of her career, during which she was the highest paid woman on television, Dickerson mothered five children. Leaving NBC in 1970 over a contract dispute, she gave political commentary for two syndicated television services and formed her own production company, Television Corporation of America, which produced news documentaries. A PBS interview with Nixon was yet another "first," and her documentary on Nixon's White House and Watergate, "784 Days that Changed America—From Watergate to Resignation," won several awards, including the Peabody. Dickerson also wrote of her 25 years in Washington in her book *Among Those Present* (1976).

In the late 1970s-early 1980s, Dickerson reported from Europe, the Middle East, and the Far East, scoring interviews with Egypt's Anwar Sadat and Israel's Menachem Begin for a 1980 special, "Nancy Dickerson, Special Assignment: The Middle East." From 1986 to 1991, she was a commentator for Fox TV News. Dickerson

had a stroke in January 1996 from which she never recovered; she died in October 1997.

Barbara Morgan,
Melrose, Massachusetts

Dickinson, Anna E. (1842–1932)

Popular American abolitionist who championed the idea of civil rights for women and blacks, achieved fame for her passionate political speeches, and helped redefine the role of women with her success. Born Anna Elizabeth Dickinson on October 28, 1842, in Philadelphia, Pennsylvania; died from cerebral apoplexy on October 22, 1932, in Goshen, New York; daughter of John Dickinson (a merchant) and Mary (Edmonson) Dickinson; received formal instruction from the Friends Select School of Philadelphia and the Westtown Boarding School until age 15; never married; no children.

Showed dedication to abolitionism and women's rights at an early age; published an anti-slavery essay at 13 (1855); started working at 15 (1857); at 17, delivered her first public speech on women's rights and within two years became the most popular female lecturer on abolition and equality of women in America (1859–61); lectured throughout the Northeast for the Republican Party (1863), which led to a profitable career in political campaigning; continued lecturing throughout the country about civil rights for women and blacks; began career as novelist in mid-20s; wrote her first novel (1868), second (1876), and third (1879); wrote plethora of plays and debuted as an actress (1876); resumed political campaigning for the Republicans (1888).

Novels: What Answer? *(1868);* A Paying Investment *(1876);* A Ragged Register (of People Places and Opinions) *(1879).* Plays: A Crown of Thorns, or, Anne Boleyn *(1876);* Laura, or True to Herself *(1876);* Aurelian *(1878);* An American Girl *(1880).*

An attractive teenager shocked an audience and sparked a heated debate at a gathering of the Pennsylvania Anti-Slavery Society when she baldly stated: "The Constitution of the United States recognizes human slavery, and makes the souls of men articles of purchase and sale." Meeting near Philadelphia in 1860, the abolitionist society had come together to discuss the precarious state of the nation and the Dred Scott decision that declared slaves as property. Although some abolitionists could not concede that America's great founding fathers condoned slavery, 18-year-old Anna Dickinson went on to assert that "if the word slave is not in the Constitution the *idea* is." Declaring that "certain fundamental ideas of

*A*nna
E.
*D*ickinson

right" were universal and the "laws of man's making which trample on these ideas are null and void," she questioned the sincerity of American democracy and demanded specific laws be designed that would curtail racial and gender discrimination. Her ideas provoked some angry reactions, but Dickinson's articulate speech and utilization of examples to defend her beliefs gained the attention and respect of many prominent reformers. This event, her first speaking engagement before a sizeable audience, revealed a talent for persuasive speech. A reporter from the *Philadelphia Press* noted that "Miss Anna E. Dickinson, . . . eloquent beyond her years, made the speech of the occasion."

As an adult, Dickinson would achieve unprecedented popularity as an orator and champion of civil rights for women and blacks in America. Throughout history, politics and public speaking were identified as masculine activities and deemed unsuitable for women. Her political involvement and unprecedented success as an orator expanded society's notion of women's intellectual capabilities and helped to remove the cultural barriers that prevented women from speaking in public.

Born in Philadelphia, Pennsylvania, on October 28, 1842, Anna Dickinson was the second daughter and fifth and last child of John and

Mary Edmonson Dickinson. Anna's devotion to abolitionism and women's rights stemmed from the ideology and activism of her family. Typical Quakers, the Dickinsons vehemently opposed slavery; often their home was utilized as a stop on the underground railroad. Anna's father, a dry goods merchant of meager means, possessed a talent for oration and devoted himself to abolitionism. Shortly after inspiring his community with a passionate anti-slavery speech, he suffered a heart attack and died. Anna, only two at the time, vaguely remembered him, but she was inspired by her mother's recounts of his dedicated activism.

Mary Dickinson also instilled the idea of gender equality in her daughter by reciting tales of Anna's ancestors. Within the Society of Friends, which encouraged female activism, her great grandmothers had served as preachers and were renowned for their eloquent and stirring sermons. Anna's parents had both descended from prominent families who had settled in America during the 17th century; despite their genteel lineage, the family was often impoverished. John Dickinson's untimely death left his family destitute and deeply in debt.

Among the women of America who have broken down the prejudice of public speaking by women none has been more eminent than Anna E. Dickinson.

—Henry Ward Beecher

Struggling to sustain the family, Mary Dickinson accepted boarders and occasionally taught privately. Because she imbued her children with the Quaker tradition, Anna received a more complete education than many women of the time. She immersed herself in classical literature, poetry, history, ethics, Shakespeare, and the Bible; reading became her favorite pastime. In addition to the classical collection chosen by her mother, Anna secretly devoured the popular verses of Lord Byron, of whom Mary disapproved. At approximately age ten, Anna attended the Friends' Select School of Philadelphia, and for a brief interval received instruction from the Westtown Boarding School. Increasingly interested in abolitionism, Anna gleaned information about the national debate over slavery from the local newspapers. When she read of a Kentucky schoolmaster who had been tarred and feathered for writing an anti-slavery letter to an Ohio newspaper, she was incensed and wrote an essay that was published by the *Liberator*,

William Lloyd Garrison's abolitionist newspaper, in 1856. "Can any man in this country . . . stand up firmly and say 'I am free,' when such evils and wrongs are constantly being enacted among us, without one word or act of denunciation?" wrote the 13-year-old.

The Dickinsons' financial problems continued, however, and at 15 Anna left school and sought employment to help support her family. (Her brothers Samuel and Edwin were both sickly and had unsuccessful careers; John taught religion and math at a college, while **Susan Dickinson**, a lover of the arts, taught for a short while before assuming the running of the household.) Briefly, Anna served as a copyist for a local law firm and publishing company; unsatisfied with this position, she embarked upon a career of teaching. "Mother wants thee, if thee can," wrote her sister Susan, nine years her senior, "to come home next seventh day prepared to pay the ice bill." During this time, Dickinson's participation in anti-slavery activities increased, and she also became an outspoken advocate for women's rights.

Raised to believe in gender equality, Dickinson was shocked by the blatant prejudice she experienced in the work force. Temporarily serving as assistant teacher in Beaver County, she applied for a full teaching position in a nearby school. Since society devalued the work of females, working women were often paid much less than men holding the same position. Inquiring about the teaching job, Dickinson was informed that a woman's salary would be $16 per month, whereas the male teacher who had held the same position earned nearly twice that amount. Outraged at the discrepancy, she wrote the school's administrator: "Are you a fool or do you take me for one? Though I am too poor today to buy a pair of cotton gloves, I would rather go in rags than degrade my womanhood by accepting anything at your hands."

Dickinson soon discovered that gender discrimination was not limited to the work force. In 1860, she attended a debate entitled, "The Rights and Wrongs of Women," sponsored by a local organization. Only 17, Anna unexpectedly became involved in her first debate when, appalled and angered by comments of a male speaker who was using his daughters and their abilities as yardsticks for womankind, she retorted:

> You say that what your daughters cannot be, no man's daughters can be; that your daughters are incapable of being doctors, lawyers, priests, businessmen, bank presidents, authors, editors. In one word, as you

yourself have summed it up, your daughters are fools! And, in heaven's name, what else is to be expected of the daughters of such a father?

This quick repartee marked the first step in her career as an orator. As 19th-century ideology relegated women into domesticity and essentially banned them from the public sphere, Dickinson's outspoken actions attracted attention. The idea of a gifted young woman aroused much curiosity; a novelty, she was invited to other local meetings. After her ringing declaration at the 1860 assembly of the Pennsylvania Anti-Slavery Society, she quickly developed a reputation as a skilled orator and devoted abolitionist. Her impromptu yet cogent speech impressed many, and soon she was befriended by *Lucretia Mott and Dr. *Hannah Longshore, distinguished reformers and active supporters of women's rights. Encouraged by her mentors, Dickinson addressed an audience of nearly 800 in the Philadelphia Concert Hall in February 1861. Her lecture, pointedly titled, "The Rights and Wrongs of Women," captivated the audience for nearly two hours and secured Anna immediate recognition in reform circles.

In spite of Dickinson's first oratorical achievement, pecuniary problems once again befell her family. The military enlistment of many men during the Civil War had created thousands of vacant jobs, and Anna easily secured employment at the U.S. Mint in Philadelphia. There, she earned $28 per month, much more than she had procured as a teacher, and, having Sundays off, she was able to attend abolitionist meetings. While addressing the Pennsylvania Anti-Slavery Society in the fall of 1861, Dickinson accused General George B. McClellan, the commander of the Army of the Potomac, of treason. McClellan's extreme military caution and well-known sympathy for slave-owners had created some speculation, but Anna's brash accusations remained unfounded. News of her speech spread, and within the week she was terminated from the mint.

After the abrupt dismissal, Dickinson visited a friend in Rhode Island and promoted abolitionism throughout New England. After hearing Anna speak on "The National Crisis" in Newport, the correspondent of the *Providence Press* proclaimed: "To witness the boldness of her manner, speech, and gesticulation, one is almost led to the conclusion that she needs only the sword, the charger, and the opportunity to become a second Joan of Arc, and . . . lead the 'grand army' on to victory and war."

Despite Dickinson's increasing popularity as a lecturer, her mother and sister remained

impoverished. Both Edwin and John would not send money, believing their sisters could care for themselves. Needing to secure substantial paid employment, Dickinson sought assistance from William Lloyd Garrison in the spring of 1862. Her eloquence had so impressed him that he arranged a series of engagements for her but warned her to speak up: "Most of the female lecturers fail for lack of voice and this has led those who are opposed to female speaking sneeringly to say, that if God had intended it, he would have given the necessary vocal powers." In April, among eminent speakers Ralph Waldo Emerson and Wendell Phillips, Dickinson addressed nearly 5,000 at Boston's Music Hall. Only 19, she argued the causes of abolitionism and women's rights before some of the most venerable reformers of the time. Once again, her powerful and emotional oratory affected many: *Susan B. Anthony, the most revered advocate of women's rights, encouraged her to speak about women, and a lasting friendship was formed.

Anna E. Dickinson

There was a side of the supremely confident Dickinson, however, that the public never saw. She had been terrified before the speech, in deep and inconsolable depression, sleeping little the night before, unable to eat the day of. Garrison wrote an abolitionist friend of hers, **Elizabeth Buffum Chace:** "It must be a great trial and even danger, to so young a person, to be the object of so much interest, to receive so much public applause, and to possess so great and happy a talent for holding and swaying the minds of large audiences." These pre-speech depressions and crises of self-confidence would eventually take a toll. But Dickinson was ecstatic over her reception, writing home: "One would suppose that 'no sich' had ever been seen in these quarters. Mr. Garrison says he has been over-run with thanks for finding me. However, I will stop blowing my own trumpet, being somewhat out of breath." To which Susan replied after suitable approbation, "Mother wants to know whether, if she gets the parlor chairs done up, a matting for our floor, and one or two little matters done up in the furniture line, thee can spare her money enough when thee comes home to pay the bill," while mother Mary advised, "Beware my child of being carried away by the voice of adulation."

Thrilled by her accomplishments, Dickinson suffered disappointment at the transience of success. Once again unemployed and broke, she returned to the family's home in Philadelphia. Scheduled to speak in Boston in the fall of 1862, she spent the summer preparing for a new speech, "Hospital Life," by interviewing wounded soldiers in army hospitals. Although she was an inexperienced female, only 20 years old, she received $100 per speech, the same amount paid to prominent male orators Henry Ward Beecher, Phillips, and Emerson. Despite Dickinson's increasing prestige and success as an orator, work was generally seasonal; immediately after a significant speech, she was often unemployed. By winter of 1862, her family, still dependent upon her for support, faced insolvency; in December, she lectured to soldiers for only $15–$20, but, by doing so, she managed to sustain herself and her family for the month.

At this time, there was unrest with the electorate throughout the United States. Many saw the war as a crusade to restore the Union, not as a conflict over slavery. Lincoln's Emancipation Proclamation may have soothed the abolitionists, but it fanned antiwar fervor, and Lincoln was a Republican. In the north, Peace Democrats were determined to fill the governorships and stop the war at the ballot box. The loss of one state meant the loss of one state's army to the Union cause.

During the spring of 1863, Anna Dickinson's luck drastically changed when Benjamin Franklin Prescott, the secretary of New Hampshire's Republican Committee, requested her assistance in the upcoming political campaign. Deeply moved by "Hospital Life," he believed that her charisma and eloquence could serve the Republicans in the upcoming gubernatorial election. Dickinson quickly exhibited persuasive skills in politics. "Her audiences are held as though they were electrified," wrote a local journalist. One of the first women to speak publicly on political issues, her characteristic pathos and wit was just what the Republicans needed to win in New Hampshire. The election was close and the governor-elect was sure that he owed his triumph to the young Miss Dickinson.

Because of her phenomenal success, she was whisked to Connecticut. Her first speech in Hartford was reported in Charles Dudley Warner's *Press* the following morning:

> The Hall, which was comfortably filled at the beginning of the address, was packed as we never saw it as the evening went on. And the audience, which began to listen in a quiet, half-critical manner, soon lost control of itself under the witchery of such a spell as a Hartford audience was never under before. . . . She spoke rapidly, her ideas evidently outrunning even her lightning-like utterance, memory and imagination both crowding her. . . . In certain powers as a speaker we have never heard her excelled.

Somewhat alarmed by Dickinson's unexpected accomplishment in New Hampshire, Democrats endeavored to sabotage her speeches. Undaunted, she often capitalized on these diversions. When the lights were sabotaged in one hall and audience and speaker were pitched into temporary darkness, Dickinson sang out: "I see that there are those here who evidently love darkness better than light, because their deeds are evil." In another instance, the Democrats stood outside yelling "Fire!" while a fire engine clanged up the street. "Yes, there *is* a fire," retorted Dickinson, "we have kindled a fire, which these people by their acts are assisting, that will never go out" until nothing is left of the Democrats, "save ashes." The *Hartford Courant*, a leading newspaper, extolled her closing speech of the Connecticut campaign; its headline dubbed Dickinson, "THE MOST REMARKABLE WOMAN OF THE AGE." This description was not inaccurate; the Republicans credited their sweeping and unexpected victory to Dickinson's oratorical abilities. Officials presented her with a gold watch, $100 for every night that she spoke, plus $400 for the closing speech. Within two years of her first speech, Anna's eloquence, passion, and persuasive talent had achieved notoriety throughout the country.

Inspired by her accomplishments, the Republicans beseeched Dickinson to speak at Cooper Union in New York. Her popularity preceded her—over 5,000 crammed into the hall, and many more were sent away. One account of her speech was printed in *The New York Times*:

> She sways the audience from the first moment of her electric utterance down to the last syllable of the ten thousand words which she must have spoken in one short hour. She is a walking encyclopedia of the events of the war, with all the pages open to you at a glance. She heaps history, fact, proverb, warning, story, appeal, and exhortation in convincing array, sweeping all before her in an avalanche of intellectual force.

As in the other states, a Republican victory followed. Once again, the party did not hesitate to credit Anna with the success; for her eloquent oratory in New York, she received $1,000 plus a request to deliver the same speech in Philadelphia. With the money, she rented a commodious house for her family, paid the bills, bought gifts for friends, donated to charities, and purchased a new wardrobe. "In her zeal to give to others," Anna "often gave more than she could afford," writes her biographer Giraud Chester.

Reformers were ecstatic with her success because her popularity gained support for the abolitionist cause. In turn, women's rights activists emphasized her importance as a pioneer; her triumphs in politics and public speaking forced society to reexamine the limited roles that women were impelled to assume. "I am thoroughly satisfied with this noble girl," commented *Elizabeth Cady Stanton. "How many life-long hopes and prayers I realized as I listened to her eloquence." As a result of her youth, passionate convictions, and effect upon audiences, many people proclaimed Dickinson the American Joan of Arc.

Anna Dickinson attracted the attention of the press for a variety of reasons. Curious, the multitude initially flocked to see her because of her age and gender, but soon she became renowned and respected for her style. Many were impressed that she spoke extemporaneously. She generally had only a few notes scribbled on a scrap of paper. Although Democratic news-

papers sporadically mocked Dickinson and called her "unsexed," most journalists praised her for her style and unique charismatic appeal. Petite, with penetrating blue eyes, and short, shiny, curling black hair, Anna's appearance and simple dress were pleasing. The *Boston Commonwealth* commented: "[I]n these days when women seem to have gone insane" adhering to fads that 'torture' and 'disfigure,' wearing 'corsets, crinolines and trailing skirts,' it is singularly refreshing to see a woman who entirely understands the art of dress. And that woman is Anna Dickinson."

Dickinson's most impressive feature, however, was her deep, rich voice and speaking style. "She was an orator to remember," writes Chester. "Her rich, vibrant voice carried to every corner of the chamber without obvious effort, yet when she dropped it to underscore an impelling point, its grim intensity made it audible to every listener. Her poise was manifest and her earnestness overwhelming. Each word bore the stamp of conviction, as if she was prepared to stake her life upon its truth." In the traditional praise-one-woman-by-disparaging-the-rest, the New York *Independent* wrote that, unlike other female orators, "Miss Dickinson is not a woman speaking like a man," and by maintaining femininity "she proves beyond all controversy that there are elements of truth, and phases of public affairs, . . . that can be given from no standpoint than the heart of a true woman." Many prominent men proposed matrimony to Dickinson, but Whitelaw Reid, a leading journalist for the *New York Tribune*, seemed to be the man most likely to marry her. The press often linked the couple's names, and for a time Reid frequented the Dickinson home. Though the two maintained a close friendship for a number of years, they became badly estranged in the 1870s. Despite the many proposals, Dickinson chose not to marry.

During the fall of 1863, the Republicans entreated her to lecture throughout the coal-mining towns of Pennsylvania, places known to be dangerous. Since the majority of the working class in this area vehemently opposed the Republicans and the conscription laws, rioting often occurred. But the Pennsylvania Republicans viewed Anna, who had been part of the working-class and sympathized with their concerns, as their only chance at victory. Officials offered her $12,000 to lecture for 12 days where no male speaker dared to tread. Agreeing, Dickinson occasionally encountered violence firsthand. Before delivering one speech, a disgruntled man shot at her; the bullet actually cut off a lock of her hair. Seemingly undaunted, she began to speak, and, impressed by her courage, the miners listened to her lecture. On the next stop, when met with loud hisses by one gentleman, she replied: "I know of but two animals that use that mode of expressing themselves, the goose and the snake. If you, sir, can sit and listen to falsehoods in a Democratic meeting, and cannot listen to plain facts now, use the mode of loco-motion designed by nature for your kind, and *get down and wriggle out!*" Reported the *Pottsville Miner's Journal:* "Not another hiss was heard." After this tour, the Republicans in Pennsylvania were victorious. Although they showered her liberally with praise and once again credited the success with her speaking, Dickinson never received the promised $12,000. From that time on, she insisted on signed contracts, but the erosion in trust in political friends would take its toll.

Dickinson continued to lecture in upstate New York, then New England and Chicago. After completing these tours, she was invited to Washington D.C. to address Congress. At first, it was to be in a local theater with Congressmen attending, but Dickinson would only agree if it was an official invitation to the Hall of Representatives. Even though no woman had ever been invited to speak there, Anna stuck to her terms. On January 16, 1864, in the House of Representatives, in a speech intended to sway Republican opponents, she attacked Southern secessionists, Democrats, the Supreme Court for the Dred Scott verdict, and President Abraham Lincoln himself for his December Amnesty Proclamation. By the end of the lecture, she had turned her criticism into a passionate demand for Lincoln's re-election. The press was ecstatic, calling "the young Quakeress" a genius. Whitelaw Reid wrote in the *Cincinnati Gazette:*

> Washington has witnessed strange scenes, betokening strange changes, in the last two years, but I can recall none so strange as that witnessed in the Hall of the House of Representatives last Saturday night. Before the largest and most distinguished audience ever assembled there, there came a young Quaker girl, eight months before a humble employee of the mint, tonight the bravest advocate for the integrity of the Republic and the demand for universal liberty throughout it. Her success has been the most remarkable won at the capitol.

However, throughout the year her opinion vacillated, and, after publicly condemning the president, she was compelled to support him after the Democrats nominated her enemy, McClelland.

(Dickinson quipped that she agreed with the little old lady who stuck up for the Civil War general: "Why will the people keep attacking poor, dear, little George McClellan? I'm sure *he* never attacked anybody.") Though still popular, these seemingly unmotivated oscillations disturbed fellow abolitionists and signaled the first of a series of actions that alienated Anna from a few reformers.

After Lincoln's re-election, Dickinson became an integral addition to the lyceum circuit. At that time, the public speeches held in various lyceums across the country provided a form of entertainment and informed the populace about contemporary news. For nearly five years, Dickinson toured the South, Midwest, and West, delivering speeches on issues of social reform almost every day. Because the Republican success enhanced her popularity, she often earned an annual salary of over $20,000, an extraordinary income for any American at that time. She was at the top of the ladder, "rivaled by only one or two men," wrote Chester.

> Anna was rich on her own earnings; she was beholden to no man; she would not be shackled by Victorian rectitude or the vestments of tradition. In an era when propriety seemingly was the foremost of virtues, she recognized no master save her impulses and her means. She was blatantly and self-consciously nonconformist, and seemed to take delight only in asserting her individuality and refusing to accept without question or protest the code of behavior that shaped the lives of her contemporaries. She dressed as she desired; she traveled where and how she willed; she delivered lectures on subjects many people felt should not even be mentioned in the presence of unmarried young ladies. As a result, she antagonized many of her former friends and supporters. Conservative newspapers now began to find fault with her and even to ridicule some of her habits and beliefs.

After encountering Mormonism in the West, her speeches often criticized polygamy, an "unmitigated despotism," which she felt stifled and degraded women.

In 1866, Dickinson met with Frederick Douglass, the celebrated abolitionist, and Theodore Tilton, editor of the *Independent*; the three formulated a Constitutional amendment that would prohibit disenfranchisement on account of race, color, or sex. As politicians revised the idea, however, the word "sex" was lost. When ratified four years later, the 15th amendment provided suffrage to men of all races, but excluded women, idiots, and criminals. Although Dickinson promoted the equality of women and maintained a friendship with Anthony and Stanton, she declined active participation within the suffrage movement.

Throughout, Dickinson dealt with frequent bouts of bronchitis, forcing her to remain in bed in strange hotels, sometimes for weeks. She also endured swings of high energy and deep depression. Having once again crossed paths with her on a lecture tour, Susan B. Anthony commented, "I found her the most weary and worn I had ever seen her, and desperately tired of the lecture field." Dickinson had peaked as an orator and political pundit, the natural next step was seeking a political life, but that was barred to her because of her gender. "An unmarried woman who must live by her labors and can expect no political office," said Dickinson, "needs to look to matters of money."

In the 1870s, the popularity of the lyceum circuit declined in America, and, tired of constant traveling, Dickinson embarked upon a new career as an author. Her first novel *What Answer?* attacked the problem of racism in American culture by defending the marriage of an interracial couple. The book was more of a social commentary than fictional work, and some critics challenged her creative ability. Respected reformer *Harriet Beecher Stowe wrote to her, praising her labors: "Well done, good and faithful Anna. . . . don't mind what anybody says about it as a work of art. Works of art be hanged! You had a braver thought than that." Dickinson likely appreciated this comment because her personal life was undergoing upheaval. Despite her considerable income, the Dickinsons were, once again, on the verge of penury. Anna's extravagance in gifts and charitable donations, and her sister Susan's poor monetary management, steadily drained any savings. In addition, their brother Samuel passed away and Edwin became severely ill. With hospital bills and debts mounting, Dickinson resumed lecturing.

During the presidential campaign of 1872, her expert oratory was sought by both the Republicans and Democrats. The former, with whom she had achieved unprecedented popularity, offered her $20,000, while the latter proposed only half that amount. Despite her previously successful affiliation with the Republicans and the larger salary, Dickinson decided to campaign for the newly formed third party, the Liberal Republican Party, and its nominee Horace Greeley, famed editor of the New York *Tribune*, because she deplored the corruption and nepotism of the Grant administration. In spite of her vehement attack of Ulysses Grant, the Republi-

cans won in a landslide victory. Gradually, Dickinson realized that her affiliation with the Democrats, who had backed Greeley, had damaged her career. Because Greeley refused to endorse women's rights, and the Republicans had a plank in their platform stating that the party was "mindful of its obligations to women," she had alienated herself from some suffragists. Furthermore, by endorsing Greeley, she disappointed many reformers and forfeited over $5,000 from cancelled lectures. She had lost much sympathy with the press who now began to demand that she "get married."

Her association with Greeley was not the only reason for cancelled lectures and a decline in popularity. While delivering a speech about "Demagogues and Workingmen" during 1871–72, Dickinson assailed industrial corporations and, in so doing, earned their disdain. In the same speech, however, she attacked trade unions and opposed the eight-hour day, and irreparably estranged the working class, who had always seen her as a hero. Antagonizing both groups also reduced her lecturing schedule and diminished her popularity. Likely disappointed by the turn of events and unaccustomed to being shunned from the limelight, Dickinson's health rapidly deteriorated. Her family was forced to move from their extravagant home to the small town of West Pittston, Pennsylvania. Desperately in need of employment, Dickinson turned again to lecturing. During 1873–74, she provided eloquent discourses about the problem of prostitution. Though she displayed remarkable insight into the problem, a woman lecturing about prostitution shocked the 19th-century code of propriety. The *Philadelphia Inquirer* advised "all respectable people to remain away" from her speeches.

After delivering a few unprofitable lectures, she wrote a second novel. *A Paying Investment*, another social commentary, demanded compulsory education, examined the roles of citizenship, and emphasized the civic responsibility to vote. Though reformers praised the text, it was not a financial success, and, Dickinson, at 30, turned to a career in the theater. Because Quakers considered the theater a vice, she risked severe maternal disapproval. In May 1876, she made her stage debut in Boston, starring in the title role of the play she had written, *Crown of Thorns or, Anne Boleyn*. Though reviews in Boston were somewhat encouraging, the New York critics were severe, ridiculing not only Dickinson's acting ability, but the script itself; the play closed after a brief continental tour.

Following the failure of *Crown of Thorns*, Anna wrote a handful of other plays that were not performed. In 1879, she wrote her final published novel, *A Ragged Register (of People Places and Opinions)*. Though the text provides an interesting, select account of Dickinson's speaking experiences, it did not become the success she had imagined. Undaunted and in need of income, within a year she produced another play. *American Girl*, the first performance in which Dickinson did not star, became her most popular production. With celebrated actress *Fanny Davenport playing the lead, the play enjoyed modest success in 1880 and received encouraging reviews. Theatrical victory, however, was ephemeral. Following a clash of egos between Dickinson and Davenport, performances ceased; Dickinson continued writing plays, but she could not produce them.

After a brief hiatus, in 1881 38-year-old Dickinson attempted to resume her acting career. This time, she shocked audiences by playing traditional male roles, such as Hamlet; as with her former sojourn in the theater, reviews were mixed. After nearly four years of touring the country with occasional dramatic work, Dickinson lost most of her belongings in a fire; she returned to stay with her mother and sister in West Pittston.

In 1888, the Republican National Committee requested that Dickinson speak on their behalf during the upcoming presidential campaign; nearly broke and bored, she quickly consented. As in previous years, her eloquent speeches proved immediately successful in Indiana and Michigan. Unfortunately, her popularity dwindled somewhat when she vehemently attacked Grover Cleveland. As she railed against the "the hangman of Buffalo," some questioned her reasoning. She proceeded to New York, but after only a limited number of speeches, her role in the campaign deteriorated. Frustrated, she returned to her family at West Pittston. Within months, her mother, who had been ill, died. Feeling stifled and out of place in the small community, Dickinson's health deteriorated both physically and mentally. Throughout her life, she had sporadically suffered from a frail constitution; now, she was seized with unbearable headaches. Rumors circulated throughout the town that she was an alcoholic, and, over time, her eccentric behavior was identified by locals as paranoia. After a reported confrontation with her sister, Dickinson was taken to the Danville State Hospital for the Insane.

After five weeks, she was re-evaluated by a different doctor and released. Befriended by this physician and his wife, she relocated to their home in Goshen, New York. Immediately following her release, she brought litigation against her sister and the doctor responsible for her commitment. The trial, held in 1895, resulted in a hung jury: two years later, the case was retried. Although Dickinson was found unquestionably sane, she was awarded only six and one-quarter cents and held responsible for court costs that were over $3,500. However, she did collect some compensation from a libel suit against the New York newspapers; in addition, the $25,000 lawsuit against the physician who had committed Dickinson to Danville was settled out of court. Dickinson lived to be nearly 90, spending the last 40 years of her life peacefully in New York. Though she continued writing plays, these were never published. Outliving most of her contemporaries, she faced obscurity and often reminisced over old newspaper clippings and letters. She died in Goshen six days before her 90th birthday. Though the new generation did not realize how Anna Dickinson's passionate speeches had expanded their role, all women are indebted to her; for her actions helped dismantle the cultural ideals that restricted women who spoke in public.

SOURCES:

Dickinson, Anna E. *A Ragged Register (of People Places and Opinions)*. NY: Harper and Brothers, 1879.

———. *A Paying Investment*. Boston: James R. Osgood, 1876.

———. *What Answer?* Boston: Fields, Osgood, 1869.

Chester, Giraud. *Embattled Maiden: The Life of Anna Dickinson*. NY: Putnam, 1951.

Venet, Wendy Hamand. *Neither Ballots nor Bullets: Women Abolitionists and the Civil War*. Charlottesville, VA: University Press of Virginia, 1991.

SUGGESTED READING:

Boase, Paul H., ed. *The Rhetoric of Protest and Reform: 1878–1898*. Athens, OH: Ohio University Press, 1980.

Yellin, Jean Fagan, and John C. Van Horne, eds. *The Abolitionist Sisterhood: Women's Political Culture in Antebellum America*. Ithaca: Cornell University Press, 1994.

COLLECTIONS:

Anna E. Dickinson Papers, Library of Congress.

Marilyn Costanzo, freelance writer
in history, Grove City, Pennsylvania

Dickinson, Emily (1830–1886)

American poet often described misleadingly as a "virgin recluse" and "partially cracked poetess" (her own phrase), who is now widely regarded as one of America's 19th-century geniuses of letters. Pronunciation: DICK-inson. *Born Emily Elizabeth Dickinson on December 10, 1830, in Amherst, Massachusetts; died also in Amherst in her own home on May 15, 1886; daugh-*

ter of Edward Dickinson (a lawyer, businessman, and treasurer of Amherst College) and Emily (Norcross) Dickinson; attended Amherst's "Primary School" beginning in 1835; in 1840, with her sister Lavinia, attended Amherst Academy, 1840–1847; attended Mt.

Holyoke Female Seminary in 1847–1848; never married; no children.

Evaded the religious revivals in the area, noting later in a poem: "I keep [the Sabbath] staying at home" (1844 and 1850); began friendship with Susan

Gilbert (1850); wrote "Brother Pegasus" letter to Austin on his engagement to Susan (1853); wrote letter: "Sue, you can go or stay" to Susan Gilbert (1854); moved back to the Homestead with family (1855); with Austin and Sue married (1856) and living in The Evergreens next door, exchanged letters between the two houses, especially with Sue (1856–86); wrote the "Master" letters during greatest poetic outpouring (1858–60s); workshopped "Safe in their Alabaster Chambers" with Sue (1861); sent her first letter to Thomas Higginson (April 15, 1862)—"Are you too deeply occupied to say if my Verse is alive?" and a second letter (April 25): "Thank you for the surgery"; wrote Higginson after publication of "A Narrow Fellow in the Grass" (1866): "It was robbed of me . . . I told you I did not print"; refused Higginson's invitation to visit in Boston, preferring to meet on her terms at her own home (1869); after her father died in Boston (1874), wrote Higginson: "His heart was pure and terrible and I think no other like it exists"; her mother was paralyzed from an illness (1875) and died (November 1882), followed by Emily's beloved nephew Gilbert Dickinson (1883); fell ill (1884); wrote to the Norcrosses her last letter (early May 1886): "Little Cousins, Called Back. Emily."

Selected publications: "I taste a liquor never brewed," under the title "The Maywine," Springfield Weekly Republican (1861); "Safe in their Alabaster Chambers," Republican (1862); "Some keep the Sabbath going to Church," Roundtable, and "Blazing in Gold and Quenching in Purple," Republican (1864); "A Narrow Fellow in the Grass," under the title "The Snake," Republican (1866); "Success is Counted Sweetest," A Masque of Poets (1879). Posthumous publication of Emily Dickinson's work began with Poems by Emily Dickinson, edited by Mabel Loomis Todd and T.W. Higginson (Roberts Brothers, Boston, 1890).

On July 18, 1862, in apparent response to Thomas Higginson's request for a photograph, Emily Dickinson wrote: "Could you believe me—without? I had no portrait now, but am small, like the Wren, and my Hair is bold, like the Chestnut Bur—and my eyes like the Sherry in the glass that the Guest leaves—would this do just as well?" The playful allusiveness of her response, her firm refusal to allow any agency, other than herself and her own language, control or categorize an idea of who she was are hallmarks of this writer's poetic and personal strategy. During an age of evangelical ardor when women of means were educated in order to do God's work, and when marriage and the management of home were her proper sphere, Emily

Dickinson chose otherwise. Because the study of women writers has been neglected, Emily Dickinson has sometimes seemed to stand completely alone in the women's section of the 19th-century canon of American Literature, in *this* solitude the myths of her peculiarities twine thickly about her—the "virginal" white dress, her withdrawal from society, the whimsy of baskets lowered from her window with gifts for children below, a disinterest in publication, and the shadow of unrequited love. But these were the elements of the female poet's personae—Dickinson played on them, and readers felt safe with them because they reinforced an image of ideal femininity. But against the rumors of the "partially cracked poetess," 20th-century poet **Adrienne Rich** imagines instead that Emily Dickinson was a woman who recognized her own gifts and "practiced the necessary economies." When Emily Dickinson mimed locking her bedroom door with an imaginary key during the visit of her niece, Martha, and said, "Matty: here's freedom," she was telling nothing less than the truth.

"I know that Emily Dickinson wrote most emphatic things in the pantry, so cool and quiet, while she skimmed the milk, because I sat on the footstool behind the door, in delight, as she read to me," said **Louise Norcross** of her cousin. "The blinds were closed, but through the green slats she saw all those fascinating ups and downs going on outside that she wrote about." Imagine Dickinson, her hands soft with flour from the bread she has been kneading, reaching quickly for the paper, the back of an envelope or a grocery list, so she can catch the ideas as they come to her and delight then in sharing them with an immediate audience. Emily Dickinson's solitary room was the best bedroom in the house, and it was filled with "a certain slant of light" that must have angled comfortably across her shoulder to illuminate the pages of her book. She wrote there, too, at a small desk with a single drawer. And later took her needle and thread and used them to bind the books of her poetry that her sister **Lavinia** would find after her death. When, in 1862, Dickinson wrote: "The Soul selects her own Society—/ Then—shuts the door," she described the fierceness of her choice to live her life according to what she knew was both true and necessary. A lyric poet for whom metaphor was a language, Dickinson's own slant truths are no more misleading than her early editors' winnowing of her nature. Her poetic subjects have been categorized as Death, Nature, and Love, and those most frequently offered to students have seemed bright, safe affirmations of "women's subjects." But Emily Dickinson wrote about nature and natural phenomena as one who had studied the sciences, and she wrote about suicide, madness, and violence, the grave and death, and language, power, and sexual ecstasy with passion and intellect. Attempts to categorize her would seem to deny the kind of language she created: moving, various and variant, something alive, still living.

"There was nothing in the parentage or direct heredity of Emily Dickinson to account for her genius," writes **Martha Dickinson Bianchi** in the first chapter of her 1924 biography of the poet. But perhaps genius is unaccountable. Emily Dickinson's family were well-to-do people whose lives were intertwined with the fortunes of the growing town of Amherst, the Academy, and the College. Her parents were well-educated: **Emily Norcross** attended boarding school in New Haven and Edward Dickinson graduated from Yale, class of 1823. Their courtship letters echo the traditional moral ideals of the time and establish the tone of their relationship that would follow "the traditional pattern of dominant husband and sweet, submissive wife," notes Richard Sewall. Edward Dickinson was a man of ambition and moral certitude. A public figure, he practiced law and brought the railroad to Amherst much as his father had been instrumental in the founding of the college; Edward served as a representative to the General Court of Massachusetts and as treasurer of Amherst College (a position his son, Austin, would later occupy).

During Emily Dickinson's lifetime, Amherst's village green was a field with a frog pond surrounded by individual houses and dirt roads radiating outward into farmland and countryside. Households drew their own water and cut their own wood for cooking and heat; after dark, reading and sewing occurred in lamplight—candles were homemade and tallow. The west half of the Homestead, a New England style brick house built by Dickinson's grandfather, and later sold and repurchased as family fortunes shifted, was small for the 13 people who lived there when Emily Dickinson was born. Her early letters to her brother Austin, "dear bedfellow," evoke the crowded household, and while her connection between literary appropriateness and proper behavior—"They shut me up in Prose—/ As when a little Girl/ They put me in a closet/ Because they liked me *still*"—may not be strictly autobiographical, it suggests that there was little room for individual idiosyncracy. Edward Dickinson has been described as a prohibitive parent: "He buys me many Books—but begs me not to read them—be-

cause he fears they joggle the Mind"—but Emily Dickinson, though professing to fear her father, seemed to have a sense of humor concerning the peculiarities of all members of her family.

Daily life in a small New England town, even for an affluent family, was exacting, serious, time-consuming business—or, in the poet's lexicon, *prose*—it necessitated conformity, something Emily Dickinson made a career of resisting. Women's work would have included the practical skills of cooking, baking, cleaning, sewing (both linens and clothing), attending to general medicinal needs, child care, early education, neighborly and social calling, and, in the Dickinson house which was a center for Amherst social and cultural activity, the responsibilities for entertaining also belonged to the woman's sphere.

Tell all the Truth but tell it slant.

—Emily Dickinson, c. 1868

The seeming paradox of Emily Dickinson's life is that she appears to have chosen a "closet" (her home, and the bedroom and pantry in which she wrote) as her method of escaping conformity. But Dickinson's "closet" opened up from the inside; the physical walls protected the flowering of her extraordinary vision, and her mother and sister bore the responsibilities of the housekeeping that nurtured her gift. "I never had a mother," Dickinson said, and scholars have speculated about a significant "break" between mother and daughter and an ensuing bitterness. Not much is known about Emily Norcross Dickinson, though her daughter's adolescent letters reflect resentment that her mother encouraged capitulation to a woman's accepted role—to the Sewing Society and the housekeeping—but these were also women whose relationships were abiding and mutable. After her mother's last illness and death, Emily Dickinson wrote: "We were never intimate Mother and Children while she was our Mother—but Mines in the same Ground meet by tunneling and when she became our Child the Affection came." Possibly "not having a mother" was an absence Emily Dickinson, who claimed herself as Eve, experienced in a literary sense— there was no precedence for her literary project, no one mother to her use of language, and "nothing to account for her genius."

Emily Dickinson's education took place in the balance between assumptions of women's subordinate status and the fervor of Amherst's intellectual growth. "God has designed nothing in vain," said the poet's grandfather, Samuel Fowler Dickinson, in reference to the education of women. The primary school that Emily Dickinson attended from 1835 to 1840 offered the rudiments of language, mathematics, and perhaps some science. But it was at Amherst Academy (founded in 1814, and out of which the college later grew) where Emily's intellectual faculties were encouraged and stimulated. In Dickinson's time, the Academy had approximately 100 girls enrolled; Emily was registered in the "English Course," and her teachers were often the talented, devoted young graduates of the college. Here Dickinson was known as a wit; she wrote comic sermons parodying the rhetoric of the local clergy, and spent her days studying and socializing in the stimulating company of other bright young men and women.

The curriculum was underscored by an understanding that religious principles were superior to all others, but the scholarship reflected by her teachers and the teachers at the adjacent college was rich in its conception and fully attuned to all the sciences of the natural world—affini-

Allison's House by Susan Glaspell, starring Eva Le Gallienne (left), was loosely based on the life of Emily Dickinson.

ties that the mature Dickinson's poetry would reflect in her specific references to geology, the seasons and weathers, and the animals and birds of her native state. In the intensity of Dickinson's language, "March is the Month of Expectation"—"his shoes are Purple"; the blue jay is a "prompt-executive Bird," the snake, "a Whiplash/ Unbraids in the Sun," and a sunset "Blaz[es] in Gold and Quench[es] in Purple."

Much has been made of Emily Dickinson's leaving Mt. Holyoke Female Seminary after only three terms: speculations include her poor health (she left once for a persistent cough), and her father's desire to have her home, but though her closer women friends were Amherst girls and women, she seems to have enjoyed the work at Mt. Holyoke and the example of *Mary Lyon, the school's leading intellect and founder. Sewall suggests that Dickinson's significant formal education had already taken place at the Academy, and further, that Dickinson herself preferred, finally, her own home library. Books were a passion and took her farther afield in her mind and imagination than the body could have traveled.

Milton was a favorite, as well as Shakespeare (Longfellow's "Kavanaugh" had to be smuggled into the house because poetry as a work of pure imagination was frivolous). Dickinson read and was nurtured throughout her life by the work of women writers: George Eliot (*Mary Anne Evans), *Elizabeth Barrett Browning, and the *Brontës. She read and considered both what was new and what was "classic"; what was "acceptable" and what was not (though she claimed never to have read the other mid-19th century genius of letters, Walt Whitman, saying, "I have heard he is disgraceful").

The 1850s were a difficult and formative decade for Dickinson. Amherst, Massachusetts was a seat for the evangelical ardor that swept through the northeast during the middle of the century. While her circle of girlhood friends, **Abiah Root**, **Abby Wood**, **Mary Wagner**, and **Jane Hitchcock** were accepted into the church at this time, Emily Dickinson "kept [the Sabbath] staying at home" despite considerable social pressure. A puritan doctrine of self-sacrifice was preached to both men and women from all the pulpits, reprinted in all the magazines, and reflected in the sentiments of society, but it had the most profound effect on women, whose sphere was already regularized. In a very real sense, a woman's salvation was in her dustrag, and in the industry of her fingers as she sewed clothing for the poor. "God keep me from what they call households," wrote Dickinson, who sewed instead her own manuscripts into books that had to wait until the world was ready for them. "Housekeeping is a prickly art," she said, then practiced the necessary economies. Her decision made her "womanhood" suspect and cost her many of her childhood friends whose decisions to accept Christ and their womanly duties as wives and mothers separated Emily from them as surely as if they spoke another language. Dickinson's poems on marriage, and her gradual withdrawal from society just as her childhood friends were coupling, have been linked to a myth of unrequited love. But in the poem that begins, "Title Divine is Mine!" the wife is "Born—Bridalled/ Shrouded—/ In a Day." The meanings are multiple and pointed. The wife is an object, here made (born) in a single day; bridalled plays on images of marriage (cultural ritual), of entrapment (harness), and resentment (to bridle). Her final silencing, "shrouded," merges death and "bride" in the same image. Contrary to unquestioned ideas about woman's preferred estate, Dickinson's "wife" is not to be envied, for she represents a ceremonious and horrifying loss of autonomy and voice that occurs in the very moment of celebration.

"We are the only poets, and everyone else is prose," Emily Dickinson wrote to **Susan Gilbert** in the early 1850s. This letter is a marker at the beginning of a long and passionate friendship that was both literary and loving. In the beginning, Austin and Emily Dickinson were friends of the Gilbert sisters, **Martha** and Susan. But for Emily Dickinson, Susan Gilbert became muse ("to be Susan is Imagination"), reader, companion, "sister," and "The Only Woman in the World." Their letters to each other continued mostly unabated for 30 years and make clear (against the stories of seclusion) that there were always visits between them. In the early letters, the young women exchange family news, ideas about books, descriptions of life, ideas, and dreams. They loved gardening and recipes and long walks. And Emily's letters to Sue are often passionate and effusive, many of the allusions specify longing and physical embrace. "Susie, will you indeed come home next Saturday, and be my own again, and kiss me as you used to?" Dickinson struggles, too, with a love she recognizes is not conventional, abjuring, "Susie, forgive me Darling, for every word I say." In 1854, after Susan Gilbert had been accepted into the church and had chosen to marry Dickinson's brother, Emily wrote to Austin: "Now Brother Pegasus, I'll tell you what it is—I've been in the habit myself of writing some few things, and it rather appears to me that you're getting away with my patent, so you'd better be somewhat careful, or I'll call the police." It is a witty, angry letter and it stakes an important claim. Austin had just written a poem (probably announcing his engagement). The possible loss of Sue is devastating to Dickinson, but she claims her poetic identity here; writing is her sole province. It is not clear whether she had hoped to have had an actual partnership or marriage with Sue herself; the angriest letter, "Sue, you can go or stay," signals hurt, and perhaps ambivalence, but it also begins their mature relationship (and the eventual exchange of letter/poems) with the inclusion of two lines of poetry:

> I have a Bird in spring
> Which for myself doth sing—

The letters that follow make it clear that "Sweet Sue" remained her muse and companion, even after she married Austin and moved to The Evergreens next door in 1856, and that throughout the early 1860s at least there were many visits between their homes, and many bright, social evenings at The Evergreens.

Dickinson's three "Master" letters to an unknown, assumed male audience, were written between 1858 and 1862. The letters are romantic and supplicatory in tone and a great deal of consideration has been given to questions of the master's identity and relevance regarding the notion that Dickinson struggled at this time with unrequited love that precipitated her withdrawal from society. (Scholars have speculated that master could have been Judge Lord, Charles Wadsworth, or Samuel Bowles, all men of considerable intellect with whom she corresponded.) But **Martha Nell Smith**'s recent holographic study of the letters calls the identity of the master as male into question, and other readings suggest that Dickinson was playing with certain conventional forms, creating, in effect, a writer's exercise. She always played with gender in her poetry, sometimes assuming a male personae, but since she also questioned the patriarchal apportionment of power, it seems imbalanced to give so much weight to three unaddressed letters (they are published in a single volume of their own) while largely ignoring the significant exchanges occurring between Sue and Emily.

In 1861, Emily Dickinson sent a draft of "Safe in their Alabaster Chambers" to Susan. She wanted the reader she trusted most, writes Martha Nell Smith, a reader she considered a fellow poet to think about these lines with her. When Dickinson wrote two alternative second stanzas for her friend, Sue replied: "You never made a peer for that verse, and I guess you[r] kingdom doesn't hold one—I always go to the fire and get warm after thinking of it, but I never *can* again." In a similar language, Dickinson apparently remarked: "If I read a book and it makes my whole body so cold no fire ever can warm me I know that is poetry. If I feel physically as if the top of my head were taken off, I know that is poetry. Is there any other way." Both women describe the effects of language as sensual, frankly eroticized, as well as intellectual, and between them, in the process of this "workshop" and others, they articulated a philosophy of poetry that insisted upon a reader's participation, and on variation which would keep a text in continuous play.

Emily Dickinson's refusal to "publish" during her lifetime has largely been interpreted as a "feminine" gesture, a modest shrinking back from public view, but Smith asserts instead that she published herself in the letter-poems, and in the 40 handsewn fascicle volumes, eschewing with lawyerly distinction not publication but print, which would (and did) have the effect of regularizing her lines and fixing what she had intended to remain mutable. In 1862, Dickinson began her correspondence with Thomas Wentworth Higginson, a noted magazine editor, who had just published his "Letter to a Young Contributor" in *The Atlantic Monthly*. "Can you tell me if my verse is alive?" she asked and sent him two poems (she had written more than 300 by this time), then "thanked him for the surgery" when he'd replied with suggestions. But though she signed herself his "scholar" in their lengthy correspondence, Dickinson rarely took his surgical advice and often needed to explain her intentions to him. When "A Narrow Fellow in the Grass" was published in 1866 (possibly because Susan had submitted it), Dickinson protested her intentions to Higginson, saying, "It was robbed of me, . . . and defeated of the third line. . . . I told you I did not print." This was not a poet without audience; this was a poet who insisted upon the fluidity of a text. Each of her variant versions of a single poem might be read as a finished draft published to a specific reader in order to create a dialogue of meaning. That she has often been mis-read, as when Higginson remarked about the erotically charged "Wild Nights, Wild Nights!" that he hesitated to print it "lest the malignant read into it more than that virgin recluse ever dreamed of putting there," is largely a factor of the truths, slant or otherwise, that readers are willing to imagine.

Her life from the 1860s on, though private, was not without turmoil. Her eyesight troubled her, necessitating several trips to Boston. Scholars have speculated that she suffered from exotropia, a misalignment of the pupils which could have made her extremely sensitive to light. And there were a number of deaths: her father, her mother, Judge Lord, her beloved nephew Gilbert, Sue's first child, and *Helen Hunt Jackson, a friend from childhood. In 1882, when Austin Dickinson began his relationship with ❦▶ Mabel Loomis Todd, the wife of a young Amherst College professor, it is likely that Emily lost the pleasure of visits with Sue, though the correspondence prevailed. Dickinson's greatest poetic outpouring had occurred in the late 1850s and throughout the '60s, but she continued to write both poetry and letters until the end of her life dealing "her pretty words like Blades—/ How glittering they shone—/ And every One unbared a Nerve/ or wantoned with a Bone." She remained fierce, witty, and physical, a poet who described her position as a woman and poet in terms of paradox and extremes: "My Life had stood—/ a Loaded Gun—."

At her death, her coffin was not carried to the cemetery through the streets she had largely eschewed for 30 years, rather across the fields, sweet with clover and the wild flowers she had loved. Upstairs, in a drawer her poems were waiting, "a letter to the world" when it was ready. Her early editors would disagree about the nature of her work and her relationships and would regularize her lines in print. But Dickinson's own slant truths prevail. In that early letter to Higginson describing her eyes "like the sherry in the glass the guest leaves," she also wrote:

> [Father] says Death might occur, and he has Molds of all the rest—but has no Mold of me, but I notice the quick wore off those things in a few days, and forestall the dishonor—you will think no caprice of me—.

No caprice, perhaps, and no mold either to contain the fluid evanescence of her mind and the quick of the voice that wrote to the bone and bared the nerves.

SOURCES:

Bianchi, Martha Dickinson. *The Life and Letters of Emily Dickinson*. Boston: Houghton Mifflin, 1924.

Johnson, Thomas H., ed. *The Complete Poems of Emily Dickinson*. Boston: Little, Brown, 1960.

Rich, Adrienne. "Vesuvius at Home: The Power of Emily Dickinson," in *On Lies, Secrets and Silence: Selected Prose: 1966–1978*. NY: W.W. Norton, 1979, pp. 157–183.

Sands, Marget. "The Revery Alone: Emily Dickinson's Poetics of Resistance and Desire," presented at The International Emily Dickinson Conference, Innsbruck, Austria, 1995.

Sewall, Richard B. *The Life of Emily Dickinson*. NY: Farrar, Straus and Giroux, 1974.

Smith, Martha Nell. *Rowing in Eden*. Austin, TX: University of Texas Press, 1992.

SUGGESTED READING:

Barker, Wendy. *Lunacy of Light: Emily Dickinson and the Experience of Metaphor*. Carbondale, IL: University of Illinois Press, 1987.

Bennett, Paula. *My Life a Loaded Gun: Female Creativity and Feminist Poetics*. Boston, MA: Beacon Press, 1986.

Cody, John. *After Great Pain: The Inner Life of Emily Dickinson*. Cambridge, MA: Belknap Press, 1971.

Howe, Susan. *My Emily Dickinson*. Berkely: North Atlantic Books, 1985.

Miller, Cristanne. *Emily Dickinson: A Poet's Grammar*. Cambridge, MA: Harvard University Press, 1987.

Narkiewicz, Beverly S. "Poets and Friends: Emily Dickinson and Helen Hunt Jackson," in *American History*. December 1995.

COLLECTIONS:

Correspondence, prose fragments, and manuscripts are located in the Frost Library at Amherst College and at the Houghton Library, Harvard University.

RELATED MEDIA:

The Belle of Amherst, a play based on the life of Emily Dickinson written by William Luce, opened on Broadway in 1976; Emily Dickinson was portrayed by *Julie Harris.

A place setting at "The Dinner Party" by **Judy Chicago**.

Susan Perry Morehouse,
Assistant Professor of Creative Writing,
Alfred University, Alfred, New York

Todd, Mabel Loomis (1858–1932)

*American poet, editor, and writer of travel books. Born Mabel Loomis on November 10, 1858, in Cambridge, Massachusetts; died on October 14, 1932; daughter of Eben J. Loomis (a poet-astronomer) and Mary Alden (Wilder) Loomis (a direct descendant of John Alden); educated privately in Washington and Boston; graduated from the Georgetown Seminary; studied music and painting in Boston; married David Todd (a professor of astronomy and director of the observatory at Amherst), in 1879; children: *Millicent Todd Bingham (1880–1968, married Walter Van Dyke Bingham).*

In the company of two astronomers (her father and husband), Mabel Loomis Todd became intrigued by the science. Todd accompanied her professor-husband David Todd to Japan in 1887 to serve as his assistant while observing the total eclipse of the sun; she then wrote of the expedition for several American newspapers and magazines. In 1889, the couple traveled to West Africa to view another eclipse. They followed the sun for almost 20 years—to Tripoli, Dutch East Indies, Chile, and Russia—while Mabel Todd continued to write of their experiences.

While living in Amherst, she cultivated a relationship with *Emily Dickinson and became romantically involved with Emily's brother Austin. Following the poet's death, and with the assistance of Austin, **Lavinia Dickinson**, and Thomas Wentworth Higginson, Todd edited and published two volumes of Dickinson's poetry (which included biographical prefaces). Mabel Todd was an accomplished pianist, singer, and lively lecturer; she was also a popular speaker on the subject of Emily Dickinson.

SUGGESTED READING:

Longsworth, Polly. *Austin and Mabel: The Amherst Affair and Love Letters of Austin Dickinson and Mabel Loomis Todd*. NY: Holt, 1984.

Dido (fl. 800 BCE)

Phoenician princess. Name variations: Elissa. Flourished 800 BCE; daughter of Belus, king of Tyre; sister of Pygmalion; married Sychaeus also known as Acerbas.

Daughter of Belus, king of the Phoenician city of Tyre, Dido allegedly founded the city of Carthage. While the accuracy of this claim is not confirmable, we do know that Tyre *did* found Carthage ("New City") on the north African coast near modern Tunis about 800 BCE. If there is any truth to the myths about Dido as reported by the Greeks and Romans hundreds of years after her day, she originally was called "Elissa" and only received her famous name upon arriving in north Africa, apparently in honor of her success there after having been exiled from her native city of Tyre. (Dido perhaps means "the Wanderer.")

*Dido on the
funeral pyre.*

As most versions of her story run, Dido's brother Pygmalion succeeded their father as the king of Tyre. Thereafter, his envy over the wealth and influence of Dido's husband Sychaeus (or Acerbas, depending on what version of the myth is followed) led Pygmalion to murder his brother-in-law. As a result, Dido is reported to have fled Tyre with a body of supporters and, after landing on the African coast of the Mediterranean, founded the city of Carthage. It is possible this event meets with a moment of historical truth, for political and financial rivalries in ancient cities led with some frequency to factional conflicts which resulted in one party's expulsion into colonial activity. If something along these lines did indeed lead to Carthage's foundation, apparently the colonists transcended their initial animosity for Tyre, for the two cities maintained lucrative trading ties for centuries.

After founding Carthage, Dido is said to have met with a tragic end. In an early version of her story, she surrendered herself to flames rather than marry a Libyan king. Later, it was believed that she committed suicide when abandoned by the Trojan hero Aeneas. As this second, better known version of Dido's story has it (thanks to Virgil's *Aeneid*), the Trojan hero Aeneas and his band (fleeing their native city upon its destruction at the hands of the Greeks led by Agamemnon, c. 1180 BCE), found themselves storm swept onto the African coast near Carthage where they went to seek sanctuary from Dido. At Carthage, in order to ensure a friendly reception for her son, the goddess Venus made Dido fall in love with Aeneas, despite Dido's previous pledge that she would ever remain faithful to her murdered first husband. For a while, as the Trojans recovered from their trials, Aeneas lived with Dido (she thought in a state of marriage) and there helped her to construct her famous city. After a time, however, propelled by the gods to abandon the woman he now loved in order to travel to Italy where he was intended to play a role in the foundation of Rome, Aeneas left Carthage and Dido without a word of explanation. (Presumably, a final confrontation with Dido would have been too painful for the dutiful Aeneas to bear.) Feeling betrayed by the lover she had saved from the sea, Dido is said thereafter to have quickly committed suicide, but not before she cursed Aeneas and his line (the eventual Romans) as her most hated enemies.

Whatever historical kernel gave rise to the Dido stories (it is particularly difficult to rationalize the 12th century BCE date of Aeneas with the 9th century date of Dido), her importance as a literary figure was manifest by the mid-2nd century BCE, when her curse was credited as the main cause of the Punic Wars (First 264–241, Second 218–201, and Third 148–146): Republican Rome's most traumatic conflicts, ending only with Carthage's absolute destruction. By Virgil's time (1st century BCE), Dido was recognized as Rome's ultimate archenemy. As such, she represented not only the cause of the Punic Wars, but also became useful in the propaganda of Caesar Augustus, Virgil's contemporary and

quasi-patron. In this latter manifestation, Aeneas (Augustus' mythological ancestor) stood for Augustus, while Dido stood for *Cleopatra VII of Egypt, the enemy (along with her Roman lover, Marc Antony) overcome by Augustus whose defeat was necessary for Rome to be "refounded" as a prosperous and successful state.

William Greenwalt, Associate
Professor of Classical History,
Santa Clara University, Santa Clara, California

Didrikson, Babe (1911–1956).

See Zaharias, Babe Didrikson.

Diebold, Laure (1915–1964)

French partisan. Name variations: Mona. Born Laure Mutschler in 1915 in the Bas-Rhin section of Alsace; married Eugene Diebold (a fellow résistant), in 1942.

Fluent in both French and German, Laure Diebold was employed as a bilingual secretary for a company in Saint-Die at the beginning of World War II. For the first year, she helped escapees elude the Nazis, until she also had to escape to the unoccupied zone. On her honeymoon in 1942, she and her husband slipped from one hotel room to another, gathering information, coding it and transmitting it to London, then decoding messages from London and disseminating them.

Within three months, they were arrested. Upon release, the Diebolds went underground. Laure adopted the name Mona and became a liaison agent. On September 1, 1942, she was appointed secretary to Jean Moulin, whom she knew as Rex. Following his capture, she moved to Paris to work for Moulin's successor Georges Bidault. In September 1943, the Diebolds were arrested and imprisoned at Fresnes. To avoid confession under torture, Laure immediately admitted to being a partisan, but maintained her insignificance as a postbox or courier, only passing on sealed messages. She withstood interrogation so well that she was believed.

In June 1944, she was sent to Auschwitz, unaware that her husband was also there. Eventually, she was transferred to Ravensbrück, then Taucha, near Leipzig. In the camps, she came down with typhus and diphtheria; she was put on the list twice for extermination and was twice saved by a Czech doctor who changed the orders. When the Americans freed the inmates of Taucha in April 1945, Laure Diebold walked out alive. She arrived in Paris on May 16; her husband arrived two days later. Though she suffered ill health the rest of her life, Diebold lived until 1964. She was awarded the *Compagnon de la Liberation*. There were many women active in the Resistance. A list would include **Elaine Mordeaux, Marie-Helene Lefaucheux** (1904–1964), **Marie-Madeleine Fourcade** (1909–1989), **Virginia Hall**, *****Danielle Casanova** (1909–1943), **Yvonne Oddon, Germaine Tillion** (1907—), and thousands more.

SOURCES:
Wilhelm, Maria. *For the Glory of France: The Story of the French Resistance*. NY: Julian Messner, 1968.

Diemer, Emma Lou (1927—)

American musician, composer of over 150 pieces, especially known for her church music. Born in Kansas City, Missouri, on November 24, 1927; daughter of George Willis and Myrtle (Casebolt) Diemer; studied with Paul Hindemith, Howard Hanson, Roger Sessions, and Ernst Toch; studied at the Kansas City Conservatory; awarded a Fulbright Fellowship to study composition and piano at the Royal Conservatory in Brussels, Belgium; received her bachelor and masters degrees from Yale University; received Doctor of Philosophy in composition from the Eastman School of Music.

While in high school, Emma Lou Diemer began to compose music. "During that time I decided to write music that avoided tonality," she wrote, "although I was not familiar with twelve tone music. So, I wrote my first piece and didn't repeat notes and it sounded very dissonant." Her musical abilities gained her admittance to Yale where she studied with Paul Hindemith and was awarded a Fulbright Scholarship to study composition. From 1959 to 1961, after receiving her Ph.D., Diemer was composer-in-residence for the Arlington, Virginia, secondary schools. She resumed this role in the Baltimore Public Schools from 1964 to 1965 while continuing to produce a steady stream of works for choral groups, orchestras, bands, solo instruments, and chamber groups.

Diemer felt that writing for non-professional musical groups was a sound discipline that helped her style. Her *Three Anniversary Choruses* performed by the South Carolina All-State Chorus in 1970 reflects this philosophy. She also maintained that the development of choruses in secondary schools throughout America was crucial to the development of musical life in the country. Her style has been described as simple and practical, singable and playable. At the same time, she was never afraid to develop new horizons. She was frequently commissioned to write compositions for many schools, churches, and special occasions. Throughout her career, Emma Lou Diemer supported herself through composition, a rare feat for composers in the 20th century.

SOURCES:
Cohen, Aaron I. *International Encyclopedia of Women Composers*. 2 vols. NY: Books & Music (USA), 1987.
Morton, Brian, and Collins, Pamela. *Contemporary Composers*. Chicago: St. James Press, 1981.

John Haag, Athens, Georgia

Dietrich, Marlene (1901–1992)

German-born film actress who became an international celebrity following her appearance in The Blue Angel. *Born Maria Magdalena Dietrich in Berlin, Germany, on December 27, 1901; died in Paris, France, on May 6, 1992, of liver and kidney failure; daughter of Louis (a lieutenant in the Royal Prussian police) and Wilhemina (Felsing) Dietrich; had an older sister, Elisabeth; married Rudolph Sieber, in 1923; children: one daughter, Maria Riva (b. 1924).*

Began her show business career as a chorus girl and was given her first substantial film role (1923); known only to German-speaking audiences until her discovery by director Josef von Sternberg, who cast her as the female lead in his The Blue Angel (1929); an international hit, the film brought her to Hollywood; continued to work with von Sternberg on a number of films before establishing professional credentials on her own and gaining international celebrity status; refused an offer by Hitler just before World War II to return to Germany and appear only in German films; instead, became a U.S. citizen, entertained U.S. troops during the war, and was awarded the National Medal of Freedom for tireless support of the Allied war effort; acting career faded (1950s), though she was much praised for work in smaller roles in such prestigious films Judgment at Nuremberg (1961); rarely appeared in public (1980s), only her voice being heard in the last film in which she participated, the biography Marlene (1984).

Filmography:

Germany: Der kleine Napoleon (1923); Tragödie der Liebe (1923); Der Mensch am Wege (1923); Der Sprung ins Leben (1924); Die Freudlose Gasse (1925); Manon Lescaut (1926); Eine Dubarry von heute (1926); Kopf hoch Charly! (1926); Madame wünst keine Kinder (1926); Der Juxbaron (1927); Sein grösser Bluff (1927); Wenn ein Weib den Weg verliert (1927); Prinzessin Olala (1928); Ich küsse ihre Hand Madame (1929); Die Frau nach der man sich sehnt (1929); Das Schiff der verlorenen Menschen (1929); Gehfaren der Brautzeit (1929); Der blaue Engel (1930).

United States: Morocco *(1930)*; Dishonored *(1931)*; Shanghai Express *(1932)*; Blonde Venus *(1932)*; Song of Songs *(1933)*; The Scarlet Empress *(1934)*; The Devil Is a Woman *(1935)*; Desire *(1936)*; The Garden of Allah *(1936)*; *(British)* Knight Without Armor *(1937)*; Angel *(1937)*; Destry Rides Again *(1939)*; Seven Sinners *(1940)*; The Flame of New Orleans *(1941)*; Manpower *(1941)*; The Lady Is Willing *(1942)*; Pittsburgh *(1942)*; The Spoilers *(1942)*; *(cameo only)* Follow the Boys *(1944)*; Kismet *(1944)*; *(French)* Martin Roumagnac *(1946)*; Golden Earrings *(1947)*; A Foreign Affair *(1948)*; *(cameo only)* Jigsaw *(1949)*; Stage Fright *(1950)*; No Highway In the Sky *(1951)*; Rancho Notorious *(1952)*; *(cameo only)* Around the World in Eighty Days *(1956)*; Monte Carlo *(1957)*; Witness for the Prosecution *(1958)*; A Touch of Evil *(1958)*; Judgment at Nuremberg *(1961)*; *(narration only)* Black Fox *(1962)*; *(cameo only)* Paris When It Sizzles *(1964)*; Just a Gigolo *(1979)*; *(voice only)* Marlene *(1982)*.

On a warm summer's day in 1997, journalist **Francine du Plessix Gray** was invited to inspect a rather modest apartment on upper Park

Marlene Dietrich

Avenue in New York. Although Marlene Dietrich had died in Paris nearly five years previously and had not lived in New York since the late 1970s, her family had maintained the apartment virtually undisturbed before finally deciding to sell and put much of its contents up for auction at Sotheby's. In opposition to Dietrich's flamboyant and sometimes controversial lifestyle, Gray reported, the *objets d'art* and furnishings were few and unassuming and of less interest than a number of smaller items, the "private tokens of a complex woman." There was a small sewing table at which Dietrich, in the later years of her career, repaired the beads and sequins of the gowns worn for her cabaret act; two ancient rotary phones with cords long enough to allow Dietrich to talk while she moved about the kitchen preparing her favorite recipes; and a cheap electric clock onto which Dietrich had pasted the telephone numbers of the daughter and husband she rarely saw. Such were the domestic icons of a woman who was, successively, a notorious Hollywood "love goddess" and rival to *Greta Garbo, a hero of the Allied war effort in World War II, a smoky-voiced cabaret singer, and, for the last 20 years of her life, a recluse who refused to be photographed even for a documentary film prepared about her.

Take my lovely illusions—some for laughs, some for tears.

—Sung by Marlene Dietrich in the film *Foreign Affair*

Such notoriety did not seem likely during Marlene Dietrich's childhood in a bourgeois Berlin household ruled by her domineering father Louis Dietrich, a lieutenant in the Royal Prussian police, and, following his wishes, her disciplinarian mother **Wilhemina Felsing Dietrich**; they had two daughters. **Elisabeth** had been born in February of 1900, a year after the couple's marriage, while Maria Magdalena, later known as Marlene, followed on December 27, 1901. Friends noted that Marlene seemed to be the more clever of the two girls, able to read by the time she was four, as well as being prettier than her older sister, with the blue eyes and clear skin of her Prussian forebears. As soon as Marlene and Elisabeth were old enough, their mother assigned them daily household tasks to help her keep their genteel home in Berlin's Schöneberg section as immaculate as any of the military barracks her husband supervised. Louis Dietrich demanded inner discipline from his daughters, too, discouraging any outward display of emotion. As an elderly woman, Dietrich would still remember the sting of her mother's slap, delivered in private after a dancing lesson during which she had refused to partner one of the boys present and had pulled a long face. "You must not show your feelings," Wilhemina reminded her. "It is bad manners." Wilhemina did not even allow her daughters, or herself, the luxury of public displays of grief when Louis Dietrich died in 1907, after a fall from a horse precipitated a heart attack.

But Wilhemina took care to reward her daughters when they had performed up to standard, taking them to Berlin's Scala Theater, which then presented the city's largest variety shows full of jugglers, clowns, singers, and impersonators, or to the State Theater, famous throughout Europe for the quality of its dramatic productions. From their grandmother Felsing, the matriarch of a long-established family of jewelers, the girls learned about current fashions and the fine art of dressing and adornment by being taken to the Felsing jewelry shop on Berlin's Unter den Linden. By the time Marlene was enrolled in a girls' school with a female staff and had begun violin and piano lessons with female teachers, her world was largely devoid of men, the few males with whom they came in contact being "old or ill, not real men," Dietrich said. Even a stepfather—Eduard von Losch, another military man whom Wilhemina married in 1911—did not intrude, for he lived in the household only eight months before being called to duty and later dying of an infection from a battle wound received early in World War I. An uncle and two cousins were also among the nearly two million Germans killed during the conflict.

Wilhemina and her two girls survived the deprivations of wartime by moving to a smaller apartment, Wilhemina finding work as a housekeeper while struggling with her depression at the loss of two husbands. Marlene found her own solace in the stories and lessons of gay Parisian life before the war which had been taught to her by a French teacher on whom she developed her first crush. When the teacher was summarily fired as anti-French sentiment swept Germany on the outbreak of war, Marlene clung to the bright visions of a world of dance halls, music, and laughter. She also began to notice during these war years that men were, by and large, unnecessary. "[German women] did not seem to suffer in a world without men," she recalled many years later. "Our life among women had become such a pleasant habit that the prospect that the men might return . . . disturbed us—men who would again take the scepter in their hands and again become lords of their households."

Matters did not seem to improve with Germany's defeat at the end of the war, when Kaiser Wilhelm II abdicated his throne and the establishment of the Socialist Republic of Germany, with its severely leftist orientation, set off street riots throughout the country culminating in the assassination of the Republic's prime minister in 1919. That same year, a new, more moderate government was formed in Weimar, long a center of Germany's intellectual and musical life. Leaving Elisabeth behind in Berlin to begin training as a teacher, Wilhemina and Marlene moved to Weimar where Dietrich, now 17, began a course of study as a classical violinist and took advantage of living in a dormitory away from her mother by embarking on her first affair with a male lover, who happened to be her violin teacher. This indiscretion may have been responsible for Wilhemina's hurried move back to Berlin barely a year later, where Marlene was enrolled at Berlin's Music Academy. But the social and intellectual ferment that marked Weimar Germany was already having its effect on Wilhemina's younger daughter. It was during these years that Marlene became passionately devoted to the theater and cabaret, where the cynical wit and amorality of a country adrift after a crushing defeat found full expression.

Flooded by immigrants displaced by the upheavals of war, Berlin during the early 1920s had become the third largest city in the world with a population of some four million. The resulting cultural fertilization was evident in the explosive growth of artistic expression on the stage, where Max Reinhardt was staging innovative, avant-garde works at the Deutsches Theater for the intellectual upper classes while cabarets, popular with the middle and lower classes, were famous for their political satire and flaunting of sexual taboos ("We say no to everything!" one of them smirked in an advertisement). The German film industry, which had been consolidated under government sponsorship during the war in the immense Universum Film Aktien Gesellschaft (Universal Film Company, or UFA) was now privately held and was producing silent films known around the world for their startling creative effects and psychologically penetrating stories. (Among the many directors who learned their craft at UFA were Alfred Hitchcock, Billy Wilder, and Ernst Lubitsch, all of whom would eventually direct Marlene Dietrich.) Along with this artistic ferment came a complete lack of censorship, so that silent film masterpieces like *The Cabinet of Doctor Caligari* and *Dr. Mabuse* jostled for screen time with *Hyenas of Lust* and *A Man's Girlhood*.

Maria Magdalena Dietrich von Losch, now permanently living apart from Wilhemina, partook enthusiastically of Berlin's frenetic social life, earning her living by day in hat shops or glove factories and spending her nights at any number of cabarets catering to every variety of political and sexual orientation. It is likely that her roommate at this time, an aspiring writer named **Gerta Huber**, became the first of many female lovers. Friends from this period remembered Dietrich as a boisterous, somewhat chubby young woman fond of a good meal and a good time. "She was anything but a sex bomb," one of them recalled. "She was much more interested, although not exclusively, in women. If she wanted a man now and then, she simply showered him with sweetness, but any direct offer would have to come from her. She forgot [casual sexual encounters] immediately."

As her independence from her mother grew, Dietrich found work not as a violinist for a respectable orchestra, but in the small ensembles that played cabarets. She also managed to get herself accepted in Max Reinhardt's acting classes at the Deutsches Theater; and, on being repeatedly complimented on her legs, began posing for commercial photographers. Films beckoned, too, although her first audition at UFA's Templehof studios did not impress the director, who predicted she had no future in films. But it was under her chosen name of Marlene Dietrich (Marlene being a contraction of her first and middle names) that she was selected from a group of fellow acting students to play a small role in a melodrama called *Tragödie der Liebe* (The Tragedy of Love), in which she was given one scene that served as a brief comic relief in an otherwise grim tale of an ill-fated romance. She was hired for the picture after the director's assistant, a handsome blond named Rudolph Sieber, urged his superior to use her. A courtship ensued, Rudi Sieber attracted by Dietrich's sensuality and Dietrich impressed by Sieber's refined manners and the fact that he had influence with film directors. The two were married in a civil ceremony on May 17, 1923, by which time Marlene was already pregnant with a daughter, ❦ **Maria (Riva)**, born in December of that year.

Sieber attempted to keep a close eye on Dietrich's nocturnal adventures and her affections for other women, but even marriage failed to reduce his wife's reputation at Berlin's cabarets, at which she often appeared wearing a monocle, a feather boa, and no underwear. Her professional talents drew attention, too, when she was cast in her first major stage role in a drama at the

See sidebar on the following page

❧ Riva, Maria (1924—)

American writer and actress. Born Maria Sieber in December 23, 1924, in Berlin, Germany; daughter of Marlene Dietrich (1901–1992) and Rudolph Sieber; married; children: three sons.

Maria Riva was born Maria Sieber in 1924, the daughter of *Marlene Dietrich and Rudolph Sieber. In 1934, she appeared as an actress in the film The Scarlet Empress. Under the name Maria Riva, she also made frequent appearances on many top shows in the early years of television, including "Hallmark Hall of Fame," "Philco Playhouse," "Armstrong Circle Theater," "Omnibus," as well as ten appearances on "Studio One," and three on "Robert Montgomery Presents." Her mother kept her date of birth so secret, that Riva did not know the year until 1976, when she found her birth certificate among her just-deceased father's papers. In 1993, Riva published her landmark biography of her mother, a work that met with critical acclaim.

Grosses Schauspielhaus called *Von Mund zu Mund* (From Mouth to Mouth). Three musical numbers were inserted into her spoken dialogue, and Dietrich mesmerized audiences with her detached, almost disinterested delivery. She later said that the half-spoken, half-sung style she adopted was modeled on two leading singer/actresses of the day—*Zarah Leander, known for her poignant delivery of romantic ballads, and **Claire Waldoff**, famous for her gruff presentation to cabaret audiences of sharp social satires. Although one reviewer at the time called Waldoff "a barrel-chested little Valkyrie" and a modern biographer felt she looked "like Mickey Rooney in drag," Waldoff and Dietrich later became lovers and often appeared in cabaret shows together.

While Dietrich's film career seemed stalled, with only three small roles during 1926 and 1927, she became an overnight sensation for her work in a musical review at Berlin's Komödie Theater in *Es Leigt in der Luft* (It's in the Air), in which she and the wife of the show's producer famously played one sketch called "Sisters" with unmistakable lesbian undertones, emphasized by bunches of violets—known to all of Berlin's *demimonde* at the time as symbols of homosexuality— pinned to their costumes. "Marlene Dietrich sings with delicacy and tired elegance," one reviewer wrote. "The number 'Sisters' goes beyond anything so cultivatedly daring we've ever seen." While the show was playing to packed houses during 1928, Dietrich's notoriety landed her the title role in the sexually satirical film *Prinzessin Olala*, in which she was first compared to Greta Garbo, whose work Dietrich much admired. Another film role that year, playing the mistress of a man who murders his wife in *Die Frau nach der man sich sehnt* (The Woman One Longs For), strengthened the similarity between herself and Garbo, although the film's director, Kurt Bernhardt, found Dietrich exasperating. "She was so aware of her face that she would not let herself be photographed in profile, because her nose turned up somewhat," he later remembered. "She never moved her head from the spotlight over the camera, facing forward and refusing to move her head to speak with other actors. She simply looked at them out of the corner of her eye. Marlene looked fantastic, but as an actress she was the punishment of God." Bernhardt would not be the last to suffer from Dietrich's preoccupation with her appearance.

By now, Berlin representatives of major Hollywood studios were sending cables to America about "the new Garbo," even though for most Berliners, Marlene Dietrich remained a stage personality. In the audience one night during her appearance in a 1929 revue called *Zwei Krawatten* (Two Neckties) was an Austrian who had immigrated to Hollywood some 20 years before to become one of Paramount's leading directors, with seven successful films to his credit. Now casting the female lead in his next production, Josef von Sternberg knew he had found her when Dietrich stepped on stage that night. "Here was the face I had sought," he later wrote, "and as far as I could tell, a figure that did justice to it." Von Sternberg's film was *Der Blaue Engel* (The Blue Angel), based on a 1902 German novel about a respected bourgeois professor whose love for an amoral cabaret singer destroys him socially and professionally. Neither the film's producer nor its male star, the great German actor Emil Jannings, thought much of Dietrich's abilities when she auditioned, but von Sternberg was so smitten with her that he threatened to quit the film if she wasn't hired to play Lola Lola. "Von Sternberg had only one idea in his head," Dietrich later wrote. "To take me away from the stage and to make a movie actress out of me, to 'Pygmalion-ize' me. I didn't know what I was doing. I just tried to do what he told me." Von Sternberg dictated her every move, every expression, every reaction during the filming, which stretched from November of 1929 to January of 1930 because each scene had to be shot twice—once in German and once in English, Dietrich's thick accent adding even more frustration to the process. She sang four songs as Lola Lola, the most famous of which became her signature, "Falling in Love Again," although it was "A Regular Man," with its sexually domineering lyrics, that became the anthem of thousands of Berlin women during the early 1930s:

How he looks, I care a lot.
I can pick him like a shot.
There's nothing to it
I have to get a man that's a man,
That's a regular man.

Dietrich complained throughout the shoot that von Sternberg was torturing her and that Jannings hated her, especially when she felt Jannings' enthusiasm during a scene in which he attempts to strangle her was needlessly energetic. She predicted that the film would ruin her future in pictures but nonetheless took care to ask von Sternberg, who by now was her lover, to arrange a contract for her with Paramount as long as it stipulated that he would direct her. Despite her expectations, the Berlin reviews for her work in *Der Blaue Engel* were ecstatic. "She is common without being common," one critic enthused, "and altogether extraordinary." The day after the Berlin opening, Dietrich set sail for America with a one-picture deal from Paramount, causing somewhat of a stir during the Atlantic crossing by propositioning the American wife of a prominent theatrical costumer. She was rebuffed in her advances, even when she explained that "in Europe, it doesn't matter if you're a man or a woman. We make love with anyone we find attractive."

America first heard Marlene Dietrich's husky, smoke-edged voice on Paramount's national radio show, the "Publix Hour," on her arrival in New York. It was followed by a carefully stage-managed arrival in Hollywood to begin *Morocco*, the first of seven American films with von Sternberg, while Dietrich carried on simultaneous affairs with one of her leading men, Gary Cooper, and with Maurice Chevalier, who denied the liaison in an unsuccessful attempt to prevent the divorce for which his wife had promptly filed. Although there was the usual difficulty with Dietrich's accent, *Morocco* premiered to great acclaim in November of 1930, quickly followed by the English version of *The Blue Angel*, the release of which Paramount had delayed to allow public attention to build for the star they promoted as their answer to Garbo ("And who is this Miss Dietrich?" Garbo disingenuously inquired when reporters asked for her opinion of her new rival.) *Morocco* was nominated for four Oscars, including one for Dietrich for her portrayal of a cabaret singer who falls in love with a wealthy entertainer. With just two pictures, von Sternberg had catapulted Dietrich to the top of the Hollywood pecking order.

Thus began one of the American film industry's most curious relationships, von Sternberg obsessed with his creation and Dietrich unwilling to work with any other director. "I am Miss Dietrich. Miss Dietrich is me," von Sternberg intoned to the press. On her return from a vacation to Germany to visit husband Rudi and bring back her daughter Maria (who was traveling to the States with her mother and Gerta Huber, who was now hired as nanny), Dietrich was served with divorce papers by von Sternberg's wife, accusing her of alienation of affections and asking for $600,000 in damages. After the divorce, von Sternberg and Dietrich kept house together, occasionally welcoming Rudi Sieber on his visits to the woman who was still legally his wife. Dietrich made no secret of her admiration and devotion to von Sternberg, whose mission, she said, was "to photograph me, make me laugh, dress me up, comfort me, advise me, coddle me, explain things to me." Such a demanding list of requirements soon began to tell on von Sternberg, who threatened at least twice to quit Paramount rather than do another picture with Dietrich but who was always wooed back into the fold by Paramount's offers of higher salaries and Marlene's persuasive outbursts.

Meanwhile, Maria was sent off to a private school. While Dietrich lavished expensive clothes and gifts on her daughter, the relationship between the two remained distant. "I always felt she wanted to be with other people," Maria Riva wrote in her biography of her mother published 60 years later. "I remember how I used to cry at night. I wasn't left alone, but I knew that the servants and bodyguards were simply there to take care of me, and I disliked them." Her happiest times were when Rudi came to visit, usually when Paramount needed to show Dietrich in a traditional family setting after her much publicized *amours*. Knowledge of Marlene's relationships with other women (notably screenwriter ✥➤ **Mercedes de Acosta** who, to Dietrich's great satisfaction, threw over Greta Garbo for her) were usually confined to Hollywood's inner circles. Dietrich's habit of dressing in trousers, tweed jackets, monocles and berets became a fad among American women and led *The Los Angeles Times* to call her "the best dressed man in Hollywood."

By the mid-1930s, Marlene Dietrich had become Paramount's biggest grossing female star under von Sternberg's meticulous eye. *Blonde Venus,* for example, earned $3 million for the studio in the first few weeks of its release. She

➤❧
de Acosta, Mercedes. See *Garbo, Greta* for sidebar.

was not without her critics in the trade press who accused her of being a mere icon and not a true actress. Perversely, Dietrich agreed with them. "I am not an actress, no," she said. "I don't like making pictures, and I haven't got to act to be happy. Perhaps that is the secret." Also numbered among her critics was the increasingly powerful Nazi party in Germany, which accused her of betraying her native country. "As long as she opts for the dollar and has shaken the dust of her Fatherland from her feet, can the new Germany place any value on the importance of her movies?" asked one party-controlled newspaper. In 1934, by which time Hitler's National Socialist Party controlled the Reichstag, Dietrich's *Song of Songs* was banned from German cinemas because it had been adapted from a novel by a Jewish writer and had been financed by "Jewish Hollywood money."

Song of Songs was the first film in six years that had not been directed by von Sternberg, after Paramount had threatened legal action against Dietrich for refusing to do the picture under Rouben Mamoulian's direction. By now, von Sternberg wanted to move on to other projects with other stars. "She is a complete artist and another director will be better for her now," von Sternberg said publicly, keeping silent about the strains in personal and professional lives and Dietrich's insecurities about working with anyone else. Their last film together was 1935's *The Devil Is a Woman*, yet another tale of a good man (Lionel Atwill's military officer) brought low by a bad woman (Dietrich's factory worker). Tensions between Dietrich and von Sternberg during filming often erupted in violent arguments. "He bawled her out in front of everyone," remembered co-star Cesar Romero, "and made her repeat difficult scenes endlessly and needlessly until she just cried and cried." To add to their crumbling relationship, the picture performed badly at the box office and was banned not only in Germany, but in Spain, where Francisco Franco's regime objected to a military officer being made a fool by a peasant girl. Paramount eventually withdrew the film completely from international release.

Early in 1935, Dietrich announced to the press that she was no longer Josef von Sternberg's protegée, making sure to point out that it was his wish to sever the relationship. "I would prefer to go on as in the past," she said. "It is so wonderful to have someone to look after your interests." Many years later, von Sternberg put their separation in plainer terms in his autobiography, *Fun in a Chinese Laundry*. Noting that Marlene would often whisper "Where are you, Jo?" into the microphone after a scene, he retorted, "Well, I'm right here, and should she be angry once more when she reads this, she might recall that she was often angry with me, and for no good reason." Von Sternberg left both Dietrich and Paramount after *The Devil Is a Woman*, suffered a nervous breakdown, and completed only seven more films over the next thirty years, none of which were successful, before his death in 1969.

As Dietrich had feared, her Hollywood star began to wane with von Sternberg's departure while her attempts to insist on arranging her own lighting and camera angles were the bane of directors. After only three films, her contract was not renewed by Paramount. From June 1937 to September 1939, she was absent from the screen completely and even appeared on a list of actresses of whom the president of the Independent Theater Owner's of America claimed Americans had grown tired. During her enforced retirement, Dietrich indulged in several well-publicized affairs, taking among her lovers Douglas Fairbanks, Jr., novelist Erich Maria Remarque (who described her as a "steel orchid"), and French actor Jean Gabin, who had come to Hollywood to film *Manpower* with her. He was the only man, Dietrich later said, with whom she was truly in love.

In June 1939, as Europe prepared for war, Dietrich answered increasingly strident Nazi demands that she return to her own country by becoming a U.S. citizen. Later that summer, novelist Remarque urged her to accept the role of an over-the-hill, dance-hall girl of the Old West in Joe Pasternak's spoof of the Western genre, *Destry Rides Again,* telling her the role of the boozy Frenchy would revive her career. He was right. Her rendition of "See What the Boys in the Back Room Will Have" made her just as famous as "Falling in Love Again" had done ten years earlier, and her scenes opposite Jimmy Stewart's gentle Tom Destry were praised for their ironic wit. The experience led to two more pictures for Pasternak, *Seven Sinners* with John Wayne and *The Spoilers* in 1942.

By now, Hollywood was going to war. Dietrich, angry at what the Nazis were doing to Germany and fearful for her mother's safety, plunged into war work with startling energy. She tirelessly entertained troops during USO shows in the United States and Europe, sometimes being so close to the front lines that she narrow-

From the movie Shanghai Express, *starring Marlene Dietrich.*

ly escaped injury on at least two occasions and had to be airlifted to safety. From England, she sang on radio broadcasts beamed to Germany, during which she urged her nation to have courage and resist Nazi tyranny. For two years, from 1942 to 1944, Dietrich remained in Europe and refused all offers of work not directly related to the war. Finally, after Germany's surrender in 1944, she was briefly reunited with her mother in June of that year. The following November, Wilhemina Felsing Dietrich von Losch died and was buried in Berlin.

Returning to America, Dietrich was awarded the Medal of Freedom for her war work and appeared in her first postwar film, *Golden Earrings*, playing a Rom (gypsy) who helps a British intelligence officer smuggle war secrets out of Germany. It was the beginning of a number of respected films for Hollywood's best directors, many of whom were themselves Europeans who had emigrated. In Billy Wilder's *A Foreign Affair*, playing the German mistress of an American officer in postwar Berlin, Dietrich is first seen with her hair unkempt, wearing hardly any makeup, and sloppily brushing her teeth—certainly a departure from her carefully cultivated screen image of the von Sternberg days and a tribute to Wilder's influence. Alfred Hitchcock, on the other hand, gave her free rein on the set of his *Stage Fright* and ignored the complaints from fellow cast members that Dietrich was directing her own lighting and performance. "Marlene was a professional star," Hitchcock later said, adding puckishly, "She was also a professional cameraman, art director, editor, costume designer, hairdresser, makeup woman, composer, producer, and director." Hitchcock's instincts were predictably correct, for Dietrich's performance as actress Charlotte Inwood in the film is generally considered among her finest, along with her performance as Christine Vole in Wilder's 1957 *Witness for the Prosecution*, in which she adopted a Cockney accent taught to her by co-star Charles Laughton. Marlene was sure her portrayal of a woman who lies on the witness stand to protect her husband would bring her a second Oscar nomination and was bitterly disappointed when it failed to materialize.

Now nearing 60 and with parts becoming more scarce, Dietrich decided to return to the stage. She had already been appearing with her own cabaret show in Las Vegas, starting in 1953, and then hired a 30-year-old Burt Bacharach to help her redesign the act and supply new material. Bacharach's suggestions paid off, for by 1958, Dietrich could command a salary of over $100,000 for a two-week engagement. But salary was hardly the issue in 1958, when Dietrich stepped onto a Berlin stage for the first time in nearly 30 years. Her Allied war work still rankled, for she was the object of several street protests and indignant editorials; and a quarter of the Titiania Palace's 2,000 seats remained empty on opening night. But the audience, led by then-chancellor Willy Brandt, rose to its feet after her last number, "I Still Have a Valise Left in Berlin," which she had carefully rehearsed to reaffirm her German heritage. She gracefully accepted 11 curtain calls. "She won

her battle from the first moment," reported Berlin's *Der Abend*. "She stood there like a queen, proud and sovereign."

By the 1970s, however, reminders of her days of glory seemed to be fading. Von Sternberg's death was followed by those of Gary Cooper, Erich Maria Remarque, Maurice Chevalier, and Mercedes de Acosta. In London preparing for her first television special, her quiet grief boiled over into anger when she snapped at the show's producer that no one knew how to light her or knew which camera angles were right for her. "I was trained by the Master, Josef von Sternberg!" she shouted imperiously. "*I'll* pick the shots I think are best!" Tempers on the set were not helped when Dietrich fell during shooting, postponing production for several weeks. By 1975, she was painfully frail and collapsed after walking on stage in Sydney, Australia, suffering a broken leg. It proved to be her last appearance on a stage.

While she recuperated in a hospital during the spring of 1976, Dietrich learned that Rudi Sieber, whom she had never divorced, had died in California. "Poor Rudi," she mourned. "I don't know how he could have put up with it, living in the shadow of a famous woman." She might have said the same of her sister Elisabeth, who died the following year. Dietrich had never spoken publicly of the older sibling who had married and lived quietly in Berlin, and Elisabeth had never revealed voluntarily her relationship to one of the world's most well-known stars.

The year of Elisabeth's death, Dietrich made her last appearance on camera, in 1977's *Just a Gigolo*. She received $250,000 for two-and-a-half days' work, playing a baroness who runs a ring of male prostitutes in Weimar Berlin. She arrived on the set for her first day's work with "her jaw set and her shoulders hunched with determination," as one crew member reported, walking with the support of her makeup artist because her eyesight was failing. Dietrich even sang on screen for the last time. It was an old, pre-World War I, German song, with the lines:

> There will come a day
> When youth will pass away.
> Then what will they say
> About me?

Hardly anyone ever saw Marlene Dietrich again after she finished work on the picture. She lived in self-imposed isolation in her Paris apartment on Avenue Montaigne, refusing all interviews and never venturing out in public except for appointments with doctors or for hospitalizations that became more frequent as the years passed. Douglas Fairbanks, Jr., telephoned several times during a stay in Paris but reported that Dietrich pretended to be the maid, or the cook, and hung up; and Billy Wilder's repeated requests for a visit while he was shooting a picture in Paris were rebuffed. There was a flurry of anticipation in 1981 when it was learned that Dietrich had agreed to be interviewed for a filmed biography being prepared by German actor Maximilian Schell; but at the last minute, she refused to be photographed and only allowed her voice to be used. Dietrich completely disappeared from view after Schell's film was released in 1982, largely forgotten until the world learned of her death in Paris on May 6, 1992, at the age of 91.

An American flag, sent by the Veterans of Foreign Wars in honor of her war service, hung alongside the French tricolor during her funeral service at Paris' Church of the Madeleine; and at her burial next to her mother and sister in Berlin, that city's flag was draped over her coffin in tribute to the woman who had forsaken her career during the war to do what she thought best for her country. Like the sturdy plastic clock and the chunky black telephones left behind in her New York apartment, Marlene Dietrich often hid her natural pragmatism under the carefully applied veneer created by von Sternberg. "I'm no romantic dreamer," her ghostly, off-camera voice scoffs in Schell's biography, *Marlene*. "I'm a logical, practical person," she says, "who has worked all her life."

SOURCES:

Gray, Francine du Plessix. "Revisiting Marlene Dietrich Through Her Homey Odds and Ends," in *The New Yorker*. August 25, 1997.

Spoto, Donald. *Blue Angel: The Life and Death of Marlene Dietrich*. NY: Doubleday, 1992.

Von Sternberg, Josef. *Fun in a Chinese Laundry*. NY: Macmillan, 1965.

SUGGESTED READING:

Riva, Maria. *Marlene Dietrich*. NY: Alfred A. Knopf, 1993.

Norman Powers, writer/producer, Chelsea Lane Productions, New York

Digby, Jane (1807–1881).

See Digby el Mesrab, Jane.

Digby, Lettice (c. 1588–1658)

English noblewoman. Name variations: Lady Digby; Baroness Offaley; Baroness Offaly. Born Lettice Fitzgerald around 1588; died in 1658 in England; daughter of Gerald Fitzgerald, earl of Kildare; married Lord Robert Digby, of Coleshill, in 1608.

Lettice Fitzgerald Digby inherited the barony of Offaly from her parents. In 1608, she married Lord Robert Digby of Coleshill, becoming one of England's wealthiest and most powerful women through the union of the two houses. Lettice's vast estates made her a prime target for insurgents during the English Civil War. Forced to defend her various castles and manors from mutinous mobs, including Geashill Castle against Irish rebels in 1642, she was known as a brave warrior.

Laura York, Riverside, California

Jane Digby el Mesrab

Digby el Mesrab, Jane (1807–1881)

English adventurer who was condemned by Victorian England for early scandals but revered among Arabs after her marriage to a Bedouin chief. Name variations: Jane Digby; Jane Digby el Mezrab; Jane Digby Law, Lady or Countess Ellenborough; Baroness von Venningen. Born Jane Elizabeth Digby on April 3, 1807, in Norfolk, England; died in Damascus, Syria, on August 11, 1881; buried in the Protestant Cemetery in Damascus; daughter of Jane Elizabeth Coke (Lady Andover, 1777–1863) and Admiral Sir Henry Digby (1763?–1842); married Edward Law, Lord Ellenbor-

ough (divorced); married Baron Karl von Venningen (divorced); married Spiro Theotoky (divorced); married Medjuel el Mesrab (a Bedouin sheik); children: (first marriage) Arthur Dudley Law (1828–1830); (with Prince Schwarzenberg) Mathilde Selden; (second marriage) Heribert von Venningen and Bertha von Venningen; (third marriage) Leonidas Theotoky.

"She was neither nymphomaniac nor courtesan," writes Jane Digby's biographer, **Margaret Fox Schmidt**, "although she has been described as both by writers who did not know the facts. Jane never used her charms to gain wealth or power; her private income was more than sufficient to live well." Rather, she was the female counterpart of the Byronic hero, suggests Schmidt, the sinner who defies the rules that seek to harness the human spirit. Intelligent in all areas except matters of the heart, she spoke nine languages and was considered a talented artist and a magnificent horsewoman. "Her attraction for men never faded; it crossed all geographical boundaries and captivated three kings (including a father and son), two princes, a German baron, an Albanian brigand general and several Bedouin sheiks to name but a few." She was grist for the works of many writers, including Honoré de Balzac and James Michener. "Part of her fascination," continues Schmidt, "stems from her refusal to fit any conventional mold."

The necessity of loving and being loved is to me as the air I breathe and the sole cause of all I have to reproach myself with.

—**Jane Digby**

Jane Digby was born in England on April 3, 1807, during the age of elegance. A descendant of two colorful houses of aristocracy, the Digbys and the Cokes, she spent her first two years at Holkham Hall, the Coke family mansion, on the Norfolk marshlands near the North Sea. The entrance hall was 50' high, the walls were adorned with paintings by Titian, Holbein, and Gainsborough, and the rooms were generally filled with guests.

Her maternal grandfather Thomas William Coke, known as Coke of Norfolk, had been a Whig member of Parliament for 56 years, even refusing a peerage to remain in the House of Commons. An outspoken opponent of Britain's war against her colonies, he drank a toast nightly to George Washington. Jane's mother ✥ **Jane Elizabeth Coke** had been married previously to the viscount Andover who was killed in a hunting accident. Preferring to be known as Lady An-

dover rather than Mrs. Digby, Jane Coke retained her titles when she married the naval hero Henry Digby, even though Digby eventually was made an admiral and knighted. Captain Digby was not a peer, but he was wealthy and had made a name for himself at the Battle of Trafalgar.

In 1809, Jane's parents moved to Forston Manor, five miles from Dorchester, in Dorset, for the birth of Jane's brother, the son and heir Edward Digby. Two years later, her brother Kenelm was born. The family divided their time between Forston Manor and Holkham, where Jane and her brothers and cousins delighted with their living quarters in one of the towers while "boldly ferreting out" the ghost of Lady **Mary Coke** who walked the corridors. There, too, intrigued by the independent ways of the gypsies, Jane wandered off for a day with a band of them. Up went a nine-mile fence around Holkham; up went a governess-for-hire sign. But the newly hired governess was soon under the spell of her young charge, for the bright and unrestrained Jane Digby was usually sorry she had caused pain with her antics. At that time, Jane's greatest ambition was to learn to shoot a pheasant from a saddle at full gallop. She would eventually be successful.

In 1823, the family moved to Harley Street and began preparation for 16-year-old Jane's debut into post-Regency London, a society that prided itself on backroom liaisons and front-room decorum. The Jane Digby who was presented at the court of George IV and ***Caroline of Brunswick** was tall and fair, with blue-violet eyes, long lashes, golden hair, elegant bearing, and "lips that would tempt one to forswear Heaven to touch them" wrote one dazzled swain. Her most ardent suitor, anxious for an heir, was the 34-year-old widower, Edward Law, Lord Ellenborough, described as handsome and vain, especially when it came to his abundant brown locks. "Young Law, Lord Ellenborough's son," wrote ✥➤ **Harriette Wilson**, "was a very smart, fine young gentleman, and his impatience of temper passed, I dare say, occasionally for quickness." Even though the beautiful Miss Digby was far more comfortable on a horse than in the drawing room, they were married on September 15, 1824.

But the marriage died aborning. The honeymoon in Brighton was a disaster, with rumors that Lord Ellenborough spent his passion on the daughter of the hotel's pastry cook rather than his unformed, teenage wife. The couple settled at Edward's country estate at Roehampton, just outside London, and Edward proceeded to occupy most of his time attending to political affairs in the city, though he had few friends in the House of Lords because of his biting tongue. At first, the young Jane enjoyed her freedom as woman of the manor and passed her days acquiring a wardrobe of ornate gowns that caused titters from the judgmental. By age 19, bored and lonely, Jane found clothes were little consolation for the cold marriage that held her prisoner. *Marguerite, the Countess of Blessington portrayed the couple under the guise of Lord and Lady Walmer in her book *The Two Friends*.

At first, Jane turned to her cousin George Anson, to whom she had been close since childhood, for loving solace. By the time she gave birth to a son, Arthur Dudley Law, on February 15, 1828, there were rumors as to paternity. But Edward, Lord Ellenborough, had realized his sole purpose for marriage. He was so delighted that, at her request, he agreed to separate bedchambers. The physical aspect of their marriage was over, and Edward turned his attention to his Cabinet post as Lord Privy Seal in Wellington's ministry.

Then, in May 1828, at one of her soirees, **Princess Esterhazy** introduced Jane to Bohemian Prince Felix Schwarzenberg, 27-year-old attaché to Prince Esterhazy at the Austrian embassy. The prince, a diplomat and captain in the Second Uhlans (mounted lancers), cut a dashing figure with his hussar jacket draped casually over one shoulder. They became lovers almost immediately. But 21-year-old Jane Digby, who knew more about horses than the fine art of extramarital finesse practiced by England's high-born, had a disastrous penchant for candor. Wrote French satirist Edmond About: "One fine morning she climbed on the rooftops and shouted distinctly to the whole of the United Kingdom, 'I am the mistress of Prince Schwarzenberg!' All the ladies who had lovers and did not say so were greatly shocked; English prudery reddened to the roots of its hair." Meanwhile, Edward, busier than ever, was made president of the Board of Control for India.

The lovers met daily. Though Edward was warned, he shook off the rumors as mindless. Then in February 1829, under the pretext of joining her son and his nursemaids for the sea air, Digby arrived at Brighton's Norfolk Hotel where she was well known. Felix arrived a little later. A hotel waiter saw Felix enter Lady Ellenborough's suite at an unfashionable hour. He then listened outside the door. The Austrian legation, uncomfortable with the rumors, called Felix home to Austria in May. By this time, Jane was three months pregnant.

Coke, Jane Elizabeth (1777–1863)

*English noblewoman. Name variations: Lady Andover. Born Jane Elizabeth Coke in 1777; died in 1863; daughter of Thomas William Coke, known as Coke of Norfolk (a Whig member of Parliament for 56 years), and Jane Dutton Coke; sister of Ann Margaret Coke (later viscountess Anson); married Charles Nevinson Howard, viscount Andover, in 1796 (died in a hunting accident, 1800); married Henry Digby (a naval admiral), on April 17, 1806; children: (second marriage) *Jane Digby el Mesrab (1807–1881); Edward St. Vincent Digby (b. 1809); Kenelm Digby (b. 1811).*

Wilson, Harriette (1786–1855)

English courtesan and writer. Born Harriette Dubochet in 1786; died in 1855 (some sources cite 1846).

Harriette Wilson was no stranger to scandal. During her long career, she was the mistress of the earl of Craven, the duke of Argyll, the marquess of Worcester, the duke of Beaufort, and the duke of Wellington. In 1825, she published what was purported to be the opening chapter of her *Memoirs of Herself and Others*. The publisher J. Stockdale, under the pseudonym Thomas Little, added a postscript that the forthcoming book "would not fail to produce the greatest moral effect on the present and future generations." Wilson then promised her coterie to keep names out, in exchange for remuneration. The duke of Wellington would not be railroaded. "Publish and be damned," he told her. Before publication, Wilson moved to Paris where she happily spent the profits of the highly successful serialization of her memoirs, all eight-volumes.

Intent on following Felix, who had written to say that though it was impossible to marry for the sake of his future, he saw no reason why they could not devote their lives to each other, Jane asked Edward for a separation. Edward, possibly out of guilt over his neglect of her, was generous financially. All concerned agreed that it would be better if the pregnant Jane were out of the country during the divorce proceedings. On August 31, accompanied by her childhood governess, she left for Basel, Switzerland, and on November 12, had a daughter, baptized Mathilde Selden. A few months later, on February 1, 1830, her son Arthur, who had remained behind, died of a convulsion.

In 19th-century England, divorce was so scandalous that it took a private act of Parliament for a marriage to be severed. Because of Edward's political stature and many enemies, their divorce, known as the Ellenborough case, played across the front page of the *Times* on April 1,

1830, while the Norfolk tryst, which took up 41 pages of the Report of the Minutes of Evidence in the House of Commons, sold for three shillings on streetcorners. "I could hear them kissing," testified the Brighton waiter, "and a noise that convinced me that the act of cohabitation was taking place between them." Jane's name became an object for satire, and ribald jokes would follow her throughout her days. Honoré de Balzac, drawing upon Digby for a character in his novel *Le Lys dans la vallée,* wrote: "Never did a nation more elaborately scheme for the hypocrisy of a married woman by placing her always between social life and death. For her there is no compromise between shame and honor; the fall is utter, or there is no fall; it is all or nothing." But Edward did not get off easily in the press, either; many felt he too was at fault. Once the dust settled, however, his career flourished.

Felix had taken up his new diplomatic post in Paris, where Jane and Mathilde joined him in February 1830. Though Felix loved Jane, he also loved his career and began to resent her sacrifice. Because of their relationship, she could not be presented at the shaky court of Charles X, soon to be the court of the Citizen King, Louis Philippe, duke of Orléans, nor accompany him to functions. Another novel, *The Exclusives,* written by Lady *Charlotte Bury, appeared in 1830, with the easily recognizable Felix and Jane portrayed under the names Lord and Lady Glenmore. By late December 1830, Felix was having an affair with Mme d'Oudenarde while Jane gave birth to their son Felix who lived only a few weeks. After a major quarrel in May 1831, Felix left Paris for Bohemia. Digby wrote a poem to her son:

"And thou, too, pity and forgive
Thy tainted birth, dishonored name.
Alas, t'is best thou dost not live
To share my destiny of shame."

Digby moved to Munich where Ludwig I, spearheading a Bavarian renaissance, was on the throne. It was at Tambosi's, a coffee house frequented by artists, musicians, and actors, that they met. Though all assumed they were lovers, Schmidt claims that the more than 70 notes and letters that passed between them "raise the intriguing possibility that Ludwig was to Jane exactly what she called him—'my best and dearest friend'—and nothing more."

For the ensuing months, August 1831 to March 1832, Jane saw Ludwig almost daily. Meanwhile, she was being ardently courted by Baron Karl von Venningen, whom she had met while riding. Felix continued to write, keeping her dangling at arm's length with over 200 letters. By March 1832, though still in love with Felix, she was pregnant with Venningen's child. Pursued by Karl, Jane went to Italy to have her child, and Heribert von Venningen was born on January 27, 1833. On November 16, Jane wed the determined Venningen in a civil ceremony in Darmstadt.

Now respectably married, she could meet Ludwig's counterpart, the Queen *Theresa of Saxony of Bavaria, and be received into Munich society. In 1834, while living in Weinheim, near Heidelberg, Jane gave birth to a daughter Bertha. (By all admittance, especially Jane's, her greatest failure was with her children: Arthur was dead; Mathilde grew up with her namesake, Felix's sister, the Princess Mathilde Schwarzenberg; and Heribert was left in Palermo with a Sicilian family for his first three years. By age 20, Bertha would be confined to an insane asylum and add fuel to the rumor that she was the child of King Ludwig, sharing the genetic strain of his grandson, the Mad king Ludwig II.)

Jane respected Venningen but "his want of *demonstration* and *warmth* of feeling," she wrote Ludwig, "stifles a passion I fain would feel." Without love, she said, "life is a dreary void." In the summer of 1835, the Venningens returned to Munich, and it was there, at the Bavarian court, that the 28-year-old Jane met 24-year-old Spiridion Theotoky, a Greek count from Corfu. Though Karl hustled her out of Munich back to Weinheim, Jane and Spiridion entered into an affair that brought more scandal. Impetuous and unwilling to be reined in by society, Digby rode her horse madly through the countryside for late-night trysts. Supposedly, Karl confronted her about the rumors, they quarreled, and she and Spiridion rode off in tandem. Then Karl caught up with their carriage, dueled with Spiridion, wounded him, and escorted his wife home.

In the spring of 1839, Jane dropped all pretenses. Leaving two more children and one more husband behind, she joined Theotoky in Paris. Amazingly, Karl genuinely wished her well and would continue a friendly correspondence for the next 30 years. In March 1840, Jane gave birth to Leonidas, Count Theotoky; two years later, in 1842, the divorce decree was handed down. For some reason, the scandal was ignored by the German press, but Digby would be romantically linked to any man she came near. She met Balzac only once, when he visited Weinheim in 1835 and had strolled with her in a park for two hours. When Jane became the basis for a character or two in his books, some were certain that they had been involved.

In March 1841, now Mrs. Theotoky, at least in the eyes of the Greek Orthodox Church, she and her French maid Eugenie accompanied Spiro to the Aegean island of Tinos where his father was governor. Expected to chafe under the primitive conditions of the island, Jane did just the opposite. She loved Spiro, became a devoted mother to her son, and cherished the informality of family life on the Greek island. Within months, she was speaking Greek fluently. In spring 1842, they moved to Corfu, where Spiro managed his father's estate at Dukades for the next two years. The Theotokys entertained lavishly, with Jane quickly taking on the customs of the area.

Then came the revolution in Athens in 1843. Greeks were demanding a constitution and the ousting of King Otto, the hand-picked British-Russian-French monarch. In 1844, when Spiro Theotoky became one of King Otto's aide-de-camps, the couple moved to Athens, and Jane quickly incurred the envy of Queen *Amalie. But Spiro was straying, and the Theotoky marriage had cooled, held together only by their son Leonidas. While vacationing at a villa in Naples in 1846, young Leonidas heard voices, ran to a balcony to see who was talking, peered over, and fell to the marble floor below. Jane watched horrified. Convinced that the death of her beloved Leonidas was penance for the way she had treated her earlier children, a shattered Jane separated from her husband. Nothing is known of her whereabouts from 1846 to 1849.

In 1849, Jane was back in Athens, holding court for the ministers of Britain and France; she had been taken under the wing of **Sophie, the duchess of Plaisance**. She was also in love with Cristos Hadji-Petros, a brigand chief and freedom fighter who had been involved in the Greek War of Independence from Turkey. When he was put in charge of the garrison at Lamia, a rugged outpost to the north, Jane went with him. Writes Schmidt: "When Athens society learned the shocking news that [Jane] Theotoky was playing blue-eyed banditti queen with Hadji-Petros in Lamia, there were screams of outrage on all sides. Most outraged was Queen [Amalie]." Amalie sacked Cristos from government employ. When Jane learned that Cristos had shown his true colors by propositioning Eugenie, she "vanished from Athens, leaving Hadji-Petros behind."

By April 1853, the 46-year-old Jane was sailing toward Syria on a horse-buying expedition with Eugenie. Landing at the port of Beirut, they decided to make a tour of the desert by caravan, south to Jerusalem, north to Damascus, then on to the city of Palmyra once ruled by *Zenobia. (Digby kept a journal of the trip, which would come into the possession of her English biographer E.M. Oddie; though the notebooks can no longer be accounted for, a substantial amount of her travel log appears in Oddie's *The Odyssey of a Loving Woman*.)

Digby, unlike her British contemporaries, fell in love with Syria and its populace. One month into the journey, she was bargaining for a thoroughbred horse in a city of Bedouin tents near the Jordan River. "My heart warms towards these wild Arabs," she wrote. "They have many qualities we want in civilized life, unbounded hospitality, respect for strangers or guests, good faith and simplicity of dealing amongst themselves, and a certain high-bred innate politeness." On her arrival in Damascus, the British consul, hearing of the beautiful Englishwoman who was determined to continue on to Palmyra, tried to warn her of the danger of a woman traveling alone through a country filled with desert tribes who would be glad to relieve her of her riches. He insisted that she at least hire an escort of Arabs who knew the route and the waterholes. So Jane engaged the protection of the Mesrabs, a poor band of the Anazeh Bedouin tribe, who had previously escorted Lady *Hester Stanhope on a similar caravan. Medjuel el Mesrab, brother of their sheik Mohammed, was chosen to negotiate with her. Lady **Anne Blount**, who later met Medjuel in Damascus, described him as a well bred, educated, and "agreeable man." He could read, write, and was an authority on desert history. Digby and Medjuel shared a love of horses and an easy command of languages.

About midway in the journey, when the caravan was raided, all but Medjuel fled. Since protectors were known to give in easily and share the bounty, Medjuel's resistance confused the marauding tribe and sent them into retreat. The escort party returned, and the caravan continued on to Palmyra. Though the Mesrab family was against Medjuel's marrying a foreigner and though the British consul in Damascus warned her that Muslim law permitted men four wives and that Anazeh tribal law punished infidelity in a wife with decapitation, Jane married Medjuel in a Muslim ceremony in late 1854.

It was a good marriage. Jane adapted so well to Bedouin ways, she was soon accepted; her official Arabic title was Sitt Mesrab. After a brief visit with her family in England in 1857, she wrote her mother: "I would gladly be as you are, but I cannot change my nature. I am different. How different I hardly realized. . . . I regret much of the past, but over the future I feel sanguine." She and Medjuel agreed to spend part of the year with his nomadic tribe in the desert and part in Damascus living a semi-Western lifestyle.

Jane renovated a house just outside the gates of Damascus to her taste: half English, half Arab. She designed a breathtaking garden with lily pond, added a greenhouse, and filled the courtyard with geese, turkeys, guinea hens, gazelles, falcons, dogs, a tamed pelican, and over 100 cats. Medjuel bred Arab horses; Jane had magnificent stables built for him. She impressed the Bedouins with her shooting skill and her way with injured animals. To allay the Arab superstition that fair hair boded evil, she dyed hers jet black.

In the desert, she dressed as a tribal woman, her head covered in a dark kerchief. She learned to milk the camels, toughened her feet in order to go barefoot, and rode horse and camel with ease. Jane helped her husband conduct English tours to Palmyra. On one such tour, she met **Emily Beaufort**, Lady Strangford, and the two became close friends. Another Englishwoman told biographer A.M.W. Stirling that when she met Jane Digby, Jane was "swathed in a veil and Arab garments, and riding at the head of a cavalcade of wild Arabs—a veritable Queen of Banditti—in surroundings that rendered her gracious, courteous manners, her air of *grande dame* and her sweet low voice more singularly impressive, even though her beauty—and but her glorious eyes—was scrupulously concealed from view."

In the summer of 1860, after a plague of worms and a bitter winter had decimated the food crops, Syrians were starving. When three Druses, a sect that was neither Christian nor Muslim, were murdered in the town of Sidon, the Druses retaliated by killing four Christians near the site. There were numerous counter-reprisals until the Druses began a full-scale uprising, and 6,000 Christians were massacred in Syria. Digby was held in such high regard that she was spared, and she risked her life venturing into the Christian quarter of the city to help others. "In defiance of Medjuel's orders," writes Schmidt, she "rode into the city" dressed as a Bedouin, "accompanied by a single terrified Arab servant who carried several leather water bottles and a basket of food and medicine. The narrow alleys through which Jane rode were littered with corpses putrefying in the sweltering heat." She also took in the Christians who appeared at her door for sanctuary and helped defray the cost for the 12,000 refugees protected in the stronghold of the Algerian Abd el Kadar.

Jane supplied Medjuel's tribe with guns for their many skirmishes with the Turks and rival tribes and, on many occasions, accompanied her husband into battle. During one particularly intense skirmish in 1873, a false rumor flashed back to Damascus that she had been killed, and the obituaries in Victorian London were not flattering. But by 1877, the 73-year-old Digby could no longer ride by Medjuel's side; her amazing energy was beginning to fade. In late July 1881, she came down with a virulent attack of dysentery; with her husband near, she died on August 11.

The day of her funeral, Medjuel agreed to endure Anglican custom and ride in the black carriage as chief mourner. Halfway to the Protestant Cemetery, however, he bolted from the carriage and fled, an act, thought those attending, of a barbarian. But as the minister was consigning the coffin to the earth, Medjuel came galloping through the gate of the cemetery astride Jane's favorite Arabian mare, gazed into the open grave, then galloped away. "Love was always the dominant theme of her life: love pursued, love won, love rejected," wrote Schmidt. "Despite her many defeats, she remained her own woman—she followed neither 'the highway of virtue nor the miry path of the courtesan.' She followed the dictates of her heart. No one has ever done that with more style than Jane Digby."

SOURCES:
Oddie, E.M. *The Odyssey of a Loving Woman.* 1936.
Schmidt, Margaret Fox. *Passion's Child: The Extraordinary Life of Jane Digby.* NY: Harper, 1976.

SUGGESTED READING:
Lovell, Mary S. *Rebel Heart: The Scandalous Life of Jane Digby.* NY: W.W. Norton, 1995.

Diggs, Annie LePorte (1848–1916)

American politician and social reformer. Born Annie LePorte in London, Ontario, Canada, on February 22, 1848; died in Detroit, Michigan, on September 7, 1916; daughter of Cornelius (a lawyer) and Ann Maria (Thomas) LePorte; attended convent and public school in New Jersey, to which the family moved in 1855; married Alvin S. Diggs (a postal clerk), on September 21, 1873, in Lawrence, Kansas; children: Fred, Mabel, and Esther.

Annie LePorte Diggs was a poll watcher in a local prohibitionist campaign in 1877 and was drawn into politics through her interest in the temperance crusade in Kansas. In August 1881, she helped form the nonpolitical Kansas Liberal Union, an inclusive group that embraced Uni-

tarians, Universalists, Free Religionists, Socialists, spiritualists, materialists, and agnostics. A
few months later, she was elected a vice president of the Free Religious Association, succeeding her idol *Lucretia Mott. With her husband
Alvin, who shared her interests and liberal
views, Diggs also published the Kansas Liberal
from her home for a short time and, during the
1880s, worked for women's suffrage and for the
establishment of a cooperative association for
farmers and workers. She wrote a column on
the Farmers' Alliance for Kansas' Lawrence
Journal and then became an associate editor of
the Alliance Advocate. Also instrumental in
turning the Kansas Farmers' Alliance into the
political People's (later Populist) Party, she became one of its most vocal advocates. Diggs
spoke at the national Populist conventions of
1890, 1891, and 1892, and she worked alongside *Mary E. Lease in the Populist election
campaigns of 1894 and 1896. In 1894, as vice
president of the Kansas Equal Suffrage Association, she helped mount an unsuccessful campaign for a woman suffrage amendment to the
Kansas constitution. (She became president of
the Association in 1899.)

In 1897, after her election as president of
the Kansas Woman's Free Silver League and as
part of the silver movement's takeover of the
Populist Party, Diggs supported a "fusion" or
joint ticket with the Democrats for the 1898
election. From 1898 to 1902, she was the state
librarian under the fusion state administration.
Her impressive leadership in guiding her ticket
to nomination in the fusion convention of 1900
led the regular Democratic politicians to denounce her "petticoat domination" and refer to
her as "Boss" Diggs.

In 1902, Diggs traveled to England to represent the Western Co-operative Association of
Kansas City at the International Co-operative
Congress. For a period of two years, she wrote
articles and newspaper stories on reform movements in England and Europe. She returned to
America in 1904 and was elected president of
the Kansas Woman's Press Association. In 1906,
she ended her work in party politics and moved
to New York City, where she joined a civic reform bureau and authored two books: The Story
of Jerry Simpson (1908), an account of a Populist hero, and Bedrock (1912), in which she
proposed that a bureau of employment be established at every educational institution. In 1912,
she moved to Detroit to live with her son and
died there in 1916.

Barbara Morgan, Melrose, Massachusetts

Diggs, Irene (1906—)

*American anthropologist who was a pioneering black
scholar in African Diaspora and Afro-Latin studies.
Born Ellen Diggs on April 13, 1906, in Monmouth,
Illinois; daughter of Henry Charles and Alice (Scott)
Diggs; University of Minnesota, B.S., 1928; Atlanta
University, M.A., 1933; doctorate from the University
of Havana, 1945.*

Born into a black working-class family in
the small college town of Monmouth, Illinois, in
the first decade of the 20th century, Irene Diggs
realized from her earliest years that education
could liberate not only individuals but an entire
class of oppressed people. An excellent student
in high school, Diggs transferred after one year
from local Monmouth College to the University
of Minnesota, earning a bachelor's degree there
in 1928. Enrolling at Atlanta University for
graduate work, she soon came to the attention
of the eminent black scholar W.E.B. Du Bois.
After receiving her master's degree in 1933 (the
first to be granted in the field of anthropology
by Atlanta University), she began to work full
time as Du Bois' chief research assistant. The
prolific and often overextended Du Bois increasingly depended on Irene Diggs to provide
him with the source materials he needed for his
many research projects. Among the projects she
was involved with during the years working
with Du Bois (1933–1943 and 1945–1947)
were editing the Encyclopedia of the Negro
(1945, 2nd edition, 1946), and serving as co-
founder of the influential journal Phylon: A Review of Race and Culture.

Having first visited Cuba in 1942 and been
deeply impressed by evidence of the continuing
impact of African culture on that island, Diggs
determined to carry out advanced research in
Afro-Caribbean traditions leading to a doctoral
degree. Awarded a Roosevelt Fellowship by the
Institute of International Education, starting in
1943 she was enrolled in a doctoral program at
the University of Havana. As a student of the
noted Cuban ethnographer Fernando Ortiz,
Diggs combined working through the published
literature of the field with extensive travels
through the island of Cuba collecting folklore,
recording village music, photographing festivals
and observing traditional Afro-Cuban dances
and rituals. Diggs was awarded her doctorate by
the University of Havana in 1945. After graduation, she spent a number of months in Montevideo, Uruguay, as an exchange scholar. Besides
carrying out archival research, she also observed
the little-known Afro-Uruguayan and Afro-Ar-

gentinean communities in Montevideo and Buenos Aires.

After a brief return to Atlanta to work again with Du Bois, Irene Diggs accepted a job offer in 1947 to join the faculty of Morgan State College (now University) in Baltimore, Maryland. Until her retirement from Morgan State in 1976, she carried a heavy teaching load, was an inspiring teacher, and continued her scholarly work under often trying circumstances. She published a significant number of important articles in scholarly journals and was also able over the decades to produce a number of well-received reference works and monographs. An underlying theme of many of Diggs' writings is the functional differences operating in race relations in the United States and in Latin America. Writing in 1971 in the *Negro History Bulletin,* she noted that in these two cultures there was a dramatic difference in how an individual human being was defined as being white or black, a fact that had an impact not only on the lives of individuals but on the culture as a whole.

The friends, colleagues and students of Irene Diggs were not only won over by her charm but by the breadth of her knowledge. An indefatigable researcher, her work took her around the world on several occasions, and she became an enthusiastic traveler. She concentrated on Latin America in the 1940s; starting in the 1950s, she visited Africa and also investigated lesser-known parts of Europe, including Cyprus, Iceland, and Finland (on which she became a respected authority). After retirement from her teaching duties, she explored the Middle and Far East and the Soviet Union in depth. She also maintained her ties with Africa, visiting many countries to expand her fund of knowledge as well as to visit old friends. A remarkable, multi-talented scholar, Irene Diggs surely deserves comparison with her great mentor W.E.B. Du Bois. In 1978, the Association of Black Anthropologists presented her with its Distinguished Scholar Award for her outstanding achievements in researching the struggles and achievements of peoples of African descent in the New World.

SOURCES:

Diggs, Irene. "Attitudes toward Color in South America," in *Negro History Bulletin.* Vol 34, 1971, pp. 107–108.

———. *Black Chronology: From 4000 B.C. to the Abolition of the Slave Trade.* Boston, MA: G.K. Hall, 1983.

———. "Color in Colonial Spanish America," in *Journal of Negro History.* Vol. 38. October 1953, pp. 403–427.

John Haag, Associate Professor of History, University of Georgia, Athens, Georgia

Dijkstra, Sjoukje (1942—)

Dutch figure skater. Born on January 28, 1942, in The Netherlands.

Won the silver medal in the Winter Olympics at Squaw Valley (1960); became World champion (1962, 1963, 1964); won the first gold medal ever for the Dutch, in the winter Olympic games in Innsbruck (1964).

The Dutch practically invented the sport of figure skating. Early Europeans used the shank bones of horses and deer as blades until the advent of the Iron Age when it was discovered that metal blades gave a superior edge. Skating blossomed, particularly in Holland where a network of canals and cold winters made it an important form of transportation as well as a means of enjoyment a la *Mary Mapes Dodge's fictional character Hans Brinker. In Holland, women as well as men raced on the ice. The first speedskating contest for women was held in Leeuwarden in 1805. But the Dutch had never won a won a gold medal in the Olympic games until the arrival of Sjoukje Dijkstra.

She began skating when she was six and according to her father "sped away immediately." Though she broke a leg on her new skates, she was back on ice as soon as the break healed. At age ten, she studied in London with Arnold Gerschwiler, a Swiss trainer. At 13, she gave up formal schooling to devote more time to her sport. Gerschwiler was a demanding taskmaster who constantly pushed Dijkstra harder. Particularly good at the compulsory figures so hated by many skaters, she was also strong in freeskating. In 1963, Dick Button would call her "probably the most powerful woman skater who has ever existed."

Dijkstra's father, a doctor in Amsterdam who was also a speed skater, encouraged her to train the long hours required to become a champion. At age 14, Dijkstra competed in her first Olympics when she placed 12th in the 1956 Games in Cortina, Italy. She won the silver at the Squaw Valley Winter Games behind *Carol Heiss-Jenkins in 1960. Two years later, she began her reign on the ice, winning three consecutive world championships from 1962 to 1964. Dijkstra was an athletic skater, known for her flying camels, double toe-loops, double axles, and flying sit spins. To her, figure skating was an athletic sport above all else and in the early 1960s her muscular frame dominated the international ice. In 1963, at the world figure-skating championship held in Cortina, the Dutch star was 59 points ahead of her closest competitor before going into the freeskating performance; she took the world title for the second year in a row.

Dijkstra had not lost a skating competition since 1961 when she entered the 1964 Innsbruck Olympics. During the competition, her compulsory figures were almost perfect, and as always her freeskating program was close to flawless. All nine judges awarded her the gold, and Queen ✧ Juliana was in the stands while the Dutch national anthem played.

SOURCES:

"How to Succeed by Trying," in *Time*. Vol. 81, no. 11. March 15, 1963, p. 78.

Markel, Robert, Nancy Brooks and Susan Markel. *For the Record. Women in Sports*. NY: World Almanac Publications, 1985.

Karin Loewen Haag, freelance writer, Athens, Georgia

Dilke, Emily (1840–1904)

English trade union leader who was an artist, art historian and critic. Name variations: Lady Dilke; Emilia Dilke; Frances Dilke; Emily Pattison; Frances Pattison; Emilia Frances Strong. Born Emily Frances Strong in Ilfracombe, Oxfordshire, England, on September 2, 1840; died in Pyrford Rough, near Woking, England, on October 24, 1904; daughter of Henry and Emily (Weedon) Strong; had private education followed by two years at South Kensington Art School, London; married Mark Pattison (1813–1884), on September 10, 1861; married Sir Charles Wentworth Dilke (1843–1911), on October 3, 1885; no children.

Joined the Women's Suffrage Union (early 1870s); was a member, Women's Protective and Provident League (WPPL), known as the Women's Trade Union League (WTUL) after 1891 (1875–1904), president (1902–1904).

Publications: Numerous articles, several books on French art, and two collections of short stories.

To many, Lady Emily Dilke was an inspiration. Her early years and first, extremely unhappy marriage to a man almost 27 years her senior inspired at least three novelists. In 1872, the most famous of the three, George Eliot (✧**Mary Anne Evans**), based her *Middlemarch* character Dorothea Brooke on Dilke, who was then a young woman known as Frances Pattison. Shortly after Lady Dilke's death, more than 40 years later, her beloved second husband Sir Charles Dilke wrote that his wife had "an overmastering sense of duty, and an unfailing courage, little short of sublime." It was that sense of duty that prompted Lady Dilke to commit the last 20 years of her life to the trade union cause. As an accomplished art critic and wife of a wealthy member of Parliament, she could have chosen to devote herself to her career as an art historian and to her social obligations as the wife of a baronet active in politics. Instead, she chose as her obligation to society the improvement of the conditions of labor for English working women.

She was born Emily Frances Strong, the middle of Henry and **Emily Weedon Strong**'s five children. Henry Strong, who had served as a British officer in India, was manager of a small bank in Oxford, England, by 1841. There, Frances, or "Fussie" as she was known to family and friends, grew up in a pleasant and politically liberal, middle-class home. Her father, despite the loss of two fingers during his army career, was an amateur artist and encouraged his daughter in her artistic interests. A family friend showed several of Frances' sketches to the renowned British artist John Ruskin. He announced she had talent, and Frances was allowed to go to London to study art over her mother's objections.

From 1859 to early 1861, Frances attended the South Kensington Art School, an intellectually stimulating environment that further defined her developing social conscience. Popular among her fellow students, she was also recognized as a promising artist by the faculty, receiving prizes in two subjects. But despite her artistic training, she had few options outside of marriage, given the social constraints of her class, and, in February 1861 she moved back to her parents' home, likely a difficult return following her days as an art student. By June, she was engaged. In September 1861, shortly after her 21st birthday, she married Mark Pattison, rector of Lincoln College, Oxford.

By contemporary accounts, Pattison was a lifeless academic, who was bitter over his apparent inability to leave behind his background as a poor cleric's son. For both husband and wife, the marriage was unhappy from the start. If marriage for Frances had seemed her only escape, she now found herself in another sort of prison. Divorce was not then the viable option for women it would later become, so she focused on her work, traveling abroad every year to study and to write. Her first published work, *The Renaissance of Art in France*, appeared in 1879. By then, she had also renewed her friendship with a former fellow art student, Charles Dilke. Three years younger than the vivacious Frances Strong, Charles had admired her from afar at South

◄✧

Juliana. See *Wilhelmina* for sidebar.

Kensington. When they met again, in Paris in 1875, he was a recent widower, a wealthy baronet, and a government official. Charles Dilke's radical Liberal politics appealed to Frances as much as his youth and charm, and the two became very close. After Mark Pattison died in 1884, they were seemingly free to marry. However, marriage was delayed for more than a year while Charles, his political career at stake, had to defend himself against charges of adultery brought up in a nasty and very public divorce case. Finally, on October 3, 1885, Emily Frances Strong Pattison and Sir Charles Wentworth Dilke married. Now known as Lady Emilia Dilke, she had the social position and the financial resources to lead a comfortable life. That she did, at the same time devoting herself to assisting women who led lives far different from her own.

Happiness in marriage seemed to provide Lady Dilke with the emotional strength to pursue interests she had long held. Although she had joined the Women's Protective and Provident League (WPPL) in 1875, it was only after her second marriage that she became truly involved in the League. Founded in 1874 by *Emma Paterson, the WPPL sought to facilitate trade unionism for English working women. After Paterson's death, Lady Dilke became in effect the head of the WPPL which in 1891 changed its name to the Women's Trade Union League (WTUL). While she was not officially elected president of the WTUL until 1902, Lady Dilke was one of its most public champions, writing numerous articles and making countless speeches. She was also one of the WTUL's most generous donors, giving an average of £100 a year.

While her husband, now a radical Liberal member of Parliament, was instrumental in the passage of protective labor legislation, Lady Dilke helped organize laundry workers, rag pickers and linen weavers. She represented the cause of working women at several Trade Union Congress (TUC) annual meetings, urging that male-dominated organization to welcome women into the TUC as equal partners. However, unlike some of her female contemporaries who stressed equality, Lady Dilke also advocated for the protective labor legislation her husband supported in Parliament. While some argued that such legislation did more harm than good by lumping women in with children as a class in need of protection, the Dilkes felt otherwise. As long as linen carders had an average life expectancy of 30 years because of harsh working conditions and starvation wages, Lady Dilke argued that both government intervention and trade unionism were needed.

Until her death in 1904, Lady Dilke helped the WTUL grow in strength and numbers. In 1876, less than 20,000 of England's working women were trade union members. By 1904, that number had risen to over 125,000, most of them textile workers. Lady Dilke's impassioned speeches as well as her social and political connections were instrumental in the growth of the WTUL. She died at her country home shortly after her 64th birthday, having helped her nation respond to the needs of its women wage earners. Her wit had been an important asset. In a play on words regarding Great Britain's turn-of-the-century preeminence as a world power, Lady Dilke's motto was: "Don't think of the Empire on which the sun never sets—think of the wage that never rises."

SOURCES:

Askwith, Betty. *Lady Dilke: A Biography*. London: Chatto & Windus, 1969.

Soldon, Norbert C. *Women in British Trade Unions, 1874–1976*. London: Gill and Macmillan, 1978.

COLLECTIONS:

Dilke Papers, British Museum, London.

Women's Trade Union League Papers, Trades Union Congress Library, London.

Kathleen Banks Nutter, Manuscripts Processor, Sophia Smith Collection, Smith College, Northampton, Massachusetts

Dimitrova, Blaga (1922—)

Bulgarian poet, novelist, political activist, and vice-president of Bulgaria, whose slow evolution from literary Stalinism to dissent is a case study in intellectual disillusionment as well as a chronicle of one writer's moral evolution. Born Blaga Nikolova Dimitrova in Biala Slatina, Bulgaria, on January 2, 1922; married Iordan Vasilev; children: one adopted daughter.

Was the best-known intellectual dissident in Bulgaria in the closing decade of the Communist regime; elected to Parliament (1990); began to serve as vice-president of Bulgaria (December 1991); resigned from that position (June 1993).

Selected writings: Because the Sea is Black: Poems of Blaga Dimitrova *(Translated by Niko Boris and Heather McHugh, Middletown, CT: Wesleyan University Press, 1989);* Journey to Oneself *(Translated by Radost Pridham, London: Cassell, 1969);* The Last Rock Eagle: Selected Poems of Blaga Dimitrova *(Translated by Brenda Walker and others, London: Forest Books, 1992);*

The collapse in Bulgaria in November 1989 of the hardline Stalinist regime of Premier Todor Zhivkov brought to world attention details of decades of not only political repression but intellectual tyranny as well. Perhaps the most talented and representative writer of the group of dissident intellectuals who were now finally able to freely voice their thoughts was the poet, novelist and playwright Blaga Dimitrova. Born in 1922 in the northern Bulgarian town of Biala Slatina, she grew up in the city of Turnovo. Dimitrova studied Slavonic philology in Sofia in 1945 and did graduate work in Moscow, receiving a degree in 1951. After graduation, she supported herself working as an editor for various publishing houses in Sofia. Although her earliest writings were critical of Bulgarian social conditions, intellectually Dimitrova was by and large a Stalinist both politically and culturally. During this phase of her life, she produced poetry and prose—including a 1950 book entitled *Verses About the Leader*—that was artistically weak but perhaps of some value as agitprop to the struggling Communist state and society that emerged after World War II.

By the 1960s, Dimitrova and a growing number of Bulgarian intellectuals found themselves increasingly unable to accept the harsh and arbitrary control of the Communist cultural bureaucracy over their artistic production. Growing confidence in her own work and disgust with the repressive Stalinism of the Zhivkov regime emboldened Dimitrova to challenge her pro-government colleagues who controlled the Writer's Union and thus were able to determine what could and could not be printed. Her first major clash with the authorities took place in the 1970s when she and her husband published two out of a projected three-volume study of the poet *Elisaveta Bagryana. Because these volumes had questioned Marxist-Leninist orthodoxy in the area of cultural and political history, they were banned immediately after publication; the third volume was denied official permission to be published.

In 1975, a harshly worded attack on authors who dared to question the official cultural line appeared in the Communist Party newspaper *Rabotnichesko Delo* (*Workers' Action*), an assault that was clearly directed against Dimitrova. Refusing to be cowed, she continued to write about issues that concerned her deeply, including the Bulgarian government's oppressive treatment of its Turkish minority. Dimitrova submitted an impassioned essay on this problem to the writers' newspaper *Literary Front*, which rejected it. When the piece was eventually published in another paper, the consequences were immediate and chilling: a crescent was painted on her door. Being branded "a friend of the Turks" was clearly a warning from the regime to immediately fall into line or be prepared for far more serious consequences.

Around this time Dimitrova had to face a major personal crisis, surgery for cancer. She recovered fully, vowing that with her restoration to health nothing would ever again stop her determination to write and disseminate the truth as she saw it. "After I met death and survived," she wrote, "I lost all my human doubts and fears. I came back ready for the battle with the system." In a 1990 interview, she recalled: "My thoughts about death helped me to overcome my slavery. I wanted to say to young people: 'Don't compromise, because later on there may be no time to say what you wanted to then.'"

In the mid-1980s, Dimitrova saw a little-publicized documentary film about the catastrophic environmental situation in the industrial city of Rousse. The film showed in terrifying detail how for years the wind had carried toxic chlorine gas from a Rumanian chemical factory directly across the Danube from Rousse. Despite the fact that the citizens of Rousse were afflicted with chronic health problems, the Bulgarian government did not protest the matter because it feared offending the Ceausescu regime. An outraged Dimitrova helped organize a Rescue Rousse Environmental Committee, which quickly gained mass support with petition drives, and a rally—the first opposition demonstration in Sofia since the end of World War II. The dictatorship of Todor Zhivkov was accused of consciously committing a crime against the citizens of Rousse. Several members of the committee lost their jobs, and Dimitrova was banned from appearing at public poetry meetings. The secret police tapped her telephone and intercepted her correspondence, but Dimitrova refused to be intimated.

In its final years, the dictatorship headed by Todor Zhivkov became more and more petty in its oppressiveness. For Dimitrova, one of the tragedies of these years was the fact that the censors who kept her writings from being published were often also her colleagues and even in some cases close friends. Displaying compassionate understanding, she noted years later that many of these censors, some of them talented poets like **Nadia Kehlibareva**, sadly died young and thus could themselves also be regarded as victims of censorship. The oppressive side of the regime made itself felt in the early 1980s, when Dimitrova's novel *Litse* (*Face*) was banned. From this point on, she was regarded both by the regime and her colleagues as a dissident. But the firmly entrenched Zhivkov regime did not regard her as an immediate threat and was content to deal with each new manuscript of hers on its own terms. Thus Dimitrova could continue to publish some if not all of her new works in Bulgaria.

In the final years of the moribund Bulgarian dictatorship, Blaga Dimitrova played an important role in signalling the dawn of a new cultural era, becoming in 1988 a founding member of the Club for Glasnost and Perestroika, an organization of intellectuals demanding that Bulgaria too embark on the road to reform launched by Mikhail Gorbachev in the Soviet Union. Although the dissidents could not always agree on exactly what they desired for Bulgaria besides the general goal of freedom, Dimitrova summed up their desire when she wrote of "the human longing for something different, a different time, a different way, and a different place."

The demise of Communism brought both promise and problems to Bulgaria. For Blaga Dimitrova, it meant that all of her writings could now be published. The novel *Litse*, which had previously only appeared in a heavily censored version, now appeared in print in its full text. Its portrait of the deformations of human decency and idealism resulting from the harsh rule of an arrogant Communist elite remained a valuable document of a difficult phase of the evolution of a nation that has suffered much throughout its long and colorful history. New challenges had to be met, particularly in public life, where Dimitrova had taken on the aura of a national hero for her principled resistance to dictatorship in years past. In 1990, she was elected to Parliament in the nation's first free elections. In December 1991, Dimitrova became vice president of Bulgaria. Not surprisingly, she chose as members of her administrative team a group of women, many of them talented writers including **Rada Sharlandjieva** and **Maria Georgieva**. But the politics of an emerging democracy was not always easily dealt with, and in less than two years Dimitrova called it quits. Accusing President Zhelyu Zhelyev of colluding with the former Communists to restore dictatorship in Bulgaria, Dimitrova protested by dramatically resigning her vice-presidential position on June 30, 1993.

Blaga Dimitrova has written in many genres including novels, plays, film scripts and reportage, and she has also produced sensitive translations from German, Swedish and Polish into Bulgarian, but her most profound thoughts have invariably appeared as poetry. Sophisticated, stylistically dense, and relentlessly demanding of the reader's intellect, her verse is characterized by its depth and compassion. In her best work, Dimitrova probes the different roles women assume in a lifetime, including the rever-

sal of roles that takes place when parents age and previous relationships are reversed. Thus we find her eloquently writing in her "Lullaby for My Mother" of the poignant situation in which:

> At night I make her bed
> in the folds of old age.
> Her skinny hand
> pulls mine into the dark.
>
> Before her dreams begin,
> from a brain erased of speech,
> a small cracked voice calls *mama*
> and I become my mother's mother.

A deep moral sense pervades the entirety of Blaga Dimitrova's work, and a passionate concern for humanity's sufferings is to be found on virtually every page of her poetry. Dimitrova's fellow Bulgarian **Julia Kristeva** has noted that "seldom has a woman's writing been at once more cerebral and more sensual."

SOURCES:

Agoston-Nikolova, Elka. "The Dilemmas of the Modern Bulgarian Woman in Blaga Dimitrova's Novel *Litse*," in *Literature and Politics in Eastern Europe: Selected Papers from the Fourth World Congress for Soviet and East European Studies, Harrogate, 1990*. NY: St. Martin's Press, 1992, pp. 74–82.

Bradbury, Malcolm. *Rates of Exchange*. NY: Alfred A. Knopf, 1983.

The Devil's Dozen: Thirteen Bulgarian Women Poets. Translated by Brenda Walker, Belin Tonchev and Svetoslav Piperov. London and Sofia: Forest Books/ Svyat, 1990.

Dimitrova, Blaga. "The future is for everyone," in *Index on Censorship*. Vol. 21, no. 9. October 1992, pp. 30–31.

———. "The Russian Legacy," in *Intellectuals and Social Change in Central and Eastern Europe: A Conference, April 1992*. Newark, NJ: Television and Radio Media Center, Rutgers, the State University Campus at Newark, 1992 [videorecording].

———. "Voices against the tide," in *Index on Censorship*. Vol. 20, no. 2. February 1991, p. 13.

Kanikova, S.I. "Blaga Dimitrova," in Celia Hawkesworth, ed. *Writers from Eastern Europe*. London: Book Trust, 1991, pp. 12–13.

Katzarova, Mariana. "Bulgaria's poet by profession, vice president by duty," in *Ms*. Vol. 3, no. 1. July 1992, pp. 16–17.

Meredith, William, ed. *Poets of Bulgaria*. Translated by John Balaban and others. Greensboro, NC: Unicorn Press, 1986.

Staitschewa, Emilia. "Die Frau und die Macht: Über die Selbstwahrnehmung der bulgarischen Dichterin Blaga Dimitrowa," in *Der weibliche multikulturelle Blick: Ergebnisse eines Symposiums*. Berlin: trafo, 1995, pp. 196–207.

John Haag, Associate Professor of History, University of Georgia, Athens, Georgia

Dimmick, Mary Scott (1858–1948).

See Harrison, Mary Scott.

Dimock, Susan (1847–1875)

American medical pioneer, whose extraordinary talent would most likely have made of her a major surgeon and medical practitioner had she not died tragically in a shipwreck at age 28. Born in Washington, North Carolina, on April 24, 1847; died in a shipwreck on May 8, 1875; daughter of Henry Dimock (a lawyer and newspaper editor) and Mary Malvina Owens Dimock.

North Carolina's first female physician, Susan Dimock was born 14 years before the start of the Civil War. Her father Henry Dimock had moved to the south from Maine after graduating from Bowdoin College; his father was a physician. Susan's mother **Mary Owens Dimock**, a native of Washington, North Carolina, was the daughter of the sheriff of Beaufort County. Henry Dimock gave up schoolteaching to take the post of editor of Washington's local newspaper, *The North State Whig*. After marrying Mary, Henry acquired the local hotel, The Lafayette, and it was here that the Dimocks' only child Susan was born on April 24, 1847. Susan's childhood was happy, and some of her most formative experiences during those years were the impressions made on her by the family physician, Dr. Solomon Samson Satchwell, who lived across the street from the hotel. Satchwell allowed Susan to read through his medical library and even took her with him when he made calls in the countryside.

A brilliant student at the local academy as well as a cheerful young girl, Susan Dimock was particularly drawn to the Latin language. To perfect her knowledge, she enjoyed translating prescriptions in one of Dr. Satchwell's ancient pharmacopoeias. Dimock's idyllic world came crashing down suddenly in 1863 when Washington was occupied by Union forces. Some of the officers of the occupying army moved into the Lafayette Hotel, and for the unreconstructed Confederates among the local population, the fact that the Dimocks not only seemed to easily accept this fait accompli but were apparently on cordial terms with the soldiers made Susan's parents much disliked in town. Only months after the surrender, Henry Dimock died. Soon after, another catastrophe struck when the hotel burned to the ground.

Daughter and mother, now penniless, faced a harsh future. They managed to get to Sterling, Massachusetts, where Mary's sister lived, and Susan immediately enrolled in a local school and qualified to become a schoolteacher. After only six months in Sterling, Susan, who was not yet 18, secured a teaching job in Hopkinton, Massachusetts. The next phase of Dimock's life evolved from her ability to make deep and lasting friendships. One of her closest friends, **Elizabeth "Bessie" Greene**, was the daughter of a wealthy Bostonian and social reformer, Colonel William B. Greene. With her and her mother's lives once again relatively stable, Susan's earlier interest in medicine returned stronger than ever. Through her friend Bessie Greene, Susan met Dr. *Marie Zakrzewska, a Polish-born Boston physician who was at the time one of the handful of female physicians in the United States. Zakrzewska suggested several medical texts for Dimock to study, and despite some misgivings voiced by her mother, her determination to become a physician became stronger with each passing day. In January 1866, Susan Dimock enrolled at the New England Hospital for Women and Children in Roxbury, Massachusetts.

Dimock's studies were supervised by Dr. Zakrzewska and Dr. *Lucy E. Sewall, highly respected female medical pioneers in New England. Susan gained valuable experience treating patients in the wards, in the dispensary and sometimes at their homes. Patients soon came to respect and love the young student who exhibited a "remarkable union of tenderness, firmness and skill." But she burned with ambition to attain the highest level of medical knowledge and applied for admission to Harvard Medical School. When that institution turned down her joint application with the British medical pioneer *Sophia Jex-Blake in spring 1867, Dimock refused to be discouraged and successfully applied for admission to Massachusetts General Hospital. Even this excellent institution did not meet Dimock's exacting standards, and she persuaded her mother and Colonel Greene to provide funds to enable her to study in Europe at the only institution that at the time allowed women to study for a medical degree, the University of Zurich.

In Zurich, Dimock was one of a group of seven extraordinary medical pioneers whose courage and tenacity, as well as their obvious intellectual abilities, made possible what the medical historian Thomas Neville Bonner has called "a revolution in women's medical education." Susan Dimock's fellow pioneers in this effort to open the doors of medicine to women included Russia's **Maria Bokova** and ⚓▶ **Nadezhda Suslova**, England's **Elizabeth Morgan** and **Louisa Atkins**, Scotland's **Eliza Walker**, and Switzerland's **Marie Vögtlin**. In this talented group, Susan Dimock stood out as a natural leader. She mastered the German language quickly and was

⚓▶ *Suslova, Nadezhda.* See Liubatovich, Olga for sidebar.

able to write her dissertation, on the different forms of puerperal fever, in a clear, easily understood style. Her professors were highly pleased with her progress and after graduating with honors in 1871 she added to her already solid medical knowledge with additional work in hospitals in Vienna and Paris.

At the time of Dimock's return to the United States in 1872, the American Medical Association declared as a body that women would forever be constitutionally incapable of carrying out the grave responsibilities of a doctor of medicine. In the same year, however, the medical society of her native state of North Carolina elected her an honorary member of the profession—"honorary" because at the time she was studying in Paris and could thus not be present for examination. Her credentials were presented by her friend of childhood, Dr. Satchwell, a physician whose words on her behalf carried much weight throughout North Carolina.

In late August 1872, Dimock took up her duties as resident physician at the New England Hospital for Women and Children. From the first day on the job, she showed extraordinary energy and imagination in carrying out the tasks assigned to her. Dimock administered the hospital for the next three years without assistance, carrying a crushing work load that included an extensive reorganization of the institution's training school. She advised her nursing staff to treat every patient "as you would wish your own sister to be treated." At the same time, she shared in the patient care in the wards and dispensary and performed virtually all of the surgery at the hospital, rapidly becoming a highly skilled practitioner of this ancient and delicate art. Amazingly, she was also able during these years to establish a considerable and highly regarded private practice.

Proud of her achievements but feeling she needed a long holiday as well as an opportunity to study the latest medical advances in Europe, Dimock requested and received permission for five months' leave of absence for the summer of 1875. Accompanied by her friends Bessie Greene and **Caroline Crane**, she sailed from New York on April 27, 1875. Their ship, the *Schiller*, was considered to be one of the best of the great iron-rigged steam vessels of the day, and the three women looked forward to a relaxing ocean voyage followed by months on the Continent. This joyous prospect turned to disaster on the night of May 7–8 when the *Schiller* entered a foggy stretch of sea off England's Cornwall and was wrecked on a granite reef off the Scilly Isles.

Most of those on board, including Susan Dimock and her friends, drowned. Colonel Greene arranged to have his daughter's body as well as that of Caroline Crane and Susan Dimock brought home to Boston, where the three were interred in Forest Hills Cemetery.

Virtually all who commented publicly at the time of Susan Dimock's tragic death noted the incalculable loss to medicine and humanity her passing represented. Several male physicians admitted that their prejudice against women studying medicine ended after they had been able to observe the extraordinary talents of this dedicated young woman. One male doctor lamented that, had she lived, she "would have become a great surgeon and would have been sure to stand . . . among those at the head of her profession." Her intelligence, modesty, and devotion to the art of healing convinced several of the most stubborn opponents of women serving as doctors that their previous attitudes needed to be drastically changed. To memorialize her life, Susan's family contributed a free bed to the New England Hospital for Women and Children (the hospital still exists in Roxbury as the Dimock Community Health Center). Washington, North Carolina, remains intensely proud of the town's greatest daughter, and her birthplace there is marked by a plaque on East Main Street.

SOURCES:
[Cheney, Edna Dow]. *Memoir of Susan Dimock, resident physician of New England Hospital for Women and Children.* Boston, MA: Press of J. Wilson, 1875 [History of Women Microfilm Collection, Reel 398, No. 2844].

Bonner, Thomas Neville. *Becoming a Physician: Medical Education in Britain, France, Germany, and the United States, 1750–1945.* NY: Oxford University Press, 1995.

——. "Medical Women Abroad: A New Dimension of Women's Push for Opportunity in Medicine," in *Bulletin of the History of Medicine.* Vol. 62, 1988, pp. 58–73.

——. "Rendezvous in Zurich: Seven Who Made a Revolution in Women's Medical Education, 1864–1874," in *Journal of the History of Medicine and Allied Sciences.* Vol. 44, no. 1. January 1989, pp. 7–27.

——. *To the Ends of the Earth: Women's Search for Education in Medicine.* Cambridge, MA: Harvard University Press, 1992.

Sherr, Lynn, and Jurate Kazickas. *Susan B. Anthony Slept Here: A Guide to American Women's Landmarks.* NY: Times Books, 1994.

John Haag, Associate Professor of History, University of Georgia, Athens, Georgia

Di Murska, Ilma (1836–1889)

Croatian soprano, a European opera star of great renown in the 19th century. Born in Zagreb on Janu-

ary 4, 1836; died in Munich, Germany, on January 14, 1889.

Ilma Di Murska's vocal range was over three octaves, powerful and memorable. She studied in Vienna before going to Paris to study with *Mathilde Marchesi and made her debut in Florence in 1862 as Lady Harriet in *Martha*. Soon, Di Murska was on the European opera circuit singing in Budapest, Berlin, Hamburg, and Vienna. In 1865, she appeared at Her Majesty's Theater in London, singing there until 1873 with Mapleson's company. She sang in the first Wagner opera heard in London, appearing as Senta in *Der fliegende Holländer*. Though particularly well known for her interpretation of Queen of the Night, Di Murska also sang Konstanze, Amina, Marguerite de Valois, Dinorah, and Ophelia. A sometimes extravagant actress, she was known for her original performances and her professional singing.

John Haag,
Athens, Georgia

Dinah (fl. 1730 BCE)

Biblical woman. Flourished around 1730 BCE; daughter of Jacob and Leah; sister of Simeon and Levi (Genesis 30:21).

In the Old Testament, Dinah was the only daughter of Jacob, father of the 12 patriarchs and ancestor of the Israelites, and his first wife *Leah. The seduction of Dinah by Shechem, son of Hivite chief Hamor, led Dinah's brothers Simeon and Levi to take revenge by putting the Shechemites to death (Genesis 34). Jacob often spoke of the tragedy of his only daughter with abhorrence and regret. Dinah in Hebrew means judged or avenged.

Dinesen, Isak (1885–1962)

Danish writer, author of tales from Africa, who was a major literary figure of the 20th century. Name variations: Karen Blixen; Karen Blixen-Finecke; (pseudonyms) Pierre Andrézel, Tania B., and Osceola. Born Karen Christentze Dinesen on April 17, 1885, in Rungsted, Denmark; died on September 7, 1962, in Rungsted; daughter of Wilhelm (an army officer and writer under his own name and his Indian name Boganis) and Ingeborg (Westenholz) Dinesen; studied English at Oxford University, 1904; studied painting at Royal Academy in Copenhagen, in Paris, 1910, and in Rome; married Baron Bror Blixen-Finecke (a big-game hunter and writer), January 14, 1914 (divorced 1921).

Awards, honors: Ingenio et Arti Medal from King Frederick IX of Denmark (1950); The Golden Laurels (1952); Hans Christian Andersen Prize (1955); Danish Critics' Prize (1957); Henri Nathansen Memorial Fund award (1957).

Writer (1907–62); with husband Baron Blixen, managed a coffee plantation in British East Africa (now Nairobi, Kenya, 1913–21); took over management until failing coffee prices forced her to give up the farm in 1931; commissioned by three Scandinavian newspapers to write a series of 12 articles on wartime Berlin, Paris, and London (1940); became one of the founding members of the Danish Academy (November 28, 1960).

Selected writings (published in Danish under name Karen Blixen, except as noted, and in English under Isak Dinesen): Sandhedens Haevn ("The Revenge of Truth," play first produced at Royal Theatre, Copenhagen, 1936); Seven Gothic Tales (Smith & Haas, 1934, Danish version published as Syv Fantastiske Fortaellinger); Out of Africa (London: Putnam, 1937, Danish version published as Den Afrikanske Farm); Winter's Tales (Random House, 1942, Danish version published as Vinter-Eventyr); (under pseudonym Pierre Andrezel) Gengaeldelsens Veje ("The Ways of Retribution," translation published as The Angelic Avengers, Putnam, 1946); Om revtskrivning 23–24 marts 1938 (Gyldendal, 1949); Daguerreotypier (two radio talks presented January, 1951, Gyldendal, 1951); Babettes Gaestebud ("Babette's Feast," Copenhagen: Fremad, 1952); Omkring den Nye Lov om Dyreforsoeg (Copenhagen: Politikens Forlag, 1952); Kardinalens tredie Historie ("The Cardinal's Third Tale," Gyldendal, 1952); En Baaltale med 14 Aars Forsinkelse ("Bonfire Speech 14 Years Delayed," Copenhagen: Berlingske Forlag, 1953); Spoegelseshestene (Fremad, 1955); Last Tales (Random House, 1957, Danish version published as Sidste Fortaellinger, Gyldendal, 1957); Anecdotes of Destiny (Random House, 1958, Danish version published as Skaebne-Anekdoter, Gyldendal, 1958); Skygger paa Graesset (Gyldendal, 1960, published as Shadows on the Grass, Random House, 1961); (introduction) Olive Schreiner's The Story of An African Farm (Limited Editions Club, 1961); On Mottoes of My Life (Copenhagen: Ministry of Foreign Affairs, 1962); Osceola (posthumously published collection of early stories and poems, Gyldendal, 1962); Ehrengard (posthumously published, Random House and Gyldendal, 1963); Karen Blixen (memorial edition of principal works, Gyldendal, 1964); Efterladte Fortallinger (Gyldendal, 1975). Contributor of short stories, articles, and reviews to Ladies' Home Journal,

Saturday Evening Post, Atlantic, Harper's Bazaar, Vogue, Botteghe Oscure, and Heretica.

Karen Blixen, better known by her pen name Isak Dinesen, remains one of Denmark's most widely acclaimed modern authors. A prose stylist who wrote skillfully in English as well as in her native Danish, Dinesen composed exotic and archaic tales that set her apart from the literary traditions of her day. Although initially snubbed by critics in her native country, she enjoyed both critical and commercial success in Britain and the United States and was twice nominated for the Nobel Prize. In addition to her considerable literary contributions, Dinesen is perhaps equally well known for her remarkable life, documented in such autobiographical works as *Out of Africa* and *Shadows on the Grass*. As David Lehman noted in *Newsweek:* "She likened herself to Scheherazade—and fully lived up to the name . . . [leading] a life as wildly improbable and flamboyantly romantic as her exotic and spellbinding tales."

I believe that life demands of us that we love it, . . . in all its forms. . . . [W]hen you mention my philosophy of life, I have no other than that.

—Isak Dinesen

Born Christenze Dinesen on April 17, 1885, in Rungsted, Denmark, in a seaside house once inhabited by Johannes Ewald (1743–1781), Dinesen was widely considered Denmark's greatest lyric poet. She led a happy childhood until tragedy shattered her comfortable existence. In 1895, her father Wilhelm hung himself. Dinesen had always been very close to her father, and his suicide was a shock. "I was ten years old when father died. His death was for me a great sorrow, of a kind which probably only children feel," she wrote in *Daguerreotypes and Other Essays*. According to **Parmenia Migel** in *Titania: The Biography of Isak Dinesen*, Dinesen later reflected: "It was as if a part of oneself had also died . . . the desolate feeling that there was no one to remember the talks on Ewald's Hill . . . suddenly one was pushed into the foremost row of life, bereft of the joy and irresponsibility of childhood." Dinesen's brother Thomas, with whom she remained close as an adult, later speculated that their father had suffered from syphilis, a disease that Dinesen herself would contract years later.

Tutored at home by a series of governesses, Dinesen showed early artistic promise and as a teenager studied drawing, painting, and languages at a private school in France. In 1903,

after a series of comprehensive exams, she was admitted into the Royal Academy of Fine Arts in Copenhagen. There she developed her affinity for painting, an affinity that would later be reflected in the rich descriptive style of her writing. According to **Judith Thurman** in *Isak Dinesen: The Life of a Storyteller*, Dinesen later wrote: "[I owe painting] . . . for revealing the nature of reality to me. I have always had difficulty seeing how a landscape looked, if I had not first got the key to it from a great painter. I have experienced and recognized a land's particular character where a painter has interpreted it to me. Constable, Gainsborough and Turner showed me England. When I travelled to Holland as a young girl, I understood all the landscape and the cities said because the old Dutch painters did me the kind service of interpreting it." Dinesen dropped out of the Academy several years later and soon thereafter took up writing. Between 1904 and 1908 she wrote the first draft of a puppet play entitled "The Revenge of Truth," as well as a series of tales she called "Likely Stories." Mario Krohn, an art historian Dinesen had met at the Academy, read her work and encouraged Dinesen to take her writing seriously. Krohn also arranged to have some of her stories read by Valdemar Vedel, editor of one of Denmark's most distinguished literary magazines, *Tilskueren*. According to Thurman, Vedel wrote to Krohn that one of Dinesen's tales, "The Hermits," was "so original . . . and so well made that I would like to take it for *Tilskueren*." The tale was published in 1907 under the pseudonym Osceola. Two years later Krohn himself became editor of *Tilskueren* and accepted Dinesen's story "The de Cats Family" in 1909.

During these years, Dinesen spent much of her time in the company of her upper-class relatives, and soon found herself deeply but unhappily involved with her second cousin, Hans Blixen-Finecke. The failed love affair had a great impact on Dinesen. According to Thurman, she later recalled: "More than anything else, a deep, unrequited love left its mark on my early youth." Extremely depressed, Dinesen left Denmark in 1910 to attend a new art school in Paris. Thurman relates that when Mario Krohn visited Dinesen in Paris and asked her about her literary ambitions she answered that she wanted "all things in life more than to be a writer—travel, dancing, living, the freedom to paint." When she returned to her family estate at Rungstedlund several months later, Dinesen turned to writing as a diversion, revising "The Revenge of Truth" and composing early versions of tales such as "Carnival" and "Peter and Rosa."

A voyage to Rome two years later did little to assuage her depression over her unrequited love, and upon her return Dinesen shocked her family and friends by announcing that she was to marry Hans' twin brother, Bror Blixen. Based on advice from relatives, the engaged couple decided to go to Africa, then thought to be a land of opportunity and excitement for young people with initiative. In 1913, Bror Blixen left for British East Africa and, with capital provided largely by Dinesen's family, purchased a 6,000-acre coffee plantation outside of Nairobi, Kenya. The following January, Dinesen joined Baron Bror Blixen; the two were married on the 14th of that month. Dinesen would not return to writing fiction for many years, but 1914 marks the beginning of her letters to her family and friends, correspondence later compiled and published as *Letters from Africa*.

The early months in Africa passed well. Dinesen enjoyed living on the plantation and accompanying her husband on safari. She was also taken with her African servants, particularly her cook, Farah, who went on to become Dinesen's friend and confidant. During her time in Africa,

Isak Dinesen

she socialized with the upper-class Europeans living there, many of whom would become models for characters in her tales. However, several months after her arrival in Kenya, Dinesen began to suffer from what she believed to be malaria but which later turned out to be a case of syphilis contracted from her husband. To receive treatment, she returned to Europe. Although the primary syphilis was arrested, Dinesen was to suffer the lingering effects of the disease throughout her life.

The next years were difficult ones for Dinesen, both personally and financially. The philandering Baron embarked on extended safaris, ignoring his duties to both the farm and his wife. Meanwhile, despite her family's continued financial support, the coffee farm was losing large amounts of money. Forced to return to Denmark for treatment of blood poisoning, Dinesen confided her marital problems to her mother and brother Thomas. These problems, combined with the ongoing financial setbacks on the farm, caused Bror's dismissal and Dinesen's appointment as the sole manager of what became known as the Karen Coffee Company. Although her family urged divorce, Dinesen agreed only to a separation from the Baron. "I would never demand a divorce or try to push it through against Bror's will. I do not know how anyone can do that unless one is quite frenzied; and even though I have occasionally been angry with Bror or, rather, perhaps, in despair over his behavior, there is far, far too much binding us together from all the years of difficulty we have shared here, for me to be able to take the initiative in putting an end to what, if nothing else, was a most intimate relationship. . . . In any case, it is my heartfelt hope that he will be happy. . . . I feel for Bror, and will until I die, the greatest friendship or the deepest tenderness that I am capable of feeling," Dinesen explained in *Letters from Africa*. In the end, however, it was the Baron who requested and received the divorce.

About this time Dinesen met Denys Finch Hatton, a handsome English pilot and hunter who was to become her companion and lover as well as the first audience for her tales. During Finch Hatton's occasional, and often unannounced, visits, Dinesen would relate to her friend stories she had thought up during his absence, weaving imaginative tales to lengthen Finch Hatton's visits.

In 1923, inspired by a debate between her mother and brother concerning sexual morality, Dinesen wrote a long essay entitled "On Modern Marriage and Other Considerations," her first formal writing effort in years. The following year, she resubmitted "The Revenge of Truth" to *Tilskueren*. When it was accepted for publication a year later, Dinesen wrote in *Letters from Africa*: "With regard to 'The Revenge of Truth.' I don't want anything in it changed; but I imagine there is little chance of it ever being published. I don't think there is anything blasphemous in it, simply that it is written from an atheist's viewpoint. I believe it would be impossible to write if one gave consideration to who is going to read one's work,—but for that matter I don't think I will be writing anything in the near future."

During the mid- and late 1920s, the Karen Coffee Company suffered enormous financial setbacks, and it soon became clear that Dinesen would be forced to sell the farm. To alleviate her anxiety, she started writing down those fantastic tales she had recounted to Hatton during his stays. She later recalled in *Daguerreotypes and Other Essays:* "During my last months in Africa, as it became clear to me that I could not keep the farm, I had started writing at night, to get my mind off the things which in the daytime it had gone over a hundred times, and on a new track. My squatters on the farm, by then, had got into the habit of coming up to my house and sitting around it for hours in silence, as if just waiting to see how things would develop. I felt their presence there more like a friendly gesture than a reproach, but all the same of sufficient weight to make it difficult for me to start any undertaking of my own. But they would go away, back to their huts, at nightfall. And I sat there, in the house, alone, or perhaps with Farah, the infallibly loyal, standing motionless in his long white Arab robe with his back to the wall, figures, voices, and colors from far away or from nowhere began to swarm around my paraffin lamp." In such a manner, Dinesen wrote two of her *Seven Gothic Tales*. By 1931, the farm had been auctioned off. While awaiting her return to Denmark, Dinesen learned that Finch Hatton had been killed when his small plane crashed in Tanganyika. She looked on Africa for the last time in May of 1931.

Once home at Rungstedlund, Dinesen began to write almost immediately, working in her father's old office. Now, however, her motives were serious. "My home is a lovely place; I might have lived on there from day to day in a kind of sweet idyll; but I could not see any kind of future before me. And I had no money; my dowry, so to say, had gone with the farm. I owed it to the people on whom I was dependent to try to make some kind of existence for myself.

Those Gothic Tales began to demand to be written," she later wrote in *Daguerreotypes and Other Essays*. Two years later, at age 48, Dinesen completed her first collection of stories, *Seven Gothic Tales*.

Although *Seven Gothic Tales* was written in English, Dinesen experienced some difficulty getting the book into print; few publishers were willing to bet on a debut work by an unknown Danish author. Several British publishers rejected the manuscript before it came across the desk of *Dorothy Canfield Fisher, a friend of Thomas Dinesen and member of the Book-of-the-Month Club selection committee. Impressed with the collection, Fisher sent it to publisher Robert Haas, who was equally impressed and released *Seven Gothic Tales* the following year.

An aura of mystery surrounded the book's publication. When it offered *Seven Gothic Tales* as its April 1934 selection, the Book-of-the-Month Club newsletter stated simply, "No clue is available as to the pseudonymic author." Dinesen herself confused matters by preceding her maiden name with a man's first name—Isak, Hebrew for "one who laughs." Her true identity was not revealed until over 50,000 copies of *Seven Gothic Tales* were in print. With this collection Dinesen began a long and rewarding relationship with American readers, as five of her books would become Book-of-the-Month Club selections.

In *Seven Gothic Tales*, Dinesen introduced stylistic and thematic motifs that are to be found throughout much of her subsequent work. She derived these motifs largely from two 19th-century literary movements—the Gothic and the decadent. As in the novels written in these genres, Dinesen's tales are often characterized by an emphasis on the emotional and spiritual, a nostalgia for the glory of past ages, a predilection for exotic characters, and an overriding sense of mystery, horror, and the supernatural. Eric O. Johannesson noted in *The World of Isak Dinesen* that "The spinechilling tale of terror, with its persecuted women, its ghosts, and its mysterious convents and castles, as well as the cruel tale, with its atmosphere of perversity and artificiality, have served as sources of inspiration for Dinesen." While critics clearly recognized Dinesen's debt to these traditions, several felt that she went beyond them. Langbaum maintained in *Isak Dinesen's Art: The Gayety of Vision* that Dinesen is "an important writer because she has understood the tradition behind her and has taken the next step required by that tradition. Like the other, more massive writers of her generation—Rilke, Kafka, Mann, Joyce, Eliot,

Yeats, . . .—she takes off from the sense of individuality developed in the course of the nineteenth-century to the point of morbidity, and leads that individuality where it wants to go. She leads it back to a universal principle and a connection with the external world."

Seven Gothic Tales also introduces Dinesen's preoccupation with the principle of interdependence, which she further develops in later works. In *Seven Gothic Tales* there are interrelationships among individual stories in the volume as well as the existence of stories within stories. Comparing such constructions to "a complex kaleidoscope," **Elizabeth Ely Fuller** wrote in the *New Boston Review* that "Each character and each event works as a little bit of mirror reflecting another character or event, and then turning slightly to catch some other reflection. To reinforce this overall plot structure, Dinesen uses mirror images and similes repeatedly as the characters muse on their own nature and on their relation to others. To any one of them, the story makes no sense, but taken as a whole, the stories, like a piece of music or a minuet, form a complete pattern of movement." The principle of interdependence works on a thematic level in *Seven Gothic Tales* as well, as such disparate concepts such as good and evil, comedy and tragedy, and art and life, are intricately linked.

In spite of poor health and repeated hospitalizations, Dinesen continued to work on a book of memoirs entitled *Out of Africa*. Considered by many to be the greatest pastoral romance of the 20th century, *Out of Africa* enjoyed immediate and lasting critical acclaim, particularly from British and American critics. In a *Chicago Tribune* review, Richard Stern called the work "perhaps the finest book ever written about Africa," claiming that "it casts over landscape, animals, and people the kind of transfixing spell 'Ulysses' casts over Dublin." Katherine Woods, writing in *The New York Times,* praised the book's absence of "sentimentality" and "elaboration" and avers, "Like the Ngong hills—'which are amongst the most beautiful in the world'—this writing is without redundancies, bared to its lines of strength and beauty." Even those critics who found fault with the book's structure commended Dinesen's style. "The tale of increasing tragedy which fills the latter half of the book seems not quite so successful as her earlier chapters," noted Hassoldt Davis in the *Saturday Review of Literature*. "But," he added, "her book has a solid core of beauty in it, and a style as cadenced, constrained, and graceful as we have today." Hudson Strode seemed to capture the sentiments of many critics when he wrote in *Books:* "The author casts enchantment over her landscape with the most casual phrases. . . . Backward, forward, she goes, a spark here, a flare there, until she has the landscape fairly lit up before you with all its inhabitants and customs in place. The result is a great naturalness."

Letters from Africa, the posthumously published compilation of Dinesen's correspondence with her family and friends, sheds a good deal of light on *Out of Africa.* Begun soon after her arrival to Africa in 1914, these letters provide the private, often painful story behind the romantic vision of life presented in her famous memoir. As these letters show, Dinesen endured a number of hardships during her 17 years in Africa. Lingering bouts of illness, marital problems, increasing loneliness, and financial worries all caused her despair. But, despite their painful revelations, these letters shed light on intermittent periods of happiness, even elation. This is particularly evident in Dinesen's descriptions of her growing attachment to the land of Africa and its people. "Immediately after lunch, Bror and I drove by car to our own farm. It is the most enchanting road you can imagine, like our own Deer Park, and the long blue range of Ngong Hills stretching out beyond it. There are so many flowering trees and shrubs, and a scent rather like bog myrtle, or pine trees, pervades everything. Out here it is not hot at all, the air is so soft and lovely, and one feels so light and free and happy," Dinesen wrote in one of her early entries in *Letters from Africa.*

Letters from Africa follows Dinesen's development from naive bride to able plantation manager to financially ruined-but-unembittered divorcée. Remarked Kathleen Chase in *World Literature Today:* "We see Dinesen unmasked in all her moods and emotions, prejudices and predilections, her thoughts, her periodic nostalgia for Denmark (always flying the Danish flag) and her idyllic relationship with the English safari leader Denys Finch Hatton." Indeed, many of these letters chart Dinesen's increasing romantic feelings for Finch Hatton. As she wrote to her brother Thomas in 1928, "That such a person as Denys does exist,—something I have indeed guessed at before, but hardly dared to believe,— and that I have been lucky enough to meet him in this life and been so close to him,—even though there have been long periods of missing him in between,—compensates for everything else in the world, and other things cease to have any significance." Though Dinesen later experienced difficulty in her relationship with Finch Hatton, most of her letters recall their friendship glowingly.

These letters also revealed a good deal about Dinesen's patrician outlook. By her own admission, she felt an affinity for the aristocracy and a general disdain for all that was bourgeois. In fact, she often called herself "God's little snob." The correspondence in *Letters from Africa* does little to change such a reputation. Isak Dinesen "was a terrible snob. Critics have long waxed ingenious in defending her short stories from charges of noblesse oblige; those defenses will be harder to make on the evidence of this collection," claimed Carl Bailey in the *Village Voice.* A *New York Times Book Review* contributor admitted that *Letters from Africa* often put Dinesen in a poor light. "Her letters reveal a difficult woman: inconsistent and often cruel in her rejection of family life, emotionally demanding and given to what she herself called 'showing off.'" However, most critics have maintained that the overall portrait of Dinesen that emerges from these letters is a positive one. Wrote **Victoria Glendinning** in the *Washington Post Book World:* "It is her will and complete lack of self-pity that make [Dinesen] so sympathetic and save her from the alienating intensity of other solitary searchers such as, for example, Simone Weil. She quotes a definition of true piety as 'loving one's destiny unconditionally.' To be able to do this without losing her resilience was part of [her] achievement." Adds Richard Stern in the *Chicago Tribune,* "If these [letters] are not as brilliant as those in her great memoir, there is at least the material for one portrait greater than all the others, that of the great human being behind them all."

In 1940, Dinesen was commissioned by the Copenhagen daily newspaper *Politiken* to spend a month in Berlin, a month in Paris, and a month in London and to write a series of articles about each city. Although the advent of World War II caused the cancellations of the Paris and London visits, Dinesen's recollections of Hitler's Germany were later compiled in the posthumous collection *Daguerreotypes and Other Essays.* About this time, Dinesen also began work on her second set of stories, but completion of the volume was delayed by complications arising from tertiary syphilis. Dinesen eventually finished this second set of tales and, in 1942, *Winter's Tales,* a book that derives its title from one of Shakespeare's plays, was published in the United States, England, and Denmark.

With *Winter's Tales* Dinesen broke from the relative realism of *Out of Africa* and returned to the highly imaginative style that characterizes *Seven Gothic Tales*. Although these two collections share a number of similarities, *Winter's Tales* is simpler in style and closer in setting to modern Denmark. "Suffused with vague aspirations toward some cloudy ideal," noted Clifton Fadiman in *The New Yorker*, "with a longing for the impossible, with a brooding delight in magnificent and absurd gestures, with a quality of sleepwalking, they are as far removed from 1943 as anything can well be." Some critics, however, found fault with Dinesen's unique writing style. In a *Commonweal* review J.E. Tobin claimed, "The characters lack even the vague shape of ghosts; the atmosphere is that of stale perfume; the writing, called quaint by some, is downright awkward." Nonetheless, the general consensus was one of commendation for both the form and content of *Winter's Tales*. Struthers Brut, writing in the *Saturday Review of Literature*, summed up such a reaction when he maintained: "Often as you read the tales you wonder why you are so interested, so constantly excited, for the tales themselves, all of them symbolic, are not espe-

cially exciting in their plots, and the characters are frequently as remote as those in fairy tales, and a great deal of the time you are wandering in a fourth dimension where nothing is clear. But the final effect is unforgettable, just as the moments of reading are unforgettable."

Winter's Tales, along with *Seven Gothic Tales* and *Out of Africa*, are generally considered to be Dinesen's masterpieces. Between their publication and the 1957 publication of *Last Tales*, there was a 15-year hiatus during which she published only one book—*The Angelic Avengers*, a thriller novel released in 1946 under the pseudonym of Pierre Andrezel. Dinesen was never proud of *The Angelic Avengers* and for many years refused to acknowledge herself as the book's author. Even after such acknowledgment, Dinesen criticized the book, claiming that she wrote it solely for her own amusement as a diversion from the grim realities of Nazi-occupied Denmark. In spite of her disclaimers, the book, a bestseller in Denmark and a Book-of-

From the movie Out of Africa, starring Robert Redford and Meryl Streep as Isak Dinesen.

the-Month Club selection in America, was generally well-received.

The primary reason for Dinesen's sparse production between 1942 and 1957 was her continual poor health. Despite a series of corrective operations, she suffered lingering bouts of illness that greatly hampered her creative output, and she spent much of the 1940s convalescing and occasionally traveling. By 1950, her health had improved, and she delivered a series of broadcasts for Danish radio in which she described her African servant and friend, Farah. These broadcasts foreshadowed some of the material that would later be included in *Shadows on the Grass.* Dinesen's 70th birthday, in 1955, was feted worldwide. In August of that same year, she underwent an operation in which several spinal nerves were severed, as well as surgery on an ulcer. After the surgery, she became an invalid, never again ate normally, and never weighed more than 85 pounds. According to Thurman, Dinesen wrote at the time: "[These] past eight months have been more horrible than I can really describe to others—such continuous, insufferable pains, under which I howled like a wolf, are something one cannot fully comprehend. I feel that I have been in an Underworld. . . . The problem for me now is how I shall manage to come back into the world of human beings. It sometimes feels practically insoluble, though I believe that if I find something to look forward to, it could be possible."

In spite of her poor health and advanced age, Dinesen experienced a great renaissance during the late 1950s and early 1960s. During this period she published three works within a four-year span—*Last Tales* in 1957, *Anecdotes of Destiny* in 1958, and *Shadows on the Grass* in 1961. By now Dinesen was hailed worldwide as a major literary figure and had been nominated for the Nobel Prize several times. When Ernest Hemingway accepted his Nobel Prize in 1954 he said that the award should have been given instead to "that beautiful Danish writer Isak Dinesen."

As in her earlier volumes, the stories in *Last Tales* vary in time and place but deal with similar character types and themes, primarily exotic, often aristocratic characters in conflict or in harmony with their destinies. Destiny, more specifically one's control over it, is one of Dinesen's major themes. In her view, such a coming to terms involves an acceptance of one's fate as determined by God. "Dinesen's tales, like the stories in the *Arabian Nights,* proclaim the belief in the all but magic power of the story to provide man with a new vision and a renewed faith in life," Johannesson wrote. "Her figures are often Hamlet figures, melancholy men and women who wait for fate to lend them a helping hand, who wait for the storyteller to provide them with a destiny by placing them in a story." Although *Last Tales* was her first set of stories in over 15 years, many critics found that Dinesen had managed to retain her artistic mastery. As a *Time* reviewer noted of *Last Tales:* "The characters are large, heroic figures and they are brought to earth with a resounding crash. Such men and women are rare in contemporary fiction; the art to make them live vitally—as Author Dinesen does—is rarer still."

A year after the release of *Last Tales, Anecdotes of Destiny* was published in both the United States and Denmark. A collection of five tales, *Anecdotes of Destiny,* with its preference for exotic locales and predominantly 19th-century settings, resembles her early work. The overall critical reaction to *Anecdotes of Destiny* was somewhat mixed. In his *Manchester Guardian* review of the book, W.L. Webb described it as "a collection of elaborate fairy tales for elderly epicures, very cold, cultured, and romantic, with a faint *Yellow Book* flavour, and belonging to no world outside of the writer's imagination." But he adds, "One can often admire their jewelled-movement ingenuity without conceding the claims of the faithful to a Larger Significance." Some critics felt that *Anecdotes of Destiny* did not quite measure up to Dinesen's other writing. "If these stories are not quite so weird as the author's earlier ones, they are also not quite so effective. . . . And occasionally they seem to sprawl somewhat carelessly," remarked Howard Blair in the *San Francisco Chronicle.* On the other hand, critic R.H. Glauber felt that the stories in *Anecdotes of Destiny* were consistent with Dinesen's previous work. "If they lack something of the complex plotting we had in earlier stories, they have a new feature that more than makes up for it—a sense of fate that hangs over the characters and toward which they rush with dignified haste," Glauber wrote in the *New York Herald Tribune Book Review.* "Babette's Feast," a short story that was later filmed as a motion picture, was ranked "with the best Dinesen has ever written."

Although now in her mid-70s and predominantly bedridden, Dinesen remained active following the publication of *Anecdotes of Destiny.* In 1961, *Shadows on the Grass,* a collection of four short essays, was released. The last of Dinesen's books published during her lifetime, it was written during a time of great suffering and was often dictated from a hospital bed a few paragraphs at a time. Like *Out of Africa* before it, *Shadows on the Grass* takes as its subject matter Dinesen's years in Africa. While it includes reminiscences about the excitement of hunting lions and the hazards of raising coffee on the equator, the book's main focus is Dinesen's recollections of her African servants. The last of Dinesen's Book-of-the-Month Club selections, *Shadows on the Grass* met with almost universal acclaim. "The four stories in 'Shadows on the Grass' are triumphantly sentimental and gently anecdotal; yet within their miniature frame they have many of the qualities of the finest story-telling," wrote William Dunlea in *Commonweal*. Critics particularly lauded Dinesen's manner in evoking memories from her past; Phoebe Adams, writing in the *Atlantic*, praised Dinesen's acuteness of perception and "ability to find an undercurrent of wonder in any situation." A *Time* reviewer concurred, claiming: "What the baroness does in this book is scarcely tangible enough to describe. She dips a branch of memory into the pool of the past until it is crystallized with insights, landscapes, literature, and animals that seem as if painted by Henri Rousseau."

Dinesen died in September of 1962, less than a year after the publication of *Shadows on the Grass*. Her legacy has been kept alive by a series of posthumously published works including *Carnival: Entertainments and Posthumous Tales* and by a major motion picture. The 1985 film *Out of Africa*, starring Klaus Maria Brandauer as Baron Blixen, Robert Redford as Finch Hatton and **Meryl Streep** as Dinesen, won a total of seven Oscars, including best picture. The film was instrumental in causing renewed interest in both Dinesen and her work; two years after its release, Vintage Books had sold over 653,000 copies of *Out of Africa*, thus making Dinesen a bestselling author almost 25 years after her death.

One of Dinesen's chief projects near the end of her life was the preservation of Rungstedlund, a 16th-century Danish inn that had been purchased by her father and in which she had been born six years later. While she would leave Rungstedlund for Africa soon after the tragic death of her father, Dinesen returned and wrote her five collections of short stories here. She established the Rungsted Foundation, a private institution that purchased the house and surrounding land and was entrusted with preserving the area as a bird reserve after her death. In July of 1958, Dinesen gave a radio talk on the future of Rungstedlund, asking listeners to donate one Danish crown to the Foundation; over 80,000 listeners complied with her request. After her death, in keeping with her wishes, Rungstedlund was preserved as a museum and bird sanctuary, which houses numerous family artifacts, and a library of over 2,000 of the author's books. Dinesen herself is buried in the sanctuary, beneath a beech tree where nightingales on their way to Africa stop to roost. The coffee plantation that lies southernmost in their path, in the Ngong Hills of Kenya, has also been turned into a museum site.

Dinesen considered herself more of a storyteller than a writer. According to Donald Hannah's *"Isak Dinesen" and Karen Blixen: The Mask and the Reality*, Dinesen once wrote: "I belong to an ancient, idle, wild and useless tribe, perhaps I am even one of the last members of it, who, for many thousands of years, in all countries and parts of the world, has, now and again, stayed for a time among hard-working honest people in real life, and sometimes has thus been fortunate enough to create another sort of reality for them, which in some way or another, has satisfied them. I am a storyteller." While she did, indeed, lead a remarkable life, it is for the translation of that life to the stuff of fiction that she will be best remembered. "Of a story she made an essence; of the essence she made an elixir," wrote *Eudora Welty in *The New York Times*, "and of the elixir she began once more to compound the story."

SOURCES:

Aiken, Susan Hardy. *Isak Dinesen and the Engendering of Narrative*. IL: University of Chicago Press, 1990.

Bjornvig, Thorkild. *The Pact: My Friendship with Isak Dinesen*. LA: Louisiana State University Press, 1974.

Contemporary Literary Criticism. Detroit, MI: Gale Research, Volume 10, 1979, Volume 24, 1984.

Dinesen, Isak. *Breve fra Africa*, Volume I: *1914–1924*, Volume II: *1925-1931*. Gyldendal, 1978, published as *Letters from Africa, 1914–1931*, edited by Frans Lasson and translated by Anne Born. IL: University of Chicago Press, 1981.

———. *Daguerreotypes and Other Essays*. Danish portions translated by P.M. Mitchell and W.D. Paden. IL: University of Chicago Press, 1979.

———. *Out of Africa*. London: Putnam, 1937, Danish translation published as *Den Afrikanske Farm*, Gyldendal, 1937.

———. *Skygger paa Graesset*, Gyldendal, 1960, published as *Shadows on the Grass*. NY: Random House, 1961.

Dinesen, Thomas. *My Sister, Isak Dinesen*. Translated from the Danish by Joan Tate. London: M. Joseph, 1975.

Donelson, Linda. *Out of Isak Dinesen in Africa: The Untold Story*. Iowa City, IA: Coulsong List, 1995.

Hannah, Donald. *"Isak Dinesen" and Karen Blixen: The Mask and the Reality*. Putnam, 1971.

Henriksen, Aage. *Isak Dinesen; Karen Blixen: The Work and the Life*. Translated by William Mishler. NY: St. Martin's, 1988.

Henricksen, Liselette. *Isak Dinesen: A Bibliography*. IL: University of Chicago Press, 1977.

Horton, Susan R. *Difficult Women, Artful Lives: Olive Schreiner and Isak Dinesen, In and Out of Africa*. Baltimore: MD: Johns Hopkins University Press, 1995.

Johannesson, Eric O. *The World of Isak Dinesen*. University of Washington Press, 1961.

Langbaum, Robert. *The Gayety of Vision: A Study of Isak Dinesen's Art*. IL: University of Chicago Press, 1964.

Migel, Parmenia. *Titania: The Biography of Isak Dinesen*. Random House, 1967.

Pelensky, Olga. *Isak Dinesen: The Life and Imagination of a Seducer*. Athens, OH: Ohio University Press, 1991.

———, ed. *Isak Dinesen: Critical Views*. Athens, OH: Ohio University Press, 1993.

Stambaugh, Sara. *The Witch and the Goddess in the Stories of Isak Dinesen: A Feminist Reading*. Ann Arbor, MI: UMI Research Press, 1988.

Svendsen, Clara, ed. *Isak Dinesen: A Memorial*. Random House, 1964.

———, ed. *The Life and Destiny of Isak Dinesen*. Random House, 1970.

Thurman, Judith. *Isak Dinesen: The Life of a Storyteller*. St. Martin's, 1982.

Trzebinski, Errol. *Silence Will Speak: A Study of the Life of Denys Finch Hatton and His Relationship with Karen Blixen*. IL: University of Chicago Press, 1977.

Whissen, Thomas R. *Isak Dinesen's Aesthetics*. Port Washington, NY: Kennikat Press, 1973.

PERIODICALS:

American Scholar. Autumn 1963.

Atlantic. June 1943; January 1947; December 1957; November 1960.

Bookmark. December 1957.

Books. April 8, 1934; March 6, 1938.

Books and Bookmen. February 1968.

Books West. Volume I, number 7, 1977.

Chicago Daily Tribune. April 21, 1934.

Chicago Sunday Tribune. December 8, 1957.

Chicago Tribune. December 27, 1985, Sec. 7, p. 37; March 30, 1986, Sec. 12, p. 10; June 4, 1986, Sec. 5, pp. 1, 3; January 5, 1987, Sec. 5, p. 3.

Chicago Tribune Book World. September 23, 1979; June 7, 1981.

Christian Science Monitor. June 5, 1943; December 23, 1960; June 13, 1963; February 11, 1980; September 14, 1981; January 21, 1986, p. 38.

Commonweal. September 28, 1934; June 18, 1943; January 31, 1947; December 13, 1957.

Harper's. March 1971.

Hudson Review. Winter 1964–65, pp. 517–530; Spring 1978; Winter 1981–82.

International Fiction Review. January 1978.

Journal of the Folklore Institute. January–April 1978, pp. 23–44.

Journal of Narrative Technique. Winter 1985, pp. 82–90.

Library Journal. May 15, 1979.

Locus. January 1992, p. 56; September 1993, p. 64.

Los Angeles Times. November 25, 1985; December 8, 1986; January 5, 1987.

Manchester Guardian. December 31, 1937; November 28, 1958.

Massachusetts Review. Summer 1978, pp. 389–406.

Modern Fiction Studies. Winter 1978, pp. 521–532.

Nation. April 18, 1934, p. 449; November 8, 1958; November 5, 1977.

New Boston Review. Spring 1978.

New Outlook. April 1934.

New Republic. June 7, 1943; January 3, 1961; October 22, 1977; March 21, 1988, pp. 26–27.

New Statesman. November 23, 1957; November 1, 1958; October 30, 1981.

New Statesman and Nation. October 20, 1934; April 17, 1943; April 19, 1947.

Newsweek. December 23, 1985.

New Yorker. May 15, 1943; November 9, 1968; December 5, 1977; November 19, 1979; September 7, 1981.

New York Herald Tribune Book Review. June 5, 1947; November 3, 1957; October 12, 1958.

New York Herald Tribune Books. June 16, 1963.

New York Herald Tribune Weekly Book Review. January 5, 1947.

New York Review of Books. May 4, 1978; July 17, 1986, p. 21.

New York Times. March 6, 1938; January 5, 1947; November 3, 1957; October 12, 1958; December 30, 1985; March 20, 1986.

New York Times Book Review. June 9, 1963; September 20, 1981; December 8, 1985; February 23, 1986, pp. 3, 37; October 16, 1987.

Observer. July 27, 1986, p. 23; January 23, 1994, p. 22.

Publishers Weekly. March 13, 1987.

San Francisco Chronicle. October 26, 1958.

Saturday Review. October 6, 1934; November 2, 1957; March 16, 1963; December 10, 1977.

Saturday Review of Literature. April 14, 1934; March 5, 1938; May 15, 1943; January 18, 1947.

Spectator. November 29, 1957; October 17, 1958.

Texas Studies in Literature and Language. Winter 1978, pp. 615–632.

Time. November 4, 1957; January 6, 1961; September 27, 1968; February 9, 1987.

Times (London). December 3, 1986.

Times Literary Supplement. March 13, 1943; January 13, 1978; July 28, 1978; April 4, 1980; September 11, 1981.

Village Voice. September 2, 1981.

Virginia Quarterly Review. Autumn 1968.

Washington Post Book World. August 9, 1981.

Wilson Library Bulletin. November 1991, p. 16.

World Literature Today. Spring 1979; Spring 1980; Spring 1981; Spring 1982.

Yale Review. Summer 1943.

RELATED MEDIA:

The Immortal Story (film), adapted by Orson Welles, Altura, 1968.

Out of Africa (film), starring Meryl Streep and Robert Redford, Universal, 1985.

Babette's Feast (film), starring *Stéphane Audran, 1987.

Lucifer's Child (play), written by William Luce, starring *Julie Harris as Dinesen, opened in New York, April 1991.

Ding Ling (1904–1985)

Leading Chinese woman writer of the modern era and important figure in Chinese Communist politics.

Name variations: Ting Ling. Born Jiang Bingzhi in Hunan province in central China in 1904 (some sources cite 1907); died of cancer in 1985; daughter of Jiang Yufeng (a Confucian scholar) and Yu Manzhen (Yü Man-chen, an early female political activist); attended progressive schools in Hunan, Shanghai and Beijing; married Chen Ming (a writer), in 1942; children: (with radical poet Hu Yuepin) a son (b. November 1930); (with Communist activist Feng Da) a daughter (b. around 1935).

Published "Miss Sophia's Diary," which defined her as a writer (1928); joined the Chinese Communist Party and rose through the party's literary ranks (1932); kidnapped and held by the Guomindang (1933); after four years under house arrest, escaped to the Communist-led base under Mao Zedong (1937); purged and exiled to Manchuria (1957); rehabilitated by the Communists (1978) and became an honored figure until her death.

Selected works, available in English translation: "Mengke" (1927); "The Diary of Miss Sophia" (February 1928); "A Woman and a Man" (1928); "Shanghai, Spring 1930" (October 1930); "Net of Law" (1932); "Mother, April 1933"; "Affair in East Village" (1936); "New Faith" (1939); "When I was in Xia Village" (1941); "Thoughts on March 8" (1942); The Sun Shines over the Sanggang River (1948); "People Who Will Live Forever in My Heart: Remembering Chen Man" (1949); "Du Wanxiang" (1978).

Walking an uneasy line between her two major roles as Communist Party activist and female writer, Ding Ling became the voice of the many Chinese women caught in their country's difficult transition from the old feudal Confucian society into the modern world. Although she always put China's political revolution ahead of the liberation of women, her inability to fully reconcile the two issues brought her into frequent conflict with authority. Over a long life in which she became the most noted Chinese woman writer of the modern era, she held many important offices and wrote numerous stories, books, and essays.

Ding Ling was born Jiang Bingzhi in 1904 to a family of the social gentry in the central Chinese province of Hunan. Her father Jiang Yufeng was a man of local power and wealth who held a degree in the Confucian civil-service system. Confucianism was the basis of the Chinese classical cultural tradition and was transmitted and in-terpreted largely through written works, making literature a critical influence in cultural and political events. The tradition was both extremely hierarchical and authoritarian, supporting a patriarchal gender system in which men held virtually all the legitimate authority; women were valued principally as wives and the mothers particularly of male children. In the long history of China, famines, wars, and other disasters were common, and the density of its population put enormous pressure on its resources. Despite its limitations, Confucianism was long found satisfactory to both men and women because it provided Chinese society with centuries of stability. The very rigidity of the system provided security and the prospect that if everybody pulled together according to assigned social roles, all might not only endure but prosper.

In the mid-19th century, however, the system began to collapse from overpopulation and the impact of the expanding Western powers—principally Great Britain, but also the United States. As the Western impact threw the weaknesses of the traditional Chinese system into sharp relief, many in China were particularly struck by the apparent strength and influence of Western women compared to their own culture. For many Chinese, both men and women, the liberation of Chinese women became an integral part of the freeing of China from Confucian control and the development of a modern, more egalitarian society. The practice of footbinding, in which the feet of young girls of good family were tightly wrapped beginning in childhood, deforming them to the point of restricting the women's mobility, is a primary example of social evils against women that survived in China into the 20th century.

As the daughter of a family of relative privilege, Ding Ling might well have had her feet bound and been married off into a family of similar status had she been born a few decades earlier. By 1904, however, a new and more liberated type of Chinese woman began to emerge, such as the rebel heroine *Qiu Jin who became a political martyr in her attempt to overthrow the decadent Manchu regime in 1907; ironically, this event occurred when the Chinese imperial throne was controlled by another woman, very powerful but also conservative, the Empress *Cixi.

Ding Ling's father, like many Chinese men, saw the value of a modern education and spent time in Japan studying modern law. Ding Ling's mother ❧▶ **Yu Manzhen** was a woman of foresight, capable of attacking the old society despite her high station within it. Inspired in part by the

❧▶

See sidebar on the following page

example of Qiu Jin, Yu Manzhen became a local activist who campaigned for political reform and entered a modern school in Changsha, the capital of Hunan province. The death of her husband, when Ding Ling was only five years old, may have influenced Manzhen to raise her as a liberated girl.

In the early 20th century, Hunan was one of the centers of ferment for political reform. Included among the local activists was Mao Zedong, who would lead the Chinese Communist Party to control all of China in 1949. Yu Manzhen was drawn to the same revolutionary doctrine of Communism as Mao, which seemed, during the Russian Revolution of 1917, to free Russia from the decadent tsarist regime, and to be a doctrine capable of bringing both political and social reform that could usher China into the modern world. In 1927, Yu Manzhen joined the Chinese Communist Party soon after its founding; she also became a noted teacher for women in the modern educational system in Hunan.

𝒟ing Ling has been one of the great survivors in modern Chinese literary history. Not only has she survived the dangers of war, exile, hard labor, and imprisonment by the governments of both right and left; she has also endured as a creative and practicing writer.

—Yi-tsi Mei Feuerwerker

In 1911, the Manchu regime ruling China fell, but a series of weak and often corrupt governments followed, sometimes dominated by military "warlord" leaders and sometimes by earnest but powerless reformers like Sun Yat-sen. At the side of her radical mother, Ding Ling lived an exciting childhood, exposed to the political chaos of the time, when suggestions for change came from all directions. In just one example, she was on hand to hear a debate on political reform in China from two great visiting Western thinkers, Bertrand Russell and John Dewey.

Ding Ling was captivated by Western literature and read translations of modern French, British, and Russian works. She was particularly influenced by Flaubert, and is said to have read his novel *Madame Bovary* more than ten times. Since the scholars who wrote and interpreted the works of the Chinese tradition were the most highly prized in Confucian society, all literary works were deemed inescapably political; even fiction was supposed to present "proper" values and behavior. In such a context, it was inevitable that contemporary Western literary works would be considered important both in discrediting that old society and in shaping radical alternatives, making Ding Ling's interest in Western literature appropriate to the times. This drawing upon Western and Soviet inspirations for their own political and social ideals by the Chinese youth came to be known as the "May Fourth Movement," after a series of nationwide demonstrations against the corrupt Chinese government. Ding Ling, like her mother and Mao Zedong, became an activist in the students' movement in Hunan.

In 1920, when she was probably 16, Ding Ling fled to Shanghai to avoid an attempt by her paternal uncles to arrange a traditional marriage for her. At the very center of the radical movement in Shanghai, she met and studied, or worked, with many of the young people who would one day be China's Communist elite. In the following years, she moved from Shanghai to Nanking, and then the capital of Beijing, where she either failed to pass the entrance exam to the University of Beijing, or simply did not attempt to formally enter the institution considered China's educational and radical political mecca. Enrolled or not, she studied with a number of China's famous intellectuals, particularly in the field of literature. In Beijing, she lived with a young poet, Hu Yuepin, a man committed as she was to both literature and reform.

In 1927, a strong government for China was temporarily achieved through the emergence of the Guomindang (Nationalist Party), unifying the country under the leadership of Chiang Kai-shek, a military man who presented himself as the successor to Sun Yat-sen. Chiang and other leaders of his Guomindang Party wanted just enough reform to strengthen China against its internal and external enemies. In contrast, the Communist Party held the belief that more thorough-going reforms were necessary, to change both the political and social systems of China, and Chinese culture itself. By 1928, party followers were engaged in a life-and-death struggle.

Ding Ling lived a bohemian life during this period, troubled by the failure of her ideals and her own lack of achievement. While maintaining

Ding Ling

a miserably poor existence in Shanghai, she drank too much and had at least one love affair outside her relationship with Hu Yuepin, but she also began to write. In 1928, she published the long story "Miss Sophia's Diary," which was to define her as a writer and be her most famous work. Tani Barlow, editor of a collection of Ding Ling's work, describes this story as "the emotional life of a tubercular woman driven to near madness by erotic passion for an unworthy man." Although the narrative drew upon elements of Ding Ling's life, it was not truly autobiographical. But the Chinese, unaccustomed to seeing such basic human drives presented so publicly, and particularly by a woman, took it as such, and Ding Ling became the notorious model of the liberated modern Chinese woman.

In the following years, Ding Ling wrote with a fierce passion, turning out collection after collection of short fiction pieces, most of which related directly to the problems of Chinese women like herself. In 1930, she had a son with her lover (some now say her husband) Hu Yuepin, and the child was sent to Hunan to live with her mother. In 1931, Hu and several other radical writers were executed by the Guomindang, and the following year Ding Ling joined the Communist Party, which treated women's issues as of major importance. The fact that she knew many of the party's leaders must have helped make the decision seem natural to her. In 1933, Ding Ling and a new lover, Feng Da, were kidnapped by the Guomindang and reportedly held under house arrest for four years; little is known of her life during this period except that she gave birth to a daughter, which her mother also took to raise, and Feng died of tuberculosis.

In 1937, Ding Ling was either freed or escaped and fled to Yanan, a Communist-based area where Mao Zedong was the leader. Although Ding Ling accepted the position of the party that all other reform movements were to be subordinated to its own seizure of power, she did not always believe that the party treated women equally. Her works during this period dealt with women's problems within a context that argued that the issues could be solved only through Communist victory. In March 1942, she published "Thoughts on March 8th," an essay relating to Women's Day (a holiday begun, ironically, but no longer widely celebrated, in the United States), in which she implied a split between theory and practice by questioning the treatment of women within the party.

Mao Zedong saw women as integral to revolution, and under his leadership the women's movement prospered. But nothing came before the victory of the revolution. In "Talks On Literature and Art at the Yanan Forum," an essay of his that followed Ding Ling's work, Mao took the hard line, stating that all art was subordinate to politics and must serve the revolution in a direct and obvious manner. Ding Ling was subjected to party discipline for presenting relationships between men and women within the party in ambiguous terms, and lost some of the power she had begun to accumulate as chief speaker for women's issues within the party. Essentially, the Communists, like the Confucians, were recognizing the power of literature to affect behavior and attempting in response to force literary content to conform to set standards.

Ding Ling's literary and political eclipse proved temporary; she wrote much in the following decades and also led entertainment troupes, edited plays and stories. In 1949, when the Chinese Communist Party triumphed over the Guomindang, her influence rose in national literary and political circles. She subsequently held many important posts in both the party and in literary organizations. Although her works could be openly didactic, they also usually presented rich characterizations amid supple and complex modes of development. Her major extended work, *The Sun Shines over the Sanggang River*, was published in 1951.

But Mao, dissatisfied with the steady pace of China's progress, launched a series of disruptive actions intended to take the country forward with unprecedented speed. Increasingly, he subordinated not only art but economic and political development to his own utopian vision. In 1957, after a series of minor writers and artists had been attacked as too individualistic and concerned with their own personal and selfish visions, Ding Ling became a target. Among other charges, she was held to have been too free in her past sexual behavior. As always, her own beliefs and activities were confused with those of the troubled heroines, like Miss Sophia, that she had created.

Sent into internal exile in Manchuria, Ding Ling attempted to keep writing while forced to do manual labor. In the final paroxysm of Mao's attempt to remold Chinese culture, the Great Proletarian Cultural Revolution (1966–76), Ding Ling was attacked by the Communist Red Guards, and the long manuscript for her sequel to *The Sun Shines over the Sanggang River* was destroyed.

With the death of Mao Zedong in 1976, and the emergence of the reform regime of Deng Xiaoping, Ding Ling reappeared from exile. Widely honored for her works and her life of struggle, she lectured throughout China, received foreign visitors, and traveled abroad. This measure of fame and security lasted until she died of cancer in 1985.

The life of Ding Ling is difficult to assess from a Western perspective. The problems of Chinese women were not, and are not, those of Western women, though there is, of course, some overlap. Although Ding Ling sometimes disagreed as to the exact value of specific marching orders, she accepted the importance of a centralized political movement and did not doubt that politics must command art; in the course of her work for the party, she also disciplined other writers and artists for their political errors. Throughout her career, political and literary life remained indistinguishable.

SOURCES:

Barlow, Tani E., with Gary J. Bjorge. *I Myself Am a Woman: Selected Writings of Ding Ling.* Boston: Beacon Press, 1989.

Feuerwerker, Yi-tsi Mei. *Ding Ling's Fiction: Ideology and Narrative in Modern Chinese Literature.* Cambridge, MA: Harvard University Press, 1982.

Isaacs, Harold R., ed. *Straw Sandals: Chinese Short Stories, 1918–1933.* Cambridge, MA: M.I.T. Press, 1974.

Klein, Donald W. and Anne B. Clark, eds. "Ting Ling," in *Biographic Dictionary of Chinese Communism, 1921–1965.* Vol II. Cambridge, MA: Harvard University Press, 1971, pp. 843–846.

Ting Ling (Ding Ling). *The Sun Shines over the Sangkan River.* Translated by Yan Hsien-yi and Gladys Yang. Peking: Foreign Languages Press, 1954.

SUGGESTED READING:

Chow Tse-tsung. *The May Fourth Movement: Intellectual Revolution in Modern China.* Stanford, CA: Stanford University Press, 1960.

Goldman, Merle. *Literary Dissent in Communist China.* Cambridge, MA: Harvard University Press, 1967.

Jeffrey G. Barlow,
Professor in the Department of Social Studies,
Pacific University, Forest Grove, Oregon

Dinh, Madame (1920–1992).

See Nguyen Thi Dinh.

Dionne Quintuplets (b. 1934)

Canada's celebrated quints, who were put on display as a major tourist attraction in Ontario during the 1930s. Name variations: The Quints; the Dionnelles. Pronunciation: DEE-yon or DEE-yown. Born on May 28, 1934, in the small village of Corbeil, north of Toronto, in Northern Ontario, Canada; daughters of Oliva and Elzire (Legros) Dionne.

Annette (b. 1934). Born Marie Lilianne Annette; studied music at the Marguerite Bourgeois; married Germain Allard (branch manager of a finance company), in the 1950s; children: Jean-François (b. November 2, 1958); Charles; Eric (b. September 1962).

Cécile (b. 1934). Born Marie Emilda Cécile; graduated as a nurse from the Hôpital Notre Dame de l'Esperance, Montreal, around 1956; married Philippe Langlois (a television technician at the CBC), around 1957 (divorced); children: Claude (b. September 15, 1958); Bertrand; Elizabeth; Patrice.

Émilie (1934–1954). Born Marie Jeanne Émilie; died of suffocation in August 1954.

Marie (1934–1970). Born Reine Alma Marie; died in February 1970; married Florian Houle (an inspector on the staff of the Quebec government), in the 1950s (separated 1966); children: Émilie (b. December 24, 1960); Monique.

Yvonne (b. 1934). Born Marie Edwilda Yvonne; graduated as a nurse from the Hôpital Notre Dame de l'Esperance, Montreal, around 1956; joined three different convents.

On May 28, 1934, quintuplets were born in the tiny village of Corbeil, Ontario, Canada. Two were delivered by midwives; three were attended by Dr. Allan Roy Dafoe, a widower, who lived in nearby Callender, an abandoned lumber town. Two months premature, weighing a combined 13 pounds, 6 ounces, the five babies were put in a wicker basket and set by the warmth of the stove. The following day, headlines in Callender heralded the most publicized births of the century: QUINTS BORN TO FARM WIFE. They would be the first quintuplets on record to survive more than a few days. When asked how she was feeling, the 25-year-old mother **Elzire Dionne**, who had five other children, managed, "Oh, pretty good."

Corbeil and Callender were still staggering from the effects of the Depression, and the French-Canadian Dionnes were extremely poor. Oliva Dionne scrambled for a living, working the fields, renting out his farm equipment, trapping foxes in the winter woods and selling their furs in North Bay. Until the birth pangs became too intense, Elzire had hoped to avoid the $20 doctor fee. The family lived in a plank farmhouse, without benefit of electricity, gas, running water, and indoor plumbing. Elzire could barely speak English.

Before fertility pills increased the chance for multiple births, the likelihood of quints being born was 57,289,761 to 1. The odds for survival were worse. Only 34 quintuplet births had been documented by 1934. Quints had been born in Lisbon, Portugal, in 1866 and in Kentucky in 1896. In 1914, **Rose Salemi** gave birth to quintuplets in Italy. In 1943, the Diligenti quints would be born in Argentina. September of 1963 would see quints born into the Prieto family of Venezuela and the Fischer family of Aberdeen, South Dakota.

The Dionne infants were initially put in the hands of **Yvonne Leroux**, a Callender resident and recent graduate of St. Joseph's Hospital in North Bay, who arrived with a hot-water bottle and kept her medical records on the back of old bills; it was her first outside case. Madame **Louise de Kiriline**, a strict disciplinarian, was brought in. In her zeal for cleanliness, de Kiriline issued edicts, demanding that gowns and masks be worn; she scrubbed, disinfected, and ordered the parental Dionnes to the household corners while the quints' five brothers and sisters were packed off to stay with relatives. Before long, reporters pulled up, hauling flashbulbs, diapers, and an incubator that could sleep three. Breast milk arrived from Toronto, Montreal, and Chicago provided by concerned mothers.

We were weighed, measured, tested, studied and examined to the heart's content of doctors and scientists, who apparently found us to be among the most fascinating females known to history.

—Dionne Quintuplets

Oliva Dionne and Dr. Dafoe resented the intrusion of the press in the first few days, although Dafoe soon came to believe that he had "no right to object to what had become a matter of continent-wide interest," and he grew increasingly grateful for the supplies and equipment generated from the publicity. Meanwhile, Oliva was frantic with concern over how to provide for his exploding family. He turned to fellow parishioners in Callender for money, but theirs was a poor parish. Mass was said in a basement. At a time when Oliva needed an angel, he got Ivan I. Spear. It was to be a catastrophic connection.

Spear, who operated the Century of Progress Tour Bureau in Chicago, wanted to sign the quints for a sideshow attraction at the Chicago World's Fair. He offered Oliva Dionne trained nurses, a luxurious private ward (with viewing windows), and a great deal of money. Thus, when the quints were barely three days old, Oliva signed a contract with Spear, giving him "exclusive rights." Though the two would later learn that the contract was null and void (in their haste, they had not asked Elzire to sign), the story evoked nasty headlines and international outrage at a time when prejudice against French-Canadians in Canada was at its height. The Canadian Parliament in Ottawa decided to appoint a board of guardians.

From the proceeds of a Red Cross fund-raising drive, a home was built across the road from the farmhouse—a nine-room nursery with electricity, plumbing, and climate control. Next to that, another two-story building was erected to house the staff; the nursery opened at the end of September 1934. "We were weighed, measured, tested, studied and examined to the heart's content of doctors and scientists, who apparently found us to be among the most fascinating females known to history," wrote the quintuplets. "We were peered at, pricked and prodded for years. . . . Every mouthful of food was counted, as well as every diaper." Dr. Dafoe wanted to have the "opportunity for unrestricted medical control in the care of the babies," while de Kiriline felt babies should be handled as seldom as possible. There were rules against kissing on the face in case of germs.

A rift occurred. In protecting the quints, the staff became a wedge between the babies and their birth mother, slowly eroding the parental-bonding process. Instead, the quints bonded with the ones who held them most—their nurses. Though their father was a regular visitor, the infants did not see the rest of the family for months at a time. The separation caused a deep wound for Elzire, who needed prompting to come to the nursery. The babies' staff, reporters, and dignitaries began to take sides; there were those who were sympathetic with the hapless Dionnes and those who championed the doctors. Process servers from both sides of the camp went back and forth, ushering in lawsuits.

But the quints recalled those early days in the nursery with affection; they were treated like five princesses. Not only did they have each other, but they also had their own doll, their own tricycle. They each slept in their own yellow crib, their name engraved on each headboard—Annette, Cécile, Émilie, Marie, and Yvonne—along with the inscription *Que le bon Jésus vous garde* ("May the good Lord watch over you"). A nurse remained in their room through the night, while a guard sat outside. Eventually there was a white dining room with three enameled tables, five small chairs, and a buffet. Though their days were organized, a new timetable of activities was put into place each month. Trips to the bathroom were carefully noted on a chart under the category Elimination Routine; other categories included "Frequency of Emotional Episodes Per Child." When teeth arrived, so did a dentist's chair and all the requisite equipment.

The little girls became as famous as *Shirley Temple (Black)*. The dominant news stories of March 1935 were the passing of a major relief bill in the U.S. Senate and the emergence of Annette's first tooth. When the quints were three, an observatory was built. Until then, the thousands that had made a pilgrimage to Corbeil to see them peered from behind a fence. Now as the children played, spectators could watch through one-way, mesh-wire windows, but the quints were aware of their presence. As the nurses exhibited them, holding up each quint and a card with their name, the quints waved and threw kisses; if Émilie was sleeping, the nurses held up Marie twice. "Most of the time we yelled and shrieked with the joy of living, and we developed a shrewd idea of what would please the crowds most," wrote the quints. The audience was delighted when "we would venture into the wading pool with shoes and socks on." Cameras were not allowed. Taking photos was the exclusive right of a U.S. feature service and the *Toronto Star* which paid $25,000 a year into the quintuplet bank account for the privilege. When Oliva Dionne once attempted to take a snapshot through a window, he was reprimanded and reminded of the contracts.

In March 1935, over the tearful protest of Elzire Dionne, Ottawa passed "An Act for the Protection of the Dionne Quintuplets": the children were now the official wards of King George V of England. The act was supposed to be in force for the first two years of their lives; in actuality, it was in force until their 18th birthdays. When the board of guardians sought to bring in more money and provide the quints with a bank account, souvenir stands popped up outside the nursery, and the quints' career in advertising began: there were quintuplet dishes, dolls, cutouts, candy, purses, and spoons. Sponsors lined up for the privilege of using their image: Libby's, Carnation, Lever Brothers, and Palmolive. "This morning the Dionne Quints had Quaker Oats," boasted one sonorous radio announcer.

Twentieth Century-Fox paid $50,000 for the right to shoot 30 minutes of footage for the 1936 film *The Country Doctor*. Before entering the nursery, the cast had their noses and throats sprayed with germicide and their clothes sterilized; those behind the cameras wore gowns and masks. The film, loosely based on the birth of the quints, was written by *Sonya Levien and

Dionne
Quintuplets

starred Jean Hersholt as a fictionalized version of Dr. Dafoe. It was so successful that Fox shot two more with Hersholt: *Reunion,* starring *Rochelle Hudson (1936), and *Five of a Kind,* starring *Claire Trevor (1938); in the latter, the quints had 18 minutes of screen time.

The Dionne Quintuplets became one of the biggest tourist attractions in Canada, competing only with Niagara Falls. "Capitalized at four percent," bragged one would-be mogul, "these Quint-inspired revenues make the Dionne girls a $500,000,000 asset to Ontario." In "Quintland," restaurants, gas stations, and land rates went up; Callender boomed. Everyone was making a fortune, and everyone was bound and determined that Oliva Dionne, whose reputation was still reeling from the early negative publicity, would not make one cent off his children.

For seven years, Oliva Dionne was portrayed in the press in unredeeming strokes while Dafoe (aided and abetted by his white uniform and the performances of Jean Hersholt) was the kindly, all-knowing country doctor. By the time the quints turned seven, the tide turned against Dafoe and Oliva Dionne began to evoke sympathy. The truth, say the quints, resided somewhere in the middle.

With the backing of the Catholic Church, Oliva Dionne began to have his way more often. His other children joined the quints for school lessons, and the quints began to cross the road on Sundays for dinners with their family. (They would later admit that it was like visiting strangers; they hated Sundays.) With the media now on the side of the Dionnes, the doctor resigned, and the government agreed to use quintuplet funds to build a new house for the entire family. The Big House (ten bedrooms, five baths, a playroom and music room) was finished the winter of 1942–43, and the Dionnes were finally under one roof.

"It was the saddest home we ever knew," wrote the quints. "The fable was that we had always felt, up to this moment, like institutional children, separated by cruel law from the rest of the family." But the nursery had been a haven for them, not a prison. In the Big House, they were paired off, two to a bedroom. Marie was separated from the other four and put in with her older non-quint sister Pauline. The quints were devastated. They were too old for change, they said. Having lived so long in sterile conditions, they had little natural physical—much less emotional—immunity and came down with numerous ailments. Émilie showed the first signs of epilep-sy; at that time, epilepsy was considered shameful, so it was kept secret and went untreated.

Their parents felt they had been spoiled and began a campaign to undo what they perceived as damage, turning the quints into scrubbing Cinderellas, while their siblings had less work. Along with guilt over the upheaval caused by their birth, the girls felt an expectation, that it was up to them to make up for all those years of loss for the family. The parents wanted their love, the quints could not manufacture it. The parents wanted the quints to mix with the family, the quints wanted to keep to themselves. Newspapers reported that the Dionne Quintuplets were becoming sullen and sad looking.

Then the nursery across the street was turned into a boarding school, the Villa Notre Dame, to be run by the Sisters of the Assumption; ten other girls were allowed in as fellow students. Since the quints only had to stay in the Big House on weekends, they loved the school. But by the end of the first year, Oliva was convinced that the nuns were out to divide the family once more, so he brought his daughters back to the Big House. They could attend classes across the way, he said, but they would sleep at home. There was no longer an outside champion; Dafoe had died when they were ten.

At age 18, the Dionne Quintuplets were still being paraded out at the bequest of advertisers, or to greet royalty, and were heavily booked on Mother's Day. They graduated from the Villa Notre Dame with the ability to speak English as well as French, a great deal of religious education, and no career skills. "I think there was too much of what is superficial in religion around us," said Cécile. "Surely the love of God should not be taught in the way a soldier is drilled." But they were also thankful for the watchful presence of the nuns and priests.

Finally to their delight, they were enrolled in Institut Familial, a Catholic college for girls in Nicolet, in the Province of Quebec. On the whole, the sisters were happy. They were back rooming together and soon learned to travel only in pairs; the sight of more than two of them tipped off onlookers and attracted enormous attention. But unlike the other students who had a decent allowance, the quints were granted only two dollars a month. They had no idea of their monetary worth. Unaware of the quintuplet bank account, they thought the money was coming out of their father's pockets.

Marie was the first to assert a pinch of independence. On her 19th birthday, she announced to her parents her intention to enter a convent. As a postulant, she became Sister Marie-Rachel, but illness would force her to leave. Then in their second college year, Yvonne entered the College Marguerite Bourgeois in Montreal as an art student, and Émilie applied and was admitted to the convent at L'Accueil Gai, near the town of St. Agathe in the Laurentian Mountains. One month later, Émilie was dead. Because the epilepsy had continued in secrecy, she died alone of suffocation during a seizure; her face had inadvertently turned downward on her pillow.

Approaching the age of 21, the four surviving sisters moved to Montreal. Annette and Marie enrolled in the College Marguerite Bourgeois, while Yvonne and Cécile entered the Hôpital Notre Dame de l'Ésperance as student nurses. Their allowance was still meager. According to the Guardianship Act, the inheritance and the properties that had been held in their name were to be handed over to them on their 21st birthday. In May 1955, Oliva summoned them to Corbeil for their birthday week and apprised them of the money. In the same conversation, he handed them trust agreements, told them they'd be better off if he remained comptroller, and asked them to sign. There was a long silence. Cécile was the first to say no, pleading for time to think about it. But family pressure weakened their resolve; within a week, all four had signed documents that kept their father in charge of over one million dollars.

The quints seemed lost. Marie returned to the convent but in short order fell ill again. Annette arrived in Quebec City to retrieve her, and they shared an apartment in Côte St.-Luc. Then Marie decided she wanted to open a flower shop, but her request for capital was denied by the Trust. Once again, Marie rebelled. With charge card in hand, she furnished her business with the help of Eaton's Department Store and other outlets and had them bill the Trust. Salon Émilie was opened on Mother's Day. Though the flower shop did not succeed, Marie's determined break for freedom was considered by the sisters well worth the price.

Yvonne entered the Convent of the Little Franciscan Sisters at Baie St. Paul, near Quebec City, where she became Sister Marie Thierry, but her stay did not work out. She tried again, entering the Convent of the Sacred Heart near Moncton, New Brunswick, as a nursing sister. Eventually, she gave up trying and left the convent.

Over the next two to three years, Annette, Cécile, and Marie were married. When Cécile gave birth to a baby boy, Claude, on September 15, 1958, Yvonne was one of the nurses in attendance. Annette's first baby was also a boy, Jean-François, born on November 2, 1958. On Christmas Eve, 1960, Marie gave birth to a baby girl; she was named Émilie. But the sisters continued to flounder. All three marriages ended in divorce.

Three years after separating from her husband in 1966, Marie, who was under psychiatric care, placed her two daughters in a home operated by Catholic sisters; shortly after, in February 1970, she was found dead in her Montreal apartment, apparently the victim of a stroke. Considered painfully shy, the surviving sisters lived as virtual recluses in genteel poverty in a Montreal suburb. When their father died in 1979, they returned home briefly but left immediately after the funeral.

In April 1995, after years of appealing to Canada's premier for help, the quints sued the province of Ontario for $10 million as compensation for a lost childhood. "From our birth," said Cécile, "we were taken hostage, deprived of personal liberty without being allowed to go out in public and financially exploited until our majority." That September, in a bid to find, they said, "inner peace," 61-year-old Annette, Cécile, and Yvonne went on Canadian television and charged that they were sexually abused by their father. They also made their case in the 1995 book *The Dionne Quintuplets: Family Secrets*. The abuse, they claim, began after they were forced to rejoin the family in the 1940s. Among other incidents, Oliva would take them on car rides in his Cadillac, one at a time, and grope them under their clothes. Though they did not tell their mother until they were 18 for fear of aggravating the situation, they did tell their school chaplain. They were directed, said Annette, to "continue to love our parents and wear a thick coat when we went for car rides."

SOURCES:

Brough, James, with Annette, Cécile, Marie and Yvonne Dionne. *"We Were Five": The Dionne Quintuplets' Story*. NY: Simon and Schuster. 1964.

Nihmey, John, and Stuart Foxman. *Time of Their Lives: The Dionne Tragedy*. NIVA, 1986.

SUGGESTED READING:

Berton, Pierre. *The Dionne Years—A Thirties Melodrama*.

Dionne, Annette, Cécile, and Yvonne, with Jean Yves-Soucy. *The Dionne Quintuplets: Family Secrets*. Canada, 1995.

RELATED MEDIA:

Canadian Broadcasting Corporation documentary, *The Dionne Quintuplets*.

"Million Dollar Babies," TV-miniseries loosely based on the Dionne story, starring **Kate Nelligan**, and Beau Bridges as Dr. Dafoe, first aired on CBS, November 20 and 22, 1994.

Diotima of Mantinea (fl. 400s BCE)

Greek priestess, philosopher, and teacher of Socrates.

Although it is questioned whether or not Diotima was a historical person, there are few reasons to doubt it. We know of her through Plato's *Symposium,* and there is some archeological evidence of her existence as well. She is the only character in Plato's work whose historicity has been challenged, and only since the 15th century. The scholars of the early middle ages, and the ancients who would have known the historicity of Diotima, did not question her existence in their references to her. It is also noteworthy that the praise given to Diotima, despite her views differing from Plato's (presented through the character of Socrates), is unusual in Plato's work and suggests a true respect.

In the *Symposium,* written some time after 389 BCE, Plato puts forth his views of his contemporaries, then uses the character of Socrates (whose own views may have differed) to present a philosophy of love. Plato's Socrates credits Diotima, a priestess of Mantinea, for inspiring his theory. She is said to have argued that the goal of love is immortality, "to give birth in beauty," either through the creation of children or beautiful things. This establishes the background against which Socrates presents Plato's case that love is the pursuit of beauty, but a more abstract beauty than Diotima's creations. From this, western culture has derived the concept of "Platonic love," an affection that is not based in bodily pleasure.

SOURCES:

Kersey, Ethel M. *Women Philosophers: a Bio-critical Source Book.* NY: Greenwood Press, 1989.

Waithe, Mary Ellen, ed. *A History of Women Philosophers, vol. 1.* Boston: Martinus Nijhoff Publications, 1987.

SUGGESTED READING:

Halperin, David M. "Why is Diotima a Woman," in *One Hundred Years of Homosexuality.* New York & London: Routledge, 1990: pp. 113–151.

Catherine Hundleby, M.A. Philosophy, University of Guelph, Guelph, Ontario, Canada

Di Robilant, Daisy, Countess

(fl. 1922–1933)

Italian feminist and activist who worked for the cause of women's and children's rights to welfare benefits both before and during the fascist dictatorship of Benito Mussolini. Pronunciation: Dee Ro-bee-lan. Little is known about di Robilant apart from the details of her involvement in fascist politics. She came from a wealthy Piedmontese noble family.

The wealthy Piedmontese noble family of Countess Daisy di Robilant was well connected to the European aristocracy and the upper reaches of Italian society. Di Robilant had a privileged upbringing and education that prepared her for an extraordinary life. Members of her family included such illustrious personalities as the Count Carlo di Robilant, who served his country from 1849 to 1887, first as a general in the Italian army, then as an ambassador to Vienna, and finally as a foreign minister.

Unwilling to pursue an idle existence, the countess devoted over 35 years of her life to public service as a philanthropist, feminist, and activist. Before the arrival of Fascism, she was a founder and president of the national Mothers' Aid Society, a charity that provided temporary shelter for homeless, single mothers. She was also an international campaigner for children's rights. Di Robilant believed that the state should enact sweeping welfare reforms to protect citizens from poverty. For years, she lobbied successive Italian prewar governments to enact legislation that would help lone mothers care for their children. She did so out of recognition that the more desperate the plight of the unsupported mother, the greater the compulsion to abort, abandon, or murder her child. Widely recognized within her own country as a major figure in public life, she was appointed to the presidency of the National Council of Italian Women in 1931, an important feminist organization that had been founded by upper-class women like herself in 1903. She also served on the governing body of the International Committee for the Protection of Children, an organization that promoted the adoption of laws to guarantee children everywhere basic rights to health, happiness, education and opportunity. In 1934, the International Congress of Women, a worldwide network of feminist leaders, also appointed her to the directorship of its department on maternity and infancy.

After the fascist seizure of power in 1922, Daisy di Robilant became a keen supporter of Benito Mussolini's social reforms and acted as a spokesperson for the regime at many international congresses throughout the period. During the dictatorship, she held a number of important government posts and served as a director of welfare and social services for unwed mothers. She also publicly endorsed the regime's attempts to prevent illegal abortions and to increase the birthrate. After 1927, she worked tirelessly and selflessly within the new institutions for women's welfare that the fascist state established. But by the early 1930s, Daisy di Robilant began to become disillusioned with Fascism's failure to implement reforms effectively. Her forthright and courageous criticisms of fascist social policy eventually provoked the indignation of Mussolini who brusquely dismissed her from high office in 1936. Her historical importance lies in the fact that she was both a feminist and a fascist. She was also one of the very few women of power and influence within an almost exclusively male-dominated fascist dictatorship.

The countess entered the most important stage of her career as an activist after Benito Mussolini and his National Fascist Party seized power in 1922. Fascism destroyed the institutions of parliamentary democracy, then determined to inaugurate a new era of Italian politics—one marked by strong and decisive action. After 1871 when the Italian kingdom was first formed, many successive governments had hoped to expand welfare provision for mothers, children, and the family, but all had hesitated to do so because of the huge cost to the treasury and the taxpayer. Italy's involvement in the First World War in the years 1915 to 1918 caused a major shift in attitudes, however. The loss of hundreds of thousands of young men at the front accentuated fears that the postwar birth and marriage rates would drop so low that the population would not replenish itself. In addition, the hardships suffered by women and children at the homefront raised awareness that the state would have to enact legislation to combat Italy's high levels of poverty and disease. In the immediate aftermath of the war, the nation was beset by unemployment and inflation that culminated in escalating labor unrest. The rise of the fascist movement after 1919 brought organized terrorism and political instability in its wake and further minimized opportunities to develop ambitious social programs. But when Mussolini became prime minister in 1922, he committed his new government to a broad range of social reforms that promised to improve the health and welfare of the nation.

The motivation behind Mussolini's purported commitment to the social betterment of the Italian people lay in Fascism's broader political agenda. The dictator outlined his aims in 1927, when he made a historic speech in Parliament. Mussolini proclaimed that a "Fecund Decade" had begun—a new age that would, he declared, see Italy transformed from a lesser economic and military power to an industrial giant and a maker of world empire. Italy needed more workers and warriors to realize Fascism's grandiose plans, so the state would have to act decisively in order to encourage a rise in fertility. Not concerned solely to increase the quantity of the population, Mussolini also sought to improve the quality of the population so that Italians would be fit enough to meet the challenges of the future. The goal of birthrate increase inspired major institutional and social reforms targeted specifically at women. Only by helping women bear and rear healthy children, Mussolini reasoned, would Fascism be able to convince them to have more babies.

The main institutional vehicle for Fascism's demographic campaign was the National Organization for the Protection of Motherhood and Infancy whose purpose was to create a health service for needy mothers and their children. Since levels of infant and child abandonment were high in such a poor country as Italy, and the mortality rate of abandoned children was almost double that for those raised within families, the new institution launched a series of initiatives aimed at persuading single mothers to care for their own children.

It is far easier to bring more babies in the world than it is to ensure that those babies survive their infancy.

—Daisy di Robilant, in a letter to Benito Mussolini

Under liberalism, the whole system of care for so-called "illegitimate" children had revolved around the foundling home, an archaic institution first created in the Middle Ages in which nuns cared for infants born out of wedlock. Many unwanted infants were simply abandoned at churches, convents, foundling homes, and hospitals. In areas equipped with such facilities, unmarried pregnant women were sometimes housed in shelters run by the Catholic Church. The church set up such charities in order to protect the lives of both the unwed expectant mother and her unborn child. It was known that women who became pregnant before marriage were sometimes killed by members of their own families. In rural communities in particular, a scandal involving accusations of the rape or seduction of a young woman could also result in a blood feud between families. Feuding families engaged in ritual violence and retribution to protect their honor. In circumstances such as these, single women often felt compelled to hide the fact that they were pregnant. Some fled the villages in which they lived. Others had abortions in order to hide their shame. And others still sought refuge with the church.

The church, however, did not wish a single mother to have any contact with her newborn child, since, according to Catholic teaching, she was a sinner who had lost her grace before God. The prime consideration of the church was to save the soul of the offspring of so-called "illicit love" by means of the ritual of baptism. Once baptized, however, the illegitimate baby faced an unsure future in impersonal and institutional care. After a brief spell in the foundling home, these infants were often farmed out to paid wet-nurses who reared them until they were old enough to be sent to the orphanages where they spent their adolescence. The entire system of relief for foundlings was based on secrecy and shame.

From the late 19th century, these traditional institutional arrangements came under increasing attack from reformers who felt that single mothers should raise their own children. By 1922, Daisy di Robilant had devoted years of service to this cause. Her long experience as a campaigner and philanthropist made her the ideal person to play a major role in Fascism's project to extend state-funded services for social welfare. In 1927, the leadership of the National Organization for the Protection of Motherhood and Infancy launched what was called an "illegitimacy campaign" to reduce levels of child abandonment and mortality. Direction of this program was given to the countess, who became head of a new experimental center in Rome that ministered to thousands of single pregnant women.

From the start of her new career as a fascist welfare activist, the countess expressed very strong views about the direction policy should take. A committed supporter of publicly funded welfare programs, she believed that the state had a moral obligation to care generously for single mothers and their children. Unmarried Italian women bringing up children alone, she realized, faced stigma and censure because the Catholic Church and social custom abhorred motherhood outside marriage. Since contraception and abortion were illegal in fascist Italy, she never hesitated to remind her colleagues, the government's own laws contributed to the social problem of child abandonment. The regime, she believed, had to help women go against convention by giving them the legal, social, medical, and financial support they needed to form stable single-parent families.

Although she never hesitated to express frank opinions, even when these might damage her career prospects, the countess was an early convert to Fascism. She completely endorsed the political objectives behind the regime's demographic campaign, going so far as to advocate that motherhood was a sort of patriotic duty owed to the nation and the state. Given the pressures on individuals to conform during the dictatorship, it was hardly surprising that she should define herself as a "fascist of true faith" in her correspondence with Mussolini and her colleagues. However, it seems likely that what motivated the countess to abandon her earlier liberalism and embrace Fascism was the promises the regime repeatedly gave that it would solve some of Italy's most serious social problems by making these top priorities in domestic politics. No previous Italian government had pledged such firm and unwavering commitment to the achievement of improved health and welfare for its people. This deeply motivated reformer believed that Fascism's rise to power did mark a new era in Italian politics—one characterized by the presence of strong leadership at a national level capable of implementing inspired policy.

She longed to have faith in the promise that Fascism would create a new and modern form of state welfare. More difficult to understand, she also believed that Fascism and feminism were not necessarily incompatible. Her brand of feminism, it has to be said, was of the moderate and reformist kind typical of a woman of her class and breeding. But even liberal and bourgeois feminists could find ample cause to oppose a regime that was so vehemently hostile to the quest for women's emancipation.

Fascism defined women purely in terms of their biological function. Women's capacity to bear children, fascists maintained, affected their personality and intelligence and made them less able than men to be active in the world outside the home. As a consequence of this belief, women faced institutionalized discrimination in all areas of public life under Fascism. Their personal, educational, and employment opportunities were severely circumscribed by a dictatorship determined to relegate women to the private sphere of family and motherhood. Fascism aggressively sought to deprive women of freedom of choice over their own bodies and political rights as citizens. But it couched its patriarchal agenda in paternalistic and protective language that aimed to make women feel that the state valued their unique contribution to society. Women's reproductive role as mothers was deemed to be of paramount political importance. The fascist government lavished much praise on women who sacrificed all for the betterment of their husbands, their children, and their nation.

Ultimately, it was the regime's professed commitment to improving the lot of women that allowed someone like the Countess di Robilant to become a follower of Fascism. Focused on the issue of welfare entitlements, her feminism had always been concerned with advancing the social rather than the political rights of women. Pragmatic and realistic, she, like many feminists of her generation, realized that the family was the pivotal institution in Italian society, one which shaped women's identity and roles. She also believed that since most Italian women did, indeed, spend the better part of their lives having and raising children, their labors should at least be recognized and rewarded. Perhaps naively, she thought that she had found in Fascism's social reforms a means to fulfill finally her highest feminist aspirations.

The countess hoped to build up the social services needed to provide unmarried mothers with medical help, free food and lodging, and financial aid. She believed strongly that social assistance to unwed mothers had to be substantial enough to support the woman during her pregnancy and to sustain a single-parent family long after birth. In particular, she was concerned to protect the most vulnerable women from a life in poverty or prostitution which, she believed, was often caused by an unwanted pregnancy. Young girls, rape victims, the homeless, and outcast women who chose to mother their children would be assisted in their endeavor by sympathetic and trained welfare workers whose prime goal was to keep families together. From the beginning of her work as an administrator, Daisy di Robilant showed a marked tendency to defy the directives of her superiors. Official policy aimed only at encouraging women to register the newborn with the appropriate authorities, thereby accepting the responsibility of parenthood, and to breast-feed the baby in its early months, thereby increasing its life chances. As an incentive, fascist welfare agencies offered single mothers a monthly cash subsidy. Any woman, moreover, who lived with a man or had a history of producing illegitimate children was denied entitlement to the benefit. The reforms that Fascism implemented aimed at making unwed mothers into responsible parents; but fascist welfare legislation completely ignored the father of illegitimate children.

Daisy di Robilant had a much more ambitious approach than other fascist reformers. She realized that in many democratic countries governments empowered courts to make the putative fathers of illegitimate offspring financially responsible for the upbringing of their children. Italian women, by contrast, were not entitled by law to seek child maintenance. The countess saw this as an injustice that served to protect men, particularly married men, from any embarrassment or responsibility. Moreover, she was motivated by a strong desire to see her women clients settled in stable marriages that might offer them some modicum of security. A lot of women who came to her for help had relationships with partners, some of whom were not the biological father of their children. These women revealed to her that their poverty was an obstacle to marriage. In order to encourage them to marry, the countess offered a different cash benefit, a marriage premium, which was substantial enough to assist a newlywed couple to set up household together. After the marriage, the countess still gave these women hardship allowances when needed.

Opposed by higher levels of fascist officialdom, di Robilant tried to implement imaginative and progressive reforms that were aimed at responding to the full range of needs of her clientele. She and the other volunteers who worked for her provided free legal advice for women, took care of all the bureaucratic maneuvering involved in welfare work, found low-cost housing and secure jobs for her clients and their partners, and coordinated all available social and medical services by means of referral. Di Robilant was attempting to go well beyond the mere provision of state handouts; she sought instead to create a comprehensive and integrated system of welfare that provided continuous and flexible support for the single mother.

Proud of the work she did, the countess claimed that she was so successful that Rome's historic foundling home was finally becoming an obsolete institution. Levels of child abandonment were decreasing, and more and more two-parent families were being formed. She attributed this success to the fact that she was offering women real support both during and after their pregnancy. Perhaps the most significant achievement of all, welfare under the countess' leadership seemed to be improving the health of single mothers and their babies. Poverty, bad housing, undernourishment and sickness all went hand in hand. Single mothers in Italy were especially disadvantaged in all these areas. The deprivations they endured made them particularly vulnerable to miscarriages and complications during pregnancy. Their children too suffered alarmingly high rates of prematurity and failure to thrive, as well as the diseases associated with poor diets and environments. But the women and children in her care received continuous medical attention, as well as free meals, and these together accounted for the improvements.

Despite her program's success in reducing levels of sickness and death among a particularly vulnerable group in society, the countess' experimental center in Rome was starved of funds. Although she achieved dramatic results, she came under increasing attack by a fascist hierarchy that disapproved of her independence of mind. In the end, her deviations from the official line cost her allies at the top of the National Organization for the Protection of Motherhood and Infancy.

The fascist regime had never fully anticipated the costs of a welfare state. By the early 1930s, the National Organization for the Protection of Motherhood and Infancy was in great financial trouble, so its leaders imposed cuts on many of its social programs. Originally conceived as a model that the rest of the nation would follow, Daisy di Robilant's experimental center in Rome was one of the first victims of the axe. Initially the size of her budget was decreased as her superiors tried to compel her to limit the scope of her services and to conform to fascist policy. By 1933, the government could no longer claim to be providing unwed mothers with any real incentive to rear their children. As her program was being dismantled despite her efforts to continue without much support from the state, the countess made repeated requests to Mussolini himself to intervene on behalf of all the children he had earlier promised to help. The dictator ignored her pleas.

The countess' attempts to salvage the illegitimacy campaign failed, and this social program fell victim to Fascism's overambition and mismanagement. Her brief experiment in Rome had shown that fascist welfare could work given enough funding and commitment. But the regime proved unable to follow her lead and sustain the momentum of reform.

SOURCES:
Di Robilant, Daisy, *L'assistenza* obbligatoria agli illegittimi *riconosciuti*: note ed apunti *di assistenza sociale.* Turin, 1937.

Quine, M.S., "From Malthus to Mussolini: The Italian Eugenics Movement and Fascist Population Policy, 1890–1938," Ph.D thesis, University of London, 1990 (published as *The Fascist Social Revolution: The Welfare State in Italy, 1922–1945,* Oxford, England: Oxford University Press, 1996).

SUGGESTED READING:
De Grazia, V. *How Fascism Ruled Women: Italy, 1922–1945.* Berkeley, CA: University of California Press, 1992.

COLLECTIONS:
Miscellaneous correspondence and papers located in the *Archivio Centrale dello* Stato (Central State Archive) in Rome.

Maria Sophia Quine,
lecturer at Queen Mary and Westfield College, University of London, and author of *Population Politics in Twentieth-Century Europe* (London, England: Routledge, 1995)

Di San Faustino, Princess (1898–1963).
See Sage, Kay.

Disney, Lillian (1899–1997)
American philanthropist. *Born Lillian Bounds in 1899; died in Los Angeles, California, age 98, on December 16, 1997; daughter of a federal marshal and a homemaker; married Walt Disney (an animator and film producer), in 1925 (died 1966); married John Truyens (a real estate developer), in 1981; children: (first marriage) Diane Disney; Sharon Disney (d. 1993).*

Born Lillian Bounds in 1899, the youngest of ten children of a federal marshal, Lillian Disney was raised on the Nez Perce Indian Reservation in Idaho. In 1923, age 24, she moved to Los Angeles, taking a job as a film-frame inker at $15 per week at the nascent Disney Studio. She married the boss in 1925. For the next 41 years, Lillian was Walt Disney's sounding board. Returning to L.A. from New York in the late 1920s, her husband showed her his sketch of a new character he was proposing, a mouse named Mortimer. "It's too formal. How about Mickey?" she said. Lillian Disney helped found the California Institute of the Arts; she also donated $50 million for an L.A. concert hall.

Disraeli, Mary Anne (1792–1872)
English viscountess. *Name variations: Viscountess Beaconsfield; Marianne or Mary Anne Evans. Born November 11, 1792, in Exeter, England; died on December 15, 1872, in Buckinghamshire, England; daughter of John Evans and Eleanor (Viney) Evans; married Wyndham Lewis, in January 1815 (died 1838); married Benjamin Disraeli (1804–1881, prime minister of England), in August 1839; no children.*

The future wife of England's prime minister, Mary Anne Evans was born into a prosperous family of Devonshire. She was the second child of John Evans, a naval officer who died in Bermuda when Mary Anne was a year old. Her widowed mother **Eleanor Viney Evans** moved into her husband's family home outside Exeter, where Mary Anne and her brother spent their childhood. At their grandfather's country manor, they grew up amid a warm and loving extended family. Probably due in part to her upbringing, Mary Anne developed a lively, cheerful, and tolerant disposition that would earn her the admiration of London society in later years.

In 1807, Eleanor relocated her teenaged children to Gloucester. After teaching Sunday school for several years, Mary Anne met and married a wealthy Welsh magistrate, Wyndham Lewis, in 1815. She was 23 and quite fond of 37-year-old Wyndham, who was deeply in love with her. They spent over 20 years together, dividing their time between his country estate in Cardiff, Wales, and, after Lewis' election to Parliament in 1820, in London. Mary Anne became a popular hostess—intelligent, charming, outgoing—and excelled in her role as a politician's wife, an asset in his business and public affairs. Keenly interested in the welfare of children and the poor, Mary Anne opened a school for the children of Greenmeadow in addition to many other charitable activities. She administered her husband's estates herself, showing a practical side of her nature previously unseen, but for the most part her life was that of a leisured aristocrat. Her husband was away from home much of the time, while Mary Anne spent her days hosting parties and entertaining their friends. And from her surviving correspondence it is evident that Mary Anne enjoyed numerous love affairs with men of her social circle, both married and single, without much comment from her elderly husband.

In 1832, she was introduced to Benjamin Disraeli. Disraeli came from an affluent family of Italian-Jewish descent which had converted to Anglicanism after settling in England. He was an elegant, moderately successful novelist who was showing some political ambition by the time he met Mary Anne. Five years later, Disraeli and Wyndham Lewis were elected to Parliament from the same town. After Lewis' death in 1838, rumors began to spread about the friendship between his wealthy widow and his young political colleague Disraeli. While her letters show that Mary Anne was grieved by her husband's death, and that her relationship with Disraeli for months was a simple friendship, the two eventually fell in love.

They married in August 1839, beginning a long and happy union that lasted until Mary Anne's death 32 years later. As she had been for her first husband, Mary Anne was an ideal companion for her "Dizzy" both personally and politically. As he rose in the British political system

from member of Parliament, to chancellor of the Exchequer, to prime minister in 1868, Mary Anne campaigned for him, criticized and edited his speeches and writings, and hosted his patrons. Husband and wife constantly exchanged loving letters, poems, and small gifts, which they carefully preserved.

The Disraelis were often invited to Queen *Victoria's court in the 1860s, as the queen was quite fond of Disraeli. Despite her failing health, including her long suffering from the stomach cancer that would kill her, Mary Anne remained a fixture in high society throughout this period. England's aristocratic women commented on her sometimes outrageous statements and social faux pas, her insistence on daring youthful fashions well into her 70s, and her scandalously affectionate behavior in public with Disraeli. Yet she always had more admirers than critics, and counted the queen as a friend. Before his first retirement as prime minister in 1868 (he served again after Mary Anne's death), Disraeli pressed the queen to honor his wife with a peerage. Queen Victoria responded by creating Mary Anne as Viscountess Beaconsfield. In the last few years of her life, Mary Anne suffered immensely from her cancer, spending every day in Disraeli's

Mary Anne Disraeli

care, but she amazed London society by her determination not to scale back her activities. She died on December 15, 1872, at age 80.

SOURCES:

Hardwick, Mollie. *Mrs Dizzy: The Life of Mary Anne Disraeli, Viscountess Beaconsfield*. London: Cassell, 1972.

Sykes, James. *Mary Anne Disraeli*. NY: Appleton, 1928.

Laura York,
Riverside, California

d'Istria, Dora (1828–1888).

See Chica, Elena.

Ditlevsen, Tove (1917–1976)

Danish writer of poems, short stories, novels and memoirs, a total of 37 works. Born in Copenhagen, Denmark, in 1917; committed suicide in March 1976; daughter of Ditlev Ditlevsen and Alfrida (Mundus) Ditlevsen; married four times; children: one daughter and two sons.

Cited as "one of the most important writers of her generation," by *Tillie Olsen, Tove Ditlevsen was born in Copenhagen, Denmark, in 1917. She grew up in a socialist working milieu in Copenhagen and left school after graduating from the eighth grade. Before marrying her first husband, the editor of *Wild Wheat*, a journal for avant-garde poetry, she held several office jobs.

Her writing concentrates on life within the family, influenced by but separate from the social and political sphere. Women and the roles through which they create their identity are her subject matter, and she measures women's quality of life by the intensity of their emotional relationships. Particularly, Ditlevsen's later works portray the loneliness of middle-class women, their emotional and social state of exposure, and their experience of sexual submission and suffering as indigenous to their lives.

Her novels, which are to some extent autobiographical, fall into two categories. The earlier works are naturalistic depictions of people and places, focusing on childhood. In the later novels, marital problems are depicted as universal concerns. She explains the *angst* that runs like an undercurrent in all her work in terms of traumatic childhood influences, which no subsequent experiences can obliterate.

As contributions to the women's literature of the 1970s, her works are particularly valuable as they dramatize the consequences of locking women into marriage, into the roles of wife and mother. She presents the opinion that a talent for writing exacts a price in the form of human relationships and that women primarily may feel the burden of the resulting loneliness.

Tove Ditlevsen's books were well received. Readers identified with her characters and responded to her warmth, sensitivity, and sense of humor. Nineteen years after her death, a new generation of Danes began to embrace her work.

SOURCES:

Ditlevsen, Tove. *Tove Ditlevsen Om Sig Selv*. Copenhagen: Gyldendahl, 1975.

Mogensen, Harald, ed. *Om Tove Ditlevsen*. Copenhagen: Forum, 1976.

Mork, Margit. *Kender Du Tove Ditlevsen*. Copenhagen: Grafisk Forlag, 1986.

Inga Wiehl, native of Denmark,
teaching in Yakima, Washington

Dittmar, Louise (1807–1884)

Self-taught German philosopher and feminist active in the 1840s who challenged the notion that there were any natural differences between the sexes, and (while also drawing on the Christian tradition) used a critique of Christianity to explore both the ideological oppression of women more generally, and to defend women's rights to sexuality. Name variations: Luise Dittmar. Born on September 7, 1807, in the German town of Darmstadt; died on July 11, 1884, in the village of Bessungen (now a part of Darmstadt); daughter of Heinrich Karl Dittmar (a higher treasury official at the court of Hesse-Darmstadt); self-taught; never married; no children.

Published nine books in the space of five years (1845–49); founded and edited Soziale Reform, *one of the five women's journals launched in Germany during the revolutions of 1848 and 1849.*

Books: Bekannte Geheimnisse *(Open Secrets, 1845);* Skizzen und Briefe *(Sketches and Letters, 1845);* Der Mensch und sein Gott *(The Human Being and His God, 1846);* Lessing und Feuerbach *(Lessing and Feuerbach, 1847);* Vier Zeitfragen *(Four Timely Questions, 1847);* Zur Charakterisierung der nordischen Mythologie *(Characterization of Nordic Mythology, 1848);* Wühlerische Gedichte *(Subversive Poems, 1848);* Brutus-Michel *(1848);* Das Wesen der Ehe nebst einigen Aufsätzen über die soziale Reform der Frauen *(The Essence of Marriage, Along with Some Essays about Women's Social Reform, 1849).*

Louise Dittmar emerged from the comfort, and claustrophobia, of unmarried daughterhood in a privileged upper-middle-class household to become Germany's most brilliant (and yet often misunderstood) feminist theorist of the 1840s—

only to die in complete obscurity four decades later. Not until the 1970s was her work rediscovered and excerpts republished; only in the 1980s and 1990s did she begin to receive the critical scholarly attention she deserves. Her work includes political satire, religious and mythological history, philosophical and theological exegesis, poetry, and journalism. It provides an important example of that peculiar hybrid blend of radical liberalism, pre-Marxist socialism, and humanist Christianity that characterized many utopian visions in 1840's France, England and Germany.

Although Dittmar's father worked at the court of Hesse-Darmstadt's grand duke, the family did not have conservative leanings. At least two of Dittmar's brothers had ties to leftist circles. One was a friend of the radical writer Georg Büchner, and one married the daughter of C.W. Leske (Karl Marx's Darmstadt publisher) in whose home many radicals gathered. These familial ties presumably reinforced Dittmar's own political instincts, and it was to these small gatherings of leftist friends that she first presented her work. But as the one daughter to remain unmarried in a family that also had eight sons, Dittmar was weighed down by many domestic duties and was unable to receive any formal education. Indeed, it is striking that it was not until after her parents' death, when she was 38 years old, that she began to publish her writings. Meanwhile, in the atmosphere of the time, female writers—especially on those "important" subjects of politics and theology in which Dittmar was most interested—were rarely taken seriously.

Consequently lacking in confidence, Dittmar published her first four books anonymously. *Bekannte Geheimnisse* and *Skizzen und Briefe,* while including scathing critiques of women's disenfranchisement, also covered a wide range of political and social issues. As these first books showed, Dittmar—much like utopian thinkers in France and England during the 1830s and 1840s—was as concerned with the role of the military, the death penalty, the growth of national and racial hatreds, the mishandling of industrial development and the growing poverty of her day, as well as the hypocrisy of a Christianity that (in Germany) still intolerantly denied political equality to Jews, as she was with the oppression of women. She embedded her critique of the extant gender relations in a critical analysis of all forms of social injustice, both along class and along religious lines, calling for a redistribution of wealth and for a radical humanism that considered Jews to be Christians'

moral equals. Her next two books were even less explicitly concerned with gender relations. Although they also contain passages that help clarify Dittmar's particular brand of feminism, *Der Mensch und sein Gott* and *Lessing und Feuerbach* are best understood as standard exemplars of the sort of rationalist and humanist religious criticism that was gaining widespread popularity in Germany.

> *And I just don't see that those many men who claim for themselves so great a right to shape the life of the world are all such geniuses.*
> —**Louise Dittmar**

Meanwhile, despite the anonymity, Dittmar's reputation was spreading within the intricate network of religious and political radicals evolving at the time, and her latter two books in particular were well-received within the then-growing movement of religious dissenters. The movement was composed of both Catholics and Protestants who were alarmed by the unexpected revival of religious conservatism in the supposedly so "enlightened" 19th century. From 1845 on, the dissenters split from the established churches and founded democratically run congregations dedicated to individual freedom of belief, cross-confessional cooperation, and the separation of church and state; the goal was to develop a humanist and tolerant form of Christianity in which individuals could combine reason and spirituality. Across the German lands, the movement reached a peak of between 100,000 and 150,000 members by 1848, making it the largest protest movement of any sort in Germany before the outbreak of revolution in 1848, and indeed many dissenters subsequently became revolutionaries. The movement also provided the seedbed for Germany's first organized women's movement, for the dissenting movement's male leaders were vocal advocates of equality between men and women within marriage, and of an expansion of women's spheres of activity into congregational and communal life.

All of the 20 or so most prominent activist women in mid-19th-century Germany had close ties to the dissenting movement and, although she never formally became a member, Dittmar was no exception. Her first invitation to speak publicly was given her in 1847 by the Mannheim Monday Club, a radical splinter group dedicated to both women's and Jewish rights. It was this group's warm reception that finally gave Dittmar the courage to acknowledge authorship of her previous works (and sign her subsequent ones), and thus ensured her place within historical memory; *Vier Zeitfragen* was the reprint of the lecture she delivered to the club. Dittmar also delivered further public lectures to audiences in Mainz, Hanau, and Darmstadt throughout 1848. In January of 1849, she founded the journal *Soziale Reform,* in which she published not only her own essays but also articles by others, the majority of which addressed women's concerns. The journal folded after only four issues, though all but one of the essays in it were reprinted, along with some new ones, in a book entitled *Das Wesen der Ehe nebst einigen Aufsätzen über die soziale Reform der Frauen.* The essays on marriage in this book, collectively entitled *Das Wesen der Ehe,* were reprinted separately in 1850, and this is the last book Dittmar ever managed to publish.

Notwithstanding the fact that her theological writings had been favorably reviewed by newspapers not only in Darmstadt and Mannheim, but also in cities as far away as Berlin and Hamburg, and that her own journal had attracted contributions from some of the leading democrats and women's rights advocates of her day, Dittmar was unable (despite repeated efforts) to find a publisher in the post-revolutionary years. During the era of political reaction following the defeat of the revolution in 1849, publishers probably found the causes she advocated simply too risky to take on. Indeed, with the exception of *Luise Otto-Peters'* *Frauen-Zeitung,* which was not forced to shut down until 1852, no women's newspaper outlasted the revolution. (Otto-Peters—less militant than Dittmar—was the most famous and successful of the mid-19th-century German women's rights activists.) Criticized also by other women's rights advocates, Dittmar eventually grew discouraged and stopped writing. From 1850 on, she lived alone, traveling occasionally, also to France and Switzerland, but feeling increasingly self-doubting and withdrawn. In 1880, she moved in with two of her nieces, dying four years later after an extended illness; the obituary mourned the passing of the "good aunt"—even her family had forgotten who she had once been.

In retrospect, what distinguished Dittmar from her contemporaries was neither her political persuasion—her political writings clearly place her within the camp of "radical liberals" or "radical democrats" to which many 1848 revolutionaries also belonged—nor her religious humanism and close ties to the religious dissenting movement, nor her advocacy of women's rights

per se. Like other women's rights advocates of her day, Dittmar defended women's rights to education, economic self-sufficiency, and participation in government. Rather, what distinguished Dittmar was her willingness (extraordinarily unusual for the time) to question the notion that there were any differences between the sexes ordained by nature. For almost all other male *and* female feminists of her time continually linked their demands for greater equality for women, and/or their efforts to expand women's sphere of activity, with concern about retaining women's femininity and difference from men. They distanced themselves—as Luise Otto-Peters put it—from "those who have brought the phrase 'emancipation of women' into discredit by degrading the woman into a caricature of the man." Dittmar, by contrast, repeatedly called attention to just how suffocating and oppressive the feminine ideal could be, and to the ways that what seemed "natural" to others was really the result of social pressure and conditioning.

For example, in her final book on marriage, Dittmar pointed out that to provide no educational opportunities for a woman—to educate her for nothing else but domesticity—"and then to say, 'that is her destiny,' does that not mean that she is being *pre*destined?" In an earlier book, she had argued that "only that which contradicts the nature of a being, is unnatural, aside from that everything that is, is natural. Whether it contradicts the external demands on it or not, in no way diminishes its inner legitimacy." Over and over again, throughout her works, Dittmar would extol *"individual peculiarity,* without which people themselves and all of life are *without charm,"* and insist that every individual "must be understood and treated as an end in himself [sic], *as he is,* while the purpose of the whole must be directed toward transforming unity into the greatest possible diversity."

Dittmar found the strongest support for her emphasis on individual peculiarity and diversity and the need to encourage the development of individual self-esteem (which she felt women in particular were lacking) in the rhetoric of religious criticism—even as her critical engagement with theology also helped her to articulate just how difficult achieving autonomous selfhood was. Dittmar, in short, was drawn to a study of Christianity because of her more general interest in the workings of ideological systems of all sorts, in the powerful hold they had on individuals' souls, and the problems individuals invariably encountered in constructing a self unbeholden to any higher authorities. This was why she was particularly attracted to the work of the philosopher Ludwig Feuerbach, and to his notion that what people worshipped as a God was really only the projected image of their own potential perfection; in projecting perfection onto a fictive being, according to Feuerbach, they denied their own worth. As Dittmar put it: "As long as we assume the existence of a 'higher' reason, so long must we naturally despise our own reason." For, as she argued, "the faith in a power that takes care of us leads to faith in a power that does our thinking for us."

In addition, Dittmar engaged critically with Christianity because of what she perceived to be the Christian legacy of disdain for the body and its claims and pleasures. This was a prevalent theme among Dittmar's progressive male contemporaries as well, but most of them tended to veil (however flimsily) their defense of their own sensual enjoyment in odes to domesticity. Dittmar, by contrast, was disgusted with women's repression within the domestic realm and outraged by her contemporaries' assumption that marriage necessarily brought women emotional or sexual happiness. In the context of her time, however, to refer to women's sexuality in any way without assuming its purpose was reproductive would have been quite scandalous; Dittmar's near-obsessive critiques of the Christian devaluation of the body in her theological writings (including a recurrent rage at Christianity's demand for "voluntary *renunciation* of earthly satisfaction" and a repeated defense of "misunderstood sensuality" and "the guiltless body") were one way to approach the unmentionable without mentioning it outright. In her final book, however, Dittmar ventured some even bolder remarks. She expressed fury that the love of women, "which springs out of the most heated yearning for satisfaction," was being squelched within "the prisonhouse of civil marriage," and she argued that within marriages as they were currently arranged—in marriages, that is, in which women were economically and legally dependent on their husbands—women were "physically and spiritually lacerating themselves, wearing themselves away." Dittmar repeatedly argued that women's capacity for sexual love was systematically distorted by her society's socialization of women ("especially in the case of women this desire is suppressed, weakened and clouded through an unnatural upbringing, through moral thumbscrews and through the most clever principle of deadening"), and she contended that "the disrespect for woman, her social repression, is most closely linked with the disrespect for and repression of the bodily senses."

Finally, however, despite all her rage at Christianity for its legacy of psychological and physiological oppression, and for providing one of human history's most successful excuses for earthly inequality, Dittmar also found a submerged strand within the Christian tradition that she could and did draw on: a belief in the equal dignity and worth of every individual, a tradition of prophetic denunciation of injustice, and a faith that a complete transformation and renewal of the world—the creation of justice on earth—was possible. This explains why, interspersed with all her near-atheism, Dittmar also relied heavily on Biblical imagery. No other language but religious language could communicate the urgency with which she felt a total revolution in social relations was both necessary and legitimate, and no other language could properly convey her sense of the sacredness of each individual's right to self-determination. Thus, for example, to underscore the legitimacy of her demand for justice for women, Dittmar concluded an essay on women's rights in her newspaper *Soziale Reform* with a passage which, for readers schooled in the New Testament, created clear echoes between women and the early Christian disciples:

> Poor and without rights, oppressed legally and in principle, physically unsuited for battle, intellectually deprived, . . . limited in her means, scorned, ridiculed, repressed and persecuted with the full weight of a life-ethic that is hostile to her—where should she gather strength, where should she plow and sow without land? . . . And yet, she will plow and sow and reap a thousand times over, like no other worker in the vineyard of the Lord!

Yet despite the widespread popularity of both religious and political radicalism in 1840's Germany, Dittmar found little support for her views. In particular, her frequent rejection of the notion that there were natural differences between the sexes was not well-received. Other activist women accused her of pursuing a path "hostile to female nature" and of promoting teachings that "strip a woman of all femininity, that make her into a man-woman, a hermaphrodite." Indeed, even in Dittmar's own journal, other feminists (both male and female) obsessively reiterated their beliefs in natural gender differences. With a few (equally embattled) exceptions, it would take more than another 100 years before feminists in the United States and Europe would finally, unabashedly raise a great many of the same issues that Dittmar had already wrestled with in the 1840s.

SOURCES:

Herzog, Dagmar. "The Feminist Conundrum," in *Intimacy and Exclusion: Religious Politics in Pre-Revolu-*

tionary Baden. Princeton, NJ: Princeton University Press, 1996.

Joeres, Ruth-Ellen Boetcher. "Spirit in Struggle: The Radical Vision of Louise Dittmar (1807–1884)," in Ruth-Ellen Boetcher Joeres and Mary Jo Maynes, eds., *Out of Line/ Ausgefallen: The Paradox of Marginality in the Writings of Nineteenth-Century German Women.* Special Issue of *Amsterdamer Beiträge zur neueren Germanistik.* Vol. 28, 1989, pp. 279–301.

Klausmann, Christina. "Louise Dittmar (1807–1884): Ergebnisse einer biographischen Spurensuche," in Ruth-Ellen Boetcher Joeres and Mary Jo Maynes, eds., *Out of Line,* p. 17–39.

Paletschek, Sylvia. *Women and Dissent.* Ann Arbor, MI: Univ. of Michigan Press.

Zucker, Stanley. *Kathinka Zitz-Halein and Female Civic Activism in Mid-Nineteenth-Century Germany.* Carbondale, IL: Southern Illinois University Press, 1991

SUGGESTED READING:

Goodman, Katherine. *Dis/Closures: Women's Autobiography in Germany between 1790 and 1914.* NY: Peter Lang, 1986.

Herzog, Dagmar. "Liberalism, Religious Dissent and Women's Rights: Louise Dittmar's Writings from the 1840s," in Konrad Jarausch and Larry Eugene Jones, eds. *In Search of a Liberal Germany: Studies in the History of German Liberalism from 1789 to the Present.* Oxford: Berg, 1990: 55–85.

Prelinger, Catherine M. *Charity, Challenge and Change: Religious Dimensions of the Mid-Nineteenth-Century Women's Movement in Germany.* NY: Greenwood, 1987.

COLLECTIONS:

Letters by Dittmar to the writer Lorenz Diefenbach, located in the Diefenbach Papers at the University of Giessen, Germany.

Dagmar Herzog, Assistant Professor of History, Michigan State University, East Lansing, Michigan

Ditzel, Nana (1923—)

Danish designer of jewelry, textiles and furniture. Born Nana Hauberg in 1923; daughter of William Hauberg and Erna (Lytzen) Hauberg; graduated from high school, 1942; graduated from the Academy of Arts and Crafts, 1946; married architect Jörgen Ditzel (died 1961); married Knud Heide.

Beginning in the early 1950s, Nana Ditzel, in collaboration with her husband Jörgen Ditzel, established herself as an imaginative and multifaceted designer. The couple initially drew attention to their work with their light and elegant basket chairs but gained even wider acclaim as designers of jewelry in silver and gold for George Jensen. The simple yet expressive shapes and the quality of execution in their work brought the Ditzels the Lunning Prize in 1956, as well as silver and gold medals from exhibits in Milan and other European cities.

After Jörgen Ditzel's death in 1961, Nana continued on her own, designing jewelry, furniture and textiles. With the intent of allowing people to move more freely in and among her furniture, she gained a reputation for untraditional designs and materials, such as foam rubber and fiberglass. She has designed children's furniture according to the same principle; one example is a high chair elegant and graceful enough to be considered a permanent fixture. Ditzel's textiles show her sure sense of color and pattern in blankets, chair covers and wall hangings. To meet heavy demands, she set up shop in London in 1968.

SOURCES:

Haard, Ulf af Segerstad. *Modern Scandinavian Furniture.* Copenhagen: Gyldendal, 1963.

Karlsen, Arne. *Dansk Möbelkunst i det 20. aarhundrede,* 2 vols. Aarhus: Christian Ejlers Forlag, 1991.

Inga Wiehl, native of Denmark, teaching in Yakima, Washington

Diver, Jenny (1700–1740)

British pickpocket. Name variations: Mary Jones. Born Mary Jones in Ireland in 1700; died on the gallows on March 18, 1740, at Tyburn, England; daughter of Harriot Jones (a maid); educated in Northern Ireland.

One of the most notorious pickpockets in criminal history, Jenny Diver (whose real name was Mary Jones) was born out of wedlock and deserted by her mother at age five. After living in several foster homes, she was finally taken to Northern Ireland, where an elderly woman cared for her and saw that she had a proper education. As a teenager, Diver moved to London, hoping to make her fortune as a seamstress. The move, however, appeared to be her undoing, for no sooner had she arrived in the city than she became involved with **Anne Murphy**, a sort of den mother to a pack of nimble-fingered street thieves. Joining the group as an apprentice pickpocket, Diver grew so adept that she promptly took over the operation. Her partners in crime were reportedly so impressed with her skills that they gave her the name Jenny Diver (*diver* being underworld parlance for pickpocket).

Diver was not only masterful with her fingers, she was a talented actress. She excelled at passing herself off as a fine lady in distress, which worked to her advantage in wealthier areas in the city. One of her favorite ploys was executed in conjunction with national holidays and royal celebrations. Stuffing her elegant gown with pillows in order to look pregnant, she would arrive by carriage at a previously designated place, attended by the gang posing as her servants. Usually able to wangle a prominent position in order to view the festivities, Diver would suddenly collapse, writhing in agony, convincing onlookers that she was in labor. While they gathered around her to offer aid, she would relieve them of their jewelry and purses, while her compatriots worked the outskirts of the crowd. With tactics such as these, she amassed a huge fortune, purchasing a large house, a fabulous wardrobe, and one of the finest carriages in London. Although Diver, who used a string of aliases to protect her identity, was occasionally caught and jailed, she was seldom proven guilty. One of her few convictions resulted in banishment to America, but her confederates managed to bribe several officials, so that instead of deportation she spent a month or so in a countryside retreat.

Eventually, Diver's advancing age, 38, affected her once nimble hands and fingers and caused her to neglect her usual elaborate preparations. In April 1738, she was caught while attempting to steal a purse, having failed to arrange for an accomplice to be nearby so she could pass off the stolen goods. Since she was using a new alias of Jane Webb at the time, authorities thought it was her first conviction and once again sentenced her to banishment in America. On June 7, 1738, she departed aboard the galley *Forward*, taking with her numerous trunks and boxes containing her fortune. But she was on her way back to Liverpool within a year, having used her considerable wealth to bribe a ship's captain. When she returned to London, however, her gang had dispersed, and she was forced to work alone in the less fashionable neighborhoods of the city. On January 17, 1740, she was caught attempting to steal the purse of a feisty young woman who put up a struggle. Diver was identified and convicted, not only of stealing, but of returning from banishment, an offense punishable by death. Sentenced to hang, she was said to have repented before her death on the gallows at Tyburn, on March 18, 1740.

Jenny Diver was immortalized in John Gay's *The Beggar's Opera* (1798), then later found her way into popular culture through the lyrics of "Mack the Knife," from the more modern version of Gay's work, *The Threepenny Opera*, written by Bertolt Brecht in 1928.

Barbara Morgan,
Melrose, Massachusetts

Dix, Dorothea Lynde (1802–1887)

American reformer who led the crusade to improve treatment of the mentally ill, built hospitals for the insane, and served as Superintendent of Army Nurses during the Civil War. Born Dorothea Lynde Dix on April 4, 1802, in Hampden, Maine; died in Trenton, New Jersey, on July 18, 1887; daughter of Joseph (a Methodist minister) and Mary (Bigelow) Dix; spent several years at private schools in Boston, but largely self-educated; never married.

At age 14, started her first school (1816); published the first of six books (1824); began work as an advocate for the mentally ill (1841); helped found, design, and expand dozens of hospitals for the mentally ill in the U.S., Europe, and Japan; served as Superintendent of Army Nurses (1861–65).

On a scorching summer day in rural Georgia in the 1840s, Dorothea Dix made her way across a field, approaching a crude log pen. She looked strangely out of place to the small group of farmers that accompanied her. They could tell she was a lady. From her simple but meticulously clean skirt and her crisp New England accent, they could tell she was an educated woman of some means. What possible interest could such a woman have, they wondered, in the wretched sight she was about to behold?

Peering through the wide gaps in the logs, this elegant visitor saw a strange animal chained inside the pen; it was a man, but his naked body was filthy, his hair long and tangled, his eyes vacant. And where his feet should have been, Dix saw only stumps. The man had been left out in the cold too long one winter, a farmer explained, and his feet had been destroyed by frostbite. To prevent that from happening again, a deep pit had been dug at the center of the pen, covered by a sturdy trap door. When cold weather approached, the prisoner was thrown into the pit, shut up "without heat, without light, without pure air" until the next spring, his groans and cries muffled within that muddy dungeon.

Dix was outraged by the sight of this "pining, miserable" creature, but she was not surprised. Over the previous few years, in poorhouses and jails, rural barns and cellars across the country, she had visited thousands of men and women who were treated in much the same way, kept in chains and darkened cells as if they were dangerous beasts. These miserable prisoners were not criminals; they were mentally ill.

Dix had also seen enough of these situations to know that their jailers were usually not cruel and sadistic people who enjoyed torturing those they called "maniacs" or "lunatics." They were mostly well-intentioned people, doing the best they could within their limited means and limited knowledge. Many she had spoken to believed that the people they were caring for were not even human beings at all. When people lost their reason, they thought, they became beasts, without a sense of decency, or even a sense of hot and cold.

I am the Hope of the poor crazed beings who pine in the cells, and stalls, and cages, and waste rooms of your poor houses. I am the Revelation of hundreds of wailing, suffering creatures, hidden in your private dwellings.

—Dorothea Dix

As soon as Dix left that field in Georgia, she recorded what she had seen in her journal, another example added to her mounting inventory of mistreatment of the mentally ill. Before long, she would weave that story into one of her public reports, using these horrifying tales to prick the conscience of legislators and citizens, urging them to correct the abuses by building modern facilities for care and treatment of the insane. For more than 40 years, Dix used this method successfully in almost every state in the nation, as well as in Europe. More than any other person in the 19th century, she was responsible for pioneering more humane treatment for the mentally ill.

Dorothea Dix had a troubled childhood, one that has tempted some biographers to trace her interest in mental illness back to her relationships with her unstable parents. She was born in Hampden, Maine, in 1802, an area that was then a sparsely settled frontier of Massachusetts. Much of the land in that part of Maine was owned by Dorothea's grandfather, Elijah Dix, a successful doctor and land speculator who lived in an impressive Boston mansion. Dr. Dix had sent his son Joseph to live in Maine, ostensibly to help sell the land that would form the new towns of Dixmont and Dixville. But he had another motive as well. Joseph had been enrolled as a divinity student at Harvard when he had fallen in love with and married **Mary Bigelow**, a woman 18 years his senior and well below his social standing. The family disapproved of the match, as did Harvard, which at the time allowed no married student to attend. In a sense, when Dr. Dix sent his son and his new bride to Maine, he was exiling them from the family.

The stresses of frontier life took their toll on Dorothea's parents. Joseph developed a drinking problem, while Mary collapsed under the strain, taking to her bed most of the time. Ignoring his responsibilities as a land broker and as a farmer,

Joseph devoted most of his time to his religious calling, working as an itinerant Methodist preacher. He was a fervent believer and a powerful speaker, but his efforts to bring the gospel to the far flung settlements of northern New England earned him little money and often carried him far from home. As the eldest child, Dorothea was left to care for her invalid mother and her two younger brothers. Years later, she summed up these experiences by saying, "I never knew childhood."

When she was 12, Dorothea ran away from home, making her way to the Dix mansion in Boston. Her grandmother, also named Dorothea, who was by now a widow, reluctantly agreed to take the child in. For the next two years, the older woman worked to mold this uneducated child from the Maine woods into a Boston gentlewoman. As biographer **Dorothy Wilson** has written, Dorothea's new life was marked by "orgies of admonition," as her grandmother trained her to a life of "industry, inflexible dignity, economy, perfection in manners, spartan discipline, puritanical piety." Dix was an eager student and an avid reader but too stubborn for her elderly grandmother's liking. At age 14, she was sent to a grand aunt's home in Worcester, Massachusetts, for the completion of her education.

While in Worcester, Dix began to exhibit some of the strong will, conscientiousness, and energy that would one day serve her as a reformer. Still only 14, she announced that she would open her own school for young children. Recruiting students from the elite families of Worcester, she taught for several years, presiding over her charges with what one student remembered as "a very stern decided expression." She demanded a great deal of her students, and even more of herself, working late into the night to prepare her lessons.

In 1820, at age 17, Dix returned to live with her grandmother in Boston. She had become a beautiful and polished young woman but took no interest in the balls, tea parties, card games, and other social events enjoyed by most young singles of her social station. To a friend, she confessed, "I look with little envy on those who find enjoyment in such transitory delights." Her delight was education, and she spent much of her time reading and attending lectures, paying particular attention to the religious disputes that were then dividing Boston. She was drawn to the preaching of one of the city's most controversial ministers, William Ellery Channing, the leading speaker of the new Unitarian movement. These

Dorothea Lynde Dix

liberal Christians rejected the traditional Calvinist view that people are born sinful and can only be saved through the miraculous interference of God's grace. Channing and his fellow Unitarians thought that this orthodox theology depicted God as an irrational tyrant who had the power to save all, but instead sent many to Hell. Rejecting this view, Channing defended what he called the "dignity of human nature." Sin was not innate and inevitable, he held. People were moral free agents, and if they only used the reason that God had given them, they could drive evil out of their own lives and become champions of "benevolence" in the world. Channing urged his followers to put this theory into practice by devoting themselves to helping those less fortunate.

Dix took Channing's preaching to heart. Not long after she had arrived back in Boston, she received word that her father had died, leaving her mother and brothers without support. To provide for them, she opened a new school in the Dix mansion, serving the children of wealthy families. At the same time, she launched a writing career, working long into the night on a children's encyclopedia that she called *Conversations on Common Things*. Published in 1824, the book was a great commercial success, with royalties going to support her mother. But, heeding Channing's call to live a life of Christian benevolence, Dix wanted to do more. Ignoring her grandmother's warnings about overworking herself, she opened a second school in the afternoons, providing a free education to children from poor families. Running two schools, and starting on a new book of religious stories for children, Dix told a friend, "what greater bliss than to look back on days spent in usefulness, in doing good to those around you, in fitting young spirits for their native skies!"

While these years in Boston were remarkably productive and exciting for Dix, they were also marked by two sorrows that would haunt her for the rest of her life. Since her earliest years in Worcester, she had been in love with Edward Bangs, a distant cousin many years her senior, who was a successful young lawyer and aspiring politician. As she grew older, their platonic friendship had grown into romantic love, and when Dix was in her early 20s, the two were secretly engaged. But Bangs expected that, after their marriage, Dix would give up teaching, writing, and public service, devoting herself full-time to the job of being his wife. When Dix refused, Bangs broke the engagement. Though she rarely mentioned the incident in later years, her biographers have sensed that the experience left a deep scar that never entirely healed. As Dorothy Wilson put it, "She would burn his letters, try to sublimate human passion in the ardor of useful service, yet never quite succeed." Though numerous men expressed a romantic interest in her through the years, there is no evidence that she ever returned their affections.

Not long after, Dix suffered a second blow, a physical collapse that her doctor described as "rheumatism of the lungs," possibly incipient tuberculosis brought on by her grueling work schedule. She was forced to close the school and head South for the winter to recuperate. The next year, with her health somewhat recovered, she gladly accepted a job as tutor of William Ellery Channing's children. The children both admired and dreaded their new teacher, a beautiful young woman who was so excited about learning, and such a demanding perfectionist. "Fixed as fate," was the way Channing's daughter later remembered her. Dix resumed her writing, publishing a book on botany that was widely admired.

After several years with the Channings, Dorothea once again turned the Dix family mansion into a school, working with paying scholars each morning and poor children in the after-noon. But she ignored her doctor's warnings about her health, pushed herself too hard, and again suffered a physical collapse. "I feel it is very possible I may never again enjoy the fragrancies of spring," she told a friend. She rallied, however, and in 1836 went to England, hoping that a sea voyage would be good for her lungs. In England, she spent more than a year convalescing at the home of William Rathbone, a friend of Channing's and a noted English politician and humanitarian. There, she mingled with some of the most important English and American writers and reformers of her day and developed a lifelong friendship with the entire Rathbone family.

While she was in England, the most important link to her own family was broken. She received word that her grandmother had died. The news was a blow to Dix; the elderly woman had become a close friend and staunch supporter, and the only real family that she had left. Returning to America, Dix found herself at a crossroad. She was now in her mid-30s, well educated and, thanks to an inheritance from her grandmother, financially secure. But she was also alone and without prospects or interest in marriage and family life. She was independent but not sure how to use this freedom. Once again her thoughts turned to Channing's call to devote one's life to Christian benevolence. "Life is not to be expended in vain regrets," she resolved. "There are duties to be performed here."

But she hesitated, not sure just what her new duties should be. In the late 1830s, Boston was experiencing a remarkable intellectual renaissance. Ralph Waldo Emerson, *Margaret Fuller, and others were promoting the strange new ideas they called "Transcendentalism," Horace Mann, *Mary Peabody Mann, and *Elizabeth Palmer Peabody were reforming the public schools, William Lloyd Garrison and *Angelina and *Sarah Grimké were agitating for the abolition of slavery, and a host of other utopian schemers promoted everything from communal living to cold-water baths as the ultimate cure for society's ills. Dix was eager to play a part, but for women, particularly of her social standing, public debate and social agitation were not considered proper. And there was the persistent problem of her health. Friends urged her to rest, not to overwork herself as she had done in the past. In the back of her mind, she must have wondered if she was sliding into a life of semi-invalidism, much like her mother had done at about the same age.

Then, in 1841, Dix was approached by a Harvard divinity student who had tried to teach Sunday School to the women convicts at the East Cambridge jail, but felt that they would respond better to a woman teacher. He asked her if she knew of a mature woman who could handle this tough assignment. "I will be there next Sunday," she replied. He had not meant for her to take the job, he protested; she was too feeble. But she insisted, and the following Sunday led services for a couple dozen women at the jail.

After services, Dix took a tour of the facilities and was shocked to find a number of mentally ill women locked up there, held without compassion, without treatment and, even worse, without heat. Dressed in filthy rags, these unfortunates were shivering, huddled together for warmth in a corner of their barren cell. When Dix asked the jailer why these women were kept in an unheated cell, she was told that a stove would be unsafe; besides, he insisted, the insane don't feel cold the way normal people do.

Her strong streak of moral righteousness aroused, Dix brought the women proper clothing and demanded that they be provided with a heated cell. When the jailer refused, she took the matter to court, exposing the pitiful conditions that she had seen. Public officials and some newspapers denounced her as a liar, a slanderer, and a woman meddling in public affairs that were none of her business. But, as it would countless times more, persecution only strengthened her resolve. With the help of the reformers Dr. Samuel Gridley Howe and Charles Sumner, who visited the jail themselves and confirmed her story, she won her first victory for the insane. The women were provided with a clean and heated cell.

Sensing that she had at last found her true calling, Dix was anxious to do more. She consulted leading experts in the field of mental illness, and learned that she was not the first to be concerned about the plight of the insane. Following the lead of French and English reformers, a few American physicians were taking a new view of mental illness. Traditionally, insanity was seen as a mysterious calamity, robbing its victims of their humanity. Because many believed it was a punishment from God for past sins, families were often ashamed of members who were ill, and locked them away in back rooms and barns. Those without a family to care for them, the "pauper insane," usually ended up in jail cells or in the poorhouse, where harsh conditions often made their illness worse. But the doctors Dix spoke with had concluded that mental illness was not a spiritual curse but a physical disease, and one that could often be cured with the right approach. They tried administering to the insane by placing them in new asylums, carefully constructed institutions often set in idyllic rural settings. There, under the watchful eye of kindly attendants, patients were released from their chains and treated with a regimen of respect, orderliness, and healthful exercise.

On the cutting edge of these reforms, Massachusetts had built one of these asylums and passed a law requiring towns to send their mentally ill citizens to the new hospital. But, as Dix found out in East Cambridge, many towns ignored the law, often for cost-saving reasons. The state could hardly complain, however, because their new asylum was already filled to capacity.

Consulting with Howe and Sumner, Dix decided that her first step should be to gather more information by conducting a survey of the treatment of the mentally ill in all of the poorhouses and jails in the state. Once the facts were gathered, she would then use them to press the state legislature into making comprehensive changes. This survey was an enormous undertaking, but she approached it with conviction and energy. Ignoring the pain in her lungs, she traveled hundreds of miles by train, coach, and horseback, visiting facilities in every county of the state. More rugged than the physical challenge was the moral one, as she descended into what historian **Helen Marshall** has called "an inferno of neglect and cruelty." She saw the insane locked into small, filthy stalls, some chained to their beds for decades, others who were beaten into submission, and many who suffered from the same cold and neglect that she had first seen in the East Cambridge jail.

Traveling for more than a year, Dix made a careful record of each case. She summarized the results into a *Memorial* to the state legislature; this document was a pioneering effort in the gathering of social welfare statistics, and a milestone in the history of American reform. After cataloging the many abuses she had seen, she made an impassioned plea to state lawmakers to expand facilities at the state's hospital for the insane. Only in such asylums, she explained, could the mentally ill escape their cruel conditions and receive the kind of scientific treatment that might cure them of their disease.

Because women were not allowed to address the state legislature, Samuel Howe presented the *Memorial* on her behalf. The speech set off a storm of controversy. Many local officials challenged her depiction of their poorhouses and jails, while other critics launched more personal attacks. A proper lady, they wrote, would never have exposed herself to such indecencies. But leading doctors and reformers came to her aid, confirming her findings and defending her character. Public opinion swayed to her side, and lawmakers agreed to expand the state asylum.

Dix's faith had moved a mountain of ignorance and apathy, and she now felt that God had chosen her to pursue this "sacred cause." She set out immediately to tour the jails and poorhouses of Rhode Island, then New York, Pennsylvania, New Jersey, and eventually most other states in the nation. Triumphing over physical pains that troubled her for the rest of her life, she traveled more than 60,000 miles in the next few years and visited many thousands of mentally ill patients in dozens of states. In the 1850s, she expanded her mission abroad, promoting better treatment for the insane in Europe, Russia, and Turkey. She even won an audience with the pope, successfully urging him to reform the Vatican's hospitals.

In each place, her method was the same. She started with an exhaustive fact-finding tour, visiting every mentally ill person she could find in an area. While she had no authority to enter and search most of these places, no jailer ever refused her, awed as they were by her forceful personality and her obvious gentility. Concluding her tour, she would then draft an eloquent memorial, which summarized the horrors she had seen, and propose the creation or expansion of hospitals for the mentally ill.

At a time when women were usually barred from public life, Dix became a widely respected, even beloved, figure. Railroads provided her with free passes as she went on her missions of mercy. She mingled freely with men in power, developing close friendships with governors, senators, and even presidents. But she was careful not to push too hard against the limits that society imposed on her because she was a woman. She rarely addressed state legislatures, for example, preferring to let a male ally speak for her in public. When lobbying for a bill, she stayed behind the scenes, quietly but forcefully making her case to male legislators, winning their support without violating the code of gentility expected of a female of her social class. Rather than challenging men for monopolizing political power, she challenged them to use that power for good. When asked how she had won so many converts to her cause, she answered: "By going to people whose duty it is

to set things right, assuming that they will do so without disturbance being made, and they generally do so."

For the same reason, Dix shunned all personal publicity, considering it unseemly for a woman to seek public honors. She never allowed her supporters to name a hospital in her honor, and when a reporter asked for an interview, she replied, "Nothing could be undertaken which would give me more pain and serious annoyance, which would so trespass on my personal rights and my perception of fitness and propriety." She avoided any controversy that might distract attention from the plight of the mentally ill. As she traveled, she lent her aid to a number of other reform causes, including penal reform, the building of lifeboats and public drinking fountains, and scholarships for young women. But she avoided the topic of women's rights and, although she hated slavery, never spoke against it publicly, fearing it might jeopardize her considerable influence in the Southern states.

While Dix was quiet about the issue of slavery, when the Civil War broke out she was anxious to do her part for the Union cause. Appointed Superintendent of Army Nurses, she organized women volunteers into a nursing corps. She worked tirelessly at the job, but some of the personal qualities that had served her so well as a reformer—her moral righteousness, her strong will, and her perfectionism—became a liability in her new job as the head of a large government bureaucracy. She often clashed with army doctors, who resented her criticisms of their practices. Even her supporters found her to be an ineffective administrator, too inflexible to compromise and unable to delegate authority. Under extremely difficult conditions, the corps of army nurses did much to alleviate suffering and improve conditions in chaotic and unsanitary army hospitals. But, at the conclusion of the war, Dix was relieved to be able to return to her work for the insane.

Dorothea Dix's single-minded commitment to the mentally ill produced remarkable results, transforming the way they were thought about and cared for in much of the world. Over the course of her 40-year career, she was personally responsible for the creation of 32 asylums in the United States, and the improvement and expansion of many more. Perhaps her favorite of these institutions was the state hospital in Trenton, New Jersey, for which she not only won funding but also helped to locate and design. That place she dubbed her "first born child." A permanent apartment was set aside for her there, and in later years this became the closest thing she knew of a home. She died there in 1887, at the age of 85.

SOURCES:

Marshall, Helen E. *Dorothea Dix: Forgotten Samaritan.* Chapel Hill, NC: University of North Carolina Press, 1937.

Schlaifer, Charles and Lucy Freeman. *Heart's Work: Civil War Heroine and Champion of the Mentally Ill, Dorothea Lynde Dix.* NY: Paragon House, 1991.

Wilson, Dorothy Clarke. *Stranger and Traveler: The Story of Dorothea Dix, American Reformer.* Boston, MA: Little, Brown, 1975.

SUGGESTED READING:

Gollaher, David L. *A Voice for the Mad: The Life of Dorothea Dix.* Free Press, 1995.

Rothman, David. *The Discovery of the Asylum: Social Order and Disorder in the New Republic.* Boston, MA: Little, Brown, 1990 (chapts. 5 and 6).

Ernest Freeberg, Ph.D. American History, Emory University, Atlanta, Georgia

Dix, Dorothy (1861–1951).

See Gilmer, Elizabeth Meriwether.

Dixie, Lady Florence (1857–1905)

English explorer and writer. Born in 1857; died in 1905; daughter of the Marquis of Queensberry; married Sir Alexander Dixie, in 1875.

Lady Florence Dixie explored Patagonia (1878–79), served as a war correspondent for the *London Morning Post* in the Boer War (1880–81), and was instrumental in securing the liberty of Cetawayo, king of Zululand. In later years, she was a champion of women's rights. Her books include: *Across Patagonia, A Defense of Zululand and its King,* and *The Child Hunters of Patagonia.*

Djahsh, Zaynab bint (c. 590–c. 640).

See Zaynab bint Jahsh.

Dlasta (fl. 8th c.).

See Valasca.

Dlugoszewski, Lucia (1925—)

American composer, pianist, teacher, writer, and inventor of percussion instruments. Pronunciation: DLOO-go-SHEV-skee. Born on June 16, 1925, in Detroit, Michigan; attended the Detroit Conservatory of Music, Wayne State University, and the Mannes School of Music.

Won the National Institute of Arts and Letters award (1966); composed and taught for the Foundation of Modern Dance.

Lucia Dlugoszewski invented over 100 percussion instruments made of plastic, metal, glass, and wood. The best known was the timbre piano which has bows and plectra in addition to a keyboard. Her musical nature found expression as early as age three when she began writing poems and songs as well as playing music. By six, she was studying under Agelageth Morrison at the Detroit Conservatory of Music, where she gave a recital playing her own music. When Dlugoszewski went to college at Wayne State University, she decided to study medicine, but in 1949 she switched to the arts and went to New York to study piano under **Grete Sultan**. She attended the Mannes School of Music from 1950 until 1951. Felix Salzer and Edgar Varese were her private tutors.

Active in many fields, Dlugoszewski won the Tompkins literary award for poetry in 1947. She was also the first woman to win the Koussevitzky Prize. In the 1960s, she began teaching at New York University and the New School for Social Research. She also began composing for the Foundation for Modern Dance. Many of her compositions were written for the instruments she invented such as *Naked Swift Music* which used the timbre piano, *Concert of Many Rooms and Moving Space* which used four unsheltered rattles, and *Orchestral Radiant Ground.*

John Haag, Athens, Georgia

Dmitrieff, Elizabeth (1851–1910)

Russian-French socialist. Name variations: Elisabeth Dmitriev or Dmitrieva. Born in Russia in 1851; died in 1910; daughter of a Russian noble; married a political prisoner.

Elizabeth Dmitrieff used her marriage to an army officer to attend a university in Switzerland. While there, she met other Russian radicals and became a Marxist. As a member of the Socialist International, she journeyed to London, where she became friends with Karl Marx. From there, she went to Paris and sent Marx detailed descriptions of events of 1870. During the Paris Commune revolt of 1871, Dmitrieff organized the Union of Women for the Defense of Paris and the Care of the Wounded, a branch of the Socialist International. With the Communards defeated, she escaped to Russia, where she married a political prisoner who had been condemned to Siberia. She remained with him in exile until she died in 1910.

Doada (fl. 990–1005)

Scottish princess who was possibly the mother of Macbeth. Name variations: Dovada; (family name) Macalpin. Flourished between 990 and 1005; daughter (or sister) of Malcolm II of Alba (1005–1034), king of Scots (some sources list her as the daughter of Kenneth II); married Findleach of Moray also known as Findlaech Mac Ruaridh (Macrory), mormaer (ruler) of Moray, around 1004; children: possibly Macbeth or Machethad, Machetad, Macbethad, often confused with MacHeth in later sources (c. 1005–1057), king of Scotland (r. 1040–1054, who married *Gruoch [Lady Macbeth]).

Macbeth's father was Findlaech Mac Ruaridh, the mormaer (ruler) of Moray, and his mother, whose identity cannot be proven, may have been Doada, a daughter (or sister) of Scotland's King Malcolm II (1005–34). In 1020, Tigernach, an Irish writer, recorded that "Findlaech . . . mormaer of Moray, was slain by the sons of his brother Maelbrigte," while another source only stated that he was "killed by his own people." Although this unadorned account does not offer any motivation for the killing of Doada's husband, it has been suggested that it represented dissatisfaction with the marriage alliance between Findlaech and Doada and the close ties this marriage entailed between these two royal houses. In any event, in 1032, Gillacomgain, one of Findlaech's nephews who had been involved in his killing and who had assumed the title of mormaer, "was burned, along with fifty of his men," according to the *Annals of Ulster,* another Irish source. Setting fire to an enemy's residence was then a common means of eliminating one's enemies, and it is possible that Macbeth killed his cousin to avenge his father's death.

Doan, Catriona Le May (b. 1970).

See Le May Doan, Catriona.

Dobravy of Bohemia (d. 977)

Duchess of Poland. Name variations: Dubravka or Dubrawka; family name Premysl. Died in 977; daughter of Boleslas or Boleslav I the Cruel, duke of Bohemia (r. 929–967); sister of Boleslav II (d. 999), duke of Bohemia (r. 967–999); married Mieczislaw also known as Burislaf or Mieszko I (c. 922–992), duke of Poland (r. 960–992); children: *Gunhilda of Poland (mother of King Canute the Great of Denmark); Boleslav Chrobry also known as Boleslaw the Brave (c. 967–1025), king of Poland (r. 992–1025); Mieszko; Swietopelk; Lambert. Mieszko I's second wife was *Oda of Germany and North Marck.

Dobson, Emily (1842–1934)

Australian philanthropist. Born Emily Lempriere on October 10, 1842, at Port Arthur, Van Diemen's Land (Tasmania); died on June 5, 1934, in Hobart; daughter of Thomas James (a public servant and artist) and Charlotte (Smith) Lempriere; married Henry Dobson (a lawyer, politician, member of the Tasmanian Legislative Assembly, 1891, and premier, 1892–94), on February 4, 1868; children: two sons and three daughters.

Emily Dobson became involved in philanthropy after her marriage to Henry Dobson, whose wealth afforded her both leisure and unlimited resources. One of her earliest campaigns was for improved sanitation (1891). Following a typhoid epidemic, she organized a petition drive for an improved sewage system and formed the Women's Sanitation Association to educate women on sanitary procedures and to instigate house-to-house visits. During the depression of the 1890s, when her husband was premier of Tasmania, she worked with the Benevolent Society and several church groups to organize a soup kitchen, which supplied up to 1,000 meals a day. In 1892, she was a founding president of the Ministering Children's League and later worked with the Society for the Protection of Children. The Society helped secure an Infant Life Protection Act in 1907, permitting inspection without notice of homes where infants were being tended for payment.

Dobson was also committed to women's social and legal rights. As a founding member of the Tasmanian National Council of Women in 1899, and as president from 1906 to 1934, she traveled at her own expense to the quinquennial conferences and was accepted as the leader of the Australian delegation for 20 years. Dobson supported numerous other causes and organizations as well, including free kindergartens, improved treatment for the blind and deaf, temperance, the Art Society, and the Girl Guides. In 1919, The Tasmanian Nation Council of Women honored her by establishing the Emily Dobson Philanthropic Prize Competition for welfare organizations.

Dobson, Rosemary (1920—)

Australian poet whose verse reflects a passion for art. Born on June 18, 1920, in Sydney, Australia; daughter of Arthur Austin Greaves Dobson (a civil engineer) *and Marjorie Caldwell Dobson; attended the University of Sydney; married Alexander Bolton (a publisher), on June 12, 1951; children: Lissant Mary; Robert Thorley; Ian Alexander.*

Published first collection of poetry (1944); won Sydney Morning Herald *poetry prize (1948); explored Europe (1966–71); received prize from Fellowship of Australian Writers (1979).*

Selected writings: In a Convex Mirror *(1944);* The Ship of Ice and Other Poems *(1948);* Focus on Ray Crooke *(1971);* Three Poems on Water-Springs, *(1973);* Greek Coins: A Sequence of Poems *(1977);* Over the Frontier *(1978);* Summer Press *(1987);* Collected Poems *(1991).*

Australian writer Rosemary Dobson is the granddaughter of a British poet, Austin Dobson, but her own verse reflects both the past—in her love of classical civilizations—as well as the modern era with its feminist consciousness. Born in 1920, in Sydney, Australia, Dobson took classes at the University of Sydney and also worked as an art teacher. During World War II, she went to work at the publishing house Angus & Robertson, and there came to know other Australian writers of her day. Her first volume of poetry, *In a Convex Mirror*, was published by her employer in 1944; her second, The *Ship of Ice and Other Poems*, won her the *Sydney Morning Herald*'s poetry prize in 1948.

In 1951, Dobson married Alexander Bolton, with whom she would have three children, and continued to write verse. She lived in London during the late 1960s when her husband worked there for Angus & Robertson, and was able to spend time traveling through Europe and visiting significant cultural sites; her poetry has often been inspired by the visual—such as paintings from Renaissance Italy, or the historical, such as life in ancient Greece. As a mid-career poet, Dobson began to inject more personal themes into her work, touching upon her roles as a wife, mother, and writer.

Her husband later founded Brindabella Press, which would issue several works of Dobson's, including *Three Poems on Water-Springs* (1973) and *Greek Coins: A Sequence of Poems* (1977). In 1979, she was honored with the Fellowship of Australian Writers' Robert Frost Award (subsequently called the Christopher Brennan Award). Her later collections of verse include the titles *Summer Press* (1987) and *Collected Poems* (1991). Dobson has also edited several anthologies of poetry and has been involved in the translation of Russian works into English,

most notably with David Campbell on *Seven Russian Poets: Imitations*, published in 1979.

SOURCES:
Contemporary Authors, Vol. 77–80. Detroit, MI: Gale Research, 1979.

Carol Brennan,
Grosse Pointe, Michigan.

Dod, Charlotte (1871–1960)

British tennis champion who was also the first superstar of women's sports as an outstanding skater, tobogganer, and field hockey player. Name variations: Lottie Dod. Born Charlotte Dod on September 24, 1871; died in a nursing home on June 26 or 27, 1960, in Bournemouth, England; fourth and youngest child of a cotton broker; grew up in Edgeworth House, in Bebington, Cheshire.

Won Wimbledon singles championship five times (1887, 1888, 1891, 1892, 1893); won Wimbledon doubles championship (1886, 1887, 1888); won Wimbledon mixed-doubles championship (1889 and 1892); at 15½, was youngest player ever to play at Wimbledon; was also the first woman to complete the Cresta bobsled run at St. Moritz; took the British women's golf championship (1904); won the silver medal for archery in the London Olympics (1908).

Long before there was a *Babe Didrikson Zaharias, Charlotte "Lottie" Dod became the first superstar of women's sports. Though the Victorian era was known for its restrictions on women, many defied convention from the outset. One such individual was Charlotte Dod (who disliked the girlish name Lottie). She entered Wimbledon in 1887 and would dominate the tournament for the next seven years. Dubbed the "Little Wonder," at age 13 Dod took on Britain's first tennis queen, *Maud Watson, and almost defeated her. Although some form of tennis had been played for years, Major Walter Wingfield introduced the modern game in 1874. Shortly thereafter, Dod's competitive play helped make it a popular sport for women.

Despite her youth (at 15½, she was the youngest player to ever enter Wimbledon), Dod had studied the men's game carefully and was much more aggressive than most other female players. When she won at Wimbledon in 1887, her competitors were wearing the customary tennis attire: lawn party dresses. Long skirts, long sleeves, and corsets (which were especially cumbersome) hardly enhanced women's athletic abilities, and it would not be until the 1920s that most women would stop wearing these restricting outfits on the court. During Dod's first Wimbledon win, she wore her school uniform, which was calf length, and eliminated the corset. Her aggressive style combined with the freedom of her clothing made her an unbeatable opponent. She won the doubles championship at Wimbledon from 1886 to 1888 and the mixed doubles in 1889 and 1892. Between 1886 and 1900, the top position in women's tennis swung back and forth between Dod and *Blanche Bingley Hillyard; between them, they could claim 11 Wimbledon singles titles. Charlotte Dod lost only five singles matches during her entire career, which is probably why she decided to cast about for tougher competition in other sports.

When she was 21, Charlotte Dod retired from the courts but not from competition. She also played golf, archery, and field hockey, loved the bobsled, and was an excellent figure skater. In 1894, she was the first woman to make the Cresta bobsled run at St. Moritz. In 1904, she won the British national golf championship at Troon, Scotland. In 1908, she took the silver medal for archery in the 1908 London Olympics. Twice, she played on England's field hockey team against Ireland, and later she became a judge in international figure-skating competitions. She was inducted into the International Women's Hall of Fame in 1986. When Charlotte Dod died in a nursing home on the southern coast of England at 88, it was said she was listening to the Wimbledon championships on the radio.

SOURCES:

Condon, Robert J. *Great Women Athletes of the 20th Century.* Jefferson, North Carolina: McFarland, 1991.

King, Billie Jean with Cynthia Starr. *We Have Come a Long Way: The Story of Women's Tennis.* NY: McGraw-Hill, 1988.

"Lottie Dod Dies at 88," in *The New York Times.* June 28, 1960, p. 31.

"Miss Lottie Dod," in *The Times* [London]. June 28, 1960, p. 15.

Young, Mark, ed. *The Guinness Book of Sports Records.* NY: Facts on File, 1992.

Karin Loewen Haag,
Athens, Georgia

Doda (fl. 1040)

*Duchess of Lower Lorraine. Flourished around 1040; married Godfrey the Bearded, duke of Lower Lorraine; children: Godfrey the Hunchback (d. 1076, who married *Matilda of Tuscany [1046–1115]); *Ida of Lorraine (1040–1113, who married Eustace II, count of Boulogne).*

Dodane (fl. 820–843).

See Dhuoda of Septimania.

Dode (b. 586)

Frankish noblewoman. Name variations: Doda; Ode de Heristal; Ode of Heristal or Heristol. Born in 586; married Arnoldus also known as Arnulf, bishop of Metz (d. 639); children: Ansegisal, mayor of Austrasia (r. 632–638).

Dodge, Mabel (1879–1962).

See Luhan, Mabel Dodge.

Dodge, Mary Abigail (1833–1896)

American author who wrote under the name Gail Hamilton. Name variations: (pseudonym) Gail Hamilton. Born in Hamilton, Massachusetts, on March 31, 1833; died in Hamilton, Massachusetts, on August 17, 1896; third daughter and the last of seven children of James Brown (a farmer) and Hannah (Stanwood) Dodge; attended schools in Hamilton and Cambridge, Massachusetts; graduated from Ipswich Female Seminary, Ipswich, Massachusetts, in 1850.

Selected writings: Country Living and Country Thinking *(1861);* Courage! *(1862);* Gala Days *(1863);* A Call to My Countrywomen *(1863);* Stumbling-Blocks *(1864);* A New Atmosphere *(1865);* Scientific Farming *(1865);* Skirmishes and Sketches *(1865);* Red Letter Days in Applethorpe *(1866);* Summer Rest *(1866);* Wool Gathering *(1868);* Woman's Wrong *(1868);* Memorial to Mrs. Hannah Stanwood Dodge *(1869);* A Battle of the Books *(1870);* Little Folk Life *(1872);* Woman's Worth and Worthlessness *(1872);* Child World *(1873);* Twelve Miles from a Lemon *(1874);* Nursery Noonings *(1875);* Sermons to the Clergy *(1876);* First Love Is Best *(1877);* What Think Ye of Christ *(1877);* Our Common School System *(1880);* Divine Guidance *(1881);* The Spent Bullet *(1882);* The Insuppressible Book *(1885);* A Washington Bible Class *(1891);* English Kings in a Nutshell *(1893);* Biography of James G. Blaine *(1893);* X-Rays *(1896);* Gail Hamilton's Life in Letters *(ed. H.A. Dodge, 1901);* Chips, Fragments and Vestiges *(ed. H.A. Dodge, 1902).*

Mary Abigail Dodge, described by her mother Hannah as a stubborn child, graduated from the Ipswich Female Seminary at age 17 and embarked on a teaching career. After several successful years in the classroom, divided between her alma mater and schools in Hartford, Connecticut, Dodge wearied of the long hours and low wages and decided to try her hand at professional writing. In 1858, she moved to Washington, D.C., where she became the governess to the children of Gamaliel Bailey, editor of the antislavery *National Era*, to whom she had sent some of her early poetry and prose. It was Bailey who launched her writing career, which gained momentum after her work appeared in several prestigious publications, including the *Atlantic Monthly*. Around this time, in what would become a lifelong effort to avoid publicity, Dodge adopted the pen name of Gail Hamilton.

From 1860 to 1868, Dodge returned home to care for her ailing mother, during which time she published two collections of essays, *Country Living and Country Thinking* and *A New Atmosphere*. In addition to her writing, she worked as an assistant editor for the children's magazine *Our Young Folks*. In 1870, she published *Battle of the Books*, a fictionalized account of her break with her first publisher, Ticknor and Fields of Boston, who had paid her less than the customary 10% royalty. By the 1880s, Dodge's essays were so much in demand that she was asking $200 per article, regardless of length.

Dodge is most noted for her writings during the 1870s, when she spent much of each year in the home of Congressman James G. Blaine, whose wife was her first cousin. Blaine—who was speaker of the house, secretary of state, and the 1884 Republican presidential candidate—recognized Dodge's literary talent and put her to work as his political ghostwriter. She is credited with many of his speeches and worked with him on his book *Twenty Years of Congress*. There are some who believe that a series of columns she wrote for the *New York Herald Tribune* in 1877 were actually a cover for Blaine's opinions.

Dodge was known for her lively, witty, and opinionated style, and much of her work is feminist in viewpoint. Proclaiming her own personal and professional independence and encouraging it in others, she had little patience with the then fashionable trend that encouraged feminine frivolity or the pretense of helplessness. In her book *Country Living and Country Thinking*, based on her own experience in running her family farm, Dodge urges women to think of careers other than marriage. In *Woman's Worth and Worthlessness*, she points out that a woman is not "supported" by a man "when she works as hard in the house as he does out of it." Although Dodge strongly defended women's right to equal educational and occupational opportunities, she opposed suffrage on the grounds that it would be too much of a burden on women whose superior role was to provide spiritual guidance to the family and to society as a whole.

In 1895, Dodge was working on the *Biography of James G. Blaine*, when she suffered a paralytic stroke that left her unconscious for several weeks. She recovered sufficiently to dictate an account of the experience (*X-Rays*) before her death in August 1896.

SUGGESTED READING:

Dodge, H. Augusta, ed. *Gail Hamilton's Life in Letters*. Vol I and II. Lee and Shepard, 1901.

Barbara Morgan,
Melrose, Massachusetts

Dodge, Mary Mapes (1831–1905)

American, known for her important contributions to children's literature, both as author of **Hans Brinker; or, The Silver Skates** *and as editor of* **St. Nicholas.** *Born Mary Elizabeth Mapes in New York City on January 26, 1831 (some sources cite 1803 or 1838); died of cancer in Onteora, New York, on August 21, 1905; daughter of James Jay Mapes (an inventor, agriculturist, chemist, artist, and editor) and Sophia (Furman) Mapes; educated at home by tutors and governesses; married William Dodge (a lawyer), on September 13, 1851; children: James ("Jamie") Mapes (b. June 20, 1852); Harrington ("Harry") Mapes (b. November 15, 1855–1881).*

After sudden death of husband of unknown causes, returned with her sons to her family home, Mapleridge, in Waverly, New Jersey (1858); became editor of her father's United States Journal *(1861); began contributing adult stories to* Harper's New Monthly Magazine *(1863); published book for boys,* The Irvington Stories *(1864); because of long standing interest in Holland, penned* Hans Brinker; or, The Silver Skates *(1865); inherited her father's considerable debts at the time of his death (1866); began writing for children's periodical, the* Riverside Magazine *(1867); published* A Few Friends and How They Amused Themselves, *a love story with descriptions of 20 games included (1868); became associate editor of weekly periodical,* Hearth and Home *(1868–73); founded and edited Scribner's children's periodical,* St. Nicholas *(1873); gained steady recognition with publication of foreign editions of* Hans Brinker *as well as four more of her books (1870s); lost Waverly property and a great deal of money in legal judgment (1881);*

Mary
Abigail
Dodge

lost youngest son to typhoid (1881); in a break from Scribner's, took Donald and Dorothy *to Roberts Brothers, which published it (1883); purchased a cottage in Onteora, New York, an artists' colony, where she spent her summers (1888); published* The Land of Pluck *and* When Life Is Young *(1894).*

Selected writings: The Irvington Stories *(1864);* Hans Brinker; or, The Silver Skates: A Story of Life in Holland *(1865);* A Few Friends and How They Amused Themselves *(1868);* Rhymes and Jingles *(1874);* Theophilus and Others *(1876);* Along the Way *(1879)* Donald and Dorothy *(1883);* The Land of Pluck: Stories and Sketches for Young Folk *(1894);* When Life Is Young: A Collection of Verse for Boys and Girls *(1894);* Poems and Verses *(1904).*

The second of five surviving children of James Jay and **Sophia Furman Mapes**, Mary Elizabeth ("Lizzie") was born on January 26, most probably in 1831, although there is some question about the exact year. Both her parents came from prominent New York families, and James Jay Mapes, who some described as a maverick genius, was an inventor, agriculturist, chemist, artist, and editor. Although talented in many fields, he was not well paid and his financial affairs were at times precarious. Both parents were devoted and provided their children with a good education at home where they were instructed by tutors and governesses. All the children's lives were enriched by a succession of literary and scientific figures who often visited their home, including Horace Greeley, William Cullen Bryant, and John Ericsson, who built the first armored turret ship, the *Monitor*, during the Civil War. From an early age, Lizzie was interested in music and art.

Around 1846, James Mapes purchased a run-down farm called Mapleridge at Waverly, New Jersey, as a place where he could demonstrate some of his agricultural methods and as a home for his family. They moved there in 1847. This purchase was financed by a friend from New York, a lawyer named William Dodge, whom

Lizzie eventually married on September 13, 1851. William was 15 years older than Lizzie, and it is assumed that their marriage was successful. The couple moved to William's family home in New York City, where several generations lived together. Two sons were born to the couple: Jamie Dodge (June 20, 1852) and Harry Dodge (November 15, 1855). Lizzie's placid family life was shattered in 1858, when William Dodge died suddenly. Exactly what occurred is uncertain, but records show death was by drowning. There is a possibility that he committed suicide. After his burial on November 11, 1858, Lizzie Dodge and her sons returned to Mapleridge and lived with her family. Devoted to her sons, she spent hours every day reading and talking to them and taking part in their activities at a special place in an old building near Mapleridge, which she called "The Den." She also used this location as a place to write. In an attempt to divert his daughter's mind from her tragedy, James Mapes urged Lizzie to begin writing, and in 1861, he purchased the *United States Journal*, adding this to a periodical he had helped to found called *Working Farmer*. Dodge became editor of this new section while continuing to write using several pseudonyms for both the *Farmer* and the *Journal*. She soon began sending articles to other publications, and in 1863, she started contributing adult stories to *Harper's New Monthly Magazine*. As suggested by James Mapes, Lizzie wrote a book for boys, and the result, *The Irvington Stories,* was published by James O'Kane in November 1864. Though this book was not a bestseller, it was popular enough to induce her to begin another book.

Although she had never been to Holland, she had always wanted to write a book about that country and had been collecting material for years. The result of her research was *Hans Brinker; or The Silver Skates*, which was published by O'Kane in December 1865, despite his reservations. This book became a bestseller (sales of 300,000 were needed at that time) in 1865, along with the American edition of Charles Dickens' *Our Mutual Friend*. The popularity of *Hans Brinker* was even greater when it was republished by Scribner's in the next decade. Dodge's philosophy of children's literature, evident in this book, was that it should provide intellectual stimulation but should discourage "emotional precocity." Dodge's happiness over the success of *Hans Brinker* was subdued by the death of her son Jamie less than a month after the book's publication.

Dodge became part of the New York literary circle, and among her friends was Horace E. Scudder, the editor of the *Riverside Magazine for*

From the television movie Hans Brinker or the Silver Skates, *based on the novel by Mary Mapes Dodge.*

Young People (published 1867–70), a quality periodical for children. She wrote an article for him reviewing toys and games, which included two card games she invented, The Protean Cards and The Stratford Game. Her interest in games culminated in a book for adults called *A Few Friends* *and How They Amused Themselves*, a combination love story with descriptions of 20 pastimes, which was published by Lippincott in November 1868. That same year, Dodge accepted the position of associate editor for a new weekly periodical, *Hearth and Home*, and remained there until

1873. At the same time she was busy working at *Hearth and Home*, she also continued to write for the *Riverside Magazine* (until its demise in 1870) and for adult periodicals such as *Scribner's Monthly* and *Atlantic Monthly*.

During the early 1870s, Mary Elizabeth Dodge began to use the name of Mary Mapes Dodge to avoid confusion with two other authors with the same name—**Mary Barker Dodge**, a poet, and *Mary Abigail Dodge (1833–1896), who wrote under the name Gail Hamilton. In 1872 yet another opportunity presented itself, when Josiah Holland and Roswell Smith, who with Charles Scribner had founded *Scribner's Monthly*, asked Dodge to contribute her thoughts about adding a children's periodical to the Scribner line. She was soon asked to found and edit such a periodical, and she left *Hearth and Home* in March 1873, devoting her energies to establishing *St. Nicholas: Scribner's Illustrated Magazine for Girls and Boys*. That same year, she and her son Harry took a long awaited trip to Europe and enjoyed sightseeing, meeting literary contemporaries and visiting the Netherlands. Upon her return, the first issue of *St. Nicholas* was published in November 1873. The magazine was successful from the start, partly because of the way Dodge involved her readers in many activities. Wonderful illustrations by artists including Reginald Birch, George Wharton Edwards, Oliver Herford, Joseph Pennell, Arthur Rackham, Frederic Remington and N.C. Wyeth were featured in the publication. *St. Nicholas* also published the work of noted authors and poets, including *Louisa May Alcott, Noah Brooks, Edward Eggleston, *Lucretia Peabody Hale, John Townsend Trowbridge, Thomas Bailey Aldrich, Bret Harte, *Sarah Orne Jewett, Horace E. Scudder, Henry Wadsworth Longfellow, John Greenleaf Whittier, and Alfred Tennyson.

During the 1870s, Dodge was at the pinnacle of her success and her work received wide recognition. *Hans Brinker* was revived again, and in 1875, a French edition of it and *Little Women* won the Montyon prize of 1,500 francs, given by the French Academy for the book that each year rendered the greatest service to humanity. The next year an Italian edition of *Hans Brinker* appeared. In addition, four other books by Dodge were published during this decade: *Rhymes and Jingles* (1874), *Baby Days: A Selection of Songs, Stories, and Pictures, for Very Little Folks* (1877), *Theophilus and Others* (1876) and *Along the Way* (1879). What could have become a major crisis for Dodge came in 1877, when Frank Stockton resigned as assistant editor

of *St. Nicholas* because of bad health. However, the position was filled ably by William Fayal Clarke, who became a close friend of Dodge and her family, even moving into the Dodges' boardinghouse where he was a part of the household for almost 20 years.

From 1879 to 1881, Dodge had a string of bad luck: she suffered from ill health, a legal judgment resulted in the loss of the Waverly property and a great deal of money, and her son Harry was plagued by poor health. In September 1879, Harry Dodge contracted typhoid and died unexpectedly in February 1881. That same year, Roswell Smith bought out Josiah Holland and Charles Scribner to form the Century Company, which took over the publication of *St. Nicholas*. During this period, Dodge began making strong demands of her publisher, which Charles Scribner was unwilling to meet. Miffed because she felt her books had not been promoted properly and upset over personal and financial problems, Dodge took her novel, *Donald and Dorothy*, to Roberts Brothers, which published it in November 1883. This book never attracted the attention of her earlier classic.

Following Harry Dodge's death, Mary Dodge's own health suffered. Overworked and ill, she took a trip to Europe for rest in 1886, and there she met *Candace Wheeler, who was promoting a colony at Onteora Park in the Catskills, a place where writers and artists could relax. In 1888, Dodge purchased a cottage at Onteora Park and spent all her summers there for the rest of her life. *St. Nicholas* continued to attract new contributors in its second and third decades, including *Frances Hodgson Burnett, Rudyard Kipling, John Bennet, Howard Pyle, Theodore Roosevelt and Mark Twain. In 1894, two of Dodge's books were published by the Century Company, *The Land of Pluck*, short works mostly culled from *St. Nicholas*, and *When Life is Young*, a book of verses. In 1898, exhausted by her own failing health and from nursing Fayal Clarke after an appendectomy, Dodge was ordered by her doctor and her employer to take a trip to Europe to recuperate. Her health, however, continued to deteriorate, and while at Onteora, Dodge died of cancer on August 21, 1905. She was buried in Evergreen Cemetery in Elizabeth, New Jersey. After her death, Clarke continued as editor at *St. Nicholas* until 1927. The magazine was sold in 1930, after which it rapidly deteriorated and finally ceased publication in 1940.

SOURCES:

Karrenbrock, Marilyn H. "Mary Mapes Dodge," in *Dictionary of Literary Biography*. Vol. 42. Detroit, MI: Gale Research, 1985, pp. 146–160.

Jo Anne Meginnes,
freelance writer, Brookfield, Vermont

Doenhoff, Marion (b. 1909).

See Dönhoff, Marion.

Dohm, Hedwig (1831–1919)

German author and influential feminist publicist.
Born Hedwig Schleh in Berlin, Germany, on September 20, 1831; died in Berlin on June 1, 1919; married (Wilhelm) Ernst Dohm (1819–1883, a journalist); children: four daughters and one son.

Selected writings: Die Antifeministen: Ein Buch der Verteidigung *(1902);* Die wissenschaftliche Emancipation der Frau *(1873);* Erinnerungen; Der Frauen Natur und Recht: Zur Frauenfrage: Zwei Abhandlungen über Eigenschaften und Stimmrecht der Frauen *(1876);* Was die Pastoren von den Frauen denken *(1872);* Wie die Frauen werden—Werde, die du bist *(1896).*

Born the 11th of 18 children, Hedwig Schleh grew up in an assimilated Jewish family in Berlin. Her father, who worked in the sales division of his family's tobacco factory and would eventually inherit the firm, only had time for his family on Sundays. Her overworked mother, quite overwhelmed by the never-ending physical and emotional demands of raising 18 children (two of whom died), often dealt with her frustrations by being verbally abusive. Fearing physical punishment and convinced that her mother had no understanding of her needs, young Hedwig often retreated for solace into her own comforting world of books and daydreams. Probably because her parents wanted to keep Hedwig at home longer in order to have her care for her younger siblings, her date of birth was given as 1833 instead of the correct year, 1831. She soon became aware of the subordinate position that she, as a young woman, had been born into when it was announced that whereas her brothers would be able to continue their educations by enrolling in Gymnasium, this path was closed to her. A major event in Hedwig Schleh's life took place in 1848 when, despite having been forbidden by her parents to walk about in a Berlin torn by revolutionary tumults, she witnessed a bloody clash between government forces and poorly armed revolutionaries. Seeing a young student die before her eyes, Hedwig was transformed by the emotionally searing event into a "foe of all armed authority and a partisan of all struggles for liberation," writes her granddaughter **Hedda Korsch**.

Hedwig Schleh escaped from the tense and stifling atmosphere of the parental home in 1853 when she married the journalist Ernst Dohm (1819–1883). Like herself from an assimilated Jewish family—his name at birth was Elias Levy—Ernst was a talented journalist and political liberal who, unlike many enemies of autocracy, decided to remain in Germany after the suppression of the revolutionary upheavals of 1848. Starting in 1848, Ernst Dohm worked on the staff of a lively humor magazine named *Kladderadatsch*. Within a year, he became editor-in-chief of this journal, quickly turning it into a rapier-like literary force that provided satirical commentary not only on social mores but on Germany's repressive political environment as well. As the mother of five children (her only son would die young), Hedwig Dohm was at first unable to be more than a passive observer of the larger stage of German public life. At home, however, she was encouraged in her literary ambitions by her husband, who recognized his wife's intellectual gifts and with whom Hedwig had countless hours of lively discussions covering the landscape of politics and the arts. Dohm's first published work, a historical study of Spanish literature, was a substantial scholarly achievement and gave her the confidence to continue writing.

By the early 1870s, the Dohm children were growing up to adulthood and their mother could now begin the literary career she had long yearned for. In 1872, she published her first political work, *Was die Pastoren von den Frauen denken* (*What the Clergy Thinks About Women*), as a response to two pamphlets by the now-forgotten authors, Philipp von Nathusius and Hermann Jacobi, conservatives who argued that access to higher education would harm women both physically and psychologically. They had also attacked contemporary advocates of women's emancipation like John Stuart Mill and Germany's *Fanny Lewald. In her spirited response, Dohm asserted that the so-called "natural laws" that restricted women to roles as *Hausfrauen* and mothers were in fact constructs devised by males to suppress female potential and serve their own selfish interests. The spheres closed to women were those that bestowed influence, status, and power to the males fortunate enough to have careers within them. Asking why an average bourgeois woman should not be allowed to earn her own living if she desired such a life, Dohm argued that along with other basic human rights, women now had a right to demand full access to advanced education and careers.

The debate and controversy touched off by Dohm's skewering of the clergy was followed two years later by an even more confident and detailed polemic discussing the same problems: *Die wissenschaftliche Emancipation der Frau* (*The Scientific Emancipation of Women*). In this book, she refuted the arguments of the renowned Munich anatomist and physiologist Theodor L.W. von Bischof who argued vociferously that women should be excluded from the study and practice of medicine. Drawing on an extensive bibliography of historical and sociological source materials, Dohm again saw the underlying arguments advanced by, in this case, a noted scholar as being little more than an attempt by powerful males to maintain lucrative and prestigious professional monopolies. Excluding women made it easier for some males to amass great wealth and power that did not have to be defended against a newly emerging cadre of talented and ambitious females. Among the reforms she advocated in this book were sex education for girls and a national system of co-educational schools. In yet another book on the same themes, *Der Frauen Natur und Recht* (*The Nature and Rights of Women*, 1876), Hedwig Dohm continued her well-researched debate with feminism's foes, arguing eloquently that in the final analysis "Human rights have no gender" ("Die Menschenrechte haben kein Geschlecht"). During these same years (in 1873 and again in 1876), she was one of the few German feminists to advocate the vote for women—at a time when the leadership of the German women's movement looked upon this demand as being essentially "premature." Although personally shy and intensely private, in 1888 Dohm founded the "Deutsche Frauenverein Reform" and from 1888 through 1901 also served on the governing board of the Verein "Frauenwohl."

Hedwig Dohm campaigned with great intellectual vigor not only as an often feared polemicist but as a novelist as well. In her 1894 Novelle, *Werde, die Du bist* (*Become Who You Are*), she showed how a woman, while having led a seemingly exemplary life as a housewife and mother, can succumb to madness because the social role chosen for her denied her love, self-fulfillment, and a positive place in the larger society outside of hearth and home. The central figure, Agnes Schmidt, only finds her way out of a mental breakdown after her husband's death and a painfully achieved level of self-awareness.

In *Sibilla Dalmar, Schicksale einer Seele,* and *Christa Roland,* an important trilogy of novels published between 1896 and 1902, Hedwig Dohm continued to explore the triumphs and tragedies of women who in her own day were struggling against ancient and powerful pa-triarchal regimes. *Schicksale einer Seele* (*Fates of a Soul,* 1899) shows how a woman who refuses to conform to society's expectations can expect to have any sense of self-worth within her soul crushed and destroyed. In excruciating detail, Dohm shows how the main character, Marlene, is drained of a positive identity at the level of ordinary daily life within the bosom of her own family. Marlene is rescued from her state of demoralization by an older woman, Charlotte von Krüger, who teaches her to view herself from a radically different (and positive) perspective. The remaining novels in Dohm's trilogy, *Sibilla Dalmar* (1896) and *Christa Roland* (1902), explore similar themes of feminine liberation and self-realization. The pressure to marry for financial considerations is examined from a critical perspective, and in the case of Sibilla her new thinking on this issue brings her to the conclusion that her own loveless marriage had essentially been little better than a thinly disguised form of prostitution. As for the character of Christa Roland, she enters into her marriage with doubts about her role, but wonders whether in fact she should not accept the traditional place of subordination. Once she is married, however, her spirits revive, she refuses to accept the old roles, and she works to develop a new conception of marriage based on a retention of individuality for each partner in the union.

Believing that she had made her points in her works of fiction, at the start of the 20th century Hedwig Dohm returned to the genre of polemical writing. Although she had now attained the age of 70, she refused to slow down. In her 1902 book *Die Antifeministen* (*The Antifeminists*), she provided her readers with a convenient anatomy of the types of male opponents to women's rights. All of these individuals, she noted, were unqualified to pass judgment on what constituted the "true nature" of women. At the same time, Dohm was not afraid to step on some female toes as well, arguing in the chapter "Woman against Woman" that some successful women collude with men to become "social males," uncritically defending and advancing a male value system that in the final analysis is destructive to all of humanity. Dohm expressed her thoughts on this issue strongly, noting that "absolutely the last thing I ever wanted to be was—a man."

In her 1903 book *Die Mütter* (*The Mothers*), an aging but still vital Hedwig Dohm addressed her fellow seniors:

> Listen, old woman, what another old woman tells you: make an effort. Have the courage to live. Don't think for a moment

about your age. Age is an enemy—fight it. Do what gives you pleasure. . . . If you like it and it is comfortable, have your white hair floating free. Join the learners. . . . There are no herbs against death but there are many herbs against the early death of woman. The most effective is unconditional emancipation for women and with it the salvation from that brutal myth that her right of existence is based on her sexuality only.

During the final decades of her long life, Hedwig Dohm remained intellectually active and enjoyed travel and visits to her daughters, grandchildren, and great-grandchildren. Her apartment in Berlin's Tiergartenstrasse was a salon frequented by many of the German capital's most influential intellectuals and politicians, including *Helene Lange, *Adele Schreiber, *Lou Andreas-Salomé, *Else Lasker-Schüler, and *Gabriele Reuter. She remained sensitive to the needs of the weak and oppressed, arguing in an article published shortly before the outbreak of World War I that a child at birth possessed basic rights. These rights were social, and included the right of every child—and its mother—to a life that was decent, humane, and materially secure.

An essential optimist, Hedwig Dohm was profoundly shaken by the start of World War I in the summer of 1914. As the war destroyed millions of lives and incalculable material and spiritual wealth, she ignored the infirmities of old age and put pen to paper. In her fiery essay "The Misuse of Death," written in 1915 but not published until 1917 in the avant-garde journal *Die Aktion,* Dohm indicted the apparatus of the modern state for ignoring the lives and hopes of the countless individuals comprising it, thus making all but inevitable the moral catastrophe that is modern total war. In late May 1919, seriously ill with influenza, Dohm penned her last literary piece. In this article, entitled "On the Deathbed," she looked back at the catastrophic war that had been recently concluded, describing it sarcastically as the "will to self-destruction." She informed her readers that the war was now making her suffocate by bringing on a "laughing fit unto death." A fighter to the end, Hedwig Dohm died of influenza in Berlin on June 1, 1919.

SOURCES:

Altbach, Edith Hoshino, *et al.,* eds. *German Feminism: Readings in Politics and Literature.* Albany, NY: State University of New York Press, 1984.

Braatz, Ilse. "Dohm, Hedwig" in Edmund Jacoby, ed. *Lexikon Linker Leitfiguren.* Frankfurt am Main: Büchergilde Gutenberg, 1988, pp. 93–94.

Brandt, Heike. *Die Menschenrechte haben kein Geschlecht: Die Lebensgeschichte der Hedwig Dohm.* Weinheim: Beltz & Gelberg Verlag, 1989.

Dohm, Hedwig. *Die Antifeministen: Ein Buch der Verteidigung.* Frankfurt am Main: Verlag Arndstrasse, 1976 (reprint of the 1902 edition published by Dümmler Verlag, Berlin).

———. *Emanzipation.* Zurich: ALA Verlag, 1977 (reprint of her *Die wissenschaftliche Emancipation der Frau* [Berlin: Wedekind & Schwieger, 1873]).

———. *Erinnerungen.* Edited by Berta Rahm. Zurich: ALA Verlag, 1980.

———. *Der Frauen Natur und Recht: Zur Frauenfrage. Zwei Abhandlungen über Eigenschaften und Stimmrecht der Frauen.* Neunkirch: ALA Verlag, 1986 (reprint of Berlin edition of 1876).

———. *Was die Pastoren von den Frauen denken.* Zurich: ALA Verlag, 1986 (reprint of the 1872 edition published by Schlingmann Verlag, Berlin).

———. *Wie die Frauen werden—Werde, die du bist.* Frankfurt am Main: Verlag Arndstrasse, 1977 (reprint of the 1896 edition published by Schottländer Verlag, Breslau).

———. *Women's Nature and Privilege.* Translated by Constance Campbell. Westport, CT: Hyperion Press, 1976.

Duelli-Klein, Renate. "Hedwig Dohm: Passionate Theorist (1833–1919)," in Dale Spender, ed. *Feminist Theorists: Three Centuries of Key Women Thinkers.* NY: Pantheon Books, 1983, pp. 165–183.

Meissner, Julia. *Mehr Stolz, Ihr Frauen! Hedwig Dohm: Eine Biographie.* Düsseldorf: Schwann Verlag, 1987.

Plessen, Elisabeth. *Frauen: Porträts aus zwei Jahrhunderten.* Stuttgart: Kreuz Verlag, 1981.

Reed, Philippa. *Alles, was ich schreibe, steht im Dienst der Frauen: Zum essayistischen und fiktionalen Werk Hedwig Dohms (1833–1919).* Frankfurt am Main and NY: Peter Lang, 1987.

Singer, Sandra L. *Free Soul, Free Woman? A Study of Selected Fictional Works by Hedwig Dohm, Isolde Kurz and Helene Bohlau.* NY: Peter Lang, 1995.

Weedon, Chris. "The Struggle for Women's Emancipation in the Work of Hedwig Dohm," in *German Life and Letters.* Vol. 47, no. 2. April 1994, pp. 182–192.

John Haag, Associate Professor of History, University of Georgia, Athens, Georgia

Doi, Takako (1928—)

Japanese political leader who was chair of the Social Democratic Party, 1986–1991. Born Takako Doi in Kobe, a port city in southwest Japan, on November 30, 1928; daughter of a physician; granted law degree from Doshisha University, Kyoto, 1958; never married; no children.

Takako Doi, chair of the Japan Socialist Party from 1986 to 1991, emerged as a national leader in a tradition-bound country where women politicians have been few and far between. In 1989, the high point of her career, she led the Socialists to a stunning victory over the ruling party in the Upper House elections, thus breaking the Liberal Democrats' monopoly on power in that chamber of Parliament. Doi's example, along with her powerful populist mes-

Takako
Doi

she successful in capturing a seat in the Lower House in the 1969 balloting, but she was returned to office in seven subsequent parliamentary contests.

Taking her place in the male-dominated Lower House, Doi impressed her colleagues with her forceful debating skills, although her self-assured manner was viewed by some as unfeminine. Even her low-pitched voice came under fire as too mannish. On the basis of her expertise in the substantive issues of foreign affairs, the environment, and constitutional law, she was promoted in 1983 to vice-chair of the party's central executive committee. It was her "common touch," however, that led party barons to support her candidacy for leadership of the Socialist Party in 1986. (Doi remained connected to her constituents by frequenting neighborhood *karaoke* bars, playing the pinball game called *pachinko* and avidly supporting the Hanshin Tigers, her home area baseball team.) Running a spirited campaign and dubbed "Madonna for the Socialist Party" (in reference to the American singer, who was embraced by Japanese youth in spite of parental objections), she easily won election to the post, thus becoming the first woman ever to head a major political organization in Japan.

Although initially her position was not taken seriously by her political rivals, Doi enjoyed a surge in the Socialist's approval rating within the first six months of her election. In addition to her successful campaign to bring more women into Japanese politics, she continued her predecessor's attempt to wean the party from its anachronistic fidelity to Marxist-Leninist ideals. She also addressed issues of concern to Japanese citizens by, among other things, denouncing the 3% consumption tax passed by the Liberal Democrats in 1988 and calling attention to the actions of certain high-ranking Liberal Democrats who had accepted stock in the Recruit-Cosmos real estate company, before it went public, in return for political favors. Although her revelations generated little excitement at first, her popularity increased in June 1989, when prime minister Noboru Takeshita, Yasuhiro Nakasone's successor, stepped down because of his involvement in the Recruit-Cosmos scandal. His successor, Sousuke Uno, shamed the country further by refusing to acknowledge allegations made by two geishas that he had accepted sexual favors from them.

As the election for the 1989 Upper House drew near, Doi utilized her position as the recognized medium through which the Japanese people could voice their concern and outrage at the

sage, inspired hundreds of politically inexperienced housewives and mothers to run for political office in the 1989 balloting and many of them were elected in the wave of "Doi fever" that swept the country. By the time Doi stepped down as chair of the Socialist Party in 1991, she had succeeded in bringing the message of empowerment to the women of her country.

Doi grew up in a household that held an unusually progressive view of women's role in society. After graduating from secondary school, she abandoned her initial plans to become a physician (the profession of her father) and entered law school at Doshisha University. Towering over her peers at 5'7", Doi was a bold, tenacious student. "She was big, loud and pushy to start with," said one of Doi's law professors in an August 1989 *Time* magazine article. "I knew from the first day she came into my office that she would make a fine politician."

However, Doi took up teaching instead, holding positions at her alma mater and later at Kansaigakuin University and Seiwa Women's University. She was rerouted into politics in 1969 when her hometown newspaper erroneously reported that she, as a member of the Socialist Party, planned to run for a seat in the Lower House of Parliament. During a visit to the mayor of Kobe made by Doi in an effort to clear up the misunderstanding, the mayor asked her, "Wouldn't it be really stupid to run in an election you know you have no chance of winning?" Outraged by the sexist remark, Doi decided at that moment to run for election. Not only was

government. She particularly focused on female voters, urging women to finally stand up and be heard. "Japanese women have persevered toward their fathers and their husbands, always walking several steps behind men," she told a gathering of women. "But the time for an end of perseverance has arrived. It is time for the women to stand up and tell the men to follow us." The electorate seemed prepared to support Doi and the party as long as there was no chance of her becoming prime minister. **Kii Nakamura**, head of the Housewives' Association, told Jim Mulvaney of *New York Newsday*: "A woman of her age, never married, no children, that would be too strange for Japanese to accept in their candidate. . . . I think she is still too masculine to be prime minister, but this time, anyway, people will support her."

When the Liberal Democrats retained its majority in the Lower House election of 1990, Doi was blamed for what she herself termed the party's "half victory." In April 1991, after the Japan Socialist Party was defeated in nationwide local elections, she stepped down as party leader but continued to serve out her eighth term in the Lower House. Although Doi downplays her accomplishments as well as comparisons to former British prime minister *Margaret Thatcher, her contribution to the women's movement in Japan is indisputable.

SOURCES:
Chicago Tribune. October 12, 1984, July 28, 1991.
Japan Quarterly. Vol. 34. January–March 1987.
Moritz, Charles. *Current Biography.* NY: H.W. Wilson, 1992.

Barbara Morgan,
Melrose, Massachusetts

Doletti, Joanna Dumitrescu (1902–1963).

See Dumitrescu-Doletti, Joanna.

Dolgorukaia, Alexandra

(1836–c. 1914)

Russian noblewoman who was briefly the mistress of Alexander II. Name variations: Aleksandra Dolgorukaya or Dolgorukova; "La Grande Mademoiselle." Born Alexandra Sergeevna Dolgorukaia in 1836; died around 1914; eldest of five daughters of Sergei Dolgorukii; married General Peter Pavlovich Al'bedinskii (governor-general of the Baltic Region), around 1861; children: one son.

Alexandra (or Alexandrine) Dolgorukaia was born in 1836, the eldest of five daughters of Sergei Dolgorukii. Once one of the most influen-

tial noble families in tsarist Russia, the Dolgorukiis had status but not wealth by the middle of the 19th century. In part for this reason, Alexandra took a position in 1853 as lady-in-waiting to *Marie of Hesse-Darmstadt, the wife of the future tsar of Russia Alexander II. Maurice Paléologue has described Alexandra as "remarkable for her intelligence and her beauty."

This combination proved irresistible to Alexander who, as one writer noted, "was particularly susceptible to female charms." A liaison between the two was apparently encouraged by some conservative members of the court who wanted to break the stabilizing influence Marie had over her weak-willed and often vacillating husband. The ploy worked in one sense in that when Marie was informed in 1857 of Alexander's affair with "La Grande Mademoiselle," as Alexandra came to be known in court circles, Marie rebuked her unfaithful husband and was momentarily estranged from him. The ploy, however, may also have been counter-productive to conservative interests in that Alexandra appears to have recognized the desperate need for agrarian reform in Russia and therefore both encouraged and supported Alexander in his efforts to emancipate the serfs. By the time the reform was finally implemented in 1861, their romance had cooled.

Dolgorukaia, with the tsar's blessing, married General Peter Pavlovich Al'bedinskii who was promptly sent off to be governor-general of the Baltic Region. She had at least one son by Al'bedinskii and long outlived her husband, dying on the eve of the First World War at the age of 77. She is perhaps best known today through Ivan Turgenev's novel *Smoke* whose heroine Irina was modeled after "La Grande Mademoiselle."

R.C. Elwood, Professor of History,
Carleton College, Ottawa, Canada

Dolgorukova, Catherine (1847–1922).

See Dolgorukova, Ekaterina.

Dolgorukova, Ekaterina

(1847–1922)

Russian noblewoman and long-time "favorite" of Tsar Alexander II whom she married in 1880. Name variations: Catherine, Katherine, or Ekaterina Dolgorukaia, Dolgorukaja, Dolgorukaya, Dolgoroukov, Dolgoruky; (after 1880) Princess Iurevskaia or Yourievski; (nickname) Katia or Katya. Pronunciation: Dol-go-RUK-of-a. Born Ekaterina Mikhailovna Dolgorukova on No-

vember 2, 1847 (o.s.), in Moscow, Russia; died in Nice, France, on February 15, 1922 (n.s.); daughter of Mikhail Mikhailovich Dolgorukov (a noble landowner) and Vera Gavrilovna (Vishnevskaia) Dolgorukova; educated at Smolny Institute, 1860–65; married Alexander II (1818–1881), tsar of Russia (r. 1855–1881), on July 6, 1880 (o.s.); children: George Iurevskii (1872–1913), who married Countess Alexandra Zarnekau); *Olga Iurevskaya (1873–1925); Boris Iurevskii (b. 1876); *Catherine Romanov (1878–1959).

Was mistress (1866–80) and then second (morganatic) wife of Alexander II; left Russia after tsar's assassination (1881); spent the rest of her life in France; published (under the name Victor Laferté) Alexandre II, Détails inédits sur sa vie intime et sa mort (Geneva and Paris, 1882).

On a sunny afternoon in early July 1880, Ekaterina Dolgorukova finally married Alexander II, Tsar of All the Russias. The ceremony, contrary to imperial Russian custom, was short, simple, and secret. It was celebrated in an unfurnished, secluded drawing room at Tsarskoe Selo, the Romanovs' chief residential palace outside of St. Petersburg, before a makeshift altar once used by a previous tsar during the battles of the Napoleonic War. The bride wore a plain beige dress; the groom, his blue Hussars uniform. Only four persons, other than the officiating clergy, witnessed the marriage of the 62-year-old tsar to his 32-year-old mistress. For Alexander, whose first wife *Marie of Hesse-Darmstadt had died the previous May, it was the fulfillment of a vow he had made to Dolgorukova 14 years earlier. For Ekaterina, who had not sought an affair with her sovereign but had given birth to four of Alexander's children without complaint, it meant that she was now "Her Serene Highness" rather than just that "gold-haired witch." Their officially sanctioned life together was both controversial and of short duration. Less than nine months after the ceremony at Tsarskoe Selo, the tsar was assassinated in St. Petersburg. His son and heir, Alexander III, who did not approve of his father's marital conduct, moved his stepmother out of the Winter Palace and was relieved when she chose to emigrate in 1882. Ekaterina Dolgorukova, or Princess Iurevskaia as she was known after her marriage, spent the last 40 years of her life in comfortable, self-imposed exile in France.

Ekaterina's origins were as noble as those of her husband. The Dolgorukovs, a minor branch of the ancient Dolgorukii family, could trace their lineage back to the 13th century and had provided many diplomats and soldiers to the subsequent rulers of the country, including the upstart Romanovs. Mikhail Dolgorukov, Ekaterina's father, had been a captain in a cavalry regiment before marrying **Vera Vishnevskaia (Dolgorukova)**, a rich Ukrainian heiress. The family had town houses in St. Petersburg and Moscow where their older daughter Ekaterina was born on November 2, 1847. Three years earlier, her mother had purchased a large estate at Teplovka near Poltava, and it was there that Ekaterina and her five siblings grew up. The three-story manor house was built in the style of a European castle and was surrounded by a luxuriant park. Her father, no longer in the army, spent his time managing or perhaps mismanaging the many serfs who labored in the adjoining fields and supplied the family with its comfortable livelihood.

The highlight of life at Teplovka was a visit by the new tsar of Russia, Alexander II, in the late 1850s. The precise date and details of this visit are in dispute, but all accounts agree that it was on this occasion that Alexander first met Ekaterina Dolgorukova. According to Maurice Paléologue, the tsar stopped at Teplovka in August 1857 while on annual army maneuvers in the south of the country. Because of an attack of asthma, the family loaned him their manor house so that he did not have to sleep in his customary tent. "One afternoon," Paléologue recounts, "as the Tsar was taking the air with his aides-de-camp under the verandah, a little girl happened to run past him. He called to her."

> "Who are you, my dear?" he asked gently. "And what are you doing here?"
>
> "I'm Catherine Michailovna and I wanted to see the Emperor."
>
> Much amused, he took her on his knee, talked to her a few minutes and then sent her back to her parents. Seeing her again the following day he was attracted by her ingenuous grace, pretty manners, and large eyes like those of a startled gazelle. In his most gracious manner . . . he begged her to show him over the garden.

Assuming that Paleologue's date is correct, Ekaterina was nine years old at the time; the tsar was thirty-nine. During the next few years, her father squandered the family fortune through gambling, extravagant living, poor estate management, and questionable investments. A year after Mikhail's death in 1860, the tsar inadvertently contributed to the Dolgorukovs' misfortunes by liberating the serfs who had previously provided much of the family's income. Vera Gavrilovna followed her husband to the grave in 1866 but not before Teplovka was destroyed by a fire that may have been intentionally set by discontented peasants.

Ekaterina
Dolgorukova

Ekaterina was fortunate that Alexander II remembered the young girl he had met on summer maneuvers. In 1860, shortly after their father's death, the tsar made Ekaterina and her sister **Marie Dolgorukova** his wards and agreed to look after their education. They were duly enrolled in the "Imperial Educational Society of Noble Maidens" or Smolny Institute, a fashionable boarding school for wellborn but often impoverished young ladies in St. Petersburg. The institute stressed the teaching of good manners and social graces along with providing a modicum of an education. All conversation and instruction, except in the Russian-language class, was in French. The girls were compelled to wear uniforms, were fed uninspired institutional cooking, and were allowed to leave the school only on specific holidays. Ekaterina did not particularly like this strict regimen, and she showed little interest in the academic side of the enterprise.

Her five years at the Smolny Institute coincided with a period of great change in Russia. Following the emancipation of the serfs in 1861, the "Tsar Liberator" implemented a series of reforms that vastly improved the Russian judiciary, rural and urban self-government, army life, and the financial structure of the country. Alexander periodically took time off from these endeavors to visit Smolny to talk to his young wards and on occasion take them on welcome excursions from the school. One suspects the orphaned girls delighted in showing off their royal surrogate parent to their classmates.

As Ekaterina grew older and more attractive—one author described her at age 15 as "tall, slim, with masses of ashen blonde hair, very dark eyes, and a flawlessly chiselled mouth"—these imperial visits grew more frequent and less familial. In 1865, a year before her scheduled graduation, Ekaterina left Smolny supposedly at the request of her mother and went to live with her older brother Mikhail in St. Petersburg. Meetings with the tsar, intentional or otherwise, increased in number. Alexander, as one of his biographers admits, was a "connoisseur of female charms." Married since 1841 to the Empress Marie of Hesse-Darmstadt and the father of eight children, his growing interest in Ekaterina was consistent with his character and male Romanov tradition. What may be surprising, given his position and persistence, was her reluctance to join his stable of "favorites." Even Ekaterina was surprised by her conduct. "I don't understand how I was able to deny him for a whole year, how I didn't fall in love with him earlier," she confided to a friend. "I think that it was only the fact of seeing him so distressed one day," after the first of many assassination attempts on his life, "that I finally succumbed and our love triumphed." The middle-aged tsar assured her that this was not another of his casual dalliances. "Today, alas, I am not free," he told her after she "succumbed" on July 1, 1866, "but at the first opportunity I shall marry you, for from now and for ever I regard you as my wife before God."

The two lovers tried to be discreet in their meetings but gossip was inevitable, especially given the disparity in their ages. In January 1867, her brother, fearing that he would be accused of abetting the affair, insisted that Dolgorukova leave the country on an extended visit to his wife's relatives in Naples. He could not prevent, however, frequent correspondence between his sovereign and his sister nor could he stop her from meeting Alexander during a state visit to Paris in June 1867. After long rides through the Bois de Boulogne and nocturnal visits to her "discreet and small hotel," the tsar convinced her to return with him to St. Petersburg. Since rendezvous in the Russian capital were difficult as long as Ekaterina lived with her brother and sister-in-law, Alexander provided her with more appropriate accommodation on Millionaires' Row close to the Winter Palace and later on the fashionable English Quay. He also made certain that she had places to stay near his summer retreats, arranged for her presence on his foreign travels, and according to several sources even took her on military maneuvers.

Many thought that this infatuation would pass as had so many in the past. But this was not to be. The aging monarch clearly found solace and comfort in his late evening visits to her various residences. His young lover listened to his problems and sympathized with the predicament of a ruler who was increasingly criticized by his own class for the sweeping nature of his reforms while at the same time was threatened in a more dangerous way by a radical intelligentsia that felt that his reforming zeal was waning. She was a pleasant escape from the burdens of being tsar. Katia, as Alexander called her, also pampered his penchant for painting by serving as the nude subject for his drawings. In time, the liaison produced children: George was born in 1872, Olga the next year, and Ekaterina in 1878. A second son, Boris, died shortly after birth in 1876. Alexander legitimized his children by giving them the surname Iurevskii in 1874, and he acknowledged his parentage by assigning them his own patronymic of Alexandrovich.

When separated by the tsar's state duties and even while living in close proximity, the two lovers corresponded on an almost daily basis. This correspondence, much of it published for the first time in 1970, was conducted in French and is revealing of the interests and personalities of the two parties. To Alexander, Katia was "my treasure," "my idol," "my adorable Imp." He discussed the weather, her health, their dogs and children, their unkind fate, and especially times spent together. His feelings may have suffered somewhat in translation when he wrote on May 6, 1870:

> Have only just got home, but I pick up my pen to tell you, dear Angel of my soul, that first of all I thank God for having given us the joy of meeting again. What I felt within me you saw for yourself, just as I saw what was happening to you. That is why we clenched each other like hungry cats both in the morning and in the afternoon, and it was sweet to the verge of madness, so that even now I still want to squeal for joy and I am still saturated in all my being.

Ekaterina's letters, which contain numerous errors in spelling and grammar, reveal what Alexandre Tarsaïdzé considers to be "her poor upbringing, the shortcomings of her education, her lack of culture and imagination." At times, she appears jealous of the tsar's other interests, possessive of his attention, and capricious. Despite the fact that she was living through the "Golden Age of Russian Culture," her often rather erotic letters show little interest in contemporary literature, music, or the arts. "I find the Russian play very pretty, but it is boring that they are always too long," she wrote on the last day of 1875. In the same breath, she continues in run-on fashion,

> I would like to give birth as soon as possible for I feel so heavy, but I am not grumbling, because it is my fault, and I confess I cannot be without your fountain, which I love so, and therefore after my six weeks are over I count on renewing my injections, for I can do nothing halfway.

Ekaterina lived a life of seclusion with her children making herself available whenever the tsar sought her company. She had no other life and no other interests. Some have accused her of being a "nefarious influence," "the evil genius behind the throne." In private, she was sometimes referred to as the "female Potemkin"—an inappropriate comparison with *Catherine II the Great's lover, influential minister and probable second husband of a century earlier. In reality, she played none of these roles except, of course, that of lover. As Norman Pereira has concluded, "there is no evidence that Katia held to any strong intellectual or political positions, much less that she tried to influence Alexander's public policy." Even Alexandre Tarsaïdzé, a sympathetic biographer, acknowledges that she was "meagerly informed politically." She was not an intriguer nor did she try to form a clique. Her detractors have argued that she sought financial benefits for her relatives and friends but this, if it did happen, was not unique in Alexander's entourage. Dolgorukova's persona did little to mitigate these negative impressions. On the rare occasions when she appeared in society, she seemed reserved, aloof, and cold. Unlike Catherine II, Ekaterina did not have an outgoing personality or a vivaciousness that might have won her much-needed allies. Indeed, in the words of Tarsaïdzé, she was "a difficult personality all around."

Ekaterina Dolgorukova's historical significance lies not in her political influence, which was negligible, but in the fact that her long affair with the tsar—a man 30 years her senior—served to discredit the monarchy, divide the royal family, and isolate Alexander from many of his subjects. The blame for this rests far more with the tsar than with his lover. As the "Tsar Liberator," he had claimed the high moral ground, but by his relations with Dolgorukova he undercut his own position. Persons who opposed his political

changes were delighted to exploit problems in his personal life. Many in the court, especially the wives of Alexander's brothers and sons, openly sympathized with the ailing Empress Marie and were hostile toward her much younger rival. For Alexander to name Ekaterina a lady-in-waiting to his wife, solely to give her an entrée to court, was tactless at best and certainly politically inept. When the influential head of the Russian police, P.A. Shuvalov, sought in 1874 to warn the tsar of the division his affair was causing, Alexander's reaction was to congratulate him on his new appointment as ambassador to the Court of St. James in London. Four years later, when terrorist attacks in Russia threatened not only the tsar but also his extended family, Alexander moved Ekaterina and their children into the Winter Palace, where security was supposedly better, and assigned them rooms directly above those of his official wife.

This insensitive behavior estranged Alexander from his highly moralistic son and heir, the tsarevich Alexander Alexandrovich, who became the center of much of the conservative opposition to his father's reign. Dolgorukova, in turn, has mistakenly been seen as a rallying point for liberals who wanted a resumption of reform and were opposed to the tsarevich and his reactionary friends. She has sometimes been seen in league with Count Loris-Melikov, the tsar's last reforming minister and another outsider in the Russian court. In reality, she understandably welcomed support and friendship from any quarter but there is no evidence that she—unlike the tsar's earlier "favorite" and her ancestral relative, *Alexandra Dolgorukaia— was actively involved in promoting political change. Political animosities, nevertheless, coalesced with private scandal to produce division within the royal household. As W.E. Mosse has concluded, "a palace revolution seemed not at all impossible."

The situation did not improve after the Empress Marie died on May 22, 1880. The tsar inopportunely chose the moment of his wife's death in St. Petersburg to be with his mistress at Tsarskoe Selo. Russian tradition called for a mourning period of one year before remarriage, a convention observed by the only two monarchs to remarry in the 18th or 19th centuries. Tradition also strongly suggested that the tsar find a bride from among royal families outside of Russia. Alexander chose to violate both conventions when he honored his pledge of 14 years earlier to marry Ekaterina Dolgorukova as soon as he was "free" and promptly did so only 46 days after the death of his first wife. Suggestions from Ekaterina and his advisors that he delay at least until his son and heir returned from a trip to Western Europe fell on deaf ears. As the fatalistic tsar informed his sister, "I would never have married before a year of mourning if not for the dangerous time we live in and for the hazardous attempts I expose myself to daily which can actually and suddenly end my life." Rumors of the secret marriage at Tsarskoe Selo on July 6 spread rapidly and were unofficially confirmed when Dolgorukova was assigned a new and luxurious suite in the Winter Palace. She was also given the title Princess Iurevskaia and an endowment of 3.3 million rubles.

These events did not bring harmony to the royal household. The women at court ostracized Ekaterina while conservatives around the tsarevich feared that Alexander II might seek to make her his empress and to change the order of succession. The tsar did in fact send an aide to Moscow to check archival records concerning procedures by which Peter the Great had designated his second wife—also named Ekaterina (*Catherine I)—as his empress and successor. Alexander spent the last year of his life in semi-seclusion, alienated from his relatives, a bitter and disillusioned man. It seemed to many that he cared only for his second family and preferred to spend his time with them rather than dealing with matters of state. Ekaterina later suggested that he seriously considered abdicating and moving to France—a step that she surely would have supported. Instead, he kept to his old routines. One of these was to drive through St. Petersburg every Sunday. On March 1, 1881, Ekaterina begged him not to follow his usual Sunday itinerary which would have taken him down the capital's main street, Nevskii Prospekt. Alexander acquiesced and thereby avoided a mine planted there by the revolutionaries. But he did not escape bombs thrown by two other terrorists. The badly wounded tsar was taken back to the Winter Palace where he died one hour later, his new wife at his side.

In one of his last letters to his eldest son, Alexander II wrote that in the case of his death "I wish that . . . the living quarters in the Winter Palace should be reserved for [Ekaterina] and her children." While this could not have been to the tsarevich's liking, he honored the request in spirit. She was allowed to stay in her apartments, but she was also offered an elegant residence elsewhere in the capital and a lifelong pension of 40,000 rubles a year. In late May, she moved into the Petit Palais Rose, much to her stepson's relief. One suspects that the 33-year-old widow did not find life in St. Petersburg very agreeable. She had lost her protector, lover, and companion of 15 years; she had little in common with his successor; and she still was an object of derision in the imperial court.

It is not surprising, therefore, that Dolgorukova-Iurevskaia packed her bags and left Russia in April 1882. She traveled in style accompanied not only by her three children but also by their tutors and governesses as well as by medical personnel, cooks, footmen, maids, a coach driver, and three dogs. Curiously, for a woman who had never shown any interest in writing and certainly had no need for money, her first act after reaching Paris was to publish a brochure entitled *Alexandre II, Détails inédits sur sa vie intime et sa mort* under the pseudonym Victor Laferté. In it, she recounted her version of the last three days of her husband's life. According to this unsubstantiated account, Alexander II had approved a liberal constitution submitted to him by her alleged ally Loris-Melikov on the morning of his death. Instead of publishing it the next day, as he had ordered, the new tsar scrapped the constitution and fired its author. The brochure predictably exacerbated Ekaterina's already strained relations with Alexander III and caused her to be forbidden to return to Russia during his lifetime.

Princess Iurevskaia lived the life of a wealthy if somewhat eccentric Russian émigrée for the next 40 years. Her Parisian houses on Avenue Kléber and in Neuilly-sur-Seine were looked after by a staff of 20. Her dinner parties and bridge games attracted many from the Russian émigré colony who probably would have shunned her earlier in St. Petersburg. In time, even visiting members of the royal family stopped by her salon. In the summer, she had her private railway carriage attached to the fast train from Paris to Biarritz or Nice where she also had villas. According to her son-in-law, Serge Obolensky, Princess Iurevskaia or "Her Highness," as she preferred to be called, "dressed in long flowing mauve dresses, [and was] very dignified and gracious; she looked exactly like what she was—the widow of one of Russia's greatest rulers." He goes on to note that she "lived entirely in the past. Life for her stopped the day the Nihilists threw the bombs that killed her royal husband." Relics of the past, including one of the fingers Alexander lost in the fatal explosion, were kept in a glass case next to her bed. Her favorite companions during these long years abroad were her dogs. She had a small villa built next to their burial place in Nice which she visited daily when on the Côte d'Azur. In 1902, she altered her will so that 40,000 rubles would be set aside for the care of her pug "Signal." One senses that while she may have "lived" in the imperial Russian past, she found more contentment and acceptance in *fin de siècle* France.

This life of what Queen *Victoria once called "busy idleness" came to an end in August 1914. The outbreak of the First World War curtailed the periodic trips she had been making to her homeland since Nicholas II became tsar two decades earlier. She turned one of her Paris residences into a hospital for wounded soldiers and for a while paid the costs of their recuperation. Nicholas' abdication in March 1917, however, meant the end of her royal pension and shortly thereafter her investments and properties in Russia were rendered worthless by the Bolshevik seizure of power. She tried to maintain the semblance of her old lifestyle by selling her possessions and properties in France one after another. "Her Highness" died in style but penniless in Nice on February 15, 1922, at the age of 74.

SOURCES:
Obolensky, Serge. *One Man in His Time*. NY: McDowell, Obolensky, 1958.
Paléologue, Maurice. *The Tragic Romance of Alexander II of Russia*. Translated from the French by Arthur Chambers. London: Hutchinson, 1927.
Pereira, N.G.O. *Tsar-Liberator: Alexander II of Russia, 1818–1881*. Newtonville, MA: Oriental Research Partners, 1983.
Tarsaïdzé, Alexandre. *Katia: Wife before God*. NY: Macmillan, 1970 (contains the previously unpublished but awkwardly translated correspondence quoted herein; inaccurate in some of its details).

SUGGESTED READING:
Almedingen, E.M. *The Emperor Alexander II*. London: The Bodley Head, 1962.
Bibesco, Marthe. *Katia* (fiction). Translated from the French by Priscilla Bibesco. London: William Heinemann, 1939.
Mosse, W.E. *Alexander II and the Modernization of Russia*. NY: Collier Books, 1962.

RELATED MEDIA:
Katia, French film with *Danielle Darrieux and John Loder, directed by F.A. Algazy (1938).

R.C. Elwood, Professor of History,
Carleton University, Ottawa, Canada

Dolgorukova, Marie (d. 1625)

Empress of Russia. Name variations: Dolgoruki. Died of poison on January 7, 1625; became first wife of Mikhail also known as Michael III (1596–1645), tsar of Russia (r. 1613–1645), on September 19, 1624.

Dolgoruky, Catherine (1847–1922).

See Dolgorukova, Ekaterina.

Dombeck, Carola (b. 1960).

See Comaneci, Nadia for sidebar.

Dominguez, Josefa Ortiz de (c. 1768–1829).

See Ortíz de Dominguez, Josefa.

Domitia Faustina (b. 147).

See Faustina II for sidebar.

Domitia Lepida (fl. 40 CE).

See Agrippina the Younger for sidebar.

Domitia Longina (fl. 80s CE)

Roman noblewoman. Married Domitian (51–96), Roman emperor (r. 81–96 CE), in 70; children: all died young.

Domitia Longina was involved in the successful plot to assassinate her husband, the emperor Domitian, in 96 CE.

Domitia Lucilla

Roman noblewoman. Married M. Annius Verus; children: Marcus Aurelius; Annia Cornificia (who married C. Ummidius Quadratus).

Domitia Paulina I (fl. 76 CE)

*Roman noblewoman and mother of Hadrian. Born a Roman matron in Gades (Cadiz) on the Atlantic coast 60 miles south of Italica; married Publius Aelius Hadrianus Afer (d. 85 CE); children: Hadrian (76-138), Roman emperor (r. 117–138); *Domitia Paulina II (fl. 80–100 CE).*

Domitia Paulina II (fl. 80–100 CE)

*Roman noblewoman. Flourished 80 to 100 CE; daughter of *Domitia Paulina I (fl. 76 CE) and P. Aelius Hadrianus Afer; sister of Hadrian, Roman emperor (r. 117–138); married L. Julius Ursus Servianus; children: Julia (who married Cn. Pedanius Fuscus).*

Domitilla.

See Flavia Domitilla.

Domna, Julia (c. 170–217 CE).

See Julia Domna.

Dona Maria (c. 1908–1938).

See Bonita, Maria.

Donahue, Hessie (fl. 1892)

American matron who knocked out heavyweight boxing champion John L. Sullivan. Born in Worcester, Massachusetts; married to boxing-school owner Charles Converse.

Hessie Donahue made sporting history with a single punch to the jaw of heavyweight boxing champion John L. Sullivan. She was one of only two boxers to ever defeat the champ, the other being Gentleman Jim Corbett. Donahue was the wife of Charles Converse, a boxing-school owner who provided sparring partners for Sullivan. In 1892, when Sullivan invited Converse to go on an exhibition tour of vaudeville theaters with him, Donahue went along. To add spice to the show, Sullivan, after sparring with all comers, would announce that he had been challenged by a woman, and Donahue would go a few rounds with him at the end of each performance. Clad in full prizefighting rig—blouse, skirt, bloomers, long stockings, and boxing gloves—Donahue would climb in the ring and trade a few harmless blows with the champ until the curtain came down. One night the fakery got out of hand when Sullivan accidentally threw an uncontrolled punch to Donahue's face. She, in turn, threw her formidable weight behind a right to his jaw that dropped him to the floor, where he remained unconscious for over a minute. The crowd went wild and the punch was included in the act for the remainder of the tour.

Donalda, Pauline (1882–1970)

Canadian soprano and tireless promoter of Canadian opera. Born Pauline Lightstone in Montreal, Quebec, Canada, on March 5, 1882; died in Montreal on October 22, 1970; studied with Edmont Duvernoy and Paul Lhérie, and with Clara Lichtenstein at the Royal Victoria College; studied in Paris on a grant from Donald Smith and adopted the name "Donalda" in his honor; married Paul Seveilhac (a French baritone), in 1906; married Mischa Léon (a Danish tenor), in 1918.

Debuted in Nice (1904) and at Covent Garden (1905); debuted in Canada and the U.S. (1906); opened a teaching studio in Paris (1922); taught hundreds of students before returning to Montreal to teach (1937); founded the Opera Guild over which she presided (1942–69); made an Officer of the Order of Canada (1967).

Pauline Donalda's parents were Jews from Poland and Russia who immigrated to Montreal, changing the family name from Lichtenstein to Lightstone. The quality of Pauline's voice attracted attention, and she was awarded a music scholarship at the Royal Victoria College. When Sir Donald Smith, Lord Strathcona, gave Pauline a grant to study in Europe, she adopted the name "Donalda" in his honor. After her London debut in 1905, she sang frequently, often when *Nellie Melba required a replacement (in this way, Donalda sang Mimi with Caruso). She married the French baritone, Paul Seveilhac, a cast member in the 1905 production of *Faust* in which Donalda sang Marguerite. She toured Russia, North America, and Europe. In February 1914, she had a huge success in Carmen in Nice.

During World War I, Donalda stayed in Canada where she organized the Donalda Sunday Afternoon Concerts. When the war ended, she returned to Paris where she married the Danish tenor Mischa Léon in 1918, after a divorce from her first husband. Subsequent to retiring from the stage, she opened a teaching studio in 1922 and taught hundreds of pupils. Donalda continued her teaching career in Montreal in 1937 and founded the Opera Guild (1942) over which she presided until 1969; the guild presented 29 operas during this time. Although her performing career was relatively short, Donalda had a great impact in the musical world as a teacher and promoter of opera. She was made an Officer of the Order of Canada in 1967 for her contributions to music.

John Haag,
Athens, Georgia

Donata

Scottish princess. Daughter of Malcolm II MacKenneth (d. 1034), king of Scotland (r. 1005–1034); married Sigurd the Stout, earl of Orkney, in 1088.

Donatella (fl. 1271)

Italian painter. Name variations: Donella. Flourished around 1271 in Bologna.

The painter Donatella of Bologna belongs to a large class of professional urban women of the 13th century. She is listed as a miniatrix, or female miniaturist, in a contract she and her husband (also a miniaturist) negotiated for the sale of their house in 1271. Donatella was not unusual or alone in her choice of occupation; many city women worked in the skilled field of manuscript illustration in the Middle Ages, as they also worked in other areas of book production. Unfortunately no other information is available about her life.

Laura York,
Riverside, California

Donella (fl. 1271).

See Donatella.

Dönhoff, Marion, Countess

(b. 1909)

German journalist, publisher, and editor-in-chief of Die Zeit, *Germany's most influential liberal weekly newspaper. Name variations; Doenhoff or Donhoff. Born Marion Hedda Ilse, Gräfin Dönhoff, at Schloss Friedrichstein near Loewenhagen, East Prussia, on December 2, 1909; daughter of August Count Dönhoff and Maria Countess von Lepel Dönhoff; had six brothers and sisters; never married.*

Served for many years in leading positions; became the first woman in post-1945 Germany to address a national—indeed international—audience, playing a major role in the reorientation of the foreign policy of the German Federal Republic in the post-Adenauer era toward greater flexibility and conciliation; was a major factor in the emergence of West Germany's Ostpolitik which transformed the political landscape of Europe in the 1970s; is universally acknowledged to be the Grand Old Lady of German journalism.

Marion Dönhoff was born in 1909, less than five years before the start of World War I, into one of the oldest and most prestigious families of the East Prussian Junker nobility, a clan whose genealogical tree branched back to the Middle Ages. As a young countess, she had the run of Friedrichstein, a splendid ancestral castle and grounds visitors often described as being "more beautiful than Versailles." Owned by the Dönhoffs since 1666, the Italian rococo architecture of the residence dominated the lakes and extensive gardens surrounding it. Tracing their blood line back to the medieval Knights of the Teutonic Order, the Dönhoff family had for centuries been soldiers, provincial governors, and substantial landowners in Lithuania, Poland, and Prussia. The high status of the family continued into the modern age, so that Marion's mother **Maria, Countess von Lepel Dönhoff**, known to all as "Ria," held the position of lady-in-waiting to German empress *Augusta of Schleswig-Holstein. Marion's stern-appearing father was a soldier and diplomat who had served in German diplomatic missions in Paris, St. Petersburg, London, Vienna, and Washington. After retiring from the diplomatic service, Count Dönhoff was elected to the German Reichstag and was often in Berlin. Born when her mother was 40 and her father 64, Marion had six brothers and sisters to play with and learn from.

Despite the splendors of the semi-feudal world in which Marion lived, which was best displayed in the magnificent reception rooms of Friedrichstein, daily life for the large Dönhoff family was in many ways simple and even Spartan. Only the parents had a bathroom and the children lived in sparsely-furnished rooms. Food was basic and by no means excessive in quantity, which meant that Marion and her siblings looked forward to those times when there were guests at Friedrichstein and only then would the table groan with luxuries. Told by their parents not to be fussy, the children held their noses when drinking the foul-smelling water that was drawn from the estate pump.

Breathtaking scenery surrounded Friedrichstein castle, and Marion developed a deep love of nature that would last a lifetime. She became an expert horsewoman, spending countless hours exploring the local countryside with her brothers and sisters and her cousins Heini and **Sissi von Lehndorff**. A stern Prussian sense of duty prevailed even on these occasions, so that when she once fell off her horse, her brother insisted she remount; only after arriving home did she learn that her arm had been badly broken. Rural pleasures could at times be as dangerous as they were thrilling. When a gun accidentally discharged like a clap of thunder during a duck hunt and Marion hit the ground, a servant was convinced that she had been shot dead. Fortunately, only her jacket was singed.

Sent to school in Berlin, Countess Marion was definitely a rebel and did her utmost to defy its strict conventions. A chance visit to a lecture on the ideas of the then-popular philosopher Count Hermann Keyserling changed the course of her life. Despite her narrow preparation by the usual succession of governesses, Dönhoff enrolled at the University of Frankfurt am Main. With Germany in social and economic crisis, many of her fellow students had been enticed by the siren songs of Adolf Hitler and the Nazi movement. Marion Dönhoff, on the other hand, displayed her lifelong spirit of intellectual independence and moved in distinctly anti-Nazi and leftist circles. Most of her friends during this period were Social Democrats, Communists, and Jews. After the Nazi seizure of power in 1933, she departed from Frankfurt to complete her studies in an intellectually free environment. Enrolling at Switzerland's University of Basel, she studied with noted economist Edgar Salin. Wishing to write a dissertation on a topic relating to Marxist philosophy, Salin persuaded her to write instead on a subject close to the traditions of the

Dönhoff family, the origins of large-scale landownership in East Prussia. Making extensive use of her family's archives, her dissertation, completed in 1935, was recognized by experts as an important study in the economic history of Eastern Europe.

War clouds began to gather on the horizon soon after Marion Dönhoff was awarded her doctorate, and although she had a strong desire to pursue a scholarly career, strong family ties eventually prevailed. Her brother insisted that she come back to Friedrichstein to learn how to administer the family lands in the event of war, which now seemed highly likely. The entire Dönhoff family looked upon Hitler and the Nazi movement with contempt and disdain. Although many Junkers first believed the Nazis could be somehow "tamed," Marion Dönhoff had few illusions about the National Socialist ideology or the aims of the Hitler dictatorship. By the late 1930s, she was convinced that the Third Reich was set on war and that Germany would lose, which meant that East Prussia was doomed. By 1943, she had gotten acquainted with all of the major conspirators against Hitler, including Count Claus von Stauffenberg. Privy to the plans of the conspiracy through her favorite cousin Heini von Lehndorff, her part in the anti-Hitler plot was to evaluate which members of the East Prussian Nazi government would be most dangerous and which might be of use to the plotters.

By the evening of July 20, 1944, it became clear to Dönhoff that the plot to kill Hitler and replace his regime had failed. During the next few weeks many of her closest friends were arrested, tortured, and executed, including Heini von Lehndorff and Heinrich Dohna von Tolksdorf, whom she had personally recruited into the conspiracy and who had been chosen to be head of the first post-Nazi East Prussian administration. Dönhoff herself was arrested and interrogated about her knowledge of the plot. Fortunately none of the other conspirators betrayed her, even under torture, and her name had not appeared on any lists of a post-Hitler government. Within a few months of the dramatic events of summer 1944, Soviet forces were penetrating deeply into East Prussian territory. At first, Dönhoff had hoped to organize an orderly evacuation of the people on her estates, but the miserable conditions of the icy roads made her decide that it would be best to remain and hope for decent treatment at the hands of the Soviet forces.

Almost at the last possible moment, in January 1945, Dönhoff decided that her only chance for survival was to attempt to escape. Mounted on her favorite bay, Alarich, she set off alone toward the west. Reaching the railroad bridge at Marienburg, she came across three gravely wounded soldiers who no longer had the strength to continue. She would describe the scene many years later in her memoirs:

> For me the end of East Prussia came down to this: three dying soldiers trying to drag themselves across Nogat Bridge to West Prussia, and a woman on horseback whose forefathers, 700 years ago, had marched from the west into the great wilderness on the other side of the stream and who now rode back again to the west—700 years of history extinguished.

Miraculously, Dönhoff arrived safely in the western sector of occupied Germany, impoverished but alive. All the male members of her family had either died in the war or been killed by the Nazis because of their involvement in the plot to kill Hitler, and her beloved Schloss Friedrichstein was now under Soviet occupation. East Prussia was no longer German, divided up between Poland and the Soviet Union. Possessing excellent educational credentials and with an unblemished record as an anti-Nazi, Dönhoff joined the staff of Hamburg's liberal newspaper *Die Zeit* in 1946. She quickly learned all aspects of newspaper work, including writing clear and convincing articles. She displayed not only journalistic skill but moral integrity as well during her first years with *Die Zeit*. In the early 1950s, the then publisher and editor-in-chief began to consult on a regular basis with the political scientist Carl Schmitt. Schmitt, an influential ideologist of dictatorial government during the final years of the Weimar Republic, had developed a body of doctrine that effectively provided Nazism with a cloak of intellectual respectability. The very thought that her employers were on close terms with a man who had greased the ways for Adolf Hitler and his brownshirts infuriated Dönhoff. When an article written by Schmitt actually was printed in *Die Zeit,* she resigned in protest. Only after the liberal-minded Gerd Bucerius became publisher in 1955 did she decide to return to *Die Zeit*. Now enjoying considerably enhanced prestige as a senior staff member, Dönhoff was vigilant in seeing to it that the paper would no longer flirt with ideas such as those of Carl Schmitt and other foes of democracy and pluralism.

Starting in the mid-1950s, Marion Dönhoff played a key role in transforming *Die Zeit* into the leading liberal newspaper of West Germany. Appointed associate editor in charge of the political section of *Die Zeit* in 1955, she became gen-

Marion Dönhoff (left) after receiving the Heine Prize in Dusseldorf.

eral editor-in-chief of the paper in 1968, consolidating her position even further in 1972 by becoming a co-owner of the paper, which by that time had achieved a universally accepted position as one of the most respected newspapers in the world. By the late 1950s, if one wanted to know what was happening in the Federal Republic of Germany, it was essential that one was a regular reader of *Die Zeit*. Starting in the early 1960s, Marion Dönhoff increasingly spoke out in favor of a more active and flexible role for West Germany in resolving the tensions that remained between the Bonn republic and the nations of Eastern Europe including the Soviet Union. In 1970, Federal Chancellor Willy Brandt was finally able to implement the more flexible policy of *Ostpolitik* that had been persuasively argued for so long in Dönhoff's articles in *Die Zeit*. When the time came, however, she decided to turn down the chancellor's invitation to accompany him on his trip to Warsaw to sign a German-Polish reconciliation agreement: it was simply too painful for her to witness the signing of a pact that confirmed once and for all the permanent loss of her beloved East Prussian homeland.

Unafraid of advancing controversial ideas, Marion Dönhoff was vilified in the 1960s by some of West Germany's more unreconstructed Cold Warriors as "the Red Countess." Although her political sympathies were generally favorable to the Social Democrats, Dönhoff remained independent of party and by the 1980s, when she took on the title of senior editor of *Die Zeit*, her political perspective had become a truly global one, more "green" than "red" in its deep concern for a rapidly deteriorating global environment. Writing in the mid-1980s, she voiced her growing concern about the prospects of a world in which "we are frittering away reserves of energy below the ground which nature has taken thousands of millions of years to accumulate." She joined the growing band of environmental activists when she presented a grim picture of a world in which, under the pressure "of either justified or artificial imperatives designed to maintain economic growth, increase consumption or satisfy it without heeding the consequences, today's generations are plundering and polluting nature."

In 1988, Countess Dönhoff published what was probably the most moving of her many books, *Kindheit in Ostpreussen*, a memoir of her magical early years growing up at Friedrichstein Castle. Published in English in 1990 as *Before the Storm: Memories of My Youth in Old Prussia*, this memoir of a vanished way of life made clear the immense losses suffered, not only by Germany, but by Western civilization, when first Nazism and then war and raging ethnic hatreds forever changed the face of Eastern Europe. A survivor of a world of aristocratic ideals of honor and privilege, Marion Dönhoff was able in her own lifetime to adjust to a radically new era, keeping alive in her career the belief that tolerance and peace were infinitely preferable to hatred and war. In 1989, she and a nephew took a journey to the former East Prussian territory, at that time still part of the Soviet Union, where Friedrichstein had once been situated. Upon her return to Hamburg, the countess could only report of her former home: "There was nothing more there, nothing at all, not even rubble."

SOURCES:

Ardagh, John. *Germany and the Germans: An Anatomy of Society Today.* NY: Harper & Row, 1987.

Baranowski, Shelley. *The Sanctity of Rural Life: Nobility, Protestantism, and Nazism in Weimar Prussia.* NY: Oxford University Press, 1995.

Dönhoff, Marion. *Before the Storm: Memories of My Youth in Old Prussia.* Translated by Jean Steinberg. NY: Alfred A. Knopf, 1990.

———. *Foe into Friend: The Makers of the New Germany from Konrad Adenauer to Helmut Schmidt.* Translated by Gabriel Annan. NY: St. Martin's Press, 1982.

———. "The roots of a growing world crisis," in *The Courier* [UNESCO]. Vol. 39. May–June, 1986, pp. 4–7.

———. *Um der Ehre willen: Erinnerungen an die Freunde vom 20. Juli.* Berlin: Siedler Verlag, 1994.

Schwarzer, Alice. *Marion Dönhoff: ein widerständiges Leben.* Cologne: Kiepenheuer & Witsch, 1996.

Tagliabue, John. "A Plucky Countess Braves the Ghosts of Prussia," in *The New York Times.* December 12, 1990, p. A4.

John Haag, Associate Professor of History,
University of Georgia, Athens, Georgia

Donnadieu, Marguerite (1914–1996).

See Duras, Marguerite.

Donnelly, Dorothy (1880–1928)

American actress, dramatist, and lyricist. Born Dorothy Agnes Donnelly in New York, New York, on January 28, 1880; died on January 3, 1928; daughter of Thomas Lester Donnelly (a manager of the Grand Opera House, New York) and Sarah (Williams) Donnelly (an actress); educated at Convent of the Sacred Heart in New York; studied classical roles with her uncle, Fred Williams.

Dorothy Donnelly made her first appearance as an actress at the Murray Hill Theater in New York in August 1898; she remained with that theater for the next three years playing juvenile and leading roles. She then portrayed Mme. Alvarez in Richard Harding Davis' *Soldiers of Fortune* in 1901–02 and appeared in the title roles of W.B. Yeats' *Kathleen na Houlihan*, 1902–03, and G.B. Shaw's *Candida*, 1903–04. Other roles include Maja in Ibsen's *When We Dead Awaken* (1905), Ruth Jordan in Channing Pollock's *Little Gray Lady* (1906), Marion Manners in **Martha Morton's** *The Movers* (1907), Jacqueline in *Madame X* (1911), and Anna Markle in *The Song of Songs* (1914). Following her appearance as Sarah Luskin in *The Bargain*, Donnelly turned to playwrighting, authoring *Flora Belle* (1916), *Fancy Free* (1918), *Forbidden* (1919) and *Poppy* (1923). She also collaborated with **Charlotte E. Wells** on *The Riddle, Woman* (1918). Most important, Donnelly wrote the book and lyrics to *Blossom Time* (also known as *Lilac Time*) which was adapted from the German in 1921, as well as *The Student Prince,* a musical version of *Old Heidelberg,* in 1924.

Donovan, Anne (1961—)

American basketball player. Born in Ridgewood, New Jersey, on November 1, 1961.

Named the 1983 Naismith College Player of the Year; was a member of the women's team that won the gold in 1984; won the first Champion Player of the Year award given by the Women's Basketball Coaches Association; became a coach at Old Dominion; inducted into the Basketball Hall of Fame (1995).

At 6'8", Anne Donovan towered over everyone, male and female, making her well suited to basketball. Her position as center used this height to her advantage. While on scholarship at Old Dominion, she totaled 2,719 points, and averaged 14.5 rebounds per game in her four-year career. In 1983, Donovan won the Naismith College Player of the Year award and the first Champion Player of the Year award given by the Women's Basketball Coaches Association. She was also named to two Kodak All-American teams as well as the 1980 Olympic team. But when the United States boycotted those games protesting the invasion of Soviet troops into Afghanistan, her opportunity to play was lost.

In 1983, Donovan was on the U.S. team at the world championship in Brazil, where she played against **Iuliana Semenova**, who at 6'10½" was even taller than Donovan. As opportunities in professional basketball for women were extremely limited, no opportunities awaited Donovan when she finished college. Like many before her, she went to Japan where her team won the Japanese championship. After playing with the 1984 national team that won a gold in the Olympics, she then returned to Old Dominion where she became a coach.

Karin Loewen Haag,
Athens, Georgia

Donska, Maria (1912–1996)

Polish-born British pianist and piano teacher, a major figure in the musical life of London for half a century, who first became popular with the public during World War II as a performer at the National Gallery lunchtime concerts. Born in Lodz, Poland, on September 3, 1912; died on December 20, 1996; never married; lived with Leonora Speyer (daughter of the violinist Leonora Speyer).

When she died in 1996, Maria Donska was one of the last survivors of the group of artists who had helped maintain the morale of London's population during the darkest days of World War II by performing at the National Gallery lunchtime concerts. Initiated by the famed pianist *Myra Hess, these concerts provided civilians and soldiers alike with a precious interlude of peace and reflection in a bomb-shattered metropolis. Born into a cultured Jewish family in the industrial city of Lodz, Poland, in 1912, Maria Donska was a prodigy who began to play the piano at the age of four. By seven, she was giving professional concerts of the music of Schubert and Schumann. At age 11, Donska gave her first performance with an orchestra, and the next year she was a fulltime conservatory student. Soon she was in Berlin studying with the renowned Austrian virtuoso Artur Schnabel. Schnabel thought so highly of his Polish pupil that he took her with him to London when he gave a noted series of Mozart and Schubert recitals that year in the British capital.

The Nazi seizure of power in 1933 compelled Donska and Schnabel to flee Germany. She returned briefly to Poland to work for Radio Warsaw, but the depth of anti-Semitic sentiments in her homeland prompted her move to London to continue her career in a freer environment. Settling in St. John's Wood with her lifelong friend and companion **Leonora Speyer** (d. 1987), the daughter of the violinist and poet *Leonora Speyer (1872–1956), Donska began working for the BBC by making a series of recordings for broadcasting. In 1936, Donska enrolled at the Royal College of Music. When asked why someone as musically gifted as she had enrolled at the RCM, she candidly replied, "To learn English so that I can play in this country."

Donska remained at the Royal Conservatory of Music until 1940, winning several gold medals for musical excellence. Early in World War II, Donska suffered a nervous breakdown over concern for the fate of her family in Poland—a fear that was justified, since none of them, including her beloved brother, survived the Holocaust. By 1943, she had recovered sufficiently to perform publicly at the National Gallery lunchtime concerts. She also recorded once more for the BBC and began teaching piano to advanced pupils at the Royal Conservatory of Music. After the war, Maria Donska was much in demand both as a teacher and as a recitalist at various festivals. In 1955, she gave a much-applauded series of recitals dedicated to the complete Beethoven piano sonatas at London's Royal Festival Hall. During this time, she met the famed sculptor Jacob Epstein, who asked her to sit for him.

Maria Donska continued playing into the 1970s, giving recitals and recording for the BBC. She finally retired from teaching at the Royal Conservatory in 1980 but gave occasional recitals as part of her schedule until 1989 when illness finally ended her long, successful musical career. In 1987, Donska's lifelong companion and friend Leonora Speyer died. Maria Donska died on December 20, 1996.

SOURCES:
"Maria Donska," in *The Times* [London]. December 23, 1996, p. 17.

John Haag, Associate Professor of History, University of Georgia, Athens, Georgia

Doolittle, Hilda (1886–1961)

A leading American poet of the first half of the 20th century. Name variations: H.D. Born Hilda Doolittle in Bethlehem, Pennsylvania, on September 10, 1886; died on September 27, 1961, at Zurich, Switzerland; daughter of Charles Leander Doolittle (a professor of astronomy) and Helen Eugenie (Woole) Doolittle; attended Bryn Mawr College, 1905–06; married Richard Aldington, in 1913 (divorced 1938): children: one daughter, Perdita (b. 1919).

Met Ezra Pound (1901); moved to Europe (1911); saw first important publication as a poet (1913); became acquainted with Bryher (1918); separated from husband (1919); published collected poems (1925); underwent psychoanalysis with Sigmund Freud (1933–34); lived in England during World War II (1939–45); received Brandeis University Creative Arts Award for Poetry (1959); received Award of Merit Medal for Poetry from American Academy of Arts and Letters (1961).

Major works: Sea Garden (1916); Collected Poems (1925); Palimpsest (1926); Hedylus (1928); Red Roses for Bronze (1931); (war trilogy) The Walls Do Not Fall (1944), Tribute to the Angels (1945), The

Flowering of the Rod *(1946)*; Tribute to Freud *(1956)*; Bid Me to Live *(1960)*; Helen in Egypt *(1961)*; *(autobiographical)* The Gift *(edited by Jane Augustine, University of Florida, 1998).*

Hilda Doolittle held an important position as an American poet and novelist from the era before World War I to the middle of the 20th century. Her work has fascinated critics in part because of the vast and varying set of influences that helped to shape her talent. For example, Doolittle's literary work owed much to her study of the ancient world. In both her poems and her novels, she tried to recreate and find new meaning there, in particular in the era of ancient Greece. Mixed with her fascination for ancient Greece was a second, anomalous element that influenced her writing: the Moravian religious heritage Doolittle received from her mother's side of the family. An additional current running through Doolittle's work was her bisexuality and feminist sensibility; their importance has received particular emphasis in the most recent studies of Doolittle's writing. Finally, her career saw her involved with such leading figures on the intellectual scene as Ezra Pound, William Carlos Williams, D.H. Lawrence, and Sigmund Freud.

Although a prolific writer who produced 15 volumes of work in several genres, Hilda Doolittle was best known for her early poetry. She stands as a leading figure—some would say as the founder—of the Imagist movement in American and English poetic writing that flourished from 1912 through World War I. The poetic world into which Doolittle entered in the early part of the 20th century was still dominated by a tradition that extended back to Henry Wadsworth Longfellow and Alfred Tennyson. It featured a heavy dose of sentimentality, verbosity, and a passion for precise meter. The Imagist movement, in which she took her place, challenged this reigning set of standards with poems that were economical in their use of language, irregular in their rhythm, and laden with new and refreshing imagery. She received her nom de plume of "H.D." from Ezra Pound upon the publication of these first Imagist poems.

Nonetheless, Doolittle's complex and extensive body of work includes novels, essays, and her own translations of classical literature. Important themes in her writing included a clear call to abandon urban society for a life spent in nature and the human inability to surrender the self in order to achieve a permanent affectionate relationship.

Hilda Doolittle was born at Bethlehem, Pennsylvania, on September 10, 1886. Her father Charles Leander Doolittle, a former soldier in the Civil War who had been educated as an engineer, was then a professor of Mathematics and Astronomy at Lehigh University. His second wife, Hilda's mother, was **Helen Woole Doolittle**. The Woole family belonged to the Moravian (or Bohemian) Brotherhood, a persecuted Protestant minority in 18th-century Germany that had found refuge in Pennsylvania. Hilda spent most of her childhood in Philadelphia after her father had received the eminent academic position of Flower Professor of Astronomy and Director of the Flower Observatory at the University of Pennsylvania. Charles Doolittle had hopes that his daughter would follow in his footsteps to become a distinguished scientist, but their tutoring sessions together soon showed Hilda's lack of aptitude in the areas where her father had done so well.

Doolittle had only a brief college experience, and she withdrew from Bryn Mawr in 1906 in her sophomore year. Some students of her life attribute this to her poor health, but another reason may have been her dismal academic performance. Over the following five years, she pursued her education at home; her passion was the literature of ancient Greece and ancient Rome. She read these works first in translation, then, as her language skills developed, in the original. Her first influential literary colleague—and her first romantic interest as well—was Ezra Pound. The two met at a Halloween party when Hilda was only 15; Pound was just a year older. The young man was already pursuing his higher education, and he frequently left the University of Pennsylvania campus to visit her. Their mutual fascination for literature helped to bring them together. William Carlos Williams, a friend of both Pound and Doolittle, later described Hilda as "tall, blond and with a long jaw but gay blue eyes," and he noted how Ezra was "wonderfully in love with her." The romance petered out, however, in large measure due to the elder Doolittles' opposition to Pound. He left for Europe in 1908. The gap Pound created in the young woman's life was soon filled by a deep, possibly physical relationship with a young woman, **Frances Gregg**. Doolittle's bisexuality, which was to play a large role in her future relationships, thus surfaced by her mid-20s.

A key turning point came in Hilda Doolittle's life in 1911. A brief vacation in Europe in the company of Frances Gregg led to her decision to settle permanently in England. Her father agreed to support her financially, and, in the end,

Hilda
Doolittle

she spent most of the remainder of her life in voluntary exile from the United States. She soon received an emotional jolt when Gregg wrote from America with news of her marriage.

Not long after settling in London, Doolittle once again entered Ezra Pound's circle. Pound had become the center of a group of young poets who shared his commitment to a new form of verse that would break away from the stale Romanticism of the 19th century. His ties to *Harriet Monroe's recently founded American magazine, *Poetry: A Magazine of Verse,* gave him the chance to promote work that he admired.

Pound led the young American woman into his group of like-minded London poets. In January 1913, Doolittle, aided by Pound, published three of her works in *Poetry*. The poems were done in the style of Imagism, and they were filled with what Vincent Quinn has called the key qualities of this important new movement: "brevity, concrete imagery, and flexible versification." In an action that has fascinated students of her life, the young American poet took Pound's suggestion to sign her verses as "H.D., Imagiste." Feminist critics such as **Janice Robinson** and **Susan Gubar** have seen this as a sign of Doolittle's abandoning her own personality under the force of Pound's strong will. Richard Aldington, a fellow poet to whom she was introduced by Pound and Doolittle's future husband, later wrote that these were the first poems to appear "with the Imagist label," and he identified her as the center of the entire movement. Doolittle went on to publish poems, once again under the pseudonym "H.D.," in Pound's anthology of Imagist poetry, *Des Imagistes*, which appeared in 1914.

Hilda Doolittle married her fellow poet, Richard Aldington, in October 1913. He had admired her poetry from the first time he had encountered it, and the two shared a passion for Greek culture and the Greek language. Although they now took their place together in the London literary scene, their marriage was shaken by Hilda's miscarriage in the spring of 1915. By this time Richard was also involved with other women. But, in the midst of these painful developments in her personal life, Hilda continued to write diligently. She published her first book, a collection of 27 early poems entitled *Sea Garden*, in 1916. When Richard was about to enter the British army to fight in World War I, she took over his responsibilities as literary editor for a monthly journal of opinion, *The Egoist*. The war years also saw her win a number of prizes from various poetry magazines, and she began to publish her translations from the Greek with *Choruses from Iphigenia in Aulis* appearing in 1916.

By the close of World War I, members of the group of Imagist poets, in which Doolittle had played so central a role, began to go their separate ways. Meanwhile, her own life had been severely disrupted by the war. Her brother was killed in France, her home in London was bombed, and Doolittle's husband was gone for long stretches of active duty. A more lasting complication came into play when her marriage to Aldington finally disintegrated as a result of his infidelity.

During the war, new personages had entered her life. D.H Lawrence and his German-born wife *Frieda Lawrence arrived in London in 1917 after being expelled from an English coastal region as potential spies. Doolittle quickly befriended them, and some biographers of Lawrence suggest that he and H.D. had a romantic liaison. There is clearer evidence of her relationship with a young Scottish composer named Cecil Gray whom she had met in the Lawrences' circle. Gray became the father of a child, her daughter **Perdita**, to whom she gave birth in March 1919. The event took place within complicated circumstances: separation from her husband and serious illness in the form of double pneumonia.

Finally, **Winifred Ellerman**, the woman who became her lifelong friend and companion, was now impelled to meet Doolittle after reading her poems. The daughter of a rich English shipowning family, "Bryher," as Winifred chose to be called, provided Doolittle with crucial emotional support over the following decades although the passionate relationship between the two women was clouded and complicated by Winifred's two marriages. After recovering her health in the aftermath of her pregnancy, Doolittle set out with Bryher on tours of Europe and the United States. By the mid-1920s, Hilda had settled in Switzerland. Her *Collected Poems* appeared in 1925, and she now began more than three decades of steady literary production, publishing five additional volumes of poetry before her death in 1961.

Throughout her career, Doolittle's passion for ancient Greece was a dominant element in her writing. Some critics found reason to fault her fiction for departing from the reality of the ancient world. As one critic, Douglas Bush, put it, she created ancient Greek characters and plots in the "soft romantic nostalgia . . . of the Victorian Hellenists." A more sympathetic assessment of her work noted that her protagonists are "too nervous in their intensity to be conventionally Attic" but credited her nonetheless with an ability to capture the longing for ancient Greece that has pervaded Western history.

The complexity of Doolittle's work as a novelist appears in *Palimpsest,* published in 1926 and her first major work of fiction. One portion of the book was set in the era of the ancient world around 75 BCE as Rome invaded Greece; a second segment of the work was an autobiographical account placed in contemporary London; the book's concluding portion takes place during a visit to contemporary Egypt. As Quinn has noted, here and in Doolittle's other works of fiction "a principal character is a sensitive woman trying amid uncongenial circumstances to remain faithful to transcendental ideals." In his view, Doolittle repeatedly presents the reader with a description of a woman who has been rejected in her efforts to find love.

A novel departure for Doolittle came in 1927 when she adapted a work by Euripides, *Hippolytus,* to produce her own three-act play entitled *Hippolytus Temporizes.* The decision to move in this direction may have been influenced by the mixed reviews her direct translations from the Greek had received. Meanwhile, her poetry in the 1920s explored and reinterpreted Greek mythology from a woman's perspective.

Doolittle's poetry, as seen in her 1931 volume *Red Roses for Bronze*, now seemed to lose much of its energy and imagination. Perhaps for that reason, she ceased to publish verse until the World War II years. Similarly, her difficulty in working in this form may have caused her to turn in 1933 to Sigmund Freud in Vienna for psychoanalysis. The initial treatment lasted for three months, and she then resumed her analysis at the hand of the noted Viennese doctor for another five weeks in 1934. A decade later, she recorded her reaction in her *Tribute to Freud*, which was published in 1956. That volume offers a glowing pen portrait of Freud that has been highly praised by Freud's biographer Ernest Jones.

Doolittle's account of her time in Vienna also offers her recollections of her state of mind at a crucial point in her writing career. The picture Doolittle presented of her psychological state in the early 1930s downplayed any suggestion of pain and pathology. She wrote in *Tribute to Freud* that she wanted to "root out my personal weeds, . . . canalize my energies." Quinn describes her central purpose as seeking aid "in overcoming doubts about the timelessness of the soul." Ironically, she found the Viennese doctor and psychoanalyst deeply skeptical about any substantial form of human immortality beyond the survival of the family line from one generation to the next. In her unpublished record of her hours with the noted psychoanalyst, Doolittle noted that they had spent some of their time together exploring her bisexuality. Freud also encouraged her to write an account of her life during the First World War, and this became the genesis of her roman à clef *Bid Me to Live*. Written between 1939 and 1949, it was published only a year before her death. Despite her deep differences with Freud over such issues as the value of a religious sensibility, she still remembered him with respect and affection. In an important study of Doolittle's work, *Psyche Reborn*, critic **Susan Stanford Friedman** wrote that the poet's psychoanalysis with Freud helped nourish "the explosion of a new kind of poetry and prose during the forties and fifties."

In the aftermath of her psychoanalysis, Doolittle turned again to translation, producing an English-language version of Euripides' *Ion* in 1937. Thereafter, she wrote poetry steadily despite the difficult circumstances of World War II, but her new work began to appear only in 1944. The war period, as Vincent Quinn notes, led her to feel that "the five years' ordeal had cleansed and strengthened her soul." In any case, in 1945 and 1946, she now presented her public with three volumes of war poems. This trilogy—*The Walls Do Not Fall, Tribute to the Angels*, and *The Flowering of the Rod*—was written from 1942 to 1944. Other works written at this time, but published only long after, were her tribute to Shakespeare and other leading English writers, *By Avon River*, and her *Tribute to Freud*.

The poetry of the war years once again displayed Doolittle's attraction to drastically new forms of writing. She now departed from her use of pure free verse to adopt the more disciplined form of free verse couplets. Instead of her customary focus on ancient Greece, the poems of her war trilogy show a new interest in Egyptian culture and the world of the Bible. The poems of *The Walls Do Not Fall, Tribute to the Angels*, and *The Flowering of the Rod* were filled with complexity. Nonetheless, their inspirational purpose was evident as she expressed a continuing belief in God and the deity's presence even in the midst of such unprecedented catastrophe.

By the closing years of her life, the distinguished poet and writer received a wave of recognition. In 1959, Brandeis University presented her with its Creative Arts Award for Poetry. The following year, Hilda Doolittle became the first woman to receive the American Academy of Arts and Letters' Award of Merit for Poetry.

Doolittle ended her writing career with the publication of two drastically different works. In her 1960 novel *Bid Me to Live*, she gave a fictionalized account of her life in the closing years of World War I. Her social relations then became dominated by the disintegration of her marriage and her growing link to D.H. and Frieda Lawrence. Julia the heroine is, like Doolittle herself, an American in wartime London married to an English writer who has left for military service. Doolittle describes how Julia's husband begins an adulterous affair, and how Julia follows suit with Frederick, a character modeled on D.H. Lawrence. In the end, Doolittle's heroine establishes a platonic relationship with a young composer.

The following year, she published *Helen in Egypt*. A lengthy and notoriously difficult work of poetry, it centers on a monologue by Helen dealing with the Trojan War. For some critics, it is Doolittle's most important work, surpassing the achievement of her early writing as an Imagist poet. It raises the startling and provocative idea that Helen was not kidnapped and carried off to Troy. Rather, she spent the years of the Trojan War in Egypt; her place in Troy was taken by a phantom whom the Greek gods placed there.

A longtime expatriate who had returned to the United States only for brief visits since 1911, Doolittle spent her last days in Zurich, Switzerland. She died there on September 27, 1961, shortly after her 75th birthday.

Evaluations of H.D.'s literary achievement vary widely. Vincent Quinn's view of her as a talented but limited writer who did her best work early on in her career remains influential. He marks the Imagist verse written between 1912 and 1917 as her best work. In his view, Doolittle had blended the imagery of nature with her own strong emotions in verse that met the Imagist ideal of "hard, clear [poetry], never blurred nor indefinite." While ranking these pieces of verse as Doolittle's supreme achievement, he also notes that they were only a limited triumph: "Like cameos and etchings, they are excellent works of art in a minor key," but he calls them lacking in the "larger intellectual and social concerns of major poetry." Thereafter, as she explored new and larger literary forms, "a luminous brevity," according to Quinn, departed from her work.

Other critics in considering the broad extent of Doolittle's work have placed a different emphasis on her work. Professor Norman Holmes Pearson of Yale University has, in contrast to Quinn, been a promoter of Doolittle's overall literary achievement. He joined a number of other critics in stressing H.D.'s development over time with such work as *Helen in Egypt* matching or exceeding her early work as a star of the Imagist movement. Finally, feminist critics such as Friedman and **Claire Buck** have found H.D. to be particularly significant as a literary voice expressing a woman's perspective. Thus, **Margaret Dickie**, writing in *The Columbia History of American Poetry*, stresses H.D.'s role as a woman writer who repeatedly employed "the metaphor of birth" and whose work was "distinguished by its exploration of female eroticism."

SOURCES:

Buck, Claire. *H.D. and Freud: Bisexuality and a Feminine Discourse*. NY: St. Martin's Press, 1991.

Doyle, Charles. *Richard Aldington: A Biography*. Houndmills, Basingstoke, Hampshire, Eng.: Macmillan, 1989

Duplessis, Rachel Blau. *H.D.: The Career of That Struggle*. Brighton, Sussex, Eng.: The Harvester Press, 1986.

Friedman, Susan Stanford. *Penelope's Webb: Gender, Modernity, H.D.'s Fiction*. Cambridge, Eng.: Cambridge University Press, 1990.

———. *Psyche Reborn: The Emergence of H.D.* Bloomington, IN: Indiana University Press, 1981.

Parini, Jay, ed. *The Columbia History of American Poetry*. NY: Columbia University Press, 1993.

Quartermain, Peter, ed. *American Poets, 1880–1945*. First Series. Detroit, MI: Gale Research, 1986.

Quinn, Vincent. *Hilda Doolittle (H.D.)*. NY: Twayne, 1967.

Robinson, Janice S. *H.D.: The Life and Work of an American Poet*. Boston, MA: Houghton Mifflin, 1982

Suchard, Alan, Fred Moramarco, and William Sullivan. *Modern American Poetry, 1865–1950*. Boston, MA: Twayne, 1989.

SUGGESTED READING:

Carpenter, Humphrey. *A Serious Character: The Life of Ezra Pound*. London: Faber and Faber, 1988.

Dickie, Margaret, and Thomas Travisano, eds. *Gendered Modernism: American Women Poets and Their Readers*. Philadelphia, PA: University of Pennsylvania Press, 1996.

Mariani, Paul. *William Carlos Williams: A New World Naked*. NY: McGraw-Hill, 1981.

Neil M. Heyman, Professor of History, San Diego State University, San Diego, California

Dora d'Istria (1828–1888).

See Chica, Elena.

Dorcas (fl. 37 CE)

Biblical woman. *Name variations: called Tabitha by the Jews. Flourished around 37 CE; a Christian woman of Joppa, a Mediterranean seaport town.*

Dorcas, whose name means *gazelle* in Greek, was a widow woman of Joppa who sewed and made clothes for the poor. Upon her death, her grieving friends sent for Jesus' disciple Peter, who laid his hands on her and restored her to life. Her revival caused many to convert to the teachings of Jesus.

Dorchester, countess of.

See Sedley, Catharine.

Doremus, Sarah Platt (1802–1877)

American philanthropist who helped found New York Woman's Hospital and shelters. Born Sarah Platt Haines on August 3, 1802, in New York City; died on January 22, 1877, in New York City as a result of a fall; daughter of Elias Haines (a businessman) and Mary Ogden; married Thomas Doremus, on September 11, 1821; children: eight daughters, one son, and a number of adoptees.

Became active in benevolent activities for the Greeks suffering under Turkish control (1828); became president of a society to promote the Grande

*Ligne Mission in Canada, organized and run by **Henrietta Feller** (1835); began working in the woman's ward of the New York City Prison (1840) which led to the formation of the Woman's Prison Association, an organization dedicated to aid recently released women; appointed manager of the City and Tract Society, an organization devoted to evangelizing among the poor (1841), and joined the City Bible Society of New York (1849) which provided them with Bibles; one of the founders of the House and School on Industry (1850), serving as president for ten years and as manager for eight; assisted in the establishment of the Nursery and Child's Hospital of New York State (1855) and during the Civil War, helped distribute supplies to hospitals in and around New York City.*

A member of the Dutch Reformed Church, the independently wealthy Sarah Platt Doremus devoted her life to many philanthropic and benevolent activities while encouraging others to do likewise. She participated in numerous and far-ranging support organizations, but her main focus became missionary work and the support of women in mission. Responding in 1834 to the appeal of the Reverend David Abell, an American member of the Dutch Reformed Church and a missionary to China, Doremus attempted to establish a branch of the Society for Promoting Female Education in the East, although officials of the American Board of Missions dismissed this plan. In response to **Frances Mason**'s plea for other women to assist her in the education of Burmese women (an action contrary to the Baptist Board of Missions' refusals to allow for female missionaries), in 1860 Doremus established the Woman's Union Missionary Society of America for Heathen Lands. She became its first president, providing her home as its headquarters. Her house soon became the staging ground for missionaries preparing to depart for abroad; it also became a rest home for those forced to return due to ill health. Within ten years, the Woman's Union Missionary Society had female missionaries in India, China, Syria, Greece, and Japan. The success of this organization soon led to the establishment of similar denominational organizations that supported and sponsored female missionaries.

Doremus' work was significant not only in the establishment and the success of the Woman's Union Missionary Society, but also in altering traditional Reformed, Baptist, and other protestant denominational resistance to women missionaries. Until Doremus and other women leaders became active in the context movements of women's rights and women's education, few

women were allowed to go on missions, and those few were almost never sanctioned representatives of mission boards. In fact, when Doremus founded her mission board, only five major and five minor boards existed; only 31 women had been allowed to become missionaries and those under special circumstances. The role of women in mission was limited to their service as wives of missionaries, carrying on the full duties of missionary work unrecognized. Doremus' organizations and boards altered prejudices against women in mission, providing not only the organizational support and funding, but a voice that stated clearly the necessity for female missionaries.

> *W*ell reported of for good works, [Sarah Doremus] hath brought up children, she hath lodged strangers, she hath washed the saints' feet, she hath relieved the afflicted, she hath diligently followed every good work.
>
> —Dr. E.P. Rogers, Funeral Sermon

SOURCES:
Deen, Edith. *Great Women of the Christian Faith*. NY: Harper and Brothers, 1959.
Hardesty, Nancy A. *Great Women of Faith*. Grand Rapids: Baker Book House, 1980.
Montgomery, Helen Barrett. *Western Women in Eastern Lands*. NY: Macmillan, 1910.

Amanda Carson Banks,
Vanderbilt Divinity School

Dorfmann, Ania (1899–1984)

Russian-American pianist who was the only woman to record a concerto with Arturo Toscanini and the NBC Symphony Orchestra. Born in Odessa, Russia, on July 9, 1899; died in New York City on April 21, 1984; taught at Juilliard in addition to concertizing.

The brilliant instrumentalist Ania Dorfmann, born in Odessa, Russia, on July 9, 1899, first appeared in public before World War I as an accompanist to Jascha Heifetz. At age 12, she was enrolled at the Paris Conservatoire where she studied with Isidor Philipp. Dorfmann left Russia in 1920, touring Europe as a concert artist. She settled in the United States in 1936 and performed with Arturo Toscanini and his NBC Symphony Orchestra in December 1939. In the last decades of her career, she taught at the Juilliard School. In 1945, Dorfmann became the only woman to record a concerto with Arturo Toscanini and his NBC Symphony, in this case the Beethoven First Piano Concerto. Among her

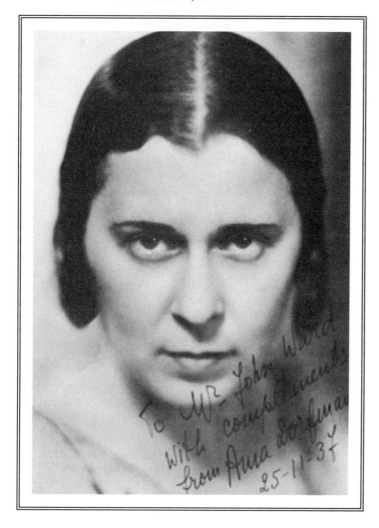

*Ania
Dorfmann*

other recordings were the complete Songs without Words of Felix Mendelssohn.

John Haag,
Athens, Georgia

Doria Shafik (1908–1975).
See Shafik, Doria.

Dori'a Shafiq (1908–1975).
See Shafik, Doria.

Dorléac, Françoise (1942–1967)

French actress. Born in Paris, France, on March 21, 1942 (some sources cite 1941); died in Nice, France, in 1967; the third of four daughters of Maurice and Renée (Deneuve) Dorléac (both actors); older sister of Catherine Deneuve.

Selected films: Mensonges *(1959);* La Fille aux Yeux d'Or *(The Girl with the Golden Eyes, 1961);* Ce Soir ou Jamais *(1961);* Le Jeu de la Vérité *(1961);* Tout l'Or du Monde *(1961);* Arsène Lupin contre Arsène Lupin *(1962);* L'Homme de Rio *(That Man from Rio, 1964);* La Chasse a L'Homme *(Male Hunt, 1964);* La Peau Douce *(The Soft Skin, 1964);* Genghis Khan *(US/UK/Ger./Yug., 1965);* Where the Spies Are *(UK, 1966);* Cul-de-sac *(UK, 1966);* Billion Dollar Brain *(UK, 1967);* Les Demoiselles de Rochefort *(The Young Girls of Rochefort, 1967).*

Françoise Dorléac, the elder sister of film star **Catherine Deneuve**, made her screen debut in 1959, after a short stage career. Talented and beautiful, Dorléac was at the height of a brilliant international career as a leading lady when she was killed in a fiery automobile crash in Nice, France. At the time of her death, she had just finished shooting *The Young Girls of Rochefort* with Deneuve, the fourth film the sisters had made together.

Dormon, Carrie (1888–1971)

American ecological pioneer whose work in the emerging discipline of ecology was highly regarded by professionals in archaeology, botany, forestry and ornithology. Name variations: Caroline Dormon. Born Caroline Coroneos Dormon at Briarwood estate, Louisiana, on July 19, 1888; died in Saline, Louisiana, on November 21, 1971; daughter of James L. Dormon and Caroline (Trotti) Dormon; sister of Virginia Dormon; never married.

Carrie Dormon, who lived to be 83, was a highly regarded botanist and ornithologist and author of six books, besides being a bona fide Southern eccentric. Regarded by many in the field as the foremost authority on wild flowers in the southern United States, in many ways she herself remained untamed and only lightly touched by society's conventions. A friend described her as:

> tall and sinewy—all whipcord and piano wire—with fresh earth on her hands and apron. There would be a cocklebur or two caught on the hem of her skirt, and bits of leaves and pine needles or wisps of cobwebs and cocoons stuck to her shoulders. Her complexion was fair. Her hair—braided into a crown or pulled back severely into a bun—was the color of straw. When you were closer you could see that her eyes were the green of chlorophyll and had a quickness about them, like the eyes of a squirrel, conditioned to detect the barest flicker of movement.

Born Caroline Coroneos Dormon on July 19, 1888, at Briarwood, the Dormon family home in Natchitoches Parish, Carrie was the sixth child and second daughter of a prosperous

Louisiana family. Her beloved "papa" was not only a lawyer but an amateur naturalist as well. Carrie was his favorite child, and James L. Dormon rarely went anywhere without her. Not only did she look forward to riding next to him in his buggy, she often accompanied him on his quail hunts, during which he would give her detailed and fascinating nature lessons. An extremely precocious child, Carrie Dormon could write at the age of three and would be a voracious reader throughout her entire life. From her mother **Caroline Trotti Dormon**, who was an amateur poet and a published author, Carrie learned to appreciate the beauty and infinite nuances of written language. On her own, and starting at an early age, Carrie began to explore and observe the natural world, both in the 135 acres of her family's Briarwood estate and in the yard of the family home in Arcadia, Louisiana. At age five, she already began to detect the immense variety of wildflowers around her home, discovering several clumps of white bluets. The same year, she began to cultivate a small wild garden in a shady corner of her home in Arcadia.

Very likely the most independent of the "wild" Dormon children, Carrie's lack of interest in social conventions concerned her father, and he determined to place her on something resembling a more traditional path of life. At age 16, she was sent off to Judson College, a Baptist girls' school in Marion, Alabama. Homesick and miserable during her first year, Dormon found things better the next year when she discovered that her way with words could win her friends. Even more important was the fact that one of her teachers discovered her great talent for identifying birds by their calls. Soon, she was teaching birdcalls to both her fellow students and some of her teachers. Carrie's father was pleased that she was being socialized, but society's norms seemed empty to Carrie and much of what she learned at Judson remained a veneer. Later, she noted, "I still belonged to the wild." Her happiest hours during these years were spent in the nearby woods of Grey's Hollow, where she discovered for the first time such priceless treasures as yellow violets, bloodroot, and hepatica.

Graduating with a bachelor's degree in 1907 in literature and art, her joy was tempered that year by the death of her mother. Starting in 1908, Carrie began to teach first grade in nearby Bienville Parish. Happiness ended for her in 1909 with the death of her beloved father. She wrote, "Papa possessed magic" and with his passing some of the magic vanished from her life. Three months later, the Dormon family home in Arca-

dia, with its large library, burned to the ground. But Briarwood remained, and Carrie and her sister **Virginia Dormon**, who had also become a teacher, would spend their summers there. In 1918, the two sisters moved to Briarwood on a permanent basis, living in a log home built from trees growing on the estate grounds. That same year, Carrie became a conservation advocate, pleading to the Southern Forestry Congress meeting in New Orleans for the preservation of Louisiana's long-leaf pine virgin forests. Her eloquence played a significant role in her being appointed state chair of conservation for the Louisiana Federation of Women's Clubs. Dormon yearned to be a forester, but was told that this was clearly not "women's work" and that she should be content to remain a teacher.

In 1919, illness prompted Carrie Dormon to ask the school superintendent to transfer her to a job in the pine woods. Fortunately a job was available, and she was sent to the forested sand hills of Kisatchie in Natchitoches Parish, which could only be reached in those days via rough

Carrie Dormon

dirt roads. She regarded the majestic long-leaf pine forests of the area as a "heaven" in which the "great pines came right to the water's edge on those lovely clear creeks, with only an occasional magnolia and dainty wild azalea and ferns." There the idea was born—this unspoiled beauty must be preserved for future generations to enjoy. Determined that nothing would stop her from achieving the preservation of this area, Dormon gave lectures and wrote newspaper articles, calling for the preservation of a virgin tract of the Kisatchie, called Odom's Falls. Her second goal was to persuade the Federal government to buy up cutover areas for a national forest. Despite the fact that Dormon was a woman, the commissioner of the Louisiana Department of Conservation, M.L. Alexander, took notice.

In September 1921, Alexander hired Dormon to carry out his department's public relations. Rising to the challenge, she lectured throughout the state and also prepared bulletins and posters making a powerful case for the economic as well as aesthetic value of trees to the state. In 1922, Dormon began working with W.W. Ashe, a land acquisitions official of the U.S. Forest Service. She made a strong impression on Ashe, who learned vast amounts from her on their many trips into the Kisatchie. The respect of Ashe for Dormon found concrete form when he named a new variety of hawthorn tree that she had discovered for her, *Craetaegus aestivales dormonae.* Carrie and her sister Virginia continued the crusade to preserve the Kisatchie, often taking other interested individuals into the area. Once during the years-long struggle, a frustrated Carrie Dormon was able to get her lawyer brother to draft an act to purchase the land. Then she lobbied with powerful state senators to see that it actually became law.

Although some of the land was in fact cut down by commercial interests and she would mourn over "[t]his beautiful forest lost to posterity," in June 1930 the Federal government finally purchased 75,589 acres of cutover land for a national forest, which was promptly named the Kisatchie National Forest. That same year, Dormon became one of the first three women to be elected an associate member of the Society of American Foresters. Politically always a liberal, she resigned in disgust when Huey Long was elected governor. If shunned in her own state during these years, in 1935 she was appointed as the only female member of the De Soto Commission established by the U.S. Congress.

But it was Dormon's work in the pine forests and flower fields that kept her busy, and

in 1934 she was finally persuaded to put her vast knowledge to paper and publish her first book, *Wild Flowers of Louisiana.* Written for amateurs like herself, it reflected her deep love of nature and was full of admonitions regarding whether or not to pick plants "freely," "sparingly," or "never." In 1941, Dormon received official recognition for her conservation efforts when she was appointed beautification consultant for the Louisiana Highway Department.

Carrie Dormon's health was frail during the last 15 years of her life. The death of her sister Virginia was also a blow, but neither fact could thwart her determination to continue to study nature and be its champion. Despite pain from angina and a crippled hip, she continued to observe birds and squirrels from her living room window. Books now flowed from her pen, including the 1958 volume *Flowers Native to the Deep South,* a book whose scope was astonishing in that it covered the entire deep South except for subtropical Florida. Of particular concern to Dormon was her hope that growing knowledge would help people to protect and preserve the native wildflowers of the region. In 1965, she published *Natives Preferred,* a chatty volume for those "who love the informality of Nature, with softly rounded masses of foliage, and flowers scattered freely by her hand." Probably her most popular book, *Natives Preferred* is also rich in autobiographical details.

Two more books appeared at the end of Dormon's life. In 1967, she published *Southern Indian Boy,* based on her lifelong interest in the Native Americans of Louisiana. From the start of her nature studies, she had discovered and mapped Indian mounds and befriended the survivors of five distinct Indian tribes in the state, gathering their lore and legends. She gave much of her data to the Smithsonian Institution's John R. Swanton, who praised her work highly.

Bird Talk, published in 1969, was Dormon's last book. An anthology of articles she published over the years in the Sunday magazine of the *Shreveport Times,* these were deeply felt personal encounters with chickadees, finches, wrens and other wild birds she had observed and admired over the decades. Despite her semi-invalid status at this stage of her life, Dormon continued to observe birds, even making new discoveries. On April 13, 1969, she noted six Cassin's finches feeding on the flat rocks outside her window; they had never before been reported in Louisiana.

Carrie Dormon's last years were rich in honors. In 1960, the Garden Club of America awarded her its Eloise Paine Luquer Medal for achievement in botany. In 1965, Louisiana State University awarded her an honorary Doctor of Science degree. The following year, the American Horticultural Society recognized Briarwood as "a sanctuary for the flora of the south." A practical measure for the preservation of Briarwood for future generations came into being with the creation of the Caroline Dormon Foundation. A remarkable life dedicated to the plants and animals of the forest ended with the death of Carrie Dormon on November 21, 1971.

SOURCES:

Bonta, Marcia Myers. *Women in the Field: America's Pioneering Women Naturalists*. College Station: Texas A&M University Press, 1991.

———, ed. *American Women Afield: Writings by Pioneering Women Naturalists*. College Station: Texas A&M University Press, 1995.

Crittenden, Bob. "Miss Caroline's Dream Became Louisiana's National Forest," in *Forests and People*. Vol. 30, 1980, pp. 24–29.

Johnson, Fran Holman. *The Gift of the Wild Things: The Life of Caroline Dormon*. Lafayette, LA: Center for Louisiana Studies, University of Southwestern Louisiana, 1990.

Rawson, Donald M. "Caroline Dormon: A Renaissance Spirit of Twentieth-Century Louisiana," in *Louisiana History*. Vol. 24, 1983, pp. 121–139.

Snell, David. "The green world of Carrie Dormon," in *Smithsonian*. Vol. 2, no. 11. February 1972, pp. 28–33.

Stringfellow, Emma L. "Caroline Dormon and Her Accomplishments" (manuscript, Northwestern State University of Louisiana, 1961).

Trissler, Alicia. "Caroline Dormon and Louisiana Archaeology of the 1930s" (M.A. Thesis, Northwestern State University of Louisiana, 1994).

John Haag, Associate Professor of History, University of Georgia, Athens, Georgia

Dorn, Erna (1912–1953)

German war criminal, concentration camp guard at Ravensbrück, and controversial participant in the Cold War. Name variations: (forged identity) Erna Brüser née Scheffler. Born Erna Kaminski in 1912; executed in Halle on October 1, 1953; daughter of Arthur Kaminski; married Erich Dorn; children: two.

Was able to avoid punishment for her activities in the Nazi period until 1951 when she was tried and convicted of war crimes in East Germany; under circumstances that are still unclear, was freed from prison during the uprising of June 17, 1953 but was recaptured and sentenced to death, a sentence that was carried out on October 1, 1953.

Many of the details of the life of Erna Dorn, who served the Nazi state with fanatical loyalty as a concentration camp guard, remain obscured by the massive propaganda unleashed by opposing forces of the Cold War in Germany. To some, she remains a war criminal as well as a possible intelligence agent of the West, pure and simple. To others, she appears to be as much a victim as a perpetrator of evil, being executed by the East German state at the height of the Cold War's often fierce tensions. Erna Kaminski's fateful encounter with the malevolent forces of history began in 1933 when she was working as a secretary in the police department of Königsberg, East Prussia (modern-day Kaliningrad, Russia). Soon after the Nazi seizure of power in Germany, her father Arthur Kaminski had become chief of the dreaded Gestapo in Königsberg. Erna began work in the Königsberg Gestapo offices. She appears to have been directly involved in the brutal measures taken against underground German Socialist and Communist organizations in the first phase of the Third Reich. In her private life, she married Erich Dorn, who began a career in the elite Nazi SS. Erna Dorn gave birth to two children.

During World War II, Erna Dorn worked for the SS in the political division of Ravensbrück, the largest concentration camp for women in Nazi Germany. She served in several other, smaller concentration camps, including Lobositz, and in the last weeks of World War II received a set of expertly forged identity papers from the commandant of Hertine, one of the subsidiary camps of Ravensbrück. Although the precise nature of the role she played in the Nazi concentration camp system remains obscure to this day, in general only high-level camp officials received officially sanctioned forged documents in the final days of Hitler's Germany. Now known as Erna Brüser née Scheffler, Erna Dorn was able to successfully hide her Nazi past in what in the spring of 1945 became the Soviet Occupation Zone of Germany. Claiming to be "a victim of Fascism," she benefited materially from her fabricated past, receiving housing, work, and financial assistance. Dorn's deception was so successful that she soon began living with a man whose anti-Fascist credentials were impeccable, being a Communist veteran of the Spanish Civil War against Franco Fascism.

Dorn's deception finally collapsed in 1951 when it became obvious that her papers were forged. A court of the German Democratic Republic (GDR), the German Communist state that had evolved out of the Soviet Occupation Zone, sentenced her to 15 years imprisonment for having been a willing participant in the Nazi concentration camp system. She was serving out her sentence in the city of Halle an der Saale when the mass uprising that convulsed the GDR began on June 17, 1953. A crowd stormed the prison, and she and other prisoners were released. Rather than disappear into the populace or attempt to flee to West Germany, Dorn appeared at an anti-GDR rally in one of Halle's main squares. She called for an overthrow of the regime, a demand that was popular with the majority of Halle's population. Within days, however, the GDR state authority was stabilized with help from Soviet occupation troops, and Erna Dorn found herself back in prison. This time, however, she was accused of high treason and sentenced to death—one of the few women ever to receive such a sentence in GDR history.

With the revolt quashed, the ruling Socialist Unity Party (SED) admitted to having committed "errors" in the recent past, making a number of conciliatory gestures to the workers and farmers of the GDR. At the same time, however, it blamed the uprising of June 17 on provocateurs and spies from the West. In a statement released on June 21, 1953, the SED Central Committee laid blame on:

> Fascist and common criminals, whose names appeared on the lists prepared at the agents' headquarters in West Berlin, [who] were temporarily released from prison. One of these was Erna Dorn, the SS Commandant [sic] of the Ravensbrück Concentration Camp for Women, who had been found guilty of bestial crimes against humanity by a democratic court. Clearly, these western agents were intent on setting up a fascist power in the German Democratic Republic, thus blocking the path to unity and peace for Germany.

On the eve of her execution in Halle on October 1, 1953, Dorn wrote a farewell letter in which she cryptically spoke of having "with forbearance taken blame for the crimes of others." After the passage of more than four decades and the collapse of the GDR, the events of 1953 as they relate to Erna Dorn have not been completely clarified. Despite extensive research, much remains unexplained about Erna Dorn. The GDR picture of her as a Nazi concentration camp sadist who later worked as an intelligence agent of the Western powers during the Cold War era, which appeared in a thinly disguised portrait of her as Hedwig Weber in Stephan Hermlin's story "Die Kommandeuse," may be an exaggeration. Indeed, after the unification of Germany took place in 1990, Hermlin was violently attacked for having written this story. Some anti-Communist Germans regarded Hermlin's "Die Kommandeuse" as a slanderous

attack on a woman, whatever her Nazi past may have been, who in fact ended her life as a genuine victim of Marxist tyranny. In 1993, the German politician Rainer Eppelmann demanded that Hermlin be denied membership in the newly created Berlin-Brandenburg Academy of the Arts because he had written and published "Die Kommandeuse" in the days of the GDR. Some public figures went so far as to advocate the reburial of Dorn's remains in the newly created "Cemetery of Honor for the Victims of Stalinist Violence" in Dresden-Tolkowitz. In death, as in life, the message of Erna Dorn's life remained shrouded in factual obscurity and ideological passions. In this sense, the changing details of her biography symbolize the immense difficulties that remain to be resolved as Germany continues to struggle with its painful past.

SOURCES:

Baring, Arnulf. *Uprising in East Germany: June 17, 1953.* Translated by Gerald Onn. NY: Cornell University Press, 1972.

Ebert, Jens, and Insa Eschebach. *Die Kommandeuse: Erna Dorn—zwischen Nationalsozialismus und Kaltem Krieg.* Berlin: Dietz Verlag, 1994.

Gerats, Josef. "Wer Erna Dorn wirklich war, wird nicht geklärt," in *Neues Deutschland.* August 26, 1994, p. 13.

Hollis, Andy. "Stephan Hermlin's 'Die Kommandeuse': A Re-Interpretation in the Light of Recent Events," in *GDR Monitor.* No. 23, 1990, pp. 27–37.

Lorey, Christoph. "Zur Innen- und Aussen-perspektive in Stephan Hermlins Erzählung 'Die Kommandeuse'," in *Seminar.* Vol. 33, no. 2. May 1997, pp. 134–148.

"Verhöhnung der Opfer," in *Süddeutsche Zeitung.* June 18, 1993.

Weringh, Koos van. "Een rasopportuniste in een verloederd Duitsland," in *Trouw.* January 13, 1995, p. 2.

John Haag, Associate Professor of History, University of Georgia, Athens, Georgia

Dornemann, Luise (1901–1992)

German reformer and author, active in the women's movement during the Weimar Republic, who became a leader of the state-sponsored women's organization in the German Democratic Republic. Name variations: *during her years in the United Kingdom, 1936–1947, spelled her name Louise Dornemann. Born in Aurich, Ostfriesland, on February 23, 1901; died on January 17, 1992; daughter of a judicial official.*

Selected writings: Alle Tage ihres Lebens: Frauengestalten aus zwei Jahrhunderten *(1988);* Clara Zetkin: Leben und Wirken *(1989);* Jenny Marx: der Lebensweg einer Sozialistin *(1980).*

Born at the start of the 20th century into a world whose stability appeared unshakable, Luise Dornemann experienced a dizzying series of wars and revolutions in her long life as well as social, technological, and ideological transformations that continued to challenge humanity at the end of that same century. Although rural and small town life remained largely intact on the windswept island of Ostfriesland where she was born, Dornemann left home and in 1921 qualified to be a teacher in the city of Aachen. Politically active, over the years she became increasingly radicalized and in 1928 joined the Communist Party of Germany (KPD). A women's rights activist, she was particularly interested in the necessity of advancing the cause of sex education and abortion rights. In 1932, she became chair of the Unified Organization for Proletarian Sexual Reform and Protection of Mothers, also serving until the Nazi seizure of power in 1933 as director of the Marriage Counseling Office in Düsseldorf. The Nazis destroyed the sexual reform movement in Germany, making already restrictive anti-abortion laws even harsher.

In 1936, Dornemann immigrated to the United Kingdom. In London, she was a member of the Communist-led Allies Inside Germany Council, and also served as a member of the executive board of the Free German Cultural League, another Communist-oriented group of German emigrés. Remaining a dedicated Communist and desiring to participate in the construction of socialism in post-Nazi Germany, in 1947 she moved to the Soviet Occupation Zone (SBZ) and joined the Socialist Unity Party, which a year earlier had absorbed the Social Democrats and claimed to be the only voice of a united working class. Dornemann also joined the mass organization created to represent women in the SBZ, the Demokratischer Frauenbund Deutschlands (Democratic Women's League of Germany or DFD), which was founded in Berlin on March 8, 1947. As a reliable and loyal KPD veteran, Luise Dornemann was chosen in 1948 for the important post of secretary of the national executive board of the DFD. In effect, chief executive officer of the DFD, Dornemann held this post until 1951. Until 1953, she also served as DFD representative to the Women's International Democratic Federation (WIDF), a Communist-dominated organization founded in Paris in 1945. After being expelled from Paris in 1951, the WIDF headquarters moved to East Berlin.

Retiring from active politics in 1953, Dornemann worked for the next decade as a research associate in East Berlin's Institute for Marxism-Leninism. Over the next decades, she wrote a number of well-received history books intended for a broad audience. Ideologically orthodox, her biographies of *Jenny Marx and *Clara Zetkin went through many editions and were available in GDR bookshops and libraries until the end of the socialist state and society in 1989–90. Dornemann's biography of Jenny Marx even appeared in Japanese (1956) and Chinese (1983) translations. Despite her advanced age, she continued to serve as a member of the DFD executive board until the collapse of the GDR dictatorship in the fall of 1989. Although there were significant achievements for women in the GDR during its 40 years of existence, and many of its 1.5 million members were active in seeking realistic solutions to women's problems, the organization never exhibited any independence vis-a-vis the state. Organizationally, it became as sclerotic as the Honecker regime itself, the best indication of this being the fact that Ilse Thiele, DFD chair who was deposed in November 1989, had held that post since 1953. Luise Dornemann died on January 17, 1992.

SOURCES:

Dornemann, Louise. *German Women under Hitler Fascism: A Brief Survey of the Position of German Women up to the Present Day.* London: "Allies Inside Germany"Council, 1943.

Dornemann, Luise. *Alle Tage ihres Lebens: Frauengestalten aus zwei Jahrhunderten.* Berlin: Dietz Verlag, 1988.

———. *Clara Zetkin: Leben und Wirken.* Berlin: 9th edition, Dietz Verlag, 1989.

———. *Jenny Marx: der Lebensweg einer Sozialistin.* Berlin: Dietz Verlag, 1980.

Herbst, Andreas, *et al. So funktionierte die DDR:* vol. 3: *Lexikon der Funktionäre.* Reinbek bei Hamburg: Rowohlt, 1994.

John Haag, Associate Professor of History, University of Georgia, Athens, Georgia

Dorothea, Princess of Lieven

(1785–1857)

Russian diplomat. Name variations: Dariya Khristoforovna; Sibyl of Europe. Born Dorothea von Benkendorff in Latvia in 1785 (some sources cite 1784); died in 1857; married Khristofor Andreevich de Lieven also known as Prince Christoph of Lieven (Russian general and ambassador at the court of Prussia), in 1800 (died 1839).

Dorothea, princess of Lieven, was born in Latvia in 1785. Her mother was a favorite of the Russian empress *Sophia Dorothea of Wurttemberg, wife of Tsar Paul I. The young Dorothea received a brilliant education and, at an early age, married Prince Christoph of Lieven, ambassador at the court of Prussia in Berlin (1811–12). Her remarkable talent for dealing with public affairs combined with her eminent social amenities to place her in control of the main springs of political action in Berlin. By her extensive official and private correspondence, she succeeded in shaping the opinions of the court of St. Petersburg. When her husband was transferred to Britain's court of St. James (1812–34), Dorothea made herself known there as she had been in Berlin and, until 1834, held a leading position in the highest social and political circles of England. After the death of her husband, she took up her residence in Paris (1839–57), and her house became a favorite resort of the chief political, literary, artistic, and social celebrities of that city. She was on terms of personal friendship with almost every eminent statesman of her time.

Dorothea Frederica of Brandenburg-Schwedt (1736–1798).

See Sophia Dorothea of Brandenburg.

Dorothea Hedwig of Brunswick-Wolfenbuttel (1587–1609)

Princess of Anhalt-Zerbst. Born on February 3, 1587; died on October 16, 1609; daughter of *Dorothea of Saxony (1563–1587) and Henry Julius, duke of Brunswick (r. 1589–1613); married Rudolf, prince of Anhalt-Zerbst, on December 29, 1605.

Dorothea of Bavaria (1920—)

Member of the Tuscan Branch of the House of Habsburg-Lorraine. Born in 1920; married Gottfried also known as Godfrey (1902–1984); children: Leopold Franz also known as Leopold Francis (b. 1942) and three daughters.

Dorothea of Brandenburg

(1430–1495)

Queen of Norway, Denmark, and Sweden. Name variations: Hohenzollern. Born in 1430; died on November 10 or 25, 1495, at Kalundborg, Denmark; daughter of John III the Alchemist, margrave of Brandenburg, and *Barbara of Saxe-Wittenberg (c. 1405–1465); sister of *Barbara of Brandenburg (1422–1481); married Christopher of Bavaria also known as Christopher III (1416–1448), king of Norway and Denmark and Sweden (r. 1439–1448), on September 12, 1445; married Christian I (1426–1481), king of Denmark, Norway, and Sweden (r. 1448–1481), on October 26 or 28, 1449; children: (second marriage) Olaf (1450–1451); Canute (1451–1455); John I, also known as Hans

(1455–1513), king of Denmark and Norway (r. 1481–1513); *Margaret of Denmark (1456–1486, who married James III of Scotland); Frederik or Frederick I (1471–1533), king of Norway and Denmark (r. 1523–1533).

The gifted Dorothea of Brandenburg married Christopher III, king of Norway, Denmark, and Sweden, at age 15. Widowed at 18, she then married Count Christian of Oldenburg (Christian I), impoverished heir to the crowns of Denmark and Norway. Christian had agreed to marry and care for her in exchange for his election to the throne. At age 13, their daughter *Margaret of Denmark was married to James III of Scotland.

Dorothea of Brandenburg

(1446–1519)

Duchess of Saxe-Lauenburg. Name variations: Dorothea von Brandenburg. Born in 1446; died in March 1519; daughter of *Catherine of Saxony (1421–1476) and Frederick II the Iron (1413–1471), elector of Brandenburg (r. 1440–1470, abdicated); married John V of Saxe-Lauenburg, duke of Saxe-Lauenburg, on February 12, 1464; children: Magnus of Saxe-Lauenburg, duke of Saxe-Lauenburg.

Dorothea of Denmark (1520–1580)

Electress Palatine. Name variations: Dorothea Oldenburg. Born on November 10, 1520; died on September 20, 1580; daughter of Christian II (1481–1559), king of Norway and Denmark (r. 1513–1523), and *Elisabeth of Habsburg (1501–1526); married Frederick II (1482–1556), elector Palatine (r. 1544–1556), on September 26, 1535.

Dorothea of Denmark (1528–1575)

Danish princess. Name variations: Dorothea Oldenburg. Born in 1528; died on November 11, 1575; daughter of *Sophia of Pomerania (1498–1568) and Frederik or Frederick I (1471–1533), king of Denmark and Norway (r. 1523–1533); married Christof von Mecklenburg, on October 27, 1573.

Dorothea of Saxe-Lauenburg

(1511–1571)

Queen of Norway and Denmark. Name variations: Lüneburg or Luneburg. Born on July 9, 1511; died on October 7, 1571, in Sonderburg; daughter of Magnus, duke of Saxe-Lauenburg, and *Catherine of

Brunswick-Wolfenbuttel (1488–1563); married Christian III (1503–1559), king of Norway and Denmark (r. 1534–1559), on October 29, 1525; children: *Anna of Denmark (1532–1585); Frederick II, king of Denmark and Norway (r. 1559–1588); Magnus, king of Livonia; Hans also known as Johann or John (1545–1622), duke of Holstein-Sonderburg; *Dorothy of Denmark (1546–1617).

Dorothea of Saxony (1563–1587)

Princess of Saxony. Born on October 4, 1563; died on February 13, 1587; daughter of *Anna of Denmark (1532–1585) and Augustus (1526–1586), elector of Saxony; married Heinrich Julius also known as Henry Julius, duke of Brunswick (r. 1589–1613), on September 26, 1585; children: *Dorothea Hedwig of Brunswick-Wolfenbuttel (1587–1609, who married Rudolf, prince of Anhalt-Zerbst). Henry Julius' second wife was *Elizabeth of Denmark (1573–1626).

Dorothea Oldenburg (1504–1547)

Duchess of Prussia. Born on August 1, 1504; died on April 11, 1547; daughter of *Anna of Brandenburg (1487–1514) and Frederick I, king of Norway and Denmark (r. 1523–1533); became first wife of Albert (1490–1568), duke of Prussia (r. 1525–1568), on July 1, 1526; children: *Anna Sophia of Prussia (1527–1591). Albert's second wife was *Anne Marie of Brunswick (1532–1568).

Dorothy of Denmark (1546–1617)

Duchess of Luneburg. Born on June 9, 1546; died on January 6, 1617; daughter of *Dorothea of Saxe-Lauenburg (1511–1571) and Christian III (1503–1559), king of Norway and Denmark (r. 1534–1559); married William the Younger (1535–1592), duke of Luneburg (1559–1592), on October 12, 1561; children: Ernest II (b. 1564), duke of Brunswick; Christian (b. 1566), duke of Brunswick; Augustus the Elder (b. 1568), duke of Brunswick; Frederick (b. 1574), duke of Brunswick; George (b. 1582), duke of Brunswick; *Sibylle of Brunswick-Luneburg (1584–1652).

Dorr, Rheta Childe (1866–1948)

American journalist and feminist who investigated conditions of women and children in industry and society, and participated in the women's suffrage movement. Born Rheta Louise Childe on November 2, 1866, in Omaha, Nebraska; died on August 8, 1948, in New Britain, Pennsylvania; daughter of Edward Payson Childe (a druggist and probate judge) and Lucie (Mitchell) Childe (a homemaker); married John Pixley Dorr, in 1892 (divorced 1898); children: one son, Julian Childe Dorr (1896–1936).

Attended University of Nebraska, (1884–85); worked as reporter for the New York Evening Post (1902–06); wrote for Everybody's magazine (1907–09); published What Eight Million Women Want (1910); wrote for Hampton's magazine (1910–12); became editor of National Women's Party newspaper, The Suffragist (1914); published Inside the Russian Revolution (1917), A Soldier's Mother in France (1918), (autobiography) A Woman of Fifty (1924), and Susan B. Anthony (1928).

While playing with her male cousin in a family cemetery, eight-year-old Rheta Childe made a discovery. Tombstones everywhere read "also Sarah, wife of the above," or "also Mary, wife of the above." As Dorr recounts in her autobiography, the sight awakened her to the position of women in society. Would she, too, like the women buried there, lose her identity as an individual? "I bet I never finish on any old gravestone as 'also Rheta, wife of the above'," she told her cousin. Dorr determined then to live so as "to claim a gravestone dedicated exclusively to myself." Her life and most of her writing reflect that commitment to independence and self-sufficiency. She would be a chronicler, a commentator, and a participant in the many changes that influenced women's place in the world from the late 19th to the mid-20th century.

Rheta Dorr grew up in the small midwestern town of Lincoln, Nebraska, in a middle-class family. She attended the Latin School of the University of Nebraska, but she claimed to have learned more from hearing *Susan B. Anthony and *Elizabeth Cady Stanton speak. She sought economic independence at an early age, defying her father's wishes and taking a job washing windows at the Nebraska State Fair Grounds. After that episode, her father insisted she enroll in the University of Nebraska, but Rheta had a limited interest in formal education. She excelled only in English, where she had an inspiring professor who introduced her to Ibsen's *A Doll's House*. That play further fired her desire for independence, and Dorr dropped out of college, against her family's wishes. She managed to get a job at the local post office where she continued her informal study of society by observing the lives of her neighbors. What Dorr saw at the post office intensified her criticism of the position of the typical married woman. Apparently a number of couples carried on illicit liaisons with the help of General Delivery. Dorr concluded that these affairs could be blamed on the lack of healthy outlets for women's energies. Trained only to be attractive to men, housewives fell back on the old romantic game, clandestinely and out of boredom. Women with jobs, she noted, did not have the time or the inclination for such behavior. After two years at the post office, Dorr became an insurance underwriter.

In 1890, she moved to New York City where she experimented with the study of art and did some free-lance writing. Two years later, she married John Pixley Dorr, a businessman from Seattle, and in 1896 her son Julian Childe was born. In 1898, Dorr left her husband, took Julian, and moved back to New York. She attributed the divorce to her realization that she and her husband held vastly different ideas about marriage and women's place. On one occasion, he read approvingly a passage from Herbert Spencer that attributed family disintegration to the weakening of the husband's authority. As Dorr recalled, she told her husband that the authority should be weakened until men and women were absolutely equal, until there was no "head of the family" at all.

After returning to New York, Dorr encountered the problems of a divorced mother trying to build a career. She had decided to seek a job as a journalist, but before finding a position with the women's section of the New York *Evening Post,* she realized that women had no place in the existing social scheme. Although pretty girls, young ladies, and protected wives had a place, independent women like herself were anomalies. While working at the *Evening Post,* Dorr covered women's clubs and charitable activities and relayed fashion and housekeeping tips. She met prominent reformers and suffragists in the U.S. and Europe, wrote about the plight of working girls, and became active in the General Federation of Women's Clubs' investigation of the conditions of women and children in industry. Dorr came to believe that public policies were needed to alleviate the inequalities among the social classes as well as between the sexes.

A variety of issues occupied the reforming women of Dorr's time—efforts to gain access to higher education, recognition in the trades and professions, attempts to secure equal pay for equal work, the rise of trade unions, the development of women's clubs, the agitation for suffrage. Dorr supported all of them and participated actively in several.

In 1907, having resigned from the *Evening Post,* Dorr researched and wrote a series of articles for *Everybody's* magazine about the effects of industrialization on women. She looked at women's historic trades—cooking, sewing, washing, canning, spinning, weaving—and tried to show how women followed these jobs from the home. Dorr hoped to describe the transformation of the trades and of the workers. She wanted to demonstrate that women are the permanent producers of wealth, and therefore should be independent human beings and citizens, not adjuncts to men and society. Following a practice of other "muckraking" investigative journalists, Dorr disguised herself as a "working girl" and took jobs in a steam laundry, a bakery, a department store, and several factories. She felt, however, that *Everybody's* betrayed the purpose of her probing investigation. The editors turned her research over to William Hand, who published the articles over his signature as coauthor. Hand compiled the material into a picture of a "triumphal army" of women invading men's jobs, rather than retaining Dorr's emphasis on the exploitation of women in industry.

After that episode, Dorr left *Everybody's* and joined the staff of *Hampton's,* a more aggressive reform magazine. There she was treated as a professional, Dorr recalled, and given "unlimited freedom to express my own ideas in my own fashion" as well as some authority in directing the magazine's policies. Every article relating to women and children, education, and women's suffrage was referred to her.

Although her articles for *Hampton's* discussed the drudgery of women's work quite forthrightly, Dorr saw a fairly optimistic prospect for improvement, especially through the efforts of women's organizations, protective legislation, and the suffrage. She wrote favorably about the Women's Trade Union League (WTUL) for the practical and democratic efforts leisure-class women made in conjunction with their "wage-earning sisters." Dorr praised the work of the Consumer's League, especially as they had helped to develop the arguments Louis Brandeis used successfully to persuade the Supreme Court to uphold protective legislation for women in the 1908 case, *Muller* v. *Oregon.* In 1910, Dorr compiled a number of her articles for *Hampton's* into *What Eight Million Women Want* where she described favorably the work of the General Federation of Women's Clubs.

Throughout these writings, Dorr emphasized the role of women as agents for social change and bemoaned the social conditioning that had led women to conform to a single type—young, beautiful, and very, very good—in order to arouse amorous emotions in men. Such conditioning prepared women to be economically dependent on men and to minimize their own intelligence and capabilities. Dorr believed that outmoded social attitudes were responsible for the oppression of women and for the other social problems she described in her writings. Like many other Progressive reformers, she believed that if the public were educated about social problems, they would respond by addressing and alleviating those problems, including such issues as child labor, juvenile delinquency, prostitution, and the double standard of morality. Although Dorr called herself a socialist during her career as a journalist, her articles did not call for public ownership of production, but rather for government regulation of industry and expanded social services.

She hoped to convince her readers that child labor was economically as well as morally wrong, as it would result in the exhaustion of future generations. Misguided industrialists who thought only of short-term profit-and-loss saw capital and labor as abstractions. Women, who saw "labor" as flesh and blood individuals, could educate capitalists to promote the larger interests of society by abolishing child labor.

The same poverty, injustice, and inequality that were responsible for child labor were also responsible for juvenile delinquency, in Dorr's view. Given such an environmental explanation, wayward youths could be reformed and rehabilitated through schools, juvenile courts, and detention homes. Well-informed citizens, led by women's groups, could implement such reforms at the local level.

Dorr had the Progressive's characteristic devotion to "scientific management," which could be applied in education as well as in business. She wrote several glowing reports of the Gary, Indiana, school system as a model for its efficiency, use of wasted space, relating the school to the life of the community, and making all the opportunities of the community available for the education of children.

As a feminist interested in the welfare of women and children, Dorr addressed problems of prostitution and the double standard. On the one hand, she blamed prostitution on the lack of decent social opportunities for working-class girls, forcing them to seek entertainment at disreputable dance halls where they were likely to be seduced. In addition, they were victimized by unscrupulous employment agencies and even by immoral employers. But Dorr also faulted the social attitudes that arrested young girls for a "fault" not punished in boys. She urged that the public must realize that "wayward" girls should not be condemned, but rehabilitated through training schools or homes that offered stability and taught useful skills.

Divorce, too, was related to the double standard and to inequality between the sexes. She saw the solution to the rising divorce rate in marriages between two equal partners, both strong, educated, and self-supporting. Such equal marriages would demand full citizenship and opportunity for women. Dorr's arguments that the most basic reform was equality of economic opportunity for women followed closely the feminist arguments of *Charlotte Perkins Gilman. Both women knew from personal experience the disabilities suffered by single mothers who had limited preparation for earning a living.

Along with her interest in women's economic status, Dorr consistently supported a woman's right to vote. In 1912, she traveled to Europe and interviewed prominent suffragists, including *Emmeline Pankhurst, leader of the movement in Great Britain. Impressed by Pankhurst's aggressive tactics, Dorr became convinced that American suffragists needed a more militant approach than that of the National American Suffrage Association. She joined the Congressional Union, led by *Alice Paul, and gave that group credit for the passage of the 19th Amendment. Dorr became editor of the Congressional Union's newspaper, *The Suffragist,* when it was founded in 1913. She argued repeatedly for a federal suffrage amendment, calling it the greatest reform since the Emancipation Proclamation. She claimed that women would create a new political situation, remake the laws, and inject a fresh point of view into American politics. She also argued that women's suffrage would enlarge the "American" pool of enlightened voters to offset the immigrants who were likely to become dupes of political bosses.

Dorr did not confine her interest in women's issues to the suffrage. From 1912 to 1917, she was part of the feminist circle, Heterodoxy, a group who took pride in their unorthodox opinions. In a sort of early consciousness-raising movement, they discussed cultural, political, and scientific innovations as well as their own personal experiences as women.

Prior to the outbreak of World War I, Dorr, like many of her contemporaries who believed in unique womanly virtues, subscribed to the theory that women had a special affinity for peace.

She argued that because women were mothers, they appreciated the cost of war in human life. War, she said, was "evidence of man's inability to govern without the help of women," the sacrifice of human interests to property interests.

World War I was the turning point in Dorr's life and thinking. By 1917, she had repudiated her former views on the subject of peace and become a rabid supporter of the war and of American involvement. She promoted these ideas as a syndicated columnist for the New York *Evening Post,* as well as in *A Soldier's Mother in France,* published in 1918. She called World War I the most righteous war in the history of the world and charged the Germans with trying to murder Christian civilization and enslave mankind. They were "beasts in human form" who would violate the young daughters of America before their parents' eyes. Dorr condemned internationalists and pacifists (her own former associates) as German propagandists and traitors.

During the time Dorr propagandized for war, she visited Russia to comment on the revolution. In *Inside the Russian Revolution,* she labelled the Bolshevik leaders German agents and "criminal lunatics." She concluded the world was not ready to create a cooperative millennium or to "hand over the work of government to the man in the street."

In 1919, Dorr was seriously injured in a motorcycle accident, which led to a long period of physical and emotional disability. She produced two significant books in the 1920s, her autobiography *A Woman of Fifty* (1924) and her biography of *Susan B. Anthony* (1928). The latter argued for a revised version of history that would recognize women's contributions, typically omitted by male historians. Organized women, she argued, had been reforming things for years and continued to work to create a new social order. In her autobiography, she continued to promote equal economic opportunity, equality in marriage, and "full citizenship" rather than special protection for women.

Dorr was a publicist of current ideas rather than an original thinker. The path of her thought parallels the mainstream—from prewar moderate liberalism, to wartime superpatriotism, to a postwar retreat from reform. During the last 20 years of her life, her activities as a journalist and feminist waned. Her health was often poor, and she was crushed by the death of her son in 1936. Rheta Childe Dorr died of a cerebral hemorrhage in 1948. She had described her own life as "a strange one for a woman," as she had chosen

to live without marriage or a permanent home but had sought happiness in her work. She believed that through her work, she had tried to make people think. In her autobiography, she claimed to have lived "vividly," a child of her times. "I had never built any towers, never any palaces," she asserted, "but surely I had laid a few stones on a corridor."

SOURCES:
Dorr, Rheta Childe. *Inside the Russian Revolution.* NY: Macmillan, 1918.
———. *A Soldier's Mother in France.* Indianapolis, IN: Bobbs-Merrill, 1918.
———. *Susan B. Anthony: The Woman Who Changed the Mind of a Nation.* NY: Frederick A. Stokes, 1928.
———. *What Eight Million Women Want.* Boston, MA: Maynard, 1910.
———. *A Woman of Fifty.* NY: Funk and Wagnalls, 1924.

SUGGESTED READING:
Cott, Nancy F. *The Grounding of Modern Feminism.* New Haven, CT: Yale, 1987.
Sochen, June. *Movers and Shakers: American Women Thinkers and Activists, 1900–1970.* NY: Quadrangle, 1973.

COLLECTIONS:
Some of Rheta Childe Dorr's correspondence related to suffrage may be found in the National Women's Party Papers, Library of Congress, Washington D.C. Her articles for *The Suffragist* are located in the National Women's Party Papers, National Museum of American History, Smithsonian Institution, Washington D.C.

Mary Welek Atwell, Associate Professor of Criminal Justice, Radford University, Radford, Virginia

Dors, Diana (1931–1984)

British actress and celebrity, presented by the media as "Britain's answer to Marilyn Monroe," who prevailed over personal problems to become both well known and admired. Born Diana Fluck in Swindon, Wiltshire, October 23, 1931; died in Windsor, Berkshire, England, on May 4, 1984; daughter of Albert Edward Sidney Fluck and Winifred Maud Mary (Payne) Fluck; married Dennis Hamilton, in 1951 (divorced 1957); married Dickie Dawson, in 1959 (divorced 1967); married Alan Lake, in 1968; children: (first marriage) two sons, Mark, Gary; (third marriage) son Jason.

Selected filmography: The Shop at Sly Corner *(1946);* Holiday Camp *(1947);* Good Time Girl *(1948);* Oliver Twist *(1948);* Here Come the Huggets *(1948);* Diamond City *(1949);* Dance Hall *(1950);* Lady Godiva Rides Again *(1951);* The Weak and the Wicked *(1954);* A Kid for Two Farthings *(1955);* Value for Money *(1955);* An Alligator Named Daisy *(1955);* Yield to the Night *(Blonde Sinner, 1956);* The Long Haul *(1957);* The Unholy Wife *(1957);* I Married a Woman *(1958);* Scent of Mystery *(1960);* On

Opposite page

Ｄiana
Ｄors

the Double *(1961)*; King of the Roaring Twenties *(1961)*; The Sandwich Man *(1966)*; Hammerhead *(1968)*; Baby Love *(1969)*; There's a Girl in My Soup *(1970)*; Dead End *(1970)*; Hannie Caulder *(1971)*; The Amazing Mr. Blunden *(1972)*; Nothing But the Night *(1972)*; Theatre of Blood *(1973)*; From Beyond the Grave *(1973)*; Adventures of a Taxi Driver *(1975)*; Adventures of a Private Eye *(1977)*; Confessions from the David Galaxy Affair *(1979)*; Steaming *(1984)*.

Selected writings: Behind Closed Dors *(London: W.H. Allen, 1979)*; Diana Dors' A-Z of Men *(London: Futura, 1984)*; Dors by Diana *(London: Macdonald Futura, 1981)*; For Adults Only *(London: W.H. Allen, 1978)*; Swingin' Dors *(London: World Distributors, 1960)*.

Born during the Great Depression in the suffocating English provincial town of Swindon, Diana Fluck dreamed as a child of becoming an actress, writing in a school essay at age nine, "I am going to be a film star, with a swimming pool and a cream telephone." At 13, physically already a woman, she pretended to be 17 and entered a local beauty contest, winning third prize. Confidently, she entertained troops at camp concerts in the closing months of World War II. At 15, Diana enrolled at the London Academy of Dramatic Art, was spotted in a production, and made her film debut in the 1946 thriller *The Shop at Sly Corner.* A ten-year contract with the J. Arthur Rank organization soon followed. Diana Fluck entered the Rank Charm School for stars and starlets and soon changed her name to Diana Dors, after her maternal grandmother.

Following appearances in a number of formulaic comedy films, Dors' contract with the Rank studios lapsed in 1950. But instead of disappearing into obscurity, her career began to blossom, not because of any significant acting achievements but rather because the British tabloid press now began transforming an actress with few prospects into a platinum-blonde, big-busted "bombshell" who was the British answer to *Marilyn Monroe and **Brigitte Bardot**. Carefully planned publicity stunts were a major part of the strategy. Much of the hype that pushed ahead Dors' career in the 1950s came from the fertile mind of her first husband, Dennis Hamilton, whom she married in 1951. The couple, who would have two sons, moved to Hollywood to advance Diana's American career. Hamilton was determined to make his wife a star, and Svengali-like, this domineering personality fed the gossip columnists of the day with countless Dors stories, many of them fabricated. The most memorable publicity stunt of this phase of Dors'

career took place in 1955, when she surfaced at the Venice Film Festival wearing a mink bikini.

Diana Dors was seen in numerous films during the 1950s, virtually all of them forgettable. One exception was her appearance in the film *A Kid for Two Farthings,* based on the Wolf Mankowitz book and directed by Carol Reed with screenplay by Mankowitz. In this charming 1955 tale, a boy in London buys a little goat and thinks it is a wish-fulfilling unicorn. Dors gave a good performance, and the film has retained much of its charm. Only rarely, however, was she able to choose a role of some substance. This was the case in the 1956 film *Yield to the Night,* in which she gave a convincing performance in the role of a condemned murderess. Virtually none of her film roles provided Dors with the opportunity to evolve into a serious actress. Of the almost two dozen forgettable films Dors made during the early 1950s, one of the most popular was *Lady Godiva Rides Again,* which prompted her to remark that she was "the only sex symbol Britain has produced since Lady *Godiva."

But it was the turmoil of her private life rather than new directions in her career, that most fans of Diana Dors read about in their tabloids. Although Dors appeared to have settled down, her marriage collapsed in a blaze of garish publicity, and the Hamiltons were divorced in 1957. Dors remained in the headlines over the next few years, often because of her colorful, and for the time rather scandalous, private life. In 1959, seeking stability, she married the British-born comedian Dickie Dawson. Virtually all of her ventures from this time, including a song recording for Columbia Records, "Swinging Dors," failed to find a public. In 1960, Dors sold her memoirs to the British tabloid *News of the World.* Racy and lurid by the standards of 1960, the series ran for 12 weeks, was read by millions, and among other things resulted in Dors being denounced by the archbishop of Canterbury as a wayward hussy.

Never able to compete successfully with Monroe, by the early 1960s Diana Dors had put on weight and was evolving from a sex symbol to a middle-aged mother figure. With her husband's earnings meager at best, Diana Dors had little choice but to become her family's sole breadwinner. In 1966, she abandoned hopes of a Hollywood career to return to the United Kingdom. Hard times compelled Dors to play Prince Charming in pantomime and work in a cabaret act in clubs outside of London. In 1967, her marriage to Dawson collapsed, and she lost custody of her two sons. The same year, Dors was

forced to declare bankruptcy. Few doubted her word when she declared herself to be quite "hopeless with money." In 1968, Dors risked marriage a third time, with the actor Alan Lake, a man of working-class origins who in 1970 was sentenced to prison for 18 months for his involvement in a bloody pub brawl. Despite some dramatic ups and downs, Dors' marriage to a man who was nine years her junior would in fact last. Lake was the father of her third son, Jason.

Dors' career revived in the early 1970s, and there were signs she was moving in new directions. In 1970, she appeared on stage at London's Royal Court Theater as the brassy widow in *Three Months Gone.* That same year, she made a favorable impression in her role in Jerzy Skolimowski's film *Deep End.* But "Queenie's Castle," a television series written with her as star, received mostly negative reviews. In 1974, she appeared as Jocasta in Sophocles' *Oedipus* at the Chichester Festival, but here too the critical response was not encouraging.

In 1974, Dors almost died from meningitis. When her acting career ended, she soldiered on as a popular guest on countless television shows, endearing herself to millions of ordinary Britishers. Dors was resilient and cheerful in the face of adversity, writing an "agony column" in a daily newspaper. Fighting her own battle with obesity, she hosted a dieting series on breakfast television and gave advice to the lovelorn on "Good Morning Britain." A true survivor in the celebrity jungle, she wrote several volumes of memoirs and spoke candidly to the media of being a cancer patient, which began in 1982. In the last years of her life, Dors was devoted to her sons and had become a solid British Mum. Having converted to Roman Catholicism, she no longer loathed Sundays as she had while growing up in Swindon. She now regarded Sunday as "a beautiful day when I like to be with my family, go to Mass, rest and spend at least some time with God."

Diana Dors lost her battle with cancer and died at the Princess Margaret Hospital, Windsor, Berkshire, on May 4, 1984. Less than a month earlier, she had finished shooting her last film, Joseph Losey's *Steaming.* Her husband was at her side when she died peacefully. He told the press, "Her last words to me before she slipped away were 'Oh my darling I love you. Take care of the boys and say farewell to everyone concerned'." Earthy and unashamed of her roots, Diana Dors was genuinely mourned by millions around the world. Her tenacity and courage in adversity won the admiration of all who came in contact with her. Alan Lake never overcame his grief over his wife's death and killed himself on October 10, 1984, the 16th anniversary of their first meeting.

SOURCES:

Barker, Paul. "Observations," in *New Statesman*. Vol. 10, no. 440. February 14, 1997, p. 54.

"Diana Dors," in *The Times* [London]. May 7, 1984, p. 14.

"Diana Dors, Actress in Britain," in *The New York Times Biographical Service*. May 1984, p. 641.

Flory, Joan, and Damien Walne. *Diana Dors: Only a Whisper Away*. London: Javelin, 1988.

Froshaug, Judy. "Tomorrow is the day of unrest," in *The Times* [London]. February 4, 1984, p. 11.

Macnab, Geoffrey. "British Cinema," in *Sight and Sound*. Vol 6, no. 7. July 1996, pp. 22–25.

Waymark, Peter. "Dors, Diana," in Lord Blake and C.S. Nicholls, eds., *The Dictionary of National Biography 1981–1985*. Oxford: Oxford University Press, 1990, pp. 119–120.

John Haag, Associate Professor of History, University of Georgia, Athens, Georgia

Dorset, countess of (1590–1676).

See Clifford, Anne.

Dorset, marquise of.

See Holland, Anne (d. 1474).
See Wotton, Margaret.

Dorsey, Sarah Anne (1829–1879).

See Davis, Varina for sidebar.

Dorziat, Gabrielle (1886–1979)

French actress. Born Gabrielle Sigrist Moppert on January 15, 1886, in Epernay, Marne, France; died in 1979; educated in Paris; studied for the stage with Mlle A. Gerlaut and at the Paris Conservatoire.

In 1900, Gabrielle Dorziat made her first stage appearance at the Parc Theatre in Brussels as Marianne in Molière's *L'Avare*. She performed at the Gymnase in Paris (1901–05); at the Vaudeville (1905–07); and at the Sarah Bernhardt Theatre, portraying Yvonne de Chazeau in *Maîtresse de Piano* (1907). Dorziat made her London debut in 1904 in the title role of *Antoinette Sabrier*, and her New York debut as Marina de Dasetta in *The Hawk* in 1914. Generally typed as the intimidating royal or aristocrat, Dorziat made approximately 70 French, English, and American films, including *L'Infante a la Rose* (1922), *Samson* (1936), *Le Mensonge de Nina Petrovna* (1937), *La Fin du Jour* (1939), *De Mayerling a Sarajevo* (*Mayerling to Sarajevo*, 1940), *Monsieur Vincent* (1947), *Ruy-Blas* (1948), *Manon* (1949), *So Little Time* (English, 1952), *Little Boy Lost* (U.S., 1953), *Madame Du Barry* (1954), *Mitsou* (1956), *Gigot* (U.S.

1962), and *Germinal* (1963). In 1936, she appeared as *Elizabeth of Bavaria (1837–1898), empress of Austria, in the film *Mayerling*.

d'Ossoli, Margaret (1810–1850).

See Fuller, Margaret.

Dostalova, Leopolda (1879–1972)

Czech actress, one of the stars of the Prague stage for more than a half-century, whose portrayals showed great emotional range and an affinity for strong, passionate women. Born in Veleslavin, near Prague, Czechoslovakia (modern-day Czech Republic), on January 23, 1879; died on June 17, 1972; daughter of an actor.

Born in 1879 in Veleslavin, a town near Prague, Leopolda Dostalova grew up in a theatrical environment, her father being an actor. She studied acting in the 1890s in Prague, and among her teachers were the leading actors and actresses of the day. The most important influence on Dostalova's evolving acting style was **Hana Kvapilova** (1860–1907), the female star of the Prague theater at the turn of the century. Hailed at her 1901 debut at Prague's National Theater as the most outstanding representative of the modern tragic style of acting, Dostalova remained a star for the rest of her extraordinarily long career.

After performing for a brief period, from 1920 through 1924, at the branch of the Prague National Theater in Vinohrady, she returned to Prague in 1924 to universal acclaim. A powerful dramatic actress, Dostalova was able to turn in a superb performance in a classic role of Sophocles one night, switching the next evening to depict a contemporary personality in a play by Karel Capek. Among her best roles were Sophocles' Antigone and Electra, Shakespeare's Lady Macbeth, Euripides' Medea, Ibsen's Hedda Gabler, and Ferdinand Bruckner's **Elizabeth I**. She was a sovereign master of roles by Slavic playwrights, including Slowacki's Balladyna, Ostrovskii's Murzavetskaia (*Wolves and Sheep*), and Tyl's Liudmila (*Dragomiry*). Exhibiting remarkable physical stamina and intellectual power, Dostalova remained a major figure of the Prague stage well into the 1950s. She was awarded the State Prize of the Czechoslovak Republic in 1946, published her memoirs in the 1960s, and died, beloved by several generations of Prague theatergoers, on June 17, 1972. A week before her death, the innovative Za Branou (Behind the Gate) theater company, of which she was doyenne, was shut down by the repressive regime installed by the Soviet Union after 1968.

SOURCES:

Dostalova, Leopolda. *Herecka vzpomina*. 2nd ed. Prague: Orbis, 1964.

Jansky, Emanuel. *Narodni umelkyne Leopolda Dostalova*. Prague: Vydavatelstvi ministerstva informaci, 1948.

Kindermann, Heinz. *Theatergeschichte Europas, X. Band: Naturalismus und Impressionismus, III. Teil*. Salzburg: Otto Müller Verlag, 1974.

"Leopolda Dostalova," *The Times* [London], June 19, 1972, p. 14.

John Haag,
Athens, Georgia

Dostoevsky, Anna (1846–1918)

Memoirist and second wife of Russian novelist Fyodor Dostoevsky. Name variations: Dostoevski or Dostoyevsky. Born in 1846; died in 1918; married Fyodor or Fedor Dostoevsky, in 1867.

Born in 1846, Anna Dostoevsky aspired to an independent life. She had just finished a course in shorthand when she was hired by Fyodor Dostoevsky to transcribe his novel *The Gambler*. At the time, the 46-year-old Fyodor was still mourning the death of his first wife **Sophie Dostoevsky** and resolving an unhappy love affair with **Polyina Suslova**. Anna, submissive and adoring, was the antithesis of Fyodor's previous paramours and quickly captured his heart.

After their marriage in 1867, the couple left Russia in order to escape their creditors. They spent three months in Dresden and Baden, during which time Anna suffered a miscarriage, and Fyodor, in a deep depression over what he perceived to be the ruin of his talent, indulged his passion for gambling. Anna began a shorthand diary in which she described the first difficult years of her marriage. Unsure of Fyodor's love, she carefully guarded her husband's ego, even to the point of encouraging him to gamble away their last 20 francs. In one entry, she describes Fyodor's contrite behavior after a losing streak at the tables. "He said pathetically that he reproached himself for his weakness for gambling, that he loved me, that I was his beautiful wife, and that he was not worthy of me. Then he asked me to give him some more money." In another entry, which illustrates Anna's growing frustration at Fyodor's contradictory behavior, she erupts when he tells her that she has been insensitive: "I was indeed pained to hear it, particularly because I always thought that Fedya was a man who understood my sensitiveness. Christ! What a number of times I could have made things unpleasant for him, if I had wished it."

After leaving Baden, the couple roamed Europe until 1871, when they returned to Russia. Fyodor had apparently broken the cycle of his gambling, and Anna had matured. "From a timid, shy girl I have become a woman of resolute character," she wrote, "who could no longer be frightened by the struggle with troubles." For the next ten years, Anna tended to her husband's needs and became an important part of his work. After his death in 1881, she continued to devote herself to the service of his writings and memory. During her final years, Anna Dostoevsky transcribed her early diaries, which she used to prepare her memoir *Reminiscences*, published after her death.

SOURCES:

Moffat, Mary Jane, and Charlotte Painter, eds. *Revelations: Diaries of Women*. NY: Random House, 1974.

Douce I (d. 1190)

Countess of Provence. Died in 1190; married Raymond Berengar I, count of Provence; children: Raymond Berengar II, count of Provence; *Berengaria of Provence (1108–1149).

Douce of Aragon (1160–1198)

Queen of Portugal. Name variations: Dulce of Aragon; Dulcia of Barcelona. Born in 1160; died on September 1, 1198, in Coimbra, Portugal; buried at Holy Cross Church, Coimbra; daughter of Raymond Berengar II, count of Provence, and *Petronilla (1135–1174), queen of Aragon; married Sancho I (1154–1211 or 1212), king of Portugal (r. 1185–1211 or 1212), in 1181; children: *Theresa Henriques (c. 1176–1250, who married Alphonso IX, king of Leon); *Sancha (c. 1178–1229); Raimundo (1180–1189); *Costanza (1182–1202); Alphonso II the Fat (1185–1223), king of Portugal (r. 1211–1223, who married *Urraca of Castile [c. 1196–1220]); Pedro (1187–1258), king of Majorca; Fernando also known as Ferdinand of Portugal (1188–1233, who married *Johanna of Flanders); Henrique (1189–c. 1191); *Branca (c. 1192–1240); *Berengaria (1194–1221), queen of Denmark; *Mafalda (c. 1197–1257).

Douglas, countess of.

See Stewart, Isabel (fl. 1371).
See Holland, Anne (fl. 1440–1462).

Douglas, Elizabeth (d. before 1451)

Countess of Orkney. Name variations: Lady Elizabeth Douglas. Died before 1451; daughter of *Margaret

Stewart (d. before 1456) and Archibald Douglas, 4th earl of Douglas; married John Stewart, 3rd earl of Buchan, in November 1413; married Sir Thomas Stewart; married William Sinclair, 3rd earl of Orkney and Caithness; children: (first marriage) Margaret Stewart, countess of Buchan (who married George Seton, 1st Lord Seton); (third marriage) *Catherine Sinclair, duchess of Albany (who married Alexander Stewart, 1st duke of Albany); William Sinclair.

Douglas, Emily Taft (1899–1994)

United States Congresswoman from 1944 to 1946.
*Born Emily Taft in Chicago, Illinois, on April 19, 1899; died in Briarcliff Manor, New York, on January 28, 1994; one of three daughters of Lorado Taft (a sculptor, art teacher, writer, and lecturer) and **Ada (Bartlett) Taft**; University of Chicago, B.A., 1920; attended the American Academy of Dramatic Art; graduate study in government and political science, University of Chicago; married Paul Howard Douglas (professor of economics and U.S. Senator from Illinois, 1949–66), in 1931; children: one daughter, **Jean Douglas**.*

Emily Taft Douglas was born in Chicago, Illinois, in 1899, and grew up wanting to be an actress. Instead, she would join *Jessie Sumner in 1945 as one of two Congresswomen elected from Illinois, and she would subsequently distinguish herself as a member of the House Foreign Affairs Committee, At the insistence of her parents, Emily finished college at the University of Chicago before pursuing her acting dream in New York. After a two-year stint in the mystery *The Cat and the Canary*, Emily returned to the University of Chicago for graduate work in government and political science. At age 32, she married economics professor Paul Howard Douglas (who would later serve in the U.S. Senate).

On a three-month trip through Europe in 1935, Douglas and her husband witnessed the rise of fascism in Europe. Visiting Rome on the day Mussolini announced he had sent his troops into Ethiopia, she described the feeling of fear and foreboding that overcame them: "Suddenly, all the things we had seen and suspected that summer fell into place. It came crystal clear to us then and there that if Hitler and Mussolini and the forces they represented were not stopped, the whole world would be engulfed." Returning home, the Douglases determined to warn Americans of the impending danger. Emily Taft Douglas organized and chaired the department of government and foreign policy of the Illinois League of Women Voters and her husband

served as alderman to the Chicago City Council. Hoping to "strengthen democracy at the grass roots," she became active in local Democratic politics. In 1942, when Paul, at age 50, enlisted as a marine private, Douglas became executive secretary of the International Relations Center in Chicago, a clearinghouse for information.

In February 1944, she was chosen as the Democratic nominee for the States Representative at Large seat in the House of Representatives. In the general election, she faced veteran incumbent Stephen Day, one of the staunchest isolationists in the House. Overcoming her self-described "quiet housewifely" persona, she campaigned on a platform of support for Roosevelt's foreign policies, and, despite the overwhelming opposition of the *Chicago Tribune*, she defeated Day by over 191,000 votes. During her term, Douglas served on the Committee on Foreign Affairs and was recognized as a highly qualified specialist in the field. In order to keep her Illinois constituents apprised of her work, she established a semi-monthly newsletter, *Win-*

Emily
Taft
Douglas

dow on Washington, which received high praise. (In one of the first issues, Douglas announced that she would hold open competitive examinations for her appointments to West Point and Annapolis.)

In August 1945, Douglas joined several committee colleagues on a visit to Europe to inspect the work of the United Nation's Relief and Rehabilitation Administration. Before the close of the year, she had co-sponsored legislation to empower the UN to control arms and outlaw the atomic bomb. She also championed federal support for libraries, especially those in rural and low-income areas. Douglas later co-sponsored a bill for bookmobile service that became the basis for the Hill-Douglas Act, which was passed by Congress under co-sponsorship of her husband.

Douglas was among 54 House Democrats ousted in the midterm election of 1946, losing to William G. Stratton. Following her husband's election to the Senate in 1948, she served as a representative to UNESCO and as a moderator for the American Unitarian Association. In later years, she devoted a great deal of time to the civil-rights movement. Douglas also wrote several books, including *Appleseed Farm* (1948), a children's story; *Remember the Ladies* (1966), biographies of women who were influential in the development of the United States; and *Margaret Sanger* (1970), a biography. Emily Taft Douglas died on January 28, 1994.

SOURCES:

Graham, Judith, ed. *Current Biography 1994*. NY: H.W. Wilson, 1994.

Office of the Historian. *Women in Congress, 1917–1990*. Commission on the Bicentenary of the U.S. House of Representatives, 1991.

Rothe, Anna, ed. *Current Biography 1945*. NY: H.W. Wilson, 1945.

Barbara Morgan, Melrose, Massachusetts

Douglas, Helen Gahagan

(1900–1980)

American actress, opera singer, and liberal Democratic Congressional representative, who ran unsuccessfully against Richard Nixon and his infamous campaign. Name variations: known as Helen Gahagan from 1900 to 1931, as Helen Gahagan Douglas after 1931. Born Helen Mary Gahagan on November 25, 1900, in Boonton, New Jersey; died on June 28, 1980; daughter of Lillian Rose (Mussen) and Walter Gahagan (a wealthy owner of a Brooklyn engineering company); attended Barnard College, 1920-22; married Melvyn Douglas (an actor), in 1931; children: Peter and Mary Helen Douglas.

Was a Broadway actress (1922–28); was an opera singer in Europe (1928–30); married Melvyn Douglas and moved to Hollywood (1931); made her only film, She *(1933); elected to Congress (1944, 1946, 1948); was a Democratic candidate for Senate (1950), defeated by Richard Nixon.*

Helen Gahagan Douglas was the first American entertainer to move from the stage and Hollywood into national politics. Her friend Ronald Reagan and many others later followed the trail she had blazed in her Congressional career. Like her famous contemporary on the other side of the political spectrum *Clare Boothe-Luce, Douglas turned her charm, wealth, and celebrity to good account in forging a political career but was, ironically, upstaged by an opponent who had none of her natural advantages, Richard Nixon, in the California senatorial election of 1950.

Helen Gahagan grew up in Brooklyn dreaming of a life on the stage; she acted in amateur productions and gave speeches on behalf of the war effort in 1918. Her father was convinced that the theater was synonymous with promiscuity and tried to forbid her from acting. At age 22, however, after two years at Barnard College, she was offered a leading role in *Dreams for Sale*, a Broadway play, along with a five-year contract. In a tense showdown with her father, director William Brady got his way, the show opened, and she proved an instant success. Critic Heywood Broun wrote in his opening night review that Gahagan was "ten of the twelve most beautiful women in America."

In the next six years, she toured extensively throughout America and Canada, becoming a premier stage actress and winning a coterie of admirers. Wealthy from her success, she spent vacations in Hungary, Italy, and Germany, usually chaperoned by her mother **Lillian Rose Gahagan**, and was twice engaged to Italian men—engagements she canceled on her return to New York. In 1926, she decided to add to her repertoire by taking voice lessons. Her mother had had an excellent voice but marriage to the family patriarch had prevented her from pursuing formal training. Helen Gahagan found a suitable teacher, **Sophia Cehenovska**, a Russian emigre, with whom she studied hard for the next three years. In 1928, she asked to be released from her second major acting contract, with George Tyler, which had four more years to run, to pursue singing full time.

Helen's operatic debut came in Ostrava, Czechoslovakia, and was followed by two years of successes in that country and in Austria, Germany, and Italy, in the operas *Tosca, Aïda, La Gioconda* and *Manon Lescaut.* Unfortunately, the onset of her operatic career coincided with the onset of the Great Depression. After losing $100,000 of her savings in the Wall Street Crash of 1929 (like many investors she had been buying shares on margin), she found it impossible to get a booking at the New York Metropolitan Opera. In 1930, when her father was diagnosed with terminal cancer, she returned from further European successes to America. That same year, she agreed to act in *Tonight or Never,* a play peculiarly well-suited to her situation since it was about an opera singer struggling for her first big break. Her leading man was Melvyn Douglas. They fell in love and were married in 1931, while the play was still going strong on Broadway.

Melvyn Douglas had been hired to a five-year contract in Hollywood, his first role being the screen version of *Tonight or Never.* *Gloria Swanson** played the female lead in the film, however, leaving Helen Douglas in the unfamiliar position of housewife in their rural San Fernando Valley home. Before long, she had found parts in Los Angeles and San Francisco plays, and, when her husband broke his film contract, they were both affluent enough to afford an eight-month round-the-world cruise. Theatrical and film successes continued when they returned to America, though they lost a great deal of money on a play they directed, starred in, and financed, *Mother Lode.* In 1933, Douglas appeared in her one and only film, a version of Rider Haggard's novel *She.* But she disliked the experience of movie acting, writing later: "I missed the audience. Without one I ran without batteries. There is a flow of energy between a theater audience and a live performance. The actor works to hold attention and the vitality required to succeed keeps the actor in a state of creative tension night after night." Now, by contrast, "I felt that everything I did . . . was out of my control." In 1936, she did a concert tour of Germany, Austria, and Czechoslovakia but found the rising Nazi movement unnerving and had to argue with the Czech concert-master about including the German lieder she had prepared on her program. Back in America, she and her Jewish husband joined the Anti-Nazi League, and from this time forward she began to turn more of her attention to politics.

Melvyn Douglas, like his wife a liberal Democrat, worked as a campaign manager for Culbert Olson, who won California's gubernatorial election in 1936, the first Democrat in that office

Helen
Gahagan
Douglas

in the 20th century. Learning during the election about the suffering of migrant farm workers, Helen Douglas volunteered as chair of the Steinbeck Committee, a relief organization to aid uprooted midwestern farmers, whose plight John Steinbeck's *The Grapes of Wrath* had made famous. This work led to meetings with first lady *Eleanor Roosevelt** and then with the president in 1938. Franklin Roosevelt appointed her to the National Advisory Committee of the Works Progress Administration (WPA) of the New Deal. Her high profile as a famous entertainer made Douglas an attractive prospect for the Democratic Party, and in 1940, while her husband was helping Roosevelt secure an unprecedented third term in office, she accepted the position of Democratic national committeewoman and vice-chair of the California Democratic Party. She planned to do more than entertain visiting Democratic dignitaries with teas and cocktail parties, the committeewoman's traditional role, and at once organized permanent offices in the north and south of the state. At her own expense, she created a staff and began to generate publicity for her causes and mobilize more Democratic women. She was keynote speaker at California's 1941 Democratic convention in Sacramento which renominated Olson for governor, and after the bombing of Pearl Harbor became co-chair of the Southern California civilian defense organization. Her greatest achievements in California politics during these early years of the Second World War were her contribution to the desegregation of war-related industries and her inclusion of women in politically important positions.

If a Balinese is oppressed by someone, the solution is mentally to discard the offender. . . . When I came to the time when I could not bear a southern bigot, Congressman John Rankin, I caused him to stop existing for me. The tactic worked so well that I could pass him in the hall and literally not see him.

—Helen Gahagan Douglas

Melvyn Douglas joined the army in 1942 and was posted to the Far East theater where he spent the war years organizing entertainments for the huge American armies there. Helen ran for U.S. Congress in 1944 at the urging of retiring Congressional representative Tom Ford, one of their friends, and, after beating out six men in Los Angeles' 14th District Democratic primary, she became California's only female Congressional representative between the 1920s and the 1960s. In the midst of her campaign, she flew to Chicago to sing the national anthem and make a speech at the Democratic convention of 1944, playing the same role for the Democrats that the equally striking and gifted playwright Clare Boothe-Luce was playing that year for the Republicans. They were two of only nine women in the 79th Congress which gathered in Washington at the beginning of 1945, and the press reduced their ideological rivalry to the "battle of the glamour queens." Despite being a freshman, Douglas was able to get an appointment to the coveted and influential Foreign Affairs Committee at once.

As a member of the House, Douglas was a consistent supporter of the New Deal at home and regretted that programs were being cut back because of wartime demands on resources. After her seven years of personal friendship with Roosevelt, she found the president's death in the last months of the Second World War a bitter blow and later wrote a warm personal memoir of Eleanor Roosevelt, with whom she remained close friends. Her biggest contribution to American politics was her joint sponsorship of the McMahon-Douglas Bill which ensured after the war that control of nuclear research and power would stay in civil rather than military hands.

In foreign policy, she took a more independent position, especially after the succession to the White House of Harry S. Truman. She would not support his anti-Communist policy in Greece and Turkey, believing that reconstruction of these newly liberated nations should be supervised by the United Nations rather than by America acting independently. Truman had appointed her as an alternate delegate to the fledgling United Nations in 1946, and from its beginnings she was a great champion of the UN. She thought much less highly of Truman than of Roosevelt, and opposed Truman's introduction of loyalty programs, the precursor of McCarthyism. Even so, she understood the importance of party solidarity, and when, in 1948, her old friend and former vice-president Henry Wallace decided to challenge Truman for the presidency she refused to join his movement. She stayed with the mainstream Truman Democrats in the face of Wallace's defection to the left and the racist Dixiecrats' defection to the right and enjoyed Truman's surprise victory in November 1948. Future allegations that she was a Communist "fellow traveler" would have carried more weight had she joined Wallace—dedicated members of the American left lined up behind Wallace's "Progressive" presidential campaign.

Meanwhile, enjoying the hectic and glamorous life of a Washington politician, Douglas had run successfully for re-election in 1946 and 1948. The Republicans ran a black candidate against her in 1946 but her strong civil rights record assured her a majority of black votes in her district. She was the first white representative to hire a black secretary on Capitol Hill and, after a confrontation over this particular woman's rights, she succeeded in abolishing segregation in the House Office Building's cafeteria. The 80th Congress, elected in 1946, was dominated by Republicans who were eager to lift most of the price-and-rent controls that the government had imposed during the war. Douglas wanted to keep the controls lest poor Americans and veterans found themselves victimized by unmanageable inflation. She posed for press photographs with a basket of groceries, claiming that as a woman she was more aware than her male Congressional colleagues of the way inflation would afflict the ordinary housewife. And in a speech on the importance of women's political education and action, she remarked: "Since government is only housekeeping on a large scale, it seems to me that women can play an important and constructive part in building world peace and healthy, sound communities at home. Who knows more about running the home than the mother? And who in the home works continuously for harmony? Again the mother."

In 1950, she decided to run for a California U.S. Senate seat. She expected to run in the Democratic primaries against the incumbent, Senator Sheridan Downey, but he retired after a few weeks of rough campaigning, citing reasons of bad health. Douglas disagreed with Downey's support for large-scale agricultural businesses that were beginning to monopolize California's irrigated farming; she stood behind the small farmers and wanted to preserve a 1902 law which limited each farmer to 160 acres of subsidized irrigation. Her remaining Democratic opponent in the senate primary, Manchester Boddy, editor of the *Los Angeles Daily News,* referred to Douglas and her liberal followers as "a small subversive clique of red hots," and Downey alleged that "she gave comfort to the Soviet tyranny by voting against aid to both Greece and Turkey." He added, unfairly, that she would not make a good senator because "she has shown no inclination, in fact no ability, to dig in and do the hard tedious work required to prepare legislation and push it through Congress."

Richard Nixon, her Republican opponent, benefitted from this divisive Democratic primary campaign and wrote later that many Democrats, including the Kennedy family, had contributed money to his campaign against her (he and John F. Kennedy had both joined Congress in 1946). Nixon felt a personal resentment towards Douglas because she had voted against funding for the House Un-American Activities Committee, through whose sensational anti-Communist allegations Nixon's name was becoming a household word. In the campaign, Nixon's staffers issued "pink sheets" in which they showed that Douglas' voting record in Congress was very similar to that of Vito Marcantonio, the only openly pro-Communist member of Congress. In a speech that became notorious in the annals of both red-baiting and sexism, Nixon, who "knew I must not appear ungallant in my criticism of Mrs. Douglas," quipped that she was "pink right down to her underwear."

The Douglas campaign unwisely tried to take the same tack and argue that *Nixon* was giving aid and comfort to the Communists, a position that it was impossible to substantiate except through deceptive propaganda. Nixon's unremitting anti-communism and his warnings that Truman's Democrats were endangering the free world got a boost during the campaign when the Korean War began, and made his election victory inevitable. The campaign degenerated into mutual smears and recriminations, but Nixon emerged the victor. It was for Helen Douglas the most serious setback of a career in which successes had until then flowed one after another.

Helen Gahagan Douglas had offers of other Congressional seats but decided that she would return to her family and to the stage. Her husband had had some well-publicized love affairs, their two children were at boarding school most of the time, and she hoped to be able to bring the family back together. The Douglases moved to the East Coast, dividing their time between Cliff Mull, Vermont, and a large apartment on New York's Riverside Drive. Offers from Broadway came in, and Douglas found she could not resist the chance to act again. She also tried to pick up her singing career once more but lukewarm critics at her long-delayed New York debut in Carnegie Hall, 1956, convinced her that she had gone too many years without practice to make an operatic career a real possibility.

Politics was still in her blood. She campaigned for Adlai Stevenson, the unsuccessful Democratic presidential candidate in 1952, and suffered the galling experience of seeing Nixon, her nemesis, elected vice-president to Dwight Eisenhower, then and for a second time in 1956. A longtime supporter of Israel, she also traveled there, spoke on behalf of American-Israeli friendship, and began a regular tour of the college lecture circuit. She also became involved in the family business that her father had run until his death in 1931 and that her brothers had been running since then. Gahagan Dredging made navigable channels in harbors and lakes, and its operations throughout North and South America had become highly profitable after the rocky years of the Depression. The company provided the land-fill on which Cape Canaveral (renamed Kennedy) Space Center in Florida was built. She even wrote a history of the company as it approached its centenary.

A strong supporter of the Democrats in 1960, Douglas campaigned for Kennedy and Johnson and worked for the Alliance for Progress which Kennedy inaugurated in 1962. Although she was now in her 60s and had suffered from recurrent bouts of heart trouble, back pain, exhaustion, and ulcers since 1946, she went on two arduous fact-finding missions to some of the remotest parts of South America. She turned against her old friend Lyndon Johnson when he escalated the war in Vietnam, and he retaliated by pretending not to know who she was during a White House reception in 1966. (In the 1940s, her close relationship with then Congressional representative Johnson had caused rumors.) She was an active member of the Women's International League for Peace and Freedom and of the Committee for a Sane Nuclear Policy, and as the Vietnam War worsened she became a regular feature on university campuses, speaking out against the war. The election of Richard Nixon as president in 1968 led to a renewed flurry of interest in the 1950 Senatorial election, and as Nixon's problems worsened in the early 1970s, culminating in the Watergate disgrace, Douglas had the dubious pleasure of witnessing his final fall from grace. A popular bumper-sticker in the Watergate era read: "Don't Blame Me: I Voted for Helen Gahagan Douglas." After campaigning unsuccessfully for George McGovern in the 1972 election, she was featured in *Ms.* magazine in 1973 and became a focal figure for anti-Nixon sentiment. She was magnanimous throughout the crisis, and journalists liked to compare her high-mindedness to the sordid tactics Nixon used as he scrambled for political survival in the summer of 1974. She took advantage of her renewed fame largely to speak on behalf of nuclear disarmament.

By then, Helen Gahagan Douglas was in her 70s and a victim of breast cancer. Ironically, one of the causes she had supported unsuccessfully in her Congressional career was for a coordinated national research effort to combat cancer, from which her father and one of her brothers had died prematurely. She endured a mastectomy in 1972 and, after a brief remission, fought a prolonged battle against other cancers through the later part of the 1970s. She died on June 28, 1980, active in writing and campaigning on peace issues almost to the end.

SOURCES:

Douglas, Helen Gahagan. *The Eleanor Roosevelt We Remember.* NY: Hill and Wang, 1963.

———. *A Full Life.* Garden City, NY: Doubleday, 1982.

Nixon, Richard. *RN: The Memoirs of Richard Nixon.* NY: Grosset and Dunlap, 1978.

Scobie, Ingrid Winther. *Center Stage: Helen Gahagan Douglas, A Life.* NY: Oxford University Press, 1992.

SUGGESTED READING:

Ambrose, Stephen. *Nixon: The Education of a Politician.* NY: Simon and Schuster, 1987.

Mitchell, Greg. *Tricky Dick and the Pink Lady: Richard Nixon vs. Helen Gahagan Douglas.* NY: Random, 1997.

Scobie, Ingrid W. "Helen Gahagan Douglas: Broadway Star as California Politician," in *California History.* Vol. 66. December 1987.

COLLECTIONS:

Helen Gahagan Douglas Papers Collection, University of Oklahoma, Norman.

Helen Gahagan Douglas, "Congresswoman, Actress, and Opera Singer," oral history edited by Amelia Fry, Bancroft Library, University of California, Berkeley.

Douglas Papers, State Historical Society of Wisconsin.

Patrick Allitt, Professor of History, Emory University, Atlanta, Georgia

Douglas, Isabel (fl. 1371).

See Stewart, Isabel.

Douglas, Lizzie (1897–1973)

American blues singer, guitarist, recording artist, and club owner, who was one of the great blues artists of all time. Name variations: Gospel Minnie; Kid; Memphis Minnie; Minnie Douglas; Minnie McCoy; Texas Tessie. Born in Algiers, Louisiana, on June 3, 1897 (some sources cite 1896); died in Memphis, Tennessee, on August 6, 1973; daughter of Abe Douglas and Gertrude Wells; married to Casey Bill Weldon, during the 1920s; married to Kansas Joe McCoy, from 1929–35; married to Little Son Je Ernest Lawlars, from 1939–61.

Lizzie Douglas, later known as Memphis Minnie, was one of 13 children born and raised on a Louisiana farm. The family moved to Walls, Mississippi, and Lizzie learned to play the banjo and guitar at ten. From 1908, she worked local parties to earn extra income, before running away from home in 1910 to work as "Kid Douglas." She ended up in Memphis, Tennessee, singing in the streets. From 1916 to 1920, she toured with the Ringling Brothers Circus, working tent shows throughout the South until returning to Tennessee to work in the saloons and bars along Beale Street in Memphis. In 1929, Douglas made her first recording on the Columbia label with Joe McCoy who became her second husband. In 1930, the couple moved to Chicago and formed their own blues group, working clubs in the Windy City. She became famous for her *Blue Monday* parties, and jazz patrons flocked to hear her sing and perform. Douglas continued to record and play Chicago clubs. In the 1940s, she led her own vaudeville troupe working throughout the South. She performed accompanied by guitar, prompting Steve LaVere and others to refer to her as a "country blues singer." In the mid-1950s, having recorded throughout her career, Douglas retired and later in the decade suffered increasingly from ill health. She died of a stroke in 1973. On a reissue of one of her albums, Charles Strachwitz wrote: "In my opinion, Memphis Minnie was without doubt the greatest of all female blues singers ever to record."

John Haag, Athens, Georgia

Lizzie
Douglas

Douglas, Margaret (b. around 1427)

Countess of Douglas and Atholl. Name variations: The Fair Maid of Galloway. Born around 1427; daughter of Archibald Douglas, count of Longueville and 5th earl of Douglas (c. 1390–1439), and *Euphemia Graham (d. 1469); married William Douglas, 8th earl of Douglas; married John Stewart (John of Balveny), 1st earl of Atholl.

Douglas, Margaret (1515–1578)

Countess of Lennox. Name variations: Lady Margaret Douglas or Douglass; Margaret Lennox. Born at Harbottle Castle, Northumberland, England, on October 8, 1515; died on March 7 or 9, 1578 (some sources cite 1577); daughter of Archibald Douglas, 6th earl of Angus, and Margaret Tudor (1489–1541); married Thomas Howard, Lord Howard; married Matthew Stuart (1516–1571), 4th earl of Lennox, on July 6, 1544; children: (second marriage) Henry Stuart (b. 1545), Lord Darnley (who married Mary Stuart, queen of Scots); Charles Stuart (b. 1555), earl of Lennox; and four daughters (names unknown); grandchildren: James VI, king of Scotland (r. 1567–1625), king of England as James I (r. 1603–1625).

Lady Margaret Douglas, countess of Lennox, was the daughter of *Margaret Tudor. Lady Margaret's maternal uncle was Henry VIII and her maternal grandfather was Henry VII. Because of her proximity to the crown, Margaret was brought up chiefly at the English court in close association with the Princess Mary Tudor (*Mary I), who would remain her close friend.

Though Margaret Douglas was high in her uncle Henry VIII's favor, she was twice discredited; first for her marriage to Lord Thomas Howard, who died in the Tower of London in 1537, and again, in 1541, for her affair with Sir Charles Howard, brother of Queen ◀ Catherine Howard. In 1544, Margaret married a Scottish exile, Matthew Stuart, 4th earl of Lennox, who was regent of Scotland in 1570–71.

During Catholic Mary I's reign, Margaret had rooms in Westminster Palace, but on Protestant *Elizabeth I's accession she moved to Yorkshire, where her home at Temple Newsam became a center for Catholic intrigue. By a series of successful maneuvers, Margaret married her son Henry Stuart, Lord Darnley, to *Mary Stuart, Queen of Scots. As a grandson of Margaret Tudor, Darnley was next in line after Mary Stuart to the English succession and their marriage on July 29, 1565, united the two nearest

claimants to the English throne. For her troubles, Margaret was sent to the Tower in 1566, but was released after the murder of Darnley the following year. Margaret was at first vocal in her condemnation of Mary Stuart but was eventually reconciled with her daughter-in-law.

In 1574, Margaret again incurred Elizabeth I's wrath when her son Charles Stuart, earl of Lennox, married *Elizabeth Cavendish (d. 1582), daughter of *Elizabeth Talbot, countess of Shrewsbury. Margaret was sent to the Tower with the countess of Shrewsbury, and was only pardoned after her son's death in 1577. Her diplomacy largely contributed to the future succession of her grandson James I to the English throne.

Douglas, Marjory (d. 1420)

Duchess of Rothesay. Died around 1420; daughter of Archibald Douglas, 3rd earl of Douglas, and Jean also known as Joan Moray; married David Stewart or Stuart (1378–1402), duke of Rothesay (r. 1398–1402), in February 1400; married Walter Haliburton, in 1403; children: John, lord Haliburton; Walter; Robert; William.

Douglas, Marjory Stoneman (1890–1998)

Influential 20th-century American environmental activist and writer whose name has become synonymous with efforts to save the Everglades. Born Marjory Stoneman in Minneapolis, Minnesota, on April 7, 1890; died, age 108, in her small cottage in Miami, Florida, where she had lived for 72 years, on May 14, 1998; daughter of Frank Bryant Stoneman (a newspaper publisher) and (Florence) Lillian (Trefethen) Stoneman; graduated from Wellesley College, 1912; married Kenneth Douglas, in 1914 (divorced 1919).

Worked as society editor and occasional general assignment editor at the Miami Herald *newspaper (1915–1918); volunteered for overseas Red Cross (1918–19); became assistant editor and editorial page columnist at* Miami Herald *(1919–24); worked as fiction writer and essayist (1924–40); served as director, University of Miami Press (1960); founded Friends of the Everglades (1969); "Marjory Stoneman Douglas Law" passed (1991); received the Presidential Medal of Freedom (1993).*

Selected publications: The Everglades: River of Grass *(1947, rev. ed., 1987);* Road to the Sun *(1952);* Freedom River *(1953);* Hurricane *(1958);* Alligator Crossing *(1959);* Florida: The Long Frontier *(1967);* Adventures in a Green World: David Fairchild and Barbour Lathrop *(1973); (with John Rothchild)* Voice

Howard, Catherine. See *Six Wives of Henry VIII.*

of the River: The Autobiography of Marjory Stoneman Douglas *(1987).*

The indefatigable Marjory Stoneman Douglas was one of 20th-century America's earliest and most influential environmentalists, devoting much of her considerable life to addressing and publicizing the severe environmental problems of her beloved adopted state of Florida. Known as the "Grandmother of the Glades," Douglas was among the first to recognize the crucial role the Everglades play in both the flow of water throughout central and southern Florida and in balancing the state's delicate ecosystem. Her later efforts to educate residents, state officials, and the wider world about the importance of Everglades conservation resulted in important changes in state environmental laws and water management policies.

She was born Marjory Stoneman on April 7, 1890, in Minneapolis, Minnesota, the only child of Frank Bryant Stoneman and **Lillian Trefethen Stoneman.** Her father was a self-educated Midwesterner and unsuccessful entrepreneur from a Quaker family. Her mother was a professionally trained musician from the East. When Douglas was three, another failed business prompted the family to move East, where they settled in Providence, Rhode Island. Frank Stoneman's unsuccessful business ventures continued, and the family lived in difficult, relatively impoverished circumstances. The economic hardship took its toll on her mother. Eventually Lillian Stoneman suffered a nervous breakdown (from which she never completely recovered), and she, with six-year-old Marjory in tow, went to live with her mother and unmarried sister at the family home in Taunton, Massachusetts.

The maternal side of Marjory's family was educated and musical, and her grandmother and aunt encouraged her intellectual curiosity; Douglas read voraciously and excelled as a student. Still, her childhood was filled with conflicts and difficulties. Her grandmother and aunt were contrary women and her mother's delicate condition forced Douglas to relinquish her childhood to play the role of nursemaid, a role she seems not to have resented. In fact, she considered her relationship with her mother the closest and most important of her life. Nevertheless, her mother's mental illness, the absence of her father, and the contentious mood of the household took its toll on young Marjory who suffered from night terrors and anxiety, an early warning of the emotional difficulties that would plague her adult years.

In 1908, she matriculated at nearby Wellesley College where the door to the intellectual world opened wide. She remembered her college years with fondness and gratitude. Douglas was an enthusiastic student and later credited three remarkable teachers with influencing her thinking: *Emily Greene Balch, the Nobel Prize-winning head of the economics department; *Mary Whiton Calkins, the pioneering professor of philosophy and psychology; and **Malvina Bennett,** the head of the Department of Expression (elocution). While at Wellesley, Douglas also became politicized and was a founding member of the Suffrage Club.

> *There is only one Marjory Stoneman Douglas, just the way there is only one Everglades.*
>
> —Helen Muir

Shortly after Douglas' graduation in 1912, her mother died of cancer. Douglas spent the next year in St. Louis before moving to Newark, New Jersey, in 1914, where she took a job in the personnel division of a department store. She soon met Kenneth Douglas, a man 30 years her senior. After a three-month, by her own account, passionless courtship, the two wed. The marriage was a disaster from the start. Kenneth Douglas turned out to be a small-time confidence man who spent time in jail for forgery shortly after the nuptials. After his release, she followed him to New York where they moved from residence to residence. Finally, her family intervened and convinced Marjory to severe the relationship. (The two were legally divorced in 1919.) Although Douglas dated and even entered into a couple of brief, unserious engagements, she never remarried, preferring instead an independent life unencumbered by marital constraints. She later reflected that her short-lived marriage was important for "getting sex and romance out of the way" so that she could carry out her "real life's work": writing and activism.

After leaving her husband in 1915, Douglas headed to south Florida where her father now lived with his second wife. Her arrival in Miami coincided with the beginning of the Florida land boom, the rapid growth of Miami, and the resulting influx of gamblers, gangsters, and entrepreneurs. "The houses were not impressive and the town was not impressive," she wrote, "but the people were impressive. Many of them were adventurers who'd worked in South America or Europe and liked Miami's position on the map, liked the tropic climate and proximity to the sea."

Moving in with her father and stepmother, Douglas began work as the interim society columnist at the *Miami Herald,* the newspaper her father had founded and now published. She quickly became the full-time society editor and also wrote features and general assignment articles. Through her father and connections at the newspaper, Douglas began taking an interest in local affairs and founded the Business and Professional Women's League. She also met and befriended a number of the influential, including William Jennings Bryan and **Mary Baird Bryan**. In 1916, in the company of suffragists, Douglas addressed the state legislature, urging ratification of the suffrage amendment which had already passed in some states. This, her first direct experience of Florida state politics, galvanized her activism: "Talking to [the legislators] was like talking to graven images. They never paid any attention to us at all. They weren't even listening."

Douglas' newspaper career was briefly interrupted when in 1918 she voyaged overseas to work on behalf of the Red Cross. After traveling extensively throughout Italy, Greece, Albania, and Bosnia, she returned to Miami in 1919 and resumed work at the newspaper, this time as an assistant editor and columnist. In her column, a voice of protest emerged, as she wrote about the plight of women and the politics and problems of South Florida. In 1922, Douglas turned her words into action and established the Baby Milk Fund, a charity that raised money to buy milk for impoverished children. She was also elected to the Everglades National Park Committee which was dedicated to acquiring public land for a national park. This grass-roots venture would eventually lead to the founding of the Everglades National Park 25 years later.

In 1924, Marjory Stoneman Douglas suffered the first of several nervous breakdowns. She left the *Miami Herald,* and her career as a journalist ended. While recuperating, she began writing and submitting stories to magazines like the *Saturday Evening Post,* and a new career as a fiction writer and essayist was born. In 1926, she had a small house built for herself across from her father's home in Coconut Grove whose design reflected her new priorities: it was composed of a sparsely furnished writing studio with a small bedroom attached. For the next 15 years, she devoted herself to magazine writing. Although her early stories were formulaic and derivative, her own distinctive voice eventually emerged as she began to paint a marvelously rich portrait of Florida, its geography, history, and unique inhabitants. Her stories often alerted readers to mounting environmental problems in Florida, like bird poaching and the destruction of the wetlands.

Douglas remained active in local politics and environmental issues throughout the 1920s and 1930s. In the early 1930s, she was hired to write a brochure advocating a proposed tropical botanical garden in Miami. The published pamphlet, "An Argument for the Establishment of a Tropical Botanical Garden in South Florida," made her a sought-after speaker on the garden club circuit. She later served as the first secretary of the board of the Fairchild Garden, the only tropical botanical garden in North America.

Through her activism and the power of her pen, she was increasingly recognized inside and outside the state as the voice of Florida. In 1942, a New York publisher accordingly commissioned Douglas to write a book on the Everglades, a project that consumed her considerable energies for the next five years. In 1947, *The Everglades: River of Grass* was published to coincide with the establishment of the Everglades National Park. Both a popular and critical success, the book forever changed the way people viewed the Everglades. It challenged the notion of the Everglades as a marshy wasteland by more accurately describing it as a river. "That was my contribution to our knowledge of Florida," she later remarked. "Before then everyone thought it was just swamps, but it's not; it is running water moving several miles an hour." In the book, she lyrically described the geography of the area, the resident birds and animals, and the almost imperceptible ebbs and flows of "the river of grass." Douglas also exposed the disastrous effects of the sugar industry, modern farming, and human encroachment on the Everglades' delicate ecosystem, and she sounded an early warning that unless current policies changed, particularly those of draining wetlands and channeling the water, the Everglades, and Florida in general, would be ruined.

Marjory Stoneman Douglas was now past middle age, yet her productivity did not slow. Over the next ten years, she published several fiction and nonfiction books, including three novels, *Road to the Sun* (1951) about the Miami real estate boom, *Freedom River* (1953) about three boys growing up near the Everglades, and *Alligator Crossing* (1959), about alligator poaching. Apart from the nonfiction *Hurricane* (1958), however, none matched the success of her 1947 classic. Douglas also spent the year of 1960 as the first director of the new University of Miami Press and, during this period, corresponded regularly with fellow Florida writer *Marjorie Kinnan Rawlings.

In 1967, Douglas applied for and received a small traveling grant from the Wellesley Alumni Association to sail to Buenos Aires and England to research a biography of W.H. Hudson, a 19th-century British writer. She spent the next year traveling, researching and writing. Though her physical health had always been excellent, her eyesight was by then rapidly deteriorating until finally she could barely see to read or write. The project was temporarily shelved in 1968, and Douglas abandoned her writing career to turn instead to full-time environmental activism. Although she had written her influential book on the Everglades more than 20 years earlier and had occasionally lobbied on its behalf, it was now that her real efforts to protect the Everglades began.

In 1969, at age 79, she founded the Friends of the Everglades, also known as "Marjory's Army," a non-profit organization that served as a clearinghouse for information on the Everglades, educated the public, initiated organized protests, and posed legal challenges to existing anti-environmental laws. Douglas spent the next two decades lecturing on behalf of Everglades conservation, lobbying state legislatures, issuing educational materials, campaigning against developers and hunters, defending the panthers and other wildlife threatened by human encroachment, and tirelessly crusading against the state's wetlands development policies. Under her stewardship, Friends of the Everglades waged and won battles to restore the Kissimmee River, to clean up Lake Okeechobee, and return the sheet flow of water to the Everglades marshes. Though Douglas wholeheartedly committed herself to conservation, her work was never tarnished with sentimentalism:

> To be a friend of the Everglades is not necessarily to spend time wandering around out there. It's too buggy, too wet, too generally inhospitable. . . . I can't say I've spent many years and months communing with the Everglades, though I've driven across it from time to time. I know it's out there and I know it's important. I suppose you could say the Everglades and I have the kind of friendship that doesn't depend on constant physical contact.

She continued actively working on behalf of the Everglades through the 1980s and was the recipient of numerous awards and honorary degrees. In 1987, at age 97, Marjory Stoneman Douglas published her autobiography. The next year *Ms.* magazine named her one of its six Women of the Year for her "continuing battle for a safe, more beautiful environment. Her 60-year fight to save the Everglades is a testament to the tenacious energy older women offer today's world." In 1991, the Florida state legislature passed an "Everglades Protection Act" also known as the "Marjory Stoneman Douglas Law," though Douglas later requested her name be removed from the bill following the legislature's addition of certain amendments. In 1993, President Bill Clinton presented the 103-year-old Douglas with the Presidential Medal of Freedom. Following the presentation, the city of Miami declared November 30 as "Marjory Stoneman Douglas Day," for her role as "a powerful crusader for women's rights, racial tolerance, and conservation of our natural resources."

Douglas issued an 11th-hour wakeup call to the state of Florida and the country, yet much irreversible damage had already been done to the Everglades and Florida's water supply. The Everglades remains an ecological disaster, crisscrossed by an enormous network of dikes, canals and pumps, and levees designed to provide drinking water to the coastal towns and cities. The water supply is contaminated by pesticides from agricultural run-off. Yet because of Marjory Stoneman Douglas' tireless efforts, new generations have taken up the crusade to protect Florida's largest and most important wetland.

SOURCE AND SUGGESTED READING:

Douglas, Marjory Stoneman. *The Everglades: River of Grass.* NY: Rinehart, 1947.

————. *Hurricane.* NY: Rinehart, 1958.

————, and John Rothchild. *Marjory Stoneman Douglas: Voice of the River.* Sarasota: Pineapple Press, 1987.

Hays, Holly M. "Marjory Stoneman Douglas: Conservationist of the Century," in *Florida Living.* August 1992, pp. 52–55.

McCarthy, Kevin, ed. *Nine Florida Stories by Marjory Stoneman Douglas.* Jacksonville, FL: University of North Florida Press, 1990.

The Miami Herald. December 1, 1993.

The New York Times. December 17, 1981, July 25, 1982.

Suzanne Smith, freelance writer and editor, Decatur, Georgia

Douglas, Minnie (1897–1973).

See Douglas, Lizzie.

Douglass, Dorothea (1878–1960).

See Chambers, Dorothea.

Douglass, Sarah Mapps (1806–1882).

See Grimké, Angelina E. for sidebar.

Doukas.

Variant of Ducas.

Dovada (fl. 990–1005).

See Doada.

Dove, Billie (1900–1997)

American actress who was a star of silents and early talkies. Born Lillian Bohny (also seen as Bohney) in New York City on May 14, 1900; died on December 31, 1997, at the Motion Picture and Television Fund retirement community in Los Angeles; married Irving Willat (a director), in 1923 (divorced 1929); married Robert Kenaston (a rancher), in 1933 (died 1973); married John Miller (an architect), around 1974 (divorced); children: son, Robert; (adopted) daughter, **Gail Adelson**.

Selected films: Get-Rich-Quick Wallingford *(1921);* At the Stage Door *(1921);* Beyond the Rainbow *(1922);* Polly of the Follies *(1922);* The Wanderer of the Wasteland *(1924);* The Black Pirate *(1926);* The Stolen Bride *(1926);* Kid Boots *(1926);* American Beauty *(1927);* The Sensation Seekers *(1927);* One Night at Susie's *(1928);* Painted Angel *(1930);* Blondie of the Follies *(1932);* (bit part) Diamond Head *(1962).*

Considered one of the most beautiful stars of the silent era, Billie Dove was an artist's model and Ziegfeld "showgirl" before entering films. After some bit parts at Cosmopolitan Studios in New York, she left for Hollywood, where she landed a featured role in *Polly of the Follies* (1922), with *Constance Talmadge. In 1926, she co-starred with Douglas Fairbanks, Sr., in one of the early color productions, *The Black Pirate.*

Although Dove starred in many silents and early sound films before retiring in 1932, she is noted as much for her brief romance with Howard Hughes as for her work. After the end of her marriage to director Irving Willat, Dove met Hughes at a Hollywood party. Hughes courted her with flowers and expensive gifts, but she later said he was much too erratic to take seriously. Dove left Hollywood to marry Robert Kenaston, a wealthy rancher, returning to the screen only briefly in 1962 for a bit part in the film *Diamond Head.*

Dowding, Angela (1919—)

English royal by marriage. Born on April 20, 1919, in Hanwell, England; daughter of Charles Stanley Dowding and **Lilian Lawlor**; became first wife of Gerald Lascelles (b. 1924, grandson of King George V and *Mary of Teck), on July 15, 1952 (divorced 1978); children: Henry Lascelles (b. 1953). Gerald Lascelles' second wife is *Elizabeth Collingwood.

Downey, June Etta (1875–1932)

American psychologist, noted for her work in the study of handwriting and personality testing. Born in

Laramie, Wyoming, on July 13, 1875; died in Trenton, New Jersey, on October 11, 1932; one of nine children of Stephen (one of first territorial delegates to Congress from Wyoming, who was instrumental in the establishment of the University of Wyoming) and Evangeline (Owen) Downey (a community organizer); attended Laramie public schools and University Preparatory School, Laramie; University of Wyoming, B.A., 1895; University of Chicago, M.A., 1898; University of Chicago, Ph.D., 1907; never married; no children.

A pioneering woman in the field of psychology and an influential teacher, June Downey graduated with a degree in classics from the University of Wyoming in 1895. She taught school for a year before beginning graduate studies in philosophy and psychology at the University of Chicago, where she received her master's degree in 1898. Downey then returned to the University of Wyoming as an instructor of English and philosophy. Her interest in psychology intensified during a summer session at Cornell University studying under Edward Bradford Titchener. In 1905, Downey achieved professorial rank at Wyoming and the following year was granted a fellowship in psychology at the University of Chicago, where she received a Ph.D. in 1907. Her dissertation on handwriting and personality was published by the *Psychological Review*. Downey was then appointed head of the department of psychology and philosophy at Wyoming, becoming the first woman to head such a department at a state university.

From 1915 on, she focused exclusively on psychology, conducting experiments in personality and creativity. Downey became an expert in the study of handwriting (particularly as an indicator of personality differences), handedness (left and right), and the influence of personality on both voluntary and involuntary movement. At a time when most psychologists were concentrating on measuring intelligence, Downey broke new ground with a personality test based on "temperament-trait" testing. Her work resulted in over 60 articles and several books, including *Graphology and the Psychology of Handwriting* (1919), *Plots and Personalities* (with Edward E. Slosson, 1922), *The Will-Temperament and Its Testing* (1923), and *Creative Imagination: Studies in the Psychology of Literature* (1929). She also wrote a book on experimental psychology for young readers called *Kingdom of the Mind* (1927), as well as a number of short stories, plays, poems, and non-scientific articles.

Highly regarded as an outstanding scholar and meticulous researcher, Downey served on the council of the American Psychological Association from 1923 to 1925. In 1929, she and *Margaret Floy Washburn were the first women elected to the Society of Experimental Psychologists. Downey, continually battling ill health, worked until her final illness. She died in 1932 at her sister's home in Trenton, New Jersey.

Barbara Morgan, Melrose, Massachusetts

Downey, Mrs. Morton (1906–1958).
See Bennett, Joan for sidebar on Barbara Bennett.

D'Oyly Carte, Bridget (1908–1985).
See Carte, Bridget D'Oyly.

Draga (1867–1903)

Queen of Serbia and consort of King Alexander, whose marriage to him in 1900 constituted a major political scandal and destabilized an already chaotic political landscape. Name variations: Draga Lunyevitza-Mashin; Draga Mashin; Lunjevica-Mashin. Most likely born in 1867 (some sources cite 1865 or 1866); murdered in a palace coup during the night of June 10–11, 1903; granddaughter of Nikola Panta Lunyevitza; had three sisters and two brothers; married Svetozar Mashin (a civil servant), in 1884 (died 1885); married Alexander Obrenovich or Obrenovitch, king of Serbia (r. 1889–1903), on July 21, 1900.

Born in 1867 into a distinguished but relatively poor family, Draga Lunyevitza was part of a clan that could boast of having played an important role in Serbia's colorful but troubled history. Her grandfather Nikola Panta Lunyevitza, a prosperous cattle breeder and Serbian patriot who bankrupted his personal holdings by financing rebellions against the Turkish occupiers, was a friend of the first king of modern Serbia, Milosh Obrenovich. Draga's father appeared to have a distinguished public career ahead of him, having already served as a popular prefect of Shabats province, but unfortunately he went insane and died in an asylum. With the death of Draga's father, the Lunyevitzas' financial situation became precarious and the large family had to struggle with very limited means. Draga dealt with the situation in a traditional fashion, by marrying at age 17. Her husband Svetozar Mashin, a mining engineer and civil servant, was also an alcoholic who cruelly abused her. After barely a year of marriage, he died in 1885 due to his imprudent lifestyle, and as a widow she once again was faced with impoverishment. In later

Opposite page

*B*illie

*D*ove

years, rumors spread in Belgrade by enemies of the king who attempted to destroy her reputation, suggesting that as a poor widow Draga Mashin had relied on payments from a number of gentlemen friends for financial survival. More likely is the fact that Draga now began to seek a safe haven from which she could make plans for the next stage of her life.

The opportunity presented itself in 1889 when she began to move in royal circles, traveling with Queen *Nathalia Keshko, consort of King Milan II. After Milan's abdication that year in favor of his and Nathalia's young son Alexander, Draga lived with Nathalia at her estate in Biarritz. Some years after this, Alexander fell head over heels in love with Draga, although she was at least a decade older than he. To complicate matters, she was a commoner and had no dowry. Politically, she also presented problems because her brother-in-law, Colonel Alexander Mashin, hated both her and young King Alexander. Mashin was a partisan of the Karageorgevitch family, which claimed the Serbian throne and hoped to overthrow the Obrenovich family which Alexander headed.

For several years, Draga was Alexander's mistress and much of Serbia seethed with hatred of both her and the king. Alexander was seen as weak, subject to the influence of his mother, father, and several foreign powers including Russia and Austria-Hungary. Stubbornly Alexander pushed ahead with his plans to marry Draga, acting in an increasingly despotic fashion and equating criticism of his marriage plans with treason. Despite overwhelming public opposition, Draga and Alexander were married on July 21, 1900. The king banned his parents from attending the ceremonies, ordering the police to prevent his father from entering Serbia and threatening to try his mother for treason in absentia for her anti-Draga activities which included writing insulting letters and postcards vilifying Alexander's beloved. Marriage to Draga did not result in any lessening of Alexander's anger toward his real or imagined political foes. Instead, his fury resulted in a purge of members of his Cabinet as well as of the court and army. Several leading politicians thought it wise to flee the country, and many army officers were pensioned off, some being forbidden to ever wear their uniforms again.

In the months following his marriage to Draga, Alexander made a number of clumsily pathetic attempts to win popularity for his new queen. Important civil and military posts were given to individuals who opportunistically declared themselves in favor of the marriage. Draga's name was given to schools, regiments, and even villages. A splendid court dress, based on medieval frescoes of long-dead Serbian queens and imitating the royal garb of ancient Byzantium was made for Draga, who, however, looked conspicuously like an actress in a modern pageant when she wore it. Only a month after their wedding, Alexander announced to his sullen nation that Draga was pregnant, and she began to wear maternity clothing. This quickly turned into a fiasco when physicians discovered that she was in fact suffering from a benign tumor. Earlier in their relationship, she had in fact had on several occasions announced what turned out to be false pregnancies.

Refusing to be frustrated, Draga told Alexander on subsequent occasions that she was pregnant. Somewhat wiser by now, and having been deeply humiliated by the earlier announcement, Alexander no longer believed her, and he ceased making public proclamations regarding a royal pregnancy. Supposedly, Draga then worked out a complex plan with her sister **Hristina**, who was married and pregnant, in which Draga feigned pregnancy to the point where she could "give birth" to a baby that was in fact her sister's. Hristina's child would be palmed off as Draga's and thus the Serbian kingdom and the Obrenovich dynasty would finally have "a legitimate heir" and with it presumably some political stability. Unfortunately, the press got wind of this plot—if it in fact ever existed in the first place—and both Alexander and Draga were now more unpopular with the Serbian people than ever before. More important, being without issue Alexander's dynasty now depended on how long he lived; inevitably, one day sooner or later his death would spell not only the end of his reign but the demise of the Obrenovich family. For many Serbian patriots, a barren queen and a resulting dynasty without an heir meant a nation profoundly at risk.

Even after this catastrophe, a desperate Alexander persisted in trying to make Draga popular with his people. He continued naming schools and hospitals after her, and went so far as to turn her birthday into a national holiday complete with parades. Women who were seen as having distinguished themselves in the service of the king, royal house, or state were awarded a special medal struck in honor of Draga. None of these measures succeeded in turning the tide of overwhelmingly hostile public opinion, which was exacerbated by Draga's relentless advancement of the interests of her family. Her two brothers, who were widely believed to be mentally unstable, were conspicuously present at court where contrary to protocol they customarily stood next to the royal couple. Draga even sought, unsuccessfully, to have them declared members of the Royal House. Had there been a royal heir, this might have been dismissed as a minor issue, but given her childlessness it aroused great anger. Rumors circulated that Draga's younger brother Nikodije would soon be adopted by Alexander and thus be placed directly in the line of succession. Only a public denial of the rumor by Alexander that Nikodije, well known in Belgrade for his drunken orgies, was not being considered as a successor was able to somewhat calm an outraged public.

Soon after the marriage of Alexander and Draga, a somber mood regarding their future had begun to emerge. A superstitious people looked for omens and often found them, including the destruction of an ancient tree at Takovo under which Milosh Obrenovich had almost 90 years before proclaimed his insurrection against the Turks. Others regarded the conversion of Queen Mother Nathalia Keshko to Roman Catholicism as not only her rejection of the Serbian Orthodox faith but a profoundly deep repudiation of her son Alexander and his Obrenovich dynasty. More disturbing signs of national disaffection included the radicalized students of Belgrade who rioted against the regime and what they regarded as its cowardice on matters of national honor. Academic youth regarded Alexander as a pitifully spineless sovereign who was the primary cause of the nation's stagnation and humiliation. As for the all-important army, Alexander unwisely neglected it. He alienated many of its officers by delaying payment of salaries for months and demoralized its enlisted soldiers with substandard uniforms and inadequate food.

As early as August 1901, a small group of junior army officers hatched a plot to murder the royal couple at the queen's birthday ball on September 24. Perhaps warned of the conspiracy, Alexander and Draga did not appear at the ball. Another plan to kill Alexander alone, while he was attending military maneuvers in the autumn of 1901, was not brought to completion. But various plans to kill the royal couple continued to be discussed and outlined by a growing number of conspirators. The individual who would most benefit from the end of the Obrenovich dynasty, Peter Karageorgevitch (Peter I), grandson of one of the founders of the Serbian state, lived in Switzerland but held aloof from

these plans. A man of principle, he did not want to ascend the throne he considered rightfully his while drenched in blood. Thus he waited patiently in exile for events to unfold in his troubled homeland.

The end of the Obrenovich dynasty came dramatically in 1903. First of all, Alexander's unrealistic foreign policy goals had needlessly alienated any possible ally, be it Austria-Hungary, Russia, Bulgaria, or even the Ottoman Empire, whom he offered a military alliance in the event of a war with Bulgaria. The impression that Alexander's foreign policy often tilted toward Austria-Hungary infuriated nationalist zealots who dreamed of a Pan-Serbian state. The grave danger of diplomatic isolation was matched on the home front by the deep hatred toward Alexander and Draga exhibited by many junior officers in the Serbian army. Several regarded the king's marriage to Draga as having brought shame to the nation. Added to their idealistic grievances were the more practical ones of shattered career plans for the numerous officers who had been denied promotion or pensioned off because of their hostility to the queen. The bond of trust linking ordinary Serbians to the crown, if indeed it ever existed, was severed on April 5, 1903. On that day, a demonstration of young workers and apprentices was bloodily suppressed by the police and army. With many of the demonstrators denouncing the royal couple and calling for a republic, the marchers were shot down without mercy. Many were left dead and wounded on the street.

With a few civilians brought into their conspiracy, a large number of officers (authorities disagree as to exactly how many there were, as few as 86 and possibly as many as 120) drew up a final plan to kill the royal couple in the spring of 1903. Alexander and Draga became aware of the evolving plot and took special steps to ensure their personal security. While Alexander rarely left the royal palace (and with enhanced security when he did so), Draga never left its confines, believing she would be safe there. The palace guard was doubled. While these precautions were put in place, Alexander organized his last, and, as it turned out, Pyrrhic victory. With the opposition boycotting the bogus elections that took place on June 1, 1903, the government-approved candidates registered a clean sweep on the basis of obviously falsified returns. With his candidates receiving 180,000 votes and the opposition only 1,500, the personal regime of King Alexander finally seemed secure. But it was to last less than a week.

The night of the planned attack, June 10–11, 1903, was the anniversary of an earlier bloody event in Serbian history, the 1868 murder of Prince Michael Obrenovich. This conspiracy was fated to be even bloodier. Among its leading members was Colonel Alexander Mashin, Draga's brother-in-law during her first brief marriage. Mashin had become embittered when after the death of King Milan in 1901 he stopped receiving royal funds and no longer was sent on diplomatic missions. Draga's indifference to his loss of royal favor turned him into her implacable enemy. Other conspirators were much less fanatical in their resolve. One of them, the royal equerry who was designated to open the outer door to the royal quarters and lead the conspirators to the royal bedchamber, had a last-minute change of heart. Instead of telling the king, he simply drank himself into a stupor, thus hoping to somehow avoid involvement in what was about to transpire.

When the door was not opened as planned, the conspirators blew it away with dynamite, alerting the royal couple and a few loyal officials. Both telephone lines and lights in the palace no longer functioned, and soon a small battle raged in the royal chambers area of the palace. In the midst of the chaos, one of the leading officers in the plot found the drunken equerry and shot him dead as a traitor. In the darkness, the royal bed was eventually discovered, and it was still warm. Where were Alexander and Draga? The king's wounded aide-de-camp, still loyal to his sovereign, lied when interrogated by the plotters about the couple's whereabouts, giving them precious time to hide. Alexander and Draga were able to find refuge in a small wardrobe room reachable only through a secret passage from their bedroom. On two occasions each of them separately attempted to rouse loyal guards below to save them; Alexander's entreaties were simply ignored, and Draga's desperate plea for help resulted in revolver shots being directed against her in the darkness. The wild shots missed her.

For about two hours, the royal couple eluded detection in their little chamber. Soon after Draga's failed effort to win over the soldiers below, one of them informed the rest of the conspirators about the location from which her voice seemed to originate. They concluded there was a secret chamber, quickly found it, and began to break down its camouflaged door with an axe. One of the conspirators asked Alexander if he would now abdicate, but he refused, crying out, "No, I am not King Milan, I am not to be overawed by a handful of officers." These words resulted in a volley of revolver shots that mortally wounded the king who fell into Draga's arms. Alexander's last words addressed one of the officers, asking him how he could do such a thing. At this moment, the revolvers were emptied into the body of Draga, who died instantly.

The officers then proceeded to strip the royal couple of the hastily improvised garb they had worn in their refuge, hacking the bodies, gashing their faces, and splitting open their bellies. The carnage was concluded when the naked, mutilated corpses were thrown out the window, intended for the gardens below. But Alexander was still barely alive and clung onto the balcony with one hand. In a murderous frenzy, one of the officers severed the king's fingers with his sword before the body finally crashed to the lawn. With his last ounce of strength, Alexander's remaining intact hand closed on some blades of grass as he breathed his last.

An appalled world read the shocking accounts of royal butchery in the Balkans in their newspapers over the next few days. Diplomatic protests attempted to bring Serbia back into what was defined as the civilized community of nations (before they initiated their own, much larger, acts of mass carnage in 1914). The new king, Peter I, who had not been part of the plot, felt compelled for reasons of state to retain some of the regicides in his government. Over time, however, he was able to ease some of the most odious among them—including Colonel Mashin—out of the circle of royal favor. Serbia continued on its difficult path of political evolution as the 20th century unfolded, earning global admiration for its fierce refusal to be conquered in two World Wars, only to be classed as barbaric once more over its genocidal policy of "ethnic cleansing" in Kosovo in 1999.

SOURCES:

Harding, Bertita. *Royal Purple: The Story of Alexander and Draga of Serbia.* London: G.G. Harrap, 1937.

Mijatovic, Cedomilj. *A Royal Tragedy, being the Assassination of King Alexander and Queen Draga of Serbia.* NY: Dodd, Mead, 1907.

Petrovich, Michael Boro. *A History of Modern Serbia 1804–1918.* 2 vols. NY: Harcourt Brace Jovanovich, 1976.

Vivian, Herbert. *The Serbian Tragedy, with Some Impressions of Macedonia.* London: G. Richards, 1904.

West, Rebecca. *Black Lamb and Grey Falcon: A Journey Through Yugoslavia.* NY: Penguin, 1994.

John Haag, Associate Professor of History, University of Georgia, Athens, Georgia

Dragoicheva, Tsola (1893–1993)

Bulgarian revolutionary, the most prominent woman in the history of Bulgarian Communism, whose political career lasted over 60 years and included several death sentences that were never carried out. Name variations: known as the Grand Old Lady of the Bulgarian Communist movement, often called the "Bulgarian La Pasionaria." Born on August 18, 1893 (some sources cite August 22, 1898, as well as 1900), in Biala Slatina, Bulgaria; died on May 26, 1993; children: one son, Chavdar Dragoichev.

Born into a working-class family in the northwestern Bulgarian city of Biala Slatina on August 18, 1893, Tsola Dragoicheva trained to become a teacher, graduating from the state institute of pedagogy in 1921. By this time, however, she was already deeply involved in the revolutionary movement, having joined the Bulgarian Communist Party (BCP) in 1919. The political and social turmoil of Bulgaria worsened in the early 1920s, encouraging the leadership of its Communist Party to attempt an armed uprising in September 1923. Dragoicheva's role dur-

ing this time was to act as liaison officer between the revolutionary committee in her home town of Biala Slatina and the surrounding villages, which contained many impoverished and radicalized peasants. After the bloody uprising was suppressed, she and many other revolutionaries were arrested and imprisoned. As punishment, she was banned for life from the teaching profession and given a 15-year prison sentence.

Freed from prison as a result of an amnesty in 1924, Dragoicheva immediately returned to her political work. In April 1925, a massive bomb blast in the Sveta Nedelia Cathedral in the capital city Sofia resulted in 123 deaths and injuries to over 300. The Communists were blamed for the atrocity, and once again Dragoicheva found herself among those subjected to the government's harsh repressive measures. Imprisoned in the city of Plovidv, she was tortured, tried, and sentenced to death. Because she was pregnant, Dragoicheva's sentence was commuted to life imprisonment at hard labor. Her child, a healthy son named Chavdar, was sent to the Soviet Union at the age of four. As a young man, Chavdar Dragoichev returned to his native country to become an eminent heart surgeon, virtually founding that medical specialization in Bulgaria.

In 1932, Tsola Dragoicheva again benefited from the changing political currents of Bulgaria and was freed by a general political amnesty. Convinced more than ever before that her country needed a sweeping social and political revolution, on the recommendation of party leader Georgi Dimitrov she left Bulgaria to continue her revolutionary training. For the next four years, she studied at Moscow's Lenin School of the Communist International and enjoyed being reunited with her son Chavdar. Having mastered both the theory and practice of Marxist revolution at the Lenin School, in 1936 she returned to Bulgaria. In 1937, she was elected to the central committee of the Bulgarian Communist Party, which during these years was carrying on a precarious illegal and underground existence. As an experienced revolutionary, Dragoicheva was well versed in conspiratorial methods (her party name was "Comrade Sonya"), and she was successful in eluding arrest by the secret police of Bulgaria's semi-Fascist regime. Her dedication to the cause and her coolheadedness under pressure earned her the respect of her fellow revolutionaries, and in 1937 she was elected to the BCP central committee. In 1940, she was elected to the BCP politburo, becoming one of the unchallenged leaders of the Bulgarian Communist movement as well as one of the few women politburo members in the world Marxist movement. Her major responsibility at this point was to regularly report to the central committee on party organizational affairs.

By 1941, Bulgaria had become an ally of Nazi Germany and thus took part in the anti-Communist crusade that served as the ideological justification for Hitler's attack on the Soviet Union in June of that year. Internally, the Bulgarian state cracked down hard on its domestic opposition, particularly the Communists. In 1941, Tsola Dragoicheva's luck finally ran out, and she was arrested and thrown into a concentration camp. Legal proceedings against her and other Communist leaders were being prepared when she was able to effect an escape. A furious regime sentenced her to death in absentia, and had she been captured, there is little doubt that this sentence would have been swiftly carried out. But this time she eluded arrest successfully. Advocating the creation of a national coalition of anti-Fascist forces, starting in 1942 Dragoicheva became the Communist representative on the umbrella organization embodying this point of view, the Bulgarian Patriotic Front. When the Patriotic Front took over the reins of government in September 1944 with the flight of German occupation forces, Dragoicheva became the Front's national secretary. As the most powerful woman in Bulgaria, in June 1945 she was elected president of the Bulgarian National Women's Union.

In December 1947, Dragoicheva joined Georgi Dimitrov's government as minister of communications, a post she would hold until 1957. The next several years would be difficult for both Dragoicheva and her country. The imposition of a hardline Communist regime brought turmoil to Bulgaria. Industrialization and modernization was a difficult process, and within the Communist movement Stalinist repression destroyed careers and lives. Tsola remained in the government Cabinet, but within the party her power was significantly eroded. In January 1948, she was demoted from full to alternate membership in the politburo and in December of that year, reflecting the harsh purge then taking place within the BCP, she lost her position in the organizational bureau of the central committee, only retaining her general membership in that body.

Joseph Stalin's death in 1953 brought little in the way of liberalization in Bulgaria but it did end the most extreme forms of terror both in the Soviet Union and its Eastern European allies. In Bulgaria, only hesitant steps toward de-Stalinization took place, but Dragoicheva was unafraid to voice her critiques within party circles. In 1956, she attacked Vulko Chervenko, secretary-general of the BCP, for his serious ideological failings. Rather than destroying her political career, her candid behavior encouraged others to call for the initiation of major reforms within the ruling party. Although she resigned her ministry of communications post in February 1957, Dragoicheva's prestige within the regime was restored in 1963 when she became vice-chair of the national committee of the Fatherland Front. Within the BCP, in 1966 she was restored to full membership within the party's politburo.

Seen in the last decades of her long life as the Grand Old Lady of Bulgarian Communism and as the La Pasionaria of the Balkans, Tsola Dragoicheva became well-known throughout the Soviet Bloc, often visiting Moscow as part of her duties as president of the Bulgarian-Soviet Friendship Association. Determined to document her long career as a revolutionary, in the 1970s she published a memoir trilogy entitled *The Call of Duty*, which appeared in translation in German- and English-language editions. In September 1973, Soviet leader Leonid Brezhnev presented her with the Order of Friendship Among Peoples. Her other awards included the Order of Lenin from the Soviet Union, as well as two Bulgarian Orders of Georgi Dimitrov. Tsola Dragoicheva lived long enough to witness not only the birth and power but also the decline and fall of Communism in Bulgaria, dramatic events on which she made no public comments. She died on May 26, 1993.

SOURCES:

Bell, John D. *The Bulgarian Communist Party from Blagoev to Zhivkov.* Stanford, CA: Hoover Institution Press, 1986.

Dragoicheva, Tsola. *Defeat to Victory: Notes of a Bulgarian Revolutionary.* Sofia: Sofia Press, 1983.

Lazitch, Branko, and Milorad M. Drachkovitch. *Biographical Dictionary of the Comintern.* Rev. ed. Stanford, CA: Hoover Institution Press, 1986.

Lukanov, Karlo. "A Jubilee of a Great Friend of the USSR," in *Culture and Life* [Moscow], 1973, no. 11, p. 17.

Oren, Nissan. *Bulgarian Communism: The Road to Power, 1934–1944.* Westport, CT: Greenwood Press, 1985.

Rothschild, Joseph. *The Communist Party of Bulgaria: Origins and Development 1883–1936.* NY: Columbia University Press, 1959.

Tourlakova, Eleonora, and Pavlina Popova. *Bulgarian Women.* Sofia: Sofia Press, 1976.

"Tsola Dragoicheva," in *The Times* [London]. June 8, 1993, p. 19.

John Haag, Associate Professor of History, University of Georgia, Athens, Georgia

Dragomir or Dragomira.

Variant of Drahomira.

Drahomira of Bohemia (d. after 932).

See Ludmila for sidebar.

Drake, Elizabeth (fl. 1625–1656)

English royalist. Name variations: Elizabeth Churchill. Flourished between 1625 and 1656; daughter of Lady Eleanor Drake (a staunch Parliamentarian and daughter of Elizabeth Villiers) and Sir John Drake; married Winston Churchill (a West Country lawyer); children: Arabella Churchill (1648–1714); John Churchill (1650–1722), 1st duke of Marlborough (a British statesman and general); Charles Churchill (1656–1714).

During the English Civil War (1642–51), Winston Churchill, a West Country lawyer, took up arms in defense of crown and his Anglican church. His fortunes fell along with those he championed. Facing destitution, the Royalist cavalry captain and his wife Elizabeth Drake took refuge with her mother, the staunch Parliamentarian Lady **Eleanor Drake**. On May 26, 1650, while living under Lady Drake's roof, Asche House in Devonshire, Elizabeth gave birth to a son, John, the future 1st duke of Marlborough.

The Churchills entertained few prospects. Elizabeth Drake's family had enjoyed a measure of social prestige. The century before, it had produced the great Elizabethan admiral, Sir Francis Drake. Through marriage, the Drakes were related to the Villiers. George Villiers, the duke of Buckingham, had been the intimate friend of both James I and Charles I.

The Stuart Restoration in 1660 produced an immediate improvement in the fortunes of Elizabeth and her husband. Elected a member of parliament for Weymouth, Winston Churchill took his seat in the Convention Parliament in 1661. Making a mark for himself, he quickly earned an entrée to Charles II's court and substantial royal preferments. In 1662, Winston became commissioner for Irish Land Claims and the following year obtained a knighthood and a posting in London. The exploits of Elizabeth and Winston's children—*Arabella Churchill and John Churchill—would be well-documented.

SOURCES:
Chandler, David. *Marlborough as Military Commander.* London, 1972.
Churchill, Winston. *Marlborough: His Life and Times.* 6 vols. London, 1933–38.

SUGGESTED READING:
Barnett, Correlli. *The First Churchill: Marlborough, Soldier and Statesman.* New York, 1974.

Drane, Augusta Theodosia
(1823–1894)

English writer. Name variations: Mother Francis Raphael. Born at Bromley, near Bow, England, on December 29, 1823; died at the Stone convent in Staffordshire, England, on April 29, 1894.

Brought up Anglican, Augusta Drane was influenced by Tractarian teaching at Torquay and joined the Roman Catholic Church in 1850. Her essay questioning the *Morality of Tractarianism,* published anonymously, was incorrectly attributed to John Henry Newman. Following a prolonged stay in Rome, she joined the third order of St. Dominic (1852), to which she belonged for over 40 years. From 1872 to 1881, Drane served as prioress of the Stone convent in Staffordshire, where she died on April 29, 1894. Her books include *The History of Saint Dominic* (1857), *The Life of St. *Catherine of Siena* (1880), *Christian Schools and Scholars* (1867), *The Knights of St John* (1858), *Songs in the Night* (1876), and the *Three Chancellors* (1859), a sketch of the lives of William of Wykeham, William of Waynflete and Sir Thomas More.

SUGGESTED READING:
Wilberforce, B., O.P., ed. *Memoir of Mother Francis Raphael, O.S.D., Augusta Theodosia Drane.* London, 1895.

Dransfeld, Hedwig (1871–1925)

German social and political leader who founded the German Roman Catholic women's movement. Born in Hacheney bei Dortmund, February 24, 1871; died in Werl, Westphalia, on March 13, 1925; daughter of Clemens and Elise (Fleischhauer) Dransfeld; never married; no children.

Hedwig Dransfeld's parents died when she was a child, and she spent most of her youth in an orphanage. Hedwig was an excellent student, enabling her enrollment in a teachers' training academy in Paderborn in 1887. Despite her precarious health, which eventually resulted in the amputation of her left arm in 1898 due to the ravages of tuberculosis of the bone, she was a well-read and ambitious young woman, teaching for a number of years at Paderborn's Ursuline Academy in Werl, Westphalia. Her ultimate goal was to be a poet, and starting in 1893 Dransfeld published the first of several volumes of verse. Her poetry was sensitive to human feelings and aspirations, and also indicated her awareness of the social issues of the day including poverty and the alienation of many men and women from traditional Christian ideals.

Having become well known in German Catholic literary and social reform circles, Dransfeld was chosen in 1905 to become editor of the journal *Die christliche Frau*. Her editorial skills raised the prestige of this journal to new heights and Hedwig Dransfeld, who was an excellent public speaker, now became well known in all strata of German Catholic public life. Emphasizing the unity of faith and social action, she continued the progressive traditions that had distinguished German Catholicism since the 1860s. By 1912, when she became chair of the *Katholischer Deutscher Frauenbund* (German Catholic Women's League; KDF), Dransfeld had become the unchallenged leader of German Catholic women. Though the KDF had been founded in 1904, the organization did not begin to benefit from strong guidance until Dransfeld became its leader.

Despite her recurring health problems that began in the summer of 1914, Hedwig Dransfeld proved to be a forceful leader during the difficult years of war, defeat and reconstruction. Emphasizing the traditional female roles of wife and mother, the KDF never addressed itself specifically to women's issues and until the collapse of the German Reich in 1918 took a markedly apolitical if essentially conservative stance on public issues. Paradoxically, its earlier "neutral" position on the issue enabled the KDF to accept without internal schisms the granting of female suffrage in the closing weeks of 1918. In January 1919, Dransfeld was among the first group of German women to be elected to the Weimar National Assembly. Elected to the Reichstag in 1920 as a candidate of the Catholic Center Party, she and four other members of the KDF represented that party and its allied party, the Bavarian People's Party, in the national Parliament. Here she quickly earned a reputation as one of the most eloquent orators in that political, often turbulent, body.

Highly regarded as an expert on cultural and educational issues, Dransfeld's books, articles, and Reichstag addresses were regarded as the authoritative voice of Germany's Catholic community. Her great prestige as a pioneer of the Catholic women's movement as well as her considerable diplomatic skills enabled her to serve as a conciliator between different factions within the Center Party. Despite the precarious state of her health, Dransfeld was active to the end of her life as an advocate for women's rights within a conservative social framework. After resigning in 1924 as head of the KDF because of rapidly failing health, she died on March 13, 1925, in Werl, Westphalia. At the time of her death, national membership in the KDF had reached a total of about 250,000; lacking Dransfeld's strong leadership, by 1928 it had declined to 198,000. The KDF would be outlawed in Nazi Germany. In November 1988, Dransfeld was honored on a postage stamp of the German Federal Republic's definitive series of famous women in the history of Germany.

SOURCES:

"Hedwig Dransfeld zum Gedächtnis," special issue of *Die christliche Frau*, 1927.

Usborne, Cornelie. *The Politics of the Body in Weimar Germany: Women's Reproductive Rights and Duties*. Ann Arbor: University of Michigan Press, 1992.

John Haag,
Athens, Georgia

Draper, Ruth (1884–1956)

American actress, performing as a solo artist in skits and playlets of her own devising, who was considered the foremost solo performer of her day. Born Ruth Draper in New York City on December 2, 1884 (not in 1889 as is sometimes found); died on December 29, 1956; daughter of William Draper (a physician) and Ruth (Dana) Draper; sister of **Muriel Draper;** *educated by private tutors and private school; never married; no children.*

Awards: Command performances before King George V and Queen Mary of Teck of England, the king and queen of Belgium, and the king and queen of Spain; honorary degree of Master of Arts from Hamilton College; honorary degree from Cambridge University; Commander, Order of the British Empire.

Made first professional appearance (1915); made first appearance on the New York stage (1916); toured the Western front in World War I; made formal professional appearance as a solo performer, London, England (1920); toured Europe and U.S. (1924–28); toured South Africa (1935); toured Far East (1938); toured Latin America (1940); toured U.S. and Canada (1940–41); toured Europe and U.S. (1946–56); gave last performances in New York (December 25–28, 1956).

Ruth Draper was born in New York City on December 2, 1884, the daughter of Dr. William Draper, a well-known New York physician, and **Ruth Dana Draper,** whose family was socially prominent, her maternal grandfather having been Charles A. Dana, the renowned editor of

Ruth Draper

the *New York Sun*. The young Ruth and her five siblings were raised in a wealthy, cultivated atmosphere in which such artists as the novelist Henry James, the painter John Singer Sargent, and the Polish piano virtuoso Ignatz Jan Paderewski were frequent visitors. Except for one year when she attended a private school, Ruth was educated by private tutors. For a time, she lived with her family in Italy.

As a young girl, Ruth Draper evinced an extraordinary talent for mimicry. By her own account, when she was a child of seven, she began to carry on long conversations with herself in which she would imagine that she was first one person and then another, all of whom were very real to her, be they fairy princesses or Indian squaws. In Draper's case, however, these imaginary friends grew in number as the years progressed and remained her intimate companions for the rest of her life, companions whom she shared with the rest of the world. Her debut as a monologist took place at a party in her teens at which each young guest was invited to contribute to the entertainment. It occurred to Draper to do the kind of a monologue she had seen performed on stage by solo artists such as ❧ **Beatrice Herford** and *Elsie Janis**. Choosing a tailor who had made some clothes for her as a subject, she then elaborated on just what such a character must be like. Later, as she repeated this first *tour de force,* the sketch began to take on a definite form that suggested still others to her. In this way, the art of Ruth Draper was born and developed over many years before she tried it on the professional stage.

By 1911, after several years of performing at home and for friends at parties, Draper began to entertain at schools, colleges, charity affairs, and clubs. By 1915, encouraged by Paderewski who recognized her genius and who predicted that one day she would have the world at her feet, she turned professional and began to earn her living through her unusual talent. In May of the following year, she made her acting debut in New York, portraying the role of a maid in the play *A Lady's Name,* which starred the celebrated *Marie Tempest**. This proved to be a false start, however, and Draper never appeared on the stage with another performer again. Several years of struggle ensued, with many managers not wishing to even audition yet another "one-

woman act" for vaudeville, as variety shows were called in those days. Her real career began only in 1918, when she performed for seven months, entertaining the troops of the American Expeditionary Force (AEF) in France during the First World War. This trip awakened in her a love of travel, and for the rest of her life she never tired of touring both in the United States and abroad.

Ruth Draper's first official professional performance took place at Aolian Hall in London in January 1920, when she was already 34 years old. But, though her career may have begun late, fame came quickly; she was soon so well known in London for her talents as a monologist that she managed several weeks at the West End Theater in 1924–25 and, in 1926, was invited to give a command performance before King George V and Queen *Mary of Teck** at Windsor Castle. In the years 1924–28, Draper toured the U.S. and Europe, during which she appeared in Paris, Brussels, Berlin, and Madrid, giving command performances before the kings and queens of Belgium and Spain, and received an honorary degree of Master of Arts from Hamilton College. At the end of her U.S. tour, she regaled audiences for an astonishing 18 consecutive weeks at the Comedy Theater in New York City (1928–29), a record for a solo performer.

By the 1930s, Ruth Draper had acquired an international reputation as one of the most, if not the most, distinguished solo performers of her time, with critics vying to find fresh superlatives to describe her art: "a unique artist and in her line unsurpassable" (*London Daily Telegraph*); "an incomparable artist who runs so true to form that there is nothing new to be said in her praise" (*London Observer*); "No one can play so many tunes on one instrument" (*The New York Times*); "Ruth Draper is a genius" (*London Daily News*).

In 1935, Draper toured South Africa and, in 1938, embarked on a Far Eastern tour that took her to India, Ceylon, Burma, the Malay States (now Malaysia), Java, Australia, and New Zealand. So enamored was she of travel that not even the Second World War curtailed her hectic tours. In 1940, prevented by the hostilities from visiting her beloved Europe, she performed throughout South America, and, in 1940–41, toured the U.S. and Canada. It was at this time that she received a second honorary degree, a Doctor of Fine Arts from the University of Maine (1941).

Draper's career was as unique as her art and was punctuated by unusual details. One man

❧▸ **Herford, Beatrice** (c. 1868–1952)

British monologist and actress. Born in Manchester, England, around 1868; died in her summer home at Little Compton, Rhode Island, on July 18, 1952; sister of Oliver Herford (1863–1935, a writer and illustrator); married Sidney Willard Hayward, in 1897.

A noted British monologist, Beatrice Herford's most famous sketches were *The Shop Girl* and *The Sociable Seamstress.* She also appeared on Broadway in *Two by Two, Cock Robin, See Naples and Die,* and *Run, Sheep, Run.*

claimed to have seen her perform 140 times; actresses went to her matinees in order to study the way in which she achieved her effects; dramatic coaches took their students to see her sketches and had them imitate her in their classes; stage hands were said to have abandoned their card games and craps shooting to watch her from the wings. Although Ruth Draper was a natural genius, who had never formally studied acting, there is no question that her monologues and character sketches had some influence on the teaching of so-called "method acting" in the U.S. with its emphasis on "improvisations" as a teaching technique. Over the years, considerable discussion ensued over exactly how to describe what Draper did on stage. Such terms as monologist, diseuse, solo performer, reciter, elocutionist, impersonator, and character actress seemed highly inadequate terms to define her art. For her own part, Draper insisted that she was simply an actress.

Always a New Yorker, Draper lived in an apartment at 66 East 79th Street when not on tour, usually vacationing in Dark Harbor, Maine. Her brother's son, Paul Draper, became a noted dancer, and on occasion she appeared with him on a double bill alternating her sketches with his own solo performances. In the course of her career, many honors came to her. She not only appeared before crowned heads but was also presented to the pope. As early as 1914, she was being painted and sketched by John Singer Sargent, and, besides her honorary degrees (one of them from Cambridge University), she received the title of Commander of the Order of the British Empire from the British government and only her lack of British citizenship prevented her from being granted the ultimate title of Dame Commander of the British Empire, which she otherwise would have certainly merited.

Over the years, Ruth Draper composed no less than 37 skits, featuring some 58 characters. Her playlets were brief and incisive, cutting away all but the essentials of the characters but nevertheless delineating them as true individuals. Taken together, her sketches would have required over eight hours to perform in their entirety and would have involved the speaking of some 30,000 words. Typically, however, an evening with Ruth Draper "and her cast of characters" was composed of seven sketches involving about 7,500 words. Her longest sketch, *Three Women and Mr. Clifford*, took just over an hour to perform and was, in effect, a one-act play in three scenes; her shortest, *A French Dressmaker*, was accomplished in four minutes.

In between, lay items of varying length such as *Love in the Balkans* and *A Cleaning Woman*, taking five minutes each; *The Dalmatian Peasant*, eight; *In a Church in Italy*, twenty-six, and *Three Breakfasts*, twenty-seven. A perfectionist who was devoted to her work, Draper honed and polished her opuscules, elaborating, expanding and adding to her bill of fare. Her scripts, however, published after her death, give only an approximation of what she actually did on the stage for they served largely as mere mnemonic devices, and she rarely performed any of her sketches the same way more than once. As she grew older, she declined to expand her repertoire with new material, claiming that it took years that she no longer had to produce a work that she considered ready for the stage.

> She is not astonishing you with the brilliance of her talent. She is modestly asking you for your interest in various characters most of whom represent her respect for the human race.
>
> —Brooks Atkinson, *The New York Times*

Ruth Draper's performances were as austere as her scripts. A chair and a table were her only props; an addition of an accessory—a hat, a shawl, a bit of lace—to her plain black gown was enough to enable her to create her character. When her hair turned grey and eventually white, she ignored it, and she never resorted to makeup; her artistry alone was all that she relied upon to create a role, even when playing young women when she was herself past 60. Her carriage was superb, and she had complete mastery over her rich and pliant voice; her ear was perfectly pitched to the subtleties of accents and to the patterns of speech of her characters. An interesting aspect of Draper's performances was her use of "foreign language." Although she performed in French or Italian when appearing in those respective countries, she thought nothing of faking a language when she needed one that she was not familiar with. Thus, her Dalmatian peasant spoke neither Croatian nor any other Balkan tongue; Draper simply and skillfully mouthed what one observer referred to as "Draperese," a gibberish that conveyed the lilt, the tone, and the feel of a Slavic language.

When once asked by someone what was the formula for her technique, Draper answered with complete ingenuousness that she had none at all. Imagination, observation and faith in her abilities were the sole ingredients of her work. Her artistic creed was sincerity. She believed with childlike simplicity in the characters that she portrayed, and she expected that acceptance from her audience, as well. In the words of Thorton Delahanty: "It is this thing that she does to her audiences, her extraordinary power of lifting them out of themselves and making each member a co-creator with her, which so distinguishes her art from that of the ordinary theater." One London critic opined in 1930 that Ruth Draper's greatest strength as an artist lay in two sources: first, her power, already fully developed, to make a general criticism of contemporary civilization by means of ironic portraiture, compelling one to criticize not only the characters that she portrayed but one's own attitudes towards them; and second, her tragic power, which she had only begun to tap. While her rivals provoked one to laughter, he felt that only Draper was capable of evoking pity:

> Her study of a Dalmatian peasant visiting her husband in a New York hospital and her wordless portrait of an unhappy woman who, when the tourists have gone, comes to pray in a Florentine church are pointers to the future development of her art. They are supremely beautiful, touching and profound. The woman capable of them is no longer to be thought of as an "entertainer"; she is potentially a tragic artist of a very high rank.

Much of the art of Ruth Draper seems to have been based on a phenomenon well known to radio producers: the ability of the audience to let its imagination run free. Yet there was more to her art than the mere conjuring up of images. Draper was a humanist who saw and felt the pain of others and who depicted her characters with understanding and compassion. Her sketches of immigrants and their plights, and those depicting the decency of simple, ordinary people were always tinged with affection, and, if her satires were mischievous and always on target, they were never concocted with malice or scorn.

Among Draper's most popular sketches were: *A Board of Managers Meeting, Breakfast in Bed, At a Children's Party, At an Art Exhibition, At an English House Party, At the Court of Philip IV, A Cleaning Woman, The Dalmatian Peasant in a New York Hospital* (her own personal favorite), *The Debutant, Doctors, A French Dressmaker, In a Church in Italy, In County Kerry, In a Railway Station on the Western Plains, The Italian Lesson, Love in the Balkans, The Miner's Wife, On a Maine Porch, Opening a Bazaar, The Return, The Scotch Immigrant at Ellis Island, Showing the Garden, Three Breakfasts, Three Generations in a Court of Human Relations, Three Women and Mr. Clifford, Visit to the Art Gallery, Vive La France, The Wives of Henry VIII*. The mood of these little plays ran the gamut from tragedy (*The Miner's Wife*) to broad satire (*Doctors*), with comedy being the most common genre in which she chose to work. All of her characters were females, though they often interacted with invisible male counterparts brought to vivid life by the magic of her art.

In *The Italian Lesson*, Draper portrayed a wealthy Park Avenue matron about to depart for a lengthy trip but who nevertheless insists on having her weekly Italian lesson. Alone on the stage, reclining on a chaise lounge, she conjured up a stageful of people all of whom were in some way connected with her departure, all the while gamely attempting to continue the constantly interrupted lesson ("Oh, Signore, I'm so glad that we're finally getting into Dante"), her non-existent "entourage" creating an invisible chaos that was hilarious.

Opening a Bazaar has been described as possessing "the sort of quiet irony which is in its nature more English than American," so much so that Draper felt obliged to caution her audience that it was not intended as a satire. A gentle caricature of a titled English woman with a strong sense of her own charitable importance, it nevertheless made a point that bordered on social commentary.

In *Doctors*, three women gather at a fashionable restaurant at the invitation of a fourth (played by Draper). All four of the ladies are on a diet, including Draper's character, but her diet consists of three chocolate eclairs which she devours, all the while going on and on about her marvelous physician and the wonderful cure he had effected on her ("I hadn't slept a wink for a year! Not a wink!"). *Showing the Garden*, depicts an English lady gamely running on and on about her garden to a visitor while having to continually apologize for its present state ("If you had just been here a week ago that whole side there would have been a mass of purple.").

One of Draper's cleverest skits was *The Wives of Henry VIII* in which she played each of the king's six wives in turn, selecting from the life of each the one scene that epitomized the particular wife's relationship with him: the middle-aged ✥ Catherine of Aragon pleading for her marriage, the alluring *Anne Boleyn, not quite as clever as she thinks she is, the coarse ✥ Anne of Cleves playing cards with Henry and outrageously beating him, and so on through to ✥ Catherine Paar, his final queen, depicted praying at his coffin.

✥▶
Catherine of Aragon, Anne of Cleves, Catherine Paar. See Six Wives of Henry VIII.

One of Draper's most touching playlets was *Three Women in a Court of Domestic Relations* in which a daughter, her mother, and her grandmother testify in turn, each giving her particular view on the question of institutionalizing the grandmother. When it comes to the grandmother's turn to speak, however, it becomes clear, even through her broken English, that institutionalization is hardly necessary; she has just become a burden to her daughter and granddaughter who simply no longer want to have her around.

The Dalmatian Peasant presents the audience with the plight of a young immigrant woman, new to America, who has just learned that her laborer husband has been injured on the job and taken to the hospital. Almost completely ignorant of English, the poor woman tries to comprehend, while unfeeling hospital employees explain to her that she is at the wrong hospital. In the end, they convince her that her husband is at Bellevue, but, as she shuffles out of the hospital muttering "Bellevue? Bellevue?," it is clear that she has no idea what Bellevue means.

Three Women and Mr. Clifford was Ruth Draper's longest and most ambitious playlet, as well as, perhaps, one of her most insightful. Wearing a plain, long-sleeved, black dress, Draper began the first scene by adding a white-lace collar and a stenographer's pad to depict Mr. Clifford's secretary. In her one-sided dialogue with Mr. Clifford, she was able to convey to the audience that the secretary, so cool and efficient, is actually in love with her employer. In the second scene, Draper removed the lace collar and replaced it with a heavy strand of pearls, a fur stole, and a perpetual pouty look of discontent to portray the wealthy, bored and unloved Mrs. Clifford. When first we see her, she is obviously standing on the curb outside of a Broadway theater waiting for Mr. Clifford to fetch a cab. Once inside the imaginary cab (a simple folding chair), Mrs. Clifford runs on and on about their son's latest escapade at college, fretting over how her husband has let the boy grow up with insufficient discipline, Draper all the while conveying through her movements the starting and the stopping of the cab at each stoplight. In the final scene, Draper sits on the arm of a chair that has its back to the audience so that we can not see its occupant. Now Mr. Clifford's mistress, she is facing the audience, laughing merrily as Mr. Clifford describes his son's latest antics at school, the very same that had earlier caused his wife such chagrin. By the end of the three short scenes, we know all that we need to know about Mr. Clifford: his insensitivity to his secretary's feelings for him, his boredom with his wife, and his want of a mistress to relieve the tedium of a moribund marriage.

Draper's sketch *Vive La France* was a particular *tour de force* for in it she not only played a young maiden but performed the entire scene in French. On a darkened stage, she conveyed—with not a word in English—that we were on a beach on the Channel coast of occupied France, where a young woman has come to see her beloved off as he embarks for England to join the Free French Forces fighting against the Nazis abroad. Although the stage was darkened and Draper wore a large shawl over her head, these artifices were scarcely necessary, for through her quick, youthful movements and the timbre of her voice, she never let you doubt that she was a woman of scarcely 20, even though she was actually past 70 the last time she performed the skit. When she ended the scene waving to her lover as his boat left the shore, crying out to him "Vive la France, Vive la France," the audience, completely swept up in the mood that she had created, would frequently cheer, so much so that Draper often used this sketch to conclude her evening's performance on a rousing note.

In her appearance, Draper was a tall, slender, handsome woman with a strong face, aristocratic features, a long aquiline nose and a bright, sunny smile. On stage, she radiated kindness and good will, and her devotees always felt that they were coming to the theater to see an old friend at work. Many of the members of her audiences were repeat attendees, and there was always a large number of theatricals in the house who considered Ruth Draper to be "an actor's actress," and who would never miss an opportunity to see her perform.

The success of Ruth Draper's solo performances encouraged other monologists to enter the field with various degrees of success, none of them enjoying the popularity of Ruth Draper. Among the better of these was the talented *Angna Enters, a gifted performer, who used no words at all. As a one-woman performer, however, only the great Canadian comedienne *Beatrice Lillie, whose solo scenes were the highlights of her London and Broadway reviews, was in the same league as Ruth Draper. To see Lillie simpering in a Japanese kimono, reducing an audience to tears as she silently arranged and rearranged a single chrysanthemum in a vase, was to enter a realm of comic genius without compare.

Apart from her performances, Ruth Draper was an author in her own right. She not only wrote all of her own sketches but, in 1933, published a translation of Lauro de Bosis' poetic drama *Iearo*. Although she was asked to appear in motion pictures or at least to allow her sketches to be filmed, Draper always refused on the grounds that what she did was only suited for performance before a live audience. In fact, it is very likely that a live audience was indispensable for her to work her magic. She also declined to appear on radio, partly for the same reason but also because much of her effect was achieved precisely because of the disparity between the nature of her characters and her own appearance. A private person, Draper avoided publicity and never gave interviews. Personally, however, she was warm and gracious and had many devoted friends. She was also a delightful houseguest, having not the slightest hesitation in giving impromptu performances for her hosts and their friends or other guests.

After World War II, Draper continued her tours, appearing repeatedly in London, where she was extraordinarily popular. She played in London for the last time in 1956 and then moved on to perform in New York, even though she had announced her "farewell performance" there two years previously. Opening at the Playhouse on Broadway on Christmas night for a four-week engagement, she received the usual rave reviews, even though, with her talents undimmed, the reviewer for *The New York Times* despaired of finding anything new to say to describe her still marvelous performance. Four days later, however, at age 72, she was found dead in her apartment by her maid. She had never married and was survived by two sisters and her nephew. Although her funeral was private, over 400 attended. A collection of her sketches appeared in 1960, and, a devoted correspondent, her letters were published in 1979.

SOURCES:
Free Library of Philadelphia, Theater Collection.
Obituary in *The New York Times*. December 31, 1956, p. 32.
Parker, John. *Who's Who in the Theater*. NY: Pitman, 1957.

SUGGESTED READING
The Art of Ruth Draper. New York, 1960.
Warren, Neilla. *The Letters of Ruth Draper*. New York, 1979.

Robert H. Hewsen, Professor of History, Rowan University, Glassboro, New Jersey

Draves, Victoria (1924—)

American diver who won the gold medal in springboard and platform diving in the 1948 Olympics, the first woman to win both. Name variations: Vickie Draves. Born Victoria Manalo in San Francisco, California, on December 31, 1924; married Lyle Draves (a diving coach); children: four sons.

When Victoria Draves began diving, her coach Phil Patterson recommended she use her mother's maiden name, Taylor, instead of her father's, Manalo, so no one would suspect she was Filipino. Patterson also enrolled her in his school so that she might not encounter prejudice, rather than have her join the Fairmont Hotel Swimming Club. When she was invited to give a diving exhibition at the exclusive men's Olympic Club in San Francisco, a breakthrough for a woman, Victoria's father was refused admission. Patterson, who worked constantly against racial bias, eventually persuaded officials to allow him in to see his daughter.

Victoria Draves made great progress as a diver until the outbreak of World War II. Then her coach joined the military, and she resigned herself to the fact that her career in diving was probably over. But after a year, she joined Charley Sava's team at the Crystal Plunge where Jimmy Hughes coached her. Draves, who had graduated from high school, took a temporary civil-service position to help pay for coaching and to help her family. When Hughes could no longer coach her, Sava suggested she go to the Athens Athletic Club in Oakland to work with Lyle Draves.

Victoria went to meet the man who would be her husband, an Iowa farm boy who had learned to dive in local fishing holes. Lyle treated her as if she were a diving novice. No one had ever told Victoria how to place her arms, how to walk the board, or how to lift up into a dive. Determined that she refine her skills, at first he would not allow her to compete. Within two years, however, she became a national champion. She also married her coach.

At the 1948 Olympic trials, Lyle was asked to fill in occasionally for Fred Cady, the Olympic diving coach who was quite ill. But when they arrived in London for the Olympics, Lyle was not allowed near Victoria because he was a family member; he got a job as a timer to be close at hand. Draves was tense when it came time for her dive. Unlike her rival Zoë Ann Olsen, a former student of Lyle's, Draves did not thrive on competition and had been having problems with her back one-and-a-half layout in practice. But Victoria Draves became the first woman in history to win Olympic gold in both springboard and platform. Turning pro after the 1948 Games, she joined Larry Crosby's Rhapsody in Swimtime and then Buster Crabbe's Aquaparades. Draves loved touring Europe and the United States. She retired to raise four sons, all divers.

SOURCES:

Carlson, Lewis H., and John J. Fogarty. *Tales of Gold.* Chicago: Contemporary Books, 1987.

Porter, David L., ed. *Biographical Dictionary of American Sports. Basketball and Other Indoor Sports.* NY: Greenwood Press, 1989.

Stump, Al J. *Champions Against Odds.* Philadelphia, PA: Macrae Smith, 1952.

Karin L. Haag, freelance writer, Athens, Georgia

Drayton, Grace Gebbie

(1877–1936)

American artist and illustrator. Name variations: Grace Gebbie; Grace Gebbie Wiedersheim. Born Grace Gebbie in Philadelphia, Pennsylvania, on October 14, 1877; died on January 31, 1936; daughter of George (Philadelphia's first art publisher) and Mary (Fitzgerald) Gebbie; married Theodore E. Wiedersheim, Jr. (divorced 1911); married W. Heyward Drayton III (divorced 1923).

One of this country's earliest illustrators, Grace Drayton developed her first cartoon, *Naughty Toodles*, for the Hearst syndicate in 1903. It was followed by her ubiquitous drawings of The Campbell Kids, which first appeared in 1905. Her characters were also seen in *Bobby Blake and Dolly Drake*, which was created for the *Philadelphia Press*, and the series *The Terrible Tales of Kaptain Kiddo*, which she created with her sister, **Margaret G. Hays**, for the *Philadelphia Sunday North American*. Its theme of children's sea voyages was similar to *The Cruise of the Katzenjammer Kids* (1907). Drayton also illustrated Mother Goose nursery rhymes and a series of verses by her sister. Her last work, *Pussycat Princess* (written by Ed Anthony), was for King Features.

Drechsler, Heike (b. 1964).

See Joyner, Florence Griffith for sidebar.

Dreier, Katherine Sophie (1877–1952).

See Dreier Sisters.

Dreier, Margaret (1868–1945).

See Dreier Sisters.

Dreier, Mary Elisabeth (1875–1963).

See Dreier Sisters.

Dreier Sisters

Labor reformers, women's suffrage activists and early leaders of the Women's Trade Union League who sought to fulfill their family legacy of philanthropy through activism.

Dreier, Katherine Sophie (1877–1952). Name variations: frequently misspelled as Drier. Born September 10, 1877, in Brooklyn, New York; died on March 29, 1952, in Milford, Connecticut, of nonalcoholic cirrhosis of the liver; daughter of Dorothea Adelheid Dreier and her cousin Theodor Dreier (an iron merchant); educated by private tutors; attended Brooklyn Art Students League, 1895–97, Pratt Institute, 1900–01; married Edward Trumball-Smith, in August 1911 (annulled 1911); no children.

Served as treasurer, German Home for Recreation for Women and Children (1900–09); was co-founder and president, the Little Italy Neighborhood Association, Brooklyn (1905); served as a delegate, Sixth Convention of the International Woman's Suffrage Alliance (1911); had first exhibit, London (1911); was an exhibitor, the New York Armory Show (1913); founded the Cooperative Mural Workshop (1914); chaired the German-American Committee, New York City's Woman's Suffrage Party (1915); was

Victoria Draves

a co-founder of the Society of Independent Artists (1916); was a co-founder of Societe Anonyme (1920); held retrospective show, New York Academy of Allied Arts (1933). Publications: numerous articles and books, including Five Months in the Argentine: From a Woman's Point of View, 1918 to 1919 *(1920),* Western Art and the New Era *(1923), and* Shawn the Dancer *(1933).*

Dreier, Mary Elisabeth *(1875–1963). Name variations: frequently misspelled as Drier. Pronunciation: DRY-er. Born September 26, 1875, in Brooklyn, New York; died in Bar Harbor, Maine, of a pulmonary embolism on August 15, 1963; daughter of Dorothea Adelheid Dreier and her cousin Theodor Dreier (an iron merchant); privately educated; lived with Frances Kellor for 45 years; never married; no children.*

Did settlement house work at Asacog House, Brooklyn (late 1890s); was a member of the Women's Trade Union League (WTUL, 1904–50), president of the New York WTUL (1906–14); was a member of the New York State Factory Investigating Commission (1911–15); served as delegate-at-large, Progressive Party convention (1912); served as chair of the New York City's Woman Suffrage Party (1916); served as chair of the New York State Committee on Women in Industry, Advisory Commission, Council of National Defense (1918–19); was a long-time member of the Industrial Department and National Board, Young Women's Christian Association (YWCA); was an antinuclear activist (1950s). Publications: Margaret Dreier Robins: Her Life, Letters and Work *(1950) and numerous articles.*

Margaret Dreier Robins

Robins, Margaret Dreier *(1868–1945). Pronunciation: DRY-er. Name variations: Gretchen; frequently misspelled as Drier. Born September 6, 1868, in Brooklyn, New York; died at Chinsegut Hill, Brooksville, Florida, of pernicious anemia and heart disease, February 21, 1945; daughter of Dorothea Adelheid Dreier and her cousin Theodor Dreier (an iron merchant); privately educated; married Raymond Robins (1873–1954, brother of Elizabeth Robins), on June 21, 1905; no children.*

Served as chair, legislative committee, the Women's Municipal League (1903–04); was a member of the WTUL (1904–44), president, Chicago WTUL (1907–13), president, National Women's Trade Union League (1907–22); served as executive board member, Chicago Federation of Labor (1908–17); was a member of the Illinois state committee of the Progressive Party (1912); was a member of the women's division, Republican Party National Committee (1919–20); served as president, International Federation of Working Women (1921–1923); was an active member, YWCA, the Red Cross, and the League of Women Voters (1920s); was a member of the White House Conference on Child Health and Protection planning committee (1929); was reelected to the NWTUL executive board (1934); was chair of the League's committee on Southern work (1937). Publications: numerous articles.

In late September 1923, Mary Dreier and her sister, Margaret Dreier Robins, were about to board ship in Rotterdam, the Netherlands. The two had spent several months in Europe, visiting friends, and had served as delegates to the Third Working Women's International Congress. The Dreier sisters had been disappointed by the tone of the conference, sponsored by the International Federation of Working Women (IFWW) which they had helped create. Rather than continue to stand alone, agitating for the rights of women workers, the IFWW now chose to work within existing male-dominated trade unions. Given the results of the conference, the Dreier sisters were eager to board ship and return home. As they were about to leave, they went from disappointment to despair. A cable arrived informing them of the death of their sister, **Dorothea Dreier** (1870–1923).

All four Dreier sisters shared the same dedication to using their family wealth to enrich humanity. Dorothea and her younger sister Katherine did so through their art. Margaret and Mary did so through labor reform. Such was the legacy of their parents, Theodor and **Dorothea Adelheid Dreier**. Yet Dorothea is the least well-known of the Dreier sisters. Her early death was due to the same crusading spirit that sustained the activities of her three better known sisters. Dorothea was an artist originally trained in the Impressionist school who later turned to Realism. Her realistic representation of workers became her expression of social concern. While painting Dutch workers in the damp homes in which they lived and worked, Dorothea came down with tuberculosis, the disease that killed her at age 52.

Theodor Dreier came to America from Bremen, Germany, in 1849. He spent several years working for Naylor, Benson and Company, iron distributors. In 1864, having secured a comfortable living, Theodor returned to his birthplace in search of a bride. He found one in his cousin, Dorothea Adelheid Dreier, the daughter of a minister. Theodore and Dorothea were part of a large, old Bremen family devoted to commercial activities and civic interests. As early as the 17th century, the Diekhoff-Dreier Fund was established by the family as a way of assisting "needy widows" and poor young people in need of vocational training. While the activities of the American Dreier sisters were very much in keeping with the reform spirit of the Progressive era in which they lived, their willingness to be reformers was also nurtured by their parents as part of the family tradition.

Both families initially objected to the marriage of Theodor and Dorothea, feeling it inappropriate for cousins to marry; Dorothea's parents were also upset at the thought of their daughter leaving for so distant a place as America. The young couple persisted, however, and after their marriage settled in the Brooklyn

Heights brownstone the Dreier family would call home for the next 25 years. Contact with the German Dreiers was maintained through regular trips to Germany as the Dreier sisters and their brother Edward grew up.

Even with the strain of providing for five children born within nine years, the Dreier household was a comfortable one. While none of the four sisters went to college, they were privately educated at home and at the Brackett School for Girls. All the children were brought up in the faith of their parents, the German Evangelical Church. An appreciation of art, music, and literature was encouraged. At the same time, an awareness of the importance of civic involvement was also stressed. As Mary Dreier would later remember in her biography of her sister, Margaret, "It was a happy family, unspoiled and ruled lovingly and understandingly by the parents."

The children—Margaret, called Gretchen by the family, Dorothea, also known as Dodo, Edward, Mary and Katherine—stayed close as

Mary Elisabeth Dreier with Frances Kellor.

adults. Together, they mourned the death of their father in 1897 and the death of their mother only two years later. Each of the Dreier children, now adults, inherited what was then the rather substantial sum of $500,000. Edward, like his father, went into business. The Dreier sisters, befitting their gender and class, could have been expected to marry and continue the charity work their family so honored. However, only one of the sisters would eventually marry and all four dedicated their lives to reform, not as an addition to familial duties but rather as a career. Their inheritance, both monetarily and in the values their parents instilled in them, prepared them for nothing less.

Margaret Dreier, attractive and popular, was apparently far more outgoing than any of her younger sisters. As a young woman, she became an active participant in the social scene of the prosperous Brooklyn Heights community in which she lived. In the midst of her busy social life, Margaret chose as her first cause the Brooklyn hospital where her father was a trustee. At age 19, she became secretary-treasurer for the Women's Auxiliary as well as the hospital's nurses training program. Yet, by the mid-1890s, as she approached her 30th birthday, Margaret came to feel that the migraine headaches from which she had suffered for years would be relieved not by rest but by action. The death of her parents, difficult as it was, provided Margaret with an independent income. Rather than concentrate on social obligations, she turned to social reform.

By the turn of the century, Margaret became a member of the State Charities Aid Association City Visiting Committee for the state institutions for the insane. Shortly after, she joined the Women's Municipal League of New York, becoming chair of the League's legislative committee and spearheading an investigation into women's employment agencies. Social reformers, such as Margaret Dreier, charged that employment agencies often exploited unsuspecting women, especially recently arrived immigrants who spoke no English. In seeking to draw attention to these agencies by lobbying for regulatory legislation, Margaret began her public career on behalf of working-class women.

At the same time, her sister Mary developed similar interests. Less outgoing than her older sister, Mary never really entered into the Brooklyn Heights social scene. Instead, at age 20, Mary began searching for socially meaningful work. Her quest brought her to a Brooklyn settlement, Asacog House. Here, in 1899, she met

*Leonora O'Reilly, a garment worker who as head of Asacog House introduced her new upper-class friend to the concerns of the working poor, especially trade unionism. Mary, like her sister Margaret, entered into the social justice movement of the Progressive era with a sincere desire to make life better for those less fortunate. However, rather than simply providing charity for the poor, Margaret and Mary Dreier sought to provide the working class, especially its women, with the tools to help themselves.

In 1903, the Women's Trade Union League (WTUL) was created as a cross-class alliance to address the needs and concerns of working-class women. Principal branches were soon established in New York, Chicago, and Boston, seeking to organize working women into trade unions, educate them as to their rights, and lobby for protective labor legislation. The Dreier sisters, at the invitation of O'Reilly, soon became active in the New York League. Within a few short years, both Margaret and Mary would rise to positions of leadership within the WTUL. Their willingness to give financial support was as critical as was their daily participation in League activities. In the WTUL, which they officially joined in 1904, the Dreier sisters found an organization that combined their interests in women and reform.

The youngest daughter, Katherine Dreier, was also influenced by the family emphasis on community work. Beginning in 1900, she served nine years as treasurer for the German Home for Recreation for Women and Children, founded by her mother a few years earlier. In 1905, Katherine became president of the Little Italy Neighborhood Association in Brooklyn, an organization she had helped establish. However, like her older sister Dorothea, Katherine was most drawn to art.

Her art education began at the age of 12 when she enrolled in a weekly class. A few years later, in 1895, Katherine began two years of study at the Brooklyn Arts Student League. In 1900, she spent a year at the Pratt Institute. Thereafter, she took private lessons with the American artist, Walter Shirlaw. The long years of study finally came to fruition in 1905 when she sold her first piece, an altar painting for the chapel of St. Paul's school in Garden City, New York.

Also in 1905, Margaret Dreier was elected president of the New York WTUL. Shortly thereafter, she met Raymond Robins, a Chicago reformer and settlement house worker, and the brother of actress and activist *Elizabeth

Robins (1862–1952). After only a six-week courtship, the two married and established a home in one of the poorest Chicago neighborhoods. There, Raymond continued his social reform work while Margaret, now known as Margaret Dreier Robins, joined the Chicago WTUL. In 1907, she was elected president of the Chicago league and president of the National Women's Trade Union League (NWTUL), a post she would hold for 15 years.

Almost 37 at the time of her wedding, Margaret had seemingly accepted that she would never marry. In Raymond, however, she found a like-minded social reformer who respected her work and her politics. During their almost 40 years together, the Robinses remained an affectionate, even passionate couple who corresponded daily when separated by the demands of their individual careers. Their only disappointment was Margaret's apparent inability to conceive a child. Nonetheless, their love for each other, their work, family and friends filled their long marriage with much joy.

As president of the NWTUL, Margaret Dreier Robins evolved into an articulate, impassioned speaker for working-class women. She saw the WTUL through internal disputes and conflicts with the male-dominated American Federation of Labor. Robins was also the driving force behind the creation of several local leagues, from Washington, D.C. to St. Louis, Missouri, during the 1910s. She was also instrumental in the establishment of the NWTUL's Training School for Women Organizers. However, Robins provided the WTUL with even more than her time and energy. Throughout her years as NWTUL president, she drew no salary and paid all her own office expenses as well as travel costs. She also financed the publication of the official NWTUL journal, *Life and Labor* (1911–21). Robins' generosity extended even beyond the immediate needs of the WTUL. She paid the court costs of Louis Brandeis for his work on the 1908 landmark Supreme Court decision in *Muller* v. *Oregon*. That case established the constitutionality of laws limiting the hours of employment for women and was seen as an advancement for working-class women.

Throughout her years in Chicago, Margaret stayed in constant touch with her sister, Mary. With Margaret's departure, Mary seemed to come into her own. In 1906, Mary Dreier was elected to the presidency of the New York WTUL, the position vacated by Margaret. As president from 1906 to 1914 of the WTUL's largest local branch, Mary Dreier was at the forefront of some of the most volatile labor actions involving working women in the pre-World War I era.

In 1909, when thousands of primarily young, immigrant female shirtwaist makers went out on strike in what came to be called "The Uprising of the Twenty Thousand," Mary Dreier was arrested on the picket line and was able to make public the police brutality towards the strikers. In the course of the strike, the shyest of the Dreier sisters developed not only her organizing abilities but her public-speaking skills. Her participation on the front lines in this often violent strike earned Mary Dreier the lifelong admiration of such working-class trade unionist women as ❧ **Pauline Newman** and *Rose Schneiderman.

Two years later, as president of the New York WTUL, Mary Dreier had the duty of leading the investigation into the Triangle Shirtwaist Company fire. On March 25, 1911, 146 workers—primarily women and children—died in the conflagration. It was later revealed that the factory doors had been locked to prevent employee theft. The WTUL, interested in protective legislation as well as union organization, saw in this tragedy the obvious need for state regulation of the workplace. In 1911, the state of New York appointed a Factory Investigating Commission with Mary Dreier as the only woman member. Examining all aspects of industrial work, from hours and wages to fire prevention, the commission eventually presented the New York State Assembly in 1915 with the most comprehensive series of labor laws ever drafted. Fellow Commission members such as Robert F. Wagner and Alfred E. Smith later remembered Mary as bringing to her work a great depth of understanding of the needs of working-class women.

Yet, in her personal relations with some of the working women she knew, class differences seemed insurmountable. Mary had long maintained a close relationship with her settlement house colleague, Leonora O'Reilly. O'Reilly, the daughter of Irish immigrants who had started work in a garment factory at age 11, brought to the WTUL years of experience as a worker and trade unionist. A self-taught woman with feminist sympathies, O'Reilly had little patience for the sometimes condescending attitudes the middle- and upper-class allies held towards the "working girls." Correspondence between Mary Dreier and O'Reilly frequently demonstrated the class tension ever-present in the WTUL despite—or perhaps due to—the lifetime annuity Mary gave to O'Reilly in 1909.

❧
Newman, Pauline. See *Miller, Frieda S.* for sidebar.

Unlike her sister, Margaret Dreier Robins seemed little bothered by class tensions within the organization she led. In her correspondence, both personal and official, Robins generally referred to the middle- and upper-class allies as women, while working-class women in the WTUL, even those in leadership positions whatever their age, were usually called girls. Mary Dreier, on the other hand, perhaps because of her close friendship with O'Reilly, often wrestled with the problem of class divisions. In 1914, she began but never finished a semi-autobiographical novel entitled *Barbara Richards,* which addresses relationships between women of different classes.

While her sisters devoted themselves to labor reform, Katherine Dreier increasingly focused on her career as an artist. She studied in Paris and London, living and working in the avant-garde art communities there. While in London, Katherine met another American painter, Edward Trumball-Smith. The two were married in the Dreier home in Brooklyn Heights, August 1911. The marriage was soon annulled, however, when it was discovered that Trumball already had a wife and children.

Katherine Dreier quickly recovered from this personal tragedy as her professional career took off. In September 1911, her first exhibition opened in London and then toured Germany where she spent a year of study. She returned to New York in time to be a part of the 1913 Armory Show. This first mass showing of modern art on American soil was greeted with much public misunderstanding and even ridicule. Katherine, whose own artistic style was based in the modern school, saw the show as an inspirational milestone in art. She would devote the rest of her public life not so much to her own art as to the effort to make modern art known and appreciated in America.

At the same time, Katherine Dreier joined her sisters in the last stages of the fight for women's suffrage. In 1911, she went as a delegate to the Sixth Convention of the International Woman Suffrage Alliance, held that year in Stockholm. In 1915, she chaired the German-American Committee of the Woman Suffrage Party in New York City. Her sister Mary chaired the New York City Woman Suffrage Party itself as well as the industrial section of the Woman Suffrage New York State Party. Margaret Dreier Robins, still based in Chicago, was active in the suffrage movement there. All three women shared the conviction that women's participation in politics would bring about much needed social reform.

During World War I, many American reformers came to see international cooperation as a way to prevent future conflict. In that spirit, the NWTUL proposed at its 1917 convention an international congress of working women to be held at war's end. Support from the British WTUL was soon won, and in 1919 the first International Congress of Working Women was held in Washington, D.C. Mary and, especially, Margaret devoted themselves to the new organization that came out of the Congress, the International Federation of Working Women (IFWW).

However, that organization proved to be shortlived when in 1923 the IFWW voted to effectively disband and become a women's department within the International Federation of Trade Unions (IFTU). Because the American Federation of Labor (AFL)—with which the NWTUL had a loose, if combative association—refused to join the IFTU due to political differences, American trade union women would lack a voice in the IFTU should it absorb the IFWW. Even more important, given their 20 years of experience with the AFL, the Dreier sisters felt strongly that the needs of working women would be best addressed through gender-specific organizations. Although both women remained members of the NWTUL, after the mid-1920s defeat of their international efforts, Mary Dreier and Margaret Dreier Robins ended their leadership of the organization they had helped create.

On the other hand, Katherine Dreier's forays into international cooperation met with more success. In the interest of promoting modern art in America, Katherine, along with Marcel Duchamp and Man Ray, founded the Societe Anonyme in New York City in 1920. It was, through lectures, exhibits, and publications "to promote the serious expression of the serious study of serious men [sic] in the art world of today." Katherine and her associates brought to America the work of leading European modernists—such as Kandinski, Klee, and Léger. During the 1920s, several major exhibits were staged by Societe Anonyme, only to be eclipsed by the opening of the New York Museum of Modern Art in 1929. While this meant that Katherine's cherished brainchild would not be the preeminent modern art museum, she continued to lecture and sponsor shows based on her extensive collection of some of the best examples of modern art. In 1934, she organized a show of 13 women artists, at the same time supporting the dance career of her friend, Ted Shawn.

Starting in the mid-1920s, the Dreier sisters—once so vital and active—slipped into less and less public involvement. In 1924, the year after her sister Dorothea's death and the disappointing end of international efforts for the WTUL, Margaret Dreier Robins and her husband "retired" to their beloved Florida home, Chinsegut Hill. Although she sat on the boards of many local and national organizations, such as the Red Cross and the National League of Women Voters, Robins leadership of the women's labor-reform movement was effectively over. Though she had become involved in the Republican Party, she became an ardent supporter of Franklin Roosevelt in 1936. By then, many of the protective labor laws Margaret Dreier Robins had fought for as head of the WTUL 30 years earlier had been enacted on a federal level by New Deal legislation. She died in 1945, at age 76, of pernicious anemia and a heart ailment and is buried on the grounds of her Florida home.

In her last years, spent in illness, Katherine Dreier prepared a catalog with Marcel Duchamp for the Societe Anonyme collection that the two had presented to Yale University in 1941. Through her efforts of time and money, Katherine did indeed bring to America the modern art she felt so vital to the 20th century. In 1952, at age 74, she died of non-alcoholic cirrhosis of the liver in her Milford, Connecticut, home.

Although Mary Dreier was just as disappointed as her sister Margaret at the inability of the WTUL to be a part of the international labor scene, she maintained an interest in international relations. During the 1930s, Mary Dreier was an outspoken foe of Nazism and an equally strong supporter of improved Soviet-U.S. relations. After World War II, she continued to advocate for international cooperation and against the proliferation of nuclear weapons. This stance during the Cold War of the 1950s, despite her advanced age, brought Mary Dreier to the attention of the FBI which investigated her as a possible subversive. While she never married, Mary Dreier had several close friendships with women, including the social reformer ❧▸ Frances Kellor with whom she lived for over 45 years. In 1963, she died a month before her 88th birthday at her summer home in Bar Harbor, Maine.

SOURCES:

Bohan, Ruth L. *The Societe Anonyme's Brooklyn Exhibit: Katherine Dreier and Modernism in America.* Ann Arbor, MI: UMI Research Press, 1982.

Dreier, Mary E. *Margaret Dreier Robins: Her Life, Letters, and Work.* NY: Island Cooperative Press, 1950.

Dye, Nancy Schrom. *As Equals and As Sisters: Feminism, the Labor Movement, and the Women's Trade*

❧▸ **Kellor, Frances Alice** (1873–1952)

American sociologist and activist. Born in 1873; died in 1952; daughter of a poor widow; graduated Cornell Law School, 1897; attended University of Chicago; lived with Mary Elisabeth Dreier (1875–1963).

Frances Kellor's entrance examination scores were so high, despite the fact that she had no high school diploma, that she was allowed admission to Cornell Law School. After securing a law degree, she entered the University of Chicago to study sociology. The two fields were neatly combined into her early specialty: the study of women criminals and the causes of crime. In 1901, Kellor wrote a series of articles on her findings.

While associated with *Jane Addams' Hull House, Kellor met *Mary Elizabeth Dreier, and the two moved to New York where they worked together on social causes for the rest of their lives. Kellor wrote books, founded the National League for the Protection of Colored Women (1906), and became secretary of the New York State Immigration Commission (1908). Her zeal to help immigrant women, especially those who traveled alone, sometimes backfired, however. In the climate of the time, when women had limited rights or means to choose a path of self-reliance, protectionist theories to safeguard women, instead of liberating them, were popular. Kellor was a proponent, for example, in detaining women who arrived in the country alone. This way, it was thought, their safety could be secured until someone arrived who would take responsibility for them.

SUGGESTED READING:

Fitzpatrick, Ellen. *Endless Crusade.* NY: Oxford University Press, 1990.

Union League of New York. Columbia, MO: University of Missouri Press, 1980.

Payne, Elizabeth Anne. *Reform, Labor, and Feminism: Margaret Dreier Robins and the Women's Trade Union League.* Urbana, IL: University of Illinois, 1988.

SUGGESTED READING:

Jacoby, Robin Miller. *The British and American Women Trade Union Leagues, 1890–1925: A Case Study of Feminism and Class.* Brooklyn, NY: Carlson, 1994.

Saarinen, Aline B. *The Proud Possessors: The Lives, Times and Tastes of Some Adventurous American Art Collectors.* NY: Vintage Books, 1968.

COLLECTIONS:

Katherine S. Dreier correspondence, papers, and memorabilia located in the Beinecke Library, Yale University.

Margaret Dreier Robins correspondence, papers, and memorabilia located in the University of Florida Library, Gainsville.

Mary E. Dreier correspondence, papers, and memorabilia located in the Schlesinger Library, Radcliffe College.

Kathleen Banks Nutter, Manuscripts Processor, Sophia Smith Collection, Smith College, Northampton, Massachusetts, and author of "Women Reformers and the Limitations of Labor Politics in Progressive Era Massachusetts," in *Massachusetts Politics* (Westfield State College, 1998)

Dressler, Marie (1869–1934)

American comedian and film star who won an Academy Award for her performance in Min and Bill. *Born Leila Marie Koerber on November 9, 1869, in Coburg, Canada; died on July 28, 1934, in Santa Bar-* bara, California; daughter of an itinerant music teacher; joined the Nevada Stock Company at the age of 14; two marriages; no children.

Selected stage performances: Robber on the Rhine (1892); The Lady Slavey (1896); Higgledy-Piggledy (1904); Tillie's Nightmare (1910).

Selected filmography: Tillie's Punctured Romance *(1914);* Tillie's Tomato Surprise *(1915);* Tillie Wakes Up *(1917);* The Scrublady *(1917);* The Cross Red Nurse *(1918);* The Agonies of Agnes *(1918);* The Callahans and the Murphys *(1927);* The Joy Girl *(1927);* Breakfast at Sunrise *(1927);* Bringing Up Father *(1928);* The Patsy *(1928);* The Divine Lady *(1929);* The Hollywood Revue *(1929);* The Vagabond Lover *(1929);* Chasing Rainbows *(1930);* Anna Christie *(1930);* The Girl Said No *(1930);* One Romantic Night *(1930);* Caught Short *(1930);* Let Us Be Gay *(1930);* Min and Bill *(1930);* Reducing *(1931);* Politics *(1931);* Emma *(1932);* Prosperity *(1932);* Tugboat Annie *(1933);* Dinner at Eight *(1933);* Christopher Bean *(1933).*

Describing herself as "too homely for a prima donna and too big for a soubrette," Marie Dressler was one of America's most endearing character actresses of the 1930s. The daughter of an impoverished music teacher, Dressler joined a stock company at age 14 and was a vaudeville headliner by the turn of the century. Her most successful turn on Broadway was as Tillie Blobbs, the daydreaming boardinghouse drudge in *Tillie's Nightmare* (1910), in which her rendition of the song "Heaven Will Protect the Working Girl" was particularly memorable. This led to a film contract with Mack Sennett and a series of "Tillie" movies, the first of which co-starred Charlie Chaplin.

Dressler never caught on in silents, and her stage career slowed during the 1920s due to her involvement in the Actor's Strike of 1919. In 1927, a close friend, screenwriter *Frances Marion, came to her rescue, fashioning the film *The Callahans and the Murphys* (1927) especially for her and then selling it to producer Irving Thalberg. Dressler and her co-star in the picture, *Polly Moran, enjoyed success in several additional films together, including *Bringing Up Father* (1928). Dressler's career was boosted once more by her surprise casting in the serious character role of Marthy, a waterfront hag, in *Anna Christie* (1930). (Frances Marion, who wrote the adaptation, convinced MGM that Dressler could handle the part.) That same year, Dressler won the Academy Award for Best Actress for her performance in another Marion screenplay, *Min and Bill*, in which Dressler ran a waterfront tavern with Wallace Beery. She and Beery, known as a delightful twosome, were together again in *Tugboat Annie* (1933). Although an unlikely star, Dressler was the No. 1 box-office attraction in the country for several years. The actress died of cancer in 1934. In a tribute, *Photoplay* called

her a star of universal appeal: "If you ever saw Marie Dressler on the screen she went straight to your heart. That was because the shining qualities that made her so beloved by everyone that knew her personally were revealed . . . in her film interpretations."

SOURCES:
Katz, Ephraim. *The Film Encyclopedia*. NY: HarperCollins, 1994.

McHenry, Robert. *Famous American Women*. NY: Dover, 1983.

Shipman, David. *The Great Movie Stars: The Golden Years*. Boston: Little Brown, 1995.

Wilmeth, Don B., and Tice L. Miller, eds. *Cambridge Guide to American Theater*. Cambridge and NY: Cambridge University Press, 1993.

SUGGESTED READING:
Dressler, Marie, with M. Harrington. *My Own Story*. New York, 1934 (an expansion of earlier autobiography, *The Life Story of an Ugly Duckling*, 1924).

Lee, Betty. *Marie Dressler: The Unlikeliest Star*. KY: University of Kentucky Press, 1997.

Barbara Morgan,
Melrose, Massachusetts

Dreux, countess of.

See Yolande de Coucy (d. 1222).
See Jeanne I (d. 1346).
See Jeanne II (r. 1346–1355).

Dreux, ruler of.

See Marguerite de Thouars (r. 1365–1377).

Drew, Georgiana Emma (1854–1893).

See Barrymore, Ethel for sidebar.

Drew, Jane (1911–1996)

British architect, among the most distinguished and respected in England, who became one of the world's leading architects, specializing in the design of structures best suited for tropical climes. Name variations: Dame Jane Beverly Drew; Mrs. Maxwell Fry. Born Joyce Beverly Drew in Thornton Heath, Surrey, England, on March 24, 1911; died on July 27, 1996, at Barnard Castle, County Durham; married James Thomas Alliston (an architect), in 1934 (divorced 1939); married E. Maxwell Fry (an architect); children: (first marriage) twin daughters Jennifer and Sarah Alliston.

Among Drew's best-known and critically acclaimed work are her designs for the New Capital City at Chandigarh, India, and the buildings for the Open University at Milton Keynes, England; her honors included being elected president of the Architectural Association (1969) and named a Dame of the British Empire (1996).

Highly talented and fiercely independent, Jane Drew chose to be an architect at a time when that profession was almost totally male-dominated. Rarely discouraged by problems or setbacks, Drew almost singlehandedly changed the course of British architecture, opening up jobs on all levels for women over a remarkable career lasting almost half a century. Born Joyce Beverly Drew (she later changed her name to Jane), she grew up in the suburban environment of Surrey. Both parents were highly educated, her father being a designer and manufacturer of surgical instruments and her mother a botanist. A passion for learning and the arts dominated the Drews' goals for their children. Both of Jane's parents were deeply idealistic. Her father was a liberal humanist who "despised the profit motive and abhorred cruelty." Founder of the British Institute of Surgical Technicians, he was adamantly opposed to the patenting of medical instruments on the grounds that this would subvert the public interest. Jane would model herself professionally after her father, inspired by his fusion of a passionate interest in his work and a high degree of humanitarian concern. Jane's mother also encouraged her daughter's independent spirit and unassailable code of ethics.

Educated at Croydon Day School, Jane Drew's idealistic impulses flourished there as she established a number of lifelong friendships. She made a secret pact with *Peggy Ashcroft, a fellow classmate who would also go on to fame. The close friends swore that they would one day pursue careers and would always use their own names. Many years later when Drew was introduced at a lecture by her married name of Mrs. Fry, she tugged at the speaker's sleeve to quietly correct him, whereupon he announced to the audience, "I'm sorry Mrs. Fry can't be with us tonight, instead Miss Jane Drew has kindly accepted to replace her."

Drew's attraction to the architectural realm began early. As a child, her parents observed her "building things" with pieces of wood and bricks. These ranged from an intricate sandcastle to a tiny model of the Acropolis. Young Jane's emerging sense of beauty and harmony was stimulated by parents who had a passion for the arts. Years later, she reminisced that she had had the good fortune to grow up in a family that never seemed to have "enough money for stair carpet but we always went to the Tate and other exhibitions."

After graduating from Croydon, Drew enrolled at London's Architectural Association School at the precocious age of 13. Showing ex-traordinary talent, she graduated with a diploma in 1929 only to face an economic depression that made jobs difficult to find for male architects and virtually impossible for females. Many firms turned down her application despite her obvious abilities, stating openly that company policy was not to employ women. In 1934, she married fellow architecture student James Thomas Alliston and started a professional partnership, Alliston Drew. Drew's early work was housing influenced by the Georgian style, but she soon was attracted to modern tendencies in architecture, particularly as exemplified in the Congres International d'Architecture Moderne (CIAM), whose guiding spirit was the innovative Swiss architect and polymath Le Corbusier.

Inspired by Le Corbusier's ideals, in the mid-1930s Jane Drew became one of the founding members and active leaders of the modernist school of British architecture, which was centered around a group naming itself Modern Architectural ReSearch (MARS), the British subsidiary of the international CIAM movement. Philosophically, MARS was grounded in the ideal of using space "for human activity rather than the manipulation of stylised convention." Immensely confident of their talents and certain of the truth of their ideals, the MARS group of architects, painters, and industrialists saw a bright future ahead. In later years, Drew characterized their attitude: "We thought we could plan the world." A passionate advocate of the modern spirit, she would defend its essentials to the end of her long life, arguing that at its best it could help liberate human beings and bring them closer to the natural environment that sustains our human essence.

By the late 1930s, Drew was juggling her personal and professional lives as the mother of twin girls. Fortunately, this phase of her career was made possible by the appearance of **Maud Hatmil**, an immigrant from British Guiana (now Guyana), who was "in need of a home and a friend." Offered a trial placement of two weeks as housekeeper, Hatmil remained for more than 40 years, raising the twins and serving Jane Drew and her family as an indispensable "Nanny, cook and friend." In 1975, Drew noted that besides the decades-long loyalty of "Maudie" Hatmil, the other factor that had made possible her successful combination of career and family was "always having my office and home in the same premises."

Drew's marriage to Alliston collapsed in the late 1930s, and they divorced in 1939. In 1940, she established her own architectural practice. A militant feminist at this stage, at first she insisted on employing only female architects. In time, she revised this attitude, choosing her colleagues on the basis of "merit, not on what sex they are." Wartime priorities changed the professional agenda of Jane Drew's firm, and during the first years of the conflict she and her fellow architects found themselves designing and supervising the construction of 11,000 air-raid shelters for children in Hackney. Her growing reputation led to Drew's being selected to serve as chair of the "Rebuilding Britain" exhibition held at London's National Gallery in 1943. Another responsibility she took on during these years was to serve as the Assistant Town Planning Advisor to the Resident Minister for the West African Colonies. In 1942, Drew's private life changed significantly with her marriage to the architect Maxwell Fry. They soon started a professional partnership that was only to be terminated with his death in 1987.

In 1944, both Drew and her husband found themselves working in several British West African colonies. Here she learned fundamental lessons about the adaptation of architectural design to tropical heat and humidity. The knowledge she absorbed during this first brief and other, longer, periods in Africa and Asia would serve her well throughout her long career. Besides investigating the specific construction challenges of each project, Drew would systematically study the climate, ecology, and regional culture of each area to be built in. She became deeply aware that an intuitive understanding of the dynamic interplay of sun, shade, and vegetation was essential to create a maximum of human comfort and well-being for those who would soon live in the structures. As she put it, "It is no good building something that would be suitable for cold Northern Europe in Africa, where you need shade."

Upon their return to London in 1945, Drew and her husband published *Village Housing in the Tropics,* the first of several major works that would be based on their rich sum of practical experiences in tropical regions. Working out of their combined home and architectural firm offices at 63 Gloucester Place in London's West End, Jane Drew and Maxwell Fry not only produced countless architectural plans but kept an open house that offered shelter to friends and acquaintances from around the world. Here they dispensed hospitality for young, unknown architects who would perfect their craft in a benevolent but demanding atmosphere. Job offers often appeared after a telephone call from Jane Drew, and it became normal for those in career crossroads to call Drew, of whom it was said, "When in need go to Jane."

Refusing to see the craft of architecture in narrow terms, Jane Drew and her husband (who was a painter as well as an architect) had many friends in the world of art. They counted among their close friends such celebrated creative spirits as *Barbara Hepworth, Julian Huxley, Henry Moore, Victor Pasmore, and Ben and *Winifred Nicholson. Drew was candid in admitting that she learned her use of color in her architectural designs from these and other artist friends, and regretted toward the end of her career that some of her younger colleagues were neglecting to use color as integral parts of each and every plan.

From 1954 through 1956, Jane Drew and Maxwell Fry embarked on their most ambitious project to date, the New Capital City in Chandigarh, India. Here they worked on-site for several years for the government of Punjab State on a collaborative project with Le Corbusier and Pierre Jeanneret to design an entire urban complex to house several hundred thousand refugees from the India-Pakistan conflict. Drew's part of the project consisted of both government and private housing, shops and shopping areas, health centers, schools and colleges. Working with a meager budget, she was able to work successfully with the limited resources available and regarded the entire project as "an exercise in what you could do without." In each design she submitted, Drew took into account the need to build housing that provided shade and shelter from the unforgiving sun of the Indian subcontinent. Her geometric designs, also responding dynamically to the relentless realities of sun and heat, resulted in attractive, yet practical, sun-protecting canopies, as well as deep, shadowed recesses, and egg-crate walls that were meant to be as pleasant to the eye as they were protective of the body.

The years in India were personally as well as professionally important for Jane Drew. Working with Le Corbusier was one of the high points of her career, and in a short memoir on her relationship with him published more than a decade after his death she referred to him as "the architect from whom I have learned most," noting that "I am writing of a man whom I greatly admire, but I recognize that I also am very attached to him." There is some evidence that the relationship between Drew and Le Corbusier in India was romantic as well as professional, but whatever the definitive story of their ties may prove to be, there can be no doubt that during those years of intense work two immensely creative personalities interacted with one another on the highest plane.

Back in London, Drew signed up for further important projects, including designing the buildings of the Open University. Approached by Labour Party leader *Jennie Lee to design the buildings of the educational experiment situated in the town of Milton Keynes, Buckinghamshire, Drew responded enthusiastically. Her design for the new architectural complex successfully harmonized with the existing, late-Georgian Walton Hall, which remained the center of the entire complex. Jane Drew's political and social instincts were brought to bear on the Open University project, which lasted from 1969 through 1977, and she worked at breakneck speed to get the project past the point of no return before any negative political intervention might sink it.

During her career, Drew designed a wide range of structures, from yacht works to hospitals. As early as 1949, she designed hospital buildings for the Kuwait Oil Company, and in 1968 she drew up imaginative plans for the Herne Hill School for the Deaf in London. A major project was her involvement in the design and building of the Torbay Hospital and Nurses' Residence in Devon. For five years ending in 1973, she worked to make this hospital complex, like others she had drawn up, one that would be "friendly, not frightening, whilst remaining efficient." As she explained it in an article published in 1975, "Far from my sex making things difficult, it enabled me to stay during my fortnightly visits as a guest in the Nurses Home and I frequently talked into the night after dinner, with the Matron, Mrs. Stamp, about the plans." Drew was able to learn much from **Mrs. Stamp**, including the psychological needs of her elderly patients and their need "to be comforted and not frightened when they had to be hospitalised." Jane Drew noted with satisfaction that she had benefitted from "equal help from men and women in the design of this hospital and experienced no difficulty because of my sex."

Drew also worked on a number of important projects in the Middle East including designing a major housing complex for the Iran Oil Company in the late 1950s. Flying to a preliminary meeting in Kuwait, Drew and her partners were met there with baffling and frustrating delays. As she soon discovered, Iran Oil executives had learned that Drew was a woman and now wanted to pull out of the contract. Fortunately the Shah of Iran's liberalizing views prevailed, and he in fact attempted to persuade her to design a palace for himself. Drew remained loyal to her contract, however, and she went on over the next decades to design a large number of structures in Iran: clinics, swimming pool complexes, and two new universities. Always more interested in the creative rather than the financial aspects heading an architectural firm, Drew found the Iranian connection to be catastrophic. The overthrow of the Iranian monarchy in 1979 ended all payments to her firm, which had to declare bankruptcy. This was at least in part due to Drew's lifelong disdain for material gain. "Business is the unpleasant part of architecture," she said. Jane and Maxwell, no longer young, had to sell their Gloucester Place building as well as a lake house in Sussex. More painful was the necessity of selling their entire art collection, although many of the works by famous artists had in fact been presented while they were struggling unknowns and could have been retained with honor by Drew and her husband.

Not only material gain but intangible honors as well meant little to Jane Drew. While fully recognizing the worth of her lifetime achievements, she nevertheless turned down a life peerage when it was offered her in the 1970s because it did not grant her husband and professional partner an equal tribute ("It leaves out Maxie"). She was honored on many occasions during the final decades of her life, including the award of numerous degrees by universities in Africa and the United Kingdom, presidency of the Architectural Association, council membership in the Royal Institute of British Architects, and a visiting professorship at Harvard University. Personal grief during these years came from the accidental death of her daughter Jennifer and the death, after 45 years of successful marriage, of her husband in 1987. After she and her husband retired, they had left London to live at Barnard Castle in County Durham. It was here that Jane Drew died on July 27, 1996. Some years earlier Lord Goodman, chair of the Arts Council, had spoken of her as:

> that rarest of creatures, a practical idealist and visionary. . . . Few architects concern themselves with the town-planning aspects of their work. Few architects see housing as an integral part of larger urban concepts. In these and other respects Jane Drew is in my view unique. . . . She is the outstanding woman architect of her generation.

SOURCES:
"Dame Jane Drew," in *The Times* [London]. August 1, 1996, p. 19.
Drew, Jane. "Le Corbusier as I Knew Him," in Russell Walden, ed., *The Open Hand: Essays on Le Corbusier*. Cambridge, MA: MIT Press, 1977, pp. 364–373.

———. "Torbay Hospital," in *A.D.: Architectural Design.* Vol. 45, no. 8. August 1975, pp. 485–486, 513.

———, and Maxwell Fry. *Architecture for Children.* London: G. Allen and Unwin, 1944.

Fry, Maxwell, and Jane Drew. *Tropical Architecture in the Dry and Humid Zones.* 2nd ed. Malabar, FL: R.E. Krieger Publishing, 1982.

Guppy, Shusha. "Dame Jane Drew," in *The Independent* [London]. August 1, 1996, p. 14.

Rowntree, Diana. "The Courage to Build and Live with Style," in *The Guardian* [London]. July 31, 1996, p. 16.

Sarin, Madhu. *Urban Planning in the Third World: The Chandigarh Experience.* London: Mansell, 1982.

Whittick, Arnold. "Drew, Jane Beverly," in Muriel Emanuel, ed. *Contemporary Architects.* 3rd ed. NY: St. James Press, 1994, pp. 260–261.

Zaknic, Ivan. *Le Corbusier: The Final Testament of Père Corbu: A Translation and Interpretation of Mise au point.* New Haven, CT: Yale University Press, 1997.

John Haag, Associate Professor of History, University of Georgia, Athens, Georgia

Drew, Louisa Lane (1820–1897)

*British actress and theater manager. Name variations: Mrs. John Drew. Born Louisa Lane on January 10, 1820, at Lambeth Parish, London, England; died in Larchmont, New York, on August 31, 1897; daughter of Eliza Trentner (an actress) and William Haycraft Lane (an actor and stage manager); married Henry Blaine Hunt, in 1836 (divorced 1846); married George Mossop; married John Drew (1827–1862, an actor), in July 1857; children: (third marriage) Louisa (whose daughter, actress **Georgiana Drew Mendum**, was a constant companion to her cousin Ethel Barrymore); John, Jr. (1853–1927); Georgiana Drew (1854–1893); (adopted) Sidney; (adopted) Adine Stevens; grandchildren: actors John, Lionel, and Ethel Barrymore.*

Famous at the turn of the century as Mrs. John Drew, Louisa Lane Drew could trace her theatrical lineage back to 1752, to a family of strolling players. She made her stage debut at 12 months, playing the part of a bawling baby. She would not be the last actor, however, to ignore stage directions. "Cry I would not," she recalled, "but at sight of the audience and the lights gave free vent to my delight and crowed aloud with joy." From that moment on, the same sight would fill her with the "most acute pleasure."

In 1827, arriving in the United States in the company of her widowed mother, actress **Eliza Trentner,** and an English stock troupe, Louisa made her American debut at the Walnut Street Theater in Philadelphia, playing the adolescent Duke of York to Junius Brutus Booth's Richard III. Her mother married a Philadelphia stage manager named John Kinlock, who was deter-

mined to turn Louisa into an "infant prodigy" like the successful *Clara Fisher (1811–1898). With her mother, Louisa joined various stock companies and toured for the next 12 years. On one of these tours to the West Indies in 1832, her stepfather caught yellow fever and died.

At 16, Louisa married Irish actor Henry Blaine Hunt, 24 years her senior. The union ended after ten years. She then wed George Mossup, an Irish comedian and singer, but the marriage had a short run that could be calculated in months. Mossup, a heavy drinker, soon died while on tour, and Louisa left him in an Albany graveyard without remorse. She found a modicum of stability in her third marriage to another Irish actor, John Drew, who had approached her for the hand of her half-sister **Georgia Kinlock,** 12 years her junior. A determined Louisa kept the man for herself, and they married in July of 1857.

When her husband John then went on an extended theatrical tour with Georgia and returned with a baby girl, Louisa promptly adopted the child and named her **Adine Stevens.** While John had been gone, Louisa had also been active, having adopted a boy named Sidney (who

Louisa Lane Drew

would be known to the Barrymore children as Uncle Googan), or so she claimed. "Mrs. Drew, of course, may say what she wishes in the matter," said her grandchild Lionel Barrymore, "but Uncle Googan certainly *looked* like her."

John Drew became a famous Irish comedian and, with Louisa's help, part lessee of the Arch Street Theater in Philadelphia. After his death at age 35 on May 21, 1862, Louisa managed the theater (reopened as Mrs. John Drew's Arch Street Theater) for 31 years, making her one of the first women in American history to run an important theater. During her tenure, she built up one of the most successful repertory companies in the history of the American stage—headliners included Edwin Booth, *Fanny Davenport, and *Helena Modjeska—while distinguishing herself as a major comedy actress. She played Lady Teazle, *Peg Woffington, as well as Mrs. Malaprop in Sheridan's *The Rivals,* her most famous portrayal. As late as 1895, she played Mrs. Malaprop in some special performances with Joseph Jefferson. Her sons, John and Sidney, and her daughter, ✤ Georgiana Drew, all became successful actors, as did her acclaimed grandchildren John, Lionel, and *Ethel Barrymore. After settling in Larchmont, New York, in 1896, Louisa died a year later and was heralded as the queen mother of the American theater. An *Autobiographical Sketch of Mrs. John Drew* was published in 1899.

✤▶
***Drew,
Georgiana.*** *See
Barrymore, Ethel
for sidebar.*

Drew, Mrs. John (1820–1897).

See Drew, Louisa Lane.

Drexel, Constance (1894–1956)

German-born American journalist who gained notoriety as a broadcaster for Nazi Germany during World War II. Born in Darmstadt, Germany, on November 28, 1894; died in Waterbury, Connecticut, on August 28, 1956; daughter of Theodor Drexel and Zela (Audeman) Drexel; never married.

Naïvely allowed herself to carry out assignments for Nazi propaganda agencies (1930s); began broadcasting from Berlin (1940); arrested by American troops in Germany (1945); had a treason indictment against her dismissed for lack of evidence (1948).

Constance Drexel was born in Germany in 1894; her father was a wealthy German from Frankfurt am Main, while her mother had been born into a wealthy Swiss family of watch manufacturers. The family moved to the United States when Constance was one year old, and in

1898 she obtained U.S. citizenship when her father became a naturalized American. Constance Drexel's early years in the town of Roslindale, Massachusetts, were pleasant, and she and her parents divided their time between America and Europe. She attended schools in four different countries, including studies at the Sorbonne.

Drexel's near-idyllic life ended, as it did for millions of others, in the summer of 1914, while she was living in France with her mother and sister. One of the first American women to volunteer her services as a French Red Cross nurse, Drexel worked in a hospital in the town of Domville. Writing of her experiences in an article published more than a decade later, she recalled the horrors trying to relieve the sufferings of mutilated and dying men: "I began to realize that this was only part of the price, that all the horrors I saw and heard were far, far easier to bear than the slow, cruel, killing price that war demands of women. When I came back to Paris late in December of that year . . . I held a firm conviction—I still hold it—that women were even heavier sufferers from war than men. I put this feeling into some magazine articles—I had begun to write for publication."

Drexel made her debut as a professional journalist in April 1915 when she traveled to the International Woman's Congress that met in the neutral Dutch city of The Hague. Working closely with *Jane Addams, head of the American delegation to the conference, Drexel sent extensive cable dispatches to the *New York Tribune.* An ardent suffragist as well as an opponent of U.S. involvement in World War I, Drexel endorsed the candidacy of Woodrow Wilson, appearing personally at the Democratic National Committee headquarters in August 1916. At the same time, her writings clearly revealed a strongly pro-German bias. She wrote admiringly of how German women of "'Kinder, Küche und Kirche' fame have shown surprising capacity in handling all sorts of relief work." By 1918, with the U.S. at war against Imperial Germany, Drexel's pro-German attitudes had become well known to federal officials, who chose to deny her a passport to travel to Europe.

Refusing to abandon her journalistic career, Drexel was finally able to travel to Europe after the signing of the armistice in November 1918. She covered the Paris peace conference, sending daily articles to the United States, at the same time also appearing in print regularly in the European edition of the *Chicago Tribune.* Working closely with several international women's organizations, her vigorous lobbying efforts made it possible for a women's equality clause to appear in article 7 of the newly adapted League of Nations Covenant. Ardently hoping as did millions of her generation that World War I had truly been "a war to end all wars," she was convinced that women would play a crucial role in the future in keeping the world from ever again committing the folly of igniting another global conflict. By the mid-1920s, however, she had become disillusioned about the extent of women's power in the political arena. In 1926, she wrote about how she "should have preferred to continue my journalistic work covering the interests of women in politics, but frankly, they were not doing enough to make it worthwhile." Announcing that she would henceforth spend at least half of her time in Europe, Drexel noted that she was particularly interested in reporting on the progress of the League of Nations.

As a freelance writer, Drexel was free to comment on any number of subjects that struck her fancy. At times, her assessment of the level reached by American civilization in the 1920s was highly critical. Writing in 1924 about an evening she spent in a Parisian restaurant, she noted that, "Hardly had we finished our coffee and liqueurs when the jazz orchestra struck up: 'Yes, we have no bananas.' There must have been 20 nationalities among those who got up to dance to that tune, everybody laughing and humming the words. . . . We may be absent from the [League of Nations] conference table, but we are present in the cabaret and the dance hall." Drexel's passionate belief in the League of Nations as a means of preventing a future world war was at the heart of her journalistic activities in the 1920s and 1930s. She was one of the best-known woman in the field of international journalism during these years and was able to combine her journalistic work with the roles of carrying out freelance writing assignments, campaigning for world peace, and being a world traveler.

The world Depression that began in 1929 with the collapse of the New York stock market did not discourage Drexel, whose career remained on track during these years. Having covered the Geneva Arms Conference in 1932, she returned to America to enjoy words of praise about her reports from such well-known public figures as Columbia University president Nicholas Murray Butler and Idaho Senator James P. Pope. Pope and Drexel remained optimists in a time of cynicism and despair, and in the spring of 1935 Senator Pope placed before the U.S. Congress a blueprint drawn up by Drexel based on the global disarmament principles of

the Kellogg-Briand Pact of some years earlier. Despite the effort that had gone into this legislative offensive, and her considerable prestige in the international press corps, Drexel's peace efforts were politely ignored by politicians as the world slid toward catastrophe.

Drexel believed, as did many others in public life, that the Versailles treaty of 1919 had been harsh and self-defeating as regards the Germans. The Nazi seizure of power in 1933 brought the question of Germany to center stage of international relations. She felt that not only her German birth but her mastery of the German language as well as an intuitive awareness of German cultural values provided her unique qualifications to assess the new situation. A critic of America's laissez-faire civilization which was now in shambles, she detected in Adolf Hitler's New Germany a society determined to bring about major social reforms based on a spirit of national unity and solidarity. Joseph Goebbels' Ministry of Public Enlightenment and Propaganda issued invitations to Drexel, who eagerly accepted. Never affluent, she welcomed the income from writing assignments from Goebbels, who saw to it that the gullible American reporter was shown only the successes of the Third Reich.

For several years, from 1937 to 1939, Drexel attempted to restore the luster of her career in the United States. But the Depression made jobs difficult to find, and her pro-German articles as well as her lack of cunning meant that her career was showing alarming signs of decline. She found work in Philadelphia with the Works Progress Administration (WPA) Writers' Project. When this assignment ended, she worked as an instructor of French on a WPA Education Project. She also was able to sell some of her pro-Nazi articles to the publisher Richard H. Waldo, an ultra-conservative who regarded Drexel as his favorite contributor to his newspaper syndicate. In 1939, Drexel left suddenly for Berlin. With travel expenses paid by the German government, she gave as an official explanation for her departure the need to care for her ailing mother, who lived in Wiesbaden.

Starting in 1940, Drexel made scheduled shortwave broadcasts every Sunday at 8:45 PM Eastern Standard Time over the German state radio. Introduced to listeners as a noted American journalist (which she no longer was) and as a member of "a socially prominent and wealthy Philadelphia family" (which was also not true), her broadcasts were largely confined to social and cultural matters. Her upbeat message to her listeners was that cultural life was flourishing as never before in Nazi Germany, even in wartime. Her message was one of order, stability, and indeed prosperity in Hitler's Third Reich, with abundant food supplies and a rich mixture of popular and elite culture available to all strata of the population of a united nation. She was grandiloquently introduced on the air as "a Philadelphia socialite heiress," but beyond earshot her cynical superiors in the Nazi radio hierarchy characterized her uncharitably as being "*wirklich dumm*" (really and truly stupid) and the quality of her work as "*schrecklich*" (terrible).

The famous reporter William L. Shirer, whose hostility to Nazism was well-known at the time, rarely socialized with Drexel in Berlin but knew enough about her to characterize her as "a sort of forlorn person and a rather shabby journalist." Shirer showed little mercy when he drew a character sketch of Drexel in Nazi Germany as:

> an insignificant, mixed-up, and ailing woman of 46 who always had a bad cold, [and who] used to tell me during the first winter of the war in Berlin that she needed money—and wouldn't I hire her as a broadcaster? But she went over to the service of Dr. Goebbels mainly because she had always been pro-German and Pan-German and since 1933 had been bitten by the Nazi bug. The money the Germans paid her no doubt was welcome, but she would have taken mine (which had an anti-Nazi taint) had I been fool enough to hire her.

After Nazi Germany declared war on the United States in December 1941, American citizens resident in the Reich were interned and repatriated by neutral nations. Constance Drexel, on the other hand, was not interned and continued to broadcast over the Nazi radio network. Although the majority of her broadcasts were relatively innocuous in content, occasionally she made what were clearly intended to be political statements. She suggested that American diplomats had encouraged the British government to declare war on Germany in 1939 and characterized President Franklin D. Roosevelt as a man whose policies had made the U.S. entrance into the world conflict all but inevitable. In August 1945, Constance Drexel was arrested by American occupation authorities in occupied Germany. Denying any wrongdoing, she defended herself by stating that during her years as a broadcaster in Nazi Germany she had been "only interested in culture, in Beethoven and music and things like that. . . . They said I was giving aid and comfort to the enemy. I was always against war. I thought that I was following President Roosevelt's line—you know, harmonizing things." She spent the next year behind bars in Germany.

Although Drexel was released from imprisonment in Germany, a legal cloud hung over her when she returned to the United States in October 1946. She was kept for a time on Ellis Island in New York harbor while legal experts debated her case. A special board of inquiry concluded that despite years of absence from America she had not forfeited her citizenship. As the months slipped by, the U.S. Department of Justice reached the conclusion that in view of the fact that their legal staff in occupied Germany had not been able to find evidence that warranted prosecution of Drexel, the decision to prosecute her would most likely not be made. The matter was finally resolved on April 14, 1948, when the treason indictment against Constance Drexel was dismissed by federal judge David A. Pine.

Drexel slipped into obscurity and semi-retirement, still writing about political issues but rarely finding a publisher. On occasion, she was able to publish pieces that were not controversial, including her edited edition of some childhood letters of Franklin D. Roosevelt to his French governess—suggesting that she had finally made peace with the ghost of her old political nemesis. A sign of American rehabilitation of Drexel—or perhaps simply an indication of forgetfulness about her past actions—was the fact that in 1956 she was appointed to the Woodrow Wilson Centennial Committee. But her enjoyment of these honors was to be of brief duration. Constance Drexel died suddenly on the morning of August 28, 1956, in the Waterbury, Connecticut, home of her cousin Frederick Drexel. A restless cosmopolitan to the end, she had planned to leave the United States for good that very afternoon to take up permanent residence with her mother's family in Geneva, Switzerland.

SOURCES:

"Constance Drexel, Ex-Newswoman, Dies; Broadcast for the Nazis During War," in *The New York Times*. August 29, 1956, p. 29.

Drexel, Constance. "Our Family Album," in *Ladies' Home Journal*. Vol. 43. January 1926, p. 26.

——. "The Woman Pays," in *Delineator*. Vol. 87, no. 19. July 1915.

Edwards, John Carver. *Berlin Calling: American Broadcasters in Service to the Third Reich*. NY: Praeger, 1991.

John Haag, Associate Professor of History, University of Georgia, Athens, Georgia

Drexel, Mary Katharine (1858–1955)

American founder of the Sisters of the Blessed Sacrament, an order devoted almost entirely to work with Native Americans and African-Americans. Name

variations: Mother Mary Katharine. Born Mary Katharine Drexel on November 26, 1858, in Philadelphia, Pennsylvania; died in Cornwall Heights, Pennsylvania, at the Motherhouse of the Sisters of the Blessed Sacrament on March 3, 1955; daughter of Francis Anthony Drexel (a banker from Austria) and Hannah Jane Langstroth, who died five weeks after Mary's birth; sister of **Elizabeth Drexel** and **Louise Drexel**; educated privately with her sisters; never married; no children.

Mary Katharine Drexel was born on November 26, 1858. Five weeks later, her mother passed away. In 1860, her father married **Emma Bouvier** who raised Mary as well as her elder sister Elizabeth and her younger sister Louise. Emma reared the Drexel children on a model of "Christian womanhood" and philanthropy, opening her home three times a week to give aid to the poor of Philadelphia. Following the death of their stepmother in 1883 and the death of their father in 1885, the Drexel sisters resolved to use their $14 million inheritance to continue their parents' philanthropic activities.

Particularly interested in relieving the plight of Native Americans, Mary Katharine Drexel sought to enhance the educational opportunities on the reservations of the American West. In 1886, she traveled to Europe to examine the latest in teaching techniques. Meeting with Pope Leo XIII in 1887, she asked for nuns and priests to work with the Native Americans. His response, "Why not, my child, yourself become a missionary?," began a process of prayer and reflection for Drexel. In 1887, she wrote her family's priest and spiritual guide, Father James O'-Connor, telling him of her resolution to join a convent and dedicate herself to Christ. The local bishop, knowing of her concerns, suggested the establishment of a new order for service to Native Americans and African-Americans. Using the Sisters of Mercy as a model, Drexel entered their novitiate in Pittsburgh on May 6, 1889. In July of 1890, Pope Leo XIII gave her his apostolic blessing, and on February 12, 1891, she took her vows as the first sister of the Sisters of the Blessed Sacrament for Indians and Colored People.

By December 1892, a novitiate and motherhouse had been established in Cornwall Heights, Pennsylvania, and in 1894 the Rules and Constitution for the Order were established. In June of that same year, the first four sisters left for St. Catherine's School, a boarding school for the Pueblo in Santa Fe, New Mexico. A Decree of Definitive Approbation was granted by the College of Cardinals in 1907.

A formal papal Decree of Approbation was granted by Pope Pius X in 1913. Drexel's order continued its work in both urban and rural settings, establishing a school for African-American girls in Virginia, a manual arts school in Arizona, and a mission in Harlem, New York. In 1915, she began work with Archbishop Francis Janssens to organize a teachers college in New Orleans for African-Americans; ten years later, in 1925, Xavier University received a charter. Following two successive heart attacks in the

1930s, Drexel began to withdraw from the administrative side of her order and turned to a contemplative life. She died on March 3, 1955, from pneumonia and heart failure, at St. Elizabeth's, the motherhouse of her order. At the time of her death, the order had 501 nuns at 51 different convents. In addition to Xavier University, the order ran 61 schools, and three social-service houses. In 1964, the Roman Catholic Church opened the cause of her beatification, and her writings were approved by the church in 1973, another step toward her possible canonization.

SOURCES:

Duffy, Consuela Marie. *Katharine Drexel: A Biography*. Philadelphia, PA: P. Reilly, 1966.

Sicherman, Barbara, and Carol Hurd Green, eds. *Notable American Women: The Modern Period*. Cambridge: The Belknap Press of Harvard University Press, 1980.

COLLECTIONS:

All of Drexel's papers are housed at St. Elizabeth's, the Motherhouse of the Sisters of the Blessed Sacrament in Cornwall Heights, Pennsylvania.

SUGGESTED READING:

Burton, Katherine. *The Golden Door: The Life of Katharine Drexel*. NY: Kennedy, 1957.

Amanda Carson Banks, Senior Information Officer, Vanderbilt Divinity School, Nashville, Tennessee

Drinker, Catherine Ann (1841–1922).

See Beaux, Cecilia for sidebar.

Drinker, Ernesta Beaux.

See Beaux, Cecilia for sidebar.

Driscoll, Clara (1881–1945)

Texas philanthropist and politician who is best known for her part in preserving the Alamo Mission in San Antonio. Name variations: Mrs. Henry Sevier. Born in St. Mary's Texas, on April 2, 1881; died in Corpus Christi, Texas, on July 17, 1945; younger of two children and only daughter of Robert (a millionaire rancher and businessman) and Julia (Fox) Driscoll; attended private schools in Texas and New York City and the Chateau Dieudonne, a French convent near Paris; married Henry Hulme ("Hal") Sevier (a journalist), in July 1906 (divorced 1937); no children.

Clara Driscoll, whose name figures prominently in the history of Texas, is best remembered for her role in preserving the Alamo Mission in San Antonio, scene of the famous battle of the Texas Revolution of 1836. The attractive, red-headed daughter of millionaire rancher Robert Driscoll, Clara spent much of her young life in private schools far removed from Texas ranch life. Upon her return from France in 1899, she was drawn into the Alamo project by **Adina De**

Zavala, a leader of the Daughters of the Republic of Texas, who for years had been actively seeking preservation of the Texas missions. The Alamo, then privately owned, was virtually lost in the midst of a run-down commercial district in San Antonio. By 1903, Driscoll had embraced the Alamo cause as her own and that year donated the bulk of the $75,000 necessary to purchase the mission site for the State. In 1905, the Texas legislature appropriated the funds to repay her and conveyed the entire Alamo site to the Daughters of the Republic of Texas. The organization then split ranks over the question of restoring or demolishing the remains of the mission. While De Zavala's supporters (the "De Zavalans") wanted to restore the adjacent buildings, the Driscoll camp (the "Driscollites") favored their demolition in order to clear the area for a memorial park. The Driscoll plan won court approval in 1910, after which work began to create the Alamo Plaza and Alamo Park. In 1925, Driscoll became president of the Daughters of the Republic of Texas and, in 1931, gave $65,000 to purchase the last remaining portion of the block of buildings in which the Alamo was located.

During the drawn out Alamo project, Driscoll wrote hundreds of pages on Texas history, which she turned into two moderately successful books and a play. Her novel, *The Girl of La Gloria,* was published in 1905 and was followed by a collection of short stories about Texas, *In the Shadow of the Alamo,* in 1906. That same year, her play *Mexicana* was turned into a musical production (written in collaboration with Robert W. Smith and composer Raymond Hubbel), and produced in New York by the Schubert brothers. (Evidently, expenditures for the lavish production rivaled the Alamo project.) Reviews were mixed, but the show ran for 82 performances.

In 1906, Driscoll married Henry Hulme ("Hal") Sevier, a former member of the Texas legislature, who was at the time a financial editor of the *New York Sun.* After a three-month honeymoon in Europe, the couple settled in New York, building an opulent home at Oyster Bay, Long Island. Driscoll continued to write, although it was the couple's social life that occupied most of her time. When her father died and her brother assumed control of the Driscoll family interests, the couple returned to Austin, Texas, where Sevier established a newspaper, the *Austin American,* in 1914. Selecting a spectacular site overlooking a lagoon on the Colorado River, they built a second home, a lavish Italian-style villa, called Laguna Gloria, which was later donated to the Fine Arts Association for use as an art gallery. Driscoll was active in various clubs, including the Pan-American Round Table, the Austin Open Forum, and the Garden Club. In 1922, she was elected the first Democratic National Committeewoman from Texas, which led to a long, personal and financial association with state and national politics. In 1929, when her brother Robert died without heirs, Driscoll assumed ownership and management of the numerous Driscoll properties composed of farmlands, ranches, and oil interests, as well as the Corpus Christi Bank and Trust Company, of which she became president. Under her skilled direction, the family businesses flourished, as did the economy of the area.

In 1932, her husband Sevier was appointed by President Franklin D. Roosevelt as ambassador to Chile, which may have had as much to do with Driscoll's support of Roosevelt's campaign as it did with Sevier's experience in Latin America. The couple resided in Chile for three years, amid growing rumors that Sevier was inept and Driscoll was in fact doing his job for him. The marriage disintegrated, and when Sevier resigned in 1935 the couple returned to Corpus Christi, taking up residence in separate hotels. Driscoll initiated the divorce, which was granted in 1937, after which she resumed her maiden name.

Clara Driscoll remained a political and financial force in Texas until her death. She built the luxurious Driscoll Hotel in Corpus Christi, where she lived for the rest of her life. (Capricious by nature, she supposedly had the hotel constructed because she was dissatisfied with the service she had received elsewhere.) In 1939, she converted a loan of $92,000 she had made to the Texas Federation of Women's Clubs to a gift for their Austin clubhouse. For her generosity, and as recognition of her work as "Savior of the Alamo," the governor proclaimed October 4, 1939, as Clara Driscoll Day.

Also in 1939, Driscoll helped launch and finance the nomination of her long-time friend John Nance Garner for president, but shifted her support to Franklin Roosevelt when he was renominated. In 1944, she headed the rump convention that split with the Texas Democratic organization in order to remain loyal to Roosevelt, who was running for a fourth term. After a bitter contest, her delegation won accreditation to the national convention that year, and she was chosen vice-chair of the national committee. During World War II, Driscoll headed the women's war-bond and stamp-sales drive in Texas.

Clara Driscoll died in Corpus Christi on July 17, 1945, of a cerebral hemorrhage. Her body lay in state in the Alamo chapel before burial in the family mausoleum at the Masonic Cemetery in San Antonio. She left a large portion of her estate for the establishment of a children's hospital in Corpus Christi, which opened in 1953. Along with the Alamo, the hospital remains a living legacy to Driscoll's spirit and generosity.

SOURCES:

Crawford, Ann Fears, and Crystal Sasse Ragsdale. *Women in Texas*. Austin, TX: State House Press, 1992.

James, Edward T. *Notable American Women*. Cambridge, MA: The Belknap Press of Harvard University Press, 1971.

McHenry, Robert, ed. *Famous American Women*. NY: Dover, 1983.

Barbara Morgan,
Melrose, Massachusetts

Driscoll, Jean (1967—)

American champion wheelchair athlete who holds five world records and won the Boston Marathon's women's wheelchair title for seven consecutive years (1990–1996). Born in Champaign, Illinois, in 1967.

On April 15, 1996, when Jean Driscoll rolled to her seventh consecutive victory in the 100th Boston Marathon, she not only tied the record for the most Boston victories in any division, but came from behind to do so. Battling back from a broken leg that slowed her training for several months, Driscoll was only in fourth place at the 11th mile of the 26-mile course. She caught up while climbing the infamous hills of Newton; these grades spell disaster to most, but are the strongest part of her race. "I love those hills," she said. "I made up ground on all of them. And I never looked back until I got to the top of each hill. That's when I knew I was doing well." Driscoll beat second place **Louise Sauvage** of Australia by only 22 seconds, while **Deanna Sodoma** of Carlsbad, California, came in third, and **Candace Cable** of Truckee, California, took fourth place.

Driscoll, a native of Champaign, Illinois, was born with spina bifida and has never had the use of her legs. After her first road race—a five-miler—she was convinced that she would never do another. However, after competing for the wheelchair track-and-field team at the University of Illinois, where she later coached, she began to race in earnest. By 1996, in addition to her seven Boston wins, Driscoll held five world records.

To prepare for a marathon, Driscoll logs 150 miles a week and does speed repetitions of three-minute miles. She uses a 17-pound aluminum wheelchair and wears what look like mini boxing gloves to punch the wheels around. A mere 112 pounds, she can bench press 200 pounds, which accounts for her remarkable power on the upward climb. Driscoll is said to have the best strength-to-weight ratio of any woman wheelchair athlete in the world. In 1995, when she and other Boston winners joined President Bill Clinton for his morning jog, the president remarked, "You have the best looking arms in America."

In 1997, Driscoll's bid for an eighth straight Boston Marathon win was derailed by a trolley track. Rolling smoothly alongside Louise Sauvage at the 23rd mile, Driscoll caught her left wheel in a track bed, causing her racing chair to veer and flip. As Sauvage sped past her, Driscoll righted herself with some assistance from race workers and police, then pressed on. "I just kept saying, 'I can't give up. . . . I've lost first . . . I can't win . . . but I've got to get second,'" she later recalled. While Sauvage took the win, Driscoll edged out Candace Cable for second place. She took her defeat in stride. "I'm a good Christian and I accept what happened," she told reporters. "Hey, I'm lucky I just scratched an elbow. Could have been worse. That's only my second accident racing."

In her limited spare time, Driscoll encourages teens to pursue their goal to win a Boston Marathon. "It bothers me that everyone says why even try," she explains. "Yes, the percentage of that happening is next to nothing. But if you are committed enough and make the sacrifices, it can happen."

SOURCES:

The Boston Globe. April 16, 1996, April 22, 1997.

Kuehls, Dave. "Wheels of Fortune," in *Runner's World*. April 1996.

Barbara Morgan,
Melrose, Massachusetts

Drobonega of Kiev (d. 1087).

See Maria of Kiev.

Droiturière, Marion la.

See French "Witches."

Droste-Hülshoff, Annette von (1797–1848)

German poet and author whose works are highly regarded for their lyrical greatness, intricate narrative structures, and insights into the position of women in society. Name variations: Nette; Annette von Droste-Hulshoff. Pronunciation: DROS-te HUELShof. Born

*Anna Elisabeth Freiin (Baroness) von Droste zu Hül-
shoff on January 10, 1797, at Castle Hülshoff near
Münster, Germany; died on May 24, 1848, in Meersburg, Germany; daughter of Clemens August, Baron
von Droste zu Hülshoff (1760-1826) and Therese
(von Haxthausen) von Droste zu Hülshoff (1772-
1853); never married; no children.*

*Wrote first poem (1804); published first collec-
tion of poetry (1838); wrote 18-to-20 ballads
(1840–41); achieved first literary success with the
novella* The Jew's Beech Tree *(1842); published second
collection of poetry (1844); first publication of collected works were released posthumously (1860).*

Selected writings—prose: (fragment) Ledwina
(1819–26); (fragment) Bei uns zu Lande auf dem
Lande *(Out at Our Country Place, 1841);* Bilder aus
Westfalen *(Pictures from Westphalia, 1842);* Die Judenbuche *(The Jew's Beech Tree, 1842).*

Poetry: Das geistliche Jahr *(Spiritual Calendar,
1820/39–40); "Schlacht im Loener Bruch" ("Battle at
the Quarry of Loenen," 1838); "Das Fräulein von Rodenschild" ("The Maiden from Rodenschild,"
1840–41); "Der zu früh geborne Dichter" ("The Poet
born too soon," c. 1841); "Am Turme" ("In the
Tower," 1841–42); "Der Knabe im Moor" ("The Boy
in the Moor," 1841–42); "Das Spiegelbild" ("The Reflection," 1842); "Lebt wohl," ("Farewell," 1844);
"Im Grase" ("In the Grass," 1845)*

Annette
von
Droste-
Hülshoff

Annette von Droste-Hülshoff is commonly
considered one of the greatest poets of the German language. Her criminal novella, *The Jew's
Beech Tree,* and many of her poems are required
reading in German schools. When the Federal Republic of Germany issued new currency in the
early 1990s, it came as no surprise when Annette
von Droste-Hülshoff adorned the new 20DM bill.
The image is striking: her hair pulled back in a
bun with signature curls on the side, her intense
eyes dominating her face (some believe due to
Graves disease), the collar of the dress close
around her neck. All known portraits of her are
similar. They evoke such an air of mystery (her
dark and fantastic ballads contributed much to
this image) that "Droste" novels abounded at the
beginning of the 20th century. Although much has
been learned about her through letters, friends'
memoirs, and her own works, much is still to be
gained by studying this multitalented writer, who
was also a painter, pianist, and composer.

Droste, as she is affectionately called by critics, was born into Catholic aristocracy on January 10, 1797, in the family's moated castle near
Münster. She grew up on the moors and heaths
of the Westphalian countryside in Northern Ger-

many as the second child of Baron Clemens August von Droste-Hülshoff (the original family
name was Deckenbroeks) and his second wife
Therese von Haxthausen (**Therese von Droste-
Hülshoff**). The two married in 1793 and already
had one daughter, Maria Anna (1795–1859),
nicknamed **Jenny**, by the time Droste was born.
Their desire for a male heir was soon realized
with Werner Konstantin's birth in 1798
(1798–1867). The youngest child, Ferdinand
(Fente), was born in 1800 (1800–1829).

Born one month early, Droste was cared for
by a wetnurse, **Maria Katharina Plettendorf**
(1763–1845), who remained a loyal member of
the household until her death. Droste fashioned
much of her self-image in terms of her premature
birth. Her poem "The Poet born too soon,"
originally written in the first person around
1841, clearly lamented being born too early into
a society that does not appreciate art. If the poet
is understood to be female, she is also bemoan-
ing her early birth into a society that allows a
woman even less artistic autonomy.

Droste's early childhood was marked by her social class, the landscape of Northern Germany, and her poor physical health. Privately tutored first by her mother and then by a tutor primarily hired to teach the boys, Droste quickly proved to be a gifted pupil, learning everything from natural sciences and mathematics to Latin, Greek, and French. She was an accomplished piano player and composer as well as a good artist. Devoted to her father, an avid naturalist, she often roamed the countryside and came to know the area surrounding the family estate intimately.

If I were a hunter on the open meadow

just one bit of a soldier

if only I were at least a man

then the heavens would guide me;

now I must sit so nice and polite

like a well-behaved child

and may only secretly loosen my hair

and let it flutter in the breeze.

—Annette von Droste-Hülshoff, from "In the Tower"

Although Droste's relationship with her father was very good, the relationship with her mother was by most accounts extremely problematic. Therese von Droste-Hülshoff was more practical, opportunistic, and energetic than her husband and was the one who ran the household with complete authority. While these were seen by many to be desirable traits, so much so that young girls were often sent to the castle to be tutored by Therese, they proved to color her relationship with her daughter. Therese believed that Droste might one day go insane due to her early maturity, especially in education, her musical and lyrical abilities as well as her excitability and rich fantasizing. She therefore greatly controlled her daughter's life, banning acting and the reading of Friedrich Schiller, while requiring walks, painting, and embroidery, occupations more appropriate for a proper young woman's development.

Droste's interest in literature and writing came very early. In fact, her first poem dates from 1804, and by 1814 she had written 50 poems that her mother bound together. Droste was drawn into the literary circle at Bökendorf, the Haxthausen family retreat. Through her mother's two older brothers, August and Werner, she was introduced to the study of the Romantics and had already met Wilhelm Grimm (1786–1859), the well-known collector of fairy tales and folksongs, in 1813. These, however, were not pleasant times, as Droste revealed to her friend, **Elise Rüdiger**, in a letter from 1844:

> We Haxthausen female cousins were forced to seek the approval of the lions the uncles brought from time to time to Bökendorf in order for them to adjust their judgement accordingly, whereby we afterward had a heaven or a hell in the house, depending upon how they [the lions] had judged us. Believe me, we were wretched animals who fought for our dear lives, and it was namely Wilhelm Grimm who, through his displeasure, scorned me so bitterly and neglected me completely for years so that I have wished death for myself a thousand times over.

Of all the different experiences and attitudes determining Droste's later life and literary production, nothing seems to have played a larger role than her *Jugendkatastrophe* (catastrophe of youth). It happened in the summer of 1820 in Bökendorf. Two of the summer guests were August von Arnswaldt (1798–1855), a noble from Hannover, and Heinrich Straube (179–1847), her uncle August von Haxthausen's collegemate in Göttingen. Droste grew very fond of Straube, and Arnswaldt attempted to test her loyalty to his friend. After Straube returned to Göttingen that summer, Arnswaldt actively courted Droste, who was certainly physically attracted to him. She quickly took back her confessions of affection for Arnswaldt and reasserted her love for Straube, but it was too late. Arnswaldt triumphantly went to Göttingen to tell Straube about this "indecisive" woman, and the two men wrote Droste a "Dear Jane" letter, ending any chance of reconciliation between Droste and Straube. Her outwardly calm acceptance of the situation confirmed her haughtiness to her family, but letters and following events illustrate the long-lasting effect the episode had on her. She did not return for 18 years to Bökendorf, which she had enjoyed so much as a second home. The estrangement between her and her uncle, who had delivered the fateful letter according to strict instructions by Arnswaldt, lasted almost 20 years. As for Straube and Arnswaldt, she never saw them again, not daring to travel to Kassel, where both men resided. Most important, she wrote very little during the years 1820–25—letters or completed works—and there are absolutely no surviving letters from 1822 to 1824. Droste has been traditionally viewed as the woman who could not decide between two suitors and tragically was left with none. **Doris Maurer** has reinterpreted this episode as a nasty trick perpetrated by Arnswaldt to expose this "haughty, unfeminine creature" and to put her in her place.

Writing took on greater importance for Droste, not just for the sake of producing but also as an avenue for self-understanding. One such example is her collection of poems for every holiday on the church calendar, *Spiritual Calendar.* Originally planned in 1819 as a book of edification for her grandmother (and long mistakenly considered merely the expression of Droste's inner religious conflict), it soon evolved into a book of self-confession. She focused to some extent on her inner desires which went against church doctrine, quite understandable after the experience at Bökendorf. Based on this new focus, she presented her mother with 25 poems (from New Year to Easter Monday) on October 8, 1820, to seek her mother's love and approval. Upon receiving the poems, her mother read them raptly, as Droste reported in a letter to her cousin Anna, but then laid the book in her wardrobe and said nothing, even when Droste removed the book from the wardrobe eight days later. In the same letter, Droste reclaimed the book, stating, "it is again my secret property." Even if one now understands the difficulty with which Droste's mother must have read the poems, completely unable to cope with her daughter's apparent rejection of Catholicism, the blow prevented Droste from working on the cycle for several years. She only took up the project again in 1834 after some urging by her good friend and sometime advisor, Christoph Bern-

hard Schlüter (1801–1884), and worked intermittently on them the rest of her life. Not surprisingly, she did not allow publication of *Spiritual Calendar* until after her death.

In the fall of 1825, Droste finally ventured on a trip to the Rhine to visit relatives, finding her way back to writing and socializing. She wrote home to ask for her manuscript of the novel *Ledwina*, which she had begun in 1819. Although never completed, *Ledwina* offers great insight into Droste's ability as a writer as well as her life—the autobiographical quality is undisputed. Like her real-life counterpart Droste, Ledwina sees herself outside the social norm, leaving the role of wife and mother to her sister Therese (whom many view as Droste's sister Jenny). Suffering from tuberculosis, Ledwina has nightmares and sees visions. Intertwined into this narrative are the family conversations, in which society and social class are questioned. The fragment breaks off when Ledwina's sister begins to see similar visions. Often viewed as an unsuccessful piece fraught with incompatible narrative strands, critics are just beginning to appreciate the intricate narrative weaving that is actually in place and how it presages the narrative greatness of Droste's masterpiece, *The Jew's Beech Tree.*

July 25, 1826, the day Droste's father died unexpectedly, marks a caesura in her life. She and her mother moved from Hülshoff to the smaller

Rüschhaus, the residence acquired earlier for just this situation. Droste would receive a modest pension from her brother, the heir to the estate, land, and title. It afforded her a small amount of independence, and she lived simply and secluded at Rüschhaus, her *Schneckenhäuschen* (little snail house), with little interruption until 1846. It was in the comfort of the Rüschhaus that she began to write again. Though Droste had a "room of her own" in which to create, the solitude and space propounded later by *Virginia Woolf, illness plagued her here too, and she suffered constantly with various maladies such as migraines, shortness of breath, sleeplessness, rheumatism, thyroid troubles, and agonizing eye problems. These difficulties seemed to increase in intensity and frequency after her younger (and favorite) brother Ferdinand's death in the summer of 1829. However, none of her illnesses stopped her friends and family from demanding much of her time as a nurse and governess whenever needed. She was, after all, an unmarried noble with time on her hands. They considered writing just another one of her pastimes.

Intellectually isolated at the Rüschhaus, Droste joined a small literary society in 1837. She had no female mentors and did not appreciate the efforts of other contemporary female writers, remaining critical of those women in the literary society who were "only passing time" and even the many revolutionary and emancipatory authors. The society brought her into contact with Levin Schücking (1814–1883), the person who would most influence her later life. Droste had met his mother **Katharina Busch**, a well-known Westphalian writer, in 1813 and again in 1829. When Schücking entered high school in 1831, he had a letter of introduction from his mother, who hoped Droste would look after her son. Droste eventually lost contact with Schücking until she joined the literary society. She was impressed with the man who could judge literature so critically and meticulously yet was such an average writer himself.

In 1839, Schücking was asked by Ferdinand Freiligrath, a well-known author, to take over writing duties on *Picturesque and Romantic Westphalia* (*Das malerische und romantische Westfalen*, 1842). Schücking hoped Droste would contribute to the collection, especially since Freiligrath was also an avid admirer of her first collection of poetry (1838). Droste contributed a great deal, for instance with detailed descriptions of the countryside and by providing poetic form to the sagas and historical material, but the finished product bore only the names of the two male co-authors. Despite Schücking's apparent lack of public gratitude, he was the one person who most motivated Droste's creative productivity. A frequent visitor at the Rüschhaus, Schücking became much closer to Droste. Her feelings for him evolved from motherly to intimate if not sexual, despite their 17-year age difference. During this intense relationship between 1840–41, she wrote a considerable number of ballads (18-to-20), which are considered among the very best of the genre and often revolve around the question of guilt and sin.

Everything seemed to fall into place when Droste helped arrange a position for Schücking as librarian in her brother-in-law's library. She had already spent one year (September 1835–September 1836) visiting her sister Jenny, who had married Joseph von Lassberg in 1834. After the couple moved to the castle at Meersburg, Droste was able to visit there, too. She went in October 1841, and Schücking followed soon after. Daily walks together and private conversations characterized their stay. Droste was shattered when Schücking left Meersburg in April 1842 to become a private tutor. She had difficulty writing after his departure but was happy to report to him that she was making progress on a new of edition of poetry and the serialized publication of *The Jew's Beech Tree,* which was to bring her the literary recognition she so deserved.

The Jew's Beech Tree was borne out of a larger Westphalian project Droste had begun in the late 1830s. The other two products of this project were the prose fragment *Out at Our Country Place* (1838–42) and *Pictures from Westphalia* (1845). Based on a true criminal story her uncle had written down, *The Jew's Beech Tree* novella chronicles the important moments in Friedrich Mergel's life: the death of his father, the appearance of his double Johannes Niemand (John Nobody), his involvement in the death of a forester, the murder of the Jew Aaron, and Friedrich's subsequent 28-year absence. After Aaron's body is found under the beech tree, the village Jews etch a prophecy into the tree: "If you draw nigh unto this spot, it will befall you as you did unto me" (Trans. by **Ursula Prideaux**). Friedrich commits suicide by hanging himself from the beech tree, thus fulfilling the prophecy. As gripping as the criminal aspect may be, the magnificence of the novella lies in the intricate narrative structure. Events are told only through the limited perspective of various characters, leaving the reader to piece together information by comparing the different narrations. In addition, the novella masterfully weaves together the fantastic elements of Late Romanticism and the detailed descriptions of Realism.

Droste had returned to the Rüschhaus in September 1842 and the six months following proved to be one of her most fruitful periods. In fact, her tremendous productivity centers around her time with Schücking and shortly thereafter. When she was with Schücking, Droste was free of the myriad of physical maladies that plagued her most of her life. By contrast, 1843 began with a six-week illness. This fact has led many critics to conclude that her physical problems were, to some degree, psychosomatic. Needless to say, she was devastated when Schücking announced his engagement and eventually married **Louise von Gall**, also a writer, on October 7, 1843. Ironically, Droste learned of the marriage while in Meersburg, Schücking having reported it among several other "events" of the day.

Droste's moderate literary success allowed her to buy a villa in Meersburg, which she visited only a couple of times due to her poor health. She did, however, meet Schücking and his wife in Meersburg in February 1844. The visit was not as Droste had hoped, but the poem she wrote upon their departure, "Farewell," reveals more than her resignation, it shows a true determination and acknowledgement of her own talents:

> Leave me on the shore of my lake
> as it rocks me with the lapping of its waves
> leave me alone with my magic word
> the spirit of the Alps and my Self.
>
> Abandoned but not lonely
> shattered but not crushed
> as long as the sacred light
> shines down on me with loving eyes
> (Trans. by U. Prideaux).

Droste finally broke off contact with Schücking in 1846 after the publication of one of his novels, in which he had indiscreetly used confidential information about Westphalian aristocracy she had provided over the years.

Droste's last years were spent very much alone at the Rüschhaus, even trips to her brother at nearby Hülshoff were seldom. She yearned to return to Meersburg and was allowed to go only after repeated pleadings to her brother, still the patriarch of the family. The revolution in Germany during the first half of 1848 unnerved Droste; she and her sister packed away valuables and important papers in case of emergency. Although Droste was fully expected to recover from her latest illness, she suddenly died of a heart attack (some say embolism) on May 24, 1848. Her remains rest not in her Westphalian home but in Meersburg, where her creative genius had had free reign.

The daguerreotype of Droste from around 1845, taken three years before her death, shows a woman remarkably unchanged in comparison to previous portraits. Once again, her hair is tightly pulled back and her clothing is restrictive. As the excerpt from the poem "In the Tower" graphically illustrates, her hairstyle symbolizes the constraints under which women lived. Just as the woman in the poem can only let down her hair in secret, so too is the woman writer limited in the public forum. Droste also seems to fit the accepted definition of a Biedermeier author, a category into which she is often placed. Originally used to explain a purely Austrian way of life in the early 1820s and 1830s, the term Biedermeier was expanded to include a type of writing that exuded the ideals of resignation, close affinity to nature and homeland, and a certain apoliticalness. This definition does not adequately describe Droste the writer. Two stanzas of her quintessential poem, "The Reflection," poignantly depict how confused Droste was by the contrast between her public image and her artistic persona seeking release:

> When you gaze at me out of the crystal, the misty circles of your eyes like dying comets, with features in which two souls strangely creep round each other like spies, then I whisper, "Phantom, you are not such as I." . . . It is certain, you are not I but a strange Being whom I approach, like, Moses, unshod; you are full of powers of which I am unaware, full of strange sorrow, strange desire; God have mercy on me if your soul slumbers in my breast! (Trans. by U. Prideaux)

These words are evocative of the Doppelgänger motif, pervasive throughout her works. She often used this motif to fictionalize the ever-present struggle between a woman defined by the patriarchal society into which she was born and the creative writer too defiant to take the literary tastes of society seriously.

SOURCES:

Heselhaus, Clemens. *Annette von Droste-Hülshoff: Werk und Leben.* Düsseldorf: August Bagel, 1971.

Mare, Margaret. *Annette von Droste-Hülshoff.* With translations by Ursula Prideaux. London: Methuen, 1965.

Maurer, Doris. *Annette von Droste-Hülshoff: Ein Leben zwischen Auflehnung und Gehorsam/ Biographie.* Bonn: Keil, 1982.

Schneider, Ronald. *Annette von Droste-Hülshoff.* Sammlung Metzler 153. Stuttgart: Metzler, 1977.

WORKS IN TRANSLATION:

An Anthology of German Poetry from Hölderlin to Rilke in English Translation, with German Originals.

Edited by Angel Flores. Garden City, NY: Doubleday, 1960 (includes eight Droste poems).

Bitter Healing: German Women Writers 1700–1830: An Anthology. Edited by Jeannine Blackwell and Susanne Zantop. Lincoln: University of Nebraska Press, 1990 (includes *Ledwina*).

Droste-Hülshoff, Annette von. *Poems.* Clarendon German Series. London: Oxford University Press, 1964.

Three Eerie Tales from 19th-Century German. Intro. by Edward Mornin. NY: F. Ungar, 1975 (includes *The Jew's Beech Tree*).

SUGGESTED READING:

Morgan, Mary. *Annette von Droste-Hülshoff: A Biography.* European University Studies Series I, German Language and Literature 701. Berne: P. Lang, 1984.

Schleimer, Gloria. *Protected Self-Revelation: A Study of Four Nineteenth-Century Women Poets, Marceline Desbordes-Valmore, Annette von Droste-Hülshoff, Elizabeth Barrett Browning, and Emily Brontë.* Diss. University of California, Irvine, 1981.

Toegel, Edith. *Emily Dickinson and Annette von Droste-Hülshoff: Poets as Women.* Potomac, MD: Studia Humanitatis, 1982.

Whitinger, Raleigh. "From Confusion to Clarity: Further Reflections on the Revelatory Function of Narrative Technique and Symbolism in Annette von Droste-Hülshoff's Die Judenbuche," in *Deutsche Vierteljahrsschrift für Literaturwissenschaft und Geistesgeschichte.* Vol. 54, 1980, pp. 259–283.

COLLECTIONS:

Correspondence, papers, and memorabilia located in Castle Hülshoff, Stiftung Preussischer Kulturbesitz in Berlin, Universitätsbibliothek/Landesmuseum Münster, and in private ownership.

The critical edition of Droste's works and correspondence: Annette von DrosteHülshoff. *Historisch-kritische Ausgabe: Werke, Briefwechsel.* Edited by Winfried Woesler. 14 vols. to date. Tübingen: Niemeyer, 1978—.

Kristina R. Sazaki, Assistant Professor of German, College of the Holy Cross, Worcester, Massachusetts

Drummond, Annabella

(1350–1401)

Queen of Scotland. Name variations: Anabil de Drummond. Born in 1350 in Scotland; died in October 1401 at Scone Palace, Perth, Tayside, Scotland; interred in Dunfermline Abbey, Fife, Scotland; daughter of Sir John Drummond of Stobhall and **Mary Montifex** (daughter of Sir William Montifex); married Sir John Stewart of Kyle, later known as Robert III (1337–1406), king of Scotland (r. 1390–1406), around 1367; children: *Elizabeth Stewart (d. before 1411, who married James Douglas, Lord of Dalkeith); *Margaret Stewart (d. before 1456, who married Archibald Douglas, 4th earl of Douglas); David Stewart (1378–1402), duke of Rothesay); Robert Stewart (died in infancy); *Mary Stewart (d. 1458); *Egidia Stewart; James I (1394–1437), king of Scotland (r. 1406–1437).

A Scottish noblewoman, Annabella Drummond became queen of her native country. Born into the petty nobility, she married the illegitimately born knight Sir John Stewart of Kyle around 1367. Her father-in-law was the earl Robert of Atholl, who was related through his mother to the Scottish royal house. Although he was not in line to the throne, Earl Robert was chosen king of Scotland by the Parliament in 1371, succeeding as Robert II. A weak and ineffectual man, Robert was also chronically ill; in 1384, his son John and daughter-in-law Annabella took over as regents of the country, ruling in Robert's name. Six years later, Robert II died and John ascended the throne as Robert III (r. 1390–1406), changing his name because there were so many disreputable King Johns in Scottish history.

Annabella thus rose from being the wife of a minor knight with a tainted birth to being queen of Scotland. She proved to be an excellent queen. Energetic and kind, she strongly advocated Scotland's right to be free from English oppression and was involved in all aspects of the administration, including creating legislation. She presided over a large court and raised her two sons, David and James (James I, r. 1406–1437), to be astute politicians. Annabella also aided in planning the defense of Scotland upon its invasion by the English in 1399. She died in 1401 during a bubonic plague epidemic.

SOURCES:

Echols, Anne, and Marty Williams. *An Annotated Index of Medieval Women.* NY: Markus Wiener, 1992.

Uglow, Jennifer. *The Continuum Dictionary of Women's Biography.* NY: Continuum, 1989.

Laura York, Riverside, California

Drummond, Flora (1869–1949)

Scottish suffragist. Name variations: General Drummond. Born in Scotland in 1869; died in 1949; grew up in the Highlands; married.

Known as "the General" because she wore a uniform and led the drum-and-fife marching band during suffragist parades, Flora Drummond arrived in London from Manchester, spurred into the movement by *Christabel Pankhurst's 1905 arrest. Imprisoned nine times, Drummond was an original: a rousing speaker, capable of handling hecklers; a doer of stunts, drawing the press' attention. With a dozen others, she once rented a boat, added bunting, and set sail up the Thames, in order to lecture Members of Parliament, including David Lloyd George, as they sat entertaining their women friends at tea on the terrace of the House of Commons.

Drummond, Margaret (d. 1375)

*Queen of Scotland. Name variations: Margaret Logie.
Died after January 31, 1375; daughter of Malcolm
Drummond; married Sir John Logie (died); became
second wife of David II (1323–1370), king of Scots (r.
1329–1370), on February 20, 1364 (divorced, March
20, 1370).*

Drummond, Margaret (fl. 1490s)

Scottish mistress. Associated with James IV
(1473–1513), king of the Scots (r. 1488–1513); children: **Margaret Stewart** (b. around 1497).

Drusilla (58 BCE–29 CE).

See Livia Drusilla.

Drusilla (15–38 CE).

See Agrippina the Younger for sidebar.

Drusilla (c. 37–c. 41 CE)

*Roman noblewoman. Name variations: Julia Drusilla.
Born around 37 CE; died around 41 CE; daughter of
Caligula (12–41), Roman emperor (r. 37–41), and
Milonia Caesonia (d. 41 CE).

Flora
Drummond

All the ancient sources speak of Roman emperor Caligula's cruelty. To demonstrate his character, Suetonius enumerates both minor malicious tricks and gross cruelties. Caligula removed canopies at the hottest time of day during the games, forbidding people to leave. He fed criminals, rather than butcher's meat, to wild animals in the arena. He made fathers attend their sons' executions and in one case invited the father to dine with him immediately afterward in jovial company. According to Suetonius, Caligula's daughter Drusilla's violent temper convinced him of his own paternity: "While still an infant she would try to scratch her little playmates' faces and eyes."

In 41 CE, a successful conspiracy against Caligula was carried out by a tribune of the Praetorian Guard who held both personal and public grievances against the emperor. Thus Caligula, writes Dio, "after doing in three years, nine months, and twenty-eight days all that has been related, learned by actual experience that he was not a god." Hatred for Caligula was so great, in fact, that after he had been assassinated his wife *Milonia Caesonia was killed as well, and his daughter Drusilla's "brains," writes Dio Cassius, "were dashed out against a wall."

Drusilla (38–79 CE)

*Herodian noblewoman. Born in 38 CE; died in the eruption of Mount Vesuvius, 79 CE; third and youngest daughter of Herod Agrippa I; sister of Herod Agrippa II and *Berenice (28–80 CE); married Azizus, the king of Emesa; children: at least one son.*

Born in 38 CE, Drusilla was the daughter of Herod Agrippa I. She was induced by Felix, the Roman procurator of Judea, to leave her husband Azizus, king of Emesa, to become Felix's adulterous companion. She was with Felix when Paul reasoned of "righteousness, temperance, and judgment to come" (Acts 24:24). Drusilla and her son died in the eruption of Mount Vesuvius.

Dryburgh, Margaret (1890–1945).

See Women POWs of Sumatra for sidebar.

Drysdale, Ann Meyers (b. 1955).

See Meyers, Ann.

du Barry, Jeanne Bécu, Comtesse (1743–1793)

French maîtresse en titre to Louis XV whose life displayed and symbolized the brilliance and decadence of the years before the French Revolution. Name variations: Comtesse du Barry; Madame du Barry; Marie Jeanne Bécu. Pronunciation: JHAN bay-COO, co-TESSE dew-BARR-ee. Born on August 19, 1743, in Vaucouleurs (Meuse), France; guillotined in Paris on December 8, 1793, and was buried in a pit by the Madeleine; daughter of Anne Bécu (1713–1788, a seamstress) and an unknown father but probably a monk, Jean-Baptiste Gomard de Vaubernier; educated at the Convent School of Saint-Aure (Paris); married Guillaume du Barry (1768–1793); children: none legitimate but possibly an illegitimate daughter Marie-Joséphine ("Betsi") Bécu.

Met Jean-Baptiste, Comte du Barry (le Roué, 1763); became Louis XV's mistress and married Guillaume du Barry (1768); presented at court as maîtresse en titre (1769); helped bring about the fall of Choiseul (1770); struggled for recognition by Marie Antoinette (1770–72); confined at the Abbey of Pont-aux-Dames after Louis XV died (1774–75); returned to Louveciennes (1776); had affair with Henry Seymour (c. 1779–80); was mistress of the Duc de Cossé-Brissac (c. 1780–92); made three trips to England to recover her stolen jewels (1791); left for England after Cossé-Brissac was lynched (1792); returned and was tried and executed (1793).

The story of Jeanne Bécu's life is a melodrama, relating the rise of an illegitimate child and prostitute to the position of mistress (*maîtresse en titre*) to the most powerful king in Europe, her Indian summer life as a wealthy and titled lady after his death, and a terrible end on the guillotine during the French Revolution. Until the late 19th century, when research began to uncover a far truer picture, she was the subject of innumerable scandal-mongering stories, pamphlets, books, and obscene songs portraying her as the most corrupt of women, a modern *Messalina, a depraved director of foul orgies and queen of a court wallowing in decadence. The truth is colorful enough, given the fetid moral atmosphere of the courts of Europe at that time, but in Madame du Barry's case, at least, it is decidedly less lurid than the tales which have shocked (and titillated) the public since her day.

Jeanne Bécu's maternal grandfather, Fabien Bécu, was a handsome cook in Paris who somehow persuaded a noblewoman, **Madame Cantigny, Comtesse de Montdidier**, to marry him. She soon ran out of money and died, but he added (illegally) the Cantigny name to his and moved back to Vaucoulers, a small town in Champagne on the Meuse River where *Joan of Arc had begun her military career. Jeanne's mother **Anne Bécu** was one of the seven children he sired in a second marriage, this to **Jeanne Humon**, a chambermaid working nearby for an exiled mistress of Louis XIV, the Madame **Marie de Ludres**. These children, to whom he passed on his good looks, mostly became servants in noble households. But Anne Bécu, or Bécu-Cantigny as she presumed to call herself, became a seamstress. A pretty young woman given to casual affairs, she was still unmarried at 30 when she gave birth to daughter Jeanne on August 19, 1743. The father is unknown, but evidence points to a local monk, Frère Ange (Brother Angel), born Jean-Baptiste Gomard de Vaubernier, who was later dismissed from his order but became a popular preacher and confessor at Saint-Eustache in Paris. He appeared on several occasions during Jeanne's life, notably at her marriage; and at various times she called herself Mlle Lange, Mlle Vaubernier, or Mlle Beauvernier.

On February 14, 1747, Anne gave birth to a son, Claude. Perhaps persuaded by a wealthy financier and munitions contractor named Billard-Dumouceaux (or Dumonceaux) who probably had met her in Vaucouleurs on his travels, she moved to Paris, where she lived with her sister Hélène, maid to the wife of the king's librarian, Arnaud-Jérôme Bignon. Claude soon died. Anne then met a servant, Nicolas Rançon, whom she married and whom Billard-Dumouceaux then set up as a munitions storekeeper for Corsica. Billard-Dumouceaux appears to have interested himself in young Jeanne, as did his mistress, a courtesan and actress named Francesca, well known around Paris as Madame **Frédérique**. It was with Francesca that Jeanne first observed Parisian high society and the life of an expensive mistress. Someone—possibly her supposed father, now attached to Saint-Eustache—decided she needed an education and enrolled her at the school of the Convent of Saint-Aure, which specialized in training deserving girls "in danger of ruin." For eight or nine years, Jeanne lived under Saint-Aure's stern regime while learning reading, writing, drawing, music, and the domestic arts. Her later love of reading and her taste for fine art may have been awakened at the convent school. Her handwriting was elegant, but her spelling and grammar were somewhat precarious—common deficiencies among even the highest nobility in that age. Her religious instruction made an impression, for she remained an observant for the rest of her life, attending mass almost daily and building chapels at her residences. Still, she emerged from school in late 1758 as a beautiful 15-year-old, lively and fun-loving, with lovely blue, roguish

(*fripon*), slanted, half-closed eyes, and ambitious to have nice things.

Aunt Hélène had her apprenticed to a young hairdresser named Lametz. The incredibly elaborate coiffeurs of that time made hairdressing a well-paying art. Jeanne spent several months learning. She and Lametz soon fell in love, but his mother, alarmed at his spending on her, went to Jeanne's mother threatening legal action against Jeanne. Anne replied with a countersuit for defamation and won. Lametz gave up and left for England. Some evidence, inconclusive, suggests that more than money was involved, that Jeanne was pregnant and gave birth about this time to a girl, **Marie-Joséphine ("Betsi") Bécu**, whose paternity was then assigned to Nicolas Bécu, Anne's brother. In later years, Betsi, who bore a strong resemblance to Jeanne, often visited her estate, Louveciennes, where she had her own room; and Jeanne played an important role in marrying her off with a large dowry to the Marquis de Boisséson in 1781.

Jeanne Bécu, Comtesse du Barry. Painting by Elisabeth Vigée-Lebrun.

Jeanne next turned up as a maid and then companion to the widow of a wealthy *fermier-général* (tax concessionaire), **Mme Delay de la Garde**, who lived in the Château de Corneuve near Paris. The widow's two married, middle-aged sons were attracted to her, as was the wife of one of them, the **Comtesse de Ligneville**. Tensions mounted, and the result was Jeanne's sudden departure early in 1761. Where she went next is unknown, but in 1762, calling herself "Mademoiselle Lange," she became a salesgirl and model at the Maison Labille, a millinery shop patronized by the aristocracy. Labille tried to keep his girls from trouble by locking them up on weeknights, but they were free to circulate on weekends. Jeanne began enjoying the colorful life of the great city, frequenting street fairs and gambling casinos. Her enemies later charged she became a common whore, selling herself on the streets for a few coins, or that she was one of the "girls" at **Madame Gourdon**'s notorious bordello. No evidence supports these tales; Madame Gourdon denied them, but police reports did mention Jeanne as sharing the company of monied men-about-town.

𝒪t is for mortals to adore your image

The original was made for the gods.

—Voltaire on Madame du Barry

It was probably in late 1763 that she met and conquered the man who set her on the road to fame and fortune. Jean-Baptiste, Comte du Barry (1723–1794), from an ancient but poor noble family near Toulouse, was for good reason known as *le Roué*. He was utterly unprincipled, a witty talker, an expert at duping others, and a champion libertine in a society boasting regiments of that ilk. After dissipating a small inheritance, he had left his wife in 1753 to go to Paris. While working with minimal success to forge a diplomatic career, he tried in 1756—with the connivance of *Madame de Pompadour, the king's *maîtresse en titre* but no longer filling the sexual role—to make a beautiful actress named Dorothée the king's mistress. Louis XV (r. 1715–1774), a bored sensualist, was interested until, perhaps fearing disease, he learned of her connection with the unsavory du Barry. The Roué did not give up the dream of making his fortune by finding a "morsel" for the king. When he met Jeanne Beauvarnier, as she was currently calling herself, he concluded he had possibly found his prize. But this time he would go slowly, preparing both her and her introduction into the royal presence.

The Prince de Ligne, who first saw Jeanne at Labille's, described her as "tall [5'5½" was tall for those days], well made and ravishingly blonde with a wide forehead, lovely eyes with dark lashes, a small oval face with a delicate complexion marked by two little beauty spots, which only made her the more *piquant*, a [small] mouth to which laughter came easily and a bosom so perfect as to defy comparison." One could add that she had beautiful small white teeth, a splendid bearing, and was very clean—this in an age when regular bathing was still not the rule. Some of her contemporaries nitpicked, mostly out of jealousy or because they opposed her rise, saying she was no true classic beauty, that her features, roguish eye, and manners betrayed her plebeian breeding. However that might be, Jeanne was a woman whose beauty drew instant attention. When yoked with a pleasant, easy-going, open, and kind nature, it made her destiny.

Exactly how the Roué met her is disputed. A plausible version says they met at the "Marquise" Dufresnoy's gambling salon, where she was (supposedly) one of those kept to attract customers. The most convincing version is more complicated. Supplying the troops in Corsica was a large operation. Rançon, Jeanne's stepfather, was in touch with contractors who included Jean-Louis Favier (1711–1784), a political writer and secret agent for the king to whom the Comte du Barry was attached as a dealer in army contracts. Hence, Jeanne probably met du Barry at her home. In a rather sordid exchange, the Rançons allowed Jeanne (legally a minor) to live with the Roué in return for some nice furniture.

She did more than live with him. The Roué was in business, using money made in his army contracts to invest in girls (*grisettes*) and young women, buying them elaborate wardrobes, teaching them high society graces, and then pimping them to nobles and monied commoners, who paid well for his services. In his stable, Jeanne became the star. She spent most of her nights with him; jaded though he was, he did not tire of her. The rest of her time was largely occupied by the men he procured for her. By the end of 1764, she was being called the Comtesse du Barry (although his wife still lived) and was much seen in public in lavish clothes and an expensive carriage. A train of prominent men frequented the splendid salon the Roué set up (July, 1, 1766) at 16, rue de Jussienne—among them the Duc de Nivernais, the Comte de Guibert, the duc de Duras, the comte de Fitz-James, both the marquis and the comte de La Tour du Pin, writers and poets Marin, La Morlière, Moncrif, Collé, Cailhava, and the Abbé Arnaud. A police agent noted drily, the demoiselle's "health is not vigorous enough to bear such heavy labor. . . . [B]eneath the surface she has a very tired air."

Jeanne's first tryst with Louis XV occurred some time early in the summer of 1768. Several versions exist. The simplest says that Lebel, the king's valet and procurer of women, tried her out at the Roué's invitation and reported to the king. Another, corresponding to the king's memory, says he saw her in a crowd while passing down a hall at Versailles (where the public had free access) and asked Lebel to find her. It appears likely, however, that the Roué had carefully set up that seemingly casual sighting but employed roundabout means because he was *persona non grata* in the king's circle. He had assigned to Jeanne monies from a contract to supply Corsica. The king's chief minister, the Duc de Choiseul (1719–1785), had begun to attack the notorious contract abuses, so at the Roué's bidding Jeanne twice went to see him to try to get the contract continued. These unusual (and documented) visits probably were set up through Lebel so as to come at times when the king was likely to be passing near Choiseul's office. The key to the plot, the man who did the arranging with Lebel, was one of the Roué's most important customers, the old Maréchal-Duc de Richelieu (1696–1788), immensely rich, one of the century's most famous libertines, and a close friend of the king. The scheme worked. The king saw Jeanne, took instant interest, and Lebel arranged the tryst after Richelieu provided him a story that she was a married woman, free of disease, whose only dalliance had been with Sainte-Foÿ.

In no time, Louis was thoroughly smitten. He told the witty Duc d'Ayen that she gave him "an enjoyment of a kind altogether new to me." "That, Sire," replied the duke slyly, "is because you have never been to a brothel." (Both knew this was not precisely true because for years the king had maintained a personal brothel, called the Deer Park, at a discreet house on the outskirts of the town of Versailles which Lebel kept supplied.) When Richelieu asked him what he found in her, Louis responded soberly, "Only this, that she is the only woman in France who makes me forget that I soon will be sixty." The king's old friend the Duc de Croÿ later observed, "At sixty years of age the King was more in love than he had ever been. He seemed rejuvenated, and I had never seen him in better spirits: in extremely good humor and far more outgoing than he had ever been."

Lebel, who expected Jeanne to be just another passing fancy (*passade*), took alarm at his master's continuing trysts and told him what he had since learned about her. Louis, angered at the deception but now utterly infatuated, raged at Lebel, possibly hastening the latter's death several weeks later on August 17. By that time the Roué and Richelieu had taken steps to ensure that Jeanne could become—as Louis soon wished her to be—the *maîtresse en titre*. To be presented at court she had to be married and show noble ancestry from before 1400. Marriage to the Roué would have meant bigamy, something even he flinched at. The solution they found was to marry her to the Roué's short, plump brother Guillaume (1732–1811), a beached naval officer vegetating in the country near Toulouse, and to fix up Jeanne's and the du Barrys' credentials. A royal dispensation cleared the 1400 obstacle, and the marriage occurred on September 1, 1768. The Roué had outdone himself. Probably with Richelieu's help, he pasted together documents "proving" the du Barrys' connections with Italian (Bari) and Irish (Barrymore) nobility. Jeanne was passed off as the daughter of "the late Sieur Jean-Jacques Gomard de Vaubernier," Madame Rançon's "first husband." The Rançons were now titled "M. and Mme. de Montrabé," while Jeanne's probable father attended as her "uncle" and was styled "Chaplain to the King." The wedding, at the little church of Saint-Laurent, was held at 5 AM. The bridal pair parted at the door. Guillaume returned to Toulouse with a 5,000 livre pension and his promise (unkept) that he would be seen no more.

The court presentation was delayed for months. Louis, timid, insecure, and given to bouts of depression, was a procrastinator and hated to make changes, give unwelcome news, or face opposition. The prospect of the parvenu Comtesse du Barry as *maîtresse en titre* aroused deep opposition. Choiseul, who had hoped to have his sister, the **Duchesse de Gramont**, become the mistress and thus secure his long reign (since 1758) as chief minister, took a violent dislike to Jeanne du Barry and hired writers to deluge the public with pamphlets and ribald ditties ridiculing her. There were others, too, who had cherished similar hopes since the death of Madame de Pompadour in 1764 only to see them dashed. The stakes were high. A *maîtresse en titre* required a huge financial outlay to support her as queen in all but title. (There was no queen, in fact, for on June 24, at the beginning of this affair, the real queen, *Marie Leczinska, had died at age 65.) Others, thus, would not get this money. Moreover, the mistress would be entitled to her own place in church and at the king's table and all court functions, an apartment in every royal château, and the possibility of being present when the king's ministers consulted with him—an unrivaled opportunity to exert influence. Yet all of this in its own way pleased Louis, for it appears he thought his ability to impose a mistress gave proof of his authority.

The ladies of court went on "strike," none willing to play the role of presenter. Eventually the **Duchesse d'Aiguillon** of the Richelieu clan, who wanted to get her son back into favor, found a needy relative, the **Comtesse de Béarn**, who agreed to do it for promotions for her two sons in the army and navy and 100,000 livres to pay her debts. The date was fixed for January 25, 1769, but at the last moment Béarn faltered and claimed she had sprained an ankle, so the affair was postponed. More delay followed when Louis badly hurt an arm in a fall from a horse while hunting. Meanwhile, in a most helpful move, the Roué had sent his witty sister Françoise, called "Chon" (1726–1809), to keep Jeanne du Barry company through months of snubs and slander and the rigid etiquette requiring her and the king to be often apart and very discreet when together; Chon remained her closest friend for many years. In time, Chon's sister "Pischi" (Jeanne, 1727–1801) joined Jeanne's intimate circle.

The day came at last on April 22, 1769, easily one of the most remarked-upon court events of the century. Du Barry kept the glittering assemblage waiting so long that Louis nearly called it off. But at the last moment she glided in, dazzling in a white gown dripping with 200,000 livres worth of diamonds, made the three required curtsies, was introduced to the king by the Comtesse de Béarn, and then flawlessly executed the three retreating curtsies, which required a deft foot to push aside her heavy train—a maneuver she had practiced a thousand times since it frequently sent ladies toppling over backward to the snickers of the crowd. Louis beamed like a young lover beholding his new bride. Despite its hostility, the court agreed she had met the test in grand style.

Henceforth, until Louis' death in May 1774, du Barry's life merged into the political, social, and artistic currents in France at the highest level. Many members of the court drifted to her side or became neutral, but her enemies remained numerous. Her hold on the king stayed strong to the end. There was even talk in 1772 and 1773 of a morganatic marriage, but, if nothing else, an annulment of du Barry's marriage promised too much trouble with the church. (Jeanne obtained a legal separation in 1772.) A semi-serious project broached in 1769–70 to marry Louis to the Archduchess *Elizabeth of Austria (b. 1743), an older sister (by 12 years) of *Marie Antoinette, posed no real threat. As much as anything, the social complications this match would have created at Versailles defeated it. Whether Louis remained entirely faithful to Jeanne is disputed; candidates for *passades* included the **Princesse de Monaco**, a **Miss Smith**, **Mme d'Armeval**, **Mme Bèche**, *Mlle Raucourt, and the **Baronne de Nieuwerkerke**. It is certain, however, that he sold the Deer Park in May 1771—a reasonably clear sign that du Barry had won.

Broadly speaking, until early 1772 Jeanne was consolidating her position and hence involved in political matters, more so than later. Two intertwined affairs dominated this period: 1) the fall of Choiseul, and 2) Jeanne's struggle to win Marie Antoinette's recognition of her position. In both cases, du Barry espoused no political agenda as such. Unlike Pompadour, she had no interest in or head for high policy. She simply wanted to be accepted socially and to enjoy the fruits of her dizzying ascent.

It would be easy to overestimate or underestimate du Barry's influence on the king in policy matters. In the case of Choiseul's fall, she probably hastened an event that would have occurred anyhow. Choiseul had been in power for a long time and thus had accumulated many enemies. He was a diplomat, highly competent, dedicated to duty, but insufferably vain. He was identified with the unpopular Austro-French alliance, which evoked memories of France's humiliation in the Seven Years' War (1756–63). He had expelled the Jesuit order, alienating the *dévots*. Most dangerously, he tended to side with the parlements—13 regional high courts of justice and administration—which were increasingly pushing their constitutional claims against the king's prerogative.

As noted, Choiseul violently opposed du Barry's ascent, probably fearing, mistakenly, that she would be another Pompadour and destroy his political influence. Also, he saw, rightly, that she was supported by his old enemy Richelieu and the duke's nephew, the Duc d'Aiguillon (1720–1788), who assiduously courted Chon. Choiseul's scurrilous press campaign against du Barry drove her finally to complain to Louis, who in turn assured Choiseul of his confidence but advised him to back off. Nothing availed. The climax came in 1770 when a long war between the parlement in Brittany and the Duc d'Aiguillon boiled over into a direct confrontation between Louis and the parlements. The degree to which Louis backed d'Aiguillon because of du Barry's persuasion cannot be known. She had secured for him the plum appointment as colonel-in-chief of the Light Horse and captain of the Royal Bodyguard against one of Choiseul's relatives and was undoubtedly interested in his advancement. But the political stakes for Louis and the monarchy far surpassed questions about d'Aiguillon. In a dramatic *lit de justice* (a formal meeting in the king's presence) on December 3, 1770, with du Barry attending, Louis ordered the Parlement of Paris to close all proceedings against d'Aiguillon, and he forbade all the parlements to take joint actions or make joint claims against his authority. When the parlements replied by going on strike, Louis, in the most dramatic act of his reign in domestic policy, had the members arrested and exiled to other locales (January 19–20), and on April 13 he announced a new system of courts to replace the parlements. Louis XV's dismissal of the parlements and Louis XVI's later restoration of them were momentous acts, for opposition by the parlements was critical in forcing Louis XVI to convoke the Estates-General, the deed that opened the way to the Revolution.

Meanwhile, Choiseul shared their fate. Louis had plainly told him he did not want war. Desperately trying to save his position, Choiseul went to the brink of war with England in order to support Spain in their quarrel over claims to the Falkland Islands. He apparently calculated that Louis would need his abilities and that the parlements would respond to his appeals for the needed money, not the appeals of the finance minister, the Abbé Terray, or of Chancellor (chief of justice) Maupeou, recent appointees who were now currying du Barry's favor. Choiseul's fate was sealed when, according to a famous but not altogether reliable story in Tallyrand's memoirs, the Roué and Favier told du Barry of a high official in the Foreign Ministry who knew of Choiseul's deceptions. She tipped off Louis, who interviewed the official and then confronted Choiseul. When he admitted ordering military movements, Louis exploded. The next day, December 24, 1770, Choiseul received a terse *lettre de cachet* ending his career and exiling him to his estate. In a postscript, on June 5, 1771, Louis yielded to du Barry's prodding and named d'Aiguillon minister of foreign affairs.

In the first months after her presentation, du Barry had won public acclaim for persuading the king to save from execution a soldier who had temporarily deserted, a woman convicted of infanticide on highly technical grounds, and an impoverished elderly noble couple who had killed two policemen while resisting handing over their château for debt. But the dismissals of Choiseul and the parlements were highly unpopular acts, and the public angrily charged she was manipulating the king at the behest of Richelieu, d'Aiguillon, and her rapacious in-laws. Ironically, when Choiseul later pleaded for money to avoid ruin, she laid siege to Louis until he grudgingly granted her defeated foe a generous settlement. Choiseul refused to thank her, likely feeling she was subtly rubbing it in.

The other grand affair, the struggle with Marie Antoinette, was on the surface a petty tale of snubs and snide remarks between a king's mistress and a spoiled, teenaged princess. It is a measure of the importance of protocol and personal relations in the courts of Europe's absolute monarchies that this homeric drawing-room brawl bore grave diplomatic implications, for at stake was the solidity of the Austro-French alliance and, thus, the balance of power.

Marie Antoinette, aged 15, daughter of Empress *Maria Theresa of Austria, arrived in May 1770 to shore up the alliance by marrying the dauphin, Louis-Auguste (the future Louis XVI). To general surprise, du Barry was invited to the most exclusive events surrounding the wedding. When Marie Antoinette naively asked what du Barry's function was, the ❦➤ Duchesse de Noailles archly replied that it was "to amuse His Majesty." Marie soon learned the truth, was shocked, and began to avoid Jeanne, writing to her mother that the comtesse was "the most stu-

---

❦➤ **Noailles, Anne Claude Laurence, duchesse de**
(d. 1793)

French duchess. Died by guillotine in 1793.

While on staff at Versailles, Anne Claude Laurence, the duchesse de Noailles, was put in charge of training the young *Marie Antoinette on her arrival in France. Marie called the rigid, punctilious Noailles, "Madame Etiquette." Once while learning to ride a donkey, Marie fell off. When friends leaned down to help her up, she replied: "Leave me on the ground. We must wait for Madame Etiquette. She will show us the right way to pick up a Dauphine who has tumbled off a donkey." Eventually, the Duchesse de Noailles would follow her former young charge to the guillotine.

pid and impertinent creature imaginable." For her part, du Barry was heard to make remarks about "that little redhead." Into this situation stepped Louis' three scheming unmarried daughters—*Sophie (1734–1782), ◀ Victoire (1733–1799), and the leader *Adelaide (1732–1800), collectively called "Mesdames." (The youngest, *Louise Marie, had become a nun to pray for her father's salvation when du Barry had come on the scene.) They despised Jeanne, and after getting Marie Antoinette under their wings, they tirelessly fed her dislike. The preliminary bouts ended in the summer of 1770 with an incident at the theater at Choisy when du Barry and several friends arrived to find their seats occupied by members of Marie Antoinette's circle led by Choiseul's sister, the Duchesse de Gramont. They refused to leave, and du Barry's party had to find other places. Jeanne complained to Louis, who banished Gramont from court. The war was now on, to the intense interest of the court and the foreign offices of Europe. All du Barry wanted was for Marie Antoinette to speak to her just once and thus acknowledge her right to be present at meals and social functions. This the headstrong, proud, spoiled—and politically naïve—princess refused to do.

Whole chapters in biographies of Madame du Barry and Marie Antoinette recount the engagements of this struggle. Suffice it to say that the fall of Choiseul in December 1770 was a blow to the pro-Austrian camp, for he was the strongest guarantee that Louis would not become so irritated by the affair that he would drop the marriage alliance. Louis in fact found himself in a hard place. He genuinely liked Marie Antoinette, which made it all the more embarrassing to go so far as to order her to accept his mistress. But her petulant defiance and du Barry's tearful complaints of her humiliation—much relished by her legions of foes—grated badly on his nerves. Most important, the discourtesy defied his authority. Maria Theresa, who had prostitutes in her own lands whipped, was increasingly worried by the implications of a possible French failure to support her in the crisis over Poland involving Prussia and Russia. Her duty to Austria came first, so she weighed in with pleas to her daughter to heed Austria's needs and speak to "the creature." At length, Louis and the Austrian ambassador agreed that at a reception on July 11, 1771, Marie Antoinette would speak to du Barry. At the critical moment, however, just as she was about to do so, Adelaide told her it was time to leave, and she retreated in confusion. The fiasco set Europe's courts buzzing. Maria Theresa, appalled,

Victoire. See Adelaide, Madame (1732–1800).

scolded her daughter roundly. At last, at the New Years' reception in the Hall of Mirrors on January 1, 1772, the deed was done. Marie Antoinette casually turned to Jeanne and said, "*Il y a bien du monde à Versailles aujourd'hui.*" ("There are a lot of people at Versailles today.") Du Barry beamed, Louis embraced the princess, and fast couriers instantly rode off to carry the news to every crowned head.

Marie Antoinette would say no more, and the snubbing went on. But she listened much less now to Mesdames, and in August 1772, with the Polish situation at a crisis, she did say a kind word to one of du Barry's friends. Also, the dauphin promised to attend suppers for du Barry and the king and by the end of the year was unusually gracious to her. In an awkward move in January 1774, du Barry tried to win over Marie Antoinette with an offer of some vastly expensive earrings, but she received no reply. The "casual" remark on January 1, 1772, however, had turned the key. Those utterly mundane words assured Maria Theresa that she could keep the balance in Eastern Europe by asking now for her share of Poland, confident that Prussia and Russia would have to let her in since she had the support of France. Thus began the partitions (1772, 1793, 1795) that wiped Poland from the map until it was reborn—in the Hall of Mirrors at Versailles—in 1919.

Notwithstanding the snubs, vicious libels, mocking songs, and her nagging worry that the fickle king would become bored and drop her if she could not find some new amusement, du Barry lived for five years in a dream world of luxury beyond imagining. She had an exquisitely decorated small apartment joined to the king's rooms below by a private staircase. In July 1769, he gave her the château of Louveciennes overlooking the Seine by the Marly waterlifters about four miles from Versailles. She refurbished this residence and added the stunning Pavilion—an entertainment-residence hall and one of the earliest examples of the neoclassical style. Later, she bought a mansion in the town of Versailles as a more sumptuous place for gatherings than her apartment. She received a monthly income of 200,000 livres which rose in time to 300,000 to keep pace with her spending. Her jewelry alone, for which she had a passion, was valued at over 2 million, one of history's major private collections. Altogether she received about 15 million livres from 1769 to 1774 plus gifts of jewels and art from the king, yet at his death she was over one million in debt. To these outlays one should probably add the hundreds of thousands in pensions and properties du Barry wheedled from an annoyed Louis for the insatiable Roué (who could subtly blackmail her) and his ever-needy relations.

Her suppliers comprised a roll of the premier artists of the day: architects Gabriel and Ledoux; sculptors Feullet, Metivier, Gois, and Pajou; painters Drouais, Vernet, Vien, Boucher, Greuze, Fragonard, and *Elisabeth Vigée-Le Brun; jewelers Aubert, Demay, Gaillard, Drais, and Rouën; goldsmiths Roettiers & August; furniture-makers Delanois, Guichard, and Carlin; engravers and gilders Beauvarlet, Cagny, and Gobert; tableware designed by Saint-Aubin; fashions designed by **Mlle Pagalle** and **Rose Bertin**; hats by Chardon, lingerie by Venot, dresses by Mmes Sigly, Montier, and Pompée, and tailoring by Carlier; porcelains by Sèvres, and tapestries by the Gobelins and the Savonnerie. Remarkably, given her humble origins, she showed excellent taste, if not quite all the refined sophistication of Pompadour. Her style, a transitional mode, combined a less ornate Louis Quinze rococo with the plainer Louis Seize neoclassical style to come.

Du Barry's star at court began to pale during the winter of 1773–74 as the king visibly aged. The event she feared began on April 26 when Louis fell sick while at Louveciennes. On the 28th, his physician ordered him to Versailles. Louis had contracted smallpox, which was ravaging the region. He had long lived in dread of dying without the sacraments. To receive them, he had to confess his sins and dismiss du Barry, who had remained at his bedside every night. Louis sent her away on May 4. After a night of tears, she was taken by d'Aiguillon to his estate at Rueil. Louis, wanting to see her once more, asked where she was. "She has gone to Rueil, Sire," was the reply. "Already? Gone as we must all go," he murmured as a tear coursed down his cheek.

On May 10, Louis died. Two days later, du Barry arrived at the grim Abbey of Pont-aux-Dames (Seine-et-Marne) to be confined pursuant to a *lettre de cachet* he had ordered on the 9th. Why? To assure Cardinal de la Roche-Aymon of his sincere repentance—and perhaps also to spare her a worse fate at the hands of Louis XVI and Marie Antoinette. (Another *lettre* ordered the Roué to the Vincennes dungeon, but he fled for a time to Lausanne.) Du Barry behaved perfectly and soon made the nuns her friends. To pay pressing debts, she sold some jewelry, including a necklace worth 450,000 livres. After he refused requests in August and November, Louis XVI released her in March 1775 on condi-

tion she stay ten leagues (about 30 miles) from the court, thus ruling out a return to Louveciennes. On April 9, she purchased the Château de Saint-Vrain with a loan from d'Aiguillon and lived there quietly until, in October 1776, the king—advised by his chief minister Maurepas, a distant relative of d'Aiguillon—consented to her return to Louveciennes. He also allowed her to keep the 40,000 livres-per-year concession she had on shop stalls at Nantes and her 105,000 in annuities (*rentes*) issued by Paris. She promptly sold Saint-Vrain and her Versailles mansion, repaid d'Aiguillon, and bought her mother and stepfather a comfortable manor house. In November 1776, she moved back to Louveciennes.

From then until her last months, du Barry lived a pleasant existence at Louveciennes, gardening, playing Lady Bountiful in the village, and entertaining a flow of court acquaintances who, now that she was no longer an object of jealousy and political machinations, felt free to enjoy the glow of her charm and hospitality. She put on a little matronly weight but remained a beautiful woman to the end, taking meticulous care of health and appearance. In May 1777, Emperor Joseph II of Austria, probably from curiosity and to spite his mother Maria Theresa and sister, Marie Antoinette, pretended to stray onto her grounds and met her. She also visited Voltaire (who liked her) on February 21, 1778, in Paris shortly before his death. She even became reconciled (to some imprecise degree) with Marie Antoinette, who was learning what it was like to be a target of slander and hatred. The finance minister Calonne quietly agreed in 1784 to convert her 50,000 livre annual pension (granted by Louis XV in 1769) to 1,250,000 livres in capital. Du Barry also helped the queen acquire Saint-Cloud. And in 1789, with the Revolution in full swing, she spontaneously offered Louveciennes and all she had should the royal family need it.

During these years, she had two affairs of the heart. One, a short, tempestuous relationship in late 1779 or 1780, was with Henry Seymour (1729–1805), nephew of the 8th duke of Somerset, who had settled nearby at the Château de Prunay with his young second wife *Louise de Ponthon (d. 1821). Du Barry was quite in love with him, but the affair ended either because he had become jealous of her friend the Duc de Cossé-Brissac or because his wife objected. Almost immediately, she began her longest affair and perhaps, her only *grande passion*. Of the bluest blood and fabulously wealthy, Louis-Hercule-Timoléon de Cossé, Duc de Brissac

(1734–1792) was married, but his wife—as was almost the rule in the aristocracy, where marriage was essentially a property arrangement—took no open offense. On July 4, 1782, du Barry made her first public appearance (at a review of a regiment just back from America) since her fall in 1774 and her first with Cossé-Brissac. They were a passionately devoted couple, spending time at Louveciennes, his Paris mansion, and his several chateaux. He was an admirable man, courageous, honest, and a liberal idealist who dreamed of a reformed monarchy ensuring a better life for all in a new age of liberty. Into this idyll burst the French Revolution.

Three deaths in 1788 ushered in the Revolution years for du Barry. On August 8, the Duc de Richelieu died; on September 1, d'Aiguillon; and on October 20, her mother. Strangely, Anne left nothing to du Barry, to whom she owed everything, giving all to Betsi, her niece (or possibly granddaughter). Du Barry kindly provided her stepfather with a small pension.

Her first close contact with the Revolution came when she sheltered two soldiers who had escaped from the mob at Versailles during the Women's March on October 5–6, 1789. In November, she sold 133,000 livres in diamonds in Amsterdam via her Paris bankers, the Vandenyvers. While living quietly at Louveciennes through 1790, she sold more jewelry abroad, probably creating a nest egg in case she had to flee. Imprudently, however, she continued to entertain noble guests, correspond with some who had become émigrés, and even asked the local government for a tax refund of 389 livres.

Then, on January 10, 1791, she returned from a party and overnight stay at Cossé-Brissac's Paris home to discover that a huge quantity of her jewels—at least 1.5 million livres' worth—had been stolen. After consulting her jeweler Rouën, she had handbills distributed describing the missing gems in detail, an understandable but foolish act, for it instantly made her a target of hatred and suspicion. On February 15, she received sudden word from one Nathaniel Parker Forth that her jewels had been recovered in London when the five burglars (three German, one French, one English) had tried to sell them to a noted diamond dealer. Besides some of the odd features of the burglary itself, there was Forth, an Irish adventurer, a dealer in horses, paintings, and information, and widely known to be an English agent. From now on du Barry had an excuse to travel to and from England and thus could be a conduit for letters and money between French and English royalists. She was later accused of arranging the theft, which seems most unlikely, but Forth's role has always aroused suspicion.

Three times in 1791 she visited London, escorted by Forth. The legal case became predictably tangled because of the absence of an extradition agreement between France and England. Meanwhile, du Barry's jewels were put under seal, but she was able to get loans on their security which financed her expensive living and entertaining in London, where she consorted with the Calonnes and other leading émigrés and British aristocrats. Her actions were closely watched by a French agent, Blache.

The political situation in France gravely deteriorated in the winter of 1791–92. Cossé-Brissac, governor of Paris, bravely accepted appointment as chief of the king's bodyguard. As events rolled toward the fall of the throne, the guard was disbanded on May 30, and on June 10 Cossé-Brissac was arrested for "treason" and imprisoned at Orléans. Du Barry, showing great courage, traveled there to visit him. When the king was overthrown on August 10, she sheltered one of Cossé-Brissac's aides at Louveciennes, but a crowd hunted him down on August 19; he died horribly in the September 2–5 prison massacres. Much worse followed. On September 9, Cossé-Brissac and 52 other prisoners were lynched in Versailles on their way to Paris. Some of the mob then marched to Louveciennes, broke in, and rolled his severed head across the floor to his swooning lover. (Many years later, a carefully preserved head was dug up on the grounds.)

Shortly afterward, on October 14, du Barry left for England on a six-week passport obtained only after she promised the president of the Convention (the government now) that she would return when her legal business was concluded. Again she socialized with the cream of the émigrés and British society, e.g., being presented to George III and Prime Minister William Pitt (the Younger). In actions which proved especially damaging to her later, she gave the cardinal-archbishop of Rouen 200,000 livres for needy émigré priests and 200,000 more to Louis-Antoine-Auguste, Duc de Rohan-Chabot (d. 1807), a friend of Cossé-Brissac and soon to be involved in the Vendée uprising against the Convention in March 1793. A single letter dating from September 1793 indicates she had an affair with Rohan-Chabot some time during late 1792 or 1793, but details are totally lacking.

Du Barry's banker urged her in November to return, but she did not. On January 21, 1793,

Louis XVI was executed, and on February 1 England declared war on France. At last, on March 1, du Barry left, arriving back at Louveciennes on the 19th after difficulties due to her expired passport. To the day of her death, she seems never to have fully grasped the danger she was in, confident always that things would turn out all right.

She found Louveciennes under seal due to a complaint lodged by George Grieve (1748–1809), now spelling his name Greive. This English radical who had spent the years 1780–83 in the American colonies during the Revolution and then come to France, had settled in the village of Louveciennes in the winter of 1792–93. He started a revolutionary club and conceived an obsessive hatred of the Comtesse du Barry. Among his informants were Salanave, one of du Barry's cooks, and her black Bengali page, Louis-Benoît Zamor, whom she had employed since his childhood from the days at Versailles and who was perhaps venting a long suppressed rage at the patronizing treatment he had received over the years as her fashionable "blackamoor" servant. A tense struggle ensued. Du Barry persuaded the departmental authorities of Seine-et-Oise to let her reoccupy her home. Greive tried to get her arrested in June, but again the department, where du Barry had an influential friend in one Lavallery, thwarted him. On July 3, he presented her case to the Convention, which ordered house arrest and an investigation. Some 59 humble citizens of Louveciennes petitioned for her release, which, with Lavallery's help, was effected on August 13. Greive, undeterred, published a pamphlet detailing her "crimes" and describing himself as the friend of Franklin and Marat and "a disorganizer of despotism in the two hemispheres for twenty years." After passage of the drastic Law of Suspects (September 17), which sent the Reign of Terror (1793–4) into high gear, he went to the Committee of General Security on September 21; it gave him an arrest warrant which he executed on the 22nd. (Coincidentally, the Roué was arrested the same day in Toulouse.) He then conveyed her to the Saint-Pélagie prison in Paris to await trial. There is some evidence that on the way he raped her, or tried to.

While Greive, ensconced in her rooms in Louveciennes, worked up an overwhelming 15-count indictment from her papers and verbal evidence, du Barry was questioned on October 30 and November 22. According to a fairly reliable story, she was approached in prison by an Irish priest in disguise who said he could get her, but not two people, out through bribery; giving up her chance, she arranged for money that effected the escape from Calais to England of Cossé-Brissac's daughter. On December 4, she was transferred to the Conciergerie, "antechamber to the guillotine." She and the three Vandenyvers were tried on December 6 and 7. Greive testified, of course, as did Blache, Salanave, Zamor, and others. Du Barry, very composed (she gave her age as 42), steadily denied she had engaged in treason and rested her case on the fact that she had always returned to France and thus was no émigré. But she had to make a devastating admission: "I cannot say how much I spent in London and gave to émigrés." Greive's bill of particulars supplied the prosecutor, Fouquier-Tinville, far more than enough to convict her given the current climate. The money for Rohan-Chabot proved particularly deadly. The jury returned the verdict in an hour at 11 PM: guilty on all counts. She was sentenced to die in the morning.

Seized now—at long last—by real fear, du Barry convinced the authorities the next morning (December 8) to delay so she could provide more information. Thinking she could now earn her release, she proceeded to recall in astounding detail the locations and exact nature of every jewel and art object she had carefully hidden on the grounds of Louveciennes. It was near 4 PM when she finished and, to her shock, the officials promptly tied her hands and took her to the tumbrel where the Vandenyvers and a Convention deputy (sentenced on unrelated charges) had been waiting in the cold. Du Barry collapsed in terror. As the cart made its long trip across the city to the former Place Louis XV, rebaptized as the Place de la Révolution (now the Concorde), she struggled and cried out to people to save her. At the scaffold, set on the spot where her royal lover's statue had once stood, she had to be wrestled up the steps. It was nearly dark and the waiting crowd had diminished. As she was strapped to the board and swung down into place, she began a terrible, animal-like screaming that ceased only when the heavy blade sliced through her throat. The crowd, usually boisterous, seemed subdued, even shaken. Her corpse, with her head between the legs, was trundled to the pit by the Madeleine, where it was heaved in to join the remains of Louis XVI, Marie Antoinette, and many others. On January 17, 1794, in Toulouse, the Roué went to his death still in character, with a joke and a disdainful smile on his lips.

Louis XV, orphaned at two and king at five, was "the handsomest man in France," intelligent, informed, gracious, and courteous. He also was timid, insecure, distrustful of his own judgment, lazy, bored, and in time obsessed by sex and a dread of death. Jeanne du Barry's ability to combine the roles of caring maternal figure, good-natured companion, and mistress proved irresistible to him. To all appearances, she loved him in return, and never spoke ill of him during or after his lifetime. She made his last five years his happiest and arguably his most personally effective as king. She spent his money lavishly but came nowhere near "ruining" the monarchy financially, as some later charged. (For that matter, most of her spending was on tangible goods of real value—art, furniture, jewels.) Expensive as the court was, money for wars past, present, and future plus interest on the debt ate up most of the budget. She could have contented herself with being the king's mistress behind the scenes, but she craved the acceptance and perquisites of a *maîtresse en titre*. She won the title, enjoyed its fruits, but inevitably, in view of her past, was the object of the vilest slanders.

Du Barry was blessed with beauty and sold it for gold and pleasures. In a more charitable assessment, her contemporary Choderlos de Laclon, author of *Les Liasons dangereuses*, wrote that "her only fault was her birth and in those who had debauched and debased her." By any account, she was impulsive, frivolous, and unheeding—fatally so. Yet she was also kind, genuine, and generous. She employed her influence to gain recognition, found allies where she could, and asked Louis' help for them. But she never used her power (as she could well have done) to harm others, to imprison, or to kill. She rejuvenated the king, however briefly, stimulating him to try to refurbish the crown's authority. Unfortunately for her and her royal lover, in the eyes of the masses she symbolized his decadence; consequently, she bears a heavy responsibility in the decline of the monarchy's credit to a level from which it never fully recovered. Child of the people though she was, she never understood the depths of the hatred they had come to bear toward her, her aristocratic friends, and the glittering world of unearned privilege they inhabited. For all her pleasures, they at last made her pay the price in blood.

SOURCES:

Castelot, André. *Madame du Barry*. Paris: Perrin, 1989.

———. *Queen of France: A Biography of Marie-Antoinette*. Translated by Denise Folliot. NY: Harper and Row, 1957.

Castries, René de la Croix, Duc de. *La Du Barry*. 2nd ed. Paris: Albin Michel, 1986.

Cronin, Vincent. *Louis and Antoinette*. NY: William Morrow, 1975.

Erickson, Carolly. *To the Scaffold: The Life of Marie Antoinette*. NY: William Morrow, 1991.

Faÿ, Bernard. *Louis XVI or The End of a World*. Translated by Patrick O'Brien. Chicago: Henry Regnery, 1968.

Gooch, G.P. *Louis XV: The Monarchy in Decline*. London: Longmans, Green, 1956.

Hardman, John. *Louis XVI*. New Haven, CT: Yale University Press, 1993.

Haslip, Joan. *Madame Du Barry: The Wages of Beauty*. NY: Grove Weidenfield, 1972.

Levron, Jacques. *Madame Du Barry ou la fin d'un courtisane*. Paris: Librairie Académique Perrin, 1973.

Loomis, Stanley. *Du Barry: A Biography*. London: Jonathan Cape, 1960.

Madame Du Barry, de Versailles à Louveciennes [Yvelines], *sous la direction de Marie-Amynthe Denis*. Paris: Flammarion, 1993.

Muller, Dominique. *Une Traine de poudre: Jeanne du Barry, la dernière favorite*. Paris: Jean-Claude Lattès, 1990.

Padover, Saul K. *The Life and Death of Louis XVI*. NY: D. Appleton Century, 1939.

Zweig, Stefan. *Marie Antoinette: The Portrait of an Average Woman*. Trans. by Eden and Cedar Paul. NY: Viking, 1933.

SUGGESTED READING:

Campan, Madame. Jeanne-Louise-Henrietta. *Memoirs of the Court of Marie Antoinette, Queen of France*. 2 vols. Boston: L. C. Page, 1900.

Douglas, R.B. *The Life and Times of Madame Du Barry*. London: L. Smithers, 1896.

Faucher-Magnan, M. *Les du Barry: Histoire d'une famille au XVIIIe siècle*. Paris: Hachette, 1936.

Fromageot, Paul. "Madame du Barry de 1791 à 1793, d'après des documents inédits," in *Revue d'histoire de Versailles*. Vol. 8, 1909.

Gerard-Doscat, Roger. *Madame Du Barry*. Lausanne: Éditions Rencontre, 1965.

Goncourt, Edmond and Jules de. *Les Maîtresses de Louis XV*. Tome II, Livre 3. Paris Firmin-Didot, 1860-.

Lambert, André. *Madame du Barry, la dernière favorite*. Kapellen (Belg.): Beckers, 1967.

Laski, Philip. *The Trial and Execution of Madame du Barry*. London: Constable, 1969.

Lenôtre, Georges. *Vieilles maisons, vieux papiers*. 6 vols. Paris: Librairie Académique Didier Perrin, 1900–35. Vols. 1,2.

Saint-André, Claude. *A King's Favourite: Madame du Barry and Her Times*. Preface by Pierre de Nolhac. NY: McBride, Nast, 1915.

Scott, Barbara. "Madame Du Barry, a Royal Favourite with Taste," in *Apollo*. January 1973, pp. 60–71.

Vatel, Charles. *Histoire de Madame du Barry d'après ses papiers personnels*. 3 vols. Versailles: Bernard, 1877–1883.

Ward, Marion. *The Du Barry Inheritance*. London: Chatto & Windus, 1967.

Welschinger, Henri. *Les Bijoux de Madame du Barry*. Paris: Charavay, 1881.

COLLECTIONS:

Bibliothèque de la Ville de Versailles; Bibliothèque nationale (ms. Fr. 8157–8160); Archives nationales (W 16, W 300); Archives du Haute-Garonne (Du Barry family). The main family papers are with the Panat family, château de l'Isle-Jourdain (Gers).

David S. Newhall, Professor Emeritus of History, Centre College, Danville, Kentucky

Dubois, Alice (d. 1918).

See de Bettignies, Louise.

Dubrawka (d. 977).

See Dobravy of Bohemia.

Duby-Blom, Gertrude (1901–1993)

Swiss-born Mexican photographer, sociologist and defender of the Lacandón Maya peoples of Chiapas State and their rapidly disappearing rain forest environment. Name variations: Queen of the Rain Forest. Born Gertrude Elisabeth Loertscher in Berne, Switzerland, in 1901; died in San Cristóbal de las Casas, Chiapas State, Mexico, on December 23, 1993; married Kurt Duby; married Frans Blom.

Celebrated by many environmental activists as the "Queen of the Rain Forest," Gertrude Duby-Blom had a long and adventurous life in both Europe and Mexico, never tiring of the struggle to achieve social justice and environmental harmony. Born in Switzerland in the first year of a new 20th century bursting with hope, Gertrude Elisabeth Loertscher grew up in a solidly conservative, middle-class milieu, her father being a pastor of the Reformed Church. But her views quickly diverged from those of her parents, not only because of her own intellectual independence but also because one of her neighbors was a leader of the Swiss railway workers union. Ideas of social justice, gender equality, and a world without war were beacons pointing to a better world for the young girl. In 1924, Gertrude married Kurt Duby, son of the radical union official. This marriage did not succeed, however, and by the late 1920s Gertrude Duby had become a political activist, organizing a Social Democratic youth movement in Zurich and working as a journalist for Swiss newspapers in several European countries. During a stay in London, she moved in circles close to the leftist Independent Labour Party and met and interviewed such political and cultural luminaries of the day as James Ramsay MacDonald, David Lloyd George, and George Bernard Shaw.

Even before the onset of the world economic depression, Trudi Duby as she was known to her friends, had become personally acquainted with the growing menace of Fascism. During a visit to Italy, the secret police looked up books she had recently checked out of a lending library and, deeming them to be subversive texts, arrested her. After hours of interrogation, she languished in jail for fully a week, but her Swiss citizenship proved to be a protective cloak, and she

was deported with a warning not to return. Trudi moved to Germany in 1928 to be closer to the front lines of the rapidly unfolding drama of who would prevail in the Weimar Republic, the forces of the working class and democracy or the reactionary legions of Adolf Hitler and his private army of brownshirts. Duby learned how to be an effective public speaker at anti-Nazi mass rallies. Realizing that there were times when it was best not to provoke one's enemies, she was skilled at calming her audiences so that they left the auditorium morally inspired but not so emotionally fired up that they might go looking for fights with local Nazi toughs. Refusing to leave Germany even after the Nazi takeover, she remained loyal to her leftist comrades and often changed apartments in order not to unnecessarily endanger them or herself. Only when the situation had become completely untenable did she flee Germany.

Moving to Paris, Trudi continued to fight against Nazism both as a journalist and political activist. Along with thousands of other aliens, she was arrested in September 1939 and spent five months in a French detention camp. Once again, her Swiss citizenship saved the day, and she was released. Disillusioned with Europe and its grim political realities, Duby decided to immigrate to the new world. At first, she spent some months in New York City helping to resettle French refugees from Nazism. But she felt that this activity was at best temporary. As a child, she had been fascinated with a far-away and exotic land, Mexico, but in reality she knew very little about either the land or its people, culture and history. When playing Indians with her childhood friends in the Swiss woods, she adopted the exotic Aztec name Popocatépetl. Now, through an accident of history, she applied for and received entry into Mexico, a land respected by anti-Nazis for its generosity toward refugees. Mexico had been one of the few countries that had sympathized with the Spanish Republic in its ill-fated struggle against Fascism, and it continued to offer asylum for political emigrés like herself.

After her arrival, Duby soon got a job as a journalist for the Ministry of Labor. Her first assignment was to compile information on the working conditions of female factory workers. The geographical diversity and rich cultural traditions of Mexico intrigued her from the start, and every new job was a voyage of discovery. One of the most important assignments of these early years involved writing a series of articles about the women who had fought in the revolutionary forces of the legendary land reformer

Emiliano Zapata. Although she had never had any interest in photography, her strong desire to document these remarkable women led her into her first venture with a camera, an old Agfa purchased from a fellow refugee.

In 1943 an event took place that would change the course of Duby's life. She received permission from the governor of Chiapas State to join a government expedition to the then-remote Lacandón jungle region near the border with Guatemala. Her interest in this area had been kindled on her sea voyage to Mexico three years earlier after reading a book by French anthropologist Jacques Soustelle, *Mexico: Tierre Indienne*. She was particularly intrigued by Soustelle's description of the Lacandónes, a people virtually unspoiled by European influences whose forbears had withdrawn to the dense interior of the rain forest to escape enslavement and cultural destruction by the Spaniards. Profoundly religious in their belief in a supreme being (Creator Hachäkyum—Our True Lord), they preserved their old ways: hunting with bows and arrows, wearing long white tunics, and never cutting their hair. More than being exposed to this strange and fascinating world and being able to make photographs, Trudi noted years later how she "fell in love with the jungle from the moment I first saw its incredible vegetation of great trees and exotic plants with leaves as big as parasols, the rare insectlike flowers, the enormous vines that hang from the tops of the trees with roots that curl around the trunks to eventually kill them so that other giant trees can grow in their places."

For a middle-aged woman who had grown up in the Calvinist culture of Switzerland, the rain forest of the Lacandónes was like a trip to the moon. Yet she realized from the start of her stay in Chiapas that this endangered region would be her world from now on, to explore, study, understand, and defend. In the rain forest, she noted, she was:

> held spellbound by the incredible musical sounds of the insects, from the highest notes to the lowest, and the singing of the frogs and all the hundreds of birds I had never seen. I listened in amazement to the peculiar cry of the howler monkey and the deafening sound of the tapir crashing through the undergrowth like a tractor. I was transfixed by the enormous flocks of parrots and the macaws describing a rainbow of colors in the sky. Then there were all the snakes of different colors slithering in between the fallen leaves on the floor of the jungle. I didn't feel any fear in the midst of this new en-

vironment: on the contrary, I felt quite at home and in my element.

Equally as important as discovering the rain forest in 1943 was Trudi's first encounter with Frans Blom. A Danish-born American anthropologist and archaeologist who had explored Mexico since 1919, he was in charge of the Chiapas expedition she had joined, and they quickly discovered that they were kindred spirits. In a diary entry, Frans described his newly acquired friend as "the kind of person with whom you can feel in close relation without having to do conversation. I like that gal." Frans had made an exception in allowing Trudi to join his expedition, a sound decision in light of what happened. He developed a severe case of malaria, and despite the fact that she was a novice in the jungle, her coolheadedness in the crisis probably saved his life when she rode on horseback for four days to get help, returning to Frans with supplies and medical assistance. Trudi and Frans quickly became inseparable, marrying in 1950. In 1951, the Bloms bought a house in San Cristóbal de las Casas, a picturesque town in the highlands of Chiapas. Immediately, they set about converting the house to a center for research. Called the Na-Bolom Center for Scientific Studies, it became part of their home. Na-Bolom means "House of the Jaguar" in the Lacandón language, and it was chosen because some Lacandónes had pronounced "Blom" as *balum*—their word for "jaguar"—or *bolom* in the language of the Tzotzil Indians of the highlands around San Cristóbal. Over the years, the Bloms' efforts resulted in the creation of a major research library containing 2,500 specialized works on Chiapas and more than 8,000 works on Mexico and Mesoamerica. Their 22-room house built around three patios but lacking plumbing or electricity became not only a research center for scholars but a place of intellectual excitement attracting artists, writers, and musicians seeking inspiration. Besides the research library, Na-Bolom would eventually encompass extensive gardens, an archaeological museum, a chapel filled with colonial art, and 14 guest rooms.

Starting in the 1950s, Gertrude and Frans made a number of perilous expeditions into the Selva Lacandona, the rain forest east of San Cristobal. Here they studied flora and fauna and got to know and deeply respect the Lacandón Maya, the indigenous people who lived there maintaining their traditional ways. Her photographs of the endangered rain forest, as well as its animals and people introduced all of them to an increasingly sympathetic outside world. Fiercely proud and remarkably independent, the

Lacandón Maya had never been conquered by the Spaniards. In time, Duby-Blom came to see her herself as the protector and patron of this group of culturally endangered people, who by the mid-1980s numbered fewer than 500 souls. At first her interest in the Lacandón native peoples was, like that of her husband, largely anthropological and sociological. They collected artifacts to prevent their loss, inoculated the Lacandón to protect them from devastating diseases from the outside world, and tried in general to shelter them from the destructive influences of that same outside world. Within a few years, however, it became clear that even if Lacandón culture might be defended in the abstract, the relentless forces of economic change were dooming these gentle people to extinction. Gertrude Duby-Blom now recognized that it would be impossible to protect the Indian way of life without also protecting the rain forests in which they lived.

In the 1950s and 1960s, she made countless trips into the rain forest, the Selva Lacandóna, to not only communicate with the various Maya tribal groups but to photograph them and the wildlife of the forest. What she documented was rapid change bordering on environmental catastrophe. Deforestation on a massive scale using chain saws and bulldozers cleared millions of acres of forest of valuable trees. Profits were immense, and the companies that carried out the clearing cut not only the valuable mahogany, ceiba, and giant cedar trees but wasted less valuable trees. The majestic ceiba, sacred tree of the Mayans, were turned into paper and plywood.

Poor peasants from elsewhere in Mexico followed in the wake of logging operations. These homesteaders slashed and burned to clear the land, whose thin topsoil had been dependent on the Lacandón forest canopy for its nutrients and fertility. With these removed, and drained by crops and cattle, the soil was generally depleted in three years. Farmers and ranchers then moved on, leaving behind a barren, eroded landscape. Ranchers, many of whom were subsidized by the U.S. cattle industry, reseeded the land with forage grasses for large herds of livestock. Soon, the delicate tropical soil was exhausted by overgrazing.

In books, articles, and lectures, Duby-Blom exposed these events in the Selva Lacandóna to the world. Her photographs sensitized people to the rapid disappearance of the largest rain forest north of the Amazon. She pointed out how a civilization that had lived in harmony with nature for many millennia was now losing both its culture and its environment. People who had once scorned money as worthless were now fascinated by what it could buy, including transistor radios and battery-operated record players. Culturally, most of the Lacandónes had become alienated from their own traditions. One group became converts to the Southern Baptist religion, another to Seventh-Day Adventism. Only the community at Najá, led by its charismatic chieftain and spiritual leader Chan K'in Viejo, kept alive the flame of traditional Mayan religion and culture. Duby-Blom became a close friend of Chan K'in, deeply respecting him for his knowledge of Mayan oral traditions and its complex morality and cosmology. Chan K'in prophesied that when the last of the mighty trees were cut down, the world would come to an end. His view of his endangered part of the world was part of a much larger organic vision of things. He repeatedly said that "the roots of all living things are tied together," so that "When you cut down a tree, a star in the heavens also falls."

For a while in the 1970s, it appeared that the tireless efforts of Trudi Duby-Blom and her husband (who had died in 1963) had finally brought at least a partial halt to the destruction of the Selva Lacandóna. Mexican President Luis Echeverria set aside 2,400 square miles of jungle, giving it to the Lacandónes people as a forest reserve.

But the results of this apparent reform were to be tragic. People living in the area were moved out, and soon lumber operators moved in to clear-cut vast tracts of rain forest. The entire scheme was apparently a ruse to get the Lacandónes to sign away the lumber rights to their own land. A reserve on paper only, the destruction of the land continued into the final decades of the 20th century. Lacandón culture also rapidly disappeared, as Chan K'in Viejo lamented that his very own sons had little interest in continuing his way of life after he died. He noted sadly that for the young Lacandónes, "The car is their new god." By the time almost 80% of the rain forest had already disappeared, in the early 1980s the Mexican government again announced a plan to provide a sanctuary for the endangered species and peoples of Chiapas. Named the Montes Azules Biosphere Reserve, it called for the preservation of 3,312 square kilometers of the Selva Lacandóna, but almost from the day of its inception it became clear that a policy that was ecologically sound on paper would never be realized on the ground. The reserve was not policed and its rules were neither honored nor enforced.

Remaining physically as well intellectually alert into extreme old age, Trudi Duby-Blom continued to preside over her world at Na-Bolom with dignity and authority. Remembering that her generation had been unable to halt Fascism in the 1930s, she often felt in her final years that she had also failed in preventing the destruction of the Selva Lacandóna and the culture of the Maya peoples who lived there. In the late 1970s, she established a tree nursery and gave away free seedlings to all those in Chiapas with an interest in reforestation. Close to Na-Bolom, the seedlings from her nursery helped to reforest the devastated highlands that had once been so green and protective of living things. Gazing through her thick eyeglasses at hundreds of saplings in her nursery, she mused, "When I was young, I thought I could change the world. Now I think I can save some trees but not the forest. But that doesn't mean I should stop fighting." Gertrude Duby-Blom died in San Cristóbal de las Casas of heart disease and pneumonia on December 23, 1993. Her dear friend Chan K'in Viejo died three years later to the day, December 23, 1996.

SOURCES:

Brunhouse, Robert L. *Frans Blom: Maya Explorer.* Albuquerque, NM: University of New Mexico Press, 1976.

"Chan K'in Viejo, 104; Led Mexican Tribe," in *The New York Times.* January 2, 1997, p. A13.

"The Death of the Lacandón Culture and Rain Forest: An Interview with Gertrude Duby Blom," in *Mexico City News.* March 18, 1983.

Duby-Blom, Gertrude, Alex Harris, and Margaret Sartor. *Gertrude Blom—Bearing Witness.* Chapel Hill: Duke University Center for Documentary Photography/ University of North Carolina Press, 1984.

"Gertrude Blom: Guardian of the Rain Forest" (Filmmakers Library/Sintra Productions, 1989) [videorecording].

Herrera, Juan Felipe. *Mayan Drifter: Chicano Poet in the Lowlands of America.* Philadelphia, PA: Temple University Press, 1997.

Hudson, A. Landis. "Falling Stars and Burning Fields: The Politics of Land Use in the Selva Lacandóna of Chiapas, Mexico" (M.S. thesis, State University of New York College of Environmental Science, 1994).

Kurlansky, Mark J. "Woman in Love with a Jungle," in *International Wildlife.* Vol. 15, no. 5. September–October, 1985, pp. 34–39.

Lyons, Richard D. "Gertrude Blom, 92, Long a Chronicler of Mayan Cultures," in *The New York Times Biographical Service.* December 1993, p. 1775.

Pappe, Silvia. *Gertrude Duby-Blom—Königin des Regenwalds: Eine Biographie.* Berne: eFeF-Verlag, 1994.

Peerman, Dean. "Gertrude Blom: Prophet Crying *for* a Wilderness," in *The Christian Century.* Vol. 102, no. 39. December 11, 1985, pp. 1146–1150.

Perera, Victor and Robert D. Bruce. *The Last Lords of Palenque: The Lacandon Mayas of the Mexican*

Rain Forest. Berkeley, CA: University of California Press, 1985.

Simonian, Lane. *Defending the Land of the Jaguar: A History of Conservation in Mexico.* Austin, TX: University of Texas Press, 1995.

John Haag, Associate Professor of History, University of Georgia, Athens, Georgia

Ducas, Irene (c. 1066–1133).

See Irene Ducas.

Ducas, Maria (fl. 1070–1081).

See Anna Dalassena for sidebar on Maria of Alania.

Du Chatelet, Gabrielle Emilie (1706–1749).

See Châtelet, Émilie du.

Duchêne, Gabrielle (1870–1954)

*French activist who was involved in left-wing, feminist, and pacifist organizations for over 50 years. Pronunciation: gah-bree-ELL du-SHEN. Born Mathilde-Denise Laforcade in Paris, France, on February 26, 1870; died in Zurich, Switzerland, on August 3, 1954; daughter of Joseph Laforcade and Rosalie (Maréchal) Laforcade; married M. Duchêne (a landscape architect); children: daughter, Suzanne-Henriette Duchêne (**Mme. Roubakine**, b. January 19, 1893).*

Named president of the Labor Section of the National Council of French Women (1913); investigated because of pacifist activities (1915); named secretary-general of the French Section of the International League of Women for Peace and Liberty (1919); active in Russian relief (1920–23); intensified her association with Communist front organizations (1927); practiced "realistic" pacifism to counter Hitler's aggression (1934–49); hid from the Gestapo and aided the Resistance (1940–44); was president of the French Section of the LIFPL (1945–54); attended the Congress of Peoples, Vienna (1952).

Gabrielle Duchêne was born into comfortable circumstances, the daughter of **Rosalie Maréchal Laforcade** and Joseph Laforcade, the Chief of Gardens of Paris. She married a landscape architect, Duchêne, and in 1893 gave birth to a daughter, Suzanne-Henriette, who was to become prominent in women's and peace organizations. The Dreyfus Affair (1894–1906) turned Gabrielle toward social activism, especially on behalf of working women. She participated in the philanthropic Welfare through Work (*Assistance par le travail*) and in 1908 founded a cooperative, Mutual Aid (*Entraide*) for laundresses (*lingères*). Drawn to the union movement, she became active in the shirt and lingerie makers union; as a result, in 1913 she was named president of the Labor Section of the National Council of French Women (CNFF) and founded the CNFF's Office for Women Domestic Workers, housed at 32, rue Fondary (Paris XV).

During the First World War (1914–18), Duchêne continued her advocacy of women's rights in the workplace. She made some progress with the Ministry of Labor on equal pay for women and worked for passage of a minimum-wage law for domestic workers (July 10, 1915). As secretary-general of her French Office of Domestic Labor, she brought several lawsuits against employers under this law. She founded (July 19, 1915) the Inter-Union Action Committee Against the Exploitation of Women and linked it to the giant General Confederation of Labor (CGT) to gain more leverage. Male unionists' resistance to women's issues, however, was strong; she fought it by agitating outside union meetings and selling participants copies of *La Voix des femmes* (The Women's Voice) and *La Lutte féministe* (The Feminist Fight). In 1917, she started the French Office of Feminine Interests, which spread information on women's issues and sundry social evils. The organization folded in two years in part because of its strong pacifist orientation.

Pacifism, in fact, had become a dominant interest of Duchêne's and remained such for the rest of her life. She supported, but could not attend, the International Congress of Women at The Hague in April 1915 inspired by *Jane Addams. In May, Duchêne founded a French section of the International Committee of Women for Permanent Peace (CIFPP), formed at The Hague but not truly launched until 1919 as the International League of Women for Peace and Liberty (LIFPL). Her group—it never numbered more than a hundred or so—won hostile notoriety as the "Rue Fondary Committee" when it distributed an unsigned, uncensored antiwar tract by Michel Alexandre, *Un Devoir urgent pour les femmes* (An Urgent Duty for Women), in November 1915. It did not call for an immediate peace, and Socialist deputies in Parliament endorsed it. Nevertheless, it caused an uproar. The police searched Duchêne's apartment and seized papers, but no arrests ensued. As a result of the affair, the group faded and the CNFF forced her to resign her Labor Section presidency. She later joined the Society for Critical and Documentary Study of the War, a peace group patronized by Romain Rolland, whom the authorities finally allowed her to visit in Switzer-

land in 1917. By the end of the war, despite setbacks, Duchêne and other radicals had won a hearing and some respect for their courage.

After the war, Duchêne was a mainstay of organizations supporting world peace and the new Soviet Union. From 1919, she was secretary-general of the French Section of the LIFPL. The section never numbered over a few thousand members, in contrast to the large American and German sections, but she was a major figure in the international organization. She lectured widely and wrote many articles for the LIFPL's magazines *S.O.S.* (1925–35) and *En Vigie* (On the Lookout, 1935–39). She attended peace conferences in, e.g., Stuttgart (1920), The Hague (1922), Frankfurt (1929), and Geneva (1932), and participated in pacifist demonstrations. On behalf of Russia, she worked hard on the Red Cross' International Russian Relief Committee during the famine of 1920–23. She never joined the Communist Party, but by 1927 she had become a dedicated fellow traveler. She founded (1927–28) a study group, the New Russia Circle, which organized many lectures; participated in the Society of Friends of the Soviet Union (1927); was a delegate from the Women's Union Section of the Communist CGTU (Unified) to the tenth anniversary celebration of the Russian Revolution; attended the Brussels congress (February 1927) which founded the League Against Imperialism and Colonial Oppression (it urged wars of liberation); and joined the Communist-directed Fraternal Union of Women Against War (1927). The French Section of the LIFPL, however, did not always share her sympathies for Communist affiliations; her political activity helped keep its membership low, and in 1936 it split apart.

In the 1930s, Duchêne's pro-Soviet activity continued unabated. The New Russia Circle became in 1936 the Association for the Study of Soviet Civilization. She was secretary-general and, as its delegate, went to the Soviet Union on a study tour. She wrote for the review *La Russie aujourd'hui* (Russia Today) and in October 1937 at the Sorbonne participated in the French Days for Peace and Friendship with the Soviet Union. As for the peace movement, the rise of Fascism and Hitler put it under great strain. The Amsterdam-Pleyel movement (1932) spawned organizations involving Duchêne. She was a member of the board of the Committee for the Fight Against War, and she belonged to the World Front. She was one of the four secretaries of the World Committee Against War and Fascism (1932), a Communist creation, and wrote for its publication, *Clarté* (Brightness). In 1935, she organized and became president of the French Section of the WCWAWF and represented it at the Brussels congress of the Universal Assembly for Peace (1935). This French Section claimed (1936) 100,000 members and 600,000 sympathizers—probably a large overestimate, but impressive nonetheless.

The February 6, 1934, rioting in Paris by right-wing organizations triggered a powerful reaction on the left which led to the Popular Front government of 1936–38 based on a coalition of the Radical, Socialist, and Communist parties. Duchêne was early into the fray, one of the first to join the Committee of Antifascist Action and Vigilance (March 1934). She supported the Popular Front and many organizations aiding victims of Fascism, e.g., Ernst Thaelmann, Ethiopia, Bulgaria, Republican Spain. She came to believe that Fascism could not be stopped by pacifist measures, that *in extremis* liberty needed to be defended by arms if peace ultimately were to prevail. As a "realist" pacifist, she condemned Hitler's occupation of the Rhineland (1936), calling for League of Nations action. Building a united front of women, however, at the International Conference of Women for the Defense of Peace, Liberty, and Democracy (Marseille, May 1938), proved illusory. With the war imminent in 1939, she opposed the ultrapacifists, who then left the LIFPL. In June 1940 came catastrophe: a defeated France surrendered to Hitler's armies.

Not surprisingly, the Gestapo had Gabrielle Duchêne on their lists. She fled to the Midi, where under an assumed name she aided refugees and the Resistance in the Aix-en-Provence region. A betrayal forced her in 1943 to find shelter with a friend, **Claire Géniaux**, in Milhars (Tarn). From the end of the war until she died in Zurich in 1954, Duchêne resumed her prewar activity on behalf of women, peace, and Communist causes. She was president of the French Section of the LIFPL until her death. She also was a member of the France-USSR National Initiative Committee (December 1944); of aid organizations for the USSR, Spain, Vietnam *et al.*; and of the "Fighters for Peace" of the National Council of the Peace Movement of the Union of French Women; and she participated in the First Consultative Congress of the International Democratic Federation of Women, and in the Congress of Peoples (Vienna, 1952).

At her death, Duchêne left a huge, invaluable archive—papers, books, brochures, newspapers, clippings, posters, dossiers—which against all odds had escaped police seizure during the war. Her daughter gave it to the Bibliothèque de documentation internationale contemporaine (University of Paris-Nanterre).

Gabrielle Duchêne, despite an evident näiveté regarding the true nature of Stalinism and the Soviet regime (which she shared with most leftists of the time), put her astonishing reserves of energy and compassion to work on behalf of a host of humane causes, above all world peace. She was an inveterate joiner, but more than that, an activist. That common label, however, seems quite inadequate when one surveys her life's work.

SOURCES:

Bard, Christine. *Les Filles de Marianne: Histoire des féminismes 1914–1940*. Paris: Fayard, 1995.

Dreyfus, Michel. "Deux fonds interessants pour les historiens à la Bibliothèque de documentation internationale contemporaine de Nanterre," in *Mouvement sociale*. [Fonds Max Lagard and Gabrielle Duchêne.] 1981, no. 116, pp. 144–146.

——, and Nicole Racine. "Duchêne, Mathilde-Denise, dite Gabrielle," in *Dictionnaire biographique du mouvement ouvrier français*. Part 4: *1914-1939*. Dir. Jean Maitron. Paris: Éditions Ouvrières, 1964—.

——. "Le Fonds féministe à la B.D.I.C.," in *Matériaux pour l'histoire de notre temps* (Nanterre) No. 1. January–March 1985, pp. 21–23.

Klejman, Laurence, and Florence Rochefort. *L'Égalité en marche: Le Féminisme sous la Troisième République*. Paris: Presses de la Fondation national des sciences politiques, 1989.

Smith, Paul. *Feminism and the Third Republic*. Oxford: Clarendon Press, 1996.

SUGGESTED READING:

Agulhon, Maurice. *The French Republic 1879–1992*. Trans. by Antonia Nevill. Oxford: Basil Blackwell, 1993.

Dreyfus, Michel. "Des femmes trotskystes et pacifistes sous le Front populaire," in *Cahiers Léon Trotsky* (Grenoble). No. 9, 1982, pp. 53–60.

Jackson, Julian. *The Popular Front in France: Defending Democracy, 1934–38*. Cambridge: Cambridge University Press, 1988.

Sowerwine, Charles. *Sisters or Comrades? Women and Socialism in France since 1876*. Cambridge: Cambridge University Press, 1982.

Weber, Eugen. *The Hollow Years: France in the 1930s*. NY: W.W. Norton, 1994.

COLLECTIONS:

Nanterre: Bibliothèque de documentation internationale contemporaine: Archives Gabrielle Duchêne. Paris: Archives Nationals: F7/12962, F7/13371.

David S. Newhall,
Pottinger Distinguished Professor of History Emeritus,
Centre College, author of
Clemenceau: A Life at War (Edwin Mellen, 1991)

Duchesne, Rose Philippine

(1769–1852)

Roman Catholic missionary who founded the U.S. branch of the Society of the Sacred Heart, and is one of three American saints (not native-born). Name varia-

tions: Saint Rose Duchesne; Quah-kah-ka-num-ad (Woman-who-prays-always). Born in Grenoble, France, on August 29, 1769; died in St. Charles, Missouri, on November 18, 1852; daughter of Pierre François (a lawyer and politician) and Rose (Perier) Duchesne; attended Convent of the Visitation, Sainte-Marie-d'en-Haut.

On September 19, 1788, against her father's wishes, Rose Philippine Duchesne followed her calling to the religious life, entering the Visitation Order at the Convent at Sainte-Marie-d'en-Haut, where she had previously received her education. In 1792, as a result of the French Revolution, she was ejected from the convent that was used as a prison by the revolutionary government and sent home to Grenoble. She spent the next ten years teaching and performing charitable work, which often included sheltering priests who were persecuted by the revolutionary government. When peace was restored, she returned to the convent of Sainte-Marie-d'en-Haut, hoping to reunite the scattered Visitandine nuns. Failing in her efforts, in 1804 she and several companions joined the Society of the Sacred Heart, founded by St. *Madeleine Sophie Barat in 1800. Thus, the convent of Sainte-Marie-d'en-Haut became the second convent of this new order.

In 1815, Duchesne was transferred to Paris and founded the first Sacred Heart convent there. Three years later, she arrived in the United States, where she established a school in St. Charles, Missouri, the first free school west of the Mississippi River for both Catholic and non-Catholic children. In 1819, she built a convent in Florissant, Missouri, which housed a free parish school, an orphanage, a boarding academy, a school for Native American girls, and the first novitiate for U.S. members of the Sacred Heart Society. In 1827, Duchesne relocated to St. Louis, where she presided over an orphanage, academy, and parish school. At the advanced age of 72, she founded a mission school for Potawatomi Indian girls at Sugar Creek, Kansas. She also nursed the sick among the tribe, who called her Quah-kah-ka-num-ad (Woman-who-prays-always). She spent her final years at St. Charles, Missouri, and died there in 1852. When Rose Duchesne was beatified on May 12, 1940, and canonized in 1988, she joined *Frances Cabrini (1946) and John Neumann (1977) as the third American saint (not native-born).

Duci, Filippa

French royal mistress. Name variations: Filippe Duc. Mistress of Henry II (1519–1559), king of France (r.

*1547–1559); children: (with Henry) *Diane de France (1538–1619).*

Rose Philippine Duchesne

Duclaux, Agnes Mary F.
(1856–1944)

English poet and critic. Name variations: Mary F. Robinson; Agnes Mary Frances Robinson; A. Mary F. Robinson; Mary Darmesteter. Born Agnes Mary Frances Robinson at Leamington, England, on February 27, 1856; educated at University College, London; married James Darmesteter (1849–1894, an Oriental scholar); married Pierre Émile Duclaux, in 1901 (died 1904).

Agnes Duclaux studied Greek literature at University College, London. She followed her first volume of poetry, *A Handful of Honeysuckle* (1879), with a translation from Euripides entitled *The Crowned Hippolytus* (1881). Duclaux also published monographs on *Emily Brontë (1883) and on *Margaret of Angoulême (1886).

The New Arcadia and Other Poems (1884) and *An Italian Garden* (1886) were said to include some of her best verses. The Orientalist James Darmesteter, then in Peshawur, became interested in her poems which he then translated into French. They married in 1888, after which much of her work was written in French. Darmesteter's *Études anglaises* was translated into English by Duclaux (1896).

She also wrote *Life of Ernest Renan* (1897); *End of the Middle Ages* (1888); *Retrospect and Other Poems* (1893); the volume on *Froissart* (1894) in the *Grands écrivains français;* essays on the Brontës, the Brownings and others, entitled *Grands écrivains d'Outre-Manche* (1901); *The Return to Nature, Songs and Symbols* (1904). After her first husband's death, in 1901 she married Émile Duclaux, the associate of Pasteur, and director of the Pasteur institute. Her *Collected Poems, Lyrical and Narrative* were published in 1902, two years before her second husband's death. The quality of her work was only gradually recognized.

Du Coudray, Angélique

(1712–1789)

French obstetrician who trained 4,000 pupils in midwifery. Name variations: Angelique du Coudray; Madame du Coudray; Marguerite le Boursier. Born in Clermont-Ferrand in 1712; died in 1789.

In an age rife with charlatans and crude techniques, Madame Du Coudray was a midwife in France who lent a scientific approach to the field of obstetrics. She was born in Clermont-Ferrand and received training in Paris at the Hôtel Dieu School. In 1740, she was licensed as an *accoucheuse*, or midwife.

Her 1759 work, *Abrégé de l'art des accouchements avec plusiers observations sur des cas singuliers*, was a revision and expansion of a 1667 midwifery textbook. She began teaching midwifery in France the same year as her publication of this text. When Louis XV provided Du Coudray with an annual salary for her teaching services in all the provinces, she arranged a class of one hundred in Auvergne. Biographer **Nina Rattner Gelbart** in *The King's Midwife: A History and Mystery of Madame du Coudray* portrays Du Coudray as a midwife who regarded her teaching as a type of patriotic duty. In order for her pupils to be able to practice deliveries, she made use of an actual foetus and invented obstetrical "machines"; these anatomical models were composed of leather which encased real pelvic bones (the bones later to be made of wicker and wood).

She is said to have trained 4,000 pupils, and to have been responsible for the training of 10,000 when including both those whom she trained as well as those who were then trained by her former students. Under Du Coudray's direction, a course in practical obstetrics was begun at the veterinary school at Alfort in 1780. Jealousy between the all-female midwives and the all-male surgeons had been reported as early as 1743, but Du Coudray was surprised by the enmity of surgeons who were staunchly opposed to her teaching. Her recognition, however, was such that the Church permitted her to baptize babies. In cases of malpractice in which a mother or a child suffered mutilation, Du Coudray was often summoned to provide assistance. Publication of her *Oeuvres* came in 1773. In her advanced years, Du Coudray received a government pension.

Duczynska, Ilona (1897–1978)

Austrian-born author and political activist, critical of both the passivity of Social Democracy and the brutality of Bolshevism, whose lifelong commitment to Socialist ideals reflected the complexities of Central European political life between the two World Wars. Name variations: Ilona Polanyi or Polányi. Born Helene Marie Duczynska in Maria Enzersdorf, Lower Austria, in 1897; died in Pickering, Canada, on April 24, 1978; daughter of Alfred Ritter von Duczynski and Hélen Békássy; married Tivadar Sugár; married Karl Polányi, in 1922; children: (second marriage) one daughter, Kári (b. 1923).

Born in a pleasantly situated suburb of Vienna in 1897, Ilona Duczynska grew up in a family dynamic that was in many ways a reflection of the complex and troubled Austro-Hungarian monarchy. Her father, a railway official of noble Polish descent who was unhappy with his lot in life, immigrated alone to the United States in 1904, dying there three years later. Her mother, who had been born into the proud Hungarian gentry class, had become estranged from her family as a result of a marriage that had been opposed from the start. These family tensions would mark Ilona for life, making her feel humiliated and rejected, feelings that were quickly transmuted into a hatred of the upper classes. Duczynska's combative temperament emerged early, and by the age of ten she already knew that in future years she would always be an individual who would choose to stand "against the world."

By the time she had entered her teens, Ilona had adopted her dead father's social radicalism, including the advocacy of atheism, anarchism and the belief that a systematic application of truths derived from the natural sciences could solve all of humanity's age-old problems. The start of World War I only made Duczynska more radical, and she was expelled from her lyceum as a subversive for having denounced the war. After receiving her leaving certificate by mail in the summer of 1915, Duczynska enrolled at the college of technology in Zurich, Switzerland. Here she was quickly drawn to the most radical anti-war circles, almost exclusively composed of Russian and Polish revolutionaries living as exiles in Switzerland. She became one of the youngest and most ardent supporters of Vladimir Lenin's Zimmerwald circle, which denounced the Social Democratic leadership of the various warring nations as "Social imperialists" and traitors to the ideals of Marxism.

In the spring of 1917, although still recovering from tuberculosis, she returned to a Vienna that was suffering from widespread malnutrition and a profound sense of war-weariness. Soon she traveled to Budapest in her mother's native Hungary, determined to make history by ridding the nation of its increasingly unpopular prime minister, István Tisza. She had been practicing with firearms while in Switzerland and was convinced that she could singlehandedly change the course of history by assassinating Tisza (she was obviously inspired by the death of Austrian prime minister Count Carl Stürgkh, who had been assassinated in a Viennese restaurant in October 1916). Fortunately, Tisza resigned before Duczynska could carry out her plans.

By this time Duczynska had become a member of the Galileo Circle, an influential group of progressive Budapest intellectuals. Within the larger circle, a small group including Duczynska who styled themselves revolutionary Socialists printed clandestine antiwar pamphlets, and Duczynska managed to throw bundles of these over the wall of a military barracks. The secret police soon got wind of the group's activities, and in January 1918 Duczynska and several of her colleagues found themselves under arrest. In June of that same year, she and her lover Tivadar Sugár were sentenced to prison terms (she received two years in jail, he three). The collapse of the Habsburg state in the autumn of 1918 resulted in the release of all political prisoners, and Duczynska and Sugár were freed. Duczynska immediately entered into the political turmoil of the day, becoming a founding member of the Communist Party of Hungary. Though there was little time for private life, within days of her release from prison she decided to marry Sugár, but the match was ill-fated and the couple went their separate ways within weeks of the nuptials.

Having barely escaped death in the influenza epidemic then sweeping the world, a still-recovering Duczynska volunteered to serve the newly established Hungarian Soviet Republic that was fighting for survival in the spring and early summer of 1919. In May 1919, she went to Zurich to serve as that revolutionary state's press representative in Switzerland, where Duczynska hoped to favorably influence both Swiss and world opinion. When the Hungarian Soviet Republic collapsed in the summer of 1919, Duczynska's Swiss friends hid her in a peasant's home so as to evade police sweeps clearing the country of undesirable foreign radicals.

The next phase of her career began in the spring of 1920 when she and several Russian revolutionaries long resident in Switzerland undertook a protracted and dangerous trip to Moscow, where they volunteered their services to the fledgling Soviet state. Within days of her arrival, the young revolutionary found herself at the center of world history in the making. Chosen to work alongside the famed revolutionary Karl Radek, she helped the Soviet leadership to prepare for the second world congress of the Communist International (Comintern). Impressed by her dedication to the revolutionary cause, Comintern leaders decided to send Duczynska to Vienna to work in the headquarters of the exiled Hungarian Communist Party. Smuggled over the border, Duczynska found refuge in Hinterbrühl, in the outskirts of Vienna, where the famous educator *Genia Schwarzwald operated a free guest house for her friends and impoverished intellectuals.

Soon after arriving at Hinterbrühl, Ilona met a Hungarian-born intellectual 11 years her senior, Karl Polányi. While the two shared the same ideals of building a better social order, Karl and Ilona differed in many ways. He was introverted and indeed had long been suffering from depression when he met the irrepressible Duczynska. On the issue of Communism, the couple also had major differences in that despite his revolutionary sympathies Karl had never agreed with the totalitarian aspects of the Hungarian Soviet regime and had in fact emigrated from Budapest to Vienna in June 1919, several months before the collapse of the ill-fated experiment in radical Socialism. Ilona, on the other hand, had until this point been an uncritical supporter of Lenin's Soviet republic, and its attempts to export revolutions into the rest of Europe. Many hours of heated discussions between the two enriched both intellectually and only strengthened their affection for one another. Polányi's depression vanished, and he became more aware of the links between political theory and practice, while Duczynska's uncritical admiration of the actual policies of Hungarian and Russian Communist leaders underwent a transformation; she became increasingly critical.

In the spring of 1922, after Duczynska's divorce from Tivadar Sugár had become final, she and Karl Polányi married. They moved into a modest apartment in one of Vienna's workers' districts. In 1923, Duczynska gave birth to her only child, a daughter named Kári. By this time, Duczynska's views had become highly critical of both Communist strategy and tactics, and given the vocal nature of her opposition, she was expelled from the small and faction-ridden Hungarian Communist group in Vienna. Duczynska joined the powerful Austrian Social Democratic Party, quickly gravitating to its left wing.

Faced with the need to earn a living for her family, she became editor of the prestigious economic journal, *Der österreichische Volkswirt*. Given the fact that this journal was essentially non-political and indeed served the "bourgeois interests" of investors and speculators, Duczynska's immense energies still needed a more sharply focused ideological outlet. This she found by also serving as editor of the journal of the leftist opposition within the Austrian Social Democratic movement, *Der linke Sozialdemokrat*. By 1929, Duczynska had become as critical of the Social Democratic leadership as she had been earlier toward the Communists, and as a consequence of her relentlessly oppositionist attitude within the party, she was expelled.

Seeking a respite from politics, Duczynska now returned to her earlier intellectual love, namely science, and worked to earn a doctorate at Vienna's College of Technology (Technische Hochschule). Within a few years, however, as the political situation in Central Europe deteriorated and Fascism loomed, her political passions were rekindled, and she became a leading member of the small but influential Gruppe Funke ("Spark Group"), a splinter organization led by Leopold and ◀⚜ **Ilse Kulcsar** that hoped to inject a more militant spirit into a seemingly paralyzed Social Democratic movement. The seizure of power by the Nazis in Germany in 1933, and the collapse of democracy in Austria soon after, alarmed Duczynska and after the bloody suppression of the Social Democrats in February 1934, she decided that the only group capable of meeting the challenge of Hitlerism were the Communists. She joined the minuscule but conspiratorially well-organized Austrian Communist Party, quickly becoming one of its leaders. Besides being a member of the *Autonomer Schutzbund* (Autonomous Protective League), she also organized an illegal radio cell and became editor of the underground journal *Der Sprecher*. In May 1935, she became a member of the group of five that ran the Viennese underground organization. Duczynska's conspiratorial cover name during this perilous period was "Anna Novotny." Thanks to her own skills and cool-headedness and those of her comrades, many illegal activities took place on a regular basis without her ever being arrested.

In February 1936, having completed her doctoral work in physics, Duczynska immigrated to England, where her husband and daughter had already been living for some time. Here she was active in organizing support for political prisoners in Austria. At the same time, she looked for work that would enable her to use her scientific expertise. Politically, Duczynska's fierce integrity again brought her into conflict with those in power. In this case, she was expelled from the Austrian Communist movement because of her critical views on the Moscow purge trials. During World War II, Duczynska found work in the British defense industry, working on the design, construction, and testing of new aircraft (she would be honored for this by being named an Associate Fellow of the Royal Aeronautical Society). At the same time, she kept her political involvement alive by becoming a leader of the leftist but non-Communist Hungarian exile movement of Count Michael Karolyi.

⚜▶ **Kulcsar, Ilse** (1902–1973)

Austrian anti-Nazi activist and author. Born Ilse Pollak in Vienna, Austria, in 1902; died in 1973; married Leopold Kulcsar; married Arturo Barea.

SUGGESTED READING:

Barea, Ilse. *Vienna: Legend and Reality.* NY: 1966.
Österreicher im Spanischen Bürgerkrieg: Interbrigadisten berichten über ihre Erlebnisse 1936 bis 1945. Vienna: Österreichischer Bundesverlag, 1986.
Pütter, Conrad. *Rundfunk gegen das "Dritte Reich": Deutschsprachige Rundfunkaktivitäten im Exil 1933–1945. Ein Handbuch.* Munich: K.G. Saur, 1986.

In 1947, after she and her husband were denied admission into the United States by immigration officials bending to emerging Cold War phobias, presumably because of their radical past, Karl and Ilona moved to Canada instead. Her husband's reputation increased over the years, particularly after the publication of his book *The Great Transformation* at the end of World War II. Ilona Duczynska, on the other hand, began to fade into history. Not until the final years of her life was she able to once again gain readers and admirers for a series of historical works that served to argue for the democratic possibilities within the Socialist view of history and society. Even before her husband's death in 1964, Duczynska regained much of her youthful optimism about the positive potentialities of Socialism. The tragic Hungarian uprising of 1956 gave her hope that the cruel despotism of the Soviet model might yet be overcome, as did the "Prague Spring" of 1968.

Starting in the 1960s, Duczynska was able once again to visit Hungary, which she continued to regard as her home as much as she did Vienna or Canada. In her last books, *Der demokratische Bolschewik* (1975) and *Workers in Arms* (1978), she wrote with youthful enthusiasm about her belief that democracy and Socialism could and indeed must inspire one another in order to survive. Her hatred of ideological dogmatism and political dictatorship made her a lifelong foe of Stalinism and party bureaucracy. Ilona Duczynska died, one of the very last survivors of Europe's classic age of revolutionary fervor, on April 24, 1978, in Pickering, Ontario, Canada. In the year of her death, the noted British historian E.J. Hobsbawm wrote "to salute her eight decades of devotion to the cause of the liberation of mankind, and her unbroken, but never uncritical, enthusiasm for socialism."

SOURCES:

Arbeitsgemeinschaft "Biografisches Lexikon der österreichischen Frau," file in Institut für Wissenschaft und Kunst, Vienna.

Buttinger, Joseph. *In the Twilight of Socialism: A History of the Revolutionary Socialists of Austria*. Translated by E.B. Ashton. NY: Frederick A. Praeger, 1953.

Congdon, Lee. *Exile and Social Thought: Hungarian Intellectuals in Germany and Austria, 1919–1933.* Princeton, NJ: Princeton University Press, 1991.

Drucker, Peter F. *Adventures of a Bystander: Memoirs.* New ed. NY: HarperCollins, 1991.

Duczynska, Ilona. *Der demokratische Bolschewik: Zur Theorie und Praxis der Gewalt.* Munich: List Verlag, 1975.

———. "Körber im Vorfebruar: Eine späte Begegnung," in Ludwig Jedlicka and Rudolf Neck, eds., *Vom Justizpalast zum Heldenplatz: Studien und Dokumentationen 1927 bis 1938.* Vienna: Österreichische Staatsdruckerei, 1975, pp. 208–211.

———. *Workers in Arms: The Austrian Schutzbund and the Civil War of 1934.* NY: Monthly Review Press, 1978.

Lewis, Jill. *Fascism and the Working Class in Austria, 1918–1934: The Failure of Labour in the First Republic.* New York and Oxford: Berg, 1991.

Pasteur, Paul. "Femmes dans le Mouvement ouvrier Autrichien 1918–1934" (Ph.D. dissertation, University of Rouen, 1986).

Szecsi, Maria. "Ilona Duczynska gestorben," in *Arbeiter-Zeitung* [Vienna], May 3, 1978.

John Haag, Associate Professor of History,
University of Georgia, Athens, Georgia

Dudach, Charlotte (1913–1985).

See Delbo, Charlotte.

Dudarova, Veronika Borisovna (1916—)

Russian conductor who was the first woman to head a major orchestra in the Soviet Union. Born on December 5, 1916, in Baku; studied piano with P.A. Serebriakov at the Leningrad Conservatory.

Became chief conductor of the Moscow State Symphony Orchestra (1960); designated a People's Artist of the USSR (1977); although she never visited the U.S. or Western Europe, achieved a considerable artistic reputation on the basis of her recordings and concert reviews.

Despite the proclamation of complete gender equality at the time of the Bolshevik Revolution in November 1917, de facto discrimination against women continued in virtually all areas of life in revolutionary Russia. With the creation of the Soviet Union in 1922 came attempts to add a new dynamic to the process of social transformation, and considerable reforms took place over the next decade. The percentage of female literacy was dramatically improved during these years, and access to the arts was greatly expanded, particularly for talented young women and men of working-class origins. Like many gifted women of this era, Veronika Dudarova was able to take advantage of the expanded opportunities during this turbulent, often creative, period. She was born in Baku on December 5, 1916, and together with her family survived the difficulties of civil war, foreign invasion and famine. By the late 1920s, it was obvious that she was a highly gifted young musician.

Starting in 1933, Dudarova began an intensive course of piano study with P.A. Serebriakov at the Leningrad Conservatory. These studies ended in 1937, at which point she began to teach and concertize. Her ultimate goal, however, was not to become a celebrated piano virtuoso or respected pedagogue, but rather to wield a baton as head of an orchestra. Such ambitions for a woman in the Soviet Union were almost as unrealistic as in the capitalist West, for in the 1930s and 1940s it was simply assumed that women were constitutionally unqualified to become conductors of any distinction. Determined to conduct, Dudarova attended countless concerts, studied all the orchestral scores she could track down, and began to organize the next phase of her career.

The Nazi invasion of the USSR in June 1941 drastically changed her plans. The 900-day siege of Leningrad ended normal musical life in that great city, and Dudarova continued her career in Moscow, which was spared from the worst effects of the war. With many male musicians at the front, she was able to pursue her conductorial goals, studying at the Moscow Conservatory with Leo Ginsburg. Her talent also came to the attention of the noted maestro Nikolai Anosov, who by 1944 felt she was ready to appear before a full symphony orchestra.

Dudarova gave her first public concert in 1947, to positive reviews. Throughout the 1950s, she rapidly expanded her repertoire and made a large number of recordings for the Soviet Melodiya recording firm, a few of which appeared on labels in the West. Her imaginative choice of repertoire was made evident by several of these recordings, including the folksy Chaikin Concerto for Accordion and Orchestra, and a recording of four of Tchaikovsky's least-known orchestral works (*The Storm, Fate, The Voyevode*, and the very early *Overture in F major*). As the highly respected chief conductor of the Moscow State Symphony Orchestra (also designated the "Moscow Region Orchestra"), she gave concerts that were well-attended and enthusiastically received by music lovers seeking an escape from life in a stagnating society.

Dudarova's achievements were first acknowledged in 1960 when she was awarded the title of People's Artist of the Russian Republic. Over the next decades, until the end of the Soviet era, she received numerous medals including the Order of the Badge of Honor. Never a political dissident, she joined the Communist Party of the Soviet Union in 1950. In 1977, she was declared a People's Artist of the USSR. Because her work was largely confined to Moscow, for most of Dudarova's career her international reputation was based on her recordings, concert reviews, and anecdotal reports of Western concert-goers who happened to attend one or more of her concerts while they were in the Soviet Union. Not until the freer atmosphere of the Gorbachev era was it possible for Dudarova to travel outside her country. One of the first of these travels, to Mexico in 1988, brought enthusiastic responses from critics and audiences.

The collapse of the Soviet Union in 1991 brought with it new artistic opportunities as well as myriad problems of daily survival. Despite her age, Dudarova continued her busy schedule of conducting. Reflecting her high status in the Russian musical world, she was chosen to conduct the memorial concert in October 1993 for the centennial of Peter Ilyitch Tchaikovsky's death, held in the town of Votkinsk, where a museum was built on the site of the great composer's former manor house. Perhaps of even greater importance for posterity, in the early 1990s she made a number of highly acclaimed recordings, often of little-known Russian symphonic works. These recordings were released not only in Russia but throughout the world.

Probably the best of these recordings was her 1992 reading of Miaskovsky's Sixth "Revolutionary" Symphony. Conducting her newly created Symphony Orchestra of Russia, Dudarova gave a powerful interpretation of this dramatic work, composed in the first years of the Soviet experiment, and received laudatory reviews from critics. Her recording of Miaskovsky's epic work (it runs to 70 minutes) introduced music lovers to a masterpiece of 20th-century music. Distilling a lifetime of musical experience, and reflecting on an artistic life lived in a society known both for its cultural brilliance and political brutality, Veronika Dudarova inspired her musicians as they played the scherzo of the Miaskovsky symphony, which depicts the wind howling through his dead aunt's apartment, where her cold corpse still remains. Equally moving, the finale of the symphony incorporates a Russian folk song, "As the Soul Departs," gently sung by the choir. Fortunately for succeeding generations, the musicality of Veronika Dudarova will remain alive in this and other recordings created under her baton.

SOURCES:

Artamonov, Alfred. "Tchaikovsky Musical Festival Opens in His Native Town," in *TASS*. October 26, 1993.

Ciechanower, Mauricio. "Sinfónica de Moscú: A los pies de una batuta femenina—Entrevista con Veronika Dudarova," in *Plural*. Vol. 18, no. 205. October 1988, pp. 59–62.

"Diaghilev Season," in *Moscow News*. No. 16, April 19, 1992.

Freed, Richard. "A Quiet 'Storm' From Veronika Dudarova," *Washington Post*. January 16, 1977, p. E5.

Kallinikov, Vasily Sergeyevich. Symphonies No. 1 in G minor, No. 2 in A [Olympia CD 511].

Miaskovsky, Nikolai. Symphony No. 6 in E flat minor, Op. 23 ("The Revolutionary") [Olympia CD 510].

Motte, Diether de la. "Neue Musik in Moskau," *Musica*, Vol. 39, no. 2, March–April 1985, pp. 178–181.

Robinson, Harlow. "Music Lightens the Rigors of Life in Moscow," in *The New York Times*. September 4, 1983, p. B13.

John Haag, Associate Professor of History,
University of Georgia, Athens, Georgia

du Deffand, marquise (1697–1780).

See Salonnières.

Dudevant, Madame (1804–1876).

See George Sand.

Dudinskaya, Natalya (1912—)

Russian ballerina who was an instrumental performer, choreographer, and instructor at Russia's famed Kirov Ballet. Name variations: Natalia. Born Natalya Mikhailovna Dudinskaya in Kharkov, Ukraine, in 1912; daughter of Natalya Tagliori (a ballet dancer and a musician); studied dance under mother's tutelage, early 1920s; attended the Leningrad School of Choreography, 1923–31; married Konstantin Sergeyev.

Joined Kirov Ballet (1931); appeared in title role of Cinderella *(1946); began teaching at the Kirov (1951); retired from dancing (1961); appeared as Carabosse in film version of* Cinderella *(1964).*

Roles created by Dudinskaya include title role in Laurencia *(1936),* Mireille de Poitiers *in* Flames of Paris, *Corali in* Lost Illusions, *Pannochka in* Taras Bulba, *title role in* Gayané, *Paragna in* Bronze Horseman *(1949), and* Sarie *in* Path of Thunder *(1957). Also appeared in* Les Sylphides, Cinderella *(1946),* Raymonda, Don Quixote, La Bayadére, Esmeralda, *and as* Titania *in* A Midsummer Night's Dream.

Natalya Mikhailovna Dudinskaya was born in 1912 in Kharkov, then the capital of the Ukraine. Her mother **Natalya Tagliori** was a dancer who ran a ballet studio in the city, and Dudinskaya began classes there at the age of eight. Around 1923, she journeyed to the city of Petrograd (now St. Petersburg) to begin classes at the Petrograd Ballet School. For the last three years of her formal training, in the late 1920s, she studied under famed ballerina *Agrippina Vaganova. Dudinskaya made her debut as Princess Florine in *Sleeping Beauty* even before her graduation in 1931, and soon after joined the company of the renowned Kirov Ballet (now the St. Petersburg Ballet). The Kirov was once

the Imperial Russian Ballet, and Vaganova herself had helped resurrect its reputation after its decline following the Bolshevik Revolution of 1917. Along with the Bolshoi Ballet, the Kirov was considered one of Russia's premier cultural institutions, and its international reputation was equally esteemed. Dudinskaya eventually became its prima ballerina. One of her first roles there was as Odette-Odile in *Swan Lake*.

Dudinskaya became romantically involved with Konstantin Sergeyev, a choreographer at the Kirov, and married him after World War II. In 1946, she created the title role in his version of Sergei Prokofiev's *Cinderella* on the Moscow stage, and he directed her in numerous other works over the years. She began teaching at the school of the Kirov Ballet in 1951 and formally retired from the stage ten years later. Having studied under Vaganova at a crucial period in her training, Dudinskaya is considered to have adapted her mistress' techniques and style to a high degree, and imparted these to a new generation of students in her classes. Later in her career, Dudinskaya choreographed some ballets together with Sergeyev, including *Hamlet* (1970), *Le Corsaire* (1973), and *Beethoven's Appassionata* (1977). For her achievements, she has been cited as a Peoples' Artist of the Union of Soviet Socialist Republics.

Carol Brennan,
Grosse Pointe, Michigan

Dudley, Amy or Amye (c. 1532–1560).

See Robsart, Amy.

Dudley, Lady Jane (1537–1554).

See Grey, Lady Jane.

Dudley, Lettice (c. 1541–1634).

See Knollys, Lettice.

Duenkel, Jenny (b. 1947).

See Ferguson, Cathy Jean for sidebar.

Duff, Alexandra (1891–1959).

See Alexandra Victoria.

Duff, Maud (1893–1945).

See Carnegie, Maud.

Duff-Gordon, Lucie (1821–1869)

English translator and travel writer whose published letters chronicled her years spent in South Africa and Egypt, presenting those cultures with keen insight and a rare understanding. Name variations: Lady Lucy Duff or Duff Gordon. Born on June 24, 1821, in Queen Square, London, England; died on July 14,

1869, of consumption in Cairo, Egypt; only child of John Austin (a jurist and author of Providence of Jurisprudence Determined*) and Sarah Taylor Austin (a translator and woman of letters); had little formal education; spent a few years at a school in Hampstead and at Miss Shepherd's School in Bromley; married Sir Alexander Duff-Gordon, on May 16, 1840; children:* **Janet Anne Duff-Gordon Ross** *(1842–1927, a writer);* Maurice *(b. March 1849);* **Urania Duff-Gordon** *(b. 1858, called Rainie).*

Spent early childhood in England; traveled to Germany with her parents, where she became fluent in the language (1826); as a teenager, attended boarding school in Bromley; made her debut in London society (1838); married at age 19 (1840); lived in London and translated many important literary and historical works (1840–50); moved with family to Weybridge, where she established a library for working men (1850); moved to Paris (1857); left England for South Africa (1861); moved on to Egypt (1862), where she lived until her death (1869).

Translations of German and French works: Barthold Niebuhr's *Studies of Ancient Greek Mythology (1839);* Wilhelm Meinhold's *Mary Schweidler: The Amber Witch (1844);* The French in Algiers, from the German and French of C. Lamping *(1845); P.J.A. von Feuerbach's* Narrative of Remarkable Criminal Trials *(1846); (with her husband) Leopold von Ranke's* Memoirs of the House of Brandenburg *(1847); A.F.L. de Wailly's* Stella and Vanessa *(1850); von Ranke's* Ferdinand I and Maximilian II of Austria *(1853); S. D'Arbouville's* The Village Doctor *(1853); Baron von Moltke's* The Russians in Bulgaria and Roumelia, 1828–1929 *(1854); (edited) H.C.L. von Sybel's* The History and Literature of the Crusades *(1861). Published letters:* Letters from the Cape *(published as part of Francis Galton's* Vacation Tourist *in 1862–1863, 1864);* Letters from Egypt, 1863–1865 *(1865);* Last Letters from Egypt *(1875).*

In her many letters from South Africa and Egypt, British "travel writer" Lady Lucie Duff-Gordon painted a vivid, compelling, and sympathetic portrait of societies and cultures at an extraordinary moment in history. In the 1860s, these societies were increasingly under the influence of European ideas and were rapidly becoming the object of European imperial ambitions. In her *Letters from the Cape* and *Letters from Egypt*, Duff-Gordon provided her readers with a sense of the rich, cultural heritage of her adopted home, and her descriptions and anecdotes convey the spirit of a woman known in her day for her independence of mind and her deeply sympathetic nature. This combination of traits also encouraged Duff-Gordon to make insightful and needed criticisms of the prejudicial and cruel elements of European imperialism. In all her work and throughout her life, Duff-Gordon was a keen student of human nature. She consistently demonstrated an abiding respect for all women and men regardless of nationality, skin color, religion, or culture.

Lady Lucie Duff-Gordon was born into a family known for its intellectual abilities and its progressive sympathies. Her parents, John Austin and ✎▶ Sarah Austin, were eager political reformers and active participants in the most exciting intellectual circles of the day. John Austin was well-known for his brilliant and vigorous mind, but he was also a sickly and humorless man whose rigid principles and perfectionism limited his ability to earn a living. John did, however, produce a book, *Providence of Jurisprudence Determined*, that established his place in legal history. He was also an important influence on the young philosopher and theorist John Stuart Mill.

Lucie Duff-Gordon's mother Sarah was a prominent translator and woman of letters. Known for her forceful personality, her devotion to reform, and her avid reading habits, Sarah carried on a voluminous correspondence with the greatest minds and political reformers of the day, including Alexis de Tocqueville, Auguste Comte, Lord Brougham, and W.E. Gladstone. Sarah Austin also had a strong sense of family. Lucie Duff-Gordon's extended family included the well-known Martineaus, who had an important influence on her as a child. One of Duff-Gordon's biographers suggested that "there was a strong sense of unity" in the clan, particularly on Lucie's mother's side of the family, and it was not uncommon for more than 60 members of the family to gather for meetings or celebrations.

Lucie was a precocious child. She displayed self-confidence and a sharp mind at an early age. The luminaries who frequented her parent's drawing room rarely brought children with them, hence Lucie's playmates were men like John Stuart Mill. At a young age, Lucie was exposed to some of the most prominent intellectuals and political leaders of her parent's generation, including James and John Stuart Mill, Jeremy Bentham, Thomas Babington Macaulay, *Mary Louisa Molesworth, and Daniel O'Connell.

Lucie had little formal education as a child, though for a short time she attended a co-educational school at Hampstead, where she probably learned Greek and possibly Latin. She also attended a German school during the year her family spent in Bonn when she was six years old. From the time she was young, Lucie received informal but valuable instruction from her mother, most likely in foreign languages. This instruction probably contributed to the close relationship Lucie maintained throughout her life with Sarah. When Lucie was older and living abroad, it was in letters to her mother that Duff-Gordon spoke the most openly about the behavior of the English in foreign countries.

The life of the Austins, though rich in intellectual stimulation, was often a financial challenge, and the family moved with some frequency in order to manage their expenses. When Lucie was 13, they relocated to the French fishing village of Boulogne. Despite their move away from London, the Austins were always active in the intellectual community, and through them young Lucie struck up a friendship with the German poet Heinrich Heine. Heine was a masterful political satirist and revolutionary poet who had fled Germany under pressure from the government. He was impressed with young Lucie's keen intellect and candor, and near the end of his life, when Heine and Duff-Gordon met again, he remembered their time in Boulogne together fondly. As a teenager, Lucie was described as curious and interesting, independent and self-possessed. Her appearance was, according to one observer, "handsome and very striking."

In 1836, the Austin family moved to Malta. This time Lucie, now 15 years old, did not relocate with her parents but instead boarded at Miss Shepherd's School at Bromley. According to most accounts, Duff-Gordon's experience at Miss Shepherd's was difficult, since she had grown used to the eclectic character of her earlier education. Her dissatisfaction with life at Bromley did not, however, dampen her independence of mind. At age 16, Lucie, a Unitarian, decided to undergo baptism and confirmation in the Church of England. She made this decision after a prolonged religious debate with one of her classmates, who was Anglican, but without consulting her parents or relations. Lucie's conversion horrified her relatives, since most of them were members of the Unitarian Church. Despite pressure from relatives, Lucie remained unswerving in her decision to convert. Duff-Gordon's years at Bromley were marked by another more disturbing legacy, for it was there that she first developed consumption, the illness that would in the years to come rob her of her health and eventually her life.

Austin, Sarah (1793–1867)

English author. Born Sarah Taylor in Norwich, England, in 1793; died at Weybridge, England, on August 8, 1867; daughter of John Taylor (a wool-stapler, who died in 1826) and Susannah Cook Taylor; married John Austin (a London barrister), in 1820 (died 1859); children: *Lucie Duff-Gordon (1821–1869).*

Sarah Austin was born into the celebrated Taylor family of Norwich, England. Her great grandfather, Dr. John Taylor (1694–1761), was the pastor of the Presbyterian church in Norwich and writer of a once famous polemical work on *The Scripture Doctrine of Original Sin* (1738), which elicited celebrated treatises by Jonathan Edwards on *Original Sin.* Her mother **Susannah Cook Taylor** was an extremely intelligent woman who contributed both beauty and talent to her daughter. The friends of Susannah and John Taylor included Henry Crabbe Robinson, Sir James Mackintosh, and Dr. Alderson and his daughter *Amelia Opie. After Sarah Taylor married John Austin in 1820, they lived in Queen Square, Westminster, and their daughter and only child *Lucie Duff-Gordon was born in 1821. Sarah, whose tastes, unlike her husband's, were decidedly social, cultivated a large circle of friends, including Jeremy Bentham, James Mill, and historians George and *Harriet Grote (1792–1878); she also befriended many Italian exiles. Austin attempted few original works, involving herself mainly with translations, of which the most important are the *Characteristics of Goëthe* (3 vols., 1833), Leopold von Ranke's *History of the Reformation in Germany* and *History of the Popes* (1840), and *Report on the State of Public Instruction in Prussia* (1834); from the French, she translated V. Cousin and F.W. Carove's *The Story without an End* (1864).

Of *History of the Popes,* her contemporary Thomas Babington Macaulay wrote: "Of this translation we need only say that it is such as might be expected from the skill, the taste, and the scrupulous integrity of the accomplished lady who, as an interpreter between the mind of Germany and the mind of Britain, has already deserved so well of both countries." Following her husband's death in 1859, Austin edited his *Lectures on Jurisprudence.* She also edited the *Memoirs of Sydney Smith* (1855) and her daughter Lucie Duff-Gordon's *Letters from Egypt* (1865). See *Three Generations of Englishwomen* (1888), by her granddaughter, **Janet Anne Duff-Gordon Ross (1842–1927).**

When Lucie's parents returned to England in 1838 after two years in Malta, she left Bromley to rejoin them and to make her formal entrance into London society. At her first ball at Lansdowne House, she met Sir Alexander Duff-Gordon, a clerk in the Treasury, and the two fell in love. Alexander's mother, the Dowager Lady Duff-Gordon, at first opposed the union because

Lucie did not have a dowry, but Alexander was determined to marry Lucie. Despite the misgivings of the dowager, they were married on May 16, 1840, and settled in London, near the residence where Lucie Duff-Gordon had spent several years as a child.

Like her parents, Lucie Duff-Gordon and her husband had many friends, and their house at No. 8 Queen Square, Westminster, became a gathering place for men and women of letters, eminent foreign visitors, and politicians. They entertained Charles Dickens, William Thackeray, Macaulay, Charles Austin, Tom Taylor, and Alfred Tennyson, among others. In 1842, Lucie gave birth to a daughter, Janet, who would grow up among the intellectual giants that peopled the Duff-Gordons' salon.

I am fully convinced that custom and education are the only real difference between one set of men and another; their inner nature is the same the world over.

—Lucie Duff-Gordon

Despite her apparently conventional life, Duff-Gordon was well-known among her acquaintances for her rejection of many Victorian mores. She smoked cigars when she went riding because they suppressed the racking coughs caused by consumption. In 1845, she defied conventions by taking in a homeless 12-year-old Nubian boy named Hassan el Bakkeet, whom she affectionately called Hatty. Hatty performed household chores, but he was less a servant than a cherished member of the family. A number of Duff-Gordon's friends expressed horror that she allowed Hatty to interact freely with their young child, but Duff-Gordon trusted Hatty completely, and he remained with the family until he died of lung congestion in 1850. In her memoirs, Duff-Gordon's daughter Janet described Hatty as her "beloved playfellow." As with her religious conversion, Duff-Gordon's forceful personality eventually either won over or silenced her critics.

Like her mother, Lucie Duff-Gordon devoted a great deal of her time and intellectual energy to translation work. She had learned German in the 1820s when she traveled with her parents to Bonn, and she was also fluent in French. Her first translation was Barthold Niebuhr's 1839 book on Greek mythology, and she produced a substantial body of translations over the next 20 years. Duff-Gordon's translations were nearly all works of history; she rarely chose to translate fiction. In 1927, J.W. Mackail, writing of Duff-Gordon's translation of Wilhelm Meinhold's *Mary Schweidler: The Amber Witch*, said that "it is of its kind a masterpiece." Duff-Gordon "achieved a rarity, a translation equal, and in some respects superior, to the original."

Those who knew Duff-Gordon were impressed not only with her intellectual abilities but also with her sympathetic nature and the natural empathy she extended to those outside her own social class. Through her friend William Bridges Adams, she met working men from London. At this time the Chartists, a British working-class movement, were demanding reforms such as universal male suffrage and the abolition of property requirements for membership in the House of Commons. In the tense atmosphere of 1848, with revolution spreading across Europe, militant Chartists threatened insurrection. Legend has it that when the Chartists marched on London in 1848, throwing much of the citizenry into a panic, nearly 40 men from the workshops came to Lady Duff-Gordon's house to ensure the safety of "their lady." The Duff-Gordon household also served for a brief time as an asylum for French Prime Minster François Guizot, a fugitive from France after the overthrow of King Louis Philippe in 1848. In 1850, when the family was living in Weybridge, Duff-Gordon established and superintended a library and reading room for workers.

In 1849, Lucie Duff-Gordon gave birth to son Maurice and soon after endured a debilitating battle with consumption. Her health was so poor that the family left the damp climate of London to stay with Lucie's parents in their cottage at Weybridge, where Lucie nearly died of bronchitis and fever. In a letter to a friend, she warned that "I fear you would think me very much altered since my illness; I have lost much of my hair, all my complexion and all my flesh look thin and old and my hair is growing grey." At the time, Duff-Gordon was just 30 years old. During the next few years, her symptoms became worse, and she found it increasingly difficult to recover from her attacks. In 1858, she gave birth to another daughter, Urania, who was called Rainie. In 1859, after the death of her father, Duff-Gordon suffered another severe attack of bronchitis. Two harsh winters passed with little improvement in her health, and, on the advice of her physician, in July 1861 Duff-Gordon set sail for the healthier climate of the Cape of Good Hope in South Africa. She stayed just over a year. The many letters documenting her experiences at the Cape would be published as part of a larger work called *Vacation Tourist* in 1864.

In 1862, Duff-Gordon moved on from the Cape to Egypt in search of even warmer temperatures and the dry air that relieved her racking cough. She settled in Luxor, described by one visitor as a "ramshackle village," where she lived in a house built over an ancient Egyptian temple. As when she lived in South Africa, Duff-Gordon maintained a prolific correspondence with her family and friends. In her letters, she described the plight of the Egyptian peasants at the time of the Khedive Ismail government, prior to the occupation of Egypt by the British.

During the 1850s and 1860s, Egypt was still formally a part of the Ottoman Empire. It was, however, virtually independent politically and becoming increasingly Western economically. Indeed, these decades saw rapid changes in Egypt as the *khedive* (the Ottoman word for viceroy) pursued Western-style reforms. Although Egypt would not officially become part of the British Empire until 1882, the transition to that state was well underway by the time Duff-Gordon moved there in 1862.

Egypt in the 1860s was a ripe target for imperial ambitions in Europe due to both its agricultural wealth and its strategic location. Economically, Egypt's wheat and cotton exports ushered the country into the British system of international trade. During the American Civil War, cotton export earnings in Egypt skyrocketed. The result was a surge of foreign businessmen and adventurers eager to extend credit to the Khedive Ismail and his government. The khedive eagerly accepted credit from the Europeans, pursuing ambitious projects intended to make Egypt into a modern imperial power. The government quickly built up an enormous debt, which by the 1870s would overcome the khedive's government. By 1882, the British ruled Egypt.

Lucie Duff-Gordon settled in Egypt in the midst of this great transition. She was known there as *Sitt el Kebeer*, the Great Lady, by the Egyptian peasants, who were called the *fellaheen*. From the beginning, she was highly critical of Khedive Ismail's government. According to speculation, Duff-Gordon's critical assessments of the Ismail government were threatening enough to cause her to be watched by Ismail's spies, and many of her letters were probably tampered with or deliberately "lost" in the mails. In letters to her husband, Duff-Gordon frequently encouraged him to make public the information she was sending him, even though it did at times contradict the official pronouncements of the British Consulate. A letter from Duff-Gordon dated May 21, 1863, revealed her loyalties:

You know that I don't see things quite as our countrymen generally do, for mine is another *standpunkt,* and my heart is with the Arabs. I care less about opening up trade with the Sudan, or about all the new railways, and I should like to see person and property safe, which no one's is here—Europeans, of course, excepted.

Two years later, in 1865, Duff-Gordon decried the "system of wholesale extortion and spoilation" that had turned Egypt into "one vast plantation where the master works his slaves without even feeding them."

Although Duff-Gordon gave considerable attention to the political activities of Europeans in Egypt, her letters also contain extensive discussions of the region's culture. She wrote knowledgeably about a broad array of subjects, including Arab architecture and Arab art, bringing to all of her descriptions the enthusiasm of a student and the acute insights of a foreigner with a deep appreciation for other cultures. One of her biographers noted that she "countered a widely held belief that Middle Eastern government was especially despotic with arguments that 'social equality' existed to a greater degree in the Levant than elsewhere." Duff-Gordon's insight was especially interesting on the subject of religion. She commented on more than one occasion that she found her Arab acquaintances more tolerant on religious questions than her "enlightened" Protestant and Roman Catholic friends in Britain. "Why do the English talk of the beautiful sentiment of the Bible," she asked in 1865, "and when they come and see the same life before them, they ridicule it?" Duff-Gordon had a rare sense of Egypt's rich and complex culture.

Tragically, Duff-Gordon's life was cut short by the consumption that had plagued her since her teenage years. In her recollections of her mother, Janet Duff-Gordon Ross noted that four of Duff-Gordon's schoolmates at Bromley Common also died of consumption at a young age. On July 14, 1869, Duff-Gordon died and was buried in Cairo at the city's English cemetery. Shortly after her death, Duff-Gordon's friend *Caroline Norton described her in an article in *Macmillan's Magazine* as "a great reader, a great thinker, very original in her conclusions, very eager in impressing her opinions." Norton concluded that "perhaps no other woman of our time . . . combined so much erudition with so much natural ability."

Duff-Gordon's literary reputation rests on the *Letters from Egypt* and *Last Letters From Egypt*, which had a wide circulation in Europe.

Most critics consider the two compilations her most interesting work. Although she is usually called a travel writer, this label is misleading. Her contributions went far beyond simply the description of her exotic surroundings. Through her eyes, the reader of her letters comes to know and respect the people of Egypt for their art, their architecture, and their political and cultural systems. Duff-Gordon, the *Sitt el Kebeer*, became a part of Egypt. She knew that "to most Europeans, the people are not real people but part of the scenery" and in her work she tried to dispel this attitude. Her enthusiasm for Middle Eastern life comes through in her work as clearly as does her disapproval of the European prejudice against other races.

Through her letters, Duff-Gordon was an insightful student of human nature and a sympathetic chronicler of people and places that most of her readers would never see. In all of her encounters with foreign peoples, Duff-Gordon was open-minded and generous, and this approach, more than anything else, made her both a discerning travel writer and, in this era of imperialism, an anomaly. Her biographer Gordon Waterfield suggested that Duff-Gordon had a quality, "an attitude of life, which makes her a member of the twentieth rather than of the nineteenth century." Surely this is one of the highest compliments a progressive and intelligent woman like Lady Lucie Duff-Gordon would wish to receive.

SOURCES:

"Lady Lucie Duff-Gordon" in *The Oxford Guide to British Women Writers*. Edited by Joanne Shattock, ed. Oxford: Oxford University Press, 1993.

"Lady Lucie Duff-Gordon," in *British Women Writers: A Critical Reference Guide*. Edited by Janet Todd. NY: Frederick Ungar,

Waterfield, Gordon. *Lucie Duff-Gordon in England, South Africa and Egypt*. NY: E.P. Dutton, 1937.

SUGGESTED READING:

Duff-Gordon, Lucie. *Last Letters From Egypt*. London: Macmillan, 1875.

Ross, Janet. *Three Generations of English Women: Memoirs and Correspondence of Susannah Taylor, Sarah Austin, and Lady Duff-Gordon*. London: T. Fisher Unwin, 1893.

Christine Stolba, Ph.D. candidate in American history, Emory University, Atlanta, Georgia

$\mathcal{L}$ucy $\mathcal{D}$uff $\mathcal{G}$ordon (1862–1935)

Duff Gordon, Lucy (1862–1935)

*English-born fashion and theatrical costume designer whose clothes were highly popular in London high society during the period from 1890 through World War I. Born Lucille Sutherland in London, England, in 1862; died of cancer in a nursing home in Putney, England, in April 1935; eldest of two daughters of Douglas Sutherland (an engineer) and Lucy (Saunders) Sutherland; sister of writer *Elinor Glyn (1864–1943); educated at a Canadian grade school and by governesses; married James Wallace (a wine merchant), on September 15, 1884 (divorced 1888); married Sir Cosmo Duff Gordon, May 24, 1900 (d. 1931); children: (first marriage) daughter Esme (who married Anthony Giffard, viscount Tiverton).*

Lucy Duff Gordon gained fame by designing "personality" dresses for wealthy women in London during the 1890s; as a result, she opened The Maison Lucille in London in 1898, and branches, known as Lucille Ltd., were established in Paris, New York, and Chicago, employing such designers as Robert Kalloch, **Shirley Barker**, Howard Greer, and Gilbert Clark. Among Duff Gordon's customers was the duchess of York, later Queen *Mary of Teck. Duff Gordon began a career as a stage designer with costumes for the London production of

The Merry Widow in 1907. One of her designs for the operetta would be copied and worn by actress **Audrey Hepburn* in the motion-picture version of *My Fair Lady*.

Along with her husband Sir Cosmo Duff Gordon, Lucy survived the *Titanic* disaster in 1912 but barely survived its aftermath. As she watched the ship slowly sink beneath the frigid waters, she had turned to her secretary aboard the half-filled lifeboat No. 1 and observed, "There is your beautiful nightdress gone." Tabloids reported this and also accused the Duff Gordons of paying mariners to row away from the scene. In May 1912, a British inquest cleared them of all charges; in actuality, Cosmo had given the mariners money to replace their lost belongings, but the damage to their reputation had been done.

Lucy began her career as a fashion journalist in 1915 and designing costumes for the *Ziegfeld Follies* in 1916. In 1917, Duff Gordon opened a mail-order dress business that was advertised in the Sears Roebuck catalog. Her film design credits include *The Misleading Lady: The Strange Case of Mary Page* (1916), *Virtuous Wives* (1920), *Way Down East* (1921), and *Heedless Moths*. Lady Lucy Duff Gordon is often confused with Lady **Lucie Duff-Gordon* (1821–1869).

Niles Holt,
Normal, Illinois

Dufferin, countess of.
See Blackwood, Helen Selina (1807–1867).

Dufferin, Helen Selina.
See Blackwood, Helen Selina.

Dufferin, Lady (1807–1867).
See Blackwood, Helen Selina.

Dufferin, Lady (fl. 1845–1891).
See Blackwood, Helen Selina for sidebar on Hariot Blackwood.

du Guillet, Pernette (c. 1523–1545).
See Labé, Louise for sidebar.

Duiveke (c. 1491–1517).
See Willums, Sigbrit for sidebar.

Dukas.
Variant of Ducas.

Dulac, Germaine (1882–1942)
French feminist journalist and pioneering director-producer whose silent films and theoretical writings were seminal in early avant-garde cinema. Name

Germaine
Dulac

variations: Charlotte Elisabeth Germaine Dulac. Pronunciation: zher-MEN du-LOCK. Born Charlotte Elisabeth Germaine Saisset-Schneider on November 17, 1882, in Amiens, France; died in July 1942, in Paris; daughter of cavalry Captain Pierre-Maurice Saisset-Schneider and Madeleine-Claire Waymel; married Marie-Louis Albert Dulac (a novelist), in 1905 (divorced 1920).

First worked as a journalist (1909–13), then turned to cinema; directed 26 films (1915–29), supervising the production of two more; produced and directed newsreels (1929–40); named an officer of the Legion of Honor.

Filmography as director: Les Soeurs ennemis (1915); Geo le mystérieux (1916); Vénus victrix (1916); Dans l'ouragan de la vie (1916); Ames de fous (1917); Le Bonheur des autres (1918); La Fête espagñole (1919); La Cigarette (1919); Malencontre (1920); La Belle Dame sans merci (1920); La Mort du soleil (1921); Werther (unfinished; 1922); La Souriante Madame Beudet (1923); Gossette (1923); Le Diable dans la ville (1924); Ame d'artiste (1925); La Folie des vaillants (1925); Antoinette Sabrier (1926); La Coquille et le clergyman (1927); L'Invitation au voyage (1927); Le Cinéma au service de l'histoire (1927); La Princesse Mandane (1928); Disque 927 (1928); Thèmes et variations (1928); Germination d'un haricot (1928); Etude cinématographique sur une arabesque (1929). Films supervised: Mon Paris (1928); Le Picador (1932).

Cinema historian Charles Ford maintained that "Germaine Dulac . . . must be considered the first among a leading group of theorists who largely defined the essence, and specified the means and limits, of the silent film." Indeed, her preeminent position in the early history of European cinema appears unassailed. Along with her countrywoman *Alice Guy-Blaché, she was only the second woman film director, an exceedingly rare vocation for the time, particularly for her gender. She was also the first to make a personal imprint on the medium, given her key position in the impressionistic school of cinematography. Her decisive role stemmed not only from her writings and films within the French avant-garde, especially during the 1930s and early 1940s, when she functioned as a major cinema critic and theorist in the area of film esthetics, but also from her untiring efforts, as president of the Fédération des Ciné-Clubs de France, to popularize the new medium. During the height of her productive period, from 1920 to 1929, Dulac directed at least one film per year, later turning to the production of newsreels. Very little in her background would have suggested such an exotic career.

𝓘f I didn't make films, I would go into politics. Yes, I have become even more feminist since the last elections, since I saw the famous posters, you know the ones, where France, Serbia, and Romania are colored black, as the only countries where we don't vote. Women must vote. Write that.

—Germaine Dulac, in *Ciné-Miroir* (1925)

Germaine Dulac was born on November 17, 1882, at 16, rue Dufour, in the northern French town of Amiens, known for its important banking center and its beautiful 13th-century Gothic cathedral. The period was one of intense nationalism and of international rivalry propelled forward on the wings of colonial aspirations, engendered by the doctrine of social Darwinism and the "New Imperialism." All through the 1880s and 1890s, France acquired colony after colony in Africa and Southeast Asia, founding a new empire to rival that of her arch-foe, Britain. In Europe, her shameful loss of Alsace-Lorraine to Germany, in 1871, still smarted, and many looked forward to revenge. On the home front, the country prospered as its economy expanded under the impact of the second industrial revolution, while politically, the nation became fragmented by a polarization of the major parties, and a rising socialist force. Such was the climate of Germaine Dulac's France.

Germaine's mother **Madeleine-Claire Waymel** stemmed from a middle-class family, composed mainly of career soldiers and industrialists. The career of her father, Pierre-Maurice Saisset-Schneider, as a captain of cavalry in the Second Army Corps largely determined the restless nature of her childhood, with its constant moving about. Typically, six months out of the year were spent in Paris, the rest either in Saint-Étienne or Compiègne (site of the 1918 armistice and the 1940 French capitulation to Germany), where Captain Saisset-Schneider served in garrison. This could not fail to create problems for Germaine's education, since she yearned to pursue serious studies and cultivate herself in the process. Finally, a solution was found, and Germaine moved to Paris permanently, where she lived with her grandmother in the rue Taitbout, subsequently devoting most of her time to the study of art, song, and music—especially Wagnerian opera—and, of course, photography. The artistic nature of her studies, in particular her love of music (Dulac was a gifted musician), were to have a profound influence on her later choice of themes, style as director, and theory of cinema.

In 1905, Germaine Saisset-Schneider married **Marie-Louis Albert Dulac**, whom sources variously describe as an agricultural engineer, novelist, or "littérateur." Immediately manifesting her later well-known independent spirit, she embarked on a career in journalism. By 1920, her marriage had ended in divorce.

Dulac began working for the feminist newspaper *La Française* in 1909, first as a journalist, later as an editor, staying on until 1913. Initially doing biographical sketches and writing up interviews with famous women, one of her first assignments was to interrogate the fashionable poet and "Muse of the Republic," the beautiful and aristocratic *Anna de Noailles. Once at the door of the countess' fashionable townhouse, however, Dulac panicked and interviewed Noailles' *valet de chambre* instead. Soon thereafter, she turned her talents towards theatrical criticism. This naturally increased her interest in cinema, for many stars of the stage, several of whom she had previously interviewed, were also making their debut on the silver screen. The analytical experience gained at this task, and contacts made within the acting community, were to prove valuable in her later career in cinema. During this period, Dulac, by now a militant suffragist, also occasionally contributed to another feminist newspaper, *Marguerite Durand's *La Fronde*.

The year 1914 not only marked a watershed for a whole generation of Europeans but was a turning-point in Dulac's career as well, for it was then that her actress friend **Stacia Napierkowska** introduced Dulac to the rudiments of filmmaking. Napierkowska invited her friend along to Rome to assist in the filming of *Caligula* for Film d'Art, an important debt Dulac later acknowledged.

Dulac's first film, *Les Soeurs ennemis,* was completed in 1915 and marked the debut of her commercial period, lasting until 1920. She herself was not happy with the results of her first directing efforts, later asserting she had "massacred" the talent of her female protagonist, *Suzanne Desprès. While her next three films, *Geo le mystérieux* (with **Jeanne Marken**), *Vénus victrix,* and *Dans l'ouragan de la vie* (starring her friend Napierkowska) attempted to walk the line between artistry and commercialism, *Ames de Fous* (1917) marked an important stage in the development of Dulac's style and theory. In the course of making this film, she realized that *atmosphere,* as against plain facts and action, was a most critical component for the emotional expression of cinema, and that the right atmosphere could be generated by using various techniques such as lighting, camera position, and editing—which she considered capital elements more important than the classical dramaturgical guidelines of theater. Charles Ford termed this appreciation a "lucid and intelligent view, rarely encountered during this period."

Louis Delluc, the leading film critic and avant-garde filmmaker who guided French cinema away from its prewar commercialism into the realm of art, wrote the script for *La Fête espagñole,* released in 1919, probably Dulac's best-known film. According to Jean Mitry, the film marked a major turning point in the history of French cinema. Whereas previous movies had always been adaptations of books or plays, this was the first film "thought in images" and based on a script conceived expressly for the medium. While critics praised the directing and screenplay, neither Dulac nor Delluc were completely satisfied with the results, since they had been unable to film completely on locale in Spain and had substituted with the French Riviera.

In December 1915, Dulac had founded her own film production company, "D.H.," or "Delia," in association with **Irène Hillel-Erlanger,** her first screenwriter. Dulac's husband had put up the initial capital of 12,000 francs and took over the administrative direction. The company was run on a shoestring budget, so that Dulac was sometimes forced to accept less than ideal scripts. With this company, she produced *La Fête espagñole, La Cigarette, Malencontre,* and *La Belle Dame sans merci.* According to Georges Sadoul—echoing the contemporary judgment of Delluc—the last of the series of films is a fine example of Dulac's work; she was "herself," not making commercialistic sacrifices to current infatuations of either the Latin or the American public. The latter, she had occasion to observe first hand in 1921, on a trip to the California movie studios to study the production methods pioneered by the American director-producer David Wark Griffith. In fact, she was not seldom disappointed and embittered by the artistic constraints placed on her work by commercial considerations. Although she dreamed of a commercial blockbuster that would buy her her artistic freedom, that blockbuster sadly never came.

Dulac's next film, *La Mort du soleil,* vigorously asserted her personal esthetics of cinema. She later claimed that it had "realized not a few of my ideas. I began to utilize what I will call technical acrobatics, since I believed that certain devices had a suggestive value equivalent to musical notes." The film itself was given only a tepid welcome by the public, who failed to appreciate her technique of psychological commentary on the state of mind of the protagonist, a scholar paralyzed by a cerebral congestion, and many movie houses simply cut out the offending sequence. Furthermore, Dulac's brilliance as a director was muted by the mediocrity of the script. In any event, the films between *La Fête espagñole* and *La Souriante Madame Beudet,* her next work, contributed significantly to the refinement of her technique as well as to her understanding of the importance of the actor's psychology.

In November 1923, *La Souriante Madame Beudet,* Dulac's 12th and most famous film outside of France, opened in Paris. The film, considered her masterpiece, was based on a drama by André Obey and Denys Amiel and starred **Germaine Dermoz,** Arquillères and **Madeleine Guitty.** Obey's drama was particularly suited to an interpretation by Dulac because Obey, himself, had developed a theory of "silent theater," in which silence replaced dialogue and the thoughts of the actors replaced their words. Dulac subscribed to a similar theory in cinema; Sadoul characterized the film as one with "no action, or little: the life of a soul." It also very much suited Dulac's temperament and feminist persuasion, for the script revolved around the Bovaryistic fantasies of a bored provincial housewife married to a rather coarse petit-bourgeois merchant. The film focuses on the atmosphere and psychology of domestic conflict, which Dulac conveyed using all the contemporary technical and pictorial devices available. Standish Lawder noted one fine example of her technical prowess in the film: "an ingenious shot into a three-way dressing-table mirror beautifully catches the anguished introspection of a woman contemplating the murder of her husband." *La Souriante Madame Beudet* is not only a work of art, but also a historical document, a commentary on contemporary middle-class mores and the condition of women at the beginning of the 20th century. According to William Van Wert, Madame Beudet is depicted as "nothing more than a showpiece for her husband. . . . She is a victim, without future, without escape." The film also marked an important turning point in the evolution of Dulac's work, which had now clearly entered into the avant-garde, which she defined as:

Germaine Dermoz in Madame Beudet, *directed by Germaine Dulac.*

> every film in which the technique, utilized with the purpose of a new expression of image and sound, breaks with the established traditions, to seek out, in the visual and auditory domains, new pathetic chords. The avant-garde film does not address itself to the simple pleasure of the crowd. It is . . .

egoistic, because [it is] the personal manifestation of a pure thought; altruistic, because [it is] disengaged from every care other than the desire for progress.

The second phase of her career in cinema had begun, and one of its characteristics was to be a willingness to compromise her avant-garde vision with hard commercial realities.

Dulac made her next film in 1923. *Gossette* was a serialized murder mystery in six episodes for Film d'Art, a purely commercial company. Though given a warm reception by contemporary critics for its superior technical production, she saw it as a compromise between cinema as art and cinema as a commercial operation. Indeed, it indicated a willingness to sacrifice some of her artistic ideals, both to popularize the avant-garde and because of her straitened financial situation. *Le Diable dans la Ville,* a medieval tale of how superstition takes hold of a whole village, soon followed. The film is notable as another example of Dulac's pioneering role in the use of new camera techniques, and Ford ob-

served that critics received it as the "conscientious work of a woman of taste."

Her next film, *Ame d'artiste,* was another financial compromise, in which Dulac agreed to work for the Franco-German film consortium run by Russian emigrants, Ciné-France-West. She directed the film, featuring **Yvette Andreyor**, **Gina Manès**, Charles Vanel, **Mabel Poulton** and Nikolas Koline, in collaboration with Alexander Wolkoff. The piece was distinctly cosmopolitan, both in style and acting (the actors were French, English, Russian, and Serbian), and with its fabulous sets was considered a European super-production to rival Cecil B. De Mille's dazzling Hollywood extravaganzas. Still, the film knew no great commercial success.

With *Antoinette Sabrier*—the story of an industrialist torn between his wife and a younger woman—directed for Paramount, Dulac finally produced a highly successful exercise in combining the demands of an artistic aesthetic with a certain popular commercialism, and the film was even praised for its profound psychology, very much in the spirit of the avant-garde cinema.

Her next film, *La Coquille et le Clergyman* (1927), is now generally considered by cinema critics and historians to be the first Surrealist film, though it was not accepted as such by Surrealists of the 1920s. The film was certainly her most controversial, and perhaps misunderstood, work. In fact, Antonin Artaud, the Surrealist actor-writer who wrote the script, allegedly rejected Dulac's film as a "perversion" of his scenario, while other contemporary Surrealists equally denounced it. Van Wert's discussion of male-dominated Surrealist cinema themes, with their prevailing exaltation of aggressive male sexual fantasies and stereotypical women, frequently portrayed as either "castrating mothers or mindless nymphomaniacs," suggest that it was Dulac's departure from such images that earned her the criticism of having "feminized" the original script. The actual artistic relationship between Artaud and Dulac, however, is still debated. Lawder reported that in 1929 even the British Board of Film Censors rejected the film, stating that it was "so cryptic as to be almost meaningless. If there is a meaning, it is doubtless objectionable." Be that as it may, *La Coquille et le Clergyman* was a tour-de-force of Dulac's cinematographic technique. Writes Lawder:

> The film is a veritable catalogue of avant-garde camera tricks, ranging from weirdly elongated images of the sexually frustrated clergyman moving in slow-motion, to shots of his hands grasping at the mirage of a

lovely lady's bare neck, to an almost painfully literal description of a split-personality neurotic, his head dividing in two.

Dulac's next few films, particularly *L'Invitation au Voyage* (inspired by the French Symbolist poet Baudelaire) and *La Princesse Mandane,* can best be described as attempts at realizing her vision of "pure cinema," or, as she described it, "a cinema free from literary subjects, and whose only subject would be lines and volumes"; ideally, this should be a cinema composed according to the rules of a "visual music." She in fact often felt stifled by the contemporary aesthetic of cinema that required films to be based on known literature or theater, and summed up her own aesthetic in 1925 in a well-known comment on the theory of cinema:

> The integral film that we dream of composing is a visual symphony made up of rhythmic images coordinated and projected on the screen solely by the feelings of an artist. A musician does not always compose under the inspiration of a story, but most frequently when inspired by a feeling.

Dulac's efforts at creating "pure" or "integral" cinema are best exemplified in her three last films as director, notably *Disque 957* (an illustration of Chopin's work), *Thèmes et Variations* (inspired by classical melodies) and *Etude cinématographique sur une arabesque* (a cinematic evocation of a Debussy partition). All of these attempted a rhythmic visualization of music. In the latter film, she used a honeycombed mirror as a device to create multiple but identical images as a visual rendering of repeated musical notes; to underscore her didactical intentions, she cut in literal images of hands playing the piano.

In 1928–29, serious health problems, and the advent of the "talkies" with their new technology and esthetics that so troubled Dulac in her conception of cinema, put an end to the second phase of her career. She could not adapt to the changed medium, rejecting sound cinema on aesthetic grounds. This watershed ushered in the third phase of Dulac's career. Combining her experience in journalism with her cinematographic expertise, she turned to newsreels, directing first for the Société Pathé-Journal and then for Gaumont, until 1940. Dulac also directed her own newsreel production company, France-Actualités, which produced a weekly newsmagazine of world events, until 1935.

Dulac made a great impact both as a popularizer and a theoretician. As early as 1922, she was elected secretary of the Ciné-Club de France, later becoming president of the Fédération des Ciné-Clubs. Subsequently, she traveled widely in France, Belgium, Switzerland, Spain, and Holland, explaining the new medium. A short documentary she made at about the same time is noteworthy because it became something of a trademark during her many speaking tours. *Germination d'un haricot* pioneered the use of time-lapse cinematography and depicted the growth of a tiny bean sprout pushing through the soil and unfolding its leaves. Ford reported that when she showed it as illustrative material at one of the many lectures given in Paris at the Vieux-Colombier, Colisée, Musée Galliéra, or Club du Faubourg, her admirers would jokingly quip, "Here comes Germaine Dulac with her beanstalk again!"

Dulac was also president of the Cinema Commission of the International Council of Women and treasurer of the Association of Film Authors. Her theoretical writings had a major impact on contemporary and later European filmmakers, notably in France, Russia, Poland and Italy, and she always militantly promoted the idea of cinema as art, sometimes incurring the enmity of those who saw this as a strict condemnation of commercial cinema. She clearly understood that a major difference between cinema and literature, or painting, was the necessity of the author to solicit major capital funding with a studio; it was a fact that the multiple consumption of the final product did sometimes necessitate certain artistic and aesthetic compromises. To make her views known, she published numerous articles on film theory and criticism in contemporary trade journals, including *Le Film, Cinémagazine, Cinéa-Ciné pour tous, Schémas, l'Art cinématographique*, and *Le Rouge et le noir*. With the Nazi occupation of France in 1940, and the censorship imposed by the *Propagandastaffel*, Dulac was forced to stop all professional activity.

A staunch feminist, Dulac battled mightily against the gender prejudices of her day in society at large. Delluc lavished praise on her first film, asserting that she was worth "more than a dozen of each of her colleagues. . . . But the cinema is full of people . . . who cannot forgive her for being an educated woman . . . or for being a woman at all." Yet Dulac was made an officer of the Legion of Honor, a particularly striking attainment for a woman of her era. She died in the last days of July 1942, following a grave illness that had sapped her energy for some years.

While a final appraisal of Germaine Dulac's life and work is still restricted by the lack of a definitive scholarly biography, Charles Ford's verdict can be considered representative of contemporary academic opinion: "Tenacious, conscientious, efficient in her work as director; ardent, passionate, revolutionary in her mission as the apostle of a new art; she fought valiantly for the 'pure cinema.' . . . Convinced feminist, seduced by the socialist doctrine, [she was also] a woman of letters enamored of the theater and of music."

SOURCES:

Bawden, Liz-Anne. *The Oxford Companion to Film*. London: Oxford University Press, 1976.

Boussinot, Roger, ed. *L'Encyclopédie du Cinéma*. 3rd ed. Vol 1. Paris: Bordas, 1989.

Ford, Charles. "Germaine Dulac," in *Anthologie du Cinéma*. Vol. 4. Paris: L'Avant-Scène, 1968.

Lawder, Standish D. *The Cubist Cinema*. NY: New York University Press, 1975.

Mitry, Jean. *Histoire du cinéma: Art et Industrie, 1915–1925*. Vol. 2. Paris: Encyclopédie universitaire, 1969.

Sadoul, Georges. *Histoire Général du Cinéma: L'Art muet 1919–1929: L'Après-Guerre en Europe*. Vol. 1. Paris: Denoël, 1975.

Thomas, Nicholas, ed. *International Dictionary of Films and Filmmakers. Vol. 2. Directors*. 2nd ed. Chicago: St. James Press, 1991.

Van Wert, William. "Germaine Dulac: First Feminist Filmmaker," in Karin Kay and Gerald Peary, eds. *Women and the Cinema: A Critical Anthology*. NY: E.P. Dutton, 1977, pp. 213–223.

SUGGESTED READING:

Ciné-Magazine. February 24, 1922; September 1927.

William L. Chew III, Professor of History, Vesalius College, Vrije Universiteit Brussel, Brussels, Belgium

Dulce.

Variant of Douce.

Dulce of Aragon.

See Douce of Aragon.

Dulcia.

Variant of Douce.

Dulles, Eleanor Lansing

(1895–1996)

American economic expert, diplomat, and author who was a major figure in the postwar economic reconstruction of Germany and whose distinguished family included three secretaries of state and a noted director of the CIA. Name variations: known as "the Mother of West Berlin." Born on June 1, 1895, in Watertown, New York; died in Washington, D.C., on October 30, 1996; daughter of Allen Macy Dulles (a Presbyterian minister) and Edith (Foster) Dulles; sister of John Foster Dulles (secretary of state), Allen Welsh Dulles (director of the Central Intelligence Agency),

Margaret Dulles, and Nataline Dulles; married David Simon Blondheim; children: David Blondheim; (adopted) Ann Blondheim.

Born into a noted family of the American WASP "ruling class," Eleanor Dulles took full advantage of the opportunities afforded her. Drawn to learning from an early age, she earned a doctorate and became a highly regarded expert on international economic issues. She was a major personality on the Washington landscape for more than half a century, always ready to share her rich knowledge of the world with friends or strangers. She played a significant role in the post-1945 economic reconstruction of West Germany and West Berlin, earning accolades as an achiever as well as a theorist in one of the greatest successes of the Cold War. Her strong personality and candor did not always serve to advance her career, but throughout her life she found telling the truth as she saw it preferable to merely sitting quietly while those she considered to be fools—almost invariably males with power—spouted nonsense. In essence, Eleanor Lansing Dulles was a remarkable human being, an American original.

Born three years before the Spanish-American war, Eleanor Lansing Dulles was less than six when the 20th century dawned in January 1901. "I remember vaguely another century," she recalled in her memoirs; "and in 1901 I was standing in the dimly lit hall of my grandfather's house at 1405 Eye Street in Washington when the telegraph boy brought the cablegram that announced the death of Queen Victoria." Eleanor grew up in an extended family that took its leading role for granted. Her father Allen Macy Dulles was a highly respected Presbyterian minister while her mother **Edith Foster Dulles** could boast of a father, John Watson Foster, who had fought in the Civil War and had a distinguished diplomatic career as the chief U.S. diplomatic representative in Mexico, Spain, and Russia, eventually achieving the post of secretary of state in the administration of Benjamin Harrison. Besides grandfather Foster, Eleanor could also point proudly to another diplomat on

Eleanor Lansing Dulles

her father's side of the family: grandfather John Welsh Dulles, who served as envoy to Great Britain during the presidency of Rutherford B. Hayes. With her extended family a part of America's Establishment, young Eleanor was an eyewitness to a good deal of contemporary history; more than seven decades later she could recall being present at the inauguration of William Howard Taft in March 1909, when the new chief executive rode in an open carriage and Washington experienced a late snowfall.

Eleanor's family, while not wealthy, was financially quite comfortable with enough resources on hand to live a pleasantly leisured life that included a summer home at Henderson Harbor by Lake Ontario. Both her parents had enjoyed tours of lands that were then distant and exotic. Despite or perhaps because of her bad eyesight, young Eleanor was drawn to books at a very early age: "I did my first traveling in books, devouring Henry M. Stanley's *Through Darkest Africa*, Dr. Fridtjof Nansen's *Farthest North*, a book about 'Hidden Shensi' in China, and several on Tibet and India." The habit of intensive reading, which remained with Dulles the rest of her life, prepared her for successful years in college. Books and libraries were simply part of "the excitement of the quest for knowledge." She enrolled at Bryn Mawr in September 1913, graduating with a degree in social science in 1917.

By that time, America was at war. Her family was closely linked to the conflict, with her uncle Robert Lansing serving as President Woodrow Wilson's secretary of state. Despite her youth and gender, Eleanor very much wanted to be "part of the action" and soon found her role in relief work. She went to Paris, first working for Shurtleff Memorial Relief and then the American Friends Service Committee, helping with refugee rehabilitation and, after the armistice was signed, with reconstruction projects. By the end of 1919, she was once again thinking about her academic career, so she enrolled at the University of London's renowned London School of Economics. Still convinced European studies were useful to her, in 1921–22 Dulles took courses at the Sorbonne. Then, however, she returned to America for a radical change of pace. She took odd jobs in the real world including running a punch press at the American Tube and Stamping Company in Bridgeport, Connecticut, and working as a payroll clerk for a hair-net company in Long Island City, Queens.

Soon Eleanor Dulles was back in college, enrolled at Radcliffe where she was awarded a master's degree in 1924. Her extensive travels and study in Europe, including her investigations of industrial methods in 75 British firms, served her well during this phase of her career, for she was able to complete her doctoral work at Harvard University, receiving her Ph.D. in 1926. Her dissertation, published in 1929 as *The French Franc, 1914–1928: The Facts and Their Interpretation,* was a superbly researched and strongly argued investigation of a major currency and its problems with inflationary pressures. Excellent reviews buoyed Dulles' spirits but the most encouraging gesture from the world of professional economists was a letter she received from leading economic theorist John Maynard Keynes, who wrote, "Congratulations, Yours is the best book on monetary inflation that I know."

A solid teaching career now began, first at Simmons College in Boston, then at Bryn Mawr, and finally at the University of Pennsylvania. A number of important books were published during these years, including studies of the French Franc, the Bank for International Settlements, and the evolution of reparations ideas. During this period, Eleanor Dulles met and fell in love with David Blondheim, an Hebraic scholar. Hopes of marriage for the couple were negated by the attitudes of her parents and family, who did not approve of her marrying Blondheim. Raised as an Orthodox Jew, he was now estranged from both his faith and family but still deeply attached to Jewish cultural values. Their love for each other persisted, however, and their relationship continued until they were finally married in 1932. But while Eleanor and David were in many ways happy to be united, Blondheim's personal demons finally triumphed when she told him that she was pregnant with their child. The prospects of being father to a child of "mixed blood" was too much for Blondheim to bear. Never having recovered from his family's rejection, he committed suicide in September 1934. Eleanor gave birth to their son David within weeks of his death. Several years later, she adopted a daughter, Ann.

Eleanor Dulles responded to the death of her husband by reverting back to her maiden name and resuming her academic career. In 1936, she became chief of the finance division of the newly founded Social Security Board, quickly earning the respect of her colleagues. After Pearl Harbor, her latent international interests asserted themselves, so that in 1942 she joined the State Department as an economics expert, becoming one of a group of pioneering women in that venerable institution. Years later, she recalled the difficulties she encountered. One of her superiors told her he would not promote her because she was a woman, while another told her male assistant that he did not have to follow her instructions. In 1958, she noted that much of the wartime prejudice still remained and that "This place is a real man's world if ever there was one. It's riddled with prejudices. If you are a woman in Government service you just have to work 10 times as hard—and even then it takes much skill to paddle around the various taboos. But it is fun to see how far you can get in spite of being a woman."

Despite the press of work and meeting the needs of her children, Dulles was able to publish a book in 1944 on the Bank for International Settlements, her second on this subject. In 1944, Eleanor Dulles' talents were recognized when she served as a prominent member of the U.S. delegation to the Bretton Woods international monetary conference, which was held in New Hampshire to create a stable financial structure for the postwar world. Around the same time, she disagreed vehemently with her brother John Foster Dulles, who believed that defeated Germany should be harshly treated and even divided up among its neighbors. Eleanor felt strongly that this was a recipe for a future catastrophe and lobbied vigorously in the State Department for more realistic policies that would create the foundations for postwar social stability and a permanent reconstruction of Europe after the destruction of the Nazi Reich.

Allied victory in Europe saw Dulles posted in Vienna as the financial attaché of the State Department. The scholarly Miss Dulles, enjoying the rank of lieutenant colonel in the Four Power Occupying Garrison, exhibited a remarkable degree of down-to-earth pragmatism in a Vienna that was demoralized and in ruins. She helped to feed the starving Viennese population by arranging the barter of horses for German cabbages and potatoes. Rejecting the idea of imposing a harsh Carthaginian peace on defeated Germany, Dulles strongly opposed Directive 1067, which mandated policies leading to a "pastoralization" of the former Reich's economy. Such policies, she was convinced, were disastrously mistaken and would result in anarchy and a likely expansion of Soviet influence. After leaving Austria in 1948, Dulles returned to Washington and quickly took a role as a key policymaker on Germany in the State Department. In 1951, her expertise in this area received an official stamp of approval when she became special assistant to the Department's Office of German Affairs.

It was as an important figure in the Office of German Affairs that Eleanor Dulles was charged with the task of advising both the American occupying authorities and West German governments on the crucial matter of economic reconstruction. Her encyclopedic theoretical knowledge of international economics combined with her pragmatic assessments of day-to-day realities empowered Dulles to give advice that enabled the fledgling Federal Republic of Germany to revitalize its economy and drastically cut down a high level of unemployment. Recognizing the crucial strategic importance of West Berlin as a bastion of Western values within Soviet-occupied East Germany, she made many trips to the beleaguered city. Eleanor Dulles admired the courage of West Berliners and did her utmost to secure funds for the city's reconstruction, somehow always finding a few million extra dollars for the construction of schools, hospitals, and the modernistic Congress Hall, which some irreverent Berliners called the "Dulleseum" and "Frau Dulles' Hut" (Mrs. Dulles' Hat); others preferred to dub it "the pregnant oyster." Over the years, she earned the unofficial title of "Mother of West Berlin," which eventually led to official tokens of recognition including an honorary doctorate from the Free University of Berlin (1957), the Ernst Reuter Plaque (1959), and the Federal Republic of Germany's Grand Cross of Merit (1962).

In Washington, D.C., a city of rumors and ceaseless intrigues, a strong-willed and outspoken individual like Eleanor Dulles was bound to make enemies. In the State Department, a bastion of male chauvinism, she had many foes as well as admirers and allies. Further complicating the situation was the fact that the Republican victory of 1952 brought her two brothers to the very heart of national and world power. Older brother John Foster Dulles, a corporate attorney with longstanding international interests, became secretary of state while younger brother Allen Welsh Dulles became director of the Central Intelligence Agency. John Foster, fearing that three Dulleses in Washington was one too many and would lead to charges of nepotism, attempted to persuade his sister to quit her job. Even when he applied pressure, she refused to budge and was successful in holding on to her job, which she felt strongly she had earned though her own merit and whose responsibilities she had carried out with distinction for years before her brothers had ever arrived in Washington. In her memoirs, this refusal throughout her career to bow to pressure from her brothers is noted with considerable satisfaction: "In the search for useful work, I did not turn to my brothers or others in the family for help. I sought rather for the support of my professors and colleagues in finding academic or government jobs."

Starting in 1953, Eleanor Dulles' bungalow house in McLean, Virginia, often served as a pleasant meeting place for her and her brothers to socialize on weekends. At the back of the house was a swimming pool that drew both Allen and John Foster to their sister's home on Sundays. Sipping highballs, CIA Director Allen and Secretary of State John Foster would discuss various facets of international relations or Washington political intrigues with their well-informed and highly opinionated sister, she in her thick glasses and they, "two middle-aged Presbyterian gentlemen sporting baggy shorts and gaudy Hawaiian shirts." Foreign diplomats fortunate enough to receive invitations to Eleanor Dulles' pool parties throughout the 1950s could report back to their capitals that they had finally been able to gain access to the very nerve center of U.S. foreign policy.

By the early 1960s, with the Democratic victory of John F. Kennedy and the passage of time, it was clear that the end of the Dulles era in Washington was at hand. John Foster Dulles had died in 1959 and his posthumous reputation as a hardline Cold Warrior had become somewhat tarnished as the world became increasingly weary of the economic burdens and inherent risks of the Cold War. The world community now desired a drastic reduction of the tensions that could by accident or miscalculation trigger global annihilation through intercontinental nuclear missiles. Rightly or wrongly, the Dulles name was increasingly linked in the public mind to the most unstable and risk-filled period of the Cold War.

Eleanor's last major assignment, with the office of intelligence and research of the State Department, was to study its foreign aid programs. To carry out this task, she showed exceptional stamina by visiting 60 foreign nations throughout the world. The Bay of Pigs fiasco of 1961 which ended the CIA career of brother Allen was handwriting on the wall, and few were surprised in 1962 when Eleanor was fired from her State Department post. Refusing to succumb to depression over this sudden end of her career in government, she accepted an offer of a temporary professorship at Duke University, moving back to Washington in 1963 for a permanent academic post in the political science department of Georgetown University.

The idea of retirement meant little to Eleanor Dulles, who remained active into the tenth decade of her life despite poor eyesight, deafness, and a weak heart. She kept on writing, penning a candid autobiography that was published in 1980. An enthusiastic outdoorswoman since childhood, she continued to summer at the family lake property, in her mid-80s sailing *The Scud,* a 14-foot wooden centerboard sloop. In her memoirs, she noted approvingly that the responsive Ackroyd dinghy, given to her in 1926 as a present for completing her Ph.D. by the aunt for whom she was named, **Eleanor Foster Lansing,** "was still going strong fifty years later." She, too, was still going strong in the final decades of her extraordinarily long and productive life, never mincing words about her accomplishments. In a 1982 interview, she told a reporter that had she been born male her career would doubtless have developed differently, "I would have been in the Cabinet. I would have earned a lot of money." During the same interview, she addressed a male photographer taking her picture, "Are you nice to women? You're nice to 'em in the evenings, but don't much like 'em during the day?" Refusing to submit to the ravages of old age, she continued to travel, met with a steadily diminishing group of old friends, and immensely enjoyed the company of her six grandchildren.

Despite having witnessed catastrophic wars, the chaos of postwar reconstruction and decades of international tensions, at the end of her life Eleanor Dulles remained essentially an optimist. In her late 80s, responding to a reporter's query as to why she continued to interest herself in international affairs, she answered crisply, "Two reasons. One is, it's fun. And the other is, I think the world needs some help."

SOURCES:

Dulles, Eleanor Lansing. *Berlin: The Wall Is Not Forever.* Chapel Hill, NC: University of North Carolina Press, 1967.

———. *Chances of a Lifetime: A Memoir.* Englewood Cliffs, NJ: Prentice-Hall, 1980.

"Eleanor Dulles," in *The Times* [London]. November 5, 1996, p. 23.

"Eleanor L. Dulles of State Dept. Dies at 101," in *The New York Times Biographical Service.* November 1996, p. 1614.

Gamarekian, Barbara. "Fiction, Reality, Dulleses," in *The New York Times Biographical Service.* February 1986, pp. 268–269.

Mosley, Leonard. *Dulles: A Biography of Eleanor, Allen and John Foster Dulles and Their Family Network.* NY: The Dial Press/ James Wade, 1978.

Rosellini, Lynn. "Eleanor Dulles, Active as Ever at 87," in *The New York Times Biographical Service.* June 1982, p. 702.

John Haag, Associate Professor of History, University of Georgia, Athens, Georgia

du Maurier, Daphne (1907–1989)

Prolific British novelist, biographer, and playwright whose gift was in story-telling and whose imagination moved her to write works of suspense, mystery, romance, and horror. Name variations: Lady Daphne Browning; (nickname) Bing. Pronunciation: doo-MOHR-ee-ay. Born on May 13, 1907, in London, England; died on April 19, 1989, in Par, Cornwall, England; daughter of Gerald du Maurier (an actor-manager in British theater) and **Muriel (Beaumont) du Maurier** *(an actress); attended Miss Tullock's day school in Oak Hill Park (1916); educated at home by governesses; attended a finishing school in Camposena, France; married Frederick Arthur Montague (Tommy) Browning, on July 19, 1932 (died 1965); children:* **Tessa Browning** *(b. July 15, 1933);* **Flavia Browning Leng** *(b. April 2, 1937); Christian, called Kit (b. November 3, 1940).*

Awards and honors: National Book Award (1938), for Rebecca; *Dame Commander, Order of the British Empire (1969); Mystery Writers of America Grand Master Award (1977).*

Published first novel, The Loving Spirit *(1931); published* Rebecca *(1938); restored and moved into Menabilly (1943); defended her authorship of* Rebecca *against charges of plagiarism (1947); suffered a coronary (1981).*

Selected writings: The Loving Spirit *(1931);* I'll Never Be Young Again *(1932);* The Progress of Julius *(1933);* Gerald: A Portrait *(1934);* Jamaica Inn *(1936);* The du Mauriers *(1937);* Rebecca *(1938);* Come Wind, Come Weather *(1940);* Frenchman's Creek *(1941);* Hungry Hill *(1943);* The Years Between *(1945);* The King's General *(1946);* September Tide *(1949);* The Parasites *(1949); (ed.)* The Young George du Maurier: A Selection of his Letters, 1860–1867 *(1951);* My Cousin Rachel *(1951);* The Apple Tree *(published in America as* Kiss Me Again Stranger, *1952);* Happy Christmas *(1953);* Mary Anne *(1954);* Early Stories *(1955);* The Scapegoat *(1957);* The Breaking Point *(1958);* The Infernal World of Branwell Bronte *(1960);* Castle Dor *(1962);* The Glass-Blowers *(1963);* The Flight of the Falcon *(1965);* Vanishing Cornwall *(1967);* The House on the Strand *(1969);* Not After Midnight *(published in America as* Don't Look Now, *1971);* Rule Britannia *(1972);* Golden Lads: Anthony Bacon, Francis and their Friends *(1975);* The Winding Stair: Francis Bacon, His Rise and Fall *(1976);* Echoes from the Macabre *(1976);* Growing Pains *(published in America as* Myself When, *1977);* The Rendezvous and Other Stories *(1980);* The Rebecca Notebook and Other Memories *(1980);* Classics from the Macabre *(1987).*

Daphne du Maurier's novel *Rebecca* begins with the words: "Last night I dreamt I went to Manderley again." That the author directs our attention to the mystery of Manderley at the very outset was perhaps inevitable. Houses always stirred du Maurier's imagination. The several she inhabited with her husband on his various military postings invariably provoked her to fantasize about the lives of their former residents. But it was Menabilly, in her beloved Cornwall, that provided one model for the fictional Manderley. For a decade, Menabilly had been her enduring passion, exciting fantasies about the family whose descendants had lived there since the 16th century. And so it would remain until the end of her life.

I was born . . . into a family of make-believe and imagination.

—Daphne du Maurier, *Enchanted Cornwall*

Du Maurier sought out Menabilly in 1928. Her interest had been aroused by guidebooks and by the strange tales of her Cornwall neighbors about a woman in blue said to appear at a side window, and the bones of a cavalier that had been discovered beneath a buttress more than 100 years earlier. Why the current owner, Dr. John Rashleigh, paid a local woman to clean and air the house once a week, but lived elsewhere and seemed unconcerned that the house was gradually falling apart, excited local speculation but no consensus. Prosaic souls accepted that the dampness was simply bad for the man's health; romantics preferred the rumor that catching his first wife entertaining a lover at Menabilly had inspired an aversion to the place. Du Maurier's first attempt to get a firsthand look, which ended in getting lost in the surrounding undergrowth as darkness fell, convinced her that Menabilly was a "house of secrets" determined to resist intruders. What she finally saw a day later when she pushed her way clear—huge unkempt lawns, long low walls covered with ivy so thick as to all but mask the empty windows—could only excite her ardor for the "house, haunting, mysterious."

Writing *Rebecca* a decade later did nothing to purge its author of her persistent fascination with Menabilly, nor did frequently wandering its grounds with Dr. Rashleigh's permission satisfy her obsession with the house. In 1943, the possibility of a lease arose. Although the house needed a new roof, had no lighting, no water, no heat; although window panes were broken and

novels, several by the popular Mrs. *Elizabeth Gaskell, achieved considerable fame for his pictures in *Punch,* where he held a staff position, and became famous as the author of three novels, the best known being *Trilby,* which featured the master manipulator, Svengali. Daphne's parents had theatrical careers. Gerald's unique style of naturalistic acting was responsible for the stage success of his Raffles, the gentleman-crook (1906), which led to a series of popular criminal roles. From 1910, Gerald, in partnership with Frank Curzon, managed Wyndham's Theater at Charing Cross in London where Gerald continued to appear on the stage. He was knighted in 1922 for his services to the theater. Although Muriel retired from the stage in 1911 before the birth of her third daughter, she does not seem to have interested herself overmuch in the rearing of her children, which she preferred to leave in the hands of a series of nurses and governesses. Perhaps Daphne was right in later ascribing Muriel's external indifference to jealousy of her daughters' close relationship with Gerald, who spent so much time with the girls that a secret language gradually developed among them.

In 1916, Gerald bought Cannon Hall in Hampstead. Among the frequent visitors to the du Maurier home were J.M. Barrie ("Uncle Jim" to the girls), who wrote *Peter Pan* for their cousins, the Llewelyn Davies boys. Another was the novelist and playwright Edgar Wallace, whose generosity in sharing the profits of *The Ringer* with Gerald, who had extensively revised the play's dialogue, enabled Gerald to purchase Ferryside in Fowey, Cornwall, where Daphne would find the solitude to write her first novel.

Daphne's childhood was typical of the Edwardian upper class. Children were briefly presented at dinner parties in which they would later learn to participate, took daily walks in the park with their nannies, passed summers in rented houses away from London, and visited the country homes of family friends. Daphne adored the freedom of the countryside. But the du Maurier childhood was also unique in ways that reflected the family's theatrical background. Daphne and her sisters especially enjoyed dressing up in costume and pretending. *Treasure Island* and a visit to the Tower of London so fired Daphne's imagination that she spent many afternoons as Jim Hawkins or Long John Silver or as the Crown's executioner repeatedly beheading her younger sister Jeanne.

As a child, Daphne wanted to be a boy because they "did all the brave things." For a girl in the Edwardian era, wanting to be a boy was

moisture had caused fungus to grow on the ceiling; although she would be pouring money into renovating a house that she could only lease rather than own; although it was war time with building materials almost impossible to get and skilled contractors even scarcer; although everyone, especially her husband, thought her "quite mad"—du Maurier wanted the house so badly she cajoled Dr. Rashleigh to lease Menabilly to her for 20 years, later extended an additional six. When the Rashleigh family decided to reclaim the house in 1969, du Maurier rented nearby Kilmarth, dower house of Menabilly, where she lived until her death in 1989.

Daphne du Maurier was born in London on May 13, 1907. The second of three daughters born to Gerald and Muriel ("Mo") du Maurier, she grew up as the child of a famous family amid Edwardian London's privileged upper class. Her grandfather, George du Maurier, forced by the loss of sight in one eye to abandon his dream of becoming a serious painter, instead illustrated

probably not unusual; both girls and women were restrained in their activities by their clothing and by society, while males were allowed to have adventures, play sports like cricket, and dress in trousers which allowed freedom of movement. In Daphne's case, however, something more seems to have been at work. Since she was aware that her father, especially after the death of his only brother Guy in World War I, deeply regretted that she was not his son and could thus carry on the family name (she could hardly have missed those sentiments since Gerald expressed them openly in a poem he wrote her), the relative freedom that she and her sisters experienced in being allowed to dress in trousers and play cricket with Gerald must have smacked as much of rejection as liberation. With the additional shock of menstruation at age 12, she not only dreamed of turning into a boy to prevent the whole process, a not unusual occurrence, but also invented an alter ego for herself named Eric Avon, captain of the cricket team at School House, Rugby, who filled her imagination with deeds of daring.

Her earliest schooling was at Miss Tullock's day school in Oak Hill Park; later, she was educated at home by governesses. Her favorite was **Maud Wadell**, nicknamed Tod, who came in 1918 when Daphne was 11 and would become a lifelong friend. After Tod went to Constantinople in 1921 to serve as governess to the children of Prince Abdul Madjid, Daphne kept in touch by letter, often begging Tod to return. In the spring of 1925, Daphne was sent to a finishing school with mostly English girls in Camposena, a village near Meudon outside of Paris, which was run by a **Miss Wicksteed**. The school's strictness (walks were permitted only on school grounds) was made even less tolerable by the Spartan conditions (cold bedrooms, no hot baths, bad food). At first, only organized outings to museums, the opera, and Versailles made life at the school more or less bearable. Then one evening, in an act of unusual daring, the normally shy Daphne joined a group of Mlle **Fernande Yvon**'s favorite students who were permitted to sit with the teacher in the evenings. Yvon was amused rather than annoyed. Soon Daphne had become Yvon's favorite, was calling her "Ferdy," and the two women were spending their summer holiday together. Daphne wrote Tod that she believed Yvon to be "Venetian," which in the du Maurier code meant lesbian.

At age 19, du Maurier, now officially finished, found herself with time on her hands, but a life that lacked direction. She read, sometimes as many as four books a week. She made trips to Europe, visited Ferdy in Paris, skied with the Edgar Wallace family, cruised the Norwegian fjords with millionaire Otto Kahn and party, socialized with Arthur Quiller-Couch, chair in English at Cambridge who had a summer home in Cornwall, and she wrote short stories, even though the constant bustle at Cannon Hall made writing difficult. In 1929, she met and had an affair with Carol Reed, later a film director. Du Maurier's parents disapproved of Reed, but then Gerald had always been possessively jealous of any man who presumed to date one of his daughters, so that alone does not explain Daphne's evasiveness when Reed began pressing for a more permanent arrangement in late 1929. For the first time, she was displaying an instinctive avoidance of commitments that threatened to disrupt the solitude she required for her writing. Having published a single short story and a poem in *The Bystander* was a modest enough accomplishment, especially since the journal was published by her uncle. But by then she had also completed most of a novel at Ferryside in Cornwall. Her father had purchased Ferryside in 1926; in 1929, she was finally allowed to stay there on her own, thus gaining the solitude she so craved for her writing.

Cornwall would also provide the material for many of her novels. Her first grew from her discovery of the *Jane Slade,* an old figureheaded schooner lying on its back in the mud; she later gained access to a box of Slade family letters, some from as early as the 19th century. When her family returned to London in October 1929, she stayed on alone. Working undisturbed, inspired by the material provided by the Slade letters, she wrote almost all of *The Loving Spirit* before dutifully returning to London for the family Christmas. By the end of January 1930, she was back in Fowey. *The Loving Spirit* was finished by March. After sending the typescript to an agent, Michael Joseph, she treated herself to a visit to Ferdy in Paris, where the news reached her that Joseph had sold the novel to Heinemann. By the time *The Loving Spirit* appeared in February 1931, she had managed to write her second novel *I'll Never Be Young Again* in a space of two months.

There is, in retrospect, something deeply ironic about du Maurier's discovery of Cornwall at the end of the 1920s. On the one hand, Cornwall not only meant for her a place and way of life that made it possible for her to develop as a novelist; it also provided both the fictional materials and the striking settings for such later works as *Rebecca, Jamaica Inn,* and *French-*

Du Maurier in Cornwall.

man's *Creek*. And yet, the modest fame that du Maurier enjoyed in the months following the publication of *The Loving Spirit* led directly to the marriage and family that would transform her most productive years into a constant struggle between the increasingly onerous responsi-

bilities of wife and mother and the demands of her art.

By early 1932, du Maurier had heard rumors of a young army officer who had been so impressed by *The Loving Spirit* that he and a fellow officer had cruised down the coast in his boat *Ygdrasil* in order to experience Cornwall firsthand and in hopes of meeting the novelist. She finally met the 31-year-old Frederick (Tommy) Browning, major in the Grenadier Guards, whom she called "Boy," in April 1932. On July 19, they were married in the church at Lanteglos near Fowey, departed at once on *Ygdrasil*, sailed along the coast to the Helford river, and moored at Frenchman's Creek. Following the honeymoon, the couple divided their time between Fowey and a cottage in Hampstead at the end of the Cannon Hall garden that du Maurier persuaded her parents to give them as a wedding present.

It was during the first decade of du Maurier's marriage that the ambivalent attitudes concerning gender and sex, which she had imbibed from both her family and society at large, began manifesting themselves in patterns of behavior that were at least eccentric, at times dysfunctional. On discovering that she was pregnant, she firmly convinced herself that she was about to present Tommy with the son that Muriel had never been able to give Gerald, then reacted to the birth of her daughter Tessa on July 15, 1933, by all but abandoning the child to the care of a nanny. The birth of a second daughter Flavia on April 2, 1937, would provoke yet again the kind of maternal indifference for which she had criticized Muriel. Not surprisingly, the long-desired son, Christian (Kit), would be the object of lavish demonstrations of affection from the moment of his birth on November 3, 1940. No less conflicted was du Maurier's reaction to the sudden death of her father, who was diagnosed with colon cancer in early 1934 and was dead by April 11. Within less than a month, du Maurier had signed a contract to write his biography, which she completed by the end of August. Though the book was warmly praised by critics for its unvarnished presentation of Sir Gerald's boyish charisma and talent, along with his eccentricities and human weaknesses, others saw du Maurier's forthright revelation of her father's extramarital affairs and occasional depression, not to mention his ambivalence toward his daughters as they passed beyond puberty, as an indiscretion, if not a betrayal.

Even in the early years of their marriage, Daphne and Tommy were anything but the inseparable couple. In fact, du Maurier made it plain rather early that she did not intend to permit her role as an officer's wife to interfere with the half-secluded, writing-centered life she could lead only in Fowey. She hated socializing on the grand scale and rebelled against expectations that she feign interest in the wives and families of the men under her husband's command, appear at dreary social functions, and participate by handing out prizes. By 1936, she was spending as much time at Ferryside as possible. By the time she finished *Jamaica Inn* in that year, she had established a routine of writing three hours in the morning, two in the afternoon, and if Tommy was not at home, yet another hour in the evening. Tessa and meals were left to the nanny and the cook.

And yet, she was an army officer's wife, whether she wanted to acknowledge it or not. *Jamaica Inn*, a Cornish tale of smugglers and villains, was her first commercial success; she now turned to another family biography, that of her grandfather, George du Maurier, which would eventually appear as *The du Mauriers*. Distractions, however, continued unabated. In 1936, after enduring the ordeal of being presented at Court for Tommy's sake, she was confronted with the news that the 2nd Battalion Grenadier Guards, which Tommy now commanded, was being transferred to Egypt. She hated Alexandria—the interminable heat, the enforced conviviality with officers' wives, the constant social circuit of an army post, and, worst of all, the impossibility of escaping to Cornwall. Having struggled to complete *The du Mauriers*, she became listless and depressed and discovered she was pregnant again. In January 1937, accompanied by Tessa and her nanny, she returned to England and gave birth to Flavia in April. The half year in England acted as a tonic; when Tommy took her back to Egypt at the end of July, she was already at work on *Rebecca*. When Tommy's tour ended in December 1937, du Maurier vowed on returning to England that she would not put up with any more foreign postings.

By the time she completed *Rebecca* in March 1938, the gathering of war clouds over Europe was probably rendering the point moot. In the summer of 1939, shortly before Germany invaded Poland, the family moved to Kent. Then in 1940, Tommy was placed in command of the 128th Hampshire Brigade, which was posted near Hertfordshire, where the wartime housing shortage forced them to take rooms in Langley's End, the home of Christopher and **Paddy Puxley**. Du Maurier became pregnant with her long yearned-for son. By the time Kit was born, Tommy's leaves had become short and infrequent and du Maurier was writing *Frenchman's Creek*. She also drifted into an affair with Christopher Puxley. Paddy discovered their affair and in April 1942 du Maurier moved to Fowey, where she rented a large cottage for herself, the three children, and their nanny because Ferryside had been requisitioned as a naval headquarters. She also rented a smaller cottage in which she and Christopher were able to continue their affair to the end of the war.

Even aside from the strain of her affair with Puxley, the last three years of the war were marked by continuous upheaval in du Maurier's private life. Tommy was seldom on leave other than during his recuperation from a glider crash, after which he was in North Africa and later India. The cottage she occupied with her three children and a nanny was cramped. The children were forever catching colds; the nanny's health was deteriorating; Tessa poisoned herself on rhododendron leaves; du Maurier had to serve as teacher for her children because the schools were closed. Though money was a constant source of concern, she managed to negotiate the 20-year lease for Menabilly and threw herself into repairs so that even Tommy was impressed when the family was able to move in time to celebrate Christmas, 1943.

For anyone not obsessed with Menabilly, the house might still have been considered unlivable. Du Maurier, however, managed to ignore both rats and bats in some of the rooms, beetles in the water pipes, and the absence of heating that in the winter months made it necessary for the family to sleep in as many clothes as they could get on. It is surely an indication of how dependent she had become on her writing as a relief from depression that, by the time the family moved in at Menabilly, she had written her longest novel, *The Hungry Hill*, a screen adaptation of it, and a stage play titled *The Years Between*. Once at Menabilly, she established a daily routine—writing from ten in the morning to one in the afternoon, having lunch at one followed by a walk with the children, and then writing until evening—and plunged into research for the novel *The King's General*, which was based on the history of Menabilly and the Rashleigh family. With the continuing illness of

From the movie Rebecca, *starring Joan Fontaine and Judith Anderson.*

Margaret, the nanny cum housekeeper, du Maurier wrote Tod, her old governess, pleading for help. Tod arrived in October 1945, and du Maurier went on writing.

The end of the war in 1945 meant that Tommy would be coming home. He was looking forward to a resumption of their old life. Du Maurier, however, feared the prospect of giving up the independence and hours of solitude she had learned to carve out for herself. Even if she had not warned him before his return that they would be sleeping in separate beds, Tommy's homecoming, as were so many after the long separations of the war, was disastrous. He arrived on July 19, 1946, to find his wife distant and his children barely recognizing him and afraid of his frequent displays of temper. Even worse, Tod, who had always irritated him, was an established member of the household. Tommy's posting as military secretary to the Minister of War probably came as a welcome relief to all concerned; it enabled a pattern to develop that would hold until Tommy's retirement in 1959, with Tommy living in a rented flat in London during the week and visiting his family at Menabilly on weekends. Tommy reacted to his failed marriage and his loneliness in London by increasing his drinking, which probably caused many of the health problems that plagued him in his last years, and by indulging in various love affairs. Du Maurier, who had ended her affair with Puxley, soon found intimacy in two curiously linked relationships with women, the first platonic, the second decidedly something more.

On November 27, 1947, accompanied by Flavia, Kit, and Tod (Tessa was in school), du Maurier set sail on the *Queen Mary* for New York, where she was to defend herself against the charge that she had plagiarized *Rebecca* from a 1924 short story ("I Planned to Murder my Husband") and a 1927 novel based on the story (*Blind Windows*) by **Edwina L. Macdonald**. Her co-defendants included Doubleday, her American publisher, and David O. Selznick, whose company had produced the Hitchcock film of *Rebecca*. Du Maurier and party were to stay at

From the movie My Cousin Rachel, starring Olivia de Haviland, Audrey Dalton, and Richard Burton.

Nelson Doubleday's Oyster Bay home. On board ship, du Maurier met Nelson's wife, **Ellen Doubleday**, to whom she developed an instant attraction. Though in court she had little difficulty in refuting the charge of plagiarism with the aid of her working notebooks to *Rebecca,* the ordeal of having to testify, together with the boundaries Ellen set to their friendship, left her ill and depressed. Back in England, du Maurier attempted to work through her crisis by writing a play (*September Tide*) whose central character, Stella, was modeled on Ellen. When *****Gertrude Lawrence** was cast as Stella, du Maurier fell at once under her spell. Their affair, with du Maurier visiting Lawrence in both Florida and New York, would continue until Lawrence's death in 1952.

Since February 1949, when she had begun her fictional portrait of a theatrical family, *The Parasites,* du Maurier had been writing in a newly erected wooden hut that stood at some distance from the main house at Menabilly. There, by the summer of 1950, amid the solitude on which she was becoming more and more dependent in order to write, the idea of a story about a widow named Rachel was forming in her imagination. *My Cousin Rachel* was finished in April 1951. But when Lawrence died the next year, du Maurier, at age 45, discovered that the solitude she had yearned for her entire adult life had been won at the price of loneliness. Tommy remained in London. Despite his drinking and philandering, he had been appointed comptroller and treasurer to HRH Princess *****Elizabeth (II)** in 1947 and now was being appointed treasurer to Prince Philip, duke of Edinburgh, following Elizabeth's coronation in 1952. Her children were away at school. She had only Tod left. And her work.

Writing now became the only cure for the depression that often threatened to overwhelm her. In January 1954, she wrote a novel based on her ancestor *****Mary Anne Clarke** (c. 1776–1852), mistress of Frederick Augustus, duke of York. *The Scapegoat,* the story of a man taking on the life of his double, an idea triggered by an incident in France in 1955, was published in 1957. But her life continued to peel away. Tessa married in March 1954 and gave birth to du Maurier's first grandchild in February 1955. Flavia married in 1956. Kit was graduated from Eton in 1958 determined to direct films. In 1957, Tommy suffered a nervous breakdown. Though Tommy was able to return to London, Daphne realized that he must soon retire, at which point he would come to live at Menabilly, intensifying the old problem of Tommy's and Tod's mutual dislike. For the sake of the husband with whom she had never come close to having a real marriage, she sacrificed her former governess and friend by setting Kit up in an apartment and sending Tod as a kind of housekeeper.

When Tommy retired in 1959, du Maurier resolved to do her duty by him, yet found ways to escape it. Her next book, a biography of Branwell Brontë, necessitated research in the British Museum and occasional trips to Yorkshire and provided relief that was absolutely necessary for her, despite the difficulty of making arrangements for Tommy's care while she was away from Menabilly. When Tommy died in March 1965, du Maurier was shocked at how much she missed him. Searching for distraction and having difficulties with writing fiction, she wrote, at her publishers suggestion, a book about Cornwall, a mother-son venture with Kit taking the photographs.

In 1969, du Maurier's lease on Menabilly at last expired, and she moved to the nearby dower house, Kilmarth. That summer, she was made Dame of the British Empire (DBE). In her later years, du Maurier turned increasingly to short stories and biography and, finally, to autobiography. By 1977, the creative juices had dried up, and her old enemy depression claimed her. After suffering a coronary in 1981, du Maurier was able to return to Kilmarth but required constant nursing care. In early 1989, she seems to have willed her death, refusing to eat, taking only liquids. On April 19, 1989, Daphne du Maurier died in her sleep.

SOURCES:

Forster, Margaret. *Daphne du Maurier: The Secret Life of the Renowned Storyteller*. NY: Doubleday, 1993.

Kelly, Richard. *Daphne du Maurier*. Boston: Twayne, 1987.

Leng, Flavia. *Daphne du Maurier: A Daughter's Memoir*. Edinburgh: Mainstream Publishing, 1994.

Shallcross, Martyn. *The Private World of Daphne du Maurier*. NY: St. Martin's Press, 1992.

SUGGESTED READING:

Du Maurier, Daphne. *Myself When Young: The Shaping of a Writer*. Garden City, NY: Doubleday, 1977.

RELATED MEDIA:

Don't Look Now, starring **Julie Christie** and Donald Sutherland, directed by Nicolas Roeg, Paramount, 1973.

Frenchman's Creek, starring *****Joan Fontaine**, Arturo de Cordova, and Basil Rathbone, directed by Mitchell Leisen, Paramount Pictures, 1944.

Hungry Hill, starring *****Jean Simmons**, *****Margaret Lockwood**, and Dennis Price, directed by Brian Desmond Hurst, Universal, 1947.

Jamaica Inn, starring Charles Laughton and *****Maureen O'Hara**, directed by Alfred Hitchcock, Paramount Pictures, 1939.

"Jamaica Inn," starring **Jane Seymour** and Patrick McGoohan, directed by Lawrence Gordon Clark, TV-movie, 1985.

My Cousin Rachel, starring *Olivia de Havilland and Richard Burton, directed by Henry Koster, Twentieth Century-Fox, 1953.

"Rebecca," starring Jeremy Brett, **Joanna David,** and **Anna Massey,** produced by BBC and Time-Life Films, presented as an eight-part miniseries on PBS-TV, 1981.

Rebecca, starring ***Joan Fontaine,** ***Judith Anderson,** and Laurence Olivier, screenplay by ***Joan Harrison** and Robert E. Sherwood, directed by Alfred Hitchcock, United Artists, 1940 (won Academy Award for Best Motion Picture).

"Rebecca" (90 min., two-part television adaptation), starring **Diana Rigg,** Charles Dance, and **Emilia Fox,** "Masterpiece Theatre," 1997.

The Birds, starring **Tippi Hedren** and Rod Taylor, directed by Alfred Hitchcock, Universal, 1963.

The Scapegoat, starring Alec Guinness and ***Bette Davis,** directed by Robert Hamer, M-G-M, 1959.

The Years Between, starring Michael Redgrave and **Valerie Hobson,** directed by Compton Bennett, Twentieth Century-Fox, 1946.

Vanishing Cornwall, narrated by Michael Redgrave, Sterling Education Films, 1968.

Carole Shelton, Adjunct Professor of History, Middle Tennessee State University, Murfreesboro, Tennessee

Dumesnil, Marie Françoise

(1713–1803)

French actress. Name variations: Mlle Dumesnil. Pronunciation: Du-may-NEL. Born Marie Françoise Marchand in Paris, France, on January 2, 1713; died at Boulogne-sur-Mer, France, on February 20, 1803.

Marie Marchand was born in Paris in 1713. Under her chosen stagename of Marie Françoise Dumesnil, she made her debut at the Comédie Théâtre Français in 1737 as Clytemnestra in *Iphigénie en Tauride,* and at once won a high place among dramatic artists of her time. Among her great parts were Athalie, Phèdre, Médéa, ***Agrippina,** and Sémiramis (***Sammuramat**). Dumesnil's imposing appearance and power gave her immense control over her audiences. It is said that during one performance those in the front seats were so overcome with horror that they fled their seats. Voltaire remarked that in his play *Mérope* she kept the audience in tears for three successive acts.

Marie Françoise Dumesnil

Although her great emotional intensity led many to rank Dumesnil above *Mlle Clairon, there were critics who resented the innovations of her forceful genius and those who felt she lacked Clairon's control. Unlike Clairon, Dumesnil had no interest in stage reform and thought the actor should always be magnificently dressed no matter what the part. When Clairon, in her memoirs, spoke ill of her, Dumesnil authorized the publication of *Mémoire de Marie Françoise Dumesnil, en réponse aux mémoires d'Hippolyte Clairon* (1800). She continued performing until 1775, when she retired upon a pension. Marie Dumesnil died at Boulogne-sur-Mer 28 years later, at the age of 90.

Dumitrescu-Doletti, Joanna
(1902–1963)

Princess of Hohenzollern. Name variations: Joanna Brana; Jeanne Lucie Dumitrescu-Tohani; assumed her grandmother's surname Doletti in 1928. Born Joanna Lucy Dumitrescu on September 24, 1902, in Bucharest, Rumania; died on February 19, 1963, in Lausanne, Switzerland; daughter of Ion Dumitrescu-Tohani and **Nella Theodoru** *or Teodoru; married Radu Saveanu, on December 11, 1924 (divorced); married Nicholas (1903–1978, son of *Marie of Rumania), prince of Hohenzollern, on October 24, 1931; children: Peter.*

Dumm, Edwina (b. 1893)

American cartoonist. Born in Sandusky, Ohio, in 1893; attended the Art Students League of New York.

Born into a newspaper family, Edwina Dumm took a correspondence course in cartooning, after which she was hired as a political cartoonist for a Columbus, Ohio, newspaper. Around 1918, while attending the Art Students League of New York, she was recruited by the George Matthew Adams Syndicate to create a comic strip about a boy and his dog. The result was *Cap Stubbs and Tippie*, for which she became well known. She also drew a dog cartoon called *Sinbad* for *Life* magazine and illustrated a one-column feature, *Alec the Great*, written by her brother.

COLLECTIONS:

Original drawings for Dumm's comics are housed in the Ohio State University Library for Communications and Graphic Arts.

Dunbar, Agnes (1312–1369)

Scottish hero and countess of Dunbar and March. Name variations: Black Agnes; Agnes of March; Agnes of Dunbar; Lady Randolph or Lady Agnes Randolph. Born in 1312 in Scotland; died in 1369 in Scotland; daughter of Sir Thomas Randolph, 1st earl of Moray; married Patrick (1285–1369, a prominent and powerful Scottish noble), 10th lord of Dunbar and 2nd earl of March, in 1324; children: at least three, including Agnes, later mistress of David II (1323–1370), king of Scotland (r. 1329–1370).

Agnes Dunbar was one of Scotland's many female participants in the war against English rule. She was probably related to the powerful warrior-king Robert I the Bruce which would have tied her to the royal house. Like Robert, Agnes had a passion for conflict and adventure as well as a loyalty to Scotland's cause. She married Lord Patrick of Dunbar, who was at first allied with England but soon switched his allegiance to his native country, no doubt in part due to Agnes' influence.

Called "Black Agnes" for her swarthy complexion, Agnes became known as an outspoken, bold woman and an inspiration to others as the war against England intensified in the 1330s. England had never accepted Scotland's claim to be an independent kingdom, and the English warrior-king Edward III sought to bring Scotland back under English rule by force. Agnes' brother was imprisoned by the English, and in 1337 Patrick left Dunbar Castle, situated on the coast near Edinburgh, to lead troops against the English invaders. The earl of Salisbury led his troops to the fortress of Dunbar in January 1338, using two Genoese galleys to cut off access by sea. Agnes refused to surrender, and the siege began.

Stories of her defense tell of Lady Agnes walking the battlements daily, yelling insults and taunts to the Englishmen below and, with her women, wiping off the damaged stones using their handkerchiefs. When Salisbury built a siege engine to batter the walls, Agnes had a stone dropped on it by a crane, destroying it. Salisbury turned the active siege into a blockade to starve her out, and the Scots were unable to send her reinforcements or try to raise the siege. She refused all offers to negotiate and refused to surrender despite the fact that food and water rations grew smaller every day and the suffering inside the castle must have been great. By late spring when the situation was critical, Scotsman Sir Alexander Ramsay of Dalwolsie and 40 followers managed to bring provisions into the fortress by boat.

Salisbury then had Agnes' brother, the earl of Moray, brought from prison in mid-April

1338, and threatened to kill him if she did not surrender. She responded that the castle belonged to her husband, and if her brother were killed then she should inherit all his property. The earl was sent back to prison. In June 1338, after a siege of nearly five months, a truce was signed between Salisbury and Agnes, and the English withdrew from Dunbar. Agnes became a Scottish hero. She and her family were amply rewarded by the Scottish king for their bravery and loyalty, making her and her descendants quite wealthy. Her diligence was commemorated in an English ditty: "Came I early, came I late, I found Agnes at the gate." Agnes Dunbar lived another 30 years.

SOURCES:

Crawford, Anne, *et al.*, eds. *The Europa Biographical Dictionary of British Women.* Detroit, MI: Gale Research, 1983.

Uglow, Jennifer, ed. *Dictionary of Women's Biography.* NY: Continuum, 1989.

Dunbar, Alice (1875–1935).

See Dunbar-Nelson, Alice.

Dunbar-Nelson, Alice (1875–1935)

African-American who earned popular acclaim as a Harlem Renaissance poet, but whose talents lay more in the discursive field than in the poetic and whose well-known marriage to Paul Laurence Dunbar was not only tumultuous but short-lived. Name variations: Alice Dunbar or Alice Moore Dunbar. Born Alice Ruth Moore on July 19, 1875, in New Orleans, Louisiana; died on September 18, 1935, of coronary complications at the University of Pennsylvania Hospital; daughter of Joseph Moore (a merchant marine) and Patricia Wright (a seamstress); graduated from Straight College (now Dillard University), New Orleans, 1892; subsequently studied at Cornell, Columbia, the Pennsylvania School of Industrial Art, and the University of Pennsylvania, specializing in English literature, English educational measurements, and psychology; married Paul Laurence Dunbar, on March 8, 1898 (separated 1902, died 1906); secretly married Henry Arthur Callis, on January 19, 1910 (divorced 1911); married Robert J. Nelson, on April 20, 1916 (died 1949); children: (third marriage) Elizabeth Nelson; Bobby Nelson.

Taught school in New Orleans (1892–96); helped found the White Rose Home for Girls in Harlem (1897–98); taught and administered at the Howard High School, Wilmington, Delaware; directed seven summer sessions for in-service teachers at State College for Colored Students (now Delaware State College) and taught two summer sessions at Hampton Institute (1902–20); wrote for and helped edit the A.M.E. Church Review (1913–14); became field organizer for the Middle Atlantic States in the women's suffrage campaign (1915); toured the South as a field representative of the Women's Committee of the Council of National Defense (1918); published poems in Crisis, Ebony and Topaz, Opportunity, Negro Poets and Their Poems, Caroling Dusk, Harlem: A Forum of Negro Life and Others (1917–28); coedited and published the Wilmington Advocate newspaper (1920–22); began her diary (1921); headed the Anti-Lynching Crusaders in Delaware fighting for the Dyer Anti-Lynching Bill (1922); directed the Democratic political campaign from New York headquarters (1924); worked as teacher and parole officer at the Industrial School for Colored Girls (1924–28); wrote column "From A Woman's Point of View" (later changed to "Une Femme Dit") in the Pittsburgh Courier (1926); wrote column "As In a Looking Glass" in the Washington Eagle (1926–30); wrote column "So It Seems to Alice Dunbar-Nelson" in the Pittsburgh Courier (1930); named executive secretary for the American Friends Inter-Racial Peace Committee (1928–31).

Selected publications: (short stories and poems) Violets and Other Tales (Boston: Monthly Review Press, 1895); (short stories) The Goodness of St. Rocque and Other Stories (NY: Dodd, Mead, 1899); "Wordsworth's Use of Milton's Description of Pandemonium" in Modern Language Notes (1909); (edited) Masterpieces of Negro Eloquence (Harrisburg, PA: Douglass, 1914) and The Dunbar Speaker and Entertainer (1920); (two-part article) "People of Color in Louisiana," in The Journal of Negro History (1916–17); (one-act war-propaganda play) Mine Eyes Have Seen (1918); (two-part article on Delaware) "These 'Colored' United States" in The Messenger (1924).

Alice Ruth Moore was born in New Orleans, Louisiana, on July 19, 1875. Her mother **Patricia (Wright) Moore**, an ex-slave, earned a living as a seamstress and her absent father worked as a sailor. Both of her parents were of mixed racial origin. This ancestry endowed Dunbar-Nelson with a light-complexion and auburn tresses and enabled her easy entrance into Creole society. Her earlier works focus on exploring and examining the intricacies of this society; they also reveal her own ambivalence about complexional differences.

Dunbar-Nelson attended public school in New Orleans, where she graduated from the two-year teacher training program at Straight

College (now Dillard University) in 1892. After graduation, she worked as a teacher, a book-keeper, and a stenographer for a black printing firm. She was also active in musical, religious, and literary arenas. She performed in amateur plays; learned to play piano and cello; wrote a column for a fraternal newspaper; and presided over a church club. In 1895, at age 20, she published her first and best-known volume *Violets and Other Tales*, a collection of short stories, poems, essays, reviews, and sketches. The next year, she moved to the northeast to continue her education, subsequently studying at Cornell, Columbia, the Pennsylvania School of Industrial Art, and the University of Pennsylvania. She specialized in English literature, psychology, and English educational measurements.

[They say] that men … prefer the soft, dainty, winning, mindless creature who cuddles into men's arms, agrees to everything they say, and looks upon them as a race of gods turned loose upon this earth for the edification of womankind. Well, maybe so, but there is one thing positive, they certainly respect the independent one, and admire her, too, even if it is at a distance, and that in itself is something.

—Alice Dunbar-Nelson

Dunbar-Nelson began teaching at *Victoria Earle Matthews' White Rose Mission (later White Rose Home for Girls) in Harlem, New York, in 1897. On March of 1898, Alice married Paul Laurence Dunbar, America's first nationally recognized black poet. Their romance had begun in 1895 when he saw a picture and poem of hers in a Boston magazine and struck up a correspondence with her. Neither of their mothers approved of the match. Dunbar-Nelson's mother and family considered Paul too dark-skinned and too provincial. Paul reveals his mother's feelings about the prospective marriage in a letter to Alice dated October 29, 1897: "Is my mother pleased at the marriage? Well, dear, to tell the truth, she doesn't hanker after it, but she is reconciled and is prepared to love you. Before I left home she had begun to enter pretty heartily into my enthusiasm." Their marriage was further burdened by their temperamental differences: Paul's medically induced alcoholism; Alice's domineering tendencies; and their infertility. After a series of separations and reconciliations, Alice left Paul in 1902 and remained estranged from him until he died on February 9, 1906. In spite of their tumultuous marriage, they respected each other and the world recognized Alice Dunbar-Nelson as Paul's wife, sending her condolences. Although her status as his widow overshadowed her own outstanding literary achievements, it increased her literary fortunes and gave her publicity.

Even before his death, she benefitted from her marriage to Paul Dunbar. They discussed their respective work, collaborated on literary projects, and his agent marketed her fiction. In 1898, her second book of short stories, *The Goodness of St. Rocque,* was not only advertised as a companion volume to Paul Dunbar's *Poems of Cabin and Field,* but also brought out by his publisher, Dodd, Mead. Her fascination with Creole culture and tradition is apparent in this volume. The title story, "The Goodness of St. Rocque," features Manuela, the tall, dark heroine visiting a voodoo priestess and the Catholic Saint Rocque to combat the charms of her rival, the blonde and petite Claralie for the attentions of a young man. The story also sketches Creole customs and provides a detailed picture of New Orleans culture. Another story in this volume examines the racial and gender problems that confront Creole women. "Sister Josepha" is a tale about a young novice who comes to the convent as an orphan. She refuses a couple's offer to adopt her when the husband's admiration of her beauty becomes too obvious. After she espies a young man, she begins to question her decision to remain in the convent and decides to run away. Her desire is thwarted when she realizes that she does not know her race, her full name, or her nationality. The story ends with her sad retreat back into the convent. Protagonists' refuge into the convent when plagued by an identity crisis was the resolution

❧► **King, Grace Elizabeth** (c. 1852–1932)

American novelist, short story writer, and historian. Born in Louisiana around 1852; died in 1932.

At the turn of the century, Grace Elizabeth King was one of the most prominent of Southern writers, and her books dealt largely with Southern subjects. Her novel *Monsieur Motte,* which first appeared in the *New Princeton Review,* was published in book form in 1888. *Balcony Stories* was then considered one of her best works, along with *Tales of a Time and Place.* King's historical writings include *New Orleans: The Place and the People,* and a life of Sieur de Bienville, the founder of New Orleans.

*A*lice
*D*unbar-
*N*elson

of several Creole stories written by white authors such as George Washington Cable, *Kate Chopin, and ◄⸘ Grace King. These stories were also embodied in the form of *Henriette Delille, who, determined not to become a white man's mistress, fled to a convent, and later, founded

the Sisters of the Holy Family, an order for women of color.

The Black critic Vernon Loggins, whose criticism of Dunbar-Nelson's first volume had been negative, commended her second collection for having "some excellent material handled with pleasing effect." He notes that she "found types in New Orleans which [Cable] had neglected, and she treated them in sketches which are frail and at the same time redolent of a delicate sympathy." Dunbar-Nelson's consideration of Creole themes in her early work betrayed a noticeable ambivalence about race. She concealed the racial identity of her Creole female protagonists, preferring to use coded terms such as "dusky-eyed" (denoting a quadroon, one-fourth black individual) to describe them. In her two-part study "People of Color in Louisiana," she explains that Creole is an ambiguous term:

> The native white Louisianian will tell you that a Creole is a white man, whose ancestors contain some French or Spanish blood in their veins. But he will be disputed by others. . . . It appears that to a Caucasian, a Creole is a native of the lower parishes of Louisiana, in whose veins some traces of Spanish, West Indian or French blood runs. The Caucasian will shudder with horror at the idea of including a person of color in the definition, and the person of color will retort with his definition that a Creole is a native of Louisiana, in whose blood runs mixed strains of everything un-American, with the African strain slightly apparent.

Dunbar-Nelson's early reticence about race shifts to a frank, nuanced discussion of the problems of Black Creoles. Published in the *Southern Workman* (August 1902), "The Pearl in the Oyster" chronicles the fall of a light-skinned Creole who rejects blacks in order to pass as a white politician. Another short story, "Stones of the Village," develops a parallel downfall for Victor Grabert, whose grandmother forbids him to play with yellow and black boys. As an adult, he passes, becomes a prominent jurist, and marries into a white family of good social standing, only to die horribly, erroneously believing that his true identity has been discovered. In an autobiographical essay written around 1929, "Brass Ankles Speaks," Dunbar-Nelson recounts her childhood experience of being rejected by darker-skinned black girls, who assailed her with taunts of "half white nigger." Her ordeal continued throughout college and at work; "Brass Ankles" was neither black enough for blacks nor white enough for whites. According to Dunbar-Nelson, the "'yaller niggers,' the 'Brass Ankles' must bear the hatred of their own and the prejudice of the white race." Given the provocative content of these stories, Dunbar-Nelson was often unable to publish them.

Dunbar-Nelson's literary interests were not confined to Creoles. She wrote stories that fea-

tured Irish and Italian immigrants and several pieces dealt with women's rights and roles. The story that most reflects Dunbar-Nelson's commitment to women's equality is "The Woman," a monologue in which the narrator delineates the advantages of being a single woman. The narrator describes the single woman's life as being one of financial, geographical, intellectual, and sexual independence, and concludes by asserting that men may marry weak women, but that they respect independent ones.

By 1902, Alice Dunbar-Nelson resided in Wilmington, Delaware, with her mother, her sister, and her sister's four little children. From 1902 to 1920, she taught at Howard High School (at the time, the only secondary school for blacks in the state) and then served as head of the English department. She supplemented her teaching and supervisory responsibilities with fundraising and playwriting. While overseeing summer sessions for teachers at State College for Colored Students (later Delaware State College), she completed her master's thesis on Milton's influence on Wordsworth at Cornell.

Following intimate liaisons with at least three prominent women, Dunbar-Nelson secretly married Henry Arthur Callis, a man who was 12 years her junior, on January 19, 1910, and divorced him a year later. On April 20, 1916, she married Robert J. Nelson (1873–1949), a race-conscious and politically oriented journalist from Harrisburg, Pennsylvania, who was widowed with two children. With "Bobbo," as she affectionately called him, she formed a lasting stable union. Together, they edited a progressive black newspaper, *The Wilmington Advocate*, from 1920 to 1922, and participated in Delaware politics. During this period, she was involved in several racial, civic, and suffrage activities. She campaigned for women's suffrage (1915), toured the South as a field representative for the Woman's Committee of the Council of National Defense (1918), and made history as the first black woman to sit on the State Republican Committee of Delaware (1920). She was one of the delegates who presented black concerns to President Warren G. Harding at the White House (1921) and headed the Delaware Crusaders for the Dyer Anti-Lynching Bill (1922). With female colleagues, she established the Industrial School for Colored Girls in Marshallton, Delaware, where she taught and worked as a parole officer from 1924 to 1928. She also joined several prominent organizations, such as the National Association of Colored Women and the Delta Sigma Theta Sorority.

Alice
Dunbar-
Nelson

Despite her versatility, sophistication, elegance, educational background, and experience, Dunbar-Nelson struggled against the societal constraints that denied opportunities for black women. In 1927, she was refused a public-school teaching position because white male physicians determined her to be medically unfit. The *Pittsburgh Courier* did not want to pay her for her column, and, in October 1920, she lost her teaching position when she attended Social Justice Day in Marion, Ohio. Her experience as executive secretary of the American Inter-Racial Peace Committee from 1928 to 1931 was marred by male insistence on monitoring her appearance for propriety. Even Robert, her usually supportive husband, expected her to juggle domestic concerns and newspaper duties.

Dunbar-Nelson allowed neither sexism nor racism to sidetrack her. She contributed articles to newspapers and journals, edited volumes illuminating black oratory, wrote plays and speeches, and received recognition as a Harlem Renaissance poet. She completed, but never published, four novels: *The Confession of a Lazy Woman* (1899), *A Modern Undine* (1901–03), *Uplift* (1930–31), and *This Lofty Oak* (1932–33). She also kept a diary that records her thoughts in 1921 and between 1926 and 1931. Prominent members of the black community welcomed her as their equal.

The financial difficulties that marked Dunbar-Nelson's life came to an end in January 1932, when her husband was appointed to the Pennsylvania State Athletic (Boxing) Commission. She and her family, composed of Robert, her sister, and her sister's children, moved into a comfortable home and enjoyed economic security. Three years later, Alice Dunbar-Nelson died of a heart condition at the University of Pennsylvania hospital on September 18, 1935.

SOURCES:

Bryan, Violet Harrington. *The Myth of New Orleans in Literature: Dialogues of Race and Gender.* Knoxville, TN: University of Tennessee Press, 1993, pp. 63–78.

———. "Race and Gender in the Early Works of Alice Dunbar-Nelson," in *Louisiana Women Writers.* Edited by Dorothy H. Brown and Barbara C. Ewell. Baton Rouge, LA: Louisiana State University Press, 1992, pp. 120–138.

Dunbar-Nelson, Alice. *Give Us Each Day: The Diary of Alice Dunbar-Nelson.* Edited by Gloria T. Hull. NY: Norton, 1984.

Hull, Gloria T. "Shaping Contradictions: Alice Dunbar-Nelson and the Black Creole Experience," in *New Orleans Review.* Vol. XV. Spring 1988, pp. 34–37.

———. *Color, Sex, and Poetry: Three Women Writers of the Harlem Renaissance.* Bloomington: Indiana University Press, 1987.

Whitlow, Roger, "Alice Dunbar-Nelson: New Orleans Writer," in *Regionalism and the Female Imagination.* Edited by Emily Toth. New York, 1985, pp. 109–125.

SUGGESTED READING:

Blassingame, John W. *Black New Orleans, 1860–1880.* Chicago, IL: University of Chicago Press, 1973.

Giddings, Paula. *When and Where I Enter: The Impact of Black Women on Race and Sex in America.* New York, 1984.

Hull, Gloria, ed. *The Works of Alice Dunbar-Nelson.* 3 vols. NY: Oxford University Press, 1988.

COLLECTIONS:

The Alice Dunbar-Nelson papers are located in Special Collections, Morris Library, University of Delaware, Newark, Delaware.

Uche Egemonye, freelance writer and graduate student in American History, Emory University, Atlanta, Georgia

Duncan, Isadora (1878–1927)

American dancer, the most prominent of her time, who invented the "New System" of improvised movements interpretive of poetry, music, and the rhythms of nature. Born Angela Isadora Duncan on May 27, 1878, in San Francisco; strangled by her shawl in a freak accident in Nice, France, on September 14, 1927; daughter of Mary Isadora (Gray) Duncan (erstwhile piano and dance teacher) and Joseph Charles Duncan (engaged in sporadic businesses); married Sergei Esenin (a poet), on May 22, 1922 (divorced); children: (with Gordon Craig) Deirdre; (with Eugene Singer) Patrick Augustus.

Went on dance tours with Loie Fuller troupe in Berlin, Leipzig, and Munich (1901); began solo performances in Vienna, Budapest (1902), Berlin, Paris, Vélizy, various German cities (1903), Athens, Vienna, Munich, Berlin (Aeschylus' The Supplicants all with Greek boys' chorus), Paris (Beethoven Soirée), Bayreuth (Tannhäuser), St. Petersburg (Chopin) (1904), St. Petersburg (Beethoven), Moscow, Kiev, Germany, Brussels, Netherlands, Stockholm (1905), Warsaw, Netherlands, Belgium, Scandinavia (1906–07), St. Petersburg (Iphigénie), London, New York (Beethoven's Seventh Symphony), Boston, Washington, D.C. (1908), Paris, U.S., (1909), Paris (Gluck's Orphée), New York (Wagner) (1911), Rome (1912), Russia, Paris (with pupils, the Isadorables, 1913), New York (with Isadorables, 1914), New York (1915), Paris, New York, South America (1916), New York (with Isadorables), San Francisco (1917), San Francisco (1918); Paris twice (second engagement with Isadorables), Athens (1920), Paris (with Isadorables), Belgium, the Netherlands, London, Soviet Union (1921), U.S., including New York, Boston, Middle West, Brooklyn (1922), New York, Paris, Moscow, other Soviet cities (1923), Ukraine, Moscow, Berlin (1924), Paris (1927).

In 1927 one of the most flamboyant autobiographies of the 1920s was written. Even the first chapter began audaciously:

> The character of a child is already plain, even in its mother's womb. Before I was born my mother was in great agony of spirit and in a tragic situation. She could take no food except iced oysters and iced champagne. If people ask me when I began to dance I reply, "In my mother's womb, probably as a result of the oysters and champagne—the food of Aphrodite."

Here one finds many of the qualities that would always mark the personality of Isadora Duncan—the precociousness, the narcissism, the sense of destiny, and above all the love of dance. For despite a life that even actress **Vanessa Redgrave** could not fully capture in the film *Isadora* (1969), it is as a dancer that Duncan must be seen. And a dancer she was, the most innovative of her time. With Duncan one had an overt celebration of the body, the use of Greek themes and symphonic music, the introduction of political and social themes. She used to tell her youthful pupils, "Listen to the music with your soul," and it was advice that she always followed. From her flowing garbs that helped revolutionize the dress of women to a platform style that centered on spontaneity, Duncan altered dance as an art form until it became politics.

Duncan's career contains many paradoxes. As biographer Walter Terry notes, she was wholly dedicated to her art but undisciplined in her life. She was a true "innocent of spirit" whose dancing and behavior were often deemed scandalous. She considered herself a revolutionary yet moved in circles filled with royalty. Her moods vacillated between laughter and depression, affection and anger, generosity and egoism.

Angela Isadora Duncan was born on May 27, 1878, in San Francisco, the second daughter and youngest of four children of **Dora Gray Duncan** and Joseph Charles Duncan. Dora grew up amid prosperous circumstances, her own father being naval officer of the Port of San Francisco and a member of the California legislature. Joseph was an adventurer *par excellence*. Thirty years older than Dora when they married, he was a divorced man with four grown children. His erstwhile occupations included running a lottery, publishing three newspapers, owning a private art gallery, and directing an auction business. When, in 1878, a bank that he had founded failed, Joseph abandoned his family for Los Angeles, where he again divorced and remarried.

During Isadora's childhood in San Francisco and Oakland, the impoverished Duncans were continually moving from one rooming house to another. Isadora later wrote, "My first recollection—a clear sensual remembrance of being thrown from a burning window to the arms of a policeman." Her mother, often pursued by landlords and grocers, earned a meager livelihood by giving piano lessons and knitting caps and mittens, which young Isadora peddled from door to door. The unsupervised Duncan children climbed walls and trees, ate and slept irregularly, and in general lived without constraint.

At age six, Isadora, already showing a talent for the dance, began teaching local children. While still young, she left school, which she considered useless, and aided the family by giving lessons in social dancing. At 13, she gave her initial dance recital, which was held at Oakland's First Unitarian Church. In 1893, Joseph, having recovered his fortune, provided Dora and her children with a San Francisco mansion possessing a tennis court, windmill, and barn (which the family converted into a theater). However, he soon suffered a financial reverse and the mansion had to be sold.

In 1895, Dora took Isadora to live in Chicago, their only possessions being a small trunk filled with their belongings, some old-fashioned jewelry, and $25 in cash. For a week, mother and daughter lived on tomatoes. Isadora became a dancer for about three weeks at the Masonic Roof Garden, earning $20 a week under the billing "The California Faun." She attracted the attention of Ivan Miroski, a 45-year-old Pole, and the couple fell in love. The romance only broke up when Isadora learned that Ivan already had a wife in London.

In Chicago, Duncan caught the eye of producer Augustin Daly, who in 1896 brought her to New York to perform in a pantomime called *Mme. Pygmalion*. Then followed two tours, which included Duncan playing a fairy in *A Midsummer Night's Dream* and a spirit in *The Tempest*. Her salary started at $15 a week, which was later raised to $25. Although Daly sent the entire troupe to London the following year, Duncan developed what she called "an ab-

Isadora Duncan

solute nausea" for the theater, and in 1898 she left the Daly Company. Encouraged by composer Ethelbert Nevin, she rented a studio in Carnegie Hall and gave individual dance performances before such socialites as Mrs. Whitelaw Reid (*Elisabeth Mills Reid, 1858–1931). While giving a series of dances illustrating *The Rubáiyát of Omar Khayyám*, the blue-eyed, auburn-haired Duncan danced with bare arms and legs, something so shocking to Victorian audiences that several walked out.

*L*ife broke her, but it never diminished her.
—Fredrika Blair

Duncan was already beginning to live out an embryonic philosophy of the art: "My dance is not a dance of the body but of the spirit. My body moves because my spirit moves it." She was much influenced by the theories of France's François Delsarte, a man who had never taught a dance student. Delsarte stressed the relationship between movement and emotion and encouraged dancing in white robes to the accompaniment of poetry. In the 1890s, however, dance was still seen as merely a fashionable entertainment, not as a genuine art form, and Isadora's career soon reached an impasse. The Duncan family was again penniless.

In 1899, Isadora, her mother, sister **Elizabeth**, and brother Raymond moved to London, traveling by cattle boat under an assumed name, O'Gorman, so as not to compromise Isadora's status as the "pet" of New York society. Almost immediately, she was discovered by Charles Hall, director of the New Gallery. By 1900, Duncan was performing before minor royalty and society matrons.

That same year, the family moved to Paris, where she and Raymond began the day by dancing in the Luxembourg Gardens. She was soon launched into the city's society. In 1901, she joined the troupe of *Loie Fuller, an American dancer who owned her own theater in Paris. As part of Fuller's entourage, Duncan was touring Central Europe. In February 1902, her real debut took place in Vienna before a highly selected artistic gathering. But she was just as popular with the less prominent. She describes, for example, her welcome in Munich:

> The students went fairly crazy. Night after night they unharnessed the horses from my carriage and drew me through the streets, singing their student songs and leaping with lighted torches on either side of my victoria [carriage]. Often, for hours, they would group themselves outside the hotel window

> and sing, until I threw them my flowers and handkerchiefs, which they would divide, each bearing a portion in their caps.

In Budapest, she entered into the first of her many love affairs, this one with Oscar Beregi, a leading young actor with the city's National Theater. Beregi recited the classical odes that served as her accompaniment. His ardor for Duncan soon cooled, however, and it was a shattered Isadora Duncan who went to Munich, where her recital was a great success: "My life has known but two motives—Love and Art—often Love destroyed Art, and often the imperious call of Art put a tragic end to Love. For these two have no accord but only constant battle."

By then, she was sponsored by the Hungarian impresario Alexander Grosz, who risked his entire capital to back her performance at Berlin's famous Kroll Opera House. She became so sought after that varied artists called her "heilige Isadora" (Saint Isadora).

In an effort to articulate verbally her unorthodox style, she gave a lecture that March at the Berlin Presse Verein that was later published in pamphlet form as "The Dance of the Future." "The dance of the future will have to become again a high religious art as it was with the Greeks," she wrote. "For art which is not religious is not art, is mere merchandise."

In 1903, after further performances in Paris and Germany, Duncan took the family to Athens, there to look for a site where—as she said—"the Clan Duncan" could "build a temple that should be characteristic of us." They bought a hill outside the city. Named Kopanos, it had belonged to five shepherds. She attempted to finance her scheme by public recitals, and indeed her final performance was attended by the nation's monarch, King George I. Once again, however, she was broke.

In 1904, she was back in Germany. That summer, she danced to Richard Wagner's *Tannhäuser* at Bayreuth with the approval of the composer's widow *Cosima Wagner. Towards the end of the year, with the aid of her sister Elizabeth, Isadora opened her first school of the dance at Grünewald, a suburb of Berlin. Twenty girls, between the ages of four and eight, enrolled. Her most gifted students would henceforth be called "the Isadorables" and go on tour with her.

Professionally, during the next decade, Duncan met with nothing but success. Tours took her throughout Europe and the United States. In the late winter of 1908, while performing in

Russia, the stronghold of ballet, she had a flirtation with Constantin Stanislavski, the innovative director of the Moscow Art Theater. That summer, she performed before the king and queen of England, Edward VII and *Alexandra of Denmark. In the fall, while appearing at New York's Metropolitan Opera House, she created controversy by dancing to Beethoven's Seventh Symphony. At a presentation held in Washington, D.C., she enchanted President Theodore Roosevelt, who praised her art.

For Duncan, however, the most important event in her life was her meeting in Berlin in December 1904 with Gordon Craig. The 32-year-old son of the famed actress *Ellen Terry was captivated when he first saw her perform at the Kroll Opera house. Already married once and the father of several children with two other women, one a young violinist named Elena Meo, he fell in love with Duncan when first introduced. Craig's conception of the stage was manifested through a simplicity of designs, which in its own way paralleled Duncan's struggle for eliminating formalism in the dance. Their affair was stormy, helped neither by her frequent absences on tour nor his refusal to sever relations with Meo, who in January 1905 gave birth to their third child. In September 1906, Duncan gave birth to their daughter Deirdre.

Craig soon found himself professionally jealous of Duncan, who refused to supply him with the funds he was always requesting. (She could never manage her finances.) He also felt guilty over his treatment of Meo. Isadora, for her part, was equally resentful of Gordon, whom she saw as always seeking to make more female conquests. She later wrote: "I could not work, I could not dance. . . . I realized that this state of things must cease. Either Craig's art or mine—to give up my Art I knew to be impossible."

In October 1907, Craig broke off the relationship. Yet within a year she had found a new lover, one whose relationship with her would be equally tempestuous. This was the 41-year-old multimillionaire (Paris) Eugene Singer, scion of the sewing-machine fortune. By this time, with highly successful engagements at the Théâtre Lyrique de la Gaité in the French capital, Duncan had reached the summit of her career. It was there, in fact, that she met Singer, whom she saw as an instrument for rescuing her now bankrupt dancing school. She remembered that when she received his calling card, "Suddenly there rang in my brain, 'Here is my millionaire.'" The handsome and cultured Singer had already been married and was the father of five children. He was

passionately in love with Duncan, taking her on a Mediterranean cruise in his private yacht and installing her new school at Beaulieu, near Nice. But Duncan was not expediential, for she was deeply attracted to the man whom in her autobiography she calls "Lohengrin."

In May 1910, their son Patrick Augustus was born in Beaulieu. Singer was anxious to marry Duncan, but she was unwilling. Moreover, while living with Singer at his château in Paignton, Devonshire, she entered into a brief affair with her accompanist, André Capelet, for whom she first had a strong physical aversion. The relationship was terminated once Singer discovered it. After an American tour early in 1911, she returned to the city of Paris and resumed her relationship with Singer. She had dreams of creating a major building devoted to the performing arts, which would have Louis Sue as architect, Craig as set designer, her brother Augustin as the leading actor, and of course Singer as the bankroller. The edifice, she hoped, would be a "meeting place and haven for all the great artists of the world." Such a combination, however, could not help but be volatile, and the project was soon aborted. By the end of 1912, Singer became disgusted with Duncan's open flirting with playwright Henri Bataille and broke with her.

In 1913, after a tour in Russia, she returned to the city of Paris. On the afternoon of April 19, while just after having lunched with Singer, she learned to her horror that her two children, together with their English governess, had drowned in the Seine en route back to their temporary quarters in Versailles. While her chauffeur was cranking up a stalled motor, the closed auto had accidentally rolled into the river. The burning of the three coffins took place before her eyes.

Though Duncan would perform many times again, henceforth she was a changed woman. Her hair suddenly turned white, something that she tried to disguise by dying it red. Indeed, she believed she had no cause for which to live. She first tried to ease her sorrow by assisting her brother Raymond in relief work among refugees of the Second Balkan War in the province of Epirus, Albania. She then began aimless wandering, initially in Switzerland, then in Italy. Her close friend *Eleanora Duse, a major Italian actress, brought her to her home in Viareggio. Obsessed with the desire to bear another child, Duncan became pregnant with the help of a young Italian sculptor. When the young man—already engaged to be married—broke off the affair, Duncan showed no anger. In August 1914, the infant son died hours after birth. Duse told her: "You must return to your art. It is your only salvation."

Duncan returned to the city of Paris, where Singer bought her a mansion in the suburb of Bellevue. Her neighbor was the sculptor Auguste Rodin, who was amazed by her capacity for recovery: "Isadora Duncan is the greatest woman I have ever known, and her art has influenced my work more than any other inspiration that has come to me. Sometimes I think she is the greatest woman the world has ever known."

In 1914, when World War I broke out, Duncan transported her pupils to the United States, installing them in an estate near Tarrytown, New York. She performed in New York and Chicago, but she could not obtain the funds needed to establish a municipal dance school in New York. Hence, she temporarily deposited her students in a Swiss boarding school, while she toured the Continent.

To the French, Duncan was more than a great dancer; she was a beloved public figure. Not only did she entertain troops and dance "The Marseillaise" with an intense patriotic fervor, she permitted Bellevue to become an army hospital. Narrates biographer **Fredrika Blair**:

> Noble, resolute, and avenging, clad in a fiery tunic, beaten to the ground to rise with superhuman strength, she seemed a whole nation at arms, and when in a final gesture of defiance, she faced the enemy with bared breast, the people rose, tears coursing down their cheeks, and shouted until the walls rang.

In 1916, Duncan toured South America, where she antagonized the Argentineans by dancing to their national anthem in a nightclub but charmed the Brazilians by her *Polonaises*. A year later, she briefly resumed her affair with Singer in New York but the inevitable break soon followed. At a small dinner party at the city's Plaza Hotel, Singer announced that he had taken up an option to buy Madison Square Garden, indeed that he was planning to install Isadora's school there. "Do you mean to tell me," Duncan said, "that you expect me to direct a school in Madison Square Garden? I suppose you want me to advertise prizefights with my dancing." Singer, enraged, left the room without a word, never seeing her again.

While touring San Francisco, she fell in love with the noted pianist Harold Bauer. Bauer was a married man, and the association was a brief one. Her loneliness did not last long, for in New York, she took on another lover, the distinguished pianist Walter Morse Rummel, ten years her junior. In 1920, Rummel and Duncan toured Greece with six of Duncan's female students. When Rummel fell in love with one of Duncan's pupils, she was again shattered. As Blair notes:

> Each love affair after the death of her children had been an attempt to regain her equilibrium, to give her life meaning, and to make it possible for her to work. Each failure, subsequently, plunged her further into despair. In every loss, she felt the ache of all previous losses as if for the first time.

Still desperate to establish her own school of dancing, in the spring of 1921 she accepted an invitation of Leonid Krassine, head of the Soviet Trade Commission, to set up an academy in Russia. In accepting his invitation, she wrote:

> I shall never hear of money in exchange for my work. I want a studio-workshop, a house for myself and pupils, simple food, simple tunics, and the opportunity to give our best work. . . . I want to dance for the masses, for the working people who need my art and have never had the money to come and see me. And I want to dance for them for nothing. . . . If you accept me on these terms I will come and work for the future of the Russian Republic and its children.

Arriving in Moscow in July 1921, Duncan soon was performing before Lenin. When she danced Tchaikovsky's *Marche Slave* at a concert marking the fourth anniversary of the Bolshevik revolution, the Russian dictator was so enamored that he stood up and shouted, "Bravo, bravo, Miss Duncan!" She was given an empty mansion in a once fashionable part of the city to teach some 50 students. Yet food and fuel were scarce, and within a month the Soviet government withdrew its support. She responded by urging the Soviets to be more revolutionary in the culture it supported while, at the same time, hoping that Herbert Hoover's American Relief Association would come to her aid.

That November, she met Sergei Esenin, a poet some 17 years her junior. The encounter was dramatic. At the home of artist Georgy Yakulov, Esenin came to the couch where she was sitting, cast himself at her feet, and called her "golden head." Soon he had moved into her quarters. Although Esenin had a record of depression and drunkenness and had already divorced one woman, he was a respected bard who had helped found the Imaginist movement. Duncan was attracted by his looks, talent, and vulnerability. Again she was entering into a volatile relationship, with Esenin sometimes treating her as an object of worship, sometimes beating and cursing her in the most vile language possible, and sometimes departing with the promise never to return.

Isadora Duncan, standing in the west door of the Parthenon (1920).

Yet in May 1922 the couple married, doing so in a civil ceremony that at the same time made her a Soviet citizen. Duncan never really learned Russian, and throughout their relationship they usually communicated through sign language and interpreters. First they journeyed through Western Europe, then in October arrived in the United States. Duncan was angry at being detained by the American immigration authorities, who suspected her of being a Communist spy. She showed her bitterness in Boston. At the end of a performance of *Marche Slave*, she seized the red scarf attached to her costume, thereby revealing more of her body than usual, and shouted: "This is red! So am I! It is the color of life and vigor. You were once wild here. Don't let them tame you."

Boston's mayor James Curley immediately banned further performances in his city and the departments of Labor, Justice, and State investigated possible Soviet ties. She justified her removal of the shawl by telling the press:

> They say I mismanaged my garments. A mere disarrangement of a garment means

nothing. . . . Why should I care what part of my body I reveal? Is not all body and soul an instrument through which the artist expresses his inner message of beauty?

Sergei did not help matters by ripping off part of Isadora's dress at a party, insulting his hosts, and using the world "Yid" (the printed text had said "Jew") in a dramatic reading. When Duncan left the United States in January 1923, she is reported to have told reporters:

> I really ought not to say a word to you newspapermen. You have succeeded in ruining my tour, when I hoped so much to earn

From the movie Isadora, *starring Vanessa Redgrave.*

money to take back to the starving children in Moscow. . . . I am not an anarchist or a Bolshevik. My husband and I are revolutionists. All geniuses worthy of the name are. Every artist has to be to make a mark in the world today. . . . Materialism is the curse of America. . . . I would rather live in Russia on black food and vodka than here in the best hotels. You know nothing of Food, of Love, of Art. . . . So goodbye America. I shall never see you again.

When the couple arrived at Paris' Crillon, Esenin smashed the hotel furniture, forcing Duncan to pay damages. By the fall, the couple was back in Moscow. Within months, Esenin had left her for a granddaughter of Leo and *Sonya Tolstoy, and in December 1925 he hanged himself.

As often with Duncan, the departure of a lover unleashed her creativity. Her special dance in honor of the recently fallen Lenin received particularly strong accolades. Still anxious concerning her school, then in a village named Litvino 50 miles from Moscow, in September 1924 she performed in Berlin. This time she found her powers waning and herself, as she said, "nearly on the verge of suicide." Overweight for a dancer and looking far older than her 47 years, she was again broke.

In her last two years, she lived in Nice, often secretly financed by such friends as Craig and Singer. Here she took on her last lover, Victor Seroff, a Russian pianist who later wrote a eulogistic biography. (The first sentence reads, "Isadora Duncan was the greatest performing artist that the United States ever produced," although the book usually has a more detached tone.) She gave her final performance in July 1927 at Paris' Théâtre Mogator in the full knowledge that this was her swan song.

That same year, Duncan's autobiography, *My Life*, was published. Although praised at the time for its candor, it is unreliable in a number of ways. She took several years off her age, exaggerated the hardships of her second visit to London (the first goes unmentioned), and probably distorted her initial meeting with Craig. She ended her account with her departure to Russia in 1921 and planned to write a sequel on her two years in the Soviet Union.

On September 14, 1927, while in Nice, Duncan took a ride in a Bugatti sports car. Although broke as usual, she pretended she was considering purchasing the auto. She bid her friends goodbye with the words, "*Adieu, mes amis. Je vais à la gloire.*" ("Farewell, my friends. I go to glory.") Just as the car started, her long-fringed shawl caught itself in the spokes of a wheel, crushing her larynx and breaking her neck. The driver sobbed, "I have killed the Madonna." Five days later, the body of Isadora Duncan was cremated, the ashes placed near those of her children in Paris' Père Lachaise cemetery.

SOURCES:

Blair, Fredrika. *Isadora: Portrait of the Artist as a Woman.* NY: McGraw-Hill, 1986.

Duncan, Isadora. *My Life.* NY: Horace Liveright, 1927.

Seroff, Victor. *The Real Isadora.* NY: Dial, 1971.

Terry, Walter. *Isadora Duncan: Her Life, Her Art, Her Legacy.* NY: Dodd, Mead, 1963.

SUGGESTED READING:

Loewenthal, Lilian. *The Search for Isadora: The Legend and Legacy of Isadora Duncan.* Pennington, NJ: Princeton Book Company, 1993.

Macdougall, A.R. *Isadora: A Revolutionary in Art and Love.* NY: Thomas Nelson, 1960.

Magriel, Paul, ed. *Isadora Duncan.* NY: Henry Holt, 1947.

McVay, Gordon. *Isadora and Esenin.* Ann Arbor, MI: Ardis, 1980.

Steegmuller, Francis, ed. *"Your Isadora": The Love Story of Isadora Duncan and Gordon Craig.* NY: Random House, 1961.

COLLECTIONS:

Craig-Duncan Collection, Irma Duncan Rogers Collection, and Dance Collections, all at the Library for the Performing Arts, Lincoln Center, New York.

Isadora Duncan file, Bibliotèque of Conservatoure de Musique, Paris.

Gordon Craig Collection, Bibliotèque Nationale, Paris.

Archive Internationale de la Danse, Bibliotèque de l'Opera, Paris.

RELATED MEDIA:

Isadora (131 min.), fictionalized account starring Vanessa Redgrave, James Fox, Jason Robards, screenplay by **Margaret Drabble**, Clive Exton, and Melvyn Bragg, Universal Pictures, London, 1969.

Justus Doenecke, Professor of History, New College of the University of South Florida, Sarasota, Florida

Duncan, Sheena (1932—)

White South African anti-apartheid activist, pacifist, and protester against capital punishment, who was twice-elected national president of the South African women's political group Black Sash. Born Sheena Sinclair in 1932 in Johannesburg, Transvaal, South Africa; daughter of Jean Sinclair (co-founding member of the Black Sash, an all-women's mostly white English-speaking organization dedicated to fighting apartheid); attended Roedean Girls School, Johannesburg, and Edinburgh College of Domestic Science (Scotland) where she qualified as a domestic science teacher (1953); married a Johannesburg architect, in 1955; children: two born between 1956 and 1963.

Worked as a Home Economist for the Johannesburg City Council Welfare Department (1953–54);

married and moved to Southern Rhodesia (now Zimbabwe, 1955); returned to Johannesburg, South Africa, to join the Black Sash as director of Johannesburg Legal Advice Office (1963); invited by U.S. government to spend six weeks there studying paralegal services (1974); served first term as national president of the Black Sash (1975–78); served for three years as chair of the Johannesburg Diocesan Challenge Group to eliminate racial discrimination within the Anglican church; invited by YWCA Conference on Human Rights to speak to delegates in Britain and Holland (1983); served second term as national president of the Black Sash (1983–86); invited by Swedish government to discuss apartheid legislation with the Swedish Foreign Affairs Ministry (1984); arrested while praying in front of the South African Parliament Building in memory of black mourners killed by police at a funeral (1985); awarded Prize for Freedom by the Liberal International Congress in Hamburg, Germany (1986); called for international economic sanctions against South Africa (1986); elected vice-president of the South African Council of Churches (1987); organized legal advice centers in churches around the country in conjunction with the Family, Home and Life Division of the South African Council of Churches; appointed to the South African Human Rights Commission (1988); as member of the South African Council of Churches, called for moratorium on all pending capital punishment executions (1988); reelected National Advice Office Co-Ordinator for Black Sash (1990); appointed member of Independent Board for Inquiry into Informal Repression (1992).

Publications: contributing editor of Sash *magazine (1966–74); wrote various brochures such as "You and the New Constitution" (1983) and "'The People,' 'These Persons,' or 'Me,'" (1993); (coauthored with A. Chaskalson)* Influx Control: The Pass Laws *(1984).*

Twice elected the national president of Black Sash, the South African English-speaking women's organization, Sheena Duncan guided the association through its most difficult times in the 1970s and 1980s. Once 10,000 strong, by the mid-1990s membership had fallen to about 2,000, a trend that reflected both the banning of the organization's outdoor political assemblies in 1977 and its struggle to redefine itself in post-apartheid South Africa as a source of expert legal advice for black South Africans. Under Duncan's leadership, the focus shifted away from organizing neatly dressed white women standing in silent protest outside government offices to assisting the black community with the convoluted apartheid laws that placed so many restrictions on their daily lives. Largely as a result of her efforts, Black Sash, once dismissed as nothing more than a white liberal feel-good organization, became a highly respected resource for a broad range of legal information.

Apartheid refers to the explicit government policies and laws put in place by the minority white Afrikaans-speaking National Party that took control of South Africa in 1948. Their policy of legalized white supremacy in South Africa was finally toppled when the human rights activist and lawyer Nelson Mandela was released in 1990 from 27 years of detention on Robben Island, a maximum-security prison near Cape Town, and later elected the first black president of South Africa in 1994.

During the apartheid era and under Duncan's leadership, Black Sash became a source of free expert legal advice for black South Africans and was especially effective in helping blacks deal with the notorious pass laws. Beginning in 1910 for men and 1956 for women, black South Africans were required to carry a pass book as a form of identification, until the pass laws were rescinded in 1986 and replaced by other means of control. Black South Africans discovered with a pass book "out of order" were immediately arrested, fined, often jailed, sometimes beaten or tortured by the hated white South African police and likely banished to the rural homelands where many faced hunger and disease. By 1982, over 200,000 black South Africans were arrested each year for pass law violations. The net effect was to severely restrict the movement of black South Africans from their homes in the poor rural areas to jobs in the mainly white urban areas.

Sheena Duncan was born in Johannesburg in 1932, the eldest of five children. Hers was a well-to-do Scottish family in which she enjoyed the privileges of her family's social and economic position. She was raised with the assistance of a white nanny and attended the private girls school, Roedean. Duncan credits her school headmistress **Ella Lemaitre** with providing her with an "introduction to things being wrong." Recalled Duncan to **Beata Lipman**: "She was a personal friend of Trevor Huddleston and of Alan Paton, so that some of my very earliest memories of becoming aware arose from visits to places like Diepkloof Reformatory, which Paton was running, and having Father Huddleston coming to talk at school and knowing what kind of work his Community of the Resurrection was doing in those days. They're the kind of churchmen who have intelligently used their compassion and their knowledge of what goes on in a wider political context."

After graduating from high school, Duncan was escorted by her mother to Edinburgh, Scotland, and delivered into the hands of her aunts for further education as a teacher of domestic science. When she returned to Johannesburg in 1953, she married her childhood sweetheart, an architect, and they relocated to Southern Rhodesia (now Zimbabwe), where their two children would be born.

But the similarities between Duncan's family and other advantaged white South African families did not run deep. Raised in "a home where conversation was conversation, not gossip," Duncan recalled that family discussions "tended to range around subjects of public interest." In an interview with *The Washington Post*, she noted: "The focus was on World War II and when we talked about injustice, we were thinking about the Jewish people." Talking with **Peggy Dye Moberg**, a writer for *The Christian Science Monitor*, Duncan said, "I cannot remember a time when I was not against apartheid. I was brought up in a house where the concept of justice was very strong. My Christianity was also a strand. The gospel demands that you heal

Sheena Duncan

the sick, feed the hungry, visit the prisons. That means more than running soup kitchens. It means curing the reasons for the sick and hungry." As a child, Duncan was taken to see Sophiatown, a black township outside Johannesburg. "That was an exceptional thing for a white child to be taken into a black town. There were hundreds and hundreds of children there, and I was a child, too. Later in the 1950s when it was announced that all the houses would be knocked down and all the black people moved (to make way for white urban growth), it meant something to me."

Black Sash was formed in 1955 in Johannesburg by Duncan's mother, **Jean Sinclair**, and four other women from the Women's League for the Defense of the Constitution. Sinclair explained, "We enlisted only women because the men were quarreling among themselves and there was a feeling that women would get on with it." These women were mainly English-speaking members of General Jan Smut's United Party which was defeated by the Afrikaans-speaking National Party in 1948. The women protested the new policy of removing people of mixed race ("coloureds") from the voters roll in the Cape region of South Africa. The women wore black sashes slung diagonally from their right shoulders, displayed placards criticizing apartheid government policies, stood in silent protest with their eyes cast down at their feet and mourned the death of democracy outside government offices. If the demonstrators did not speak out loud, they could not be arrested or prosecuted for an illegal public display. Although they lost this first fight, they gained their name, Black Sash, and broadened their campaign to defend the civil rights of those who suffered the most disenfranchisement under the intensified apartheid legislation of the National Party—black South Africans. The group's early protest strategy included very organized stands. Protesters who were standing alone had a support person within view, whose job it was to draw away any member of the public who attempted to engage the woman holding a placard in conversation. This strategy was intended to keep the protester from being accused of involvement in an illegal gathering.

Black Sash was one of the first white organizations to call for universal voting and the abolition of the death penalty. They also maintained contact with banned organizations that were fighting for the same issues but using civil-disobedience tactics declared illegal under apartheid. According to **Kathryn Spink**, by the

late 1960s the press would telephone Black Sash offices whenever an incident occurred:

> Through its advice office work the Black Sash could keep a unique finger on the pulse of what was happening in the black communities even when restrictions on the media denied such information to other parties. . . . The advice office could thus mobilize and "conscientise" both those who worked in them and the people who came for assistance. . . . This was the starting point for various strategies employed to force the government to act, strategies in which the essential ingredient was public knowledge. The initial step was invariably to inform the public of carefully substantiated facts of which, in segregated South African society, it might otherwise be totally unaware, and so raise public concerns about a particular grievance.

To this end they collected petitions challenging the three pillars of the apartheid National Party government: (1) physical removal of blacks to "homelands" where they were confined on less than 14% of the total land in South Africa, (2) a system of passes and laws designed to keep blacks from moving permanently into the white urban areas, and (3) a political structure that stripped South African citizenship from millions of blacks.

As a result of this change in Black Sash's agenda and an increasingly hostile political atmosphere, membership that peaked at 10,000 in the 1960s soon dwindled to a fifth of this number. Michael Hornsby, writing for *The Times* (Johannesburg), notes, "It was one thing for middle-class ladies of English background to be asked to protest against the unconstitutional machinations of a Boer government, it was quite another to expect them to campaign for equal citizenship with blacks." In her 1990 article, Duncan recalled, "They called each other 'Mrs.' and wore hats. But those women in the early days were considered communists by their peers." In response to accusations by whites that women like Duncan were dishonest communists, and that a militant grouping existed within Sash, Duncan remarked, "It's very hard to make white people know and understand the truth. They have no dealings with black people." She wrote in 1990: "We are simply a human rights organization."

Despite their political activities, most Black Sash members escaped punishment and prosecution by the National Party. In *Cry Amandla! South African Women and the Question of Power*, **June Goodwin** quotes Duncan: "We're not banned because the government doesn't think we're effective enough to worry about, that is, because we're women. We're immune because we're unequal. . . . Women's lack of equality in the Nationalist Afrikaaner society is extraordinary." In 1985, Duncan wryly commented to Andie Tucher that Black Sash "has certain advantages in pressing for reform, and that to some extent women protesters are protected by their sex. . . . We have a very old-fashioned government that does not take women seriously. And it is quite an advantage to be regarded as an ornament." In the same year, she told *The Washington Post*, "Just as the visibility of Bishop Desmond Tutu gives him greater protection, being white gives us more protection. But that in turn gives us greater responsibility."

According to Duncan, a key factor in avoiding the ire of the apartheid government was Black Sash's refusal to advocate civil disobedience. She explained to Goodwin, "One of the earliest national conference resolutions was that Black Sash would protest by all lawful means. That decision was made at a time when it was perfectly possible to do what they wanted by lawful means. In those days they could have mass marches, ten abreast."

However, by 1977, all outdoor political "assemblies" were illegal, and at the moment when membership was shrinking Black Sash was forced to develop new methods of peaceful demonstration. Under Duncan's leadership, the group's tactics expanded to include the distribution of posters, pamphlets, letters and handouts, to workshops and public meetings around the country, to press statements and international speaking tours. The group evolved into a sophisticated organization with an arsenal of peaceful weapons to force the government to change its policies of strict racial segregation under apartheid. With the belief that if the white community adopted these strategies they could make a positive influence on government action, Duncan explained to Spink: "One can seek action in court that will lead to an order being made that will instruct government to do something. One can force government to do things by raising sufficient pressure in the electorate and amongst members of parliament for policy to be changed. For example—to induce the government to provide houses for the homeless. Boycotting elections, signing petitions, silent vigils and demonstrations, and letter writing campaigns all need to involve the white community in order to expose the truth about pass laws and the homelands."

During the apartheid era, one of the group's main roles was the "support and encouragement and counseling" of blacks who became entangled in South Africa's intricate maze of pass laws and other discriminatory legislation. Black Sash worked to resolve cases of unfair dismissal, wrongful eviction, and applications for citizenship by arming clients with the necessary documentation and then directing them to the proper government offices. Speaking in 1985 to **Dorothy Gilliam** of *The Washington Post*, Duncan explained, "We play a limited supporting role to blacks. We never go to a community, but we wait for them to ask us. If, for example, a community is being removed to a homeland, they may ask us to help set up a press conference. People ask for help with all sorts of problems." When it comes to dealing with fellow whites, however, the Sash was more aggressive: "We try to be a catalyst by explaining to white South Africans what apartheid really means, to show them that civil war is inevitable on the current path." Tucher has called Duncan "particularly skilled at the important task of what she calls 'nagging and pushing and shoving' South African leaders, as well as the more sober business of providing an analysis of what's really happening and what different things mean for the international community."

> Our task is to find non-violent ways in which power can be transferred to the powerless thereby creating a society of true peace and justice.
>
> —Sheena Duncan

Often even legal training could not render the frequently amended pass laws decipherable because of their obscure provisions and tortuous language. "Outside of Sash," Goodwin writes, "nobody in this country—except the government's Black Affairs Department—understands that the pass laws and all that goes with them are the foundation, the cornerstone of the whole structure [of apartheid]. Sash has a broad vision of the system because of its day-to-day work at the advice offices. Almost no lawyers understand it; they never handle these cases."

Duncan compiled the brochure *You and the New Pass Laws*, which was distributed to 50,000 black South Africans in the 1980s and was widely recognized as the definitive explanation of the devastating implications of the pass laws which took from eight million black people the most basic civil rights. Spink notes that, no longer able to claim a share to the land and wealth of South Africa, blacks could be deported to the homelands, had no right to a South African passport, and were subject to arrest if caught in an urban area without a permit.

By the early 1980s, the tactics Duncan developed for addressing the inequities of the apartheid system were beginning to fail. In a 1983 interview with Joseph Lelyveld of *The New York Times,* Duncan admitted that she was "ready to give up work because she found that much of her time was either devoted to counseling those who were actually beyond her help or devising ways where people who have some rights can finally get them." The government had effectively closed many of the loopholes in the pass laws with new legislation, and Black Sash found it could no longer make a real difference in the lives of the blacks who sought assistance against many types of discrimination.

After the government rescinded the pass laws in 1986 by passing even more restrictive legislation, Duncan refocused her political tactics on organizing the successful 1986 "Free the Children" campaign to release more than 1,000 black children aged 10 to 17 from prisons. She noted, "There is more concern voiced for pets on state-run radio than for children." Black Sash estimated that at least 8,000 children were imprisoned during the nationwide State of Emergency in the first year, 1986. Duncan's organization delivered food to children in jail and organized national and international pressure to release them.

Regarding the main function of Black Sash as political pressure, "which we carry out through educating the black community," Duncan rededicated her efforts in the post-pass laws era to providing free legal advice at several Black Sash office locations around South Africa. Michael Getler of *The Washington Post* described Duncan's downtown Johannesburg office in 1987: "Scores of black people fill a small complex of offices while the overflow crowd lines up patiently in the corridor and down the steps from the offices of Sheena Duncan. . . . More than 16,000 persons were helped here last year, an estimated 30,000 nationwide." Goodwin adds, "Duncan sits at a small table. . . . At her side, a black woman translates. In one afternoon she dealt with these issues: how to obtain pensions; how to transfer a house to a child; how to get one's name on the 22,000 person waiting list for a house in Soweto; women who need help because their husbands have deserted them." Duncan's work with women was widespread. She reported to Lipman: "In the South African Council of Churches we find as we go about the country with our work that women are often the strongest members of a local community, so that most of my work in the Council lies in

teaching women's groups. You do find that the people involved at the grass roots in the rural areas tend to be women. . . . There's a sort of power of endurance in women. . . . Their sense of close responsibility for their children doesn't appear to be so easily destroyed by the dreadful social conditions."

One of Black Sash's central goals was to reach the white South African community without resorting to violence. "I am a staunch pacifist," said Duncan to Spink, "whose avowed aim is to find non-violent ways in which power can be transferred to the powerless, not out of any desire for the defeat or subjugation of the currently powerful, but in the true longing for a society in which equal distribution of powers would lead to peace and justice preserved in that creative tension which exists between conflicting interests of equal strengths."

Duncan credited her religious nature with her commitment to improving the circumstances of those not born to privilege. The church in South Africa, however, was not always a source of strength for her. "I was a child during the Second World War," she remarked to Goodwin. "I remember the glamour of uniforms. . . . And today, Christianity props up the system. . . . The church supports all sorts of militaristic functions in our society. The church prays for our white soldiers, but there is no suggestion that blacks on the other side are also Christian youth in need of our prayers." Perhaps it was this ultimate betrayal of her faith by the South African church that led Duncan in her 1986 presidential address to the Black Sash national conference to reveal a change in her position on civil disobedience. Spink reprinted part of her speech:

> I believe that there is one small hope left in South Africa and that lies in those political movements and black communities who have withdrawn and are withdrawing their cooperation from the apartheid state. The withdrawal of cooperation entails civil disobedience. Civil disobedience is not to be taken lightly but only in deep respect for the idea of law. All societies need a framework of law in which people can know what it is to be free. It is the law which is necessary to uphold justice and democracy and peace in free societies. Civil disobedience must not be entered into when the law can offer redress. It is a last resort. In South Africa the law does not offer redress for the many gross violations of civil liberties and human rights which are part of the laws of this country.

The printed version of Duncan's speech was seized by the South African police before it could be distributed to the public.

SOURCES:

Duncan, Sheena. "Forced Removals Mean Genocide." in *Lives of Courage: Women for a New South Africa.* NY: Basic Books, 1989, pp. 312–328.

———. "The Rights of Ordinary People," in *Values Alive: A Tribute to Helen Suzman.* Edited by Robin Lee. Johannesburg: Jonathan Ball, 1990, pp. 53–61.

Gastrow, Shelagh. "Sheena Duncan" in *Who's Who in South African Politics.* Johannesburg: Ravan Press, 1985, pp. 78–80.

Getler, Michael. "Scenes of Irony Abound in a Land Defined by Race: Blacks and Whites Inhabit Two Worlds," in *The Washington Post.* February 11, 1987.

Gilliam, Dorothy. "Apartheid Resistance," in *The Washington Post.* July 29, 1985.

Goodwin, June. *Cry Amandla! South African Women and the Question of Power.* NY: Africana Publishing, 1984 (see especially chapter 14).

Hornsby, Michael. "Resistance Born from the Death of a Constitution," in *The Times* (Johannesburg). January 31, 1986.

Lelyveld, Joseph. "A White Women's Group Counters Apartheid," in *The New York Times.* February 27, 1983.

Lipman, Beata. "Sheena Duncan." in *We Make Freedom: Women in South Africa.* London: Pandora Press, 1984, pp. 131–135.

Moberg, Peggy Dye. "Sheena Duncan," in *Christian Science Monitor.* October 31, 1985.

"Sheena Duncan." *Washington Post.* July 28, 1985.

Spink, Kathryn. *Black Sash: The Beginning of a Bridge in South Africa.* London: Methuen, 1991.

Tucher, Andie. "Human Rights: South African Women Fight Apartheid," in *Inter Press Service.* October 11, 1985.

SUGGESTED READING:

Lazar, Carol (photographs by Peter Magubane). *Women of South Africa: Their Fight for Freedom.* Boston: Bulfinch Press (Little, Brown), 1993.

Lazerson, Joshua. *Against the Tide: Whites in the Struggle Against Apartheid.* Boulder, CO: Westview Press, 1994.

Walker, Cherryl. *Women and Resistance in South Africa.* London: Onyx Press, 1982.

RELATED MEDIA:

"Women of South Africa" (2-part series), produced by Britain's Channel 4 (interview with Sheena Duncan in "Part 2: South Africa Belongs to Us"), 1986.

Kearsley Alison Stewart, Lecturer, Department of Anthropology and Women's Studies Program, University of Georgia, Athens, Georgia

Dunham, Katherine (1909—)

African-American choreographer, anthropologist, and social activist who first introduced Afro-Caribbean dance to American audiences and created the first African-American dance troupe in the U.S. Name variations: (pseudonym) Kaye Dunn. Born Katherine Dunham on June 22, 1909, in Glen Ellyn, Illinois; daughter of Albert Millard Dunham and Fanny June (Taylor) Dunham; had one older brother, Albert, Jr., who died in 1949; attended University of Chicago and received a degree in social anthropology in 1936; married Jordis McCoo, in 1931 (divorced 1939); married Thomas Pratt, in 1939 (died 1986); children: one adopted daughter, Marie-Christine.

Co-founded the Ballet Negre in Chicago (1929) and, later, the Negro Dance Group; traveled to Trinidad, Jamaica, and Haiti (1935–36) and adapted Afro-Caribbean dance rhythms to her own ballets; created the Katherine Dunham Dance Company (1938), which appeared on stage and film to great acclaim (1940s–50s); established the Katherine Dunham Performing Arts Training Center in East St. Louis, Illinois, for urban African-American youth (1967); active in civil-rights movement and social causes, staging a 47-day hunger strike in protest of U.S. treatment of Haitian refugees fleeing political and economic strife (1992).

Choreography: (stage) Negro Rhapsody, L'Ag'YA, Tropics, Le Jazz Hot, Tropical Review, Carib Song, Windy City, Bal Negre, Caribbean Rhapsody, Los Indios, Shango, Bambouche, Aïda (for the Metropolitan Opera Company); (film) Carnival of Myth, Star Spangled Banner, Pardon My Sarong, Mumbo, Cakewalk, Green Mansions.

While those who knew her were alarmed, few were surprised when Katherine Dunham, on a chill afternoon in late January of 1992, announced her protest of the U.S. government's policy toward Haitian refugees by embarking on a hunger strike. For most of her 82 years, Dunham's passion for social justice had run high, particularly when it came to her beloved Haiti; and for the next 47 days, as Dunham refused to take anything but cranberry juice and tea, notables as diverse as film director Jonathan Demme and the Reverend Jesse Jackson came to the shabby, two-story house in East St. Louis, Illinois, to pay their respects to the woman whom choreographer Alvin Ailey once called "the mother of us all."

Born to a middle-class family in rural Glen Ellyn, Illinois, in 1909, Katherine Dunham had early on felt a strong attraction to music and rhythm, which would prove to be unlikely catalysts for her social crusading. In her fictionalized autobiography *A Touch of Innocence,* published in 1959, Dunham would remember her mother's harp and organ playing. **Fanny Taylor Dunham**, a French-Canadian who claimed a Native-American heritage, died when Katherine was only three; and, as Dunham recalled in the third person, "with her father alone, there was seldom music." Albert Dunham, a dry cleaner and dyer, moved his daughter and son Albert, Jr.—some years older than Katherine—to Joliet, Illinois, where they were left in the care of an aunt. From then on, the two children would see little of their father, who later remarried.

It was music that remained Katherine's chief joy in school, even when she caused a stir by refusing to sing an old Southern song taught to her class by a white music teacher, who particularly relished the lyric: "Came to a river and I couldn't get across/ Jumped on a nigger 'cuz I thought he was a hoss." Letters from family friends, and personal visits to the school principal by her aunt and her father, led the school to quietly suggest the music teacher drop that particular ballad from the repertoire. By the time she was eight years old, Dunham had successfully organized a cabaret to raise money for her church, writing and performing most of the music and dances, and adding $32 to the church's coffers.

I used to want the words "She tried" on my tombstone. Now, I want "She did it."

—Katherine Dunham

Dunham's other great comfort was her brother Albert. The two grew close during those lonely times in Joliet, especially afternoons after school, when Albert would read to her from science-fiction magazines and tell her about his dreams of attending school in Chicago. When he finally left Joliet for the University of Chicago, Dunham followed him to the city as soon as she graduated from high school, finding work in department stores, attending ballet school, and plunging eagerly into Chicago's lively arts community of the mid-1920s. Albert founded the Cube Theater, an experimental venture that featured the work of African-American writers and performers. It was here that Dunham met playwright Langston Hughes, actor Canada Lee, composer W.C. Handy, and appeared on stage professionally for the first time, taking a dramatic role in *The Man Who Died at Twelve O'-Clock*. It was also at this time that she met poet, painter, and dancer Mark Turbyfill, who invited her to help him set up his Ballet Negre, modelled on Serge Diaghilev's Ballets Russes. It would be the country's first completely African-American dance troupe, with Turbyfill rehearsing the dancers to Dunham's choreography. As she would find out throughout her professional life, money was a problem. The Ballet Negre gave only one public performance, at Chicago's Beaux Arts Theatre, before disbanding in 1931, after two years. Shortly afterward, Katherine married Jordis McCoo, whom she had met through her work at the Cube.

Although the success of the Ballet Negre had been less than spectacular, the idea of an all-black dance troupe intrigued Katherine Dunham. It wasn't long before her Negro Dance Group set up shop in an unheated loft, and Dunham began researching the roots of the urban dances upon which she based much of her choreography—the Lindy, the cake walk, the black bottom. With the advice and guidance of an anthropologist at the university, she was soon immersed in African dance traditions, which she incorporated into her own work. The Dance Group gave its first, scantily attended, performances in the early 1930s; and, in 1934, at the Chicago World's Fair, Dunham made her own professional debut dancing *La Guiablesse* (The She-Devil), a dance created by her friend *Ruth Page, based on a folk tale from Martinique.

While the Negro Dance Group's future seemed as uncertain as that of the Ballet Negre, one audience member was impressed enough to contact Dunham with an invitation. *Edith Rosenwald Stern happened to serve on the board of the Rosenwald Foundation, which provided grants for academic research. The board may not have been prepared for the type of proposal that Dunham gave them by stripping off her prim two-piece suit and performing an African war dance in her rehearsal tights. Nonetheless, the Foundation gave her a grant for research in social anthropology, and, in 1935, Dunham began a year-and-a-half project studying the local dance traditions of the Caribbean.

She traveled in Martinique, Trinidad, Jamaica, and, finally, Haiti, with whose people and culture she would form a deep and abiding relationship. Living in remote villages in Haiti's back-country, she found a rich source of material in the dances and ritual of *voudun,* into which she was initiated. She would later tell how she had lain on her side for three days as part of the initiation rites, her hair full of eggshells and feathers, and announced that she had taken the snake god Dumballa as her personal deity. In years to come, she would take care to sprinkle the stage with perfume before every performance to appease him. Her research, she said, was intended to find out "what we are really like, [instead of] what we have been made into by slavery and/or colonialism."

Based on her work in the Caribbean, Dunham received her bachelor's degree in social anthropology in 1936 from the University of Chicago and was offered a Rockefeller scholarship to allow her to work toward her master's degree. But by now she had decided to make dance her

Katherine
Dunham

career, though she continued to write scholarly articles under the name Kaye Dunn throughout the 1930s and 1940s. "You can learn more about people from their dances than from almost anything else about them," she said, and she set out to show the world what she had discovered.

Her dance group's New York debut came in March 1937, at a "Negro Dance Evening" organized by the YWHA in Manhattan. The next year, she staged her first full-scale choreographic work, *L'Ag'YA,* based on folklore from Martinique, and was named dance director for the

WPA's Federal Dance Project in Chicago. By 1939, she was back in New York, choreographing *Pins and Needles* at the Labor Stage for the International Ladies Garment Workers' Union and presenting two more of her original works, *Tropics* and *Le Jazz Hot.* Before the year was out, she had divorced McCoo and married John Pratt, a white man who had joined her company as a costume and set designer two years earlier. The marriage, while troubled at times, would last until Pratt's death in 1986. The company, now called the Katherine Dunham Dancers, attracted attention from major supporters with their appearance in the 1940 Broadway musical *Cabin in the Sky,* in which they danced to George Balanchine's choreography. Co-starring with *Ethel Waters, Dunham played the wily Georgia Brown. When Dunham's own *Tropical Revue* opened on Broadway in 1944, the box office was soon taking in $17,000 a week—a record for its time.

Over the next decade, the Dunham company gained an international reputation for presenting works of startling originality, establishing a fertile ground for the growth of what came to be regarded as "modern" dance—even though much of her work was based on material that was centuries old. She was, in fact, often accused of plagiarizing a cultural heritage for her own ends. In 1957, Richard Buckle, editor of the English magazine *Ballet,* called her *Caribbean Rhapsody* "a disconcerting mixture of revived folk dance and ritual," and said it was as if "Dunham had explored a whole culture and resuscitated a whole corpus of age-old, obsolescent tradition only to use them as sauce and stuffing to an ephemeral entertainment." But Dunham was not to be denied the same creative impulse that had inspired West Indian slaves to turn the staid, courtly dances of their French and British masters into a body of dance and movement full of color, rhythm and vitality. "I'd not consider myself too terribly talented," she rejoined, "if I only reproduced what I saw elsewhere." She was frequently charged, too, with ignoring other cultures' dance traditions by limiting herself strictly to Afro-Caribbean dance. But she told *Dance* in 1956, "I don't see any color in what we do. I see human emotions. It's only a fortunate accident that I've hit upon and used material chiefly of people with Negro background."

Even though she tried to use the troupe's multiethnic composition as an example of racial harmony, Katherine Dunham was continually confronted with racial prejudice during her company's touring life. The State Department routinely turned down her offers to form an American cultural program for overseas audiences, refusals she would later brand as racist; the troupe was often denied accommodation at major hotels, leading to successful lawsuits against two of them, in Chicago and Cincinnati; and she once told an all-white audience in Lexington, Kentucky, who had just warmly received the company's performance, that they would not be appearing there again because the theater's management refused "to let people like us sit next to people like you."

By the mid-1950s, strains began to pull the Katherine Dunham Dancers apart. Dunham had been touring nearly constantly at home and abroad, had battled discriminatory practices from Broadway to Hollywood (where she had been told that her troupe would never appear in films because there weren't enough "pale-skinned" dancers in the company), struggled to keep the company financed and her school in New York open, all the while creating and mounting new productions. There were troubles in her personal life, too. Her beloved brother Albert had died in 1949 after a nervous breakdown, and her marriage to John Pratt had become troubled, leading Pratt to quit the company in the middle of an Asian tour. In 1957, after a performance in Japan, Dunham announced she was disbanding the troupe and retiring from public performance. After recuperating in Japan, Dunham returned to her beloved Haiti, where she had purchased a former plantation, Habitacion LeClerc. During the next several years, she established a medical clinic for poor Haitians and donated some of her land to the nation as a botanical garden, bird sanctuary, and an outdoor theater. In 1959, Haiti's then-president, François "Papa Doc" Duvalier, made her a Commander and Grand Officer of his Legion Of Honor.

But dance remained her first love. Before long, she had established a studio at Habitacion LeClerc; and in 1962, she began to put the Katherine Dunham Dance Company back together, finally opening in New York with a new work, *Bambouche,* in October of 1962 and setting up a new dance studio on 42nd Street, where *Eartha Kitt and even Marlon Brando came to learn her technique. The next year saw the premiere of her controversial choreography for the Metropolitan Opera's production of *Aïda,* sensual and opulent even by the Met's standards; and, in 1965, she presented an equally provocative staging of *Faust* at Southern Illinois University (SIU), setting Goethe's medieval story in World War II Germany.

While she was rehearsing *Faust,* Dunham happened to visit nearby East St. Louis, Illinois, across the Mississippi River from St. Louis, Missouri. Shocked by the lack of proper health, educational, and housing resources in the primarily black city, not to mention a total lack of any cultural opportunities, she immediately wrote a proposal to provide such services, built around what she called a "cultural village." Although Buckminster Fuller designed and built one of the village's proposed domes, the project never advanced further.

Nonetheless, Dunham could not forget the poverty, hopelessness, and anger she had seen, even more so when they exploded into riots during the troubled summer of 1967. That year, as an artist in residence at SIU, she set up a cultural arts program at the university, which included three community centers and a small performing arts group, which she called the Performing Arts Training Center. The Center's first presentation—a staging of Langston Hughes' *Dreams Deferred*—was performed in parks and schools throughout East St. Louis, aspiring to build a sense of identity and community, and leading to further programs in the cultural arts. "If they didn't want to learn dance," Dunham recalled for an interviewer, "we taught them judo and karate and percussion."

The real test came the following year. In April of 1968, when news of the assassination of Dr. Martin Luther King, Jr., reached East St. Louis, anger flared into violence, as it did in so many African-American communities across America. Dunham remained in the midst of it, managing to persuade some of East St. Louis' young people to vent their anger through the drumming she had learned 30 years earlier in Haiti. For 12-to-14 hours a day, for days on end, the drumbeats pounded throughout the city. Dunham was fearless in venturing out into the streets, and, while trying to prevent the innocent from being rounded up in random police raids and sent to jail, she was herself arrested and imprisoned until officials of SIU intervened for her release. She later persuaded the authorities to free many of those arrested, and even set up a program to transport young people in police cars and vans to classes and rehearsals at her Training Center.

"I've never known what it's like to believe a thing cannot be done," Dunham once said, and the years since 1968 in East St. Louis have borne that statement out. Dunham went on to create the Katherine Dunham Fund for Research and Development of Cultural Arts and counseled drug addicts, set up nutritional programs, and worked with senior citizens—just some of the activities that brought her the 1979 Albert Schweitzer Award "for a life dedicated to music and devoted to humanity."

Approaching her ninth decade of life, Katherine Dunham refused to rest on past accomplishments or give up her devotion to social justice. "I'd rather lose my body than my morality," she once said. The 1992 hunger strike in support of Haitian refugees was followed by her outspoken advocacy of the Reverend Bertrand Aristide's claim to Haiti's presidency—a position she has seen vindicated after her equally public support for the use of U.S. troops in Haiti to establish that claim.

Dunham then turned to fighting to save her own work. Her modest home in East St. Louis was badly in need of repair, with her personal archives, comprising 50 years' worth of work, threatened by dampness and leaks, to say nothing of the perilous state of the Dunham Center for the Performing Arts. Dunham told *Dance* in 1995 that the Center had received no funds from Southern Illinois University or anyone else for several years, and that she would be unable to support it with her own resources much longer. (SIU's Katherine Dunham Dancers merely used her name, with Dunham's permission, and was not under her direction or control.) In those later years, a reporter who visited Dunham, taking note of the wheelchair in which she was confined and looking over the photographs from her endangered collection, asked her when she stopped dancing. "Never," she retorted, then added sweetly, "because you dance inside yourself."

SOURCES:
Beckford, Ruth. *Katherine Dunham: A Biography.* NY: Marcel Dekker, 1979.
Ben-Itzak, Paul. "Dunham Legacy Stands at Risk," in *Dance Magazine.* Vol. 69, no. 1. January 1995.
Buckle, Richard. "Adventures of a Ballet Critic: Concerning the Dunham Dancers," in *Ballet Magazine.* Vol. 2. June–September 1958.
Campbell, Bebe Moore. "The 1990 Essence Awards," in *Essence.* Vol. 21, no. 6. October 1990.
Dunham, Katherine. *A Touch of Innocence.* NY: Harcourt Brace, 1959.
Glieck, Elizabeth. "Hunger Strike: Dance Legend Katherine Dunham Ends Her Fast for the People of Haiti," in *People Weekly.* Vol. 37, no. 12. March 30, 1992.

RELATED MEDIA:
Dance in America: Divine Drumbeats, produced by WNET-TV, originally broadcast on PBS, April 1990.

Norman Powers, writer-producer, Chelsea Lane Productions, New York, New York

Duniway, Abigail Scott (1834–1915)

American writer, editor, and businesswoman who was a leader in the women's suffrage movement. Born Abigail Jane Scott (nicknamed Jenny) on October 22,

1834, in a log cabin in Groveland, Tazewell County, Illinois; died on October 11, 1915, in Portland, Oregon; second daughter and third child of John Tucker Scott (a farmer and sawmill owner) and Ann (Roelofson) Scott; schooled mostly at home and self-taught; had less than a year of formal education; married Benjamin C. Duniway, on August 2, 1853 (died 1896); children: **Clara Belle Stearns** *(1854–1886);* Willis *(1856–1913);* Hubert *(b. 1859);* Wilkie Collins *(b. 1861);* Claude Augustus *(b. 1866);* Ralph *(b. 1869).*

Immigrated to Oregon via the Oregon Trail (1852); published first novel, Captain Gray's Company *(1859); founded and began teaching at Lafayette Union School (1862); helped found Oregon State Equal Suffrage Association (1870); established* New Northwest *weekly newspaper (1871); went on first lecture tour, in company of suffragist Susan B. Anthony (1871); women's suffrage referendum passed in Oregon (1912).*

Selected publications: Captain Gray's Company; or Crossing the Plains and Living in Oregon *(1859);* My Musings *(1875);* David and Anna Matson *(1876);* From the West to the West: Across the Plains to Oregon *(1905);* Path Breaking: An Autobiographical History of the Equal Suffrage Movement in Pacific Coast States *(1914).*

Abigail Scott Duniway hated patchwork quilts. "Nobody but a fool," she wrote in 1880, "would spend so much time in cutting bits of dry goods into yet smaller bits and sewing them together again, just for the sake of making believe that they were busy at practical work." For Duniway, the quilt was a symbol of woman's unpaid subjection within a male-dominated society, a situation she was determined to change.

> *When woman's true history shall have been written, her part in the upbuilding of this nation will astound the world.*
> —Abigail Scott Duniway

Born in a log cabin on October 22, 1834, in newly settled Tazewell County, Illinois, Abigail Jane Scott, whom the family nicknamed Jenny, was the second daughter and third child of the twelve children of John Tucker Scott and **Ann Roelofson Scott**. Their first child, a boy, had died within four months of his birth, and they grieved when Abigail was born, so great was their disappointment over the birth of another girl. Abigail's behavior during her childhood did not help her cause. She was a wild, difficult, and dreamy child.

Abigail's parents were farmers, who believed in hard work. Abigail had many household du-

ties, including washing dishes, milking cows, making butter, planting and hoeing corn and potatoes, and helping her younger brother, Harvey, gather and chop wood. She also picked wool by hand (her most hated task), and then spinned, spooled, reeled, and hanked it. Later, in her first serialized novel, and her only novel dealing with early childhood experience, Duniway chose wool picking as prime punishment for the female child character. Despite her dislike for the numerous chores, Abigail worked herself harder than her parents demanded and suffered numerous ailments as a result, including rheumatoid arthritis, which affected her throughout her life.

Largely due to her fragile health, Duniway was unable to spend much time in a formal educational setting. Though she attended lessons at nearby Pleasant Grove schoolhouse for about five months and in 1850 was enrolled in a school she later described as "an apology for an academy," she received most of her education at home. Newspapers were important to those on the frontier. For Abigail, they were valuable tools for improving her reading skills. She also relied upon a Webster's Elementary Spelling book which she so valued that she later carried it across the plains to Oregon.

The Scott family experienced financial ups and downs. In 1840, John Scott lost their farm and in 1842 was forced to declare bankruptcy. Family fortunes improved in 1846, however, when John borrowed money and was able to purchase the first circular sawmill west of Ohio. This enabled the family to move from their log cabin into a larger home. The Scotts lived in the path of the emigration to the West, and John had for years been longing to join the migration to Oregon. By 1850, he was financially able to consider such a move. Though Ann Scott was reluctant to make the long journey, John believed that a move to the temperate Oregon climate would benefit her health. She had recently become an invalid following the difficult birth and loss of her twelfth child. Thus, the Scott family was among the emigrants making up the migration of 1852, the largest in American history.

The overland journey to Western Oregon began April 2, 1852, and ended on October 1. The six months were filled with wonder, hardship, and tragedy for the Scott family. Believing she was best qualified, they assigned Abigail the task of keeping a journal to chronicle their experiences along the way. She also wrote to family left behind in Illinois.

Duniway saw slavery for the first time when the family crossed into Missouri. Offering the family's opinion of the institution, she wrote, "Slavery is a withering blight upon the prospects happiness and freedom of our Nation." Less than a month after leaving home, she wrote her grandfather, describing the trip and detailing family illnesses and difficulties of the journey, but adding, "I never enjoyed myself so well before and never had as good health before in my life." But tragedy soon struck. On June 20, 1852, Ann Roelofson Scott died suddenly of "plains cholera," an illness characterized by violent cramps and diarrhea. Hardships continued as the family lost oxen, a horse, a wagon, and the family savings along the way. On July 30, 1852, a young man, believed to be Abigail's sweetheart, drowned while attempting to recover cattle that had stampeded into the Snake River. Abigail's three-year-old brother, Willie, also died on the journey.

The remaining nine members of the Scott family arrived in Western Oregon penniless, exhausted, and grieving. They settled in Lafayette, Oregon, at that time the seat of Yamhill County. Shortly after their arrival, John Tucker Scott purchased an inn, the Oregon Temperance House, which housed regular boarders as well as the traveling elite. Like proprietors of other 19th-century temperance houses, Scott promoted the consumption of the milder intoxicants: cider, beer, and wine.

In March 1853, John Scott married **Ruth Eckler Stevenson**, who had also been widowed during the journey to Oregon, while Abigail left home to teach in the village of Cincinnati (present-day Eola). Her one-room log-cabin school was one of the first in Oregon, but her tenure was short-lived. On August 2, 1853, Abigail married Benjamin Duniway, a young man she had first met in Eastern Oregon when he greeted new arrivals to the territory.

It was not long after her marriage that Duniway began to consider housekeeping a drudgery. Though he was a gentle man, Ben was not happy when she refused to perform tasks he expected of a wife. She later said that she regretted doing "heavy work for hale and hearty men," which often compelled her to neglect her children. Despite her protests, Abigail Duniway was a hard worker, often driving herself to exhaustion, sickness, and attacks of rheumatoid arthritis.

The Duniways' first child, Clara Belle, was born nine months after their marriage. Their second child, and the first of five sons, Willis, was born in February 1856. Duniway almost died during the difficult birth and was not well for a

number of months thereafter. To quietly pass the time, she began to write poems and stories. With encouragement from her husband, she submitted a poem, "The Burning Forest Tree," to the *Oregon City Argus* under the pseudonym "Jenny Glen." The newspaper printed the poem and several others that soon followed, but the editor suggested that her talents might be better spent writing prose.

Duniway took the editor's advice and, at age 23, began to write a novel, drawing from her experiences while journeying to Oregon and as a resident of the Oregon territory. The novel, *Captain Gray's Company, or Crossing the Plains and Living in Oregon*, was published in April 1859, and is believed to be the first book published in Portland. Duniway's views on the plight of frontier women, and women in general, were revealed through her female characters, especially through her heroine Ada, who advocated improved conditions and health care for women. But it was not just in her novel that Duniway was expressing her thoughts regarding the rights of women. She also became embroiled in a more public debate over the issue.

In 1857, a controversy emerged over women's rights when the Oregon Constitutional Convention debated the issue. Only one delegate, Republican David Logan, favored female suffrage, but the issue of a woman's right to hold separate property from her husband had more backers and won conditional approval from the delegates. Women's rights continued to be debated in Oregon's leading newspapers during 1858–59, and Duniway joined in. An issue that especially stirred her was that of wife abuse; she was outspoken in her scorn for laws that allowed an abusive and/or drunken husband to keep custody of the children in the event of separation or divorce.

But women's rights were not Duniway's only concern. From 1859 to 1862, under the pseudonym "A Farmer's Wife," she became a regular contributor to the *Oregon Farmer*, in which she discussed the economic crisis faced by farmers and offered solutions, including encouraging women to buy Oregon products rather than send their money out of state. Her column was, for the most part, non-controversial, except for her advocacy of hiring help for farmers' wives.

Throughout their early years of marriage, the Duniways suffered a number of financial ups and downs. In June 1855, a storm, possibly a tornado, destroyed their home and furnishings. Friends and neighbors helped them rebuild, but in 1856 their cabin burned down. Family financial problems led Duniway to return to teaching several times in addition to earning a small income from her writing. Just when the Duniways were beginning to see some improvement in their finances, Ben, ignoring the pleas of his wife to avoid risking their economic future, co-signed for a loan to an acquaintance. Soon Ben discovered he had made a poor decision, as the borrower left him responsible for the debt. Despite desperate attempts to earn more money, the Duniways were forced to give up their Lafayette farm in 1862 to pay the debts. Legend has it that Abigail never forgave her husband for his folly. Although she publicly expressed only respect for him, she vented her anger through her fictional characters, this episode being reenacted in the first serial novel in her *New Northwest* newspaper. Shortly after losing the farm, Ben suffered an injury when a team of horses knocked him down and pulled a wagon over his back. From then on, his physical condition was poor, and he was incapable of performing farm labor. The weight of the Duniway family's financial support thus shifted to Abigail's shoulders.

She opened a small school, Lafayette Union School, in her home, and took in "young lady" boarders. In 1865, she sold the school and opened a new one in Albany, but, in partnership with another woman, she converted the school into a millinery shop the following year. Duniway's decision was a profitable one. In the post-Civil War boom, the demand for clothing, hats, and notions was high. The millinery shop made quick profits, and soon she was able to buy out her partner's share of the business.

By this time, Duniway's teaching, writing, and millinery shop brought her name recognition throughout the sparsely settled state of Oregon and the Pacific Northwest. Women knew, also, that Abigail Scott Duniway was a woman they could rely on in times of need. She was frequently visited by women who told of their lives with abusive husbands or of husbands who had deserted them and left them penniless. Duniway helped them as best she could, offering advice and occasionally advancing small loans. One evening, when she returned home frustrated over yet another incident that reminded her of how few rights women had, Ben responded, "Don't you know it will never be any better for women until they have the right to vote?" Abigail forever credited Ben's response as the impetus that launched her championship of women's suffrage.

It has been said that Abigail Duniway was not happy in her marriage. In addition to causing their financial woes, she found that Ben did not share her intellectual interests. But, according to biographer **Ruth Barnes Moynihan**, Abigail realized that it served her interests to maintain an image as a dutiful wife who was forced by necessity to enter the public arena. And while Duniway appeared to be a self-confident, secure woman as she campaigned for women's rights, she knew the price, in loss of material security and public esteem, that she might have to pay were she to disregard the wishes of her husband and the accepted duties of a 19th-century wife.

In 1870, Abigail Duniway helped found the Oregon State Equal Suffrage Association, and in December 1870 she traveled as an Oregon delegate to a suffrage convention in San Francisco. While in California, she gave her first public lecture, receiving praise from both her audience and newspaper reporters, and was offered a salary for a speaking tour of the state. When she wrote Ben of her success, he sent a telegram advising that she was needed back in Oregon. Fearing an emergency, she hurried home, turning down the lecture tour and missing the last two weeks of the convention. When she arrived home, she was angered to find that there was no special reason for Ben's request for her return.

For several years, Abigail had been wanting to establish a newspaper, and the disappointment over the lecture tour seemed to serve as impetus. Over the next three months, she moved her family to Portland, by now the largest city in the Northwest, and established the weekly *New Northwest* newspaper. Her paper, she said, was "not a Woman's Rights, but a Human Rights organ." Duniway's brother, Harvey Scott, who had achieved success since his arrival in Oregon as editor of the *Portland Oregonian* and President Ulysses Grant's recently appointed customs inspector for the area, gave Ben a job in the Portland customs house.

In 1871, Duniway convinced national suffragist *Susan B. Anthony to accompany her on a two-month lecture tour of the Pacific Northwest. Abigail had asked *Elizabeth Cady Stanton to join her also and was disappointed when Stanton turned her down. Although the tour met with mixed success and the often primitive living conditions along the way were uncomfortable for Anthony, Duniway was inspired by the experience. These tours helped her gain stories as well as new subscribers for the *New Northwest*.

Duniway's newspaper exposed injustices toward women due to their inequality under the law, such as a woman's failure to be judged by a

jury of her peers since women were not permitted to sit on juries, and the hardships a woman must face if divorced, including the possibility of never again seeing her children. She also advocated birth control through abstinence, a not unusual stand for the time, but a controversial one:

abstinence often meant a woman must disobey her husband, a stand that angered both men and many women. She believed that too many children contributed to poverty and illiteracy among children and made a drudge out of a wife. She spoke out against prostitution but sympathized with prostitutes, whom she saw as victims of the double standard, leaving women to take the blame for indiscretions involving both sexes. Ambivalent over the issue of divorce, she preferred that women help establish laws that would prevent child marriages or marriage to "drunkards" so that divorce could be avoided. Duniway did not, however, shun divorcees, as was the common practice among her contemporaries. Her activities and reputation as an outspoken suffragist resulted in ridicule and circulation of gossip and rumors about her personal life, including accusations that she was a smoker and heavy drinker and that her husband was "hen pecked."

Duniway regularly attended the annual National Woman Suffrage Association conventions, which were often held on the East Coast. She was away at one of these conventions when her only daughter Clara eloped with Don Stearns, a man Duniway did not consider suitable. Abigail was further grieved when Clara died of consumption in 1886, at age 31. Her elder sons also caused her worry. Willis was developing a reputation as a womanizer, Hubert was responsible for the pregnancy of an 18-year-old boarder whom he was forced to marry, and Wilkie was known for his associations with a gambling crowd. Duniway apparently sought relief in her writing, venting her frustrations through the characters in her novels.

During the years she published the *New Northwest,* she remained a controversial figure. In conservative Oregon, her openmindedness often brought her into conflict with fellow citizens. Her associations and friendships with divorcees, Jews, and Unitarians induced criticism, but her stand on the temperance issue engendered such controversy that she eventually sold the *New Northwest* to escape the heat.

The early temperance movement was dominated by men, including many anti-suffragists, with women members following their lead. It was not until temperance workers came to realize that votes for women could help their cause that they came to support women's suffrage. Duniway, however, felt it was wrong to give women the ballot based solely upon using them as a means to achieve prohibition. Also, she had long believed that the answer to problems associated with liquor, such as drunkenness and resultant wife abuse, was through education and temperance—not through laws that would dictate prohibition. In her mind, laws of the proposed prohibition type were contrary to the American spirit and the American Constitution. Her views thus conflicted with those who defined "temperance" as "prohibition" and led to charges that she had "sold out to liquor" interests.

In 1872, Duniway appeared before the state legislature on behalf of women's rights and submitted suffrage petitions to every legislature thereafter. In 1880, when a women's suffrage amendment to the Oregon constitution was finally introduced and received legislative approval, Duniway organized a ratification jubilee and claimed credit for the victory. To become law, however, the amendment needed to pass the legislature a second time in 1892 and then receive approval in a general referendum in 1894. Election dirty tricks, such as bribes to needy immigrants willing to vote against suffrage or distribution of purposely defective ballots with the suffrage amendment crossed out or marked "no," helped defeat the measure by a 5-to-2 margin.

Duniway also campaigned for women's suffrage in the Washington territory and spoke regularly to the territorial legislature, and suffrage in the late 1870s and early 1880s came close to being passed several times. But when she arrived in Olympia in October 1883 to voice further support for suffrage, she found Washington women suffragists afraid that the many controversies surrounding Duniway would lose the vote for them. At first, she acceded to their wishes but later returned to Olympia to speak before the legislature, where the suffrage bill passed. Four years later, Washington women lost their vote in a rigged court case and did not get it back for 21 years.

In 1886, Duniway's family convinced her to sell her newspaper. In doing so, she lost what political influence a female non-voter could have. Funds from the sale of the Duniway Publishing Company enabled her sons and co-owners, Willis and Wilkie, to buy ranch land in Idaho. Ben Duniway moved with them, and Abigail planned to settle there the following year, once the *New Northwest* completed its final months of publication. As matters turned out, she only spent summers on the Idaho ranch. The ranching venture ended in failure, and by the mid-1890s both her sons and husband were back in Portland.

Abigail, long desiring to be free of financial worries and able to spend her time writing, proposed a "trust" arrangement whereby her sons could support her and, in turn, her invalid husband. The early arrangement was that she would turn ownership of her property over to her sons who would guarantee $100 per month support. The plan did not work out, however, as the Depression of 1893 made the arrangement unsatisfactory and payments to their mother had to be lowered. Duniway's letters of the 1890s are said to be full of complaints over her lack of money and resentment over having to support Ben, blaming him for misuse of her profits from the Duniway Publishing Company. She reluctantly nursed him until he died in 1896.

Her poor financial straits caused her to be careful with money and cognizant of payments for lectures and expenses incurred while working for women's suffrage. Other, more affluent suffragists had little understanding of her financial woes and considered her a money-grubber, excluding her from leadership positions. Nevertheless, she kept up her fight. A vote on suffrage in Oregon in 1900 was close, failing 28,402 to 26,265. Duniway's brother Harvey, who had promised his support, left town at the height of the campaign, while his newspaper, the *Portland Oregonian*, launched a campaign against the amendment two weeks before the election.

Following the suffrage referendum, Abigail suffered episodes of illness, almost dying following a mastoidectomy in 1903. She did not give up her fight for the ballot, however, and prepared for another vote in 1906. Arguments with other leading suffragists, particularly over the prohibition issue, caused her to be snubbed at the national convention held in Oregon in 1905. She was again ignored in 1906 when leaders traveled to Oregon to campaign for suffrage as a tribute to the recently deceased Susan B. Anthony. The 1906 campaign was an expensive failure and left the Oregon State Woman Suffrage Association in debt. Duniway blamed the national organization and its association with prohibition issues for the failure, and the national leaders blamed Duniway.

Duniway led another campaign in 1908, which was again defeated. A printing error on the 1910 ballot led to confusion and another defeat. In 1912, public support for women's suffrage in Oregon was much stronger, probably influenced by the fact that neighboring Washington and California had obtained women's suffrage in 1910 and 1911, respectively, and the death of Harvey Scott in 1910 put an end to opposition in the *Oregonian*. With the help of loyal supporters, Duniway again obtained petitions and submitted the amendment in January 1912. Shortly thereafter, however, she became gravely ill, suffering from pneumonia and then blood poisoning in her leg. Her family thought she would die, but she vowed to live to see victory. In the spring of 1912, she directed the campaign from her bed.

Women's suffrage finally won in Oregon, although by a small majority. Duniway also lived to see prohibition become an Oregon law in 1914. Nevertheless, she continued to believe that prohibition was wrong and correctly predicted that the law would only be temporary because it was sure to be disobeyed.

Abigail Duniway died in 1915, the result of a recurrence of the infection she had suffered in 1912. Without antibiotics, there was little doctors could do to help. While she lived, Duniway was a speaker for women, particularly those on the Western frontier. Her controversial stands created enemies, but she called attention to important issues of the day. Duniway emphasized the important role women played, working together with men to civilize the West, and she had a vision of the future with women playing major roles in the shaping of society. In her autobiography, *Path Breaking*, written in 1914, Duniway wrote that "the world is moving and woman is moving with it—not always in the same direction, maybe, in the best chosen paths, for we are no wiser than our brothers—but always moving onward, in some direction toward a higher goal."

SOURCES:

Duniway, Abigail Scott, *Captain Gray's Company: or Crossing the Plains and Living in Oregon*. Portland, OR: S.J. McCormick, 1859.

———. *David and Anna Matson*. NY: S.R. Wells, 1876.

———. *Path Breaking: An Autobiographical History of the Equal Suffrage Movement in Pacific Coast States*. 1914.

Moynihan, Ruth Barnes. *Rebel for Rights: Abigail Scott Duniway*. New Haven, CT: Yale University Press, 1983.

Smith, Helen Krebs. *The Presumptuous Dreamers: A Sociological History of the Life and Times of Abigail Scott Duniway (1834–1915)*. Vols I and II. Lake Oswego, OR: Smith, Smith and Smith, 1974.

COLLECTIONS:

Oregon Historical Society, Portland, Oregon, file on Abigail Scott Duniway includes journal of trip to Oregon, ledgers of Duniway Publishing Co. and Oregon State Woman Suffrage Association. *New Northwest*, 1871–87, *Oregon City Argus*, 1855–60 and *Oregon Farmer*, 1859–62, on microfilm.

June Melby Benowitz, Ph.D., Instructor of American History, Keiser College, Sarasota, Florida

Dunkeld, Ada (c. 1145–1206)

Countess of Holland. Born around 1145; died on January 11, 1206; daughter of Henry Dunkeld, first earl of Huntingdon, and *Adelicia de Warrenne (d. 1178); sister of William I (r. 1165–1214) and Malcolm IV (r. 1153–1165), both kings of Scotland; married Florence also known as Floris III (d. 1190), count of Holland, in 1161 or 1162.

Dunkeld, Ada (c. 1195–after 1241)

*English noblewoman. Born around 1195; died after 1241; daughter of David Dunkeld, 1st earl of Huntingdon, and *Maude of Chester (1171–1233, d. of Hugh, third earl of Chester); married Henry Hastings, 1st baron Hastings, before June 7, 1237; children: three, including Henry Hastings and Eleanor (Hillaria) Hastings.*

Dunkeld, Isabel.

See Isabel (fl. 1225).

Dunkeld, Margaret (d. 1228).

See Margaret, countess of Huntingdon.

Dunkeld, Margaret (d. 1259).

See Margaret de Burgh.

Dunkeld, Margaret (1261–1283).

See Margaret of Norway.

Dunlop, Florence (c. 1896–1963)

Canadian teacher and pioneer in education for children with special needs. Born in Ottawa, Ontario, Canada, around 1896; died in Ottawa in 1963; graduated from Ottawa Normal School, 1916; attended Queens University; Columbia University, M.A. and Ph.D., New York.

Florence Dunlop, one of Canada's educational pioneers, graduated from the Ottawa Normal School in 1916. She began her teaching career in a rural community in northern Ontario, where she was intrigued with the variations in learning abilities and personality types she encountered in the classroom. Upon returning to Ottawa, Dunlop continued teaching and enrolled in advanced studies at Queens University. She focused on children outside the norm and entered an exchange-teacher program that allowed her to teach and observe in London for a year. There, and in subsequent travels to South Africa, Australia, and New Zealand, she visited schools, talked to teachers, and studied programs for students with special needs. Returning to Ottawa in 1927, she was appointed supervisor of Special Education.

Dunlop painstakingly worked out a system for the early identification and treatment of both physically and psychologically challenged students within Ottawa's public-school system. "My aim," she said, "is to give every child the best education possible—regardless of his abilities or handicaps." Working with physicians and using her own talents as a psychologist, she developed a system of special education to meet the myriad needs of children in the community. In addition to special classes for children with physical difficulties, including deafness and blindness, she set up vocational schools for those who could not manage an academic program and organized a corps of visiting teachers for children confined by chronic illness. During the summers, she attended Columbia University's summer sessions, eventually earning both her M.S. and her Ph.D. She then stayed on at the university as a member of the summer-school faculty.

Dunlop also traveled widely, both to observe psychology clinics and special classes and to lecture on her own work in Ottawa. She was part of the group of prominent educators who organized the International Council for the Study of Exceptional Children. She also made a number of trips to the United States, where she advised the U.S. Office of Education in Washington and worked as a consultant in Maryland, Ohio, and California. In recognition of her work, President Dwight D. Eisenhower invited her to attend the 1960 White House Conference on Children and Youth. At the age of 65, hoping to share her knowledge with younger teachers, Dunlop accepted a post as professor of special education at San Francisco State College. Illness, however, forced her return to Ottawa in 1962, where she died a year later.

SOURCES:
Fleming, Alice. *Great Women Teachers.* Philadelphia, PA: J.B. Lippincott, 1965.

Barbara Morgan,
Melrose, Massachusetts

Dunlop, Jane (1904–1964).

See Davis, Adele.

Dunn, Kaye (b. 1909).

See Dunham, Katherine.

Dunn, Tricia (1974—).

See Team USA: Women's Ice Hockey at Nagano.

Dunne, Irene (1898–1990)

American stage and film actress, nominated five times for an Academy Award as Best Actress, who moved easily from serious drama to musicals to "screwball comedy" and was best remembered for her roles in The Awful Truth, Anna and the King of Siam, *and* I Remember Mama. *Born Irene Marie Dunn in Louisville, Kentucky, on December 20, 1898 (and not 1901, 1902, 1904, or 1907, as often given); died of heart failure in Hollywood, California, on September*

4, 1991, at age 91; daughter of Joseph John Dunn and Adelaide Antoinette (Henry) Dunn; attended local schools, a music conservatory in Indianapolis, and the Chicago Musical College; married Francis J. Griffin (a New York dentist), in 1927 (died 1965); children: daughter, **Mary Frances Griffin** (adopted, 1936).

Awards: nominated for Academy Award for Best Actress for Cimarron (1931), Theodora Goes Wild (1936), The Awful Truth (1937), Love Affair (1939), and I Remember Mama (1948); granted honorary degree of Doctor of Music from Chicago Music College; named honorary member of the music fraternity, Sigma Alpha Iota; received University of Notre Dame's Laetare Medal for her work for Catholic charities; chosen honorary National Commander of the American Cancer Society volunteer army; named chair of the National Women's Committee of the American Heart Association, chair of the Sponsor's Committee of the Hebrew University Rebuilding Fund, and by the National Conference of Christians and Jews as the woman who has done most to promote better understanding of peoples of all faiths (1948).

First appeared on stage in Irene (on tour, 1920); made New York debut in The Clinging Vine (1922); appeared in Lollipop (1924) and The City Chap (1925); toured in Sweetheart Time (1926); appeared on Broadway in Yours Truly (1927), She's My Baby (1928); appeared in Chicago in Show Boat (1929); made last stage appearance in New York in Luckee Girl (1930).

Filmography: Leathernecking (also known as Present Arms, 1930); Cimarron (1930); Bachelor Apartment (1931); Consolation Marriage (Married in Haste, 1931); The Great Lover (1931); Symphony of Six Million (Melody of Life, 1932); Back Street (1932); Thirteen Women (1932); No Other Woman (1933); The Secret of Madame Blanche (1933); The Silver Cord (1933); Ann Vickers (1933); If I were Free (Behold We Live, 1933); This Man is Mine (1934); Stingaree (1934); The Age of Innocence (1934); Sweet Adeline (1935); Roberta (1935); Magnificent Obsession (1935); Show Boat (1936); Theodora Goes Wild (1936); High, Wide and Handsome (1937); The Awful Truth (1937); Joy of Living (1938); Love Affair

Irene Dunne

(1939); Invitation to Happiness *(1939);* When Tomorrow Comes *(1939);* My Favorite Wife *(1940);* Penny Serenade *(1941);* Unfinished Business *(1941);* Lady in a Jam *(1942);* A Guy Named Joe *(1943);* The White Cliffs of Dover *(1944);* Together Again *(1944);* Over 21 *(1945);* Anna and the King of Siam *(1946);* Life With Father *(1947);* I Remember Mama *(1948);* Never a Dull Moment *(1950);* The Mudlark *(1950);* It Grows on Trees *(1952).*

Irene Dunne was born Irene Marie Dunn in Louisville, Kentucky, on December 20, 1898. Her paternal grandfather, of Irish descent, had been a builder of boats on the Ohio River; her father Joseph John Dunn was a supervisory inspector of steamships for the federal government; her mother **Adelaide Hunt Dunn** was a musician. Dunne was educated at the Loretta Academy, a private school in Louisville, before her father died when she was 11. Following his death, Adelaide and Irene moved in with her parents in Madison, Indiana. Realizing that her daughter had inherited her own musical talent, Adelaide saw to it that Irene studied violin and piano under private teachers, but it was soon clear that Irene's greatest talent lay in her voice. Her mother's fondest dream, then, was that her daughter become an opera singer, and, in fact, the young Irene earned her first salary singing in a church choir. She then went on to study for a year at a musical conservatory in Indianapolis after which she secured an appointment to teach music and art in a high school in East Chicago, Indiana. While en route by train to this job, Dunne read about a competition for a scholarship to the Chicago Musical College and disembarked at Chicago in order to enter. She won the competition and, with her scholarship, was able to study at the school for an entire year.

Leaving the Chicago Music College in 1919, Dunne secured a job in Atlanta singing Gilbert and Sullivan with a company of young singers from the Metropolitan Opera. Flushed with enthusiasm, she left for New York as soon as her season in Atlanta was over, hoping to be accepted at the Met. After failing an audition there, however, she added an *e* to her surname and turned to the legitimate stage, landing the lead in a touring company of the popular musical comedy *Irene* that had starred the French musical star *Irene Bordoni* in New York. Thereafter, Dunne appeared regularly in New York in straight plays such as *The Clinging Vine* (1922), *Lollipop* (1924), and *The City Chap* (1925), although she actively sought out singing roles as well, finding parts in minor musicals such as *Sweetheart Time*

(1926) and *She's My Baby* with Clifton Webb and *Beatrice Lillie* (1928). In between plays, Dunne continued to take courses at the Chicago Musical College, graduating with honors in 1926. In 1927, she married Francis J. Griffin, a New York dentist, to whom she remained wed for 37 years until his death in 1965.

By 1929, Dunne was a recognized Broadway actress. That same year, after a chance encounter, the producer Florenz Ziegfeld, renowned for his eye for unusual beauty, engaged her to play the leading role of Magnolia in the touring company of his production of the Jerome Kern-Oscar Hammerstein musical *Show Boat,* adapted from a novel by *Edna Ferber*. It was this tour that made Irene Dunne a stage star. For 72 weeks, she appeared in virtually every city in the eastern half of the country, receiving rave reviews from the critics and accolades from cheering audiences, especially in Chicago, where her appearance was a triumph that secured her a contract from RKO Studios. Thereafter, for the next 20 years, Irene Dunne appeared in one film after another—41 in all—never featured as less than a star and, in the course of her career, playing an astonishing variety of roles.

Her first film, *Leathernecking,* was an insignificant musical about a marine who poses as an officer to impress a Honolulu socialite, but the studio liked her performance and almost immediately cast her in the western *Cimarron,* another Ferber novel, which won the Academy Award for Best Picture of the year and which has since been refilmed twice. Again, Dunne's performance, as an Oklahoma homesteader who ends as a congresswoman and who ages 50 years in the course of the film, showed that RKO had not gambled foolishly. *Cimarron* not only made her a film star but also secured her the first of her five Academy Award nominations for Best Actress. She lost to *Norma Shearer* who had starred in *The Divorcee.* This was the era when silent films had just given way to talking pictures and Hollywood studios had a pressing need not only for actors who knew how to talk, but for singers who could perform in the rash of musicals ("all talking, all dancing, all singing") that were then being made.

Her next film, *Symphony for Six Million,* in which Dunne portrayed a handicapped woman, was undistinguished, but her performance in *Back Street,* based on the melodramatic novel of marital infidelity by *Fannie Hurst*, in which she played the role of mistress of a married man, established her as a serious actress. The film was an enormous popular success and broke the previous box-office record set by *All Quiet on the Western Front* in 1930.

Dunne followed her dramatic triumph in *Back Street* with several other tear-jerkers in 1932–33, and, as her reputation as one of the finest dramatic actresses in Hollywood grew, she was cast opposite some of the most popular leading actors of the day, co-starring with Joel McCrae in *The Silver Cord* (1932) as a woman who must struggle against a domineering mother-in-law to save her marriage, and with the new and extremely popular Robert Taylor in *Magnificent Obsession* (1935). This film about a young doctor who kills a man and blinds the man's wife in an automobile accident, and then becomes a great surgeon in order to heal her, was one of Irene Dunne's greatest successes.

But ever determined to avoid typecasting, Dunne continued to seek new challenges and was finally able to secure roles in two musicals, *Sweet Adeline* (1934) and *Roberta* (1935), although neither of these films added to her luster as a musical-comedy star. The film version of the Broadway musical *Roberta* was a celebration of the Paris world of *haute couture*, with its ritual fashion show climax so *de rigeur* in 1930s' movie musicals, and featured Dunne in the unlikely role of an expatriate Russian princess. Unfortunately, Fred Astaire and *Ginger Rogers stole the film, even though it gave Dunne the opportunity to sing "Smoke Gets in Your Eyes," one of the classic Broadway show tunes of the day. Dunne recouped, however, in 1936 with her stunning performance in the enormously popular film version of *Show Boat*. Widely considered to be the best of the three screen versions of this classic, this film proved that Irene Dunne was not only a fine actress but also an enchanting musical-comedy star and a gifted comedienne. Although some critics thought Dunne too mature for the part of Magnolia (she was then 38, claiming to be 34, and playing 21), audiences were captivated by her singing of "Make Believe" with Alan Jones.

During these early years in Hollywood, Dunne regularly commuted to New York between pictures to be with her husband, but, in 1936, Francis Griffin gave up his New York practice to join her in California, where they built a nine-room, French provincial home in Holmby Hills and adopted an infant daughter whom they named Mary Frances. At same time, her seven-year contract at RKO came to an end, and, through the shrewdness of her agent, Charles Feldman, Dunne pioneered the non-exclusive, three-year contract that enabled her to make one picture a year each for Paramount, Columbia, and RKO, an arrangement that struck the first blow to the traditional seven-year contract that had reduced film stars to indentured servants of the studio bosses. It was only after her release from exclusive contract to RKO and the start of her virtual freelancing that Dunne, now close to 40, saw her career begin to soar.

> [Comedy] demands more timing, pace, shading and subtlety of emphasis. It is difficult to learn, but once it is acquired it can be easily slowed down and it becomes an excellent foundation for dramatic acting.
>
> —Irene Dunne

The revelation of Dunne's comic talents came at a most opportune moment, for these were the years when Hollywood was perfecting a new genre of light screen entertainment that came to be known as "screwball comedy," a delightful concoction of foam and wit somewhere between standard comedy and farce, alongside of whose chief interpreters—*Carole Lombard, *Constance Bennett, or *Myrna Loy for example—Dunne proved more than capable of holding her own. Originally, however, she had doubted her ability to handle a completely comic role and even went so far as to take a trip to Europe when the studio offered her *Theodora Goes Wild* (1937), hoping that someone else would have been cast in it by the time she returned. On the contrary, the studio had held the picture for her, and, against her better judgment, she undertook to make the best of it. The film, co-starring the popular Melvyn Douglas, a master at sophisticated comedy, was about a staid New England woman who, without her family knowing it, secretly writes a naughty book and then attempts to live up to the role thrust upon her after the book becomes a bestseller. In this film, Dunne turned out to have an instinctive comic flair of the type described as "captivating," "scintillating," and "sparkling" and *Theodora Goes Wild* was an instant success that earned her her second Oscar nomination. This time she lost to *Luise Rainer who had portrayed *Anna Held in *The Great Ziegfeld*.

Nevertheless, Dunne had received such rave reviews for her talents as a comedienne, that she suddenly found herself switched from dramatic parts to comic ones and, after the largely forgotten *High, Wide and Handsome* (1937), was never given another musical role. Though already one of the most popular, most sought after, and most highly paid leading ladies in Hollywood, her popularity soared as she was cast in the smash hit *The Awful Truth* (1938) opposite Cary Grant. One of the most popular films of the decade, *The Awful Truth* dealt with a married couple who decide to divorce only to discover that they cannot live without each other, and garnered for Dunne her third Academy Award nomination. She again lost to Rainer for the latter's role as a Chinese wife in *The Good Earth*. Another comedy, the less successful *Joy of Living* with Douglas Fairbanks, Jr., followed.

In 1939, Dunne returned to serious roles when she was co-starred with the popular French romantic lead, Charles Boyer, in the film *Love Affair* (which would be remade with *Deborah Kerr as *An Affair to Remember*). The story of two people who fall in love aboard an ocean liner, *Love Affair* won Dunne a fourth Academy Award nomination, her second in a row, but this time she lost to *Vivien Leigh, almost undefeatable as Scarlett O'Hara in *Gone With the Wind*. The chemistry between Dunne and Boyer was immediately appreciated by audiences every-

where, and the two were paired again the following year in *When Tomorrow Comes*. She then played yet another romantic role opposite Fred MacMurray in *Invitation to Happiness* (1939). This film was followed by a return to "screwball comedy," when she was again cast opposite Cary Grant in *My Favorite Wife* (1940) in which she played a woman lost in a shipwreck and thought dead, who suddenly returns to disrupt her husband's life. In years to come, Grant was to recall that Dunne had the best sense of timing of anyone he had ever worked with—and he had worked twice with *Mae West who was legendary for her timing.

By 1940, Irene Dunne had had no less than 18 of her films open at the Radio City Music Hall in New York, then the most prestigious film theater in the country, an all-time record at that time. In 1941, she made yet another film with Grant, *Penny Serenade,* a sentimental drama that dealt with the woes and tribulations of a couple attempting to adopt a child, a story that touched a nerve with Dunne, who, unable to

From the movie Anna and the King of Siam, *starring Irene Dunne.*

conceive, had only recently gone through the adoption process. As in *Magnificent Obsession* and *Love Affair*, Dunne's performance raised the film above the cloying level that a film of this type could so easily have fallen to, and the critics and the public were both impressed.

For all her success as a dramatic actress and a comedienne, however, Dunne still hankered for a musical career. Unfortunately, with her lyric soprano voice, her talents would have been best served by operettas on the order of those dominated by *Jeanette MacDonald but these, however, were giving way to the flashy period musicals best suited to *Alice Faye and *Betty Grable. Thus, after the undistinguished film *Unfinished Business* (1941), Irene Dunne took a brief sojourn from Hollywood to appear as a guest artist with the Chicago Symphony Orchestra (1941–42). She returned to the screen to do the now-forgotten *Lady in a Jam* followed, however, by two wartime films that added significantly to her stature as an actress. *A Guy Named Joe* (1943) in which she played opposite the enormously popular Spencer Tracy, was a fantasy about love and death; *The White Cliffs of Dover* (1944) dealt with a woman whose life spanned both World Wars. Both films were typical of many produced in the mid-'40s, glittering as they were with all-star casts that featured, in the former, Van Johnson, Lionel Barrymore, and *Esther Williams in one of her rare non-swimming roles, and in the latter, veteran comedian Frank Morgan and the youthful Roddy McDowall, Van Johnson and Peter Lawford. Both were box-office as well as critical successes.

After World War II, Dunne's career began to wane, but she still had three important films ahead of her that would add considerable luster to a brilliant film career. In 1946, she essayed the role of *Anna Leonowens, opposite the English actor Rex Harrison, in the film version of the novel *Anna and the King of Siam*. Based on the true story of a Welsh schoolmarm who, in the 1860s journeys to the court of Siam, now Thailand, to serve as governess to the king's horde of children, the film later served as the inspiration for the Broadway and Hollywood musical extravaganza, *The King and I*. Then in 1947, Dunne shrewdly chose to play the role of a middle-aged Norwegian immigrant mother in *I Remember Mama*, the film version of the extremely successful play that had starred *Mady Christians on Broadway. A story, written by ❧ **Kathryn McLean**, set at the turn of the century and filled with warmth and gentle humor, the film version stands as one of the most memorable testimonies

to Irene Dunne's skill as a dramatic actress. With no big scenes or opportunities for histrionics, Dunne's basic talent and her long years of mastering her craft came together to enable her to bring an integrity to the interpretation of the role that was outstanding for its sincerity and lack of artifice. It was a tribute to Dunne that, even though she did not win this, her fifth Academy Award nomination (it went to *Jane Wyman for *Johnny Belinda*), the industry to which she had devoted herself for almost 20 years at least recognized and appreciated the quiet triumph that she had achieved. Finally, in 1948, Dunne starred as the wife of William Powell in the film version of *Life With Father*, a role that had been created by *Dorothy Stickney on Broadway not long before.

The same year, 1948, Irene Dunne reprised several of her famous roles for "The Lux Radio Theater," one of the prestige radio programs of the day, later becoming host for the "Schlitz Playhouse of Stars," another program with a similar format. In the 1950s, she tried television but, ever conscious of her image, made occasional appearances only on the more distinguished dramatic programs such as "Ford Theater," "The Playhouse of Stars," "The Loretta Young Show," "The June Allyson Show," and the "General Electric Theater."

Through her willingness to play parts suited to a woman of her advancing age (aided by her youthful appearance and the discreet and regu-

❧➤ **McLean, Kathryn** (1909–1966)

American author and short story writer. Name variations: Kathryn Forbes. Born in San Francisco, California, on March 10, 1909; died on May 15, 1966; daughter of Leon Ellis and Della (Jesser) Anderson; graduated Mount View High School in San Francisco; married Robert McLean (a contractor), in 1926 (divorced, May 1946); children: Robert, Jr., and Richard.

Under the pseudonym Kathryn Forbes, Kathryn McLean wrote her semi-autobiographical *Mama's Bank Account*. With gentle humor, the episodic book centers around her Norwegian-American family stretching their earnings to pay expenses in turn-of-the-century San Francisco. Dramatized by John Van Druten as *I Remember Mama*, it was produced by Richard Rodgers and Oscar Hammerstein for Broadway in 1944. The story also evolved into a highly popular television series, produced by CBS from 1949 to 1957, starring *Peggy Wood and childstar-turned-feminist **Robin Morgan**.

SUGGESTED READING:

Current Biography. NY: H.W. Wilson, 1944 and 1966.

lar reassignment of her birth year), Dunne was able to prolong her career until she was well into her 50s. In 1950, she appeared as Queen *Victoria in *The Mudlark* opposite the English actor Alec Guinness, and was teamed once more with Fred MacMurray in *Never a Dull Moment*. After her last film, however, *It Grows on Trees* (1952), Dunne retired from films on her own initiative, and, except for an occasional appearance on television, her acting career came to a close.

A devout Roman Catholic, Irene Dunne steered clear of both the more glamorous and the less savory aspects of Hollywood life, devoting herself to her family and to her philanthropic work, especially to St. John's Hospital in Santa Monica, her pet charity. At home, she lived as Mrs. Griffith, her only concession to her status as a film star being her resolve never to be seen unless she was looking her best. A woman with a canny clothes sense, she was known for her poise and dignified bearing, was regarded as one of the best dressed women in Hollywood, and was always among the few actresses whose names were considered for the title "first lady of the screen." A staunchly conservative Republican, she became increasingly active in party affairs once her film career came to an end and in 1957–58 was appointed by President Dwight Eisenhower to serve as alternate U.S. delegate to the United Nations General Assembly in New York. In 1965, she was invited to serve on the board of directors of Technicolor, Inc. Although an Academy Award may have eluded her, Dunne was honored for her life's work by the American Film Institute at its tenth anniversary celebration in 1977. Her last public appearance was at the Kennedy Center Honors held in Washington, D.C., in December 1985, when she was to be saluted for her life's achievement along with the comedian Bob Hope, the opera singer *Beverly Sills and the composer Alan Jay Lerner. Unfortunately, Dunne collapsed after the group photographic session and thus became the first honors recipient to miss taking part in the televised gala that followed the next evening. She died of heart failure in Hollywood on September 4, 1991, at age 91.

Irene Dunne was one of the most enduring and versatile stars of the motion picture during the period that has come to be known as the "Golden Age" of Hollywood. Whether in serious drama, which she always preferred, musical, screwball, or light comedy, historical dramas, or what were then known as "women's pictures," she seemed to have no difficulty in producing whatever was required of her by her directors. A tribute to her shrewdness at selecting her scripts

can be seen by how many of them were remade as vehicles for others: *Love Affair* in the '50s with **Deborah Kerr**, *Cimarron* with *Maria Schell, *The Awful Truth* and *Magnificent Obsession* with Jane Wyman, and *Show Boat* and *Roberta* with *Kathryn Grayson. *Back Street* was remade twice, first with *Margaret Sullivan and then with *Susan Hayward; Steven Spielberg's film *Always* was a remake of *A Guy Named Joe*. As a dramatic actress, she was noted for the sincerity that she brought to her roles, carefully cultivating the natural catch in her voice to convey the most varied emotions in a subtle way that was highly effective. As a comedienne, it was the interplay between her innate dignity and her inner sense of fun that made her so deliciously funny in "screwball" roles: "Can you imagine Irene Dunne doing this?" was all part of the joke.

Never a great beauty even in her youth, Dunne was nevertheless a pretty girl with warm brown eyes, light brown hair and a dazzling smile, who matured into a handsome woman. As the years advanced after her retirement, however, she held her age less well than such contemporaries as *Loretta Young and *Claudette Colbert and, unwilling to destroy the public's memory of her on screen, declined an opportunity to appear in a photographic tribute to legendary screen actresses offered to her by *Life* magazine. Although her passing created far less stir than did those of some her contemporaries, this was due in part to the fact that she really retired long before she had to but also to her desire for privacy and her lack of public flamboyance. Her position in the history of the first 25 years of talking films is, however, firmly secure. A tribute to her uniqueness as an actress was offered by James Waters, who wrote in *The New York Times* on September 20, 1990: "Imagine Claudette Colbert as Queen Victoria in *The Mudlark* or Joan Crawford doing *I Remember Mama* or *Jean Arthur in *Show Boat*. And while Constance Bennett, Carole Lombard or Myrna Loy might have molded nicely into *The Awful Truth* or *Theodora Goes Wild*, aren't we glad they didn't?"

SOURCES:
Current Biography. NY: H.W. Wilson, 1945.
Free Library of Philadelphia, Theater Collection.
The International Dictionary of Films and Filmakers, Vol. III, *Actors and Actresses.*
Waters, James. "Irene Dunne: No Oscar, Just Love," in *The New York Times.* September 20, 1990.

Robert Hewsen, Professor of History, Rowan University, Glassboro, New Jersey

Dunne, Margaret Abbott (1878–1955).

See Abbott, Margaret.

Dunning, Emily (1876–1961).

See Barringer, Emily Dunning.

Dunnock, Mildred (1900–1991)

American character actress of stage, film, and television who originated the part of Linda Loman in Death of a Salesman. *Born Mildred Dorothy Dunnock on January 25, 1900 (some sources cite 1904), in Baltimore, Maryland; died in Massachusetts on July 5, 1991; daughter of Walter (president of the Dumari Textile Company), and Florence (Saynook) Dunnock; attended Public School 59 and Western High School, Baltimore; Goucher College, Baltimore, A.B.; attended Johns Hopkins and Columbia University; studied acting with Lee Strasberg and Elia Kazan; married Keith Urmy (a banker); children: daughter,* **Linda McGuire** *(actress); granddaughter,* **Patricia McGuire Dunnock** *(actress).*

Selected plays: The Corn Is Green *(1940);* Lute Song *(1946);* Another Part of the Forest *(1946);* Death of a Salesman *(1949);* The Wild Duck *(1951);* In the Summer House *(1953);* Cat on a Hot Tin Roof *(1955);* The Milk Train Doesn't Stop Here Anymore *(1962);* Trojan Women *(1963);* A Place without Doors *(1970);* Days in the Trees *(1976).*

Selected filmography: The Corn Is Green *(1945);* Kiss of Death *(1947);* Death of a Salesman *(1951);* I Want You *(1951);* Viva Zapata! *(1952);* The Girl in White *(1952);* The Jazz Singer *(1953);* Bad for Each Other *(1953);* The Trouble with Harry *(1955);* Love Me Tender *(1956);* Baby Doll *(1956);* Peyton Place *(1957);* The Nun's Story *(1959);* The Story on Page One *(1960);* Butterfield 8 *(1960);* Something Wild *(1961);* Sweet Bird of Youth *(1962);* Behold a Pale Horse *(1964);* Youngblood Hawke *(1964);* Seven Women *(1965);* What Ever Happened to Aunt Alice? *(1969);* The Spiral Staircase *(UK, 1975);* One Summer Love *(Dragonfly, 1976);* The Pick-Up Artist *(1987).*

Mildred Dunnock, who for 50 years excelled in supporting character roles (mostly mothers and eccentrics) on stage, screen, and television, thought of herself as more of a schoolteacher than an actress. By her own admission, she was "burned by a footlight fire" in college, but she went into teaching to please her father, who objected to her going to New York to pursue a career in the theater. While teaching school in Baltimore and later in New York, Dunnock remained active in community theater and summer stock, eventually finding her way into a few short-lived Broadway plays. In 1940, she won acclaim for her portrayal of a Welsh schoolteacher in *The Corn Is Green*, which ran for 477 performances. While performing nightly, Dunnock maintained her teaching schedule, from 8:30 AM to 4:35 PM on all but matinee days. "People don't think you can act if you're a schoolteacher," she told Peter Kihss of the *New York World-Telegraph*, "but teaching is something I intend to keep up. . . . The arrangement is only possible because I have such an understanding headmistress. It's a good thing, too, my husband likes the theater." Dunnock repeated her role in the 1945 film version of *The Corn Is Green* with *Bette Davis.

Mildred Dunnock

Once established, Dunnock played a number of memorable roles on Broadway, including the semi-crazed Lavinia in ***Lillian Hellman**'s *Another Part of the Forest*, and the beleaguered wife Linda Loman in *Death of a Salesman* (1949), which Brooks Atkinson of *The New York Times* called "the performance of her career." (She repeated the role in the 1951 film and the 1966 television adaptation.) Her portrayal of Big Mama in *Cat on a Hot Tin Roof* (1955), though different from the pathetic or timorous women she usually played, was equally well received. Walter Kerr of the *New York Herald Tribune* called her "startlingly fine in an unfamiliar sort of role: the brash, gravel-voiced outspoken matron." Dunnock played both classical and modern roles with the American Shakespeare Festival and, in 1965, directed *Graduation* on Broadway. Dunnock continued on the stage and films, well into her 70s, and also appeared on television series and specials, including "Studio One," "Kraft Television Theater," and "Philco Playhouse." Playwright Arthur Miller, who authored some of her finest roles, called her "a fiercely dedicated artist." She was nominated for an Academy Award for her performance in the films *Death of a Salesman* (1951) and *Baby Doll* (1956).

SOURCES:
Candee, Marjorie Dent, ed. *Current Biography 1955.* NY: H.W. Wilson, 1955.
Hartnoll, Phyllis, and Peter Found. *The Concise Oxford Companion to the Theater.* Oxford: Oxford University Press, 1993.

The Seller of
Tisane, *painting
by Françoise
Duparc.*

Katz, Ephraim. *The Film Encyclopedia.* NY: Harper-Collins, 1994.
Wilmeth, Don B., and Tice L. Miller. *Cambridge Guide to American Theater.* Cambridge: Cambridge University Press, 1993.

Barbara Morgan,
Melrose, Massachusetts

Duparc, Françoise (1726–1778)

French portrait and genre painter. Born in Murcie, Spain, on October 15, 1726; died in Marseilles, France, on October 11, 1778; daughter and one of several children of Antoine Duparc (a sculptor) and Gabrielle Negrela.

The life of painter Françoise Duparc is poorly documented. Of the 41 paintings that were in her studio at the time of her death, only four remain that are positively attributed to her hand. They were bequeathed in her will to the town hall of Marseilles and are now housed in the *Musée des Beaux-Arts.* Although they are considered to be of high quality and have appeared in several exhibitions, they have not yet generated enough interest to lift the artist from obscurity.

It is believed that Duparc, whose family returned to Marseilles from Spain in 1730, began her art studies in her father's studio. There is also evidence, however, that she studied with Jean Baptiste van Loo (1684–1745), who was in Marseilles from 1735 to 1736 and again from 1742 and 1745. According to one source, Duparc copied a van Loo portrait so well that he had trouble distinguishing it from his original. Duparc resided with her sister in Paris and also may have lived in London for a time, as there are records of paintings exhibited there in 1763 and 1766. She moved back to Marseilles by 1771, where she was made a member of the local artists' academy in 1776. She died in 1778, at age 52.

The four documented Duparc works are a blend of portraiture and genre, each a single half-length portrait of a working-class man or woman—an old man carrying a sack (*Man with a Sack*), a woman knitting (*Knitter*), a young woman selling herb tea (*The Seller of Tisane*), and an old woman seated with her arms crossed (*Old Woman*). The paintings, with their layered surfaces and naturalistic portrayals, are compared to the work of Jean-Baptiste-Siméon Chardin (1699–1799); inspired by the Dutch genre painters of the 17th century, Chardin was considered one of the finest genre painters of 18th-century France. Unlike Chardin, however, Duparc concentrated completely on the human figure, to the exclusion of implied narrative or elements of the setting. According to some critics, the failure of her works to entertain or instruct explains her lack of success in her lifetime. Other paintings by Duparc, as described in her will, were religious in nature (a Virgin and Child and a miniature of Magdaline) or were portraits. It is assumed that most of her paintings are now hanging unnoticed in private collections in the south of France.

SOURCES:
Harris, Ann Sutherland, and Linda Nochlin. *Women Artists: 1550–1950.* NY: Alfred A. Knopf, 1976.

Barbara Morgan,
Melrose, Massachusetts

Dupin, Amandine Aurore Lucie (1804–1876).
See Sand, George.

Duplessis, Lucile (1771–1794).
See Desmoulins, Lucile.

Duplessis, Marie (1824–1847).
See Plessis, Alphonsine.

Du Pont, Margaret Osborne (b. 1918).
See Osborne, Margaret.

du Pré, Jacqueline (1945–1987)

English cellist, one of the most talented of the 20th century, who ranks with Pablo Casals, Guilhermina Suggia, and Mstislav Rostropovich, and is especially known for her interpretations of the works of Sir Edward Elgar. Name variations: Du Pre. Pronunciation: Du-PRAY. Born on January 26, 1945, in Oxford, England; died on October 20, 1987, in London, of multiple sclerosis; daughter of Derek du Pré (an accountant) and Iris (Greep) du Pré (a pianist and composer); sister of Hilary du Pré (a flutist) and Piers du Pré (a clarinetist); entered Herbert Wallen's Cello School in London at age six; began studying with William Pleeth at age ten; studied with Pablo Casals and then with Mstislav Rostropovich; married Daniel Barenboim (a pianist and conductor), on June 15, 1967; no children.

Became interested in cello at age four (1949); won the Suggia Cello Award (1956); performed for BBC television at age 12 (1957); won Guildhall's Gold Medal as well as the Queen's Prize at age 15 (1960); made her concert debut at Wigmore Hall in London at age 16 (1961); continued to concertize, establishing a worldwide reputation; married and converted to Judaism in Jerusalem (1967); performed often in concert with husband but began to suffer from major symptoms of multiple sclerosis in her late 20s; disease destroyed her career and eventually took her life at age 42 (1987).

Night after night, from January to May 1966, two cellists were hard at work in Moscow. One was the famous Russian musician Mstislav Rostropovich; the other was a tall, long-haired blonde Englishwoman. Despite the girl's youth and because of her great talent, Rostropovich viewed her almost as his equal and had agreed to fit her lessons into his busy schedule. It wasn't unusual for the two to begin as late as 10:30 PM. Week by week, the great Russian performer watched the power of the young woman's playing grow. She was "the most natural player that I have ever seen, in all my life," he said later. "[H]er thoughts flowed straight from mind to cello without pause." At only 21, Jacqueline du Pré was already recognized as one of the world's finest cellists.

She was born in Oxford, England, on January 26, 1945. Her father Derek was an accountant who played the piano and accordion for entertainment. His family came from the Channel Islands off England's south coast, which had been home to the du Prés since William the Conqueror invaded Britain in 1066. Jacqueline's mother was **Iris Greep**, a fine pianist and a composer who had studied at the Royal Academy in London. The Greeps were dockers from Devon, perhaps of Dutch extraction. Jacqueline was the second of three children; her older sister **Hilary du Pré** was a flutist and her younger brother Piers played the clarinet.

Jacqueline was still an infant when her mother noticed that she listened carefully to her lullabies. At age four, after hearing a cello played on "The Children's Hour," a BBC-radio program, she told her mother she wanted the instrument that "made that noise." On her fifth birthday, her parents gave her a three-quarter cello, which was still large enough to make it difficult for the child to reach the high notes. Her mother composed little tunes, with illustrated lyrics about elves and witches, and featuring notes slightly beyond Jacqueline's reach in order to stretch her technical skills. At age six, she became a student at Herbert Wallen's Cello School in London, where she was provided with a smaller cello. At age seven, she made her first public appearance, performing Schubert's *Moments Musicales*. The young girl was fiercely serious about music. One day as she began to tune her cello, she asked her uncle, Wilfrid du Pré, to play a middle C on the piano. Wilfrid, thinking his niece would not know the difference, simply struck the first note that came to hand. An insulted Jacqueline pitched a sizeable fit for which she later apologized.

> To ask what more she might have done is sad and pointless; it is like asking how much more a young Schubert might have composed had he lived another five years. There is no end to talent like this.
>
> —William Pleeth

The life of Jacqueline du Pré was centered around music. She often said that until age 17 the cello was her best friend. At age ten, she began to study with William Pleeth, whom she called her "cello daddy"; at age 11, she won the Suggia Cello Award, an important international prize that paid her tuition fees at the Guildhall School of Music for the next five years. At age 12, she was invited to perform on BBC television, and at 15 she won Guildhall's Gold Medal as well as the Queen's Prize for British instrumentalists under 30. She went to Zermatt, Switzerland, to attend classes with the great master of the cello, Pablo Casals, and commented later that his classes were "like getting a punch in the stomach" because Casals set down dogmatic rules for playing. At age 16, she made her concert debut at Wigmore Hall in London. Although she was shy, du Pré loved performing. Unlike some nervous performers, she was jubilant on stage. About this time, a gift from an anonymous donor made it possible for her to acquire a Stradivarius cello dated 1673; in 1964, she was able to acquire a second Stradivarius, the famous Davidov cello, dated 1712.

It is rarely possible for a young genius to live a normal life, but du Pré briefly enjoyed a relatively youthful period between her studies and her ascent to international stardom. She lived on her own, dated, and traveled. One night, returning from rehearsal with her friend, Hugh Maguire, she felt extremely animated and longed to avoid the solitude of her Holland Park apartment. Maguire invited her to come home with him. She stayed six months. Hugh Maguire's home was a veritable musical conservatory, where many musicians, almost all male, dropped by and often performed impromptu chamber music concerts. Many were attracted to the tall blonde cellist, and one, conductor and pianist Daniel Barenboim, would become her husband. Maguire remembered times when Jackie, full of natural gaiety and high spirits, would play her cello while lying on her bed roaring with laughter.

Like most great cellists, du Pré created an almost physical bond between herself and her instrument. Throwing herself into her performance, she instantly communicated her delight in the music she was playing, and her style was impassioned and grainy. She also had a marvelous memory, which contributed to the speed of her development. Her main problem was technique. She had a freak left hand, on which the first and index fingers were the same length, meaning that she was unable to finger the strings conventionally. But her warmblooded, romantic approach made her a worldwide favorite on concert stages.

In time, du Pré became most famous for her performances of the music of Sir Edward Elgar, particularly his *Cello Concerto*. Except for the widely known *Pomp and Circumstance Marches*, Elgar's music had been infrequently performed since his death in 1934. In 1965, music critic Edward Greenfield wrote of one of du Pré's performances, "Not since Master Yehudi Menuhin recorded Elgar's Violin Concerto with the composer has a young artist played with such profound dedication on record as Jacqueline du Pré."

De Pré converted to Judaism and married Daniel Barenboim in Jerusalem, on June 15, 1967, a year after their first meeting. Three days later, the Six Day War broke out in the Middle East, and the newlyweds soon went on a concert tour of North America with the Israel Philharmonic Orchestra to raise funds for the Israeli cause. When they were not on tour, the couple lived in a small apartment in London near Baker Street, and du Pré and Barenboim often gave joint concerts. When asked what it was like to accompany his wife on the piano, Barenboim once replied, "Difficult. It doesn't dawn on her sometimes that we mortals have difficulties in following her."

When they were not on tour, du Pré enjoyed cooking the spicy food her husband liked. Unlike Barenboim, who had grown up in the bright Israeli sun, she loved swimming and walking in the rainy countryside. The young couple shared a large circle of musician friends, including Artur Rubinstein, Zubin and **Nancy Mehta**, Itzhak and **Toby Perlman**, Vladimir Askenazy, Pinchas and **Eugenia Zukerman**, and Christopher and **Diana Nupen**. "Whenever I think about Jacqueline du Pré," said Itzhak Perlman, "I always imagine a shooting star shining brightly in the night for an instant and then disappearing. Her career, which lasted a mere ten years, revealed to the public that she was indeed a shining star."

No one knows when du Pré first sensed that something was wrong. Several incidents—sudden unexplained falls, memory lapses, extreme fatigue, disorientation—were later remembered. She and her husband were widely sought in concert halls throughout the world, and her schedule was grueling. While playing had once been a welcome release, persistent fatigue had now begun to make performing a source of anxiety. In its early stages, multiple sclerosis is extremely difficult to diagnose, and many reasons were given for the cellist's new difficulties—exhaustion, psychological problems, even stage fright. She began seeing a therapist. Especially baffling was the fact that her symptoms came and went. At times, her playing was unsurpassed, but it could also deteriorate suddenly, sometimes in the middle of a performance.

By 1970, although her commitments were greater than ever, du Pré found her strength and endurance dwindling even further and thought she was losing her mind. For six months, she stopped playing, then picked up her cello again that December; it was as if she had never stopped playing. She began to make recordings, of Chopin's *Cello Sonata in G minor, Op. 65* and a transcription of Franck's *Violin Sonata in*

Jacqueline
du Pré

A, then again stopped playing. After signs of improvement, she began to perform again in concert, but her playing now became increasingly erratic. On January 25, 1973, she was performing the Brahms Double Concerto under the direction of her husband at Philharmonic Hall in New York when all sensation in her fingers went dead. She could not feel the strings of her cello.

When the diagnosis was multiple sclerosis, du Pré was emotionally unprepared for what followed. Relieved at first to learn that her symptoms were physical and not psychological, she discovered in time just how devastating the disease can be. She proved to be among the 15% of MS patients whose bodies are ultimately destroyed by the crippling condition. Losing control of her fingers and then of her body, she was confined to a wheelchair and then to bed. But her interest in music remained as acute as ever, and for a time she was able to teach master classes. Since she could no longer play, she whistled the musical parts and explained the fingering to her students.

Surrounded by friends, she built a semblance of a life, hosting dinner parties and attending concerts in a wheelchair, beautifully dressed in evening clothes and maintaining her sunny disposition. As the years passed, however, it became harder and harder for her to speak. Robert Anderson said that for a period of time they spoke French together, because the sounds were easier for her to articulate. As the disease progressed, her eyesight also began to fail.

Locked out of the world of music, du Pré gradually grew apart from her husband. Barenboim saw that du Pré had every comfort and made regular visits to see her, but, since she did not want his musical career as well as hers to be sacrificed to the disease, he continued his concert tours. He also established a life with **Helena Bachkirev**, a Russian pianist who became the mother of his two children. Still, he was frequently at his wife's bedside as the bond between these two musicians was never broken.

On October 20, 1987, Jacqueline du Pré died in London at age 42 and was laid to rest at the Golders Green Jewish Cemetery. A few months later, a Thanksgiving Ceremony was held in her memory, attended by Charles, prince of Wales and *Katherine (Worsley), duchess of Kent. Hundreds gathered to hear Barenboim perform Mozart's *Piano Concerto no. 20 in B flat Major* and the English Chamber Orchestra played Elgar's *Serenade for Strings Opus 20 in E minor*. Although she had not appeared on a concert stage for more than 14 years, du Pré had left the world with a wealth of sound. Year after year, recordings of her performances are re-released, allowing new generations of music lovers to enjoy her extraordinary talent.

In 1999, the controversial film *Hilary and Jackie* was released, based on Piers and Hilary du Pré's book, *A Genius in the Family*. The movie starred **Emily Watson** as Jacqueline du Pré and **Rachel Griffiths** as Hilary (both actresses received Academy Award nominations for their performance).

SOURCES:

"Du Pré show," in *London Times*. January 7, 1988, p. 3.

Dyer, Richard, "Jacqueline du Pré's tragic story," in *Boston Globe*. May 28, 1990, p. 33.

Easton, Carol. *Jacqueline du Pré: A Life*. NY: Summit, 1989.

Greenfield, Edward. "Joyful Memories of Jacqueline," in *Manchester Guardian*. June 9, 1989, p. 32.

James, Brian. "She never lost patience. She permitted herself a few tears," in *London Times*. October 21, 1987, p. 20.

————. "A Silent Farewell to a Cellist," in *London Times*. October 22, 1987, p. 2.

McLellan, Joseph. "Making a Case for Laser Disc, Sight and Sound," in *Washington Post*. May 26, 1991, sec G., p. 1.

Murdin, Lynda. "Simple service for cellist," in *London Times*. October 21, 1987, p. 2.

Oulton, Charles. "Family Anger at du Pré Book," in *Sunday Times*. March 20, 1988, p. A5.

Potter, Tully. "The Recordings of Jacqueline du Pré," in *The Strad*. Vol. 99, no. 1174. February 1988, pp. 134–135.

"Remembering Jacqueline du Pré," in *The Strad*. Vol. 99, no. 1174. February 1988, pp. 126–134.

Shawe-Taylor, Desmond. "Joyous Legacy of a Tragic Prodigy," in *Sunday Times*. October 25, 1987, p. 63.

"Thanksgiving Ceremony: Dr. Jacqueline du Pré," in *London Times*. January 27, 1988, p. 14.

Wordsworth, William. *Jacqueline du Pré. Impressions*. NY: Vanguard, 1983.

SUGGESTED READING:

Wilson, Elizabeth. *Jacqueline du Pre: Her Life, Her Music, Her Legend*. Arcade, 1999.

RELATED MEDIA:

Hilary and Jackie (film), starring Emily Watson as Jacqueline du Pré and Rachel Griffiths as Hilary du Pré, directed by Anand Tucker, screenplay by Frank Cottrell Boyce, based on the book by Piers and Hilary du Pré, *A Genius in the Family*, 1999.

Karin Loewen Haag,
freelance writer, Athens, Georgia

Durack, Fanny (1889–1956)

Australia's first female Olympic gold medalist, who once held every world record in women's swimming from 100 yards to 1 mile. Name variations: Sarah Durack. Born Sarah Durack in Sydney, Australia, on October 27, 1889; died of cancer in Stanmore, Australia, on March 20, 1956; third daughter and sixth child of Thomas Durack (a Sydney publican) and Mary (Mason) Durack; married Bernard Martin Gately (a horse trainer), on January 22, 1921.

Won the gold medal in the 100-meter freestyle in Stockholm Olympics (1912); broke 12 world records (1912–18).

Fanny Durack, Australia's first female Olympic gold medalist, may also have held a record for the number of controversies surrounding her competitions. She was born in Sydney in 1889, one of six children of Thomas and **Mary Mason Durack**. She learned to swim at the Coogee and Wylie baths, where she trained in the breast stroke, which was then the only style used in women's competition. She won her first State title in 1906, while still a schoolgirl.

In Durack's era, competitive swimming for women was still in its infancy. The first recorded women's world swimming record was set in 1908 by **Martha Gerstung** of Germany in 100-meter freestyle competition. By 1911, Durack had changed her stroke to the American crawl, now considered a competitive stroke for women as well as men. Along with fellow Australian ❧▶ **Wilhelmina Wylie**, Fanny was poised to enter the Stockholm Olympic Games of 1912, the first year that swimming and diving for women were introduced to the Olympics. At this juncture the problems began. First, the men in charge of the Australian team thought it a waste of time and money to send women to the Games. Second, the possibility of women performing athletics in front of men caused great controversy. Durack and Wylie were being sponsored by the Sydney branch of the New South Wales Ladies' Amateur Swimming Association (NSWLSA), which in 1912 did not allow women to compete in front of male spectators. The prevalent theory responsible for this policy—held also by Pierre de Coubertin, father of the Olympics—was that male spectators would come to women's competitions for salacious reasons rather than to watch the women compete. Sports for women, concluded another Olympic organizer, was considered "morally questionable," a position which denied women the right to compete due to men's perceived inability to consider women as anything other than objects for their viewing pleasure. *Rose Scott, president of the NSWLSA Sydney branch, was both a powerful feminist and an ardent believer in social purity. She was also publicly adamant that the women not compete in front of a mixed crowd but for a subtly different reason. "I think it is disgusting," she was quoted as saying, "that men should be allowed to attend" at all.

Following a public outcry, the rule was rescinded, Scott resigned her presidency, and Durack and Wylie were on their way, but only when they agreed to pay for their own trips. Funds were raised to send Durack, while Wylie's family footed the bill for her travel. (Durack and Wylie, intense rivals, traveled separately. Chaperoned by her sister Mary, Durack traveled on a French mail steamer, the *Armand Behie*; Wylie, accompanied by her father, was on board the RMS *Malvia*.)

The 1912 Stockholm Games provided one individual swimming event for women, the 100-meter freestyle, and a team relay event, the 400 meters. During the first heat of the 100-meter freestyle, Durack, wearing a long woollen swimsuit with a skirt, beat **Daisy Curwen**'s world record with a time of 19.8 seconds. In the second heat, Durack even beat Curwen who was then hastily transported out of the building on a stretcher for a date with an appendectomy. On July 15, despite running into the side wall of the pool, Durack won the freestyle and the gold medal handily in 1:22.2 (her time was the same as the men's winner that year), while Wylie came in second. ❧▶ **Jennie Fletcher** of Great Britain, whose life included a 72-hour work week in a textile factory in Leicester with little time for training, came in third. The event was a clean sweep for the Commonwealth nations. There was no American women's swim team in Stockholm; America's female swimmers had been effectively blocked from competing by James Sullivan, chief organizer of the American team.

After the Olympics, Durack and Wylie showcased their skills on tours throughout Europe and the U.S., causing further controversy. When they arrived in America without official sanction in 1918, they were banned by the Amateur Swimming Union of Australia. The following year, they faced suspension of their amateur status when they refused to swim until their manager's expenses were paid. The tour ended for good after Durack jumped the starter's gun during a swim in Chicago.

Durack was unable to defend her title in the 1920 Antwerp Olympics, because she underwent her own appendectomy a week before the team's departure. However, between the years of 1912 and 1918, she broke 12 world records and

❧▶ **Wylie, Wilhelmina** (b. 1892)
Australian swimmer. Name variations: Mina Wylie. Born Wilhelmina Wylie in Australia in 1892. Won the silver medal in the 100-meter freestyle in Stockholm Olympics of 1912.

❧▶ **Fletcher, Jennie** (1890–1968)
British swimmer. Name variations: Jenny. Born in Great Britain on March 19, 1890; died in 1968. Won the bronze medal in the 100-meter freestyle and the gold medal in the 4x100-meter freestyle relay in Stockholm Olympics of 1912.

Fanny
Durack

did a great deal to promote women's swimming. She retired from competition after her marriage in 1921 but continued to coach and to serve on the New South Wales Women's Amateur Swimming Association. Fanny Durack died of cancer on March 20, 1956. In 1967, she was posthu-mously elected to the International Swimming Hall of Fame. In December 1990, a headstone was placed at her unmarked grave in Waverley Cemetery in Sydney.

Barbara Morgan,
Melrose, Massachusetts

Durack, Mary (1913–1994)

Australian author known for her biographies of the Durack family, Kings in Grass Castles *and* Sons in the Saddle. *Name variations: Dame Mary Durack. Born Mary Durack on February 20, 1913, in Adelaide, Australia; died in 1994 in Australia; daughter of Bessie Ida Muriel (Johnstone) and Michael Durack; sister of Elizabeth Durack (painter and illustrator); educated at Loreto Convent (graduated 1929); married Horace Clive Miller (an airline operator), on December 2, 1938; children: (Patricia)* **Mary Miller Millett***; **Robin Elizabeth Miller Dicks** (deceased);* **Juliana Miller Rowney** *(deceased); Andrew Clive Miller;* **Marie Rose Miller Megaw***; John Christopher Miller.*

Selected writings: (with Florence Rutter) Child Artists of the Australian Bush *(Harrap, 1952); (novel)* Keep Him My Country *(Constable, 1955); (family history)* Kings in Grass Castles *(Constable, 1959);* The Rock and the Sand *(Constable, 1969); (editor) M.L. Skinner,* The Fifth Sparrow *(Sydney University Press, 1972); (with Ingrid A. Drysdale)* The End of Dreaming *(Rigby, 1974);* Swan River Saga *(two-act play; first produced in Perth, Australia, 1971, published by Service Printing Co., 1975); (biography of Eliza Shaw)* To Be Heirs Forever *(Constable, 1976); (novel)* Sons in the Saddle *(Constable, 1983); (with Olsen, Serventy, Dutton, and Bortignon)* The Land beyond Time *(Macmillan, 1984); (with Mahood, Williams, Willey, Sawrey, Iddon, and Ruhen)* The Stockman *(Lansdowne-Rigby, 1984).*

Selected writings for children: Little Poems of Sunshine by an Australian Child *(R.S. Sampson, 1923);* All-About: The Story of an Aboriginal Community on Argyle Station, Kimberley *(Endeavour Press, 1935);* Chunuma *(Endeavour Press, 1936);* Son of Djaro *(Endeavor Press, 1938),* The Way of the Whirlwind *(Consolidated Press, 1941, reprinted, Angus & Robertson, 1979); (poems)* Piccaninnies *(Offset Printing, 1943); (poems)* The Magic Trumpet *(Cassell, 1944); (poems)* Kookanoo and Kangaroo *(Rigby, 1963, and Lerner, 1966);* To Ride a Fine Horse *(St. Martin's, 1963);* The Courteous Savage: Yagan of Swan River *(Thomas Nelson, 1964, published as* Yagan of the Bibbulmun, *1976);* An Australian Settler *(Clarendon Press, 1964, published as* A Pastoral Emigrant, *Oxford University Press, 1964);* Tjakamarra: Boy between Two Worlds *(Vanguard Service Printing, 1977).*

"I was never aware of having an ambition to write books," said Mary Durack, "though I seem to have been a compulsive writer from the time I could form words on paper. . . . Perhaps the compulsion arose from the genes of Celtic

ancestors who were frustrated by lack of opportunity, education, or encouragement." The second of six children, Durack was the daughter of a rancher and grew up in the Kimberley region of Western Australia, enjoying station life. When she and her older brother reached school age, the family moved to Perth where better educational opportunities awaited the Durack children. Mary completed school at the Loreto Convent at age 16 and by her own decision returned to Kimberley. She was joined there by her sister **Elizabeth Durack**, who was two years younger than she, as soon as Elizabeth had also graduated. The pair shared cooking duties and salary on their father's Ivanhoe station. With Mary as writer and Elizabeth as illustrator, they began a collaboration, and the children's book *Chunuma* (1936) was their first publication together. After seven years, they had saved enough money to travel to Europe, where they remained for a year.

Following their travels, the sisters parted ways, and Mary Durack returned to Western Australia to write for the *Western Mail*. A suc-

ℳary ℒurack

cessful freelance writer, she married Horace Miller, an airline operator. The couple settled in Perth and had six children, and Durack flew west often to the family's second home in Broome.

Although she was also a novelist, Durack's greatest success came with her children's books and her biographies of the Durack family, including *Kings in Grass Castles* and *Sons in the Saddle*. "That the greater part of my literary output has been of a documentary or historical nature," remarked Durack, "was a matter of chance rather than of choice. For preference I would have concentrated on fiction or drama, but my inheritance or chance acquisition of historical documents decided otherwise." In addition to her published works, Durack was also the writer of several unpublished plays, three of which were produced in Australia: "Dalgerie" (libretto for one-act opera), "The Ship of Dreams" (two-act for children), and "The Way of the Whirlwind" (two-act ballet for children). Her two-act play *Swan River Saga* was first produced in Perth in 1971 and was published by Service Printing Company in 1975.

Durack strove for accuracy in her histories: "Bearing in mind Napoleon's definition of history as 'a fiction agreed upon,' I try to assure that there is as little fiction as possible in my interpretation and to remember that my characters, enmeshed in their time and circumstances, should not be casually judged by standards imposed by different backgrounds and other generations." She was awarded the Order of the British Empire (OBE) in 1966, and made Dame of the British Empire (DBE) in 1978. Dame Mary Durack died in Australia in 1994.

SOURCES:

Hetherington, John. *42 Faces*. Melbourne: F.W. Cheshire, 1962.

Metzger, Oprida, and Deborah A. Straub. *Contemporary Authors, New Revision Series, Volume 17*. Detroit: Gale Research, 1986.

Wilde, William H., Joy Hooton, and Barry Andrews. *Oxford Companion to Australian Literature*. Melbourne: Oxford, 1985.

RELATED MEDIA:

Six of Durack's "Kookanoo" stories were recorded on an album released by Admark (1973).

Durand, Marguerite (1864–1936)

French actress and feminist journalist. Pronunciation: mar-GREET dew-RAWN. *Born Marguerite-Charlotte Durand de Valfère in Paris, France, on January 24, 1864; died in Paris on March 16, 1936; daughter of Anna-Alexandrine-Caroline Durand de Valfère and General Alfred Boucher or possibly Auguste Clésinger; married Georges Laguerre, in 1888 (divorced 1895); children: (with Antonin Périvier) son, Jacques Périvier (b. 1896).*

Marguerite Durand and her half-brother Charles (d. 1909) were born out of wedlock to **Anna-Alexandrine-Caroline Durand de Valfère**. Anna had been born to a comfortable and cultivated family in Frankfurt-am-Main; her father, Charles Durand de Valfère, was a friend of, and attorney for, Benjamin Constant. Anna's mother was **Octavie Bouquié**, a reader for the Grand Duchess *Helena of Russia at the Imperial Court in St. Petersburg, where Anna was raised.

Marguerite's father was a Royalist colonel in the French army, Alfred Boucher (d. 1885), who fought in the African, Crimean, Italian, and Mexican campaigns and was promoted to general and Officer in the Legion of Honor. For unknown reasons, Boucher did not marry Anna; but he treated Marguerite as his daughter, and she kept up relations with him and his family. Nevertheless, the sculptor Auguste Clésinger (1814–1883) has sometimes been regarded as her father, for he lived with Anna for a long time, was a witness at Marguerite's birth declaration, and "married" Anna in church, a marriage annulled because he had been married to and separated from **Solange**, the daughter of *George Sand; divorce was not legal at that time.

Little is known of Marguerite's childhood and youth. For whatever reasons, her mother found herself obliged to raise her two children alone, and it was a hard struggle. She supported herself, apparently, by writing under pseudonyms, notably for newspapers. She also wrote a book (unpublished) on the diplomat Viel-Castel and a dictionary of famous women, which was incomplete when she died in 1911. Marguerite received a strict Catholic upbringing and was educated in the convent school of the Dames Trinitaires in Paris. Possibly in an act of rebellion, in 1879 she joined Professor Regnier's class at the Conservatory of Dramatic Art. She flourished there, winning the first honorable mention (*accessit*) on July 28, 1880, and the first prize for comedy on July 27, 1881. On September 1, 1881, she joined the Comédie-Française. She debuted as Marcelle in *Demi-Monde* (Dumas fils), on January 21, 1882, and for several years enjoyed a sparkling reputation in plays such as *Les Femmes Savantes* and *L'Avare* (Molière), *Le Mariage de Figaro* (Beaumarchais) and *Les Honnêtes femmes* (Becque).

In 1886, however, she suddenly left the stage to marry Georges Laguerre (1858–1912), a rapidly rising lawyer-politician (a deputy in Parliament since 1883) who had won a reputation defending social revolutionaries, including Blanquist demonstrators, Prince Kropotkin, and *Louise Michel, and was close to the Radical leader Georges Clemenceau. In 1887, Laguerre became a leader of the Republican Committee of National Protest supporting General Georges Boulanger's political ambitions after he had been dropped as minister of war. "If Boulangism had its birth anywhere," wrote Maurice Barrès, "it was in the home of Laguerre." Marguerite, dubbed "the Madame Roland of Boulangism," played host and was an animating force behind Laguerre's Boulangist tabloid, *La Presse*, where she first came in contact with the world of journalism. Apparently she acquired doubts about the role of royalist money and bribery in the movement, for she was known as a staunch Republican afterward. In any case, she never spoke or wrote about the Boulangist triumph and crash (1888–91), and in 1891 she separated from Laguerre; they divorced in 1895 but remained on friendly terms. Laguerre's career plummeted. At his death in 1912, she took care of his sickly orphaned daughter (by a second marriage), **Georgette Laguerre**, but was finally forced to put her in a sanitarium.

The year she left Laguerre, Durand joined the prestigious *Le Figaro*, writing a woman-about-town column on fashions, trends, and political gossip. Antonin Périvier, the literary director, had hired her, and in time (August 14, 1896) she gave birth to their son, Jacques, of whom little is known save that he was always in poor health. Périvier, a married man, recognized but did not support Jacques; he did, however, retain Durand as a columnist.

In 1896, she was sent to cover the Fourth French International Feminist Congress (April 8–12). Durand went merely looking for a good story but came away converted to the feminist cause by **Marie Pognon** and the intelligent, dedicated women she found in attendance. She then set about to launch a major, unique enterprise: a daily newspaper written, administered, and printed entirely by women. *La Fronde*—named for the sling David used to kill Goliath and for a 17th-century insurrection—appeared on December 9, 1897, with an initial run of 200,000 copies. It lasted until March 16, 1905, having become a monthly supplement to *L'Action* in September 1903. Durand recruited her close friend *Séverine (Caroline Rémy), the only top-flight woman journalist in France, and mobilized a large galaxy of collaborators and contributors, including Pognon, *Jane Misme, *Jeanne Schmahl, *Hubertine Auclert, *Clémence Royer, *Nelly Roussel, Marie Bonneviale, *Aline Valette, Eliska Vincent, Jeanne Brémontier, Daniel Lesueur (Jeanne Loiseau Lapauze), Judith Claudel, Pauline Kergomard, Hélène Sée, *Dorothea Klumpke, Clotilde Dessard, Mary Léopold Lacour, Louise Debor, Marie-Louise Néron, Odette Laguerre, *Myriam Harry, Lucie Delarue-Mardrus, Marcelle Tinayre, Camille Bélilon (Ernestine Tournemine), Harlor (Thérèse Hammer), Marie Maugerat, Isabelle Bogelot, Marie Martin, *Maria Vérone, Mathilde Méliot, and *Avril de Saint-Croix.

La Fronde was a first-class operation, the clerical staff neatly turned out in velvet, white-cuffed dresses and set up in a fine mansion on the rue Saint-Georges. Not surprisingly, finances were strained from the start. The subscription list settled at about 12,000 in its best years—mainly "female intellectuals," Durand admitted—a decent showing but insufficient for the scale of the operation. Where and how Durand obtained money for the paper—and, indeed, for her fairly lavish lifestyle—has never been altogether clear. She had many friends in high places (more than just friends, rumor said), including Alphonse and Gustave Rothschild and even Kaiser Wilhelm II; René Viviani, a wealthy lawyer, sometime minister, and premier (1914–15), almost certainly was a major benefactor. Many years later, however, Durand wrote to Jane Misme that she had started the paper solely from her own sources, e.g., selling her pearls one by one. She said she provided (at considerable trouble) a daily review of the world press to an "important Parisian personality" for a thousand francs per day, but she denied ever having had a patron (*commanditaire*) or accepting aid from anyone whomsoever. Rumors that the "Jewish syndicate" had bankrolled her to support the case in favor of Captain Dreyfus, for example, were utterly false.

La Fronde was not a paper devoted solely to women's interests but rather a comprehensive newspaper with numerous rubrics and features— "*Le Temps* in petticoats," as a snide witticism put it. This involved, for example, winning for female reporters the right to enter hitherto exclusively male domains such as the Chamber of Deputies, the Senate, the Paris Municipal Council, the Bourse, and the Association of Parliamentary Journalists. Durand herself was the first woman admitted to the Union of Newspaper Directors. By its very existence as well as its content, *La Fronde* endeavored to popularize a new image of women as being fit to engage in every sphere of public and private life—active, financially independent, cultivated, sporting; and it even ran a women's employment office. At the same time, it also projected a new image of feminism, not as seeking to ape men's dress and manner, as the public so often perceived its adherents as doing, but instead as thoroughly feminine, "feminism in lace." The paper aimed to rise above party and faction, giving voice to various shades of opinion, while, however, firmly defending the Republic. With regard to feminism, for example, it carried writings by women ranging from the socialist left to the Roman Catholic right. *La Fronde* was, nevertheless, one of the first and most consistent upholders of the right of Captain Alfred Dreyfus to receive a fair trial on his treason charge. In the heat of the Dreyfus Affair battles (1897–1900), the paper became more leftish and stridently anticlerical (not just laic), was accordingly the target of much anti-Dreyfusard abuse, and saw its circulation suffer.

In the domain of women's issues, *La Fronde* regularly campaigned for abolition of the Napoleonic Code's strictures making women perpetual minors before the law. It fought for equal wages for men and women, opening of all the professions and the School of Fine Arts to women, equal consideration of women for the Legion of Honor, abolition of legalized prostitution, passage of a seat law for salesclerks, and ending of the exploitation of orphans by charitable or religious institutions. It also promoted the "science of motherhood" (*puériculture*), which trod on sensitive ground because of the connection between sex education and contraception. Likewise, its advocacies of a "right to die" and of the international peace movement (hence friendliness with Kaiser Wilhelm's Germany) touched issues that alienated many would-be subscribers.

By 1903, *La Fronde* was facing financial ruin. Durand, for reasons she never made clear, answered a plea from a failing paper, Henri Bérenger and Victor Charbonnel's rabidly anticlerical *L'Action,* to merge resources. *La Fronde* would continue, after September 1, as a monthly supplement. The doomed marriage of two ailing papers lasted until March 1, 1905. Durand later expressed regret that she had agreed to the merger. Her wry verdict on *La Fronde*'s eventual failure was that it was judged "too bourgeois by the socialists, too serious by the Parisians, and too Parisian by the provinces."

Founding and running *La Fronde* brought Durand into contact with the issue of women workers and unions. Laws "protecting" women

by forbidding night work made it illegal for a morning paper like *La Fronde* to employ women typesetters. While litigating the question, and having received no support from the Federation of Book Workers which opposed admission of women printers, she founded a Union of Women Printers, which was admitted to the Labor Exchange on February 3, 1900, and the Women Printers' Cooperative Society (November 22, 1900), the first women's cooperative in France. The following year, she became heavily involved in the strike of the Berger-Levrault printing firm in Nancy when she allowed eight typesetters from *La Fronde* to offer to replace strikers. Berger-Levrault had previously shown sympathy to the women's movement and had refused to fire female typesetters at the Federation's demand. The infuriated Federation got the Labor Exchange to expel the Union of Women Printers on January 7, 1902, but Durand contested the action and ultimately won reinstatement by the courts in 1905. It proved to be a Pyrrhic victory, for it only fed a long-standing hostility of the French labor movement toward union memberships for women. The issue came to a head in the Couriau Affair of 1913; once again the Federation of Book Workers was at the center, and Durand—now co-director of *Les Nouvelles*—was prominent in the dispute as a journalist.

In the meantime, Durand also organized unions of flower-makers and feather sellers, stenographer-typists, cashier-bookkeepers, and midwives. In 1900, in conjunction with the Paris Exposition, she was secretary-general of the Fifth International Congress on the Conditions and Rights of Women (September 5–8) and headed the section on legislative questions. The Congress was highly successful in drawing official and international support but failed to attract many working women delegates. In 1907, with Viviani as minister of labor, she was named president of the new Office of Women's Work and convened a Congress of Women's Work (March 25–28), but the result was analogous to 1900; the few representatives of working women were put in the shade by a bejewelled and begowned Marguerite Durand and her bourgeois supporters. The General Labor Confederation (CGT) denounced her and the whole affair, and the Office itself soon became ephemeral. Undeterred, she organized with **Jeanne Oddo-Deflou** and Eliska Vincent the National Congress on the Rights and Suffrage of Women (June 26–28, 1908) and presided over the sessions on labor issues.

In 1908, Durand joined Jacques Stern and William Tournier as a co-director of *Les Nou-*

Marguerite
Durand

velles. Not a feminist paper per se and tending not to take pronounced stands, it offered concise news in two daily editions but ceased publication at the outbreak of the World War (1914–18). Meanwhile, in 1910, Durand ran (illegally, of course) in Paris IX for Parliament, get-ting 403 write-in votes. Her platform featured women's rights and equal pay, safety laws, the eight-hour day, but not yet votes for women. Women should be able to run for and hold of-fice, but—ardent anticlerical that she was—she thought votes for women would only strengthen the Catholic Church's political influence and thus endanger the Republic. (*La Fronde* had never campaigned for women in suffrage.) Moreover, the violent tactics being used by the English suffragists, she said in 1910, "would quickly be stopped by the ridicule" if tried in France. Yet by 1914 she had given way on this point, for she was, with Séverine, a principal organizer of a street rally on July 5 honoring the 18th-century *philosophe* Marquis de Condorcet, an advocate of women's rights, and calling for the vote. Some 6,000 marchers participated, the largest such demonstration France had seen. Most of the public viewed it as scandalous.

Also in 1914, Durand made an ill-timed effort to revive *La Fronde*. It appeared as a weekly one week before the June 28 assassination of the Archduke Franz Ferdinand, and when the war began in August it tried to rally women "to carry out their social duties." The German invasion led to *La Fronde*'s closing on September 3. During the war, Durand was rather circumspect because her prewar friendship with the kaiser, visits to Germany, and the pacifist tenor of *Les Nouvelles* raised suspicions about her patriotism. Her only public involvement in the war effort was as a member, principal speaker, and money-raiser for the Feminine Automobile Club, which employed about 20 cars to transport wounded and convalescent soldiers. She quit the organization in 1916, however, as a result of a power struggle with the president. That same year, she also spoke out to the government about low morale among female workers in the war industries due to mistreatment by their bosses and the unions. She asked for a Women's Labor Bureau to study the situation and propose remedies, but Premier Aristide Briand resigned before he could fulfill his promise to institute the bureau. Also, in 1918 she testified in defense of a left-wing pacifist, *Hélène Brion, accused of subverting the war effort.

After the war, which converted her to seeking full political, not just civil, rights for women including the suffrage, Durand played the role of *grande dame* of the feminist movement, speaking at banquets promoting women's rights, international disarmament, and the League of Nations. In 1922, she organized the Exposition of Celebrated Women of the Nineteenth Century, partly to raise money for a retirement home for female journalists, which became a reality in 1928 when she bought Séverine's residence at Pierrefonds (Oise), "Les Trois marches," before the latter's death there in 1929. And once again she revived *La Fronde* for a short run, from May 1926 to July 1928, and won a personal triumph

in 1927 when she and Séverine were admitted to the sacrosanct Association of Journalists (*la Maison des journalistes*). The new *La Fronde* differed from the original because it employed many men; it was partly undertaken to prepare her candidacy for the Paris Municipal Council in 1927. Since 1914, she had evolved toward a moderate socialism and was now a member of the Republican Socialist Party. Cautiously, her platform advocated only the municipal, not a general, suffrage for women, probably to conform to the party's position. She was ruled ineligible, however, and gave her support to a Socialist candidate. In 1930, she became a member of the administrative commission of the Republican Socialist Party.

Durand's last contribution to feminism was to give to the city of Paris her extensive library of feminist documents and history. She spent her last years organizing this material in a building across the street from the Panthéon, dying there of a heart attack on March 16, 1936, while working alone on her collection. The newspapers paid little attention and, a sad irony, mostly commented on her role in the Boulanger affair.

Marguerite Durand was an original, striking, and influential figure in journalism and feminism. Elegant in attire and manner and thoroughly worldly, she helped to change some of the popular misconceptions of feminists as disheveled revolutionaries, amazons, or puritanical busybodies. Due to her stage training, she was a fine speaker with "almost a seductive quality" when before an audience. She was intensely ambitious to hold center stage and be regarded as *the* leader of the women's movement. Her ambition helped her achieve what she did but also not infrequently alienated people. She pioneered women's labor unions, for example, but she expected "her" unionists to take her direction and tolerate her overweening, patronizing airs while they chanted their eternal gratitude. On the other hand, she was by no means heartless. She was compassionate toward suffering, and her sympathy extended, too, to animals. One of her original ideas was a cemetery for pets. In 1899, she founded one at Asnières on an island in the Seine which still exists. (It also proved to be an important source of income for her.) Self-confident in the highest degree, she was intelligent, wonderfully courageous, and in the midst of difficulties utterly serene: "She was truly the chief," remarked Séverine once when recalling the struggles at *La Fronde*. Moreover, she was, wrote Léon Abensour, a fine journalist, "another Madame Roland . . . a natural writer."

In the end, her greatest accomplishment was, indeed, *La Fronde*. This enterprise, unprecedented and still unique, involved an enormous effort, and its contribution to the progress of feminism was likewise huge. Wrote Abensour, it was "through *La Fronde* that the country began to view feminism not as a species of literary curiosity issuing from a rebellious, whimsical writer, but under its large and human aspect." As if speaking of the effort and her own struggle, Durand wrote to Jane Misme in October 1903, "It is not really a question of women's rights; it is a question of *human dignity and worth.*"

Her greatest permanent legacy was her library. The Bibliothèque Marguerite Durand in Paris remains the most important repository of materials on the history of the women's movement in France and is one of the most valuable collections of its kind in the world.

SOURCES:

Abensour, Léon. *Histoire générale du féminisme: Des origines à nos jours.* Paris: Resources, 1921; Slatkine Reprints, 1979.

Albistur, Maïté and Daniel Armogathe. *Histoire due féminisme français, du moyen âge à nos jours.* Paris: Éditions des Femmes, 1977.

Colin, Madeleine. *Ce n'est pas d'aujourd' hui . . . : Femmes, syndicats, luttes de classe.* Paris: Éditions sociales, 1975.

Dictionnaire de biographie française. A. Balteau, M. Barroux, M. Prévost *et al.*, directeurs. Paris: Letouzey et Ané, 1933-.

Dizier-Metz, Annie. *La Bibliothèque Marguerite Durand: Histoire d'une femme, mémoire des femmes.* Paris: Mairie de Paris-Agence Culturelle de Paris, 1992.

Goliber, Sue Helder. "The Life and Times of Marguerite Durand: A Study in French Feminism." Ph.D. diss., Kent State University, 1975.

Hause, Steven C., with Anne R. Kenney. *Women's Suffrage and Social Politics in the French Third Republic.* Princeton, NJ: Princeton University Press, 1984.

Historical Dictionary of the Third French Republic. 2 vols. Patrick H. Hutton, ed. NY: Greenwood Press, 1986.

Klejman, Laurence, and Florence Rochefort. *L'Égalité en marche. Le féminisme sous la Troisième République.* Paris: Presses de la Fondation nationale des sciences politiques, 1989.

McMillan, James F. *Housewife or Harlot: The Place of Women in French Society 1870–1940.* NY: St. Martin's Press, 1981.

Rabaut, Jacques. *Histoire des féminismes français.* Paris: Stock, 1978.

Stewart, Mary Lynn. *Women, Work, and the French State: Labour Protection and Social Patriarchy 1879–1919.* Kingston, Ont.: McGill-Queen's University Press, 1989.

Sowerwine, Charles. *Sisters or Citizens? Women and Socialism in France Since 1876.* NY: Cambridge University Press, 1982.

David S. Newhall, Professor Emeritus of History, Centre College; author of *Clemenceau: A Life at War* (Edwin Mellen Press, 1991)

Durant, Ariel (1898–1981)

Russian-born American author and historical researcher. Born in 1898 as Ida Appel Kaufman in Prosurov, Russia; died in Hollywood Hills, California, on October 25, 1981, two weeks before the death of Will Durant, who was never told of her passing; married William James (Will) Durant; children: Ethel Durant; Louis Durant.

Played a crucial role in the writing of the best-selling 11-volume series The Story of Civilization, *first as her husband's research assistant, then as his full partner and collaborator; with husband, jointly awarded the Pulitzer Prize (1968) and the Presidential Medal of Freedom (1977).*

Although the 11 volumes of *The Story of Civilization*, which appeared in print in leisurely fashion from 1935 through 1975, never received accolades from professional historians, its authors Will and Ariel Durant created a work of popular history that continues to impress readers with its sincerity and deep humanity. Born into a Jewish family in a small town in Tsarist Russia, Ida Appel Kaufman was brought to New York by her family as an infant. Barely into her teens, she met and fell in love with her teacher at the anarchist-sponsored Francisco Ferrer School. Will Durant, a Roman Catholic ex-seminarian and an enthusiastic Socialist, also found the lively immigrant girl entrancing. At age 15, Ida, whom Will first called "Puck" and later Ariel, was "strong and brave as a boy." The name Ariel, taken from the imp in Shakespeare's "The Tempest," later became Ida Durant's legal first name. On their wedding day in 1913, Ariel "roller-skated all the way down from Harlem to City Hall."

Determined to succeed as an author, Will turned his detailed academic knowledge of the Western philosophical tradition into a book for the masses, *The Story of Philosophy*. Published in 1926, and made highly entertaining and readable because of its clear style and numerous colorful anecdotes, the book became a hit with sales of more than two million in the first three years after publication (total sales by the late 1970s were over three million copies). Since Ariel had assisted with the research for *The Story of Philosophy*, it became clear that the collaboration of husband and wife was fruitful, leading as it did to their financial independence. The young couple began to plan a new, more ambitious, project. Starting in 1927, Will and Ariel Durant began to gather materials for a vast panoramic history of mankind which they eventually chose to entitle *The Story of Civilization*.

Will retired from teaching at Manhattan's adult education Labor Temple School, and with Ariel assisting him, the couple began to write the first volume of their ambitious project.

Appearing in 1935 as *Our Oriental Heritage,* their incredibly ambitious undertaking was now launched; it would not be completed until 40 years later with the appearance of *The Age of Napoleon,* the 11th and last volume of the series. Popular with the public and usually panned by academic historians, *The Story of Mankind* was conceived of by the Durants not as traditional "drums and trumpets" military-political-economic history but rather as a grand tapestry of mankind's cultural achievements. Speaking jointly, they noted that history was:

> above all else the creation and recording of the intellectual, moral and aesthetic heritage of mankind; progress is the increasing abundance, use, preservation and transmission of that heritage. To those of us who study history not merely as a warning reminder of man's follies and crimes but also as a re-

membrance of generative souls, the past ceases to be a depressing chamber of horrors; it becomes a celestial city, a spacious country of the mind, wherein a thousand saints, statesmen, inventors, scientists, poets, artists, musicians, philosophers and lovers still live and speak, teach and carve and sing.

Although the Durants and their two children lived in comfort in a Spanish-style home in the Hollywood Hills, their life from the mid-1930s on was based on a strictly followed regimen of work and study. In order to keep to their schedule of producing another volume in the *Story of Mankind* series every four years or so, they worked seven days a week from 8 in the morning to 10 at night. For each volume, they read about 500 books from cover to cover, mostly secondary sources, jotting down citations on green slips and significant ideas and commentaries on white pads. Next in the process was to string the notes in order beside a drafting board that rested across the arms of Will's rocking chair. It was there that he would consult the notes and reference sources, writing down his daily quota of text in a notebook that would be typed up at a later time.

The Durants' loyal readers, many of whom purchased their volumes of *The Story of Mankind* through their membership in the Book-of-the-Month-Club, eagerly awaited each new volume of the ambitious series begun in 1935 in the depths of the Great Depression. On the eve of World War II in 1939, *The Life of Greece* appeared, followed in 1944 by *Caesar and Christ*, and by *The Age of Faith* in 1950. Refusing to make concessions to their age, the Durants worked at a furious pace and so were able to publish *The Renaissance* ahead of schedule in 1953, following it up in 1957 with *The Reformation*. In 1961, when they published *The Age of Reason Begins,* Ariel's name began to appear on the title page as a co-author with her husband. This well-earned credit for her co-authorship would continue for the succeeding volumes of the series: *The Age of Louis XIV* (1963), *The Age of Voltaire* (1965), and *Rousseau and Revolution* (1967).

By the time *Rousseau and Revolution* appeared in 1967, many of the Durants' loyal readers made the reluctant conclusion that the advanced age of both Will and Ariel precluded any more books by them. The couple had themselves noted that the years since 1789 would have to be written about by "fresher spirits." Fortunately, the pessimists were mistaken when the Durants were able to uncover new reserves of energy that

Ariel and Will Durant.

enabled them to publish two final books. One volume, *The Age of Napoleon*, which appeared in conjunction with Will's 90th birthday celebrations, ended the *Story of Mankind* as the 11th volume in the series. The other jointly written book, entitled *A Dual Autobiography*, appeared in 1977 as the couple's record of an extraordinary marriage and intellectual partnership. Although professional historians continued to disparage their work, the Durants received several major awards in their final decades, including a Pulitzer Prize in 1968 and the Presidential Medal of Freedom in 1977. After suffering a serious stroke, Ariel Durant died at her Hollywood Hills home on October 25, 1981. Will, in fragile health at age 96, had undergone surgery and was in intensive care at the time of her death. He was never informed of her passing, and died less than two weeks after she did, thus ending a truly unique partnership.

SOURCES:

"Ariel Durant, Historian, Is Dead; Wrote 'The Story of Civilization'," in *The New York Times Biographical Service*. October 1981, p. 1338.

Durant, Will and Ariel. *A Dual Autobiography*. NY: Simon and Schuster, 1977.

Frey, Raymond. "William James Durant: An Intellectual Biography" (Ph.D. dissertation, Drew University, 1989).

"Historian Will Durant Dies; Author of 'Civilization' Series," in *The New York Times Biographical Series*. November 1981, pp. 1491–1493.

Murphy, Cullen. "The Venerable Will," in *Atlantic Monthly*. Vol. 256, no. 5. November 1985, pp. 22, 24.

RELATED MEDIA:

Snyder, Robert. "Journey: Will and Ariel Durant," Masters & Masterworks videocassette, 1969.

"Will and Ariel Durant: The famous historians discuss their life and career with James Day" (audio cassette), Center for Cassette Studies.

John Haag, Associate Professor of History,
University of Georgia, Athens, Georgia

Duras, Marguerite (1914–1996)

French author and filmmaker born and raised in French Indochina whose work crosses traditional boundaries of fiction and autobiography, blurring the lines between self and other, reality and imagination, absence and desire. Name variations: Marguerite Donnadieu. Pronunciation: du-RAS. Born Marguerite Donnadieu on April 4, 1914, in Gia-Dinh, near Saigon, in French Indochina; died in Paris, France, on March 3, 1996; daughter of French colonial settlers Henri Donnadieu (taught mathematics and made a brief career for himself in the colonial government) and Marie Legrand Donnadieu (trained as an elementary school teacher in France and taught at a school for indigenous children in Indochina);

*M*arguerite *D*uras

completed high school in Saigon; studied law and political science in Paris; married Robert Antelme, in 1939 (divorced 1946); children: (with Dionys Mascolo) son, Jean Mascolo (b. 1947).

Grew up in Indochina; returned to France with family (1932); chose name Marguerite Duras when her first book, Les Impudents, *was published (1943); entered the French Resistance movement; joined the Communist Party (1944), which she then left (1950); actively protested against the war in Algeria (1955–60); published over 40 novels as well as numerous essays, stories, plays, films, and interviews; awarded the Goncourt prize for literature for her novel* The Lover *(1984).*

Selected novels: Un Barrage contre le Pacifique *(1950, translated as* The Sea Wall, *1986);* Moderato Cantabile *(1958, translated as* Moderato Cantabile *in* Four Novels by Marguerite Duras, *1965);* Le Ravissement de Lol V. Stein *(1964, translated as* The Ravishing of Lol V. Stein, *1986);* L'Amant *(1984, translated as* The Lover, *1985);* La douleur *(1985, translated as* The War: A Memoir, *1987);* Yann Andréas Steiner *(1992).*

Films: Hiroshima mon amour *(1960),* Nathalie Granger *(1972),* India Song *(1974),* Le Camion *(*The Truck, *1977).*

Her life focused on her writing, her writing delved into her life: fiction and autobiography are virtually inseparable in the works of Marguerite Duras. Her many books and films refer back to her youth in Indochina, the wartime years in France, the relationship with her mother and brothers. Intimate, personal experience surfaces like a favorite literary trope as the author probes for potential meanings and new understandings. Marguerite Duras remains, however, an elusive figure for potential biographers: chronologies of her life vary from source to source. During her lifetime, Duras rarely spoke of the dates and facts related to her own biography and conflicting references to her life's events dot several of her novels. How, then, can we reconstruct the life of Marguerite Duras? Weaving together Duras' childhood in Indochina and her adult life in France with the literary and ideological currents of her fiction, a telling picture can be painted of one of the most successful and important French literary figures in the second half of the 20th century.

The story of my life doesn't exist. Does not exist. There's never any center to it. No path, no line. There are great spaces where you pretend there used to be someone, but it's not true, there was no one.

—**Marguerite Duras,** *The Lover*

Marguerite Duras was born Marguerite Donnadieu on April 4, 1914, in the French colony of Indochina (modern-day Vietnam and Cambodia). At the time of her birth, the French still held multiple colonies all over the globe—colonies typically exploited for their natural resources. Indochina was certainly no exception: in search of petroleum, rubber, and arable farm land, the French brought their colonial organization, the Catholic religion, and Western traditions to Southeast Asia, coolly displacing thousands of years of rich cultural heritage. In the French colonial society of Indochina, white men typically controlled money and power, embedding the notions of class and race into the social hierarchy. Marguerite Duras' parents enlisted separately as foot soldiers in this proverbial colonial army: both had been lured to Indochina by French propaganda for the colonies. Marguerite's mother **Marie Legrand Donnadieu** went to Indochina to teach indigenous children, a low-level position within the colonial establishment, and there she met her husband Henri Donnadieu. A math teacher who went on to a more important position in the colonial establishment, Henri Donnadieu did not live long enough to earn his family the fabled wealth of the colonies. Named to a governmental post in Phnom Penh in 1918, he soon fell ill and returned to France where he died shortly thereafter. The family went to France to settle his estate and, two years later, returned to Indochina where Marie Donnadieu took a teaching position.

As members of a poor, white family in Indochina, Marguerite, her two brothers, Pierre and Paulo, and her mother, did not fit neatly into the colonial hierarchy. Their poverty alienated them from the colonial elite, yet their white skin entitled them to certain privileges in the eyes of that same government. As a child and adolescent in this society, Marguerite Duras was doubly marginalized: a white girl with no money and an uncertain future, she had neither power nor position. She spoke Vietnamese and played with indigenous children, but was not Vietnamese; at the same time, little more than the French language and her parents' families connected her to France. Indeed, the sense of privilege instilled upon her by her French nationality ran contrary to the sense of exclusion from the community that grew out of her economic and gender status. Her Creole origins thus became fundamental to Duras' literary search for self.

This constant conflict fueled by class, race, and gender manifested itself in the family's daily life and in Duras' work: sometime between 1924 and 1926, Duras' mother bought a "concession," or farmlands, from the colonial government with her savings. Naive and unaware of the corruption that riddled the colonial bureaucracy, Marie Donnadieu did not know that good land could only be bought by bribing the proper officials. With all of their money invested in the purchase of their bungalow and the lease of the surrounding land for rice farming, the family soon discovered that the land was flooded by the China Sea every summer and thus unsuitable for cultivation. The mother briefly reassured Marguerite and her brothers that all would be remedied by the construction of a series of dikes along the perimeter of the property: when these collapsed, the family was forced to acknowledge that the land was worthless, and that they would never recover their investment.

This episode is recounted in detail in several of Duras' books, including *The Sea Wall* and *The Lover*. Stylistically very different, these two novels examine and reexamine the plight of an adolescent girl in a poor, white family in Indochina. *The Sea Wall*, with its realistic account of Suzanne, Joseph, and their mother, details their desperate and somehow pathetic struggle to save a concession doomed to failure: "Then, in July, the sea had risen as usual, in an assault on the plain. The sea walls had not been strong enough. The logs had been eaten through by the dwarf crabs of the paddies. In one single night the sea walls had collapsed." The struggle against nature has already been lost, and what remains is a struggle against time, an eternal wait for something to happen, for the savior to arrive. Suzanne waits for a man, Joseph waits for a woman, the mother waits for death. *The Lover* comments more obliquely on the same story, abandoning realist tendencies for a select series of images that piece by piece construct the unnamed narrator's story. The doomed concession, the eternal wait, and the forbidden love all return in a changed context. Even the crumbled sea walls of the concession are present, yet transformed: "All around her are wildernesses, wastes. The sons are wildernesses, they'll never do anything. The salt land's a wilderness too, the money's lost for good, it's all over. The only thing left is this girl, she's growing up, perhaps one day she'll find out how to bring in some money." Returning to the same events, reconstructing mirror images, Duras gradually colors in the dimmed lines of childhood through her fiction.

At 16, Marguerite went to Saigon to study, and around this time she met the Chinese man who would become her lover and the unnamed protagonist of her novel, *The Lover*. Two years later, at age 18, she and her family left for France: Duras would never return to Indochina again. In France, Duras began studying politics and law, and during this time met Robert Antelme, a fellow law student. They married in 1939 and lived in an apartment on the rue Saint-Benoît in Paris, where Duras remained until she died. In 1942, she learned of her brother Paulo's death in Saigon; during that same year, she lost a child at birth, in part because a doctor could not reach her in time because of the German Occupation. In 1943, Duras and her husband joined the French Resistance movement: a year later, Robert Antelme was arrested and deported by the Nazis to Dachau for his participation in the Resistance. Duras explores the trials of the long wait for Antelme in her book *The War: A Memoir*. During her husband's absence, Duras joined the Communist Party, a decision that she attributes in *The War* to a personal need for connection rather than to specific political ideals. Indeed, she left the party six years later. Upon Antelme's return to Paris in 1945, Duras nursed her husband back to health but had already decided to divorce him in order to have a child with her companion, Dionys Mascolo. Despite this change of heart, she and Antelme remained friends and continued to collaborate on projects. Duras' son Jean Mascolo was born in 1947.

During this period of political and personal commotion, Marguerite Donnadieu became Marguerite Duras with the publication of her first novel, *Les Impudents*. Following the war, Duras received major critical acclaim for *The Sea Wall* and embarked upon a literary career that would span six decades. With the publication of *Moderato Cantabile* in 1958, she assured herself a certain degree of financial stability and established herself as one of the premier novelists in France, often categorized with the "new novelists" like **Nathalie Sarraute*. Duras' minimalist style, developed in *The Square* and *Moderato Cantabile,* remains more difficult to define according to genre and style: novels may read like theater or scenarios, the subjectivity of the "I" is ever vacillating. Indeed, through her innovative use of narrative, she created a unique niche for herself on the literary stage.

During this time of literary development, Duras' political activism is well-defined. She protested actively with French intellectuals against the war in Algeria, where the French fought to hold onto their colony. She wrote for the leftist paper *Libération,* as well as for *France-Observateur* and the feminist journal *Sorcières* (*Witches*). Her position on feminism, however, proves difficult to pinpoint: Duras wrote and rewrote women's stories, giving them voices where they had previously gone unheard; yet these female voices often completed male paradigms of love and desire. Duras is hailed by some as a feminist, as a master of *écriture féminine,* and labeled by others as a conservative, unable to disengage her narratives from the confines of Western, heterosexual discourse. Take, for example, *Moderato Cantabile,* the story of Anne Desbaresdes, told by an unnamed narrator loosely associated with the protagonist. Anne Desbaresdes is the wife of a wealthy factory owner and the mother of a young boy, whose care is entrusted uniquely to her. Bored and depressed by her bourgeois lifestyle, Anne searches for distraction and ultimately liberation, which gradually evolves from a singular event: after accompanying her son to his piano lesson, she witnesses the aftermath of a crime of passion. Anne watches in fascination as a man cradles the head of his lover in his arms while blood trickles from her mouth. Anne then enters a nearby café, embarking on the first step in her own passionate love story, one that she is about to create. She and Chauvin, an unemployed factory worker, meet daily in the café to recreate the crime verbally, to fill in the gaps that they did not witness. They create their own violent, albeit bloodless, affair that terminates in Anne's narrative death; the development of Duras' narration proves to be as dangerous as the opening crime scene. As Marilyn Schuster writes in *Marguerite Duras Revisited:* "Fiction in *Moderato Cantabile* becomes an instrument of desire and death. Anne does not tell this story with Chauvin's help in order to understand or to escape the person she had become but to kill her, to live as fully as she can the story of fatal passion that she discovers when she witnesses the crime." Duras thus crafts a novel that is stylistically fascinating and innovative. At the same time, she repeats the age-old tale of the lover's quarrel, culminating in the death of the woman. This complex configuration of narration, at once daring and conservative, characterizes much of Duras' fiction.

Duras' novels go on to shape and express her views on feminism and the world throughout the 1960s. In particular, *The Ravishing of Lol V. Stein* presents an excellent example of *écriture féminine*, as the author displaces traditional chronological narrative with one characterized by its gaps, absences, and holes. Indeed, in order to read the story, the reader must invent the missing details and slowly reconstruct the story of Lol. V. Stein. As such, the reader functions much like the biographer who must continually fill the empty spaces in the life of the author, Marguerite Duras.

In the 1970s, Duras the writer engineered another twist in her personal story, turning to filmmaking as a primary occupation. In 1959, she had already written the scenario for Alain Resnais' *Hiroshima, mon amour*: this experience had introduced her to the production process and assured her a small but serious following in the cinema. Her 1970s' productions, including *Nathalie Granger, India Song*, and *The Truck*, appeared in print and on the screen, and met with mixed critical reviews. *India Song*, considered by critics to be her finest film, revisits the Lol V. Stein narrative, bringing together all of its diverse elements. Duras' cinematic productions, like her narrations, are characterized by innovative approaches, such as the stark separation of soundtrack and visual images.

The 1980s and 1990s were marked by health problems and various detoxification treatments related to Duras' long-term addiction to alcohol. In October 1988, she was hospitalized in the American Hospital in Neuilly and, for reasons that the doctors were unable to deter-

Marguerite Duras and Jeanne Moreau on the set of Nathalie Granger.

mine, went into a coma that lasted for five months. She remained hospitalized until June 1989; a tracheotomy left her with a breathing apparatus in her throat. Despite her failing health, Duras returned to writing: she had become a worldwide celebrity in 1984 with the publication of *The Lover,* for which she won the prestigious Goncourt prize. During this time, Yann Andréa, a homosexual student from Caen, became her companion and helped her through the difficulties associated with her illness. She details the story of their meeting in her last book, *Yann Andréas Steiner.* In this narrative, she merges the identities of Yann Andréas and Aurélie Steiner, the Jewish, female protagonist of her film *Aurélie Steiner.* In the process, Duras confounds gender and sexuality, once again blurring the lines between fiction and reality.

Marguerite Duras continued to inspire interest and debate throughout her later years. In particular, an article written for the *Libération* in 1985 proved especially controversial: in the article, Duras accused a mother of murdering her young son but went on to declare the woman's innocence, claiming to recognize in the woman's gaze the look of insanity caused by an abusive marriage. Duras was ridiculed by critics for having termed the murder sublime: some criticized her for having condemned a woman who proclaimed her innocence, others for having arrogantly spoken in the name of all women. Duras stood by her interpretation of the events, despite these reproaches. Throughout her career, her staunch disregard for public opinion permitted Marguerite Duras to express herself in any situation. No doubt that this self assurance also allowed her to put forth the narrative innovations and interpretive strategies that characterize her work.

Marguerite Duras died on March 3, 1996, in Paris, one month before her 82nd birthday, bringing to an end 50 years of authorship and publication. The literary and cinematic world mourned the passing of one of their most lauded yet controversial figures. An astonishing woman, she never strayed from her vision of living and writing. Indeed, with each novel, film, and article, Marguerite Duras inscribed the pages of her very being, one in which life, love, and writing prove to be integral elements of a single story.

SOURCES:

Duras, Marguerite. *The Lover.* Translated by Barbara Bray. NY: Pantheon, 1985.

———. *Moderato Cantabile* in *Four Novels by Marguerite Duras.* Translated by Richard Weaver. NY: Grove Press, 1965.

———. *The Sea Wall.* Translated by Herma Briffault. NY: Farrar, Strauss and Giroux, 1952.

———. *The War: A Memoir.* Translated by Barbara Bray. NY: Pantheon, 1986.

Schuster, Marilyn R. *Marguerite Duras Revisited.* NY: Twayne, 1993.

SUGGESTED READING:

Hewitt, Leah D. *Autobiographical Tightropes: Simone de Beauvoir, Nathalie Sarraute, Marguerite Duras, Monique Wittig, and Maryse Condé.* Lincoln: University of Nebraska, 1990.

Hill, Leslie. *Marguerite Duras: Apocalyptic Desires.* London: Routledge, 1993.

RELATED MEDIA:

Duras, Marguerite. *Hiroshima mon amour.* Translated by Richard Weaver. NY: Grove Press, 1961. Film made by Alain Resnais in 1959, distributed by Zenith International Film Corporation.

———. *India Song.* (120 min.) color film, 1974.

Sara Steinert Borella, Assistant Professor of French, Pacific University, Forest Grove, Oregon

Durbin, Deanna (1921—)

Canadian-born actress and singer whose voice entertained the world through the years of World War II. Born Edna Mae Durbin in Winnipeg, Manitoba, Canada, on December 4, 1921; second and youngest daughter of James and Ada (Read) Durbin; studied voice at Ralph Thomas' Academy in Los Angeles, California; married Vaughn Paul, in 1941 (divorced); married Felix Jackson (a movie producer), in 1945 (divorced); married Charles David (a film executive), in 1950; children: (second marriage) daughter Jessica; (third marriage) son Peter.

Films: Every Sunday (short, 1936); Three Smart Girls (1936); Hundred Men and a Girl (1937); Mad About Music (1938); That Certain Age (1938); Three Smart Girls Grow Up (1939); First Love (1939); It's a Date (1940); Spring Parade (1940); Nice Girl? (1941); It Started with Eve (1941); The Amazing Mrs. Holliday (1943); Hers to Hold (1943); Her Butler's Sister (1943); Christmas Holiday (1944); Can't Help Singing (1944); Lady on a Train (1945); Because of Him (1946); I'll Be Yours (1947); Something in the Wind (1947); Up in Central Park (1948); For the Love of Mary (1948).

Deanna Durbin, whose wholesome sweetness and superb singing voice saved Universal Studios from bankruptcy, was one of the top box-office attractions of the late 1930s and the 1940s. Starring in 24 movies and making numerous recordings and radio appearances, she abruptly left Hollywood at age 27, saying that she hated all the trappings of stardom. Although critics and film historians remain perplexed about the popularity of her films, she is credited

Deanna
Durbin

with enriching America's culture by introducing its youth to classical music.

She was born Edna Mae Durbin in Winnipeg, Manitoba, Canada, on December 4, 1921, but was raised in California from infancy.

Durbin displayed an early talent for music, although it was not until her older sister **Edith** went to work as a schoolteacher that the family could afford singing lessons. At age 14, Durbin was recommended to MGM by a talent agent who was astounded with the maturity of her soprano voice. The studio cast her with another newcomer, *Judy Garland, in the musical short *Every Sunday* (1936), but MGM later dropped her in favor of Garland. Picked up by Universal, Durbin proved to be a moneymaker from her first film, *Three Smart Girls* (1936), with **Nan Grey** and **Barbara Reed**. In this film about three young sisters trying to reconcile their battling parents, Durbin sang a number of songs, including "Someone to Care for Me," which she further popularized on Eddie Cantor's weekly NBC radio show. The success of *Three Smart Girls* salvaged Universal's plummeting stock and catapulted Durbin to a popularity that rivaled that of *Shirley Temple (Black). Durbin's second movie, *One Hundred Men and a Girl* (1937), which included some classical as well as popular songs, solidified her reputation.

In 1938, Durbin was given a special Academy Award with Mickey Rooney for "bringing to the screen the spirit and personification of youth." She also became the first female to be sworn into the Boy Scouts. After her box-office hit *Nice Girl?* (1941), featuring Stephen Foster's "Old Folks at Home" and the patriotic "Thank You America," she was a guest at the White House for President Franklin D. Roosevelt's birthday.

In the spring of 1941, Durbin married Vaughn Paul in a lavish Hollywood ceremony. Following *It Started with Eve* (1941) with Charles Laughton, she took a brief hiatus while the studio grappled with the problem of moving her into more adult roles. She stayed busy, however, singing for soldiers at USO clubs and appearing on a number of radio shows. Durbin returned to the screen with *The Amazing Mrs. Holliday* (1943), about a missionary trying to get nine Chinese orphans into the United States. Around this time, producer Felix Jackson (whom she would later marry) took over her career, starring her in the wartime drama *Hers to Hold* (1943). In 1944, she made her only color film, *Can't Help Singing*, which contained some of Jerome Kern's lesser tunes.

Also in 1944, Durbin—desperately wanting to attempt a dramatic role—pressured the studio into starring her in Somerset Maugham's *Christmas Holiday*, an adult story about a young woman who marries a killer and is forced to perform in a New Orleans dive. In spite of Durbin's more than adequate acting (and lovely renditions of the songs "Always" and "Spring Will Be a Little Late This Year"), her loyal fans did not like the change. She grudgingly returned to her standard fare with *Can't Help Singing* (1944),

followed by the comedy-murder *Lady on a Train* (1945), in which she plays a devout murder-mystery fan who observes a killing from a train window. Around 1947, when Durbin was the highest-paid female star in Hollywood, Universal began to undergo some corporate changes that led them to cut the budgets of her subsequent movies as a way to improve their profit margins. As a result, her last three films suffered in production values. The only saving grace in her final movie *For the Love of Mary* (1948) was her still marvelous singing voice.

Durbin, who had divorced Vaughn Paul, married film producer Felix Jackson in 1945. The couple had a daughter in 1946, shortly before they separated and subsequently divorced. In 1950, she was married for a third time to Pathé Films executive Charles David. Although Durbin appeared to have abandoned her career prematurely, she may have realized that she could not sustain the screen persona her public had grown to demand. Before she retired to France, she told her mentor and friend Eddie Cantor, "I don't want to have anything to do with show business ever." True to her word, the woman who had been Universal's bread and butter has granted few interviews and never returned to the screen.

Barbara Morgan,
Melrose, Massachusetts

Durgautti or Durgavati (d. 1564).

See Durgawati.

Durgawati (d. 1564)

Rani and regent of India's Gondwana who militarily opposed the Mughal expansion. Name variations: Durgautti or Durgavati; Maharani or Maharanee of Gurrah. Birth date unknown; took her own life in the battle of Narhi in 1564; daughter of Salwahan, the raja of Rath and Mahoba; married Dalpat Sa Garha Mandala, the raja of Gondwana; children: Bir Narayan.

Raja Dalpat of Gondwana died (1548); became regent of Gondwana (1548); Akbar ascended the throne as emperor of the Mughal imperial (1562); border raids by Asaf Khan; Adhaz Kayastha negotiated with Akbar the Great in Agra; invasion of Gondwana by Asaf Khan (1564); battle of Narhi (1564).

In 1398, Tamerlane raided and sacked Delhi for the first time. It was, however, left to his descendant, Babar, to conquer the Sultanate in 1526. By the time of Babar's death in 1530, the empire that he had left to his sons stretched from Badakshan to Bengal in the southwest. It was an empire dominated by Persian culture, tastes, ideas, and attitudes. But as a political entity it was beset by rebellion and instability. In 1562, Akbar the Great ascended the throne and quickly moved to consolidate his vast inheritance. He faced several potent foes, whose independence was threatened by the very existence of the Mughal Empire. One of these adversaries was Rani (queen) Durgawati of Gondwana. Located just outside the southern boundaries of the Mughal Empire, sooner or later Gondwana's proximity to Akbar's possessions was bound to bring the two states into conflict.

Almost nothing is known of Durgawati's birth and early life. She was the daughter of Raja Salwahan, ruler of Rath and Mahoba. Raised in the court of her father, she is reputed to have combined beauty and refinement with inexhaustible energy, intelligence, and bravery. The Gonds were a group of Dravidian tribes that made up the original inhabitants of this region of India. Durgawati was a princess of the Chandel Dynasty, which figured prominently in the political and social history of India from the 9th to the 16th centuries.

In Indian society, the offering of a daughter in marriage was considered a sign of the social superiority of the groom's family. This, however, did not apply to royal marriages. Thus, Durgawati was married at an early age to the Raja Dalpat Sa Garha Mandala of Gondwana, a strikingly handsome prince. To suit her, he changed the location of his capital from Singaurgarh to Chanragarh.

During the 16th century, the role of elite women in India was in transition. Unlike royal women of a preceding age, the mothers, wives and sisters of monarchs began to exercise increasing influence on the course of government policy. The Rani Durgawati was a case in point. Durgawati's husband died in 1548, four years after their marriage, and she became the regent of Gondwana, ruling successfully in the name of her young son Bir Narayan. Noted for her religious devotion, Durgawati patronized many religious figures, including the Brahmin Vitthaleshvara, and she built seven religious houses for the well-known devotee of Krishna. When Vitthaleshvara traveled abroad, he was always escorted by a large contingent of Durgawati's troops.

Durgawati ruled Gondwana for 16 years, with the assistance of her two able ministers, Adhaz Kayastha and Man Brahman. Known as a moderate and skillful monarch, she excelled at both diplomacy and conquest. During her reign, the kingdom prospered economically. Gondwana could field a well-equipped army of 20,000 calvary and 1,000 war elephants, along with an indeterminate number of infantry. However, the Mughal Empire controlled access to the best horses imported from Iran, central asia and Arabia, thus in this regard opponents like Gondwana were at a distinct disadvantage.

The rani followed in the footsteps of her predecessors by enlarging the size of her domain. She was noted for her martial skills and qualities as a general. Of the 23,000 villages in her kingdom, 12,000 were under the control of the crown, while the remainder were administered by her vassals. As Abul Fazl, the 16th-century intellectual, noted:

> She was not lacking in any of the essentials of bravery and effort, and did great things by dint of her far-seeing abilities. She had great contests with Baj Bahador [of Malwa] and the Mianas [Afghans of Sironj in Malwa] and was always victorious. . . . She was a good shot with gun and arrow, and continually went a-hunting, and shot animals of the chase with her gun. It was her custom that whenever she heard that a tiger had made his appearance, she did not drink water till she shot him. There are stories current in Hindustan of her exploits in the assemblies of peace and in the fields of battle.

Asaf Khan, who had led a successful military expedition against Raja Ramchand of Pannah, was appointed as the Mughal governor of Kara Manipur, a province on the border of Gondwana. Initially, he encouraged peaceful trade with the rani's subjects. However, the wealth of Gondwana soon attracted his interest. By various means, Asaf Khan attempted to force Durgawati into acknowledging Akbar the Great's sovereignty over Gondwana. The governor sent spies into Gondwana to ascertain the strength of its army and the size of its treasury. Next, he employed a policy of destabilization, by raiding villages along the border. The rani sent her minister Adhaz Kayastha to negotiate with Emperor Akbar, but this proved unsuccessful. Akbar seems to have demanded the cession of certain territories, but Durgawati's ambassador refused.

In retaliation for the Mughal raids into Gondwana, Durgawati sent her own forces across the border into Pannah. A wasting border war soon erupted. In 1564, acting upon his own initiative, but with the Emperor Akbar's permission, Asaf Khan invaded Gondwana with an army of 50,000 troops.

Durgawati did not expect a full-scale invasion that year. Many of her cavalry defected to the Mughal imperial side, led by the petty chiefs of Garha. The rest of her army was dispersed; she had only 500 troops with her in the capital of Chanragarh. Before she could gather more of her military strength, however, she marched against the invaders, much to the dismay of her ministers Man Brahman and Adhaz Kayastha. Durgawati blamed Adhaz Kayastha for the mismanagement of her military forces. She is reputed to have answered his objections by saying, "How could I, who have for years governed the country, think of flight? It is better to die with glory than to live with ignominy."

Although Asaf Khan suggested a negotiated settlement, Durgawati refused the offer, considering it an insult that she should deal with a mere governor. Had the emperor come in person, the outcome might have been different. A game of cat and mouse began. Dogged by the Mughal imperial army, Durgawati marched her army swiftly around the countryside, seeking to gain time, hoping to enlarge her force by local recruiting and a general call to arms. She received scant support, however, since many of the local chiefs were intimidated by the approach of the massive Mughal force.

Proceeding through dense forest and difficult terrain, Durgawati led her small army to the town of Garh. Then she moved north, to Narhi. The village of Narhi was surrounded by mountains and bordered by the Gaur and Narmade rivers on both sides, natural obstacles that made Narhi an excellent defensive position of great strategic value. The only possible access to the town was through a narrow and difficult mountain pass. Durgawati was advised by her ministers to avoid battle, partly to win time in order to raise more troops. But she was outraged by the suggestion. "How long am I to shelter among the trees?" she replied.

Asaf Khan's army attacked through the mountain pass protecting Narhi. Donning armor and mounting an elephant, Durgawati surprised the enemy with her troops, holding the pass and driving them back down the other side. The Mughals retreated, pursued by the rani's troops, who took bloody revenge on the fleeing soldiers of Asaf Khan's army.

Durgawati's next maneuver was to suggest a preemptive strike on the Mughal imperial camp during the night. But the majority of her chiefs were against such a risky undertaking, and so she relented, privately grumbling as to their lack of courage. Without a night attack, Asaf Khan easily recaptured the cliffs overlooking the pass the next morning. After a brief skirmish, he then fortified them with artillery. Canons were one of the factors that accounted for the military superiority of Mughals, and much of their knowledge had been acquired from the Turks.

Riding her war elephant and accompanied by her son Bir Narayan, Durgawati faced the Mughal army on the following day. Asaf Khan's troops employed mounted archers against her elephants. A two-day battle ensued. Outnumbered, Durgawati and her troops repulsed three imperial attacks. On the second day, Bir Narayan was wounded, and he was escorted from the battlefield by a large contingent of the rani's soldiers. His removal from the battlefield caused a panic, which left Durgawati with only 300 troops. Weakened, her demoralized army was soon overpowered in a bloody melee. Durgawati was wounded by two arrows, and, rather than suffer capture, she asked Adhaz Kayastha to take her life. He refused to obey, however, and promised to carry her from the battlefield. She is said to have beseeched him, crying:

> It is true we are overcome in war, but shall we also be vanquished in honor? Shall we, for the sake of a lingering ignominious life, lose the reputation and virtue we have been so solicitous to acquire? No! let your gratitude now repay that service, for which I lifted up your head, and which I now require at your hands. Haste—let your dagger save me from the crime of putting an end to my own existence!

Adhaz Kayastha still refused. Instead, Durgawati raised the dagger to her chest and plunged it in, taking her own life. The Rani of Gondwana was buried in a narrow defile some 12 miles from Jabalpur.

Asaf Khan now marched upon the capital. Due to his losses in the battle of Narhi, he did not besiege Chanragarh for nearly two months. Durgawati's son Bir Narayan held the celebrated fortress that dominated the city. He sallied forth from the fort with the remainder of the Gondwanan army and died in battle. The treasure inside the fortress included incalculable amounts of gold, silver and jewels, and Asaf Khan seems to have kept much of the booty for himself. **Kamlavati**, the sister of the rani, was also captured, along with the Gondwanan court.

As O.P. Kejarival has noted, there is some dispute as to whether Gondwana was entirely annexed as a result of Durgawati's defeat. It may well be that it became a tributary of the

Mughal Empire, retaining some of its regional autonomy. Douglas Streusand, however, stressed the long-term implications of Gondwana's eventual conquest:

> It fits the general pattern of Mughal expansion: resistance to the end meant destruction; submission, even at the last moment . . . meant survival. The heroism of Rani Durgawati is beyond doubt; one also cannot doubt that it led only to her death and the extinction of her dynasty and principality.

Durgawati exhibited all the attributes of leadership so widely valued in 16th-century India. She was a renowned beauty and a fierce, but fair, ruler. Along with her religious piety, she proved herself a resourceful negotiator and diplomat, a skilled trader and financial manager, and a determined general and warrior.

The Rani of Gondwana fits the emerging pattern of Indian princesses of the day. Elite women increasingly claimed the right to rule and did so successfully. Not only did they resist incursions into their territory, but they also struck strategic alliances with other Indian states for their own benefit. Not all of the ranis resisted the expansion of the Mughal Empire, however, and many retained their positions as vassals of the Great Mughal. But none seems to have asserted her right to independence as fiercely as Durgawati, rani of Gondwana.

SOURCES:

Dunbar, Sir George. *A History of India.* London: Nicholson and Watson, 1943.

Kejariwal, O.P. *The Asiatic Society of Bengal and the Discovery of India's Past.* New Delhi: Oxford University press, 1988.

Mahnmud, S.F. *A Concise History of Indo-Pakistan.* Oxford: Oxford University press, 1988.

Savarbar, V.D. *Six Glorious Epochs of Indian History.* Bombay: Bal Savarbar, 1971.

Streusand, Douglas E. *The Formation of the Mughal Empire.* New Delhi: Oxford University Press, 1988.

SUGGESTED READING:

Srivasta, A.L. *Akbar the Great.* Agra: Shival Lal Agarwala, 1962.

Hugh A. Stewart, M.A.,
University of Guelph, Guelph, Ontario, Canada

Durham, Dianne (1968—)

African-American gymnast. Born in Gary, Indiana, in June 1968. First African-American gymnast to become a national champion.

Dianne Durham saw her career cut short by injury. One of America's best gymnasts, she began taking gymnastics at a local Y when she was four years old. By 1981, Durham was the junior elite champion, a title she would successfully defend in 1982. In 1983, at her first senior national championship, she became the first African-American to win a national gymnastics competition, earning the gold medal in all-around, balance beam, vault, and floor exercises; she tied for a silver medal in the uneven bars. That year, Durham also won a silver in the McDonald's International Championships.

She had planned to enter the 1983 World Championships, but surgery on an injured knee prevented her. Durham was back in December, competing in the Chunichi Cup competition in Japan where she finished third all-around. Her knee, however, continued to bother her during the 1984 American Cup meet, and later that spring she left coach Bela Karolyi. A strong contender for the 1984 U.S. Olympic team, Durham had to withdraw due to a further injury.

Karin Loewen Haag,
Athens, Georgia

Durieux, Tilla (1880–1971)

Grand dame of the German stage who introduced the works of George Bernard Shaw to Germany, was regarded as the best exponent of the femmes fatales found in the plays of the Expressionists, and fought as a partisan in Yugoslavia during World War II. Born Ottilie Godeffroy on August 18, 1880, in Vienna, Austria, into a family of Croatian and French ancestry; died in West Berlin on February 21, 1971; daughter of a professor at Vienna's Museum of Technology and Crafts; married Eugen Spiro (a painter), in 1904 (divorced 1906); married Paul Cassirer (1871–1926, an art dealer and publisher), in 1906 (divorced 1926); married Ludwig Katzenellenbogen, in 1930 (killed 1944).

Began to study acting (1899); made her stage debut (1901); quickly became a star of the Berlin stage; was labeled an enemy of traditional German values and therefore of the Nazis who claimed to champion conservative ideals; with third husband Katzenellenbogen, fled Germany (1933) but Nazis killed him (1944); survived in Yugoslavia, joining the partisan forces; returned to Germany (1952); despite age, resumed her acting career to great acclaim, reigning as the leading actress of the German stage to the end of her long and extraordinary life.

Tilla Durieux was born into a comfortable bourgeois family on August 18, 1880, in Vienna, the heart of the vast multinational Habsburg empire. Her background was typical of many citizens of the city. Of mixed French and Croatian-Hungarian ancestry, Durieux's heritage reflected the nature of the polyglot empire with its cultural goulash of German, Slavic, Jewish, and Magyar ingredients. Her father, a professor at Vienna's Museum of Technology and Crafts, was a remote figure who died of cancer in 1895, leaving the family in difficult financial straits. Musically gifted, Durieux planned for a career as a concert pianist, but a single event changed the course of her life forever. In 1895, *Sarah Bernhardt** made a guest appearance in Vienna, and young Tilla decided that she, too, would be an acclaimed actress.

The aspiring actress chose the maiden name of her paternal grandmother, becoming Tilla Durieux. Despite the precarious state of the family finances, she enrolled in the theater school of Karl Arnau, a noted actor of the day, where she studied both acting and singing. By October 1899, Durieux was considered to be sufficiently prepared to appear in a one-act musical "genre picture," *Kurmärker und Picarde,* by the now-forgotten Louis Schneider. The young actress, who depended more on talent than on beauty, was chosen to appear in virtually all of the plays presented by the Arnau school. When she made her last appearance in May 1901, her future seemed secure.

Tilla Durieux made her professional stage debut on September 26, 1901, at the Royal Municipal Theater in Olmütz, Austrian Moravia (present-day Olomouc, Czech Republic). She played the minor role of a Tyrolian youth in Karl Zeller's naïvely charming operetta *Der Vogel-händler.* Despite a tiny salary and the fierce intrigues of theater life, the 21-year-old was full of energy and enthusiasm. In the summer of 1902, she performed at two theaters in Stuttgart, one at a spa in the suburbs of the Swabian capital. The next season, Durieux appeared in Breslau, German Silesia (present-day Wroclaw, Poland), where she performed in three different theaters. For the first time, she played a number of significant roles in classic plays by Shakespeare (*Richard III*), Lessing (*Emilia Galotti*), Goethe (*Goetz von Berlichingen*), and Schiller (*Die Piccolomini*). Durieux also performed in plays by contemporary authors including Gerhart Hauptmann (*Der arme Heinrich*), Hugo von Hofmannsthal (*Hochzeit der Sobeide*) and Maxim Gorki (*Nachtasyl*).

By 1903, Tilla Durieux's talent was well established in theatrical circles in major German cities. Max Reinhardt, the powerful Berlin theater director, had recognized her remarkable personality and magnetic stage presence. Durieux's debut as Oscar Wilde's Salomé (*Salome III*) at

Berlin's Deutsches Theater on September 8 was nothing short of sensational. Her passionate portrayal of Salomé was the talk of the town. Leading critic Alfred Kerr described her as "a doe who has swallowed paprika." Compared with **Gertrud Eysoldt**, a leading lady of the German stage, Durieux's presence, energy, and clear diction were universally praised. Critics raved about her powerful and original portrayals of the female protagonists in Kleist's *Kätchen von Heilbronn,* Hebbel's *Judith,* and also his *Gyges und sein Ring,* as well as Schiller's *Don Carlos.* Writing in *Die Schaubühne,* the influential critic Siegfried Jacobsohn praised Durieux's unique ability to portray "a mixture of serpentine spirit, of coqueterie, of erotic heat and passion, of authentic mendacity and jealousy, all without forgetting to reproduce the true tonalities and teeming emotions of the original verse."

The move to Berlin brought about significant changes in Durieux's personal life. In 1904, she married the painter Eugen Spiro, a union that lasted only two years. Not long after divorcing her first husband, she married the art dealer and publisher Paul Cassirer (1871–1926). Now Durieux lived in a sumptuous villa in Berlin's most prestigious residential area whose walls

Tilla
Durieux

were hung with superb paintings by Cézanne and van Gogh. She presided over a salon that included some of Europe's most brilliant and creative men and women. An independent superstar able to choose virtually any role she wanted, she ended her relationship with Max Reinhardt's Deutsches Theater in 1910.

At barely 30 years of age, she could chart her own future. Years later in her memoirs, she reflected on what had happened to her almost overnight: "How was it that I, the little daughter of a professor who was supposed to become a piano teacher, found myself surrounded by all these beautiful things? It must have been a dream, one that I would suddenly one day find myself awakened from." Tilla Durieux moved from success to success. The poet and playwright Max Dauthendey wrote the role of Empress *Catherine II the Great for her in his *Spielereien einer Kaiserin*, a play that opened to enthusiastic reviews in 1911. In this piece, she portrayed an energetic and ruthless Empress Catherine who rose from barracks whore to tsarina. Durieux had a unique ability to portray women with boundless willpower and surging, unbridled erotic energy. She became a symbol of the cultural and intellectual freedom in Berlin, challenging traditional concepts of the feminine role.

Her artistic connections during this period were important as well. Durieux and Cassirer entertained not only the artistic radicals of the day but the political nonconformists as well at their palatial home. She and her husband were indefatigable advocates of a new aesthetic vision, popularizing the works of the French impressionists and German modernists. Cassirer supported the Berlin Secession movement of avant-garde painters and sculptors, founding a publishing firm that issued not only books but a superbly produced art journal, *Pan*. His determination to overturn stuffy traditionalism in painting and sculpture was reinforced by Durieux who worked to accomplish the same goal on stage. Many of Europe's greatest artists asked Tilla to pose for them, including Renoir, Liebermann, Slevogt, Kokoschka, and Corinth. Auguste Renoir's portrait of Durieux in her Eliza Doolittle costume, entitled "Unknown Woman" (Metropolitan Museum of Art, New York), prompted Tilla many years later to comment, "It is called 'Unknown Woman', but it is I."

Inevitably, Durieux was drawn into the artistic and political conflicts that convulsed Berlin on the eve of World War I. Two successive issues of *Pan* printed the first German translation of erotic passages from Gustave Flaubert's Egyptian diary.

Both issues were declared obscene and banned by Berlin's police chief, Traugott von Jagow. During this time, von Jagow and the municipal censor visited a play rehearsal at a municipal theater where he met Durieux. Enchanted by the actress, the conservative police chief sent her a note suggesting a private meeting that weekend. Tilla's husband promptly challenged the police chief to a duel, declaring that "as an ancient Hebrew I believe in an eye for an eye, a tooth for a tooth." Von Jagow backed off from the challenge, sending a guards captain in dress uniform to Cassirer's office to proffer his apologies, which were accepted. The incident unleashed an avalanche of articles from the liberal press which condemned the hypocrisy of self-declared upholders of traditional morality like von Jagow who confiscated issues of *Pan* while at the same time seeking to initiate erotic relationships with desirable women like Durieux.

From 1911 to 1914, Durieux was the star attraction at Berlin's Lessing Theater, rarely disappointing audiences who expected an evening of powerfully projected acting. Her wardrobe was copied by the public who considered her to be the "most elegant lady" in Berlin's theatrical world. Her sharply etched portraits of complex modern women such as Ibsen's Hedda Gabler enhanced her reputation. She introduced the role of Eliza Doolittle in the German premiere of George Bernard Shaw's *Pygmalion* in 1913. The critic for the influential *Berliner Tageblatt* praised her for using a jargon "created in a masterly fashion from the various provinces of Austria and Germany, to provide for herself a dialect uniquely her own." The coming of war in August 1914 destroyed the stable order of European society, and Tilla quickly threw herself into humanitarian activities, working as a nurse. Politically, she and her husband found themselves strongly opposed to the regime of Kaiser Wilhelm II and the industrialist-landowning elite that had recklessly steered Germany into the cataclysm; one of Tilla's closest friends during these years, and one with whose ideas she sympathized with, was the brilliant Marxist theorist and antiwar activist, *Rosa Luxemburg.

After World War I, Durieux became a champion of the innovative playwright Frank Wedekind, whose bold explorations of sexuality shocked conservative circles. Her portrayal of Countess Weidenfels in *Der Marquis von Keith* in 1920 received near-universal praise. Never conventionally beautiful and now no longer young, she dominated the Berlin stage through her extraordinary talent and the sheer force of her multifaceted personality. Despite the fact that she did not act in English, she appeared in New York in a German-language version of Dario Nicodemi's mediocre play *The Shadow* in 1923. The *New York Times* critic conceded that while the play was weak, the evening was a stimulating one because it contained "long scenes in which Mme. Durieux made it seem real, alive, important, a triumph of dramaturgy." When she returned the next year to appear in Victorien Sardou's *Fedora,* the same paper heaped more praise on the German actress' performance, describing it as "artistically beautiful throughout."

These professional triumphs were clouded by personal tragedy, however. Her husband, who had never been in good health, endured severe bouts of intense, disabling pain in the early 1920s. By late 1925, he learned he was suffering from cancer and had only months to live. Durieux, emotionally unable to witness Cassirer's physical and psychological decline at close hand, divorced him. Shattered by her abandonment, he committed suicide in 1926. For the rest of her life, Durieux regretted her decision to leave her ailing husband. Cassirer's suicide threw her into a period of despondency and guilt. One

Madame Tilla Durieux, *painting by Pierre-Auguste Renoir (1914).*

of her close friends, the artist *Käthe Kollwitz, encouraged her to begin a new life with different activities. Durieux began taking English lessons from one of Kollwitz's American friends, the writer and political radical, *Agnes Smedley. In her memoirs, Durieux described Smedley wearing "a simple dress, [with] wild blondish hair and a pair of enormous blue-gray eyes."

Within a short time, the Durieux-Smedley relationship deepened. Durieux not only provided funds so that Smedley would have uninterrupted time to complete a book manuscript; she also saw to it that the aspiring young author's manuscript was circulated among influential friends in the publishing world. Ignoring Smedley's testy personality, Durieux detected her potential talent, spending considerable amounts of money to finance her writing career. She offered to support Smedley if she chose to study for a doctoral degree at the University of Berlin. With Durieux's generous backing, Smedley enrolled in courses and became active in Berlin's social life, attending the theater and countless dinner parties. Writing to a friend about her patron, Smedley said, "When I have to go anyplace, Frau Durieux sends her car these days and I feel like a princess."

Tilla Durieux's friendship with Agnes Smedley reinforced her long-established interest in the political aspects of art. Convinced that the 20th century needed new ideas in the arts as well as in politics, she experimented with emerging methods of communication. In 1925, she appeared on the Berlin Radio. She also appeared in experimental plays by Bertolt Brecht and worked with innovative directors Erwin Piscator, Erich Engel and Leopold Jessner. During the mid-1920s, Durieux began a relationship with Ludwig Katzenellenbogen, who would become her husband. His generosity enabled her to provide a subsidy of 400,000 marks for Erwin Piscator's new theater, the *Theater am Nollendorfplatz*, in 1927. Durieux acted in a number of new and exciting plays, including *Rasputin*, which were either enthusiastically praised or condemned by Berlin's lively press. Ex-Kaiser Wilhelm II joined the fray from his exile in the Netherlands, criticizing Durieux's appearance in plays that undermined German *Kultur* and spread "Bolshevik propaganda." Although the Piscator theater received high praise for its bold and radical experimentation, it was too costly a venture and was forced to close its doors in 1929.

Tilla married Katzenellenbogen in 1930 and difficult times lay ahead for the couple. A wealthy industrialist, his enterprises were severely affected by the Depression when he lost much

of his capital. Ludwig was Jewish, so weeks after Hitler's accession to power in late March 1933, the couple fled Germany with two suitcases and 200 marks. They stayed briefly in Prague before settling in Switzerland where she earned enough money to permit them to live a modest life. For the next two decades, Durieux would live in exile. Her reputation enabled her to secure top roles in Switzerland, Austria, Czechoslovakia, Alsace, the Netherlands, and Scandinavia. Katzenellenbogen's financial problems clouded their life, however, and soon after they settled in Switzerland, a warrant was issued for his arrest. Although Tilla could remain in Switzerland, her husband had to leave. Yugoslavia was one of the few countries that would accept them both as refugees. Fortunately, Ludwig owned significant shares of Yugoslav stock which could provide economic sustenance. Durieux's maternal grandfather had gone to school in Zagreb, the city in which they now settled, so she felt linked to her new home. By chance, she met a distant relative, Countess Zlata Lubienski, who helped the refugees settle in. Throughout the 1930s, Tilla and her husband struggled to survive. She toured countless European cities while he tried his hand at various business schemes, including part-ownership of a hotel. Durieux spent countless hours making the hotel presentable to tourists, but the venture proved to be a drawback. Since all of their funds were invested in the hotel, they were unable to flee to America after 1938 when it became obvious a war would soon break out.

The couple moved to Belgrade, where they resided when Nazi Germany attacked Yugoslavia on Easter Sunday, 1941. The German occupation of Yugoslavia was harsh, becoming even more brutal when a partisan movement under Josip Broz Tito gathered strength. Although she was German, Durieux joined the Yugoslav resistance. Not long afterward, her husband was arrested and taken to Germany where he was imprisoned at the Oranienburg concentration camp before dying at Berlin's Jewish Hospital in 1944. This personal loss made Tilla more fearless still. She established contacts with German anti-Nazis within the occupation regime and acted as treasurer for the "Red Aid" organization, keeping large sums of money in her bedroom to aid the partisans. Although capture by the Nazis would have meant death, she was determined to participate personally in the overthrow of Hitlerism.

Tilla Durieux was in her mid-60s at the end of World War II, her theatrical career in a shambles. She stayed in Yugoslavia where she worked for a number of years as a seamstress for a puppet theater in Zagreb, sewing and repairing puppets. In 1951, the aging actress was rediscovered, and she returned to Germany the following year and immediately resumed her acting career. Despite her age, she appeared on stage, in films, and on television, celebrated in both West and East Germany. Her stamina was astounding, and, at age 85, she starred in the role of Madame Karma in André Roussin's *The Clairvoyant*, in which she was on center stage for most of the play. Her appearance as an old peasant woman in the 1954 motion picture *The Last Bridge* showed Durieux at her best. In 1965, Deutsche Grammophon released her recording of selected scenes from plays long associated with her career. Five years later, the East German firm VEB Deutsche Schallplatten issued her recorded reminiscences. By the 1960s, Durieux was the undisputed doyenne of the German stage. The oldest active actress in that divided nation, she was one of the few artists equally respected and loved in East and West. On her 90th birthday in 1970, the Federal Republic of Germany awarded her the Grand Federal Cross of Merit (*Grosses Bundesverdienstkreuz*) while her colleagues in East Berlin named her an honorary member of the Deutsches Theater ensemble. For Tilla Durieux, there was no Berlin Wall.

In late January 1971, she appeared on stage for the last time. Soon after a fall, she underwent surgery. While in the hospital, Tilla Durieux sent two telegrams, one to East Berlin, the other to Wiesbaden, assuring her colleagues that she was on the mend and would fulfill her engagements. This was not to be. She died in West Berlin on February 21, 1971, which was Paul Cassirer's 100th birthday.

SOURCES:

Bab, Julius. *Schauspieler und Schauspielkunst.* 4th ed. Berlin: Oesterheld, 1928.

Durieux, Tilla. *Eine Tür fällt ins Schloss: Roman.* Berlin-Grünewald: Horen-Verlag, 1928.

———. *Eine Tür steht offen: Erinnerungen.* Berlin-Grünewald: F.A. Herbig, 1954.

———. *Meine ersten neunzig Jahre: Erinnerungen.* Munich: F.A. Herbig, 1971.

———. *Spielen und Träumen; mit fünf Radierungen von Emil Orlik.* Berlin: Verlag der Galerie Flechtheim, 1922.

Fontana, Oskar Maurus. "Ein Wiedersehen mit Tilla Durieux," in *Die Neue Zeitung.* Nr. 291, 1951.

"Frau Tilla Durieux: Shakespeare in German," in *The Times* [London]. February 25, 1971, p. 16.

Harta, F.A. *Tilla Durieux. 12 Steinzeichnungen.* Leipzig and Vienna: Thyrsos Verlag, 1923.

Ihering, Herbert. *Von Reinhardt bis Brecht: Vier Jahrzehnte Theater und Film.* 2 vols. Berlin: Aufbau-Verlag, 1958, 1961.

Kienzl, Florian. *Die Berliner und Ihr Theater.* Berlin: Haude & Spener, 1967.

MacKinnon, Janice R. and Stephen R. MacKinnon. *Agnes Smedley: The Life and Times of an American Radical.* London: Virago Press, 1988.

Oppenheimer, Max. *Menschen finden ihren Maler.* Zurich: Oprecht, 1938.

Paret, Peter. *The Berlin Secession: Modernism and Its Enemies in Imperial Germany.* Cambridge, MA: Belknap Press of Harvard University Press, 1980.

Piscator, Erwin. *The Political Theatre: A History, 1914–1929.* Translated by Hugh Rorrison. NY: Avon Books, 1978.

Preuss, Joachim Werner. *Tilla Durieux: Porträt der Schauspielerin/ Deutung und Dokumentation.* Berlin: Rembrandt Verlag, 1965.

"Register," in *Der Spiegel.* Vol. 25, no. 10. March 1, 1971, p. 190.

"Tilla Durieux 18.8.1880–21.2.1971," in *Theater heute.* Vol. 12, no. 4. April 1971, pp. 52–53.

"Tilla Durieux, Grand Old Lady of German Stage, Dead at 90," in *The New York Times Biographical Edition.* February 25, 1971, p. 503.

Willett, John. *The Theatre of Erwin Piscator: Half a Century of Politics in the Theatre.* London: Eyre Methuen, 1978.

John Haag, Associate Professor of History, University of Georgia, Athens, Georgia

Düringsfeld, Ida von (1815–1876)

German writer. Name variations: Duringsfeld; (pseudonym) Thekla. Born at Militsch, in Lower Silesia, Prussia, on November 12, 1815; died at Stuttgart, Wurttemberg, on October 25, 1876; married Otto von Reinsberg, in 1845.

A German poet, storyteller, and novelist, Ida von Düringsfeld published her *Poems* (1835) and a cycle of stories entitled *The Star of Andalusia* (1838) under the pseudonym Thekla. Subsequent volumes appeared annually and were also released pseudonymously or anonymously. In 1845, the year she married Otto von Reinsberg, she published *The Women of Byron* under her own name. Her extensive travels gave rise to highly prized works: numerous stories, collections of national songs, descriptions of national usages, including *Proverbs of German and Rumanian Speech* (2 vols., 1872–75) and *The Wedding Book: Usages and Beliefs Regarding the Wedding among the Christian Nations of Europe* (1871). Her other works include *Skizzenaus der vornehmen Welt* (1842–45) and *Antonio Foscarini* (1850).

Durova, Nadezhda (1783–1866)

Russian author and military veteran, the first woman to hold officer's rank in the Russian Empire and the first to be awarded the Cross of St. George, whose

most important work, The Cavalry Maiden, *describes her adventures disguised as a man while serving for nine years in the Russian Imperial cavalry during the Napoleonic Wars. Name variations: Nadezha; while serving in the Imperial Russian Army she used the name Aleksander Andreievich Aleksandrov. Born Nadezhda Andreevna Durova in September 1783 in Kherson, Russia; died on March 21, 1866, in Elabuga, Russia; daughter of Andrei Vasil'evich Durov and Nadezhda Ivanonvna Durova; sister of Vasily Andreievich,* Evgeniia Andreievna, *and* Kleopatra Andreievna; *married V.S. Chernov; children: one son.*

The daughter of a cavalry captain in the Imperial Russian Army, Nadezhda Durova was born in Kherson but in 1789 moved with her parents to the town of Sarapul when her father received an appointment as governor there. Attracted from her childhood to the military life, young Nadezhda loved to ride horses during all seasons and hated the restrictive attitudes of her mother, who looked ahead to her daughter becoming a wife and mother. At age 18, Nadezhda married a young jurist, V.S. Chernov. Soon it became clear to her that while she had escaped from a repressive mother her marriage was loveless and her husband indifferent to her emotional needs. After three years with Chernov, she returned home with her young son. But the desire for freedom was too strong, and on September 17. 1806, dressed in men's clothes, Durova joined a troop of Cossacks moving west. Despite her lack of papers, she was accepted and after three years was able to transfer to an Uhlan regiment which fought in the Prussian campaign. Most if not all of her fellow soldiers must have suspected that she was not a man, given the fact that she was unable to grow a gallantly twirling mustache, the fashion of the day. During these years, she served first in a Polish Uhlan regiment in Grodno, then was attached to the Mariupol Hussars regiment and, from 1811, to a Lithuanian Uhlan regiment.

Durova's father attempted to track down his daughter and in time the Russian tsar, Alexander I, received reports on her case. Won over by her war record and her impassioned pleas, the tsar decided not to send her home; instead, in December 1807, he granted her a commission and the right to officially call herself Aleksander Andreievich Aleksandrov. After several years of peace, Russia again found itself at war when Napoleonic France invaded her vast territory in 1812. Excited by the opportunity to once again be in combat, Durova participated in the bloody battle of Borodino, receiving a foot wound. After

her recovery, she was appointed an orderly to Field Marshal Mikhail Kutuzov and was able to participate in the Russian pursuit of the defeated French-led forces into Western Europe. In 1816, with Russia victorious and at peace, Durova retired from the cavalry, receiving a Captain's pension. Before her retirement, she was awarded the prestigious Cross of St. George—the first Russian woman to receive this honor.

Although she had received little formal education, Nadezhda Durova's command of the Russian language was more than adequate, and she kept extensive diaries during her military career. In the mid-1830s, more than two decades after the Napoleonic Wars, her writings came to the attention of Russia's great poet, Alexander Pushkin. Deeply impressed by her literary talent and her skill at evoking the chaos of war, he was instrumental in editing and publishing her war memoirs in his journal *Sovremennik* (*The Contemporary*), for which he wrote a highly laudatory introduction. In book form, Durova's war memoir was published as *The Cavalry Maiden: It Happened in Russia.* The much-feared and powerful literary critic Vissarion Belinsky was convinced that because of its literary quality, this work had to have been written by Pushkin. When Durova began to publish works of fiction starting in 1837, her literary reputation soared and her memoirs, which had not sold well at first, became a bestseller. In 1839, she published additional material from her war diaries under the title *Aleksandrov's Notes: More about the Cavalry Maiden.*

Recognized by her contemporaries in Russia as a remarkable commentary on the phenomenon of war, *The Cavalry Maiden* has been increasingly viewed by modern critics as a major literary portrait of human conflict in wartime. Before battle, Durova is filled with abstract love of nation and the Russian soil, determined to die in battle come what may, and utterly unafraid of the future. Once the battle begins, however, she finds herself to be cold, tired, hungry and confused by the utter turmoil that is warfare. She finds herself at times to hate and resent her superior officers almost as much as the foe. It is this utter honesty that makes her book take its place in the ranks of such classic portrayals of the chaos of war as Stendhal's *Charterhouse of Parma* and Stephen Crane's *Red Badge of Courage.* Although her prose style is often awkward and artless, certain passages including her description of the accidental death of her beloved horse Alcides, are genuinely moving in their folk-like lyrical pathos: "You who carried me on your spine so obediently in my childhood years, who passed with me across the bloody fields of honor, glory, and death; who shared my rigors, dangers, hunger, cold, joy, and contentment! You, the only creature of the animal kingdom who loved me! You are no more. You exist no longer." Returning to Russia after victories in the West, Durova concludes her memoir on a gloomy note. Departing from its comfortable billets in the German province of Holstein, she and her regiment reach the impoverished town of Vitebsk where she writes sorrowfully: "Here we are back on our native soil again. I am not at all pleased, I can't forget Holstein."

Nadezhda Durova's novels and stories—*Fate's Toy* (1837), *Elena, the Belle of T.* (1837), *Gudishki* (1839), *The Summer House* (1839), *Sulphur Spring* (1839), *Nurmeka* (1839), *Buried Treasure* (1840), *Yarchuk, the Dog Who Saw Ghosts* (1840), and *The Corner* (1840)—are written in the grand tradition of European Romanticism. The plots are convoluted, often Gothic in character, and range in subject matter from the tragic chronicle of a woman who died of a syphilitic infection received from her dissolute husband (*Fate's Toy*), to the conflict of Christian and pagan cultures in medieval Lithuania (*Gudishki*), to the mysterious tale of a Polish priest's love for his ward and its eventual bloody result (*The Summer House*). At first, Durova was lionized by the literary elite of St. Petersburg but the novelty of inviting the new literary celebrity from the provinces wore thin. She recorded her disillusionment over the comet-like nature of her fame in a memoir entitled *A Year of Life in Petersburg, or The Disadvantages of the Third Visit.* Here she noted how during the first visit to the elite salons of Russia's intelligentsia she had been fawned over. The mood changed considerably during the second visit, when she was usually treated no more than politely. The third visit found her generally being ignored, with herself sitting quite neglected in a corner of the room. **Mary Fleming Zirin**, a leading expert on Durova, has suggested that these insights into the nature of literary celebrity remain valid and can with justice be codified as Durova's Law of Lionization.

By 1840, the plaudits for Durova had ended, and she returned to live in the remote town of Elabuga in the Ural Mountains. Whether she had found herself uninspired and incapable of discovering new artistic inspirations or, as is more likely, she had become thoroughly disillusioned by the transitory nature of fame, Durova ceased to write at this point in

what would turn out to be a long life. Once again obscure, she ended her days as an amiable eccentric. She continued to dress as a man, and insisted that she be addressed as "Aleksander Andreievich." In 1858, eight years before her death, she wrote one last essay (never published) in which she voiced not only her patriotic sentiments but also her passionate belief that women must play a larger role in the modern world:

In our times a woman who is bored, who cannot find a way to occupy herself, and who languishes in inactivity, is more out of place than ever. Now more than ever Russian society needs active, hard-working women who sympathize judiciously with the great events taking place around them and are capable of adding their might to the structure of social welfare and order which is being erected by common efforts. Now Russian society has more need than ever not of women-cosmopolites but of Russian women in all the fine sense of the word.

Throughout the many years she lived in Elabuga, Nadezhda Durova's generosity to those who were poor and ill invariably reached the point of endangering her own survival. At her death of 1866, her estate consisted of only one ruble, despite the fact that she had received a generous pension of 1,000 rubles annually since

Nadezhda Durova

1824. She was buried with full military honors, and the local populace retained fond memories of her long after her death; in 1901, a new monument was erected over her grave.

Given the fact that she had been proud to be a loyal subject of her tsar, Durova's reputation was in eclipse during the first 25 years of Soviet rule. During World War II, however, a new form of Soviet patriotism rehabilitated many of the military heroes of the tsarist era, and by 1942 biographies and plays about this remarkable woman, the first to hold officer rank in Russia's armed forces, were being published in the Soviet Union. In 1957, an opera based on her life was written, and the film *Ballad of a Hussar*, celebrating her exploits, was produced in 1962. The same year a marble bust in the park near the cemetery where she is buried was unveiled in Elabuga. As late as the early 1960s, Soviet abhorrence of tsarism still motivated omissions from editions of her memoirs, and Durova's rhapsodic description of her interview with Alexander I was purged from the 1960 and 1962 editions of her best-known work. Not until 1983, when her birthday was celebrated with considerable enthusiasm in the Soviet Union, was a complete and unabridged edition of *The Cavalry Maiden* made available to the reading public.

SOURCES:.

Durova, Nadezhda. *The Cavalry Maiden: Journals of a Russian Officer in the Napoleonic Wars.* Translated by Mary Fleming Zirin. Bloomington: Indiana University Press, 1988.
———. "My Childhood Years," in Domna C. Stanton, ed., *The Female Autograph.* Translated and edited by Mary Fleming Zirin. Chicago, IL: University of Chicago Press, 1987, pp. 119–142.
Heldt, Barbara. "Nadezhda Durova: Russia's Cavalry Maid," in *History Today.* Vol. 33. February 1983, pp. 24–27.
———. *A Terrible Perfection: Women and Russian Literature.* Bloomington: Indiana University Press, 1987.

John Haag, Associate Professor of History,
University of Georgia, Athens, Georgia

Durr, Françoise (1942—)

French tennis player. Name variations: Francoise; (nickname) Frankie. Born in Algiers in 1942; married Boyd Browning (an American); lives in Phoenix, Arizona.

Born a French national in Algiers during the years of World War II, Françoise Durr was a tennis-crowd favorite for her intensity, temperament, and eclectic style: she had a Western-grip forehand, an unorthodox backhand, and suffered from a weak serve. In 1967, Durr was the first Frenchwoman in 19 years to win the singles title at her home court of Roland Garros after successively routing Brazil's *Maria Bueno, England's **Ann Hayden Jones**, and Australia's *Lesley Turner. That same year, Durr won the German singles title and was a semifinalist at Forest Hills. Though she never had another year like 1967, and never again won a major singles title, Durr was a formidable doubles player throughout the 1960s and 1970s. For five years, she won the French doubles title, partnering **Gail Sherriff** (1967, 1970, 1971) and Ann Jones (1968, 1969). In America, she won the U.S. doubles twice, with *Darlene Hard** in 1969 and with the Netherlands' **Betty Stove** in 1972. Though she never took a doubles match at Wimbledon, Durr reached the finals six times. She also won the French mixed doubles with **Jean Claude Barclay** in 1968, 1971, 1973, before retiring in 1980.

Durriyah Shafiq (1908–1975).

See Shafik, Doria.

Duse, Eleonora (1858–1924)

First international stage actress and the most charismatic and honored actress of her time who was renowned for the subtlety, depth, and psychological insights of her stage portrayals. Born Eleonora Giulia Amalia Duse on October 3, 1858, in the town of Vigevano, Italy; died in Pittsburgh, Pennsylvania, on April 21, 1924; daughter of Alessandro Duse (an actor) and Angelica Cappelletto Duse; married Teobaldo Marchetti Checchi, in 1881 (estranged after 1885); children: (with Martino Cafiero) a son who died within a week of his birth; (with husband) daughter **Enrichetta Checchi** (b. 1882).

Appeared on stage at age four in a production of Victor Hugo's Les Miserables (1862); joined the company of Cesare Rossi (1879); triumphed in a production of Emile Zola's Thérèse Raquin (1879); became prima donna in the Rossi company (1881); attended performances of Sarah Bernhardt in Italy (1882); became estranged from husband during tour of South America (1885); formed her own company (1886); first performed Heinrik Ibsen's A Doll's House (1891); made successful theatrical tours in Russia, Vienna, and Berlin (1891-92); met Gabriele D'Annunzio (1894); performed in U.S. (1893, 1896, 1902); performed in London, including a command performance for Queen Victoria (1895); performed in Ibsen's Hedda Gabler (1898); triumphed in her own production of D'Annunzio's Francesca da Rimini (1904); retired from the stage (1909); made silent film

Cenere (1916); resumed acting (1921); performed in London and U.S. (1923).

To many in Europe and the United States, the Italian actress Eleonora Duse was "the incomparable Duse," a stage artist of unsurpassed dramatic power. As the first international stage actress, she gave performances which drew plaudits from George Bernard Shaw, invitations to a reception at the White House, and a command performance at Windsor Castle before Queen *Victoria. Her triumphant tours of European capitals and the United States drew raves from critics and audience members alike. "She was a revelation of dramatic art to me," wrote one member of her audience. "She was unique—the juggler of human emotions." "The reason why Duse in the greatest actress in the world," responded another critic, "is that she has a more subtle nature than any other actress. . . . No play has ever been profound enough . . . for this actress to say everything she has to say in it."

Eleonora Duse was born into the world of the theater. Her family traveled constantly in Italy, for a time as part of a theatrical troupe owned by the Duse family. Her father Alessandro Duse was enthralled with acting, although not highly successful at it. Her mother **Angelica Cappelletto Duse**, who was less enthusiastic, performed female roles when needed by the family's traveling theatrical company; stricken with tuberculosis, she often could not perform at all. It was not unusual for the family to leave Duse's mother behind, resting in a hospital or guest house, when the troupe moved on to another Italian town. There is speculation that the "weak lungs" which afflicted Duse throughout her life were the result of the same disease that eventually killed her mother.

Although some of Duse's biographers perpetuated the romantic myth that she was actually born in a train approaching that small Italian town of Vigevano, there was no train line to Vigevano at the time; Vigevano itself is accepted as the town of her birth. Her childhood was lonely and terror filled. An only child, she was able to attend school only when the family remained in the same place for any period of time. Wherever she went to school, she noticed that she was treated by the other children as an outsider. Sensitive and quiet, she also suffered in the constant turmoil of the acting world—the rivalries, the tantrums, and the continual financial uncertainties of the family. Some biographers believe that such a childhood made Duse "introspective" and contributed to her remarkable talent as an actress to convey inner turmoil by subtle gestures or tones of voice.

Duse saw her childhood slightly differently, believing that it caused strong emotions that she kept in check as a child but revealed as an adult in her stage art. "The outlines of my art," she wrote, "developed themselves in that condition of anguish and weariness, of fever and repugnance, in which my sensibility became a manner almost plastic, like the incandescent material we saw glass workers holding at the end of their tubes. . . . On certain evenings, on a wall covered with copper saucepans, I could see myself as in a mirror, in an attitude of pain and rage, with a face I could not recognize."

Duse's first appearance on stage came at age four, when she played Cosette in a stage adaptation of Victor Hugo's *Les Miserables*. Some of the theatrical companies her family worked for were very respectable; some were distinctly second rate. She was only 14 when she was handed a telegram as she came offstage during a performance. It contained the news that her mother had died in another town, where she had been left by the family because she was too ill to travel.

> *From 1884 to 1924 the name [Duse] stood for the most potent magic of which the theater is capable. To those her saw her—and thank God, I am old enough to be one of them—that magic still remains undiminished and unsurpassed. . . . I saw the stage take on an added dimension. I felt the vast audience grow still and sit as though mesmerized in the presence of a frail, worn woman. . . . I saw "the impossible" come true.*
>
> —Eva Le Gallienne

Father and daughter continued to act in a variety of companies. When Duse was 21, the theatrical entrepreneur Giovanni Emanuel saw her perform and hired her as part of his troupe for the Teatro dei Fiorentini in Naples. She became the second female lead, subordinate to the actress **Giacinta Pezzana**, who was noted for her diction and beautiful voice. Far from resenting Duse, Pezzana proved to be a generous mentor; Duse scored her first success in 1879 in Naples, playing opposite Pezzana in Emile Zola's *Thérèse Raquin*.

That same year, the entrepreneur Cesare Rossi, who favored more natural styles of acting than the "heroic" or flamboyant styles popular at the time, hired Pezzana and Duse for his company in Turin. When Pezzana left the company in 1881, Duse became "prima donna." She began to acquire more confidence in her acting and made a success of the younger Alexandre Dumas' *The Princess of Baghdad,* which had been one of Pezzana's failures. Duse came to enjoy some of her roles, writing of her performance in *Romeo and Juliet,* "Words slipped from me with strange ease, almost involuntarily in delirium. When I fell lifeless on the body of Romeo, the howl of the crowd . . . was so violent that I was frightened."

She also began an affair with an audience regular, the newspaper editor Martino Cafiero. At 38 years of age, Cafiero was more than 15 years her senior, but he was able to introduce her into the fashionable world of Naples, including yachting clubs and museums. The affair ended when Duse told Cafiero that she was pregnant, and he left her. The child, a boy, died only a week after his birth. In 1881, Duse agreed to marry an actor in the Rossi troupe, Teobaldo Checchi, who declared that he desired to give Duse respectability and to protect her from Rossi, who had a predatory reputation toward the women in his troupe. A daughter, Enrichetta, who was born in 1882, was often left in the care of an older couple when Duse went on tour.

Duse and her husband became permanently estranged during a theatrical tour of South America in 1885, when she began a shipboard romance with her leading man, Flavio Ando. By some accounts, Checchi discovered Duse and Ando together in Ando's stateroom. The affair did not last long—Duse commented that Ando "was pretty, but dumb"—but Duse told her husband she did not need his money. Divorce was impossible for them, but, when Duse returned to Italy, Checchi remained behind in South America.

The incident evoked negative publicity for Duse in Italy and may have contributed to the tendency of the Italian theatergoers to be cooler to her talents than audiences throughout the rest of Europe. Newspapers charged that she had abandoned her husband; Checchi complained that he was impoverished and "banished from the land of my birth." Duse worked to see that her daughter retained a relationship with her father, however, and when Checchi became Argentine counsel in England, Enrichetta was sent there for periodic visits.

Even before Duse announced in 1886 that she would form her own company, she had begun to develop a distinctive style of acting. A significant influence on her was Arrigo Boito, a composer and poet with whom she had her most long-lasting and professionally rewarding relationship. When they met, she was 25 and he was 40. Boito knew the world of the theater better than Duse, and he was a friend of luminaries such as Victor Hugo and Giuseppe Verdi (for whom he was a librettist). He wrote her often, encouraging her to persevere despite her frequent bouts of ill-health and depression.

In addition to promoting "naturalness" in acting, Boito also encouraged Duse to view the theater in terms of achieving lofty ideals, of perfecting oneself, and of "cultivating the spirit." Encouraged by Boito to read a wide range of literature, she also began an intense study of foreign languages (although, throughout her career, she would perform only in Italian). In 1888, she appeared as *Cleopatra (VII) in his translation (done specifically for Duse) of Shakespeare's *Antony and Cleopatra.* Even after the Duse-Boito relationship cooled, they kept in contact, and she was devastated by his death in 1918.

Another influence on Duse was the appearance in Italy in 1882 of the famous French actress *Sarah Bernhardt. Declaring that Bernhardt's performances were "an emancipation," Duse began to show more confidence in her acting and abandoned many of the standard Italian plays of the day, which were essentially dramatized novels or opera librettos transformed into plays. She incorporated into her repertoire works by the major French playwrights, such as the older and younger Alexandre Dumas and Victorien Scribe. By adopting plays which were a large part of Bernhardt's repertoire (which Duse used in Italian translations), Duse was virtually inviting comparisons between her acting ability and that of Bernhardt, particularly since she usually opened her theatrical tours with a performance as Marguerite Gautier (*Alphonsine Plessis) in *The Lady of Camelias,* which was a Bernhardt standard.

Critics began to compare Duse's style of acting, which was subtle and often emphasized the psychological nuances of the characters she played, with the performances of Bernhardt, who often let her own personality show through whatever roles she played. When Duse performed in Paris in 1897, Bernhardt graciously made her own theater available, but on opening night, when Duse seemed excessively nervous, Bernhardt drew most of the attention by receiving a constant stream of visitors to her box in the theater. Although the two also performed (in separate portions of plays) at a joint benefit,

they did not become confidants or even friends. In fact, in her memoirs, Bernhardt wrote of Duse, "Eleonora Duse is an actress more than an artist. . . . [S]he walks in paths that have been traced out by others. . . . [S]he is a great actress, but she is not an artist."

Duse's tour of Russia in 1891 was the beginning of her career as a celebrated international star; between 1892 and 1902, she gave more than 100 performances in Berlin, Vienna, Paris, Russia, and made three trips to the United States. Her finely nuanced performances or "quiet acting," which was initially less impressive than other acting styles, began to have an impact. Her performance of *The Lady of the Camelias* in Vienna was hailed as a major triumph over Bernhardt. One member of her audience in Russia noted that at the beginning of a play, Duse seemed "insignificant and the voice nothing special" but that by the third act, much of the audience was "sobbing."

Duse spoke in an ordinary, everyday voice most of the time on stage. Though her stage voice was seldom described as beautiful, she used it to project subtle changes in her character's emotion. "Her voice was not an actor's voice," wrote one member of her audience. "Like everything else about Duse it was natural; not the pseudo-naturalness acquired in a classroom or studio, but true naturalness." "Her acting is entirely quiet acting," added another critic. "She does not roar or shout, nor does she throw herself up and down the stage, like a demented steamroller."

One writer was impressed that "the outline of the motionless face is remarkably mobile, capable of endless nuance." "Here was a young woman," wrote still another critic, "who could grip your heart night after night in the theater and crumple it like a handkerchief." She had an ability both to cry and to blush at will; audiences marveled at seeing a slight pink color appear on her face, darken, and then spread across her face and neck (an effect which was quite obvious to most in the audience, since Duse generally wore little, or no, stage makeup).

"There were," wrote one member of her audience, "periods in the play in which she enabled us to dispense with language. It was not necessary for us to understand what she was saying, because we understood what she was feeling. The greatest feat which an actor can perform is to take the audience beyond the barriers of speech." Still another insisted that "she is absolutely unrivalled at playing hysterical and nervous parts. I have never seen anything like her on stage, with the exception of **Sada Jacco**, the Japanese actress." "Across her face flit the 'agonies' . . . of the modern, anaemic, overwrought woman," commented one of her admirers. "She excels in the delineation of listless, nervous, hysterical half-mad souls."

Seeking to expand beyond the available French and Italian repertoire, Duse found that she had a special affinity for the women portrayed in the plays of Henrik Ibsen. She incorporated translations of Ibsen's plays into her work,

including productions of *A Doll's House* in 1891 and *Hedda Gabler* in 1905. It was said that her acting of Ibsen's heroines implied that she was always holding something in reserve, that she understood personality quirks that the characters in his plays chose not to reveal.

Such achievements did not come easily, as became clear when the diary of a young actor in her troupe was published. It portrayed a demanding, irritable Duse—the diary generally referred to her as "Madame"—who was ever fearful that things would go wrong onstage and was often nervous and imperious in dealing with others in her troupe. The actress *Eva Le Gallienne called her a mystic driven by a desire for perfection, but she added that this observation did not mean that Duse was an exemplary woman. "Many people thought of her—with good reason, as intolerant, spoiled, and selfish," she wrote. "To me she was not only the greatest actress I have ever seen but a rare, generous, and extraordinary human being."

Duse's generosity became legendary. Asked what her fee would be to perform in a benefit, she asked about the pay that would be given to a child actor with a very minor role. Then she requested the same amount: 10 francs. When the famous dancer *Isadora Duncan lost both of her children in a drowning accident, Duse sought her out to try to comfort her during Duncan's visit to Italy in 1913. And Duse could be courageous. She was the first to perform Ibsen's plays in Italy and dared to perform Ernst Renan's *L'Abesse du Juarre*, which concerned an abbess who, when condemned to death, decides to give herself to her childhood sweetheart shortly before her scheduled execution.

From 1894 to 1904, Duse maintained an intense professional and personal relationship with the poet and dramatist Gabriele D'Annunzio. Accounts of their first meeting differ, the most dramatic being that D'Annunzio blocked her path as she came offstage after a performance and shouted praise for her performance. She was 39; he was five years younger. They traveled together when she performed in other countries, including a joyous journey to Egypt and Corfu.

Others saw D'Annunzio as a vain womanizer of short stature, narrow shoulders, and an "androgynous softness." Duse saw a sensuous poet of animalistic intensity who would raise Italian drama to unprecedented levels. As a young actress, Duse had been content to do the available melodramatic plays, believing that

Duse
(1891)

their very banality gave her opportunities to be creative. The more mature Duse lamented the dearth of quality plays, complaining that, "Once more, I am the bearded lady, squeezing my soul over the framework of rotten vulgar pieces." The playwright Luigi Pirandello, who saw Duse perform in his youth and whose plays would later revolutionize the Italian theater, remarked that the story of her career was that she had either failed to find the right author or found the wrong author.

Duse financially supported D'Annunzio, giving him money to rehabilitate his villa; the profit from a single performance by her paid the rent on his villa for a year. "I love you—I love you—I love you," she wrote him.

When friends suggested that D'Annunzio was undeserving of her love, she replied, "I have two arms, one's called Enrichetta, the other Gabriele D'Annunzio. I cannot cut off one without dying."

The years with Duse proved the most creative of D'Annunzio's life, but he gave very little of his work to her. When he wrote *La Citta Morta* (1897), she returned from a tour eager to play the lead, but he gave the play to Bernhardt instead. When Duse begged him to write for her, he produced *Sogno d'un Mattino di Primavera,* an inferior drama. Although Bernhardt was unable to make *La Citta Morta* a success, Duse placed it in her repertoire and performed it until audiences came to accept this tale of a brother's passion for his sister. She spent 400,000 lires of her own money mounting a production of his play **Francesca da Rimini*, taken from Dante's *Divine Comedy*. Although it was unsuccessful in Italy—there was a near riot during the performance in Rome—Duse kept the production going until it was hailed in Berlin and Vienna.

Duse rehearsed for D'Annunzio's next play, *La Figlia di Iorio*, completed in 1903, more than she had rehearsed for any other. When she fell ill, he promised to give her more time to prepare for the part, then gave the part, instead, to a younger actress, **Irma Gramatica**, who would have great success with the role. Duse believed that she had been robbed of the chance to give D'Annunzio a complete dramatic triumph.

D'Annunzio exploited his partnership with Duse in his most profitable writing, the novel *Il Fouco* (*The Flame of Life*, 1900), which portrayed an aging actress obsessively in love with a much younger poet. Duse read the story in manuscript, offered her suggestions, and refused to condemn the book publicly. "I thought of it as true art," she said. "I tried to defend it." In 1904, D'Annunzio ended the relationship when he transferred his affections to a younger woman, the Marchesa **Alessandra di Carlotti Rudini**.

Duse's trip to the United States in 1893 had not been a great success, largely because she canceled a number of performances for reasons of poor health and because American critics were initially baffled by her "quiet" acting. On arrival in America, she had written that she saw "not a gleam of art, but only railways, cars, and business." "I thought," she wrote, "of trusting myself to the sea again and going straight back to Italy." She balked at the constant requests for publicity photographs and interviews. "Will you tell me," she asked one interviewer, "why women workers who work during the day have the right to rest at night while I, who work at night, cannot dispose of my own afternoons?"

Her 1896 and 1902 tours in the United States were much more successful, drawing President Grover Cleveland and his Cabinet to many of her performances and culminating in a special reception for her at the White House. A London tour in 1895 was also a major triumph, eliciting not only an invitation to perform before Queen Victoria at Windsor Castle but also rapturous praise from George Bernard Shaw, who declared that "I should say without qualification that it is the best modern acting I have ever seen. The extraordinary richness of her art can only be understood by those who have never studied the process by which an actress is built up."

Eleonora Duse retired in 1909, only five years before the start of World War I. During the war, she suffered financially, because the two nations that usually accounted for most of her income, Germany and Austria, were "enemy" countries. She was also seriously injured when her face slammed into a car windshield during a 1916 automobile accident. She rejected an invitation to travel to America in 1916 to make a film with the famed director D.W. Griffith—his *Birth of Nation* struck her as having "Nothing beautiful in it"—but she agreed to appear in a silent film, *Cenere*, made in Italy. The picture was a financial flop, possibly because of her prematurely graying hair but also because her subtle methods of acting did not translate well to the silent screen.

In 1921, she resumed acting. A triumphant tour of major Italian cities was a source of special satisfaction, since she had always won more recognition in other countries than in her native Italy. Increased costs ate up most of the profits, however, and she added tours of London and the States to her itinerary in 1923. The new Italian government of Benito Mussolini offered her a lifelong retirement pension, but she refused, requesting instead that the government reimburse the members of her acting troupe should something happen to her during her tour abroad.

It was almost a premonition: choosing to walk from her hotel in Pittsburgh to a nearby theater, she was caught in a freezing rain when she and an assistant could not find an unlocked stage door. By the time an unlocked door was located on the other side of the theater, she was exhausted. She was able to complete her performance but returned to her hotel room with a high fever. Newspapers reported that her "perennial lung problem" had reappeared. On April 21, 1924, she died in Pittsburgh of pneumonia.

What followed made clear that she had become an international treasure. A brief funeral service was held in Pittsburgh. Then a train bore her body north to New York, where so many people wanted to file past her coffin that tickets had to be issued. The boat that took her body back to her native Italy landed at Naples, but her coffin was taken by train over much of Italy—past silent crowds in Florence, Bologna, and Rome (where another funeral was held). She was buried at the cemetery of Sant' Anna. In accordance with her wishes, her gravestone was inscribed simply with the words "Eleonora Duse 1858–1924."

SOURCES:

Harding, Bertita. *Age Cannot Wither: The Story of Duse and d'Annunzio.* Philadelphia, PA: J.B. Lippincott, 1947.

Le Gallienne, Eva. *The Mystic in the Theatre: Eleonora Duse.* London: Bodley Head, 1966.

Pontiero, Giovanni, ed. and trans. *Duse on Tour: Guido Noccioli's Diaries, 1906-07.* Amherst, MA: University of Massachusetts, 1982.

Symons, Arthur. *Eleonora Duse.* NY: Benjamin Blom, 1927 (reprinted 1969).

Weaver, William. *Duse: A Biography.* NY: Harcourt Brace Jovanovich, 1984.

SUGGESTED READING:

Carlson, Marvin. *The Italian Stage from Goldoni to D'Annunzio.* Jefferson, NC: McFarland, 1981.

Rheinhardt, E. A. *The Life of Eleonora Duse.* London: Martin Secker, 1930.

COLLECTIONS:

Duse's voluminous correspondence is widely scattered. Much of her correspondence is housed in the Fondazione Giorgio Cini in Venice, Italy. Her letters to D'Annunzio are in the Il Vittoriale degli Italiani, Gardone, Italy. In the U.S., there is some material in the Humanities Research Center, Austin, Texas. Her letters to Boito were published in Paul Radice, ed. *Eleonora Duse Arrigo Boito: Lettre d'amore.* (Milan: Il Saggiatore, 1979).

Niles R. Holt, Professor of History, Illinois State University, Normal-Bloomington, Illinois

Dustin, Hannah (1657–c. 1736)

Colonial American hero. Name variations: Hannah Duston or Dustan. Born Hannah Emerson in Haverhill, Massachusetts, on December 23, 1657 (some sources cite 1659); died in Ipswich, Massachusetts, probably in early 1736; married Thomas Dustin (or Duston or Dustan), in December 1677 (died 1732); children: nine.

Had Hannah Dustin not been carrying the scalps of ten Abnakis when she returned by canoe to Haverhill, Massachusetts, on April 21, 1697, the tale of her captivity and escape might not have been believed. At a time when the French incited Native Americans to raid English Settlements during King William's War (1689–1697), Dustin was one among many victims of a raid on Haverhill by a band of Abnakis on March 15, 1697. Dustin's husband Thomas and seven of their eight children escaped the raid, in which 27 women and children were killed. Less than a week from childbed, Hannah along with her infant daughter and her nurse **Mary Neff** were taken prisoner.

Dustin's house was put to flame and she watched her infant killed by an Indian who bashed the baby's head against a tree. Hannah was wearing only one shoe as she and Mary were marched some hundred miles to an island in the confluence of the Merrimack and Contoocook rivers (near present-day Concord, New Hampshire). They were put to work for one of their captor's family of 12 and told that they would soon be traveling to another village where they would be stripped, whipped, and forced to run the gauntlet. In desperation, Dustin wove her escape plan.

She prompted fellow captive Samuel Lennardson (or Leonardson), an English boy who had been kidnapped from Worcester more than a year earlier, to ask the chief how best to murder someone with a tomahawk. When the chief demonstrated, Dustin had the knowledge she required. During the morning of March 30, she and Lennardson came upon their sleeping captors and attacked them with proficiency. One Indian escaped with wounds, and a boy, whom they had befriended and intended to spare, ran off, while the remaining ten were murdered in their sleep, one by Lennardson and nine by Dustin.

Dustin, Lennardson, and Neff took off in one of the Abnakis' canoes and had not traveled far before Dustin realized that she needed proof of the event. She turned back and scalped the ten corpses before arriving safely in Haverhill on April 21. Dustin continued on to Boston, where she and her companions were lauded. A sum of £25 was awarded to "Thomas Dustan of Haverhill, on behalf of Hannah his wife," and £12½ were awarded to the others. A generous gift was also sent by Francis Nicholson, the royal governor of Maryland after he heard of Dustin's massacre.

The remainder of Dustin's life was lived quietly as a colonial farm wife. She had another child and moved to Ipswich, Massachusetts, after the death of her husband in 1732. Dustin died, probably in 1736, in Ipswich. Late in the 19th century, monuments that portrayed Dustin with a raised tomahawk were placed in Haverhill and at the site of the massacre, now called Dustin's Island.

Dutt, Toru (1856–1877)

Indian poet and translator. Born in Calcutta in 1856; died in 1877 of tuberculosis; daughter of Govin Chunder Dutt (a justice of the peace).

Selected works: A Sheaf Gleaned in French Fields (1875); Bianca; or the Young Spanish Maiden (posthumous, 1878); (novel) Le Journal de Mlle. d'Avers (The

See illustration on the following page

Monument to Hannah Dustin in Penacooh, New Hampshire.

Diary of Mille d'Avers, posthumous, 1879); Ancient Ballads and Legends of Hindustan *(posthumous, 1882).*

The daughter of a justice of the peace, Toru Dutt was born in Calcutta to a family of high-caste cultivated Hindus, and her parents were

converts to Christianity. She received a broad education at home with her sister **Aru**. At 13, she and her sister were sent to France to study for a few months and attended a convent in Nice. The family moved to Cambridge, England, in 1871, and the sisters heard lectures that the philosopher Henry Sidgwick and other liberal dons had begun for women. The family returned to India in 1873, and as Dutt resumed her studies she began learning Sanskrit. With a strong affinity for the French character and an aptitude for the French language, she undertook a study of French romantic poetry and produced essays on Leconte de Lisle and Joséphin Soulary as well as a series of English translations of poetry. In 1876, the translations were collected in *A Sheaf Gleaned in French Fields*. Her collection *Ancient Ballads and Legends of Hindustan* was selected from work left unpublished at the time of her early death, and these English versions of native Indian legends have been said to show strong original power. After Dutt's death of tuberculosis while in her early 20s, her novel, written in French and entitled *Le Journal de Mlle. d'Avers*, was published in 1879. Dutt is regarded as a pioneer for her writings in an age when few Indian women published.

Duval, Enna (1818–1892).

See Brewster, Anne Hampton.

d'Uzes, Anne, Duchesse (1847–1933).

See Uzès, Anne, Duchesse d'.

Dwyer, Doriot Anthony (1922—)

American flutist who was the first woman to hold a principal chair in a major American symphony orchestra. Born March 6, 1922, in Streator, Illinois; daughter of Edith (Maurer) Anthony and William C. Anthony.

Was first flutist for the Boston Symphony Orchestra (1952–89).

Until the middle of the 20th century, symphony orchestras were exclusively male enclaves, reflecting the belief that had been held for centuries that men should play in public and women should play at home. Unionization of musicians both helped and hindered women. Unions demanded that all auditions be held behind curtains so that the judges would not be able to tell the gender of the musician playing. In this way, women were often admitted to orchestras. At the same time, however, unions espoused seniority, and in symphony orchestras those with seniority were inevitably men. As the 20th century progressed, women increasingly joined orchestras, and those in small towns and cities, whose musicians were often unpaid, sometimes were composed of one-third to one-half women members. Gradually women worked their way into over 30 major symphony orchestras in the United States. Doriot Anthony Dwyer was one such musician.

Doriot Anthony was born in Streator, Illinois, in 1922. Recognizing the exceptional talent of his daughter, William Anthony inquired of her flute teacher about Doriot's chances for an orchestra career. The teacher replied they were nil, saying, "There are no women in symphony orchestras." In the 1930s, women were not even allowed to audition so membership in these all white male clubs remained concretely exclusive. Doriot Dwyer, however, was a great niece of *Susan B. Anthony, who was also a musician, and it appears their pioneering spirits were matched. "I liked symphony music," said Dwyer. "I liked being in touch with conductors and soloists and I was absolutely determined not only to be in a first-rate orchestra but also to lead the flute section—to be a principal player." Mastering the flute was one thing, entering an orchestra another. For seven years, Dwyer lived in California and wrote to major Eastern orchestras, believing that male conductors there were more enlightened. Finally, she heard from Charles Munch at the Boston Symphony.

Munch's decision to audition women was more or less a lark. Several were invited to try out on what was known as "Ladies' Day." Dwyer worked for that audition as if she were working to pass her doctorate in music. She memorized all her pieces, determined to play the perfect audition. Munch was stunned by the level of playing he discovered at "Ladies' Day." Dwyer was asked to audition a second time, but she refused, stating that her first audition should adequately demonstrate her talent. She was hired, but the management kept it a secret so as not to upset members and patrons of the orchestra; at that time, many felt that the only reason conductors hired female musicians was to sleep with them. In 1952, Dwyer's appointment as a principal player for the Boston Symphony Orchestra made national headlines, because the event was so unusual. She went on to have a long and distinguished career with the orchestra, and, as the century neared its close, women were increasingly featured in orchestras throughout the world.

SOURCES:
Epstein, Helen. "Notes from the Orchestra Pit," in *Ms.* Vol 5, no. 10. April 1977, pp. 106, 108, 110–111.

John Haag,
Athens, Georgia

Dwyer, Florence Price (1902–1976)

U.S. Representative, a Republican from New Jersey, who served in Congress from 1957 to 1973. Born Flo-

Florence
Price
Dwyer

of the Legislative Reorganization Act of 1970, she authored an amendment requiring the recording of individual votes. Under the presidency of her fellow Republican Richard Nixon, she urged the appointment of more women to federal office. Dwyer, who was never seriously challenged for her seat, retired from politics in 1972. She died in Elizabeth, New Jersey, on February 29, 1976.

Dyer, Louise (1884–1962).

See Hanson-Dyer, Louise.

Dyer, Mary Barrett (c. 1591–1660)

American Quaker and religious martyr who was a companion of Anne Hutchinson. Name variations: Dyar. Born Mary Barrett in England around 1591; hanged on June 1, 1660, in Boston, Massachusetts Bay Colony; married William Dyer (date unknown); children; six survived infancy.

Mary Barrett Dyer and her husband William emigrated from England and settled in the Massachusetts Bay Colony in 1635, becoming members of Boston's First Church. Dyer's delivery of a stillborn and deformed child in 1837 was cited by authorities as evidence of the unfitness of both Dyer and her midwife, *Anne Hutchinson, in the eyes of the Lord. When Hutchinson was excommunicated and exiled from the colony in 1639, Mary Dyer followed her out of the church in a show of support. Dyer was also excommunicated and banished, and she and her family moved to the Rhode Island (Newport) area.

In 1652, the Dyers returned to England with Roger Williams, the founder of the Rhode Island Colony, and other Rhode Island leaders in order to secure a formal charter. When her husband returned to America in 1652, Dyer stayed in England for four more years, during which time she was converted to membership in the Society of Friends, or the Quakers. She returned to America in 1657 and set about trying to change the attitude of the Congregationalist Church about the role of women as missionaries and voices of the spirit. Enroute to Rhode Island, she was imprisoned in Boston along with her companion, **Ann Burden**, another Quaker.

In response to specific Boston and Massachusetts Bay laws about Quakers, Dyer was exiled from Boston in 1657 and from New Haven in 1658. When she returned to Boston in 1659 to visit two Quakers imprisoned there, she was arrested and, in September, was banished to Rhode Island. Dyer quickly returned to Boston where she was imprisoned again and sentenced

rence Louise Price in Reading, Pennsylvania, on July 4, 1902; died in Elizabeth, New Jersey, on February 29, 1976; briefly attended the University of Toledo, Toledo, Ohio.

A 16-year veteran of the House of Representatives, Florence Dwyer moved to New Jersey after her marriage and worked on the 1940 campaign of presidential candidate Wendell Willke. In 1950, after several years as a lobbyist for the New Jersey Business and Professional clubs, she was elected to the state assembly, where she won passage of a law guaranteeing equal pay for women and helped established the first minimum salary schedule for New Jersey teachers. She won election to the House in 1956, defeating Democrat Harrison Williams, who later served as a U.S. senator. As a representative, Dwyer concentrated on issues of consumer protection, women's equality, and procedural reform within the House. She was a chief sponsor of the act creating the Consumer Protection Agency and a staunch supporter of the Equal Rights Amendment. During consideration

to hang for being a Quaker. Her two Quaker friends were hanged, and Dyer, due to her husband's intervention, was reprieved at the gallows on October 27, 1659. Spending the winter in Rhode Island, she returned to Boston in the Spring of 1660. Arrested and sentenced to death, she was hanged on June 1, 1660.

SOURCES:
Deen, Edith. *Great Women of the Christian Faith*. NY: Harper & Brothers, 1959.
Plimpton, Ruth Talbot. *Mary Dyer: Biography of a Rebel Quaker*. Boston: Branden, 1994.

SUGGESTED READING:
Crawford, Deborah. *Four Women in a Violent Time: Anne Hutchinson (1591-1643), Mary Dyer (1591?-1660), Lady Deborah Moody (1600-1659), and Penelope Stout (1622 -1732)*. NY: Crown Publishers, 1970.
Rogers, Horatio. *Mary Dyer of Rhode Island the Quaker martyr that was hanged on Boston Common, June 1, 1660*. Providence: Preston and Rounds, 1896.

Amanda Carson Banks,
Lecturer, Vanderbilt Divinity School, Nashville, Tennessee

Dympna (fl. 650 CE)

Martyr and patron saint of mental illness, epilepsy, possession by the devil, and sleepwalkers. Name variations: Dimpna. Born the daughter of a pagan Irish, British or Armorican king and a Christian princess.

Buried in two marble sarcophagi, the bodies of St. Dympna and St. Gerebernus were discovered in Gheel, 25 miles from Antwerp, in the 13th century. Dympna's body now rests in a silver reliquary located in a church that bears her name. Gerebernus' head also resides there, separated from his other remains which were relocated to Sonsbeck in the diocese of Münster. The folklore of many European countries recounts a story of Dympna that describes her as the daughter of a pagan king (Irish, British or Armorican) and a Christian princess. Dympna was baptized and instructed in the Christian faith before her mother died when Dympna was still very young. The king had idolized his wife, and as Dympna grew up her remarkable resemblance to her mother is said to have invoked an incestuous lust in her father. St. Gerebernus, her confessor, advised her to flee so as to suffer no more danger.

Dympna was accompanied by St. Gerebernus and attended by the court jester and his wife when she boarded a ship en route to Antwerp. It would only be a matter of time, however, before the king would track them down. Once ashore, Dympna's party headed southeast over wild forest country until arriving at a small oratory dedicated to St. Martin. There, they built a site that

is now the location of the town of Gheel, and prepared to live as solitaries.

Dympna's father in the meantime arrived in Antwerp. From there, he sent out spies who located the fugitives by way of the coins, similar to those that the spies offered, used by Dympna's group. The king came upon his daughter by surprise and attempted to convince her to return with him. Dympna, supported by St. Gerebernus, refused. Ordered by the king to kill them both, his attendants murdered the priest, then hesitated. The king's own hand held the sword that then cut off his daughter's head. Left exposed, the bodies were then buried by unknown hands, thought by some to be angels.

It is said that when the relics of St. Dympna were elevated, many epileptics and people suffering from possession who visited her shrine were restored to normal health. Since that time, Dympna has been regarded as the patron saint of the mentally ill and those suffering from epilepsy. As mental illness was at one time associated with diabolical possession, she has been invoked to help those suffering from possession by the devil, and because sleepwalking was likewise attributed to possession by evil spirits she has also been invoked against this condition as well.

The inhabitants of Gheel have become known for the care they have taken of the mentally ill. An infirmary was built to serve those so afflicted as early as the 13th century, and an excellent state sanatorium was located in Gheel for their care and supervision. Residing in the homes of farmers and local residents to whom they give their labor and with whom they share family life, the majority of the mentally ill in Gheel were said to lead contented, productive lives.

Dysart, countess of (c. 1626–1698).
See Murray, Elizabeth.

Dyveke (c. 1491–1517).
See Willums, Sigbrit for sidebar.

Dzerzhinska, Sofia (1882–1968)

Polish-born Russian revolutionary leader who survived both tsarism and Stalinism, publishing her memoirs when she was in her 80s. Name variations: Zofia Dzierzynska; Sofia Dzerzhinskaia; Zosia Dzerzhinskaya. Born Sofia Sigizmundovna Muszkat in Warsaw, Russian Poland, on December 4, 1882 (or November 22 in the Julian calendar still in use in Russian Poland); died in Moscow on February 27, 1968; daughter of Zygmunt Muszkat; married Feliks

Dzerzhinsky (a close associate of V.I. Lenin and founder of the Cheka—the Soviet secret police); children: son, Jan.

Born into an assimilated family of the Polish-Jewish bourgeoisie in Warsaw on December 4, 1882, Sofia Muszkat was drawn in her early years into progressive and revolutionary circles. Harsh Russification measures and repression of both the Polish nationalist and labor movements by tsarist officials only strengthened the determination of the Polish intellectual classes to struggle against the forces of foreign oppression. A gifted music student at the Warsaw Conservatory, Sofia spent much of her time working for the most important Marxist revolutionary organization in Russian Poland, the Social Democracy of the Kingdom of Poland and Lithuania (SDKPiL). In 1905, Sofia, known to her SDKPiL comrades as "Zosia," met Feliks Dzerzhinsky, a veteran of the revolutionary movement, and was soon attracted to him. Born into a family of the Polish gentry (*szlachta*), Dzerzhinsky had been a full-time member of the anti-Russian underground since his late teens. A figure like those found on the pages of Russian novels, young Feliks was dedicated to the goals of national liberation and social revolution and was the embodiment of Lenin's ideal of the professional revolutionary. He had devoted his life to the joint causes of freeing Poland from tsarist oppression and the workers from the fetters of capitalism.

In the real world, however, the overwhelming power of a Russian officialdom that had crushed many Polish uprisings in the previous century made only too clear that the hopes of young revolutionaries like Sofia and Feliks were fragile indeed. As part of a Russian crackdown, she and Feliks were arrested in 1906. Both were incarcerated in Warsaw's notorious Ratusz municipal prison. In the female section of Ratusz, Sofia Muszkat found herself in an overcrowded, filthy situation, with over 100 criminals and prostitutes as well as political prisoners like herself confined to cells originally meant to accommodate no more than 30 women. After her release, an undeterred Sofia returned to her illegal work in a number of Polish cities, but in 1909 she was once again arrested in Warsaw. After three months of imprisonment, she was expelled from Russian Poland. Settling in Austrian Poland, she continued her revolutionary activities in the ancient city of Cracow. Here she again met Feliks Dzerzhinsky, who had recently returned from exile in Siberia.

Feliks and Sofia worked together in Cracow, strengthening the party organization. They spent long hours copying materials sent from Berlin where the SDKPiL executive committee was headquartered. Sofia often went on dangerous trips carrying contraband documents from Cracow to Warsaw, where they would eventually appear in the SDKPiL illegal newspaper *Czerwony Sztandar* (*Red Banner*), which was printed at an underground printing press. Sofia's work was highly regarded in the party, not only by Feliks Dzerzhinsky. But in time their relationship became more than a comradely one, and in August 1910 they were married. The couple spent a short honeymoon in the Tatra mountains, away from secret police and internal party squabbles. Soon after, in November 1910, Sofia Dzerzhinska was sent by the party to carry out underground work in Warsaw. Within a few weeks, in December of that year, she was arrested.

Although she was pregnant at the time of her arrest, Sofia Dzerzhinska remained in prison and in June 1911 she gave birth to her only child, a son named Jan. Born prematurely, Jan almost died of convulsions soon after his birth and was sickly during his infancy. For the first eight months of his life, Jan—affectionately called "Janek" (Johnny) by his mother—remained with his mother in her cell in the women's (called by its inmates the "Serbian") section of Warsaw's Pawiak prison. After Sofia Dzerzhinska was sentenced in November 1911 to a life of exile in Siberia, she decided that Janek would not survive being with her. Janek, whose health remained fragile, was taken to a children's home in Warsaw. Fortunately, Sofia's uncle **Marian Muszkat**, a respected physician, took care of the child and in time his health improved dramatically. In March 1912, Janek's father eluded the Russian police and was able to see his son for the first time. Feliks described him to a party colleague as "a tall boy, but dreadfully thin."

In the late summer of 1912, Sofia Dzerzhinska was able to escape her Siberian exile. Her husband had enabled her flight by sending her a forged passport and 100 rubles. She made her way to Cracow, hoping there to rejoin Feliks and then reclaim their son in Warsaw. Sofia arrived safely in Cracow on September 26, 1912, only to learn that Feliks had been arrested for the sixth time in his revolutionary career on September 1. First imprisoned in the Warsaw Citadel, later in the Russian town of Orel and finally in Moscow, he would not see his wife and child again until 1918, after the Bolshevik Revolution. Sofia, on the other hand, returned to Cracow to continue her party work as secretary of the foreign sections bureau of the SDKPiL.

After the Bolshevik Revolution of November 1917, in which her husband played a leading role, Sofia Dzerzhinska moved to Switzerland to assist Russian and Polish revolutionaries in their plans to return home. In 1918, she was a key member of the Soviet delegation in the Swiss capital, Berne. In 1919, she went to Moscow, working for some time in the People's Commissariat of Education. At the same time, Feliks Dzerzhinsky assisted Vladimir Lenin by serving as chair of the All-Russian Extraordinary Commission. Known universally as the Cheka, this was the much-feared secret police that crushed all those accused of "counter-revolutionary thoughts or deeds." Both Feliks and Sofia were deeply disappointed in the summer of 1920 when the Polish army under Jozef Pilsudski triumphed over the Red Army and all hopes of establishing a Communist society in Poland had to be abandoned.

After her husband's sudden death in July 1926, Sofia Dzerzhinska continued her work as a Communist activist. Among the positions she held during the 1920s were posts in the Polish Bureau of the Communist Party of the Soviet Union and at the Communist University of National Minorities of the West. She also served as executive secretary of the Polish bureau of the Soviet Communist party central committee's department of propaganda and agitation. She generally avoided becoming embroiled in internal conflicts of the Polish Communist émigrés living in Moscow, and in 1929 was able to largely withdraw from active political affairs by becoming a research scholar as well as editor-in-chief at Moscow's prestigious Marx-Engels-Lenin Institute. In 1937, at a time when Joseph Stalin was engaged in mercilessly purging the Polish Communist Party (in 1938 it was the only Communist party to be abolished for being "infected by Fascism"), Sofia Dzerzhinska assumed a post in the executive committee of the Communist International (Comintern). Her son Jan also worked for the Comintern until it was dissolved by Stalin in 1943 as a conciliatory gesture to his wartime allies in the West. During World War II, Sofia served as a director of the Radio Kosciuszko, which broadcast the Soviet view of world affairs to German-occupied Poland. Dzerzhinska also worked during the war years in the Moscow headquarters of the Bureau of Polish Communists.

After her retirement in 1946, Dzerzhinska remained in Moscow collecting materials for her autobiography, which finally appeared in print in 1964. A Polish version was published in Warsaw in 1969. One of the more intriguing aspects of the Polish edition is the fact that it makes no mention of Dzerzhinska's Jewish ancestry; Poland underwent a virulent wave of anti-Semitism in 1968 which resulted in the expulsion or emigration of thousands of its remaining Jewish population. Proud to the end of her long life of her remarkable career of revolutionary activism, Sofia Dzerzhinska died in Moscow on February 27, 1968. She was one of the most highly decorated revolutionary veterans of the Soviet era, having been awarded the Order of Lenin on three occasions as well as several other high decorations.

SOURCES:

Blobaum, Robert. *Feliks Dzierzynski and the SDKPiL: A Study of the Origins of Polish Communism.* Boulder, CO: East European Monographs, 1984.

Dzierzynska, Zofia. *Lata wielkich bojow: wspomnienia.* Warsaw: Ksiazka i Wiedza, 1969.

Feliks Dzerzhinsky: A Biography. Translated by Natalia Belskaya. Moscow: Progress Publishers, 1988.

Latka, Jerzy S. *Krwawy apostol: Feliks Dzierzynski, 1877–1926.* Cracow: Klub Przyjaciol Turcji, 1993.

Toranska, Teresa. *"Them": Stalin's Polish Puppets.* Translated by Agnieszka Kolakowska. NY: Harper & Row, 1987.

John Haag, Associate Professor of History, University of Georgia, Athens, Georgia

ACKNOWLEDGMENTS

Photographs and illustrations appearing in *Women in World History, Volume 4,* were received from the following sources:

Courtesy of Les Archives Photographiques d'Art et d'Histoire: **p. 606**; Photo by Jitendra Arya: **p. 567**; Photo by Clive Bardo: **p. 875**; Photo by Baron: **p. 499**; Photo by Jerry Bauer: **p. 81**; Painting by Gustave Boulanger: **p. 129**; Photo by Gloria Branfman: **p. 443**; Courtesy of the Caroline Dormon Nature Preserve: **p. 719**; Portrait by Jules Cayron (1897): **p. 883**; Painting by A.E. Chalon, R.A: **p. 675**; Courtesy of the Children's Television Workshop: **p. 89**; Engraving by A. Closs; painting by E. Keller: **p. 626**; Photo by Coffin: **p. 826**; Columbia Broadcasting System: **p. 610**; Courtesy of Nadia Comaneci: **p. 41**; Courtesy of the Carl A. Kroch Library, Rare and Manuscript Collections, Cornell University Library, Ithaca, New York: **p. 57**; Courtesy of Michael Dark (N.S.W., Australia): **p. 317**; Courtesy of Laurent Dassault: **p. 341**; From Julia de Burgos, *Antologia Poetica,* Courtesy of Angela Davis: **p. 379**; Editorial Coqui, San Juan de Puerto Rico, 1979: **p. 433**; From *Having Our Say,* reprinted by permission of the Delany family: **pp. 464, 465**; Courtesy of the Disney Channel: **p. 581**; Courtesy of Elite International Sports Marketing: **p. 578**; Courtesy of Emmalyn II Productions Co., Inc.: **p. 441**; Courtesy of Flair Photography Ltd.: **p. 167**; Courtesy of the Service de Presse et d'Information Division, Embassy of France, Washington, D.C.: **p. 449**; Courtesy of French Embassy Press and Information Division, © France Presse: **p. 447**; Photo by

Arnold Genthe: **p. 907**; Courtesy of Girton College, Cambridge, England; painting by Rudolph Lehmann: **p. 361**; Detail from an anonymous portrait of Grace Darling, Grace Darling Museum, Bamburgh, England: **p. 320**; Courtesy of Gyldendal Norsk Forlag: **p. 20**; Photo by Philippe Halsman: **p. 345**; Watercolor by Jules Hebert: **p. 302**; Painting by J.B. Hilair, 1787: **p. 536**; Courtesy of the Imogene Cunningham Trust; photograph by Imogene Cunningham, © 1978, 1996: **p. 251**; Courtesy of the International Museum of Photography at the George Eastman House: **pp. 85, 93, 753**; Courtesy of the International Swimming Hall of Fame: **pp. 262, 576, 878**; Courtesy of the Japanese Embassy: **p. 698**; From *Marion Dönhoff: ein widerständiges Leben,* Cologne: Verlag Kiepenheuer and Witsch, 1996: **p. 709**; Photo by Ove Kjeldsen: **p. 653**; Courtesy of Professor Noeline J. Kyle (with permission from David family): **p. 347**; From the painting by Jules Lefebvre: **p. 34**; Courtesy of the Library of Congress: **pp. 3, 30, 187, 257, 271, 413, 683, 855**; Courtesy of The Louvre, Paris: **p. 481**; Courtesy of the Manassas Museum: **p. 419**; Photo by Manuel: **p. 11**; Courtesy of the Maureen Connolly Brinker Tennis Foundation, Dallas, Texas: **p. 67**; Photo by Angus McBean: **p. 495**; Photo by Marian Meade: **p. 154**; Courtesy of Mercury/RKO: **p. 49**; Courtesy of Metro-Goldwyn-Mayer: **pp. 16 (1958), 47 (1952)**; From the oil portrait by Pierre Mignard: **p. 545**; Courtesy of the Mount Vernon Ladies' Association: **pp. 243–244**; Photo by Nadar: **p. 544**; Courtesy of the National Archives, National Publicity Studios Collection, National Library of New Zealand, Alexander Turnbull Library (F-40058-1/2): **p. 103**; © National Endowment for the Arts: **p. 667**; Courtesy of the National Park Service, Washington, D.C.: **p. 37**; Courtesy of the Nobel Foundation: **p. 477**; Courtesy of Jerry Ohlinger: **pp. 589, 598**; Courtesy of the Oklahoma State University Library, Angie Debo Papers, Stillwater, Oklahoma: **p. 424**; Courtesy of Paramount, 1932: **p. 635**; Polish postage stamp issued December 30, 1969: **p. 281**; Courtesy of the Queen's University Archives, Ontario, Canada: **p. 513**; Courtesy of the Schlesinger Library, Radcliffe College: **pp. 517, 559, 761**; Courtesy of the Smithsonian Institution, Center for Folklife and Cultural Heritage; photo by Diana Davies: **p. 149**; Courtesy of RKO, 1934: **p. 387**; Courtesy of RKO-Radio: **pp. 487**, photo by Ernest A. Bloch: **489**; Photo by Paul Rockett: **p. 467**; Photo by Sarony, New York: **p. 26**; Courtesy of the Schomburg Center for Research in Black Culture: **p. 837**; Courtesy of Selznick International: **p. 830**; Courtesy of Seven Arts-Warner Bros., 1962: **p. 390**; Courtesy of the

ACKNOWLEDGMENTS

Archives of the Sisters of the Blessed Sacrament, Bensalem, Pennsylvania: **p. 775**; Courtesy of the Sophia Smith Collection, Smith College, Northampton, Massachusetts: **p. 211**; Courtesy of the Society of the Sacred Heart, National Archives: **p. 803**; Detail of a fresco in the church of St. Panteleimon at Boyana: **p. 555**; Photo by Edward Steichen: **pp. 137, 845**; Portrait by Josef Stieler: **p. 637**; Painting by Titian: **p. 126**; Courtesy of Twentieth Century-Fox: **p. 299** (1954), **831, 868** (1952); Courtesy of the U.S. House of Representatives: **pp. 28, 733, 914**; Courtesy of United Artists, 1932: **p. 199**; United Press International: **p. 259**; Courtesy of Universal Studios: **pp. 657** (1984), **846** (1968), **892**, photo by Ray Jones; Courtesy of the University of Texas at Austin, Harry Ransom Humanities Research Center: **p. 235**; Courtesy of the University of Wales, Gregynog: **pp. 366–367**; Courtesy of the University of Washington Libraries, Seattle: **p. 208**; Photo by Vandamm, New York: **p. 141**; Courtesy of Walt Disney Productions, © MCM-LXI: **p. 693**; Courtesy of Warner Bros.: **pp. 201** (1945), **411** (1953), **520** (1967); Courtesy of Western Michigan University Archives and Regional History Collections: **p. 191**; Courtesy of WGBH-TV, Boston, Massachusetts: **p. 229**.

ISBN 0-7876-4063-8

90000